THE THIRTEENTH MENTAL
MEASUREMENTS YEARBOOK

EARLIER PUBLICATIONS IN THIS SERIES

THE THIRTEENTH MENTAL MEASUREMENTS YEARBOOK

JAMES C. IMPARA and BARBARA S. PLAKE

Editors

LINDA L. MURPHY
Managing Editor

The Buros Institute of Mental Measurements
The University of Nebraska-Lincoln
Lincoln, Nebraska

1998
Distributed by The University of Nebraska Press

LC 39-3422
ISBN 910674-44-2

Manufactured in the United States of America.

The paper used in this publication meets the minimum requirements of American National Standard for Information Sciences—Permanence of Paper for Printed Library Materials, ANSI Z39.48-1984.

Note to Users

The staff of the Buros Institute of Mental Measurements has made every effort to ensure the accuracy of the test information included in this work. However, the Buros Institute of Mental Measurements and the Editors of *The Thirteenth Mental Measurements Yearbook* do not assume, and hereby expressly and absolutely disclaim, any liability to any party for any loss or damage caused by errors or omissions or statements of any kind in *The Thirteenth Mental Measurements Yearbook*. This disclaimer also includes judgments or statements of any kind made by test reviewers, who were extended the professional freedom appropriate to their task. The reviews are the sole opinion of the individual reviewers and do not necessarily represent any general consensus of the professional community or any professional organizations. The judgments and opinions of the reviewers are their own, uninfluenced in any way by the Buros Institute or the Editors.

All material included in *The Thirteenth Mental Measurements Yearbook* is intended solely for the use of our readers. None of this material, including reviewer statements, may be used in advertising or for any other commercial purpose.

TABLE OF CONTENTS

INTRODUCTION

The publication of *The Thirteenth Mental Measurements Yearbook* (*13th MMY*) comes during the year in which the Buros Institute of Mental Measurements celebrates its 60th anniversary. This volume continues the historic mission of the Buros Institute of Mental Measurements to provide test users with descriptive information, references, and critical reviews of tests. Criteria for inclusion of a test in the *13th MMY* are that the test be (a) new or revised since last reviewed in the *MMY* series, (b) commercially available, and (c) published in the English language. Descriptive information about the contents and use of the newest Buros Institute of Mental Measurements publication is provided below.

THE THIRTEENTH MENTAL MEASUREMENTS YEARBOOK

The *13th MMY* contains reviews of tests that are new or significantly revised since the publication of the *12th MMY* in 1995. Reviews, descriptions, and references associated with many older tests can be located in other Buros publications: *MMY*s and *Tests in Print IV*.

Content. The contents of the *13th MMY* include: (a) a bibliography of 369 commercially available tests, new or revised, published as separates for use with English-speaking subjects; (b) 693 critical test reviews by well-qualified professional people who were selected by the editors on the basis of their expertise in measurement and, often, the content of the test being reviewed; (c) bibliographies of references for specific tests related to the construction, validity, or use of the tests in various settings; (d) a test title index with appropriate cross-references; (e) a classified subject index; (f) a publishers directory and index, including addresses and test listings by publisher; (g) a name index including the names of authors of all tests, reviews, or references included in this *MMY*; (h) an index of acronyms for easy reference when a test acronym, not the full title, is known; and (i) a score index to refer readers to tests featuring particular scores of interest to them.

Because the Institute's overarching mission is improvement in the development and use of tests, we have also included a copy of the Code of Professional Responsibilities in Educational Measurement. This code is reproduced in its entirety at the end of this volume.

Organization. The volume is organized like an encyclopedia, with tests being ordered alphabetically by title. If the title of a test is known, the reader can locate the test immediately without having to consult the Index of Titles.

The page headings reflect the encyclopedic organization. The page heading of the left-hand page cites the number and title of the first test listed on that page, and the page heading of the right-hand page cites the number and title of the last test listed on that page. All numbers presented in the various indexes are test numbers, not page numbers. Page numbers are important only for the Table of Contents and are indicated at the bottom of each page.

TESTS AND REVIEWS

The *13th MMY* contains descriptive information on 369 tests as well as 693 test reviews by 408 different authors. The reviewed tests have generated 3,222 references in the professional literature (gathered since the 1995 publication of the *12th MMY*) and reviewers have supplied 1,140 additional references in their reviews.

Statistics on the number and percentage of tests in each of 18 major classifications are contained in Table 1.

TABLE 1
TESTS BY MAJOR CLASSIFICATIONS

Classification	Number	Percentage
Personality	75	20.3
Vocations	73	19.8
Miscellaneous	46	12.5
Achievement	23	6.2
Developmental	22	6.0
Behavior Assessment	21	5.7
English	21	5.7
Intelligence and Scholastic Aptitude	18	4.9
Education	14	3.8
Neuropsychological	13	3.5
Reading	13	3.5
Speech and Hearing	13	3.5
Mathematics	6	1.6
Foreign Languages	4	1.1
Sensory-Motor	4	1.1
Fine Arts	1	.3
Science	1	.3
Social Studies	1	.3
Total	369	100.0

TABLE 2
NEW AND REVISED OR SUPPLEMENTED TESTS BY MAJOR CLASSIFICATIONS

Classification	Number of Tests	Percentage New	Revised
Achievement	23	65.2	34.8
Behavior Assessment	21	81.0	19.0
Developmental	22	68.2	31.9
Education	14	85.7	14.3
English	21	66.7	33.3
Fine Arts	1	0.0	100.0
Foreign Languages	4	100.0	0.0
Intelligence and Scholastic Aptitude	18	72.2	27.8
Mathematics	6	66.7	33.3
Miscellaneous	46	93.5	7.7
Neuropsychological	13	92.3	7.7
Personality	75	66.7	33.3
Reading	13	53.8	46.2
Science	1	100.0	0.0
Sensory-Motor	4	75.0	25.0
Social Studies	1	0.0	100.0
Speech and Hearing	13	69.2	30.8
Vocations	73	80.8	19.2
Total	369	75.3	24.7

The percentage of new and revised or supplemented tests according to major classifications are contained in Table 2. Overall, three-fourths of the tests included in the *13th MMY* are new and have not been listed in a previous *MMY* although many descriptions were included in *Tests in Print IV* (1994). The Index of Titles can be consulted to determine if a test is new or revised.

Test Selection. Our goal is to include reviews of virtually all English language, commercially published tests that are new or revised. No minimal standards exist and inclusion of a test in the *MMY* does not mean that a test has met any standard of "goodness." We attempt to gather all tests, good and bad alike. We select our reviewers carefully and let them and well-informed readers decide for themselves about the quality of the tests. Some new or revised tests are not included because they were received too late to undergo the review process and still permit timely publication, or because some reviewers did not meet their commitment to review the test.

There are some new or revised tests for which there will be no reviews although all these tests are described in *Tests in Print IV* and/or will be described in *Tests in Print V*. In the *10th* and *11th MMY*s, a number of tests were included without reviews but with descriptive information. The absence of reviews occurred for a variety of reasons including: We could not identify qualified reviewers, the test materials were incomplete so reviews were not possible, the tests were sufficiently obscure that reviews were deemed unnecessary, or the tests were published in South Africa during the time we felt morally obligated to boycott their products. Descriptions of all these tests still in print were published in *TIP IV*. There continue to be some tests that meet the above conditions that are not reviewed in this volume. Descriptions of the tests may be found in *TIP IV*.

A new policy for selecting tests for review will be effective for the *14th MMY* (expected publication in 2000). The new policy for selecting tests for review requires at least minimal information be available regarding test development. The requirement that tests have such minimal information does not assure the quality of the test, it simply provides reviewers with a minimum basis for critically evaluating the quality of the test.

Reviewer Selection. The selection of reviewers was done with great care. The objective was to secure measurement and subject specialists who represent a variety of different viewpoints. It was also important to find individuals who would write critical reviews competently, judiciously, fairly, and in a timely manner. Reviewers were identified by means of extensive searches of the professional literature, attendance at professional meetings, and recommendations from leaders in various professional fields. Perusal of reviews in this volume will also reveal that reviewers work in and represent a cross-section of the places in which tests are taught and used: universities, public schools, businesses, and community agencies. These reviewers represent an outstanding array of professional talent, and their contributions are obviously of primary importance in making this *Yearbook* a valuable resource. A list of the individuals reviewing in this volume is included at the beginning of the Index section.

Readers of test reviews in the *13th MMY* are encouraged to exercise an active, analytical, and evaluative perspective in reading the reviews. Just as one would evaluate a test, the readers should evaluate critically the reviewer's comments about the test. The reviewers selected are competent professionals in their respective fields, but it is inevitable that their reviews also reflect their individual perspectives. The *Mental Measurements Yearbooks* are intended to stimulate critical thinking about the selection of the best available test for a given purpose, not the passive acceptance of reviewer judgment. Active, evaluative reading is the key to the most effective use of the professional expertise offered in each of the reviews.

REFERENCES

This yearbook lists a total of 4,362 references related to the development, psychometric quality, and use of specific tests. The "Reviewer's References" section groups the reviewer's references in one convenient listing for easy identification and use by the reader. Of the total of 4,362 references, 3,222 are included under "Test References" and 1,140 are included under "Reviewer's References."

All references listed under "Test References" have been selected by Buros Institute staff who searched through hundreds of professional journals. Because of the great proliferation of tests in recent years, it was decided to increase test and review coverage but to limit the increase in references by not including theses, dissertations, books, book chapters, or presentations at professional meetings.

Buros Institute publications traditionally list all references chronologically and then alphabetically by author within year. Our format for references in journals is author, year, title, journal, volume, and page numbers; for books it is author, year, title, place of publication, and publisher. A large number of additional references are listed in *Tests in Print IV*, published in 1994.

All tests in this yearbook that generated 10 or more references are listed in Table 3. Within the table the tests are also rank-ordered according to number of references. The references are valuable as additions to our cumulative knowledge about specific tests, and they are also a useful resource for further research into test quality.

TABLE 3
NUMBER OF REFERENCES FOR MOST
FREQUENTLY CITED TESTS

NAME OF TEST	NUMBER OF REFERENCES
Beck Depression Inventory [1993 Revised]	1026
Child Behavior Checklist	556
Revised Hamilton Rating Scale for Depression	382
Bayley Scales of Infant Development, Second Edition	130
California Achievement Tests, Fifth Edition	113
Iowa Tests of Basic Skills, Forms K,L, and M	110
Beck Hopelessness Scale [Revised]	83
Millon Clinical Multiaxial Inventory—III	81
Stanford Achievement Test, Ninth Edition	80
Beck Anxiety Inventory [1993 Edition]	73
Benton Visual Retention Test, Fifth Edition	66
California Verbal Learning Test, Research Edition, Adult Version	57
Nelson-Denny Reading Test, Forms G and H	52
State-Trait Anger Expression Inventory, Revised Research Edition	52
Parenting Stress Index, Third Edition	51
The Self-Directed Search, Form E—1990 Revision	48
Hamilton Depression Inventory	43
Self-Description Questionnaire—I, II, III	42
Tennessee Self-Concept Scale, Second Edition	41
Clinical Evaluation of Language Fundamentals, Third Edition	38
Mill Hill Vocabulary Scale	30
Preschool Language Scale—3	26
Cognitive Abilities Test, Form 5	23
Jackson Personality Inventory—Revised	21
State Trait-Depression Adjective Check Lists	21
Stuttering Severity Instrument for Children and Adults, Third Edition	21
Career Development Inventory [Consulting Psychologists Press, Inc.]	17
Composite International Diagnostic Interview	17
Wechsler Individual Achievement Test	17
Test of Written Language—Third Edition	16
Beck Scale for Suicide Ideation	14
MacArthur Communicative Development Inventories	14
Defense Mechanisms Inventory [Revised]	12
Minnesota Test for Differential Diagnosis of Aphasia	10

INDEXES

As mentioned above, the *13th MMY* includes six indexes invaluable as aids to effective use: (a) Index of Titles, (b) Index of Acronyms, (c) Classified Subject Index, (d) Publishers Directory and Index, (e) Index of Names, and (f) Score Index. Additional comment on these indexes is presented below.

Index of Titles. Because the organization of the *13th MMY* is encyclopedic in nature, with the tests ordered alphabetically by title throughout the volume, the test title index does not have to be consulted to find a test if the title is known. However, the title index has some features that make it useful beyond its function as a complete title listing. First, it includes cross-reference information useful for tests with superseded or alternative titles or tests commonly (and sometimes inaccurately) known by multiple titles. Second, it identifies tests that are new or revised. Third, it may cue the user to other tests with similar titles that may be useful. It is important to keep in mind that the numbers in this index, like those for all *MMY* indexes, are test numbers and not page numbers.

Because no *MMY* includes reviews of all tests currently in print, a particular test of interest may not be reviewed in this volume. To learn if a commercially published test has been reviewed in this or an earlier volume of the *MMY*, users may access the Buros page on the World Wide Web (http://www.unl.edu/buros). In addition to other information about Buros products or services, there is a "Test Review Locator" that will indicate if a test has been reviewed and the *MMY* in which the review can be found.

Index of Acronyms. Some tests seem to be better known by their acronyms than by their full titles. The Index of Acronyms can help in these instances; it refers the reader to the full title of the test and to the relevant descriptive information and reviews.

Classified Subject Index. The Classified Subject Index classifies all tests listed in the *13th MMY* into 18 major categories: Achievement, Behavior Assessment, Developmental, Education, English, Fine Arts, Foreign Language, Intelligence and Scholastic Aptitude, Mathematics, Miscellaneous, Neuropsychological, Personality, Reading, Science, Sensory-Motor, Social Studies, Speech and Hearing, and Vocations. Each test entry in this index includes test title, population for which the test is intended, and test number. The Classified Subject Index is of great help to readers who seek a listing of tests in given subject areas. The Classified

Subject Index represents a starting point for readers who know their area of interest but do not know how to further focus that interest in order to identify the best test(s) for their particular purposes.

Publishers Directory and Index. The Publishers Directory and Index includes the names and addresses of the publishers of all tests included in the *13th MMY* plus a listing of test numbers for each individual publisher. This index can be particularly useful in obtaining addresses for specimen sets or catalogs after the test reviews have been read and evaluated. It can also be useful when a reader knows the publisher of a certain test but is uncertain about the test title, or when a reader is interested in the range of tests published by a given publisher.

Index of Names. The Index of Names provides a comprehensive list of names, indicating authorship of a test, test review, or reference.

Score Index. The Score Index is an index to all scores generated by the tests in the *13th MMY*. Test titles are sometimes misleading or ambiguous, and test content may be difficult to define with precision. But test scores often represent operational definitions of the variables the test author is trying to measure, and as such they can define test purpose and content more adequately than other descriptive information. A search for a particular test is most often a search for a test that measures some specific variable(s). Test scores and their associated labels can often be the best definitions of the variable(s) of interest. The Score Index is a detailed subject index based on the most critical operational features of any test—the scores and their associated labels.

HOW TO USE THIS YEARBOOK

A reference work like *The Thirteenth Mental Measurements Yearbook* can be of far greater benefit to a reader if some time is taken to become familiar with what it has to offer and how it might be used most effectively to obtain the information wanted.

Step 1: Read the Introduction to the *13th MMY* in its entirety.

Step 2: Become familiar with the six indexes and particularly with the instructions preceding each index listing.

Step 3: Use the book by looking up needed information. This step is simple if one keeps in mind the following possibilities:

1. Go directly to the test entry using the alphabetical page headings if you know the title of the test.

2. Consult the Index of Titles for possible variants of the title or consult the appropriate subject area of the Classified Subject Index for other possible leads or for similar or related tests in the same area, if you do not know, cannot find, or are unsure of the title of a test. (Other uses for both of these indexes were described earlier.)

3. Consult the Index of Names if you know the author of a test but not the title or publisher. Look up the author's titles until you find the test you want.

4. Consult the Publishers Directory and Index if you know the test publisher but not the title or author. Look up the publisher's titles until you find the test you want.

5. Consult the Score Index and locate the test or tests that include the score variable of interest if you are looking for a test that yields a particular kind of score, but have no knowledge of which test that might be.

6. If after following the above steps you are not able to find a review of the test you want, go to the Buros web page (http://www.unl.edu/buros) and use the test locator service to identify the *MMY* that contains the description and any available reviews of the test of interest.

7. Once you have found the test or tests you are looking for, read the descriptive entries for these tests carefully so that you can take advantage of the information provided. A description of the information provided in these test entries is presented later in this section.

8. Read the test reviews carefully and analytically, as suggested above. The information and evaluation contained in these reviews are meant to assist test consumers in making well-informed decisions about the choice and applications of tests.

9. Once you have read the descriptive information and test reviews, you may want to order a specimen set for a particular test so that you can examine it firsthand. The Publishers Directory and Index has the address information needed to obtain specimen sets or catalogs.

Making Effective Use of the Test Entries. The test entries include extensive information. For each test, descriptive information is presented in the following order:

a) TITLES. Test titles are printed in boldface type. Secondary or series titles are set off from main titles by a colon.

b) PURPOSE. For each test there is a brief, clear statement describing the purpose of the test. Often these statements are quotations from the test manual.

c) POPULATION. This describes the groups for which the test is intended. The grade, chronological age, semester range, or employment category is usually given. For example, "grades 1.5–2.5, 2–3, 4–12, 13–17" means that there are four test booklets: a booklet for the middle of first grade through the middle of the second grade, a booklet for the beginning of the second grade through the end of third grade, a booklet for grades 4 through 12 inclusive, and a booklet for undergraduate and graduate students in colleges and universities.

d) PUBLICATION DATE. The inclusive range of publication dates for the various forms, accessories, and editions of a test is reported.

e) ACRONYM. When a test is often referred to by an acronym, the acronym is given in the test entry immediately following the publication date.

f) SCORES. The number of part scores is presented along with their titles or descriptions of what they are intended to represent or measure.

g) ADMINISTRATION. Individual or group administration is indicated. A test is considered a group test unless it may be administered *only* individually.

h) FORMS, PARTS, AND LEVELS. All available forms, parts, and levels are listed.

i) MANUAL. Notation is made if no manual is available. All other manual information is included under Price Data.

j) RESTRICTED DISTRIBUTION. This is noted only for tests that are put on a special market by the publisher. Educational and psychological restrictions are not noted (unless a special training course is required for use).

k) PRICE DATA. Price information is reported for test packages (usually 20 to 35 tests), answer sheets, all other accessories, and specimen sets. The statement "$17.50 per 35 tests" means that all accessories are included unless otherwise indicated by the reporting of separate prices for accessories. The statement also means 35 tests of one level, one edition, or one part unless stated otherwise. Because test prices can change very quickly, the year that the listed test prices were obtained is also given. Foreign currency is assigned the appropriate symbol. When prices are given in foreign dollars, a qualifying symbol is added (e.g., A$16.50 refers to 16 dollars and 50 cents in Australian currency). Along with cost, the publication date and number of pages on which print occurs is reported for manuals and technical reports (e.g., '93, 102 pages). All types of machine-scorable answer sheets available for use with a specific test are also reported in the descriptive entry. Scoring and reporting services provided by publishers are reported along with information on costs. In a few cases, special computerized scoring and interpretation services are noted at the end of the price information.

l) FOREIGN LANGUAGE AND OTHER SPECIAL EDITIONS. This section concerns foreign language editions published by the same publisher who sells the English edition. It also indicates special editions (e.g., Braille, large type) available from the same or a different publisher.

m) TIME. The number of minutes of actual working time allowed examinees and the approximate length of time needed for administering a test are reported whenever obtainable. The latter figure is always enclosed in parentheses. Thus, "50(60) minutes" indicates that the examinees are allowed 50 minutes of working time and that a total of 60 minutes is needed to administer the test. A time of "40–50 minutes" indicates an untimed test that takes approximately 45 minutes to administer, or—in a few instances—a test so timed that working time and administration time are very difficult to disentangle. When the time necessary to administer a test is not reported or suggested in the test materials but has been obtained from a catalog or through correspondence with the test publisher or author, the time is enclosed in brackets.

n) COMMENTS. Some entries contain special notations, such as: "for research use only"; "revision of the ABC Test"; "tests administered monthly at centers throughout the United States"; "subtests available as separates"; and "verbal creativity." A statement such as "verbal creativity" is intended to further describe what the test claims to measure. Some of the test entries include factual statements that imply criticism of the test, such as "1990 test identical with test copyrighted 1980."

o) AUTHOR. For most tests, all authors are reported. In the case of tests that appear in a new form each year, only authors of the most recent forms are listed. Names are reported exactly as printed on test booklets. Names of editors generally are not reported.

p) PUBLISHER. The name of the publisher or distributor is reported for each test. Foreign publishers are identified by listing the country in brackets immediately following the name of the publisher. The Publishers Directory and Index must be consulted for a publisher's address.

q) FOREIGN ADAPTATIONS. Revisions and adaptations of tests for foreign use are listed in a separate paragraph following the original edition.

r) SUBLISTINGS. Levels, editions, subtests, or parts of a test available in separate booklets are sometimes presented as sublistings with titles set in small capitals. Sub-sublistings are indented and titles are set in italic type.

s) CROSS REFERENCES. For tests that have been listed previously in a Buros Institute publication, a test entry includes—if relevant—a final item containing cross references to the reviews, excerpts, and references for that test in those volumes. In the cross references, "T4:467" refers to test 467 in *Tests in Print IV*, "8:1023" refers to test 1023 in *The Eighth Mental Measurements Yearbook*, "T3:144" refers to test 144 in *Tests in Print III*, "7:637" refers to test 637 in *The Seventh Mental Measurements Yearbook*, "P:262" refers to test 262 in *Personality Tests and Reviews*, "2:1427" refers to test 1427 in *The 1940 Yearbook*, and "1:1110" refers to test 1110 in *The 1938 Yearbook*. In the case of batteries and programs, the paragraph also includes cross references—from the battery to the separately listed subtests and vice versa—to entries in this volume and to entries and reviews in earlier *Yearbooks*. Test numbers not preceded by a colon refer to tests in this *Yearbook*; for example, "see 45" refers to test 45 in this *Yearbook*.

ACKNOWLEDGMENTS

The publication of the *13th Mental Measurements Yearbook* could not have been accomplished without the contributions of many individuals. The editors acknowledge gratefully the talent, expertise, and dedication of all those who have assisted in the publication process. Particular and special recognition is due to Jane Conoley, our friend and colleague, who edited many of the reviews in this volume before assuming a dean's job at another university. She is missed.

Linda Murphy, Managing Editor, is the glue that binds us together. Her dedication and level of effort are inspirational. In addition to her strong work ethic, she provides a historical base and a knowledge level that keeps us from making many errors we might make without her wise counsel. She makes our job as editors much more palatable than it would otherwise be. Nor would the publication of this volume be possible without the efforts of Gary Anderson, Editorial Assistant, and Rosemary Sieck, Clerical Assistant. As always, their efforts go far beyond that required as part of normal job responsibilities. Jane Gustafson, our Marketing Coordinator, has continued to provide conventional and innovative strategies for making users aware of the *MMY* series. Janice Nelsen's (Institute Secretary) helpful attitude, pleasant demeanor, and breadth of competence contributes greatly to our success. We appreciate all the efforts of these permanent staff, each of whom contributes more than their share to the development and production of all of the Buros Institute's products.

This volume would not exist without the substantial efforts of the test reviewers. We are very grateful to the many reviewers who have prepared test reviews for the Buros Institute. The willingness of these reviewers to take time from their busy professional schedules to share their expertise in the form of thoughtful test reviews is appreciated. *The Mental Measurements Yearbook* would not exist were it not for their efforts.

The work of many graduate students helps make possible the quality of this volume. Their efforts have included writing test descriptions, fact checking reviews, looking for test references, and innumerable other tasks. We thank Ted Carter, Jorge Gonzalez, Jessica Jonson, Gary Loya, Annie Mitchell, Heidi Paa, Robert Spies, Elisabeth Sundermeier, Suthakaran Veerasamy, and Yang Yongwei for their assistance.

Appreciation is also extended to our National and Departmental Advisory Committees for their willingness to assist in the operation of the Buros Institute and for their thought-provoking suggestions for improving the *MMY* series and other publications of the Buros Institute of Mental Measurements. During the period in which this volume was prepared the National Advisory Committee has included Gary Melton, Anthony Nitko, Charles Peterson, Lawrence Rudner, and Frank Schmidt.

The Buros Institute is part of the Department of Educational Psychology of the University of Nebraska-Lincoln and we have benefited from the many departmental colleagues who have contributed to our Departmental Advisory Committee. The current members are John Creswell, Terry Gutkin, Harold Keller, Lisa Larson, and Greg Schraw. We are also grateful for the contribution of the University of Nebraska Press, which provides expert consultation and serves as distributor of the *MMY* series.

SUMMARY

The *MMY* series is a valuable resource for people interested in studying or using tests. Once the process of using the series is understood, a reader can gain rapid access to a wealth of information. Our hope is that with the publication of the *13th MMY*, test authors and publishers will consider carefully the comments made by the reviewers and continue to refine and perfect their assessment products.

James C. Impara
Barbara S. Plake
March 1998

Tests and Reviews

[1]
AAMR Adaptive Behavior Scale—Residential and Community, Second Edition.

Purpose: To determine "an individual's strengths and weaknesses among adaptive domains and factors."

Population: Persons with disabilities in residential and community settings.

Publication Dates: 1969–1993.

Acronym: ABS-RC:2.

Scores, 23: 18 domain scores (10 part one domain scores: Independent Functioning, Physical Development, Economic Activity, Language Development, Numbers and Time, Domestic Activity, Prevocational/Vocational Activity, Self-Direction, Responsibility, Socialization; 8 part two domain scores: Social Behavior, Conformity, Trustworthiness, Stereotyped and Hyperactive Behavior, Sexual Behavior, Self-Abusive Behavior, Social Engagement, Disturbing Interpersonal Behavior); 5 factor scores (Personal Self-Sufficiency, Community Self-Sufficiency, Personal-Social Responsibility, Social Adjustment, Personal Adjustment).

Administration: Individual.

Price Data, 1994: $89 per complete kit including examiner's manual ('93, 76 pages), 25 examination booklets, and 25 profile/summary forms; $39 per 25 examination booklets; $18 per 25 profile/summary forms; $35 per examiner's manual; software scoring and report system available ($79 for Apple or IBM and $89 for Macintosh).

Time: Administration time not reported.

Authors: Kazuo Nihira, Henry Leland, and Nadine Lambert.

Publisher: PRO-ED, Inc.

Review of the AAMR Adaptive Behavior Scale—Residential and Community, Second Edition by KAREN T. CAREY, Associate Professor of Psychology, California State University, Fresno, Fresno, CA:

The American Association on Mental Retardation's (AAMR) Adaptive Behavior Scale—Residential and Community, Second Edition (ABS-RC:2) was developed for persons through 79 years of age and is a revision of the AAMR Adaptive Behavior Scales. The scale is designed to meet the 1992 AAMR definition of mental retardation that includes limitations in two or more of the "critical" areas, an intelligence quotient of 70–75 or below, and an age of onset below 18 years. The authors use Heber's (1961) definition of adaptive behavior: "the manner in which people cope with the natural and social demands of their environments" (manual, p. 1), and define impairments of adaptive behavior as described by Grossman (1983) as "significant limitations in an individual's effectiveness in meeting the standards of maturation, learning, personal independence, and/or social responsibility that are expected for his or her age level and cultural group, as determined by clinical assessment, and usually standardized scales" (manual, p. 1).

The ABS-RC:2 is divided into Part One, which includes the areas of personal independence and responsibility in daily living, and Part Two, which focuses on social behaviors. Ten domains are included in Part One: Independent Functioning, Physical Development, Economic Activity, Language Development, Numbers and Time, Domestic Activity, Prevocational/Vocational Activity, Self-Direction, Responsibility, and Socialization. Within each domain are subdomains that include specific areas such as "Care of Clothing" under the Independent Functioning domain. The subscales in Part Two include Social Behavior, Self-Abusive Behavior, Social Engagement, and Disturbing Interpersonal Behavior. Points are obtained for each domain by summing item points within each domain. Percentile ranks, standard scores, and age equivalents (for Part One only) can then be obtained for each domain. Factor analyses of the domains revealed three factors for Part One and two factors for Part Two. Part One factors are Personal Self-Sufficiency (which includes the Independent Functioning and Physical Development Domains), Community Self-Sufficiency (which includes the domains of Independent Functioning, Economic Activity, Language Development, Numbers and Time, and Domestic Activity), and Personal Social Responsibility (which includes the domains of Prevocational/Vocational Activity, Responsibility, and Socialization). Part Two factors are Social Adjustment (from the domains of Social Behavior, Conformity, and Trustworthiness) and Personal Adjustment (which includes the domains of Stereotyped and Hyperactive Behavior, Sexual Behavior, and Self-Abusive Behavior). Item raw scores from each of the domains that make up the factors are summed, resulting in standard scores, percentile ranks, and age equivalents (for Part One).

The scale is completed by the examiner him/herself or through an interview format based on another's knowledge of the individual being assessed. Most domains consist of subdomains within which there are a series of items. For example, in Part One of the Independent Functioning Domain there are eight subdomains that include Eating, Toilet Use, Cleanliness, etc. Within each subdomain there are a series of items (e.g., for the subdomain of Eating there are four items that include use of table utensils, eating in public, drinking, and table manners). Some items consist of statements that are arranged in order of difficulty (i.e., 3, 2, 1, 0) from most difficult to least difficult and the examiner circles the appropriate number of the statement that refers to what the individual can "usually" manage. The difficulty number is then recorded in a box adjacent to the item for easy summing upon completion of the scale. Other items require the examiner to read statements and circle either "yes" or "no." The total number of "no" responses are summed for each item and recorded in the adjacent box.

For items in Part Two, the examiner identifies the frequency of occurrence of each behavior. For example, a "0" is circled if the individual never engages in a behavior, a "1" is circled if the behavior occurs occasionally, and a "2" is circled if the behavior occurs frequently. The points for each item are recorded in the adjacent item box. An "other" line is provided for additional problem behaviors the examiner may observe.

The sum of the item scores for both Parts One and Two are then totaled and placed on the Profile/Summary Form. The Profile/Summary Form also includes a worksheet for computing the factor scores, a profile of scores page, and a comments/recommendations section. A software scoring and report system is available from the publisher.

Standard scores for the scale are based on a mean of 10 and a standard deviation of 3; factor scores are based on a mean of 100 and a standard deviation of 15. Age equivalents for Part One are based on the raw scores of a sample of "normal" individuals from 3 to 17 years. The Scale was standardized on 4,103 individuals with "developmental disabilities" in 46 states and the District of Columbia. The norming sample was selected to represent the national population with developmental disabilities. Although the sample is well represented by Whites and African Americans, percentages are somewhat lower for the Hispanic population (percentage of sample = 3.8; percentage of nation = 8.2) and Asians (.8 for the sample and 5.2 for the nation). Persons included in the sample had additional disabilities of blindness, deafness, emotional disturbance, learning disability, physical impairments, and speech/language impairments.

Reliability was examined in several different ways. First, all of the subjects in the sample served as subjects for internal consistency studies using coefficient alpha. Results ranged from .80 to .99 for both Parts One and Two. Stability was investigated with 45 individuals employed in a sheltered workshop (median age = 42 years). The ABS-RC:2 was initially completed by the individuals' supervisors and completed a second time by the same persons 2 weeks later. Correlation coefficients for Parts One and Two ranged from .81 to .99. Interscorer reliability was examined by having two graduate students independently score 16 protocols, resulting in correlations ranging from .83 to .99 for both parts.

A series of validation studies was also completed. For item analysis, subjects in the norming group served as subjects. Item discrimination coefficients ranged from .29 to .79. Criterion-related validity was investigated in two studies. In the first study, 63 individuals in the standardization sample were also given the Vineland Adaptive Behavior Scales. Information related to the ages of these individuals is not provided in the manual. Correlations ranged from nonsignificant on the domains of Prevocational/Vocational Activity, Self-Direction, and all scales of Part Two except for Self-Abusive Behavior (a -.30 correlation was found for this domain) to .71. A second study was conducted with 30 "students" (no information is provided on the ages of this sample) who were also given the Adaptive Behavior Inventory. Correlation coefficients range from nonsignificant on Part Two to .67 on Part One. The authors explain the nonsignificant correlations for both studies by stating that the Vineland Adaptive Behavior Scale and the Adaptive Behavior Inventory measure *adaptive* behavior, whereas Part Two of the ABS-RC:2 measures maladaptive behaviors.

Construct validity evidence was provided by interrelations of the domain and factor scores using the norming sample. Intercorrelations for Part One range from .47 to .88. Intercorrelations between Part One and Part Two were significantly lower and the authors offer a caveat stating "one would not expect the Part One and Part Two domains and factors to intercorrelate very highly with one another because they are measuring different constructs" (manual, p. 37).

Correlation coefficients were also calculated for subjects in the sample who had been administered standardized intelligence tests. These tests included the Stanford Binet (n = 545), the Leiter International Performance Scale (n = 116), the Slosson Intelligence Test (n = 290), and the Wechsler Adult Intelligence Scale—Revised (n = 1,046). Correlation coefficients indicated that Part One of the ABS-RC:2 correlates with traditional intelligence tests (ranges from .27 to .73). Correlation coefficients between these intelligence tests and Part Two were significantly lower (ranging from -.25 to .22).

Ecological validity included having supervisors and parents/guardians complete the scale with the 45 employees from the sheltered workshop. Correlation coefficients ranged from .25 to .88 on Part One and from .07 to .85 on Part Two.

The manual of the ABS-RC:2 is clearly written and the Scale appears easy to use for those familiar with standardized tests. Appendices include norm tables for converting raw scores to standard scores, percentile ranks, and age equivalents, and a sample printout of the software scoring and report system.

In summary, it appears the scale could be quite useful for those attempting to assess the adaptive and maladaptive behaviors of individuals with disabilities. The scale is technically adequate for such assessments

and provides items not available on other instruments.

REVIEWER'S REFERENCES

Heber, R. (1961). A manual on terminology and classification on mental retardation (2nd ed.). *Monograph Supplement to the American Journal on Mental Deficiency.*

Grossman, H. J. (Ed.). (1983). *Classification in mental retardation.* Washington, DC: American Association on Mental Deficiency.

Review of the AAMR Adaptive Behavior Scale— Residential and Community, Second Edition by PATTI L. HARRISON, Professor and Chair, Educational and School Psychology Program, The University of Alabama, Tuscaloosa, AL:

The AAMR Adaptive Behavior Scale—Residential and Community, Second Edition (ABS-RC:2) is a comprehensive rating scale designed for assessment of individuals with developmental disabilities. The ABS-RC:2 is the latest revision of a widely used instrument. The manual notes that the ABS-RC:2 represents the results of numerous item analyses and modifications of the 1969 and 1974 versions, but describes few specific differences between the current and earlier versions. The manual also fails to note differences between the ABS-RC:2 and its companion, the Adaptive Behavior Scale—School, Second Edition (ABS-S:2; Lambert, Nihira, & Leland, 1993; 2). Because the ABS-RC:2 and ABS-S:2 are almost identical, it would have been helpful for the authors to provide information about the type of clients, informants, etc., for which each instrument should be used.

TECHNICAL DATA. The ABS-RC:2 was standardized with a sample of 4,103 adults, aged 18–60+ years, with developmental disabilities. The manual lists demographic characteristics of the sample and provides evidence of good representation. National data are reported for comparison with some variables (e.g., ethnicity, urban/rural), but the manual does not indicate if the national data were based on the total U.S. population or only adults with developmental disabilities. Three characteristics of the norm sample have implications for scoring and interpretation. First, about 80% of the sample resided in small community facilities or large residential facilities and only 20% resided with parents or lived independently. These data suggest that the functioning of many adults in the sample was low enough to require relatively significant amounts of professional support. Second, the ABS-RC:2 does not include a norm sample of adults with typical functioning, and most norm-referenced scores only indicate a client's relative standing in comparison to adults with developmental disabilities. Third, the manual indicates that age equivalents for the ABS-RC:2 were generated using normative data for children without mental retardation gathered during development of the ABS-S:2.

The manual provides an array of reliability and validity data. Internal consistency coefficients range from .80–.98 for domains and .92–.99 for factors. A small sample of 45 employees of a sheltered workshop yielded stability coefficients in the .80s and .90s. Two graduate students computed final scores for 16 protocols and had high interscorer agreement.

Item, criterion, and construct validity data are reported and, although some studies are characterized by small samples, data provide solid evidence of the ABS-RC:2's validity. Item discrimination power appears to be adequate. Correlations between the ABS-RC:2 and Vineland and Adaptive Behavior Inventory for a small sample of 30 students range from .31–.71. Age differentiation data indicate that scores increase with age for children without developmental disabilities but do not increase for adults with developmental disabilities. Correlations between adaptive behavior domains and factors on the ABS-RC:2 and mental ability tests for large samples of adults with developmental disabilities are generally in the moderate range. Comparison of mean scores between groups with and without developmental disabilities and between groups residing in community versus large residential settings support the scale's discriminant validity. Correlations between two informants (parents and supervisors) for a small group of sheltered workshop employees range from .07–.88. Although fairly high intercorrelations raise questions about the specificity of individual adaptive behavior domain and factor scores, confirmatory factor analysis provides support for the five factors of the ABS-RC:2. The manual also lists references for many research studies conducted with earlier versions of the instrument.

ADMINISTRATION. The ABS-RC:2 consists of a large number of items measuring behaviors in both adaptive and maladaptive domains. Two item types are included in Part One of the questionnaire booklet and could be confusing for inexperienced informants. One item type lists behaviors in order of difficulty (e.g., "uses no money" through "taking complete care of his or her money"), and the informant selects only the highest level of behavior exhibited by the client. The other item type lists a large number of related behaviors, and informants indicate "yes" or "no" in response to each behavior.

The manual indicates that the instrument may be completed by a trained professional who has direct knowledge of the client or through an interview by a trained professional with a third party informant. However, the manual provides no guidance for interviewing, and appropriate techniques are often critical when interviewing parents or nonprofessionals. The manual also provides limited instructions for addressing a major problem in administration of rating scales: Even the most knowledgeable informants are often unable to respond to some of the items because they have insufficient opportunities to observe the client. The manual notes that an alternative informant should be used when the initial informant has insufficient knowledge, but does not describe how to score an item when even the best informant has no knowledge to rate the item.

SCORING AND INTERPRETATION. Item scores are summed to yield domain raw scores that can be transformed to norm-referenced percentile ranks, standard scores ($M = 10$; $SD = 3$), and age equivalents. Determination of factor scores requires complex calculations with both item and domain scores, and the accompanying computer scoring program is useful for determining factor scores. Norm-referenced factor scores include percentile ranks, standard scores ($M = 100$; $SD = 15$), and age equivalents.

The nature of the norm sample, described above, results in some important implications—and potential confusion—when interpreting scores for the ABS-RC:2. The manual gives only limited cautions about these implications. First, interpretation must always acknowledge that percentile ranks and standard scores indicate a client's relative standing compared to *a norm group of adults with developmental disabilities*, primarily adults in small and large residential facilities. Unlike scores from intelligence tests and other measures that often indicate a person's standing relative to people with typical development, ABS-RC:2 standard scores and percentile ranks do not suggest strengths or deficits relative to the general norm for adults. A standard score of 120 on an ABS-RC:2 factor indicates that the client is above average, compared to people with developmental disabilities, but gives no information about the person's standing compared to adults with "normal" functioning.

Second, given the restrictions of the norm sample, the entire range of standard scores is not possible for some domains and factors of the ABS-RC:2. For example, the lowest possible standard score for both the Economic Activity and the Numbers and Times domains is 6. For 60+-year-olds, the lowest possible standard score for the Personal Self-Sufficiency factor is 63. Professionals may find these standard scores unexpectedly high for a client, for example, whose IQ is below 40 and whose adaptive functioning seems very limited.

Third, the age equivalents, based on the ABS-RC:2 scores of a norm sample of children with no mental retardation, can be misleading. Age equivalents are problematic for any instrument, as noted in the manual, but these problems are magnified when professionals attempt to interpret age equivalents along with the standard scores and percentile ranks on the ABS-RC:2. Sample scores for a 33-year-old client, presented on pages 12–14 in the manual, illustrate the problems. For example, on the Personal-Social Responsibility Factor, the sample client obtained a standard score of 101, suggesting average functioning in relation to other people with developmental disabilities, but an age equivalent of 3–9, suggesting functioning well below expectations for a 33-year-old.

CONCLUSIONS. The ABS-RC:2 has many features that enhance the assessment of adults with developmental disabilities. It is a comprehensive instrument and provides extensive coverage of many important adaptive and maladaptive behaviors. The manual reports the results of many reliability and validity studies, and these data, along with a wealth of research with earlier versions, provide ample support for using the instrument. Only two major problems are obvious, and these should be taken into account by professionals using the instrument. The manual does not provide enough information about administration and interviewing techniques. Interpretation is hindered by inclusion of norm-referenced comparisons with adults with developmental disabilities only and failure to include norm-referenced comparisons with the general adult population. The authors are encouraged to address these problems in subsequent revisions of the instrument.

REVIEWER'S REFERENCE

Lambert, N., Nihira, K., & Leland, H. (1993). Adaptive Behavior Scale—School, Second Edition. Austin, TX: PRO-ED, Inc.

[2]
AAMR Adaptive Behavior Scale—School, Second Edition.

Purpose: "Used to assess adaptive behavior."
Population: Ages 3–21.
Publication Dates: 1981–1993.
Acronym: ABS-S:2.

Scores, 21: 16 domain scores (9 part one domain scores: Independent Functioning, Physical Development, Economic Activity, Language Development, Numbers and Time, Prevocational/Vocational Activity, Self-Direction, Responsibility, Socialization; 7 part two domain scores: Social Behavior, Conformity, Trustworthiness, Stereotyped and Hyperactive Behavior, Self-Abusive Behavior, Social Engagement, Disturbing Interpersonal Behavior), 5 factor scores (Personal Self-Sufficiency, Community Self-Sufficiency, Personal-Social Responsibility, Social Adjustment, Personal Adjustment).
Administration: Individual.
Price Data, 1994: $89 per complete kit including examiner's manual ('93, 118 pages), 25 examination booklets, and 25 profile/summary forms; $39 per 25 examination booklets; $18 per 25 profile/summary forms; $35 per examiner's manual; software scoring and report system available ($79 for Apple or IBM, $89 for Macintosh).
Time: Administration time not reported.
Comments: Previously called AAMD Adaptive Behavior Scale.
Authors: Nadine Lambert, Kazuo Nihira, and Henry Leland.
Publisher: PRO-ED, Inc.
Cross References: See T4:2 (42 references); for a review of an earlier edition by Stephen N. Elliot, see 9:3 (9 references); see also T3:6 (55 references); for reviews of an earlier edition by Morton Bortner and C. H. Ammons and R. B. Ammons, see 8:493 (25 references); see also T2:1092 (3 references); for reviews of an earlier edition by Lovick C. Miller and Melvyn I. Semmel, see 7:37 (9 references).

TEST REFERENCES

1. Lovett, D. L., & Harris, M. B. (1987). Identification of important community living skills for adults with mental retardation. *Rehabilitation Counseling Bulletin, 31,* 34–41.
2. Perry, A., & Factor, D. C. (1989). Psychometric validity and clinical usefulness of the Vineland Adaptive Behavior Scales and the AAMD Adaptive Behavior Scale for an autistic sample. *Journal of Autism and Developmental Disorders, 19*(1), 41-55.
3. Henderson, D., & Vandenberg, B. (1992). Factors influencing adjustment in the families of autistic children. *Psychological Reports, 71,* 167–171.
4. Rousey, A., Best, S., & Blacher, J. (1992). Mothers' and fathers' perceptions of stress and coping with children who have severe disabilities. *American Journal on Mental Retardation, 97,* 99-109.
5. Cheramie, G. M. (1994). The AAMD Adaptive Behavior Scale—School Edition, Part Two: Test-retest reliability and parent-teacher agreement in a behavior disordered sample. *Perceptual and Motor Skills, 79,* 275-283.
6. Macmillan, D. L., Siperstein, G. N., & Gresham, F. M. (1996). A challenge to the viability of mild mental retardation as a diagnostic category. *Exceptional Children, 62,* 356–371.

Review of the AAMR Adaptive Behavior Scale— School, Second Edition by ROBERT G. HARRINGTON, Professor of Educational Psychology and Research, University of Kansas, Lawrence, KS:

The primary use of the Adaptive Behavior Scale—School, Second Edition (ABS-S:2) is to assess the adaptive functioning of school-age children who may be mentally retarded; however, it also has been utilized to evaluate adaptive behavior characteristics of autistic children (Perry & Factor, 1989) and to identify behavior-disordered children (Cheramie & Edwards, 1990). Heber (1961) has defined adaptive behavior as the manner in which individuals cope with the natural and social demands of their environment, and more recently, Grossman (1983) has elaborated on this basic definition to include standards of maturation, learning, personal independence, and/or social responsibility in reference to age peers and cultural group. Adaptive behavior in combination with significantly below average intellectual functioning continues to play a major role in identifying individuals with mental delays as exemplified in the *1992 Diagnosis, Classification, and System of Supports* (American Association on Mental Retardation, 1992).

The ABS-S:2 is the 1993 revision of the 1975 and 1981 AAMD Adaptive Behavior Scales. Part 1 of the scale focuses on personal independence behaviors grouped into nine domains. Part 2 deals with social behaviors grouped into seven domains. The ABS-S:2 can be completed by professionals with direct information about the target child or can be administered in interview fashion by a third party. In this latter case, good interviewing skills are a prerequisite. The ABS-S:2 is relatively easy for the experienced professional to administer, score, and interpret. The instrument comes complete with a comprehensive, easy-to-follow examination booklet and a separate profile summary form. The ABS-S:2 renders a combination of 16 domain scores with a standard score mean of 10 and standard deviation of 3 and three factor scores on Part 1 and two factor scores on Part 2 with standard score means of 100 and standard deviations of 15. In total, the ABS-S:2 yields five types of scores including raw scores, percentiles, domain standard scores, factor standard scores, and age equivalents. Norms are provided for a normal sample and for a sample of children with mental retardation. Unlike the previous edition of the test there are no separate norms for individuals who are trainable mentally retarded. Although interest scores can be compared using a regression procedure, the clinician is cautioned to never compare domain and factor scores because domain scores are contained in the factor scores.

The scale was normed using a stratified random sampling procedure on 2,074 persons with mental retardation and 1,254 persons without mental retardation from a national U.S. sample. Items were selected for inclusion on the ABS-S:2 based upon careful review of items from previous versions of the

test and based upon their interrater reliability and ability to discriminate groups varying with respect to adaptive behavior levels. Because the ABS-S:2 contains relatively few item changes from previous versions, earlier studies of item reliability are relied upon heavily by the authors to support the item reliability of the current test (Bensberg & Irons, 1986; Brulle & Hoernicke, 1984; Givens, 1980; Givens & Ward, 1982; Lambert & Windmiller, 1981; Mayfield, Forman, & Nagel, 1984).

In an internal consistency study of the standardization samples the factor scores were found to be the most reliable, yielding coefficients in excess of .90 in most instances for both standardization groups. The standard errors of measurement for the ABS-S:2 scores were uniformly low reflecting a high degree of scale reliability. In one test-retest reliability study of 25 male and 20 female employees in a sheltered workshop, results supported the stability of the test with correlations generally in the .90 range and above (Nihira, Leland, & Lambert, 1993), but in a second test-retest study in which high school teachers completed protocols on 45 students with emotional disturbances in grades 9 through 11, three of the subtests received coefficients in the .70 range and most were at least in the .80 range. A reliability coefficient of at least .80 is considered minimal and thus this second study is somewhat disappointing leading one to question whether the reduced test reliability might be attributed to the sample of children with emotional disturbances under study. In an interscorer reliability study two trained professionals tabulated the raw scores for each domain and factor for 15 completed protocols. Partial correlations were in the high .90 range demonstrating excellent interscorer agreement for simply calculating standard scores from raw scores. Unfortunately, however, no interscorer agreements are reported for interviewers deriving raw scores for individual items, which of course is the more subjective scoring task. The unanswered question of whether two independent interviewers would agree on how to score a response to individual items on the test is a serious omission to the examiner's manual.

The validity of the ABS-S:2 is based heavily upon previous research on earlier versions of the scale (Cheramie & Edwards, 1990; Lambert & Windmiller, 1981) and some recent research into its content, criterion-related, and construct validity. Content validity of Part 1, the Adaptive Behavior Scale, was established through a critical review of domains and items in other existing behavior rating scales, through item analyses to determine which items discriminated between groups of individuals judged to be functioning at different adaptive behavior levels, and by the degree to which correlations showed each item measured adaptive behavior independent of intelligence. Part 2, The Maladaptive Behavior Scale, was developed based upon descriptions of types of behavior considered unacceptable or beyond the tolerance threshold of those with daily contact with individuals with mental retardation. Median item discrimination coefficients that were generated for the domains and factors as a result of item analysis using the point-biserial correlation technique were, on the average, substantially above the .20 minimum recommended by Garrett (1965) for discriminating power or item validity at all ages assessed by the scale. In several small sample studies of the criterion-related validity of the ABS-S:2 with the Vineland Adaptive Behavior Scale (Sparrow, Balla, & Cichetti, 1984; Nihira, Leland, & Lambert, 1993), and the ABS-S:2 with the short form of the Adaptive Behavior Inventory (ABI; Brown & Leigh, 1986) results showed that Part 1, the Adaptive Behavior Scale, correlated moderately well with these other adaptive behavior scales, but Part 2, the Maladaptive Scale, correlated poorly with these measures of adaptive behavior. This finding is to be expected and provides support for the criterion-related validity of the ABS-S:2.

Because adaptive behavior is an age-related construct the test developers tested whether scores increased with age for samples of 3- to 17-year-olds with and without mental retardation, and a sample of adults with developmental disabilities. Mean raw scores rose steadily with the normal subjects, were less pronounced with the subjects with mental retardation, and the increases were almost nonexistent for the adults with developmental disabilities. Correlation coefficients between raw scores and age confirmed these results. This progression of scores for the three groups sampled provides support for the age-related nature of adaptive behavior. A review of an intercorrelation matrix for the ABS-S:2 domains and factors from Part 1 and Part 2 of the scale shows moderate to strong correlations for those domains and factors contained in Part 1 and those in Part 2, but as expected, little correlation between domains and factors on Part 1 and Part 2. This finding supports the contention that the domains and factors on the two separate parts of the scale are related. To evaluate the relationship between the ABS-S:2 and mental ability tests several studies were conducted and reported in the examiner's manual comparing the ABS-S:2 with the Stanford-Binet Intelligence Scale (Terman & Merrill, 1972); the Leiter International Performance Scale (Levine, 1982), the Slosson Intelligence Test (Slosson, 1971), the Wechsler Adult Intelligence Scale—Revised (WAIS-R; Wechsler, 1981), the Wechsler Intelligence Scale for Children—Revised (WISC-R; Wechsler, 1974), the Peabody Picture Vocabulary Test—Revised (PPVT-R; Dunn & Dunn, 1981), and the General Mental Ability Quotient of the Detroit Tests of Learning Aptitude—3 (DTLA-3; Hammill, 1992). Results showed moderate positive correlations between domain and factor scores on Part 1 and these measures of mental ability, but nonsignificant positive correlations and even negative correlations between the domain and factor scores on Part 2 and the mental ability tests. These results are as expected and provide support for the construct validity of the scale.

Visual analyses of descriptive differences in mean raw scores among adults with mental retardation, young people with mental retardation, and young people without mental retardation are presented in tabular form as evidence of the discriminative validity of the ABS-S:2, but the authors present no statistical tests to better make their case. The authors concede the ABS-S:2 has less discriminative validity at the younger age levels due to the fact that both normal children and children with mental retardation are developing new skills in adaptive behavior. A LISREL VII analysis was conducted as a confirmatory factor analysis of the factor structure of the ABS-S:2 of students with mental retardation. Standardized path coefficients depicting the factor loadings associated with each component were fairly large and positive showing support for the factorial validity of the ABS-S:2. Finally, as a test of the ecological validity of the scale 50 teachers and 50 teacher aides completed ABS-S:2 protocols on 50 students with emotional disabilities. Correlations between these two groups are in the .50 to .90 range showing a good relationship between the observations of respondents and demonstrating that respondents report similar behavior patterns across environments.

In summary, there are still some outstanding questions left unanswered about the reliability and validity of the ABS-S:2. Some of the reliability coefficients are below the desirable .90 level needed for making critical diagnostic decisions about the adaptive functioning status of children. Furthermore, there is some evidence that Part 1 of the scale is probably inappropriate for children with physical disabilities, sensory impairments, emotional disabilities, and for very young children. In particular, there is evidence that in evaluating the adaptive behavior levels of deaf-blind children, the language development items (Domain IV) of the ABS-S:2 should be modified to allow credit to be given for alternative methods of communication, such as sign language, Braille, and finger spelling as has been suggested previously (Suess, Cotten, & Sisson, 1983). Otherwise these children will be penalized and scores will represent an underestimate of their true adaptive behaviors in the Language Development domain.

In future research the test developers must show evidence for the interscorer reliability of test items. Furthermore, they should demonstrate statistically the discriminative validity of the scale. More independent research using larger sample sizes should be conducted on the validity of the instrument. It is clear the test developers are overrelying upon research from the two previous versions of the test to bolster their position for the reliability and validity of the current scale.

Previous versions of the ABS have been among the most widely used measures (Allen-Meares & Lane, 1983; Cantrell, 1982; Coulter & Morrow, 1978). When compared to other available measures of adaptive behavior such as the Scales of Independent Behavior (SIB; Bruininks, Woodcock, Weatherman, & Hill, 1984) and the Vineland Adaptive Behavior Scales (VABS; Sparrow, Balla, & Cicchetti, 1984), it is clear that the ABS-S:2 does make a contribution to the area of adaptive behavior assessment. It is a very comprehensive scale that covers not only adaptive behaviors but maladaptive behaviors as well. However, it is unclear what role the Maladaptive Behavior Scale should play in the identification of children with mental retardation or emotional disturbances. It has considerable item coverage. It is easy to score and administer. It is adapted for use by teachers in public school classrooms and can be computer scored. Unfortunately, no interpretive case studies are provided in the Examiner's Manual. When deciding among the various available adaptive behavior scales it is probably best for the examiner to ask the following important questions: Does the adaptive behavior scale cover areas that I am interested in assessing? Does the adaptive behavior scale have a sufficient floor given the age level and adaptive

behavior level of the client I am assessing? Can the assessment results be translated into useful intervention plans? The answers to these questions will vary with the referred individual, and for this reason no general recommendation can be made for any adaptive behavior scale. The ABS-S:2 is, however, a major improvement over the previous version of the scale given that it has addressed many of the criticisms mentioned by Sattler (1988) and should be given serious consideration whenever the adaptive behavior of a school-age subject must be evaluated for possible mental retardation or whenever independent functioning skills need to be assessed as a part of a multifaceted assessment.

REVIEWER'S REFERENCES

Heber, R. (1961). A manual on terminology and classification on mental retardation (2nd ed.). *Monograph Supplement to the American Journal of Mental Deficiency* (now Retardation).

Garrett, H. (1965). *Testing for teachers* (2nd ed.). New York: American Book Company.

Slosson, R. L. (1971). Slosson Intelligence Test. East Aurora, NY: Slosson Educational Publications.

Terman, L. M., & Merrill, M. A. (1972). Stanford-Binet Intelligence Scale, 1972 Norms Edition. Boston: Houghton-Mifflin.

Wechsler, D. (1974). Wechsler Intelligence Scale for Children—Revised. San Antonio: The Psychological Corporation.

Coulter, W. A., & Morrow, H. W. (1978). Requiring adaptive behavior measurement. *Exceptional Children, 45*, 133–135.

Givens, T. (1980). Scorer reliability on the AAMD Adaptive Behavior Scale—Public School Version Part One. *Psychology in the Schools, 17*, 335–338.

Dunn, L. M., & Dunn, L. M. (1981). Peabody Picture Vocabulary Test—Revised. Circle Pines, MN: American Guidance Service.

Lambert, N. M., & Windmiller, M. (1981). AAMD Adaptive Behavior Scale—School Edition. Monterey, CA: Publishers Test Service.

Wechsler, D. (1981). Wechsler Adult Intelligence Scale—Revised. San Antonio: The Psychological Corporation.

Cantrell, J. K. (1982). Assessing adaptive behavior: Current practices. *Education and Training of the Mentally Retarded, 17*, 147–149.

Givens, T., & Ward, L. C. (1982). Stability of the AAMD Adaptive Behavior Scale—Public School Version. *Psychology in the Schools, 19*, 166–169.

Levine, M. N. (1982). Leiter International Performance Scale. Los Angeles: Western Psychological Services.

Allen-Meares, P., & Lane, B. A. (1983). Assessing the adaptive behavior of children and youths. *Social Work, 28*, 297–301.

Grossman, H. J. (Ed.). (1983). *Classification in mental retardation.* Washington, DC: American Association on Mental Deficiency (now Retardation).

Suess, J. F., Cotten, P. D., & Sisson, G. F. P., Jr. (1983). The American Association on Mental Deficiency—Adaptive Behavior Scale: Allowing credit for alternative means of communication. *American Annals of the Deaf, 128*, 390–393.

Bruininks, R. H., Woodcock, R. W., Weatherman, R. F., & Hill, B. K. (1984). Scales of Independent Behavior (SIB). Chicago, IL: The Riverside Publishing Co.

Brulle, A. R., & Hoernicke, F. A. (1984). A brief report on the reliability of the public school version of the AAMD Adaptive Behavior Scale. *Mental Retardation and Learning Disability Bulletin, 122*, 115–118.

Mayfield, K. L., Forman, S. G., & Nagel, R. J. (1984). Reliability of the AAMD Adaptive Behavior Scale—Public School Version. *Journal of School Psychology, 22*, 53–61.

Sparrow, S. S., Balla, D. A., & Cicchetti, D. V. (1984). Vineland Adaptive Behavior Scales. Circle Pines, MN: American Guidance Service.

Bensberg, G. J., & Irons, T. (1986). A comparison of the AAMD Adaptive Behavior Scale and the Vineland Adaptive Behavior Scale within a sample of persons classified as moderately and severely mentally retarded. *Education and Training of the Mentally Retarded, 21*, 220–229.

Brown, L., & Leigh, J. E. (1986). Adaptive Behavior Inventory. Austin, TX: PRO-ED, Inc.

Sattler, J. M. (1989). *Assessment of children.* San Diego, CA: Sattler Publishing Co.

Perry, A., & Factor, D. C. (1989). Psychometric validity and clinical usefulness of the Vineland Adaptive Behavior Scales and the AAMD Adaptive Scales for an autistic sample. *Journal of Autism and Developmental Disorders, 19*, 42–55.

Cheramie, G. M., & Edwards, R. P. (1990). The AAMD ABS-SE Part Two: Criterion-related validity in a behavior-disordered sample. *Psychology in the Schools, 27*, 186–195.

American Association on Mental Retardation. (1992). *Mental retardation: Definition, classification, and systems of support* (9th ed.). Washington, DC: American Association on Mental Retardation.

Hammill, D. D. (1992). Detroit Tests of Learning Aptitude—Third Edition. Austin, TX: PRO-ED, Inc.

Nihira, K., Leland, H., & Lambert, N. (1993). Adaptive Behavior Scale—Residential and Community: Second Edition. Austin, TX: PRO-ED, Inc.

Review of the AAMR Adaptive Behavior Scale—School: Second Edition by TERRY A. STINNETT, Associate Professor of Applied Behavioral Studies in Education, Oklahoma State University, Stillwater, OK:

The AAMR Adaptive Behavior Scale—School: Second Edition (ABS-S:2) is the most recent revision of the 1975 AAMD Adaptive Behavior Scale, Public School Version (ABS-PSV). The ABS-PSV was first revised in 1981 and the scale was renamed the AAMD Adaptive Behavior Scale, School Edition (ABS-SE). The ABS-SE was a notable improvement over the first version of the scale (Elliott, 1985) and the ABS-S:2 revision has improved the scale further.

The authors of the ABS-S:2 define the adaptive behavior construct as the individual's typical performance in coping with environmental demands. The scale is designed to measure school-age children's personal and community independence and adaptive qualities that are associated with personal and social performance and adjustment. Those qualities are reflected by the specific domains and factors included on the instrument. The authors propose the scale to be useful for determining an individual's strengths and weaknesses in specific adaptive behavior domains and factors, for identifying students who are significantly below their peers in adaptive functioning, for documenting an individual's progress and assessing the effects of intervention programs, and for research. The ABS-S:2 likely will be used to diagnose persons with developmental disabilities in conjunction with individually administered intelligence measures.

The ABS-S:2 is appropriate for use with individuals through 21 years of age. Adaptive behavior ratings can be obtained first person when the rater has personal knowledge of the individual being rated or through a third party informant interview. The third party informant should be a person who knows the individual well. If the informant does not have information to give answers to all items, then additional or alternate informants must be obtained. However, information from several individuals should not be combined into a single rating.

The ABS-S:2 has been logically divided by its authors into two parts. Part 1 contains nine behavior domains with 18 subdomains intended to measure personal independence and personal responsibility in daily living. Part 2 contains seven domains that pertain to behaviors that relate to personality and behavior disorders. The Part 1 domains include Independent Functioning (24 items), Physical Development (6 items), Economic Activity (6 items), Language Development (10 items), Numbers and Time (3 items), Prevocational/Vocational Activity (3 items), Self-Direction (5 items), Responsibility (3 items), and Socialization (7 items with one supplemental item for females). The Part 2 domains include Social Behavior (7 items), Conformity (6 items), Trustworthiness (6 items), Stereotyped and Hyperactive Behavior (5 items), Self-Abusive Behavior (3 items), Social Engagement (4 items), and Disturbing Interpersonal Behavior (6 items with one supplemental item).

Part 1 items are presented in two different formats. One format presents a number of separate component behaviors ordered by difficulty level within each item for the overall adaptive skill that is being assessed (e.g., table manners). The rater picks a single option from the list of behaviors for the item that represents the highest level of the task the person can usually achieve. Because the options within the items are ranked and assigned point values by difficulty level, higher point values indicate performance of higher adaptive level. These items can have different maximum point values based on the number of options within each item. For example, an item with three options could have a maximum of 3 points, whereas an item with six options could have 6 points value. Other Part 1 items are formatted so that the rater indicates by circling "yes" or "no" whether the person can accomplish tasks. Socially acceptable behaviors are give 1 point and inappropriate behaviors are given zero points. These different item types are scattered throughout Part 1 so users should be vigilant to ensure the protocol is correctly completed. The different item formats could especially be a problem if a first party rater completes the protocol instead of having an experienced user of the scale collect the data through interview.

Part 2 items are of a third type. The rater responds to a 3-point Likert that typifies the frequency the individual performs certain behaviors (i.e., "N" never, "O" occasionally, and "F" frequently). There is also space on the protocol for raters to write in additional behaviors that are not included in the item; hence, Part 2 can reflect idiosyncrasies of the person being rated.

The ABS-S:2 raw scores are the total number of points obtained on the scale's items within the specific domains. A positive feature of the scale is that there are Mental Retardation Norms or Non-Mental Retardation norms available for users to select at their discretion. However, the authors do not provide suggestions to help users determine which norm set to use. Raw scores can be converted to standard scores (M = 10, SD = 3), percentile rank scores, and age equivalent scores for all nine Part 1 domains. Similarly, standard scores and percentile rank scores can also be derived for the seven Part 2 domains. Age equivalents are not available for the Part 2 domains. The authors report performance on the Part 2 domains is not age related, that is the raw scores for these domains did not increase or decrease with age sufficiently to calculate age equivalent scores. Rating labels are available for all domains (e.g., Very Superior to Very Poor). Finally, three factor scores can be calculated from Part 1 items: Personal Self-Sufficiency, Community Self-Sufficiency, and Personal-Social Responsibility. Part 2 items can yield two factor scores: Social Adjustment and Personal Adjustment. Part 1 factor scores can be converted to standard scores (M = 100, SD = 15), percentile ranks, and age equivalent scores. Part 2 factors render similar scores except for age equivalents. Users are advised to transfer raw scores from the examination booklet to a separate Profile/Summary form. The Profile/Summary form contains a workspace for computing the factor scores, a comments/recommendations section, and a profile page for graphic presentation of the individual's adaptive functioning. The Profile/Summary form is well designed and should facilitate the interpretive process. An ABS-S:2 Software Scoring and Report System is also available (Bryant, Lynn, and Pearson, 1993) in Apple II, Macintosh, and IBM PC and compatible formats.

NORMATIVE SAMPLES AND STANDARDIZATION. The ABS-S:2 has an improved standardization sample from earlier versions of the scale. There are separate norms for people with mental retardation (N = 2,074) and for those without mental retardation (N = 1,254). Both samples include a more diverse geographic representation than earlier versions of the scale (40 states for the MR sample and 44 for the Non-MR sample). The authors indicate that in some instances they were able to compare the sample demographics to the nation as a whole and the manual has tables that contain the percentage of demographic characteristics in the school-aged population versus the sample for comparative purposes. However, no description of the source of the population estimates is presented for users. Nevertheless, the samples are of good size and diversity to be suited for most applications and are certainly improved over earlier versions of the scale.

The ABS-S:2 reports percentages of students in the Mental Retardation sample group by IQ score (e.g., 12% [IQ<20], 48% [20–49], and 40% [50–70]). However, the IQ ranges reported in the MR sample do not include people with mental retardation who have intellectual functioning from 71 to 75 even though the intellectual functioning criterion in the 1992 AAMR definition of Mental Retardation specifies the upper limit IQ cutoff at 75. Gresham, MacMillan, and Siperstein (1995) note that shifting the IQ criterion from 70 and below to 75 and below could result in twice as many people being eligible for the diagnosis of mental retardation (using the IQ criterion alone). "There are more cases falling in the range of 71 to 75 (2.80%) than in the entire range associated with mild mental retardation, which is IQs ranging from 55 to 70 (2.51%)" (Gresham et al., 1995, p. 5). This could make use of the MR norms problematic for those individuals with IQs in the range of 71 to 75. Because the MR norms are collapsed across all of the reported IQ ranges and those persons with IQs from 71 to 75 were omitted, estimates of adaptive behavior for these individuals could be higher than if they had been included in the norms. Although users of the instrument should not view this as a serious problem with the norms, it is an instance of the scale not being consistent with the new AAMR definition of mental retardation (American Association on Mental Retardation, 1992).

RELIABILITY. Internal consistency estimates (alpha coefficients) are reported separately by age and averaged for all ages for all domains and factors for both the Mental Retardation and the Non-Mental Retardation samples. Homogeneity among items within each domain and factor for both norm groups is excellent. The coefficient alphas are higher for the Mental Retardation sample. Alphas (averaged across ages using z-transformation) ranged from .98 (Independent Functioning domain, Personal Self-Sufficiency factor, and Community Self-Sufficiency factor) to .82 (Prevocational/Vocational Activity domain). The majority of the averaged coefficients were in the range of .90 (17 of 21 alphas ≥.90) and at the specific age groups most alphas were also in the .90s. The lowest internal consistency estimates were for the Prevocational/Vocational Activity domain (5-year-, 8-year-, and 9-year-olds, .80) and the Self-Abusive Behavior domain (19-year- and 21-year-olds, .80).

For the Non-Mental Retardation group the averaged alphas ranged from .97 (Social Behavior domain) to .82 (Prevocational/Vocational Activity domain) [9 of 21 alphas ≥.90]. At specific age groups, all coefficients equalled or exceeded .80, except for 5-year-olds (.79, Prevocational/Vocational Activity domain), 6-year-olds (.79, Responsibility domain), 7-year-olds (.79, Economic Activity domain), and 13-year-olds (.79, Economic Activity domain).

Standard Errors of Measurement, derived from the internal consistency reliability estimates, are presented for all domains and factors for each age group and averaged across the ages. The *SEMs* are available for both sets of norms.

Test-retest reliability data are reported from two studies; both used a 2-week time interval between the ratings. In Study 1, supervisors of individuals employed in a sheltered workshop setting rated the individuals with the Adaptive Behavior Scales—Residential and Community: Second Edition (ABS-RC:2). The ABS-S:2 is a shortened version of the ABS-RC:2. The items that comprise the ABS-S:2 were extracted from the ABS-RC:2 to calculate the ABS-S:2 estimates. However, the individuals who were rated were older than individuals who might be assessed with the ABS-S:2 (i.e., the median age of those who were rated in the study was 42 years). The stability coefficients were corrected to remove error variance associated with internal consistency and corrected and uncorrected estimates are presented. Uncorrected estimates ranged from .98 (Economic Activity domain, Community Self-Sufficiency factor) to .82 (Stereotyped and Hyperactive Behavior domain, Personal Adjustment factor), whereas corrected estimates ranged from .99 (Independent Functioning, Trustworthiness, Self-Abusive Behavior, Social Engagement domains) to .85 (Personal Adjustment factor). Although these estimates are of sufficient magnitude to demonstrate temporal stability (in the short term), a study of the scale using a greater interval between test and retest is needed before users can be confident the test has long-term stability. Also, it would be helpful if such a study was based on individuals of the appropriate age for the ABS-S:2.

In Study 2, Florida high school teachers rated 9th through 11th grade students who were receiving services for emotional disturbance. Uncorrected es-

timates ranged from .89 (Self-Abusive Behavior domain) to .42 (Economic Activity domain). Corrected estimates ranged from .98 (Social Behavior domain) to .72 (Personal Self-Sufficiency factor). The reliabilities for the Independent Functioning domain, the Personal Self-Sufficiency factor, and the Community Self-Sufficiency factor were inadequate with this sample of students (.75, .72, and .78 respectively). Also the estimates for the Socialization domain, Social Engagement domain, and the Personal Adjustment factor were marginal (.80, .80, and .81).

The authors also have included interscorer reliability estimates. Two professionals trained in the use of the scale scored the same 15 completed ABS-S:2 protocols. There was a high degree of agreement between the scorers; *r*s ranged from .95 to .99 across the domains and factors of the scale.

Because the ABS-S:2 is likely to be administered to several parties as part of an adaptive behavior assessment, interrater reliability becomes critical for the scale. A study of interrater reliability is included in the validity section of the manual and referred to as ecological validity. Fifty students with emotional disturbance who were attending school in Florida were rated with the ABS-S:2. The students' teacher and the teacher's aide completed the scale. There was a high degree of agreement between the teachers and aides. Part 1 domain/factor *r*s ranged from .49 to .92 and Part 2 domain/factor *r*s ranged from .53 to .88. The scale has excellent interrater reliability.

VALIDITY. The ABS-S:2 contains relatively few item changes and the authors suggest validity studies of earlier versions of the scale might be of interest. Reports of these studies are in an appendix in the ABS-S:2 manual. The ABS items have been analyzed over time with different groups known to vary in their level of adaptive functioning and have been demonstrated to have discriminative power (e.g., Cheramie & Edwards, 1990; Gully & Hosch, 1979). As the scale was developed, items were retained based on interrater reliability and discriminative power with various groups in different settings.

ITEM CHARACTERISTICS. For this revision (ABS-S:2) an item analysis was conducted by computing item-total correlations (point-biserial correlations of each item with domain and factor scores at each age group). The authors selected .30 as their standard for acceptable item validity. Tables in the manual contain the *median* item to domain/factor score correlations for both the MR and the Non-MR samples. Although it is not completely clear, it appears that these correlations are the median of all item correlations within a domain or factor. Unfortunately, the individual item-total correlations are not presented, which makes evaluation of individual items impossible. Because medians are reported in the tables, one-half of the individual item correlations would have fallen below each of the reported table values (and one-half also would have fallen above the reported coefficient). This suggests that some items (e.g., those with correlations below the medians in the range of .30) would have marginal item validity. Adding to the confusion in this section of the manual, the authors state the developmentally disabled sample served as subjects for the analysis; however, correlation tables are presented for both samples. One analysis was based on ABS-S:2 ratings of the developmentally disabled individuals who represent the MR norms. Although not reported in the manual, a communication with the scale's publisher confirmed the same procedure was also applied to the ratings of the individuals who represented the Non-MR norms (see Tables 6.3 and 6.4 in the ABS-S:2 manual). In spite of these problems, the median item point-biserial correlations reported for domains and factors for the MR norms demonstrate the ABS-S:2 items (on average) are related to and account for variance in the domain and factor scores. The item-total correlations with the Non-MR sample were lower and thus do not predict the domain/factor scores as well for this group. The authors declare these results provide evidence of item validity, but sagacious users likely will find these data unclear.

CRITERION-RELATED VALIDITY. Reports of three studies of the criterion-related validity for the ABS-S:2 are in the manual. In Study 1, individuals in the standardization sample (n = 63) of the ABS-RC:2 were also administered the Vineland Adaptive Behavior Scales (VABS; Sparrow, Balla, & Cicchetti, 1984). The appropriate items for the ABS-S:2 were extracted from the ABS-RC:2. Part 1 domain and factor scores of the ABS-S:2 were correlated with the VABS: rs ranged from .71 (Physical Development domain) to .31 (Socialization domain). The correlation between the ABS-S:2 Pre-Vocational/Vocational Activity domain and the VABS was not significant, nor was the correlation between the Self-Direction domain and the VABS. The Part 2 domain and factor scores were not significantly related to the VABS, except for the Self-Abusive Behavior Domain (r = -.30).

In Study 2 the relationship of the ABS-S:2 with the Adaptive Behavior Inventory was examined (ABI: Brown & Leigh, 1986). Thirty students with mental retardation from a central Florida school district were evaluated with both scales. Correlations for the Part 1 domains/factors ranged from .67 (Community Self-Sufficiency factor) to .37 (Responsibility domain) with the ABI. No Part 2 domains/factors were significantly related to the ABI.

Study 3 examined the relationship of the ABS-S:2 with the VABS. Twenty-nine students from the standardization sample of the ABS-S:2 were also administered the VABS. Correlations for the Part 1 domains/factors ranged from .65 (Language Development domain) to .37 (Responsibility domain) with the VABS. The Economic Activity domain and the Prevocational/Vocational domain were not significantly related to the VABS nor were any of the Part 2 domains/factors.

The correlations were generally in the moderate range between the Part 1 domains/factors and criterion measures across the three reported studies and provide evidence of the scale's criterion-related validity. This suggests that the ABS-S:2, the VABS, and the ABI to a degree all measure adaptive behavior, but also that each scale is measuring something unique from the others. Users should not consider each of the instruments to reflect similar aspects of the adaptive behavior construct. It is not clear in the manual exactly what scores were used for the criterion measures, but it appears that only the total scores were used. Stronger support for the scale's criterion-related validity might have been evident if the ABS-S:2 domain and factor scores had been correlated with the VABS domain scores in addition to the VABS Adaptive Behavior Composite score and likewise with the ABI subtest scores. The Part 2 domain/factor scores do not appear to reflect adaptive behavior and the authors contend that these items represent maladaptive behaviors. The items obviously describe maladaptive behaviors, but the authors do not provide any empirical evidence other than the high internal consistency estimates and the high intercorrelations among the Part 2 domain/factors.

CONSTRUCT VALIDITY. Construct validity for the ABS-S:2 was assessed by examining the relationship of the domains/factors with age, the scale's relation with a variety of mental ability tests, the pattern of intercorrelation among the scale's domains/factors, and through confirmatory factor analysis.

Raw scores of three groups were examined to determine whether they were age related: (a) students without mental retardation aged 3 to 17 years; (b) students with mental retardation aged 3 to 17 years; and (c) adults with developmental disabilities. As expected, age was related to adaptive behavior functioning for the students without mental retardation (rs ranged from .22 to .56). Examination of the Part 1 raw score means for this group generally revealed a pattern of higher scores associated with increasing age. Adaptive behavior was less related to age for the other two groups; rs for the adult group ranged from -.04 to .10 and for the group of students with mental retardation rs ranged from .10 to .23. The maladaptive behavior domains and factors generally were not related to age for any of the groups (most rs were nonsignificant or negligible).

The authors also presented the domain/factor intercorrelations for the Mental Retardation sample and the Non-Mental Retardation sample. The Part 1 domains/factors are intercorrelated as are the Part 2 domains/factors for both groups. Furthermore, the Part 1 scores are inversely related to the Part 2 scores as would be predicted because Part 1 and Part 2 are supposed to measure constructs that are somewhat opposing (i.e., adaptive vs. maladaptive behaviors). These data could be analyzed further with exploratory factor analysis, but this type of analysis was not conducted. Because the test's authors present an interpretive model for examining strengths and weaknesses across the domains and factors of the ABS-S:2, data from exploratory factor analyses could also be used to examine the specific variance (subtest specificity) for domains and factors. It would be helpful if users had estimates of each domain's unique variance before interpreting domains as separate adaptive behavior strengths and weaknesses. Until those data are available users should be cautious about interpreting relative adaptive behavior strengths and weaknesses on the ABS-S:2.

A confirmatory factor analysis of the ABS-S:2 is presented in the manual but is not described in sufficient detail to be critically evaluated. The data seem to fit well the 5-factor model proposed by the authors. However, the factor-loading coefficients (standardized path coefficients) associated with each component of the factors are blanked (not displayed, see Table 6.20) except for the factor on which they loaded. To exacerbate this problem, no cutoff criterion is reported in the manual. Users have no way of determining whether the components loaded on other factors in addition to the one that was reported.

A series of studies reported in the manual examined the relationship of the ABS-S:2 with mental ability tests. The Part 1 domains/factors were found to be moderately related to the Wechsler Adult Intelligence Scale—Revised (WAIS-R; Wechsler, 1981) (rs ranged from .27 to .73), the Slosson Intelligence Test (SIT; Slosson, 1971) (rs ranged from .41 to .67), the Stanford-Binet Intelligence Scale (S-B; Terman & Merrill, 1972) (rs ranged from .47 to .71), the Leiter International Performance Scale (LIPS; Levine, 1982) (rs ranged from .35 to .71), the Wechsler Intelligence Scale for Children—Revised (WISC-R; Wechsler, 1974) (rs ranged from .28 to .61), the Peabody Picture Vocabulary Test—Revised (PPVT-R; Dunn & Dunn, 1981) (rs ranged from .37 to .58), and the Detroit Tests of Learning Aptitude—3 (DTLA-3; Hammill, 1992) (rs ranged from .38 to .72 with the Responsibility domain not significant). The majority of the correlations between the mental ability tests and the Part 2 domains/factors were not significant or negligible with the exception of the Social Engagement domain and the DTLA-3 ($r = -.33$).

SUMMARY. The ABS-S:2 is a timely revision of an important instrument and it has been improved from earlier forms. Based on careful review of the scale, I recommend it for use with some reservations. The scale has an excellent standardization sample and should be appropriate for use with a wide variety of individuals. The scale's psychometric qualities are good. However, further validity research is needed, especially construct validity. There is also a need for subtest specificity estimates to guide users of the scale in making empirically based interpretations regarding relative strengths and weaknesses. In sum, the ABS-S:2 is recommended for use. It has been and remains one of the best available scales for assessment of adaptive behavior.

REVIEWER'S REFERENCES

Slosson, R. L. (1971). Slosson Intelligence Test. East Aurora, NY: Slosson Educational Publications.

Terman, L. M., & Merrill, M. A. (1972). Stanford-Binet Intelligence Scale, 1972 Norms Edition. Boston, MA: Houghton-Mifflin.

Wechsler, D. (1974). Wechsler Intelligence Scale for Children—Revised. San Antonio, TX: The Psychological Corporation.

Gully, K. J., & Hosch, H. M. (1979). Adaptive Behavior Scale: Development as a diagnostic tool via discriminant analysis. American Journal of Mental Deficiency, 83, 518–523.

Dunn, L., & Dunn, L. (1981). Peabody Picture Vocabulary Test—Revised. Circle Pines, MN: American Guidance Service.

Wechsler, D. (1981). Wechsler Adult Intelligence Scale—Revised. San Antonio, TX: The Psychological Corporation.

Levine, M. N. (1982). Leiter International Performance Scale. Los Angeles, CA: Western Psychological Services.

Sparrow, S., Balla, D., & Cicchetti, C. (1984). Vineland Adaptive Behavior Scales. Circle Pines, MN: American Guidance Service.

Elliott, S. N. (1985). [Review of the AAMD Adaptive Behavior Scale]. In J. V. Mitchell, Jr. (Ed.), The ninth mental measurements yearbook (pp. 2–5). Lincoln, NE: Buros Institute of Mental Measurements.

Brown, L., & Leigh, J. (1986). Adaptive Behavior Inventory. Austin, TX: PRO-ED, Inc.

Cheramie, G. M., & Edwards, R. P. (1990). The AAMD ABS-SE Part Two: Criterion-related validity in a behavior-disordered sample. *Psychology in the Schools, 27*, 186–195.

American Association on Mental Retardation. (1992). *Mental Retardation: Definition, classification, and systems of supports* (9th ed.). Washington, DC: Author.

Hammill, D. (1992). Detroit Tests of Learning Aptitude—Third Edition. Austin, TX: PRO-ED, Inc.

Bryant, B. R., Lynn, G., & Pearson, N. (1993). ABS-S:2 Software Scoring and Report System. Austin, TX: PRO-ED, Inc.

Gresham, F. M., MacMillan, D. L., & Siperstein, G. N. (1995). Critical analysis of the 1992 AAMR definition: Implications for school psychology. *School Psychology Quarterly, 10*, 1–19.

[3]
Accounting Aptitude Test.

Purpose: Designed to assess aptitude for an accounting career.
Population: First-year college students.
Publication Dates: 1982–1992.
Scores, 3: Communication Skills, Quantitative Skills, Problem-Solving Skills.
Administration: Group or individual.
Price Data, 1994: $50 per examination kit including Form Z test booklet, Ready-Score answer document, and administrator's handbook ('92, 22 pages); $28 per 10 test booklets; $60 per 20 answer documents; $35 per administrator's handbook.
Time: 50(55) minutes.
Author: The Psychological Corporation.
Publisher: The Psychological Corporation.

Review of the Accounting Aptitude Test by JoELLEN CARLSON, Director of Testing Standards, New York Stock Exchange, Inc., New York, NY:

The Accounting Aptitude Test consists of 60 multiple-choice questions, each with four answer options, and is group administered in 50 minutes. The test comprises three parts: I. Verbal—27 questions in vocabulary, grammar, and reading comprehension; II. Quantitative—13 questions covering addition, subtraction, multiplication, division, and "algebraic manipulation"; and III. Problem Solving—20 questions consisting of analogies, recognition of relevant data, and logic. The publisher states that the test "measures those skills and abilities considered important for success in the study of introductory accounting and non-accounting finance-related jobs such as assistant bookkeeper and accounting clerk" (p. 5).

The only materials provided by the publisher for this review were the Administrator's Handbook, a copy of one form of the test, and an answer sheet. In the materials provided, the discussion of test development fails to describe procedures followed in developing the content outline, selecting question writers and reviewers, preparing and trying out the questions, or developing the test forms. The Administrator's Handbook indicates that certified public accountants (CPAs) in academe, public practice, government, and industry develop the content. It also states that "the test is developed according to carefully derived content outlines that include the skills and abilities relevant to entry-level accounting positions or accounting study" (p. 13), but does not offer supporting detail. Unfortunately, the publisher concludes that generating test questions to sample all aspects of the outlines assures relevance to actual knowledge and practice of accounting. No evidence of this is provided.

As would be expected and is appropriate for an aptitude test, none of the content is specific to the field of accounting. This reviewer fails to see the appropriateness of having CPAs develop questions to test non-accounting-specific vocabulary, grammar, reading comprehension, and much of the other content of test. Although these subject-matter experts would be appropriate for developing a test of achievement in accounting, and certainly may be useful in guiding the development process for a test of this sort, it would seem that a test of verbal aptitude is most appropriately developed by those whose expertise is in language.

Apparently only a single form of the test, Form Z, is in use. A reference to "currently available forms dating from 1981" is puzzling, given that all other information seems to indicate a single form.

Four correspondence tables are provided, relating raw scores to percentile ranks. The four reference groups are described as: (a) enrolled students with no previous accounting study, (b) enrolled students with up to one year of accounting study, (c) enrolled students with more than one year of accounting study, and (d) employees in entry-level accounting positions. All are based on all first-time examinees tested between January 1, 1988 and December 31, 1991. No information is provided on how the samples were selected, the sizes of the samples, or the conditions under which data were collected. The publisher states that data available for several similar groups were combined to form larger normative samples, but does not provide information on which to judge the appropriateness of doing so.

Basic characteristics of the test are reported based on results for 7,075 examinees, indicated to be all first-time examinees tested between January 1, 1988 and December 31, 1991. One might assume that the data are for all of the groups indicated as the norming groups, but inconsistencies in the data would indicate otherwise. The three subtest means in the table are identical to those of the first of the four tables of percentile equivalents, suggesting that the reliability data may be based on enrolled students with no previous accounting study. One of the standard deviations, however, is different. Further, the means reported in the two tables for total score differ. Curiously, neither of those means is the sum of the subtest means, as would be expected. This reviewer concludes that the data are described so incompletely that they are useless for evaluating the test and suspects that these tables were compiled rather carelessly.

An extended section of the manual discusses what constitutes test validity and describes strategies that would be appropriate for demonstrating content, criterion-related, and construct validity. Reported "validity" evidence is limited to several correlational studies. One study was a limited graduate student project not described as a dissertation study. The other studies are based on institutional data from a research project in Illinois and three universities. Correlations with course grades and other information reported from these studies are of no value for potential users of this test because of a lack of adequate description of samples, discussion of why the particular data were correlated with Accounting Aptitude test results, and other important facets of validation studies.

Apparently each institution using the test is responsible for its own test administration and scoring. The Administrator's Handbook provides specific directions for all aspects of test center preparation, test administration, security, and follow-up, and stresses the importance of following the directions exactly as given in the manual. No information is given about what is communicated to examinees either before or after the test. The directions to be read to the examinees are precise and clear, but there is no mention of what to communicate to examinees about how they will be notified of their scores or what will be done with the scores. The statement that the publisher "encourages universities and employers to provide examinees with their test results" (p. 12) is troublesome in its shortcoming.

Among the suggestions and claims made regarding uses of the test, an especially disturbing one is that "test results may be useful in assisting with personnel decisions regarding employment of new staff as well as training, placement, and promotion of permanent staff" (p. 13). Although some of these uses may be appropriate uses of a content-related test, they are certainly not appropriate uses of an *aptitude* test of this sort.

The publisher encourages users to conduct local validation studies to "establish appropriate evidence linking the examination to the attributes necessary for success in accounting studies" (p. 20). This, however, does not mitigate the publisher's responsibility to provide appropriate evidence of its suggested uses of the test and interpretations of the scores.

As a final comment, a cursory examination of some of the items in the verbal subtest reveal major ambiguities in the items themselves. This test cannot be recommended.

Review of the Accounting Aptitude Test by BIKKAR S. RANDHAWA, Professor of Educational Psychology, University of Saskatchewan, Saskatoon, Canada:

The Accounting Aptitude Test (AAT) was published in 1982. It was developed by certified public accountants in public practice, academe, government, and industry but their identity is unknown to the user. To our knowledge, there is no entry of this test either in previous *Mental Measurements Yearbooks* or in any book listing tests in print (prior to *Tests in Print IV* in 1994), or in a journal that reviews tests. Hence, this test has been a well-kept secret. I wonder if this test was marketed only through the test catalogue of the publisher. If that is the case, I wonder how widely it has been used.

The only materials available to users are the items listed in the price data (i.e., Form Z test booklet, Ready-Score answer document, and Administrator's Handbook, published in 1992). The AAT test booklet consists of 60 four-option multiple-choice items. The verbal or Communication Skills subtest has 27 items, which test the knowledge of synonyms (15 items), sentence construction (3 items), word or phrase usage (3 items), and reading comprehension (6 items based on two passages with 3 items on each).

The Quantitative Skills subtest consists of 13 items. These items emphasize the use of fundamental operations involving decimal fractions, percents, integers, and mixed numbers (a whole number with a simple fraction). Three items on this test are based on a graph. There is one item involving the simplification of an exponential expression. One item is on the yield of a given stock. However, the definition of yield accompanying this item is not absolutely correct. The yield expected is a percentage value but the answer obtained, given the definition, will provide a proportion. Including this item, there are four simple problems in this test. This test is taken by examinees without a calculator, a feature that may not be consistent with contemporary instructional approaches in mathematics.

The Problem-Solving Skills subtest is made up of 11 items on verbal analogies, four items on numerical reasoning, and five items on verbal and logical reasoning. In my view, the label of this subtest is inappropriate. Only nine items, 52 to 60, could be considered problem-solving items in the conventional sense.

The test format is columnar, presumably an attempt at space conservation but this is not really realized because there are many unused portions on several pages. A single column per page throughout, as is usually the case in most standardized tests, would probably require more pages than in the present format, but it would be easier for examinees to follow.

Although the test consists of three parts or subtests, 50 minutes time allowance for the total test is provided. This procedure for test administration may shortchange or misrepresent the measurement of the third part, Problem Solving. Usually, when distinct subcomponents of ability are measured, each subcomponent or subtest is allotted an amount of time such that about 90% of the examinees from the target population are able to finish the test.

The 1992 edition of the Administrator's Handbook contains a brief description of the test, its development, directions for administration, interpretation of test results, and norms. It is my impression that technical information included in this handbook was not based on data specifically collected in order to provide appropriate and representative norms for users. Rather the test users' data were assembled and analyzed for inclusion. The sampling frames for the normative groups are not described. An interesting but questionable statement that precedes the tables of norms is:

> The norms reported in this Handbook represent four groups of examinees. Data available for several similar groups were combined, when appropriate, to form larger, yet still well-defined, normative samples. The increased sample size that results from combining smaller samples contributes to a degree of stability in the normative information that would not otherwise be possible. (p. 14)

However, an examination of the tables of norms clearly indicates that they were prepared from the data of examinees tested between January 1, 1988 and December 31, 1991. The examinees tested would not have been a part of the standardization and validity study for this instrument because testing took place over a long period of time. Many sources of error over such a length of time would make scores of examinees included in the preparation of norms unreliable. For this reason, it is not surprising to note that there were no discernible observed differences in the means and standard deviations of the three groups of examinees who were enrolled students, whatever that means, with "no previous accounting study," with "up to one year of accounting study," and with "more than one year of accounting study." Therefore, I do not see the appropriateness of three separate tables of norms. As mentioned earlier, this instrument does not discriminate among these three different groups.

Each table of norms for enrolled students was based on fairly large numbers of examinees (3,125; 1,515; and 1,477 for Tables 1, 2, and 3, respectively). As these tables were based on whoever was tested with this instrument within the testing period of 4 years and whoever met the definition of "similar groups," that is probably the reason for such unexplainable differences in the number of examinees in these norming groups. This point is reinforced by the number of examinees ($N = 142$) on whose data Table 4 is based. This table of norms is supposed to be used for interpreting results of prospective employees in entry level accounting positions. Such a sample size cannot be representative of examinees in the United States for entry level accounting placements. Except for the Quantitative subtest, the summary statistics for this group appear to be different from the other three groups.

The handbook makes unsubstantiated claims based on undocumented testimonies. For example:

> Accounting educators and counselors have found test results valuable in advising students considering a career in accounting and comparing the aptitude of their students with *national student norms* [italics added]. Employers of accounting personnel in public accounting firms, business organizations, and government agencies have found that the test provides *valuable information* [italics added] when used in conjunction with other relevant information. Test results may be *useful* [italics added] in assisting with personnel decisions regarding employment of new staff, as

well as training, placement, and promotion of permanent staff. (p. 13)

There is no evidence available in the handbook to back up any of these claims.

The *Standards for Educational and Psychological Testing* (AERA, APA, & NCME, 1985) require that for any claims made by the author of a test, clear and unequivocal supporting information must be available to users. Furthermore, in precisely the same spirit, Messick (1991) suggests that, as a part of the validation of a test, evidential and consequential information should be available for both the use and interpretation of scores. In these respects, the AAT does not measure up at all. The internal consistency reliability estimates (KR-20) for the three subtests and the total test are based on all first-time examinees tested in 4 years ($N = 7,075$). For the verbal, quantitative, and problem-solving subtests reliability coefficients are .73, .68, and .74, respectively. However, the total number of examinees used for providing four sets of norms for the first-time examinees is 6,259. I do not see the value of this reliability evidence for the interpretation of group-specific normative percentiles because reliability estimates are based on a different pool of examinees than those used for providing the tables of norms. Also, it is not known how stable the scores are over time. Therefore, this test may not be useful for the study of change. My basic concern is that no specific validation plan was used to provide appropriate and useful information for test users.

The section on summary of validity studies in the handbook lists a number of correlational studies in which the total score was used to predict course grades and achievement test scores. The range of r is .22 to .62. It appears that these studies were not focused to address validity issues but rather those issues that were considered important by other researchers for various reasons and who happened to use the AAT in those endeavors. The test authors have not convinced me that the three subtests included here serve any purpose in predicting incrementally one's performance in accounting. There is no study documenting the use of this test for entry-level accounting employees' selection and performance effectiveness. In the absence of this kind of evidence, claims in the handbook are spurious and misleading.

In summary, it is critical to know whether the AAT is a specific accounting aptitude test or a general aptitude or reasoning test. An examination of the items in the three subtests does not convince me that it is a specific accounting aptitude test. In the absence of evidence on discriminant, concurrent, and construct structure of the test, any claims of its utility have to be at best modest. The reliability evidence is not appropriate for proper use and interpretation of the test. Also, in spite of the increased variability in the combined group used for establishing internal consistency reliabilities of the subtests and the total tests, reported reliabilities are low. No other reliability estimates are provided. Therefore, much systematic evidence on this test is needed before it is recommended for use.

REVIEWER'S REFERENCES

American Educational Research Association, American Psychological Association, & National Council on Measurement in Education. (1985). *Standards for educational and psychological testing.* Washington, DC: American Psychological Association, Inc.

Messick, S. (1989). Validity. In R. L. Linn (Ed.), *Educational measurement* (3rd ed.; pp. 13–103). New York, NY: Macmillan Publishing Company.

[4]

ACCUPLACER: Computerized Placement Tests.

Purpose: Designed to assist colleges in determining student entry skills in reading, writing, mathematics, and levels of English proficiency; scores aid in the appropriate placement of students into entry level courses.

Population: Entry level students in 2-year and 4-year institutions.

Publication Dates: 1985–1993.

Acronym: CPTs.

Administration: Individual.

Price Data, 1995: Annual licensing fee and per student fee, cost available from publisher.

Time: Untimed.

Comments: Administered on computer adaptively.

Author: The College Board.

Publisher: The College Board.

a) READING COMPREHENSION.

Comments: Each student is administered a fixed number of items which are selected adaptively depending on student responses to prior items.

Price Data: $1 per test.

b) WRITING.

Scores: Total score only.

Comments: Each student is administered a fixed number of items which are adaptively delivered.

Price Data: $1 per test.

c) ARITHMETIC.

Scores: Total score only.

Comments: Each student is administered a fixed number of items which are adaptively delivered.

Price Data: $1 per test.

d) ELEMENTARY ALGEBRA.

Scores: Total score only.

Comments: Each student is administered a fixed number of items which are adaptively delivered.

Price Data: $1 per test.

e) COLLEGE LEVEL MATHEMATICS.
Comments: Each student is administered a fixed number of items covering the areas of Intermediate Algebra, College Algebra and Precalculus.
Price Data: $2 per test.
f) LEVELS OF ENGLISH PROFICIENCY.
Scores: 3 modules: Language Usage, Sentence Meaning, Reading Skills.
Comments: Designed to identify the English proficiency levels of students; each student takes a fixed number of items; the 3 tests are administered separately.
Price Data: $2 per test.

Review of the ACCUPLACER: Computerized Placement Tests by MARTIN A. FISCHER, Associate Professor and Program Director, Program in Communication Disorders, Department of Human Services, Western Carolina University, Cullowhee, NC:

SUMMARY. The ACCUPLACER is a computer program designed to facilitate the evaluation and placement of college students into appropriate courses. The ACCUPLACER is composed of four sections: Computerized Placement Tests (CPTs), Computerized Placement Advising and Management Software (CPAMS), Placement Validation and Retention Service (PVRS), and School to College Placement Articulation Software Service (PASS).

COMPUTERIZED PLACEMENT TESTS. The CPTs are made up of six test areas and several supplemental skills tests. Each test is designed to evaluate a student's ability in a specific academic area. Test areas include: Reading Comprehension, Sentence Skills, Arithmetic, Elementary Algebra, College-Level Mathematics, and Levels of English Proficiency. Supplementary Skill tests include: Arithmetic and Elementary Algebra. All of the tests consist primarily of multiple-choice questions with some open-ended questions.

Each test is designed to evaluate a specific ability as follows:
Reading Comprehension (RC) is made up of 17 questions. The questions contain either a passage followed by a question based on its content, or two sentences in which the examinee answers a question about the relationship between them.
Sentence Skills (SS) contains 17 questions of two types. "Sentence correction" questions require that the examinee demonstrate an understanding of sentence structure by choosing the most appropriate word or phrase to substitute for the underlined portion of a given sentence. "Construction shift" questions require that a sentence be rewritten according to specifications while retaining essentially the same meaning as the original.
Arithmetic Test includes 16 questions drawn from three broad categories including: operations with whole numbers and fractions, operations with decimals and percents, and applications and problem solving.
Elementary Algebra Test includes 12 questions drawn from three categories including: operations with integers and rationales; operations with algebraic expressions; and solutions of equations, inequalities, and word problems.
College-Level Mathematics Test (CLM) is an optional test that consists of 35 to 40 questions from six general categories including: algebraic operations, solution of equations and inequalities, coordinate geometry, applications and other algebra topics, functions, and trigonometry.
Levels of English Proficiency Test (LOEP) is designed to assess the English skills of students who have learned English as a second language or who are native English speakers with limited proficiency. The major use of the test is in determining the appropriate placement of students into English as a second language and developmental courses at the time of college entry. Tests include 20 questions each evaluating reading skills, sentence meaning, and language use.

COMPUTERIZED PLACEMENT ADVISING AND MANAGEMENT SOFTWARE. The CPAMS is a computer system for evaluating information obtained from the CPTs and recommending student placement into courses best suited for them. It is also designed to track student progress and maintain records. "The system is designed primarily for incoming students" (p. 2-1). CPAMS features individual student and roster reporting options. Reports available include course assignment listings, test scores, and data based on variables specified by the operator. These variables specify which data are to be included in the reports. The system is designed to run as a standalone or networked using IBM or compatible microcomputers.

THE PLACEMENT VALIDATION AND RETENTION SERVICE. The PVRS is offered by the College Board to users of the ACCUPLACER system. The purpose of the service is to help colleges use the CPT results more effectively in placing incoming students into the appropriate courses. The PVRS provides analysis of data supplied by the college to determine the relationship between student's placement test scores and their grades in college courses.

RELIABILITY AND VALIDITY. Overall reliability and validity appeared to be quite good. Three reliability indices were used including: standard errors of measurement conditional on score level (CSEM), test-retest reliability (based on 2-week to 2-month intervals), and a measure of the consistency of placement decisions. Simulations conducted on 1,800 hypothetical examinees resulted in CSEMs with a high degree of score accuracy for the CPTs as well as high reliability coefficients ranging from .86 to .92. Test-retest reliability resulted in correlation coefficients ranging from .76 to .96. Reliability of classification estimated for selected CPTs ranged from .91 to .96. Throughout the CPTs, significant steps were made to minimize item bias including analysis for cultural and linguistic bias. Both content and predictive validity were evaluated and appeared to be adequate.

EVALUATION. The ACCUPLACER manual is comprehensive and contains an excellent set of instructions for both installation and operation of the CPTs. Also in the manual is a series of background readings that include an introduction to CPTs, guides for implementing the CPT, and information on validating the CPT results.

The manual suggested that no computing skills or knowledge of CPTs are required for installation or administration. This proved to be the case. The program was easily installed in less than 10 minutes from four floppy disks onto an IBM-compatible (DOS) computer (it can also be installed onto a network). Once installed, the instructions for customizing the CPTs were clear and comprehensive. Similarly, the on-screen (menu driven) instructions for students taking the CPTs were unambiguous.

The CPTs were easy to customize by following the on-screen help commands. Each testing session began with a series of questions about the student's academic and linguistic background. From these questions, using the Seamless Serial Testing feature, the CPTs automatically adjusted to the level to the examinee. Subsequent questions were automatically selected based on performance as the test proceeded. The order of CPT presentation was easily preset by the examiner and the sequence was simple to modify. On-screen directions allowed the examinee to complete each test in approximately 15 minutes (the tests are untimed). Each answer needed to be confirmed before the next question was presented. This made it easy to change errors or impulsive responses. Following completion of the CPTs, test results were compiled on several reports for analysis. The reports were comprehensive and could be combined with information such as major field of study, advisors, and placement rules to generate course assignments. Data were easily transferred to floppy disks that could be sent to the College Board's Placement Validation and Retention service for further analysis.

CONCLUSION. The ACCUPLACER appears to be an excellent system for providing CPT evaluation and placement of students in appropriate courses. The system is easy to install and operate and is extremely flexible. Results appeared reliable and can be evaluated and reported in a variety of ways. Subsequent reports can be generated and sent to the Placement Validation and Retention Service for in-depth analysis.

Review of the ACCUPLACER: Computerized Placement Tests by STEVEN V. OWEN, Professor of Educational Psychology, University of Connecticut, Storrs, CT:

The ACCUPLACER is a test management and reporting system developed jointly by the College Entrance Examination Board and Educational Testing Service. The ACCUPLACER has four main parts, only one of which—Computerized Placement Tests (CPTs)—is reviewed here. CPTs are to be used for assessing basic skills to assist in course placement decisions for college students. The skills covered by the CPTs include arithmetic, basic algebra, college-level mathematics, sentence skills, and reading comprehension. More recent versions of the ACCUPLACER also include a computerized test termed "Levels of English Proficiency," or LOEP. LOEP is meant for students whose native language is something other than English, or whose native English is substandard.

Item pools were developed and refined based on analyses from item response theory. Using between 12,000 and 30,000 students to collect calibration data for each test, ETS employed a 3-parameter IRT model to develop item difficulty and discrimination estimates. The Rasch difficulty estimates are used by the computer to create the adaptive testing routine.

Before computerized testing begins, the student responds to several biographical questions, such as years of English and mathematics in high school, whether or not English is the first language, and how many years since the last mathematics course. Each of the CPTs is adaptive, which means that different students will answer different questions based on their answers on previous questions. At the beginning of any CPT, an item is selected randomly from an item set of moderate difficulty. The student's response to the initial test item sets in motion the adaptive process. Generally speaking, an incorrect answer will bring up an easier item; a correct response delivers a more difficult question. The software is constrained by content, however. New items are chosen in order to maintain content validity for each test. In mathematics, the starting options are more varied. Here the test administrator may choose a beginning test (e.g., arithmetic or basic algebra), or the student may choose, or the computer will select a starting point based on the student's earlier responses to background questions. The adaptive testing situation makes for an extremely efficient assessment; although tests are untimed, student typically spend only 15 or 20 minutes per test.

There are additional advantages to a computerized operation. The tests are self-instructional and little proctor assistance is needed. If the tests are loaded on a network, multiple test takers can be served simultaneously, each taking different tests at different speeds. Finally, CPTs provide almost immediate feedback to students. At the conclusion of testing, personalized score reports can be printed. Scores may also be aggregated across students, stored in a computer file, and summarized and printed in various ways for college personnel.

The ACCUPLACER's Technical Data Supplement (College Entrance Examination Board, 1993) gives summaries of psychometric information for the CPTs. Instead of reporting overall (and misleading) standard errors of measurement, ETS reports estimated standard errors for each possible score within each test. Two-week stability estimates (for very small samples) range from .73 to .96. Reliability estimates of cut-scores across the various tests range from .91 to .96.

The Technical Data Supplement also reports content and predictive validity evidence for the CPTs. The content validation process involved panels of experts who offered advice about item content and wording. Tables of specifications were used to assure representative sampling of item within domains. For predictive validity, 50 colleges were recruited over a 2-year period. For each CPT, teacher-awarded

grades from relevant courses were regressed against CPT scores. (For example, English composition grades were correlated with Sentence Skills scores.) Median validity coefficients (uncorrected for restriction of range) were fairly low for language arts CPTs: Reading Comprehension, .18; Sentence Skills, .15 to .20. Without explanation, no validity coefficients are reported for Writing. The various mathematics CPTs fared generally better, with median coefficients between .19 and .49. For the LOEP measure, correlations with various English-as-a-second-language courses ranged from .09 to .48.

Norm tables are complete and easy to follow. Instructions for installation on a computer or computer network are simple as well. The summary score reports, for individual students and for administrative aggregates, are easy to arrange and to read. Working through the computer menus is not much challenge, even for computer novices. The CPTs run very quickly. I tested the programs on an ancient IBM 386 computer and on a Pentium-133 without discernible differences in program speed. Loading the maximum number of tests onto a computer hard drive does not require mountains of memory.

What could be better about the ACCUPLACER's CPTs? Several things. Although a newer version is available, the earlier version 4.0 was the one made available for review. The ACCUPLACER is DOS-based, which is out of step with an increasingly Windows-based computer universe. Computer literate students accustomed to a point-and-click operation may be puzzled by having to use arrow keys to move through menus. And the screen graphics are poorly done. I tested the program with various monitor resolutions, but nothing would make the print inviting. Clunky looking words will probably not depress CPT scores, but they give the impression of dated software and are irritating while reading. But even with their technological backwardness, the ACCUPLACER's CPTs have much to recommend them.

REVIEWER'S REFERENCE

College Entrance Examination Board. (1993). *ACCUPLACER Computerized Placement Tests technical data supplement.* Princeton, NJ: Author.

[5]

Achievement Test for Accounting Graduates.

Purpose: Constructed to assess achievement in accounting for use in selecting applicants or placing and training of current personnel.
Population: Accounting job applicants or employees.
Publication Dates: 1989–1992.

Acronym: ATAG.

Scores, 6: Financial Accounting, Auditing, Cost and Managerial Accounting, Information Systems, Taxation, Total.

Administration: Group or individual.

Forms, 2: T, V.

Restricted Distribution: Distribution restricted and test administered at licensed testing centers; details may be obtained from publisher.

Price Data, 1996: $50 per examination kit including Form V test booklet, Ready-Score answer document, and administrator's handbook ('92, 20 pages); $38 per 10 test booklets (specify Form T or V); $35 per administrator's handbook.

Time: 120(125) minutes.

Author: The Psychological Corporation.

Publisher: The Psychological Corporation.

Review of the Achievement Test for Accounting Graduates by JoELLEN CARLSON, Director of Testing Standards, New York Stock Exchange, Inc., New York, NY:

The Achievement Test for Accounting Graduates (ATAG) is intended to be an objective measure of advanced (post-baccalaureate) accounting knowledge. It consists of 115 multiple-choice questions, each with four answer options, and is group-administered in 2 hours. The test covers five areas: Financial Accounting, Cost and Managerial Accounting, Auditing, Taxation, and Information Systems. The publisher's stated purposes of the test are selection of students for graduate study, placement and training of job applicants, and evaluation for accounting educators and the accounting profession.

The only materials provided by the publisher for this review were the Administrator's Handbook, a copy of one form of the test, and an answer sheet. In the materials provided, the discussion of test development fails to describe procedures followed in selecting content experts, developing the content outline, preparing and trying out the questions, or developing the test forms. The Administrator's Handbook indicates that certified public accountants (CPAs) in public practice, industry, and education have been consulted, have had some involvement in specifying the content to be included, and perhaps have even been involved in question-writing. Although the handbook includes statements such as, "The test is developed according to carefully derived content outlines that include the skills and abilities relevant to entry-level professional accounting positions" (p. 12), there is no supporting detail.

Two forms of the test are in use—a primary form (Form V) and an alternate form (Form T). The publisher mentions that these forms are considered equivalent forms and each is linked statistically to a third, previous form of the test. No details are given regarding the linking or its adequacy. Note, however, that only raw scores are reported.

Basic characteristics of the test are reported based on results from 7,829 examinees for Form V and 918 for Form T, but no information is given about the backgrounds of these examinees or the means for collecting the data. The mean of Form V is reported as 59.6, with a standard deviation of 16.2 and a standard error of measurement of 4.8. For Form T, the reported mean is 57.5, with a standard deviation of 21.1 and a standard error of measurement of 4.6. The KR20 reliability estimates reported for the total test are .91 for Form V and .95 for Form T. For Form V, reliability estimates for the subtests range from .77 to .81, and from .72 to .89 for Form T. No other reliability estimates are provided.

The Administrator's Handbook provides two sets of percentile ranks corresponding to raw scores for each of the two forms. One set is for "enrolled students with more than two years of accounting study tested between 7/1/86 and 6/30/92" (p. 14), and one set is for "entry-level accountants with less than two years of experience tested between 7/1/86 and 6/30/92" (p. 17). No information is provided on how the samples were selected, the sizes of the samples, or the conditions under which data were collected. The publisher states that data available for several similar groups were combined to form larger normative samples, but does not provide information on which to judge the appropriateness of doing so.

Although it appears that the items would measure academic achievement in accounting, no evidence of the validity of any score interpretation is provided. An extended section of the manual discusses what constitutes test validity and describes strategies that would be appropriate for demonstrating content, criterion-related, and construct validity. Unfortunately, the discussion concludes with a statement that the publisher "has not conducted any validity studies for the ATAG" (p. 19). The discussion seems to imply that the involvement of CPAs from "a variety of professional settings" and the *intention* to measure knowledge, skills, and abilities "representative of the job domain for entry-level accountants" are evidence of some type(s) of validity.

Further suggestions and claims are made regarding uses of the test. For example, the suggestion is made that "test results may be useful in assisting with personnel decisions regarding employment of new staff as well as training, placement, and promotion of permanent staff" (p. 12). Although not necessarily untrue, this suggestion may be inappropriate without supporting data or guidance for the user as to how to determine such usefulness. Another disturbing suggestion the publisher makes is that the results of this test have been found valuable in evaluating the effectiveness of accounting faculty. Given the problems and issues inherent in such a practice, and in the absence of any data to support such a claim, this would seem a totally inappropriate use of these scores.

The publisher does encourage users who plan to use the ATAG as part of an employee selection to establish evidence linking the test to the attributes needed for success in the position for which a person is being tested. Users are also told that they must set their own performance standards; at a minimum, the publisher must be responsible for giving guidance about appropriate interpretations of the scores. Certainly, encouraging the user to set standards and conduct validation studies is not sufficient.

Apparently each institution using the test results is responsible for its own test administration and scoring. The Administrator's Handbook provides specific directions for all aspects of test center preparation, test administration, security, and follow-up, and stresses the importance of following the directions exactly as given in the manual. No information is given about what is communicated to examinees either before or after the test. The directions to be read to the examinees are precise and clear, but there is no mention of what to communicate to examinees about how they will be notified of their scores or what will be done with the scores. The statement that the publisher "encourages universities and employers to provide examinees with their test results" (p. 12) is troublesome in its shortcoming, particularly if the results are being used to make such high-stakes decisions as employment and job retention or promotion.

This test cannot be recommended for use for its intended purposes in the absence of the usual types of information routinely provided in a technical manual. Given the lack of useful information about test development, standardization procedures, norming groups, equating methods, and psychometric characteristics, and of evidence to support the validity of any interpretation of test scores, it would be irresponsible to use the ATAG for admissions decisions, and completely inexcusable to use it in making personnel decisions about accountants or accounting faculty.

Review of the Achievement Test for Accounting Graduates by THOMAS F. DONLON, Director, Test Development and Research, Thomas Edison State College, Trenton, NJ:

The Achievement Test for Accounting Graduates (ATAG) is a 115-question multiple-choice survey of accounting knowledge, requiring 2 hours for administration. It has five subscores, the so-called F-A-C-I-T scores, based on subsets of items as follows: Financial Accounting (38 items), Auditing (18 items), Cost and Managerial Accounting (23 items), Information Systems (18 items) and Taxation (18 items). Two forms of the test, Form T and Form V, are currently available. Provision is made for the administration of the individual FACIT subtests; specific time limits for these sections are described, and separate norms are developed.

Norms are available for the two forms and their subtests separately, and in each case for two groups: (a) Enrolled Students with More Than Two Years of Accounting Study and (b) Entry-Level Accountants with Less than Two Years of Experience Tested. In each case, the normative testings were carried out between 7/1/86 and 6/30/92. There are disparities in the sizes of the norms groups: Ns of 117 and 715 for Form T Students and Entry-Level Accountants, respectively, and Ns of 5,594 and 6,863 for the analogous Form V groups. The Administrator's Handbook states that "Form V is considered the primary form; Form T is used as an alternate" (p. 12).

The user is told that Forms V and T, though separately normed, are "considered equivalent forms" (p. 12). Buttressing this, the user is told that "Each form is linked statistically to a previously published form (Form R)" (p. 12). How this linking is done, and why, is not stated. No data are provided. The language suggests there is a common-items equating of V and T to R, and a judgment that things equal to the same thing are equal to each other. But the whole matter is little discussed, and in any case, the user is explicitly told that scores "*cannot* be compared across different test forms" (p. 12). Exactly what the user is to conclude about "equivalence" is ambiguous. This reviewer thinks that the user would be advised to take the alleged equivalence with a grain of salt.

In the section on Interpreting Test Results, the user is reminded that "to interpret the meaning of a percentile rank, it is imperative that test users understand the composition of the available norm groups" (p. 12). That is probably good advice for any statistic, and so it was a jolt to see the Reliability section, where Kuder-Richardson Formula #20 reliabilities are estimated for each total form and subtest. The reliability groups are not characterized as Students or Entry-Level Accountants. Whoever they are, they do a lot less well on the ATAG than the norming samples have done. The reliability sample mean on Form T is 57.5, versus the means of 65.9 and 65.7 for the Students and Entry-Level Accountants in the norms groups. The reliability sample mean on Form V is somewhat closer: 59.6 versus the means of 63.7 and 63.2 for the norms groups. But the differences are large enough to require explanation, and none is provided. The reliability sample sizes are also odd: 918 for Form T, and 7,829 for Form V. Because about 12,000 cases are in the Form V norms groups combined, it is hard to know what has gone on in establishing reliability samples.

The mysteriously different properties of the reliability sample are even more startling for the variabilities. Norms group total score standard deviations on Form T were 10.7 (Students) and 13.9 (Entry-Level Accountants). The Form T standard deviation for the reliability sample is a whopping 21.1. Form V norms groups show smaller differences, 13.0 and 13.2, versus 16.2 for the reliability sample. The mysteries are particularly annoying because the use of groups with greater variability will increase the reliability estimates. The reported reliabilities are adequate, around .80 for the subtests, over .90 for the total tests, but the failure to clarify the sample and its adequacy casts a shadow on these results.

The Psychological Corporation states in the manual that it has developed the ATAG "to measure an individual's knowledge of accounting at the advanced level (post-baccalaureate)" (p. 12). However, it has conducted no validity studies on the ATAG, relying on the contributions of consultant certified public accountants in "public practice, industry, and education" (p. 12) to establish the relevance of content. The 35 elements in the fully elaborated FACIT content outline will permit a knowledgeable person to get a sense of the intended coverage of the test. However, the Handbook assertion that "Colleges and universities have found the test results valuable" (p. 12) and "Employers of professional accountants … have found that the test provides valuable information" (p. 12) seems oddly vague and unsubstantiated. Whoever finds the test information "valuable" has, in a sense, validated it in some context. Why not say who they are and what use they made?

Curiously, the test takers are not told the scoring system (Rights Only), although they are instructed to guess. No data on an Omit score or a Not Reached score are provided. On the Cost and Managerial subtest and the Taxation subtest there are substantial percentages of performances among the norms groups that are not greater than mean chance level. This is not the case for the 117 students taking Form T, but for the other groups these percentages range around 8% to 10%. Similarly, the average item on these subtests is typically harder than the average item on the other subtests. There are no intercorrelation data provided.

If the work of the accountant-consultants is accepted, the ATAG is a potentially useful survey test of basic accounting knowledge. Its length, both in numbers of items and in the time allowed, seems to be practical. The provisions for subtests seem very appropriate. The Ready-Score answer sheet has a two-ply construction that permits the user to easily score the test by opening it up and seeing the test-taker's marks in the context of key information.

Overall, the test has no obvious salient flaws but there is a dearth of information about its validity and of adequate information about its reliability. The Psychological Corporation should be encouraged to do more work on the norming and validation and to improve the psychometric description of the test.

[6]
Achieving Behavioral Competencies.

Purpose: To develop a program of instruction in social/emotional skills.
Population: "Students who are seriously emotionally disturbed, closed head injured, juvenile offenders, learning disabled, or at-risk for school drop-out."
Publication Date: 1992.
Acronym: ABC.
Scores, 24: Relating to Others (Building Friendships, Maintaining Friendships, Apologizing, Compromising/Negotiating, Giving/Accepting Praise or Criticism, Total), Personal Responsibility (Goal Setting, Decision Making, Assuming Responsibility, Promptness, Asking for Assistance, Total), Coping with Stress (Handling Frustration, Coping with Anger, Dealing with Stress, Accepting Authority, Resisting Peer Pressure, Total), Personal/Affective Development (Building Self-Esteem, Coping with Depression, Coping with Anxiety, Controlling Impulsivity, Sensitivity to Others, Total).
Administration: Group.
Editions, 2: Individual Student Report, Class Report.
Price Data, 1994: $137.50 per set including curriculum, 25 rating forms, and computer program (IBM/Compatibles, Macintosh, and Apple).

Time: Administration time not reported.
Comments: Computer reports generated from teacher ratings.
Authors: Lawrence T. McCarron, Kathleen McConnell Fad, and Melody B. McCarron.
Publisher: McCarron-Dial Systems.

Review of the Achieving Behavioral Competencies by SALLY KUHLENSCHMIDT, Associate Professor of Psychology, Western Kentucky University, Bowling Green, KY:

Achieving Behavioral Competencies (ABC) is composed of two parts: (a) a teacher rating scale of four categories of behavior judged important for social/emotional coping in a school or vocational setting, and (b) a curriculum to improve those behaviors. The four areas are Relating to Others (primarily peer relationships), Personal Responsibility (primarily work habits), Coping with Stress, and Personal/Affective Development. Three types of scores (Average ABC Factor Score, four Factor Scores, and unit scores) are available for individual students or across students in a class. Easy-to-use software (PC or Mac) does the score calculations and generates reports. Most items are clearly written to focus on specific behaviors. Items incorporate qualitative aspects of behavior and are positively phrased, setting a constructive tone for working with students. However, the phrasing may prevent inclusion of primarily negative behaviors, for example, "avoiding responsibilities" or "hallucinating." The teacher responds on a 5-point Likert scale, *never* (1) to *always* (5), and takes about 10 minutes to complete the form. The curriculum was designed for secondary students who are learning disabled, seriously emotionally disturbed, closed-head injured, juvenile offenders, or at risk for school drop out.

TEST DEVELOPMENT. The development of the four scales is incompletely described in the manual. Three domains (Coping Skills, Work Habits, Peer Relationships) were "consistently recognized" (p. 1) by teachers as identified by a varimax rotation factor analysis but there is insufficient information to interpret this study (e.g., what population of teachers was used?). Fad and Ryser (1993) developed the first version of the ABC rating form beginning with 125 items divided into five domains. Teachers in Texas (the number is not stated) provided 125 student ratings (no other student information). The authors used the factor analysis to obtain the three principal factors present in the current form. The number of ratings is grossly inadequate to

obtain a stable factor structure (the bare minimum is five per item). Cross-validation of these results on adequate samples is absolutely necessary for any valid conclusions.

The final Teacher Rating Form includes the 20 items loading highest in the 1993 study although only the top 10 for each factor are listed. The authors added the Personal/Affective Development factor because the target populations "often manifest affective disorders" (p. 3). Again, no other information on development was provided so the source of these items is a mystery.

RELIABILITY AND VALIDITY. Information on the reliability and the validity of the ABC is inadequate. The sample used for the alpha reliability coefficients on the factor scales is not described in the manual but is probably the Fad and Ryser sample (1993). The manual states that the reliability coefficients were ".957, .968 and .958 for work habits, coping skills, and peer relationships, respectively" (p. 3). No coefficient is reported for the Personal/Affective Development Scale. Coefficients are not reported for the unit scores nor are scale means or standard deviations for the sample. The Standard Error of Measurement definition provided is incorrect. Confidence interval tables would be useful.

The test user must rely on the software to score and interpret the test. The scores appear to be weighted additions of ratings with no comparison to a standardization sample and no age, grade, sex, or disability norms. The numbers reflect simple frequency observations, added in various unknown ways. The unit scores apparently consist of about four items each. However, which items contribute to a unit score are not listed. Thus, the adequacy of the unit labels cannot be judged. No validity data are presented in the manual other than the original factor analysis.

CONCEPTUAL PROBLEMS. Cut scores for referral to remediation and selective remediation are provided, a poor practice because of measurement error. Nor is the basis for those specific cuts explained. The authors persistently recommend using pre-post measures of change. Change scores (pre-post) should not be used to evaluate progress because they are notoriously unstable. The authors also suggest that the unit scores (based on a few items) will be more sensitive to change than the group scores (based on many items). However, the fewer items, the less reliable the score is likely to be. Change perceived on the basis of cut scores, pre-post measures, or unit scores is untrustworthy.

CURRICULUM. The easy-to-follow curriculum occupies the vast majority of the attractive folder and comes with activities and handouts. The four sections may be approached in any order, according to the authors. The overall scheme for each section is nicely planned beginning with generating student self-awareness regarding the issue being studied, followed by teacher instruction and demonstration. Students are then encouraged to explore the topic through peer interaction. Finally, students are explicitly taught to manage the behavior independently and to generalize it to other settings, a step too often overlooked in other training programs. In the body of the curriculum are several self-tests for the student (Building Self-Esteem, Assuming Responsibility, Coping with Depression, and Coping with Anxiety). No information is provided about the source or adequacy of these measures. The relation between specific test items and curricular material also needs to be demonstrated.

As students may not have volunteered for the class, the manual should fully address issues of confidentiality and sensitivity to student disclosures. Only those with above average clinical skills should lead this instruction because of potential dangers. For example, the depression section contains no guidance concerning suicide. Some material in the Personal/Affective Development section is incorrect or potentially misleading, specifically the desensitization and relaxation procedures and the discussion of rational self-talk. However, most topics have been well constructed to fit classroom and teacher needs. Suggestions for moderating the content given particular populations would be very helpful.

RECOMMENDATIONS. Without adequate psychometric data, I cannot recommend the Achieving Behavioral Competencies Teacher Rating Form. I fear it is worse than a simple checklist because of psychometric inaccuracies that encourage misinterpretation and misapplication of the numbers from the rating form. The curriculum materials may be useful with cautious application and prior appropriate training. The literature does support several related instruments as measures for these areas (e.g., the Child Behavior Checklist [55], peer nominations, Beck Depression Inventory [31], State-Trait Anxiety Inventory [T4:2563]). They could be used to guide curriculum choices. I hope the authors will conduct appropriate psychometric studies and build a quality product of demonstrated use, rather than settle for appearances.

REVIEWER'S REFERENCE

Fad, K. S., & Ryser, G. R. (1993). Social/behavioral variables related to success in general education. *RASE: Remedial and Special Education, 14*(1), 25–35.

Review of the Achieving Behavioral Competencies by ROBERT A. LEARK, Clinical Professor of Psychology, Pacific Christian College, Fullerton, CA:

The Achieving Behavioral Competencies (ABC) is not a test although it incorporates a testing procedure within its design. The ABC is a three-prong approach to assessing, teaching, and analyzing social/emotional behavior. The three prongs are the ABC—Teacher Rating Scale (ABC-TRS), a computer software program, and curriculum. The ABC does utilize an 80-item Likert rating scale model questionnaire completed by the teacher to rate the student's behavior. The ABC-TRS is the anchor point for measuring behavioral intervention outcomes.

The ABC social/emotional curriculum is beyond the scope of this review, however, it does merit comment. The authors, well known in the development of rehabilitation and educational material, have done a solid job of providing the classroom teacher with differential material that breaks down social and emotional behavior into simple operational tasks. These tasks can be useful for the brain-injury rehabilitation staff, development disorder classroom teacher, or classrooms for emotionally disturbed individuals. Because brain injury can regress adult behavior, the tasks may be appropriate for those providing rehabilitation to brain-injured adults.

The curriculum consists of 20 teaching units intended to produce skill mastery in social/emotional behaviors. The teaching units include strategies for using the material to assure generalization of skills. The basic paradigm for the skill mastery is based upon a five-strategy incremental approach: self-awareness, teacher instruction, teacher demonstration, student interaction, and self-management and generalization of skill. The authors' curriculum includes demonstration student outcomes such as absenteeism, discipline referrals, or behavioral incident reports. Each of the domains is covered by items on the ABC-TRS.

At this point, it is important to turn to the actual instrument, the ABC-TRS. The ABC-TRS is an 80-item Likert rating scale to be completed by the classroom teacher. The 80 items are statements describing individual student behaviors in the classroom. The teacher rates the student on a 5-point Likert scale (1 = *Never* to 5 = *Always*). Each of the four curriculum domains is represented by 20 items on the ABC-TRS. Expected time to complete the questionnaire is about 10 minutes.

The third prong of the ABC is the software to be used by the teacher to record test item responses for each student. The software itself is simple to use and easily installed by the most fearful computer user. The software allows the teacher to organize class files (i.e., students within each classroom). Within each classroom file, the software user can record test items response for each student within that classroom. Individual profiles for each student can be printed, on paper or on computer screen. Additionally, the teacher can analyze the entire class as a group and receive an analysis by paper or computer screen. These aspects of the software make the software a valuable tool for the classroom teacher. The software is easily used to add students or to delete students from the class (actually from the software, not from the actual classroom!).

The three-prong approach of the instrument package is attractive. The simplicity of the software and the 80-item instrument that is clearly linked to behavioral interventions is ideal for the classroom teacher. It is not ideal for the routine practitioner, nor should the ABC be seen as an individual psychological test, as it clearly is not.

PSYCHOMETRIC PROPERTIES OF THE ABC-TRS. The manual does not provide a normative table. There is no description of the normative sample used to derive the reliability or validity data. Further, the test does not utilize a mean score or standard deviation transformation of the raw data. Rather, raw scores are used to provide a total score for any particular domain. Thus, the test user is only provided with a raw value of items for the four curriculum domains of social/emotional behavior. Each of the four domains is analyzed by the items comprising the domain. Because each domain is represented by 20 items, individual domains are represented by 2 items per topic within domain.

The test can only be scored by the computer software included with the product. The software is easy to use and follows an intuitive flow of information. The scoring provides the teacher with a rating for each individual item within each domain. Because each item is rated from a score of 1 to 5, the topics are scored 2 to 10. Lower scores, 2 to 4, are reported as "Remediation recommended," scores of 5 to 8 are reported as "Selective remediation" and score values of 9 to 10 are described by the phrase "appears adequate."

The authors provide information on how the ABC-TRS was developed in line with the curriculum. One study is reported (and at the time of the publication of the instrument, that article was "in press"). This sole study provided data supporting the three-factor solution of the original 80 items. Only 30 of the 80 items are represented by the factor analysis. Within the three factors (Coping Skills, Work Habits, Peer Relationships), loadings ranged from .66 to .89. Only the top 10 items with the highest factor loadings for each factor structure were included. These three factors were then further compared to the top 5 items, with this factor loading ranging from .80 to .92. However, there is no indication of the sample size used to develop the factor structure in the manual. The factor structure data tables fail to provide the basic information necessary to arrive at independent conclusions regarding the analysis.

Estimates of the ABC-TRS reliability were reported in the manual, with the same caveat given for the normative and validity data: No indication of the sample size, ages, distribution, etc., is given. Alpha reliability coefficients of .975, .968, and .958 are reported for the three factors.

At this point the test authors indicate that the initial ABC-TRS and curriculum were not complete because students with social/emotional problems are reported as having "self-esteem" problems. So, the authors included a fourth segment, Personal/Affective, to the curriculum.

From the calculated alpha reliability coefficients for the 80-item instrument, standard error of measurement (*SEM*) coefficients are provided. But, without an adequate understanding of the distribution and transformation, the use of the *SEM* is misleading.

Essentially, that represents the psychometric properties reported in the manual. This makes the manual inadequate in its design. It does not meet the *Standards for Educational and Psychological Testing* (AERA, APA, & NCME, 1985) because normative data are not provided to the reader. Such basic information as sample size is missing, there are no standard scores generated, and no test mean scores nor standard deviation. The test is designed for use on an individual student basis. However, no test-retest reliability is given. Although test-retest reliability may not always be an adequate description of the reliability of test scores, there was no attempt by the authors to indicate why test-retest reliability was not investigated. Given that this questionnaire is a pre-test/post-test design outcome measure, its test-retest reliability should be of concern.

TEST SCORING. Responses to the 80 items are recorded on the rating scale form. The test user then enters the individual rating responses for each item into the software program. The software program establishes classroom files allowing for the entry of each student to the file. The individual files include demographic information, then the items are entered in sequential order. The software program provides an individual analysis of the items, presenting rating scores according to factor structure. Each of the factors is further analyzed in the report to include the specific behavioral domain within each factor.

The scoring is either for the class as a group (or selected students) or by individual report. Individual reports can be by individual or average over two test scenarios. The user can selectively print out all factor or unit profiles.

SUMMARY COMMENTS. The ABC-TRS is not for general psychological use. It is limited to those situations where behavioral management is important. Classroom and rehabilitation situations are best suited for this instrument. In this sense, the instrument is not a psychological measure. It is a comprehensive evaluation of an instructional program using a pre- and post-test design. The authors have designed the package for these situations. Within this design, the manual is lacking in expected representation of normative data and test development. Given the publisher's history in producing quality products, this is surprising and disappointing.

REVIEWER'S REFERENCE

American Educational Research Association, American Psychological Association, & National Council on Measurement in Education. (1985). *Standards for educational and psychological testing*. Washington, DC: American Psychological Association, Inc.

[7]
Adaptive Style Inventory.

Purpose: "Designed to assess individuals' ability to adapt to different learning situations."
Population: Junior high through adult.
Publication Date: 1993.
Acronym: ASI.
Scores, 16: 4 scores: Concrete Experience, Reflective Observation, Abstract Conceptualization, Active Experimentation in each of 4 situations: Acting Situation, Deciding Situation, Thinking Situation, Valuing Situation.
Administration: Group.
Price Data, 1993: $59 per complete kit including 10 questionnaires, 10 profiles and interpretive notes (14 pages), and 10 scoring booklets.

Time: Administration time not reported.
Comments: Self-scored inventory.
Authors: Richard E. Boyatzis and David A. Kolb.
Publisher: McBer & Company.

Review of the Adaptive Style Inventory by THOMAS R. KNAPP, Professor of Nursing and Education, The Ohio State University, Columbus, OH:

For this review I was provided with three documents pertaining to The Adaptive Style Inventory (ASI): (a) a copy of the inventory itself; (b) directions for scoring and interpreting the scores; and (c) something called "Scoring Sheet and Profiles," which actually consists of a scoring key and several diagrams upon which to record the scores. There are apparently no test manual, no norms, and no validity or reliability data. The remainder of this review will therefore concentrate on a number of personal observations regarding the inventory itself.

The ASI is a rather unusual measuring instrument. In the instructions to the respondent on the first page, the inventory is said to be designed "to help you assess the ways you adapt to different situations" (p. 1). That's fine. But the inventory consists of eight clusters of six possible combinations of four statements taken two at a time, necessitating 48 choices on the part of the respondent. For example, the first cluster is headed "When I start to do something new" and the respondent is asked to choose one response from each of the six pairs of the four statements "I rely on my feelings to guide me," "I set priorities," "I try out different ways of doing it," and "I observe the situation." It is not obvious to me why that particular forced-choice format was adopted.

The "items" (there are 8 of them if you count each cluster as an item, 48 if you count each pair of statements as an item) are attractively presented. The respondent is asked to write down in the space provided for each item some of his (her) own experiences regarding a phenomenon (e.g., starting something new), with the actual stimuli for the paired comparisons listed beneath that space. In the scoring, which is straightforward, the points for the responses to various pairs of *clusters* are summed to yield scores on Concrete Experience, Reflective Observation, Abstract Conceptualization, and Active Experimentation for each of four "situations" (Acting, Valuing, Deciding, and Thinking) and a "kite" profile. (The respondent's experiences are not scored.) The interpretations provided for the various scores are heavily jargon-bound and are outside of the purview of my expertise. I therefore cannot judge whether or not such interpretations are justified.

Concrete Experience, Reflective Observation, Abstract Conceptualization, and Active Experimentation are said to be "learning styles," with "adaptive style" being the individual respondent's particular combination of learning styles. Reference is made to Kolb and Boyatzis' Learning Style Inventory (LSI; T4:1438)—not to be confused with other inventories of that same name or with other instruments bearing similar titles. Respondents who have completed that inventory are asked to compare their ASI scores with their LSI scores.

Further research on this instrument is necessary if its psychometric characteristics are to be properly evaluated.

Review of the Adaptive Style Inventory by ERICH P. PRIEN, President, Performance Management Associates, Memphis, TN:

The subject of management style has been a focus of research periodically in past years. Throughout this period, it has also been intensely addressed in consulting practice as a determinant of managerial success as well as being linked to overall organization effectiveness. However, attempts to "validate" an optimum strategy or approach have not been fruitful. Generally, the conclusions support each individual achieving a level of self-understanding and then designing and refining a style that works for them.

The Adaptive Style Inventory (ASI) is designed as a tool for practitioners to use in the practice of counseling and coaching managers to improve their performance. It is a self-administered, self-scoring inventory that produces results that are specifically unique to the individual.

The essence of the inventory is captured in the frame of reference for each of the eight items representing four types of situations; these are: Acting, Deciding, Thinking, and Valuing. For each of the eight items comprising the inventory, the individual must select several examples that represent situations or circumstances from their own experience corresponding to the general frame of reference for the item. For example, for Item 1, the frame of reference is the statement "when I start to do something new:" (Inventory, p. 3). The individual must select three different situations corresponding to that general frame of reference. For example, the situations might be *buying a new automobile* or *learning to use a new computer software routine*. Thus, the situation will be unique to the individual, but the responses then are in terms of a subset of phrases representing

a style or approach in a pair-comparison format. Thus, for buying a new car, the individual would respond to (a) I rely on my feelings to guide me or (b) I set priorities. This pair-comparison format is then repeated using statements representing four different learning styles (Concrete Experience, Reflective Observation, Abstract Conceptualization, and Active Experimentation).

The scoring of the ASI results in a description of relative emphasis of four different learning styles for the four types of situations. This is a rather complex instrument, and the final product in terms of scores is essentially a fourfold table that characterizes the individual's learning style in four different types of situations. The assumption is that by characterizing learning style, the individual improves their personal insight and understanding and, thus, will be in a better position to respond to their environment and, as a result, improve their effectiveness.

Because the reference for the inventory is unique to the individual, normative data would be meaningless. No information is provided as to reliability, although given the brevity of the scales, any such estimates would be reasonably speculative. Utility of the inventory is based on the assumption that different styles of learning are more appropriate for different types of situations. But in the manual the authors essentially provide the user carte blanche with a variety of phrases indicating that the final choice is up to the individual, and the most appropriate style depends upon the specific situation and the preferences of the individual.

The ASI may be a stimulating and informal instrument to use in coaching and counseling, when working with groups or with individuals to get them to focus attention on how they approach different situations. However, the value of the profile is limited to that informal encounter. The issue of validity of either the styles of learning called *adaptive types* (construct validity) or the reaction of types to an external criterion of individual performance effectiveness is not addressed or even mentioned.

The results of this review would not support using the instrument for any dedicated purpose in management training and development, although it might serve a catalyst function in certain settings.

[8]
Adolescent Coping Scale.
Purpose: Assesses 18 possible coping strategies used by adolescents and young adults in dealing with stress.

Population: Ages 12–18.
Publication Date: 1993.
Acronym: ACS.
Scores, 18: Seek Social Support, Focus on Solving the Problem, Work Hard and Achieve, Worry, Invest in Close Friends, Seek to Belong, Wishful Thinking, Not Coping, Tension Reduction, Social Action, Ignore the Problem, Self-Blame, Keep to Self, Seek Spiritual Support, Focus on the Positive, Seek Professional Help, Seek Relaxing Diversions, Physical Recreation.
Administration: Group.
Price Data, 1993: A$90 per complete kit including manual (48 pages) and all required material in a notebook; $2.20 per questionnaire; $20 per 10 questionnaires (short form); $10 per 10 scoring sheets; $10 per 10 profile charts; $45 per manual.
Time: 10 minutes for Long Form; 3 minutes for Short Form.
Authors: Erica Frydenberg and Ramon Lewis.
Publisher: Australian Council for Educational Research Ltd. [Australia].

Review of the Adolescent Coping Scale by FREDERICK T. L. LEONG, Associate Professor of Psychology, The Ohio State University at Columbus, Columbus, OH:

One of the strengths of the Adolescent Coping Scale is the authors' recognition of the complexity of the stress and coping relationship. In response to this complexity, the authors have developed two versions of the scale—a Specific Form, which includes a respondent nominated stressor and a General Form with reference to stress in general. In addition, the Adolescent Coping Scale comes in a Regular Form (80 items) and a Short Form (19 items). These four versions—Specific Regular, General Regular, Specific Short, and General Short—provide a certain amount of flexibility to the test user. The scale also has the advantage of both self-scoring and computer scoring.

The scale measures 18 coping styles ranging from Seeking Social Support to Ignoring the Problem to Physical Recreation. In developing the scale, the authors used responses from over 643 senior students in high schools in Melbourne, Australia to select the final items. The authors used both item analysis and factor analysis in order to develop the scale. They also provided some information about the relationships between the Regular and the Short Forms with correlations between the two versions of the same coping style subscale (e.g., Seek Social Support) ranging from .75 to .92.

Despite the above mentioned strengths, the Adolescent Coping Scale suffers from several major problems. One major problem includes the fact that the authors make reference to the need for an adolescent coping scale within an Australian context in the manual and yet provided no specific information about what is unique about the Australian context and why such an instrument would be necessary given the other coping styles instruments that are already available. Logically, following this argument, the appropriate procedure would have been to use the Adolescent Coping Scale in contrast to some other common measures of coping styles to demonstrate the superior or incremental validity of the former instrument in its use with Australian participants. Yet, no such test was conducted to support the authors' claim for the need of a coping styles measure that takes into account the Australian context. This same problem also pertains to the authors' argument of a need for an adolescent coping scale. Although the argument makes sense, the authors provide little or no evidence of how the current scale is uniquely suited for adolescents. In my assessment, simply deriving items from an adolescent sample does not make it a scale designed for adolescents, especially when the items and factor scales end up replicating scales developed for adult populations. Relatedly, the authors do not refer to other existing coping style measures and, therefore, fail to provide a justification of why the current coping style scale is needed. The authors neither discuss the problems in previous coping scales, which the current one may be aimed at correcting, nor how the current scale may be different or superior to previous scales because it addresses new domains not covered in previous scales. Hence, one is left with the concern of the reinvention of the wheel given that there are already well-established coping scales such as Lazarus and Folkman's Ways of Coping Questionnaire (T4:2936).

Other problems with the scale also include the unusual ways in which the statistical analyses were conducted for the reliability. For example, test-retest reliability was done on an item level and because many of the items were not correlated .32 and above, the authors provide a criterion that is unusual stating that if at least 70% of the respondents chose responses within one item point from each other then that is acceptable. This is a rather unusual procedure for assessing test-retest reliability. Furthermore, although the authors claim that the scale was developed by factor analysis, there are 18 scales in the final version and the various factor analyses that were conducted keep producing only six factors, which is another major problem in the development of the scale.

In addition, relatively little evidence is provided for the validity of the ACS. The authors mention the continuing work to develop validity information but the lack of a basic level of validity evidence at this point generates some concern in terms of the utility of the instrument, which is why it is still considered a research edition. For example, no concurrent validity information is provided for the Regular version of the Adolescent Coping Scale (e.g., how does it correlate with other established measures of coping styles?). Indeed, I was surprised to find a separate section on the validity of the Short Form with no information on the validity of the Regular Form. Furthermore, this information on validity of the Short Form was basically correlations with the Regular Form and yet little or no validity work has been done on the Regular Form. The only validity information provided in the manual was labeled as "item validity" (p. 33), which consisted of whether certain items loaded in the expected factors. Although factor analysis is an important step in evaluating the factorial validity of an instrument, the lack of information on the scale's concurrent validity, predictive validity, and other aspects of external validity seems quite troublesome. Another unusual aspect to the ACS is the authors' claim that this scale should be used in an idiographic rather than a nomothetic version. Given all the development work that has gone into it, I am uncertain as to the value of providing solely idiographic information to the student or the client with regard to coping styles and the lack of a nomothetic approach is problematic given the purpose of the coping scale.

In conclusion, the major problems in the Adolescent Coping Scale give me considerable reservations about using it as a measure of adolescent coping styles whether in Australia or elsewhere. This conclusion is further supported by the fact that there are other coping styles measures with much more evidence of their validity.

Review of the Adolescent Coping Scale by JUDY J. OEHLER-STINNETT, Associate Professor of Applied Behavioral Studies, Oklahoma State University, Stillwater, OK:

The Adolescent Coping Scale (ACS) was developed as a research and clinical tool for use with adolescents age 12 to 18 years of age. It represents an effort to assess an important but frequently over-

looked area, that of positive as well as less adaptive coping styles in youth. In the manual overview, the instrument is described as a research and clinical instrument. By clinical the authors mean use of the instrument as a counseling, self-help tool to help adolescents become more aware of and to change their coping strategies as needed. The manual does not provide normative information and the scale is not intended for use as a diagnostic instrument of pathological coping styles. However, the scale is described as a psychological instrument and is recommended for use by psychologists and other trained professionals.

The ACS attempts to measure both general coping styles and strategies being used for current problems by utilization of two forms, a General Form, which asks respondents to indicate how they cope across a variety of concerns, and a Specific Form, in which respondents are instructed to complete the instrument with a current concern in mind. There is no control in the scoring for the type of problem elicited by the instructions for the Specific Form. Therefore, it is unclear whether across a normative sample adolescents might respond more typically with a certain coping strategy for social versus academic problems, for example. Rather than general and specific, it may be that the two forms can be conceptualized as measures of trait versus state coping strategies. However, the data reported in the manual for both forms are so similar that it is difficult to determine any significant difference between the two forms. Also, earlier studies by the authors indicated a few gender, age, and ethnic differences in responses that are not accounted for in the current scoring and interpretation scheme.

Each form consists of 18 coping strategies with 3–5 items in each subscale. The 18 strategies range from Focus on Solving the Problem to Ignore the Problem. There are Short Forms of both the General and the Specific Form, which consist of 18 items representing one item for each subscale. Raw scores are weighted for number of items and then plotted on an individual profile sheet. Interpretation is based on frequency of strategies used and an "eyeball look" at relative frequency of each coping strategy. Although earlier published works by the authors indicate three major styles of coping derived from factor-analytic studies, Problem-Focused Coping, Coping by Reference to Others, and Non-Productive Coping, the current manual does not provide scoring for these composite subconstructs on the protocols (there is such scoring for the Short Form in the manual). This is unfortunate as the psychometric properties of these composites are more acceptable than those for the 18 coping strategies that are scored and interpreted on the profile sheet (Frydenberg & Lewis, 1990, 1993).

Although the authors are obviously familiar with the underlying dimensions of the coping construct and could easily have written items based on this knowledge, they took a novel approach in scale/item development by developing items based on pooled responses of 643 Australian adolescents to open-ended questions pertaining to their coping strategies. They were not able to differentiate items based on the General/Specific dichotomy, and items for both forms are identical. Through conceptual grouping of responses, 156 items were written. Utilizing a sample of 500 Year 7 and 11 students (which does not cover the full range of students for whom the scale is recommended), further refinement was conducted through factor analysis and item examination. These procedures are only briefly described in the manual and it is not clear what specific factor analytic criteria were used to exclude items. However, at this point the scale, consisting of 50 items, was again subjected to factor analysis resulting in 13 subscales. In order to represent another five coping styles, 29 new items were added.

Further factor analyses are problematic. Due to perceived sample size difficulties, the scale was divided into three sections and three separate factor analyses were performed, with the result being the current 18 subscales. However, it does not appear that similar subscales were grouped together in the three analyses, and it is a strong possibility that fewer than 18 factors would have emerged in a single analysis. Also, although reported item factor loadings for the scored coping strategy are high, loadings across other factors are not reported in the manual. An oblimin solution in which factors were correlated was appropriate, but there are not enough data to determine the subtest specificity of each coping strategy. Subtest intercorrelations were not reported. A description indicates that 12% were above .40, but no significance levels were given. Alpha levels for the 18 scales ranged from .62 to .87 for the Specific Form and .54 to .85 for the General Form, with correlations generally in the .70s; these results do not lend support to the internal consistency of the scored subscales. No concurrent or predictive validity studies are reported. Test-retest reliabilities for the 18 strategies on the Long Forms are also below accept-

able levels. On the Specific Form, the range is .49 to .82, with a mean of .68; for the General Form, the range is .44 to .84, with a mean of .69.

The Short Forms of the General and Specific scales consist of 18 items, with one item per strategy, as noted. Selection of these items was based on face validity, primarily, and the items' relationship to the relevant subscale, secondarily. Correlations of the items with their respective scale ranged from .61 to .86, with a mean for the Specific Form of .77 and for the General Form, .78. Nonselected item-subscale correlations were not reported. An examination of the three separate factor analyses indicates that these items did not have the highest factor loadings on the coping strategy they represent. Item test-retest correlations for selected items are unacceptable, ranging from .22 to .85 with all but two below .70. Use of the Short Forms to represent 18 distinct coping strategies cannot be recommended. One strength of the Short Forms is that factor analyses of the items yielded a three-factor solution for both the General and Specific Forms. These three factors correspond to the three conceptual categories of Solving the Problem (Problem-Focused Coping), Reference to Others (Relationship-Focused Coping), and Non-Productive Coping (Emotion-Focused Coping/Denial). The authors state that these major categories mask important strategy selection differences, and the alphas for the three factors are still below acceptable levels (.50–.69). Future studies employing a single factor analysis of all the Long-Form items and the subtest specificity statistics would assist in the determination of the appropriate number of interpretable strategies. As a counseling tool, it is useful to have the social area separated into seeking help from authority figures as opposed to friends even if these load together on a factor. It is refreshing to see seeking social support treated as a positive coping strategy rather than as pathological dependence. It is also interesting that coping through spirituality is included, a component of adaptive functioning that is important to many adolescents but ignored frequently by professionals. The most confounded strategy is Tension Reduction, which includes both expression of emotion (which can be positive) with non-productive strategies such as taking drugs or taking things out on others.

Overall, this instrument represents a good start in delineating important coping functions of adolescents, and the authors state further work is needed. It would have been nice if they had completed that work prior to publication. Due to the described psychometric limitations, it cannot be recommended as a measure of distinct modes of coping at this time. Given the paucity of instruments in this area, however, it may have appropriate uses. Because the scale is described as a self-help tool, the appropriate applied emphasis would be use as an adjunct to an interview rather than as a scorable instrument. The scale needs further psychometric refinement in order to be utilized in research studies quantifying coping strategies. The potential is there for the three major coping styles to delineate mastery and relationship motivation, as well as a helpless style, in relationship to stressors and should be further investigated. The studies that have been conducted set the ACS apart from other coping instruments, which have even less psychometric work completed to support them. Another instrument similar to the ACS, which has been investigated, is the Adolescent-Coping Orientation for Problem Experiences Scale (Plancherel & Bolognini, 1995).

REVIEWER'S REFERENCES

Frydenberg, E., & Lewis, R. (1990). How adolescents cope with different concerns: The development of the Adolescent Coping Checklist (ACC). *Psychological Test Bulletin, 3*, 63–73.
Frydenberg, E., & Lewis, R. (1993). Boys play sport and girls turn to others: Age, gender and ethnicity as determinants of coping. *Journal of Adolescence, 16*, 253–266.
Shulman, S. (1993). Close relationships and coping behavior in adolescence. *Journal of Adolescence, 16*, 267–283.
Plancherel, B., & Bolognini, M. (1995). Coping and mental health in early adolescence. *Journal of Adolescence, 18*, 459–474.

[9]
Adult Attention Deficit Disorder Behavior Rating Scale.

Purpose: Designed to "identify behavior that will support a diagnosis of Attention Deficit Disorder (ADD)."
Population: Ages 16 and above.
Publication Date: 1993.
Acronym: AADDBRS.
Scores, 10: Inattention, Impulsivity, Hyperactivity, Anger Control, Academics, Anxiety, Confidence, Aggressiveness, Resistance, Social.
Administration: Individual.
Price Data, 1993: $35 per complete kit including manual (23 pages), 25 rating sheets, and 25 profile sheets; $9.50 per 25 replacement forms (rating sheets and profile sheets).
Time: (15–30) minutes.
Comments: An extension of the Attention Deficit Disorder Behavior Rating Scales (21).
Authors: Ned Owens and Betty White Owens.
Publisher: Ned Owens Inc.

Review of the Adult Attention Deficit Disorder Behavior Rating Scale by ROBERT J. MILLER, Associate Professor of Special Education, Mankato State University, Mankato, MN:

The Adult Attention Deficit Disorder Behavior Rating Scale (AADDBRS) "was designed, specifically, to identify behavior that will support a diagnosis of Attention Deficit Disorder (ADD)" (manual, p. 2). The instrument was "not meant to be a diagnostic instrument and should not be used as such" (manual, p. 2). This instrument is suggested as a screening device to gather information for a medical diagnosis of Attention Deficit Disorder and the manual authors suggest it is to be used in conjunction with test results from the Wechsler Adult Intelligence Scale (WAIS) and the Bender Visual Motor Gestalt Test.

The adult instrument consists of 50 items related to the behavior of the subject with 5 items in each of 10 factors. These 10 factors are suggested by the authors as important for diagnosing ADD. The factors are divided into organic factors including Inattention, Impulsivity, and Hyperactivity; and, environmental factors including Anger Control, Academics, Anxiety, Confidence, Aggressiveness, Resistance, and Social. The organic factors are considered primary to the diagnosis of Attention Deficit Disorder. The environmental (secondary) factors are "precipitated" by the organic factors.

Each of the 50 items on the Scale is gender neutral and consists of a simple statement or phrase of two to eight words. Instructions for the adult completing the Scale are to rate each of the 50 behaviors with the use of a Likert-type scale ranging from a rating of 1 = *You have not exhibited this behavior as a child or an adult*; 2 = *You have exhibited this behavior as a child or an adult to a slight degree*; 3 = *You have exhibited this behavior as a child or an adult to a considerable degree*; 4 = *You have exhibited this behavior as a child or adult to a large degree*; and, 5 = *You have exhibited this behavior as a child or an adult to a very large degree*. The Adult Attention Deficit Disorder Behavior Rating Scale uses the same format as the previously published Child Scale and the same Scale Profile sheet is used for both scales. The Adult Scale is to be completed by the examinee. It is also recommended that other people who are familiar with the adult complete the Scale. The AADDBRS is untimed and simple to administer. The administration time of the scale is suggested to be from 15 minutes to 30 minutes.

Cumulative raw scores from the completed AADDBRS are to be transferred and charted for each factor on the Adult Attention Deficit Disorder Behavior Rating Scale Profile with cumulative raw score in each factor of 1—7 rated as "normal," 8—16 identified as "at risk," and 17—25 identified as "very high risk." The authors suggest that adults scoring 8 or more points on the Inattention and Impulsivity factors meet the behavior criteria for Attention Deficit Disorder without Hyperactivity and should be referred to their medical doctor for the possibility of medical intervention. According to the test Profile, adults scoring 8 or more on Inattention, Impulsivity, and Hyperactivity factors meet the criteria for Attention Deficit Disorder with Hyperactivity and should be referred to their medical doctor for the possibility of medical intervention. There is no discussion in the manual of the rationale for the score of 8 or higher as representative of ADD or ADHD. No empirical justification for a score of 8 or more as significant to a diagnosis of ADD or ADHD is provided in the manual.

Additional information provided regarding the Adult Attention Deficit Disorders Behavior Rating Scale is woefully inadequate. Information on a single study of 50 adults who had been diagnosed and treated for ADD was included in the manual as supportive documentation. The age range of the subjects was 16 to 55 and a profile of the "average" scores of the 50 adults on each of the 10 factors is included in the manual. Additionally, average IQ scores for this group and average WAIS subtests scores are provided for the group of 50 adults.

No demographic information is included regarding the gender, socioeconomic status, or distribution of ages of the sample of this study. No information was included regarding minority group representation or whether the sample was gathered from rural, urban, or suburban locations. No information was provided regarding subjects not currently identified as ADD who might have completed the Scale. This lack of the ability to compare the results of a profile to some sort of larger norm group including adults without ADD limits the usefulness of the instrument and brings into question the raw score of "eight or more" as a meaningful construct in gathering information for the diagnosis of ADD or ADHD. Presenting a chart of mean scores of 50 adult subjects is of limited value and any broad generalizations based on this single study of adults would be inappropriate. Finally, no information is included in the manual regarding either the reliability or the validity of the AADDBRS for adults or children.

The manual contains a comparison of the 50 adults' scores using the Adult Scale to scores of 50 children using the Child Scale. In their comparison of the test results of these groups, the authors chart the "average child" and "average adult" score on the AADDBRS Profile. They also compare the mean scores of adults on the WAIS, with children on the Wechsler Intelligence Scale for Children (WISC-R) as well as providing mean subtest scores for the adult sample on the WAIS and the children's sample on the WISC-R. The authors include no information concerning the 50 children used as a comparison group. The authors appear to be attempting to convince the examiner that "average" scores of adults and "average" scores for children change little on the AADDBRS and on subtests of intelligence tests over time. The comparison of these groups given the amount of information furnished in the manual is inappropriate.

According to the test manual authors, each adult completing the test "should be told to be sure to include his childhood behaviors as well as his adult behavior" (manual, p. 18). I am concerned about the wisdom and value of these instructions. The rationale for using both childhood remembrances and current behavior is flawed. Childhood behavior may, or may not, have much relevance to the current behavior of that adult. As a child, I may perceive myself as: "Fail to complete assigned tasks" (Item 1) to a "very large degree" and scoring myself as "5." However, I may be confident that I no longer exhibit this behavior as an adult. How will I rate myself? Under the current directions of the Scale, I must rate myself a "5" because I demonstrated that behavior as a child. As a result of this rating of my behavior my Scale score may be inappropriately inflated. My initial score of "5" on Item 1 and four additional scores of "1" on the total of five foils places my raw score at "9" even if I do not believe I have any concerns regarding my behavior as an adult. I would not recommend the use of the Adult Attention Deficit Disorders Behavior Rating Scale as a screening device for ADD or ADHD.

Review of the Attention Deficit Disorder Behavior Rating Scale by JAMES C. REED, Chief Psychologist, St. Luke's Hospital, New Bedford, MA:

The Adult Attention Deficit Disorder Behavior Rating Scale is based on a previous scale that was developed for children. In fact, the same profile sheet is used for both scales. The scale consists of 50 items, and the person taking the test rates each item on a scale from 1 to 5: 1. "you have not exhibited this behavior as a child or an adult" … 5. "you have exhibited this behavior as a child or an adult to a very large degree." The columns are summed and the scores are referred to a normative table. For each of the 10 factors a score between 8 and 16 indicates that the person is at risk for the behavior, and a score between 17 and 25 places the person at very high risk. The authors report that the adult scale had been administered to 50 adults who have been diagnosed as having attention deficit disorder and as having been treated with success. The age range was from 16 to 55.

In the manual the directions on page 18 for the administration of the adult scale refer to page 11 for the diagnosis of attention deficit disorder. Page 11, however, is in the section of the manual that pertains to children. Consequently, the inference can be made that one uses the same interpretive procedures for the adults as one does for the children. In the children's section it is stated, "The first three behaviors, Inattention, Impulsivity, and Hyperactivity, are required for a diagnosis of Attention Deficit Disorder with Hyperactivity. These behaviors are classified on the profile sheet as Primary/Organic behaviors, because they are organically, or neurologicallly caused" (p. 2). The manual authors also state the disorder is a chemical disorder and neurological weaknesses need to be explored. For adults the implication is strongly present, if not directly stated, that the Wechsler Adult Intelligence Scale (WAIS), should be used to explore the neurological basis.

In considering this scale for use, there are several factors to be reviewed. From a positive standpoint, it might be said that the scale has face (perhaps a better word would be "faith") validity. The 50 items represent behaviors that most would consider, in one form or another, to be indicative of an ADD. However, these behaviors could also be indicative of a number of other behavioral and/or psychiatric problems, and nowhere in the manual do the authors present any information concerning the uniqueness of these behaviors to attention deficit disorder. In other words, there are no objective indications of validity. The sample of 50 adults is not specified with respect to any defining characteristic. It is impossible for the reader to know how the diagnosis was made of attention deficit disorder for these adults. It is also unknown, or at least not given, as to the population from which they were drawn.

Another limitation of the scale is that there is no information presented about the independence of the 10 factors. No reliability coefficients are reported, no correlation coefficients between the factors are given, and no evidence is presented to show these factors will differentiate ADD persons from other behaviorally disordered groups.

The authors stated that ADD is a chemical disorder, but the basis for this statement or evidence in support of it is not presented. They recommend the use of the WAIS to detect subtle neurological disorders. It is highly questionable whether the WAIS is a suitable instrument for detecting subtle neurological disorders, and the available literature suggests that it is not. Furthermore, the pattern analysis recommended by the authors is not explicit and it fails to consider the low reliability of the WAIS subtests. For example, in the manual, the authors indicate the score on the Information subtest for ADD persons is often relatively lower than that of Comprehension and Similarities because "the person can not sit still or pay attention long enough to acquire the information" (p. 19). What constitutes relative lowness is not stated. Other equally undefined pattern interpretations for the WAIS are also given.

In summary, the scale consists of 50 items that many observers would agree are characteristic of ADD to some extent or another. However, the psychometric limitations of the scale are compelling. There are no reliability or validity coefficients. The adult population on which the test was developed is not defined. Validating data for the risk and the high risk categories are not presented. The test appears to be lacking in psychometric characteristics that specialists in test construction deem important. At present the scale might be regarded as an exploratory instrument, for it is only recently, as the authors point out, that the concept of an attention deficit disorder among adults has come into existence.

[10]

Alcohol Clinical Index.

Purpose: "To identify alcohol problems among patients."
Population: Adults at-risk for alcohol problems.
Publication Date: 1987.
Administration: Individual.
Price Data, 1990: $9.75 per user's booklet (31 pages); $9.95 per 50 questionnaires (specify test).
Time: Administration time not reported.
Authors: Harvey A. Skinner and Stephen Holt.
Publisher: Addiction Research Foundation [Canada].
    a) CLINICAL SIGNS.
    Scores, 6: Hand, Head, Abdomen, Body, Locomotor Function, Total.
    b) MEDICAL HISTORY.
    c) ALCOHOL USE.

d) RISK FACTORS.
Scores, 2: Early Indicators, Risk Factors.

Review of the Alcohol Clinical Index by STEVEN I. PFEIFFER, Professor and Director of School Psychology, Farleigh Dickinson University, Teaneck, NJ:

The Alcohol Clinical Index (ACI) was designed as a brief and economic screening instrument for use by physicians and allied health care professionals to identify alcohol use problems among patients in primary care settings. The ACI consists of two components: a 17-item clinical signs checklist (CSC) and a 13-item Medical History Questionnaire (MHQ).

The test authors, Drs. Skinner and Holt, advocate administering laboratory tests (e.g., serum gamma-glutamyl-transferase and mean corpuscular volume) and brief alcohol questionnaires (e.g., CAGE questionnaire, Alcohol Dependence Scale) to corroborate a positive finding on the ACI.

The ACI was derived from a comprehensive set of 108 clinical indicators of alcohol abuse (Skinner, Holt, Sheu, & Israel, 1986; also test manual). It is recommended that the 17 clinical signs should be elicited by a physician or nurse as part of a physical examination (illustrative items: "rhinophyma-varying degrees of epithelial thickening, dilation of sebaceous follicles and bluish-red discoloration of the distal portion of the nose"; "gynecomastia-male only, glandular and fatty tissue enlargement of both breasts").

The 13 Medical History items can either be self-completed by the patient or administered by the physician or nurse. Illustrative items include: "Do you often wake up with headache?" and "Do you find it hard to remember recent events?"

The manual reports the diagnostic rule that if either clinical signs or Medical History is greater than or equal to four then there is a "high likelihood of alcohol abuse or dependence" (p. 6). The manual recommends, however, as mentioned above, corroboration using laboratory tests and alcohol questionnaires. Although a decision rule is provided, the manual offers no evidence to support the diagnostic sensitivity, specificity, or predictive power of the ACI.

Similarly, the manual includes no information to suggest that any estimates of reliability or validity were obtained. Also, it is uncertain what type, if any, of pilot testing or validation was undertaken, and basic information on the sample used for test development is sorely missing. There are no norms in the manual, and one has no idea if the test or test items are biased across different racial, ethnic, or geographic regional groups.

A study by Skinner and Holt, along with two coinvestigators, reports a higher predictive power for the ACI than with laboratory tests in distinguishing an outpatient group with alcohol problems from social drinkers (Skinner, Holt et al., 1986). This same investigation provides the data that led to the diagnostic rule reported in the test manual (88%–90% accuracy was achieved by the decision rule of clinical signs or medical history of four or more).

However, a recently published validity study with lower socioeconomic alcohol-dependent men obtained overall predictive values for the ACI not nearly as favorable as those reported by the test authors. For example, The Clinical Signs Checklist yielded 70% accuracy regardless of cutoff point (ranging from 1 through 5). The Medical History questionnaire generated somewhat better outcomes, with an overall accuracy of 84% (Alterman, Gelfund, & Sweeney, 1992).

The ACI is a brief, economical, and easy-to-administer screening instrument to identify primary care patients with alcohol problems. The authors appropriately recognized the need for future investigators to evaluate the diagnostic sensitivity and specificity of the index (Skinner, Holt et al., 1986). Research is also needed to evaluate sources of measurement error and estimates of reliability, content and construct validity, and possible test and item bias (e.g., one item on the clinical signs checklist inquires about tattoos). Until these much needed reliability, validation, and norming steps are undertaken, the ACI should be restricted to use as a research tool and not in individual clinical decision making.

REVIEWER'S REFERENCES

Skinner, H. A., Holt, S., Sheu, W. J., & Israel, M. (1986). Clinical versus laboratory detection of alcohol abuse: The Alcohol Clinical Index. *British Medical Journal, 292,* 1703–1708.

Alterman, A. I., Gelfund, L. A., & Sweeney, K. K. (1992). The Alcohol Clinical Index in lower socioeconomic alcohol-dependent men. *Alcoholism: Clinical and Experimental Research, 16,* 960–963.

Review of the Alcohol Clinical Index by WILLIAM I. SAUSER, JR., Professor and Executive Director for Outreach, College of Business, Auburn University, Auburn, AL:

The Alcohol Clinical Index consists of 13 objective medical history questions that can be answered "yes" or "no," plus 17 observable clinical signs that could be recognized easily by trained health care professionals. According to the manual, it is intended for use as a low-cost screening device, administered by primary care physicians or nurses, "to identify patients who drink excessively but who do not consider themselves 'alcoholics.' The basic strategy is to intervene with brief counseling before the patient has developed major symptoms of alcohol dependence" (p. 2).

In the manual, the test developers cite epidemiological evidence from the U.S.A. and Canada indicating that roughly 5% of North American adults are alcoholics, 20% are problem drinkers, 60% are social drinkers, and 15% abstain from consuming alcohol. There are a number of clinical assessment devices available to identify alcoholics (Ingram, Sauser, & Owens, 1989); a purpose of the Alcohol Clinical Index, however, is to distinguish between social drinkers and problem drinkers, the latter group being defined in the manual as those individuals who "do *not* show major symptoms of alcohol dependence … [but] drink at levels that have increased health risk and … may have accrued some consequences related to drinking in the recent past" (p. 1).

It is these problem drinkers who the test developers view as a rich target audience for early detection and intervention programs. They argue that such early detection and intervention might curb the incidence of alcohol-related problems, which have staggering economic and social-psychological costs. Skinner, Holt, and Israel (1981) note that in the United States "alcohol-related problems cost nearly $43 billion in 1975 as a result of lost production, motor vehicle accidents, crime, social problems, and demands for health care services. Indeed, over 12% of the total expenditure on health care for adults … was for alcohol-related medical service" (p. 1142).

The Alcohol Clinical Index is very simple and straightforward. Literate patients could complete the medical history in a matter of minutes; illiterate or visually impaired patients would have no difficulty responding to the questions administered orally. Similarly, a medical professional could easily detect the presence or absence of the clinical signs during the course of a routine physical examination. The Alcohol Clinical Index, when administered alongside other simple questionnaires recommended by the test developers (and included within the manual), appears to be effective for use as a screening device for identifying problem drinkers.

Despite its simplicity, the Alcohol Clinical Index is built upon significant scientific research. The authors cite 11 of their published research articles (readily available in most medical libraries) substantiating the effective use of the Alcohol Clinical Index in the manner they recommend. Most impressive is a study of 131 outpatients with alcohol problems, 131 social drinkers, and 52 patients from family practice (Skinner, Holt, Sheu, & Israel, 1986), which found "a probability of alcohol abuse exceeding 0.90 … if four or more clinical signs or four or more medical history items from the index were present" (p. 1703). This study serves as the basis for the diagnostic rule given in the manual, "If Clinical Signs ≥4 or Medical History ≥4 then there is a high likelihood of alcohol abuse or dependence. Investigate further using the laboratory tests and alcohol questionnaires" (p. 6).

One warning is in order: Personnel specialists and human resource managers must recognize that the Alcohol Clinical index is a medical examination that leads to medical diagnosis and intervention. It should *not* be used as a routine employment screening device lest the potential employing organization run afoul of the Americans with Disabilities Act (Veres & Sims, 1995).

In summary, the Alcohol Clinical Index is a short, easily administered medical screening device that may be used by primary care physicians and nurses to detect problem drinkers, who may be further examined and targeted for early intervention programs. Although presented in a simple, easy-to-understand manual, the Alcohol Clinical Index is the product of rigorous scientific study.

REVIEWER'S REFERENCES

Skinner, H. A., Holt, S., & Israel, Y. (1981). Early identification of alcohol abuse: I. Critical issues and psychosocial indicators for a composite index. *Canadian Medical Association Journal, 124*, 1141–1152.
Skinner, H. A., Holt, S., Sheu, W. J., & Israel, Y. (1986). Clinical versus laboratory detection of alcohol abuse: The Alcohol Clinical Index. *British Medical Journal, 292*, 1703–1708.
Ingram, J. J., Sauser, W. I., Jr., & Owens, C. A. (1989). Assessment: Determination of client needs and progress. In D. R. Self (Ed.), *Alcoholism treatment marketing: Beyond TV ads and speeches* (pp. 207–223). New York: Haworth.
Veres, J. G., III, & Sims, R. R. (Eds.). (1995). *Human resource management and the Americans with Disabilities Act.* Westport, CT: Quorum.

[11]

Aphasia Diagnostic Profiles.

Purpose: "Provides a systematic method of assessing language and communication impairment associated with aphasia."

Population: Adults with acquired brain damage.

Publication Date: 1992.

Acronym: ADP.

Scores: Behavioral Profile Score plus 9 subtests: Personal Information, Writing, Reading, Fluency, Naming, Auditory Comprehension, Repetition, Elicited Gestures, Singing.

Administration: Individual.

Price Data, 1997: $179 per complete kit including 25 record forms, manual (55 pages), stimulus cards/letterboard/pointer, and carrying case; $45 per 25 record forms; $50 per manual; $49 per stimulus cards/letterboard/pointer; $24.99 per carrying case.

Time: (40–50) minutes.
Author: Nancy Helm-Estabrooks.
Publisher: Applied Symbolix.

Review of the Aphasia Diagnostic Profiles by WILFRED G. VAN GORP, Associate Professor of Psychology in Psychiatry and Director, Neuropsychology Assessment Program, Cornell University Medical College, White Plains, NY:

The Aphasia Diagnostic Profiles (ADP) is a standardized assessment measure of language function for individuals with brain damage and provides "a systematic method of assessing language and communication impairment associated with aphasia resulting from acquired brain damage" (p. 1). It can be administered by speech-language pathologists, neuropsychologists, and others trained in assessing and working with patients with aphasia. Patients without the ability to speak (such as that resulting from severe spinal cord injuries) can also be assessed. Individual subtest scores are obtained, as well as an overall Aphasia Severity Score, which allows the classification of overall level of impairment.

The test manual is well written and the test stimuli seem appropriate and well designed. The author has appropriately included scales for assessment of Writing, Reading, Fluency, Naming, Comprehension, Repetition, Gesturing, and Singing, and these scales appear reasonably comprehensive for individuals with known or suspected aphasia. The instructions for the patient are well written in a conversational tone, which is useful (if not required) to elicit maximal understanding and cooperation from aphasic patients. Individuals seeking a literature on others' use of the instrument, including external validation and reliability studies, will be disappointed, as this reviewer could not identify a body of literature as yet on this test outside of what is reported in the test manual.

The author (Helm-Estabrooks) has also included assessment of a "behavioral profile" to assess the patient's functioning in the behavioral, nonaphasic realm. Although the inclusion of a rating system to assess functioning in the behavioral realm is a distinct positive feature of this test, one must be careful not to conclude that information from the behavioral profile can be used to characterize neurocognitive status, as is sometimes implied by the author.

The manual also contains instructions on how one may calculate an "Index of Wordiness" (p. 19).

This is potentially a very useful feature of the ADP. The author recommends that this Index be used "only for comparisons across different administrations to the same patient" (p. 20), but it seems that there are other potential uses of such a scale. Normative data for patients with different disorders producing an aphasia (such as Alzheimer's disease) may produce distinct profiles of "wordiness" and, as such, offer potential diagnostic utility. For instance, the patient with Alzheimer's disease may produce a large or normal verbal output but with very low content, whereas the patient with vascular dementia may produce a restricted output with normal content. As such, the Index of Wordiness may have potential use beyond that described in the test manual.

The psychometric features of the ADP, as described in the manual, may be sufficient for an initial introduction of the test into the literature, but they are thus far quite limited. Although a relatively large sample of individuals with cerebrovascular accidents (CVA) is included in the standardization sample and information regarding age, gender, and education on the subjects in the sample is included, no information on subjects' ethnicity is provided. Content and criterion validity are not conclusively demonstrated by the data reported in the test manual. For instance, the author clearly defines content validity, but she does not provide independent, empirical assurance that this was actually achieved. Although she refers the reader to portions of the manual that discuss the rationale for selection of test items or scales, there is no attempt psychometrically to demonstrate content validity, such as by having raters blindly sort test items into the domains they feel the items measure.

There are difficulties with criterion-related validity, as well. Evidence of criterion validity is attempted through an analysis showing that patients with left hemisphere CVAs (and bilateral CVAs) perform worse on the ADP scales than the normal controls. This may establish that the items adequately identify patients with strokes, but without the inclusion of other groups, we cannot determine the specificity of these items/scales for patients with left hemisphere damage, or aphasic disturbances in patients with other neurologic disorders (such as Alzheimer's disease, Parkinson's disease, etc.). A better approach might have been to have a clinician use another aphasia battery or clinical examination as the gold standard, and rate patients' abilities in these domains. Patients' scores on the ADP scales could then be validated against the "gold standard" test battery.

The authors do report useful data on construct validity, demonstrating relatively high intercorrelations (many of which are $r = .50$ or above) among ADP subscales (as would be expected, because all tests are measures of language function in a language-impaired population). Additionally, a factor structure revealed conceptually meaningful factors. Hence, there is reasonable evidence for adequate construct validity of the ADP, though no external validation measures were used.

Test-retest reliability data are reported (ranging from $r = .64-.91$) based on a test-retest interval of within 30 days. The test user must exercise considerable caution in interpreting these data because the conclusions are based upon retesting of only 19 subjects. Additionally, there is a discussion of interrater agreement, though no data are presented to actually support any conclusions regarding interrater reliability on the ADP.

In sum, the ADP seems to hold promise as a clinical tool to assess various aspects of language functioning in individuals with aphasic disorders. Adequate reliability and validity, however, have yet to be fully established, and as such, this test cannot be recommended over other standard language batteries used to assess aphasia, such as the Boston Diagnostic Aphasia Examination (T4:207) or the Western Aphasia Battery (T4:2949). These latter tests have not only been standardized by their authors, but there is now a published literature on them upon which the test user can refer to make conclusions regarding test validity and reliability in different clinical settings. The ADP is still waiting for this stage to occur.

Review of the Aphasia Diagnostic Profiles by RICHARD G. WHITTEN, Clinical Assistant Professor of Psychiatry, University of South Dakota Medical School, Sioux Falls, SD:

Aphasia is communication impairment due to brain damage. The Aphasia Diagnostic Profiles (ADP) is a systematic means for assessing residual strengths and weaknesses in communication following a stroke or some other brain trauma. In common with other aphasia test batteries, the ADP is made up of subtests and normed against a representative (though very small) sample of subjects. The ADP also includes a method for classifying communication performance into specific aphasia syndromes (Broca's aphasia, conduction aphasia, etc.). The ADP will be of interest to speech therapists, psychiatrists, neurologists, and psychologists involved with rehabilitation and training.

The ADP kit contains a well-written manual, a deck of 25 black-and-white line-drawing stimulus cards, a letter board, and a very detailed record form. The simplicity and portability of the materials is completely suitable for hospital bedside administration although use of a tape recorder is sometimes needed. Administration time depends upon patient characteristics, but the manual suggests 40–50 minutes is sufficient.

The nine subtests are administered in a specific order and elicit different communication skills. These subtests should be familiar to examiners who have used the Boston Diagnostic Aphasia Examination (BDAE; T4:207) or the Multilingual Aphasia Examination (MAE). The ADP subtests are Personal Information, Writing, Reading, Fluency, Naming, Auditory Comprehension, Repetition, Elicited Gestures, and Singing. Errors in speech performance (paraphasias) can be noted and scaled on the Error Profiles. The examiner can also attempt to describe specific patient behavioral and emotional difficulties which could interfere with performance (Disinhibition, Unconcerned, etc.) with a 10th subtest called the Behavioral Profile.

Correct performances on individual items within a subtest are typically summed and then can be transformed into standard scores and percentile rankings. Combinations of certain subtests in turn make up three Composite Scores: Lexical Retrieval, Aphasia Severity, and Alternative Communication. Subtest scores can also be used in a decision tree analysis to classify the speaker's performance into a specific aphasia syndrome.

Although the majority of subtests are straightforward, the ADP measure of spontaneous speech or Fluency is quite involved and certainly one of the ADP's strengths. Ironically, although the differentiation of fluent and nonfluent speech output has traditionally been a basis for aphasia syndrome classification, definitions vary and interrater reliability can be quite marginal. Unfortunately, no information on interrater reliability for the ADP Fluency measure is published.

Psychometrically, the ADP is a somewhat mixed bag. About 290 right-handed, presumably native-English-speaking subjects, ages 20–99 years were administered the ADP at 42 North American sites. Both normal subjects ($n = 40$) and potentially aphasic subjects were tested and their results lumped together ($n = 222$) to form one set of norms. Separate age and education norms are not published. The author has recognized the necessity for norming performance against a relevant group of subjects (the elderly), but unfortunately, only 11 "normal" subjects over 60 years of age were included. The 168 over-60 subjects were aphasic or potentially aphasic referrals to speech therapists. Consistent with the high risk population, about 75% of those subjects reporting an education level have fewer than 12 years of education, but surprisingly we are not given information on the relationship between education and subtest performance. The failure to explore how premorbid abilities (education, IQ, learning disabilities, etc.) affect current performance is a serious drawback for many aphasia test batteries, like the ADP, and can lead to overdiagnosis and overtreatment.

Similarly, although the manual's published reliability figures on subtest score stability over time are quite adequate (test-retest $r = .68–.91$) and the reported subtest interitem consistency is adequate (Cronbach's alpha $= .73–.96$), no interrater reliability figures are published. This is a serious drawback because personal experience and judgment are still necessary to administer the exam, despite the thoroughly detailed directions in the manual. Interrater reliability on the Behavioral Profile can certainly be expected to be marginal because few concrete behavioral "anchors" are available to judge "Discouragement," "Suspiciousness," and other undefined descriptors.

ADP validity was explored using a discriminant function analysis to classify subjects into diagnostic (Right CVA vs. Bilateral CVA vs. Normal) groups. Sensitivity and specificity appear adequate at this level of diagnosis. A principal components analysis and factor analysis (oblique rotation) were also undertaken. The ADP is certainly a multifactorial exam, with what looks like a primary, general aphasia factor subsuming the majority of subtests, an attention or distractibility factor, and a phrase length or fluency factor. Factor-based scales have not been published, however, and the Composite Scores (made up of subtest scores) are not consistent with the published factors. Finally, although one very exciting and significant advantage of the ADP is an aphasia syndrome decision tree based on subtest scores, no reliability or validity studies of this system are presented.

Hence, the ADP is a highly ambitious undertaking which offers in one portable and efficient package the opportunity to elicit enormous amounts of detailed, clinically relevant data during a brief bedside or treatment room exam. Unfortunately, it cannot be recommended as an alternative to the BDAE or MAE, or as the primary language evaluative system, because the normative sample needs to be enlarged, the effects of age and education need to be published, and interrater reliability needs to be established. Alternative factor-based composite scores should be offered, and the validity of its aphasia syndrome classification system needs to be explored. Even given its limitations, it is an exciting battery with which anyone evaluating and treating aphasia should be familiar.

[12]
Aprenda: La Prueba De Logros en Español.

Purpose: Designed as a "norm-referenced achievement test for Spanish-speaking students."
Publication Date: 1990–1991.
Administration: Group.
Price Data, 1996: $23 each examination kit (Primary 1—Intermediate 3) including test booklet and directions for administering ('90, 47 pages), practice test and directions, and hand-scorable answer folder (Preprimer—$22); $15 for 25 practice tests and directions; $109 for machine-scorable test booklets and $74.50 for hand-scorable test booklets (Preprimer through Primary 3); $74.50 for reusable test booklets and $17 for hand- and machine-scorable answer folders (Intermediate 1—3); $30.50 per norms booklet; $23.50 per index of instructional objectives; $41.50 per technical data report; $56 per multilevel norms booklet ('91, 173 pages); price data for scoring services available from publisher.
Foreign Language Edition: Test booklets written in Spanish.
Author: The Psychological Corporation.
Publisher: The Psychological Corporation.
a) PREPRIMER (NIVEL PREPRIMARIO).
Population: Grades K.5–1.5.
Scores, 7: Sounds and Letters, Word Reading, Sentence Reading, Total Reading, Listening to Words and Stories, Mathematics, Total.
Time: (145) minutes.
b) PRIMARY 1 (PRIMER NIVEL PRIMARIO).
Population: Grades 1.5–2.5.
Scores, 11: Word Reading, Reading Comprehension, Total Reading, Language, Spelling, Listening, Concepts of Numbers, Mathematics Computation, Mathematics Applications, Total Mathematics, Total.
Time: (235) minutes.
c) PRIMARY 2 (SEGUNDO NIVEL PRIMARIO).
Population: Grades 2.5–3.5.
Scores, 11: Reading Vocabulary, Reading Comprehension, Total Reading, Language, Spelling, Lis-

tening, Concepts of Numbers, Mathematics Computations, Mathematics Applications, Total Mathematics, Total.

Time: (230) minutes.

d) PRIMARY 3 (TERCER NIVEL PRIMARIO).

Population: Grades 3.5–4.5.

Scores, 14: Reading Vocabulary, Reading Comprehension, Total Reading, Language Mechanics, Language Expression, Total Language, Study Skills, Spelling, Listening, Concepts of Number, Mathematics Computation, Mathematics Applications, Total Mathematics, Total.

Time: (275) minutes.

e) INTERMEDIATE 1 (PRIMER NIVEL INTERMEDIO).

Population: Grades 4.5–5.5.

Scores, 14: Reading Vocabulary, Reading Comprehension, Total Reading, Language Mechanics, Language Expression, Total Language, Study Skills, Spelling, Listening, Concepts of Numbers, Mathematics Computation, Mathematics Applications, Total Mathematics, Total.

Time: (285) minutes.

f) INTERMEDIATE 2 (SEGUNDO NIVEL INTERMEDIO).

Population: Grades 5.5–6.5.

Scores: Same as *e* above.

Time: Same as *e* above.

g) INTERMEDIATE 3 (TERCER NIVEL INTERMEDIO).

Population: Grades 6.5–8.9.

Scores: Same as *e* above.

Time: Same as *e* above.

Review of the Aprenda: La Prueba De Logros en Español by MARIA MEDINA-DIAZ, Assistant Professor of Educational Measurement and Evaluation, School of Education, University of Puerto Rico, Rio Piedras, PR:

Aprenda: La Prueba De Logros en Español "was developed to respond to concerns about the assessment of academic achievement of Spanish-speaking students" (p. 9) in the United States who "lack the English-language skills required for demonstrating their achievement on English-language tests" (p. 9). It is a norm-referenced test designed to measure achievement of those students from Kindergarten through grade 8 whose primary language of instruction is Spanish and "to provide information upon which decisions for improving instruction can be made" (p. 9).

Aprenda items reflect mostly the content measured by the Stanford Achievement Test Series, Eighth Edition and cover additional objectives re-

lated with the domain and usage of the Spanish language. The test items comprising Mathematics Computation, which are independent of language, are the same items that are in corresponding levels of the Stanford Battery ("Cálculos matemáticos"). No information is provided in the technical manual regarding who participated in writing the items and how the test specifications were prepared.

The tryout items were reviewed by Spanish-speaking content experts and editors, measurement specialists, and teachers of bilingual education programs. An advisory panel of eight bilingual educators reviewed the tryout items to detect item bias (i.e., gender, ethnic/class, and regional caused by language differences among Hispanic populations) and stereotypes. In addition, statistical procedures for detecting item bias by gender groups were applied and items exhibiting large differences were flagged for possible exclusion from the pool of tryout items. No information on the criterion used to flag items, nor on the number of items flagged and excluded was supplied in the technical report.

The authors advise that the items were checked for readability and vocabulary by comparing the items with Spanish-language instructional materials. No detailed procedures and statistical indexes related to the readability levels of the test were reported in the technical manual. Despite the authors' efforts, I think there are regional differences among Spanish-speaking people for some of the vocabulary words on the test. For example, the following words have different meanings among Spanish-speaking students: "mecate," "maceta," "sonajas," "cuadras," "pelotas," "soccer," "armijo," "pastel," "puré," calcetín," "chamarra," "pila," "lumbre," "calificaciones," "cuadernos," "tinaja," "revista," "pegadura," and "cubeta." The semantic structure of the stem, the content, and vocabulary included in the test items are most consistent with Mexican-American population usage in the United States.

In addition, a careful examination of the pictures and activities of the children show stereotyped messages. For example, in the Preprimer test most of the girls are wearing ribbons and in some items are the passive figures. Also, the usage of Hispanic-origin names gives the misleading impression that all Spanish-speaking children have names such as "Lupita," "Pepe," and "Lola."

NORMS. The samples for the spring and fall 1989 standardization and normalization procedures were selected to represent the national Spanish-speaking school population in terms of region of the United States and country of origin based on the 1980s U.S. Census data. Districts with bilingual programs were selected from 15 states around the country. "Approximately 7000 students from 94 school districts participated in the spring standardization, with another 1800 students" in grades 1 through 6 in the "equating levels program and 1000 in the equating to the Stanford" (p. 23) test. Approximately 3,000 students participated in the fall standardization. Sufficient details about how the sample was selected are not provided in the technical manual. No data of the sample characteristics by school grade levels were reported.

VALIDITY. The specific procedures for developing the test blueprint and the tryout items are not detailed in the technical manual. Evidence in support of content validity can be found by comparing the test content and the Aprenda's Index of Instructional Objectives (IIO), which includes specific item-by-item objectives and p-values (difficulty indexes) calculated with the national sample of students. Each instructional objective is represented by 1 through 18 items across the different subtests. The items that measure the same clusters of skills (or content cluster) were grouped together for analyzing the student's performance in comparison with the norms. Common content objectives across test levels include: (a) Number Concepts (whole numbers and fractions), (b) Number Calculations (whole numbers), (c) Mathematical Applications (problem solving, geometry/ measurement), and (d) Listening (vocabulary and listening comprehension). The same content objectives are found in the three intermediate test levels. A good addition are the subtests of Study Skills and Thinking Skills in Primary 3 and Intermediate tests. The Thinking Skills are embedded throughout the battery and an individual's score is reported.

In order to use the test data meaningfully, the authors recommend users compare local curriculum objectives with the behavior called for in the test items and what is included in the IIO. According to the authors "Aprenda uses the same stringent criteria as those established for the Stanford series and assesses important instructional objectives at each grade [level] from Kindergarten to Grade 8" (p. 9). There is no additional information, however, about the match of the test to frequently used textbooks or any attempt to link the test to various state-level objectives.

Subtest and total scores increase from fall to spring of the same school years supporting the au-

thors' claim that the Aprenda is sensitive to developmental instructional sequences. However, this claim should be taken cautiously because the mean p-values in some instances (particularly in the intermediate levels) for the subtests and the total battery in the spring administration for the previous grade level were greater than in the fall administration of the next grade level. Overall, there is a very small increment in the mean difficulty values (p-values) across grade levels suggesting the test items are a bit easier for the students from one grade level to another. The p-values for content clusters provide useful information about the item-objectives difficulty levels with the national sample.

RELIABILITY. Kuder-Richardson 20 reliability coefficients, mean, standard deviations, and standard errors of measurement for fall and spring standardization samples (i.e., national school and Spanish-speaking school populations) for each test, subtests, and grade level are presented in tables. The reliability coefficients for all grades for the subtests ranged from .661 to .966 with the national sample and ranged from .695 to .961 with the Spanish-speaking sample. For the basic battery for every grade level and group, the reliability estimates exceeded .95. Kuder-Richardson 21 reliability coefficients were also calculated for the cluster content of each subtest. A great variation is found in these estimates across content cluster and grade levels. Alternate-form reliability coefficients were not reported. Correlations between subtests ranged from .43 to .86. These reliability-related estimates are quite acceptable for a test battery of this kind.

TEST ADMINISTRATION. For each test level, there is a booklet entitled *Directions for Administering* that includes two versions: students' directions in Spanish and directions for the administrator in English (English/Spanish); and students' directions in Spanish and directions for the administrator in Spanish (Spanish/Spanish). This booklet also contains a brief description of the subtests and the test materials. Test administration should be divided in several sittings and the total time allocated to each one is reported. The total testing time suggested is 75 minutes. The administration of a complete battery can take 2 or 3 days.

Students in kindergarten through grade 3 take the test in machine-scorable booklets. Separate answer sheets are used by students in grades 4 through 8. A Practice test is included to be administered to all students a week before the test.

In the Preprimer ("Nivel Primario") and Primary 1 ("Primer Nivel Primario") tests, the instructions and test items are read to the students. Guidelines for the time for pausing between each item are not provided. The inclusion of a Listening subtest at all levels is a distinct feature of the battery, but the administration procedures raise some concern. Although the teacher's familiar voice may be comforting to the students, the threat to standardization could be substantial across various teachers. Two additional concerns are the length of the tests (Preprimer, 195 items; Primary 1, 265 items; Primary 2, 284 items; Primary 3, 355 items; Intermediate levels, 357 items) and the number of items of the same type (18 items in some cases) that the student should answer related to each objective. This may affect students' fatigue, motivation, and anxiety for answering the tests, particularly in kindergarten and first grade.

TEST REPORTING. Aprenda can be hand scored or machine scored. Individual test results are reported using raw scores and norm-referenced scores (i.e., percentile ranks, stanines, grade equivalents, and scaled scores). Procedures for converting raw scores to scaled scores, and scaled scores to obtain percentile ranks, stanines, and grade equivalents are well explained in the Multilevel Norms Booklet. Norms tables are included by reference group (National School Population or Spanish-speaking School Population), grade (K—8), and time of the year (spring or fall).

Individual and class reports also provide raw scores in the content cluster of the subtests in the battery. This may be helpful in identifying students' strengths and weaknesses in specific objectives within a content area. For individual students, the raw score on a particular content cluster is converted to a stanine and then to a performance category (Below average, Average, and Above average). This provides a comparison with the performance of the national sample of the students at the same grade level and time of year. The percent of students in each of the performance categories can be determined for groups of students.

SUMMARY. Most of the criticisms of the Aprenda test battery result of the absence of specific and essential information about its construction and support for validity. Fine differences in vocabulary and instructional experiences among these students are not quite captured in this instrument or any other achievement test yet designed. Deficiencies can be reduced, however, by further revisions. As an achievement battery, its reliability and difficulty indexes are quite acceptable. The individual and class reports provide useful information for instructional purposes. The potential user must check the purposes, objectives, and content carefully to be assured of a match between the test and the contexts in which it is used.

Review of the Aprenda: La Prueba De Logros en Español by SALVADOR HECTOR OCHOA, Assistant Professor of Educational Psychology, Texas A&M University, College Station, TX:

The Aprenda: La Prueba De Logros en Español is designed to assess the achievement of students who receive instruction in Spanish. The Aprenda was designed to closely correlate with the content of the Stanford Achievement Test Series. Although the Aprenda is not a direct translation of the Stanford Achievement Test Series, it was designed to equate to the Stanford Achievement Test Series, Eighth Edition "in order to maintain the capability for tracking growth when students exit a bilingual program" (p. 26 of technical manual).

The Aprenda standardization sample and its description have limitations. First, the test publishers conducted a fall and spring standardization procedure. The sample for the spring standardization consisted of 7,000 students; and the Fall standardization was made up of 3,000 pupils. No reason is given in the technical manual as to why the size of the standardization samples differed so significantly.

Second, the technical manual author states that "94 school districts ... participated in the Spring standardization sample" (p. 23), but Appendix 6 lists only 49 school districts. Appendix 6, however, does list an additional 45 school districts that were included in the fall standardization sample. It appears that there is a clerical error on page 23 of the manual.

Third, the test publisher reports that both standardization samples represented "the national Spanish-speaking school population in terms of region of the United States and country of origin" (p. 23). Data provided on Table 3 of the technical manual, however, indicate that this is not the case. On Table 3, the test publishers report the West geographical region has 30% of the total U.S. Spanish-speaking school enrollment. The percentages of students in the spring and fall standardization samples from the West geographical region of the United States, however, were 68% and 82%, respectively. The Northeast, Midwest, and South regions were not adequately represented. Similarly, on Table 3, the test publishers report that Cubans constitute 6% of the total U.S. Spanish-speaking school enrollment. The percentage of students in both standardization samples whose country of origin is Cuba was zero. Fourth, no information is provided in the manual concerning the gender, age, grade level, and socioeconomic status characteristics of the sample. Thus, one is unable to discern if a sufficient number of students were included across all age and grade levels.

With respect to the sample used to equate the Aprenda with the Stanford, the manual author reports it consisted of 1,000 students who were "identified by their school districts as being equally proficient in English and in Spanish" (p. 26). The manual does not contain, however, necessary information with respect to gender, age, grade level, socioeconomic status, country of origin, and geographical region. Moreover, the test publishers fail to provide the criteria school districts used to identify students who were balanced bilinguals in English and Spanish. This is especially critical given that it is difficult to find students who are truly balanced bilingual students across reading, writing, listening, and speaking. All four of these domains influence achievement.

With respect to reliability, the manual contains information only about internal consistency. The Kuder-Richardson Formula 20 coefficients reported for the total battery across all grade levels on all seven levels of the Aprenda are in the mid to high .90s. This is quite good. An overwhelming majority of the cluster scores across all grade levels on all seven levels of the Aprenda are above .80 and are more than acceptable. The manual, however, did not include any information pertaining to test-retest reliability.

The manual does contain a discussion of the three major types of validity. With respect to content validity, the national norms booklet author states, "the Aprenda was constructed to match those objectives of the Stanford Achievement Test Series that are appropriate for students receiving most of their instruction in Spanish" (p. 11). Five thousand items were field tested with 8,500 bilingual school children who were from the United States, Mexico, and Puerto Rico. Only items that had a biserial correlation coefficient of .35 or greater and a mid-range level of difficulty were included in the final form. Criterion-related validity was demonstrated by showing progression "[across] differing points in the instructional sequence" (i.e., from Fall to Spring) (p. 36). Construct validity was demonstrated by correlating corresponding subtests at adjacent levels (i.e.,

Nivel Preprimario/Preprimer with Primer Nivel Primario/Primary 1; Primer Nivel Primario/Primary 1 with Segundo Nivel Primario/Primary 2; etc.).

With respect to test administration, the Aprenda has a separate test administration booklet for all seven battery levels. This booklet provides sufficient information pertaining to test administration. The Spanish instructions that are read to students are succinct, clear, and grammatically correct. The layout of test items in the test booklets is appropriate. Moreover, the national norms booklet provides sufficient information on how to use the tables of norms.

With respect to item bias, the manual contains a list of personnel who served as the minority advisory panel. This panel reviewed items for possible gender, regional, and ethnic/class bias.

The Aprenda test helps to address the need for measures to assess the academic achievement of pupils with limited English proficiency in the United States. One primary strength of the Aprenda is that it uses the Stanford Achievement Test, English Edition as its model for test content. Moreover, it is not a translation of the Stanford Achievement Test. This is an important advantage of the Aprenda because translating English tests into Spanish can be problematic given that psychometric properties and item-difficulty levels can change in these situations. Many commercial instruments in Spanish are mere translations of English instruments. The primary limitation of the Aprenda is its standardization sample. The test publisher's efforts to obtain a nationally representative sample of Spanish-speaking school students in the United States is commendable given that many instruments in Spanish are not normed on students with limited English proficiency. The standardization sample of the Aprenda, however, does not reflect the Spanish-speaking school-age population of the United States. Examiners should proceed with caution when using the Aprenda with Spanish-speaking students from different geographical regions and different countries of origin than those represented in the norm population.

[13]

The APT Inventory.

Purpose: Designed to measure an individual's relative strength on each of ten personal traits.
Population: Adults.
Publication Date: 1992.
Scores, 10: Communication, Analytical Thinking, Administrative, Relating to Others, Influencing, Achieving, Empowering, Developing, Leadership, Ethics.

Administration: Individual or group.
Manual: No manual.
Price Data, 1992: $100 per 20 sets (each set includes assessment, response sheet, and interpretation booklet).
Time: (40) minutes.
Comments: Self-administered; self-scored.
Author: Training House, Inc.
Publisher: Training House, Inc.

Review of The APT Inventory by E. SCOTT HUEBNER, Professor of Psychology, University of South Carolina, Columbia, SC:

The Assessment of Personal Traits (APT Inventory) was purportedly designed to assess traits of importance to occupational success. The front cover of the test protocol implies that questions such as "How apt are you for the job you hold?" and "Do you have the aptitude to perform the work easily and effectively?" can be addressed through the use of the instrument.

The APT Inventory consists of 100 statements to which the individual and/or knowledgeable others respond with one of five choices (from "strong fit; always applies" to "never applies; there is no fit"). The items are subsequently summed to reveal raw score ratings on 10 traits: Communication, Thinking, Administrative, Relating, Influencing, Achieving, Empowering, Developing, Leadership, and Ethics. Normative scores are not available, nor has any apparent attempt been made to collect normative data.

Scoring and interpretation procedures are described briefly in an eight-page document that accompanies the protocol. The user is provided with directions for self-scoring and encouraged to gather responses from three or four other people who know her/him well for comparison purposes. Validity issues are addressed by the unusual suggestion to "ignore any statements that are not descriptive of a trait that is part of the behavioral area you are checking" (p. 5). Also, in the case that observer and self-reports differ, it is recommended simply "to adjust (weigh) your totals to be more in line with others" (p. 5).

After calculating the raw score totals for each trait, the user is encouraged to assign a rank to each score so that a "1" reflects the individual's strongest area and a "10" reflects the individual's weakest area. In order to address the match between their behavioral traits and the demands of their jobs, it is suggested that individuals then rank order each trait in terms of its importance. The individual's rankings of their trait strengths are then to be compared with the importance rankings to yield a measure of goodness to fit.

The APT Inventory has no manual that describes the theoretical foundation of the instrument nor any data related to its psychometric properties. No information is provided about item development or analyses. For example, this reviewer wonders what criteria support the placement of the item "empowers others to be and to do more than they ever realized they were capable of" on the Leadership subscale rather than the Empowering subscale. Similar questions arise with respect to other items on the scale. No evidence of reliability or validity is provided.

In short, the APT Inventory represents an instrument without a clear theoretical rationale, without normative data for self- or other-ratings, and without any evidence of reliability and validity. Hence, until appropriate evidence is available, this instrument should not be used for any purpose, including research purposes.

Review of The APT Inventory by JAYNE E. STAKE, Professor of Psychology, University of Missouri, St. Louis, MO:

The Assessment of Personal Traits (APT) Inventory was designed to educate managers about the personal qualities, behaviors, and skills necessary for successful management and to help them gain perspective on their own relative strengths and weaknesses in these areas. The instrument includes 100 items that pertain to management-related traits and aptitudes. Although the inventory was clearly designed for people in management positions, the purpose of the measure is described much more broadly in the inventory pamphlet as a tool for evaluating one's suitability for one's present job. This description of the test is misleading; people who are not in management will find many of the items to be unrelated to their job responsibilities, and the inventory is not appropriate for them.

The APT Inventory was developed on the basis of suggestions from human resource directors from 26 business corporations. These consultants suggested 10 categories of traits important for successful management: Communication, Thinking, Administrative, Relating, Influencing, Achieving, Empowering, Developing, Leadership, and Ethics. Ten items were written for each of the 10 categories based on the definitions of the traits provided by the consultants. No evaluation of test items has been undertaken, so there is no information about the internal consistency, distinctness, or stability of the 10 scales. Based on a review of item content, it appears that, in many cases, items within scales have low intercorrelations and items targeted for different scales are highly correlated; thus, the internal consistency and distinctiveness of the scales are very much in question. The problem here is that the constructs purportedly being measured are vague and loosely defined, comprising diverse types of skills and behaviors. For example, the Communication scale includes items that pertain to interpersonal sensitivity, language usage and grammar, public speaking, and writing skill. Because item content within scales is so broad, identical scores for two people on the same scale could represent quite different patterns of strengths and weaknesses.

The APT Inventory was designed to be self-administered and scored. Managers may describe themselves on the inventory as a means of assessing their self-perceptions of their management ability, or a set of people may rate a target manager to help that individual gain insight into others' views of his/her management performance. Test-takers rate on a 5-point scale how often an aptitude, trait, or behavior applies to themselves or to a target person. The instructions do not indicate to which setting the test-taker should refer in making these ratings. Some items are explicitly relevant to management situations only (e.g., "Uses meetings as an opportunity to strengthen teamwork and commitment among work group members," p. 3), but other items are not (e.g., "Shows empathy and sensitivity to the feelings, needs, and personal interests of others," p. 3). On the latter items, test-takers may be confused about what life setting they should refer to in making their judgments and may rate themselves or others in reference to nonmanagement situations. To the extent this occurs, the validity of the inventory as a measure of management ability and performance would be weakened.

In regard to test interpretation, there are no norms for test scores nor any evidence for the predictive or construct validity of the inventory. Test users are expected to evaluate the validity of the measure for themselves. They are instructed to read descriptions of each of the 10 areas measured and to decide (a) whether items that make up the scale for the domain represent valid aspects of that domain and (b) whether ratings made by the self or others are accurate. When test users believe that three or more items on a scale are not indicative of the intended domain, they are to reject their score in this area as invalid by their definition of the domain. In assessing the validity of ratings from others, a set of scores that vary widely from one another are to be interpreted as less valid than ratings that coincide more closely. In addition, test users are instructed to rate the importance of each trait for the job they currently hold and then to compare the pattern of their importance ratings to the pattern of their own scores.

This process of test evaluation and interpretation may be useful in management training sessions to convey ideas about good management practices and to stimulate self-evaluation and self-insight regarding job performance in management. Because the test user is directly involved in evaluating the meaning and validity of test items and scores, misinterpretation of test results should be minimized. It must be emphasized, however, that there are no psychometric data to support the reliability or validity of any of the 10 APT Inventory scales; hence, it should not be used in management selection or other personnel decisions.

[14]

Aptitude Interest Inventory.
Purpose: To develop a plan for career exploration.
Population: High school to adult.
Publication Date: 1993–1996.
Acronym: Aii.
Administration: Group.
Restricted Distribution: Distribution restricted to licensed sites.
Price Data: Available from publisher.
Comments: Previously entitled Career Assessment Program; tests must be computer administered and scored (Windows format).
Author: Educational Technologies, Inc.
Publisher: Invest Learning.
   a) APTITUDE BASED CAREER DECISION TEST.
   Purpose: "Used to assist individuals in selecting a career based on their aptitudes."
   Acronym: ABCD.
   Scores, 7: Clerical Perception, Vocabulary, Numerical Computation, Numerical Reasoning, Spatial Visualization, Inductive Reasoning, Analytical Reasoning.
   Time: (100) minutes.
   b) INTEREST BASED CAREER DECISION TEST.
   Purpose: "Used to assist individuals select a career based on their interests."
   Acronym: IBCD.
   Scores: Ratings grouped into 3 areas: Data, People, Things.
   Time: (30–45) minutes.
   Comments: Self-report survey.

Review of the Aptitude Interest Inventory by ALBERT M. BUGAJ, Associate Professor of Psychology, University of Wisconsin—Marinette, Marinette, WI:

The Aptitude Interest Inventory (Aii) (previously entitled Career Assessment Program) is a two-part, computer-administered test and test-result management program. The first part, the Aptitude Based Career Decision Test (ABCD), is designed to assist individuals in selecting careers based on their aptitudes. Part Two, the Interest Based Career Decision Test (IBCD), helps test takers select careers based on their interests. The tests are suitable for high schoolers and adults. Both can be purchased separately, and are also available in paper-and-pencil form, which can be scanned and imported into the results-management program.

The Aii comes with a 427-page manual, if one counts all appendices and tables. The manual is easy to read and highly informative. As with most manuals for computerized programs, it begins with an explanation of how to load the Aii onto a DOS-based network or stand-alone computer with hard drive (required for the program). Loading the Aii can be easily and quickly performed.

The program itself is menu driven, and can be quickly mastered by a person with a working knowledge of packaged software programs. The Aii is designed to be operated by a system administrator, teachers, and students. The administrator performs such tasks as establishing files for classes, teachers, and students; managing data storage; and printing reports. Teachers maintain their own class files and assign tests. The program can be accurately described as "user friendly" for the administrator, teachers, and the students taking the tests. The menus thoroughly direct the administrator, teacher, or student through his or her particular part of the program or test. The administrator's manuals for both the computerized and paper-and-pencil versions of the ABCD and the IBCD are equally thorough, explicit, and easy to read.

The counselor's manuals for the ABCD contains complete explanations of the uses of the test, the nature of the test reports and scores, and how to interpret them. Wisely, periodic cautions are given that the scores should be interpreted for the test taker by a trained counselor. The manual also points out that other sources of data (e.g., SAT scores or school subject competency scores in combination with ABCD scores) should also be used, to determine the accuracy of scores for the individual case and whether

retesting might be necessary. This should not be taken as an indication of the weakness of the test, but rather of the care the test developers have taken to be sure an accurate assessment of the individual is made. Norms are provided for various age groups, as well as separately for males and females.

A detailed technical manual for the ABCD is provided. Here a knowledge of test construction and statistics are required for understanding. The ABCD technical manual includes data comparing the machine-scored test to an earlier hand-scored version (the average correlation between the two forms being an acceptable .6), and item analyses for each scale (most item-total correlations falling in the moderate range). One failing of the manual is in the presentation of the reliability of the ABCD. The manual refers to a table showing split-half and test-retest reliability. However, only one set of statistics is given (these are high, ranging from .71 to .98). Data presented several pages later, during a discussion of validity, seems to indicate these are test-retest reliabilities over a 6-week interval. It is unfortunate that this is not specified in the section on reliability, and that the split-half reliabilities are absent. In the same discussion, test-retest reliabilities (over a 4-year interval) are lower, ranging from .39 to .88.

The validity of the ABCD was determined in a variety of ways. Factor analysis was performed to determine the orthogonality of the separate scales. To measure concurrent validity, the ABCD, Comprehensive Ability Battery, and Differential Aptitude Test were administered to two separate groups of subjects. Correlations between appropriate scales ranged from .07 to .87. Summaries of a number of published tests of criterion-related validity are provided. In general, these indicate that the ABCD can differentiate between practitioners in a variety of fields (e.g., carpentry, horticulture, accounting). The validity and norms of the ABCD were developed with a large sample, with care taken to establish a good cross-section of the population based on age, race, and gender.

The technical manual of the IBCD begins with a detailed survey of the test's history, and provides an excellent example of gathering evidence through construct validation. However, most of the narrative and data provided concern the earlier Cleff Job Matching System, the Audio-Visual Job Matching System, Job Matching II, and related tests. Although these earlier tests appear reliable and valid, the IBCD is presented without validity and reliability figures, probably because of its relatively recent evolution (being developed in 1988).

Overall, the Aptitude Interest Inventory, in general, and the Aptitude Based Career Decision Test, in particular, can be highly recommended. The program is easy to use, and provides useful output. The Aii also serves as an excellent data management system for tracking changes in student interests and ability over time. The ABCD has been carefully constructed, and appears to have good evidence of validity and reliability. The more recent Interest Based Career Decision test is harder to recommend because no validity and reliability information is provided. Perhaps this latter test could be used as a preliminary exploration of career interest.

Review of the Aptitude Interest Inventory by DONALD THOMPSON, Dean, and Professor of Counseling and Psychology, Troy State University Montgomery, Montgomery, AL:

The Aptitude Interest Inventory (Aii) (originally published as the Career Assessment Program) is a computer-assisted test management system that includes an aptitude battery with seven subtests (ABCD; Aptitude Based Career Decision Test), and an interest inventory (IBCD: Interest Based Career Decision Test). The tests are administered and scored by computer, and the computer then generates separate diagnostic reports for interests and aptitudes. There is also a paper-and-pencil version of the Aii that has an answer sheet that allows the responses to be scanned into a computer to generate a report; however, this review focuses on only the computer-administered version.

The test package is delivered on three 3.5-inch floppy disks (only an MS-DOS version is currently available), and the package contains a complete test management system that allows the purchaser to manage multiple test sites, teachers, classrooms, test takers, etc. The package must be installed on a computer hard drive and requires about 2.4 MB of disk space. The package is not copy protected, which eliminates many problems that have historically been associated with testing software. The purchaser of the software is authorized to use the software on one machine (or multiple machines for site licenses) for unlimited administrations of the tests. The package includes a single large user's guide divided into four sections (user's manual, test administrator's manual, counselor's manual, and technical manual). The installation process is straightforward and trouble free. However, the instructions for setting up classrooms, sites, teachers, and test takers are somewhat cumbersome, and the manual does not provide a good rationale or overview as to what the end product is to be. Fortunately, the publisher also provides a training video that provides excellent instructions for program setup and the test administration process.

Both the aptitude battery and interest inventory can be group or individually administered. As noted earlier, there are seven aptitude subtests in the ABCD. The time allotted for the entire aptitude battery is 1 hour and 44 minutes. The ABCD is designed to be a total aptitude testing system that provides specific scores on seven aptitudes, and identifies potential for success in 66 occupational families. The report information is keyed to, and correlated with, the *Guide for Occupational Exploration* (G.O.E.) and the *Dictionary of Occupational Titles* (D.O.T.).

On the IBCD (interest inventory) the test taker responds to 200 written descriptions of specific job activities (each statement is also accompanied by a picture depicting the activity). The 200 statements are grouped (for scoring purpose only) into 20 dimensions. The statements and accompanying pictures are examples of real life activities or situations (e.g., "take photographs," "fill out application form"). The test taker is asked to indicate how much he or she likes or dislikes doing the particular type of activity. The IBCD is not timed and can usually be completed in about 30 minutes. The authors report that it is appropriate for all populations and for ages from high school through adult. The scoring of the IBCD provides occupational recommendations in 66 G.O.E. clusters, and also matches individuals to local training programs.

The seven aptitude tests and the interest inventory can be taken in any order, and the computer maintains a log of the completed tests. A test taker could take the eight tests at different times, or could complete the entire battery in one testing.

The Aii aptitude tests evolved from earlier paper-and-pencil tests contained in the Ball Aptitude Battery (T4:238). Considerable empirical work has been done to analyze item content and factor structure to insure that the seven aptitude tests were measuring the intended dimensions and provided meaningful predictive data. The technical manual indicates good psychometric properties for the ABCD (or at least for the Ball Aptitude Inventory), and there is extensive research addressing the reliability and validity of the different aptitude measures. Reliability coefficients range from .71 to .98, and predictive validity evidence is provided between the ABCD and various academic and vocational criteria for success. Concurrent validity evidence is provided with the Comprehensive Ability Battery (CAB), Differential Aptitude Tests (DAT), and General Aptitude Test Battery (GATB).

Norms are based on a large sample of high school seniors, and research is reported regarding the use with other populations. However, it does not appear that the empirical data regarding validity and reliability are based on the computer version of the test. For the most part, computer-based administration of the tests would not appear to be substantially different from the paper-and-pencil process; however, some researchers have found differences when tests are administered by computer. Although it might be assumed that the tests have acceptable evidence or reliability and validity when administered by computer, it would be prudent for the publisher to conduct studies directly assessing these factors for the computer-based version.

The empirical data regarding the IBCD leave much to be desired. The manual does present reliability and validity information, but the data refer to several studies conducted more than 15 years ago. Reference is made to longitudinal studies that began in 1979 and 1981, which were to be completed in 10 years, yet no final reporting of these data is included in the manual. No specifics regarding the norm sample are provided in the technical manual. Because none of the four manuals include an index, it is often difficult to find particular information.

In general, it is this reviewer's conclusion that the Aii is a reasonably good computer-based test administration and management system. However, the psychometric properties of the aptitude and interest tests leave much to be desired. The tests appear to be simple conversions of paper-and-pencil instruments to computer-based administration.

There are several positive features of the Aii. It is inexpensive, because once the initial purchase is made, there is no additional cost for each test administered. The test management system works well and there were no technical problems with the software during multiple uses. The empirical evidence suggests that the aptitude and interest test results may provide data to assist clients in making sound career decisions in conjunction with good career counseling.

There are several problems with the current version of the Aii. The empirical evidence regarding both tests is somewhat dated, and is limited for the interest test. Clearly the tests do not take full advantage of the capabilities of the computer for test administration. The test presentation is much the same as it would be with paper and pencil. Many computer-based aptitude batteries have been converted to adaptive tests. The Aii technical manual indicates that computer adaptive versions of several of the aptitude subtests are planned, but do not appear to be coming soon. Also, on the interest inventory, the pictures are low resolution monochrome line drawings as opposed to photographic quality pictures. Many pictures are difficult to interpret because of poor resolution. The publisher indicated to this reviewer that a Windows-based version of the software with photographic quality pictures is planned. The computer generates a comprehensive report that can be an effective tool for guidance and counseling, and the profiles and report match individuals to local training programs. However, although the reports are thorough and informative, they are definitely not designed to be used directly by the test taker, as they are overly complex and need the expertise of a counselor to interpret.

Certainly there are better computer-based aptitude and interest test products (such as Psychological Assessment Resource's (PAR) Self-Directed Search [SDS; 285] for interests and Psychological Corporation's Differential Aptitude Tests—Computerized Adaptive Edition [DAT Adaptive; 12:117]), but few software packages come with both. The test management aspect of the Aii is a very useful feature found in few packages. The Aii could be a very effective test system if and when the appropriate empirical data are available and the software is enhanced to improve the presentation.

[15]
Arousal Seeking Tendency Scale.

Purpose: Designed to "assess individual differences in preference for change, novelty, and risk taking."
Population: Ages 15 and older.
Publication Dates: 1978–1994.
Acronym: MAST.
Scores: Total score only.
Administration: Group or individual.
Price Data, 1994: $28 per test kit including scale, scoring directions, norms, and manual ('94, 6 pages).
Time: (10–15) minutes.
Comments: Previously listed as Measure of Arousal Seeking Tendency.
Author: Albert Mehrabian.

Publisher: Albert Mehrabian.
Cross References: For reviews by Norman S. Endler and Jon D. Swartz of an earlier edition, see 9:677; see also T3:1438 (1 reference).

Review of the Arousal Seeking Tendency Scale by GREGORY J. BOYLE, Professor of Psychology, Bond University, Gold Coast, Queensland, Australia:

This 32-item self-report inventory is intended to quantify the level of arousal seeking tendency in individuals aged 15 years and older (although younger adolescents might also be quite capable of providing valid responses to the scale items). The response format is a 9-point scale ranging from +4 (*very strong agreement*) to -4 (*very strong disagreement*). Clearly, use of such an elaborate scoring system has the definite advantage of approximating interval level measurement data, thereby facilitating the validity of subsequent statistical analyses. The scale includes 16 positively and also 16 negatively worded items to counteract "response bias." Respondents' total raw scores are converted to standardized *z*-scores for ease of comparison—but unless normalized, there can be no certainty that the transformed scores are directly comparable, given expected demographic differences for different samples. Other than the basic assessment of arousal seeking tendency, the current brief test manual does not elaborate on other possible uses of the scale.

Evidently, pilot testing was undertaken using samples of undergraduate students. An early version of the Arousal Seeking Tendency Scale (Mehrabian, 1978) was administered to a sample of 325 University of California undergraduates. Mehrabian (1978) pointed out that this scale "shows a consistent set of effects for preferred settings—compared to low-arousal seekers, high-arousal seekers exhibit more approach, work, and affiliation in preferred settings" (p. 730). Because the instrument was designed primarily for use with undergraduate student samples, questions about its external validity, to the general adult population at large, necessarily remain unanswered.

Normative data provided in the test manual include the mean score of 32 and the standard deviation of 29, apparently based on undergraduate student respondents. Additional information about the demographic characteristics of the normative sample would be useful. Consequently, it remains somewhat unclear as to whether or not the reported mean and standard deviation is appropriate for different population samples. It would be helpful if a range of mean scores and standard deviations were reported corresponding to different sociodemographic

samples and subgroups. For example, what is the relationship between age and scores on the scale? What effect does formal education have on obtained scores? What differences are there in item responses and scores with respect to gender, socioeconomic status, family background, and so on? Such normative data could then be presented in tabular form, allowing a more precise assessment of any particular individual's score on the scale.

Given the discernible transparency of items generally included in self-report scales, it would be expected that the problems of motivational and response distortion due to lack of adequate self-insight, response sets, or even deliberate faking, might influence the way in which individuals respond to the various items in the Arousal Seeking Tendency Scale (MAST), thereby possibly reducing predictive validity (cf. Boyle, 1985).

Information provided on reliability indicated that the Arousal Seeking Tendency Scale has a high internal consistency reliability of .93 (Mehrabian, 1978, p. 724). However, high item homogeneity coefficients may also indicate a corresponding high level of item redundancy—with concomitant reduced breadth of measurement—and may bear little necessary relationship to test-retest reliability—response consistency over time (cf. Boyle, 1991a). It would be helpful if data were provided on test-retest reliability, over both the immediate short term (dependability), and longer term (stability). At present, we do not know where this scale stands on the state-trait continuum (cf. Boyle, 1987).

The importance of multivariate assessment cannot be overstated (cf. Boyle, 1991b). Any experimental treatment/manipulation, or therapeutic intervention may cause changes not only to an individual's arousal seeking tendency, but also on measures of other related states that covary with this construct. Many multidimensional instruments also include a measure of arousal (e.g., the Stress-Arousal Inventory; the IPAT Eight State Questionnaire; the Menstrual Distress Questionnaire, and Zuckerman's Sensation-Seeking Scale—all of which have been subjected to an extensive body of empirical research).

Under the section on validity, the test manual refers the reader to several published articles. For example, Steenkamp and Baumgartner (1992), in an extensive investigation of the MAST in relation to other measures of stimulus/arousal seeking, including the Change Seeker Index (CSI), the Sensation Seeking Scale (SSS), and the Novelty Experiencing Scale

(NES), reported that the MAST compared very favorably in terms of reliability and validity (cf. Baumgartner & Jan-Benedict (1994). Steenkamp and Baumgartner (1992) concluded that both the CSI and MAST "loaded highly on the underlying construct of OSL in the LISREL analysis and yielded the most convincing evidence with respect to factorial structure" (p. 446). However, it would be helpful if a summary of these validity findings were presented in the test manual, especially an overview of the findings pertaining to concurrent, discriminative, construct, and predictive validity. For example, what is the factor analytic dimensionality of the scale? Is the scale truly unidimensional, or does it comprise separate factors/subscales?

Relationships between the arousal seeking tendency construct and Mehrabian's pleasure-arousability-dominance or PAD temperament model wherein arousability is viewed as a trait characteristic have been investigated. Mehrabian (1996a, b) reported PAD analyses of the MAST along with Jackson's Change, Play, and Sentience scales. It was found that arousal seeking and related personality traits were weighted most by dominance, next by arousability, and finally by pleasantness of temperament. Evidently, arousal seekers strive for mastery over difficult and risky situations, which once achieved, results in feelings of dominance, further boosting arousal levels.

In summary, it would be useful if future versions of the manual for the Arousal Seeking Tendency Scale (MAST) were to provide a more extensive literature review; more detailed empirical data such as correlations with other established instruments; normative data for differing samples and subgroups; additional data pertaining to reliability, validity, and utility; as well as information about the factor analytic dimensionality of the scale. Although a number of published articles relating to the usefulness of the scale in various studies are included, it would be beneficial if the manual were to be thoroughly revised, expanded, and updated. Despite the limitations of the current prefatory version of the manual, the Arousal Seeking Tendency Scale appears to be a useful psychometric measure. Nevertheless, until additional empirical data are incorporated into the manual, and its relationship to Mehrabian's PAD temperament model is spelled out in more detail, this scale probably should be restricted as a research instrument only.

REVIEWER'S REFERENCES

Mehrabian, A. (1978). Characteristic individual reactions to preferred and unpreferred environments. *Journal of Personality, 46,* 717–731.
Boyle, G. J. (1985). Self-report measures of depression: Some psychometric considerations. *British Journal of Clinical Psychology, 24,* 45–59.
Boyle, G. J. (1987). Review of the (1985) "Standards for educational and psychological testing: AERA, APA and NCME." *Australian Journal of Psychology, 39,* 235–237.
Boyle, G. J. (1991a). Does item homogeneity indicate internal consistency or item redundancy in psychometric scales? *Personality and Individual Differences, 12,* 291–294.
Boyle, G. J. (1991b). Experimental psychology does require a multivariate perspective. *Contemporary Psychology, 36,* 350–351.
Steenkamp, J. E. M., & Baumgartner, H. (1992). The role of optimum stimulation level in exploratory consumer behavior. *Journal of Consumer Research, 19,* 434–448.
Baumgartner, H., & Jan-Benedict, E. M. (1994). An investigation into the construct validity of the Arousal Seeking Tendency Scale, Version II. *Educational and Psychological Measurement, 54,* 993–1001.
Mehrabian, A. (1996a). Analysis of the Big Five personality factors in terms of the PAD temperament model. *Australian Journal of Psychology, 48,* 86–92.
Mehrabian, A. (1996b). Pleasure-arousal-dominance: A general framework for describing and measuring individual differences in temperament. *Current Psychology: Development, Learning, Personality, Social, 14,* 261–292.

[16]

ASIST: A Structured Addictions Assessment Interview for Selecting Treatment.

Purpose: To assess alcohol and drug use for the purpose of selecting treatment.
Population: Adults.
Publication Dates: 1984-1990.
Acronym: ASIST.
Scores: 12 sections: Identifying Information, Basic Information, Alcohol Use, Psychoactive Drug Use, Health Screening, Other Life Areas, Previous Treatment, Client Preference for Treatment, Treatment Assessment Summary, Treatment Plan, Actual Referrals, Assessment Worker's Observation.
Administration: Individual.
Price Data, 1994: $25 per 10 questionnaires; $35 per Assessment Handbook ('90, 200 pages).
Foreign Language Edition: Questionnaire available in French.
Time: Administration time not reported.
Author: Addiction Research Foundation.
Publisher: Addiction Research Foundation [Canada].

Review of the ASIST: A Structured Addictions Assessment for Selecting Treatment by WESLEY E. SIME, Professor of Health and Human Performance, University of Nebraska-Lincoln, Lincoln, NE:

The ASIST is a structured interview designed to aid therapists and administrators in determining the severity of need and the best treatment intervention for individuals who exhibit alcohol and/or drug abuse symptoms. The ASIST is more than an instrument, rather it includes a very comprehensive manual that could serve as a procedures model for developing a new program for establishing a community-based referral system.

The instrument itself assesses four different categories that include alcohol use, drug use, physical and emotional health, and "other life" areas. Other life areas include accommodation, family issues, social issues, education/training, work, financial, leisure, and legal concerns. Each of these four areas contains a standard sequence of inquiry that includes questions about "what concerns do you have," "do you feel that you need help" in order to control this area, "what behavioral disturbances do you experience," "how important now is help to you," and finally "what is the severity of the rating" as viewed by the therapist (p. 23). It also includes a determination of all previous treatment, specifically defining which was most helpful. A treatment assessment form elicits the client's preference for treatment compared with the assessment worker's preference for treatment followed by the agreed upon treatment plan (usually a compromise).

The treatment plan contains an assessment of the problem, the goals to be accomplished, the recommended interventions, a specific section for client responsibility and therapist or assessment worker responsibility, and finally, case manager responsibilities. In comparison to other similar instruments, the last three items (listed above) seem to be the most salient elements in structuring a viable treatment plan.

The physical health screening questions include a variety of medical disorders of which two (rheumatic fever and tuberculosis) seem to be irrelevant to substance abuse and others such as the pulmonary disorders related to smoking and/or infectious diseases and the neurological disorders related to long-term substance abuse are notably absent. Certainly this part of the instrument could be more useful if it included a more comprehensive and relevant list of medical disorders related to substance abuse.

The procedural manual for this instrument includes a thorough description of intake assessment references in the community, treatment guidelines, case management, a clinical procedural policy regarding crisis emergencies, withdrawal, and security issues. It also provides an interesting and useful procedure for developing a community resource directory.

The appendix includes three articles on substance use, all of which were published by the Addiction Research Foundation 10–15 years ago, making them somewhat outdated.

My major concern about this instrument is its general utility for others in the field. Unfortunately, the instrument is regionally and nationally specific. The manual is prepared in accordance with statutes from the province of Ontario and the Ministry of Health for Canada. The Ontario Health Insurance Program (OHIP) requirements punctuate the entire

document and specific terms such as "are useful only in Canada" appear frequently. The spelling of terms (e.g., centre) is generic to the King's English and terms such as HMRI (Health Ministries Regional District Codes) and HSC (homes for special care) in the Ministries of Health and Victorian Order of Nurses are applicable only for current Canadian and/or Ontario users. Standards for blood alcohol content (.08) at the legal limit may not be uniform across other provinces or in some U.S. states where the legal limit is .10. In addition, the limit for percent of alcohol in beer in Ontario is known to be 5% whereas many of the U.S. beers are 3.2%. Finally, there is reference to Canadian laws on patient records.

Demographic questions specify two alternative language response options (French and English only). For more universal usage, Spanish language options should be included. It is unfortunate that the authors did not take the time to prepare a separate version of the workbook and the instrument, which would be applicable to other populations beyond those in Ontario or Canada.

A more serious issue of attending to detail is noted in two sections of the ASIST where typographical errors have apparently persisted throughout the past 10 to 12 years of usage (this instrument came out in 1984 and was edited again in 1989). The word aggressive is misspelled in Section 3.12, and the term "now" was misspelled as "know" in Section 5.6 under physical health. [Editor's note: Both of these errors have been corrected in the most recent printing of the revised version.]

I am very concerned that no data are reported regarding the functional utility of this instrument after 10–12 years of usage. In the ASIST, client recommendations are found on a risk-o-graph (p. 8), which defines the amount of drinks per day against body weight for males and females. There is a criterion line for three different levels of risk, but these have not been defined nor data provided supporting the validity of such criteria. It should also be noted that there are no measures of reliability regarding the instrument and no assessment of the instrument's predictive or construct validity to make appropriate referrals of treatment outcome based on those referrals.

This instrument is hand scored with no extra provision for machine scoring. There is no description of how the instrument was formulated and how it has been revised over the years. Although the validity remains essentially undetermined and there is no way of assessing the advantage of this instrument over other available options in the area of substance abuse, it is, however, a very practical tool for identifying the severity of symptoms for clients. It should be noted that the instrument is designed for case managers and administrators who need a relatively simple and nonclinical device for assessing need for therapy. By using this instrument to make client needs assessments, it would appear that trained and experienced clerical workers could function as well as mental health counselors.

Review of the ASIST: A Structured Addictions Assessment Interview for Selecting Treatment by NICHOLAS A. VACC, Professor and Chairperson, Department of Counseling and Educational Development, and GERALD A. JUHNKE, Assistant Professor of Counseling and Educational Development, School of Education, The University of North Carolina at Greensboro, Greensboro, NC:

A Structured Addictions Assessment Interview for Selecting Treatment (ASIST) was designed to structure the assessment and referral process for alcohol- and drug-abusing clients and to propose a treatment selection. The ASIST is a structured interview, which includes recommendations at specific points in the interview for possibly administering the Alcohol Dependence Scale (ADS; T4:145) and the Drug Abuse Screening Test (DAST; see the Drug Use Questionnaire, 104), respectively. Also available is an Assessment Handbook, which is equivalent to a technical manual, that includes procedures for addictions assessment/referral services including ASIST.

The interview format provides data relating to 12 areas: Identifying Information (e.g., client name, address), Basic Information (e.g., date of birth, referral source), Alcohol Use (e.g., family drinking history, personal drinking history), Psychoactive Drug Use (e.g., drug types and amounts used), Health Screening (e.g., medical history), Other Life Areas (e.g., relationship, employment, or legal problems), Previous Treatment, Client Preference for Treatment (e.g., client-identified goals), Treatment Assessment Summary, Treatment Plan, Actual Referrals, and Assessment Workers' Observation Form. The same format is used for both males and females. No indication is given within the ASIST or the Assessment Handbook concerning the average completion time for the interview.

The ADS and DAST are independent instruments and are recommended as an element of the ASIST assessment and referral process; these instruments are not included in the ASIST booklet. However, the Assessment Handbook provides both scoring and interpretation guidelines for the use of the ADS and DAST. The instruments appear integral to the ASIST interview process, and they are also available from the agency, Addiction Research Foundation, which produced the Assessment Handbook and the ASIST.

The ADS has 25 questions presented in a multiple-choice self-report format (Personal communication, Linda Omerea, May 17, 1996). Although the purpose of the ADS is not clearly indicated within the Assessment Handbook or the ASIST, it seems to reflect the respondent's alcohol use. The Handbook includes an ADS scoring key and interpretation guide. The ADS score is determined by first matching the client's responses to the respective item scores indicated in the ADS scoring key, and then summing the matching scores to provide an ADS score, which is interpreted using the ADS interpretation guide. This guide is broken into four quartiles and provides a suggested interpretation of alcohol dependence (i.e., low, moderate, substantial, severe) and general clinical guidelines (e.g., "Abstinence is probably the only reasonable treatment goal" [p.H.3.8]).

The DAST is a 20-question screening instrument presented in a dichotomous, yes-no, self-report format. Although the purpose for the administration of the DAST is not specifically stated within the Assessment Handbook of the ASIST, directions given to the client suggest that the instrument will reflect the client's current involvement with drugs other than alcohol. The Handbook contains a sample of the DAST, a scoring scheme, and a DAST scoring table that reports drug-abuse severity ranging from 0 for "None Reported" to 20 for "Severe Level." The score is obtained by summing the number of client scores that correspond with the scoring scheme.

The Assessment Handbook indicates that formal validity studies regarding the ASIST interview procedure have been conducted only on the ADS and DAST, but information regarding these studies is not provided. However, Skinner and Allen (1982) and Ross, Gavin, and Skinner (1990) reported validity and reliability data for the ADS, and Skinner (1983) and Saltstone, Halliwell, and Hayslip (1994) presented validity and reliability estimates for the DAST. Validity estimates range between .06 and .86 for the ADS and the Alcohol-Related Measures items (Horn, Wanberg, & Foster, 1974), and were found to be .69 (Skinner & Allen, 1992) and .79

(Ross, Gavin, & Skinner, 1990) for the ADS and the Michigan Alcoholism Screening Inventory (MAST). Validity estimates range from -.38 to .55 for the DAST and a variety of relevant indices (Skinner, 1983), and a correlation of .41 was found for the DAST and the MAST (Saltstone, Halliwell, & Hayslip, 1994). Reliability estimates for the DAST and ADS are high with both being above .90. Subjects initially used for the development of the DAST (i.e., 223 subjects [Skinner, 1983]) and the ADS (i.e., 225 subjects [Skinner & Allen, 1982]) were volunteers who sought help at the Clinical Institute of the Addiction Research Foundation in Toronto, Canada. The subjects were overwhelmingly male (72% and 80%, respectively); no indications were noted as to ethnic or racial distributions.

The Assessment Handbook was designed for the Canadian Ministry of Health Addictions Services, and a substantial amount of the information and forms included were intended to match the services requirement format of the Canadian Ministry of Health Information Services, thus having limited utility outside such governmental agencies. In general, some sections of the handbook are elementary and limited in usefulness to all but the least experienced addictions professionals. The Assessment Handbook includes suggestions regarding topics such as client cancellations, no-shows, subpoenas, and evening appointments. Yet, omitted in the Assessment Handbook are important topics such as information about the age range and needed reading competencies of clients completing the DAST and ADS.

The authors have attempted to create a broad-spectrum alcohol and other drug-intake procedure to accommodate the assessment of all clients. However, the proposed clinical guidelines are very general and too nonspecific to be of substantial value to most addiction professionals. Also, the print quality of the ASIST is lower than expected for a commercial instrument. Despite these many limitations, the ASIST has some qualities that make it a useful instrument. First, it provides a thorough intake format that requires the joint identification of specific client goals. Second, basic life needs related to health, food, shelter, and social interactions are identified. Third, the treatment assessment summary provides the addictions professional and the client with an "urgency rating." Based upon the client's self-report, this rating indicates the most pressing issues facing the client. Thus, counselor and client can rank order the immediacy of presenting concerns. Fourth, the ASIST provides the client and counselor with a list of identified goals and their corresponding responsibilities. The DAST and ADS appear to hold clinical merit as brief initial assessment tools to provide a measure of alcohol and drug misuse.

In summary, the ASIST interview has some merit, particularly because it addresses a population for which comprehensive instruments are needed. However, it is impossible to judge adequately the potential value of the instrument because of the lack of sufficient information. This instrument could best be classified as being in the research or developmental stage. As an "in-house" procedure to aid an agency in the assessment and referral process for alcohol- and drug-abusing clients, the ASIST offers some promise. Yet, much needs to be done before it reaches the criterion of *The Standards for Educational and Psychological Testing* (American Educational Research Association, American Psychological Association, & National Council on Measurement in Education, 1985).

REVIEWER'S REFERENCES

Horn, J. L., Wanberg, K. W., & Foster, F. M. (1974). The Alcohol Use Inventory. Denver, CO: Center for Alcohol Abuse Research and Evaluation.

Skinner, H. A. (1983). The Drug Abuse Screening Test. *Addictive Behaviors, 7*, 363-371.

Skinner, H. A., & Allen, B. A. (1982). Alcohol dependence syndrome: Measurement and validation. *Journal of Abnormal Psychology, 91*, 199-209.

American Educational Research Association, American Psychological Association, & National Council on Measurement in Education. (1985). *Standards for educational and psychological testing.* Washington, DC: American Psychological Association, Inc.

Ross, H. E., Gavin, D. R., & Skinner, H. A. (1990). Diagnostic validity of the MAST and the Alcohol Dependence Scale in the assessment of DSM-III alcohol disorders. *Journal of Studies on Alcohol, 51*, 506-513.

Saltstone, R., Halliwell, S., & Hayslip, M. A. (1994). A multivariate evaluation of the Michigan Alcoholism Screening Test and the Drug Abuse Screening Test in a female offender population. *Addictive Behaviors, 19*, 455-462.

[17]

Assessment Inventory for Management.

Purpose: "For screening candidates for insurance field sales management positions."

Population: Managers.

Publication Dates: 1991–1993.

Acronym: AIM.

Scores, 19: 7 Job Task Areas [Basic Task Areas (Staffing/Recruiting and Selection, Training, Performance Management—Supervision, Total); Advanced Task Areas (Business Management, Field Office Development, Total)]; 12 Job Behaviors [Interpersonal Relations (Communicating, Counseling, Supporting), Leadership (Delegating, Motivating, Rewarding, Team Building, Networking), Organization (Coordinating, Monitoring, Planning, Problem-Solving and Decision-Making)].

Administration: Group.

Price Data, 1993: $35 per complete kit including test booklet, manual ('93, 22 pages), answer booklet, 2 management questionnaires, 2 management selection interview guides, and sample feedback report; $10 per test booklet; $10 per manual; $1 per answer booklet/return envelope; $150 per scored answer booklet.

Foreign Language Edition: French Canadian edition ('92) available.

Time: (120–180) minutes.

Comments: Mail-in scoring.

Author: LIMRA International.

Publisher: Life Insurance Marketing and Research Association, Inc.

Review of the Assessment Inventory for Management by CONNIE KUBO DELLA-PIANA, Assistant Professor of Communication, and GABRIEL M. DELLA-PIANA, Director of Evaluation, El Paso Collaborative for Academic Excellence, University of Texas at El Paso, El Paso, TX:

The Assessment Inventory for Management (AIM) is a paper-and-pencil test that "enables you to identify candidates who have the greatest potential for success in field sales management" (manual, p. 2). The title is slightly misleading because the test is "the result of two years of extensive research with 22 life insurance companies" (manual, p. 2). It is said to possess validity evidence that "incumbents who score high on the test are more successful managers as a whole than managers who have low scores" (manual, p. 17). One page titled "Technical information about AIM" (manual, p. 17) refers to a criterion-related validity study that "shows that AIM is a valid tool for assessing probability of success in field management" and a cross-validation "to ensure that the validity estimates were stable and would apply to other groups of candidates" (manual, p. 17). This review describes the test and points out some areas where a user might want evidence and a rationale or argument to support claims.

The purpose of the AIM is "to measure the probability for success in field management" (manual, p. 4) and to be "a selection tool designed to help solve the persistent managerial selection problem" (manual, p. 2). However, the section on interpreting AIM results (manual, pp. 14–16) suggests that it is also to be used for classification decisions (e.g., decisions about whether to proceed with the candidate through subsequent steps in management selection, or to provide training for those whose behavior ratings fall into the bottom 50% on any job behaviors; manual, p. 16). Thus, the purpose is selection and classification with limited validity or reliability evidence to support these test uses.

Test items were developed through a "comprehensive job analysis" that included three stages: identifying job task areas, analyzing the job behaviors necessary to complete the job tasks, and identifying the cognitive abilities and personal characteristics needed to perform the job tasks and job behaviors (manual, pp. 4–6). Results of the job analysis are reported, but procedures for conducting the analysis are not described or referenced in the manual or elsewhere in the kit.

Seven job task areas were identified: (1) Staffing (Recruiting and Selecting), (2) Training, (3) Performance Management, (4) Business Management, (5) Field Office Development, (6) Administration, and (7) Sales Assistance and Support. A sample "Feedback Report" provides a graphic representation of "probability of successful performance" for the first three areas, the first three combined; Areas 4 and 5 separately; and all five areas, but not Areas 6 and 7. The "Feedback Report" also provides a check-off of job behavior areas (see below) with "development opportunities" or "strengths."

Twelve job behavior areas are defined under three categories (Interpersonal Relations, Leadership, and Organization) but there is no rationale to connect these to the seven job tasks.

The criterion to be predicted is "how well the manager performs the job tasks and the job behaviors" (p. 6). There is a self-assessment of tasks, skills, and abilities (on a scale of *outstanding* to *below average*) for all the job tasks and job behaviors identified in the task analysis. No judgments by supervisors or managers with whom the person works or has worked are called for. This reliance on self-reports by the person tested as the sole measure of the criterion without making use of multiple measures seriously limits the validity evidence for the criterion to be predicted. Even the "Interview Guide" for management selection (to be used after receiving the AIM results) is a report from the management candidate only with no information from people who have worked with the candidate. Furthermore, if the AIM is to be used with other measures or information (such as the interview), the manual should provide some guidance for how to combine inferences from test results (Feedback Report) with other information in coming to understandings and decisions.

To predict the criterion, the AIM provides a series of test items or questions "designed to measure the [cognitive] abilities, personal characteristics, and 'street smarts' [or situational judgment] needed to perform successfully as a field manager" (manual, p. 7). These are multiple-choice questions of four types: biographical (105 items); cognitive ability (problem sensitivity, inductive, and deductive reasoning), which appears to be heavily loaded on reading comprehension (52 items); an adjective check list to assess self-descriptions of personal characteristics (146 items) to be rated on a scale of "not at all like me" to "definitely like me"; and situational judgment tapping how one would or would not act in given circumstances (40 items). How items were derived from the domains that grew out of the job and task analysis is not specified. Nor is there any construct validity evidence to support the item selection such as in a comparison of known groups of successful and less successful performers. There is no information on item selection or revision based on preliminary trials. Also, no scores reported for the predictor variables are in the illustrative "Feedback Report."

The four-page section on "Administering AIM" is skimpy with respect to coverage and detail. For example, the test is for group administration but the instructions refer mostly to "the candidate" (p. 11). As a test that will take an estimated 120 to 180 minutes (though untimed), there are no instructions for dealing with variable completion times in group administration nor any instructions to the test takers as to how much time the test might take. The test is presumably relatively unmonitored according to the instructions. Also, it presumably requires no specific ability or training because it can be administered by "Anyone in your organization who has thoroughly read this manual" (manual, p. 10). For the relatively high stakes involved it is unusual to offer such little help in test administration even if direct training is not seen as necessary.

The AIM test in its current form is not recommended for high stakes use in selection because of the lack of reported validity and reliability evidence on which to make a decision on test use or to inform one's use of the test. When used informally along with other information or conducting one's own validity studies (always a good idea) the test may serve some users well.

Review of the Assessment Inventory for Management by CYRIL J. SADOWSKI, Professor of Psychology, Auburn University Montgomery, Montgomery, AL:

The Assessment Inventory for Management (AIM) was developed to predict performance of field managers in the insurance industry. It is available in both English and French. Four predictor domains are addressed in the paper-and-pencil portion: Cog-

nitive Abilities, Personality Characteristics, Biodata, and Situational Judgments. An interview schedule also is available, but information about its technical merits is not available in the administration manual.

The multiple-choice items and descriptive adjectives were selected for appropriate content by industry representatives and managers. An initial screening was conducted by mailing the instrument to 1,218 managers. Although the initial reliabilities for the ability items and biodata were low, this might have been due to the low return rates, 28.8% for the ability items and 22.3% for the biodata items. Initial reliabilities for the personal characteristics were much more substantial.

The validity study was based on a mail-out of 2,600 managers and their supervisors. Returns were obtained from 1,086 managers and 1,457 performance appraisals were garnered. Alpha reliabilities for the 4 Cognitive Abilities scales ranged from .62 to .73, for the 7 Biodata dimensions from .60 to .75, and for the 12 Adjective scales from .63 to .86. Raw multiple correlations between the AIM scales and areas of performance appraisal ranged from .17 to .37. "Predicted task performance validity coefficients for the AIM test ranged from .10 to .32" (p. 12).

Two types of feedback are provided. First is an overall assessment of potential performance in the general performance domains. There also is information provided regarding candidates' strengths and areas for development. Thus, the instrument seems useful in identifying a pool of candidates not only for selection into field management but also for targeting training needs.

The AIM scales appear to be reasonably reliable predictors that were carefully selected. The content validity of the measures and the performance criteria substantially adds to their credibility as an industry-specific predictor. Moreover, the AIM appears not to have adverse impact with respect to women and nonwhites. Although the AIM is well conceived and well constructed, it would benefit from further validity studies that use better sampling techniques and include more women and nonwhites. It would also be beneficial to determine the equivalence of the English and French versions of the test.

[18]

Assessment of Chemical Health Inventory.

Purpose: "Designed to evaluate the nature and extent of adolescent and adult chemical use and associated problems."

Population: Adolescents, adults.

Publication Dates: 1988–1992.

Acronym: ACHI.

Scores: 9 factors (Chemical Involvement, Alienation, Family Estrangement, Personal Consequence, Depression, Family Support, Social Impact, Self Regard, Family Chemical Use) yielding Total score.

Administration: Individual.

Price Data, 1993: $179.95 per starter set including microcomputer disk containing 25 administrations and user manual ('92, 119 pages); $9 per 10 response forms; $5.75 (sold in multiples of 50) per microcomputer disk to administer and score ACHI; $29.95 per manual.

Time: (15–25) minutes.

Comments: Requires 4th grade reading level; may be taken and scored on computer (or administered on paper); mail-in service available.

Authors: Daniel Krotz, Richard Kominowski, Barbara Berntson, and James W. Sipe.

Publisher: RENOVEX Corporation.

Review of the Assessment of Chemical Health Inventory by PHILIP ASH, Director, Ash, Blackstone and Cates, Blacksburg, VA:

The Assessment of Chemical Health Inventory is a 128-item self-administered computer-based instrument intended to assist chemical dependency counselors in evaluating the nature and extent of adolescent and adult substance (alcohol and other drugs) abuse. Both an adolescent form and an adult form are available; both come on disk for computer administration and in a paper-and-pencil machine-scannable version that must be entered into a computer for scoring and analysis. Most of the items in the two versions are identical; a few reflect adolescent/adult differences (e.g., among the biodata items, the adolescent version asks "With whom do you live?" whereas the adult version asks for level of educational attainment).

The first six items inquire as to biographical data (e.g., age, ethnicity, religion, sex, and living arrangements or educational level). The remaining 122 items are cast in a Likert-type five-choice response format (*Strongly Agree* to *Strongly Disagree*), scored in ascending or descending order so that the highest weight is assigned to the most negative or pathological response, yielding higher scores for the more serious abusers. In obtaining composite (factor or subtest) scores, however, each item is differentially weighted, and the factor scores are also differentially weighted to obtain the overall assessment score (user manual, p. 4). The source or method of arriving at these differential weights is not described. The resultant factor scores and the ACHI Assessment Score are transformed to standard scores, which are presented in the Assessment Report.

The computer-generated Assessment Report yields means and standard deviations for the standard scores for 11 measures: ACHI Assessment Score [total], Berntson Social Desirability Scale, and nine "factor" scores including Use Involvement, Personal Consequences, Family Estrangement, Alienation, Social Impact, Family Chemical Use, Self Regard/Abuse, Depression, and Family Support, as well as a Validity Check, a list of Critical Life Items if any of a particular subset of items is responded to in a significantly deviant fashion, a discussion ("ASSESSMENT SCORE") of the meaning of the respondent's ACHI Assessment Score, and a RECOMMENDATION as to further work with the respondent.

According to information received from Dr. James W. Sipe, one of the main authors of the instrument and a member of the staff of RENOVEX, which distributes the inventory, the ACHI is no longer advertised nor included in any catalog, and the company that developed the software is no longer in business. RENOVEX sells copies of administration materials to previous and current users, but apparently no new customers are added.

The main and probably only source of information about the Inventory is contained in the user manual. A computer-based search of the psychological and social sciences literature (January 1974—September 1995) failed to reveal a single reference to the ACHI, or to a book or paper authored by any of the named authors of the Inventory, or even to any reference in which any of them were cited.

For purposes of administration, use, and interpretation, the main parts of the manual include a summary "Characteristics of ACHI" (p. 1); "ACHI: Abstract and Review" (pp. 2–7), outlining general measurement principles with limited reference to any characteristics of the ACHI itself; "ACHI: The Development Stages" (pp. 8–11); "Validation Protocols," describing four "validation" projects (pp. 13–15); "Research and Design" (pp. 16–41); and six sections dealing with actual application: "ACHI Installation," "Administrative Guidelines," "ACHI Tutorial," a sample Assessment Report, "Clinical Interpretation," and "Clinical Applications" (pp. 42–88). The first four sections were apparently written by Dr. Sipe. The "Research and Design" chapter was written by Barbara and Bruce Berntson and Bryan Davis. No authorship is given for the applications sections or chapters.

Overall, the manual is not very well written, including misspellings (e.g., "expirimental" is repeatedly used; "randon" for "random"; "compromising" for "comprising"), and apparent typographical or clerical errors. More importantly, however, there are significant inconsistencies both within the sections authored by Drs. Sipe and Berntson et al., and among the differently authored sections.

ITEM SOURCES. We are told (Validation Project 1, p. 13) that "Subject matter experts from Minnesota identified 508 questions assumed to have value in distinguishing among chemical use, abuse, and dependency" *or that* "this study was designed to identify …items, taken from four existing questionnaires consisting of 255 items" (Research and Design, p. 16). Validation Project I involved the administration of the 508 items to two adolescent samples (N = 416), on the basis of which 255 items were selected to have "good construct validity" (p. 13) "through face validation" (p. 9) decided upon by the participating substance abuse counselors.

FACTOR ANALYSES. At least two factor analyses are reported. The first, based upon the 255 items selected by face validity analysis of the original pool of 508 items, yielded (principal components analysis with varimax rotation) 30 (or 29, depending upon who wrote the sections) composites. This was apparently followed by a principal components with varimax rotation of 100 items (how selected?). It should be noted, however, the output of "merely a numerical technique with no direct clinical or substantive significance" (p. 20) was "scrutinized from a clinical perspective in an attempt to achieve composite indices that, while being empirically verified, were also meaningful and of clinical usefulness" (p. 20)! These procedures "culminated in ten composites" (p. 20). However, detailed data are provided for only eight (pp. 22–26), and only nine are included in the assessment report printout.

ITEM DISTRIBUTION. The final instrument contains 128 items on the paper-and-pencil forms, as indicated in the summary sheet. It should be noted, however, that in the Research and Design (R&D) chapter the ACHI is referred to as "a 100 item questionnaire" (p. 16). The item content (of only eight) of the nine "factors," of the Berntson Social Desirability Scale, and of the Critical Life Items, are given in the R&D chapter. Analysis of the list found that at least *26* item numbers did not occur in any of the lists (although some may belong in Factor 7 [Self Regard/Abuse], for which item data were missing). About 80 items were each included in only one of the lists, and about 19 items were each included in two

lists. The list for Factor 3 (Family Estrangement) was obviously in error, with the array "8, 23, 26, 27, 30, 21, 23, 27 …." Item 6, a biodata item (adult/Educational Level; adolescent/Family Living Arrangement) was also included in the group of items for Factor 2 (Personal Consequences). To add to the confusion, the factor numbers given with the factor definitions (pp. 40–41) are different from the factor numbers assigned to the "Composite Characteristics" table (Table II, pp. 22–26).

NORMS. The summary (p. 1) indicates case numbers for the samples used: adults/150 nonclinical, 100 clinical; adolescents/1,288 nonclinical, 688 clinical. All the adults came from one (Minneapolis) sample, and the summary agrees with the text. However, the numbers for adolescents came from three samples. Adding the sample numbers for adolescents in these three studies (no study involved both adults and adolescents) yields totals discrepant with those given in the summary: 1,088 nonclinical, 619 clinical. Where the higher numbers in the summary came from is not explained. Furthermore, the user manual contains no norms tables of any sort.

RELIABILITY. The reliabilities reported in the summary are coefficient alpha internal consistency estimates (.74–.94), and based upon data from Validation Research Project II—Salt Lake City (pp. 13–14), which involved administration of a prior 255-item questionnaire to 981 adolescents (851 control and 130 exp*i*rimental [*sic*]). Alpha coefficients were also reported (Table II, pp. 22–26) for eight of the nine factors for a combined sample derived from Validation Project II (Salt Lake City) plus Validation Project III (Detroit, or Michigan). These factor alphas were in about the same range as reported in the summary.

No coefficient alpha data were presented for the adult sample. Furthermore, no other reliability measures (test-retest, alternate forms) are reported in the user manual.

VALIDITY. At least four approaches to validation are claimed in the manual.

The first is "concurrent validity" based on a correlation between a score (ACHI Assessment Score?) and "staff assessment" (p. 1), with r = .82. This is mentioned in one line on the summary (p. 1), but not referred to or elaborated upon anywhere else in the manual.

The second is "face validity," apparently based upon the item selection and reduction from 508 to 255 items in Validation Project I (p. 13).

The third is discriminant analysis, done on 29 (p. 14) or 30 (p. 18) "composites," in which percent of correct identification as between clinical and nonclinical samples yielded "hit" rates usually above 90% in Validation Projects II, III, and IV. Discriminant function analysis, however, is a suboptimal approach to validation. As Tatsuoka and Tiedeman (1954) point out, discriminant function analysis may be used to (a) identify group differences, (b) study and understand such differences, and (c) classify people. There is nothing in the technique that implies prediction, such as a statement that a person with this score will, if untreated, exhibit substance abuse behavior. Rulon (1951) presents a satirical fable about classifying a hexagon as a square or a circle. For most psychological testing purposes, regression equations against appropriate criteria provide a more effective technique (Anastasi, 1988, p. 191). Other substance abuse scales have reported criterion-related validities based upon number of different substances used, frequency of use, incidence of hospitalization or legal offenses while "under the influence," and similar measures. What the summary describes as "concurrent validity" (p. 1) would probably qualify as a criterion-based approach, but no information on the claim cited is available.

The fourth approach to validity claimed by the authors is by way of canonical correlations. Typically, in canonical correlation a correlation matrix of predictors (e.g., test scores) is correlated with a matrix of quantified criteria (observed or rated behaviors) for a defined sample of subjects. The manual authors nowhere describe the input to the canonical correlations reported for Validation Projects III and IV (pp. 14–15), and no mention is made of canonical correlation in the summary. It is this reviewer's understanding, however, that the two correlation matrices used were (a) the correlation matrix among the item responses for the clinical sample and (b) the item intercorrelation matrix for the nonclinical sample. Unlike in its usual application, therefore, the two matrices each consisted of the same variables, but based upon different human samples. The very high (above .90) resulting canonical correlations would therefore be expected, and would not reflect any aspect of the *validity* of the instrument. In fact, it seems to be a methodologically inappropriate use of canonical correlation.

In short, evidence supporting the validity of the ACHI for assessing substance abuse seems to be thin to negligible. The manual contains a Level of Care guide (pp. 82–87), based primarily upon the ACHI Assessment Score, providing "rules of thumb" (p. 82) that range from in-patient candidacy; through out-patient candidacy; to education, counseling, and contracting, but without any explicit data showing why the recommendations move by standard deviations above and below the mean.

In summary, since its inception as a 508-item experimental inventory much effort seems to have been expended in collecting and analyzing sample data on abusers and nonabusers. However, the user manual is poorly organized, carelessly written, and afflicted with many internal inconsistencies. The data supporting reliability and validity concerns are, at best, weak. As noted above, although the summary provides number of cases for norms, no tables of norms are presented in the manual. Self-administration of the ACHI by computer is not difficult, although a couple of glitches were noted in the program as this reviewer took it. The format of the printed assessment report is not easy to follow and far from optimum in design. In this reviewer's opinion current users should take the time to evaluate the instrument again, and possibly consider other inventories such as the Personal Experience Inventory (PEI; T4:1971) (Winters & Henly, 1989), the Chemical Dependency Assessment Survey (Oetting, Beauvais, Edwards, & Waters, 1984), and the Drug Use Screening Inventory (Tarter, 1990).

REVIEWER'S REFERENCES

Rulon, P. J. (1951). The stanine and the separile: A fable. *Personnel Psychology, 4*, 99–114.
Tatsuoka, M. M., & Tiedeman, D. V. (1954). Discriminant analysis. *Review of Educational Research, 24*, 402–420.
Oetting, E., Beauvais, F., Edwards, R., & Waters, M. (1984). The Drug and Alcohol Assessment System. Fort Collins, CO: Rocky Mountain Behavioral Sciences Institute.
Anastasi, A. (1988). *Psychological testing* (6th ed.). New York: Macmillan Publishers.
Winters, K. C., & Henly, G. A. (1989). Personal Experience Inventory. Los Angeles: Western Psychological Services.
Tarter, R. (1990). Evaluation and treatment of adolescent drug abuse: A decision-tree method. *American Journal of Drug and Alcohol Abuse, 16*, 1–46.

Review of the Assessment of Chemical Health Inventory by BETSY WATERMAN, Assistant Professor, Counseling and Psychological Services Department, State University of New York at Oswego, Oswego, NY:

The Assessment of Chemical Health Inventory (ACHI) was developed to assess chemical misuse among adolescents and adults. This instrument is designed to be self-administered and is an attempt to provide a more objective look at chemical use than many other current measures provide. The 128 test items were developed from within a Disease Model theoretical orientation and reflect the criterion outlined in the *DSM-III-R*. It appears there are two forms, one for adolescents and one for adults, although this is not clearly stated in the manual. The authors indicate that approximately 20 minutes is required for administration. Reading level is reported to be at the fourth grade level. Use with special populations (e.g., poor or nonreaders) is discussed briefly and the authors indicate the items can be read aloud to those who cannot read adequately.

Administration procedures are outlined in the manual, including standardized verbal instructions. The inventory can be administered on a computer or by having the individual fill in the appropriate circles on a response form. There are opportunities for practice trials to familiarize the respondent with the computerized format. The manual also includes instruction for using the software program. Testing administration is generally straightforward and requires individuals to respond to a statement, such as, "I use drugs or alcohol to change the way I feel" (p. 35), by selecting from among five choices (*Strongly Disagree, Disagree, No Opinion, Agree,* or *Strongly Agree*). The computer format allows for immediate scoring. The printed profile presents client identifying information, demographic data, and validity checks including "paired opposites" (p. 52) items and the Berntson Social Desirability Scale.

ACHI scores range from 1.00 to 9.00. They are presented on a graph and compared with the means of chemically dependent individuals. "Levels of care" (e.g., inpatient treatment) are suggested in the manual as they relate to the score earned. Scores between 1.00 and 5.07 are considered to be typical ranges of substance use and scores above 6.08 indicate possible need for treatment. Nine factor scores are presented in a profile (Chemical Involvement, Alienation, Family Estrangement, Personal Consequences, Depression, Family Support, Social Impact, Self-Regard, and Family Chemical Use) and compared to the means of nonclinical groups. Critical items (e.g., suicidal ideation) that may require immediate attention are also identified on the printout.

The ACHI was constructed and validated in four separate phases and in four locations: Minnesota, Salt Lake City, Detroit, and Minneapolis, respectively. During Phase I, 508 original items were identified by experts in the chemical dependency field. Subjects ranged in age between 14 and 20 years and were in outpatient (N = 116) or inpatient (N = 300) treatment programs. Of the original 508 items, 255 were identified by the authors as having good

"construct" validity, although it appears they are actually referring to face validity in this case.

In Phases II to IV, validity studies were conducted in which the ACHI was used to distinguish between users and nonusers of chemical substances. A total of 981 adolescents between the ages of 13 and 18 provided the sample in Phase II. It was not clear how gender and racial groups were reflected in experimental and control samples. Three hundred and ten adolescents, aged 13 to 18, served as the sample in Phase III with equal numbers of white and black subjects reflected in the pool. Two hundred and fifty adults participated in Phase IV. It should be noted that the control sample in this final phase included 150 individuals attending a community college. No age range or mean was given for this group of individuals. This sample may not be very different in age than the upper end of the previous adolescent group samples. The ACHI was reported as able to classify correctly 94% to 99% of nonusers and 74% to 88% of those who were chemically dependent.

Data from both Salt Lake City and Michigan were combined and analyzed, and, according to the authors, resulted in 10 composites or factors. Only 8 were reported in the validation study itself: Chemical Use Involvement, Social Impact, Personal Consequence, Family Chemical Use, Family Estrangement, Depression, Alienation, and Family Support. A ninth factor is reported elsewhere in the manual as Self Regard/Abuse. Cronbach alphas and standardized item alphas for the ACHI ranged between .74 and .94 across items within factors. There was no information about test-retest reliability in the manual.

The ACHI is an instrument designed to identify individuals who are chemically dependent. It is easy to administer and can be taken on a computer allowing for quick scoring and interpretation. Although the instrument appears to have an adequate ability to discriminate substance users from nonusers, a number of annoying problems exist. The manual is difficult to use and appears to have been constructed in a fragmented way. Information regarding the norming samples was extremely hard to follow and terms such as face validity and construct validity appear incorrectly used. The manual is not integrated into a coherent format, omits key pieces of information (such as the years when the validation studies were completed), and includes conflicting pieces of information. Numbers do not add up and clear explanations regarding missing data are not included. Although not conceptually problematic, numerous misspellings and typographical errors are distracting.

The computer-assisted feature is appealing but the software is outdated. The software included with the instrument was available on a 5.25-inch floppy disk that will run only on older IBM or compatible PCs. Most 486 and Pentium computers cannot use the current disk included in the package. The directions assume that the computer boots up on a floppy drive, which is not consistent with most modern computers and, overall, instructions were not easily generalizable to different computer setups. The authors would be encouraged to include both size disks (3.5-inch and 5.25-inch) with the test manual and it would be useful to have Windows, DOS, and Macintosh versions available.

In spite of the annoying problems related to this instrument the instrument appears to have been reasonably well constructed. Although norming information is confusing, it does seem that the instrument is effective in discriminating between users and nonusers a majority of the time. Problems related to "faking good" exist with this instrument as they do with other measures of this type, and it is unlikely that the ACHI has overcome this difficult problem. Overall, this instrument appears to have value in identifying those who are chemically dependent as well as determining possible family, social, or emotional factors that may be negatively impacting upon the individual. Revising the manual, integrating and extending the norming information, and updating the computer software would enhance this instrument's utility.

[19]
Assessment of Interpersonal Relations.

Purpose: "Developed to assess the quality of relationships children have with the individuals who are most important in their lives—their mothers, fathers, male peers, female peers, and teachers."
Population: Ages 9-0 to 19-11.
Publication Date: 1993.
Acronym: AIR.
Scores, 6: Mother, Father, Male Peers, Female Peers, Teachers, Total Relationship Index.
Administration: Group.
Price Data, 1994: $64 per complete kit; $39 per 50 record booklets; $27 per manual (78 pages).
Time: (20–25) minutes.
Author: Bruce A. Bracken.
Publisher: PRO-ED, Inc.

TEST REFERENCES

1. Crain, R. M., & Bracken, B. A. (1994). Age, race, and gender differences in child and adolescent self-concept: Evidence from a behavioral-acquisition, context-dependent model. *School Psychology Review, 23,* 496–511.

Review of the Assessment of Interpersonal Relations by PATRICIA B. KEITH, Assistant Professor of School Psychology, Alfred University, Alfred, NY:

GENERAL DESCRIPTION. The Assessment of Interpersonal Relations (AIR) is an instrument developed to measure the quality of the relationships of children and adolescents with parents, peers, and teachers. Interpersonal relationships are defined "as the unique and relatively stable behavioral pattern that exists or develops between two or more people as a result of individual and extraindividual influences" (manual, p. 6). Behavioral aspects of relationships, environmental influences, and similarity of characteristics (e.g., sex, age) are included in this definition.

This norm- and ipsative-referenced instrument is composed of five relationship scales (Mother, Father, Male Peers, Female Peers, and Teachers) and a Total Relationship Index (TRI). Each scale contains the same 35 items, which are well organized in an eight-page test booklet containing an identification section, directions, scales, and data summary page. Using a 4-point Likert scale the examinee is asked to mark how they honestly feel about identified relationships. Relationship characteristics measured are: companionship, emotional support, guidance, emotional comfort, reliance, trust, understanding, conflict, identification, respect, empathy, intimacy, affect, acceptance, and shared values. Raw scores are calculated, summed, and converted into standard scores that can be graphically presented. Also, confidence intervals, categorical classification systems, percentile ranks, and difference scores are found.

THEORETICAL MODEL. Many interpersonal relationship theories form the theoretical foundation for the AIR (manual, pp. 2–3). These theories generally suggest that interpersonal relationships of children and adolescents are influenced by and related to their functioning in many different settings and often predict later psychosocial adjustment. Relationships between the children and their peers (same and different-sex) and adults (parents and teachers) are important. Additionally, interindividual (e.g., physical attractiveness and health, the ability to express humor, perceived social competence) and intraindividual factors (e.g., birth order, parenting styles and practices, family dynamics) also influence interpersonal relationships.

Seven theoretical and definitional characteristics influenced the instrument's development. Using the work of Shavelson, Hubner, and Stanton (1976) the AIR emphasizes the organizational structure, multifaceted nature, hierarchical dimensionality, stability, developmental characteristics, evaluative underpinnings, and construct differentiality of self concept. Organizational structure contributes to interpersonal relationships because relationships are organized according to behavioral principles (i.e., specific and generalized response patterns are the result of direct and indirect feedback). Although interpersonal relationships take place in three principal environmental contexts (family, social, and academic) these contextual domains are not mutually exclusive and therefore this construct is multifaceted in nature. Despite the existence of a general pattern of interpersonal relationships, it is believed that some relationships are more important to individual children and adolescents, thus interpersonal relationships will have a hierarchical dimension. Although individuals' social networks change, it is postulated that these relationship patterns evolve gradually; consequently this construct is considered stable. Additionally, developmental characteristics must be considered in determining interpersonal relationships. Evaluations and generalizations of interpersonal relationships take place within and across domains. Finally, interpersonal relationships are one facet of general affect; it is related to concepts such as self concept, social skills, and family dynamics but can be differentiated from anxiety and locus of control.

Using these theoretical foundations, the AIR and the Multidimensional Self Concept Scale (MSCS; Bracken, 1992) were co-developed and co-normed. Bracken identified six contexts in which children and adolescents most customarily function (social, competence, affect, academic, family, and physical), along with three relationship domains (social, family, and academic). These contexts and domains form the MSCS and the AIR respectively. Reviews of the MSCS can be found in *The Twelfth Mental Measurements Yearbook* (Archambault, 1995; Willis, 1995).

ADMINISTRATION, SCORING, AND INTERPRETATION. Individuals with experience in psychometrics, personality theory, individual human differences, and developmental psychology will find the AIR easy to administer and score after several practice sessions. Directions are short and stress the importance of the examinee rating each statement honestly, as there are no right or wrong answers. If the examinee does not live with their mother or father, a box is checked, and a reason is given for completing the scale (death, separation, divorce, or other). Although a third grade reading level is required to complete this instrument, the examiner can define any words that are unfamiliar to the examinee. Twenty minutes is said to be the average length of time needed to complete the instrument; however, time required to complete the instrument will depend upon the examinees' abilities to process their thoughts and feelings about their parents, peers, and teachers and then rate them. Individual or group administrations can be done by paraprofessionals with training in test administration.

The AIR is scored using a differential scoring procedure. Positively worded items are scored from *strongly agree = 4* to *strongly disagree = 1*, whereas items with negative connotations are scored *strongly agree = 1* to *strongly disagree = 4*. Although Bracken has placed all negative connotative items on multiples of five (5, 10, 15, 20, 25, 30, 35), the examiner must be careful to apply the correct scoring procedure. Failure to use the correct scoring procedure will likely influence the usefulness of this instrument. After raw scores are calculated, they are converted to standard scores based on the examinee's age and gender. Next, confidence intervals (ranging from 85% to 99%), classifications of score ranges (very positive, moderately positive, average, moderately negative and very negative), and percentile ranks are found. If an examinee does not complete a scale, scores can be prorated.

Interpreting the AIR is done in two ways (norm-referenced and ipsative), and should be context-dependent and part of a larger evaluation battery. In norm-referenced interpretation the examinees' scores are compared to the standardization sample ($M = 100$). Interpretations generally suggest if the examinee deviates significantly from their "normal" peers (e.g., average adjustment, well adjusted, less well adjusted). Statements can be made about the examinee's general relationship pattern (TRI) and relationship patterns with their mother, father, male peers, female peers, and teachers. Ipsative interpretation contrasts performance on each subscale with overall performance in the AIR. Using this type of interpretation scheme, interpersonal relationships measured by the subscales can be viewed as strengths, weaknesses, or average.

PSYCHOMETRIC CHARACTERISTICS OF THE AIR. A national sample of 2,501 children, in grades 5 to 12 and ranging from 9 years to 19 years, was used for norming. Children were from regular and special education classes and attend schools in rural, urban (major cities and small towns) or suburban school districts. School districts participating in the standardization were from across the United States. Children from intact, reconstituted, single-parent families or who were living in foster home placements were well represented in the sample, along with students from both genders.

Chapter 5 of the manual is especially well written and straightforward in presenting information about the AIR's reliability, validity, ceiling, floor, and item gradient. Briefly, all subscales and TRI scores have internal consistency scores of 93% or better across all age and gender levels. Test-retest reliability coefficients over a 2-week interval for all subscales and TRI scores range from .94 to .98. Content validity is strong for this instrument, as the AIR's design was based on sound psychological theories, research, and literature support. Additionally, factor analysis results yield seven "meaningful" factors with eigenvalues from 25.83 to 3.59. Standard scores have a mean of 100 and a standard deviation of 15 (same as IQ scales). Special care was taken to be sure that ceiling, floor, and item gradient would not adversely affect standard scores more than 1/3 of a standard deviation. Standard errors of measurement for the five subscales range from 3.00 to 3.97; the TRI has a standard error of measurement of 3.0.

In summary, the AIR is an extremely valuable addition for psychologists, counselors, educators, and others who are interested in interpersonal relationships of children and adolescents. Based on a strong theoretical foundation, exceptional psychometric properties, and ease of administration and interpretation, this instrument is recommended for use. The examiner's manual is especially well written, although more information about age, race, and gender "comparative analyses" would be good.

REVIEWER'S REFERENCES

Shavelson, R. J., Hubner, J. J., & Stanton, G. C. (1976). Self-concept: Validation of construct interpretations. *Review of Educational Research, 46*, 407–441.

Bracken, B. A. (1992). Multidimensional Self Concept Scale. Austin, TX: PRO-ED, Inc.

Archambault, F. X. (1995). [Review of the Multidimensional Self Concept Scale]. In J. C. Conoley & J. C. Impara (Eds.), *The twelfth mental measurements yearbook* (pp. 647–649). Lincoln, NE: Buros Institute of Mental Measurements.

Willis, W. G. (1995). [Review of the Multidimensional Self Concept Scale]. In J. C. Conoley & J. C. Impara (Eds.), *The twelfth mental measurements yearbook* (pp. 649–650). Lincoln, NE: Buros Institute of Mental Measurements.

Review of the Assessment of Interpersonal Relations by FREDERIC J. MEDWAY, Professor of Psychology, University of South Carolina, Columbia, SC:

The Assessment of Interpersonal Relations (AIR) is a multidimensional, context-dependent scale designed to assess the quality of children's social relationships with individuals most important in their lives—their parents, peers, and teachers. The scale goes beyond traditionally sociometric methods to assess how children feel about their interpersonal relationships. The need for such a measure is based on the notion that children's psychological adjustment can be enhanced if relationship difficulties can be identified early and steps taken to improve them. Because a large number of children referred for child guidance problems do have faulty interpersonal relationships, the need for such a measure is well justified.

The AIR was co-developed and co-normed with the Multidimensional Self Concept Scale (MSCS, Bracken, 1992; 12:246). Together these scales are designed to assess children's and adolescents' self-perceptions within six critical contexts—Social, Competence, Affect, Academic, Family, and Physical. The AIR assesses stable relationship patterns within three contexts in which children spend most of their time—Social, Family, and Academic domains. Items measure emotional support, companionship, reliance, guidance, trust, understanding, empathy, intimacy, conflict, affect, acceptance, shared values, identification, emotional comfort, and respect. The construct of interpersonal relations is not thoroughly tapped by any existing measure and the AIR is the most well-developed measure of its type. In developing the AIR, Bracken sought to devise a measure that (a) employed standard scores for ease of interpretation and score integration across various other psychoeducational and achievement batteries, (b) permitted interchild (normative) and intrachild (ipsative) interpretations, and (c) would be appropriate for nearly all school-age children. This instrument will be very useful to school psychologists, neuropsychologists, and others who do multidisciplinary team assessments of students' academic and behavior problems. Although the AIR does not measure why a child gives a certain rating, these reasons can be assessed in a follow-up interview.

There are 35 items comprising each of the five domains or subscales: mother, father, male peers, female peers, and teachers. Each item presents a statement about relationships that the respondent rates for agreement-disagreement on 4-point Likert scales. An illustrative item is "It is important that I am accepted by my … (parents, teacher, etc.)." To avoid response sets of central tendency, the examinee must choose either "strong agree," "agree," "disagree," or "strongly disagree." Seven items on each subscale describe a negative interpersonal situation (e.g., difficulty being oneself in others' presence); for these items, scoring is reversed.

The AIR provides a global measure of children's interpersonal relations (Total Relationship Index) and a measure of specific relationships in each of the five domains. Administration time is brief, it can be group administered, and a psychometrically sophisticated examiner is not required. The AIR can be administered by a classroom teacher (or mental health worker or paraprofessional) without taking away much instructional time.

The AIR yields raw scores, standard scores based on an IQ metric with a mean of 100 ($SD = 15$), T scores ($M = 50$, $SD = 10$), confidence intervals, classification categories, and percentiles. Subscales with incomplete items can be prorated. The AIR classification system merely describes the extent to which interpersonal relations are positive or negative (from very negative to very positive). This classification system can be easily understood by parents and teachers, and does not label a child. The test can be interpreted as a norm-referenced instrument comparing the examinee with the standardization sample or can be interpreted looking at the child's relationship strengths and weaknesses across the five domains relative to his or her overall relationship performance. The AIR manual adequately covers interpretive issues such as differences in ratings across gender and type of interpersonal relationship so that the examiner has some understanding of relationship normality. Bracken appropriately notes that such relationships are complex and users of the scale should be cautioned that this area requires additional research study.

Both field testing and standardization of the AIR were appropriate. The AIR was standardized on more than 2,500 children in grades 5 through 12 varying in gender, geographic region, ethnicity, and family background so as to match U.S. Census statistics. Exceptional children were included in the standardization sample and the scale is nondiscriminatory.

Besides being easy to administer and score, the AIR is psychometrically very sound. The last chapter of the manual presents information regarding internal consistency, test-retest reliability (2-week interval), content and discriminant validity, and factor analysis. Test reliability estimates exceed .90 for each of the five scales and the Total Relationship Index. The AIR shows a moderate correlation of .55 with the MSCS. Whereas the underlying construct of interpersonal relationship perceptions shares some variance with self-image perceptions, the AIR does appear to measure a unique and similarly important construct.

In summary, the AIR is a well-conceived and developed instrument that provides a straightforward method of measuring children's important social networks. Its developer was well aware of the theoretical underpinnings of these relationships and of important test evaluation criteria. As with other self-report measures there remains the problem that certain examinees may not understand some of the more abstract relationship concepts. No evidence of possible social desirability influences on scores is reported and, unfortunately, the AIR was correlated with only one self-concept measure and no other measure of interpersonal behavior. At its best the scale can only be used by clinicians as a generic measure of interpersonal relations. Because the test was not designed to determine the nature or cause of a high or low score, follow-up interviewing will be necessary before interventions can be planned. With this understanding of the test's limitations and an understanding that children's interpersonal relations themselves are not presently well understood, both practitioners and researchers will find this test a useful asset when a quick and reliable measure of children's interpersonal relations is needed.

REVIEWER'S REFERENCE

Bracken, B. A. (1992). Multidimensional Self Concept Scale. Austin, TX: PRO-ED, Inc.

[20]

Assessment of Living Skills and Resources.

Purpose: Assesses "daily tasks that require a high level of cognitive function," or Instrumental Activities of Daily Living (IADLs), "in community-dwelling elders."
Population: Community-dwelling elders.
Publication Date: 1991.
Acronym: ALSAR.
Scores: 11 task scores: Telephoning, Reading, Leisure, Medication Management, Transportation, Shopping, Meal Preparation, Laundering, Housekeeping, Home Maintenance.
Administration: Individual.
Price Data, 1994: $5 per master of the reproducible ALSAR; $55 for each of two instructional videotapes ("An Overview of IADL Assessment" and "Administration of the ALSAR"); master of the ALSAR included in the latter videotape.
Time: (15–20) minutes.
Comments: Incorporates assessment of Instrumental Activities of Daily Living (IADL); administered by health professionals from any discipline.
Authors: Theresa J. K. Drinka, Jane H. Williams, Martha Schram, Jean Farrell-Holtan, and Reenie Euhardy.
Publisher: Madison Geriatric Research, Education, and Clinical Center, VA Medical Center.

Review of the Assessment of Living Skills and Resources by CAMERON J. CAMP, Research Scientist, Myers Research Institute of The Menorah Park Center for the Aging, Beachwood, OH:

The Assessment of Living Skills and Resources (ALSAR) is described as an instrument developed to help professionals assess Instrumental Activities of Daily Living (IADLs) in community-dwelling elders. It can purportedly be administered by health professionals of any discipline, and focuses on 11 IADL tasks: Telephoning, Reading, Leisure Activity, Medication Management, Money Management, Transportation, Shopping, Meal Preparation, Laundering, Housekeeping, and Home Maintenance. These content areas correspond with content found in most measures of IADLs. The ALSAR has a unique feature in that it measures both skills and resources in determining risk of disability (i.e., inability to complete a task).

Skill is defined as accomplishment of a task by an older adult. This is done either by performing a task by themselves or by procurement, defined in turn as the task being accomplished by another person "if the patient takes responsibility for procurement" (p. 85). Probe questions are provided to help assess skill for a particular IADL. For example, probes for skill at Telephoning include "Can you hear the phone ringing?" and "Do you make calls or only use the phone if someone calls you?" Each task is given a skill rating using scores of 0 (Consistent Performance/Independent), 1 (Partial Performance or Procurement/Partially Independent), or 2 (Patient Takes No Responsibility for Doing the Task or Procurement/Dependent). A rating of 2 is also used if the older adult claims to be able to do the task but appearances suggest otherwise. This is a unique aspect of the ALSAR in comparison to other IADL measures, and addresses the distinction Bould, Smith, and Longino (in press) characterize as the difference between "help" and "care." Help implies that the older person is in charge and can decide what services he or she needs; care has the connotation of dependency.

Resource is defined as a support for doing a task that is extrinsic to the individual and may be either human or technical, formal or informal. Probe questions for resources in telephoning include "Any special devices on your phone?—large scale numbers on dial?" and "Can you get to the phone if it's ringing?" Again, a resource score of 0 indicates adequate resources are available to accomplish the task. A score of 1 indicates that needed resources are inconsistent, unstable, unreliable, or that the caregiving environment provides resources but their use causes strain. A rating of 2 means that resources are insufficient to accomplish the task, are not being used, or are about to be lost. Thus, the ALSAR can detect effects of interventions designed to increase IADL performance through environmental modification and accommodation of disabilities, which is another important and relatively unique aspect of this test.

For each item, the skill and resource scores are added to create a combined risk score. For this task risk score, 0 or 1 indicates low risk for not accomplishing the task, 2 represents moderate risk, and 3 or 4 represents high risk. The sum of the 11 task risk scores is known as the R-Score. An article describing validation and initial testing of the ALSAR has been published (Williams et al., 1991). However, a master form with instructions along with two instructional videotapes are commercially available. It is important to have such material because the initial article describing the ALSAR does not contain the detailed probe questions for each item found in the instructions.

The ALSAR validation sample consisted of 75 Hospital Based Home Care patients (72 men, 3 women) receiving treatment at a VA hospital in Madison, WI. Patients ranged in age from 51 to 94 years; over 90% were over the age of 60, and 29% were over age 80. Half of the patients were married, and 78% lived in their own home or apartment. The sample size was, therefore, small as validation samples go, and the fact that males predominated the sample is a serious deficiency.

The Barthel Index (Mahoney & Barthel, 1965) was used to assess patients' capacity to perform Activities of Daily Living (ADLs). The Mini-Mental Status Exam (MMSE; Folstein, Folstein, & McHugh, 1975) was used to assess cognitive status, and the Carroll Rating Scale (CRS; Carroll, Feinberg, Smouse, Rawson, & Greden, 1981) was given as a self-assessed measure of depression. Average scores of the sample indicated that a proportion of the sample was at some risk for loss of independence, mild depression, and possible early stage dementia. A physical or occupational therapist administered 88% of the ALSARs, though instructions accompanying a test manual state that the ALSAR can be administered by any health professional.

For R-Scores, the Cronbach alpha coefficient was .91. Average interrater agreement on ratings for Skills was 86% (range = 72%–94%), and for Resources was 95% (range = 78%–100%). Fifteen of the

22 kappa coefficients were .7 or above, and other kappas ranged from .27 to .69. Items were, therefore, internally consistent and generated moderate to good interrater reliability.

With regard to concurrent validity, a Pearson product-moment r of -.58 (p<.001) was calculated between R-Score and the Barthel Index. With regard to predictive validity, patients were tracked for a 6-month period after initial assessment with the ALSAR. The sample was categorized as to whether, over 6 months, patients had or had not: changed to a more supportive living arrangement; changed to a more structured living arrangement; been placed in a nursing home; been hospitalized; or died. Initial ALSAR scores were significantly different between each of these outcome categories. The R-Score was not significantly correlated with the CRS dysphoria measure.

In summary, the ALSAR is a relatively easy-to-administer test of IADL functioning that addresses important issues not assessed in most other instruments—procurement of services by the disabled person and level of environmental support. Its major weakness is the rather small and nonrepresentative sample used in its initial validation. If its psychometric properties can be verified across larger and more representative samples across a variety of settings, the ALSAR could prove to be a very useful measure.

REVIEWER'S REFERENCES

Mahoney, F. S., & Barthel, D. W. (1965). Functional evaluations: The Barthel Index. *Maryland State Medical Journal, 14,* 61–65.

Folstein, M. F., Folstein, S. E., & McHugh, P. R. (1975). Mini-Mental State—A practical method for grading the cognitive state of patients for the clinician. *Journal of Psychiatric Research, 12,* 189–198.

Carroll, B. J., Feinberg, M., Smouse, P. E., Rawson, S. G., & Greden, J. F. (1981). The Carroll rating scale for depression. I. Development, reliability, and validation. *British Journal of Psychiatry, 138,* 194–200.

Williams, J. H., Drinka, T. J. K., Greenberg, J. R., Farrell-Holtan, J., Euhardy, R., & Schram, M. (1991). Development and testing of the Assessment of Living Skills and Resources (ALSAR) in elderly community-dwelling veterans. *The Gerontologist, 31,* 84–91.

Bould, S., Smith, M. H., & Longino, C. F., Jr. (in press). Ability, disability, and the oldest old. *Journal of Aging and Social Policy.*

Review of the Assessment of Living Skills and Resources by ANITA M. HUBLEY, Assistant Professor of Psychology, University of Northern British Columbia, Prince George, British Columbia, Canada:

The Assessment of Living Skills and Resources (ALSAR) is designed to evaluate the ability of older adults to accomplish 11 tasks considered essential for independent living in the community. Unlike most measures of instrumental activities of daily living (IADLs), the ALSAR rates not only patient skill in performing or procuring each task, but also the resource level available to the patient to accomplish each task. It is the combination of skill and resources that determines risk—or the likelihood that the pa-

tient currently will be unable to accomplish the task at hand.

Administration of the ALSAR appears to be quite straightforward. The authors provide a list of suggested skill and resource questions for each task on the back of the record sheet that should prove useful in guiding an interview. However, the record sheet itself would benefit from some revisions that would incorporate the suggested questions and some space for notes on a page separate from the actual scoring of skills, resources, and risk.

Scoring of the ALSAR is also straightforward, but does involve an element of subjective judgment, which is, of course, based upon the particular questions asked in the interview. Skills are scored as independent (0), partially independent (1), or dependent (2). Resources are scored as consistently available (0), inconsistently available (1), or not available or in use (2). The risk score for each task is simply the sum of the skill and resource scores for that task. An "R" score, which is the sum of the 11 task risk scores, is also provided. Interrater agreement for the skill and resource scores was obtained by two trained clinicians who independently interviewed and rated 32 patients. The average interrater agreement across the 11 tasks was 86% on skills and 95% on resources. Kappa coefficients (which correct for chance agreement), however, ranged from .53 to .90 on skills and from .27 to 1.00 on resources. Overall, the interrater agreement is adequate for an interview-based checklist such as the ALSAR.

The risk ratings assessed for each task, according to the authors, are meant to be used to identify patient needs, to identify areas of IADL risk, and to prioritize treatment goals. However, the authors do not clearly state the purpose of the "R" score. Although this score is used to assess the reliability (i.e., internal consistency) and validity of the ALSAR, there are no specific recommendations for its use by the clinician. It appears that all of the goals and decisions proposed by the authors are made at the item level. If, in fact, the "R" score is intended to be used as an overall measure of independent living risk and used in decision making, normative data (using a larger sample size and equal numbers of men and women) need to be provided and cut-scores considered.

It is essential to know at what level (i.e., "R" score vs. item level) inferences will be made using the ALSAR before one can properly evaluate any evidence for reliability and validity. The authors should note that it is these inferences that are being validated (see Hubley & Zumbo, 1996). Internal consistency, as measured by Cronbach's alpha, is reported to be .91; however, it is difficult to interpret precisely what coefficient alpha means unless the intention is to actually use a total score, such as the "R" score, in practice. More important will be information regarding test-retest reliability and the ability of the ALSAR (again at the appropriate scale or item level) to assess stability and change in risk.

Similar problems concerning the level of inferences used apply to the evaluation of validity. There is some preliminary evidence available regarding construct validity using the "R" score as a measure of overall risk. For example, the "R" score was found to be negatively correlated with the Barthel Index, a measure of basic activities of daily living ($r = -.58$, $p <.001$) and the Mini-Mental State Examination, a screening instrument used to assess cognitive functioning ($r = -.26$, $p <.05$). Other nonsignificant correlations with measures of patient depression and caregiver strain may reflect smaller sample sizes and/or reduced variability or less problematic levels. More research is needed to provide evidence regarding convergent and discriminant validity. There is good evidence for the predictive validity of ALSAR "R" scores in differentiating among patients who experience a change in living arrangement or environment, nursing home placement, hospitalization, or death, at 6-months follow-up. However, because many of the clinicians in the study would likely have been involved in patient care, it is not clear what role the initial "R" scores might have played (either directly or indirectly) in initiating these changes. It should also be noted that the assessment of skills and resources in the ALSAR relies upon the self-report of the patient or family member(s) during the interview and is not based on a functional or observational assessment. Clearly, the accuracy of the source of any information will have an impact on the predictive validity of the "R" scores.

SUMMARY. In summary, the Assessment of Living Skills and Resources shows promise as a measure of instrumental activities of daily living. The administration and scoring of the ALSAR appear straightforward. Interrater reliability is adequate. Thus far, there appears to be some good evidence supporting the use of the "R" score in identifying older adults who may be at risk and unable to safely maintain independent living in the community. However, the ALSAR is presented more as a useful template for ascertaining risk level for 11 key tasks of instrumental activities of daily living. The authors need to direct more attention to identifying the level at which test inferences should be made.

At the present time, it appears that only one study has been published providing information regarding the development and psychometric properties of the ALSAR (Williams et al., 1991). Notably, although instructions regarding the administration and scoring of the ALSAR are provided in both written and video format, because there is no formal test manual, anyone planning to use this measure should read the article. Finally, far more research is needed before it can be determined if the ALSAR will prove to be competitive with other well-established measures of IADLs such as Lawton and Brody's (1969) Instrumental Activities of Daily Living Scale.

REVIEWER'S REFERENCES

Lawton, M. P., & Brody, E. M. (1969). Assessment of older people: Self-maintaining and instrumental activities of daily living. *The Gerontologist, 9*, 179–186.
Williams, J. H., Drinka, T. J. K., Greenberg, J. R., Farrell-Holtan, J., Euhardy, R., & Schram, M. (1991). Development and testing of the Assessment of Living Skills and Resources (ALSAR) in elderly community-dwelling veterans. *The Gerontologist, 31*, 84–91.
Hubley, A. M., & Zumbo, B. D. (1996). A dialectic on validity: Where we have been and where we are going. *The Journal of General Psychology, 123*, 207–215.

[21]
Attention Deficit Disorder Behavior Rating Scales.

Purpose: Designed to help school personnel and psychologists make proper ADD referrals.
Population: School personnel and psychologists.
Publication Dates: 1982–1993.
Acronym: ADDBRS.
Scores, 10: Inattention, Impulsivity, Hyperactivity, Anger Control, Academics, Anxiety, Confidence, Aggressiveness, Resistance, Social.
Administration: Individual.
Editions, 2: Child, Adult.
Price Data, 1993: $65 per complete kit including 25 rating sheets, 25 profile sheets, manual ('93, 14 pages), and three audiotapes (Attention Deficit Disorder, Kids on Medication, Does Your Child Have Learning Disabilities?); $30 per 25 rating scales, 25 profile sheets and manual; $9 per 25 rating sheets and 25 profile sheets; $11.50 per audiotape; $20 per set of 20 teacher information and parent information handout sheets and instructions; $35 per adult version including 25 rating sheets, 25 profile sheets, and manual.
Time: Administration time not reported.
Authors: Ned Owens and Betty White Owens.
Publisher: Ned Owens, Inc.

Review of the Attention Deficit Disorder Behavior Rating Scales by E. JEAN NEWMAN, Assistant

Professor of Educational Psychology, University of South Alabama, Mobile, AL:

The Attention Deficit Disorder Behavior Rating Scales (ADDBRS) is a 50-item checklist of behaviors. Each item is rated on a 5-point scale according to frequency, varying from (1) "You have not noticed this behavior before" to (5) "to a very large degree," with intervening levels annotated as "slight degree," "considerable degree," and "large degree." The scale was first published in 1982, and revised in 1993.

In the manual, the authors state that the instrument was designed to identify behavior supporting a diagnosis of Attention Deficit Disorder in children ages 6 through 16. Although the authors present the instrument as limited to use for screening, and not as a diagnostic tool, they recommend the instrument for persuading parents, teachers, and medical doctors of the need for intervention.

The authors state that a study was conducted of the behaviors common to children diagnosed as ADD, resulting in the rating scale. Of 10 behaviors targeted by the authors, 3 (Inattention, Impulsivity, Hyperactivity) are listed in the *Diagnostic and Statistical Manual of Mental Disorders, Fourth Edition (DSM-IV)* as criteria for being diagnosed Attention Deficit/Hyperactivity Disorder (American Psychiatric Association, 1994). The remaining 7 behaviors listed are Anger Control, Academics, Anxiety, Confidence, Aggressiveness, Social, and Resistance. These behaviors were taken from observations in private practice, with children who had been diagnosed attention deficit (personal communication, August 23, 1996).

The scale is formatted with five items for each behavior, and the rater or counselor may total the raw score for each observed behavior. The manual provides a profile with three score ranges: normal, at risk, and very high risk. The instrument is simple to complete, score, and categorize using the profiles provided. In the original pilot study, the norming sample consisted of 100 children diagnosed with Attention Deficit Disorder, who were showing improvement in school while on medication. This is a small sample for determining reliability and validity evidence. Although the sample included students aged 6 through 16, no statistics or descriptions are furnished regarding number in the sample by age, range of scores, or method of AD/HD diagnosis. The norming sample for the revised 1993 scale consisted of 200 children. However, even less information was supplied about them, other than an assurance from the authors that there were no significant differences between the two sets of results.

In both studies, the authors used the Wechsler Intelligence Scale for Children—Revised (WISC-R) to confirm that the children were in the normal range of intelligence. In the 1982 study, 47% of the children were reported as having scores at or above 110, and 47% were in the average range. That leaves only 6% of the normative sample in the lower levels of the intelligence distribution and represents a major limitation of the instrument. Many students with ADD function in the bottom half of the IQ distribution and appear to be underrepresented in the norm group. The fact that the scale was normed on students already being treated further limits its utility. If we use the norms properly, the ADDBRS should only be used when assessing students with WISC-R IQs above 90 who are already responding well to medication. It has not been normed on those with IQs of 90 or below who are not on medication—a group of students who are most at risk.

Use of the Bender Visual Motor Gestalt Test and the WISC-R to bolster the authors' contention of validity is not helpful in evaluating the ADDBRS. No information is provided regarding how the Bender was scored, the range of scores, or what statistical analyses were performed using these instruments.

Similarly, no assessment of validity was reported. The authors claim high validity because use of the instrument resulted in an ADD diagnosis for all students assessed, with subsequent improvement both academically and behaviorally. However, the children had already been diagnosed and medicated before the instrument was administered; therefore the claim for validity is circular at best.

There are no reports of predictive validity evidence. In the case of content validity, the authors did include items they say tap into inattention, impulsivity, and hyperactivity. However, there are no reports from comparative item analysis, construct validation, or comparisons with other scales. Additionally, the lack of information regarding the other seven variables assessed by the instrument leaves many questions about the validity of the instrument. In relation to construct validity, the authors claim that the items assessing Inattention, Impulsivity, and Hyperactivity cumulatively define "Primary/Organic behaviors" (p. 2), and their cause is organic or neurological. The remaining seven variables are considered secondary, or caused by the first three. Further, they explain that Inattention is organic, often due to poor auditory processing, and that Hyperactivity is the least problematic of the three, especially because very few children are truly "hyperkinetic" (p. 10). The strong emphasis on organic origin could mislead both parents and educators to see the child's difficulties as being irreparable. The implications of such a narrowed focus could have serious ramifications toward attempts at intervention. Items included as organically caused relate to task completion, organization skills, time and attention on task, and inability to sit still, listen or concentrate. Because there is much evidence that these behaviors can be controlled and mastered with motivation, supervision, medication, and persistence, they are obviously vulnerable to intervention. Consequently, the claim for construct validity, presenting the constructs as organic and secondary, may be too restrictive and may result in a misinterpretation of both the instrument and the disorder.

The author reports (personal communication, August 13, 1996) that no item analysis was conducted, and that the scale was not changed in any way; the revision process was procedural, using a larger sample to confirm earlier findings.

SUMMARY. The Attention Deficit Disorder Behavior Rating Scales has a clear and simple format. Its intended uses, for screening and pattern description only, are clear. The instructions for completion by teachers and parents are clear. The scoring is simple and straightforward, requiring little training. In short, the instrument seems to offer pertinent information with the minimal involvement of time, expertise, or expense.

However, when assessed for the rigors of analyses required to deem the ADDBRS valid, reliable, or methodologically sound, the instrument falls short. The authors have not shown its consistency over time, consistency with similar instruments, generation of appropriate range of scores, inclusion of differential samples, or of large enough samples for statistical power. Likewise, the authors have furnished no evidence of validity, either in predicting the presence of attention deficit behaviors or in measuring the variables described. Thus, there is no support for its construct validity, content validity, or criterion validity. Although the test may be a useful and helpful tool, there are no empirical data to substantiate any such claims. For an alternate choice, the reader is encouraged to consider the Attention Deficit Disorders Evaluation Scale (ADDES), School Version (McCarney & Bauer, 1990; 12:38). With a

norming sample of 4,876 students, which includes both attention-deficit and non-attention-deficit children from 19 states across the United States, the manual provides substantive data by sex, age, race, socioeconomic status, and geographical region. Coefficients for test-retest reliability, internal consistency, and interrater reliability are well documented and substantially high. Details of content validity, item analysis, and factor analysis for construct validity and predictive validity reflect a thorough psychometric analysis, as well as documentation of the instrument as a useful and acceptable tool for assessment.

REVIEWER'S REFERENCES
McCarney, S. B., & Bauer, A. M. (1990). *Attention Deficit Disorders Evaluation Scale.* Columbia, MO: Hawthorne Educational Services, Inc.
American Psychiatric Association. (1994). *Diagnostic and statistical manual of mental disorders* (4th ed.). Washington, DC: Author.

[22]
Auditory Continuous Performance Test.

Purpose: "Designed to help … identify children who have auditory attention disorders … Also yields information that will help diagnose children as having Attention Deficit/Hyperactivity Disorder."
Population: Ages 6–0 to 11–11.
Publication Date: 1994.
Acronym: ACPT.
Scores, 4: Inattention Errors, Impulsivity Errors, Total Error Score, Vigilance Decrement.
Administration: Individual.
Price Data, 1995: $75 per complete kit including examiner's manual (52 pages), test audiocassette, and 12 record forms; $11 per 12 record forms; $32 per examiner's manual; $40 per 1 test audiocassette.
Time: (15) minutes.
Author: Robert W. Keith.
Publisher: The Psychological Corporation.

Review of the Auditory Continuous Performance Test by NADEEN L. KAUFMAN, Professor of Clinical Psychology, California School of Professional Psychology, San Diego, CA and ALAN S. KAUFMAN, Senior Research Scientist, Psychological Assessment Resources, Inc. (PAR), Odessa, FL:

The Auditory Continuous Performance Test (ACPT) is an individually administered, continuous performance test, given by audiocassette, that is normed for children ages 6 years 0 months to 11 years 11 months. It is an auditory vigilance task that was developed to measure children's auditory skills "to help you determine if an attention problem is one of the underlying factors contributing to a child's learning problems" (examiner's manual, p. 1). The ACPT was intended to measure auditory attention, as distinct from auditory processing skills, which the author claims can be measured with his 1986 test, SCAN: A Screening Test for Auditory Processing Disorders (T4:2336). The author indicates in the Introduction that differential diagnosis between auditory attentional problems and auditory processing deficiencies is important, and can be conducted by comparing test results on the ACPT and SCAN; he does not, however, offer guidelines for making such a comparison or provide joint data on the two tests.

In addition to identifying children with auditory attention disorders, the "ACPT also yields information that will help diagnose children as having Attention Deficit/Hyperactivity Disorder (ADHD)" (examiner's manual, p. 1). Indeed, the use of the ACPT for ADHD assessment is so pervasive throughout the brief manual that even the two possible scores a child can obtain on the ACPT (Pass or Fail) are defined in terms of ADHD. For example, "Fail" is defined as follows: "The score obtained is most similar to the scores of children in the standardization sample who were identified as having ADHD" (examiner's manual, p. 7). In fact, that statement makes no sense at all because the standardization sample is subsequently defined as "children between the ages of 6 and 11 years who had not been diagnosed as having ADHD" (examiner's manual, p. 27). Such carelessness is common in this manual, which begins with a misspelled Foreword ("Forward").

Additional purposes of the ACPT are for verifying "a clinician's or teacher's observations of poor attending behaviors," measuring "the effects of behavioral modification programs," and "the effects of stimulant medication" for children diagnosed as having ADHD, and as a research tool for differentiating "children who have learning disabilities or language disorders from children who have central auditory processing disorders" (examiner's manual, pp. 1–2). None of these purposes are addressed in the section on validity. Whereas parent's ratings of attention are compared to ACPT scores, no ratings by teachers or clinicians are provided. Similarly, an ADHD sample was tested on the ACPT, but no data are presented on the effects of behavior modification programs or stimulant medication. And no data are offered on the ACPT scores of children with known learning problems or with any exceptionality other than ADHD. In general, the author shows little awareness of the burgeoning research on ADHD or understanding of the prevalence of the comorbidities that exist within the ADHD population.

The ACPT requires the child to listen to an audiocassette tape of a man who speaks rapidly and in a monotone, but with a pleasant voice and good articulation. The man says a 96-word list of 20 common monosyllables (e.g., room, drop, else, five); he then repeats, without pausing, the same 96-word list an additional five times. The six trials take about 11 minutes; an extra 4 minutes are needed for set-up and a brief warm-up exercise for an estimated total testing time of 15 minutes. The child is listening for a single target word (dog) that appears 20 times per 96-word trial, and responds to each target word by raising his or her thumb. Children can make either errors of Inattention (not giving a "thumbs up" to dog) or Impulsivity (giving a "thumbs up" to a wrong word). The Total Error Score equals the sum of these two types of errors, and this score is converted to Pass or Fail based on a norms-based criterion score that ranges from 38 errors required to fail at age 6 years to only 16 errors at ages 10–11. Examiners also compute a Vigilance Decrement Score for each child, which equals the number of correct "dog" responses on Trial 1 minus the number of correct "dog" responses on Trial 6. Unusual Vigilance Decrement Scores are appropriately determined from distributions of such scores; those decrements that occur less than 10% of the time in the normal population are considered unusual.

Although administration of the ACPT is easy, scoring is not. The voice on the tape speaks so rapidly that the *examiner* must be quite vigilant to note each correct or incorrect "thumbs up" on the record form. The notations must be made with extreme rapidity to ensure that the examiner does not miss an incorrect "thumbs up" that follows closely on the heels of a correct response. The examiner's task is made more difficult by an unnecessarily small 5.5 x 8.5-inch record form with small print and small boxes for recording check marks. The objectivity of scoring that is possible with computerized continuous performance tests as the Gordon Diagnostic System (132), Conner's Rating Scales (T4:636), Test of Variables of Attention (TOVA; 336), or Intermediate Visual and Auditory Continuous Performance Test (IVA, Sandford & Turner, 1994) is just not feasible with an audiocassette administration; neither is the recording of more subtle aspects of the response such as response latency.

The standardization sample, though small (*N* = 510) is very well stratified by age (85 for each year of age between 6 and 11), gender, race/ethnicity, geographic region, and parent education level. The main concern about the standardization is a change that was made *after* standardization. The word "dark," though included among the list of stimulus words during standardization, was deleted from the audiocassette tape when it was revealed that too many normal children confused "dog" with "dark." (No other words sound even remotely like "dog.") Elimination of items based on standardization data is common practice and usually of no particular concern. In this instance, however, the stimulus is like one long 11-minute item. It would seem to make quite a difference whether this long list of words does or does not include a distractor word that is very similar to the target word. One might speculate that elimination of all of the "dark" stimuli would have affected the number of errors of inattention or impulsivity that the children in the norms group made to the other stimuli. The elimination of such an obviously similar-sounding word also raises other questions that are not addressed in the manual: Why were normal children's difficulties with "dark" not noticed during the three pilot studies that preceded standardization? Did the author initially intend to measure auditory processing or discrimination, as well as attention, when the test was originally designed?

Reliability data are meager and unimpressive. The author correctly does not report measures of internal consistency on this one-item test, but the appropriate type of reliability—test-retest—is offered only for 46 7-year-olds ($r = .67$) and 40 9-year-olds ($r = .74$). How does one determine the stability for children of other ages? How does one have confidence in test results that suggest inadequate reliability? Why are correlations reported between error scores on the test and retest, when the only scores reported are Pass and Fail? Why are no stability data presented for these categorical scores?

The one construct validity study was quite good, as the author offers data for 220 children diagnosed with ADHD, who were tested off medication, versus data for a sample of 220 normal individuals who were matched on the basis of age, race, and gender. Presumably the latter group was taken from the normative sample, but this was not stated. The mean Total Error Scores for the ADHD sample were significantly higher than the mean scores for normal children, and the mean Vigilance Decrement Scores were significantly higher for ADHD children for each age except 11. However, the author does not indicate whether the differences in Total Error Scores were significant for each age or for the total sample, or whether an appropriate correction was made for multiple comparisons in either analysis. A discriminant analysis was also conducted with these samples, and the resultant hit rates of 68% to 76% (median = 69%) are not particularly impressive. The values are inflated to some extent by the experimental design; the author investigated three different criterion scores and only reported data for the one that produced the best discrimination. Also, no mention is made whether or not the percents obtained for each age were significantly better than chance.

The one concurrent validity study used a curious choice of criterion: the six-item Attention Scale on the Devereux Scales of Mental Disorders. The Devereux is not frequently used for ADHD populations, whereas other checklists, such as Conners' or Achenbach's behavior rating scales, are commonly used in ADHD research and include reliable attentional scales.

Overall, the ACPT has the advantage of measuring auditory attention, in contrast to the numerous available measures of visual attention. The ACPT has better norms than most computerized continuous performance tests, but the norms for the ACPT are compromised by a substantial change from the standardization to the final version of the test (deleting the word "dark," which closely resembled the target word "dog"). Scoring is subjective because of the human error that is introduced by the audiocassette format, and this format also cannot take advantage of computer technology, which permits recording of response latencies. Reliability data for the ACPT are largely lacking, and the data that are presented indicate inadequate stability of the error scores. A good construct validation study of ADHD children was conducted, but the analyses were not reported in sufficient detail to permit full evaluation of the construct validity.

For examiners who wish to evaluate children's attention, the various computerized continuous performance tests such as the Gordon, TOVA, Conners, and IVA are to be preferred to the ACPT. If auditory attention is an important aspect of the assessment, then examiners are encouraged to use the IVA (which alternates auditory with visual stimuli and gives separate scores and comparisons for each) instead of the ACPT.

REVIEWER'S REFERENCE
Sanford, J. A., & Turner, A. (1994). *Intermediate Visual and Auditory Continuous Performance Test*. Richmond, VA: Braintrain.

Review of the Auditory Continuous Performance Test by JOSEPH G. LAW, JR., Associate Professor of Behavioral Studies and Educational Technology, University of South Alabama, Mobile, AL:

The Auditory Continuous Performance Test (ACPT) was developed in order to provide a standardized tool for assessing auditory attention problems. The author's hope was to improve differentiation of children with auditory figure-ground problems from those with Attention Deficit/Hyperactivity Disorder (ADHD). The ACPT consists of tape-recorded stimuli that are presented to the child. In each of the six test presentations 20 monosyllabic words such as *drop* and *low* are repeated and reorganized so that the total items in each presentation is 96. Embedded within these words is the target word, *dog*. The child is asked to raise his or her thumb whenever the target word is presented. A trial word list using the same stimuli is administered up to three times in order to verify the child correctly understands the instructions prior to actual testing.

The manual contains specific examples and directions for administration of both the trial and test word lists. One-page folded record forms, an audio cassette, and the examiner's manual are provided in the test kit. The ACPT is quite easy to administer and to score. Impulsivity and Inattention errors are summed to make an error score that is then placed on the first page of the record form. The criterion scores for the child's age group is obtained from a table on the front page of the record form. The child's success is noted by circling either the words *Pass* or *Fail* on the cover.

The format of the record form enables easy recording of demographic information, the child's correct responses and errors, as well as analysis of inattention and impulsivity errors. There is adequate room to make behavioral observations, record the results of prior hearing tests, and keep diagnostic records about prior assessment for ADHD.

The 46-page manual contains 16 pages of information on the design, development, and technical characteristics of the test as well as information on the sample. There were three pilot studies using a total of 48 children in the early development of the ACPT and the standardization group consisted of 510 children aged 6 to 11 years. None had been diagnosed with ADHD. These children were tested at 72 sites and the racial and ethnic proportions of the sample regarding whites, African-Americans, Hispanics and others was roughly equivalent to that of the 1990 census. There were six age levels from 6 years 0 months to 11 years 11 months and 85 children in each of the six age ranges.

To establish cutoff scores, 220 of the children in the standardization sample were compared to a like number who were diagnosed as having ADHD. These children were matched on the basis of gender, race, and age. Those who were taking stimulant medication were tested when not on medicine. A signal detection model was used in a discriminant analysis to determine the number of hits, misses, correct rejections, and false alarms. The ACPT accurately discriminated between children with and without ADHD about 70% of the time for all ages combined. The rate at which the ACPT incorrectly placed ADHD children in the pass category ranged from 18% to 29%. The overall rate at which the normal students were mislabeled as having ADHD was 2% to 8%.

Validity studies are reported in the manual. For 528 children tested, correlations between the Attention scale of the child form of the Devereux Scales of Mental Disorders and the ACPT averaged .41, indicating a moderately strong relationship between the two instruments. In another study, Keith and Engineer (1991) studied 20 children diagnosed with ADHD and found the ACPT to be very sensitive to the effects of stimulant medication.

A test-retest reliability study of 86 children is reported. The between-test interval averaged 5.9 days. Test retest reliability for 46 children aged 7 to 7 years 11 months was .67 and for children ranging from 9 years to 9 years 11 months was .74. Unfortunately, such data for children older than 10 years of age were not included.

This is a promising new test of auditory attention. It has better documentation of reliability and validity in the manual than the Auditory Discrimination and Attention Test (Carey, 1995) and considerably more test items. Test-retest reliability seems adequate for the ages tested. Norms and technical data reported in the manual are adequate.

The ACPT is a short, easily administered test with good psychometric properties. The upper age limit of 11 years 11 months limits its use to a certain extent. How well it correlates with visual continuous performance tests in the assessment of ADHD is an empirical question much in need of research. Although it promises to be an excellent research and clinical instrument, more research on its validity is needed before routine use for diagnosis or assessment of treatment effectiveness in clinical populations.

REVIEWER'S REFERENCES

Keith, R. W., & Engineer, P. (1991). Effects of methylphenidate on the auditory processing abilities of children with attention deficit-hyperactivity disorder. *Journal of Learning Disabilities, 24*(10), 630–636.

Carey, K. T. (1995). [Review of the Auditory Discrimination and Attention Test.] In J. C. Conoley & J. C. Impara (Eds.), *The twelfth mental measurements yearbook* (p. 40). Lincoln, NE: Buros Institute of Mental Measurements.

[23]
Auditory Selective Attention Test.

Purpose: "To measure selective attention."
Population: Adults.
Publication Date: 1993.
Acronym: ASAT.
Scores: Total Errors.
Administration: Individual.
Price Data, 1993: $100 per test (cassette tape); $5 per manual (15 pages).
Time: 30(35) minutes.
Comments: Stereo tape player and a pair of stereo headphones must be supplied by the examiner.
Authors: Winfred Arthur, Jr., Gerald V. Barrett, and Dennis Doverspike.
Publisher: Barrett and Associates, Inc.

Review of the Auditory Selective Attention Test by WILLIAM W. DEARDORFF, Clinical Faculty, U.C.L.A. School of Medicine, Los Angeles, CA:

Auditory selective attention is an information-processing construct that represents a person's ability to selectively attend to auditory messages in the presence of other competing messages (manual, p. 1). Selective attention has been identified as a construct underlying performance in a variety of information-processing tasks. The Auditory Selective Attention Test (ASAT) is a version of a dichotic listening task.

The materials required to administer the test include the ASAT, a stereo tape player, stereo headphones, the answer sheet, and pencils. The beginning of the tape explains the nature of the test to the test taker. After the instructions, there are a few practice trials to familiarize the test taker with the procedure. The practice trials are followed by the 24 actual test messages.

The framework of the messages is as follows: (a) A message number is announced, which the test-taker repeats to the examiner. (b) After each message number, the test-taker is instructed to attend to the right or left ear. (c) Sixteen pairs of numbers and letters are then presented to both ears at a rate of two per second. (d) The test-taker's task is to repeat aloud the digits presented to the relevant ear immediately upon hearing them.

There is a second part to each message, which is similar in format but with a different amount of numbers and letters. The test manual is comprehensive and includes sections on test development and construction, administration, scoring, reliability, criterion-related validity, construct-related validity, norms, and references. The ASAT can be scored in a variety of ways, including correct responses and errors. Scores can be obtained for Part One, Part Two, Right or Left Ear, Omissions, or Intrusions, among others.

The test shows reasonable reliability, criterion-related validity (for such things as flying, monitoring and maintenance tasks, and driving), and construct-related validity. It is designed for use with adults. It takes approximately 30–35 minutes to administer. Test takers must be screened for hearing loss prior to taking the ASAT.

Review of the Auditory Selective Attention Test by JUDY R. DUBNO, Professor, Department of Otolaryngology and Communicative Sciences, Medical University of South Carolina, Charleston, SC:

The Auditory Selective Attention Test (ASAT) was designed to test the ability to selectively attend to an auditory message in the presence of additional competing auditory messages and to respond quickly and accurately. The test materials consist of a stereo audio cassette tape recording and test booklet. The test booklet contains information on test development, instructions for administering and scoring the test, an answer sheet, and normative data for several groups of subjects. The test taker listens to the tape using a stereo tape player and a pair of stereo headphones. The test is administered on an individual basis and takes approximately 30 minutes. At the beginning of the audio tape, instructions are given to the test taker, which may be supplemented by the examiner.

The tape consists of 24 "messages" spoken by a male. Each message is a random list of letters and numbers, one list presented to the left ear and a different list presented to the right ear. Before each list, the test taker is instructed to attend to the left or right ear. The task of the test taker is to repeat each of the numbers spoken to the indicated ear, while ignoring letters in the indicated ear and the entire message in the other ear. There are two parts to each message, one containing a long list of letters and numbers and the other containing a short list. In some cases, after the first list, the test taker is instructed to switch attention to the opposite ear. Letters and numbers are presented at the rate of two per second. A series of practice trials is used to familiarize test takers and to adjust the volume of the tape output. A correct response requires the numbers presented to the relevant ear to be repeated in the correct order. Incorrect responses are recorded as omissions and intrusions (numbers or letters not in the relevant message or reported out of sequence). According to the test booklet, previous research supports the use of the Total Error Score (omissions plus intrusions).

Normative data for the ASAT were obtained by combining results from several studies, with sample sizes in each study ranging from 60 to 280 (total number of subjects was 1,191). Subjects' age and background (not defined) were diverse, but mean age was about 36 years; females represented 40% of the sample. The normative values for the general population are reported as percentile ranks for 10-point intervals of error totals. There was a modest correlation between age and error score, so a set of normative values are given for subjects older than 40 years. Separate norms are also provided for college students and professional drivers. There were no gender-related differences reported in ASAT results. Results for children are not known.

The ASAT has been shown to be fairly reliable, as measured on a group of 20 undergraduate students tested two times over 2 weeks, but there is some improvement in performance with repeated test administrations. The test-retest results were fairly consistent for omissions and total errors, but there was poor reliability for intrusions. Internal consistency was inferred from correlations among the various error scores; these ranged from about .2 to .8. These results suggest that caution should be applied in repeated administrations of the test, and that there may be a lack of consistency among the error measurements. The test manual did not provide split-half reliabilities or interrater reliability coefficients.

Criterion-related validity was addressed by determining how well the ASAT predicts performance on other tasks that require selective attention. For example, driving a car and flying an airplane are both tasks that require processing of information from a variety of sources and demand selective attention. Results of several published studies suggest that the ASAT predicts performance on driving, flying, and certain monitoring and maintenance tasks. Similarly, the ASAT has been shown to be among the best predictors of involvement in driving accidents. Construct validity was evaluated by comparing results

with other information-processing or dichotic listening tests. Results on the ASAT are correlated with choice reaction time but not with simple reaction time. Significant relationships with the ASAT have also been observed with visual selective attention and with a measure of preference for pace of presentation.

The strengths of the ASAT are its ease of administration, good test construction, good quality tape recording, and appropriate validity information. There are several disadvantages noted. The first is its somewhat poor reliability and differences in performance observed with repeated measurements. The second relates to the test administration. The taped directions provided to the test taker are somewhat redundant and repetitive, making the test appear to be more complex than necessary. There is also some question of the use of an oral rather than a written response. When test takers respond orally, it is likely that their responses will interfere with the ability to hear the next few test items, unless their entire response is given at the end of the list. The option to respond at the end of the list was not stated explicitly in the instructions. Although a written response appears to be a good alternative, this is not noted in the instructions. The third disadvantage relates to the feasibility of the test for all older individuals and for any person with hearing loss. The test instructions state that test takers may be screened for hearing loss by "self-report." This procedure is likely to underestimate the number of test takers whose hearing loss will affect test results, especially for older test takers. Indeed, the trend of decreasing scores with age may be related to the prevalence of hearing loss among older test takers. It should also be made clear that raising the level of the test items will not surmount the confounding effects of hearing impairment on a dichotic auditory selective attention task.

In summary, the ASAT has utility as a tool to evaluate the ability of normal-hearing adults to process auditory information and respond quickly and accurately in the presence of competing auditory messages.

[24]
Autism Screening Instrument for Educational Planning, Second Edition.

Purpose: "Designed to help professionals identify individuals with autism and to provide information needed to develop appropriate educational plans."

Population: Autistic individuals ages 18 months to adult.

Publication Dates: 1978–1993.

Acronym: ASIEP-2.

Administration: Individual.

Price Data, 1994: $149 per complete kit including manual ('93, 81 pages), 25 summary booklets, 25 Autism Behavior Checklist Forms, 25 Sample of Vocal Behavior Record Forms, 25 Interaction Assessment Record Forms, 25 Educational Assessment Forms, 25 Prognosis of Learning Rate Forms, toys, manipulatives, stand, and coding audiotape for Interaction Assessment; $18 per 25 summary booklets; $44 per toys, manipulatives, and stand; $9 per coding audiotape for Interaction Assessment; $32 per examiner's manual.

Time: Administration time not reported.

Comments: Subtests administered depends on results of Autism Behavior Checklist and purpose of assessment.

Authors: David A. Krug, Joel R. Arick, and Patricia J. Almond.

Publisher: PRO-ED, Inc.

  a) AUTISM BEHAVIOR CHECKLIST.
  Scores, 6: Sensory, Relating, Body and Object Use, Language, Social and Self Help, Total.
  Price Data: $11 per 25 record forms.
  b) SAMPLE OF VOCAL BEHAVIOR.
  Scores, 5: Repetitive, Noncommunicative, Babbling, Unintelligible, Total.
  Price Data: $11 per 25 record forms.
  c) INTERACTION ASSESSMENT.
  Scores, 4: Interaction, Independent Play, No Response, Negative.
  Price Data: $11 per 25 record forms.
  d) EDUCATIONAL ASSESSMENT.
  Scores, 6: In Seat, Receptive Language, Expressive Language, Body Concept, Speech Imitation, Total.
  Price Data: $11 per 25 record forms.
  e) PROGNOSIS OF LEARNING RATE.
  Scores, 5: Hand-Shaping, Random Position–A, Fixed Position–B, Fixed Position–C, Random Position–D.
  Price Data: $11 per 25 record forms.

Cross References: See T4:235 (1 reference); for reviews by Lawrence J. Turton and Richard L. Wikoff of an earlier edition, see 9:105 (1 reference).

TEST REFERENCES

1. Kamps, D. M., Dugan, E. P., Leonard, B. R., & Daoust, P. M. (1994). Enhanced small group instruction using choral responding and student interaction for children with autism and developmental disabilities. *American Journal on Mental Retardation, 99,* 60–73.

2. Capps, L., Sigman, M., & Yirmiya, N. (1995). Self-competence and emotional understanding in high-functioning children with autism. *Development and Psychopathology, 7,* 137-149.

3. Yirmiya, N., Solomonica-Levi, D., & Shulman, C. (1996). The ability to manipulate behavior and to understand manipulation of beliefs: A comparison of individuals with autism, mental retardation, and normal development. *Developmental Psychology, 32,* 62–69.

Review of the Autism Screening Instrument for Educational Planning, Second Edition by D. JOE OLMI, Assistant Professor, School Psychology Program, and Director, School Psychology Service Center, Department of Psychology, University of Southern Mississippi, Hattiesburg, MS:

The Autism Screening Instrument for Educational Planning, Second Edition (ASIEP-2) is an individually administered screening and diagnostic battery designed to assess children suspected of having autism. It consists of five subtests including the Autism Behavior Checklist (ABC), the Sample of Vocal Behavior, the Interaction Assessment, the Educational Assessment, and the Prognosis of Learning Rate. The ASIEP-2 is designed to be used throughout the referral to placement process from general screening to diagnosis to educational program planning to program evaluation. The kit includes record forms for each subtest, the ASIEP-2 summary booklet, the examiner's manual, the coding tape for the Interaction Assessment, various toys and items used during administration, and the response tray. Other items such as a stopwatch, audio cassette player, masking tape, preferred food and drink items, and play area with other toys are also needed for administration. It may be advisable to have another adult assist with the administration of some items or subtests of the ASIEP-2. The following is a brief description of each subtest.

The Autism Behavior Checklist (ABC) is a 57-item checklist of behavioral characteristics where each item is circled if it is descriptive of the behavior of the target individual. The ABC is to be filled out by individuals, typically parent(s) and teacher(s), who know the referred child and have spent time with him or her. Each item is weighted from 1 to 4. Items fall into five classes of behaviors including Sensory, Relating, Body and Object Use, Language, and Social and Self Help. A total score is obtained by summing all circled items. Each of the five class scores and the total score are plotted on the reverse side of the record form for interpretive purposes. Scores of less than 54 are an indication that no further assessment is necessary. A score of 68 suggests "high-probability" (p. 27) for autism, and a score in the 54–67 range suggests individuals who are high functioning but who display some of the behavioral characteristics of autism. In each of these two latter cases assessment should continue.

The Sample of Vocal Behavior (SVB) is an assessment of characteristics of preverbal and emerging spontaneous expressive language. Areas of assessment include Repetitiveness, Noncommunication, Intelligibility, and Babbling. Administration using two adults (one to elicit vocalizations and one to record) or one adult with an audio cassette recorder for later analysis is recommended. The goal is to elicit 50 vocalizations from the child. If 50 utterances are not obtained within an initial 30-minute period, a second 30-minute session is allowed, but no more. Scoring categories include Variety (first-use versus repetitive), Function (communicative versus noncommunicative), Articulation (intelligibility), and Length (number of words in utterance). Each utterance is to be scored along each applicable category. The authors recommend scoring all utterances along one category at a time. This reviewer suggests following the recommendation. Scoring is difficult and practice is necessary in order to become relatively competent on this subtest. Summing errors were noted in the Sample of Vocal Behavior record form appearing on page 11, Figure 2.2 of the manual. Optional analyses in Vocalization Complexity and parts of Speech are suggested for further diagnostic information and program planning. Again, this reviewer stresses that reliable scoring and interpretation of this subtest requires skill and practice.

Two people are required to administer the Interaction Assessment competently. One individual interacts with the child in the play setting, while the other individual records/codes the interactions. The authors of the examiner's manual indicated a training videotape was available for this subtest, but that tape was unavailable for this review. The Interaction Assessment requires the examiner to use time sampling observation procedures with a cueing audiotape indicating the beginning and ending of the recording period. The assessment is composed of three phases—Active Modeling, Passive No Initiation, and Direct Cues—that last 4 minutes each with 16 observation intervals. Student response behaviors, which must be overt, can be recorded in one of four categories—Interaction, Constructive Independent Play, No Response, and Aggressive Negative. Each and every recording interval carries a coded student response behavior. If no student response behavior occurred within an interval, a "No Response" behavior is recorded.

The Educational Assessment is administered and scored by a special education teacher in less than 20 minutes. It is designed to assess the child's ability in five areas including Staying In Seat, Receptive Language, Expressive Language, Body Concept, and Speech Imitation. In order to administer this subtest the child must not exhibit behaviors disruptive to a

testing session such as out-of-seat, nonattending, and noncompliant behaviors. There are 12 items in each of the last four sections of the subtest. Items are scored "1" (correct) or "0" (incorrect). Until the items are mastered or memorized by the administrator, it will be necessary to use the examiner's manual as a cue. Administration is simple and straightforward.

The Prognosis for Learning Rate takes approximately 20 minutes to administer and is designed to assess the child's ability to acquire or learn newly presented information based on reinforcement procedures and without verbal and physical cues. The child must be able to sit in a chair at a table for a period of time for administration. Part 1 (handshaping) entails having the child place a chip on a tray, when instructed, for 24 trials with the criterion being independent placement on four of five consecutive trials. Review of the record form suggests this segment serves as a "pretraining" phase. Part 2, Step A requires the child to place the black circle plastic chip on the tray when offered a choice of the black chip and a white square chip. The criterion is 15 consecutive correct trials. A posttest follows, cueing the child to shape and color. Optional learning tasks are available for administration. Repetition and practice are necessary to administer this subtest smoothly.

On each of the subtests, raw scores are easily converted to standard scores using the tables provided in the examiner's manual. These are plotted on the summary booklet. The ASIEP-2 summary booklet also allows for recommendations and interpretation across subtests. Scoring and interpretation are straightforward, but practice is necessary. Technically, the ASIEP-2 is sound. Content, concurrent, and criterion-related validity for the ABC were well established with intrarater reliability of .87 for split-half procedures and interrater reliability of .95. Sound psychometric support was found for the SVB, the Interaction Assessment, the Educational Assessment, and the Prognosis of Learning Rate. Great care was taken during the standardization process to differentiate behaviors consistent with autism from behaviors consistent with other disabilities having overlapping characteristics.

In summary, the ASIEP-2 is a well-developed screening and assessment tool that can be valuable to assessment and instructional personnel who work with children suspected of having autism. The ASIEP-2 is probably best used in an interdisciplinary or transdisciplinary assessment format by various members of the team, as advocated by the authors of the instrument. Rest assured, competent administration of the ASIEP-2 takes skill and practice. No shortcomings are noted, but inclusion of the training tapes mentioned in the examiner's manual would be beneficial to anyone learning to administer the ASIEP-2.

Review of the Autism Screening Instrument for Educational Planning, Second Edition by DONALD P. OSWALD, Assistant Professor of Psychiatry, Medical College of Virginia/Virginia Commonwealth University, Richmond, VA:

The Autism Screening Instrument for Educational Planning, Second Edition (ASIEP-2) is intended to assist professionals in the identification of individuals with autism and in the development of appropriate educational plans for these students. The ASIEP-2 consists of five component tests: the Autism Behavior Checklist (ABC), the Sample of Vocal Behavior (SVB), the Interaction Assessment (IA), the Educational Assessment (EA), and the prognosis of Learning Rate (PLR). The complete instrument is intended for use with students whose language and social age equivalents fall between 3 months and 49 months; the Autism Behavior Checklist, however, may be used as a stand-alone instrument for the assessment of characteristics of autism, regardless of the chronological age or functioning level of the individual. The ASIEP-2 is intended to be used by professional educators who are familiar with the syndrome of autism.

This edition of the instrument represents a revision of earlier versions of the ASIEP; it incorporates feedback from users regarding organization and some additional data in the standardization section. No further information is offered in the manual regarding new or updated aspects of the instrument.

The ABC is the most widely used component of the original ASIEP. It has proven valuable in clinical, educational, and research applications and is unchanged in the second edition of the ASIEP. Item development for the ABC involved an extensive content validation procedure that yielded a set of 57 items grouped into five symptom areas: Sensory, Relating, Body and Object, Language, and Social and Self Help. Each of the 57 items is assigned a weight ranging from 1 to 4, based on the item's strength in predicting autism in the standardization sample.

Psychometric and normative studies on the ABC involved three samples: (a) 1,049 individuals,

ages 18 months to 35 years, 172 of whom were previously diagnosed with autism; (b) 62 individuals, ages 3 years to 23 years, all of whom were previously diagnosed with autism; and (c) 953 individuals, ages 21 years to 68 years, 95% of whom had been diagnosed with severe mental retardation. The total number of persons with autism involved in the standardization of the instrument is relatively small; nonetheless, validity studies of the total score as an indicator of autism have been supportive.

The SVB employs a standard language sample method widely used in research and clinical settings. A sample of 50 utterances is collected and scored along the dimensions of Variety, Function, Articulation, and Length. The procedure yields a raw score that may be converted to a Language Age ranging from 9 months to 48 months. SVB validation studies demonstrated that students with autism produced more repetitive, noncommunicative, and babbling utterances than a matched sample of students without autism. Psychometric studies of the SVB are generally positive, although they are somewhat less rigorous than those applied to the ABC, typically involving much smaller samples.

The Interaction Assessment (IA) is a time-sample observation procedure consisting of three, 4-minute phases that vary in terms of the level of initiation of the student's interaction partner. Student behaviors are coded as Interaction, Constructive Independent Play, No Response (including self-stimulatory behavior), and Aggressive Negative; a code is recorded every 15 seconds. IA standardization sample group means (autistic and nonautistic, preschool and school-age) are offered for each behavior in each phase, providing a point of reference for individual subject scores. The IA yields an Autistic Interaction Score that may be converted to a percentile based on either an autistic or nonautistic normative sample. Rater reliability is likely to be dependent on training and experience; the authors of the examiner's manual indicate a videotape and standard completed record form are available for a reliability check.

The Educational Assessment (EA) is intended to measure the child's functioning level in five areas: In-Seat Behavior, Receptive Language, Expressive Language, Body Concept, and Speech Imitation. All of the items are in the repertoire of a typical child by age 48 months. Raw scores may be converted to percentiles for the content areas, using either the autistic or nonautistic normative sample and a total score percentile may be computed based on the autistic sample.

Finally, the prognosis of Learning Rate (PLR) is an attempt to assess the student's learning rate on a new task. The test involves administering up to 48 trials of a discrimination task based on color. A subject's score may be compared to autistic or nonautistic normative groups and converted to a percentile.

The second edition of the ASIEP-2 appears to offer few substantive revisions to the original. The changes may improve ease of use slightly but they are largely cosmetic. The ABC continues to be a respected and widely used screening instrument for the assessment of characteristics of autism. It has a considerable track record in the research literature but the authors have failed to take advantage of this fact in revising the ASIEP; as a result, interpretation is still hindered by the limitations of the original standardization sample size.

The SVB and the IA offer a nicely structured observation method under reasonably controlled conditions. Results of these subscales may be of maximum utility when used in a within-subject design as pre- and posttest measures. The EA is a screening tool for a relatively small set of early developmental tasks. The authors acknowledge in the examiner's manual that "for programming purposes, the student should be evaluated with a more comprehensive developmental instrument" (p. 35). Interpretation of the PLR score is somewhat difficult; the task is too restricted to serve as a generalized estimate of learning potential. The authors maintain that PLR scores reflect "ability to perform well in a language curriculum" (p. 39). However, the data cited to support this claim are unconvincing and users would be well-advised to view the PLR with caution.

In sum, the ASIEP-2 appears to retain virtually all of the strengths and weaknesses of the original instrument. It is best viewed as a screening tool for the purposes of evaluation of characteristics of autism, and language, social, and early educational assessment but cannot be said to replace a more comprehensive evaluation in any of these areas.

[25]
The Balanced Emotional Empathy Scale.

Purpose: To measure an individual's vicarious emotional response to perceived emotional experiences of others.
Population: Ages 15 and older.
Publication Dates: 1972–1996.
Acronym: BEES.
Scores: Total score only.

Administration: Group or individual.
Price Data, 1996: $28 per test kit including scale, scoring directions, norms, manual ('96, 12 pages), and literature review.
Time: (10–15) minutes.
Comments: Replaces The Emotional Empathic Tendency Scale.
Author: Albert Mehrabian.
Publisher: Albert Mehrabian.

Review of The Balanced Emotional Empathy Scale by RICHARD W. JOHNSON, Director of Training at Counseling & Consultation Services of the University Health Services and Adjunct Professor of Counseling Psychology, University of Wisconsin—Madison, Madison, WI:

The Balanced Emotional Empathy Scale (BEES) was published in 1996 as a replacement for the Emotional Empathic Tendency Scale (EETS), which was first published by Albert Mehrabian in 1972. Much of the item content is similar on the two instruments; however, all of the items for the BEES have been newly prepared.

The BEES (as the EETS before it) has been designed to measure "individual differences in the tendency to feel and vicariously experience the emotional experiences of others" (p. 2). It is primarily a measure of emotional, not cognitive, empathy. According to research reported by Mehrabian, Young, and Sato (1988), emotional empathy has a strong genetic component. Cognitive empathy (ability to assume the perspective of another person, such as that noted by Carl Rogers) is a more teachable characteristic.

Although the manual does not clearly specify the uses of the BEES, research conducted with the EETS suggests that it may be helpful in understanding individual differences in a wide range of behaviors including child-rearing practices, altruism, social skills, and interpersonal effectiveness.

The BEES, which consists of 30 items, employs a nine-step response format ranging from *very strong agreement* (+4) through *very strong disagreement* (-4). The origin of the items for the scale is unclear. No information on item selection or item analysis is provided. In general, respondents are asked to rate the degree to which they identify with the feelings of others in a variety of situations. Based on research conducted with the EETS, scores on the BEES appear to be independent of one's tendency to make socially desirable responses.

The normative data consist of mean scores and standard deviations for men, women, and a combined sample of men and women. The samples of men and women used to provide these data are not described in regard to size, composition (e.g., age, education, socioeconomic background, race), nor the manner in which they were chosen. Other than means and standard deviations, no information regarding the nature of the score distributions has been provided.

As a rule, women score much higher on the BEES than do men. The size of the difference between the mean scores for men and women represents more than one standard deviation. The author suggests that the combined norms should be sufficient for most purposes; however, this point seems debatable. It would seem desirable to use separate norms to take into account social conditioning in most situations. Some of the items used to indicate emotional empathy (e.g., crying at weddings and movies) show large sex differences that should be interpreted differently for men and women. The differential meaning of the scores for men and women is an empirical question that needs further research.

The BEES possesses adequate internal consistency according to one study (Cronbach's alpha = .87); however, no information is provided concerning the sample upon which this study was based. No test-retest reliability studies are reported. It would be instructive to study the stability of empathy scores over time, especially if one wishes to use the variable for predictive purposes.

Construct validity of the BEES has been studied in terms of three factors (pleasure, arousal, and dominance) specified in Mehrabian's (1980) personality model. Scores on the BEES can be predicted with a regression equation weighted equally on the pleasure and arousal factors, that is, individuals with high emotional empathic scores tend to be both pleasant (positive) and arousable (reactive). The author considers the BEES to be superior to the EETS in that its scores are more equally weighted ("balanced") in regard to pleasure and arousal factors than in the EETS. The author does not clearly indicate why such balance is important.

Most of the validity for the BEES has been derived from validity studies conducted on the EETS, with which it is highly correlated ($r = .77$). Studies conducted with the EETS found that individuals who scored high on the scale were more likely to demonstrate empathic behavior in their relationships with others and to show greater arousal of their autonomic nervous system in response to emotional stimuli than were those who scored low on this scale. Individuals with high scores on the EETS, compared with those with low scores, showed more altruism, less aggressiveness, greater affiliation, and a greater likelihood to volunteer to help others (Mehrabian et al., 1988). It should be noted that very few validity studies have been conducted with the BEES itself.

To clarify the meaning of scores on the BEES, especially for use in clinical situations, it would be helpful to study the relationship between its scores and scores on other self-report measures of empathy such as the Empathy scale of the California Psychological Inventory (T4:361) and the Feeling score on the Myers-Briggs Type Indicator (T4:1702).

Based on research conducted with the EETS, the BEES can be viewed as an adequate measure of emotional empathy for research purposes. Further research based on the BEES itself must be undertaken before it can qualify as a clinical instrument for use with individuals. Additional information is needed concerning item analysis, test norms, test-retest reliability, predictive validity, and construct validity.

REVIEWER'S REFERENCES

Mehrabian, A. (1980). *Basic dimensions for a general psychological theory: Implications for personality, social, environmental, and developmental studies.* Cambridge, MA: Oelgeschlager, Gunn & Hain.

Mehrabian, A., Young, A. L., & Sato, S. (1988). Emotional empathy and associated individual differences. *Current Psychology: Research & Reviews,* 7(3), 221–240.

Review of The Balanced Emotional Empathy Scale by SUSANA URBINA, Associate Professor of Psychology, University of North Florida, Jacksonville, FL:

The Balanced Emotional Empathy Scale (BEES) is made up of 30 statements to which test takers respond by indicating the extent of their agreement or disagreement, using a 9-point, Likert-style format. The BEES is designed to help assess the emotional—as opposed to the cognitive—aspects of empathy. It is aimed at differentiating individuals who are more likely to experience the feelings of others from those who are less responsive to such emotions.

To reduce bias due to acquiescence, 15 of the BEES items are worded as positive instances of presence of empathic feelings and 15 are worded as indications of the absence of such feelings. No explanation is provided concerning the provenance of the statements nor the bases on which they were selected. If one reads through the entire scale, the intention of the items is fairly transparent and the direction of the scoring is easy to guess. Moreover, the content of the statements is often redundant and unimaginative. Consider, for example, the following pair: "It is difficult for me to experience strongly the feelings of characters in a book or a movie" and "I am rarely moved to tears while reading a book or watching a movie." These are just two of the six items that deal with one's reactions to movies, books, or song lyrics. One of the statements ("I have difficulty feeling and reacting to the emotional expressions of foreigners") seems unnecessarily chauvinistic and naive in its implications and could seriously interfere with rapport for some respondents. Other items rely on the use of additional stereotypes, such as "helpless old people," that many may find offensive.

The manual for the BEES is flimsy and singularly uninformative, even for an instrument that is, presumably, meant to be used exclusively in research. Out of a total of 12 photocopied pages in the manual, one is a title page, two contain the items themselves, and two more list the scoring direction for each one; the remaining seven pages contain a very limited amount of information about the scale. For instance, the section that deals with norms simply gives the means and the standard deviations for a female group, a male group, and a combined-sex group, followed by a half-page of information on converting z scores to percentiles. No other data about the norms are presented, not even the number of persons (N) from whom the norms were derived, let alone how their scores were distributed. Similarly, the section on reliability—which consists of only two sentences—states that the internal consistency coefficient alpha for the BEES is .87, without any indication about when or how the coefficient was obtained.

In addition to the BEES, Albert Mehrabian coauthored the Questionnaire Measure of Emotional Empathy (QMEE, Mehrabian & Epstein, 1972), a 33-item scale that is very similar to the BEES in content and style. In between the QMEE and the BEES, Mehrabian (1994) also published a seven-page manual for a measure entitled the Emotional Empathic Tendency Scale (EETS), which was identical to the QMEE in all discernible respects. The QMEE, which was developed with some attention to psychometric principles, has been used—both by Mehrabian and others—in a number of empirical studies of empathy. Many of these are reviewed by Bryant (1987) and by Chlopan, McCain, Carbonell, and Hagen (1985).

In the BEES manual, the main evidence cited with regard to the validity of the scale is its correlation of .77 with the EETS. Once again, no information is supplied about the sample used to obtain this validity coefficient, nor about when or how it was

obtained. In this context, Mehrabian also cites an unpublished paper, written by him, which provides some evidence that the BEES compares favorably to the EETS in at least one respect. Apparently, the Balanced scale is more evenly weighted than the EETS on Arousability and Pleasantness, two of the traits that—according to Mehrabian—characterize emotionally empathic individuals.

SUMMARY. The BEES *may* be an appropriate tool to help assess self-reported tendencies toward empathic emotional experiences. Its manual, however, falls far short of providing an adequate empirical foundation for evaluating the scale. In this reviewer's opinion, a single question—asking respondents to indicate, on a Likert-type scale, the extent to which they tend to experience the feelings of others as if they were their own—may be just as informative for most purposes as administering the complete BEES. Furthermore, regardless of the possible merits—or lack of merit—of the BEES itself, much of the literature on the assessment of emotional empathy suggests that paper-and-pencil measures of this construct are quite problematic. The most critical issues concern the definition of the construct itself and the extent to which it can be considered as a unitary, generalized phenomenon, as opposed to a multidimensional and context-sensitive set of characteristics. Other problems include the potential influence of the social desirability factor and the possible confusion of emotional empathy, which is typically construed as a positive attribute, with the less desirable phenomena of projection or maladaptive emotional disinhibition (Bryant, 1987; Chlopan et al., 1985; Levenson & Ruef, 1992).

REVIEWER'S REFERENCES
Mehrabian, A., & Epstein, N. (1972). A measure of emotional empathy. *Journal of Personality, 40,* 525–543.
Chlopan, B. E., McCain, M. L., Carbonell, J. L., & Hagen, R. L. (1985). Empathy: Review of available measures. *Journal of Personality and Social Psychology, 48,* 635–653.
Bryant, B. K. (1987). Critique of comparable questionnaire methods in use to assess empathy in children and adults. In N. Eisenberg & J. Strayer (Eds.), *Empathy and its development* (pp. 361–373). Cambridge, England: Cambridge University Press.
Levenson, R. W., & Ruef, A. M. (1992). Empathy: A physiological substrate. *Journal of Personality and Social Psychology, 63,* 234–246.
Mehrabian, A. (1994). *Manual for the Emotional Empathic Tendency Scale (EETS).* (Available from Albert Mehrabian, 1130 Alta Mesa Road, Monterey, CA 93940).

[26]
BASIS-A Inventory [Basic Adlerian Scales for Interpersonal Success—Adult].

Purpose: Designed "to help understand how an individual's life-style, based on beliefs developed in early childhood, contributes to one's effectiveness in social, work, and intimate relationships."

Population: Adults.
Publication Date: 1993–1997.
Acronym: BASIS-A.
Scores, 10: BASIS scales (Belonging-Social Interest, Taking Charge, Going Along, Wanting Recognition, Being Cautious); HELPS scales (*Harshness, Entitlement, Liked By All, Striving for Perfection, Softness*).
Administration: Group or individual.
Price Data, 1997: $95 per introductory kit including 15 test booklets, technical manual ('97, 87 pages), interpretive manual ('97, 61 pages), and 15 copies of interpretive guide; $85 per 25 test booklets; $34 per technical manual and interpretive manual; $7 per sampler kit including test booklet and BASIS-A interpretive guide; $35 per 25 BASIS-A interpretive guides.
Foreign Language Edition: Test items and instructions available in Spanish and German.
Time: (10–15) minutes.
Comments: Self-scored.
Authors: Mary S. Wheeler, Roy M. Kern, and William L. Curlette.
Publisher: TRT Associates.

Review of the BASIS—A Inventory [Basic Adlerian Scales for Interpersonal Success—Adult Form] by JAMES P. CHOCA, Chief, Psychology Service, Lakeside Medical Center, Department of Veterans Affairs, Chicago, IL:

The Basic Adlerian Scales for Interpersonal Success—Adult Form (BASIS-A) attempts to systematize the ideas of Alfred Adler (1956) with regards to personality styles. Adler's approach was to describe a person's *life style* on the basis of the family history and early recollections. For example, after a thorough evaluation, an individual who was born several years after the birth of his or her siblings, and who was the "baby" of the family, can be seen as having a strong sense of entitlement. Having decided that he or she has a right to be treated in a special manner, such a person may have difficulty when the expected treatment is not forthcoming. Done in this manner, the formulation of the person's life style reflects the uniqueness and individuality of that person because the description would not apply to many other individuals.

The original Adlerian approach, however, presents several inherent problems. There is, for instance, the issue of the validity and reliability. When two different clinicians interview the same person, the information they obtain may not be the same, and the two clinicians may arrive at different formulations of a person's life-style. In fact, it could be that a clinician, upon seeing the individual on two differ-

ent occasions, may arrive at a somewhat different conceptualization of the person's psychological essence. Tied in with these validity and reliability issues is the question of how much of the conceptualized life-style is a product of what the client is presenting, as opposed to being an imaginative fabrication or a counter-transference on the part of the clinician.

Thus, in spite of the appeal that Adler's ideas have had, the system he proposed for assessing the life style lacked objectivity by today's standards. The BASIS-A Inventory attempts to correct that problem. The instrument turns Adler's ideas, with the refinements of other thinkers such as Harold Mosak, into measurable constructs that can characterize the individual in a scientifically replicable manner.

In order to accomplish its task, the BASIS-A Inventory measures five themes (Belonging-Social Interest, Going Along, Taking Charge, Wanting Recognition, and Being Cautious) representing Adlerian constructs. Several factor analyses of previous pools of items were used to augment and purify the item pool. The inventory also includes five additional scales, referred to as the HELPS scales (Harshness, Entitlement, Liked by All, Striving for Perfection, and Softness). The interpretative test manual does not fit the HELPS constructs into a model or global scheme, such as what has been used by other theoreticians (e.g., Leary's Circumplex or Millon Polarities).

Consistent with Adlerian theory, examinees are instructed to complete the inventory using their recollections of how they felt as a child. The use of a 5-point scale (from *strongly disagree* to *strongly agree*) is thought to allow a wider range of projection than the true-false format. The test items are well written and the test form offers a reasonable way to complete and score the test. The briefness of the test (65 items) can also be noted as advantageous.

Any time a system of classification is developed, one must accept the fact that many individuals need to be bent to fit the categories, and that the sense of uniqueness that the individual presents must be forfeited to some degree. In my opinion, use of the inventory does not fully reveal the Adlerian sense of how the life style came to be, which was usually part of what was derived from the history and early recollections. The BASIS-A Inventory could also be criticized for not precisely following an overall theoretical scheme to derive the scales used. Still, the five themes and HELPS scales that comprise the inventory involve personality concepts often seen in the literature and undoubtedly represent important elements of a person's life style. The themes of Going Along or Being Cautious, for instance, are pointedly represented in other personality inventories, such as the Millon Clinical Multiaxial Inventory (Millon, 1994; 201) or the NEO-PI (Costa & McCrae, 1985; 12:330).

The good descriptions of the different scales offered in the interpretive manual allow the user to characterize individuals with high scores on a particular scale. The descriptions, however, were seemingly theoretically derived and occasionally appeared to go beyond the concept involved.

A technical manual for this test offers a great deal of research support accumulated since the first items became available in 1978. The presentation is well organized and readable. The magnitude of the reliability estimates presented in this manual are acceptable. Validity was examined through correlations between the scales of this inventory and other scales presumed to measure similar constructs. Many of these correlations show only a modest relationship between the two scales in question. Of course, such modest correlations were to be expected because different scales are not typically designed to measure exactly the same construct. That may leave us, nevertheless, wanting more reassurance that the scales measure what they are supposed to measure.

Finally, it should be noted that practically no studies using this test have been published in journals outside of the Adlerian publication (*Individual Psychology*). Future publications in good refereed journals would increase our confidence in the value of the data being reported.

REVIEWER'S REFERENCES
Adler, A. (1956). The style of life. In H. L. Ansbacher & R. R. Ansbacher (Eds.), *The individual psychology of Alfred Adler: A systematic presentation in selections from his writings* (pp. 172–203). New York: Basic Books.
Costa, P. T., & McCrae, R. R. (1985). *The NEO Personality Inventory manual: Form S and Form R.* Odessa, FL: Psychological Assessment Resources.
Millon, T. (1994). *Manual for the MCMI-III.* Minneapolis, MN: National Computer Systems.

Review of the BASIS-A Inventory [Basic Adlerian Scales for Interpersonal Success—Adult Form] by PEGGY E. GALLAHER, Assistant Professor of Psychology, Baruch College of the City University of New York, New York, NY:

Professionals who practice Adler's Individual Psychology will find the BASIS-A to be an acceptable screening instrument for assessing five fundamental constructs from that system, including Social Interest. The test authors caution that the instrument should not be used to replace the more comprehensive life-style assessment interview that is typically used within therapeutic and educational settings.

The inventory has gone through several waves of development. The five thematic scales were identified through exploratory factor analysis; I would suggest that the authors confirm the dimensionality of the instrument through confirmatory factor analysis on a new sample of examinees. The reliability of the scales, which was estimated using both internal consistency and test-retest methodology, appears to be excellent.

The raw scores are converted to *T*-scores on a self-scoring profile. The standardized scores are obtained from a normative sample of 1,083 undergraduate and graduate students, clinical patients, teachers, and "other occupations" from the southeastern United States. No other information is given on the composition of the norm group, which is a serious shortcoming for users who plan to interpret scores to examinees.

A great deal of concurrent validity research has been conducted on the BASIS-A. One glaring omission from this work is any mention of the Big-5 dimensions of personality. Given the prominence of that taxonomy in present-day personality research, it would be extremely helpful to know how the five thematic dimensions measured by the BASIS-A are related to the Big-5. [Editor's Note: The test authors advise that this research has recently been completed but was not yet available at the time the review was prepared.]

To summarize some of the findings (correlations greater than .50), Social Interest is related to extraversion and social support and negatively associated with depression. Going Along is negatively related to aggression. Taking Charge is related to dominance, and Wanting Recognition is related to a measure of parent's perception of how effectively he or she communicates with a child in a variety of situations. The fifth thematic scale, Being Cautious, is related to depression and a history of child abuse. Being Cautious and Social Interest have a high negative (-.52) correlation with each other, and both appear to be tapping into depression as measured by the Beck Depression Inventory.

The inventory also includes validity scales. The Harshness and Softness scales assess faking bad and faking good, respectively. They were developed by instructing a group of examinees to fake good or bad on the inventory and identifying items that were highly correlated with the Marlow-Crowne Social Desirability Scale and differentiated the faking groups from a group tested under normal conditions. The Softness and Harshness scales are correlated with the Being Cautious (-.62 and .48, respectively) and Social Interest scales (.61 and -.53, respectively), although they have no items in common. The interpretive manual takes pains to remind users that validity scales must be examined as a first step in test-score interpretation. The manual is also strong in its suggestions for giving feedback.

The BASIS-A appears to be a responsibly developed test that could be improved by: (a) increasing the size of its norm group and further specifying its composition and (b) providing more evidence for the discriminant validity of the scales. The user needs to know what information this inventory is supplying that cannot be obtained using more widely used instruments. For the Adlerian, this is the screening measure of choice. The test developers appear to be serious about producing a reliable and valid instrument of what they consider to be critical individual differences in social behavior. If they can target their validity research in such a way to more convincingly specify what the scales are measuring, the inventory might find users outside of Individual Psychology.

[27]
Batería Woodcock-Muñoz-Revisada.

Purpose: Designed to assess achievement and "cognitive abilities, scholastic aptitudes, and Spanish oral language."
Population: Spanish speaking ages 2 and over.
Publication Dates: 1982–1996.
Acronym: Batería-RCOG.
Administration: Individual.
Scores: 7 standard battery test scores plus one cluster score: Memoria para Nombres, Memoria para Frases, Pareo Visual, Palabras Incompletas, Integración Visual, Vocabulario Sobre Dibujos, Análisis Síntesis, Amplia Habilidad Cognitiva; and 14 supplementary battery scores: Aprendizje Visual-Auditivo, Memoria para Palabras, Tachar, Integración de Sonidos, Reconocimiento de Dibujos, Vocabulario Oral, Formación de Conceptos, Memoria Diferida-Memoria para Nombres, Memoria Diferida-Aprendizaje Visual Auditivo, Inversión de Numeros, Configuración de Sonidos, Relaciones Especiales, Comprensión de Oraciones, Analogías Verbalis; plus 14 supplemental battery cluster scores derived from combinations of standard and supplemental scores: Recuperación a Largo Plazo (Glr), Memoria a Corto Plazo (Gsm), Rapidez en el Procesamiento (Gs),

Procesamiento Auditivo (Ga), Procesamiento Visual (Gv), Comprensión Conocimiento (Gc), Razonamiento Fluido (Gf), Amplia Habilidad Cognitiva-Escala Extendida, Aptitud en Lectura, Aptitud en Matemáticas, Aptitud en Languaje Escrito, Aptitud en Concocimiento.
Administration: Individual.
Price Data: Available from publisher.
Time: (30–40) minutes for standard battery; (40) minutes additional for Supplemental battery.
Comments: Parallel Spanish version of the Woodcock-Johnson Tests of Cognitive Ability—Revised, a component of the Woodcock-Johnson Psycho-Educational Battery—Revised (12:415); revision of the Batería Woodcock Psico-Educativa en Español.
Authors: Richard W. Woodcock and Ana F. Muñoz-Sandoval.
Publisher: The Riverside Publishing Company.
Cross References: For reviews of the Woodcock-Johnson Psycho-Educational Battery—Revised by Jack A. Cummings and by Steven W. Lee and Elaine Flory Stefany, see 12:415 (36 references); see also T4:2973 (90 references) and T3:2639 (3 references); for reviews of an earlier edition of the Woodcock-Johnson Psycho-Educational Battery by Jack A. Cummings and Alan S. Kaufman, see 9:1387 (6 references).

Review of the Batería Woodcock-Muñoz—Revisada by ROBERT B. FRARY, Professor and Director Emeritus, Office of Measurement and Research Services, Virginia Polytechnic Institute and State University, Blacksburg, VA:

The Batería Woodcock-Muñoz: Pruebas de Habilidad Cognitiva—Revisada (Batería—R COG) and the Batería Woodcock-Muñoz: Pruebas de Aprovechamiento (Batería—R APR) expand and supplant the Batería Woodcock Psico-Educativa en Español (Woodcock, 1982). The two new batteries are designed as parallel Spanish-language versions of the Woodcock-Johnson Tests of Cognitive Ability—Revised (WJ-R COG; 1989) and the Woodcock-Johnson Tests of Achievement—Revised (WJ-R ACH, 1989). As such, they share the complex structure of the Woodcock-Johnson (12:415) batteries, which comprise 35 separate tests providing norm-referenced scores, combinations of which yield a number of additional scores. Any evaluation of the Batería-R batteries is in part dependent on the qualities of the WJ batteries. In this regard, the reader should consult reviews by Webster (1994), Cummings (1995), and Lee and Stefany (1995). These reviews (especially the review by Webster) describe the characteristics of the WJ batteries and the theory underlying their development in some detail. Because this information applies as well to the Batería-R batteries, what follows is only an overview.

Like their parent batteries, the Batería-R COG and APR provide a comprehensive set of individually administered tests of abilities and achievement spanning a wide range of ages (2 to 90). They are not intended to be administered in their entireties but selectively according to the needs of the individual examinees. Indeed, it might take 2 to 3 days to administer all 35 tests in both batteries to an individual. Each battery is divided into a "standard" set of tests and a "supplementary" set. Combinations of tests from within these groupings yield up to 30 additional scores. For example, the Batería-R COG tests for Memoria para Frases (Memory for Sentences), Pareo Visual (Visual Matching), Integración de Sonidos (Sound Blending), and Vocabulario Oral (Oral Vocabulary) yield a "cluster" score, Aptitud en Lectura (Reading Aptitude). The development of the WJ-R COG (and hence the Batería-R COG) battery was based on the Horn-Cattell model of intellectual processing (Horn & Cattell, 1966). There are seven standard Batería-R COG tests, each of which represents one of the abilities delineated by Horn and Cattell. The WJ-R ACH (and hence the Batería-R APR) battery is organized from a theoretical standpoint that distinguishes tasks according to their complexity and whether they require connected discourse or unitary responses. Again, combinations of tests yield cluster scores. For example, the Science, Social Studies, and Humanities tests yield a Broad Knowledge score.

The following features distinguish the Batería-R from the WJ-R:

1. A brief preliminary Language Use Survey collects information useful in interpreting testing outcomes.

2. A Comparative Language Index may be determined for examinees who take both the Batería-R and the WJ-R. This index not only indicates the relative strength of the examinee in Spanish versus English but also indicates a norm-based level of proficiency in each language.

3. The Batería-R COG cluster score, Oral Language, may be transformed into the five-level scale of Cognitive-Academic Language Proficiency (Cummins, 1984).

4. A Supplemental Manual accompanies each Batería-R battery. The features just listed are explained extensively in these manuals.

The Supplemental Manuals refer to a computer program, Report Writer for the Batería-R, which has not been produced. Instead, capability to handle data from the Batería-R has been incorporated into the Woodcock Scoring and Interpretative Program (Schrank & Woodcock, 1997), which also handles data from the WJ-R (B. Wendling, personal communication, September 6, 1997). It generates score reports and narrative interpretative reports including comparative language information. These reports are in English except for a summary report available in both languages. This program is available from the publisher ($395) separately from either of the Batería-R (or WJ-R) batteries. It operates on a Windows© platform; a Macintosh© version is anticipated.

Administration of the Batería-R is essentially the same as for the WJ-R, which requires substantial experience in the testing of individual subjects and strong familiarity with the administration and scoring procedures for each of the 35 tests. Moreover, for the Batería-R, the examiner must be fluent in Spanish. Because need for the Batería-R may occur in settings where a fully qualified Spanish-speaking examiner is not available, each Supplemental Manual provides comprehensive instructions for the training and utilization of ancillary Spanish-speaking examiners. The manuals make a sharp contrast between simply using such a person as an interpreter as opposed to requiring more active involvement with the measurement process.

It was the consensus of the reviewers cited earlier that the WJ-R embodied a high level of quality and that it had the potential to yield reliable and valid scores when properly used for its intended purposes, such as provisional placement in academic programs and diagnosis of learning deficiencies. They viewed the norming of the WJ-R as an especially strong point, given the size and comprehensiveness of the norming sample. The extent to which these qualities extend to the Batería-R constitutes the focus of this review.

A complex test development and equating procedure was undertaken as described in each Supplemental Manual. For each WJ-R test, equating items were identified. These were items that could be adopted directly (nonverbal or mathematical items) or translated unambiguously into Spanish and which spanned a wide range of difficulty based on Rasch model calibration of the responses of the WJ-R norming sample. Additional items were written in

Spanish, both to cover English items that resisted translation and to produce additional Spanish items for strictly verbal tests. The resulting Spanish item bank was administered in several countries, including the U.S., to nearly 4,000 monolingual subjects from 2 years of age through university graduate students (age unspecified). The equating procedures permitted creating raw-score to Rasch (W) ability tables consistent with the U.S. norms. Thus, a raw score on a Batería-R test can be evaluated for percentile rank, grade-equivalence, etc., by entering the appropriate U.S. norms table with the corresponding transformed Rasch ability measure. A more detailed description of this process is found in Woodcock and Muñoz-Sandoval (1993).

Though the development/equating process would probably be endorsed by most measurement specialists, its success must be judged in terms of the tests themselves and the psychometric characteristics of their scores. One of the most important concerns is content validity, especially given the possibility of content changes associated with translation. Many Batería-R tests are virtually or largely identical to those of the WJ-R. These are the nonverbal and mathematics-based tests, for which only the instructions and brief item wordings had to be translated. The Spanish translations or adaptations for these tests appear to be entirely adequate. Tests with more extensive verbal stimuli contain many items completely different from the WJ-R. In some cases, these changes were intentional so that administration of a Batería-R test would not give away the content of the corresponding WJ-R test for bilingual examinees taking both. In other cases, the changes reflect adaptation to Spanish language or culture. The new items and items that underwent fairly extensive changes in translation employ standard Spanish in a manner that should be readily understandable across a wide variety of backgrounds for speakers of this language. Moreover, with some exceptions to be noted, the content, tone, and character of the translated items is very similar to those of the WJ-R that they replace.

One pair of tests that clearly measure different constructs are the WJ-R Letter-Word Identification test as contrasted with Identificación de Letras y Palabras in the Batería-R APR. The latter items of both of these tests require the subject to read and then state orally words of increasing complexity. In English, this task requires knowledge of a highly complex and illogical set of orthographic/pronuncia-tion rules and exceptions, to say nothing of the need to know how specific words are pronounced. In Spanish, however, one needs only to know a small set of consistent rules. Memory and vocabulary level must be major determinants of success for the English test but not for the Spanish. Therefore, it would be inappropriate to say that Anglophone and Hispanophone subjects attaining the same percentile rank on these tests are somehow equivalently endowed with respect to the task at hand. Nevertheless, the differing demands of this task in English and Spanish may not be a serious impediment to interpreting the scores in a clinical setting. In contrast, if the results were to be used comparatively, perhaps for program evaluation, the potential for misinterpretation is much greater.

It would have been reasonable to expect content/construct differences between the corresponding Social Studies tests of the Batería-R and WJ-R, inasmuch as the latter has some orientation toward U.S. institutions and history. For example, the WJ-R contains questions requiring knowledge of why the Pony Express was discontinued and the name of the branch of the U.S. federal government responsible for law enforcement. Contrary to what might have been expected, similar questions are found in the Batería-R APR test, Estudios Sociales, in which examinees are asked to identify the work of George Washington Carver and name the country that gave the Statue of Liberty to the U.S. Accordingly, examiners need to be aware that the Batería-R Social Studies score represents to some extent achievement in social studies as they might be taught or presented in the U.S., not what may have been learned in a Spanish-speaking country. However, the proportion of such U.S.-oriented questions is relatively small in either test and should not influence scores to an extreme extent.

In contrast to the amount of U.S.-dependent content in the Batería-R Social Studies test, there is essentially none in the Batería-R Humanities test. There are only a few U.S.-dependent questions in the WJ-R Humanities test (e.g., concerning the theme of *The Yearling* and the author of *Tom Sawyer*), and these or similar ones do not appear in the corresponding Batería-R test.

Another problem associated with cross-national interpretation of testing outcomes is revealed in the work of Fletcher and Sabers (1995), who analyzed norming data from several countries for the Batería Woodcock Psico-Educativa en Español

(Woodcock, 1982), which contains tests highly similar to some of the Batería-R. Fletcher and Sabers found that means based on cluster scores from the Batería Woodcock varied substantially and quite irregularly across countries and grade levels. They conjectured that this outcome was due to differences among educational systems. Again, clinical judgment should prevent serious misinterpretation of the scores of an individual. However, knowledge of intercountry educational differences may be more than can be expected of many clinicians.

Perusal of the items of the various tests revealed a moderate number of item-writing or other editing lapses. For the most part, these problems stem from overly restrictive decisions about correct answers or problems with translations of words or picture meanings from English to Spanish. These oversights need not be considered flaws, especially if clinicians are sufficiently knowledgeable and flexible in scoring. The publisher should be sensitive to these issues in future printings.

The Supplemental Manuals provide information about reliability and validity. Internal consistency reliability coefficients reported are generally good. However, these coefficients are reported for only 9 of the 21 tests in the Batería-R COG, whereas all tests in the Batería-R APR are covered. Validity evidence reported in the Supplemental Manuals is meager. An unpublished study involving 70 U.S. kindergarten students found substantial correlations between scores from the Oral Language cluster of the Batería-R COG and other measures of oral fluency in Spanish. Another unpublished study of 120 U.S. second grade students found moderate correlations, again between Batería-R Oral Language scores and other measures of oral language.

SUMMARY. In spite of very limited empirical evidence of the adequacy of the Batería-R COG and APR and the flaws noted above, there are, nevertheless, considerable grounds for recommending these batteries. They are the only thoroughly comprehensive ones suitable for evaluation of Spanish-speaking students in U.S. schools and could well be used in other English-speaking educational settings. Tying score outcomes to U.S. norms argues to some extent against their use in strictly Hispanic settings as does the use of U.S. money, U.S. time zones, U.S. ZIP codes, and the English system of measurement in a number of items. The testing materials are well organized and of good physical quality. Most impor-

tant, profiting from experience with the WJ-R, the authors have produced tests that should be substantially functional for use with their intended population.

REVIEWER'S REFERENCES

Horn, J. L., & Cattell, R. B. (1966). Refinement and test of the theory of fluid and crystallized general intelligences. *Journal of Educational Psychology, 57*, 253–270.
Woodcock, R. W. (1982). Batería Woodcock Psico-Educativa en Español. Itasca, IL: The Riverside Publishing Co.
Cummins, J. (1984). *Bilingualism and special education: Issues in assessment and psychology.* San Diego: College Hill Press.
Woodcock, R. W., & Johnson, M. B. (1989). Woodcock-Johnson Tests of Achievement—Revised. Itasca, IL: The Riverside Publishing Co.
Woodcock, R. W., & Johnson, M. B. (1989). Woodcock-Johnson Tests of Cognitive Ability—Revised. Itasca, IL: The Riverside Publishing Co.
Woodcock, R. W., & Muñoz-Sandoval, A. F. (1993). An IRT approach to cross-language test equating. *European Journal of Psychological Assessment, 9*, 233–241.
Webster, R. E. (1994). Review of Woodcock-Johnson Psychoeducational Test Battery—Revised. In D. J. Keyser & R. C. Sweetland (Eds.), *Test critiques* (vol. X, pp. 804–815). Austin, TX: PRO-ED, Inc.
Cummings, J. A. (1995). [Review of the Woodcock-Johnson Psychoeducational Battery—Revised.] In J. C. Conoley & J. C. Impara (Eds.), *The twelfth mental measurements yearbook* (pp. 1111–1116). Lincoln, NE: The Buros Institute of Mental Measurements.
Fletcher, T. V., & Sabers, D. L. (1995). Interaction effects in cross-national studies of achievement. *Comparative Education Review, 39*, 455–467.
Lee, S. W., & Stefany, E. F. (1995). [Review of the Woodcock-Johnson Psychoeducational Battery—Revised.] In J. C. Conoley & J. C. Impara (Eds.), *The twelfth mental measurements yearbook* (pp. 1116–1117). Lincoln, NE: The Buros Institute of Mental Measurements.
Schrank, F. A., & Woodcock, R. W. (1997). *Woodcock scoring and interpretive program.* Itasca, IL: The Riverside Publishing Co.

Review of the Batería Woodcock Psico-Educativa en Español by MARIA PRENDES LINTEL, Assessment Coordinator, Lincoln Family Practice Program, Lincoln, NE:

[Editor's Note: This review is based on the Batería Woodcock Psico-Educativa en Español, which is the earlier edition of the Batería Woodcock-Muñoz described above.]

The Batería Woodcock Psico-Educativa en Español (Batería) was developed in 1982 and according to the manual has been widely used since its development. However, it is extremely difficult to evaluate this test, which purports to have an extensive variety of applications in educational and noneducational settings. The reason for this is that the manual does not discuss validity of any type or reliability factors but does state that a future publication of the technical manual is planned. However, that was in 1982 and in 1996 the manual was not among the components available. There are other concerns aside from those previously listed. One major concern is the norming sample, the other is the translation of the Batería to Spanish.

NORMS. The norms for the Batería, according to the manual, are based on a composite sample gathered during January to July of 1980 from typical urbanized areas in Costa Rica (San Jose), Mexico (Chihuahua and Guadalajara), Peru (Lima), Puerto Rico (Ponce), and Spain (Madrid). There were 802 subjects in the sample drawn from kindergarten, grade 1, grade 3, grade 5, grade 8 (2 secundaria), and grade 11 (2 bachillerato, 3 BUP). The manual indicated that "General Spanish Norms provide functional and instructional information regarding how well a subject is faring compared with native Spanish speakers across the Spanish speaking world" (manual, Woodcock, 1982, p. 28). The Batería is said to have a common norm base, meaning the same group of people provided all the normative data for the Batería. The above statement suggests scores from this test would be valid for anyone in the Spanish-speaking world regardless of linguistic bias, cultural uniqueness, history, and conceptual differences. Such statements are of concern and are perhaps reflective of the times in which this test was developed. However, given the *Standards for Educational and Psychological Testing* (AERA, APA, & NCME, 1985) and the American Psychological Association's (1990) *Guidelines for Providers of Services Ethnic, Linguistic, and Culturally Diverse Populations*, testing psychologists should not assume the appropriateness of results from using this test.

I will briefly summarize the reasons why the Batería should not be used. First, the manual does not discuss how the test was developed or translated into Spanish. There are issues of conceptual meaning and understanding as well as ethnic and linguistic bias that are totally absent from the manual. Second, it is inappropriate to use a test normed on a population other than the one being tested (e.g., normed on Spanish children from other countries) as such norms are not representative of Hispanic children in the United States. Third, the manual does not address nor present any validity or reliability information. A better practice for testing the Hispanic population in the United States includes but is not limited to: (a) A review of test items for appropriateness of content, editorial accuracy, and ethnic and linguistic bias; (b) the test should be normed on a representative sample of the various Hispanic minorities population in the United States, including geographic representation; (c) there should be a test manual where appropriate levels of reliability, validity, and statistical analysis are fully described and reported.

It is my understanding that a new version of the Batería will soon be introduced. Because I have not had the opportunity to review the new version I can only hope that it is not like its predecessor. The Batería is questionable for use even in those countries in which it was normed because it is still missing vital information (e.g., reliability, validity) necessary for a testing psychologists to have in order to make a professionally responsible decision regarding the use of this test. The Batería test developers are referred to the Spanish Assessment of Basic Education, Second Edition (291) for a model of appropriate test development and measurement with the Hispanic population of the United States.

REVIEWER'S REFERENCES
Woodcock, R. W. (1982). *Examiner's manual* Batería Woodcock Psico-Educativa En Español, Woodcock Spanish Psycho-Educational Battery. Itasca, IL: The Riverside Publishing Co.
American Educational Research Association, American Psychological Association, & National Council on Measurement in Education. (1985). *Standards for educational and psychological testing.* Washington, DC: APA, Inc.
American Psychological Association. (1990). *Guidelines for providers of services ethnic, linguistic, and culturally diverse populations.* Washington, DC: Author.

[28]
Bayley Infant Neurodevelopmental Screener.

Purpose: "Designed to identify infants between the ages of 3 and 24 months who are developmentally delayed or have neurological impairments."

Population: Ages 3–24 months.

Publication Dates: 1992–1995.

Acronym: BINS.

Scores: 4 areas: Basic Neurological Functions/Intactness, Receptive Functions, Expressive Functions, Cognitive Processes; one total test score.

Administration: Individual.

Levels, 6: 3–4 months, 5–6 months, 7–10 months, 11–15 months, 16–20 months, 21–24 months.

Price Data, 1998: $219.50 per complete kit including 25 record forms, manual ('95, 105 pages), stimulus card, and necessary manipulables in soft-sided carrying case; $25 per 25 record forms; $60 per manual; $12 per stimulus card; $56 per training video.

Time: (10) minutes.

Comments: Includes a subset of items from the Bayley Scales of Infant Development—Second Edition (BSID–II; 29), as well as items that assess neurological functioning.

Author: Glen P. Aylward.

Publisher: The Psychological Corporation.

Review of the Bayley Infant Neurodevelopmental Screener by JAMES K. BENISH, School Psychologist, Helena Public Schools, Adjunct Professor of Special Education, Carroll College, Helena, MT:

The Bayley Infant Neurodevelopmental Screener (BINS) is a tool for screening infants who may be developmentally delayed or neurologically impaired. The BINS utilizes a subset of items from the Bayley Scales of Infant Development—Second Edition (BSID-II; 29); however, the authors stipulate that "it is *not* an abbreviated form of the BSID-II, but rather a tool for screening infants to identify them for further diagnostic testing" (manual, p. 1). This is an important function to consider, because the BINS is inadequate as a comprehensive diagnostic tool.

The BINS was designed to be administered to infants between the ages of 3 and 24 months. The BINS assesses four conceptual areas: Basic Neurological Functions/Intactness, Receptive Functions, Expressive Functions, and Cognitive Processes. There are 11 to 13 test items in each of the six age levels. The BINS is fairly easy to administer and score, but requires some specific prior training. User qualifications necessitate knowledge of infant development including experience in handling infants. A graduate level program with a background in standardized assessment and infant development is recommended by the authors. The examiner must be completely familiar with test items to prevent disruption of the flow in administering the BINS. Total testing time is about 10 minutes depending on infant age and temperament.

STANDARDIZATION AND NORMS. The Early Neuropsychologic Optimality Rating Scales "served as the tryout version of the BINS" (manual, p. 1). Clinical and nonclinical samples were included in the standardization to develop the norms. A sample of 600 nonclinical cases was collected based on age, sex, race/ethnicity, geographic region, and parent education level. "The BINS nonclinical sample was stratified according to five demographic variables and represents percentages based on the 1988 update of the U.S. census (U.S. Bureau of the Census, 1988)" (p. 7). The clinical samples comprised 303 infants at 3, 6, 9, 12, 18, and 24 months. Complications of infants sampled included low birth weight, respiratory distress syndrome, and prematurity. Other, less frequent, complications also existed in the nonclinical sample. Clear, concise tables of demographic data were included for the nonclinical sample population; however, descriptions of the clinical samples were listed without tables. Aside from identifying infants at medical risk, the criteria for sampling the clinical population was not elaborated.

RELIABILITY. Internal consistency reliability was calculated using Cronbach's alpha for both clinical and nonclinical samples. Alpha coefficients were listed as ranging from .73 to .85. Of the six age groups, four were above .80, but the 3-month and 12-month age groups were only .73. Test-retest reliability was calculated by readministering the BINS to a group of 150 infants previously assessed. The test-retest correlation was marginal at the 3-month group (.71), but respectable with the 9- and 18-month groups (.83 and .84 respectively). Mean number of days between tests was 3.9. Although interrater reliability was only .79 at the 6-month-old group, it was quite high at the 12-month-old group (.91) and the 24-month-old group (.96), indicating very acceptable interrater scoring agreement.

VALIDITY. A convergent validity study was conducted by comparing the BINS and the BSID-II. Cut score comparison between the two resulted in highest agreement when the lowest BINS cut score was used. When the highest cut score was used, overidentification occurred, resulting in infant scores in the moderate or high-risk range on the BINS, but with scores in normal limits on the BSID-II. Conversely, there was also a trend to underidentify infants when the lowest cut score was used on the BINS, although not nearly so often. When the BINS was compared with the Battelle Developmental Inventory, similar findings were obtained when using highest and lowest cut scores in regard to over- and underidentifying risk factors. Such findings raise questions regarding potential problems in concluding whether risk factors found with the BINS merit further assessment with the BSID-II, the Battelle Developmental Inventory, or another assessment instrument. Both appear to have better predictive validity than the BINS when the highest cut scores are used.

SUMMARY. The BINS could be utilized as a quick screening or surveillance tool if used with caution. The authors emphasize that the BINS is not a substitute for a more comprehensive evaluation in identifying developmental delay or neurological impairment. Test findings with the BINS should not be used for treatment decisions. The test's strengths include a fairly good normative sample, good organization of areas assessed, and clear scoring procedures. Weaknesses are its classification agreements with the BSID-II and the Battelle Developmental Inventory in terms of cut scores and risk factors. The knowledge and evaluator experience needed to use the BINS may limit it in nonclinical settings where infant referrals are low. This is a tool that requires careful adherence to its directions, and may not be the test of choice for some. However, as a screener or surveillance tool, it should be given consideration.

Review of the Bayley Infant Developmental Screener by DAMON KRUG, University Professor, College of Education, Governors State University, University Park, IL and BRANDON DAVIS, School Psychologist, Arbor Clinic, Muncie, IN:

The Bayley Infant Neurodevelopmental Screener (BINS) is an instrument designed to combine neurological assessment with developmental assessment. The combination of neurological and developmental assessments was expected to produce a brief screening instrument that would effectively identify infants from age 3 months to 24 months who were in need of further neuropsychological testing. The BINS was not only designed to identify children in need of further neuropsychological testing but could also be used to track the development of an at-risk child through repeated administrations.

The BINS, although named after the Bayley Scales of Infant Development—Second Edition (BSID-II; 29), is not a shortened version of the BSID-II. It is an independent instrument designed to screen a large number of infants in a short period of time. The screener is reported to take only 10 minutes to administer and is designed to be administered by professionals who have knowledge of infant development and experience handling infants. These can include "developmental pediatricians, psychologists, pediatric nurse practitioners, occupational and physical therapists, and early childhood specialists" (manual, p. 3). The need for a trained professional to administer the test is appropriate. Part of the screener calls for assessment of muscle tone, thus the administrator must have knowledge of what is appropriate muscle tone for an infant and how to handle and approach an infant to perform such an assessment.

The norms for the BINS are appropriate and well developed. The norms include both a nonclinical sample and a clinical sample. The nonclinical sample was carefully matched by geography, parental education level, gender, and ethnicity to the 1988 U.S. Census. The clinical sample was also carefully planned. The sample included infants suffering from a variety of neurological and developmental difficulties. The collection of the normative data appears to be appropriate and scientifically sound.

The extensive norms were also used to analyze item bias and item discriminability. The manual describes an extensive analysis to eliminate items that were ethnically biased or had insufficient item discriminability in separating infants with neurological or developmental delays and normally developing infants.

The manual reports three forms of reliability: internal consistency, test-retest reliability, and interrater reliability. The reported internal consistency coefficients ranged from .73 to .85. Coefficients in this range are expected and appropriate. The test-retest reliability coefficients ranged from .71 to .84 and were lowest for infants 3 months of age. Although the coefficients are significant and of respectable size, the time interval between the first and second testing is questionable. The manual reports the mean number of days between the first and second testing was 3.9 days with a standard deviation of 3.8. Although this time period is shorter than the recommended 2 weeks, the reviewer agrees with the developer's rationale: "At this young age it was not believed that there would be a significant practice effect or increase in scores during the second testing. The greatest concern was for maturation of the infant" (manual, p. 57). The development of an infant, at the ages appropriate for this screener, can change daily, thus the restricted range is acceptable for this instrument.

The interrater reliability coefficients ranged from .79 to .96. The high coefficients strongly suggest that two independent people can administer the test and get very similar results. However, the manual does not address intrarater reliability—how consistent a rater can be with him or herself. This is relevant because the test is designed to be administered by a single individual to a large number of infants in a short period of time. Thus, it is important that an examiner will not underrate one child based on the superior performance of the previous child. The underrating of a child may lead to overidentification of children suspected of having neurological or developmental difficulties. Thus, the lack of intrarater reliability cautions the use of the instrument to screen a large number of infants in a short period of time.

Regarding validity, the manual reported two forms of validity—convergent and concurrent. For convergent validity, the identification of at-risk children by the BINS was compared to the identification of at-risk by the BSID-II and the Battelle Developmental Inventory. In comparison to both instruments, the BINS was most successful in identifying low- to moderate-risk children who were developing normally. However, the BINS also identified infants developing normally as infants at moderate to high risk, range of disagreement 3% to 50%. The manual also reported the BINS was compared to the Denver II. However, no calculations regarding accuracy of classification could be calculated due to almost all of the infants receiving a pass score on the Denver II. Thus, it appears the BINS, although demonstrating good ability in accurately identifying low- to moderate-risk infants, also may categorize normal infants as moderate- to high-risk infants. By incorrectly identifying normal infants as high- to moderate-risk infants, the BINS may lead to infants being subjected to long, involved, and unnecessary testing.

With respect to concurrent validity, the BINS shows high accuracy in identifying high- to moderate-risk infants, which supports the convergent validity data. However, the concurrent data also show that the BINS identifies some normally developing infants as moderate- to high-risk infants. This also supports the convergent validity data. Again, this implies the BINS may overidentify at-risk infants and may lead to some infants being subjected to long, involved, and unnecessary testing.

The main criticism of the validity data presented for the BINS is the lack of predictive validity data. The lack of predictive validity is listed as a criticism of other screening instruments in the rationale for the BINS (manual, p. 1). Thus, it was expected that the BINS would attempt to respond to the lack of predictive validity. The lack of any predictive validity data is disappointing.

The administrative instructions for the varying age-specific sections of the BINS are exceptional. The directions provided in the manual are clear and precise. The directions include infant position, materials necessary, procedural directions, and scoring guidelines. Further, the test kit provides all necessary materials except for the stairs. However, guidelines are presented for the size of the stairs and directions for building stairs if necessary.

Overall, the BINS is a well-researched and carefully developed instrument. Although the lack of intrarater reliability and predictive validity data is disappointing, it does not seriously impair the viability of the test. The BINS was designed to be a screening instrument to determine if more extensive testing was necessary. In a setting where there are a large number of infants being screened every day, the brief administration time and high validity at identifying infants at high to moderate risk makes this test a viable option. However, in a setting where there is less time pressure and/or fewer clients, a careful structured observation and good clinical interview would probably be equally effective.

[29]

Bayley Scales of Infant Development, Second Edition.

Purpose: "Assesses the current developmental functioning of infants and children."
Population: Ages 1–42 months.
Publication Dates: 1969–1993.
Acronym: BSID-II.
Scores, 2: Mental, Motor, plus 30 behavior ratings.
Administration: Individual.
Price Data, 1996: $760 per complete kit including 25 Mental Scale record forms, 25 Motor Scale record forms, 25 Behavior Rating Scale record forms, visual stimulus cards, map, manipulatives, carrying case, stimulus booklet, and manual ('93, 374 pages); $31 per 25 Mental Scale record forms, $26.50 per 25 Motor Scale record forms; $24 per 25 Behavior Rating Scale record forms; $61 per stimulus booklet; $61 per manual.
Time: (25–60) minutes.
Author: Nancy Bayley.
Publisher: The Psychological Corporation.
Cross References: See T4:266 (58 references); for reviews by Michael J. Roszkowski and Jane A. Rysberg of an earlier edition, see 10:26 (80 references); see also 9:126 (42 references) and T3:270 (101 references); for a review by Fred Damarin, see 8:206 (28 references); see also T2:484 (11 references); for reviews by Roberta R. Collard and Raymond H. Holden, see 7:402 (20 references).

TEST REFERENCES

1. Siegel, L. S. (1984). A longitudinal study of a hyperlexic child: Hyperlexia as a language disorder. *Neuropsychologia, 22,* 577–585.
2. Marcus, J., Hans, S. L., Nagler, S., Auerbach, J. G., Mirsky, A. F., & Aubrey, A. (1987). Review of the NIMH Israeli Kibbutz-City study and the Jerusalem infant development study. *Schizophrenia Bulletin, 13,* 425–438.
3. Matheny, A. P., Jr. (1989). Children's behavioral inhibition over age and across situations: Genetic similarity for a trait during change. *Journal of Personality, 57,* 215–235.
4. Power, T. J., & Radcliffe, J. (1989). The relationship of play behavior to cognitive ability in developmentally disabled preschoolers. *Journal of Autism and Developmental Disorders, 19*(1), 97–107.
5. Melhuish, E. C., Lloyd, E., Martin, S., & Mooney, A. (1990). Type of childcare at 18 months: II. Relations with cognitive and language development. *Journal of Child Psychology and Psychiatry and Allied Disciplines, 31,* 861–870.
6. Melhuish, E. C., Mooney, A., Martin, S., & Lloyd, E. (1990). Types of child care at 18 months: I. Differences in interactional experience. *Journal of Child Psychology and Psychiatry and Allied Disciplines, 31,* 849–859.
7. Kochanek, T. T., Kabacoff, R. I., & Lipsitt, L. P. (1990). Early identification of developmentally disabled and at-risk preschool children. *Exceptional Children, 56,* 528–538.
8. Seoman, J., Bellinger, D. C., & Krentzel, C. P. (1990). Infantile colic and transient developmental lag in the first year of life.. *Child Psychiatry and Human Development, 21,* 25-36.
9. van Baar, A. (1990). Development of infants of drug dependent mothers. *Journal of Child Psychology and Psychiatry and Allied Disciplines, 31,* 911-920.
10. DiPietro, J. A., & Allen, M. C. (1991). Estimation of gestational age: Implications for developmental research. *Child Development, 62,* 1184–1199.
11. Dunbar, S. B., Jarvis, A. H., & Breyer, M. (1991). The transition from nonoral to oral feeding in children. *The American Journal of Occupational Therapy, 45,* 402-408.

12. Dyer, K., Williams, L., & Luce, S. C. (1991). Training teachers to use naturalistic communication strategies in classrooms for students with autism and other severe handicaps. *Language, Speech, and Hearing Services in Schools, 22,* 313–321.

13. Fewell, R. R. (1991). Trends in the assessment of infants and toddlers with disabilities. *Exceptional Children, 58,* 166-173.

14. Fish, M., Stifter, C. A., & Belsky, J. (1991). Conditions of continuity and discontinuity in infant negative emotionality: Newborn to five months. *Child Development, 62,* 1525–1537.

15. Lyons-Ruth, K., Repacholi, B., McLeod, S., & Silva, E. (1991). Disorganized attachment behavior in infancy: Short-term stability, maternal and infant correlates, and risk-related subtypes. *Development and Psychopathology, 3,* 377-396.

16. Murray-Branch, J., Udavari-Solner, A., & Bailey, B. (1991). Textured communication systems for individuals with severe intellectual and dual sensory impairment. *Language, Speech, and Hearing Services in Schools, 22,* 260–268.

17. Nath, P. S., Borkowski, J. G., Whitman, T. L., & Schellenbach, C. J. (1991). Understanding adolescent parenting: The dimensions and functions of social support. *Family Relations, 40,* 411-420.

18. Nugent, J. K. (1991). Cultural and psychological influences on the father's role in infant development. *Journal of Marriage and the Family, 53,* 475–485.

19. Poulson, C. L., Kymissis, E., Reeve, K. F., Andreatos, M., & Reeve, L. (1991). Generalized vocal imitations in infants. *Journal of Experimental Child Psychology, 51,* 267-279.

20. Saudino, K. J., & Eaton, W. O. (1991). Infant temperament and genetics: An objective twin study of motor activity level. *Child Development, 62,* 1167–1174.

21. Sigman, M., McDonald, M. A., Neumann, C., & Bwibu, N. (1991). Prediction of cognitive competence in Kenyan children from toddler nutrition, family characteristics and abilities. *Journal of Child Psychology and Psychiatry and Allied Disciplines, 32,* 307-320.

22. Brandt, P., Magyary, D., Hammond, M., & Barnard, K. (1992). Learning and behavioral-emotional problems of children born preterm at second grade. *Journal of Pediatric Psychology, 17,* 291–311.

23. Burack, J. A., & Volkmar, F. R. (1992). Development of low- and high-functioning autistic children. Journal of Child Psychology and Psychiatry and Allied Disciplines, 33, 607-616.

24. Case-Smith, J. (1992). A validity study of the posture and fine motor assessment of infants. *The American Journal of Occupational Therapy, 46,* 597-605.

25. Crittenden, P. M. (1992). Children's strategies for coping with adverse home environments: An interpretation using attachment theory. *Child Abuse & Neglect, 16,* 329-343.

26. Diamond, K. E., & LeFurgy, W. G. (1992). Relations between mothers' expectations and the performance of their infants who have developmental handicaps. *American Journal on Mental Retardation, 97,* 11-20.

27. Einarsson-Backes, L. M., & Stewart, K. B. (1992). Infant neuromotor assessments: A review and preview of selected instruments. *The American Journal of Occupational Therapy, 46,* 224-232.

28. Emde, R., Plomin, R., Robinson, J., Corley, R., DeFries, J., Fulker, D. W., Reznick, J. S., Campos, J., Kagan, J., & Zahn-Waxler, C. (1992). Temperament, emotion, and cognition at fourteen months: The MacArthur longitudinal twin study. *Child Development, 63,* 1437–1455.

29. Feldman, H. M., Evans, J. L., Brown, R. E., & Wareham, N. L. (1992). Early language and communicative abilities of children with periventricular leukomalacia. *American Journal on Mental Retardation, 97,* 222-234.

30. Gowen, J. W., Johnson-Martin, N., Goldman, B. D., & Hussey, B. (1992). Object-play and exploration in children with and without disabilities: A longitudinal study. *American Journal on Mental Retardation, 97,* 21-38.

31. Jacobson, S. W., Jacobson, J. L., O'Neill, J. M., Padgett, R. J., Frankowski, J. J., & Bihun, J. T. (1992). Visual expectation and dimension of infant information processing. *Child Development, 63,* 711–724.

32. Louis, B., & Lewis, M. (1992). Parental beliefs about giftedness in young children and their relation to actual ability level. *Gifted Child Quarterly, 36,* 27-31.

33. Murray, L. (1992). The impact of postnatal depression on infant development. *Journal of Child Psychology and Psychiatry and Allied Disciplines, 33,* 543-561.

34. Phillips, W., Baron-Cohen, S., & Rutter, M. (1992). The role of eye contact in goal detection: Evidence from normal infants and children with autism or mental handicap. *Development and Psychopathology, 4,* 375-383.

35. Riese, M. L. (1992). Visual and auditory orienting responses in preterm infants: A comparison of three cohorts over time. *The Journal of Genetic Psychology, 153,* 155-164.

36. Rouet, J. F., Ehrlich, R. M., & Sorbara, D. L. (1992). Neurodevelopment in infants and preschool children with congenital hypothyroidism: Etiological and treatment factors affecting outcome. *Journal of Pediatric Psychology, 17,* 187–213.

37. Schery, T. K., & O'Connor, L. C. (1992). The effectiveness of school-based computer language intervention with severely handicapped children. *Language, Speech, and Hearing Services in Schools, 23,* 43–47.

38. Steffens, M. L., Oller, D. K., Lynch, M., & Urbano, R. C. (1992). Vocal development in infants with Down syndrome and infants who are developing normally. *American Journal on Mental Retardation, 97,* 235-246.

39. Tannenbaum, A. (1992). Early signs of giftedness: Research and commentary. *Journal for the Education of the Gifted, 15,* 104-133.

40. Brooks-Gunn, J., Klebanov, P. K., Liaw, F., & Spiker, D. (1993). Enhancing the development of low-birthweight, premature infants: Changes in cognition and behavior over the first three years. *Child Development, 64,* 736-753.

41. Jacobson, S. W., Jacobson, J. L., Sokol, R. J., Martier, S. S., & Ager, J. W. (1993). Prenatal alcohol exposure and infant information processing ability. *Child Development, 64,* 1706-1721.

42. Krauss, M. W. (1993). Child-related and parenting stress: Similarities and differences between mothers and fathers of children with disabilities. *American Journal on Mental Retardation, 97,* 393-404.

43. Lyons-Ruth, K., Alpern, L., & Repacholi, B. (1993). Disorganized infant attachment classification and maternal psychosocial problems as predictors of hostile-aggressive behavior in the preschool classroom. *Child Development, 64,* 572-585.

44. McCall, R. B., & Carriger, M. S. (1993). A meta-analysis of infant habituation and recognition memory performance as predictors of later IQ. *Child Development, 64,* 57-79.

45. McCardle, P., & Wilson, B. (1993). Language and development in FG syndrome with callosal agenesis. *Journal of Communication Disorders, 26,* 83–100.

46. McEvoy, R. E., Rogers, S. J., & Pennington, B. F. (1993). Executive function and social communication deficits in young autistic children. *Journal of Child Psychology and Psychiatry and Allied Disciplines, 34,* 563-578.

47. Miller, L. J., & Roid, G. H. (1993). Sequence comparison methodology for the analysis of movement patterns in infants and toddlers with and without motor delays. *The American Journal of Occupational Therapy [Special Issue], 47,* 339-347.

48. Moffitt, T. E., Caspi, A., Harkness, A. R., & Silva, P. A. (1993). The natural history of change in intellectual performance: Who changes? How much? Is it meaningful? *Journal of Child Psychology and Psychiatry and Allied Disciplines, 34,* 455-506.

49. Morris, R. D., Krawiecki, N. S., Wright, J. A., & Walter, L. W. (1993). Neuropsychological, academic, and adaptive functioning in children who survive in-hospital cardiac arrest and resuscitation. *Journal of Learning Disabilities, 26,* 46–51.

50. Palthe, T. W., & Hopkins, B. (1993). A longitudinal study of neural maturation and early mother-infant interaction: A research note. *Journal of Child Psychology and Psychiatry and Allied Disciplines, 34,* 1031-1041.

51. Passino, A. W., Whitman, T. L., Borkowski, J. G., Schellenbach, C. J., Maxwell, S. E., Keogh, D., & Rellinger, E. (1993). Personal adjustment during pregnancy and adolescent parenting. *Adolescence, 28,* 97-122.

52. Paul, R., & Alforde, S. (1993). Grammatical morpheme acquisition in 4-year-olds with normal, impaired, and late-developing language. *Journal of Speech and Hearing Research, 36,* 1271–1275.

53. Paul, R., & Smith, R. L. (1993). Narrative skills in 4-year-olds with normal, impaired, and late-developing language. *Journal of Speech and Hearing Research, 36,* 592–598.

54. Phelps, L., & Cox, D. (1993). Children with prenatal cocaine exposure: Resilient or handicapped? *School Psychology Review, 22,* 710-724.

55. Plomin, R., Kagan, J., Emoe, R. N., Reznick, J. S. Braungart, J. M., Robinson, J., Campos, J., Zahn-Waxler, C., Corley, R., Fulker, D. W., & DeFries, J. C. (1993). Genetic change and continuity from fourteen to twenty months: The MacArthur longitudinal twin study. *Child Development, 64,* 1354-1376.

56. Spiker, D. Ferguson, J., & Brooks-Gunn, J. (1993). Enhancing maternal interactive behavior and child social competence in low birth weight, premature infants. *Child Development, 64,* 754-768.

57. Weismer, S. E., Murray-Branch, J., & Miller, J. F. (1993). Comparison of two methods for promoting productive vocabulary in late talkers. *Journal of Speech and Hearing Research, 36,* 1037–1050.

58. Yoder, P. J., Kaiser, A. P., Alpert, C., & Fischer, R. (1993). Following the child's lead when teaching nouns to preschoolers with mental retardation. *Journal of Speech and Hearing Research, 36,* 158–167.

59. Bagnato, S. J., & Neisworth, J. T. (1994). A national study of the social and treatment "invalidity" of intelligence testing for early intervention. *School Psychology Quarterly, 9,* 81-102.

60. Bendersky, M., & Lewis, M. (1994). Environment risk, biological risk, and developmental outcome. *Developmental Psychology, 30,* 484-494.

61. Bernstein, V. J., & Hans, S. L. (1994). Predicting the developmental outcome of two-year-old children born exposed to methadone: Impact of social-environmental risk factors. *Journal of Clinical Child Psychology, 23,* 349-359.

62. Black, M. M., Hutcheson, J. J., Dubowitz, H., & Berenson-Howard, I. (1994). Parenting style and developmental status among children with nonorganic failure to thrive. *Journal of Pediatric Psychology, 19,* 689-707.

63. Black, M. M., Nair, P., & Harrington, D. (1994). Maternal HIV infection: Parenting and early child development. *Journal of Pediatric Psychology, 19,* 595-616.

64. Brinker, R. P., Baxter, A., & Butler, L. S. (1994). An ordinal pattern analysis of four hypotheses describing the interactions between drug-addicted, chronically disadvantaged, and middle-class mother-infant dyads. *Child Development, 65,* 361–372.

65. Brinker, R. P., Seifer, R., & Sameroff, A. J. (1994). Relations among maternal stress, cognitive development, and early intervention in middle- and low-SES infants with developmental disabilities. *American Journal on Mental Retardation, 98,* 463–480.

66. Campbell, F. A., & Ramey, C. T. (1994). Effects of early intervention on intellectual and academic achievement: A follow-up study of children from low income families. *Child Development, 65,* 684–698.

67. Ducharme, J. M., Pontes, E., Guger, S., Crozier, K., Lucas, H., & Popynick, M. (1994). Errorless compliance to parental requests II: Increasing clinical practicality through abbreviations of treatment parameters. *Behavior Therapy, 25,* 469–487.

68. Eaves, L. C., Ho, H. H., & Eaves, D. M. (1994). Subtypes of autism by cluster analyses. *Journal of Autism and Developmental Disorders, 24,* 3-22.

69. Gerken, K. C., Eliason, M. J., & Arthur, C. R. (1994). The assessment of at-risk infants and toddlers with the Bayley Mental Scale and the Battelle Developmental Inventory: Beyond the data. *Psychology in the Schools, 31,* 181-187.

70. Gyurke, J. S. (1994). A reply to Bagnato and Neisworth: Intelligent versus intelligence testing of preschoolers. *School Psychology Quarterly, 9,* 109-112.

71. Kaler, S. R., & Freeman, B. J. (1994). Analysis of environmental deprivation: Cognitive and social development in Romanian orphans. *Journal of Child Psychology and Psychiatry and Allied Disciplines, 35,* 769-781.

72. Kobe, F. H., Mulick, J. A., Rash, T. A., & Martin, J. (1994). Nonambulatory persons with profound mental retardation: Physical, developmental, and behavioral characteristics. *Research in Developmental Disabilities, 15,* 413-423.

73. Laucht, M., Esser, G., & Schmidt, M. H. (1994). Contrasting infant predictors of later cognitive functioning. *Journal of Child Psychology and Psychiatry and Allied Disciplines, 35,* 649-662.

74. Lavigne, J. V., Arend, R., Rosenbaum, D., Sinacore, J., Cicchetti, C., Binns, H. J., Christoffer, K. K., Hayford, J. R., & McGuire, P. (1994). Interrater reliability of the DSM-III-R with preschool children. *Journal of Abnormal Child Psychology, 22,* 679-690.

75. Leadbeater, B. J., & Bishop, S. J. (1994). Predictors of behavioral problems in preschool children of inner-city African-American and Puerto Rican adolescent mothers. *Child Development, 65,* 638–648.

76. Mellins, C. A., Levenson, R. L., Jr., Zawadzki, R., Kairam, R., & Weston, M. (1994). Effects of pediatric HIV infection and prenatal drug exposure on mental and psychomotor development. *Journal of Pediatric Psychology, 19,* 617-628.

77. Molfese, V. J., Holcomb, L., & Helwig, S. (1994). Biomedical and social-environmental influences cognitive and verbal abilities in children 1 to 3 years of age. *International Journal of Behavioral Development, 17,* 271-287.

78. Moss, H. A., Browers, P., Wolters, P. L., Wiener, L., Hersh, S., & Pizzo, P. A. (1994). The development of a Q-Sort behavioral rating procedure for pediatric HIV patients. *Journal of Pediatric Psychology, 19,* 27–46.

79. Nellis, L., & Gridley, B. E. (1994). Review of the Bayley Scales of Infant Development—Second Edition. *Journal of School Psychology, 32,* 201-209.

80. Osterling, J., & Dawson, G. (1994). Early recognition of children with autism: A study of first birthday home videotapes. *Journal of Autism and Developmental Disorders, 24,* 247-257.

81. Owen, M. T., & Mulvihill, B. A. (1994). Benefits of a parent education and support program in the first three years. *Family Relations, 43,* 206-212.

82. Pianta, R. C., & Egeland, B. (1994). Predictors of instability in children's mental test performance at 24, 48, and 96 months. *Intelligence, 18,* 145-163.

83. Poehlmann, J. A., & Fiese, B. H. (1994). The effects of divorce, maternal employment, and maternal social support on toddlers' home environments. *Journal of Divorce & Remarriage, 22*(1/2), 121-135.

84. Pollitt, E. (1994). Poverty and child development: Relevance of research in developing countries to the United States. *Child Development, 65,* 283–295.

85. Raggio, D. J., Massingale, T. W., & Bass, J. D. (1994). Comparison of Vineland Adaptive Behavior Scales—Survey Form age equivalent and standard score with the Bayley Mental Development Index. *Perceptual and Motor Skills, 79,* 203-206.

86. Rauch-Elnekave, H. (1994). Teenage motherhood: Its relationship to undetected learning problems. *Adolescence, 29,* 91-103.

87. Restall, G., & Magill-Evans, J. (1994). Play and preschool children with autism. *The American Journal of Occupational Therapy, 48,* 113-120.

88. Shapiro, E. G., McPhee, J. T., Abbott, A. A., & Sulzbacher, S. I. (1994). Minnesota Preschool Affect Rating Scales: Development, reliability, and validity. *Journal of Pediatric Psychology, 19,* 325–345.

89. Skuse, D., Pickles, A., Wolke, D., & Reilly, S. (1994). Postnatal growth and mental development: Evidence for a "sensitive period." *Journal of Child Psychology and Psychiatry and Allied Disciplines, 35,* 521-545.

90. Stewart, S. M., Kennard, B. D., Waller, D. A., & Fixler, D. (1994). Cognitive function in children who receive organ transplantation. *Health Psychology, 13,* 3-13.

91. Urquiza, A. J., Wirtz, S. J., Peterson, M. S., & Singer, V. A. (1994). Screening and evaluating abused and neglected children entering protective custody. *Child Welfare, 73,* 155–171.

92. van Beek, Y., Hopkins, B., Hoeksma, J. B., & Samson, J. F. (1994). Prematurity, posture and the development of looking behaviour during early communication. *Journal of Child Psychology and Psychiatry and Allied Disciplines, 35,* 1093-1107.

93. Vaughn, B. E., Goldberg, S., Atkinson, L., Marcovitch, S., MacGregor, D., & Seifer, R. (1994). Quality of toddler-mother attachment in children with Down Syndrome: Limits to interpretation of strange situation behavior. *Child Development, 65,* 95-108.

94. Weismer, S. E., Murray-Branch, J., & Miller, J. F. (1994). A prospective longitudinal study of language development in late talkers. *Journal of Speech and Hearing, 37,* 852–867.

95. Wolters, P. L., Brouwers, P., Moss, H. A., & Pizzo, P. A. (1994). Adaptive behavior of children with symptomatic HIV infection before and after zidovudine therapy. *Journal of Pediatric Psychology, 19,* 47–61.

96. Yoder, P. J., Davies, B., & Bishop, K. (1994). Adult interaction style effects on the language sampling and transcription process with children who have developmental disabilities. *American Journal on Mental Retardation, 99,* 270–282.

97. Yoder, P. J., Davies, B., Bishop, K., & Munson, L. (1994). Effect of adult continuing wh-questions on conversational participation in children with developmental disabilities. *Journal of Speech and Hearing Research, 37,* 193–204.

98. Yoder, P. J., Warren, S. F., Kim, K., & Gazdag, G. E. (1994). Facilitating prelinguistic communication skills in young children with developmental delay II: Systematic replication and extension. *Journal of Speech and Hearing Research, 37,* 841–851.

99. Biringen, Z., Emde, R. N., Campos, J. J., & Appelbaum, M. I. (1995). Affective reorganization in the infant, the mother, and the dyad: The role of upright locomotion and its timing. *Child Development, 66,* 499-514.

100. Burt, D. B., Loveland, K. A., Chen, Y-W., Chuang, A., Lewis, K.R., & Cherry, L. (1995). Aging in adults with Down Syndrome: Report from a longitudinal study. *American Journal on Mental Retardation, 100,* 262–270.

101. Campbell, F. A., & Ramey, C. T. (1995). Cognitive and school outcomes for high-risk African-American students at middle adolescence: Positive effects of early intervention. *American Educational Research Journal, 32,* 743–772.

102. Davidson, D. A. (1995). Physical abuse of preschoolers: Identification and intervention through occupational therapy. *The American Journal of Occupational Therapy, 49,* 235–243.

103. Heller, K. W., Alberto, P. A., & Romski, M. A. (1995). Effect of object and movement cues on receptive communication by preschool children with mental retardation. *American Journal on Mental Retardation, 99,* 510–521.

104. Lozoff, B., Park, A. M., Radan, A. E., & Wolf, A. W. (1995). Using the HOME Inventory with infants in Costa Rica. *International Journal of Behavioral Development, 18,* 277–295.

105. McCune, L. (1995). A normative study of representational play at the transition to language. *Developmental Psychology, 31,* 198-206.

106. Mundy, P., Kasari, C., Sigman, M., & Ruskin, E. (1995). Nonverbal communication and early language acquisition in children with Down Syndrome and in normally developing children. *Journal of Speech and Hearing, 38,* 157–167.

107. Phelps, L. (1995). Psychoeducational outcomes of fetal alcohol syndrome. *School Psychology Review, 24,* 200–212.

108. Plomin, R. (1995). Genetics and children's experiences in the family. *Journal of Child Psychology and Psychiatry and Allied Disciplines, 36,* 33-68.

109. Schatz, J., & Hamdam-Allen, G. (1995). Effects of age and IQ on adaptive behavior domains for children with autism. *Journal of Autism and Developmental Disorders, 25,* 51-60.

110. Segal, L. B., Oster, H., Cohen, M., Caspi, B., Myers, M., & Brown, D. (1995). Smiling and fussing in seven-month-old preterm and full-term black infants in the still-face situation. *Child Development, 66,* 1829–1843.

111. Slater, A. (1995). Individual differences in infancy and later IQ. *Journal of Child Psychology and Psychiatry and Allied Disciplines, 36,* 69-112.

112. Ulrich, B. D., & Ulrich, D. A. (1995). Spontaneous leg movements of infants with Down syndrome and nondisabled infants. *Child Development, 66,* 1844–1855.

113. van den Boom, D. C. (1995). Do first-year intervention effects endure? Follow-up during toddlerhood of a sample of Dutch irritable infants. *Child Development, 66,* 1798–1816.

114. Yoder, P. J., Spruytenberg, H., Edwards, A., & Davies, B. (1995). Effect of verbal routine contexts and expansions on gains in the mean length of utterance in children with developmental delays. *Language, Speech, and Hearing Services in Schools, 26,* 21–32.

115. Zelazo, P. R., Kearsley, R. B., & Stuck, D. M. (1995). Mental representations for visual sequences: Increased speed of central processing from 22 to 32 months. *Intelligence, 20,* 41-63.

116. Burchinal, M. R., Follmer, A., & Bryant, D. M. (1996). The relations of maternal social support and family structure with maternal responsiveness and child outcomes among African American families. *Developmental Psychology, 32,* 1073–1083.

117. Dittrichová, J., Brichácek, V., Mandys, F., Paul, K., Sobotková, D., Tautermannová, M., Vondrácek, J., & Zezuláková, J. (1996). The relationship of early behaviour to later developmental outcome for preterm children. *International Journal of Behavioral Development, 19,* 517–532.

118. Molfese, V. J., DiLalla, L. F., & Lovelace, L. (1996). Perinatal, home environment, and infant measures as successful predictors of preschool cognitive and verbal abilities. *International Journal of Behavioral Development, 19,* 101–119.

119. Moss, H. A., Wolters, P. L., Browers, P., Hendricks, M. L., & Pizzo, P. A. (1996). Impairment of expressive behavior in pediatric HIV-infected patients with evidence of CNS disease. *Journal of Pediatric Psychology, 21,* 379–400.

120. Riksen-Walraven, J. M., Meij, J. T., Hubbard, F. O., & Zevalkink, J. (1996). Intervention in lower-class Surinam-Dutch families: Effects on mothers and infants. *International Journal of Behavioral Development, 19,* 739–756.

121. Robinson, B. F., & Mervis, C. B. (1996). Extrapolated raw scores for the second edition of the Bayley Scales of Infant Development. *American Journal on Mental Retardation, 100,* 666–671.

122. Ross, G., Boatright, S., Auld, P. A. M., & Nass, R. (1996). Specific cognitive abilities in 2-year-old children with subependymal and mild intraventricular hemorrhage. *Brain and Cognition, 32,* 1–13.

123. Ross, G., Lipper, E., & Auld, P. A. M. (1996). Cognitive abilities and early precursors of learning disabilities in very-low-birthweight children with normal intelligence and normal neurological status. *International Journal of Behavioral Development, 19,* 563–580.

124. Teo, A., Carlson, E., Mathieu, P. J., Egeland, B., & Sroufe, L. A. (1996). A prospective longitudinal study of psychosocial predictors of achievement. *Journal of School Psychology, 34,* 285–306.

125. Waterhouse, L., Morris, R., Allen, D., Dunn, M., Fein, D., Feinstein, C., Rapin, I., & Wing, L. (1996). Diagnosis and classification in autism. *Journal of Autism and Developmental Disorders, 26,* 59–86.

126. Watson, J. E., Kirby, R. S., Kelleher, K. J., & Bradley, R. H. (1996). Effects of poverty on home environment: An analysis of three-year outcome data for low birth weight premature infants. *Journal of Pediatric Psychology, 21,* 419–431.

127. Harcovitch, S., Goldberg, S., Gold, A., Washington, J., Wasson, C., Krekewich, K., & Handley-Derry, M. (1997). Determinants of behavioural problems in Romanian children adopted in Ontario. *International Journal of Behavioral Development, 20,* 17–31.

128. Lyons-Ruth, K., Easterbrooks, M. A., & Cibelli, C. D. (1997). Infant attachment strategies, infant mental lag, and maternal depressive symptoms: Predic-

tors of internalizing and externalizing problems at age 7. *Developmental Psychology, 33*, 681–692.

129. Molfese, V. J., & Acheson, S. (1997). Infant and preschool mental and verbal abilities: How are infant scores related to preschool scores? *International Journal of Behavioral Development, 20*, 595–607.

130. Phillips, K., & Matheny, A. P., Jr. (1997). Evidence for genetic influence on both cross-situation and situation-specific components of behavior. *Journal of Personality and Social Psychology, 73*, 129–138.

Review of the Bayley Scales of Infant Development: Second Edition by CARL J. DUNST, Research Scientist, Orelena Hawks Puckett Institute, Asheville, NC:

The Bayley Scales of Infant Development: Second Edition (BSID-II) is an individually administered scale assessing a number of aspects of both the mental and motor development of children from birth to 42 months of age. The instrument also includes a Behavior Rating Scale permitting the measurement of a number of different aspects of behavior style and motor quality. The Bayley scales are perhaps the best known and most widely used infant scales, and the long awaited revision provides a much needed contemporary assessment tool for measuring emerging infant and toddler intellectual and psychomotor functioning.

The Mental and Motor scales are formatted much like their predecessor with age levels being used to order and group the items. The Mental scale includes 64 new items and the Motor scale has 44 new items. Twenty-nine and 8 items, respectively, have been deleted from the Mental and Motor scales. The Behavior Rating Scale is a new instrument and replaces the Infant Behavior Record. The recording forms for all three scales are formatted in a user-friendly manner, including enough information to aid in proper administration, yet are not so busy as to be distracting.

The manual is at first glance a bit intimidating, but is actually a major improvement over the manual for the first edition of the scale. Information pertaining to the history of the scale, development and standardization of the revision, administration and interpretation, and reliability and validity is extensive and extremely useful in providing a complete picture of the instrument.

The care taken in both the standardization of the instrument and the establishment of the reliability and validity of the scales is to be commended. Taken together, the psychometric evidence reported in the manual as well as that now being reported independently (Goldstein, Fogle, Wieber, & O'Shea, 1995) far exceeds generally accepted standards (American Educational Research Association, American Psychological Association, & National Council on Measurement in Education, 1985).

Notwithstanding the accolades of this reviewer and others (e.g., Nellis & Gridley, 1994), the revision does have certain problems and limitations. One limitation, as was the case with the first edition, is the inability to calculate Mental and Motor development indices (MDIs and PDIs) below 50 although methods have been developed for estimating MDIs and PDIs that fall below this score (Robinson & Mervis, 1996). This seems especially problematic in light of the claims made about the value of the scales for assessing children with disabilities (manual, pp. 4–5). Much more problematic is the implicit assertion that the scales have value for *developing* Individualized Family Service Plans (IFSPs) required for children participating in early intervention programs as part of the Individuals with Disabilities Education Act (Public Law 101-476). Whereas the scale clearly has utility as a diagnostic tool, it is not viewed as an appropriate assessment instrument having treatment utility (Neisworth & Bagnato, 1996) nor is it currently recognized as an intervention tool as part of recommended practices in early intervention and early childhood special education (Odom & McLean, 1996). This reviewer has administered hundreds of Bayley Scales and has overseen the administration of the scales by psychologists with children participating in several early intervention programs, and the scales simply have limited value as a tool for informing practice. Normative scales like the BSID-II may be useful for monitoring changes in the mental and motor status of children participating in early intervention programs, but they are not appropriate as instruments for identifying behavior goals for intervention. The BSID-II was not designed for this purpose, and its use for this purpose is not warranted.

The BSID-II will most likely be widely used as the instrument of choice for assessing infant development in clinical settings and for research purposes. As long as the scales are used for the purposes for which they were designed, they are highly recommended.

REVIEWER'S REFERENCES

American Educational Research Association, American Psychological Association, & National Council on Measurement in Education. (1985). *Standards for educational and psychological testing.* Washington, DC: American Psychological Association, Inc.

Nellis, L., & Gridley, B. E. (1994). Review of the Bayley Scales of Infant Development—second edition. *Journal of School Psychology, 32*, 201–209.

Goldstein, D., Fogle, E., Wieber, J., & O'Shea, T. M. (1995). Comparison of the Bayley Scales of Infant Development—second edition and the Bayley Scales of Infant Development with premature infants. *Journal of Psychoeducational Assessment, 13*, 391–396.

Neisworth, J. T., & Bagnato, S. J. (1996). Assessment for early intervention: Emerging themes. In S. Odom & M. McLean (Eds.), *Early intervention/early childhood special education: Recommended practices* (pp. 23–57). Austin, TX: PRO-ED, Inc.

Odom, S. L., & McLean, M. E. (Eds.) (1996). *Early intervention/early childhood special education: Recommended practices.* Austin, TX: PRO-ED, Inc.

Review of the Bayley Scales of Infant Development, Second Edition by MARK H. FUGATE, Assistant Professor of School Psychology, Alfred University, Alfred, NY:

The Bayley Scales of Infant Development, Second Edition (BSID-II) is an individually administered instrument designed to measure the current developmental functioning of infants and children ages 1 to 42 months (3 1/2 years). The BSID-II is a revision of the Bayley Scales of Infant Development (1969) and contains many structural similarities to the previous scale.

Upon initial inspection the BSID-II appears much the same as the original Bayley Scales of Infant Development (BSID). Similar to the original scale the BSID-II consists of three scales: the Mental scale, the Motor scale, and a behavior rating scale. As is often typical of test revisions the authors of the BSID-II have updated the normative data, improved items and stimulus materials, and improved the utility of the BSID, while maintaining the basic properties of the original instrument. The most significant changes evident in the BSID-II include: a substantial revision of the Behavior Rating Scale (BRS; previously the Infant Behavior Record); more extensive content coverage in the Motor and Mental scales; and an expansion of the age range to 42 months (an extension of 12 months beyond the BSID).

The Mental scale should not be considered an "IQ" measure as the items are not generally concerned with functions generally measured by intelligence scales. Prior to 12 months of age, the Mental scale of the BSID-II essentially measures the sensory and perceptual development. Items are highly dependent upon auditory and visual skills, although early vocalization, memory, and social skill development are also assessed. Beyond 12 months, the mental scale becomes more oriented toward vocalization and language skill development, problem solving, generalization, classification, social skills, and the development of early number concepts.

The Motor scale of the BSID-II measures the development of both gross and fine motor skills. Prior to 12 months of age the Motor scale assesses basic arm and leg movement, and motor skills associated with rolling, crawling, sitting, standing, and cruising. Beyond age 12 months, the Motor scale becomes more oriented toward the development of fine motor skills such as hand control, grasping, and the manipulation of objects, although there is continued evaluation of gross motor skills such as walking, running, and jumping. In both the Mental and Motor scales items are arranged in a hierarchical manner where later occurring items are more difficult than earlier items.

The Behavior Rating Scale evaluates qualitative aspects of the child's behavior during assessment. Prior to 6 months of age the BRS is primarily oriented toward the functions of attention and arousal. Beyond age 6 months the BRS becomes increasingly concerned with orientation toward, and interactions with, the examiner and caregiver, quality of movement, and emotional regulation. In addition to a composite Total Score, the BRS also estimates behavioral qualities across four factors: Attention/Arousal (ages 1 to 5 months), Orientation/Engagement (ages 6 to 42 months), Emotional Regulation (ages 6 to 42 months), and Motor Quality (ages 1 to 42 months). Information from the BRS is designed to supplement information from the Mental and Motor scales, and all three scales are believed to make complementary, yet somewhat independent, contributions to the assessment process.

MATERIALS. Stimulus materials for the BSID-II include a variety of toys, blocks, shapes, form boards, common household articles, and a stimulus booklet. Care has been taken to provide materials that are safe for use with young children. In addition to materials found in the test kit, the examiner needs to provide paper, a stopwatch, facial tissues, plastic bags, and a set of stairs. Directions for the construction of the stairs are provided in the manual. This complex inventory of stimulus materials fits neatly into trays and pockets within the test case. With the exception of the stairs, the entire test kit is reasonably portable. Overall, stimulus materials are attractive, appropriately engaging for children, well organized, and easy to use.

The 374-page manual is generally well organized and complete. The authors explain the nature and purpose of the BSID-II; there is extensive information concerning the administration, scoring, and interpretation; norms tables and other interpretive aids are well organized and quickly located within the manual; and appropriate attention is devoted to the development, standardization, reliability, and validity of the scale. Additionally, the BSID-II record forms are easy to follow, provide appropriately detailed administration guides, and include a number of spaces for recording clinical observations.

ADMINISTRATION, SCORING, AND INTERPRETATION. Estimated administration time for the BSID-II is 25 to 35 minutes for children under 15 months old and up to 60 minutes for children from 16 to 42 months. The time expectation will push the attention limits of many infants and young children; as a result it may be necessary to take multiple breaks in administration or complete the assessment across multiple sessions. Individual behavior categories on the BRS are rated using a 5-point scale. Behavioral definitions are given for each item in an attempt to increase the consistency of ratings.

For the Mental and Motor scales there is a specified "item set" and order of presentation for each age group. However, flexibility in administration order is permitted if necessary to help maintain the child's interest. Directions for administration and scoring of individual items are clearly outlined in the manual, as are the basal and ceiling rules for each item set. The item sets established for the BSID-II are the result of the Rasch scaling approach used in test construction. Examiners who are unfamiliar with this "item set" approach should give particular attention to the directions for administration in cases where basal and ceiling limits are not met (see manual, p. 42). Administration of items in the Mental and Motor scales is generally uncomplicated. Some items require the assistance of the child's caregiver in an attempt to elicit required responses.

For the Mental and Motor scales, raw scores are converted into the Mental Developmental Index (MDI) and Psychomotor Developmental Index (PDI) respectively. The indexes are presented as standard scores (M = 100, SD = 15). Confidence intervals (90% and 95%) are also presented in the norms tables. Raw scores for the BRS Total Score and individual factor score are converted into percentile ranks. Interpretation and presentation of the results would be enhanced if percentile ranks were also provided for the Mental and Motor scales, and if standard scores were provided for the BRS. The BSID-II also provides a mechanism for estimating developmental scores. However, caution should be used when interpreting these scores (see discussion in manual, pp. 49, 229, & 324).

Interpretation of the BSID-II should begin with the MDI, PDI, and BRS total score, as these are the most reliable scores available. The manual (p. 228) also provides general classification guidelines relative to MDI and PDI scores. Significant differences between MDI and PDI scores are not uncommon (see manual, pp. 198–199) and should be interpreted carefully. Because the subscores of the BRS tend to be somewhat less reliable than the total score, factor scores for the BRS should be interpreted more tentatively than the total score. The examiner also needs to proceed with extreme caution if he/she chooses to interpret facet scores on the Motor and Mental scales or responses to individual items. In general, the administration, item scoring, and interpretation of the BSID-II will be enhanced if the examiner is experienced in the assessment of young children and has a thorough understanding of child developmental research methodology and theoretical constructs.

TEST CONSTRUCTION AND STANDARDIZATION. According to the manual, the BSID-II was not developed to reflect any individual theory of early childhood development. In contrast, items for the BSID-II were drawn from a broad range of child developmental research. Individual items of the BSID-II represent contemporary concepts regarding infant recognition memory and habituation of attention, infant and childhood visual preference and perception, language development, personal and social development, the development of problem-solving skills, and the development of number concepts. In some cases individual items represent practical adaptation of actual experimental paradigms. Other items may reflect more conceptual adaptations. In either case, the BSID-II appears to be well grounded in current theory and research regarding infant and child development. Individual items were analyzed for ethnic bias using review by a panel of experts, partial correlation analyses, and the Rasch Parameter Estimation Technique (see manual, pp. 23–24). Items that demonstrated significant group bias were removed from the final edition of the BSID-II.

The BSID-II was standardized on 1,700 infants and children between the ages of 1 and 42 months. The sample spanned 17 age levels and contained 100 individuals (50 males and 50 females) at each level. Age intervals occur monthly up to 12 months (with the exception of ages 7, 9, and 11) and every 3 months thereafter to the age of 30 months, and then at 6-month intervals. The standardization sample closely approximates the regional, ethnicity, and parent education characteristics of children 1 to 42 months of age as determined by the 1988 U.S. Census data. There was a conscious effort on the part of test developers to limit the standardization sample to children who were not diagnosed with medical, psychological, or behavioral problems. This choice was made to enable examiners to compare individual child performance to that of normal developing peers (Gyurke, 1994). Overall, the standardization sample is more than adequate.

RELIABILITY. The BSID-II has moderate to high internal consistency reliability coefficients for the Mental scale (average .88; range .78 to .93), Motor scale (average .84; range .75 to .87), and Behavior Rating Scale Total Score (average .88; range .82 to .92) across the 17 age groups represented in the standardization sample. Compared to the BRS Total Score, there is a decrease in the internal consistency reliability coefficients for the BRS factors across all age groups: Attention/Arousal (average .74; range .64 to .82); Orientation/Engagement (average .87; range .84 to .90); Emotional Regulation (average .84; range .73 to .90); and Motor Quality (average .82; range .75 to .86). Test-retest reliability coefficients are more variable. BRS coefficients are consistently lower than stability coefficients for the Mental scale and Motor scale (testing intervals ranged from 1 to 16 days; median interval was 4 days). These test-retest results are not surprising as the behavior and day-to-day functioning of infants and young children is generally quite variable. Although the reliability estimates for the BSID-II are within an acceptable range as compared to other measures of early childhood development, these estimates are somewhat marginal relative to established criteria for making individual diagnostic decisions (Salvia & Ysseldyke, 1991). Therefore, one should interpret the results of the BSID-II carefully, noting that scores represent behavior and responses for a give day or time.

VALIDITY. The BSID-II manual presents extensive information regarding the construct and criterion validity of this instrument. The construct validity evidence consists of intercorrelation data for the Mental and Motor scales, exploratory factor analysis of the BRS, and intercorrelations of MDI and PDI scores with other measures of preschool cognitive functioning. Intercorrelations between items on the Mental and Motor scales suggest that items appear to be more highly correlated with items

within the scale in which the item is placed than with the opposite scale. Similarly, correlations between the MDI and PDI are reported to be in the low to moderate range. Data are also presented that demonstrate the MDI tends to correlate more highly with other measures of preschool cognitive functioning (WPPSI-R, MSCA, DAS; manual, pp. 216–218) than the PDI. These data support the assumption that the Mental and Motor scales are measuring separate and somewhat unrelated abilities. The strong correlations between the MDI, WPPSI-R (.73), and MSCA (.79) provide evidence of criterion validity for children at the older age range (36 to 42 months) of the BSID-II.

The manual presents data from exploratory factor analysis of the BRS to support the construct validity of the rating scale. This analysis appears to support the 2-factor assumption for young infants (1 to 5 months) and the 3-factor solution for older infants and children (6 to 42 months). Data are also provided from a series of studies with children demonstrating a variety of developmental disabilities. These results seem to support the discriminant validity of the BSID-II. Collectively, the validity information provided in the manual tends to support the construct and criterion-related validity of the BSID-II. However, the evidence is thin in some respects. Exploratory factor analysis of the Mental and Motor scales would be helpful, as would confirmatory factor analysis of the entire BSID-II. Also, further study of the validity of the scale for younger children (1 to 30 months) and children with special needs would be advantageous.

SUMMARY. The Bayley Scales of Infant Development, Second Edition is an individually administered test designed to assess the current developmental functioning of children ages 1 to 42 months. The items included in the Mental and Motor scales are well grounded in theory and research, and appear sufficiently interesting to maintain the attention of young children. The test is well standardized and has good reliability to fulfill its purposes. As is typical of instruments designed to assess children, reliability of BSID-II results appears to be affected by the natural variability for children's behavior and functioning. Therefore, care should be exercised when interpreting the BSID-II. Evidence for the validity of the BSID-II presented in the manual provides initial support for the use of the instrument; however, additional research regarding the validity of the BSID-II is required.

REVIEWER'S REFERENCES

Salvia, J., & Ysseldyke, J. E. (1991). *Assessment* (5th ed.). Boston: Houghton Mifflin.

Gyurke, J. S. (1994). Psychological Corporation responds to concerns about Bayley Scales. *NASP Communique, 23*(1), 30.

[30]
Beck Anxiety Inventory [1993 Edition].

Purpose: "Measures the severity of anxiety in adults and adolescents."

Population: Adults and adolescents.

Publication Dates: 1987–1993.

Acronym: BAI.

Scores: Total score only.

Administration: Group or individual.

Price Data, 1994: $46 per complete kit including 25 record forms and manual ('93, 23 pages); $25.50 per 25 record forms; $22.50 per manual.

Foreign Language Edition: Also available in Spanish.

Time: (5–10) minutes.

Authors: Aaron T. Beck and Robert A. Steer.

Publisher: The Psychological Corporation.

Cross References: See T4:267 (2 references).

TEST REFERENCES

1. Sokol, L., Beck, A. T., Greenberg, R. L., Wright, F. D., & Berchick, R. J. (1989). Cognitive therapy of panic disorder: A nonpharmacological alternative. *The Journal of Nervous and Mental Disease, 177*, 711-716.

2. Middleton, H. C. (1990). An enhanced hypotensive response to clonidine can still be found in panic patients despite psychological treatment. *Journal of Anxiety Disorders, 4*, 213-219.

3. Middleton, H. C. (1990). Cardiovascular dystonia in recovered panic patients. *Journal of Affective Disorders, 19*, 229-236.

4. Beck, A. T., & Steer, R. A. (1991). Relationship between the Beck Anxiety Inventory and the Hamilton Anxiety Rating Scale with anxious outpatients. *Journal of Anxiety Disorders, 5*, 213-223.

5. Dyck, M. J. (1991). Positive and negative attitudes mediating suicide ideation. *Suicide and Life-Threatening Behavior, 21*, 360–373.

6. Clark, D. B., Leslie, M. I., & Jacob, R. G. (1992). Balance complaints and panic disorder: A clinical study of panic members of a self-help group for balance disorders. *Journal of Anxiety Disorders, 6*, 47-53.

7. Fydrich, T., Dowdall, D., & Chambless, D. L. (1992). Reliability and validity of the Beck Anxiety Inventory. *Journal of Anxiety Disorders, 6*, 55-61.

8. Öst, L. G., Hellström, K., & Kåver, A. (1992). One versus five sessions of exposure in the treatment of injection phobia. *Behavior Therapy, 23*, 263–282.

9. Otto, M. W., Pollack, M. H., Sachs, G. S., & Rosenbaum, J. F. (1992). Hypochondriacal concerns, anxiety, sensitivity, and panic disorder. *Journal of Anxiety Disorders, 6*, 93-104.

10. Borden, J. W., Lowenbraun, P. B., Wolff, P. L., & Jones, A. (1993). Self-focused attention in panic disorder. *Cognitive Therapy and Research, 17*, 413-425.

11. Gidycz, C. A., Coble, C. N., Latham, L., & Layman, M. J. (1993). Sexual assault experience in adulthood and prior victimization experiences. *Psychology of Women Quarterly, 17*, 151-168.

12. Jacob, R. G., Woody, S. R., Clark, D. B., Lilienfeld, S. O., Hirsch, B. E., Kucera, G. D., Furman, J. M., & Durrant, J. D. (1993). Discomfort with space and motion: A possible marker for vestibular dysfunction assessed by the Situational Characteristics Questionnaire. *Journal of Psychopathology and Behavioral Assessment, 15*, 299–324.

13. Jolly, J. B. (1993). A multi-method test of the cognitive content-specificity hypothesis in young adolescents. *Journal of Anxiety Disorders, 7*, 223-233.

14. Jolly, J. B., Aruffo, J. F., Wherry, J. N., & Livingston, R. (1993). The utility of the Beck Anxiety Inventory with inpatient adolescents. *Journal of Anxiety Disorders, 7*, 95-106.

15. Osman, A., Barrios, F. X., Aukes, D., Osman, J. R., & Markway, K. (1993). The Beck Anxiety Inventory: Psychometric properties in a community population. *Journal of Psychopathology and Behavioral Assessment, 15*, 287–297.

16. Steer, R. A., Ranieri, W. F., Beck, A. T., & Clark, D. A. (1993). Further evidence for the validity of the Beck Anxiety Inventory with psychiatric outpatients. *Journal of Anxiety Disorders, 7*, 195-205.

17. Beck, J. G., & Zebb, B. J. (1994). Behavioral assessment and treatment of panic disorder: Current status, future directions. *Behavior Therapy, 25*, 581–611.

18. Borden, J. W. (1994). Panic disorder and suicidality: Prevalence and risk factors. *Journal of Anxiety Disorders, 8*, 217-225.

19. Brown, H. D., Kosslyn, J. M., Breiter, H. C., Baer, L., & Jenike, M. A. (1994). Can patients with obsessive-compulsive disorder discriminate between percepts and mental images? A signal detection analysis. *Journal of Abnormal Psychology, 103*, 445-454.

20. Burgess, E., & Haaga, D. A. F. (1994). The Positive Automatic Thoughts Questionnaire (ATQ-P) and the Automatic Thoughts Questionnaire—Revised (ATQ-RP): Equivalent measures of positive thinking? *Cognitive Therapy and Research, 18*, 15-23.

21. Clark, D. A., Beck, A. T., & Beck, J. S. (1994). Symptom differences in major depression, dysthymia, panic disorder, and generalized anxiety disorder. *American Journal of Psychiatry, 151*, 205-209.

22. Clark, D. A., Steer, R. A., & Beck, A. T. (1994). Common and specific dimensions of self-reported anxiety and depression: Implications for the cognitive and tripartite models. *Journal of Abnormal Psychology, 103*, 645-654.

23. Clark, D. M., Salkovskis, P. M., Hackmann, A., Middleton, H., Anastasiades, P., & Gelder, M. (1994). A comparison of cognitive therapy, applied relaxation and imipramine in the treatment of panic disorder. *British Journal of Psychiatry, 164*, 759-769.

24. Cox, B. J., Direnfeld, D. M., Swinson, R. P., & Norton, G. R. (1994). Suicidal ideation and suicide attempts in panic disorder and social phobia. *American Journal of Psychiatry, 151*, 882-887.

25. Durham, R. C., Murphy, T., Allan, T., Richard, K., Treliving, L. R., & Fenton, G. W. (1994). Cognitive therapy, analytic psychotherapy and anxiety management training for generalized anxiety disorder. *British Journal of Psychiatry, 165*, 315-323.

26. Goldstein, A. J., & Feske, U. (1994). Eye movement desensitization and reprocessing for panic disorder: A case series. *Journal of Anxiety Disorders, 8*, 351-362.

27. Joiner, T. E., Jr. (1994). Contagious depression: Existence, specificity to depressed symptoms, and the role of reassurance seeking. *Journal of Personality and Social Psychology, 67*, 287-296.

28. Jolly, J. B., Dyck, M. J., Kramer, T. A., & Wherry, J. N. (1994). Integration of positive and negative affectivity and cognitive content-specificity: Improved discrimination of anxious and depressive symptoms. *Journal of Abnormal Psychology, 103*, 544-552.

29. Jolly, J. B., & Dykman, R. A. (1994). Using self-report data to differentiate anxious and depressive symptoms in adolescents: Cognitive content specificity and global distress? *Cognitive Therapy and Research, 18*, 25-37.

30. Jolly, J. B., & Kramer, T. A. (1994). The hierarchical arrangement of internalizing cognitions. *Cognitive Therapy and Research, 18*, 1-14.

31. Kaspi, S. P., Otto, M. W., Pollack, M. H., Eppinger, S., & Rosenbaum, J. F. (1994). Premenstrual exacerbation of symptoms in women with panic disorder. *Journal of Anxiety Disorders, 8*, 131-138.

32. Khawaja, N. G., Oei, T. P. S., & Baglioni, A. J. (1994). Modification of the catastrophic cognitions questionnaire (CCQ-M) for normals and patients: Exploratory and LISREL analyses. *Journal of Psychopathology and Behavioral Assessment, 16*, 325–342.

33. Lecci, L., Karoly, P., Briggs, C., & Kuhn, K. (1994). Specificity and generality of motivational components in depression: A personal projects analysis. *Journal of Abnormal Psychology, 103*, 404-408.

34. McDermut, W., & Haaga, D. A. F. (1994). Cognitive balance and specificity in anxiety and depression. *Cognitive Therapy and Research, 18*, 333-352.

35. Rifai, A. H., George, C. J., Stack, J. A., Mann, J. J., & Reynolds, C. F. (1994). Hopelessness in suicide attempters after acute treatment of major depression in late life. *American Journal of Psychiatry, 151*, 1687-1690.

36. Sobell, L. C., Toneatto, T., & Sobell, M. (1994). Behavioral assessment and treatment planning for alcohol, tobacco, and other drug problems: Current status with an emphasis on clinical applications. *Behavior Therapy, 25*, 533–580.

37. Solomon, A., & Haaga, P. A. F. (1994). Positive and negative aspects of sociotropy and autonomy. *Journal of Psychopathology and Behavioral Assessment, 16*, 243–252.

38. Steer, R. A., Clark, D. A., & Ranieri, W. F. (1994). Symptom dimensions of the SCL-90-R: A test of the tripartite model of anxiety and depression. *Journal of Personality Assessment, 62*, 525-536.

39. Stein, M. B., Asmundson, G. J. G., Ireland, D., & Walker, J. R. (1994). Panic disorder in patients attending a clinic for vestibular disorders. *American Journal of Psychiatry, 151*, 1697-1700.

40. Alford, B. A., & Gerrity, D. M. (1995). The specificity of sociotropy-autonomy personality dimensions to depression vs. anxiety. *Journal of Clinical Psychology, 51*, 190-195.

41. Alford, B. A., Lester, J. M., Patel, R. J., Buchanan, J. P., & Giunta, L. C. (1995). Hopelessness predicts future depressive symptoms: A prospective analysis of cognitive vulnerability and cognitive content specificity. *Journal of Clinical Psychology, 51*, 331-339.

42. Carter, A. S., Grigorenko, E. L., & Pauls, D. L. (1995). A Russian adaptation of the Child Behavior Checklist: Psychometric properties and associations with child and maternal affective symptomatology and family functioning. *Journal of Abnormal Child Psychology, 23*, 661–684.

43. Dugas, M. J., Letarte, H., Rheaume, J., Freeston, M. H., & Ladouceur, R. (1995). Worry and problem solving: Evidence of a specific relationship. *Cognitive Therapy and Research, 19*, 109-120.

44. Freeston, M. H., Ladouceur, R., Provencher, M., & Blais, F. (1995). Strategies used with intrusive thoughts: Context, appraisal, mood, and efficacy. *Journal of Anxiety Disorders, 9*, 201-215.

45. Gidycz, C. A., Hanson, K., & Layman, M. J. (1995). A prospective analysis of the relationships among sexual assault experiences. *Psychology of Women Quarterly, 19*, 5-29.

46. Gillis, M. M., Haaga, D. A. F., & Ford, G. T. (1995). Normative values for the Beck Anxiety Inventory, Fear Questionnaire, Penn State Worry Questionnaire, and Social Phobia and Anxiety Inventory. *Psychological Assessment, 7*, 450–455.

47. Haaga, D. A. F., Fine, J. A., Terrill, D. R., Stewart, B. L., & Beck, A. J. (1995). Social problem-solving deficits, dependency, and depressive symptoms. *Cognitive Therapy and Research, 19*, 147–158.

48. Joiner, T. E. (1995). The price of soliciting and receiving negative feedback: Self-verification theory as a vulnerability to depression theory. *Journal of Abnormal Psychology, 104*, 364-372.

49. Joiner, T. E., Jr., & Metalsky, G. I. (1995). A prospective test of an integrative interpersonal theory of depression: A naturalistic study of college roommates. *Journal of Personality and Social Psychology, 69*, 778–788.

50. Kumar, G., & Steer, R. A. (1995). Psychosocial correlates of suicidal ideation in adolescent psychiatric inpatients. *Suicide and Life-Threatening Behavior, 25*, 339–346.

51. Miguel, E. C., Coffey, B. J., Baer, L., Savage, C. R., Rauch, S.L., & Jenike, M. A. (1995). Phenomenology of intentional repetitive behaviors in obsessive-compulsive disorder and Tourette's disorder. *Journal of Clinical Psychiatry, 56*, 246–255.

52. Neron, S., Lacroix, D., & Chaput, Y. (1995). Group vs. Individual cognitive behaviour therapy in panic disorder: An open clinical trial with a six month follow-up. *Canadian Journal of Behavioural Science, 27*, 379–392.

53. Pawluk, L. K., Hurwitz, T. D., Schluter, J. L., Ullevig, C., & Mahowald, M. W. (1995). Psychiatric morbidity in narcoleptics on chronic high dose methylphenidate therapy. *The Journal of Nervous and Mental Disease, 183*, 45-48.

54. Reynolds, W. M., & Kobak, K. A. (1995). Reliability and validity of the Hamilton Depression Inventory: A paper-and-pencil version of the Hamilton Depression Rating Scale clinical interview. *Psychological Assessment, 7*, 472–483.

55. Riley, W. T., McCormick, M. G. F., Simon, E. M., Stack, K., Pushkin, Y., Overstreet, M. M., Carmona, J. J., & Magakian, C. (1995). Effects of alprazolam doses on the induction and habituation processes during behavioral panic induction treatment. *Journal of Anxiety Disorders, 9*, 217-227.

56. Romach, M., Busto, U., Somer, G., Kaplan, H. L., & Sellers, E. (1995). Clinical aspects of chronic use of alprazolam and lorazepan. *American Journal of Psychiatry, 152*, 1161–1167.

57. Steer, R. A., Beck, A. T., & Beck, J. S. (1995). Sex effect sizes of the Beck Anxiety Inventory for psychiatric outpatients matched by age and principal disorders. *Assessment, 2*, 31-38.

58. Steer, R. A., Clark, D. A., Beck, A. T., & Ranieri, W. F. (1995). Common and specific dimensions of self-reported anxiety and depression: A replication. *Journal of Abnormal Psychology, 104*, 542–545.

59. Steer, R. A., Kumar, G., Ranieri, W. F., & Beck, A. T. (1995). Use of the Beck Anxiety Inventory with adolescent psychiatric outpatients. *Psychological Reports, 76*, 459–465.

60. Stein, M. B., Kirk, P., Prabhu, V., Grott, M., & Terepa, M. (1995). Mixed anxiety-depression in a primary-care clinic. *Journal of Affective Disorders, 34*, 79-84.

61. Watson, D., Weber, K., Assenheimer, J. S., Clark, L. A., Strauss, M. E., & McCormick, R. A. (1995). Testing a tripartite model: I. Evaluating convergent and discriminant validity of Anxiety and Depression Symptom Scales. *Journal of Abnormal Psychology, 104*, 3-14.

62. Borrelli, B., Niaura, R., Keuthen, N. J., Goldstein, M. G., DePue, J. D., Murphy, C., & Abrams, D. B. (1996). Development of major depressive disorder during smoking-cessation treatment. *Journal of Clinical Psychiatry, 57*, 534–538.

63. Clark, D. A., Steer, R. A., Beck, A. T., & Snow, D. (1996). Is the relationship between anxious and depressive cognitions and symptoms linear or curvilinear? *Cognitive Therapy and Research, 20*, 135–154.

64. Horowitz, M., Sonneborn, D., Sugahara, C., & Maercker, A. (1996). Self-regard: A new measure. *American Journal of Psychiatry, 153*, 382–385.

65. Jacob, R. G., Furman, J. M., Durrant, J. D., & Turner, S. M. (1996). Panic, agoraphobia, and vestibular dysfunction. *American Journal of Psychiatry, 153*, 503–512.

66. Jolly, J. B., & Wiesner, D. C. (1996). Psychometric properties of the Automatic Thoughts Questionnaire—Positive with inpatient adolescents. *Cognitive Therapy and Research, 20*, 481–498.

67. Kumar, G., Steer, R. A., & Deblinger, E. (1996). Problems in differentiating sexually from nonsexually abused adolescent psychiatric inpatients by self-reported anxiety, depression, internalization, and externalization. *Child Abuse & Neglect, 20*, 1079–1086.

68. McKellar, J. D., Malcarne, V. L., & Ingram, R. E. (1996). States-of-mind and negative affectivity. *Cognitive Therapy and Research, 20*, 235–246.

69. Schwartz, J. A. J., & Koenig, L. J. (1996). Response styles and negative affect among adolescents. *Cognitive Therapy and Research, 20*, 13–36.

70. Stein, M. B., Baird, A., & Walker, J. R. (1996). Social phobia in adults with stuttering. *American Journal of Psychiatry, 153*, 278–280.

71. Taylor, S., Koch, W. J., Woody, S., & McLean, P. (1996). Anxiety sensitivity and depression: How are they related? *Journal of Abnormal Psychology, 105*, 474–479.

72. Trappler, B., & Friedman, S. (1996). Posttraumatic stress disorder in survivors of the Brooklyn Bridge shooting. *American Journal of Psychiatry, 153*, 705–707.

73. Wetherell, J. L., & Areán, P. A. (1997). Psychometric evaluation of the Beck Anxiety Inventory with older medical patients. *Psychological Assessment, 9*, 136–144.

Review of the Beck Anxiety Inventory by E. THOMAS DOWD, Professor of Psychology, Kent State University, Kent, OH:

Aaron T. Beck, M.D., and his associates have designed well-constructed and widely-used tests for years, with the twin virtues of simplicity and brevity. The Beck Anxiety Inventory (BAI) is no exception. At 21 items, it is certainly short and easy to understand as well. Each of the 21 items represents an anxiety symptom that is rated for severity on a 4-point Likert scale (0–3), ranging from *Not at all* to *Severely; I could barely stand it.* The scoring is easy, as the points for each item are simply added to form the total score.

The test kit I received contained a brief manual, several answer sheets for the BAI as well as for the BDI and the BHS, and a complete computer-scoring package. Although not stated as such, I suspect that the instrument can be ordered without the computer scoring package.

The manual, which is quite short, appears to have been written for a clinician rather than a researcher. The guidelines for administration and scoring are quite adequate, as are the data on reliability and validity. But the description of the scale development is inadequate, as it refers the reader to the original Beck, Epstein, Brown, and Steer (1988) article. In addition, the descriptions of other studies on the instrument are unacceptably brief.

The BAI was originally developed from a sample of 810 outpatients of mixed diagnostic categories (predominantly mood and anxiety disorders). Two successive factor analyses on different samples then reduced the number of items to 21, with a minimum item-total correlation of .30. The original development appears to have been very well done and is described in detail in Beck et al. (1988).

The reliability and validity data are thorough and informative but are based only on three studies: Beck et al. (1988), Fydrich, Dowdall, and Chambless (1990), and Dent and Salkovskis (1986). Of these, the first used a mixed diagnostic group, the second used patients diagnosed with *DSM-III-R* anxiety disorders, and the third used a nonclinical sample. The manual authors quite appropriately caution the reader the instrument was developed on a psychiatric population and should be interpreted cautiously with nonclinical individuals. The normative data tables are very thorough and informative, including means, standard deviations, coefficient alpha reliabilities, and corrected item-total correlations for five anxiety diagnostic groups with the highest representation in the sample. This apparently unpublished clinical sample consists of 393 outpatients who were seen at the Center for Cognitive Therapy in Philadelphia between January 1985 and August 1989.

Internal consistency reliability coefficients are uniformly excellent, ranging between .85 and .94.

Test-retest reliability data from Beck et al. (1988) showed a coefficient of .75 over one week. The validity data are quite comprehensive, including content, concurrent, construct, discriminant, and factorial validity. In general, the data show excellent validity, even regarding the difficult problem of untangling anxiety and depression. Especially interesting to this reviewer were the factorial validity data. One factor analysis (Beck et al., 1988) found two factors (r = .56, p < .001) that seemed to reflect somatic and cognitive/affective aspects of anxiety, respectively. A cluster analysis on the clinical sample showed four clusters that are labeled Neurophysiological, Subjective, Panic, and Autonomic. The separate clusters showed acceptable reliability, considering the small number of items in each, and discriminant function analyses found some significant differences among the clusters.

Two demographic variables, gender and age, appear to be significantly related to anxiety. Women were found to be more anxious than men and younger people were found to be more anxious than older people. Because of this, the authors caution users to adjust scores somewhat on interpretation, though how much is a little vague.

As I mentioned earlier, a computer-scoring package came with the BAI, including large and small disks and a very detailed instruction manual. According to the manual, this package provides three modes of test administration and interpretive profiles for the Beck Depression Inventory (BDI; 31), The Beck Hopelessness Scale (BHS; 32), the Beck Anxiety Inventory (BAI; 30), and the Beck Scale for Suicide Ideation (BSSI; 33) separately and together. The profile includes clinical group references and a history of the patient's scores on previous administrations, in addition to data on that test. However, the package I received (as indicated in the manual and the README file) included only the separate profile reports and the BDI, BAI, and BHS. A note at the end of the manual suggested that some of this material would not be available until December 1992, so apparently I received an older version of the computer-scoring package. [Editor's note: A 1994 version of the computer-scoring package is now available and produces integrative narrative reports.] Scoring of each test is not free once the package has been purchased. Credits must be purchased for the Use Counter (included) that is installed between the computer and the printer.

In summary, the Beck Anxiety Inventory is another of the useful instruments designed by Beck and his colleagues. There are only a few deficits. First, the manual is too brief to give as much information as many users might like (though the computer scoring manual is very comprehensive). Second, there have been too few studies conducted on the BAI, with the result that it rests on an uncomfortably small data base. This is particularly apparent for the gender and age differences. The clusters of anxiety disorders identified thus far appear to be especially promising and further research should be conducted here. Clinicians, however, will find this a very useful test, especially when combined with the other Beck instruments into a comprehensive computer-scored interpretive profile.

REVIEWER'S REFERENCES

Dent, H. R., & Salkovskis, P. M. (1986). Clinical measures of depression, anxiety and obsessionality in nonclinical populations. *Behavioral Research and Therapy*, *24*, 689–691.

Beck, A. T., Epstein, N., Brown, G., & Steer, R. A. (1988). An inventory for measuring clinical anxiety: Psychometric properties. *Journal of Consulting and Clinical Psychology, 56*, 893–897.

Fydrich, T., Dowdall, D., & Chambless, D. L. (1990, March). *Aspects of reliability and validity for the Beck Anxiety Inventory.* Paper presented at the National Conference on Phobias and Related Anxiety Disorders, Bethesda, MD.

Review of the Beck Anxiety Inventory by NIELS G. WALLER, Associate Professor of Psychology, University of California, Davis, CA:

While describing the development of the Beck Anxiety Inventory, Beck et al. (Beck, Epstein, Brown, & Steer, 1988) note that a number of studies have reported correlations greater than .50 between widely used anxiety and depression scales. Similar findings have been reported by others (Lovibond & Lovibond, 1995), and formal reviews of this topic (Clark & Watson, 1991; Dobson, 1985) conclude that anxiety and depression scales frequently correlate between .40 and .70. No one expects these scales to be uncorrelated because of the high comorbidity rates of anxiety and mood disorders (Maser & Cloninger, 1990). Yet many researchers (Riskind, Beck, Brown, & Steer, 1987) feel uncomfortable when measures of conceptually distinct constructs correlate as highly as .50.

The Beck Anxiety Inventory (BAI; Beck & Steer, 1990; Beck, Epstein, Brown, & Steer, 1988) is a brief self-report scale that was designed "to measure symptoms of anxiety which are minimally shared with those of depression" (Beck & Steer, 1990, p. 1). The 21 symptoms on the BAI were selected from three existing measures: (a) The Anxiety Check List (Beck, Steer, & Brown, 1985), (b) the PDR Check List (Beck, 1978), and (c) the Situational Anxiety Check List (Beck, 1982). The item pools of these scales were combined and winnowed using Jackson's (1970) method of scale construction. After eliminating identical or highly similar items, Beck and his colleagues used factor analysis to cull items for the final scale. Scales that are developed by this method often have high reliabilities, and coefficient alpha (Cortina, 1993) for the BAI is typically in the mid-.90s (Beck, Epstein, Brown, & Steer, 1988; Jolly, Aruffo, Wherry, & Livingston, 1993; Kumar, Steer, & Beck, 1993).

The BAI items are measured on a 4-point Likert scale that ranges from *Not at all* (0 points) to *Severely; I could barely stand it* (3). The instructions for the test ask subjects to "indicate how much you have been bothered by each symptom during the PAST WEEK, INCLUDING TODAY, by placing an X in the corresponding space in the column next to each symptom" (manual, p. 4). Notice these instructions focus on a 2-week time frame; and consequently, the BAI should measure state anxiety better than trait anxiety. Beck et al. (1988) report a 1-week test-retest correlation of .75 for the BAI, whereas Creamer, Foran, and Bell (1995) report a 7-week correlation of .62.

The factor structure of the BAI has been investigated in clinical (Beck, et al., 1988; Hewitt & Norton, 1993; Kumar et al., 1993) and nonclinical (Creamer et al., 1995) samples. Many studies have found two correlated dimensions (r = approximately .55) that have been interpreted as measuring somatic (example markers: *Feelings of choking, Shaky*) and subjective (example markers: *Fear of the worst happening, Fear of losing control*) symptoms of anxiety. A similar structure emerged in a recent factor analysis of data from the computer-administered BAI (Steer, Rissmiller, Ranieri, & Beck, 1993).

The underlying structure of the BAI has also been investigated with cluster analysis. The BAI manual authors report that a centroid cluster analysis of clinical data uncovered four symptom clusters representing (a) neurophysiological, (b) subjective, (c) panic, and (d) autonomic symptoms of anxiety. Interestingly, a similar structure was uncovered in a recent factor analysis of the scale (Osman, Barrios, Aukes, Osman, & Markway, 1993). Regarding the cluster solution, Beck and Steer (1990) have suggested the cluster subscales "may assist the examiner in making a differential diagnosis" (p. 6) and that "profile analyses of BAI subscales appear promising" (p. 18). In my opinion, neither of these statements is supported by the data. The BAI subscales are highly correlated; consequently, subscale profiles will almost certainly be unreliable for most test takers.

For example, from data reported in Table 5 of the BAI manual, it is easy to calculate the reliabilities for the cluster-subscale difference scores. For some of these scores the reliabilities are as low as .50. In other words, it is difficult to obtain reliable profiles when scales are composed of only four or five items.

Because of the goals of the BAI authors, it is appropriate to ask how strongly the BAI correlates with popular depression scales, such as The Beck Depression Inventory (BDI; Beck & Steer, 1993; 31). In clinical samples, correlations between the BAI and BDI have ranged from .48 to .71 (Beck et al., 1988; Fydrich, Dowdall, & Chambless, 1992; Hewitt & Norton, 1993; Steer, Ranieri, Beck, & Clark, 1993). A Bayesian (Iversen, 1984, p. 41–44) posterior estimate for these data suggests that r = .587 with a 95% probability that the population correlation lies between .545 and .626. In nonclinical samples (Creamer et al., 1995; Dent & Salkovskis, 1986), correlations between the BAI and BDI have ranged from .50 to .63. The Bayesian estimate of r for these data is .591 with a 95% probability that the population correlation lies between .548 and .631.

In conclusion, it appears that Beck was not successful in developing an anxiety scale with high discriminant validity. Nevertheless, he did develop a highly reliable scale that can be administered in 5 to 10 minutes. Thus, the BAI appears to be a useful addition to the growing number of clinical anxiety measures.

REVIEWER'S REFERENCES

Jackson, D. N. (1970). A sequential system for personality scale development. In C. D. Spielberger (Ed.), *Current topics in clinical and community psychology* (vol. 2, pp. 61–96). New York: Academic Press.

Beck, A. T. (1978). *PDR Check List*. Philadelphia: University of Pennsylvania, Center for Cognitive Therapy.

Beck, A. T. (1982). *Situational Anxiety Check List (SAC)*. Philadelphia: University of Pennsylvania, Center for Cognitive Therapy.

Iversen, G. R. (1984). *Bayesian statistical inference*. Beverly Hills, CA: Sage.

Beck, A. T., Steer, R. A., & Brown, G. (1985). *Beck Anxiety Check List*. Unpublished manuscript, University of Pennsylvania.

Dobson, K. S. (1985). The relationship between anxiety and depression. *Clinical Psychology Review, 5*, 307–324.

Dent, H. R., & Salkovskis, P. M. (1986). Clinical measures of depression, anxiety, and obsessionality in non-clinical populations. *Behaviour Research and Therapy, 24*, 689–691.

Riskind, J. H., Beck, A. T., Brown, G., & Steer, R. A. (1987). Taking the measure of anxiety and depression: Validity of reconstructed Hamilton scales. *Journal of Nervous and Mental Disease, 175*, 475–479.

Beck, A. T., Epstein, N., Brown, G., & Steer, R. A. (1988). An inventory for measuring clinical anxiety: Psychometric properties. *Journal of Consulting & Clinical Psychology, 56*, 893–897.

Beck, A. T., & Steer, R. A. (1990). *Manual for the Beck Anxiety Inventory*. San Antonio, TX: The Psychological Corporation.

Maser, J. D., & Cloninger, C. R. (Eds.). (1990). *Comorbidity of mood and anxiety disorders*. Washington, DC: American Psychiatric Press.

Clark, L. A., & Watson, D. (1991). Theoretical and empirical issues in differentiating depression from anxiety. In J. Becker, & A. Kleinman (Eds.), *Psychosocial aspects of depression*. Hillsdale, NJ: Erlbaum.

Frydrich, T., Dowdall, D., & Chambless, D. L. (1992). Reliability and validity of the Beck Anxiety Inventory. *Journal of Anxiety Disorders, 6*, 55–61.

Beck, A. T., & Steer, R. A. (1993). *Beck Depression Inventory, manual*. San Antonio, TX: The Psychological Corporation.

Cortina, J. M. (1993). What is coefficient alpha? An examination of theory and applications. *Journal of Applied Psychology, 78*, 98–104.

Hewitt, P. L., & Norton, G. R. (1993). The Beck Anxiety Inventory: A psychometric analysis. *Psychological Assessment, 5,* 408–412.

Jolly, J. B., Aruffo, J. F., Wherry, J. N., & Livingston, R. (1993). The utility of the Beck Anxiety Inventory with inpatient adolescents. *Journal of Anxiety Disorders, 7,* 95–106.

Kumar, G., Steer, R. A., & Beck, A. T. (1993). Factor structure of the Beck Anxiety Inventory with adolescent psychiatric inpatients. *Anxiety, Stress, and Coping, 6,* 125–131.

Osman, A., Barrios, F. X., Aukes, D., Osman, J. R., & Markway, K. (1993). The Beck Anxiety Inventory: Psychometric properties in a community population. *Journal of Psychopathology and Behavioral Assessment, 15,* 287–297.

Steer, R. A., Rissmiller, D. J., Ranieri, W. F., & Beck, A. T. (1993). Structure of the computer-assisted Beck Anxiety Inventory with psychiatric inpatients. *Journal of Personality Assessment, 60,* 532–542.

Steer, R. A., Ranieri, W. F., Beck, A. T., & Clark, D. A. (1993). Further evidence for the validity of the Beck Anxiety Inventory with psychiatric outpatients. *Journal of Anxiety Disorders, 7,* 195–205.

Creamer, M., Foran, J., & Bell, R. (1995). The Beck Anxiety Inventory in a non-clinical sample. *Behavior Research and Therapy, 33,* 477–485.

Gillis, M. M., Haaga, D. A. F., & Ford, G. T. (1995). Normative values for the Beck Anxiety Inventory, Fear Questionnaire, Penn State Worry Questionnaire, and Social Phobia and Anxiety Inventory. *Psychological Assessment, 7,* 450–455.

Lovibond, P. F., & Lovibond, S. H. (1995). The structure of negative emotional states: Comparison of the Depression Anxiety Stress Scales (DASS) with the Beck Depression and Anxiety Inventories. *Behaviour and Therapy Research, 33,* 335–343.

[31]
Beck Depression Inventory [1993 Revised].

Purpose: "Designed to assess the severity of depression in adolescents and adults."

Population: Adolescents and adults.

Publication Dates: 1961–1993.

Acronym: BDI.

Scores: Total score only; item score ranges.

Administration: Group or individual.

Price Data, 1994: $46 per complete kit including 25 record forms and manual ('93, 24 pages); $25.50 per 25 record forms; $22.50 per manual.

Foreign Language Edition: Also available in Spanish.

Time: (5–15) minutes.

Authors: Aaron T. Beck and Robert A. Steer.

Publisher: The Psychological Corporation.

Cross References: See T4:268 (660 references); for reviews by Collie W. Conoley and Norman D. Sundberg of a previous edition, see 11:31 (286 references).

TEST REFERENCES

1. Phil, B. M. (1983). Depression and hostility in self-mutilation. *Suicide and Life-Threatening Behavior, 13,* 71–84.

2. Wallace, J. E., Becker, J., Coppel, D. B., & Cox, G. B. (1983). Anticonformity aspects of depression in mild depressive states. *Journal of Personality, 51,* 640–652.

3. Gilbert, M. J., & Cervantes, R. C. (1986). Patterns and practices of alcohol use among Mexican Americans: A comprehensive review. *Hispanic Journal of Behavioral Sciences, 8,* 1–60.

4. Smith, K., & Crawford, S. (1986). Suicidal behavior among "normal" high school students. *Suicide and Life-Threatening Behavior, 16,* 313–325.

5. Dunn, S. E., Putallaz, M., Sheppard, B. H., & Lindstrom, R. (1987). Social support adjustment in gifted adolescents. *Journal of Educational Psychology, 79,* 467–473.

6. Merkel, W. T., & Wiener, R. L. (1987). A reconsideration of the Willoughby Personality Schedule with psychiatric inpatients. *Journal of Behavior Therapy and Experimental Psychiatry, 18,* 13–18.

7. Prezant, D. W., & Neimeyer, R. A. (1988). Cognitive predictors of depression and suicide ideation. *Suicide and Life-Threatening Behavior, 18,* 259–264.

8. Strauman, T. J., & Higgins, E. T. (1988). Self-discrepancies as predictor of vulnerability to distinct syndromes of chronic emotional distress. *Journal of Personality, 56,* 685–707.

9. Arena, J. G., Goldberg, S. J., Saul, D. L., & Hobbs, S. H. (1989). Temporal stability of psychophysiological response profiles: Analysis of individual response stereotypy and stimulus response specificity. *Behavior Therapy, 20,* 609–618.

10. Barlow, D. H., Craske, M. G., Cerny, J. A., & Klasko, J. S. (1989). Behavioral treatment of panic disorder. *Behavior Therapy, 20,* 261–282.

11. Blanchard, E. B., Kolb, L. C., Taylor, A. E., & Wittrock, D. A. (1989). Cardiac response to relevant stimuli as an adjunct in diagnosing post-traumatic stress disorder: Replication and extension. *Behavior Therapy, 20,* 535–543.

12. Blanchard, E. B., McCoy, G. C., Berger, M., Musso, A., Pallmeyer, T. P., Gerardi, R., Gerardi, M. A., & Pangburn, L. (1989). A controlled comparison of thermal biofeedback and relaxation training in the treatment of essential hypertensional IV: Prediction of short-term clinical outcome. *Behavior Therapy, 20,* 405–415.

13. Chibnall, J. T., & Tait, R. C. (1989). The Psychosomatic Symptom Checklist revisited: Reliability and validity in a chronic pain population. *Journal of Behavioral Medicine, 12,* 297-307.

14. Clark, L. A., Watson, D., & Leeka, J. (1989). Diurnal variation in the positive affects. *Motivation and Emotion, 13,* 205–234.

15. Cooper, N. A., & Clum, G. A. (1989). Imaginal flooding as a supplementary treatment for PTSD in combat veterans: A controlled study. *Behavior Therapy, 20,* 381–391.

16. Craighead, L. W., & Blum, M. D. (1989). Supervised exercise in behavioral treatment for moderate obesity. *Behavior Therapy, 20,* 49–59.

17. Earls, C. M., & David, H. (1989). A psychosocial study of male prostitution. *Archives of Sexual Behavior, 18,* 401–419.

18. Fantuzzo, J. W., Dimeff, L. A., & Fox, S. L. (1989). Reciprocal peer tutoring: A multimodal assessment of effectiveness with college students. *Teaching of Psychology, 16,* 133-135.

19. Feehan, M., & Marsh, N. (1989). The reduction of bruxism using contingent EMG audible biofeedback: A case study. *Journal of Behavior Therapy and Experimental Psychiatry, 20,* 179–183.

20. Freedman, M., & Oscar-Berman, M. (1989). Spatial and visual learning deficits in Alzheimer's and Parkinson's disease. *Brain and Cognition, 11,* 114-126.

21. Gannen, L., & Pardie, L. (1989). The importance of chronicity and controllability of stress in the context of stress-illness relationships. *Journal of Behavioral Medicine, 12,* 357-372.

22. Joffe, R. T., & Regan, J. J. (1989). Personality and response to tricyclic antidepressants in depressed patients. *The Journal of Nervous and Mental Disease, 177,* 745-749.

23. Keane, T. M., Fairbank, J. A., Caddell, J. M., & Zimering, R. T. (1989). Implosive (flooding) therapy reduces symptoms of PTSD in Vietnam combat veterans. *Behavior Therapy, 20,* 245–260.

24. Kennedy, S. H., Craven, J. L., & Roin, G. M. (1989). Major depression in renal dialysis patients: An open trial of antidepressant therapy. *The Journal of Clinical Psychiatry, 50,* 60–63.

25. King, A. C., Taylor, C. B., Haskell, W. L., & DeBusk, R. F. (1989). Influence of regular aerobic exercise on psychological health: A randomized, controlled trial of healthy middle-aged adults. *Health Psychology, 8,* 305–324.

26. LaKey, B. (1989). Personal and environmental antecedents of perceived social support developed at college. *American Journal of Community Psychology, 17,* 503-519.

27. Lahmeyer, H. W., Reynolds, C. F., III, Kupfer, D. J., & King, R. (1989). Biologic markers in borderline personality disorder: A review. *The Journal of Clinical Psychiatry, 50,* 217–225.

28. Louks, J., Hayne, C., & Smith, J. (1989). Replicated factor structure of the Beck Depression Inventory. *The Journal of Nervous and Mental Disease, 177,* 473-479.

29. Lynch, P. M., & Zamble, E. (1989). A controlled behavioral treatment study of Irritable Bowel Syndrome. *Behavior Therapy, 20,* 509–523.

30. Marmar, C. R., Gaston, L., Gallagher, D., & Thompson, L. W. (1989). Alliance and outcome in late-life depression. *The Journal of Nervous and Mental Disease, 177,* 464-472.

31. Marsh, K. L., & Weary, G. (1989). Depression and attributional complexity. *Personality and Social Psychology Bulletin, 15,* 325–336.

32. McNamee, G., O'Sullivan, G., Lelliott, P., & Marks, I. (1989). Telephone-guided treatment for housebound agoraphobics with panic disorder: Exposure vs. relaxation. *Behavior Therapy, 20,* 491–497.

33. Miller, I. W., Norman, W. H., Keitner, G. I., Bishop, S. B., & Dow, M. G. (1989). Cognitive-behavioral treatment of depressed inpatients. *Behavior Therapy, 20,* 25–47.

34. Niederche, G., & Yoder, C. (1899). Metamemory perceptions in depressions of young and older adults. *The Journal of Nervous and Mental Disease, 177,* 4-14.

35. Otto, M. W., Dougher, M. J., & Yeo, R. A. (1989). Depression, pain, and hemispheric activation. *The Journal of Nervous and Mental Disease, 177,* 210-218.

36. Sachs, G. S., Gelenberg, A. J., Bellinghausen, B., Wojcik, J., Falk, W. E., Farhadi, A. M., & Jenike, M. (1989). Ergoloid mesylates and ECT. *The Journal of Clinical Psychiatry, 50,* 87–90.

37. Schmidt, U., & Marks, I. M. (1989). Exposure plus prevention of bingeing vs. exposure plus prevention of vomiting in bulimia nervosa: A crossover study. *The Journal of Nervous and Mental Disease, 177,* 259-266.

38. Slavin, L. A., & Compas, B. E. (1989). The problem of confounding social support and depressive symptoms: A brief report on a college sample. *American Journal of Community Psychology, 17,* 57-66.

39. Slife, B. D., Sasscer-Burgos, J., Froberg, W., & Ellington, S. (1989). Effect of depression on processing interactions in group psychotherapy. *International Journal of Group Psychotherapy, 39,* 79–104.

40. Sohlberg, S., Norring, C., Holmgren, S., & Rosmark, B. (1989). Impulsivity and long-term prognosis of psychiatric patients with anorexia nervosa/bulimia nervosa. *The Journal of Nervous and Mental Disease, 177,* 249-258.

41. Sokol, L., Beck, A. T., Greenberg, R. L., Wright, F. D., & Berchick, R. J. (1989). Cognitive therapy of panic disorder: A nonpharmacological alternative. *The Journal of Nervous and Mental Disease, 177,* 711-716.

42. Stiffman, A. R. (1989). Suicide attempts in runaway youths. *Suicide and Life-Threatening Behavior, 19,* 147–159.

43. Stravynski, A., Lesage, A., Marcouiller, M., & Elie, R. (1989). A test of the therapeutic mechanism in social skills training with avoidant personality disorder. *The Journal of Nervous and Mental Disease, 177,* 739-744.

44. Tschann, J. M., Johnston, J. R., & Wallerstein, J. S. (1989). Resources, stressors, and attachment as predictors of adult adjustment after divorce: A longitudinal study. *Journal of Marriage and the Family, 51,* 1033-1046.

45. Vitaliano, P. P., Maiuro, R. D., Russo, J., & Mitchell, E. S. (1989). Medical student distress: A longitudinal study. *The Journal of Nervous and Mental Disease, 177,* 70-76.

46. Wilson, A., Passik, S. D., Faude, J., Abrams, J., & Gordon, E. (1989). A hierarchical model of opiate addiction: Failures of self-regulation as a central aspect of substance abuse. *The Journal of Nervous and Mental Disease, 177,* 390-399.

47. Zemore, R., & Veikle, G. (1989). Cognitive styles and proneness to depressive symptoms in university women. *Personality and Social Psychology Bulletin, 15,* 426–438.

48. Agras, W. S., Taylor, C. B., Feldman, D. E., Losch, M., & Burnett, K. F. (1990). Developing computer-assisted therapy for the treatment of obesity. *Behavior Therapy, 21,* 99–109.

49. Anderson, I. M., Parry-Billings, M., Newsholme, E. A., Poortmans, J. R., & Cowen, P. J. (1990). Decreased plasma tryptophan concentration in major depression: Relationship to melancholia and weight loss. *Journal of Affective Disorders, 20,* 185-191.

50. Baer, L., Jenike, M. A., Ricciardi, J. N., II, Holland, A. D., Seymour, R. J., Minichiello, W. E., & Buttolph, M. L. (1990). Standardized assessment of personality disorders in obsessive-compulsive disorder. *Archives of General Psychiatry, 47,* 826-830.

51. Beitman, B. D., Kushner, M., Lamberti, J. W., & Mukerji, V. (1990). Panic disorder without fear in patients with angiographically normal coronary arteries. *The Journal of Nervous and Mental Disease, 178,* 307-312.

52. Bless, H., Bohner, G., Schwarz, N., & Strack, F. (1990). Mood and persuasion: A cognitive response analysis. *Personality and Social Psychology Bulletin, 16,* 331-345.

53. Breslau, N. (1990). Does brain dysfunction increase children's vulnerability to environmental stress? *Archives of General Psychiatry, 47,* 15–20.

54. Brown, T. A., & Cash, T. F. (1990). The phenomenon of nonclinical panic: Parameters of panic, fear, and avoidance. *Journal of Anxiety Disorders, 4,* 15-29.

55. Bulik, C. M., Carpenter, L. L., Kupfer, D. J., & Frank, E. (1990). Features associated with suicide attempts in recurrent major depression. *Journal of Affective Disorders, 18,* 29-37.

56. Caldwell, C. B., & Gottesman, I. I. (1990). Schizophrenics kill themselves too: A review of risk factors for suicide. *Schizophrenia Bulletin, 16,* 571–589.

57. Christensen, A. J., Smith, T. W., Turner, C. W., Holman, J. M., Jr., & Gregory, M. C. (1990). Type of hemodialysis and preference for behavioral involvement: Interactive effects on adherence in end-stage renal disease. *Health Psychology, 9,* 225-236.

58. Christensen, L., & Burrows, R. (1990). Dietary treatment of depression. *Behavior Therapy, 21,* 183–193.

59. Clark, D. C., Sommerfeldt, L., Schwarz, M., Hedeker, D., & Watel, L. (1990). Physical recklessness in adolescence: Trait or byproduct of depressive/suicidal states? *The Journal of Nervous and Mental Disease, 178,* 423-433.

60. Craighead, W. E. (1990). There's a place for us: All of us. *Behavior Therapy, 21,* 3–23.

61. Deutscher, S., & Cimbolic, P. (1990). Cognitive processes and their relationship to endogenous and reactive components of depression. *The Journal of Nervous and Mental Disease, 178,* 351-359.

62. Devins, G. M., Mandin, H., Hons, R. B., Burgess, E. D., Klassen, J., Taub, K., Schorr, S., Letourneau, P. K., & Buckle, S. (1990). Illness, intrusiveness, and quality of life in end-stage renal disease: Comparison and stability across treatment modalities. *Health Psychology, 9,* 117-142.

63. Devins, G. M., Mann, J., Mandin, H., Paul, L. C., Hons, R. B., Burgess, E. D., Taub, K., Schorr, S., Letourneau, P. K., & Buckle, S. (1990). Psychosocial predictors of survival in end-stage renal disease. *The Journal of Nervous and Mental Disease, 178,* 127-133.

64. Dykstra, S. P., & Dollinger, S. J. (1990). Model competence, depression, and the illusion of control. *Bulletin of the Psychonomic Society, 28,* 235–238.

65. Egeland, B., Kalkoske, M., Gottesman, N., & Erickson, M. F. (1990). Preschool behavior problems: Stability and factors accounting for change. *Journal of Child Psychology and Psychiatry and Allied Disciplines, 31,* 891-909.

66. Ellis, H. C., Seibert, P. S., & Herbert, B. J. (1990). Mood state effects on thought listening. *Bulletin of the Psychonomic Society, 28,* 147–150.

67. Ferrarese, C., Appollonio, J., Frigo, M., Meregalli, S., Piolti, R., Tamma, F., & Frattola, L. (1990). Cerebrospinal fluid levels of diazepam-binding inhibitor in neurodegenerative disorders with dementia. *Neurology, 40,* 632–635.

68. Freedman, M. (1990). Object alternation and orbitofrontal system dysfunction in Alzheimer's and Parkinson's disease. *Brain and Cognition, 14,* 134-143.

69. Ganzini, L., McFarland, B. H., & Cutler, D. (1990). Prevalence of mental disorders after catastrophic financial loss. *The Journal of Nervous and Mental Disease, 178,* 680-685.

70. Garvey, M., DeRubeis, R. J., Hollon, S. D., Evans, M. D., & Tuason, V. B. (1990). Does 24-h urinary MHPG predict treatment response to antidepressants? II. Association between imipramine response and low MHPG. *Journal of Affective Disorders, 20,* 181-184.

71. Gelenberg, A. J., Wojcik, J. D., Falk, W. E., Baldessarini, R. J., Zeisel, S. H., Schoenfeld, D., & Mok, G. S. (1990). Tyrosine for depression: A double-blind trial. *Journal of Affective Disorders, 19,* 125-132.

72. Hartley, L., Lebovits, A. H., Paddison, P. L., & Strain, J. J. (1990). Issues in the identification of premenstrual syndromes. *The Journal of Nervous and Mental Disease, 178,* 228-234.

73. Heimberg, R. G., Hope, D. A., Dodge, C. S., & Becker, R. E. (1990). DSM-III-R subtypes of social phobia: Comparison of generalized social phobics and public speaking phobics. *The Journal of Nervous and Mental Disease, 178,* 172-179.

74. Ingram, R. E., Atkinson, J. H., Slater, M. A., Saccuzzo, D. P., & Garfin, S. R. (1990). Negative and positive cognition in depressed and nondepressed chronic-pain patients. *Health Psychology, 9,* 300-314.

75. Jackson, J. L., Calhoun, K. S., Amick, A. E., Maddever, H. M., & Habif, V. L. (1990). Young adult women who report childhood intrafamilial sexual abuse: Subsequent adjustment. *Archives of Sexual Behavior, 19,* 211-221.

76. Johnson, C., Tobin, D., & Enright, A. (1989). Prevalence and clinical characteristics of borderline patients in an eating-disordered population. *The Journal of Clinical Psychiatry, 50,* 9–15.

77. Kleinman, P. H., Miller, A. B., Millman, R. B., Woody, G. E., Todd, T., Kemp, J., & Lipton, D. S. (1990). Psychopathology among cocaine abusers entering treatment. *The Journal of Nervous and Mental Disease, 178,* 442-447.

78. Lerner, M. S., & Clum, G. A. (1990). Treatment of suicide indicators: A problem-solving approach. *Behavior Therapy, 21,* 403–411.

79. Lewinsohn, P. M., Clarke, G. N., Hops, H., & Andrews, J. (1990). Cognitive-behavioral treatment for depressed adolescents. *Behavior Therapy, 21,* 385–401.

80. Littlefield, C. H., Rodin, G. M., Murray, M. A., & Craven, J. L. (1990). Influence of functional impairment and social support on depressive symptoms in persons with diabetes. *Health Psychology, 9,* 737-749.

81. Lowe, C. F., & Chadwick, P. D. J. (1990). Verbal control of delusions. *Behavior Therapy, 21,* 461–79.

82. Mattick, R. P., Andrews, G., Hadzi-Pavlovic, D., & Christensen, H. (1990). Treatment of panic and agoraphobia: An integrative review. *The Journal of Nervous and Mental Disease, 178,* 567-576.

83. Mavissakalian, M. R., Jones, B., & Olson, S. (1990). Absence of placebo response in obsessive-compulsive disorder. *The Journal of Nervous and Mental Disease, 178,* 268-270.

84. McCullough, J. D., Braith, J. A., Chapman, R. C., Kasnetz, M. D., Carr, K. F., Cones, J. H., Fielo, J., & Roberts, W. C. (1990). Comparison of dysthymic major and nonmajor depressives. *The Journal of Nervous and Mental Disease, 178,* 596-597.

85. McCullough, J. P., Braith, J. A., Chapman, R. C., Kasnetz, M. D., Carr, K. F., Cones, J. H., Fielo, J., Shoemaker, O. S., & Roberts, W. C. (1990). Comparison of early and late onset dysthymia. *The Journal of Nervous and Mental Disease, 178,* 577-581.

86. McNally, R. J., Cassiday, K. L., & Calamari, J. E. (1990). Taijin-kyofu-sho in a Black American woman: Behavioral treatment of a "culture-bound" anxiety disorder. *Journal of Anxiety Disorders, 4,* 83-87.

87. Meneese, W. B., & Yutrzenka, B. A. (1990). Correlates of suicidal ideation among rural adolescents. *Suicide and Life-Threatening Behavior, 20,* 206–212.

88. Middleton, H. C. (1990). An enhanced hypotensive response to clonidine can still be found in panic patients despite psychological treatment. *Journal of Anxiety Disorders, 4,* 213-219.

89. Middleton, H. C. (1990). Cardiovascular dystonia in recovered panic patients. *Journal of Affective Disorders, 19,* 229-236.

90. Moos, R. H. (1990). Depressed outpatients' life contexts, amount of treatment, and treatment outcome. *The Journal of Nervous and Mental Disease, 178,* 105-112.

91. Neimeyer, R. A., & Feixas, G. (1990). The role of homework and skill acquisition in the outcome of group cognitive therapy for depression. *Behavior Therapy, 21,* 281–292.

92. Nelson, G. M., & Beach, S. R. H. (1990). Sequential interaction in depression: Effects of depressive behavior on spousal aggression. *Behavior Therapy, 21,* 167–182.

93. Nutt, D. J., Glue, P., Lawson, C., & Wilson, S. (1990). Flumazenil provocation of panic attacks. *Archives of General Psychiatry, 47,* 917-925.

94. O'Leary, K. D., Riso, L. P., & Beach, S. R. H. (1990). Attributions about the marital discord/depression link and therapy outcome. *Behavior Therapy, 21,* 413–422.

95. Pennebaker, J. W., Czajka, J. A., Cropanzano, R., Richards, B. C., Brumbelow, S., Ferrara, K., Thompson, R., & Thyssen, T. (1990). Levels of thinking. *Personality and Social Psychology Bulletin, 16,* 743-757.

96. Pollard, C. A., Detrick, P., Flynn, T., & Frank, M. (1990). Panic attacks and related disorders in alcohol-dependent, depressed, and nonclinical samples. *The Journal of Nervous and Mental Disease, 178,* 180-185.

97. Rabbitt, P., & Alison, V. (1990). "Lost and Found": Some logical and methodological limitations of self-report questionnaires as tools to study cognitive ageing. *British Journal of Psychology, 81,* 1-16.

98. Renneberg, B., Goldstein, A. J., Phillips, D., & Chambless, D. L. (1990). Intensive behavioral group treatment of avoidant personality disorder. *Behavior Therapy, 21,* 363–377.

99. Roy-Byrne, P. P., Cowley, D. S., Greenblatt, D. J., Shader, R. I., & Hommer, D. (1990). Reduced benzodiazepine sensitivity in panic disorder. *Archives of General Psychiatry, 47,* 534–538.

100. Self, C. A., & Rogers, R. W. (1990). Coping with threats to health: Effects of persuasive appeals on depressed, normal, and antisocial personalities. *Journal of Behavioral Medicine, 13,* 343-357.

101. Sheehan, D. Y., Raj, A. B., Harnett-Sheehan, K., Soto, S., & Lewis, C. P. (1990). Adinazolam sustained release formulation in the treatment of generalized anxiety disorder. *Journal of Anxiety Disorders, 4,* 239-246.

102. Smith, T. W., Peck, J. R., & Ward, J. R. (1990). Helplessness and depression in rheumatoid arthritis. *Health Psychology, 9,* 377-389.

103. Starkstein, S. E., Preziosi, T. J., Bolduc, P. L., & Robinson, R. G. (1990). Depression in Parkinson's disease. *The Journal of Nervous and Mental Disease, 178,* 27-31.

104. Steketee, G. (1990). Personality traits and disorders in obsessive-compulsiveness. *Journal of Anxiety Disorders, 4,* 351-364.

105. Stinson, D., & Thompson, C. (1990). Clinical experience with phototherapy. *Journal of Affective Disorders, 18,* 129-135.

106. Tang, C. S., & Critelli, J. W. (1990). Depression and judgment of control: Impact of a contingency on accuracy. *Journal of Personality, 58,* 717–727.

107. van den Burg, W., Bouhuys, A. L., van den Hoofdakker, R. H., & Beersma, D. G. M. (1990). Sleep deprivation in bright and dim light: Antidepressant effects on major depressive disorder. *Journal of Affective Disorders, 19,* 109-117.

108. Vitaliano, P. P., Maiuro, R. D., Russo, J., Katon, W., DeWolfe, D., & Hall, G. (1990). Coping profiles associated with psychiatric, physical health, work, and family problems. *Health Psychology, 9,* 348-376.

109. Webster-Stratton, C., & Hammond, M. (1990). Predictors of treatment outcome in parent training for families with conduct problem children. *Behavior Therapy, 21,* 319–337.

110. Weddington, W. W., Brown, B. S., Haertzen, C. A., Cone, E. J., Dax, E. M., Herring, R. I., & Michaelson, B. S. (1990). Changes in mood, craving, and sleep during short-term abstinence reported by male cocaine addicts. *Archives of General Psychiatry, 47,* 861-868.

111. Whitaker, A., Johnson, J., Shaffer, D., Rapoport, J. L., Kalikow, K., Walsh, B. T., Davies, M., Braimen, S., & Dolinsky, A. (1990). Uncommon troubles in young people: Prevalence estimates of selected psychiatric disorders in nonreferred adolescent population. *Archives of General Psychiatry, 47,* 487–496.

112. Williams, K. E., & Chambless, D. L. (1990). The relationship between therapist characteristics and outcome of in vivo exposure treatment for agoraphobia. *Behavior Therapy, 21,* 111–116.

113. Williamson, D. A., Prather, R. C., McKenzie, S. J., & Blown, D. C. (1990). Behavioral assessment procedures can differentiate bulimia nervosa, compulsive overeater, obese, and normal subjects. *Behavioral Assessment, 12,* 239-252.

114. Barkley, R. A., Fischer, M., Edelbrock, C., & Smallish, L. (1991). The adolescent outcome of hyperactive children diagnosed by research criteria: III. Mother-child interactions, family conflicts and maternal psychopathology. *Journal of Child Psychology and Psychiatry and Allied Disciplines, 32,* 233-255.

115. Baum, J. G., Clark, H. B., & Sandler, J. (1991). Preventing relapse in obesity through posttreatment maintenance systems: Comparing the relative efficacy of two levels of therapist support. *Journal of Behavioral Medicine, 14,* 287-302.

116. Becker, J. V., Kaplan, M. S., Tenke, C. E., & Tartaglini, A. (1991). The incidence of depressive symptomatology in juvenile sex offenders with a history of abuse. *Child Abuse & Neglect, 15,* 531-536.

117. Beckham, J. C., Keefe, F. J., Caldwell, D. S., & Roodman, A. A. (1991). Pain coping strategies in rheumatoid arthritis: Relationships to pain, disability, depression and daily hassles. *Behavior Therapy, 22,* 113–124.

118. Boggiano, A. K., & Barrett, M. (1991). Gender differences in depression in college students. *Sex Roles, 25,* 595-605.

119. Boggiano, A. K., Barrett, M., Silvern, L., & Gallo, S. (1991). Predicting emotional concomitants of learned helplessness: The role of motivational orientation. *Sex Roles, 25,* 577-593.

120. Boyce, P., Hickie, I., & Parker, G. (1991). Parents, partners or personality? Risk factors for post-natal depression. *Journal of Affective Disorders, 21,* 245-255.

121. Burnette, M. M., Koehn, K. A., Kenyon-Jump, R., Hutton, K., & Stark, C. (1991). Control of genital herpes recurrences using progressive muscle relaxation. *Behavior Therapy, 22,* 237–247.

122. Catanzaro, S. J. (1991). Adjustment, depression, and minimal goal setting: The moderating effect of performance feedback. *Journal of Personality, 59,* 243–261.

123. Corrigan, P. W. (1991). Social skills training in adult psychiatric populations: A meta-analysis. *Journal of Behavior Therapy and Experimental Psychiatry, 22,* 203–210.

124. Costello, E. J. (1991). Married with children: Predictors of mental and physical health in middle-aged women. *Psychiatry, 54,* 292–305.

125. Cox, B. J., Endler, N. S., & Swinson, R. P. (1991). Clinical and nonclinical panic attacks: An empirical test of a panic-anxiety continuum. *Journal of Anxiety Disorders, 5,* 21-34.

126. Craske, M. G., Brown, T. A., & Barlow, D. H. (1991). Behavioral treatment of panic disorder: A two-year follow-up. *Behavior Therapy, 22,* 289–304.

127. Cutler, S. E., & Nolen-Hoeksema, S. (1991). Accounting for sex differences in depression through female victimization: Childhood sexual abuse. *Sex Roles, 24,* 425-438.

128. Denham, S. A., Zahn-Waxler, C., Cummings, E. M., & Iannotti, R. J. (1991). Social competence in young children's peer relations: Patterns of development and change. *Child Psychiatry and Human Development, 22,* 29-44.

129. Dyck, M. J. (1991). Positive and negative attitudes mediating suicide ideation. *Suicide and Life-Threatening Behavior, 21,* 360–373.

130. Edwards, M. C., Finney, J. W., & Bonner, M. (1991). Matching treatment with recurrent abdominal pain symptoms: An evaluation of dietary fiber and relaxation treatments. *Behavior Therapy, 22,* 257–267.

131. Fairburn, C. G., Jones, R., Peveler, R. C., Carr, S. J., Solomon, R. A., O'Connor, M. E., Burton, J., & Hope, R. A. (1991). Three psychological treatments for bulimia nervosa. *Archives of General Psychiatry, 48,* 463-469.

132. Field, T., Morrow, C., Healy, B., Foster, T., Adlestein, D., & Goldstein, S. (1991). Mothers with zero Beck Depression scores act more "depressed" with their infants. *Development and Psychopathology, 3,* 253-262.

133. Fischer, S., & Gillman, I. (1991). Surrogate motherhood: Attachment, attitudes and social support. *Psychiatry, 54,* 13–38.

134. Free, M. L., Oei, T. P. S., & Sanders, M. R. (1991). Treatment outcome of a group cognitive therapy program for depression. *International Journal of Group Psychotherapy, 41,* 533–547.

135. Gabardi, L., & Rosén, L. A. (1991). Differences between college students from divorced and intact families. *Journal of Divorce & Remarriage, 15*(3/4), 175-191.

136. Gelernter, C. S., Uhde, T. W., Cimbolic, P., Arnkoff, D. B., ViHone, B. H., Tancer, M. E., & Bartko, J. J. (1991). Cognitive-behavioral and pharmacological treatments of social phobia. *Archives of General Psychiatry, 48,* 938-945.

137. Günther, V., & Kryspin-Exner, I. (1991). Ergopsychometry in depressive patients. *Journal of Affective Disorders, 23,* 81-92.

138. Harris, E. S. (1991). Adolescent bereavement following the death of a parent: An exploratory study. *Child Psychiatry and Human Development, 21,* 267-281.

139. Haviland, M. G., Hendryx, M. S., Cummings, M. A., Shaw, D. G., & MacMumary, J. P. (1991). Multidimensionality and state dependency of alexithymia in recently sober alcoholics. *The Journal of Nervous and Mental Disease, 179,* 284-290.

140. Hayne, C. H., & Louks, J. L. (1991). Dysphoria in male alcoholics with a history of hallucinations. *The Journal of Nervous and Mental Disease, 179,* 415-419.

141. Jarrett, R. B., Giles, D. Z., Gullion, C. M., & Rush, A. J. (1991). Does learned resourcefulness predict response to cognitive therapy in depressed outpatients? *Journal of Affective Disorders, 23,* 223-229.

142. Kerns, R. D., Haythronthwaite, J., Rosenberg, R., Southwick, S., Giller, E. L., & Jacob, M. C. (1991). The Pain Behavior Checklist (PBCL): Factor structure and psychometric properties. *Journal of Behavioral Medicine, 14,* 155-167.

143. Kuch, K., Cox, B. J., Woszczyna, C. B., Swinson, R. P., & Shulman, I. (1991). Chronic pain in panic disorder. *Journal of Behavior Therapy and Experimental Psychiatry, 22,* 255–259.

144. Levitt, A. J., Joffe, R. T., & MacDonald, C. (1991). Life course of depressive illness and characteristics of current episode in patients with double depression. *The Journal of Nervous and Mental Disease, 179,* 678-682.

145. Loranger, A. W., Lenzenweger, M. F., Gartner, A. F., Susman, V. L., Herzig, J., Zammit, G. K., Gartner, J. D., Abrams, R. C., & Young, R. C. (1991). Trait-state artifacts and the diagnosis of personality disorders. *Archives of General Psychiatry, 48,* 720-728.

146. Lucas, J. A., Telch, M. J., & Bigler, E. D. (1991). Memory functioning in panic disorder: A neuropsychological perspective. *Journal of Anxiety Disorders, 5,* 1-20.

147. Maes, M., Bosmans, E., Suy, E., Vandervorst, C., Dejonckheere, C., & Raus, J. (1991). Antiphospholipid, antinuclear, Epstein-Barr and cytomegalovirus antibodies, and soluble interleukin-2 receptors in depressive patients. *Journal of Affective Disorders, 21,* 133-140.

148. Magnusson, A., & Kristbjarnarson, H. (1991). Treatment of seasonal affective disorder with high-intensity light. *Journal of Affective Disorders, 21,* 141-147.

149. Mark, M. M., Sinclair, R. C., & Wellens, T. R. (1991). The effect of completing the Beck Depression Inventory on self-reported mood state: Contrast and assimilation. *Personality and Social Psychology Bulletin, 17,* 457-465.

150. McCullough, J. D. (1991). Psychotherapy for dysthymia: A naturalistic study of ten patients. *The Journal of Nervous and Mental Disease, 179,* 734-740.

151. McGorry, P. D., Chanen, A., McCarthy, E., Van Riel, R., McKenzie, D., & Singh, B. S. (1991). Posttraumatic stress disorder following recent-onset psychosis: An unrecognized postpsychotic syndrome. *The Journal of Nervous and Mental Disease, 179,* 253-258.

152. Meesters, Y., Lambers, P. A., Jansen, J. H. C., Bouhuys, A. L., Beersma, D. G. M., & van den Hoofdakker, R. H. (1991). Can winter depression be prevented by light treatment? *Journal of Affective Disorders, 23,* 75-79.

153. Morrow, K. B. (1991). Attributions of female adolescent incest victims regarding their molestation. *Child Abuse & Neglect, 15,* 477-483.

154. Morse, C. A., Dennerstein, L., Farrell, E., & Varnavides, R. (1991). A comparison of hormone therapy, coping skills training, and relaxation for the relief of premenstrual syndrome. *Journal of Behavioral Medicine, 14,* 469-489.

155. Nelson, L. J., & Hekmat, H. (1991). Promoting healthy nutritional habits by paradigmatic behavior therapy. *Journal of Behavior Therapy and Experimental Psychiatry, 22,* 291–298.

156. Nirenberg, T. D., Wincze, J. P., Bansal, S., Liepman, M. R., Engle-Friedman, M., & Begin, A. (1991). Volunteer bias in a study of male alcoholics sexual behavior. *Archives of Sexual Behavior, 20,* 371-379.

157. O'Hara, M. W., Schlechte, J. A., Lewis, D. A., & Wright, E. J. (1991). Prospective study of postpartum blues. *Archives of General Psychiatry, 48,* 801-806.

158. Ollo, C., Johnson, R., & Grafman, J. (1991). Signs of cognitive change in HIV disease: An event-related brain potential study. *Neurology, 41,* 209–215.

159. Öst, L. G., Salkovskis, P. M., & Hellström, K. (1991). One-session therapist-directed exposure vs. self-exposure in the treatment of spider phobia. *Behavior Therapy, 22,* 407–422.

160. Perry, S., Fishman, B., Jacobsberg, L., Young, J., & Frances, A. (1991). Effectiveness of psychoeducational interventions in reducing emotional distress after human immunodeficiency virus antibody testing. *Archives of General Psychiatry, 48,* 143-147.

161. Peselow, E. D., Corwin, J., Fiere, R. R., Rotrosen, J., & Cooper, T. B. (1991). Disappearance of memory deficits in outpatient depressives responding to imipramine. *Journal of Affective Disorders, 21,* 173-183.

162. Piper, W. E., Azim, H. F. A., Joyce, A. S., & McCallum, M. (1991). Transference interpretations, therapeutic alliance, and outcome in short-term individual psychotherapy. *Archives of General Psychiatry, 48,* 946-953.

163. Piper, W. E., Azim, H. F. A., Joyce, A. S., McCallum, M., Nixon, G. W. H., & Segal, P. S. (1991). Quality of object relations versus interpersonal functioning

as predictors of therapeutic alliance and psychotherapy outcome. *The Journal of Nervous and Mental Disease, 179,* 432-438.

164. Reiter, S. R., Otto, M. W., Pollack, M. H., & Rosenbaum, J. F. (1991). Major depression in panic disorder patients with comorbid social phobia. *Journal of Affective Disorders, 22,* 171-177.

165. Rubin, K. H., Both, L., Zahn-Waxler, C., Cummings, E. M., & Wilkinson, M. (1991). Dyadic play behaviors of children of well and depressed mothers. *Development and Psychopathology, 3,* 243-251.

166. Sagar, H. J., Sullivan, E. V., Cooper, J. A., & Jordan, N. (1991). Normal release from proactive interference in untreated patients with Parkinson's disease. *Neuropsychologia, 29,* 1033–1044.

167. Schneider, M. S., Friend, R., Whitaker, P., & Wadhwa, N. K. (1991). Fluid noncompliance and symptomatology in end-stage renal disease: Cognitive and emotional variables. *Health Psychology, 10,* 209-215.

168. Simonds, J. F., McMahon, T., & Armstrong, D. (1991). Young suicide attempters compared with a control group: Psychological, affective, and attitudinal variables. *Suicide and Life-Threatening Behavior, 21,* 134–151.

169. Smith, S. S., Joe, G. W., & Simpson, D. D. (1991). Parental influences on inhalant use by children. *Hispanic Journal of Behavioral Sciences, 13,* 267-275.

170. Souza, F. G. M., Mauder, A. J., Foggo, M., Dick, H., Shearing, C. H., & Goodwin, G. M. (1991). The effects of lithium discontinuation and the non-effect of oral inositol upon thyroid hormones and cortisol in patients with bipolar affective disorder. *Journal of Affective Disorders, 22,* 165-170.

171. Spring, B., Wurtman, J., Gleason, R., Wurtman, R., & Kessler, K. (1991). Weight gain and withdrawal symptoms after smoking cessation: A preventive intervention using d-finfluramine. *Health Psychology, 10,* 216-233.

172. Stanton, A. L., Burker, E. J., & Kershaw, D. (1991). Effects of researcher follow-up of distressed subjects: Tradeoff between validity and ethical responsibility? *Ethics & Behavior, 1,* 105–112.

173. Stein, M. B., & Uhde, T. W. (1991). Endocrine, cardiovascular, and behavioral effects of intravenous protirelin in patients with panic disorder. *Archives of General Psychiatry, 48,* 148-156.

174. Steketee, G., Quay, S., & White, K. (1991). Religion and guilt in OCD patients. *Journal of Anxiety Disorders, 5,* 359-367.

175. Sternberger, L. G., & Burns, G. L. (1991). Obsessive compulsive disorder: Symptoms and diagnosis in a college sample. *Behavior Therapy, 22,* 569–576.

176. Stotland, S., & Zuroff, D. C. (1991). Relations between multiple measures of dieting self-efficacy and weight change in a behavioral weight control program. *Behavior Therapy, 22,* 47–59.

177. Strain, E. C., Stitzer, M. L., & Bigelow, G. E. (1991). Early treatment time course of depressive symptoms in opiate addicts. *The Journal of Nervous and Mental Disease, 179,* 215-221.

178. Taylor, S., & Rachman, S. J. (1991). Fear of sadness. *Journal of Anxiety Disorders, 5,* 375-381.

179. Teti, D. M., & Gelfand, D. M. (1991). Behavioral competence among mothers of infants in the first year: The mediational role of maternal self-efficacy. *Child Development, 62,* 918–929.

180. Thase, M. E., Bowler, K., & Harden, T. (1991). Cognitive behavior therapy of endogenous depression: Part 2: Preliminary findings in 16 unmedicated patients. *Behavior Therapy, 22,* 469–477.

181. Thase, M. E., Simons, A. D., Cahalane, J. F., & McGeary, J. (1991). Cognitive behavior therapy of endogenous depression: Part 1: An outpatient clinical replication series. *Behavior Therapy, 22,* 457–467.

182. Thase, M. E., & Wright, J. H. (1991). Cognitive behavior therapy manual for depressed inpatients: A treatment protocol outline. *Behavior Therapy, 22,* 579–595.

183. Townsley, R. M., Beach, S. R. H., Fincham, F. D., & O'Leary, K. D. (1991). Cognitive specificity for marital discord and depression: What types of cognition influence discord? *Behavior Therapy, 22,* 519–530.

184. Vallejo, J., Gasto, C., Catalan, R., Bulbena, A., & Menchon, J. M. (1991). Predictors of antidepressant treatment outcome in melancholia: Psychosocial, clinical and biological indicators. *Journal of Affective Disorders, 21,* 151-162.

185. VanAmeringen, M., Mancini, C., Styan, G., & Donison, D. (1991). Relationship of social phobia with other psychiatric illness. *Journal of Affective Disorders, 21,* 93-99.

186. Wagner, W. G. (1991). Depression in mothers of sexually abused vs. mothers of nonabused children. *Child Abuse & Neglect, 15,* 99-104.

187. Warner, P., Bancroft, J., Dixson, A., & Hampson, M. (1991). The relationship between perimenstrual depressive mood and depressive illness. *Journal of Affective Disorders, 23,* 9-23.

188. Webster-Stratton, C., & Spitzer, A. (1991). Development, reliability, and validity of the Daily Telephone Discipline Interview. *Behavioral Assessment, 13,* 221-239.

189. Welch, G. W., & Ellis, P. M. (1991). FACTOREP: A new tool to explore the dimensions of depression. *Journal of Affective Disorders, 21,* 101-108.

190. Whipple, E. E., & Webster-Stratton, C. (1991). The role of parental stress in physically abusive families. *Child Abuse & Neglect, 15,* 279-291.

191. Whitley, B. E., Jr., Michael, S. T., & Tremont, G. (1991). Testing for sex differences in the relationship between attributional style and depression. *Sex Roles, 24,* 753-758.

192. Wilson, K. G., Sandler, L. S., Asmundson, G. J. G., Larsen, D. K., & Ediger, J. M. (1991). Effects of instructional set on self-reports of panic attacks. *Journal of Anxiety Disorders, 5,* 43-63.

193. Wollersheim, J. P., & Wilson, G. L. (1991). Group treatment of unipolar depression: A comparison of coping, supportive, bibliotherapy, and delayed treatment groups. *Professional Psychology: Research and Practice, 22,* 496–502.

194. Agostinelli, G., Sherman, S. J., Presson, C. C., & Chassin, L. (1992). Self-protection and self-enhancement biases in estimates of population prevalence. *Personality and Social Psychology Bulletin, 18,* 631-642.

195. Arndt, I. O., Dorozynsky, L., Woody, G. E., McLellan, A. T., & O'Brien, C. P. (1992). Desipramine treatment of cocaine dependence in methadone-maintained patients. *Archives of General Psychiatry, 49,* 888-893.

196. Asle, H., & Torgersen, S. (1992). Mental health locus of control in first-degree relatives of agoraphobic and depressed inpatients. *Psychological Reports, 71,* 579-586.

197. Bagby, R. M., Cox, B. J., Schuller, D. R., Levitt, A. J., Swinson, R. P., & Joffe, R. T. (1992). Diagnostic specificity of the dependent and self-critical personality dimensions in major depression. *Journal of Affective Disorders, 26,* 59-64.

198. Barber, J. P., & DeRubeis, R. J. (1992). The ways of responding: A scale to assess compensatory skills taught in cognitive therapy. *Behavioral Assessment, 14,* 93-115.

199. Barkley, R. A., Anastopoulos, A. D., Goevremont, D. C., & Fletcher, K. E. (1992). Adolescents with attention deficit hyperactivity: Mother-adolescent interactions, family beliefs and conflicts and maternal psychopathology. *Journal of Abnormal Child Psychology, 20,* 263-288.

200. Barlow, D. H., Rapee, R. M., & Brown, T. A. (1992). Behavioral treatment of generalized anxiety disorder. *Behavior Therapy, 23,* 551–570.

201. Beach, S. R. H., & O'Leary, K. D. (1992). Treating depression in the context of marital discord: Outcome and predictors of response of marital therapy versus cognitive therapy. *Behavior Therapy, 23,* 507–528.

202. Beer, J., & Beer, J. (1992). Burnout and stress, depression, and self-esteem of teachers. *Psychological Reports, 71,* 1331-1336.

203. Beer, J., & Beer, J. (1992). Depression, self-esteem, suicide ideation, and GPAs of high school students at risk. *Psychological Reports, 71,* 899-902.

204. Benson, L. T., & Deeter, T. E. (1992). Moderators of the relation between stress and depression in adolescents. *The School Counselor, 39,* 189–194.

205. Berenbaum, H. (1992). Posed facial expressions of emotion in schizophrenia and depression. *Psychological Medicine, 22,* 929-937.

206. Bernstein, G. A., & Garfinkel, B. D. (1992). The Visual Analogue Scale for Anxiety—Revised: Psychometric properties. *Journal of Anxiety Disorders, 6,* 223-239.

207. Boyacioglu, G., & Karanci, A. N. (1992). The relationship of employment status, social support, and life events with depressive symptomotology among married Turkish women. *International Journal of Psychology, 27,* 61–71.

208. Brand, E., & Clingempeel, W. G. (1992). Group behavioral therapy with depressed geriatric inpatients: An assessment of incremental efficacy. *Behavior Therapy, 23,* 475–482.

209. Brewerton, T. D., Mueller, E. A., Lesem, M. D., Brandt, H. A., Quearry, B., George, D. T., Murphy, D. L., & Jimerson, D. C. (1992). Neuroendocrine response to M-chlorophenylpiperazine and L-tryptophan in bulimia. *Archives of General Psychiatry, 49,* 852-861.

210. Brown, T. A., & Deagle, E. A. (1992). Structured interview assessment of nonclinical panic. *Behavior Therapy, 23,* 75–85.

211. Brubeck, D., & Beer, J. (1992). Depression, self-esteem, suicide ideation, death anxiety, and GPA in high school students of divorced and nondivorced parents. *Psychological Reports, 71,* 755-763.

212. Burnett, K. F., Taylor, C. B., & Agras, W. S. (1992). Ambulatory computer-assisted behavior therapy for obesity: An empirical model for examining behavioral correlates of treatment outcome. *Computers in Human Behavior, 8,* 239–248.

213. Carroll, K. M., & Rounsaville, B. J. (1992). Contrast of treatment-seeking and untreated cocaine abusers. *Archives of General Psychiatry, 49,* 464-471.

214. Chambless, D. L., Renneberg, B., Goldstein, A., & Gracely, E. J. (1992). MCMI-diagnosed personality disorders among agoraphobic outpatients: Prevalence and relationship to severity and treatment outcome. *Journal of Anxiety Disorders, 6,* 193-211.

215. Chan, D. W. (1992). Coping with depressed mood among Chinese medical students in Hong Kong. *Journal of Affective Disorders, 24,* 109-116.

216. Clark, D. B., Leslie, M. I., & Jacob, R. G. (1992). Balance complaints and panic disorder: A clinical study of panic symptoms in members of a self-help group for balance disorders. *Journal of Anxiety Disorders, 6,* 47-53.

217. Clarke, G., Hops, H., Lewinsohn, P. M., Andrews, J., Seeley, J. R., & Williams, J. (1992). Cognitive-behavioral group treatment of adolescent depression: Prediction of outcome. *Behavior Therapy, 23,* 341–354.

218. Clarke, G. N., Lewinsohn, P. M., Hops, H., & Seeley, J. R. (1992). A self-and parent-report measure of adolescent depression: The Child Behavior Checklist Depression Scale (CBCL-D). *Behavioral Assessment, 14,* 443-463.

219. Cole, P. M., Barrett, K. C., & Zahn-Waxler, C. (1992). Emotion displays in two-year-olds during mishaps. *Child Development, 63,* 314–324.

220. da Roza Davis, J. M., Sharpley, A. L., Solomon, R. A., & Cowen, P. J. (1992). Sleep and 5-HT^2 receptor sensitivity in recovered depressed patients. *Journal of Affective Disorders, 24,* 177-182.

221. Diamond, R., White, R. F., Myers, R. H., Mastromauro, C., Koroshetz, W. J., Butters, N., Rothstein, D. M., Moss, M. B., & Vasterling, J. (1992). Evidence of presymptomatic cognitive decline in Huntington's disease. *Journal of Clinical and Experimental Neuropsychology, 14,* 961-975.

222. Evans, M. D., Hollon, S. D., DeRubeis, R. J., Piasecki, J. M., Grove, W. M., Garvey, M. J., Tugson, V. B. (1992). Differential relapse following cognitive therapy and pharmacotherapy for depression. *Archives of General Psychiatry, 49,* 802-808.

223. Fahy, T. J., O'Rourke, D., Brophy, J., Schazmann, W., & Sciascia, S. (1992). The Galway study of panic disorder I: Clomipramine and lofepramine in DSM-III-R panic disorder: A placebo controlled trial. *Journal of Affective Disorders, 25,* 63-76.

224. Florin, I., Nostadt, A., Reck, C., Franzen, U., & Jenkins, M. (1992). Expressed emotion in depressed patients and their partners. *Family Process, 31,* 163–172.

225. Fydrich, T., Dowdall, D., & Chambless, D. L. (1992). Reliability and validity of the Beck Anxiety Inventory. *Journal of Anxiety Disorders, 6,* 55-61.

226. Garske, G. G., & Thomas, K. R. (1992). Self-reported self-esteem and depression: Indexes of psychosocial adjustment following severe traumatic brain injury. *Rehabilitation Counselor Bulletin, 36,* 44–52.

227. Geisser, M. E., Robinson, M. E., & Pickren, W. E. (1992). Differences in cognitive coping strategies among pain-sensitive and pain-tolerant individuals on the cold-pressor test. *Behavior Therapy, 23,* 31–41.

228. George, C. E., Lankford, J. S., & Wilson, S. E. (1992). The effects of computerized versus paper-and-pencil administration on measures of negative affect. *Computers in Human Behavior, 8,* 203–209.

229. Goldstein, M. J. (1992). Commentary on "expressed emotion in depressed patients and their partners." *Family Process, 31,* 172-174.

230. Hatch, J. P., Moore, P. J., Bocherding, S., Cyr-Provost, M., Boutros, N. N., & Seleshi, E. (1992). Electromyographic and affective responses of episodic tension-type headache patients and headache-free controls during stressful task performance. *Journal of Behavioral Medicine, 15,* 89-112.

231. Hay, D. F., Zahn-Waxler, C., Cummings, E. M., & Iannotti, R. J. (1992). Young children's view about conflict with peers: A comparison of the daughters and sons of depressed and well women. *Journal of Child Psychology and Psychiatry and Allied Disciplines, 33,* 669-683.

232. Hibbard, M. R., Gordon, W. A., Stein, P. N., Grober, S., & Sliwinski, M. (1992). Awareness of disability in patients following stroke. *Rehabilitation Psychology, 37,* 103–119.

233. Hollon, S. D., DeRubeis, R. J., Evans, M. D., Wiemer, M. J., Garvey, M. J., Grove, W. M., & Tuason, V. B. (1992). Cognitive therapy and pharmacotherapy for depression: Singly and in combination. *Archives of General Psychiatry, 49,* 774-781.

234. Hops, H., & Seeley, J. R. (1992). Parent participation in studies of family interaction: Methodological and substantive considerations. *Behavioral Assessment, 14,* 229-243.

235. Hutchinson, R. L., Tess, D. E., Gleckman, A. D., & Spence, W. C. (1992). Psychosocial characteristics of institutionalized adolescents: Resilient or at risk? *Adolescence, 27,* 339-356.

236. Jack, D. C., & Dill, D. (1992). The silencing the self scale: Schemas of intimacy associated with depression in women. *Psychology of Women Quarterly, 16,* 97-106.

237. Kaplan, R. F., Meadows, M.-E., Vincent, L. C., Logigan, E. L., & Steere, A. C. (1992). Memory impairment and depression inpatients with Lyme encephalopathy: Comparison with fibromyalgia and nonpsychotically depressed patients. *Neurology, 42,* 1263–1267.

238. Kerr, J., & Beer, J. (1992). Specific and diversive curiosity and depression in junior high school students of divorced and nondivorced parents. *Psychological Reports, 71,* 227-231.

239. Kettlewell, P. W., Mizes, J. S., & Wasylyshyn, N. A. (1992). A cognitive-behavioral group treatment of bulimia. *Behavior Therapy, 23,* 657–670.

240. Kirkpatrick-Smith, J., Rich, A. R., Bonner, R., & Jans, F. (1992). Psychological vulnerability and substance abuse as predictors of suicide ideation among adolescents. *Omega, 24,* 21–33.

241. Krejci, R. C., Sargent, R., Forand, K. J., Vreda, J. R., Saunders, R. P., & Durstine, J. L. (1992). Psychological and behavioral differences among females classified as bulimic, obligatory excercisor and normal control. *Psychiatry, 55,* 185–193.

242. Laberge, B., Gauthier, J., Coteé, G., Plamondon, J., & Cormier, H. J. (1992). The treatment of coexisting panic and depression: A review of the literature. *Journal of Anxiety Disorders, 6,* 169-180.

243. Lam, R. W., Buchanan, A., Mador, J. A., Corral, M. R., & Remick, R. A. (1992). The effects of ultraviolet-A wavelengths in light therapy for seasonal depression. *Journal of Affective Disorders, 23,* 237-244.

244. Leadbeater, B. J., & Linares, O. (1992). Depressive symptoms in Black and Puerto Rican adolescent mothers in the first 3 years postpartum. *Development and Psychopathology, 4,* 451-468.

245. Leahy, J. M. (1992). A comparison of depression in women bereaved of a spouse, child, or a parent. *Omega, 26,* 207–217.

246. Lee, S., Chow, C. C., Shek, C. C., Wing, Y. K., & Chen, C-N. (1992). Folate concentration in Chinese psychiatric outpatients on long-term lithium treatment. *Journal of Affective Disorders, 24,* 265-270.

247. Lester, D., & Anderson, D. (1992). Depression and suicidal ideation in African-American and Hispanic American high school students. *Psychological Reports, 71,* 618.

248. Loas, G., Salinas, E., Guelfi, J. D., & Samuel-Lajeunesse, B. (1992). Physical anhedonia in major depressive disorder. *Journal of Affective Disorders, 25,* 139-146.

249. MacKinnon-Lewis, C., Lamb, M. E., Arbuckle, B., Baradaran, L. P., & Volling, B. L. (1992). The relationship between biased maternal and filial attributions and the aggressiveness of their interactions. *Development and Psychopathology, 4,* 403-415.

250. McCance, E. F., Marek, K. L., & Price, L. H. (1992). Serotonergic dysfunction in depression associated with Parkinson's disease. *Neurology, 42,* 1813–1814.

251. McKnight, D. L., Nelson-Gray, R. O., & Barnhill, J. (1992). Dexamethasone suppression test and response to cognitive therapy and antidepressant medication. *Behavior Therapy, 23,* 99–111.

252. Miller, S., & Watson, B. C. (1992). The relationship between communication attitude, anxiety, and depression in stutterers and nonstutterers. *Journal of Speech and Hearing Research, 35,* 789–798.

253. Mintz, J., Mintz, L. I., Arruda, M. J., & Hwang, S. S. (1992). Treatments of depression and the functional capacity to work. *Archives of General Psychiatry, 49,* 761-768.

254. Moes, D., Koegel, R. L., Schreibman, L., & Loos, L. M. (1992). Stress profiles for mothers and fathers of children with autism. *Psychological Reports, 71,* 1272-1274.

255. Moran, P. B., & Eckenrode, J. (1992). Protective personality characteristics among adolescent victims of maltreatment. *Child Abuse & Neglect, 16,* 743-754.

256. Mulhern, R. K., Fairclough, D. L., Smith, B., & Douglas, S. M. (1992). Maternal depression, assessment methods, and physical symptoms affect estimates of depressive symptomatology among children with cancer. *Journal of Pediatric Psychology, 17,* 313–326.

257. Öst, L. G., Hellström, K., & Kåver, A. (1992). One versus five sessions of exposure in the treatment of injection phobia. *Behavior Therapy, 23,* 263–282.

258. Otto, M. W., Pollack, M. H., Sachs, G. S., & Rosenbaum, J. F. (1992). Hypochondriacal concerns, anxiety, sensitivity, and panic disorder. *Journal of Anxiety Disorders, 6,* 93-104.

259. Perry, S., Fishman, B., Jacobsberg, L., & Francis, A. (1992). Relationships over 1 year between lymphocyte subsets and psychosocial variables among adults with infection of Human Immunodeficiency Virus. *Archives of General Psychiatry, 49,* 396-401.

260. Philips, H. C., Fensta, H. N., & Samson, D. (1992). An effective treatment for urinary incoordination. *Journal of Behavioral Medicine, 15,* 45-63.

261. Politano, P. M., Stapleton, L. A., & Correll, J. A. (1992). Differences between children of depressed and non-depressed mothers: Locus of control, anxiety and self esteem: A research note. *Journal of Child Psychology and Psychiatry and Allied Disciplines, 33,* 451-455.

262. Pop, V. J., Komproe, I. H., & van Son, M. J. (1992). Characteristics of the Edinburgh Post Natal Depression Scale in the Netherlands. *Journal of Affective Disorders, 26,* 105-110.

263. Renneberg, B., Chambless, D. L., & Gracely, E. J. (1992). Prevalence of SCID-diagnosed personality disorders in agoraphobia outpatients. *Journal of Anxiety Disorders, 6,* 111-118.

264. Riggs, D. S., Hiss, H., & Foa, E. B. (1992). Marital distress and the treatment of obsessive compulsive disorder. *Behavior Therapy, 23,* 585–597.

265. Robinson, P. J., & Fleming, S. (1992). Depressotypic cognitive patterns in major depression on conjugal bereavement. *Omega, 25,* 291–305.

266. Rousey, A., Best, S., & Blacher, J. (1992). Mothers' and fathers' perceptions of stress and coping with children who have severe disabilities. *American Journal on Mental Retardation, 97,* 99-109.

267. Rubin, R. T., Heist, E. K., McGeoy, S. S., Hanada, K., & Lesser, I. M. (1992). Neuroendocrine aspects of primary endogenous depression. *Archives of General Psychiatry, 49,* 558-567.

268. Sanchez-Bernardos, M. L., & Sanz, J. (1992). Effects of the discrepancy between self-concepts on emotional adjustment. *Journal of Research in Personality, 26,* 303-318.

269. Sandler, L. S., Wilson, K. G., Asmundson, G. J. G., Larsen, D. K., & Ediger, J. M. (1992). Cardiovascular reactivity in nonclinical subjects with infrequent panic attacks. *Journal of Anxiety Disorders, 6,* 27-39.

270. Scheffers, M. K., Johnson, R., Grafman, J., Dale, J. K., & Straus, S. E. (1992). Attention and short-term memory in chronic fatigue syndrome patients: An event-related potential analysis. *Neurology, 42,* 1667–1675.

271. Shek, D. T. L. (1992). Meaning in life and psychological well-being: An empirical study using the Chinese version of the Purpose in Life Questionnaire. *The Journal of Genetic Psychology, 153,* 185-200.

272. Siblerud, R. L. (1992). A comparison of mental health of multiple sclerosis patients with silver/mercury dental fillings and those with fillings removed. *Psychological Reports, 70,* 1139-1151.

273. Startup, M., Rees, A., & Barkham, M. (1992). Components of major depression examined via the Beck Depression Inventory. *Journal of Affective Disorders, 26,* 251-260.

274. Stein, M. B., Tanar, M. E., & Uhde, T. W. (1992). Heart rate and plasma norepinephrine responsivity to orthostatic challenge in anxiety disorders: Comparison of patients with panic disorder and social phobia and normal control subjects. *Archives of General Psychiatry, 49,* 311-317.

275. Stein, P. N., Gordon, W. A., Hibbard, M. R., & Sliwinski, M. J. (1992). An examination of depression in the spouses of stroke patients. *Rehabilitation Psychology, 37,* 121–130.

276. Stuart, S., Simons, A. D., Thase, M. E., & Pilkonis, P. (1992). Are personality assessments valid in acute major depression? *Journal of Affective Disorders, 24,* 281-290.

277. Sung, H., Lubin, B., & Yi, J. (1992). Reliability and validity of the Korean Youth Depression Adjective Check List (Y-DACL). *Adolescence, 27,* 527-533.

278. Thornton, B., & Leo, R. (1992). Gender typing, importance of multiple roles, and mental health consequences for women. *Sex Roles, 27,* 307-317.

279. Wetzel, R. D., Murphy, G. E., Carney, R. M., Whitworth, P., & Knesevich, M. A. (1992). Prescribing therapy for depression: The role of learned resourcefulness, a failure to replicate. *Psychological Reports, 70,* 803-807.

280. Whatley, S. L., & Clopton, J. R. (1992). Social support and suicidal ideation in college students. *Psychological Reports, 71,* 1123-1128.

281. Wierson, M., & Forehand, R. (1992). Family stressors and adolescent functioning: A consideration of models for early and middle adolescents. *Behavior Therapy, 23,* 671–688.

282. Yeaworth, R. C., McNamee, M. J., & Pozehl, B. (1992). The Adolescent Life Change Event Scale: Its development and use. *Adolescence, 27,* 783-802.

283. Zakowski, S. G., McAllister, C. G., Deal, M., & Baum, A. (1992). Stress, reactivity, and immune function in healthy men. *Health Psychology, 11,* 223–232.

284. Zamble, E. (1992). Behavior and adaptation in long-term prison inmates. *Criminal Justice and Behavior, 19*, 409–425.

285. Ackerman, M. D., D'Attilio, J. P., Antoni, M. H., Rhamy, R. K., Weinstein, D., & Politano, V. A. (1993). Patient-reported erectile dysfunction: A cross-validation study. *Archives of Sexual Behavior, 22*, 603-618.

286. Addington, D., Addington, J., & Maticka-Tyndale, E. (1993). Rating depression in schizophrenia: A comparison of a self-report and an observer report scale. *The Journal of Nervous and Mental Disease, 181*, 561-565.

287. Ahles, T. A. (1993). Cancer pain: Research from multidimensional and illness representation models. *Motivation and Emotion, 17*, 225–243.

288. Albright, J. S., Alloy, L. B., Barch, D., & Dykman, B. M. (1993). Social comparison by dysphoric and nondysphoric college students: The grass isn't always greener on the other side. *Cognitive Therapy and Research, 17*, 485-509.

289. Alden, J. D., & Harrison, D. W. (1993). An initial investigation of bright light and depression: A neuropsychological perspective. *Bulletin of the Psychonomic Society, 31*, 621–623.

290. Allen, H. I., Liddle, P. F., & Frith, C. D. (1993). Negative features, retrieval processes and verbal fluency in schizophrenia. *British Journal of Psychiatry, 163*, 769-775.

291. Andrew, B., Hawton, K., Fagg, J., & Westbrook, D. (1993). Do psychosocial factors influence outcome in severely depressed female psychiatric in-patients? *British Journal of Psychiatry, 163*, 747-754.

292. Baron, P., & Campbell, T. L. (1993). Gender differences in the expression of depressive symptoms in middle adolescents: An extension of earlier findings. *Adolescence, 28*, 903-911.

293. Beck, A. T., Steer, R. A., Beck, J. S., & Newman, C. F. (1993). Hopelessness, depression, suicidal ideation, and clinical diagnosis of depression. *Suicide and Life-Threatening Behavior, 23*, 139-145.

294. Beck, A. T., Steer, R. A., & Brown, G. (1993). Dysfunctional attitudes and suicidal ideation in psychiatric outpatients. *Suicide and Life-Threatening Behavior, 23*, 11-20.

295. Birchwood, M., Mason, R., MacMillan, F., & Healy, J. (1993). Depression, demoralization and control over psychotic illness: A comparison of depressed and non-depressed patients with a chronic psychosis. *Psychological Medicine, 23*, 387-395.

296. Brent, D. A., Perper, J. A., Moritz, G., Liotus, L., Schweers, J., Roth, C., Balach, L., & Allman, C. (1993). Psychiatric impact of the loss of an adolescent sibling to suicide. *Journal of Affective Disorders, 28*, 249-256.

297. Brewer, B. W. (1993). Self-identity and specific vulnerability to depressed mood. *Journal of Personality, 61*, 343–364.

298. Byrne, B. M., & Baron, P. (1993). The Beck Depression Inventory: Testing and cross-validating a hierarchical factor structure for nonclinical adolescents. *Measurement and Evaluation in Counseling and Development, 26*, 164-178.

299. Carro, M. G., Grant, K. E., Gotlib, I. H., & Compas, B. E. (1993). Postpartum depression and child development: An investigation of mothers and fathers as sources of risk and resilience. *Development and Psychopathology, 5*, 567-579.

300. Carroll, K. M., Power, M. D., Bryant, K., & Rounsaville, B. J. (1993). One-year follow-up status of treatment-seeking cocaine abusers: Psychopathology and dependence severity as predictors of outcome. *The Journal of Nervous and Mental Disease, 181*, 71-79.

301. Channon, S., Baker, J. E., & Robertson, M. M. (1993). Working memory in clinical depression: An experimental study. *Psychological Medicine, 23*, 87-91.

302. Channon, S., Jones, M., & Stephenson, S. (1993). Cognitive strategies and hypothesis testing during discrimination learning in Parkinson's disease. *Neuropsychologia, 31*, 75-82.

303. Christensen, L., Bourgeois, A., & Cockroft, R. (1993). Electroencephalographic concomitants of a caffeine-induced panic reaction. *The Journal of Nervous and Mental Disease, 181*, 327-330.

304. Connelly, B., Johnston, D., Brown, J. D. R., Mackay, S., & Blackstock, E. G. (1993). The prevalence of depression in a high school population. *Adolescence, 28*, 149-158.

305. Conway, M., Grannopoulos, C., Csank, P., & Mendelson, M. (1993). Dysphoria and specificity in self-focused attention. *Personality and Social Psychology Bulletin, 19*, 265-268.

306. Cooper, J. A., & Sagar, H. J. (1993). Incidental and intentional recall in Parkinson's disease: An account based on diminished attentional resources. *Journal of Clinical and Experimental Neuropsychology, 15*, 713-731.

307. Cooper, J. A., Sagar, H. J., & Sullivan, E. V. (1993). Short-term memory and temporal ordering in early Parkinson's disease: Effects of disease chronicity and medication. *Neuropsychologia, 31*, 933-949.

308. Corcoran, R., & Thompson, P. (1993). Epilepsy and poor memory: Who complains and what do they mean? *British Journal of Clinical Psychology, 32*, 199-208.

309. Dahlquist, L. M., Czyzewski, D. I., Copeland, K. G., Jones, C. L., Taub, E., & Vaughan, J. K. (1993). Parents of children newly diagnosed with cancer: Anxiety, coping, and marital distress. *Journal of Pediatric Psychology, 18*, 365–376.

310. David, A. S. (1993). Spatial and selective attention in the cerebral hemispheres in depression, mania, and schizophrenia. *Brain and Cognition, 23*, 166-180.

311. deBears, E., Lange, A., Blonk, R. W. B., Koele, P., van Balkom, A. J. L. M., & van Dyck, R. (1993). Goal attainment scaling: An idiosyncratic method to assess treatment effectiveness in agoraphobia. *Journal of Psychopathology and Behavioral Assessment, 15*, 357–373.

312. de Man, A. F., Leduc, C. P., & Labréche-Gauthier, L. (1993). Correlations of suicidal ideation in French-Canadian adolescents: Personal variables, stress, and social support. *Adolescence, 28*, 819-830.

313. de Man, A. F., Leduc, C. P., & Labréche-Gauthier, L. (1993). A French-Canadian scale for suicide ideation for use with adolescents. *Canadian Journal of Behavioural Science, 25*, 126-134.

314. Derry, P. A., Chovaz, C. J., McClachlan, R. S., & Cummings, A. (1993). Learned resourcefulness and psychosocial adjustment following temporal lobectomy in epilepsy. *Journal of Social and Clinical Psychology, 12*, 454–470.

315. Dorman, A., O'Connor, A., Hardiman, E., Freyne, A., & O'Neil, H. (1993). Psychiatric morbidity in sentenced HIV-positive prisoners. *British Journal of Psychiatry, 163*, 802-805.

316. Dunn, G., Sham, P., & Hand, D. (1993). Statistics and the nature of depression. *Psychological Medicine, 23*, 871-889.

317. Dura, J. R. (1993). Educational intervention for a Huntington's disease caregiver. *Psychological Reports, 72*, 1099-1105.

318. Fairburn, C. G., Jones, R., Peveler, R. C., Hope, R. A., & O'Connor, M. (1993). Psychotherapy and bulimia nervosa: Longer-term effects of interpersonal psychotherapy, behavior therapy, and cognitive behavior therapy. *Archives of General Psychiatry, 50*, 419-428.

319. Fals-Stewart, W., Marks, A. P., & Schafer, J. (1993). A comparison of behavioral group therapy and individual behavior therapy in treating obsessive-compulsive disorder. *The Journal of Nervous and Mental Disease, 181*, 189-193.

320. Fitzgerald, H. E., Sullivan, L. A., Ham, H. P., Zucker, R. A., Bruckel, S., Schneider, A. M., & Noll, R. B. (1993). Predictors of behavior problems in three-year-old sons of alcoholics: Early evidence for the onset of risk. *Child Development, 64*, 110-123.

321. Flick, S. N., Roy-Byrne, P. P., Cowley, D. S., Shores, M. M., & Dunner, D. L. (1993). DSM-III-R personality disorders in a mood and anxiety disorders clinic: Prevalence, comorbidity, and clinical correlates. *Journal of Affective Disorders, 27*, 71-79.

322. Ford, J. G., Lawson, J., & Hook, M. (1993). Further development of the public-private congruence technique. *Psychological Reports, 73*, 872-874.

323. Fremouw, W., Callahan, T., & Kashden, J. (1993). Adolescent suicide risk: Psychological, problem solving, and environmental factors. *Suicide and Life-Threatening Behavior, 23*, 46-62.

324. Gidycz, C. A., Coble, C. N., Latham, L., & Layman, M. J. (1993). Sexual assault experience in adulthood and prior victimization experiences. *Psychology of Women Quarterly, 17*, 151-168.

325. Gillis, J. S. (1993). Effects of life stress and dysphoria on complex judgements. *Psychological Reports, 72*, 1355-1363.

326. Gonman, J., Leifer, M., & Grossman, G. (1993). Nonorganic failure to thrive: Maternal history and current maternal functioning. *Journal of Clinical Child Psychology, 22*, 327-336.

327. Goodman, S. H., Brogan, D., Lynch, M. E., & Fielding, B. (1993). Social and emotional competence in children of depressed mothers. *Child Development, 64*, 516-531.

328. Gould, R. A., Clum, G. A., & Shapiro, D. (1993). The use of bibliotherapy in the treatment of panic: A preliminary investigation. *Behavior Therapy, 24*, 241–252.

329. Grubb, H. J., Sellers, M. I., & Waligroski, K. (1993). Factors related to depression and eating disorders: Self-esteem, body image, and attractiveness. *Psychological Reports, 72*, 1003-1010.

330. Hagopian, L. P., & Slifer, K. J. (1993). Treatment of separation anxiety disorder with graduate exposure and reinforcement targeting school attendance: A controlled case study. *Journal of Anxiety Disorders, 7*, 271-280.

331. Haller, D. L., Knisely, J. S., Dawson, K. S., & Schnoll, S. H. (1993). Perinatal substance abusers: Psychological and social characteristics. *The Journal of Nervous and Mental Disease, 181*, 509-513.

332. Haslam, N., & Beck, A. T. (1993). Categorization of major depression in an outpatient sample. *The Journal of Nervous and Mental Disease, 181*, 725-731.

333. Horowitz, M., Stinson, C., Fridhandler, B., Milbrath, C., Redington, D., & Ewert, M. (1993). Vivid representation of psychotherapeutic processes: Pathological grief: An intensive case study. *Psychiatry, 56*, 356–374.

334. Hortacsu, N., Cesur, S., & Oral, A. (1993). Relationship between depression and attachment styles in parent- and institution-reared Turkish children. *The Journal of Genetic Psychology, 154*, 329-337.

335. Huzel, L. L., Delaney, S. M., & Stein, M. B. (1993). Lymphocyte A B-adrenergic receptors in panic disorder: Findings with highly selective ligand and relationship to clinical parameters. *Journal of Anxiety Disorders, 7*, 349-357.

336. Jackson, H. J., & Pica, S. (1993). An investigation into the internal structure of DSM-III antisocial personality disorder. *Psychological Reports, 72*, 355-367.

337. Jacob, R. G., Woody, S. R., Clark, D. B., Lilienfeld, S. O., Hirsch, B. E., Kucera, G. D., Furman, J. M., & Durrant, J. D. (1993). Discomfort with space and motion: A possible marker for vestibular dysfunction assessed by the Situational Characteristics Questionnaire. *Journal of Psychopathology and Behavioral Assessment, 15*, 299–324.

338. Jacobs, G. D., Benson, H., & Friedman, R. (1993). Home-based central nervous system assessment of a multifactor behavioral intervention for chronic sleep-onset insomnia. *Behavior Therapy, 24*, 159–174.

339. Jacobs, K. W., & Boze, M. M. (1993). Correlations among scales of the Beck Depression Inventory and the Profile of Mood States. *Psychological Reports, 73*, 431-434.

340. Jacobson, S. W., Jacobson, J. L., Sokol, R. J., Martier, S. S., & Ager, J. W. (1993). Prenatal alcohol exposure and infant information processing ability. *Child Development, 64*, 1706-1721.

341. James, L. D., Thorn, B. E., & Williams, D. A. (1993). Goal specification in cognitive-behavioral therapy for chronic headache pain. *Behavior Therapy, 24*, 305–320.

342. Jolly, J. B. (1993). A multi-method test of the cognitive content-specificity hypothesis in young adolescents. *Journal of Anxiety Disorders, 7*, 223-233.

343. Kenardy, J., & Dei, T. P. S. (1993). Phobic anxiety in panic disorder: Cognition, heart rate, and subjective anxiety. *Journal of Anxiety Disorders, 7*, 359-371.

344. King, A. C., Taylor, C. B., & Haskell, W. L. (1993). Effects of differing intensities and formats of 12 months of exercise training on psychological outcomes in older adults. *Health Psychology, 12,* 292–300.

345. Kirkham, M. A. (1993). Two-year follow-up of skills training with mothers of children with disabilities. *American Journal on Mental Retardation, 97,* 509-520.

346. Lakey, B., Baltman, S., & Bentley, K. (1993). Dysphoria and vulnerability to subsequent life events. *Journal of Research in Personality, 27,* 138-153.

347. Lapp, W. M., & Collins, R. L. (1993). Relative/proportional scoring of the Ways of Coping Checklist: Is it advantageous or artifactual? *Multivariate Behavioral Research, 28,* 483–512.

348. Lester, D. (1993). Depression, suicidal preoccupation and scores on the Rokeach Value Survey: A correction. *Psychological Reports, 73,* 1202.

349. Lester, D. (1993). Functional and dysfunctional impulsivity and depression and suicidal ideation in a subclinical population. *The Journal of General Psychology, 120,* 187-188.

350. Lester, D., & Schaeffler, J. (1993). Self-defeating personality, depression, and suicidal ideation in adolescents. *Psychological Reports, 73,* 113-114.

351. Linden, W., Chambers, L., Maurice, J., & Lenz, J. W. (1993). Sex differences in social support, self-deception, hostility and ambulatory cardiovascular activity. *Health Psychology, 12,* 376-380.

352. Lubin, B., Whitlock, R. V., Schemmel, D. R., & Swearingin, S. E. (1993). Evaluation of a brief measure of depressive mood for use in a university counseling center. *Psychological Reports, 72,* 379-385.

353. Maddock, R. J., Gietzen, D. W., & Goodman, T. A. (1993). Decreased lymphocyte beta-adrenoreceptor function correlates with less agoraphobia and better outcome in panic disorder. *Journal of Affective Disorders, 29,* 27-32.

354. Marcel, B. B., Samson, J., Cole, J. O., & Schatzberg, A. F. (1993). Discrimination of facial emotion in depressed patients with visual-perceptual disturbances. *The Journal of Nervous and Mental Disease, 181,* 583-584.

355. McCormick, R. A. (1993). Disinhibition and negative affectivity in substance abusers with and without a gambling problem. *Addictive Behaviors, 18,* 331-336.

356. McGreal, R., & Joseph, S. (1993). The Depression-Happiness Scale. *Psychological Reports, 73,* 1279-1282.

357. Meesters, Y., Jansen, J. H. C., Beersma, D. G. M., Bouhuys, A. L., van den Hoofdakker, R. H. (1993). Early light treatment can prevent an emerging winter depression from developing into a full-blown depression. *Journal of Affective Disorders, 29,* 41-47.

358. Meesters, Y., Jansen, J. H. C., Lambers, P. A., Bouhuys, A. L., Beersma, D. G. M., & van den Hoofdakker, R. H. (1993). Morning and evening light treatment of seasonal affective disorder: Response, relapse, and prediction. *Journal of Affective Disorders, 28,* 165-177.

359. Miller, D. A. F., McCluskey-Fawcett, K., & Irving, L. M. (1993). Correlates of bulimia nervosa: Early family mealtime experiences. *Adolescence, 28,* 621-635.

360. Mindell, J. A., & Durand, V. M. (1993). Treatment of childhood sleep disorders: Generalization across disorders and effects on family members. *Journal of Pediatric Psychology, 18,* 731–750.

361. Moore, R. G., & Blackburn, I. (1993). Sociotropy, autonomy and personal memories in depression. *British Journal of Clinical Psychology, 32,* 460-462.

362. Morano, C. D., Cisler, R. A., & Lemerond, J. (1993). Risk factors for adolescent suicidal behavior: Loss, insufficient familial support, and hopelessness. *Adolescence, 28,* 851-865.

363. Morrissette, D. L., Skinner, M. H., Hoffman, B. B., Levine, R. E., & Davidson, J. M. (1993). Effects of antihypertensive drug atenolol and nifedipine on sexual function in older men: A placebo-controlled, crossover study. *Archives of Sexual Behavior, 22,* 99-109.

364. Nixon, C. D., & Singer, G. H. S. (1993). Group cognitive-behavioral treatment for excessive parental self-blame and guilt. *American Journal on Mental Retardation, 97,* 665-672.

365. Nofzinger, E. A., Thase, M. E., Reynolds, C. F., III, Frank, E., Jennings, R., Garamoni, G. L., Fasiczka, A. L., & Kupfer, D. J. (1993). Sexual function in depressed men: Assessment by self-report, behavioral and nocturnal penile tumescence measures before and after treatment with cognitive behavior therapy. *Archives of General Psychiatry, 50,* 24-30.

366. Ollendick, T. H., Lease, C. A., & Cooper, C. (1993). Separation anxiety in young adults: A preliminary examination. *Journal of Anxiety Disorders, 7,* 293-305.

367. Page, S., & Bennesch, S. (1993). Gender and reporting differences in measures of depression. *Canadian Journal of Behavioural Science, 25,* 579-589.

368. Park, C. L., & Cohen, L. H. (1993). Religious and nonreligious coping with the death of a friend. *Cognitive Therapy and Research, 17,* 561-577.

369. Persons, J. B., Burns, D. D., Perloff, J. M., & Miranda, J. (1993). Relationships between symptoms of depression and anxiety and dysfunctional beliefs about achievement and attachment. *Journal of Abnormal Psychology, 102,* 518-524.

370. Pibernik-Okanovil, M., Roglic, G., Prasek, M., & Metelko, Z. (1993). War-induced prolonged stress and metabolic control in type 2 diabetic patients. *Psychological Medicine, 23,* 645-651.

371. Pincus, T., Pearce, S., McClelland, A., & Turner-Stokes, L. (1993). Self-referential selective memory in pain patients. *British Journal of Clinical Psychology, 32,* 365-374.

372. Pinto, A., & Francis, G. (1993). Cognitive correlates of depressive symptoms in hospitalized adolescents. *Adolescence, 28,* 661-672.

373. Poulakis, Z., & Wertheim, E. H. (1993). Relationships among dysfunctional cognitions, depressive symptoms, and bulimic tendencies. *Cognitive Therapy and Research, 17,* 549-559.

374. Prince, J. D., & Berenbaum, H. (1993). Alexithymia and hedonic capacity. *Journal of Research in Personality, 27,* 15-22.

375. Raj, B. A., Corvea, M. H., & Dagon, E. M. (1993). The clinical characteristics of panic disorder in the elderly: A retrospective study. *Journal of Clinical Psychiatry, 54,* 150–155.

376. Rierdan, J., & Koff, E. (1993). Developmental variables in relation to depressive symptoms in adolescent girls. *Development and Psychopathology, 5,* 485-496.

377. Rokke, P. D. (1993). Social context and perceived task difficulty as mediators of depressive self-evaluation. *Motivation and Emotion, 17,* 23–40.

378. Rosenblatt, A., & Attkisson, C. C. (1993). Assessing outcomes for sufferers of severe mental disorder: A conceptual framework and review. *Evaluation and Program Planning, 16,* 347–363.

379. Rosenfarb, I. S., Burker, E. J., Morris, S. A., & Cush, D. T. (1993). Effects of changing contingencies on the behavior of depressed and nondepressed individuals. *Journal of Abnormal Psychology, 102,* 642-646.

380. Roy, A. (1993). Features associated with suicide attempts in depression: A partial replication. *Journal of Affective Disorders, 27,* 35-38.

381. Rude, S. S., & Burnham, B. L. (1993). Do interpersonal and achievement vulnerabilities interact with congruent events to predict depression? Comparison of DEQ, SAS, DAS, and combined scales. *Cognitive Therapy and Research, 17,* 531-548.

382. Rugle, L., & Melamed, L. (1993). Neuropsychological assessment of attention problems in pathological gamblers. The *Journal of Nervous and Mental Disease, 181,* 107-112.

383. Saddler, C. D., & Sacks, L. A. (1993). Multidimensional perfectionism and academic procrastination: Relationships with depression in university students. *Psychological Reports, 73,* 863-871.

384. Sanders, M. R., Patel, R. K., LeGrice, B., & Shepherd, R. W. (1993). Children with persistent feeding difficulties: An observational analysis of the feeding interactions of problem and non-problem eaters. *Health Psychology, 12,* 64-73.

385. Schmidt, P. J., Grover, G. N., & Rubinow, D. R. (1993). Alprazolam in the treatment of premenstrual syndrome. *Archives of General Psychiatry, 50,* 467-473.

386. Schotte, C., Maes, M., Beuten, T., Vandenbossche, B., & Cosyns, P. (1993). A videotape as introduction for cognitive behavioral therapy with depressed inpatients. *Psychological Reports, 72,* 440-442.

387. Schultz, G., & Melzack, R. (1993). Visual hallucinations and mental state: A study of 14 Charles Bonnet Syndrome hallucinators. *The Journal of Nervous and Mental Disease, 181,* 639-643.

388. Schwab, K., Grafman, J., Salazar, A. M., & Kraft, J. (1993). Residual impairments and work status 15 years after penetrating head injury: Report from the Vietnam Head Injury Study. *Neurology, 43,* 95–103.

389. Senra, C., & Polaino, A. (1993). Concordance between clinical and self-report depression scales during the acute phase and after treatment. *Journal of Affective Disorders, 27,* 13-20.

390. Shagle, S. C., & Barber, B. K. (1993). Effects of family, marital, and parent-child conflict on adolescent self-derogation and suicidal ideation. *Journal of Marriage and the Family, 55,* 964–974.

391. Shaw, D. S., & Vondra, J. I. (1993). Chronic family adversity and infant attachment security. *Journal of Child Psychology and Psychiatry and Allied Disciplines, 34,* 1205-1215.

392. Silverman, R. J., & Peterson, C. (1993). Explanatory style of schizophrenic and depressed outpatients. *Cognitive Therapy and Research, 17,* 457-470.

393. Simons, A. D., Angell, K. L., Monroe, J. M., & Thase, M. E. (1993). Cognition and life stress in depression: Cognitive factors and the definition, rating, and generation of negative life events. *Journal of Abnormal Psychology, 102,* 584-591.

394. Smith, J. E., Waldorf, V. A., & McNamara, C. L. (1993). Use of implosive therapy scenes to assess the fears of women with bulimia in two response modes. *Behavior Therapy, 24,* 601–618.

395. Soloff, P. H., Cornelius, J., George, A., Nathan, S., Perel, J. M., & Ulrich, R. F. (1993). Efficacy of phenelzine and haloperidol in borderline personality disorder. *Archives of General Psychiatry, 50,* 377-385.

396. Spangler, D. L., Simons, A. D., Monroe, S. M., & Thase, M. (1993). Evaluating the hopelessness model of depression: Diathesis-stress and symptoms components. *Journal of Abnormal Psychology, 102,* 592-600.

397. Spencer, M. B., Cole, S. P., DuPree, D., Glymph, A., & Pierre, P. (1993). Self-efficacy among urban African American early adolescents: Exploring issues of risk, vulnerability, and resilience. *Development and Psychopathology, 5,* 719-739.

398. Spoov, J., Suominen, J. Y., Lahdelma, R. L., Katile, H., Kymáláinen, O., Isometsa, E., Liukko, H., & Aurinen, J. (1993). Do reversed depressive symptoms occur together as a syndrome? *Journal of Affective Disorders, 27,* 131-134.

399. Steer, R. A., Ranieri, W. F., Beck, A. T., & Clark, D. A. (1993). Further evidence for the validity of the Beck Anxiety Inventory with psychiatric outpatients. *Journal of Anxiety Disorders, 7,* 195-205.

400. Steiger, H., Leung, F., Thibaudeau, J., & Houle, L. (1993). Prognostic utility of subcomponents of the borderline personality construct in bulimia nervosa. *British Journal of Clinical Psychology, 32,* 187-197.

401. Stein, M. B., Enns, M. W., & Kryger, M. H. (1993). Sleep in nondepressed patients with panic disorder: II. Polysomnographic assessment of sleep architecture and sleep continuity. *Journal of Affective Disorders, 28,* 1-6.

402. Stevens-Ratchford, R. G. (1993). The effect of life review reminiscence activities on depression and self-esteem in older adults. *The American Journal of Occupational Therapy, 47,* 413-420.

403. Telch, C. F., & Agras, W. S. (1993). The effects of a very low calorie diet on binge eating. *Behavior Therapy, 24,* 177–193.

404. VanAmeringen, M., Mancini, C., & Streiner, D. L. (1993). Fluoxetine efficacy in social phobia. *Journal of Clinical Psychiatry, 54,* 27–32.

405. VanHasselt, V. B., Null, J. A., Kempton, T., & Bukstein, O. E. (1993). Social skills and depression in adolescent substance abusers. *Addictive Behaviors, 18,* 9-18.

406. Waterman, J., & Lusk, R. (1993). Psychological testing in evaluation of child sexual abuse. *Child Abuse & Neglect, 17,* 145-159.

407. Whitley, B. E., Jr., & Gridley, B. E. (1993). Sex role orientation, self-esteem, and depression: A latent variable analysis. *Personality and Social Psychology Bulletin, 19*, 363-369.

408. Wiederman, M. W., & Allgeier, E. R. (1993). The measurement of sexual-esteem: Investigation of Snell and Papini's (1989) Sexuality Scale. *Journal of Research in Personality, 27*, 88-102.

409. Wilson, T. D., & Kraft, D. (1993). Why do I love thee?: Effects of repeated introspections about a dating relationship on attitudes toward the relationship. *Personality and Social Psychology Bulletin, 19*, 409-418.

410. Zane, G., & Williams, S. L. (1993). Performance-related anxiety in agoraphobia: Treatment procedures and cognitive mechanisms of change. *Behavior Therapy, 24*, 625-643.

411. Addeo, R. R., Greene, A. F., & Geisser, M. E. (1994). Construct validity of the Robson Self-Esteem Questionnaire in a college sample. *Educational and Psychological Measurement, 54*, 439-446.

412. Agras, W. S., Rossiter, E. M., Arnow, B., Telch, C. F., Raeburn, S. D., Bruce, B., & Koran, L. M. (1994). One-year follow-up of psychosocial and pharmacologic treatments for bulimia nervosa. *The Journal of Clinical Psychiatry, 55*, 179-183.

413. Agras, W. S., Telch, C. F., Arnow, B., Eldredge, K., Wilfley, D. E., Raeburn, S. D., Henderson, J., & Marnell, M. (1994). Weight loss, cognitive-behavioral, and desipramine treatments in binge eating disorder: An additive design. *Behavior Therapy, 25*, 225-238.

414. Alden, L. E., Bieling, P. J., & Wallace, S. T. (1994). Perfectionism in an interpersonal context: A self-regulation analysis of dysphoria and social anxiety. *Cognitive Therapy and Research, 18*, 297-316.

415. Alfano, M. S., Joiner, T. E., & Perry, M. (1994). Attributional style: A mediator of the shyness-depression relationship. *Journal of Research in Personality, 28*, 287-300.

416. Alford, B. A., & Correia, C. J. (1994). Cognitive therapy of schizophrenia: Theory and empirical status. *Behavior Therapy, 25*, 17-33.

417. Allen-Burge, R., Storandt, M., Kinscherf, D. A., & Rubin, E. H. (1994). Sex differences in the sensitivity of two self-report depression scales in older depressed inpatients. *Psychology and Aging, 9*, 443-445.

418. Arndt, I. O., McLellan, T., Dorozynsky, L., Woody, G. E., & O'Brien, C. P. (1994). Desipramine treatment for cocaine dependence: Role of antisocial personality disorder. *The Journal of Nervous and Mental Disease, 182*, 151-156.

419. Asmundson, G. J. G., & Stein, M. B. (1994). Selective processing of social threat in patients with generalized social phobia: Evaluation using a dot-probe paradigm. *Journal of Anxiety Disorders, 8*, 107-117.

420. Atkinson, S. D. (1994). Grieving and loss in parents with a schizophrenic child. *American Journal of Psychiatry, 151*, 1137-1139.

421. Atlas, G., & Morier, D. (1994). The sorority rush process: Self-selection, acceptance criteria, and the effect of rejection. *Journal of College Student Development, 35*, 346-353.

422. Basoglu, M., Marks, I. M., Kilic, C., Swinson, R. P., Noshirvani, H., Kuch, K., & O'Sullivan, G. (1994). Relationship of panic, anticipatory anxiety, agoraphobia, and global improvement in panic disorder with agoraphobia treated with alprazolam and exposure. *British Journal of Psychiatry, 164*, 647-652.

423. Basoglu, M., Paker, M., Paker, O., Ozmen, E., Marks, I., Incesu, C., Sahin, D., & Sarimurat, N. (1994). Psychological effects of torture: A comparison of tortured with nontortured political activists in Turkey. *American Journal of Psychiatry, 151*, 76-81.

424. Bazin, N., Perruchet, P., DeBonis, M., & Feline, A. (1994). The dissociation of explicit and implicit memory in depressed patients. *Psychological Medicine, 24*, 239-245.

425. Beach, S. R. H., Whisman, M. A., & O'Leary, K. D. (1994). Marital therapy for depression: Theoretical foundation, current status, and future directions. *Behavior Therapy, 25*, 345-371.

426. Beck, J. G., & Zebb, B. J. (1994). Behavioral assessment and treatment of panic disorder: Current status, future directions. *Behavior Therapy, 25*, 581-611.

427. Benkelfat, C., Ellenbogen, M. A., Dean, P., Palmour, R. M., & Young, S. N. (1994). Mood-lowering effect of tryptophan depletion: Enhanced susceptibility of young men at genetic risk for major affective disorders. *Archives of General Psychiatry, 51*, 687-697.

428. Berman, W. H., Heiss, G. E., & Sperling, M. B. (1994). Measuring continued attachment to parents: The Continued Attachment Scale—Parent Version. *Psychological Reports, 75*, 171-182.

429. Blood, G. W., Blood, I. M., Bennett, S., Simpson, K. C., & Susman, E. J. (1994). Subjective anxiety measurements and cortisol responses in adults who stutter. *Journal of Speech and Hearing, 37*, 760-768.

430. Boone, D. E. (1994). Validity of the MMPI-2 depression content scale with psychiatric inpatients. *Psychological Reports, 74*, 159-162.

431. Borden, J. W. (1994). Panic disorder and suicidality: Prevalence and risk factors. *Journal of Anxiety Disorders, 8*, 217-225.

432. Boumann, C. E., & Yates, W. R. (1994). Risk factors for bulimia nervosa: A controlled study of parental psychiatric illness and divorce. *Addictive Behaviors, 19*, 667-675.

433. Bromberger, J. T., Wisner, K. L., & Hanusa, B. H. (1994). Marital support and remission of treated depression: A prospective pilot study of mothers of infants and toddlers. *The Journal of Nervous and Mental Disease, 182*, 40-44.

434. Brown, H. D., Kosslyn, J. M., Breiter, H. C., Baer, L., & Jenike, M. A. (1994). Can patients with obsessive-compulsive disorder discriminate between percepts and mental images? A signal detection analysis. *Journal of Abnormal Psychology, 103*, 445-454.

435. Bruch, M. A., & Heimberg, R. G. (1994). Differences in perceptions of parental and personal characteristics between generalized and nongeneralized social phobics. *Journal of Anxiety Disorders, 8*, 155-168.

436. Burgess, E., & Haaga, D. A. F. (1994). The Positive Automatic Thoughts Questionnaire (ATQ-P) and the Automatic Thoughts Questionnaire—Revised (ATQ-RP): Equivalent measures of positive thinking? *Cognitive Therapy and Research, 18*, 15-23.

437. Burgess, M., Marks, I. M., & Gill, M. (1994). Postal self-exposure treatment of recurrent nightmares. *British Journal of Psychiatry, 165*, 388-391.

438. Burns, D. D., Rude, S., Simons, A. D., Bates, M. A., & Thase, M. E. (1994). Does learning resourcefulness predict the response to cognitive behavioral therapy for depression? *Cognitive Therapy and Research, 18*, 277-291.

439. Burns, D. D., Sayers, S. L., & Moras, K. (1994). Intimate relationships and depression: Is there a causal connection? *Journal of Consulting and Clinical Psychology, 62*, 1033-1043.

440. Butler, L. D., & Nolen-Hoeksema, S. (1994). Gender differences in responses to depressed mood in a college sample. *Sex Roles, 30*, 331-346.

441. Calamari, J. E., Faber, S. D., Hitsman, B. L., & Poppe, C. J. (1994). Treatment of obsessive compulsive disorder in the elderly: A review and case example. *Journal of Behavior Therapy and Experimental Psychiatry, 25*, 95-104.

442. Carmichael, M. S., Warburton, V. L., Dixen, J., & Davidson, J. M. (1994). Relationships among cardiovascular, muscular, and oxytocin responses during human sexual activity. *Archives of Sexual Behavior, 23*, 59-79.

443. Carroll, K. M., Rounsaville, B. J., Gordon, L. T., Nich, C., Jatlow, P., Bisighini, R. M., & Gawin, F. H. (1994). Psychotherapy and pharmacotherapy for ambulatory cocaine abusers. *Archives of General Psychiatry, 51*, 177-187.

444. Chadwick, P. D. J., Lowe, C. F., Horne, P. J., & Higson, P. J. (1994). Modifying delusions: The role of empirical testing. *Behavior Therapy, 25*, 35-49.

445. Cheng, W. C., Shuckers, P. L., Hauser, G., Burch, J., Emmett, J. G., Walker, B., Law, E., Wakefield, D., Boyle, D., Lee, M., & Thyer, B. A. (1994). Psychosocial needs of family caregivers of terminally ill patients. *Psychological Reports, 75*, 1243-1250.

446. Chouinard, G., Saxena, B. M., Nair, N. P. V., Kutcher, S. P., Bakish, D., Bradwejn, J., Kennedy, S. H., Sharma, V., Remick, R. A., Kukha-Mohamad, J. A., Belanger, M. C., Snaith, J., Beauclair, L., Pohlmann, H., & D'Souza, J. (1994). A Canadian multicentre placebo-controlled study of a fixed dose of brofaromine, a reversible selective MOA-A inhibitor, in the treatment of major depression. *Journal of Affective Disorders, 32*, 105-114.

447. Christensen, A. J., Wiebe, J. S., Smith, T. W., & Turner, C. W. (1994). Predictors of survival among hemodialysis patients: Effect of perceived family support. *Health Psychology, 13*, 521-525.

448. Christenson, G. A., Faber, R. J., deZwaan, M., Raymond, N. C., Specker, S. M., Ekern, M. D., Mackenzie, T. B., Crosby, R. D., Crow, S. J., Eckert, E. D., Mussell, M. P., & Mitchell, J. E. (1994). Compulsive buying: Descriptive characteristics and psychiatric comorbidity. *The Journal of Clinical Psychiatry, 55*, 5-11.

449. Clark, D. A., Beck, A. T., & Beck, J. S. (1994). Symptom differences in major depression, dysthymia, panic disorder, and generalized anxiety disorder. *American Journal of Psychiatry, 151*, 205-209.

450. Clark, D. A., & Steer, R. A. (1994). Use of nonsomatic symptoms to differentiate clinically depressed and nondepressed hospitalized patients with chronic medical illnesses. *Psychological Reports, 75*, 1089-1090.

451. Clark, D. A., Steer, R. A., & Beck, A. T. (1994). Common and specific dimensions of self-reported anxiety and depression: Implications for the cognitive and tripartite models. *Journal of Abnormal Psychology, 103*, 645-654.

452. Clark, K., Dinsmore, S., Grafman, J., & Dalakas, M. C. (1994). A personality profile of patients diagnosed with post-poliosyndrome. *Neurology, 44*, 1809-1811.

453. Clark, M. E. (1994). Interpretive limitations of the MMPI-2 anger and cynicism content scales. *Journal of Personality Assessment, 63*, 89-96.

454. Cloitre, M., Shear, M. K., Cancienne, J., & Zeitlin, S. B. (1994). Implicit and explicit memory for catastrophic associations to bodily sensation words in panic disorder. *Cognitive Therapy and Research, 18*, 225-240.

455. Cohan, C. L., & Bradbury, T. N. (1994). Assessing responses to recurring problems in marriage: Evaluation of the Marital Coping Inventory. *Psychological Assessment, 6*, 191-200.

456. Cohen, D. S., Friedrich, W. N., Jaworski, T. M., Copeland, D., & Pendergrass, T. (1994). Pediatric cancer: Predicting sibling adjustment. *Journal of Clinical Psychology, 50*, 303-319.

457. Cowen, P. J., Power, A. C., Ware, C. J., & Anderson, I. M. (1994). 5-HT$_{1A}$ receptor sensitivity in major depression: A neuroendocrine study with buspirone. *British Journal of Psychiatry, 164*, 372-379.

458. Cox, B. J., Direnfeld, D. M., Swinson, R. P., & Norton, G. R. (1994). Suicidal ideation and suicide attempts in panic disorder and social phobia. *American Journal of Psychiatry, 151*, 882-887.

459. Craig, A. R., Hancock, K. M., & Dickson, H. G. (1994). Spinal cord injury: A search for determinants of depression two years after the event. *British Journal of Clinical Psychology, 33*, 221-230.

460. Crews, W. D., Jr., & Harrison, D. W. (1994). Cerebral asymmetry in facial affect perception by women: Neuropsychological effects of depressed mood. *Perceptual and Motor Skills, 79*, 1667-1679.

461. Crews, W. D., Jr., & Harrison, D. W. (1994). Functional asymmetry in the motor performance of women: Neuropsychological effects of depression. *Perceptual and Motor Skills, 78*, 1315-1322.

462. Crittenden, P. M., Claussen, A. H., & Sugarman, D. B. (1994). Physical and psychological maltreatment in middle childhood and adolescence. *Development and Psychopathology, 6*, 145-164.

463. Crocker, J., Luhtanen, R., Blaine, B., & Broadnax, S. (1994). Collective self-esteem and psychological well-being among White, Black, and Asian college students. *Personality and Social Psychology Bulletin, 20*, 503-513.

464. Cross, S. E., & Markus, H. R. (1994). Self-schemas, possible selves, and competent performance. *Journal of Educational Psychology, 86,* 423-438.

465. Damos, D. L., & Parker, E. S. (1994). High false alarm rates on a vigilance task may indicate recreational drug use. *Journal of Clinical and Experimental Neuropsychology, 16,* 713-722.

466. DeLuca, J., Barbieri-Berger, S., & Johnson, S. K. (1994). The nature of memory impairments in multiple sclerosis: Acquisition versus retrieval. *Journal of Clinical and Experimental Neuropsychology, 16,* 183-189.

467. de Man, A. F., & Leduc, C. P. (1994). Validity and reliability of a self-report suicide ideation scale for use with adolescents. *Social Behavior and Personality, 22,* 261-266.

468. DeSimone, A., Murray, P., & Lester, D. (1994). Alcohol use, self-esteem, depression, and suicidality in high school students. *Adolescence, 29,* 939-942.

469. Dumas, J. E., & Serketich, W. J. (1994). Maternal depressive symptomatology and child maladjustment: A comparison of three process models. *Behavior Therapy, 25,* 161–181.

470. Durham, R. C., Murphy, T., Allan, T., Richard, K., Treliving, L. R., & Fenton, G. W. (1994). Cognitive therapy, analytic psychotherapy and anxiety management training for generalized anxiety disorder. *British Journal of Psychiatry, 165,* 315-323.

471. Ehlers, A., Hofmann, S. G., Herda, C. A., & Roth, W. T. (1994). Clinical characteristics of driving phobia. *Journal of Anxiety Disorders, 8,* 323-339.

472. Engel, N. A., Rodrigue, J. R., & Geffken, G. R. (1994). Parent-child agreement on ratings of anxiety in children. *Psychological Reports, 75,* 1251-1260.

473. Fagerström, R. (1994). Correlation between depression and vision in aged patients before and after cataract operations. *Psychological Reports, 75,* 115-125.

474. Fallon, B. A., & Nields, J. A. (1994). Lyme disease: A neuropsychiatric illness. *American Journal of Psychiatry, 151,* 1571-1583.

475. Fals-Stewart, W., & Lucente, S. (1994). The effect of cognitive rehabilitation on the neuropsychological status of patients in drug abuse treatment who display neurocognitive impairment. *Rehabilitation Psychology, 39,* 75–94.

476. Fava, M., Bless, E., Otto, M. W., Pava, J. A., & Rosenbaum, J. F. (1994). Dysfunctional attitudes in major depression: Changes with pharmacotherapy. *The Journal of Nervous and Mental Disease, 182,* 45-49.

477. Fear, C. F., Littlejohns, C. S., Rouse, E., & McQuail, P. (1994). Propofol anaesthesia in electroconvulsive therapy. *British Journal of Psychiatry, 165,* 506-509.

478. Fichter, M. M., Quadflieg, N., & Rief, W. (1994). Course of multi-impulsive bulimia. *Psychological Medicine, 24,* 591-604.

479. Fimm, B., Bartl, G., Zimmerman, P., & Wallesch, C. (1994). Different mechanisms underly [*sic*] shifting set on external and internal cues in Parkinson's disease. *Brain and Cognition, 25,* 287-304.

480. Fishbein, D. H., & Reuland, M. (1994). Psychological correlates of frequency and type of drug use among jail inmates. *Addictive Behaviors, 19,* 583–598.

481. Flannery, R. B., Jr., Perry, J. C., Penk, W. E., & Flannery, G. J. (1994). Validating Antonovsky's sense of coherence scale. *Journal of Clinical Psychology, 50,* 575-577.

482. Fox, K. M., & Gilbert, B. O. (1994). The interpersonal and psychological functioning of women who experienced childhood physical abuse, incest, and parental alcoholism. *Child Abuse & Neglect, 18,* 849-858.

483. Frueh, B. C., Mirabella, R. F., Chobot, K., & Fossey, M. D. (1994). Chronicity of symptoms in combat veterans with PTSD treated by the VA mental health system. *Psychological Reports, 75,* 843-848.

484. Fuller, K. H., Waters, W. F., & Scott, O. (1994). An investigation of slow-wave sleep processes in chronic PTSD patients. *Journal of Anxiety Disorders, 8,* 227-236.

485. Gallagher-Thompson, D., & Steffen, A. M. (1994). Comparative effects of cognitive-behavioral and brief psychodynamic psychotherapists for depressed family categories. *Journal of Consulting and Clinical Psychology, 62,* 543-549.

486. Garety, P. A., Kuipers, L., Fowler, D., Chamberlain, F., & Dunn, G. (1994). Cognitive behavioural therapy for drug-resistant psychosis. *British Journal of Medical Psychology, 67,* 259–271.

487. Garvey, M. J., Hollon, S. D., & DeRubeis, R. J. (1994). Do depressed patients with higher pretreatment stress levels respond better to cognitive therapy than imipramine? *Journal of Affective Disorders, 32,* 45-50.

488. George, M. S., Kellner, C. H., Bernstein, H., & Goust, J. M. (1994). A magnetic resonance imaging investigation into mood disorders in multiple sclerosis: A pilot study. *The Journal of Nervous and Mental Disease, 182,* 410-412.

489. Gilbert, P., Pehl, J., & Allan, S. (1994). The phenomenology of shame and guilt: An empirical investigation. *British Journal of Medical Psychology, 67,* 23–36.

490. Glover, H., Ohlde, C., Silver, S., Packard, P., Goodnick, P., & Hamlin, C. L. (1994). Vulnerability scale: A preliminary report of psychometric properties. *Psychological Reports, 75,* 1651-1668.

491. Goldstein, A. J., & Feske, U. (1994). Eye movement desensitization and reprocessing for panic disorder: A case series. *Journal of Anxiety Disorders, 8,* 351-362.

492. Goodale, T. S., & Stoner, S. B. (1994). Sexual abuse as a correlate of women's alcohol abuse. *Psychological Reports, 75,* 1496-1498.

493. Gournay, K., & Brooking, J. (1994). Community psychiatric nurses in primary health care. *British Journal of Psychiatry, 165,* 231-238.

494. Greene, B., & Blanchard, E. B. (1994). Cognitive therapy for irritable bowel syndrome. *Journal of Consulting and Clinical Psychology, 62,* 576-582.

495. Greif, G. L., & Hegar, R. L. (1994). Parents who abduct: A qualitative study with implications for practice. *Family Relations, 43,* 283-288.

496. Gruen, R. J., Gwadz, M., & Morrobel, D. (1994). Support, criticism, emotion and depressive symptoms: Gender differences in the stress-depression relationship. *Journal of Social and Personal Relationships, 11,* 619-624.

497. Gruen, R. J., Schuldberg, D., Nelson, E. A., Epstein, L., Weiss, L., & Quinlan, D. M. (1994). Network orientation and depressive symptomatology: Development of the Network Utilization Scale. *Journal of Social and Clinical Psychology, 13,* 352–365.

498. Hardy, G. E., & Barkham, M. (1994). The relationship between interpersonal attachment styles and work difficulties. *Human Relations, 47,* 263–281.

499. Harnish, M. J., Beatty, W. W., Nixon, S. J., & Parsons, O. A. (1994). Performance by normal subjects on the Shipley Institute of Living Scale. *Journal of Clinical Psychology, 50,* 881-888.

500. Haslam, N., & Beck, A. T. (1994). Subtyping major depression: A taxometric analysis. *Journal of Abnormal Psychology, 103,* 686-692.

501. Hayward, P., Ahmad, T., & Wardle, J. (1994). Into the dangerous world: An in vivo study of information processing in agoraphobics. *British Journal of Clinical Psychology, 33,* 307-315.

502. Hegel, M. T., Ravaris, C. L., & Ahles, T. A. (1994). Combined cognitive-behavioral and time-limited alprazolam treatment of panic disorder. *Behavior Therapy, 25,* 183–195.

503. Henriques, J. B., Glowacki, J. M., & Davidson, R. J. (1994). Reward fails to alter response bias in depression. *Journal of Abnormal Psychology, 103,* 460-466.

504. Heppner, P. P., Kivlighan, D. M., Good, G. E., Roehlke, H. J., Hills, H. I., & Ashby, J. S. (1994). Presenting problems of university counseling center clients: A snapshot and multivariate classification scheme. *Journal of Counseling Psychology, 41,* 315-324.

505. Hermas, S. L., & Lester, D. (1994). Physical symptoms of stress, depression, and suicidal ideation in high school students. *Adolescence, 29,* 639-641.

506. Hertel, P. T., & Milan, S. (1994). Depressive deficits in recognition: Dissociation of recollection and familiarity. *Journal of Abnormal Psychology, 103,* 736-742.

507. Hetherington, M. M., & Burnett, L. (1994). Ageing and the pursuit of slimness: Dietary restraint and weight satisfaction in elderly women. *British Journal of Clinical Psychology, 33,* 391-400.

508. Hewitt, P. L., Flett, G. L., & Weber, C. (1994). Dimensions of perfectionism and suicide ideation. *Cognitive Therapy and Research, 18,* 439-460.

509. Hill, C. R., & Safran, J. D. (1994). Assessing interpersonal schemas: Anticipated responses of significant others. *Journal of Social and Clinical Psychology, 13,* 366–379.

510. Hiss, H., Foa, E. B., & Kozak, M. J. (1994). Relapse prevention program for treatment of obsessive-compulsive disorder. *Journal of Consulting and Clinical Psychology, 62,* 801-808.

511. Hjelle, L. A., & Bernard, M. (1994). Private self-consciousness and the retest reliability of self-reports. *Journal of Research in Personality, 28,* 52-67.

512. Holroyd, S., Rabins, P. V., Finkelstein, D., & Lavrisha, M. (1994). Visual hallucinations in patients from an ophthalmology clinic and medical clinic population. *The Journal of Nervous and Mental Disease, 182,* 273-276.

513. Ingram, R. E., Bernet, C. Z., & McLaughlin, S. C. (1994). Attentional allocation processes in individuals at risk for depression. *Cognitive Therapy and Research, 18,* 317-332.

514. Ingram, R. E., Partridge, S., Scott, W., & Bernet, C. Z. (1994). Schema specificity in subclinical syndrome depression: Distinctions between automatically versus effortfully encoded state and trait depressive information. *Cognitive Therapy and Research, 18,* 195-209.

515. Ivanoff, A., Jang, S. J., Smyth, N. J., & Linehan, M. M. (1994). Fewer reasons for staying alive when you are thinking of killing yourself: The Brief Reasons for Living Inventory. *Journal of Psychopathology and Behavioral Assessment, 16,* 1-13.

516. Ivarsson, T., Lidberg, A., & Gillberg, C. (1994). The Birleson Depression Self-Rating Scale (DSRS). Clinical evaluation in an adolescent inpatient population. *Journal of Affective Disorders, 32,* 115-125.

517. Jarrett, R. B., & Rush, A. J. (1994). Short-term psychotherapy of depressive disorders: Current status and future directions. *Psychiatry, 57,* 115–132.

518. Joiner, T. E., Jr. (1994). Contagious depression: Existence, specificity to depressed symptoms, and the role of reassurance seeking. *Journal of Personality and Social Psychology, 67,* 287-296.

519. Joiner, T. E., Schmidt, K. L., & Metalsky, G. I. (1994). Low-end specificity of the Beck Depression Inventory. *Cognitive Therapy and Research, 18,* 55-68.

520. Jolly, J. B., Dyck, M. J., Kramer, T. A., & Wherry, J. N. (1994). Integration of positive and negative affectivity and cognitive content-specificity: Improved discrimination of anxious and depressive symptoms. *Journal of Abnormal Psychology, 103,* 544-552.

521. Jolly, J. B., & Kramer, T. A. (1994). The hierarchical arrangement of internalizing cognitions. *Cognitive Therapy and Research, 18,* 1-14.

522. Joseph, S. (1994). Subscales of the Automatic Thoughts Questionnaire. *The Journal of Genetic Psychology, 155,* 367-368.

523. Kaspi, S. P., Otto, M. W., Pollack, M. H., Eppinger, S., & Rosenbaum, J. F. (1994). Premenstrual exacerbation of symptoms in women with panic disorder. *Journal of Anxiety Disorders, 8,* 131-138.

524. Katz, I. M., & Campbell, J. D. (1994). Ambivalence overemotional expression and well-being: Nomothetic and idiographic tests of the stress-buffering hypothesis. *Journal of Personality and Social Psychology, 67,* 513–524.

525. Kazdin, A. E., & Mazurick, J. L. (1994). Dropping out of child psychotherapy: Distinguishing early and late dropouts over the course of treatment. *Journal of Consulting and Clinical Psychology, 62,* 1069-1074.

526. Keenan, K., & Shaw, D. S. (1994). The development of aggression in toddlers: A study of low-income families. *Journal of Abnormal Child Psychology, 22,* 53-77.

527. Kinderman, P. (1994). Attentional bias, persecutory delusions and the self-concept. *British Journal of Medical Psychology, 67,* 53–66.

528. Kirkby, R. J. (1994). Changes in premenstrual symptoms and irrational thinking following cognitive-behavioral coping skills training. *Journal of Consulting and Clinical Psychology, 62,* 1026-1032.

529. Kirkpatrick, B., Buchanan, R. W., Breier, A., & Carpenter, W. T. (1994). Depressive symptoms and the deficit syndrome of schizophrenia. *The Journal of Nervous and Mental Disease, 182,* 452–455.

530. Koenig, L. J., Isaacs, A. M., & Schwartz, J. A. J. (1994). Sex differences in adolescent depression and loneliness: Why are boys lonelier if girls are more depressed. *Journal of Research in Personality, 28,* 27–43.

531. Kogan, E. S., Kabacoff, R. I., Hersen, M., & VanHasselt, V. B. (1994). Clinical cutoffs for the Beck Depression Inventory and the geriatric depression scale with older adult psychiatric outpatients. *Journal of Psychopathology and Behavioral Assessment, 16,* 233–242.

532. Kopelman, M. D., Christensen, H., Puffett, A., & Stanhope, N. (1994). The great escape: A neuropsychological study of psychogenic amnesia. *Neuropsychologia, 32,* 675–691.

533. Kopelman, M. D., Green, R. E. A., Guinan, E. M., Lewis, P. D. R., & Stanhope, N. (1994). The case of the amnesic intelligence officer. *Psychological Medicine, 24,* 1037–1045.

534. Kranzler, H. R., Burleson, J. A., Del Boca, F. K., Babor, T. F., Korner, P., Brown, J., & Bohn, M. J. (1994). Buspirone treatment of anxious alcoholics: A placebo-controlled trial. *Archives of General Psychiatry, 51,* 720–731.

535. Kranzler, H. R., Kadden, R. M., Babor, T. F., & Rounsaville, B. J. (1994). Longitudinal, expert, all data procedure for psychiatric diagnosis in patients with psychoactive substance use disorders. *The Journal of Nervous and Mental Disease, 182,* 277–283.

536. Kring, A. M., Smith, D. A., & Neale, J. M. (1994). Individual differences in dispositional expressiveness: Development and validation of the Emotional Expressive Scale. *Journal of Personality and Social Psychology, 66,* 934–949.

537. Kuyken, W., & Brewin, C. R. (1994). Stress and coping in depressed women. *Cognitive Therapy and Research, 18,* 403–412.

538. Lakey, B., & Dickinson, L. G. (1994). Antecedents of perceived support: Is perceived family environment generalized to new social relationships? *Cognitive Therapy and Research, 18,* 39–53.

539. Lakey, B., & Ross, L. T. (1994). Dependency and self-criticism as moderators of interpersonal and achievement stress: The role of initial dysphoria. *Cognitive Therapy and Research, 18,* 581–599.

540. Lankford, J. S., Bell, R. W., & Elias, J. W. (1994). Computerized versus standard personality measures: Equivalency, computer anxiety, and gender differences. *Computers in Human Behavior, 10,* 497–510.

541. Law, W. A., Martin, A., Mapou, R. L., Roller, T. L., Salazar, A. M., Temoshok, L. R., & Rundell, J. R. (1994). Working memory in individuals with HIV infection. *Journal of Clinical and Experimental Neuropsychology, 16,* 173–182.

542. Leadbeater, B. J., & Bishop, S. J. (1994). Predictors of behavioral problems in preschool children of inner-city African-American and Puerto Rican adolescent mothers. *Child Development, 65,* 638–648.

543. Lecci, L., Karoly, P., Briggs, C., & Kuhn, K. (1994). Specificity and generality of motivational components in depression: A personal projects analysis. *Journal of Abnormal Psychology, 103,* 404–408.

544. Leddy, M. H., Lambert, M. J., & Ogles, B. M. (1994). Psychological consequences of athletic injury among high-level competitors. *Research Quarterly for Exercise and Sport, 65,* 347–354.

545. Lee, D. Y., & Uhlemann, M. R. (1994). Development of an instrument to assess clinicians' recognition memory using a videotaped stimulus interview. *Journal of Clinical Psychology, 50,* 802–809.

546. Lennings, C. J. (1994). Time perspective, mood disturbance, and suicide liberation. *Omega, 29,* 153–164.

547. Lenzenweger, M. F., & Korfine, L. (1994). Perceptual aberrations, schizotypy, and the Wisconsin Card Sorting Test. *Schizophrenia Bulletin, 20,* 345–357.

548. Lester, D. (1994). Depression and suicidal preoccupation in high school and college students. *Psychological Reports, 75,* 984.

549. Lightsey, O. R., Jr. (1994). "Thinking positive" as a stress buffer: The role of positive automatic cognitions in depression and happiness. *Journal of Counseling Psychology, 41,* 325–334.

550. Lightsey, O. R., Jr. (1994). Positive automatic cognitions as moderators of the negative life event-dysphoria relationship. *Cognitive Therapy and Research, 18,* 353–365.

551. LoPresto, C. T., Sherman, M. F., & DiCarlo, M. A. (1994). Factors affecting the unacceptability of suicide and the effects of evaluator depression and religiosity. *Omega, 30,* 205–221.

552. Lubin, B., & Whitlock, R. V. (1994). Development of a critical item scale for the Depression Adjective Check Lists. *Journal of Clinical Psychology, 50,* 841–846.

553. Lyness, S. A., Eaton, E. M., & Schneider, L. S. (1994). Cognitive performance in older and middle-aged depressed outpatients and controls. *Journal of Gerontology: Psychological Sciences, 49*(Pt.1), P129–P136.

554. Lyon, H. M., Kaney, S., & Bentall, R. P. (1994). The defensive function of persecutory delusions: Evidence from attribution tasks. *British Journal of Psychiatry, 164,* 637–646.

555. MacGillivray, R. G., & Baron, P. (1994). The influence of cognitive processing style on cognitive distortion in clinical depression. *Social Behavior and Personality, 22,* 145–156.

556. MacLeod, A. K., & Tarbuck, A. F. (1994). Explaining why negative events will happen to oneself: Parasuicides are pessimistic because they can't see any reason not to be. *British Journal of Clinical Psychology, 33,* 317–326.

557. Malla, A. K., & Norman, R. M. G. (1994). Prodromal symptoms in schizophrenia. *British Journal of Psychiatry, 164,* 487–493.

558. Matson, N. (1994). Coping, caring and stress: A study of stroke carers and carers of older confused people. *British Journal of Clinical Psychology, 33,* 333–344.

559. McClennan, H., Joseph, S., & Lewis, C. A. (1994). Causal attributions for marital violence and emotional response by women seeking refuge. *Psychological Reports, 75,* 272–274.

560. McCullough, J. D., McCune, K. J., Kaye, A. L., Braith, J. A., Friend, R., Roberts, W. C., Belyea-Caldwell, S., Norris, S. L. W., & Hampton, C. (1994). Comparison of community dysthymia sample at screening with a matched group of nondepressed community controls. *The Journal of Nervous and Mental Disease, 182,* 402–407.

561. McCullough, J. D., McCune, K. J., Kaye, A. L., Braith, J. A., Friend, R., Roberts, W. C., Belyea-Caldwell, S., Norris, S. L. W., & Hampton, C. (1994). One-year prospective replication study of an untreated sample of community dysthymia subjects. *The Journal of Nervous and Mental Disease, 182,* 396–401.

562. McDermut, W., & Haaga, D. A. F. (1994). Cognitive balance and specificity in anxiety and depression. *Cognitive Therapy and Research, 18,* 333–352.

563. McFarland, C., & Miller, D. T. (1994). The framing of relative performance feedback: Seeing the glass as half empty or half full. *Journal of Personality and Social Psychology, 66,* 1061–1073.

564. McKean, K. J. (1994). Using multiple risk factors to assess the behavioral, cognitive, and affective effects of learned helplessness. *The Journal of Psychology, 128,* 177–183.

565. Meadows, M.-E., Kaplan, R. F., & Bromfield, E. B. (1994). Cognitive recovery with vitamin B12 therapy: A longitudinal neuropsychological assessment. *Neurology, 44,* 1764–1765.

566. Molock, S. D., Kimbrough, R., Lacy, M. B., McClure, K. P., & Williams, S. (1994). Suicidal behavior among African American college students: A preliminary study. *The Journal of Black Psychology, 20,* 234–251.

567. Moore, R. G., & Blackburn, I-M. (1994). The relationship of sociotropy and autonomy to symptoms, cognition, and personality in depressed patients. *Journal of Affective Disorders, 32,* 239–245.

568. Morin, C. M., Stone, J., McDonald, K., & Jones, S. (1994). Psychological management of insomnia: A clinical replication series with 100 patients. *Behavior Therapy, 25,* 291–309.

569. Munford, M. B. (1994). Relationship of gender, self-esteem, social class, and racial identity to depression in Blacks. *The Journal of Black Psychology, 20,* 157–174.

570. Naidoo, P., & Pillay, Y. G. (1994). Correlations among general stress, family environment, psychological distress, and pain experience. *Perceptual and Motor Skills, 78,* 1291–1296.

571. Napholz, L. (1994). Sex role orientation and psychological well-being among working Black women. *The Journal of Black Psychology, 20,* 469–482.

572. Nelson, L. D., Cicchetti, D., Satz, S. M., & Mitrushina, M. (1994). Emotional sequelae of stroke: A longitudinal perspective. *Journal of Clinical and Experimental Neuropsychology, 16,* 796–806.

573. Ness, R., Handelsman, L., Aronson, M. J., Hershkowitz, A., & Kanof, P. D. (1994). The acute effects of a rapid medical detoxification upon dysphoria and other psychopathology experienced by heroin abusers. *The Journal of Nervous and Mental Disease, 182,* 353–359.

574. Nolan, R., & Willson, V. L. (1994). Gender and depression in an undergraduate population. *Psychological Reports, 75,* 1327–1330.

575. O'Connor, B. P., & Vallerand, R. J. (1994). Motivation, self-determination, and person-environment fit as predictors of psychological adjustment among nursing home residents. *Psychology and Aging, 9,* 189–194.

576. Okasha, A., Bishry, A., Khalil, A. H., Darwish, T. A., Sief el Dawla, A., & Shohdy, A. (1994). Panic disorder: An overlapping or independent entity? *British Journal of Psychiatry, 164,* 818–825.

577. Olmsted, M. P., Kaplan, A. S., & Rockert, W. (1994). Rate and prediction of relapse in bulimia nervosa. *American Journal of Psychiatry, 151,* 738–743.

578. Organista, K. C., Muñoz, R. F., & González, G. (1994). Cognitive behavioral therapy for depression in low-income and minority medical outpatients: Description of a program and exploratory analyses. *Cognitive Therapy and Research, 18,* 241–259.

579. Orloff, L. M., Battle, M. A., Baer, L., Ivanjack, L., Pettit, A. R., Buttolph, M. L., & Jenike, M. A. (1994). Long-term follow-up of 85 patients with obsessive-compulsive disorder. *American Journal of Psychiatry, 151,* 441–442.

580. Palosaari, U., & Aro, H. (1994). Effect of timing of parental divorce on the vulnerability of children to depression in young adulthood. *Adolescence, 29,* 681–690.

581. Patrick, M., Hobson, R. P., Castle, D., Howard, R., & Maughan, B. (1994). Personality disorder and the mental representation of early social experience. *Development and Psychopathology, 6,* 375–388.

582. Peterson, C., & Ulrey, L. M. (1994). Can explanatory style be scored from TAT protocols? *Personality and Social Psychology Bulletin, 20,* 102–106.

583. Pianta, R. C., & Egeland, B. (1994). Predictors of instability in children's mental test performance at 24, 48, and 96 months. *Intelligence, 18,* 145–163.

584. Pianta, R. C., & Egeland, B. (1994). Relation between depressive symptoms and stressful life events in a sample of disadvantaged mothers. *Journal of Consulting and Clinical Psychology, 62,* 1229–1234.

585. Power, M. J., Katz, R., McGuffin, P., Duggan, C. F., Lam, D., & Beck, A. T. (1994). The Dysfunctional Attitude Scale (DAS). A comparison of Forms A and B and proposals for a new subscaled version. *Journal of Research in Personality, 28,* 263–276.

586. Preasser, K. J., Rice, K. G., & Ashby, J. S. (1994). The role of self-esteem in mediating the perfectionism-depression connection. *Journal of College Student Development, 35,* 88–93.

587. Prodromidis, M., Abrams, S., Field, T., Scafidi, F., & Rahdert, E. (1994). Psychosocial stressors among depressed adolescent mothers. *Adolescence, 29,* 331–343.

588. Rathus, J. H., Reber, A. S., Manza, L., & Kushner, M. (1994). Implicit and explicit learning: Differential effects of affective states. *Perceptual and Motor Skills, 79,* 163–184.

589. Ravindran, A. V., Welburn, K., & Copeland, J. R. M. (1994). Semi-structured depression scale sensitive to change with treatment for use in the elderly. *British Journal of Psychiatry, 164,* 522–527.

590. Reed, M. K. (1994). Social skills training to reduce depression in adolescents. *Adolescence, 29,* 293-302.

591. Richards, M. H., & Duckett, E. (1994). The relationship of maternal employment to early adolescent daily experience with and without parents. *Child Development, 65,* 225-236.

592. Richman, H., & Nelson-Gray, R. (1994). Nonclinical panicker personality: Profile and discriminative ability. *Journal of Anxiety Disorders, 8,* 33-47.

593. Rifai, A. H., George, C. J., Stack, J. A., Mann, J. J., & Reynolds, C. F. (1994). Hopelessness in suicide attempters after acute treatment of major depression in late life. *American Journal of Psychiatry, 151,* 1687-1690.

594. Robbins, P. R., & Tanck, R. H. (1994). Depressed mood and early memories: Some negative findings. *Psychological Reports, 75,* 465-466.

595. Roemer, L., & Borkovec, T. D. (1994). Effects of suppressing thoughts about emotional material. *Journal of Abnormal Psychology, 103,* 467-474.

596. Roesler, T. A. (1994). Reactions to disclosure of childhood sexual abuse: The effect of adult symptoms. *The Journal of Nervous and Mental Disease, 182,* 618–624.

597. Roesler, T. A., & McKenzie, N. (1994). Effects of childhood trauma on psychological functioning in adults sexually abused as children. *The Journal of Nervous and Mental Disease, 182,* 145-150.

598. Rohde, P., Lewinsohn, P. M., & Seeley, J. R. (1994). Responses of depressed adolescents to cognitive-behavioral treatment: Do differences in initial severity clarify the comparison of treatments? *Journal of Consulting and Clinical Psychology, 62,* 851-854.

599. Romney, D. M. (1994). Cross-validating a causal model relating attributional style, self-esteem, and depression: An heuristic study. *Psychological Reports, 74,* 203-207.

600. Rose, D. T., Abramson, L. Y., Hodulik, C. J., Halberstadt, L., & Leff, G. (1994). Heterogeneity of cognitive style among depressed inpatients. *Journal of Abnormal Psychology, 103,* 419-429.

601. Rosen, R. C., Kostis, J. B., Jekelis, A., & Taska, L. S. (1994). Sexual sequelae of antihypertensive drugs: Treatment effects on self-report and physiological measures in middle-aged male hypertensives. *Archives of Sexual Behavior, 23,* 135-152.

602. Rosenfarb, I. S., Becker, J., & Khan, A. (1994). Perceptions of parental and peer attachments by women with mood disorders. *Journal of Abnormal Psychology, 103,* 637-644.

603. Rosenfarb, I. S., Becker, J., Khan, A., & Mintz, J. (1994). Dependency, self-criticism, and perceptions of socialization experiences. *Journal of Abnormal Psychology, 103,* 669-675.

604. Russo, J. (1994). Thurstone's scaling model applied to the assessment of self-reported depressive severity. *Psychological Assessment, 6,* 159-171.

605. Salamero, M., Marcos, T., Gutiérrez, F., Rebull, E. (1994). Factorial study of the BDI in pregnant women. *Psychological Medicine, 24,* 1031-1035.

606. Santor, D. A., Ramsay, J. O., & Zuroff, D. C. (1994). Nonparametric item analyses of the Beck Depression Inventory: Evaluating gender item bias and response option weights. *Psychological Assessment, 6,* 255-270.

607. Santor, D. A., & Zuroff, D. C. (1994). Depressive symptoms: Effects of negative affectivity and failing to accept the past. *Journal of Personality Assessment, 63,* 294-312.

608. Sanz, J., & Avia, M. D. (1994). Cognitive specificity in social anxiety and depression: Self-statements, self-focused attention, and dysfunctional attitudes. *Journal of Social and Clinical Psychology, 13,* 105–137.

609. Schaaf, K. K., & McCanne, T. R. (1994). Childhood abuse, body image disturbance, and eating disorders. *Child Abuse & Neglect, 18,* 607-615.

610. Scheier, M. F., Carver, C. S., & Bridges, M. W. (1994). Distinguishing optimism from neuroticism (and trait anxiety, self-mastery, and self-esteem): A reevaluation of the Life Orientation Test. *Journal of Personality and Social Psychology, 67,* 1063-1078.

611. Schill, T., & Sharp, M. (1994). Self-defeating personality, depression, and pleasure from activities. *Psychological Reports, 74,* 680-682.

612. Schwartz, L., Slater, M. A., & Birchler, G. R. (1994). Interpersonal stress and pain behaviors in patients with chronic pain. *Journal of Consulting and Clinical Psychology, 62,* 861-864.

613. Shapiro, D. A., Barkham, M., Rees, A., Hardy, G. E., Reynolds, S., & Startup, M. (1994). Effects of treatment duration and severity of depression on the effectiveness of cognitive-behavioral and psychodynamic-interpersonal psychotherapy. *Journal of Consulting and Clinical Psychology, 62,* 522-534.

614. Shaw, D. S., Vondra, J. I., Hommerding, K. D., Keenan, K., & Dunn, M. (1994). Chronic family adversity and early child behavior problems: A longitudinal study of low income families. *Journal of Child Psychology and Psychiatry and Allied Disciplines, 35,* 1109-1122.

615. Shear, M. K., Pilkonis, P. A., Cloitre, M., & Leon, A. C. (1994). Cognitive behavioral treatment compared with nonprescriptive treatment of panic disorders. *Archives of General Psychiatry, 51,* 395-401.

616. Siblerud, R. L., Motl, J., & Kienholz, E. (1994). Psychometric evidence that mercury from silver dental fillings may be an etiological factor in depression, excessive anger, and anxiety. *Psychological Reports, 74,* 67-80.

617. Smith, T. W., Christensen, A. J., Peck, J. R., & Ward, J. R. (1994). Cognitive distortion, helplessness, and depressed mood in rheumatoid arthritis: A four-year longitudinal analysis. *Health Psychology, 13,* 213-217.

618. Smyth, N. J., Ivanoff, A., & Jang, S. J. (1994). Changes in psychological maladaptation among inmate parasuicides. *Criminal Justice and Behavior, 21,* 357–365.

619. Sobell, L. C., Toneatto, T., & Sobell, M. (1994). Behavioral assessment and treatment planning for alcohol, tobacco, and other drug problems: Current status with an emphasis on clinical applications. *Behavior Therapy, 25,* 533–580.

620. Soloff, P. H., Liss, J. A., Kelly, T., Cornelius, J., & Ulrich, R. (1994). Risk factors for suicidal behavior in borderline personality disorder. *American Journal of Psychiatry, 151,* 1316-1323.

621. Solomon, A., & Haaga, D. A. F. (1994). Positive and negative aspects of sociotropy and autonomy. *Journal of Psychopathology and Behavioral Assessment, 16,* 243–252.

622. Spicer, K. B., Brown, G. G., & Gorell, J. M. (1994). Lexical decision in Parkinson disease: Lack of evidence for generalized bradyphrenia. *Journal of Clinical and Experimental Neuropsychology, 16,* 457-471.

623. Spiegel, D. A., Bruce, T. J., Gregg, S. F., & Nuzzarello, A. (1994). Does cognitive behavior therapy assist slow-taper alprazolam discontinuation in panic disorder? *American Journal of Psychiatry, 151,* 876-881.

624. Startup, M., & Edmonds, J. (1994). Compliance with homework assignments in cognitive-behavioral psychotherapy for depression: Relation to outcome and methods of enhancement. *Cognitive Therapy and Research, 18,* 567–579.

625. Steer, R. A., Clark, D. A., & Ranieri, W. F. (1994). Symptom dimensions of the SCL-90-R: A test of the tripartite model of anxiety and depression. *Journal of Personality Assessment, 62,* 525-536.

626. Steer, R. A., Rissmiller, D. J., & Beck, A. T. (1994). Use of the computer-administered Beck Depression Inventory and Hopelessness Scale with psychiatric patients. *Computers in Human Behavior, 10,* 223–229.

627. Stein, M. B., Asmundson, G. J. G., Ireland, D., & Walker, J. R. (1994). Panic disorder in patients attending a clinic for vestibular disorders. *American Journal of Psychiatry, 151,* 1697-1700.

628. Stephens, G. C., Prentice-Dunn, S., & Spruill, J. C. (1994). Public self-awareness and success-failure feedback as disinhibitors of restrained eating. *Basic and Applied Social Psychology, 15,* 509-521.

629. Stiles, W. B., & Shapiro, D. A. (1994). Disabuse of the drug metaphor: Psychotherapy process-outcome correlations. *Journal of Consulting and Clinical Psychology, 62,* 942-948.

630. Strong, J., Ashton, R., & Stewart, A. (1994). Chronic low back pain: Toward an integrated psychosocial assessment model. *Journal of Consulting and Clinical Psychology, 62,* 1058-1063.

631. Sunderland, T., Cohen, R. M., Molchan, S., Lawlor, B. A., Mellow, A. M., Newhouse, P. A., Tariot, D. N., Mueller, E. A., & Murphy, D. L. (1994). High-dose selegiline in treatment-resistant older depressive patients. *Archives of General Psychiatry, 51,* 607-615.

632. Sutker, P. B., Uddo, M., Brailey, K., Vasterling, J. J., & Errera, P. (1994). Psychopathology in war-zone deployed and nondeployed Operation Desert Storm troops assigned graves registration duties. *Journal of Abnormal Psychology, 103,* 383-390.

633. Tan, J. C. H., & Stoppard, J. M. (1994). Gender and reactions to dysphoric individuals. *Cognitive Therapy and Research, 18,* 211-224.

634. Thase, M. E., Reynolds, C. F., Frank, E., Jennings, J. R., Nofzinger, E., Fasiczka, A. L., Garamoni, G., & Kupfer, D. J. (1994). Polysomnographic studies of unmedicated depressed men before and after cognitive behavioral therapy. *American Journal of Psychiatry, 151,* 1615-1622.

635. Thase, M. E., Reynolds, C. F., Frank, E., Simmons, A. D., McGeary, J., Fasiceka, A. L., Garamoni, G. G., Jennings, R., & Kupfer, D. J. (1994). Do depressed men and women respond similarly to cognitive behavior therapy? *American Journal of Psychiatry, 151,* 500-505.

636. Tomarken, A. J., & Davidson, R. J. (1994). Frontal brain activation in repressors and nonrepressors. *Journal of Abnormal Psychology, 103,* 339-349.

637. Tremblay, P. F., & King, P. R. (1994). State and trait anxiety, coping styles, and depression among psychiatric inpatients. *Canadian Journal of Behavioural Science, 26,* 505–519.

638. Troop, N. A., Holbrey, A., Trowler, R., & Treasure, J. L. (1994). Ways of coping in women with eating disorders. *The Journal of Nervous and Mental Disease, 182,* 535–540.

639. Upmanyu, V. V., & Upmanyu, S. (1994). Depression in relation to sex role identity and hopelessness among male and female Indian adolescents. *The Journal of Social Psychology, 134,* 551-552.

640. Vaughan, K., Armstrong, M. S., Gold, R., O'Connor, N., Jenneke, W., & Tarrier, N. (1994). A trial of eye movement desensitization compared to image habituation training and applied muscle relaxation in post-traumatic stress disorder. *Journal of Behavior Therapy and Experimental Psychiatry, 25,* 283–291.

641. Vera, M. N., Vila, J., & Godoy, J. F. (1994). Cardiovascular effects of traffic noise: The role of negative self-statements. *Psychological Medicine, 24,* 817-827.

642. Waelde, L. C., Silvern, L., & Hodges, W. F. (1994). Stressful life events: Moderators of the relationships of gender and gender roles to self-reported depression and suicidality among college students. *Sex Roles, 30,* 1–22.

643. Wall, J. E., & Holden, E. W. (1994). Aggressive, assertive, and submissive behaviors in disadvantaged, inner-city preschool children. *Journal of Clinical Child Psychology, 23,* 382-390.

644. Wallston, K. A., Stein, M. J., & Smith, C. A. (1994). Form C of the MHLC Scales: A condition-specific measure of locus of control. *Journal of Personality Assessment, 63,* 534-553.

645. Weary, G., & Edwards, J. A. (1994). Individual differences in causal uncertainty. *Journal of Personality and Social Psychology, 67,* 308-318.

646. Webber, E. M. (1994). Psychological characteristics of binging and nonbinging obese women. *The Journal of Psychology, 128,* 339-351.

647. Webster-Stratton, C. (1994). Advancing videotape parent training: A comparison study. *Journal of Consulting and Clinical Psychology, 62,* 583-593.

648. Wegner, D. M., & Zanakos, S. (1994). Chronic thought suppression. *Journal of Personality, 62,* 615–640.

649. Westefeld, J. S., & Liddell, D. L. (1994). The Beck Depression Inventory and its relationship to college student suicide. *Journal of College Student Development, 35,* 145-147.

650. Wind, T. W., & Silvern, L. (1994). Parenting and family stress as mediators of the long-term effects of child abuse. *Child Abuse & Neglect, 18*, 439-453.

651. Wong, J. L., & Whitaker, D. J. (1994). The stability and prediction of depressive mood states in college students. *Journal of Clinical Psychology, 50*, 715-722.

652. Yee, C. M., & Miller, G. A. (1994). A dual-task analysis of resource allocation in dysthymia and anhedonia. *Journal of Abnormal Psychology, 103*, 625-636.

653. Young, A. H., Sharpley, A. L., Campling, G. M., Hockney, R. A., & Cowen, P. J. (1994). Effects of hydrocortisone on brain 5-HT function and sleep. *Journal of Affective Disorders, 32*, 139-146.

654. Zuroff, D. C. (1994). Depressive personality styles and the five-factor model of personality. *Journal of Personality Assessment, 63*, 453-472.

655. Agras, W. S., Telch, C. F., Arnow, B., Eldredge, K., Detzer, M. J., Henderson, J., & Marnell, M. (1995). Does interpersonal therapy help patients with binge eating disorder who fail to respond to cognitive-behavioral therapy? *Journal of Consulting and Clinical Psychology, 63*, 356-360.

656. Akillas, E., & Efran, J. S. (1995). Symptom prescription and reframing: Should they be combined? *Cognitive Therapy and Research, 19*, 263-279.

657. Albright, J. S., & Henderson, M. C. (1995). How real is depressive realism? A question of scales and standards. *Cognitive Therapy and Research, 19*, 589-609.

658. Alford, B. A., & Gerrity, D. M. (1995). The specificity of sociotropy-autonomy personality dimensions to depression vs. anxiety. *Journal of Clinical Psychology, 51*, 190-195.

659. Alford, B. A., Lester, J. M., Patel, R. J., Buchanan, J. P., & Giunta, L. C. (1995). Hopelessness predicts future depressive symptoms: A prospective analysis of cognitive vulnerability and cognitive content specifity. *Journal of Clinical Psychology, 51*, 331-339.

660. Arnold, E. H., & O'Leary, S. G. (1995). The effect of child negative affect on maternal discipline behavior. *Journal of Abnormal Child Psychology, 23*, 585-595.

661. Baer, L., Rauch, S. L., Ballantine, T., Martuza, R., Cosgrove, R., Cassem, E., Girionas, I., Manzo, P. A., Dimino, C., & Jenike, M. A. (1995). Cingulotomy for intractable obsessive-compulsive disorder: Prospective long-term follow-up of 18 patients. *Archives of General Psychiatry, 52*, 384-392.

662. Baker, J. D., Williamson, D. A., & Syloe, C. (1995). Body image disturbance, memory bias, and body dysphoria: Effects of negative mood induction. *Behavior Therapy, 26*, 747-759.

663. Ball, S. A., Carroll, K. M., Babor, T. F., & Rounsaville, B. J. (1995). Subtypes of cocaine abusers: Support for a Type A-Type B distinction. *Journal of Consulting and Clinical Psychology, 63*, 115-124.

664. Baran, S. A., Weltzin, T. E., & Kaye, W. H. (1995). Low discharge weight and outcome in anorexia nervosa. *American Journal of Psychiatry, 152*, 1070-1072.

665. Barber, J. P., Luborsky, L., Crits-Christoph, P., & Diguer, L. (1995). A comparison of core conflictual relationship themes before psychotherapy and during early sessions. *Journal of Consulting and Clinical Psychology, 63*, 145-148.

666. Bartelstone, J. H., & Trull, T. J. (1995). Personality, life events, and depression. *Journal of Personality Assessment, 64*, 279-294.

667. Basoglu, M., Marks, M., Sengun, S., & Marks, I. M. (1995). The distinctiveness of phobias: A discriminant analysis of fears. *Journal of Anxiety Disorders, 9*, 89-101.

668. Basoglu, M., & Parker, M. (1995). Severity of trauma as predictor of long-term psychological status in survivors of torture. *Journal of Anxiety Disorders, 9*, 339-350.

669. Bauserman, S. A. K., Arias, I., & Craighead, W. E. (1995). Marital attributions in spouses of depressed patients. *Journal of Psychopathology and Behavioral Assessment, 17*, 231-249.

670. Beatty, S., & Hewitt, J. (1995). Affective reactions to failure as a function of effort and depression. *Perceptual and Motor Skills, 80*, 33-34.

671. Beatty, W. W., Paul, R. H., Wilbanks, S. L., Hames, K. A., Blanco, C. R., & Goodkin, D. E. (1995). Identifying multiple sclerosis patients with mild or global cognitive impairment using the Screening Examination for Cognitive Impairment (SEFCI). *Neurology, 45*, 718-723.

672. Beebe, D. W., Holmbeck, G. N., Albright, J. S., Noga, K., & Decastro, B. (1995). Identification of "binge-prone" women: An experimentally and psychometrically validated cluster analysis in a college population. *Addictive Behaviors, 20*, 451-462.

673. Bentall, R. P., Kaney, S., & Bowen-Jones, K. (1995). Persecutory delusions and recall of threat-related, depression-related, and neutral words. *Cognitive Therapy and Research, 19*, 445-457.

674. Betz, N. E., Wohlegmuth, E., Serling, D., Harshbarger, J., & Klein, K. (1995). Evaluation of a measure of self-esteem based on the concept of unconditional positive regard. *Journal of Counseling and Development, 74*, 76-83.

675. Bierhals, A. J., Frank, E., Prigerson, H. G., Miller, M., Fasiczka, A., & Reynolds, C. F. (1995). Gender differences in complicated grief among the elderly. *Omega, 32*, 303-317.

676. Blaine, B., & Crocker, J. (1995). Religiousness, race, and psychological well-being: Exploring social psychological mediators. *Personality and Social Psychology Bulletin, 21*, 1031-1041.

677. Blanchard, E. B., Hickling, E. J., Taylor, A. E., & Loos, W. (1995). Psychiatric morbidity associated with motor vehicle accidents. *The Journal of Nervous and Mental Disease, 183*, 495-504.

678. Blatt, S. J., Quinlan, D. M., Pilkonis, P. A., & Shea, M. T. (1995). Impact of perfectionism and need for approval on the brief treatment of depression: The National Institute of Mental Health Treatment of Depression Collaborative Research Program revisited. *Journal of Consulting and Clinical Psychology, 63*, 125-132.

679. Blatt, S. J., Zohar, A. H., Quinlan, D. M., Zuroff, D. C., & Mongrain, M. (1995). Subscales within the dependency factor of the Depressive Experiences Questionnaire. *Journal of Personality Assessment, 64*, 319-339.

680. Bonanno, G. A., Keltner, D., Holen, A., & Horowitz, M. J. (1995). When avoiding unpleasant emotions might not be such a bad thing: Verbal-autonomic

response dissociation and midlife conjugal bereavement. *Journal of Personality and Social Psychology, 69*, 975-989.

681. Bouhuys, A. L., Bloem, G. M., & Groothuis, T. G. G. (1995). Induction of depressed and elated mood by music influences the perception of facial emotional expressions in healthy subjects. *Journal of Affective Disorders, 33*, 215-226.

682. Brackney, B. E., & Karabenick, S. A. (1995). Psychology and academic performance: The role of motivation and learning strategies. *Journal of Counseling Psychology, 42*, 456-465.

683. Bradley, B. P., Mogg, K., Millar, N., & White, J. (1995). Selective processing of negative information: Effects of clinical anxiety, concurrent depression, and awareness. *Journal of Abnormal Psychology, 104*, 532-536.

684. Brand, E. F., LaKey, B., & Buman, S. (1995). A preventative, psychoeducational approach to increased perceived social support. *American Journal of Community Psychology, 23*, 117-135.

685. Brown, C., Schulberg, H. C., & Madonia, M. J. (1995). Assessing depression in primary care practice with the Beck Depression Inventory and the Hamilton Rating Scale for Depression. *Psychological Assessment, 7*, 59-65.

686. Brown, E. J., Heimberg, R. G., & Juster, H. R. (1995). Social phobia subtype and avoidant personality disorder: Effect on severity of social phobia, impairment, and outcome of cognitive behavioral treatment. *Behavior Therapy, 26*, 467-486.

687. Brown, G. P., Hammen, C. J., Craske, M. G., & Wickens, T. D. (1995). Dimensions of dysfunctional attitudes as vulnerabilities to depressive symptoms. *Journal of Abnormal Psychology, 104*, 431-435.

688. Brown, W. A., & Harrison, W. (1995). Are patients who are intolerant to one serotonin selective reuptake inhibitor intolerant to another? *Journal of Clinical Psychiatry, 56*, 30-34.

689. Bunce, S. C., Larsen, R. J., & Peterson, C. (1995). Life after trauma: Personality and daily experiences of traumatized people. *Journal of Personality, 63*, 165-188.

690. Burch, J. W. (1995). Typicality range deficit in schizophrenics' recognition of emotion in faces. *Journal of Clinical Psychology, 51*, 140-152.

691. Carroll, K. M., Nich, C., & Rounsaville, B. J. (1995). Differential symptom reduction in depressed cocaine abusers treated with psychotherapy and pharmacotherapy. *The Journal of Nervous and Mental Disease, 183*, 251-259.

692. Carter, A. S., Grigorenko, E. L., & Pauls, D. L. (1995). A Russian adaptation of the Child Behavior Checklist: Psychometric properties and associations with child and maternal affective symptomatology and family functioning. *Journal of Abnormal Child Psychology, 23*, 661-684.

693. Carter, M. M., Hollon, S. D., Carson, R., & Shelton, R. C. (1995). Effects of a safe person on induced distress following a biological challenge in panic disorder with agoraphobia. *Journal of Abnormal Psychology, 104*, 156-163.

694. Cash, T. F., & Szymanski, M. L. (1995). The development and validation of the Body-Image Ideals Questionnaire. *Journal of Personality Assessment, 64*, 466-477.

695. Castonguay, L. G., Hayes, A. M., Goldfried, M. R., & DeRubeis, R. J. (1995). The focus of therapist interventions in cognitive therapy for depression. *Cognitive Therapy and Research, 19*, 485-503.

696. Chambless, D. L., & Williams, K. E. (1995). A preliminary study of African Americans with agoraphobia: Symptom severity and outcome of treatment with in vivo exposure. *Behavior Therapy, 26*, 501-515.

697. Chochinov, H. M., Wilson, K. G., Enns, M., Mowchun, N., Lander, S., Levitt, M., & Clinch, J. J. (1995). Desire for death in the terminally ill. *American Journal of Psychiatry, 152*, 1185-1191.

698. Christensen, A. P., & Oei, T. P. S. (1995). The efficacy of cognitive behaviour therapy in treating premenstrual dysphoric changes. *Journal of Affective Disorders, 33*, 57-63.

699. Christensen, A. P., & Oei, T. P. S. (1995). Correlates of premenstrual dysphoria in help-seeking women. *Journal of Affective Disorders, 33*, 47-55.

700. Christensen, L., & Duncan, K. (1995). Distinguishing depressed from nondepressed individuals using energy and psychosocial variables. *Journal of Consulting and Clinical Psychology, 63*, 495-498.

701. Conway, K. (1995). Miscarriage experience and the role of support systems: A pilot study. *British Journal of Medical Psychology, 68*, 259-267.

702. Cournoyer, R. J., & Mahalik, J. R. (1995). Cross-sectional study of gender role conflict examining college-aged and middle-aged men. *Journal of Counseling Psychology, 42*, 11-19.

703. Coyne, J. C., & Calarco, M. M. (1995). Effects of the experience of depression: Application of focus group and survey methodologies. *Psychiatry, 58*, 149-163.

704. Crowson, J. J., & Cromwell, R. L. (1995). Depressed and normal individuals differ both in selection and in perceived tonal quality of positive-negative messages. *Journal of Abnormal Psychology, 104*, 305-311.

705. Dalack, G. W., Glassman, A. H., Rivelli, S., Covey, L., & Stetner, F. (1995). Mood, major depression, and fluoxetine response in cigarette smokers. *American Journal of Psychiatry, 152*, 398-403.

706. Dalgleish, T., Cameron, C. M., Power, M. J., & Bond, A. (1995). The use of an emotional priming paradigm with clinically anxious subjects. *Cognitive Therapy and Research, 19*, 69-89.

707. Davies, F., Morman, R. M. G., Cortese, L., & Malla, A. K. (1995). The relationship between types of anxiety and depression. *The Journal of Nervous and Mental Disease, 183*, 31-35.

708. De Beurs, E., van Balkom, A. J. L. M., Lange, A., Koele, P., & van Dyck, R. (1995). Treatment of panic disorder with agoraphobia: Comparison of fluvoxamine, placebo, and psychological panic management combined with exposure and of exposure in vivo alone. *American Journal of Psychiatry, 152*, 683-691.

709. DeMan, A. F., & Leduc, C. P. (1995). Suicidal ideation in high school students: Depression and other correlates. *Journal of Clinical Psychology, 51*, 173-181.

710. Dobson, K. S., & Pusch, D. (1995). A test of the depressive realism hypothesis in clinically depressed subjects. *Cognitive Therapy and Research, 19,* 179–194.

711. Dugas, M. J., Letarte, H., Rheaume, J., Freeston, M. H., & Ladouceur, R. (1995). Worry and problem solving: Evidence of a specific relationship. *Cognitive Therapy and Research, 19,* 109-120.

712. Dumas, J. E., & Wekerle, C. (1995). Maternal reports of child behavior problems and personal distress as predictors of dysfunctional parenting. *Development and Psychopathology, 7,* 465–479.

713. Eckhardt, M. J., Stapleton, J. M., Rawlings, R. R., Davis, E. Z., & Grodin, D. M. (1995). Neuropsychological functioning in detoxified alcoholics between 18 and 35 years of age. *American Journal of Psychiatry, 152,* 53-59.

714. Ehlers, A. (1995). A 1-year prospective study of panic attacks: Clinical course and factors associated with maintenance. *Journal of Abnormal Psychology, 104,* 164-172.

715. Ehlers, A., & Breuer, P. (1995). Selective attention to physical threat in subjects with panic attacks and specific phobias. *Journal of Anxiety Disorders, 9,* 11-31.

716. Eitel, P., Hatchett, L., Friend, R., Griffin, K. W., & Wadhwa, N. K. (1995). Burden of self-care in seriously ill patients: Impact on adjustment. *Health Psychology, 14,* 457–463.

717. Ethier, L. C., Lacharité, C., & Couture, G. (1995). Childhood adversity, parental stress, and depression of negligent mothers. *Child Abuse & Neglect, 19,* 619–632.

718. Everson, S. A., Matthews, K. A., Guzick, D. S., Wing, R. R., & Kuller, L. H. (1995). Effects of surgical menopause on psychological characteristics and lipid levels: The healthy women study. *Health Psychology, 14,* 435–443.

719. Feske, U., & Chambless, D. L. (1995). Cognitive behavioral versus exposure only treatment for social phobia: A meta-analysis. *Behavior Therapy, 26,* 695–720.

720. Field, T., Fox, N. A., Pickens, J., & Nawrocki, T. (1995). Relative right frontal EEG activation in 3- to 6-month-old infants of depressed mothers. *Developmental Psychology, 31,* 358-363.

721. Field, T., Pickens, J., Fox, N. A., Nawrocki, T., & Gonzalez, J. (1995). Vagal tone in infants of depressed mothers. *Development and Psychopathology, 7,* 227-231.

722. Flett, G. L., Vredenburg, K., & Krames, L. (1995). The stability of depressive symptoms in college students: An empirical demonstration of regression to the mean. *Journal of Psychopathology and Behavioral Assessment, 17,* 403–415.

723. Foa, E. B., Riggs, D. S., & Gershuny, B. S. (1995). Arousal, numbing, and intrusion: Symptom structure of PTSD following assault. *American Journal of Psychiatry, 152,* 116-120.

724. Frasure-Smith, N., Lespérance, F., & Talajic, M. (1995). The impact of negative emotions on prognosis following myocardial infarction: Is it more than depression? *Health Psychology, 14,* 388–398.

725. Freeston, M. H., Ladouceur, R., Provencher, M., & Blais, F. (1995). Strategies used with intrusive thoughts: Context, appraisal, mood, and efficacy. *Journal of Anxiety Disorders, 9,* 201-215.

726. Gershuny, B. S., & Sher, K. J. (1995). Compulsive checking and anxiety in a nonclinical sample: Differences in cognition, behavior, personality and affect. *Journal of Psychopathology and Behavioral Assessment, 17,* 19–38.

727. Gidycz, C. A., Hanson, K., & Layman, M. J. (1995). A prospective analysis of the relationships among sexual assault experiences. *Psychology of Women Quarterly, 19,* 5-29.

728. Ginter, G. G. (1995). Differential diagnosis in older adults: Dementia, depression, and delirium. *Journal of Counseling and Development, 73,* 346-351.

729. Godding, P. R., McAnulty, R. D., Wittrock, D. A., Britt, D. M., & Khansur, T. (1995). Predictors of depression among male cancer patients. *The Journal of Nervous and Mental Disease, 183,* 95-98.

730. Goldman, L., & Haaga, D. A. F. (1995). Depression and the experience and expression of anger in marital and other relationship. *The Journal of Nervous and Mental Disease, 183,* 505–509.

731. Goldsmith, D. F., & Rogoff, B. (1995). Sensitivity and teaching of dysphoric and nondysphoric women in structured versus unstructured situations. *Developmental Psychology, 31,* 388-394.

732. Golombok, S., Cook, R., Bish, A., & Murray, C. (1995). Families created by the new reproductive technologies: Quality of parenting and social and emotional development of the children. *Child Development, 66,* 285-298.

733. Goodnick, P. J., Henry, J. H., & Buki, V. M. V. (1995). Treatment of depression in patients with diabetes mellitus. *Journal of Clinical Psychiatry, 56,* 128–136.

734. Grant, G. M., Salcedo, V., Hynan, L. S., Frisch, M. B., & Poster, K. (1995). Effectiveness of quality of life therapy for depression. *Psychological Reports, 76,* 1203–1208.

735. Grant, J. R., & Cash, T. F. (1995). Cognitive-behavioral body image therapy: Comparative efficacy of group and modest-contact treatment. *Behavior Therapy, 26,* 69–84.

736. Green, M. W., & Rogers, P. J. (1995). Impaired cognitive functioning during spontaneous dieting. *Psychological Medicine, 25,* 1003–1010.

737. Griffin, K. W., Friend, R., & Wadhwa, N. K. (1995). Measuring disease severity in patients with end-stage renal disease: Validity of the Craven et al. ESRD Severity Index. *Psychological Medicine, 25,* 189-193.

738. Haaga, D. A. F., Ahrens, A. H., Schulman, P., Seligman, M. E. P., DuRubeis, R. J., & Minarik, M. L. (1995). Metatraits and cognitive assessment: Application to attributional style and depressive symptoms. *Cognitive Therapy and Research, 19,* 121-142.

739. Haaga, D. A. F., Fine, J. A., Terrill, D. R., Stewart, B. L., & Beck, A. J. (1995). Social problem-solving deficits, dependency, and depressive symptoms. *Cognitive Therapy and Research, 19,* 147–158.

740. Halberstadt, A. G., Cassidy, J., Stifter, C. A., Parke, R. D., & Fox, N. A. (1995). Self-expressiveness within the family context: Psychometric support for a new measure. *Psychological Assessment, 7,* 93-103.

741. Hammen, C. L., Burge, D., Daley, S. E., Davila, J., Paley, B., & Rudolph, K. D. (1995). Interpersonal attachment cognitions and prediction of symptomatic responses to interpersonal stress. *Journal of Abnormal Psychology, 104,* 436–443.

742. Handlin, D., & Levin, R. (1995). Dreams of traditional and nontraditional women: Are dream aggression and hostility related to higher levels of waking well-being? *Sex Roles, 33,* 515–530.

743. Hannon, R., Adams, P., Harrington, S., Fries-Dias, C., & Gipson, M. T. (1995). Effects of brain injury and age on prospective memory self-rating and performance. *Rehabilitation Psychology, 40,* 289–298.

744. Hedlund, S., & Rude, S. S. (1995). Evidence of latent depressive schemas in formerly depressed individuals. *Journal of Abnormal Psychology, 104,* 517–525.

745. Hobfoll, S. E., Ritter, C., Lavin, J., Hulsizer, M. R., & Cameron, R. P. (1995). Depression prevalence and incidence among inner-city pregnant and postpartum women. *Journal of Consulting and Clinical Psychology, 63,* 445-453.

746. Hodges, J. R., & Patterson, K. (1995). Is semantic memory consistently impaired early in the course of Alzheimer's disease? Neuroanatomical and diagnostic implications. *Neuropsychologia, 33,* 441–459.

747. Hoffart, A. (1995). Psychoanalytical personality types and agoraphobia. *The Journal of Nervous and Mental Disease, 183,* 139-144.

748. Hofmann, S. G., Newman, M. G., Ehlers, A., & Roth, W. T. (1995). Psychophysiological differences between subgroups of social phobia. *Journal of Abnormal Psychology, 104,* 224-231.

749. Ingram, R. E., Fidaleo, R. A., Friedberg, R., Shenk, J. L., & Bernet, C. Z. (1995). Content and mode of information processing in major depressive disorder. *Cognitive Therapy and Research, 19,* 281–293.

750. Ito, L. M., DeAraudjo, L. A., Hemsley, D. R., & Marks, I. M. (1995). Beliefs and resistance in obsessive-compulsive disorder: Observations from a controlled study. *Journal of Anxiety Disorders, 9,* 269–281.

751. Jackman, L. P., Williamson, D. A., Netemeyer, R. G., & Anderson, D. A. (1995). Do weight-preoccupied women misinterpret ambiguous stimuli related to body size? *Cognitive Therapy and Research, 19,* 341–355.

752. Johnson, J. G. (1995). Event-specific attributions and daily life events as predictors of depression symptom change. *Journal of Psychopathology and Behavioral Assessment, 17,* 39–49.

753. Johnson, J. G., Williams, J. B. W., Rabkin, J. G., Goetz, R. R., & Remien, R. H. (1995). Axis I psychiatric symptoms associated with HIV infection and personality disorder. *American Journal of Psychiatry, 152,* 551-554.

754. Johnson, W. G., Schlundt, D. G., Barclay, D. R., Carr-Nangle, R. E., & Engler, L. B. (1995). A naturalistic functional analysis of binge eating. *Behavior Therapy, 26,* 101–108.

755. Joiner, T. E. (1995). The price of soliciting and receiving negative feedback: Self-verification theory as a vulnerability to depression theory. *Journal of Abnormal Psychology, 104,* 364-372.

756. Joiner, T. E., Jr., & Blalock, J. A. (1995). Gender differences in depression: The role of anxiety and generalized negative affect. *Sex Roles, 33,* 91–108.

757. Joiner, T. E., Jr., & Metalsky, G. I. (1995). A prospective test of an integrative interpersonal theory of depression: A naturalistic study of college roommates. *Journal of Personality and Social Psychology, 69,* 778–788.

758. Kagan, N. I., Kagan, H., & Watson, M. G. (1995). Stress reduction in the workplace: The effectiveness of psychoeducational programs. *Journal of Counseling Psychology, 42,* 71-78.

759. Kalichman, S. C., Sikkema, K. J., & Somlai, A. (1995). Assessing persons with human immunodeficiency virus (HIV) infection using the Beck Depression Inventory: Disease processes and other potential confounds. *Journal of Personality Assessment, 64,* 86-100.

760. Kashubeck, S., & Christensen, S. A. (1995). Parental alcohol use, family relationship quality, self-esteem, and depression in college students. *Journal of College Student Development, 36,* 431–443.

761. Kelly, A. E., & Achter, J. A. (1995). Self-concealment and attitudes toward counseling in university students. *Journal of Counseling Psychology, 42,* 40-46.

762. Koenig, L. J., & Wasserman, E. L. (1995). Body image and dieting failure in college men and women: Examining links between depression and eating problems. *Sex Roles, 32,* 225–249.

763. Kok, R. M., Heeren, T. J., Hooijer, C., Dinkgreve, M. A. H. M., & Rooijmans, H. G. M. (1995). The prevalence of depression in elderly medical inpatients. *Journal of Affective Disorders, 23,* 77-82.

764. Kranzler, H. R., Burleson, J. A., Korner, P., Del Boca, F. K., Bohn, M. J., Brown, J., & Liebowitz, N. (1995). Placebo-controlled trial of fluoxetine as an adjunct to relapse prevention in alcoholics. *American Journal of Psychiatry, 152,* 391-397.

765. Kroeger, D. W. (1995). Self-esteem, stress, and depression among graduate students. *Psychological Reports, 76,* 345-346.

766. Kubany, E. S., Abueg, F. R., Owens, J. A., Brennan, J. M., Kaplan, A. S., & Watson, S. B. (1995). Initial examination of a multidimensional model of trauma-related guilt: Applications to combat veterans and battered women. *Journal of Psychopathology and Behavioral Assessment, 17,* 353–376.

767. Kuch, K., Cox, B. J., & Direnfeld, D. M. (1995). A brief self-rating scale for PTSD after road vehicle accident. *Journal of Anxiety Disorders, 9,* 503–514.

768. Kumar, G., & Steer, R. A. (1995). Psychosocial correlates of suicidal ideation in adolescent psychiatric inpatients. *Suicide and Life-Threatening Behavior, 25,* 339–346.

769. Kuyken, W., & Dalgleish, T. (1995). Autobiographical memory and depression. *British Journal of Clinical Psychology, 34,* 89-92.

770. Lam, R. W., Gorman, C. P., Michalon, M., Steiner, M., Levitt, A. J., Corral, M. R., Watson, G. D., Morehouse, R. L., Tam, W., & Joffe, R. T. (1995). Multicenter, placebo-controlled study of fluoxetine in seasonal affective disorder. *American Journal of Psychiatry, 152,* 1765–1770.

771. Law, W. A., Mapou, R. L., Roller, T. L., Martin, A., Nannis, E. D., & Temoshok, L. R. (1995). Reaction time slowing in HIV-1-infected individuals: Role of the preparatory interval. *Journal of Clinical and Experimental Neuropsychology, 17,* 122–133.

772. Lehmicke, N., & Hicks, R. A. (1995). Relationships of response-set differences on Beck Depression Inventory scores of undergraduate students. *Psychological Reports, 76,* 15-21.

773. Lester, D., & Akande, A. (1995). Depression in Nigerian and American students. *Psychological Reports, 76,* 906.

774. Lester, D., & Akande, A. (1995). Gender and depression in undergraduates: A comment. *Psychological Reports, 76,* 22.

775. Lippa, R. (1995). Gender-related individual differences and psychological adjustment in terms of the big five and circumplex models. *Journal of Personality and Social Psychology, 69,* 1184–1202.

776. Loss, N., Beck, S. J., & Wallace, A. (1995). Distressed and nondistressed third- and sixth-grade children's self-reports of life events and impact and concordance with mothers. *Journal of Abnormal Child Psychology, 23,* 397–409.

777. Lundy, A., Gottheil, E., Serota, R. D., Weinstein, S. P., & Sterling, R. C. (1995). Gender differences and similarities in African-American crack cocaine abusers. *The Journal of Nervous and Mental Disease, 183,* 260–266.

778. Lyubomirsky, S., & Nolen-Hoeksema, S. (1995). Effects of self-focused rumination on negative thinking and interpersonal problem solving. *Journal of Personality and Social Psychology, 69,* 176–190.

779. Macdiarmid, J. I., & Hetherington, M. M. (1995). Mood modulation by food: An exploration of affect and cravings in "chocolate addicts." *British Journal of Clinical Psychology, 34,* 129-138.

780. MacLeod, A. K., & Cropley, M. L. (1995). Depressive future-thinking: The role of valence and specificity. *Cognitive Therapy and Research, 19,* 35-50.

781. Malone, K. M., Haas, G. L., Sweeney, J. A., & Mann, J. J. (1995). Major depression and the risk of attempted suicide. *Journal of Affective Disorders, 34,* 173-185.

782. Mancini, C., VanAmeringen, M., & Macmillan, H. (1995). Relationship of childhood sexual and physical abuse to anxiety disorders. *The Journal of Nervous and Mental Disease, 183,* 309–314.

783. Manne, S. L., Lesanics, D., Meyers, P., Wollner, N., Steinherz, P., & Redd, W. (1995). Predictors of depressive symptomatology among parents of newly diagnosed children with cancer. *Journal of Pediatric Psychology, 20,* 491–510.

784. Markowitz, J. C., Klerman, G. L., Clougherty, K. F., Spielman, L. A., Jacobsberg, L. B., Fishman, B., Frances, A. J., Kocsis, J. H., & Perry, S. W. (1995). Individual psychotherapies for depressed HIV-positive patients. *American Journal of Psychiatry, 152,* 1504–1509.

785. Mavissakalian, M. R., Hamann, M. S., Haidar, S. A., & De Groot, C. M. (1995). Correlates of DSM-III personality disorder in generalized anxiety disorder. *Journal of Anxiety Disorders, 9,* 103-115.

786. McClain, L., & Abramson, L. Y. (1995). Self-schemas, stress, and depressed mood in college students. *Cognitive Therapy and Research, 19,* 419–432.

787. McKnight, J. D., & Glass, D. C. (1995). Perceptions of control, burnout, and depressive symptomatology: A replication and extension. *Journal of Consulting and Clinical Psychology, 63,* 490-494.

788. Mendelberg, H. E. (1995). Inpatient treatment of mood disorders. *Psychological Reports, 76,* 819–824.

789. Meszaros, A., Engelsmann, F., Meterissian, G., & Kusalic, M. (1995). Computerized assessment of depression and suicidal ideation. *The Journal of Nervous and Mental Disease, 183,* 487–488.

790. Mghir, R., Freed, W., Raskin, A., & Katon, W. (1995). Depression and posttraumatic stress disorder among a community sample of adolescent and young adult Afghan refugees. *The Journal of Nervous and Mental Disease, 183,* 24-30.

791. Miguel, E. C., Coffey, B. J., Baer, L., Savage, C. R., Rauch, S. L., & Jenike, M. A. (1995). Phenomenology of intentional repetitive behaviors in obsessive-compulsive disorder and Tourette's disorder. *Journal of Clinical Psychiatry, 56,* 246–255.

792. Mogg, K., Bradley, B. P., & Williams, R. (1995). Attentional bias in anxiety and depression: The role of awareness. *British Journal of Clinical Psychology, 34,* 17-36.

793. Moilanen, D. L. (1995). Validity of Beck's cognitive theory of depression with nonreferred adolescents. *Journal of Counseling and Development, 73,* 438–442.

794. Morris, S. J., & Kanfer, F. H. (1995). Self-evaluation, self-description, and self-standards in subclinical depression. *Journal of Psychopathology and Behavioral Assessment, 17,* 261–282.

795. Muñoz, R. F., Ying, Y. W., Bernal, G., Pérez-Stable, E. J., Sorensen, J. L., Hargreaves, W. A., Miranda, J., & Miller, L. S. (1995). Prevention of depression with primary care patients: A randomized control trial. *American Journal of Community Psychology, 23,* 199–222.

796. Nezu, C., Nezu, A. M., Rothenberg, J. L., Dellicarpini, L., & Groag, I. (1995). Depression in adults with mild mental retardation: Are cognitive variables involved? *Cognitive Therapy and Research, 19,* 227–239.

797. Noor, N. M. (1995). Work and family roles in relation to women's well-being: A longitudinal study. *British Journal of Social Psychology, 34,* 87–106.

798. Nurmi, J., Onatsu, T., & Haavisto, T. (1995). Underachievers' cognitive and behavioral strategies: Self-handicapping at school. *Contemporary Educational Psychology, 20,* 188-200.

799. Oei, T. P. S., & Free, M. L. (1995). Do cognitive behaviour therapies validate cognitive models of mood disorders? A review of the empirical evidence. *International Journal of Psychology, 30,* 145–180.

800. Ogles, B. M., Lambert, M. J., & Sawyer, J. D. (1995). Clinical significance of the National Institute of Mental Health Treatment of Depression Collaborative Research Program Data. *Journal of Consulting and Clinical Psychology, 63,* 321-326.

801. Oldman, A., Walsh, A., Salkovskis, P., Fairburn, C. G., & Cowen, P. J. (1995). Biochemical and behavioural effects of acute tryptophan depletion in abstinent bulimic subjects: A pilot study. *Psychological Medicine, 25,* 995–1001.

802. Pace, T. M., & Trapp, M. D. C. (1995). A psychometric comparison of the Beck Depression Inventory and the Inventory for Diagnosing Depression in a college population. *Assessment, 2,* 167-172.

803. Parra, E. B., Arkowitz, H., Hannah, M. T., & Vasquez, A. M. (1995). Coping strategies and emotional reactions to separation and divorce in Anglo, Chicana, and Mexicana women. *Journal of Divorce & Remarriage, 23,* 117–129.

804. Pawluk, L. K., Hurwitz, T. D., Schluter, J. L., Ullevig, C., & Mahowald, M. W. (1995). Psychiatric morbidity in narcoleptics on chronic high dose methylphenidate therapy. *The Journal of Nervous and Mental Disease, 183,* 45-48.

805. Paykel, E. S., Ramana, R., Cooper, Z., Hayhurst, H., Kerr, J., & Barocka, A. (1995). Residual symptoms after partial remission: An important outcome in depression. *Psychological Medicine, 25,* 1171–1180.

806. Park, S., Holzman, P. S., & Lenzenweger, M. F. (1995). Individual differences in spatial working memory in relation to schizotypy. *Journal of Abnormal Psychology, 104,* 355-363.

807. Parry, B. L., Cover, H., Mostofi, N., Leveau, B., Sependa, P. A., Resnick, A., & Gillin, J. C. (1995). Early versus late partial sleep deprivation in patients with premenstrual dysphoric disorder and normal comparison subjects. *American Journal of Psychiatry, 152,* 404-412.

808. Perry, W., McDougall, A., & Viglione, D. (1995). A five-year follow-up on the temporal stability of the ego impairment index. *Journal of Personality Assessment, 64,* 112-118.

809. Peterson, C., & De Avila, M. E. (1995). Optimistic explanatory style and the perception of health problems. *Journal of Clinical Psychology, 51,* 128-132.

810. Philpot, V. D., Holliman, W. B., & Madonna, S. (1995). Self-statements, locus of control, and depression in predicting self-esteem. *Psychological Reports, 76,* 1007–1010.

811. Pincus, T., Pearce, S., McClelland, A., & Isenberg, D. (1995). Endorsement and memory bias of self-referential pain stimuli in depressed pain patients. *British Journal of Clinical Psychology, 34,* 267-277.

812. Potthoff, J. G., Holahan, C. J., & Joiner, T. E., Jr. (1995). Reassurance seeking, stress generation, and depressive symptoms: An integrative model. *Journal of Personality and Social Psychology, 68,* 664–670.

813. Power, M. J., Duggan, C. F., Lee, A. S., & Murray, R. M. (1995). Dysfunctional attitudes in depressed and recovered depressed patients and their first-degree relatives. *Psychological Medicine, 25,* 87-93.

814. Ramana, R., Paykel, E. S., Cooper, Z., Hayhurst, H., Saxty, M., & Surtees, P. G. (1995). Remission and relapse in major depression: A two-year prospective follow-up study. *Psychological Medicine, 25,* 1161–1170.

815. Rapaport, M. H., Thompson, P. M., Kelsoe, J. R., Golshan, S., Judd, L. L., & Gillin, J. C. (1995). Gender differences in outpatient research subjects with affective disorders: A comparison of descriptive variables. *Journal of Clinical Psychiatry, 56,* 67–72.

816. Rauch, S. L., Savage, C. R., Alpert, N. M., Miguel, E. C., Baer, L., Brieter, H. C., Fischman, A. J., Manzo, P. A., Moretti, C., & Jenike, M. A. (1995). A positron emission tomographic study of simple phobic symptom provocation. *Archives of General Psychiatry, 52,* 20–28.

817. Reynolds, W. M., & Kobak, K. A. (1995). Reliability and validity of the Hamilton Depression Inventory: A paper-and-pencil version of the Hamilton Depression Rating Scale clinical interview. *Psychological Assessment, 7,* 472–483.

818. Ricciardi, J. N., & McNally, R. J. (1995). Depressed mood is related to obsessions, but not to compulsions, in obsessive-compulsive disorder. *Journal of Anxiety Disorders, 9,* 249-256.

819. Richards, A., French, C. C., & Dowd, R. (1995). Hemisphere asymmetry and the processing of emotional words in anxiety. *Neuropsychologia, 33,* 835–841.

820. Robins, C. J., Hayes, A. M., Block, P., Kramer, R. J., & Villena, M. (1995). Interpersonal and achievement concerns and the depressive vulnerability and symptom specificity hypotheses: A prospective study. *Cognitive Therapy and Research, 19,* 1-20.

821. Rogers, J. H., Widiger, T. A., & Krupp, A. (1995). Aspects of depression associated with borderline personality disorder. *American Journal of Psychiatry, 152,* 268-270.

822. Rudd, M. D., Joiner, T. E., Jr., & Rajab, M. H. (1995). Help negation after acute suicidal crisis. *Journal of Consulting and Clinical Psychology, 63,* 499-503.

823. Rudd, M. D., & Rajab, M. H. (1995). Specificity of the Beck Depression Inventory and the confounding role of comorbid disorders in a clinical sample. *Cognitive Therapy and Research, 19,* 51-68.

824. Rude, S. S., & Burnham, B. L. (1995). Connectedness and neediness: Factors of the DEQ and SAS dependency scales. *Cognitive Therapy and Research, 19,* 323-340.

825. Ryan, R. M., Plant, R. W., & O'Malley, S. (1995). Initial motivations for alcohol treatment: Relations with patient characteristics, treatment involvement, and dropout. *Addictive Behaviors, 20,* 279–297.

826. Sachdev, P., & Hay, P. (1995). Does neurosurgery for obsessive-compulsive disorder produce personality change? *The Journal of Nervous and Mental Disease, 183,* 408–413.

827. Sanders, B., & Becker-Lausen, E. (1995). The measurement of psychological maltreatment: Early data on the Child Abuse & Trauma Scale. *Child Abuse & Neglect, 19,* 315–323.

828. Santor, D. A., Zuroff, D. C., Ramsay, J. Q., Cervantes, P., & Palacios, J. (1995). Examining scale discriminability in the BDI and CES-D as a function of depressive severity. *Psychological Assessment, 7,* 131-139.

829. Satel, S. L., Krystal, J. H., Delgado, P. L., Kosten, T. R., & Charney, D. S. (1995). Tryptophan depletion and attenuation of cue-induced craving for cocaine. *American Journal of Psychiatry, 152,* 778-783.

830. Savournin, R., Evans, C., Hirst, J. F., & Watson, J. P. (1995). The elusive factor structure of the Inventory of Interpersonal Problems. *British Journal of Medical Psychology, 68,* 353–369.

831. Schmidt, N. B., & Harrington, P. (1995). Cognitive-behavioral treatment of body dysmorphic disorder: A case report. *Journal of Behavior Therapy and Experimental Psychiatry, 26,* 161–167.

832. Schneider, B., & Varghese, R. K. (1995). Scores on the SF-36 Scales and the Beck Depression Inventory in assessing mental health among patients on hemodialysis. *Psychological Reports, 76,* 719–722.

833. Schumaker, J. F., Warren, W. G., Carr, S. C., Schreiber, G. S., & Jackson, C. C. (1995). Dissociation and depression in eating disorders. *Social Behavior and Personality, 23,* 53-58.

834. Segal, Z. V., Gemar, M., Truchon, C., Guirguis, M., & Horowitz, L. M. (1995). A priming methodology for studying self-representation in major depressive disorder. *Journal of Abnormal Psychology, 104,* 205-213.

835. Seiner, S. H., & Gelfand, D. M. (1995). Effects of mothers' simulated withdrawal and depressed affect on mother-toddler interactions. *Child Development, 66,* 1519–1528.

836. Senra, C. (1995). Measures of treatment outcome of depression: An effect size comparison. *Psychological Reports, 76,* 187-192.

837. Sequin, M., Lesage, A., & Kiely, M. C. (1995). Parental bereavement after suicide and accident: A comparative study. *Suicide and Life-Threatening Behavior, 25,* 489–498.

838. Shapiro, D. A., Rees, A., Barkham, M., Hardy, G., Reynolds, S., & Startup, M. (1995). Effects of treatment duration and severity of depression on the maintenance of gains after cognitive-behavioral and psychodynamic-interpersonal psychotherapy. *Journal of Consulting and Clinical Psychology, 63,* 378-387.

839. Sharpe, M. J., Heppner, P. P., & Dixon, W. A. (1995). Gender role conflict, instrumentality, expressiveness, and well-being in adult men. *Sex Roles, 33,* 1–18.

840. Shaw, D. S., & Vondra, J. I. (1995). Infant attachment security and maternal predictors of early behavior problems: A longitudinal study of low-income families. *Journal of Abnormal Child Psychology, 23,* 335-357.

841. Shean, G. D., & Heefner, A. S. (1995). Depression, interpersonal style, and communication skills. *The Journal of Nervous and Mental Disease, 183,* 485–487.

842. Siegrist, M. (1995). Inner speech as a cognitive process mediating self-consciousness and inhibiting self-deception. *Psychological Reports, 76,* 259-265.

843. Sigmon, S. T., Stanton, A. L., & Snyder, C. R. (1995). Gender differences in coping: A further test of socialization and role constraint theories. *Sex Roles, 33,* 565–587.

844. Simons, A. D., Gordon, J. S., Monroe, S. M., & Thase, M. E. (1995). Toward an integration of psychologic, social, and biologic factors in depression: Effects on outcome and course of cognitive therapy. *Journal of Consulting and Clinical Psychology, 63,* 369-377.

845. Smith, W. P., Compton, W. C., & West, W. B. (1995). Meditation as an adjunct to a happiness enhancement program. *Journal of Clinical Psychology, 51,* 269-273.

846. Solomon, S., Greenberg, J., Pyszczynski, T., & Pryzbylinski, J. (1995). The effects of mortality salience on personally-relevant persuasive appeals. *Social Behavior and Personality, 23,* 177–190.

847. Spencer, T., Wilens, T., Biederman, J., Faraone, S. V., Ablon, S., & Lapey, K. (1995). A double-blind, crossover comparison of methylphenidate and placebo in adults with childhood-onset attention deficit hyperactivity disorder. *Archives of General Psychiatry, 52,* 434–443.

848. Steer, R. A., Clark, D. A., Beck, A. T., & Ranieri, W. F. (1995). Common and specific dimensions of self-reported anxiety and depression: A replication. *Journal of Abnormal Psychology, 104,* 542–545.

849. Steer, R. A., Kumar, G., Ranieri, W. F., & Beck, A. T. (1995). Use of the Beck Anxiety Inventory with adolescent psychiatric outpatients. *Psychological Reports, 76,* 459–465.

850. Stein, M. B., Kirk, P., Prabhu, V., Grott, M., & Terepa, M. (1995). Mixed anxiety-depression in a primary-care clinic. *Journal of Affective Disorders, 34,* 79-84.

851. Stiles, W. B., & Shapiro, D. A. (1995). Verbal exchange structure of brief psychodynamic-interpersonal and cognitive-behavioral psychotherapy. *Journal of Consulting and Clinical Psychology, 63,* 15-27.

852. Stiles, W. B., Shapiro, D. A., Harper, H., & Morrison, L. A. (1995). Therapist contributions to psychotherapeutic assimilation: An alternative to the drug metaphor. *British Journal of Medical Psychology, 68,* 1–13.

853. Stout, J. C., Salmon, D. P., Butters, N., Taylor, M., Peavy, G., Heindel, W. C., Delis, D. C., Ryan, L., Atkinson, J. H., Chandler, J. L., Grant, I., & The HNRC Group. (1995). Decline in working memory associated with HIV infection. *Psychological Medicine, 25,* 1221–1232.

854. Streichenwein, S. M., & Thornby, J. I. (1995). A long-term double-blind, placebo-controlled crossover trial of the efficacy of fluoxetine for trichotillomania. *American Journal of Psychiatry, 152,* 1192–1196.

855. Sullivan, M. J. L., Bishop, S. R., & Pivik, J. (1995). The Pain Catastrophizing Scale: Development and validation. *Psychological Assessment, 7,* 524–532.

856. Sutker, P. B., Davis, J. M., Uddo, M., & Ditta, S. R. (1995). Assessment of psychological distress in Persian Gulf troops: Ethnicity and gender comparisons. *Journal of Personality Assessment, 64,* 415-427.

857. Sutker, P. B., Davis, J. M., Uddo, M., & Ditta, S. R. (1995). War zone stress, personal resources, and PTSD in Persian Gulf War returnees. *Journal of Abnormal Psychology, 104,* 444-452.

858. Swanson, S. C., Templer, D. I., Thomas-Dobson, S., Cannon, W. G., Streiner, D. L., Reynolds, R. M., & Miller, H. R. (1995). Development of a three-scale MMPI: The MMPI-TRI. *Journal of Clinical Psychology, 51,* 361-374.

859. Teasdale, J. D., Taylor, M. J., Cooper, Z., Hayhurst, H., & Paykel, E. S. (1995). Depressive thinking: Shifts in construct accessibility or in schematic mental models? *Journal of Abnormal Psychology, 104,* 500–507.

860. Teichman, Y., Bar-El, Z., Shor, H., Sirota, P., & Elizor, A. (1995). A comparison of two modalities of cognitive therapy (individual and marital) in treating depression. *Psychiatry, 58,* 136–148.

861. Teti, D. M., Gelfand, D. M., Messinger, D. S., & Isabella, R. (1995). Maternal depression and the quality of early attachment: An examination of infants, preschoolers, and their mothers. *Developmental Psychology, 31,* 364-376.

862. Thomas, A. M., Forehand, R., & Neighbors, B. (1995). Change in maternal depressive mood: Unique contributions to adolescent functioning over time. *Adolescence, 30,* 41–52.

863. Tidswell, P., Dias, P. S., Sagar, H. J., Mayes, A. R., & Battersby, R. D. E. (1995). Cognitive outcome after aneurysm rupture: Relationship to aneurysm site and perioperative complications. *Neurology, 45,* 875–882.

864. Tivis, L. J., & Parsons, O. A. (1995). An investigation of verbal spatial functioning in chronic alcoholics. *Assessment, 2,* 285–292.

865. Tran, G. Q., & Chambless, D. L. (1995). Psychopathology of social phobia: Effects of subtype and of avoidant personality disorder. *Journal of Anxiety Disorders, 9,* 489–501.

866. Trief, P. M., Carnrike, C. L. M., Jr., & Drudge, O. (1995). Chronic pain and depression: Is social support relevant. *Psychological Reports, 76,* 227-236.

867. Trull, T. J. (1995). Borderline personality disorder features in nonclinical young adults: I. Identification and validation. *Psychological Assessment, 7,* 33-41.

868. Tucker, D. D., & Schlundt, D. G. (1995). Selective information processing and schematic content related to eating behavior. *Journal of Psychopathology and Behavioral Assessment, 17,* 1–17.

869. Varnado, P. J., Williamson, D. A., & Netemeyer, R. (1995). Confirmatory factor analysis of eating disorder symptoms in college women. *Journal of Psychopathology and Behavioral Assessment, 17,* 69–79.

870. Viglione, D. J., Lovette, G. J., & Gottlieb, R. (1995). Depressive Experiences Questionnaire: An empirical exploration of the underlying theory. *Journal of Personality Assessment, 65,* 91–99.

871. Vlaeyen, J. W. S., Haazen, I. W. C. J., Schuerman, J. A., Kole-Snijders, A. M. J., & van Eek, H. (1995). Behavioural rehabilitation of chronic low back pain: Comparison of an operant treatment, an operant-cognitive treatment and an operant-respondent treatment. *British Journal of Clinical Psychology, 34,* 95-118.

872. Vrana, S. R., Roodman, A. & Beckham, J. C. (1995). Selective processing of trauma-relevant words in posttraumatic stress disorder. *Journal of Anxiety Disorders, 9,* 515–530.

873. Wallace, J., & Pfohl, B. (1995). Age-related differences in the symptomatic expression of major depression. *The Journal of Nervous and Mental Disease, 183,* 99-102.

874. Watson, D., Weber, K., Assenheimer, J. S., Clark, L. A., Strauss, M. E., & McCormick, R. A. (1995). Testing a tripartite model: I. Evaluating convergent and discriminant validity of Anxiety and Depression Symptom Scales. *Journal of Abnormal Psychology, 104,* 3-14.

875. Weekes, J. R., Morison, S. J., Millson, W. A., & Fettig, D. M. (1995). A comparison of native, metis, and caucasian offender profiles on the MCMI. *Canadian Journal of Behavioural Science, 27,* 187–1908.

876. Weiner, J., Harlow, L., Adams, J., & Grebstein, L. (1995). Psychological adjustment of college students from families of divorce. *Journal of Divorce and Remarriage, 23,* 75–95.

877. Weizman, A., Burgin, R., Harel, Y., Karp, L., & Gavish, M. (1995). Platelet peripheral-type benzodiazepine receptor in major depression. *Journal of Affective Disorders, 33,* 257-261.

878. Wells, P. A., Willmoth, T., & Russell, R. J. H. (1995). Does fortune favour the bald? Psychological correlates of hair loss in males. *British Journal of Psychology, 86,* 337–344.

879. Whisman, M. A., Miller, I. W., Norman, W. H., & Keitner, G. I. (1995). Hopelessness, depression in depressed inpatients: Symptomatology, patient characteristics, and outcome. *Cognitive Therapy and Research, 19,* 377–398.

880. Woody, G. E., McLellan, A. T., Luborsky, L., & O'Brien, C. P. (1995). Psychotherapy in community methadone programs: A validation study. *American Journal of Psychiatry, 152,* 1302–1308.

881. Woolfolk, R. L., Novalany, J., Garz, M. A., Allen, L. A., & Polino, M. (1995). Self-complexity, self-evaluation, and depression: An examination of form and content within the self-schema. *Journal of Personality and Social Psychology, 68,* 1108–1120.

882. Worling, J. R. (1995). Adolescent sibling-incest offenders: Differences in family and individual functioning when compared to adolescent nonsibling sex offenders. *Child Abuse & Neglect, 19,* 633-643.

883. Yager, J., Rorty, M., & Rossotto, E. (1995). Coping styles differ between recovered and nonrecovered women with bulimia nervosa, but not between recovered women and non-eating disordered control subjects. *The Journal of Nervous and Mental Disease, 183,* 86-94.

884. Yang, B., & Clum, G. A. (1995). Measures of life stress and social support specific to an Asian student population. *Journal of Psychopathology and Behavioral Assessment, 17,* 51–67.

885. Yin, Z., Zapata, J. T., & Katims, D. S. (1995). Risk factors for substance use among Mexican–American school–age youth. *Hispanic Journal of Behavior Sciences, 17,* 61–76.

886. Zeitlin, S. B., & Polivy, J. (1995). Coprophagia as a manifestation of obsessive-compulsive disorder: A case report. *Journal of Behavior Therapy and Experimental Psychiatry, 26,* 57–63.

887. Zettle, R. D., & Herring, E. L. (1995). Treatment utility of the sociotropy/autonomy distinction: Implications for cognitive therapy. *Journal of Clinical Psychology, 51,* 280-289.
888. Ali, A., & Toner, B. B. (1996). Gender differences in depressive response: The role of social support. *Sex Roles, 35,* 281–293.
889. Baker, M., Milich, R., & Manolis, M. B. (1996). Peer interactions of dysphoric adolescents. *Journal of Abnormal Child Psychology, 24,* 241–255.
890. Berthiaume, M., David, H., Saucier, J-F., & Borgeat, F. (1996). Correlates of gender role orientation during pregnancy and the postpartum. *Sex Roles, 35,* 781–800.
891. Blazina, C., & Watkins, C. E., Jr. (1996). Masculine gender role conflict: Effects on college men's psychological well-being, chemical substance usage, and attitudes toward help-seeking. *Journal of Counseling Psychology, 43,* 461–465.
892. Bornelli, B., Niaura, R., Keuthen, N. J., Goldstein, M. G., DePue, J. D., Murphy, C., & Abrams, D. B. (1996). Development of major depressive disorder during smoking-cessation treatment. *Journal of Clinical Psychiatry, 57,* 534–538.
893. Breitbart, W., Rosenfeld, B. D., & Passik, S. D. (1996). Interest in physician-assisted suicide among ambulatory HIV-infected patients. *American Journal of Psychiatry, 153,* 238–242.
894. Bromberger, J. T., & Matthews, K. A. (1996). A "feminine" model of vulnerability to depressive symptoms: A longitudinal investigation of middle-aged women. *Journal of Personality and Social Psychology, 70,* 591–598.
895. Cameron, R. P., Grabill, C. M., Hobfoll, S. E., Crowther, J. H., Ritter, C., & Lavin, J. (1996). Weight, self-esteem, ethnicity, and depressive symptomatology during pregnancy among inner-city women. *Health Psychology, 15,* 293–297.
896. Cash, T. F., & Labarge, A. S. (1996). Development of the Appearance Schemas Inventory: A new cognitive body-image assessment. *Cognitive Therapy and Research, 20,* 37–50.
897. Catanzaro, S. J. (1996). Negative mood regulation expectancies, emotional distress, and examination performance. *Personality and Social Psychology Bulletin, 22,* 1023–1029.
898. Chacko, R. C., Harper, R. G., Gotto, J., & Young, J. (1996). Psychiatric interview and psychometric predictors of cardiac transplant survival. *American Journal of Psychiatry, 153,* 1607–1612.
899. Channon, S. (1996). Executive dysfunction in depression: The Wisconsin Card Sorting Test. *Journal of Affective Disorders, 39,* 107–114.
900. Cheung, E. C. (1996). Cultural differences in optimism, pessimism, and coping: Predictors of subsequent adjustment in Asian American and Caucasian American college students. *Journal of Counseling Psychology, 43,* 113–123.
901. Clark, D. A., Steer, R. A., Beck, A. T., & Snow, D. (1996). Is the relationship between anxious and depressive cognitions and symptoms linear or curvilinear? *Cognitive Therapy and Research, 20,* 135–154.
902. Clark, M. E. (1996). MMPI-2 negative treatment indicators content and content component scales: Clinical correlates and outcome prediction for men with chronic pain. *Psychological Assessment, 8,* 32–38.
903. Clark, M. M., Niaura, R., King, T. K., & Pera, V. (1996). Depression, smoking, activity level, and health status: Pretreatment predictors of attrition in obesity treatment. *Addictive Behaviors, 21,* 509–513.
904. Coleman, M. J., Levy, D. L., Lenzenweger, M. F., & Holzman, P. S. (1996). Thought disorder, perceptual aberrations, and schizotypy. *Journal of Abnormal Psychology, 105,* 469–473.
905. Corbitt, E. M., Malone, K. M., Haas, G. L., & Mann, J. J. (1996). Suicidal behavior in patients with major depression and comorbid personality disorders. *Journal of Affective Disorders, 39,* 61–72.
906. Dahlquist, L. M., Czyzewski, D. I., & Jones, C. L. (1996). Parents of children with cancer: A longitudinal study of emotional distress, coping style, and marital adjustment two and twenty months after diagnosis. *Journal of Pediatric Psychology, 21,* 541–554.
907. Davila, J., Hammen, C., Burge, D., Daley, S. E., & Paley, B. (1996). Cognitive/interpersonal correlates of adult interpersonal problem-solving strategies. *Cognitive Therapy and Research, 20,* 465–480.
908. Davis, J. M., Adams, H. E., Uddo, M., Vasterling, J. J., & Sutker, P. B. (1996). Physiological arousal and attention in veterans with posttraumatic stress disorder. *Journal of Psychopathology and Behavioral Assessment, 18,* 1–20.
909. Deffenbacher, J. L., Oetting, E. R., Thwaites, G. A., Lynch, R. S., Baker, D. A., Stark, R. S., Tacker, S., & Elswerth-Cox, L. (1996). State-trait anger theory and the utility of the Trait Anger Scale. *Journal of Counseling Psychology, 43,* 131–148.
910. Delahanty, D. L., Dougall, A. L., Schmitz, J. B., Hawken, L., Trakowski, J. H., Jenkins, F. J., & Baum, A. (1996). Time course of natural killer cell activity and lymphocyte proliferation in response to two acute stressors in healthy men. *Health Psychology, 15,* 48–55.
911. Dimitrov, M., Grafman, J., & Hollnagel, C. (1996). The effects of frontal lobe damage on everyday problem solving. *Cortex, 32,* 357–366.
912. Donohue, B., Acierno, R., & Kogan, E. (1996). Relationship of depression with measures of social functioning in adult drug users. *Addictive Behaviors, 21,* 211–216.
913. Dykman, B. M. (1996). Negative self-evaluations among dysphoric college students: A difference in degree or kind. *Cognitive Therapy and Research, 20,* 445–464.
914. Fastenau, P. S., Denburg, N. L., & Abeles, N. (1996). Age differences in retrieval: Further support for the resource-reduction hypothesis. *Psychology and Aging, 11,* 140–146.
915. Fishbein, D. H. (1996). Female PEP-using jail detainees: Proneness to violence and gender differences. *Addictive Behaviors, 21,* 155–172.
916. Foa, E. B., Franklin, M. E., Perry, K. J., & Herbert, J. D. (1996). Cognitive biases in generalized social phobia. *Journal of Abnormal Psychology, 105,* 433–439.
917. Giesler, R. B., Josephs, R. A., & Swann, W. B., Jr. (1996). Self-verification in clinical depression: The desire for negative evaluation. *Journal of Abnormal Psychology, 105,* 358–368.
918. Glennerster, A., Palace, J., Warburton, D., Oxbury, S., & Newsum-Davis, J. (1996). Memory in myasthenia gravis: Neuropsychological tests of central cholinergic function before and after effective immunologic treatment. *Neurology, 46,* 1138–1142.
919. Gould, R. A., Ball, S., Kaspi, S. P., Otto, M. W., Pollack, M. H., Shekhar, A., & Fava, M. (1996). Prevalence and correlates of anger attacks: A two site study. *Journal of Affective Disorders, 39,* 31–38.
920. Grafman, J., Schwab, K., Warden, D., Pridgen, A., Brown, H. R., & Salazar, A. M. (1996). Frontal lobe injuries, violence, and aggression: A report of the Vietnam Head Injury Study. *Neurology, 46,* 1231–1238.
921. Greene, J. D. W., Baddeley, A. D., & Hodges, J. R. (1996). Analysis of the episodic memory deficit in early Alzheimer's disease: Evidence from the Doors and People Test. *Neuropsychologia, 34,* 537–551.
922. Grissett, N. I., & Fitzgibbon, M. L. (1996). The clinical significance of binge eating in an obese population: Support for BED and questions regarding its criteria. *Addictive Behaviors, 21,* 57–66.
923. Haack, L. J., Betalsky, G. I., Dykman, B. M., & Abramson, L. Y. (1996). Use of current situational information and causal inference: Do dysphoric individuals make "unwarranted" causal inferences? *Cognitive Therapy and Research, 20,* 309331.
924. Hewitt, P. L., Flett, G. L., & Ediger, E. (1996). Perfectionism and depression: Longitudinal assessment of a specific vulnerability hypothesis. *Journal of Abnormal Psychology, 105,* 276–280.
925. Horneffer, K. J., & Fincham, F. D. (1996). Attributional models of depression and marital distress. *Personality and Social Psychology Bulletin, 22,* 678–689.
926. Horowitz, M., Sonneborn, D., Sugahara, C., & Maercker, A. (1996). Self-regard: A new measure. *American Journal of Psychiatry, 153,* 382–385.
927. Hudziak, J. J., Boffeli, T. J., Kriesman, J. J., Battaglia, M. M., Stanger, C., & Guze, S. B. (1996). Clinical study of the relation of borderline personality disorder to Briquet's Syndrome (hysteria), somatization disorder, antisocial personality disorder, and substance abuse disorder. *American Journal of Psychiatry, 153,* 1598–1606.
928. Jacob, R. G., Furman, J. M., Durrant, J. D., & Turner, S. M. (1996). Panic, agoraphobia, and vestibular dysfunction. *American Journal of Psychiatry, 153,* 503–512.
929. Jacobvitz, D. B., & Bush, N. F. (1996). Reconstructions of family relationships: Parent-child alliances, personal distress, and self-esteem. *Developmental Psychology, 32,* 732–743.
930. Johnson, S. K., DeLuca, J., & Natelson, B. H. (1996). Depression in fatiguing illness: Comparing patients with chronic fatigue syndrome, multiple sclerosis and depression. *Journal of Affective Disorders, 39,* 21–30.
931. Joiner, T. E., Jr., & Rudd, M. D. (1996). Disentangling the interrelations between hopelessness, loneliness, and suicidal ideation. *Suicide and Life-Threatening Behavior, 26,* 19–26.
932. Joiner, T. E., Jr., & Rudd, M. D. (1996). Toward a categorization of depression-related psychological constructs. *Cognitive Therapy and Research, 20,* 51–68.
933. Jolly, J. B., & Wiesner, D. C. (1996). Psychometric properties of the Automatic Thoughts Questionnaire—Positive with inpatient adolescents. *Cognitive Therapy and Research, 20,* 481–498.
934. Kelly, V. A., & Myers, J. E. (1996). Parental alcoholism and coping: A comparison of female children of alcoholics with female children of nonalcoholics. *Journal of Counseling and Development, 74,* 501–504.
935. Kinderman, P., & Bentall, R. P. (1996). Self-discrepancies and persecutory delusions: Evidence for a model of paranoid ideation. *Journal of Abnormal Psychology, 105,* 106–113.
936. King, T. K., Clark, M. M., & Pera, V. (1996). History of sexual abuse and obesity treatment outcome. *Addictive Behaviors, 21,* 283–290.
937. Kissane, D. W., Bloch, S., Dowe, D. L., Snyder, R. D., Onghena, P., McKenzie, D. P., & Wallace, C. S. (1996). The Melbourne Family Grief Study, I: Perceptions of family functioning in bereavement. *American Journal of Psychiatry, 153,* 650–658.
938. Kissane, D. W., Bloch, S., Onghena, P., McKenzie, D. P., Snyder, R. D., & Dowe, D. L. (1996). The Melbourne Family Grief Study, II: Psychosocial morbidity and grief in bereaved families. *American Journal of Psychiatry, 153,* 659–666.
939. Koivisto, M., Portin, R., & Rinne, J. O. (1996). Perceptual priming in Alzheimer's and Parkinson's diseases. *Neuropsychologia, 34,* 449–457.
940. Kolko, D. J. (1996). Clinical monitoring of treatment course in child physical abuse: Psychometric characteristics and treatment comparisons. *Child Abuse & Neglect, 20,* 23–43.
941. Kopper, B. A., & Epperson, D. L. (1996). The experience and expression of anger: Relationships with gender, gender role socialization, depression, and mental health functioning. *Journal of Counseling Psychology, 43,* 158–165.
942. Kubany, E. S., Haynes, S. N., Abueg, F. R., Manke, F. P., Brennan, J. M., & Stahura, C. (1996). Development and validation of the Trauma-Related Guilt Inventory (TRGI). *Psychological Assessment, 8,* 428–444.
943. Kumar, G., Steer, R. A., & Deblinger, E. (1996). Problems in differentiating sexually from nonsexually abused adolescent psychiatric inpatients by self-reported anxiety, depression, internalization, and externalization. *Child Abuse & Neglect, 20,* 1079–1086.
944. Lassiter, G. D., Koenig, L. J., & Apple, K. J. (1996). Mood and behavior perception: Dysphoria can increase and decrease effortful processing of information. *Personality and Social Psychology Bulletin, 22,* 794–810.
945. Leadbeater, B. J., Bishop, S. J., & Raver, C. C. (1996). Quality of mother-toddler interactions, maternal depressive symptoms, and behavior problems in preschoolers of adolescent mothers. *Developmental Psychology, 32,* 280–288.

946. Lester, D., & Whipple, M. (1996). Music preference, depression, suicidal preoccupation, and personality: Comment on Stack and Gundlach's papers. *Suicide and Life-Threatening Behavior, 26*, 68–70.

947. Maes, M., Smith, R., Christophe, A., Cosyns, P., Desnyder, R., & Meltzer, H. (1996). Fatty acid composition in major depression: Decreased omega 3 fractions in cholesteryl esters and increased C20: 4 omega 6/C20: 5 omega 3 ratio in cholesteryl esters and phospholipids. *Journal of Affective Disorders, 38*, 35–46.

948. Mancini, C., & VanAmeringen, M. (1996). Paroxetine in social phobia. *Journal of Clinical Psychiatry, 57*, 519–522.

949. McDermott, P. A., Alterman, A. I., Brown, L., Zaballero, A., Snider, E. C., & McKay, J. R. (1996). Construct refinement and confirmation for the addiction severity index. *Psychological Assessment, 8*, 182–189.

950. McKellar, J. D., Malcarne, V. L., & Ingram, R. E. (1996). States-of-mind and negative affectivity. *Cognitive Therapy and Research, 20*, 235–246.

951. McNally, R. J., Amir, N., & Lipke, H. J. (1996). Subliminal processing of threat cues in posttraumatic stress disorder. *Journal of Anxiety Disorders, 10*, 115–128.

952. Miller, S. M., Rodoletz, M., Schroeder, C. M., Mangan, C. E., & Sedlacek, T. V. (1996). Applications of the mentoring process model to coping with severe long-term medical threats. *Health Psychology, 15*, 216–225.

953. Minarik, M. L., & Ahrens, A. H. (1996). Relations of eating behavior and symptoms of depression and anxiety to the dimensions of perfectionism among undergraduate women. *Cognitive Therapy and Research, 20*, 155–169.

954. Monroe, S. M., Roberts, J. E., Kupfer, D. J., & Frank, E. (1996). Life stress and treatment course of recurrent depression: II. Postrecovery associations with attrition, symptom course, and recurrence over 3 years. *Journal of Abnormal Psychology, 105*, 313–328.

955. Moore, R. G., & Blackburn, I. (1996). The stability of sociotropy and antonomy in depressed patients undergoing treatment. *Cognitive Therapy and Research, 20*, 69–80.

956. Moretti, M. M., Segal, Z. V., McCann, C. D., Shaw, B. F., Miller, D. T., & Vella, D. (1996). Self-referent versus other-referent information processing in dysphoric, clinically depressed, and remitted depressed subjects. *Personality and Social Psychology Bulletin, 22*, 68–80.

957. Morris, S. J. (1996). Processing strategies used by dysphoric individuals: Self-derogating, non-self-embarrassing, or schematic. *Cognitive Therapy and Research, 20*, 213–233.

958. Nunn, K. P., Lewin, T. J., Walton, J. M., & Carr, V. J. (1996). The construction and characteristics of an instrument to measure personal hopefulness. *Psychological Medicine, 26*, 531–545.

959. Partonen, T., Sihvo, S., & Lönngvist, J. K. (1996). Patients excluded from an antidepressant efficacy trial. *Journal of Clinical Psychiatry, 57*, 572–575.

960. Peterson, L., Johannson, V., & Carlsson, S. G. (1996). Computerized testing in a hospital setting: Psychometric and psychological effects. *Computers in Human Behavior, 12*, 339–350.

961. Power, M. J., Comeron, C. M., & Dalgleish, T. (1996). Emotional priming in clinically depressed subjects. *Journal of Affective Disorders, 38*, 1–11.

962. Radcliffe, J., Bennett, D., Kazak, A. E., Foley, B., & Phillips, P. C. (1996). Adjustment in childhood brain tumor survival: Child, mother, and teacher report. *Journal of Pediatric Psychology, 21*, 529–539.

963. Reynolds, C. F., III, Frank, E., Perel, J. M., Mazumdar, S., Dew, M. A., Begley, A., Houck, P. R., Hall, M., Mulsant, B., Shear, M. K., Miller, M. D., Cornes, C., & Kupfer, D. (1996). High relapse rate after discontinuation of adjunctive medication for elderly patients with recurrent major depression. *American Journal of Psychiatry, 153*, 1418–1422.

964. Richards, A., French, C. C., & Randall, F. (1996). Anxiety and the use of strategies in the performance of sentence-picture verification task. *Journal of Abnormal Psychology, 105*, 132–136.

965. Roberts, J. E., & Kassel, J. D. (1996). Mood state dependence and cognitive vulnerability to depression: The roles of positive and negative affect. *Cognitive Therapy and Research, 20*, 1–12.

966. Robinson, B. B. E., & Bacon, J. G. (1996). The "If only I were thin" treatment program: Decreasing the stigmatizing effects of fatness. *Professional Psychology: Research and Practice, 27*, 175–183.

967. Rothschild, A. J. (1996). The diagnosis and treatment of late-life depression. *Journal of Clinical Psychiatry, 57*, 5–11.

968. Roy-Byrne, P., Wingerson, D. K., Radant, A., Greenblatt, D. J., & Cowley, D. S. (1996). Reduced benzodiazepine sensitivity inpatients with panic disorder: Comparison with patients with obsessive-compulsive disorder and normal subjects. *American Journal of Psychiatry, 153*, 1444–1449.

969. Rush, A. J., Gullion, C. M., Basco, M. R., Jarrett, R. B., & Trivedi, M. H. (1996). The Inventory of Depressive Symptomatology (IDS): Psychometric properties. *Psychological Medicine, 26*, 477–486.

970. Saigh, P. A., Yule, W., & Inamdar, S. C. (1996). Imaginal flooding of traumatized children and adolescents. *Journal of School Psychology, 34*, 163–183.

971. Schwartz, J. A. J., & Koenig, L. J. (1996). Response styles and negative affect among adolescents. *Cognitive Therapy and Research, 20*, 13–36.

972. Sebastian, S. B., Williamson, D. A., & Blouin, D. C. (1996). Memory bias for fatness stimuli in the eating disorders. *Cognitive Therapy and Research, 20*, 275–286.

973. Shaw, D. S., Owens, E. B., Vondra, J. I., Keenan, K., & Winslow, E. B. (1996). Early risk factors and pathways in the development of early disruptive behavior problems. *Development and Psychopathology, 8*, 679–699.

974. Showers, C. J., & Kling, K. C. (1996). Organization of self-knowledge: Implications for recovery from sad mood. *Journal of Personality and Social Psychology, 70*, 578–590.

975. Simon, L., Greenberg, J., Harmon-Jones, E., Solomon, S., & Pyszczynski, T. (1996). Mild depression, mortality, salience, and defence of the worldview:

Evidence of intensified terror management in the mildly depressed. *Personality and Social Psychology Bulletin, 22*, 81–90.

976. Smith, D. W., & Frueh, B. C. (1996). Compensation seeking, comorbidity, and apparent exaggeration of PTSD symptoms among Vietnam combat veterans. *Psychological Assessment, 8*, 3–6.

977. Spalletta, G., Troisi, A., Saracco, M., Ciani, N., & Pasini, A. (1996). Symptom profile, Axis II comorbidity and suicidal behavior in young males with DSM–III–R depressive illnesses. *Journal of Affective Disorders, 39*, 141–148.

978. Stein, M. B., Baird, A., & Walker, J. R. (1996). Social phobia in adults with stuttering. *American Journal of Psychiatry, 153*, 278–280.

979. Stroebe, W., Stroebe, M., Abakoumkin, G., & Schut, H. (1996). The role of loneliness and social support in adjustment to loss: A test of attachment versus stress theory. *Journal of Personality and Social Psychology, 70*, 1241–1249.

980. Stunkard, A., Berkowitz, R., Tanrikut, C., Reiss, E., & Young, L. (1996). d-Fenfluramine treatment of binge eating disorder. *American Journal of Psychiatry, 153*, 1455–1459.

981. Taylor, S., Koch, W. J., Woody, S., & McLean, P. (1996). Anxiety sensitivity and depression: How are they related? *Journal of Abnormal Psychology, 105*, 474–479.

982. Terry, D. J., Mayocchi, L., & Hynes, G. J. (1996). Depressive symptomatology in new mothers: A stress and coping perspective. *Journal of Abnormal Psychology, 105*, 220–231.

983. Trappler, B., & Friedman, S. (1996). Posttraumatic stress disorder in survivors of the Brooklyn Bridge shooting. *American Journal of Psychiatry, 153*, 705–707.

984. VanAmeringen, M., Mancini, C., & Wilson, C. (1996). Buspirone augmentation of selective serotonin reuptake inhibitors (SSRIs) in social phobia. *Journal of Affective Disorders, 39*, 115–121.

985. Waldstein, S. R., Polefrone, J. M., Fazzari, T. V., Manuck, S. B., Jennings, J. R., Ryan, C. M., Muldoon, M. F., & Shapiro, A. P. (1996). Hypertension and neuropsychological performance in men: Interactive effects of age. *Health Psychology, 15*, 102–109.

986. Watkins, P. C., Vache, K., Verney, S. P., Muller, S., & Mathews, A. (1996). Unconscious mood-congruent memory bias in depression. *Journal of Abnormal Psychology, 105*, 34–41.

987. Wilens, T. E., Biederman, J., Prince, J., Spencer, T. J., Faraone, S. V., Warburton, R., Schleifer, D., Harding, M., Linehan, C., & Geller, D. (1996). Six-week, double-blind, placebo-controlled study of desipramine for adult attention deficit hyperactivity disorder. *American Journal of Psychiatry, 153*, 1147–1153.

988. Yost, J. H., & Weary, G. (1996). Depression and the correspondent inference bias: Evidence for more effortful cognitive processing. *Personality and Social Psychology Bulletin, 22*, 192–200.

989. Zlotnick, C., Shea, T., Pilkonis, P. A., Elkin, I., & Ryan, C. (1996). Gender, type of treatment, dysfunctional attitudes, social support, life events, and depressive symptoms over naturalistic follow-up. *American Journal of Psychiatry, 153*, 1021–1027.

990. Zucker, R. A., Ellis, D. A., Fitzgerald, H. E., Bingham, C. R., & Sanford, K. (1996). Other evidence for at least two alcoholisms II: Life course variation in antisociality and heterogeneity of alcoholic outcome. *Development and Psychopathology, 8*, 831–848.

991. Avissar, S., Nechamkin, Y., Roitman, G., & Schreiber, G. (1997). Reduced G Protein functions and immunoreactive levels inmononuclear leukocytes of patients with depression. *American Journal of Psychiatry, 154*, 211–217.

992. Beardslee, W. R., Salt, P., Versage, E. M., Gladstone, T. R. G., Wright, E. J., & Rothberg, P. C. (1997). Sustained change in parents receiving preventative interventions for families with depression. *American Journal of Psychiatry, 154*, 510–515.

993. Beardslee, W. R., Versage, E. M., Wright, E. J., Salt, P., Rothberg, P. C., Drezner, K., & Gladstone, T. R. G. (1997). Examination of preventive interventions for families with depression: Evidence of change. *Development and Psychopathology, 9*, 109–130.

994. Bjorck, J. P., Lee, Y. S., & Cohen, L. H. (1997). Control beliefs and faith as stress moderators for Korean American versus Caucasian American Protestants. *American Journal of Community Psychology, 25*, 61–72.

995. Black, D. W., Kehrberg, L. L. D., Flumerfelt, D. L., & Schlosser, S. S. (1997). Characteristics of 36 subjects reporting compulsive sexual behavior. *American Journal of Psychiatry, 154*, 243–249.

996. Cheng, C. (1997). Assessment of major life events for Hong Kong adolescents: The Chinese Adolescent Life Event Scale. *American Journal of Community Psychology, 25*, 17–33.

997. Chochinov, H. M., Wilson, K. G., Enns, M., & Lander, S. (1997). "Are you depressed?" Screening for depression in the terminally ill. *American Journal of Psychiatry, 154*, 674–676.

998. Codori, A-M., Slavney, P. R., Young, C., Miglioretti, D. L., & Brandt, J. (1997). Predictors of psychological adjustment to genetic testing for Huntington's Disease. *Health Psychology, 16*, 36–50.

999. Cohan, C. L., & Bradbury, T. N. (1997). Negative life events, marital interaction, and the longitudinal course of newlywed marriage. *Journal of Personality and Social Psychology, 73*, 114–128.

1000. Covey, L. S., Glassman, A. H., & Stetner, F. (1997). Major depression following smoking cessation. *American Journal of Psychiatry, 154*, 263–265.

1001. Deale, A., Chalder, T., Marks, I., & Wessely, S. (1997). Cognitive behavior therapy for chronic fatigue syndrome: A randomized controlled trial. *American Journal of Psychiatry, 154*, 408–414.

1002. Doyon, J., Gaudreau, D., Laforce, R., Jr., Castonguay, M., Bédard, P. J., Bédard, F., & Bouchard, J-P. (1997). Role of the striatum, cerebellum, and frontal lobes in the learning of a visuomotor sequence. *Brain and Cognition, 34*, 218–245.

1003. Durns, J. W., Wiegner, S., Derleth, M., Kiselica, K., & Pawl, R. (1997). Linking symptom-specific physiological reactivity to pain severity in chronic low back pain patients: A test of mediation and moderation models. *Health Psychology, 16*, 319–326.

1004. Enns, M. W., Inayatulla, M., Cox, B., & Cheyne, L. (1997). Prediction of suicide intent in aboriginal and non-aboriginal adolescent inpatients: A research note. *Suicide and Life-Threatening Behavior, 27*, 218–224.

1005. Fastenau, P. S., Denburg, N. L., & Domitrovic, L. A. (1997). Intentional and incidental memory: Order effects in clinical testing. *Professional Psychology: Research and Practice, 28*, 32–35.

1006. Foster, G. D., Wadden, T. A., & Vogt, R. A. (1997). Body image in obese women before, during, and after weight loss treatment. *Health Psychology, 16*, 226–229.

1007. Hawkins, C. A. (1997). Disruption of family rituals as a mediator of the relationship between parental drinking and adult adjustment in offspring. *Addictive Behaviors, 22*, 219–231.

1008. Herschbach, P., Duran, G., Waadts, S., Zettler, A., Amm, C., & Marten-Mittage, B. (1997). Psychometric properties of the Questionnaire on Stress in Patients with Diabetes—Revised (QSD-R). *Health Psychology, 16*, 171–174.

1009. Johnson, D. E., Waid, L. R., & Anton, R. F. (1997). Childhood hyperactivity, gender, and Cloninger's personality dimensions in alcoholics. *Addictive Behaviors, 22*, 649–653.

1010. Madill, A., & Barkham, M. (1997). Discourse analysis of a theme in one successful case of brief psychodynamic-interpersonal psychotherapy. *Journal of Counseling Psychology, 44*, 232–244.

1011. Marziali, E., Monroe-Blum, H., & McCleary, L. (1997). The contribution of group cohesion and group alliance to outcome of group psychotherapy. *International Journal of Group Psychotherapy, 47*, 475–497.

1012. McCallum, M., Piper, W. E., & O'Kelly, J. (1997). Predicting patient benefit from a group-oriented, evening treatment program. *International Journal of Group Psychotherapy, 47*, 291–314.

1013. McFarland, C., & Buehler, R. (1997). Negative affective states and the motivated retrieval of positive life events: The role of affect acknowledgement. *Journal of Personality and Social Psychology, 73*, 200–214.

1014. Metha, A., & McWhirter, E. H. (1997). Suicide ideation, depression, and stressful life events among gifted adolescents. *Journal for the Education of the Gifted, 20*, 284–304.

1015. Murphy, T. K., Goodman, W. K., Fudge, M. W., Williams, R. C., Jr., Ayoub, E. M., Dalal, M., Lewis, M. H., & Zabriskie, J. B. (1997). B lymphocyte antigen D8/17: A peripheral marker for childhood-onset obsessive-compulsive disorder and Tourette's syndrome? *American Journal of Psychiatry, 154*, 402–407.

1016. Nouwen, A., Gingas, J., Talbot, F., & Bouchard, S. (1997). The development of an empirical psychosocial taxonomy for patients with diabetes. *Health Psychology, 16*, 263–271.

1017. Roitman, S. E. L., Cornblatt, B. A., Bergman, A., Obuchowski, M., Mitropoulou, V., Keefe, R. S. E., Silverman, J. M., & Siever, L. J. (1997). Attentional functioning in schizotypal personality disorder. *American Journal of Psychiatry, 154*, 655–660.

1018. Sallee, F. R., Vrindavanam, N. S., Deas-Newsmith, D., Carson, S. W., & Sethuraman, G. (1997). Pulse intravenous clomipramine for depressed adolescents: Double-blind, controlled trial. *American Journal of Psychiatry, 154*, 668–673.

1019. Salmela-Aro, K., & Nurmi, J-E. (1997). Goal contents, well-being, and life context during transition to university: A longitudinal study. *International Journal of Behavioral Development, 20*, 471–491.

1020. Schafer, J., & Fals-Stewart, W. (1997). Spousal violence and cognitive functioning among men recovering from multiple substance abuse. *Addictive Behaviors, 22*, 127–130.

1021. Shackelford, T. K., & Larsen, R. J. (1997). Facial asymmetry as an indicator of psychological, emotional, and physiological distress. *Journal of Personality and Social Psychology, 72*, 456–466,.

1022. Sklar, S. M., Annis, H. M., & Turner, N. E. (1997). Development and validation of the drug-taking confidence questionnaire: A measure of coping self-efficacy. *Addictive Behaviors, 22*, 655–670.

1023. Spinelli, M. G. (1997). Interpersonal psychotherapy for depressed antepartum women: A pilot study. *American Journal of Psychiatry, 154*, 1028–1030.

1024. Walsh, B. T., Wilson, G. T., Loeb, K. L., Devlin, M. J., Pike, K. M., Roose, S. P., Fleiss, J., & Waternaux, C. (1997). Medication and psychotherapy in the treatment of bulimia nervosa. *American Journal of Psychiatry, 154*, 523–531.

1025. Wang, L., Heppner, P. P., & Berry, T. R. (1997). Role of gender-related personality traits, problem-solving appraisal, and perceived social support in developing a mediational model of psychological adjustment. *Journal of Counseling Psychology, 44*, 245–255.

1026. Wetherell, J. L., & Areán, P. A. (1997). Psychometric evaluation of the Beck Anxiety Inventory with older medical patients. *Psychological Assessment, 9*, 136–144.

Review of the Beck Depression Inventory by JANET F. CARLSON, Associate Professor, Counseling and Psychological Services Department, State University of New York at Oswego, Oswego, NY:

The Beck Depression Inventory (BDI) is a well-known and widely used self-report inventory that taps overall severity of depression in adolescents and adults. The original BDI was developed by Beck and his associates in 1961 (Beck, Ward, Mendelson, Mock, & Erbaugh, 1961) and revised in 1971, at which time it was introduced at the Center for Cognitive Therapy (CCT) of the University of Pennsylvania Medical School where a large portion of research bearing on the BDI has been conducted. The current edition consists of 21 symptoms and attitudes, which the subject rates on a 4-point scale of severity. Test takers are asked to rate the items for the past week, including the day on which the test is taken. The items cover cognitive, affective, somatic, and vegetative dimensions of depression, although the inventory itself was developed atheoretically. Collectively, the items correspond reasonably well to the symptoms of depression listed in the *Diagnostic and Statistical Manual of Mental Disorders* (4th ed.) (*DSM-IV*, American Psychiatric Association, 1994).

APPLICATIONS. The use of the BDI has expanded well beyond its original intended application with psychiatric populations. In addition to its continued use among this population, it is accepted and commonly used by clinicians as a screening instrument among normal populations. The test authors are careful to avoid endorsing the use of the BDI for purposes other than those for which it was developed, and simply acknowledge that many practitioners have found the inventory useful in these other contexts. The test authors indicate the vast amount of research and attending literature has supported the use of the BDI in myriad applications, from research, to screening, to assessment of therapeutic outcomes. Despite the extensive body of research bearing on numerous aspects of the BDI, the test manual itself contains only "an overview of the published information on the revision" despite noting that "specific characteristics of the revised BDI have not previously been described in detail" (p. 1).

ADMINISTRATION, SCORING, AND INTERPRETATION. The BDI may be administered individually or in group format, in written or oral form. Instructions to the test taker were modified slightly from the previous edition, as the current version directs test takers to described themselves or their feelings over the past week, including the present day. Thus, the 1993 edition taps more trait aspects of depression whereas the earlier version appears to have measured state aspects of depression. The test manual authors indicate that total administration time is no more than 15 minutes, irrespective of the mode of administration. A total score is obtained by simply summing the ratings given by the test taker on all items. Interpretation is based on the total score, which may range from 0 to 63. Among depressed patients, scores in the 0–9 range denote "Minimal" depression, 10–16 suggest "Mild" depression, 17–29 are considered "Moderate", and scores in the 30–63 range indicate "Severe" levels of depression. Within the normal population, total scores above 15 may be indicative of possible depression, although further assessment would be essential in order to confirm the presence of depression. Computer software is available from The Psychological Corporation, which offers the Beck Computer Scoring program (Beck & Steer, 1992). The program scores and interprets the BDI, as well as the several other instruments developed by Beck.

The test authors note that in addition to the total score, responses to individual items should be considered in an effort to understand and extract clinically meaningful data. In particular, the clinical relevance of Item 2, which the authors term the pessimism/hopelessness item, and Item 9, the suicide ideation item, is noted. Because the severity of depression, as assessed by the BDI, is independent of symptom types, the test authors suggest that overall patterns of responses be considered in order to ascertain whether the individual patient demonstrates symptoms that are more cognitive, more somatic, more vegetative, or more affective. Elucidating the nature of the most prominent symptoms may have important treatment implications.

TECHNICAL ASPECTS. The section of the test manual that covers psychometric characteristics presents information from six normative-outpatient samples used by the CCT to establish reliability estimates and provide evidence of scale validation. The total normative sample consisted of 944 outpatients with mixed diagnoses ($n = 248$), single episodes of major depression ($n = 113$), recurrent episodes of major depression ($n = 168$), Dysthymic disorder ($n = 99$), alcoholism ($n = 105$), or heroine addiction ($n = 211$). Gender and race distributions of the six normative samples are presented in the test manual, as are means, standard deviations, percentages of item endorsement, and item-total correlations.

Alpha reliability coefficients across the six samples ranged from .79 to .90. Item-total correlations ranged from .07 to .68, with most values being in the .30 or better range. The authors cite several studies related to the stability of BDI scores over

time, using patient and nonpatient groups. It appears that nonpsychiatric samples demonstrate somewhat more stable BDI scores (in the .60 to .90 range) than patient samples (in the .48 to .86 range). These results are not unexpected, given that depressed individuals who are undergoing treatment are expected to improve.

Validation evidence for the BDI is provided in the test manual under the headings of content, discriminant, construct, and concurrent validity. The test authors report on two studies that compared the content of the revised BDI to *DSM-III* criteria for affective disorders and found that two-thirds of the criteria were addressed by the BDI items. The authors note that the lack of items related to the omitted criteria was intentional, and provide an appropriate rationale for not including items that reflected these criteria. The test authors cite several studies bearing on the ability of the BDI to differentiate psychiatric patients from normals, patients with Dysthymic Disorder from those with Major Depressive Disorder, and patients with Generalized Anxiety Disorders from those with Major Depressive Disorder. Based on research findings, the test authors extracted two subscales that can be calculated by summing the ratings for appropriate items. Items 1 through 13 comprise the cognitive-affective subscale, and Items 14 through 21 comprise the somatic-performance subscale. A score greater than 10 on the cognitive-affective subscale indicates moderate depression. Correlation coefficients between the BDI and the Beck Hopelessness Scale and the Hamilton Rating Scale for Depression ranged from .38 to .76 and from .40 to .87, respectively, across the six normative-outpatient samples. Among patients with mixed depressive disorders, correlation coefficients between the BDI and the Symptom Checklist-90-Revised and the Minnesota Multiphasic Personality Inventory-Depression scale were .76 and .61, respectively.

Factor analyses with clinical and nonclinical samples have been conducted. Some of the findings are presented briefly in the test manual. The test authors note the number of factors extracted varied with the characteristics of the samples used, and with the method of extraction employed. Brown, Schulberg, and Madonia (1995) indicate that the many factor analyses of the BDI have found anywhere from three to seven factors and note that "[s]tudies using latent structure analysis suggest that the BDI represents one general syndrome of depression that subsumes three highly inter-correlated factors ... reflect[ing] negative attitudes toward self, performance impairment, and somatic disturbance, as originally described by Beck and Lester" (p. 59). Compared to other measures of depression, the BDI appears to tap more of the cognitive or cognitive-affective components of depression than other instruments such as the Hamilton Rating Scale for Depression (263) and the Zung Self-Rating Scale (e.g., Brown, Schulberg, & Madonia, 1995; Lambert, Hatch, Kingston, & Edwards, 1986; Santor, Zuroff, Ramsay, Cervantes, & Palacios, 1995).

Because so much additional information concerning the psychometric properties of the BDI is contained in the literature and is not contained in the test manual, potential users would be well advised to consult the literature for further information. Prior reviews of the earlier editions of the BDI have indicated the importance of doing so as well. One previous reviewer (Conoley, 1992) summarized the findings of a reference that the reviewer found particularly useful, in that it presents a review and meta-analysis of the reliability and validity literature for the BDI (Beck, Steer, & Garbin, 1988). Readers are referred to these sources for elaboration.

CRITIQUE. In general, the information referenced in the test manual and elsewhere is favorable and supportive of the BDI as far as its use with the intended population and, perhaps, others (Brown, Schulberg, & Madonia, 1995; Conoley, 1992; Santor, Zuroff, Ramsay, Cervantes, & Palacios, 1995; Stehouwer, 1985; Sundberg, 1992). The BDI has been widely used over at least the last 25 years, and has been recognized for its solid contributions to the measurement of depression. Potential users must be prepared, however, to ferret out some information beyond that presented in the test manual that may affect their choice of instruments. In particular, test users should bear in mind that the BDI is not intended to be a diagnostic instrument. Thus, in clinical applications, it is best regarded as a screening instrument for depression or as an indicator of the extent of depression, and should not serve as the sole means by which depression is assessed.

The availability of software to score and interpret the BDI makes its use as a screening and/or research instrument quite practical and it seems likely that the BDI will continue to enjoy widespread applications in these venues. In situations where the ratings given to somatic or performance items could be attributable to another cause (e.g., a medical condition where fatigue is a symptom or side effect of treatment), the use of the cognitive-affective subscale may be particularly helpful, although further evidence of the validity and reliability of the subscale is needed. Similarly, validity and reliability evidence to establish the probity of various modifications to administration noted in the test manual would be useful additions.

All items on the BDI contribute to the total score (i.e., there are no filler items) and items clearly are aimed at assessing aspects of depression. The four response options presented for each item are numbered from 0 to 3, in order of increasing severity, and scoring blanks are presented on each side of the test form. These characteristics make administration, scoring, and interpretation straightforward and, for many users, probably contribute to the appeal of this instrument. But these traits make faking rather easy as well. In cases where test takers might be motivated to deceive (e.g., competency to stand trial, custody hearings, involuntary commitment procedures, social desirability), the test user is advised to use additional or less transparent means of assessment.

SUMMARY. The BDI has made, and is likely to continue making, a noteworthy contribution to the assessment of depression. The expansion of its use beyond that originally intended by the test authors is likely attributable to its obvious strengths. Working in its favor are the facts that it is a simple measure that is easily and rapidly administered, encompasses the majority of symptoms associated with depression, has been well researched, can be scored and interpreted via computer software, and can be considerably less expensive than other screening or research tools that require individual administration.

REVIEWER'S REFERENCES

Beck, A. T., Ward, C. H., Mendelson, M., Mock, J., & Erbaugh, J. (1961). An inventory for measuring depression. *Archives of General Psychiatry, 4,* 561–571.

Stehouwer, R. S. (1985). [Review of Beck Depression Inventory]. In D. J. Keyser & R. C. Sweetland (Eds.), *Test critiques* (Vol. II) (pp. 83–87). Kansas City, MO: Test Corporation of America/Westport Publishers.

Lambert, M. J., Hatch, D. R., Kingston, M. D., & Edwards, B. C. (1986). Zung, Beck, and Hamilton rating scales as measures of treatment outcome: A meta-analytic comparison. *Journal of Consulting and Clinical Psychology, 54,* 54–59.

Beck, A. T., Steer, R. A., & Garbin, M. G. (1988). Psychometric properties of the Beck Depression Inventory: Twenty-five years of evaluation. *Clinical Psychology Review, 8,* 77–100.

Beck, A. T., & Steer, R. A. (1992). *Beck computer scoring.* San Antonio, TX: The Psychological Corporation.

Conoley, C. W. (1992). [Review of the Beck Depression Inventory (Revised Edition)]. In J. J. Kramer & J. C. Conoley (Eds.), *The eleventh mental measurements yearbook* (pp. 78–79). Lincoln, NE: The Buros Institute of Mental Measurements.

Sundberg, N. D. (1992). [Review of the Beck Depression Inventory (Revised Edition)]. In J. J. Kramer & J. C. Conoley (Eds.), *The eleventh mental measurements yearbook* (pp. 79–81). Lincoln, NE: The Buros Institute of Mental Measurements.

American Psychiatric Association. (1994). *Diagnostic and statistical manual of mental disorders* (4th ed.). Washington, DC: Author.

Brown, C., Schulberg, H. C., & Madonia, M. J. (1995). Assessing depression in primary care practice with the Beck Depression Inventory and the Hamilton Rating Scale for Depression. *Psychological Assessment, 7,* 59–65.

Santor, D. A., Zuroff, D. C., Ramsay, J. O., Cervantes, P., & Palacios, J. (1995). Examining scale discriminability in the BDI and CES-D as a function of depressive severity. *Psychological Assessment, 7*, 131–139.

Review of the Beck Depression Inventory by NIELS G. WALLER, Associate Professor of Psychology, University of California, Davis, CA:

The Beck Depression Inventory (BDI) is a brief self-report measure of depressive symptoms in adolescents and adults. It has been a clinical mainstay for more than 35 years (Beck, Ward, Mendelson, Mock, & Erbaugh, 1961) and, not surprisingly, the BDI has spawned a rich and extensive research literature. To date, the BDI—in one form or another—has been used in over 3,000 studies. Most of these have used a 21-item long form (Beck, Ward, Mendelson, Mock, & Erbaugh, 1961), although authorized (Beck & Beck, 1972) and unauthorized short forms have also been used. A new edition of the BDI, called the BDI-II (Beck, Steer, & Brown, 1996) is scheduled for release in 1996. At the time of this writing the BDI-II was not available; thus my review focuses on the BDI, although I also discuss some promised features of the BDI-II.

The BDI can be administered via paper and pencil, a computer, or orally in approximately 5–15 minutes. In other words, in less time than it takes to drink a cup of coffee, a clinician or researcher can gather information on 21 signs of depression severity: (1) Sadness, (2) Pessimism, (3) Sense of Failure, (4) Dissatisfaction, (5) Guilt, (6) Punishment, (7) Self-dislike, (8) Self-accusations, (9) Suicidal ideas, (10) Crying, (11) Irritability, (12) Social withdrawal, (13) Indecisiveness, (14) Body Image Change, (15) Work difficulty, (16) Insomnia, (17) Fatigability, (18) Loss of Appetite, (19) Weight Loss, (20) Somatic Preoccupation, and (21) Loss of Libido. These symptoms were not selected to reflect any particular theory of depression. The items of the BDI-II, on the other hand, are tailored to the current criteria of depression as outlined in the *Diagnostic and Statistical Manual of Mental Disorders, Fourth Edition (DSM-IV)*.

BDI items comprise four self-descriptive statements. For example, Item 10—which measures Crying—reads as follows: "(0) *I don't cry any more than usual;* (1) *I cry more now than I used to;* (2) *I cry all the time now;* (3) *I used to be able to cry, but now I can't cry even though I want to*" (p. 1, BDI Questionnaire). Notice that each statement is preceded by a scoring weight. The weights range from 0 to 3; consequently BDI total scores range from 0 to 63.

The scoring weights were rationally derived such that higher weights signify greater symptom severity in clinical populations. For some items, as discussed below, the scoring weights are not appropriate for nonclinical samples. All items are face valid (transparent) and scored in the same direction. Thus, BDI scores can be easily distorted with respect to faking (Beck & Beamesderfer, 1974; Dahlstrom, Brooks, & Peterson, 1990; Lees-Haley, 1989); obviously, the scale should be administered only to cooperative examinees with no motivation to malinger.

The BDI was originally designed to measure the severity of depressive symptoms in clinical samples. Nevertheless, it is frequently used as a screening instrument in nonclinical samples (Barrera & Garrison-Jones, 1988) even though the manual author warns "there is considerable debate concerning the use of the BDI for screening" (p. 2). Santor, Ramsay, and Zuroff (1994) have recently shown why the BDI can perform nonoptimally in nonclinical populations. Using a nonparametric item response model (Ramsay, 1991), these authors compared the BDI item-scoring weights in clinical and nonclinical samples. They found the estimated and original (rationally derived) weights were similar in their clinical sample but that "differences implied by the a priori weights may not be warranted for some options in the nonpatient college sample" (p. 266). For example, regarding Item 10, their analyses indicated that "*at any level of depression,* it is more likely that an individual [from a nonclinical sample] will choose Option 3 than Option 2" (p. 259, italics added).

The aforementioned scoring problems *may* be alleviated in the BDI-II. The product bulletin notes that "Dr. Beck … used Item Response Theory (IRT) to examine how well the four response options are differentiated from each other, and how well the set of response options measures the underlying dimension (latent trait) of self-reported depression. Based on these analyses … several response options were reworded and subsequently tested on a large clinical sample (N = 500)." By relying on IRT while revising the BDI, Beck and his colleagues have set a new standard for clinical test revision. I hope Beck or other researchers will publish IRT item parameter estimates (Reise & Waller, 1990) for the BDI and BDI-II so that these scales can be administered by a computerized adaptive test (Waller & Reise, 1989).

The BDI manual contains a weak and inadequate summary of the scale's properties. Rather than reviewing the psychometric characteristics of the BDI in sufficient detail, the manual directs readers elsewhere for more comprehensive reviews (e.g., Beck, Steer, & Garbin, 1988). Much of the manual is a presentation of BDI summary statistics—such as item means, standard deviations, endorsement percents, and item-total correlations—for six normative outpatient samples: (a) mixed diagnostic; (b) major depression, single episode; (c) major depression, recurrent episode; (d) dysthymic disorder; (e) alcoholism; and (f) heroin addiction. Data from nonclinical samples are conspicuously absent. For the clinical samples, the BDI reliabilities are uniformly high (mean coefficient alpha = .86). The product bulletin promises that the BDI-II is even more reliable.

The weakest parts of the manual are the sections on test validity. Five types of validity are discussed: (a) content, (b) discriminant, (c) construct, (d) concurrent, and (e) factorial. The content and organization of these sections leaves much to be desired. Consider, for example, that under the heading: Discriminant Validity, we find evidence that the BDI *discriminates* psychiatric patients from normal controls. This is surely a desiderata, but it does not speak to the discriminant validity of the instrument. As Campbell and Fiske (1959) remind us, tests are invalidated when they yield high correlations with other tests purporting to measure *different* things. In other words, they are invalidated when they fail to *discriminate* between conceptually distinct constructs—such as depression and anxiety (Clark & Watson, 1991). I hope a future manual will report correlations between the BDI and scales that are not designed to measure depression, such as the Beck Anxiety Inventory (Beck & Steer, 1990; 30).

Our review materials also included a copy of the Beck Computer Scoring Program (BCS, version 1). This stand-alone product can be used to (a) administer, (b) score, and (c) interpret the BDI and several other Beck scales (The Beck Hopelessness Scale [32], the Beck Anxiety Inventory [30], and The Beck Scale for Suicide Ideation [33]). Overall, the program passed a very rigorous test: I was able to load the program, take the BDI, and generate an interpreted report without opening the manual. Noteworthy features of the BCS include (a) the ability to return to previously administered items and (b) the ability to display the test instructions during any point of the scale administration. I found the interpretive summaries to be both useful

and conservative, though they err on the side of redundancy. For example, a sample report for Jane Doe concludes that: "Ms Doe expresses higher levels of hopelessness and anxiety than depression. Viewed together, the moderate hopelessness, severe anxiety, and mild depression indicate that she views the future with considerable hopelessness and anxiety but is not very depressed by this view." Scores on the computer-administered BDI are comparable to those from the paper-and-pencil version (Steer, Rissmiller, Ranieri, & Beck, 1994).

As a clinician trained in psychometric theory, I am skeptical of 5-minute assessment scales. Nevertheless, as a Minnesota-trained dust-bowl empiricist, I also listen to the data. In the case of the BDI, the data speak loud and clearly. The BDI is an excellent measure of depressive symptoms when it is used *in clinical samples with cooperative subjects*. The BDI-II promises to be a useful screening measure in nonclinical samples. In situations where subjects may be motivated to malinger, other scales with validity checks, such as the Minnesota Multiphasic Personality Inventory—2 (MMPI-2) (Butcher, Dahlstom, Graham, Tellegen, & Kaemmer, 1989; T4:1645) should provide more trustworthy data.

REVIEWER'S REFERENCES

Campbell, D. T., & Fiske, D. W. (1959). Convergent and discriminant validation by the multitrait-multimethod matrix. *Psychological Bulletin, 56,* 81–105.

Beck, A. T., Ward, C. H., Mendelson, M., Mock, J., & Erbaugh, J. (1961). An inventory for measuring depression. *Archives of General Psychiatry, 4,* 561–571.

Beck, A. T., & Beck, R. W. (1972). Screening depressed patients in a family practice. *Postgraduate Medicine, 52*(6), 81–85.

Beck, A. T., & Beamesderfer, A. (1974). Assessment of depression: The depression inventory. In P. Pichot (Ed.), *Modern problems in pharmacopsychiatry* (pp. 151–169). Basel, Switzerland: Karger.

Barrera, M., & Garrison-Jones, C. V. (1988). Properties of the Beck Depression Inventory as a screening instrument for adolescent depression *Journal of Abnormal Child Psychology, 16*(3), 263–273.

Beck, A. T., Steer, R. A., & Garbin, M. G. (1988). Psychometric properties of the Beck Depression Inventory: Twenty-five years of evaluation. *Clinical Psychology Review, 8,* 77–100.

Butcher, J. N., Dahlstrom, W. G., Graham, J. R., Tellegen, A., & Kaemmer, B. (1989). *Minnesota Multiphasic Personality Inventory—2 (MMPI-2): Manual for administration and scoring.* Minneapolis: University of Minnesota Press.

Lees-Haley, P. R. (1989). Malingering traumatic mental disorder on the Beck Depression inventory: Cancerphobia and toxic exposure. *Psychological Reports, 65,* 623–626.

Waller, N. G., & Rise, S. (1989). Computerized adaptive personality assessment: An illustration with the Absorption scale. *Journal of Personality and Social Psychology, 57,* 1051–1058.

Beck, A. T., & Steer, R. A. (1990). *Manual for the Beck Anxiety Inventory.* San Antonio, TX: The Psychological Corporation.

Dahlstrom, W. G., Brooks, J. D., & Peterson, C. D. (1990). The Beck Depression Inventory: Item order and the impact of response sets. *Journal of Personality Assessment, 55,* 224–233.

Reise, S. P., & Waller, N. G. (1990). Fitting the two-parameter model to personality data. *Applied Psychological Measurement, 14,* 45–58.

Clark, L. A., & Watson, D. (1991). Tripartite model of anxiety and depression: Psychometric evidence and taxonomic implications. *Journal of Abnormal Psychology, 100,* 316–336.

Ramsay, J. O. (1991). Kernel smoothing approaches to nonparametric item characteristic curve estimation. *Psychometrika, 56,* 611–630.

Santor, D. A., Ramsay, J. O., & Zuroff, D. C. (1994). Nonparametric item analyses of the Beck Depression Inventory; Evaluating gender item bias and response option weights. *Psychological Assessment, 6,* 255–270.

Beck, A. T., Steer, R. A., & Brown, G. (1996). Beck Depression Inventory II. San Antonio, TX: Harcourt Brace & Company, The Psychological Corporation.

[32]
Beck Hopelessness Scale [Revised].

Purpose: Measures "the extent of negative attitudes about the future (pessimism) as perceived by adolescents and adults."

Population: Adolescents and adults.

Publication Dates: 1978–1993.

Acronym: BHS.

Scores: Total score only.

Administration: Group or individual.

Price Data, 1997: $49.50 per complete kit including 25 record forms and manual ('93, 29 pages); $27.50 per 25 record forms; $24 per manual; $6.50 per scoring key.

Foreign Language Edition: Also available in Spanish.

Time: (5–10) minutes.

Authors: Aaron T. Beck and Robert A. Steer.

Publisher: The Psychological Corporation.

Cross References: See T4:269 (37 references); for reviews by E. Thomas Dowd and Steven V. Owen of an earlier edition, see 11:32 (13 references).

TEST REFERENCES

1. Topol, P., & Reznikoff, M. (1982). Perceived peer and family relationships, hopelessness and locus of control as factors in adolescent suicide attempts. *Suicide and Life-Threatening Behavior, 12,* 141–150.

2. Ramsay, R., & Bagley, C. (1984). The prevalence of suicidal behaviors, attitudes and associated social experiences in an urban population. *Suicide and Life-Threatening Behavior, 14,* 151–167.

3. Bonner, R. L., & Rich, A. R. (1987). Toward a predictive model of suicidal ideation and behavior: Some preliminary data in college students. *Suicide and Life-Threatening Behavior, 17,* 50–63.

4. McLeavey, B. C., Daly, R. J., Murray, C. M., O'Riordan, J., & Taylor, M. (1987). Interpersonal problem-solving deficits in self-poisoning patients. *Suicide and Life-Threatening Behavior, 17,* 33–49.

5. Rich, A. R., & Bonner, R. L. (1987). Concurrent validity of a stress-vulnerability model of suicidal ideation and behavior: A follow-up study. *Suicide and Life-Threatening Behavior, 17,* 265–270.

6. Prezant, D. W., & Neimeyer, R. A. (1988). Cognitive predictors of depression and suicide ideation. *Suicide and Life-Threatening Behavior, 18,* 259–264.

7. Bonner, R. L., & Rich, A. R. (1990). Psychosocial vulnerability, life stress, and suicide ideation in a jail population: A cross-validation study. *Suicide and Life-Threatening Behavior, 20,* 213–224.

8. Caldwell, C. B., & Gottesman, I. I. (1990). Schizophrenics kill themselves too: A review of risk factors for suicide. *Schizophrenia Bulletin, 16,* 571–589.

9. Devins, G. M., Mandin, H., Hons, R. B., Burgess, E. D., Klassen, J., Taub, K., Schorr, S., Letourneau, P. K., & Buckle, S. (1990). Illness, intrusiveness, and quality of life in end-stage renal disease: Comparison and stability across treatment modalities. *Health Psychology, 9,* 117–142.

10. Lerner, M. S., & Clum, G. A. (1990). Treatment of suicide indicators: A problem-solving approach. *Behavior Therapy, 21,* 403–411.

11. Rudd, M. D. (1990). An integrative model of suicidal ideation. *Suicide and Life-Threatening Behavior, 20,* 16–30.

12. Biblarz, A., Biblarz, D. N., Pilgrim, M., & Baldree, B. F. (1991). Media influence on attitudes toward suicide. *Suicide and Life-Threatening Behavior, 21,* 374–384.

13. Dyck, M. J. (1991). Positive and negative attitudes mediating suicide ideation. *Suicide and Life-Threatening Behavior, 21,* 360–373.

14. Rabkin, J. G., Williams, J. B. W., Remien, R. H., Goetz, R., Kertzner, R., & Gorman, J. M. (1991). Depression, distress, lymphocyte subsets, and human immunodeficiency virus symptoms on two occasions HIV-Positive homosexual men. *Archives of General Psychiatry, 48,* 111–119.

15. Schneider, S. G., Taylor, S. E., Kemeny, M. E., & Hammen, C. (1991). AIDS-related factors predictive of suicidal ideation of low and high intent among gay and bisexual men. *Suicide and Life-Threatening Behavior, 21,* 313–328.

16. Simonds, J. F., McMahon, T., & Armstrong, D. (1991). Young suicide attempters compared with a control group: Psychological, affective, and attitudinal variables. *Suicide and Life-Threatening Behavior, 21,* 134–151.

17. Brackney, B. E., & Westman, A. S. (1992). Relationships among hope, psychosocial development, and locus of control. *Psychological Reports, 70,* 864–866.

18. Bromet, E. J., Schwartz, J. E., Fennig, S., Geller, L., Jandorf, L., Kovasznay, B., Lavelle, J., Miller, A., Pato, C., Ram, R., & Rich, C. (1992). The epidemiology of psychosis: The Suffolk County Mental Health Project. *Schizophrenia Bulletin, 18,* 243–255.

19. Cole, D. E., Protinsky, H. O., & Cross, L. H. (1992). An empirical investigation of adolescent suicidal ideation. *Adolescence, 27,* 813–818.

20. Diamond, R., White, R. F., Myers, R. H., Mastromauro, C., Koroshetz, W. J., Butters, N., Rothstein, D. M., Moss, M. B., & Vasterling, J. (1992). Evidence of presymptomatic cognitive decline in Huntington's disease. *Journal of Clinical and Experimental Neuropsychology, 14,* 961–975.

21. Kirkpatrick-Smith, J., Rich, A. R., Bonner, R., & Jans, F. (1992). Psychological vulnerability and substance abuse as predictors of suicide ideation among adolescents. *Omega, 24,* 21–33.

22. Page, R. M. (1992). Feelings of physical unattractiveness and hopelessness among high school students. *The High School Journal, 75,* 150–155.

23. Whatley, S. L., & Clopton, J. R. (1992). Social support and suicidal ideation in college students. *Psychological Reports, 71,* 1123–1128.

24. Yeaworth, R. C., McNamee, M. J., & Pozehl, B. (1992). The Adolescent Life Change Event Scale: Its development and use. *Adolescence, 27,* 783–802.

25. Zamble, E. (1992). Behavior and adaptation in long-term prison inmates. *Criminal Justice and Behavior, 19,* 409–425.

26. Beck, A. T., Steer, R. A., Beck, J. S., & Newman, C. F. (1993). Hopelessness, depression, suicidal ideation, and clinical diagnosis of depression. *Suicide and Life-Threatening Behavior, 23,* 139–145.

27. Morano, C. D., Cisler, R. A., & Lemerond, J. (1993). Risk factors for adolescent suicidal behavior: Loss, insufficient familial support, and hopelessness. *Adolescence, 28,* 851–865.

28. Overholser, J. C., Schubert, D. S. P., Foliart, R., & Frost, F. (1993). Assessment of emotional distress following a spinal cord injury. *Rehabilitation Psychology, 38,* 187–198.

29. Shorkey, C. T., & Whiteman, V. L. (1993). Development of the Ego and Discomfort Anxiety Inventory: Initial validity and reliability. *Psychological Reports, 73,* 83–95.

30. Steer, R. A., Kumar, G., & Beck, A. T. (1993). Hopelessness in adolescent psychiatric inpatients. *Psychological Reports, 72,* 559–564.

31. Terkuile, M. M., Linssen, A. C. G., & Spinhoven, P. (1993). The development of the Multidimensional Locus of Pain Control Questionnaire (MLPC): Factor structure, reliability, and validity. *Journal of Psychopathology and Behavioral Assessment, 15,* 387–404.

32. VanHasselt, V. B., Null, J. A., Kempton, T., & Bukstein, O. E. (1993). Social skills and depression in adolescent substance abusers. *Addictive Behaviors, 18,* 9–18.

33. Borden, J. W. (1994). Panic disorder and suicidality: Prevalence and risk factors. *Journal of Anxiety Disorders, 8,* 217–225.

34. Boone, D. E. (1994). Validity of the MMPI-2 depression content scale with psychiatric inpatients. *Psychological Reports, 74,* 159–162.

35. Crocker, J., Luhtanen, R., Blaine, B., & Broadnax, S. (1994). Collective self-esteem and psychological well-being among White, Black, and Asian college students. *Personality and Social Psychology Bulletin, 20,* 503–513.

36. Dulit, R. A., Fyer, M. R., Andrew, C. L., Brodsky, B. S., & Frances, A. J. (1994). Clinical correlates of self-mutilation in borderline personality disorder. *American Journal of Psychiatry, 151,* 1305–1311.

37. Edelman, R. E., Ahrens, A. H., & Haaga, D. A. F. (1994). Inferences about the self-attributions, and overgeneralization as predictors of recovery from dysphoria. *Cognitive Therapy and Research, 18,* 551–566.

38. Gage, M., Noh, S., Polatajko, H. J., & Kaspar, V. (1994). Measuring perceived self-efficacy in occupational therapy. *The American Journal of Occupational Therapy, 48,* 783–790.

39. Ivanoff, A., Jang, S. J., Smyth, N. J., & Linehan, M. M. (1994). Fewer reasons for staying alive when you are thinking of killing yourself: The Brief Reasons for Living Inventory. *Journal of Psychopathology and Behavioral Assessment, 16,* 1–13.

40. MacLeod, A. K., & Tarbuck, A. F. (1994). Explaining why negative events will happen to oneself: Parasuicides are pessimistic because they can't see any reason not to be. *British Journal of Clinical Psychology, 33,* 317–326.

41. Marshall, G. N., Wortman, C. B., Vickers, R. R., Jr., Kusulas, J. W., & Hervig, L. K. (1994). The five-factor model of personality as a framework for personality-health research. *Journal of Personality and Social Psychology, 67,* 278–286.

42. McLeavey, B. C., Daly, R. J., Ludgate, J. W., & Murray, C. M. (1994). Interpersonal problem-solving skills training in the treatment of self-poisoning patients. *Suicide and Life-Threatening Behavior, 24,* 382–394.

43. Page, R. M., & Tucker, L. A. (1994). Psychosocial discomfort and exercise frequency: An epidemiological study of adolescents. *Adolescence, 29,* 183–191.

44. Rabkin, J. G., Rabkin, R., Harrison, W., & Wagner, G. (1994). Effect of imipramine on mood and enumerative measures of immune status in depressed patients with HIV illness. *American Journal of Psychiatry, 151,* 516–523.

45. Range, L. M., & Penton, S. R. (1994). Hope, hopelessness, and suicidality in college students. *Psychological Reports, 75,* 456–458.

46. Reed, G. M., Kemeny, M. E., Taylor, S. E., Wang, H-Y. J., & Visscher, B. R. (1994). Realistic acceptance as a predictor of decreased survival time in gay men with AIDS. *Health Psychology, 13,* 299–307.

47. Sahs, J. A., Goetz, R., Reddy, M., Rabkin, J. G., Williams, J. B. W., Kertzner, R., & Gorman, J. M. (1994). Psychological distress and natural killer cells in gay men with and without HIV infection. *American Journal of Psychiatry, 151,* 1479–1484.

48. Schrader, G. (1994). Chronic depression: State or trait? *The Journal of Nervous and Mental Disease, 182,* 552–555.

49. Shearer, S. L. (1994). Dissociative phenomena in women with borderline personality disorder. *American Journal of Psychiatry, 151,* 1324–1328.

50. Smyth, N. J., Ivanoff, A., & Jang, S. J. (1994). Changes in psychological maladaptation among inmate parasuicides. *Criminal Justice and Behavior, 21,* 357–365.

51. Thackston-Williams, L., Compton, W. C., & Kelly, D. B. (1994). Correlates of hopelessness on the MMPI-2. *Psychological Reports, 75,* 1071–1074.

52. Upmanyu, V. V., & Upmanyu, S. (1994). Depression in relation to sex role identity and hopelessness among male and female Indian adolescents. *The Journal of Social Psychology, 134*, 551-552.

53. Yang, B., & Clum, G. A. (1994). Life stress, social support, and problem-solving skills predictive of depressive symptoms, hopelessness, and suicide ideation in an Asian student population: A test of a model. *Suicide and Life-Threatening Behavior, 24*, 127-139.

54. Alford, B. A., Lester, J. M., Patel, R. J., Buchanan, J. P., & Giunta, L. C. (1995). Hopelessness predicts future depressive symptoms: A prospective analysis of cognitive vulnerability and cognitive content specificity. *Journal of Clinical Psychology, 51*, 331-339.

55. Blaine, B., & Crocker, J. (1995). Religiousness, race, and psychological well-being: Exploring social psychological mediators. *Personality and Social Psychology Bulletin, 21*, 1031-1041.

56. Clum, G. A., & Yang, B. (1995). Additional support for the reliability and validity of the Modified Scale for Suicide Ideation. *Psychological Assessment, 7*, 122-125.

57. Engström, G., Alsen, M., Regnell, G., & Träskman-Bendz, L. (1995). Serum lipids in suicide attempters. *Suicide and Life-Threatening Behavior, 25*, 393-400.

58. Haaga, D. A. F., Ahrens, A. H., Schulman, P., Seligman, M. E. P., DuRubeis, R. J., & Minarik, M. L. (1995). Metatraits and cognitive assessment: Application to attributional style and depressive symptoms. *Cognitive Therapy and Research, 19*, 121-142.

59. Hays, R. D., Cunningham, W. E., Ehi, M. K., Beck, C. K., & Shapiro, M. F. (1995). Health-related quality of life in HIV disease. *Assessment, 2*, 363-380.

60. Joiner, T. E., & Rudd, M. D. (1995). Negative attributional style for interpersonal events and the occurrence of severe interpersonal disruptions as predictors of self-reported suicidal ideation. *Suicide and Life-Threatening Behavior, 25*, 297-304.

61. Kumar, G., & Steer, R. A. (1995). Psychosocial correlates of suicidal ideation in adolescent psychiatric inpatients. *Suicide and Life-Threatening Behavior, 25*, 339-346.

62. MacLeod, A. K., & Cropley, M. L. (1995). Depressive future-thinking: The role of valence and specificity. *Cognitive Therapy and Research, 19*, 35-50.

63. Malone, K. M., Haas, G. L., Sweeney, J. A., & Mann, J. J. (1995). Major depression and the risk of attempted suicide. *Journal of Affective Disorders, 34*, 173-185.

64. Pillay, A. L., & Wassenaar, D. R. (1995). Psychological intervention, spontaneous remission, hopelessness, and psychiatric disturbance in adolescent parasuicides. *Suicide and Life-Threatening Behavior, 25*, 386-392.

65. Reynolds, W. M., & Kobak, K. A. (1995). Reliability and validity of the Hamilton Depression Inventory: A paper-and-pencil version of the Hamilton Depression Rating Scale clinical interview. *Psychological Assessment, 7*, 472-483.

66. Rudd, M. D., Joiner, T. E., Jr., & Rajab, M. H. (1995). Help negation after acute suicidal crisis. *Journal of Consulting and Clinical Psychology, 63*, 499-503.

67. Rudd, M. D., & Rajab, M. H. (1995). Specificity of the Beck Depression Inventory and the confounding role of comorbid disorders in a clinical sample. *Cognitive Therapy and Research, 19*, 51-68.

68. Shek, D. T. L. (1995). Chinese adolescents' perceptions of parenting styles of fathers and mothers. *The Journal of Genetic Psychology, 156*, 175-190.

69. Watson, D., Weber, K., Assenheimer, J. S., Clark, L. A., Strauss, M. E., & McCormick, R. A. (1995). Testing a tripartite model: I. Evaluating convergent and discriminant validity of Anxiety and Depression Symptom Scales. *Journal of Abnormal Psychology, 104*, 3-14.

70. Weiner, J., Harlow, L., Adams, J., & Grebstein, L. (1995). Psychological adjustment of college students from families of divorce. *Journal of Divorce and Remarriage, 23*, 75-95.

71. Yang, B., & Clum, G. A. (1995). Measures of life stress and social support specific to an Asian student population. *Journal of Psychopathology and Behavioral Assessment, 17*, 51-67.

72. Anderson, R. L., Klein, D. N., Riso, L. P., Ouimette, P. C., Lizardi, H., & Schwartz, J. E. (1996). The subaffective-character spectrum subtyping distinction in primary early-onset dysthymia: A clinical and family study. *Journal of Affective Disorders, 38*, 13-22.

73. Breitbart, W., Rosenfeld, B. D., & Passik, S. D. (1996). Interest in physician-assisted suicide among ambulatory HIV-infected patients. *American Journal of Psychiatry, 153*, 238-242.

74. Corbitt, E. M., Malone, K. M., Haas, G. L., & Mann, J. J. (1996). Suicidal behavior in patients with major depression and comorbid personality disorders. *Journal of Affective Disorders, 39*, 61-72.

75. MacLeod, A. K., & Byrne, A. (1996). Anxiety, depression, and the anticipation of future positive and negative experiences. *Journal of Abnormal Psychology, 105*, 286-289.

76. Ouimette, P. C., Klein, D. N., & Pepper, C. M. (1996). Personality traits in the first degree relatives of outpatients with depressive disorders. *Journal of Affective Disorders, 39*, 43-53.

77. Raudin, L. D., Hilton, E., Primeau, M., Clements, C., & Barr, W. B. (1996). Memory functioning in lyme borreliosis. *Journal of Clinical Psychiatry, 57*, 282-286.

78. Segerstrom, S. C., Taylor, S. E., Kemeny, M. E., Reed, G. M., & Visscher, B. R. (1996). Causal attributions predict rate of immune decline in HIV-seropositive gay men. *Health Psychology, 15*, 485-493.

79. Young, M. A., Fogg, L. F., Scheftner, W., Fawcett, J., Akiskal, H., & Maser, J. (1996). Stable trait components of hopelessness: Baseline and sensitivity to depression. *Journal of Abnormal Psychology, 105*, 155-165.

80. Codori, A-M., Slavney, P. R., Young, C., Miglioretti, D. L., & Brandt, J. (1997). Predictors of psychological adjustment to genetic testing for Huntington's Disease. *Health Psychology, 16*, 36-50.

81. Rabkin, J. G., Goetz, R. R., Remien, R. H., Williams, J. B. W., Todak, G., & Gorman, J. M. (1997). Stability of mood despite HIV illness progression in a group of homosexual men. *American Journal of Psychiatry, 154*, 231-238.

82. Sklar, S. M., Annis, H. M., & Turner, N. E. (1997). Development and validation of the drug-taking confidence questionnaire: A measure of coping self-efficacy. *Addictive Behaviors, 22*, 655-670.

83. Tibben, A., Timman, R., Bannick, E. C., & Duivenvoorden, H. J. (1997). Three-year follow-up after presymptomatic testing for Huntington's Disease in tested individuals and partners. *Health Psychology, 16*, 20-35.

Review of the Beck Hopelessness Scale [Revised] by EPHREM FERNANDEZ, Associate Professor of Clinical Psychology, Southern Methodist University, Dallas, TX:

The Beck Hopelessness Scale or BHS is a 20-item self-report instrument for assessing hopelessness, particularly in relation to the risk of suicide. It evolved out of the Beck Depression Inventory (BDI; Beck, Ward, Mendelson, Mock, & Erbaugh, 1961) but clearly outperforms the latter in accounting for suicidal ideation; when vegetative and other symptoms of depression are controlled for, hopelessness remains a significant predictor of suicidality; conversely, when hopelessness is partialled out, depression does not correlate with suicidality. This is what makes the BHS unique and valuable as a complement to measures of depression. The BHS is now available as a separate test within a set of multiple instruments from the publisher.

The concept of hopelessness invites the obvious question, "hopeless about what?" One may not feel suicidal over the perceived hopelessness of ever becoming a millionaire but one may get suicidal over loss of income. Thus, Obayuwana et al. (1982) have delineated multiple areas of functioning (from family support to economic assets) that enter into the equation for hope. Yet, many BHS items (e.g., Items 9, 14) are phrased in general terms that do not orient the test taker to the significant personal goals by which hope and hopelessness are calibrated.

The state-trait debate is also relevant to the assessment of hopelessness, as noted by Glanz, Haas, and Sweeney (1995). Pessimistic attitudes or traits may be less life threatening (because they have been held for a long time) as opposed to newly arisen cognitions of hopelessness, which are likely to exert a greater destabilizing effect on the individual. In that sense, sudden crises may lead to desperation and feelings of inescapability that culminate in suicidality, whereas dispositional pessimism and feelings of resignation may be far less life threatening. Many of the BHS items (e.g., Items 10, 11, 12, 13, 14, 18) pertain to mild pessimism or uncertainty that endures over time.

Hopelessness is a future-oriented concept. The authors of the BHS present it as a measure of the extent of negative attitudes about the future that supposedly indicate suicidal risk. First of all, this only holds inasmuch as one possesses a concept of the future; the younger the individual, the less likely this is the case. Hence, the BHS is less appropriate for youth than it is for adults. Moreover, depression and suicidality can arise not only out of despondency (towards the future) but also pain and suffering (in the present) or even remorse (over the past). Acute pain and suffering in the present (regardless of its implications for the future) can be so unbearable as to lead to suicide; this is commonly observed among victims of torture. Extreme trauma in the past can also be a cause of depression, as witnessed in cases of bereavement and other profound losses. Therefore, as a measure of suicidal risk, the BHS is limited by its temporal frame of reference.

The BHS is an indirect predictor of eventual suicide. Beck, Steer, Kovacs, and Garrison (1985) reported that BHS scores of 9 or more predicted eventual suicide in depressed suicide ideators within 5–10 years of discharge from the hospital. Such predictions that suicide will occur sooner or later in those already known to be suicidal are of limited utility. A test of suicidal contemplation (e.g., the Suicidal Intent Scale) would serve as a more direct measure. Besides, a greater achievement than predicting eventual suicide is to predict imminent suicidal attempts, when or how soon they are likely to occur, so that help can be provided in a timely fashion.

The authors of the BHS acknowledge the varying relationship between hopelessness and socially desirable self-presentation, depending on the particular test used to assess social desirability. The correlation coefficients have been of a negative magnitude that is difficult to ignore: -.64 when the Edwards Social Desirability Scale was used (Fogg & Gayton, 1976), and as high as -.71 in the case of the Desirability Scale of the Jackson Personality Research Form used by Mendonca, Holden, Mazmanian, and Dolan (1983). In the BHS manual, it is concluded that social desirability factors lead to overestimation of suicidal risk, which is supposedly less serious of an error than underestimation. On the contrary, socially desirable responding can just as readily lead to "faking good," especially if a patient is unwilling to have his or her suicidal plans discovered or thwarted; such cases would lead to false negatives or misses, which can be of dire consequence. There-

fore, although Beck and colleagues dismiss the need to administer social desirability scales in conjunction with the BHS, it is recommended that social desirability be taken into account in interpreting scores on the BHS. Boyle, Stankov, and Cattell (1995) have outlined some valuable approaches to handling this and the wider problem of motivational bias in responding to tests.

Most notable among the psychometrics of the BHS are the high internal consistency as indexed by KR-20 coefficients mostly in the .90s, retest reliability in the high .60s, and concurrent validity with clinicians' ratings of hopelessness ($r = .74$). High scores (exceeding 9) generally predict about 90% of suicide completers, but not without false alarms (about 6%); low scores are insensitive to suicidality and merely suggest the lack of hopelessness rather than an abundance of hope. Sensitivity and specificity are reportedly optimized at a BHS score of 9 and a BDI score of 23. The manual underscores that a high BHS score along with a declining BDI score are especially indicative of suicide risk.

Factor analytic studies have uncovered anywhere between one to five factors in the BHS. Usually, a core of affective, motivational, and cognitive factors has emerged. Of these, it is the affective factor "feelings about the future" that accounts for the bulk of variance in BHS scores, thus raising some uncertainties about the multidimensionality of the scale. The factor structure also changes with the type of population investigated.

In conclusion, little doubt exists that the BHS is a useful departure from the BDI as far as suicide risk assessment is concerned. However, more light needs to be shed on the construct of hopelessness, specifically its presumed multifactorial structure, the targets of hope/hopelessness, and its state-trait variations. Although there has been cross-validation in clinical groups such as substance abusers, inmates, and those with depressive disorders, cross-cultural validation has been limited. Incremental utility against competing instruments such as the Reasons for Living Inventory (Linehan, Goodstein, Nielsen, & Chiles, 1983) is also a matter of interest. Finally, the possible influence of social desirability and motivational bias in BHS results remains an issue in need of systematic research.

REVIEWER'S REFERENCES

Beck, A. T., Ward, C. H., Mendelson, M., Mock, J., & Erbaugh, J. (1961). An inventory for measuring depression. *Archives of General Psychiatry, 4,* 561–571.

Fogg, M. E., & Gayton, W. F. (1976). Social desirability and the Hopelessness Scale. *Perceptual and Motor Skills, 43,* 482.

Obayuwana, A. O., Collins, J. L., Carter, A. L., Rao, M. S., Mattura, C. O., & Wilson, S. B. (1982). Hope Index Scale: An instrument for the objective assessment of hope. *Journal of the National Medical Association, 74*, 761–765.

Linehan, M. M., Goodstein, J. L., Nielsen, S. L., & Chiles, J. A. (1983). Reasons for staying alive when you're thinking of killing yourself: The Reasons for Living Inventory. *Journal of Consulting and Clinical Psychology, 51*, 276–286.

Mendonca, J. D., Holden, R. R., Mazmanian, D., & Dolan, J. (1983). The influence of response style on the Beck Hopelessness Scale. *Canadian Journal of Behavioral Science, 15*, 237–247.

Beck, A. T., Steer, R. A., Kovacs, M., & Garrison, B. (1985). Hopelessness and eventual suicide: A 10-year prospective study of patients hospitalized with suicidal ideation. *American Journal of Psychiatry, 142*, 559–563.

Boyle, G. J., Stankov, L., & Cattell, R. B. (1995). Measurement and statistical models in the study of personality and intelligence. In D. H. Saklofske & M. Zeidner (Eds.), *International handbook of personality and intelligence* (pp. 417–446). New York: Plenum.

Glanz, L. M., Haas, G. L., & Sweeney, J. A. (1995). Assessment of hopelessness in suicidal patients. *Clinical Psychology Review, 15*, 49–64.

[33]
Beck Scale for Suicide Ideation.

Purpose: "To detect and measure the severity of suicidal ideation in adults and adolescents."

Population: Adults and adolescents.

Publication Dates: 1991–1993.

Acronym: BSS.

Scores: Total score only; item score ranges.

Administration: Group or individual.

Price Data, 1994: $46 per complete kit including 25 record forms and manual ('93, 24 pages); $25.50 per 25 record forms; $22.50 per manual.

Foreign Language Edition: Spanish forms available.

Time: (5–10) minutes.

Comments: Computer scoring available.

Authors: Aaron T. Beck and Robert A. Steer.

Publisher: The Psychological Corporation.

TEST REFERENCES

1. Beer, J., & Beer, J. (1992). Depression, self-esteem, suicide ideation, and GPAs of high school students at risk. *Psychological Reports, 71*, 899–902.

2. Brubeck, D., & Beer, J. (1992). Depression, self-esteem, suicide ideation, death anxiety, and GPA in high school students of divorced and nondivorced parents. *Psychological Reports, 71*, 755–763.

3. Whatley, S. L., & Clopton, J. R. (1992). Social support and suicidal ideation in college students. *Psychological Reports, 71*, 1123–1128.

4. De Wilde, E. J., Kienhorst, C. W. M., Diekstra, R. F. W., & Wolters, W. H. G. (1993). Social support, life events, and behavioral characteristics of psychologically distressed adolescents at high risk for attempting suicide. *Adolescence, 29*, 49–60.

5. Morano, C. D., Cisler, R. A., & Lemerond, J. (1993). Risk factors for adolescent suicidal behavior: Loss, insufficient familial support, and hopelessness. *Adolescence, 28*, 851–865.

6. Clum, G. A., & Febbraro, G. A. R. (1994). Stress, social support, and problem solving appraisal/skills: Prediction of suicide severity within a college sample. *Journal of Psychopathology and Behavioral Assessment, 16*, 69–83.

7. Ivanoff, A., Jang, S. J., Smyth, N. J., & Linehan, M. M. (1994). Fewer reasons for staying alive when you're thinking of killing yourself: The Brief Reasons for Living Inventory. *Journal of Psychopathology and Behavioral Assessment, 16*, 1–13.

8. Molock, S. D., Kimbrough, R., Lacy, M. B., McClure, K. P., & Williams, S. (1994). Suicidal behavior among African American college students: A preliminary study. *The Journal of Black Psychology, 20*, 234–251.

9. Clum, G. A., & Yang, B. (1995). Additional support for the reliability and validity of the Modified Scale for Suicide Ideation. *Psychological Assessment, 7*, 122–125.

10. DeMan, A. F., & Leduc, C. P. (1995). Suicidal ideation in high school students: Depression and other correlates. *Journal of Clinical Psychology, 51*, 173–181.

11. Engström, G., Alsen, M., Regnell, G., & Träskman-Bendz, L. (1995). Serum lipids in suicide attempters. *Suicide and Life-Threatening Behavior, 25*, 393–400.

12. Kumar, G., & Steer, R. A. (1995). Psychosocial correlates of suicidal ideation in adolescent psychiatric inpatients. *Suicide and Life-Threatening Behavior, 25*, 339–346.

13. Malone, K. M., Haas, G. L., Sweeney, J. A., & Mann, J. J. (1995). Major depression and the risk of attempted suicide. *Journal of Affective Disorders, 34*, 173–185.

14. Pine, D. S., Trautman, P. D., Shaffer, D., Cohen, L., Davies, M., Stanley, M., & Parsons, B. (1995). Seasonal rhythm of platelet [3H] imipramine binding in adolescents who attempted suicide. *American Journal of Psychiatry, 152*, 923–925.

Review of the Beck Scale for Suicide Ideation by KARL R. HANES, *Consultant Psychologist, and Director, Vangard Publishing, Carlton, Victoria, Australia:*

The Beck Scale for Suicide Ideation (BSS) is a 21-item self-report instrument that was developed as a self-administered variation of the earlier Scale for Suicidal Ideation (SSI; Beck, Kovacs, & Weissman, 1979). The BSS is well constructed; easy to administer; has high face, convergent, and construct validity; and scores from this scale have acceptable levels of internal consistency. The test is appropriate for use with English-speaking populations of average intelligence. The manual does provide clear instructions on administration and scoring of this instrument, although the significance of specific responses or of actual scores on this measure is not explored in any great detail.

Despite this, there are a few specific points of concern. The manual provides scant details regarding the development of this measure, appearing to rely on the longevity and status of its parent instrument. This is not very helpful for those who are not familiar with the earlier measure. Some further information regarding the specific items on this test and background material on test-relevant previous research in this field would be helpful. Moreover, the requirement of a self-administered variation of the SSI is not convincingly demonstrated, with the statement that the authors "saw a need for a self-report version of the SSI" (manual, p. 3) not being terribly informative. Providing such a rationale would seem to be of particular importance in this case, given the strong requirement for clinical evaluation and the strong possibility of concealment and provision of misleading information in those at high risk for suicide.

The test's intended population is not totally clear. Although the descriptive information for this test emphasizes its use with adults and adolescents, the normative sample, which is otherwise satisfactorily large, appears to contain an insufficient number of adolescents and, in fact, the manual implies that its use in adolescents may not be entirely appropriate because no validity or reliability data are available with an adolescent population. It is possible that potential users of this product may be misled by the descriptive information and, as a result, be uncertain as to whether to employ this test with adolescents.

The test-retest reliability data provided are meaningless because patients were retested after treatment. Also, the predictive validity of the test is poor, few demographic data for the normative sample are provided, and there are no comparative normative data with nonpsychiatric patients.

Although the test's clinical applicability is probably quite limited if it is promoted as a test for use with psychiatric populations alone, it would seem to have a place as an instrument for detecting suicidal ideation in the psychiatric, psychological, and allied health areas, particularly given its time-efficient administration. It is especially recommended for use by inexperienced clinicians, who may lack the experience to recognize suicidal tendencies in their patients, and in circumstances where formal clinical evaluation is not possible. The potential for use of such an instrument in nonclinical, yet at-risk populations (e.g., incarcerated subjects) would seem to be considerable, but is obviously limited by the unavailability of appropriate normative data or the requirement that its scoring and administration be limited to professionals with "appropriate clinical training and experience" (p. 5). Although this is a necessary and important requirement for using tests of this kind, might it be possible, in the interests of saving lives, to permit use of such an instrument in circumstances where the presence of a clinician may not be possible? This is certainly a direction in which further development of this measure might be possible. Another good product from a well-credentialed test-development team, the BSS is an ambitious and well-designed test that is probably the leader in a field that has few competing instruments.

REVIEWER'S REFERENCE

Beck, A. T., Kovacs, M., & Weissman, A. (1979). Assessment of suicidal intention: The Scale for Suicide Ideation. *Journal of Consulting and Clinical Psychology, 47,* 343–352.

Review of the Beck Scale for Suicide Ideation by JAY R. STEWART, Assistant Professor and Director, Rehabilitation Counseling Program, Bowling Green State University, Bowling Green, OH:

GENERAL DESCRIPTION. The Beck Scale for Suicide Ideation (BSS) is a self-report instrument designed to aid clinicians in assessing the presence and severity of suicidal ideation in adolescents and adults. Each item contains three statements, graded in intensity from 0 to 2.

The scale is divided into three parts. The first part, containing the first five items, is a screen for the patient's attitudes toward living and dying: Wish to live, Wish to die, Reasons for living or dying, Active suicide attempt, and Passive suicide attempt. If the patient indicates no contemplation of a suicide attempt, they are instructed to skip the second part

(Items 6 through 19) and complete the third part. Those who indicate contemplating a suicide complete the entire instrument.

The second part investigates the suicidal ideation and the patient's anticipated reactions to those thoughts. This part measures frequency, duration, and acceptance of suicide ideation; control over suicide ideation; and the deterrents and reasons for suicide. The patient's anticipated reactions to the suicidal ideation include planning, opportunity, capacity, expectation, and actual preparation for committing suicide; suicide note and post-suicide arrangements; and deception about their suicidal ideation. The third part identifies the number of previous suicide attempts and the seriousness of intent to die during the last suicide attempt.

THEORETICAL MODEL AND TEST DEVELOPMENT. Beck's (1976) cognitive model of psychopathology is the foundation for the BSS. In this model, behaviors result from cognitions; treatment involves detecting, assessing, and modifying pathological cognitions. To Kovacs and Beck (1977), suicidal behavior is linked to an internal struggle between the suicidal ideator's wish to live and wish to die; each is a separate subjective experience measured by the BSS.

Beck, Kovacs, and Weissman (1979) first developed the Scale for Suicide Ideation (SSI). The 19-item scale investigated suicidal intent and risk. The therapist completed the SSI with patient answers obtained in a semistructured interview. The ultimate risk for suicide was a combination of patient's intent to die and his or her ability to overcome deterrents to committing suicide, such as religious beliefs. The SSI items were changed to self-reported statements, and the SSI self-report version was renamed the Beck Suicide Scale.

STANDARDIZATION. The BSS was standardized on 178 adults receiving psychiatric services and identified as suicide ideators (individuals who have current plans and wishes to commit suicide, but no recent suicide attempts); 126 were inpatients of a suburban general hospital and 52 were receiving outpatient psychiatric services. The inpatient sample, mean age 37.4 years, consisted of 50% females, 81% Caucasians, 15% African Americans, and 4% Asian Americans. This sample had a variety of severe mental disorders with 40% having a mood disorder diagnosis. The outpatient sample, mean age 34.1 years, consisted of 60% females, 88% Caucasians, and 12% African Americans.

RELIABILITY. Reliability data are limited to the first 19 items on the BSS. The inpatient sample produced a coefficient alpha reliability estimate of .90, and the outpatient sample produced an alpha of .87, indicating high internal consistency for both samples. Test-retest stability was performed on 60 inpatients and a correlation of .54 ($p<.01$) was found between tests administered one week apart, indicating moderate test-retest reliability. For a sample of 108 adolescent inpatients, ages 12 to 17, a coefficient alpha of .95 was estimated, indicating a high level of internal consistency (Steer, Kumar, & Beck, 1993).

VALIDITY. The validity of the BSS has correlated with the SSI .90 ($p<.01$) for an inpatient sample and .94 ($p<.001$) for an outpatient sample, providing concurrent validity for the BSS. Additional concurrent validity was ascertained through an inpatient suicide ideators sample on the Beck Depression Inventory (BDI) .48 ($p<.01$), Beck Hopelessness Scale (BHS) .48 ($p<.001$), and previous suicide attempts .32 ($p<.01$). A sample of outpatient suicide ideators produced similar results.

Construct validity was investigated through the significant correlation with assessment scores on the BDI and BHS. Depression and hopelessness were theorized to be factors in suicide risk. Through principal component analysis of the BSS scores of 126 suicide ideators, Beck, Kovacs, and Weissman (1979) identified and labeled three significant factors: (a) Active Suicide Desire, (b) Preparation, and (c) Passive Suicide Desire.

A prospective study by Beck, Steer, Kovacs, and Garrison (1985) found that the BHS did, but the SSI did not, predict eventual suicide. In another study (Beck & Steer, 1991), outpatients were asked to complete the SSI as if they were in the worst period of their mental disorder. SSI scores for those who eventually committed suicide were significantly higher than those who did not.

INSTRUMENT ADMINISTRATION AND INTERPRETATION. Clinicians familiar with the BDI will recognize the similarity of the BSS in ease of administration and scoring. Berchick and Wright (1992) suggest administering the BDI to potentially suicidal patients before every counseling session. If the Hopelessness or Suicidal Ideation items have two or three ratings, then the BHS and the BSS should be administered.

The test's authors do not provide cutoff scores. Instead, the clinician is directed to look at total score and each item's score for warnings of suicidal risk.

Clinicians can discuss test item scores during therapy sessions. Clinicians should be prepared to respond to the patient's suicidal ideation.

CONCLUSIONS. The BSS is a valuable tool in assessing suicide risk. Easily administered and used in treatment sessions, the instrument can provide an additional safeguard for clinicians concerned about patient suicide risk. The validity, reliability, and pragmatic approach help explain why suicide assessment reviewers (Range & Knott, 1997) highly recommend the instrument. However, it should not be considered a solitary tool for working with suicidal patients, and it is not intended to unerringly detect hidden suicidal risk. Instead, it monitors quality and quantity changes of ongoing suicidal ideation.

REVIEWER'S REFERENCES

Beck, A. T. (1976). *Cognitive therapy and emotional disorders.* New York: Meridian.
Kovacs, M., & Beck, A. T. (1977). The wish to die and the wish to live in attempted suicide. *Journal of Clinical Psychology, 33,* 361–365.
Beck, A. T., Kovacs, M., & Weissman, A. (1979). Assessment of suicidal intention: The Scale for Suicide Ideation. *Journal of Consulting and Clinical Psychology, 47,* 343–352.
Beck, A. T., Steer, R. A., Kovacs, M., & Garrison, B. (1985). Hopelessness and eventual suicide: A 10-year prospective study of patients hospitalized with suicidal ideation. *American Journal of Psychiatry, 142,* 559–563.
Beck, A. T., & Steer, R. A. (1991). *Manual for the Beck Scale for Suicide Ideation.* San Antonio, TX: The Psychological Corporation.
Berchick, R. J., & Wright, F. D. (1992). Guidelines for handling the suicidal patient: A cognitive perspective. In B. Bonger (Ed.), *Suicide: Guidelines for assessment, management, and treatment* (pp. 179–186). New York: Oxford University Press.
Steer, R. A., Kumar, G., & Beck, A. T. (1993). Self-reported suicidal ideation in adolescent psychiatric inpatients. *Journal of Consulting & Clinical Psychology, 61,* 1096–1099.
Range, L. M., & Knott, E. C. (1997). Twenty suicide assessment instruments: Evaluation and recommendations. *Death Studies, 21,* 23–58.

[34]

Behavior Assessment System for Children.

Purpose: "To aid in the identification and differential diagnosis of emotional/behavior disorders in children and adolescents."

Population: Ages 4–18.

Publication Date: 1992.

Acronym: BASC.

Subtests: Available as separates.

Price Data, 1997: $75 per starter set including manual (290 pages), one sample each of the hand-scored forms for all levels of the Teacher Rating Scales, Parent Rating Scales, and Self-Report of Personality, the Structured Developmental History, and the Student Observation System; $226 per IBM BASC Enhanced ASSIST software (unlimited use).

Authors: Cecil R. Reynolds and Randy W. Kamphaus.

Publisher: American Guidance Service, Inc.

a) TEACHER RATING SCALES.

Price Data: $26 per 25 hand-scored forms; $16.95 per 25 computer-scored forms.

Time: (10–20) minutes.

1) *Teacher Rating Scales—Preschool.*

Population: Ages 4–5.

Scores, 14: Externalizing Problems (Aggression, Hyperactivity), Internalizing Problems (Anxiety, Depression, Somatization), Attention Problems, Atypicality, Withdrawal, Adaptive Skills (Adaptability, Social Skills), Behavioral Symptoms Index.

2) *Teacher Rating Scales—Child.*
Population: Ages 6–11.
Scores, 19: Externalizing Problems (Aggression, Hyperactivity, Conduct Problems), Internalizing Problems (Anxiety, Depression, Somatization), School Problems (Attention Problems, Learning Problems), Atypicality, Withdrawal, Adaptive Skills (Adaptability, Leadership, Social Skills, Study Skills), Behavioral Symptoms Index.

3) *Teacher Rating Scales—Adolescent.*
Population: Ages 12–18.
Scores, 18: Externalizing Problems (Aggression, Hyperactivity, Conduct Problems), Internalizing Problems (Anxiety, Depression, Somatization), School Problems (Attention Problems, Learning Problems), Atypicality, Withdrawal, Adaptive Skills (Leadership, Social Skills, Study Skills), Behavioral Symptoms Index.

b) PARENT RATING SCALES.
Price Data: $26 per 25 hand-scored forms; $16.95 per 25 computer-scored forms.
Foreign Language Edition: Spanish translation available; pricing, time, age ranges, and scores are same as for English version and can be scored with BASC Enhanced ASSIST and the BASC Plus.
Time: (10–20) minutes.

1) *Parent Rating Scales—Preschool.*
Population: Ages 4–5.
Scores, 14: Same as *a-1* above.

2) *Parent Rating Scales—Child.*
Population: Ages 6–11.
Scores, 16: Externalizing Problems (Aggression, Hyperactivity, Conduct Problems), Internalizing Problems (Anxiety, Depression, Somatization), Attention Problems, Atypicality, Withdrawal, Adaptive Skills (Adaptability, Leadership, Social Skills), Behavioral Symptoms Index.

3) *Parent Rating Scales—Adolescent.*
Population: Ages 12–18.
Scores, 15: Externalizing Problems (Aggression, Hyperactivity, Conduct Problems), Internalizing Problems (Anxiety, Depression, Somatization), Attention Problems, Atypicality, Withdrawal, Adaptive Skills (Leadership, Social Skills), Behavioral Symptoms Index.

c) SELF-REPORT OF PERSONALITY.
Price Data: $26 per 25 hand-scored forms; $16.95 per 25 computer-scored forms.
Time: (25–35) minutes.

1) *Self-Report of Personality—Child.*
Population: Ages 8–11.
Scores, 16: Clinical Maladjustment (Anxiety, Atypicality, Locus of Control, Social Stress), School Maladjustment (Attitude to School, Attitude to Teachers), Depression, Sense of Inadequacy, Personal Adjustment (Relations with Parents, Interpersonal Relations, Self-Esteem, Self-Reliance), Emotional Symptoms Index.

2) *Self-Report of Personality—Adolescent.*
Population: Ages 12–18.
Scores, 18: Clinical Maladjustment (Anxiety, Atypicality, Locus of Control, Social Stress, Somatization), School Maladjustment (Attitude to School, Attitude to Teachers, Sensation Seeking), Depression, Sense of Inadequacy, Personal Adjustment (Relations with Parents, Interpersonal Relations, Self-Esteem, Self-Reliance), Emotional Symptoms Index.

d) STRUCTURED DEVELOPMENTAL HISTORY.
Price Data: $34 per 25 history forms.

e) STUDENT OBSERVATION SYSTEM.
Price Data: $29 per 25 observation forms.
Time: [20] minutes.

TEST REFERENCES

1. Riccio, C. A., & Hynd, G. W. (1993). Developmental language disorders in children: Relationship with learning disability and attention deficit hyperactivity disorder. *School Psychology Review, 22,* 696-709.
2. McNamara, J. R., Hollmann, C., & Riegel, T. (1994). A preliminary study of the usefulness of the Behavior Assessment Systems for Children in the evaluation of mental health needs in a head start population. *Psychological Reports, 75,* 1195-1201.
3. Flanagan, R. (1995). A review of the Behavior Assessment System for Children (BASC): Assessment consistent with the requirements of the Individuals with Disabilities Education Act (IDEA). *Journal of School Psychology, 33,* 177-186.
4. Flanagan, D. P., Alfonso, V. C., Primavera, L. H., Povall, L., & Higgins, D. (1996). Convergent validity of the BASC and SSRS: Implications for social skills assessment. *Psychology in the Schools, 33,* 13–23.

Review of the Behavior Assessment System for Children by JONATHAN SANDOVAL, Professor and Acting Director, Division of Education, University of California, Davis, Davis, CA:

The Behavior Assessment System for Children (BASC) is an integrated set of self-reports of personality (SRP), teacher rating scales (TRS), parent rating scales (PRS), a developmental history (SDH), and an observation protocol (SOS), all designed to assess children for the differential diagnosis and educational treatment of emotional and behavior disorders. The focus is on both adaptive and maladaptive behavior, and different sources and methods are available for the user to determine an estimate of functioning. It is one of the first systems of this sort and represents a significant advance in the assessment of children.

The SRP, the TRS, and the PRS yield scores in *T*-score units and percentiles based on either a national norm group, by gender in the norm group, or in comparison to a group of seriously emotionally disturbed children. The ratings produce various scales and composites, which may be contrasted and compared to identify relative strengths and weaknesses.

The SDH is a rationally laid out developmental history cataloging important life events and developmental milestones. The SOS is a time-sampling observation protocol that also provides space for free observations and anecdotes. These are among the first widely published developmental histories and observation systems and their utility remains to be established, although locally developed measures of this sort have been employed by clinicians for many years. Users of the observation scale probably should have training and supervision in observation techniques and practice with this category system because the SOS is somewhat more complicated to use than the other components of the BASC.

Both the SDH and the SOS have no norms and little specific guidance for how they are to be interpreted, relying on the users' professional training. These two parts of the BASC system will be commented on no further except to praise their inclusion and to warn of the general problem of recording and interpreting very low frequency behaviors to be found on both measures.

Technical Qualities of Ratings and Self-Report Measures.

TEST DEVELOPMENT AND THEORY. The BASC has been carefully developed and represents a synthesis of what is known about developmental psychopathology and personality development. The items for all of the components have been derived from a review of the relevant literature and clinical experience.

Each of the clinical scales on the TRS and PRS have established constructs and items with high content validity. The three dimensions of difficulty, Externalizing Problems, Internalizing Problems, and School Problems are found in several studies of emotional development.

In addition, the Adaptive scales on both the TRS and PRS focus on positive aspects of behavior. The importance of these positive behaviors has also been supported by a substantial literature. Many raters will appreciate the opportunity to catalogue strengths as well as weaknesses. Having a measure of adaptive behavior is a welcome feature of the BASC for those concerned with the identification of mental retardation.

Sophisticated data reduction methods have been used throughout test development. All items were required to contribute to only one scale, and to serve across ages and across measures on the rating scales. Prior to standardization, pilot items were subjected to careful item analysis designed to assure that they contributed to measurement and discrimination. After standardization, covariance structure analysis was used to evaluate the placement and functioning of each item. Studies were also done to ensure that the items had strong correlations with hypothetical latent variables. Each of the scales and composites were similarly established using contemporary latent trait analyses techniques and factor analyses. The items were also subjected to bias analyses to detect gender and ethnic discrepancies in performance so that the final version of the scale contained no biased items. The items are appropriately worded and should be easily understood by the intended reporter. The care taken by the authors in test development is exemplary.

NORMING—STANDARDIZATION PROCEDURES. A sufficient number of subjects were available at each age level to provide useful general norms. Minority children were overrepresented at the younger ages, but scores were weighted to create norms characteristic of the U.S. population. Weighting was also done to make the sample match the population with respect to maternal education, geographical region, and special educational placement.

A clinical norm sample was also included consisting of children with identified emotional and behavioral problems, the most prevalent of which were behavior disorder and attention deficit hyperactivity disorder. The clinical norms were collected for the TRS on 693 children, for the PRS on 401 children, and for the SRP on 411 children from 39 North American sites. This sample was not adjusted, and males and whites were overrepresented. The sample is described by gender, age, race/ethnicity, and geographic region.

The standardization of the instruments was quite good for measures of this sort. It should be noted, however, that a large number of the schools participating were private Catholic institutions or associated with universities. To the extent these institutions are selective, there may be a bias in the norms. In this norming, as in many others, children with a Spanish-speaking family background are lumped together as Hispanic. Both this and the category of Asian may be too heterogencous to be of use in the future as these groups grow in size in the U.S.

The user has a choice of the general, the clinical, and within these, gender-based norms. Although the manual presents a rationale for general rather than gender norms it may be that gender norms will be more useful to clinicians in the long run.

RELIABILITY. The manual reports internal consistency and test-retest reliabilities for the PRS, TRS, and SRP, and interrater reliabilities for the rating scales. Internal consistency reliability is quite good. The alpha coefficients increase slightly with the age of the child and are typically in the mid .80s to .90 for adolescents. Reliabilities are similar across gender. The internal consistency reliabilities for the clinical sample are similar to the general sample. The composites are more reliable than the scales, with almost all alpha coefficients falling in the low to mid .90s. The picture is similar across measures; almost all scales and all composites have high enough reliability to use to make individual decisions about individuals. The least reliable scales tended to be Somatization and Anxiety for the younger ages on the TRS and Atypicality and Conduct Problems for the PRS.

One-month test-retest reliabilities are also quite high, in some cases exceeding the alpha estimates, except on the SRP where they were slightly lower. These test-retest estimates, too, are typically in the mid .80s to the mid .90s over a one-month period. The pattern of correlations matched the pattern in the internal consistency estimates. The lowest reliabilities (low .70s) were for the adolescent level of the PRS.

The interrater reliabilities for the TRS were reasonably high for the child version but low on some scales of the preschool version. The composite values on the child TRS ranged from .69 (Internalizing Problems) to .89 (School Problems). Comparing ratings from parents on the PRS, as would be expected from other studies, yielded only moderate correlations, with median values of .46, .57, and .67 for the preschool, child, and adolescent forms respectively. The lowest values were for Internalizing Problems, Adaptability, and Adaptive Skills. The preschool reliabilities may not be high enough for the scores to be profiled accurately. The user should exercise caution in the use of the BASC with the very young.

VALIDITY. As mentioned previously, the authors have used sophisticated modern techniques to construct their scales and study the structure of relationships between scales. They started out with a model of relationships and modified it using the data provided by the standardization sample. The confirmatory factor analytic techniques have vali-

dated the authors' conceptualization of what is being measured, but future studies on different samples will be needed to further validate the model of Internalizing, Externalizing, and Adaptive Skills.

The BASC manual reports correlational studies between the TRS and five other well-known teacher report forms: Achenbach's Teacher's Report Form, Quay and Peterson's Revised Behavior Problem Checklist, Conners' Teacher Rating Scales, Burks' Behavior Rating Scales, and the Teacher Rating Scale of the Behavior Rating Profile. The correlations between the TRS and the Achenbach scales are quite high, in the .80s and .90s. The correlations are lower with the other scales, but still relatively high in parallel areas, particularly the measures of externalizing and school behavior.

The PRS is correlated fairly highly with the Child Behavior Checklist, particularly on the externalizing scales (.71 to .84), and is moderately correlated with the Personality Inventory for Children—Revised and with the Conners' Parent Rating Scales (PRS Hyperactivity and Externalizing both correlate .56 with the Conners' Hyperactivity Index). These are the three most commonly used parent ratings of children's problems.

The SRP has been correlated with the Minnesota Multiphasic Personality Inventory (MMPI), Achenbach's Youth Self-Report, the Student Rating Scales of the Behavior Rating Profile, and the Children's Personality Questionnaire. The correlations between the SRP composites and selected MMPI scales are reasonably high for an adolescent population. The SRP composites correlate reasonably well with the Youth Self-Report, but other correlations suggest the two measures are measuring somewhat different constructs. The same is true of the Student Rating Scales but not of the Children's Personality Questionnaire. The correlations between the SRP and the Children's Personality Questionnaire are only moderately high suggesting these two measures are different.

The validity of the BASC is also supported by the performance of carefully diagnosed groups of children with Conduct Disorder, Behavior Disorder, Depression, Emotional Disturbance, Attention Deficit Hyperactivity Disorder, Learning Disability, Mild Mental Retardation, and Autism. On balance, the profiles of the groups on the various BASC measures, using the general norms, make sense and support the construct validity of the scale. Interestingly, the SRP measures do not differentiate Attention Deficit,

Learning Disabled, or retarded children very well, although the PRS and TRS do.

Finally, additional convergent and discriminant validity is addressed by presenting the correlation matrix for the TRS and PRS and for the SRP and both the TRS and PRS. There are many reasons why the various sources of information in the system may not agree and there are other methods besides correlation to investigate agreement. Nevertheless, the data in the manual support the use of the test. There are low to moderate correlations between the student self-reports and ratings by parents and teachers and fairly good agreement between teacher and parent ratings except at the preschool age.

UTILITY. In general, the materials are very easy to use in the school situation. The manual is "user-friendly" in the way it is organized and employs graphics well to convey technical information.

The parent rating scales can be readily understood and completed by parents with minimal assistance from the professional administering the scale. The protocols are efficiently arranged and attractive. The rating scales are easy to score but volume users will opt for the computer program to save time and increase accuracy of scoring. Having the summary table and profile chart on the same page is a useful feature. The scores derived from the various components of the system are familiar and seem consistent with theory and other measures.

The reading ability level and vocabulary demanded for 8- to 11-year-olds on the SRP may be difficult for some subjects. Younger children may need some terms defined or words read to them by the examiner.

One of the few places where the BASC does not live up to its promise is in providing a way to compare all of the data collected systematically. There is no easy way to integrate the information obtained from the rating scales with the observational protocol or with the developmental history. This shortcoming greatly limits the advantage of having an all-encompassing assessment system because the components cannot be readily and easily compared. On the other hand, no system should be established that excuses psychologists from thinking and making careful judgments about the individuals they are assessing.

It is the case that data obtained from the parent and teacher rating scales can be easily compared if the user has also purchased the computer program. These differences cannot be examined statistically by the handscorer. In any case, the self-report data cannot be compared statistically to the parent and teacher ratings.

SUMMARY. The Behavior Assessment System for Children (BASC) is a well-designed and useful set of measures for the assessment and identification of school-aged children with emotional disturbances and behavioral disorders. In combining information from a variety of sources into an integrated system, the BASC uniquely attempts to provide a multidimensional understanding of a child. Although there are shortcomings, the BASC is made up of some of the best measures of their kind and represents an approach of choice for identifying children with emotional and behavioral disorders in schools. Of the different components of the BASC, the parent and teacher reports appear to be the most valuable for practitioners, but the self-report measure should not be overlooked. The measures are not radically different from familiar rating and self-report instruments and break no new ground; instead they represent a refinement of current technology. The one caution is that the use of the BASC with preschoolers should be carefully done. The measures for this age range are not as psychometrically sound as they are for older children and adolescents.

Review of the Behavior Assessment System for Children by JOSEPH C. WITT, Professor of Psychology, Louisiana State University, Baton Rouge, LA, and KEVIN M. JONES, Assistant Professor of Psychology, Eastern Illinois University, Charleston, IL:

The Behavior Assessment System for Children (BASC) is a comprehensive attempt to quantify the qualitative judgments made about a particular child's behavior. The BASC is a multimethod, multiinformant, and multidimensional instrument used to assess both adaptive and maladaptive behavior in children aged 4 to 18 years. The system includes separate parent, teacher, and child self-report scales, a student observation system, and a structured developmental history. The BASC rating scales include unique features, such as adaptive *and* maladaptive scales, normative data across informants, norms based on both large representative samples and clinical subpopulations, and validity checks. When judged by traditional psychometric standards, the BASC compares favorably or exceeds the standardization quality of similar, existing instruments (see Adams & Drabman, 1994; Hoza, 1994). We believe it is only a matter of time before the BASC will supplant many of its competitors, and become synonymous with the practice of interpreting informant ratings on multiple psychological dimensions.

Our criticisms, in fact, will focus less on nipping at the heels of such a formidable instrument, and focus more on the contribution of the BASC to our current assessment technology. Because this review is simply a structured assessment of informant (i.e., our) perceptions about the instrument, we will accordingly rate our perceptions of the BASC assumptions along similar dimensions.

The BASC provides a multimethod assessment *some of the time*. The BASC has been called a *system* in the same manner that many insects have been called *centipedes*; not because they have 100 legs but because most people cannot count past 25. Although the BASC manual reports the distinct advantage of using multiple measures (informant ratings, observation), to our knowledge the relationship between all five BASC components has *never* been demonstrated. During the development and standardization of the BASC, the authors did not employ two of the five components, the Classroom Observation or the Developmental History.

The BASC is a reliable instrument *some of the time*. Psychometric qualities are generally quite good, with important exceptions. For example, internal consistency coefficients for individual scales (e.g., conduct problems) fall below the criterion of .90 offered by Salvia and Ysseldyke (1991) for diagnostic decisions. This is especially true for the Parent Rating Scale, with average coefficients in the mid to upper .70s. Also, the manual reports low to moderate levels of interrater agreement between teachers and parents, although children's self-reports tend to disagree with parents, teachers, and other child self-report scales. Given these limitations, users may often find themselves attempting to integrate a rather ambiguous series of behavioral profiles, similar to a projective personality test. We caution users to avoid making clinical judgments based more on theoretical orientation than the referral complaint itself.

The BASC is an accurate measure of behavior *some of the time*. An informant's ratings may be an honest attempt to describe actual behavior. However, most people are not familiar with quantifying their perceptions according to one of four descriptors. Because behavior varies across settings, parents or teachers may find the forced-choice format difficult to interpret. For example, a child may "never" cry around her father but "always" cries during thunderstorms. Does the compromise, "sometimes," reflect something meaningful about the child? Even the most sensitive validity indices (i.e., lie scales) cannot

discriminate whether values obtained on individual scales reflect the child's actual behavior or simply the standards and tolerances of each informant. Certainly the same behavior might be rated differently depending on whether the informant anticipates positive or negative outcomes (e.g., medication, special education pull-out programs). Alternatively, different frequencies of behavior may be rated similarly; for example, the parent may perceive 15 episodes of "teases others" as equal in severity to 1 or 2 episodes of "plays in toilet."

After wrestling with their own biases, interpretation problems, and situational specificity, the scores derived from informants are somehow integrated by the clinician to make diagnostic decisions. Unfortunately, the veracity of the resulting diagnoses is an unattainable goal; unlike cards in a deck or plastic dinosaurs, we cannot turn the child upside down to double check our diagnosis. Acting on the assumption that there *is* a problem, however, and that problems should be categorized in some manner, the clinician confidently makes judgments based on indirect measures of parent or teacher behavior, which may or may not be related to the child's actual behavior.

The BASC produces valid inferences based on scores *some of the time*. The BASC manual provides ample evidence of concurrent validity with other rating scales (with the possible exception of the child self-report scale) and factor analyses indicate a statistical and logical degree of fit among BASC domains. Treatment validity, or the degree to which assessment data contribute to treatment, remains an important issue. Unlike many other rating scales, the BASC is beneficial because it includes adaptive behaviors that may be targeted for intervention. The insufficient overlap on specific items across the three informant scales, however, make it difficult for the clinician to isolate specific target behaviors that occur *across* settings.

The most critical link to treatment is the identification of manipulable conditions (e.g., task demands) that are functionally related to the child's behavior. In order to identify these variables, assessment must isolate specific behaviors and monitor variability across conditions. In other words, assessment should document "some of the behavior all of the time." This approach appears antithetical to the goal of the BASC, which is to document "all of the behavior some of the time."

The Student Observation System (SOS), an important strength of the BASC, could potentially offer descriptive information about observed teacher-student interactions. However, the authors recommend using a momentary time-sampling procedure, which may be limited because consistent patterns cannot be established between child behavior and common classroom contingencies during such brief (3-second) intervals. It is unclear exactly how seriously the BASC developers consider this component, given the absence of standardization data and the impoverished amount of space dedicated to interpretation (less than one page) in the BASC manual. We interpret the SOS as a cry for help, a faint plea for behavior *analysis* within an otherwise circuitous assessment system. We would encourage users to routinely employ a variation of the SOS, using continuous intervals and an abbreviated behavior code specific to the child's referral problems.

SUMMARY. In sum, we contend that "for a person who likes this type of test, this is the type of test this person will like" (Jones & Witt, 1994). Because of their efficiency and objectivity, structured rating scales are popular among both practitioners and researchers (Witt, Heffer, & Pfeiffer, 1990), and the BASC will solve some of the problems inherent in educational and psychological assessment. Without direct observations of behavior and its antecedents and consequences (Neef & Iwata, 1994), however, assessment will yield very little information directly related to treatment decisions. Unfortunately, it is increasingly clear that the problem-solving role in psychological practice has become departmentalized, so that the goal of assessment is often to produce a diagnosis that is protected from the falsifiability inherent in producing treatments. Users are advised there may be a logical point at which the convenience of assessment obviates the utility of this information.

REVIEWERS' REFERENCES

Witt, J. C., Heffer, R. W., & Pfeiffer, J. (1990). Structured rating scales: A review of self-report and informant rating processes, procedures, and issues. In C. R. Reynolds & R. W. Kamphaus (Eds.), *Handbook of psychological and educational assessment of children* (pp. 364–394). New York: Guilford.
Salvia, J., & Ysseldyke, J. E. (1991). *Assessment* (5th ed.). Boston: Houghton Mifflin.
Adams, C. A., & Drabman, R. C. (1994). BASC: A critical review. *Child Assessment News, 4,* 1–5.
Hoza, B. (1994). Review of the Behavior Assessment System for Children. *Child Assessment News, 4,* 5, 8–10.
Jones, K. M., & Witt, J. C. (1994). Rating the ratings of raters: A critique of the Behavior Assessment System for Children. *Child Assessment News, 4,* 10–11.
Neef, N. A., & Iwata, B. A. (1994). Current research on functional analysis methodologies: An introduction. *Journal of Applied Behavior Analysis, 27,* 211–214.

[35]

Behavior Rating Instrument for Autistic and Other Atypical Children, 2nd Edition.

Purpose: Designed to evaluate the status of autistic, atypical, and other developmentally delayed children by assessing their present levels of functioning and measuring changes in their behavior.

Population: Autistic children.
Publication Dates: 1977–1991.
Acronym: BRIAAC.
Scores, 9: Relationship to an Adult, Communication, Drive for Mastery, Vocalization and Expressive Speech, Sound and Speech Reception, Social Responsiveness, Psychobiological Development, Expressive Gesture and Sign Language, Receptive Gesture and Sign Language.
Administration: Individual.
Price Data, 1994: $124.50 per complete kit including manual ('91, 140 pages) and report form masters with permission to reproduce 50 copies; $49.50 per manual; $75 per reproducible masters and permission to make 50 copies.
Time: Untimed.
Authors: Bertram A. Ruttenberg, Enid G. Wolf-Schein, and Charles Wenar.
Publisher: Stoelting Co.
Cross References: See T4:280 (1 reference); for a review by Edward Workman of an earlier edition, see 9:129; see also T3:272 (1 reference).

Review of the Behavior Rating Instrument for Autistic and Other Atypical Children, 2nd Edition by DOREEN WARD FAIRBANK, Assistant Professor of Psychology, Director, Meredith College Autism Program, Meredith College, Raleigh, NC:

The Behavior Rating Instrument for Autistic and Other Atypical Children (BRIAAC) was originally published in 1977 as an observational instrument used to assess the status of children with autism, atypical, and other low-functioning disabilities. This revised edition was completed for four reasons according to the BRIAAC manual: "1) To clarify and elaborate upon the scales ...; 2) to expand the applicability of BRIAAC to include severely developmentally delayed, deaf, blind and deaf-blind children; 3) To report additional data on the psychometric properties of BRIAAC as well as updating publications concerned with its use as a research and assessment instrument; and 4) To present a BRIAAC checklist to be used for observational reporting and interview purposes" (p. 2).

The BRIAAC was designed as a behavioral observation and rating system for children with the following disabilities: "'early infantile autism,' 'autistic disorder' (DSM-III-R), 'pervasive developmental disorders not otherwise specified (NOS)' (DSM-III-R), 'atypical child', and 'low-functioning deaf, blind and deaf-blind'" (p. 11). The BRIAAC is also useful in assessing children who are regarded as "untestable" because it does not depend on the child's cooperation, but observes the child in his/her natural environment.

The BRIAAC consists of seven scales that describe the areas of behavior most characteristic of autistic and atypical children: Relationship to an Adult, Communication, Drive for Mastery, Vocalization and Expressive Speech, Sound and Speech Reception, Social Responsiveness, and Psychobiological Development. The Body Movement scale from the 1977 edition has been eliminated. Two supplementary scales that evaluate children whose principal means of communication is non-vocal were added: Expressive Gesture and Sign Language, and Receptive Gesture and Sign Language. A Composite score (Cumulative Total Score) is also available. Each scale describes 10 levels of functioning, beginning with the most severely disturbed behavior and progressing to a ceiling behavior that is roughly comparable to a normal 3- to 4-year-old. The levels within each scale follow a developmental sequence and therefore can reflect the changes in the children's behavior as they progress in psychological functioning. The weighted scores range from 10 to 100 and can be totaled to give an overall measure of the severity of the disturbance.

The BRIAAC is based on a representative sample of observations from the child's typical day and the minimum observation period is 2 hours. Scoring must be completed on only observed behavior and not on the basis of inferred behavior. Two methods of scoring are available. The first method involves obtaining a weighted score and the second uses a checklist. The weighted score is completed by the rater distributing the 10 points proportionately among the levels, weighting the points according to observed frequency, intensity, and duration. The checklist method is appropriate for the individual who does not have the opportunity to do the more complete observation but wants the information covered by the BRIAAC. The rating for the checklist is a (2) for characteristic/frequent behaviors, a (1) for occasional/intermittent, and a (0) for not observed/no opportunity. The BRIAAC can be used by raters after they have been adequately trained in observational procedures by a certified BRIAAC trainer and have achieved an acceptable degree of interrater reliability.

The BRIAAC manual describes several concurrent validity studies. [Editor's Note: The technical manual does provide data on a number of studies. However, these studies are all for the original edition

of the BRIAAC that includes the Body Movement scale. There are no reliability or validity studies reported for the scales included only in the second edition (seven scales plus two supplemental scales).] The first study ranked BRIAAC scores for 26 autistic and atypical children against an expert clinician's rankings. The authors report significant positive Pearson product-moment correlations for Total Score ($r = .64$), Relationship ($r = .43$), Vocational and Expressive Speech ($r = .65$), Sound and Speech Reception ($r = .65$), and Drive for Mastery ($r = .83$). A second study found a correlation of .95 when comparing a clinician's ranking of degree of autism and the Cumulative score on the BRIAAC. A third study reported concurrent validity of the BRIAAC scored for 70 visually handicapped and blind children between 3 and 6 years of age and rankings of the children by clinicians. All of the Spearman rank correlation coefficients were significant and ranged from .57 for vocalization to .94 for Body Movement.

A study of the intercorrelation of the scales and a factor analysis with varimax rotation was conducted on a sample of 52 children with autism and other atypical disabilities. The manual states that: "The results of the intercorrelations indicate that the various scales are tapping a common complex entity, but that each scale is sufficiently distinct to warrant inclusion" (p. 103). The results of the factor analysis indicate that there is one common factor that the authors labeled "Reality Participation."

Interrater reliability was assessed by trained teams of three to five raters observing 113 children with autism. Spearman rank correlation coefficients ranged from .84 for Vocalization to .93 for Body Movement with an average correlation of .88 across all eight scales. This would suggest that the BRIAAC has adequate interrater reliability for trained raters. The authors of the BRIAAC found significant Pearson rank correlation coefficients for all scales in an interrater reliability study conducted with a sample of 26 low-functioning, deaf-blind children.

A study of test-retest reliability of the BRIAAC was conducted on a sample of 20 children with autism and atypical disabilities. The Spearman rank correlational coefficients ranged from .61 for Psychobiological to a high of .91 for Social Responsiveness with an average correlation of .81 across all eight scales and the Total Score. All correlations were reported to be significant. A test-retest (average time interval was 8.2 months) reliability study was conducted with a sample of 30 low-functioning deaf-blind children. Again, all of the correlations were statistically significant (ranging from .40 to .83).

The BRIAAC seems to be a reliable, valid, and sufficiently sensitive instrument for assessing the status of children with autism, atypical, and other low functioning disabilities. The proposed goals for the second edition appear to have been accomplished.

[36]
Benton Visual Retention Test, Fifth Edition.

Purpose: "To assess visual perception, visual memory, and visuoconstructive abilities."

Population: Age 8–adults.

Publication Dates: 1946–1992.

Acronym: BVRT.

Scores, 9: Omissions, Distortions, Perseverations, Rotations, Misplacements, Size Errors, Total Left, Total Right, Total.

Administration: Individual.

Forms, 3: C, D, E in a single booklet.

Price Data, 1994: $101.50 per complete set including stimulus booklet (all 30 designs), scoring template, 25 response booklets, record form, and manual ('92, 108 pages); $48 per stimulus booklet; $27 per 25 response booklets—record form; $5.50 per scoring template; $43 per manual.

Time: (5–10) minutes.

Author: Arthur L. Benton.

Publisher: The Psychological Corporation.

Cross References: See T4:293 (62 references), 9:140 (30 references), T3:283 (27 references), 8:236 (32 references), T2:543 (71 references), and 6:543 (22 references); for a review by Nelson G. Hanawalt, see 5:401 (5 references); for reviews by Ivan Norman Mensh, Joseph Newman, and William Schofield of the original edition, see 4:360 (3 references); for an excerpted review, see 3:297.

TEST REFERENCES

1. La Rue, A., D'Elia, L. F., Clark, E. O., Spar, J. E., & Jarvik, L. F. (1986). Clinical test of memory in dementia, depression, and healthy aging. *Psychology and Aging, 1,* 69-77.
2. Sinnott, J. D. (1986). Prospective/intentional and incidental everyday memory: Effects of age and passage of time. *Psychology and Aging, 1,* 110-116.
3. Vilkki, J. (1989). Perseveration in memory for figures after frontal lobe lesion. *Neuropsychologia, 27,* 1101–1104.
4. Fletcher, C. M., & Prior, M. R. (1990). The rule learning behavior of reading disabled and normal children as a function of task characteristics and instruction. *Journal of Experimental Child Psychology, 50,* 39-58.
5. Graff-Radford, N. R., Damasio, A. R., Hyman, B. T., Hart, M. N., Tranel, D., Damasio, H., Van Hoesen, G. W., & Rezai, K. (1990). Progressive aphasia in a patient with Pick's disease: A neuropsychological, radiologic, and anatomic study. *Neurology, 40,* 620–626.
6. Green, J., Morris, J. C., Sandson, J., McKeel, D. W., & Miller, J.W. (1990). Progressive aphasia: A precursor of global dementia? *Neurology, 40,* 423–429.
7. Harper, R. G., Kotik-Harper, D., & Kirby, H. (1990). Psychometric assessment of depression in an elderly general medical population: Over- or underassessment? *The Journal of Nervous and Mental Disease, 178,* 113-119.
8. Hollander, E., Schiffman, E., Cohen, B., Rivera-Stein, M. A., Rosen, W., Gorman, J. M., Fyer, A. J., Papp, L., & Liebowitz, M. R. (1990). Signs of central nervous system dysfunction in obsessive-compulsive disorder. *Archives of General Psychiatry, 47,* 27–32.
9. de Sonneville, L. M. J., Njiokiktjien, C., & Hilhorst, R. C. (1991). Methylphenidate-induced changes in ADDH information processors. *Journal of Child Psychology and Psychiatry and Allied Disciplines, 32,* 285-295.

10. Klonoff, H., Clark, C., Oger, J., Paty, D., & Li, D. (1991). Neuropsychological performance in patients with mild multiple sclerosis. *The Journal of Nervous and Mental Disease, 179,* 127-131.
11. Lucas, J. A., Telch, M. J., & Bigler, E. D. (1991). Memory functioning in panic disorder: A neuropsychological perspective. *Journal of Anxiety Disorders, 5,* 1-20.
12. Stern, Y., Marder, K., Bell, K., Chen, J., Dooneief, G., Goldstein, S., Mindry, D., Richards, M., Sano, M., Williams, J., Gorman, J., Ehrhardt, A., & Mayeux, R. (1991). Multidisciplinary baseline assessment of homosexual men with and without human immunodeficiency virus infection. *Archives of General Psychiatry, 48,* 131-138.
13. Anderson, S. W., Damasio, H., Damasio, A. R., Klima, E., Bellugi, U., & Brandt, J. P. (1992). Acquisition of signs from American Sign Language in hearing individuals following left hemisphere damage and aphasia. *Neuropsychologia, 30,* 329–340.
14. Dartigues, J. F., Gagnon, M., Mazaux, J. M., Baberger-Gateau, P., Commenges, D., Lettenneur, L., & Orgogozo, J. M. (1992). Occupation during life and memory performance in nondemented French elderly community residents. *Neurology, 42,* 1697–1701.
15. Meyers, C. A., & Abbruzzese, J. L. (1992). Cognitive functioning in cancer patients: Effect of previous treatment. *Neurology, 42,* 434–436.
16. Sakurai, Y., Kurisaki, H., Takeda, K., Iwata, M., Bandoh, M., Watanabe, T., & Momose, T. (1992). Japanese crossed Wernicke's aphasia. *Neurology, 42,* 144–148.
17. Tatemichi, T. K., Desmond, D. W., Mayeux, R., Paik, M., Stern, Y., Sano, M., Remien, R. H., Williams, J. B. W., Mohr, J. P., Hauser, W. A., & Figueroa, M. (1992). Dementia after stroke: Baseline frequency, risks, and clinical features in a hospitalized cohort. *Neurology, 42,* 1185–1193.
18. Tatemichi, T. K., Desmond, D. W., Prohovnik, I., Cross, D. T., Gropen, T. I., Mohr, J. P., & Stern, Y. (1992). Confusion and memory loss from capsular genu infarction: A thalamocortical disconnection syndrome? *Neurology, 42,* 1966–1979.
19. Young, A. W., Robertson, I. H., Hellawell, D. J., DePauw, K. W., & Pentland, B. (1992). Cotard delusion after brain injury. *Psychological Medicine, 22,* 799-804.
20. Benke, T. (1993). Two forms of apraxia in Alzheimer's disease. *Cortex, 29,* 715-725.
21. Celano, M. P., & Geller, R. J. (1993). Learning, school, performance, and children with asthma: How much at risk? *Journal of Learning Disabilities, 26,* 23–32.
22. Corcoran, R., & Thompson, P. (1993). Epilepsy and poor memory: Who complains and what do they mean? *British Journal of Clinical Psychology, 32,* 199-208.
23. Crockett, D. J. (1993). Cross-validation of WAIS-R prototypical patterns of intellectual functioning using neuropsychological test scores. *Journal of Clinical and Experimental Neuropsychology, 15,* 903-920.
24. Dodrill, C. B., Arnett, J. L., Sommerville, K. W., & Sussman, N. M. (1993). Evaluation of the effects of vigabatrin on cognitive abilities and quality of life epilepsy. *Neurology, 43,* 2501–2507.
25. Dvara, R., Lopez-Alberola, R. F., Barker, W. W., Loewenstein, D.A., Zatinsky, M., Eisdorfer, C. E., & Weinberg, G. B. (1993). A comparison of familial and sporadic Alzheimer's disease. *Neurology, 43,* 1377–1384.
26. Krupp, L. B., Masur, D. M., & Kaufman, L. D. (1993). Neurocognitive dysfunction in the eosinophilia-myalgia syndrome. *Neurology, 43,* 931–936.
27. Larrabee, G. J., Youngjohn, J. R., Sudilovsky, A., & Crook, T. H. (1993). Accelerated forgetting in Alzheimer-type dementia. *Journal of Clinical and Experimental Neuropsychology, 15,* 701-712.
28. Markowitsch, H. J., von Cramon, D. Y., & Schuri, U. (1993). Mnestic performance profile of a bilateral diencephalic infarct patient with preserved intelligence and severe amnesic disturbances. *Journal of Clinical and Experimental Neuropsychology, 15,* 627-632.
29. Meador, K. J., Moore, E. E., Nichols, M. E., Abney, O. L., Taylor, H. S., Zamrini, E. Y., & Loring, D. W. (1993). The role of cholinergic systems in visuospatial processing and memory. *Journal of Clinical and Experimental Neuropsychology, 15,* 832-842.
30. Rothlind, J. C., Bylsma, F. W., Peyser, C., Folstein, S. E., & Brandt, J. (1993). Cognitive and motor correlates of everyday functioning in early Huntington's disease. *The Journal of Nervous and Mental Disease, 181,* 194-199.
31. Roxborough, H., Muir, W. J., Blackwood, D. H. R., Walker, M. T., & Blackburn, I. M. (1993). Neuropsychological and P300 abnormalities in schizophrenics and their relatives. *Psychological Medicine, 23,* 305-314.
32. Ryan, L., Clark, C. M., Klonoff, H., & Paty, D. (1993). Models of cognitive deficit and statistical hypotheses: Multiple sclerosis, an example. *Journal of Clinical and Experimental Neuropsychology, 15,* 563-577.
33. Anderson, S. W., & Rizzo, M. (1994). Hallucinations following occipital lobe damage: A pathological activation of visual representations. *Journal of Clinical and Experimental Neuropsychology, 16,* 651-663.
34. Bylsma, F. W., Peyser, C. E., Folstein, S. E., Folstein, M. L., Ross, C., & Brandt, J. (1994). EEG power spectra in Huntington's disease: Clinical and neuropsychological correlates. *Neuropsychologia, 32,* 137–150.
35. Diamond, B. J., Valentine, T., Mayes, A. R., & Sandel, M. E. (1994). Evidence of covert recognition in a prosopagnosic patient. *Cortex, 30,* 377-393.
36. Duffy, L., & O'Carroll, R. (1994). Memory impairment in schizophrenia—a comparison with that observed in the Alcoholic Korsakoff Syndrome. *Psychological Medicine, 24,* 155-165.
37. Dywan, J., Segalowitz, S. J., & Williamson, L. (1994). Source monitoring during name recognition in older adults: Psychometric and electrophysiological correlates. *Psychology and Aging, 9,* 568-577.

38. Farlow, M., Murrell, J., Ghetti, B., Unverzagt, F., Zeldenrust, S., & Benson, M. (1994). Clinical characteristics in a kindred with early-onset Alzheimer's disease and their linkage to a G->T change at position 2149 of the amyloid precursor protein gene. *Neurology, 44,* 105–111.

39. Gottschalk, L. A. (1994). The development, validation, and applications of a computerized measurement of cognitive impairment from the content analysis of verbal behavior. *Journal of Clinical Psychology, 50,* 349-361.

40. Rapcsak, S. Z., Polster, M. R., Comer, J. F., & Rubens, A. B. (1994). False recognition and misidentification of faces following right hemisphere damage. *Cortex, 30,* 565-583.

41. Sobell, L. C., Toneatto, T., & Sobell, M. (1994). Behavioral assessment and treatment planning for alcohol, tobacco, and other drug problems: Current status with an emphasis on clinical applications. *Behavior Therapy, 25,* 533–580.

42. Tomer, A., Larrabee, G. J., & Crook, T. H. (1994). Structure of everyday memory in adults with age-associated memory impairment. *Psychology and Aging, 9,* 606-615.

43. Vilkki, J., Ahola, K., Holst, P., Öhman, J., Servo, A., & Heiskanen, O. (1994). Prediction of psychosocial recovery after head injury with cognitive tests and neurobehavioral ratings. *Journal of Clinical and Experimental Neuropsychology, 16,* 325-338.

44. Webster, J. S., Rapport, L. J., Godlewski, M. C., & Abadee, P. S. (1994). Effect of attentional bias to right space on wheelchair mobility. *Journal of Clinical and Experimental Neuropsychology, 16,* 129-137.

45. Becker, J. T., Lopez, O. L., & Boller, F. (1995). Understanding impaired analysis of faces by patients with probable Alzheimer's disease. *Cortex, 31,* 129-137.

46. Carmelli, D., Swan, G. E., & Cardon, L. R. (1995). Genetic mediation in the relationship of education to cognitive function in older people. *Psychology and Aging, 10,* 48-53.

47. Giambra, L. M., Arenberg, D., Zonderman, A. B., Kawas, C., & Costa, P. T. (1995). Adult life span changes in immediate visual memory and verbal intelligence. *Psychology and Aging, 10,* 123-139.

48. Graf, P., Uttle, B., & Tuokko, H. (1995). Color- and Picture-Word Stroop Tests: Performance changes in old age. *Journal of Clinical and Experimental Neuropsychology, 17,* 390-415.

49. Helmstaedter, C., Pohl, C., & Elger, C. E. (1995). Relations between verbal and nonverbal memory performance: Evidence of confounding effects particularly in patients with right temporal lobe epilepsy. *Cortex, 31,* 345-355.

50. Hokkanen, L., Launes, J., Vataja, R., Valanne, L., & Iivanainen, M. (1995). Isolated retrograde amnesia for autobiographical material associated with acute left temporal lobe encephalitis. *Psychological Medicine, 25,* 203-208.

51. Jacobs, D. M., Marder, K., Cote, L., Sano, M., Stern, Y., & Mayeux, R. (1995). Neuropsychological characteristics of preclinical dementia in Parkinson's disease. *Neurology, 45,* 1691-1696.

52. Jacobs, D. M., Sano, M., Dooneief, G., Marder, K., Bell, K. L., & Stern, Y. (1995). Neuropsychological detection and characterization of preclinical Alzheimer's disease. *Neurology, 45,* 957-962.

53. Koivisto, K., Reinikainen, K. J., Hänninen, T., Vanhanen, M., Helkala, E.-L., Mykkänen, L., Laakso, M., Pyörälä, K., & Riekkinen, P. J. (1995). Prevalence of age-associated memory impairment in a randomly selected population from eastern Finland. *Neurology, 45,* 741-747.

54. LaRue, A., O'Hara, R., Matsuyama, S. S., & Jarvik, L. F. (1995). Cognitive changes in young-old adults: Effect of family history of dementia. *Journal of Clinical and Experimental Neuropsychology, 17,* 65-70.

55. LaRue, A., Swan, G. E., & Carmelli, D. (1995). Cognition and depression in a cohort of aging men: Results from the western collaborative group study. *Psychology and Aging, 10,* 30-33.

56. Migliorelli, R., Petracca, G., Tesón, A. Sabe, L., Leiguarda, R., & Starkstein, S. E. (1995). Neuropsychiatric and neuropsychological correlates of delusions in Alzheimer's Disease. *Psychological Medicine, 25,* 505–513.

57. Migliorelli, R., Teson, A., Sabe, L., Petracchi, M., Leiguarda, R., & Starkstein, S. E. (1995). Prevalence and correlates of dysthymia and major depression among patients with Alzheimer's Disease. *American Journal of Psychiatry, 152,* 37-44.

58. Rasmusson, D. X., & Brandt, J. (1995). Instability of cognitive asymmetry in Alzheimer's disease. *Journal of Clinical and Experimental Neuropsychology, 17,* 449-458.

59. Resnick, S. M., Trotman, K. M., Kawas, C., & Zonderman, A. B. (1995). Age-associated changes in specific errors on the Benton Visual Retention Test. *Journal of Gerontology: Psychological Sciences, 50B,* P171-P178.

60. Silver, H., Geraisy, N., & Schwartz, M. (1995). No difference in the effect of biperiden and amantadine on Parkinsonian- and Tardive Dyskinesia-type involuntary movements: A double-blind crossover, placebo-controlled study in medicated chronic schizophrenic patients. *Journal of Clinical Psychiatry, 56,* 167–170.

61. Takahashi, N., Kawamura, M., Hirayama, K., Shiota, J., & Isono, O. (1995). Prosopagnosia: A clinical and anatomical study of four patients. *Cortex, 31,* 317-329.

62. Temple, C. M., & Carney, R. A. (1995). Patterns of spatial functioning in Turner's syndrome. *Cortex, 31,* 109-118.

63. Tison, F., Dartigues, J. F., Auriacombe, S., Letenneur, L., Boller, F., & Alperovitch, A. (1995). Dementia in Parkinson's disease: A population-based study in ambulatory and institutionalized individuals. *Neurology, 45,* 705–708.

64. Tuokko, H. Kristjansson, E., & Miller, J. (1995). Neuropsychological detection of dementia: An overview of the neuropsychological component of the Canadian study of health and aging. *Journal of Clinical and Experimental Neuropsychology, 17,* 325-373.

65. Rasmusson, D. X., Carson, K. A., Brookmeyer, R., Kawas, C., & Brandt, J. (1996). Predicting rate of cognitive decline in probable Alzheimer's disease. *Brain and Cognition, 31,* 133–147.

66. Schofield, P. W., Marder, K., Dooneief, G., Jacobs, D. M., Sano, M., & Stern, Y. (1997). Association of subjective memory complaints with subsequent cognitive decline in community-dwelling elderly individuals with baseline cognitive impairment. *American Journal of Psychiatry, 154,* 609–615.

Review of the Benton Visual Retention Test, Fifth Edition by ANITA M. HUBLEY, Assistant Professor of Psychology, University of Northern British Columbia, Prince George, British Columbia, Canada:

The Benton Visual Retention Test (BVRT) consists of a series of 10 designs measuring visual perception, visual memory, and visuoconstructive abilities. There are three nearly equivalent forms (Forms C, D, & E) of the BVRT. Alternate form reliability is adequate but not strong. Although Benton (1974) reports correlation coefficients ranging from .79 to .84 among the three forms, this information does not appear in the current edition of the manual. The presence of alternate forms is a particular strength of this test and provides an advantage over similar tests when retesting is needed to assess the effect of treatment, surgery, or time on visuospatial ability.

Four methods of administration (A, B, C, & D) are available: In Administrations A and B, the examinee views each design for 10 seconds (A) or 5 seconds (B) before reproducing it from memory. In Administration D, a 15-second delay interval is used before the examinee is permitted to reproduce the design. Administration C is a copy trial. When used together, these administration procedures permit a closer examination of visuoconstructive abilities, immediate visuospatial recall, and delayed visuospatial recall. Surprisingly, no mention is made in the manual of Forms F and G or Administration M (the four-choice recognition or multiple-choice formats) or the reasons why they are no longer available or perhaps recommended.

Overall, the instructions for administration of the BVRT are clearly written and, because they are presented in the manual using a different colored ink, easily followed as well. Several commonly asked questions regarding the administration of the test (e.g., can the examinee make corrections? is size important?) are specifically and appropriately addressed in the manual. One consideration for future revisions of the test is that it may be particularly useful if the main instructions were also presented in the stimulus booklet (e.g., on the examiner's side of the divider page).

In scoring the BVRT, there are two main scores used: Number Correct Score, in which each of the 10 designs are judged on an all-or-none basis as either correct or incorrect, and Number Error Score, in which the total number of errors made and their type are recorded. There are six major categories of errors: Omissions, Distortions, Perseverations, Rotations, Misplacements, and Size Errors. The scoring of this test is somewhat cumbersome. However, detailed descriptions of the various types of errors are provided and numerous examples of correct and incorrect reproductions are provided with brief descriptions of the specific error made. Many of the recommendations made by Swan, Morrison, and Eslinger (1990) to improve scoring consistency and agreement have been specifically addressed in this edition of the manual.

Interscorer reliability for the BVRT with respect to total scores on Administration A is very high with reliabilities ranging from .90 to .97 for the Number Correct Score and from .94 to .98 for the Number Error Score according to the manual. Not reported in the manual is research by Randall, Dickson, and Plasay (1988) wherein slightly lower interscorer reliabilities of .85 for Number Correct and .93 for Number Error are reported. Interrater agreement for the six error categories varies with high kappa coefficients for Omissions (.976), Perseverations (.881), Distortions (.892), and Rotations (.884), and lower coefficients for Misplacements (.850) and Size Errors (.737) (Swan et al., 1990).

Surprisingly, there is no information provided in the manual regarding test-retest reliability. Studies described by Lezak (1995) suggest inconsistent results when intact individuals are assessed. Lezak reports concordance coefficients (W) of .74 for Number Correct and .77 for Number Error among three administrations given 6 and 12 months apart. Botwinick, Storandt, and Berg (1986) found essentially no change in Number Correct scores for older adults across four administrations given 1 and 1 1/2 years apart whereas Larrabee, Levin, and High (1986) observed an increase in Number Error Scores in older adults tested after 10–13 months. More recent research by Youngjohn, Larrabee, and Crook (1992) found 3-week test-retest reliabilities of only .57 for Number Correct and .53 for Number Error for a wide age range of subjects.

A considerable amount of normative information is available for the BVRT. Unfortunately, the presentation of the normative data and the description of the samples used is a weak point of the manual. For example, for the Administration A norms, the overall sample sizes are reported for only two of the three studies cited. Moreover, although the two cited studies report large overall sample sizes of 600+ and 769 subjects each, no breakdown of the sample sizes is provided by age group, gender (except one study which included only men), socioeconomic status, or education for either the individual studies or the combined norms reported in the manual. Similar problems arise with the norms provided for each of the administration methods and for older adults.

One difficulty that arises with using the norms provided in the manual is that an IQ score, or an estimated premorbid IQ score, is required. Although it is ideal to have such information, there are times when IQ information is simply not known or available, or it is not easily or reasonably obtained. In such cases, the clinical neuropsychologist usually takes into consideration the education level of the patient. However, the manual does not describe the relationship between education level and the BVRT scores. Although intelligence level may be a better predictor of BVRT scores than education, it would be useful to have education-based norms provided in the manual. Two sets of adult norms using education are available in the literature, although the education levels of the samples are quite high. Robertson-Tchabo and Arenberg (1989; also reported in Spreen & Strauss, 1991) provide Number Error Score norms based on 1,643 subjects by age group (seven 10-year age groups ranging from 20–89 years), education level ("no degree" and "college degree" groups), and gender. Youngjohn, Larrabee, and Crook (1993) provide both Number Correct Score and Number Error Score norms based on 1,128 subjects by age group (five age groups ranging from 18–84 years) and education level (12–14 years, 15–17 years, and 18+ years).

SUMMARY. The Benton Visual Retention Test is recommended as a brief, flexible measure of visuospatial perception, construction, and memory. Instructions for administration and scoring are easy to follow and the test materials are easy to use. The multiple forms of the test are useful when retesting is needed and practice effects are to be avoided. Interscorer reliabilities are very high for the two BVRT summary scores and moderate to high for the error categories. Test-retest reliabilities, based on studies with intact adults, are inconsistent with reports varying from essentially no change in scores over a longer period of time (e.g., 1 1/2 years) to low test-retest reliabilities reported over a shorter test interval (e.g., 3 weeks). Extensive normative data do appear to be available for both children and adults. Finally, there does appear to be good evidence for construct validity of this test as a measure primarily of visuospatial perception and construction, and secondarily of visuospatial memory. As such a measure, the BVRT has been shown to be useful in helping to differentiate the performance of intact individuals from those with evidence of cerebral disease, dementia, and schizophrenia.

The primary weakness of the BVRT is the manual itself. The Fifth Edition of the test boasts a number of revisions, including (a) presentation of extensive post-1974 normative data, particularly for older adults; (b) recent reliability data; (c) simplified, more explicit scoring with more helpful examples; (d) a review of clinical and research applications; and (e) an analysis of the cognitive factors underlying the test and the test's role in neuropsychological assessment. The administration and scoring sections of the manual are very well presented. However, when it comes to the norms, it is not clear which versions of the BVRT were used in each case and what impact this might have on the norms. Nor is enough detail provided about the samples comprising the norms. This lack of detail also extends to the sections on the history and development of the test and to descriptions of the samples used in the reliability studies. Information on interscorer reliability has been updated, but no information on test-retest reliability is provided at all. Finally, although revisions (d) and (e) were technically available, one has to wade through study after study to evaluate evidence for construct validity and to find useful snippets of interpretive information. Although the manual contains a good description of the factors that need to be considered for the valid interpretation of results, it is, in fact, Lezak (1995, p. 483) who provides the kind of interpretative guidelines for the BVRT that were expected, but not found, in the manual.

REVIEWER'S REFERENCES

Benton, A. L. (1974). Revised Visual Retention Test (4th ed.). New York: The Psychological Corporation.

Botwinick, J., Storandt, M., & Berg, L. (1986). A longitudinal, behavioral study of senile dementia of the Alzheimer type. Archives of Neurology, 43, 1124–1127.

Larrabee, G. J., Levin, H. S., & High, W. M. (1986). Senescent forgetfulness: A quantitative study. Developmental Neuropsychology, 2, 373–385.

Randall, C. M., Dickson, A. L., & Plasay, M. T. (1988). The relationship between intellectual function and adult performance on the Benton Visual Retention Test. Cortex, 24, 277–289.

Robertson-Tchabo, E. A., & Arenberg, D. (1989). Assessment of memory in older adults. In T. Hunt & C. Lindley (Eds.), Testing older adults. Austin, TX: PRO-ED, Inc.

Swan, G. E., Morrison, E., & Eslinger, P. J. (1990). Interrater agreement on the Benton Visual Retention Test. The Clinical Neuropsychologist, 4, 37–44.

Spreen, O., & Strauss, E. (1991). A compendium of neuropsychological tests. New York: Oxford University Press.

Youngjohn, J. R., Larrabee, G. J., & Crook, T. H. (1992). Test-retest reliability of computerized everyday memory measures and traditional tests. The Clinical Neuropsychologist, 3, 276–286.

Youngjohn, J. R., Larrabee, G. J., & Crook, T. H. (1993). New adult age- and education-correction norms for the Benton Visual Retention Test. The Clinical Neuropsychologist, 7, 155–160.

Lezak, M. D. (1995). Neuropsychological assessment (3rd ed.). New York: Oxford University Press.

Review of the Benton Visual Retention Test, Fifth Edition by CYNTHIA A. ROHRBECK, Associate Professor of Psychology, The George Washington University, Washington, DC:

The Benton Visual Retention Test (BVRT), Fifth Edition is a figure-drawing task that measures spatial relations and memory for visually learned material. It has been useful in research and has been used as a screener for brain damage or dysfunction in both children and adults.

The Fifth Edition has three alternate forms (C, D, and E), with 10 designs each, many of which have more than one figure. The test can be administered in four different ways (A, B, C, and D). Depending on the type of administration, the subject either copies each design while looking at it or reproduces a design from memory. Administration A, the method most often used, involves a 10-second exposure to the stimulus, the design is then covered, and the subject immediately reproduces it by memory. Administration B is the same, but with a 5-second exposure. In Administration C, there is no time limit, and the stimulus design remains in front of the subject, who copies it. In Administration D, there is a 10-second exposure, next the stimulus is covered, and after a 15-second delay, the stimulus is reproduced by memory.

The BVRT is simple to administer and instructions for administering the test in the manual are clear. Unlike the Bender Visual-Motor Gestalt Test, the BVRT stimulus book can be folded into an easel that presents the material at a 60-degree angle to the surface of the table. The test takes approximately 5 minutes to administer. The examinee's responses and record of correct designs and number of errors can be included in a response booklet. The BVRT kit also includes a template for measuring the examinee's drawings or noting the angles of drawings, when necessary, to determine errors. Once a tester has learned how to score the BVRT, he or she should be able to score a BVRT in about 3–15 minutes (depending on the number of errors and the scorer's familiarity with error categories).

Scores include both the number correct (0 or 1 for each design, so a range of 0–10 for all 10 designs) and the number of errors. The manual includes examples of incorrect and correct responses for each design in each form. Fifty-six specific error types can be grouped into six categories—Omissions, Distortions, Perseverations, Rotations, Misplacements, and Size Errors. Errors can be further categorized as central, left, or right (e.g., omission of right major figure, or perseveration of left peripheral figure). An incorrect reproduction may contain as many as 4 specific errors, although the manual notes that the upper limit for number of errors is about 24. Eight types of errors from the Fourth Edition were deleted because they "were nondiscriminating, rarely used, and cumbersome to assess" (manual, p. 12). The manual presents compelling evidence for the need to record the number of errors. In addition, it presents research suggesting that Omission and Size Errors are particularly noticeable in reproductions from memory by patients with cerebral disease. It is not clear, however, why the other types of errors are important, or whether the specification of right or left figure errors is necessary.

It should be noted (and is clearly stated in the manual) that BVRT scores may suggest cognitive dysfunction, but cannot be used to definitively diagnose such impairment. The BVRT is best used as one part of a battery of tests to assess neurological difficulties. The manual also notes that other explanations for poor performance on the BVRT should be excluded before further investigating the possibility of cerebral dysfunction. Such factors could include lack of adequate effort on the task, serious depression, lack of education, etc.

Performance on the BVRT is related to age; the number of correct responses increases from age 8 to 14 or 15, and remains steady from 14 or 15 until the mid 40s. Beginning in the 50s, performance begins to decline. Perhaps for this reason, norms for children are based on ages 8–14, with adult norms beginning at age 15. Norms for both children and adults are available for A, B, and C administrations, but not D. Because performance on the BVRT is also correlated with intellectual functioning, subgroup norms are available for different age and IQ ranges. In general, scores 2 points lower than the norms (for correct designs) are said to raise the possibility of impairment, with scores 3 or 4 points lower more strongly suggesting impairment. Similarly, scores that are 3 points greater than the expected error scores may indicate impairment, with scores that are 4 or 5 points higher more strongly suggesting impairment. For Administration B, research suggests that norms should be about 1 point lower than the norms for Administration A. The

Fifth Edition includes normative data in addition to that in the Fourth Edition (1974), especially for Administration A and for older subjects.

The Fifth Edition also includes more recent data on reliability and interrater agreement in scoring. Interrater agreement has ranged from .94 to .98 for the number of correct responses and the number of error scores. Agreement (kappas) for identifying specific types of errors has ranged from .74 to .98. In response to earlier critiques, the Fifth Edition includes more scoring samples that illustrate errors than in the past.

With regard to validity, the BVRT has been significantly correlated with several Wechsler Adult Intelligence Scale (WAIS) subtests, including Digit Span, Block Design, Digit Symbol, and Object Assembly. According to the BVRT manual, factor analytic studies suggest that the BVRT Administration A reflects a "short-term memory ability and a visuoperceptual analytic ability" whereas Administration C reflects a "visuoconstructional ability" (p. 94). The manual summarizes research that suggests that the BVRT, when used in combination with other neurological tests, has successfully differentiated patients with dementia from normal controls. Discrimination has not been as strong for children.

In summary, the BVRT was designed to measure specific types of cognitive impairment. Several decades of research support its clinical and research utility, reliability, and validity. Its advantages include its brevity and its precise scoring system. On the other hand, when diagnosing cognitive or neurological impairment, it should be only one part of a larger battery of tests. Future research should provide additional normative data (for example, normative data for children on Form C are only based on children with average IQs). In addition, the next revision should better specify the subject populations that have been used in the cited reliability and validity studies. It is likely that most of that work has been based on adult samples; future reliability and validity studies should include child samples.

[37]

BEST Instruments.

Purpose: A series of learning instruments designed to help managers and employees understand their behavior.
Population: Adults.
Publication Dates: 1989–1994.
Acronym: BEST.
Administration: Group.

Price Data, 1993: $25 per sample pack; $15 per user's guide ('89, 16 pages); $149 per user's kit.

Comments: Subtests available as separates.

Author: James H. Brewer.

Publisher: Associated Consultants in Education.

a) MY BEST PROFILE.

Purpose: "To promote positive interpersonal relations."

Publication Date: 1989.

Scores: 4 personality types: Bold, Expressive, Sympathetic, Technical.

Price Data: $4.95 per profile; $99.95 per computer software.

Time: (15–20) minutes.

b) MY BEST COMMUNICATION STYLE.

Purpose: "To improve communication skills."

Publication Dates: 1989–1990.

Scores: 4 styles: Bold, Expressive, Sympathetic, Technical.

Price Data: $2.95 per inventory.

Time: (15–20) minutes.

c) MY BEST LEADERSHIP STYLE.

Purpose: "To improve leadership skills."

Publication Dates: 1989–1994.

Scores: Same as *a* above.

Price Data: $4.95 per profile; $99.95 per computer software.

Time: (15–20) minutes.

d) LEADERSHIP/PERSONALITY COMPATIBILITY INVENTORY.

Purpose: "To promote more productive leadership in organizations."

Acronym: L/PCI.

Scores: Same as *a* above plus 4 Leadership Role Characteristics: Active/Competitive, Persuasive/Interactive, Precise/Systematic, Willing/Steady.

Publication Dates: 1990–1994.

Price Data: $5.95 per profile.

Time: (15–20) minutes.

e) WORKING WITH MY BOSS.

Purpose: "To improve the productive relationship between employee and supervisor."

Publication Date: 1989.

Scores: Same as *a* above.

Price Data: $4.95 per profile.

Time: (10—15) minutes.

f) PRE-EVALUATION PROFILE.

Purpose: "To prepare supervisors for performance evaluations of employees without personality type bias."

Acronym: PEP.

Publication Date: 1989.

Scores: Same as *a* above.

Price Data: $4.95 per profile.

Time: (15–20) minutes.

Comments: Supervisor completes profile for self and employee.

g) OUR BEST TEAM.

Purpose: "To build a more productive team."

Publication Date: 1989.

Scores: Same as *a* above.

Price Data: $6.95 per profile.

Time: (20–30) minutes.

Comments: Ratings of all team members are combined for a composite profile.

h) MY TIMESTYLE.

Purpose: "To develop more productive time usage."

Publication Date: 1990.

Scores: 4 time styles: Road Runner, Race Horse, New Pup, Tom Cat.

Price Data: $2.95 per profile.

Time: (10–15) minutes.

i) MY BEST PRESENTATION STYLE.

Purpose: "To assist individuals in making more effective presentations."

Publication Date: 1989.

Scores: Same as *a* above.

Price Data: $4.95 per profile.

Time: (15–20) minutes.

j) SALES STYLE.

Purpose: "To sharpen sales skills."

Publication Date: 1990.

Scores: 4 sales styles: Quick-Sell, Persistent-Sell, Talkative-Sell, Precise-Sell.

Price Data: $2.95 per profile.

Time: (10–15) minutes.

k) MY TEACHING STYLE.

Purpose: "To help teachers understand learning style."

Publication Date: 1989.

Scores: Bold, Expressive, Sympathetic, Technical.

Price Data: $4.95 per profile.

Time: (15–20) minutes.

l) NEGOTIATING STYLE.

Purpose: "To build productive negotiating strategies."

Publication Date: 1991.

Scores: 4 negotiating styles: Pushy, Stand Pat, Buddy, Check All.

Price Data: $2.95 per profile.

Time: (10–15) minutes.

m) CAREER/PERSONALITY COMPATIBILITY INVENTORY.

Purpose: "To improve career selection."

Publication Date: No date on materials.

Acronym: C/PCI.

Scores: Bold, Expressive, Sympathetic, Technical.

Price Data: $5.95 per profile; $345 per computer software.

Time: (20–30) minutes.

Review of the BEST Instruments by MARY A. LEWIS, Director, Human Resources, Chlor-Alkali and Derivatives, PPG Industries, Inc., Pittsburgh, PA:

The BEST Instruments are a collection of 13 learning instruments designed to be easy to administer, score, and understand. All 13 instruments are supported by the same User's Guide, which provides several pages of introduction to the concept of personality typing. The work of Marston and Herrmann is discussed as the foundation for the theory used to develop the four personality types measured in various ways by the BEST Instruments. These types are B - Bold, E - Expressive, S - Sympathetic, and T - Technical. Each of the 13 instruments included in this review measures these four traits using in some cases identical instruments, and in others using situational items more tailored to the purpose of the specific tool. These instruments are clearly designed to be used as teaching tools, and the descriptions of each instrument in the battery discuss the learning points intended. The author, in fact, included a disclaimer in the User's Guide that specifically states that the instruments are not intended for uses other than training and development. With training and development as their primary intent, perhaps the most efficient way to review these instruments is to review MY BEST PROFILE in depth and then point out similarities and differences in the other instruments.

MY BEST PROFILE is described as the most basic of the BEST instruments. It consists of a 17-item word association list in which the individual marks one of four words that "best fits" their behavioral style, and a 15-item situation analysis questionnaire in which the individual indicates which of four options is their response to a situational item stem. Each of the four options is associated with one of the four BEST styles. The questionnaire is a two-part form, and is scored by removing the top page and counting the number of Bs, Es, Ss, and Ts marked. These counts are recorded, and the higher the number, the more dominant the style. Means and standard deviations for style scores are not provided; however, the manual does indicate that a number of 15 or higher is considered dominant.

The Technical Information section of the User's Guide describes the process by which the style scales were developed. Data were collected over a 4-year period on 1,217 study group participants in various occupational groups in a range of U.S. locations. Coefficient alpha reliabilities ranged from .86 for Sympathetic to .97 for Technical. Validity of the scales was supported in three ways. The first was that participants thought their real personality was represented by the instruments. However, this information does not address the appropriateness of what is being delivered other than in layman's perceptions. To the extent that what is measured is a Barnum statement, most participants will agree with their assessment. Therefore, this source of validity evidence is more a comfort factor for the participant rather than a true test of validity in the classic sense. However, in a training environment, this is a good start because buy-in of students is a key to learning.

The User's Guide then asserts that construct validity was demonstrated by reviewing the types with six seminar presenters who were familiar with personality types. These individuals were successful in selecting descriptive words that described the categories. In addition, the author cites his experience in observing others, which confirms the construct validity of the BEST system. Unfortunately, no psychometric data are provided to support these assertions. For example, the author could have at least indicated that the six persons were able to categorize correctly some percentage of the statements, or that observation was able to confirm dominant style type in some percent of the cases.

In the part of the technical section on concurrent validity, the author cites a "similar research base" (p. 12) as a source for determining concurrent validity with the BEST system and other instruments that use the four-type personality system. Concurrent validity typically refers to administering an instrument and collecting a criterion measure at the same time, using an estimate of the validity (usually a correlation). In this case, I would assume the author was defining the other measures of four-type personality as the criterion. Although a number of specific four-type systems are cited, no psychometric link is provided. Further, such links would more appropriately be called construct validity rather than concurrent validity. This lack of psychometric data could be more troubling if the BEST instruments were designed for a purpose other than training and development. It is refreshing that the author acknowledges that these measures of validity and reliability are not exact. The User's Guide does an excellent job in making clear the limitations of the studies and the appropriate use of the instruments.

CAPSULE SUMMARIES OF THE BEST INSTRUMENTS. The BEST consists of a series of 13 instruments, many of which are assessed using the 17-item work association questionnaire and the 15-item situational questionnaire (Profile, Leadership

Style, Leadership Personality Compatibility, Working with My Boss, Our Best Team, Presentation Style, and Career Personality Compatibility). Teaching Style uses the 17-item word association questionnaire coupled with 14 questions on teaching situations. The remaining instruments (Communication Style, Pre-Evaluative Profile, My Timestyle, Sales Style, and Negotiating Style) all use other measurements, mostly consisting of 16 or more situational items. Several of the instruments that use the word association and situational questionnaires are also supplemented with other measurements specific to the topic.

Each of the instruments in the series is presented in a brochure format. Most have two-part forms, similar to the Profile, for scoring. They are all self-report tools, which can be administered and scored in less than 30 minutes. All use a simple counting scoring procedure. The brochures are self-contained teaching tools. They include complete instructions that can be easily followed, a simple process for scoring, and instructional points for the use of each instrument.

I recommend that training professionals consider these as possible tools to add to their instructional kits. Deciding on the appropriateness of their use for a particular course of instruction is as simple as ordering a set of instruments and reviewing the materials. The decision should be based on how well the content of the specific tool fits the instructor's training goals. My view is that the author has done an excellent job in meeting the clearly described goals of developing cost-effective instruments that are easy to understand, administer, and score. As the author said: They are "educational and fun—not heavy psychological measurements of abnormal behavior." In that context, they succeed very well.

Review of the BEST Instruments by FRANK SCHMIDT, Professor, College of Business, University of Iowa, Iowa City, IA:

The BEST Instrument is a self-administered, self-scored personality test intended for use in work settings for training and development purposes. The manual states (p. 13) that the BEST is not intended to be used as a predictor of job performance, for employee selection, or as a performance evaluation scale.

The theoretical basis of the instrument is several old and sometimes obscure personality theories, but it is not clear from the manual exactly how these theories guided the construction of the BEST. Theorists mentioned include Adler, Jung, Allport, Marston,

and Herrmann. Of these, a reference is given only for Marston. Other references are to such popular publications as *McCall's, Redbook,* and *U.S. News and World Report.* There is no mention of any recent research in personality, and, in particular, no mention of any of the recent research based on the widely accepted Big Five model of personality. Yet the dates of publication of the manual and test materials range from 1989 to 1991.

After a review of these theories, the author wrote and selected items, based on judgment rather than item analysis, that he believed measure four basic personality types. The first type, the Bold Personality, is said to be adventure- and power-seeking. The second type is Expressive, a type with much in common with the high end of the Extroversion trait in the Big Five model. The third is the Sympathetic type, which seems similar to the high end of the Agreeableness trait in the Big Five. The fourth type is called Technical; this type seems similar to the high end of the Conscientiousness trait in the Big Five. The BEST Instrument is said to define a typology, but in actuality it appears to measure four traits on continuous scales.

My BEST Profile consists of 32 items, divided into two sections. The "Word Association" section consists of 17 items requiring the test taker to select the one of four words that "best fits your behavior style." The "Situation Analysis" section has 15 multiple-response items with stems like "When I am under pressure, I feel" (p. 2) followed by four adjectives.

SCORING AND INTERPRETATION. The manual presents clear and detailed instructions for administering the instrument, including instructions for helping the test taker through the self-scoring process. Based on these instructions, each test taker plots his or her 4-point profile, with each point representing one of the four basic personality types. According to the manual, most people are characterized by a mix of the four types. However, a score of 15 or more on any type scale is said to indicate that "your behaviors are most likely dominated by that type" (p. 1).

The My BEST Profile Interpretation presents characteristics, strengths, and developmental needs of each of the four personality types. For example, it is said that the Bold personality types need to learn to be sensitive to the needs of other people, and Expressive types may tend to delegate too much and may be overly optimistic.

The same instrument is interpreted in slightly different ways for a variety of other developmental purposes. The My BEST Leadership application describes the test taker's leadership style as suggested by his or her personality profile. The Our BEST Team application describes the profile of a work team, based on average scores of its members; and this information is used to deduce at what sort of tasks the team will excel. There is another application that purports to describe the oral presentation style of the individual. In the PEP Pre-Evaluation application, the supervisor fills out the BEST Instrument on both himself or herself and the subordinate to be evaluated, in an attempt to understand the similarities and differences in their personalities. In the Working With My Boss application, one uses the instrument to describe his or her boss, with a view to understanding and improving their relationship. And there are several other applications of this sort.

RELIABILITY. Coefficient alpha reliabilities are presented, but it is not clear on what sample these are based. These values are high, however, ranging from .86 for the Sympathetic Personality Type to .97 for the Technical Personality Type. Apparently only one form of this instrument exists, so no parallel forms reliabilities are presented. There are also no test-retest reliability estimates. Hence, reliability information is quite limited.

VALIDITY. No criterion-related validity data are presented. More surprisingly, basic data related to construct validity are not presented. For example, the correlations among the four scales are not provided, nor are the results of any factor analyses (either at the scale or item level). No correlations with other personality scales are reported, so the reader has no empirical evidence indicating how these four scales relate to established personality inventories and constructs.

The manual states (pp. 12–13) that the BEST was compared rationally *on a content basis* to nine other instruments "using a similar research base" (p. 12). The conclusion was: "While differences exist, one can see the similar personality typing used in each of these instruments" (p. 13). Not many informed people would accept this as evidence of content or construct validity.

The manual states that face validity was assessed by asking test takers to rate their perceptions of the BEST's accuracy, a highly dubious procedure. In previous studies, it has been found that such accuracy ratings are high even if all participants are given exactly the same personality descriptions. The author found that 76% of test takers rated the BEST as accurate. But in any event, face validity is of marginal importance.

The following quotation illustrates the flavor of the section in the manual on construct validity:

> In determining construct validity, several methods were used.
> The four BEST personality types were described to six seminar presenters who had knowledge of personality types. They were successful in selecting descriptive words and statements in the four personality categories. (p. 12)

It is hard to give much credibility to such "construct validity evidence." Another form of construct validity evidence is the following:

> [T]he author and assistants have observed the actions of others in various situations related to the BEST system since 1984. These recorded observations confirm the construct validity of the BEST system. (p. 12)

Here we have a testimonial by the author and his associates presented as evidence of construct validity.

SUMMARY. Obviously, the scientific foundations of the BEST are weak. Its theoretical basis is unclear and obscure; in constructing the BEST, the author apparently completely ignored the large volume of recent high quality personality research and theory in the scientific literature. Only very limited information is presented on reliability, and essentially no validity evidence is presented.

On the positive side, the BEST is specifically not advocated for use in personnel selection, performance appraisal, or promotion decisions; it is recommended only for use in developmental activities. One of its purposes may be said to be the stimulation of reflection and thought about the role of personality in work settings, and it may achieve this objective. (Unfortunately, it is presented as providing "understanding," rather than just stimulating thought.)

What about alternatives to the BEST? The instrument most commonly used for these purposes is the Myers-Briggs Type Indicator (T4:1702), which does have a much more extensive research base than does the BEST. However, this reviewer knows of no validity studies conducted on the Myers-Briggs specifically for developmental and self-insight uses. However, if one feels compelled to use a personality measure for developmental purposes, the Myers-Briggs would probably be a better choice than the BEST. In the judgment of this reviewer, though, one of the newer instruments based on the Big Five model of personality would be far better than either.

Booker Profiles in Mathematics: Numeration and Computation.

Purpose: "Designed to pinpoint strengths and weaknesses in basic mathematical knowledge."
Population: Ages 7–16.
Publication Date: 1994.
Scores, 2: Numeration and Computation.
Administration: Individual.
Price Data: Available from publisher.
Time: (45) minutes.
Author: George Booker.
Publisher: Australian Council for Educational Research Ltd. [Australia].

Review of the Booker Profiles in Mathematics: Numeration and Computation by RICHARD C. PUGH, Professor of Educationand Director of Education Technology Services, Indiana University, Bloomington, IN:

The Booker Profiles in Mathematics: Numeration and Computation consists of two test components, Numeration and Computation. The major purpose of the Numeration test component is to pinpoint and diagnose specific difficulties with number concepts and skills. The major purpose of the Computation test component is to pinpoint and diagnose specific difficulties with computational understanding and skills. The test components contain a series of test questions designed to identify strengths and weaknesses in basic mathematical knowledge. These criterion-referenced tests are intended to serve a wide range of examinees varying from early school learners through high school and college students. Among the stated general uses of the Profiles are (a) classroom assessments in primary and secondary schools, (b) analysis of individual student needs, (c) information for determining appropriate career or study options, and (d) diagnoses of learning disabilities. The tests are presented as useful in diagnosing why an individual may be experiencing mathematical difficulties and can be administered in follow-up to a referral of a student who has been observed as having classroom learning problems in mathematics.

The Profile kit of materials includes (a) an easel of test questions containing sections on Numeration and Computation; (b) a set of laminated blackline masters containing the Cover, Response, Record, and Summary sheets to be copied; and (c) a manual containing directions for administration, methods for recording the responses, and suggestions for interpretations and reteaching. Several manipu-

lative materials such as blocks and numeral cards, which are required for several items, are not included in the test materials and must be supplied by the user.

The development of the Profiles was based on experience gained from providing mathematics assistance to learners for a 15-year period at the Kelvin Grove College of Advanced Education, Queensland, Australia. Further development resulted from studying the learning difficulties in mathematics. More recent development took place in a variety of school and clinic settings including the Brisbane College of Advanced Education and the Institute of Learning In Mathematics and Language at Griffith University, Queensland. During 1990 and 1991, it is reported that seven groups of approximately 25 final year undergraduate students and teachers administered the initial instrument to an individual child or adolescent between 7 and 16 years of age, analyzed the information collected, and developed a profile of the respondent's strengths and weaknesses in mathematics. This profile was then incorporated into a program of reteaching that was designed for the individual's needs.

In 1992, information gained from the initial field trial was used to revise the tests. The cycle of field test followed by revision continued through several iterations. The manual reflects this development process in its sections on (a) profiling strengths and weaknesses, (b) describing likely difficulties, and (c) overcoming difficulties. The Summary of Profile Result Forms provide guidelines for interpretations.

TECHNICAL. The validity argument for the Profiles is dependent upon content validity. The domain of content for the Numeration and Computation tests defines the content validity for the Profiles. There is a clear statement of the universe of knowledge reported in the manual. Users, whose instructional setting is consistent with this universe of knowledge domain, will find the Profiles to be content valid.

The reliability of the results from the profiles was not discussed in the manual. It is apparent that judgment is involved in the interpretation of the Profiles. A consistency study would have been helpful.

CONTENT. The test questions are based on the underlying components of Numeration and Computation for whole numbers including problem solving. The Numeration component test questions are arranged into subsets identified as name, read, write, interpret, and process one-digit, two-digit, three-digit, four-digit, five-digit, six-digit, and seven-digit numbers. The Computation component test questions are arranged into four sections corresponding to the operations of addition, subtraction, multiplication, and division with each section classified into subsets that are labeled concept, basic number facts, algorithms, and problem solving. These subsets serve to define the domain used for constructing and selecting items. The tests are criterion-referenced as opposed to norm-referenced. There is a complete absence of any norms for comparison of scores with a distribution of scores. Rather, the scoring, which is a compilation of the proportion of errors across the various content categories, reflects the level of competence in each test subset of the domain. The domain definitions appear to be defined adequately so that users can judge the relation of the items to the subsets of the domain they represent. The number of items in each of the Numeration and Computation sections and subsets are reported in the manual. They vary from as few as three items for the Computation concept and problem solving subsets to as many as 30 for the Computation basic facts and algorithm subsets for addition, subtraction, multiplication, and division.

ADMINISTRATION. The manual gives the rationale for the test and states very clearly the recommended uses of the test. The manual includes directions for test administration in a clear manner. The easel format provides for an individually administered test setting and is illustrated in the manual. Although the amount of time required to administer the Profiles varies somewhat, it is reported that 45 minutes is usually sufficient to present as many questions as needed to give a comprehensive report on the Numeration knowledge and understanding and approximately 45 more minutes to give a comprehensive report on Computation knowledge and understanding. It is estimated that an additional 10–15 minutes will be needed to prepare a summary sheet for either the Numeration or Computation summary sheet. Additionally the manual recommends that no more than one hour of testing be undertaken at any single sitting.

SCORING. For both Numeration and Computation, the major purpose is to generate information on those aspects of knowledge that are found to be causing difficulties in test responses. On a Summary of Profile Results sheet, incorrect answers are marked and used twice in the preparation of a profile by totaling the number of errors across rows and columns; that is, (1) across each aspect of Numeration or Computation and (2) across the particular

number range. An indication of strengths and weaknesses comes from the Summary of Profile Results sheet by reviewing row and column totals. Several common profiles are described in the manual to assist the test user in interpreting results. Whether sufficient detail and clarity to maximize the accuracy of interpretation is provided in the manual is not clear. Experience with the use of the Profiles appears to be associated with obtaining dependable and accurate results. The experience gained by the test developers over a considerable length of time is well integrated into their examples of profile interpretations. Whether a new user will be as successful as the original developers in interpreting Summary of Profile Results sheets is an open question.

SUMMARY. The Booker Profiles in Mathematics: Numeration and Computation was created to serve as a diagnostic instrument for individuals who experience difficulty in learning mathematics. The kit for the Profiles is very attractive and appears to be very useful for the stated purpose. Technically, the Profiles are criterion referenced and are defined by the knowledge domain of their content. The potential user is advised to compare actual test content to their objectives and instruction and if they are found consistent to consider using the Profiles for their stated purpose.

Review of the Booker Profiles in Mathematics: Numeration and Computation by JAMES P. VAN HANEGHAN, Associate Professor of Behavioral Studies and Educational Technology, College of Education, University of South Alabama, Mobile, AL:

The Booker Profiles in Mathematics: Numeration and Computation (BPMNC) is a diagnostic assessment of number concepts and arithmetic operations with whole numbers of one to seven digits. The instrument is constructed to help design instruction, to diagnose learning difficulties, or to be part of portfolio assessment.

According to the manual, the test can be used for classroom assessments, analysis of student needs, assistance in choosing career paths, and the diagnosis of learning disabilities. The age range suggested for using the test is early elementary students through adults. The suggested range of uses and ages seems overly broad and may create problems in using the test. The manual focuses on test administration, difficulties students might have in these areas, and suggested teaching activities for remediation. The authors leave it up to the test user to link test information to curricula, job characteristics, or other criteria. For example, there is no information in the manual on what patterns of errors would be diagnostic of a learning disability in mathematics. One might be able to use the information from the test to support inferences from other assessments, but there are no data to support claims that the test can diagnose a learning disability in mathematics. Perhaps the most reasonable use of the test based on the test items and the score sheets is as a tool for determining the course of action for remediating students who have been exposed to but have not learned numeration and computation concepts. This was the purpose for developing the test and its main use in Australia where it was constructed.

The test is given individually, and items are presented using an easel that includes the testers' scripts, questions to the student, and hints about coding strategies, affect, and other qualitative information on one side and information presented to the student on the other side. Also included with the test are the manual and scoring masters. Not included, but also needed, are counters, base-ten materials, and numbers written on index cards.

The easel is nicely designed, especially the hints for coding qualitative information. As will be noted below, BPMNC interpretation requires clinical judgment and the hints help make such judgments easier. Although it is likely that most users will have access to manipulatives, the inclusion of manipulatives in the test kit would be more convenient.

Assessments can be made of each area (Numeration and Computation) or both can be assessed. The Numeration test examines the following concepts: alternate representations of number, place value, sequencing, comparison, counting, rounding, and exponents. The computation test examines: conceptual understanding (represent an operation concretely), times recall of basic facts (e.g., 2 + 2), algorithms (e.g., borrowing across zero), and problem solving (word problems).

The starting point for the assessment depends on the history of the student and clinical judgment. For example, with older children and adults, the starting point for Numeration may be at 2 or 3 digit numbers, whereas for younger children one might start at the beginning. The manual does not give specific basal or ceiling rules. It notes that even if a child makes many errors in numeration, it may be worth continuing to learn the basis for the errors. Aside from the general heuristics, the starting and

stopping point chosen is largely a clinical judgment. This degree of flexibility allows the user to adapt the test for different levels and purposes, but it introduces dependence on tester judgment that the appropriate items have been answered.

Most of the items on the test seem to have reasonable face and content validity. However, in some areas, items could be added or changed. For example, word problems are included, but only a few basic types. There is only one item per operation asking students to represent an operation concretely. Only one item at a particular digit size is used to assess rounding. Additionally, the word problems may be too difficult computationally for younger school-age children who may be able to understand the problem conceptually, but have not acquired the algorithmic skill to carry out the computation efficiently with larger numbers.

There are a few items that could be potentially confusing. For example, in the division section, students are asked to make up a division problem for a picture where five children are playing with blocks. The blocks are scattered all over the picture and the student could easily become distracted counting the blocks in the picture or searching for patterns in the picture. A division question where the student is asked to represent a problem concretely could also serve as source of confusion. It is worded, "Five children have enough money to buy 15 apples. When they share them out, how many will each child get?" The problem never states that the children bought the apples, and uses too many pronouns. Although it is probable that children might be able to pick out key words and solve the problem, it may present difficulties irrelevant to the child's ability to represent division concretely. This would be especially true for poorer students who will probably be the most likely to take the test.

Scores are the number of errors students made on problems of particular types. The scores are complemented by clinical information gained from comments about student work placed on the score sheets. For example, for the test of basic facts, the types of strategies and degree of confidence expressed by a student is recorded. The combination of clinical information and error patterns then serve as the basis for making judgments.

Although there is evidence in the manual of content validity, virtually no psychometric reliability and validity evidence is presented in the manual. The author undertook a reasonable rationale task analysis and solicited expert advice in revising and updating the test to establish content validity. Nevertheless, other types of reliability and validity of this tool are important. Questions such as whether testers would draw similar conclusions about the strengths and weaknesses of a student based on the data drawn from the BPMNC, and whether the BPMNC scores correlate with other tests of computation and numeration are important to answer.

Two distinguishing features of the BPMNC in its favor are the broad coverage provided and the clinical information that can be gained by looking at strategies, confidence, and other nonquantitative factors. However, more work needs to be done to show that information can be interpreted in light of some of the suggested uses. Only then will the information gained from the test have utility beyond what can be learned from teacher-made tests, assignments, and other diagnostic tests that are easier to administer.

[39]
Brief Test of Head Injury.

Purpose: Designed to provide information about cognitive, linguistic, and communicative abilities of patients with severe head trauma.
Population: Acute and long-term head-injured adults.
Publication Dates: 1989–1991.
Acronym: BTHI.
Scores, 8: Orientation/Attention, Following Commands, Linguistic Organization, Reading Comprehension, Naming, Memory, Visual-Spatial Skills, Total.
Administration: Individual.
Price Data, 1991: $148.98 per complete kit including 24 record forms, manual ('91, 85 pages), manipulatives package, stimulus cards and letter board, and carrying case; $24 per 24 record forms; $9.99 per manipulatives package; $45 per stimulus cards and letter board; $24.99 per carrying case; $45 per manual.
Time: (25–30) minutes.
Authors: Nancy Helm-Estabrooks and Gillian Hotz.
Publisher: The Riverside Publishing Company.

Review of the Brief Test of Head Injury by DEBORAH D. ROMAN, Director, Neuropsychology Laboratory, and Assistant Professor, Departments of Physical Medicine and Rehabilitation and Neurosurgery, University of Minnesota, Minneapolis, MN:

The Brief Test of Head Injury (BTHI) is designed to assess patients with severe head injuries. It can be used to determine brain injury severity, to gauge recovery, and as a first step in planning more in-depth assessments and rehabilitation treatment. The BTHI can be administered in 25 to 30 minutes

at bedside. The authors note that the test can be used with patients who are physically limited or unable to vocalize.

The BTHI consists of 50 items divided into seven clusters: (a) Orientation/Attention, (b) Following Commands, (c) Linguistic Organization, (d) Reading Comprehension, (e) Naming, (f) Memory, and (g) Visuo-Spatial Skills. Results yield seven cluster scores as well as a total raw score that is converted into a standard score and percentile rank, used to reach a severity rating.

Items are scored along three dimensions: (a) Response Modality (linguistic or gestural), (b) Communication Quality (on a scale of 0 to 3), and (c) Perseveration (the presence or absence of a perseverative response). Because scores are based in part on a judgment as to the quality of the response, the scoring system is somewhat subjective and would require practice to master. The authors report high agreement among raters who carefully study the manual's scoring criteria, but provide no data on interrater reliability.

The final version of the test was standardized on a sample of 265 head injury patients undergoing treatment in acute or rehabilitative units in 25 sites in the U.S. and Canada. Thirty-two normal controls were also tested, but were not included in the normative data. Subjects ranged in age from 10 to 89, with a median age of 28. Over two thirds of the sample were males. They were tested between zero and more than 56 days after injury. About 60% were tested within 2 months of injury. Educational and vocational sample characteristics are provided in the manual.

BTHI Total score and the seven cluster scores are converted into standard scores and percentile ranks, with the head injury standardization sample serving as the normative comparison group. Severity scores, derived from raw total scores, range from severe (a raw score of 0 to 17) to borderline (a raw score of 43 to 48).

Reliability was assessed using test-retest (mean retest time is 19.1 days) and by determining interitem consistency. A *t*-test analysis comparing initial and follow-up testings of patients showed a significant improvement in scores from the first to the second administration. The authors interpreted this as evidence of functional recovery over time, and did not feel that the inconsistent performance constituted inadequate reliability. Interitem reliability coefficients (Cronbach's alpha) ranged from .65 to .86 for cluster raw and standard scores, and was .95 for

BTHI Total raw or Total standard scores. The standard error of measurement for the BTHI Total raw score was 2.7.

Predictive validity was examined using discriminate analysis. A cutoff score of 43 correctly classified 100% of the 32 normals and 85% of 61 head-injured patients (injured within 1 month of testing). But only 64% of a second head-injury sample, tested within 7 days of injury, were correctly classified. It was assumed that this sample had milder injuries, permitting earlier testing.

In a study designed to assess concurrent validity, BTHI scores were compared to scores on the Glasgow Coma Scale (GCS) and the Rancho Los Amigos Levels of Cognitive Functioning (Rancho). First, the 53 head-injury subjects were divided into severe, moderate, and mild groups using GCS severity ratings. Significance tests based on BTHI Total scores were significant for the severe versus mild groups and for the mild versus moderate groups, but not for the moderate versus severe groups. These findings replicated for the larger standardization group ($n = 153$). Comparisons of Rancho and BTHI scores ($n = 193$) were also significant for most groups (except for Rancho Levels VI and V, which approached statistical significance). The BTHI was positively correlated with the Rancho (.75) and the GCS (.29).

In conclusion, the BTHI is a useful screening tool in assessing patients with severe head injury. It briefly evaluates several cognitive domains commonly affected by head injury. The items are relatively easy, and each domain is not assessed in great detail. The test was designed to detect gross deficits and is not appropriate for use in illuminating subtle or mild impairments. Accordingly, it should be used as a screening instrument and should not be considered a conclusive, comprehensive measure of brain functioning. Most appropriately, it can be used in conjunction with other inventories such as the GCS (Teasdale & Jenett, 1974), Galveston Orientation and Amnesia Test (GOAT; Leun, O'Donnell, & Grossman, 1979), and Rancho (Hogan, 1982).

The test offers adequate evidence of predictive and concurrent validity, with respect to Total raw scores. However, reliability has not been firmly established. Momentary fluctuations in attention or wakefulness could have a significant affect on test scores, particularly attention, orientation, and memory items. As such, further studies, reevaluating the same patients over a shorter period of time, would be desirable. Also, given the somewhat subjective nature of the scoring system, the authors should provide data on interrater reliability.

REVIEWER'S REFERENCES

Teasdale, G., & Jenett, B. (1974). Assessment of coma and impaired consciousness: A practical scale. *Lancet, 2,* 81–84.

Leun, H. S., O'Donnell, V. M., & Grossman, R. G. (1979). The Galveston Orientation and Amnesia Test: A practical scale to assess cognition after head injury. *Journal of Nervous and Mental Disorders, 167,* 675–684.

Hagen, C. (1982). Language cognitive disorganization following closed head injury: A conceptualization. In L. E. Trexler (Ed.), Cognitive rehabilitation: Conceptualization and intervention (pp. 131–151). New York: Plenum Press.

Review of the Brief Test of Head Injury by MICHAEL LEE RUSSELL, Director, Neuropsychology Fellowship, Tripler Regional Medical Center, Honolulu, HI:

Professionals working in acute care and inpatient rehabilitation settings have need for a standardized instrument that can perform rapid bedside cognitive screening of acute head injury and stroke. Most such tests are essentially efforts to standardize or elaborate upon a behavioral neurologists' clinical examination. The most widely used instrument for this purpose today is the Neurocognitive Status Examination (COGNISTAT; Northern California Neurobehavioral Group, 1995). The Brief Test of Head Injury (BTHI) is designed for a similar population, but offers some unique features. The BTHI is designed as a bedside screening tool for the rapid assessment of head-injured patients with scores between III and VIII on the Ranchos Los Amigos Levels of Cognitive Functioning (Malkmus, Booth, & Kodimer, 1980). An advantage of the BTHI is that, unlike the COGNISTAT, it can be used with intubated patients who cannot speak.

The principal author of the BTHI, Nancy Helm-Estabrooks, is a speech-language pathologist, and the manual states that the BTHI was modeled on an earlier test by the same author, the Boston Assessment of Severe Aphasia (Helm-Estabrooks, Ramsburger, Morgan, & Nicholas, 1989; 12:52). The BTHI assesses many of the same domains as the COGNISTAT, but with heavier weighting to language functions, and no formal coverage of Executive function. Seven cognitive functions (clusters) are addressed by the BTHI: (a) Orientation/Attention, (b) Following Commands, (c) Linguistic Organization, (d) Reading Comprehension, (e) Naming, (f) Memory, and (g) Visual-Spatial Skills.

This edition of the BTHI was normed on 273 head-injured patients and 32 noninjured subjects, at several sites in the United States and Canada. The clinical sample is problematic: It includes patients ranging in age from 10 to 89 years old, of mixed gender, with twice as many males as females. Further, the BTHI was administered anywhere from the day of injury to more than 18 months post injury. It would have been desirable to see some breakdown of scores by sex, age, or education, and acute versus long term injury; however, the author states "the BTHI norms group was not divided into subgroups by any variables … because none of these by themselves are meaningful for grouping patients" (manual, p. 53). It strains credibility to argue that a 10-year-old and 89-year-old are essentially equivalent subjects for any cognitive test. It is also well established that acute and long term patients perform quite differently on such measures. An even more important stratification of data would be with the noninjured sample, to address meaningfully the normal performance of a noninjured patients at different levels of development (i.e., a 10-year-old) on this test. Unfortunately, the nonclinical sample is far too small for any such analysis. The authors' assertion that these variables are unimportant hardly needs to be debated, as most psychological tests stratify by age, education, and gender for good reason.

The author estimates the BTHI administration time to be 25 to 30 minutes, which is probably accurate for a skilled administrator, although in initial practice it took us somewhat longer to give the entire instrument. The scoring system is also somewhat awkward, necessitated by the need to score for both linguistic or gestural responses. Both types of response are rated on a 5-point scale from *Refusal or Rejection* to *Fully Communicative Response*. Scoring of the Gestural component using such a fine gradient seemed particularly problematic. Unfortunately, interrater reliability of this method is not available.

The BTHI does not appear to be a particularly sensitive measure for certain groups. For example, 58% of the acutely injured sample were correctly classified by the suggested cutting score (which means 42% were not). Surprisingly, there is essentially no difference in the BTHI total scores between Moderate and Severe Head Injury (Mild = 35.2, Moderate = 28.8, Severe = 28.9), which is likely a product of the problematic normative sample—more of the mild to moderate head injuries likely came from the acute settings, more of the severe patients from long term rehabilitation settings, illustrating the danger of pooling such diverse data. Although the initial number of 273 patients in the normative sample sounds sufficient, the diversity of the sample causes problems whenever it is broken down.

That the BTHI items and clusters were clinically, rather than empirically, derived is clear from the high intercorrelation of the cluster scores: For example the Memory Scale correlates .74 with the Linguistic Organization Scale, indicating that either the BTHI's Memory scale is very dependent on linguistic organization, or the linguistic organization scale is very dependent on memory. The authors' factor analysis shows that the seven clusters are really accounted for by only two factors, the major of which appears to be auditory comprehension (p. 62).

The materials used in the test are of reasonable quality, and utilize many of the standard items seen in a typical noncommercial bedside interview (i.e., an eraser, a key, and quarters, dimes, nickels, and pennies for naming and multistep commands). There are two line drawings of common objects (as in the Boston Naming Test) and three photographs to name (as in the Famous Faces Test). The choice of Michael Jackson as one of these photos is perhaps somewhat unfortunate in that it dates from the 1980s and does not resemble the performer today. A picture arrangement task is much like that seen in the Wechsler Adult Intelligence Scale—Revised (WAIS-R). Little is unfamiliar, as the BTHI is composed of analogues of pieces of many common tests. As with any bedside screen, some of the subsections do seem inadequate in terms of number of items—perhaps the full 55 items of the Boston Naming Test is excessive, but a two-item version is equally likely to not be enough.

The BTHI is a short bedside screening instrument for patients suspected of head injury. In comparing the BTHI with its closest rival, the COGNISTAT, the BTHI requires more time, is harder to administer, and yields little additional information. Its normative sample is problematic. Further, its item content is too heavily weighted toward speech assessment to fully justify itself as a test of all aspects of cognitive function. It does have a unique advantage in that it is able to work with patients who are either expressively aphasic or intubated, and for that reason alone might warrant a place in a clinician's tool kit. It is hoped that future editions of this test refine its normative sample and include a larger noninjured standardization sample.

REVIEWER'S REFERENCES

Malkmus, D., Booth, B. J., & Kodimer, C. (1980). *Rehabilitation of the head injured adult: Comprehensive Cognitive Management.* Downey, CA: Professional Staff Association of Ranchos Los Amigos Hospital, Inc.

Helm-Estabrooks, N., Ramsburger, G., Morgan, A. R., & Nicholas, M. (1989). Boston Assessment of Severe Aphasia. Chicago: Riverside.

The Northern California Neurobehavioral Group. (1995). *Manual for COGNISTAT (The Neurobehavioral Cognitive Status Examination).* Fairfax, CA: Author.

[40]
California Achievement Tests, Fifth Edition.

Purpose: "Designed to measure achievement in the basic skills taught in schools throughout the nation."

Population: Grades K.0–K.9, K.6–1.6, 1.6–2.2, 1.6–3.2, 2.6–4.2, 3.6–5.2, 4.6–6.2, 5.6–7.2, 6.6–8.2, 7.6–9.2, 8.6–10.2, 9.6–11.2, 10.6–12.9.

Publication Dates: 1957–1993.

Acronym: CAT/5.

Administration: Group.

Levels: 13 overlapping levels.

Forms, 4: Complete Battery A, B; Survey A, B.

Price Data, 1994: $19.20 per 30 locator tests with directions and answer sheets (specify grades 1–6 or grades 6–12); $32.15 per set of 3 hand-scoring stencils for complete and basic skills batteries for use with CompuScan answer sheets (specify Level 14, 15, 16, 17, 18, 19, 20, or 21/22); $21.50 per set of 2 hand-scoring stencils for Survey tests for use with CompuScan answer sheets (specify Level 14, 15, 16, 17, 18, 19, 20, or 21/22); $24.50 per 50 CompuScan answer sheets, Levels 14–21/22 (specify Complete Battery or Survey tests); $18 per 25 SCOREZE answer sheets (specify form, subject area, and indicate Level 14–21/22); $612 per 1,250 continuous form transoptic answer sheets (specify form and indicate Level 14–21/22); $1.20 per class record sheet for hand-recording; $30 per 100 student diagnostic profiles (specify Level); $20.70 per test coordinator's handbook; $12.45 per technical bulletin; $19.50 per Class Management Guide; $8.85 per Multi-Level Norms book (specify Fall, Winter, or Spring); scoring service available from publisher.

Author: CTB Macmillan/McGraw-Hill.

Publisher: CTB Macmillan/McGraw-Hill

a) LEVEL K.

Population: Grades K.0–K.9.

Scores, 5: Reading (Visual Recognition, Sound Recognition, Vocabulary, Comprehension), Mathematics Concepts and Applications.

Price Data: $7.20 per 30 practice tests; $8.85 per Form A Complete Battery Examiner's Manual; $51.90 per 30 Form A Complete Battery hand-scorable booklets including examiner's manual; $82.80 per 30 Form A Complete Battery reflective machine-scorable booklets including examiner's manual; $84.30 per 30 Form A Complete Battery transoptic booklets including examiner's manual.

Time: (87) minutes.

b) LEVEL 10.

Population: Grades K.6–1.6.

Scores, 4: Reading (Word Analysis, Vocabulary, Comprehension), Mathematics Concepts and Applications.

Price Data: $7.20 per 30 practice tests; $8.85 per Complete Battery examiner's manual (select Form) ('93, 45 pages); $51.90 per 30 Form A Complete Battery hand-scorable booklets including examiner's

manual; $82.80 per 30 Complete Battery reflective machine-scorable booklets including examiner's manual (select Form); $84.30 per 30 Complete Battery transoptic machine-scorable booklets including examiner's manual (select Form).

Time: (88) minutes.

c) LEVEL II.

Population: Grades 1.6–2.2.

Scores, 9: Reading (Word Analysis, Vocabulary, Comprehension), Language (Mechanics, Expression), Mathematics (Computation, Concepts and Applications), Science, Social Studies.

Price Data: $7.50 per 30 practice tests; $8.85 per Complete Battery examiner's manual ('93, 61 pages); $58.50 per 30 Complete Battery Form A hand-scorable booklets including examiner's manual; $90.30 per 30 Complete Battery reflective machine-scorable booklets including examiner's manual (select Form); $91.20 per 30 Complete Battery transoptic machine-scorable booklets (select Form).

Time: (217) minutes.

d) LEVEL 12.

Population: Grades 1.6–3.2.

Scores, 10: Reading (Word Analysis, Vocabulary, Comprehension), Spelling, Language (Mechanics, Expression), Mathematics (Computation, Concepts and Applications), Science, Social Studies.

Price Data: $8.40 per 30 practice tests; $8.85 per examiner's manual ('93, 60 pages) (select Complete Battery, Form A or B, or Survey Form A); $58.50 per 30 Complete Battery Form A hand-scorable booklets including examiner's manual; $90.30 per 30 Complete Battery reflective machine-scorable booklets including examiner's manual (select Form A or B); $82.50 per 30 Survey Form A reflective machine-scorable booklets including examiner's manual; $91.20 per 30 Complete Battery transoptic machine-scorable booklets including examiner's manual (select Form A or B); $84 per 30 Survey Form A transoptic machine-scorable booklets including examiner's manual.

Time: (292) minutes.

e) LEVEL 13.

Population: Grades 2.6–4.2.

Scores, 10: Same as *d* above.

Price Data: Same as *d* above.

Time: (330) minutes.

f) LEVEL 14.

Population: Grades 3.6–5.2.

Scores, 10: Reading (Vocabulary, Comprehension), Spelling, Language (Mechanics, Expression), Mathematics (Computation, Concepts and Applications), Study Skills, Science, Social Studies.

Price Data: $9.60 per 30 practice tests; $78.60 per 30 Complete Battery reusable test booklets (select Form A or B); $76.20 per 30 Survey Form A reusable test booklets; $8.85 per examiner's manual for Levels

14–21/22 ('93, 35 pages) (select Complete Battery Form A and B or Survey).

Time: (330) minutes.

g) LEVEL 15.

Population: Grades 4.6–6.2.

Scores, 10: Same as *f* above.

Price Data: Same as *f* above.

Time: Same as *f* above.

h) LEVEL 16.

Population: Grades 5.6–7.2.

Scores, 10: Same as *f* above.

Price Data: Same as *f* above.

Time: Same as *f* above.

i) LEVEL 17.

Population: Grades 6.6–8.2.

Scores, 10: Same as *f* above.

Price Data: Same as *f* above but without practice tests.

Time: Same as *f* above.

j) LEVEL 18.

Population: Grades 7.6–9.2.

Scores, 10: Same as *f* above.

Price Data: Same as *i* above.

Time: Same as *f* above.

k) LEVEL 19.

Population: Grades 8.6–10.2.

Scores, 10: Same as *f* above.

Price Data: Same as *i* above.

Time: Same as *f* above.

l) LEVEL 20.

Population: Grades 9.6–11.2.

Scores, 10: Same as *f* above.

Price Data: Same as *i* above.

Time: Same as *f* above.

m) LEVEL 21/22.

Population: Grades 10.6–12.9.

Scores, 10: Same as *f* above.

Price Data: Same as *i* above.

Time: Same as *f* above.

Cross References: See T4:352 (52 references); for reviews by Peter W. Airasian and James L. Wardrop of the 1985 edition, see 10:41 (68 references); for reviews by Bruce G. Rogers and Victor L. Willson of the 1978 edition, see 9:180 (19 references); see also T3:344 (68 references); for reviews by Miriam M. Bryan and Frank Womer of the 1970 edition, see 8:10 (33 references); for reviews by Jack C. Merwin and Robert D. North of the 1957 edition, see 6:3 (19 references); for a review by Charles O. Neidt, see 5:2 (10 references); for reviews by Warren G. Findley, Alvin W. Schindler, and J. Harlan Shores of the 1950 edition, see 4:2 (8 references); for a review by Paul A. Witty of the 1943 edition, see 2:1193 (1 reference); for a review by D. Welty Lefever and an excerpted review by E. L. Abell, see 7:876. For reviews of subtests, see 8:45 (2 reviews), 8:257 (1 review), 8:719 (2 reviews), see 6:251 (1 review), 5:177 (2 reviews), 5:468 (1 review), 4:151 (2 reviews), 4:411 (1 review), 4:530 (2 reviews, 1 excerpt), 2:1292 (2 reviews), 2:1459 (2 reviews), 2:1563 (1 review), 1:893 (1 review), and 1:1110 (2 reviews).

TEST REFERENCES

1. Scott-Jones, D. (1987). Mother-as-teacher in the families of high- and low-achieving low-income Black first-graders. *Journal of Negro Education, 56,* 21–34.

2. Scruggs, T. E., Mastropieri, M. A., McLoone, B. B., Levin, J. R., & Morrison, C. R. (1987). Mnemonic facilitation of learning disabled students' memory for expository prose. *Journal of Educational Psychology, 79,* 27–34.

3. Haynes, N. M., Comer, J. P., & Hamilton-Lee, Muriel. (1988). The school development program: A model for school improvement. *Journal of Negro Education, 57,* 11–21.

4. Nicholsonne, M. R. (1988). Strides toward excellence: The Harford Heights model. *Journal of Negro Education, 57,* 282–291.

5. Sizemore, B. A. (1988). The Madison elementary school: A turnaround case. *Journal of Negro Education, 57,* 243–266.

6. Young, R., Jr. (1988). A process for developing more effective urban schools: A case study of Stowe middle school. *Journal of Negro Education, 57,* 307–334.

7. Baker, L. (1989). Developmental change in readers' responses to unknown words. *Journal of Reading Behavior, 21,* 241-260.

8. Baker, L., & Zimlin, L. (1989). Instructional effects on children's use of two levels of standards of evaluating their comprehension. *Journal of Educational Psychology, 81,* 340–346.

9. Bauman, K. E., Koch, G. G., & Fisher, L. A. (1989). Family cigarette smoking and test performance by adolescents. *Health Psychology, 8,* 97–105.

10. Bean, R. M., & Wilson, R. M. (1989). Using closed captioned television to teach reading to adults. *Reading Research and Instruction, 28,* 27–37.

11. Ebmeier, H., & Schmulbach, S. (1989). An examination of the selection practices used in the Talent Search Program. *Gifted Child Quarterly, 33,* 134–141.

12. Graham, S., & Harris, K. R. (1989). Components analysis of cognitive strategy instruction: Effects on learning disabled students' compositions and self-efficacy. *Journal of Educational Psychology, 81,* 353–361.

13. Jenkins, J. R., Matlock, B., & Slocum, T. A. (1989). Two approaches to vocabulary instruction: The teaching of individual word meanings and practice in deriving word meaning from context. *Reading Research Quarterly, 24,* 215-235.

14. Mantzicopoulos, D., Morrison, D. C., Hinshaw, S. P., & Carte, E. T. (1989). Nonpromotion in kindergarten: The role of cognitive, perceptual, visual-motor, behavioral, achievement, socioeconomic, and demographic characteristics. *American Educational Research Journal, 26,* 107-121.

15. Reuman, D. A. (1989). How social comparison mediates the relation between ability-grouping practices and students' achievement expectancies in mathematics. *Journal of Educational Psychology, 81,* 178–189.

16. Reutzel, D. R., Oda, L. K., & Moore, B. H. (1989). Developing print awareness: The effect of three instructional approaches on kindergartners' print awareness, reading readiness and word reading. *Journal of Reading Behavior, 21,* 197-217.

17. Scarborough, H. S. (1989). Prediction of reading disability from familial and individual differences. *Journal of Educational Psychology, 81,* 101–108.

18. Schunk, D. H., & Hanson, A. R. (1989). Self-modeling and children's cognitive skill learning. *Journal of Educational Psychology, 81,* 155–163.

19. Aydelott, S. T. (1990). The status of secondary reading programs in American-sponsored overseas schools. *Journal of Reading, 34,* 170-173.

20. Bauer, R. H., & Peller-Porth, V. (1990). The effect of increased incentive on free recall by learning-disabled and nondisabled children. *The Journal of General Psychology, 117,* 447-462.

21. Clements, D. H. (1990). Metacomponential development in a logo programming environment. *Journal of Educational Psychology, 82,* 141–149.

22. Lynch, S., & Mills, C. J. (1990). The Skills Reinforcement Project (SRP): An academic program for high potential minority youth. *Journal for the Education of the Gifted, 13,* 364–379.

23. Mills, J. R., & Jackson, N. E. (1990). Predictive significance of early giftedness: The case of precocious reading. *Journal of Educational Psychology, 82,* 410–419.

24. Morrow, L. M., O'Connor, E. M., & Smith, J. K. (1990). Effects of a story reading program on the literacy development of at-risk kindergarten children. *Journal of Reading Behavior, 22,* 255-275.

25. Nelson-LeGall, S., Kratzer, L., Jones, E., & DeCooke, P. (1990). Children's self-assessment of performance and task-related help seeking. *Journal of Experimental Child Psychology, 49,* 245-263.

26. Slavin, R. E., Madden, N. A., Kurweit, N. L., Livermon, B. J., & Dolan, L. (1990). Success for all: First-year outcomes of a comprehensive plan for reforming urban education. *American Educational Research Journal, 27,* 255-278.

27. Sowell, E. J., Zeigler, A. J., Bergwall, L., & Cartwright, R. M. (1990). Identification and description of mathematically gifted students: A review of empirical research. *Gifted Child Quarterly, 34,* 147-154.

28. Van Haneghan, J. P. (1990). Third and fifth graders use of multiple standards of evaluation to detect errors in word problems. *Journal of Educational Psychology, 82,* 352–358.

29. Zigmond, N., & Baker, J. (1990). Mainstream experiences for learning disabled students (Project MELD): Preliminary report. *Exceptional Children, 57,* 176-185.

30. Zinar, S. (1990). Fifth-graders' recall of propositional content and causal relationships from expository prose. *Journal of Reading Behavior, 22,* 181-199.

31. Bauer, R. H., & Newman, D. R. (1991). Allocation of study time and recall by learning disabled and nondisabled children of different ages. *Journal of Experimental Child Psychology, 52,* 11-21.

32. Bean, R. M., Cooley, W. W., Eichelberger, T., Lazar, M. K., & Zigmond, N. (1991). In class or pullout: Effects of setting on the remedial reading program. *Journal of Reading Behavior, 23,* 445-464.

33. Clements, D. H. (1991). Enhancement of creativity in computer environments. *American Educational Research Journal, 28,* 173-187.

34. Gambrell, L. B., & Chasen, S. P. (1991). Explicit story structure instruction and the narrative writing of fourth- and fifth-grade below-average readers. *Reading Research and Instruction, 31*(1), 54-62.

35. Garcia, G. E. (1991). Factors influencing the English reading test performance of Spanish-speaking Hispanic children. *Reading Research Quarterly, 26,* 371-392.

36. Konopak, B. C., Williams, N. L., Granier, D. M., Aveh, S., & Wood, K. E. (1991). Elementary students' use of imagery in developing meaning in literary text. *Yearbook of National Reading Conference, 40,* 247-254.

37. Parker, R. I., Tindal, G., & Hasbrouck, J. (1991). Progress monitoring with objective measures of writing performance for students with mild disabilities. *Exceptional Children, 58,* 61-73.

38. Purcell-Gates, V., & Dahl, K. L. (1991). Low-SES children's success and failure at early literacy learning in skills-based classrooms. *Journal of Reading Behavior, 23,* 1-34.

39. Stevens, R. J., & Slavin, R. E. (1991). When cooperative learning improves the achievement of students with mild disabilities: A response to Taleyama-Sniezek. *Exceptional Children, 57,* 276-280.

40. Thorkildsen, T. A. (1991). Defining social goods and distributing them fairly: The development of conceptions of fair testing practices. *Child Development, 62,* 852–862.

41. Vaughn, V. L., Feldhusen, J. F., & Asher, J. W. (1991). Meta-analysis and review of research on pull-out programs in gifted education. *Gifted Child Quarterly, 35,* 92-98.

42. Watson, S. B. (1991). Cooperative learning and group educational modules: Effects on cognitive achievement of high school biology students. *Journal of Research in Science Teaching, 28,* 141-146.

43. Willerman, M., & MacHarg, R. A. (1991). The concept map as an advance organizer. *Journal of Research in Science Teaching, 28,* 705-711.

44. Williams, N. L., Konopak, B. C., Wood, K. D., & Avett, S. (1991). Middle school students' use of imagery in developing meaning in expository text. *Yearbook of National Reading Conference, 40,* 261-267.

45. Dowaliby, F. J. (1992). The effects of adjunct questions in prose for deaf and hearing students at different reading levels. *American Annals of the Deaf, 137,* 338-344.

46. DuPont, S. (1992). The effectiveness of creative drama as an instructional strategy to enhance the reading comprehension skills of fifth-grade remedial readers. *Reading Research and Instruction, 31*(3), 41-52.

47. Fitzgerald, J., & Stamm, C. (1992). Variation in writing conference influence on revision: Two cases. *Journal of Reading Behavior, 24,* 21-50.

48. Gallagher, S. A., & Johnson, E. S. (1992). The effect of time limits on performance of mental rotations by gifted adolescents. *Gifted Child Quarterly, 36,* 19-22.

49. Garrison, W., Dowaliby, F., & Long, G. (1992). Reading comprehension test item difficulty as a function of cognitive processing variables. *American Annals of the Deaf, 137,* 22-30.

50. Matthew, J. L., Golin, A. K., Moore, M. W., & Baker, C. (1992). Use of SOMPA in identification of gifted African-American children. *Journal for the Education of the Gifted, 15,* 344-356.

51. Truesdell, L. A., & Abramson, T. (1992). Academic behavior and grades of mainstreamed students with mild disabilities. *Exceptional Children, 58,* 392-398.

52. Alexander, C. L., Entwisle, D. R., & Dauber, S. L. (1993). First-grade classroom behavior: its short- and long-term consequences for school performance. *Child Development, 64,* 801-814.

53. Audette, R., Algozzine, R., & Warden, M. (1993). Mobility and school achievement. *Psychological Reports, 72,* 701-702.

54. Brantley, D. C., & Webster, R. E. (1993). Use of an independent group contingency management system in a regular classroom setting. *Psychology in the Schools, 30,* 60-66.

55. Camilli, G., Yomamoto, K., & Weing, M. (1993). Scale shrinkage in vertical equating. *Applied Psychological Measurement, 17,* 379-388.

56. Celano, M. P., & Geller, R. J. (1993). Learning, school, performance, and children with asthma: How much at risk? *Journal of Learning Disabilities, 26,* 23–32.

57. Feingold, A. (1993). Cognitive gender differences: A developmental perspective. *Sex Roles, 29,* 91-112.

58. Freeman, V. S., & Morss, J. (1993). Study habits and academic achievement among Asian students. *College Student Journal, 27,* 352-355.

59. Fuller, G. B., & Vance, B. (1993). Comparison of the Minnesota Percepto-Diagnostic Test—Revised and Bender-Gestalt in predicting achievement. *Psychology in the Schools, 30,* 220-226.

60. Graham, S., Schwartz, S. S., & MacArthur, C. A. (1993). Knowledge of writing and the composing process, attitude toward writing, and self-efficacy for students with and without learning disabilities. *Journal of Learning Disabilities, 26,* 237–249.

61. Hart, L. C. (1993). Some factors that impede or enhance performance in mathematical problem solving. *Journal for Research in Mathematics Education, 24,* 167-171.

62. Ialongo, N., Edelsohn, G., Werthamer-Larsson, L., Crockett, L., & Kellam, S. (1993). Are self-reported depressive symptoms in first-grade children developmentally transient phenomena? A further look. *Development and Psychopathology, 5,* 433-457.

63. Kusché, C. A., Cook, E. T., & Greenberg, M. T. (1993). Neuropsychological and cognitive functioning in children with anxiety, externalizing, and comorbid psychopathology. *Journal of Clinical Child Psychology, 22,* 172-195.

64. Lupkowski-Shoplik, A. E., & Assouline, S. G. (1993). Identifying mathematically talented elementary students: Using the lower level of the SSAT. *Gifted Child Quarterly, 37,* 118-123.

65. Lynch, S. J., & Mills, C. J. (1993). Identifying and preparing disadvantaged and minority youth for high-level academic achievement. *Contemporary Educational Psychology, 18,* 66-76.

66. May, D. C., & Kundert, D. K. (1993). Pre-first placements: How common and how informed? *Psychology in the Schools, 30,* 161-167.

67. McKeown, M. G. (1993). Creating effective definitions for young word learners. *Reading Research Quarterly, 28,* 17-31.

68. Miller, S. D., Adkins, T., & Hooper, M. L. (1993). Why teachers select specific literacy assignments and students' reactions to them. *Journal of Reading Behavior, 25,* 69-95.

69. Mouw, J. T., & Khanna, R. K. (1993). Prediction of academic success: A review of the literature and some recommendations. *College Student Journal, 27,* 328-336.

70. O'Connor, R. E., Jenkins, J. R., Cole, K. N., & Mills, P. E. (1993). Two approaches to reading instruction with children with disabilities: Does program design make a difference? *Exceptional Children, 59,* 312-323.

71. Speck, C., & Prideaux, D. (1993). Fundamentalist education and creation science. *Australian Journal of Education, 37,* 279-295.

72. Spencer, S. L., & Fitzgerald, J. (1993). Validity and structure, coherence, and quality measures in writing. *Journal of Reading Behavior, 25,* 209-231.

73. Stoddard, K., Valcante, G., Sindelar, P., O'Shea, L., & Algozzine, R. (1993). Increasing reading rate and comprehension: The effects of repeated readings, sentence segmentation, and intonation training. *Reading Research and Instruction, 32*(4), 53-65.

74. Stouthamer-Loeber, M., Loeber, R., Farrington, D. P., Zhang, Q., van Kammen, W., & Maguin, E. (1993). The double edge of protective and risk factors for delinquency: Interrelations and developmental patterns. *Development and Psychopathology, 5,* 683-701.

75. Vaughn, S., Schumm, J. S., & Gordon, J. (1993). Which motoric condition is most effective for teaching spelling to students with and without learning disabilities. *Journal of Learning Disabilities, 26,* 191–198.

76. Wyman, P. A., Cowen, E. L., Work, W. C., & Kerley, J. H. (1993). The role of children's future expectations in self-system functioning and adjustment to life stress: A prospective study of urban at-risk children. *Development and Psychopathology, 5,* 649-661.

77. Alexander, K. L., Entwisle, D. R., & Bedinger, S. D. (1994). When expectations work: Race and socioeconomic differences in school performance. *Social Psychology Quarterly, 57,* 283-299.

78. Bramlett, R. K. (1994). Implementing cooperative learning: A field study evaluating issues for school-based consultants. *Journal of School Psychology, 32,* 67-84.

79. Carr, M., & Kurtz-Costes, B. E. (1994). Is being smart everything? The influence of student achievement on teachers' perceptions. *British Journal of Educational Psychology, 64,* 263–276.

80. Cox, B. D. (1994). Children's use of mnemonic strategies: Variability in response to metamemory training. *The Journal of Genetic Psychology, 155,* 423-442.

81. Flynn, J. M., & Rahbar, M. H. (1994). Prevalence of reading failure in boys compared with girls. *Psychology in the Schools, 31,* 66-71.

82. Jones, M. G., & Carter, G. (1994). Verbal and nonverbal behavior of ability-grouped dyads. *Journal of Research in Science Teaching, 31,* 603–619.

83. Kellam, S. G., Rebok, G. W., Mayer, L. S., Ialongo, N., & Kalodner, C. R. (1994). Depressive symptoms over first grade and their response to a developmental epidemiologically based preventive trial aimed at improving achievement. *Development and Psychopathology, 6,* 463-481.

84. Maag, J. W., Irvin, D. M., Reid, R., & Vasa, S. F. (1994). Prevalence and predictors of substance use: A comparison between adolescents with and without learning disabilities. *Journal of Learning Disabilities, 27,* 223–234.

85. Meyer, L. A., Stahl, S. A., & Wardrop, J. L. (1994). Effects of reading storybooks aloud to children. *The Journal of Educational Research, 88,* 69–85.

86. Mills, C. J., Ablard, K. E., & Gustin, W. C. (1994). Academically talented students' achievement in a flexibly paced mathematics program. *Journal for Research in Mathematics Education, 25,* 495-511.

87. Needels, M. C., & Knapp, M. S. (1994). Teaching writing to children who are underserved. *Journal of Educational Psychology, 86,* 339-349.

88. O'Melia, M. C., & Rosenberg, M. S. (1994). Effects of cooperative homework teams on the acquisition of mathematics skills by secondary students with mild disabilities. *Exceptional Children, 60,* 538-548.

89. Pearl, R., & Bryan, T. (1994). Getting caught in misconduct: Conceptions of adolescents with and without learning disabilities. *Journal of Learning Disabilities, 27,* 193–197.

90. Rauch-Elnekave, H. (1994). Teenage motherhood: Its relationship to undetected learning problems. *Adolescence, 29,* 91-103.

91. Rech, J. F. (1994). A comparison of the mathematics attitudes of Black students according to grade level, gender, and academic achievement. *The Journal of Negro Education, 63,* 212–220.

92. Reid, R., Maag, J. W., Vasa, S. F., & Wright, G. (1994). Who are the children with attention deficit-hyperactivity disorder? A school-based survey. *The Journal of Special Education, 28,* 117–137.

93. Russo, M. F., Loeber, R., Lahey, B. B., & Keenan, K. (1994). Oppositional defiant and conduct disorders: Validation of the DSM-III-R and an alternative diagnostic option. *Journal of Clinical Child Psychology, 23,* 56-68.

94. Sawyer, R. J., & Dubowitz, H. (1994). School performance of children in kinship care. *Child Abuse & Neglect, 18,* 587-597.

95. Wiig, E. H., & Wilson, C. C. (1994). Is a question a question? Passage understanding by preadolescents with learning disabilities. *Language, Speech, and Hearing Services in Schools, 25,* 241–250.

96. Zentall, S. S., Smith, Y. N., Lee, Y. B., & Wieczorek, C. (1994). Mathematical outcomes of attention deficit hyperactivity disorder. *Journal of Learning Disabilities, 27,* 510–519.

97. Benton, S. L., Corkill, A. J., Sharp, J. M., Downey, R. G., & Khramtsova, I. (1995). Knowledge, interest, and narrative writing. *Journal of Educational Psychology, 87,* 66-79.

98. Crone, L. J., Lang, M. H., Teddlie, C., & Franklin, B. J. (1995). Achievement measures of school effectiveness: Comparison of model stability across years. *Applied Measurement in Education, 8,* 353–365.

99. Eno, L., & Woehlke, P. (1995). Use of the Lollipop Test as a predictor of California Achievement Test scores in kindergarten and transitional first-grade status. *Psychological Reports, 76,* 145-146.

100. Entwisle, D. R., & Alexander, K. L. (1995). A parent's economic shadow: Family structure versus family resources as influences on early school achievement. *Journal of Marriage and the Family, 57,* 399–409.

101. Felner, R. D., Brand, S., DuBois, D. L., Adan, A. M., Mulhall, P. F., & Evans, E. G. (1995). Socioeconomic disadvantage, proximal environmental experiences, and socioemotional and academic adjustment in early adolescence: Investigation of a mediated effects model. *Child Development, 66,* 774-792.

102. Ialongo, N., Edelsohn, G., Werthamer-Larsson, L., Crockett, L., & Kellam, S. (1995). The significance of self-reported anxious symptoms in first grade children: Prediction to anxious symptoms and adaptive functioning in fifth grade. *Journal of Child Psychology and Psychiatry and Allied Disciplines, 36,* 427-437.

103. Joshi, R. M. (1995). Assessing reading and spelling skills. *School Psychology Review, 24,* 361–375.

104. Linn, R. L., & Kiplinger, V. L. (1995). Linking statewide tests to the National Assessment of Educational Progress: Stability of results. *Applied Measurement in Education, 8,* 135–155.

105. Marston, D., Deno, S. L., Kim, D., Diment, K., & Rogers, D. (1995). Comparison of reading intervention approaches for students with mild disabilities. *Exceptional Children, 62,* 20–37.

106. Martens, B. K., Steele, E. S., Massie, D. R., & Diskin, M. T. (1995). Curriculum bias in standardized tests of reading decoding. *Journal of School Psychology, 33,* 287–296.

107. Miller, K. E., & Niemi, K. A. (1995). Gifted and talented: Fourth-, fifth- and sixth-grade students' evaluation of a gifted program. *The Journal of Genetic Psychology, 156,* 167–174.

108. Rellinger, E., Borkowski, J. G., Turner, L. A., & Hale, C. A. (1995). Perceived task difficulty and intelligence: Determinants of strategy use and recall. *Intelligence, 20,* 125–143.

109. Shell, D. F., Bruning, R. H., & Colvin, C. (1995). Self-efficacy, attribution, and outcome expectancy mechanisms in reading and writing achievement: Grade-level and achievement-level differences. *Journal of Educational Psychology, 87,* 386–398.

110. Stevens, R. J., & Slavin, R. E. (1995). The cooperative elementary school: Effects on students' achievement, attitudes, and social relations. *American Educational Research Journal, 32,* 321–351.

111. Espin, C. A., & Foegen, A. (1996). Validity of general outcome measures for predicting secondary students' performance on content-area tasks. *Exceptional Children, 62,* 497–514.

112. Shepard, L., Smith, M. L., & Marion, S. F. (1996). Failed evidence on grade retention. *Psychology in the Schools, 33,* 251–261.

113. Southard, N. A., & May, D. C. (1996). The effects of pre-first-grade programs on student reading and math achievement. *Psychology in the Schools, 33,* 132–142.

Review of the California Achievement Tests, Fifth Edition by ANTHONY J. NITKO, Professor of Education, School of Education, University of Pittsburgh, Pittsburgh, PA:

The California Achievement Tests (CAT/5) measures students' educational development in Reading, Spelling, Language, Mathematics, Study Skills, Science, and Social Studies using multiple-choice and constructed-response question formats. There are two multiple-choice versions: the Survey Battery and the Complete Battery. The Survey version is shorter and is used only to obtain norm-referenced information about students. It spans grades 1.6 through 12.9.

The Complete Battery spans grades K.0 through 12.9. The Complete Battery is about one and one-half times as long as the Survey Battery. It includes the items from the Survey. All the items in the Complete Battery are used to obtain scaled scores. Because the Complete Battery is longer, scores for curriculum-referenced objectives are also provided, each score based on four or more items.

A Performance Assessment is available as a supplemental component. It assesses through paper-and-pencil constructed-response items the areas of language arts, mathematics, science, and social studies. Some items require reading one or more selections that are contained in a separate "reader," which accompanies the response booklet. The results from the performance tasks can be integrated with the results from the multiple-choice tests. A separate writing assessment is available, also as a supplemental component.

ITEMS AND CONTENT. The materials accompanying the CAT/5 do an excellent job of describing how the items were developed. The processes of development, from curricular analyses, content and bias review, through final tryout and selection are well documented and well done. Items that finally appeared on the tests met both content and statistical specifications.

The objectives and subskills that each item is intended to assess are identified in the Class Management Guide. This material allows local school officials to review more thoroughly the test content in relation to the local curriculum's emphasis. From this reviewer's perspective, the items appear to measure the objectives and subskills the publisher intended to measure. Also, as was intended, items often measure the ability of a student to use several subskills in order to reach the correct answers.

The test developers are to be commended for making deliberate efforts in the planning, writing, and selection of the items to assess students' ability to integrate information and apply more complex thinking processes. For example, some reading passages may include social studies content. Thus, reading scores will measure a student's ability to comprehend this thematic material.

THINKING PROCESSES FRAMEWORK. The CAT/5 developers used a thinking process framework to help balance the types of thought processes students would be required to use when responding to all items in the multiple-choice batteries. This framework is a modification of the Rankin-Hughes Framework (Rankin & Hughes, 1987). Items for all CAT/5 subtests are classified into six thinking process categories: gathering information, organizing information, analyzing information, generating ideas, synthesizing elements, and evaluating outcomes. Several tables of classified items are presented to allow school officials to evaluate the thinking process coverage against their local curricular emphasis.

A further modification of this framework is used to create six scores that reflect each student's performance in each thinking skills category. These scores are derived from the multiple-choice items from several subtests and the performance assessments. As a group, these six scores are referred to as Integrated Outcomes Scores.

INTEGRATED OUTCOMES SCORES. The Integrated Outcomes scores and associated subtests from which the items come are: (a) Uses information to demonstrate understanding (Vocabulary, Comprehension, Study Skills); (b) understands writing conventions, structures, and applications (Spelling, Language Mechanics, Language Expression); (c) demonstrates content and concept knowledge (Mathematics Concepts and Applications, Science, Social Studies); (d) demonstrates knowledge of processes, skills, and procedures (Mathematics Concepts and Applications, Science, Social Studies); (e) uses applications and problem-solving strategies (Mathematics Concepts and Applications, Science, Social Studies); and (f) examines and applies meaning (Vocabulary, Comprehension, Study Skills).

CONTENT RECENCY AND EMPHASIS. The content specifications and test items of the CAT/5 were developed in the late 1980s. The test developers did an admirable job in reflecting both the then-current and possible-future curriculum practices. In some states and school districts, curriculum changes may have been more rapid than anticipated by the CAT/5 developers. It is important for local school officials, therefore, to review carefully the CAT/5 items to determine whether their content and emphasis matches the local curriculum at each grade level.

NORMING AND SCALING. National standardization occurred in 1991. Spring standardization was based on 115,888 K through 12 students; Fall standardization on 109,825 K through 12 students; and Winter standardization on 4,161 grade 1 students. (Winter norms are interpolated for other grade levels.) Public, Catholic, and private (non-Catholic) schools were stratified on the basis of geographic region (4), U.S. census community type (4), and size of school (2). Public schools were further stratified by socioeconomic status (2). The

demographics for the spring and fall standardization samples are compared to the 1988 U.S. Census and 1990 National Center for Educational Statistics data. Spring and fall standardization samples have somewhat different characteristics, especially in the representation of African Americans. The spring sample has between 7% and 8% African Americans, whereas the fall sample has 17% to 20%. The U.S. Census percentage is 11%. This is likely to make fall-to-spring comparisons problematic. Schools that switch testing dates from fall to spring also may need to monitor their results carefully.

The CAT/5 continues the tradition of its earlier edition in applying item response theory (IRT) models for scaling items and developing scaled scores. The IRT scale is the basis for deriving other norm-referenced scores that describe a student's performance. In the materials accompanying the CAT/5, IRT scoring is explained as "pattern scoring" and is contrasted with number-correct or raw scores. This discussion, which is found in the Classroom Management Guide, is a good nontechnical discussion of IRT scoring.

As indicated previously, scores are provided for each objective when the Complete Battery is administered. The scores, called Objective Performance Indices (OPI), are reported within intervals in some of the student reports: not mastered (.00–.49), partially mastered (.50–.74), and mastered (.75–.99). The intention of reporting these scores is to offer classroom teachers some details on which objectives to focus instruction. The OPI score is an estimate of a student's true proportion correct score on the cluster of items that measure an objective. This estimate is based on both the items themselves and on the student's overall test performance on the subtest containing the items measuring the objective. A Bayesian prior technique is used in which the standard error of the overall score of the subtest is used to weight this score's influence in relation to the score from only those few items that measure the objective. The smaller the standard error, the more the total subtest score influences the estimated objective mastery score. Those using the OPI score must keep in mind that it is not simply the proportion correct score on those few items that measure each objective. This Bayesian method of calculating OPI should be more reliable than the score based on only the few items defining each objective.

VALIDITY AND RELIABILITY. Several aspects of the CAT/5 that bear on the validity of its scores have been identified above. First, each school should match the CAT/5 items and objectives to its local curriculum. This will be especially important if innovative and nontraditional curricula have been put in place in recent years. The CAT/5 materials provide descriptions of the objectives as well as the thinking processes assessed by various clusters of items. These, too, should be studied against the goals and objectives of the local curriculum. It is possible that a local curriculum emphasizes some objectives and thinking processes more than does the CAT/5. This may lead to invalid local interpretations of the results. Thus, emphasis in the local curriculum should also be checked.

Some technical features of the CAT/5 scores and items support their use for measuring students' progress and growth. Scores increase in each curriculum area with increased schooling, as would be expected when students learn. There is also an increase within subtests from fall to spring. Studies on speediness indicate that 95% or more of the students are able to finish the subtests within the prescribed time limits.

The intercorrelations among the subtest scaled scores are generally high, in the .5 to .8 range. This indicates that general educational development cannot be so easily separated into curriculum subtest areas. That is, there is considerable overlap between a student's ability to perform in one subject and the student's ability to perform in another. The pattern of intercorrelations are generally what would be expected, however. For example, Spelling has lower intercorrelations with all the subtests except Language and Reading; Mathematics Computation has lower intercorrelations with all subtests except Mathematics Concepts and Applications; and Vocabulary and Reading Comprehension are among the highest of intercorrelations. Educators need to be cautious, however, so they do not overinterpret differences in a student's performance on different subtests: Always corroborate information from the CAT/5 about a student's curricular strengths and weaknesses with classroom performance data about the student.

The CAT/5's internal consistency (KR20) reliabilities are higher for the Complete Battery than for the Survey Battery. The Survey Battery subtests have KR20s that are generally in the .70 to .80 range; the Complete Battery subtests' KR20s are generally in the .80 to .90 range. The CAT/5 developers do tell educators not to use the Survey Battery subtest scores to make serious educational decisions about individual differences: The Complete Battery is

better suited for such decision making. The Survey Battery total scores (e.g., Total Reading) do have somewhat higher KR20s than the corresponding subtests, but these are generally in the .85 to .90 range. The Complete Battery total scores have KR20s that are in the .90–.95 range. Estimated KR20s are also reported for the Complete Battery's item pattern (or IRT) scaled scores. These are generally .02 to .03 higher than the corresponding number right KR20s described above.

Standard errors of measurement are generally in the 1.5 to 2.5 range for Survey Battery subtests and generally about 2.7 for the total scores. For the Complete Battery, the standard errors of measurement are about .5% higher, as would be expected because this battery is longer. These standard errors of measurement are tolerable, but they do point to the need for educators not to overinterpret small differences among different students or among one student's subtest scores. Corroboration with classroom data is necessary before educational decisions are made. (Of course, this is true of all standardized tests.)

The CAT/5 uses an IRT-derived scaled score as a yardstick to measure students' educational development over time. This scale has a 0 to 999 range. These scaled scores are most reliable when a student scores in the middle range of scores for the test level that matches his or her functional educational placement. Students whose scaled scores are very low or very high for the grade-level norm group to which they are being compared may be measured quite inaccurately. The IRT scaled scores' standard errors of measurement for students in the middle ranges of their norm group are approximately 10 to 15 scaled score points. However, those students at the extremely low or extremely high end of their norm group distribution may have standard errors of measurement of 70 scaled score points or more. Because grade equivalents are obtained from scaled scores, this caution for interpretation applies to grade equivalents as well.

SUMMARY. The CAT/5 continues the tradition of the earlier editions of the California Achievement tests by producing a technically solid achievement assessment tool. The addition of the supplemental performance tasks, if used, will give educators a more balanced assessment of students' strengths and weaknesses than if the multiple-choice version is used alone. Educators should follow the publisher's advice and not use the Survey version for serious decisions about individual students. Before purchasing the CAT/5, however, be sure to very carefully match the test's items and objectives with the local curriculum. The curricular emphasis of the CAT/5 is that which was prevalent in schools in the late 1980s. If a school district has made important curricular changes in recent years, and if these changes result in instructional objectives that do not match the emphases of the CAT/5 items, it would be wise to look at other test products.

REVIEWER'S REFERENCE

Rankin, S. C., & Hughes, C. S. (1987). The Rankin-Hughes Framework and how computing can help (pp. 1–13). *Michigan Association for Computer Users in Learning, Developing thinking skills across the curriculum.* Westland, MI: author.

Review of the California Achievement Tests, Fifth Edition by ROBERT F. McMORRIS, Professor of Educational Psychology & Statistics, University at Albany, State University of New York, Albany, NY, and WEI-PING LIU, Head Test Librarian, University at Albany, State University of New York, Albany, NY, and ELIZABETH L. BRINGSJORD, Assistant Professor, Division of Nursing, Russell Sage College, Troy, NY:

The California Achievement Tests, Fifth Edition (CAT/5), published in 1992, is a nationwide test series designed to measure basic academic skills in seven curriculum areas: Reading, Language, Spelling, Mathematics, Study Skills, Science, and Social Studies. Thirteen overlapping levels, Level K to Level 21/22, are appropriate for grades ranging from kindergarten through grade 12. The CAT has been revised to reflect the directions and content found in current curriculum and text series.

TEST MATERIALS. Two test configurations, the Survey and the Complete Battery, are developed to measure the same content with items of closely matched difficulty. Each configuration has two forms, A and B, and allows for norm-referenced interpretation. The longer Complete Battery also allows for criterion-referenced interpretation, known on this test as curriculum referencing. The Survey contains 20 items for each subtest whereas the Complete Battery contains 24–50 items per subtest.

Two locator tests (Test 1 for grades 1–6 and Test 2 for grades 6–12) are available for use with the CAT/5 to match students in the same grade with different levels of the test series; each test consists of 20 vocabulary and 20 mathematics items. The test developers recommend that the locator test should be given several days, if not weeks, prior to the administration of an appropriate-level achievement test so that it will not act as a pretest.

To minimize the problem of students' limited test-taking experience, six practice exercises for the CAT/5 provide students opportunity to become familiar with the form and administration procedure of a standardized test. Because practice tests were administered throughout the norming procedure used for grades K through 6, the developers appropriately recommend their use, particularly in these early grade levels.

CONTENT DEVELOPMENT. Consistent with most contemporary battery/survey-type achievement tests, the CAT/5 was developed with the intent that it be broadly based and integrative. The developers employed a systematic, multi-pronged approach toward achieving this aim—including the development of a computerized curriculum taxonomy—during the early phase of test development. The developers claim that this data base greatly facilitated the process of test development. Norm-referenced scores represent a global measure of domains. The developers strove for more integrative items in this version of the CAT; many items were designed to test multiple content areas, skills, and/or cognitive processes simultaneously.

TEST DEVELOPMENT. After the basic skills and objectives were identified through the review of current curriculum guides, recently published textbooks, and instructional programs, a group of experienced teachers wrote about twice as many items as would be needed. All items were edited based on recognized principles of test construction, written in language appropriate for the various testing levels and diverse test-taker populations, and tried out in schools throughout the country. The accuracy, validity, and grade-appropriateness of the items for all test areas were evaluated by teachers and other curriculum experts. Based on the tryout data, items were selected for the final forms of the Complete Battery and the Survey. A three-parameter Item Response Theory (IRT) model was also used in test development and norming.

The publishers provide blueprint follow-up information; in the Handbook of Instructional Objectives and Outcomes—with one handbook for each level or set of levels—each item is classified by performance description, objective, and either thinking skill (multiple-choice items) or integrated outcome (performance assessment items).

INTERNAL CONSISTENCY RELIABILITY. The Kuder-Richardson Formula 20 (KR20) was used to estimate the internal consistency of two forms for both the Complete Battery and Survey for Fall and Spring standardizations. KR20s were computed for the total battery score, for each content area total (e.g., total Reading), and for each subtest. Because of the influence of the number of items, reliability coefficients should be higher for the Complete Battery than for the Survey, higher for the total battery than for the content area totals, and higher for the content area totals than for the subtests. These expectations are confirmed.

For the total battery, KR20s ranged from .94 to .98, with a median of .96. For the content area totals, KR20s for the Complete Battery ranged from .86 to .96, with a median of .94; corresponding KR20s for the Survey ranged from .79 to .91, with a median of .87. For both the Complete Battery and the Survey, the content area and total battery scores show a high degree of internal consistency.

For subtests of the Complete Battery, KR20s ranged from .63 to .94, with a median of .88. For the Survey, KR20s ranged from .58 to .87, with a median of .78. Results for the Spring standardization were slightly higher than those for Fall. In both the Survey and the Complete Battery, the subtests of Science and Social Studies had lower KR20s than did other subtests, perhaps a result of items covering heterogeneous content.

ITEM-PATTERN KR20. A newer measure of reliability, the "item-pattern KR20," was used by the CAT/5 test developers to increase the score reliability. Item-pattern scoring, which takes into account the particular items that an examinee answered correctly, was somewhat more reliable than number-correct scoring.

STABILITY AND EQUIVALENCE RELIABILITY. Reliability coefficients using alternate forms with a 2-week interval were computed for Complete Battery A and B. These conservative estimates of reliability were computed for the three content area totals and the six component (corresponding) subtests. For the subtests, these coefficients ranged from .25 to .90, with a mean of .75. For the content area totals, the coefficients ranged from .27 to .93, with a mean of .82.

MASTERY OF OBJECTIVES. The Complete Battery allows criterion-referenced interpretation. Students are designated as having *mastery* if they answer 75% of the items correctly, *partial knowledge* with 50% correct, and *nonmastery* otherwise. Such designations are based on a minimum of 4 items for an objective; the majority of objectives are measured with 4 items, although occasionally the count does go as high as 13.

The test publishers note appropriately the arbitrariness of the mastery cutoffs plus the limited reliability likely using only four items. Percentages of students attaining mastery differs considerably across objectives. We have not found any reliability coefficients or percentage of consistent labeling of students across forms, and we urge caution when using such volatile and only partially defensible designations.

On a brighter note, if the tests are scored by CTB, the mastery designations are based on a Bayesian approach, which incorporates overall test performance. Further, CTB can express the estimates in mastery confidence intervals—a helpful way to express reliability information for an individual's score.

PERFORMANCE ASSESSMENT. Students may also take constructed-response items in Language Arts, Mathematics, Science, and Social Studies. The median coefficient alpha reliability estimate for those subtests is .80. Coefficients range from .52 up to .94. Reliabilities for the higher grades tend to run somewhat higher than they do for the lower grades.

We have not found interrater reliability information, always a concern with constructed responses, and compounded when the tests are locally scored. For the tryout data reported above, however, such reliability could not have been a major problem given the decent coefficient alphas.

INTEGRATED OUTCOMES. Reliability coefficients are given at each test level for each of the six integrated outcomes (e.g., Uses Information to Demonstrate Understanding; Examines and Applies Meaning), where selected items from multiple subtests contribute to these scores. Coefficients are computed for the multiple-choice and the constructed-response outcomes/formats separately and combined.

For the multiple-choice tests, KR20 coefficients range from .68 to .97, with a median of .82. Most of the coefficients in the .90s were for older ages; most of the .70s were for younger ages.

For the open-ended items of the performance assessments, the analogous coefficient alphas were somewhat lower, not surprising given these scores suffer from fewer items and more flexibility in scoring. The median coefficient was .79; the range was from .37 to .91.

When the multiple-choice and open-ended performances were combined, however, reliabilities increased. The median alpha was .89 with the range from .75 to .97. Note that these integrated outcomes are based on items across subject matter and across cognitive levels, so such heterogeneity places some upper limits on what we could expect and even desire for KR20s and alphas. We admit also to wondering, if a factor structure were estimated for the whole test, whether factors would fall out according to the subtests, to the integrated outcomes, to multiple choice versus constructed response, or just to a general ability factor (e.g., *g*). On a simpler note, would the pattern of item intercorrelations support the use of the integrated outcomes, a question that has implications for validity as well as for reliability.

STANDARD ERRORS OF MEASUREMENT. The test publishers provide appropriate explanations for standard error of measurement (see especially the Class Management Guide) to accompany summary numerical values. The tabled standard errors are based on the more optimistic KR20s rather than on alternate-form reliability estimates, as noted by Rogers (1985) for a previous edition.

CTB provides several possible report forms; these forms differ in whether their use would encourage interpretation using intervals rather than points. The Individual Test Record is a commendable report in portraying percentile confidence bands for norm referencing and mastery bands for referencing on objectives.

PROFILES AND UNDERACHIEVEMENT. Profiles are provided for displaying and comparing scores within the CAT/5. Nevertheless, the Technical Report did not include reliabilities of differences for score comparisons. Such reliabilities of differences would tend to be considerably less than the reliabilities of the component measures. However, there is some assistance available for the test user dealing with profiles; when CTB provides results using the Individual Test Record form, the percentile bands can help incorporate reliability information in the interpretation.

Developers of achievement batteries frequently couple their batteries with aptitude measures to produce discrepancy scores and computer-generated reports for identifying so-called "underachievers." The CAT/5 is coupled with the Test of Cognitive Skills (TCS/2) to produce Anticipated Achievement Scores based on the discrepancy between predicted and observed CAT scores. Reliabilities of these difference scores are not reported, but such scores are notoriously unreliable. Although the Technical Report does not include consideration of Anticipated Achievement scores under the reliability section, elsewhere the report contains standard errors of estimate, 80% confidence intervals, and intercorrelations between the achievement and aptitude batteries.

CONTENT VALIDITY. According to the developers, content validity for the CAT/5 was established by analyzing a comprehensive sample of curriculum materials from all over the country. From the blueprint that was generated, test questions were developed to assess achievement within specific domains. The test developers clearly acknowledge that the content tested on the CAT/5 represents only sampling rather than exhaustive coverage of the domains. However, because tests are broad and representative in their coverage, inferences can still be made about overall achievement in those domains, as noted in the Class Management Guide. The developers also made use of textbooks and major basal series to verify "that the content and format of the items were appropriately targeted to the grades in which the associated skills are typically taught" (Technical Report, p. 15). Content validity was further supported through active participation of classroom teachers and curriculum experts.

CONSTRUCT AND CRITERION-RELATED VALIDITY. Carney and Schattgen (1994) noted in their critique of the CAT/5 that "issues of construct and criterion-related validity need more coverage" (p. 118). With regard to construct validity, Carney and Schattgen noted that reviews of previous CAT editions have found "substantial" overlap between the CAT and its companion ability measure, the Test of Cognitive Skills. Although Carney and Schattgen called on the CAT/5 developers to discuss this issue, it does not appear from our reading of the latest technical materials that they have yet done so.

The CAT/5 developers have responded, albeit modestly, to the question of criterion-related validity. In both Technical Bulletin 3 and the latest Technical Report, results from "predictive" validity studies are reported. Actually, two of the studies reported were done with previous editions of the CAT and/or the Comprehensive Test of Basic Skills (CTBS).

USEFULNESS. The CAT/5 was developed to provide test users with information to guide instruction and improve learning. For example, the developers provide score reports for the Complete Battery that include criterion-referenced performance indicators based on level of mastery of specific educational objectives. Individual and group performance is reported with the Objective Performance Index (OPI), an index that represents the average percent correct on items for specific objectives.

It does appear from our review of items, tests, and various score reporting options that the CAT/5 developers provide substantial information related to academic achievement. However, we suggest the developers (or others) consider an evaluative plan to further substantiate the usefulness of the test. Debriefing teachers who have used the CAT/5 would certainly shed light on questions relevant to useful-ness. The developers could also debrief students and/or parents after testing and score reporting to determine what sorts of interpretations are made and how these interpretations relate to study behaviors, course/school selection, career planning, and later achievement.

Although the developers encourage use of the performance-based components of the test to make instructional decisions, empirical support is lacking. As stated above, we recommend the developers conduct follow-up interviews and/or surveys with teachers (and perhaps students and parents as well) to determine both how the performance-based assessments have been used and how useful the interpretations are perceived to be.

With regard to the issue of time, if a district or school chooses to use both the Complete Battery and the performance-based assessments, there is a considerable time commitment. Fortunately, the developers provide many flexible options for combining the component tests. Obviously, a standardized achievement test (or combination of tests) that sacrifices breadth for depth will have to face validity concerns for some interpretations. The fidelity—bandwidth dilemma remains crucial.

Use of curriculum (a.k.a. domain or criterion) referencing to specify mastery also raises issues of appropriate determination of passing scores, the dependability of designations for individual students, and the use of these designations.

DIFFERENTIAL PERFORMANCE. CTB sought to minimize any bias across gender or ethnic groups by using care in item development and extensive item review by panels of judges plus statistical review using differential item functioning (DIF) methodology.

Obvious care was taken in item development and selection to present balanced and appropriate sets of items. Items were reviewed by panels of professionals from the educational community representing a diversity of ethnic backgrounds. We salute the developers for their diligence in recruiting a respectable number of bias reviewers; it strikes us as prudent, particularly given the cultural sensitivity issues that continue to plague the standardized testing environment.

Item responses were analyzed for differential item functioning (DIF) using the Linn and Harnisch (1981) procedure. Comparisons were made by gender and ethnicity, with Blacks and Hispanics as two of the focal groups.

Although the CAT/5 performance-based assessments are relatively brief in duration, students who have had frequent exposure to both extended and brief performance-based assessments likely would have an advantage over those who have not. Indeed, Baker, O'Neil, and Linn (1993) warn that there is tremendous variation in the extent to which students have prior experience with performance-based assessment. Unlike the multiple-choice portion of the test, the CTB Performance Assessment components were not assessed for differential item functioning (DIF) across ethnic groups, only across gender. We assume the sizes of the ethnic groups available for analysis were insufficient to allow dependable estimates using the IRT-based technique.

Given the fact that the developers analyzed DIF for the CTB Performance Assessment Component only across gender, we recommend caution in interpreting scores on this portion of the test.

NORM REFERENCING. Spring and Fall standardizations each involved scores from over 100,000 students from approximately 260 public schools and 100 private or parochial schools. Sampling stratifications included four regions and two sizes (for all schools), four community types (for public and Catholic schools), and two socioeconomic levels (for public schools only).

Rather than collecting norming data directly on each of the two forms for both the Complete Battery and the Survey, CTB chose to use a single test, the Benchmark, the same Benchmark test used for norming the CTBS/4. Anchor items and IRT methods were used in equating the forms, helping to minimize any errors due to content differences, time differences, and statistical manipulations. Their use of a separate sample of students for calibrating items once items had been selected is reassuring.

Representativeness of the norm groups depends on the schools' willingness to cooperate. The proportion of first-choice schools who participated in norming is not provided, nor are procedures for and success with obtaining back-up schools. This concern is not new for the CAT; note reviews by Airasian (1989), Rogers (1985), and Wardrop (1989).

Considerable description of the sample, available in the Technical Report, was obtained using a "School Characteristics Questionnaire" sent to each participating school and to which 94% of those schools responded. Some means are given as percentages, such as percentage of Blacks in the public schools (7% in the Fall, 20% in the Spring), some are given as counts, such as school size (454 in the Fall, 579 in the Spring). The counts for special education categories might have been easier to interpret as percentages.

Tests may be hand scored or machine scored. When CTB scores the tests, they normally use pattern (IRT) scoring, which would give slightly more reliable scores than would number-correct scoring. Either approach provides scale scores for the subtests, where scale scores are supposedly (i.e., assumed to be) equal-interval scores stretching from K–12. One bonus with the scale scores: For each score, the standard error of measurement is provided for number-correct and for pattern scoring.

Scale scores are the basis for the various derived scores including percentile ranks, normal curve equivalents, stanines, and grade equivalents. The Norms Books provide a convenient way to translate from scale scores to any of these derived scores, although CTB-generated reports following from machine scoring are even more convenient. The Class Management Guide provides many suggestions for interpretation and illustrates possible reports, including the Individual Test Record, which presents these derived scores along with confidence bands.

SUMMARY. One of the parents in the Family Circus cartoon, referring to their busy children, wonders with the other parent: "I thought I knew all the answers, but they keep thinking up new questions." Many comments concerning the CAT/5 relate to this new-questions sentiment. For example, the test questions on the CAT/5, and the ways they have been combined, have evolved to meet additional questions and directions that users see for tests. Many such test questions—both multiple-choice and constructed response—deal with problem solving, interpretation, judgment, application, and other above-knowledge-level skills. Performance on individual questions is combined by objective, by subtest, by content area, by total of the three content areas, and by integrated outcome.

CTB has provided considerable assistance to test interpreters with the Class Management Guide, the Administrators Handbook, the Test Coordinator's Handbook, the 700-page Technical Report, and various other publications. Glossary definitions and discussions are worthwhile. Machine scoring can result in a variety of reports, some even generated locally if desired, and a couple of reports even portraying interval interpretations. The norms are dependent on the assumptions of the IRT model being met—probably the assumptions are met quite well. The quality of the information for assessing mastery learning is perhaps more suspect; certainly users might be aware of the arbitrary decisions made for setting mastery levels and the fairly small number of items per objective as well as CTB's new response to improve the quality of such information using Bayesian and IRT methods to incorporate a broader base of performance for judging competence.

Reliability tends to be quite high when a large number of items are involved (e.g., for the content totals, the total battery scores, and the integrated outcomes when based on multiple-choice and constructed-response items combined). Interpretation for an individual's scores may be difficult especially for Survey subtests, mastery designations, differences profiled within the CAT/5, and the Anticipated Achievement Scores, especially if any of the scores are unaccompanied by confidence intervals.

The information concerning validity is some same old, some new, and somewhat reassuring. Considerable effort was exerted to develop plans and items consistent with current curriculum and instruction, and content validity was considered carefully, although we would like to have seen more content-area experts used. Also, considerable effort was given to minimizing inappropriate differential performance across gender and ethnic groups, and some attention was given to criterion-related and construct validity.

As Airasian (1989) observed in his review of the previous edition, the CAT has been "a well-respected test battery for over 50 years. The latest version … represents an improvement on an already creditable test battery" (p. 126). These supportive comments remain applicable with the CAT/5.

REVIEWERS' REFERENCES

Linn, R. L., & Harnisch, D. L. (1981). Interactions between item content and group membership on achievement test items. *Journal of Educational Measurement, 18,* 109–118.

Rogers, B. G. (1985). [Review of the California Achievement Tests, Forms C and D.] In J. V. Mitchell, Jr. (Ed.), *The ninth mental measurements yearbook* (pp. 243–246). Lincoln, NE: The Buros Institute of Mental Measurements.

Airasian, P. W. (1989). [Review of the California Achievement Tests, Forms E and F.] In J. C. Conoley & J. J. Kramer (Eds.), *The tenth mental measurements yearbook* (pp. 126–128). Lincoln, NE: The Buros Institute of Mental Measurements.

Wardrop, J. L. (1989). [Review of the California Achievement Tests, Forms E and F.] In J. C. Conoley & J. J. Kramer (Eds.), *The tenth mental measurements yearbook* (pp. 128–133). Lincoln, NE: The Buros Institute of Mental Measurements.

Baker, E. L., O'Neil, H. F., Jr., & Linn, R. L. (1993). Policy and validity prospects for performance-based assessment. *American Psychologist, 48,* 1210–1218.

Carney, R. N., & Schattgen, S. F. (1994). [Review of] California Achievement Tests, fifth edition. In D. J. Keyser & R. C. Sweetland (Eds.), *Test critiques, 10* (pp. 110–119). Austin, TX: PRO-ED, Inc.

[41]
California Verbal Learning Test, Children's Version.

Purpose: "Designed to assess multiple components of verbal learning and memory."

Population: Ages 5–16.

Publication Dates: 1989–1994.

Acronym: CVLT-C.

Scores: List A Trials 1–15 Total, List B Free-Recall Trial, Short Delay Free Recall, Short-Delay Cued Recall, Long-Delay Free Recall, Long-Delay Cued Recall, Semantic Cluster Ratio, Perseverations, Free-Recall Intrusions, Cued-Recall Intrusions, Recognition Hits, Discriminability, False Positives.

Administration: Individual.

Price Data, 1996: $295 per complete kit including comprehensive manual ('94, 147 pages), 25 record forms, scoring assistant disk, and user's guide (Macintosh ['94, 115 pages] or Windows 1.0 ['94, 186 pages] version); $100.50 per set including manual and 25 record forms; $34 per 25 record forms; $78 per manual; $221 per scoring assistant including disk, user's guide, and keyboard overlay (Macintosh or Windows).

Time: (55) minutes.

Comments: CVLT-C Scoring Assistant User's Guide available for Macintosh and Windows.

Authors: Dean C. Delis, Joel H. Kramer, Edith Kaplan, and Beth A. Ober; Alan J. Fridlund, and Dean C. Delis (Scoring Assistant User's Guide).

Publisher: The Psychological Corporation.

TEST REFERENCES

1. Brugge, K. L., Nichols, S. L., Salmon, D. P., Hill, L. R., Delis, D. C., Aaron, L., & Trainer, D. A. (1994). Cognitive impairment in adults with Down's Syndrome: Similarities to early cognitive changes in Alzheimer's disease. *Neurology, 44,* 232–238.

2. Yeates, K. O., Enrile, B. G., Loss, N., & Blumenstein, E. (1995). Verbal learning and memory in children with myelomeningocele. *Journal of Pediatric Psychology, 20,* 801–815.

Review of the California Verbal Learning Test, Children's Version by BILLY T. OGLETREE, Assistant Professor of Communication Disorders, College of Education and Allied Professions, Western Carolina University, Cullowhee, NC:

The purpose of the California Verbal Learning Test, Children's Version (CVLT-C) is to assist with the diagnosis and treatment of memory impairments in children between 5 and 16 years of age. The CVLT-C test packet includes a manual, two computerized scoring assistant user guides with software for Macintosh and Windows), and test forms. The examiner's manual describes the test's composition and provides guidelines specific to administration, scoring, and score interpretation. The CVLT-C's design, use, and technical aspects are described below.

The CVLT-C was designed to evaluate clinically relevant components of verbal memory and learning. It also isolates deficient strategies contributing to specific learning problems and assists with the design of remediation programs based upon learning strengths and weaknesses. The CVLT-C assesses verbal memory and learning within the context of an everyday memory task (i.e., the recall of two hypothetical shopping lists presented to the child as

List A [Monday's list] and List B [Tuesday's list]). List A consists of 15 items from three different semantic categories (i.e., clothing, toys, and fruits). List B is described as an interference list and contains 15 items from two semantic categories (i.e., food items and furniture). Words were carefully chosen to make the two lists as comparable as possible. Two criteria were used: the frequency of each word's occurrence in the English language and its rank order as an exemplar of a semantic category.

The examiner begins the CVLT-C by introducing the test in language appropriate for the child's age. To avoid unnecessary anxiety, examiners are cautioned not to refer to the CVLT-C as a "memory" or "learning" test. In the first five trials, List A is read by the examiner at an approximate rate of one word per second. Afterwards, the child is asked to recall as many words as possible. These five trials are followed by one interference trial using List B. The test concludes with five additional trials using List A including a Short-Delay Free-Recall trial, a Short-Delay Cued-Recall trial, a Long-Delay Free-Recall trial, a Long-Delay Cued-Recall trial, and a Recognition trial. Short- and Long-Delay Free-Recall trials are preceded by the request to repeat words on List A. In contrast, Short- and Long-Delay Cued trials occur after instructions to repeat items from the three semantic categories (e.g., "Tell me all the things from the Monday shopping list that are things to wear"). During the recognition trial, 45 words are read to the child and he/she is asked to indicate which items appeared on List A.

A 20-minute delay occurs before Long-Delay trials. Single prompts (e.g., "Tell me anything else you can") and encouraging comments are allowed during all trials. Examiners are to note where prompts were used by recording a Q on the record sheet.

The CVLT-C should be administered by professionals with graduate-level training in the use of individually administered educational or psychological instruments. The manual notes that a trained technician can administer the test under supervision. The supervising professional, however, must be responsible for test interpretation. The CVLT-C is reported to require 30 minutes to administer excluding the 20-minute delay interval preceding the Long-Delay trials. To administer the CVLT-C examiners must have a watch or access to a clock to time the delay interval. The CVLT-C must be administered in one sitting with no breaks other than the above-mentioned delay interval.

Following administration of the CVLT-C, examiners have the choice of using hand or computerized scoring. When computerized scoring is chosen, the examiner follows directions provided in the Scoring Assistant User's Guide. Software provided will automatically compute raw and scaled scores for all of the key CVLT-C indices. Computerized scoring is recommended given the difficulty with hand scoring for a number of indices.

Hand scoring for the CVLT-C is divided into three sections. In Section 1, examiners classify and record response types. Response types include "correct," "perseveration," and "intrusion." Definitions and examples of the latter two of these types are provided in the examiner's manual. Examiners are also asked to convert raw scores to scaled scores (normalized T scores and z scores) and to calculate contrast measures. The second section of hand scoring consists of calculations of the "Learning Characteristics" indices of List A, trials 1 through 5. Semantic cluster ratios are calculated from observed and expected values. A sample calculation is provided. The ratios of observed to expected semantic cluster scores are then calculated and recorded. These raw scores are converted to scaled scores (z scores). If desired, observed and serial cluster scores can also be calculated. Other scores derived from List A, trials 1 through 5, include calculations of correct responses from the primacy, middle, and recency regions of Word List A, calculation of learning slope, and calculations of recall consistency. Formulas are provided in the manual for the calculation of learning slope and percentage or recall consistency. Section 3 of hand scoring outlines the computation of "Recognition Measures" including correction recognition hits, discriminability index, false positive rate, and response bias.

Specific interpretive guidelines for all of the above-mentioned scores are provided in chapter 5 of the examiner's manual. In addition, this chapter provides three case studies illustrating the clinical use of the CVLT-C. According to the CVLT-C manual, the above-mentioned procedures/interpretive scoring guidelines should generate test results useful in the quantification of the following parameters: (a) levels of recall and recognition on all trials; (b) different learning strategies (e.g., semantic clustering); (c) serial-position effects; (d) learning rate across trials; (e) consistency of item recall across trials; (f) degree of vulnerability to proactive and retroactive interference; (g) retention of information over short and longer delays; (h) enhancement of recall performance by category cueing and recognition testing; (i) indices of recognition performance (discriminability and response bias) derived from signal-detection theory; (j) perseverations and intrusions in recall; and (k) false positives in recognition.

Technical aspects of the CVLT-C are clearly presented in the examiner's manual. These include complete discussions of standardization, validity, and reliability. The standardization sample for the CVLT-C included 920 children divided into 12 age groups of comparable size, ranging from 5 through 16 years of age. The sample reflected national and regional trends specific to age, sex, and parents' educational level.

Evidence for content validity, criterion-related validity, and construct validity is provided in the CVLT-C examiner manual. Content validity is supported by the test's solid research foundation. This is discussed at length in chapter 4 of the manual. Criterion-related validity is supported, in part, by the reported correlation between CVLT-C scores and Wechsler Intelligence Scale for Children—Revised (WISC-R) vocabulary standard scores. Correlations indicated a "mild but significant" relationship (coefficients from .32 to .40). The authors suggest that this degree of correlation suggests that the CVLT-C evaluates "a domain of cognition different from verbal I.Q., given that only 9 to 16 percent of the variance is shared by the two tests" (p. 91). Finally, construct validity for the CVLT-C is supported by factor analyses indicating that the multiple indices of the CVLT-C cluster into theoretically meaningful factors consistent with the experimental constructs they are intended to measure.

Reliability for the CVLT-C is reported across trials, semantic categories, and words. Standard errors of measurement and test-retest stability are also reported. Across trials consistency was evaluated by calculating correlations. Odd-even reliability coefficients were used due to the number of trials. Coefficients ranged from .84 to .91 with an average coefficient of .88 (based upon Fischer's z transformation). The coefficient alpha reliability coefficients ranged from .81 to .88 with an average of .85. Across semantic category consistency was evaluated by considering item sets that were semantically unrelated. Alpha coefficients were calculated based upon the three category scores. Reliability coefficients ranged from .64 to .80 with an average of .72. Across word consistency was based on the total score for each of the 15 stimulus words in List A (these could appear five times). The average odd-even correlation was

.83 and the average coefficient alpha correlation was .81. Standard errors of measurement reported for List A, trials 1 through 5 are reasonably low indicating relatively stable individual test scores. The authors note that all of the measures reported thus far are strong indicators of the CVLT-C's internal consistency.

Test-retest stability on the CVLT-C was examined by testing 106 children of the original standardization sample twice with a median retest interval of 28 days. Some improvement in recall of words from both lists was noted for all ages tested. Recognition hit rates improved for one age group, whereas perseveration responses increased slightly across all age groups. Intrusion rates remained the same. The authors suggest that "these modest levels of reliability are within expected limits given the nature of the test" (p. 89).

In summary, this reviewer finds the CVLT-C to be a valid, reasonably quick diagnostic tool useful in the identification of components of verbal learning and memory for children between 5 and 16 years of age. Its strengths include a strong theoretical base, a comprehensive format, a clear presentation of information specific to the interpretation of findings (guidelines and case studies in chapter 5 of the manual), and an inclusion of computerized scoring materials and guides. Furthermore, technical aspects of development (i.e., the standardization sample, and information specific to validity and reliability) appear appropriate for the test's purposes.

The CVLT-C's weaknesses include an examiner's manual that periodically lacks clarity. This may be a serious problem for "first time users" who are less familiar with comparable measures. It may be minimized, however, if the authors' user recommendations are followed (i.e., graduate-level training in the use of individually administered instruments). A second potential weakness is the assumption that shopping is an everyday memory task for young children. This reviewer's experiences suggest that this is not true. At any rate, the repeated presentation of a shopping list, as occurs with the CVLT-C, is not an everyday occurrence with children. Finally, the hand scoring of the CVLT-C is detailed, cumbersome, and difficult to follow. Repeated calculations and score recording is necessary making examiner errors possible. Although this weakness is noted by the authors and computerized scoring is recommended, this reviewer would not recommend the CVLT-C to examiners who do not have access to a computer for scoring purposes.

Review of the California Verbal Learning Test, Children's Version by LeADELLE PHELPS, Professor of School Psychology, Department of Counseling and School Psychology, State University of New York at Buffalo, Buffalo, NY:

The California Verbal Learning Test, Children's Version (CVLT-C) is a standardized individually administered battery designed to assess verbally mediated memory and learning strategies. Normed for children ages 5–16, the CVLT-C is designed to assist professionals in the diagnosis and treatment of verbal memory handicaps secondary to learning disabilities, aphasia or related language dysfunctions, attention deficit hyperactivity disorder (ADHD), developmental disorders, traumatic brain injuries, and/or various other neuropsychological impairments. Requiring approximately 30 minutes to administer, the battery evaluates a respondent's: (a) immediate free recall of a 15-item shopping list, (b) learning curve over five presentations of the list, (c) short-delay (i.e., approximately 2–3 minutes) free recall of the items following the introduction of a second shopping list (i.e., an interference task), (d) short-delay cued-recall, (e) long-delay (i.e., 20-minutes) free recall, (f) long-delay cued-recall, and (g) long-delay recognition recall. The test items are all related to the shopping lists. The *cued* response procedure prompts the respondent by asking for recall of items that were: (a) things to wear (e.g., sweater, belt), (b) things to play with (e.g., puzzle, blocks), and (c) fruits (e.g, peaches, strawberries). The recognition procedure requires the respondent to indicate whether or not 45 items were contained within the original shopping list.

In addition to recall, recognition, and learning curve scores, the procedure assists in the identification of learning strategies (e.g., semantic clustering), effects of proactive and retroactive interference, serial position effects, consistency of item recall, cueing enhancement, and the presence of perseveration or intrusion errors. All these quantitative data are then used to identify memory/learning deficits, isolate deficient learning strategies, and develop remediation programming.

The CVLT-C manual is clearly written with explicit instructions regarding: (a) standardized testing instructions and procedures; (b) recording of responses; (c) determination and scoring of intrusion and perseveration errors; and, (d) calculation of learning slope, recall consistency, false positives, correct recognition, and semantic strategy cluster scores. Normative data based on chronological age provide standard scores for immediate free recall, short-delay free recall, short-delay cued recall, long-delay free recall, and long-delay cued recall. Although hand scoring the CVLT-C can take up to an hour, user-friendly scoring software with versions for both Windows and Macintosh (the *Scoring Assistant*) is available. Finally, an entire chapter of the CVLT-C manual is devoted to interpretative guidelines followed by three illustrative case studies.

The item development, standardization procedures, and psychometric properties of the CVLT-C are exemplary. The test was normed on 920 children closely matching 1988 U.S. Census race/ethnicity, parental education, and geographical region data. Reliability coefficients are well within the acceptable range, averaging .88 (split-half), and .85 (coefficient alpha) across the age spans. Construct validity was demonstrated via a principal component factor analysis with a six-factor solution similar to the Adult CVLT being identified. Unfortunately, no concurrent validity studies comparing the CVLT-C with other child memory/learning tests such as the Children's Auditory Verbal Learning Test-2 (CAVLT-2; 12:76; Talley, 1993), Children's Memory Scale (CMS; Cohen, 1997), Test of Memory and Learning (TOMAL; 330; Reynolds & Bigler, 1994), or the Wide Range Assessment of Memory and Learning (WRAML; T4:2957; Sheslow & Adams, 1990) are reported.

The sole, yet significant, drawback of the CVLT-C is the exclusive focus on verbal mediation. As the test does not provide for the assessment of cross modality competencies (i.e., verbal vs. visual), the battery is restricted to usefulness with disabilities related to language and verbal functioning. In contrast, competing batteries such as the CMS, TOMAL, and WRAML allow for *modality specific assessment and contrast* by evaluating the memory and learning of both auditory and visual information. Such a broadened assessment is likely to be of more value in the identification and treatment of nonverbal learning disabilities, right hemisphere or global head injuries, generalized cerebral vascular accidents, ADHD, and developmental disorders. For this reason, the CVLT-C may be most useful *not as an initial screening measure*, but as an in-depth tool to generate specific treatment recommendations, evaluate the efficacy of remediation activities via pre-post comparisons, and promote research protocols with children experiencing specific language-based memory and/or learning impairments.

REVIEWER'S REFERENCES

Sheslow, D., & Adams, W. (1990). Wide Range Assessment of Memory and Learning. Wilmington, DE: Wide Range.
Talley, J. L. (1993). Children's Auditory Verbal Learning Test-2. Odessa, FL: Psychological Assessment Resources.
Reynolds, C. R., & Bigler, E. D. (1994). Test of Memory and Learning. Austin, TX: PRO-ED, Inc.
Cohen, M. (1997). Children's Memory Scale. San Antonio, TX: The Psychological Corporation.

[42]
California Verbal Learning Test, Research Edition, Adult Version.

Purpose: Assesses "multiple strategies and processes involved in learning and remembering verbal material."

Population: Adolescents and adults.

Publication Dates: 1983–1987.

Acronym: CVLT.

Scores, 5: Semantic Clustering, Serial Clustering, Correct, Perseverations, Intrusions.

Administration: Individual.

Price Data, 1998: $42 per 25 record forms; $129.50 per set including 25 record forms and manual (91 pages); $96 per manual.

Time: (15) minutes plus a 20-minute delay when nonverbal testing may occur.

Comments: 2 lists (A and B) administered in various combinations using Immediate Free Recall, Short-Delay Free Recall, Cued Recall, and Long Delay Testing.

Authors: Dean C. Delis, Joel H. Kramer, Edith Kaplan, and Beth A. Ober.

Publisher: The Psychological Corporation.

Cross References: See T4:364 (12 references).

TEST REFERENCES

1. Barr, W. B., Goldberg, E., Wasserstein, J., & Novelly, R. A. (1990). Retrograde amnesia following unilateral temporal lobectomy. *Neuropsychologia, 28*, 243–255.
2. Dupont, R. M., Jernigan, T. L., Butters, N., Delis, D., Hesselink, J. R., Heindel, W., & Gillin, J. C. (1990). Subcortical abnormalities detected in bipolar affective disorder using magnetic resonance imaging. *Archives of General Psychiatry, 47*, 55–59.
3. Gur, R. E., Gur, R. C., & Saykin, A. J. (1990). Neurobehavioral studies in schizophrenia: Implications for regional brain dysfunction. *Schizophrenia Bulletin, 16*, 445–451.
4. Heilman, K. M., Bowers, D., Watson, R. T., Day, A., Valenstein, E., Hammond, E., & Duara, R. (1990). Frontal hypermetabolism and thalamic hypometabolism in a patient with abnormal orienting and retrosplenial amnesia. *Neuropsychologia, 28*, 161–169.
5. Taylor, A. E., Saint-Cyr, J. A., & Lang, A. E. (1990). Memory and learning in early Parkinson's disease: Evidence for a "frontal lobe syndrome". *Brain and Cognition, 13*, 211-232.
6. Tompkins, C. A., Holland, A. L., Ratcliff, G., Costello, A., Leahy, L. F., & Cowell, V. (1990). Predicting cognitive recovery from closed head-injury in children and adolescents. *Brain and Cognition, 13*, 86-97.
7. Akshoomoff, N. A., Courchesne, E., Press, G. A., & Iragui, V. (1992). Contribution of the cerebellum to neuropsychological functioning: Evidence from a case of cerebellar degenerative disorder. *Neuropsychologia, 30*, 315-328.
8. Hoff, A. L., Riordan, H., O'Donnell, D., Stritzke, P., Neale, C., Boccio, A., Anand, A. K., & DeLisi, L. E. (1992). Anomalous lateral sulcus asymmetry and cognitive function in first-episode schizophrenia. *Schizophrenia Bulletin, 18*, 257–273.
9. Kaplan, R. F., Meadows, M.-E., Vincent, L. C., Logigan, E. L., & Steere, A. C. (1992). Memory impairment and depression in patients with Lyme encephalopathy: Comparison with fibromyalgia and nonpsychotically depressed patients. *Neurology, 42*, 1263-1267.
10. Shear, P. K., Tallal, P., & Delis, D. C. (1992). Verbal learning and memory in language impaired children. *Neuropsychologia, 30*, 451-458.
11. Swirsky-Sacchetti, T., Mitchell, D. R., Seward, J., Gonzales, C., Lublin, F., Knobler, R., & Field, H. L. (1992). Neuropsychological and structural brain lesions in multiple sclerosis: A regional analysis. *Neurology, 42*, 1291–1295.
12. Chouinard, M. J., & Braun, C. M. J. (1993). A meta-analysis of the relative sensitivity of neuropsychological screening tests. *Journal of Clinical and Experimental Neuropsychology, 15*, 591-607.

13. Goldberg, T. E., Hyde, T. M., Kleinman, J. E., & Weinberger, D. R. (1993). Course of schizophrenia: Neuropsychological evidence for a static encephalopathy. *Schizophrenia Bulletin, 19*, 797–804.

14. Krupp, L. B., Masur, D. M., & Kaufman, L. D. (1993). Neurocognitive dysfunction in the eosinophilia-myalgia syndrome. *Neurology, 43*, 931–936.

15. Markowitsch, H. J., von Cramon, D. Y., & Schuri, U. (1993). Mnestic performance profile of a bilateral diencephalic infarct patient with preserved intelligence and severe amnesic disturbances. *Journal of Clinical and Experimental Neuropsychology, 15*, 627-632.

16. Trueblood, W., & Schmidt, M. (1993). Malingering and other validity considerations in the neuropsychological evaluation of mild head injury. *Journal of Clinical and Experimental Neuropsychology, 15*, 578-590.

17. Beers, S. R., Goldstein, G., & Katz, L. J. (1994). Neuropsychological differences between college students with learning disabilities and those with mild head injury. *Journal of Learning Disabilities, 27*, 315–324.

18. Buytenhuijs, E. L., Berger, H. J. C., Van Spaendonck, K. P. M., Horstink, M. W. I. M., Borm, G. F., & Cools, A. R. (1994). Memory and learning strategies in patients with Parkinson's disease. *Neuropsychologia, 32*, 335–342.

19. Crossen, J. R., & Wiens, A. N. (1994). Comparison of the Auditory-Verbal Learning Test (AVLT) and the California Verbal Learning Test (CVLT) in a sample of normal subjects. *Journal of Clinical and Experimental Neuropsychology, 16*, 190-194.

20. Damos, D. L., & Parker, E. S. (1994). High false alarm rates on a vigilance task may indicate recreational drug use. *Journal of Clinical and Experimental Neuropsychology, 16*, 713-722.

21. Deweer, B., Ergis, A. M., Fossati, P., Pillon, B., Boller, F., Agid, Y., & Dubois, B. (1994). Explicit memory, procedural learning, and lexical priming in Alzheimer's disease. *Cortex, 30*, 113-126.

22. Gold, J. M., Hermann, B. P., Randolph, C., Wyler, A. R., Goldberg, T. E., & Weinberger, D. R. (1994). Schizophrenia and temporal lobe epilepsy: A neuropsychological analysis. *Archives of General Psychiatry, 51*, 265-272.

23. Kohler, S. (1994). Quantitative characterization of verbal learning deficits in patients with Alzheimer's disease. *Journal of Clinical and Experimental Neuropsychology, 16*, 749-753.

24. Lyness, S. A., Eaton, E. M., & Schneider, L. S. (1994). Cognitive performance in older and middle-aged depressed outpatients and controls. *Journal of Gerontology: Psychological Sciences, 49*(Pt.1), P129-P136.

25. Meadows, M.-E., Kaplan, R. F., & Bromfield, E. B. (1994). Cognitive recovery with vitamin B12 therapy: A longitudinal neuropsychological assessment. *Neurology, 44*, 1764–1765.

26. Millis, S. R., & Ricker, J. H. (1994). Verbal learning patterns in moderate and severe traumatic brain injury. *Journal of Clinical and Experimental Neuropsychology, 16*, 498-507.

27. Peavy, G., Jacobs, D., Salmon, D. P., Butters, N., Delis, D. C., Taylor, M., Massman, P., Stout, J. C., Heindel, W. C., Kirson, D., Atkinson, J. H., Chandler, J. L., Grant, I., & The HNRC Group. (1994). Verbal memory performance of patients with human immunodeficiency virus infection: Evidence of subcortical dysfunction. *Journal of Clinical and Experimental Neuropsychology, 16*, 508-523.

28. Pillon, B., Deweer, B., Michon, A., Malapani, C., Agid, Y., & Dubois, B. (1994). Are explicit memory disorders of progressive supranuclear palsy related to damage to striatofrontal circuits? Comparison with Alzheimer's, Parkinson's, and Huntington's disease. *Neurology, 44*, 1264–1270.

29. Simon, E., Leach, L., Winocur, G., & Moscovitch, M. (1994). Intact primary memory in mild to moderate Alzheimer disease: Indices from the California Verbal Learning Test. *Journal of Clinical and Experimental Neuropsychology, 16*, 414-422.

30. Smits, R. C. F., Emmen, H. H., Bertelsmann, F. W., Kulig, B. M., vanLoenen, A. C., & Polman, C. H. (1994). The effects of 4-aminopyridine on cognitive function in patients with multiple sclerosis: A pilot study. *Neurology, 44*, 1701–1705.

31. Sobell, L. C., Toneatto, T., & Sobell, M. (1994). Behavioral assessment and treatment planning for alcohol, tobacco, and other drug problems: Current status with an emphasis on clinical applications. *Behavior Therapy, 25*, 533–580.

32. Strauss, M. E., & Summerfelt, A. (1994). Response to Serper and Harvey. *Schizophrenia Bulletin, 20*, 13–21.

33. Trueblood, W. (1994). Qualitative and quantitative characteristics of malingered and other invalid WAIS-R and clinical memory data. *Journal of Clinical and Experimental Neuropsychology, 16*, 597-607.

34. VanderPloeg, R. D., Schinka, J. A., & Retzlaff, P. (1994). Relationships between measures of auditory verbal learning and executive functioning. *Journal of Clinical and Experimental Neuropsychology, 16*, 243-252.

35. Weinstein, C. S., Seidman, L. J., Ahern, G., & McClure, K. (1994). Integration of neuropsychological and behavioral neurological assessment in psychiatry: A case example involving brain injury and polypharmacy. *Psychiatry, 57*, 62–76.

36. Yeates, K. O., & Mortensen, M. E. (1994). Acute and chronic neuropsychological consequences of mercury vapor poisoning in two early adolescents. *Journal of Clinical and Experimental Neuropsychology, 16*, 209-222.

37. Becker, J. T., Caldararo, R., Lopez, O. L., Dew, M. A., Dorst, S. K., & Banks, G. (1995). Qualitative features of the memory deficit associated with HIV infection and AIDS: Cross-validation of a discriminant function classification scheme. *Journal of Clinical and Experimental Neuropsychology, 17*, 134-142.

38. Bondi, M. W., Salmon, D. P., Monsch, A. U., Galasko, D., Butters, N., Klauber, M. R., Thal, L. J., & Saitoh, T. (1995). Episodic memory changes are associated with the APOE-e4 allele in nondemented older adults. *Neurology, 45*, 2203–2206.

39. Bortz, J. J., Prigatano, G. P., Blum, D., & Fisher, R. S. (1995). Differential response characteristics in nonepileptic and epileptic seizure patients on a test of verbal learning and memory. *Neurology, 45*, 2029–2034.

40. Delis, D. C., Peavy, G., Heaton, R., Butters, N., Salmon, D. P., Taylor, M., Stout, J., Mehta, P., Ryan, L., White, D., Atkinson, J. H., Chandler, J. L., McCutchan, J. A., Grant, I., & HNRC Group. (1995). Do patients with HIV-associated minor cognitive/motor disorder exhibit a "subcortical" memory profile? Evidence using the California Verbal Learning Test. *Assessment, 2*, 151-165.

41. Dupont, R. M., Jernigan, T. L., Heindel, W., Butters, N., Shafer, K., Wilson, T., Hesselink, J., & Gillin, J. C. (1995). Magnetic resonance imaging and mood disorders: Localization of white matter and other subcortical abnormalities. *Archives of General Psychiatry, 52*, 747–755.

42. Fischer, R. S., Alexander, M. P., D'esposito, M., & Otto, R. (1995). Neuropsychological and neuroanatomical correlates of confabulation. *Journal of Clinical and Experimental Neuropsychology, 17*, 20-28.

43. Gold, M., Adair, J. C., Jacobs, D. H., & Heilman, K. M. (1995). Right-left confusion in Gerstmann's Syndrome: A model of body centered spatial orientation. *Cortex, 31*, 267-283.

44. Millis, S. R. (1995). Factor structure of the California Verbal Learning Test in moderate and severe closed-head injury. *Perceptual and Motor Skills, 80*, 219-224.

45. Millis, S. R., Putnam, S. H., Adams, K. M., & Ricker, J. H. (1995). The California Verbal Learning Test in the detection of incomplete effort in neuropsychological evaluation. *Psychological Assessment, 7*, 463–471.

46. Yehuda, R., Keefe, R. S. E., Harvey, P. D., Levengood, R. A., Gerber, D. K., Geni, J., & Siever, L. J. (1995). Learning and memory in combat veterans with posttraumatic stress disorder. *American Journal of Psychiatry, 152*, 137-139.

47. Barrett, D. H., Green, M. L., Morris, R., Giles, W. H., & Croft, J. B. (1996). Cognitive functioning and post-traumatic stress disorder. *American Journal of Psychiatry, 153*, 1492–1494.

48. Brugger, P., Monsch, A. U., Salmon, D. P., & Butters, N. (1996). Random number generation in dementia of the Alzheimer type: A test of frontal executive functions. *Neuropsychologia, 34*, 97–103.

49. Galloway, S., Malloy, P., Kohn, R., Gillard, E., Duffy, J., Rogg, J., Tung, G., Richardson, E., Thomas, C., & Westlake, R. (1996). MRI and neuropsychological differences in early- and late-life-onset geriatric depression. *Neurology, 46*, 1567-1574.

50. Harvey, P. D., Stokes, J. L., Lord, J., & Pogge, D. L. (1996). Neurocognitive and personality assessment of adolescent substance abusers: A multidimensional approach. *Assessment, 3*, 241–253.

51. Hermann, B. P., Seidenberg, M., Wyler, A., Davies, K., Christeson, J., Moran, M., & Stroup, E. (1996). The effects of human hippocampal resection on the serial position curve. *Cortex, 32*, 323–334.

52. Jeste, D. V., Heaton, S. C., Paulsen, J. S., Ercoli, L., Harris, M. J., & Heaton, R. K. (1996). Clinical and neuropsychological comparison of psychotic depression with nonpsychotic depression and schizophrenia. *American Journal of Psychiatry, 153*, 490–496.

53. Pillon, B., Dubois, B., & Agid, Y. (1996). Testing cognition may contribute to the diagnosis of movement disorders. *Neurology, 46*, 329–334.

54. Raudin, L. D., Hilton, E., Primeau, M., Clements, C., & Barr, W. B. (1996). Memory functioning in lyme borreliosis. *Journal of Clinical Psychiatry, 57*, 282–286.

55. Tierney, M. C., Szalai, J. P., Snow, W. G., Fisher, R. H., Nores, A., Nadon, G., Dunn, E., & St. George-Hyslop, P. H. (1996). Prediction of probable Alzheimer's disease in mentally-impaired patients: A prospective longitudinal. *Neurology, 46*, 661–665.

56. Tierney, M. C., Szalai, J. P., Snow, W. G., Fisher, R. H., Tsuda, T., Chi, H., McLachlan, D. R., & St. George-Hyslop, P. H. (1996). A prospective study of the clinical utility of Apo E genotype in the prediction of outcome in patients with memory impairment. *Neurology, 46*, 149–154.

57. Mendez, M. F., Cherrier, M. M., & Perryman, K. M. (1997). Differences between Alzheimer's disease and vascular dementia on information processing measures. *Brain and Cognition, 34*, 301–310.

Review of the California Verbal Learning Test, Research Edition, Adult Version by RAY FENTON, Supervisor of Assessment and Evaluation, Anchorage School District, Anchorage, AK:

The California Verbal Learning Test (CVLT) is a brief, individually administered measure of "multiple strategies and processes involved in learning and remembering verbal material" (manual, p. 1). The CVLT has had extensive use as a measure of verbal learning and memory based on the presentation of lists of common English words. The test can be administered within about 40 minutes including a 20-minute time delay to allow forgetting.

Sixteen words over five trials (four words from each of four semantic categories) are presented to assess immediate recall, short-delay recall, and de-layed recall. The responses of clients are coded as "C" for the correct recall of a word, "I" for the recall of a word not on the list that is considered an intrusion, or "P" for perseveration or the repetition of any response on the same trial.

Scoring may be done using either paper and pencil or the CVLT Administration and Scoring Software, that will automatically compute the ex-pected and chance scores and ratio of expected to chance scores. When hand scoring the examiner counts types of responses and enters counts into formulas included as part of the 12-page booklet used for recording performance. The record booklet re-minds the test administrator to consider examinee history including neurological injury, developmental learning disability, medical illness, psychiatric disor-der, loss of consciousness, and substance abuse.

The CVLT Research Edition Manual Version 1 provides a clear introduction to the purposes of the test and introduction to the prior research upon which the test is based. Chapter 3, Theoretical and Empirical Foundations of the CVLT Indices, pro-vides a good description of common errors and typical experiences with examinees. There are gen-eral interpretive guidelines for the use of various scores including Recall Measures: Immediate Free Recall (Lists A and B), Short-Delay Free Recall, Cued Recall, Long-Delay Testing; Learning Char-acteristics: Semantic Clustering, Serial Clustering, Percentage of total Recall from Primacy, Middle, and Recency Regions, Slope (increment in words recalled per trial over trials), Consistency of Item Recall from Trial to Trial; Recall Errors: Perseverations and Intrusions; and Recognition Mea-sures: Correct Target Recognitions (Hits), False Positives, Discriminability, and Response Bias. Scor-ing also produces various ratios that allow consider-ation of the role of interference and retention over time.

Norms development is based on a relatively small group of 273 neurologically intact individuals with a mean age of 58.93 drawn from research projects across the country. Individuals were screened for a history of neurological or psychological disor-ders that might affect memory. Information is presented suggesting that age and sex affect learning and retention.

Consistency of performance was estimated with a split-half correlation of .63 and an estimated total test reliability of .77. Coefficient alpha reliability, based on the four category scores, is .74. Internal consistency reliability coefficients presented include within trials (odd-even) (.92) and semantic categories (split-half) (.77). Item totals across five trials with two samples had correlations of .70 and .85.

Limited test-retest reliability information was available at the time of publication of the Research Edition Manual Version 1. Test-retest reliability for a sample of 21 normal adults over a year on the various CVLT scores showed correlations ranging from .12 to .79 with most correlations above .55. Correlations are .60 and above for Short Delay Cued Recall, Long Delay Free Recall, Long Delay Cued Recall, Percent Primacy Recall, Perseverations, Free-Recall Intrusions, and Discriminability. Ad-ditional information is needed on test-retest reli-ability.

Validity is discussed in terms of factor analysis of scores and performance with selected neurological groups. Groups showing the expected patterns of impairment included chronic alcoholics, patients di-agnosed with idiopathic Parkinson's Disease, Mul-tiple Sclerosis, Huntington's Disease, and Alzheimer's disease. The CVLT has a successful history of use with a variety of populations (Delis, Freeland, Kramer, & Kaplan, 1988; Kramer & Delis, 1991; Millis, Putnam, Adams, & Ricker, 1995).

CONCLUSION. The CVLT is an easy-to-use and well-designed measure of multiple strategies and processes involved in learning and remembering ver-bal material. The Research Edition has retained the positive features of other versions of the CVLT and will prove useful in screening and clinical assessment. The test may be of special interest to practitioners who must concern themselves with individuals who, because of self-interest, may exhibit incomplete effort (Millis et al., 1995) or with members of the selected neurological groups identified above.

REVIEWER'S REFERENCES

Delis, D. C., Freeland, J., Kramer, J. H., & Kaplan, E. (1988). Integrating clinical assessment with cognitive neuroscience: Construct validation of the Califor-nia Verbal Learning Test. *Journal of Consulting and Clinical Psychology, 56*, 123–130.
Kramer, J. H., & Delis, D. C. (1991). Interference effects on the California Verbal Learning Test: A construct validation study. *Journal of Consulting and Clinical Psychology, 3*, 299–302.
Millis, S. R., Putnam, S. H., Adams, K. M., & Ricker, J. H. (1995). The California Verbal Learning Test in the detection of incomplete effort in neuropsychological evaluation. *Psychological Assessment, 7*, 463–471.

[43]
Campbell Interest and Skill Survey.

Purpose: "Measures self-reported interests and skills."
Population: Ages 15 years to adult.
Publication Dates: 1989–1992.
Acronym: CISS.

Scores, 99: 7 Orientation Scales (Influencing, Organizing, Helping, Creating, Analyzing, Producing, Adventuring), 29 Basic Scales (Leadership, Law/Politics, Public Speaking, Sales, Advertising/Marketing, Supervision, Financial Services, Office Practices, Adult Development, Child Development, Counseling, Religious Activities, Medical Practice, Art/Design, Performing Arts, Writing, International Activities, Fashion, Culinary Arts, Mathematics, Science, Mechanical Crafts, Woodworking, Farming/Forestry, Plants/Gardens, Animal Care, Athletics/Physical Fitness, Military/Law Enforcement, Risks/Adventure), 60 Occupational Scales (Attorney, Financial Planner, Hotel Manager, Manufacturer's Representative, Marketing Director, Realtor, CEO/President, Human Resources Director, School Superintendent, Advertising Account Executive, Media Executive, Public Relations Director, Corporate Trainer, Secretary, Bank Manager, Insurance Agent, Retail Store Manager, Hospital Administrator, Accountant/CPA, Bookkeeper, Child Care Worker, Guidance Counselor, Religious Leader, Teacher K–12, Social Worker, Psychologist, Nurse (RN), Nursing Administrator, Commercial Artist, Fashion Designer, Liberal Arts Professor, Librarian, Musician, Translator/Interpreter, Writer/Editor, Restaurant Manager, Chef, Physician, Chemist, Medical Researcher, Engineer, Math/Science Teacher, Computer Programmer, Statistician, Systems Analyst, Carpenter, Electrician, Veterinarian, Airline Mechanic, Agribusiness Manager, Landscape Architect, Architect, Police Officer, Military Officer, Ski Instructor, Test Pilot, Athletic Coach, Athletic Trainer, Emergency Medical Technician, Fitness Instructor), 2 Special Scales (Academic Focus, Extraversion), 3 Procedural Checks (Response Percentage Check, Inconsistency Check, Omitted Items Check).

Administration: Group.

Price Data, 1997: $39.95 per hardcover manual; $24.95 per softcover manual; $2.95 per CISS Career Planner; $9.95 per 50 interest/skill pattern worksheets; $15 per 25 Microtest Q System answer sheets; $5.25 per Microtest Q System report; $24.95 per 100 report cover sheets; $39.95 per preview package including soft cover manual and 25 answer sheets; $6.25 per mail-in answer sheet/report.

Time: (35) minutes.

Comments: Each scale contains both an interest and a skill score; combined gender scales allow for broadest interpretation of survey results; workshops available.

Author: David Campbell.

Publisher: NCS Assessments.

Cross References: See T4:368 (1 reference).

Review of the Campbell Interest and Skill Inventory by RICHARD C. PUGH, Professor of Education, and Director of Education Technology Services, Inc., Indiana University, Bloomington, IN:

The development of the Campbell Interest and Skill Survey (CISS) was enriched by the extensive background of more than 35 years with the domain of vocational interests during the legendary career of David P. Campbell. The domain of the CISS Survey includes the generation of scores for both self-reported interests and self-reported skills. It is argued in the encyclopedic manual that scores on both self-reported interests and self-reported skills are relevant to a person's career planning. The purpose of the Survey is to assist individuals in gaining a better understanding of their interests and skills in making career decisions. It is one of three surveys (the other two are the Campbell Organizational Survey [12:60] and the Campbell Leadership Index [12:59]) in the Campbell Development Survey (CDS) Battery, which are designed for use in settings such as educational institutions, human resource departments, training and development programs, and in individual counseling sessions.

The CISS consists of 200 interest items in which examinees are asked to rate their level of interest and 120 skill items in which examinees are asked to rate their level of skill. The manual states that scores on the interest items reflect the person's attraction for an occupational area and scores on the skill items are an estimate of a person's self-confidence in performing in the area. The self-reported interest and skill scores are organized into the following types: Orientation Scales (7 scales), Basic Scales (29 scales), Occupational Scales (58 scales), Special Scales (2 scales), and Procedural Checks (3 checks). For each type of score, the manual reports statements of rationale, developmental histories, technical merits including estimates of reliability and validity, and intended uses. The self-reported interests and skills scores for all the CISS scales are reported and compared in an individually prepared computer-generated, multi-page CISS Individual Profile.

In the generation of items for the CISS, guiding principles for item selection included (a) good response distributions, (b) clustering into homogeneous sets that discriminated between individuals in different occupations, and (c) a conceptually simple wording and clear style. Items were also screened to avoid offending anyone by the item content or grammar. It is reported in the manual that a few hundred people were used to try out early versions of items.

A 6-point item-response format was chosen after considering several other alternatives. It is argued that this provided a wide range for examinees to express a variety of choices yet the absence of a middle-point caused a mild stand to be taken. Further, an ambiguous meaning associated with a middle-point type response was avoided. In the development of the norms a standard score with a mean of 50 and a standard deviation of 10 was adopted because of the familiarity. Through this scaling, a comparison of scores in the same profile was permitted.

Reasons were given for including skill items on the Survey. It was felt that self-perceptions about skills play an important role in determining career choices and a better picture of an individual's skill levels would be gained. The manual emphasizes that the scores on skill scales should be interpreted as a measure of an examinee's belief about how well he or she can perform a range of occupational activities. The interpretation of the skill scale scores is judged more appropriate if the scores are considered a measure of an examinee's self-confidence in the skill area. Evidences were presented to demonstrate the validity of self-reported skills. One type of evidence was the report of self-reported skill scores of workers in different occupations. The rank-order of occupations tended to correspond to one's expectation. Correlations between the skill scores and interests scores for the Orientation and Basic Scales were reported, which indicated a substantial amount of common variance between them. For example, the median Orientation correlation was .70 between interest and skill scores across the seven orientations with a range from a low of .66 for the Orientation scale of Helping to a high of .76 for the Orientation scale of Influencing, indicating substantial overlap between the measure of one's vocational interest and the measure of one's confidence to perform (i.e., self-reported skill) in the same area.

The interest and skill items of the CISS are organized into 7 pairs (i.e., one interest and one skill scale) of Orientation scales and 29 pairs of Basic scales grouped within an Orientation scale. The argument is made that there are similarities between the CISS Orientations and the Holland Themes and a comparison is presented. Differences are also pointed out but the conclusion is reached that the similarities are more evident than differences. This reviewer tends to agree. A statement of rationale for each of the scales is presented. For each orientation scale a table is presented listing the written text of the item along with a corrected correlation between each item and the scale score. Based on a reported diverse sample of employed adults numbering 4,842 the item correlations with scale were mostly at the .50 to .60 level, which reflected the principal component analysis that was used in their formulation. The authors

report that the Orientation Scales were constructed using a combination of statistical information and logical reasoning. The norms were generated for the Orientation Scales by calculating a raw score mean of male examinees ($N = 3,435$) and a raw score mean was calculated for females ($N = 1,790$) and the two means were averaged to generate a mean used in the raw score to standard score conversion formula. This procedure was followed in order to give each gender equal weight in the norms. The norms have a general population mean of 50 and standard deviation of 10.

Evidence for the validity of the Orientation scales includes intercorrelations between interest and skill scores, which were lower among orientation scales and higher between interest and skill scores within an Orientation scale. Another source of validity evidence is the relationship between 58 occupational samples and Orientation Scale scores. A table of means of each occupational group is presented for each Orientation Scale. The conclusion is reached by the authors that the pattern of means portray a rational, straightforward trend. My conclusion is that they seem to follow one's expectations. Both internal consistency and test-retest reliability coefficients are reported. The median internal consistency estimate is .87 and median test-retest correlation (over approximately 90 days) was .87 for interest scores and .81 for skill scores for the Orientation Scales. The types of validity and reliability evidence reported for the Basic Scales are similar to the types of evidence reported for the Orientation Scales. In general, the Basic Scale intercorrelations were higher between the interest and skill scores within a Basic Scale than across Basic Scales and the pattern of means for 58 occupational samples for the 29 Basic Scales argued for their validity. The median internal consistency coefficient was .86 for interest scores and .79 for skill scores. The median test-retest correlations were .83 for interest scores and .79 for skill scores. Given that some of the Basic Scale scores are based on as few as three items, these reliability estimates are quite high.

In contrast to the Orientation and Basic Scales, the CISS Occupational Scales were developed empirically by administering the Survey to workers in a wide range of occupations and comparing each occupation's item responses with the responses of a General Reference Sample. Items were selected that best discriminated between the occupational sample and the general reference sample. As a result the items are not as homogeneous as for the Orientation and Basic Scales. They were generated empirically without an emphasis placed on whether the items followed a logical pattern. The development of these scales followed the pattern for the Strong-Campbell Interest Inventory except the CISS uses a 6-point response format in contrast to the 3-point response format of the SCII. A second difference is that the CISS uses combined-gender scales rather than separate male and female scales for each occupation. In building the occupational scoring scales, the general reference sample statistics were weighted to reflect the male/female ratio in whichever occupational sample was being analyzed. Evidence is presented supporting the use of unisex scales. The validity of the Occupational Scales is based on the discrimination between people in an occupation and people not in the occupation. For reliability estimates, only measures of test-retest stability were presented because measures of internal consistency were judged as not appropriate. The median test-retest correlation for interest scores was .87 and for skill scores was .79.

The CISS Special Scales include both interest and skill scores for academic focus, extraversion, and variety. The Academic Focus Scale scores refer to the self-reported interests and skills related to the demands of academic environments. The Extraversion Scale scores indicate the examinee's interest and self-confidence in working with people. The Variety Scales are designed to measure one's variety of interests and skills. The manual provides information on the development of the scales, norming procedures, and evidences for their validity and reliability. The Academic Focus and Extraversion Scales are fully developed and ready for use whereas the Variety Scale remains under development and should only be used in that context.

Procedural checks for interest and personality inventories should be presented on the extent to which scores are susceptible to examinee's responding atypically to the items. The CISS provides three Procedural checks, namely, a Response Percentage Check, an Inconsistency Check, and an Omitted Items check. Cutoffs are defined for each of the three Procedural Checks for screening for aberrant item response patterns.

The CISS Profile is a comprehensive computer-generated report of an examinee's scores. Multiple examples of individual profiles are presented in the manual. A Profile consists of the scores for each of Scales within the Orientation Scales, Basic Scales, and Occupational Scales. The scores are reported by listing and plotting the interest and skill scores on the standard score scale with a mean equal to 50 and a standard deviation equal to 10. A written interpretation is generated, which elaborates the meaning of the Orientation Scales and the meaning of the Basic and Occupational Scales within Orientation Scales. In addition an interest/skill pattern is reported as well as a plot of the middle 50% of the people in the occupation. This Profile report appears to be very useful to the examinee with one exception. The exception is with the Interest/Skill pattern report which classifies a set of interest and skill scores for each scale into one of four quadrants and labels the results with the words (a) pursue, (b) avoid, (c) develop, or (d) explore. For the "pursue" quadrant, both the interest and skill scores are at least 55, the set of scores indicating that this is an area worth strong consideration because both scores are at least .5 standard deviations above the mean. Similarly, if both scores are 45 or below the set of scores is labeled "avoid" indicating that both the levels of interest and skill are low on the particular scale. The other two quadrants are defined by either the interest or skill score at 55 or above when the other one is 54 or below. That is, if the interest score is 55 or above but the skill score is 54 or below the set of scores is labeled "develop" but if the set of scores is reversed the set of scores is labeled "explore." When attention is drawn to the difference between the interest and skill scores, questions regarding the reliability of their difference becomes an issue. It is apparent that very small differences in the interest and skill scores might be reported differently. For example, suppose the interest score was 55 and the corresponding skill score was 54, the set of scores would be labeled "develop" but if they were reversed with the interest score 54 and the skill score 55 they would be labeled "explore." In actuality, there probably is no real difference between these two sets of scores given the relatively lower reliabilities of their differences and the accompanying increase in their standard errors of measurement. Much caution should be exercised when interpreting sets of scores labeled either "develop" or "explore" on the profile.

In summary, the CISS has a very extensive and comprehensive manual and has been developed following and often exceeding the *Standards for Educational and Psychological Testing* (AERA, APA, & NCME, 1985). Even though the CISS has only recently been available, it has accumulated a very rich amount of validity and reliability information. As a result, the CISS is projected to become an extensively used and researched survey of self-reported interests and skills.

REVIEWER'S REFERENCE

American Educational Research Association, American Psychological Association, & National Council on Measurement in Education. (1985). *Standards for educational and psychological testing*. Washington, DC: American Psychological Association, Inc.

Review of the Campbell Interest and Skill Survey by MICHAEL J. ROSZKOWSKI, Associate Professor of Psychology/Director of Marketing Research, The American College, Bryn Mawr, PA:

The Campbell Interest and Skill Survey (CISS) is a career interest inventory intended to help people make informed occupational choices by identifying the type of work they would enjoy (Interest) and could confidently perform (Skill). The specified possible applications for the CISS include educational and occupational planning, learning about the interests and skills associated with different occupations, determining the causes of job dissatisfaction, team building, improving child-parent communications regarding career plans, and facilitating interaction at conferences and retreats. The CISS is said to be appropriate for most adults and even adolescents as young as 15 years old, provided they can understand the vocabulary used in the questions. The reading level of the instrument is reported to be sixth-grade.

The CISS consists of 320 items listing occupations, school subjects, and work-related activities. As implied by its name, the questionnaire is divided into two parts: Interest (Part I) and Skill (Part II). The first 200 items are Interest items, and the rest are Skill items. Three types of items form the Interest portion of the survey: (a) an occupational title, (b) school subjects, and (c) specific work activities. The Skills portion consists of items specifying occupational activities, similar to Items 12–200 in the Interest portion, but phrased in different language.

The CISS uses 6-point response formats. On the Interest items listing an occupational title or activity, the respondent has to indicate his or her degree of attraction or aversion to it (strongly like, like, slightly like, slightly dislike, dislike, strongly dislike). The school subjects are rated on a scale involving three degrees of "yes" and three degrees of "no." On the Skill items, the individual indicates his or her self-assessed ability to perform the activity by assigning himself or herself a skill level (expert, good, slightly above average, slightly below average, poor, none) for a particular task. It is reported that the Skill items should be considered measures of "self-confidence" rather than skill per se.

The 320 items form three types of scales, expressed as T-scores: 60 Occupational scales, 29 Basic scales, and 7 Orientation scales. (Not all items are used on the orientation scales: only 75 interest and 69 skill items are used.) For each scale, both interest and skill scores are provided. The level of abstractness increases as one progresses from the Occupational scales through the Orientation scales. In addition, scores on three special scales are computed: Academic Focus, Extraversion, and Variety. (The Variety scale is still experimental.)

The Occupational scales (e.g., Attorney) were developed by comparing the scores that satisfied workers from different occupations received on each item to scores from a reference group of workers in general. Items that differentiated between an occupational group and the reference sample of general workers were retained as part of that Occupational scale. The occupational samples ranged in size from 35 (Athletic Coach) to 199 (School Superintendent), with a median sample size of 75 persons per occupation. Data were collected primarily by mail from 5,225 people (3,435 males and 1,790 females) representing more than 60 occupations. The cooperation rate is not indicated (i.e., how many of those contacted agreed to participate). The Basic scales (e.g., Public Speaking), which are more general in nature than the Occupational scales, were formed by grouping together items that measured homogenous content. The most abstract are the orientation scales, which subsume the Basic scales; each of the 29 Basic scales falls into one of the 7 Orientation scales. The CISS Orientation scales build on Holland's six basic work personality types, or work "themes." The names of the orientations on the CISS differ from Holland's typology, but conceptually they are similar, with some exceptions. The names of all orientations were changed to be gerunds rather than adjectives so that they would appear more action oriented.

Scoring is done by the publisher. The scoring process includes three procedural checks to detect patterns of response that may indicate distorted answers of dubious validity. A computer-generated 11-page interpretive report is produced for the respondent, presenting a graphic profile of the respondent's interest and skill scores for all Orientation, Basic, and Occupational scales. The report explains the nature of each orientation and graphs the person's Interest and Skill scores. There is a two-page Report Summary for the counselor, which condenses the information provided to the respondent. Interest and Skill scores on each Occupational, Basic, and Orientation scale are compared and can be placed into one of four quadrants. An action-oriented label is used to identify each of these quadrants: (a) High Interest (55 or above) and High Skill (55 or above) = Pursue, (b) High Interest (55 or above) and Low Skill (54 or below) = Develop, (c) Low Interest (54 or below) and High Skill (55 or above) = Explore, and (d) Low Interest (45 or below) and Low Skill (45 or below) = Avoid. If the scores are mid-range (do not fall into a quadrant) in many or most areas, the report suggests that the person may not have enough experience to form strong preferences.

The studies of the CISS's reliability consist of both internal consistency and temporal stability checks. However, no data on the internal consistency reliability of the Occupational scales are available because Campbell does not believe that one should expect these scales to be internally consistent.

The internal consistency reliability of the Interest portion of the Basic scales, based on 4,842 employed adults, ranges from a low of .69 (Adult Development) to a high of .92 (Religious Activities), with a median internal consistency reliability of .86. On the Skill portion, the internal consistency reliability ranges from .62 (Performing Arts) to .87 (Religious Activities), with a median internal consistency reliability of .79. The reported correlations between the items and their respective Basic scales are acceptable for both Skills and Interests, but these correlations are lower for Skills. Considering that the item-Basic scale correlations are lower on the Skill portion, and that there are fewer Skill than Interest items, the lower internal consistency reliability of the Skill Basic scales is not surprising. A substantial number of both the Interest and the Skill Basic scales reliability estimates are below .85. Given the relatively high item-to-scale correlations of the existing items, the only way to increase internal consistency reliability of the Basic scales would be to increase the number of items, because the problem is not one of having inappropriate items on the scales.

The internal consistency of the Interest portion of the Orientation scales ranged from .82 (Creating) to .93 (Analyzing), with a median internal consistency reliability of .87. The median internal consistency reliability of the Skills portion of these scales was also .87, but with a larger range: 76 (Creating) to .89 (Influencing). The Creating Ori-

entation Scale has the weakest internal consistency reliability of the Orientation scales on both interest and skill.

The test-retest reliability analysis was based on a sample of 324 individuals in 54 occupations who took the CISS twice, 3 months apart. The median test-retest reliability for the Occupational scales was .87 on the Interest domains and .79 on the Skill domains. The Basic scales had a median reliability of .83 (range .75 to .90) and .79 (range .74 to .86) on the Interest and Skill portions, respectively. The Orientation Interest scales' test-retest reliability ranged from .81 to .88, with a median of .87. The Skill portion of the Orientation scales had a median reliability of .81, ranging from .75 to .84. In general, Skill scores appear to be less reliable than the Interest scales at all levels of the CISS, probably because (as Campbell explains) they are shorter. There is no discussion of the reliability of the classification into the four quadrants.

The test manual's discussion of the CISS's validity involves (a) consideration of the intercorrelations among the various scales and (b) the pattern of mean scores for the different occupational groups. The factor analysis conducted in support of the development of the seven Orientations, although not presented under validity in the manual, also bears on the instrument's validity. The correlation pattern between the Occupational and Orientation scales is said to indicate that the Occupational scores correlate most highly with their appropriate orientation. With a few exceptions, the data provided in the manual support this contention.

Next, evidence is presented to show that the Occupational scales discriminate between workers in a particular occupation and the general population. The median difference on an Occupational scale between people in a particular occupation and workers from other occupations is about 2 standard deviations. The difference between the scores of people working in the occupation and those who do not is called the "validity index" for each occupational scale. In addition, the tables in the manual present, for each Occupational scale, the three highest scoring and the three lowest scoring occupations relative to the criterion occupation; as noted by Campbell, the patterns appear to make sense.

The validity of the Basic scales is inferred from the "drop-line" charts, which show the mean Basic interest and skill scores for each of 58 occupations on all the Basic scales. The pattern is said to "correspond to reasonable expectations." Further validity evidence is said to be found in the extent of overlap between the Interest and Skill portions of the Basic scales. The median correlation is .68 (based on 5,391 working adults). Furthermore, Occupational groups that scored below or above the general population norm on a given Basic interest scale scored correspondingly lower or higher on that skill scale as well. Rarely was the discrepancy in corresponding mean Interest and Skill Basic scores as large as 5 points (1/2 of a standard deviation).

The authors claim that the Orientation scales are valid based on the fact that the intercorrelations between them are low, which means that they are measuring different dimensions.

The nature of the correlations between corresponding interest and skill scores on the orientation scales is also offered as evidence for the validity of the Orientation scales. Data from three samples are presented: 88 high school students, 157 college students, and 5,391 employed adults. The median correlations were .65, .70, and .70, respectively. Correlations between the items and the Orientation scales are also furnished as proof of validity. The 75 Interest items and the 69 Skill items that form the Orientation scales correlate at a median of .59 (Interest) and .58 (Skill) with their respective Orientation scales. The last line of evidence is a graphical presentation of the mean orientation scores for the 58 occupational samples, which shows a match between a particular occupation and orientation.

Some further comments on the interest-skill correlations are warranted. Campbell and his coauthors note that previous research found low correlations between these two dimensions. In contrast, the correlations between the interest and skill scores on the CISS are substantial. These findings support what I intuitively would expect, namely that people gravitate toward those areas that they feel they have competence to perform, and shy away from things for which they have low levels of skill, especially if improvements in skill are perceived to be impossible (e.g., innate ability) or difficult to bring about. If one were to correct the correlations between the CISS Interest and Skill scores for unreliability, some of these correlations would be of a size that could cause one to question the value of the skill dimension, given its high degree of redundancy with interest. Further practical experience with this instrument will probably allow us to better answer this question in the future. (Campbell acknowledges that "not as much is known about this domain," preface, p. iv.)

In summary, I consider the CISS to be a valuable addition to the category of empirically key interest inventories, one that could provide information not available from the other interest inventories. The reliability and validity data on the CISS are not as extensive as that on the SCII, but then it has not been around for as long. I am sure further psychometric studies will be published on this scale by its users as well as its authors. The major weakness of the CISS is the less-than-ideal level of reliability on some scales, a problem common to most interest inventories. It might prove difficult to obtain a higher level of reliability without increasing the number of items to a point where it becomes impractical due to length. One way of increasing the size of the skill item pool without sacrificing practicality would be to have the examinee rate the same exact items for both interest and skill, rather than having separate interest and skill items. (I'm not sure why this approach was not used in the construction of the CISS, but perhaps there are reasons.) The test materials and reports are very attractive, user-friendly, and colorful. Test users should find them quite appealing.

[44]
Canadian Achievement Tests, Second Edition.

Purpose: Designed to measure achievement in the basic skills in reading, language, spelling, mathematics, and study skills.
Population: Grades 2.6–12.9.
Publication Dates: 1981–1995.
Acronym: CAT/2.
Administration: Group.
Price Data, 1996: C$75 per 35 consumable test booklets and examiner's manual (specify Level 12 or 13); $95 per 35 reusable test booklets with examiner's manual (specify Level 14–19); $1 for scoring keys (specify level); $58 per 50 machine-scorable answer sheets (specify level); $28 per 25 hand-scorable U-Score answer sheets (specify test and level); $17 per 50 student diagnostic profile sheets (specify level); $1 per class record sheet; $35 per 35 Parent's Guide to CAT Results; $8 per examiner's manual (specify level); $32 per norms book ('92, 109 pages); $32 per technical bulletin ('92, 139 pages); $21 per handbook for test coordinators ('92, 95 pages); $26 per class management guide ('95, 256 pages); $90 per training videotape; $48 per Multi-Level specimen set (grades 2.6–12.9) including Introduction to CAT/2, 1 copy each of Level 13 (consumable) and Levels 15 and 18 (reusable) booklets, examiner's manual (Levels 13, 14–16, and 17–19), Level 13 and Levels 14–16 practice test, Levels 14–16 machine-

scorable answer sheet, Levels 17–19 U-Score answer sheet, Level 16 Student Diagnostic Profile Sheet, class record sheet, and sample scoring reports; $21 per Primary specimen set (grades 2.6–4.2); $21 per Junior specimen set (grades 4.0–7.2).

Comments: Norm group and "criterion referenced"; "cross-linked" with Canadian Test of Cognitive Skills (45); hand scored or machine scored by the Canadian Test Centre.

Author: Canadian Test Centre, Educational Assessment Services.

Publisher: Canadian Test Centre, Educational Assessment Services [Canada].

a) LOCATOR TESTS.

Population: Grades 2–6, Grades 6–12.

Scores, 2: Vocabulary, Mathematics.

Price Data: $21 per Test 1 or Test 2 with directions and 35 answer sheets; $21 per 50 additional answer sheets; $7 per additional directions.

Time: (23) minutes.

b) LEVEL 12.

Population: Grades 2.6–3.2.

Scores, 8: Reading (Word Analysis, Vocabulary, Comprehension); Spelling, Language (Language Mechanics, Language Expression); Mathematics (Mathematics Concepts and Applications, Mathematics Computation).

Time: (170) minutes.

c) LEVEL 13.

Population: Grades 3.0–4.2.

Scores, 8: Same as *b* above.

Time: (185) minutes.

d) LEVEL 14.

Population: Grades 4.0–5.2.

Scores, 8: Same as *b* above without Word Analysis and the addition of Study Skills.

Time: (211) minutes.

e) LEVEL 15.

Population: Grades 5.0–6.2.

Scores, 8: Same as *d* above.

Time: Same as *d* above.

f) LEVEL 16.

Population: Grades 6.0–7.2.

Scores, 8: Same as *d* above.

Time: Same as *d* above.

g) LEVEL 17.

Population: Grades 7.0–8.2.

Scores, 8: Same as *d* above.

Time: (199) minutes.

h) LEVEL 18.

Population: Grades 8.0–10.2.

Scores, 8: Same as *d* above.

Time: (199) minutes.

i) LEVEL 19.

Population: Grades 10.0–12.9.

Scores, 8: Same as *d* above.

Time: (199) minutes.

Cross References: See T4:371 (3 references); for a review by L. A. Whyte of an earlier edition, see 9:187.

TEST REFERENCES

1. Lemoine, H. E., Levy, B. A., & Hutchison, A. (1993). Increasing the naming speed of poor readers: Representations formed across repetitions. *Journal of Experimental Child Psychology, 55,* 297-328.
2. Wilkinson, S. C. (1993). WISC-R profiles of children with superior intellectual ability. *Gifted Child Quarterly, 37,* 84-91.

Review of the Canadian Achievement Tests, Second Edition by JOHN HATTIE, Chair, Educational Research Methodology, University of North Carolina at Greensboro, Greensboro, NC:

The Canadian Achievement Tests, Second Edition (CAT/2) is designed to measure the achievement of grades 2.6 to 12.9 Canadian students in Reading, Spelling, Language, Study Skills, and Mathematics. Although not tied to a particular instructional program, each test has subscores aimed to assist in diagnosing strengths and weaknesses across various curricula objectives. Further, the CAT/2 is intended to measure students' thinking skills in applying information and in thinking critically. The Reading test assesses Word Analysis, Vocabulary, and Comprehension; Spelling assesses vowels, consonants, and structural units of words; Language assesses Mechanics and Expression; and Mathematics assesses Concepts and Applications and Computation. Two locator tests, of 20 reading and 20 math items, can be used to best estimate the appropriate grade level test to administer to a student.

The package includes a Parents' Guide, a Handbook for Test Coordinators, an Examiner's Manual, and a Class Management Guide of Instructional Activities for Teachers. The CAT/2 is used by Statistics Canada to track achievement over time, and thus the tests often are used for high stakes testing. There is a caution to not concentrate instruction on the specific content of the test, as this can have the effect of narrowing the curriculum, distorting the conclusions to be drawn from test results, and ultimately shortchanging students in terms of the richness and breadth of their educational experience.

The items were field tested using a sample of 5,000 students, and the final standardization sample comprised 50,000 students drawn by stratified random sampling from the public, separate, private, and bank schools, by geographic region, degree of urbanization, and by school level. The scaled scores are developed in an exemplary manner, albeit within the classical test model. Given that there are so few items at each objective (within the various subtests; e.g., for word analysis within the reading test), a score conditioned on the students' total score is calculated, and this adds much credibility to the meaning of these scores.

The norms are impressive, although grade equivalent scores and percentiles are used (and these are notoriously misinterpreted). The estimates of reliability for the scale scores are reasonable, although the stability of the objective scores is sometimes very low. This test may have a major role in Canada, but barely scrapes through satisfying minimum test standards. Although the test package is over 3 inches thick, there is almost no mention of validity. There are tables of intercorrelations, but no factor analyses or interpretations. It is claimed that the development of the items are related to Canadian curricula, but there is no evidence to defend this claim. It is stated that the test is relevant to assess curricula coverage but no validity evidence is provided relating to this claim.

In short, this test has misplaced precision in its standardization and norms, could profit from a healthy dose of item response procedures, and there is a misplaced absence of the primary concerns of test validity. For a test based originally on the California Achievement Tests (40), and in its second edition, the absence of validity evidence is a major impediment to meaningful interpretation of the scores. The test must be considered "still under construction."

Review of the Canadian Achievement Tests, Second Edition by LESLIE EASTMAN LUKIN, Assessment Specialist, Lincoln Public Schools, Lincoln, NE:

The Canadian Achievement Tests, Second Edition (CAT/2) is an achievement battery that is designed to measure basic skills in Reading, Spelling, Language, Study Skills, and Mathematics. The tests can be administered to groups of students and utilizes a multiple-choice format.

Reading is broken down into Word Analysis (lower grades only), Reading Comprehension, and Vocabulary. Word analysis is only included in Levels 12 and 13 (grades 2, 3, or 4). This test measures a student's ability to identify correctly or understand the meaning of consonant/vowel sounds, compound words/syllables/contractions, roots, and affixes. Vocabulary includes understanding of synonyms, antonyms, affixes, word definitions, multimeaning words, and words in context. Multimeaning words and words in context are measured using a cloze procedure (having the student identify the missing word in a sentence or paragraph). Reading Comprehension utilizes excerpts from traditional and contemporary literature and requires students to demonstrate recall

or comprehension of stated information within the text, passage analysis, central thought, written forms/techniques, and critical assessment.

The Spelling test requires students to identify the correct spelling of vowel/consonant sounds in words and structural units in words. The items included in the Spelling test attempt to provide context for spelling by imbedding the word within a short sentence or a phrase.

Language includes both Mechanics and Expression. Mechanics focuses on the correct use of capitalization and punctuation. There are four major forms within which students are asked to demonstrate their knowledge: sentences/phrases/clauses, quotations/dialogue, writing conventions, and using editing skills. Language Expression measures a student's knowledge of the correct use of nouns/pronouns, verbs, adjectives/adverbs, sentence formation, combining sentences, topic sentences, and paragraph structure/coherence.

The items on the study skills test are organized in thematic units (hypothetical student projects). Items on this test measure a student's knowledge about or ability to use library materials, interpret graphs, organize/summarize information, and analyze/assess/interpret information.

The mathematics test contains a section on Concepts and Applications and a separate section for Computation. The section on Concepts includes numeration, number theory, data interpretation, pre-algebra concepts, measurement concepts, and logical reasoning/geometry.

A number of supplementary materials are available to support the use of the CAT/2, such as: instructional materials for teachers, information for parents about the test and preparing for the test, information for test coordinators, and practice tests.

LOCATOR TESTS. The two locator tests (one for grades 2 through 6 and another for grades 6 through 12) are designed to help test administrators select the most appropriate level of the test to administer to an individual student. Each locator test consists of 20 vocabulary items and 20 mathematics items. No psychometric information is available on either form of the locator test.

NORMS. Norms expressed in terms of percentile ranks and stanines are available for each level of the CAT/2 for grades 2 through 12 (fall, winter, and spring of the school year). Grade-equivalent and scale scores are also provided. A large norming sample (50,000) was drawn from public, separate, private, and band schools across Canada. A stratified random sampling technique was employed using geographical region and urbanization as the selection criteria. Only schools where English is the language of instruction were considered for inclusion in the sample. Neither ethnicity nor socioeconomic status were specifically considered during the selection of the sample.

In order to be able to adequately describe the norming sample, each school that participated was asked to complete a school characteristics questionnaire. Results from the questionnaire are reported in the technical manual and include information about school type (public/private), geographical region, community size, and various indices of socioeconomic status. No demographic information was provided for the individual students who participated in the norming. It is difficult to draw any conclusions about the inclusion of students from various ethnic backgrounds based on the information provided.

As for the inclusion of special needs students, information was solicited from the participating districts concerning the participation rates for special needs students in district testing. Districts were instructed to include all students in norming who would normally be included in district testing. Based on the information reported, the authors concluded that approximately one-half to three-quarters of the identified special needs students in participating districts were included in the norming.

RELIABILITY. Internal consistency estimates of reliability were reported for each test and associated subtest by level and by grade. In addition, estimates of reliability were also reported for each of the major objectives associated with each test. The estimates of reliability for the major tests were in the acceptable range, from .73 (Level 19, grade 10—Spelling) to .98 (Level 14, grade 5—Total Battery). Most of the coefficients were in the .8 to .9 range, with the major exception being the test of Spelling (44% of the reported coefficients in the .70 to .79 range). The Spelling test was by far the briefest test included in the CAT/2 battery.

As one might expect, the estimates of reliability for the objectives were quite a bit lower than the estimates of reliability for the overall tests. The values ranged from .08 (Level 18, grade 8.7—Language Mechanics: writing conventions) to .89 (Level 12, grade 2.7/3.7—Mathematics Computation: multiply whole numbers). Although most of these estimates were in the .5 to .6 range, a fairly large number of these estimates were unacceptably low (lower than .49). The areas of Language Mechanics and Expression were particularly problematic having 44% and 29% (respectively) of the associated objectives exhibiting low estimates of reliability.

VALIDITY. A fair amount of information about test development is provided in the technical manual. The CAT/2 is based on the Comprehensive Tests of Basic Skills, Fourth Edition (CTBS/4). The items from the CTBS/4 were reviewed by Canadian educators and those items that were judged to be relevant were retained (or revised). One thousand additional items were generated by Canadian teachers. An item tryout was conducted in May 1991 with approximately 5,000 Canadian students. Items were retained that met technical requirements and fit content coverage needs. In addition, all items were reviewed for bias. Specifically, reviewers focused on both individual items and the balance of the overall test, looking for examples of ethnic, regional, socioeconomic, or gender bias. No information is provided about the characteristics of the reviewers, other than they were educators from various ethic groups. No empirical studies of bias were conducted. The authors provide information about the inclusion of both males and females in the test content, and the social roles depicted in Table 9 of the technical manual. The authors claim that this information is proof of the "balance" achieved on the CAT/2. It is notable that no males were depicted in traditional female tasks on four of the eight levels of the CAT/2.

Very little additional information concerning the validity of potential interpretations/uses for CAT/2 scores is provided in the technical manual. Under a section entitled "Descriptive Statistics," information is provided about p-values, means, standard deviations, and correlations between CAT/2 tests. Little interpretation of this information is offered, except to say that the expected patterns are generally demonstrated.

SUMMARY. The CAT/2 appears to be a relatively well-constructed measure of basic academic skills. The major strengths of this instrument include the content coverage within each of the major academic areas, the reliability of the major tests (with the exception of Spelling), and the definition of terms and appropriate cautions provided for potential users. There are also a number of notable weaknesses. The lack of any specific information about the inclusion of students from various ethnic backgrounds in the norming and the lack of any empirical study of bias is particularly problematic. In addition, the internal consistency estimates of reliability were unacceptably low for many of the objectives. This appears to be another attempt to build a test that yields both norm-referenced and criterion-referenced information. Unfortunately, the criterion-referenced information (objectives) often is not reliable enough to be useful. Finally, not enough attention has been paid to providing evidence to support the intended use and interpretation of the scores associated with this test.

[45]
Canadian Test of Cognitive Skills.

Purpose: Designed to assess the academic aptitude important for scholastic success of students in grades 2 through 12.
Population: Grades 2–12.
Publication Dates: 1992–1996.
Acronym: Canadian TCS.
Scores, 4: Sequences, Memory, Analogies, Verbal Reasoning.
Administration: Group.
Levels, 5: Level 1 (Grades 2–3); Level 2 (Grades 4–5); Level 3 (Grades 6–7); Level 4 (Grades 8–9); Level 5 (Grades 10–12+).
Price Data, 1996: C$75 per 35 consumable test booklets (Level 1); $95 per 35 reusable test booklets (specify Level 2–5); $12 per 35 practice tests including directions; $58 per 50 machine-scorable answer sheets (specify level); $28 per 25 U-Score answer sheets; $1 per scoring keys (specify level); $17 per 50 individual record sheets; $1.50 per class record sheet; $8 per examiner's manual ('92, 26 pages; specify level); $32 per norms book ('92, 154 pages); $21 per handbook and technical bulletin ('96, 87 pages); $48 per Multi-Level specimen set; $21 per Primary, Junior, or Senior specimen set.
Time: (52) minutes for Level 1; (55) minutes for Level 2–5.
Comments: A Practice Test (15–20 minute administration time) is available and is recommended to be administered at least one day prior to the actual testing session; adapted from Test of Cognitive Skills, Second Edition (325).
Author: Canadian Test Centre, Educational Services.
Publisher: Canadian Test Centre, Educational Assessment Services [Canada].

Review of the Canadian Test of Cognitive Skills by MARTINE HÉBERT, Assistant Professor, Department of Counseling, Administration and Evaluation, Université Laval, Quebec, Canada:

The Canadian Test of Cognitive Skills (Canadian TCS), a Canadian adaptation of the Test of Cognitive Skills, Second Edition (TCS/2; 325), is intended to evaluate selected verbal, nonverbal, and memory abilities that are considered important to scholastic success. Four subtests—Sequences, Analogies, Memory, and Verbal Reasoning—are included to measure the academic aptitude of pupils in grades 2 through 12. Each subtest contains 20 items and five different levels of the test are provided according to grade range. As with the TCS/2, the Canadian TCS has modified the item format of the Memory subtest (for Levels 2 to 5), using nonsense words instead of low-frequency words, thus responding to one criticism voiced in a review of the earlier American version (see Sternberg, 1985).

The Canadian TCS is group administered and requires, on the average, one hour of testing. Two practice tests (according to test level) are available, and should, following the publisher's suggestion, be administered at least one day before the testing session to familiarize students with item formats and the tasks. In addition, sample items are provided for each subtest.

The Canadian TCS is accompanied by an examiner's manual, a norms book, and a handbook and technical bulletin. The examiner's manual is clearly written and provides relevant information as to the administration instructions as well as general guidelines for ensuring standard testing conditions. The norms book presents instructions for hand scoring (machine scoring is also provided by the publisher), provides norm tables to obtain derived scores, and explains the various types of scores available. At the present time, only a working draft version of the handbook and technical bulletin is available.

Unfortunately, the interested test user might find it difficult to retrieve the specific information he or she needs at first glance. Some information is repeated or presented partially in different sections of the accompanying documents. The biggest concern lies with the present version of the handbook and technical bulletin. One would expect the latter to provide a brief review of the original American test and its predecessor versions, a section describing the rationale for each subtest, and a detailed description of the content and types of items included. The potential test user would also appreciate finding references to the pertinent empirical literature.

Some information regarding test development is also presently lacking. Authors report that review procedures were applied to ascertain content and accuracy of items and to identify items reflecting possible gender or ethnic bias. Although they mention that "statistical evidence of bias was also included in the item selection criteria" (p. 1), no further information is presented in the handbook as to the statistical procedures employed. In order to evaluate the appropriateness of the items, such valuable information as item difficulty level and discrimination indices should be included in the handbook.

The Canadian TCS yields seven scores. Raw scores for the four subtests are obtained by computing the number of correct responses and converting them to subtest scale scores. Tables are provided to transform scores into both grade- and age-based stanines and percentiles. Grade norms are detailed for the fall, the midyear, and the spring period. A Nonverbal score is obtained by averaging the scaled score of the Sequences and Analogies subtests. The Total score is similarly computed by averaging the scaled scores of all four subtests. A Cognitive Skills Index (CSI), an indicator of a student's overall cognitive ability relative to children of similar chronological age, is also given as an age-based standard score (mean = 100, standard deviation = 16). The authors accurately caution the test user regarding the analysis of the latter score, as it may not have the same interpretation at various age levels, given the selective retention of pupils in the school environment. Scores may also be used to compute a predicted achievement score and the discrepancy between predicted and obtained achievement, if children are simultaneously administered the Canadian Achievement Test, Second Edition (CAT/2).

The normative sample for the Canadian TCS included approximately 36,000 grade 2 through 12 students from 195 Canadian schools where English was the language of instruction, who were tested in the spring of 1992. The sample was drawn by stratified random sampling procedures, on the basis of geographic region and community type, and contains between 2,700 and 3,900 children for each grade level. All children had completed the appropriate practice test before actual testing. A background questionnaire was used to compile characteristics (e.g., socioeconomic, special education) of the participating schools and tables provided in the handbook efficiently summarize this information.

Internal consistency reliability based on Kuder-Richardson 20 coefficients is reported by grade and test level. Reliability coefficients for the Sequences subtest fall mostly in the high .70s (range: .69 to .81). KR-20 coefficients were found to be mostly in the high .70s/low .80s for the Analogies (range: .62 to

.83) and the Verbal Reasoning (range: .68 to .81) subtests. Internal consistency reliability estimates for the Memory subtest are higher; all but one coefficient falls above .80 (range: .78 to .92). Standard errors of measurement are generally slightly less than two raw score units. No information is given concerning total score reliability. The working draft version of the handbook does not present any data on the test-retest reliabilities of the Canadian TCS. Such data would be pertinent to help interpretation of the possible practice effects if retesting is necessary.

Information on the validity of the Canadian TCS is scantily addressed in the available documentation. The authors report having conducted a factor analysis on an unspecified sample: "The factor structure of the Cdn. TCS consists of three distinct abilities—verbal ability, non-verbal ability and memory" (p. 44); however, no further details are given. Such information would help clarify the apparent overlap in the constructs evaluated, as intercorrelations suggest that Sequences, Analogies, and Verbal Reasoning subtests share common variance (r = .50 to .63), whereas the Memory task appears more distinct from the other three subtests (r = .16 to .48).

Concurrent validity was examined in some small-scale studies, using different criterion measures across different grade levels. For example, for Level 1, the Verbal Reasoning subtest scores of the Canadian TCS were correlated with the similar subtest of the TCS in a sample of 32 grade 2 students (r = .58). A weak correlation (.30) was obtained between the total score of the Canadian TCS and IQ from the WISC-R in a group (N = 49) of grade 3 students. Data are also provided on a sample of grade 9 students (N = 119) tested with Level 4 of the Canadian TCS and the Differential Aptitude Test (DAT), and indicated shared variance between pertinent subtests of the two measures.

In conclusion, the Canadian TCS appears to be a promising test. The instrument's ease of administration and its potential to provide predictive information, if used in combination with an achievement test, make it a pertinent tool for evaluating school-related abilities. Unfortunately, as of yet, the handbook and technical bulletin presents insufficient information regarding the psychometric properties of the Canadian TCS. Fortunately, this weakness may be corrected in the final version of the handbook.

REVIEWER'S REFERENCE

Sternberg, R. J. (1985). [Review of the Test of Cognitive Skills.] In J. V. Mitchell, Jr. (Ed.), *The ninth mental measurements yearbook* (pp. 1556–1557). Lincoln, NE: Buros Institute of Mental Measurements.

Review of the Canadian Test of Cognitive Skills by SUSAN J. MALLER, Assistant Professor of Educational Measurement and Research, University of South Florida, Tampa, FL:

The Canadian Test of Cognitive Skills (Canadian TCS) is a group-administered norm-referenced test designed to assess the academic aptitude important for success of students in grades 2 through 12. The Canadian TCS does not assess academic achievement or all aspects of cognitive ability; rather, the Canadian TCS measures verbal and nonverbal cognitive ability of an abstract nature. All five levels of the Canadian TCS (grades 2–3, 4–5, 6–7, 8–9, and 10–12+) include four tests (Sequences, Memory, Analogies, Verbal Reasoning). The Canadian TCS norms book describes various ways that results can be used, including classroom and administrative applications (e.g., identifying and planning for individual students with special needs, communicating to parents, evaluating educational programs).

Practice tests are administered at least one day prior to Canadian TCS testing. Separate practice tests, requiring approximately 20 minutes, are given for either Levels 1 or 2–5. The Canadian TCS requires an examiner be trained by the test coordinator, who is a testing director, assistant superintendent, or supervisor, and requires approximately 52 minutes to administer, including directions read from the examiner's manual.

Each test includes 20 items. The Sequences test requires the examinee to complete a pattern of letters, numbers, or figures. The Memory test requires the examinee to recall either picture pairs (Level 1) or nonsense words (Levels 2–5) defined during the beginning of the examination session. The Analogies test requires the examinee to infer relationships between two sets of two pictures by examining the first set of pictures and then choosing a picture that completes the second set of pictures. Although most of the artwork is clear, there are some items, especially in the Level 5 test, that are too detailed and ambiguous. The Verbal Reasoning test consists of several types of items; the examinee selects a word or statement that: (a) names a necessary part of a stimulus word; (b) is most like a stimulus set of words, does not belong with the others, or is related to a second set of words in a manner similar to a first set of words; and (c) must be true given the stimulus statements. The sample items, however, are limited in terms of format and do not cover all types of items presented in the actual test, thus potentially causing some confusion for examinees.

Examinees taking Level 1 record answers in the test booklet, whereas examinees taking Levels 2–5 record answers on separate answer sheets. The Canadian TCS can either be hand or machine scored. Hand scoring is completed by the examiner. Level 1 test booklets or Levels 2–5 answer sheets are sent to the CTT Scoring Service for machine scoring.

Scores are reported in various metrics, including stanine scores, percentile ranks, and age-based standard scores referred to as the Cognitive Skills Index (CSI; $M = 100$, $SD = 16$). Scale scores for Levels 1–5 are on the same scale, making it possible to compare scaled scores across levels.

The standardization sample ($N = 36,000$) was intended to be representative of all students in Canada attending schools where English is the language of instruction. A multistage cluster random sampling method (first stage was school district and second stage was school), stratified on geographic region and degree of urbanization, was used to select a representative sample. Socioeconomic status (SES) was not a stratification variable, because the technical manual (a working draft as of September 1996) states that SES data were not available from the Canadian Census. Of the participating districts, 88.7% returned a "School Characteristics Questionnaire" that reported background information (e.g., number of students served, average family income). The technical manual presents the characteristics of the standardization sample without comparison to the Canadian Census data. Thus, it is impossible to assess the actual representativeness of the standardization sample. Furthermore, data regarding ethnicity are not reported.

Reliability was reported across grades in terms of internal consistency (Kuder-Richardson 20) coefficients, which ranged from .69 to .81 for Sequences, .62 to .83 for Analogies, .78 to .92 for Memory, and .68 to .81 for Verbal Reasoning. Standard errors of measurement by grade and Canadian TCS test are reported for raw scores only. Machine-scored reports include CSI confidence intervals based on one standard error. Because test-retest reliability coefficients were not reported, it is impossible to assess Canadian TCS score stability over time.

The Canadian TCS was adapted from the Test of Cognitive Skills, Second Edition (325). According to the manual, educators, who were professional item writers, developed three times more items than necessary. Items were reviewed by educational and cognitive psychologists. No data were provided regarding results of item analyses (using either classical or item response theory methods) or methods used for final item selection. Items were evaluated for bias by educators representing both genders and various ethnic groups. Although the manual states that statistical investigations of bias were conducted to determine item selection, no data were provided regarding results of these investigations.

Evidence of construct and criterion-related validity is weak. Low to moderate intercorrelations between the Canadian TCS tests were reported across grade levels. The Nonverbal scale was correlated highly with the Sequences and Analogies tests. Concurrent validity was evaluated by correlating the Canadian TCSC Verbal Reasoning Test with the TCS Verbal Reasoning Test using a sample of 32 grade 2 students resulting in a moderate correlation ($r = .557$). The correlations of the Level 5 Canadian TCS with the Differential Aptitudes Test, Canadian Edition (Form A) ranged from .005 to .635 for a sample of 119 grade 9 students. A correlation of .30 between the Wechsler Intelligence Scale for Children—Revised (WISC-R) Full Scale IQ (FSIQ) and the total battery of the Canadian TCS was obtained for a sample of 49 children; however, the manual suggested that this correlation was attenuated due to restriction of range, without providing the reason for the lack of variability. Another study reported that 13 out of 161 grade 8 referred children, qualified for gifted placement on the basis of their Canadian TCS scores and other criteria, also obtained WISC-R FSIQs in the High Average to Superior ranges. Finally, the correlation between the Verbal Reasoning tests of the Canadian TCS and the Canadian Cognitive Abilities Test (CCAT) was .34, whereas the correlation between the Canadian TCS Verbal Reasoning and CCAT Nonverbal Reasoning tests was -.08.

Sufficient evidence, using representative samples, is not presented to demonstrate that the Canadian TCS either measures constructs that are consistent with other tests of cognitive ability or predicts future academic performance. For this reason, as well as the lack of information regarding (a) the representativeness of the standardization sample, (b) the stability of test scores over time, and (c) investigations of test and item bias, the Canadian TCS cannot be recommended, even as a screening instrument. It is hoped the publisher will provide additional information regarding the psychometric properties of the Canadian TCS in the final version of the technical manual.

[46]
Career Anchors: Discovering Your Real Values, Revised Edition.

Purpose: Designed to help a person identify their career anchor, uncover their real values, and use them to make better career choices.
Population: Adults.
Publication Date: 1990.
Scores, 8: Technical/Functional Competence, General Managerial Competence, Autonomy/Independence, Security/Stability, Entrepreneurial Creativity, Service/Dedication to a Cause, Pure Challenge, Lifestyle.
Administration: Group.
Price Data, 1993: $24.95 per complete kit including instrument (67 pages) and trainer's manual (20 pages); $9.95 per instrument.
Time: (180–240) minutes.
Comments: Self-rating plus interview with a partner.
Author: Edgar H. Schein.
Publisher: Pfeiffer and Company, International Publishers.

Review of the Career Anchors: Discovering Your Real Values, Revised Edition by MICHAEL B. BUNCH, Vice President, Measurement Incorporated, Durham, NC:

Although Career Anchors may be considered a test in the sense that it yields eight scores, it may be more effectively viewed as a diagnostic or self-help tool to be used by individuals mapping a career or going through mid-career adjustments either with or without the assistance of a counselor. The eight scores are keyed to eight career anchors: Technical/Functional Competence, General Managerial Competence, Autonomy/Independence, Security/Stability, Entrepreneurial Creativity, Service/Dedication to a Cause, Pure Challenge, and Lifestyle. These anchors clearly have more to do with attitudes and work style than with the choice of specific occupational titles. There are no norms; nor are there any fixed cutoffs for the scores. A person's highest score presumably identifies his or her primary anchor, and lower scores identify lesser anchors. Some people may have only one clearly defined anchor; others may have more than one.

The eight anchors are well defined in terms accessible to the likely user. Each is described in general terms and in terms of pay and benefits, promotion systems, and types of recognition. The background information should be very useful to the novice and to the mid-career incumbent. The exercises, from the initial response to the 40 statements, to the structured interviews with a partner, are extremely well crafted and thought provoking. Even without the scores, the exercises may well be worth the time and money invested.

The test is the evolutionary product of over 30 years of research by the author, which included longitudinal studies of 44 alumni of a graduate business school. The content of the test and the interpretations of the anchors mark this test as one primarily for managers or those aspiring to management positions. The manual provides a frank and refreshing discussion of career development, defining 10 steps (including disengagement and retirement). At every step and with every explanation, there is evidence of some research base.

If Career Anchors has one potential drawback, it is the brevity of the inventory. The 40 items are evenly divided among the eight anchors, yielding 5 items per anchor. To decide on a career in general management rather than as a technical line manager on the basis of 10 items (5 for each) seems a bit risky. Fortunately, however, the author and publishers do not stop there. The inventory yields an initial map of the examinee's anchor system, which is then subjected to rather intense scrutiny through the structured interviews. The final pages of the manual provide space to record anchor rankings based on the interviews and the inventory, along with a final ranking. This triangulation should be sufficient to yield stable results.

In summary, the inventory has some grounding in research. The accompanying manual reflects that research, is very well written, and affords the user a wealth of beneficial information. Individuals contemplating a mid-career shift or industrial psychologists looking for a tool to match individuals to career paths within their organizations would do well to consider Career Anchors.

Review of the Career Anchors: Discovering Your Real Values, Revised Edition by GARY J. ROBERTSON, Vice President, Research and Development, Wide Range, Inc., Tampa, FL:

The Career Anchors uses two major activities presented in a workshop format to identify a participant's Career Anchor, defined as the occupational self-concept composed of self-perceived abilities, motives, and values. An individual's Career Anchor is described as the one thing a person would refuse to give up if forced to make a choice among alternative occupational pursuits. The outcome of the activities is the identification of a Career Anchor

which, it is hoped, will increase an individual's self-understanding and guide future career decisions. Developed by Edgar Schein, the concept has evolved over the past 25 years as Schein has conducted follow-up studies with various groups of alumni of the Massachusetts Institute of Technology Sloan School of Management (Sloan School) and other groups. To date, eight career anchor categories have been identified: Technical/Functional Competence, General Managerial Competence, Autonomy/Independence, Security/Stability, Entrepreneurial Creativity, Service/Dedication to a Cause, Pure Challenge, and Lifestyle.

THE CAREER ANCHORS CONSTRUCT. Five of the eight Career Anchor types first emerged from Schein's follow-up study of 44 male graduates of the Sloan School's master's degree program in management; the remaining three Career Anchor types were added later. Of the 14 studies cited in the trainer's manual, six were with Sloan School alumni, seven were with middle and upper-level managers, and one was with physicians in managerial positions. Thus, the research base underlying the construct is restricted to individuals with above-average educational and occupational status. The type of self-analysis required to determine one's career anchor places considerable emphasis on verbal-analytical abilities typically present in the more highly educated professional and managerial occupations. This characteristic should be kept in mind by possible users because no data are presented to support the generalizability of the Career Anchor construct to other occupational groups. According to the theory, a person's Career Anchor gradually crystallizes from direct work experiences so use of the instrument is restricted to those individuals whose work experience is such that they have an experiential base from which to develop self-knowledge of what is most important and what is not (Schein, 1978, p. 171). The idea of an internalized core of abilities, motives, and values that acts as an anchor to keep an individual "on course" in an occupation that is congruent with this core self is intuitively appealing and seemingly useful for career counseling. More research is needed, however, to determine the utility of the Career Anchors construct in occupations outside the professional and managerial groups.

THE ASSESSMENT PROCESS. The two major components of Career Anchors are the Career Orientations Inventory (COI) and the Career Anchor Interview (CAI). The COI is a paper-and-pencil 40-item Likert-type rating scale, with 5 items allocated to each of the eight Career Anchor types. The participant's Career Anchor on the COI is the area with the highest average rating (each of the 40 items is rated on a 6-point rating scale). The CAI employs a fairly unstructured format, with pairs of workshop participants taking turns interviewing one another. The broad, general questions in the CAI offer no guidelines for following up responses to get at the information most essential for determining the respondent's Career Anchor type. Presumably, whatever information emerges from the interview will be sufficient to enable the interviewer and interviewee to complete the culminating activity of giving a preferential ranking to the eight Career Anchor types. Thus, the CAI lacks a standardized administration procedure other than the broad, general biographical questions outlined in the work text. The absence of any criteria for evaluating the responses is a serious weakness of the CAI that raises questions about the generalizability of CAI results. This weakness becomes even more problematic in light of the advice given for evaluating discrepancies between COI and CAI Career Anchor type ratings. Respondents are told to give preference to the CAI ranking: "The interview information is more reliable because it is based on your actual biography, whereas the inventory scores could be based on your need to see yourself in a certain way" (trainer's manual, p. 60). No data are presented to substantiate this claim; moreover, one wonders why the author did not take steps in developing the COI to deal with the social desirability of responses if this was indeed a problem. The author's ambivalence on the appropriate point in the workshop at which to introduce and define the eight Career Anchor types undoubtedly confounds the interpretation of COI results because users can present this information *either* before or after the COI but *always* before the CAI. To this reviewer, it would seem best to postpone the explanation of the Career Anchor types until after both the administration of the COI and the CAI. Presentation at this point minimizes the possibility of the explanation influencing responses in an unintended way. A more explicit procedure for handling ties on the COI scales is also needed.

ADEQUACY OF THE MATERIALS. Components of Career Anchors include a trainer's manual and a participant work text titled Career Anchors/Discovering Your Real Values. The trainer's manual presents two options for conducting the

workshop: a 2-hour and a 4-hour format. Although this reviewer has not actually conducted a workshop, he feels that the 2-hour format is inadequate to achieve the stated workshop goals. Based on the time required to complete the COI and CAI plus summarizing and analyzing the results, a minimum of 4 hours seem necessary. Both the trainer's manual and the work text are attractive, well designed, and clearly written. The trainer's manual lacks information about the intended target audience for Career Anchors and about the qualifications needed by workshop leaders. Individuals wanting more background information about the Career Anchor concept can consult chapters 10–12 of Schein's text *Career Dynamics: Matching Individual and Organizational Needs* (1978, pp. 124–172).

TECHNICAL ADEQUACY. Career Anchors was developed primarily by using qualitative research methodology applied to in-depth case studies. Schein stated (personal communication, February, 1997) that the COI, in particular, was never intended to be a psychometric instrument embracing quantitative research methodology. The decision to avoid the quantitatively based psychometric test development model is unfortunate because most psychological assessment instruments embody *both* qualitative and quantitative development methodology. Many of the lingering technical questions about both the COI and CAI could and should have been addressed by applying the appropriate psychometric methodology. For example, basic information is needed about the reliability of the eight COI scales, their intercorrelations, and their factor structure. In view of the preponderance of men in the research reported to date, more data are needed to establish the viability of Career Anchors for women, especially those outside professional and managerial careers. In another personal communication (February, 1997), Schein indicated that only 20 women are included in the research reported to date. Despite this small number, the author maintains that occupation, not gender per se, is the important factor in determining one's Career Anchor. Reliability data are also needed for the CAI to evaluate the author's claim that the CAI is more reliable than the COI and that CAI should override COI results in resolving discrepancies between the two sets of Career Anchor ratings. The single table of data in the trainer's manual is valuable because it shows the distribution of the eight Career Anchor types for 328 individuals (308 men and 20 women) in 14 different research groups available as of the 1990 publication date. In fact, the table provides some serendipitous construct validity data in that 57% of the professionals-managers in the groups studied demonstrated either Technical/Functional or Managerial Career Anchors just as one might hypothesize. The relatively low incidence of the other six Career Anchor types (1.9–11.1%) underscores the need for broadening the research base.

SUMMARY. Career counseling and organization development personnel who work with early midcareer managers may find Career Anchors helpful. Effective use of the material definitely requires a workshop leader with considerable background and familiarity with the Career Anchors concept and experience in conducting this type of workshop. Certainly, Schein has produced what appears to be a valuable contribution spanning a significant portion of his career as an I/O psychologist; however, Career Anchors would be a much stronger product had the appropriate psychometric methods been employed when needed at various stages in the development process. At a minimum, the basic technical information outlined earlier should be added to the trainer's manual or issued in a technical supplement in order to strengthen Career Anchors and possibly broaden its user base.

REVIEWER'S REFERENCE

Schein, E. H. (1978). *Career dynamics: matching individual and organizational needs.* Reading, MA: Addison-Wesley Publishing Company.

[47]
Career Attitudes and Strategies Inventory: An Inventory for Understanding Adult Careers.

Purpose: "Developed to assess some common attitudes, feelings, experiences, and obstacles that influence the careers of employed and unemployed adults."
Population: Adults seeking vocational counseling.
Publication Dates: 1992–1994.
Acronym: CASI.
Scores: 9 scales: Job Satisfaction, Work Involvement, Skill Development, Dominant Style, Career Worries, Interpersonal Abuse, Family Commitment, Risk-Taking Style, Geographical Barriers.
Administration: Individual.
Price Data, 1996: $68 per kit including manual ('94, 53 pages), 25 inventory booklets, 25 handscorable answer sheets, and 25 interpretive summary booklets.
Time: (35) minutes.
Comments: Also includes Career Obstacles Checklist designed to assess "personal problems that may influence an individual's job situation."
Authors: John L. Holland and Gary D. Gottfredson.
Publisher: Psychological Assessment Resources, Inc.

Review of the Career Attitudes and Strategies Inventory: An Inventory for Understanding Adult Careers by MICHAEL B. BROWN, Assistant Professor of Psychology, East Carolina University, Greenville, NC:

The Career Attitudes and Strategies Inventory (CASI) is a relatively brief, self-scoring assessment of adult career attitudes and behaviors. It is intended to provide an assessment of job stability, and it is suggested that the profile of scores provides a status report on the positive and negative aspects of clients' career adjustment. The nine scales of the CASI measure areas related to career adaptation. Examples of scales include Job Satisfaction, Work Involvement, Family Commitment, and Geographical Barriers. Following in the tradition of John Holland's Self-Directed Search (282) the inventory is meant to be completed and scored by the client. Clients use a questionnaire containing 130 items, indicating their self-rating on a separate self-scoring answer sheet. The answer sheet also contains a separate career obstacle checklist listing 21 potential career obstacles. Clients follow the directions on the answer sheet to obtain raw scores, transferring the raw score to a profile sheet in the four-page Interpretive Summary. The Interpretive Summary also includes brief interpretive statements for each scale.

MATERIALS. The materials are attractively done. The four-page test booklet is well designed and easy to read. The separate one-page answer sheet is a two-part carbonless form that is used for self-scoring. The answer sheet requires the client to indicate an answer of True, Mostly True, Mostly False, or False for each item on the inventory. The two true responses are both designated by an upper case letter "T," with a darker colored T to be circled for True and the lighter colored T circled for Mostly True. A similar system using an upper case letter "F" is used to indicate False or Mostly False. This answer system, combined with the compact layout of the answer sheet, may prove confusing for some clients. Professionals who use the CASI must ensure clients understand the directions for answering and are able to maintain their place as they complete the survey. The manual authors state the client must be able to do "simple math" to self-score the inventory. Again, some clients may need more guidance to follow the directions for scoring. The four-page Interpretive Summary has a profile on which to plot scores, and three interpretive statements for each scale. Each interpretation corresponds to one of three ranges of raw score distribution. The interpretive summaries are clearly written but very brief. These interpretations may require more detailed explanation and integration by the professional, particularly for clients with less education and verbal sophistication.

MANUAL. The manual is very brief (only 45 pages) but clearly written and organized. Practical applications of the CASI and scoring procedures are concisely described. Interpretive information includes a description of each scale along with 14 case profiles. The illustrative profiles are helpful and include persons with a range of ages and occupations, although occupations that require more education and training seem to predominate. The major limitation of the illustrative profiles is the brevity of case material and corresponding interpretations. There is a section on becoming a competent user of the inventory that is well done, and there is a short "test" to help the user assess understanding of the basic concepts of the CASI. The major concern about this section is that it implies the inventory has greater psychometric sophistication than is warranted by the technical characteristics of the instrument.

TECHNICAL CHARACTERISTICS. There are significant limitations in the technical characteristics of the CASI that must be considered when using this inventory. The current version of the CASI is the third version in the development of the inventory and was derived from item analyses of previous versions. The normative sample consists of 747 persons ranging in age from 17 to 77 years of age. Women are overrepresented in the norm group (64% women, 36% men), although the manual authors point out there appears to be little substantive difference in the scores of men and women. The majority of the group is composed of persons with some education beyond high school (only 10% of the sample had 12 or fewer years of education). It is difficult to ascertain the actual ethnic identification of the group, as over one-third of the group were not asked to provide an ethnic identification. There is no indication of the geographical or socioeconomic status of the sample. Normative data for career obstacles are considered "approximate" (p. 36) as identical instructions were not given to each group used in the norming process.

Internal consistency reliability coefficients for the CASI scales ranged from .76 to .92, which is adequate for this type of inventory. Test-retest reliability was assessed using a small group of working adults. The average interval was 13 days, and test-retest reliabilities ranged from .66–.94.

Validity is inferred through a number of means. One of the difficulties in assessing the validity of the CASI is that different versions were used at different points during its development to assess validity. Caution is suggested in interpretation of validity because both the norm group and the CASI itself appear to have undergone substantial changes from the first to the third version. Validity is addressed through correlation of the CASI and the Hoppock Job Satisfaction Blank, a two-item indicator of general happiness, career search activities, and measures of vocational identity and personality type. The CASI and the Hoppock Job Satisfaction Blank have a correlation of .86, whereas the CASI and the measure of general happiness have a correlation of .71. Construct validity is inferred through an examination of the intercorrelations between various CASI scales, which are said to "appear predictable from the scale titles" (p. 28). As an example, the Job Satisfaction Scale is negatively correlated with the Career Worries and Interpersonal Abuse Scales.

OVERALL EVALUATION. The CASI has serious drawbacks presented by the lack of adequate norms and limitations in the determination of its validity. The structure and appearance of the materials give it a look of psychometric sophistication that exceeds its present technical state. This is of particular importance when used with client self-scoring and interpretation, when there is the danger the client would consider the results to be more exact than warranted. I recommend that its use by a client be preceded by a discussion of the limitations of the instrument and the meaning of its scale scores. The CASI may be most useful to the career counselor or vocational psychologist when used as a checklist to obtain a client's self-rating in a number of areas that are relevant to career adjustment. As such it can be used to rapidly "screen" for client opinions and attitudes and generate information for discussion between client and counselor. I would certainly find it useful as a pre-interview survey, a device to generate discussion, or to identify potentially problematic areas that would benefit from further exploration. It should be used in an ipsative rather than normative fashion until better psychometric data are produced. When detailed information in specific domains of the client's career attitudes or strategies is necessary, additional inventories (such as the Adult Career Concerns Inventory [12:18] or the Salience Inventory [T4:2321]) should be considered.

Review of the Career Attitudes and Strategies Inventory: An Inventory for Understanding Adult Ca-

reers by RICHARD T. KINNIER, Associate Professor, Counseling Psychology Program, Arizona State University, Tempe, AZ:

The Career Attitudes and Strategies Inventory (CASI) was designed "to assess some common attitudes, feelings, experiences, and obstacles that influence the careers" of adults (manual, p. 1). The CASI consists of 130 items in nine scales related to the test taker's career. They are: Job Satisfaction, Work Involvement, Skill Development (motivation to improve one's work performance), Dominant Style (leader versus follower), Career Worries, Interpersonal Abuse (experienced at work), Family Commitment (as it relates to career commitment), Risk-Taking Style (willingness to take or experience risk), and Geographic Barriers (extent to which one is motivated to stay in or move to a geographical location). A separate item asks test takers to check (from a list) any career obstacles they are currently experiencing. According to the authors, the test should be used to supplement (not supplant) other career-relevant information such as the client's abilities and interests. The results should be used in counseling to stimulate further career-related thinking and exploration by the client.

Each of the 130 items is answered on a 4-point scale consisting of the categories, "False," "Mostly False," "Mostly True," and "True" as they relate to the test taker. The items are clearly written. The test booklet and answer sheet are clearly presented and easy to use. All responses fit on one side of the answer sheet. The instructions are clear. According to the authors, the test takes about 35 minutes to complete.

The CASI is self-administered and can be self-scored. The directions for scoring are clear and easy to follow. To score, individuals remove the top layer of the answer sheet. On the revealed bottom sheet, responses are numbered. Those numbers are simply summed for each scale. Raw scores are then entered and plotted on a profile sheet. Raw score plots are clearly displayed for each scale and raw scores are easily transformed to *T*-scores listed at the bottom of the profile sheet.

The authors describe the test as "self interpreted" but they also state that "most clients will also require or want help with the interpretation of the profiles from a counselor" (p. 3). I would recommend the test be used only in conjunction with counseling. Although the interpretation of each scale seems fairly straightforward, the implications of the scores for a person's career development and choice are more complex and best addressed in counseling.

The interpretive guide for the scales consists of verbal descriptions of three levels (the top 25%, the middle 50%, and the bottom 25% of the norms). The verbal descriptions are clearly written. One slight annoyance is that the profile sheet is on the back page of the interpretive guide, which does not allow the test taker to look at both simultaneously. Having a separate page for the profile sheet would be preferable, in my opinion. The authors provide 14 illustrative profiles with brief descriptions of the test takers. Having a few illustrative cases seems useful for practice in interpretation but all 14 do not seem needed. The sections in the manual on "Becoming a Competent User" and "Some Practical Applications" are brief and helpful guides for counselors who may consider using the CASI. Overall, the manual is well organized and well written. Also, its brevity makes for easy reading and quick familiarity with the test.

TEST DEVELOPMENT. The CASI was developed by two highly respected theoreticians in the area of career counseling and testing. The development of their test followed a typical path of tests of this type. First, items were constructed on the basis of theoretical criteria and common sense. Several people contributed potential items. Next, items were deleted or refined on the basis of factor and item analyses. In the manual, the authors refer to the analyses but the actual data from those analyses are not in the manual. The current version of the CASI is the third version of refined items.

NORMS. The standardization sample consisted of 747 adults. About 64% are women and 34% are men (a few did not report their sex). The mean age was 38 (*SD* = 11 years). The ethnic makeup of the sample is predominantly European American (i.e., 79%). They are a highly educated sample (about 90% went beyond high school, over 50% graduated from college, and over 25% obtained a postgraduate degree). The authors claim the sample is heterogeneous in age and education but in comparison with national norms, this sample seems slightly more female, more European American, and more educated. Also, although there is a wide range of occupations represented in the sample, "a few occupations were overrepresented" (p. 33), according to the authors. Apparently there was an overrepresentation of career counselors. The authors claim they reduced the influence of overrepresentation by "reconstituting" the sample, presumably by removing subjects so that "no more than 30 individuals from a single occupation were included in the final normative groups" (p. 33). Unfortunately, 30 is still a large number in terms of proportionality. However, in spite of the slight bias of the sample on the basis of sex, education, ethnicity, and occupation, I think the sample is still a reasonable norm group for this type of test and its intended use.

The authors report they combined samples from the second and third versions of the test to create their final norm group. This procedure can be problematic if some items were changed or deleted between Versions 2 and 3, which apparently did happen. However, for practical purposes this may not be significant because the authors recommend broad-band interpretation anyway. In my opinion, the broad-band interpretation guide is a strength of the measure.

RELIABILITY. Reliability was evaluated by internal consistency and test-retest correlational analyses. Cronbach alphas were computed on each of the scales for several samples. According to the authors, "alphas for version 3 are based on samples of 564 to 596 persons" (p. 29). It is not clear to what the range of 564 to 596 refers, perhaps it reflects differential completion of the scales. The authors should clarify that. Alpha coefficients ranged from .76 to .92. Alphas on another sample of about 40 "working adults" ranged from .77 to .95. A test-retest correlational analysis was also computed on that sample (range of time period = 6 to 21 days). The coefficients ranged from .66 to .94. Overall, the scales seem to be internally consistent and fairly stable over a short period of time. I would characterize the evidence of reliability as fairly good in comparison with other similar kinds of measures.

VALIDITY. Validity was evaluated mainly by correlational analyses. Scales were correlated with each other and with other relevant variables. The authors claim the correlations are generally supportive of both convergent and discriminant validity. I would concur the results are generally supportive. But I would hasten to add that this measure is still in an early stage of development and refinement. Certainly more independent research is needed to establish real confidence in its validity. Also, at this time validity has been more clearly demonstrated in some scales than in others. For example, the scale Job Satisfaction correlates highly with Hoppock's Job Satisfaction Blank ($r = .84$) and correlates negatively with the scale Career Worries ($r = -.21$) as would be predicted. There seems to be good evidence that both Job Satisfaction and Career Worries are valid scales.

In contrast, although the scale Interpersonal Abuse correlates negatively with Job Satisfaction ($r = -.41$) as would be expected, it also correlates nega-

tively with measures of Extraversion, Agreeableness, and Emotional Stability; and it correlates positively with Family Commitment. Of course, conclusions about causation must be speculative but the pattern does raise the question: To what extent is the scale a measure of actual abuse from others or more a reflection of psychological instability, dislike of work, or antisociability of the individual. I am also troubled by the fact that so many different kinds of unpleasant social encounters (i.e., sexual harassment; prejudice on the basis of race, sex, or other condition or preference; power abuses; and unfriendliness or meanness of fellow employees) are categorized under Interpersonal Abuse. One score on Interpersonal Abuse may be too general to be practically informative as to what is actually going on at work.

The scales that I think have the most compelling face validity and empirical support at this time are: Job Satisfaction, Skill Development, Dominant Style, Career Worries, Risk-taking Style, and Career Obstacles.

CONCLUSION. The CASI is a self-administered and self-scored measure of perceptions individuals have about their careers. The test consists of 130 items and takes approximately 35 minutes to take. The test booklet and answer sheet are clearly presented, the booklet and manual are easy to read, and the test is easy to take and to score. Although the interpretation of the nine scale scores is fairly straightforward, the implications of the scores for a person's career development and choice are more complex and best addressed in the context of counseling. The norms are adequate given the way the scores are supposed to be interpreted (i.e., broad bands). The scales are fairly reliable. Tests of validity (mainly convergent and discriminant correlations) are generally encouraging.

At this early stage of development, some scales seem more valid and useful than others. Future research might address this. In the meantime, the CASI can serve as a useful supplement to the conventional self-assessment interventions for career counseling. It is a unique measure in that, unlike most other career-related tests, it assesses perceptions the test-taker has about his or her current job and career.

[48]
Career Development Inventory [Consulting Psychologists Press, Inc.]

Purpose: "Measures several affective and cognitive aspects of the earlier stages of career development."

Population: Grades 8–12, college.

Publication Dates: 1979–1984.

Acronym: CDI.

Scores, 8: Career Planning, Career Exploration, Decision Making, World-of-Work Information, Knowledge of Preferred Occupational Group, Career Development Attitudes, Career Development Knowledge and Skills, Total.

Administration: Group.

Levels, 2: School Form, College and University Form.

Price Data, 1993: $30 per sampler set including user's manual ('81, 27 pages) and supplement ('84, 20 pages), test booklet, and prepaid answer sheets for both high school and college and university inventories; $23 per 25 reusable high school test booklets; $48 per 10 prepaid high school answer sheets; $45 per 25 reusable college and university test booklets; $48 per 10 prepaid college and university answer sheets; $19 per user's manual; $22 per technical manual ('84, 47 pages); $35 per complete manual set.

Time: (55–65) minutes.

Authors: Donald E. Super, Albert S. Thompson, Richard H. Lindeman, Jean P. Jordaan, and Roger A. Myers.

Publisher: Consulting Psychologists Press, Inc.

Cross References: See T4:391 (20 references); for a review by James W. Pinkney, see 9:195 (4 references).

TEST REFERENCES

1. Blustein, D. L. (1987). Decision-making styles and vocational maturity: An alternative perspective. *Journal of Vocational Behavior, 30,* 61-71.

2. Blustein, D. L. (1987). Social cognitive orientations and career development: A theoretical and empirical analysis. *Journal of Vocational Behavior, 31,* 63-80.

3. Nevill, D., & Super, D. E. (1988). Career maturity and commitment to work in university students. *Journal of Vocational Behavior, 32,* 139-151.

4. King, S. (1990). Background and family variables in a causal model of career maturity: Comparing hearing and hearing-impaired adolescents. *Career Development Quarterly, 38,* 240-260.

5. Orstein, S., & Isabella, L. (1990). Age vs. stage models of career attitudes of women: A partial replication and extension. *Journal of Vocational Behavior, 36,* 1-19.

6. Biller, E. F., & Horn, E. E. (1991). A career guidance model for adolescents with learning disabilities. *The School Counselor, 38,* 279-286.

7. Luzzo, D. A. (1992). Ethnic group and social class differences in college students' career development. *Career Development Quarterly, 41,* 161-173.

8. Gassin, E. A., Kelly, K. R., & Feldhusen, J. F. (1993). Sex differences in the career development of gifted youth. *The School Counselor, 41,* 90–95.

9. Luzzo, D. A. (1993). Reliability and validity testing of the Career Decision-Making Self-Efficacy Scale. *Measurement and Evaluation in Counseling and Development, 26,* 137-143.

10. Hess, W. D., & Winston, R. B., Jr. (1995). Developmental task achievement and students' intentions to participate in developmental activities. *Journal of College Student Development, 36,* 314–321.

11. Luzzo, D. A. (1995). Gender differences in college students' career maturity and perceived barriers in career development. *Journal of Counseling and Development, 73,* 319-322.

12. Luzzo, D. A. (1995). The relative contributions of self-efficacy and locus of control to the prediction of career maturity. *Journal of College Student Development, 36,* 61-66.

13. Jackson, G. C., & Healy, C. C. (1996). Career development profiles and interventions for underrepresented college students. *The Career Development Quarterly, 44,* 258–269.

14. Luzzo, D. A., & Hutcheson, K. G. (1996). Causal attributions and sex differences associated with perceptions of occupational barriers. *Journal of Counseling and Development, 75,* 124–130.

15. Ohler, D. L., Levinson, E. M., & Barker, W. F. (1996). Career maturity in college students with learning disabilities. *The Career Development Quarterly, 44,* 278–288.

16. Savickas, M. L., & Hartung, P. J. (1996). The Career Development Inventory in review: Psychometric and research findings. *Journal of Career Assessment, 4,* 171–188.

17. Smallman, E., & Sowa, C. J. (1996). Career maturity levels of male intercollegiate varsity athletes. *The Career Development Quarterly, 44,* 270–277.

Review of the Career Development Inventory by DONNA L. SUNDRE, *Associate Assessment Specialist/ Associate Professor of Psychology, James Madison University, Harrisonburg, VA:*

GENERAL INFORMATION. The Career Development Inventory (CDI) represents an assessment outcome of more that 40 years of research on adolescent career decision-making readiness, development, and maturity. According to the User's Manual, the CDI is designed to measure "career development and vocational or career maturity" (p. 1). In its present form, the authors contend the instrument can be used for "individual counseling, group assessment, and program evaluation and planning" (p. 3). Two forms are available intended for different audiences. The School Form is designed for students in grades 8–12, and the College and University Form is designed for higher education use. The latter form was modified to fit a college context and to address occupations more common to college students.

Both forms of the CDI produce eight scales: Career Planning (CP); Career Exploration (CE); Decision Making (DM); World of Work Information (WW); Knowledge of Preferred Occupation (PO), a cognitive scale; Career Development Attitudes (CDA), a conative scale that combines CP and CE; Career Development Knowledge and Skills (CDK), a cognitive scale that combines DM and WW; and Career Orientation Total (COT), the combination of CP, CE, DM, and WW. The instrument is divided into two parts: Part I—Career Orientation; and Part II—Knowledge of Preferred Occupation. When using the School Form, the Preferred Occupation (PO) scale is considered useful only for grade 11–12 students given the advanced terms, ideas, and maturity expected to be a part of development of occupations and choice.

PRACTICAL EVALUATION. Test booklets for both forms are reusable and durable. Administration of the instruments is straightforward, and the manual contains excellent directions and guidance. Hand scoring is not recommended for a variety of reasons: Reports use standard scale scores rather than raw scores; the CE scale score is calculated using differential item weights; and the Knowledge of Preferred Occupation (PO) scale requires a different key for each of the 20 occupational groups. Hand scoring may not be an option for this instrument.

The User's Manual Volume I, published in 1981, contains development information related to both forms and statistical and measurement findings related to the School Form; it is exceptionally well written and organized. Great care has been taken in its development and presentation. An extensive reference section and appendix including norming tables, scale statistics, and factor analysis results are also provided. The manual will be very useful to many counselors; this reviewer was particularly impressed with Chapter III: Uses of CDI Results. Users will find cogent advice for planning meaningful activities to engage individual clients, organizing guidance programs, and designing evaluation and research. Regarding uses of the instruments with individuals, the individual item responses for the career planning and career exploration scales would be very useful for working with individuals. The score reporting program provides group item response patterns; however, the individual responses are not available. The Supplement to the User's Manual (1982) contains eight sections and an appendix. Most of this information describes minor variations and supplementation for the College and University (CU) Form compared to the School (S) Form. A presentation of case studies was a thoughtful addition. The section on norms, reliability, and validity included in this manual pertains solely to the CU Form.

Subsequent to the publication of the User's Manual (1981) and the Supplement (1982) the scoring service and computer-generated reports appear to have been revised in 1986 in two important ways. First a graphic percentile rank profile is now displayed. It is nice to have such a straightforward result presentation; however, there is some danger in overreliance on normative data with this type of data. For example, the authors cite research indicating that many senior students are not well prepared for the transition to work or to college and know very little about their preferred occupations. Average scores on many of these scales should be cause for concern and counseling rather than calm. The second improvement in the score report is the addition of a local norms column alongside the national norms. This is an important improvement.

There is also a somewhat more recently published (1984) Technical Manual that contains greater detail on the development of the instrument and its earlier forms as well as additional reliability and validity studies, uses of the CDI, and a more extensive reference section.

NORMS. The authors of the User's Manual are forthright in indicating that the norms are not representative of the target population. As mentioned earlier, the 1986 revisions to the computerized score reports have augmented the earlier reports with a local norm option, a fine addition. The School Form is intended for grades 8–12. The answer sheets also provide scoring for grades 7, 8, and junior college, yet the norming samples do not include representatives of these groups. It is unclear how norms for these groups were generated, and for junior college students using the School Form, the appropriateness of some of the items is also in question.

The College and University (CU) norms are based on a small ($N = 1,345$), underrepresentative sample of students spanning first year through seniors. A total of 13 institutions participated in the norming, and, of these, two had to be eliminated because the grade level of the participants was not specified. Due to the small overall number of subjects and overrepresentation of a single institution, graduate students were not included in the standardization sample. The authors note that the sample is not representative. In addition, the local norm option on the score report mentioned earlier will be beneficial.

RELIABILITY. The School Form User Manual (1981) contains internal consistency and standard errors of measurement (*SEM*) indicators of reliability for grades 9–12 for total groups and by gender. In general, these reliabilities are sufficient; however, two scales, Decision Making (DM) and Preferred Occupation (PO) are problematic, particularly for females. The authors mentioned the discrepancy but did not address it. The authors also indicate the reliability for the PO scale improves in the 11th and 12th grades when compared to reliabilities observed for the 9th and 10th grades. However, I did not find this conclusion borne out by the coefficients; for females grades 9–12 the Cronbach alpha coefficients were .53, .53, .67, and .57 respectively; the coefficients for males grades 9–12 were .61, .55, .64, and .71. The *SEM*s, of course, correspond with the reliabilities, and are considerably larger for DM and PO than the other scales. The manual contains useful guidance to users on interpretation and application of *SEM*s, and the final chapter has realistic caveats concerning use of particular scale scores with individuals. The technical manual contains 3-week test-retest reliabilities for the School Form from two high school samples; the overall reliabilities for three scales—Decision Making (.70 at School L and .69 at School T), World of Work (.67

and .68), and Preferred Occupation (.61 and .63)—appeared fairly unstable. All other scales were adequate.

In the Supplement to the User Manual (1982) the authors address the CU Form regarding internal consistency via Cronbach's alpha and *SEM*s. The alphas, in general, appear adequate; however, the presentation of alphas by class level for the cognitive subscales (DM, WW, and PO) is not reported due to lack of variability, which constricted the interitem correlations, and according to the authors, rendered the alphas inappropriate. Although all the raw score means and standard deviations are not presented, the example provided suggests a very significant reduction in variability. The alphas reported for these scales for the total group and by gender are considerably lower than the other scales. Further, the *SEM*s reported for all three of these scales are in double digits, indicating low reliabilities. Because a primary purpose of using the instrument is for work with individuals, these findings are troubling. The authors' contention that the alphas were rendered inappropriate due to lack of variance seems to beg the question of the appropriateness of the instrument's design and item development. An assumption is made that career maturity is developmental in nature; one would also assume there will be variation on this maturity and that if grade level norms are desired and appropriate, there will be sufficient variance with which to estimate this maturation. This is not the case for these subscales, at least not with this item pool. Upon review of the means and standard deviations reported for the entire group in Table 1, there is some evidence for the presence of a ceiling effect for the DM and WW scales. Although the authors cite Anastasi (1982) to support the inappropriateness of reporting alphas when the variance is restricted, my interpretation differs; at no time does Anastasi suggest that the alphas are rendered inappropriate. She clearly indicates that, "For tests designed to cover a wide range of age or ability, the test manual should report separate reliability coefficients for relatively homogenous subgroups within the standardization sample" (Anastasi, 1988, p. 132). If the score reports provide normative differences by college year, and they do, it follows that the alphas should also be reported and considered appropriate. In the Technical Manual the authors reported 2-week test-retest reliabilities for the College Form; again, the cognitive scales appeared fairly unreliable over a very brief period of time with the following coefficients

reported: Decision Making, .65; World of Work, .43, and Preferred Occupation, .62. Clearly, caution should be advised regarding use of these scales, particularly with individuals.

VALIDITY. Validity is without question the essential attribute of any measure. The authors present evidence for content and construct validity and suggest that criterion validity will be addressed in subsequent work. The item content for both forms of the instrument is derived from past research and explication of Super's model for career maturity. The current forms of the instruments were generated from preliminary forms.

The construct validity was investigated through testing for theoretically expected subgroup performance (sex, grade, and academic program) differences and factor analysis. Separate hypotheses are advanced for the two forms and will be discussed separately.

For the School Form, construct validity was explored through observation of predicted subgroup differences by year of school, sex, academic program, and factor structure. The general absence of sex differences was considered consistent with expectations, although in the 11th and 12th grades females begin to outperform males on the cognitive scales. The authors suggest this result would be expected. The general pattern in the School Form of somewhat increasing total and scale scores over grades is consistent with theory. In fairness, the research shows almost as great career development differences within grades as between. A more appropriate and rigorous assessment of the model would incorporate repeated measures of scales over an extended period of time. This is precisely the design the authors describe as in progress in the final chapter of the User's Manual; however, the Technical Manual published in 1984 indicated that this study is still underway. Differences observed by curricular program also appear to make sense, although the observed differences are generally small.

For the College Form, construct validity was reviewed using the same general techniques as for the School Form: year in college, sex, and major field differences. Observed increases in scale scores by years in college were largely not evident and certainly not compelling. The differences observed over the 4-year period amount to approximately one half a standard deviation or less, and sometimes the direction of change is not discernible. In contrast to the School Form, at the college level, the existence of sex differences on the cognitive scales, with girls outperforming boys, was taken to be evidence of construct validity; however, the observed differences are *considerably* smaller than one *SEM*. Major field differences were, for some scales, quite large, and these results were considered consistent with expectations.

Reports of a series of discriminant analyses using linear combinations of the five scales, and canonical correlation analyses using the conative and cognitive sets of scales, conducted for both forms of the instrument are included in the Technical Manual. Although significant findings are apparent, because the scales will not be used or reported as linear combinations or sets, these results are not helpful to users. The use of more powerful statistical techniques and subsequent significant findings does not render the generally meager scale score differences observed and reported in the earlier manuals of more practical significance. The theoretical grounds for these analyses and logic supporting the expectations are not well explicated in the Technical Manual, and the interpretations of the results were unconvincing, particularly for the College Form.

Of more interest and practical utility is the presentation of correlations of CDI scales with other recognized assessment instruments. These results demonstrated consistent positive correlations between the cognitive subscales and measures of academic abilities such as the Differential Aptitude Battery and the Iowa Tests of Educational Development as well as some moderate correlations of the conative subscales with attitudinal measures from other career maturity scales such as the Salience Inventory (SI) from the Work Importance Study. It was also reassuring to see that socioeconomic status did not impact the CDI scales for either form of the instrument. The results of the analyses supported the two-factor structure upon which the instrument was designed.

The factor analysis results are consistent with those predicted. Across both forms of the instrument, the predicted two-factor structure consistently emerges. The first factor has all of the cognitive scales (DM, WW, and PO) loading on it, and the second factor, conative in nature, is defined by the two attitudinal scales (CE and CP). This factor structure appears to be quite stable across sex and over years in school. A minor qualm regarding the report of factor analysis as evidence of construct validity will be mentioned here. This reviewer considers factor structures and their stability as indicators of content validity rather than construct validity; the

issue of construct validity addresses the issue of factor score meaning, not composition.

A final consideration regarding the factor structure is that if there are only two underlying dimensions consistently identified, why use five subtests? Obviously, the authors have attempted to design the scales around Super's model; however, given the low reliabilities for the cognitive subscales, it would seem prudent to use the more reliable and discernible factors to assess hypothesized career maturity. Interestingly, the Technical Manual contains study results using profile types based upon the composite scales (CDA, attitudinal and CDK, knowledge and skills) indicating such applications have promise.

SUMMARY EVALUATION. The essential question in construct validity is whether or not the inferences we wish to make about career development and maturity on the basis of these scores are warranted. The same issue is central to selection of an instrument. At this stage of development for the CDI, the standardization sample is not adequate for either form of the instrument, the reliability of several scales is quite questionable in regard to item homogeneity as well as stability over fairly brief periods of time, and the validity of inferences counselors would like to make regarding individuals has not been well established. Clearly, the collection of validity evidence is a cumulative and ongoing process, and users of the instrument will contribute to the establishment of better norms and validity evidence than are currently provided by the publisher.

REVIEWER'S REFERENCES
Anastasi, A. (1982). *Psychological testing* (5th ed.). New York: Macmillan Publishing Company.
Anastasi, A. (1988). *Psychological testing* (6th ed.). New York: Macmillan Publishing Company.

[49]
The Career Exploration Inventory.

Purpose: Designed to measure both work and leisure interests.
Population: Adults.
Publication Date: 1992.
Acronym: CEI.
Scores, 15: Mechanical, Animal Care, Plants, Physical Sciences, Life Sciences, Artistic, Literary Arts, Social Service, Physical Performing, Personal Service, Persuading/Influencing, Protecting, Leading, Clerical, Financial Detail.
Administration: Group.
Manual: No manual.
Price Data: Available from publisher.
Time: Administration time not reported.
Comments: Self-administered and self-scored.

Author: John J. Liptak.
Publisher: JIST Works, Inc.

Review of the Career Exploration Inventory by BERT A. GOLDMAN, Professor, School of Education, University of North Carolina at Greensboro, Greensboro, NC:

John Liptak's Career Exploration Inventory (CEI) is designed to identify one's level of interest in 15 interest clusters. Next to each interest cluster, Liptak presents lists of related occupations, typical leisure activities, and related education and training so that one can identify work, leisure, and learning activities that are related to one's interest clusters. He also identifies several sources from which one may locate additional information about these three activity areas.

The CEI format is attractive and arranged in an easily followed nine-step set of directions. These step-by-step directions clearly lead one through administering the test, scoring the responses, and interpreting the results followed by suggesting sources from which one may locate additional information concerning relative work, leisure, and learning activities. The last step provides a worksheet designed to enable one to develop an action plan for work, leisure, and learning during the next 30 days to 5 years.

There is no manual or technical report to accompany the test. Although a test user should have no difficulty administering the instrument, scoring the responses, or interpreting the results given the easy-to-follow step-by-step directions clearly printed on the test, the discerning potential user would certainly want to review technical aspects of the instrument such as validity, reliability, and norms before deciding upon its use. The fact that there is no manual or technical report to accompany the test presents a very strong deterrent to its use.

This reviewer did receive, along with the CEI, a copy of an article written by John Liptak entitled "The Career Exploration Inventory: Expanding Options for the Unemployed," which appeared in the *Journal of Employment Counseling,* 29 (June), 1992, 60–68. In this article, Liptak reports that test-retest reliability coefficients over a 3-month period ranged from .80 to .92 (*N* = 55) for the 15 interest categories with a mean reliability of .84. No information concerning the sample was given other than to state that it comprised adults. The reported reliability is satisfactory and according to Liptak, comparable to that of existing instruments.

In this article Liptak goes on to discuss the CEI's validity. He cites a study involving an adult population of 210, which includes 106 employees who had attended the Employee Career Development Program at a local state university and 104 unemployed adults who participated in the Job Training Partnership Act program sponsored by the Private Industry Council of Westmoreland/Fayette, Inc., in southwestern Pennsylvania. Liptak states that "The CEI most accurately measured leisure interest in the present (79%) and leisure interests in the past (77%) ... Using the top score for each category, the CEI obtained 'hit' rates (from 43% to 51%) that were comparable to the data obtained from other interest inventories" (p. 64). The meaning of this latter statement as a reflection of suitable validity remains unclear to this reviewer.

Further, in this article Liptak indicates that the CEI's construct validity was determined by comparing it to Holland's Self-Directed Search (SDS) and to the Myers-Briggs Type Indicator (MBTI). Liptak states that based on a sample of 59 adults there were high correlations between the CEI and the SBS, but he presents only two correlations (i.e., the Social [.931] and Business [.984] areas). Similarly, Liptak says there were high correlations between the CEI and the MBTI; but again he cites only two correlations (i.e., MBTI's Extrovert vs. CEI's Persuading and Influencing [.822], and MBTI's Sensing vs. CEI's Artistic [.93]). These limited examples of construct validation leave much to be desired in this reviewer's mind.

Also in this article Liptak contends that the CEI is unique because not only does it measure work interests, but it measures leisure interests as well.

Step 9, the last step in the test format, is labeled "An Action Plan" intended to enable the test taker to plan one's work, leisure, and learning activities over the next 30, 60, and 90 days and 1, 2, and 5 years based on what one has learned from the CEI.

Is it likely that someone would seriously lay out a plan for work, leisure, and learning for the next 30 days to 5 years based on the results of the CEI? Furthermore, should they? Although the introduction to using the CEI cautions the user that the CEI does not measure ability or motivation, which are important factors in career selection and success, such caution is not repeated in Step 9, the Action Plan. Instead, in Step 9, which is the final step, test users are encouraged to lay out their work, leisure, and learning plans over the next 30 days to 5 years based upon the CEI results.

In sum, this reviewer finds the Career Exploration Inventory to possess an attractive format arranged in easily followed steps for self: administration, scoring, and interpretation of results. However,

Step 9, the final step—the Action Plan, may be a "pipe dream" in addition to not including a cautionary note concerning its use. By far, the major deterrent to using this test is the fact that there is no manual or technical report informing the user of the instrument's validity, reliability, or norms. John Liptak may well have created a unique instrument for measuring both work and leisure interests, but if he wishes to compete with authors of other interest tests he will do well to prepare an appropriate manual or technical report to accompany the CEI. Until such a publication is available, one should carefully consider whether to use the CEI.

Review of the Career Exploration Inventory by DOUGLAS J. McRAE, Educational Measurement Specialist, Monterey, CA:

PURPOSE. The Career Exploration Inventory is designed to help the responder explore and plan three major areas: work activities, leisure activities, and education or learning.

DESCRIPTION. The CEI consists of 120 items, grouped into 8 items each for 15 major clusters of interest. The responder indicates *past, current,* and/or *future* interest for the activity described in each item. Hence, for each area of interest there is a maximum possible score of 24 points. The 15 areas of interest are Mechanical, Animal Care, Plants, Physical Science, Life Science, Artistic, Literary Arts, Social Service, Physical Performing, Personal Service, Persuading/Influencing, Protecting, Leading, Clerical, and Financial Detail. The CEI leads the responder through a self-scoring process that results in an identification of highest areas of interest. Finally, the CEI provides information on occupations, leisure activities, and education/training for each area of interest.

RATIONALE. The CEI is based on a theoretical rather than an empirical rationale. The clusters of interests are modeled after categories suggested by Super and Bowlsbey in 1979. No particular rationale is given for relating items to interest cluster. No rationale is provided for cut scores defining high, medium, or low interest for each cluster. Support materials indicate the CEI differs from other interest inventories by its focus on leisure activities as well as work activities.

TECHNICAL INFORMATION. No technical information on the CEI is published with the instrument itself. The only technical information available to the reviewer was a brief article published

in the June 1992 *Journal of Employment Counseling.* Information included results from a pilot study involving 15 participants, a field test involving 210 adults, a concurrent validity study involving 59 adults relating the CEI to the Self-Directed Search, and a test-retest study involving 55 adults. Results from these studies were modestly positive.

EVALUATION. The Career Exploration Inventory is very easy to administer, and it provides a quick look at relative interests based on both work and leisure activities. It does not have a strong empirical rationale or validation. As such, use should be limited to situations that involve exploratory directions in contrast to higher stakes career decisions.

[50]
Career Exploration Series, 1992 Revision.

Purpose: Designed for career guidance using "a series of six job interest inventories that focus on specific occupational fields."

Population: Grades 7–12 and college and adults.

Publication Dates: 1979–1992.

Acronym: CES.

Scores: 6 areas: Agriculture—Forestry—Conservation, Science—Mathematics—Health, Business, Industrial, Consumer Economics, Design—Art—Communications.

Administration: Group.

Price Data, 1993: $45 per class set of 30 inventories (5 of each title); $249 per complete CES software set (6 programs); $40 per 25 reusable booklets (specify title); $8.75 per 25 answer folders (specify title); $49.95 per software package (specify title, computer type, and disk size).

Time: (50–60) minutes.

Comments: Self-administered and self-scored interest inventories.

Authors: Arthur Cutler, Francis Ferry, Robert Kauk, and Robert Robinett.

Publisher: CFKR Career Materials, Inc.

Cross References: For reviews by Mark Pope and William I. Sauser, Jr., see 11:60; for reviews by Bruce R. Fretz and Robert B. Slaney of the original edition, see 9:196.

Review of the Career Exploration Series, 1992 Revision by HERBERT C. RUDMAN, Emeritus Professor of Measurement and Quantitative Methods, Michigan State University, East Lansing, MI:

The Career Exploration Series (CES) was first introduced as a general career interest inventory in 1970, and was copyrighted in its present configuration in 1979. Its basic format has not changed significantly since that time, although the authors have made an attempt to keep current with traditional and emerging occupations. The publisher has introduced an optional computer disk that is programmed to match a student's current occupational interests with a description of the skills needed for specific occupations. Although this computerized feature adds an appearance of being "modern," it serves mostly to enhance a sense of "face validity" and does not offer any more information to the student than do the more traditional self-scored booklets of the CES system.

INVENTORY CONTENT. The CES Series consists of six self-administered and self-scored inventories that cover broad career areas: agricultural occupations (AG-O); business-related occupations including clerical, sales, office, and administrative skills (BIZ-O); consumer- and home-economics-related occupations (CER-O); design, art, and communications occupations (DAC-O); industrial career areas including construction, technical, mechanical, transportation, and design occupations (IND-O); and a "new, updated" scientific-mathematical-and-health-occupations booklet that "contains 15 of the 20 fastest growing occupations of the 90's PLUS many of the 225 most popular jobs today" (SCI-O). Unfortunately, the booklet fails to identify these new occupations and popular jobs for the student.

Ancillary materials consist of a user's guide and expendable answer folders used by the student and tailored to each of the six booklets. The user's guide is described by the publisher as a general guide to the use of all six instruments in the Career Exploration Series. It is designed to provide basic information needed to understand the test's background and format well enough to administer the instruments and use the results with students.

The CES system uses the same format for each of the six career area instruments. Each career "family" (AGO-O, BIZ-O, CER-O, DAC-O, IND-O, and SCI-O) has its own reusable booklet. Answer inserts (a four-page folder) are used by the student for self-assessment and comparison of his or her responses to the items contained in the reusable booklet. The authors have inserted a caveat at the end of each booklet, which assures the students that the experience they have just had is with a *sample* of jobs that are possible in the career area, and that further exploration might yield a job of more interest than those listed.

Detailed instructions for administering the interest inventories are available in the four-page user's guide. Basically, the administration of the inventory consists of the students responding to a series of questions posed in the booklets, matching their responses to the 60 jobs listed, and recording the number of matches between these jobs and their responses. The students are instructed to analyze all of those job titles that appear to have a high number of matches and to choose up to 12 jobs of interest to them. The U.S. Department of Labor's *Occupational Outlook Handbook* serves as a major source for job titles used in the CES inventories.

The time needed to complete *each* of the six occupational area instruments is estimated to be between 45 to 50 minutes. Because this time frame is common to many secondary school academic periods it would take six periods to complete the entire CES series of inventories.

TECHNICAL ASPECTS. Attempts by this reviewer to gain more technical information about the Career Exploration Series than that contained in the brief four-page user's guide resulted in the publisher sending material that dealt with a parallel program entitled JOB-O, which also used the same six "families" of occupations used in the CES. Not only was this confusing, but it verified previous reviewers' impressions that the work done over 20 years was characterized by a "carelessness of quality of some of the materials, which should make the user suspicious about less obvious aspects of the CES" (Pope, 1992). I would concur with this observation. The authors and publishers appear to have limited technical information to share with those interested in either of the two programs.

The Career Exploration Series fails to meet the *Standards for Educational and Psychological Testing* for test use in counseling as established by the American Educational Research Association, American Psychological Association, and the National Council on Measurement in Education (1985). Its authors offer little or no research data to support their assertions for the validity of interpretations of student responses, nor do they offer reliability data concerning the stability of student interests at any stage in their development from high school to higher education.

Other reviewers have described the publisher's stance that because the CES is one that uses inventories rather than *tests* the *Standards* are not applicable to the CES. However, the *Standards* do apply to the use of inventories that are used as diagnostic tools in planning job and career development for individuals. The stated purposes of the Career Exploration Series do indeed appear to relate to

Chapter 9 (Test Use in Counseling) and Chapter 10 (Employment Testing) of the *Standards*.

The authors of the CES have shown a modicum of sensitivity to previous reviews of their work. But it is clear that a persistent criticism of the CES has not been addressed since this measure was reviewed in the *Ninth* and *Eleventh Mental Measurements Yearbooks* (1985, 1992). If students are to explore possible future occupations in light of their present interests, some data concerning predictive validity are essential. It simply is not enough to claim face validity based upon sales figures and ignore such issues as construct and content validity. The publisher of these materials, CFKR Career Materials, claims that the CES has been used by 9,000,000 students in the past 20 years. How stable are these expressed interests over time? Test-retest reliability studies over some identifiable cohorts would have been useful during the two decades or more that the Career Exploration Series has been developed. However, this four-page guide in no way offers the user of the CES the validity or reliability data needed to interpret accurately the information yielded.

Missing from the Career Exploration Series is any indication of the role that past experiences, gender differences, economic opportunities, and the like play in the perceptions of students and their aspirations for job skills and careers. The necessity of this information is well articulated in Chapter 9 of the AERA, APA, and NCME *Standards* (1985). Yet no mention of group membership is made in the user's guide of the CES. Hence, its use with students is severely limited.

SUMMARY. The Career Exploration Series has had a long use. It has been reviewed now for the third time since 1985. Some attempts were made by the authors and publisher, CFKR Career Materials, to update and modify its materials in the light of these and other reviews. However, whatever was done to improve the materials was minor, and errors persisted even to typographical errors in subsequent editions. This review of the CES will most likely be its last. As a representative of CFKR wrote in a letter to me, "We do provide the CES Series for those customers who wish to continue the program. However, we do not plan to revise the program to meet the School-to-Work educational reform act" (personal communication, May 24, 1996).

REVIEWER'S REFERENCES

American Educational Research Association, American Psychological Association, & National Council on Measurement in Education. (1985). *Standards for educational and psychological testing*. Washington, DC: APA, Inc.

Pope, M. (1992). [Review of the Career Exploration Series, 1988 Revision.] In J. J. Kramer & J. C. Conoley (Eds.), *The eleventh mental measurements yearbook* (pp. 151–152). Lincoln, NE: The Buros Institute of Mental Measurements.

[51]

Career Interest Inventory.

Purpose: "Designed to assist students in making decisions concerning their educational and vocational plans."

Publication Dates: 1989–1991.

Administration: Group.

Price Data, 1994: $11.50 per examination kit including Level 1 machine-scorable answer document, Level 2 hand-scorable booklet, directions for administering, and student profile; $32.50 per counselor's manual ('91, 120 pages); $11.50 per 25 Exploring Interests: An Introduction to the Career Interest Inventory; $4.50 per directions for administering ('90, 29 pages); $1.62 scoring charge per Level 1 answer document; $.59 for first copy and $.17 per each additional copy of individual report; $.56 for first copy and $.05 per each additional copy of counselor's report (by Teacher/Counselor or School); $.53 for first copy and $.18 per each additional copy of student record label; $.42 for first copy and $.10 per each additional copy of occupational interest report (by School); $.27 for first copy and $15.58 per set of career planning summary (by Teacher/Counselor); $.20 for first copy and $15.58 per set of career planning summary (by School); $.15 for first copy and $13.35 per set of career planning summary (by District); $70 (not refundable) plus $.28 per pupil for student data tape; $.35 per pupil for student data diskette; $12.50 for first 1,000 and $3.20 per each additional 1,000 for return of test booklets; $6.39 for first 1,000 plus $1.74 per each additional 1,000 for return of answer documents; $10.47 for first 1,000 plus $3.20 per each additional 1,000 for return of mixed documents.

Time: (30–40) minutes.

Author: The Psychological Corporation.

Publisher: The Psychological Corporation.

a) LEVEL 1.

Population: Grades 7–9.

Scores, 47: 15 Occupational Interests (Social Science, Clerical Services, Health Services, Agriculture, Customer Services, Fine Arts, Mathematics and Science, Building Trades, Educational Services, Legal Services, Transportation, Sales, Management, Benchwork, Machine Operation), 16 High School Subject Interests (Speech or Drama, Metal Shop or Woodworking, Mathematics, Auto Repair, Science, Cooking or Sewing, Art or Music, Farming or Livestock Care, Newspaper Writing, Typing or Office Machines, Social Studies, Health Care, Creative Writing, Computers, English or Literature, Bookkeeping or Office Practices), 16 High School Activity Interests (Mathematics Club, Farming Club, Speech or Debate Team, School Library Aide, School Play, Automobile Club, Science Fair, Teacher's Aide, Student Government, Office Helper or Assistant,

School Literary Magazine, School Officer, Photography Club, Business Club, School Newspaper, Computer Club).

Price Data: $37.50 per 25 hand-scorable booklets; $37.50 per 25 Type 1 machine-scorable answer documents; $37.50 per 25 Type 2 machine-scorable answer documents.

b) LEVEL 2.

Population: Grades 10–12 and adults.

Scores, 35: 15 Occupational Interests (same as Level 1), 20 Post-High School Course Interests (Marketing or Sales, Computer Programming, Electronics or Electrical Trades, Plumbing or Welding, Automotive Repair, Carpentry or Home Building, Word Processing or Typing, Haircutting or Styling, Bookkeeping or Office Practices, Cooking or Sewing, Music or Art, Farming or Livestock Care, Mathematics or Science, English or Foreign Language, Business Law or Management, Creative Writing, Speech or Drama, Photography, Health Care, Newspaper Writing).

Price Data: $40.50 per 25 hand-scorable booklets; $40.50 per 25 Type 1 machine-scorable answer documents; $40.50 per 25 Type 2 machine-scorable answer documents.

Review of the Career Interest Inventory by WILLIAM D. SCHAFER, Associate Professor of Measurement, Statistics, and Evaluation, University of Maryland at College Park, College Park, MD:

The Career Interest Inventory (CII) was designed to assess interest in activities linked to 15 occupational groups representative of the spectrum of career fields described in the U.S. Department of Labor's (1977, 1986) *Dictionary of Occupational Titles* (DOT). It is available in two levels. Level 1, recommended for students in grades 7–9, contains 120 work activity statements, 16 school subject areas (course-taking activities), and 16 extra-curricular school activities (152 items). Level 2, recommended for students in grades 10–12 and adults, contains 150 work activity statements and 20 school subject areas (170 items). Examinees are to respond to a 5-point scale indicating the degree to which they would like or dislike doing the activity. It may be administered to groups; although it is not timed, examinees are expected to complete the CII in about 40 minutes, including administrative time, which is consistent with the time structure of most schools. It may be hand scored by the examinees, also in groups, or machine scored. The materials used depend on the type of scoring. The CII may be used in conjunction with the Differential Aptitude Tests (DAT; 12:118)

with a combined report produced if machine scoring is elected.

The manual for administering the CII, with modifications for either format, is clear. It contains the statements to be read in black type and explanatory material with activity directions in red. It gives directions for examinees to score their own responses if hand scoring is used. Also available are a folder to be used to help students think about career choice issues, including work values, in preparation for the CII; a workbook for use in career exploration; and a counselor's manual that contains test-development and technical information and presents useful recommendations for interpretation and use in practice.

Scoring the CII is straightforward. Responses to the 8 (Level 1) or 10 (Level 2) job activity statements are summed separately within each of the occupational groups to yield 15 scores that range from 8 to 40 (Level 1) or 10 to 50 (Level 2). A consistency index is used to assess the degree that responses are differentiated within each occupational group, but few suggestions appear in the counselor's manual about its use. Subject area and school activity (Level 1 only) scores are not combined but are keyed to the occupational groups.

The occupational groups were designed to represent similar work activities and educational needs within each group as well as to span combinations of activities dealing with data (intangibles), people (or animals), or things (inanimate tangibles) and the nine primary occupational categories as described by the DOT. They are keyed to the U.S. Department of Labor's (1979) *Guide for Occupational Exploration* (GOE) interest areas.

Examinees are also asked to indicate their educational plans after high school from among four choices (none, vocational/technical, college or university, or military) or undecided. Appropriateness of these plans, based on expert judgment, is related to each of the 15 occupational groups. Although helpful, this information seems particularly prone to misuse and the cautions in the counselor's manual about overinterpreting it should be emphasized.

The CII was developed using a nationally representative sample of participants who completed developmental versions that oversampled items in each occupational group. Each item was written to summarize a DOT description of an occupation and was reviewed for vocabulary level (fifth grade at most) and absence of bias or stereotyping. The final scales were constructed based on item-scale correlations for males, females, and the total group, and on breadth of occupational group representation. Internal consistency reliability coefficients (alphas) of the scales range from .82 to .94 for Level 1 and from .87 to .94 for Level 2. These are certainly adequate. Overestimation that would be expected when the same sample is used to select items and to estimate alphas is not severe in this case because each coefficient was estimated with over 34,000 participants. Yet, the fact that a consistency index is calculated for each scale implies the interests each represents may not be as homogeneous as the alpha coefficients suggest. No data on stability are available.

Correlations among the 15 scales ranged from .00 to .84 for Level 1. The largest correlation was between Building Trades and Machine Operation, which becomes .93 when corrected for attenuation. For Level 2, the correlations ranged from .01 to .86, the largest, again for Building Trades and Machine Operation, becomes .92 after correction. Other notably large correlations were between Machine Operation and Transportation (.80 for Level 1, .82 for Level 2), Building Trades and Transportation (.77 for Level 1, .79 for Level 2), Management and Sales (.76 for Level 1, .70 for Level 2), Benchwork and Building Trades (.69 for Level 1, .75 for Level 2), Benchwork and Transportation (.62 for Level 1, .71 for Level 2), Clerical Services and Management (.70 for both levels), Clerical Services and Educational Services (.70 for Level 1, .69 for Level 2), and Customer Services and Educational Services (.70 for level 1, .68 for Level 2). The absence of any negative correlations is more indicative of some of the difficulties in assessing interests than a criticism of the CII.

Principal components factor analysis and varimax rotation were applied to each level item-by-item correlation matrix. At Level 1, an 8-factor solution was judged best, with all but 2 factors having high loadings with items from two or fewer scales. The 2 factors that had strong loadings with more than two scales' items were called Working with Hands or Things and Helping People. At Level 2, the best solution was for 10 factors, 7 of which with high loadings with items from two or fewer scales. The other 3 were called Working with Hands or Things, Helping People, and Business. These results seem consistent with the large interscale correlations noted earlier between Benchwork, Building Trades, Machine Operation, and Transportation (Working with Hands or Things) and between Clerical Services, Customer Services, and Educational Services

(Helping People). Perhaps these scales do not represent interests that are as distinct from each other as those of the other scales.

Other than internal structure, validity evidence is available through correlations with judgmentally matched scales of the Ohio Vocational Interest Survey Second Edition (OVIS II). Correlations were generally strong with the exception of the CII Health Services scale, which correlated .10 with the OVIS II Medical Services scale and .08 with the OVIS II Health Services scale. Correlations with other inventories should be studied in future research as should predictive validity of the CII for such outcomes as effectiveness of career exploration, career choice, and career satisfaction.

In practice, the 15 occupational group interest results are interpreted as raw scores and compared with each other. It is claimed the occupational group scales are directly comparable because they are raw scores, and that because both males and females were included in the representative population they are sex fair. Each of these claims deserves consideration.

Although interests across the 15 occupational groups may actually differ in the general population, it seems reasonable to compare observed occupational group differences to evaluate whether the CII raw scores should be compared with each other. This may be done by estimating Cohen's (1988) effect size index, $d = |M1 - M2|/s$. According to Cohen, a large effect size is $d = .80$, approximately the difference between "college graduates and persons with a 50–50 chance of passing an academic high school curriculum" (p. 27).

Means, standard deviations, and ns are available in the manual for each grade level from 7 though 12 on each of the 15 occupational group scales. The difference between the highest and lowest means produces effect size estimates that range from .92 to 1.03. For each grade, Fine Arts ranks among the top three occupational group scale means and Machine Operation is lowest. Other popular (high mean) occupational scales are Educational Services, Legal Services, Mathematics/Science, Management, and Health Services, whereas other comparatively unpopular occupational scales are Transportation, Building Trades, and Benchwork.

Means, standard deviations, and ns are also available by sex at each grade level. The largest effect size estimate between sexes at each grade level is for Machine Operation, with the larger means for males. Also favoring males, in approximate decreasing effect-size order are Building Trades, Transportation, Benchwork, Mathematics/Science, Sales, and Agriculture. Scales favoring females are, in approximate decreasing effect-size order, Educational Services, Customer Services, Clerical Services, Social Science, Health Services, Legal Services, Fine Arts, and Management. Interestingly, the least popular occupational groups overall are those with the largest effect-size differences favoring males.

In the light of these effect sizes, claims of sex fairness and raw score comparability may be questionable. Of course, comparisons based on some form of scaled scores by grade within sex and occupational group may also lead to questionable interpretations. Perhaps several approaches (e.g., raw scores and scaled scores overall and within subpopulations) should be considered as a way to enhance meaningful career exploration in actual use, but no convenient way to facilitate that beyond the information discussed above is provided in the manual.

The CII is an attractive and easy-to-use tool for career exploration. The link with the DAT is a helpful feature. However, the evidence supporting its validity is both sparse and mixed and the information it provides to counselors and examinees may be oversimplified for use in career exploration, which is a very complex process.

REVIEWER'S REFERENCES

United States Department of Labor. (1977). *Dictionary of occupational titles* (4th ed.). Washington, DC: Government Printing Office.

United States Department of Labor. (1979). *Guide for occupational exploration* (4th ed.). Washington, DC: Government Printing Office.

United States Department of Labor. (1986). *Dictionary of occupational titles* (4th ed. Supplement). Washington, DC: Government Printing Office.

Cohen, J. (1988). *Statistical power analysis for the behavioral sciences* (2nd ed.). Hillsdale, NJ: Lawrence Erlbaum Associates.

Review of the Career Interest Inventory by SHELDON ZEDECK, Chair and Professor of Psychology, Department of Psychology, University of California, Berkeley, CA:

The Career Interest Inventory (CII) is designed to be a career-guidance instrument that assists students in making decisions concerning their educational and work plans. It is designed to provide information that links interests to occupations that are described in the *Dictionary of Occupational Titles* (4th ed.) (United States Department of Labor, 1977) as well as designed to provide information concerning students' interests in a variety of school activities and/or subjects.

There are 120 job activity and 32 high school subject and activity statements on Level 1 (designed for grades 7–9) and 150 job activity and 20 post-high

school course statements on Level 2 (designed for grades 10–12 and adults) of the CII. Examples of statements are "take a course in government and economics," "research new ways to drill for oil," and "run a printing press."

The items are clear and nonbiased. The 5-point response scale ranges from "1" or "dislike the activity a great deal" to "5" or "like the activity very much."

For purposes of interpreting the results and for guidance, the user is referred to a number of ancillary materials such as the Counselor's Manual for Interpreting the Career Interest Inventory, the Guide to Careers Student Workbook, and the Exploring Interests: An Introduction to the Career Interest Inventory. Students are encouraged to work through the latter booklet prior to completing the CII: This booklet gets the student thinking about careers, values, likes, and dislikes, either by open-ended questions or checklists to which the student responds. The "Directions for Administering" the CII are quite exhaustive and easy to follow. The directions lay out a script for administering and scoring the inventory.

Results from the CII are used to counsel students about educational and occupational alternatives; by measuring students' interests in 15 occupational groups, the test provides insight into careers described in other sources such as the *Guide for Occupational Exploration* (United States Department of Labor, 1979) and the *Occupational Outlook Handbook* (United States Department of Labor, 1990). In addition, if students' abilities are also assessed, such as by the Differential Aptitude Tests (12:118), information about students' interests can be linked to abilities and aptitudes. The CII Score Report provides profiles and graphic results for the occupational groups, subject areas, and school activities; the student is also presented with a narrative that highlights his or her interests, likes, and dislikes. An available option is to obtain a group report that summarizes the results for, as an example, a class or school.

The Counselor's Manual for Interpreting the Career Interest Inventory is quite detailed, informative, and easy to understand. Information is presented on the history of interest measurement, how to score the instrument, how to interpret the results—raw scores and profiles, and how to use the results for career exploration and planning. Valuable sections of the manual address the way in which the CII can be used with students at risk of dropping out of school as well as those who are disadvantaged or handicapped.

In addition to providing a student's raw score for an occupational group, a useful scoring feature is a consistency index. This index is used to differentiate identical raw scores between those that reflect indifference (i.e., responding to some likes and some dislikes for the items in an occupational group), and those that indicate being undecided (i.e., responding with a midpoint value to most, if not all, of the statements within the occupational group).

The manual also contains sections on the development of the instrument as well as on reliability and validity. The sample of approximately 100,000 that participated in the initial stages of development are representative of the population in terms of geographic region, socioeconomic status, urban classification, and ethnicity. Items were retained on the inventory if they met item-scale correlation criteria. The primary criterion was that the scale should be homogeneous (the coefficient alphas for the scales are all in the .80s or .90s). The argument for content validity is made on the basis of the instrument's representation of the world of work. Statements were written to cover activities in the *Dictionary of Occupational Titles* (United States Department of Labor, 1977) or interests in the *Guide for Occupational Exploration* (United States Department of Labor, 1979). Factor analytic results are presented to support the claim that there is homogeneity of items within an occupational group and that the groups are relatively independent of each other. In addition, evidence is presented for the correlation between the CII and the Ohio Vocational Interest Survey, a measure also based, in part, on the *Dictionary of Occupational Titles* (United States Department of Labor, 1977).

What is most obviously missing, however, is any empirical evidence of a link between test results and satisfaction or performance in any occupational group or subject. Without such information, the utility of the instrument is diminished. Furthermore, no information is offered on the instrument's comparison to more popular interest inventories such as the Strong Interest Inventory (12:374).

In conclusion, the first edition of the CII requires further data collection. In addition, due to its linkage to several occupational sources, such as the *Dictionary of Occupational Titles* (U.S. Department of Labor, 1977), the items used on the instrument should be monitored for appropriateness, relevance, and timeliness. The CII will require modification when the *Dictionary* is revised.

REVIEWER'S REFERENCES

United States Department of Labor. (1979). *Guide for occupational exploration* (4th ed.). Washington, DC: Government Printing Office.
United States Department of Labor. (1977). *Dictionary of occupational titles* (4th ed.). Washington, DC: Government Printing Office.
United States Department of Labor. (1990). *Occupational outlook handbook* (1990–91 edition). Washington, DC: Government Printing Office.

[52]

The Career Profile System, Second Edition.

Purpose: "Predicts an individual's probability of success in an insurance sales career."

Population: Insurance sales representatives and candidates for insurance.

Publication Dates: 1983–1992.

Administration: Individual.

Price Data: Available from publisher.

Foreign Language Editions: English-speaking Canada and French-speaking Canada editions available; U.S. Spanish edition of Initial Career Profile available in 1994.

Time: (55–65) minutes.

Comments: Profiles processed by publisher.

Author: Life Insurance Marketing and Research Association, Inc.

Publisher: Life Insurance Marketing and Research Association, Inc.

a) STUDENT CAREER PROFILE.

Population: High school—college.

Scores: Total score and ratings in 3 areas: Industry Contacts, Achievement Orientation, Economic Maturity.

1) *Candidate Self-Assessment.*

Scores: 11 areas: Motivating Goals (External Goals, Internal Goals, Nonwork Goals), Knowledge and Expectations of the Career (Knowledge of the Career, Expectations of the Commitment Required, Expectations of Sales Process, Income Expectations), The Candidate's Concerns (Acceptance as a Sales Representative, Potential Drawbacks of Career, Impact on Social Relationships, Income).

b) INITIAL CAREER PROFILE.

Population: Inexperienced candidates.

Scores: Total score and ratings in 6 areas: Commitment to Present Situation, Belief in the Value of Insurance, Financial Situation, Income Expectations, Career Expectations, Work History.

1) *Candidate Self-Assessment.*

Scores: Same as *a*-1 above.

c) ADVANCED CAREER PROFILE.

Population: Experienced candidates.

Scores: Total score and ratings in 5 areas: Position Familiarity, Professional Involvement, Belief in the Value of Insurance, Insurance Earnings, Income Needs and Expectations.

1) *Candidate Self-Assessment.*

Scores: 11 areas: Satisfaction with Present Insurance Sales Career (Training and Support,

Compensation, Evaluation of Products, Evaluation of Current Agency, Administrative Issues), Sales Results (Number of Sales, Total Annualized Premiums, Persistency), Insurance Income (Income History, Income Needs, Income Expectations).

Review of The Career Profile System, Second Edition by AYRES G. D'COSTA, Associate Professor, The Ohio State University, Columbus, OH:

The Career Profile was developed and is serviced by the Life Insurance Marketing and Research Association (LIMRA), a major international organization serving the life insurance agent industry. This Career Profile is designed as a service to insurance organizations engaged in the selection of candidates as salespersons. It is *not* intended as a counseling device for persons interested in career exploration, as its somewhat generic title might suggest.

The administrative manual (2nd edition, 1992) describes the Career Profile as a "selection questionnaire that provides an assessment of a candidate's probability of success in insurance sales" (p. 3). This biodata-based assessment is usually a first step in the agent selection process; and it is conducted at a member insurance agency office, either via computer linkup to LIMRA, or in paper-and-pencil mode with the answer sheets going to LIMRA for scoring and interpretative reporting. The Career Profile is available in three forms: Student, Initial, and Advanced. All three are available for Canadian use, including a French-language version. Agencies wanting to use the Career Profile must typically be members of LIMRA, or receive special permission. All materials, scoring services, reports, and support services are directly provided by LIMRA.

LIMRA provides a special Administrator's Kit for each type of client. Each kit includes the questionnaire forms (if not administered by computer), an administrator's manual, and a selection guide. These materials provide clear and well-written instructions on what to expect of the Career Profile, how to administer it, what reports are provided by LIMRA as feedback, and how these reports can be utilized in selection and follow-up training work with each candidate.

As expected, the Initial and Advanced Career Profile Questionnaires have several similar work-experience-related items, and the Student Version is somewhat different in that it is appropriately tailored to persons without real work experience. The number of items in each questionnaire is 162. Although there is no time limit, there were no specific guide-lines provided in the administrative manuals pertaining to any adaptations that might be permissible to make for candidates under the Americans with Disabilities Act of 1990 (e.g., persons with reading problems). Presumably, these guidelines are provided by LIMRA as needed by the agency administrator. All three questionnaires posted a prominent Equal Employment Opportunity Commission notification recognizing that "it is illegal to discriminate in employment against qualified individuals with disabilities, or on the basis of race, color, religion, national origin, sex, or age." Marital status, incidentally, was not included.

One of the strengths of the Career Profile is the quality of the materials and the professional guidance provided to users. The administrative manual and the selection guide provide a nice overview of a good selection process, and how the reports provided by the Career Profile may be utilized.

The Career Profile Report provides an Overall Probability of Success rating on a scale of 1 to 19. For example, for the Initial Career Profile, a rating of 19 indicates a 27.6% probability of success in U.S. Home service work; a 10 would indicate 16.6%; and 1 would indicate 5.5%. The corresponding probabilities for the Advanced Career Profile would be 31.6%, 20.6%, and 9.6%, respectively.

Following the Overall rating are Candidate Profile Summary ratings (High/Moderate/Low) on "several areas that comprise the overall Career Profile" (administrative manual, p. 8). Although Appendix B of the administrative manual provided an example with six areas: Work History, Commitment to Situation, Belief in Insurance, Financial Situation, Income Expectations, and Career Expectations, it was not clear to this reviewer whether these are the only areas considered, nor how these specific areas were arrived at. What is nice is that all ratings are accompanied by a descriptive paragraph that explains the rating to the recruiting officer.

For example, Appendix B provides the following paragraph:

> J. Smith rated low in this area. This indicates a general lack of personal experience with insurance products and their associated benefits. This will make it more difficult for J. Smith to analyze prospect's insurance needs and to convince them of the value of owning insurance. Since this belief has not been demonstrated, development in this area will be needed if you continue with the selection process. (p. 18)

The second report is the Candidate's Self-Assessment on several areas important to selling insurance; for example, career goals, knowledge of career, expectations, etc. The administrative manual suggests that these ratings be used in conjunction with the appropriate LIMRA Interview Guide.

Finally, a Monthly Environmental Adequacy Report is provided to offices using the computer-based mode, on testing distractions, visual conditions, faulty equipment, lack of privacy, and lack of assistance.

The technical information about the Career Profile is available in several reports instead of a special technical manual. The test-retest reliability study was reported in a McManus and Mitchell (1987) paper using subjects who were administered the instrument twice within the same company. Although the study sample is relatively small (N = 158) and differs from the normative sample (N = 11,892) in that it is older and less educated, rs ranging from .63 to .92 were reported. The authors conclude that "it is the scored items, which tend to tap factual information in contrast to many of the softer items which tap attitudes and opinions, that exhibit the highest reliabilities."

This reviewer did not find any internal measures, such as Cronbach's alpha, reported for the Career Profile overall rating. This is surprising. In particular, it would have been useful to see some index of reliability for the summary ratings reported for the several areas comprising the Career Profile. Ordinarily, when subscores are reported, it is expected that these subareas are also checked for reliability and validity. Although a factor analysis study was reported, there was no information specifically linking those factors to the selected subareas.

The validity of the Career Profile is based upon LIMRA's extensive experience in developing selection biodata instruments for the industry (McManus, 1993). A job analysis was first conducted in 1984 utilizing descriptions of the agent's job provided by some 2,000 agents and 1,000 field management personnel. Like most job analyses, this initial study examined the importance and the amount of time spent on 26 tasks identified as comprising the agent's job. In addition, this study studied the importance of 34 personal characteristics for success in this job.

Biodata-based job analysis is the unique thrust of LIMRA's approach to developing the Career Profile. This is the key to analyzing the validity of this instrument. The unit of analysis is not what a worker actually does on the job, it is not work outcomes or tasks completed, it is not job-related behaviors, it is not human attributes enabling the worker to be effective; but rather, it is "the life-history antecedents to success in the job" (Crosby, 1988, p. 5). This requires the retrospective gathering of information from agents and their supervisors about important (past) life events/facts that are believed to have been important for present success on the job. Biodata items are then written to measure these predictor constructs. Crosby (1988) claims that this "approach introduces rationality early in the biodata predictor development process," and provides several advantages both empirical and administrative.

One criticism that has not been mentioned here is the possible adverse impact on nontraditional candidates whose backgrounds may be different from the mainstream ones that provided the biodata norms and items for such predictor constructs. There is the danger that minority candidates might be eliminated early in the selection process just because their biodata did not fit the normed constructs and the traditional early career profile.

A second criticism relates to the tenuous relationship between early predictors and later job success. Although school grades are usually reasonably good predictors of college grades, later job success is quite another matter. Personnel selection assessment has been justified on the basis of the high costs of on-the-job training; and needless to say, even a small percentage validity gain is translated into significant financial advantages, which could be crucial in a highly competitive market place. Moreover, given that applicant information gathering is the norm for job selection processes, the systematic use of biodata in personnel selection is to be commended.

These criticisms are not intended to deny the innovative and pioneering nature of LIMRA's methodology. A rational approach to gathering and interpreting candidate biodata is undoubtedly better than one based on manager subjectivity and lack of expertise. Biodata has the advantage of being readily available, although somewhat fakeable; and when it is properly interpreted and utilized, it could provide a company with an important basis for designing effective training for its prospective agents. A major asset in this approach is the claimed built-in understanding linking biodata to future job success, thereby enabling managers to help candidates to take advantage of their past experiences or to knowingly seek and develop new opportunities and different skills to remediate past deficiencies.

The technical report on the validity of the Career Profile by McManus (1993) utilizes the reporting structure specified for criterion-related validity studies in the Uniform Guidelines on Employee Selection procedures (1978). This validity study involved all new agents contracted in 1990 by 43 U.S. (*n* = 9,780) and 19 Canadian (*n* = 1,046) companies participating with LIMRA. The criterion of success was insurance business productivity for the year. To control for company differences, all measures were standardized within company to a mean of 500 and a *SD* of 100. These standardized values were then adjusted for individual company quality using agent survival rate as the basis for increasing the production measure.

McManus (1993) asserts that "LIMRA conducts ongoing validation studies of The Career Profile system" (p. 5); however, no updates since this 1993 report were made available to this reviewer. It is possible that these ongoing studies are less formal and only internally reported.

Studies of the relationship of the Career Profile overall rating to the career success measures (adjusted for setting differences) are reported. In addition to means and standard deviations for the predictor rating and for the success criterion, McManus (1993) reports raw correlations (Pearson *r*s) ranging from .09 to .16 for the larger study groups. Similar correlations were reported for females and for three minority groups, although a couple of negative *r*s showed up here. All *r*s were tested for statistical significance and *p*-values of less than .03 reported to imply that these correlations are significant and therefore significant predictive validity has been achieved in most instances.

Another set of problems is due to lack of homoscedasticity and linearity. Brown, Stout, Dalessio, and Crosby (1988) analyzed these data and concluded that "errors in prediction are quite low for low test scores and are very high for high test scores" (p. 740). This suggests that the overall rating from the Career Profile may be "very useful for identifying candidates who are potential failures, but less useful for predicting who will be successful."

These studies and findings are typical of the knotty problems inherent in prediction studies. The nature of the predictor-criterion relationship is unknown and can be assumed to be complicated. This is particularly true for predictions based on biodata because of the likely discontinuity in the constructs being tracked, even assuming that LIMRA has developed understandings of such construct linkages. Although the effort is indeed worthy, caution is called for, especially where predictions of success are claimed with *r*s that can only be claimed to explain 2% of the variance at best.

Administrators responsible for selection procedures in field offices should be warned not to use the expectancy tables in Appendix A of the administrative manual for predictions of future success of agents (as implied in the administrative manual), but rather as a guideline for not taking risks with seriously deficient candidates. McManus (1993) notes that LIMRA's member companies individually set policies regarding its use and application. She also states that "LIMRA recommends administering the Career Profile questionnaire as a preliminary screen in the selection process to identify high-risk candidates." However, she proceeds to state that "candidates rated highly are evaluated as having a higher probability of succeeding as agents than candidates who receive low ratings" (p. 13). This is overstating the case, given the Brown et al. (1988) admonition.

In addition to urging caution in the use of the current instrument, there is need to train member company administrators to look for nontraditional indicators of potential, especially where minority candidates are concerned, or else this selection procedure could unwittingly result in systematically keeping out promising minority candidates with backgrounds that do not match the traditional. Given that clients with insurance needs have diverse backgrounds, this approach would also be a wise business decision for the industry. There is also a need to examine gender differences in biodata predictors to make sure that women are not adversely impacted by this selection procedure. Although McManus (1993) does compare regression slopes for different special groups concluding that there is no evidence of bias, and does indicate that alternative assessment procedures are continuously being investigated by LIMRA, there is need to document efforts that minority concerns were attended to in the development of the Career Profile, instead of merely examining regression slopes in a criterion study after the fact. Much depends in such studies on the relevance of the biodata indicators and of the success criterion to minority groups. No such research efforts were made available to this reviewer.

In general, the Career Profile is a reasonable personnel selection device, and merits cautious attention from the insurance industry.

REVIEWER'S REFERENCES

Uniform guidelines on employee selection procedure. (1978). *Federal Register*, *43*(166), 38290–38309.

McManus, M. A., & Mitchell T. W. (August, 1987). *Test-retest reliability of the Career Profile*. Hartford, CT: Life Insurance Marketing and Research Association. Mimeo.

Brown, S. H., Stout, J. D., Dalessio, A. T., & Crosby, M. M. (1988). Stability of validity indices through test score ranges. *Journal of Applied Psychology, 73*, (4), 736–742.

Crosby, M. M. (1988). *A biodata-based job analysis of the life insurance sales job*. Technical Report MRR3-1988. Hartford, CT: Life Insurance Marketing and Research Association. Mimeo.

McManus, M. A. (1993). *Validity of the Career Profile*. Technical Report MRR7-1993. Hartford, CT: Life Insurance Marketing and Research Association. Mimeo.

Review of The Career Profile System, Second Edition by MICHAEL S. TREVISAN, Assistant Professor, Department of Educational Leadership and Counseling Psychology, Washington State University, Pullman, WA:

The Career Profile System is a set of screening instruments used to assess the probability for success of candidates pursuing careers selling life insurance. By comparing a candidate's score on a Career Profile questionnaire to the performance of thousands of life insurance sales people with the same score, an actuarial assessment of the candidate is provided, which conveys information about the risk a company would incur if the candidate is hired.

Previously known as the Aptitude Battery Index, The Career Profile System has been in existence for over 50 years. The system is composed of three questionnaires that are administered to candidates depending on where they are in their careers. The Student Career Profile Questionnaire was developed from 1984–1989 but not marketed until 1992. This questionnaire is administered to high school, college, or university students or those who graduated within the past 3 months. The Initial Career Profile Questionnaire was developed in 1990 and is administered to candidates who have never worked as a life insurance agent, and the Advanced Career Profile Questionnaire is administered to those candidates who have worked up to 5 years in the industry. (No information was available regarding when the development took place for the Advanced Career Profile.) There is a Canadian version of each questionnaire both in English and French, as well as a version that is administered on a personal computer (PC).

FORMAT AND SCORE REPORTS. All three questionnaires consist of 162 selected response items. The number of alternatives per item ranges from 2 to 21. These items were constructed from a thorough search of the literature for factors that affect a candidate's probability for success as an insurance agent. A Candidate Profile Report is supplied for each administration of the Career Profile. A rating score ranging from 1 to 19 is provided in the report; the higher the number the greater the probability for success as an agent. Low, Moderate, and High descriptions of factors affecting the rating are also provided. The combined data provides a company and candidate with good information about the candidate's qualities and prospects as an insurance agent.

ADMINISTRATION AND SCORING. Companies choosing to purchase and use The Career Profile System will find a fairly simple instrument to administer and a useful strategy for assessing candidates. Administration of the questionnaire is clearly documented and straightforward. Documentation accompanying the questionnaire outlines a complete selection framework, placing the questionnaire as one of several steps in an accurate, defensible selection strategy. All scoring is conducted by the publisher. Ways of appropriately discussing the results of the Career Profile with prospective candidates are provided in the administration manuals. Missing from the manuals, however, is information about whether the Career Profile can be individually administered, group administered, or both. Also, the administration manual does not discuss good test user practice for administration of the Career Profile, such as establishing rapport with the candidate, avoiding test administrator bias, orienting the test taker with the Career Profile, and conducting the assessment in an environment conducive to concentration and intellectual work. In order to avoid mismeasurement and enhance the validity of test results, clarity regarding the two aforementioned issues should be provided in subsequent administration manuals.

RELIABILITY. Limited discussion regarding the internal consistency of data derived from the Student Career Profile was provided with the review materials but the presentation is not clear. Further reliability information for data obtained from this instrument or any of the other instruments was not provided with the original package of materials but generally referred to in a technical document. A call by this author to the publisher requesting reliability information did result in securing a copy of the reference document. However, the reliability data provided in the additional report refer only to test-retest reliability data and given the 1987 publication date, presumably refer to the previous edition of The Career Profile System. No reliability data are available for the PC version or either Canadian version.

Moreover, the publishers refer to the reliability of the Career Profile, which is not entirely correct. Reliability is a characteristic of data obtained from an instrument. Consequently, data obtained from different instruments, samples of people, or time may have different reliability characteristics. It is recommended that reliability be estimated for data obtained from each instrument and version and that a rationale be provided for the type of reliability. This information should be clearly discussed in reference documents provided with the Career Profile in a nontechnical manner. This will help to foster informed decisions by companies needing selection instruments but that may not have access to technical personnel with expertise in test development.

VALIDITY. Validity of data obtained from the Career Profile is established through compliance with the *Uniform Guidelines on Employee Selection Procedures* (1978). The research base used to develop and refine the Career Profile provides companies with a legally defensible component of a larger candidate selection strategy. However, the 1978 *Uniform Guidelines* are becoming antiquated and, therefore, due for revision. The publishers are urged to consider current and emerging trends in testing and assessment, with attention to employee selection and revise the Career Profile as needed. In addition, although an instrument is validated according to the *Uniform Guidelines,* if rejection rates for underrepresented groups are discrepant from other groups, a company must take steps to rectify the discrepancy. Thus, the publishers of the Career Profile are also urged to discuss ways companies might use the instrument in the context of an overall, fair, unbiased selection strategy, particularly in light of affirmative action or similar policies. Also, the different language versions as well as the PC version warrant a series of validity studies to determine whether data obtained from these versions of the Career Profile are comparable.

RECOMMENDATION AND SUMMARY. In addition to the previous recommendations, the publishers are urged to document clearly the development of each version and type of instrument, particularly the dates. It is not clear in the review documentation, for example, when the first edition started and ended, when the second edition started, and whether the three instruments that constitute The Career Profile System were part of the first edition. The aforementioned limitations aside, the longevity of The Career Profile System and its use by

several dozen insurance companies illustrates its usefulness as part of a company candidate selection process. Given the competitive environment for insurance sales and the often difficult dual task for companies to select individuals who will increase profits on the one hand while not discriminating against an individual or group of people on the other, The Career Profile System is a set of tools worthy of consideration.

REVIEWER'S REFERENCE

Uniform guidelines on employee selection procedures. (1978). *Federal Register, 43*(166), 38290–38309.

[53]

Career Values Card Sort.

Purpose: Defines factors that affect career satisfaction, the intensity of feelings about these factors, determines areas of value conflict and congruence, helps make career decisions.
Population: Adults.
Publication Dates: 1993–1994.
Scores: No scores.
Administration: Group or individual.
Price Data, 1994: $8 per complete kit including manual ('93, 19 pages) and set of cards; $4 per set of cards; $5 per manual.
Time: (20–30) minutes.
Comments: Self-administered.
Authors: Richard L. Knowdell.
Publisher: Career Research & Testing, Inc.

Review of the Career Values Card Sort by ESTHER E. DIAMOND, Educational and Psychological Consultant, Evanston, IL:

The Career Values Card Sort Planning Kit by Richard L. Knowdell is designed to help adults define those factors likely to affect their satisfaction in the career they eventually will choose. A 19-page manual contains the rationale for the kit and the directions for a series of activities to help the individual obtain a picture of his or her career value pattern, including areas of conflict and how they might be resolved.

An overview introduces the question of what one wants in a career—values such as where to live and work, what kind of work is appealing, what kind of coworkers would be kindred spirits, working conditions desired, comfortable level of responsibility, salary level, and so on. The basic factors of a value are described as something prized, that is chosen from several alternatives, and that one is willing to support or act on. Clarification of career values is described as a task "drawing deeply from the well of experiences in both work and personal life" (p. 2).

The Card Sort activity involves sorting 41 work values into five groups denoting the individual's intensity of feeling about them: *Always Valued, Often Valued, Sometimes Valued, Seldom Valued,* and *Never Valued.* The definitions of the values themselves, according to a note in the manual (p. 4), first appeared in *PATH: A Career Workbook for Liberal Arts Students,* by Howard E. Figler, copyright 1979, and adapted by permission of the publisher, Carroll Press.

A sample summary sheet of prioritized values illustrates the interrelationship among the 41 values and their importance to the individual's tentative career decision. Prioritized values are then related to a Career Values Worksheet on which the prioritized work values are listed next to statements about their applicability to the career decision, perceived areas of conflict, and means by which the conflicts might be resolved. Finally, any changes in plans resulting from learning on the Values Card Sort are noted.

For greater depth in considering career values and the role they play in shaping one's future, five supplementary activities are suggested. The results can be shared and discussed with a counselor, a group facilitator, a classmate, or a friend.

Recalling past events in the Memory Scan brings to mind events in which *Always Valued* factors were exercised very freely. At the same time, situations where there has been little or no support for exercising *Always Valued* factors will come to mind. Analyzing one's role in the development of both kinds of situations is explored and value conflicts and their effects on decision-making patterns are examined.

The activity Growing Person/Changing Values emphasizes the fact that as one grows, circumstances change and, inevitably, values change accordingly. To anticipate these changes, the respondent considers three stages of life—10 years earlier, the present, and 10 years from now. What key incidents brought about changes in values in the last 10 years? What circumstances (for example, graduation, marriage, parenting, divorce, job or career change, and so on) might bring about even more changes in the next 10 years? The respondent is asked, also, to consider the psychological gains and losses experienced as a result—"the people, places, things, and organizations left behind" and "the new people, places, things, and organizations added" (p. 16).

The New Career/Life Landscapes activity asks the reader to consider how his or her career and life might differ if all the *Always Valued* factors were realized. Would one's sense of self be affected? What changes would there be in one's relationships and in one's job duties and working conditions? And

how would allocations of time to work and to personal life change? This activity seems rather static and forced. It does not challenge the imagination as the earlier two activities do. It does not add insights or further the understanding of the very important way in which career values can impact all of one's life.

The fourth activity asks the individual how in charge they feel of building thier *Alway Valued* factors into their life and career. They are to copy their prioritized *Always Valued* and rate from *1 - not at all* to *5 - completely* how in charge they feel of building the factor into their career.

The fifth activity, Career Values Diary, helps the individual trace how closely day-to-day activities accommodate those values listed as *Always Valued.* Conflicts are more easily detected and ways to resolve them determined. Even here, only one suggestion hints at the importance of integrating all the information involved in sorting, reexamining, and revising one's *Always Valued* list. That suggestion involves keeping a free-flowing narrative of feelings about careers considered and processing it periodically to note factors that bring one joys and sadness, hope and frustration—factors that cannot always be easily separated. The diary, however, should help the individual integrate all the complex bits of information identified in the earlier card sort activities into a realistic, manageable career plan in which values play their appropriate role.

The Career Values Card Sort Planning Kit is clearly not a test. It is a workbook, but one that is very uneven in style and audience level. The word level and the diction range from condescendingly elementary to highly sophisticated and possibly beyond the reading and comprehension level of the average adult. (Remember that the definitions of the 41 values originated in a career workbook for liberal arts students, whose reading level can be assumed to have been higher than that of the average adult.) A number of the exercises are extremely mechanical and repetitious of earlier exercises, without consistently integrating what has been learned up to that point to create a more comprehensive picture of the individual's "career self" (p. 4).

Beyond the brief statement in the manual about the origin of the 41 career values definitions, no information is given about how the instrument was developed, the population on whom it has been tried out, reliability, content and construct validity, freedom from bias, and results of item analysis. There are no scores.

In a telephone conversation with the author, Richard Knowdell, he stated that he had no technical information, that the kit is mainly "a learning tool" that has face validity and has been used with thousands of clients. He is not planning to produce any further material about its development and use.

The test user looking for a career values instrument of established worth had better look elsewhere. A number of career guidance tests deal with values, but in a more complete context, and they provide technical information to support much of their claim about the utility of their instrument. The Career Values Card Sort Planning Kit might be useful as a purely exploratory "learning tool," with exercises that one could choose or reject to build a unique "career-self" profile, but there is no empirical evidence of its actual usefulness in planning for a satisfying career.

Review of the Career Values Card Sort by RICH-ARD T. KINNIER, Associate Professor, Counseling Psychology Program, Arizona State University, Tempe, AZ:

The Career Values Card Sort was designed to help individuals identify or clarify their career-related values. It consists of 41 cutout cards. Each card is approximately 3 inches by 2 inches. Value labels (e.g., "INDEPENDENCE," "SECURITY," "FAST PACE") are printed on each card in bold, capitalized letters. Under each value label is a brief definition of the value. For example, under the label of "SECURITY" are the words, "Be assured of keeping my job and a reasonable financial reward." The author does not report how that particular value list was constructed (which is a problem that I will discuss later). Nevertheless, the number of values (41) seems manageable, the list seems representative of the career values found in other career value assessments, and the definitions are clearly written.

In addition to the 41 value-labeled cards, 5 same-sized cutout cards labeled, "ALWAYS VALUED," "OFTEN VALUED," "SOMETIMES VALUED," "SELDOM VALUED," and "NEVER VALUED" are included. These are to be used as column headings. I think that it would be preferable to have the category cards look different from the 41 value-label cards (perhaps be bigger and a different color for easier sorting).

Individuals using the Card Sort are instructed to "deal your cards into the appropriate column" (manual, p. 3). Individuals are further instructed to: "Lay your cards out so that you can see all your choices in one glance. Move quickly, follow your

feelings" and "your ALWAYS VALUED column should have no more than eight cards in it" (manual, p. 3).

After the cards are laid out, individuals are instructed to rank order the values and to transcribe them onto a summary sheet of prioritized values in order to have a more permanent record of their rankings. A summary sheet sample and a blank summary sheet are included in the manual. The basic self-administration and the transcription of the sortings are fairly straightforward and clearly described procedures.

There is no scoring system other than the transcription of rank-ordered value labels onto a summary sheet. Beyond that the author provides several additional exercises or activities for the user. These activities are similar to the values clarification or self-assessment exercises found in numerous career-development workbooks or textbooks published during the past two decades. They include activities such as considering one's values in light of an imminent career decision. For another activity the author suggests that participants keep logs of their work activities for a week at a time and then consider how their highest values are accommodated. In another the author asks participants to complete the sentence, "As a result of my learnings on the Values Card I plan to …" (manual, p. 4). Worksheet samples and blank worksheets for completing some of the exercises are found inside the manual.

Some individuals may find some of the activities helpful. However, I found a few of the activities to be less than inspiring or engaging. For example, I found some of the instructions for the Career Values Diary activity to be tedious and I thought the Career Values Worksheet sample was somewhat unclear. Unfortunately, in my opinion, the practice of overstocking career development manuals and assessments with superficially developed exercises is commonplace. In these kinds of manuals or assessments I would rather see a shorter list of critically and popularly acclaimed activities or at least some guidance from the author(s) about which activities are most highly recommended.

TEST DEVELOPMENT AND NORMS. The author provides no information on how the Card Sort was developed. A list of four "Objectives" is found on page 3 and a brief overview of career values is presented on page 1. The overview is basically a brief reference to the criteria of a clarified value (from the values clarification literature). There are no norms for this assessment device.

RELIABILITY AND VALIDITY. No formal procedures were used (and/or reported in the manual) on how the list was constructed. In my opinion, the list does have good face validity but a more formal validation procedure is needed.

No reliability studies were reported in the manual. The most appropriate type of reliability probably would be test-retest. Evidence that individuals' sortings are fairly stable over a short period of time would be a good indication that the Card Sort was reliable and would provide some support for the validity of that particular list of values.

CONCLUSION. The Career Values Card Sort is a self-administered card sort designed to help individuals identify or clarify their career-related values. It consists of 41 values, each printed and defined on separate cards. The cards are nicely formatted and the directions for how to sort the cards and transcribe the values are clear.

I think that the exercise of sorting and thinking about the implications of the rankings can be an effective intervention for helping individuals with their career decision making. I was less impressed with the quality and clarity of some of the supplemental activities. I would encourage the author to be more selective in his recommendation of activities.

The Card Sort has good face validity but more psychometric work is needed. Specifically, the list of values should be more formally validated. One way to do this would be to construct the list from established measures (e.g., the Rokeach Value Survey [12:334]) and then to have expert judges refine the list. Additionally, a test-retest study could provide us with an indication of the Card Sort's temporal reliability.

In the meantime, the Card Sort appears to be a useful device. For most people the assessment would probably be an enjoyable and helpful experience.

[54]
CAT/5 Listening and Speaking Checklist.

Purpose: "Designed to help the teacher in evaluating two important aspects of the reading/language arts domain: listening and speaking."
Population: Grades K–12.
Publication Date: 1993.
Scores: Overall Rating Index.
Administration: Group.
Levels, 3: Grades K–3, 4–8, 9–12.
Price Data, 1994: $16.95 per review kit including sample copy of each of the 3 levels, teacher's guide (28 pages), and class summary folder; $21 per classroom package including 30 checklists, teacher's guide, and class summary folder; $9.55 per teacher's guide; $1.65 per class summary folder.
Time: Administration time not reported.
Comments: Student self-evaluation forms, a checklist assessment plan, and a letter to parents are also available.
Authors: CTB Macmillan/McGraw-Hill.
Publisher: CTB Macmillan/McGraw-Hill.

Review of the CAT/5 Listening and Speaking Checklist by GERALD S. HANNA, Professor of Educational Psychology and Assessment, Kansas State University, Manhattan, KS:

The CAT/5 Listening and Speaking Checklist is an informal oral language measure for grades K through 12. It was designed to help teachers to (a) determine if additional evaluation is needed, (b) monitor instruction and help in planning lessons, and (c) facilitate reporting to parents. This reviewer agrees with the developers of the checklist that listening and speaking outcomes are often underevaluated and that the above goals are important.

Each level of the checklist contains a useful list of listening and speaking outcomes common to curricula at its level. The checklist also provides for customization by means of adding local outcomes and omitting outcomes that do not reflect local curricula. Examination of the varied outcomes listed would seem a helpful way for teachers to avoid overlooking important skills.

Table 1 of the teacher's guide provides a contrast of formal and informal evaluation methods. Several of the contrasts seem questionable. One is the contention that formal evaluation is designed for comparative measurement whereas informal evaluation is designed for diagnostic measurement and classroom instruction. This contrast does not hold up under scrutiny. Criterion-referenced (i.e., noncomparative) interpretations are frequently appropriate for formally secured assessment data and for informally gathered information. Moreover, norm-referenced instruments are often designed and used to enhance classroom instruction.

Perhaps the most worrisome contrast is the contention that the quality of formal evaluation is judged by validity and reliability whereas the quality of informal evaluation is judged by effect on instruction. Is not some degree of consistency of data an absolute prerequisite to utility for any purpose, including diagnosis and instruction? And is effect upon instruction not a fundamental validity consideration?

Yet the CAT/5 Listening and Speaking Checklist is offered without validity information, as though being an informal instrument rendered issues of score utility irrelevant. Along these lines, the teacher's guide does not adequately report the rationale or procedures of instrument development. This falls short of prevailing professional standards as, for example, detailed in *Standards for Educational and Psychological Testing* (AERA, APA, & NCME, 1985).

The overall rating index and the cut points are reported to be based on a field trial "in classrooms across the country in Grades K through 12" (p. 10). Unfortunately the number of classrooms, their locations, and the qualifications of their teachers are not reported.

Teachers are wisely advised in the teacher's guide to observe students on multiple occasions because "a single observation is a far less reliable indicator of true performance than are repeated observations of the same behavior" (p. 10). Thus, reliability is correctly recognized as an important attribute of assessments.

Nonetheless, the teacher's guide provides no information concerning the reliability of the scores or the errors of measurement. The professional standards reflected in the *Standards for Educational and Psychological Testing* (AERA, APA, & NCME, 1985) state very clearly that "for each total score, subscore, or combination of scores that is reported, estimates of relevant reliabilities and standard errors of measurement should be provided in adequate detail to enable the test user to judge whether scores are sufficiently accurate for the intended use of the test" (p. 20). Without some indication of the consistency of scores produced by a typical teacher who would use the instrument, reliance on the scores is not justified.

Ratings of 3 are to be given for "maximal ability of mastery," whereas a rating of 2 represents only minimal or rudimentary ability. One wonders how consistent the meaning of these numbers would be from teacher to teacher. In rating such skills as "demonstrates appropriate telephone skills," interrater consistency would be enhanced at each level if it were clear just which skills were deemed appropriate. Would teachers in a given school agree? Similarly in rating such listening skills as "applies understanding to new situations," what basis of judgment is to be used in rating adequacy of application to various situations? It seems likely that teachers would differ greatly in the standards they apply to such ratings. If so, how meaningful would reports to parents be? It is unfortunate that there are no data concerning these reliability issues.

Because interpretations are made in a (rather unusual) criterion-referenced manner, the meaning of the interpretations requires a clear description of the content domains to which they are referenced. In this reviewer's judgment, the domains are not adequately described to render criterion-referenced interpretations meaningful.

In summary, the CAT/5 Listening and Speaking Checklist provides a highly flexible list of outcomes that teachers may rate with unknown reliability to make criterion-referenced interpretations of student achievement in inadequately described content domains. The overall lack of attention to reporting the instrument's technical quality makes it impossible for this reviewer to recommend it for purposes other than research.

REVIEWER'S REFERENCE

American Educational Research Association, American Psychological Association, & National Council on Measurement in Education. (1985). *Standards for educational and psychological testing.* Washington, DC: American Psychological Association, Inc.

Review of the CAT/5 Listening and Speaking Checklist by RICHARD M. WOLF, Professor of Psychology and Education, Teachers College, Columbia University, New York, NY:

The CAT/5 Listening and Speaking Checklist was developed to assist teachers in appraising their students' performance in listening and speaking. It can be used for informal assessment of student performance or in a more formal way such as judging the quality of an oral presentation. Three levels of the instrument are available: (a) kindergarten through grade 3, (b) grades 4 through 8, and (c) grades 9–12. The levels differ in the amount of complexity that is to be appraised. A teacher's guide is provided to acquaint the user with the importance of appraising these unquestionably important educational outcomes. Some discussion is provided as to what constitutes listening and speaking to assist the teacher on not only the importance of these two areas, but also some idea of what they are. The actual instrument is intended to be used with one student at a time. That is, the teacher is to focus on a target student and render the needed appraisals. The teacher may use each section, listening and speaking, separately. Suggestions are provided for teachers on how to complete the checklist.

The actual items comprising the checklist seem fairly reasonable although no evidence is provided to justify them. Unfortunately, the instrument is not a checklist but a series of rating scales that call for ratings from 1 (minimal or rudimentary ability) to 3 (maximal ability or mastery). Unfortunately, these are neither defined further nor are examples given as to what constitutes each level. This is left to the teacher to decide. A procedure is presented for aggregating the ratings and for determining whether the overall rating represents further evaluation/instruction suggested, basic, proficient, or advanced proficiency. No justification for the index needed to achieve a particular level is provided. This is unfortunate. Presumably, some analysis of speaking and listening was carried out to establish content validity, but this is not mentioned. No evidence is provided about the reliability of the scores produced by the instrument.

Of the two sections of the instrument, the listening section is the most problematic. It presumes that the teacher will ask the student a series of questions to determine whether he or she has correctly comprehended orally presented material. The basis for this statement is the presence of such items as "recalls events and details," "describes story characters," and "predicts outcomes from story." The implication is that this section of the instrument will be administered in an individual testing session. Whether teachers will be able to do so during regular class sessions is problematic.

The speaking section is not without problems either. Although the speaking behavior section of the instrument seems reasonable, the section on participation is questionable. Items such as "takes turns," "listens to others," and "is considerate of others' ideas and feelings" are questionable for inclusion in an instrument designed to measure speaking proficiency.

In summary, this instrument is intended for teachers to use in an informal or formal way to assess the listening and speaking performance of students. Although it is called a checklist, it is actually a series of rating scales with ill-defined scale points and an unjustified way of determining an overall index of speaking or listening proficiency. No evidence is supplied to support either the validity or reliability of the scores. Despite this, teachers may find some parts of the instrument useful in appraising student performance in these critical areas. However, caution should be exercised in making inferences about student proficiency on the basis of the numerical values obtained. There is no basis provided for that. Also, each teacher will need to decide what constitutes each level of each rating scale.

[55]
Child Behavior Checklist.

Purpose: To assess the competencies and problems of children and adolescents through the use of ratings and reports by different informants.

Population: Ages 2–18.

Publication Dates: 1980–1994.

Price Data, 1994: $10 per 25 Child Behavior Checklists (specify Ages 2–3 or Ages 4–18); $10 per 25 CBCL profiles (specify age and sex); $7 per CBCL scoring templates (specify level); $10 per 25 Teacher's Report Forms; $10 per 25 TRF profiles; $7 per TRF templates; $10 per 25 Youth Self-Report Forms; $7 per YSR templates; $10 per 25 YSR profiles; $10 per 25 Direct Observation Forms; $10 per 25 SCICA protocol forms; $10 per 25 combined SCICA observation and self-report scoring forms; $10 per 25 profiles for handscoring SCICA; $25 per CBCL/2–3 manual ('92, 210 pages); $25 per CBCL/4–18 manual ('91, 288 pages); $25 per TRF manual ('92, 214 pages); $25 per YSR manual ('91, 221 pages); $25 per SCICA manual ('94, 210 pages); $110 per SCICA videotape; computer programs available for computer scoring and profiling; $25 per Empirically Based Taxonomy ('93, 212 pages).

Comments: Behavior checklists; forms available as separates.

Author: Thomas M. Achenbach.

Publisher: Thomas M. Achenbach, Ph.D.

a) CHILD BEHAVIOR CHECKLIST.

Purpose: "To record in a standardized format the behavioral problems and competencies of children . . . as reported by their parents or others who know the child well."

Comments: Ratings by parents.

1) *Ages 2–3.*

Population: Ages 2–3.

Publication Dates: 1986–1992.

Acronym: CBCL/2–3.

Scores: 6 scales: Withdrawn, Anxious/Depressed, Sleep Problems, Somatic Problems, Aggressive, Destructive.

Time: (15) minutes.

2) *Ages 4–18.*

Population: Ages 4–18.

Publication Dates: 1980–1991.

Acronym: CBCL/4–18.

Parts: 2 profiles: Boys Aged 4–18, Girls Aged 4–18.

Scores: 15 scales: Syndrome Scales (Withdrawn, Somatic Complaints, Anxious/Depressed, Social Problems, Thought Problems, Attention Problems, Aggressive Behavior, Delinquent Behavior), plus Internalizing, Externalizing, Total Problems, Competence Scales (Activities, Social, School, Total Competence).

Time: (15) minutes.

b) TEACHER'S REPORT FORM.

Purpose: "To obtain teachers' reports of their pupils' problems and adaptive functioning in a standardized format."

Population: Ages 5–18.

Publication Dates: 1982–1991.

Acronym: TRF.

Forms: 2 profiles: Boys Aged 5–18; Girls Aged 5–18.

Scores, 13: Same as CBCL/4–18 above plus Academic Performance, Adaptive Functioning.

Time: (15) minutes.

Comments: Ratings by teachers.

c) YOUTH SELF-REPORT.

Purpose: "To obtain 11- to 18-year-olds' reports of their own competencies and problems in a standardized format."

Population: Ages 11–18.

Publication Dates: 1983–1991.

Acronym: YSR.

Scores, 14: Same as CBCL/4–18 above without School Scale.

Time: (15) minutes.

Comments: Ratings by self.

d) DIRECT OBSERVATION FORM.

Purpose: "To obtain direct observational data in situations such as school classrooms, lunchrooms, recess, and group activities."

Population: Ages 5–14.

Publication Date: 1981–1986.

Acronym: DOF.

Scores, 10: Behavior Problems, Internalizing, Externalizing, Withdrawn-Inattentive, Nervous-Obsessive, Depressed, Hyperactive, Attention-Demanding, Aggressive, On-Task Behavior.

Time: (10) minutes for each observation period.

Comments: Ratings by trained observer.

e) SEMISTRUCTURED CLINICAL INTERVIEW FOR CHILDREN AND ADOLESCENTS.

Purpose: "To advance the application of empirically based assessment to clinical interviews."

Population: Ages 6–12.

Publication Date: 1994.

Acronym: SCICA.

Scores: 8 syndrome scales: Aggressive Behavior, Anxious, Anxious/Depressed, Attention Problems, Family Problems, Resistant, Strange, Withdrawn.

Time: (60–90) minutes.

Comments: Videotape and IBM computer scoring program available.

Cross References: See T4:433 (135 references); for reviews by Sandra L. Christenson and Stephen N. Elliott and R. T. Busse of the Teacher's Report Form and the Youth Self-Report, see 11:64 (216 references); for additional information and reviews by B. J. Freeman and Mary Lou Kelley, see 9:213 (5 references).

TEST REFERENCES

1. Faulstich, M. E., Moore, J. R., Roberts, R. W., & Collier, J. B. (1988). A behavioral perspective on conduct disorders. *Psychiatry, 51,* 398–416.

2. Gallucci, N. T. (1988). Emotional adjustment of gifted children. *Gifted Child Quarterly, 32,* 273–276.

3. Schnayer, R., & Orr, R. R. (1988). A comparison of children living in single-mother and single-father families. *Journal of Divorce, 12*(2/3), 171–184.

4. Shybunko, D. E. (1988). Effects of post-divorce relationships on child adjustment. *Journal of Divorce, 12*(2/3), 299–313.

5. Tanaka, J. S., & Westerman, M. A. (1988). Common dimensions in the assessment of competence in school-aged girls. *Journal of Educational Psychology, 80,* 579–584.

6. Walsh, P. E., & Stolberg, A. L. (1988). Parental and environmental determinants of children's behavioral, affective and cognitive adjustment to divorce. *Journal of Divorce, 12*(2/3), 265–282.

7. Akkok, F., & Askar, P. (1989). The adaptation and standardization of the teacher version of the Child Behavior Profile: Turkish boys aged 7–12. *International Journal of Psychology, 24,* 129–136.

8. Birenbaum, L. K., Robinson, M. A., Phillips, D. S., Stewart, B. J., & McCown, D. E. (1989–90). The response of children to the dying and death of a sibling. *Omega, 20*(3), 213-228.

9. Forgatch, M. S. (1989). Pattern and outcome in family problem solving: The disrupting effect of negative emotion. *Journal of Marriage and the Family, 51,* 115-124.

10. Kane, M. T., & Kendall, P. C. (1989). Anxiety disorders in children: A multiple-baseline evaluation of a cognitive-behavioral treatment. *Behavior Therapy, 20,* 499–508.

11. Links, P. S., Boyle, M. H., & Offord, D. R. (1989). The prevalence of emotional disorder in children. *The Journal of Nervous and Mental Disease, 177,* 85-91.

12. Palace, E. M., & Johnston, C. (1989). Treatment of recurrent nightmares by the dream reorganization approach. *Journal of Behavior Therapy and Experimental Psychiatry, 20,* 219–226.

13. Stiffman, A. R. (1989). Suicide attempts in runaway youths. *Suicide and Life-Threatening Behavior, 19,* 147–159.

14. Tschann, J. M., Johnston, J. R., Kline, M., & Wallerstein, J. S. (1989). Family process children's functioning during divorce. *Journal of Marriage and the Family, 51,* 431-444.

15. Webster-Stratton, C. C. (1989). The relationship of marital support, conflict, and divorce to parent perceptions, behaviors, and childhood conduct problems. *Journal of Marriage and the Family, 51,* 417-430.

16. Wolfe, V. V., Gentile, C., & Wolfe, D. A. (1989). The impact of sexual abuse on children: A PTSD formulation. *Behavior Therapy, 20,* 215–228.

17. Benjamin, R. S., Costello, E. J., & Warren, M. (1990). Anxiety disorders in a pediatric sample. *Journal of Anxiety Disorders, 4,* 293-316.

18. Berden, G. F., Althaus, M., & Verhulst, F. C. (1990). Major life events and changes in the behavioural functioning of children. *Journal of Child Psychology and Allied Disciplines, 31,* 949-959.

19. Bray, J. H., & Berger, S. H. (1990). Noncustodial father and paternal grandparent relationships in stepfamilies. *Family Relations, 39,* 414-419.

20. Campbell, S. B., & Ewing, L. J. (1990). Follow-up of hard-to-manage preschoolers: Adjustment at age 9 and predictors of continuing symptoms. *Journal of Child Psychology and Psychiatry and Allied Disciplines, 31,* 871-889.

21. Coleman, D. J., & Kaplan, M. S. (1990). Effects of pretherapy videotape preparation on child therapy outcomes. *Professional Psychology: Research and Practice, 21,* 199–203.

22. Compas, B. E., & Williams, R. A. (1990). Stress, coping and adjustment in mothers and young adolescents in single- and two-parent families. *American Journal of Community Psychology, 18,* 525-545.

23. Durrant, J. E., Voelker, S., & Cunningham, C. E. (1990). Academic, social, and general self-concepts of behavioral subgroups of learning disabled children. *Journal of Educational Psychology, 82,* 657–663.

24. Egeland, B., Kalkoske, M., Gottesman, N., & Erickson, M. F. (1990). Preschool behavior problems: Stability and factors accounting for change. *Journal of Child Psychology and Psychiatry and Allied Disciplines, 31,* 891-909.

25. Elliot, D. J., & Tarnowski, K. J. (1990). Depressive characteristics of sexually abused children. *Child Psychiatry and Human Development, 21,* 37-48.

26. Erhardt, D., & Baker, B. L. (1990). The effects of behavioral parent training on families with young hyperactive children. *Journal of Behavior Therapy and Experimental Psychiatry, 21,* 121–132.

27. Gensheimer, L. K., Roosa, M. W., & Ayers, T. S. (1990). Children's self-selection into prevention programs: Evaluation of an innovative recruitment strategy for children of alcoholics. *American Journal of Community Psychology, 18,* 707-723.

28. Gottfried, A. E. (1990). Academic intrinsic motivation in young elementary school children. *Journal of Educational Psychology, 82,* 525-538.

29. Hepperlin, C. M., Stewart, G. W., & Rey, J. M. (1990). Extraction of depression scores in adolescents from a general-purpose behaviour checklist. *Journal of Affective Disorders, 18,* 105-112.

30. Hodges, W. F., London, J., & Colwell, J. B. (1990). Stress in parents and late elementary age children in divorced and intact families and child adjustment. *Journal of Divorce & Remarriage, 14*(1), 63-79.

31. Kearney, C. A., & Silverman, W. K. (1990). Treatment of an adolescent with obsessive-compulsive disorder by alternating response prevention and cognitive therapy: An empirical analysis. *Journal of Behavior Therapy and Experimental Psychiatry, 21,* 39–47.

32. Kruesi, M. J. P., Rapoport, J. L., Hamburger, S., Hibbs, E., Potter, W. Z., Lenane, M., & Brown, G. L. (1990). Cerebrospinal fluid monoamine metabolites,

aggression, and impulsivity in disruptive behavior disorders of children and adolescents. *Archives of General Psychiatry, 47*, 419–426.

33. Lewinsohn, P. M., Clarke, G. N., Hops, H., & Andrews, J. (1990). Cognitive-behavioral treatment for depressed adolescents. *Behavior Therapy, 21*, 385–401.

34. Philippot, P., & Feldman, R. S. (1990). Age and social competence in preschoolers' decoding of facial expression. *British Journal of Social Psychology, 29*, 43-54.

35. Tschann, J. M., Johnston, J. R., Kline, M., & Wallerstein, J. S. (1990). Conflict, loss, change and parent-child relationships: Predicting children's adjustment during divorce. *Journal of Divorce, 13*(4), 1-22.

36. Vandvik, I. H. (1990). Mental health and psychosocial functioning in children with recent onset of rheumatic disease. *Journal of Child Psychology and Psychiatry and Allied Disciplines, 31*, 961-971.

37. Wagner, B. M., & Compas, B. E. (1990). Gender, instrumentality, and expressivity: Moderators of the relation between stress and psychological symptoms during adolescence. *American Journal of Community Psychology, 18*, 383-406.

38. Webster-Stratton, C., & Hammond, M. (1990). Predictors of treatment outcome in parent training for families with conduct problem children. *Behavior Therapy, 21*, 319–337.

39. Abelsohn, D., & Saayman, G. S. (1991). Adolescent adjustment to parental divorce: An investigation from the perspective of basic dimensions of structural family therapy theory. *Family Process, 30*, 177-191.

40. Almagor, M. (1991). The relationship among fathers' physical disability, agreement regarding marital satisfaction, and perception of children's emotional state. *Rehabilitation Psychology, 36*, 241–254.

41. Barnett, B., Schaafsma, M. F., Guzman, A. M., & Parker, G. B. (1991). Maternal anxiety: A 5-year review of an intervention study. *Journal of Child Psychology and Psychiatry and Allied Disciplines, 32*, 423-438.

42. Beitchman, J. H., Zucker, K. J., Hood, J. E., Da Costa, G. A., & Akman, D. (1991). A review of the short-term effects of child sexual abuse. *Child Abuse & Neglect, 15*, 537-556.

43. Benbenishty, R., & Oyserman, D. (1991). A clinical information system for foster care in Israel. *Child Welfare, 70*, 229–242.

44. Brown, R. T., Madan-Swain, A., & Baldwin, K. (1991). Gender differences in a clinic-referred sample of attention-deficit-disordered children. *Child Psychiatry and Human Development, 22*, 111–128.

45. Capaldi, D. M. (1991). Co-occurence of conduct problems and depressive symptoms in early adolescent boys: I. Familiar factors and general adjustment at grade 6. *Development and Psychopathology, 3*, 277-300.

46. Costello, E. J., Loeber, R., & Stouthamer-Loeber, M. (1991). Pervasive and situational hyperactivity—confounding effect of informant: A research note. *Journal of Child Psychology and Psychiatry and Allied Disciplines, 32*, 367-376.

47. Crowell, J. A., O'Connor, E., Wollmers, G., Sprafkin, J., & Rao, U. (1991). Mothers' conceptualization of parent-child relationships: Relation to mother-child interaction and child behavior problems. *Development and Psychopathology, 3*, 431-444.

48. DeMaso, D. R., Campis, L. K., Wypji, D., Bertram, S., Lipshitz, M., & Freed, M. (1991). The impact of maternal perceptions and medical severity on the adjustment of children with congenital heart disease. *Journal of Pediatric Psychology, 16*, 137–149.

49. Edwards, M. C., Finney, J. W., & Bonner, M. (1991). Matching treatment with recurrent abdominal pain symptoms: An evaluation of dietary fiber and relaxation treatments. *Behavior Therapy, 22*, 257–267.

50. Ellwood, M. S., & Stolberg, A. L. (1991). A preliminary investigation of family systems' influences on individual divorce adjustment. *Journal of Divorce & Remarriage, 15*(1/2), 157-174.

51. Finney, J. W., Riley, A. W., & Cataldo, M. F. (1991). Psychology in primary health care: Effects of brief targeted therapy on children's medical care utilization. *Journal of Pediatric Psychology, 16*, 447–461.

52. Floyd, F. J., & Zmich, D. E. (1991). Marriage and the parenting partnership: Perceptions and interactions of parents with mentally retarded and typically developing children. *Child Development, 62*, 1434–1448.

53. Gersten, J. C., Beals, J., & Kallgren, C. A. (1991). Epidemiology and preventive interventions: Parental death in childhood as a case example. *American Journal of Community Psychology, 19*, 481-500.

54. Greenberg, M. T., Speltz, M. L., Derlyen, M., & Endriga, M. C. (1991). Attachment security in preschoolers with and without externalizing behavior problems: A replication. *Development and Psychopathology, 3*, 413-430.

55. Groze, V., & Gruenewald, A. (1991). PARTNERS: A model program for special-needs adoptive families in stress. *Child Welfare, 70*, 581–589.

56. Harris, E. S. (1991). Adolescent bereavement following the death of a parent: An exploratory study. *Child Psychiatry and Human Development, 21*, 267-281.

57. Jensen, A. M., & Harper, D. C. (1991). Correlates of concern in parents of high-risk infants at age five. *Journal of Pediatric Psychology, 16*, 429–445.

58. Jensen, P. S., Xenakis, S. N., Wolf, P., & Bain, M. W. (1991). The "Military Family Syndrome" revisited: "By the numbers." *The Journal of Nervous and Mental Disease, 179*, 102-107.

59. Jouriles, E. N., Murphy, C. M., Farris, A. M., Smith, D. A., Richters, J. E., & Waters, E. (1991). Marital adjustment, parental disagreements about child rearing and behavioral problems in boys: Increasing the specificity of the marital assessment. *Child Development, 62*, 1424–1433.

60. Kim, W. J., Hahn, S. U., Kish, J., Rosenberg, L., & Harris, J. (1991). Separation reaction of psychiatrically hospitalized children: A pilot study. *Child Psychiatry and Human Development, 22*, 53-67.

61. Kline, M., Johnston, J. R., & Tschann, J. M. (1991). The long shadow of marital conflict: A model of children's postdivorce adjustment. *Journal of Marriage and the Family, 53*, 297–309.

62. Kolko, D. J., & Kazdin, A. E. (1991). Motives of childhood firesetters: Firesetting characteristics and psychological correlates. *Journal of Child Psychology and Psychiatry and Allied Disciplines, 32*, 535-550.

63. Leckman, J. F., Hardin, M. T., Riddle, M. A., Stevenson, J., Ort, S. I., & Cohen, D. J. (1991). Clonidine treatment of Gilles de la Tourette's Syndrome. *Archives of General Psychiatry, 48*, 324-328.

64. Machida, S., & Holloway, S. D. (1991). The relationship between divorced mothers' perceived control over child rearing and children's post-divorce development. *Family Relations, 40*, 272-278.

65. McGee, R. (1991). Social competence in adolescence: Preliminary findings from a longitudinal study of New Zealand 15 year-olds. *Psychiatry, 54*, 281–291.

66. Morison, P., & Masten, A. S. (1991). Peer reputation in middle childhood as a predictor of adaptation in adolescence: A seven-year follow-up. *Child Development, 62*, 991–1007.

67. Noam, G. G., Recklitis, C. J., & Paget, K. F. (1991). Pathways of ego development: Contributions to maladaptation and adjustment. *Development and Psychopathology, 3*, 311-328.

68. Rosenthal, J. A., Groze, V., & Aguilar, G. D. (1991). Adoption outcomes for children with handicaps. *Child Welfare, 70*, 623–636.

69. Sandler, I., Wolchik, S., Brauer, S., & Fogas, B. (1991). Stability and quality of life events and psychological symptomatology in children of divorce. *American Journal of Community Psychology, 19*, 501-520.

70. Snyder, J. (1991). Discipline as a mediator of the impact of maternal stress and mood on child conduct problems. *Development and Psychopathology, 3*, 263-276.

71. Vuchinich, S., Teachman, J., & Crosby, L. (1991). Families and hazard rates that change over time: Some methodological issues in analyzing transitions. *Journal of Marriage and the Family, 53*, 898–912.

72. Walker, L. S., & Greene, J. W. (1991). The Functional Disability Inventory: Measuring a neglected dimension of child health status. *Journal of Pediatric Psychology, 16*, 39–58.

73. Webster-Stratton, C., & Spitzer, A. (1991). Development, reliability, and validity of the Daily Telephone Discipline Interview. *Behavioral Assessment, 13*, 221-239.

74. West, S. G., Sandler, I., Pillow, D. R., Baca, L., & Gersten, J. C. (1991). The use of structural equation modeling in a generative research: Toward the design of a preventative intervention of bereaved children. *American Journal of Community Psychology, 19*, 459-480.

75. Whipple, E. E., & Webster-Stratton, C. (1991). The role of parental stress in physically abusive families. *Child Abuse & Neglect, 15*, 279-291.

76. Wolfe, V. V., Gentile, C., Michienzi, T., Sas, L., & Wolfe, D. A. (1991). The Children's Impact of Traumatic Events Scale: A measure of post-sexual-abuse PTSD symptoms. *Behavioral Assessment, 13*, 359-383.

77. Adam, B. S., Everett, B. L., & O'Neal, E. (1992). PTSD in physically and sexually abused psychiatrically hospitalized children. *Child Psychiatry and Human Development, 23*, 3–8.

78. Altepeter, T. S., & Breen, M. J. (1992). Situational variation in problem behavior at home and school in attention deficit disorder with hyperactivity: A factor analytic study. *Journal of Child Psychology and Psychiatry and Allied Disciplines, 33*, 741-748.

79. Anastopoulos, A. D., Goevremont, D. C., Shelton, T. L., & DuPaul, G. J. (1992). Parenting stress among families of children with attention deficit hyperactivity disorder. *Journal of Abnormal Child Psychology, 20*, 503-520.

80. Barakat, L. P., & Linney, J. A. (1992). Children with physical handicaps and their mothers: The interrelation of social support, maternal adjustment, and child adjustment. *Journal of Pediatric Psychology, 17*, 725–739.

81. Barkley, R. A., Anastopoulos, A. D., Goevremont, D. C., & Fletcher, K. E. (1992). Adolescents with attention deficit hyperactivity: Mother-adolescent interactions, family beliefs and conflicts and maternal psychopathology. *Journal of Abnormal Child Psychology, 20*, 263-288.

82. Bederman, J., Faraone, S. V., Keenan, K., Benjamin, J., Krifcher, B., Moore, C., Sprich-Buckminster, S., Ugaglia, K., Jellinek, M. S., Steingard, R., Spencer, T., Norman, D., Kolodny, R., Kraus, I., Perrin, J., Keller, M. B., & Tsuang, M. T. (1992). Further evidence for family-genetic risk factors in attention deficit hyperactivity disorder: Patterns of comorbidity in probands and relatives in psychiatrically and pediatrically referred samples. *Archives of General Psychiatry, 49*, 728-738.

83. Brandt, P., Magyary, D., Hammond, M., & Barnard, K. (1992). Learning and behavioral-emotional problems of children born preterm at second grade. *Journal of Pediatric Psychology, 17*, 291–311.

84. Brodzinsky, D. M., & Brodzinsky, A. B. (1992). The impact of family structure on the adjustment of adopted children. *Child Welfare, 71*, 69–76.

85. Capaldi, D. M. (1992). Co-occurrence of conduct problems and depressive symptoms in early adolescent boys: II. A 2-year follow-up at grade 8. *Development and Psychopathology, 4*, 125-144.

86. Caspi, A., Block, J., Block, J. H., Klopp, B., Lynam, D., Moffitt, T. E., & Stouthamer-Loeber, M. (1992). A "common language" version of the California Child Q-Set for personality assessment. *Psychological Assessment, 4*, 512–523.

87. Christensen, A., Margolin, G., & Sullaway, M. (1992). Interparental agreement on child behavior problems. *Psychological Assessment, 4*, 419–425.

88. Clarke, G. N., Lewinsohn, P. M., Hops, H., & Seeley, J. R. (1992). A self-and parent-report measure of adolescent depression: The Child Behavior Checklist Depression Scale (CBCL-D). *Behavioral Assessment, 14*, 443-463.

89. Cornwall, A. (1992). The relationship of phonological awareness, rapid naming, and verbal memory to severe reading and spelling disability. *Journal of Learning Disabilities, 25*, 532–538.

90. Daltroy, L. H., Larson, M. G., Eaton, H. M., Partridge, A. J., Pless, I. B., Rogers, M. P., & Liang, M. H. (1992). Psychosocial adjustment in juvenile arthritis. *Journal of Pediatric Psychology, 17*, 277–289.

91. Donders, J. (1992). Premorbid behavioral and psychosocial adjustment of children with traumatic brain injury. *Journal of Abnormal Child Psychology, 20,* 223-246.

92. Downey, G., & Walker, E. (1992). Distinguishing family-level and child-level influences on the development of depression and aggression in children at risk. *Development and Psychopathology, 4,* 81-95.

93. Eckblad, G., & Vandvik, I. H. (1992). A computerized scoring procedure for the Kuebaek Family Sculpture Technique applied to families of children with rheumatic diseases. *Family Process, 31,* 85-98.

94. Engstrom, I. (1992). Mental health and psychological functioning in children and adolescents with inflammatory bowel disease: A comparison with children having other chronic illnesses and with healthy children. *Journal of Child Psychology and Psychiatry and Allied Disciplines, 33,* 563-582.

95. Floyd, F. J., & Saitzyk, A. R. (1992). Social class and parenting children with mild and moderate mental retardation. *Journal of Pediatric Psychology, 17,* 607–631.

96. Frankel, F., Hanna, G. L., Cantwell, D. P., Shekim, W., & Ornitz, E. (1992). Cluster analysis of Child Behavior Checklists of 6 to 11-year-old males with varying degrees of behavior disorders. *Child Psychiatry and Human Development, 23,* 69–85.

97. Fristad, M. A., Topolosky, S., Weller, E. B., & Weller, R. A. (1992). Depression and learning disabilities in children. *Journal of Affective Disorders, 26,* 53–58.

98. Grych, J. H., Seid, M., & Fincham, F. D. (1992). Assessing marital conflict from the child's perspective: The Children's Perception of Interparental Conflict Scale. *Child Development, 63,* 558–572.

99. Hamlett, K. W., Pellegrini, D. S., & Katz, K. S. (1992). Childhood chronic illness as a family stressor. *Journal of Pediatric Psychology, 17,* 33–47.

100. Hanson, C. L., De Guire, M. J., Schinkel, A. M., Henggeler, S. W., & Burghen, G. A. (1992). Comparing social learning and family systems correlates of adaptation in youths with IDDM. *Journal of Pediatric Psychology, 17,* 555–572.

101. Hibbard, R. A., & Hartman, G. L. (1992). Behavioral problems in alleged sexual abuse victims. *Child Abuse & Neglect, 16,* 755-762.

102. Hops, H., & Seeley, J. R. (1992). Parent participation in studies of family interaction: Methodological and substantive considerations. *Behavioral Assessment, 14,* 229-243.

103. Hotte, J. P., & Rafman, S. (1992). The specific effects of incest on prepubertal girls from dysfunctional families. *Child Abuse & Neglect, 16,* 273-283.

104. Jones, R. N., Sloane, H. N., & Roberts, M. W. (1992). Limitations of "don't" instructional control. *Behavior Therapy, 23,* 131–140.

105. Jouriles, E. N., & Farris, A. M. (1992). Effects of marital conflict on subsequent parent-son interactions. *Behavior Therapy, 23,* 355-374.

106. Kliewer, W., & Sandler, I. N. (1992). Locus of control and self-esteem as moderators of stressor-symptom relations in children and adolescents. *Journal of Abnormal Child Psychology, 20,* 393-413.

107. Koenig, L. J., & Bornstein, R. A. (1992). Psychopathology in boys with Tourette syndrome: Effects of age on the relationship between psychological and physical symptoms. *Development and Psychopathology, 4,* 271-285.

108. Koot, H. M., & Verhulst, F. C. (1992). Prediction of children's referral to mental health and special education services from earlier adjustment. *Journal of Child Psychology and Psychiatry and Allied Disciplines, 33,* 717-729.

109. Kruesi, M. J. P., Hibbs, E. D., Zahn, T. P., Keyser, C. S., Hamburger, S. D., Bartko, J. J., & Rapoport, J. L. (1992). A 2-year prospective follow-up study of children and adolescents with disruptive behavior disorders: Prediction by cerebrospinal fluid 5-hydroxyindoleacetic acid, homovanillic acid, and autonomic measures? *Archives of General Psychiatry, 49,* 429-435.

110. LaFreniere, P. J., & Dumas, J. E. (1992). A transactional analysis of early childhood anxiety and social withdrawal. *Development and Psychopathology, 4,* 385-402.

111. LaFrenière, P. J., Dumas, J. E., Capuano, F., & Dubeau, D. (1992). Development and validation of the Preschool Socioaffective Profile. *Psychological Assessment, 4,* 442–450.

112. Lustig, J. L., Wolchik, S. A., & Braver, S. L. (1992). Social support in chumships and adjustment in children of divorce. *American Journal of Community Psychology, 20,* 393-399.

113. Mabe, P. A., Treiber, F. A., & Riley, W. T. (1992). The relationship of anger and child psychopathology. *Child Psychiatry and Human Development, 22,* 151–164.

114. MacLean W. E., Jr., Perrin, J. M., Gortmaker, S., & Pierre, C. B. (1992). Psychological adjustment of children with asthma: Effects of illness severity and recent stressful life events. *Journal of Pediatric Psychology, 17,* 159–171.

115. Mazur, E., Wolchik, S. A., & Sandler, I. N. (1992). Negative cognitive errors and positive illusions for negative divorce events: Predictors of children's psychological adjustment. *Journal of Abnormal Child Psychology, 20,* 523-542.

116. Montgomery, M. J., Anderson, E. R., Hetherington, E. M., & Clingempeel, W. G. (1992). Patterns of courtship for remarriage: Implications for child adjustment and parent-child relationships. *Journal of Marriage and the Family, 54,* 686–698.

117. Mulhern, R. K., Fairclough, D. L., Smith, B., & Douglas, S. M. (1992). Maternal depression, assessment methods, and physical symptoms affect estimates of depressive symptomatology among children with cancer. *Journal of Pediatric Psychology, 17,* 313–326.

118. Myers, H. F., Taylor, S., Alvy, K. T., Arrington, A., & Richardson, M. A. (1992). Parental and family predictors of behavior problems in inner-city black children. *American Journal of Community Psychology, 20,* 557-576.

119. Northam, E., Bowden, S., Anderson, V., & Court, J. (1992). Neuropsychological functioning in adolescents with diabetes. *Journal of Clinical and Experimental Neuropsychology, 14,* 884-900.

120. Panak, W. F., & Garber, J. (1992). Role of aggression, rejection, and attributions in the prediction of depression in children. *Development and Psychopathology, 4,* 145-165.

121. Pett, M. A., Wampold, B. E., Vaughan-Cole, B., & East, T. D., IV. (1992). Consistency of behaviors within a naturalistic setting: An examination of the impact of context and repeated observations on mother-child interactions. *Behavioral Assessment, 14,* 367-385.

122. Power, T. J. (1992). Contextual factors in vigilance testing of children with ADHD. *Journal of Abnormal Child Psychology, 20,* 579-593.

123. Prichard, S., & Epting, F. C. (1992). Children and death: New horizons in theory and measurement. *Omega, 24,* 271–274.

124. Quiggle, N. L., Garber, J., Panak, W. F., & Dodge, K. A. (1992). Social information processing in aggressive and depressed children. *Child Development, 63,* 1305–1320.

125. Rait, D. S., Ostroff, J. S., Smith, K., Cella, D. F., Tan, C., & Lesko, L. M. (1992). Lives in a balance: Perceived family functioning and the psychosocial adjustment of adolescent cancer survivors. *Family Process, 31,* 383-397.

126. Rey, J., & Morris-Yates, A. (1992). Diagnostic accuracy in adolescents of several depression rating scales extracted from a general purpose behavior checklist. *Journal of Affective Disorders, 26,* 7-16.

127. Rogosch, F. A., Mowbray, C. T., & Bogat, G. A. (1992). Determinants of parenting attitudes in mothers with severe psychopathology. *Development and Psychopathology, 4,* 469-487.

128. Rose, S. A., Feldman, J. F., Rose, S. L., Wallace, I. F., & McCarton, C. (1992). Behavior problems at 3 and 6 years: Prevalence and continuity in full-terms and preterms. *Development and Psychopathology, 4,* 361-374.

129. Rossman, B. B. R., & Rosenberg, M. S. (1992). Family stress and functioning in children: The moderating effects of children's beliefs about their control over parental conflict. *Journal of Child Psychology and Psychiatry and Allied Disciplines, 33,* 699-715.

130. Sandler, I. N., West, S. G., Baca, L., Pillow, D. R., Gersten, J. C., Rogosch, F., Virdin, L., Beals, J., Reynolds, K. D., Kallgren, C., Tein, J. Y., Kriege, G., Cole, E., & Ramirez, R. (1992). Linking empirically based theory and evaluation: The family bereavement program. *American Journal of Community Psychology, 20,* 491-521.

131. Sawyer, M. G., Baghurst, P., & Mathias, J. (1992). Differences between informants' reports describing emotional and behavioral problems in community and clinic-referred children: A research note. *Journal of Child Psychology and Psychiatry and Allied Disciplines, 33,* 441-449.

132. Scholte, E. M. (1992). Identification of children at risk at the police station and the prevention of delinquency. *Psychiatry, 55,* 354–369.

133. Sinclair, E., & Alexson, J. (1992). Special education placements of language disordered children in a psychiatric population. *Child Psychiatry and Human Development, 23,* 131–143.

134. Spiker, D., Kraemer, H. C., Constantine, N. A., & Bryant, D. (1992). Reliability and validity of behavior problem checklists as measures of stable traits in low birth weight, premature preschoolers. *Child Development, 63,* 1481–1496.

135. Sullivan, P. M., Scanlan, J. M., Brookhouser, P. E., & Schulte, L. E. (1992). The effects of psychotherapy on behavior problems of sexually abused deaf children. *Child Abuse & Neglect, 16,* 297-307.

136. Taylor, H. G., & Schatschneider, C. (1992). Academic achievement following childhood brain disease: Implications for the concept of learning disabilities. *Journal of Learning Disabilities, 25,* 630–638.

137. Thompson, R. W., & Nichols, G. T. (1992). Correlations between scores on a continuous performance test and parents' ratings of attention problems and impulsivity in children. *Psychological Reports, 70,* 739-742.

138. Tiedemann, G. L., & Johnston, C. (1992). Evaluation of a parent training program to promote sharing between young siblings. *Behavior Therapy, 23,* 299–318.

139. Toth, S. L., Manly, J. T., & Cicchetti, D. (1992). Child maltreatment and vulnerability to depression. *Development and Psychopathology, 4,* 97-112.

140. Verhulst, F. C., & Van der Ende, J. (1992). Six-year stability of parent-reported problem behavior in an epidemiological sample. *Journal of Abnormal Child Psychology, 20,* 595-610.

141. Walker, L. S., Van Slyke, D. A., & Newbrough, J. R. (1992). Family resources and stress: A comparison of families of children with cystic fibrosis, diabetes, and mental retardation. *Journal of Pediatric Psychology, 17,* 327–343.

142. Walker, L. S., & Zeman, J. L. (1992). Parental response to child illness behavior. *Journal of Pediatric Psychology, 17,* 49–71.

143. Weiss, B., Dodge, K. A., Bates, J. E., & Pettit, G. S. (1992). Some consequences of early harsh discipline: Child aggression and a maladaptive social information processing style. *Child Development, 63,* 1321–1335.

144. Weiss, B., Dodge, K. A., Bates, J. E., & Pettit, G. S. (1992). Some consequences of early harsh discipline: Child aggression and a maladaptive social information processing style. *Child Development, 63,* 1321–1335.

145. Weiss, B., & Nurcombe, B. (1992). Age, clinical severity, and the differentiation of depressive psychopathology: A test of the orthogenetic hypothesis. *Development and Psychopathology, 4,* 113-124.

146. Achenbach, T. M. (1993). Implications of multiaxial empirically based assessment for behavior therapy with children. *Behavior Therapy, 24,* 91–116.

147. Achenbach, T. M. (1993). Taxonomy and comorbidity of conduct problems: Evidence from empirically based approaches. *Development and Psychopathology, 5,* 51-64.

148. Ackerman, P. T., & Dykman, R. A. (1993). Phonological processes, confrontational naming, and immediate memory in dyslexia. *Journal of Learning Disabilities, 26,* 597–609.

149. Austin, J. K., & Huberty, T. J. (1993). Development of the Child Attitude Toward Illness Scale. *Journal of Pediatric Psychology, 18,* 467–480.

150. Bank, L., Duncan, T., Patterson, G. R., & Reid, J. (1993). Parent and teacher rating in the assessment and prediction of antisocial and delinquent behaviors. *Journal of Personality, 61,* 693–709.

151. Biederman, J., Faraone, S. V., Doyle, A., Lehman, B. K., Kraus, I., Perrin, J., & Tsuang, M. T. (1993). Convergence of the Child Behavior Checklist with structured interview-based psychiatric diagnoses of ADHD children with and without comorbidity. *Journal of Child Psychology and Psychiatry and Allied Disciplines, 34,* 1241-1251.

152. Bronstein, P., Clauson, J., Stoll, M. F., & Abrams, C. L. (1993). Parenting behavior and children's social, psychological, and academic adjustment in diverse family structures. *Family Relations, 42,* 268-276.

153. Brooks-Gunn, J., Klebanov, P. K., Liaw, F., & Spiker, D. (1993). Enhancing the development of low-birthweight, premature infants: Changes in cognition and behavior over the first three years. *Child Development, 64,* 736-753.

154. Carpentieri, S. C., Mulhern, R. K., Douglas, S., Hanna, S., & Fairclough, D. L. (1993). Behavioral resiliency among children surviving brain tumors: A longitudinal study. *Journal of Clinical Child Psychology, 22,* 236-246.

155. Carro, M. G., Grant, K. E., Gotlib, I. H., & Compas, B. E. (1993). Postpartum depression and child development: An investigation of mothers and fathers as sources of risk and resilience. *Development and Psychopathology, 5,* 567-579.

156. Celano, M. P., & Geller, R. J. (1993). Learning, school, performance, and children with asthma: How much at risk? *Journal of Learning Disabilities, 26,* 23–32.

157. Cicchetti, D., Rogosch, F. A., Lynch, M., & Holt, K. D. (1993). Resilience in maltreated children: Processes leading to adaptive outcome. *Development and Psychopathology, 5,* 629-647.

158. Cole, P. M., Usher, B. A., & Cargo, A. P. (1993). Cognitive risk and its association with risk for disruptive behavior disorder in preschoolers. *Journal of Clinical Child Psychology, 22,* 154-164.

159. Conrad, M., & Hammen, C. (1993). Protective and resource factors in high- and low-risk children: A comparison of children with unipolar, bipolar, medically ill, and normal mothers. *Development and Psychopathology, 5,* 593-607.

160. Craig, H. K. (1993). Clinical forum: Language and social skills in the school-age population. Social skills of children with specific language impairment: Peer relationships. *Language, Speech, and Hearing Services in Schools, 24,* 206–215.

161. Craig, H. K., & Washington, J. A. (1993). Access behaviors of children with specific language impairment. *Journal of Speech and Hearing Research, 36,* 322–337.

162. Cuccaro, M. L., Holmes, G. R., & Wright, H. H. (1993). Behavior problems in preschool children: A pilot study. *Psychological Reports, 72,* 121-122.

163. D'Abate, D. (1993). The role of social network supports of Italian parents and children in their adjustment to separation and divorce. *Journal of Divorce & Remarriage, 20*(1/2), 161-187.

164. DeGangi, G. A., Wietlisbach, S., Goodin, M., & Scheiner, N. (1993). A comparison of structured sensorimotor therapy and child-centered activity in the treatment of preschool children with sensorimotor problems. *The American Journal of Occupational Therapy, 47,* 777-786.

165. Doll, B. (1993). Evaluating parental concerns about children's friendships. *Journal of School Psychology, 31,* 431-447.

166. Dykman, R. A., & Ackerman, P. T. (1993). Behavioral subtypes of attention deficit disorder. *Exceptional Children, 60,* 132-141.

167. Easterbrooks, M. A., Davidson, C. E., & Chazan, R. (1993). Psychosocial risk, attachment, and behavior problems among school-aged children. *Development and Psychopathology, 5,* 389-402.

168. Egeland, B., Carlson, E., & Sroufe, L. A. (1993). Resilience as process. *Development and Psychopathology, 5,* 517-528.

169. Egeland, B., Pianta, R., & O'Brien, M. A. (1993). Maternal intrusiveness in infancy and child maladaptation in early school years. *Development and Psychopathology, 5,* 359-370.

170. Eisenstadt, T. H., Eyberg, S., McNeil, C. B., Newcomb, K., & Funderburk, B. (1993). Parent-child interaction therapy with behavior problem children: Relative effectiveness of two stages and overall treatment outcome. *Journal of Clinical Child Psychology, 22,* 42-51.

171. Elliot, S. N., Busse, R. T., & Gresham, F. M. (1993). Behavior rating scales: Issues of use and development. *School Psychology Review, 22,* 313-321.

172. Fitzgerald, H. E., Sullivan, L. A., Ham, H. P., Zucker, R. A., Bruckel, S., Schneider, A. M., & Noll, R. B. (1993). Predictors of behavior problems in three-year-old sons of alcoholics: Early evidence for the onset of risk. *Child Development, 64,* 110-123.

173. Floyd, F. J., & Phillippe, K. A. (1993). Parental interactions with children with and without mental retardation: Behavior management, coerciveness, and positive exchange. *American Journal on Mental Retardation, 97,* 673-684.

174. Friedman, A. G., Campbell, T. A., & Evans, I. M. (1993). Multi-dimensional child behavior therapy in the treatment of medically-related anxiety: A practical illustration. *Journal of Behavior Therapy and Experimental Psychiatry, 24,* 241–247.

175. Friedrich, W. N. (1993). Sexual victimization and sexual behavior in children: A review of recent literature. *Child Abuse & Neglect, 17,* 59-66.

176. Friedrich, W. N., Shurtleff, D. B., & Shaeffer, J. (1993). Cognitive abilities and lipomyelomeningocele. *Psychological Reports, 73,* 467-470.

177. Gest, S. D., Neemann, J., Hubbard, J. J., Masten, A. S., & Tellegen, A. (1993). Parenting quality, adversity, and conduct problems in adolescents: Testing process-oriented models of resilience. *Development and Psychopathology, 5,* 663-682.

178. Goodman, S. H., Brogan, D., Lynch, M. E., & Fielding, B. (1993). Social and emotional competence in children of depressed mothers. *Child Development, 64,* 516-531.

179. Greenberg, M. T., Speltz, M. L., & DeKlyen, M. (1993). The role of attachment in the early development of disruptive behavior problems. *Development and Psychopathology, 5,* 191-213.

180. Hagopian, L. P., & Slifer, K. J. (1993). Treatment of separation anxiety disorder with graduate exposure and reinforcement targeting school attendance: A controlled case study. *Journal of Anxiety Disorders, 7,* 271-280.

181. Halperin, J. M., Newcorn, J. H., Schwartz, S. T., McKay, K. E., Bedi, G., & Sharma, V. (1993). Plasma catecholamine metabolite levels in ADHD boys with and without reading disabilities. *Journal of Clinical Child Psychology, 22,* 219-225.

182. Harris, J., Tyre, C., & Wilkinson, C. (1993). Using the Child Behaviour Checklist in ordinary primary schools. *British Journal of Educational Psychology, 63,* 245–260.

183. Healy, J. M., Jr., Stewart, A. J., & Copeland, A. P. (1993). The role of self-blame in children's adjustment to parental separation. *Personality and Social Psychology Bulletin, 19,* 279-289.

184. Hoffman, M. A., Leng-Shiff, R., & Ushpiz, V. (1993). Gender differences in the relation between stressful life events and adjustment among school-aged children. *Sex Roles, 29,* 441-455.

185. Howe, G. W., Feinstein, C., Reiss, D., Molock, S., & Berger, K. (1993). Adolescent adjustment to chronic physical disorders-I. Comparing neurological and non-neurological conditions. *Journal of Child Psychology and Psychiatry and Allied Disciplines, 34,* 1153-1176.

186. Jagers, R. J., & Mock, L. O. (1993). Culture and social outcomes among inner-city African American children: An Afrographic exploration. *The Journal of Black Psychology, 19,* 391-405.

187. Kearney, C. A., & Silverman, W. K. (1993). Measuring the function of school refusal behavior: The School Refusal Assessment Scale. *Journal of Clinical Child Psychology, 22,* 85-96.

188. Kelley, S. J., Brant, R., & Waterman, J. (1993). Sexual abuse of children in day care centers. *Child Abuse & Neglect, 17,* 71-89.

189. Kolko, D. J., & Kazdin, A. E. (1993). Emotional/behavioral problems in clinic and nonclinic children: Correspondence among children, parent and teacher reports. *Journal of Child Psychology and Psychiatry and Allied Disciplines, 34,* 991-1006.

190. Korhonen, T. T., Vähä-Eskeli, E., Sillanpää, M., & Kero, P. (1993). Neuropsychological sequelae of perinatal complications: A 6-year follow-up. *Journal of Clinical Child Psychology, 22,* 226-235.

191. Koverola, C., Pound, J., Heger, A., & Lytle, C. (1993). Relationship of child sexual abuse to depression. *Child Abuse & Neglect, 17,* 393-400.

192. Kurtz, L., & Derevensky, J. L. (1993). The effects of divorce on perceived self-efficacy and behavioral control in elementary school children. *Journal of Divorce & Remarriage, 20*(3/4), 75-94.

193. Kusché, C. A., Cook, E. T., & Greenberg, M. T. (1993). Neuropsychological and cognitive functioning in children with anxiety, externalizing, and comorbid psychopathology. *Journal of Clinical Child Psychology, 22,* 172-195.

194. Little, S. S. (1993). Nonverbal learning disabilities and socioemotional functioning: A review of recent literature. *Journal of Learning Disabilities, 26,* 653–665.

195. Loeber, R., Wung, P., Keenan, K., Giroux, B., Stouthamer-Loeber, M., Van Kammen, W. B., & Maughan, B. (1993). Developmental pathways in disruptive child behavior. *Development and Psychopathology, 5,* 103-133.

196. Lothar, S. S., Doernberger, C. H., & Zigler, E. (1993). Resilience is not a unidimensional construct: Insights from a prospective study of inner-city adolescents. *Development and Psychopathology, 5,* 703-717.

197. Lumley, M. A., Melamed, B. G., & Abeles, L. A. (1993). Predicting children's presurgical anxiety and subsequent behavior changes. *Journal of Pediatric Psychology, 18,* 481–497.

198. Macmann, G. M., Barnett, D. W., & Lopez, E. J. (1993). The Child Behavior Checklist 14–18 and related materials: Reliability and validity of syndromal assessment. *School Psychology Review, 22,* 322-333.

199. Martens, B. K. (1993). Social labeling, precision of measurement, and problem solving: Key issues in the assessment of children's emotional problems. *School Psychology Review, 22,* 308-312.

200. Martinez, P., & Richters, J. E. (1993). The NIMH community violence project: II. Children's distress symptoms associated with violence exposure. *Psychiatry, 56,* 22–35.

201. McConaughy, S. H. (1993). Advances in empirically based assessment of children's behavioral and emotional problems. *School Psychology Review, 22,* 285-307.

202. McConaughy, S. H., & Skiba, R. J. (1993). Comorbidity of externalizing and internalizing problems. *School Psychology Review, 22,* 421-436.

203. McKinney, J. D., Montague, M., & Hocutt, A. M. (1993). Educational assessment of students with attention deficit disorder. *Exceptional Children, 60,* 125-131.

204. Minde, K., Popiel, K., Leos, N., Falkner, S., Parker, K., & Handley-Derry, M. (1993). The evaluation and treatment of sleep disturbances in young children. *Journal of Child Psychology and Psychiatry and Allied Disciplines, 34,* 521-533.

205. Morris, R. D., Krawiecki, N. S., Wright, J. A., & Walter, L. W. (1993). Neuropsychological, academic, and adaptive functioning in children who survive in-hospital cardiac arrest and resuscitation. *Journal of Learning Disabilities, 26,* 46–51.

206. Mulhern, R. K., Carpentieri, S., Slema, S., Stone, P., & Fairclough, D. (1993). Factors associated with social and behavioral problems among children recently diagnosed with brain tumor. *Journal of Pediatric Psychology, 18,* 339–350.

207. Osofsky, J. D., Wewers, S., Haun, D. M., & Fick, A. C. (1993). Chronic community violence: What is happening to our children? *Psychiatry, 56,* 36–45.

208. Passino, A. W., Whitman, T. L., Borkowski, J. G., Schellenbach, C. J., Maxwell, S. E., Keogh, D., & Rellinger, E. (1993). Personal adjustment during pregnancy and adolescent parenting. *Adolescence, 28,* 97-122.

209. Pettit, G. S., Bates, J. E., & Dodge, K. A. (1993). Family interaction patterns and children's conduct problems at home and school: A longitudinal perspective. *School Psychology Review, 22,* 403-420.

210. Polaino-Lorente, A., & Domenech, E. (1993). Prevalence of childhood depression: Results of the first study in Spain. *Journal of Child Psychology and Psychiatry and Allied Disciplines, 34,* 1007-1017.

211. Radke-Yarrow, M., & Brown, E. (1993). Resilience and vulnerability in children of multiple-risk families. *Development and Psychopathology, 5,* 581-592.

212. Radovanovic, H. (1993). Parental conflict and children's coping styles in litigating separated families: Relationships with children's adjustment. *Journal of Abnormal Child Psychology, 21,* 697-713.

213. Richters, J. E., & Martinez, P. E. (1993). Violent communities, family choices, and children's chances: An algorithm for improving the odds. *Development and Psychopathology, 5,* 609-627.

214. Rodrigue, J. R., Geffken, G. R., & Morgan, S. B. (1993). Perceived competence and behavioral adjustment of siblings of children with autism. *Journal of Autism and Developmental Disorders, 23*(4), 665-674.

215. Ross, C. K., Lavigne, J. V., Hayford, J. R., Berry, S. L., Sinacore, J. M., & Pachman, L. M. (1993). Psychological factors affecting reported pain in juvenile rheumatoid arthritis. *Journal of Pediatric Psychology, 18,* 561–573.

216. Rovet, J. F. (1993). The psychoeducational characteristics of children with Turner syndrome. *Journal of Learning Disabilities, 26,* 333–341.

217. Salzinger, S., Feldman, R. S., Hammer, M., & Rosario, M. (1993). The effects of physical abuse on children's social relationships. *ChildDevelopment, 64,* 169-187.

218. Sandberg, D. E., Meyer-Bohlburg, H. F. L., & Yager, T. J. (1993). Feminine gender role behavior and academic achievement: Their relation in a community sample of middle childhood boys. *Sex Roles, 29,* 125-140.

219. Schuman, W. B., Armstrong, F. D., Pegelow, C. H., & Routh, D. K. (1993). Enhanced parenting knowledge and skills in mothers of preschool children with sickle cell disease. *Journal of Pediatric Psychology, 18,* 575–591.

220. Shagle, S. C., & Barber, B. K. (1993). Effects of family, marital, and parent-child conflict on adolescent self-derogation and suicidal ideation. *Journal of Marriage and the Family, 55,* 964–974.

221. Stanger, C., & Lewis, M. (1993). Agreement among parents, teachers, and children on internalizing and externalizing behavior problems. *Journal of Clinical Child Psychology, 22,* 107-115.

222. Stice, E., Barrera, M., & Chassin, L. (1993). Relation of parental support and control to adolescents' externalizing symptomatology and substance use: A longitudinal examination of curvilinear effects. *Journal of Abnormal Child Psychology, 21,* 609-629.

223. Stouthamer-Loeber, M., Loeber, R., Farrington, D. P., Zhang, Q., van Kammen, W., & Maguin, E. (1993). The double edge of protective and risk factors for delinquency: Interrelations and developmental patterns. *Development and Psychopathology, 5,* 683-701.

224. Szajnberg, M. D., Krall, V. K., Davis, P., Treem, W., & Hyams, J. (1993). Psychopathology and relationship measures in children with inflammatory bowel disease and their parents. *Child Psychiatry and Human Development, 23,* 215–232.

225. Szatmari, P., Saigal, J., Rosenbaum, P., & Campbell, D. (1993). Psychopathology and adaptive functioning among extremely low birthweight children at eight years of age. *Development and Psychopathology, 5,* 345-357.

226. Taylor, H. G., Barry, C. T., & Schatschneider, C. (1993).School-age consequences of haemophilus influenzae Type b meningitis. *Journal of Clinical Child Psychology, 22,* 196-206.

227. Teja, S., & Stolberg, A. L. (1993). Peer support, divorce, and children's adjustment. *Journal of Divorce & Remarriage, 20*(3/4), 45-64.

228. Tems, C. L., Stewart, S. M., Skinner, J. R., Hughes, C. W., & Emslie, G. (1993). Cognitive distortion in depressed children and adolescents: Are they state dependent or traitlike? *Journal of Clinical Child Psychology, 22,* 316-326.

229. Timko, C., Baumgartner, M., Moos, R. H., & Miller, J. J., III. (1993). Parental risk and resistance factors among children with juvenile rheumatic disease: A four-year predictive study. *Journal of Behavioral Medicine, 16,* 571-588.

230. Trupin, E. W., Tarico, V. S., Low, B. P., Jemelka, R., & McClellan, J. (1993). Children on child protective service caseloads: Prevalence and nature of serious emotional disturbance. *Child Abuse & Neglect, 17,* 345-355.

231. Tubman, J. G. (1993). A pilot study of school-age children of men with moderate to severe alcohol dependence: Maternal distress and child outcomes. *Journal of Child Psychology and Psychiatry and Allied Disciplines, 34,* 729-741.

232. Tubman, J. G. (1993). Family risk factors, parental alcohol use, and problem behaviors among school-age children. *Family Relations, 42,* 81-86.

233. Utens, E. M. W. J., Verhulst, F. C., Meijboom, F. J., Duivenvoorden, H. J., Erdman, R. A. M., Bos, E., Roelandt, J. T. C., & Hess, J. (1993). Behavioural and emotional problems in children and adolescents with congenital heart disease. *Psychological Medicine, 23,* 415-424.

234. Vandvik, I. H., & Eckblad, G. F. (1993). FACES III and the Kuebaek Family Sculpture Technique as measures of cohesion and closeness. *Family Process, 32,* 221-233.

235. Varni, J. W., Katz, E. R., Colegrove, R., Jr., & Dolgin, M. (1993). The impact of social skills training on the adjustment of children with newly diagnosed cancer. *Journal of Pediatric Psychology, 18,* 751–767.

236. Verhulst, F. C., & Van der Ende, J. (1993). "Comorbidity" in epidemiological sample: A longitudinal perspective. *Journal of Child Psychology and Psychiatry and Allied Disciplines, 34,* 767-783.

237. Vuchinich, S., Vuchinich, R., & Wood, B. (1993). The interparental relationship and family problem solving with preadolescent males. *Child Development, 64,* 1389-1400.

238. Wadsworth, S. J., DeFries, J. C., & Fulker, D. W. (1993). Cognitive abilities of children at 7 and 12 years of age in the Colorado Adoption Project. *Journal of Learning Disabilities, 26,* 611–615.

239. Waterman, J., & Lusk, R. (1993). Psychological testing in evaluation of child sexual abuse. *Child Abuse & Neglect, 17,* 145-159.

240. Weisz, J. R., Sigman, M., Weiss, B., & Mosk, J. (1993). Parent reports of behavioral and emotional problems among children in Kenya, Thailand, and the United States. *Child Development, 64,* 98-109.

241. Westerman, M. A., & Schonholtz, J. (1993). Marital adjustment, joint parental support in a triadic problem-solving task, and child behavior problems. *Journal of Clinical Child Psychology, 22,* 97-106.

242. Wherry, J. N., Paal, N., Jolly, J. B., Adam, B., Holloway, C., Everett, B., & Vaught, L. (1993). Concurrent and discriminant validity of the Gordon Diagnostic System: A preliminary study. *Psychology in the Schools, 30,* 29-36.

243. Zametkin, A. J., Liebenaver, L. L., Fitzgerald, G. A., King, A. C., Minkonas, D. V., Herscovitch, P., Yamada, E. M., & Cohen, R. M. (1993). Brain metabolism in teenagers with attention-deficit hyperactivity disorder. *Archives of General Psychiatry, 50,* 333-340.

244. Zucker, K. J., Wild, J., Bradley, S. J., & Lowry, C. B. (1993). Physical attractiveness of boys with gender identity disorder. *Archives of Sexual Behavior, 22,* 23-36.

245. Ackerman, P. T., Dykman, R. A., & Ogesby, D. M. (1994). Visual event-related potentials of dyslexic children to rhyming and nonrhyming stimuli. *Journal of Clinical and Experimental Neuropsychology, 16,* 138-154.

246. Ackerman, P. T., Dykman, R. A., Oglesby, D. M., & Newton, J. E. O. (1994). EEG power spectra of children with dyslexia, slow learners, and normally reading children with ADD during verbal processing. *Journal of Learning Disabilities, 27,* 619–630.

247. Adams, C. D., Hillman, N., & Gaydos, G. R. (1994). Behavioral difficulties in toddlers: Impact of sociocultural and biological risk factors. *Journal of Clinical Child Psychology, 23,* 373-381.

248. Anastopoulos, A. D., Spisto, M. A., & Maher, M. C. (1994). The WISC-III freedom from distractibility factor: Its utility in identifying children with attention deficit hyperactivity disorder. *Psychological Assessment, 6,* 368-371.

249. Archer, R. P., & Krishnamurthy, R. (1994). A structural summary approach for the MMPI-A: Development and empirical correlates. *Journal of Personality Assessment, 63,* 554-573.

250. Attar, B. K., Guerra, N. G., & Tolan, P. H. (1994). Neighborhood disadvantage, stressful life events, and adjustment in urban elementary-school children. *Journal of Clinical Child Psychology, 23,* 391-400.

251. Barber, B. K., Olsen, J. E., & Shagle, S. C. (1994). Associations between parental psychological and behavioral control and youth internalized and externalized behaviors. *Child Development, 65,* 1120-1136.

252. Bates, J. E., Marvinney, D., Kelly, T., Dodge, K. A., Bennett, D. S., & Pettit, G. S. (1994). Child-care history and kindergarten adjustment. *Developmental Psychology, 30,* 690-700.

253. Bendell, D., Field, T., Yando, R., Lang, C., Martinez, A., & Pickens, J. (1994). "Depressed" mothers' perceptions of their preschool children's vulnerability. *Child Psychiatry and Human Development, 24,* 183–190.

254. Black, M., Dubowitz, H., & Harrington, D. (1994). Sexual abuse: Developmental differences in children's behavior and self-perception. *Child Abuse & Neglect, 18,* 85-95.

255. Bradely, R. H., Whiteside, L., Mundform, D. J., Casey, P. H., Caldwell, B. M., & Barrett, K. (1994). Impact of the infant health and development program (IHDP) on the home environments of infants born prematurely and with low birthweights. *Journal of Educational Psychology, 86,* 531-541.

256. Bradely, R. H., Whiteside, L., Mundfrom, D. J., Casey, P. H., Kelleher, K. J., & Pope, S. K. (1994). Contribution of early intervention and early caregiving experiences to resilience in low-birthweight, premature children living in poverty. *Journal of Clinical Child Psychology, 23,* 425-434.

257. Brier, N. (1994). Targeted treatment for adjudicated youth with learning disabilities: Effects on recidivism. *Journal of Learning Disabilities, 27,* 215—222.

258. Buitelaar, J. K., Swinkels, S. H. N., de Vries, H., van der Gaag, R. J., & van Hooff, J. (1994). An ethological study on behavioural differences between hyperactive, aggressive, combined hyperactive/aggressive and control children. *Journal of Child Psychology & Psychiatry & Allied Disciplines, 35,* 1437-1446.

259. Campbell, S. B. (1994). Hard-to-manage preschool boys: Externalizing behavior, social competence, and family context at two-year followup. *Journal of Abnormal Child Psychology, 22,* 147-166.

260. Chen, W. J., Faraone, S. V., Biederman, J., & Tsuang, M. T. (1994). Diagnostic accuracy of the Child Behavior Checklist scales for attention-deficit hyperactivity disorder: A receiver-operating characteristic analysis. *Journal of Consulting and Clinical Psychology, 62,* 1017-1025.

261. Cohen, D. S., Friedrich, W. N., Jaworski, T. M., Copeland, D., & Pendergrass, T. (1994). Pediatric cancer: Predicting sibling adjustment. *Journal of Clinical Psychology, 50,* 303-319.

262. Colegrove, R. W., Jr., & Huntzinger, R. M. (1994). Academic, behavioral, and social adaptation of boys with hemophilia/HIV disease. *Journal of Pediatric Psychology, 19,* 457-473.

263. Compas, B. E., Worsham, N. L., Epping-Jordan, J. E., Grant, K. E., Mireault, G., Howell, D. C., & Malcarne, V. L. (1994). When mom or dad has cancer: Markers of psychological distress in cancer patients, spouses, and children. *Health Psychology, 13,* 507-515.

264. Cook, E. T., Greenberg, M. T., & Kusche, C. A. (1994). The relations between emotional understanding, intellectual functioning, and disruptive behavior problems in elementary-school-aged children. *Journal of Abnormal Child Psychology, 22,* 205-219.

265. Cornell, D. G., Delcourt, M. A. B., Bland, L. C., Goldberg, M. D., & Oram, G. (1994). Low incidence of behavior problems among elementary school students in gifted programs. *Journal for the Education of the Gifted, 18,* 4-19.

266. Coster, W. J., Haley, S., & Baryza, M. (1994). Functional performance of young children after traumatic brain injury: A 6-month follow-up study. *The American Journal of Occupational Therapy, 48,* 211-218.

267. Cross, T. P., DeVos, E., & Whitcomb, D. (1994). Prosecution of child sexual abuse: Which cases are accepted? *Child Abuse & Neglect, 18,* 663-677.

268. Cummings, E. M., Hennessy, K. D., Rabideau, G. J., & Cicchetti, D. (1994). Responses of physically abused boys to interadult anger involving their mothers. *Development and Psychopathology, 6*, 31-41.

269. Day, D. M., Factor, D. C., & Szkiba-Day, P. J. (1994). Relations among discipline style, child behaviour problems, and perceived ineffectiveness as a caregiver among parents with conduct problem children. *Canadian Journal of Behavioural Science, 26*, 520-533.

270. Dodge, K. A., Pettit, G. S., & Bates, J. E. (1994). Effects of physical maltreatment on the development of peer relations. *Development and Psychopathology, 6*, 43-55.

271. Dodge, K. A., Pettit, G. S., & Bates, J. E. (1994). Socialization mediators of the relation between socioeconomic status and child conduct problems. *Child Development, 65*, 649-665.

272. Dumas, J. E., & Serketich, W. J. (1994). Maternal depressive symptomatology and child maladjustment: A comparison of three process models. *Behavior Therapy, 25*, 161-181.

273. Dunn, J., Slomkowski, C., Beardsall, L., & Rende, R. (1994). Adjustment in middle childhood and early adolescence: Links with earlier and contemporary sibling relationships. *Journal of Child Psychology and Psychiatry and Allied Disciplines, 35*, 491-504.

274. Eddowes, E. A., Aldridge, J., & Culpepper, S. (1994). Primary teachers' classroom practices and their perceptions of children's attention problems. *Perceptual and Motor Skills, 79*, 787-790.

275. El-Sheikh, M. (1994). Children's emotional and psychological responses to interadult angry behavior: The role of history of interparental hostility. *Journal of Abnormal Child Psychology, 22*, 661-678.

276. El-Sheikh, M., Ballard, M., & Cummings, E. M. (1994). Individual differences in preschoolers' physiological and verbal responses to videotaped angry interactions. *Journal of Abnormal Child Psychology, 22*, 303-320.

277. Erhardt, D., & Hinshaw, S. P. (1994). Initial sociometric impressions of attention-deficit hyperactivity disorder and comparison boys: Predictions from social behaviors and from nonbehavioral variables. *Journal of Consulting and Clinical Psychology, 62*, 833-842.

278. Estroff, D. B., Yando, R., Burke, K., & Snyder, D. (1994). Perceptions of preschoolers' vulnerability by mothers who had delivered preterm. *Journal of Pediatric Psychology, 19*, 709-721.

279. Evans, D. W. (1994). Self-complexity and its relation to development, symptomatology and self-perception during adolescence. *Child Psychiatry and Human Development, 24*, 173-182.

280. Fallon, T., & Schwab-Stone, M. (1994). Determinants of reliability in psychiatric services of children aged 6-12. *Journal of Child Psychology & Psychiatry & Allied Disciplines, 35*, 1391-1408.

281. Fields, J. H., Grochowski, S., Lindenmayer, J. P., Kay, S. R., Grosz, D., Hyman, R. B., & Alexander, G. (1994). Assessing positive and negative symptoms in children and adolescents. *American Journal of Psychiatry, 151*, 249-253.

282. Fitzgerald, H. E., Zucker, R. A., Maguin, E. T., & Reider, E. E. (1994). Time spent with child and parental agreement about preschool children's behavior. *Perceptual and Motor Skills, 79*, 336-338.

283. Frankel, F., & Myatt, R. (1994). A dimensional approach to the assessment of social competence in boys. *Psychological Assessment, 6*, 249-254.

284. Frick, P. J., O'Brien, B. S., Wootton, J. M., & McBurnett, K. (1994). Psychopathy and conduct problems in children. *Journal of Abnormal Psychology, 103*, 700-707.

285. Friman, P., Larzelere, R., & Finney, J. W. (1994). Exploring the relationship between thumb-sucking and psychopathology. *Journal of Pediatric Psychology, 19*, 431-441.

286. Fritz, G. K., Spirito, A., & Yeung, A. (1994). Utility of the repressive defense style construct in childhood. *Journal of Clinical Child Psychology, 23*, 306-313.

287. Furstenberg, F., & Doyal, G. (1994). The relationship between emotional-behavioral functioning and personal characteristics on performance outcomes of hearing impaired students. *American Annals of the Deaf, 139*, 410-414.

288. Giedd, J. N., Castellanos, F. X., Casey, B. J., Kozuch, P., King, A. C., Hamburger, S. D., & Rapoport, J. L. (1994). Quantitative morphology of the corpus callosum in attention deficit hyperactivity disorder. *American Journal of Psychiatry, 151*, 665-669.

289. Goodwin, D. A. J., Boggs, S. R., & Graham-Pole, J. (1994). Development and validation of the Pediatric Oncology Quality of Life Scale. *Psychological Assessment, 6*, 321-328.

290. Granger, D. A., Weisz, J. R., & Kauneckis, D. (1994). Neuroendocrine reactivity, internalizing behavior problems, and control-related cognitions in clinic-referred children and adolescents. *Journal of Abnormal Psychology, 103*, 267-276.

291. Greenbaum, P. E., Dedrick, R. F., Prange, M. E., & Friedman, R. M. (1994). Parent, teacher, and child ratings of problem behaviors of youngsters with serious emotional disturbances. *Psychological Assessment, 6*, 141-148.

292. Groot, A. D., Koot, H. M., & Verhulst, F. C. (1994). Cross-cultural generalizability of the Child Behavior Checklist cross-informant syndromes. *Psychological Assessment, 6*, 225-230.

293. Hagglund, K. J., Clay, D. L., Frank, R. G., Beck, N. C., Kashani, J. H., Hewett, J., Johnson, J., Goldstein, D. E., & Cassidy, J. T. (1994). Assessing anger expression in children and adolescents. *Journal of Pediatric Psychology, 19*, 291-304.

294. Halperin, J. M., Sharma, V., Siever, L. J., Schwartz, S. T., Matier, K., Wornell, G., & Newcorn, J. H. (1994). Serotonergic function in aggressive and nonaggressive boys with attention deficit hyperactivity disorder. *American Journal of Psychiatry, 151*, 243-248.

295. Harrest, A. W., Pettit, G. S., Dodge, K. A., & Bates, J. E. (1994). Dyadic synchrony in mother-child interaction: Relation with children's subsequent kindergarten adjustment. *Family Relations, 43*, 417-424.

296. Hubbs-Tait, L., Osofsky, J. D., Hann, D. M., & Culp, A. M. (1994). Predicting behavior problems and social competence in children of adolescent mothers. *Family Relations, 43*, 439-446.

297. Huesmann, L. R., Eron, L. D., Guerra, N. G., & Crawshaw, V. B. (1994). Measuring children's aggression with teachers predictions of peer nominations. *Psychological Assessment, 6*, 329-336.

298. Hutton, C. J., & Bradley, B. S. (1994). Effects of sudden infant death on bereaved siblings: A comparative study. *Journal of Child Psychology and Psychiatry and Allied Disciplines, 35*, 723-732.

299. John, O. P., Caspi, A., Robins, R. W., Moffitt, T. E., & Stouthamer-Loeber, M. (1994). The "little five": Exploring the nomological network of the five-factor model of personality in adolescent boys. *Child Development, 65*, 160-178.

300. Kaufman, J., Cook, A., Arny, L., Jones, B., & Pittinsky, T. (1994). Problems defining resiliency: Illustrations from the study of maltreated children. *Development and Psychopathology, 6*, 215-229.

301. Kazdin, A. E., & Mazurick, J. L. (1994). Dropping out of child psychotherapy: Distinguishing early and late dropouts over the course of treatment. *Journal of Consulting and Clinical Psychology, 62*, 1069-1074.

302. Knight, G. P., Virdin, L. M., & Roosa, M. (1994). Socialization and family correlates of mental health outcomes among Hispanic and Anglo American children: Consideration of cross-ethnic scalar equivalence. *Child Development, 65*, 212-224.

303. Kurtz, L., & Derevensky, J. L. (1994). Family configuration and maternal employment: Effects on family environment and children's outcomes. *Journal of Divorce & Remarriage, 22*(1/2), 137-154.

304. Lachiewicz, A. M., Spiridigliozzi, G. A., Bullion, C. M., Rausford, S. N., & Rao, K. (1994). Aberrant behaviors of young boys with fragile X syndrome. *American Journal on Mental Retardation, 98*, 567-579.

305. Lambert, M. C., Knight, F. Taylor, R., & Achenbach, T. M. (1994). Epidemiology of behavioral and emotional problems among children of Jamaica and the United States: Parent reports for ages 6 to 11. *Journal of Abnormal Child Psychology, 22*, 113-128.

306. Lavigne, J. V., Arend, R., Rosenbaum, D., Sinacore, J., Cicchetti, C., Binns, H. J., Christoffer, K. K., Hayford, J. R., & McGuire, P. (1994). Interrater reliability of the DSM-III-R with preschool children. *Journal of Abnormal Child Psychology, 22*, 679-690.

307. Leadbeater, B. J., & Bishop, S. J. (1994). Predictors of behavioral problems in preschool children of inner-city African-American and Puerto Rican adolescent mothers. *Child Development, 65*, 638-648.

308. Liaw, F., & Brooks-Gunn, J. (1994). Cumulative familial risks and low-birthweight children's cognitive and behavioral development. *Journal of Clinical Child Psychology, 23*, 360-372.

309. Luthar, S. S., & Ripple, C. H. (1994). Sensitivity to emotional distress among intelligent adolescents: A short-term prospective study. *Development and Psychopathology, 6*, 343-357.

310. Manly, J. T., Cicchetti, D., & Barnett, D. (1994). The impact of subtype, frequency, chronicity, and severity of child maltreatment on social competence and behavior problems. *Development and Psychopathology, 6*, 121-143.

311. Mann, B. J., & Sanders, S. (1994). Child dissociation and the family context. *Journal of Abnormal Child Psychology, 22*, 373-388.

312. Mannarino, A. P., Cohen, J. A., & Berman, S. R. (1994). The Children's Attributions and Perceptions Scale: A new measure of sexual abuse-related factors. *Journal of Clinical Child Psychology, 23*, 204-211.

313. Mannarino, A. P., Cohen, J. A., & Berman, S. R. (1994). The relationship between preabuse factors and psychological symptomatology in sexually abused girls. *Child Abuse & Neglect, 18*, 63-71.

314. Martin, C. S., Earleywine, M., Blackson, T. C., Vanyukov, M. M., Moss, H. B., & Tarter, R. E. (1994). Aggressivity, inattention, hyperactivity, and impulsivity in boys at high and low risk for substance abuse. *Journal of Abnormal Child Psychology, 22*, 177-203.

315. McConaughy, S. H., & Achenbach, T. M. (1994). Comorbidity of empirically based syndromes in matched general population and clinical samples. *Journal of Child Psychology and Psychiatry and Allied Disciplines, 35*, 1141-1157.

316. McConaughy, S. H., Mattison, R. E., & Peterson, R. L. (1994). Behavioral/emotional problems of children with serious emotional disturbances and learning disabilities. *School Psychology Review, 23*, 81-98.

317. McGraw, K. O., Gordjé, S., & Wong, S. P. (1994). How many subjects to screen? A practical procedure for estimating multivariate normal probabilities for correlated variables. *Journal of Consulting and Clinical Psychology, 62*, 960-964.

318. Moore, K. J., Osgood, D. W., Larzelere, R. E., & Chamberlain, P. (1994). Use of pooled time series in the study of naturally occurring clinical events and problem behavior in a foster care setting. *Journal of Consulting and Clinical Psychology, 62*, 718-728.

319. Moss, H. B., Majumder, P. P., & Vanyukov, M. (1994). Familial resemblance for psychoactive substance use disorders: Behavioral profile of high risk boys. *Addictive Behaviors, 19*, 199-208.

320. Mott, P., & Krane, A. (1994). Interpersonal cognitive problem-solving and childhood social competence. *Cognitive Therapy and Research, 18*, 127-141.

321. O'Brien, B. S., Frick, P. J., & Lyman, R. D. (1994). Reward dominance among children with disruptive behavior disorders. *Journal of Psychopathology and Behavioral Assessment, 16*, 131-145.

322. Okun, A., Parker, J., & Levendosky, A. A. (1994). Distinct and interactive contributions of physical abuse, socioeconomic disadvantage, and negative life events to children's social, cognitive, and affective adjustment. *Development and Psychopathology, 6*, 77-98.

323. Pearson, D. A., & Aman, M. G. (1994). Rating hyperactivity and developmental indices: Should clinicians correct for developmental level? *Journal of Autism and Developmental Disorders, 24*, 395-411.

324. Pearson, D. A., & Lachar, D. (1994). Using behavior questionnaires to identify adaptive deficits in elementary school children. *Journal of School Psychology, 32,* 33-52.

325. Pett, M. A., Vaughan-Cole, B., & Wampold, B. E. (1994). Maternal employment and perceived stress: Their impact on children's adjustment and mother-child interaction in young divorced and married families. *Family Relations, 43,* 151-158.

326. Phares, V., & Danforth, J. S. (1994). Adolescents', parents', and teachers' distress over adolescents' behavior. *Journal of Abnormal Child Psychology, 22,* 721-732.

327. Pianta, R. C., & Egeland, B. (1994). Predictors of instability in children's mental test performance at 24, 48, and 96 months. *Intelligence, 18,* 145-163.

328. Pianta, R. C., & Lothman, D. J. (1994). Predicting behavior problems in children with epilepsy: Child factors, disease factors, family stress, and child-mother interaction. *Child Development, 65,* 1415-1428.

329. Prinz, R. J., Blechman, E. A., & Dumas, J. E. (1994). An evaluation of peer coping-skills training for childhood aggression. *Journal of Clinical Child Psychology, 23,* 193-203.

330. Prinz, R. J., & Miller, G. E. (1994). Family-based treatment for childhood antisocial behavior: Experimental influences on dropout and engagement. *Journal of Consulting and Clinical Psychology, 62,* 645-650.

331. Quamma, J. P., & Greenberg, M. T. (1994). Children's experience of life stress: The role of family social support and social problem-solving skills as protective factors. *Journal of Clinical Child Psychology, 23,* 295-305.

332. Reid, M. J., O'Leary, S. G., & Wolff, L. S. (1994). Effects of maternal distraction and reprimands on toddlers' transgressions and negative affect. *Journal of Abnormal Child Psychology, 22,* 237-245.

333. Resta, S. P., & Eliot, J. (1994). Written expression in boys with attention deficit disorder. *Perceptual and Motor Skills, 79,* 1131-1138.

334. Rosenberg, L. A., Brown, J., & Singer, H. S. (1994). Self-reporting of behavior problems in patients with tic disorders. *Psychological Reports, 74,* 653-654.

335. Rosenthal, J. A., & Groze, V. K. (1994). A longitudinal study of special-needs adoptive families. *Child Welfare, 73,* 689-706.

336. Rotto, P. C., & Kratochwill, T. R. (1994). Behavioral consultation with parents: Using competency-based training to modify child noncompliance. *School Psychology Review, 23,* 669-693.

337. Rouet, J., & Ireland, L. (1994). Behavioral phenotype in children with Turner Syndrome. *Journal of Pediatric Psychology, 19,* 779-790.

338. Russo, M. F., Loeber, R., Lahey, B. B., & Keenan, K. (1994). Oppositional defiant and conduct disorders: Validation of the DSM-III-R and an alternative diagnostic option. *Journal of Clinical Child Psychology, 23,* 56-68.

339. Schwab-Stone, M., Fallon, T., Briggs, M., & Crowther, B. (1994). Reliability of diagnostic reporting for children aged 6–11 years: A test-retest study of the Diagnostic Interview for Children—Revised. *The American Journal of Psychiatry, 151,* 1048-1054.

340. Shaw, D. S., Keenan, K., & Vondra, J. I. (1994). Developmental precursors of externalizing behavior: Ages 1 to 3. *Developmental Psychology, 30,* 355-364.

341. Shaw, D. S., Vondra, J. I., Hommerding, K. D., Keenan, K., & Dunn, M. (1994). Chronic family adversity and early child behavior problems: A longitudinal study of low income families. *Journal of Child Psychology and Psychiatry and Allied Disciplines, 35,* 1109-1122.

342. Sheebar, L. B., & Johnson, J. H. (1994). Evaluation of a temperament-focused, parent-training program. *Journal of Clinical Child Psychology, 23,* 249-259.

343. Shields, A. M., Cicchetti, D., & Ryan, R. M. (1994). The development of emotional and behavioral self-regulation and social competence among altered school-age children. *Development and Psychopathology, 6,* 57-75.

344. Silberg, J. L., Erickson, M. T., Meyer, J. M., Eaves, L. J., Rutter, M. L., & Hewitt, J. K. (1994). The application of structural equation modeling to maternal ratings of twins' behavioral and emotional problems. *Journal of Consulting and Clinical Psychology, 62,* 510-521.

345. Snyder, J., Edwards, P., McGraw, K., Kilgore, K., & Holton, A. (1994). Escalation and reinforcement in mother-child conflict: Social processes associated with the development of physical aggression. *Development and Psychopathology, 6,* 305-321.

346. Song, L-Y., Singh, J., & Singer, M. (1994). The Youth Self-Report Inventory: A study of its measurement fidelity. *Psychological Assessment, 6,* 236-245.

347. Spense, S. H. (1994). Practitioner review: Cognitive therapy with children and adolescents: From theory to practice. *Journal of Child Psychology and Psychiatry and Allied Disciplines, 35,* 1191-1229.

348. St. James-Roberts, I., Singh, G., Lynn, R., & Jackson, S. (1994). Assessing emotional and behavioural problems in reception class school-children: Factor structure, convergence and prevalence using the PBCL. *British Journal of Educational Psychology, 64,* 105-118.

349. Stanford, L. D., & Hynd, G. W. (1994). Congruence of behavioral symptomatology in children with ADD/H, ADD/WO, and learning disabilities. *Journal of Learning Disabilities, 27,* 243-253.

350. Stanger, C., Achenbach, T. M., & Verhulst, F. C. (1994). Accelerating longitudinal research on child psychopathology: A practical example. *Psychological Assessment, 6,* 102-107.

351. Stein, J. A., & Newcomb, M. D. (1994). Children's internalizing and externalizing behaviors and maternal health problems. *Journal of Pediatric Psychology, 19,* 571-594.

352. Stoolmiller, M. (1994). Antisocial behavior, delinquent peer association, and unsupervised wandering for boys: Growth and change from childhood to early adolescent. *Multivariate Behavioral Research, 29,* 263-288.

353. Summerville, M. B., Kaslow, N. J., Abbate, M. F., & Cronan, S. (1994). Psychopathology, family functioning, and cognitive style in urban adolescents with suicide attempts. *Journal of Abnormal Child Psychology, 22,* 221-235.

354. Thurber, S., & Hollingsworth, D. K. (1994). Neurological impairment and hypersensitivity among psychiatrically disturbed adolescents. *Journal of Counseling and Development, 73,* 85-87.

355. Tomporowski, P. D., Tinsley, V., & Hager, L. D. (1994). Visuospatial attentional shifts and choice responses of adults and ADHD and non-ADHD children. *Perceptual and Motor Skills, 79,* 1479-1490.

356. Trickett, P. K., McBride-Chang, C., & Putnam, F. W. (1994). The classroom performance and behavior of sexually abused females. *Development and Psychopathology, 6,* 183-194.

357. Urquiza, A. J., Wirtz, S. J., Peterson, M. S., & Singer, V. A. (1994). Screening and evaluating abused and neglected children entering protective custody. *Child Welfare, 73,* 155–171.

358. van Eldik, T. Th. (1994). Behavior problems with deaf Dutch boys. *American Annals of the Deaf, 139,* 394-399.

359. Verbaten, M. N., Overtoom, C. C. E., Koelega, H. S., Swaab-Barneveld, H., van der Gaag, R. J., Buitelaar, J., & van Engeland, H. (1994). Methylphenidate influences on both early and late ERP waves of ADHD children in a continuous performance test. *Journal of Abnormal Child Psychology, 22,* 561-578.

360. Verhulst, F. C., Koot, H. M., & Van der Ende, J. (1994). Differential predictive value of parents' and teachers' reports of children's problem behavior: A longitudinal study. *Journal of Abnormal Child Psychology, 22,* 531-546.

361. Vostanis, P., Nicholls, J., & Harrington, R. (1994). Maternal expressed emotion in conduct and emotional disorders of childhood. *Journal of Child Psychology and Psychiatry and Allied Disciplines, 35,* 365-376.

362. Vuchinich, S., Wood, B., & Vuchinich, R. (1994). Coalitions and family problem solving with preadolescents in referred, at-risk, and comparison families. *Family Process, 33,* 409-424.

363. Wall, J. E., & Holden, E. W. (1994). Aggressive, assertive, and submissive behaviors in disadvantaged, inner-city preschool children. *Journal of Clinical Child Psychology, 23,* 382-390.

364. Webster-Stratton, C. (1994). Advancing videotape parent training: A comparison study. *Journal of Consulting and Clinical Psychology, 62,* 583-593.

365. White, J. L., Moffitt, T. E., Caspi, A., Bartusch, D. J., Needles, D. J., & Stouthamer-Loeber, M. (1994). Measuring impulsivity and examining its relationship to delinquency. *Journal of Abnormal Psychology, 103,* 192-205.

366. Wolfe, D. A., & McGee, R. (1994). Dimensions of child maltreatment and their relationship to adolescent adjustment. *Development and Psychopathology, 6,* 165-181.

367. Wolfe, D. A., Sas, L., & Wekerle, C. (1994). Factors associated with the development of posttraumatic stress disorder among child victims of sexual abuse. *Child Abuse & Neglect, 18,* 37-50.

368. Adler, N. A., & Schutz, J. (1995). Sibling incest offenders. *Child Abuse & Neglect, 19,* 811–819.

369. Allen, K., & Prior, M. (1995). Assessment of the validity of easy and difficult temperament through observed mother-child behaviours. *International Journal of Behavioral Development, 18,* 609–630.

370. Allison, D. B. (1995). When is it worth measuring a covariate in a randomized clinical trial? *Journal of Consulting and Clinical Psychology, 63,* 339-343.

371. Arnold, E. H., & O'Leary, S. G. (1995). The effect of child negative affect on maternal discipline behavior. *Journal of Abnormal Child Psychology, 23,* 585–595.

372. Beidel, D. C., Turner, S. M., & Morris, T. L. (1995). A new inventory to assess childhood social anxiety and phobia: The Social Phobia and Anxiety Inventory for Children. *Psychological Assessment, 7,* 73-79.

373. Bergman, A. J., & Walker, E. (1995). The relationship between cognitive function and behavioral deviance in children at risk for psychopathology. *Journal of Child Psychology and Psychiatry and Allied Disciplines, 36,* 265-278.

374. Braungart-Rieker, J., Rende, R. D., Plomin, R., DeFries, J. C., & Fulker, D. W. (1995). Genetic mediation of longitudinal associations between family environment and childhood behavior problems. *Development and Psychopathology, 7,* 233-245.

375. Butler, S. M., Mackay, S. A., & Dickens, S. E. (1995). Maternal and adolescent ratings of psychopathology in young offender and non-clinical males. *Canadian Journal of Behavioural Science, 27,* 333–342.

376. Campbell, S. B. (1995). Behavior Problems in preschool children: A review of recent research. *Journal of Child Psychology and Psychiatry and Allied Disciplines, 36,* 113-149.

377. Carlson, E. A. Jacobvitz, D., & Sroufe, L. A. (1995). A developmental investigation of inattentiveness and hyperactivity. *Child Development, 66,* 37-54.

378. Carlson-Greene, B., Morris, R. D., & Krawiecki, N. (1995). Family and illness predictors of outcome in pediatric brain tumors. *Journal of Pediatric Psychology, 20,* 769–784.

379. Carter, A. S., Grigorenko, E. L., & Pauls, D. L. (1995). A Russian adaptation of the Child Behavior Checklist: Psychometric properties and associations with child and maternal affective symptomatology and family functioning. *Journal of Abnormal Child Psychology, 23,* 661–684.

380. Caselli, L. T., & Motta, R. W. (1995). The effect of PTSD and combat level on Vietnam veterans' perceptions of child behavior and marital adjustment. *Journal of Clinical Psychology, 51,* 4-12.

381. Chamrad, D. L., Robinson, N. M., & Junos, P. M. (1995). Consequences of having a gifted sibling: Myths and realities. *Gifted Child Quarterly, 39,* 135–145.

382. Clay, D. L., Wood, P. K., Frank, R. G., Hagglund, K. J., & Johnson, J. C. (1995). Examining systematic differences to chronic illness: A growth modeling approach. *Rehabilitation Psychology, 40,* 61–70.

383. Curtner-Smith, M. E., Bennett, T. L., & O'Rear, M. R. (1995). Fathers' occupational conditions, values of self-direction and conformity, and perceptions of nurturant and restrictive parenting in relation to young children's depression and aggression. *Family Relations, 44,* 299–305.

384. de Paúl, J., & Arruabarrena, M. I. (1995). Behavior problems in school-aged physically abused and neglected children in Spain. *Child Abuse & Neglect, 19*, 409–418.

385. DiBiase, R., & Waddell, S. (1995). Some effects of homelessness on the psychological functioning of preschoolers. *Journal of Abnormal Child Psychology, 23*, 783–792.

386. Dishion, T. J., Andrews, D. W., & Crosby, L. (1995). Antisocial boys and their friends in early adolescence: Relationship characteristics, quality, and interactional process. *Child Development, 66*, 139-151.

387. Drotar, D., Stein, R. E. K., & Perrin, E. C. (1995). Methodological issues in using the Child Behavior Checklist and its related instruments in clinical child psychology research. *Journal of Clinical Child Psychology, 24*, 184-192.

388. Dumas, J. E., & Wekerle, C. (1995). Maternal reports of child behavior problems and personal distress as predictors of dysfunctional parenting. *Development and Psychopathology, 7*, 465–479.

389. Dykens, E. M. (1995). Measuring behavioral phenotypes: Provocations from the "New Genetics." *American Journal on Mental Retardation, 99*, 522–532.

390. Edelbrock, C., Rende, R., Plomin, R., & Thompson, L. A. (1995). A twin study of competence and problem behavior in childhood and early adolescence. *Journal of Child Psychology and Psychiatry and Allied Disciplines, 36*, 775–785.

391. Egeland, B., & Hiester, M. (1995). The long-term consequences of infant day-care and mother-infant attachment. *Child Development, 66*, 474-485.

392. Eltz, M. J., Shirk, S. R., & Sarlin, N. (1995). Alliance formation and treatment outcome among maltreated adolescents. *Child Abuse & Neglect, 19*, 419–431.

393. Farmer, J. E., & Peterson, L. (1995). Injury risk factors in children with attention deficit hyperactivity disorder. *Health Psychology, 14*, 325–332.

394. Farmer, J. E., & Peterson, L. (1995). Pediatric traumatic brain injury: Promoting successful school reentry. *School Psychology Review, 24*, 230–243.

395. Feldman, R. S., Salzinger, S., Rosario, M., Alvarado, L., Caraballo, L., & Hammer, M. (1995). Parent, teacher, and peer ratings of physically abused and nonmaltreated children's behavior. *Journal of Abnormal Child Psychology, 23*, 317-334.

396. Ferdinand, R. F., & Verhulst, F. C. (1995). Psychopathology from adolescence into young adulthood: An 8-year follow-up study. *American Journal of Psychiatry, 152*, 1586–1594.

397. Flaks, D. K., Ficher, I., Masterpasqua, F., & Joseph, G. (1995). Lesbians choosing motherhood: A comparative study of lesbian and heterosexual parents and their children. *Developmental Psychology, 31*, 105-114.

398. Fletcher, J. M., Brookshire, B. L., Landry, S. H., Bohan, T. P., Davidson, K. C., Francis, D. J., Thompson, N. M., & Miner, M. E. (1995). Behavioral adjustment of children with hydrocephalus: Relationships with etiology, neurological, and family stress. *Journal of Pediatric Psychology, 20*, 109-125.

399. Friedrich, W. N., & Schafer, L. C. (1995). Somatic symptoms in sexually abused children. *Journal of Pediatric Psychology, 20*, 661–670.

400. Fuhrman, T., & Holmbeck, G. N. (1995). A contextual-moderator analysis of emotional autonomy and adjustment in adolescence. *Child Development, 66*, 793-811.

401. Galvin, M., Eyck, R. T., Shekhar, A., Stilwell, B., Fineberg, N., Laite, G., & Karwisch, G. (1995). Serum dopamine beta hydroxylase and maltreatment in psychiatrically hospitalized boys. *Child Abuse & Neglect, 19*, 821–832.

402. Gnys, J. A., Willis, W. G., & Faust, D. (1995). School psychologists' diagnoses of learning disabilities: A study of illusory correlation. *Journal of School Psychology, 33*, 59-73.

403. Goldberg, S., Gotowiec, A., & Simmons, R. J. (1995). Infant-mother attachment and behavior problems in healthy and chronically ill preschoolers. *Development and Psychopathology, 7*, 267-282.

404. Gotlib, I. H., Lewinsohn, P. M., & Seeley, J. R. (1995). Symptoms versus a diagnosis of depression: Differences in psychosocial functioning. *Journal of Consulting and Clinical Psychology, 63*, 90-100.

405. Gracia, E. (1995). Visible but unreported: A case for the "not serious enough" cases of child maltreatment. *Child Abuse & Neglect, 19*, 1083–1093.

406. Greenberg, M. T., Kusche, C. A., Cook, E. T., & Quamma, J. P. (1995). Promoting emotional competence in school-aged children: The effects of the PATHS curriculum. *Development and Psychopathology, 7*, 117-136.

407. Guralnick, M. J., Connor, R. T., & Hammond, M. (1995). Parent perspective of peer relationships and friendships in integrated and specialized programs. *American Journal on Mental Retardation, 99*, 457–476.

408. Guralnick, M. J., Connor, R. T., Hammond, M., Gottman, J. M., & Kinnish, K. (1995). Immediate effects of mainstreamed settings on the social interactions and social integration of preschool children. *American Journal on Mental Retardation, 100*, 359–377.

409. Haraldsson, E. (1995). Personality and abilities of children claiming previous-life memories. *The Journal of Nervous and Mental Disease, 183*, 445–451.

410. Harnish, J. D., Dodge, K. A., & Valente, E. (1995). Mother-child interaction quality as a partial mediator of the roles of maternal depressive symptomatology and socioeconomic status in the development of child behavior problems. *Child Development, 66*, 739-753.

411. Haskett, M. E., Myers, L. W., Pirrello, V. E., & Dombalis, A. O. (1995). Parenting style as a mediating link between parental emotional health and adjustment of maltreated children. *Behavior Therapy, 26*, 625–642.

412. Hazzard, A., Celano, M., Gould, J., Lawry, S., & Webb, C. (1995). Predicting symptomatology and self-blame among child sex abuse victims. *Child Abuse & Neglect, 19*, 707–714.

413. Hegar, R., & Scannapieco, M. (1995). From family duty to family policy: The evolution of kinship care. *Child Welfare, 74*, 200–216.

414. Hickey, J. E., Suess, P. E., Newlin, D. B., Spurgeon, L., & Porges, S. W. (1995). Vagal tone regulation during sustained attention in boys exposed to opiates in utero. *Addictive Behaviors, 20*, 43-59.

415. Hinshaw, S. P., Simmel, C., & Heller, T. L. (1995). Multimethod assessment of covert antisocial behavior in children: Laboratory observations, adult ratings, and child self-report. *Psychological Assessment, 7*, 209-219.

416. Holmbeck, G. N., & Faier-Routman, J. (1995). Spinal lesion level, shunt status, family relationships, and psychosocial adjustment in children and adolescents with spina bifida myelomeningocele. *Journal of Pediatric Psychology, 20*, 817–832.

417. Kearney, C. A., Eison, A. R., & Silverman, W. K. (1995). The legend and myth of school phobia. *School Psychology Quarterly, 10*, 65-85.

418. Krol, N. P. C. M., DeBruyn, E. E. J., & Van Den Bercken, J. H. L. (1995). Intuitive and empirical prototypes in childhood psychopathology. *Psychological Assessment, 7*, 533–537.

419. Kuczynski, L., & Kochanska, G. (1995). Function and content of maternal demands: Developmental significance of early demands for competent action. *Child Development, 66*, 616-628.

420. Kumar, G., & Steer, R. A. (1995). Psychosocial correlates of suicidal ideation in adolescent psychiatric inpatients. *Suicide and Life-Threatening Behavior, 25*, 339–346.

421. Lahey, M., & Edwards, J. (1995). Specific language impairment: Preliminary investigation of factors associated with family history and with patterns of language performance. *Journal of Speech and Hearing Research, 38*, 643–657.

422. Lanktree, C. B., & Briere, J. (1995). Outcome of therapy for sexually abused children: A repeated measures study. *Child Abuse & Neglect, 19*, 1145–1155.

423. Lovett, B. B. (1995). Child sexual abuse: The female victim's relationship with her nonoffending mother. *Child Abuse & Neglect, 19*, 729–738.

424. Luthar, S. S. (1995). Social competence in the school setting: Prospective cross-domain associations among inner-city teens. *Child Development, 66*, 416-429.

425. Manne, S. L., Lesanics, D., Meyers, P., Wollner, N., Steinherz, P., & Redd, W. (1995). Predictors of depressive symptomatology among parents of newly diagnosed children with cancer. *Journal of Pediatric Psychology, 20*, 491–510.

426. McCloskey, L. A., Figueredo, A. J., & Koss, M. P. (1995). The effects of systemic family violence on children's mental health. *Child Development, 66*, 1239–1261.

427. McDermott, P. A., Watkins, M. W., Sichel, A. F., Weber, E. M., Keenan, J. T., Holland, A. M., & Leigh, N. M. (1995). The accuracy of new national scales for detecting emotional disturbance in children and adolescents. *The Journal of Special Education, 29*, 337–354.

428. McGee, R. A., Wolfe, D. A., Yuen, S. A., Wilson, S. K., & Carnochan, J. (1995). The measurement of maltreatment: A comparison of approaches. *Child Abuse & Neglect, 19*, 233–249.

429. McKelvey, R. S., & Webb, J. A. (1995). A pilot study of abuse among Vietnamese Amerasians. *Child Abuse & Neglect, 19*, 545–553.

430. Mcguire, S., Dunn, J., & Plomin, R. (1995). Maternal differential treatment of siblings and children's behavioral problems: A longitudinal study. *Development and Psychopathology, 7*, 515–528.

431. Messer, S. C., & Gross, A. M. (1995). Childhood depression and family interaction: A naturalistic observation study. *Journal of Clinical Child Psychology, 24*, 77-88.

432. Naglieri, J. A., & Gottling, S. H. (1995). Use of the Teacher Report Form and the Devereux Behavior Rating Scale—School Form with learning disordered/emotionally disordered students. *Journal of Clinical Child Psychology, 24*, 71-76.

433. Oram, G. D., Cornell, D. G., & Rutemiller, L. A. (1995). Relations between academic aptitude and psychosocial adjustment in gifted program students. *Gifted Child Quarterly, 39*, 236–244.

434. Paternite, C. E., Loney, J., & Roberts, M. A. (1995). External validation of oppositional disorder and attention deficit disorder with hyperactivity. *Journal of Abnormal Child Psychology, 23*, 453–471.

435. Patterson, C. J. (1995). Families of the lesbian baby boom: Parents' division of labor and children's adjustment. *Developmental Psychology, 31*, 115-123.

436. Patterson, G. R., & Forgatch, M. S. (1995). Predicting future clinical adjustment from treatment outcome and process variables. *Psychological Assessment, 7*, 275–285.

437. Phelps, L. (1995). Psychoeducational outcomes of fetal alcohol syndrome. *School Psychology Review, 24*, 200–212.

438. Plomin, R. (1995). Genetics and children's experiences in the family. *Journal of Child Psychology and Psychiatry and Allied Disciplines, 36*, 33-68.

439. Radke-Yarrow, M., McCann, K., DeMulder, E., Belmont, B., Martinez, P., & Richardson, D. T. (1995). Attachment in the context of high-risk conditions. *Development and Psychopathology, 7*, 247-265.

440. Reid, R. (1995). Assessment of ADHD with culturally different groups: The use of behavioral rating scales. *School Psychology Review, 24*, 537–560.

441. Rey, J. M., Starling, J., Wever, C., Dossetor, D. R., & Plapp, J. M. (1995). Inter-rater reliability of global assessment of functioning in a clinical setting. *Journal of Child Psychology and Psychiatry and Allied Disciplines, 36*, 787–792.

442. Richards, C. M., Symons, D. K., Greene, C. A., & Szuszkiewicz, T. A. (1995). The bidirectional relationship between achievement and externalizing behavior problems of students with learning disabilities. *Journal of Learning Disabilities, 28*, 8–17.

443. Roberts, J. E., Burchinal, M. R., & Clarke-Klein, S. M. (1995). Otitis media in early childhood and cognitive, academic, and behavior outcomes at 12 years of age. *Journal of Pediatric Psychology, 20*, 645–660.

444. Robinson, N. S., Garber, J., & Hilsman, R. (1995). Cognitions and stress: Direct and moderating effects on depressive versus externalizing symptoms during the junior high school transition. *Journal of Abnormal Psychology, 104*, 453–463.

445. Rubin, K. H., Coplan, R. J., Fox, N. A., & Calkins, S. D. (1995). Emotionality, emotion regulation, and preschoolers' social adaptation. *Development and Psychopathology, 7*, 49-62.

446. Schuerholz, L. J., Harris, E. L., Baumgardner, T. L., Reiss, A. L., Freund, L. S., Church, R. P., Mohr, J., & Denckla, M. B. (1995). An analysis of two

discrepancy-based models and a processing-deficit approach in identifying learning disabilities. *Journal of Learning Disabilities, 28,* 18–29.

447. Schweitzer, J. B., & Sulzer-Azaroff, B. (1995). Self-control in boys with Attention Deficit Hyperactivity Disorder: Effects of added stimulation and time. *Journal of Child Psychology and Psychiatry and Allied Disciplines, 36,* 671-686.

448. Serra, M., Minderaa, R. B., van Geert, P. L. C., Jackson, A. E., Althaus, M., & Til, R. (1995). Emotional role-taking abilities of children with a pervasive developmental disorder not otherwise specified. *Journal of Child Psychology and Psychiatry and Allied Disciplines, 36,* 475-490.

449. Shaw, D. S., & Vondra, J. I. (1995). Infant attachment security and maternal predictors of early behavior problems: A longitudinal study of low-income families. *Journal of Abnormal Child Psychology, 23,* 335-357.

450. Snyder, J. J., & Patterson, G. R. (1995). Individual differences in social aggression: A test of a reinforcement model of socialization in the natural environment. *Behavior Therapy, 26,* 371–391.

451. Solomon, J., George, C., & DeJong, A. (1995). Children classified as controlling at age six: Evidence of disorganized representational strategies and aggression at home and at school. *Development and Psychopathology, 7,* 447–463.

452. Spaccarelli, S. (1995). Measuring abuse stress and negative cognitive appraisals in child sexual abuse: Validity data on two new scales. *Journal of Abnormal Child Psychology, 23,* 703–727.

453. Spaccarelli, S., & Kim, S. (1995). Resilience criteria and factors associated with resilience in sexually abused girls. *Child Abuse & Neglect, 19,* 1171–1182.

454. Speltz, M. L., DeKlyen, M., Greenberg, M. T., & Dryden, M. (1995). Clinic referral for oppositional defiant behavior: Relative significance of attachment and behavioral variables. *Journal of Abnormal Child Psychology, 23,* 487–507.

455. Stein, M. A., Szumowski, E., Blondis, T. A., & Roizen, N. J. (1995). Adaptive skills dysfunction in ADD and ADHD children. *Journal of Child Psychology and Psychiatry and Allied Disciplines, 36,* 663-670.

456. Stice, E., & Barrera, M., Jr. (1995). A longitudinal examination of the reciprocal relations between perceived parenting and adolescents' substance use and externalizing behaviors. *Developmental Psychology, 31,* 322-334.

457. Stocker, C. M. (1995). Differences in mothers' and fathers' relationships with siblings: Links with children's behavior problems. *Development and Psychopathology, 7,* 499–513.

458. Strassberg, Z. (1995). Social information processing in compliance situations by mothers of behavior-problem boys. *Child Development, 66,* 376-389.

459. Summers, J. A., Allison, D. B., Lynch, P. S., & Sandler, L. (1995). Behavior problems in Angelman syndrome. *Journal of Intellectual Disability Research, 39,* 97–106.

460. Swenson, C. C., & Kennedy, W. A. (1995). Perceived control and treatment outcome with chronic adolescent offenders. *Adolescence, 30,* 565–578.

461. Taylor, H. G., Hack, M., Klein, N., & Schatschneider, C. (1995). Achievement in children with birth weights less than 750 grams with normal cognitive abilities: Evidence for specific learning disabilities. *Journal of Pediatric Psychology, 20,* 703–719.

462. Thurber, C. A. (1995). The experience and expression of homesickness in preadolescent and adolescent boys. *Child Development, 66,* 1162–1178.

463. Tildesley, E. A., Hops, H., Ary, D., & Andrews, J. A. (1995). Multitrait-multimethod model of adolescent deviance, drug use, academic, and sexual behaviors. *Journal of Psychopathology and Behavioral Assessment, 17,* 185–215.

464. Tordjman, S., Anderson, G. M., McBride, P. A. Hertzig, M. E., Snow, M. E., Hall, L. M., Ferrari, P., & Cohen, D. J. (1995). Plasma androgens in autism. *Journal of Autism and Developmental Disorders, 25,* 295–304.

465. Treadwell, K. R. H., Flannery-Schroeder, E. C., & Kendall, P. C. (1995). Ethnicity and gender in relation to adaptive functioning, diagnostic status, and treatment outcome in children from an anxiety clinic. *Journal of Anxiety Disorders, 9,* 373-384.

466. Tucker, M. A., & Fox, R. A. (1995). Assessment of families with mildly handicapped and nonhandicapped preschoolers. *Journal of School Psychology, 33,* 29-37.

467. van den Boom, D. C. (1995). Do first-year intervention effects endure? Follow-up during toddlerhood of a sample of Dutch irritable infants. *Child Development, 66,* 1798–1816.

468. van den Oord, E. J. C. G., Koot, H. M., Boomsma, D. I., Verhulst, F. C., & Orlebeke, J. F. (1995). A twin-singleton comparison of problem behaviour in 2-3-year-olds. *Journal of Child Psychology and Psychiatry and Allied Disciplines, 36,* 449-458.

469. Vasey, M. W., Daleiden, E. L., Williams, L. L., & Brown, L. M. (1995). Biased attention in childhood anxiety disorders: A preliminary study. *Journal of Abnormal Child Psychology, 23,* 267-279.

470. Victor, S. B., & Fish, M. C. (1995). Lesbian mothers and their children: A review for school psychologists. *School Psychology Review, 24,* 456–479.

471. Vostanis, P., & Nicholls, J. (1995). Nine-month changes of maternal expressed emotion in conduct and emotional disorders of childhood: A follow-up study. *Journal of Child Psychology and Psychiatry and Allied Disciplines, 36,* 833–846.

472. Walker, L. S., Garber, J., Van Slyke, D. A., & Greene, J. W. (1995). Long-term health outcomes in patients with recurrent abdominal pain. *Journal of Pediatric Psychology, 20,* 233–245.

473. Wallander, J. L., & Venters, T. L. (1995). Perceived role restriction and adjustment of mothers of children with chronic physical disability. *Journal of Pediatric Psychology, 20,* 619–632.

474. Weine, A. M., Phillips, J. S., & Achenbach, T. M. (1995). Behavioral and emotional problems among Chinese and American children: Parent and teacher reports for ages 6 to 13. *Journal of Abnormal Child Psychology, 23,* 619–639.

475. Weisz, J. R., Chaiyasit, W., Weiss, B., Eastman, K. L., & Jackson, E. W. (1995). A multimethod study of problem behavior among Thai and American children in school: Teacher report versus direct observations. *Child Development, 66,* 402-415.

476. Worling, J. R. (1995). Adolescent sibling-incest offenders: Differences in family and individual functioning when compared to adolescent nonsibling sex offenders. *Child Abuse & Neglect, 19,* 633–643.

477. Wright, J. C., Binney, V., & Smith, P. K. (1995). Security of attachment in 8–12-year-olds: A revised version of the Separation Anxiety Test, its psychometric properties and clinical interpretations. *Journal of Child Psychology and Psychiatry and Allied Disciplines, 36,* 757–774.

478. Zahn-Waxler, C., Cole, P. M., Welsh, J. D., & Fox, N. A. (1995). Psychophysiological correlates of empathy and prosocial behaviors in preschool children with behavior problems. *Development and Psychopathology, 7,* 27-48.

479. Achenbach, T. M., & McConaughy, S. H. (1996). Relations between DSM-IV and empirically based assessment. *School Psychology Review, 25,* 329–341.

480. Acker, M. M., & O'Leary, S. G. (1996). Inconsistency of mothers' feedback and toddlers' misbehavior and negative affect. *Journal of Abnormal Child Psychology, 24,* 703–714.

481. August, G. J., Realmuto, G. M., MacDonald, A. W. III, Nugent, S. M., & Crosby, R. (1996). Prevalence of ADHD and comorbid disorders among elementary school children screened for disruptive behavior. *Journal of Abnormal Child Psychology, 24,* 571–595.

482. Baker, B. L., & Heller, T. L. (1996). Preschool children with externalizing behaviors: Experience of fathers and mothers. *Journal of Abnormal Child Psychology, 24,* 513–532.

483. Bandura, A., Barbaranelli, C., Caprara, G. V., & Pastorelli, C. (1996). Mechanisms of moral disengagement in the exercise of moral agency. *Journal of Personality and Social Psychology, 71,* 364–374.

484. Barrett, P. M., Rapee, R. M., Dadds, M. M., & Ryan, S. M. (1996). Family enhancement of cognitive style in anxious and aggressive children. *Journal of Abnormal Child Psychology, 24,* 187–203.

485. Beidel, D. C., Fink, C. M., & Turner, S. M. (1996). Stability of anxious symptomatology in children. *Journal of Abnormal Child Psychology, 24,* 257–269.

486. Bickett, L. R., Milich, R., & Brown, R. T. (1996). Attributional styles of aggressive boys and their mothers. *Journal of Abnormal Child Psychology, 24,* 457–472.

487. Boetsch, E. A., Green, P. A., & Pennington, B. F. (1996). Psychosocial correlates of dyslexia across the life span. *Development and Psychopathology, 8,* 539–562.

488. Briggs-Gowan, M. J., Carter, A. S., & Schwab-Stone, M. (1996). Discrepancies among mother, child, and teacher reports: Examining the contributions of maternal depression and anxiety. *Journal of Abnormal Child Psychology, 24,* 749–765.

489. Bronstein, P., Duncan, P., D'Ari, A., Pieniadz, J., Fitzgerald, M., Abrams, C. L., Frankowski, B., Franco, O., Hunt, C., & Oh Cha, S. Y. (1996). Family and parenting behaviors predicting middle school adjustment: A longitudinal study. *Family Relations, 45,* 415–426.

490. Butler, R. W., Rizzi, L. P., & Handwerger, B. A. (1996). Brief report: The assessment of posttraumatic stress disorder in pediatric cancer patients and survivors. *Journal of Pediatric Psychology, 21,* 499–504.

491. Campbell, S. B., Pierce, E. W., Moore, G., Marakovitz, S., & Newby, K. (1996). Boys externalizing problems at elementary school age: Pathways from early behavior problems, maternal control, and family stress. *Development and Psychopathology, 8,* 701–719.

492. Celano, M., Hazzard, A., Webb, C., & McCall, C. (1996). Treatment of traumagenic beliefs among sexually abused girls and their mothers: An evaluation study. *Journal of Abnormal Child Psychology, 24,* 1–17.

493. Chassin, L., Curan, P. J., Hussong, A. M., & Colder, C. R. (1996). The relation of parent alcoholism to adolescent substance use: A longitudinal follow-up study. *Journal of Abnormal Psychology, 105,* 70–80.

494. Contos, A. L., Gries, L. T., & Sliss, V. (1996). Correlates of therapy referral in foster children. *Child Abuse & Neglect, 20,* 921–931.

495. Deater-Deckard, K., Dodge, K. A., Bates, J. E., & Pettit, G. S. (1996). Physical discipline among African American and European American mothers: Links to children's externalizing behaviors. *Developmental Psychology, 32,* 1065–1072.

496. de Groot, A., Koot, H. M., & Verhulst, F. C. (1996). Cross-cultural generalizability of the youth self-report and teacher's report from cross-informant syndromes. *Journal of Abnormal Child Psychology, 24,* 651–664.

497. Doll, B. (1996). Prevalence of psychiatric disorders in children and youth: An agenda for advocacy by school psychology. *School Psychology Quarterly, 11,* 20–47.

498. Dukewich, T. L., Borkowski, J. G., & Whitman, T. L. (1996). Adolescent mothers and child abuse potential: An evaluation of risk factors. *Child Abuse & Neglect, 20,* 1031–1047.

499. Egeland, B., Pianta, R., & Ogawa, J. (1996). Early behavior problems: Pathways to mental disorders in adolescence. *Development and Psychopathology, 8,* 735–749.

500. El-Sheikh, M., Cummings, E. M., & Reiter, S. (1996). Preschoolers' responses to ongoing interadult conflict: The role of prior exposure to resolved versus unresolved arguments. *Journal of Abnormal Child Psychology, 24,* 665–679.

501. El-Sheikh, M., & Reiter, S. L. (1996). Children's responding to live interadult conflict: The role of form of anger. *Journal of Abnormal Child Psychology, 24,* 401–415.

502. Epkins, C. C. (1996). Cognitive specificity and affective confounding in social anxiety and dysphoria in children. *Journal of Psychopathology and Behavioral Assessment, 18,* 83–101.

503. Fahrenfort, J. J., Jacobs, E. A. M., Miedema, S., & Schweizer, A. T. (1996). Signs of emotional disturbance three years after early hospitalization. *Journal of Pediatric Psychology, 21,* 353–366.

504. Feigin, A., Kurlan, R., McDermott, M. P., Beach, J., Dimitsopulos, T., Brower, C. A., Chapieski, L., Trinidad, K., Como, P., & Jankovic, J. (1996). A controlled trial of deprenyl in children with Tourette's syndrome and attention deficit hyperactivity disorder. *Neurology, 46,* 965–968.

505. Feiring, C., & Lewis, M. (1996). Finality in the eye of the beholder: Multiple sources, multiple time point, multiple paths. *Development and Psychopathology, 8,* 721–733.

506. Forsyth, B. W. C., Horwitz, S. M., Leventhal, J. M., & Burger, J. (1996). The Child Vulnerability Scale: An instrument to measure parental perceptions of child vulnerability. *Journal of Pediatric Psychology, 21,* 89–101.

507. Fox, N. A., Schmidt, L. A., Calkins, S. D., Rubin, K. H., & Coplan, R. J. (1996). The role of frontal activation in the regulation and dysregulation of social behavior during the preschool years. *Development and Psychopathology, 8,* 89–102.

508. Hart, J., Gunnar, M., & Cicchetti, D. (1996). Altered neuroendocrine activity in maltreated children related to symptoms of depression. *Development and Psychopathology, 8,* 201–214.

509. Howard, B. L., & Kendall, P. C. (1996). Cognitive-behavioral family therapy for anxiety-disordered children: A multiple evaluation. *Cognitive Therapy and Research, 20,* 423–443.

510. Jacobsen, L. K., Giedd, J. N., Vaituzis, A. C., Hamburger, S. D., Rajapakse, J. C., Frazier, J. A., Kaysen, D., Lenane, M. C., McKenna K., Gordon, C. T., & Rapoport, J. L. (1996). Temporal lobe morphology in childhood-onset schizophrenia. *American Journal of Psychiatry, 153,* 355–361.

511. Jensen, P. S., Wantabe, H. K., Richters, J. E., Roper, M., Hibbs, E. D., Salzberg, A. D., & Liu, S. (1996). Scales, diagnoses, and child psychopathology: II. Comparing the CBCL and the DISC against external validators. *Journal of Abnormal Child Psychology, 24,* 151–168.

512. Johnston, C. (1996). Parent characteristics and parent-child interactions in families of nonproblem children and ADHD children with higher and lower levels of oppositional-defiant behavior. *Journal of Abnormal Child Psychology, 24,* 85–104.

513. Leadbeater, B. J., Bishop, S. J., & Raver, C. C. (1996). Quality of mother-toddler interactions, maternal depressive symptoms, and behavior problems in preschoolers of adolescent mothers. *Developmental Psychology, 32,* 280–288.

514. Leffert, J. S., & Siperstein, G. N. (1996). Assessment of social-cognitive processes in children with mental retardation. *American Journal on Mental Retardation, 100,* 441–455.

515. Lengua, L. J., & Sandler, I. N. (1996). Self-regulation as a moderator of the relation between coping and symptomatology in children of divorce. *Journal of Abnormal Child Psychology, 24,* 681–701.

516. Ligezinska, M., Firestone, P., Manion, I. G., McIntyre, J., Ensom, R., & Wells, G. (1996). Children's emotional and behavioral reactions following the disclosure of extrafamilial sexual abuse: Initial effects. *Child Abuse & Neglect, 20,* 111–125.

517. Manion, I. G., McIntyre, J., Firestone, P., Ligezinska, M., Ensom, R., & Wells, G. (1996). Secondary traumatization in parents following the disclosure of extrafamilial child sexual abuse: Initial effects. *Child Abuse & Neglect, 20,* 1095–1109.

518. McConaughy, S. H., & Achenbach, T. M. (1996). Contributions of a child interview to multimethod assessment of children with EBD and LD. *School Psychology Review, 25,* 24–39.

519. Mizuta, I., Zahn-Waxler, C., Cole, P. M., & Hiruma, N. (1996). Across-cultural study of preschoolers' attachment: Security and sensitivity in Japanese and U.S. dyads. *International Journal of Behavioral Development, 19,* 141–159.

520. Moore, B. D., Slopis, J. M., Schomer, D., Jackson, E. F., & Levy, B. M. (1996). Neuropsychological significance of areas of high signal intensity on brain MRI's of children with neurofibromatosis. *Neurology, 46,* 1660–1668.

521. O'Brien, B. S., & Frick, P. J. (1996). Reward dominance: Associations with anxiety, conduct problems, and psychopathy in children. *Journal of Abnormal Child Psychology, 24,* 223–240.

522. Oosterlaan, J., & Sergeant, J. A. (1996). Inhibition in ADHD, aggressive, and anxious children: A biologically based model of child psychopathology. *Journal of Abnormal Child Psychology, 24,* 19–36.

523. Pine, D. S., Wasserman, G. A., Coplan, J., Fried, J. A., Huang, Y.-Y., Kassir, S., Greenhill, L., Shaffer, D., & Parsons, B. (1996). Platelet Seratonin 2A (5-H T2A) receptor characteristics and parenting factors for boys at risk for delinquency: A preliminary report. *American Journal of Psychiatry, 153,* 538–544.

524. Power, T. J., & Ikeda, M. J. (1996). The clinical utility of behavior rating scales: Comments on the diagnostic assessment of ADHD. *Journal of School Psychology, 34,* 379–385.

525. Radcliffe, J., Bennett, D., Kazak, A. E., Foley, B., & Phillips, P. C. (1996). Adjustment in childhood brain tumor survival: Child, mother, and teacher report. *Journal of Pediatric Psychology, 21,* 529–539.

526. Roberts, R. E., Solovitz, B. L., Chen, Y. W., & Casat, C. (1996). Retest stability of DSM-III-R diagnoses among adolescents using the Diagnostic Interview Schedule for Children (DISC-2.1c). *Journal of Abnormal Child Psychology, 24,* 349–362.

527. Robins, R. W., John, O. P., Caspi, A., Moffitt, T. E., & Stouthamer-Loeber, M. (1996). Resilient, overcontrolled, and undercontrolled boys: Three replicable personality types. *Journal of Personality and Social Psychology, 70,* 157–171.

528. Rund, B. R., Oie, M., & Sundet, K. (1996). Backward-masking deficit in adolescents with schizophrenic disorders or attention deficit hyperactivity disorder. *American Journal of Psychiatry, 153,* 1154–1157.

529. Schill, M. T., Kratochwill, T. R., & Gardner, W. I. (1996). An assessment protocol for selective mutism: Analogue assessment using parents as facilitators. *Journal of School Psychology, 34,* 1–21.

530. Schuerholz, L. J., Baumgardner, T. L., Singer, H. S., Reiss, A. L., & Denckla, M. B. (1996). Neuropsychological status of children with Tourette's syndrome with and without attention deficit hyperactivity disorder. *Neurology, 46,* 958–964.

531. Schwartz, C. E., Snidman, N., & Kagan, J. (1996). Early childhood temperament as a determinant of externalizing behavior in adolescence. *Development and Psychopathology, 8,* 527–537.

532. Shaw, D. S., Owens, E. B., Vondra, J. I., Keenan, K., & Winslow, E. B. (1996). Early risk factors and pathways in the development of early disruptive behavior problems. *Development and Psychopathology, 8,* 679–699.

533. Stanger, C., MacDonald, V. V., McConaughy, S. H., & Achenbach, T. M. (1996). Predictors of cross-informant syndromes among children and youths referred for mental health services. *Journal of Abnormal Child Psychology, 24,* 597–614.

534. Stormshak, E. A., Bellanti, C. J., & Bierman, K. L. (1996). The quality of sibling relationships and the development of social competence and behavioral control in aggressive children. *Developmental Psychology, 32,* 79–89.

535. Thompson, L. L., Riggs, P. D., Mikulich, S. K., & Crowley, T. J. (1996). Contribution of ADHD symptoms to substance problems and delinquency in conduct-disordered adolescents. *Journal of Abnormal Child Psychology, 24,* 325–347.

536. van den Oord, E. J. C. G., Verhulst, F. C., & Boomsma, D. I. (1996). A genetic study of maternal and paternal ratings of problem behaviors in 3-year-old twins. *Journal of Abnormal Psychology, 105,* 349–357.

537. van der Meere, J., Gunning, W. B., & Stemerdink, N. (1996). Changing a response set in normal development and in ADHD children with and without tics. *Journal of Abnormal Child Psychology, 24,* 767–786.

538. Vermande, M. M., van den Bercken, J. H., & De Bruyn, E. E. (1996). Effects of diagnostic classification systems on clinical hypothesis-generation. *Journal of Psychopathology and Behavioral Assessment, 18,* 49–70.

539. Whiteside-Mansell, L., Pope, S. K., & Bradley, R. H. (1996). Patterns of parenting behavior in young mothers. *Family Relations, 45,* 273–281.

540. Worden, J. W., & Silverman, P. R. (1996). Parental death and the adjustment of school-age children. *Omega, 33,* 91–102.

541. Zahn-Waxler, C., Schmitz, S., Fulker, D., Robinson, J., & Emde, R. (1996). Behavior problems in 5-year-old monozygotic and dizygotic twins: Genetic and environmental influences, patterns of regulation, and internalization of control. *Development and Psychopathology, 8,* 103–122.

542. Beardslee, W. R., Versage, E. M., Wright, E. J., Salt, P., Rothberg, P. C., Drezner, K., & Gladstone, T. R. G. (1997). Examination of preventive interventions for families with depression: Evidence of change. *Development and Psychopathology, 9,* 109–130.

543. Crick, N. R. (1997). Engagement in gender normative versus nonnormative forms of aggression: Links to social-psychological adjustment. *Developmental Psychology, 33,* 610–617.

544. Feldman, M. A., & Walton-Allen, N. (1997). Effects of maternal mental retardation and poverty on intellectual, academic, and behavioral status of school-age children. *American Journal on Mental Retardation, 101,* 352–364.

545. Fisher, L., Ames, E. W., Chisholm, K., & Savoie, L. (1997). Problems reported by parents of Romanian orphans adopted to British Columbia. *International Journal of Behavioral Development, 20,* 67–82.

546. Goldsmith, H. H., Gottesman, I. I., & Lemery, K. S. (1997). Epigenetic approaches to developmental psychopathology. *Development and Psychopathology, 9,* 365–387.

547. Gottman, J. M., Guralnick, M. J., Wilson, B., Swanson, C. C., & Murray, J. D. (1997). What should be the focus of emotional regulation in children? A nonlinear dynamic mathematical model of children's peer interaction in groups. *Development and Psychopathology, 9,* 421–452.

548. Guralnick, M. J. (1997). Peer social networks of young boys with developmental delays. *American Journal on Mental Retardation, 101,* 595–612.

549. Harcovitch, S., Goldberg, S., Gold, A., Washington, J., Wasson, C., Krekewich, K., & Handley-Derry, M. (1997). Determinants of behavioural problems in Romanian children adopted in Ontario. *International Journal of Behavioral Development, 20,* 17–31.

550. Hoksbergen, R. A. C. (1997). Turmoil for adoptees during their adolescence. *International Journal of Behavioral Development, 20,* 33–46.

551. Huesmann, L. R., & Guerra, N. G. (1997). Children's normative beliefs about aggression and aggressive behavior. *Journal of Personality and Social Psychology, 72,* 408–419.

552. Hughes, J. N., Cavell, T. A., & Grossman, P. B. (1997). A positive view of self: Risk or protection for aggressive children? *Development and Psychopathology, 9,* 75–94.

553. Mathijssen, J. J. J. P., Koot, H. M., Verhulst, F. C., De Bruyn, E. E. J., & Oud, J. H. L. (1997). Family functioning and child psychopathology: Individual versus composite family scores. *Family Relations, 46,* 247–255.

554. McGee, R. A., Wolfe, D. A., & Wilson, S. K. (1997). Multiple maltreatment experiences and adolescent behavior problems: Adolescents' perspectives. *Development and Psychopathology, 9,* 131–149.

555. Mouton-Simien, P., McCain, A. P., & Kelley, M. L. (1997). The development of the toddler behavior screening inventory. *Journal of Abnormal Child Psychology, 25,* 59–64.

556. Stranger, C., Achenbach, T. M., & Verhulst, F. C. (1997). Accelerated longitudinal comparisons of aggressive versus delinquent syndromes. *Development and Psychopathology, 9,* 43–58.

Review of the Child Behavior Checklist by BETH DOLL, Associate Professor of School Psychology, University of Colorado at Denver, Denver, CO:

The Child Behavior Checklist/4–18 and 1991 Profile (CBCL/4–18) combines a 113-item behavior problems checklist with a seven-part social competency checklist. A preschool version of the checklist, the Child Behavior Checklist/2–3 (CBCL/2–3) is composed solely of a 100-item behavior problems checklist. Parental responses to both checklists provide accurate and comprehensive descriptions of their children's behavior that clinicians can use to distinguish between typical children and those having significant behavioral disturbances. Items on the behavior problems checklists are clustered into behavioral syndromes that are similar to diagnostic categories of the *Diagnostic and Statistical Manual of the American Psychiatric Association—Fourth Edition* (DSM-IV; American Psychiatric Association, 1994). Unlike the DSM diagnoses, the CBCL syndromes were entirely empirical in their derivation, based upon repeated and comprehensive analyses of parent ratings of children's behaviors. The checklists are part of a larger effort by Achenbach (1993) to create an empirical taxonomy of behavioral disturbance in which syndromes describe features of behavior that co-occur in children, and profiles represent combinations of syndromes that occur at greater than chance levels. The clinical utility of the profiles emerging from Achenbach's work is not yet well tested. Still, the CBCL checklists and syndromes have become a standard against which many other clinical decision-making tools are compared (Edelbrock & Costello, 1988).

The CBCL/4–18 is a revision of the 1983 version of the CBCL and improves upon it in several respects: The checklist was renormed on a nationally representative sample, the norms were extended to include 17- and 18-year-olds, the wording of some items was slightly modified to be inclusive of subjects as old as 18, the behavioral syndromes were reformulated to be uniform across gender and age, and titles of the syndromes were rephrased to be less provocative. In most other respects, the two versions are very much the same, and only a single problem item was revised for the 1991 checklist. This is the first publication of a CBCL/2–3 manual, although descriptions of an earlier version appeared in professional journals (Achenbach, Edelbrock, & Howell, 1987). The CBCL/4–18's behavioral taxonomy, clinical cutoff scores, and T-scores were derived from two samples of children: an exemplary sample of typical children and a less satisfactory sample of children receiving mental health services because of behavioral disturbances. The typical sample is a balanced representation of the 48 continental states with respect to SES, ethnicity, region, and urban-suburban-rural residence. Children who had re-

ceived mental health services in the previous year were excluded, leaving the sample somewhat more behaviorally adjusted than U.S. children as a group. Likewise, the CBCL/2–3's typical sample was formed from 2- and 3-year-olds living in the same homes as the CBCL/4–18 sample. In contrast, the CBCL/4–18 referred sample, a cumulative sample of all referred children used to develop the current and earlier profiles, underrepresents the Western and Southwestern regions of the United States and is predominantly (89%) white. Similarly, the referred sample of the CBCL/2–3 underrepresents the Midwestern United States and is 82% white. Because the less-representative referred samples were used to derive the scales' clinical syndromes as well as their elevated T-scores, the scales' representation of behavioral disturbances may be more appropriate to some ethnic groups or regions of the country than others.

The behavior problems checklist is the CBCL's strongest feature. Its items use simple, unambiguous words to describe the behavior problems that most concern parents and mental health professionals. With some minor exceptions, the CBCL/4–18 items are the same ones that were developed for the 1983 profile of the CBCL through a painstaking process of polling parents and professionals for item nominations and confirming item intelligibility in repeated trials. Items on the CBCL/2–3 were drawn predominantly from the checklist for older children with additional items derived from parent interviews. Item intelligibility is still a problem for 17 interview items of the CBCL/4–18 and the 12 interview items of the CBCL/2–3. These items are either nonspecific (i.e., "Strange behavior") or have a precise professional meaning that may be unfamiliar to a lay person (e.g., "Repeats certain acts over and over; compulsions" should only be endorsed when children engage in ritualistic acts that relieve the anxiety of obsessions). Users of the CBCL often overlook their responsibility for checking with parents and correcting responses when they misinterpret interview items. The need to do so merits more emphasis in the manual because failure to check these items may artificially elevate certain scales.

Items were only included on the Behavior Problems checklists if they significantly discriminated between referred and typical children. Higher behavior problems scores signify that a child has more behaviors in common with referred children and thus is more likely to be behaviorally disordered. This is counterintuitive to most users' expectations that higher scores signify a more severe "case" of the disorder and that confusion leads to frequent misinterpretations of the scores. Behavioral syndromes were derived from a principal components analysis of the behavior problems of referred children, and syndrome titles were assigned based on each syndromes' item content. The 1991 titles are more carefully phrased than were the 1983 syndrome titles (e.g., "Hostile Withdrawal" has been renamed simply "Withdrawn").

Where these empirically derived syndromes do not converge with the diagnostic categories of the DSM-IV, the exceptions represent the new understandings of behavioral disorders (Achenbach, 1993). Still, an artifact of the factor analytic origins of the syndromes is that their titles, although appropriate to group patterns of behavior, may not be accurate for a particular child's individual profile. For example, a child could be given a rating at the 98th percentile on the Withdrawn scale with endorsements of "secretive," "stares," "sulks," and "underactive," yet this particular combination of behaviors is not necessarily an example of withdrawn behavior. Users interpreting individual profiles will need to examine carefully the meaning of a syndrome score given the items endorsed for that child.

For each syndrome, standardized T-scores were based upon a composite of typical and referred norms. Below $T = 70$, scores were assigned based on the norms of typical children and scores above $T = 70$ were derived from norms of referred children. Because most typical children received few problem endorsements, the scale makes only minimal distinctions among different levels of normalcy and problem behaviors scores do not extend below the mean. The resulting syndrome scores on both the CBCL/4–18 and the CBCL/2–3 are moderately reliable with one-week test-retest reliabilities generally falling above .8 and internal consistency coefficients averaging .8. Still, like all behavioral rating scales, the reliability of the syndrome scores depends heavily upon the raters, and interparent agreement coefficients average a very modest .66 on the CBCL/4–18 and somewhat lower on the CBCL/2–3. At this level of reliability, profiles of high and low syndrome scores must be interpreted with caution because differences among syndromes may reflect rater variations rather than true differences in the child. On both scales, the reliability of composite behavior problems scores (Internalizing, Externalizing, and Total Problems scores) is exemplary with internal consistency and one-week test-retest coefficients above .89. Thus, practitioners should generally rely on the composite scores to support diagnostic or treatment decisions.

The Competence Scale of the CBCL/4–18 presents special problems. Most typical children scored very high on the Competence items, and its scores start at $T = 55$ and go lower. T-scores below 33 were derived from the referred sample with the paradoxical result that the CBCL/4–18's Competence scores do a better job of discriminating among degrees of incompetence than of competence. Likewise, the reliability of the competence checklist is less satisfactory. The internal consistency reliabilities of the subscales hover around .5, although the test-retest reliabilities and interparent agreement coefficients were similar to those of the Behavior Problems checklist. In a similar way, only the composite competence score has the exemplary reliability necessary to support clinical decision making.

Directions for hand scoring the CBCL are included in the manual, but hand scoring is highly tedious and most examiners make at least one or two minor errors on every protocol. It is easy to misrecord items because they do not transfer in sequence to the profile form and sometimes load on more than one scale. Moreover, the Internalizing and Externalizing composites are not a simple total of their respective syndromes. CBCL users are well-advised to purchase the computer-scoring program for more facile and accurate scoring. The CBCL manuals should emphasize this option to users.

CBCL/4–18 is intended to be one component of a broad, multi-informant assessment of a child's behavioral adjustment. In addition to the parent rating form (the CBCL/4–18), Achenbach has developed parallel Youth Self-Report and Teacher Report forms with 89 items common to all three checklists. Using separate principal components analyses, the combined pool of items was divided into eight syndromes of a cross-informant scale. Results of this analysis are highly similar but not identical to those conducted for each separate checklist. The converged ratings from cross-informant analyses have the potential to support clinical decisions that are far more reliable and less rater-dependent than those from any single checklist. Because of the complexity of their derivation, scores for this multi-axial behavior rating scale are only available through the computer-scoring program. Their availability is one of the essential strengths of the CBCL/4–18. Significant and meaningful correlations between the CBCL and other behavior rating scales are well-documented in Achenbach and Brown (1991).

One difficulty in interpreting these studies is that the CBCL is acknowledged generally to be a criterion measure for evaluating the validity of most behavior problems checklists, and low correlations with related scales are generally attributed to less satisfactory aspects of the other scales. Thus, the most convincing evidence of the CBCL's validity is its demonstrated relationship to clinical diagnoses, referral for behavioral disturbances, and poor social outcomes, all described briefly in the checklist's manual. In many respects the development of the CBCL checklists has been one long validity study, extending from the mid-1960s into the present, deriving an empirically defensible description of the behaviors that distinguish between children with and without behavioral disturbances.

SUMMARY. The CBCL is essentially an empirically derived research instrument that has become recognized as an important clinical tool. Its origins in empiricism represent both its greatest strength and its most striking weaknesses. Its empirical development provides the CBCL with an impressive accumulation of validity information.

Simultaneously, its empirical roots predispose it to be an occasionally awkward clinical tool. The scale's clinical utility is diminished by the CBCL's tedious and error-prone hand-scoring procedures, rather limited assessment of behavioral competence, duplication of items across some scales, and minor misalignments with the DSM-IV diagnostic categories. When these features are especially important, practitioners might want to consider using the Behavior Assessment System for Children instead (BASC; Reynolds & Kamphaus, 1991; 34). Like the CBCL, the BASC is a broad, well-standardized behavioral rating survey having parallel forms for parent, teacher, and students. The reliabilities of the two scales are very similar. However, because it was developed as a clinical assessment tool, the BASC is more closely linked to the DSM definitions of behavioral disturbances. More importantly, the BASC's competence scales are lengthier and more reliable than those of the CBCL. Still, the BASC's empirical validity research is nowhere near as extensive as that of the CBCL, leaving the latter the preferred behavioral rating scale for most research purposes and certain clinical purposes.

REVIEWER'S REFERENCES

Achenbach, T. M., Edelbrock, C., & Howell, C. T. (1987). Empirically based assessment of the behavioral/emotional problems of 2- and 3-year-old children. *Journal of Abnormal Child Psychology, 15*, 629–650.

Edelbrock, C., & Costello, A. J. (1988). Convergence between statistically derived behavior problem syndromes and child psychiatric diagnoses. *Journal of Abnormal Child Psychology, 16*, 219–231.

Achenbach, T. M., & Brown, J. S. (1991). *Bibliography of published studies using the Child Behavior Checklist and related materials: 1991 edition.* Burlington, VT: University of Vermont Department of Psychiatry.

Reynolds, C. R., & Kamphaus, R. W. (1992). Behavior Assessment System for Children. Circle Pines, MN: American Guidance Services.

Achenbach, T. M. (1993). Implications of multiaxial empirically based assessment for behavior therapy with children. *Behavior Therapy, 24*, 91–116.

American Psychiatric Association. (1994). *Diagnostic and statistical manual of mental disorders* (4th ed.). Washington, DC: Author.

Review of the Child Behavior Checklist by MICHAEL J. FURLONG, Associate Professor, Graduate School of Education, and MICHELLE WOOD, Researcher, Graduate School of Education, University of California, Santa Barbara, Santa Barbara, CA:

The Child Behavior Checklist (CBCL/4–18), a general measure of child and adolescent emotional and behavioral problems, is designed to be completed by parents and parent surrogates (including adoptive parents, foster parents, or other adults who live with the child such as care workers in residential settings). The CBCL/4–18 is part of an integrative web of assessment tools including: (a) the preschool version CBCL/2–3; (b) the Teacher Report Form (TRF); (c) the Youth Self-Report (YSR); (d) the Direct Observation Form (DOF); and (e) the Semistructured Clinical Interview for Children (SCIC). Achenbach (1991) advocates that the information from the profile should be integrated with other data such as observations in natural settings, interviews, standardized tests of abilities, medical diagnostic procedures, and self-reports to provide a comprehensive "multiaxial" picture of the child. Because the YSR and TRF were developed from the CBCL/4–18 and share 89 common items, they provide critical supplementary information from additional informants. Considering these tools have also been especially well validated in empirical research, it is advised that professionals utilize all three of these checklists as an integrative unit where appropriate for the age of the youth.

1991 VERSION. Although the pre-1991 scales were normed for youths ages 4 to 16 years, the 1991 edition contains national norms through the age of 18. Some small changes in wording (mainly deletion of the words "child" and "children" to make the instrument more appropriate for 17- to 18-year-olds) were made in the 1991 edition, but these do not affect the scoring. In fact, all pre-1991 editions can be scored using the 1991 profile.

Some of the syndrome subscales have changed in content or name. A syndrome designated as "Cruel" was included in the pre-1991 profiles for 6- to 11- and 12- to 16-year-old girls. Some evidence of a similar syndrome was found in the factor analyses of girls for the 1991 profile, but it was inconsistent among analyses for 4- to 5-, 6- to 11-, and 12- to 18-year-old girls. Because most of the items were also on the Aggressive syndrome scale, Cruel was not retained in the 1991 profile. Other syndrome subscale names were changed from the previous psychiatric terms or labels to more descriptive categories: for instance, the Schizoid and Obsessive-Compulsive scales are now called Thought Problems; the Unpopular syndrome on the pre-1991 TRF and YSR has been renamed Social Problems; and the Nervous-Overactive and Inattentive syndromes are called Attention Problems.

Correlations between the raw scores on the pre-1991 and 1991 counterpart scales for referred and nonreferred samples of youths were generally in the .90s, indicating that youths would produce very similar patterns of results using the two versions. However, t tests showed significant differences between the absolute magnitude of scores obtained by the same youths on most of the pre-1991 and 1991 versions, reflecting the differences between the scales in the number and content of their items. Thus, a scale score on the earlier version is not necessarily equivalent to the same score on the 1991 counterpart. Due to these differences and improvements in the versions, it is advised that interested users obtain the latest versions and all supporting materials.

ADMINISTRATION. The instructions for the CBCL/4–18 state that the parents should respond to the items based on their child's behavior "now or within the past 6 months." No empirical evidence is cited to justify this time frame, yet the manual (Achenbach, 1991) does state that, compared to shorter rating periods such as 3 months, "the standard 6-month rating period may pick up a few more reports of low frequency but important and memorable behaviors, such as suicide attempts, running away from home, and firesetting" (p. 75). On the CBCL/2–3, respondents are instructed to rate the child on each item that describes the child now or within the previous 2 months. The 2-month rating period was chosen "to take account of the rapid changes characterizing ages 2 to 3" (Achenbach, 1992, p. 3). Related materials use similar timeframes: The TRF is based on the teacher's perceptions of the child's behavior in the classroom within the preceding 2 months; the YSR is based on the child's self-perceptions of behavior within the past 6 months. But whether these time periods were chosen for empirical reasons or are more arbitrary in nature is unclear. Further research or clarification in the manual should discuss whether the appearance of a specific behavior for 6 months may constitute a trait or a condition (dependent on the child's developmental status) and, in this

context, whether this time frame is a suitable measurement period to determine outcome-based research. The use of different time frames for the CBCL/4–18 and the TRF may also contribute to the generally low levels of parent-teacher agreement found in research (Stanger & Lewis, 1993).

In a similar vein, there is a short discussion in the manual concerning the phenomenon of "practice effects" on the CBCL/4–18. The tendency for problem scores to decline over brief test-retest intervals (about 7 days) has been documented on this instrument and others, although the declines in the CBCL/4–18 were small (2% of the variance in scale scores). Practically, however, the mean decrease in problem scale scores was 10.7% from a Time 1 to Time 2, with mean scores significantly declining on the following scales: the Withdrawn, Anxious/Depressed, Attention, Internalizing, and Total Problems subscales for boys; the Somatic Complaints, Anxious/Depressed, Aggressive Behavior, Internalizing, Externalizing, and Total Problems subscales for girls. Although a 7-day interval would most likely be deemed inappropriate for any posttest analysis, and 6 of these 11 documented declines may be due to chance alone, it is important to recognize this could be the result of routine regression toward the mean in subscale scores when using the CBCL/4–18 for outcome-based research, at least over brief time periods.

RESPONSE SCALE. The checklist uses a three-option response scale (0/1/2) for each problem item: 0 = *not true of their child*; 1 = *somewhat or sometimes true*; and 2 = *very true or often true*. Although Achenbach and associates have documented that more finely gradiented response scales do not increase discriminative power of ratings of emotional and behavioral problems (Achenbach & Edelbrock, 1978; Achenbach, Howell, Quay, & Conners, 1991), the response scale may be contextually challenging for particular problem items. The three-option scale, although convenient and economical, assumes that these responses are equally meaningful for all items. For some items of extreme concern and lower prevalence (e.g., "cruel to animals"), a youth may only have to exhibit this behavior once or twice in the preceding 6 months to receive a rating of 2; whereas for a behavior of higher prevalence and less developmental concern (e.g., "cries a lot"), a child may have to exhibit this behavior one to two times a day to get the highest rating. Therefore, it is important to think about responses in context of the items, to do a thorough item-by-item analysis during scoring and interpretation, and to consider that each item is weighed equally in subscale scores. Clinically, administrators may want to get a sense of the caregivers' understanding of these categories in terms of their implied frequency and tolerance/intolerance of the specific behaviors.

CONTENT AND SCORING. The scoring profile for the CBCL/4–18 includes: (a) three competence scales (Activities, Social, and School); (b) a total competence scale score; (c) eight syndrome scales (Aggressive Behavior, Attention Problems, Delinquent Behavior, Social Problems, Somatic Complaints, Thought Problems, Anxious/Depressed, and Withdrawn); (d) an Internalizing problem scale score; (e) an Externalizing problem scale score; and (f) a Total problem scale score. Raw scores and their corresponding T scores for each subscale may be hand-tallied and graphed on a profile using templates, or computer-scoring programs may be purchased that will score the profiles based on key-entered or machine-read forms. The hand-scoring templates are well constructed and easy to use, but it is imperative for users to be well acquainted with the manual's procedures. For example, administrators must be cognizant of the appropriate forms to be used for a child's sex, that competence scales are not scored for 4- to 5-year-olds, and that T scores must be computed with respect to the age of the child being scored (4 to 11 or 12 to 18).

A few notes of caution about scoring the profiles deserve recognition. Twenty items on the CBCL/4–18 are scored rather subjectively. When parents' descriptions of the behaviors indicate to the administrator that they have rated an item inappropriately or scored more than one item for the same behavior, administrators must use proper discretion to adjust the scoring. For example, if a parent were to mark a "2" on Item #66 (*compulsions*) indicating that a child "runs away from home" and additionally scores Item #67 (*runs away from home*) with "2," administrators must rescore Item #66 as a "0." An appendix contained in the manual (Achenbach, 1991) is very specific about which items require special scoring attention, but in practice, raters may not always do this. Proper use requires a thorough review of all item responses prior to any hand or computer scoring. The Thought Problems syndrome scale is especially affected by the subjective scoring procedures because it contains a majority of items that call for administrator clarification of parents' responses.

Another issue is that the scoring procedures do not provide error bands. Error bands could poten-

tially communicate the magnitude of errors of measurement based on the confidence intervals of each subscale's reliability, thereby highlighting the fluctuations that are known to characterize any test score. Achenbach (1991) reports that the standard errors of measurement are generally small and that, on the average, the range of scores represented by a particular score is relatively narrow. Nonetheless, routine application of bands of error to CBCL/4–18 scores would encourage less rigid interpretation of the actual values earned and help to thwart misinterpretation.

NORMS. Normative data for the CBCL/4-18 competence and problem scales were drawn from a subset of youths without disabilities in a national sample assessed in 1989. These 2,368 children were chosen to be representative of the 48 contiguous states with respect to ethnicity, SES, geographical region, and urban-suburban-rural residence. The normative sample was constructed by drawing from a pool of 4- to 18-year-olds all children who had not received professional help for behavioral/emotional problems within the preceding 12 months; thus, they are termed the "nonreferred" group as compared to the "referred" sample who had received referral for mental health services or special education classes for behavioral/emotional problems within the year. Demographic distribution tables are contained in the manual, and the normative sample is composed of approximately 73% Caucasian, 16% African American, 7% Latino, and 3% other ethnicities, and a slightly high representation from middle class SES and southern region respondents. In about 82% of the cases, the child's mother was the respondent. The CBCL/2–3 is not equivalent to its older sibling the CBCL/4–18, because it has only recently been created, has limited empirical information to support its factor structure, and has a small norm sample (just 368).

The authors recognize that there are some debatable issues with the chosen normative population. The referral criterion used to distinguish the two samples (nonreferred vs. referred) may fail to exclude children who have significant problems that have not received professional attention (the in-process-of-being referred children). Due to this inevitable error variance in the definition of the population, it is not that unusual for an "unhealthy" youth to receive scores in the normal to borderline range, even though the CBCL/4–18 has been shown to discriminate well between referred and nonreferred children on most of the scale scores. The checklist identifies extreme behavioral and emotional problems better than moderate or mild problems because it is not sensitive to the transition from normal to moderate problems. In fact, false-negative statistics show that 17.7% of the youths are considered "normal" when they are actually from the clinical, referred population. Therefore, all elevated scores merit follow-up; and a few youths who have CBCL/4–18 below the clinical range may still need professional services for emotional and behavioral concerns.

Some research has brought into question the normative findings of the nonclinical standardization sample. For example, Sandberg, Meyer-Bahlburg, and Yager (1991) found that the mean total behavior problem scores in a community sample of 530 parents of 6- to 10-year-olds who completed the CBCL/4–18 were dramatically higher than the norm group. In addition, the researchers found significant race/ethnicity effects in their male subsample. These results raise doubts about the appropriateness of using the CBCL/4–18 norms as a yardstick for sample comparisons. Establishing local norms within a community may be critical when using the CBCL/4–18 for widespread research and outcome-based studies, particularly with diverse populations.

RELIABILITY. Whichever form of reliability or stability is used, the CBCL/4–18 fares quite favorably. Across all age/gender groups, including the preschool version (CBCL/2–3), the internal consistencies of the Externalizing and Total Problems scores were in the .92 to .96 range, and the reliability of the Internalizing scale was nearly as strong, .88 to .92. Among the syndrome scales, the internal consistency of the Aggressive scale was strong, .92 for all age/gender groups. Adequate reliability indices are reported in the manual for the Anxious-Depressed (.86 to .88 for CBCL/4–18) and Attention (.83 to .84) scales.

Users are cautioned that the reliability of the Thought Problems syndrome scale is inadequate (lower than .70 across age/gender groups). This is likely attributable to the fact that all of the items on the cross-informant version of this scale require the administrator to use the subjective scoring procedures described above. The Sex Problems syndrome scale for ages 4 to 11 also has inadequate internal consistency (.54 for girls and .56 for boys), and given its mixed content, should be interpreted quite cautiously and always contextualized so that parents and others do not react inappropriately to its label.

The Social Competence scale is a commendable attempt to integrate strength-based assessment content into the CBCL/4–18 (this scale is not included in the CBCL/2–3). Unfortunately, it requires additional development as shown by the low internal consistency coefficients of .57 to .64 across age/gender groups. Within the Social Competence scale, the Activities subscale has clearly inadequate internal consistency estimates (.42 to .54).

VALIDITY. The CBCL/4–18 is the standard in the field of child psychopathology against which the validity of other instruments is often measured. For this reason, it is somewhat difficult to assess its validity using traditional measures of concurrent validity. Nonetheless, Achenbach provides multiple indices that demonstrate high concurrent correlations with related instruments (e.g., Conners' Parent Rating Scale and the Quay Problem Behavior Checklist) and strong discriminant validity as demonstrated by the ability of the Total Problems and Social Competence scores, alone and in combination, to appropriately classify matched groups of referred and nonreferred youths. Youths who obtain Total Problem T-scores above 75 are extremely likely (greater than 95%) to be from a referred sample. The CBCL/4–18 results in relatively few false positives compared with false negatives regardless of the classification algorithm used. However, even in a nonreferred sample, 30% of the youths obtained a score in the clinical range on either the Total Competence or the Total Problems scales. As is true of most rating scales, the scores that are the most stable and highly associated with youths' emotional and behavioral problems are the broad band Internalizing, Externalizing, and the Total Problems scores. Individual syndrome subscales should be interpreted cautiously.

AREAS OF STRENGTHS. The CBCL/4–18 and the CBCL/2–3 are critical components of a complex, evolving, and continually improving assessment package that has clearly become a collection of benchmark instruments. Over 1,700 empirical studies have employed one or more of these instruments, the assessment package has gained international recognition, and it has also been used in national evaluation studies such as the Fort Bragg and the Center for Mental Health Services system of care projects. Consequently, the measurements are endorsed and validated by hundreds of researchers and have been translated into 50 different languages (translated versions should be carefully checked for appropriate local use). As a research and descriptive tool, the CBCL/4–18 is unquestionably the most well articulated and well established of its kind. In addition, the materials associated with the assessment tools (i.e., manuals, scoring procedures, reports, computer programs) are easy to use, in language appropriate for both professionals and non-professionals, and very affordable. The authors of this integrative package should be applauded for their efforts to continually improve the efficiency and practicality of these instruments while also avoiding unnecessary commercial ventures that hike up prices.

AREAS OF CONCERN. Despite the fact that the CBCL/4–18 is accepted as the premiere instrument of parent-reported emotional and behavioral problems of their children, there are some important weaknesses of the assessment tool that need to be recognized.

The Achenbach instruments lack a strength-based approach: There is a great need to develop the Social Competence scales more completely. Although the CBCL/4–18 Social Competence portion purports to measure positive aspects (strengths) of a youth's behavior, it falls short of this objective. It would be more accurate to label this scale "social incompetence" because its norms differentiate among low competence much more effectively than high competence. If the CBCL instruments neglect to demonstrate more strengths on the social/emotional level, they will inevitably fail to meet new expectations in the fields of ecological, strength-based assessment.

Achenbach (1991, p. 237) maintains that in the desire "to restrict the CBCL/4–18 to items that are meaningful in themselves," items designed to detect social desirability sets or lying were not added. Although this desire to maintain face validity is quite important, it is our opinion that there is a greater need to avoid the situation where the scale is perceived as vulnerable to raters' potential impulses and deceptions, a condition that is very important, for example, in research involving juvenile offenders who might be motivated to minimize their problems. Notwithstanding these issues, the CBCL/4–18 continues to be the standard for other broad band parent rating scales.

REVIEWERS' REFERENCES

Achenbach, T. M., & Edelbrock, C. S. (1978). The classification of child psychopathology: A review and analysis of empirical efforts. *Psychological Bulletin, 85,* 1275–1301.

Achenbach, T. M. (1991). *Manual for the Child Behavior Checklist/4–18 and the 1991 Profile.* Burlington, VT: University of Vermont Department of Psychiatry.

Achenbach, T. M., Howell, C. T., Quay, H. C., & Conners, C. K. (1991). National survey of problems and competencies among 4- to 16-year-olds: Parents' reports for normative and clinical samples. *Monographs of the Society for Research in Child Development, 56*(3), Ser. No. 225.

Sandberg, D. E., Meyer-Bahlburg, H. F. L., & Yager, T. J. (1991). The Child Behavior Checklist nonclinical standardization samples: Should they be utilized as norms? *Journal of the American Academy of Child and Adolescent Psychiatry, 30*(1), 124–134.

Achenbach, T. M. (1992). *Manual for the Child Behavior Checklist/2–3 and the 1992 Profile.* Burlington, VT: University of Vermont Department of Psychiatry.

Stanger, C., & Lewis, M. (1993). Agreement among parents, teachers, and children on internalizing and externalizing behavior problems. *Journal of Clinical Child Psychology, 22*(1), 107–115.

[56]
Child Development Inventory.

Purpose: "Designed to provide systematic ways of obtaining in-depth developmental information from parents."

Population: Ages 1–3 to 6–3.

Publication Dates: 1968–1992.

Acronym: CDI.

Scores, 9: Social, Self Help, Gross Motor, Fine Motor, Expressive Language, Language Comprehension, Letters, Numbers, General Development.

Administration: Individual.

Price Data, 1993: $55 per complete set including 10 test booklets, 25 answer sheets, 25 CDI profiles, and manual ('92, 44 pages) with scoring template; $13 per 10 test booklets; $9 per 25 answer sheets; $9 per 25 CDI profiles; $25 per manual with scoring template; $27 per specimen set.

Time: [30–50] minutes.

Comments: Formerly called the Minnesota Child Development Inventory.

Author: Harold Ireton.

Publisher: Behavior Science Systems, Inc.

Cross References: See T4:436 (14 references); for a review of an earlier edition by Jane A. Rysberg, see 9:712; see also T3:1492 (6 references); for a review by William L. Goodwin, see 8:220 (3 references).

Review of the Child Development Inventory by JEAN POWELL KIRNAN, Associate Professor of Psychology, and DIANA CRESPO, Research Assistant, Trenton State College, Trenton, NJ:

The Child Development Inventory (CDI) was developed in 1992 as a replacement for the Minnesota Child Development Inventory (MCDI). The purpose of the inventory has remained the same: the involvement of the parent(s) in the collection of information for the purpose of identifying and assessing children for developmental problems. The need for parental involvement is obvious in that they provide a unique perspective of the child in environments and situations not observable to teachers and other professionals. Additionally, the involvement of the parent(s) at the assessment stage eases the way for involvement in later stages should remediation be warranted.

The CDI differs from the MCDI in several ways: (a) the addition of items to increase comprehensiveness of the inventory; (b) deletion of poor items; (c) update and improvement of the normative sample; and (d) modification of the dimensions that are measured. Specifically, the Situation Comprehension and Personal-Social scales were dropped. Three scales (Letters, Numbers, and Social) were added, as well as 30 problem items related to health and growth. Thus, the CDI provides a user with eight scale scores (Social, Self-Help, Gross Motor, Fine Motor, Expressive Language, Language Comprehension, Letters, and Numbers), a General Development score, and a checklist of problems. Additionally, the MCDI covered ages 1 to 6 years whereas the CDI covers ages 15 months to 6 years.

The items for the CDI trace their development back to the MCDI. Approximately 2,000 statements were developed through a survey of the literature and psychological tests for preschool-age children. These were then reduced to 673 on the basis of whether the statement: (a) described developmental skills in children; (b) was observable by parents; (c) was descriptive and clear; and (d) was potentially age discriminating.

These 673 items were then further reduced on the basis of their age discriminating power. Age discrimination was determined by analyzing the responses of a group of white children ($N = 887$ for the MCDI and $N = 568$ for CDI). Items that showed an increasing percentage passing with increasing age were selected. These data were also used to determine the age level of the items. Age level was defined as the age at which at least 75% of the parents had answered "Yes."

The CDI yields separate scores on eight scales along with a measure of general development. The author states the scales were not derived through factor analysis. It is unclear exactly how the scales were determined. At a minimum, the use of a panel of subject matter experts (SMEs), consisting of educators, child development professionals, and parents, would support the integrity of the scales. Most of the items appear face valid; however, there are some troubling issues. For example, two of the items in the Social scale refer to playing a game with rules. This might be perceived as a social or a cognitive skill. Additionally, several of the scales have very few items in the higher age groups. From age 4 to age 6 and 1/2, there are only three additional items in the Social scale. Again the development of the items and scales without the input of several experts leaves the instrument open to criticism.

A major criticism of the MCDI still characteristic of the CDI is the normative sample. The normative sample for the CDI consists of 568 primarily white children from a working-class neighborhood in Minneapolis-Saint Paul. The lack of geographical, socioeconomic, and ethnic diversity is disturbing. Additionally, no date is given as to the year when data were collected.

The author recognizes the restrictive nature of the sample but suggests the behaviors measured are descriptive of most children in the country. Again, the opinion of objective SMEs would strengthen this claim. The development of local norms is suggested for any user who is working with children who differ substantially from the normative group. However, the determination of "substantial differences" is left to the reader.

Completion of the CDI requires that the parent possess a good command of the English language (a 7th to 8th grade reading level). Should there be difficulty in understanding the items or otherwise completing the form, the author suggests the use of the Child Development Review (CDR), which is an interview alternative to the CDI. Such advice should not be given without providing data on the comparability of the two instruments, the CDI and the CDR.

The Child Development Inventory is administered in a reusable booklet with a separate optically scannable answer sheet. Background information about the child and family is requested on the answer sheet.

There are 300 items on the test; however, there are 320 available spaces on the answer sheet. The instruction booklet explains that the test was trimmed, yet, the answer sheet was not. The questions themselves are divided into different categories dealing with various abilities. Despite this division, the items within each category are not ordered chronologically. For example, a question about jumping over objects with two feet might be followed by an item assessing the ability to sit without being aided.

The respondent answers according to whether the child partakes in the activity. Respondents answer either "Yes" or "No" to the items. The author instructs the test-taker to respond "No" if the child does not engage in the activity, has just begun to engage in the activity, or only engages in the activity sometimes. A "Yes" response should be indicated when the child currently demonstrates the activity or used to engage in the activity.

Some of the questions are vague. For example, one item questions if the child directs other children. It is unclear if this is intended in a helpful manner or in a negative, directive fashion. Interpretation by the reader could leave various respondents with a different understanding of the item. The result would be that the test-takers are answering different questions.

There is a potential problem for leniency in responses. The respondents, normally parents, may be hesitant to admit to difficulties faced by their child. The use of a wider response range than the dichotomous "yes/no" might allow for a perception of greater flexibility in responding. A 3-point or 5-point scale ranging from "rarely" to "frequently" might increase response accuracy. Finally, a social desirability scale could be added to identify "suspicious" forms.

The administration is approximately 40 minutes. However, this does not include the scoring. The scoring of the test takes about 25 minutes and is accomplished by placing a template, which is provided, over the scantron sheet. The score for each section is simply the number of "Yes" responses for that section. The General Development score is derived by adding the "Yes" responses to select items representing each of the separate scales.

The score for each of the eight scales is then plotted on a separate CDI profile sheet. A line signifying the child's age is drawn. This is accomplished after completing an age calculation described in the manual. The chronological age line serves as a high point. Those areas that exceed this line are the situations in which the child excels. Using a table in the manual, the examiner then marks the age levels that are 25% and 30% below the child's chronological age. These age guides provide a lower boundary for the norm. It allows the person interpreting the results to be easily aware of the problem areas for the child. Those scales that dip below the 30% line (known as delay scores) should be of concern to the test taker.

The test author states that often children age 4 or older achieve a delay score due to the fact that so few items exist in some of the scales at these age levels. In these cases, one is directed to look to other evidence to support or refute this finding. This shortcoming suggests that certain scales are not valid for these upper age groups.

Interpretation of the problem items is nonsystematic at best. This scale is not scored and appears on the profile in a format for the user to "mark" those problems identified by the respondent. Frequency with which these problems were endorsed by the normative group is presented by sex and age in Table 6 in the manual. However, the utility of these data is questionable. The author reports that the frequency of problems cited for 5-year-olds is rela-

tively low, probably due to the fact that parents of this age group were given the option of responding to this section of the questionnaire. Additionally, one problem was endorsed by more than 50% of the respondents. The author suggests that this may not be a problem but a "challenge" to parents. Why, then, is it still included? Could there be other statements that may not necessarily indicate problem areas? Again, the inclusion of a panel of experts would help resolve some of these issues.

The author notes the MCDI used separate male and female norms for scoring; however, the CDI uses combined norms. The problem with this attempt to achieve simplicity is that the gender differences still exist. The difference between this test and the former is that now the administrator has to keep in mind that the differences are there. In the user's manual, gender differences are listed by item within scales for 32 items. It is unclear how the user is to take these differences into account when interpreting the scores.

The reliability of the CDI was demonstrated using Cronbach's coefficient alpha measure of internal consistency. Coefficients were calculated for the separate scales at each age level and demonstrate a wide range from .33 to .96. Within each scale, the lower coefficients tend to appear in the higher age groups reflective of the previously noted problem of few additional items in these ages. This problem raises the question of the validity of these measures for the older ages. No measures of test-retest reliability are presented.

The validity of the CDI was assessed in a variety of ways. Measures of developmental traits may be analyzed for their relationship with age. According to theory, scores on the trait should increase with age; thus, a positive relationship should exist whereby the mean score increases for each scale as age increases. The author presents data that partially supports the developmental nature of the scales.

A study of 132 kindergarten students demonstrated a relationship between CDI scores and scores on math and reading skills tests. Although some of these correlations were nonsignificant, the Expressive Language, Language Comprehension, Letters, Numbers, and General Development scales all showed significant correlations with both skills tests in the range of .31 to .69.

Intercorrelations are also presented. The high correlations between scales in some age groups suggest that the scales are not measuring unique developmental factors. For example, in the lowest age group (2 to 2 and 1/2 years old), the Number scale correlates .82 and .84 with Expressive Language and Language Comprehension, respectively, Again, the lack of factor analysis in scale development and the small number of items in the lower age group raise questions about the validity of the CDI Number scale in young children.

Too many issues are left to the user to decide: accuracy of parental responses, interpretation of gender differences, interpretation of the problem items, validity of the scales at different ages, and the usefulness of the normative sample. Additionally, the lack of objective decision making via statistical means or by use of a panel of judges in the item writing, item selection, and scale development raises issues regarding the comprehensiveness of the scales. Norms are nonrepresentative and reliability and validity statistics support the weaknesses in higher age groups for some scales and lower age groups for others. The availability of other instruments (such as the Battelle Developmental Inventory [T4:263; reviewed by Harrington, 1985]) with greater reliability and validity, representative norms, and clearer interpretation of results, leave these reviewers unable to recommend the CDI.

REVIEWERS' REFERENCE

Harrington, R. G. (1985). [Review of the Battelle Developmental Inventory.] In D. J. Keyser & R. C. Sweetland (Eds.), *Test critiques*, (vol. 2). Kansas City, MO: Test Corporation of America.

Review of the Child Development Inventory by STEPHANIE STEIN, Associate Professor of Psychology, Central Washington University, Ellensburg, WA:

The Child Development Inventory (CDI) is a questionnaire intended to identify developmental concerns in children ages "15 months to six years of age and for older children who are judged to be functioning in the one to six-year range" (manual, p. 2). The questionnaire consists of 270 developmental items and 30 problem items that address parental concerns about the hearing, vision, health, behavior, and emotional development of their child. The parent responds to each developmental item by marking a YES or NO and by marking a YES next to any relevant problem item. The author suggests the questionnaire requires a seventh to eighth grade reading level.

The CDI is a 1992 revision of the Minnesota Child Development Inventory (MCDI). According to the author, the changes in the newly revised inventory include (a) a revision of items to make them more comprehensive and to "eliminate poor items" (p. 2), and (b) more contemporary norms. The author also states that the CDI is "simpler and easier to use" (p. 2), although he does not explain what makes it so. In addition, the scales of the CDI have been reformulated from the MCDI, eliminating the scale Situation Comprehension and restructuring the Comprehension-Conceptual scale into three scales called Language Comprehension, Letters, and Numbers. Finally, the CDI has 30 problem items, which do not make up a scale and are not normed but are intended to "complement the results from the inventory scales" (p. 3). The manual for the CDI is well written and sufficiently detailed in the description of the items within each scale and the scoring procedures. Several case examples are given to help the examiner understand how to interpret the results.

The author explains that the items for the MCDI were selected from 2,000 initial items developed through reviews of the literature and relevant tests as well as generated by the author to fill in "gaps in the literature" (p. 2). After reducing the item pool to 673 statements, the "age discriminating power of these items was then determined on an item validation sample of 887 white children" (p. 2) who were roughly equal between the sexes and ranged in age from 1 month to 6 and a half years. An age level was assigned to each item, indicating "the age at which at least 75 percent of parents answered YES to the statement" (p. 2). Unfortunately, the author does not explain how the new CDI items were developed, only that they "included most of the MCDI items" (p. 2). A review of the items by age grouping indicates there are relatively few items at the older ages (above 5 years). Finally, in developing the nine inventory scales, the author made the questionable decision to forgo factor analysis. Consequently, the moderate to high scale intercorrelations suggest the individual scales may not necessarily be measuring distinctly different skills.

The reliability data presented for the CDI consist of Cronbach's alpha internal consistency correlations for each scale by age grouping. The coefficients range from a weak .33 in the Gross Motor scale for ages 5-0 to 5-5 to a high of .96 in the Expressive Language scale for ages 2-0 to 2-5. The mean coefficients for the various scales range from about .67 in Gross Motor to about .84 in Language Comprehension and across scales within age group from .58 for the 5-0- to 5-5-year-olds to about .85 for ages 12–17 months. Although the manual author states that "this is an acceptable set of scale reliabilities" (p. 38), the inventory does not appear to be sufficiently reliable at the older ages (5 years and above), with the exception of the Letters scale. In addition, the author would be advised to either completely eliminate the Gross Motor scale for children above the age of 4–5 years or to increase or revise the items to make a more reliable measure at the older ages. It would also be helpful to collect reliability data on both test-retest reliability to determine the stability of this measure and interjudge reliability of ratings by both parents.

The information in the manual supporting the validity of the CDI is provided by three sources. First, the author claims that the age-scaling of the inventory adequately differentiates "younger children from more developed, more skilled older children" (p. 36). He further states that, "among the norm group children, low scores for age are relatively infrequent, especially for the General Development Scale" (p. 37). In addition, two validity studies are briefly described. In one, the CDI scores for 132 beginning kindergarten students were compared to their group-administered reading and math scores on a first grade pretest. The reading scores correlated moderately (.56 to .69) with the Letter, Number, and General Development scales. In the second study, CDI results were obtained on 26 children (ranging from 2 to 6 years) enrolled in an early intervention program in Saint Paul. Seventy-three percent of the children (*n* = 19) "had CDI Profiles that were delayed in one or more areas" (p. 38). Although these studies provide a good start in establishing the validity of the CDI, further validity evidence should be provided before the test user can use the inventory with confidence, knowing that it measures what it is supposed to measure.

The test user might surmise that the dropping of the word "Minnesota" from the title of the CDI means that the norms are more nationally representative than the MCDI. This conclusion would be incorrect. The norm group for the CDI consists entirely of 568 children from South Saint Paul, Minnesota, most of them white (95%) and apparently middle class (the only CDI data given is parent education level which averages around 13.4). The geographically, racially, and culturally narrow norm group is perhaps the biggest weakness of this instrument. In addition, there are only 19 children in the norm group ages 6-0 to 6-2, making the norms very questionable for the older children.

Overall, the CDI appears to be a useful rough screening device for identifying possible developmental problems in young children. However, it does not have adequate reliability, validity, or norm-group representativeness to be used in the actual *diagnosis* of developmental delays or *placement decisions*. The reliability coefficients and norms suggest that this instrument is more appropriate for assessing developmental concerns in children below the age of 5-5 years than in older children.

[57]
Children at Risk Screener: Kindergarten and Preschool.

Purpose: Designed as a "screening tool for cognitive development ... to assist in the identification of children who are at risk for educational failure for cognitive developmental delay."

Population: Ages 24–83 months.

Publication Date: 1991.

Acronym: CARS.

Scores: Total score only.

Administration: Individual.

Price Data, 1994: $89.25 per kit; $18.50 per 25 hand-scorable score sheets; $12.60 per manual (21 pages); $12.60 per technical report (40 pages); $8.40 per 4 magnetic balls.

Time: (5–10) minutes.

Comments: Research edition; includes "a ten-item pretest [which] familiarizes the child with test terminology."

Author: May Aaronson.

Publisher: CTB Macmillan/McGraw-Hill.

Review of the Children at Risk Screener: Kindergarten and Preschool by GLEN P. AYLWARD, Professor of Pediatrics, Psychiatry, and Behavioral and Social Sciences, Southern Illinois University School of Medicine, Springfield, IL:

The Children at Risk Screener: Kindergarten and Preschool (CARS), formerly the Preschool Preposition Test (PPT), is a 23-item receptive language test for children from 2 to 6 years of age. The purpose of the CARS is to identify children who are at risk for educational failure or "cognitive developmental delay" (manual, p. 1). The ability to follow directions, skills in abstract reasoning and spatial relationships, and receptive language are assessed. The CARS is reportedly based on Nancy Bayley's work on the Berkeley Growth Study, where knowledge of prepositions was associated with early verbal and spatial abilities and later intelligence test scores.

The basic components of the CARS are (a) a 6-block x 10-block yellow test board grid; (b) a raised, red figure of a child; (c) a raised green car figure; and (d) four magnetized, halved red balls. The child is requested to place the ball on the grid or figures in response to prepositions or locative terms such as "into," "in back," "high," "against," "on," or "next to." In addition, there is a two-page score sheet in which the examiner places an "x" on the top sheet in the location that matches the child's placement of the ball on the test board. This mark also is transferred (by means of a carbon format) to the second sheet which, in turn, includes shaded areas indicative of where the correct responses are located on the grid. A 10-item pretest is also included.

The CARS takes approximately 5 to 10 minutes to administer. All children start with Item 1, and continue until all 23 items are administered. The order of presentation does not correspond to item difficulty; therefore, there is no discontinuation or ceiling rule. This could prove frustrating for children with delays, or, conversely, initially be too easy for more advanced preschoolers. Raw scores are converted to percentiles for 10 age groups (based on 6-month intervals) and to score ranges (above average, average, below average) for 8 age groups (the 72–77 and 78–83 month groups are not included).

The normative sample consists of a total of 985 children drawn from 14 subsamples (ns ranging from 17–294). These samples include African-American and White children from urban, suburban, and rural areas, and from lower and middle class socioeconomic status households. The normative sample does not appear to match general census proportions. Moreover, Head Start groups comprise almost 25% of the normative sample, but only in the 30- to 68-month age range. In some respects, the normative population represents a "convenience sample," and various ethnic groups, socioeconomic statuses, or geographic areas are not represented adequately. Moreover, the normative data were collected prior to 1980. Therefore, it can be expected that the normative sample would be skewed towards poorer language performance, simply by virtue of many children being enrolled in Head Start and at environmental risk. In addition, a total sample of 354 children with mental retardation or other "handicapping" conditions is included for comparative purposes. The 8 subsamples that comprise the total comparative sample (ns 10–92) include children from "homeless institutionalized," "autistic-like special classes," or "severely emotionally disturbed-day treatment center" (p. 7) groups. Specific characteristics of these populations are not described.

The psychometric aspects of the test are difficult to gauge because of the sampling issues outlined above. Internal consistency, evaluated with the Kuder-Richardson (KR20) formula, is $r = .86$ (apparently using the entire sample). Individual items significantly correlate with the total item score ($p<.005$), but the correlations are not reported. Test-retest reliability figures are presented for four samples ($ns = 17–92$) with either 1 or 7 months between testing sessions. Correlations for the 1-month retest groups are .82–.86; for those with a 7-month test-retest interval, .64–.65.

Construct validity is assessed by correlating the total CARS score with ages in months for the normative sample of 985 children. However, the CARS has a low ceiling, even using a substantial number of children at environmental risk. As a result, the relationship between increases in raw scores and age diminish by 53 months. At this age, skewedness and kurtosis coefficients deviate from the normal distribution. This "topping out" issue suggests that the test may not be appropriate for children older than 4 1/2 years of age, unless they are significantly delayed. Criterion-related validity is reportedly measured with at least 18 other tests; unfortunately, not all of these are found in the tables of the Technical Report. The Boehm Test of Basic Concepts is one such omission. Nonetheless, correlations with the Peabody Picture Vocabulary Test (not the revised version) range from .30 (PPVT IQ score) to .72 (PPVT raw score), based on an n of 122 children. Correlations with the Stanford-Binet (Form LM) range from .52–.74, depending on the sample. Long term data in terms of prediction of third-grade and eighth-grade aptitude test scores are difficult to interpret, due to small sample sizes (ns of 22–37), gender differences, and lack of consideration of other intervening variables.

In summary, there are several features of the CARS that are attractive: (a) it is very simple in design and administration, (b) the test procedure would be appealing to young children, and (c) the receptive skills that are assessed involve abstract concepts rather than concrete objects or actions. Conversely, the screening test norms are in need of updating, and more rigor is required in terms of sample selection. CARS items should be listed in terms of difficulty, and ceiling rules need to be specified. The age range of the test may need to be more restricted as well. Finally, relationships with more current test measures are needed to document criterion-related validity.

Review of the Children at Risk Screener: Kindergarten and Preschool by ANNIE W. WARD, Emeritus Professor, University of South Florida, Daytona Beach, FL:

DESCRIPTION. This is a simple screening test for young children that can be administered in 5 to 10 minutes using attractive manipulative materials, consisting of a magnetized board and a cutout of a car and a child. There are four magnetized half-balls, which the child is to manipulate according to instructions. The skill tested is *receptive language,* and the task for the child is to demonstrate an understanding of prepositions by placing one of the balls in the position relative to a cutout of a car and a child as indicated by the oral instructions. It was formerly known as the Preschool Preposition Test (PPT). It is unfortunate that the acronym CARS for the current name leads to confusion with a very different instrument with the same acronym, the Childhood Autism Rating Scale (T4:439).

There is a pre-test of 10 items to be sure the child understands the nouns used, and the test cannot be used with non-English-speaking children. Furthermore, the child must also process phrases and sentences of varying length and complexity and follow directions.

DEVELOPMENT. The author cites Nancy Bayley's work with the Berkeley Growth Study as the basis for the development of the CARS. It has been used in many studies in the Washington, DC and Montgomery County, Maryland school districts, and much of the testing has involved children in Head Start and Special Education classes.

ADMINISTRATION AND SCORING. The directions and score sheet are clear, concise, and well written. There are 23 items, and recording the responses to each item is simply a matter of placing an X on a picture to indicate where the child places the ball. Correct positions are shaded on the pictures, so scoring involves only counting the Xs in the shaded areas.

A graph of mean scores for 6-month age groups for Head Start and Non-Head Start groups is provided to assist in identifying children who need further evaluation for "possible developmental delay or risk of educational failure" (manual, p. 8).

The demographic make-up of the norms groups is presented in the Technical Report, but there is no information as to how these groups were selected so it is impossible to judge their representativeness. In the other data table, all the *N*s are quite small and it cannot be determined the extent to which these students represent the target population.

TECHNICAL INFORMATION. As a measure of reliability, a KR20 value of .86 is reported, but there is no information about the size or makeup of the sample on which this is based. Two test-retest correlations are also reported, one with a 1-month interval, the other with a 7-month interval. These correlations were greater than .80 for the 1-month study, which used an autistic-like sample, and appropriately .64 for the 7-month study, which used one group of Head Start children and another group of mentally retarded children. An alternative form of the test is not available, but it would be quite useful to have and should be fairly simple to develop.

The manual for the CARS states that the test for the validity of an instrument is whether it functions as it is intended to function. Because the CARS is intended to be used as a screening instrument, the ultimate test of its validity is some measure of how well it serves the screening function. The CARS has been found to correlate with age and with teachers' ratings; both are essential if it is to be useful in identifying children who need further study. It also correlates moderately with widely used intelligence and behavior scales. The technical manual cites studies that found correlations of from .52 to .72 with scores on the Stanford-Binet and the Peabody Picture Vocabulary Test. In addition, the relative difficulty of the items on the CARS scale was found to be fairly similar for normal, mentally retarded, and institutionalized children.

These data suggest that the CARS has the potential to be a simple, fast, and useful screening device. However, additional data should be collected, using carefully selected samples that are representative of various groups, with well-designed follow-up studies.

[58]

Children's Apperception Test [1991 Revision].

Purpose: A projective "method of investigating personality by studying the dynamic meaningfulness of the individual differences in perception of standard stimuli."
Population: Ages 3–10.
Publication Dates: 1949–1992.
Acronym: C.A.T.

Scores: No scores.

Administration: Individual.

Editions, 3: Animal, Human, Supplement, plus Short Form.

Price Data, 1993: $85 per C.A.T.—A, C.A.T.—S, C.A.T.—H, manual ('91, 24 pages), 30 recording and analysis blanks, and 10 copies of Haworth's Schedule of Adaptive Mechanisms in C.A.T. Responses; $23.50 per C.A.T.—A or C.A.T.—H; $27.50 per C.A.T.—S; $9.30 per 25 recording and analysis blanks (short form); $9.30 per 30 Haworth's Schedules.

Time: (15–20) minutes.

Authors: Leopold Bellak and Sonya Sorel Bellak.

Publisher: C.P.S., Inc.

Cross References: See T4:444 (4 references); for reviews by Clifford V. Hatt and Marcia B. Shaffer of an earlier edition, see 9:219 (1 reference); see also T3:396 (1 reference), T2:1451 (23 references), and P:419 (18 references); for reviews by Bernard L. Murstein and Robert D. Wirt, see 6:206 (19 references); for reviews by Douglas T. Keeny and Albert I. Rabin, see 5:126 (15 references); for reviews by John E. Bell and L. Joseph Stone and excerpted reviews by M. M., Genn, Herbert Herman, Robert R. Holt, Laurance F. Shaffer, and Adolf G. Woltmann, see 4:103 (2 references).

TEST REFERENCES

1. Cramer, P. (1987). The development of defense mechanisms. *Journal of Personality, 55,* 597–614.
2. McNeil, T. F., & Kaij, L. (1987). Swedish high-risk study: Sample characteristics at age 6. *Schizophrenia Bulletin, 13,* 373–381.
3. Jarvelin, M. R., Moilanen, I., Vikevainen-Tervonen, L., & Huttunen, N. (1990). Life changes and protective capacities in enuretic and non-enuretic children. *Journal of Child Psychology and Psychiatry and Allied Disciplines, 31,* 763-774.
4. Heinze, M. C., & Grisso, T. (1996). Review of instruments assessing parenting competencies used in child custody evaluations. *Behavior Sciences and the Law, 14,* 293–313.

Review of the Children's Apperception Test [1991 Revision] by HOWARD M. KNOFF, Professor of School Psychology, Department of Psychological Foundations, University of South Florida, Tampa, FL:

The Children's Apperception Test (CAT) is a projective personality assessment instrument, consisting of 10 pictures showing different animals engaged in various "human," relationship-oriented interactions. The CAT was designed to elicit and provide insight into how children from ages 3 to 10 perceive, interpret, respond to, and resolve different developmental problems from a psychodynamic and/ or psychosexual perspective. Extending Henry Murray's theoretical orientation and work with the Thematic Apperception Test with adults, and based on the untested (at least from a contemporary perspective) assumption that animals are children's preferred identification figures, the authors selected the pictures and themes for the 10 cards based on their own experience and their belief that the clinical success of the instrument was all the validation necessary for these choices. The authors state that the CAT can be clinically useful to any psychologically trained professional in "determining what dynamic and structural factors might be related to a child's behavior and problems in a group, in school or kindergarten, or at home" (manual, p. 2), and they suggest, without empirical support, that the instrument is culture-fair and also can be used in child development research or as a therapeutic play technique. Besides the 10 pictures, the CAT comes with a manual, separate interpretive protocols, and an additional manual with 10 additional puzzle-like cards that constitute a "supplement" to the CAT.

TEST ADMINISTRATION AND SCORING. Introduced as a game rather than a test in order to develop rapport, the CAT is administered by presenting the child with the stimulus cards, one at a time and in a specified order, asking him or her to tell a story about the picture by including (a) what is going on in the picture, (b) what the animals are doing, (c) what happened before in the story, and (d) what will happen later. Prompting (but not suggesting responses to) the child is encouraged if necessary. Clinicians record all of the child's responses verbatim, and they can go over selected (or all of the) stories after the administration to probe for elaboration on specific points. Critically, with no other structured directions noted in the manual, the CAT uses, at most, a quasi-structured administration process that is too dependent on the clinician for an objective and unbiased assessment of the child—even prior to interpretation. That is, without a standardized posttest inquiry, the potential that a clinician could self-select specific conflict areas for elaboration, based on the background or referral reasons of a case, and bias both these additional responses and the interpretation of the instrument, is likely. Moreover, many of the assumptions inherent in the suggested administration directions are untested or, at least, no research is cited by the authors to validate their recommended procedures.

Assuming that children's interpretation of the CAT cards "must be a function of continually present psychological forces which at that moment manifest themselves in relation to the given stimulus material" (manual, p. 4), the 10 cards presumably address the following issues: feeding problems, oral problems, sibling rivalry, attitudes toward parents, relationships to parents as (sexual) couples, jealousy toward same-gender parent figures, fantasies about aggression, acceptance by the adult world, fear or loneliness at night, and toileting behavior and parents' response to it. Relative to interpretation, it is recommended that the child's responses to the "latent content" of the cards be analyzed, across and within the cards, using a structured CAT protocol that considers 10 variables: (a) the Main Theme, (b) the Main Hero, (c) the Main Needs and Drives of the Hero, (d) the child's Conception of the Environment, (e) how the child sees and reacts to the figures in the cards, (f) Significant Conflicts described, (g) the Nature of the Child's Main Anxieties, (h) the child's Main Defenses, (i) the Adequacy of Superego as Manifested by "Punishment" for "Crime," and (j) the Integration of the Child's Ego. Significantly, although these variables are described in the manual, the empirical basis for the descriptions and their validity, through independent research, are not. Further, although four CAT case studies are provided, they demonstrate nothing relative to the psychometric integrity of the instrument other than its subjective, potentially biased nature.

In addition to the primary CAT test materials, scoring protocol, and interpretive guidelines, the authors' manual suggests the possible use of (a) a short form of the CAT, (b) an alternative interpretive approach analyzing 12 ego functions from an "ego psychological" perspective, (c) another interpretive approach focusing on defense mechanisms and the psychoanalytic process of identification, and (d) the CAT-Supplement. All of this discussion, and the accompanying protocols or materials, are consistent with other parts of the manual in the absence of an empirical foundation, a dependence on an untested psychodynamic perspective, and a belief that "a projective test does not need validation and the establishment of norms" (manual, p. 17). Moreover, as noted above, the CAT-Supplement has different stimulus materials and its own manual, which describes its purpose, administration and scoring, and interpretation. The Supplement is, in essence, a separate instrument; it has all of the same assumptions and weaknesses of the CAT itself, it does not add to the clinical utility of the CAT, and its inclusion in the CAT materials is confusing and questionable.

PSYCHOMETRIC PROPERTIES. Although the authors allude to the development of norms for the CAT along with issues of reliability and validity, no psychometric data for the instrument are reported in the manual. The authors, however, do cite references to some work that has addressed this area, but

much of this research is largely nonempirical and case-study-oriented, of questionable methodological and technical integrity, and lacking in convergent and discriminant validity with most clinical populations (e.g., Knoff, 1993; Knoff, Batsche, & Carlyon, 1993). As noted above, the authors state that the CAT, along with other projective tests, need not demonstrate such properties because "the individual case can stand by itself" (p. 17). This statement is indefensible and, in the end, leaves the CAT largely untested, putting any clinical interpretations or decisions derived from it in doubt. The psychometric integrity of the CAT must be established. However, the question still remains as to whether this projective instrument, given its underlying psychological orientation and assumptions, can ever be sensitive and efficacious enough to be useful as a clinical assessment or intervention tool.

OTHER CONCERNS. A number of critical issues already have been addressed; however, some additional critique is warranted and described below:

1. As noted earlier, a number of forms related to interpretation are presented in the manual. Although some of these forms lack explicit instructions and guidelines, the presence of these many forms is confusing both from a theoretical and a practical use perspective. A single systematic and objective scoring and interpretive approach to the CAT is greatly needed if the instrument is to demonstrate any clinical utility. The next edition of the manual should present this approach and exclude other superfluous or unvalidated forms or approaches.

2. In the section of the manual that describes "typical" themes of responses to each of the CAT cards, no information is provided to indicate how "typical" was determined. That is, no empirical, normative, or even developmental data were presented to validate the assertions. Once again, the subjective nature of this instrument's development, scoring, and interpretation is apparent, and concerns about its clinical use are reinforced.

3. The lack of an objective scoring approach and norms for this instrument means that a number of potential developmental and demographic differences across the 3- through 10-year-old age span cannot be tested. For example, differences across age, gender, socioeconomic status, expressive language output, race, and others need to be assessed so that any differences that arise can be integrated into scoring and interpretative procedures. In the manual, the authors note that "statements made about the

CAT are thus far based on approximately 200 records of children between the ages of three and ten inclusive" (p. 17). However, they fail to elaborate on this assertion, providing no data, documentation, or critical analysis. The CAT remains largely untested, despite the large number of articles published on its use.

4. Finally, the CAT was first published in 1949, and the manual reviewed was the eighth revised edition. This manual's bibliography, however, is largely outdated. Indeed, many of the 83 references included are from 1960 or earlier. Future editions of this manual should completely update the current CAT, and should present a critical review of the research such that the psychometric integrity of the instrument and its clinical utility can be fairly appraised.

CONCLUSIONS. The authors' claim that there is no need to validate or norm projective instruments such as the CAT represents the strongest rationale to dismiss this test as a viable personality assessment measure. Indeed, the absence of empirical data supporting its use renders the CAT a research tool at best, and certainly not an instrument that should contribute to clinical diagnosis or intervention development. A great deal of test development and research demonstrating the CAT's reliability and validity is needed before this instrument can even approach the claims made by the authors. Despite its following, the CAT should not be available to clinicians in its present form. The CAT is an historical anachronism. It is now outdated in the context of contemporary personality assessment with children.

REVIEWER'S REFERENCES

Knoff, H. M. (1993). The utility of Human Figure Drawings in personality and intellectual assessment: Why ask why? *School Psychology Quarterly, 8*, 191–196.
Knoff, H. M., Batsche, G. M., & Carlyon, W. (1993). Projective techniques and their utility in child psychotherapy. In T. R. Kratochwill & R. J. Morris (Eds.), *Handbook of psychotherapy with children and adolescents* (pp. 9–37). Hillsdale, NJ: Lawrence Erlbaum Associates.

Review of the Children's Apperception Test [1991 Revision] by ROBERT C. REINEHR, Professor of Psychology, Southwestern University, Georgetown, TX:

The Children's Apperception Test (CAT) was designed in 1949 as a projective technique for use with children ages 3–10 years. It is a direct descendant of the Thematic Apperception Test (T4:2824) and is presented as a method of studying "the dynamic meaningfulness of the individual differences in perception of standard stimuli" (manual, p. 1).

The CAT consists of 10 pictures, each occupying an entire 8.5 by 11-inch card. Each picture is a line drawing depicting animals in various activities, chosen to suggest the most important life situations of children. The choice of these situations is frankly psychoanalytic: Orality, identification with parental and sibling figures, and primal scene fears are all listed as target situations. One picture depicts a mature dog spanking a puppy in a room where a toilet is the only other prominent feature.

The Supplement to the Children's Apperception Test (CAT-S) is a further collection of 10 pictures intended to elicit material concerning problems that are more specific to a given child: concerns with physical disability, for example, or about the mother's pregnancy. These pictures are also line drawings, although smaller than the pictures in the CAT, each page containing three or four pictures. They are printed on heavy cardboard and each may be popped out for individual presentation. The pop-outs are irregular in shape, although all are rounded in a manner resembling the bubbles used for dialogue in comic strips.

Separate manuals are provided for the CAT and the CAT-S. The CAT manual contains descriptions of and typical responses to the pictures, a section suggesting variables to be considered when interpreting the responses to the pictures, a recording and analysis blank, and a checklist (the Haworth Schedule of Adaptive Mechanisms) to be used as an aid in interpretation. There is also some discussion of the use of a shorter method of interpretation, some examples of responses taken from sample records, and a brief discussion of a "research aspect," in which is stated the authors' belief that a projective test does not need validation and the establishment of norms to the extent required by other tests. It is their opinion that the individual case can stand by itself and that normative information, although useful for special situations, is not necessary.

The manual for the CAT-S contains a description of and typical responses to each of the pictures, some discussion of the possible use of normative information, and the partial results of two small studies of thematic frequency. For the basic principles of interpretation, the reader is referred to the CAT manual.

Neither manual meets the standards recommended in the American Psychological Association *Standards* (American Educational Research Association, American Psychological Association, & National Council on Measurement in Education, 1985). There is no information regarding internal consistency, retest reliability, or interscorer reliability. There is no validity information of any kind. Clinical speculation and the unsupported opinion of the test interpreter are the basis for the evaluation of CAT stories.

Whatever the value of the argument that projective techniques should not be subject to the same standards as other tests, it is certainly necessary that test developers provide at least some evidence that different interpreters of the test data will draw the same or similar conclusions and that these conclusions will be of the sort that may be verified outside the testing situation. The CAT and CAT-S manuals do not address these issues in any way.

Although some reviewers have argued that the long history of usage by clinicians suggests that the CAT can serve as a valuable clinical tool in the hands of a skilled examiner, there is no evidence to this effect. There is, in fact, no objective evidence to suggest that the responses to these pictures can be interpreted in a manner that is useful in any scientific sense. The CAT is at best an aid to a system of clinical inference that is itself highly suspect. The use of the technique as a method of developing a personality description is entirely unjustified by any scientific standard.

REVIEWER'S REFERENCE

American Educational Research Association, American Psychological Association, & National Council on Measurement in Education. (1985). *Standards for educational and psychological testing.* Washington, DC: American Psychological Association, Inc.

[59]
Children's Category Test.

Purpose: "Designed to assess non-verbal learning and memory, concept formation, and problem-solving abilities."
Population: Ages 5-0 to 16-11.
Publication Date: 1993.
Acronym: CCT.
Scores, 6: Subtest I, Subtest II, Subtest III, Subtest IV, Subtest V, Total.
Administration: Individual.
Levels, 2: Level 1 (Ages 5 to 8), Level 2 (Ages 9 to 16).
Price Data, 1994: $280 per complete kit including manual (72 pages), 25 Level 1 record forms, 25 Level 2 record forms, stimulus booklet, and color response cards (1 for each level); $17.50 per 25 record forms; $35 per manual; $120 per Level 1 stimulus booklet; $95 per Level 2 stimulus booklet; $9 per 2 response cards.
Time: (15–20) minutes.
Author: Thomas Boll.
Publisher: The Psychological Corporation.

Review of the Children's Category Test by MARK D. SHRIVER, Assistant Professor, University of Nebraska Medical Center, Omaha, NE:

The Children's Category Test (CCT) is an adaptation of the Category Test, which is a part of the Halstead-Reitan Neuropsychological Test Battery. The CCT was "designed to assess non-verbal

learning and memory, concept formation, and problem-solving abilities" (p. 1). "In addition, the CCT directly assesses the cognitive processes required for successful academic achievement by measuring the child's ability to learn, to solve problems, and to develop, test, and modify hypotheses" (p. 1). Also, "the task itself is a learning experience rather than a demonstration of acquired skills, ability, or knowledge. Second, the test does not require a verbal or a motor response and it does not have a strict time limit" (p. 1). The appropriateness of an author's purposes or stated applications for a test is dependent upon the supporting reliability and validity evidence provided. This review will discuss the CCT's reliability and validity given the test's stated purposes.

There are two levels to the CCT. Level 1 is for children 5.0 to 8.11 years old and Level 2 is for children and adolescents 9.0 to 16.11 years old. Specific directions for standardized administration of the CCT are provided in chapter 3 and are easy to read and follow. Administration of the CCT takes approximately 15–20 minutes and examiners are strongly encouraged not to take longer than 25 minutes (p. 5). The manual states that examiners should adhere carefully to standardized administration and verbal directions as "Changes in the phrasing or presentation of a test item or other deviations from standard subtest directions could reduce the validity of test results" (p. 10). However, it is noted on page 8 of the manual that the examiner should attempt to attain the child's best performance and "If the child appears confused or does not understand the task, repeat and elaborate upon the instructions but do not reveal the underlying principle of the subtest…. You may also ask the child to carefully study each picture, to describe the stimulus, to recall how pictures change, and to think of the possible reason for a correct response." The manual does not include a discussion of how this type of support from the examiner or differences in administration from standard directions between examiners may affect individual student performance and affect the reliability and validity of the resultant scores.

It should be noted that page 14 of the manual, in the section describing the directions for Level 1, shows a picture of the Level 2 materials (Figure 3.1). In addition, the test author claims in at least two places in the manual (p. 1 and p. 48) that the test "requires neither a verbal response nor a motor response"; however, obviously one or the other is required if the examiner is to determine the examinee's response.

User qualifications are provided on page 2 of the manual and state that, "Although a trained technician can administer and score the CCT under supervision, responsibility for interpreting the results must lie with those who have appropriate graduate or professional training and experience in neuropsychological assessment." According to the Acknowledgments in the manual, it appears that part of the reason for developing the CCT was to increase its use in schools (p. iii). The user qualifications for this test, however, may disqualify many school psychologists who do not have supervised training in neuropsychological assessment.

The CCT record forms are easy to complete. Scoring consists primarily of counting and summing the number of errors across the subtests for each level. A standard score (T score) with a mean of 50 and standard deviation of 10 is computed based on the total number of errors across all the level subtests. A 90% and 95% confidence interval and percentile rank for the standard score are also provided in the manual.

TEST DEVELOPMENT. It is not clear from the manual how the CCT was developed from the Category Test. It does appear that the CCT was 1 of 12 shortened versions initially generated from the Category Test and subsequently examined for their respective degree of correlation with the Category Test. The CCT (1 of the 12) apparently met criteria for having higher correlations with the original measure than the other shortened tests. Level 2 of the CCT "was chosen based on its number of items and the distribution of those items across the 6 subtests of the original Category Test" (p. 27). Level 1 "contains the same number of items (80) distributed across the same number of subtests (5) as the Reitan-Indiana Neuropsychological Test Battery for Young Children" (p. 27). The manual refers the test user to Reeder and Boll (1992) for more detailed information. The manual would be more user-friendly, however, if it provided more detailed information for the potential test user. For example, how were items chosen to be included on each of the 12 shortened tests? Was there a cut-off for correlations between the shortened tests and original test to determine if the tests may be measuring the same construct? What were the correlations that were found between the shortened tests and the original test? In addition, no information is provided in the manual describing if the test has been analyzed for differential validity across groups (e.g., ethnic, cultural, gender).

STANDARDIZATION. A stratified random sampling plan was used to ensure appropriate representation of children across age, gender, race/ethnicity, parent education, and geographic region. For the entire standardization sample ($n = 920$), these goals were generally met in comparison with 1988 U.S. Census data. The norming sample is reported to be representative of the educational mainstream. Special education students being served in mainstream classrooms were not excluded so that 7% of the sample consists of children identified as learning disabled, speech/language impaired, emotionally disturbed, or physically impaired and 5.2% of the sample were in gifted and talented programs. Although representation of the children across demographic variables looks good, there are only 70 or 80 children at each one-year age level, which limits comparisons of an individual child with the norm group at each year of age. Also, it should be noted that only English-speaking children are included in the norms, and it is unclear if there are children with *severe* motor deficits or language disorders in the standardization sample, a population with which the manual indicates this test may be particularly useful (pp. 1 and 48).

RELIABILITY. Level 1 and Level 2 were each divided into equivalent halves and Spearman-Brown correlations were computed to evaluate internal consistency. Internal consistency correlations averaged .88 for Level 1 across one-year age levels (range = .86–.91) and averaged .86 for Level 2 (range = .81–.89) across the one-year age levels (p. 33). These reliabilities are good, but suggest that additional assessment information be used when making decisions about an individual.

Standard errors of measurement are provided in the manual and for Level 1 average 3.46 with a range or 3.00 to 3.74 across the one-year age levels, and for Level 2 average 3.74 with a range of 3.32 to 4.36 across the one-year age levels (p. 33). These *SEM*s comprise approximately a 2/3 standard deviation around the standard score, and computed confidence intervals at 95% comprise greater than a standard deviation around the standard score (range = 5 to 8 points across all ages) (p. 62). These are higher than desired for using this test to make decisions about individuals.

Test-retest reliabilities across 10 to 42 days were only computed at ages 8, 12, and 16 years with about 30–40 children at each age (p. 35). Reliabilities are moderate averaging .75 (p. 35). Given that this test is purported to assess actual learning within the subtests, it would be expected that error scores decrease with additional administrations of the test, and they did. However, the learning that takes place during and between administrations of the CCT also decreases reliability or stability of the test over time. The author states that a lack of changes in error scores over time is "an indicator of abnormality in most instances" (p. 49). This "abnormality" apparently is perceived to lie within the child. Evidence for this statement is not provided in the manual, however. In other words, it is unclear if changes or lack of changes in errors on the CCT are reflective of neurological impairments or ineffective teaching or both.

VALIDITY. Correlations are presented between the CCT and the Vocabulary subtest of the Wechsler Intelligence Scale for Children—Revised (WISC-R) ($N = 920$); the Performance, Verbal, and Full Scale scores of the Wechsler Intelligence Scale for Children—Third Edition (WISC-III) for 26 children with Attention Deficit Hyperactivity Disorder; and the California Verbal Learning Test—Children's Version (CVLT-C), a neuropsychological measure that assesses verbal learning and memory ($N = 920$). Low negative correlations (some statistically significant) were found in comparison with the WISC-R Vocabulary subtest and the CVLT-C, suggesting that the CCT is measuring something different from these tests. These correlations do not provide evidence, however, of what the CCT is purported to measure. Low positive correlations (.22, .14, and .27) were found in comparison with the Full Scale, Verbal, and Performance scores of the WISC-III (p. 39). In addition, evidence is presented that children make fewer errors on the CCT as they mature (p. 41).

The criterion-related evidence presented includes significant correlations for the current Level 1 (.881) and Level 2 (.716) total scores with the original CCT total scores for the two levels (p. 42) for 110 children referred for a neuropsychological evaluation. The manual states that these correlations suggest that the current CCT and the original CCT are "parallel forms" (p. 42); however, approximately 25% of the variance for Level 1 and approximately 50% of the variance for Level 2 are not explained by the correlation between the current and original CCT. The manual also indicates that there are consistent significant differences between the performance of children with neurological impairments and normal children on the CCT; however, the studies cited to support this statement are from 1977 and earlier, so it is difficult to determine if the manual is referring to the current CCT or the original CCT (p. 43). Evidence for one version of the test is not necessarily evidence for the other version.

Predictive validity evidence is presented for 313 children and reveals low to moderate correlations with group-administered academic achievement test scores for reading (overall correlation = -.28) and math (overall correlation = -.34) (p. 44) and for teacher assigned grades for math (-.20), spelling, (-.38), and reading (-.20) (p. 45). The correlations for predictive validity are lower than those for widely used intelligence tests and suggest that if prediction of academic performance is the primary reason for an evaluation then review of past academic performance (i.e., grades) and administration of an intelligence test (e.g., WISC-III) are still most appropriate.

SUMMARY. The reliability and validity evidence presented in the manual does not support the intended stated purposes and applications of this test. This test is meant to serve as a measure of a student's ability to learn, and it was developed to facilitate more wide-spread use in the schools. However, this measure should only be administered by someone as part of a comprehensive neuropsychological battery and interpreted by a individual with training in neuropsychology. In addition, it is unclear if the learning context of this instrument represents or correlates significantly with the typical classroom context in which students learn. Minimal evidence is provided regarding the construct validity of this instrument. It still appears that if an examiner wants to assess how a child learns in the classroom, then the examiner should observe the child performing with the academic curriculum in the classroom. Short of this, the examiner may observe the child performing in the academic curriculum in a clinical context, or conduct a direct skills assessment with content similar to the child's actual curriculum (Shapiro, 1996). Additional research is needed to determine what information the CCT provides over and above such a complete psychoeducational evaluation.

REVIEWER'S REFERENCES

Reeder, K. P., & Boll, T. J. (1992). A shortened intermediate version of the Halstead Category Test. *Archives of Clinical Neuropsychology, 7*, 53–62.
Shapiro, E. S. (1996). *Academic skills problems: Direct assessment and intervention* (2nd ed.). New York: The Guilford Press.

Review of the Children's Category Test by NICHOLAS A. VACC, Professor and Chairperson, Department of Counseling and Educational Development, School of Education, The University of North Carolina at Greensboro, Greensboro, NC:

The Children's Category Test (CCT) was designed as a measure of nonverbal learning ability for children between the ages of 5.0 to 16.11. The author intended that the CCT would (a) assess diversified groups of individuals for whom many existing psychometric procedures may not be usable and (b) offer the option of being administered to individuals with limited verbal ability and restricted motor activity. The CCT, which is individually administered, is designed to assess nonverbal learning and memory, concept formation, and problem-solving abilities. The author reports that the CCT provides information on a child's ability to change problem-solving strategies, to develop alternate solutions, and to profit from previous experience. An attribute of the CCT is its lack of reliance on expressive language skills, thus increasing the utility of the instrument for diverse groups of individuals. The author purports that a primary value of the CCT is that it assesses the "learning experience" (p. 1) as opposed to being a measure of acquired skills, ability, or knowledge. The underlying assumption is that the CCT assesses cognitive processes required for successful achievement, by measuring a child's ability to learn and solve problems. The instrument is intended not to be affected by learning disorders, verbal or motor deficits, neurological deficits, or emotional handicaps. In essence, the instrument is attempting to provide information on a child's cognitive ability to learn.

The CCT was derived through a series of assessment transformations that began with the Halstead-Reitan Neuropsychological Test Battery (T4:1119), which employed the Category Test. The Category Test was modified and named the Short Category Test (T4:2455), with its primary distinction being the absence of the equipment required for assessment in the Category Test and a corresponding reduction in the amount of time to administer the instrument. The primary purpose of the tests remained the same: to assess an individual's ability to solve problems that require abstract concept formation based on the presentation of geometric shapes and configurations. The CCT was developed as a children's form of the Short Category Test, which was recommended as an assessment instrument for use with individuals aged 15 years through adulthood.

The author states that "a trained technician can administer and score the CCT under supervision" (p. 2). He recommends, however, that assessment professionals who are involved in education or neuropsychological assessment and who have an educational background at the graduate level would be best suited for administering the test and interpreting the results. The test contains two parts: Level 1 for children between the ages of 5.0 years to 8.11 years,

and Level 2 for children between the ages of 9.0 years to 16.11 years. Level 1 contains 80 items and Level 2 has 83 items. The CCT follows the same theoretical tradition as the Category Test with stimuli presented following several established principal ideas. The test materials comprise four components: a reusable Level 1 test booklet, a reusable Level 2 test booklet, a manual, and separate record forms for each level. All materials provided are attractive, user friendly, and nicely developed. The manual is particularly helpful in providing (a) a contextual backdrop for the CCT; (b) a clear presentation for administration and scoring procedures; (c) standardization, reliability, and validity data; and (d) a section on clinical applications and interpretations. The test booklets for Levels 1 and 2 are functional and easy to use, and they correspond well with the record form, which is clearly formatted. The front-page information provides a general overall description of the child to be assessed, including behavioral observations and summary score information that is parallel to the structure of the test booklet.

The CCT requires approximately 20 minutes to administer. However, the author advises test administrators to complete a level of the CCT within 25 minutes; longer intervals could impact performance negatively because concepts are learned and each of the subtests are accumulative. Test administrators need the manual, the Level 1 or Level 2 stimulus book, the Level 1 or Level 2 record form, and either the color response card for Level 1 or the number response card for Level 2. The author advises establishing rapport with the examinee, and provides specific suggestions for prompting and providing general statements such as "That was a hard one, but let's try the next one now" (p. 9) or "I think you can do it" (p. 9). Although the CCT is designed to be administered in a standard format, such prompting varies the conditions and may have an effect on test performance depending on the skill of the test administrator.

Standardization of the CCT was developed using children based on the March 1988 U.S. Bureau of Census report, with consideration given to the variables of age, gender, race, ethnicity, geographic region, and parent-education level. The total sample of 920 children ranged in age from 5 to 16 years. Approximately 7% were children who had been identified as having a learning disability. The proportion of males and females was approximately 50%. Race and ethnicity backgrounds included African Americans, Hispanic, Caucasian, and a small group classified as Others, which included Asian Americans and Native Americans. Parents' level of education was subdivided as follows: less than high-school education, high-school education (which was the predominant group), 13 to 15 years of education, and 16+ years of education. The number of children from each geographic region (i.e., northeast, north central, south, and west) was in accordance with the proportions living in each area as specified in the Census data. Based on the characteristics of the standardization sample, standard scores were developed with the distribution of raw scores for each age converted to a scale with a mean of 50 and a standard deviation of 10.

Reliability was estimated using the Spearman-Brown formula, with estimates ranging from .87 to .91 for Level 1 and from .81 to .89 for Level 2. The standard error of measurement varied by age from 3.00 to 3.74 for Level 1 and from 3.32 to 4.36 for Level 2. Test-retest stability was reported for testing over a period of time of 10 to 42 days with a subsample of 106 children; retest coefficients by age groups varied from .70 to .79.

Validity of the CCT was examined by construct and criterion-related validity. Construct validity information was obtained by investigating the relationship between the CCT and the Wechsler Intelligence Scale for Children—Revised (WISC-R) Vocabulary Subtest, the Wechsler Intelligence Scale for Children—Third Edition (WISC-III), and the California Verbal Learning Test—Children's Version (CVLT-C). Correlations between the CCT and the WISC-III ranged from .14 to .27. Correlations between the CCT and the CVLT-C ranged from .15 to -.27 for a subsample of 320 children for Level 1 and from -.10 to -.37 for a subsample of 600 children for Level 2.

Criterion-related validity evidence is also presented in the manual comparing the CCT and the Category Test, which yielded correlations of .02 to .88 for Level 1 and from .28 to .72 for Level 2. The degree of relationship between these two tests is rather dispersed. The relationship for full-scale scores for Levels 1 and 2 (i.e., .88 and .72, respectively), however, is convincing. The author also presents comparisons between the CCT and achievement test scores and school grades. In each situation, negative correlations existed ranging between -.08 and -.59, based on age-group analyses. Generally speaking, there is a negative correlation between achievement and performance on the CCT, and positive correlations between the CCT and the Category Test.

However, in using the Category Test as a criterion, the authors have viewed prediction in a broad sense.

Within the manual section on clinical applications and interpretations, the author points out that the CCT is unique in that it can offer a measure of a child's learning capacity that is independent of previously acquired knowledge and skill, thus tending to be more a measure of verbal ability that includes receptive or expressive aspects of learning. Accordingly, the CCT is purported to be able to provide a new dimension in evaluating a child's potential that could be viewed as independent of (a) the educational environment of the child and (b) effects due to extreme emotional pathology. In the same regard, the CCT is an assessment tool that is recommended for use with children with neurological injury or deterioration. The assumption underlying the CCT's use is that the CCT requires neither verbal nor motor responses and does not have a strict time limit. Although it is well known that more traditional achievement and ability tests are good predictors of a child's achievement in school, the CCT provides an alternate source of information concerning the child's capacity to learn. Again, the intent of the CCT is to go beyond evidence of knowledge acquisition by testing learning and other types of cognitive processes that are viewed as important in functioning. Accordingly, performance on the CCT is an index of a child's ability to learn (i.e., to benefit from trial and error experiences and to sort out elements in a given specified situation).

In summary, if assessment is viewed as a comprehensive process of gathering information about a child across developmental areas with strengths rather than deficits being emphasized, then the CCT adds another dimension to the assessment process. I believe the CCT would be helpful in obtaining a multidimensional, integrated understanding of a child's learning. I recommend its use as part of a battery of instruments when doing a comprehensive assessment of a child.

[60]
Children's Personality Questionnaire, 1985 Edition.

Purpose: Designed to measure personality traits to predict and evaluate the course of personal, social, and academic development.
Population: Ages 8–12.
Publication Dates: 1959–1985.
Acronym: CPQ.
Scores, 14 to 18: 14 primary factors [Cool vs. Warm (A), Concrete Thinking vs. Abstract Thinking (B), Affected by Feelings vs. Emotionally Stable (C), Phlegmatic

vs. Excitable (D), Obedient vs. Dominant (E), Sober vs. Enthusiastic (F), Expedient vs. Conscientious (G), Shy vs. Bold (H), Tough-Minded vs. Tender-Minded (I), Vigorous vs. Guarded (J), Forthright vs. Shrewd (N), Self-Assured vs. Apprehensive (O), Undisciplined Self-Conflict vs. Controlled (Q3), Relaxed vs. Tense (Q4)]; 4 optional secondary factors (Extraversion, Anxiety, Tough Poise, Independence).

Administration: Group.

Forms, 4: A, B, C, D.

Price Data, 1994: $29.25 per handscoring introductory kit including test booklet (Form A) and technical handbook with scoring keys ('85, 79 pages); $14 per technical handbook; $18 per 25 reusable test booklets (Form A or B); $24.25 per 25 reusable test booklets (Form C or D); $10.75 per 50 answer sheets; $15 per 50 answer-profile sheets; $10.75 per 50 profile sheets; $13.50 per scoring key (separate scoring keys required for Forms A/C and B/D); $20.25 per 25 machine-scorable answer sheets; $23.75 per computer interpretation introductory kit including test booklet (Form A), technical handbook, and machine-scorable answer sheet; $20 or less per computer interpretation.

Foreign Language Editions: German and Spanish editions available (Forms A and B, 1963); South African edition available from Human Sciences Research Council in Pretoria, South Africa.

Time: (30–60) minutes per form.

Comments: Test booklet is entitled "What You Do and What You Think."

Authors: Rutherford B. Porter and Raymond B. Cattell.

Publisher: Institute for Personality and Ability Testing, Inc.

Cross References: See T4:454 (9 references); for reviews by Steven Klee and Howard M. Knoff, see 9:222 (11 references); see also T3:1129 (60 references); for a review by Harrison G. Gough, see 8:520 (46 references); see also P:38 (14 references); for reviews by Anne Anastasi, Wilbur L. Layton, and Robert D. Wirt of the 1963 edition, see 6:122 (2 references).

TEST REFERENCES

1. Marjoribanks, K. (1992). Ability and personality correlates of children's attitudes and aspirations. *Psychological Reports, 71*, 847-850.
2. Waterman, J., & Lusk, R. (1993). Psychological testing in evaluation of child sexual abuse. *Child Abuse & Neglect, 17*, 145-159.
3. Kurian, M., Verdi, M. P., Caterino, L. C., & Kulhavy, R. W. (1994). Relating scales on the Children's Personality Questionnaire to training time and belt rank in ATA taekwondo. *Perceptual and Motor Skills, 79*, 904-906.

Review of the Children's Personality Questionnaire, Second Edition by ROSA A. HAGIN, Professor Emeritus, Fordham University—Lincoln Center, New York, NY:

The Children's Personality Questionnaire (CPQ) was designed as a psychometric measure of personality traits in children, ages 8 through 12 years. The publication date of the test is 1975, although the *Children's Personality Questionnaire Handbook* on which much of this review is based, was revised in 1985 to incorporate information from previous editions, norm tables, and additional references.

According to the handbook (1985), the CPQ's theoretical basis lies in the work of Cattell (1957), whose research identified objectively determined source traits believed to comprise personality structure and to be of potential importance in clinical, educational, and counseling practice. The test's authors believe these traits remain relatively consistent throughout the lifespan and, therefore, can be recognized and measured in comparable tests at other ages. In the Institute for Personality and Ability Testing series adjoining the CPQ are the Early School Personality Questionnaire (ESPQ; T4:843) for ages 6–8, the High School Personality Questionnaire (HSPQ; T4:1159) for adolescents, and the Sixteen Personality Factor Questionnaire (16PF; 12:354) for adults.

Suggested users of the CPQ include (a) schools and camps to screen out for individual attention and guidance children who need help with emotional conflicts and behavior disorders, (b) school and occupational counselors to raise the accuracy of estimates of scholastic promise, (c) clinicians whose work requires a diagnostic instrument dealing with basic personality concepts, and (d) school psychologists to keep developmental records of emotional maturity of students. The test authors emphasize the comprehensive and unitary nature of the CPQ. Unlike what they call special-purpose tests that deal with only single dimensions of personality, the CPQ is said to address the major dimensions factor-analytically demonstrable in research on personality by R. B. Cattell and colleagues.

Four forms of the test are available; each form consists of two parts, containing a total of 140 forced-choice items. The authors suggest that each form should be given in two sittings, not longer than 50 minutes. Authors state that the items are expressed in language within the reading vocabulary of an average child of 8 years, but the items may be read aloud and words may be explained if necessary. It is generally recommended that more than one form of the test be used and that interpretation be made on the composite score for each factor. Norms are available for girls, boys, and for mixed gender groups. Raw scores can be transformed into n-stens (a normalized standard-ten scale) and percentiles. Directions for computation of s-stens (standard deviation stens) for special purposes are also included. Stencils are provided for hand scoring. Computerized scoring with a brief computerized interpretive report is also available.

The CPQ measures a set of 14 factorially independent dimensions of personality (or source traits) identified by letters, technical names (e.g., threctia/parmia or sizothymia/affectothymia), and popular descriptions (e.g., shy/adventurous, reserved/warmhearted). Four secondary order factors can be calculated from equations utilizing combinations of the sten scores for the primary factors: Extraversion, Anxiety, Tough Poise, and Independence.

Although the theoretical foundations of the CPQ are well explained in the handbook, data concerning the technical characteristics of the test are incomplete for the applications the authors have proposed. These inadequacies are apparent in the description of normative samples, as well as in evidence for reliability and validity.

The sections of the handbook dealing with test design and construction describe principles for "good" test construction, but fail to show how these principles were applied in the design of the CPQ. For example, although authors of Appendix D acknowledged the need for sampling based on a stratification of age, gender, socioeconomic, and geographic factors, no data are provided on the composition of the normative sample except the size of the sample for each set of norms and the total number of answer sheets analyzed (15,000). Given that the age range of the test extends from latency into early adolescence, the omission of age distributions is a particularly serious omission.

Although the handbook authors clearly state the four forms of the test are equivalent, the equivalence coefficients in Table 5 raise questions about this statement. With Forms A and B, coefficients (even with Spearman-Brown corrections) range as low as .37 and with Forms C and D as low as .33. Considering the importance placed on the interpretation of single factors, test-retest data also raise questions. Most test-retest coefficients for single forms range between .50 and .70, and some are as low as .37. When two forms are combined, as suggested in the handbook, coefficients range from .46 to .87, but are generally on the order of .62 to .79. These coefficients imply the need to ask a child to read and reply to 240 items, as much as 200 minutes of testing time, to obtain marginally reliable responses.

The handbook's discussions of validity data rest heavily on the construct validity implicit in the hypothesized structure of personality based on Cattell's factor analyses. Although Table 6 of the handbook contains CPQ Direct Validity Coefficients, no explanation of it is provided. Also absent is information on the selection of items and systematic evidence of their relationship to the factor used to describe them. The section of the handbook describing criterion relationships useful in educational, clinical, and social psychology presents some more sophisticated evidence of what the authors call concrete validity. However, this evidence consists of individual studies scattered through the literature of the years 1960–1970, rather than any recent systematic studies with the normative samples.

To summarize, the CPQ is a personality measure with familiar theoretical foundations in the psychometric study of personality structure. However, its handbook does not contain sufficient information about its technical characteristics to justify its use in decision making in school, counseling, or clinical settings. Information is needed about the characteristics of the standardization sample and the methods for selection of items. Improved reliability is needed if the 14 factors are to be used as individual measures of traits. Finally, systematic longitudinal research is necessary to determine the stability of the factors across ages, an assumption that has been made both within the CPQ and in relation to adjoining tests of the IPAT series, the ESPQ and HSPQ.

REVIEWER'S REFERENCE

Cattell, R. B. (1957). *Personality and motivation structure and measurement.* New York: World Book Company.

Review of the Children's Personality Questionnaire, 1985 Edition by TERRY A. STINNETT, Associate Professor of Applied Behavioral Studies in Education, Oklahoma State University, Stillwater, OK:

The Children's Personality Questionnaire (CPQ) is a self-report inventory intended to measure unitary personality traits in children between the ages of 8 and 12 years. The CPQ is one in a series of tests that includes the Early School Personality Questionnaire (ESPQ; T4:843), the High School Personality Questionnaire (HSPQ; T4:1159), and the Sixteen Personality Factor Questionnaire (16 PF; 12:354). The CPQ overlaps by one year with the HSPQ (age 12) and with the ESPQ (age 8) at the upper and lower ends of its age range. However, the authors offer no suggestions to guide users for selecting one test over another at the overlapping ages in the CPQ manual. Nonetheless, because all of these tests measure the same personality factors that are purported to be consistent across the lifespan, the authors suggest they can be used to make developmental comparisons for children across a wide age range. There is also a reference in the 1985 handbook, that was apparently also in earlier versions of the CPQ materials, to the Pre-School Personality Questionnaire (PSPQ). To date this instrument has not been published, but the reference to it in the current manual remains. This illustrates a major criticism of the current CPQ; the manual is shamefully outdated and in need of revision. For example, perusing the reference lists and bibliographic supplements in the manual reveals the most recent citations are from 1977! The only change from the 1975 edition to the current version appears to be that the manual and the norms have been compiled into one document. In all previous versions the norm tables for the CPQ were published separately from the handbook (manual); in this revision the norms are contained in the manual. The CPQ handbook desperately needs revision and updating. A very brief PsychLit search covering the time period from 1974 to 1996 yielded 25 articles in which the researchers used the CPQ. An updated manual is needed badly and should summarize a current literature review related to the test.

The authors of the CPQ state five purposes for the instrument: (a) for screening the personality functioning of those children suspected to have emotional and behavioral disorders who might need individual attention and guidance; (b) to provide personality data useful for predicting scholastic achievement and creativity for school and occupational purposes; (c) for delineating basic personality traits in children who might be referred for clinical practice to provide developmental data that reflect response to treatment, etc.; (d) for measurement of personality and emotional development associated with the child's educational experience; and (e) to provide an objective basis for discussing and comparing the personality functioning of children with parents and teachers. There is a well-written interpretive section in the manual (Chapter 9: Criterion Relations useful in Educational, Clinical, and Social Psychology) that can be used to guide users in interpretation of CPQ scores in relation to the test's stated purposes. But like most other aspects of the manual, the material is clearly dated and in need of substantial revision. Such a revision should also include applications in school psychology.

The CPQ was designed to measure 14 primary dimensions or "source traits" that reflect Cattell's conceptualization of personality. These personality traits are labeled with the letters of the alphabet, have technical names, and also are presented with more understandable clinical descriptions for use in communicating with laypersons. Four broad second-order personality factors can also be derived by combining various scores from the primary traits in specified ways. The test has four equivalent forms (A, B, C, and D), which are divided into two sections each (e.g., A_1 and A_2 comprise Form A, B_1 and B_2 comprise Form B, etc.). Each section contains 70 items; thus, each form has a total of 140 items. Users should find the administration and scoring procedures straightforward. However, children with low intellectual ability or poor reading skills will likely have difficulty completing the protocols unassisted. Raw scores from the CPQ can be converted to "n-stens," "s-stens," and percentile rank scores. Users may wonder why the revised CPQ does not use a more common standard score transformation. Interpretation might be made easier for users if the T-score (mean = 50, standard deviation = 10) or the typical deviation score metric (mean = 100, standard deviation = 15) were adopted in place of the sten. There are separate standard score tables provided for gender (boys, girls, and combined) by form (A, B, C, D, A + B, C + D, and A + B + C + D). The equivalent forms and section format of the CPQ allow test users the flexibility of administering the questionnaire in short sessions if needed. The authors also suggest that the parallel forms can allow users to administer different versions of the questionnaire immediately without worrying about retest effects in the same form were used repeatedly. They recommend that at least two complete forms (or all four forms) be administered for the most precise assessment of personality. As would be expected, the combined forms have higher test-retest reliabilities than any single form in isolation. Use of combined forms, however, will significantly increase the time needed for administration of the CPQ.

Reliability estimates are presented based on the 1975 edition of the CPQ. Test-retest reliabilities of the 14 factors, based on a 1-week interval, ranged from .46 to .87 (median r = .71) for combined Forms A + B and from .62 to .84 (median r = .765) for Forms C + D. Test-retest reliabilities for all four forms combined are not presented in the manual. In general, the test-retest reliabilities of the CPQ are too low for users to have much confidence in the test's temporal stability. Internal consistency reliabilities are not reported for single forms of the test, but combined forms yielded KR_{21} coefficients ranging from .32 to .79 (median = .71) for Forms A + B, .26 to .71 (median = .625) for Forms C + D, and .49 to .86 (median = .80) for Forms A + B + C + D. Clearly some of the factors are not homogeneous.

The authors also report correlations of the 14 factors between Forms A + B and C + D as estimates of alternate-form reliability. They did not present the other possible form comparisons. The rs (after Spearman-Brown correction) ranged from .37 to .75 (median = .615) for Forms A + B and from .33 to .72 (median = .545) for Forms C + D. These equivalence coefficients are quite low considering the forms are supposed to be parallel. As a result, users should not consider results derived from one form to the next as directly comparable.

A number of other serious problems that confront potential users of the CPQ need to be addressed. The standardization sample is not described in sufficient detail for objective evaluation. In Appendix D in the handbook the authors reported the sample reflected children from four geographic regions, three ethnic groups, three levels of socioeconomic status, and two levels of community size, but the exact sampling design demographics are not reported. The Ns that comprise the separate norm tables are simply included as notes under each table. The current handbook is also unclear as to when these data were collected.

The test's development is not adequately described and the handbook does not contain detailed information regarding the CPQ's validity. In terms of construct validity, this is a glaring omission, especially for a test that has been derived through factor analyses. Because fundamental psychometric information is omitted from the manual, a thorough technical evaluation of the scale is impossible. As a result, the scale cannot be recommended for use. The CPQ needs to be completely revised or it should be retired.

[61]

Children's Role Inventory.

Purpose: "A measure assessing the roles played by children in their alcoholic families."
Population: Adult children of alcoholics.
Publication Date: 1988.
Acronym: CRI.
Scores: 4 role categories: Hero, Mascot, Lost Child, Scapegoat.
Administration: Group.
Manual: No manual.

Price Data: Available from publisher.
Time: Administration time not reported.
Authors: Ann E. Potter and Dale E. Williams.
Publisher: Dale E. Williams (the author)

TEST REFERENCES

1. Williams, D. E., & Potter, A. E. (1994). Factor structure and factorial replication of the Children's Roles Inventory. *Educational and Psychological Measurement, 54*, 417-427.

Review of the Children's Role Inventory by STEPHEN N. AXFORD, *Psychologist, Pueblo School District No. Sixty, Pueblo, CO, and University of Phoenix, Southern Colorado Campus, Colorado Springs, CO:*

The Children's Role Inventory (CRI), as described by its authors, is a "measure assessing the roles played by children in their alcoholic families" (p. 71). In fact, the instrument, contrary to what its name may convey, is apparently designed to be used with adult children of alcoholics rather than juveniles. This assumption is based on the fact that all subjects used in the validation of the instrument were self-reported adult children of alcoholics. The CRI specifically is designed to measure self-esteem and use of social support. The authors suggest that the CRI may have utility in "isolating those [adult] children who may be at risk for developing esteem and alcohol-related problems" (p. 77).

The group-administered CRI comprises 60 items employing a 5-point Likert scale. Materials include: a research article (Potter & Williams, 1991) describing the construction and validation of the instrument; the scale or protocol sheet used by the examinee to rate items (e.g., "When I was a child, I ... was an achiever"); and a scoring key with items arranged in four categories: Hero, Mascot, Lost Child, and Scapegoat. Administration instructions are limited to a brief statement on the single-page scale, simply stating, "Circle the number that best fits how each word or phrase describes how you were or how you acted in the family in which you were raised."

Although no technical manual currently exists for the CRI, the authors, in personal correspondence with the Buros Institute, indicated that development of such a manual is a goal of theirs. Nevertheless, normative scores are not provided. Also absent, outside the limited information provided in the research article, are instructions for interpreting data. Of course, this places limitations on the CRI for clinical use at the present time.

Three studies are reported by the authors, related to the development and validation of the CRI. In general, the authors were diligent and appropriately cautious in terms of attention to issues related to theoretical conceptualization, research design and methodology, and interpretation of results. The authors are off to a good start in developing and validating the CRI.

The first of the studies focused on item development and selection. The authors employed children of alcoholics to generate items. Subjects were 140 self-declared adult children of alcoholics participating in a support group, Adult Children of Alcoholics (ACA). Five psychologists specializing in alcohol addiction reviewed the 100 items generated and employed a rating system for assigning items with "best" fit to categories. Eighty-two items were selected for the first version of the CRI. Adequate levels of internal consistency (Cronbach's alpha ranged from .89 to .95) were observed.

The second study focused on cross-validating the internal consistency and construct validity of the first study. Subjects included 142 ACA members, 28 men and 114 women. Ranging from .90 to .95, internal consistency was observed to be within quite acceptable limits. However, given that all subjects were members of a support group, although "data were collected anonymously and within a 2-week time span," there does seem to be the potential of cohort contamination of results. In any case, through item analysis/item deletion, employing a rank-ordering system using corrected item-total correlation, 15 items for each subscale or category were retained.

The third study was conducted to: "(1) obtain convergent and discriminant validity evidence for the CRI and (2) compare the responses of self-identified adult children of alcoholics with a control sample" (p. 71). One-hundred-thirty-eight ACA subjects (27 men, 111 women) were employed. As acknowledged by the authors, these subjects were not screened and thus there was the possibility that subjects may have participated in the previous two studies. All ACA subjects chosen for participation "scored above the recommended cut off indicative of parental drinking problems on the Children of Alcoholics Screening Test" (pp. 73–74). A comparison sample of 105 adult subjects (24 men, 81 women) denying parental alcoholism and scoring below the recommended cut-off on the Children of Alcoholics Screening Test was employed. For both the clinical and comparison samples, "CRI subscales were differentially predictive of self-esteem as well as size of and satisfaction with one's social support network" (p. 70). Also, reliability results were replicated for both samples. Internal

consistency for both samples was observed to be adequate (with correlations ranging from .89 to .92).

The authors acknowledge several limitations related to their research: In completing the inventory, subjects were required to recall childhood memories; the clinical samples were all solicited from the ACA support group (thus, it is uncertain as to whether the obtained results can be generalized to the larger population of children of alcoholics); and subjects were not screened for prior participation, which may have contaminated results for the second and third studies. In addition, all subjects were recruited from a limited geographic region (Omaha/Council Bluffs metro area, and Lincoln, NE). Ethnicity is not addressed. Nevertheless, the authors appear to have conducted their research carefully. The results from the studies reported are encouraging and warrant continued research using the CRI.

In summary, the initial research in developing and validating the CRI is encouraging. However, as the authors seem to acknowledge, additional research is needed before interpretive results can be generalized beyond the clinical sample (i.e., ACA support group members) used in the study, in terms of differential diagnosis and preventative care. Thus, it is not recommended that the CRI be used as a primary method, within a clinical context, for gathering diagnostic information regarding children of alcoholics. The CRI may be useful, however, as an adjunct or supplementary measure when working with children of alcoholics. However, the CRI does seem to possess ample technical merits to be used in research. Also, with additional validation and standardization, the CRI has potential to be used as an important clinical tool.

REVIEWER'S REFERENCE

Potter, A. E., & Williams, D. E. (1991). Development of a measure examining children's roles in alcoholic families. *Journal of Studies on Alcohol, 52*, 70–77.

Review of the Children's Role Inventory by KATHLEEN D. PAGET, *Division Director, The Center for Child and Family Studies, College of Social Work, University of South Carolina, Columbia, SC:*

The Children's Role Inventory (CRI) is an adult self-report scale designed to measure the roles played by children in their families. Comprising 60 adjectives, the measure requires respondents to rate themselves retrospectively on a Likert scale from 0 ("Strongly disagree or very unlike me") to 4 ("Strongly agree or very like me"). The scale is based on the popular conceptualization that children growing up in families affected by alcoholism assume "roles or defensive behavior patterns in response to the parental alcoholism and the imbalanced family system" (Potter & Williams, p. 70). The four roles that form the foundation for the measure were described more than 10 years ago as the Hero, Mascot, Lost Child, and Scapegoat (Black, 1981; Wegscheider, 1981). According to the test developers, "all children of alcoholics are thought to assume one or more of these roles" (Potter & Williams, p. 70).

The genesis of the scale suggests that it was developed as a tool for research purposes rather than as an instrument to be marketed for use by practitioners. No manual accompanies the scale; instead, supporting documentation results from three studies conducted by the test developers and published in the same article (Potter & Williams, 1991). In the first study, items were generated and responded to by adult children of alcoholics, and their responses were used to refine the measure. The second study incorporated a refined measure to cross-validate internal consistency findings. The third study resulted in convergent and discriminant validity evidence through a comparison of self-identified adult children of alcoholics with a comparison sample. In reporting the results of these studies, the test developers used scoring procedures that compiled items into the four categories, but they did not detail how specific numerical ratings were incorporated into the final scores. Thus, in contrast to many measures marketed for practical use and supported by extensive supporting documentation, the CRI is in the very early stages of development, a reality that results in more questions than answers about its practical use. In addition to the basics of scoring, questions arise about administration, norming, and interpretation when the measure's accompanying materials are perused.

Administration procedures appear to be very easy, and the time period to complete the items is very short, possibly as short as 5 minutes. The procedures are based on certain assumptions, however, that leave the user unguided about some important aspects of the measure. Instructions are as follows: "The following words or phrases describe behaviors and characteristics of children. Circle the number that best fits how each word or phrase describes how you were or how you acted in the family in which you were raised." The lack of a more circumscribed frame of reference leaves respondents struggling to define their own temporal and relational context: Some will focus on their memories as young children whereas others will reflect more on their adolescence; some will emphasize interactions with an adult family member and others will think more often of sibling interactions. In addition, the assumption that people grow up in one family ignores the increasing number of adults who, as children, experienced multiple-family situations as a result of foster care and divorce. Moreover, although the directions ask for how the respondent "acted in the family," some respondents will extend the context to include situations outside the family. Despite the range of contexts that respondents may create for themselves when completing the items, this information is not known because the directions do not request it. In short, the vagueness of the measure's directions combine with the general scope of the trait-based adjectives to cry out for more situational specificity to the items. Information on the consistency of results across time and respondents would help temper these concerns, but at the present time, test-retest and interrater reliability coefficients are missing from the materials that accompany the measure.

Specific information about the measure's validity also is missing. Before results from the CRI can be interpreted to support the four roles that it purports to measure, more work must be done to collect construct validity information. The inter-item and inter-subscale reliability coefficients provided by the test developers are a necessary but not sufficient prerequisite to empirically derived construct validity. This is especially true because the sample used to generate items comprised individuals ("adult children of alcoholics") who had begun counseling and may have been exposed to information regarding the four roles. A factor analysis based on a priori questioning of the original clustering of items is needed. Through the use of a comparison sample and a discriminant analysis, the test developers are beginning to address the important issue that some individuals who do not grow up in families characterized by alcoholism may exhibit behavioral patterns similar to those who do. Also, in studying convergent and predictive validity, they have begun to address possible gender differences in response patterns on the CRI. Missing from published information, however, is the consideration of possible racial/ethnic differences in response patterns on the CRI. In describing the four samples used across the three published studies, no mention is made of the racial composition of the samples. Given the diversity of the American population, such information is sorely needed.

Although increased psychometric documentation has been collected and recorded over time by the developers of the CRI, the instrument is not ready for application and public use. If the developers wish for it to be, then continued refinement of the measure is needed with respect to administration, scoring, validation, and interpretation prior to the preparation and printing of a manual.

REVIEWER'S REFERENCES

Wegscheider, S. (1981). *Another chance: Hope and health for the alcoholic family.* Palo Alto, CA: Science and Behavior Books, Inc.

Black, C. (1981). *It will never happen to me.* Denver, CO: MAC Publishing.

Potter, A. E., & Williams, D. E. (1991). Development of a measure examining children's roles in alcoholic families. *Journal of Studies on Alcohol, 52,* 70–77.

[62]
Chinese Proficiency Test.

Purpose: "Designed to evaluate the proficiency in Chinese listening and reading comprehension attained by Americans and other English-speaking learners of Chinese."

Population: Adults.

Publication Date: 1988.

Acronym: CPT.

Scores, 4: Listening Comprehension, Structure, Reading, Total.

Administration: Group.

Price Data: Available from publisher.

Time: 120(180) minutes.

Comments: Mail-in scoring.

Author: Center for Applied Linguistics.

Publisher: Center for Applied Linguistics.

Review of the Chinese Proficiency Test by CHI-WEN KAO, Assistant Assessment Specialist and Assistant Professor of Psychology, Office of Student Assessment, James Madison University, Harrisonburg, VA:

The Chinese Proficiency Test (CPT) was designed to measure proficiency in Chinese listening and reading comprehension for Americans and other English-speaking learners of Chinese. The language of the test is focused on that used in contemporary real-life settings rather than Chinese literature. There are a total of 150 four-choice multiple-choice questions with 60 items in Listening Comprehension and 90 items in Reading Comprehension. The two subtests are meant to be administered together, and the actual testing time is about 2 hours.

In the Listening Comprehension section, the examinee listens to a number of single statements/questions; short or long dialogues; and longer passages such as a news broadcast or an announcement by native speakers of Chinese. Following the Chinese message, each question stem is presented in spoken English, and the response options are printed in English in the test booklet. The Reading Comprehension section has two subsections: Structure and Reading. The Structure section consists of 35 items of two types. In the first type of question, the examinee selects from four possible positions within a sentence for a word that is left out in a sentence. In the second type of question, the examinee selects the correct word from a list of options to fill in the blank of a sentence. The Reading subsection comprises 55 items. The reading text in each item could range from a few words such as street signs or newspaper headlines to longer passages such as excerpts from newspapers or magazines. The reading text is presented in Chinese but the questions and options are both posed in English. Recognizing that different learners of Chinese are exposed to different types of Chinese written characters, complicated or simplified forms, both forms of Chinese characters are presented in the Reading Comprehension section.

The CPT is administered by the Center for Applied Linguistics (CAL), and individuals may only register through local CPT test centers or a Chinese-teaching institution, which determines the testing dates.

A total and three subtest raw scores are the only scores available. All tests are scored by CAL, and the examinees' test results are sent from CAL to the testing centers, where examinees obtain their results. Tables of percentile ranks matched with the raw scores are provided in the examinee's handbook, which can be used to interpret the standing of the examinee's performance relative to the normative population. A puzzling omission is percentile ranks for the total scores.

The standard error of measurement (*SEM*) for total and subtest scores are reported in the Test Interpretation Manual. The use of *SEM* to interpret a true score and the significant differences between two scores is clearly explained in the Test Interpretation Manual, which, however, is not available to the examinee. It would be welcome to see that students are also aided with interpretive information that assures understanding of their score meaning.

The user population for this test is not well specified. The manual authors claim that the test is "appropriate to differentiate among students who have completed at least one year of regular college-level instruction in Chinese or an equivalent number of contact hours in high school" (p. 1). However, the descriptions are ambiguous about the number of hours in Chinese instruction that the potential users have received. This problem is worsened and becomes more confusing to readers from the authors' explanation that "the CPT was designed primarily for intermediate and advanced students of Chinese" (p. 9). First of all, the manual does not provide definitions of performance criteria for learners with different proficiencies. Second, there is no evidence provided for this claim.

As to the purpose of using the CPT, the manual authors claim that the "CPT is to provide an objective measure of an individual's general proficiency in Chinese" (p. 2); however, no information about the validity of this claim is provided in the manual. On the contrary, the manual authors suggest that validation for any purposes of using the CPT should be the user's responsibility rather than that of the test developers (p. 2). This is not in congruence with the *Standards for Educational and Psychological Testing* (AERA, APA, & NCME, 1985) which states that test developers should recommend the appropriate use of a test and provide validity evidence for the recommended use of the test.

NORMS. The normative data were collected from 479 subjects at around 60 institutions in the United States and abroad between 1984 and 1987. No information is available about the sampling procedure or the composition of the standardization sample. The manual reports a preliminary norming study involving 617 subjects in 1983 and more than 700 subjects in the subsequent 4 years. It is unclear how the 479 students selected for the standardization sample were derived or their relation, if any, to the preliminary studies.

RELIABILITY. The Kuder Richardson 20 formula was employed to estimate internal reliability. The reliability coefficients for Listening, Structure, Reading, and Total were reported as .89, .83, .93, and .96, respectively. Because the normative data were divided into three proficiency groups, it would have been useful to have the reliability coefficients reported for each of the proficiency subgroups. Obviously, the reliability estimates would decrease, but the information would be useful.

VALIDITY. Definitions of the content domains for the measures of the Listening and Reading tests were clearly explained and provided in the manual. However, the manual lacks evidence of procedures used to verify whether item content reflects the defined domains. No definition is available about the content domain of the measure of Structure. Instead, readers are given a description of the item format of the Structure section in the content validity section (p. 7). This information seems more appropriate for the test format section. It is unclear why the procedures for development of the content domain for the Structure were not described in the manual.

The concurrent validity was examined by comparing the degree of agreement between the self-reported language levels of examinees in the standardization sample with the means of test total scores made by these three proficiency groups. Although the mean scores reported for the three proficiency groups appear different, no further statistical analysis is provided. It is not clear whether score means are different from one another either statistically or educationally. The effect sizes should have been reported. This reviewer would argue that the idea of using self-reported course history as a criterion measure is fallible. Clearly, more appropriate criteria can be identified, for example, other well-established Chinese proficiency tests or course grades.

The normative sample was divided into three levels of proficiency based on self-reports of highest level of Chinese instruction. No validity for the self-reported information was reported via comparison with actual course enrollments. Furthermore, there is no information about why the norms were divided into three levels. If the CPT was meant to provide indices for proficiency levels, a more sophisticated methodology should be involved in providing cutscores for different proficiency groups. The test would have greater utility if the levels of proficiency were well defined and the test was empirically validated by external measures that display satisfactory validity and reliability evidence.

SUMMARY. From a psychometric point of view, much information that could have defended the validity of this test was missing. For example, no evidence of item content validity was provided even though the content domain for a few dimensions was well defined. The concurrent validity evidence presented was not compelling. The test purposes are not well specified nor validated. The representativeness of the standardization sample is in question. This reviewer would reserve a recommendation to use the CPT until the missing information is provided, and the instrument development procedures and technical qualities meet the *Standards for Educational and Psychological Testing* (AERA, APA, & NCME, 1985).

REVIEWER'S REFERENCE

American Educational Research Association, American Psychological Association, & National Council on Measurement in Education. (1985). *Standards for Educational and Psychological Testing*. Washington, DC: American Psychological Association, Inc.

Review of the Chinese Proficiency Test by ANTONY JOHN KUNNAN, Assistant Professor of Education, Division of Educational Foundations and Interdivisional Studies, California State University, Los Angeles, CA:

The purpose of the Chinese Proficiency Test (CPT) is "to evaluate the level of proficiency in (Mandarin) Chinese attained by American and other English-speaking learners of Chinese" (Test Interpretation Manual, p. 1). The test is intended for students at a range of proficiency levels from those who have completed one year of Chinese language instruction at the college or university level up through the maximum level of proficiency normally attained by Chinese majors at the completion of their program. The uses of the test could include, among others: admission to, placement within, or exemption from a Chinese study program; application for scholarship or appointment; competency testing upon exit from a Chinese program; or certification of Chinese language proficiency for occupational purposes (p. 2).

FEATURES. The CPT contains a total of 150 four-option multiple-choice items divided into two sections, Listening Comprehension and Reading Comprehension. In the Listening Comprehension section, the test taker listens to a number of dialogues between two or more native speakers and longer single-speaker passages in Mandarin Chinese. Following each passage, the test taker is asked one or more questions for which he or she must choose the correct answer from the four-option multiple choices printed in the test booklet in English.

In the Reading Comprehension section, the Structure section assesses the test takers' ability to recognize correct structural patterns in written Chinese in 35 items, and the Reading section assesses comprehension in a variety of printed texts. The 55 items in this section deal only with factual content of the passages and require no background in Chinese literature. In addition, in order to make the test equally fair to test takers whose exposure to written Chinese has been based on either traditional or simplified characters, all material in this section is provided in both character systems.

TEST DEVELOPMENT. The manual does not specifically outline the procedures in the development of the CPT. However, in the section on content validity, the manual notes that in constructing test items "certain content domains were postulated as appropriate to the proficiency of an English-

speaking learner of Chinese" (p. 7). Representative items were then constructed for each of the domains representing increasing levels of proficiency in Chinese as a second language.

The CPT is a norm-referenced test and the norming population consists of 479 test takers who took the test between 1984 and 1987 at 60 institutions in the U.S. and abroad. The norming group was identified into three norming groups: beginning, intermediate, and advanced. In the manual, a CPT Percentile Rank Table with the rank data on the three groups of students is presented so that test takers can compare their performance with the performance of the norming population. In the Examinee Handbook this table is called the CPT National Norms Table.

RELIABILITY. Reliabilities and standard error of measurement (*SEM*) of the CPT based on the 1984–1987 data indicate that the test consistently measures performance. The total test reliability (based on KR-20) and *SEM* reported were .96 and 5.14, respectively.

VALIDITY. In terms of concurrent validity, the manual reports CPT score patterns obtained by test takers at three self-reported proficiency levels (beginning, intermediate, and advanced) as an external criterion that appears to corroborate and reflect the self-reported proficiency levels.

A content validity discussion of the test is also presented. As mentioned above, test items are constructed based on content domains and levels of proficiency. The levels of proficiency postulated are: Level 1 (Survival), Level 2 (Tourist resident in Chinese society), and Level 3 (Foreign professional in Chinese society). For each of these levels, the target language-use situations and topics are as follows. For Level 1, Listening Comprehension materials include understanding oral language heard in a grocery store, train station, etc., and Reading Comprehension materials include street signs, storefront designations, and other "sight" vocabulary. For Level 2, Listening Comprehension materials include short conversations between two people involving a single conversation turn on topics such as planned trips, family problems, etc., and Reading Comprehension materials include newspaper headlines, printed announcements, and simple newspaper and magazine descriptions. For Level 3, Listening Comprehension materials include oral discourse involving two conversational turns dealing with general academic topics such as current events, health care, etc., and

Reading Comprehension materials include passages on a wide variety of daily topics such as results of an opinion poll, job descriptions, vacation travel, etc. Questions at Level 3 may deal with authors' opinions and attitudes, and may require inference. With regard to the Structure section, the manual does not provide a listing of type of items for each content domain and level of proficiency.

Though this attempt to match the test materials and the corresponding target language-use situations the test takers are expecting to encounter is valuable, it is unclear how the levels of proficiency are linked to the content domain. This is a problem because a mere listing of target language-use situations and topics cannot indicate the level of proficiency required to be successful in those situations. But what can resolve this problem is a detailed content analysis of the grammatical, textual, functional, and sociolinguistic features of the test items and the expected response that could reveal the abilities necessary for success on those items at each of the levels (see Bachman, Kunnan, Vanniarajan, & Lynch, 1988).

Another serious problem with regard to the validity of the test is that no construct validation study is reported. A factor-analytic study (Hale, Rock, & Jirele, 1989), or a latent trait model analysis (Embretson, 1985), or a structural modeling study (Muthen, 1988; Kunnan, 1994) would be considered essential to claim that the CPT is a construct-valid test. Additionally, no case is made for the total reliance on the multiple-choice test method, now a major debate in measurement literature (see Bennett & Ward, 1993).

SUMMARY. The CPT is a well-designed and promising test with respectable reliability but its total reliance on the multiple-choice test method and its validity claims are both problematic. Additional studies that address these problems can set aside critical validation concerns that linger at present.

REVIEWER'S REFERENCES

Embretson, S. E. (1985). Multicomponent latent trait models for test design. In S. E. Embretson (Ed.), *Test design: Development in psychology and psychometrics* (pp. 195–218). Orlando, FL: Academic Press.

Bachman, L. F., Kunnan, A. J., Vanniarajan, S., & Lynch, B. (1988). Task and ability analysis as a basis for examining content and construct comparability in two EFL proficiency test batteries. *Language Testing, 5,* 128–159.

Muthen, B. (1988). Some uses of structural equation modeling in validity studies: Extending IRT to external variables. In H. Wainer & H. Braun (Eds.), *Test validity* (pp. 213–238). Hillside, NJ: Lawrence Erlbaum Associates.

Hale, G. A., Rock, D. A., & Jirele, T. (1989). *Confirmatory factor analysis of the TOEFL.* TOEFL Research Report 32. Princeton, NJ: Educational Testing Service.

Bennett, R. E., & Ward, W. C. (1993). *Construction versus choice in cognitive measurement: Issues in constructed response, performance testing, and portfolio assessment.* Hillside, NJ: Lawrence Erlbaum Associates.

Kunnan, A. J. (1994). Modelling relationships among some test taker characteristics and performance of EFL tests: An approach to construct validation. *Language Testing, 11,* 225–252.

Chinese Speaking Test, 1995 Edition.

Purpose: "To evaluate the level of oral proficiency in Chinese attained by American and other English-speaking learners of Chinese."

Population: Adults.

Publication Dates: 1988–1994.

Acronym: CST.

Scores: Total score only.

Administration: Individual or group.

Forms, 3: A, B, C.

Price Data, 1995: $60 per examinee for full length test; $45 per examinee for short form.

Time: (45) minutes full length; (25) minutes short form.

Comments: Examinee responses recorded on test tape scored by publisher; short form is first 25 minutes of full length test.

Author: Staff of the Division of Foreign Language Education and Testing.

Publisher: Center for Applied Linguistics.

Review of the Chinese Speaking Test, 1995 Edition by JAMES DEAN BROWN, Professor, Department of ESL, and TE-FANG HUA, Ph.D. Candidate, University of Hawaii at Manoa, Honolulu, HI:

This review focuses on the 1989 version of the Chinese Speaking Test (CST). A newer version of the CST is in preparation, but parts of that version are still in draft form. The 1989 CST includes one Examinee Handbook, four Examinee Test Booklets, a master tape, and one Official Test Manual.

The Examinee Handbook contains the test's purpose, its timing (45 minutes), how to register and prepare, what to expect at the test, how the CST looks, and how scoring logistics work. In general, the Examinee Handbook is straightforward, clear, and complete, though more information about the scoring scale would help examinees.

Each of the four Examinee Test Booklets contains seven parts or subtests including personal conversation, giving directions, detailed description, picture sequences, topical discourse, and situations. Only the first subtest (which is not scored) has taped prompts in Chinese; all others have written and taped directions in English. Examinees are required to perform all speaking tasks in Chinese, but need not understand much spoken Chinese, which the authors say is justified because the CST is designed to measure only speaking ability. This approach has two drawbacks: first, spoken discourse seldom occurs in a vacuum without listening; and second, directions in English are appropriate only for learners of Chinese who also speak English (thus excluding large numbers of other learners of Chinese).

The Official Test Manual contains: (a) *general information* (test format, test content, appropriate uses for the test, and laudably, a brief argument for local validation and standard setting); (b) *preparation procedures* (registering, collecting fees, maintaining test security, reporting scores, getting test materials, checking them, distributing Examinee Handbooks, and securing a test site); (c) *setup procedures*; (d) *procedures for language laboratory administrations*; (e) *procedures for individual administrations*; and (f) *technical information*. The first five sections provide ample information for proctors to set up and administer the CST effectively, and commendably, all directions that proctors must read to students are clearly blocked out and easy to identify.

The remainder of this review will focus on the Technical Information section (which includes discussions of the development process, level of difficulty, speededness issues, reliability, standard error of measurement, and validity). The authors begin this section by saying that the CST is a semidirect test of oral proficiency based on the American Council on the Teaching of Foreign Languages/Interagency Language Roundtable (ACTFL/ILR) standards. They then refer the reader to an earlier explanation of the CST adaptation of the ACTFL/ILR guidelines, which included paragraph-length descriptions in combinations of English and pinyin of the Chinese abilities of examinees at novice, novice-high, intermediate-low, intermediate-mid, intermediate-high, advanced, advanced high, and superior levels. These descriptions are adequate for test users to understand what the CST levels mean, but not to understand how points are assigned for each level. In any case, readers are told that the tests must be sent to the publisher for scoring.

The authors next explain how the CST was developed. First, a preliminary version was piloted in 1984 and 1985 using 27 students of Chinese at five institutions. Then, the four final CST forms were developed, and "a formal study of the reliability and validity of these forms was carried out in Spring, 1986" (manual, p. 19) using 32 students, who were selected from a group of *volunteers* "so as to provide a wide and ... rectangular distribution of proficiency levels" (Clark & Li, 1986, p. 3). The sample sizes and selection methods raise serious questions about the generalizability of this study.

The authors then refer readers to Clark and Li (1986) for descriptive characteristics of the sample, raw data, and "more in-depth statistical analyses" (manual, p. 20). Readers must refer to this document (not included in the testing materials) to understand that only two raters were used to score all 32 examinees. Unfortunately, results based on just two raters may be idiosyncratic to them, and other raters might produce quite different results.

The authors next point out that the CST is not appropriate for examinees who are at novice-low, novice-mid, or novice-high levels on the ACTFL scale. Because the largest number of students of Chinese in U.S. universities fall into these levels, the applicability of the test is seriously limited.

Reliability is discussed in terms of both interrater reliability, which ranged from .89 to .96 for the four forms, and parallel forms reliability, which ranged from .90 to .99. The authors apparently overlooked the need to establish equivalent means and variances before making claims that the "four forms of the CST are parallel." To the authors' credit, they do discuss the standard error of measurement, but in terms of it being .25 on the 0—5 ILR scale (the first mention of this 0—5 scale). Indeed, there is no indication of what an examinee's score might look like. Will it be a verbal descriptor like "intermediate-high"? Or is it a number? The manual authors do not say.

In addition, no descriptive statistics are presented, no information about norms, and no description of how numerical scores are related to the scale descriptors. Elsewhere (Clark & Li, 1986), we deduced that the seven categories in the scale descriptors were converted to an 8-point 4—11 scale (with the 11th point assigned to examinees above the high-superior level).

Validity is discussed from four perspectives. First, construct validity is discussed briefly, then sidestepped with the comment that "a great deal has been written elsewhere about the construct validity of the OPI [oral proficiency interview], and no attempt is made to review this evidence here" (manual, p. 23). Second, the content validity of the CST is defended in terms of the systematic way in which the types of contents in the six subtests were developed and arranged. Insofar as test users find those particular contents representative of what they want to test, the CST is probably content valid. Third, the authors address the issue of face validity by asking the examinees if the questions "adequately probed their maximum level of speaking ability" (manual, p. 24) (*Yes* = 70%, *No* = 30%). Fourth, criterion-related validity is defended on the basis of correlations between the CST and live oral proficiency interviews, coefficients that ranged from .86 to .98 for various combinations of raters and forms, indicating that, insofar as the live interviews are valid, the CST probably is too.

To summarize, we found most of the information in the Examinee Handbook and Official Test Manual to be adequate for examinees and proctors to successfully negotiate the test administration (as long as those examinees speak English). However, the Technical Information section is much weaker: (a) the scale and its relationship to scoring are never adequately explained; (b) the small sample sizes and selection procedures limit generalizability; (c) the lack of descriptive statistics makes it difficult to interpret all statistics; (d) the inability to assess the abilities of novice-low, novice-mid, and novice-high students (the levels of most students in U.S. universities) severely limits the CST's usefulness; (e) claims for four parallel forms overlook the need for equivalent means and variances; and (f) the validity arguments are convincing only under certain fairly prescribed circumstances. Perhaps most problematic, throughout the CST documentation, references are made to other documents (e.g., Clark & Li, 1986) for information that should have been provided in the testing materials themselves.

REVIEWER'S REFERENCE

Clark, J. L. D., & Li, Y. C. (1986). *Development, validation, and dissemination of a proficiency-based test of speaking ability in Chinese and an associated assessment model for other less commonly taught languages.* Washington, DC: Center for Applied Linguistics.

Review of the Chinese Speaking Test, 1995 Edition by ANTONY JOHN KUNNAN, Assistant Professor of Education, Division of Educational Foundations and Interdivisional Studies, California State University, Los Angeles, CA:

The purpose of the Chinese Speaking Test (CST) is "to evaluate the level of oral proficiency in Chinese attained by American and other English-speaking learners of Chinese" (manual, p. 1). The CST is intended for students at proficiency levels from Intermediate to Superior following the guidelines developed by the American Council on the Teaching of Foreign Languages (ACTFL). The uses of the test could include, among others, admission to, placement within, or exemption from a Chinese study program; application for scholarship or appointment; competency testing upon exit from a Chinese program; or certification of Chinese language proficiency for occupational purposes (manual, p. 3).

FEATURES. The CST is a semidirect test, which means the test is administered via an audiotaped recording and a test booklet that contains written materials, maps, and pictures, and the test taker's responses are recorded on another audio-tape and then rated. It can be administered individually or to a large group in a language laboratory in two forms: The long form lasts 45 minutes and consists of four types of questions designed to elicit speech samples of about 20 minutes duration; the short form lasts about 25 minutes and elicits speech samples of about 15 minutes duration. In Part 1 of the test, the respondent takes part in a personal conversation through several questions about his or her family and education; in Part 2 the test taker is instructed to answer and ask questions, describe a place or activity, give directions, and narrate a story based on a series of pictures; in Part 3 the test taker is instructed to talk about five different topics (two in the short form); and in Part 4 (only in the long form) the test taker is instructed to carry out a specific task based on real life situations.

The recorded speech samples are scored by specially trained raters. The score report contains the test taker's oral proficiency rating, generally based on the ACTFL proficiency guidelines and scale, ranging from Novice to Superior.

TEST DEVELOPMENT. The test manual contains the procedures adopted for the development of the CST, such as the administration of the preliminary version of the four different forms to two groups of students of Chinese, and the minor modifications made to the overall format and content. The test was revised in 1994 to include more contextualized clues. However, it is unclear how the authors arrived at the four parts to the test; whether they based their decisions on content validity, whether they followed the Oral Proficiency Interview (OPI) format, or whether they had corroboration from any statistical procedures. With regard to level of difficulty, the manual authors state the long form of the test is most appropriate for learners between the levels of Intermediate-High and Superior and the short form for learners between the levels of Novice-High to Intermediate-High on the ACTFL scale. In terms of speededness, responses to questionnaires collected from validation studies indicated that adequate time is allotted for most test takers to respond to each question.

VALIDITY. Three types of validity evidence were gathered: content validity, criterion-related validity, and construct validity. Evidence for content validity was found in the tasks: Test takers are asked to speak in Chinese, they are not required to decode

Chinese, and the tasks closely parallel the OPI format. In a validation study, test takers were asked to indicate on a questionnaire if the questions in each of the tests (the OPI and the CST) adequately probed their maximum level of speaking ability: for the CST, 70% said "yes" and 30% said "no"; for the OPI, 74% said "yes" and 26% said "no," thus providing evidence of the content validity of the CST as a surrogate OPI.

Evidence for criterion-related validity of the 1988 version of the test was offered through correlations obtained from ratings of test performance by two raters who provided independent ratings of the four forms of the CST with the OPI; these correlations ranged from .92 to .98. In a further study, correlations were obtained from ratings by one rater who rated test performance of a test taker on the CST and another rater on the OPI; these slightly lower correlations ranged from .86 to .93. For these two sets of studies, sample sizes were 15 or 16 subjects. No direct correlational study has yet been reported for the revised test.

With regard to construct validation, no separate study of the CST is reported. Instead, the manual authors note that evidence from the content validation and criterion validation studies is sufficient to support the construct validation of the test as a measure of speaking proficiency. In addition, the reader is directed to construct validation studies of the OPI reported in journals.

Despite this excellent case for test validation, a major concern still exists: Why does the test use different tasks? This question should be asked as it is left unclear whether the test developers believe the oral discourse expected is going to be significantly different in each of the tasks. For example, is the oral discourse of giving directions different from giving detailed descriptions or is oral topical discourse different from oral discourse in a specific situation? The manual authors do not provide any discussion on this matter. One empirical method that could be used to establish the basis for the four tasks is to conduct an exploratory factor analysis of test performance data and to interpret the factors (see Kunnan, 1992; Bachman, Davidson, Ryan, & Choi, 1995).

RELIABILITY. Interrater reliability information was collected for the four parallel forms: The reliabilities were uniformly high ranging from .89 to .97. Parallel form reliability information was also collected: For Forms A and B the reliabilities were .95 and .99 for two raters and .90 for different raters; and for Forms C and D the reliabilities were .95 and

.93 for two raters and .91 for different raters. Both these studies indicate that the test yields consistent results and trained raters are able to use the scoring guidelines consistently. In addition to these classical interrater reliability studies, a generalizability study with facets such as age, gender, native language, a decision-study with varying numbers of raters, and a many-facet Rasch measurement (examining relative severity of different raters and relative difficulty of different tasks) would have enhanced the technical strengths of the test (see Bachman, Lynch, & Mason, 1995; Lumley & McNamara, 1995).

SUMMARY. The CST is a reasonably efficient alternative to a direct test. Its validity and reliability are somewhat well established, although the sample sizes are small. Support from additional studies will enhance the confidence with which the test can be used.

REVIEWER'S REFERENCES
Kunnan, A. J. (1992). An investigation of a criterion-referenced test using G-theory, and factor and cluster analyses. *Language Testing, 9*, 30–49.
Bachman, L. F., Davidson, F., Ryan, K., & Choi, I-C. (1995). *An investigation into the comparability of two tests of English as a foreign language.* Cambridge: Cambridge University Press.
Bachman, L. F., Lynch, B. K., & Mason, M. (1995). Investigating variability in tasks and rater judgements in a performance test of foreign language speaking. *Language Testing, 12*, 238–257.
Lumley, T., & McNamara, T. F. (1995). Rater characteristics and rater bias: Implications for training. *Language Testing, 12*, 54–71.

[64]
Christensen Dietary Distress Inventory.

Purpose: Designed to provide an objective assessment of the probability of diet contributing to emotional distress.

Population: Ages 18 and above.

Publication Date: 1990.

Acronym: CDDI.

Scores: Total score only.

Administration: Group.

Price Data: Available from publisher.

Time: (10–15) minutes.

Comments: Self-report inventory.

Author: Larry Christensen.

Publisher: Pro-Health Publications.

Cross References: See T4:460 (1 reference).

TEST REFERENCES
1. Christensen, L., & Burrows, R. (1990). Dietary treatment of depression. *Behavior Therapy, 21*, 183–193.

Review of the Christensen Dietary Distress Inventory by RICHARD F. FARMER, Assistant Professor of Psychology, Idaho State University, Pocatello, ID:

The Christensen Dietary Distress Inventory (CDDI) is a 34-item self-report questionnaire designed to diagnose persons whose emotional distress is partially or completely due to the intake of specific dietary substances, namely refined sucrose and caffeine. The development of this inventory was premised on the notion that persons who experience "a dietary induced emotional distress exhibit responses which differentiate them from individuals whose emotional distress arises from sources other than diet" (manual, p. 1).

The 34 items of the CDDI assess a variety of physical symptoms and psychological complaints. Directions for the CDDI ask the respondent to read each inventory item and to determine if the item is applicable to him or her. If the item is not applicable, the respondent is instructed to go on to the next item. If the item is applicable, the respondent is asked to choose one of four or five response options that seems most accurate or applicable. The CDDI is designed for persons 18 years or older, can be administered to individuals or groups, and takes about 10 minutes to complete. The manual cautions against the use of this measure with bipolar patients and persons on psychotropic medication because elevated CDDI scores may be due to these conditions rather than diet.

Items were selected for inclusion in the CDDI based on their ability to discriminate dietary responders (i.e., those whose mood disturbance decreased following dietary intervention and returned with reinstatement of pretreatment dietary intake pattern) from dietary nonresponders (i.e., those whose mood disturbance was not modified by dietary intervention). Item response options are weighted -1, 0, 1, or 2 in accordance with their ability to discriminate these two groups (see Christensen, Krietsch, & White, 1989). A total score for the measure (range: -2 to 39) is derived from the sum of the weighted values of the items endorsed. A scoring template is available to assist in scoring.

There are no normative data provided for this measure based on the rationale that the CDDI "is designed to be used for diagnostic purposes as opposed to measuring psychological constructs" (manual, p. 3). Rather, a list of potential cutoff scores is provided along with associated sensitivity and specificity indices. The test user is instructed to use the cutoff score that best meets the needs of the user (e.g., detect actual cases or minimize false classifications). The manual recommends, however, that test users select a cutoff score that maximizes the correct classification of true positives at the cost of also selecting some false positives. The manual does not contain any information on how these sensitivity and specificity values were derived other than to refer the

test user to a previously published article where these values were first reported (Christensen et al., 1989). Reference to this report reveals that sensitivity and specificity indices were based on a small sample ($n = 16$ total; 7 dietary responders and 9 nonresponders) recruited from newspaper advertisements. The use of a small, unrepresentative normative sample in conjunction with an absence of data on the estimated true prevalence rate of dietary-induced emotional distress in the population suggests that these sensitivity and specificity indices should be employed with extreme caution.

Test-retest reliability data are presented for two samples ($ns = 51$ and 22) for whom the retest interval was 10 and 8.4 days, respectively. The manual reports a test-retest reliability value of .87 for both samples, presumably based on the CDDI summary scores. Absent is a mention of the degree of diagnostic concordance across testing occasions, which would appear to be a more appropriate index of this measure's reliability as it is presented as a diagnostic instrument.

The manual cites one report supportive of the measure's validity (Christensen et al., 1989), where CDDI scores were compared with the subjects' classification as dietary responders or nonresponders. The manual states that a "relationship of 0.48 [was found] between these two variables" (manual, p. 7), without further indicating who the subjects were, how they were selected, how many there were, or what method was employed for arriving at the validity coefficient. The manual goes on to provide group means on the CDDI (without standard deviations) for dietary responders ($M = 17.3$) and nonresponders ($M = 13.1$) as further indication of the measure's validity. The mean of the nonresponder sample (13.1), however, is virtually the same value as the suggested cutoff (13.0) for discriminating between persons whose emotional distress is due to diet versus some other cause. This is particularly disconcerting given that the manual instructs the test user to inform respondents who exceed a selected cutoff score that "their mood disturbance is in all probability due in part or totally to their consumption of refined sucrose and/or caffeine" (manual, p. 9). Other validity-related research by the author (Christensen & Burrows, 1991) published after the publication of the CDDI manual indicates that CDDI means for dietary responders ($n = 41$, $M = 20.2$, $SD = 4.9$) were greater than those of psychology clinic outpatients ($n = 39$, $M = 12.6$, $SD = 4.8$) and college students enrolled in an introductory psychology course (n = 144, M = 10.0, SD = 4.3). Although such data are encouraging, it does cast some doubt on the CDDI's differential diagnostic abilities when used in accordance with instructions provided in the manual, as the mean for the emotionally distressed outpatient group in the 1991 study (12.6) is almost the same as the suggested cutoff (13.0) for diagnosing dietary-induced mood distress.

In summary, the CDDI is presented as a diagnostic and research tool for the identification of persons whose emotional distress may be the result of dietary factors, specifically the intake of refined sucrose and caffeine. Limited psychometric data presented in the test manual appear inconclusive as to the CDDI's ability to accomplish its stated goal. Additional cross-validation research on the sensitivity and specificity indices with larger and more representative normative samples is urgently needed, as is additional work on the discriminative ability of the CDDI item set. Conceptual concerns related to the formatting of CDDI items warrant further consideration, such as asking respondents to speculate about the origins of their physiological symptoms and psychological complaints, as do almost half of the CDDI items. Can respondents perform such a task accurately? A related problematic aspect of this measure is that many "deviant" response options (i.e., those that contribute to a diagnosis of dietary-influenced emotional distress) indicate the respondent's uncertainty about the origin of a particular symptom or complaint. Furthermore, response options within a set at times seem poorly differentiated (e.g., "every other day" versus "several times a week") despite differential weighting. Given the present limitations of this measure, users should exercise extreme caution when making diagnostic inferences related to the cause of a given examinee's emotional distress based on CDDI scores.

REVIEWER'S REFERENCES

Christensen, L., Krietsch, K., & White, B. (1989). Development, cross-validation, and assessment of reliability of the Christensen Dietary Distress Inventory. *Canadian Journal of Behavioural Science, 21,* 1–15.

Christensen, L., & Burrows, R. (1991). Criterion validity of the Christensen Dietary Distress Inventory. *Canadian Journal of Behavioural Science, 23,* 245–247.

Review of the Christensen Dietary Distress Inventory by SANDRA D. HAYNES, Assistant Professor of Human Services, Metropolitan State College of Denver, Denver, CO:

The Christensen Dietary Distress Inventory (CDDI) is designed to assess the effects of dietary habits on psychological well-being. The inventory was developed to investigate the proposition that persons with emotional distress may experience hypoglycemic-type symptoms which aggrandize mood symptoms. If such difficulties could be identified, the author reasoned, these individuals might enjoy relief of some psychological symptoms, specifically improvement in mood, by relieving hypoglycemic symptoms via changes in diet. Research using the CDDI supported the hypothesis that persons with mood symptoms may experience hypoglycemic symptoms and further research led to the refinement of the instrument to include the ability to discriminate between those individuals who might benefit from dietary refinements from those who might not.

As it currently stands, the test can be used for adults 18 years of age or older. The instrument can be administered individually or in groups and can be completed in approximately 10 minutes. Scoring is likewise quick and easy, accomplished with a single scoring template. The resulting total score is a composite of the assigned weights for the selected responses; weights are given on the scoring template. Confusion, however, may exist for individuals taking the test. There are five possible responses for each item. Each response represents different physiological states and individuals may experience several of the states listed. Although examinees are instructed to select the single, most accurate response, selection may be difficult and confusing. This may be especially true for assessment of persons with eating disorders for whom bodily states are often denied or undetected. Thus, although items were developed in this way to discriminate between "dietary responders" versus "dietary non-responders" (i.e., those whose mood symptoms improve with changes in diet versus those whose mood symptoms do not improve), the test might not be useful with eating-disordered populations for whom concurrent mood disorders are frequent. Interpretation of the test results are likewise not clear cut. The stated purpose of the CDDI is primarily diagnostic and thus scores are not compared to a normative sample. Instead a cutoff score is used. The author, however, does not provide a specific comparison score to be used but rather leaves this decision to the individual user. The selected cutoff score is based on the percentage of false positives and false negatives the user is willing to tolerate. Suggestions for cutoff score selection are offered and a table is provided in the manual listing scores along with their calculated sensitivity and specificity. Scoring is nonetheless relatively ambiguous and the user must make assiduous effort to communicate the rationale used in selecting the cutoff score used to all persons concerned with the test results.

Subjects selected for test construction research and reliability and validity assessment were small in number and little effort was made to include comparisons between different *DSM-IV* (*DSM-III-R* at the time of test publication) diagnosis. Regardless, reliability of the CDDI was assessed via test-retest (interval of 10 days or less) reliability measures and was found to be relatively high (approximately .87). Appropriate to the test's stated use, criterion-related validity was evaluated and was deemed adequate (.48). Content validity appears satisfactory as the method of test construction seems well construed and in line with the current literature in the area related to hypoglycemia and to mood disorders. The research was sound, outside of the noted small sample size, based on an extensive literature review and empirical testing.

It is clear that much data is needed relative to distinguishing between the influence of dietary habits on *DSM-IV* diagnostic categories. The only attempt at differentiation listed in the test manual was for bipolar mood disorder. The author reported that such subjects tended to test as dietary responders but did not, in fact, respond positively when put on a control diet. Such an omission of research is, however, understandable given that this is one of the only attempts to date to quantify the influence of diet on psychological disorders and serves to underscore the necessity of further research in this important area. At the same time, the user must remain cognizant of the fact that the test was designed for use with depressed individuals and that use outside this realm may not be appropriate. It is recommended that test manual revisions include such a statement.

The most disquieting aspect of this instrument is the recommendation of a diet at the end of the test manual. Although the recommendations are reasonable in quelling the symptoms of hypoglycemia, the diet is limited in scope and could amplify other psychological symptoms when used with certain populations (e.g., persons with eating disorders who regularly attempt diets and fail or who already engage in dietary restriction in a detrimental fashion). This points to the need for a user qualification statement in the test manual, a item that is lacking in the current publication of the manual.

The premise of the CDDI is timely given the increased interest in physiological influences on psy-

chological states and in more "natural" remedies for psychological difficulties This instrument, however, appears limited in application especially among persons with eating disorders and concurrent mood disorders. More research is needed to identify the effect of dietary habits on *DSM-IV* diagnoses other than mood disorders. Nonetheless, the efforts of the author of the CDDI warrant applause.

[65]
The City University Colour Vision Test, Second Edition 1980.

Purpose: To assess defects of color vision.
Population: Adults and children.
Publication Date: 1980.
Scores, 3: Chroma Four, Chroma Two, Overall.
Administration: Individual.
Manual: No manual (introductory notes and instructions included in binder of test plates).
Price Data, 1992: $163 per complete kit including profile sheets, 10 test pages, and instructions.
Time: Administration time not reported.
Author: Robert Fletcher.
Publisher: Keeler Instruments, Inc.

Review of The City University Colour Vision Test, Second Edition 1980 by KAREN T. CAREY, Associate Professor of Psychology, California State University, Fresno, Fresno, CA:

The City University Colour Vision Test was developed to assess color vision deficits involving red, green, and yellow. Eleven plates are provided in the spiral-bound binder. Each plate consists of five colored circles with one in the center and four surrounding the center circles. The center circle is the stimulus item and examinees are asked to identify "which spot looks most near in colour to the one in the center" (manual, p. 1) The first plate (A) is used for demonstration purposes and Plates 1 through 10 make up the actual test.

No information is provided within the binder related to norming samples, technical adequacy, or other necessary information about how the test was developed. Information is provided in the notes section of the binder regarding proper illumination of the plates, three brief paragraphs on interpretation, and a recommendation that children and mentally handicapped adults use a "Q-tip pointer" in order that the colored circles on the plates not be touched.

Protocols for administration are provided within the binder and consist of a one-page record form. The examiner should note whether the examinee uses the right eye, left eye, or both eyes and then circle the examinee's response based on whether the examinee identified the circle at the top, bottom, left, or right of the center circle. The number of errors the examinee makes (two or more) suggests borderline color vision problems, with more errors indicating more serious color vision problems.

In summary, there is simply not enough information provided to determine whether the test is valid or reliable. The examiner wanting to assess color vision is advised to select other devices with appropriate technical adequacy.

[66]
The Classroom Communication Skills Inventory: A Listening and Speaking Checklist.

Purpose: Evaluates "oral communication skills that have been determined to be important for listening and speaking in the school setting and are essential for classroom learning."

Population: Students.

Publication Date: 1993.

Acronym: CCSI.

Scores: 10 ratings: Basic Speech and Hearing Processes (Auditory Perception, Speech), Classroom Communication (Attention, Class Participation), Language Content and Structure (Vocabulary, Grammar, Organization of Language), Interpersonal Classroom Communication (Using Language for a Variety of Purposes, Conversing Effectively, Using Appropriate Nonverbal Communication Skills).

Administration: Individual.

Price Data, 1993: $25 per teacher manual (51 pages) and 25 record forms.

Time: (10–15) minutes.

Author: The Psychological Corporation.

Publisher: The Psychological Corporation.

Review of The Classroom Communication Skills Inventory: A Listening and Speaking Checklist by LINDA CROCKER, Professor of Foundations of Education, University of Florida, Gainesville, FL:

The Classroom Communication Skills Inventory (CCSI) is a checklist of listening and speaking skills and behaviors, designed for use by a classroom teacher. The behaviors and skills domains sampled by items on this checklist are intended to allow the administrator to draw inferences about the examinee's abilities to be an active listener and participant in normal classroom instructional settings, to identify areas of strengths and weaknesses in these classroom communication skills, and to suggest underlying reasons for identified weaknesses.

The authors describe the source of items for this checklist as a variety of disciplines such as education, speech-language pathology, psychology, linguistics, and developmental psycholinguistics. No particular theoretical posture has been assumed in development or selection of the items included on the checklist, and no individual authors are named for this instrument.

Although the 52-item checklist is simple and straightforward to use and requires no special training for administration, the administrator must be familiar with the examinee's behavior in the natural classroom setting over a reasonable time period in order to render the types of judgments required by a number of items (e.g., "The student learns vocabulary taught in class lessons and uses the words appropriately in class assignments" or "The student converses with the teacher in one-on-one situations"). In addition, many of the items require the administrator to make subjective judgments about the examinee's performance that have an implied normative basis. For example, an administrator would need to be familiar with behavior of many students at a given grade level in order to judge whether "The student talks neither too much nor too little in class," "The student has an adequate vocabulary size," or "The student's voice is appropriate for age and gender." All items in the Basic Speech and Hearing Process are rated using a 3-point scale: "The behavior has not been observed," "The student appears to exhibit normal behavior," or "The student appears to exhibit below-normal behavior." For other subscales, the scale is expanded to 4 points to include scores for average and above average ability. Obviously, individual classroom teachers may employ substantially different standards in rating examinees on such items. This could result in students with similar levels of performance receiving different scores due to the rater's perspective and base of experience.

A positive feature of the teacher's administration manual is the generous use of examples of classroom strategies to assist students when deficiencies are detected. However, there are no other guidelines for score interpretation. The manual authors suggest that the score for each item on the checklist be interpreted individually.

The information on the sample used to estimate means, standard deviations, reliability coefficients, and standard errors of measurement is sparse. Sample sizes range from 254 for grade 3 to 467 for grade 9. The manual states that the "CCSI was administered in Fall 1992 to a random sample of students in grades 1 through 12 across the nation" (p. 34). This suggests that the authors of the manual have taken some license with the technical definition of "random sample" because it seems highly unlikely that a true random sample could have been drawn from all of the nation's school children for this test administration.

Coefficient alpha reliability coefficients are reported for each subtest and grade-level. It was surprising to note that in most instances, the shortest subtests displayed the highest reliability although according to test theory, we would predict that the longer subtests should be more reliable. In general these coefficients ranged from the mid .70s to the low .80s for sample sizes from 254 to 467 at different grades. Test retest reliability was estimated for a larger sample (n = 1,586) ranging from .28–.88, with a median of .82. These coefficients, however, may be inflated due to the apparent use of a more heterogeneous sample created by combining subjects across multiple grade levels.

Evidence of the construct validity of the scores is limited to the patterns of intercorrelations among the subtest and cluster scores and to results of factor analysis. This analysis also appears to have been applied to a combined sample over multiple grade levels (n = 4,805). These results generally provide evidence of the structural integrity of the scoring scheme; however, there is no evidence of relationship of CCSI scores to an external criterion, such as school achievement.

In summary, the primary strengths of the CCSI lie in its ease of use and the inclusion of instructional strategies to implement when an examinee's ratings for an item or set of items indicate a problem in communication skills. Weaknesses include subjectivity in scoring, limited validity evidence, a discrepancy between the types of reliability coefficients reported and the scoring guidelines, and lack of scoring guides to facilitate teachers' normative judgments. Use of this information for decision making about individual student placement or selection for special programs cannot be supported based on the psychometric data presented to date. The CCSI items, however, may provide classroom teachers with a more detailed and extensive breakdown of behaviors and skills involved in assessing student communication skills than they would think to observe informally.

Review of The Classroom Communication Skills Inventory: A Listening and Speaking Checklist by DOLORES KLUPPEL VETTER, Professor of Communicative Disorders, University of Wisconsin—Madison, Madison, WI:

The Classroom Communication Skills Inventory (CCSI) identifies a number of behaviors that are exemplars of communicative competence and classroom etiquette. The major value of the inventory is that it is a fairly exhaustive list of the skills and abilities required for good communication. In addition, it can be useful in organizing the observations of the classroom teacher. Should the teacher follow the advice in the CCSI teacher's manual and prepare an inventory for each student in the class, the resulting perspective would allow the teacher to plan activities or to arrange seating that should facilitate communication.

The content of the CCSI encompasses four broad categories: Basic Speech and Hearing Processes, Classroom Communication, Language Content and Structure, and Interpersonal Classroom Communication Skills. The CCSI uses the same scales and items for students in grades 1 through 12. There are 3 to 11 items on each scale (i.e., a total of 42 items) and guidelines are provided regarding typical expectations. Teachers, however, are encouraged to use the expectations they have developed from prior experience. They may make their actual ratings from direct observations or from their recall of students' behaviors.

The items on two of the scales, Auditory Reception and Speech, are scored as normal, below normal (referral), or not observed. A plus sign is assigned for normal performance, a minus for below normal, and 0 is assigned when a behavior is not observed. Items on the remaining scales are scored using 4 points (above expectation = 3, average = 2, below expectation = 1, or not observed = 0). When performance is rated below expectation on Auditory Reception, Speech, and Attention, the manual encourages the classroom teacher to refer the student(s) for evaluation by an appropriate specialist (e.g., speech/language pathologist, physician, or special educator).

The means, standard deviations, and standard errors of measurement are provided for random samples of students by grades (approximately 4,800 distributed from grade 1 through grade 12). These statistics require a measurement scale that is at least interval in nature (Reckase, 1984). However, the scaling used for the inventory is ordinal. Therefore, the descriptive statistics provided are not interpretable. The CCSI teacher's manual contains additional statistics that were calculated to provide evidence for internal consistency (coefficient alpha), test-retest reliability (Pearson r), and construct validity (principle-factors factor analysis with an oblique rotation). Again, however, many of these statistics require (arguably) an interval or ratio measurement scale. So, these statistics also are of little value in characterizing test performance.

Another problem becomes apparent if the teacher ignores these measurement problems and attempts a comparison of a student's scores to the descriptive statistics. The CCSI teacher's manual does not contain sufficient information for the user to determine how scores were transformed when the descriptive statistics were calculated. For example, the mean given for the scale Speech, derived from 375 grade 1 students, is 9.25. There is no information about how numbers were assigned to the plus and minus ratings of behaviors nor how to treat ratings of 0 (not observed). Therefore, the CCSI teacher's manual does not provide sufficient guidance to the teacher for making comparisons between a student's ratings and those of the reference group.

When the descriptive statistics in the CCSI teacher's manual are compared across grades, the means and standard deviations for the scales change little in magnitude (e.g., grade 1 Vocabulary mean is 7.22 with a *SD* of 2.03 whereas the grade 12 Vocabulary mean is 7.58 with a *SD* of 2.24). This would indicate that the development (or the acquisition) of vocabulary normally expected throughout elementary and secondary school is not reflected in scores derived from the use of the CCSI. Therefore, it is not clear how to follow the recommendation in the CCSI teacher's manual that the inventory be used to monitor performance changes over time.

Given the nature of the measurement scales and the consequent erroneous descriptive statistics as well as the erroneous evidence for reliability and validity, it is not possible for the data gathered through the use of the CCSI to be used to determine the "students' strengths and weaknesses, as well as to identify possible underlying reasons for those weaknesses" (manual, p. 5). Its only value is as a list of skills and abilities related to good communication around which a classroom teacher can organize observations of students.

REVIEWER'S REFERENCE

Reckase, M. D. (1984). Scaling techniques. In G. Goldstein & M. Hersen (Eds.), *Handbook of psychological assessment* (pp. 38–53). New York: Pergamon Press.

[67]
Clinical Evaluation of Language Fundamentals—Preschool.

Purpose: "Measures a broad range of expressive and receptive language skill in preschool-aged children."
Population: Ages 3-0 to 6-11.

Publication Dates: 1991–1992.
Acronym: CELF-Preschool.
Scores, 9: Receptive Language (Linguistic Concepts, Sentence Structure, Basic Concepts, Total), Expressive Language (Recalling Sentences in Context, Formulating Labels, Word Structure, Total), Total.
Administration: Individual.
Price Data, 1994: $157.50 per complete kit including examiner's manual ('92, 120 pages), 25 record forms, and 3 stimulus manuals; $31.50 per examiner's manual; $26.25 per 25 record forms; $84 per stimulus manual 1; $21 per stimulus manual 2 or stimulus manual 3.
Time: (30–45) minutes.
Comments: A downward extension of the Clinical Evaluation of Language Fundamentals—Revised (T4:521).
Authors: Elisabeth H. Wiig, Wayne Secord, and Eleanor Semel.
Publisher: The Psychological Corporation.

TEST REFERENCES

1. Feldman, H. M., Holland, A. L., & Brown, R. E. (1992). A fluent language disorder following antepartum left-hemisphere brain injury. *Journal of Communication Disorders, 25,* 125–142.
2. Tager-Flusberg, H., & Sullivan, K. (1994). Predicting and examining behavior: A comparison of autistic, mentally retarded and normal children. *Journal of Child Psychology and Psychiatry and Allied Disciplines, 35,* 1059-1075.

Review of the Clinical Evaluation of Language Fundamentals—Preschool by JANET A. NORRIS, Professor of Communication Sciences and Disorders, Louisiana State University, Baton Rouge, LA:

The Clinical Evaluation of Language Fundamentals—Preschool (CELF-Preschool) is a standardized test instrument designed to assess performance in aspects of language that are fundamental to the development of effective communication skills. These are defined as receptive and expressive language abilities in the areas of word meanings (semantics), word and sentence structure (morphology and syntax), and recall of spoken language (auditory memory). The six subtests are standardized for ages 3 years through 6 years 11 months. The information obtained is recommended for use in identifying language disorders, determining eligibility for treatment or special services programs, analyzing relative strengths and weaknesses in language, and identifying areas of language in need of more extensive testing. The results of the CELF-Preschool are to be considered as one source of data used in making diagnostic or treatment decisions in conjunction with personal and educational history, observations of behavior, results of other formal and informal assessments, and information provided by individuals familiar with the child in a variety of communicative situations.

The stated goal of the CELF-Preschool is not to measure all of the variables that may contribute to or explain a child's language delay or disability. Instead, the test is intended to evaluate language skills, and to use the resulting profile of abilities to differentiate normal from disordered development, and generalized deficits from receptive or expressive language deficits. Three of the subtests are receptive, and three are primarily expressive. These subtests parallel the test format and content of a related instrument, the Clinical Evaluation of Language Fundamentals—Revised (CELF-R; Semel, Wiig, & Secord, 1987; T4:521), and are considered a downward extension of that instrument, which is designed for school-aged children. The skills assessed by the CELF-Preschool reportedly examine the prerequisites of those language abilities measured by the CELF-R.

The test manual provides a detailed discussion of test administration and scoring, test interpretation, standardization, adaptations that may be made for children who are difficult to test, and additional test instruments that may be used to explore any of the language abilities assessed by the six subtests in greater depth when conducting follow-up testing. In addition, appendices provide examples of scored protocols that may be used to practice scoring, and a comprehensive chart highlighting dialectal variations of morphology and syntax that should not be scored as errors. The manual is clearly written and sufficiently detailed to provide anyone knowledgeable about language and principles of assessment with enough information to administer, score, and interpret the test.

One weakness of the CELF-Preschool is the lack of any theoretical justification for the language abilities assessed. Only general statements are given to explain the selection of subtests or their component items, such as "to assess areas of relevant linguistic development in 3- through 6-year-old children" (p. 39), or to evaluate "early acquired linguistic concepts" (p. 39). Furthermore, minimal information is provided regarding item selection or evaluation during test construction phases. The manual indicates which categories of items are included for each subtest, but not how or why those were selected. Therefore, although content validity is claimed, no demonstration is provided that this was achieved. The manual does indicate that items were deleted when shown to have poor content, discriminating power, or when they demonstrated bias for any gender or racial/ethnic group, but not how this was determined.

The lack of a theoretical basis for subtest and item selection may be a contributing factor to problems with construct validity exhibited by the CELF-Preschool. The manual describes a study comparing the performance of groups of children with identified language disorders to children without language disorders. The CELF-Preschool was only moderately effective in discriminating between the two groups. When the performance criteria of 1.5 standard deviations below the mean was used, the CELF-Preschool correctly identified children as having or not having language disorders only 71% of the time, or an incorrect identification for greater than one out of every four test administrations. However, even this represented an overestimate of the test's effectiveness. Performance on the CELF-Preschool selected fewer than half of the children tested (i.e., 38 out of 80) who had identified language disorders. Consequently, the test cannot be confidently used for the purposes for which it was developed, including identifying children with language disorders and determining eligibility for treatment or special services programs. Use of the CELF-Preschool is particularly problematic for the Receptive Language composite, which has a large standard error of measurement (*SEM*). At the 90% confidence level, the interval recommended by the test for eligibility and placement decisions, the range of scores within which a child's "true" score may fall is more than one standard deviation at most of the age intervals.

Reliability for the CELF-Preschool was estimated by calculating internal test consistency and test-retest reliability coefficients, with mixed results. Internal consistency was measured by an alpha coefficient for each of the six subtests for each of the eight 6-month age intervals. Only 3 out of 48 coefficients were above .90 with the majority being between .61 and .89. A small sample of 57 children was employed to measure test-retest reliability. Although the composite (Receptive, Expressive, and Total/Language) scores were sufficiently high to warrant the use of the CELF-Preschool for evaluation and placement purposes, none of the six subtests met the minimum .90 criterion recommended for diagnostic decisions (Salvia & Ysseldyke, 1988). The test-retest reliability coefficient of the Sentence Structure subtest was .64, the remaining subtests had coefficients between .81 and .89. Because of the relatively low test-retest reliability of the Sentence Structure subtest, and because this subtest also had among the lowest coefficient alphas, scores should be interpreted with caution.

Several measures of concurrent validity were obtained for the CELF-Preschool, including tests of language, intelligence, and cognition and achievement. The CELF-Preschool is described as a downward extension of the CELF-R, with each subtest of the CELF-Preschool assessing prerequisite parallel skills of the CELF-R. The two tests have overlapping age norms for the interval between 5 years and 6 years, 11 months. Eighty children in this age interval with diagnosed language disorders were administered both tests. Correlations between performance on the two tests was low to moderate for individual subtests (range .27 to .84) and moderate for composite scores (range .63 to .93). These results suggest that the two instruments assess related language skills but not parallel abilities. High correlations, ranging from .73 to .90, were obtained when the CELF-Preschool was compared to another measure of oral language, the Preschool Language Scale-3 (PLS-3; Zimmerman, Steiner, & Pond, 1992), indicating that the two tests measured similar skills. However, no description of the language status of children included in this study is provided, and the reported mean standard scores (all close to 100) suggest that primarily children with normal language development were compared. Only moderate correlations were obtained when performance on the CELF-Preschool was compared to tests of intelligence and to tests of cognition and achievement, indicting that related but different abilities were assessed by these instruments. Overall, concurrent validity for the CELF-Preschool was shown to be good.

The normative sample on which the standard scores were derived was representative of preschool students in the U.S. The norming sample comprised 800 children stratified for age, gender, race/ethnicity, geographic region, and mother's educational level. The recommended number of 100 subjects per age interval (Salvia & Ysseldyke, 1988) was maintained. It is assumed that the scoring instructions regarding acceptability of dialectal variations were followed, suggesting that bias related to cultural differences in language form was minimized.

Test materials are well constructed and thoughtfully designed. Pictures are colorful and attractive to preschool-aged children. Children from a range of race/ethnic groups are depicted in the drawings. The record form is well organized with many features designed to maximize the accuracy and efficiency of test administration and scoring. For example, small sketches of the pictures are included on the record

form so that the order in which pictures are pointed to can be recorded when two- to three-part commands are given.

In summary, the CELF-Preschool has many positive features in its test design and scoring. Considerable effort was made to create a language test that could be used reliably to make initial decisions regarding the presence or absence of a language disorder in preschool children. However, findings of construct validity suggest that the test may not adequately discriminate between populations of children with and without language disorders, rendering this test of limited use for its stated purposes.

REVIEWER'S REFERENCES

Semel, E. M., Wiig, E. H., & Secord, W. A. (1987). Clinical Evaluation of Language Fundamentals—Revised. San Antonio, TX: The Psychological Corporation.

Salvia, J., & Ysseldyke, J. E. (1988). Assessment in special and remedial education (4th ed.). Boston: Houghton Mifflin.

Zimmerman, I. L., Steiner, V. G., & Pond, R. E. (1992). Preschool Language Scale-3. San Antonio, TX: The Psychological Corporation.

Review of the Clinical Evaluation of Language Fundamentals—Preschool by NORA M. THOMPSON, Neuropsychologist, Center on Human Development and Disabilities, University Hospital, Seattle, WA:

PURPOSE. The Clinical Evaluation of Language Fundamentals—Preschool (CELF-Preschool), a downward extension of the widely used Clinical Evaluation of Language Fundamentals—Revised (CELF-R; T4:521), is an individually administered test designed to identify, diagnose, and perform follow-up evaluations of language deficit in preschool children. Language form and content are assessed through subtests measuring semantics, morphology, syntax, and auditory memory. Summary standard scores reflecting receptive, expressive, and total language performance are derived. The test is designed to be administered by preschool education professionals (e.g., speech-language pathologists, child psychologists, and special educators) to children 3 years through 6 years, 11 months of age.

ADMINISTRATION AND SCORING. Average time to administer the CELF-Preschool ranges from 30 to 45 minutes, depending on the child's age and cooperation. The Examiner's Manual outlines in sufficient detail the standardized instructions for test administration. The new user must allow sufficient time to practice administration of all subtests to administer them in a standardized fashion. The test materials are colorful and interesting to preschool children. All six subtests have trial items that allow the examiner to teach the task through verbal and, if necessary, physical feedback. The Response Booklet is designed for ease in recording responses with examiner prompts and sufficient space to write verbatim responses or observations. The scoring process and derivation of standard scores are well explained in the Examiner's Manual and supplemented with practice scoring samples and dialectal variations. Interpretive information presented in the manual is complete and illustrated by case material. Extensive information is provided regarding extension testing and developing instructional objectives.

RELIABILITY AND VALIDITY. The provided normative data are based on a nationally representative standardization sample (n = 800), stratified on the basis of age (100 children at each of eight 6-month intervals), gender, race and ethnicity, parent education level, and geographic region. Internal consistency, test-retest reliability, and interrater reliability are acceptable, ranging from r = .30 to r = .97. Correlations between the CELF-Preschool and the Preschool Language Scale-3 are robust, from r = .73 to r = .90. Moderate correlations are reported with measures of general cognitive ability (r = .45 to r = .72).

SUMMARY. The CELF-Preschool provides the educational specialist a carefully designed and well-developed method for systematically evaluating basic language skills of preschool children. Although some time is needed to master the administration procedures, this is made up for by the ease of use, the appeal of the materials to the child, and solid normative data. This is a test that can be used with confidence in the identification of language deficit during the preschool years.

[68]
Clinical Evaluation of Language Fundamentals, Third Edition.

Purpose: Constructed as a "clinical tool for the identification, diagnosis, and follow-up evaluation of language skill deficits."

Population: Ages 6.0–21.11.

Publication Dates: 1980–1995.

Acronym: CELF—3.

Administration: Individual.

Price Data: Available from publisher.

Time: (30–45) minutes.

Authors: Eleanor Semel, Elisabeth H. Wiig, and Wayne A. Secord.

Publisher: The Psychological Corporation.

a) CELF—3, AGES 6–8.

Population: Ages 6–8.

Scores, 12: Receptive Language (Sentence Structure, Concepts and Directions, Word Classes); Expressive Language (Word Structure, Formulated Sen-

tences, Recalling Sentences); Total Language; Supplementary Subtests (Word Associations, Listening to Paragraphs); Rapid/Automatic Naming [optional].

b) CELF—3, AGES 9+.

Population: Ages 9–21.11.

Scores, 12: Receptive Language (Concepts and Directions, Word Classes, Semantic Relationships); Expressive Language (Formulated Sentences, Recalling Sentences, Sentence Assembly); Total Language; Supplementary Subtests (Word Associations, Listening to Paragraphs); Rapid/Automatic Naming [optional].

Cross References: See T4:521 (5 references); for reviews by Linda Crocker and David A. Shapiro of an earlier edition, see 11:72; for a review by Dixie D. Sanger of an earlier edition, see 9:233 (2 references); see also T3:474.

TEST REFERENCES

1. Bedrosian, J. L., & Willis, T. L. (1987). Effects of treatment on the topic performance of a school-age child. *Language, Speech, and Hearing Services in Schools, 18*, 158–167.
2. Fujiki, M., Brinton, B., & Dunton, S. (1987). A grammatical judgement screening test for young elementary school-aged children. *Language, Speech, and Hearing Services in Schools, 18*, 131–143.
3. Hall, P. K., & Jordan, L. S. (1987). An assessment of a controlled association task to identify word-finding problems in children. *Language, Speech, and Hearing Services in Schools, 18*, 99–111.
4. Frisk, V., & Milner, B. (1990). The relationship of working memory to the immediate recall of stories following unilateral temporal or frontal lobectomy. *Neuropsychologia, 28*, 121–135.
5. Fujiki, M., & Brinton, B. (1991). The verbal noncommunicator: A case study. *Language, Speech, and Hearing Services in Schools, 22*, 322–333.
6. Miniutti, A. M. (1991). Language deficiencies in inner-city children with learning and behavioral problems. *Language, Speech, and Hearing Services in Schools, 22*, 31–38.
7. Wilson, K. S., Blackmon, R. C., Hall, R. E., & Elcholtz, G. E. (1991). Methods of language assessment: A survey of California public school clinicians. *Language, Speech, and Hearing Services in Schools, 22*, 236–241.
8. Aram, D. M., Morris, R., & Hall, N. E. (1992). The validity of discrepancy criteria for identifying children with developmental language disorders. *Journal of Learning Disabilities, 25*, 549–554.
9. Lawrence, C. W. (1992). Assessing the use of age-equivalent scores in clinical management. *Language, Speech, and Hearing Services in Schools, 23*, 6–8.
10. Lewis, B. A. (1992). Pedigree analysis of children with phonology disorders. *Journal of Learning Disabilities, 25*, 586–597.
11. Lewis, B. A., & Freebairn, L. (1992). Residual effects of preschool phonology disorders in grade school, adolescence, and adulthood. *Journal of Speech and Hearing Research, 35*, 819–831.
12. Lorsbach, T. C., Sodoro, J., & Brown, J. S. (1992). The dissociation of repetition priming and recognition memory in language/learning-disabled children. *Journal of Experimental Child Psychology, 54*, 121–146.
13. Mack, A. E., & Warr-Leeper, G. A. (1992). Language abilities in boys with chronic behavior disorders. *Language, Speech, and Hearing Services in Schools, 23*, 214–223.
14. Craig, H. K., & Evans, J. L. (1993). Pragmatics and SLI: Within-group variations in discourse behaviors. *Journal of Speech and Hearing Research, 36*, 777–789.
15. Masterson, J. J., Evans, L. H., & Aloia, M. (1993). Verbal analogical reasoning in children with language-learning disabilities. *Journal of Speech and Hearing Research, 36*, 76–82.
16. Bellaire, S., Plante, E., & Swisher, L. (1994). Bound-morpheme skills in the oral language of school-age, language-impaired children. *Journal of Communication Disorders, 27*, 265–279.
17. Ghaziuddin, M., Bolyard, B., & Alessi, N. (1994). Autistic disorder in Noonan syndrome. *Journal of Intellectual Disability Research, 38*, 67–72.
18. Murphy, D. G. M., Allen, G., Haxby, J. V., Largay, K. A., Daly, E., White, B. J., Powell, L. M., & Schapiro, M. B. (1994). The effects of sex steroids and the X chromosome on female brain function: A study of the neuropsychology of adult Turner syndrome. *Neuropsychologia, 32*, 1309–1323.
19. North, K., Joy, P., Yuille, D., Cocks, N., Mobb, E., Hutchins, P., McHugh, K., & deSilva, M. (1994). Specific learning disability in children with neurofibromatosis type 1: Significance of MRI abnormalities. *Neurology, 44*, 878–883.
20. Tager-Flusberg, H., & Sullivan, K. (1994). A second look at second-order belief attributions in autism. *Journal of Autism and Developmental Disorders, 24*, 577–586.
21. Gillam, R. B., Cowan, N., & Day, L. S. (1995). Sequential memory in children with and without language impairment. *Journal of Speech and Hearing Research, 38*, 393–402.

22. Gillon, G., & Dodd, B. (1995). The effects of training phonological, semantic, and syntactic processing skills in spoken language on reading ability. *Language, Speech, and Hearing Services in Schools, 26,* 58–68.

23. Johnson, C. J. (1995). Expanding norms for narration. *Language, Speech, and Hearing Services in Schools, 26,* 326–341.

24. Lahey, M., & Edwards, J. (1995). Specific language impairment: Preliminary investigation of factors associated with family history and with patterns of language performance. *Journal of Speech and Hearing Research, 38,* 643–657.

25. Liles, B. Z., Duffy, R. J., Merritt, D. D., & Purcell, S. L. (1995). Measurement of narrative discourse ability in children with language disorders. *Journal of Speech and Hearing Research, 38,* 415–425.

26. Montgomery, J. W. (1995). Sentence comprehension in children with specific language impairment: The role of phonological working memory. *Journal of Speech and Hearing Research, 38,* 187–199.

27. Oetting, J. B., Rice, M. L., & Swank, L. K. (1995). Quick incidental learning (QUIL) of words by school-age children with and without SLI. *Journal of Speech and Hearing Research, 38,* 434–445.

28. Rustin, L., & Cook, F. (1995). Parental involvement in the treatment of stuttering. *Language, Speech, and Hearing Services in Schools, 26,* 127–137.

29. Schloss, P. J., Alper, S., Young, H., Arnold-Reid, G., Aylward, M., & Dudenhoeffer, S. (1995). Acquisition of functional sight words in community-based recreation settings. *The Journal of Special Education, 29,* 84–96.

30. Scott, C. M., & Stokes, S. L. (1995). Measures of syntax in school-age children and adolescents. *Language, Speech, and Hearing Services in Schools, 26,* 309–319.

31. Taylor, H. G., Hack, M., Klein, N., & Schatschneider, C. (1995). Achievement in children with birth weights less than 750 grams with normal cognitive abilities: Evidence for specific learning disabilities. *Journal of Pediatric Psychology, 20,* 703–719.

32. Tomblin, J. B., Abbas, P. J., Records, N. L., & Brenneman, L. M. (1995). Auditory evoked responses to frequency-modulated tones in children with specific language impairment. *Journal of Speech and Hearing Research, 38,* 387–392.

33. Fujiki, M., Brinton, B., & Todd, C. M. (1996). Social skills of children with specific language impairment. *Language, Speech, and Hearing Services in Schools, 27,* 195–202.

34. McFadden, T. V. (1996). Creating language impairments in typically achieving children: The pitfalls of "normal" normative sampling. *Language, Speech, and Hearing Services in Schools, 27,* 3–9.

35. Sabers, D. L. (1996). By their tests we will know them. *Language, Speech, and Hearing Services in Schools, 27,* 102–108.

36. Schneider, P., & Watkins, R. V. (1996). Applying Vygotskian developmental theory to language intervention. *Language, Speech, and Hearing Services in Schools, 27,* 157–170.

37. Ward-Lonergan, J. M., Liles, B. Z., & Owen, S. V. (1996). Contextual strategy instruction: Socially/emotionally maladjusted adolescents with language impairments. *Journal of Communication Disorders, 29,* 107–124.

38. Wiig, E. H., Jones, S. S., & Wiig, E. D. (1996). Computer-based assessment of word knowledge in teens with learning disabilities. *Language, Speech, and Hearing Services in Schools, 27,* 21–28.

Review of the Clinical Evaluation of Language Fundamentals, Third Edition by RONALD B. GILLAM, Assistant Professor of Communication Sciences and Disorders, The University of Texas at Austin, Austin, TX:

The Clinical Evaluation of Language Fundamentals, Third Edition (CELF-3) was developed for identifying, diagnosing, and providing follow-up evaluations of language skills in individuals between 6 and 21 years of age. The CELF-3 consists of 11 subtests, but only 6 of the 11 are needed to obtain Receptive Language, Expressive Language, and Total Language Scores.

Like the original edition of the CELF and its first revision (the CELF-R), the CELF-3 was designed to assess language content and form in listening (receptive) or speaking (expressive) domains. Three subtests—Concepts and Directions, Word Classes, and Word Associations—assess language content in tasks that minimize syntactic complexity. Two subtests—Sentence Structure and Word Struc-

ture—assess language form in tasks that minimize vocabulary and semantic complexity. Five subtests—Listening to Paragraphs, Semantic Relationships, Sentence Assembly, Recalling Sentences, and Formulated Sentences—assess form-content interactions in tasks that place heavy demands on each domain and on working memory. A final subtest—Rapid, Automatic Naming—measures accuracy and speed of naming colors and shapes.

Examiners who are familiar with the CELF-R will note that the subtests on the CELF-3 are somewhat shorter (six subtests can be completed in about 30–45 minutes), and the materials are more colorful and engaging. Like the CELF-R, the CELF-3 is relatively easy to learn and use. The Formulated Sentences subtest has been improved by having children create sentences that correspond with color pictures, but this subtest still poses scoring challenges. The authors provide ample scoring support in the form of directions, examples, and practice items.

The CELF-3 was normed on 2,450 students; 200 students in each year between the ages of 6:0 and 16:0, and 50 students in each year between the ages of 17:0 and 21:11. The norming sample was stratified to represent the U.S. population of individuals between the ages of 6 and 21 years with respect to age, gender, race/ethnicity, geographic region, and parent education level. Unfortunately, the normative sample was limited to normally achieving children. This poses interpretation problems for those who wish to use the test for identifying children with language impairments. If only normally achieving children were tested, and the entire range of scores presented in the manual were obtained by children who were "normal," what would constitute an abnormal score? A better approach to selecting participants for norming would have been to sample randomly from the population of interest.

The reliability of the CELF-3 was evaluated through measures of internal consistency, test-retest reliability, and interrater reliability. Tests of internal consistency revealed that the Receptive Language, Expressive Language, and Total Language composite scores (M = .91, range .83–.95) are more reliable than the individual subtest scores (M = .77, range = .54–.91). Reliability for the Listening to Paragraphs subtest (M = .66, range = .55–.77) was particularly low. Test-retest reliability was assessed by repeated administration of the CELF-3 with 152 examinees between the ages of 7 and 13 years. This group evidenced consistently higher scores on the second administration. Stability quotients across ages were .90 or higher for only one subtest, Recalling Sentences. Interrater reliability was assessed for the Formulated Sentences and Word Associations subtests by correlating the subtest total raw scores from two different raters. Correlations ranged from .70 to .99. The better procedure, however, would have been to assess interrater reliability by correlating item-by-item scores rather than total raw scores. In summary, the CELF-3 suffers from a variety of reliability problems.

Three interrelated types of validity were considered in the validation of the CELF-3: content validity, construct validity, and concurrent validity. The authors support the content validity of the CELF-3 by pointing out that the language skills that are sampled on the test are well documented in the child language development and disorders literature. This is true, and numerous examples of the subtest tasks can be found in the literature as well.

Construct validity was assessed by factor analysis and discriminant analysis studies. Results of factor analysis calculations indicated that one factor accounted for approximately 50% of the variance of the scores. No other factor accounted for more than 10% of the variance. Thus, the CELF-3 measures one dominant skill, which the authors call language ability. Another study compared Total Language scores earned by age- and gender-matched children who had or had not been previously diagnosed with a language disorder. Mean scores for the previously identified children were lower than mean scores for the nonidentified group, but standard deviations indicated that there was a great deal of overlap between scores of the two groups. Even with an extremely liberal cutoff score of 1 SD below the mean, the CELF-3 misclassified 29% of the children. Most of the classification errors related to children who had been identified as language impaired by their school system, but who did not score 1 or more standard deviations below the mean on the CELF-3. It does not appear that the CELF-3 assesses language form separately from language content or receptive language separately from expressive language, and it is not a powerful instrument for distinguishing between normal and disordered language performance.

Concurrent validity of the CELF-3 was assessed by investigating relationships between CELF-3 and CELF-R scores and between CELF-3 and WISC-III (Wechsler Intelligence Scale for Children—Third Edition) scores. One would expect two versions of the same test to correlate highly, so correlations between the CELF-R and the CELF-3 say little about validity. Strong correlations between the CELF-3 and the WISC-III ($r = .75$) add additional support to the idea that the CELF-3 measures general verbal ability. However, tests of concurrent criterion-related validity (correlating results of the CELF-3 with results from another language test) and predictive criterion-related validity (correlating results of the CELF-3 with results from a test of academic ability) would have been more convincing.

In conclusion, the CELF-3 should be used with caution. This test was developed to assess language form and content in receptive and expressive domains, and to diagnose language impairment in students between the ages of 6 and 21 years. Neither the design nor the purpose of the CELF-3 are supported by the reliability and validity studies reported in the technical manual. Factor analysis results indicate that the CELF-3 assesses general language ability predominantly. This finding, in combination with low subtest reliability results, suggests that examiners should not reach conclusions about the specific nature of language difficulties or generate instructional objectives based on subtest performance. Finally, because of its low discriminative power, examiners who base diagnostic decisions about language impairment on CELF-3 results risk underidentifying students who may, in fact, evidence significant language difficulties. This would be especially problematic for states or school districts with 1.5 SD or lower cutoff requirements. Use of the CELF-3 should be limited to contexts in which the examiner wishes only to determine a student's overall language ability with reference to a large sample of "normal" children. The CELF-3 should not be used to diagnose language impairment.

Review of the Clinical Evaluation of Language Fundamentals, Third Edition by JOHN MacDONALD, School Psychologist, North Kitsap School District, Kingston, WA:

The authors intend the Clinical Evaluation of Language Fundamentals, Third Edition (CELF-3) to identify individuals with language disabilities, diagnose the nature and degree of a language disability, identify strengths and weaknesses, identify areas for more extensive assessment, and plan intervention. The CELF-3 has updated norms, revised subtests and items, and color stimuli.

Materials are pleasant and interesting. Few authors document tests so well. They provide extensive rationales for each subtest. Scoring guides include clear objectives and sample answers. A chapter on "Extension Testing," similar to testing-the-limits, describes extra diagnostic procedures, instructional objectives, and instructional resources for each subtest. An appendix describes dialectal variations and another includes training exercises for two difficult-to-score subtests.

Standardization norms were collected from 2,450 individual in 12 age groups, representative of the 1988 U.S. Census population survey for gender, ethnicity, region, and parental education. A panel of 10 experts in speech and language pathology and test bias reviewed all materials for gender, ethnic, and regional biases.

Internal consistency is disappointing. Coefficient alphas for Sentence Structure are in the .60s, Word Structure .80s, Concepts and Directions .59 to .88, Formulated Sentences .54 to .91, Word Classes .67 to .88, Recalling Sentences .83 to .90, Sentence Assembly .73 to .88, Semantic Relationships .67 to .85, Word Association .65 to .83, and Listening to Paragraphs .55 to .77. Individual subtests should be interpreted cautiously, and not interpreted at all when reliability is low. A ceiling effect would reduce score variability, limiting reliability. Such an effect is most likely in the upper developmental ranges of a test. Examining Table 3.1 in the technical manual suggests this is the case for Concepts and Directions, Formulated Sentences, Word Classes, and Listening to Paragraphs.

Internal consistency for Composite scores is barely adequate—.83 to .91 for Receptive Language, .84 to .94 for Expressive Language, and .91 to .95 for Total Language.

The authors provide computed 68% and 90% confidence intervals in the examiner's manual. These use the obtained score as the midpoint, rather than the estimated true score. It is surprising, given that other Psychological Corporation tests (e.g., the Wechsler Intelligence Scale for Children, Third Edition [WISC-III]) provide confidence intervals based on the estimated true score as the midpoint. With high-reliability tests, this error can be ignored without much damage. But the CELF-3 has less than high reliability. A 14-year-old obtaining a Receptive Language composite scores of 69 has an estimated true score of 72—that is, even chances of obtaining a score above or below 72 on retesting. A 68% confidence interval for the true score would be 67 to 77, not 64 to 74 as given in the manual.

Test-retest reliability varies from .52 for Sentence Structure to .90 for Recalling Sentences, and .80, .86, and .91 for Receptive, Expressive, and Total language Composites. Retest intervals were 1 to 4 weeks.

Admirably, the authors include extensive training sets for scoring Formulated Sentences and Word Associations subtests. This appears to pay off— interrater agreement varies from .97 and .99 for Word Associations and is as high as .91 for Formulated Sentences at age 6. Agreement drops off to .85 at age 11 and .70 at age 16, possibly due to a ceiling effect on this subtest, as variance in raw scores drops off at higher ages.

There is developmental validity for most subtests, with the exception of Listening to Paragraphs. There is little growth in mean raw scores on most subtests from age 11 to 21, with more variance within one-year age groups than between age groups.

Principal components analysis indicates a single factor accounts for half the variance in CELF-3 subtest scores. Second, third, and fourth factors account for less than 10% of the variance each. Correlations between the CELF-3 and CELF-R range from .42 to .75 on equivalent subtests, and from .72 to .79 on Composite scores. CELF-R scores were 3 points lower on Receptive Language, 9 points lower on Expressive Language, and 5 points lower on Total Language.

The correlation between CELF-3 Total language and WISC-III Full Scale is .75, comparable to the correlation between CELF-3 and CELF-R Total Language scores. Along with the finding of a strong single factor underlying CELF-3 subtests, this begs the question of whether the CELF-3 subtests are measuring anything other than general intellectual ability. CELF-3 Total scores do correlate more highly with WISC-III Verbal (.75) than with WISC-III Performance (.60) scales.

The CELF-3 correctly classified 85% of school-district-identified students without language disorders, and 57% of students with language disorders.

This is an interesting test. It has excellent norms and the authors have done a model job of documentation. Unfortunately, it suffers from marginal subtest reliability, which limits ability to individually interpret subtest scores, particularly at adolescent and young adult age ranges. It seems to be measuring intellectual ability as much as oral language skills. In the hands of a competent, observant, and resourceful speech and language pathologist it appears useful. The extension testing procedures appear especially valuable.

Clinical Evaluation of Language Fundamentals—3 Screening Test.

Purpose: "Designed to screen school age children, adolescents, and young adults for language disorders."
Population: Ages 6-0 to 21-11.
Publication Dates: 1995–1996.
Acronym: CELF-3 Screening Test.
Scores: Total score only.
Administration: Individual.
Price Data, 1996: $125.50 per kit including examiner's manual ('96, 55 pages), stimulus manual, and 25 record forms; $35 per examiner's manual; $64.50 per stimulus manual; $30 per 25 record forms; $52.50 for a briefcase (available separately from kit).
Time: (10–15) minutes.
Comments: A test in the CELF series of language testing instruments; administered orally with visual stimuli; not for diagnostic use; "criterion-referenced."
Authors: Eleanor Semel, Elisabeth H. Wiig, and Wayne A. Secord.
Publisher: The Psychological Corporation.
Cross References: For reviews by Linda M. Crocker and Jon F. Miller of an earlier edition, see 9:234.

TEST REFERENCES

1. Masterson, J. J. (1993). The performance of children with language-learning disabilities on two types of cognitive tasks. *Journal of Speech and Hearing Research, 36,* 1026–1036.

Review of the Clinical Evaluation of Language Fundamentals—Revised Screening Test by BILLY T. OGLETREE, Assistant Professor of Communication Disorders, College of Education and Allied Professions, Western Carolina University, Cullowhee, NC:

[Editor's Note: This review is based on the CELF–R Screening Test and was prepared before the new CELF–3 Screening Test materials were available.]

The purpose of the Clinical Evaluation of Language Fundamentals—Revised (CELF-R) Screening Test is to identify children between the ages of 5 and 16 who are at risk for language disorders. The CELF-R Screening Test packet includes an examiner's manual, stimulus materials, and test forms. The examiner's manual describes the test's development and provides guidelines specific to administration, scoring, and score interpretation. Stimulus materials include an easel cover and black-and-white stimulus pictures. The CELF-R Screening Test's design, use, and technical aspects are described below.

The CELF-R Screening Test is designed to present, in condensed form, those aspects of the CELF-R (Semel, Wiig, & Secord, 1987) that best differentiate age levels and language abilities of school-age children. Step-wise discriminant analytic procedures and item analyses were used to identify critical items within the CELF-R. These items, then, served as the models from which parallel items were constructed for the screening version.

The CELF-R Screening Test is composed of six standard and two supplemental sections. Section 1 consists of 13 items that parallel those presented in the CELF-R's Word Structure subtest. Each item uses a carrier phrase format to elicit a response expressing a morphological rule. Target forms include irregular noun plurals, possessives, third person present tense, regular and irregular past tense, regular and irregular comparative and superlative adjectives, and reflexive pronouns. Section 2 consists of 8 items combining features of CELF-R's Linguistic Concepts and Oral Directions subtests. Items address one-, two-, and three-level verbal commands and modifiers indicating orientation, size, and/or color. Section 3 consists of 8 items designed to parallel content from CELF-R's Recalling Sentences subtest. Noun modification, coordination of phrases and clauses, subordination of clauses with "after," and relativization are addressed. Section 4 consists of 8 items that parallel those presented in CELF-R's Word Classes subtest. Items address associative relationships based upon class, space, and time. Section 5 consists of 8 items that parallel content from CELF-R's Semantic Relationships subtest. Comparative, passive, spatial, and temporal relationships are addressed. Finally, Section 6 consists of 8 items paralleling content from CELF-R's Sentence Assembly subtest. Items address simple sentences with direct and indirect objects, coordination of clauses with "and," negation, subordination of clauses with "after" and "even though," and relativization.

The two supplemental sections of the CELF-R Screening Test address oral and written expression. The Oral Expression subtest consists of two stories following conventional story lines. Written Expression consists of three single paragraphs designed for different age groups.

Both professionals and trained paraprofessionals can serve as examiners for the CELF-R Screening Test. Paraprofessionals are encouraged to administer the test 10 times under supervision before using results independently. Prior to administration, the examiner determines which sections of the CELF-R Screening Test are appropriate for the child based upon chronological age. For all standard sections of the test, one stimulus item is presented at a time beginning with trial items. When administering Sections 1, 5, and 6, items can be repeated once if requested by the child or if the child does not respond within 10 seconds. No repetitions are allowed for other sections including supplemental sections. Oral and Written Expression sections are optional and administered only if information is desired in these areas. Appropriate administration of the Oral Expression section requires examiners to be familiar with the schema and details of stimulus stories. Guidelines to assist with examiner familiarization are provided. Administration of this section involves the presentation of the story picture and the careful reading of the story. Afterwards, the child is encouraged to look at the picture and retell the story. When administering the Written Expression subtest, the examiner selects and becomes familiar with the paragraph corresponding to the child's chronological age. The examiner then instructs the child to write down as much of the paragraph as possible after it is read. Although the record form provides space for written samples, examiners are encouraged to have additional writing materials on hand.

The CELF-R Screening Test should be administered in one sitting; however, if children are clearly not performing due to frustration/fatigue, the test can be discontinued and finished at a later date. If this occurs, it should be noted on the record form. The CELF-R Screening Test is untimed with the exception of the Written Expression subtest. Administration of the standard subtests should take no more than 10 minutes.

Examiners are encouraged to consider dialectal variations (provided in Appendix A of the examiner's manual) when scoring the CELF-R Screening Test. For Sections 1, 2, 4, 5, and 6, a correct response receives a score of 1, an incorrect response receives a score of 0, and a stimulus item not responded to receives a score of "NR." For Section 3, responses are scored 0 to 3 with 0 signifying no response. A score scale of 1–4 is used for the supplemental sections. Scoring keys are provided for these sections.

Raw scores for each standard section are summed and recorded in spaces provided on the record form. These scores are then transferred to the Scoring Summary section of the record form and tallied. Finally, this total raw score is compared to a criterion score based upon the child's age. A total score below the criterion score is used as support for a complete diagnostic evaluation. Holistic scoring is

used for supplemental sections. According to the authors, holistic scoring necessitates judgments of acceptability against internalized models of intactness. The examiner's manual provides holistic scoring guidelines and scoring examples specific to the Written Expression subtest. Scores from the supplemental sections are recorded at the bottom of the record form. Performance patterns indicating weaknesses and referral options are also provided in the examiner's manual.

The technical aspects of the CELF-R Screening Test are clearly presented in the examiner's manual. These include complete discussions of standardization, validity, and reliability. The CELF-R Screening Test and CELF-R were administered concurrently to 2,273 children from across the United States of America. This sample reflected national and regional trends specific to age, sex, racial origin, and parental occupation. Criterion scores were established for each age level based upon the relationship between raw scores on the CELF-R Screening Test and composite standard scores on the CELF-R. Specifically, criterion scores were selected to identify 100% of children scoring at or below a standard score of 70 on the CELF-R and 70% of children scoring at or below a standard score of 85.

Evidence for content validity, criterion-related validity, and construct validity is provided in the examiner manual. Content validity is supported by the screening test's relationship to the CELF-R, a valid measure of language. Criterion-related validity is supported by correlation coefficients reported between CELF-R Screening Test scores and CELF-R Total Language raw scores. Correlations varied across age groups ranging from .66 to .87. Correlations for 10 of 12 age groups were .75 or higher. The authors note that validity of a screening test should be described in terms of the measure's ability to correctly identify "at risk" subjects. There was only a 4% false-negative rate reported in the manual. That is, only 4% of the sample passed the CELF-R Screening Test yet failed the CELF-R. The vast majority of false negatives were reported among younger members of the sample. Finally, construct validity for the CELF-R Screening Test is supported by "strong" correlations between the screening sections and related CELF-R subtests. Correlations from .61 to .78 were reported.

Reliability for the CELF-R Screening Test was obtained through a test-retest study involving 128 subjects of the original sample who participated in retesting 1 to 2 weeks after initial test administration. This group was drawn from three age groups including 6-, 10-, and 14-year-olds. Results indicated stability of rank-ordered scores with relatively low standard errors of measurement.

Interrater reliability was reported for the Written Expression supplemental subtest. Specifically, six trained raters scored 10 papers selected for each of the three written paragraphs. For each paragraph, each rater was paired with all other raters to obtain the percentage of agreement and correlation between scores. Correlations ranged from .33 to .88 with 8 of 12 correlations reported being equal to or less than .67.

In summary, this reviewer finds the CELF-R Screening Test to be a viable, quick screen useful in the identification of children at risk for language disorders between 5 and 16 years of age. In general, its administration, scoring, and interpretation are simple and conveyed precisely in the examiner's manual. This presentation is augmented with an abundance of examples. Technical aspects of the test's development (i.e., the standardization sample, and information specific to validity and reliability) appear appropriate for the test's purposes and are clearly presented in the examiner's manual.

Examiners considering the CELF-R Screening Test are cautioned to use it only as a screening tool. Use of the test for broader diagnostic purposes is clearly ill-advised and inappropriate. Furthermore, this reviewer suggests that scoring and interpretation of supplemental sections (i.e., Oral and Written Expression) should be limited to professionals knowledgeable with respect to normal parameters of oral and written language. Although this suggestion contrasts with the authors' claim that the CELF-R Screening Test can be administered by "trained" paraprofessionals, it would appear prudent given the somewhat low interrater reliability reported from trained examiners scoring written samples.

REVIEWER'S REFERENCE

Semel, E., Wiig, E. H., & Secord, W. (1987). Clinical Evaluation of Language Fundamentals—Revised. San Antonio, TX: The Psychological Corporation.

Review of the Clinical Evaluation of Language Fundamentals—3 Screening Test by MARCEL O. PONTON, Director, Neuropsychology Clinic, Harbor-UCLA Medical Center, and Assistant Clinical Professor, Department of Psychiatry, UCLA School of Medicine, Los Angeles, CA:

The Clinical Evaluation of Language Fundamentals—3 Screening Test was designed to screen school-age children, adolescents, and young adults (6 years 0 months through 21 years 11 months) for language

disorders. The test's only function is to help the clinician decide whether a more in-depth language evaluation is needed. Thus, although the CELF-3 Screening Test has six subtests, none can identify specific weaknesses or strengths in the patient's language, nor can they diagnose a language disability. That is actually left to the parent test, the CELF-3. The authors contend that "If possible, every child should be screened for potential language problems early in her/his school career" (manual, p. 2). The intended market for the test is quite large, it includes speech pathologists, school psychologists, special educators, learning-disabilities specialists, classroom teachers, paraprofessionals, teaching aides, and "other professionals."

The test is to be administered individually, using the colored stimuli that come in an easel format. These color images are in contrast to the black-and-white stimuli from the CELF-3 Screening Test, and very much in keeping with the publisher's use of color in all of their new tests.

Depending on their age, subjects will be tested with Items 1–30 (6 years 0 months to 8 years 11 months) or Items 10–45 (9 years 0 months to 21 years 11 months). The younger group basically has four subtests dealing with basic morphological rules (Items 1–9), receptive language skills (Items 10–16), sentence repetition (Items 17–24), and conceptual relationships between words (Items 25–30). The older group is exposed to five subtests, which include receptive language skills (Items 10–16), sentence repetition (Items 17–24), conceptual relationships between words (Items 25–30), grammatical/syntactic construction (Items 31–37), and interpretation of semantic relationships (Items 38–45). There are no basal or ceiling rules; the examiner is expected to administer all test items corresponding to the subject's age group. Most of the items are scored 0, 1, or NR (no response). For Items 25–30, the correct answers are highlighted in red on the record form. Items 31–45 offer a multiple-choice format for the examiner to circle the correct responses in the record form.

The test yields a single summated "Total Score," which is then compared to a predetermined criterion score. These scores appear on the record form, and therefore do not need to be calculated from the manual. Ages 6.0–6.5 and 6.6–6.11 have different criterion scores. There is a criterion score for each age group from ages 7 through 16. Ages 17.0 through 21.11 are combined into a single group and have one criterion score. These criterion scores were developed by determining the prevalence of the total test scores for the CELF-3 Screening Test for intervals ranging from -2, -1.5, -1 standard deviations from the mean, the mean, and above the mean for CELF-3 Total Language scores. If a child fails the minimal criteria for his or her age group (i.e., has a score lower than the criterion), he or she is then referred to further evaluation, presumably with the CELF-3. The CELF-3 Screening Test was standardized on a sample of 1,900 individuals ranging in age from 6.0 to 21.11 years, and representing a national sample, which matched the U.S. Census for geographical and ethnic distribution. The sample was evenly distributed by gender. It is noted that the CELF-3 Screening Test and then the CELF-3 were administered to the same subjects.

The manual refers the reader to the CELF-3 technical manual for data on the content validity of the CELF-3 as a measure of language. For criterion validity the total scores of the CELF-3 Screening Test were compared to the Total Language scores of the CELF-3. The correlation coefficients ranged "from .68 to .88, providing sufficient evidence of concurrent validity" (manual, p. 37). The sensitivity of the test is given as further evidence of criterion-related validity. The false positive rate was lower among the younger children. The rate of correct hits/misses ranged from a low of 73.3% among the 6.6–6.11 age group to a high of 92% among the 10-year-olds. The overall sensitivity of the CELF-3 Screening Test was 83.5%, which is acceptable.

Unfortunately, factor analytic data comparing the structure of this test and the CELF-3 are absent from the construct validity section of the manual. Instead, two tables of correlations between the item groups of the CELF-3 Screening Test and the CELF-3 are provided. These correlations ranged from .39 to .79 in the younger group (6.0- to 8.11-year-olds), and from .39 to .72 in the older group (9.0- to 21.11-year-olds). Test-retest reliability (1- to 2-week intervals) was obtained from a subsample of 200 subjects. Test-retest reliability coefficients ranged from .83 to .93, which are well within acceptable limits.

The test's strength lies in its ease of use and its appealing presentation. The manual contains useful and concise information. The test kit is compact and the record form is well designed, with appropriate notations regarding administration rules that facilitate its use.

Some issues deserve attention. Despite its handsome design, the test appears to offer very limited clinical information to grant an independent edition. The basic idea of a pass/fail criterion as the major contribution of this test places it in the penumbra of its parent test (CELF-3). It can never shine on its own. In the most ideal of scenarios, the examiner (paraprofessional or clinician) could administer the test, find a "fail" criterion score, and then: (a) refer the child for more in depth assessment, or (b) test the child him or herself with a larger battery of language tests, which, it is hoped, includes the CELF-3. Reality eludes these possibilities, however, because the era of shrinking budgets and managed care demands efficiency and specificity from assessment. Clearly, the test was not designed to be used exclusively by people in clinical settings, rather it was intended to be used by a wide array of people ranging from paraprofessionals to clinicians. The entrepreneurial design of the test is plausible. However, the implications of this issue are somewhat troubling. Although the authors must have carefully pondered the many advantages of having this test in the hands of such a large potential market, none were clearly verbalized, other than to say that "the potential gains through early identification must be carefully considered" (manual, p. 2). If the authors' recommendation is to be followed (i.e., children should be screened early in their academic careers), at least one in every four 6-year-olds will be a false positive. Second, the potential of misidentifying ESL children with this test is very high, especially if paraprofessionals are involved. Third, neither the accuracy nor the urgency of such recommendation will guarantee further testing under the current climate, thus creating more of a problem than solving it.

The usefulness of this test will increase when it is included as part of the overall CELF-3 (e.g., as is done with the Wide Range Assessment of Memory and Learning [WRAML; T4:2957]). If problems are found, the full administration of the test follows immediately, and the question of what kind of language problem is present can be satisfactorily answered. The clinician, the patient, and the third-party payor all save time and money. A potentially penurious solution, indeed; but a clinically sound solution, nonetheless. A set of guidelines as to what constitutes a "paraprofessional" and "other professionals" is also in order.

[70]
Coaching Process Questionnaire.

Purpose: "Provides managers with an assessment of their coaching ability."
Population: Managers and employees.
Publication Date: 1992.
Acronym: CPQ.
Administration: Group.

Time: Administration time not reported.
Comments: Self-scored instrument.
Author: McBer & Company.
Publisher: McBer & Company.

a) PARTICIPANT VERSION.
Population: Managers.
Scores, 5: Diagnostic Skills, Coaching Techniques, Coaching Qualities, Coaching Model, Overall CPQ score.
Price Data, 1993: $60 per complete kit including 10 questionnaires, and 10 profiles and interpretive notes.

b) EMPLOYEE VERSION.
Population: Employees.
Scores, 5: Diagnostic Skills, Coaching Techniques, Coaching Qualities, Coaching Model, Overall Employee score.
Price Data: $25 per 10 questionnaires.

Review of the Coaching Process Questionnaire by PATRICIA A. BACHELOR, Professor of Psychology, California State University at Long Beach, Long Beach, CA:

The Coaching Process Questionnaire (CPQ) is designed as a self-administered and self-scored assessment of a manager's coaching ability. Coaching, in this context, is the two-way conversation between employees and managers designed to improve employee performance and commitment. The four elements of the coaching process, as defined by this instrument, are (a) Diagnostic Skills, (b) Coaching Qualities, (c) Coaching Techniques, and (d) Coaching Model. Diagnostic Skills assess the manager's ability to prepare for a coaching session. Coaching Techniques assess the manager's ability to communicate in a meaningful way. Coaching Qualities are personal attitudes and beliefs supportive to the coaching process. The Coaching Model is the ability to structure the coaching session so that developmental opportunities will be understood and pursued.

The CPQ has two versions—an Employee Version and a Manager Version. The Employee Version comprises 40 items designed to assess the four aforementioned dimensions of the manager's coaching skills, behaviors, and techniques. Each statement is answered on a 5-point Likert-type scale evaluating the degree to which the employee perceives that his/her manager demonstrates the specific coaching behavior. The Manager Version consists of 40 statements that are designed to assess a manager's coaching performance and employee development. The manager responds on a 5-point Likert-type scale evaluating the degree to which he or she demon-strates a particular coaching behavior. All of the items on the Manager form of the CPQ are parallel to those on the Employee Version. For example, Question 14 on each form involves rewards for results. That is, the employee responds to the statement "My manager rewards me for achieving desired results," whereas the manager is asked to respond to "I reward employees for achieving desired results."

The employee test booklet also provides instructions for scoring the ratings on four dimensions. Each dimension, labeled only as A, B, C, and D, consists of the sum of scores on each of the 10 indicated items. These dimension scores are not explained further. The manager uses the profile and Interpretive Notes Booklet to score his or her CPQ, compare scores with other managers, and interpret feedback about the manager's coaching behavior. Areas of strength and weakness in coaching are, thereby, identified. A Coaching Process Profile is obtained by plotting, on a tear-out grid, the manager's scores on each of the four coaching dimensions as well as the Overall (total) score. This visual presentation of the manager's assessment can be compared to the preprinted 50th percentile of "more than 400 managers in a variety of industries" (p. 3, profile). No more details are provided about this norm group. The Employee average and total scores can also be plotted on this chart to provide contrasts in perceptions. Discrepancies of more than 20 points are indicative of weakness on that dimension. No additional interpretative information is provided in the materials that accompany the test booklets. The remaining pages in the manual describe the four dimensions of the coaching profile. The language is clear but written at a low level that at times seemed condescending. Most managers would certainly possess expertise that surpassed the treatment presented in the CPQ manual.

Unfortunately, a technical manual does not exist for this test. Thus, there is no mention of test development and/or modification, estimates of reliability coefficients, validity studies, or standardization and/or norm groups. Without such information about the psychometric properties of the CPQ, test users would be unable to evaluate if the test is appropriate for a specific application or interpret performances with any confidence. Nor can test consumers assess claims of accuracy or dependability of test scores for specific purposes. These qualities are essential for competent and legitimate test use.

Without some type of evaluation regarding the stability, consistency, and accuracy of test scores for appropriate purposes, test users would be unable to defend their use of this test. Test examiners are ethically bound to select, administer, and interpret test scores in keeping with the test developer's standards for appropriate use of the test. The test authors are encouraged to read and promptly prepare a technical manual in conformance with the *Standards for Educational and Psychological Testing* (AERA, APA, & NCME, 1985). Thus, the present form of the Coaching Process Questionnaire can, at best, be considered in the development/research phase and its use limited only to stimulating a discussion of the coaching process among employees and their managers.

REVIEWER'S REFERENCE

American Educational Research Association, American Psychological Association, & National Council on Measurement in Education. (1985). *Standards for educational and psychological testing*. Washington, DC: American Psychological Association, Inc.

Review of the Coaching Process Questionnaire by GENEVA D. HAERTEL, Senior Research Associate, EREAPA Associates, Livermore, CA:

The Coaching Process Questionnaire (CPQ) provides managers with an assessment of their skills, techniques, and behaviors in coaching employees. There are two versions of the questionnaire: the Participant Version and the Employee Version. The Participant Version, taken by the manager, provides a self-assessment of the manager's strengths and weaknesses in coaching employees during performance reviews and employee development activities. The Employee Version, taken by a subordinate(s) of the manager, provides feedback on the manager's coaching skills, techniques, and behaviors. Both versions of the questionnaire provide scores on four elements: Diagnostic Skills, Coaching Techniques, Coaching Qualities, Coaching Model, and an overall CPQ score. In order to identify managers' strengths and weaknesses, their scores on the four coaching elements can be compared with those of a norming sample of over 400 managers and employees from a variety of industries. In addition, the results of the manager's self-assessment can be compared with his or her own employees' scores. A substantial difference of 20 or more points between the manager's score on a coaching element and his or her employees' average score on the same element signifies a weakness in the manager's use of that coaching element. (This interpretation assumes that the employees rate the manager less favorably than the manager rates him or herself.)

There are 40 items presented in the Participant Version of the CPQ. Each of the items describes a coaching behavior. When answering each item, the manager or participant is directed to recall their experiences with employees in coaching sessions. The participant rates the degree to which he or she typically demonstrates each coaching behavior on a 5-point rating scale; a rating of "1" is designated "to a small degree" and "5" is designated "to a large degree." Scores are calculated for each of the four coaching process elements: (1) Diagnostic Skills, (2) Coaching Techniques, (3) Coaching Qualities, (4) Coaching Model, and the total CPQ. Each element comprises 10 items, which are intermixed with items from the other elements. The test-taking instructions are concise and clearly written.

Like the Participant Version, the Employee Version of the CPQ has 40 items representing the four coaching process elements. An employee rates the degree to which his or her manager demonstrates each coaching behavior. The content of these 40 items matches that used in the Participant Version. However, items in the Participant Version are written in the first person, whereas in the Employee Version the employee is rating "my employer." The 40 items are rated on the same 5-point rating scale used in the Participant Version. Scores on the four elements can be calculated using a form on the back cover of the test booklet. The test-taking instructions are well written.

The CPQ Profile and Interpretive Notes, which is 11 pages in length, is the manual that accompanies the questionnaire. It states the purpose of the questionnaire and defines commonly used terms. A step-by-step scoring process is presented so that a manager can compare his or her own coaching scores with the norming population. In addition, a manager can plot his or her employees' average scores on each of the four elements and compare them with his or her own scores.

The questionnaire's conceptual framework is addressed in the manual. Each of the coaching elements is described using figures, a table, and lists of skills and attributes involved in coaching. The coaching process is depicted in a seven-step flowchart accompanied by one-to-five sentence descriptions of each step. An interesting feature of the manual is a page of commonly asked questions about the CPQ and the coaching process itself. Each question is followed by a one- or two-paragraph answer. Although the answers provide helpful direction, some lack the level of specificity needed to be truly useful. The final entry in the manual is the coaching process profile on which the manager plots his or her raw scores and the employees' average scores and converts them to percentiles based upon the norming population. Overall, the manual is clearly written, appropriate examples of coaching skills are provided, and coaching qualities are described in explicit terms. However, the manual fails to provide any information on the questionnaire's reliability or validity and little information is provided on the questionnaire's norming population.

The lack of psychometric information on the CPQ is problematic. Upon request the questionnaire publisher provided a page of information containing reliability and validity information on several instruments supported by their company. Based on the supplementary statistical information, the norming group for the CPQ was composed of 214 participants (managers) and 576 subordinates or employees. No further breakdown of characteristics of the norming group was provided. In order for consumers of the CPQ to determine the appropriateness of the questionnaire for their circumstances, more information must be provided on the norming group. It would be helpful if the following characteristics of the norming group were reported: types of industries on which the norms were developed, the managers' years of experience, ages of managers and employees, and numbers of males and females. The supplementary statistical information also provided a range of reliability estimates for the participant version (.68–.78) and for the employee version (.81–.87). Unfortunately, the type of reliability estimate calculated was not specified. Although the magnitude of the reliability estimates is satisfactory, consumers need to know whether these are test-retest or internal consistency estimates.

No validity information was presented on the questionnaire as a measure of a manager's coaching skill. However, inspection of the questionnaire reveals its face validity. Its content is focused on behaviors employed in the coaching process—such as communication and diagnostic skills. The instrument has some content validity. The questionnaire developers have presented a model of the coaching process and developed items rating each of the four elements of the model. However, the origin of the coaching model was not described, nor were there citations of empirical studies providing information about the use and characteristics of the model and the

CPQ. There was no definitive statement of the universe of coaching content to be covered, nor were the processes used to generate the 40 items specified. The questionnaire's construct and criterion validity were not addressed.

In summary, the Coaching Process Questionnaire provides industry with a measure of a manager's coaching skills. The CPQ is easy to administer and score and is face valid. The questionnaire provides useful information comparing a manager's self-assessment of coaching performance with (a) a norming group of over 200 managers, and (b) employees' assessments of the manager's coaching ability. A profile of the manager's performance on the four coaching elements and overall coaching performance is available. Although the two versions of the questionnaire are clearly written, the profile and interpretive notes need to be further developed. This attractive instrument would be enhanced by providing data on the origin and use of the coaching model and questionnaire. In addition, psychometric information about the questionnaire's norming group, reliability, and content, criterion, and construct validity must be provided. As it stands, the CPQ can be used to provide insights to managers about their own performance, as a starting point for managers' professional development activities, and for research purposes, but its psychometric characteristics have not been sufficiently documented to make it a viable instrument for the high stakes decision making required in personnel evaluation.

[71]
Cognitive Abilities Test, Form 5.

Purpose: Designed "to assess the pattern and level of students' development in reasoning and problem solving with verbal, quantitative, and spatial symbols."

Population: Grades K–3, 3–12.

Publication Dates: 1954–1997.

Acronym: CogAT.

Administration: Group.

Price Data, 1997: $37.50 per examination kit including information on primary assessments and Grades 3–12 assessments for CogAT, inservices, ancillaries, and score reports; $40 per norms booklet for hand scoring for all levels; $6 per Interpretive Guide for Teachers and Counselors; $25 per Interpretive Guide for School Administrators; $29 per Research Handbook.

Comments: Scoring service available from publisher.

Authors: Robert L. Thorndike and Elizabeth P. Hagen.

Publisher: The Riverside Publishing Company.

   a) PRIMARY BATTERY.

   Population: Grades K–3.

Publication Dates: 1979–1997.

Scores, 4: Verbal, Quantitative, Nonverbal, Composite.

Levels, 2: Primary Battery, Level 1 and Primary Battery, Level 2.

Price Data: $15.75 per 25 practice tests (Levels 1 and 2); $73 per 25 test booklets with directions (specify level); $6.50 per scoring keys (specify level); $6 per Preparing for Testing manual.

Time: Untimed, approximately 120 minutes in 3 sessions.

b) MULTILEVEL EDITION

Population: Grades 3–12.

Publication Dates: 1979–1997.

Scores, 4: Verbal, Quantitative, Nonverbal, Composite.

Levels: 8 overlapping levels: Level A through Level H.

Price Data: $16.75 per 25 practice tests (Levels A—H); $56 per 25 test booklets with directions (specify level); $34 per 50 answer documents for Levels A—H; $13.50 per scoring keys for Levels A—H; $6 per Preparing for Testing manual.

Time: (180) minutes in 3 sessions.

Cross References: See T4:537 (19 references); for reviews by Anne Anastasi and Douglas Fuchs of an earlier edition, see 10:66 (13 references); for a review by Charles J. Ansorge of an earlier edition, see 9:240 (5 references); see also T3:483 (32 references), for reviews by Kenneth D. Hopkins and Robert C. Nichols, see 8:181 (12 references); for reviews by Marcel L. Goldschmid and Carol K. Tittle and an excerpted review by Richard C. Cox of the primary batteries, see 7:343.

TEST REFERENCES

1. Holmes, B. C. (1987). Children inferences with print and pictures. *Journal of Educational Psychology, 79,* 14–18.
2. Keane, K. J., & Kretschmer, R. E. (1987). Effect of mediated learning intervention on cognitive task performance with a deaf population. *Journal of Educational Psychology, 79,* 49–53.
3. Graham, S., & Harris, K. R. (1989). Components analysis of cognitive strategy instruction: Effects on learning disabled students' compositions and self-efficacy. *Journal of Educational Psychology, 81,* 353–361.
4. Renick, M. J., & Harter, S. (1989). Impact of social comparisons on the developing self-perceptions of learning disabled students. *Journal of Educational Psychology, 81,* 631–638.
5. Atwater, M. M., & Alick, B. (1990). Cognitive development and problem solving of Afro-American students in chemistry. *Journal of Research in Science Teaching, 27,* 157–172.
6. Cooper, D. H., & Speece, D. L. (1990). Maintaining at-risk children in regular education settings: Initial effects of individual differences and classroom environments. *Exceptional Children, 57,* 117–126.
7. Hoover, S. M., & Feldhusen, J. F. (1990). The scientific hypothesis formulation ability of gifted, ninth-grade students. *Journal of Educational Psychology, 82,* 838–848.
8. Speece, D. L., & Cooper, D. H. (1990). Ontogeny of school failure: Classification of first-grade children. *American Educational Research Journal, 27,* 119–140.
9. Swanson, H. L. (1990). Influence of metacognitive knowledge and aptitude on problem solving. *Journal of Educational Psychology, 82,* 306–314.
10. Mulholland, D. J., Watt, N. F., Philpott, A., & Sarlin, N. (1991). Academic performance in children of divorce: Psychological resilience and vulnerability. *Psychiatry, 54,* 268–280.
11. Emery, D. W., & Milhalevich, C. (1992). Directed discussion of character perspectives. *Reading Research and Instruction, 31*(4), 51–59.
12. Schack, G. D. (1993). Effects of a creative problem-solving curriculum on students of varying ability levels. *Gifted Child Quarterly, 37,* 32–38.
13. Swanson, H. L. (1993). An information processing analysis of learning disabled children's problem solving. *American Educational Research Journal, 30,* 861–893.
14. Waterman, B., & Lewandowski, L. (1993). Phonologic and semantic processing in reading-disabled and nondisabled males at two age levels. *Journal of Experimental Child Psychology, 55,* 87–103.
15. Borduin, B. J., Borduin, C. M., & Manley, C. M. (1994). The use of imagery training to improve reading comprehension of second graders. *The Journal of Genetic Psychology, 155,* 115–118.
16. McCormick, C. E., Stoner, S. B., & Duncan, S. (1994). Kindergarten predictors of first-grade reading achievement: A regular classroom example. *Psychological Reports, 74,* 403–407.
17. Sawyer, R. J., & Dubowitz, H. (1994). School performance of children in kinship care. *Child Abuse & Neglect, 18,* 587–597.
18. Stone, B. J. (1994). Group ability test versus teachers' ratings for predicting achievement. *Psychological Reports, 75,* 1487–1490.
19. Cahan, S., & Ganor, Y. (1995). Cognitive gender differences among Israeli children. *Sex Roles, 32,* 469–484.
20. Chamrad, D. L., Robinson, N. M., & Junos, P. M. (1995). Consequences of having a gifted sibling: Myths and realities. *Gifted Child Quarterly, 39,* 135–145.
21. Kundert, D. K., May, D. C., & Brent, D. (1995). A comparison of students who delay kindergarten entry and those who are retained in grades K–5. *Psychology in the Schools, 32,* 202–209.
22. Sweeney, N. S. (1995). The age position effect: School entrance age, giftedness, and underachievement. *Journal for the Education of the Gifted, 18,* 171–188.
23. Robinson, N. M., Abbott, R. D., Berninger, V. W., & Busse, J. (1996). The structure of abilities in math-precocious young children: Gender similarities and differences. *Journal of Educational Psychology, 88,* 341–352.

Review of the Cognitive Abilities Test, Form 5 by BERT A. GOLDMAN, Professor, School of Education, University of North Carolina at Greensboro, Greensboro, NC:

The Cognitive Abilities Test (CogAT), Form 5 by Thorndike and Hagen is based upon Vernon's and Cattell's theoretical models of human abilities. Central to these theories and consequently to CogAT is the major factor, *g*, representing general overall reasoning skills. Also included in the theories and incorporated in the CogAT are specific group factors that are measured by the Verbal, Nonverbal, and Quantitative Batteries. The total score is a composite of the Verbal, Quantitative, and Nonverbal Batteries providing a measure of *g*. The Nonverbal Battery was included to measure general abstract reasoning ability by means of items containing geometric shapes and figures that are less influenced by cultural factors and schooling than are the verbal and quantitative tasks of the other two batteries.

In 1954 a battery of tests known as the Lorge-Thorndike Intelligence Tests was published. The first revision of these tests was published in 1968 as the Lorge-Thorndike Tests. Note that the word *Intelligence* was no longer included in the test title. The authors indicate that they have renamed the instrument the Cognitive Abilities Test (CogAT) because they say experts are not in agreement on the meaning of intelligence and the new title is a more accurate description of what is being measured. This reviewer notes with interest that the theoretical basis for the CogAT appears to be the same theoretical basis that the CogAT authors used for revising a well-known test entitled the Stanford-Binet Intelligence Scale, Fourth Edition (T4:2553).

In preparing the present 1993 version of the CogAT, the authors replaced one of the Verbal Battery, Levels 1 and 2 subtests and developed new items for all of the batteries' subtests. Also a total score, called a composite, is now provided.

To measure the level of development of general and specific cognitive skills of students from kindergarten through grade 12, the CogAT employs a Primary Battery consisting of Levels 1 and 2 and a Multilevel Battery consisting of Levels A through H. The entire CogAT battery covers ages 5 through 18+ years. The Primary Battery may be administered to beginning kindergarten through grade 2 students and to grade 3 students slow in cognitive development. The Multilevel Battery is used for grades 3 through 12 students and for grade 2 students whose rate of cognitive development is more rapid than their age peers. Neither the CogAT Interpretive Guide for Teachers and Counselors, nor the CogAT Directions for Administration reveals for which specific grade each of the Levels 1, 2, and A–H is to be used. However, when one reaches page 12 of the Research Handbook or page 30 of the Interpretive Guide for School Administrators, one finds recommended CogAT levels for each grade (and also on page 7 of Preparing for Testing). With this exception, the Directions for Administration are clear and easily followed. Also, considerable information is provided in the Interpretive Guide for Teachers and Counselors to enable one to interpret test results.

The Primary Battery consists of Verbal, Quantitative, and Nonverbal batteries, each containing two tests that are orally administered, require no reading skills, and are in multiple-choice format containing four pictorial choices. The tests have no time limits, but approximate testing time is 2 hours.

The Multilevel Battery consists of Verbal, Quantitative, and Nonverbal batteries, each containing three tests with specific time limits totaling 1 1/2 hours (actual test administration time is approximately 2 1/2 hours). The batteries are in a five-choice, multiple-choice format with the exception of the Quantitative Relations subtest, which has three choices.

Care was taken in reviewing all items to ensure that their content is appropriate for various socioeconomic backgrounds, racial and ethnic groups, and both genders.

In 1992 a sample of approximately 160,000 K–12 students was selected from public, Catholic, and private non-Catholic schools to establish a national standardization of the CogAT. A detailed description of the selection procedure that was used to ensure national representation of the sample is given in the norms booklet and also in the Research Handbook.

The norms booklet clearly explains how to: convert raw scores to Universal Scale Scores (for comparing a raw score on one level of the test to a raw score on any other level), obtain Standard Age Scores (for determining students' cognitive development patterns and for identifying students at either extreme of the range of scores who may thus be eligible for special programs), obtain Grade Percentile Ranks (for comparing students' scores within the same grade), and obtain Stanines (for obtaining patterns of cognitive ability and for providing a relatively easy way to report results to both students and their parents).

Reliability estimates are provided in the form of Kuder-Richardson Formula 20 reliabilities and are reported in the CogAT Research Handbook along with Standard Errors of Measurement. The average K-R 20 reliabilities for the Verbal, Quantitative, and Nonverbal Batteries of Levels 1 and 2 ranged from .81 to .93 and for Levels A through H they ranged from .92 to .95. Although these reliability estimates, in general, are quite good one must understand that they are only estimates of reliability based upon internal consistency. There are no data showing actual reliability over time.

The CogAT was designed to measure kindergarten through grade 12 students' general and specific cognitive skills regarded as essential for achieving the instructional objectives of each grade level. Thus, this general abilities test was devised to predict future school success. The authors of the CogAT provide evidence of their test's validity by providing correlations between K–12 students' CogAT scores and their scores on one of three achievement tests concurrently standardized with it (i.e., Iowa Tests of Basic Skills [K–8] and Iowa Tests of Educational Development or the Tests of Achievement and Proficiency [9–12]). The results revealed correlations with the Iowa Tests of Basic Skills ranging, on the average, from .71 for the Nonverbal Battery to .83 for the Verbal Battery, and with the Iowa Tests of Educational Development ranging, on the average, from .70 for the Nonverbal Battery to .84 for the Verbal Battery. Although these correlations between aptitude and achievement appear to be substantial, one must be cautioned that in the words of the test authors "Since the tests were given concurrently" the correlations "represent prediction only in the statistical sense, and do not forecast achievement over time" (p. 64, CogAT Research Handbook).

The authors have included with their test clearly written instructions for its administration, a number of well-written, easily understood, and very informative publications such as the: Preparing for Testing manuals, Norms Booklet, Interpretive Guide for Teachers and Counselors, Interpretive Guide for School Administrators, and Research Handbook.

In sum, this reviewer finds the CogAT, Form 5 to be a carefully crafted instrument. The weaknesses, which should not deter its use, are the lack of both reliability and validity data over time. However, the types of reliability and validity data that are presented do encourage the use of this instrument. Perhaps the authors will collect such information in the future.

Review of the Cognitive Abilities Test, Form 5 by STEPHEN H. IVENS, Vice President, Research & Development, Touchstone Applied Science Associates, Brewster, NY:

The Cognitive Abilities Test (CogAT) is a well-known and respected test battery designed to measure both general and specific cognitive abilities of students in grades K–12. The most recent version of this instrument, Form 5, consists of two editions: The Primary Battery, Levels 1 & 2, for grades K through 3 and the Multilevel Battery, Levels A–H, for grades 3 through 12. Each level consists of a Verbal, Quantitative, and Nonverbal section. Student performance is reported for each section of the battery. Composite scores are now reported for the entire battery even though the publisher stated for Form 4 that total scores could give a "misleading picture of the cognitive development of an individual whose cognitive skills in one area are much more highly developed than in the other areas" (Form 4 Examiner's Manual—Multilevel as quoted by Fuchs, 1989, page 194).

The Primary Battery is orally administered and untimed. All items are multiple choice using pictures for the response options. Students respond directly in the test booklets. The Multilevel Battery has separately timed sections. All items are multiple-choice with five response options except for the quantitative relations items, which are three choice items. Students respond on separate machine-scorable answer documents. The Directions for Administration for each level are attractive, clear, and thorough.

For each of the sections, and the composite score, seven types of scores are produced: (a) Standard Age Score, (b) Percentile rank by age, (c) Stanine by age, (d) Universal Scale Score, (e) Percentile rank by grade, (f) Stanine by grade, and (g) Normal Curve Equivalents. The raw score and the number of items attempted are also reported for each section. The age and grade norms provide identical or nearly identical information for students whose age is typical for their grade placement. For students who are much younger than the typical student in the grade, the age norms will be higher than the grade norms. Similarly, students who are much older than the typical student in the grade will receive higher grade norms than age norms.

The theory and rationale underlying the development of the CogAT is presented in the manual entitled Interpretive Guide for School Administrators. This manual is excellent and should be readily available for all users of the CogAT. The chapter on norms and types of score reports, and the chapters covering the interpretation and uses of score reports, are thorough and well written. The section on checking score reports, which discusses the integrity of score information, should be required reading for users of all educational tests.

Reliability coefficients (K-R 20) for Levels 1–2 range from the low to mid .80s for the Verbal section to the low .90s for the Quantitative and Nonverbal sections. The corresponding values for Levels A–H in grades 3 through 12 are in the low to mid .90s. These values are acceptably high. Test-retest and alternate form reliability coefficients are not reported.

The logical and rational component of construct validity is discussed in both the Interpretive Guide for School Administrators and the CogAT Research Handbook. Although there is little empirical evidence of validity in the materials reviewed, there is a large corpus of published research in the professional journals supporting the validity of the CogAT. The bottom line, however, is that validity is situationally specific and the ultimate responsibility for documenting the validity of the instrument for a specific purpose rests with the user.

As a stand-alone battery, the CogAT is an excellent measure of the cognitive development of students in grades K–12. The primary value of the CogAT for many users, however, comes from the joint standardization in 1992 of the CogAT with the Iowa Tests of Basic Skills (ITBS), the Tests of

Achievement and Proficiency (TAP), and the Iowa Tests of Educational Development (ITED). Extensive technical data on the 1992 standardization of these instruments are published in the CogAT Research Handbook and the CogAT Norms Booklet.

The norming of the CogAT consisted of a national probability sample of approximately 160,000 students in the Spring of 1992. Separate public school, Catholic school, and private non-Catholic school samples were drawn. Within each stratification category, sample percents were weighted to compensate for missing categories and the fact that some schools tested more or fewer students than called for in the sampling plan. Although the sampling procedures are carefully described and quite acceptable, the acceptance rate of schools invited to participate in the standardization is not reported.

The CogAT is an excellent instrument for assessing the cognitive development of students. When combined with the ITBS, and either the ITED or TAP, schools can reliably compare a student's level of cognitive development to his or her level of academic achievement.

REVIEWER'S REFERENCE

Fuchs, D. (1989). [Review of the Cognitive Abilities Test, Form 4]. In J. C. Conoley & J. J. Kramer (Eds.), *The tenth mental measurements yearbook* (pp. 193–197). Lincoln, NE: Buros Institute of Mental Measurements.

[72]
College Adjustment Scales.

Purpose: Identifies developmental and psychological problems experienced by college students.
Population: College and university students.
Publication Date: 1991.
Acronym: CAS.
Scores, 9: Anxiety, Depression, Suicidal Ideation, Substance Abuse, Self-Esteem Problems, Interpersonal Problems, Family Problems, Academic Problems, Career Problems.
Administration: Individual or group.
Price Data, 1996: $69 per complete kit including manual (25 pages), 25 reusable item booklets, and 25 answer sheets; $25 per 25 reusable item booklets; $25 per 25 answer sheets; $28 per manual.
Time: (15–20) minutes.
Authors: William D. Anton and James R. Reed.
Publisher: Psychological Assessment Resources, Inc.
Cross References: See T4:544 (1 reference).

TEST REFERENCES

1. Street, S., Kromrey, J. D., Reed, J., & Anton, W. (1993). A phenomenological perspective of problems experienced by high school seniors. *The High School Journal, 76,* 129–138.
2. Tloczynski, J. (1994). A preliminary study of opening-up meditation, college adjustment, and self-actualization. *Psychological Reports, 75,* 449–450.

3. Turner, P. R., Valtierra, M., Talken, T. R., Miller, V. I., & DeAnda, J. R. (1996). Effect of session length on treatment outcome for college students in brief therapy. *Journal of Counseling Psychology, 43,* 228–232.

Review of the College Adjustment Scales by WILLIAM E. MARTIN, JR., Professor of Educational Psychology, Northern Arizona University, Flagstaff, AZ:

According to Anton and Reed, the College Adjustment Scales (CAS) were developed "to provide a rapid method of screening college counseling clients for common developmental and psychological problems" (manual, p. 1). The CAS is a 108-item self-report measure with the following nine scales (12 items per scale): Anxiety, Depression, Suicidal Ideation, Substance Abuse, Self-Esteem Problems, Interpersonal Problems, Family Problems, Academic Problems, and Career Problems. Test takers are asked to respond to each item, based on its accuracy, using a 4-point scale ranging from *Not At All True* to *Very True.* The entire process for completing, scoring, and profiling the CAS is estimated by the test authors to take a maximum of 24 minutes.

DEVELOPMENT OF THE SCALES. The initial CAS scales were derived from problems encountered in the college population. Specifically, approximately 2,000 students presenting at a college counseling center for services completed an intake problems checklist. Based on their responses, two principal components factor analyses were conducted resulting in a 9-factor and a 7-factor solution. Information for which solution was retained was not provided.

The derived factors, along with additional adjustment problem areas, were used in a survey of assessment needs completed by 73 professionals from nine counseling centers. The survey findings of professionals, paired with the analyses of problems associated with students seeking services, resulted in the nine scales of the CAS. Next, a literature review was conducted to identify behavioral expressions for each of the scales. This resulted in an item pool of 181 items. These items were subsequently reviewed for bias by an expert panel; 14 items, which were determined to be biased, were rewritten. The internal consistency of items for each scale was derived from a study of 224 college students enrolled at four universities located in the Southeastern United States. Items were retained in the item pool based on three criteria (see manual) resulting in a final pool of 108 items. Final internal consistency reliability coefficients for the nine scales ranged from .80 to .92 with an average of .86.

VALIDITY OF THE SCALES. The reported test validity is based upon one group differences study and four convergent and discriminant validity studies that were conducted at several universities throughout the United States. In the first study, CAS scores were compared between a group receiving university counseling services and students not receiving services. The recipient group evidenced significantly higher scores on the CAS when compared to the nonrecipient group with Anxiety and Suicidal Ideation reflecting the most characteristic dimensions of the recipient group.

Independent samples from 33 university counseling centers were used to measure the convergent and discriminant validity of the CAS. The CAS subscales were correlated with subscales of several frequently used standardized tests measuring psychological constructs including anxiety, depression, hopelessness, personality, interpersonal problems, substance abuse, self-esteem, family adaptability, and career development. The procedure design was primarily multitrait-monomethod (self-report instruments). The findings reflected high correlations among scales measuring similar constructs (convergent validity) and low correlations among dissimilar constructs (discriminant validity). For example, the NEO Personality Inventory (NEO-PI) Neurotocism scales were correlated with the CAS subscales in three studies. On two similar subscales across the studies, correlations were high moderate or high. The correlations for Anxiety were .80, .71, and .80 and for Depression they were .64, .69, and .74. For dissimilar measures, low correlations, as illustrated by comparisons of the Openness subscale on the NEO-PI and all of the CAS subscales, were obtained throughout the three studies.

ADMINISTRATION, SCORING, AND INTERPRETATION. Standardized instructions for administration are provided in the CAS manual. The test-taking materials include a four-page item booklet written at a fifth grade reading level. Additionally, there is an answer sheet printed on carbonless white paper with the CAS Profile sheet on the reverse side that lists raw scores, percentiles, and T scores.

Ninety percent of the normative sample ($N = 1,146$) consisted of college and university students aged 17–30. The students were reasonably equally proportioned from first year through seniors. However, only 2% of the total sample were graduate students. The sample reflected national college enrollment proportions according to gender and ethnicity. The majority (54%) of the sample were raised in the Southeast compared to other regions of the United States: Northeast (13%), Midwest (10%), West (13%), and outside the United States (5%). Information was not available for the remainder of the sample.

Percentile scores and normalized T scores derived for each scale from the raw score frequency distributions of the standardization sample are used for interpretation of the results. As the authors found weak associations among gender and ethnic group and the CAS scores, no normative data are provided based on these variables. The authors suggest that when a student scores at or above a T score of 60 on any scale, further evaluation, and possibly intervention, are warranted in the area of adjustment difficulty. In addition to normative comparisons, brief descriptive guidelines are provided for interpretation of each scale. Three case illustrations are presented in the manual.

SUMMARY. The CAS is a useful screening tool for college and university counseling professionals to identify possible adjustment difficulties among students. It must be emphasized, however, that it is a screening tool. With only 12 items per major adjustment difficulty (e.g., suicidal ideation, career problems), there is room for diagnostic errors.

The methodology to develop the scales was reasonably sound and there is evidence for the validity of the scales. However, more validity studies are needed, especially concurrent validity studies related to profile interpretations examining the relationship between the CAS and other major psychological disturbance assessment instruments (e.g., Minnesota Multiphasic Personality Inventory—2 [MMPI–2; T4:1645]; and Millon Clinical Multiaxial Inventory [MCMI–III; 201]). Additionally, both the descriptive guidelines for each scale and the number of case illustrations could be expanded.

Normative data are not available for students from various ethnic groups. Given specific reported college adjustment difficulties related to ethnocultural factors (Negy & Woods, 1992; Solberg, Ritsma, Davis, Tata, & Jolly, 1994), it may be valuable to generate percentile scores and T scores by ethnic group.

REVIEWER'S REFERENCES

Negy, C. R., & Woods, D. J. (1992). Mexican Americans' performance on the Psychological Screening Inventory as a function of acculturation level. *Journal of Clinical Psychology, 48*, 315–319.

Solberg, V. S., Ritsma, S., Davis, B. J., Tata, S. P., & Jolly, A. (1994). Asian-American students' severity of problems and willingness to seek help from university counseling centers: Role of previous counseling experience, gender, and ethnicity. *Journal of Counseling Psychology, 41*, 275–279.

Review of the College Adjustment Scales by ED-WARD R. STARR, Assistant Professor of Counseling Psychology, State University of New York at Buffalo, Buffalo, NY:

The College Adjustment Scales (CAS) is a 108-item inventory designed as a quick and economical screening device for clinicians providing counseling services to college and university students. The authors attempt to provide clinicians with data regarding the most common developmental and psychological problems in this population. The inventory comprises nine subscales: Anxiety, Depression, Suicidal Ideation, Substance Abuse, Self-Esteem Problems, Interpersonal Problems, Family Problems, Academic Problems, and Career Problems. Subscales reflect many of the problems most frequently raised by college and university students, thus increasing its clinical relevance and utility. Notably absent among the subscales, though, is one related specifically to eating disorders.

The manual contains a brief and general introduction to the CAS and discusses the test materials, their use, administration, and scoring. The materials themselves are convenient, economical, and straightforward, requiring of respondents only a fifth grade reading level and a pen or pencil. The four-page item booklet is reusable, with responses recorded by students on a separate answer sheet. Raw data can be hand scored and plotted into a profile in less than 5 minutes. The profile form provides percentile scores, relative to the standardization sample, and *T*-score conversions. The CAS can be administered and scored by individuals without formal training in psychology. Training in its use and interpretation, however, requires graduate level training in an appropriate subdiscipline in psychology.

STANDARDIZATION. The CAS was standardized on 1,146 college and university students, ages 17 to 65 (although less than 10% of the sample is older than 30 years) from throughout the U.S. The sample is well represented with respect to geographic region and gender. However, with regard to race, although the sample closely reflected racial patterns in college enrollment nationally, due to the extraordinarily low college enrollments of certain minorities in the U.S. (e.g., Pacific Islanders and Native Americans) some oversampling of minority groups may have been more appropriate. Normative data for each subscale are provided in the manual.

RELIABILITY. Only measures of internal consistency are reported in the CAS manual. Reliability coefficients range between .80 and .92, with a mean of .86. Reliability estimates based on alternative forms of the CAS or test-retest procedures are not available.

VALIDITY. Five validation studies of the CAS are reported in the manual. The first study compared the standardization sample to 198 students reporting current involvement in counseling for personal, academic, or career concerns. Significant differences on the subscales were obtained using multivariate ANOVA and discriminant function analysis. The remaining four studies compared specific CAS subscale results, using moderately sized samples of college students either requesting or receiving services from a college or university counseling center, to a variety of other well-established measures of the relevant constructs (e.g., the State-Trait Anxiety Inventory, Beck Depression Inventory, Beck Hopelessness Scale, NEO-Personality Inventory, Michigan Alcoholism Screening Test, Drug Abuse Screening Test, Multidimensional Self-Esteem Inventory, Family Adaptability and Cohesion Evaluation Scales III, Career Decision Scale, and the Self-Expression Inventory). Results in each study, based on correlational analysis, are consistent with predictions, with subscales having sufficient discriminant and predictive validity.

SUMMARY. There is a clear need for screening devices for this population and very little attention has been given to the development of reliable and valid instruments. In spite of some of its limitations, the CAS is certainly a solid step in the right direction. Further research should help establish its utility.

Until further data can be generated regarding its use in cross-cultural contexts, the CAS should probably be used with some caution. Although the manual authors state the available research and normative data indicate the CAS is unbiased with respect to gender and ethnic group membership, the data provided are not particularly compelling. The CAS assumes concept equivalence in cross-cultural contexts, which may cause some problems in interpreting the meaning of results. For example, the construct self-esteem, as reflected in the CAS is one that is limited to Euro-American notions of self that give primacy to the individual, without concern for a more collective sense of identity as is typical, for instance, of Native American communities.

Given the CAS was developed and standardized exclusively on a college population, its use in other clinical settings cannot be recommended. Although it is not intended for use as a diagnostic aid, the CAS may be most effectively used adjunctively as part of a battery of assessment measures to rule out potential comorbidity.

The authors aptly note that because only about 10% of the standardization sample were over age 30, the CAS should be used cautiously with older students. When using the CAS to screen for eating disorders, one should analyze results at the item level to obtain specific data. This should be augmented with other methods of evaluation. Given the incidence, prevalence, and significance of eating disorders, particularly among women college students, a separate subscale would have been justified.

A major strength of the CAS is that it was developed for use in either individual or group settings. With the current proliferation of prevention programs, personal development workshops, and training groups open to the general student population on most campuses, it may be particularly well suited for use in identifying at-risk students attending these group experiences for counseling referrals. Overall, the CAS is a promising screening device in an area of indicated need. Its real utility awaits further research and clinical application.

[73]
College Outcome Measures Program.

Purpose: To help "colleges define and assess general education outcomes of college."
Population: College students.
Publication Dates: 1976–1991.
Acronym: COMP.
Administration: Group.
Restricted Distribution: Distribution restricted to colleges.
Price Data, 1993: $50 per complete package including specimen copies of all tests, support materials package, and technical materials package including report ('92, 180 pages); $15 per specimen copies of all instruments (1 each); $20 per support materials package including college assessment planning book, COMPguide 1 (directions) ('91, 31 pages), COMPguide 2 (support) ('91, 60 pages), guide for matching COMP outcomes to program outcomes, good practices in general education, increasing student competence and persistence, and relevant articles; $15 per 1982–1992 technical report ('92, 180 pages); $15 per Appendices A–E; $10 per 1976–1981 technical report ('82, 96 pages); $4 per increasing student competence and persistence.

Comments: "Developed to assist in program evaluation"; 6 tests available as separates.
Authors: American College Testing Program, Aubrey Forrest (1976–1981 technical manual), and Joe M. Steele (1982–1991 technical manual).
Publisher: American College Testing Program.
  a) THE OBJECTIVE TEST.
  Scores, 7: Process Areas (Communicating, Solving Problems, Clarifying Values), Content Areas (Functioning within Social Institutions, Using Science and Technology, Using the Arts), Total.
  Price Data: $7.50–$19 per student (depending on number tested per year).
  Time: (150–160) minutes.
  b) THE COMPOSITE EXAMINATION.
  Scores, 9: Process Areas (Communicating, Solving Problems, Clarifying Values), Content Areas (Functioning within Social Institutions, Using Science and Technology, Using the Arts), Performance Areas (Writing, Speaking), Total.
  Price Data: $11–$25 per student (depending on number tested per year).
  Time: (390–400) minutes.
  c) SPEAKING SKILLS ASSESSMENT.
  Scores, 4: Audience, Discourse, Delivery, Total.
  Price Data: $3–$6 per student (depending on number tested per year).
  Time: (15–20) minutes.
  d) WRITING SKILLS ASSESSMENT.
  Scores, 4: Audience, Organization, Language, Total.
  Price Data: Same as *c* above.
  Time: (80–90) minutes.
  e) ASSESSMENT OF REASONING AND COMMUNICATING.
  Scores, 4: Reasoning, Writing, Speaking, Total.
  Price Data: Same as *a* above.
  Time: (120–130) minutes.
  f) THE ACTIVITY INVENTORY.
  Scores, 7: Same as *a* above.
  Price Data: $2–$5 per student (depending on number tested per year).
  Time: (90–100) minutes.
Cross References: See T4:587 (1 reference).

Review of the College Outcome Measures Program by ROBERT D. BROWN, Carl A. Happold Distinguished Professor Emeritus of Educational Psychology, University of Nebraska-Lincoln, Lincoln, NE:

The purpose of the College Outcome Measurements Program (COMP) instruments is to measure and evaluate the knowledge and skills: (a) that undergraduate college students are expected to acquire through their general education programs, and (b) that are important to function effectively in adult society. The complete program includes an objective test that focuses on six areas: Communicating, Solving Problems, Clarifying Values (which are considered process areas), and Functioning with Social Institutions, Using Science Technology, and Using the Arts (which are considered as content areas); performance assessments of Writing and Speaking; and an Activity Inventory that assesses student involvement in out-of-class activities related to the same six areas. Because these assessments overlap and because institutions may have different purposes and needs, it is possible for institutions to select measures most appropriate for their intents. Test content focuses on assessing students' ability to apply knowledge rather than on what factual knowledge they have acquired within specific traditional content domains. The objective test is scored only by ACT but the performance assessments can be scored by local faculty or by ACT. Guidelines are available for faculty training in scoring. An institution can add items to the package. ACT scores the Objective Test and provides information for each institution's faculty to score the Writing and Speaking assessments.

It is essential to note that the COMP program is designed for use in making judgments about the quality of general education programs rather than about the performance of individual students. Scores can be made available by the institution for feedback to individual students, but ACT does not recommend use of the scores by the institution to make academic judgments or recommendations about individual students. This distinction is important for evaluating the psychometric attributes of the COMP instruments. Costs will vary depending upon the tests selected and the student sample size. If institutions provide the ACT scores of the tested students, ACT will provide various analyses of results using the students' ACT scores as one factor.

COMP is unique in several ways. It includes an Objective Test, which employs a multiple-choice format, but unlike most such formats, each item includes two correct answers and two incorrect answers for which there is a penalty for guessing correction. It also includes a Composite Examination covering the same content as the Objective Test, but with the inclusion of writing and speaking samples. Both the Composite and the Objective Test give allegiance to the authentic test movement by including simulation activities based on "realistic stimulus materials drawn from contemporary adult society" (Comp. Guide 1, p. 6). These include materials from magazine articles, television, music, art prints, and short stories.

The COMP program has two Guides: Guide 1 describes the instruments and provides suggestions for planning to use the COMP (e.g., sampling issues), implementing COMP use, and utilizing COMP results. Guide 2 provides normative tables for freshmen and sophomores, and suggestions and examples of procedures for recruiting students and interpreting results. Both Guides provide helpful information for institutional personnel responsible for selecting and using the COMP program. The guides include little technical psychometric information. Information regarding the psychometric properties of the COMP tests are included in the COMP Technical Report 1982–1991: Clarifying and Assessing General Education Outcomes of College, ACT, 1992 and its supplements. The Technical Report and its supplements could serve as a model for its comprehensiveness concerning test development, reliability information and issues, and validity information and issues. On the other hand, the entire package of reports and supplements could be substantially improved. Much of the information is most accessible to those familiar with sophisticated measurement terminology. This reviewer wonders about the usefulness of this presentation for faculty and administrators making decisions about selecting the COMP tests and using them at their institution. A succinct and straightforward summary of this information in one of the Guides and an index and/or outline of what can be found in the technical reports would be beneficial.

RELIABILITY. As the Technical Report notes, Cronbach alpha reliability estimates for the Objective Test (Total score of .84, for six subtests it ranged from .63 to .68) and for the Composite Examination (Total score = .87, subtests .62 to .76) are not high enough to justify interpretation and decision making about individual students. As the COMP tests are intended for use in making decisions about the performance of groups of students rather than individual student performance, the most relevant reliability information is about group means. Reported reliability coefficients of the group means for the six subtests of the Objective Tests range from .97 to .98 with an average standard error of .80. The standard error of the mean for the six subtests ranged from .29 to .36. These data suggest the Objective Tests are sufficiently reliable for assessment of group differences and changes over time for purposes of program evaluation. The same pattern holds for the Speaking, Writing, and Reasoning tests. They are more than adequately reliable for making judgments about group performance, but not about individual students. Critical for use of these instruments is the extent of interrater agreement because of the subjective nature of the tasks and scoring. Apparently scoring guidelines are adequate. Reported interrater reliabilities are in the .90s.

Intercorrelations for the subtests of the Composite Examination are reported to be in the mid .50s and .60s, for the Objective Test they are in the mid .40s to mid .50s. This leaves about 75% of the variance unexplained, which suggests the subtests are sufficiently independent to warrant assessment of different subtest outcomes for different student groups (e.g., students in one program compared to another). As might be expected, the Speaking and Writing measures are moderately correlated with each other but sufficiently independent to use in program evaluation to determine if some student groups write well but do not speak well or vice versa. The Activity Inventory has a reported total score Cronbach alpha reliability estimate of .94 with the subscales reported at .75 to .88. Subscales are moderately correlated with each other but appear to be measuring independent activity patterns.

VALIDITY. It is particularly important to note and comment on two aspects of validity: (a) traditional psychometric evidence provided by longitudinal and criteria studies, and (b) validity as determined by its use by a specific institution. The Technical Report provides substantial indications of the traditional psychometric evidence for validity. These include indications of improved scores from first year of college to senior year, differential improvement by curriculum emphasis, and significant correlations and multiple regression coefficients between COMP scores and ratings by job supervisors in a variety of professions. It is noteworthy that subscales of the Activity Inventory add significantly to the multiple regressions equations used for predicting job supervisor ratings, thus supporting those who suggest that student involvement is an important educational goal.

The Report also candidly confronts issues that must be considered whenever outcome assessments are used to evaluate programs. Among these issues are questions like: Does initial skill level affect subsequent measured growth? Are the instruments sufficiently sensitive to determine whether or not changes in program or curriculum make a difference in scores? Are there differential outcomes for student subgroups such as age, gender, and ethnicity? What impact does student motivation play in the validity of the results? How much should students be expected to improve? The studies highlighted and summarized in the Report, for the most part, support the validity of the COMP instruments, but each institution must confront these questions, the provided evidence, and their relevance for its particular context.

Validity of a test depends upon its use; this is particularly relevant for the COMP. Administrators with any integrity will not want to rely on external experts alone for judgments regarding the appropriateness of the COMP test domains and test content to assess what they believe the outcomes should be for their students. Different institutions have different requirements and expectations for their students. The COMP test designers are highly cognizant of this issue and throughout the manual and other materials, test users are continually advised to have faculty, students, and relevant administrators review carefully the appropriateness of the test content for their specific institution and its purposes. Much value could accrue to the institution by engaging in the process of thinking through its goals, describing expected student outcomes, and determining the appropriateness of the fit of the COMP tests to the institution's goals.

Another unique validity issue arises because the COMP is intended to provide information for use in assessing accomplishment of institutional goals rather than for assessing individual students. High motivation of students to perform well on the tests is not automatic. Not all students would customarily be expected to take the battery and often there would be no sanctions for an individual student doing poorly. The test manual includes a special section devoted to brainstorming different ways to motivate students to do well such as paying them and notes psychometric ways to determine if certain students perform below expectations. This is an important, but sticky issue; one not easily resolved. If seniors perform better than they did as first year students, test users want to be able to say it is because they have learned new knowledge and developed new skills, not that they sloughed off on the test when they were first year students. If the seniors, on the other hand, do less well than expected, test users want to be sure that it is an accurate indicator of student knowledge and skills and not because they did not take the test seriously.

NORMS. Hundreds of postsecondary institutions have given the COMP to thousands of students. Norm groups are provided for 2-year and 4-year institutions by grade level. Most of the 4-year groups are fairly wide-ranging with public state universities included with small private colleges. Most institutions will likely find these norms helpful as a broad gauge basis for comparison with the performance of their own students, but many will wish they had purer peer comparison groups. One possible different format would be to have norms based on student performance on the ACT College Entrance Examination (Enhanced ACT Assessment, 12:139).

SUMMARY COMMENT. The College Outcome Measures Program represents a worthy response to increasing calls for higher education to be accountable for student learning in general education and to provide concrete evidence of student writing and speaking skills. Postsecondary institutions, for the most part, have been slow, if not resistant, to be responsive to these calls. Faculty and campus administrators have traditionally relied on accreditation studies as evidence of program quality, unlike their K–12 counterparts who for decades have reported standardized achievement test scores of their students (e.g., California Achievement Test, Iowa Test of Basic Skills) to their boards, parents, and to the larger community. As a minimum, the COMP provides postsecondary institutions with a start toward an authentic and reliable assessment of whether or not students are achieving the outcomes the institutions describe in their college bulletins and mission statements. Some campuses will profit by having key administrators and faculty read the COMP guides and reports, think about the issues, and design their own assessment program. Other campuses may decide to use parts of the COMP to test their students and evaluate their programs. Still others may participate fully in ongoing, longitudinal evaluation of their general education programs through use of the full complement of the COMP instruments and the accompanying services.

All campuses should at least examine the COMP for its relevance to their programs. Key faculty and administrators should discuss carefully the potential value of an assessment program like the COMP. They need to consider the relevance of important validity issues (e.g., relevance of content to college's goals, student motivation) to their campus. Vital to this discussion is the potential use of the information garnered. Is it going to be used solely for validation of student accomplishments as they pertain to the institution's goal or is the information going to be used for making decisions about how to improve programs? It is also important that each institution weigh the relative merits and cost of designing its own procedures and instruments versus using the available, ready-made COMP package or parts of the package. The college or university cannot help but benefit from involving a broad spectrum of persons (faculty, administrators, alumnae, students, employers) in considering these choices. Given the unique validity issues, it is essential that a person with professional competence in measurement issues be a consultant to this process.

ACT has contributed a significant service to higher education by providing the COMP as a starting place for campus discussions and by providing assessment instruments that can serve as a useful core evaluation tool to many institutions.

Review of the College Outcome Measures Program by CLEBORNE D. MADDUX, Professor of Special Education and Educational Technology, University of Nevada, Reno, NV:

The American College Testing Program (ACT) developed the College Outcome Measures Program (COMP) in 1976, and it has been controversial ever since. The manual states that the purpose of the materials is to help colleges evaluate their general education program by providing a commercial, nationally standardized set of measures of the cognitive outcomes of general education in order to demonstrate to the public that general education successfully prepares students to function well in adult society.

Predictably, some faculty and others rebelled at the idea that the state of the art of standardized assessment was sufficiently advanced for a norm-referenced device or set of devices to provide a more valid and useful assessment of cognitive effects than could be obtained through a less formal and more highly individualized evaluation tailored to specific institutions. Nevertheless, by 1988, more than 450 institutions had administered one or more of the early COMP instruments. The manual states that as of 1991, this number had risen to over 500 institutions that have used one or more of the assessment instruments, and 1,500 that have used some of the other materials produced by ACT. A printed supplementary leaflet (one of many) states that about 600 institutions have administered the assessment instruments.

COMP instruments are intended to measure cognitive outcomes organized around three process areas and three content areas. Processes include Communicating, Solving Problems, and Clarifying Values, and the content areas are Functioning Within Social Institutions, Using Science and Technology, and Using the Arts. The manual recommends selecting a random sample of students and offering whatever material rewards for participation the institution can provide.

The literature that accompanies the COMP material is poorly organized, often redundant, confusing, and sometimes outdated or contradictory. The booklet that appears to be the main COMP manual is pretentious and sometimes downright silly. For example, it begins as follows:

> Many metaphors are implied by the name DIRECTIONS. One metaphor related to DIRECTIONS is that of a physical fitness regimen to keep the body in top shape. (American College Testing Program, 1991, p. 1)

Such pseudointellectual posturing is unwelcome to the bewildered reader who opens the manual in the hope of finding a clear statement of purpose, a description of materials, and directions for administration. It is not until page 3 that the manual finally includes a paragraph stating the purpose of the COMP. Such convoluted writing is typical of the COMP documentation and is found throughout the voluminous printed material that includes bound volumes; slick, commercially printed brochures; and an array of photocopied inserts and sheets produced with a personal computer and printer. One possible explanation for the lack of organization of the printed material is that it has obviously been written by many different individuals over a long period of time.

THE COMPOSITE EXAMINATION. The Composite Examination is the main instrument, making use of 15 group-administered simulation activities, requiring 4 and one-half hours for administration, and yielding six subtest scores corresponding to the three processes and contents outlined above, as well as a score for Writing, a score for Speaking, and a Total score. A confusing aspect of the various documentation supplied with the COMP materials is that the Writing and Speaking Assess-

ment instruments are sometimes referred to as separate instruments, yet are treated as subtests of the Composite Examination.

The format of the examination requires short written responses, longer expository written responses, audiotaped oral responses, and multiple-choice responses. For three of the items, students view a supplied videotape with short vignettes ranging in length from 2 to 4 minutes. Three items require listening to a supplied audiotape with short segments from 2 to 5 minutes in length. Scoring involves using standardized rating scales by a team of five faculty members, requiring 60 minutes per student to complete the task. Training materials for faculty are provided as well as an offer of a service to rescore for assessment of interrater reliability.

Validity data are aimed at convincing the reader that those skills measured by the examination are important to adults, and that they can be improved through instruction. Studies are cited that provide some moderate evidence for these contentions. Test-retest reliability studies (14–16-week intervals) were conducted at several different institutions and produced coefficients that ranged from .66 to .88. These are incorrectly referred to as "large" (Ns ranged from 29 to 41).

THE OBJECTIVE TEST. The Objective test is a greatly abbreviated version of the Composite Examination requiring 2 and one-half hours for administration. Scoring has also been greatly simplified and relies totally on a multiple-choice, machine-scorable format. The same 15 simulation activities are employed as those used in the Composite Examination. The test yields three scores for Process, three for Content, and a total score, as does the Composite Examination. However, there are no writing and speaking scores.

Scores are equated raw scores and percentiles, and normative data are available for a variety of subpopulations including college freshmen, sophomores, and seniors; freshmen and sophomores enrolled at 2-year institutions; and those at 4-year institutions. There are also separate norms for college seniors at institutions with mean ACT scores both above and below 21.4.

The main validity information consists of correlation coefficients reflecting the relationship to scores on the Composite Examination. These range from .64 to .88. All but two, calculated separately for freshmen, seniors, and total group, were .73 or higher. Although these are referred to as "high" by the

COMP documentation, it should be noted that the correlation of .64 for seniors taking both the Composite Examination and the Objective Test reflects only about 41% of shared variance. Although the two instruments are clearly related, such correlations should not be referred to as more than "low" to "moderate," particularly because none of the 21 reported coefficients exceeded .88, and the majority fell in the .70s or lower. Internal reliability was estimated with Cronbach's alpha and range from .66 to .84, with six of the seven indices in the .60–.68 range.

WRITING SKILLS ASSESSMENT, SPEAKING SKILLS ASSESSMENT, AND ASSESSMENT OF REASONING AND COMMUNICATING. Although the Writing Skills Assessment and Speaking Skills Assessment are subtests of the Composite Examination, they are each bound and priced separately. The Assessment of Reasoning and Communicating is a rescoring of these instruments and is treated in one section of the technical reports together with the Writing Skills Assessment and the Speaking Skills Assessment.

For the Writing Skills Assessment, students are asked to write a letter or a memo after listening to a taped commentary on family closeness, a taped radio broadcast on the topic of nuclear waste disposal, and a recording of selections of music. The letters or memos are to respond to specific questions or topics related to the presentation. Scoring is done by a committee of faculty members who rate each writing sample on a 5-point scale with regard to Audience, Organization, Language, and Total.

For the Speaking Skills Assessment, students are presented with three activities and told that they are to prepare to give a 3-minute oral response at a time and place to be announced. They are told that they may read anything that they think will be helpful, but are not to discuss the topics with anyone. Brief note cards are permitted, but extensive notes are not allowed. They are then presented with a paragraph about community response to pornography, instructions to persuade a friend to eat fewer sweet foods, and a color art reproduction and instructions to prepare a talk about this painting. Faculty read and rate responses in one of five categories reflecting quality with regard to Audience, Discourse, Delivery, and Total.

The Assessment of Reasoning and Communicating instrument makes use of the Writing Skills Assessment and Speaking Skills Assessment and scores the results on a 5-point scale for several categories within each of the following areas: social, scientific, and artistic reasoning in speaking and writing tasks.

With regard to validity, the manual states that faculty experts in communication were consulted to help decide on important writing and speaking outcomes to be measured. In addition, six studies conducted between 1976 and 1981 are summarized. These studies were designed to show that the outcomes measures are important in the work world and included volunteers, bank employees, business/criminal justice management personnel, practice teachers, and student nurses. In addition, a search of the literature in various journals was conducted to gather information on status indices and prestige hierarchies. A number of interrater reliability studies are presented. For Speaking, the average coefficient was .92, for Writing, .94, and for Reasoning Skills, .99. Internal consistency (Cronbach's alpha) studies are listed producing coefficients of .89 to .92 for Speaking, .78 to .79 for Writing, .74 to .75 for Reasoning, and .88 to .90 for Total Score.

THE ACTIVITY INVENTORY. The Activity Inventory consists of 54 multiple-choice questions designed to measure student involvement in various out-of-class activities. Students are presented with an activity and are asked to mark A, B, C, D, or E, with A indicating the highest level of participation and E the lowest. The inventory yields a total score and six subscores corresponding to the three areas and three processes.

Validity information consists of studies designed to demonstrate that the activities included are those that distinguish students with varying levels of education and that are common to adults who are judged to be functioning well in society. Internal consistencies (Cronbach's alpha) reported included .94 for total and the statement that all others were .75 or higher.

SUMMARY. The College Outcome Measures Program (COMP) is a highly ambitious project with extensive materials and documentation. A complete analysis of these materials is far beyond the scope of this brief review.

The usefulness of these materials hinges on the question of whether or not an institution might be better served by a more qualitative and individualized approach to the evaluation of its general education program. However, if a commercial, standardized approach is decided upon, the COMP could be useful.

The manual and other documentation for the COMP are poorly organized and poorly written, and should be improved. Discussions concerning reliability, validity, and norming are spread throughout the literature and the materials; these discussions need to be consolidated into one up-to-date volume. Although reliability and validity appear to be as good as could be expected for such an ambitious and varied instrument, claims reflecting value judgments about the technical characteristics need to be toned down considerably.

Although the instruments are not as well conceived or executed as claimed in the documentation, they have nevertheless undergone extensive development over a period of years. For institutions desiring a norm-referenced approach to evaluating general education programs, the COMP may be of interest.

[74]
Collegiate Assessment of Academic Proficiency.

Purpose: Designed to assess general education skills typically attained by the end of the first two years of college.

Population: Students in the first 2 years of college.

Publication Dates: 1989–1992.

Acronym: CAAP.

Administration: Group.

Restricted Distribution: Available to institutions signing a participation agreement and paying a participation fee.

Price Data, 1993: $175 per year institutional participation fee; test module prices (including scoring and reporting) available from publisher.

Time: 40(50) minutes per test.

Author: American College Testing.

Publisher: American College Testing.

a) WRITING SKILLS.
Publication Date: 1990.
Scores, 3: Usage/Mechanics, Rhetorical Skills, Total.

b) MATHEMATICS.
Publication Date: 1989.
Scores, 2: Algebra, Total.

c) READING.
Publication Date: 1989.
Scores, 3: Arts/Literature, Social Studies/Sciences, Total.

d) CRITICAL THINKING.
Publication Date: 1989.
Scores: Total score only.

e) SCIENCE REASONING.
Publication Date: 1989.
Scores: Total score only.

f) WRITING (ESSAY).
Publication Date: 1990.
Scores: Total score only.
Comments: Total of 3 individual essays.
Cross References: See T4:589 (1 reference).

TEST REFERENCES
1. Pascarella, E., Bohr, L., Nora, A., Desler, M., & Zusman, B. (1994). Impacts of on-campus and off-campus work on first year cognitive outcome. *Journal of College Student Development, 35,* 364-370.
2. Bohr, L., Pascarella, E. T., Nora, A., & Terenzini, P. T. (1995). Do Black students learn more at historically Black or predominantly White colleges? *Journal of College Student Development, 36,* 75-85.
3. Springer, L., Terenzini, P. T., Pascarella, E. T., & Nora, A. (1995). Influences on college students' orientations toward learning for self-understanding. *Journal of College Student Development, 36,* 5-18.

Review of the Collegiate Assessment of Academic Proficiency by STEVEN V. OWEN, Professor of Educational Psychology, University of Connecticut, Storrs, CT:

Fueled partly be accountability pressures, interest in collegiate institutional assessment surged in the 1980s. The American College Testing Program (ACT) responded by building, over a 5-year period, the Collegiate Assessment of Academic Proficiency (CAAP). The result is a collection of short tests that are meant to assess general educational skills developed over the first 2 years of college. ACT claims that scores from these tests might serve a wide variety of aims:

Evaluating program effectiveness in particular skill areas. Here, the focus is on whether the institution is meeting certain educational goals. Scores may thus be used to examine pre-to-post change, or to gauge achievement against existing standards or other institutions.

Giving diagnostic advice about individual students. Scores might indicate, for example, the need for remedial work, or readiness for more advanced coursework.

Using individual student scores as screening devices. Here, scores might signal that a student is not eligible for an upper division course, is ready for the junior year, or (with other evidence) does not qualify to graduate.

These are all high stakes decisions, and ACT warns that using CAAP scores for most of these purposes should be justified by local research.

Six tests comprise the CAAP:

Science Reasoning (45 items covering eight passages), aiming at data representation, understanding research summaries, and reconciling conflicting ideas.

Mathematics (35 items; no passages), which covers algebra, coordinate geometry, trigonometry, and calculus. The test items are meant to reflect mathematical reasoning instead of formula memorization. In addition to a total score, a separate algebra score is reported.

Reading (36 items over four passages), focusing on reading comprehension of implicit meaning and drawing conclusions from written discourse. Passages are drawn from prose, humanities, social studies, and natural sciences. Complementing the total score are two subscores for arts/literature and for social/natural sciences.

Writing Skills (72 items across seven passages). Here, the intent is to measure broad areas of diction, mechanics, and rhetorical skill. After a total score, there are subscores in usage/mechanics and rhetorical skill.

Essay Writing (two short prompts ask respondents to take a position about a proposed policy change). The Technical Handbook includes the claim that respondents must "explain … why the position taken is the better (or best) alternative" (p. 18). However, nothing in the prompts themselves states that elaboration of reasons counts heavily in the holistic scoring rubric.

Critical Thinking (32 items over three passages), which revolves around argument: analyzing, evaluating, and extending the argument.

The CAAP tests put a premium on speed. Each has a 40-minute time limit, and the proportion of students not able to finish the tests range from .05 to .24. Efficiency in testing is usually a virtue, but the time limits may extract a penalty for the proficient but more reflective student.

PSYCHOMETRIC EVIDENCE FOR CAAP. For content validation and item construction, "nationally known" specialist panels gave advice about topics and their proportions within tests. ACT then recruited college faculty as item writers; over several iterations, a final item pool was assembled for pilot testing. Item analyses helped to narrow the item pool by tossing out items that were too easy or difficult, or that had weak part-whole correlations. The resulting item difficulties (averaging around .60, with Mathematics lower at around .38) will come close to maximizing the spread of scores. This objective is time tested for norm-referenced applications, but the CAAP orientation seems mainly criterion referenced. One wonders why ACT did not use construction standards (e.g., masters vs. nonmasters) more suited to its criterion-referenced claims.

Reliability evidence is given as KR-20 coefficients and standard errors of measurement. KR-20 estimates are satisfactory, ranging from .78 (Mathematics) to .93 (Writing Skills). (These were calculated by averaging separate coefficients for various subgroups reported in the CAAP Technical Handbook.) No reliability estimates are given for various subscores within tests. Neither are there interrater reliabilities reported for the scores of the Essay Writing test. And although there are parallel forms of the CAAP, no equivalence reliability estimates are reported. Stability estimates are available (over 2-year intervals) but ACT reports none of these.

Standard errors, chronically underused by practitioners, are so large as to create serious doubt about the use of CAAP scores to make decisions about individual students. As an example, consider the Mathematics standard error reported for one subgroup: 2.47 (CAAP Technical Handbook, p. 31; this is at odds with the figure of 1.96 in the CAAP User's Guide, p. 24). Developing a .95 confidence interval around an average raw Mathematics score of 15.2 gives a band of 10.3 to 20.1. If we wish to translate the bandwidth to comparable percentile ranks, we are stuck. In its norm tables (User's Guide, Appendix D), ACT gives only translations from scale scores to percentile ranks; raw score equivalents are omitted. Assuming a normal distribution of scores, we can nevertheless estimate percentile ranks from raw scores. Plain talk summary: The 95% confidence band places this person's math score somewhere between the 18th and the 82nd percentile rank. This band does not give much confidence about developing useful cutpoints (e.g., for eligibility for an advanced course). ACT's only acknowledgement about how fragile individual decisions can be comes in the discussion of the use of change scores (e.g., pre to post) (User's Guide, p. 31). This is a wise caution, because the feeble reliabilities of the CAAP change scores range from .31 to .40.

ACT provides an assortment of criterion-related validity coefficients for the various CAAP tests. Coefficients from predicting same-year GPA are modest, ranging from .34 to .38. Predicting next-year GPAs deliver predictably lower correlations, between .23 and .35.

Construct validity evidence takes a different guise. CAAP scores are said to represent "the academic skills and knowledge acquired by students during the first two years of college" (CAAP Technical Handbook, p. 44). One way of examining this is by assessing change in CAAP scores from the beginning of the freshman year to the end of the sophomore year. ACT's evidence is very slim. One gets the hint that growth in skills is small from the item analysis data: Test difficulties are not very different for freshmen and sophomores. Using both longitudinal and cross-sectional data, ACT reports gain scores over a 2-year period (but does not say whether the gains are in raw or scaled scores). Assuming raw scores, effect sizes are not very impressive: .07 to .21 standard deviation improvement in CAAP scores over 2 years. CAAP scores, whatever they measure, are durable.

WHAT I THINK. There are two obvious hypotheses about why CAAP scores do not change much. One is that the colleges involved in the validity studies did not impart the skills measured by CAAP. Certainly college faculty would argue against this interpretation.

A second hypothesis is that the construct CAAP taps is general aptitude, which is not easily manipulable in a 2-year period. The CAAP Technical Handbook shows test intercorrelations ranging from .46 to .75 (Science and Essay Writing data were unavailable and not printed in the Handbook). For each of the two parallel forms of the CAAP, I ran the intercorrelations through a principal factor analysis; this is crudely analogous to a second-order factoring. For both forms of the CAAP, a single factor emerged, explaining 98% and 99% of the test covariation. Each test loaded in the .80s except for Mathematics, which was around .60. An internal consistency estimate for each factor was .86. Except to improve the internal consistency, I suspect that the addition of Science and Essay Writing to the factor procedure would not change the results much. What shall we call the single, strong factor? Charles Spearman would have suggested "g," and perhaps that is still a useful term. Unfortunately, g is not what ACT had in mind in constructing CAAP.

In summary, institutions should consider carefully whether the CAAP tests will deliver results that are useful in planning, program evaluation, policy development, design of interventions, and diagnosis of student progress. Institutions that already have some proxy for g (e.g., SAT or ACT scores) should ask whether another assessment will give additional useful advice. For ACT's part, they should expand what seem now like draft versions of the CAAP Technical Handbook and the CAAP User's Guide. At the very least, they should develop a convincing argument with, for instance, a multitrait, multimethod approach, that CAAP measures something more malleable than general aptitude.

Review of the Collegiate Assessment of Academic Proficiency by JEFFREY K. SMITH, Professor of Educational Psychology and Associate Dean, Graduate School of Education, Rutgers The State University of New Jersey, New Brunswick, NJ:

The Collegiate Assessment of Academic Proficiency (CAAP) is a set of six tests designed to provide colleges with indicators of the academic performance of their students for purposes of program evaluation and assessment of individual students. The skills measured are argued to be general educational foundation skills necessary for success in the final 2 years of an undergraduate curriculum. The tests measure Reading, Mathematics, Science Reasoning, Critical Thinking, and Writing (both through multiple-choice and essay formats). All tests employ a four-choice multiple-choice format except for the essay-based Writing test.

The Reading test consists of four passages of roughly 900 words each with nine items relating to each passage. One passage is fiction; the remaining three are drawn from the humanities, social sciences, and natural sciences. All passages are taken from published material. The Critical Thinking test contains pairs of essays presenting different points of view on various topics. Questions are based on comparisons of the arguments made by the two essays. The Mathematics test ranges from pre-algebra to introductory calculus. There is a mix of story items and solutions of equations. The Writing Skills test consists of a series of passages with underlined segments that have possible editing changes made for them. A "no change" option is included for each item. The Science Reasoning test contains passages and diagrams from biology, chemistry, physics, and the physical sciences. A series of questions is related to each of the passages. The Writing essay test consists of two 20-minute prompts consisting of a brief paragraph. The Writing test is scored holistically on a 6-point scale.

The CAAP appears to be a well-conceptualized and executed effort to measure many of the academic skills related to the type of learning that occurs in college. A review of the CAAP indicates clearly that the tests are at an appropriate level and provide strong coverage of the six areas measured. The development of the measures was based on research conducted by ACT and items were written by college faculty in the various disciplines. Norms are available based on testing from approximately 75,000 students at colleges and universities using the

CAAP. There are norms for first and second year students from public and private schools, and from 2- and 4-year institutions. ACT provides scoring services and a variety of score reports.

Extensive reliability information is provided on the CAAP, but there is only modest information concerning validity, especially for an assessment program that is well-established. Reliabilities (KR20) for the multiple-choice measures range from .76 to .95. The KR20 reliabilities are quite satisfactory for reporting group results, but are only consistently strong enough for individual level scores for the Writing Skills multiple-choice test. No test-retest or parallel form reliability information is provided. A section reporting completion rates for the measures indicates that the measure suffer from speededness. A study of 2,000 examinees found that between 5% and 16% did not complete the last five items of the tests they were taking. Although the manual argues that these reflect high completion rates, it is difficult to agree with this conclusion based on the data (e.g., in Reading, up to 20% did not reach the last 5 items of a 36-item measure).

The validity section of the technical manual is quite brief, and the data provided are not particularly encouraging. There is no information with regard to content validity except the suggestion that each institution should conduct its own content validity assessment. Although it is true that test users should judge a test for their specific purposes, this does not mean that a study of the opinions of college faculty and administrators with regard to the appropriateness of the CAAP would not be useful in helping others decide whether to use the measures. A major concern regarding content validity of the CAAP relates to the coverage of the CAAP to what is taught in college. If college disciplines can be organized into the humanities, the social sciences, and the natural sciences (including Mathematics), it would seem that the natural sciences and the humanities are well covered in the CAAP, but the social sciences are not. There are skills measures that are certainly important to the social sciences, but the work and tools of the social scientist (hypothesis generation and testing, interpretation of statistical data, the search for alternative explanations of findings, etc.) are fundamentally absent from the assessment.

A series of studies from 58 institutions regarding the relationship between CAAP scores and college grades is summarized in the technical manual. Concurrent correlations between CAAP scores and GPAs are modest (median correlations ranging from .34 to .38), and predictive correlations between second year CAAP scores and third year (GPA were even more modest (ranging between .23 and .32). (No correlations are provided for the Writing essay or the Science Reasoning test.) In a second series of studies, CAAP scores for students entering their first year of college were compared to scores of these students when they completed their second year. Gains ranged from .6 scale points to 2.3 scale points. These translate to gains of roughly .15 to .50 standard deviations. This seems to be very little growth over the course of 2 years.

The validity data do not argue strongly for the utility of the CAAP, but these results need to be put in context. First, although the correlations reported in these studies are modest, it should be kept in mind that college grade-point averages are notoriously unreliable. Second, the small gains found over time may reflect the general nature of the measures as opposed to the frequently very specific nature of college courses. Third, motivation to perform well on the part of examinees may be clouding the picture. This is a topic mentioned frequently in the materials provided with the tests.

To summarize, the CAAP presents users with a solid, traditionally conceived, set of measures of skills related to college learning. The level of difficulty is appropriate, norms are provided for comparison purposes, and scoring and reporting services are available. Reliability is solid for group comparisons, but generally not adequate for individual decisions without supporting information. Validity information is problematic, but not unusually so for a measure of this type. The CAAP provides a potentially useful alternative to locally developed measures for evaluation of college programs and as a component of a program for student placement and assessment.

[75]
The Common-Metric Questionnaire.

Purpose: "Designed to describe, analyze, and evaluate jobs of all types from both public and private sector organizations."

Population: Job incumbents, supervisors, job analysts.

Publication Dates: 1990–1992.

Acronym: CMQ.

Scores: 6 sections: General Background, Contacts With People, Making Decisions, Physical and Mechanical Activities, Work Setting, Selection Test Scores.

Administration: Group.

Price Data, 1994: $75 per complete kit including CMQ Booklet, Directions for Administering the CMQ ('92, 99 pages, and Guide to Using the CMQ for Human Resource Applications ('92, 113 pages); $25 per CMQ Booklet; $35 per Directions for Administering the CMQ; $35 per Guide to Using the CMQ for Human Resource Applications; $750 per Selection Test Validation Report; $28 per 25 Selection Test Validation Criterion Forms; $69 for CMQ Reporting Software; $2500 per Market-Capturing Equation; $10 per Reporting Software user's manual.

Time: (180–240) minutes.

Comments: When individually administered, the CMQ is mailed to the rater who completes it on his/her own time and returns it; The CMQ should only be individually administered to executive, managerial, and professional level employees; small group administration is recommended.

Authors: Robert J. Harvey (questionnaire) and The Psychological Corporation (manuals).

Publisher: Robert J. Harvey (the author).

Review of the Common-Metric Questionnaire by GERALD A. ROSEN, Consulting Psychologist, Huntingdon Valley, PA:

The Common-Metric Questionnaire (CMQ) is a "worker-oriented" (p. 9) job analysis inventory that has been designed for the description of jobs that may be highly dissimilar on a common profile of tasks or activities. Much of the motivation for developing the CMQ came from the author's dissatisfaction with other job analysis instruments. Some of these tests limit their scope to either managerial or nonmanagerial jobs, but not both. Others, it is asserted, employ too high a reading level for use with some incumbents, or use items that are vague, or rating scales with undefined anchors and rating points. The CMQ, in contrast, is intended for use with incumbents, supervisors, and job analysts for the collection of behaviorally specific data on almost all jobs regardless of level. The development efforts for the CMQ have been largely successful in meeting these goals.

The CMQ describes jobs on four dimensions derived from factor analyses of older instruments including the Position Analysis Questionnaire and Job Element Inventory. Scores are reported on 4 variables called categories of work characteristics (Interpersonal Activities, Decision-Making Activities, Mechanical and Physical Activities, and Work Context Activities). Within each category, subscores are provided on from 2 to 6 variables—a total of 19 in all. These scores are based on responses to 242 items written in the form of statements. The instrument employs a "matrix" format such that for each of the 242 items, the respondent first determines if the statement applies to the job being analyzed. If it does, several additional responses are required. If it does not apply, the respondent goes on to the next item.

The test administration manual is 99 pages long and will require much time and attention from the human resource department generalists, for whom it is written, to fully understand. This is due to several factors: First, the CMQ is a fairly complex instrument that seeks to collect data for many purposes (job description, performance appraisal, selection test validation, and compensation). Second, the test can only be processed by the publisher, so there are all of the usual instructions for use of scannable documents, interacting with the scoring service, ordering materials, etc. Third, the manual includes instructions for both individual and large group administration. And fourth, there is a 26-page chapter on the CMQ test booklet. Complexities of the instrument aside, the manual is a comprehensive document that goes well beyond the minimum requirements for providing the information necessary for proper standardized test administration.

The test booklet is 32 pages long, 20 pages of which are the actual test items. However, it is not the length of the test booklet, but its layout that presents a problem. In order to keep the booklet from being even longer, the 20 pages of test responses employ a visually difficult format. The booklet is held vertically so that the crease between facing pages is horizontal. The top page contains the response categories (e.g., "Hourly to many times each hour," "Every few hours to daily," p. 14), for the items (e.g., "Coordinate or schedule work activities?" p. 15) on the bottom page. Responses are bubbled in rows to the right of the items on the bottom page. To ensure that responses are bubbled into the proper spaces, the participant must follow a shaded line from a response category across the top page to a point where it turns 90 degrees downward and then follow it down the top page and into the bottom page to the appropriate bubble to the right of an item. Although the verbal description of this process makes it sound more complex than it is, it can be an extremely visually fatiguing task with possible negative consequences for test completion and accuracy of responses. This may be one reason why the test administration manual requires the use of "subject matter experts" as "checkers" to verify the completeness and accuracy of the collected data.

A user's guide is also supplied with the CMQ. It is a 113-page document that, like the test administration manual, is written with the human resource generalist in mind. It will challenge many test users. It is part basic job analysis textbook, part test usage guide, and part, perhaps the largest part, blatant marketing tool for the various reports available from the publisher's scoring service. From a careful reading of the manual, the CMQ user will gain some understanding of the instrument's underlying perspective on job analysis, its intended uses, dimensions measured, and sample reports. Given the complexity of the CMQ and the many uses for which it is advertised, it is apparent from reading the user's guide that some in its intended audience will not be equipped to make an informed decision on whether it will meet their particular need.

An in-depth description of the development of the CMQ is contained in a research monograph not supplied with the test materials, but available at no charge from the publisher. Although not all of the data presented are as comprehensive as might be desired (e.g., no cross-validation for the discriminant analysis on exempt/nonexempt status), the document contains the necessary information to answer most questions apt to be posed by technically oriented test users. For example, it includes reliability data on internal consistencies of the scales (coefficient alpha). Also, the demonstration of the instrument's ability to differentiate exempt from nonexempt jobs provides some interesting validity data. The user's guide and research monograph seem to work best when used in conjunction with each other.

SUMMARY. The CMQ is a job analysis inventory that describes dissimilar jobs on the same dimensions; hence the name, "Common-Metric." The advantage of such a scheme is comparability across jobs. The disadvantage is lack of specificity within jobs. Although this is less true of the CMQ than other worker-oriented instruments, it remains an issue to be considered when selecting tests for specific human resource purposes. For example, one item asks if knowledge of sheet-metal work, welding, electrical work, carpentry, plumbing, and/or construction are used, and, if so, how often and how important that knowledge is and where it was acquired. On the one hand, the item lumps together a very broad array of knowledge and, on the other hand, fails to obtain any data on the depth of the knowledge required. Hence, the utility of the CMQ for job descriptions may be limited in some cases. However, the CMQ's common-metric methodology should prove particularly useful for compensation studies.

In an organization that finds comparisons among and between clerical, blue-collar, supervisory, managerial, and/or executive positions useful, the value of the approach taken by the CMQ cannot be underestimated. Furthermore, the CMQ is a thoughtfully developed instrument with acceptable reliability for the purposes for which it is intended. The "matrix" model of item response results in more comprehensive and specific data than would customarily be obtained with this type of instrument. The CMQ, therefore, is a viable choice among job analysis instruments and an improvement over many previously developed tools.

[76]
Communication and Symbolic Behavior Scales.

Purpose: "A standardized method of examining communicative and symbolic behaviors of children."
Population: 9 months to 6 years.
Publication Date: 1993.
Acronym: CSBS.
Scores, 7: Communicative Functions, Gestural Communicative Means, Vocal Communicative Means, Verbal Communicative Means, Reciprocity, Social-Affective Signaling, Symbolic Behavior.
Administration: Individual.
Price Data: Available from publisher.
Time: (60–70) minutes.
Comments: Assessments videotaped for analysis.
Authors: Amy M. Wetherby and Barry M. Prizant.
Publisher: Applied Symbolix.

TEST REFERENCES

1. Crais, E. R., & Roberts, J. E. (1991). Decision making in assessment and early intervention planning. *Language, Speech, and Hearing Services in Schools, 22,* 19–30.
2. Warren, S. F., & Abbeduto, L. (1992). The relation of communication and language development to mental retardation. *American Journal on Mental Retardation, 97,* 125-130.
3. Warren, S. F., Yoder, P. J., Gazdag, G. E., Kim, K., & Jones, H. A. (1993). Facilitating prelinguistic communication skills in young children with developmental delay. *Journal of Speech and Hearing Research, 36,* 83–97.

Review of the Communication and Symbolic Behavior Scales by STEVEN H. LONG, Assistant Professor of Communication Sciences, Case Western Reserve University, Cleveland, OH:

The Communication and Symbolic Behavior Scales (CSBS) is intended for the assessment of children up to 6 years of age whose functional communication age is between 8 months and 2 years. It uses a structured interaction with a child to gather information about communicative, social-affective, and symbolic abilities.

TEST MATERIALS. The CSBS includes a kit of toys and books that are used to tempt children into communicative interactions or to engage them in various types of symbolic play. A few items are edible or disposable and must be replaced after each administration of the test. Many items can be mouthed and will require sterilization.

A manual contains the procedures for administering, scoring, and interpreting the CSBS. These procedures are further illustrated on two instructional videotapes that accompany the test. Responses from a child are coded on a set of 10 score sheets. In addition, two forms are provided for the caregiver, one to describe the child prior to the assessment and the other to rate representativeness of behavior afterwards.

Because the CSBS evaluates many behaviors that must be judged visually, the examination session must be videotaped. Furthermore, it is important that the camera be properly positioned in order to capture the behaviors of interest, should they occur. If videorecording problems occur, nearly all assessment information would be lost.

TEST ADMINISTRATION. The interaction with the child is carefully organized so that materials are presented in sequence and a fixed amount of time is allowed to observe the child's play with or use of those materials. The CSBS puts the examiner in the role of introducing materials and giving direction to the child's caregiver. The behavioral sample is taken, for the most part, from the child's interaction with the caregiver rather than with the examiner. The interaction begins with a warm-up of 10–15 minutes. For the next 10–20 minutes, the child is encouraged to communicate by offering a series of alluring toys (balloons, bubbles), simple dyadic games (peek-a-boo), and mild frustrations (toys in a sealed plastic bag). This is followed by book sharing for 5 minutes, symbolic play with representational toys for 10 minutes, probes of the child's comprehension for 5 minutes, and probes of the child's play with construction toys (blocks, rings, cups) for 5 minutes. From the videotape, the form and function of all child communicative behaviors is noted on the scoring sheets, which list possible categories. Similarly, the child's social/affective signaling (e.g., shifts in gaze) is noted as well as the symbolic behavior evident during the play sequences and the conversation probes. These behaviors are then summed, weighted, and scored according to guidelines provided in the manual.

PSYCHOMETRIC ADEQUACY. The content validity of the CSBS is based on the view that language emerges as the result of interacting social, affective, cognitive, and linguistic factors. Thus, it is logical to assess behaviors in all of these domains in order to form a profile that might highlight one or more areas of development that are incommensurate with the others. Evidence for the construct validity of the CSBS appears in the age-related increases in scores shown by children in the standardization group on nearly all of the instrument's 22 scales. Adequate predictive validity is claimed on the basis of discriminant analyses of CSBS scores. These analyses show that the instrument classified children into normal, pervasive developmental disorder, and speech-language impaired groups with accuracy ranging from 60% to 98%.

Statistical analysis of reliability is quite thorough. Six of the CSBS's seven scales showed high internal consistency. Repeated administrations of the instrument to 66 children showed that scores did not differ on retesting when it occurred after an interval of less than 2 months but that differences emerged with intervals longer than that. Interexaminer reliability was .83 or better in pairwise comparison of three different raters.

The standardization group for CSBS consisted of 282 child scores distributed from 8 to 24 months. The manual authors refer to 282 "children" but the discussion makes it clear that there were actually only 216 individuals tested, of whom 66 were retested and their second scores added to the standardization sample. The authors justify adding the second scores to the norms because "they increase the relevance of the norms to their intended use and reduce the error that would be associated with estimates of developmental improvement based on different children at different ages" (p. 64). Roughly half of the 282 normative scores placed the children at a "prelinguistic" stage, the other half at a "linguistic" stage that subsumed individuals at early one-word, late one-word, and multiword levels of development. A weighting procedure was used to adjust the norms for the slight differences in the monthly distribution of the sample. Other weightings were used to adjust for gender, race, and Spanish origin so that the final norms are more in line with characteristics of the national population. The result of these weightings was to create equal representation (5.92%) at all monthly intervals except the first two. The weighted percentage of girls in the standardization sample was 48.7%; the weighted percentage of African American children, 12.1%; and the weighted percentage of children of Spanish origin, 9.4%.

Norms are reported in a series of tables, each table corresponding to one of the six CSBS scales or to a composite of several scales. The norms are expressed both as standard scores and percentile ranks, broken down (a) monthly from 8 to 24 months, and (b) by language stage. The standard error of measurement is reported for each table.

SUMMARY. The CSBS uses a structured interaction to examine early symbolic and communicative behavior in children with a functional communication age between 8 months and 2 years. The entire interaction with the child is scripted to take between 45 and 60 minutes. Scoring is accomplished through careful review of the child's videotaped behavior and categorization of all communicative, social-affective, and symbolic acts. In the design of the instrument and in its standardization, considerable thought was given to matters of reliability and validity and the CSBS can make strong claims in those areas.

Those who would consider using the CSBS must be aware of three conditions. First, the instrument requires the involvement of the child's caretaker to complete questionnaires before and after the interaction and to participate along with the child in the interaction itself. Second, the interaction must be videotaped. Third, the procedure is lengthy. The authors do not offer an estimate of how long it will take most examiners to administer, tally, and interpret the CSBS (they do suggest 90 minutes to code). Assuming, however, that it will take at least 2 minutes to review and code every minute of videotape, then administration and coding will require 2.25 to 3 hours. Tallying the 10 worksheets may take another hour and lookup of norms an additional 15 minutes. Thus, the procedure may demand from 3.5 to 4.25 hours to complete.

Review of the Communication and Symbolic Behavior Scales by DOLORES KLUPPEL VETTER, Professor of Communicative Disorders, University of Wisconsin—Madison, Madison, WI:

The Communication and Symbolic Behavior Scales (CSBS) was designed to identify children who have or who are at risk for developing a communicative disorder. In addition, data from it may be used to establish a profile of communicative, social-affective, and symbolic functioning that will allow the monitoring of children's behavioral changes over time. It is designed for children who have a functional communication age between 8 and 24 months and whose chronological age is between 9 months and 6 years.

The CSBS uses action-based toys, books, and play materials appropriate for very young children.

The evaluator, the child, and the child's caregiver are present during the assessment. Behaviors of the child are sampled during activities (i.e., communicative temptations) that range in the degree of structure provided. The activities are designed with the purpose of optimizing the occurrence of spontaneous communicative and play behaviors. Minimal interaction or direction is provided by the evaluator and the child's caregiver is requested to interact spontaneously and not to direct the child's activities. The evaluation session generally takes about one hour. It is videotaped and is scored at a later time. Finally, information is also requested from the caregiver through the use of a questionnaire and a form on which the caregiver provides ratings of the child's behaviors during the assessment. The Caregiver Questionnaire may be completed in advance, or at the time of the evaluation, and the Caregiver Perception Form is completed immediately following the evaluation.

In the CSBS manual the authors state that a trained examiner is able to score the videotape in about one hour. This may be an optimistic time estimate; the evaluation session will yield a videotape of approximately one hour's length and the behaviors that are scored involve judgments and decisions. Training for an examiner, however, will require a substantial investment of time and energy prior to the use of the CSBS. Although the administration of the procedure should be straightforward for any professional proficient in assessing developmentally young children, learning how to score the various communicative and symbolic behaviors likely will require practice. For example, while viewing the videotape, the examiner must first identify that a single communicative act has occurred by answering three questions affirmatively (i.e., Was the act a gesture, vocalization, or verbalization? Was the act directed toward the adult? Did the act serve a communicative function?). When a communicative act has been identified, it is then rated for one of three communicative functions (i.e., behavior regulation, social interaction, or joint attention), or the examiner determines that the communicative function is unclear. Each of these decisions may initially necessitate a replaying of the videotape and a rereading of the definitions before a decision can be reached regarding a single communicative act.

Information and examples are provided in the CSBS manual to assist the examiner in learning to score behaviors on the videotape. In addition, the authors prepared two videotapes that were used to train examiners for the scoring of the behaviors of the normative sample; these are provided with the CSBS to make the sampling procedures and the scoring criteria explicit.

The information obtained from the CSBS results in 18 scales that represent observed communicative behaviors (e.g., conventional use of gestures, inventory of different words) and four scales that reflect aspects of symbolic behavior (e.g., constructive play). The authors then devised seven cluster scores that reflect the child's abilities in broader domains (e.g., a cluster score for communicative functions was constructed from the individual scales of behavior regulation, social interaction, and joint attention) and that have the advantage of being more reliable than individual scales. Finally, there is a communication composite score that was constructed of the 18 communicative behavior scales. Tables are provided in the CSBS manual from which standard score equivalents for cluster and composite scores (at 1-month age intervals) may be determined; tables with percentile ranks are also given. The CSBS manual contains a detailed tutorial on the interpretation of the various types of scores, and confidence intervals are provided for the appropriate interpretation of the cluster and composite scores. The authors stress the desirability of comparing the scaled values of the scores within and among children through the use of the CSBS Profile.

The depth and extent of the information provided relevant to the standardization of the CSBS is impressive. Detailed demographic information (i.e., age, linguistic state, gender, and ethnic status) is presented for the standardization sample of 242 children. Descriptive statistics for the individual scales, and the cluster and communication composite scores are also contained in the CSBS manual. Reliability is addressed through the evaluation of (a) internal consistency of the cluster and composite scores by age and language stage of the children, (b) test-retest stability of the individual scales at two time intervals, (c) interrater reliability of the individual scales among three pairs of raters, and (d) the standard errors of measurement for cluster scores and the communication composite score. As might be expected there was some variability among the reliability estimates, but taking everything together, the CSBS yields very adequate reliability. Persuasive evidence also was presented for content, ecological, criterion-related, and construct validity. When a discriminant function analysis was applied to three groups of children (i.e., the standardization sample, a group with pervasive developmental disorders, and

one with speech-language impairments), 98% of the standardization sample, 85% of the children with pervasive developmental disorders, and 60% of children with speech-language impairments were accurately classified.

In summary, the CSBS provides a procedure for evaluating early communicative and symbolic behaviors in children. The rationale for the scales is well developed and the standardization information is extensive. Examiners will have to use the video training tapes and engage in substantial practice in order to achieve reliable and valid administration, scoring, and interpretation of the information acquired through the use of the CSBS. The information obtained from a child should provide results that will facilitate comparisons with the standardization sample, that will track development within the child, and that will provide directions for intervention when necessary.

[77]
Composite International Diagnostic Interview.

Purpose: "For use in epidemiological studies of mental disorders."
Population: Adults.
Publication Date: 1993.
Acronym: CIDI.
Scores, 18: Demographics, Tobacco Use Disorder, Somatoform Disorders, Panic Disorder, Generalized Anxiety, Phobic Disorders, Major Depressive Episode and Dysthymia, Manic Episode, Schizophrenic and Schizophreniform Disorders, Eating Disorders, Alcohol Abuse and Dependence, Obsessive Compulsive Disorder, Drug Abuse and Dependence, Organic Brain Syndrome, Psychosexual Dysfunctions, Comments by the Respondent and the Interviewer, Interviewer Observations, Interviewer Rating.
Administration: Individual.
Price Data: Available from publisher.
Time: (75–95) minutes.
Author: World Health Organization.
Publisher: American Psychiatric Press, Inc.

TEST REFERENCES

1. Rogler, L. H. (1993). Culturally sensitizing psychiatric diagnosis: A framework for research. *The Journal of Nervous and Mental Disease, 181*, 401-408.
2. Asherson, P., Walsh, C., Williams, J., Sargeant, M., Taylor, C., Clements, A., Gill, M., Owen, M., & McGuffin, P. (1994). Imprinting and anticipation: Are they relevant to genetic studies or schizophrenia? *British Journal of Psychiatry, 164*, 619-624.
3. Eaton, W. W., Kessler, R. C., Wittchen, H. U., & Magee, W. J. (1994). Panic and panic disorder in the United States. *American Journal of Psychiatry, 151*, 413-420.
4. Le, F., Mitchell, P., Vivero, C., Waters, B., Donald, J., Selbie, L. A., Shine, J., & Schofield, P. (1994). Exclusion of close linkage of bipolar disorder to the Gs-alpha subunit gene in nine Australian pedigrees. *Journal of Affective Disorders, 32*, 187-195.
5. Sobell, L. C., Toneatto, T., & Sobell, M. (1994). Behavioral assessment and treatment planning for alcohol, tobacco, and other drug problems: Current status with an emphasis on clinical applications. *Behavior Therapy, 25*, 533–580.

6. Dettling, M., Heinz, A., DuFeu, P., Rommelspacher, H., Graf, K.-L., & Schmidt, L. G. (1995). Dopaminergic responsivity in alcoholism: Trait, state, or residual marker? *American Journal of Psychiatry, 152*, 1317–1321.

7. Garfinkel, P. E., Lin, E., Goering, P., Spegg, C., Goldbloom, D. S., Kennedy, S., Kaplan, A. S., & Woodside, B. (1995). Bulimia nervosa in a Canadian community sample: Prevalence and comparison of subgroups. *American Journal of Psychiatry, 152*, 1052-1058.

8. Gureje, O., Aderibigbe, Y. A., & Obikoya, O. (1995). Three syndromes in schizophrenia: Validity in young patients with recent onset of illness. *Psychological Medicine, 25*, 715–725.

9. Kessler, R. C., Foster, C. L., Saunders, W. B., & Stang, P. E. (1995). Social consequences of psychiatric disorders, I. Educational attainment. *American Journal of Psychiatry, 152*, 1026-1032.

10. Peters, L., & Andrews, G. (1995). Procedural validity of the computerized version of the Composite International Diagnostic Interview (CIDI—Auto) in the anxiety disorders. *Psychological Medicine, 25*, 1269–1280.

11. Sartorius, N., Ustun, T. B., Korten, A., Cooper, J. E., & van Drimmelen, J. (1995). Progress toward achieving a common language in psychiatry, II: Results from the international field trials of the ICO—10 Diagnostic Criteria for Research for Mental and Behavioral Disorders. *American Journal of Psychiatry, 152*, 1427–1437.

12. Nelson, C. B., Little, R. J. A., Heath, A. C., & Kessler, R. C. (1996). Patterns of DSM-III-R alcohol dependence symptom progression in a general population survey. *Psychological Medicine, 26*, 449–460.

13. Parikh, S. V., Wasylenki, D., Goering, P., & Wong, J. (1996). Mood disorders: Rural/urban differences in prevalence, health care utilization, and disability in Ontario. *Journal of Affective Disorders, 38*, 57–65.

14. Schuckit, M. A., Tipp, J. E., Anthenelli, R. M., Bucholz, K. K., Hesselbrock, V. M., & Nurnberger, J. I. (1996). Anorexia nervosa and bulimia nervosa in alcohol-dependent men and women and their relatives. *American Journal of Psychiatry, 153*, 74–82.

15. Thompson, L. L., Riggs, P. D., Mikulich, S. K., & Crowley, T. J. (1996). Contribution of ADHD symptoms to substance problems and delinquency in conduct-disordered adolescents. *Journal of Abnormal Child Psychology, 24*, 325–347.

16. Tiemens, B. G., Ormel, J., & Simon, G. E. (1996). Occurrence, recognition, and outcome of psychological disorders in primary care. *American Journal of Psychiatry, 153*, 636–644.

17. Williams, L. M. (1996). Cognitive inhibition and schizophrenic symptom subgroups. *Schizophrenia Bulletin, 22*, 139–151.

Review of the Composite International Diagnostic Interview by MARY MATHAI CHITTOORAN, UC Foundation Assistant Professor of School Psychology and Special Education, The University of Tennessee at Chattanooga, Chattanooga, TN:

The Composite International Diagnostic Interview (CIDI), Version 1.1 is a comprehensive, standardized, and structured interview for the assessment of mental disorders in adults. Appropriate for use in a variety of cultures with respondents of diverse educational backgrounds, the core version of the CIDI is currently available in 16 languages. Although the CIDI was designed to be used in epidemiological studies of mental disorders, it is finding increased acceptance in clinical and research circles.

The CIDI had its inception in 1980, when questions from the National Institute of Mental Health Diagnostic Interview Schedule (NIMH-DIS) and the ninth edition of the Present State Examination (PSE-9) were combined to form a draft version. Since then, items have been modified, added, and structured to correspond to the criteria for mental disorders outlined in two major diagnostic systems— the *International Classification of Diseases* (ICD-10) and the American Psychiatric Association's *Diagnostic and Statistical Manual—Third Edition, Revised* (*DSM-III-R*). According to the authors of the manual, feasibility and cross-cultural acceptability were established in field trials conducted in sites around the world and the CIDI was determined to have "excellent interrater reliability (kappa >.90 in almost all diagnostic categories) and good test-retest reliability" (p. 10). Subsequent field trials confirmed previous findings and suggested a high degree of diagnostic concordance between CIDI and clinical ICD-10 and DSM-III-R diagnoses.

Test materials consist of a Researcher's Manual, an Interviewer's Manual, a 105-page Interview protocol, a Computer Manual, and an IBM-compatible computer diskette that includes data cleaning and entry programs as well as scoring programs for both *ICD-10* and *DSM-III-R* diagnoses. A computer-administered version of the CIDI, the CIDI-Auto, is also available and an abbreviated version, the CIDI-Quick, is under development.

The CIDI may be administered by both clinicians and nonclinicians and all interviewers undergo rigorous training sessions offered by a CIDI training center. Interview questions are standardized and are designed to elicit descriptive information about the frequency, severity, onset, and recency of symptoms. The interviewer is responsible for gathering the information, coding it appropriately, and submitting it to the editor for data cleaning, computer entry, and scoring. A positive diagnosis is made when (a) *all* criteria for a disorder are met *AND* when (b) all *positive* criteria—as distinguished from exclusionary criteria—for that disorder are met.

COMMENTARY. The CIDI has a number of excellent features. It is the result of a large-scale collaborative project that was developed over a 13-year period, with an impressive number of field trials in international settings. Content validity appears to be adequate as interview questions were constructed upon the recommendations of an international panel of experts who also judged its cross-cultural acceptability. Interrater reliability ranges from good to excellent. Test materials are sturdy, attractive, and of good quality. The CIDI offers a highly structured format with explicit directions to interviewers, which combined with the training program (arguably one of the CIDI's greatest strengths), adds to ease of administration and minimizes a significant source of potential error. Additionally, computer-generated diagnoses may obviate concerns about human error in data entry and scoring.

The CIDI is subject to the limitations of all interviews in that its results are dependent on the skills of the interviewer but this may be especially problematic if the interviewer is a nonclinician. Respondents may display behaviors that escape the nonclinician but that could be critical to an accurate diagnosis, and decision-making, particularly with borderline cases, is often heavily influenced by clinical experience. Similarly, the generation of computer diagnoses, although advantageous in many ways (Wittchen, 1993), disregards the value of human experience in decision making.

Although the CIDI does address the use of self-descriptive phrases such as "excessive," "sickly," or "a lot of trouble," other phrases like "worried a lot" are left vague and undefined. Also of concern is the fact that the interviewer is asked to comment on respondent behaviors such as the existence of neologisms, and to determine whether the respondent is "essentially normal, a little abnormal, or very abnormal" (p. 86). These are tasks that may well be beyond the capabilities of a nonclinician and although the authors recognize the need for special training in this area, there are no formal guidelines available. There is also the danger, inherent in all interviews, that questions in sensitive areas (e.g., those dealing with sexuality or drug use) may be refused or not answered truthfully. The accuracy of the CIDI's computer diagnoses cannot be evaluated in the absence of critical materials such as the computer manual and the computer programs, which were repeatedly requested from, but not provided by, the publisher.

Although the authors of the CIDI manual address the cultural acceptability of certain items, there are still a number of questions that may pose problems in certain cultures, for example, items in which a nonnative speaker of English is asked to repeat a Western colloquialism, "No if's and's or but's" (pp. 77–78) or to remember three objects, among them a penny. Respondents in foreign countries may not recognize drugs by their formal names and so may provide inaccurate information about drug use. Yet another item uses a cutoff of 140 pounds for men and 125 pounds for women as one of the preliminary criteria in determining the existence of an eating disorder; although this weight might be significant in the Western world, a slight build is the norm in many countries. The inclusion of such items is puzzling, given that the CIDI is specifically intended to be used with a cross-cultural population.

One of the greatest drawbacks of the CIDI is the lack of technical information offered to potential users. The Researcher's manual contains vague descriptions about the composition of samples used in field studies and only very sketchy information about the outcome of such studies. Limited data about the CIDI's reliability and validity are provided and the vagueness of terms such as "almost all diagnostic categories" and "good" reliability is misleading. Further, because the diagnostic utility of some of these mental disorders is still open to question, the validity of tests based on these classifications may be correspondingly poor. Additional information is also needed about criterion-related validity and the congruence between English-language versions and other versions. The advent of *DSM-IV* in 1994 also renders sections of the CIDI obsolete, at least until further revisions are undertaken.

An independent review of 53 studies abstracted in PSYCLIT (e.g., Wittchen, 1994) indicated that the CIDI is used most often to diagnose depression and alcohol and drug-related disorders, and that test-retest and interrater reliability range from moderate to good. A limited number of studies (e.g., Lyketsos, Aritzi, & Lyketsos, 1994) provide support for the inclusion of the CIDI in clinical decision making.

The CIDI, Version 1.1 is an ambitious attempt to develop a structured interview with cross-cultural acceptability that can be used for the diagnosis of mental disorders in adults. It is suggested that the CIDI be used primarily as a measure for epidemiological research, and that its use in clinical settings be limited, at least until the authors are able to provide additional technical information as well as support for its use in clinical settings. The CIDI's sister measure, the Schedules for Clinical Assessment in Neuropsychiatry, also developed by the WHO, may serve as an alternative measure in clinical settings (Janca, Ustun, & Sartorious, 1994). The CIDI may also be profitably used in a comprehensive battery that includes a complete history, norm-referenced measures of social-emotional functioning, behavioral observations, and clinical decision making.

REVIEWER'S REFERENCES

Wittchen, H. U. (1993). Computer scoring of CIDI diagnoses: Special Issue: The WHO Composite Diagnostic Interview. *International Journal of Methods in Psychiatric Research, 3*(2), 101–107.

Janca, A., Ustun, T. B., & Sartorious, N. (1994). New versions of World Health Organization instruments for the assessment of mental disorders. *Acta Psychiatrica Scandinavica, 90*(2), 73–83.

Lyketsos, C. G., Aritzi, S., & Lyketsos, G. C. (1994). Effectiveness of office-based psychiatric practice using a structured diagnostic interview to guide treatment. *Journal of Nervous and Mental Disease, 182*(12), 720–723.

Wittchen, H. U. (1994). Reliability and validity studies of the WHO-Composite International Diagnostic Interview (CIDI): A critical review. *Journal of Psychiatric Research, 28*(1), 57–84.

Review of the Composite International Diagnostic Interview by JANICE G. WILLIAMS, Associate Professor of Psychology, Clemson University, Clemson, SC:

The Composite International Diagnostic Interview (CIDI) is a comprehensive structured interview for making psychiatric diagnoses consistent with the *Diagnostic and Statistical Manual—Third Edition, Revised* (*DSM-III-R*) and the *International Classification of Disease* (*ICD-10*). The instrument was developed from other structured interviews, including the Diagnostic Interview Schedule, the Present State Examination, and a structured interview based on the *ICD-10* diagnostic criteria. The CIDI is intended for epidemiological research on psychiatric diagnoses, but the manual author indicates that it can be used for other clinical and research purposes, as well. The instrument can be administered by trained interviewers with no other clinical background. Training for administering the interview is a 5-day process.

Development of the CIDI was a joint project of the World Health Organization and the National Institutes for Health. A unique feature of the CIDI is its availability in 16 languages. Development included field trials to examine reliability and validity of the instrument in different countries. The CIDI has undergone a number or revisions that have addressed its comprehensiveness, its length, and its adequacy of measurement of substance abuse and dependence. Additionally, the CIDI should be undergoing current revision to incorporate changes from *DSM-III-R* to *DSM-IV*.

RELIABILITY AND VALIDITY. References cited in the CIDI indicate adequate reliabilities for most CIDI sections. Both test-retest and interrater reliabilities have been examined. A lack of test-retest reliability has been noted for CIDI time-related items, such as age at onset of symptoms. This lack of reliability might be expected, as interviews are based solely on patient recall. However, these items have been revised since those findings.

The CIDI was constructed for content validity. Items are based on the diagnostic criteria for the *DSM-III-R* and the *ICD-10*. A major shortcoming of the CIDI Researcher's Manual is failure to provide a summary of the available information on reliability and validity. References to published works are provided, but many of the journals in which they are published will not be found in the typical library. Psychometric properties of the scales are difficult to determine because of the frequency with which the sections have been revised. Currently, a new version of the CIDI should be in preparation in response to the publication of *DSM-IV*.

The most appropriate use of the CIDI is for research. Certainly the instrument would be valuable for epidemiological research on mental disorders, as well as for research on correlates of such diagnoses. Development of the instrument in 16 languages makes it a potentially pivotal instrument for advancing cross-cultural research on mental disorders. As more information is accumulated on the reliability and validity of the CIDI in the diverse languages, it may become a standard measure for study of cross-cultural issues in psychiatric diagnosis.

Currently, the CIDI should be used with some caution. At best, the CIDI can be only as useful as the classification systems on which it is based. As controversies, criticisms, and revisions of these systems continue, the same issues and arguments will apply to the CIDI. One limitation of the CIDI is its reliance on patient self-report. Although the manual states that the CIDI could be used for clinical diagnosis, it seems inappropriate to base diagnosis on an interview by an individual without a clinical background. However, the CIDI would serve as a useful adjunct to other sources of diagnostic information.

SUMMARY. The CIDI is a comprehensive interview for making diagnoses based on the *DSM-III-R* and *ICD-10*. Reliability and validity appear adequate for research purposes, although the manual does not provide enough information about psychometric properties of the scales. The CIDI has been developed in 16 languages, making it a potentially useful instrument for cross-cultural research on mental disorders.

[78]
Comprehensive Adult Student Assessment System.

Purpose: Used for "assessing adult basic skills within a functional context" to "place learnees into appropriate instructional levels, diagnose learners' needs, monitor progress, and certify mastery of functional basic skills."
Population: Adults.
Publication Dates: 1980–1993.
Acronym: CASAS.
Administration: Group.
Restricted Distribution: Agency training is required before tests can be provided.
Price Data: Available from publisher.
Time: (60) minutes per test.
Comments: The CASAS system "currently offers more than 80 standardized assessment instruments including multiple choice, written response, and performance-based assessment ... has the capacity to customize assessment to measure specific competencies and learner outcomes."
Author: CASAS.
Publisher: CASAS.

a) APPRAISAL TESTS.
1) *Life Skills Appraisal.*
Scores: 2 tests: Reading, Math.
2) *ESL Appraisal (English as a Second Language).*
Scores: 4 tests: Reading, Listening, Writing, Oral.
Comments: Places students into a Level A, B, or C pretest of the CASAS Listening Series.
3) *GAIN Appraisal (Greater Avenues for Independence).*
Scores: 3 tests: Reading, Math, Listening.
4) *ECS Appraisal (Employability Competency System).*
Scores: 2 tests: Reading, Math.
Comments: Places students into Levels A, B, or C of the CASAS Basic Skills for Employability pretests.
5) *Workplace Appraisal.*
Scores: 2 tests: Reading, Reading/Math.
Comments: Not a pre-employment test; designed to be used at worksite to provide an initial assessment of workers' functional reading skills of materials encountered at the worksite.
6) *IRCA Pre-Enrollment Appraisal.*
Scores: 4 tests: Reading, Listening, Writing, Oral.
Comments: "Designed for use with the amnesty population, it may also be used with non-amnesty ESL students."

b) CASAS TESTS FOR MONITORING PROGRESS.
Comments: All tests serve as pre/post-tests.
1) *Life Skills Survey Achievement Tests.*
(*a*) Reading.
Levels: 4 levels (A, B, C, D), each with 2 forms.
(*b*) Math.
Levels: 4 levels (A, B, C, D), each with 2 forms.
(*c*) Listening Comprehension (for ESL students).
Levels: 3 levels (A, B, C), each with 2 forms.
2) *Basic Skills for Employability Tests.*
(*a*) Reading.
Levels: 3 levels (A, B, C), each with 2 forms.
(*b*) Math.
Levels: 3 levels (A, B, C), each with 2 forms.
(*c*) Listening Comprehension (for ESL students).
Levels: 3 levels (A, B, C), each with 2 forms.

c) CASAS TESTS FOR SPECIAL POPULATIONS.
Population: Developmentally disabled students.

Levels: 3 levels (AA, AAA, AAAA), each with 2 forms.
Comments: Pretests and corresponding posttests are available.

d) CASAS CERTIFICATION TESTS.
Comments: "Designed to determine if a student is ready to move to a higher level of instruction or to be certified as completing a program of instruction."
1) *Life Skills Certification (Exit) Tests.*
Scores: 1 test: Reading/Math.
Levels: 3 levels (A, B, C), each with 1 form.
2) *Employability Certification (Exit) Tests.*
Scores: 2 tests: Reading, Math.
Levels: 2 levels (B, C), each with 1 form for each test.
3) *GAIN Certification (Exit) Tests.*
Scores: 3 tests: Basic Skills Certification Reading/Math, ESL Certification Listening/Reading, ESL Certification Applied Performance Test.
Comments: Available only to California County Welfare Departments for use with GAIN participants.

e) CASAS TEST FOR WRITING ASSESSMENT.
Purpose: "Measures a student's functional writing skill abilities within a life skills context."
Comments: Pretest and posttest are available.

f) OCCUPATION SPECIFIC TESTS.
Purpose: "Assess whether a person is ready to enter an occupational training program."
Scores: 5 areas: Auto Mechanic, Clerical, Food Service, Health Occupations Level B, Health Occupations Level C.

g) CASAS SECONDARY DIPLOMA TESTS.
Scores: 8 areas: Math, Economics, American Government, United States History, English/Language Arts, World History, Biological Science, Physical Science.
Comments: Tests are available for pretesting and posttesting.

TEST REFERENCES

1. Frager, A. M. (1991). Adult literacy assessment: Existing tools and promising developments. *Journal of Reading, 35*, 256-259.
2. Askov, E. N. (1993). Approaches to assessment in workplace literacy programs: Meeting the needs of all the clients. *Journal of Reading, 36*, 550-554.

Review of the Comprehensive Adult Student Assessment System by RALPH O. MUELLER, Associate Professor of Educational Research, and PATRICIA K. FREITAG, Assistant Professor of Educational Research, Department of Educational Leadership, Graduate School of Education and Human Development, The George Washington University, Washington, DC:

OVERVIEW. The Comprehensive Adult Student Assessment System (CASAS) is an integrated, hierarchical array of more than 80 instruments that measure adult "basic skills in a functional context" (technical manual, p. 4). The instruments can be customized from a large item bank to be closely aligned with life skills, employability, high school completion, or English-as-a-Second-Language (ESL) curricula for adult learners. According to the authors, each assessment instrument requires about 60 minutes to be administered. The primary purpose of the instruments is to provide for "learner-centered curriculum management, assessment, and evaluation" (technical manual, p. 2). Intended applications of the instruments include (a) diagnostic placement of adult learners in appropriate program levels (although it is not clear whether or not this diagnostic function is restricted to just CASAS-based curricula); (b) progress and monitoring assessment of learners; (c) outcome measures and competency certification of adult learners in life skills, employability, or ESL training programs; and (d) reporting mechanisms for data at the local, state, and federal levels.

The major strengths of the CASAS system are (a) the explicit links from diagnostic program placement to instruction and ultimately to assessment of learner outcomes for CASAS-based adult learning programs (however, the assessment manuals are somewhat vague concerning the relationships between these three components for other adult curricula) and (b) the breadth of competency areas and assessment functions covered by CASAS (e.g., the availability of instruments for use in adult ESL and linked, multi-level assessments for use in adult special needs programs). A weakness of the CASAS system seems to be that instruments designed to measure different competencies in different learner groups are based on a number of overlapping items, making the distinction between and the selection of appropriate instruments for use in non-CASAS based programs difficult.

DOCUMENTATION. Each assessment includes supporting documentation consisting of the CASAS technical manual, test administration directions, and scoring packets. This review is based on these documents; additional materials pertinent to specific instruments, program curriculum, and student assessment are available from the publisher upon request.

The technical manual contains an overview of the adult student assessment system and is written clearly to meet the needs of program managers and instructors. The Rasch model of Item Response Theory is reviewed extensively, perhaps at the expense of detailed validity and reliability information, which is reported toward the end of the manual.

In the Test Administration Directions and the Scoring Packet, the reader finds clearly written guidelines for test administration and form-specific scoring keys. Item codes include: content area, competency area, competency outcome, and specific task format that allow for curriculum alignment, group or individual progress charts, and competency certification. Scoring keys are easy to follow and score scale conversion charts indicate, according to the authors, (a) "accurate" score ranges and (b) the relationship between instrument levels within each competency area. Instruments in each area are constructed in hierarchical levels with overlapping items. However, the documentation lacks specifications for instrument construction or models for customizing tests to be aligned with an existing curriculum.

The authors suggest a pre-post test design for instructors to "provide standardized information about learning gains" (Test Administration Directions, p. 3). The post-test described in the Test Administration Directions is used to monitor instruction with a "certification test" recommended to "confirm the learner's skill level" (Test Administration Directions, p. 3). The time period between assessments is not specified, but one must assume the items for the certification test would be similar but not identical to those used for instruction and achievement testing.

The items include appropriate diagrams, charts, graphs, tables, reading passages, and oral components to the relevant functional contexts. However, the machine-scored answer sheets and selected response formats seem to limit the performance aspect of the tests. Clearly, reading comprehension, mathematical skills, listening comprehension, writing, speaking, and problem solving are important indicators of adult life skills and employability. The ability to think critically, problem solve, and appropriately apply these skills in complex situations may be underrepresented by CASAS items. Although the documented item bank is extensive, the number of content areas and competencies covered by CASAS, with multiple instruments at each level in each content area, places a tremendous demand on item development and field testing.

VALIDITY AND RELIABILITY. "The CASAS Item Bank provides statistically reliable and externally validated test items for the construction of instruments that measure basic skills in a functional context for youth and adults" (technical manual, p. 7). To justify this claim, two sections of the technical manual are devoted to evidence of the validity and reliability of CASAS tests. From the manual it is not clear whether or not the data in these sections were obtained from the calibration sample that is characterized broadly by the following statistics (p. 23); age range: 16–85 with 40% in the 21–30 group; ethnicity: 54% Hispanic, 18% Asian, 12% Chinese, 9% White, 4% Black; and gender: 50% female. Information on the sampling procedures used and the SES, learning abilities, and residency of participants that might be relevant to assess the "appropriate use of test instruments for specific populations" (p. 1) is not provided in the supplied manuals. Thus, although relevant data might be available in unpublished CASAS reports, these could not be reviewed.

VALIDITY. It seems that great care was taken during item-bank development to ensure the content validity of CASAS tests. With regard to the construct-related validity, the manual authors claim that "adult life skills problem-solving is the unobservable trait or ability assumed to underlie performance" (technical manual, p. 37). Unfortunately, no supporting empirical evidence is presented, constituting a violation of Standards 1.8 through 1.10 in *Standards for Educational and Psychological Testing* (American Educational Research Association, American Psychological Association, & National Council on Measurement in Education, 1985, p. 15). Similarly, contrary to Standards 1.11 through 1.13 (p. 16) specific evidence of the criterion-related validity is not provided to substantiate that, indeed, "[t]he instructional level indicated by a CASAS test depicts the learner's probability of success in accomplishing a given learning activity and related competency" (technical manual, p. 38). This is significant for adult learners in non-CASAS adult basic education. Gain scores estimated by CASAS instruments for adult learners in other education programs will likely have lower reliability than those reported in the test manuals.

Other validity evidence consists of data on three key CASAS claims that in 1993 were evaluated and supported by the Program Effectiveness Panel of the U.S. Department of Education. The claims are that "learners within educational programs that have adopted the key elements [of CASAS] (1) demonstrate significant learning gains, (2) demonstrate increased hours of participation, and (3) achieve increased goal attainment compared to programs that have not adopted the key elements" (technical manual, p. 32). The manual contains statistical analyses from various state and national studies, based on samples ranging in size from $n = 32$ to $n = 1,326$. No detailed information on the validation samples is provided in the manual, which constitutes a violation of the *Standards* (Standard 1.5, p. 14). Although the reported data seem supportive of the above claims, note again that conclusions are based on analyses of gain scores that are known to have lower reliabilities than their raw score counterparts.

RELIABILITY. Internal consistency coefficients and IRT-based standard errors of estimate for tests from the anchor series (Forms 71 through 77) are reported in the reliability subsection of the manual (evidence of equivalence and stability reliability is not provided). KR-20 reliability coefficients for CASAS Forms 71, 72, and 74 through 77 are mostly above .80. The internal consistency data are presented separately for subgroups of students speaking various native languages ($n = 31$, Form 76, Laotian; to $n = 385$, Form 74, Spanish) as well as across the subgroups ($n = 199$, Form 77 to $n = 1,000$, Form 71). Further, IRT-based standard errors of estimate are reported for CASAS Reading Forms 74 through 77. However, it is not clear whether the calibration or some other sample was used to obtain the results nor how "local agency personnel" (technical manual, p. 1) unfamiliar with IRT are to interpret them (in partial violation of Standards 2.1 through 2.3; *Standards*, p. 20).

SUMMARY. The Comprehensive Adult Student Assessment System (CASAS) offers diagnostic, achievement, and competency tests in many content areas related to adult basic skills and employability. The broad array of instruments available are reliable indicators of learner achievement in CASAS-based adult learning programs. It is possible for these instruments to be customized to meet the assessment needs in other adult education programs as well. Empirical evidence to support construct and criterion-related validity claims would strengthen the interpretation of score data as well as promote the general use of these instruments across adult basic education programs. Similarly, a more complete description of the calibration and validation samples would improve the assessment documentation. In our opinion, more thorough descriptions of study samples, clear specifications for instrument construction, and analysis of data from field tested "performance measures" are needed. These additions would facilitate the general use of this extensive system for adult learner assessment and strengthen the program links among placement, instruction, and assessment.

REVIEWER'S REFERENCE

American Educational Research Association, American Psychological Association, & National Council on Measurement in Education. (1985). *Standards for educational and psychological testing*. Washington, DC: American Psychological Association, Inc.

Review of the Comprehensive Adult Student Assessment System by WILLIAM D. SCHAFER, Associate Professor of Measurement, Statistics, and Evaluation, University of Maryland at College Park, College Park, MD:

The Comprehensive Adult Student Assessment System (CASAS) consists of several series of tests that can be used to measure fundamental skills adults need to function productively in society. They are appropriate for both native speakers of English and English-as-a-Second-Language examinees. Taken together, over 80 tests using several item formats (selected-response, extended response, and performance assessment) are included in CASAS. Machine scoring and reporting are available and computer versions exist for some of the series of tests.

CASAS is designed to be used as part of an agency's educational program and is targeted to adults functioning at the high school level and below. The tests measure skills included in series of specific curricula that are part of an instructional package that also includes instructional materials and competency descriptions. Training in the use of CASAS is available in three phases: initial implementation, technical assistance, and ongoing program development. Agencies must engage in training as a precondition to using the CASAS tests.

The tests assess skills that are tied to the U.S. Department of Labor's Secretary's Commission on Achieving Necessary Skills (SCANS) competencies. Tests in a given series are equated. Results are scaled to a mean of 200 and range from 150 to 250 on a latent ability scale estimated using the Rasch (one-parameter logistic) model. As a point of reference, students scoring at least 225 are viewed as able to study a high school curriculum and perhaps transition to post-secondary programs.

The CASAS tests are designed to be used to place students into programs, to monitor progress, and to certify program completion. Special tests exist for developmentally disabled students. An attractive feature of CASAS is that each test measures skills in realistic contexts. An adult examinee should be motivated by the test itself to perform well both on the test and in an educational program articulated with it because the items present situations that are commonly encountered in daily living.

Since its inception in 1980, CASAS has become quite popular, having been implemented in 49 states. Data are presented in the technical manual indicating that students who participate in a CASAS program show increased learning, persistence, and goal attainment on CASAS tests. Although these are modest criteria because they extend to neither external measures nor outcomes following program completion, they are important elements in reports agencies must prepare to document effectiveness to funding sources.

Initial item bank development and calibration for the anchor series of life skills tests, which are the foundation of the instruments CASAS uses, was performed with adult basic education, English-as-a-Second-Language, and high school completion populations. The sample was predominantly Hispanic (54%), between the ages of 21 and 30 (40%), and about evenly split between men and women. No data on geographic representation or urbanicity are reported in the technical manual. The item calibration sample sizes ranged from 203 to 1,258 over pairs of forms at each of three levels of difficulty. The items were written by field-based practitioners following training and screening and were pretested in classroom contexts. New item development, item calibration, and equating of test forms is ongoing and involves data generated at sites currently using the CASAS program.

The numbers of items on the six anchor life skills tests range from 31 to 44 and their alpha coefficients range from .81 to .89. Reported in another table are alpha coefficients for language and ethnic subpopulations, which also appear adequate. Some minor numerical discrepancies between these two tables in the technical manual should be resolved. The standard errors of the two intermediate and the two advanced tests are reported by score level and range from just over 10 scaled-score units at the extremes to under 4 near the centers of the test-score ranges. The use of item-response-curve methods and reporting of standard errors by test scores are attractive technical features of CASAS. Unfortunately, similar information about the other content areas and test forms is not included in the technical manual.

Evidence from several sources is presented to support the validity of the CASAS life skills tests. The studies mentioned earlier showing that students who have studied the CASAS competencies perform at higher levels on these tests provide construct-related validity evidence, as do factor analyses that support their unidimensionality and data on parameter invariance that support the application of the Rasch model as appropriate. Use of competencies within a taxonomy of life skills in the areas of basic skills in reading and math, listening comprehension, and life-skill problem solving, judged appropriate and translated into items by adult educators, constitutes content-related evidence. Criterion-related evidence is presented showing that students with increasing CASAS test scores have increasing probabilities of passing GED subtests and that students with increasing degrees of retardation have decreasing mean achievement on the CASAS scale.

Although items were subjected to review by experts for sources of bias, no statistical analyses of differential item or test functioning are presented. Also, other than in the life-skills area, the technical adequacy of the CASAS tests is not documented in the technical manual, nor are procedures used to scale the other series described.

CASAS should be judged as a system, including curriculum and instructional support materials, and not just as a series of tests. Indeed, the tests are neither designed nor used as stand-alone instruments. Ongoing work is being used to improve CASAS and the methods used for the life-skills tests, for which scoring is dichotomous, seem appropriate and well informed by research. Unfortunately, there was no documentation to judge the methods used with extended-response and performance-assessment items, for which scoring is polytomous. It is hoped that, over time, more evidence will become available with which to evaluate the full range of tests in the system.

[79]
Comprehensive Behavior Rating Scale for Children.

Purpose: A teacher rating scale designed to measure various dimensions of a child's school functioning.
Population: Ages 6–14.
Publication Date: 1990.
Acronym: CBRSC.
Scores: 9 scales: Inattention-Disorganization, Reading Problems, Cognitive Deficits, Oppositional-Conduct Disorders, Motor Hyperactivity, Anxiety, Sluggish Tempo, Daydreaming, Social Competence.
Administration: Individual.
Price Data, 1994: $69.50 per complete kit including manual (10 pages), 25 profile and questionnaire forms, and scoring key; $14.50 per 25 profile and questionnaire forms; $37.50 per manual; $22.50 per scoring key.
Time: (10–15) minutes.
Authors: Ronald Neeper, Benjamin B. Lahey, and Paul J. Frick.
Publisher: The Psychological Corporation.

TEST REFERENCES
1. Frick, P. J., O'Brien, B. S., Wootton, J. M., & McBurnett, K. (1994). Psychopathy and conduct problems in children. *Journal of Abnormal Psychology, 103,* 700-707.

Review of the Comprehensive Behavior Rating Scale for Children by WAYNE C. PIERSEL, Associate

Professor of Educational Psychology, University of Nebraska—Lincoln, Lincoln, NE:

The Comprehensive Behavior Rating Scale for Children (CBRSC) is a norm-referenced assessment instrument designed to evaluate the perceived behavior of children aged 6 through 14. This is a single instrument that can be completed by a teacher or other knowledgeable adult who has direct contact with the child being evaluated. Although the manual does not provide any information regarding the length of time required to complete or score the CBRSC, this reviewer in an informal trial found that two teachers were able to complete this scale in approximately 15 minutes with another 10 to 15 minutes required to score and convert raw scores to *T*-scores and percentiles.

The current version of the CBRSC consists of 70 items intended to assess school functioning across nine domains or scales. Each item is rated on a 5-point scale ranging from *not at all* (1) to *very much* (5). The scales include Inattention-Disorganization (11 items), Reading Problems (9 items), Cognitive Deficits (9 items), Oppositional-Conduct Disorder (12 items), Motor Hyperactivity (4 items), Anxiety (12 items), Sluggish Tempo (4 items), Daydreaming (3 items), and Social Competence (6 items). If an item is not completed, the manual provides instructions for prorating of raw scores on affected scales. The test authors note that the nine scales were derived through factor analysis with each scale measuring a different dimension of school functioning. The authors further state that the CBRSC was designed to address areas neglected by other teacher rating scales. Specifically, the authors comment that Reading Problems, Cognitive Deficits, Sluggish Tempo, and Day Dreaming domains have no counterparts on other teacher rating scales. The authors are unique in noting that rating scales including their scale provide a view of the child as "he or she is seen through the eyes of the teacher" (manual, p. 5). This important point is frequently overlooked by most other rating scales leaving much of the professional public treating the resulting scores as measures or ratings of actual behavior.

Administration and scoring of the CBRSC is explained well and is easy to accomplish. After the 70 items are rated by the teacher, scoring templates are used to sum the ratings for the items comprising each of the nine scales. The scoring and entry of numbers in appropriate columns is relatively straightforward. The user then utilizes one of the norm tables in the back of the manual to convert the raw score for each scale to a T score and a percentile. Users have a choice of norm groups for converting raw scores to T-scores. The total normative sample, normative sample by gender for all ages, or normative sample by gender and age (6–7, 8–12, 9–12, 13–14) may be utilized. The authors note that they had initially intended the CBRSC to be applicable for ages 5 to 16. However, limited samples at the two ends of the age distribution resulted in the current age ranges.

Development of the CBRSC is described in chapter 4 of the manual. It appears that an initial version consisting of 60 items was completed by 26 teachers in three elementary schools prior to 1984. Following analysis of this initial version, a second version consisting of 102 items was used to rate 678 children ranging in age from 5 to 15. Subsequently, the third version containing 81 items was used in a national standardization in 1985. Data collection was coordinated by 21 school psychologists resulting in a standardization sample of 1,163 males and 990 females ranging in age from 6 to 14. Each of the trial versions was subjected to factor analyses to determine the number of factors and item loadings. Finally, a fourth and final version with 70 items was adopted. This 70-item version was not subjected to standardization or analysis. It is not clear precisely how the final 70-item version was established (i.e., was a final factor analysis conducted using just 70 items?). In fact, one of the major problems with this scale is that the norming, norm tables, reliability, and validity indicators are based on the 81-item scale. The authors not that further study is needed on the final 70-item version. No explanation is offered as to why the 81-item scale was used in the standardization and data analysis while publishing a 70-item scale that was not subject to separate data collection and analysis.

There are numerous additional problems concerning the CBRSC. Although the manual is well organized and descriptive, it is unclear regarding which version of the instrument and the exact number of items utilized in various analyses. For example as already noted, the authors indicate that reliability estimates were performed on the earlier version containing 102 items. No reliability estimates are provided for the current version of the CBRSC containing 70 items.

The authors indicate that the final 70-item version of the CBRSC was based on factor analytic techniques. The information reported in the manual indicates that a decision rule of .45 or greater loading on at least one factor was used. The manual does not contain a complete factor matrix showing the loading of each item on all nine factors. It is not clear if the final version (70-item version) was factor analyzed or if the loadings from other versions were utilized in the final item-to-scale match. In addition, as noted above, three of the scales (Motor Hyperactivity, Sluggish Tempo, and Daydreaming) have four or fewer items comprising that scale. The discussion of the items dropped such as "Seems depressed," "Seems very sad," and "Rarely seems to have a good time" because of loadings on more than one scale (Anxiety and Depression) ignores some of the research suggesting that anxiety and depression may be very similar if not the same construct (King, Ollendick, & Gullone, 1991). The authors claim that their scale is unique in assessing domains not assessed by other rating scales. Although some limited data using an outpatient clinic sample are present, there is a lack of convergent and discriminant validity to support the authors' claim. The data presented indicate that ratings on various scales can distinguish between clinic and nonreferred samples, but more refined discriminations were not demonstrated.

The norm tables in the appendix provide the sample size for each set of norms (total sample, age, gender). It is important to note that the tables list different sample size for each scale within the same norm table. For example, in Table A-3 (females) the N for Inattention-Disorganization is 990 whereas the sample size is 2,149 for Anxiety. Based on the data presented on pages 38–40, it appears that norm tables are reporting total sample for each gender rather than the actual sample for that specific gender or age. The number 2,149 represents the approximate number in the total sample for the standardization. No explanation is provided for the differing sample sizes for each scale within a specific norm table. All norm tables have this characteristic of varying sample sizes across the nine scales. One would assume that there would be the same size N for each scale with a particular norm group because the teacher would have completed the entire scale. Again, no explanation is provided.

In their chapter on interpretation of the scale scores (domains), the authors provide concise, clear descriptions of the item content and what the scale is believed to represent. However, they provide only limited concurrent and no predictive or discriminant validity for any of the scales. The validity is primarily face or content in nature. The claims the CBRSC may be useful for screening, contribute to a comprehensive evaluation, and facilitate treatment planning including development of individual treatment plans and individual education plans (IEPs) are not supported. It needs to be noted that these claims are ubiquitous among various assessment instruments including rating scales. Although this and other scales may be useful for screening and classification, it remains very unclear and possibly incorrect to imply that this and other similar scales are useful for developing IEPs and planning treatments. The authors ignore an extensive body of research demonstrating that the factor structure on rating scales is strongly influenced by gender and age (Achenbach, 1985; Achenbach & McConaughy, 1987). The failure of the authors to provide factor loadings by age and gender prevents the user from ascertaining that the factor structure remained invariant across age and gender. Indeed, the authors report significant gender differences for eight of the nine scales (no differences on Anxiety scale) across different age groups. Males were rated higher (more deviant). The four case studies provided in the manual do not provide convincing demonstrations regarding the scale's usefulness.

In the chapter on reliability and validity, the authors attempt to demonstrate that the CBRSC can discriminate between clinic samples and normal samples. However, they do not conduct the types of analyses that would permit answering this question thoroughly and do not provide empirical data supporting the scales' ability to discriminate between different psychiatric categories. Further, the validation samples were composed primarily of males (91%) in out-patient settings. The authors leave the reader with the suggestion that the scale may be useful as an adjunct for diagnosing or classifying individuals but again fail to provide needed empirical data. The manual does present data on test-retest reliability over a 2-week period ranging from .84 to .97 for the tryout sample. Unfortunately, seven scales do not match the scales in the final 70-item version. They do not report any interrater reliability data.

In this reviewer's opinion this scale should be used with caution. There is missing information and incorrect information. Most importantly, much of the data present in the manual are derived from an earlier larger version of the scale. There are no data presented on the current 70-item version. There are other comprehensive behavior rating scale systems available that are better developed and validated. Two such comprehensive systems are the Child Behavior Checklist (Achenbach, 1991; 55) and the Behavior Assessment System for Children (Reynolds & Kamphaus, 1991; 34). The Child Behavior Checklist includes Teacher, Parent, and Youth Self-Report

(11–16) forms. It also includes a semistructured interview and a structured observation form. The Behavior Assessment System for Children includes teacher, parent, and self-rating scales, structured developmental history, and student observation system. These two comprehensive systems are much better developed and validated than many other rating scale packages.

REVIEWER'S REFERENCES

Achenbach, T. M. (1985). Assessment and taxonomy of child and adolescent psychopathology. In A. E. Kazdin (Series Ed.), *Developmental clinical psychology and psychiatry series* (vol. 3). Beverly Hills, CA: Sage.
Achenbach, T. M., & McConaughy, S. H. (1987). *Empirically based assessment of child and adolescent psychopathology: Practical applications.* Newbury Park, CA: Sage.
Achenbach, T. M. (1991). Child Behavior Checklist. Burlington, VT: University of Vermont College of Medicine.
King, N. J., Ollendick, T. H., & Gullone, E. (1991). Negative affectivity in children and adolescents: Relations between anxiety and depression. *Clinical Psychology Review, 11,* 441–459.
Reynolds, C. R., & Kamphaus, R. W. (1992). *Behavior Assessment System for Children* manual. Circle Pines, MN: American Guidance Service.

[80]
Comprehensive Receptive and Expressive Vocabulary Test.

Purpose: "Measures both receptive and expressive oral vocabulary."
Population: Ages 5-0 to 17-11.
Publication Date: 1994.
Acronym: CREVT.
Scores, 3: Receptive Vocabulary, Expressive Vocabulary, Total.
Administration: Individual.
Price Data, 1994: $114 per complete kit; $29 per 25 profile record forms (specify Form A or B); $34 per photo album picture book; $26 per manual (49 pages).
Time: (20–30) minutes.
Authors: Gerald Wallace and Donald D. Hammill.
Publisher: PRO-ED, Inc.

TEST REFERENCES

1. Nippold, M. A. (1995). School-age children and adolescents: Norms for word definition. *Language, Speech, and Hearing Services in Schools, 26,* 320–325.

Review of the Comprehensive Receptive and Expressive Vocabulary Test by ALAN S. KAUFMAN, Senior Research Scientist, Psychological Assessment Resources, Inc. (PAR), Odessa, FL, and NADEEN L. KAUFMAN, Professor of Clinical Psychology, California School of Professional Psychology, San Diego, CA:

The Comprehensive Receptive and Expressive Vocabulary Test (CREVT) is an untimed individually administered test that is suitable for children as young as 4 years 0 months (Receptive) or 5 years 0 months (Expressive), and is intended for adolescents as old as 17 years 11 months (both sections). It is intended to measure the kinds of vocabulary abilities indicated by its title, and its purported uses are for identifying deficiencies in oral vocabulary, identifying discrepancies between receptive and expressive vocabulary, documenting progress in instructional programs, and serving as a research tool. It yields standard scores (mean = 100, standard deviation = 15) for Receptive Vocabulary, Expressive Vocabulary, and a combination of the two (general vocabulary). The authors state that the CREVT should be used with individuals who speak English and not used for those who are deaf or speak no English; they fail to mention its administration to bilingual students, an important group of potential referrals for assessment. They do, however, address test interpretation for people learning English as a second language.

The CREVT comes in two forms, A and B, and the testing time is reported to be 20 to 30 minutes for the Receptive and Expressive portions of a single form. In view of the brief testing time and the caution by the authors that "additional informal and formal assessment will be necessary before making any definitive conclusion about an individual's oral vocabulary status" (p. 5, examiner's manual), the test seems misnamed with the word "Comprehensive." Perhaps "Screening" would have been a better choice.

The stimuli for the CREVT Receptive Vocabulary subtest appear in a well-constructed, attractive "Photo Album Picture Book." Both forms of the test use the same Picture Book, which includes six high-quality photos on each of 10 pages. Each page is on a specific topic, such as animals, occupations, foods, and household appliances. Most receptive questions are phrased, "Put your finger on _____." This format makes sense when examinees are asked the noun depicted in the photo (sedan, surgeon, trousers), but it seems awkward for adjectives or verbs (carnivorous, squeezed, organize), and downright unfair and confusing for words that are not in the picture at all (the child is told, "Put your finger on *aviator*," but the photo shows a pilotless airplane).

Although the photos are attractive and have nice color and contrast, some of the photos seem old-fashioned (e.g., sewing machine, telephone, clock), two depend to some extent on reading labels (most notably a milk carton), some of the categories have narrow definitions (e.g., the very broad category of "recreation" has a *baseball* and *baseball bat* as two of the six photos), and there is apparent gender bias both in the choice of photos (four of the six "occupations" are depicted by white males) and topics ("tools"). Data presented on item bias by gender and race (in a one-half page chapter on p. 39 of examiner's manual) suggest no bias, but sufficient details on the bias study are not presented, so no definitive conclu-

sions are possible. Only a single Delta coefficient (an index used to help detect item bias) is presented for each section of each form of the test, so it may be that the coefficients of .98–.99 were spuriously inflated by performing the bias analysis on the total sample, ranging from preschool to high school students, instead of on more homogeneous age groups.

The Receptive Vocabulary items are administered for one topic at a time, which creates an apparent chasm between the easiest and hardest items for each topic. For example, the six "clothing" items start with "sneakers" and end with "bodice." Each topic has its own discontinue rule, as the items go from easy to hard on each page, which may create frustration for young children. Also, perusal of the photos and the items for the Receptive Vocabulary section of both Form A and Form B suggest that there is insufficient "top" for bright adolescents. Examination of the data supports that belief, as mean scores for ages 14–17 years range from 50 to 54 out of 61 possible points. Standard deviations for 16- and 17-year-olds are relatively large (9 to 11 points) such that it is impossible for those older adolescents to obtain scores more than 1 SD above the mean; for age 17, the highest score would be about +.7 SD above the mean. That did not stop the authors, however, from stretching the top such that standard scores as high as 119 to 123 are obtainable at ages 16 and 17. Even at ages 14 and 15, where scores of about 130 can be earned, the data do not support going more than about 1 SD above the mean. There is the illusion of top for the CREVT Receptive Vocabulary standard score, but this section of the test seems best suited for children between the ages of 4 and 10 or 11 years, unless the goal is to assess below average to average students.

The Expressive Vocabulary section of each form includes 25 words that are scored 1–10 and are administered in the typical Wechsler-Binet Vocabulary format ("Tell me what 'janitor' means"). Examiners are told to query responses that are vague, incorrect, or incomplete, which seems to suggest that all wrong responses except "don't know" should be queried. In fact, about a half-dozen responses per item are listed as requiring a query, but the guidelines for compiling these lists of questionable responses, unfortunately, are vague and the lists are incomplete. Like the items in Receptive Vocabulary, the words chosen for Expressive Vocabulary lack apparent top for bright adolescents. Again, this perception is borne out by data; it is not possible to score more than 1 *SD* above the mean at ages 15–17 years. And again, the authors stretch the norms more than seems reasonable by awarding standard scores as high as 128 at ages 15–16 and 123 at age 17. There is also poor bottom on expressive vocabulary for young children as raw scores of 1 convert to standard scores in the 80s for ages 5 through 6.11 years, and raw scores of 2 yield standard scores in the 80s for 7-year-olds.

The norms for the CREVT are good. The total sample includes 1,920 individuals ages 4 to 17 years, and the sample is nicely stratified on the variables of gender, race, ethnic group, geographic region, urban-rural residence, and disability status. The matches of the sample percents to census figures are good for the total sample and adequate for five age groupings between 4–6 and 16–17 years. Forms A and B were given to everyone in the normative sample, but readers are not told this important information until the reliability chapter. Additionally, the manual does not indicate whether the order of administration of the forms was counterbalanced, and only vague indications are presented regarding the methods for constructing the alternate forms.

Reliability data for the CREVT indicate good internal consistency, alternate-forms reliability, and stability. Coefficients alpha average .92–.93 for Receptive Vocabulary, .91 for Expressive Vocabulary, and .95 for general vocabulary. Alternate-forms coefficients average .92 for Receptive Vocabulary, .90 for Expressive Vocabulary, and are inexplicably not given for general vocabulary. Test-retest coefficients are provided for two small samples of kindergarten (N = 27) and grade 12 (N = 28) students over 2 month (kindergarten) and 2 week (grade 12) intervals. Values for the three scales on Forms A and B ranged from .79–.87 (median = .84) for kindergarten and from .79–.94 (median = .87) for grade 12. The authors are to be commended for reporting reliability coefficients (alphas) for separate groups of learning disabled, speech-language impaired, and mentally retarded students. The values were good, typically in the low- to mid-.90s. They should not, however, have reported these coefficients only for homogeneous age groups within each exceptionality, because some of the sample sizes were too small (e.g., 9 or 18).

Evidence for content validity is provided, but it remains unclear why the 10 particular content categories chosen were any better than other possible categories, or why a category system was used at all. Validity data for the CREVT are meager. Correlations are presented between the CREVT and four

language tests, such as the Peabody Picture Vocabulary Test—Revised (PPVT-R; T4:1945), but the samples are generally small in these studies (*N*s of 15, 20, 27, and 40) and the subjects are not described. Further, means and *SD*s are *not* presented for any measures; the actual coefficients are *not* presented in favor of coefficients that were already corrected for range restriction and attenuation; and coefficients that failed to reach significance were eliminated from the table. No correlations are provided with the most pertinent criterion for expressive vocabulary, namely the Vocabulary subtest on the Wechsler Intelligence Scale for Children—Third Edition (WISC-III; 12:412). Construct validity is limited to age differentiation of the raw scores, and group differentiation of the Receptive and Expressive Vocabulary standard scores (learning-disabled children averaged 87–90, speech-language impaired children averaged 82–83, and mentally retarded children averaged 62–67). No predictive validity data are provided, and no evidence is given to support the value of the difference between a child's Receptive versus Expressive Vocabulary.

The authors provide some interpretive guidelines for comparing scores in the two areas and some appropriate cautions regarding test interpretation. They do not make any unusual claims for the test, such as its possible use as an intelligence test, and provide a straightforward rationale for its practical uses and applications, and for the value of vocabulary tests in general.

In sum, the CREVT is a reliable and stable test with good norms and attractive pictorial stimuli. Its main problems are in the specific items and administration format for the Receptive Vocabulary section; the lack of top for adolescents on both sections and the lack of bottom for 5- to 7-year-olds on Expressive Vocabulary; and the inadequate evidence of validation for the whole test. The use of six photos per page for Receptive Vocabulary reduces the influence of chance guessing, which is an advantage over the four-choice PPVT-R. Despite that positive feature and the attractiveness of the CREVT stimuli, the PPVT-R is a much better choice for measuring receptive vocabulary. The PPVT-R has better bottom and top, much better evidence of validity, and a less confusing format for administering items. The WISC-III Vocabulary subtest offers much better top, bottom, and validity than the CREVT Expressive Vocabulary, and is a much better choice. The receptive versus expressive comparison obtained from PPVT-R and WISC-III Vocabulary is much preferred to the CREVT comparison even though the latter test has a common set of norms for both measures. Even for examiners who are not qualified to give the WISC-III, the Expressive Vocabulary section of the CREVT cannot be recommended for anything other than research use until its validity has been supported by additional studies.

Review of the Comprehensive Receptive and Expressive Vocabulary Test by MARY J. McLELLAN, Assistant Professor of Educational Psychology, Northern Arizona University, Flagstaff, AZ:

The Comprehensive Receptive and Expressive Vocabulary Test (CREVT) was published in 1994 by PRO-ED. The authors, Gerald Wallace and Donald Hammill, both have an extensive list of test publications to their credit. The CREVT is presented to the test user in a format familiar to past users of PRO-ED products, in that the directions for test administration are on the test protocol. This test is very easy to administer, comes with two forms (A and B), and this reviewer found that the testing time claims stated in the test manual of 20 to 30 minutes were accurate. The CREVT is simple to learn and attractively packaged with color photographs as the stimuli for the Receptive Vocabulary responses.

The Receptive Vocabulary section is presented to the students as areas of understanding, such as animals, transportation, and occupations. Within each area of receptive understanding, one item typically asks for a concrete representation, then the stimulus words shift to more abstract representation (e.g., neigh for horse). Each area of understanding has an individual area score. There is, however, no discussion of the statistical interpretability, or clinical relevance of these individual area scores.

The Expressive Vocabulary section is a standard oral vocabulary test. The student is asked to tell what each word means. The directions provide an example for guidance to the test taker, and this reviewer found this example helpful. The words presented are standard vocabulary words and they are scored as 1 (correct) or 0 (incorrect) point answers. Examples of correct responses are provided on the test protocol, in addition to examples of responses that should be queried.

The rationale and overview section of the test manual provides the test user with information about oral vocabulary and a description of the CREVT. The authors present a rationale for combining the receptive and expressive scores to obtain a general vocabulary score. In fact, the authors conclude that "the CREVT can be described as a test of both the receptive and expressive aspects of semantics (specifically, oral vocabulary)" (p. 2). Combining the receptive and vocabulary aspects into a unified concept of oral language is cited as a concept that is agreed upon by "most professionals in the area of language development or language disorders" (p. 2). There are, however, no references cited to support this claim.

The standardization sample of the CREVT consisted of 1,920 students. The manual indicates that the sample characteristics compare to 1990 census figures. There was no description of when the standardization data were collected. The standard methods of establishing standard scores, percentiles, and age equivalents were used. Test reliability and validity are described in the test manual in a comprehensive fashion. There is a separate table that provides reliability quotients for a population of students with disabilities and confirms satisfactory reliability for the use of this test with children with disabilities. The psychometric properties of the CREVT should come as no surprise to the test users because tests of vocabulary typically have very high reliability quotients.

The validity of the CREVT is discussed in chapter 7 of the test manual and further rationale is provided regarding the choice of the test format. A point of interest to the test users is Table 7.4 (p. 35). In this table the correlations with selected comparable tests is presented. It is interesting to note the correlations reported for the Expressive One Word Picture Vocabulary Test—Revised. The correlations with the receptive vocabulary scores of the CREVT are noticeably higher than the correlations with expressive vocabulary scores. This does not appear to be consistent with the overall rationale the authors are presenting. No explanation of these results is provided in the manual.

Test users are encouraged to review carefully the conversion of raw scores to standard scores and attend to the raw scores required to obtain scores within the "average range." At age 5, a raw score of "0" on the Expressive Vocabulary section yields a standard score of 87. It is critical to understand that a statistically valid test score may, in fact, be derived from a shamefully limited sample of the subject's language.

A recent article in *School Psychology Review* by Kitendra and Rohena-Diaz (1996) presents an excellent discussion of the development of language and how we, as evaluators of children, must be familiar with many aspects of a student's language usage before any determination of their language competence can be made. Although the article specifically discusses children who are linguistically diverse, information is applicable to language assessment in general. The CREVT is an example of a test that has reasonable statistical properties and conforms to standards of testing that should be familiar to consumers. However, the sophisticated evaluator must be sensitive to the limitations such tests present.

In summary, the CREVT is easy to use and nicely packaged. The consumers of this product should be cautious of the low raw scores needed, in some cases, to support adequate language development. In addition, the Receptive Vocabulary measures provide limited evaluation of a child's ability to identify concrete representations as opposed to abstract representations of words.

REVIEWER'S REFERENCE

Jitendra, A. K., & Rohena-Diaz, E. (1996). Language assessment of students who are linguistically diverse: Why a discrete approach is not the answer. *School Psychology Review, 25*, 40–56.

[81]

Comprehensive Scales of Student Abilities: Quantifying Academic Skills and School-Related Behavior Through the Use of Teacher Judgments.

Purpose: To provide "a quick teacher rating scale of student ability."
Population: Ages 6–0 to 17–0.
Publication Date: 1994.
Acronym: CSSA.
Scores, 9: Verbal Thinking, Speech, Reading, Writing, Handwriting, Mathematics, General Facts, Basic Motor Generalizations, Social Behavior.
Administration: Individual.
Price Data, 1994: $64 per complete kit including 100 profile/record forms and manual (52 pages); $39 per 100 profile/record forms; $27 per manual.
Time: (5–10) minutes.
Authors: Donald D. Hammill and Wayne P. Hresko.
Publisher: PRO-ED, Inc.

Review of the Comprehensive Scales of Student Abilities: Quantifying Academic Skills and School-Related Behavior Through the Use of Teacher Judgments by JENNIFER J. FAGER, Assistant Professor, Education and Professional Development, Western Michigan University, Kalamazoo, MI:

DESCRIPTIVE INFORMATION. The Comprehensive Scales of Student Abilities (CSSA) is designed, according to the authors, to address the needs teachers have for a "quick teacher rating scale of student ability that satisfies the psychometric criteria usually applied to norm-referenced, standardized measures" (p. 2). Thus, the instrument developers created an instrument for the purpose of identifying strengths and weaknesses for intervention, determining specific needs prior to referral for evaluation or services, measuring student abilities for research purposes, aiding in prereferral screening of large groups of students, documenting educational progress, and providing evidence of the need for referral (p. 3).

The CSSA is composed of 68 items that are grouped into nine scales designed after review of "several taxonomies of mental abilities" (p. 2). These scales include: Verbal Thinking, Speech, Reading, Writing, Handwriting, Mathematics, General Facts, Basic Motor Generalizations, and Social Behavior. Descriptions of each scale's intended measurements and the interpretation of low and high scores for each scale are defined in the examiner's manual. Each scale includes between four and eleven 9-point Likert-type items that use a rating system where *poor* is the lowest level and *good* is at the top of the continuum.

The intended population for whom the instrument is designed includes students in the United States between the ages of 6 and 17 in grades 1 through 11. The authors acknowledge that students with cultural differences such as non-English speaking or conditions such as recent family trauma might receive low scores by teachers using the instrument. It is suggested in the examiner's manual that there is a place for this information provided on the Profile/Record Form.

Teachers are to be the only raters in the process, which should take approximately 10 minutes as suggested by the instrument developers. When completing the CSSA, teachers are to respond to all of the 68 items, which will provide an overall picture of the student in relation to his or her peers. When this reviewer examined each of the 68 items it was noted that nearly half appear inappropriate for students at all levels. For example, one statement addresses the student's ability to read fluently. Some first graders of average ability may not have learned to decode words let alone read fluently. In addition, current secondary school structures also interfere with teachers' ability to complete each item with appropriate knowledge. The General Facts Scale purports to measure "knowledge of science, social studies, and everyday facts that are usually taught in a school's general curriculum" (p. 15). A high school biology teacher may have difficulty responding to the statement that addresses social studies knowledge. Teachers in self-contained classrooms would be far better equipped to respond accurately to all 68 items.

Although teachers are to be the sole raters, they can, however, solicit the assistance of others to help score and interpret the results. Many teachers are unfamiliar or uncomfortable with the measurement practices that are necessary to interpret scores and convey results to parents and other interested parties (Plake, Impara, & Fager, 1993). If a teacher is going to use the CSSA for the purposes outlined, that teacher should understand the usefulness of the information as well as the potential misuses of such data. The CSSA is to be administered on a student-by-student basis only when a need has been identified. The teachers using the CSSA should be familiar with the instrument and able to rate a student compared to typical performance of the student's peers. Results are reported in terms of raw scores, scale standard scores, and percentile ranks to allow for comparisons to be made with other instruments measuring student ability. The authors suggest the results be treated as a hypothesis that needs to be investigated further rather than as a final analysis of the child's abilities.

SAMPLING AND NORMING PROCEDURES. The instrument developers attended carefully to appropriate norming procedures. Census data from the U.S. 1990 Census were used as criteria to stratify the norm group. The CSSA was normed on a sample representing students across the country and stratified by geographical region, gender, race, residence, and ethnicity.

RELIABILITY AND VALIDITY. Reliability issues are thoroughly addressed in the examiner's manual. The instrument developers used sound theoretical bases when determining reasonable levels of internal consistency. The coefficient alphas for each of the nine scales and for the overall instrument are all over .90 and the *SEM* is small. Interrater reliability issues are also considered and meet statistical standards for instruments designed for individual student decision-making procedures. This reviewer is concerned with the reliability of a few of the scales due to the small number of items included in those scales. The "General Facts" Scale includes six items that are to measure the student's "knowledge of science, social studies, and everyday facts that are usually taught in a school's general curriculum" (p. 15). One would be hard pressed to summarize the

general curriculum of a school into six statements. Besides the low number of items addressing broad constructs, the issue of reliability as it relates to individual teachers is of concern. The procedures to ensure that the instrument is administered are useful in increasing its reliability; however, if a teacher does not possess the knowledge of a student on each item and has to guess, reliability is reduced.

Appropriate attention was given to issues of validity. Content, criterion, and construct validity were examined and meet standards set in the measurement field. The constructs that serve as the foundation for the nine scales come from an examination of the literature on developmentally appropriate levels of ability for children ages 6 years through 17 years 11 months. Concerns of this reviewer are in the content of the items and how they parallel the curriculum practices of school districts. A student may receive a low score on the mathematics scale because he or she has not been introduced to the math concepts necessary to demonstrate the ability being assessed.

Beyond the concerns and cautions expressed earlier in this review it should be noted that the overall CSSA is constructed in a usable fashion. Unfortunately, many issues related to appropriateness of items for all levels, teachers' abilities to accurately report and use the results, and low numbers of items used to measure broad constructs could interfere with the use of this instrument. The authors suggested that teachers expressed a need for this type of instrument. If it is used as a stand-alone document, decisions regarding a student's placement could be inaccurately made. Although the reliability and validity data are impressive, it should be noted that all items may not apply to all students being evaluated. Students could benefit from the results as long as it is used as intended by the instrument developers. If not, it may be used as a device for labeling students without providing supportive evidence or the assistance necessary to overcome the deficiencies identified.

REVIEWER'S REFERENCE
Plake, B. S., Impara, J. C., & Fager, J. J. (1993). Assessment competencies of teachers: A national survey. *Educational Measurement: Issues and Practice, 12*(4), 10–12.

Review of the Comprehensive Scales of Student Abilities: Quantifying Academic Skills and School-Related Behavior Through the Use of Teacher Judgments by BLAINE R. WORTHEN, *Professor of Psychology, and* XITAO FAN, *Assistant Professor of Psychology, Utah State University, Logan, UT:*

The Comprehensive Scales of Student Abilities (CSSA) is an individually administered and norm-referenced rating instrument consisting of "objective rating scales ... designed to help quantify teacher judgments about student competencies in a variety of abilities manifested in academic settings" (examiner's manual, p. 1). Teachers using the CSSA rate each student's abilities in nine school-related areas: Verbal Thinking, Speech, Reading, Writing, Handwriting, Mathematics, General Facts, Basic Motor Generalizations, and Social Behaviors. The CSSA is intended for obtaining teachers' ratings of students of 6 to 17 years of age (grades 1 through 11).

The purposes of the CSSA are: (a) to identify strengths and weaknesses for intervention; (b) to determine specific needs prior to referral for evaluation or services; (c) to serve as a measurement device in research studies; (d) to be used as a tool in the prereferral screening of large groups of students; (e) to assist in documenting educational progress; and (f) to be used as evidence of the need for referral. The CSSA is intended to serve as a quick rating instrument of student abilities that satisfies psychometric criteria typically required of norm-referenced, standardized measures, so that the potential of such teacher perceptions can be fully tapped for the six purposes listed above.

TEST CONTENT AND ADMINISTRATION. The CSSA includes an examiner's manual and individual Profile/Record Form. Each form is used to record a teacher's ratings of a student on a total of 68 items intended, collectively, to cover the nine areas noted above. The number of items for each of the nine scales ranges from 4 to 11. As specified in the manual, the raters should be classroom teachers who have intimate knowledge about the student(s) to be rated. Each individual item is rated on a 9-point Likert-type rating scale ranging from *Poor* to *Good*, with the mid-point (5) indicating *Average*.

Nine scale scores are generated for each student; the instrument does not have a total score. The nine scales are standardized with means of 100 and standard deviation of 15. The raw score on a scale is the simple arithmetic sum of the scores of the items for that particular scale, and such raw scores can easily be transformed to both standard and percentile scores using the tables provided in the examiner's manual. The Profile/Record Form layout is such that it is easy to score items and to add item scores into scale scores.

The administration of the instrument appears to be reasonably straightforward and efficient; the examiner's manual states that a teacher can rate each student on all 68 items in about 10 minutes. The front page of the Profile/Record Form provides a section for a summary of the results in transformed scores (standard scores and percentile ranking), and another section for a Diagnostic Profile, which provides a visual display of a student's standing in the nine areas assessed. In general, the Profile/Record Form is well designed, making the administration of the instrument easy and clear.

Some items seem likely to trouble the thoughtful rater. For example, Item 36 gives "physical strength" as its descriptor, but adds "(can compete with other children in sports and play)" as further descriptive information intended to provide clarity for the rater. The rater who recognizes that flexibility, speed, and skill have more to do with success in most sports than does strength, per se, is left to wonder whether to rate Johnny's *strength* (as in weight lifting or shot put) or *competitive* success in sports (which may have more to do with agility). Other items are vague (#29), contain editorial errors (#33 and #34), or raise questions as to what basis the teacher has for rating (e.g., Item 56, intended to rate the student's "ability to think without words").

TECHNICAL CONSIDERATIONS. The rationale for developing the CSSA appears to be sound. The examiner's manual provides adequate information about instrument scoring and interpretation on the scale scores. The authors' cautionary notes concerning the correct interpretation of CSSA scores are especially appropriate for CSSA users with little or no training in educational and psychological measurement. Users are reminded about (a) noncomparability of raw scores from different scales, (b) difficulties in interpreting percentile scores, (c) the limitations and tentativeness of CSSA scores, and (d) the inability to infer causation or diagnosis from CSSA scores. Indeed, the presentation of information in the examiner's manual is relevant, accurate, well documented, and possesses a degree of clarity and completeness not seen in most test manuals. Technical issues are explained clearly in terms likely to be understood by most users.

NORMS. Normed on a sample of nearly 2,500 students from 33 states, the normative process seems to be well established for students. The characteristics of the normative sample relative to race/ethnicity, gender, urban-rural residence, and geographical region are reasonably representative of those characteristics in the intended population, as reflected in U.S.

Census Bureau data. The raters, however, may be less representative of teachers at large, because (a) bias due to volunteerism may exist (370 of the 4,000 contacted volunteered to rate students in the norming process), and (b) an unspecified number of undescribed "professional colleagues" of the CSSA authors rated students "in their geographic area" (p. 19), yielding ratings of 521 students in the normative sample whose scores may be suspect because they apparently were generated by those lacking the intimate and extensive knowledge of the students necessary to provide valid ratings.

RELIABILITY. Three types of reliability estimates are provided: test-retest, interrater reliability, and internal consistency (Cronbach's coefficient alpha), with the accompanying standard error of measurement (*SEM*) estimates for each scale.

The internal consistency estimates are impressively high, ranging from .88 to .99 for different age groups on different scales. This degree of consistency among CSSA items appears to be sufficient to warrant their use in making decisions about students.

Test-retest reliability estimates, with intervals from 14 to 21 days between administration, are also very high, ranging from .86 to .95. These reliability estimates, however, were derived on a much smaller sample (75 subjects from 7 to 17 years old) from only one private school. This sampling limitation reduces the generalizability of such reliability estimates.

Interrater reliability estimates for the CSSA are also extremely high for such a rating scale, ranging from .92 to .97. Due to the subjective nature of rating, interrater reliability is an important type of reliability estimate for the CSSA. Unfortunately, the interrater reliability estimates are by far the least trustworthy of all reliability estimates provided for the CSSA. This is so because the sample on which interrater reliability was estimated only consisted of 25 students *with learning disabilities*, ages 13–15, drawn from one private school in Texas. This severely limits any claims about the generalizability of interrater reliability estimates for the general student population.

The manual advises users to average the three types of reliability estimates (internal consistency, test-retest, and interrater) to obtain an overall estimate of the CSSA's reliability. The logic underlying this advice is flawed, however. As Anastasi (1988, pp. 126–127) has explained, the three types of reliability estimates relate to three different error sources, each independent of the other two. As such, they should not be averaged. Instead, to obtain an esti-

mate for true score variance (reliability), which is stable over time (test-retest), consistent over items (internal consistency), and free from interscorer difference (interrater), these three sources of error should be additive, rather than being averaged.

VALIDITY. Three types of validity evidence are presented in the examiner's manual: content-related validation, criterion-related validation, and construct validation. The authors correctly point out that (a) validity is related to test use and test score interpretation, not to the test itself; and (b) as a process of evidence accumulation, validity is not dichotomous (i.e., it is not a matter of being valid or invalid, but rather, it is a matter of degree).

Several types of evidence related to content validation are presented: (a) previous empirical evidence about the relationship between teacher rating and other types of assessment results (e.g., standardized tests); (b) the use of an established taxonomy to guide the development of scale categories; and (c) use of accepted item selection procedures in decisions about item inclusion. Of the three types of evidence presented, the first two are both relevant and appear to be adequate. The authors should be commended for the extensive research related to the first type of evidence. However, the careful and accurate coverage typical of the examiner's manual is lacking in this section, as evidenced by an erroneous reference to the National Council on Measurement in Education (NCME) as the "National Council for Mathematics Education" (p. 27).

A greater concern is the reported use of the "point-biserial correlation technique" (p. 31) to obtain the item discrimination coefficients (correlation of each item score with the total raw score for the scale) when, in fact the items are not dichotomously scored. Our assumption that these are actually mislabeled Pearson product-moment correlations is supported by their magnitude; of 117 median item discrimination coefficients reported, 64 range between .90 and .96, 48 fall between .80 and .89, and the remaining 3 are .75, .76, and .76. It would be difficult to obtain such high correlations with the attenuation the point-biserial imposes on one variable (being dichotomous). Further, inclusion of items with such high item discrimination coefficients violates the test authors' selection criterion that "the magnitude of the coefficients had to be between .30 and .80" (manual, p. 31); 112 of the 117 coefficients fall above the suggested cutoff of .80. Discrimination indices of such magnitudes are not only rather rare (at least in our experience), but also perplexing. Statistically, if an item correlates .95 with a scale, the item and the scale are essentially providing the same information. Then why use the scale, because using only the item essentially provides the same information much more efficiently?

Criterion-related validity evidence is very important for a rating scale such as the CSSA because subjective ratings of students' abilities in areas such as Reading, Mathematics, or Verbal Thinking are more indirect than administering established ability tests in these areas. Thus, the validity of CSSA ratings must be established by demonstrating that this indirect mode of assessment is closely related to the more direct, traditional modes of assessing student abilities in these areas. And here the evidence presented in the examiner's manual is not convincing. Although the CSSA scale scores were correlated with subtest scores on five existing instruments, the relatively small sample sizes (ranging from 31 to 72) were drawn from the same one-school sample of *learning disabled* students cited earlier as inadequate for establishing the CSSA's interrater reliability. Claiming that results obtained with such a special sample provide any evidence of the CSSA's criterion-related validity with the general student population is simply untenable. Moreover, some of the intercorrelations of CSSA scales with the subtests in the criterion measures do little to strengthen the claims of criterion-related validity. For example, the mathematics subtest of the Diagnostic Achievement Test for Adolescents correlates nearly as well with the CSSA Writing scale (.60) as with the CSSA Math scale (.67). The Test of Adolescent Language "Speaking" subtest is equally correlated with the CSSA Speech scale (.44) and Reading scale (.43), and its Writing subtest correlates less with CSSA's Writing scale (.70) than with CSSA's Math (.83) and Reading (.90) scales.

Several types of construct validity evidence are presented: exploratory factor analysis results, intercorrelations of CSSA scales, correlations of CSSA scales with intelligence tests, and comparison of CSSA scale scores across several groups classified with varying forms of exceptionality. Overall, the construct validation process is well conceived but, unfortunately, the actual data presented do not provide a convincing case for the construct validity of the CSSA's scales.

First, the factor analysis results are equivocal. It is unclear how items are classified into different scales because nine items are placed in scales on which they have equal or lower factor loadings than they do on other scales. For example, Item 56 loads .79 on the General Facts Scale but only .68 on the Math Scale in which it is placed. Item 46 is placed on the Handwriting Scale with a loading of .70, but loaded higher on four other factors (.75, .76, .80, and .92). Apparently some other rationale for placing items on scales occasionally overrode the factor analysis.

Second, the intercorrelations among the nine CSSA scales are so high (.54–.95, with nearly half above .80) as to cast doubt on the claim that the nine scales are measuring *different* constructs. The CSSA manual indicates that the relationship among all nine scales was unexpected, hypothesizing that this overlap may be attributable to teachers' ratings of student abilities being global and holistic. To test this, the present authors conducted a factor analysis (principal component as the factor extraction method) using the intercorrelation matrix presented in the manual. Even applying liberally the accepted criteria for extracting factors, only one factor emerged, and it accounts for 82% of the total variance. Such a potent general factor suggests that the nine scales are measuring something *in common* rather than measuring *different* constructs.

A third source of proffered validity evidence is the relationship between CSSA scales and those of the Wechsler Intelligence Scale for Children—Revised (WISC-R). Again, the evidence appears to be weak. For example, the CSSA Verbal Thinking and Reading scales have lower correlations with the WISC-R Verbal Scale (.32 and .33) than does the CSSA Math Scale (.51), whereas the opposite would be expected. This sample was restricted to students classified by Texas as having learning disabilities, thus further limiting the usefulness of these data.

A final well-conceived effort to establish construct validity is determining whether or not the instrument can successfully differentiate between or among groups of students who have already been identified (by some other means) as possessing different levels of the specific school-related abilities tapped by the CSSA. But for this purpose, only students with various types of *learning disabilities* or other types of impairment were used. Comparisons that also included students with normal and high abilities would be much more meaningful. In the absence of such comparisons, the mean scores of students with *learning disabilities* appear to be too high (most within one standard deviation of the mean) to warrant their being identified as students with serious problems. If the CSSA cannot reliably identify students already classified as *learning disabled*, it is unclear how low a student's ability must be before it is flagged by the CSSA.

SUMMARY. The CSSA has a clear rationale for its development and application. The administration, scoring, and interpretation aspects of the instrument are clearly explained and easy to implement. The norming procedures appear to have been appropriately carried out in a psychometrically sound fashion. Internal consistency reliability data are adequate, test-retest reliability estimates are equivocal, and interrater reliability data are unconvincing. The "Achilles' heel" of the CSSA, however, is its weak evidence of validity. Although some aspects of content validity evidence appear to be reasonable, the evidence of criterion-related and construct validity is unconvincing.

In spite of these shortcomings, the CSSA may be useful for "low-stakes" assessment situations, such as for exploratory research and initial rough screening of students. The shortcomings of the CSSA, especially those related to validity, should be addressed; if its inadequacies are corrected, the CSSA should prove to be useful in the various situations envisioned by its authors, who have noted that, "Further data gathered from varied samples of students throughout the country would add significantly to assumptions pertaining to the test's usefulness" (examiner's manual, p. 37). Until that happens, however, the CSSA must be considered as purely an experimental measure.

REVIEWER'S REFERENCE

Anastasi, A. (1988). *Psychological testing* (6th ed.). New York: Macmillan.

[82]
Comprehensive Test of Nonverbal Intelligence.

Purpose: Constructed to measure "nonverbal intellectual abilities."
Population: Ages 6–0 to 18–11.
Publication Date: 1996.
Acronym: CTONI.
Scores, 9: 6 subtest scores (Pictorial Analogies, Geometric Analogies, Pictorial Categories, Geometric Categories, Pictorial Sequences, Geometric Sequences), 3 composite scores (Nonverbal Intelligence Quotient, Pictorial Nonverbal Intelligence Quotient, Geometric Nonverbal Intelligence Quotient).
Administration: Individual.
Price Data, 1996: $239 per complete kit including manual (92 pages), analogies picture book, categories picture book, sequences picture book, and 25 profile/

examiner record forms in storage box; $28 per 25 profile/examiner record forms; $39 per manual; $59 per picture book (specify Analogies, Categories, or Sequences).
Time: (40–60) minutes.
Authors: Donald D. Hammill, Nils A. Pearson, and J. Lee Wiederholt.
Publisher: PRO-ED, Inc.

Review of the Comprehensive Test of Nonverbal Intelligence by GLEN P. AYLWARD, Professor of Pediatrics, Psychiatry, and Behavioral and Social Sciences, Southern Illinois University School of Medicine, Springfield, IL:

The Comprehensive Test of Nonverbal Intelligence (CTONI) is a battery of six subtests, designed to measure different aspects of nonverbal intellectual abilities from ages 6-0 to 18-11. Uses outlined by the authors include assessment of intellectual ability of individuals for whom other intelligence tests are not appropriate, comparison of verbal and nonverbal intellectual abilities, or application in research studies. The higher-order nonverbal skills of problem solving, reasoning, and abstract thinking are assessed using the context of pictured objects and geometric designs. The test "model" enables evaluation of the *abilities* of analogical reasoning, categorical classifications, and sequential reasoning in both *contexts* (pictorial and geometric), thereby providing a wide breadth of measurement, and perhaps even addressing to some degree the problem of subvocalization on nonverbal tests.

The six subtests that comprise the CTONI are: (a) Pictorial Analogies (employing a 2 x 2 matrix to measure the ability to recognize the relationship of two objects to each other and to find a similar relationship between two different objects), (b) Geometric Analogies (the same, using geometric designs instead of pictures of objects), (c) Pictorial Categories (measures the ability to deduce the relationship between two stimulus figures and select from five choice items the one that shares the same relationship with the stimulus figures), (d) Geometric Categories (geometric designs are used instead of pictures of objects in the same format), (e) Pictorial Sequences (problem solving format in which the "rule" guiding the progression of figures must be identified), and (f) Geometric Sequences (the same as in the pictorial subtest but using geometric figures). In addition, a Pictorial Nonverbal Intelligence Composite (formed by combining the standard scores of the three Pictorial subtests), a Geometric Nonverbal Intelligence Composite (formed from the combination of the three geometric design subtests), and a

Nonverbal Intelligence Composite (derived by combining the standard scores of all six CTONI subtests into a summary nonverbal intelligence score) are produced. The multidimensional Nonverbal Intelligence Quotient is considered the most stable and clinically useful score produced by the CTONI, because it represents a blend of the cognitive abilities of analogical reasoning, categorical classifying, and sequential reasoning, best approximating the concept of "*g*." The Pictorial Nonverbal Intelligence Quotient is an index of problem solving and reasoning, using representational pictures of familiar objects; verbal skills and mediation are most likely involved. The Geometric Nonverbal Intelligence Quotient employs unfamiliar designs in problem solving and reasoning, thereby limiting the tendency to use verbalization strategies.

Each subtest of the CTONI contains 25 items; because there is no basal age, all examinees begin with Item 1, and continue until the ceiling is achieved, this being failure of 3 out of 5 items in a row. Mean raw scores show a definite developmental trend, ranging from 2–8 at 6 years of age to 15–17 at age 18 years. Resultant correlations with age range from .45 to .66. Low mean raw scores in Pictorial Analogies, Geometric Analogies, and Geometric Sequences at younger ages suggest that item sampling may be restricted. The entire test reportedly takes from 40–60 minutes (depending on age), with individual subtests requiring 5–10 minutes. Instructions can be delivered orally or by pantomime. Instructions for the pictorial and geometric subtests are identical.

Raw scores, percentiles, age equivalents, and standard scores are derived. Raw scores are converted to percentiles and standard scores, based on yearly increments. The mean standard score is 10 ($SD = 3$), and the mean composite scores is 100 ($SD = 15$). This allows comparison to other tests, particularly verbally based instruments. Prorated composite scores may also be produced.

The CTONI was normed on 2,129 children and adolescents from 23 states. Students were enrolled in general classes, but those with disabilities who were mainstreamed were also included. The sample was proportionately matched to census data in terms of gender, ethnicity, and geographic area. At any age group, the sample ranged from 101 to 286 students, with the lowest numbers being in the 6- and 18-year groups, and the most in the 8-, 9-, and 10-year age groupings.

In regard to estimating reliability, coefficient alphas for subtests range from .86–.92; for composite scores, .93–.97. Internal consistency in selected subgroups (based on ethnicity, gender, deafness, or learning disabilities) ranges from .85–.95 for individual subtests, and .93–.98 for composite quotients. SEMs range from .9–1.1 for subtests, and 2.6–4.2 for composite quotients. Test-retest reliability estimates (measured over a 1-month interval) in samples ranging from 30 to 63 students are .79–.94. Reliability estimates for interexaminer scoring for 50 protocols ranged from .95–.99.

The authors qualitatively justify content validity requirements by indicating that the abilities measured on the CTONI are congruent with abilities measured by most intelligence tests, as outlined by Salvia and Ysseldyke (1995). Moreover, content also is compatible with Cattell and Horn's concept of fluid intelligence, Das' simultaneous and successive processing, Jensen's cognitive level of intelligence (transformation of stimulus input), and Wechsler's concept of the Performance Intelligence Quotient (PIQ). Item analysis utilizing point biserial correlations produced median discriminating powers of .00–.67, with the lowest correlations (.00, .21, and .24) being at age 6 years. Median item difficulties ranged from .00–.71, with the lowest being at 6 and 7 years of age. Item bias values are acceptable.

Criterion-related validity evidence was presented by comparing CTONI scores with the Wechsler Intelligence Scale for Children—Third Edition (WISC-III), the Test of Nonverbal Intelligence—Second Edition (TONI-2), and the Peabody Picture Vocabulary Test—Revised (PPVT-R), in a sample of 43 "elementary-level" students attending a school that exclusively serves learning disabled students. Geometric Analogies, Pictorial Sequences, and Geometric Sequences had the highest correlations with the WISC-III PIQ ($rs = .32–.44$); Pictorial Sequences had the highest correlation with the PPVT-R ($r = .53$). As expected, CTONI composite quotients had higher correlations with both subtest and composite criterion IQ scores. The Pictorial Nonverbal Intelligence Quotient had a particularly low correlation with the TONI-2 Quotient (.43), in comparison to the Geometric Nonverbal Intelligence Quotient or the Nonverbal Intelligence Quotient (.84 and .82, respectively).

Principal components factor analysis using the normative sample produced one factor, this being best represented by the Nonverbal Intelligence Quotient (factor loadings ranging from .50 to .71). Subgroup analyses also routinely produced a single factor.

In summary, the CTONI has several distinct assets. The use of both pictorial and geometric content, and the separation of the processes involved into analogies, categories, and sequences are useful in the overall evaluation of nonverbal intelligence. The type of nonverbal skills are of a "higher-order" nature, namely, they do not rely solely on concrete properties of objects (size, color, shape) or perception/perceptual-motor integration.

It also appears that the content of the task is less critical than the process involved in solving a task, along the lines of Naglieri and Das (1988). Along these lines, however, one might want to consider combinations of both pictorial and geometric analogies, pictorial and geometric categories, and pictorial and geometric sequences (versus grouping all three processes by content); this is particularly true because intercorrelations of subtests outlined in the manual are generally higher based on the process (analogies, categories, sequences), versus the content (pictorial/geometric). It appears that first order interpretation must involve the composite quotients, and sometimes diagnostic information is lost with compiled scores. This might not be a major problem if the examiner's primary interest is to obtain an overall nonverbal IQ measure. The use of the CTONI in conjunction with other instruments is a good suggestion, and without doubt, there are fewer intervening variables than found on other tests or batteries such as the WISC-III PIQ.

The test seems particularly useful in testing bilingual students, and those with language deficits, auditory processing problems, motor impairments, or in children from socially disadvantaged households. However, examiners should be aware that the type of "fluid" functions assessed with the CTONI and other tests of nonverbal intelligence may be affected more than verbal functions in children at biological risk, thereby yielding a lower IQ estimate. The combination of pictorial and geometric content, absence of purely perceptual-performance matching or gestalt closure tasks, or better normative data are potential advantages over existing nonverbal tests such as Raven's Progressive Matrices (Raven, 1947; T4:2208), the TONI and TONI-2 (Brown, Sherbenou, & Johnsen, 1990; T4:2775), or the Matrix Analogies Test—Extended Form (Naglieri, 1985; T4:1566). Conversely, the amount of time required, weakness in normative data at the youngest ages (particularly age 6), and the need to further substantiate test profiles and discrepancies in clinical populations are

potential drawbacks, though not necessarily insurmountable ones.

REVIEWER'S REFERENCES

Raven, J. C. (1947). Coloured Progressive Matrices. London: H. C. Lewis.
Naglieri, J. A. (1985). Matrix Analogies Test—Expanded Form. San Antonio: The Psychological Corporation.
Naglieri, J. A., & Das, J. P. (1988). Planning-arousal-simultaneous-successive (PASS): A model for assessment. Journal of School Psychology, 26, 35–48.
Brown, L., Sherbenou, R. J., & Johnsen, S. K. (1990). Test of Nonverbal Intelligence, Second Edition. Austin, TX: PRO-ED, Inc.
Salvia, J., & Ysseldyke, J. E. (1995). Assessment (6th ed.). Boston: Houghton Mifflin.

Review of the Comprehensive Test of Nonverbal Intelligence by GABRIELE van LINGEN, Lecturer, Department of Psychology, The University of Hong Kong, Hong Kong:

The Comprehensive Test of Nonverbal Intelligence (CTONI) consists of six subtests designed to "measure different but interrelated nonverbal intellectual abilities" (p. 7). According to the authors, three higher order cognitive abilities—analogical reasoning, categorical classification, and sequential reasoning—are measured in two different contexts of pictorial objects and geometric designs. The CTONI is intended for three principal uses: (a) to assist in the assessment of the intellectual ability of individuals for whom other tests may be either inappropriate or biased, such as those with language and fine motor difficulties; (b) to allow for comparisons between nonverbal and verbal abilities; and (c) to conduct research on nonverbal abilities. The test materials are attractively presented. However, some of the drawings are detailed and small, making the test inappropriate for the visually impaired, as the authors note, and possibly affecting the test performance of younger examinees (6- to 7-year-olds). The CTONI does not have alternate forms.

ADMINISTRATION AND SCORING. This test has no time limits. The examiner's manual has an overall format that is clear and well written. Especially helpful is a first chapter providing definitions and basic concepts related to the testing of nonverbal intelligence. The manual also presents all aspects of the test's administration and scoring in clear detail. Instructions for both pantomime and oral directions are given, with information for appropriate use. The Profile/Examiner Record Form is well designed. Identifying and referral information is easily recorded, and a completed example is displayed in the manual. Ease of scoring of the individual items for each subtest is assured. However, providing parallel identifying information (appropriate letters) for item options in the picture books would have been helpful. The CTONI subtests have no basals, but the manual provides clear examples on calculating ceilings and scoring when no ceiling is reached. Standard scores for each subtest (mean = 10, standard deviation = 3) are easily obtained and interpreted. Three composite scores or "quotients" (mean = 100; standard deviation = 15) are calculated—the Pictorial Nonverbal Intelligence Quotient (PNIQ), the Geometric Nonverbal Intelligence Quotient (GNIQ), and the Nonverbal Intelligence Quotient (NIQ). The authors provide a theoretical basis for the different constructs of PNIQ and GNIQ, while appropriately cautioning the user that the clinical connotations of a significant difference between them must be determined by future research. The record form also allows for reporting other intelligence test scores and calculating a CTONI equivalent score for easy comparison. A table relating various standard scores and percentile ranks is an added convenience for interpreting the CTONI scores and relating them to other test scores. Age equivalents, with appropriate caveats on their use, are also given. Overall, the manual provides a clear overview of the scores, their meaning and interrelationships, and appropriate cautions on the use of the results. It does not, however, furnish illustrative case studies or other information designed to assist the user in developing interventions based on test results.

STANDARDIZATION AND NORMING. The CTONI was normed on a sample of 2,129 individuals. The subgroup sizes at each age level are 101 and larger. The manual reports, with appropriate tables, that the sample is representative of the general population with regard to geographic region, gender, race, residence, ethnicity, family income, educational attainment of parents, and disabling condition. Disabilities are limited to learning disability, speech-language disorder, mental retardation, and other handicap. Representativeness appears to hold for each age group covered by the test's norms; however, some of these subgroups are quite small.

RELIABILITY. Information related to the CTONI's reliability is based on Cronbach's coefficient alpha for internal consistency, delayed (1-month interval), test-retest using the same form, and interrater reliability based on two independent raters. Coefficient alphas are also presented for relevant subgroups. All three types of reliability estimates have acceptably high coefficients for both subtest and composite scores. Interrater reliability estimates are the highest, ranging from .95 to .99, whereas test-retest reliability estimates are the lowest, but still within acceptable ranges (.79 to .94).

Measures of average reliability, computed from all three measures, range from .92 to .96.

VALIDITY. The manual provides information for content, criterion, and construct validity. Several sources of information are provided as evidence of content validity. One source relates to item selection, for which the authors used an extensive content analysis of existing nonverbal intelligence measures. They also document the relationship of item content to several models of intelligence (Das, 1972; Horn & Cattell, 1966; Jensen, 1980; Salvia & Ysseldyke, 1995; Wechsler, 1991). Classical item analysis, using acceptable criteria for item discrimination and item difficulty, was used to retain items. However, tables displaying the results of a final item analysis using the entire normative sample suggest that these criteria may not have been met consistently for the youngest age groups (6-0 to 7-11). The authors took an additional step related to content validity by using Item Response Theory (IRT) and Delta Scores. Results from these analyses for five dichotomous groups (male/female, African American/non-African American, ESL/non-ESL, American Indian/non-American Indian, Learning Disabled/non-Learning Disabled) suggest that the CTONI items contain little bias in these groups.

Evidence of criterion-related validity was provided by two correlational studies using other intelligence tests. In the first, the CTONI scores of 43 children with learning disabilities were correlated with their scores from the Wechsler Intelligence Scale for Children—Third Edition (WISC-III), the Test of Nonverbal Intelligence—Second Edition (TONI-2), and the Peabody Picture Vocabulary Test—Revised (PPVT-R). The resulting table of significant intercorrelations ($p < .05$) is not impressive in overall values, except for two subtests (Similarities, Object Assembly) on the WISC-III and the NIQ (.81 and .92, respectively), the WISC-III Full Scale IQ and the NIQ (.81), and the TONI-2 Quotient with the NIQ (.82) and the GNIQ (.84). The second study, using the CTONI scores and the WISC-III performance IQ of 32 deaf students aged 8–18, resulted in somewhat higher correlations (from .85 to .90).

The evidence for construct validity is based on the finding that performance on the CTONI is highly correlated to chronological age, as predicted by the "developmental nature of intelligence" (p. 59). Additional evidence is based on the dramatically lower CTONI performance of a mentally retarded subgroup compared to other subgroups. A third line of evidence is derived from the results of factor analysis, for which the CTONI subtests loaded on a single factor for the entire sample and for various subgroups.

The examiner's manual also specifically addresses the issue of test bias, which is important when considering the applicability of a nonverbal intelligence test. Relevant results obtained from the reliability and validity studies are used to support the position that the "CTONI items contain little or no bias in the groups studied" (p. 68).

SUMMARY. The CTONI presents a welcome addition to measures of nonverbal intelligence, and the reviewer is excited about its appearance on the market. The CTONI's model of nonverbal intelligence holds promise and is more clearly delineated than for similar tests such as Raven's Progressive Matrices and the TONI-2. Both manual and record forms are well designed for ease of use. The manual provides easily understood information about aspects of nonverbal intelligence, issues of reliability, validity, and test bias. The CTONI has minor weaknesses related to item presentation that may present problems for younger test takers. Other issues, such as limited evidence on validity, will be amended as investigators conduct further research using the CTONI.

REVIEWER'S REFERENCES

Horn, J. L., & Cattell, R. B. (1966). Refinement and test of the theory of fluid and crystallized general intelligences. *Journal of Educational Psychology, 57,* 253–270.
Das, J. P. (1972). Patterns of cognitive ability in nonretarded and retarded children. *American Journal of Mental Deficiency, 77,* 6–12.
Jensen, A. R. (1980). *Bias in mental testing.* New York: Free Press.
Wechsler, D. (1991). Wechsler Intelligence Scale for Children—Third Edition. San Antonio: The Psychological Corporation.
Salvia, J., & Ysseldyke, J. E. (1995). *Assessment* (6th ed.). Boston: Houghton Mifflin.

[83]
Comprehensive Testing Program III.

Purpose: "Designed to measure attainment of major educational objectives regardless of particular curriculum programs and methods."
Population: Grades 1–2, 2–3, 3–4, 4–6, 6–8, 8–12.
Publication Dates: 1974–1996.
Acronym: CTPIII.
Administration: Group.
Forms, 2: 1, 2.
Price Data: Available from publisher.
Comments: "All quantitative ability and mathematics tests are written to the NCTM standards; where applicable, items intended to tap higher-order thinking skills are included and are identified on reports"; previously listed as ERB Comprehensive Testing Program.
Author: Educational Records Bureau.
Publisher: Educational Testing Service.

a) ACHIEVEMENT TESTS, LEVEL A.
Population: Grades 1–2.
Scores, 4: Auditory Comprehension, Reading Comprehension, Word Analysis, Mathematics.
Time: (155–235) minutes in several sessions.
b) ACHIEVEMENT TESTS, LEVEL B.
Population: Grades 2–3.
Scores, 5: Auditory Comprehension, Reading Comprehension, Word Analysis, Writing Mechanics, Mathematics.
Time: (190–290) minutes in several sessions.
c) ABILITY/ACHIEVEMENT TEST, LEVEL C.
Population: Grades 3–4.
Scores, 7: Ability (Verbal, Quantitative), Auditory Comprehension, Reading Comprehension, Writing Mechanics, Writing Process, Mathematics.
Time: 310(330) minutes in several sessions.
d) ABILITY/ACHIEVEMENT TEST, LEVEL D.
Population: Grades 4–6.
Scores, 7: Ability (Verbal, Quantitative), Vocabulary, Reading Comprehension, Writing Mechanics, Writing Process, Mathematics.
Time: (290) minutes in several sessions.
e) ABILITY/ACHIEVEMENT TEST, LEVEL E.
Population: Grades 6–8.
Scores, 8: Ability (Verbal, Quantitative), Vocabulary, Reading Comprehension, Writing Mechanics, Writing Process, Mathematics, Algebra I [optional end-of-course test].
f) ABILITY/ACHIEVEMENT TEST, LEVEL F.
Population: Grades 8–12.
Scores, 10: Ability (Verbal, Quantitative), Vocabulary, Reading Comprehension, Writing Mechanics, Writing Process, Mathematics (Algebra I, Algebra II, Geometry [optional end-of-course tests]).
Cross References: For a review by Kathleen Barrows Chesterfield of an earlier edition, see 9:397.

Review of the Comprehensive Testing Program III by STEVEN J. OSTERLIND, Professor, University of Missouri—Columbia, Columbia, MO:

The Comprehensive Testing Program III (CTPIII) is a battery of standardized assessment instruments covering an array of school-achievement and ability areas, including Verbal Ability, Auditory Comprehension, Reading Comprehension, Word Analysis, Vocabulary, Writing Mechanics, Writing Process, Quantitative Ability, Mathematics, and several end-of-course tests. Most of the battery's tests are available in several, increasingly difficult levels (labeled A to F), which can correspond to achievement benchmarks, grades, or age. The CTPIII is designed for group administration in school settings, whether public or independent.

A brief rationale for the CTPIII's development is proffered by the publisher in the Technical Report, citing the impetus for updating the test as the "changing needs of the client population and by the larger issue of education reform" (p. 6). Of course, having an articulated rationale for developing a test is commendable, but one wishes this rationale had been thoroughly developed. As it is, the rationale only hints at, rather than explains, employing various educational pedagogies and practices as theory upon which the test is built. Because deliberately infusing any particular outlook on education in the developmental process can profoundly influence the interpretations yielded by the test's scores, this lack of a clearly developed rationale leaves test users uncertain about exactly what is the approach being taken for the assessment.

Still, some useful information is given in the rationale. It specifically mentions two policy decisions taken to ensure that particular philosophies were infused in the test. These are: (a) employing approaches of the whole language movement in the English Expression test and the Writing Process tests, and (b) using the NCTM (National Council of Teachers of Mathematics) Standards in the Mathematics Achievement tests. The practical implications of these policy decisions are difficult to see directly in the multiple-choice items of the language arts area (the passages used are grade-level appropriate); but, they are more directly observable in the quantitative test items, which emphasize concepts and mathematical relationships over rote recall.

From careful inspection of the mathematics items, they appear to offer a range and variety of challenges to examinees that is not seen in some other comparable tests. Further, throughout most tests in the battery the items appear to have been well conceived and thoughtfully constructed.

The CTPIII includes an Instructional Objectives Manual: Relating the CTPIII to Curriculum. This manual has two parts for each test, one that describes content specifications and another that identifies particular test items by content category. Upon close inspection, one is left with concerns about the utility of these parts. The first part is superficial and too cursory in its description of the included content to be of much use to teachers or administrators. Instead of meaningful description of instructional objectives, it presents simple general statements (e.g., "the content domain from Word Analysis" is drawn from "Word recognition/analysis skills included in representative state and local curricula," p. 1). As with the test rationale, here one is

also left with the gleanings of a good, useful idea only to find substance lacking. On the plus side, however, the second part for each test could be helpful to teachers and others who wish to inspect implementation in the items of a given specification.

The CTPIII's main student report—labeled the Individual Student Report—seems well conceived and carefully developed, for it offers much useful information. Students are provided several transformed scores, including percentile ranks, stanines, and normed scores. NCEs can also be reported. Especially useful is the Student Profile portion. This area of the report displays error bands giving a picture of a range of achievement that is more realistic than would be a single take-it-or-leave-it score. The Score Interpretation Folder gives readable explanations to teachers, parents, administrators, and other test users of the report data.

The CTPIII offers full-scale norms for both Fall and Spring. As schools vary the time at which the test may be administered, this offering is especially laudatory, as are the worksheets for school personnel to build their own local norms. The norms are for all schools in the sample population, suburban schools, and independent schools, the last being a major audience for the CTPIII. Likely, the CTPIII offers the largest and most carefully developed sample of independent school norms available. This feature alone makes the CTPIII worthy of consideration for adopting in other-than-public-school settings.

Technically, the development of CTPIII norms is adequate but not exemplary. The sample populations range from about 1,000 to more than 10,000 for different tests within the battery. But, there is an uneven mix of school types. This is probably a consequence of using convenience sampling over statistical sampling, an unfortunate fact of life in real-world standardization studies.

Reliability indexes are given only for internal consistency by KR 20. They appear to be within reasonable ranges, with most tests in the mid .60s to mid .80s range and some tests greater than .90. With the sample sizes and norming procedures, however, one would also expect some traditional temporal stability coefficients such as test-retest. Given Fall and Spring norms and the expectation that some schools may administer the tests more than once to the same students, such indexes would have provided especially useful information.

The CTPIII is equated both horizontally and vertically (by classical test theory methods), a laudable feature for a comprehensive school-based test battery. As with many other technical characteristics, however, the procedures employed are adequate for building a national test but could have been much stronger by also using the more modern and psychometrically robust Item Response Theory scaling.

Construct validity is a difficult aspect to evaluation in any test for it is the sum of all the parts of a test, especially the effort put into development and interpretation of scores yielded. It leads directly to the confidence one has in making proper interpretations of the scores yielded by the assessment. Here, one wishes for much more from the CTPIII. For example, no studies on the test factor structure are reported, nor are there indications of how experts reviewed the content congruence of items.

In sum, the CTPIII has much to recommend it, particularly to independent schools. By industry standards, it is above average in useability and reporting features, and it is acceptable in its psychometric characteristics. Unquestionably, it is adequate for its intended purposes. One wishes, however, that for a major testing program like the CTPIII much more technical work could have been done to make it even stronger.

Review of the Comprehensive Testing Program III by DARRELL L. SABERS, Professor of Educational Psychology, University of Arizona, Tucson, AZ:

The Comprehensive Testing Program III (CTPIII) is an unusual test battery in that it is not designed for the general population of students in the nation. Rather, the CTPIII is designed for students (and schools) where achievement is far enough above average so that the more popular batteries will not discriminate among the achievement levels of the students. It is intentionally designed for the schools that are members of the Educational Records Bureau (ERB), and those schools have an active role in determining the specifications for the tests in the battery.

The CTPIII is as much a new test as a revision of CTPII. Although ERB member schools were involved in reviewing the tests' specifications, the committees charged with developing the rationale and content for the test battery were not restricted by previous decisions regarding CTPII except that the new battery retain the multiple-choice format. The goal was to provide measures that were relevant to the user schools rather than to an undefined national curriculum.

VALIDITY. A separate document, the Instructional Objectives Manual, is devoted to the content validity of the achievement component of the

CTPIII. The domain and targeted skills for each achievement test are described, and the content category for each item is identified. Each specification identifies the items that measure higher-order thinking skills, which are emphasized heavily after the lowest test levels. No test specifications or other rationale are presented for the ability tests.

Very little discussion of validity is provided to help the potential user interpret the correlations with the DCAT/NAT (National Achievement Test) or the tables of intercorrelations among the tests. The following evaluation is based on the data in tables and an examination of the items themselves.

The great emphasis on process behaviors in what is tested in the CTPIII is both a strength and a weakness. The items can be praised for the degree to which they measure higher-order thinking. However, when this type of item is used in both ability and achievement tests, there is little to differentiate the underlying constructs of ability and achievement, and the similarity is evident in both the verbal and quantitative portions of the test. It is easier to differentiate Vocabulary and Reading Comprehension tests from each other than it is to differentiate either from the Verbal Ability test. From Level D to Level F, for groups from grades 4 through 11, the correlation between Verbal Ability and one of these tests is hardly ever lower than the correlation between the two achievement measures. The magnitude of these correlations is not surprising given that the Verbal Ability measure includes items using the same format as the Vocabulary and the Reading Comprehension tests, and perhaps all tap the same competencies.

The correlations between Mathematics Achievement and Quantitative Ability are about the same magnitude as are the reliability coefficients for the two tests. The Quantitative Ability test could be considered a parallel form of the Mathematics tests because there is so little differentiation between what these tests measure. About the only consistent difference between the two types of measures is that the Quantitative Ability tests are more highly speeded than the achievement measures (there is no explanation given for the inclusion of the speed factor). The content and method similarities in the achievement and ability tests are not surprising given that the emphasis on NCTM (National Council of Teachers of Mathematics) objectives were the basis for both, and both types of tests were assigned to the same committee for developing the specifications. Terwilliger (11:254; 1992) commented on the lack of distinction of ability and achievement in the CAP, which was used as an equating test for the CTPIII, and his comments apply equally well to the CTPIII. There is no distinction between ability and achievement based on the data. In the materials provided to this reviewer there is no mention of comparing ability to achievement; if Quantitative and Verbal abilities are considered to be additional achievement measures there may be no problem with these tests except that there are no data to support their validity. The available data support the criticism that the one dominant global achievement factor includes the ability tests as well as the achievement tests.

RELIABILITY. Internal consistency coefficients are reported by single grade levels for all tests for three separate samples (equating and scaling, suburban schools, and independent schools). Standard errors of measurement (in raw score units; not by score level) are reported for these analyses. Alternate forms coefficients are available for three single grades and three combinations of two grades each (4–5, 6–7, & 8–9). The coefficients are high enough to satisfy potential users for those grade levels for which the data are provided.

SCALING AND STANDARDIZATION. The two forms of the CTPIII were equated using both vertical and horizontal equating in what appears to be a conscientious effort to ensure that the scale scores are meaningful. For most uses the member schools are likely to make, the precision of this scaling is adequate, especially because raw scores (not scaled scores) were used in the equating described below.

The CTPIII battery was equated to the CAP tests (NAT/DCAT) for the purpose of obtaining national norms; thus the standardization sample for the CAP is described as the national norming sample (the care taken in selection and weighting of that sample was judged to be appropriate by Terwilliger in 11:254). The questions regarding national norms for the CTPIII are limited to issues of equating nonparallel tests. The developers decided to equate to existing norms rather than administer the CTPIII to a representative sample of students across the nation because the CTPIII, being designed for higher achieving students, would be too difficult for many students in a representative sample. The procedures for equating to the NAT/DCAT are described in a section of the Technical Report headed "Norms Development and Uses" whereas "Equating and Scaling" refers to equating Forms 1 and 2 within the CTPIII.

NORMS. Three types of norm samples are used for providing a basis for score interpretation: national norms, suburban schools, and independent schools. The latter two categories of norms are compiled from user norms; that is, the norms are derived from data obtained from those who used the test (possibly, but not defined as, member schools of ERB). Both of these categories of norms are made more reliable by use of a 3-year rollover sampling base; that is, using a 3-year sample where after 3 years the oldest year's data are replaced by the new year's data. For example the 1992 data were replaced by the 1995 data and combined with the 1993 and 1994 data to provide the basis for reporting 1996 scores. This type of user norm is preferred to a simple 1-year sample, and is similar to how the Graduate Record Examination (GRE) percentile scores are reported. Fall and spring norms are available in separate booklets.

There is a potential problem with rolling norms in that a change in the group tested could distort the norms and make it difficult to track the progress of students. However, there is no evidence of a problem in the 1996 norms even though there was some change in the number of students tested in the previous years. The stability of the norms is evident by comparing the 1995 and 1996 Fall Norms booklets, which are very similar. The national norms do not change annually.

One might wonder whether equating to a test designed for a different level of the student population provides legitimate norms. Member schools might not care about this issue given that their more appropriate comparisons would be to schools in their own classifications: suburban schools or independent schools. The CTPIII provides a unique opportunity for making comparisons to the group that best fits the user, with the added benefit that these comparisons are based on measures of more challenging items than would be used for in-level testing with competing batteries.

Critics of the CTPIII might suggest that the comparisons of interest could be made using out-of-level tests from competing batteries, but member schools are unlikely to agree with that suggestion. The CTPIII tests have adequate ceiling and yet cover the intended content and processes for the target grade level, although the good discussion of this topic (p. 23, Technical Report) may apply only to mathematics.

TECHNICAL REPORT. It is difficult to determine who was the intended reader for the Technical Report. Simple terms (mean and median) are defined, but the Orshansky Index is not. Positive aspects of the Technical Report include extensive reporting of descriptive data on difficulty, speededness, and internal consistency for both user groups. Negative aspects include the lack of information on how much time was taken by the students who completed the untimed tests at the early grades. Also, there are some grades for which no reliability data are reported, and no explanation given why there is the omission.

CONCLUSION. Even if the national norms are considered suspect for this battery, it is easy to recommend the achievement tests for those schools with above average populations. The items are well written and are likely to prove challenging to higher-ability students. The discussion of interpreting scores in the student report suggests adequate caution regarding possible error in measurement. The criticisms aimed at the construct validity of the CTPIII might apply to any competing battery developed to measure ability and achievement.

Given the emphasis on verbal and quantitative ability that many college-bound students in ERB schools will face in the SAT (College Board SAT I Reasoning Test; T4:564), this reviewer would support administering the ability measures if there were adequate information to support the validity of those measures. In fact, when the SAT is the college admissions test of choice, there may be more reason to give the CTPIII ability tests than the achievement tests. However, using the ability measures to differentiate potential from achievement is not justified.

REVIEWER'S REFERENCE

Terwilliger, J. (1992). [Review of the National Achievement Test (Second Edition).] In J. J. Kramer & J. C. Conoley (Eds.), *The eleventh mental measurements yearbook* (pp. 590–591). Lincoln, NE: Buros Institute of Mental Measurements.

[84]

Coping Resources Inventory for Stress.

Purpose: "Designed to measure coping resources which are believed to help lessen the negative effects of stress."
Population: Adults.
Publication Dates: 1988–1993.
Acronym: CRIS.
Scores, 16: Self-Disclosure, Self-Directedness, Confidence, Acceptance, Social Support, Financial Freedom, Physical Health, Physical Fitness, Stress Monitoring, Tension Control, Structuring, Problem Solving, Cognitive Restructuring, Functional Beliefs, Social Ease, Coping Resource Effectiveness.
Administration: Group or individual.
Price Data, 1997: $2.95 per test booklet; $16.95 per manual ('93, 65 pages); $19.95 per interpretive report; $8.95 per profile report; $29.95 per specimen set including

test booklet, manual, pre-paid answer sheet, and interpretive report; $399 per PC-CRIS test administration and scoring program (with PC-CRIS manual); $5.95 to $11.95 per PC-CRIS Interpretive or Profile report (depending on quantity purchased); $9.95 per PC-CRIS test administration program.
Foreign Language Edition: Spanish edition available.
Time: (45–90) minutes.
Comments: Computer (PC-CRIS) administration and software package available.
Authors: Kenneth B. Matheny, William L. Curlette, David W. Aycock, James L. Pugh, and Harry F. Taylor.
Publisher: Health Prisms, Inc.
Cross References: See T4:650 (3 references).

Review of the Coping Resources Inventory for Stress by SHARON L. WEINBERG, Professor and Head, Program of Quantitative Methods, School of Education, New York University, New York, NY:

Based on the theory that stress arises from the inequality between perceived demands and perceived resources, the Coping Resources Inventory for Stress (CRIS) is designed to measure a person's coping resources, including personal behaviors, attitudes, and beliefs, in addition to physical being and financial resources. These perceived resources are those that "are believed to lessen the likelihood that demands will turn into stressors" (p. 4). For example, one such personal trait measured is confidence in that "a confident person should experience less arousal when confronting a stressful situation than a less confident person in the same situation" (p. 4).

The CRIS is a carefully constructed and thoroughly tested inventory consisting of 260 items in a true-false format clustered into 15 coping resources scales and 5 test-taking attitude scales that provide information on the accuracy of the other scores. The 260 items were selected from 700-plus items analyzed on more than 3,500 individuals utilizing factor analysis, item analysis, reliability analysis, and group and item bias studies. The 15 coping resources scales are: Self-Disclosure, Self-Directedness, Confidence, Acceptance, Social Support, Financial Freedom, Physical Health, Physical Fitness, Stress Monitoring, Tension Control, Structuring, Problem Solving, Cognitive Restructuring, Functional Beliefs, and Social Ease. A global Coping Resource Effectiveness Score based on the full complement of 280 items is also provided.

The CRIS may be given in either individual or group format using a machine-scorable answer sheet that must be sent to the publisher for scoring. A

Score Report and a comprehensive Interpretive Report are provided by the publisher in return. Alternatively, the CRIS may be administered and scored using a personal computer version available from the publisher. The software that supports the computer version requires an IBM-compatible computer with at least 125 K RAM. Both Score and Interpretive Reports are produced directly by the computer version.

Strong support for the validity of the CRIS comes from the more than 50 validity studies in which the CRIS has been used. Scales on the CRIS have been found to predict illness, to correlate negatively with measures of emotional distress, to correlate with personality type, to discriminate drug abstainers from relapsers, and to correlate with acculturation and life satisfaction. More recently, six scales of the CRIS were utilized in a study to test the instrument's convergent/divergent validity. The results of this study, like the others, support the construct validity of the CRIS. Reports of internal consistency and test-retest reliability are also quite favorable. Based on a sample of 814 individuals, per scale alpha coefficient internal consistency reliabilities are reported to range from .84 to .97. On a smaller sample of only 34 undergraduates, per scale test-retest reliability using a 4-week interval is reported to range from .76 to .95.

The centiles reported in the Score and Interpretive Reports are based on a sample of 1,897 individuals weighted for sex, age, race, and education level to be representative of the United States population. In addition, separate norms are available for particular populations, such as corporate executives and middle level government managers.

The CRIS has been used widely in a variety of settings and on a broad range of individuals. The delimiting factor for use in a particular population is whether the inventory "can be read and understood by the test taker" (p. 29). According to one formula for determining grade level readability, the CRIS has a readability index of the seventh grade level. The CRIS may be used to assess personal coping resources in: corporate training programs; high stress jobs where burnout is prevalent; substance abuse programs; mental health treatment programs; individual, family, couples psychotherapy or counseling; eating disorders or nutrition programs, and senior high schools or colleges.

In summary, the CRIS is a well-conceptualized instrument producing psychometrically sound results that provides a way to assess personal coping resources and to identify habits and conditions that interfere with a healthy lifestyle. Important strengths of the CRIS are that it has been used extensively in both clinical and research settings and that much data have been collected, analyzed, and documented on the utility of the inventory in exploring vulnerability to stress.

Review of the Coping Resources Inventory for Stress by PAUL D. WERNER, Professor, California School of Professional Psychology, Alameda, CA:

On the Coping Resources Inventory for Stress (CRIS, eighth edition), 12 primary scales provide coverage of domains that have emerged from many researchers' analyses of stress and coping: specific ways of dealing with stressors (e.g., Stress Monitoring, Tension Control), broader aspects of personality (Confidence, Acceptance), contextual factors (Social Support, Financial Freedom), and variables representing physical status (Physical Health, Physical Fitness). These variables are synthesized into three Composite scales and one global Coping Resource Effectiveness scale, allowing the CRIS and its narrative report to provide assessments of coping resources at three levels of specificity. Five appropriately derived validity scales usefully gauge the impact of factors such as social desirability, random responding, and uncommon response patterns on CRIS scale scores.

The CRIS was developed by an extensive, painstaking, and thoughtful iterative process in which a combination of rational, empirical, and factor analytic procedures was used with successively collected samples. Of particular note was the developers' attention to ethnic and gender bias in items, through input from expert judges and statistical analysis of item difficulty data. The developers' willingness to revamp and improve the measure based on successive results has been rewarded. First, both alpha coefficients and retest reliabilities (4-week interval) of the current CRIS scales are excellent. Second, the CRIS scales show expectable relationships with relevant criteria in many domains. The clearest of these validity results come from the many studies correlating the scales of the CRIS with other questionnaire scales (e.g., the MMPI and the Problem Solving Inventory). Additionally of note is validity evidence showing associations between CRIS scores and health-related categorizations (e.g., bulimics vs. normal eaters; high-illness vs. low-illness groups). The developers of the CRIS have broad ambitions for its use, foreseeing its adoption by clinicians, trainers in the world of organizational psychology, school counselors, and teachers of "healthy lifestyle" courses. Results to date, and the vitality of current research with the CRIS—especially with varied socioeconomic, ethnic, and linguistic groups—suggest that such ambitions may be realistic ones.

A number of matters of concern should also be noted, as these both limit the measure's current usefulness and provide directions for future work. Four concerns may be raised about the manual itself. First, for claimed reasons of "test security," no list is provided to show the assignment of items to scales. Users thus cannot employ information about scales' item content as a basis for learning about the meaning of each scale score, and for improving their own interpretative understandings of the scales. The authors' de-emphasis on interpretation by test administrators and their corresponding focus of the narrative report is suggested by the allocation of only a page and a half in the manual to discussion of how testers can help respondents use their scores.

In light of the authors' emphasis on use of the narrative in counseling and intervention planning, a second weakness in the manual may be noted: Too little information is given about the procedures used in developing the report and about the validity of its components. For example, we are told that each composite and primary subscale is subdivided into between three and five subscales (the names of which the manual does not provide), scores on which are translated into statements about specific "strengths and weaknesses" (p. 13) of the respondent. These interpretations appear to be based on item content only, and no evidence is provided documenting the concurrent validity of these subscale scores.

My third concern about the manual also bears on our confidence in the interpretive report. An extensive list of references in the "Professional Bibliography Supporting the Interpretive Report" includes many books and articles predating work on even the earliest version of the CRIS. These references are largely to others' work on the constructs that the CRIS attempts to measure, work in which these constructs were assessed by procedures other than the CRIS. Only by a circuitous (and to this reviewer's thinking, inappropriately optimistic) logic can "support" be found in this literature for drawing interpretations and implications from CRIS scores.

My fourth (and a more minor) concern about the manual has to do with the section on normative data. On the positive side, it is stated that the computerized scoring system compares respondents'

scale scores with norms for a sample weighted for sex, age, and race, based on 1,897 cases in a representative sample of the United States population. Of concern, the tables of scale means and standard deviations in this section of the manual are implied by the text to be based on a different normative sample ($N = 814$). If, indeed, this is not the weighted normative sample, the authors need to elaborate on this sample's composition, and to explain why it, rather than the larger sample, was used to develop the tables of descriptive statistics.

A number of issues arise when considering the validity evidence that is presented concerning the CRIS scales. First, much of the evidence given in the manual's section on construct validity, impressive as it is, consists of analyses of earlier versions of the CRIS that were used to refine the CRIS and to bring it to its present point. Thus, additional evidence directly pertaining to construct validity with reference to the current scales is needed.

Second, there appears to be little evidence, beyond that from studies using other questionnaires as criteria, about each scale's concurrent validity for assessing the specific construct that it claims to measure. For example, validity claims for the CRIS Self-Disclosure scale would be enhanced by the finding of positive correlations between this scale and variables measuring self-disclosure from non-questionnaire measurement perspectives (e.g., peer ratings of self-disclosure, or performance measures of self-disclosure). Evidence such as this is needed to reassure prospective users that each scale indeed measures what its name indicates, rather than some kindred construct or questionnaire method variance. The manual indicates that results of this sort are beginning to appear (e.g., the finding that, among Black students with a family history of hypertension, CRIS Tension Control scores are negatively correlated with systolic blood pressure responses to stressful conditions); more such analyses vis-a-vis nonquestionnaire criteria are needed.

Relatedly, discriminant validity concerns are raised by the observation that (a) many CRIS scores are associated with the same criterion and (b) correlations among many CRIS scales are significantly larger than zero, with the maximum correlation between each of the 12 primary scales and the other 11 scales ranging from .35 to .66. It should be acknowledged that the test developers would argue that such correlational results are not worrisome, and indeed "would be expected for variables from the same domain" (CRIS manual, p. 40). However, results such as these highlight the need for a more solid foundation of concurrent validity evidence about each scale, relating to its accuracy for assessment of the particular construct implied by the scale's name.

CONCLUDING SUMMARY. The product of a substantial, thoughtful, and growing program of research, the eighth version of the Coping Resources Inventory for Stress (CRIS) is a noteworthy measure warranting use by researchers studying stress and coping. In order to better establish the inventory's appropriateness for drawing differentiated inferences about individual clients in clinical, counseling, and educational/training settings, more evidence is needed pertaining to discriminant validity, and to the concurrent validity of each scale of the CRIS as a measure of the construct implied by its name.

[85]

Course Finder 2000.

Purpose: Assesses "students' interests and preferences, and identifies suitable higher education courses at appropriate universities/colleges in Great Britain."
Population: Students entering higher education.
Publication Date: 1992–1993.
Acronym: CF2000.
Administration: Group.
Price Data: Available from publisher.
Time: (45–60) minutes.
Comments: For use in Great Britain.
Authors: Malcolm Morrisby, Glen Fox, and Mark Parkinson.
Publisher: The Morrisby Organisation [England].

Review of the Course Finder 2000 by COLIN COOPER, Lecturer, School of Psychology, The Queen's University of Belfast, Belfast, United Kingdom:

This questionnaire has been designed to help school-leavers discover which United Kingdom university (and other "higher-education") courses may match their interests, educational qualifications, and existing careers plans. It does not cover U.K. "further education" courses (non-degree, often vocational courses in local colleges). Entrance to all U.K. degree courses is via a central clearing house (UCAS), which allows students to apply for only a small number of courses. The purpose of the Course Finder 2000 questionnaire is to help students to identify which degree courses may best fit their interests and qualifications prior to applying to universities via UCAS.

Applicants spend approximately 45 minutes completing a substantial questionnaire detailing their qualifications, any geographical preferences, their level of interest in various (potentially subject-relevant) concepts, such as "the environment" and "how computers work," any existing preferences for a particular subject-area, and more detailed study interests. A teacher then enters the student's likely grades for examinations that have not yet been taken, and mails the form to the publishers. They generate a 27-page individual report that estimates the applicant's strength of interest in 20 main areas of study (computer science, law and politics, etc.) together with a brief resumé of what studying these topics actually *involves* and the career opportunities that a degree in each will offer.

The system claims to hold all the information about entrance-requirements (at "A-level" and GCSE standard) for all courses (including "joint" or "combined" degrees where two or more subjects are studied in depth), and so it is able to suggest a number of courses at different universities that might appeal to the student's interests, geographical preferences, and existing and predicted educational qualifications. This list shows the grades typically required for entry into the course, its duration, any other features such as an industrial placement year, and the proportion of applicants who are accepted by each course. The list is quite extensive: In the example provided for review the student showed some interest in 11 of the 20 main areas of study, and the system identified 225 courses that may be of interest, spread across 73 universities.

Questions of reliability and validity naturally arise when considering a measure such as this; unfortunately, despite the presence of some data in the "adviser's manual," it is not entirely obvious how these can be established. Section B of the questionnaire asks 120 questions about the student's main interests, using a small degree of ipsatisation, so that a student could not express a strong degree of interest in *all* areas. These are scored to form 20 six-item scales, and the reliability of these is given in the manual. However, I am not sure that these mean very much because many of the words are near synonyms. How could someone who expressed a strong interest in "medical techniques" possibly express anything other than a strong interest in "the problems of the human body," for example? So although the reliability of all but one of the six-item scales is quite acceptable, it really is difficult to see how it could be otherwise.

Section D of the questionnaire provides 94 two-item scales exploring specific interests (e.g., interest in "animal life" and "large mammals," "the construction of ships," and "the design of ships"). All the correlations between the pairs of items are above .45. (Coefficient alpha is not defined for two-item scales, so just the correlations are reported.) But again, given the meanings of the words, it would be amazing if the correlations were *not* large.

Section C of the questionnaire simply asks students to rate their degree of interest in the 20 main areas of study that run through the questionnaire: The correlation between this and the scores from the 200 interest-items in Section B is .93 (uncorrected for reliability) in a sample of 1,680 students, indicating that these two sections measure essentially the same thing. Although this reviewer is obviously in favor of measures that show high construct validity, this can be carried to extremes: In the present case it is difficult to see why both sections are retained in the questionnaire. No information is given about the temporal stability (test-retest reliability) of any section of the questionnaire, which seems to be an unfortunate omission.

Some other aspects of the test can really only be taken on trust. For example, there is no way of checking that the database of courses is both comprehensive and up-to-date (in terms of entry requirements, etc.). Nor is it known how the responses to the various sections are weighted and combined to lead to overall recommendations for particular courses. Unfortunately, it is not easy to establish the predictive validity of the questionnaire. In one attempt, university students were asked to express an interest in between one and three university courses. The system returned the actual courses that the students were studying in 88% of the cases. However, as the system produces rather large lists of courses, this is perhaps rather less impressive than it appears at first sight. It would be more valuable to conduct follow-up studies in which interest strength is related to academic performance, rated happiness with the chosen course, dropping out/changing course, and so on—though this would perhaps be beyond the scope of a single test publisher.

One key assumption of the entire questionnaire is that university courses can be divided into 20 homogeneous groups, each of which reflect broadly similar interests. It is not obvious where this taxonomy came from, or whether it has any basis in fact. Indeed, some groupings surprised this reviewer. For example, history and philosophy are combined into one category, law and politics into a second, and the whole of social sciences into a third. A factor analysis of the items in Section B of the questionnaire would show whether the taxonomy of interests is actually supported by the data.

Despite this last problem and the difficulties in establishing the questionnaire's predictive validity, it seems likely that the very act of completing this detailed questionnaire will encourage pupils to think in some detail about their interests and needs when selecting a degree course, and about the types of careers that may result. It provides a useful list of courses that may be of interest (and which match the student's academic results), and would seem to be a useful adjunct to careers counseling.

[86]
Creative Styles Inventory.

Purpose: "Identifies an individual's preference for assimilating information using either an intuitive or a logical style."
Population: High school (advanced).
Publication Date: 1986.
Acronym: CSI.
Scores: Total score only.
Administration: Group.
Price Data, 1993: $49 per complete kit including 10 inventories and 10 interpretive booklets (4 pages).
Time: (10–15) minutes.
Comments: Self-scored inventory.
Author: Bernice McCarthy and Excel, Inc.
Publisher: McBer & Company.

Review of the Creative Styles Inventory by KWONG-LIEM KARL KWAN, Assistant Professor of Educational Studies, College of Education, Purdue University, West Lafayette, IN:

The Creative Styles Inventory (CSI) is designed for test-takers to understand their preferred mode (i.e., logical or intuitive) of learning, decision making, and problem solving. This is a self-administering and self-scoring inventory with 32 pairs of items presented in two columns (Column A & Column B), each of which has the options of *A Lot* or *Somewhat*. For each pair, test-takers are instructed to choose either the item in Column A or that in Column B, and to choose either *A Lot* or *Somewhat* within the column. Each item endorsement carries a numerical value of either -2, -1, +1, or +2, which is computed to yield a total score that is then compared to a raw-score profile that ranges from -60 to +60. More negative scores indicate a more *Logical/Analytic* mode, whereas more positive scores indicate a more *Intuitive* mode. Scores between ±2 to ±8 are considered "balanced."

To test-takers, the CSI is a brief instrument (it took two high-school-educated university clerical staff and the test reviewer about 20 minutes to complete rating and scoring the items). In general, the CSI's rating instructions are easy to follow; however, an explicit statement that informs test-takers to choose the *preferred* item in each pair is necessary. Most of the items were clearly worded, except for item-pairs #6 and #7 in which the word "like" could be ambiguous in the context. In Item #29, quotation marks are needed for both made-up words (i.e., "lumper" & "splitter"; both clerical staff and the test reviewer consulted the dictionary first). The test author made an attempt to randomly counterbalance item-pairs that are indicative of the respective logical-intuitive modes. Item content, however, is obvious enough for discerning test-takers to produce a skewed or invalid profile. The scoring instructions appear self-explanatory. The scoring key for item-pair #18, however, is not compatible with the overall scoring profile. According to the scoring key, items representative of the Logical/Analytic Mode were negatively scored whereas those of the Intuitive Mode were positively scored. For item-pair #18, which was "abstract-concrete," such scoring was reversed. Theoretically speaking, however, "abstract" appears indicative of the Intuitive Mode (i.e., +ve score) whereas "concrete" is more representative of the Logical/Analytic Mode (i.e., -ve score).

To test administrators, the CSI is simple to understand and interpret (only four pages of Profile and Interpretive Notes). Such simplicity, however, presents several major test validity and reliability issues that test administrators should seriously consider.

First, the major constructs (i.e., creative styles, logical/analytic mode, and intuitive mode) of the inventory are not formally and sufficiently operationalized, although the constructs of Logical/Analytic mode and Intuitive mode are somewhat illustrated by the Creative Styles Characteristics as well as the respective mode's Strengths and Weaknesses as listed in the Profile and Interpretive Notes. An inherent assumption of the CSI is that creative styles are related to an individual's ability to employ both logical and intuitive modes of information processing. It is doubtful, however, that the Logical-Intuitive mode is the only dimension that constitutes *creative styles*, which is the inventory's name. In addition to the "balanced" Logical-Intuitive mode, creative styles can be manifested in and measured by a "balanced" approach in other dimensions. In fact,

instead of the ability to employ both modes "cooperatively," there may be an underlying or overarching dimension of "flexibility-rigidity" (which the Logical-Intuitive dimension and other dimensions could subsume) that is more indicative of creative styles. The CSI's unidimensional approach, therefore, could be delimiting the definition and misleading test users' conception of creative styles.

A second major issue pertains to the lack of psychometric procedures and empirical references in item construction, sampling, scoring, and profile interpretation. No literature (beyond a statement that "[t]he inventory is based on extensive psychological research establishing the connection between the two modes of information processing and the two hemispheres of the brain") was identified to justify the sampling and content validity of test items. No standardization procedures were reported to indicate the reliabilities of items that constituted the Logical and Intuitive modes of information processing, the robustness of the Logical, Intuitive, and Creative Styles constructs, and the discriminant and predictive validities of these constructs. No normative samples were described to support the target population for whom the inventory is intended; and no normative data were presented to explain the construction and, hence, the meaning and meaningfulness of the scoring system (i.e., the raw-score profile). An attempt was made to gather such information from the publisher who notified the test reviewer that no normative data are available.

Despite its brevity and ease to use, no psychometric information (i.e., normative sample, standardization procedure, item reliability, construct and predictive validity) were provided in the CSI's test materials. Without this empirical information, the inventory remains at best a conceptual instrument. Test-users who want an understanding of subjects' information-processing preference may explore the compatibility of the Logical-Intuition dimension of the CSI and the Sensing-Intuition dimension of the Myers-Briggs Type Indicator (T4:1702).

Review of the Creative Styles Inventory by SHEILA MEHTA, Assistant Professor of Psychology, Auburn University at Montgomery, Montgomery, AL:

This group-administered verbal test purports to identify an individual's hemispherical preference for processing information (i.e., preferred learning or problem-solving style). The Creative Styles Inventory (CSI) was designed for people with at least a high school education and it can be administered, scored, and interpreted by the test taker. The test yields one score from 32 Likert-type verbal items. No other information is included regarding for whom and for what purpose the test was designed. However, it seems to be intended for business managers to use on their subordinates to assist the managers in working with their employees individually and to facilitate selection of work groups. The CSI could also be used on post-secondary students so that teachers can assess their preferred learning mode or style.

Each test comes with two booklets: a test Inventory and a Profile and Interpretive Notes. Both booklets are attractive, durable, and easy to use. The first page of the Inventory contains simple, easy-to-follow instructions, an example, and the 32 test items arranged with right and left anchor columns. Each item has a left anchor, such as "bases decisions on facts" and a right anchor, such as "bases decisions on feelings." For every item the taker chooses either "a lot" or "somewhat" for the right or left anchor, by placing an O in the appropriate column. The second page of the inventory is the scoring page. For each item a carbon-like reproduction of the O appears on a whole number from -2 to +2. Instructions guide the test taker through the simple, three-step scoring process that involves totaling the minus numbers, totaling the plus numbers, and adding the two subtotals together. Test takers are instructed to use the Profile and Interpretive Notes booklet to plot their Creative Styles profile and to understand what it means.

The three-page interpretive booklet explains the Creative Styles (logical/analytical versus intuitive mode preference), characteristics of the two modes, how to plot the score on the profile, strengths and weaknesses of the modes, how to develop rational versus intuitive capabilities, how to apply what test takers learn about themselves, and how to integrate the modes more effectively. The interpretative booklet is especially informative.

There are a few minor improvements that could be made in regard to the format of the inventory booklet. For instance, the example in the instructions is worded, "I prefer dogs 'a lot' or 'somewhat'—or—I prefer cats 'a lot' or 'somewhat.'" The actual inventory items, however, are worded without a subject, and more importantly, the verbs are in the third person. Because the test taker is presumably completing the inventory for him or herself, it would be better to have the items stems, if they begin with a verb, in the first person form. Furthermore, one anchor of an item (14) begins with a verb in the first person form, whereas its opposite anchor and all the other item stems are in third person. These inconsistencies are a bit confusing. Finally, many people may not know what is meant by community versus agency, terms used in the anchors of one item (26), and indeed this item correlates relatively low with the total scale. Finally, the scoring sheet can be seen through the inventory page.

Positive features of the inventory regarding content are its face validity and apparently non-biased content. Test takers will not be put off by the language and they will feel that the test is measuring what they have been told it is measuring. Although there is no documentation in the technical manual of steps taken to minimize the influence of cultural factors on individual test scores, there do not appear to be items that are offensive or biased with regard to race, sex, native language, ethnic origin, geographic region, etc.

Although the CSI deserves praise for its appearance and ease of administration, scoring, and interpretation, it is difficult to evaluate its technical merit. A number of obstacles existed in obtaining the information needed to thoroughly assess the CSI. First, no information regarding norms, reliability, and validity accompany the CSI. Second, it was difficult to obtain this information. A search for it began with the publisher who referred me to a company owned by the test author. Some confusion existed regarding the test name, as the publisher had renamed it, and whether and where a manual for it existed. As it turns out, some information is available through Excel in the form of a nine-page report on The Hemispheric Mode Indicator (the original name of the CSI), and written by Marcus G. Lieberman, Ph.D., in 1987. Unfortunately, this report is seriously limited in the technical information it yields.

Regarding norms, the only information available is that approximately 2,000 educators, mostly teachers and a few administrators, make up the standardization sample. There is no indication of how this sample was selected and the only demographic information on the respondents is age and sex.

Two types of reliability were assessed: internal consistency and test-retest. Internal consistency was assessed by calculating Cronbach's alpha for 76 respondents (no information regarding how this sample was obtained), resulting in a coefficient of .90. This coefficient indicates good internal consistency, not so high as to suggest that every item is measuring the same aspect of the construct, and not so low as to suggest that the items are measuring entirely different constructs. The Pearson Product Moment Correlation coefficient was used to measure temporal stability of the CSI. A sample of 47 respondents (again no information regarding how they were obtained) took the CSI approximately 2 months apart, an appropriate delay interval. The resulting coefficient of .90 indicates that the trait being measured is stable over time, as would be expected with approaches to learning and problem solving.

Two types of validity were assessed: content and concurrent. After a review of the literature in the area of brain hemisphere dominance, which included only six sources, the test author prepared 40 items that the various scholars had attributed to right or left hemispheric laterality. These items were tested (no information appears in the report regarding the type or size of the sample) by correlating each item with the total with the item in question removed. From these 40 items, 32 were selected. Problems in this procedure are that there is no clear statement of the behaviors represented by the CSI and that a relatively small number of items were culled from the literature.

Concurrent validity was assessed by correlating the 32 items with a measure called Style of Learning and Thinking (SOLAT-C) (Torrance & Reynolds, 1980). The subjects for this step were obtained from 49 attendees of a workshop of learning styles and hemispheric laterality. No information is given regarding characteristics of this sample. For these subjects two correlations were calculated: the Spearman rank correlation was .819 and the Pearson product-moment correlation was .659. Although no information regarding the expected network of relationships between the CSI and other constructs is provided in the technical report, these results suggest that the CSI is related to the SOLAT-C, as would be expected, but is not identical to it. The CSI appears to be measuring something different and not duplicating the related measure. The problem with this procedure is that the validity of various forms of the SOLAT has been questioned. The adult version, now called the Human Information Processing Survey, was said by its reviewer to have no empirical or theoretical basis (10:144). The elementary and youth forms of the SOLAT were not considered to be reliable or valid by two sets of reviewers (11:390).

No mention of the construct validity of the CSI is made in its technical report. The most serious problem with the CSI is its lack of a theoretical basis. Are the left and right hemispheres of the brain responsible for different thoughts and behaviors? This popularized idea is not well supported by the scientific literature.

In summary, the CSI appears to be a unique and possibly useful instrument for business settings. Unfortunately, its application in schools is limited by being able to use it only on advanced high school levels and beyond and by its questionable validity. Moreover, the paucity of information provided in the technical manual compromises the reviewer's ability to thoroughly assess the instrument. Adequate information regarding norms, standardization samples, construct validity, and a theoretical rationale are lacking. However, despite these shortcomings, the reviewer does see a limited use for the CSI in business settings, given its quick and easy administration, scoring and interpretation, and the fact that it will be used to facilitate working groups rather than for selection or clinical purposes.

REVIEWER'S REFERENCE

Torrance, E. P., & Reynolds, C. E. (1980). Preliminary norms—technical manual for Style of Learning and Thinking—Form C. Athens, GA: Georgia Studies of Creative Behavior, University of Georgia.

[87]

CTB Portfolio Assessment System.

Purpose: Designed to require the use of higher-order thinking skills in Language Arts and Mathematics to complete real-life tasks.

Population: Grades 1 & 2, 3, 4, 5 & 6, 7 & 8.

Publication Date: 1992.

Administration: Group.

Price Data, 1995: $82.60 per portfolio assessment classroom module including portfolio box, guide for using portfolios, administration manual (19–24 pages), scoring manual (20–25 pages), 35 individual student portfolio folders, and class record sheet (specify level and subject); $17.70 per 35 individual student portfolio folders; $17.70 per guide for using portfolios; $23.60 per administration manual (select level and subject); $23.60 per scoring manual; $1.15 per class record sheet.

Time: Administration time not reported.

Comments: Portfolio assessment; administered four times throughout school year.

Author: CTB Macmillan/McGraw-Hill.

Publisher: CTB Macmillan/McGraw-Hill.

a) INTEGRATED LANGUAGE ARTS.

Population: Grades 1 & 2, 3, 4, 5 & 6, 7 & 8.

Levels: 5.

Scores, 5: Reading Comprehension, Writing, Speaking, Listening Comprehension, Participation.

b) INTEGRATED MATHEMATICS.

Population: Grades 3, 4, 5 & 6, 7 & 8.

Levels: 4.

Scores, 4: Mathematical Content and Concepts, Mathematical Reasoning, Mathematical Communication, Participation.

Review of the CTB Portfolio Assessment System by TERRY ACKERMAN, Associate Professor, Department of Educational Psychology, University of Illinois, Champaign, IL:

This portfolio assessment system covers Language Arts for grades 1 through 8 and Mathematics for grades 3 through 8. There are five Language Arts assessment levels designed for grades 1 & 2, 3, 4, 5 & 6, and 7 & 8. The Mathematics program is broken up into four levels: grades 3, 4, 5 & 6, and 7 & 8.

PURPOSE. The purpose of the portfolio is to provide a means by which students can assume responsibility for their own learning experiences by participating in a series of comprehensive, creative activities. All of the students' work is kept in colorful portfolio folders provided by CTB. The program divides the school year into four equal periods or stages. In most cases, stages involve several interrelated activities. At the end of each quarter students are asked to engage in performance assessment activities that require the students to integrate the newly learned skills and competencies. Throughout the assessment activities students are challenged to complete everyday "real-life" tasks requiring higher order thinking skills.

The Integrated Language Arts tasks require students to integrate their reading, writing, speaking, and listening skills. Many of the Language Arts tasks involve popular children's stories, plays, or books. At each grade level a comprehensive two-way table of specifications is provided. This table identifies the particular activities within each stage and what areas of skill are being scored by the particular activity. In Language Arts, five main skill areas are assessed: Reading Comprehension, Writing, Speaking, Listening Comprehension, and Participation. The skills being scored vary with the activity and stage.

The Integrated Mathematics portfolio requires students to employ their mathematics content knowledge to solve problems, make predictions and judgments, and draw conclusions. The four skill areas that are scored are Mathematical Content and Concepts, Mathematical Reasoning, Mathematical Communication, and Participation. Mathematical Content and Concepts is broken down into seven specific topics: number theory/relations, patterns and functions, probability and statistics, geometry and spatial

sense, measurement, decimals and fractions, and computation and estimation. The particular topics that are scored also vary with activity and stage.

Each activity results in either a written or oral performance that the teacher can observe and evaluate. Although each student is asked to perform the same task, the portfolio approach enables the teacher to collect many different kinds of data that represent a multidimensional profile of each student's abilities, strengths, and weaknesses.

PORTFOLIO PACKET CONTENTS. Each portfolio assessment contains several components: a guide for using portfolios, an administration manual, a scoring manual, a portfolio box (designed to hold the students' portfolios), portfolio folders, and a class record sheet (for recording results of up to 35 students).

ADMINISTRATION DIRECTIONS. Assessment at each of the four stages begins with the teacher introducing the context for the assessment. Directions for each of the activities are then provided to the class. For each activity suggested, administration directions for what the teacher is to say are provided. In this respect the assessment is standardized. Students may work alone, in pairs, or in small groups. The teacher is expected to act as a guide or coach, encouraging and helping students find their way to knowledge. Some of the activities have optional project sheets that can be copied and used to help students complete the activities. Students can work at their own pace. No specific timelines for completion are provided.

The Integrated Language Arts assessments are all based upon well-known books. One problem that may arise is obtaining multiple copies of the book being studied. For some activities it is assumed that each student has a copy of the book.

SCORING. Activities in both Language Arts and Mathematics can be scored in one of two ways. There is a trichotomous, holistic rubric (e.g., satisfactory, unsatisfactory, not observed) or an analytical scoring procedure that uses a checklist. A check would indicate that a specified criterion has been met. Checks can be summed to produce an overall activity total. Scoring should be completed at the stage level after all of the activities for each stage have been completed.

Teachers are strongly encouraged to have conferences with each student to assess the completed activities and share an insight. These conferences are intended to help the student understand that the teacher is a partner in the learning process. Students are encouraged to take risks and develop creative solutions. Students manage their own portfolio and are prompted to add any notes, reflections, anecdotes, summaries, or suggestions. The guide for using portfolios suggests that the portfolios be passed along to the student's net teacher or school if the child transfers.

There are both advantages and disadvantages to this recommendation. Regarding the information a portfolio may provide about students' abilities, creativity, and likes and dislikes may be quite advantageous in preparing curriculum materials or placing a student in a particular level of instruction. Realistically, however, teachers may not want to spend the time looking over student work from the previous year, particularly given the fact that another teacher may have subjectively scored the work differently.

RELIABILITY. Portfolio assessment does not lend itself to typical measures of reliability. No discussion about measurement or assessment accuracy was provided. Although it is tempting to compute some type of coefficient based on either the holistic scores or the analytical scores, the multidimensional nature of the task would suggest that any measure of internal consistency (e.g., coefficient alpha) would be inappropriate. Interrater reliability involving the consistency of different teachers or observers (e.g., parents and teachers) although possible may not be practical.

Research by Shavelson, Gao, and Baxter (1991) has suggested that at least eight products over different areas may be needed to measure portfolio performance accurately. Inasmuch as the analytical ratings are based upon several different components of each activity, the number of activities within each stage falls short of this suggested number.

VALIDITY. Validity is never discussed. This indeed is a shortcoming of the portfolio for it raises several questions that the developers of the program could and should easily address. For instance, why were the selected activities chosen? What was the process for selection of activities? Were they curriculum based? Must the stages be followed in a particular order? If so, why? Were they based on suggested state guidelines? How do teachers integrate these assessments into their curriculum? How does one really know if higher order skills are being tested? No guidelines or suggestions are provided.

Should these assessment activities be counted as part of the student's overall evaluation or course grade? Programs of assessment should be designed to both serve and enhance instruction. Whereas the portfolio clearly does this, the authors need to advise teachers how portfolio results can be recycled back into instruction. Diagnostic guidelines need to be established for this assessment program to help identify learning disabilities as well as gifted and talented students.

NORMS. There is no normative information provided. Ideally, before being marketed, either quantitative or qualitative data that provides a comparative basis for subsequent users to judge their class performance against should be collected, analyzed, and reported.

SUMMARY CONTENTS. The CTB Portfolio Assessment appears to be well thought out and carefully written. The creators have designed the activities well. Activities appear to be easy to implement and should stimulate student participation. However, major weaknesses exist. The authors do not provide any information concerning the precision or validity of the program. In addition, no guidelines on how to integrate the program into the regular classroom curriculum or how to recycle results to improve instruction are provided. Like a new airplane, the CTB Portfolio Assessment looks sleek, but until we are provided with previous performance results, we cannot be convinced that it can really fly.

REVIEWER'S REFERENCE

Shavelson, R., Gao, X., & Baxter, G. (1991). *Design theory and psychometrics for complex performance assessment.* Los Angeles: UCLA.

Review of the CTB Portfolio Assessment System by BRUCE G. ROGERS, *Professor of Educational Psychology, University of Northern Iowa, Cedar Falls, IA:*

The CTB Portfolio Assessment (CTB/PA) was designed to assess the ability of pupils to "use higher-order thinking skills in real-world activities" (Guide, p. 1). Those skills are assessed in the areas of Language Arts (for grades 1–8) and Mathematics (for grades 3–8). Students are asked to work both individually and in groups as they write, discuss, and perform. Led through a variety of activities, pupils make written responses, which are later filed in their portfolios. These portfolios can then be used by the pupil, the teacher, and the parents to examine student progress over time.

The CTB/PA is a 1990s product, so, unlike many standardized tests, it does not have the benefit of years of research into its reliability and validity characteristics. This reviewer anticipates that such evidence will soon be gathered in a technical manual for future revisions. An administrator's manual and a scoring manual are available for both subject areas at each grade level. Teachers are also provided with several forms for recording scores.

The CTB/PA has some notable strengths. First, suggestions for explaining the activities to students are given in the administrator's manual. They appear to be written clearly as are the directions for administering the activities. Second, forms for the students to use are provided. The teacher can copy them directly or adapt them as desired. Third, a scoring guide is provided showing a sample of a check list and a rating scale with a scoring rubric for each exercise. These materials were designed specifically to help the teacher to implement the program in an efficient manner.

The limitations of this instrument relate primarily to the lack of technical information about the test. There is virtually no evidence provided that relates to commonly used standards in test development. There is no description of the technical rationale for instrument development, no discussion of any procedures for assessing validity, no evidence from reliability studies, and no normative data. The absence of such evidence is troublesome for a reviewer. One could go through the test materials in detail to find fault with them. However, it appears to this reviewer that a more positive approach is to propose certain considerations that may be of benefit both to those who are potential adopters of the instrument and to the authors of the instrument.

It is often said that the first principle of item writing is to begin with an important idea. Toward that goal, test developers prepare aids such as instructional objectives and tables of specifications. Because none of these are to be found in the administrator's manual, teachers will need to construct their own statements of objectives and then apply them to the activities in the manual. Some teachers might ask how these activities compare with national standards. For example, to what extent does the Mathematics Assessment sequence coordinate with the well-known standards prepared by the National Council of Teachers of Mathematics? Such questions about the content validity of this instrument would seem to be a reasonable request of potential users.

Teachers may also want a discussion as to how the activities were developed and justified. Because the authors emphasize "real-world activities" in the description of the test, some teachers may look at the activities in that context. For example, in the Grade 4 Language Arts, the teacher selects an editorial from a local newspaper and reads it to the students. Each

pupil writes a letter to the editor in response. There is considerable controversy among both educators and the public in general as to the appropriateness of asking students to express their own opinions on a matter versus evaluating their understanding of written material. In the "real world," grade 4 students seldom write letters to the editors of the local newspaper, but they often do read excerpts in the newspaper with the expectation of understanding it. Therefore, in assessing the evidence for the content validity of this instrument, presenting information relating to the "real-life" applications of the activities would appear to be appropriate.

The authors enumerate several types of student records that are frequently contained in cumulative records, including standardized test scores. That immediately suggests an investigation of the relationship of scores from those instruments with those from the CTB/PA, as confirmation of construct validity. Teachers may also wish to see some evidence of these relationships in schools where this program has already been adopted, because such is not contained in the current manuals.

The scoring manual gives clearly written suggestions for evaluating the written or oral performance for each activity. Both holistic scoring and analytical scoring methods are described. Because these scoring methods involve subjective judgments, potential users of these instruments may ask for evidence from reliability studies. Internal consistency estimates, test-retest indices, and measures of interrater reliability would provide very useful information for both users and developers.

The scoring manuals contain detailed directions on how to assign points to each activity. Some teachers may want to compare the resulting scores of individual pupils with the distribution of scores from some meaningful group. However, the manuals do not contain normative data. For the purposes of many teachers, percentiles within grades would seem appropriate. Although national norms are expected for major standardized tests, even restricted area norms would be an important beginning point for this instrument.

In summary, the CTB/PA provides a set of activities that appear to be constructed as well, if not better, than sets of activities in most textbooks and activity books used in the elementary grades. Those teachers who desire to incorporate portfolios in their classrooms may find these instruments convenient to use. However, they should be concerned about the lack of supporting technical data. CTB/Macmillan McGraw-Hill has an outstanding reputation for psychometric expertise. Members of its staff have excellent training and continually make major contributions to the professional educational measurement organizations. The authors are encouraged to use this expertise to create technical manuals that provide information about how the instruments were constructed and how typical students have scored on them. In addition, evidence relating to both validity and reliability of the instruments should be included. If such data were gathered (perhaps it is in process at the time of this writing), this reviewer believes that the authors would probably make some valuable revisions in the test as they examine both content validity and construct validity. When such technical information is available, both reviewers and potential users can then make informed decisions about the usefulness of this instrument.

[88]
CTB Writing Assessment System.

Purpose: "Includes direct and indirect writing measures to aid educators in evaluating writing programs and students' writing abilities."
Population: Grades 2.0–12.9.
Publication Date: 1993.
Scores, 6: Holistic, Analytic (Content, Organization, Sentence Construction, Vocabulary/Grammar, Spelling/Capitalization).
Administration: Group.
Levels, 4: 12–13 (grades 2.0–4.2), 14–16 (grades 3.6–7.2), 17–19 (grades 6.6–10.2), and 20–22 (grades 9.6–12.9 and adults).
Price Data, 1994: $33.65 per examination kit including 1 sample writing book for each prompt (includes examples of reading-related and independent prompts, sample administration and scoring manual, Writing Assessment Guide (83 pages), and Student Information and Score Sheet); $31.15 per 30 books with reading passages; $24.50 per 30 books without reading passages; $13.25 per 50 Student Information and Score Sheets; $14.85 per 50 Optional Writing answer sheets; $9.55 per manual; $19.65 per Writing Assessment Guide; $4.61 per student for Holistic or Analytic Scoring by publisher; $5.84 per student for holistic scoring combined with 1 analytic score (Professional Reports from local scoring); $.61 per student's Individual Test Record/Writing; $.34 per class record sheet/writing; $.46 per frequency distribution/writing.
Comments: Includes books 1–32 with a writing assignment called a "prompt"; each book comes with its own manual; books are available as separates; overall guide is entitled *Writing Assessment Guide*.
Author: CTB Macmillan/McGraw-Hill.
Publisher: CTB Macmillan/McGraw-Hill.

a) LEVEL 12–13.
Population: Grades 2.0–4.2
Time: 30–35 (35–40) minutes.
Comments: 4 books (Personal Expression—Descriptive [Books 1 & 4], Personal Expression—Narrative [Books 2 & 3]) available as separates.
b) LEVEL 14–16.
Population: Grades 3.6–7.2.
Time: 30–35 (35–40) minutes.
Comments: 8 books (Personal Expression—Descriptive [Books 5 & 8], Personal Expression—Narrative [Books 6 & 7], and Informative [Books 9–12]) available as separates.
c) LEVEL 17–19.
Population: Grades 6.6–10.2.
Time: 40–45 (45–50) minutes.
Comments: 10 books (Personal Expression—Narrative [Books 13 & 14], Informative [Books 15–18], Persuasive [Books 19–22]) available as separates.
d) LEVEL 20–22.
Population: Grades 9.6–12.9.
Time: 40–45 (45–50) minutes.
Comments: 10 books (Personal Expression—Narrative [Books 23 & 24], Informative [Books 25–28], Persuasive [Books 29–32]) available as separates.

Review of the CTB Writing Assessment System by GEORGE ENGELHARD, JR., *Professor of Educational Studies, Emory University, Atlanta, GA:*

The CTB Writing Assessment System (WAS) provides direct and indirect measures for evaluating students' writing abilities. Indirect measures of writing skills based on multiple-choice items are available from CTB as a part of the language arts subtests of CTB's norm-referenced tests. The focus of this review is on the evaluation of the direct writing component of the WAS; the WAS has not been reviewed previously in a *Mental Measurements Yearbook*. The manual also provides some suggested activities for teaching writing that are not reviewed here.

The WAS was designed for use in evaluating writing programs and students' writing ability. It consists of 32 prompts (called books in the manual) designed to measure writing ability from grade 2.0 through grade 12.9 and adults. Three modes of discourse are represented: personal expression (descriptive and narrative), informative, and persuasive. Some of the prompts include a reading passage (reading-related prompts), whereas other prompts do not include a reading passage (independent prompt).

Holistic scoring on 4-point, 6-point, and 8-point scales is available, as well as Analytic scoring on a 4-point scale for the following domains: Content,

Organization, Sentence Construction, Vocabulary/ Grammar, and Spelling/Capitalization. Even though several scoring options are available, the 6-point scale receives the most attention in the manual; for example, it is the only scoring system with norms and information regarding rater agreement. According to the manual, the Holistic scores are obtained from two raters and averaged, whereas the Analytic scores are usually obtained from one rater. The recommended use of a single rater for the Analytic scores is a concern. Because the Analytic scores are more likely to be used for individual evaluation and feedback, these scores require a high level of precision and accuracy.

The score reports are nicely organized with descriptive phrases used to illustrate the meaning of the score points. Ratings of "0" are assigned to papers that are illegible, off topic, primarily in another language, and insufficient sample to evaluate, whereas papers with no response are not scored. The use of a "0" rating may be problematic because it does not mean that the examinee has no writing ability. It should not be a problem for individual assessments, but it may be a problem if summary statistics (e.g., means and standard deviations) are used to evaluate a writing program. Information regarding the standard error of measurement should be added to the score reports for individual examinees.

National percentiles, NCEs, and stanines are only provided for the 6-point Holistic scores on each prompt. These normative data were obtained from a CTB norming study conducted in 1991. The prompts were administered along with the CTBS/4 Language Expression test. Each prompt was calibrated using the 2 Parameter Partial Credit (2PPC) model. The 2PPC model is a two-facet IRT model (writing ability and prompt facets) that includes a scale or "item discrimination" parameter. According to the manual, each prompt was placed on a Language Expression scale. Insufficient detail is provided regarding the design of this normative study. Given the difficulties of equating performance assessments (Gordon, Engelhard, Gabrielson, & Bernknopf, 1996), much more detail is needed on how the prompts included in the WAS were calibrated and equated. Some of the questions that are not addressed in the manual are as follows: Were the prompts randomly assigned to students within classrooms? How were the prompts equated? How successful was the calibration? Were the multiple-choice items and prompts jointly calibrated onto the Language Expression scale? In addition to these questions, information regarding model-data fit is required in order to evaluate the adequacy of the 2PPC for these data. No indices of model-data fit are provided in the manual. Information regarding model-data fit is essential because the norms are not based on observed scores but on an estimated frequency distribution of scores. No demographic information is supplied regarding the normative sample.

The manual reports rater agreement indices for holistic scoring that are typical of those obtained in large-scale direct writing assessments. The proportion of perfect rater agreement ranges from .41 to .75 with a median of .58, whereas adjacent score agreement between raters ranged from .93 to 1.00 with a median of .98. The correlations between rater scores (interrater reliability) ranged from .50 to .82 with a median of .71. No information is provided for the analytic scores regarding rater agreement or interrater reliability.

Scores in writing assessment may be affected by a variety of factors in addition to student writing ability. Some of the factors that may influence student scores are variation in prompt difficulty, rater severity, and student characteristics related to subgroup membership. Generalizability theory provides one conceptual framework for examining the influences of these additional variables (Cronbach, Linn, Brennan, & Haertel, 1997). Rasch measurement theory provides another framework for examining multifaceted direct writing assessment systems (Du & Wright, 1997; Engelhard, 1992). Potential users of the WAS should have this type of psychometric information to aid in the evaluation of the WAS.

Establishing the validity of the scores obtained from direct writing assessments is challenging. In support of the validity of the scores, the manual provides the intercorrelations between Holistic scores on three prompts with reading scores (Vocabulary, Comprehension, and Total) and language scores (Mechanics, Expression, Total) from the CTBS/4. Sample sizes range from about 400 to 700 depending on the grade level and prompt. The obtained correlations are comparable to what would be expected for these types of validity coefficients. For example, the median correlation of the 6-point holistic scores with Language Total scores was .50, and with Reading Total scores, .49. The median correlation among the prompt scores was .54. The potential user should note that some of the correlations reported are not based on the final prompts included in the WAS. No evidence regarding the consequential validity is provided. No information is provided on whether or not the prompts were statistically examined for bias related to race, sex, native language, ethnic origin, or geographic region.

Appropriate guidelines are provided for the sound administration of the WAS. Each prompt has a separate administration and scoring manual. The directions to the teachers are easy to understand and give enough detail to allow the examiner to replicate the standardized conditions used to obtain the norms and validity data. Directions and training are also available for local scoring of papers. Only one anchor paper is provided for each score point (6-point Holistic scale). This is an insufficient number of anchor papers to train raters; no anchor papers are provided to illustrate the 4-point Analytic scales. Overall, the administration and scoring manual is clearly written and should be easy even for a novice to follow.

In summary, the WAS reflects sound professional test development, administration, and scoring strategies, and offers a useful direct measure of writing ability. However, missing technical information, such as how the prompts were equated and a clear description of the demographic characteristics of the normative sample, makes it difficult to evaluate the psychometric quality of the WAS. In spite of these weaknesses, the WAS offers a viable alternative to users who are not able to invest in the local development of a direct writing system. As with other standardized assessments, the user should carefully consider the match between local instructional goals for student writing and the WAS.

REVIEWER'S REFERENCES

Engelhard, G. (1992). The measurement of writing ability with a many-faceted Rasch model. *Applied Measurement in Education, 5*(3), 171–191.

Gordon, B., Engelhard, G., Gabrielson, S., & Bernknopf, S. (1996). Conceptual issues in equating performance assessments: Lessons from writing assessment. *Journal of Research and Development in Education, 29*(2), 81–88.

Cronbach, L. J., Linn, R. L., Brennan, R. L., & Haertel, E. (1997). Generalizability analysis for performance assessments of student achievement or school effectiveness. *Educational and Psychological Measurement, 57*, 373–399.

Du, Y., & Wright, B. D. (1997). Effects of student characteristics in a large-scale direct writing assessment. In M. Wilson, G. Engelhard, & K. Draney (Eds.), *Objective measurement: Theory into practice* (vol. 4), 1–24. Norwood, NJ: Ablex.

Review of the CTB Writing Assessment System by JOE B. HANSEN, Executive Director, Planning, Research and Evaluation, Colorado Springs School District Eleven, Colorado Springs, CO:

The publisher, CTB Macmillan/McGraw-Hill presents this writing assessment as a "system" rather than a test, because it provides both direct and indirect (multiple-choice) measures of writing performance, if and only if the writing assessment is administered with one of CTB's other multiple-choice language tests. It is difficult to ascertain exactly why it warrants the designation of system, when either component can be used independently of the other. The Writing Assessment System (WAS) comes with a comprehensive guide (79 pages), administration and scoring manual, and 32 writing books for use with various prompts and grade levels. The guide contains descriptive information about the assessment and preparing students to become better writers and test takers.

DESCRIPTION. The purpose of the WAS is not only to assess student proficiency in written composition, but also to provide diagnostic data for instructional use. The Holistic ratings can be used to assess individual and group performance, and the Analytic scores are intended for use in identifying specific strengths and weaknesses for individuals and groups. Given this complex purpose, the design characteristics of the WAS was generally consistent with expectations, based on other available writing assessment products. The Holistic scoring guide makes use of a 6-point scale, whereas the Analytic scoring guide uses a 4-point scale. Both scoring guides have well-written descriptors that appear to be relatively easy to teach from or to use in local scoring sessions.

The WAS has four levels covering grades 2.0 through 12.9 and adults. Administration times vary from 30 to 45 minutes depending on prompt, category, and level. It covers three categories of writing: personal expression, which includes both narrative and descriptive; informative/expository; and persuasive. Although scoring options include both Holistic and Analytic, norms are available for Holistic scoring only.

NORMS AND SCORING OPTIONS. Norms were produced as part of the 1991 CTB norming study and are included in the Writing Assessment Guide. The 2 Parameter Partial Credit Model (2PPC) was used to scale the responses on CTB's Language Expression Scale. The norms tables provide percentile ranks, stanines, and NCEs for each raw score point, 0 through 6. A zero score is awarded only if a response is off topic, illegible, provides an insufficient sample to evaluate, or is in a language other than English.

The norming information provided in the Writing Assessment Guide, which also serves as the technical manual, does not include any information on sampling procedure, sample sizes, participation rates, sampling error, or any other information necessary to evaluate the representativeness, or the demographic or geographic characteristics of the norming sample. Therefore, the user is missing information crucial to the evaluation and selection process. Readers are referred to the CAT-5 Technical Study for this information. This lack of information about the norming process is annoying at best and could be viewed by some potential users of the WAS as an attempt to discourage an analysis of the norming sample and procedure.

The availability of norms for holistic scoring is advantageous, but more information should be made available to potential users about the norming sample. It is not clear from the information provided in either The Guide or the CAT-5 Technical Manual exactly how the WAS norms were derived. The sampling procedures for norming the CAT-5 appear to be more than adequate for obtaining a nationally representative sample, but no specific information is provided on how the WAS norms were derived.

Prompts were field tested on a sample of 13,000 students in the fall of 1991. Each normed prompt was tried out on approximately 500 students and each non-normed prompt was tried out on approximately 150 students, according to the Guide.

RELIABILITY. The Guide provides three indices of interrater agreement, one showing the proportion of cases for which the two primary raters were in perfect agreement on the 7-point scale; a second showing the proportion of cases for which the raters differed by no more than 1 point; and a third showing the product moment correlation between the two ratings. Zero scores are not included in the calculations of the indices.

The proportion of cases receiving perfect agreement range from .408 to .752, with a median of .584. Agreement within one score point ranges from .926 to 1.000, with a median of .983. When the product moment correlation is used as the reliability index, the range is .501 to .821 with a median of .710. The question of whether these reliability indices are high enough is largely a matter of judgment. Holistic scoring may result in slightly lower interrater agreement than Analytic, due to the need to address a broader range of factors in the scoring process, thereby introducing more error variance due to increased subjectivity. In general, these indices appear to be within the expected ranges for holistically scored writing assessments.

VALIDITY. The Guide provides intercorrelations between Holistically scored prompts and scores on the Language and Reading tests of the CTBS/4. These could be viewed as validity indices, although the publisher is careful to avoid labeling them as such.

Nevertheless, they are the only data available to the potential user for evaluating validity. The median of 48 correlations with the CTBS/4 Language test was .50. The median correlation with Reading was .49. Of course, one would not expect extremely high correlations between writing, a constructive cognitive process, and performance on these more traditional assessments of language knowledge and use. Unfortunately, no data are provided on the relationship between performance on this writing assessment and other direct writing assessments. Therefore, the potential user must accept on faith the precept that this assessment is appropriate and technically adequate as a measure of writing proficiency.

Also missing from the data provided is any analysis of differential performance across ethnic or gender groups. Because direct writing assessment is often thought of as the quintessential performance assessment, this is a potential concern for users. Once again, this concern would be easier to address if the norming sample data and subpopulation statistics were provided with the rest of the product information.

TEST ADMINISTRATION. Extensive, detailed instructions are provided for answer sheet preparation for either local or publisher scoring. The instructions include scheduling advice for effective testing (e.g., don't schedule on Monday or Friday, avoid days just before or after major school functions). They also include instructions for preparing the students for the testing experience. The instructions are clear and easy to follow, and a copy of a blank answer sheet is included for reference. However, in one or two instances, it would be helpful for the person filling in the identification information to have a completed example rather than a blank form.

Administration directions are well scripted and easy to follow. The sample kit evaluated included an administration and scoring manual for Level 17–19, which corresponds to grade levels 6.6 to 10.2. The language and sentence length used in the script seem appropriate for the intended student audience. Appropriate information is provided on timing and the handling of materials.

SCORING AND REPORTING. Two scoring and reporting options are provided. The user may elect to: (a) have the publisher score and report results, or (b) score locally, but send the results to the publisher for reporting. There is no provision for local scoring and reporting. If local scoring is chosen extensive training is needed. The Administration and

Scoring Manual provides detailed instructions for organizing and conducting the training. These instructions are quite thorough and include sample materials to be copied and used in the training.

SUMMARY. The CTB WAS is designed to provide both individual diagnostic data and group performance data on writing proficiency for grades 2 through adult. It makes use of both direct (constructed response) and indirect (multiple-choice) measures to accomplish its purposes. Writing exercises may be scored either holistically or analytically. Reliability appears to be adequate, although not particularly high, especially for the Holistic scoring approach.

Limited availability of data on validity makes independent evaluation of validity difficult. Lack of information on norming procedures is also a problem for those wanting to evaluate the quality of the norms.

Both local and publisher scoring options are available, although users should be advised that local scoring requires extensive training. This is often the case for direct writing assessments.

Direct writing assessment (dwa) can be a valuable instructional tool. Unfortunately, the number of commercially available dwas is small compared to other basic skills assessments. The CTB WAS would seem to offer an acceptable alternative for schools or districts who do not wish to develop their own.

[89]
Defense Mechanisms Inventory [Revised].

Purpose: To "measure and predict responses to conflict and threat."
Population: Adults and college students.
Publication Dates: 1968–1993.
Acronym: DMI.
Scores, 5: Turning Against Object, Projection, Principalization, Turning Against Self, Reversal.
Administration: Individual.
Forms: 2 forms (Male, Female) for each of 3 versions (Adolescent, Adult, Elderly).
Price Data, 1997: $129 per DMI Introductory Kit including administration manual ('93, 147 pages), clinical manual ('93, 126 pages), 20 reusable adult test booklets (10 male and 10 female), 25 answer sheets, set of 5 scoring keys, 25 adult profile forms, and the supplementary bibliography; $31 per 10 male and 10 female reusable test booklets (specify Adult [A], Elderly [E], or Adolescent [Y]); $11 per 25 answer sheets; $14 per 25 profile forms (specify Adult or College); $14 per 5 scoring templates; $14 per supplemental bibliography.
Time: (30–45) minutes.
Comments: Title of administration manual is Defense Mechanisms: Their Classification, Correlates, and Mea-

surement with the Defense Mechanisms Inventory; title of clinical manual is Defenses in Psychotherapy: The Clinical Application of the Defense Mechanisms Inventory.
Authors: David Ihilevich and Goldine C. Gleser.
Publisher: Psychological Assessment Resources, Inc.
Cross References: See T4:723 (15 references); for a review by James J. Hennessy of the earlier edition, see 10:79 (8 references); see also T3:665 (14 references), 8:534 (30 references), and T2:1152 (5 references); for a review by James A. Walsh, see 7:63 (4 references).

TEST REFERENCES
1. Labourie-Vief, G., Hakim-Larson, J., & Hobart, C. J. (1987). Age, ego level, and the life-span development of coping and defense processes. *Psychology and Aging, 2*, 286-293.
2. Noam, G. G., Recklitis, C. J., & Paget, K. F. (1991). Pathways of ego development: Contributions to maladaptation and adjustment. *Development and Psychopathology, 3*, 311-328.
3. Aronoff, J., Stollak, G. E., & Woike, B. A. (1994). Affect regulation and the breadth of interpersonal engagement. *Journal of Personality and Social Psychology, 67*, 105-114.
4. Fukunishi, I., Numata, Y., & Hattori, M. (1994). Alexithymia and defense mechanisms in myocardial infarction. *Psychological Reports, 75*, 219-223.
5. Juni, S. (1994). Measurement of defenses in special populations: Revision of the Defense Mechanisms Inventory. *Journal of Research in Personality, 28*, 230-244.
6. Juni, S., & Grimm, D. W. (1994). Sex roles as factors in defense mechanisms and object relations. *The Journal of Genetic Psychology, 155*, 99-106.
7. Tasca, G. A., Russell, V., & Busby, K. (1994). Characteristics of patients who choose between two types of group therapy. *International Journal of Group Psychotherapy, 44*, 499–508.
8. Woike, B. A., Aronoff, J., Stollak, G. E., & Loraas, J. A. (1994). Links between intrapsychic and interpersonal defenses in dyadic interaction. *Journal of Research in Personality, 28*, 101-113.
9. Recklitis, C. J., Yap, L., & Noam, G. G. (1995). Development of a short form of the adolescent version of the Defense Mechanisms Inventory. *Journal of Personality Assessment, 64*, 360-370.
10. Whyne-Berman, S. M., & McCann, J. T. (1995). Defense mechanisms and personality disorders: An empirical test of Millon's theory. *Journal of Personality Assessment, 64*, 132-144.
11. Diehl, M., Coyle, N., & Labouvie-Vief, G. (1996). Age and sex difference in strategies of coping and defense across the life span. *Psychology and Aging, 11*, 127–139.
12. Layman, M. J., Gidycz, C. A., & Lynn, S. J. (1996). Unacknowledged versus acknowledged rape victims: Situational factors and posttraumatic stress. *Journal of Abnormal Psychology, 105*, 124–131.

Review of the Defense Mechanisms Inventory [Revised] by KEVIN D. CREHAN, Associate Professor of Educational Psychology, University of Nevada—Las Vegas, Las Vegas, NV:

The Defense Mechanisms Inventory [Revised] (DMI) is a paper-and-pencil test designed to yield scores on five groupings of ego-defense strategies. The scales are labeled Turning Against Object (TAO), Projection (PRO), Principalization (PRN), Turning Against Self (TAS), and Reversal (REV). The inventory consists of 10 popular conflict scenarios related to authority, independence, competition, sexual identity, and situations. Two of each type of conflict situation are presented in brief narratives. Respondents are asked to reply to the scenarios by selecting their most and least likely reaction as to what is projected they would actually do, what they would (in fantasy) impulsively do, what thought might occur to them, and how they would feel. Five optional responses are provided with each alternative keyed to one of the five ego-defense groupings (i.e., TAO, PRO, PRN, TAS, and REV). Total scores for each ego-defense grouping are determined by awarding 2 points for the defense reaction selected as most likely, 1 point for the three reactions not selected, and zero points for the reaction selected as least likely. A total ipsative score for each of the five ego-defense groupings is determined by summing over the four projections (i.e., actual, impulsive, thought, and feel). The profile that emerges among the five defense mechanism groupings is the primary focus of interpretation. Six versions of the instrument target male and female subjects at three age levels: youth, adult, and elderly. The six versions differ only in that the scenarios are altered to be sex and age appropriate for the target population.

The DMI is designed for clinical use by therapists familiar with "the psychoanalytic theory of defense mechanisms" (p. 1). In support of this application, a clinical manual is provided, which focuses on implications of DMI profiles for therapeutic intervention with emotionally disturbed, nonpsychotic adult outpatients. The clinical manual provides interpretations for profiles high on each of the five defense mechanisms and for five profiles high on two of the defense scales. An additional seven interpretations are furnished for profiles categorized as moderate, low, or flat. The basis for the profiles is a disaggregation of data from 221 male and 259 female outpatients from two samples. Separate profiles are given for males and females. In addition to the DMI profiles, MMPI and 16PF profiles are presented for each profile type. Sample sizes for the MMPI and 16PF profiles are smaller because not all subjects responded to these instruments. The discussion of each of the 10 profiles characterized as high on one or two defense scales includes a profile analysis, a composite clinical picture, a dynamic formulation, guidelines for therapeutic intervention, and contraindicated therapeutic interventions.

In addition to the clinical manual, the authors provide a separate document that presents an extensive review of theoretical and empirical literature on defense mechanisms and measures of defense mechanisms including the DMI among others. This document includes DMI administration and scoring procedures in an appendix.

A common criticism of the DMI is the ipsative nature of scoring. For example, Cooper and Kline (1982) observed that the forced-choice format of the DMI causes the five defense scales to be interdependent. Because the sum of the five subscale scores is always 200, the score on any one subscale can be determined by the remaining four subscale scores. Correlations among the subscales taken together are, therefore, negative. Cooper and Kline point out that this problem clouds the interpretation of intercorrelations among DMI scales and confounds interpretation of correlations of DMI scores with other measures. The DMI authors address this concern in their monograph. They explain their preference of forced-choice over free-choice formats by pointing out their desire to provide a profile of defense mechanisms rather than a level of defensiveness. The DMI authors also cite the difficulty of acquiescent response sets as a concern with the free-choice format.

Norms are provided for male and female samples of high school students, college students, and "general" adults. Raw scores are converted to standard T scores (not normalized) on the profile sheets. The authors acknowledge the obvious problems of using ipsative scores to develop norm tables but offer arguable justification for doing so. The adult norms were used to provide cut scores for the profile classifications presented in the clinical manual. The general adult male ($n = 558$) and female ($n = 438$) norms consist of an aggregate of subjects from a number of nonrandom data collections in a variety of locations. The male norm group averages 42 years old and the female group averages 30 years old. Differences in level of education between the genders also appear to exist with males having a higher level. The effect of the happenstance nature of the samples used for the norms on profile classification is undetermined.

A number of studies reported reliability estimates of internal consistency and/or stability for the five defense mechanism scales. These internal consistency reliability estimates are generally acceptable for a self-report measure of typical behavior ranging from around .80 for the TAO scale to around .60 for the PRO scale. However, because the clinical manual provides interpretive recommendations for profiles, the stability of profile classification is the important consideration. One study of repeatability of profile classification is reported in the clinical manual. Ninety-four women were observed three times with 6-month intervals between observations. Only 18% of profile classifications were the same on all three occasions, 52% were the same on two of three occasions, and the remaining 30% were different on all occasions.

The monograph's validity chapter presents a variety of studies related to direct and indirect evidence of validity for the DMI. Content evidence includes two studies where judges classified DMI responses by defense type. Satisfactory agreement between judges' classification of responses keyed to the PRN, TAS, and REV scales was observed. Percent agreement for these three scales ranged from 61% to 80% over the two studies. Agreements in judges' classifications and responses keyed to the TAO and PRO scales were 45% or lower.

The factor structure of the DMI is investigated by a principal-component analysis reported in the monograph. The results of this analysis support a two-factor empirical structure for the DMI rather than the nominal five-factor theoretical model. Other researchers (e.g., Juni, 1994) report factor analytic results that fail to replicate the theoretical five-scale structure.

The monograph's validity chapter continues with summarization of a number of studies that are, at best, loosely related to the intended clinical application of DMI profile interpretation. Although the reported studies provide correlational evidence of correspondence between DMI scale scores and other measures of similar constructs, there are also correlations that are inconsistent with expectations. In summary, the validity evidence is equivocal.

A separate monograph chapter addresses predictive evidence of the DMI for the outcomes of: alcoholics remaining in outpatient treatment, continuation in treatment and weight loss for obese subjects, survival of coronary patients, and symptom reduction for patients with acute stress reaction. The reported results of these studies were either not in support of the predictive power of the DMI or appear to be flavored with post hoc interpretation.

The major addition to the DMI since it was last reviewed by Hennessy (1989; 10:79) is the clinical manual. The DMI authors provide guidelines for therapeutic interventions and contraindicated interventions with each of the major DMI profile interpretations. In their introduction, the authors appropriately claim no validity for these guidelines. The profile types are based on a median of 8 subjects for the male profiles and 12 subjects for the female profiles and, as noted earlier, evidence of profile stability is weak. In their concluding remarks, the DMI authors characterize the clinical descriptions and therapeutic recommendations as preliminary and suggestive. This reviewer would add premature as descriptive of these recommendations because there is insufficient evidence to support the profile interpretations and suggested interventions provided in the clinical manual.

The DMI is ambitious in its attempt to measure the likely subconscious defensive reactions to frustrating situations using a paper-pencil self-report instrument. A considerable amount of research on the psychometric characteristics of the instrument has been conducted. Several of these studies have suggested revisions in scoring and/or scale interpretations. The DMI authors might be advised to look to efforts toward revision rather than expanded clinical utilization of their instrument. The DMI remains a tool for research applications.

REVIEWER'S REFERENCES

Cooper, C., & Kline, P. (1982). A validation of the Defence [sic] Mechanism Inventory. *British Journal of Medical Psychology, 55*, 209–214.
Hennessy, J. J. (1989). [Review of the Defense Mechanisms Inventory]. In J. C. Conoley & J. J. Kramer (Eds.), *The tenth mental measurements yearbook* (pp. 226–228). Lincoln, NE: Buros Institute of Mental Measurements.
Juni, S. (1994). Measurement of defenses in special populations: Revision of the Defense Mechanisms Inventory. *Journal of Research in Personality, 28*, 230–244.

Review of the Defense Mechanisms Inventory [Revised] by LIZANNE DeSTEFANO, Professor of Educational Psychology, University of Illinois at Urbana-Champaign, Champaign, IL:

INTRODUCTION. The purpose of the Defense Mechanisms Inventory [Revised] (DMI) is to measure and predict adults' defensive responses to conflict situations. Whereas prior editions were appropriate for research purposes only, the authors support the use of the revised DMI for use with clinical populations. Based on psychoanalytic theory and the work of Lazarus and Folkman (1984), Haan (1977), French, Doehrman, Davis-Sacks, and Vinokur (1983), Menninger (1963), Caplan (1966), Horowitz (1976), and the research of the authors (Ihilevich & Gleser, 1971), the DMI uses a two-tiered conceptual model to classify responses to threat. Responses first are analyzed in terms of three global categories: problem-solving responses, coping strategies, and defense mechanisms. Problem-solving responses are further separated into two categories: those aimed at changing oneself and those aimed at changing the environment. The DMI produces a profile of five defense styles: Turning Against Object (TAO), Projection (PRO), Principalization (PRN), Turning Against Self (TAS), and Reversal (REV). In addition to the adult form, restricted use research versions of the DMI for adolescents and senior citizens are available.

ADMINISTRATION, SCORING, AND INTERPRETATION. The first volume of the DMI manual, *Defense Mechanisms: Their Classification, Correlates, and Measurement with the Defense Mechanism Inventory*, serves as a technical guide. The volume contains information on the administration, standardization, validity, and reliability of the DMI. The second volume, *Defenses in Psychotherapy: The Clinical Application of the Defense Mechanism Inventory*, presents a preliminary classification of standard score profiles, comparison with MMPI and Cattell's 16 PF profiles, and suggestions for therapeutic interventions. Limited administration and scoring instructions are included in Appendix A of the technical guide. The DMI consists of 10 brief vignettes (2 vignettes for each of five areas of conflict) followed by four standard questions: What would your actual reaction be? What would you impulsively (in fantasy) want to do? What thought might occur to you? How would you feel and why? The questions represent different levels of defense: actual behavior, feeling, fantasy behavior, and thought. Conflicts portrayed are: situational, authority, independence, competition, and masculinity/femininity. Examinees are required to read each vignette and indicate one of five responses to each question as most representative of how they would react and another as least representative.

Administration of a full DMI takes from 30 to 45 minutes. Hand scoring can be completed in approximately 5 minutes using a set of templates. T-scores for each of the five scales are obtained easily by plotting the raw scores on the profile sheet. Separate profiles are available for males and females. The DMI Profile serves as the basis for test interpretation.

Norms are presented for different groups defined by age and sex. The authors address the criticism of the use of norms with a forced-choice test, but they do not discuss the severe limitations of their norming process and the resulting norms. DMI norms were obtained by aggregating the results of several independent research studies conducted between 1968 and 1982 by different investigators at different universities with different samples. Little information is presented about the samples, although most were made up of undergraduate students. Norms based on even smaller samples of high school students and the "general population" are also presented as are norms based on a very small and oddly composed group of black and white participants. Norms are presented as unweighted means and standard deviations for each of the five scales. Although there is some consistency in central tendency and variability across the many subsamples that constitute the norms, the tremendous limitations of the norm group render the norms useless for anything but the most gross group interpretation. They have no clinical use for individual diagnosis.

The profiles presented in the second volume were based primarily on two sources: outpatients seen at community mental health centers in Ohio and Michigan from 1965 to 1972 and patients seen in private practice by one of the authors from 1987 to 1990. A group of 94 clients seen at a Planned Parenthood clinic make up a third source for the female profiles. Once again, the arbitrary nature of the samples severely limits the utility of the profiles for clinical use. The formation of these profiles seems somewhat arbitrary and without clear psychometric, clinical, or theoretical justification.

Chapters III through XII of the second volume present, for each defense style defined by a profile: summaries of research studies; comparisons with MMPI, Cattell's 16 PF, and other assessment data based on very small samples; clinical interpretations; and guidelines for intervention.

STANDARDIZATION AND PSYCHOMETRIC PROPERTIES. As stated earlier, the DMI did not undergo formal standardization. Norms in the form of unweighted means and standard deviations are based on aggregated data from several research studies conducted on diverse samples over a considerable period of time. Internal consistency of the scale scores was investigated in six studies, producing an overall mean of .72. Test-retest reliability of scale scores (over a 2- to 4-week period) was investigated in four studies, yielding an overall mean of .73. Stability of profiles over time is quite poor, especially for middle range profiles.

Large numbers of research studies by the authors and others are presented as evidence of the content, construct, concurrent, and criterion-related validity of the instrument. Factor analytic studies support the conceptualization and classification of defenses that underlie the DMI. Studies that investigate the relationship between the various scales of the DMI and other psychological constructs, assessment information, clinical conditions, adaptive functioning, or demographic variables are so numerous and involve such diverse (clinical and nonclinical) samples that clear implications are difficult to draw. It does appear, however, that there is substantial research evidence to support the concurrent validity of the DMI classification system and individual DMI scales. Most of these studies involve the use of individual scale scores, so the validity of profiles or norms remains largely untested. There is very little evidence supporting the predictive validity of the DMI.

SUMMARY. The classification system and scale scores of the DMI have been used extensively in research with clinical and nonclinical populations as a measure of responses to perceived threats. The relationship between the various scales of the DMI and other psychological constructs, assessment information, clinical conditions, adaptive functioning, or demographic variables is well documented in the research literature. However, the clinical profiles and the norms upon which they are based are technically flawed, severely limiting their use for individual diagnosis and treatment planning. The DMI profiles are based on very small and unrepresentative samples. They do not meet generally accepted standards for stability over time. Much more research is needed before these profiles can be used for clinical purposes.

REVIEWER'S REFERENCES

Menninger, K. (1963). *The vital balance.* New York: Viking Press.
Caplan, G. (1964). *Principles of preventive psychiatry.* New York: Basic Books.
Ihilevich, D., & Gleser, G. C. (1971). Relationship of defense mechanisms to field dependence-independence. *Journal of Abnormal Psychology, 77,* 296–302.
Horowitz, M. J. (1976). *Stress response syndromes.* New York: Jason Aronson.
Haan, N. (1977). *Coping and defending.* New York: Academic Press.
French, J. R. P., Doehrman, S. R., Davis-Sacks, M. L., & Vinokur, A. (1983). *Career change in mid-life: Stress, social support, and adjustment.* Ann Arbor, MI: Institute for Social Research.
Lazarus, R. S., & Folkman, S. (1984). *Stress, appraisal and coping.* New York: Springer.

[90]
Degrees of Word Meaning.

Purpose: Developed to "assess the size of students' reading vocabularies by measuring their understanding of the meaning of words in naturally occurring contexts."
Population: Grades 3–8.
Publication Date: 1993.
Acronym: DWM.
Scores: Total score only.
Administration: Group.
Levels: 6 overlapping levels.
Price Data, 1994: $31.25 per user's manual (96 pages); $15.75 per 5 test administration procedures; $41 per 30 test booklets (select level); $10.50 per 30 practice booklets; $13.25 per 30 NCS answer sheets; $12.25 per scoring key (select level).
Time: Untimed.
Author: Touchstone Applied Science Associates (TASA), Inc.
Publisher: Touchstone Applied Science Associates (TASA), Inc.

Review of the Degrees of Word Meaning by DAVID P. HURFORD, Director of the Center for the Assessment and Remediation of Reading Difficulties and Associate Professor of Psychology and Counseling, Pittsburg State University, Pittsburg, KS:

The Degrees of Word meaning (DWM) along with its companion test, the Degrees of Reading Power (DRP; 12:101), form the assessment component of the Degrees of Literacy Power Program. This program is designed to assess students' development of literacy with regard to: (a) ability to comprehend surface meaning of increasingly difficult textual material; (b) ability to analyze, evaluate, and extend the ideas that are presented in increasingly difficult textual material; and (c) reading vocabulary.

The goal of the Degrees of Literacy Power Program is to assist in increasing literacy and comprehension by providing teachers, parents, and administrators with information concerning a student's literacy and strategies for increasing the student's abilities. As an example, Touchstone Applied Science Associates (TASA) created the Parent Involvement Program that parents can use to promote literacy based on their child's score(s) from the DWM and/or DRP.

The DWM is specifically concerned with measuring reading vocabulary, which it does by assessing a student's knowledge of the meaning of a word as it appears within its naturally occurring context. That is, the test has been constructed so that word meaning must be determined by reading a sentence with the target word embedded therein. The rationale for this type of test rests with the concept of *effectiveness measures,* which is strongly concerned that measures tap an individual's ability to perform in the "real world." Given the present concern with education's ability to prepare students for careers, the business world, and higher education, the goal of tapping real world behavior seems justified and long overdue. In addition, vocabulary development in students has long been associated with academic success and achievement. The DWM relates test performance to real world measures, which is defensible as an outcomes measure.

The DWM has six levels of Form M, which are available for grades 3 through 8 along with a practice form (Y-7) to acquaint the student with the format of the test. The suggested levels for Form M for each grade are as follows: M-7, grades 3 and 4; M-6, grades 4 and 5; M-5, grades 5 and 6; M-4, grades 6 and 7; M-3, grades 7 and 8; and M-2, grades 8 and above. The levels are approximate in that any level of the DWM can be given to any grade level, providing that there are enough difficult items to assess the higher achieving students and enough easy items to assess the lower achieving students. The results of all levels of the DWM are reported on the same scale. The DWM is intended to be group administered and it has no time limit. The authors suggest that most students will be able to complete the DWM in approximately 45 minutes. However, it was strongly emphasized that some students may not be able to complete the test within that time frame. These students must be provided the opportunity to finish the test, preferably with a single, but extended session. Each of the DWM tests consists of 40 multiple-choice items. Each item has nine response choices. All DWM test booklets are reusable and can be either hand or machine scored.

One of the most impressive aspects of the DWM pertains to its development. The developers of the DWM conducted the most recent and comprehensive word frequency count to date: the American Printed School English Corpus. This corpus includes 17 million tokens (total number of words) and 164,000 types (number of different words). Each word was then assigned a Standard Frequency Index (SFI) score, which indicates the frequency of the word relative to the number of different content areas in which the word can be found. The words "the," "and," and "is," for example, have SFI scores of 80 and have approximate frequencies of 10,000 per million words. On the other extreme, "acclimate," "orthogonal," and "spatulate" have SFI scores of less than 20 and have frequencies per million words of .01. SFI scores can be used to estimate the size of an individual's reading vocabulary. Because larger scores are typically assumed to reflect better test performance, the SFI scores are transformed ([100 - SFI] x 10). For example, higher frequency words with SFIs of 80 would have DWM test scores of 200 [(100-80) x 10]; lower frequency words with SFIs of 20 would have DWM test scores of 800 [(100-20) x 10]. With the use of a table, DWM scores are easily derived from raw scores and range approximately between 200 and 800. The test manual has tables that provide the estimated size of reading vocabulary, percentile ranks, normal curve equivalents, and stanines for each DWM score. Raw scores less than 5 are highlighted on the raw score to DWM score conversion table to emphasize that scores this low, essentially at chance performance, might be indicative of guessing.

Approximately 16,500 students, fourth through the eighth grade, were involved with the norming study. Each student in the norming sample took the eight calibration test forms. The standardization sample was created by taking a random, stratified sample of New York State schools rather than including several states; however, the standardization sample was similar to the national census for ethnicity, socioeconomic status, and percentage of students in private versus public education.

The primary source of establishing validity was that of construct validity. The DWM was created to determine the approximate size of an individual's reading vocabulary. The DWM scores, as reported above, are linear transformations that reflect the SFI score and thus, the estimated size of one's reading vocabulary. Given the careful construction of the American Printed School English Corpus, and the use of SFI scores, it would seem that construct validity evidence is intact. However, examinations of the relationship between the DWM and other tests that purport to assess reading vocabulary were not reported. Estimates of internal consistency reliabilities for each grade level (4–8) and calibration test form ranged from .83 to .94 (M = .89.9) and split-half reliability coefficients by grade and calibration form from .84 to .96 (M = 91.0). The DWM was also assessed for test-biased items. Each item has been assessed for test bias for gender, ethnicity, socioeconomic status, and student ability. In addition, the DWM test scores were assessed with the Rasch model. Item difficulty fit very well across the various groups with the Rasch model, suggesting that there was little support for test bias. The range of Rasch item difficulty correlations across the groups was .96 to .99 (M = .98).

One of the strengths of the DWM is its overall fit with the Degrees of Literacy Power Program, which is geared toward helping to assess a student's literacy skills and then providing parents, teachers, and administrators with strategies to assist in literacy development. The DWM also has a user-friendly manual. The manual provides information concerning all aspects of the test including its development, administration, scoring, and interpretation. The manual defines technical terms in an easily understood manner. The section "using DWM test results" profiles student performances on the test. There are suggestions for interpreting student performance, which include protocols for determining if performance was a result of guessing. There is a warning that if a student leaves the last item on a test blank it may indicate that the student accidentally skipped an item in the test booklet, alerting the examiner to possible misscoring. If the test administrator determines that this is the case, then it is recommended that the test answers be adjusted. These types of instructions are quite useful, not only for the test administrator and scorer, but are better indicators of true performance.

In summary, the DWM estimates reading vocabulary assessing a student's knowledge of the meaning of a word as it appears in its naturally occurring context. The test was carefully constructed from the development of the most recent and comprehensive corpus of word frequencies. From this corpus test items were identified, their SFI scores were determined, and then a linear transformation of this score resulted in the DWM score. Evidence of construct validity seems well established, although no work was reported with other tests. Reliability coefficient estimates were quite strong. The DWM would be an excellent test not only for assessing reading vocabulary, but to use with programs that need to reflect outcomes based on contextual abilities.

Review of the Degrees of Word Meaning by JUDITH A. MONSAAS, Associate Professor of Education, North Georgia College & State University, Dahlonega, GA:

The Degrees of Word Meaning Tests (DWM) are primarily designed to measure word knowledge for students in grades 3 through high school. The authors also state that the DWM can be used as part of a battery to identify, place, and evaluate the progress of college students or with adult students in Adult Basic Education (ABE), GED programs, or placement in remedial programs. There are six levels of one test form (Form M) and a practice test that can be used to help familiarize students with the test format and item types. This is recommended because the authors have developed a test that is somewhat different from traditional vocabulary tests. Because the six levels are fairly broad based, and the items are arranged in order of difficulty, the authors state that the use of a particular test level is not restricted to particular grades; however, it is probably still wise to use the test form for the appropriate grade. Because all levels of the test are tied to the same scale, any student can take any test as long as there are enough easy or difficult items to put them on the scale. In the DWM manual, the authors alternately refer to test *form* and *levels* using these terms somewhat interchangeably. The descriptive information about the DWM refers to "Form/Level" M-2 through M-7 (six levels), but the reliability and validity sections refer to Forms A–H (eight forms). This leads one to question whether or not the technical data refer to the final test forms/levels.

The DWM is part of a larger battery of tests called the Degrees of Literacy Power program, which includes the Degrees of Reading Power (12:101) and the DWM test. The DWM reports traditional norm-referenced test scores but word frequency studies are used to support estimates of the size of students' reading vocabulary as well as examples of books that the student should be able to read. This information should ultimately be more useful to teachers than the traditional NRT scores. The several score reports for teachers, parents, and administrators are well thought out and useful for teachers in estimating students' vocabulary, selecting reading material, and planning instruction. The authors also point out that direct instruction in vocabulary is not effective because vocabulary is picked up through reading in "naturally occurring contexts."

The authors have attempted to develop an "authentic" assessment of word meaning and seem to have succeeded as well as possible within an objective testing framework. This test differs from traditional vocabulary tests in several ways. The words are presented in a "naturally occurring" context; this means that the words are presented in sentences in which they are most likely to be seen in text. The word knowledge required to answer the question is consistent with what it means in the adult sense. And test items are designed to measure how well students are able to derive the meaning from the context based on their knowledge of the word. That is, if the student knows the word they should be able to answer correctly but if they do not know the word, there are not sufficient context cues for them to answer correctly. Finally, 9 answer choices that are grammatically correct, semantically plausible, and relatively independent are provided for each item. According to the authors, this reflects more accurately the generative process used in reading and reduces the likelihood that students would get the question correct just by guessing. The use of 9 answer choices was not sufficiently justified in the manual. Why 9 rather than 8 or 10? It is possible that the traditional 4 or 5 answer choices are not enough to reflect the generative process involved in reading, but the choice of 9 seems somewhat arbitrary.

NORMING. The DWM tests are criterion referenced but because they may be used for some testing purposes that require norms, they have been normed for students in spring for grades 3–8. As part of the Degrees of Reading Program, the scale was normed rather than the test forms so that as items are tried out they can be incorporated into the item bank. Because there are several forms and special secure forms can be developed for individual user groups, this seems wise. The decision to use a random, stratified sample of New York State schools that demographically matches the nation may limit the use of the normative data. The authors argue that school participation rates are a problem in national norming studies and that their participation rate exceeded that reported by other publishers. A modest national norming study might have convinced this reviewer that the New York sample obtained similar results to that of a national norm group. Most studies show regional differences in achievement in most subject areas making the New York sample somewhat suspect.

The norm-referenced score reporting methods include percentile ranks, normal curve equivalents, and stanines as well as DWM scores that are calibrated across all the levels of the test. The authors, wisely, chose not to report grade equivalent scores. Criterion-referenced scores are reported in terms of the estimated size of the reading vocabulary, which is a range of number of words known based on word frequency studies. This is tied to the calibrated DWM scores. Examples of words at the different scale points are also reported. For example, a student with a DWM score of 600 has an estimated reading vocabulary of 19,900–22,100 words and sample words at this scale point are "converge, frank, and reel" (pp. 9–10). These scale points can also be tied back to the norms for each grade level.

RELIABILITY. Coefficient alphas and split-half estimates of reliability were computed for each DWM "form/level" and for each grade level. Coefficients for each form across grade levels were all in the .90s and for each form within grade levels were in the .80s and .90s. These are all quite good. Unfortunately, it is unclear if these data refer to the six levels of the DWM because coefficients are reported for eight forms of the DWM. No alternate forms reliability studies were conducted, but because all test forms were calibrated to the same scale, this should not be a problem. A more serious limitation is that standard errors of measurement were not reported for the scores on the DWM.

VALIDITY. Construct validity evidence is reported for the DWM. Word frequency studies were used to develop the test forms. A statistic known as the Standard Frequency Index (SFI), a method of expressing word frequency (number of times per million a word appears in text) weighted by the number of different content areas in which the word appears, is used to define the scale. Validity evidence cited demonstrates a strong correlation between the SFI scale and the Rasch difficulty index, which is used to calibrate the DWM scale. Partial correlations between the dominant and secondary meanings of the words, after controlling for student ability, were near zero providing justification for including both meanings of words on the test. The data provide evidence that a scale exists and that it can be used to assess the size of students' vocabulary.

Data on test fairness are reported by racial/ethnic group (Blacks, Whites, and Hispanics), gender, and SES (high SES and low SES). Rasch model data fit statistics and correlations of Rasch item difficulties for these groups are all similar indicating that the model data fit comparably across groups and that the order of item difficulties were invariant across all groups. Again, these data are for the mysterious eight forms not the six levels of the DWM.

Criterion-related validity evidence supporting specific test uses would provide useful additional validity evidence. Also, because the authors argue that this test is different from and more authentic than traditional vocabulary tests, correlations of DWM scores and traditional vocabulary test scores would provide evidence regarding this assertion.

SUMMARY. Overall, this test appears to be a welcome addition to vocabulary assessment. The authors convincingly argue that the tests are more authentic than traditional tests and that they can be used to estimate students' vocabulary. Score reports for teachers can be very useful for planning, instruction, and working with individual students. The reliability evidence is strong and construct validity evidence is adequate but needs to be reported for the current levels of the test. Caution remains with respect to using the norms in regions of the country other than the northeast, and users await additional criterion-related validity evidence.

[91]

Depression and Anxiety in Youth Scale.

Purpose: Designed to help professionals identify depression and anxiety in children and youth.

Population: Ages 6-0 to 19-0.

Publication Date: 1994.

Acronym: DAYS.

Administration: Group.

Price Data, 1994: $89 per complete kit including 50 student rating scales, 50 teacher rating scales, 50 parent rating scales, 50 profile/record forms, scoring keys, and manual (39 pages); $17 per 50 record forms; $17 per 50 profile/record forms; $26 per manual.

Authors: Phyllis L. Newcomer, Edna M. Barenbaum, and Brian R. Bryant.

Publisher: PRO-ED, Inc.

a) STUDENT SELF-REPORT SCALE (SCALE S).

Scores, 2: Depression, Anxiety.

Time: (15–20) minutes.

b) TEACHER RATING SCALE (SCALE T).

Scores, 2: Depression, Anxiety.

Time: (5–10) minutes.

c) PARENT RATING SCALE (SCALE P).

Scores, 3: Depression, Anxiety, Social Maladjustment.

Time: (6–10) minutes.

Review of the Depression and Anxiety in Youth Scale by GLORIA MACCOW, School Psychologist, Guilford County Schools, Greensboro, NC:

The authors describe several features of the Depression and Anxiety in Youth Scales (DAYS) that should make it useful for professionals in mental health and school settings. On the first page of the manual, readers learn they can use the instrument with confidence because of its ease of administration, high reliability and validity, good standardization, and simplicity in scoring and interpretation. In some respects, the instrument lives up to its advance billing.

The DAYS is useful as a screening measure to identify single symptoms (or clusters of symptoms) of depression and/or anxiety in children and youth. The paper-and-pencil rating scales can be used by mental health professionals in private or school settings. Data are collected about an individual's thoughts, feelings, and behavior from multiple informants—teachers, parents, and students' self-ratings. Users of the DAYS should have knowledge of professional and ethical guidelines, statistics, and the symptoms of depression and anxiety.

The categories Major Depressive Disorder and Overanxious Disorder in the *Diagnostic and Statistical Manual* (III-R) provided the theoretical foundation for the development of the DAYS. The items reflect available research including the finding that multidimensional assessment procedures are necessary to obtain a "valid indicator of depression and anxiety in children and youth" (p. 3). The authors discuss at length the difficulties with diagnostic accuracy that could result from using a battery of different instruments standardized on different samples. To increase diagnostic efficiency, the authors constructed

the DAYS as a "multidimensional instrument consisting of three scales—student self-report, teacher (and/or teacher alternate) rating, and parent (or parent surrogate) rating—each standardized on the same population" (p. 3).

The students who are the focus of the ratings should be between 6 years 0 months and 19 years 0 months. For the Student Self-Report (Scale S), respondents use a 4-point Likert-type response format in completing the 22 statements—11 each measuring Anxiety and Depression. The students indicate if they have experienced the symptom *Not at All* (1), *Sometimes* (2), *Often* (3), or *Almost All the Time* (4). The words anxiety and depression are not used when providing the instructions to the students. Instead, students are told each statement measures how they feel. Scale S can be administered to individuals in professional offices or to whole classes of students in schools. To read the items themselves, students should be able to comprehend at the level of the typical fourth grader. A scoring form is provided to determine the raw scores. The items are listed on the left and two columns—one for Depression and one for Anxiety—are on the right. The user records the number selected by the student for each item and adds the numbers in each column.

The Teacher Rating Scale (Scale T) consists of 20 items, of which 13 measure Depression and 7 measure Anxiety. The teacher or teacher alternate responds to each descriptive statement by circling either T for True or F for False. The responses are hand scored by placing a scoring key over the responses. The number of marks are summed separately for Anxiety and Depression. The higher the score, the greater the level of pathological symptomatology. Scale T takes about 5 minutes to complete and should be completed no more than 5 days after the student completes Scale S.

The Parent Rating Scale (Scale P) consists of 28 descriptive statements, also with a True-False response format. The items measure three constructs: Anxiety, Depression, and Social Maladjustment. The scale can be completed in 6 to 10 minutes, and can be mailed to parents or completed during a parent conference. The Parent Rating Scale should be completed within 3 to 5 days after the student completes the Student Rating Scale. The ratings yield raw scores, which are computed using scoring keys. The sum is computed for the items on each of the three constructs. The raw scores on all three scales can be converted to standard scores and percentile ranks using tables in the manual. The standard scores have a mean of 100 and a standard deviation of 15. The scores are listed and plotted on the Profile/Record Form.

The technical properties of the rating scales are adequate. For standardization, the authors selected participants from the four major census districts. Participants in the sample were similar to the general population in terms of demographic characteristics. The manual does not describe the overlap among the samples for the different scales. The omission is striking because of the authors' intent to standardize the three scales on the same subject samples. Based on the dates the scales were administered, there seems to be no overlap between the student sample and either the teacher or parent samples. Scale S was completed by 2,176 students in 12 states between August and November, 1989. Teacher and Parent scales were completed on 1,285 (1,286) students in 9 (6) states between August 1990 and April 1992. Another concern about the sample is that there were fewer than 100 participants for several of the 13 age groups.

The average internal consistency reliability coefficients for the scales are at least .80, which is the minimum reliability required for individually administered screening tests. There is no discussion of interrater reliability, which is important for standardized rating scales. The authors used professional judgment and item analysis to establish content validity. There is a need for factor analysis to confirm that the identified items do indeed load on either Anxiety, Depression, or Social Maladjustment. From a professional judgment perspective, several items seem to be assigned incorrectly. For example, on the Student scale "I have trouble sleeping" and "I don't feel like eating" are listed on the Anxiety construct. However, according to the DSM-III-R, disturbances in appetite and sleep are characteristics of Major Depressive Disorder.

For criterion-related validity, only one of six samples had more than 100 participants. Concurrent validity was established with several measures of anxiety and depression. No studies were reported on the predictive validity of the DAYS. The authors report several studies in support of construct validity. One study found the intercorrelations among the constructs on the three scales were generally above the acceptable level of .30. Although the authors present some evidence for variation in scores with age and gender, the manual does not provide mean scores for age and gender. A later study (Newcomer, Barenbaum, & Pearson, 1995) found no interaction effects by gender and age.

In summary, the rating scales of the DAYS indeed are easy to administer, score, and interpret. The development of the scales was based on a sound theoretical framework, and internal consistency reliability and intercorrelations among the constructs are adequate for a screening measure. In spite of these characteristics that make the DAYS appealing, there are several shortcomings related to standardization. First, there is a need for data on interrater reliability and factor analysis. Second, and most importantly, the three scales were not standardized on the same subject samples. This is contrary to the original intent of the authors. Additionally, because of the lack of overlap among the samples, the authors did not deliver on their promise to improve diagnostic accuracy.

REVIEWER'S REFERENCE

Newcomer, P. L., Barenbaum, E., & Pearson, N. (1995). Depression and anxiety in children and adolescents with learning disabilities, conduct disorders, and no disabilities. *Journal of Emotional and Behavioral Disorders, 3*, 27–39.

Review of the Depression and Anxiety in Youth Scale by JANET V. SMITH, Assistant Professor of Psychology and Counseling, Pittsburg State University, Pittsburg, KS:

The Depression and Anxiety in Youth Scale (DAYS) is designed to help identify depression and anxiety in children and adolescents aged 6-0 to 19-0 years. The authors state that the test is designed for use in both a school setting and mental health settings, although there is a clear bias throughout the manual for use in an educational setting.

The DAYS consists of three separate scales. The Student scale (Scale S) is a 22-item self-report scale with a 4-point Likert-type response format. The Teacher Rating Scale (Scale T) is a 20-item true/false rating scale. Scale T can also be completed by a "teacher alternative" such as a school counselor or mental health professional. The Parent scale (Scale P) is a 28-item true/false rating scale. Each scale yields separate scores for Depression and Anxiety. Scale P yields an additional score for Social Maladjustment. There is a low correlation between scores on the Student, Teacher, and Parent scales. However, this does not represent a problem for the DAYS as it is common to find that children' and adolescents' ratings of their own behavior differ significantly from other's ratings of their behavior.

The DAYS manual is extremely well organized and information is presented in a very clear, simple manner. In addition, test materials are well designed and are very easy and quick to administer and score. However, the simplicity and brevity of the scales present difficulties for the test. Items have a high face validity and may be very easy to fake. A more serious threat to the usefulness of the DAYS is that subscale scores are based on a very small number of items with range on some subscales as low as 7 points. This makes it difficult for reliable and meaningful discriminations to be made between levels of symptomatology.

The DAYS Depression subscale items are based on the DSM-III-R criteria for Major Depressive Disorder. The Anxiety subscale items are based on DSM-III-R criteria for overanxious disorder. Item selection consisted initially of expert evaluation to determine those items that were considered to be measuring only depression and only anxiety. These items were then submitted to item analysis to develop the final version of the subscales. Test development procedures for the Anxiety and Depression subscales appear appropriate, although it would have been useful to provide information on factor analysis to verify the existence of separate subscales. Little rationale is provide for the Social Maladjustment subscale.

Norms are based on nonclinical samples of schoolchildren and are representative in terms of major geographic regions, urban/rural setting, gender, race, and ethnicity, based on 1985 U.S. Census data. Overall, normative samples are large, with total sample sizes ranging from 1,286 to 2,176. However, younger age groups are somewhat underrepresented in the normative samples.

The manual provides tables to convert easily raw scores into percentile ranks as well as to standard scores with a mean of 100 and standard deviation of 15. Only one set of tables is presented, with norms collapsed across age groups and gender. Given the large developmental span covered by the DAYS as well as gender differences in depression and anxiety, it would have been highly desirable to separate norms by different age groups and gender.

Reliability of the DAYS is variable, depending on the scale used and the attribute being measured. Internal consistency reliability was estimated using 50 protocols from each 1-year age interval. Coefficients alpha ranged from .61 to .93, with internal consistency highest for total scale scores and lowest for the Social Maladjustment subscale score. Test-retest reliability was found to be in the .7 range for all subscales on the Student scale, using a nonclinical sample of 75 children and a test interval of 4 days.

Interrater reliability for the Teacher scale produced considerably higher reliability coefficients in the .9 range for all subscales. No information regarding test-retest reliability nor interrater reliability was provided for the Parent scale. Standard errors of measurement were provided for each age group, and ranged from 4 to 9 (based on standard scores). Again, scores were most accurate for total scale scores and least accurate for the Social Maladjustment subscale.

The manual describes several studies to support the validity of scores for the DAYS. In three separate studies, scores on the Student scale were correlated with other questionnaire measures of depression and anxiety. Significant correlations were found between both of the subscales and the Reynolds Children Depression Scale, the Reynolds Adolescent Depression Scale (RADS), and the Children's Manifest Anxiety Scale (CMAS). Correlation coefficient values ranged between .55 and .90. However, despite the very high correlations found with the external measures, these studies do not validate that the two subscales of the DAYS are indeed measuring Depression or Anxiety separately. The CMAS was found to be equally related to scores on the Depression subscale ($r = .71$) as scores on the Anxiety subscale ($r = .70$). Similarly, external measures of depression were mostly equally related to scores on both the Depression and Anxiety subscales. In one study, the correlation between the RADS and the DAYS Anxiety subscale (.80) was actually higher than the correlation between the RADS and the Depression subscale (.63). Further support for the validity of the Student scale is provided by two studies showing that scores obtained by a clinical inpatient sample were higher than those of nondisordered students and that scores obtained by emotionally disturbed special education students were higher than those obtained by typical learners.

Support for the Depression and Anxiety subscales of the Teacher and Parent scales is provided by three studies correlating teachers' and parents' ratings of students with the adult rating scales of the CMAS and the Child Depression Scale (CDS). Correlations ranged from .42 to .87, but again did not differentiate between Depression and Anxiety subscales. No support is offered for the validity of the Social Maladjustment subscale.

In summary, the DAYS is very easy and quick to administer and score. As such, it may have value in the screening of large groups of students or for research purposes. However, the authors are wise to caution that the DAYS should not be used alone for diagnostic purposes. Even as part of a test battery, it is unlikely to provide much useful information. Psychometric support for the Parent scale is sparse, with no validity provided for the Social Maladjustment scale. Therefore, use of the Parent scale is not recommended at this time.

[92]
Derogatis Psychiatric Rating Scale.

Purpose: Multidimensional psychiatric rating scale for use by clinician to assist in validating patient-reported results.
Population: Adults and adolescents.
Publication Dates: 1974–1992.
Acronym: DPRS.
Administration: Individual.
Comments: Formerly called Hopkins Psychiatric Rating Scale (9:483).
Author: Leonard R. Derogatis.
Publisher: NCS Assessments.

    a) BRIEF DEROGATIS PSYCHIATRIC RATING SCALE.
    Acronym: B-DPRS.
    Scores, 10: Primary Dimensions (Somatization, Obsessive-Compulsive, Interpersonal Sensitivity, Depression, Anxiety, Hostility, Phobic Anxiety, Paranoid Ideation, Psychoticism) and Global Pathology Index.
    Price Data, 1994: $30 per 100 forms; $50 per 50 scannable forms.
    Time: (1–2) minutes.
    b) DEROGATIS PSYCHIATRIC RATING SCALE.
    Acronym: DPRS.
    Scores, 18: Same as brief edition plus Sleep Disturbance, Psychomotor Retardation, Hysterical Behavior, Abjection-Disinterest, Conceptual Dysfunction, Disorientation, Excitement, Euphoria.
    Price Data: $32 per 100 forms.
    Time: (2–5) minutes.
Cross References: See 9:483 (1 reference).

TEST REFERENCES

1. Glass, T. A., Seeman, T. E., Herzog, A. R., Kahn, R., & Berkman, L. F. (1995). Change in productive activity in late adulthood: MacArthur studies of successful aging. *Journal of Gerontology: Social Sciences, 50B*, S65-S76.

Review of the Derogatis Psychiatric Rating Scale by SAMUEL JUNI, Professor, Department of Applied Psychology, New York University, New York, NY:

Presenting a tool to clinicians without an accompanying manual inevitably results in trouble for the struggling practitioner who is trying to be true to undefined requirements. It also affects the scale's integrity, which is sure to suffer because errors are apt to find their way into the instrument's design. Such errors may well have been caught in time as the test features were explored, highlighted, explained, and then modified as the manual was constructed for the professional consumer. In terms of user-friendliness, a manual is also helpful to put the developmental aspects of the scale in context. As a personal curiosity, for example, I would have liked to know the relationship of the current scale to its predecessors (the Hopkins and SCL scales), which have been in the literature for some time.

Before one even examines the specifics of the instruments, questions arise that remain unanswered to the very end. For whom is the instrument intended and who did the author have in mind as potential consumers of this product? Is it intended for any specific type of patient or therapy client? Are there any expectations, qualifications, or assumptions about the rater? Are there any specifications or prescriptions about the relationship between the rater and the patient? Furthermore, the characteristics of the data base are undefined. Is it based on observation (as it is referenced in published studies), self-report, charted historical data, retrospective, or results of medical/psychological examinations? This is to name some of a myriad of options.

The Derogatis Rating Scale presents a potpourri of traits, symptoms, and styles. As a clinician, I felt very comfortable with the comprehensiveness of the symptoms on an intuitive level. Each of the rating scales also features a Global Pathology Index. I would personally be quite content with such a comprehensive inventory, as I am with the various other available psychiatric rating scales reviewed by Derogatis and DellaPietra. I also see no conceptual advantages or disadvantages of the Global Pathology Index as compared with other available indices. For example, the Global Assessment of Functioning Scale from *DSM* seems just as comprehensive, and its annotation for different parts of the continuum is certainly more elaborate.

Psychometrically, however, there are a host of inadequacies and problems with the scales. It is not at all clear what the inclusionary or exclusionary criteria are for the various symptoms and rating foci. No comprehensive rationale comes to mind why these specific symptoms are featured, as opposed to others often seen on psychiatric inventories. Are these supposed to be the most common? Are they perhaps more aligned to, or indicative of, basic (versus peripheral) functioning difficulties? Scaling methodology typically utilizes one of two approaches: (a) a theoretical approach, where different items correspond to theoretically derived indices; or (b) an empirical approach, where observations yield common events that are deemed relevant to the measure at hand. There is no hint from the scale content if either of these approaches were used for devising or validating the scales.

Some of the categories overlap. Consider Anxiety and Phobic Anxiety. There is no rationale provided for why anxiety should be given additional weighing, by choosing a specific subdivision and giving it its own item. Why are other symptom categories not broken down into subsets as well?

In addition, the very definitions of the symptoms seem to lack theoretical uniformity. Consider, for example, anxiety that is defined deliberately as diffuse and based on emotional state, with symptoms given as "signs" indicating the presence of anxiety. Contrast this definitive mode with that of depression, which is annotated primarily based on symptomatology, with the mood aspects seemingly presented as being on equal footing with other symptoms, but not at all pathognomic of the construct. There is a definite impression here that the symptoms lists of descriptors or the symptoms were not subject to quality control.

The two forms of this test (the extended scale of 17 primary symptoms and the brief scale with 9 symptoms), as well as the Global Pathology Index, show inconsistencies in construction. Although this is not a theoretical obstacle, it certainly is bound to disorient the clinician who attempts to use them together. Furthermore, there are actual psychometric contradictions in item rationale and item construction which pose serious challenges to the integrity of the scales. One gets the impression that these scales were not conceived a priori, but rather concatenated from previously existing units, with undue attention to their synthesis.

It is noteworthy that the composition of items forming the Global Index seems to discriminate among the Psychiatric Scale items, overstressing some, eliminating others altogether, and even introducing new ones that are not alluded to in the symptom scales. For example, in the *severe* category alone, the Global Index features Mood Disorders (which can be easily located in the Symptom Scale), Hallucinations (which is only marginally present—as a detail in the Psychoticism Scale), and Poor Self-Care and Being a Risk to Self or Others—two items that are nowhere to be found in the Symptom Scales. Of course, one can expect the clinician to deduce such factors from symptoms. Without a formula, however, the value of

the measurement instrument, over and above an intuitive clinical qualitative statement, is minimal.

The Global Pathology Index refers to functioning within the last 7 days. We are not given a rationale for this time period at all. Furthermore, the clinician is instructed to base his or her ratings on the lowest level of functioning within that time period. The psychiatric symptom scales have no temporal frame of reference at all. Nor is it specified if the ratings are to be based on the patient's typical functioning or the lowest level of functioning. If the test booklet were printed in reverse, at least, we might have hoped for consistency of the clinician, who might be expected to use the 7-day and lowest functioning criteria. But because the Psychiatric Rating Scales come first in the booklets, there is no way to guess which criteria the clinician is using from the symptom ratings. One can also question, from a judgmental perspective, how a clinician who chose to use a 2-day time period and modal functioning criteria for the symptom ratings, for example, would then manage to change gears into the 7-day/lowest functioning mode of the global scale. Would there then be a realignment of rating severities, as the time frame and modal perspective change?

The Psychiatric Rating Scale items feature a 7-point response format. The numerical values of 0 through 6 are indexed respectively with the following descriptors: *absent, slight, mild, moderate, marked, severe, extreme.* For some unexplained reason, there is a bold triangle drawing emphasis (and probably encouraging the likelihood of choice) for points 1, 3, and 5, the only options that also have actual phrases detailing examples that mandate such choices. The Global Pathology Index has a response format ranging from 0 to 8, indexed with the following respective descriptors: *absent, minimal, slight, moderate, substantial, marked, severe, extreme.* For this scale, bold triangles and example phrases are given for points 1, 3, 5, and 7 only. The unnecessary response differences are sure to disorient the serious clinician who is intent on being true to the scaling requirements when switching from one scaling mode to another. Regardless of whether we focus on one or the other of these competing classificatory schemes, I have an overall linguistic uncertainty about the specific ordinal nature of the verbal descriptors, which becomes downright troubling if the scaling is then to be used to yield numerical ratio-type values.

There are even more serious measurement errors explicit in the scaling inconsistencies. Juxtaposing the two scale markers, we find symmetrical congruence with respect to the end points and center (i.e., each scale begins with "absent," has "moderate" as a midpoint, and ends with "extreme"). It is at the intermediate points that the symmetry falls apart, and actually renders values contradictory from one scale to another. Specifically, in the symptom scales, *slight* is symmetrical with *severe* (1 vs. 5) whereas *mild* is symmetrical with *marked* (2 vs. 4). In the Global Pathology Index, *minimal* is inserted into the continuum before *slight*, whereas *substantial* is inserted before *marked*. This results in a total implicit redefinition of the choice markers. Whereas *slight* is the polar opposite of *severe* in the Psychiatric Rating Scales, and *mild* is the polar opposite of *marked*, both of these markers get pushed higher on the continuum on the global scale equivalent, in addition to their redefinition as nonsymmetrical.

In the style of classic multiscale inventories, the Global Pathology Index features a grid allowing the plotting of scale points. Although there is no harm to this option, there clearly is no method for profile interpretation that even comes close to those of other inventories (e.g., the Minnesota Multiphasic Personality Inventory [MMPI] or the Wechsler Scales), especially in view of the rather atheoretical structure of this scale. Furthermore, it is misleading to offer such a grid, implying that the pattern of between-scale variance is visually interpretable, based on some inherent scheme of sequencing the scales.

In conclusion, these scales are an addition to the psychiatric rating literature, which may prove useful in specific areas or with specific populations. A manual describing development and scale usage would be most helpful to expound the details of the scales and to standardize their use.

Review of the Derogatis Psychiatric Rating Scale by PAUL RETZLAFF, Professor, Psychology Department, University of Northern Colorado, Greeley, CO:

The Derogatis Psychiatric Rating Scale (DPRS) is a very brief, clinician-endorsed instrument assessing dimensions similar to those of the patient-endorsed Symptom Checklist-90-Revised (SCL-90-R; T4:2674) and Brief Symptom Inventory (BSI; T4:324). The DPRS is apparently the old Hopkins Psychiatric Rating Scale renamed. As such, the DPRS and B-DPRS (the brief version) provide a rating system for the dimensions of Somatization, Obsessive-Compulsive, Interpersonal Insensitivity, Depression, Anxiety, Hostility, Phobic Anxiety, Para-

noid Ideation, and Psychoticism. Additionally, and beyond the usual SCL-90-R and BSI scales, the DPRS (but not the B-DPRS) includes Sleep Disturbance, Psychomotor Retardation, Hysterical Behavior, Abjection-Disinterest, Conceptual Dysfunction, Disorientation, Excitement, and Euphoria. Most would probably agree that these are important clinical and research variables.

Both the paper-and-pencil and computer forms of the DPRS consist of the dimension name, a description of the dimension, and a single 0 to 6 response scale for each dimension. The single 7-point response scale is anchored from a low of "absent" to a high of "extreme." In addition, points 1, 3, and 5 have further dimension-specific anchoring. The dimension definitions, response scaling, and anchors appear to be fairly well done.

There is no manual for the DPRS. There is only an extremely brief mention of the "test" in the SCL-90-R manual. There are no norms for the test. The "scoring," either by hand or computer, simply restates the endorsements made by the clinician.

No reliabilities are presented. The most obvious type of reliability would be an interjudge consistency. A second useful statistic would be a short-term stability (test-retest) correlation that could infer evidence of reliability. Along that same line, there are no longer-term stability coefficients. Such would be useful to infer appropriate temporal stability of the judges and constructs.

No validities are provided. Certainly these authors could have calculated and presented the intercorrelations between similar SCL-90-R and DPRS scales. Winokur, Guthrie, Rickels, and Nael (1982) presented a very small ($N = 20$) study. They only found four of the nine main scales to have correlations above chance using the Hopkins versions of these tests.

Also there is no intercorrelation matrix for the DPRS scales. Such information would be helpful to determine the specificity of the scales, an important feature for this type of instrument.

The scales are most flawed by the use of, in essence, a single item per scale. No matter how well defined and no matter how many points are on the scale, it is still a single item.

In sum, the Derogatis Psychiatric Rating Scale (DPRS) is a poorly documented test and probably a poor test. It is poorly conceived and executed from a psychometric perspective. Further, there is a remarkable lack of data presented including norms, reliabilities, and validities given the statures of the author and publisher. Although some may say that the DPRS is simply a "checklist" or "rating scale," the fact is that the laws of physics and psychometrics still apply.

REVIEWER'S REFERENCE

Winokur, A., Guthrie, M. B., Rickels, K., & Nael, S. (1982). Extent of agreement between patient and physician ratings of emotional distress. *Psychosomatics, 23*, 1135–1146.

[93]
Derogatis Stress Profile.

Purpose: "Designed to assess and represent stress at three distinct but related levels of measurement."
Population: Adults.
Publication Date: 1984–1986.
Acronym: DSP.
Scores: 3 domains: Environmental Events, Emotional Response, Personality Mediators; 11 dimensions: Time Pressure, Driven Behavior, Attitude Posture, Relaxation Potential, Role Definition, Vocational Satisfaction, Domestic Satisfaction, Health Posture, Hostility, Anxiety, Depression; 2 global scores: Subjective Stress, Total Stress.
Administration: Group.
Price Data, 1993: $50 per 50 tests; $17.50 per 50 score profile forms; $8 per summary report and scoring instructions ('86, 14 pages); $75 per 50 uses of computer scoring program.
Time: 10(15) minutes.
Author: Leonard R. Derogatis.
Publisher: Clinical Psychometric Research, Inc.
Cross References: See T4:747 (1 reference).

TEST REFERENCES

1. Simonds, J. F., McMahon, T., & Armstrong, D. (1991). Young suicide attempters compared with a control group: Psychological, affective, and attitudinal variables. *Suicide and Life-Threatening Behavior, 21*, 134–151.
2. Chaffin, M. (1992). Factors associated with treatment completion and progress among intrafamilial sexual abusers. *Child Abuse & Neglect, 16*, 251–264.
3. Chang, E. C., D'Zurilla, T. J., & Maydew-Olivares, A. (1994). Assessing the dimensionality of optimism and pessimism using a multimeasure approach. *Cognitive Therapy and Research, 18*, 143–160.
4. Nussbaum, P. D., & Goreczny, A. J. (1995). Self-appraisal of stress level and related psychopathology. *Journal of Anxiety Disorders, 9*, 463–472.

Review of the Derogatis Stress Profile by MARIELA C. SHIRLEY, Assistant Professor of Psychology, University of North Carolina at Wilmington, Wilmington, NC:

The Derogatis Stress Profile (DSP) is a "multidimensional psychological self-report scale which serves as a screening and outcome measure of stress" (manual, p. 1). The author states that the DSP is based on Lazarus' interactional model of stress. The DSP measures three construct levels of stress: primary dimensions, secondary domains, and superordinate global constructs. These in turn form a "hierarchical" model that defines the individual's overall stress experience. The 77 items yield 11 primary dimensions (i.e., specific stress foci): Time Pressure, Driven Behavior, Attitude Posture, Relaxation Potential, Role Definition, Vocational Environment, Domestic Environment, Health Environment, Hostility, Anxiety, and Depression. These primary dimensions are subsumed under three primary domains (Environmental Events, Personality Mediators, Emotional Response) and lead to a global estimate of the individual's current stress experience (Total Stress Score).

Items and domains were selected based on their hypothesized etiological relevance to the stress-illness relationship and empirical evidence supporting the characteristic as related to one or more stress-related illnesses (e.g., Time Pressure, Driven Behavior). The author is explicit in indicating that dimensions and domains assessed by this instrument are not exhaustive of those identified in the stress literature. However, the author does not indicate how the final sample of 77 items was obtained. Were these derived from a larger pool of items? If so, what procedures were used for this derivation? In addition, a single-item visual analog measure of the individual's subjective evaluation of their stress experience (Subjective Stress Score) is obtained. Whether or not a single item is sufficient to measure perceived stress (based on Lazarus' principles of primary and secondary appraisal) is questionable. Although the manual does not specify administration procedures, it appears that this test can be given in both individual or group formats.

To each of the 77 items on the DSP individuals respond on a scale of 0 (*not at all true of me*) to 4 (*extremely true of me*). Primary dimension subscale scores are computed based on the sum of the 7 items that comprise each subscale. Approximately half the items on the DSP involve calculating "reflected" scores (i.e., subtracting the item score from 4 before adding it to the subscale raw score total) to correct for response sets. *T*-scores are then obtained from a table of standardized area *T*-scores. The three domain scores are a sum of the relevant dimension subscale *T*-scores. The two global scores are computed as follows: (a) The Total Stress Score (TSS) is a sum of the 11 dimension *t*-scores; (b) the Subjective Stress Score (SSS) is an analogue 100 mm line on which the respondent indicates their current level of stress.

Stress summary profiles can be generated to plot individual subscales, primary domains, and global scores. Although an evaluation of the individual subscales allows for fine-grained analyses of the differential role that certain characteristics may contribute to the individual's stress response, the three domain and TSS scores are based on an addition of the subscales relevant to the domain in question. This assumes that various dimensions of stress contribute equally to determine the three domains and the overall global score. An interaction model of stress may not necessarily be additive in nature. The stress literature does not suggest an additive model of stress, nor does the author's principal components analysis as the items significantly correlate with one another and are therefore not orthogonal. An additive model does not take into account the relative valence individuals may assign to particular characteristics, effects of prior stress experiences on current stress responses, other individual difference factors (e.g., psychopathology), and how these characteristics contribute to their experience of stress.

The test manual contains explicit information regarding the uses of the test, composition of the instrument, and scoring procedures. The author conducted statistical testing of the instrument; however, normative, reliability, validity, and structural composition information is provided in a document separate from the test manual (see Derogatis, 1987). This is a weakness of the manual in conforming to guidelines of the *Standards for Educational and Psychological Testing* (AERA, APA, & NCME, 1985). The standardization sample was based on 867 individuals who were employees of 12 corporations. No information was provided on ethnic breakdown. Separate analyses by age range were conducted to evaluate differential responses among males and females. The results indicated differences within genders regarding which dimensions are most stressful for specific age ranges. It is likely that these differences may also vary dependent on the populations sampled (e.g., Solis, 1991). Test-retest reliability (7-day interval; r ranged from .72 to .92) and internal consistency reliability (alpha coefficients ranged from .79 to .93) are both high.

The structure of the DSP was evaluated by principal components analysis using a criterion of an eigenvalue of .90 or greater. This resulted in four factors: Personality Mediators Domain (40% variance), Emotional Response Domain (12% variance), Domestic/Vocational Environment (9% variance), and Health Environment (8% variance). Principal components analysis is not an appropriate model to test the structure of this questionnaire related to an interactional model of stress. A factor analysis would have been a more appropriate procedure that would

also test the hierarchical stress model the author puts forth. Half of the standardization sample ($N = 867$) could have been randomly selected for an initial factor analysis with the second half of the sample used for a confirmatory factor analysis test of the hierarchical model (Cudeck & Browne, 1983). This alternative analytic method would allow for the subscales to be correlated and for testing of their relationship to the three primary domains to determine the best model.

Predictive validity, or the extent to which DSP stress dimensions could discriminate among diabetics' glycemic control (good vs. poor), was assessed in a sample of 43 "brittle diabetics." These results showed that four of the subscales were able to discriminate between groups of diabetics. It is not clear if the author used the classification procedure in discriminant function analysis (Huberty, 1984). Further evaluation on larger samples, accounting for base rates, is needed.

The author clearly states that the DSP is not intended as a measure of psychological or psychiatric diagnosis. However, how predisposing factors such as other psychiatric illness (e.g., major depression, generalized anxiety disorder) may affect responses to the DSP is not addressed. Nussbaum and Goreczny (1995) evaluated dispositional influences or individuals' reactions to stressors among male veterans. In addition to the DSP, the authors included the SCL-90-R and the Minnesota Multiphasic Personality Inventory (MMPI). Although the results indicated there were no differences on measures of psychopathology between stress deniers, stress augmenters, and accurate stress appraisers, these investigators found that higher levels of subjective stress were accompanied by higher levels of psychopathology. Thus, self-report measures of stress may reflect bias due to the individual's coexisting psychopathology as well as self-efficacy, coping style, and health belief expectations.

Individual responses indicating a difference of 8 points or more between the SSS and the TSS (manual, p. 9) are considered to be indications of stress denial or stress augmentation. It is unclear how this criterion was derived. In the case of "denial," elevated T-scores accompanied by a low SSS may simply reflect individuals who are not bothered by their level of stress versus denial of stress. The fact that individual test items relate more to trait variables whereas the SSS relates to situational stress variables may explain this discrepancy. Although generally elevated state scores correspond to elevated trait scores, assuming that this *will* occur at the individual level is a false assumption. The DSP should have been validated against other instruments assessing defensiveness.

Overall, the DSP is potentially useful to health professionals in identifying individuals' stress levels. In this context, the DSP may be useful in screening out individuals who may benefit from stress management interventions as well as a method of assessing outcome from the use of these interventions. Questions arise regarding the psychometric properties of the DSP and how these were obtained. Construct validity was not addressed by the analyses conducted after the development of the scale. This then raises validity questions as to how the initial items were obtained and what procedures were used to yield the final sample of 77 items. A primary concern lies in the fact that although stress is defined as an interaction between the individual's current environment, long-standing personality style, and emotional responses to stress, the DSP operationalizes this as an additive model. Appropriate factor analyses were not conducted to test a hierarchical model of stress. The DSP in its current format may simply be a measure of general distress. A second concern is that the test manual is incomplete in its provision of the full psychometric standardization, reliability, and validity information of this instrument. Further documentation is needed in the test manual as well as information on the interpretation of the results.

REVIEWER'S REFERENCES

Cudeck, R., & Browne, M. W. (1983). Cross-validation of covariance structures. *Multivariate Behavioral Research, 18*, 147–167.

Huberty, C. J. (1984). Issues in the use and interpretation of discriminant analysis. *Psychological Bulletin, 95*, 156–171.

American Educational Research Association, American Psychological Association, and National Council on Measurement in Education (Joint Committee). (1985). *Standards for educational and psychological testing*. Washington, DC: APA, Inc.

Derogatis, L. R. (1987). The Derogatis Stress Profile (DSP): Quantification of psychological stress. *Advances in Psychosomatic Medicine, 17*, 30–54.

Solis, S. (1991). Psychosocial stress in Marine Corps officers. *Military Medicine, 156*, 223–227.

Nussbaum, P. D., & Goreczny, A. J. (1995). Self-appraisal of stress level and related psychopathology. *Journal of Anxiety Disorders, 9*, 463–472.

Review of the Derogatis Stress Profile by PAUL D. WERNER, Professor, California School of Professional Psychology, Alameda, CA:

Appealing in its link to interactional and transactional conceptions of stress, the Derogatis Stress Profile (DSP) aspires to assess three elements of stress that have been emphasized in such models. These are the impact of environmental events, the individual's personality, and aspects of emotional response. The questionnaire is engagingly written, and inspection of its items suggests that they would be viewed as relevant to assessment of stress by lay test takers and as content valid by professionals.

The DSP's first 77 items are scored for 11 subscales, *T*-scores on which are combined three domain scores, and an overall Total Stress Score. A final item, yielding the Subjective Stress Score, presents a 100 mm line on which the respondent indicates his or her current level of stress. Thus, this brief measure has the potential for rapidly assessing stress-related dimensions at three levels of specificity, as well as respondents' current levels of stress.

The DSP's publisher does not provide a manual, but rather a brief "Summary Report" as well as a bibliography listing publications based on research using the measure. About half of the Summary Report is devoted to describing the DSP's scales and their linkage to the test developer's theory of stress. The scales' definitions are, for the most part, clearly articulated. One feels that Derogatis has thought deeply about linkages between them and both everyday and clinical issues pertaining to stress. The remainder of the Summary Report details scoring procedures, provides *T*-score conversion tables, and describes a computer program that facilitates scoring and profiling of results.

Notably missing in the Summary Report is technical information that readers need to make an informed choice about whether to employ the DSP, and, if they employ it, to validly interpret its scores. For fundamental information concerning reliability and validity, and even a description of the DSP's normative group, one must, then, turn to the items on the bibliography or to more recent articles. A paper by Derogatis (1987) gives the fundamental results cited in most articles using the measure: (a) The DSP has excellent 7-day retest correlations—with values ranging form .72 to .92—and fine internal consistency coefficients—alphas ranging from .79 to .93—in samples of corporate employees; (b) Factor analysis suggests that the 11 basic dimensions do sort out into the expected personality, emotional, and environment domains, although there is also considerable association among domains.

Validity results are often encouraging, particularly when the DSP is studies in relation to other questionnaire measures, but these results are not uniformly positive. Illustrative of the strength of positive results, Dobkin, Pihl, and Breault (1991) found a correlation of .80 between DSP Anxiety scores and Anxiety scores on the Jenkins Activity Survey, as well as a correlation of -.50 between DSP

Depression and the Profile of Mood States—Bipolar (POMS-B) Elation-Depression scale. A sampling of other findings obtained by Dobkin et al. illustrates the puzzling negative results sometimes obtained: DSP Hostility correlated -.09 with the POMS-B Agreeable-Hostile score, and DSP Environmental domain scores were unassociated with scores on both the Daily Hassles Scale and the Life Experiences Survey. Indeed, of the 10 studies that I read in preparing this review, 7 reported one or more unexpected or counterintuitive results involving the DSP. Of course, such results could be due to problems in the other measures in these studies, or in their authors' theoretical conceptualizations. But they do suggest that there are construct validity issues pertaining to the DSP and the measurement of stress more generally that need attention as work continues on the DSP.

More research is needed in a number of areas to permit greater confidence in and understanding of the DSP, both as a research tool and as a counseling aid. For example, there apparently has been no research on correlations between measures of response style and DSP scores. These factors may be critical to understanding the responses of employees and others who complete the DSP in settings where they believe that test scores may lead to differential treatment. Additionally, evidence is needed on the measure's reliability and factor structure in more varied groups than those studied to date. Although there has been attention to age as a correlate of DSP scores, information is lacking on how DSP scores relate to other demographic variables such as ethnicity and socioeconomic status. Similarly, because the DSP's normative group consists of people in the world of work, the DSP may be of little interpretive relevance to members of other groups, such as students, the unemployed, or the retired. At this point, the DSP may be recommended for no more than exploratory research use with such groups.

SUMMARY. An advantage of the DSP is that this easily administered questionnaire assesses stress-related dimensions, from an interactional perspective, at three levels of specificity. Results to date suggest that its scales are reliable and that they often relate as expected to criterion variables and to one another. On the other hand, because unexpected findings have been prevalent, further construct validity studies are called for. The instrument should be used interpretively with individuals only with the utmost caution.

REVIEWER'S REFERENCES

Derogatis, L. R. (1987). The Derogatis Stress Profile (DSP): Quantification of psychological stress. *Advances in Psychosomatic Medicine, 17,* 30–54.
Dobkin, P. L., Pihl, R. O., & Breault, C. (1991). Validation of the Derogatis Stress Profile using laboratory and real world data. *Psychotherapy and Psychosomatics, 46,* 185–196.

[94]
Developmental Challenge Profile: Learning from Job Experiences.

Purpose: "Designed to encourage managers and executives to think about their jobs from a developmental perspective."
Population: Managers.
Publication Date: 1993.
Scores: 16 developmental components: Transitions (Unfamiliar Responsibilities, Proving Yourself), Creating Change (Developing New Directions, Inherited Problems, Reduction Decisions, Problems with Employees), High Level of Responsibility (High Stakes, Managing Business Diversity, Job Overload, Handling External Pressure), Non-authority Relationships (Influencing Without Authority), Obstacles (Adverse Business Conditions, Lack of Top Management Support, Lack of Personal Support, Difficult Boss), Support (Supportive Boss).
Administration: Individual or group.
Price Data, 1993: $20 per profile.
Time: Administration time not reported.
Comments: Used in conjunction with BENCH-MARKS (12:50) which assesses managerial strengths and weaknesses.
Authors: Patricia J. Ohlott, Cynthia D. McCauley, and Marian N. Ruderman.
Publisher: Center for Creative Leadership.

TEST REFERENCES

1. McCauley, C. D., Ruderman, M. N., Ohlott, P. J., & Morrow, J. E. (1994). Assessing the developmental components of managerial jobs. *Journal of Applied Psychology, 79,* 544-560.
2. Ohlott, P. J., Ruderman, M. N., & McCauley, C. D. (1994). Gender differences in managers' developmental job experiences. *Academy of Management Journal, 37,* 46–67.

Review of the Developmental Challenge Profile: Learning from Job Experiences by JEAN POWELL KIRNAN, Associate Professor of Psychology, and KRISTEN WOJCIK, Research Assistant, Trenton State College, Trenton, NJ:

The Developmental Challenge Profile (DCP) is a self-development tool aimed at helping managers identify learning and challenging opportunities in their *current* jobs. Thus, the emphasis is on the current job only and not previous positions. Developed by the Center for Creative Leadership (CCL), the DCP is based on the hypothesis that hands-on experiences and challenges provide one of the best methods to learn managerial and organizational skills necessary for effective leadership.

This hypothesis suggests that unlike classroom or assessment center type training, experiential learning has the benefit of a high level of motivation, and immediate and meaningful feedback of one's actions. However, as with any learning experience, the degree to which individual development occurs is dependent not only on the opportunity to learn, but on the capability of the individuals to learn from the situation, their career history, their motivation to learn, and even their personality.

The instrument may be used alone (for individual development and/or as an assessment of organizational opportunities/challenges) or in conjunction with BENCHMARKS (12:50) a CCL product designed to identify managerial practices in "need of attention." A developmental training program is available from the CCL for those human resource professionals interested in using these instruments.

The DCP measures 16 job developmental components grouped into six broad categories: Transitions (changes in job content, status, or location), Creating Change (working in ambiguity to introduce new concepts/operations or revise existing ones), High Levels of Responsibility (increased impact of decisions), Non-Authority Relationships (ability to build relationships with people not under their authority), Obstacles (reduce discomfort from people and business related problems), and Support from immediate boss (receive advice, feedback, recognition, and new opportunities).

The development of both the DCP and BENCHMARKS can be traced back to two studies involving the use of in-depth interviews with successful executives. The initial study consisted of a sample of 86 predominantly male executives, whereas the second study utilized a sample of 76 female executives. The primary topic of discussion in the interview was the identification of critical events that led to lasting change in the way these executives manage and what was learned from these critical experiences.

Teams of researchers worked individually and then in groups to identify themes in the qualitative data. This content analysis resulted in the 16 event types measured by the DCP. The initial generation of types was based on the first sample. The female sample was used to supplement these findings by providing additional items for those developmental components found to be more specific to women. More information on the gender similarities and differences in developmental components might be of interest to some users.

During the in-depth interviews, respondents were also asked to indicate what was learned from these events. This information is used in the DCP report as a method of suggesting what a respondent might learn from their current job.

Both empirical and theoretical criteria were used in the development of the 16 components. Factor analysis, item-total correlations, and a confirmatory analysis with a new sample of managers supported these 16 factors.

The Developmental Challenge Profile is a paper-and-pencil test consisting of three sections. Section I of the reusable questionnaire booklet requests the test taker's name, the date he/she started in the position, and background information on the job. Section II comprises 113 items that represent the 16 individual job components. Section III asks for the respondent's indication of his/her growth while in that position and the job's challenge level.

All responses are recorded on a separate one-page optically scannable answer sheet. Six response options are provided for the respondent to indicate the degree to which each item is characteristic of the job or manager: *not at all descriptive, slightly descriptive, moderately descriptive, quite descriptive, extremely descriptive,* and *cannot answer.*

The items in the profile cover challenges and concerns of the position, the organization, or the individual interspersed among each other. For example, an item like "The business is competitive" might be followed by "You must manage a diverse workforce." It might be less confusing for the respondent if the items were grouped together for clearer meaning.

The Developmental Challenge Profile may be administered on an individual basis or in a group setting (e.g., training programs). The instructions are simple and straightforward. About 20 to 30 minutes are needed to complete the questionnaire. Although not specifically stated in the manual, it would appear the answer sheets are mailed to the publisher for scoring, as a sample score report is provided in the manual.

In the score report, results for each job component are presented as a number ranging from 1 (not descriptive of the job) to 5 (extremely descriptive of the job). These figures are reached by averaging the responses from items on the test that correspond with each job component. There is a corresponding bar chart ranging from low to high for the "relative score." This is the respondent's score relative to that of other managers. For example, if a respondent scored low in the "Job Overload" component, it means that the manager has less job overload relative to other managers. A separate numerical and relative score is provided for each of the 16 developmental components. No score is reported for a component if an insufficient number of questions were answered.

Also included in the score report are skills that interviewed managers who scored high on the same components learned from experience in their jobs. First, the highest rated components of the respondent are listed, then the skills from other managers. These are well detailed and organized; however, it is unclear which skills match with which component. Several steps are presented to help the individual understand his/her score report. These include discussing goals, scores, and the developmental opportunities in the position.

A norm group for the DCP is used so managers taking the test can compare their scores to a relevant sample. Updated periodically, the sample's last update was in December 1992. The current norm group consists of 1,049 managers of which 68% were male, 26% were female, and 6% did not indicate their sex. In terms of ethnic background, 85% of the norm group were Caucasian, 3% were Black, 2% Hispanic, 1% Asian, 1% American Indian, 1% some other race, and 7% did not respond. The mean age for the sample was 41.59 years.

The reliability of the DCP is reported utilizing both test-retest and internal measures of consistency. Test-retest reliabilities for the 16 components are good ranging from about .78 to .93. Careful readers will note some discrepancies between coefficients in the tables and those reported in the text. The differences are, however, slight. Alpha measures of internal consistency ranged from .52 to .80. The small number of items in some of the components may contribute to these low internal estimates. The publishers have added items in the hope of increasing the coefficients.

By the very nature of what it purports to measure, developmental opportunities in the current job, the DCP is difficult to validate. The publishers have conducted a series of studies where they have compared the DCP with aspects of on-the-job learning and characteristics of the jobs themselves hypothesized to provide different developmental challenges.

The 16 components of the DCP were compared to two measures of learning and development: (a) management responses to a 5-point scale of a global question of how much their current job was contributing to growth as a manager; and (b) an index of learning derived from managers' ratings of the degree to which they are learning 33 different

lessons on their current jobs. In the first comparison, 7 of the 16 components were positively correlated, 3 were negatively correlated, and 6 showed no relationship with the overall measure of growth. In the comparison to the learning index, 13 components were positively correlated, 1 was negative, and 2 showed no relationship. It was the less attractive components of Adverse Business Conditions, Lack of Top Management Support, Lack of Personal Support, and Difficult Boss that showed either no relationship or a negative relationship with one or both of the learning measures. For example, individuals identifying a Difficult Boss on the DCP reported less development and learning on the job than those who did not have a difficult boss.

The publishers point out that although these components do not show a relationship with the overall measures, early studies with Benchmarks had tied them to the learning of specific skills. Additionally, they hypothesized that negative experiences may not be realized for their learning value while one is currently experiencing them. It would be interesting to test this hypothesis by reassessing the degree of learning after the negative experience has passed. A later study of stressful aspects of the work situation showed a relationship between these components and harmful stress. These findings support the perceived negative aspects of these four components and call for their continued research as contributors to managerial growth.

The second group of validation studies describes the relationships between the 16 components with job characteristics presumed to be related to these components. For example, individuals reporting a transition of "first time working with top executives" (p. 18) had higher scores on the transition components of Unfamiliar Responsibilities and Proving Yourself than did individuals not experiencing this transition. Further analyses are presented for job characteristics such as organizational level, primary job mission, line versus staff position, and domestic versus foreign operations with similar findings.

The research findings presented would appear to provide support that individuals reporting learning on the job score higher on the job components than those not reporting learning. Additionally, scores on the components tend to increase and decrease with job characteristics in a theoretically expected manner. A study of the DCP in use with Benchmarks would be helpful. A measurement of the individual's weaknesses could be made initially utilizing Benchmarks along with a measure of the job's challenge areas with the DCP. After a specified amount of time on the job, a follow-up administration of Benchmarks could determine if change had occurred in the areas identified by the DCP.

The usefulness of the DCP alone is questionable. What can be gained by knowing the challenges a job offers for development without knowing if the individual needs development in these areas? Additionally, one must ask the question of whether the DCP is comprehensive in its coverage of job components. Are the 16 components equally essential for all jobs and are all essential components included in the DCP? What if one needs development in areas not identified by the DCP?

Improvement to internal consistency is needed and is being pursued by the publishers. Further investigation of the negative components, continuing validation studies of the instrument in-use, and additional information on females and ethnic minorities is recommended with increasing use and larger databases of respondents. The DCP most likely will prove useful to those individuals already involved with BENCHMARKS as it is a natural extension of this measure and program. Its utility as a stand-alone instrument is questionable.

Review of the Developmental Challenge Profile: Learning from Job Experiences by EUGENE P. SHEEHAN, Associate Professor of Psychology, University of Northern Colorado, Greeley, CO:

The premises underlying the Developmental Challenge Profile: Learning from Job Experiences (DCP) are that employees learn from job experiences and that these experiences are most likely to induce learning when the employee is faced with challenging job situations. The purpose of the DCP is to examine components of managerial jobs that enable and foster learning for the job incumbent. To accomplish this, the profile measures opportunities for learning, referred to as the developmental components of jobs.

The DCP was developed from critical incident interviews with 86 executives in which they identified events or episodes that resulted in lasting change in their approach to management. These interviews generated 16 developmental components of jobs clustered into six broad categories (Transitions, Creating Change, High Levels of Responsibility, Non-Authority Relationships, Obstacles, and Support). This clustering is uneven as the number of components in each category varies from one (Support) to four (Creating Change, High Levels of Responsibility,

and Obstacles). The profile uses 113 items to assess the 16 developmental components. Respondents indicate on a 5-point scale the degree to which each item is indicative of the job they currently hold. Item distribution across the 16 developmental components varies between 2 and 11.

Managers who complete the DCP receive a summary report that describes the job components. They also receive information on how their scores on each component compare with the scores of other managers in the norm group, along with information on how to interpret their scores. The authors of the DCP suggest three uses for the profile. First, the profile can provide managers with information regarding learning opportunities available in their jobs. Second, it can provide organizations with a profile of the types of development opportunities available throughout the organization and the jobs that contain these opportunities. Third, the profile can be used in combination with BENCHMARKS (12:50), an instrument also developed at the Center for Creative Leadership and designed to assess the strengths and weaknesses of managers. The combination of the two instruments should permit managers to identify whether the opportunities for development in their jobs are compatible with their strengths and weaknesses and their own personal developmental goals. Of course, the identification of learning opportunities does not mean that managers will avail themselves of such opportunities.

The DCP manual contains extensive psychometric data. Procedures used to develop and refine both individual items and the 16 developmental components are appropriate and grounded in psychometric theory. Internal consistencies of the developmental components are generally acceptable, although some give cause for concern. Eleven of the 16 alphas are .70 or higher, whereas 5 are below .67. The lowest alpha (.52) was obtained on the Proving Yourself component. Short-term test-retest reliabilities are good, ranging from .78 to .93, with the majority greater than .80.

Developmental component intercorrelations are presented, and they range from -.44 (Difficulties with Boss and Supportive Boss) to .55 (Problems with Employees and Inherited Problems). Interpretation of such a large correlation matrix (120 correlations) is difficult—data from a factor analysis would have been useful.

The validity evidence for the DCP is most impressive. The authors summarize several studies that provide validity support for the DCP. For example, most of the developmental components have statistically significant correlations with perceptions of on-the-job learning. Additionally, the developmental components behaved in different but predictable ways when compared with measures of work experience or when tested on different groups of managers.

The job components and the individual items demonstrate good face validity as indicators of a job's potential to serve as a learning experience for the employee. For example, one would assume that managers learn when they take on unfamiliar responsibilities or when they encounter and deal with adverse business conditions.

The profile was developed and validated using a sample of 692. Subsamples were used in some of the validation studies. Norms were developed using a sample of 1,049. Inadequate data are provided on these groups. Although age, sex, race, and years of managerial experience are useful descriptors, they are also rather broad. It would also be useful to know more about the type of industry and managerial responsibilities of the individuals around whom the DCP is based. This is especially pertinent in the case of the norm group, about which little descriptive data are provided.

The DCP is attractively designed with clear and easily followed instructions. The manual and trainer's guide is comprehensive, containing in-depth descriptions of the job components, information on development of the profile, psychometric data, a sample DCP summary report with discussion cases and suggestions for helping managers interpret their report, and research references.

Overall, the DCP is an interesting instrument designed to assess the opportunities for development in managerial positions. The profile has an impressive developmental background and solid psychometric support. The combination of the items and the summary report should cause managers to reflect on the learning opportunities available in their position. The psychometric data argue for the validity of the instrument and suggest that the profile will serve its intended purpose.

[95]
Developmental Observation Checklist System.

Purpose: "For the assessment of very young children with respect to general development (DC), adjustment behavior (ABC), and parent stress and support (PSSC)."
Population: Birth to age 6.
Publication Date: 1994.
Acronym: DOCS.

Scores, 12: Developmental Checklist (Cognition, Language, Social, Motor, Total); Adjustment Behavior Checklist (Mother, Father, Both Parents, Teacher); Parental Stress and Support Checklist (Mother, Father, Both Parents).
Administration: Individual.
Parts, 3: Developmental Checklist, Adjustment Behavior Checklist, Parental Stress and Support Checklist.
Price Data, 1994: $84 per complete kit including manual (91 pages), 25 profile/record forms, 25 DC profile/record forms, 25 ABC profile/record forms, and 25 PSSC profile/record forms; $28 per manual; $9 per 25 profile/record forms; $34 per 25 DC profile/record forms; $9 per ABC or PSSC profile/record forms; $89 per Macintosh PRO-SCORE system; $79 per IBM PRO-SCORE system.
Time: Administration time not reported.
Authors: Wayne P. Hresko, Shirley A. Miguel, Rita J. Sherbenou, and Steve D. Burton.
Publisher: PRO-ED, Inc.

Review of the Developmental Observation Checklist System by FRANK M. BERNT, Associate Professor of Health Services, St. Joseph's University, Philadelphia, PA:

The Developmental Observation Checklist System (DOCS) is a screening device for identifying younger children who may be at-risk (as a function of developmental delays, family system stressors, or both) and who might, therefore, need additional assessment or referral. It is also intended to be an instrument for measuring educational progress and for use in research studies. The DOCS is appropriate for children ages 6 years and younger living in the United States whose parents' dominant language is English. All portions of the DOCS are completed by the child's parent (or by a teacher or caretaker who is very familiar with the child), with minimal guidance from a test administrator. Instructions and items are written to be understood by adults with a fourth grade reading level. In cases where parents cannot read at this level, administrators are advised to provide assistance by reading instructions and items aloud.

The first portion of the DOCS (Developmental Checklist, or DC scale) consists of 475 statements describing skills or behaviors found in young children. Parents (caretakers) indicate whether the child is performing the particular behavior by checking either "yes" or "no." Respondents do not complete all 475 items; the statements are ordered in a developmental sequence (from easiest to most difficult), so that respondents begin at an entry point based upon the child's age (the test administrator helps the respondent get started). Respondents progress through the items to establish a basal level (the highest point at which five answers in a row receive a "yes" response) and a ceiling level (the point at which five answers in a row receive a "no" response). All items below the basal level are scored as correct, and no items above the ceiling level are scored as correct (sufficient examples with computation are provided in the manual to make such calculations very simple). The DC scale takes about 20 minutes to complete.

The Adjustment Behavior Checklist (ABC) consists of 25 items using a 4-point rating system (from *very much like* to *not at all like*); the Parental Stress and Support Checklist (PSSC) consists of 40 items using a 4-point rating system (from *highly agree* to *do not agree*). All items for these two tests are to be completed regardless of the child's age. It takes about 10 minutes to complete both scales.

RELIABILITY AND VALIDITY. Description of the development and standardization of the DOCS is thorough; documentation of its reliability and validity is impressive. Internal consistency estimates (coefficient alpha) range from .94 to .99 for Language, Motor, Social, Cognitive, and Overall scales on the DC. It is not clear which items were used for each age group; consequently, it is difficult to determine whether such estimates might have been an artifact of including items below the basal level not actually answered by parents (based on the scoring assumptions reported in the manual). For the ABC, internal consistency estimates are slightly lower but still well within acceptable range (.81 for the youngest group and .88–.90 for older groups). Alpha values for the PSSC ranged from .90 to .94.

Test-retest reliabilities ranged from .85 to .96 for three separate age groups on all components of the DC, on the ABC, and on the PSSC (14–21 days between administrations). Interrater reliability was examined for a group of 30 children ages 4 to 5 years, using parents and caregivers as raters. Coefficients for component and overall scores on the DC ranged from .91 to .94. Interrater reliabilities for the ABC and PSSC were not reported.

Examination of concurrent validity involved numerous separate studies using sample sizes ranging from 20 to 35 for age groups of 3–4 years and older. Correlations between the total scale score for the DC and comparable scales were high: for example, .72 with the McCarthy Scale, .74 with Denver-R, and .71 with the Slosson Intelligence Test (Revised). Correlations between subscales of the DC and analogous subscales

from other tests were slightly lower but still very supportive of concurrent validity (mean rs for correlations with each of the four subscales range from .52 to .58).

The ABC was highly correlated with the Test of Early Socioemotional Development and the Vineland Adaptive Behavior Scale ($r = .65$ and .69, respectively). The PSSC was highly correlated with the Parental Stress Inventory ($r = -.72$, reverse scoring).

Examination of the intercorrelations among DC, ABC, and PSSC components indicated that the four DC subscales were virtually perfectly correlated with each other (rs ranging from .97 to .99). This may reflect a combination of peculiarities of the test. Perhaps most importantly, a large number of the items contribute to more than one subscale score. Given this and test characteristics, it is difficult to say whether the subscales really serve any purpose separate from one another. None of the DC components were significantly correlated to either the ABC or the PSSC; ABC and PSSC scales were moderately correlated ($r = .44$).

SUMMARY. The development of the DOCS is thorough and has yielded an assessment instrument with very satisfactory reliability and validity. The manual provides strong evidence to support its suitability as a screening/initial assessment device for the three broad areas that it measures: social-developmental level of the child, family support and stress, and social adjustment. It appears to have strong potential as a research tool and as an instrument for measuring developmental progress and instructional effectiveness. The suggestion that it might serve as a source of directing instructional practice and of facilitating referral seems sensible but is (by virtue of its recent publication) not yet empirically established.

Given its concurrent validity relative to similar tests of child development, the DOCS appears to offer several advantages over alternatives. It is easy to complete; it is largely self-administered, so that it lends itself to group administration. The DOCS has been standardized using a much more representative norm sample than most alternatives, including the Receptive-Expressive Emergent Language Test and the Denver II. Its inclusion of a Parental Stress scale adds a systems component that is not found in other developmental scales. Its validity and reliability evidence is much more extensive than is found in most other cases.

In summary, the DOCS has much to recommend it. Perhaps the only aspect of the DOCS that begs more careful attention is the untested assumption that items are ordered from least to most difficult. Although the description of test development indicates that experts in child development were consulted to execute this ordering, it seems that the credibility of using the basal-ceiling approach would be enhanced substantially if some type of multidimensional scalogram analysis of the DC subtest were done. Once the cumulative nature or hierarchical ordering of items on this scale is established, its advantages over other similar tests—even the Denver II (12:103)—will make it a very appealing alternative.

Review of the Developmental Observation Checklist System by GENE SCHWARTING, Project Director, Early Childhood Special Education, Omaha Public Schools, Omaha, NE:

INTRODUCTION. The Developmental Observation Checklist System (DOCS) was developed to serve as a screening instrument for children below the age of 6 years to identify potential developmental delays. The major components, all of which utilize a parent-report format, are a Developmental Checklist (DC), an Adjustment Behavior Checklist (ABC), and a Parent Stress and Support Checklist (PSSC).

The DC consists of 475 items for which the parent responds "yes" or "no" to descriptions of specific behaviors to assess current skills in Cognitive, Language, Social, Motor, and Overall development. Suggested starting points based on the child's chronological age are given, with basals and ceilings of five consecutive positive or negative responses respectively. The ABC involves 25 descriptions of negative behaviors of children, to which the parent responds on a 4-point Likert-type scale. The PSSC includes 40 items describing parental needs and concerns, again expressed on a 4-point scale. Tables in the manual are used to translate the raw scores into percentiles, standard scores, normal curve equivalent (NCE) scores, and age equivalents.

None of the scales are timed; however, it is estimated that parents will complete the three forms in 30 minutes. Examiners who score and interpret the instrument should have some exposure to tests and measurement strategies as well as developmental assessment techniques.

TEST DEVELOPMENT. At its inception, the authors identified several purposes for the DOCS, developed constructs for these purposes, and created items to measure these constructs. The original version, with 1,060 items, was administered to a sample of 200 parents and the results used to revise

the items and their sequence, with this revision administered to a second sample of 100 prior to the norming process.

The actual standardization was done in 30 states over the period from 1989 to 1992. Subjects were recruited whose demographics matched their community, and the resultant norm group of 1,094 reflects a close approximation to the general population in terms of ethnicity, gender, urban/rural status, and geographic location. Information is not presented as to socioeconomic status of the parents.

VALIDITY AND RELIABILITY. Internal consistency, using coefficient alpha, is .99 for the DC subtests and overall score for almost every age group (range is .94–.99). The ABC varies from .81 to .90 and the PSSC from .90 to .94 by age cohort. Interrater reliability on a single sample ($r = 30$) of the DC, comparing parent and caregiver scores, is greater than .90 for the subtests as well as the total score. And, test-retest reliability varies from .85 to .96 for all components of the DC, ABC, and PSSC on three samples of parents of 2- to 5-year-old children.

Construct validity evidence is provided by comparison of scores with chronological age and the intercorrelations of the sections of the DC with ABC and PSSC, with all correlations being significant. A number of criterion-related validity studies were conducted (sample sizes of 20–35) among the DOCS components, comparing them to various intelligence, language, and adaptive behavior measures with correlations varying from -.41 to .83.

SUMMARY AND COMMENTS. Scoring the developmental checklist requires some care, as an item may score for one or all of the scale components, requiring the use of a straightedge to line up the item with the response blanks. In dealing with children functioning well below age level, the floor may not be adequate as standard scores do not go below 64.

The DOCS is dependent on both the parent's ability to be objective and their reading skills, with some items being vague and dependent on parent interpretation (i.e., "protects toys and personal objects"). Responses on the ABC and PSSC are arbitrarily weighted, with "somewhat like" receiving a score of 2 and "not much like" a score of 3, assuming a linear relationship in the scoring of responses. Overall, the DOCS seems to be a well-developed instrument with adequate norms, validity, and reliability. It appears to have promise as a screening measure for young children, to be followed as needed by direct assessment.

[96]
Devereux Behavior Rating Scale—School Form.

Purpose: To evaluate "behaviors typical of children and adolescents with moderate to severe emotional disturbance."
Population: Ages 5–18.
Publication Dates: 1990–1993.
Acronym: BRSS.
Scores, 4: Interpersonal Problems, Inappropriate Behaviors/Feelings, Depression, Physical Symptoms/Fears.
Administration: Individual.
Forms, 2: Children, Adolescents.
Price Data, 1994: $95 per complete kit including manual ('93, 42 pages), 25 answer documents 5–12, and 25 ready score answer documents 13–18; $50 per manual; $22.50 per 25 ready score answer documents 5–12; $22.50 per 25 ready score answer documents 13–18.
Time: (5–10) minutes.
Comments: Ratings by parents and teachers.
Authors: Jack A. Naglieri, Paul A. LeBuffe, and Steven I. Pfeiffer.
Publisher: The Psychological Corporation.
Cross References: For additional information on the Devereux Adolescent Behavior Rating Scale, see T3:702 (1 reference); for a review by Carl F. Jesness, see 7:66; see also P:60 (1 reference). For additional information on the Devereux Child Behavior Rating Scale, see T3:203 (6 references); see also T2:1158 (1 reference); for a review by Allan G. Barclay, see 7:67; see also P:61 (3 references).

TEST REFERENCES

1. Weintraub, S. (1987). Risk factors in schizophrenia: The Stony Brook high risk project. *Schizophrenia Bulletin, 13,* 439–450.
2. Renken, B., Egeland, B., Marvinney, D., Mangelsdorf, S., & Sroufe, L. A. (1989). Early childhood antecedents of aggression and passive-withdrawal in early elementary school. *Journal of Personality, 57,* 257–281.
3. Pianta, R. C., & Egeland, B. (1994). Predictors of instability in children's mental test performance at 24, 48, and 96 months. *Intelligence, 18,* 145-163.
4. Safran, S. P., Safran, J. S., & Rich, C. E. (1994). What disturbs students? An examination of age and gender differences. *The Journal of Special Education, 28,* 138–148.
5. Masten, A. S., Coatsworth, J. D., Neemann, J., Gest, S., Tellegen, A., & Garmezy, N. (1995). The structure and coherence of competence from childhood through adolescence. *Child Development, 66,* 1635–1659.
6. McDermott, P. A., Watkins, M. W., Sichel, A. F., Weber, E. M., Keenan, J. T., Holland, A. M., & Leigh, N. M. (1995). The accuracy of new national scales for detecting emotional disturbance in children and adolescents. *The Journal of Special Education, 29,* 337–354.
7. Naglieri, J. A., Bardos, A. N., & LeBuffe, P. A. (1995). Discriminant validity of the Devereux Behavior Rating Scale—Short Form for students with serious emotional disturbance. *School Psychology Review, 24,* 104–111.
8. Naglieri, J. A., & Gottling, S. H. (1995). Use of the Teacher Report Form and the Devereux Behavior Rating Scale—School Form with learning disordered/emotionally disordered students. *Journal of Clinical Child Psychology, 24,* 71-76.

Review of the Devereux Behavior Rating Scale—School Form by LISA BLOOM, Associate Professor of Special Education, Western Carolina University, Cullowhee, NC:

DESCRIPTION AND PURPOSE. The Devereux Behavior Rating Scale—School Form is a behavior rating scale used for assessing maladjustment in children and adolescents. This instrument can be used for several purposes. It can be used to (a) screen for children or adolescents who may need more in-depth evaluation, (b) determine behavioral aspects that are more atypical than others (i.e., depression), (c) identify specific problem behaviors, and (d) monitor and evaluate progress over time.

The instrument includes two rating scales, one for ages 5–12 and the other for ages 13–18. Each scale includes four subscales that correspond to four areas of the federal definition for Serious Emotional Disturbance, Interpersonal Problems, Inappropriate Behaviors/Feelings, Depression, and Physical Symptoms/Fears.

The Devereux School Form represents a revision of the Devereux Child Behavior Rating Scale (T3:703) and the Devereux Adolescent Behavior Rating Scales (T3:702). The revisions include the following. First, the Devereux child and adolescent scales were combined into one scale with two levels for two age groups. These two levels overlap by 55%. Second, the items were revised. Many items were simplified, outdated terms and phrases were eliminated, and the use of jargon was minimized. Third, modifications were made in the format to make it easier to administer, score, and interpret. Fourth, items are now organized into areas that represent types of difficulties consistent with the federal definition of Serious Emotional Disturbance. Fifth, items were selected to effectively differentiate normal children and adolescents from those with moderate to severe emotional disturbance. A new standardization sample was included to ensure the scale accurately depicts behavioral functioning of contemporary children and adolescents. Finally, evidence of reliability and validity are presented.

ADMINISTRATION AND SCORING. The Devereux School Form is easy to score and use. Items and directions are written at about a fifth to sixth grade level. Both scales contain 40 items. The responder is prompted to focus on the past 4 weeks, and identify on a 5-point scale from *never* to *very frequently* how often the child engages in specific behaviors. Subsequent questions include phrases such as "annoy others," and "fail to show pride in his or her accomplishments." The examiner is encouraged to obtain ratings from several sources including parents, several teachers, and teacher's aides.

Item raw scores are obtained directly from the record. Scores for each subscale are determined by adding the scores for each item included in the respective subscale. Total scores are computed by totaling scores on all items. Clear directions and tables are provided for converting total raw scores and subscale raw scores to standard scores. Confidence intervals and cutoff scores for determining that a child or adolescent should be described as having a significantly high score on the Devereux—School Form are provided. Directions are also given to identify particular behaviors that warrant specific interventions or further investigation.

ITEM SELECTION AND STANDARDIZATION. Item selection involved a review of items from the original scales. These items, as well as new items developed, were based on a review of the literature, the diagnostic criteria in the *DSM-III-R*, comparisons to other rating scales, reviews by noted experts in the field, and field tests.

The test was standardized on 3,153 children and adolescents aged 5–18 years. This sample was representative of the U.S. population in terms of age, gender, geographic region, race, ethnicity, socioeconomic status, community size, and educational placement.

PSYCHOMETRIC PROPERTIES. With regard to reliability, adequate data on internal reliability, test-retest reliability, and interrater and intrarater reliability were reported. Internal consistency was determined with Cronbach's alpha. The total scale internal reliability coefficients range form a low of .92 to a high of .97. The coefficients for the four subscales range from a low of .70 for parents rating females aged 13–18 on Inappropriate Behavior/Feelings to a high of .94 for teachers' ratings for males aged 5–12 on the Inappropriate Behavior/Feelings subscales.

Two test-retest reliability studies were conducted, one with a clinical sample and one with a regular education sample. The correlation coefficients obtained from these studies ranged from a low of .34 (a 4-week interval on the Physical Symptoms/Fears subscale) from the clinical sample to a high of .85 for the total scale with the regular education sample (a 1-week interval).

Two interrater studies show a total scale reliability of .40 and .53 (*p*<.01). The subscale coefficients ranged from .36 to .60. For one of the interrater studies, teacher ratings were compared with residential counselor ratings. One would expect these coefficients to be lower because the children and adolescents were observed in different settings and context. For the other interrater study, teacher and teacher's aide ratings were compared. The lower coefficients obtained here (.40 to .60) are somewhat bothersome because those raters observed the children and adolescents in the same setting.

Intrarater studies show a total scale reliability of .57 and .78 (*p*<.01). One would expect lower intrarater reliability because as much as 70 days elapsed between ratings (enough time for behavioral improvements to occur).

The standard errors of measurement for the Total Scale standard score range from a low of 2.65 (teacher ratings for females 5–12) to a high of 4.22 (parents ratings for females aged 13–18) with an average of 3.45.

Authors also report on content-related, construct-related, and criterion-related validity. With regard to content validity, the authors report selecting items from a large pool so that behaviors in each of the four subscales are adequately represented. Construct validity was determined by calculating the correlations of the items to the total score. All item-total correlations are significant (*p*>.01) and most are greater than .50. Criterion-related validity was assessed by determining the extent to which ratings discriminated between normal and clinically diagnosed groups. To that end, six studies were completed. For ages 5–12 years, the lowest accuracy rate was 73.2% and the highest 79.2%. For ages 13–18 the highest was 93% and the lowest was 60.2%. The averages were 75.3% for ages 5–12 and 77.5% for ages 13–18.

STRENGTHS AND WEAKNESSES. The strength of the Devereux School Form is that it can provide the examiner with information regarding children and adolescents from several sources including parents and teachers. The items are written in clear simple language with an emphasis on how often behaviors occurred in the past 4 weeks. Many of the items are written in observable terms. This type of format may lend itself well to gaining information from a variety of settings and responders at different intervals. Thus, it may be a useful tool for screening as well as documenting improvement during the course of a treatment program. Additionally, the manual provides sufficient technical information and is well written.

One weakness of the Devereux School Form, as with many behavior rating scales, is that the items exclusively describe negative behaviors. Therefore, they are not useful in identifying student strengths and would be difficult to use in formulating positively oriented observable behaviors for goals and objectives.

Another weakness is that interrater reliability was low for the subscales and criterion-related reliability data were not reported for them. Additionally, each subscale contains only 10 items. This number does not appear to be sufficient. Therefore, caution should be used in determining a diagnosis for the subareas using the Devereux School Form.

As long as the user is aware of these limitations, the Devereux School Form may be a reasonable tool for individuals working with children and with youth "at risk" for serious emotional disturbance. It may assist with identification, planning, and progress monitoring.

Review of the Devereux Behavior Rating Scale— School Form by RICHARD F. FARMER, Assistant Professor of Psychology, Idaho State University, Pocatello, ID:

The Devereux Behavior Rating Scale—School Form (Devereux—School Form) was designed to assess the degree to which a child or adolescent displays behaviors that are indicative of moderate to severe emotional disturbance. The two levels of the Devereux—School Form (for children ages 5–12 and adolescents ages 13–18) represent substantive revisions of the Devereux Child Behavior Rating Scale (Spivack & Spotts, 1966; T3:703) and the Devereux Adolescent Behavior Rating Scale (Spivack, Spotts, & Haimes, 1967: T3:702). Each of the two new forms contains 40 behaviorally referenced items that are rated along a 5-point continuum (0 = *never* to 4 = *very frequently*) according to frequency of occurrence over the past 4 weeks. Scale items, written at the 6th grade level, are rated by persons who have sufficient opportunities to observe the child or adolescent across a variety of settings (e.g., parents, teachers, vocational trainers, inpatient counselors). The entire scale requires about 5 to 10 minutes to complete. Total Scale standard scores ($M = 100$, $SD = 15$) and standardized Subscale Scores ($M = 10$, $SD = 3$) can be derived from item raw scores. Specific problem behaviors can also be identified from the rating sheet, which denotes scores for individual items that are equal to or exceed 1 SD above the mean.

A number of modifications were made in the revised form, including changes in content coverage, item formatting, and scoring. Item selection was primarily guided by federal definitions for serious emotional disturbance. The content domains of the four, 10-item subscales found in both versions of the Devereux—School Form (Interpersonal Problems, Inappropriate Behaviors/Feelings, Depression, and Physical Symptoms/Fears) correspond to areas included in these federal definitions. The inability to learn not accounted for by physiological, health, or intellectual impairments, another component of the federal guidelines, is not included in the Devereux—School Form as the test developers correctly assert that this area is best evaluated through direct assessments of academic achievement.

The national normative standardization sample consisted of 2,042 children and 1,111 adolescents who attended regular education classes. Demographic characteristics of the normative sample are representative of the larger U.S. population in terms of gender, community size (i.e., urban, suburban, rural), race, and ethnicity as indexed by 1990 and 1991 U.S. Census data. Each of the ages from 5 to 18 years was adequately sampled, as were the various geographic regions of the U.S. Self-reported educational attainment of parents of the normative sample was somewhat higher than U.S. Census figures, however (e.g., some college or college graduate: 52.3% for sample versus 39.9% for population). Separate norms are provided for each age group, with these two sets of norms further subdivided by child or adolescent gender and rater (i.e., teacher or parent).

Reliability of the Devereux—School Form was assessed with multiple methods. Median internal consistency values ranged between .94 and .96 for the Total Score and .82 to .85 for the four subscales. Test-retest correlations based on a 1-week retest interval for the Total Score ranged between .69 and .85 for adolescents and children, respectively, in regular education settings. For clinical samples, test-retest correlations ranged between .75 for a 24-hour retest interval and .52 for a 4-week interval. Subscale test-retest reliability coefficients for all samples demonstrated more variability, but generally revealed adequate levels of stability (i.e., $r \geq .50$) across temporal periods up to 4 weeks. Total score interrater reliability (rs = .53 and .40 for the general education and clinical samples, respectively) and intrarater reliability (rs = .78 and .57 for the educational and clinical samples, respectively) also appeared satisfactory. Indeed, the presentation of separate reliability values for general education and clinical samples likely resulted in attenuated reliability values due to range restriction of scores.

The validity of the Devereux—School Form is largely supported by demonstrations of criterion-related validity using the known groups method. Six studies are presented in the test manual, which compared behavior ratings for samples of emotionally disturbed children and adolescents against matched controls. Using the criterion of a Test Score $\geq +1$ *SD* as indicative of emotional disturbance, 75.3% of children and 77.5% of adolescents across the six studies were correctly classified as belonging to the clinical or control samples. Overall, correct classification rates were better for the control sample, with false negative rates tending to be higher than false positive rates. Clinical samples that were characterized by relatively severe emotional disturbance by virtue of their placement (e.g., those receiving treatment in a psychiatric hospital) tended to be more accurately classified than those who evidenced less disturbance (e.g., those who were clinically diagnosed and receiving special education services).

In summary, the Devereux—School Form is presented as a measure designed to assess the presence of moderate to severe emotional disturbance in children and adolescents. This measure can also be used to identify specific problem areas as represented by the four subscales and specific problem behaviors through an examination of individual item ratings. Other applications such as the evaluation of the appropriateness of special education classes and the effectiveness of intervention strategies through repeated assessments are also possible. Strengths of the Devereux—School Form include the use of large and representative normative samples, sound standardization procedures, ease of test use and scoring, and adequate reliability. This measure appears to be most valid for identifying emotional disturbance among children and adolescents with relatively severe emotional problems. Users will also find the test manual well-written and informative. Relative weaknesses include the absence of specific behavioral guidelines for making behavioral frequency ratings (e.g., what constitutes "occasionally" or "very frequently"?), invariance in the direction of item keying, and an absence of data on individual item reliabilities necessary to support the utility of individual item ratings for identifying specific behavioral problem areas. Given the high Total Scale internal consistency coefficients, one must also wonder about the degree to which each of the four subscales measures different constructs. The test manual does not provide intercorrelations among subscale scores or other data that would further support the validity of the subscales (e.g., factor analysis of scale items, correlations between individual subscales and other measures that purport to measure the same construct). As such, some degree of caution should be exercised in interpretation of subscale scores despite the apparent face validity of items when considered in conjunction with their associated subscale labels. Apart from these few relative weaknesses, the Devereux—School Form appears to be a sound measure of severe emotional disturbance for child and adolescent populations.

REVIEWER'S REFERENCES

Spivack, G., & Spotts, J. (1966). Devereux Child Behavior Rating Scale. Devon, PA: The Devereux Foundation Press.
Spivack, G., Spotts, J., & Haimes, P. E. (1967). Devereux Adolescent Behavior Rating Scale. Devon, PA: The Devereux Foundation Press.

[97]
Diagnosing Organizational Culture.

Purpose: "Designed to help consultants and organizational members identify the shared values and beliefs that constitute an organization's culture."
Population: Adults.
Publication Dates: 1992–1993.
Scores: 5 scores (Power, Role, Achievement, Support, Total) in each of two areas: Existing Culture, Preferred Culture.
Administration: Group.
Price Data, 1993: $24.95 per complete kit including trainer's manual ('93, 58 pages) and instrument ('92, 30 pages); $8.95 per instrument.
Time: (45–60) minutes.
Authors: Roger Harrison and Herb Stokes (instrument only).
Publisher: Pfeiffer & Company International Publishers.

Review of Diagnosing Organizational Culture by JOHN W. FLEENOR, *Director of Research, Mediappraise Corp., Raleigh, NC:*

Diagnosing Organizational Culture is a 15-item questionnaire developed to measure the four components of Harrison's (1972) model of organizational culture. The four components of this model are Power orientation, Role orientation, Achievement orientation, and Support orientation. In a Power-oriented organization, there is an inequality in access to resources; people higher in the organization have more access to resources than do lower-level employees. In a Role-oriented organization, structures and procedures are substituted for power among the leaders. In an Achievement-oriented organization, employees are motivated by intrinsic rewards, such as the work itself, rather than by external rewards. In a Support-oriented organization, the climate is based on mutual trust between the individual and the organization, and the employees believe they are valued as individuals, rather than just as cogs in a machine. According to Harrison, every organization has some combination of these four components, which are only partially compatible with one another. The benefits of one component can only be achieved at the expense of the other components. Harrison recommends using Diagnosing Organizational Culture for organizational assessment and diagnosis to help raise the awareness of employees on issues related to organizational culture.

The initial version of Diagnosing Organizational Culture was developed in the 1970s by Harrison. During the 1980s, the instrument was revised by Harrison with the assistance of Stokes. The current version was published in 1992.

MANUAL. In addition to the instrument booklet, a trainer's manual also is provided. In the trainer's manual, Harrison describes the ways the instrument can be used, the model on which the instrument is based, and basic psychometric properties of the instrument. He describes how to conduct a workshop on organizational culture using the results from this instrument. This manual also includes masters for transparencies to be used in this workshop, which should be helpful to workshop presenters.

ADMINISTRATION AND SCORING. The instrument is self-scored by the respondents. On each of 15 items, the respondents rank four possible alternatives according to how well each describes the existing culture in their organization (4 = high, 1 = low). On each item, the "a" alternative refers to Power-orientation (P), the "b" alternative to Role-orientation (R), the "c" alternative to Achievement-orientation (A), and the "d" alternative to Support-orientation (S). For each item, the respondents also rank the four alternatives as to how well each describes their preferred culture. Scores are calculated by adding the ranks individually for each of the four orientations. In addition to the orientation scores, a total score is provided for both the existing culture and the preferred culture. Known as the culture index, the total score is calculated by using the following formula: A + S - P - R.

RELIABILITY. In a study of the reliability of Diagnosing Organizational Culture, the instrument was administered to 231 employees in a large company. Split-half reliabilities of the four orientations, corrected by the Spearman-Brown formula, were calculated. Apparently, each alternative was considered as a separate item, which resulted in 60 items being used in this analysis (four alternatives for each of 15 items). The obtained reliabilities were .90 for Power, .87 for Support, .86 for Achievement, .64 for Role, and .85 for the Culture Index.

VALIDITY. As evidence of validity, Harrison correlated scores from Diagnosing Organizational Culture with scores from another measure of organizational culture developed by Janz (undated). The Janz questionnaire was designed to measure values, power, and rules. The Power scale from Diagnosing Organizational Culture correlated .79 with the power scale from the Janz questionnaire. Additionally, Role correlated .40 with the rules scale, and Achievement correlated .69 with the values scale. Janz had previously reported that his instrument was related to measures of organizational performance. This led Harrison to contend that these findings provide indirect evidence of validity for Diagnosing Organizational Culture, because of the correlation between the two instruments.

CONCLUSION. Diagnosing Organizational Culture was designed to be a relatively quick, easy, and inexpensive method of measuring self-perceptions of organizational climate. It appears, to a large extent, that the questionnaire meets these objectives. Because it provides measures of both actual and preferred organizational climates, the instrument may be useful as a self-awareness tool in training sessions on organizational climate. The instrument allows the respondents to see how well their current organizations meet their expectations of work-place climate. Much of the trainer's manual is devoted to the use of Diagnosing Organizational Culture in training sessions on organizational climate.

However, because of the transparent nature of the items, the self-scoring method, and the rather perfunctory reliability and validity analyses, the instruments cannot be recommended for full-scale organizational change efforts. Additionally, no evidence is presented to support the additive model used to calculate the Climate Index, and the reported reliability of the Role scale is below acceptable standards. If one wishes to conduct an organizational change effort, it is recommended that a more sophisticated measure of organizational climate be used—one that includes, for example, respondent anonymity, demonstrated validity and reliability, and a detailed feedback report.

REVIEWER'S REFERENCES

Janz, T. (undated). *The reliability, construct, and criterion validity of a compact measure of organization culture.* Calgary, Canada: Human Performance Systems.
Harrison, R. (1972). Understanding your organization's character. *Harvard Business Review*, May–June, 119–128.

[98]

Diagnostic Achievement Test for Adolescents, Second Edition.

Purpose: To provide "examiners with an estimate of students' listening and speaking skills and their knowledge of information commonly taught in schools."
Population: Ages 12–0 to 18–11.
Publication Dates: 1986–1993.

Acronym: DATA-2.

Scores, 22: 13 subtest scores (Receptive Vocabulary, Receptive Grammar, Expressive Grammar, Expressive Vocabulary, Word Identification, Reading Comprehension, Spelling, Writing Composition, Math Calculation, Math Problem Solving, Science, Social Studies, Reference Skills) and 9 composite scores (Listening, Speaking, Reading, Writing, Math, Spoken Language, Written Language, Achievement Screener, Total Achievement).

Administration: Individual.

Price Data, 1994: $104 per complete kit including examiner's manual ('93, 73 pages), 25 student response forms, 25 profile/examiner record forms, and a student booklet; $29 per examiner's manual; $18 per 25 student response forms; $39 per 25 profile/examiner record forms; $22 per student booklet; $89 per Macintosh PRO-SCORE; $79 per IBM PRO-SCORE.

Time: (60—120) minutes.

Authors: Phyllis L. Newcomer and Brian R. Bryant.

Publisher: PRO-ED, Inc.

Cross References: For reviews of an earlier edition by Randy W. Kamphaus and James E. Ysseldyke, see 10:92.

TEST REFERENCES

1. Vallicorsa, A. L., & Garriss, E. (1990). Story composition skills of middle-grade students with learning disabilities. *Exceptional Children, 57,* 48-54.

Review of the Diagnostic Achievement Test for Adolescents, Second Edition by JERRILYN V. ANDREWS, Assistant for Assessment and Data Collection, Office of School Administration, Montgomery County Public Schools, Rockville, MD:

The Diagnostic Achievement Test for Adolescents, Second Edition (DATA—2) includes all nine subtests that were part of the first edition of the DATA as well as four new ones: Receptive Vocabulary, Receptive Grammar, Expressive Grammar, and Expressive Vocabulary. The addition of the four subtests is accompanied by the addition of four new composite scores: Listening, Speaking, Spoken Language, and Written Language, added to the original five in DATA. DATA—2 offers considerably broader coverage of skills of interest at the secondary school level than other individually administered achievement tests. With an estimated testing time of only 1 to 2 hours, the DATA—2 provides a wide range of information for a minimal time investment. Like the first edition, the DATA—2 materials are easy to manage, the examiner instructions are clear, and the test itself is easy to administer and score. DATA—2, like the earlier edition, offers raw scores, percentiles, and standard scores for subtests and composites.

Unfortunately, many of the weaknesses found in the original DATA have been carried forward to the second edition. The psychometric properties of the test still do not seem to have been rigorously investigated.

From the manual, it appears the original DATA items and subtests are unaltered and the norms for them are still based on the original, Phase 1, norming sample (1985–86). A second norming group, referred to as Phase 2 (1990–91), was used for the new subtests. It is not clear from the manual whether the Phase 2 norming sample was given the entire DATA—2 or given only the new subtests. Further, it appears that the norms for the new subtests and their associated composite scores are based only on the Phase 2 sample. The manual authors state that the combined Phase 1 and 2 samples include 2,085 students from 19 states; Phase 1 alone contained 1,035 students from 15 states. From that information, it is impossible to tell how many states are represented in Phase 2. The initial list from which both samples were generated was the PRO-ED customer file so it is possible that some students are in both samples. The description of these samples and how they have been used is not adequate.

The authors assert the combined norming sample is a good demographic match to the national school-aged population. The only percentage distributions included in the manual are race (white, black, other), ethnicity (African American, American Indian, Asian, Hispanic, other), gender, region, age, and residence (rural, urban). These demographic variables have not been cross-tabulated; the user cannot tell, for example, how the percentage of African American males compares to the percent in the school-aged population. Comparing the race and the ethnicity data, it appears the racial category "white" is the summation of the ethnic categories "Hispanic" and "other" and that the racial category "other" is the summation of the ethnic categories "American Indian" and "Asian." The lack of any SES data comparing the norm group to the national population remains a major weakness. Although the test has norms for students through age 18, only 90 18-year-olds are included in the combined norming sample.

The discussion of test reliability in the examiner's manual is brief. The manual does contain coefficient alphas calculated for each of the subtests and for the composite scores; these were based on a random sample of 50 protocols from each age, 12 through 18 years. The coefficients calculated individually for each age for each of the subtests and composites were averaged over all ages; these average alphas all exceed .8, which is commendable. Standard errors of measurement are also presented and appear reasonable. There is no mention, however, of test-retest reliability. The original DATA manual contained some information on test-retest reliability but the results were rather weak. Although the DATA—2 manual contains much of the original psychometric information from the DATA, the test-retest reliability data are no longer included in the manual, and no new data on this have been added.

With the exception of content validity, the validity data are rather weak. Predictive validity has not been examined. Concurrent validity of the DATA—2 was assessed by administering it and the Wide Range Achievement Test—Revised (WRAT—R) to a total of 30 students from Austin, Texas. The ages of the students and dates of testing are not reported. All other data reported regarding concurrent validity are from the original publication of the DATA and do not include the new subtests. Exact correlations are reported only when they are significant. Potential test users should be provided with all correlations. (For a detailed discussion of the weaknesses found in the validation of the DATA, the reader is referred to the reviews by Kamphaus and by Ysseldyke in 10:92.)

The authors provide some very appropriate cautions on interpreting DATA—2 scores. They are to be particularly commended for strongly emphasizing that low scores on the DATA—2 do not mean a student has a learning disability. In their words "Low scores merely mean that a student has had difficulty with the contents of this test" (p. 36). Because individually administered achievement tests are used most often with students who are not experiencing academic success, these warnings are important.

In summary, the DATA—2 has some very strong points compared to other individually administered achievement tests. Most notable are its broad coverage of academic skills taught at the secondary level, the inclusion of subtests assessing listening and speaking skills, reasonable test administration time, and straightforward directions for administration and scoring. Its psychometric properties, however, are not adequately documented. Potential users who plan to use test norms would be well advised to use great caution or administer a test with stronger psychological underpinnings.

Review of the Diagnostic Achievement Test for Adolescents, Second Edition by GERALD E. DeMAURO, Director, Bureau of Assessment, New Jersey State Department of Education, Trenton, NJ:

The Diagnostic Achievement Test for Adolescents, Second Edition (DATA—2) is designed to provide an evaluation of students' listening and speaking skills and knowledge of acquired information. The stated purposes of the DATA—2 are to: Identify students in need of instructional intervention, identify individuals' strengths and weaknesses, document student progress in response to intervention, and serve as a research tool (manual, p. 6).

The DATA—2 is individually administered and takes between 1 and 2 hours to complete, depending upon individual student requirements. Basal and ceiling response patterns for all subtests except Writing Composition and Reference Skills are recommended.

The DATA—2 consists of 10 core and 3 optional subtests, some of which can be combined to yield an additional nine composite scores. The subtests range from having a single essay (Writing Composition) or 30 short questions (Expressive Grammar) to 45 questions (Word Identification, Math Calculation, Math Problem Solving, Spelling, Science, Social Studies, and Reference Skills). Science, Social Studies, and Reference Skills are optional. Composite scores are Listening (Receptive Vocabulary and Receptive Grammar), Speaking (Expressive Grammar and Expressive Vocabulary), Reading (Word Identification and Reading Comprehension), Writing (Spelling and Writing Composition), Math (Math Calculation and Math Problem Solving), Spoken Language (Listening and Speaking), Written Language (Reading and Writing), Achievement Screener (Word Identification, Math Calculation, and Spelling), and Total Achievement (the 10 required subtests). All DATA—2 items are short answers, with the exception of Writing Composition, and all subtests except Spelling, Writing Composition, Math Calculation, and Math Problem Solving require oral responses.

DEVELOPMENT. The development of the original instrument (DATA) was based on a literature related to a taxonomy of content areas, spoken language, textbook reviews, subject matter vocabulary, spelling software, and a variety of curricular materials.

The original item pool was field tested in 1984 and 1985 among junior and senior high school students in West Virginia. Items were selected that had point biserial values of .3 or higher and reasonable p-values (.15 to .85).

The revised test, DATA—2, was field tested on 150 junior and senior high school students in

Austin, Texas, using the same item discrimination and difficulty analyses. Median point biserial values indicate better discrimination among older students and generally high values for all subtests but Receptive Grammar where the median values for 12- and 13-year-olds were less than .30. Receptive Grammar (range = .33 to .44), Expressive Vocabulary (range = .15 to .40), Reading Comprehension (range = .38 to .43), and Social Studies (range = .11 to .49) had the lowest median item p-values across age groups.

STANDARDIZATION. The DATA—2 was standardized using 2,085 students in 19 states in two phases. The samples were chosen from PRO-ED customer files. Phase I occurred in 1985 and 1986 and Phase 2 occurred in 1990 and 1991.

Subtest scores are scaled to have a mean of 10 and a standard deviation of 3. Composite scores are scaled to have a mean of 100 and standard deviation of 15. These composite distributions are given for the numbers of subtests combined rather than for specific subtests. The varying correlations between the subtests would be an important factor for interpreting the standard scores for these composites. Scores for age groups in each half year from 12-0 to 18-11 are represented in the subtests normative tables derived from raw score means and standard deviations and then smoothed for each of the 13 subtests.

RELIABILITY. Cronbach's alpha is used to estimate internal consistency of the subtests of seven age groups, 12 to 18 years. The coefficients range from .76 to .98. Receptive Grammar (.84) has the lowest average coefficient across age groups, and Spelling and Writing Composition (.97) has the highest, using r to z transformations for averaging. Writing Composition uses an analytic method to generate scores on an essay.

CONCURRENT VALIDITY. Scores from the earlier form of DATA—2 were correlated with the Stanford Diagnostic Reading Test (n = 33), the Stanford Diagnostic Mathematics Test (n = 38), the Iowa Test of Basic Skills (n = 67), and the Iowa Test of Educational Development (n = 96). There is some evidence of convergence with related measures (e.g., Iowa Test of Basic Skills Spelling correlates well with DATA Spelling, .66).

The DATA—2 concurrent validity is estimated through the correlations of subtest scores with scores of 30 students on the Wide Range Achievement Test—Revised (Jastak & Wilkinson, 1984). Of 66 possible disattenuated correlations, 50 exceeded .35.

CONSTRUCT VALIDITY. DATA scores for 67 students are correlated with scores on the Short Form Test of Academic Aptitude (Sullivan, Clark, & Tiegs, 1974). The coefficients range from .31 (Written Composition) to .58 (Reading Comprehension) for subtests.

Age-standardized DATA scores from 40 students are correlated to scores from the Scholastic Aptitude Scale (Bryant & Newcomer, 1991), the Detroit Tests of Learning Aptitude—3 (Hammill, 1991), and the Test of Nonverbal Intelligence—2 (Brown, Sherbenou, & Johnsen, 1990). The correlations are disattenuated to correct for unreliability. Of 660 correlations, 370 exceed .35.

The authors report results supporting the DATA—2 as an achievement measure in its general correlation to age, high interrelationships among subtests (based on 100 subjects randomly sampled from the normative sample), and relationship to aptitude measures.

DATA—2 scores are also lower for students with learning disabilities, as would be expected of an achievement measure. The authors claim that high item-to-test correlations are evidence of construct validity, although this naturally would depend on the inferences that would be supported by the total test scores.

CONCLUSION. The DATA—2 is an interesting instrument in its attention to individual administration as well as its attention to computation, mechanical, and analytical skills. Clearly, there is a place for an instrument with this focus.

The test would benefit from expansion of the samples on which the validity investigations are based, as well as careful delineation of the inferences permitted by the scores. This is the central validity issue.

Although the convergent properties are well documented, evidence to support the discriminative properties of the subtests would help the interpretation of scores and the rationale for combining some scores with others to yield composites. For example, although Expressive Grammar and Expressive Vocabulary combine to form the Speaking composite, Expressive Vocabulary actually has higher correlations with Receptive Vocabulary, Receptive Grammar, and Reading Comprehension. Attention to these relationships may well recommend different weighting or combining strategies.

Finally, the focus and administrative procedures of this instrument have much to offer. Perhaps item banking strategies would improve its usefulness as a tool that could be used repeatedly. Further work is encouraged.

REVIEWER'S REFERENCES

Sullivan, E. T., Clark, W. W., & Tiegs, E. W. (1974). *Short Form Test of Academic Aptitude.* Monterey, CA: CTB/McGraw-Hill.

Jastak, S., & Wilkinson, G. S. (1984). *Wide Range Achievement Test (revised edition).* Wilmington, DE: Jastak Associates.

Brown, L., Sherbenou, R. J., & Johnsen, S. K. (1990). *Test of Non-verbal Intelligence: A Language-free Measure of Cognitive Ability (2nd edition).* Austin, TX: PRO-ED, Inc.

Bryant, B. R., & Newcomer, P. (1991). *Scholastic Aptitude Scale.* Boca Raton, FL: Psycho-Educational Services.

Hammill, D. D. (1991). *Detroit Tests of Learning Aptitude (3rd edition).* Austin, TX: PRO-ED, Inc.

[99]
Diagnostic Inventory for Screening Children.

Purpose: A diagnostic screening tool used to identify developmental delays in preschool children.
Population: Birth–5 years.
Publication Dates: 1984–1988.
Acronym: DISC.
Scores, 8: Fine Motor, Receptive Language, Expressive Language, Gross Motor, Auditory Attention and Memory, Visual Attention and Memory, Self-Help, Social.
Administration: Individual.
Price Data, 1994: $563 per complete kit; $29 per manual ('88, 163 pages); $86 per 40 record forms; $13 per 40 summary Sheet A; $12 per 40 summary Sheet B; $12 per 40 item performance summary sheets; $14.50 per training videotape manual; $13 per age equivalents profile.
Time: (1545) minutes.
Authors: Jeanette Amdur, Marian Mainland, and Kevin Parker.
Publisher: The Psychological Corporation.
Cross References: See T4:780 (3 references).

Review of the Diagnostic Inventory for Screening Children by GENE SCHWARTING, Project Director, Early Childhood Special Education, Omaha Public Schools, Omaha, NE:

INTRODUCTION. The Diagnostic Inventory for Screening Children (DISC) is to be used as a "diagnostic screening tool" for ages birth to 5 years, and is described as the middle of a three-sieve system, following a broad general screen and preceding a full assessment. The DISC provides a developmental profile in eight areas, with results available as age scores, percentiles, and categorization as average or delayed within one's age cohort. It is to be individually administered by a trained examiner with minimal credentials of a 2-year college diploma in early childhood.

The test kit consists of a large canvas bag containing balls, puzzles, a pegboard and formboard, crayons, picture books, and many other items. The examiner must provide a ticking clock and a mirror. A test manual provides specific directions and scoring criteria comparable to most instruments designed for this age group, and a 34-page protocol and several summary sheets are available to record scores. Items are not time-limited, and may be administered out of sequence. The record form indicates suggested starting points, with basal and ceiling established by passing or failing all items at an age level. Items are scored as "yes," "no," or "report" (for those limited times when parent report can be used).

TEST DEVELOPMENT. In the late 1970s the need for a screening instrument of this type was noted at the Child and Family Centre at Kitchener-Waterloo Hospital in Kitchener, Ontario. A large number of items were selected, often from already-existing developmental assessments, and administered to an initial sample of 400 children. The final version consists of 27 items in each of the eight scales, spread over 27 age levels. Items are arranged within the scales in order of difficulty, being placed at the age where 75% of the standardization group passed them. Norming was completed (date not specified) on 573 children residing in three counties in Ontario, Canada. This group was categorized as English, French, and "other" with data also provided as to occupation of head of household (over one-third were managerial) and marital status (91% were two-parent households).

RELIABILITY AND VALIDITY. Reliability of .99 is reported for both split-half internal consistency and interrater scoring across the scales and age levels, whereas test-retest (one-week interval) with a small sample (n = 47) varies from .94 to .98. Intercorrelations of the scales vary from .07 to .91, with many falling in the .60–.80 range and raising questions as to the discreteness of the skills being measured. Factor analysis indicates two major factors, described as cognition/motor and social/personality, accounting for most of the variance. Predictive and concurrent validity information is not presented.

COMMENTS AND SUMMARY. The DISC appears to have good face and content validity, which is not surprising based upon its origin, and adequate reliability. The test materials themselves are not up to contemporary standards, as the line drawings are rather crude, a number of small objects such as buttons and a penny could be ingested by young children, and one puzzle did not fit together. Concerns also exist as to the durability of the items when subjected to the abuse expected from young children and the disinfecting required after objects are manipulated and mouthed.

One-half of the scales have limited ceilings, as by age 43–48 months the average scores were 24 passes of the 27 items. Furthermore, the age placement of some items may be different on the DISC than on other developmentally sequenced instruments. The dearth of validity studies, and the norm group previously described, raise questions as to the applicability of the instrument for other populations. The authors recommend the development of local norms.

Finally, one could question the need for the DISC at all. The instrument involves the manipulation of 11 containers of objects and six envelopes of forms, requires individual administration by a trained examiner, and still needs to be followed up by another evaluation to obtain a standard score. The time might be better spent using a broad-based screening instrument such as the Denver II (12:103), the Revised Brigance Diagnostic Inventory of Early Development (12:326), or proceeding directly to a more formal assessment instrument that will provide standard scores.

Review of the Diagnostic Inventory for Screening Children by T. STEUART WATSON, Associate Professor of Educational Psychology, and CARLEN HENINGTON, Instructor in Educational Psychology, Mississippi State University, Starkville, MS:

The authors describe the Diagnostic Inventory for Children (DISC) as a "diagnostic screening tool" (p. 9, quotes included in text) to be used, following a large-group screening, with children determined to be at-risk for developmental delay. The DISC attempts to identify developmental delays in eight domains: (a) Fine Motor skills (voluntary, controlled, and guided movements of small muscles); (b) Gross Motor skills (coordination of large muscles in movement, balance, and motor patterns); (c) Receptive Language (ability to understand and respond appropriately to verbal interaction); (d) Expressive Language (ability to produce appropriate verbalizations); (e) Visual Attention and Memory (ability to attend to visual cues/tasks and to recall, recognize, or retain visual experiences); (f) Auditory Attention and Memory (ability to attend to auditory cues/tasks and to recall, recognize, or retain auditory experiences); (g) Self-Help skills (ability to aid oneself in personal care); and (h) Social skills (ability to engage in appropriate interpersonal behaviors).

TEST CONTENT. The DISC is similar in format (i.e., layout, procedure, administration time) to the Bayley Scales of Infant Development—Second Edition (29; BSID-II, Bayley, 1993). For example, the Language, and Attention and Memory scales of the DISC can be compared to the Mental Scales of the BSID-II. Both instruments also assess fine and

gross motor skills. A key difference is that the BSID-II is promoted as an intelligence instrument and yields a Mental Development Index and a Psychomotor Developmental Index, whereas the authors of the DISC emphasize that it does not yield an overall (IQ-like) score.

The manual indicates that 27 age ranges are represented within the test. However, only 27 items assess skills in each of the eight scales across 11 delineated age ranges in approximately 5-month segments. Some age ranges contain as many as four items, whereas others contain as few as two items. This may not be a sufficient number of items to discriminate between children with and without developmental delay within some age ranges.

The materials used in the assessment come in a large zippered duffel bag and are easily transportable. The assessment materials are described as common items that may be familiar to the child and are interesting, durable, transportable, relatively inexpensive, and in most cases washable. Many pieces (e.g., the wheels on the cars, dolls with detachable head and tiny shoes) are small enough to be a potential choking or ingestion hazard. Although the manual encourages the examiner to allow the child to play with some materials to establish rapport, these pieces require close supervision when presented to the child and should not be viewed as toys. Some items are not durable. For example, the storybook has paper pages, the doll has removable limbs that may be lost, and the rattle is breakable plastic. Regarding diversity, the puzzle pieces contain only white male figures, the dolls are white females, and the storybook, *Cinderella*, contains only white characters and depicts stereotyped role models. Additionally, the kit was developed in Canada and many materials (e.g., Canadian coin, Canadian flag) are specific to that country and may not have validity in the United States. Visual and auditory attention and memory materials (e.g., the picture booklet and stimulus cards) are abstract, often complex, black-and-white line drawings. In some cases, the drawings are disproportionally drawn. These characteristics may affect the child's responding.

The DISC kit does not provide the necessary materials for certain test items. For example, one of the Gross Motor items requires stairs, a Self-Help item requires eating utensils and food, a Social Skills item requires a mirror, and an Auditory Attention and Memory item requires a ticking clock. Food items are to be determined on an individual basis. The administration manual lists the necessary materials for each item and the location provided (e.g., container #1). Commonly, the containers are resealable sandwich-type bags. Although not durable, they are replaceable and allow for visibility of enclosed materials. However, without a systematic arrangement of materials, pieces may be misplaced or it may be difficult to locate a specific piece during administration.

ADMINISTRATION AND SCORING. The DISC can be administered and interpreted by a professional, other than a psychologist or psychometrist, with a 2-year college degree in Early Childhood Education, Child Development, or the equivalent. Most of the items are based on child performance; however, parental report is accepted for all of the Self-Help and most of the Social Skills, and for children 24 months or younger on some Expressive Language items. The scales may be administered in any order. If the child spontaneously responds to an item out of order, credit is usually given. The authors suggest that examiners familiarize themselves with the test and possess an understanding of the skill or task being assessed and the bases or "process(es) involved in completion of the task" (p. 51). A training tape is available, but was not provided for review.

Scoring the DISC is straightforward and similar to the BSID-II. A check mark is placed in one of three columns on the protocol ("Y" for yes or pass, "N" for no or fail, and "R" for refused). Other scoring in the "R" column may include "Rpt" for parent or adult report and "No Opp" for no opportunity. In many situations, a mastery criterion is required for an item. For example, if the examiner is to administer the item four times, the child must respond correctly three of the four times. The examiner is cued on the protocol and in the manual regarding this requirement. Most items are not timed, with the exception of three items on the Attention and Memory scales. Usually the examiner can demonstrate a failed item. However, additional demonstration is not allowed on the two Attention and Memory scales due to the nature of the skills being assessed.

Basal and ceiling rules apply to each scale. The raw score for each scale is computed based on the number of items passed. Those items below the basal are considered passed. Interpretation of the scores is based on normative data for children of the same age. No standard score is obtained. The child obtains an "A" for average/above average (i.e., percentile score of 25 or above), "P" for possible delay (i.e., percentile of 10 to 24), or "D" for probable delay (i.e., percentile

score less than 10). Although the authors discourage their use, age equivalents can be calculated and plotted on a graph.

MANUAL. The spiral-bound manual is organized by scale and is, for the most part, relatively user-friendly. However, the durability of the manual is questionable given that the separator pages and cover are card stock. Repeated use will likely result in damaged and/or lost pages. Instructions for administration and scoring are clear and succinct. Some items have a comment or note section to provide special instructions or to provide a cue for related items on other scales. The authors briefly describe the suggested assessment environment, but leave most of the general assessment suggestions and strategies to other sources. Given the population for whom this test is intended (i.e., minimally qualified personnel administering to young children), relying on outside sources to teach basic assessment skills is especially problematic and may lead to test results fraught with error.

STANDARDIZATION AND NORMS. Two separate standardization studies were conducted: one to select items for inclusion on the final version of the test and one to establish normative data. Only the standardization regarding norming will be reviewed. There are numerous problems with the standardization sample. First, the total number of children at each range is too low (range 39–70) with males overrepresented at three ranges (i.e., 4–6 months, 25–30 months, and 37–42 months). Second, only children from three counties in Ontario were included, making use of the test for Canadian children outside of these counties highly suspect and invalidating the test for use in the United States. Third, the ethnic groups in the sample obviously reflect the Canadian population (e.g., English, French, other) and not the ethnic composition of the United States. Fourth, children with developmental delays were excluded from the sample; this is highly curious given the primary objective of the test to differentiate delayed from nondelayed children. With the number and magnitude of problems in the standardization sample, this test is invalid and, therefore, useless for its stated purpose and target population.

RELIABILITY. Three kinds of reliability were assessed: interrater, test-retest, and internal consistency. The authors provide an easy-to-read table on page 34 of the manual summarizing all three reliabilities across each of the eight scales. Reliability coefficients ranged from .94–.99 with low *SEM*s. These coefficients appear to indicate that the DISC is a reliable instrument. However, a couple of points must be considered before drawing definitive conclusions regarding the reported coefficients. First, one study of 30 children to establish interrater reliability and one study of 47 children to establish test-retest reliability are insufficient for demonstrating reliability. Second, inspection of the corrected split-half reliabilities (internal consistency) for each scale at various ages seems to indicate that the test is generally more reliable for children at the middle age ranges (i.e., 13–36 months) than for younger or older children.

VALIDITY. The construct validity of the DISC was assessed through factor analyses and item-scale correlations. A two-factor solution most consistently emerged across all age ranges. These factors were labeled cognitive/motor skills and interpersonal skills. No method is presented for deriving factor scores. Content validity evidence was provided through the first standardization procedure by only choosing items that corresponded to predetermined criteria. Most problematic and limiting, the authors present no data regarding concurrent, predictive, or discriminant validity. It is imperative that the authors provide data showing that the DISC discriminates between delayed and nondelayed children in the areas assessed. Without such information, this test has little value.

SUMMARY AND CONCLUSIONS. The DISC has some very noticeable and profound shortcomings. The two most significant problems are the psychometric properties and materials provided in the assessment kit. First, the lack of adequate representation in the standardization sample and absence of validity data renders this test useless for its intended purpose. Second, the materials are not safe, durable, or reflective of racial and gender diversity. Although other instruments used to assess infants and toddlers also have this weakness (i.e., materials) to varying degrees, one of these, the BSID-II, is a psychometrically sound, well-researched instrument that fulfills the need the authors used to justify this test. In view of these significant limitations, this test offers nothing beyond what is already available in existing instruments. There are a couple of potential advantages to the DISC, notably extending the age range of the BSID-II both downward and upward and providing scores in specific domains. These potential advantages, however, are unrealized because of the rather severe psychometric deficiencies of the test.

REVIEWER'S REFERENCE

Bayley, N. (1993). Bayley Scales of Infant Development, Second Edition. San Antonio, TX: The Psychological Corporation.

[100]

The Diagnostic Screening Batteries.

Purpose: Designed to provide clinicians with a structured intake interview procedure that samples a broad range of clinical possibilities in a systematic fashion.
Population: Ages 2 to adults.
Publication Dates: 1984–1989.
Scores: No scores.
Administration: Individual.
Editions, 3: Child, Adolescent, Adult.
Price Data: Available from publisher.
Time: Administration time not reported.
Comments: Computer administration; IBM and Apple versions available.
Authors: James J. Smith, Joseph M. Eisenberg, and Joseph M. Ferraro.
Publisher: Reason House, Ltd.

Review of The Diagnostic Screening Batteries by BRIAN F. BOLTON, University Professor, Rehabilitation Research and Training Center, University of Arkansas, Fayetteville, AR:

The Diagnostic Screening Batteries consist of parallel diagnostic instruments designed for three age groups: children (aged 2–17), adolescents (aged 13–17), and adults (aged 18+). The three batteries use similar formats and procedures. Each battery includes a questionnaire to be completed by the patient (except that a parent completes the child questionnaire) and a questionnaire to be completed by the clinician.

The authors describe the batteries as tools to facilitate the clinician's initial exploration of the patient's presenting complaints and concerns. The term "screening" in the title refers to the clinician's initial attempt to gain insight and understanding into the patient's difficulties and problems. The batteries were constructed to provide "direction and consistency" (p. 1) to the intake/diagnostic phase of the patient evaluation process.

The patient and clinician questionnaires can be administered on-line or using paper and pencil. The adult patient questionnaire consists of 37 required questions and 14 follow-up (contingent) questions. The response format ranges from yes/no (17 questions) to lists of problems/symptoms of varying lengths (34 questions). The typical list includes six problems/symptoms with the patient instructed to check all that apply. Depending on the patient's reading level and severity of impairment, completion of the questionnaire takes between 15 and 25 minutes.

The adult clinician questionnaire consists of 13 basic questions and 12 follow-up questions. Two questions require written responses, two require ratings of global functioning, and one question requires an IQ estimate. The clinician questionnaire assumes that a brief interview has been conducted, medical and psychiatric records are available, and some psychological tests have been administered. The focus of the clinician questionnaire is on intellectual functioning, possible organicity, and symptoms of schizophrenia and personality disorders.

The Diagnostic Screening Batteries were designed to review systematically the "total number of diagnostic possibilities" (p. 1) presented in the *Diagnostic and Statistical Manual: Third Edition—Revised (DSM-III-R)*. After the patient's and clinician's responses are entered into the computer program, a printout with some two dozen possible diagnoses is produced, followed by a shorter list of about one dozen "refined diagnostic possibilities" (p. 1).

The authors stipulate that the goal of the program is not to generate a specific and final differential diagnosis, but rather to give the clinician an overview of diagnostic possibilities. They suggest that by carefully examining the list of diagnostic possibilities generated, in conjunction with a review of the responses to the questionnaires, the clinician will be ready "to begin a detailed exploration of specific clinical entities and the patient's personal concerns" (p. 1). Whether or not this recommended strategy would be useful is a matter for clinicians to decide.

However, the authors' caution to users that "it is up to the qualified clinician to determine which diagnoses are most valid and appropriate for each patient" (p. 3) is not just a matter of preference or style. In fact, it would be impossible for a clinician to assess the validity of the diagnoses without knowing details about the development of the instruments and the computer program. Specifically, how were the diagnostic criteria in the *DSM-III-R* translated into questions for the patient and clinician questionnaires? How were the resulting response profiles compared to "each and every diagnosis" in the *DSM-III-R*?

In other words, the user needs to know how the *DSM-III-R* diagnostic categories were operationalized in the Diagnostic Screening Batteries? What constitutes a "configuration of responses" to the questionnaires? How were phrases like "even remotely possible," "strongly resemble," and "vigorous scoring criteria" quantified? The authors state that the patient's and clinician's questionnaire responses are compared to all possible diagnoses found in the *DSM-III-R*. This is a claim that should be documented.

The manual should explain how the interview questions were derived from the *DSM-III-R* diagnostic criteria. Were the "boxed" diagnostic criteria used as guidelines? A map that shows the translation of criteria into questions would be helpful. Likewise, an explanation of the statistical routine that compares the response configurations to the various *DSM-III-R* diagnostic categories is needed. Were the decision trees for differential diagnosis incorporated into the computer program?

Without this essential information about the Diagnostic Screening Batteries, potential users simply cannot make intelligent decisions about the utility of the instruments and the computer program for clinical applications. It is unreasonable to expect psychologists to take on faith the appropriateness and suitability of the rationale and procedures that the authors followed in constructing the batteries. The manual should present necessary information to answer the questions posed in preceding paragraphs.

In summary, The Diagnostic Screening Batteries consist of questionnaires for patients in three age groups with parallel questionnaires for clinicians and computer programs that generate lists of possible *DSM-III-R* diagnoses. Although the idea is good, it is not possible to recommend the batteries for clinical use at this time. This is because the manual does not provide any details about how the patient and clinician questionnaires operationalize *DSM-III-R* diagnostic criteria, nor is there any description of the statistical procedures that translate the obtained diagnostic data into tentative diagnoses. The authors have the obligation to prepare a technical manual that gives potential users sufficient information to enable them to evaluate the validity and utility of the batteries.

Review of The Diagnostic Screening Batteries by RONALD J. GANELLEN, Director, Neuropsychology Service, Department of Psychiatry, Michael Reese Hospital and Medical Center, and Associate Professor, Northwestern University Medical Center, Chicago, IL:

The Diagnostic Screening Batteries (DSB) presents a semistructured interview format to explore systematically the symptoms a client experiences to generate possible *DSM-III-R* diagnoses. The authors state their goal in creating the DSB was to develop a tool "to facilitate the clinician's initial exploration and to reduce part of the tedium involved when one works with a similar activity or a repetitive nature over an extended period of time" (p. 1).

Three versions of the DSB are presented, one for adults, one for children, and one for adolescents. The DSB can be administered in several different formats, including a clinical-interview situation in which the clinician asks a client whether they have experienced specific symptoms, a paper-and-pencil-administered self-report format in which a patient identifies which symptoms he or she has experienced, or a computer-administration format in which the patient responds to questions about their symptoms as they appear on the computer screen. No guidelines are presented to assist the clinician in deciding which format to use in a particular clinical situation.

Several serious limitations of the DSB exist. First, the data collected during the DSB's semistructured interview are used to generate *DSM-III-R* rather than *DSM-IV* diagnoses. Even though there is considerable continuity between *DSM-III-R* and *DSM-IV* diagnoses, since the *DSM-IV* was released in 1994 clinicians who provide direct clinical service or who are involved in research are obligated to present *DSM-IV* diagnoses when communicating with other mental health professionals, determining appropriate treatment interventions, and submitting information to insurance carriers. Use of an outdated version of the *DSM* carries the risk of appearing to be behind the times or of being denied payment for services. Of course, a clinician could translate the *DSM-III-R* diagnosis generated by the DSB into the appropriate *DSM-IV* diagnosis, but this adds several additional steps as the criteria in parallel *DSM-III-R* and *DSM-IV* diagnoses have changed in some instances and this involves extra work on the part of the clinician to look up the correct code.

Before using an assessment instrument in clinical practice a clinician should be assured that the instrument measures what it purports to measure and does so consistently, either across time or when used by different clinicians. In other words, before selecting a particular tool, such as a semistructured clinical interview for a particular task, such as establishing an appropriate diagnosis, evidence of the tool's validity and reliability should be provided.

No information concerning the DSB's psychometric properties is presented in the brief DSB manual and no mention is made in the manual of any research that has been conducted supporting the DSB's utility for the purposes for which it was developed. It is regrettable that the authors apparently have not examined interrater reliability, test-retest reliability, correspondence of results generated by different versions of the DSB, or the construct validity of the DSB. Although the DSB possesses face validity as the items address specific *DSM-III-R* criteria, the extent to which results based on the DSB agree with other methods for obtaining diagnoses (convergent validity) or aid in distinguishing between different clinical conditions (discriminant validity) has not been determined. As a result, it is not at all clear how useful the results of the DSB are. The absence of this information sorely limits the confidence potential users of the DSB can have in it as a reliable, efficient, and meaningful component of an assessment battery.

The DSB manual is quite brief. It offers no clear or specific instructions for administering any of the three versions of the DSB, face-to-face interview, paper-and-pencil self-report, or computer self-report formats. Although the authors may have assumed that the DSB would be used only by experienced clinicians who would provide appropriate guidance to their clients when presenting the DSB, the lack of instructions for administration runs a substantial risk that the DSB will be used in widely varying ways by different professionals. The lack of standardized administration procedures increases the likelihood that discrepant results will be obtained if the same individual is administered the DSB under different circumstances.

In summary, serious limitations of the DSB exist including linking the output from the DSB to the *DSM-III-R* rather than the *DSM-IV*; the absence of research establishing its reliability and validity; and the lack of clear, detailed instructions for test administration. Unfortunately, there is little basis to justify the time and expense involved in administering, scoring, and interpreting the DSB because its developers present no evidence showing that the DSB does what it was developed to do. Given these limitations, the DSB cannot be recommended either for routine clinical practice or for use as a research tool.

[101]
Diagnostic Test of Library Skills—Advanced Edition.

Purpose: To evaluate students' current knowledge of library skills.
Population: Grades 9–12.
Publication Date: 1993.
Acronym: DTLS-A.
Scores: Total score only.
Administration: Group.
Price Data, 1993: $29.95 per complete kit including 50 test booklets, 100 answer sheets, scoring key, teacher's guide, and reorder form for individual components.

Time: (30) minutes.
Comments: Upward extension of Diagnostic Test of Library Skills (T4:795); computer version available for Apple, Macintosh, IBM (and compatible) computers.
Author: Susan E. Bailey.
Publisher: Learnco Inc.

Review of the Diagnostic Test of Library Skills— Advanced Edition by MARK H. DANIEL, Senior Scientist, American Guidance Service, Circle Pines, MN:

This is a multiple-choice test of high-school students' skills in using a library and extracting information from library reference materials. The 50 items fall into seven categories: use of reference books (15 items); use of the card catalog (12); definitions of terms (10); "arrangement" (i.e., use of the Dewey Decimal System) (7); "location" (i.e., where in the library certain materials may be found) (4); table of contents (1); and author (1). The test consists of a reusable four-page question booklet, a consumable answer sheet, and two loose sheets entitled "Visual Materials for Questions" (examples of catalog cards, excerpts from reference books, etc.), which the examinee must refer to in order to answer about half of the questions. The only other materials are a one-page "Teacher's Guide" describing the test's purpose and administration procedures, an answer key, and an "Item Analysis Sheet" on which the teacher can record the number of students in a class failing each item; this sheet shows the content category to which each item belongs.

Because the purpose of the Diagnostic Test of Library Skills—Advanced Edition (DTLS-A) is to help the teacher identify topics that need to be taught or reviewed, the test's content is the most important consideration in evaluating the instrument. No information is provided on how the content domain was defined or how the items were selected and developed. In the absence of such information, the reviewer must rely on inspection of the content.

The DTLS-A is written entirely for a noncomputerized library. There is no mention of the computerized resources that in many libraries have replaced such materials as card catalogs and the Reader's Guide. Students who use library computers to find books or to conduct subject-matter searches may find much of the DTLS-A content to be unfamiliar.

The test would be easier for students to use, and there would be less likelihood of clerical errors, if the visual materials were printed with the questions in the test booklet rather than on separate pages.

The test items have not been carefully edited for punctuation, grammar, or typography. For example, in a list of books and their authors, one author's name is printed in bold as if it were part of the title. The excerpts from the Reader's Guide presented as visual materials are not formatted like the actual reference, and as a result are more difficult to interpret. In addition, some of the content is of questionable accuracy. Contrary to one question, magazine articles are not found "in" the Reader's Guide—references to them are. Another question refers to an "excerpt" from the Reader's Guide (in the visual materials) that is, in fact, a combination of an excerpt and an explanation, something that is not apparent on first look. According to another question, college catalogs are kept in a vertical file, yet this is not a standard practice.

There are also problems with content selection. Some questions in the middle of the test measure basic information (e.g., what "author" or "illustration" means) that earlier questions presume the student knows. At the other extreme, a few questions are arcane, such as the number of "subject areas" in the Dewey Decimal System, or whether an author's name is John Doe or Doe, John. Quite a few of the questions depend on the student's general knowledge (e.g., when Charles Dickens lived, what the periodic table is) or other academic skills (e.g., how to read a numerical table) rather than library skills.

No information on the development or psychometric properties of the DTLS-A is provided. Given the test's purpose, the lack of reliability and validity data is not a serious shortcoming. However, normative information and data on the relative difficulty of items would help the test user interpret results and identify important knowledge gaps. Also, an indication that the items had been subjected to statistical item analysis would give the potential user greater confidence that the items function as intended.

In summary, the DTLS-A cannot be recommended for general use. Its psychometric characteristics are unknown, and it does not appear to have been subjected to standard development procedures. A conscientious teacher or librarian could, with a reasonable amount of effort, construct a test for identifying instructional needs that would be more accurate in its details. Furthermore, such a locally developed test would have the advantage of assessing content that today's students need to know.

Review of the Diagnostic Test of Library Skills— Advanced Edition by ERNEST W. KIMMEL, Executive Director, Office of Public Leadership, Educational Testing Service, Princeton, NJ:

The Teacher's Guide tells us that "This test is designed to tell you precisely who needs what ... to evaluate students' current knowledge in the following areas: library terms; use of title page; table of contents; card catalog; library arrangement; reference books; etc." (p. 1). The test consists of 50 four-choice questions. Over half of the questions require the test-taker to refer to visual materials that are printed on separate sheets of paper—an unnecessary logistical complication during the administration of the test. Printing the stimulus material adjacent to the applicable question(s) would be much easier for the test-taker and would be consistent with good practice in test publishing. Many of the questions are definitional in nature, requiring no application. For certain of the questions, the "correct" answer is based on common practice—but the questions refer to practices that may, in fact, vary with the policies of a particular library (e.g., "Which materials may be used only in the library?"). Similarly, many of the questions would seem anachronistic to a student whose experience was limited to a library that uses electronic media extensively. A thorough editing of the test could have eliminated such problems as the stem of one question providing the answer for another.

Responses to the questions are recorded on an answer sheet that must be scored manually. There is no suggestion or recommendation of a score or score pattern that can be considered to represent a satisfactory level of individual performance. Rather, we are told that "An examination of individual answer sheets will indicate individual student needs" (p. 1).

At a class or group level, the teacher or librarian using the tests is given an "Item Analysis Sheet" for tabulating the number of students choosing an incorrect answer for each question. The one-page Teacher's Guide indicates "After the number wrong for each question has been counted, you will be able to determine areas which require your attention" (p. 1). To aid in making that determination, the "Item Analysis Sheet" categorizes each question into one of the following: Definition, Author, Card Catalog, Use of Reference Books, Location, Arrangement, or Table of Contents. These categories are not defined, described, or explained, so that it is not possible to know the content/skills domain to which one can make inferences. This underscores a fundamental problem with this test—there is no documentation! No information is provided as to how the domain of library skills was defined nor why these categories were chosen as the framework for inter-preting the areas in which students need help. Does this framework solely reflect the judgment of the test author or did a panel of librarians and language arts teachers develop a consensus that these categories reflect the knowledge and skills needed by secondary school students? Similarly, there is no evidence that the questions included in each category provide a basis for generalization. As a test that purports to be diagnostic, one would expect to find evidence that (a) the knowledge and skills included can be improved through instruction, and (b) a strong performance on the test is related to a student's demonstrated ability to use a library in an effective manner.

In summary, this test should be used with the same caution that one would give to a test developed by the teacher in the next classroom. It may provide some useful information for planning instruction but no evidence is provided to support any but the most direct inferences about students' skills in using a library.

[102]

Discourse Comprehension Test.

Purpose: To assess "comprehension and retention of stated and implied main ideas and details in a set of stories."

Population: Aphasic or head injured adults.

Publication Date: 1993.

Acronym: DCT.

Scores, 9: Number of Words, Number of Unfamiliar Words, Number of Sentences, Mean Sentence Length, Number of Minimal Terminal Units, Ratio of Clauses to Terminal Units, Listening Difficulty, Number of Unfamiliar Words, Reading Difficulty.

Administration: Individual.

Price Data, 1994: $65 per complete kit including manual (108 pages), audio tape, 12 story cards, and vinyl carrying case.

Time: Administration time not reported.

Comments: Stories can be read aloud, heard on tape, or read silently.

Authors: Robert H. Brookshire and Linda E. Nicholas.

Publisher: Communication Skill Builders.

[Editor's Note: The publisher advised in September 1997 that this test is now out of print.]

Review of the Discourse Comprehension Test by RALPH G. LEVERETT, Professor of Education/Special Education, Union University, Jackson, TN:

This assessment was designed to measure "spoken narrative discourse" (manual, p. 3). This distinguishes it from related instruments that evaluate listening comprehension. The Discourse Comprehension Test (DCT) utilizes a story format and yes/

no questions. Similar measures of comprehension typically use single words and isolated sentences rather than discourse. Performance on single words and isolated sentences "is not likely to predict ... comprehension of multiple-sentence messages (discourse)" (p. 3). The tasks required in comprehension of discourse require the examinee to consider relationships among sentences and ideas. Additionally, discourse tasks more nearly represent situations "encountered in daily life" (p. 4). Adults with aphasia, right brain lesions, and traumatic head injury are the target populations for the DCT.

A second use of the DCT is as a measure of silent reading comprehension. Use of this format allows comparison of listening skills and reading skills. Caution is advised, however, in overinterpreting the results of this comparison. In the listening format, the examinee hears the information a single time. In silent reading, sentences may be reread for clarity. An additional difference between the two is that in the recorded or live voice presentation, words related to the questions are given additional stress by the speaker. This may provide an advantage for the listener over the reader. However, possible advantages of that format are not explored in the manual. The listening format is controlled by the examiner. The reading format is controlled by the examinee. Reading passages are written at a 5th to 6th grade level. This represents a "functional level for adult readers" (p. 26).

Regardless of the version, listening comprehension or silent reading, the nature of the test material requires the examinee to respond to questions related to stated or implied main ideas and stated or implied details. Each of these categories is scored separately, and a total score is provided for main ideas and details. Sample activities are provided to familiarize the examinee with the task.

This test is functional in nature. Its use is both diagnostic and therapeutic. The design of the test is to determine specific auditory comprehension deficits, direct the therapist in the selection of goals, provide baseline and intermediate measures of changes in performance during therapy, and inform those who communicate with persons who have comprehension deficits.

The authors provide extensive information on test development. They identify performance differences among the three target groups. Considering the technical nature of the literature on auditory comprehension deficits, the manual provides the examiner with information that is readily understood. Extensive statistical information is provided for each of the crucial variables in test content and among target groups. Statements on validity and reliability are complete.

The section on validity is especially helpful to the examiner. The various types of reliability are discussed in relationship to the test, and a brief definition of each type of validity is provided. This is a useful feature to remind the examiner of key test components and the nature of careful test construction. Throughout the test manual, the DCT is compared to respected tests. Among these are the Boston Diagnostic Aphasia Examination (BDAE), the Porch Index of Communicative Ability (PICA), and the Western Aphasia Battery (WAB).

The authors' discussion of reliability explores the administration of the DCT generally and under both slow (110–130 wpm) and fast (190–210 wpm) rates of administration. The discussion of this entire section is presented with the same candor seen throughout the manual. Candor is also seen in the discussion on the effects of prior knowledge on performance. This is explored under a section on "passage dependency" (p. 19). The authors are honest in their comparison of the DCT with similar tests. When no similar tests are available, that fact is stated.

Materials provided with the DCT include both printed cards of stories (Forms A and B) and an audiotape of stories and questions. Instructions are provided for the use of live voice whenever a tape recorder is unavailable or whenever the examiner deems that the recorded presentation will "adversely affect" (p. 34) performance. Recorded material should be presented at a "comfortable listening level" (p. 12).

The manual specifies three criteria for the appropriate examinee in both uses of the DCT. Under the Listening Comprehension version, the candidate would possess adequate hearing, "intelligible and reliable yes and no responses (either spoken, by head nods, or pointing ...)" (p. 33), and correct responses to "at least half" of the yes/no responses on the Auditory Verbal Comprehension subtest of the Western Aphasia Battery (WAB). When the Silent Reading Comprehension version is used, adequate vision is the crucial criterion. The two remaining criteria are the same as for the listening version.

A reproducible response form is included in the manual. The manual includes a scored sample of this form. Included on the form is a list of behaviors that may affect the examinee's performance. Recording of responses is simple.

The authors distinguish the DCT from similar tests; however, they appear to respect these other measures of neurological deficits. The results of this test would be seen as supplementary to these measures and providing information unattainable by their use alone. This test provides a practical measure of language as it occurs in daily life—spoken discourse rather than single words or isolated sentences.

Review of the Discourse Comprehension Test by GARY L. MARCO, Executive Director, Educational Testing Service, Princeton, NJ:

The Discourse Comprehension Test (DCT) is an individually administered test designed to assess the comprehension and retention of narrative discourse likely to occur in natural spoken communication. Listening comprehension and silent reading comprehension versions are available. The test is intended for use with adults who are known to have aphasia, right-brain damage, or traumatic brain injury. The test is *not* intended to distinguish between adults with brain damage and adults with no brain damage. Possible uses of the test results include (a) identifying deficits in discourse comprehension of daily-life communication, (b) guiding treatment selection, (c) assessing changes in discourse comprehension, and (d) counseling those in communication with brain-damaged individuals.

TEST DEVELOPMENT. The test developers, Robert Brookshire and Linda Nicholas, are members of the Speech Pathology Section, Department of Veterans Affairs Medical Center, Minneapolis. They have studied communication disorders in brain-damaged adults (see, for example, Brookshire & Nicholas, 1984). They state that other tests designed to test reading and listening comprehension among brain-damaged adults assess comprehension of single words and isolated sentences.

Stimulus material. The stimulus material for the DCT consists of 10 humorous stories. The stories, which are at the 5th and 6th grade reading levels, are controlled for such factors as number of words, mean sentence length, and several measures of text difficulty.

The 10 stories were divided into two parallel sets of five stories each based on the performance of 20 test takers with no brain damage. Eight yes/no questions are asked about each story: two on stated main ideas, two on implied main ideas, two on stated details, and two on implied details. The test questions are controlled for number of words, number of unfamiliar words, a measure of grammatical complexity, and passage dependency. The stories and questions for the listening version may be administered via audiotape.

TEST ADMINISTRATION. The test manual clearly specifies the test administration procedures for an individual administration and provides an excellent Response Record Form for recording score and qualitative information on the test taker. The test manual recommends that the DCT be administered to adults who answer at least half of the questions correctly on the screening test of the Sentence Comprehension Test, or alternatively, on the Western Aphasia Battery (Kertesz, 1982). One or two practice stories followed by a set of eight questions are used for test familiarization. The test taker is instructed not to hurry and to guess when unsure of the answer. The actual test administration consists of five stories from Set A and five stories from Set B. Each story is followed by eight questions.

The test administrator starts with Set A and may discontinue testing after this set if the test taker's performance is relatively stable. The test administrator is advised, however, that giving all 10 stories will improve the stability of the score.

In the listening comprehension mode the stories and associated questions are played one story at a time and then the questions for that story are played one at a time. In the reading comprehension mode the test taker reads each story silently and then answers the questions with the story script removed.

Rest periods are allowed between questions as necessary, and testing may take place at two different sittings if the test taker becomes fatigued.

At the end of the testing session, the test administrator fills out a Response Record Form for the test taker. Scores as well as observations regarding performance patterns and styles (for example, difficulty attending to stories, noise build-up, or fatigue) are recorded.

PSYCHOMETRIC CONSIDERATIONS.

Normative data. Performance data are available on 40 non-brain-damaged and 60 brain-damaged adults (aphasia, right-brain damage, or traumatic brain injury) for listening comprehension and on 20 non-brain-damaged adults for reading comprehension. The 25 non-brain-damaged males and 15 non-brain-damaged females who took the listening comprehension test ranged from 55 to 75 years in age and 8 to 18 in years of education. The reading comprehension test sample (10 males and 10 females) ranged from 42 to 73 years in age and from 6 to 17 in years of education.

Cutoff scores. Cutoff scores were developed for listening comprehension on the basis of the performance of 40 non-brain-damaged ("normal") adults. No cutoffs were established for reading comprehension. The cutoff scores were set at two standard deviations below the mean for type of question (stated main idea, implied main idea, stated detail, implied detail) subscores and for overall score—all within each of the three discourse sets (A, B, A+B). Small sample sizes plus the easiness of the test for the non-brain-damaged adults make the cutoff scores suspect. In addition, the procedure used for setting cutoffs does not consider information on brain-damaged test takers.

Score comparability. Scores on reading comprehension will not necessarily be comparable to those on listening comprehension because of test administration differences. Nor will scores on alternate forms be comparable. A full-scale equating study involving larger samples would be necessary to establish comparability.

Reliability. From a generalizability perspective, one can question why the test maker relied completely on humorous stories as stimulus material. Such stories represent only a small sample of adult discourse in daily life. The generalizability of scores on the DCT to the full range of adult discourse has not been established.

The test makers did find high test-retest (2- to 3-week intervals) reliabilities for the DCT listening test, but again based on small samples—14 adults with aphasia ($r = .87$) and 7 right-brain-damaged adults ($r = .95$). The test manual also cites the similarity of the average performance of 40 adults with no brain damage on the two alternate story sets as evidence of split-half reliability, but no correlations are reported because of the very high test scores obtained by the test takers. Clearly, more reliability data on brain-damaged adults are needed.

Validity. The test maker provided considerable evidence of the content validity of the test. For example, 7 of 10 judges had to agree that the questions dealing with stated or implied information and main idea or detail were categorized appropriately. Another content validity investigation (based on only 10 non-brain-damaged adults) used the Passage Dependence Index (Tuinman, 1974) to show that passage information was required to answer the questions.

In terms of construct validity, the DCT pattern of use for the 10,000 most frequently used English words more closely resembled that of adult conversation than of newspapers (based on comparative data from Hayes, 1989). Moreover, the average listening performance of 100 test takers appeared to confirm the distinctness of the dimensions related to main idea versus details and stated information versus implied information.

In terms of criterion-related validity, the DCT scores of 20 listeners with aphasia correlated to a moderate degree (.53–.76) with scores on the auditory comprehension subtests of the Boston Diagnostic Aphasia Examination and two other measures. These correlations, though based on a small sample, indicate that the DCT, although tapping some of the same underlying abilities as the other tests, is also measuring something different.

These data do not, however, address the essential validity question: Can the test identify brain-damaged adults with discourse comprehension problems? An appropriate validity study to determine the test's effectiveness would distinguish brain-damaged adults who have little or no comprehension deficit from those who do.

CONCLUSION. The DCT may very well be a useful measure of discourse comprehension of stories used in daily adult conversation among brain-damaged adults, but its norms, cut scores, score comparability, generalizability, reliability, and validity are not well established. Until more definitive data are available on larger samples, users should combine their own knowledge of the individuals with test score information to help determine whether discourse comprehension problems are evident.

REVIEWER'S REFERENCES

Tuinman, J. J. (1974). Determining the passage dependency of comprehension questions in 5 major tests. *Reading Research Quarterly, 2,* 206–223.
Kertesz, A. (1982). The Western Aphasia Battery. New York: Grune & Stratton.
Brookshire, R. H., & Nicholas, L. E. (1984). Comprehension of directly and indirectly stated main ideas and details in discourse of brain-damaged and non-brain-damaged listeners. *Brain and Language, 21,* 21–36.
Hayes, D. P. (1989). *Guide to the lexical analysis of texts* (Technical Report No. 89-6). Ithaca, NY: Department of Sociology, Cornell University.

[103]
Draw-a-Story: Screening for Depression and Age or Gender Differences.

Purpose: Designed to identify depression.
Population: Ages 5 and over.
Publication Dates: 1987–1993.
Acronym: DAS.
Scores: 2 task scores: Draw-A-Story, Stimulus Drawing Task.
Administration: Group or individual.
Forms, 2: A, B.
Price Data, 1993: $25 per test including manual ('93, 111 pages).
Time: (5–15) minutes.
Comments: Previous edition titled Draw-a-Story: Screening for Depression and Emotional Needs.
Author: Rawley Silver.
Publisher: Ablin Press Distributors.

Cross References: See T4:817 (1 reference); for reviews of the earlier edition by Walter Katkovsky and David Lachar, see 11:115.

TEST REFERENCES

1. Silver, R. (1996). Sex differences in the solitary and assaultive fantasies of delinquent and nondelinquent adolescents. *Adolescence, 31,* 543–550.

Review of the Draw-a-Story: Screening for Depression and Age or Gender Differences by DENNIS C. HARPER, Professor of Pediatrics and Rehabilitation Counseling, University of Iowa Hospitals and Clinics, Iowa City, IA:

The Draw-a-Story by Silver is presented as a screening measure for depression in children and adults, ages 5 through adulthood. The author presents this as a screening instrument based upon the role of art in the drawings of depressed individuals listed in a few research studies (Gantt, 1990; multiple studies by Silver, 1981, 1982, 1983, 1986, 1987, 1988, 1989, 1990, 1991, in press a, in press b). The Draw-a-Story (DAS) is reported to be an instrument used for semistructured interview in the assessment of depression. An earlier instrument by this author, the Silver Drawing Test of Cognitive Skills and Assessment (1990; T4:2462), focused on cognitive and adjustment status. The instrument under review is reported to expand the number of stimulus drawings in order to improve validity and increase data. A broader range of drawings is also presented to "provide access to fantasies" (p. 10). The author also explores the relationship of age and gender differences in the attitudes toward self and others as a reported goal of the DAS.

The instrument itself consists of two series of stimulus drawings. Form A consists of 14 stimulus drawings selected from both the Silver Drawing Test and Stimulus Drawings and Techniques because they "seem to have prompted negative fantasies in earlier studies" (p. 11) according to the author. The test author notes that Form B has been included to "offset the negativity of Form A, to expand the range of choices, and to provide a second scored response" (p. 11). Individuals completing the drawing task are asked to choose two drawings from a display of stimulus drawings, imagine something happening between the subjects they have chosen, and then in drawings of their own display what is going on. When the drawings are finished, titles are requested, discussed, and then scored on a 5-point rating scale shown in the manual. The age range is reported to be from 5 years to adults, there is no time limit, and the manual indicates that the material can be scored by teachers, art therapists, psychologists, and other clinicians. Administration can be done individually or to groups. Individual administration is recommended for children and adults who have difficulty in understanding directions. Specific suggestions are given for working with young children.

The manual consists of a series of drawings and specific recommendations regarding scoring and samples. Two chapters (4 and 5) discuss reliability and studies on depression. Finally, chapter 6 discusses data and research of previous studies with regard to age and gender differences in attitudes toward self and others. The reliability data are presented examining interrater agreement (Form A and Form B), test-retest reliability on the content scale, evaluation of the relationships between DAS and Stimulus Drawing measures at tow times, and also alternate form reliability. Interscorer reliability (between judges) for Forms A and B on a sample of 40 responses from five groups of children or adolescents resulted in correlations of .81 to .74. Test-retest reliability (1-week interval and no interval) on Form A for the Stimulus Drawings on 31 children ranged between .22 and .93. Alternate form reliability data were reported but the author indicates the sample was too small for a meaningful interpretation. The author's data suggest that scores from Form A are reliable; however, the interscorer reliability for Form B needs further evaluation. Although the data reported on reliability seem to be reasonable given this type of task, the specific capabilities of the raters are not articulated. Highly qualified raters who are familiar with the rest would obviously do better with this particular test as well as the technique, depending upon their experience.

As noted in chapter 5, Screening for Depression, the fundamental question of the DAS is whether or not it can be used to identify individuals who may be depressed. The author's rationale is that negativity in drawings reflects depression. Several articles are cited from the literature to support this contention. The research study by Silver (1988) is presented from a published text of the author. Data reviewed present strongly negative themes noted in children who are depressed. To a lesser degree depressive themes are noted in learning-disabled adolescents as well as depressed adults. The 1993 study focusing on adults with the DAS is also presented and no significant differences are reported between male and female adults who were depressed. The author concludes that strongly negative responses to the DAS are associated with childhood depression and may be associated with depression among adolescents and men. Theoretically, the implied definition of depression is primarily cognitive and fails to consider a broader and more contemporary understanding of this disorder.

The major questions left unanswered by these studies presented by Silver relate to the credentials and capabilities of the raters or judges and the validity of the instrument in detecting depression. Without specific information on rater capabilities one is unable to evaluate the sensitivity of this instrument in identifying depression. Data on discriminating depression are meager at best. Several studies are reported in chapter 6 exploring the relationship between age and gender differences among children and adults in their response to the DAS.

Returning to the author's initial contention of the instrument. Can drawings be used to uncover depressive illness? This question remains unanswered on the basis of the material presented in the Draw-a-Story. This method would appear to be an interesting technique to elicit further information from children depending upon the qualifications and the sophistication of the rater of the instrument. It is acknowledged that it is a difficult task to evaluate depression in younger children. Formal techniques of assessment for older children and adults are well known (Beck, Reynolds, Kovacs) and are available with proven reliability and validity. This is largely a projective instrument with some guided suggestions on the interpretation of particular drawings as they relate to negative themes generally. This technique might be a useful adjunct in the interview process, especially for young children where emotional disturbance and/or depression is suspected. Earlier reviews (Crehan, 1991; Ward, 1992) of the Silver Drawing Test have raised multiple concerns about validity and reliability issues. These have not been resolved in the Draw-a-Story. Caution in interpretation is clearly warranted.

REVIEWER'S REFERENCES

Silver, R. A. (1981, 1982, 1986, 1989). *Stimulus drawings and techniques in therapy, development and assessment.* New York: Ablin Press.

Silver, R. A. (1983). Silver Drawing Test of Cognitive and Creative Skills. Seattle: Special Child Publications.

Silver, R. A. (1987). Sex differences in the emotional content of drawings. *Art Therapy, 4,* 67–77.

Silver, R. A. (1988). Draw A Story: Screening for depression and emotional needs. New York: Ablin Press.

Gantt, L. (1990). *A validity study of the Formal Elements Art Therapy Scale (FEATS) for diagnostic information in patient's drawings.* Unpublished doctoral dissertation, University of Pittsburgh.

Silver, R. A. (1990). Silver Drawing Test of Cognitive Skills and Adjustment. New York: Ablin Press.

Silver, R. A. (1991). *Stimulus drawings and techniques in therapy, development and assessment.* Sarasota, FL: Ablin Press.

Crehan, K. D. (1992). [Review of the Silver Drawing Test of Cognitive Skills and Adjustment]. In J. J. Kramer & J. C. Conoley (Eds.), *The eleventh mental measurements yearbook* (pp. 827–828). Lincoln, NE: Buros Institute of Mental Measurements.

Ward, A. W. (1992). [Review of the Silver Drawing Test of Cognitive Skills and Adjustment]. In J. J. Kramer & J. C. Conoley (Eds.), *The eleventh mental measurements yearbook* (pp. 828–829). Lincoln, NE: Buros Institute of Mental Measurements.

Silver, R. A. (in press, a). Age and gender differences expressed through drawings: A study of attitudes toward self and others. *Art Therapy.*

Silver, R. A. (in press, b). Assessing the emotional content of drawings by older adults: Research findings and implications. *American Journal of Art Therapy.*

Review of the Draw-a-Story: Screening for Depression and Age or Gender Differences by JOSEPH C. WITT, Professor of Psychology, Louisiana State University, Baton Rouge, LA, and FRANK M. GRESHAM, Professor, School of Education, University of California—Riverside, Riverside, CA:

This instrument is ostensibly a projective test of depression designed for art therapists. Administration and interpretation of the instrument follow a standard format: The therapist asks the child to make up a story and then the therapist makes up a story about the child's story. The new wrinkle here is that in addition to writing a story in response to a picture, the child also must draw the story. Presumably, this double-barreled approach would make it virtually impossible for the subject to hide any intrapsychic disease, disturbance, or depression from the in-depth probing of the art therapist. This approach may, in fact, be the MRI of art therapy where even the most minor elements of sadness and gloom show up as clearly to the therapist as would three kilograms of unsealed heroin to the keen nose of a drug-sniffing dog in a quiet Turkish airport. On the other hand, perhaps the minor waver of the lines in a child's drawing is merely poor perceptual-motor coordination and the sad "themes" simply reflect the child's logical disdain for a therapist making seemingly irrelevant requests.

The Draw-a-Story (DAS), like most of its projective predecessors, suffers from the same fundamental problems of questionable psychometric quality: illusory correlation, absence of incremental validity, and impossibility of disconfirmation. Each of these problems will be reviewed next.

ILLUSORY CORRELATION. Most professionals utilize projective tests such as the DAS because they have come to believe that accurate descriptions of personality and predictions of cognitive and behavioral functioning can be made from such procedures. This belief stems from the perception that predictions made by "experts" are more accurate and valid than predictions made by lay persons.

Interpretation of projective measures such as the DAS are prone to the phenomenon of the *illusory correlation*. An illusory correlation refers to the relationship between test responses and symptoms/ behavior that are based on verbal associations rather than valid observations (Kurtz & Garfield, 1978). Chapman (1967) illustrated that an illusory correlation was the reputed correlation between two events that are: (a) unrelated, (b) related to a lesser extent than reported, or (c) related in the opposite direction from the verbal report.

A number of empirical studies have found evidence for illusory correlations using a variety of projective measures (see Gresham, 1993 for a brief review). In addition, many studies have demonstrated that the illusory correlation is a robust phenomenon that is highly resistant to change. Moreover, a number of investigations have shown that psychologists highly experienced in figure drawings were no more accurate than inexperienced psychologists in differentiating normal from disturbed children and in making psychiatric diagnoses (Gresham, 1993). Based on the well-established findings regarding the salience and persistence of illusory correlations, it is not surprising that many psychologists hold strong opinions that they can make valid predictions of behavior or accurate descriptions of personality using figure drawings. The author of the DAS presents no empirical evidence that this measure is not subject to illusory correlational biases.

INCREMENTAL VALIDITY ISSUES. Some would defend the use of measures such as the DAS because these measures are helpful in supporting assessment results and/or hypotheses derived from other assessment procedures (e.g., tests, observations, historical information). Given paltry validity evidence for figure drawing tests, it is rather strained logic to believe that one could use a less valid measure such as figure drawings to "validate" or otherwise support the results obtained from more valid measures (Motta, Little, & Tobin, 1993). Previous work using human figure drawings has shown that these procedures function at no better than chance levels in discriminating known groups of emotionally disturbed from nonemotionally disturbed children (Motta et al., 1995; Naglieri & Pfeiffer, 1992; Prewett, Bardos, & Naglieri, 1989). In short, figure drawing measures such as the DAS have little, if any, incremental validity because they do not add a significant amount of variance in describing personality, predicting behavior, or in discriminating known groups of individuals above chance levels.

Another argument often made for the use of figure drawings such as the DAS is that they are frequently interpreted as validating overt behavior. For instance, a teacher refers a student for exhibiting highly aggressive and dangerous behavior such as hitting, using a knife to threaten others, and throwing objects in the classroom. A school psychologist might administer the DAS in which the student draws a seven-headed green dragon breathing fire at another child. His story about this might be that the dragon will set the child on fire with his breath and then eat the child. Obviously, this drawing and story confirm what the teacher and others knew already based on overt behavior—the referred child has a tendency to exhibit aggressive behavior. This simple-minded interpretation is, of course, redundant with what is already known and therefore does not result in any incremental validity.

IMPOSSIBILITY OF DISCONFIRMATION. Measures like the DAS and their interpretations perhaps are used because figure drawing interpretations cannot be disconfirmed. Given that one never "proves" the null hypothesis, many may take this as evidence for the validity of measures like the DAS. Needless to say, arguments regarding sample representativeness, base rates, and statistical hypothesis testing often fall on deaf ears.

A valuable lesson can perhaps be learned from those who develop projective tests. Many in psychology are interested in how to have the new behavior patterns learned in therapy maintain over time. These instruments, which have been so soundly criticized in the literature, persist over time. In the face of incredible reasons not to use them people use them. This aspect deserves some study. Perhaps it has something to do with the partial reinforcement effects. That is, by chance alone some interpretations will be consistent with a child's behavior. Knowing the effects of partial reinforcement on the persistence of behavior, it is not surprising that the use of figure drawings continues in spite of this rather lean schedule of partial reinforcement. Coupled with this is a confirmatory bias in which instances wherein DAS interpretations confirm one's hypothesis are recalled and instances in which DAS interpretations disconfirm one's hypotheses are forgotten. Hence, their use may have nothing to do with the instrument, but more to do with the professional facade of the user who offers insights dredged from the deep psychic depths, insights which are unverifiable and therefore impossible to refute and therefore impossible to impugn the expertise to the seer.

CONCLUSIONS. The DAS is a projective instrument that combines the worst of projective assessment strategies: figure drawings and accompanying thematic apperception stories. The DAS authors have spliced two questionable assessment procedures, thereby creating a hybrid typifying what is most distressing in psychological assessment "instrumentation." Information obtained from the DAS is tautological to what already would be known regarding a child's behavior and interpretations may lead to illusory correlations between the DAS and behavior, false beliefs in incremental validity, and faulty hypothesis-testing strategies.

The DAS represents an assessment technique whose time has passed. It has poor psychometric properties, few data to support its intended use, and the potential for more abuse than appropriate use in making decisions for children. Based on the evidence reviewed herein, there is not a single scientific reason for using the DAS. Its advocated use is surely based more on convenience than on solid empirical evidence. The DAS, along with virtually all projective instruments, belongs in a museum chronicling the history of simple-minded assessment practices along with mood rings, phrenology, tarot cards, and horoscopes.

REVIEWERS' REFERENCES

Chapman, L. (1967). Illusory correlation in observational report. *Journal of Verbal Learning and Verbal Behavior, 6*, 151–155.

Kurtz, R. M., & Garfield, S. L. (1978). Illusory correlation: A further exploration of Chapman's paradigm. *Journal of Consulting and Clinical Psychology, 46*, 1009–1015.

Prewett, P. N., Bardos, A. N., & Naglieri, J. A. (1989). Assessment of mentally retarded children with the Matrix Analogies Test—Short Form, Draw a Person: A Quantitative Scoring System, and the Kaufman Test of Educational Achievement. *Psychology in the Schools, 26*, 254–260.

Naglieri, J. A., & Pfeiffer, S. I. (1992). Performance of disruptive behavior disordered and normal samples on the Draw A Person: Screening Procedure for Emotional Disturbance. *Psychological Assessment, 4*, 156–159.

Gresham, F. M. (1993). "What's wrong in this picture?": Response to Motta et al.'s review of human figure drawings. *School Psychology Quarterly, 8*, 182–186.

Motta, R. W., Little, S. G., & Tobin, M. I. (1993). The use and abuse of human figure drawings. *School Psychology Quarterly, 8*, 162–169.

[104]
Drug Use Questionnaire.

Purpose: To assess "potential involvement with drugs."
Population: Clients of addiction treatment.
Publication Date: 1982.
Acronym: DAST-20.
Scores: Total score only.
Administration: Group.
Price Data: Available from publisher.
Foreign Language Edition: Available in French.
Time: (5–10) minutes.
Comments: Self-report inventory; manual is entitled "Directory of Client Outcome Measures for Addiction Treatment Programs"; previously entitled Drug Abuse Screening Test.
Author: Harvey A. Skinner.
Publisher: Addiction Research Foundation [Canada].

Review of the Drug Use Questionnaire by PHILIP ASH, Director, Ash, Blackstone and Cates, Blacksburg, VA:

The Drug Use Questionnaire (DAST-20) is a 20-item yes-no response, single score inventory derived from an earlier 28-item version, the Drug Abuse Screening Test (Skinner, 1982). It should be noted, however, that although the individual copies of the inventory use the title "Drug Use Questionnaire (DAST-20)," in the manual this 20-item inventory is entitled "Drug Abuse Screening Test (DAST)," and nowhere in the nine pages of the manual is the title "Drug Use Questionnaire" used or referred to. A briefer (10-item) version is also said to have been developed, as well as an adolescent version in which the word "work" has been replaced by "school," but no reports have been published on the psychometric properties of these scales.

Modeled after the Michigan Alcoholism Screening Test (MAST; Selzer, 1971), the DAST (and/or DAST-20) is intended to help in evaluating the seriousness of an individual's drug involvement, both for client assessment and in treatment evaluation research. Focusing on features of drug dependence such as inability to stop using drugs, withdrawal symptoms, and "other consequences relating to the use or abuse of prescribed, over-the-counter and illicit drugs" (p. 82), it asks respondents to indicate "whether they have experienced each drug-related problem in the past 12 months" (p. 82).

The manual consists mostly of summaries of research previously reported for the original 28-item DAST. It should be noted, however, the *Directory of Client Outcome Measures for Addictions Treatment Programs*, in which the manual for the DAST occupies a mere nine pages, contains a rich collection of information about a large number of substance (including alcohol) abuse measures as well as measures in other life areas. The *Directory* is well worth perusing for its own value.

Reliability and validity data are based primarily upon studies of the original 28-item DAST, but Skinner's (1982) original report also studies the 20-item subset, and found that the two versions were "almost perfectly" (p. 83) correlated ($r = .99$).

Internal consistency estimates for both versions were high. Cronbach alpha estimates for the 28-item DAST were .92 for a sample including both alcohol and drug users, and .95 for the 20-item DAST. For a subsample of drug abusers, alpha = .86 for each version. The number of cases involved is not reported. In another study (Skinner & Goldberg, 1986), for a sample of 105 narcotics users, alpha = .74. No test-retest reliability estimates are reported.

No validity data are presented for the DAST-20 as such. For the original 28-item DAST, correlations of total score with frequency of use of specific drugs varied as follows: cannabis ($r = .55$), barbiturates ($r = .47$), amphetamines ($r = .36$), opiates other than heroin ($r = .35$). In a sample of narcotics users, DAST scores were related to the number of drugs currently used ($r = .29$), cannabis use ($r = .55$), and similar issues ($r = .30$ to $.38$). Correlations between .74 and .75 were found between DAST scores and DSM-II diagnosis of lifetime and current drug abuse/dependence (Gavin, Ross, & Skinner, 1989). Skinner (1982) found only modest correlations between response bias measures and DAST scores. Scores on the DAST were also found to be correlated positively with measures of impulsive and reckless behaviors ($r = .42$) and deviant attitudes ($r = .54$).

The only "norms" offered include the "average DAST [28-item] score" (p. 86) for four groups: clients with (a) alcohol problems (4.5); (b) drug and alcohol problems (15.2); (c) drug problems only (17.8); and (d) narcotics users seeking treatment (12.8). In none of the reported studies were control (nondrug-user) groups employed.

Two factor analyses yielded disparate results. One principal components analysis (Skinner, 1982) based upon a sample including both alcohol and drug abusers yielded a "strong" single underlying drug abuse factor. The second study (Skinner & Goldberg, 1986), based upon a sample of narcotics users, yielded five dimensions (factors): drug dependence, social problems, medical problems, polydrug abuse, and previous treatment.

In summary, as a quick and dirty screen of young to middle-aged adults seeking treatment for substance abuse, the Drug Use Questionnaire (DAST-20) may serve a useful purpose in identifying at least the two extremes of minimal users (whose major problem may not be substance abuse) and very heavy users. However, one must retain a measure of skepticism with respect to the stability of data such as validity coefficients when the number of items in the scale to which they are applied has been reduced by almost a third under the scale upon which they were calculated. Even the authors state that it is only highly likely the longer scale statistics apply to the DAST-20. Also, nowhere is the rationale or related data for the deletion of 8 items of the original version

given. Finally, the name change from DRUG ABUSE SCREENING TEST to DRUG USE QUESTIONNAIRE on the forms given to examinees is confusing. At the minimum, an independent manual for the 20-item DRUG USE QUESTIONNAIRE would seem to be required to meet the standards for good psychometric practice. Also, validity data and norms specific to the DAST-20 are needed.

For much more comprehensive assessment of *how* and *why* a client appears for substance abuse treatment, much more detailed and sophisticated instruments may be found, such as the Personal Experience Inventory (PEI; T4:1971; Winters and Henly, 1989), the Personal Experience Inventory for Adults (PEI-A; 225; Winters, 1994), the American Drug and Alcohol Survey (Oetting, Beauvais, & Edwards, 1989), and the Drug Use Screening Inventory (Tarter, 1990).

REVIEWER'S REFERENCES

Selzer, M. L. (1971). The Michigan Alcoholism Screening Test: The quest for a new diagnostic instrument. *American Journal of Psychiatry, 127,* 1653–1658.

Skinner, H. A. (1982). The American Drug Abuse Screening Test. *Addictive Behaviors, 7,* 383–371.

Skinner, H. A., & Goldberg, A. E. (1988). Evidence for a drug dependence syndrome among narcotic users. *British Journal of Addiction, 81,* 479–484.

Gavin, D. R., Ross, H. E., & Skinner, H. A. (1989). Diagnostic validity of the Drug Abuse Screening Test in assessment of DSM-III drug disorders. *British Journal of Addiction, 84,* 301–307.

Oetting, E., Beauvais, F., & (1989). The Drug and Alcohol Survey. Fort Collins, CO: Rocky Mountain Behavioral Sciences Institute.

Winters, K. C., & Henly, G. A. (1989). Personal Experience Inventory. Los Angeles: Western Psychological Services.

Tarter, R. E. (1990). Evaluation and treatment of adolescent substance abuse: A decision tree method. *American Journal of Drug and Alcohol Abuse, 16,* 1–46.

Winters, K. C. (1995). Personal Experience Inventory for Adults. Los Angeles: Western Psychological Services.

Review of the Drug Use Questionnaire by JEFFREY S. RAIN, Assistant Professor and Chairman, Industrial/Organizational Psychology Program, School of Psychology, Florida Tech, Melbourne, FL:

The Drug Use Questionnaire (entitled Drug Abuse Screening Test [DAST-20] in the manual) is a 5-minute self-report instrument purported to measure the "seriousness of drug involvement for both clinical case findings during assessment and use in treatment evaluation research" (p. 82). Items cover symptoms of drug dependence and consequences of drug use. Respondents indicate if they agree or disagree with each statement by circling "yes" or "no." The Michigan Alcoholism Screening Test (MAST; Selzer, 1971) formed the basis of the 28-item original DAST, the predecessor of the DAST-20. An adolescent version, a 10-item brief version, and a French version were developed also; however, no data were presented on which they could be reviewed. The DAST-20 is presented as one of the measures in the

Directory of Client Outcome Measures for Addictions Treatment Programs.

Potential users of self-report measures in general, including the DAST-20, should first take into consideration those conditions under which overall validity is likely to be enhanced. Specific to alcohol and drug self-report measures, the availability of corroborating indices of drug use, the establishment of rapport with the client, the motivation of the client not to distort responses, and the length of time between current use of drugs and the assessment session each could function to reduce the usefulness of the data collected. These factors should still be considered even though research studies, in general, suggest that self-report measures can provide reliable and valid data.

Specific to the self-report issues, responses to some of the items may be dependent on the circumstances under which the DAST-20 is given and may cause a negative reaction by the client. Clients may be voluntary inpatients, court mandated participants, or individuals in crisis. Wording indicating the client's use is "abuse" (Item #3) or asking them to determine certain outcomes as being caused "because of your use of drugs" (Item #11) may provoke a reaction by the client. Clients may not be prepared to describe themselves as having "abused" drugs prior to treatment. Likewise, they may be unwilling to acknowledge the impact of their drug use/abuse on family or work before or during therapy. It should be noted that response bias analyses indicated low to moderate potential bias, though significance levels and sample sizes were not presented.

The reliability and validity data presented for the DAST-20 suggest it has the foundation to be a worthwhile screening or tracking instrument. Most of the concerns raised in reviewing the DAST-20's technical information might be answered if the *Directory of Client Outcome Measures for Addictions Treatment Programs* provided more space and thus more detailed information could have been presented. A test manual following the *Standards for Educational and Psychological Testing* (AERA, APA, & NCME, 1985) should be developed.

Reliability statistics presented were based on an earlier 28-item version of the DAST-20. Internal consistency reliabilities from the 28-item version were .86 or higher, which is very good. The only study reported that used the 20-item version yielded a coefficient alpha of .74, a substantial drop in reliability. The reliability decrease could be explained by the fact that reliability tends to decrease as the number of test items decrease. Extending this relationship, the adequacy of the reliability of the 10-item "brief" DAST must also be questioned.

Further, the level of reliability could be inflated by the number of "no" responses; the average score from the original sample was approximately 9.2, leaving half the items as "no." If "no" responses are interpreted as "not applicable" then the reliability may be in large part based on nonapplicability of an item. Disaggregating reliability by sample population would be instructive. The average score for individuals with only drug problems was 17.8 and may provide a better evaluation of reliability of the whole test.

As with the reliability examples above, validity findings raised further questions. The data suggested the 28-item version possessed elements of criterion-related and construct validity. Data for the DAST-20 were less specific; more of the data were based on the 28-item version. As with the reliability data, reporting significance levels and sample sizes would be helpful. Analyses where sufficient detail was presented indicate that the DAST is able to differentiate between individuals with alcohol only, drug and alcohol, and drug only problems.

A potential strong point of the DAST-20 may be its ability to measure change across time. The time frame may be varied from 6 months, 12 months, to 24 months. Used in this manner, it may provide a quick drug use symptoms and consequences screen on a case-by-case basis. In particular, test-retest reliabilities should be conducted to support this application.

Administration and scoring of the DAST-20 is very simple and straightforward. It is also very inexpensive. Comparison to norms and sample disaggregations was limited to data from three studies totaling 829 subjects.

In short, the DAST-20 has a good beginning and the association with its developmental underpinnings (i.e., MAST). However, more psychometric detail must be presented and additional studies conducted to increase its normative base before more definitive conclusions are drawn. Publication in the *Directory of Client Outcome Measures for Addictions Treatment Programs* may have limited the space to address some of the above issues with available validation studies. Depending on the veracity of the responses required, the DAST-20 should be used in conjunction with other indices and by experienced staff/professionals.

REVIEWER'S REFERENCES

Selzer, M. L. (1971). The Michigan Alcoholism Screening Test: The quest for a new diagnostic instrument. *American Journal of Psychiatry, 127,* 1653–1658.

American Educational Research Association, American Psychological Association, & National Council on Measurement in Education. (1985). *Standards for educational and psychological testing.* Washington, DC: American Psychological Association, Inc.

[105]
The Early Childhood Behavior Scale.

Purpose: Designed to assess behaviors related to early childhood emotional disturbance and behavior disorder.
Population: 36–72 months.
Publication Dates: 1991–1992.
Acronym: ECBS.
Scores, 4: Academic Progress, Social Relationships, Personal Adjustment, Total.
Administration: Individual.
Price Data, 1993: $55 per complete kit including technical manual ('92, 36 pages), intervention manual ('91, 130 pages), and 50 ratings forms; $10 per technical manual; $20 per intervention manual; $25 per 50 rating forms.
Time: (15–20) minutes.
Comments: Ratings by teachers or parents.
Author: Stephen B. McCarney.
Publisher: Hawthorne Educational Services, Inc.

Review of The Early Childhood Behavior Scale by KATHLEEN D. PAGET, Division Director, The Center for Child and Family Studies, College of Social Work, University of South Carolina, Columbia, SC:

The Early Childhood Behavior Scale (ECBS) is a 53-item rating scale designed to assess behaviors related to early childhood emotional disturbance and behavior disorders. Normed on a population of children from 36 to 72 months of age, the scale yields scores in the three areas of Academic Progress, Social Relationships, and Personal Adjustment as well as a total score. According to the technical manual, teachers are the primary raters, and administration time is 15 to 20 minutes. Teachers rate the frequency of behaviors exhibited by children in their classrooms on a 7-point Likert scale from 0 (*Not in My Presence*) to 6 (*More Than Once an Hour*) and then use the accompanying intervention manual to write goals and objectives and apply intervention strategies to the problem behaviors. A reading of the technical manual suggests that the test developer attended to many details related to assuring the psychometric soundness of the instrument; nevertheless, significant caveats must be raised to the prospective user of the ECBS. These caveats include concerns about the context in which the test was developed, the recency of the measure in light of current policy, and the deficit orientation of the identification process.

The provisions of Public Law 94-142 pertaining to emotional disturbance and behavior disorders guided the development of the scale. Rather than create an appropriate developmental context for the ECBS, the author took an existing assessment and

intervention model for school-age children and applied it, in its entirety, to young children. Although the developer went to great lengths to validate the instrument, no amount of attention to reliability and validity coefficients tempers the concern that an approach for school-age children was simply extended downward. The manual contains no mention of a developmental context in which young children should be viewed, and the language describing the data in the tables and figures could just as well apply to older children.

Details of the norming process do little to temper concerns about an appropriate developmental context. The technical manual states, "normative data were gathered from identified behaviorally disordered and regular education children, ages 3 up to 6 years, from 68 public school systems in 17 states" (p. 7). To determine discriminant or diagnostic validity, "196 randomly selected students from the normative sample [were chosen as a comparison for] a corresponding group of identified behaviorally disordered students who were receiving services" (p. 14). Logical analysis of these statements reveals that behaviorally disordered and regular education students were never separated out for comparison purposes, and the question must be raised as to whether the ECBS clearly discriminates typically developing children from those with atypical development. The lack of predictive validity information makes it all the more important to raise this question.

The conceptual questions raised above are related to current policy and practice issues. There is no mention in either the assessment or intervention manual of the passage of Public Law 99-457 in 1986 or its reauthorization as Public Law 102-119, the Individuals with Disabilities Education Act in 1991. Given the extent of recent political activity and its implications for developmentally appropriate practice, this oversight is surprising. An outdated reference list combines with this oversight to suggest that the ECBS has not kept pace with the recent literature in early childhood education. Although the assessment-intervention connection advanced by the intervention manual is consistent with current best practice, the lack of parent involvement in the assessment-intervention process clearly is not. Parents could be the raters who appropriately complete this instrument, but the manual does not explicitly mention this possibility. Instead, the manual's language describing the primary rater as "anyone familiar with the child's behavior patterns" (p. 18) is followed by the specific exemplars of preschool/ elementary level teachers (p. 18) and educators with primary educational opportunities. The potential user of the measure is left to wonder where parents fit in as primary information sources and intervenors with their young children, especially those as young as 3 years of age. Moreover, current best practice related to comprehensive assessment is superseded by an emphasis on efficiency, with statements such as "It is not appropriate to consult with other personnel to get information which is not observed by the rater" (p. 18) and "information [is] easily gathered with a minimum of time and personnel resource allocation" (p. 27). Although the situational specificity of ratings on the ECBS is laudable (and the option of "Not in My Presence" is an improvement over other behavior rating scales in this respect), the language of the manual encourages ratings from classroom settings only. The potential lack of input from parents and other professionals greatly increases the risk of errors in the identification process.

It is an interesting paradox that a measure's greatest strengths can also be its greatest weaknesses. At the same time that quantitative data support the soundness of the ECBS in identifying behavior disorders and emotional disturbance in young children, the numbers do nothing to assist the user in viewing a young child within a normal or typical developmental perspective. At the same time that the author provides technical guidance as to who should complete the ratings on the instrument, the central issues of parent involvement and comprehensive, interdisciplinary assessment are completely overlooked. An instrument that combines a careful quantitative approach with sensitivity to the nuances of young children's development is needed. If revised and interpreted within a developmental context consistent with current policy, the ECBS could meet this need.

Review of The Early Childhood Behavior Scale by JONATHAN SANDOVAL, *Professor and Acting Director, Division of Education, University of California, Davis, Davis, CA:*

The Early Childhood Behavior Scale is a teacher rating scale designed to identify children between 3 and 6 years of age with behavior disorders and emotional disturbance, making it one of a small but growing number of measures of this type for this age group. The scale consists of 53 negatively framed statements of child behaviors grouped under three headings: Academic Progress (AP), Social Relationships (SR), and Personal Adjustment (PA). The

teacher rates each behavior for frequency of occurrence on a 7-point scale. The ratings are summed for a raw score in each of these areas. More than half of the items are included on the PA scale. Accompanying the scale is The Early Childhood Behavior Intervention Manual (ECBIM), which lists goals, objectives, and intervention strategies for addressing each of the 53 test items (behaviors).

The scale's purpose is to identify children for special education intervention. It was developed from educational definitions found in the Education for All Handicapped Children Act of 1975 (Public Law 94-142) rather than psychiatric perspective as found in, for example, the *Diagnostic and Statistical Manual of the American Psychiatric Association.* The author also recommends the scale be used to measure change following school-based intervention.

The test items were selected by the author and reviewed by an unspecified group of "diagnosticians and educators" who approved the content as being appropriate to children with behavior disorders. The test was normed on a poorly described sample of 1,314 children rated by 289 teachers (average of one teacher to 4.5 children) in 17 states. Some of the children tested were previously identified as behaviorally disordered and an unknown number were not. Details of how the children were selected are missing from the manual although some demographic data are included that suggest the sample is somewhat similar to the U.S. population. Raw scores are converted to standard scores with a mean of 10 and a standard deviation of 3, although the distribution of behaviors is markedly skewed.

The three subscales are similar to the dimensions found on other measures and seem to have reasonable reliability. The test-retest correlation over a 30-day period for a random group of children in the norm group was .86 for the total score and ranged from .81 for SR to .91 for PA. There is no reporting of stability by age, information that would be useful. The interrater reliability based on 101 pairs of teachers is reported for 12 age groups; the median correlation is .84. This level of agreement is good at this age level. Internal consistency reliabilities for the three subscales are in the low .90s, suggesting that the items on these scales do measure the same underlying entities. Standard errors of measurement are reported by gender and various age groups but it is unclear which reliability estimates were used in their calculation.

The subscale item-total correlations are reported, and most are above .50. An exploratory factor analysis supports the subscale structure of the test to some extent, but a confirmatory factor analysis was not reported. The three-factor solution from varimax rotation reported in the manual indicates that a number of items load significantly on more than one factor. The PA scale items load on all three factors. In fact, all three subscales are correlated with each other, and the total score may be more valid than the subscales.

Correlations among the three subscales and a total score for one of two Child Behavior Checklist total scores for 57 behaviorally disordered children is reported in the manual as evidence of concurrent validity. These correlations are between .62 and .71, which are reasonably high, but this sample may have had extreme scores on the measures. The manual also presents data indicating that children in regular education score (remarkably) at the mean for the test and that behaviorally disordered children score several standard score points lower. This evidence suggests the measures may have validity for some purposes but much more evidence must be collected on this measure. The psychometric data reported in the manual are skimpy, not always appropriate, and are overinterpreted. The evidence presented does not inspire confidence. Users should proceed with caution until more evidence on this scale is reported. Other scales such as the Child Behavior Checklist (55) and the Behavior Assessment System for Children (34) have been more carefully constructed and are attractive alternatives.

Although subscale and total scores are produced by the test, the guidelines in the manual suggest that the user identify items with high raw scores on subscales on which a child has scored one standard deviation or more below the mean. These items, then, become the basis for intervention as suggested in the ECBIM. It should be pointed out that this item-by-item interpretation has not been justified by the data presented in the manual and that we have no data about the effectiveness or validity of the suggested strategies.

In summary, this scale probably meets the minimum standards for measures of its kind, but it is not the best measure available for identifying emotionally disturbed or behaviorally disturbed children. Some users may be interested in the accompanying ECBIM, which does contain a number of suggestions for helping young children. Having ratings for each behavior and including them on a scale, although novel, does not necessarily increase the validity of the intervention. More data should be collected on this measure.

[106]

Early Childhood Physical Environment Observation Schedules and Rating Scales.

Purpose: "Intended for the systematic assessment of the quality of the physical environment of child care centers and related early childhood environments."

Population: Directors and staff of child care centers, early childhood teachers.

Publication Dates: 1982–1994.

Scores: 9 scales: Early Childhood Teacher Style and Dimensions of Education Rating Scales (Early Childhood Teacher Style Rating Scale, Early Childhood Dimensions of Education Rating Scale, Teacher Style and Dimensions of Education Validity Check), Early Childhood Physical Environment Scales (Pattern 905: Spatial Organization, Pattern 908: Behavior Settings), Playground and Neighborhood Observation Behavior Maps (Playground Observation Behavior Map, Neighborhood Observation Behavior Map, Neighborhood Observation Supplementary Coding Sheet), Environment/Behavior Observation Schedule for Early Childhood Environments.

Administration: Group.

Price Data, 1994: $12 per complete kit including manual ('94, 80 pages), technical report, and specimen sets.

Time: [10–30] minutes per scale.

Comments: For research purposes only.

Author: Gary T. Moore.

Publisher: Center for Architecture and Urban Planning Research, University of Wisconsin—Milwaukee.

Review of the Early Childhood Physical Environment Observation Schedules and Rating Scales by LISA G. BISCHOFF, Associate Professor of School Psychology, Indiana State University, Terre Haute, IN:

The Early Childhood Physical Environment Observation Schedules and Rating Scales are a set of "preliminary procedures" designed to describe and assess physical aspects of childcare environments. According to Gary Moore, the author, the scales were developed and initial validation research was conducted in 1982 as part of a doctoral dissertation in environmental psychology. The author states that the scales in their current form are appropriate "for research purposes only" and that development of "a more complete and more methodologically rigorous set of scales for the description and evaluation of child care physical environments" (p. vi) is currently underway.

The Early Childhood Physical Environment Observation Schedules and Rating Scales are designed to assess the quality of early childhood childcare settings using five sets of scales. The first two sets of scales are designed to assess center size and philosophy (Early Childhood Center, Children, and Teacher Profiles) and caregiver style (Early Childhood Teacher Style and Dimensions of Education Rating Scales) and the third set of scales (Early Childhood Physical Environment Scales) addresses center layout and ambiance. These three sets of scales are described as measures of independent variables. Two sets of behavior maps and observation schedules provide a description of the physical and social environment and the behavior of participants within the childcare setting. These two sets of behavior maps and observation schedules are described as measures of dependent variables.

The first set of scales is designed to assess center size and educational philosophy as well as demographic characteristics of children and childcare providers in order to "factor out" the effect of such variables from the effects of physical environment. Philosophy of the center is categorized as representing one of five philosophical viewpoints including open education, individualized instruction, traditional education, other specialized programs (e.g., Montessori), or eclectic program. Categorization is based on a statement of center philosophy by the director of the center, analysis of published brochures, and director response to six Likert-type items related to educational philosophy. Procedures for determining category and psychometric information regarding this set of profiles are not included in the manual.

The second set of scales is designed to assess teacher style and approach to education. The first two instruments contain statements to which teachers respond using a 5-point Likert-type scale. The Early Childhood Teacher Style Rating Scale was developed based on a factor analytic study of early childhood teacher behavior patterns. The Early Childhood Dimensions of Education Rating Scale was developed from the Dimensions of Schooling (DISC) Questionnaire (Traub, Weiss, Fisher, & Musella, 1972). To validate these scales, an instrument was developed for completion by center directors regarding teacher philosophy and approach to children. Results of the scales were compared with results of the validity check with a sample from 16 centers. Paired samples t-tests were conducted with results indicating $p > .10$ on five of six dimensions.

The third set of scales is designed to assess variables in the physical environment. The first instrument was developed to assess the organization and space of the childcare environment as a whole and is based on dimensions of spatial organization critical for a "modified open plan" childcare facility, which Moore (manual) states is the organizational

plan most conducive to cognitive and social development. The second instrument is designed to assess the organization and character of specific behavior settings within the environment and is based on dimensions of well-defined behavior settings provided for particular developmental activities. Each scale includes 10 statements to be rated on a 5-point Likert scale by an observer outside the childcare center. Construct validity evidence for these scales is addressed through research-based definitions of organizational patterns upon which the scales are based as well as quasi-experimental research supporting the constructs upon which the scales are based. Interrater reliability was assessed through independent rating of 16 childcare centers by three judges. Mean percent exact agreement between judges was 52%.

The fourth set of scales includes two structured observation instruments (behavior maps) and a supplementary coding sheet. These instruments provide an observation format and coding system designed to facilitate description of physical and social environmental variables as well as description of behavior in playground, or planned play settings, and in neighborhood, or spontaneous play settings. The coding sheet provides definitions and instructions relevant to use of the behavior maps. Procedures for use of the maps suggest observation be conducted in 2- to 2 1/2-hour sessions. Construct validity of these scales is addressed through inclusion of observation components based on research in environmental psychology and attention to relevant child and behavior variables identified in developmental literature and preliminary observation. Interrater reliability was assessed through independent rating by two trained observers. Exact agreement between judges was 84%.

The final set of scales includes an observation schedule and grid as well as instructions, definitions, and coding information designed to assess child and teacher behavior in childcare settings. Construct validity of these scales is addressed through attention to categories of child behavior identified in child development literature. Interrater reliability was assessed through independent rating by two trained observers. Exact agreement between judges was 85% and Cohen's kappa coefficients calculated for all items on the scales provided an average k of .86.

In summary, The Early Childhood Physical Environment Observation Schedules and Rating Scales provide a useful set of instruments for researchers interested in measuring physical environmental variables in childcare and related environments. Although variables related to physical environment are included in other scales such as the Home Observation for Measurement of the Environment (HOME; Caldwell & Bradley, 1984; T4:1172) and the Infant/Toddler Environment Rating Scales (ITERS; Harms, Cryer, & Clifford, 1990; 12:188), such variables are often confounded by social and behavioral content. Furthermore, the full range of environmental variables is not addressed. The current scales appear to address these issues. The instruments are described as "preliminary procedures" and are recommended for "research purposes only." Psychometric information provided supports these statements. Suggestions for use of the instruments in research are provided relative to each set of scales. The published manual provides information regarding instrument development, theoretical bases, and instructions for use with more detailed information provided in Moore (1983). Further, the author invites questions and comments and provides telephone, fax, email, and postal addresses to facilitate such communication.

REVIEWER'S REFERENCES

Traub, R. E., Weiss, J., Fisher, C. W., & Musella, D. (1972). Closure on openness: Describing and quantifying open education. *Interchange, 3,* 69–84.

Moore, G. T. (1983). Some effects of physical and social environmental variables on children's behavior: Two studies of children's outdoor play and child care environments. *Dissertation Abstracts International, 44*(2), 626B. (University Microforms No. DA83-13216)

Caldwell, B. M., & Bradley, R. H. (1984). Home Observation for Measurement of the Environment. Little Rock, AR: University of Arkansas, Center for Child Development and Education.

Harms, T., Cryer, D., & Clifford, R. M. (1990). The Infant/Toddler Environment Rating Scale. New York: Columbia University Press.

Review of the Early Childhood Physical Environment Observation Schedules and Rating Scales by PATRICIA B. KEITH, Assistant Professor of School Psychology, Alfred University, Alfred, NY:

The Early Childhood Physical Environment Observation Schedules and Rating Scales manual is based on the hypothesis that a relation exists between the physical environment of child care centers and children's social behavior and cognitive development. Using the author's 1982 environmental psychology doctoral dissertation materials, the manual contains a series of forms for gathering information that may be of assistance to those interested in evaluating early child centers. Because the number of early childhood centers has expanded significantly in the past 20 years and is likely to continue to expand in number, research concerning children's social and cognitive development in out-of-home centers may be important. Children's experiences in early childhood centers is likely to influence their academic readiness, proficiency in following directions, and abilities to establish relationships with teachers and other children in primary school.

The manual recommends that materials be used for research purposes only and if interested in evaluation of early childhood centers, these materials could be reviewed. But, researchers should have background knowledge and resources available to them in several areas that are not presented in this manual (e.g., early childhood development, human resource management, teacher training, curriculum development) to develop a good research project. Countless typographical errors and awkward writing styles will be encountered, yet, these materials can be used as a starting point for new projects. Twelve dollars spent on these materials will most likely save researchers much time in deciding what to do and what not to do. The psychometric properties of the observation schedules and rating scales are in need of further development and refinement. References found in the manual may help researchers in their preliminary review of the literature.

[107]
Early Intervention Developmental Profile.

Purpose: Designed to yield information for planning comprehensive developmental programs for children with all types of handicaps.

Population: Children with handicaps who function at the 0–35-month age level.

Publication Dates: 1977–1991.

Scores, 8: Perceptual/Fine Motor, Cognition, Language, Social/Emotional, Self-Care (Feeding, Toileting, Dressing), Gross Motor.

Administration: Individual.

Price Data: Available from publisher.

Time: (50–60) minutes.

Comments: Stimulation activities manual included; also available in Spanish; see Preschool Developmental Profile (239) for extended ages.

Authors: D. Sue Schafer, Martha S. Moersch, Sally J. Rogers, Diane B. D'Eugenio, Sara L. Brown, Carol M. Donovan, and Eleanor Whiteside Lynch.

Publisher: The University of Michigan Press.

Cross References: See T4:835 (1 reference).

TEST REFERENCES

1. Beckman, P., Lieber, J., & Strong, B. (1993). Influence of social partner on interactions with mothers and familiar playmates. *American Journal on Mental Retardation, 98,* 378–389.

Review of the Early Intervention Developmental Profile by BARBARA A. ROTHLISBERG, Professor of Psychology in Educational Psychology and Director of the M.A./Ed.S. Program in School Psychology, Ball State University, Muncie, IN:

The Early Intervention Developmental Profile (hereafter called the Profile) is less an assessment device than it is a programming tool designed to chart the progress of children aged 0–35 months in six domains of behavior: Perceptual/Fine Motor, Cognition, Language, Social/Emotional, Self-Care, and Gross Motor development. As the second "volume" in a five-volume series addressing the needs of infants and young children, the Profile offers a method for a multidisciplinary team (or occasionally a single trained examiner) to estimate a child's relative performance in different skill areas in a comprehensive manner and devise individualized objectives to encourage growth in domains where current performance is lagging and sustain growth in areas where progress is developmentally appropriate. The companion volumes to the Profile offer descriptive information and programming suggestions for infants and/or preschoolers.

The Profile was developed because of the Early Intervention Project for handicapped Infants and Young Children and is designed to be a supplemental measure, never meant to supplant standardized instruments constructed to diagnose and/or predict behavior. In fact, the authors state that the Profile has *not* been standardized on either a normal or exceptional population. Instead, items were derived based on nonspecified research- and theory-based developmental sequences to indicate a child's status and determine what specific skills should emerge next. Items were ordered on the individual subscales according to their placement on other, standardized measures of infant and preschool behavior. As a check on the validity of item placement, the Profile scores of 14 children with disabilities were correlated with standardized tests such as the Bayley Scales of Infant Development (Bayley, 1969), the Vineland Social Maturity Scale (Doll, 1953), and the Receptive-Expressive Emergent Language Scale (Bzoch & League, 1971); coefficients for the Profile subscales appeared to relate strongly to the standardized instruments. No other reliability or validity studies were offered. The correlation information on the sample of 14 is the only support for the subscales' technical merits.

The Profile's comprehensive nature suits the use of multidisciplinary team involvement. Its intent is to provide the respective professionals involved in assessment and programming for a child a common measure from which to explore the very different domains of early development. Each professional would "assess" in their areas of expertise (psychologist in Cognitive, speech therapist in Language, etc.) but

could then provide the group and the parents of the child with a disability a means of representing and comparing growth across the different domains. The Profile is designed so that each record form will accommodate the scoring and results of four different evaluations, suggested at 3-month intervals. Results based on the success of the child with the item sets can be plotted on a graph based on age spans to detect relative strengths and weaknesses in behavioral areas. Each domain is represented as a subscale with items organized according to 3- or 4-month age spans from 0–2 months to 32–35 months. The number of items administered to the infant/preschooler varies with the age span and the domain to be explored. Generally, the youngest age levels sample the fewest behaviors. The child's behavior is observed in the presence of a parent or caretaker and either the infant is asked to perform an activity or the adult reports on the child's success at items. Evaluation of all domains can take up to one hour.

It is suggested that the evaluation commence with the Perceptual/Fine Motor domain and end with the Gross Motor subscale. A lengthy list of materials is included but the materials are not provided. Therefore, whereas the questions asked of the child or caretaker may be somewhat standard, the materials to be used are not. Basal and ceiling rules are given to help the evaluators minimize the number of items to be administered to any given child (extensive item descriptions are furnished in Volume 1: Developmental Programming for Infants and Young Children: Assessment and Application [Rogers & D'Eugenio, 1981]). Basals consist of six consecutive items passed or passes across two consecutive age levels; ceilings consist of six consecutive items failed or failures across two consecutive age levels. Graphing of a child's performance is determined by the highest item number of a sequence of passes for each subscale.

Given the global nature of the Profile's construction and its attempt to offer a sweeping overview of infant progress, it is appropriate that this measure does not supplant others for diagnostic purposes; however, its developmental orientation does provide to the multidisciplinary team and other educational programmers a comprehensive overview of early child development. The Profile is best used in displaying the child's current level of functioning across different behavioral domains and offers direction as to further educational and developmental planning. The child's performance can be operationalized into a set of instructional objectives and programming can be assisted by the comprehensive set of stimulation activities offered in Volume 3 of the set (Brown & Donovan, 1981). Because it is designed to give a global estimate of development across behavioral domains, the ability of the intervention team to plot out the success of the child's individualized objectives on the Profile can give early intervention projects a means of measuring progress in the developing child and suggest areas for further work.

In summary, the Profile is not a diagnostic tool but a means by which the relative developmental progress of a young child may be plotted in six behavioral domains to help in determining the success and direction of intervention programming. The behavioral objectives that result from analysis of the Profile can help educators and parents evaluate the child's current level of progress and plan what types of behavioral change should be anticipated for the future. The Profile provides an estimate of developmental growth that can be useful to parents and professionals interested in intervention planning for infants who are disabled or who are at risk for developmental deficits.

REVIEWER'S REFERENCES

Doll, E. A. (1953). *The measurement of social competence: A manual for the Vineland Social Maturity Scale.* Minneapolis: American Guidance Service.

Bayley, N. (1969). The Bayley Scales of Infant Development. New York: The Psychological Corporation.

Bzoch, K. R., & League, R. (1971). The Bzoch-League Receptive-Expressive Emergent Language Scale for the Measurement of Language Skill in Infancy. Gainesville, FL: Tree of Life Press.

Brown, S. L., & Donovan, C. M. (1981). Volume 3: Stimulation activities. In D. S. Schafer & M. S. Moersch (Eds.), *Developmental programming for infants and young children* (rev. ed.). Ann Arbor, MI: University of Michigan Press.

Rogers, S. J., & D'Eugenio, D. B. (1981). Volume 1: Assessment and application. In D. S. Schafer & M. S. Moersch (Eds.), *Developmental programming for infants and young children* (rev. ed.). Ann Arbor, MI: University of Michigan Press.

Review of the Early Intervention Developmental Profile by GARY J. STAINBACK, Senior Psychologist I, Department of Pediatrics, East Carolina University School of Medicine, Greenville, NC:

The Early Intervention Developmental Profile is an infant-based assessment instrument designed for children who function below a 36-month level. The profile is composed of six scales, providing developmental norms and milestones for the following areas: Perceptual/Fine Motor, Cognition, Language, Social/Emotional, Self-Care, and Gross Motor development. It reportedly can be administered in less than an hour by an experienced clinician or multidisciplinary team. The main purpose for administering the scale is for supplementary information to be used in conjunction with standard psychological, motor, and language assessment. The authors make it very clear the scale was not designed for

predictive purposes nor for diagnosing handicapping conditions. Rather, the intent is to identify the relative strengths and weaknesses of the child and provide guidance for what developmental skills are expected to emerge next.

The Early Intervention Developmental Profile contains 299 items, 48 of which are devoted to the Perceptual/Fine Motor area, 46 for the Cognitive area, 41 for the Language area, 38 for the Social/ Emotional area, 50 for Self-Care, and 76 for the Gross Motor area. Items selected for the profile had two criteria for inclusion; the item must have either appeared in at least two recognized scales, or must be an original item. Items were also screened for inclusion by the project staff member most trained in that area (e.g., psychology for Cognition, physical therapist for Gross Motor) to determine if the item marked an important developmental milestone. Lastly, items were needed for each age range appearing in the profile: 0 to 2, 3 to 5, 6 to 8, 9 to 11, 12 to 15, 16 to 19, 20 to 23, 24 to 27, 28 to 31, and 32 to 35, although no consistent attempt was made to arrange items in a developmental sequence within each age group.

A specific weakness for the profile is that it has not been standardized. Items were assigned to specific age ranges based on standardization or research from other instruments. One does not know, however, how many "new" items were added to the scale, or the number of items in each area that did not have standardized support for inclusion in the profile.

Validation studies from 1973–76 project activities were cited for concurrent validity in the manual. Results were compared by "correlating each of the six profile scales with standardized, widely used evaluation instruments" (p. 2). Fourteen handicapped students were mentioned in the manual, but it is not known if this constituted the entire concurrent validity study or if additional children were utilized and these 14 are mentioned because of their handicapping conditions. In addition, there is no description of the characteristics of these 14 students, or the nature of their handicapping conditions. The six developmental scales were correlated against the Bayley Scales of Infant Development (Mental and Motor scales), Vineland Social Maturity Scale, Receptive-Expressive Emergent Language scale, and the Clinical Motor Evaluation. Correlations ranged from .33 (between a dissimilar instrument and area of development) to .96 between Cognition and the Bayley Mental Scale. The relationship between the profile's six scales and individual performance was also explored, and correlation coefficients ranged from ".59 among the language, self-care, and gross motor scales to a high of .95 between cognition and social/emotional scales" (p. 3). These findings should be interpreted with caution, however, because of the small sample size.

Interrater reliability was reportedly demonstrated through videotaping of three profile assessments, with nine raters trained in the profile administration and experienced in assessment of young children. Percent of agreements ranged from 80% to 97%, with a mean of 89% agreement. Test-retest data were also reported with 15 children given the profile three times at 3-month intervals. Results (.83 to .96 for 3-month retest; .77 to .93 for 6-month retest) were significant at the .01 or .001 level between initial scores and each retest score.

Test materials are not a part of the package for the profile. One will receive Booklet 1 (Assessment and Application), Booklet 2 (Early Intervention Developmental Profile, or record booklet), and Booklet 3 (Stimulation Activities). Recommended materials, all of which are easily obtainable, must be obtained by the examiner(s). Administration usually begins following a brief observation time. Basal and ceiling rules are either six consecutive items passed or failed or all items in two consecutive age ranges. It is suggested by the authors that the Perceptual/Fine Motor scale be administered first, followed by the Cognitive, Social/Emotional, Language, Self-Care, and Gross Motor scales. Items are scored either pass (P), fail (F), omitted (0), or pass-fail (PF) for emerging skills. Omitted items are scored as failure; however, no mention is made about how to credit PF scored items. Developmental criteria for scoring each item are presented in the manual. On the inside back cover of the record booklet, the examiner can profile the child's performance by marking the highest item number of a sequence of passes earned in each section, and then connecting the points. This profiling is to represent the child's highest success, without consideration of intermittent failures.

Generally there are three to four items for each age range, with the exception of the Gross Motor scale, which averages seven to eight items per age range. There are four areas, however, in which only one or two items compose the domain age range; two fall in the language scale (0–2 and 32–35), the 0–2 age range on the Self-Care scale, and 20–23 months on the Gross Motor scale. Total number of items administered to a child for the six scales was considered sufficient for the purpose of this instrument by this reviewer.

Of particular value for individuals utilizing the Early Developmental Profile is the third booklet consisting of stimulation activities. These can be very useful for programming purposes. For individuals who may find it difficult to write program goals and objectives, the authors also provided a chapter for Program Development, which orients the reader to the process of writing behavioral objectives and goals for children.

In summary, the Early Intervention Developmental Profile can prove useful in providing supplementary information for programming purposes for children already identified as possessing special needs. The profile lacks technical data, and should certainly not be used for diagnostic purposes. Its value to add to diagnostic tests may also be quite limited, and is only recommended to be used for programming purposes following multidisciplinary diagnostic assessment.

[108]
Early Language Milestone Scale, Second Edition.

Purpose: To assess speech and language development during infancy and early childhood.
Population: Birth to 36 months.
Publication Dates: 1983–1993.
Acronym: ELM Scale—2.
Scores, 4: Auditory Expressive, Auditory Receptive, Visual, Global Language.
Administration: Individual.
Price Data, 1994: $89 per complete kit including manual ('93, 95 pages), object kit, and 100 records; $29 per manual; $29 per 100 record forms; $34 per object kit.
Time: (1–10) minutes.
Author: James Coplan.
Publisher: PRO-ED, Inc.
Cross References: For a review of an earlier edition by Ruth M. Noyce, see 10:99 (2 references).

Review of the Early Language Milestone Scale, Second Edition by PHILIP BACKLUND, Associate Dean and Professor of Speech Communication, Communication Department, Central Washington University, Ellensburg, WA, and SHERWYN MORREALE, Chair, Center for Excellence in Oral Communication, University of Colorado at Colorado Springs, Colorado Springs, CO:

The original purpose of the Early Language Milestone (ELM) Scale was to serve as a screening test capable of detecting language-delayed children as early and as rapidly as possible. The scale was developed as a tool for assessing language development from birth to 36 months of age and intelligibility of speech from 18 to 48 months of age. It is not meant to substitute for formal diagnostic assessment of the language-delayed child, but identifies and quantifies language delay in very young children so that these children may receive definitive care as promptly as possible.

The 43-item scale is divided into three categories of skills: Auditory Expressive, Auditory Receptive, and Visual. Each category contains age-related benchmark skills that a child at a particular age normally would be expected to demonstrate. For example, in Auditory Expressive, one behavior called for is the child's ability to express two-word sentences, a behavior normally expected of children aged 20–24 months. Each item can be elicited through one (or more) of three different ways: parental history, direct testing, or incidental observation. Some item responses are obtained only on the basis of history or incidental observation as there would be no reliable method to induce direct response from a very young child. High stimulus items, such as orienting to a bell, are measured only through direct testing. The cutoff point for passing the scale is the age by which 90% of children in the population would be expected to demonstrate the behaviors. Therefore, the ELM Scale-2 identifies the lowest 10% of children with respect to speech and language development. Administration of the scale can be accomplished in 1 to 10 minutes depending on the response of the child and the number of items that need to be administered.

The first edition of this scale was published with a scoring method that required the examiner to determine the child's basal level only by administering items at or slightly below the child's chronological age. The basal score is calculated at the point where the child has three demonstrated appropriate responses on consecutive items. The first edition added a single forced-choice question related to unclear speech, as unclear speech is the most obvious sign of language disability.

The second edition of the scale made minor modifications to the items in the scale to improve accuracy, but the major change was the addition of instructions on how to determine an "optional point" score. The rationale for this change was, in part, due to the utility of describing a child's language in more detail than simply *pass* or *fail*. The author suggests that if the child is at risk developmentally, if the caretaker has specific concerns about the child's language development, or if detailed information is needed to determine eligibility for remedial service, to monitor progress, or for use in research, then a point score is useful. The point score is determined by first calculating the basal score, and then determining the child's ceiling level (three successive failures on consecutive items) in each skill category. Point scores can be converted to percentile values, standard score equivalents, or chronological age equivalents. High-risk children are more appropriately assessed using the point-scoring method. Failing the ELM Scale-2 by the pass/fail method automatically shifts the child from low-risk to high-risk; in such instances, the examiner is encouraged to seek more data.

The manual that comes with the scale is well developed. It includes a brief section on language development, extensive instructions on administering the test including numerous examples of patterns of item scoring at different age levels, and explicit instructions on using item prompts and determining response to prompt. The instructions for use are very clear. The scale can be administered by examiners with varying degrees of knowledge of early language development. The manual also includes an interesting and informative history of the development of the scale together with information on validation and reliability. The appendices include a number of clinical examples that illustrate the use of the scale and conversion scales to determine percentile scores, standard score equivalents, and age equivalents.

The instrument and manual are accompanied by scoring sheets and the necessary items for administering the scale, including a cup, bell, spoon, crayon, and block.

Normative data were originally obtained on the first edition of the scale using 191 pediatric patients from birth to 3 years of age and subsequently validated on several groups of developmentally delayed children. An item related to the intelligibility of speech was added in 1987 using data gathered from a sample of 235 low-risk children based on parental report (Coplan & Gleason, 1988). The point-scoring method was developed during the late 1980s with mean score and percentile distributions published in 1990 (Coplan & Gleason, 1990). The manual includes a description of a series of validation studies that compared ratings on the ELM Scale-2 with similar instruments. These studies support the ELM Scale-2 as a valid and discriminating measure of linguistic development. Reliability studies are also reported using test-retest and interobserver studies. Reported results range from .93 to .99 for interobserver reliability and .74 to .94 for test-retest reliability. The final part of this section of the manual describes the ELM Scale-2 as it fits into the broader conceptual framework of screening and infant developmental testing. This information is useful in understanding how the results are to be interpreted.

The ELM Scale-2 is a unique instrument. It facilitates routine developmental screening of very young children and permits early detection of potential problems. The addition of the point-scoring method increases the instrument's usefulness. The pass/fail method of scoring is most effectively used with low-risk subjects. High-risk, delayed, or research populations are more effectively assessed using the point-scoring method. Based on comparisons with similar instruments, the ELM Scale-2 has been shown to be equivalent to or more discriminating than similar instruments. This instrument fills a need for a discriminating, dependable, screening device that can be used routinely by a range of trained administrators without excessive demands on time or administration.

REVIEWER'S REFERENCES

Coplan, J., & Gleason, J. R. (1988). Unclear speech: Recognition and significance of unintelligible speech in preschool children. *Pediatrics, 82*, 447–452.

Coplan, J., & Gleason, J. R. (1990). Quantifying language development from birth to 3 years using the Early Language Milestone Scale. *Pediatrics, 86*, 963–971.

Review of the Early Language Milestone Scale, Second Edition by BETSY WATERMAN, Assistant Professor, Counseling and Psychological Services Department, State University of New York at Oswego, Oswego, NY:

The Early Language Milestone Scale, Second Edition (ELM Scale—2), was designed to screen for language or speech delays as early as possible in a child's development. It measures language development in infants from birth to 36 months of age and speech development in children from 1 1/2 to 4 years of age. The author suggests that this instrument can be used as part of "well-child care" (p. v), as a screening tool for large groups of children, as a means of identifying children at risk for speech and language delays, and as a research tool. A discussion with the author indicates this measure has been primarily used as a screening tool when working with low or high risk children in medical settings. It takes approximately 1 to 10 minutes to administer the scale.

The ELM Scale—2 has 43 items that are divided into three sections: Auditory Expressive (AE), Auditory Receptive (AR), and Visual (V). The author also identifies seven item clusters: Babbling, Orients to bell, One-step commands, Gesture games, Single words, name and use of objects, and Intelligibility, consisting of from 2 to 4 items each. Items are elicited by direct testing (T), caretaker report (history or H), or direct observation (O). Scoring can be done in either of two ways: a Pass/Fail method or in a point-scoring system. The latter system has been added in the new edition of the ELM Scale. The pass/fail method is intended primarily for screening. The child must pass all three divisions (Auditory Expressive, Auditory Receptive, and Visual) and must not fail any critical items, those items that 90% of children have attained, in order to pass the ELM Scale—2 as a whole.

The point-scoring method is designed for use with children at higher risk for language delays, for obtaining more precise information about the child's abilities, and for use in research. In this method, the child generally receives one point for every item or part of an item that is passed. Raw scores are determined for each division and for the test as a whole and these can be converted to percentiles, standard scores, or age equivalents. The scoring system is based on a hierarchy of skills within clusters and the passing of an item in the cluster results in the passing of all lower items. Likewise, the failure of an item results in a failure of all higher items.

During the initial construction of the ELM, 57 items were administered to 191 typical children between the ages of 0 and 36 months. Eighty percent of this population were white and 20% were nonwhite. When possible, items were tested by all three methods, parent report, direct observation, and direct testing. When data obtained by the different methods of testing were discrepant from each other, the parent report was used. A logistic model was used to generate curves that were ultimately converted to bar graphs. Intelligibility questions were added in 1987 and normed on 235 low-risk children.

Validation studies of the original version of the ELM were conducted with over 1,500 children and with both high- and low-risk populations. Sensitivity, the proportion of the sample population correctly identified as speech/language delayed when compared with other measures of language, ranged between 83% and 100%. Specificity, the proportion of the sample population correctly identified as typical learners, was reported between 68% and 100% for all populations. Positive Predictive Values, the proportion of subjects identified by the ELM as delayed learners who then showed delays at the time of formal diagnostic testing, were reported between 67% and 95%. Negative Predictive Values, the proportion of children passing the screening test who were actually typical learners, ranged between 95% and 100%. The Bayley Scales of Infant Development (BSID), Stanford-Binet Intelligence Scale (SBIS), Peabody Picture Vocabulary Test—Revised (PPVT—R), Receptive-Expressive Emergent Language Test (REEL), Preschool Language Scale (PLS), Leiter International Performance Scale, Sequenced Inventory of Communication Development (SICD), and Illinois Test of Psycholinguistic Abilities (ITPA) were used as concurrent measures of language abilities in the young subjects in various studies.

The ELM Scale—2 point-scoring system was validated on a sample of 50 low-risk subjects. Concurrent validity, at 30 months of age, with the PPVT—R, and, at 36 months with the SBIS and ITPA ranged from .51 to .66. A test-retest correlation coefficient of .28 was reported between testing at 9 and 18 months.

One hundred subjects (57 male and 43 female) were used as the sample for reliability studies. Seventy-three White, 18 Black, 5 Hispanic, and 4 other or of unknown racial or ethnic background were included. Children at three age levels were included: 0—12 months (n = 49), 12—24 months (n = 25), and 24—36 months (n = 26). Interobserver reliability was reported at 98% and test-retest reliability (mean interval of 7.4 days) at 96% for the pass/fail method. Interobserver coefficients ranging from .93 to .99 and test-retest reliability ranging from .77 to .94 were reported for the point-scoring method.

The ELM Scale—2 is a quick and easy-to-administer instrument designed to identify young children (between 0 and 36 months) who may be at risk for language or speech impairment. The point-scoring system that has been added appears to enhance the sensitivity of the measure. Validation studies appear adequate although a few mild concerns exist. Although the author indicates that the instrument can be used with children over 36 months of age, no validation or reliability studies have been conducted with this age group. Information about the number of subjects across racial, ethnic, gender, and age variables in the validity samples is also not consistently reported in the manual. As with other instruments that rely heavily on the reporting of parents, findings may be affected by a desire to create a particular image of their child (good or bad) or by inaccurate memory of behaviors. The manual is quite comprehensive and generally "reader friendly" with many examples available to aid the examiner in administration and scoring. Terms such as Sensitiv-

ity and Specificity, however, were presented before their definitions, making the validation section somewhat confusing to interpret. The scoring form was not easy to follow with item numbers placed inconsistently in front of, or at the end of, the bar graph. Problems, however, are minor and this instrument appears to be an excellent one for what it is intended—the screening of children for at-risk language and speech development. It appears to be particularly useful with the youngest population of children (0 to 12 months) when compared with other similar instruments.

[109]
Early Memories Procedure.

Purpose: "Method of exploring personality organization, especially current life concerns, based on an individual's memory of the past."

Population: Ages 10 and over with at least a fourth-grade reading level.

Publication Dates: 1989–1992.

Scores: No scores.

Administration: Group.

Price Data, 1994: $63 per 10 test booklets; $4 per manual.

Time: (90–240) minutes.

Comments: Instrument may be interpreted according to a Freudian, Adlerian, Ego-Psychological or Cognitive-Perceptual model.

Author: Arnold R. Bruhn.

Publisher: Arnold R. Bruhn and Associates.

Cross References: See T4:840 (1 reference).

Review of the Early Memories Procedure by KARL R. HANES, Consultant Psychologist, and Director, Vangard Publishing, Carlton, Victoria, Australia:

The Early Memories Procedure (EMP) is a projective test of personality organization that utilizes 21 probes to uncover pertinent early memories of an individual. The use of actual past events as a seemingly neutral medium within which to explore current psychological disposition is a novel approach that appears, on the face of it, to defy the spirit of the projective methodology, which presumes the presentation of largely ambiguous stimuli in a nondirective format. Like many unorthodox developments that appear to run contrary to current world views in general and, more specifically, to conventional paradigms of clinical practice and psychometric evaluation, the EMP makes an easy target for censure. Many would suggest that this inventory is lengthy, that its validity ultimately relies on the fate of the cognitive-perceptual theory developed by its creator (see Bruhn, 1990), and that it will probably have little appeal to those who do not favor the use of projective methods to assess personality or who are not adherents of the psychodynamic or psychoanalytic schools of psychology.

However, in the opinion of this reviewer, condemning this inventory on the basis of disagreement with its underlying philosophical and theoretical premises runs the risk of perpetuating the kind of scientific skirmishes that have probably stifled scientific advancement and that emanate from the view that there is a single right way to solve human problems.

The EMP is a unique inventory, the only projective measure that assesses autobiographical memory, and is based on the idea that what is revealed in memory are affect-laden schemas of experience that mirror significant current attitudes and perceptions. In actual fact, this view is not inconsistent with much of what is known about memory for past events, which is thought to be composed in part of the actual experiences but may also be colored by fantasy, other possibly similar or related encounters, and motivational factors (see Loftus, 1979).

This notwithstanding, there are obvious aspects of this inventory that are in need of further development. The purpose of the measure, its intended population and limitations, and its relationship to other similar measures such as the Rorschach (T4:2824) and Thematic Apperception Test (T4:2292), are clearly outlined and the manual provides unequivocal guidelines for its administration. Scoring criteria for this measure are well elaborated in an accompanying document, the Comprehensive Early Memory Scoring System Manual—Revised (CEMSSR; Last & Bruhn, 1992), but require considerable persistence to decipher. The care and attention to detail that have gone into the construction of the EMS questionnaire and its scoring accompaniment, the CEMSS, is admirable and shows an attempt to apply considerable scientific rigour to an area of personality assessment where such considerations have not been greatly emphasized.

However, personally, I would like to see an integrated manual that incorporates development, administration, scoring criteria, and other information in the one package. Normative data are nonexistent, though this is true of most projective methods. Though reliability and validity data have never been a high priority in the projective assessment tradition, I wonder whether it might not be possible to assess the convergent validity of this measure—as compared to, for example, more longstanding projective instruments such as the Rorschach, as well as to provide some interrater and test-retest

reliability data. For example, one could administer this inventory to subjects who are depressed, grieving, or ruminating over an obvious current concern—the responses these subjects make should be consistent with their current problems or concerns.

Some of the items on the questionnaire are excellent and have high face validity. However, I do think the probes that merely ask for memories without attention to their significance could be revised. For example, the first school memory is considered to provide attitudes toward achievement, mastery, and independence—it is possible, however, that this probe could conjure up relatively innocuous or trivial memories that do not bear upon these issues at all. It may be more advantageous to probe subjects for memories they consider to be significant, associated with profound emotions, and so forth. I would consider this inventory to be particularly valuable in cases where early life experiences are suspected of being intrusive or relevant to current concerns (e.g., sexual abuse, family breakup) and one that could be easily incorporated into a self-administered history-taking questionnaire for use at an early stage of the counseling or psychotherapeutic process.

The EMP is an important addition to the range of projective techniques for assessment of psychological disposition and possible behavioral maladjustment that would make a valuable inclusion within the armamentarium of the psychodynamic or psychoanalytic therapist. Its orientation is exploratory rather than strictly psychometric, it is reasonably priced, but I would wait for the next version, complete with scoring details, before investing in this promising measure.

REVIEWER'S REFERENCES

Loftus, E. F. (1979). The reality of repressed memories. *American Psychologist, 48,* 518–537.
Bruhn, A. R. (1990). Cognitive-perceptual theory and the projective use of autobiographical memory. *Journal of Personality Assessment, 55,* 95–114.
Last, J., & Bruhn, A. R. (1992). The Comprehensive Early Memories Scoring System—Revised. (Available from A. R. Bruhn, 7910 Woodmont Ave., Suite 1300, Bethesda, MD 20814.)

Review of the Early Memories Procedure by LeADELLE PHELPS, Professor of School Psychology, Department of Counseling and Educational Psychology, State University of New York at Buffalo, Buffalo, NY:

The Early Memories Procedure (EMP) is a projective method utilizing elicited autobiographical memories as a technique to: (a) identify significant unresolved issues, and (b) obtain an assessment of global personality organization. Similar to the Thematic Apperception Test (T4:2824) or the Rorschach (T4:2292) but without the cards, the technique is intended to uncover unconscious needs, interests, attitudes, and perceptions of self. Memories are reported using a self-administered 31-page response booklet. The author indicates that the procedure requires the equivalent of a fourth grade writing ability. Children younger than 10 years of age or individuals lacking the requisite writing competencies may dictate their responses into an audio tape recorder.

Respondents are asked to recall six *spontaneous memories*: first, the earliest childhood memory one can recall, four additional childhood memories, and finally, a particularly clear or important memory from any period within the lifespan. Next, 15 *directed* memories are solicited, focusing first on memories of school, punishment, sibling(s), and family, followed by the clearest lifetime memories of one's mother, father, an admired person, happiest event, most traumatic event, parental fighting, parental use of alcohol/drugs, incident in which one felt most ashamed, physical or emotional abuse, inappropriate sexual experience, and a fantasy event. Last, the respondent is asked to "interpret" a memory of her or his choosing. These memories are then rated on a Likert-type rating scale based on: (a) clarity of recall (5-point scale), (b) quality of generated affect (i.e., pleasantness of the memory rated on a 7-point scale), (c) potential for aggressiveness (3-point scale), (d) reality orientation (5-point scale), and (e) quality of interpersonal relationships (4 levels). In addition, the examiner may probe further by asking the client how a recalled event would be changed or altered if such were possible.

Memories are interpreted based on how the events are construed by the respondent (e.g., blame, responsibility, cause and effect, beliefs, attitudes, introspection). More specifically, memories may be evaluated based on content, passivity of response, and type, breadth, and depth of emotional response. The author and associates provide three separate scoring manuals, two of which are simply photocopied reproductions. As a result, it is difficult to obtain a lucid, succinct overview of recommended scoring procedures to facilitate the stated purposes of the procedures (i.e., identification of significant unresolved issues and assessment of global personality organization).

The procedure and scoring suggestions have not been standardized or subjected to rigorous psychometric evaluation. No data regarding reliability or validity are given. For this type of procedure, interrater, test-retest, and interitem reliability indices are a mainstay. Likewise, no indication of content, criterion, or construct validity is given. Until such data are provided, the EMP is not recommended for generalized use.

[110]
Early School Inventory.

Population: Ages 5–7.
Publication Dates: 1986–1987.
Acronym: ESI.
Price Data, 1994: $46 per ESI manual for interpretation and use ('87, 222 pages) including normative information, 1 ESI-D, and 1 ESI-P skill record.
Time: Administration time not reported.
Authors: Joanne R. Nurss and Mary E. McGauvran.
Publisher: The Psychological Corporation.

a) EARLY SCHOOL INVENTORY—DEVELOPMENTAL.
Purpose: "Provides a systematic method for gathering information about a child's development for use in planning effective instruction."
Acronym: ESI-D.
Scores, 4: Physical Development, Language Development, Cognitive Development, Social-Emotional Development.
Price Data: $36.50 per 35 self-scoring checklists and directions for administering; $3 per ESI-D skill record.
Administration: Group.

b) EARLY SCHOOL INVENTORY—PRELITERACY.
Purpose: Provides information about "a child's progress in acquiring the preliteracy skills needed when learning to read and write."
Acronym: ESI-P.
Scores, 3: Print Concepts, Writing Concepts, Story Structure.
Price Data: $44.50 per 35 self-scoring sheets, directions, and one set of 4 cards; $32 per 35 self-scoring sheets; $3.50 per directions; $15 per cards; $3 per ESI-P skill record.
Administration: Individual.

Review of the Early School Inventory by DAMON KRUG, University Professor, College of Education, Governors State University, University Park, IL, and BRANDON DAVIS, School Psychologist, Arbor Clinic, Muncie, IN:

The Developmental and Preliteracy Early School Inventories were developed to help teachers learn more about their students' development and preliteracy skills. The inventories are a list of behaviors that can be rated by teachers. By examining the profile, teachers can use recommended activities to enhance their students' skills.

The norms are based on students from classrooms participating in the Metropolitan Readiness Test (MRT). Teachers were asked to choose two or three students who fairly represented the students in their classrooms (manual, p. 11). This yielded a total norm group of 2,146 students ranging in age from 60 to 84 months. This norm group appears to be appropriate in size. However, there is no description of the sample regarding gender, ethnicity, or parental socioeconomic status. The above listed factors would likely influence development and preliteracy skills. Further, preschool experience would also likely influence the mastery of the behaviors listed on the inventories. By not incorporating the previously mentioned student characteristics, it is impossible to evaluate the appropriateness of the norms in interpreting an individual's performance.

With respect to item analysis and possible item bias, there is no description of any procedure to examine items for possible gender or ethnic bias. It is possible that the developers believe that the behaviors included in the inventories are essential regardless of gender or ethnicity. Thus, it would be less important to examine for gender or ethnic bias. However, this is not stated and in the current arena of multiculturalism, it is not advisable to make assumptions regarding ethnic and gender issues.

With respect to reliability, the manual reports on both internal consistency and interrater reliability. Regarding the Developmental Inventory, the reported internal consistency coefficients are rather low ranging from .21 to .69. However, because the Developmental Inventory assesses a variety of skills within two different domains, Physical and Language, internal consistency coefficients would not be expected to be high. For example, expecting large muscle development to be consistent with written language development is not realistic. Many young children will develop large muscle skills well before they develop written language skills. Thus, scores on items within these areas may not be consistent with each other. Internal consistency would have been better if calculated for each domain or subdomain separately, which was done for the Preliteracy Inventory.

With respect to the Preliteracy Inventory, the internal consistency coefficients ranged from .75 to .86. The internal consistency coefficients are much higher and more acceptable than those for the Developmental Inventory.

Interrater reliability is important for any instrument based on behavioral observation. The manual refers to interrater reliability but provides no data and instead refers the reader to a paper available from The Psychological Corporation. It would have been better if the developers at least summarized the

interrater data and referred readers more interested in the details to the paper. The omission of this data disallows efficient evaluation of these inventories.

The manual makes no mention of test-retest reliabilities. This is surprising because the manual devotes 140 pages to activities that could be used to assist students in learning behaviors they have not mastered. Further, in the directions for administering the Developmental Inventory, it is suggested that teachers use repeated administrations to track student progress. However, without evidence of sufficient test-retest reliability the inventories should not be used for repetitive assessments.

With respect to validity, the manual reports on both content and concurrent validity. For both the Developmental and Preliteracy Inventories content validity is substantiated through extensive literature reviews during the development of the inventories. The concurrent validity of the Developmental Inventory was established by comparing the mean preliteracy scores from Levels 1 and 2 of the MRT for students for whom each behavior was observed versus students for whom a behavior was not observed. These comparisons were made for four different age groupings: 60–65 months, 66–71 months, 72–77 months, and 78–84 months. The overwhelming number of comparisons favored students for whom behaviors were observed, thus concurrent validity for the Developmental Inventory was established.

For the Preliteracy Inventory, concurrent validity was established by correlating the total scores from the Print Concept and Story Structure areas with Level 1 and Level 2 scores from the MRT. The correlations were higher for the Print Concept area (.43 to .63) as compared to results for the Story Structure area (.22 to .42). The lower correlations for the Story Structure area are likely due to the restricted range of the Story Structure scores. Thus, the correlations are acceptable for establishing concurrent validity.

The administration guidelines provided for both inventories are easily read and complete enough to insure correct administration of the inventories. However, the Developmental Inventory protocol provides some practical difficulties. The protocol is a double-page width two-ply form with carbon paper between the two plys. The double-page width makes the form cumbersome to handle during the observation. Also, if the form is folded as recommended any mark made on one side is transferred by the carbon paper to both sides of the second ply. As a result, each page of the second ply will have marks from both pages of the first ply; thus, the second ply is very difficult to read and understand. The difficulty introduced by the carbon paper is significant because the second ply is designed to be used for parent consultation. One way to solve the problem is to insert a page-size piece of cardboard or a clipboard between the folded sheets. The suggested solution does, however, make the form even more cumbersome and awkward. It would have been better to print the rating form as one double-sided page and have a separate summary page for parents. The proposed changes would not only make the rating form more user-friendly but would also lessen the possibility of misinterpretation of the raw data by parents.

The Early School Inventories—Developmental and Preliteracy were designed to assist teachers in becoming more familiar with their students' development and preliteracy skills. Teachers are expected to use this information to alter instruction to better meet the needs of their students. The inventories do assist teachers in becoming more familiar with their students. However, insufficient description of the norm group, lack of easily accessible interrater reliability data, lack of test-retest reliability data, and cumbersome protocols limit the viability of wide-scale use of the Developmental and Preliteracy Inventories. Further, equal information could be gathered through carefully structured observations and curriculum-based measurements.

Review of the Early School Inventory by CAROL WESTBY, Professor of Communicative Disorders and Sciences, Wichita State University, Wichita, KS:

The Early School Inventory—Developmental, the Early School Inventory—Preliteracy, and the accompanying manual for interpretation and use are intended to be used in conjunction with the Metropolitan Readiness Assessment Program and *Handbook of Skill Development Activities for Young Children.* The ESI—Developmental is designed to assist teachers of kindergarten and first grade students in learning more about children's development. The ESI—Preliteracy provides information about the children's understanding of concepts of print, written expression, and story structure. Each inventory relies on teachers' observations of children in the classroom setting.

The ESI—Developmental consists of 20 behaviors in each of the four developmental areas. Physical Development includes subcategories of large muscle, fine muscle, sensory development, and general health conditions. Language Development includes subcategories of speech, vocabulary, sentences and stories, and awareness of written language conventions. Cognitive Development includes subcategories of information, awareness of details, memory, and temporal and spatial concepts. Social-Emotional Development includes intrapersonal and interpersonal skills. All items are listed on an 11-inch by 17-inch sheet with a carbon copy for parents. Teachers are to indicate the date the child was observed and whether or not each behavior was observed. The teacher provides one of three ratings for each item—proficient in the skill, in the process of developing the skill, or in need of help to develop the skill.

The ESI—Preliteracy consists of three sections. For Section I, the children are shown pictures and asked what someone would read in the pictures and why they would read it. They are shown a page with a picture and print and asked to point to a letter, a word, a numeral, a period, where one would begin reading, the direction one would read, and where one would finish reading. For Section II, the child is given a piece of paper and asked to write a story or note and his/her name. The message- and name-writing tasks are scored holistically based on the degree to which they represent readable, conventional spelling. For Section III, the child is asked to retell the story of Goldilocks and the Three Bears. Points are awarded for reporting elements of the story such as the setting, specific character names, a sequence of three or more events, or what happened at the end of the story. Scores on each section of the Preliteracy Inventory are converted to performance ratings similar to the Developmental Inventory—proficient, in the process of developing, and in need of help to develop.

The authors report that the items on the two inventories were determined on the basis of an extensive review of the literature related to early school learning and were reviewed by experts in early education and by teachers. They do not, however, provide any citations. Many of the items on the Preliteracy Inventory are similar to skills identified by researchers investigating emergent literacy. The expected responses for the Preliteracy Inventory are clearly defined and guidelines are provided for scoring.

The Developmental Inventory is more problematic. It is not clear how items on the Developmental Inventory were selected for each category. Some items appear in more than one category (e.g., naming colors, sizes, and shapes is listed under Cognitive Development and describing objects in terms of color, sizes, and shapes is listed under Language Development). A number of the items are quite vague (e.g., "understands language of school," "tolerates reasonable amount of frustration"). There are no guidelines in the manual on how to interpret each of the items and what a child must specifically do to qualify as exhibiting proficiency or development in a skill.

Limited information is provided on reliability and validity of the inventories. Reliability measures of internal consistency are provided for both inventories. The authors state that interrater reliability was conducted for both inventories, but they do not report any of the data in the manual, stating, instead, that the data are available in a separate paper from the publisher. Because a number of the items on the Developmental Inventory are vague and no scoring guidelines are provided for this inventory, it may be difficult to establish high interrater reliability on the Developmental scale.

The authors claim that content validity is present because the items are important to early learning. Although that likely is true, the authors provide no supporting literature references. Concurrent validity is justified by the correlations between the inventories and the Metropolitan Readiness Tests.

The normative sample for the inventories consisted of 2,500 children who participated in the Metropolitan Readiness Testing standardization programs. Teachers were asked to rate two or three students in their classroom who fairly represented the students in their classrooms in terms of ability. Percentages of children who demonstrated each behavior are given for each 6-month interval from 5 years 0 months to 7 years, 0 months. The percentile information is not, however, essential for interpretation of children's performance on the inventories. The authors' view is that children in the 5- to 7-year age range need to be proficient in all the items listed. The majority of the manual is devoted to specific activities to use to develop the skills assessed by the inventories. The discussion of how to select activities based on a child's performance on the inventories is, however, confusing.

The advantage of the Developmental and Preliteracy Inventories is that they are keyed to the Metropolitan Readiness Assessment Program. For that reason, they may be useful to teachers who want more specific information on individual children and activities to facilitate their acquisition of specific skills related to readiness testing. The lack of specific description for what constitutes performance of skills on the Developmental Inventory gives that inventory questionable test-retest and interrater reliability, and

hence, questionable usefulness. A variety of other developmentally based criterion-reference assessments would be easier to use and would have greater reliability and validity. The Preliteracy Inventory would appear to be better supported by research literature and its greater explicitness should give it greater reliability than the Developmental Inventory.

[111]
Eating Inventory.

Purpose: To assess "three dimensions of eating behavior found to be important in recognizing and treating eating-related disorders: cognitive control of eating, disinhibition, and hunger."
Population: Ages 17 and older.
Publication Dates: 1983–1988.
Scores, 3: Cognitive Restraint of Eating, Disinhibition, Hunger.
Administration: Group.
Price Data, 1994: $83 per complete kit including 25 questionnaires, 25 answer sheets, and manual ('88, 37 pages); $24 per 25 questionnaires; $34.50 per 25 answer sheets; $34.50 per manual.
Time: (15–20) minutes.
Authors: Albert J. Stunkard and Samuel Messick.
Publisher: The Psychological Corporation.
Cross References: See T4:848 (1 reference).

TEST REFERENCES
1. Craighead, L. W., & Blum, M. D. (1989). Supervised exercise in behavioral treatment for moderate obesity. *Behavior Therapy, 20,* 49–59.
2. Macdiarmid, J. I., & Hetherington, M. M. (1995). Mood modulation by food: An exploration of affect and cravings in "chocolate addicts." *British Journal of Clinical Psychology, 34,* 129-138.
3. Shide, D. J., & Rolls, B. J. (1995). Information about the fat content of preloads influences energy intake in healthy women. *Journal of the American Dietetic Association, 95,* 993–998.

Review of the Eating Inventory by LISA BLOOM, Associate Professor of Special Education, Western Carolina University, Cullowhee, NC:

DESCRIPTION AND PURPOSE. The Eating Inventory is a questionnaire designed to assess three dimensions of eating behavior. These dimensions are referred to as factors and include Cognitive Restraint of Eating, Disinhibition, and Hunger. This inventory can be used with both adults and adolescents for a variety of purposes. It can be used to measure restrained eating, to assess eating disorders and obesity before and after treatment, and to determine the effects of quitting smoking or other conditions that have implications for weight change.

The instrument includes a two-part questionnaire. The first part contains 36 true/false items such as "When I feel blue, I often overeat." The second part includes 15 rating scale items such as "eat whatever you want when you want" to which the respondent indicates on either a 4- or 6-point scale the extent to which the statement describes his/her behavior.

ADMINISTRATION AND SCORING. The Eating Inventory is very easy to administer and score. Clients complete the self-report items by filling in a circle on an answer sheet. The answer sheet has a built-in scoring system. After the questionnaire is completed, the examiner tears the perforated slip on the answer sheet. On the inside, each of the three factors is coded so that the examiner simply counts the number of responses for each factor to obtain a raw score.

Directions and tables are provided for determining how raw scores compare with scores from normal and obese populations. A table for normative guidelines for interpreting raw scores is also provided. The manual also suggests that professional judgment is needed in interpreting the scores because of the relatively small amount of normative data available.

ITEM SELECTION AND STANDARDIZATION. Items were chosen from three sources: the Restraint Scale (Herman & Polivy, 1980), the Latent Obesity Questionnaire (Pudel, Metzdorff, & Oetting, 1975), and clinical experience of the first author. After initial administration to a sample of 220 subjects, items were revised.

PSYCHOMETRIC PROPERTIES. With regard to reliability, internal consistency was estimated with Cronbach's alpha. The questionnaire was administered to 98 subjects: 53 restrained eaters and 45 unrestrained eaters. For each of the 3 factors, Cognitive Restraint, Disinhibition, and Hunger, reliability coefficients were reported for the combined sample, restrained eaters, and unrestrained eaters. Coefficients ranged from .93 for the combined sample-Cognitive Restraint to .79 for the restrained eaters-Cognitive Restraint.

Authors also report on content-related, construct-related and criterion-related validity. With regard to content validity, the authors report using an extensive review of literature as a basis for developing drafts of a large number of items that were subsequently refined and included in the questionnaire. For construct validity and criterion-related validity, the authors report studies of clinical and control groups that demonstrate that scores on each of the three factor-based scales differentiate between groups in ways predicted by theory and research on eating behavior.

STRENGTHS AND WEAKNESSES. The strength of the Eating Inventory is that it can be easily administered and scored. The items are written in clear simple language. Additionally, the manual is well written and includes case studies to demonstrate how the questionnaire can be used in developing treatment programs.

One weakness of the Eating Inventory is that it has not been standardized on a normative population sample. Therefore, as the authors note, results must be interpreted with caution.

REVIEWER'S REFERENCES

Pudel, V. E., Metzdorff, M., & Oetting, M. X. (1975). Zur Persoehnlichkeit Adipoeser in psychologischen Tests unter Beruecksichtigung latent Fettsuechtiger. (The personality of the adipose fat person under consideration of latent obesity factors in psychological testing.) *Zeitschrift fuer Psychosomatishe Medizin und Psychoanalyse, 21,* 345–350.

Herman, C. P., & Polivy, J. (1980). Restrained eating. In A. J. Stunkard (Ed.), *Obesity* (pp. 208–225). Philadelphia: Saunders.

Review of the Eating Inventory by SANDRA D. HAYNES, Assistant Professor of Human Services, Metropolitan State College of Denver, Denver, CO:

The Eating Inventory "is designed to assess three dimensions of eating behavior: (a) cognitive restraint of eating, (b) disinhibition, and (c) hunger" (manual, p. 1). The first dimension, Cognitive Restraint of Eating, refers to the ability of individuals to respond to information concerning caloric balance, nutrition, and behavioral strategies for control of eating. Disinhibition, when applied to eating behavior, refers to the tendency to consume more food after consuming a food such as a milk shake or a disinhibiting substance such as alcohol or in response to unpleasant emotional states. The third dimension, Hunger, refers to the individual's hunger and satiety signals. It is postulated that especially obese individuals may have an impairment in the mechanism of satiety and thus feel more hunger than persons of normal weight. Although initially developed to investigate the concept of "restrained eating" (i.e., food intake restriction in order to control body weight), the inventory has been shown to be an effective tool in assessing weight change outcomes in bulimic, depressed, and obese patients, and patients who are relinquishing smoking.

The Eating Inventory can be used with adolescents and adults. Administration can be accomplished by trained, supervised paraprofessionals and can be performed in groups or with individuals in approximately 10 to 15 minutes. The instructions are clearly written and easily understood. The Eating Inventory is divided into two parts. Part I consists of 36 true/false statements and Part II consists of 15 questions answered by selecting a response from a 4- or 6-point Likert-type scale. Scoring is accomplished by calculating a score for each of the three scales of the Eating Inventory, Factor I—Cognitive Restraint of Eating, Factor II—Disinhibition, and

Factor III—Hunger. The Ready-Score answer sheet makes for simple scoring with no need for additional scoring tools such as templates. The authors are careful to note that interpretation must be done by a trained professional and should be supplemented with other information such as clinical interviews, observation, and personal history. Integrating such information with the three scales of the inventory allows for the development of individualized treatment programs based on the area or areas identified to cause difficulties.

Normative guidelines are provided for interpreting raw scores although such guidelines are provisional in nature given the small amount of normative data available at the time of the manual was written. Scores falling into the "clinical range" are interpreted differently for each scale. Factor I scores in this range are considered positive as they indicate that the individual has a good deal of cognitive control with regard to eating behavior. For Factors II and III, however, elevated scores are considered negative with treatment being recommended. Such differences may lead to confusion in interpretation and it is, therefore, essential that the user be very aware of these differences in score interpretation. Additionally, although studies cited in the test manual report treatment success for persons with Factor I scores in the clinical range, certain modern theories in the treatment of eating disorders discourage the use of strict cognitive control over eating and encourage greater sensitivity to bodily sensations (e.g., intuitive eating).

Normative data for the Inventory were developed using an adequate sample with regard to size and heterogeneity of subjects. Results indicated that the instrument sufficiently differentiated among subsamples (i.e., restrained versus nonrestrained eaters) and allowed for identification of gender differences. The three scales were developed using an extensive literature review and factor analysis.

Internal consistency (coefficient alpha) was relatively high for each of the two groups mentioned above and a combined group estimate. Test/retest reliability was conducted over a 1-month interval using a different, smaller sample and was found to be high as well. These results must be considered in light of the small sample size used in the analysis.

The extensive literature review conducted in test development provides evidence of content validity. Construct validity of the Inventory is evidenced by a coherent set of three constructs (identified using factor analysis) that differentiate among groups. Likewise, criterion-related validity evidence for Factors II and III is repre-

sented by correlation with a similar scale developed by Gormally, Black, Daston, and Rardin (1982). Scores consistently differentiated between groups used in test construction and norming studies in the predicted direction (i.e., restrained eaters scored higher on Factor I and lower on Factors II and III than nonrestrained eaters).

The test manual provides good references regarding test construction and offers a good resource for test interpretation. In future revisions it might be helpful to include more of this information directly in the manual. Additionally, some research appears outdated and inconsistent with eating disorder treatments that encourage intuitive eating. Thus, the test user must be clear that the theoretical rationale used in treatment matches the theoretical rationale of the test. It is recommended that the Eating Inventory be tested with samples from eating disorder programs that encourage intuitive eating, perhaps indicating a need for a revision in norms and test interpretation.

REVIEWER'S REFERENCE

Gormally, J., Black, S., Daston, S., & Rardin, D. (1982). The assessment of binge eating severity among obese persons. *Addictive Behaviors, 7*, 47–55.

[112]

Ego Function Assessment.

Purpose: Designed as a "mental status examination" to assess ego function.
Population: Adults.
Publication Date: 1989.
Acronym: EFA.
Scores, 12: Reality Testing, Judgment, Sense of Reality, Regulation and Control of Drives, Object Relations, Thought Processes, Adaptive Regression in the Service of the Ego, Defensive Functions, Stimulus Barrier, Autonomous Functions, Synthetic Functions, Mastery-Competence.
Administration: Individual.
Price Data, 1993: $12 per manual (64 pages); $9.50 per 10 blanks.
Time: Administration time not reported.
Author: Leopold Bellak.
Publisher: C.P.S., Inc.

Review of the Ego Function Assessment by BETH DOLL, Associate Professor of School Psychology, University of Colorado at Denver, Denver, CO:

The Ego Function Assessment (EFA) is a semistructured interview that attempts to operationally define and reliably assess ego functions. Ten questions are provided to assess each of 12 different functions of the ego; questions are scored on a scale from 1 (poor) to 7 (excellent) or, alternatively, on a scale from 1 (poor) to 13 (excellent). A manual provides users with an alternative form of the interview and with an alternate response rating protocol written by another author.

Although the conceptual origins of the EFA are clearly grounded in psychodynamic theory, its procedural heritage is linked to the verbal subtests of individually administered intelligence tests. Bellak's intent is to provide users with an interview that is both conceptually accurate and sufficiently standardized to be reliable. On the first point, he has succeeded. In systematically defining the EFA interview questions, Bellak has created a typology of self-regulating ego functions that is both succinct and articulate. Because the assessment of ego function underlies most psychoanalytic treatment decisions, a reliable assessment of ego functioning would hold special utility for psychoanalytic practice. On the second point, however, Bellak has been less successful. The standardization of the EFA is threatened by diverse forms of the interview, unclear response rating conventions, and limited information about the procedure's empirical reliability and validity.

The EFA manual includes two forms of the interview: Bellak's original 12-function format, with 10 questions for each function, and Gruber's (1984) 11-function format. Although many of Bellak's interview items are closed "yes-no" questions, Gruber's are open questions that invite elaboration. The EFA record form includes two extra functions (for a total of 14) with anywhere from one to three questions listed for each function. Although the record form refers readers to the EFA manual for a more comprehensive description of the interview, some questions listed on the form do not appear in either of the manual's versions of the interview. Moreover, a fourth form of the EFA published in Bellak, Hurvich, and Gediman (1973) is not entirely consistent with any of the other three forms. Consequently, at the most basic level of standardization, it is not clear which EFA questions potential interviewers should use.

As described in the manual, EFA scoring is a very approximate activity. Bellak urges clinicians to rate responses according to their own clinical experience, using either a 7-point or a 13-point scale. Gruber's rating format, also published in the manual, provides more detail by describing six to seven levels of adaptation (1 through 7) for each of the ego functions. Still, Gruber's rating does not entirely match the questions asked in either the EFA manual or the Record Form version of the interview. A comprehensive description of a 7-point scale for each function can be found in Bellak et al. (1973), and has been reprinted as an appendix in Bellak and Gold-

smith (1984); this appendix appears to represent the original scoring protocol for the EFA. The manual includes no information about the reliability of scoring under these conditions. However, a few references to the rather inadequate reliability of EFA function scores can be found in Bellak and Goldsmith (1984). One study published here documents very modest interrater correlations ranging from .56 to .87 for individual EFA functions with an average correlation of .76 (Coyne et al., 1984). A second study reports very inadequate interrater correlations falling below .5 for all but three functions of the EFA (Dahl, 1984). A necessary conclusion is that the EFA scores are not sufficiently reliable to support clinical decision making.

Given their questionable reliability, the validity of the EFA function scores should be questioned. Again, the EFA manual provides no documentation of the measure's agreement with important indices of mental health. Varying levels of success in using the EFA to document treatment gains were discussed in over a dozen chapters of Bellak and Goldsmith (1984). Neither the EFA manual nor other sources compile this information into a broad cross-study examination of the scale's validity.

SUMMARY. In the final analysis, the EFA remains a noble but unfinished attempt to measure reliably the psychoanalytic concepts of ego function. A minimum of four different forms of the scale exist, without clear indication of which is the finished version. Scoring protocols are described in Bellak et al. (1973) and Bellak and Goldsmith (1984), but are not included in the EFA manual. In this and other respects, the EFA manual is incomplete in its description of the measure and its features. Interested users will not be able to use the EFA without consulting the 1973 and 1984 volumes, but only the latter is still in print and available from publishers. The minimal evidence that does exist regarding the EFA's reliability and validity suggests that these are modest at best, with some studies showing them to be quite unsatisfactory.

REVIEWER'S REFERENCES

Bellak, L., Hurvich, M., & Gediman, H. K. (1973). *Ego functions in schizophrenics, neurotics, and normals: A systematic study of conceptual, diagnostic and therapeutic aspects.* New York: Wiley.

Bellak, L., & Goldsmith, L. A. (Eds.) (1984). *The broad scope of ego function assessment.* New York: John Wiley & Sons.

Coyne, L., Schroeder, P. J., Frieswyk, S., Cerney, M., Newsom, G., & Novotny, P. (1984). Ego function assessment—its relationship to psychiatric hospital treatment outcome and follow-up adjustment: The factor analytic study. In L. Bellak & L. A. Goldsmith (Eds.), *The broad scope of ego function assessment* (pp. 82–101). New York: John Wiley & Sons.

Dahl, A. A. (1984). A study of agreement among raters of Bellak's ego function assessment test. In L. Bellak & L. A. Goldsmith (Eds.), *The broad scope of ego function assessment* (pp. 160–166). New York: John Wiley & Sons.

Review of the Ego Function Assessment by SAMUEL JUNI, Professor, Department of Applied Psychology, New York University, New York, NY:

OVERVIEW OF THE EGO FUNCTION ASSESSMENT (EFA). Dr. Bellak's approach to psychodiagnostics is central to the field. Contemporary approaches in projective testing invariably incorporate his classic orientation to personality analysis, and his annotated case studies are part and parcel of informed teaching of psychological testing and assessment.

The EFA as a system is ambitious and comprehensive. The measurement facet of the EFA has its origin in an attempt to specify characteristics of schizophrenia and to contrast them with those of other psychiatric classifications (Bellak, Hurvich, & Gediman, 1973).

The EFA essentially represents a developmental project that has evolved from Bellak's elaboration of elements in egopsychology within the general psychoanalytic framework. In his work, Bellak has attempted to synthesize solid conceptualization and clinical erudition into a unified product, elaborating important aspects at each end of the synthesis. Based on a comprehensive analysis of the psychoanalytic literature, notably modern ego psychology, the ego is conceptualized in terms of a specification of principal ego functions. The major EFA literature has been anthologized by Bellak and Goldsmith (1984) in a book that has come to be the primary reference for the system. (In this review, I shall refer to this work as the *sourcebook*.) Although this review will focus on the manual and the record blank as the product being offered to the consumer and the testing community, the general evaluation is necessarily based on the sourcebook as well as significant elements of the literature published subsequently.

Evaluating the EFA is complex. Its status as a nosological and conceptual system can serve as the focus for a lengthy thesis. Second, the methods of ascertaining data to be used for the assessment are subject to critique. Third, there are numerous studies in the literature regarding the reliability and validity of the technique. Finally, specific instruments designed for use with the EFA need to be evaluated.

THE EFA AS A CLASSIFICATORY SYSTEM. There is definitely a solid theoretical base for the dimensions of the EFA. It is not clear, however, what criteria were used by Dr. Bellak to elevate some constructs as veritable dimensions, whereas others are subsumed in a group to form other dimensions. In essence, the conceptual integrity of each function is

not firmly established. As Goldsmith writes in her chapter in the sourcebook, "Bellak has always acknowledged that such classifications are in ways arbitrary but yet flexible and open to change" (p. 61).

One can deduce from the variety of study contexts in published papers that the EFA is robust as a system with regard to time frame objectives. Some of the studies use the EFA to define the patient's best functioning period; some, to define the patient's worst functioning (often at time of hospital admission); some, to define current or recent functioning; some, to define typical functioning.

In research addressing reliability, acceptable interrater reliability is generally demonstrated in each study for half or more of the functions. However, the functions for which reliability is confirmed vary from study to study. As a rule, Sense of Reality, Adaptive Regression in the Service of the Ego, Defensive Functioning, and Stimulus Barrier seem to come through often as unreliable, as does Autonomous Functioning in some studies. It is unfortunate for the overall evaluation of the EFA that some authors decided to include or exclude functions in their studies based on these inconsistent data.

Studies are inconsistent in their use of subscale scores for the various functions. Moreover, there are also alternate factor analytic studies that reduce the EFA into competing factor structures. One set of three factors includes: Freedom from Thought Disorder, Judgement and Impulse Control, and Superego Functioning. Another set of four includes: Thought Organization, Object Relations, Judgement, and Drive Regulation. There is no significant overlap, overall, between the factor structures of the different studies.

A significant part of the sourcebook elaborates EFA theory and describes specific aspects of the functions. Major chapters present studies intended to support the reliability and validity of the EFA system and to define its hegemony. The bulk of these are correlational studies: some observational, some outcome studies, some case studies, and some statistical.

There is no doubt that the cumulative evidence tends to support the EFA as a powerful approach. There are, however, specific methodological flaws in many of the studies. In addition, the methods, approaches, conceptualizations, and measures are inconsistent from study to study. Moreover, data collections forming the basis of EFA formulation are idiosyncratic, varying from study to study in terms of method, time frame, specific EFA functions measured, and subscale scoring. All in all, it is impossible to come up with any unequivocal conclusion about reliability or validity, other than the generally favorable impression about the EFA based on the sheer weight of the collective data.

Besides the validity studies presented in the sourcebook, predictive validity of the scales measuring the system in general has subsequently been demonstrated in delineating psychiatric features of Crohn's disease (Hartkamp, Davies, Standke, & Heigl, 1993); differentiating among neurotics, schizophrenics, and controls (Basu, 1993); differentiating between borderline personality and eating disorder patients (Smith, Burkey, Nawn, & Reif, 1991); and predicting spiritual maturity levels (Brokaw & Edwards, 1994; Hall & Brokaw, 1995). The growing literature plots out validation pairings of specific functions and their effects or correlates, but with a wide variety of interview data collection formats, differing lengths of time and reference periods for the diagnostics, a variety of scales and subscales, and different composite factors of the EFA. It must be said that a good representation of solid case studies has been annotated as well, which buttress the utility of the instrument from the clinical perspective.

Fascinating and clinically useful as ego function may be as a classificatory system, its assessment component has been inextricably linked to the interview technique in its elaboration by Dr. Bellak. This has left the technique at the mercy of the vagaries of open-ended questioning and creative nonstandardized interpretation. Consequently, there is no consistent method to evaluate the psychometrics of such a complex, dynamic, and unoperationalized entity.

In sum, there exists an impressive compendium of validity and interrater reliability data for different functions of the EFA, used in various combinations and with alternate measurement methods. As a whole, this complex amalgam of evidence leaves one with an intuitive sense that the system is useful for the diagnostician. It is, unfortunately, impossible to come up with a more definitive evaluation of the approach due to glaring inconsistencies in standardization from one study to another and a general lack of operationalization of measurement strategies in almost all of the studies.

EFA PSYCHOMETRICS—THE MANUAL AND ITS TESTS. The manual is a sparse document. By right, the major aspects of the sourcebook should have been abridged and incorporated into the manual, especially Bellak's chapter titled "The Flexibility of the EFA." Evaluating the EFA without studying these primary sources is an impossible task.

The manual presents very little information about ego function theory or its conceptualization, no reliability or validation data on the assessment approach, and very limited instruction to the examiner who wishes to use the instrument. Factor scores and subscale scores that dot the literature are totally ignored in the manual and the record blank.

The manual as a document is too terse, very abridged, and highly complex. The various approaches and measurement options cannot be understood well after one or two readings. It begins by outlining EFA rationale, and then refers to various forms of the scales, which takes some sorting out. Although stating that the manual should suffice for clinical purposes, it strongly suggests using, as well, the original 1973 interview guide and the 1984 sourcebook for research use. The 12 Ego Functions are listed in a table, and several components are enumerated for each of them. The Record Blank essentially includes this table (with the surprising addition of two Functions—Superego and Drive), and offers several sample questions to elicit each function. The manual reports that this instrument is not easily learned and is cumbersome to use. The reader is not informed of any specific method to use in ascertaining the required information about the patient. The Record Blank also includes a Graphic Representation Grid (containing only the 12 original functions), and a 19-item General History Questionnaire. It would seem that this questionnaire is the essence of the Modified EFA (EFA-M) referred to in the manual.

A further modification of the instrument, devised by Gruber, is then offered in the manual and is purported to be simpler and less demanding. In contrast to the one-page table for the original scale, this modified scale is printed as a multipage document in the second half of the manual and features specific interview questions for each function, including detailed scoring criteria for each as well as suggested additional data sources. It is important to note that Gruber drops the Thought Processes function and adds the Superego function in his modification.

In the remaining part of the manual, Dr. Bellak presents a detailed multipage questionnaire for the EFA. Recognizing the loss of richness and complexity in the non-interview approach, the instrument is offered as merely adjunctive to the interview. Because the instrument was originally constructed with a low-functioning population, the author cautions that it is of limited value at the upper ends of the scale and more suited for those with pathological problems.

In the style of classic multiscale inventories, the EFA scale features a grid allowing the plotting of scale points. Although there is no harm to this option, there is no method for profile interpretation that approaches those of other inventories (e.g., the MMPI or the Wechsler Scales), especially in view of the rather atheoretical structure of this scale. In this context, the use of a 13-point scale for the grid, instead of the 7-point scale used for the individual functions, is disconcerting.

THE QUESTIONNAIRE. This review will now address the aspect of EFA that comes closest to a test as such—the questionnaire version. Strictly speaking, the psychometric basis of the instrument, in its current form, is nonexistent. Its validity and reliability are dependent, by extrapolation, on those of the original and Gruber scales. Inasmuch as these differ significantly from the questionnaire, such supportive psychometric features are merely suggestive, at best.

Each function is assessed by 10 items, each of which is rated on a 3-point continuum (*often, rarely, sometimes*). These markers are noteworthy for the absence of *always* and *never*, glaring omissions for any personality inventory.

The manual then provides a score for each function, computed by summing its 10 respective items. Psychometrically, the summing of items without the statistical demonstration of internal consistency is totally unacceptable.

The interviewer is then asked to supply an overall global rating for each function, on a scale of 1 to 7. Because no formula is devised for a composite measure, the clinician is forced to utilize undefined intuitive techniques in combining heterogeneous items into one overall rating. Analytically, one can well envision reducing each symptom to the degree to which it disrupts social functioning, or perhaps, the degree to which it makes the patient feel uncomfortable. Such a proposed algorithm still would leave glaring subjective holes, but it would nonetheless provide a heuristic for the clinician on how to arrive at a unitary commonalty. Alas, the manual offers no such heuristic for abstraction, rendering the overall measure unreliable by its very design.

SUPPLEMENTARY QUESTIONNAIRE DATA. The questionnaire offers regular and supplementary sections for some constructs. No method for the differential use of these indices, or for their combination with the questionnaire results, is offered.

The supplementary sections for each dimension are typically fraught with problems—both conceptual and psychometric. Although the manual assures the reader of the operational and descriptive nature of the measures, this guarantee apparently does not hold true for the supplementary sections. Instead, projective data are repeatedly recommended here, particularly specific TAT cards, dream elicitation, Rorschach scores, psychoanalytic inferences from WAIS responses, and Figure Drawing nuances. Some of these augmentations are based on findings of questionable validity. Perhaps more disturbing is the likelihood that such supplementary information will confound the ability of the rater to come to a unitary conclusion about any function, as it now must be based on a nonhomogeneous synthesis of observation and projectively based inferences. Yes, the two polarities can be synthesized in an evaluation that is based on commentary and prose, but not in an instrument that portends numericism as its goal.

Clearly, astute and seasoned clinical skills are crucial to a proper EFA. As such, the cogent pointers and suggestions in the manual for soliciting ancillary information are left to the skills of the potential instrument user. Such use is bound to defy standardization because supervision/training in synthesizing and prioritizing psychometric data is often quite inconsistent, varied, and inadequate, as anyone familiar with training institutes and doctoral programs will confirm.

CONCLUSION. The EFA is first and foremost a synthesis of theory as it is conceptualized into a clinical system that can be used to understand, and work with, a variety of patients. As such, it is excellent, and highlights the insights of psychoanalytic theory, ego psychology, and object relations conceptualization. The secondary goal of the EFA to evolve into a measurement instrument is less than successful, in that the interview process that it prescribes is inherently undefined in many areas. The ultimate attempt to establish an objective questionnaire assessment tool falls very short because many subjective elements are included in the final product.

The construction of a conceptually derived measure requires first and foremost a clear presentation of the key elements of the theoretical system. The EFA is exemplary in that respect. The second phase is one of operationalization. This must involve compromise—compromise between the goals of including as much of the conceptual model as possible into the instrument and the deference to measurement limitations due to reliability and validity constraints. The latter are apt to make the instrument a less than perfect measure of the construct.

The EFA as an approach is very impressive. The interview is likely to be useful to clinicians as a vehicle for prescription of dynamics. However, the nuances and vague definitions of the specifics of the interview as an assessment tool make it impossible to confirm the reliability or validity of the approach. The questionnaire method suffers from the same inherent problems, as it is adjunctive to these same unoperationalized procedures. Taken as a pure questionnaire, the tool suffers foremost in its inability to reflect the richness of the system.

If we are willing to accept the limitations in richness and accuracy toward the end of having a tool that is operationally defined, the questionnaire method is a potential measure of EFA. However, first all adjunctive data must be excluded and the global assessment for each function must be eliminated. Only then, can studies be initiated to determine the reliability of the ratings. This should also be accompanied by a serious consideration of the conceptual basis for the delineation of the precise number of functions, as well as the merit of the specific questions for each function—within the domain of content validity. Finally, factor analysis and internal consistency studies will be effective in pruning down the instrument to yield a questionnaire that is efficient in measuring those aspects of EFA that are measurable by a questionnaire approach.

REVIEWER'S REFERENCES

Bellak, L., Hurvich, M., & Gediman, H. (1973). *Ego functions in schizophrenics, neurotics, and normals: A systematic study of conceptual, diagnostic, and therapeutic aspects.* New York: John Wiley & Sons.

Bellak, L., & Goldsmith, L. A. (Eds.). (1984). *The broad scope of ego function assessment.* New York: John Wiley & Sons.

Smith, T. E., Burkey, N. A., Nawn, J., & Reif, M. C. (1991). A comparison of demographic, behavioral, and ego function data in borderline and eating disorder patients. *Psychiatric Quarterly, 62,* 19–33.

Basu, J. (1993). Applicability of the Ego Function Assessment Scale as a guided interview schedule on schizophrenics, neurotics and normals: A preliminary report. *Psychological Studies, 38*(3), 119–124.

Hartkamp, N., Davies, O. S., Standke, G., & Heigl, E. A. (1993). [Crohn Disease, addiction, and neurosis: A comparison of ego functions]. *Psychotherapie, Psychosomatik, Medizinische Psychologie, 43,* 75–81.

Brokaw, B. F., & Edwards, K. J. (1994). The relationship of God image to level of objective relations development. *Journal of Psychology and Theology, 22,* 352–371.

Hall, T. W., & Brokaw, B. F. (1995). The relationship of spiritual maturity to level of object relations development and God image. *Pastoral Psychology, 43,* 373–391.

[113]

Ekwall/Shanker Reading Inventory—Third Edition.

Purpose: "Designed to assess the full range of students' reading abilities."

Population: Grades 1–9.
Publication Dates: 1979–1993.
Acronym: ESRI.
Administration: Individual.
Price Data: Available from publisher.
Authors: Eldon E. Ekwall and James L. Shanker.
Publisher: Allyn and Bacon.

a) GRADED WORD LIST.
Purpose: "To obtain a quick estimate of the student's independent, instructional, and frustration reading levels."
Acronym: GWL.
Scores, 3: Independent Reading Level, Instructional Reading Level, Frustration Level.
Time: (5–10) minutes

b) ORAL AND SILENT READING.
Purpose: To obtain an assessment of the student's independent, instructional, and frustration reading levels in oral and silent reading.
Scores, 3: 3 scores (Independent Reading Level, Instructional Reading Level, Frustration Level) in each of two areas (Oral, Silent Reading).
Time: (10–30) minutes.

c) LISTENING COMPREHENSION.
Purpose: "To obtain the level at which a student can understand material when it is read to him or her."
Score: Listening Comprehension Level.
Time: (5–10) minutes.

d) THE BASIC SIGHT WORDS AND PHRASES TEST.
Purpose: To determine basic sight words and basic sight word phrases that can be recognized and pronounced instantly by the student.
Scores, 2: Basic Sight Words, Basic Sight Phrases.
Time: (5–12) minutes.

e) LETTER KNOWLEDGE.
Purpose: "To determine if the student can associate the letter symbols with the letter names."
Scores, 2: Letters (Auditory), Letters (Visual).
Time: Administration time not reported.

f) PHONICS.
Purpose: "To determine if the student has mastered letter-sound (phonics)."
Scores, 9: Initial Consonants, Initial Blends and Digraphs, Ending Sounds, Vowels, Phonograms, Blending, Substitution, Vowel Pronunciation, Application in Context.
Time: Administration time not reported.

g) STRUCTURAL ANALYSIS.
Purpose: "To determine if the student can use structural analysis skills to aid in decoding unknown words."
Scores, 10: Hearing Word Parts, Inflectional Endings, Prefixes, Suffixes, Compound Words, Affixes, Syllabication, Application in Context (Part I, Part II, Total).
Time: Administration time not reported.

h) KNOWLEDGE OF CONTRACTIONS TEST.

Purpose: "To determine if the student has knowledge of contractions."

Scores, 3: Number of Words Pronounced, Number of Words Known, Total.

Time: Administration time not reported.

i) EL PASO PHONICS SURVEY.

Purpose: "To determine if the student has the ability to pronounce and blend 90 phonic elements."

Scores, 4: Initial Consonant Sounds; Ending Consonant; Initial Consonant Clusters; Vowels, Vowel Teams, and Special Letter Combinations.

Time: Administration time not reported.

j) QUICK SURVEY WORD LIST.

Purpose: "To determine quickly if the student has mastered phonics and structural analysis."

Score: Comments.

Time: Administration time not reported.

k) READING INTEREST SURVEY.

Purpose: "To assess the student's attitude toward reading and school, areas of reading interest, reading experiences, and conditions affecting reading in the home."

Score: Comments.

Time: Administration time not reported.

Cross References: See T4:872 (3 references); for reviews by Lynn S. Fuchs and Mary Beth Marr of an earlier edition, see 9:380.

TEST REFERENCES

1. McCabe, P. P., Margolis, H., & Mackie, B. (1991). The consistency of reading disabled students' instructional levels as determined by the Metropolitan Achievement Test and the Ekwall Informal Reading Inventory. *Reading Research and Instruction, 30*(3), 53-62.

2. Miller, S. D., & Yochum, N. (1991). Asking students about the nature of their reading difficulties. *Journal of Reading Behavior, 23,* 465-485.

Review of the Ekwall/Shanker Reading Inventory—Third Edition by KORESSA KUTSICK MALCOLM, School Psychologist, Augusta County Public Schools, Fishersville, VA:

The third edition of the Ekwall/Shanker Reading Inventory provides materials and procedures for a very comprehensive assessment of a student's reading skills. The purpose of each of the tests is well defined. Examiners may choose to administer all, or selected, tests from the inventory. Skills that can be evaluated by this instrument include letter identification, various levels of phonetic skills, structural analysis skills, sight word recognition, silent and oral reading levels, reading comprehension, and listening comprehension. A reading interest inventory is also provided that enables examiners to obtain information from subjects regarding their attitudes about reading and learning. Alternate forms of the tests are available, which would allow for the retesting of students in order to monitor their skill progressions with interventions.

The authors provide detailed information regarding the procedures followed to develop this test. They cite some research that guided the test's development and likely used their extensive experiences in various reading clinics as further development support. This experience has enabled the authors to create a set of tests that should address most diagnosticians' needs in their reading assessment endeavors.

Straightforward lists of particular tests and related materials are provided to help potential examiners plan for the assessment of a student. The authors provide clear instructions on the preparation of materials. Advice about caring for frequently used materials is also provided.

Scoring procedures given for the various tests are rather typical of informal reading inventories. Various codes are used to mark errors and difficulties a student exhibits while reading particular passages or word lists. Although detailed instructions for the use of these codes are provided, a good bit of practice would be needed for an examiner to become fluent in their use.

All of the reading materials needed to administer the Ekwall/Shanker Inventory are provided in the manual. Other materials, such as tape recorders and stop watches, are to be supplied by examiners. Most of the reading materials seem appropriate in terms of type size for various reading levels. Some of the materials did appear to be visually cluttered. This might be an issue for individuals who are poor readers. More spacing and better page placement might enhance the appearance of the provided reading materials.

Unlike most informal reading inventories, the authors of this edition of the Ekwall/Shanker Reading Inventory attempt to address statistical properties of their instrument. Some minimal information is provided regarding the reliability of the instrument. One study involving interscorer reliability was reported which had moderately high correlations. Additional research into the reliability and validity of this inventory, as with most informal reading inventories, is greatly needed.

In summary, the Ekwall/Shanker Reading Inventory was found to be one of the more comprehensive, and potentially useful, instruments of its kind. Additional research into the reliability and validity of the tests that comprise this instrument would strengthen its application of placing students into reader categories. As it is presented, this inventory provides users with techniques that elicit comprehensive information regarding an individual's reading skills, such information could guide instructional programs to remediate any identified skill weaknesses.

Review of the Ekwall/Shanker Reading Inventory—Third Edition by BLAINE R. WORTHEN, Professor of Psychology, Utah State University, Logan, UT, and RICHARD R. SUDWEEKS, Associate Professor of Instructional Science, Brigham Young University, Provo, UT:

The Ekwall/Shanker Reading Inventory (ESRI) is an informal reading inventory (Johnson, Kress, & Pikulski, 1987) consisting of 11 tests for use by classroom teachers, reading specialists, and school psychologists in assessing students' reading abilities. One advantage of such inventories is that the student is expected to perform an authentic task: to read to someone else and interpret meaning in context. Another advantage is the opportunity provided to observe directly a student's performance on a varied range of reading tasks in a one-on-one setting. One disadvantage is that the results are dependent upon the examiner's ability to accurately observe, code, and rate the examinee's performance.

TEST CONTENT AND ADMINISTRATION. The core of the ESRI is a series of graded passages, ordered in terms of readability, with a series of comprehension questions accompanying each passage. The student is given a passage and asked to read orally while the teacher or examiner observes the student's performance and records any errors (omissions, insertions, substitutions, mispronunciations, or repetitions). The examiner then asks a series of prescribed questions to assess the student's comprehension. In a similar fashion, other graded passages are used to assess students' abilities to read silently. The results of both tasks are interpreted by describing the level of passages that the student can read without outside help (the independent level), the level at which they can succeed only with help from the teacher (the instructional level), and the level at which the material becomes too difficult for the student to read (the frustration level). Hence, the results are interpreted descriptively rather than normatively. The listening comprehension level is determined by reading a different set of passages to the student and determining the highest level of passage the student can listen to and successfully answer 70% of the comprehension questions.

The ESRI includes four sets of graded passages. Each set consists of nine passages ordered in difficulty from preprimer through ninth grade levels. Sets A and C are designated for assessing students' abilities to read orally. Sets B and D are designated for assessing their abilities to read silently. The corresponding passages in all four sets are intended to be equivalent in terms of readability and the difficulty of the comprehension questions.

The ESRI also includes a graded word list consisting of 10 words at each level of difficulty from preprimer through ninth grade level. The manual authors advocate using this list to determine an appropriate entry point for a student to start the oral and silent reading passages. They include an important warning that this test by itself is an inadequate measure of a student's reading ability.

The battery also includes eight optional tests for use in diagnosing specific strengths and weaknesses of individual students. Tests 4–9 assess knowledge of sight words and phrases, decoding skills, and phonics skills. Test 10 may be used as a pretest to determine which, if any, of these optional diagnostic tests need to be administered. Test 11 is designed to assess students' reading interests.

INTERPRETATION AND USE. In general, the test manual is well done. It contains helpful directions for administering the various tests plus scoring sheets for recording students' responses. The manual authors identify the various kinds of errors to assess and provide procedures for coding and counting them. Helpful guidelines for interpreting and counting repetitions and meaningful substitutions are included; for example, pauses and self-corrected errors should not be counted.

The table on the scoring sheet for each oral passage is especially helpful. However, the manual authors acknowledge that interpretations are not as algorithmic as these tables imply and that teacher judgment is needed to classify borderline performances. Users must prepare their own flash cards for the Basic Sight Words and Phrases Test. They also must duplicate sufficient copies of the scoring sheets and may choose to use stopwatches and/or tape recorders. Otherwise, all necessary materials are included in the test manual.

Some of the prescribed comprehension questions are erroneously worded or mistyped (e.g., Question 1 in Set 4D and Question 1 in Set 5B). These errors are confusing and misleading.

TECHNICAL CONSIDERATIONS. The Harris-Jacobsen Readability Formula (Harris & Sipay, 1981) was used to establish the readability level for most of the passages. The two main variables in this formula are the number of "hard words" in the passage and the average sentence length. The authors report that both of these variables were adjusted in the passages to obtain the desired level of readability for each grade level. Because readability estimates are not reported for any of the passages, the skeptical user must either personally compute the readability of the various passages or accept the authors' judgment that the passages within each set are appropriately scaled and that corresponding passages across sets are equivalent.

The most serious weakness of the ESRI is the absence of empirical evidence of validity. Another serious weakness is the narrow definition of comprehension represented by the questions posed to the students. Comprehension is more than the ability to answer questions. Asking students to retell or summarize what they have read would provide a more insightful view of how they constructed and organized meaning. It would also provide a more direct assessment of the student's ability to comprehend the meaning of the passage as a whole.

Except at the preprimer level, each graded passage is accompanied by 10 comprehension questions. Generally, one question corresponds to each sentence in the passage. In all passages above the second grade level, the question set includes one about vocabulary and one intended to assess students' abilities to draw defensible inferences. The other 8 are factual questions designed to assess literal recognition or recall. No attempt is made to assess students' understanding of the main idea, and the inferences that are tested are very simple.

Unless the correct answers to the questions are dependent upon having read the passage, there is no assurance that the questions assess comprehension rather than background knowledge. Inspection of the passages at Levels 4 and 5 led us to conclude that at least 3 of the 10 questions for each passage were not passage dependent. Many vocabulary questions (e.g., "What is a herd?" [Set 5A] and "What does the word 'survive' mean?" [Set 4C]) are not passage dependent.

The only reliability estimates reported are the results of one "preliminary study" involving 40 students from grades 1 through 9. Half of the students received the A and B forms first, and then received the C and D forms several days later. The other half received the same forms in the reverse sequence. The reported reliability coefficients were .82 for the oral forms (A and C) and .79 for the silent forms (B and D).

Because one examiner administered all four forms to students in grades 1 through 4, and another examiner administered the forms to students in grades 5 through 9, the authors claim that the reported correlation coefficients are measures of "intrascorer reliability." However, this claim overlooks the fact that differences between the raters are confounded with differences in the forms. Informal reading inventories are dependent upon the observational skills and judgment of the examiners; thus, the question of intrascorer consistency is important, but interscorer consistency also needs to be investigated. A well-designed generalizability study that isolated that main effects due to differences in passages, examiners, and testing occasions and the interactions among these error sources would be much more informative (Shavelson & Webb, 1991). Given the complete lack of validity data and the tentative nature of the reported reliability coefficients, the reliability and validity of the ESRI are not yet established.

SUMMARY. The Ekwall/Shanker Reading Inventory is neither a substantial improvement over the previous editions produced by Ekwall nor over other commercially published informal reading inventories. If a teacher is willing to accept the narrow definition of comprehension represented by the prescribed questions, then this inventory may be useful for obtaining an "informal" assessment of a student's reading level as a basis for making placement and grouping decisions. But we question its use by anyone interested in obtaining a comprehensive diagnosis of a student's reading strengths and weaknesses.

REVIEWER'S REFERENCES

Harris, A. A., & Sipay, E. R. (1981). *How to increase reading ability: A guide to developmental and remedial methods* (7th ed.). New York: David McKay.
Johnson, M. S., Kress, R. A., & Pikulski, J. J. (1987). *Informal reading inventories* (2nd ed.). Newark, DE: International Reading Association.
Shavelson, R. J., & Webb, N. M. (1991). *Generalizability theory: A primer.* Newbury Park, CA: Sage.

[114]
Electrical Maintenance Trainee.

Purpose: "To measure the knowledge and skills required for electrical maintenance."

Population: Applicants for jobs requiring electrical knowledge and skills.

Publication Date: 1991.

Scores: Total score only.

Administration: Group.

Price Data, 1993: $498 per complete kit including 10 reusable test booklets, 100 answer sheets, manual (14 pages), and scoring key.

Time: (150–210) minutes.

Authors: Roland T. Ramsay.

Publisher: Ramsay Corporation.

Review of the Electrical Maintenance Trainee by DAVID C. ROBERTS, Consultant, Personnel Decisions International, Dallas, TX:

The Electrical Maintenance Trainee test consists of 121 four-option multiple-choice items. This instrument was designed for use as an employee selection and placement tool for jobs in which electrical knowledge and skills are required. Items were written to cover the following content categories: Motors (12 items), Digital Electronics (6), Analog Electronics (7), Schematics and Electrical Print Reading (13), Control (8), Power Supplies (10), Basic AC/DC Theory (18), Power Distribution (5), Test Instruments (10), Mechanical (4), Computer and PLC (6), Hand and Power Tools (2), Electrical Maintenance (7), Construction and Installation (4), Equipment Operation (2), and Transducers (5).

Test administration and scoring instructions are provided in the manual. There is a 210-minute time limit for the test; however, the manual states that most examinees can finish the test in 150 minutes or less. The multiple-choice answer sheet is scored by hand, producing a single score that represents number of correct answers.

The manual lists areas and subareas of knowledge and skill identified by the publisher as required in electrical maintenance jobs and used as a starting point for item development. Nine maintenance supervisors served as subject matter experts to provide "percent of time spent" (p. 4) and relative importance ratings of the knowledge and skill areas; no demographic, organizational, or industry information is provided for the sample of subject matter experts (SMEs). These ratings were used to determine the number of test items written to cover each area. No other information on item development is provided.

The test was administered to a sample of 33 students and item statistics calculated. Item difficulty ranged from .09 to .79 (mean = .39); point biserial discrimination coefficients ranged from -.22 to .74 (mean = .28). Internal consistency of the test in this sample was estimated to be .90, with a standard error of measurement of 4.8 (mean = 46.76, SD = 15.32); no information on test-retest reliability is reported. Raw score to percentile equivalents for the student sample are also reported; this is the only normative information provided in the manual.

The manual provides no information regarding construct or criterion-related validity of the test; the publisher argues that a content validation strategy be used to support test use. No adverse impact or fairness evaluations are reported.

The items comprising this test could be useful in assessing the requisite knowledge and skill required in electrical maintenance jobs. The items demonstrate face validity: Many require mathematical operations, reading of schematics, or knowledge of electrical terminology. However, given the insufficient information regarding relevance across jobs or organizations, psychometric properties across samples, or criterion-related validity, its use without supporting work should be avoided. Given the publisher's content-driven argument for the test's job relevance, it is especially disconcerting that limited information is provided regarding the job analyses that drove item development. The information that is provided would be inadequate in determining if the test is appropriate for electrical maintenance jobs in organizations other than the one(s) involved in test development. Organizations considering use of the test should, at a minimum, ensure its job relevance through a confirmatory task analysis and establish locally derived norms using a sample of sufficient size to ensure stability.

Although test development sample sizes are small enough to question stability of the data, the trends that are reported indicate that further work with this test would most likely allow for a better instrument. Sixteen items have negative point biserial correlations with total score; an additional 25 have point biserial correlations of .20 or lower. If these trends hold in additional samples, the test might be shortened without a loss in internal consistency. In addition, the usefulness of the test in organizations might be expanded if investigation of the instrument's internal structure were undertaken. Identification and scoring of subscales assessing specific knowledge areas would provide diagnostic insight about incumbent or applicant knowledge and skills. This information could be used to guide targeted training or remediation of distinct competencies that fall under the electrical knowledge and skill domains.

[115]
Electromechanical Vocational Assessment Manuals.

Purpose: Designed to evaluate a variety of work abilities (tasks) of blind or visually impaired persons.
Population: Blind or visually impaired adults.
Publication Date: 1983.
Scores, 6: Fine Finger Dexterity Work Task Unit, Foot Operated Hinged Box Work Task Unit, Hinged Box Work Task Unit, Index Card Work Task Unit, Multifunctional Work Task Unit, Revolving Assembly Table Work Task Unit.
Administration: Individual.

Price Data: Available from publisher.
Time: 50(60) minutes for any one task unit.
Comments: Special administration equipment required.
Author: Rehabilitation Research and Training Center in Blindness and Low Vision.
Publisher: Rehabilitation Research and Training Center in Blindness and Low Vision.

Review of the Electromechanical Vocational Assessment Manuals by JOHN GEISLER, Professor, Department of Counselor Education and Counseling Psychology, Western Michigan University, Kalamazoo, MI:

This review was not written for the purpose of assessing the adequacy of particular instruments, but was written for the sole purpose of reviewing the information contained in six 1983 manuals published by the Rehabilitation Research and Training Center on Blindness and Low Vision for the National Industries for the Blind. They were developed as a result of a grant to Mississippi State University from the National Institute for Handicapped Research, U.S. Department of Education. No claim is made here as to the adequacy of the instruments themselves. The manuals were developed to assist in the assessment of visually impaired and blind persons in the area of electromechanical vocational abilities and were developed to be utilized by persons charged with the task of assessing the skills of persons seeking employment in this field.

The six manuals are to be used with six different assessment activities and instruments: Fine Finger Dexterity, Foot Operated Hinged Box Work, Hinged Box Work (table top), Index Card Work, Multifunctional Work, and Revolving Assembly Table Work. Each of these activities and instruments require different and specific equipment, materials, timers, and scoring procedures. Each manual contains a description of the assessment (work unit), the abilities being assessed, instructions to the examinee, a description of the instruments (and their set-up), and scoring procedures.

The description of the skills and abilities being assessed in all six areas is very well written and thorough although it is suggested that the ability labeled "Frustration Tolerance" be included in every manual (it is not included in three of the manuals) and that it be placed in a separate category because it is not a "Work Ability" per se, but rather is a measure of attitudes toward the tasks being performed.

The examinee orientation sections are very detailed and the demonstration and practice sections are very complete, thorough, and detailed. The authors are to be commended for the exactness

associated with these sections. Administrators will find these sections are particularly helpful and well conceived. However, the sentence in the introductory directions, which tells the examinees that they will be assessed on their emotional reactions to the tasks (mad, bored, tired, etc.), probably should be removed because this could cause the candidates to stifle any overt demonstrations of their emotional reactions.

The scoring sections of the manuals could be improved by having an example provided. The scoring protocol is not clearly written and part of it refers to other sections of the manuals. It is assumed that the percent of correct responses by any examinee could be over, under, or equal (+, -, or =) to standard criteria that have been set by sighted persons. Also, the method of establishing the standards for the six instrument is highly questionable. Using only three sighted persons (out of five) for the criterion group is not acceptable. Expanded normative groups, both sighted and visually impaired, are needed. Using a percentage of responses compared to an inadequate criterion group is not the best scoring method. Means, standard deviations, standard errors of measurement, standard scores (with different normative groups), and related data (reliability and validity) need to be developed.

It is also suggested that a standard protocol be developed for assessing subjective reactions for all six sections, just as one was included for the last of the six tasks (Revolving Assembly Table). Such a protocol would necessarily have to be empirically validated and have demonstrated reliability. Such evidence was not reported for the rating sheet for the last of the six tasks.

In summary, the materials presented in the manuals were clear, concise, and worthwhile. They need improvement in terms of measuring the subjective reactions of the examinees. Scoring also needs to be explained more fully and perhaps changed. When reliability, validity, and norm group information and other data are established it is expected that the six instruments will be a welcome addition for the vocational assessment of blind and visually impaired persons.

Review of the Electromechanical Vocational Assessment Manuals by ROBERT JOHNSON, Assistant Professor of Educational Research, University of South Carolina at Columbia, Columbia, SC:

The purpose of the six task units in the Electromechanical Vocational Assessment Manuals (EVAM) is "to provide a flexible system of evaluating a variety of work abilities" of adults who are blind or visually impaired (p. 1). The skills primarily assessed in the units are manual dexterity, bi-manual and hand-foot coordination, and kinesthetic memory. Each task unit is described in a self-contained manual, and the six manuals are assembled in a larger notebook. Each manual follows the same general format and provides documentation about the development of the unit and instructions for preparing the work environment, administering the task, and scoring the performance. Each task requires special equipment for assembly, and most of the tasks require time and accuracy counts for the performance.

The six tasks are modeled on small-unit assembly work performed in factories. For example, in the Fine Finger Dexterity Task Unit the client's manual dexterity is assessed when the examinee constructs a "product" by inserting pins into a predrilled, plastic form. In the Foot Operated Hinged Box Work Task Unit, an assessment of hand and foot coordination, the client joins a nut and screw, presses a foot lever to open a storage box, deposits the "product," and releases the foot lever to begin the next cycle. The Hinged Box Work Task Unit, an assessment of the client's bi-manual coordination, requires the client to pick up an index card with one hand, pick up a plastic bag in the other hand, insert the card into the bag, and place the completed product in a box. In another measure of the client's bi-manual coordination, the Index Card Work Task Unit, the client places two index cards on the surface of a work unit that is divided into a left and right side. The cards are pushed under a counter at the end of the unit and "stamped." The client then moves the card on the left side of the unit to the right side, and the card on the right side of the unit is placed into a box as a completed product. A new card is placed on the left side of the unit and the process repeated. The Multifunctional Work Task Unit is an assessment of bi-manual coordination and material control. In this task the client uses each hand to simultaneously fit two wooden dowels inside a t-shaped template (ostensibly for drilling holes); the "completed" products are removed from the template and stored in barrels on each side of the work area. The Revolving Assembly Table Work Task Unit measures the client's bi-manual coordination, kinesthetic memory, and ability to work with others. In the task the client works with others to assemble nut and bolt units and package the assemblages into vials. One client places empty bottles on a revolving table; the next client places the nut and bolt assembly into the bottle; and

once filled, the first client removes and caps the bottle.

Each performance session is standardized by providing directions in the form of a script for the examiner to read when administering the assessment. Lists of equipment and diagrams provide information for the administrator to prepare the work environment. Prior to the assessment the evaluator guides the examinee through the task, and the examinee then practices the task three times. In a final practice session the client repeats the task for 10 minutes. The actual performance session last 50 minutes. The administration time and count of errors and successfully completed tasks are recorded by a work pace timer. To establish the proficiency of the visually impaired examinee, the client's performance on the assessment (i.e., number of total responses minus the number of errors) is compared with that of five sighted individuals who completed the task. The "sighted" standard was established by discarding the scores of the highest and lowest performances of the sighted individuals and then averaging the remaining three performances; no rationale was provided for discarding performances in the establishing of performance standards.

The EVAM was originally published in 1983; a relevant question would be whether the work samples that are embedded in the assessments are current. The manuals detailed little about the development of the exercises or the validity and reliability of the assessments. The statement that the National Industries for the Blind sponsored the development of the tasks lends some credence to the content validity of the exercises. A study of the reliability and validity of the manuals was mentioned in each manual, but no results were presented.

Per the request of this reviewer, the Rehabilitation and Training Center on Blindness and Low Vision provided for review the document the *Electromechanical Vocational Assessment Technology for the Evaluation of Industrial Work Abilities of Blind and Visually Impaired Persons: Executive Summary* (Bagley, Graves, & Machalow, 1985). The authors stated that the tasks in the EVAM were developed to assess work skills of blind and visually impaired adults who are employed in sheltered workshop settings. Their statement that the units were designed to assess work abilities that were identified by the National Industries for the Blind lends additional credence to the content validity of the units.

Bagley et al. (1985) directly addressed issues of reliability and validity in the report. The authors indicated adequate test-retest reliability for the Multifunctional, Index Card, Fine Finger Dexterity, and the Foot Operated Hinged Box task units; however, no supporting empirical evidence was provided. The authors reported there was evidence to support the content validity of the Index Card and Foot Operated Hinged Box assessments. The authors also reported there was evidence to support the concurrent validity of the Index Card and Fine Finger Dexterity assessments and the predictive validity of the Multifunctional, Index Card, and Foot Operated Hinged Box assessments. Again, no statements about the validity of the task units were supported with empirical evidence.

Bagley et al. (1985) recommended that the Hinged Box and the Revolving Assembly Table assessments be redesigned. The Hinged Box assessment was considered to lack face validity and mechanical problems with the Revolving Assembly Table assessment did not allow for testing under appropriate conditions. The review copy of the EVAM sent to this reviewer contained both work units; so it appears that the tasks remain in the collection. In addition, the 1983 publication date of the manuals leaves the impression that the Hinged Box assessment was not updated. Whether the mechanical problems with the revolving table were resolved is undocumented.

Until several changes are made to the Electromechanical Vocational Assessment manuals, this reviewer considers the value of the assessments questionable. Although issues of content validity were reviewed in 1985, more than a decade has passed and the content of the EVAM should be revisited to determine if the task units remain relevant in employment training for the visually impaired. The manuals should be updated to contain the reliability and validity information referenced in the executive summary. In addition, any supporting empirical data should be included to allow the consumer to assess any claims made by the test producer. The two tasks that were questioned by Bagley et al. (1985) should either be removed from the assessment package, or documentation should be included that addresses whether the concerns raised by the authors were addressed.

REVIEWER'S REFERENCE

Bagley, M., Graves, W., & Machalow, S. (1985). *Electromechanical vocational assessment technology for the evaluation of industrial work abilities of blind and visually impaired persons: Executive summary.* Mississippi State, MS: Rehabilitation Research and Training Center in Blindness and Low Vision.

[116]
Electronics Test—Form G2.

Purpose: "To measure the knowledge and skills required for electronics jobs."
Population: Electronics employees and applicants for electronics jobs.
Publication Dates: 1987–1994.

Scores: Total score only.
Administration: Group.
Price Data, 1993: $498 per 10 reusable test booklets, manual ('94, 13 pages), scoring key, and 100 blank answer sheets.
Time: (120) minutes.
Author: Roland T. Ramsay.
Publisher: Ramsay Corporation.

Review of the Electronics Test—Form G2 by KEITH HATTRUP, Assistant Professor of Psychology, San Diego State University, San Diego, CA:

The Electronics Test—Form G2 is a paper-and-pencil test of knowledge in the area of electronics. It includes 125 multiple-choice items designed to assess 13 separate knowledge areas, including Motors, Digital Electronics, Analog Electronics, Radio Control, AC/DC Theory, Power Distribution, etc. The test is not timed, but examinees are instructed they should complete the test within 2 hours. According to the test manual, the test should be administered individually or in groups of up to 20 examinees per examiner.

Internal consistency reliability of the 125 items is high (alpha = .95), as might be expected given the large number of items. Item-total correlations ranged from -.19 to .65, with an average of .36. The test manual also reports the standard error of measurement; however, the manual does not describe how the *SEM* should be interpreted or used in constructing and evaluating confidence intervals. This information would be a useful addition to any test manual. Additional evidence of this test's retest reliability would contribute to supporting inferences about the consistency of test scores across time, test content, and testing situations.

The test was developed to provide a content valid measure of achievement in the area of electronics knowledge. A panel of six subject matter experts (electrical maintenance supervisors) independently rated the amount of time job incumbents spend using each of several categories of electronics knowledge. An attempt was then apparently made to write relatively more items for more important categories of electronics knowledge. As a result, the development of test items contributes to the test's content validity as a general test of knowledge of job-relevant electronics facts and principles. Unfortunately, the test manual does not indicate the job types or levels for which the knowledge assessed by the test is most applicable. The items assess a level of knowledge that is clearly above that of most high school graduates, but it is not clear from the manual how much extra training is required to answer test items correctly. None of the items assesses abstract, content-free, or fluid reasoning abilities; instead, the items all measure crystallized intelligence that must be developed through systematic training. Unfortunately, the population of examinees for whom this test is most appropriate is poorly defined in the manual.

Assuming an appropriate population of examinees could be identified, the objectivity and specificity of the measure as a test of advanced electronics knowledge probably represent both the most significant strengths and limitations of the instrument. On one hand, the large number of clear factual items, and the research conducted to document the job-relevance of knowledge assessed by the measure, contribute to arguments supporting the instrument's content validity. However, the difficulty of the test and its reliance on factual information about electronics means that the instrument is likely to be relevant in only a limited number of circumstances. Hunter (1983) has shown that one of the most direct predictors of job performance is an incumbent's job-specific knowledge. However, it is only appropriate to test and screen for high levels of job knowledge among applicants if the job requires newly hired incumbents to perform tasks with little job-specific training. A more general test of cognitive ability would be far more useful in selecting job applicants who would be expected to develop high-level electronics knowledge on the job. In other words, the Electronics Test would be appropriate for testing and selection of already-trained applicants for jobs requiring high levels of electronics knowledge, whereas a test of general mental ability would be more appropriate for use in selecting applicants who would be expected to benefit from job-relevant training. Some discussion of these issues in the test manual would help test users evaluate the trade-offs between testing for high-level job-specific knowledge versus more general reasoning and learning abilities.

Aside from evidence supporting the test's content validity, no studies have been conducted to assess criterion-related validity or other aspects of the test's construct validity. Criterion-related validity coefficients, correlations of the test with other achievement and aptitude tests, and correlations with other psychological and demographic variables would contribute to a better understanding of the sources of variance contributing to scores on the Electronics Test. Studies of mean differences, adverse impact,

and differential prediction across sex and race groups would also help support inferences about the test's appropriateness when used for members of diverse groups. It should also be noted that 30 of the 125 items are also included in the Technician Electrical Test—Form A2 (318) by the same publisher. Some discussion of the similarities and differences of these two tests would help test users choose between them, particularly given the high degree of similarity in the constructs measured by the instruments.

The test manual provides clear and detailed recommendations for test administration and hand scoring of test responses. Experienced test administrators should have no difficulty setting up, administering, and scoring the Electronics Test. Interpretation of test scores is likely to prove much more difficult. The only normative information provided in the test manual are the means, standard deviations, and percentile equivalents of observed scores for a sample of 91 "applicants for electronics jobs" (p. 8). Unfortunately, the normative data are for an earlier version of the Electronics Test (Forms F and G), rather than the present test (Form G2), which retained approximately 98% of the items from the earlier form. From the information presented in the manual, it is impossible to determine the education, experience, and demographic backgrounds of the 91 "applicants for electronics jobs" who were included in the norming and reliability studies. Therefore, it is impossible to determine whether the normative data presented in the manual are representative of what might be observed in any particular setting. Normative information for various demographic groups (e.g., sex, race, geographic region, education, etc.) and various job levels or types (e.g., recent graduates, entry-level trainees, apprentices, journey-level trades workers, different industries, etc.) would also be helpful. Users of this test are urged to collect evidence supporting the test's reliability and validity in the setting in which it is to be used.

In summary, the Electronics Test (Form G2) was carefully developed based on an analysis of the electronics knowledge needed in the performance of jobs that involve electronics work. The factual nature of the items and their representativeness in sampling a well-defined knowledge domain provide support for the test's content validity. Much more detailed information is needed about the norming sample and the population of examinees for whom the test is appropriate to guide test users in selecting this test and evaluating test scores. Until additional psychometric evidence is made available, use of the Electronics Test (Form G2) can only be recommended for applications in which psychometric issues are secondary, such as in facilitating the identification of training needs or training content. Additional research, either done locally by test users or by the test authors, is needed to support the test's use in employment decision making.

REVIEWER'S REFERENCE

Hunter, J. E. (1983). A causal analysis of cognitive ability, job knowledge, job performance, and supervisory ratings. In F. Landy, S. Zedeck, & J. Cleveland (Eds.), *Performance measurement and theory* (pp. 257–275). Hillsdale, NJ: Erlbaum.

Review of the Electronics Test—Form G2 by EUGENE (GENO) PICHETTE, *Assistant Professor in the Division of Rehabilitation Psychology and Counseling, University of North Carolina at Chapel Hill, Chapel Hill, NC:*

The Electronics Test—Form G2 was developed by the Ramsay Corporation as a test to be used in employee selection. It is a test that reportedly assesses the applicant's and/or incumbent's level of knowledge and skills in electronics. The author indicates this test is part of a series of skill tests used in employee selection. The test was first introduced in 1987, with revisions occurring in June of 1988 and June of 1990. Accordingly, 98% of the test items remain the same.

The instrument consists of 125 items that measure knowledge and skill in 13 different areas in electronics. These areas are: Motors, Digital Electronics, Analog Electronics, Schematics and Print Reading, Radio Control, Power Supplies, Basic AC/DC Theory, Test Instruments, Mechanical, Computer and PLC, Regulators, Electronic Equipment, and Power Distribution. The test is group administered. Test items are in a multiple-choice format, presented in the test manual, and the examinees are required to choose the best answer and place their answer on a separate answer sheet. These 13 knowledge areas were independently ranked by maintenance supervisors on the estimated percentage of time spent working in each of the different areas. As a result, each area has a different number of questions associated with it.

The administration and scoring of the Electronics Test—Form G2 is easy to follow and presented in a straightforward manner. The manual states that the examiner can allow as much time as necessary in order for individuals to complete the test, but the manual contradicts itself by indicating in the directions that time limits specified should be observed. Also, the manual suggests that the examiner should have taken the tests in order to become familiar with the test items and testing procedures. Scoring is accomplished by using the hand scoring keys, and a total score consisting of the number correct is recorded on the answer sheet.

Reliability is provided in the manual and is derived from a relatively small sample size ($N = 91$) with limited representativeness. The manual indicates that the reliability coefficient is .95 and is produced on the basis of both Form F and G. Other psychometric data include a mean score of 68.37, standard deviation of 20.36, and a standard error of measurement of 4.6. Also, item analysis data for each of the 125 items are provided.

The manual states that experts in the electronics area have independently ranked the knowledge areas for the percentage of time spent working in each of the 13 different areas. No information is given on the qualifications or affiliations of the experts consulted. A major weakness of this test is the lack of normative data, a shortcoming that undermines the contention of this test being an employee selection test for the electronics area.

The manual provides a brief descriptive overview of content, criterion-related, and construct validity; however, it provides no data. The author does provide percentile equivalents for Forms F and G based upon a restricted sample. The test publishers indicate that normative data on tests facilitates comparisons of a person's scoring at a given level with a reference group; however, the test developers offer very little with regard to producing adequate norms for different normative groups.

SUMMARY. The Electronics Test—Form G is a test used in employee selection for electronics jobs. Significant to this test is the lack of normative data that supports its contention of measuring knowledge and skills required for electronics jobs. Specifically, the sample used may not be a representative sample and of sufficient size. To the benefit of the test publishers, many of the test items do appear to have face validity.

This test is a quick and easily administered test that attempts to screen applicants and/or incumbents for jobs in electronics. However, due to very limited reliability and validity information, further development is needed before that test is used to screen applicants for selection into jobs in electronics.

[117]
Emotional or Behavior Disorder Scale.

Purpose: Designed to identify behavior problems of students in the home or school environment.
Population: Ages 4.5 to 21.
Publication Dates: 1991–1992.
Acronym: EBDS.
Scores, 4: Academic, Social Relationships, Personal Adjustment, Total.
Administration: Individual.

Price Data, 1993: $86 per complete kit including School Version technical manual ('92, 33 pages) and 50 rating forms, Home Version technical manual ('92, 31 pages) and 25 rating forms, and intervention manual ('91, 202 pages); $22 per intervention manual.

Time: (15–20) minutes.

Author: Stephen B. McCarney.

Publisher: Hawthorne Educational Services, Inc.

a) SCHOOL VERSION.

Price Data: $10 per technical manual; $30 per 50 rating forms.

b) HOME VERSION.

Price Data: $10 per technical manual; $14 per 25 rating forms.

Review of the Emotional or Behavior Disorder Scale by PATTI L. HARRISON, Professor and Chair, Educational and School Psychology Program, The University of Alabama, Tuscaloosa, AL:

The Emotional or Behavior Disorder Scale is a brief rating instrument designed to assist in early identification and provision of services for children and adolescents with emotional or behavior disorders. The Home Version has a total of 59 items, and the School Version has a total of 64 items. Both versions include three subscales; the Academic Progress and Social Relationships subscales have fewer items than the Personal Adjustment subscale. Each item describes a behavior problem such as not turning in homework, having few interactions with peers, and speaking in a bizarre way. Item scores indicate the frequency of the rater's observations of the behavior (e.g., 2 = only one time; 4 = more than one time a month up to one time a week; 7 = more than once an hour, etc.). The rater may record a score of 1 to indicate "not in my presence," which could indicate either that the behavior is never exhibited or that the rater has not observed the behavior.

DEVELOPMENT AND STANDARDIZATION. The test manuals indicate that the Emotional or Behavior Disorder Scale was based on the earlier Behavior Disorders Identification Scale, but provide no additional discussion of how items from the earlier instrument were used. Item development included generation and reduction of an initial item pool based on review of literature and input from parents and educators. The manuals do not provide information about pilot studies or other prenorming studies, studies that can be very important for analysis of item bias, selection of the most reliable and valid items, and inclusion of items with maximum discrimination between children with and without problem behaviors.

The Home and School Versions were standardized in a large number of public school systems and states across the United States, with no apparent co-norming. If home and school scales are used in an integrated fashion, as might be expected with this instrument, then co-norming of parent-teacher versions and data comparing results of the two versions should be provided. A total of 1,769 students and 1,845 parents/guardians were involved in the norming for the Home Version, and 3,188 students and 867 teachers were involved in the norming for the School Version.

Several characteristics of the norm samples raise serious questions and concerns. No explanation is offered about the inclusion of more parents than students in the norming for the Home Version. For the School Version, the manuals do not report the average number of students rated by each teacher. The manuals indicate that students in regular education and students with behavior disorders were included in the norm samples, but do not report the actual numbers of students with behavior disorders, except to point out that 200 additional students with behavior disorders were included in the School Version norm sample. The manuals provide data about sex, race, residence, geographic area, and parental occupation for the samples, and the data suggest failure to match the U.S. population on important characteristics. For example, white children were overrepresented. Parental occupations are listed as white collar, blue collar, and other; no definitions for these three groups are provided.

RELIABILITY AND VALIDITY. The manuals for the Home and School Versions include an array of reliability and validity data. Reliability data included classical test-retest, interrater, and internal consistency (alpha) estimates. All reliability coefficients for the three subscales are reported to be higher than .85, with the exception of coefficient alphas in the .70s for Academic Progress and Social Relationship subscales for the Home Version. Interrater data are reported across 13 age groups, with inadequate, small samples of each age group.

The manual lists mean item scores and mean subscale scores, and the means imply that the distribution of scores is highly skewed, as is typical with problem behavior rating scales. Mean item scores suggest a strong likelihood of raters selecting "not in my presence" for most items. The author attempts to support a sufficient amount of variation in the scores, in spite of the skewed distribution, by noting that, for most of the items, ratings other than "not in my presence" were selected for at least 10% of the subjects. However, variation in only 10% of the subjects—and the possibility of scoring "not in my presence" based on the absence of the behavior or lack of opportunity to observe the behavior—raise questions about the norm distributions and resulting scores for the instrument.

Limited validity data are reported, and the data raise many concerns about the validity for score interpretation. The manuals report moderate correlations between the scale and the Behavior Rating Profile and Behavior Evaluation Scale for small samples of students previously identified as having behavior disorders. Principal components factor analyses fail to support the three subscales of the instrument for either the Home Version on the School Version. For example, items from both the Social Relationships and Personal Adjustment subscales loaded on the first factor and items from Academic Progress and Personal Adjustment loaded on the second factor on the School Version. In spite of the results of factor analyses and additional data about strong intercorrelations among the subscales, the author concludes that the three subscales are distinctive and can be used separately in decision making. Studies comparing subscale scores from groups of examinees randomly selected from the norm sample and students receiving services for emotional or behavior disorders found that mean scores for the two groups were significantly different. Although the author concludes that these data support the diagnostic validity of using the instrument for identifying students with behavior disorders, comprehensive discriminant function analyses are needed to support diagnostic validity.

SCORING AND INTERPRETATION. Normative scores are available for several age and sex groups. Standard scores with a mean of 10 and standard deviation of 3 may be obtained for the subscales, and higher standard scores indicate fewer problem behaviors. Subscale scores may be summed and used to obtain a percentile score for the total scale. As noted earlier in this review, the highly skewed score distributions for the norm sample have important implications for interpreting standard scores. For example, the highest possible standard score on the School Version is 13. (The graph on the rating form is misleading and allows test users to plot subscale standard scores from 1 to 20.) The subscale standard scores are not based on a normal distribution, and, thus, do not have the same interpretation and

association with percentile ranks as do normally distributed standard scores. On the School Version, a female, age 15–21 years, who obtains a standard score of 10 on every subscale will obtain a total percentile rank of 28, and not the percentile rank of about 50 that would be found in a normal distribution. It is recommended that percentile ranks, instead of standard scores, may have been more appropriate for subscale scoring.

The author indicates that subscale standard scores are sensitive and objectively represent serious problems. The author recommends that subscale standard scores below 7, or more than one standard deviation below the mean, should be used to determine the areas of serious problems because "the student is demonstrating significant behavior deviance in the educational environment and may be far more successful with a specialized support system" (Home Version manual, p. 22). The author further recommends that a score below 7 on any one subscale is sufficient to qualify a student for special services, along with other documentation. The author specifically notes, "Because the subscales are broad and encompassing, they each represent a measure of behavior disorder in and of themselves" (Home Version manual, p. 22).

This reviewer has serious concerns about the author's recommendations for interpreting and using scores from the Emotional and Behavior Disorders Scale and planning interventions. Validity data do not support any of the recommendations, including using a score of 7 or below to identify behavioral deviance or qualify a student for special services or interpreting any one of the three subscales as a measure of behavior disorders. No studies have addressed the treatment validity of the instrument, which are necessary before recommending that the items of the scale have validity in planning effective interventions. Most importantly, professional standards for the use of educational and psychological tests recommend comprehensive approaches to assessment that integrate information from numerous sources, settings, and methods of assessment. A recommendation to interpret a single score from a single instrument as an indication of significant deviance is inconsistent with professional standards.

SUMMARY. Although the Emotional or Behavior Disorder Scale, with its brevity, simple scoring system, and extensive lists of intervention activities, may be appealing to many tests users, it is not recommended for use. Data about the development, norm sample, reliability, and validity suggest highly questionable psychometric properties. The author's recommendations for using scores to identify behavior deviance and planning interventions are not supported by validity studies or professional standards of assessment. Other instruments, such as the Child Behavior Checklist (Achenbach, 1991; 55), Behavior Assessment System for Children (Reynolds & Kamphaus, 1992; 34), and Conners' Rating Scales (Conners, 1990; T4:636), which have extensive research support, should be used instead.

REVIEWER'S REFERENCES

Conners, C. K. (1990). Conners' Rating Scales. Toronto, Canada: Multi-Health Systems.
Achenbach, T. M. (1991). Manual for the Child Behavior Checklist/4–18 and 1991 Profile. Burlington, VT: University of Vermont, Department of Psychiatry.
Reynolds, C. R., & Kamphaus, R. W. (1992). Behavior Assessment System for Children. Circle Pines, MN: American Guidance Service.

Review of the Emotional or Behavior Disorder Scale by STEVEN W. LEE, Associate Professor & Coordinator, School Psychology Program, Department of Educational Psychology and Research, University of Kansas, Lawrence, KS:

The Emotional or Behavior Disorder Scale (EBDS) was developed to "contribute to the early identification and service delivery for students with emotional or behavior disorders" (manual, p. 3). The EBDS has both a Home and School Version and is promoted as an ecological assessment of behavior disorders in children from 4.5 to 21 years of age. Both versions of the scale are reportedly based on the federal definition for severely emotionally disturbed/behaviorally disordered children (P.L. 94-142) making it a practical instrument for use in the school for diagnosis and intervention. Unfortunately, the P.L. 94-142 definition was politically derived and uses imprecise descriptors that are difficult if not impossible to operationalize effectively. In addition to the P.L. 94-142 definition, the manual states that the EBDS is also "based on the most recently approved definition (of emotional/behavior disorder) developed by the National Mental Health and Special Education Coalition" (p. 3). These two definitions are not identical, calling into question the foundation upon which the test was created.

The actual instruments include a 64-item School Rating Form and a 59-item Home Rating Form. Both versions use a 7-point Likert scale for rating descriptions of student's behavior in the Academic, Social Relationships, and Personal Adjustment areas. Items are rated on the Likert scale using estimates of occurrence. Raw scores are summarized by domain and converted to standard scores and percentile ranks based on the normative sample. The

norm tables are divided by gender with each having three ages groups roughly corresponding to elementary, middle, and high school age groupings. Both versions use identical format, scoring, and transformation approaches.

The standardization sample for the School Rating Form utilized 867 teachers' ratings of 2,988 students in 71 school systems from 23 states. Procedures for selecting the teachers and the teachers' selection of the students were not mentioned. In this vein, it was unclear whether emotionally disturbed or behaviorally disordered students were included in the sample. Although data on the teachers/respondents were not provided, the student sample was underrepresented by Afro-American students and not well balanced by age. For example, the range of sample size by age yields a difference of 275 students (age 16 = 117 students vs. age 12 = 392 students). Indices of interrater, test-retest, and internal-consistency reliability for the School Rating Form were generally good.

The content validity information presented in the manual includes an item analysis of the scale and item ratings by "diagnosticians and educators" to determine if an item was "inappropriate for a representation of behavior disorders" (p. 10). It was on the item analysis and ratings from the professionals that the final 64-item set was derived. Indices of construct and criterion-related validity were provided in the manual. Two studies seemed to show that the EBDS successfully differentiated behavior disordered from regular students as mean differences were provided. However, more powerful statistical techniques such as discriminant analyses, which take into account sample variability, would have provided a more convincing argument for differential diagnosis validity. Data from the manual indicate that the intercorrelations between the Social Relationships and the Personal Adjustment subscales may be measuring the same dimension, as a .907 correlation between the two subscales was reported. Finally, a concurrent validity study (n = 57) compared EBDS scores with the Behavior Evaluation Scale (McCarney, Leigh, & Cornbleet, 1983). These correlations fell into the moderate range for each of the subscales.

The psychometric properties of the Home Rating Form of the EBDS are similar to the School Rating Form except that concurrent validity estimates for the Home Rating Form were compared with the Behavior Rating Profile (Brown & Hammill, 1978) in a small sample of ratings for 49 students. The correlations between these tests ranged from .55

(Academic subscale) to .61 (Social Relationships subscale) indicating moderate to weak shared variance. Not only could the Behavior Rating Profile (BRP) be called into question as a criterion measure (Posey, 1989; Bacon, 1989), but the BRP does not possess a factor structure that is similar to the Home Rating Form, leaving the criterion-related validity of the instrument unknown.

The administration and scoring of the instruments is fairly straightforward except that the qualifications of the raters are not clearly specified. Although "any number" of individuals may rate a student, the guidelines for interpreting these multiple ratings say no more than "Should any one rater prove less than professionally objective in completing the EBDS, it would be readily apparent when compared to those of other personnel" (p. 24). This statement ignores several alternative reasons for a divergent rating, not the least of which is that the student acts differently in different situations. In diagnostic situations this may be precisely what we want to know, as most behavior is context dependent rather than the reverse.

One of the most disturbing aspects of the EBDS manual was the grandiose, contradictory, and confusing language used to describe the instruments. For example, the EBDS is described as a theoretically derived instrument, even though it was based upon a federal definition for emotional and behavioral disorders. Further, the author states that "subscales of the EBDS ... can be viewed independently of one another" (p. 24), even though the intercorrelations between the subscales suggest a strong overlap between subscales. Assertions like these, when unaccompanied by clear scientific evidence, diminish the credibility of the instrument.

In summary, the development of the Home and School Rating Forms of the EBDS was based on the definition of emotional/behavior disorder developed by the National Mental Health and Special Education Coalition. Indices of reliability of the instruments appear to be good; however, estimates of validity provided in the manual are not sufficient to declare the EBDS valid for its intended use. More information on administration and interpretation (especially for multiple raters) of the EBDS should have been provided in the manual.

REVIEWER'S REFERENCES
Brown, L. L., & Hammill, D. D. (1978). Behavior Rating Profile. Austin, TX: PRO-ED, Inc.
McCarney, S. B., Leigh, J. E., & Cornbleet, J. E. (1983). Behavior Evaluation Scale. Columbia, MO: Educational Services.
Bacon, E. H. (1989). [Review of the Behavior Rating Profile]. In J. C. Conoley & J. J. Kramer (Eds.), *The tenth mental measurements yearbook* (pp. 84–86). Lincoln, NE: Buros Institute of Mental Measurements.
Posey, C. (1989). [Review of the Behavior Rating Profile]. In J. C. Conoley & J. J. Kramer (Eds.), *The tenth mental measurements yearbook* (pp. 86–87). Lincoln, NE: Buros Institute of Mental Measurements.

[118]
Emotional Problems Scales.

Purpose: "To assess emotional and behavioral problems in individuals with mild mental retardation or borderline intelligence."
Population: Ages 14 and over.
Publication Dates: 1984–1991.
Acronym: EPS.
Price Data, 1997: $7955 per complete kit including manual ('91, 31 pages), 25 BRS test booklets, 25 SRI test booklets, SRI scoring keys, and 25 profile forms; $28 per manual; $20 per 25 profile forms; $345 per IBM computer report.
Comments: Previous editions titled Prout-Strohmer Personality Inventory and Strohmer-Prout Behavior Rating Scale.
Authors: H. Thompson Prout and Douglas C. Strohmer.
Publisher: Psychological Assessment Resources, Inc.
a) BEHAVIOR RATING SCALES.
Acronym: BRS.
Scores, 12: Thought/Behavior Disorder, Verbal Aggression, Physical Aggression, Sexual Maladjustment, Distractibility, Hyperactivity, Somatic Concerns, Depression, Withdrawal, Low Self-Esteem, Externalizing Behavior Problems, Internalizing Behavior Problems.
Administration: Individual.
Price Data: $20 per 25 test booklets.
Time: (20–25) minutes.
b) SELF-REPORT INVENTORY.
Acronym: SRI.
Scores, 7: Positive Impression, Thought/Behavior Disorder, Impulse Control, Anxiety, Depression, Low Self-Esteem, Total Pathology.
Administration: Individual.
Price Data: $20 per 25 test booklets; $15 per scoring keys.
Time: (30–35) minutes.
Cross References: For reviews by Richard Brozovich and Ernest A. Bauer and by Peter F. Merenda of the Prout-Strohmer Personality Inventory, see 11:311.

Review of the Emotional Problems Scales by S. ALVIN LEUNG, Associate Professor of Educational Psychology, The Chinese University of Hong Kong, Hong Kong:

The Emotional Problems Scales (EPS) is specifically designed to help mental health practitioners assess individuals with mild mental retardation and borderline intellectual abilities for possible maladaptive behavior and emotional problems. The instrument is appropriate for individuals whose age is 14 or older, and whose standardized IQ score is between 55 and 83. The EPS consists of two separate instruments. The first is the Behavior Rating Scales (BRS), which is to be completed by one or more professional mental health providers on a target client. The second is the Self-Report Inventory (SRI), which is to be completed by a target client.

According to the EPS Professional Manual, a "rational/empirical" model was used to develop the EPS items (p. 17). Based on a review of relevant literature and interviews with professionals, the test authors identified a number of problem and behavior concerns for mildly retarded individuals. These concerns were conceptualized into 12 clinical scales for the BRS, and 5 clinical scales and 1 validity scale for the SRI. An item pool was developed for each scale and experts (consisting of psychologists, practitioners, and graduate students) were asked to rate each item to determine if its content matched the intended meaning of the scale. Item-scale correlation coefficients (r>.60 for the BRS, and r>.20 for the SRI) were used to determine final item assignment.

The resultant BRS consists of 135 items (e.g., thinking appears mixed up or confused), using a 4-point scale (0 to 3, 0 = almost never, 3 = often). The 12 clinical scales of the BRS are Thought/Behavior Disorder, Verbal Aggression, Physical Aggression, Sexual Maladjustment, Noncompliance, Distractibility, Hyperactivity, Somatic Concerns, Anxiety, Depression, Withdrawal, and Low Self-Esteem. Four BRS scales (Verbal Aggression, Physical Aggression, Noncompliance, and Hyperactivity) are combined to form the externalizing behavior problems scale, and three scales (Anxiety, Depression, and Low Self-Esteem) are combined to form the internalizing behavior problems scale.

The SRI consists of 147 items that were written to not exceed a fourth-grade reading level. The five clinical scales of the SRI are Thought/Behavior Disorder, Impulse Control, Anxiety, Depression, and Low Self-Esteem. A Total Pathology score can be computed by aggregating the scores of the five clinical scales. A Positive Impression scale is used as a validity scale to measure a tendency to minimize problems and symptoms. There are also four validity indicators that can be used to detect response sets that may reduce the validity of the test scores. The SRI used a yes/no answer format.

The BRS items are arranged easily for handscoring, and the SRI can be scored by using stencils available from the publisher. The BRS and

SRI scores are reported in both percentile scores and *T*-scores. Demographic information on the normative samples is summarized in the EPS Professional Manual. The sample size of the BRS and SRI are 673 and 746, respectively. The manual does not describe how the subjects in the normative samples were identified. More than 60% of the subjects came from the northeast area of the United States, and slightly over 80% of them were White. The mean age was about 30 years for both samples. All the subjects were identified as mildly retarded with standardized IQ test scores between 55 and 83, with a mean of about 69, and they were all recipients of special educational services at the time of testing.

Cronbach's alpha coefficients for the BRS clinical scales ranged from .90 to .97, indicating a high degree of internal consistency. The interrater reliability for all the clinical scales ranged from .79 to .94, except for the Sexual Maladjustment scale, for which the correlation is .24. The authors explained this low correlation in terms of a restricted range of scores in the normative sample. For the SRI, the alpha coefficients for the five clinical scales and the Positive Depression scale ranged from .81 to .96, and the test-retest coefficients (4- to 6-weeks interval) ranged from .65 to .92, with a mean of .83. Overall, the BRS and SRI scales appear to be consistent and stable measures.

Only several research studies (three studies on the BRS and two studies on the SRI) on the validity of the EPS are described in the Professional Manual, and most of them are not published research. These studies are described only briefly, and important information, such as the age and cognitive functioning of the participants, and how the participants were recruited and tested, are missing. Therefore, it is not clear whether the studies are rigorous research.

Indeed, a major weakness of the EPS is that there is a lack of empirical research data to support the validity of the clinical scales. First, as indicated above, only a few research studies have been done to examine its validity, and the quality of these studies is questionable. Second, although there is some evidence showing that the BRS and SRI clinical scales are related to other scales measuring similar constructs, more evidence is needed to show that each scale accurately measures its intended construct. Third, there is no evidence to support the utility and validity of the externalizing and internalizing composite scales of the BRS and the total pathology scale of the SRI, yet users are encouraged to compute and interpret these composite scales. Fourth, a distressful finding is the low correlation between the equivalent clinical scales of the BRS and SRI (e.g., between the depression scales of the two instruments). One would expect at least moderate correlation between corresponding scales of the two inventories because they are designed to measure similar constructs from two different frames of reference. Fifth, the SRI has a set of validity indicators and a positive impression scale as validity checks, yet their validity has not been researched.

The item selection process of the EPS seems to be systematic. However, the appropriateness of the statistical procedure used to assign items into clinical scales is questionable. The authors used "corrected item-to-total scale scores correlations" (p. 18) to determine if an item was to be included in a clinical scale. Items were first assigned to a clinical scale and then item-scale correlation coefficients were computed. Two different correlation coefficient cutoffs were used for the BRS and SRI (.6 for the BRS and .2 for the SRI), but the authors provided no justification on why different cutoffs were selected. The EPS Professional Manual reported that confirmatory factor analyses of the items were conducted for both the BRS and SRI (p. 18). Confirmatory factor analysis would be an appropriate method to examine the item structure of the clinical scales. However, the results were not reported in the manual.

In summary, there is not enough evidence to support the validity of the EPS. More research studies on the construct validity of the instrument must be conducted before the EPS can be used by mental health professionals in their clinical work with individuals with mild cognitive deficits.

Review of the Emotional Problems Scales by JOHN A. MILLS, Professor/Psychologist, Counseling and Student Development, Indiana University of Pennsylvania, Indiana, PA:

The Emotional Problems Scales (EPS) is a pair of instruments designed specifically for the measurement of behavioral problems with individuals 14 years old and older who fall in the mildly mentally retarded to borderline range of intelligence. The manual reports the rationale for a separate measure for emotional problems for persons of borderline intelligence. It also established three areas of concern to which the instrument responds, specifically the need to address problems of comorbidity of limited intellectual ability and psychiatric problems, concerns of the "diagnostic overshadowing" of limited intellectual functioning over emotional problems, and problems in the psychometric and practical problems in assessment of emotional problems with persons in the mentally retarded to borderline range of intellectual functioning. The manual for the instrument is clear about the target population as well as the minimum qualifications of the user. This is particularly critical with the Behavior Rating Scales (BRS), which is a 135-item observational instrument that should only be administered in a clinical situation by qualified professionals who are already acquainted with the examinee.

The EPS was developed using a carefully described and well-justified procedure that began with reviews of the literature, interviews with relevant professionals, and a review of existing instruments designed to measure similar and related constructs. The initial step of instrument development led to the specification of the content areas of scales and the range of item content within scales. The manual is careful to specify constructs well. After initial scale development, there were a series of refining steps en route to the final set of scales, item content, and instrument format. Concerns about the manual's treatment of instrument development are not critical to the usefulness of the final instrument. Specifically, the "experts" used to review the content of the items may not have represented the same level of expertise as those used to develop items at initial stages. In addition, the determination of the nature and number of scales was partly rational, though a confirmatory factor analysis was conducted without reporting the results.

Support for the reliability of the EPS is strong. The internal consistency reliability coefficients for the Behavior Rating Scales (BRS) and Self-Report Inventory (SRI) are high. Interrater reliability and the association between raters and alternate situations for the BRS are strong for scales other than "Sexual Maladjustment," a scale that appears to have problems with restricted range. This is an important source of strength for a behavioral measure. Test-retest measures (over 4–6 weeks) for the SRI are also strong.

The validation procedures for the two scales of the EPS seem uneven. The convergent and discriminant validity of the BRS is evidenced through comparison of scale performance between the BRS and appropriate scales on the AAMD Adaptive Behavior Scale, the Child Behavior Checklist, and measures of work adjustment. These are appropriate measures for validation of the EPS. The manual presented specific data in a series of table to support the argument for the validity of the BRS. Validation of the SRI was attempted by comparison to the BRS. The modest connection between scores on the two scales was compared to the prevailing problem in literature reports of comparisons between self-report and observational scales. Two subsequent samples were used to obtain evidence of the validity of the BRS. This is an area that requires further development and the careful professional will be cautious with interpretation of results that are supported only by scores on the BRS. There is no information presented about the predictive validity of either the BRS or SRI. In spite of the difficulties with reliability and validity evidence presented, a clinician may make responsible interpretations as a result of scale scores in combination with other information.

The standard administration of the EPS is well-suited to the target population and is described clearly in the manual. This reviewer was particularly encouraged to see descriptions of alternative methods of administration in specific situations in which the standard administration is impossible or not in accordance with the specific demands of the situation. In particular, the BRS may be administered with alternate raters in differing situations, it may be used with locally determined comparisons, or may even be used as a behavioral checklist. The SRI is administered orally, requiring no reading for the examinee, but requiring the examinee to have normal hearing and the ability to comprehend spoken English. The reading level of the instrument was appropriately limited to make the instrument understandable to the possibly examinee. Normative samples include a wide range of ages, and because there was not a significant influence of demographic variables, the normative data are not separated for gender, race, or IQ. There is no discussion of cultural or other ethnic concerns, and this economy in reporting of norms may not be entirely supported on the basis of existing evidence. Normalized T-scores are used for scale score interpretation. Interestingly, the entire normative sample comprised persons who were receiving services. The manual does not mention this as a specific matter for interpretation, but it seems to this reviewer that this fact of the normative sample should be considered in making recommendations.

The EPS is a highly usable and psychometrically promising instrument designed to address the emotional difficulties of mentally retarded and borderline intellectual functioning persons from ages 14 through adulthood. The manual is well organized and clear. The instructions for administration, scoring, and interpretation are useful and thorough. The presentation of scale scores is somewhat complex, but clear. A sample interpretation is provided to help the examiner understand how the scale relationships might be considered in the interpretive process. There is some need for more work in validation, particularly in the SRI, but the EPS represents a generally effective and sound instrument with good quality supporting documentation.

[119]
Empowerment Inventory.

Purpose: To identify actions that individuals, managers, and work teams can take to raise one's level of empowerment.
Population: Work team members/employees.
Publication Date: 1993.
Acronym: EI.
Scores, 4: Choice, Competence, Meaningfulness, Progress.
Administration: Group or individual.
Price Data, 1994: $6.25 per inventory.
Time: (20) minutes.
Comments: Self-scored.
Authors: Kenneth W. Thomas and Walter G. Tymon.
Publisher: XICOM, Inc.

Review of the Empowerment Inventory by LESLIE EASTMAN LUKIN, Assessment Specialist, Lincoln Public Schools, Lincoln, NE:

The Empowerment Inventory consists of 24 statements of feelings that an individual might have about his/her job. Test takers are asked to mark each statement using a 7-point rating scale that ranges from *strongly disagree* to *strongly agree*. Directions are provided in the manual for converting the ratings on individual items to four scores: Choice, Competence, Meaningfulness, and Progress. The authors report that these four scores represent empowerment feelings as related to performing job-related tasks.

The authors provide little to no information concerning the intended audience or the intended purpose and use of the Empowerment Inventory. The general suggestion appears to be that individuals use this inventory to determine their current level of empowerment. Test takers are encouraged to make sense of their scores by using the limited normative data that are provided in the test manual. Finally, the authors recommend that individuals use the provided lists of "building blocks" to take action to empower themselves.

NORMS. A table of percentile ranks for each of the four scores is provided by the authors to help test takers interpret their scores. The authors indicate that the norming sample used to generate these percentile ranks consisted of "a set of managers who have already taken the Empowerment Inventory" (manual, p. 5). The only other information provided about this sample is that these managers scored "moderately high" on feelings of empowerment. Without any additional information, it is hard to imagine how these norms add anything to the interpretation of performance on the Empowerment Inventory. At the very least, the authors need to provide information about the size of the sample, how the sample was drawn, and descriptive information about the sample that would allow test takers to judge the appropriateness of this sample for comparative purposes.

RELIABILITY AND VALIDITY. The authors provide no evidence of the reliability of the scores associated with this inventory. At a minimum, it would have been appropriate to report estimates of internal consistency. In addition, the authors provide no evidence to support the proposed interpretation and use of these scores. The authors should have at least provided some content-related evidence of validity in the form of providing clear definitions of the construct being measured by the inventory and how the individual statements were selected for inclusion in the inventory. Without estimates of score reliability and evidence of validity, it is impossible to judge whether these scores provide any interpretable information.

In summary, because of the complete lack of psychometric information about this inventory we cannot conclude that this inventory does indeed measure feelings of empowerment. There would be no use of this inventory that would be supported by the current information provided in the manual by the authors.

Review of the Empowerment Inventory by PATRICIA SCHOENRADE, Professor of Psychology, William Jewell College, Liberty, MO:

The Empowerment Inventory is an easy-to-understand, 24-item scale designed to assess the respondent's sense of empowerment at work, and to help identify strategies for increasing empowerment. The authors subdivide the construct into respondents' perceptions of Choice, Competence, Meaningfulness, and Progress. The scale requires only a few minutes to complete, is easily self-scored, and is followed by suggestions for actions by individuals and work teams that may increase the sense of empowerment.

Empowerment, for the authors, is the experience of people when they are "energized by the tasks they perform" (manual, p. 8). The manual guides the respondent through scoring and graphing the scores, and offers interpretive aids that further explain the four feelings assessed. The manual concludes with lists of "building blocks" translated into "team actions" and "personal actions" for enhancing each of the four components. The respondent is invited to identify those that seem potentially helpful, particularly with respect to components on which a low score was attained.

Perhaps because the inventory and the manual are combined into one document for general use, the manual contains surprisingly little quantitative information about the test. Scores are graphed in comparison to those of "390 practicing managers who rated their entire jobs" (p. 7), but we are not told how the managers were selected, what they managed, or when the normative data were gathered. Moreover, although the authors suggest the scale may be used with respect to a part of a job, a specific task, or a team role, the only normative information presented for comparison is that of the entire-job ratings of the 390 managers.

Reliability information is absent from the manual. Both test-retest and internal consistency information would seem important if responses are to be considered representative of the current perspective on one's job, rather than a snapshot of how one feels at the particular moment.

With regard to content validity, the statements seem to be reasonable reflections of the terms identifying the four components. There is, however, no description of the processes used in developing items, with the exception of a single reference to a 1990 article (Thomas & Velthouse, 1990) and to a 1992 "working paper." (The former article deals with a model of empowerment, but not with this scale in particular.) The authors state that the scale is a "third-generation refinement" of the original inventory (p. 9), but do not explain anything about the refinement process.

Construct validity may be difficult to assess because "empowerment" is still a very popular and variously defined term, but factor analyses might help the reader to determine how well the scale items reflect the four components; unfortunately, none are reported in the manual. There is no mention of predictive validity in the manual, and it seems unlikely that data are currently available on that point.

The Empowerment Inventory may prove a useful discussion-starter for managers, employees, and work groups who wish to focus feelings about the work situation; the action plans may offer certain helpful suggestions. The scale cannot, however, be assumed to assess a significant psychological construct or to predict work-related attitudes or behavior without considerably more research and supporting information.

REVIEWER'S REFERENCE

Thomas, K. W., & Velthouse, B. A. (1990). Cognitive elements of empowerment: An "interpretive" model of intrinsic task motivation. *Academy of Management Review, 15,* 666–681.

[120]
Entrepreneurial Style and Success Indicator.

Purpose: Assesses variables thought to be related to entrepreneurial success and increase understanding of entrepreneurial style.
Population: Adults.
Publication Dates: 1988–1989.
Acronym: ESSI.
Scores, 4: Behavioral Action, Cognitive Analysis, Interpersonal Harmony, Affective Expression, plus 28 Success Factors.
Administration: Group.
Price Data, 1993: $15 per test booklet; $10 per interpretations booklet ('88, 42 pages); $15 per audiotape (Business With Style); $35 per professional's guide ('89, 73 pages).
Time: (120–180) minutes for Basic; (360–720) minutes for Advanced.
Comments: May be self-administered.
Authors: Howard L. Shenson, Terry D. Anderson, Jonathan Clark, and Susan Clark.
Publisher: Consulting Resource Group International, Inc.

Review of the Entrepreneurial Style and Success Indicator by STEPHEN F. DAVIS, Professor of Psychology, Emporia State University, Emporia, KS:

"The Entrepreneurial Style and Success Indicator (ESSI) is a scientifically developed, self-administered, self-scored, learning and communication instrument" (Professional's Guide, 1989, p. 2). The three-part ESSI was developed to assist adults achieve a fuller understanding of their business acumen, skills, and potential.

Parts One and Two begin with a brief questionnaire that serves to establish entrepreneurial style (Part One) and determine the strength of entrepreneurship (Part Two). The remainder (majority) of these sections is devoted to an in-depth discussion and explanation of the scores of these questionnaires. For example, four basic entrepreneurial styles (Action, Expression, Analysis, and Harmony), their accompanying behavioral characteristics, and how the examinee's score relates to these styles are presented in Part One. In Part Two the Foundations of Entrepreneurship scores are compared to normative scores and the examinee is prompted to consider a set of 28 factors that are ostensibly related to entrepreneurial success.

In Part Three the examinee matches the Part One score with 1 or more of 21 interpretative summaries to help isolate his or her entrepreneurial style more accurately. Based on these matches the examinee is directed to consider specific patterns in the In-Depth Interpretations manual. A consideration of the various styles also introduces the concepts of style shifting, style matching, and developing a plan for increased entrepreneurial potential.

The self-administration of the ESSI takes approximately 2 hours. Several options are available for enhancing the information gleaned from the basic ESSI administration. For example, a separate booklet presenting in-depth interpretations of 21 different entrepreneurial profiles is available to assist examinees in more accurately determining their specific entrepreneurial style. Shenson and Anderson (the authors) indicate that "over 90% of the comments contained in each pattern are perceived to have greater than 90% accuracy for the average person who has a particular pattern" (inside cover of In-Depth Interpretation manual). (Unfortunately, further information about the source and nature of these data is not provided.) For those individuals interested in turning the basic entrepreneurial clarification experience into a 1- or 2-day workshop, the 73-page Professional's Guide provides all the necessary ingredients, including several ready made charts that are suitable for use as overhead transparencies.

Clearly, the ESSI package contains a wide array of options and appears capable of achieving its goal of providing information and stimulating communication. However, there are several notable drawbacks.

The most noticeable problems associated with the ESSI concern its almost complete lack of statistical support and verification. Although the Professional's Guide indicates the ESSI correlates positively with self-reported measures ($r = .87$), other-reported measures ($r = .79$), and independent-measured success ($r = .81$) from a group of 4,000 self-reported entrepreneurs, no additional information about these participants and their data is presented. Likewise, no measures of reliability and only scant normative data are presented. The normative data appear as a guide for assigning scores on the Foundations of Entrepreneurship Assessment (Part Two) questionnaire to "Low," "Medium," and "High" categories. However, no information concerning the origin and derivation of these norms or the 28 factors characteristic of successful entrepreneurs is provided. Anticipating such concerns, Shenson and Anderson indicate the ESSI "is designed to be a learning and communication tool" (Professional's Guide, p. v), not "produce a psychometric evaluation" (Professional's Guide, p. v) or a "finite assessment" (Professional's Guide, p. v). Moreover, the authors appeal to the *ipsative* (nonindependent) nature of the Part One scores as a reason why normative data are not, and cannot, be presented. Despite these protestations against the need for empirical support for the development of the ESSI, Shenson and Anderson indicate that "Although this instrument was not designed to be a psychological test, questions of reliability and validity nonetheless apply … Clearly, then, a major step in developing and refining the ESSI is to subject it to rigorous empirical study" (Professional's Guide, p. 9). One can only wonder why such rigorous empirical study was not conducted during the development of the ESSI. Moreover, the Personal Style Theory from which Part One of the ESSI was developed deserves more than a passing glance. The work of Carl Jung, which reportedly forms the cornerstone of this theory, is augmented by theoretical concepts from Marston, Lewin, Horney, Fromm, and Merrill and Reid. Unfortunately, the exact nature and extent of the contributions of each theorist are not presented. As with the ESSI, the Personal Style Theory lacks empirical support; no measures of validity and reliability and no normative data are presented. Finally, the lack of standardized administration procedures will be problematic to some potential examiners. The provision of such empirical data and standardized administration procedures would strengthen one's confidence in the entire ESSI package and its scientific development.

These issues notwithstanding, the ESSI has several strengths. Albeit lengthy, especially if the In-Depth Interpretations booklet is used, examinees will have no trouble reading and comprehending the items, instructions, and discussion. The ESSI appears capable of facilitating an assessment of self-perceived entrepreneurial tendencies and opening lines of communication in this area. If these are your goals, then the ESSI may be well suited to your needs.

[121]
EPS Sentence Completion Technique.

Purpose: "A semi-projective instrument specifically designed for use with individuals in the mildly mentally retarded and borderline intelligence ranges."
Population: Mildly mentally handicapped ages 14 and over.

Publication Dates: 1989–1991.
Scores: Interpretation on 4 levels: Individual Items, Problem Areas (Interpersonal Relationships, Psychological Functioning, Work/School, Independence, Sexuality, Family, Residential Living and Adjustment, Behavior, Health), Thematic Interpretation, Specific Questions/ Clinical Hypotheses.
Administration: Individual.
Editions, 2: School, nonschool.
Price Data, 1994: $18 per complete kit including user's guide ('91, 4 pages) and 50 test booklets.
Time: (10–15) minutes.
Authors: Douglas C. Strohmer and H. Thompson Prout.
Publisher: Psychological Assessment Resources, Inc.

Review of the EPS Sentence Completion Technique by CHARLES A. PETERSON, Director of Training in Psychology, Department of Veterans Affairs, Minneapolis Medical Center, and Associate Clinical Professor of Psychology, University of Minnesota, St. Paul, MN:

INTRODUCTION. Intelligence is an organ of adaptation (Hartmann, 1958/1939), enabling the species to individually and collectively live within its *Umwelt*. In broad generalities, higher intelligence is associated with greater resources for problem solving, so that thought becomes experimental action (Freud, 1911/1958) instead of preemptory trial-and-error. What with restricted access to symbolization and abstract problem solving, lower intelligence offers fewer resources for adaptation. Comprehension, contemplation, and expression, along with other mental functions, are compromised. Not counting a sizable amount of time devoted to the intellectual assessment and classification of intelligence, and despite the fact that not everyone is blessed with high intelligence, psychologists, with few exceptions (e.g., Wagner, 1983, pp. 36–37), have held little interest in the description of personality and the prediction of behavior in individuals in the mentally retarded and borderline intelligence ranges.

Intent on redressing this wrong, the EPS (Emotional Problems Scale) SCT (Sentence Completion Technique) is described as a "semi-projective test" for use with low IQ individuals who frequently have the "inability to express emotional concerns" (p. 1). It is presumed that the (fairly simple and straightforward) sentence completion technique (4th grade reading level) is well-suited for the low IQ testee.

TEST CONSTRUCTION. The nine problem domains comprising the EPS-SCT reflect an "intuitive rational" strategy (Hase & Goldberg, 1967) derived from a sample of problems "professionals" encountered in their work with low IQ patients. After sifting the wheat from the chaff, 40 stems were chosen. (Why 40? Numerology? Or the magic number from the Rotter Incomplete Sentences Blank? [Rotter, 1950].) Two of the stems demand critical comment. Not the first to confuse the two, the authors regard Item 4, "Love is," as a "Sex" stem. Item 38, "What I don't understand about love and sex," is almost tragicomic in that the healthiest individuals could fill a small volume on the subject, spending much of their life trying to disentangle the two (Freud, 1912/1957). A stem such as "My body" might be more useful. The test manual (four pages!) contains no mention of several issues typically addressed in the construction of sentence completion tests:

1. First-person or third-person stems? It may be that low IQ individuals show differential ability to identify or project based on "person" of the stem used.

2. Instruction? Most sentence completion tests use one brief instruction that, variously, urges the respondent to complete the sentences as quickly as they can, to complete the sentences with the first thing that comes to mind, or to finish the sentences in whatever way they wish, as openly and honestly as possible because there are no right or wrong answers. The EPS-SCT uses a shotgun melange of all three. Do low IQ individuals benefit from a torrent of instructions or from one simple instruction?

3. Length of stem? The manual does not address this issue but the EPS-SCT does have a reasonable spread of stem lengths, varying from 2–10 words. However, some investigation of how low IQ individuals differentially use different length stems seems warranted. The answer blank provides barely adequate space for response. The answer blank also provides a key adjacent to each stem to facilitate interpretation so that the tester knows whether the stem addresses "sexuality," "work/school," or one of the other nine problem areas. If the higher IQ tester needs a key to figure out the problem domain, one wonders if the lower IQ test subject will reliably respond within the parameters of the stem. Further, there are some problem domains (e.g., Health, with only one stem), whereas others (e.g., Interpersonal Relationships) have seven stems. Because scale reliability inescapably varies with the number of items (a seven-item scale is always more reliable than a one-item scale), the different domains will have different degrees of predictive validity. Things get worse from this point on: The manual contains no information on the test's reliability or validity.

ADMINISTRATION AND INTENDED TEST SUBJECT. The test may be administered to the test subject by someone without formal graduate training in psychology. The "tester" first reads sample stems to the test subject, and after any necessary clarifications, reads the remainder of the stems and records the responses verbatim. Respondents with some reading ability may read the items and write the answers in the space provided on the SCT booklet. The authors state that the test may be used with subjects having a Full Scale or Verbal IQ between 55 and 83 "on a standardized intelligence test" (p. 2). The authors should be more specific here, as one cannot comfortably equate an IQ derived from a Shipley-Hartford with one derived from the Wechsler scales. The authors, to their credit, do insist that graduate training in psychology or related fields is necessary to interpret the EPS-SCT.

INTERPRETATION. The authors state that the test is a "semi-projective test" designed for "low-inference behaviorally oriented interpretations" (p. 1). What is "semi-projective"? Does this translate as "semi-objective" and thereby become psychometrically more respectable to those who would otherwise avoid a projective test? Although the distinction between objective and projective tests is a fuzzy one (Peterson & Schilling, 1983), simply calling something "semi-projective" neither solves the taxonomic dilemma (Peterson, Johanson, & Waller, 1993) nor does it guarantee that "low-inference behaviorally oriented interpretation(s)" are more valid than deeper inferences. So-called low-inference interpretations are perhaps easier to observe and validate but they run the risk of banality. For example, the patient who completes the stem "I HATE" with "work," may be said to, guess what, hate work. Unwittingly celebrating Schafer's (1954, p. xi) wisdom, "No matter how helpful a clinical tool it might be, no psychological test does its own thinking," the authors point out that the EPS-SCT can be interpreted at a variety of different levels.

SUMMARY. The EPS-SCT, admirably, is aimed at a neglected clinical population, borderline and mentally retarded individuals who may have some difficulty expressing themselves. If, in fact, low IQ individuals have trouble expressing their concerns, it is neither intuitively clear nor empirically demonstrated that a sentence completion format will overcome the respondent's problems in expression. Given the premise of the test, this is a crucial omission. Until then, it may be appropriate to summon Allport's (1953) criticism of testing-based inferences: If you want to know something about someone, sometimes it is best to just ask. Further, the authors have provided absolutely no reliability or validity data in support of this test. In keeping with the test's structure and aim, one could finish the stem, THIS TEST, with "*is kinda flawed.*"

REVIEWER'S REFERENCES

Freud, S. (1911/1958). Formulations on the two principles of mental functioning. In J. Strachey (Ed. & Trans.), *The standard edition of the complete psychological works of Sigmund Freud* (vol. 12, 213–226). London: Hogarth (originally published 1911).

Freud, S. (1912/1957). On the universal tendency towards debasement in the sphere of love. In J. Strachey (Ed. & Trans.), *The standard edition of the complete psychological works of Sigmund Freud* (vol. 11, 178–190). London: Hogarth (originally published 1912).

Rotter, J. B. (1950). The Incomplete Sentences Blank—Adult Form [test]. New York: The Psychological Corporation.

Allport, G. W. (1953). The trend in motivational theory. *American Journal of Orthopsychiatry, 25,* 107–119.

Schafer, R. (1954). *Psychoanalytic interpretation in Rorschach testing.* New York: Grune & Stratton.

Hartmann, H. (1958). *Ego psychology and the problem of adaptation.* New York: International Universities Press (originally published 1939).

Hase, H. D., & Goldberg, L. R. (1967). Comparative validity of different strategies of constructing personality inventory scales. *Psychological Bulletin, 67,* 231–248.

Peterson, C. A., & Schilling, K. M. (1983). Card pull in projective testing. *Journal of Personality Assessment, 47,* 265–275.

Wagner, E. E. (1983). *The Hand Test manual.* Los Angeles: Western Psychological Association.

Peterson, C. A., Johanson, T. T., & Waller, N. G. (1993). A taxonomy of psychological tests. *British Journal of Projective Psychology, 38,* 63–70.

Review of the EPS Sentence Completion Technique by ROBERT C. REINEHR, Professor of Psychology, Southwestern University, Georgetown, TX:

The EPS Sentence Completion Technique (SCT) consists of 40 sentence stems designed for use with individuals with mild mental retardation or borderline intelligence. The items are constructed with fourth-grade reading and vocabulary levels. The technique is intended for use either as an independent instrument or as a part of a comprehensive assessment battery such as the Emotional Problems Scales (EPS; 118). Although respondents who possess adequate reading comprehension and writing skills may be permitted to record their own answers, the usual procedure is to have the examiner both read the items and record the answers. The materials are presented in a four-page booklet that contains the sentence stems and room to record the response to each.

The authors refer to the SCT as a "semi-projective" (p. 1) instrument because, although using a conventional projective technique for gathering data, the interpretation strategies provided are said to yield low-inference, behaviorally oriented interpretations. This approach purports to accept responses at face value, to relate them to actual situations, and to minimize the interpretations of unconscious determinants of emotions and behaviors.

Each sentence stem was chosen to elicit information regarding one of nine problem areas: Inter-personal Relationships, Psychological Functioning, Work or School, Independence, Sexuality, Family, Residential Living and Adjustment, Behavior, and Health. These areas are based on a list of problems reported by counselors to be frequently encountered during counseling of individuals in the borderline intelligence and mentally retarded ranges. The problem areas are represented by different numbers of test items. Interpersonal Relationships and Psychological Functioning are each represented by seven items, for example, but there are only three items related to Residential Living and Adjustment and there is only one item related to Health.

It is suggested that interpretation may be conducted on four levels: Individual Items, Problem Areas, Thematic Interpretation, and Specific Questions or Clinical Hypotheses. In the interpretation of Individual Items, "items that are deemed clinically significant by the clinician are treated as 'critical items'" (p. 3). No method for the objective identification of critical items is presented. Interpretation at the level of Problem Areas involves identifying these clinically significant responses within the nine problem areas of the SCT. Although this area would seem to offer promise for the development of a method for objective interpretation of responses, the procedure suggested in the manual for this type of interpretation is entirely dependent on the judgment of the clinician.

The procedure for Thematic Interpretation involves identifying systematic themes in SCT responses. A systematic theme is one in which responses consistent in topic are given to items representing different SCT problem areas. As with Individual Item or Problem Area interpretation, "themes deemed to be clinically significant should be explored further …. Clinicians with questions about specific problems the client may be experiencing … can examine the SCT item responses for relevant data" (p. 3). It is pointed out that "both supportive and disconfirming evidence should be noted and evaluated when deciding whether or not a problem exists" (p. 3).

Most recommendations for the interpretation of answers to the SCT are similarly vague and are of little practical value. A brief sample interpretation contributes very little useful information: Responses judged clinically significant and useful are listed but the other responses from the sample protocol are not shown and no information is provided regarding the criteria by which responses were judged to be clinically significant.

The manual is only four pages in length and does not meet any of the *Standards for Educational or Psychological Testing* (AERA, APA, & NCME, 1985).

There is no normative information and no information concerning reliability or validity. Although the SCT purports to be only "semi-projective," the authors do not provide any guidelines that are of substantial value in making interpretations more objective. The SCT has few of the characteristics of an objective test; it is essentially an aid to clinical interview, and at the current stage of development is almost entirely without scientific merit.

REVIEWER'S REFERENCE

American Educational Research Association, American Psychological Association, & National Council on Measurement in Education. (1985). *Standards for educational and psychological testing.* Washington, DC: American Psychological Association, Inc.

[122]
ERB Writing Assessment.

Purpose: "Provides a direct measure of writing ability."
Population: Grades 3, 4–6, 7–9, 10–12.
Publication Date: 1989–1997.
Scores, 8: Overall Development, Organization, Support, Sentence Structure, Word Choice, Mechanics, Total, Scale.
Administration: Group.
Price Data, 1997: $6.50 per student for test materials in packages of 5, 10, and 20 plus shipping; $27 per computer disk (IBM only); $50 per data tape; $4.75 per additional set of anchor papers; $7.50 per perusal set (per level).
Comments: Writing samples scored by Measurement Incorporated.
Author: Educational Records Bureau.
Publisher: Educational Records Bureau, Inc.
a) PRIMARY LEVEL.
Population: Grade 3.
Time: (60) minutes (2 sessions).
b) LEVEL I.
Purpose: To assess student's descriptive writing.
Population: Grades 4–6.
Time: (50) minutes (2 sessions).
c) LEVEL II.
Purpose: To assess student's expository writing.
Population: Grades 7–9.
Time: (50) minutes (2 sessions).
d) LEVEL III.
Purpose: To assess student's persuasive writing.
Population: Grades 10–12.
Time: (50) minutes (2 sessions).
[Editor's Note: The following reviews are based on test materials published prior to 1994. The publisher has advised that several changes have been made and these will be reviewed in a future *MMY*.]

Review of the ERB Writing Assessment Program by G. MICHAEL POTEAT, Associate Professor of Psychology, East Carolina University, Greenville, NC:

The Educational Records Bureau (ERB) Writing Assessment Program is presented as a direct measure of writing ability. The materials provided to the test reviewer consisted of (a) a brief instruction manual, (b) a writing booklet, (c) a one-page set of scoring guidelines, (d) an anchor set containing sample essays and assigned scores, (e) a sample report of student results, and (f) a short Questions and Answers booklet. No technical manual was provided. Most of the evaluative information about the ERB Writing Assessment Program was contained in the "Questions and Answers" booklet. The ERB Writing Assessment is designed to assess the writing ability of students at three levels: Level I for grades 4–6, Level II for grades 7–9, and Level III for grades 10–12 [Editor's note: There are now four levels with the addition of a Primary Level for grade 3]. The instrument is administered in two group sessions in which students write and revise a response to a provided topic. The writing assessment is completed using a three-page, lined writing booklet. The written responses are then mailed to ERB for scoring. The writing samples are evaluated by evaluators described as a "team of trained readers" (p. 1).

A different style of prompt requiring different forms of writing is used for each of the three levels. For Level I (grades 4–6) the mode of writing is described as descriptive, for Level II (grades 7–9) the mode is expository, and for Level III (grades 10–12) the mode is persuasive. Students at grades 4–6 are given two 34–40 minute sessions, and students in higher grades are given two 45–50-minute sessions. Students produce a rough draft during the first session and complete the writing assignment during the second session, which may be on the same or a consecutive day. A four-page, test administrator's manual is provided to facilitate administration. Students are to be furnished with a dictionary and/or thesaurus to help with proofreading their work.

Each essay is scored by two readers described as being "experienced in analytic scoring" (p. 3). Analytical scoring is designed to provide detailed information on specific diagnostic information to allow the evaluation of students and programs over time. Six areas are evaluated using a 6-point scale ranging from 1 (low) to 6 (high). The areas evaluated include: Topic Development, Organization, Support, Sentence Structure, Word Choice, and Mechanics. Readers are reported to have backgrounds in education and to have experience in scoring writing samples during the past 3 years. Ratings provided by the two initial readers that differ by more than one point are reviewed by a scoring supervisor.

The results include raw and percentile scores for each student based on standards for each level. Percentile ranks are provided for each student compared to other students in the same grade who have taken the test in previous years. Schools are also able to request norms based on "independent," "suburban," or "composite" (a combination of both independent and suburban) schools. No other information about norms or the conversion of raw scores to percentiles was provided. Stanines were not discussed in the test materials but are provided on the sample report of student results.

Although the direct assessment of writing using an analytical approach has some intuitive appeal, the evaluation of the ERB Writing Assessment Program is difficult. The paucity of information provided by the publisher prevents a critical evaluation of the merits of the instrument. No information is provided about interrater (reader) reliability other than the statement that differences of more than one point are referred to a supervisor. Information about both interrater reliability and temporal stability are of critical importance. A similar objection can be raised concerning validity. The instrument can be argued to have prima facie evidence for content validity but empirical evidence comparing the ERB Writing Assessment to other instruments and classroom writing would be very valuable in evaluating the instrument. The lack of information about norms, about how percentile ranks are obtained, and the absence of any form of meaningful standard score limit the usefulness of the ERB Writing Assessment for both psychologists and educators.

In summary, the ERB offers a method for assessing written expression that appears to be relatively objective and based on a set of defined criteria. However, the lack of psychometric information means that the instrument must be regarded as an educational classroom work sample. It cannot be considered as a true educational test. It probably does provide some useful information but—in the competitive, standard driven educational systems of today—most psychologists, principals, teachers, and school administrators will want an instrument with demonstrated sound psychometric properties, with well-defined norms, and which provides reliable standard scores. The publisher of the ERB Writing Assessment program should develop a technical manual that addresses these issues.

Review of the ERB Writing Assessment by WAYNE H. SLATER, Associate Professor of Curriculum and Instruction, University of Maryland, College Park, MD:

The authors of the ERB Writing Assessment Program state that it provides a direct measure of writing ability at three levels: Level I: Descriptive Writing (grades 4–6), Level II: Expository Writing (grades 7–9), and Level III: Persuasive Writing (grades 10–12). For each of the three levels tested, a different writing prompt is used and a different mode of discourse must be used by the students to develop their essays. The authors then argue for the modes selected by stating, "The National Council of Teachers of English currently recognizes four different modes of discourse (methods of development or types of writing): Narrative, Descriptive, Expository, and Persuasive" (p. 1). Because they do not provide a reference for this quote, one is at a loss to understand why they decided to exclude Narrative from their assessment, especially given the emphasis on narrative writing and reading at the elementary school level (Graves, Watts, & Graves, 1994). In addition, because they use the global mode label Expository, one may legitimately conclude that the authors of this assessment have an oversimplified understanding of the modes of written discourse that may not serve them or their clients well (Britton, Burgess, Martin, McLeod, & Rosen, 1979; Corbett, 1990; Hillocks, 1986; Kellogg, 1994; Kinneavy, 1980; Mullis, et al., 1994).

Student testing is completed in two sessions. In the first session, students generate a rough draft. They write their final composition during the second testing session. Each school participating in the ERB Writing Assessment Program may decide whether both testing sessions should occur on the same day. Students in grades 4–6 are tested in two 35–40-minute sessions; grades 7–9 and 10–12 complete their work in two 45–50-minute sessions. The final draft of the student compositions is returned and evaluated. Schools are supplied with test materials for students' rough drafts and final compositions. Test administrator manuals are also provided for each group of students being tested. The authors state that dictionaries and thesauruses should be available in the classroom so that students may proofread and edit their work. Although the test administrator manuals are straightforward and the topics for writing are field tested and sufficiently generic to meet the needs of most students, one needs to question the authors' suggestion that schools may decide whether testing should occur on the same day (a morning and an afternoon session) or on two consecutive days. Given the need for internal consistency across samples for normative purposes and a concern for student fatigue, especially at the elementary school level, the authors need to provide compelling data that such a recommendation would have no impact on the results of their writing assessment.

The student final drafts are scored analytically. Each writing sample is scored in six different areas on a scale from 1 (low) to 6 (high). These areas include Topic Development, Organization, Support, Sentence Structure, Word Choice, and Mechanics. According to the manual, each writing sample is evaluated independently by two readers experienced in analytic scoring. The readers are trained for the specific writing prompt with sets of anchor papers. If the two readers' initial ratings in any characteristic differ by more than one point, the sample is read by a scoring supervisor who decides on a final score. The papers are scored by Measurement Incorporated, Durham, North Carolina.

The authors argue against the use of holistic assessment because it only provides some idea of how each student scored in relation to the other students in the class, but does not indicate the individual strengths and weaknesses of each student. They also argue against the use of primary trait scoring for similar reasons. Given what we have learned from writing research and assessment over the past 30 years, the authors' arguments against using holistic and primary trait assessments are uninformed (Braddock, Lloyd-Jones, & Schoer, 1963; Cooper & Odell, 1977; Mosenthal, Tamor, & Walmsley, 1983; Kellogg, 1994).

Two types of data are provided for every student taking the ERB Writing Assessment: raw scores and percentile ranks. The authors claim that the raw score indicates how a student performs at the level tested, based on the standard used to evaluate papers at that level. They claim that raw scores provide valid comparisons among individual students and also show growth across grades within a specific level. The authors also claim (manual, p. 2) that if a student takes the test the first year as a fourth grader and then takes it again the following year as a fifth grader, that student's raw scores will increase if his or her writing has improved. Because the prompts and modes of discourse are different for each testing level, however, it is not possible to compare raw scores across levels. Percentile ranks are also provided for

every student, allowing comparisons to be made between that student and all the other students at the same grade level who took the test in previous years at other ERB schools.

Because the authors of the ERB Writing Assessment do not provide a technical manual that includes norms (type and standardization sample), reliability (types and procedure, scorer), and validity (validation procedures, size and nature of samples) data, there is no information to review in assessing the authors' claims. For example, the authors state, "if a student takes the test the first year as a fourth grader and then takes it again the following year as a fifth grader, that student's raw scores will increase if his or her writing has improved" (p. 2). Research suggests that one writing sample, which is what the ERB requires, will not be sufficiently sensitive to detect improvement, especially in one year (Beach & Bridwell, 1984; Bereiter & Scardamalia, 1987; Cooper & Odell, 1977; White, 1994). The authors also state that schools can request percentile ranks based on Independent School Norms, Suburban School Norms, or Composite Norms (Independent and Suburban Schools). Because no technical manual is provided, one has no information on the independent and suburban schools selected. For example, did the authors use a proportional stratified random sample of independent and suburban schools? Without this information, a client will be unable to make valid comparisons between his or her school and the schools used in the ERB's norms. In addition, the ERB will provide composite norms (Independent and Suburban Schools). However, it is not clear why composite norms are important for this assessment and why they would be needed.

To conclude, this reviewer has major reservations about recommending the use of the ERB Writing Assessment Program. This writing assessment program does not assess narrative writing; lacks consistency in administration (same day or two consecutive days); provides only an analytical assessment of students' final drafts, while not providing any holistic or primary trait assessments; does not provide a technical manual that includes norms, reliability, and validity data; and apparently focuses on independent and suburban schools while not including urban school participation. Given these significant limitations, the reviewer would recommend instead the Stanford Writing Assessment Program, Second Edition (295), or other similar, well-established writing assessment programs.

REVIEWER'S REFERENCES

Braddock, R., Lloyd-Jones, R., & Schoer, L. (1963). *Research in written composition.* Champaign, IL: National Council of Teachers of English.

Cooper, C. R., & Odell, L. (1977). *Evaluating writing: Describing, measuring, judging.* Urbana, IL: National Council of Teachers of English.

Britton, J., Burgess, T., Martin, N., McLeod, A., & Rosen, H. (1979). *The development of writing abilities (11–18).* London: Macmillan Education Ltd.

Kinneavy, J. (1980). *A theory of discourse.* New York: W. W. Norton.

Mosenthal, P., Tamor, L., & Walmsley, S. A. (Eds.). (1983). *Research on writing: Principles and methods.* New York: Longman.

Beach, R., & Bridwell, L. S. (Eds.). (1984). *New directions in composition research.* New York: The Guilford Press.

Hillocks, G., Jr. (1986). *Research on written composition: New directions for teaching.* Urbana, IL: National Conference on Research in English and ERIC Clearinghouse on Reading and Communication Skills.

Bereiter, C., & Scardamalia, M. (1987). *The psychology of written composition.* Hillsdale, NJ: Lawrence Erlbaum.

Corbett, E. P. J. (1990). *Classical rhetoric for the modern student* (3rd ed.). New York: Oxford University Press.

Graves, M. F., Watts, S., & Graves, B. (1994). *Essentials of classroom teaching: Elementary reading.* Boston: Allyn and Bacon.

Kellogg, R. T. (1994). *The psychology of writing.* New York: Oxford University Press.

Mullis, I. V. S., Dossey, J. A., Campbell, J. R., Gentile, C. A., O'Sullivan, C., & Latham, A. S. (1994, July). *National Center for Education Statistics: Report in brief: NAEP 1992 trends in academic progress: Achievement of U.S. students in science, 1969 to 1992; mathematics, 1973 to 1992; reading, 1971 to 1992; writing, 1984 to 1992: Report No. 23-TR01.* Washington, DC: U.S. Department of Education, Office of Educational Research and Improvement.

White, E. M. (1994). *Teaching and assessing writing* (2nd ed.). San Francisco: Jossey-Bass Publishers.

[123]
ETS Tests of Applied Literacy Skills.

Purpose: To measure adult literacy.

Population: Adults.

Publication Date: 1991.

Scores, 3: Total score for each of 3 subtests: Quantitative Literacy, Document Literacy, Prose Literacy.

Administration: Group.

Forms, 2: Forms A and B for each test.

Price Data: Available from publisher.

Time: 6(20) minutes for the battery; 2(20) minutes of any one subtest.

Authors: Educational Testing Service, Irwin J. Kirsch (manual), Anne Jungeblut (manual), and Anne Campbell (manual), with contributions from Norman E. Freeberg, Robert J. Mislevy, Donald A. Rock, and Kentaro Yamamoto.

Publisher: Simon & Schuster, Higher Education Group.

Review of the ETS Tests of Applied Literacy Skills by ROGER A. RICHARDS, Adjunct Professor of Communication, Bunker Hill Community College, Boston, MA, and Consultant, Massachusetts Department of Education, Malden, MA:

The ETS Tests of Applied Literacy Skills are presented as "refinements of the instruments used in several large-scale assessments of adult literacy" (manual, p. 1-1)—namely, those of the National Assessment of Education Progress, the Workplace Literacy Assessment project sponsored by the U.S. Department of Labor, and the National Adult Literacy Survey of the National Center for Education Statistics.

Unlike its antecedents, which "were designed to estimate accurately and reliably group distributions of literacy skills," the present tests are "designed to estimate the proficiency levels of individuals" (p. 1-1). A number of specific uses are clearly spelled out:

> to assist program providers and staff in estimating the literacy proficiencies of individuals applying for or receiving services; to assist in placing individuals into appropriate existing programs; and to provide a means for assessing learner progress over time. (manual, p. 1-1)

A defining characteristic of the tests is that they combine the competency-based approach and the profile approach to the measurement of literacy. The former represents a departure from school-based content to include "a range of materials more like those that adults typically encounter at home, at work, or while traveling or shopping within their community" (p. 1-4), as emphasized by the word *Applied* in the title. (There is, by the way, no reason why the tests could not be used in a school or college setting to lend a practical tone where it is often badly needed.) The profile approach replaces a single literacy score with scores for "three distinct and important aspects of literacy—prose, document, and quantitative" (p. 1-6), as reflected in the designation of the instrument as *Tests* rather than *Test.*

There are two forms of each of the three tests: Prose Literacy, Document Literacy, and Quantitative Literacy. Each form consists of two 20-minute sections—both of which must be completed—each including 9 to 13 tasks. The Prose forms contain 24 items each; the Document forms, 26; and the Quantitative forms, 23. Although no information is given on the percentage of examinees who actually complete the tests, the time allowances seem generous. The examiner is not required to give all three tests to any given client, but may select the most appropriate.

The tests are a series of simulation tasks, well selected in terms of the structure of stimulus material, the content and/or context represented, and the nature of response required. The stimulus materials are all "real-life" sources such as actual newspaper and magazine articles, voting instructions, maps, tables of data, a routine application, and advertisements, among others. The content of these sources draws on six "adult contexts" (p. 2-1): home and family, health and safety, community and citizenship, consumer economics, work, and leisure and recreation. The response required varies from underlining sentences or graphic elements in text, to writing out answers in provided spaces, to filling out forms.

There are no multiple-choice questions; all are open-ended. Despite this fact, the scoring has straightforward guidelines that can be easily followed by nonprofessional staff members. High interscorer agreement is reported. The standards for acceptable answers are quite liberal; frequently the examinee is required to give only two or three points of five or six covered by the material. In several cases, the scoring instructions even accept an answer if it is underlined in its text instead of being written on the answer page. Clearly the intention is to give credit for what individuals can do, rather than to trip them up on technicalities.

The test content is likely to be interesting and nonintimidating to most examinees. It offers good variety and a quick pace. Because most sources require only two or three tasks to be performed, examinees are not likely to become bogged down on a single passage they find boring or difficult. The format and typography are attractive and clear, making the tests easily accessible to a wide range of examinees.

The directions for administering the test are a model of standardized procedure and of clarity. A well-written, easily understood script appropriate to the population likely to be tested is provided for the test administrator.

There is a marked contrast between the testing materials and parts of the documentation. The manual shifts from lucid exposition for the nontechnical reader to discussion of esoteric statistical theory. There is a shortage of the kinds of information that many test users have come to expect of a publisher. Some of the information is there, but hidden in out-of-the-way places. Useful data are buried in two paragraphs of a section entitled "Assembling the Test Forms," where we're told that:

> traditional item statistics ... produced, including the percentage responding correctly to the item, an estimate of how well each task related to the set of tasks in its block, as well as estimates of the internal consistency or reliability of each block. (p. 2-5)

Most of these statistics are not shared with the reader. The examiner whose own literacy skills are well developed will perhaps be startled to learn the average difficulty of the subtests: .65 and .67 for the two Prose forms, .76 and .73 for the Document forms, and .53 for both forms of Quantitative. Equivalent-forms reliability is estimated at approximately .90 for all tests.

The manual leaves some fundamental questions unanswered. For example, are the tests suitable for the full range of adult clients? We are told that the Tests of Applied Literacy Skills have been linked to the young adult literacy scales of previous tests (p. 5-3). That being the case, are the results meaningful when used with older adults? For that matter, to what population is an individual's performance on these tests being compared? A table entitled "Demographic Characteristics of Respondents Receiving New Tasks and NAEP Tests" (p. 2-4) gives minimal statistics by gender, race/ethnicity, and level of education, but provides no breakdown on the ages of the participants nor other information that would help users to know the kind of population to which their clients are being compared.

The meaning of the scores is obscure. Score conversion tables are provided for each form of each test. Converted scores range variously from 170 to 400 and 160 to 390 for Prose Forms A and B, respectively; 130 to 370 and 120 to 390 for Document Forms A and B, respectively; and 160 to 410 for both Quantitative forms (pp. 3-8 to 3-10). But what does a score of 310, for example, mean? Does it correspond to a particular percentile? We assume that the scoring system is based upon a given mean and given standard deviation. But what are these values? We know only that in the linking process cited above, means and standard deviations for the young adult literacy items were in the range of 282–292 and standard deviations just under 48 (p. 5-3). Are we to infer that the mean of the converted scores is approximately 290 and the standard deviation approximately 48? The tables do not lend themselves to this interpretation. On the Quantitative tests, for example, only 14 of the 156 scores presented on the conversion table would equal or exceed 1 *S.D.* above the mean, whereas 34 scores would fall under 1 *S.D.* below the mean.

The conversion tables are confusing in other ways. To obtain a converted score, we sum the number of right answers on the two sections of the test. On Quantitative Form A, a converted score of 300 corresponds to the following combinations of scores for Sections 1 and 2, respectively: 11+2, 10+3, 9+4, 9+5, 8+6, 8+7, 7+7, 7+8, 6+8, 5+9, 4+9, 3+10, 1+11. Not understanding how raw scores ranging from 12 to 15 can all receive the same converted score, most test users will regard all this as so much statistical sleight-of-hand. A lengthy section entitled "Interpreting the Scores" contains an excellent account of the mental operations required to perform different kinds of tasks and of the variables that determine the ease or difficulty of any given task, but as an elucidation of the scores for the layperson, it falls short.

No guidance is provided, either, on what range of scores might indicate that an individual does or does not need to enter a literacy program. There are no suggestions concerning what kinds of scores might qualify clients for jobs of various levels and types. And no guidance is given to help users determine what level of improvement in scores following participation in a literacy program is significant. Users are apparently on their own to develop local standards as they gain experience with the tests. Initially, however, they may well be at a loss to know what the performance of their clients means relative to any benchmark or criterion.

The evidence of the tests' validity is limited. The most persuasive form of validity is their obvious face validity. The correlations among the literacy scales range from .59 to .62, thereby supporting the authors' contention that the scores yielded by the test do, in fact, measure different sets of skills. A report of efforts "to minimize construct irrelevant variance" by comparing performance of Whites, Blacks, and Hispanics indicates that the efforts were successful. The manual does not deal with other forms of validity. For example, there are no studies that compare scores on the test with performance on jobs that require various levels of literacy.

The manual displays a kind of split personality, as though it was written by two different people with very different orientations and purposes. Much of it will be of little help to practitioners who do not have a solid background in psychometrics. Few, for example, are likely to be enlightened by such explanations as "a Bayesian posterior distribution of proficiency was calculated using a diffuse prior, taking into account only performance on items they had reached" (p. 5-3). Although such passages are no doubt of interest to the specialist, one wishes that more of the manual had been devoted to the needs of the nonspecialist. Perhaps the manual could be separated into a user's guide and a psychometric monograph.

The ETS Tests of Applied Literacy Skills appear to be a welcome addition to the tools available for measuring adult literacy in a variety of settings. They are adaptable to needs of individual clients, well constructed, easy to administer, objective to score, and of practical interest to the population for which they were designed. Their use of a profile differentiates among different kinds of literacy needed in the workplace. We look forward to the accumulation and publication of additional information that will permit users to gain a fuller understanding of the data the tests yield.

Review of the ETS Tests of Applied Literacy Skills by HERBERT C. RUDMAN, Emeritus Professor of Measurement and Quantitative Methods, Michigan State University, East Lansing, MI:

The ETS Tests of Applied Literacy Skills are a well-crafted set of tests designed to assess the quality of adult literacy along three dimensions: *Prose* (editorials, news stories, poems and the like); *Document interpretation* (job applications, payroll forms, transportation schedules, maps, tables, indexes, etc.); and *Quantitative knowledge and applications* (balancing a checkbook, figuring an appropriate amount for a tip, completing an order form, deducing the amount of interest from a loan advertisement).

These tests have their roots in several large-scale assessments of adult literacy: the young adult literacy survey published in 1986 by the National Assessment of Educational Progress (NAEP); the National Adult Literacy Survey conducted by the National Center for Educational Statistics for the U.S. Department of Education and the U.S. Department of Labor (1988); and by further investigations by the authors of the present ETS Tests of Applied Literacy Skills (TALS).

The TALS represents one end point on a content continuum that reflects daily situations faced by adults. At the other end of the continuum we would find content normally taught in schools (spelling, vocabulary, reading comprehension, mathematics, English grammar and punctuation, etc.). The authors of the TALS point out that the concept of literacy varies across historical time periods, social settings, levels of technology, and characteristics of adult populations. Just as some would argue that there is no single *g* factor of intelligence so do the studies underlying the TALS suggest that literacy is not a single-factor concept.

TEST CONTENT. The Administration and Scoring Manual that accompanies the ETS Tests of Applied Literacy Skills (TALS) presents an excellent rationale for the content used in Forms A and B of each of the three sets of literacy skills assessed and sets the basis for content and construct validity. The TALS consists of three test booklets. One test assesses Document Literacy, another Prose Literacy, and the third booklet measures Quantitative Literacy. The fundamental principle underlying the measurement of these three types of literacy is that demonstrated performance on any given task (test item) reflects the interactions among the *structure* of the stimulus materials used (e.g., narrative, graph, map, checkbook, and the like), the *context* from which these stimulus materials have been drawn (the workplace, home, the community), and the *nature of the task* or the mental processes that the individual is asked to perform. These interactions in varying forms affect the difficulty of a task and place it on a scale of difficulty in relation to other tasks.

The contexts of the adult tasks sampled for inclusion in the TALS are identified as: (a) home and family, (b) health and safety, (c) community and citizenship, (d) consumer economics, (e) the work-place, and (f) leisure and recreation.

Each of the three test booklets is organized into two sections. The authors caution those admin-istering the tests to adhere strictly to a 20-minute testing period for each section so that all test-takers begin and end each section together. Both sections are to be completed in one sitting. Test administra-tors are instructed to constantly monitor the tests during these two 20-minute sessions to ensure that all students are working in the same section. If users do not adhere to these time limits, proper interpreta-tion of test results cannot be made.

TECHNICAL ASPECTS. The Tests of Ap-plied Literacy Skills reflect the long history of stan-dardized test development within the Educational Testing Service. Its target populations are clearly defined, samples from these populations are carefully drawn, and stimulus materials are well matched to the types of literacy measured. As with other ETS standardized tests, field testing included a sensitivity review of symbols, words, and phrases to avoid sexist, racist, or other potentially offensive language.

Item (task) analysis utilized a spiraled matrix sampling procedure that put samples of content from each of the three scales (Prose, Document, and Quantitative Literacy) into six booklets. A random sample was drawn from various adult populations in which the two final forms of the ETS Tests of Applied Literacy Skills could be used. These populations repre-sented "adult basic education, community college, em-ployment service/unemployment insurance, job train-ing, and correctional institution programs" (p. 2-3). The field test was conducted in 30 states across the country and included 106 sites. The field test design that was followed called for testing new tasks written for TALS, as well as tasks previously used in Na-tional Assessment of Educational Progress (NAEP) studies. The new tasks were tested on 3,105 adults and the NAEP tasks were tested on 1,421 adults. All told, 4,526 adults were tested.

Up to this point, the tests were constructed in much the same way that standardized tests have been normally developed by test authors and publishers. The scoring of the TALS, however, was a more complex task. Given the nature of the test, scoring was not based on only the correct response, but on three categories: a clearly correct response, an incor-rect response, and no response (blank). An answer was identified as a Category 1 if it was clearly correct, a Category 2 if it was incorrect, and a Category 0 if no response was given. The last two categories were used to differentiate between an incorrect response and a nonresponse. Scoring tables were constructed so that a raw score could only be a Category 1 (correct response). The authors assumed that a nonresponse did not neces-sarily mean that the test taker simply did not know the correct response. Elaborate scoring guides were framed on the basis of approximately 500 responses for each item. The authors warn of overinterpretation if the scoring guides are not carefully followed.

After considerable training within the ETS staff, the raw score results were entered into data files and traditional item statistics were used. These included percent correct (P-value) for each task, estimates of internal consistency (coefficient alpha), and the number of tasks by scale and form. Item statistics for Forms A and B are quite similar. The Prose scale mean difficulty of Form A is .65 and of Form B is .67; both forms have an equal number of items or tasks. The Document scale yields mean P-values of .76 for Form A and .73 for Form B; both forms contain 26 tasks. The Quantitative scale is the most difficult of the three scales with mean difficulty values of .53 for both Forms A and B. Estimated reliability indices for both forms range from a high of .92 to a low of .88.

SUMMARY. The authors of the ETS Tests of Applied Literacy Skills are to be commended for the care taken in the construction of these tests. The administra-tion and scoring manual that accompanies the TALS is a comprehensive document and, on the whole, clearly written and detailed. It offers the reader a clear rationale for the content used and the standardization procedures followed. However, the elaborate and complex scoring guides contained in the manual raise doubt about the value of such guides for interpretation of the test results by users of the TALS.

The scoring of these tests introduces an ele-ment of subjectivity among the judges who will determine in which category a response will fall. In addition, judgements must be made by those scoring the test about the test takers' (a) level of knowledge, and (b) his or her proficiency in applying a set of literacy skills to selected materials that come from a variety of contexts. The Administration and Scoring Manual contains numerous tables to aid scorers and users in making these judgements but the tables may, instead, confuse rather than aid.

It is clear to this reviewer that the weakest link in the ETS Tests of Applied Literacy Skills lies not in the tests themselves, but in the scoring and interpretation portion of the Administration and Scoring Manual. Its explanation of scoring procedures to be followed, although detailed, is not helpful for interpreting and using the results. In fact, it adds an element of confusion not seen in other parts of the manual. The problems likely to be encountered by users of the TALS are not uncommon for performance assessment measures. The notion that multiple-choice tests do not yield information from a study of distractors chosen has increased the use of the analytic and interpretive activities noted in the Administration and Scoring Manual of TALS. If the scoring of the tasks used in the ETS Tests of Literacy Skills have only one correct answer, and if the contents of the stimulus materials are similar to that used in some standardized tests employing multiple-choice formats, and if traditional statistics are used to describe test results, why make scoring and interpretation so complex? If future revisions of the TALS are contemplated, and they should be, some mechanism for interpreting the performance of test takers other than that presently used should be contemplated.

REVIEWER'S REFERENCES

Kirsch, I. S., & Jungeblut, A. (1986). *Literacy: Profiles of America's young adults* (NAEP Report No. 16-PL-02). Princeton, NJ: Educational Testing Service.

U.S. Department of Education, & U.S. Department of Labor. (1988). *The bottom line: Basic skills in the workplace.* Washington, DC: Office of Public Information, Employment and Training Administration.

[124]
Examining for Aphasia, Third Edition.

Purpose: "For evaluating possible aphasic language impairments and other acquired impairments that are often closely related to language functions."
Population: Adolescents and adults.
Publication Dates: 1946–1994.
Acronym: EFA.
Scores, 41: Agnosias (Common Objects, Pictures, Colors, Geometric Forms, Numerals, Letters, Printed Words, Almost Alike Pictures, Printed Sentences, Non-verbal Noises, Object Identification, Total); Aphasias (Word Identification, Comprehension of Sentences, Comprehension of Multiple Choice, Oral Paragraphs, Silent Reading Sentences, Silent Reading Paragraphs, Total); Apraxias (Body Parts, Simple Skills, Pretend Action,

Numerals, Words, Sentences, Total), Aphasios (Automatic Speech, Writing Numerals, Writing Letters, Spelling, Writing from Dictation, Naming Body Parts, Word Finding, Arithmetic Computations, Arithmetic Problems, Total); Composites (Receptive, Expressive, Subaphasic, Aphasia, Total).
Administration: Individual.
Price Data, 1994: $114 per complete kit including 25 examiner record books, 25 Profile/Response forms, picture book, examiner's manual ('94, 35 pages), and object kit; $34 per 25 examiner record booklets; $18 per 25 Profile/Response forms; $29 per picture book; $27 per examiner's manual; $11 per object kit.
Time: (30–120) minutes.
Comments: Shortened version of test may be administered for screening purposes.
Author: Jon Eisenson.
Publisher: PRO-ED, Inc.
Cross References: See T4:940 (2 references), T2:2071 (3 references), and P:76 (2 references); for excerpted reviews by Louis M. DiCarlo and Laurance F. Shaffer, see 5:52 (3 references); for a review by D. Russell Davis and excerpted reviews by Nolan D. C. Lewis and one other, see 4:42; for a review by C. R. Strother and an excerpted review, see 3:39.

Review of Examining for Aphasia, Third Edition by HELEN KITCHENS, Associate Professor, Division of Counseling, Education, and Psychology, Troy State University—Montgomery, Montgomery, AL:

Examining for Aphasia (EFA-3) is designed to evaluate "possible aphasic language impairments and other acquired impairments ... closely related to language functions" (manual, p. 5). According to the examiner's manual, the EFA-3 can be used by the clinician to gather information in order to plan the rehabilitation of the aphasic person. Eisenson also states in the manual that the EFA-3 reveals "both the assets and the deficits of the subject at the time of the evaluation" (p. 5), and allows the clinician to chart the patient's progress through reevaluation.

As in previous editions of the EFA-3, the examiner's manual, which contains administration, scoring, and interpretative data, is excellent. Eisenson also provides the clinician with basic information about aphasia, related impairments, causes, and related disturbances. A glossary provided at the end of the manual defines key terms used in the EFA-3 manual and also defines terms used more broadly in the literature on aphasia.

The EFA-3 is divided into two main parts: Part I—Receptive and Evaluative (Decoding) Impairments and Part II—Expressive and Productive (Encoding) Impairments. Part I assesses agnosias through visual, auditory, and tactile tasks, and aphasias through auditory verbal and silent reading comprehension passages. Part II assesses apraxias and dyspraxias. Some items in this section ask the patient to perform a pretended action in order to predict the patient's ability to deal with abstract situations particularly where language is involved. Part II also assesses aphasias through items that examine the patient's type and level of symbolic dysfunction (i.e., automatic speech, writing numbers and letters, writing from dictation, spelling, word finding, arithmetic processes, oral reading comprehension, and story telling).

If one evaluates the EFA-3 based on *The Standards for Educational and Psychological Testing* (AERA, APA, & NCME, 1985), some major concerns arise. As Eisenson acknowledges, the EFA-3 is not a norm-referenced test. No reliability or validity data are offered. Eisenson writes:

> In the second edition of Examining for Aphasia, I took the position that persons with aphasia are so inconsistent in their test responses that formal norm-referenced procedures could not be meaningfully applied. However, recently published tests do suggest that the performance of a person with aphasia can be quantified with reasonable reliability. Nevertheless, I continue to caution that the purpose of assessment is to inform clinicians not only how to obtain quantifiable scores, but also how to obtain information … of the person's language and related abilities and disabilities, in order to establish bases for the initiation, direction, and continuation of therapy. (manual, pp. 20–21)

No one would argue with Eisenson as to the value of providing bases for therapy; however, that does not negate the necessity for accumulating data regarding the validity and reliability of the EFA-3. As most other major instruments used in assessing aphasia provide such information, this is a serious drawback for the EFA-3.

Examiners will find the EFA-3 easy to administer with simple, concise direction. It is composed of many different subtests that allow the examiner to assess potential areas of deficits. Subtests are arranged in a logical pattern from simple to more difficult as well as from receptive to expressive. However, there were too few items in the subtests; and in the receptive section, items were repeated too frequently, enabling the patient to develop a learned response (possibly memorizing the same group of functional items).

High-functioning aphasic patients will find the EFA-3 enjoyable and interesting to take. Being tested in the various modes (expressive, receptive,

reading, and writing) provides welcome variety. However, low-functioning aphasic patients may have limited interest in the exam due to their receptive and expressive language deficits.

Examiners are instructed to score the EFA-3 by entering a plus mark when the examinee makes a correct response (examinee may either respond verbally or by pointing to the correct response), a check mark for a delayed response, and a minus sign when the examinee fails to respond or responds incorrectly. This scoring procedures is not sufficient in demonstrating the most effective cues for the individual patient. This system does not give the examiner and/or other interpreter enough information regarding the appropriate level of cues for the patient (i.e., phonemic, semantic, gestural) to establish a complete treatment plan, beginning at the appropriate level in the hierarchy of cues. As there is no space provided on the test protocol to note cueing level, the therapist will be unable to determine whether the patient responded verbally or by gesturing. Additionally, when you reevaluate a patient, a score of 90% may not be comparable to the original score of 90% as different cueing levels may have been used; however, the score will not reflect that.

The test protocol is user friendly with percentiles and levels of severity easy to calculate. The graphs are easy to follow, and when looking at the scoring sheet, overall severity rating is easy to locate on the graph.

In summary, the EFA-3 is best used as a screening instrument. It provides the clinician with a quick, overall screen of a patient's assets and deficits.

REVIEWER'S REFERENCE

American Educational Research Associate, American Psychological Association, & National Council on Measurement in Education. (1985). *Standards for educational and psychological testing.* Washington, DC: American Psychological Association, Inc.

[125]
Family Risk Scales.

Purpose: Designed to be used as a standardized measure of a child's risk of entering foster care.
Population: Families.
Publication Date: 1987.
Scores: 26 scales: Habitability of Residence, Suitability of Living Conditions, Financial Problems, Adult Relationships, Family's Social Support, Parents' Physical Health, Parents' Mental Health, Knowledge of Child Care, Parents' Substance Abuse, Parents' Motivation, Attitude to Placement, Cooperation, Preparation for Parenthood, Supervision Under Age 10, Parenting Age 10 and Up, Physical Punishment, Verbal Discipline, Emotional Care Under Age 2, Emotional Care Age 2 and Up, Physical Needs of Child, Sexual Abuse, Child's Physical Health,

Child's Mental Health, School Adjustment, Delinquent Behavior, Home-Related Behavior.

Administration: Individual.

Price Data: Available from publisher.

Time: (20–30) minutes.

Authors: Stephen Magura, Beth Silverman Moses, and Mary Ann Jones.

Publisher: Child Welfare League of America, Inc.

TEST REFERENCES

1. Groze, V., & Gruenewald, A. (1991). PARTNERS: A model program for special-needs adoptive families in stress. *Child Welfare, 70,* 581–589.

2. Pecora, P. J., Fraser, M. W., & Haapala, D. A. (1992). Intensive home-based family preservation services: An update from the FIT Project. *Child Welfare, 71,* 177–188.

3. Thieman, A. A., & Dail, P. W. (1992). Family preservation services: Problems of measurement and assessment of risk. *Family Relations, 41,* 186-191.

4. Doueck, H. J., English, D. J., DePanfilis, D., & Moote, G. T. (1993). Decision-making comparison of selected risk-assessment systems. *Child Welfare, 72,* 441–452.

5. DePanfilis, D., & Scannapieco, M. (1994). Assessing the safety of children at risk of maltreatment: Decision-making models. *Child Welfare, 73,* 229-245.

Review of the Family Risk Scales by DAVID N. DIXON, Professor and Doctoral Training Director, Department of Counseling Psychology, Ball State University, Muncie, IN:

The Family Risk Scales are the result of a funded project by the three authors, supported by an advisory board from a number of private and public child preventive service agencies. The scales are intended to assist in the assessment of parental characteristics and family conditions that are predictive of maltreatment or other harm to children. A booklet/manual describes the development of the scales, recommends administration and scoring procedures, and provides limited reliability and validity information.

The scales are intended to be completed by a professional service provider, typically a social worker, and reflect an analysis and synthesis of all information available to the professional. As such, the data collection phase is not standardized, resulting in differing sources, amounts, and complexity of information with different cases.

There are 26 scales, with Scales 1–5 all scored for the entire family, Scales 6–13 all scored separately for the primary caretaker and secondary caretaker, and Scales 14–26 scored separately for each child in the home. The authors suggest that the scales can be completed in approximately 20 minutes, excluding data gathering. Twelve of the scales use a 1–4 scale for categorization, 12 use a 1–5 scale, and 2 use a 1–6 category scale. The categories for each scale are described well in the manual providing guidelines for coding. A 90-minute training session is recommended before using the scales.

The procedures used to develop the scales were intended to maximize content validity. The authors initially drafted 53 rating scales based on concerns of child preventive services, sent these scales out for reactions from service agencies primarily in New York City, received recommendations from the advisory committee, and piloted the items with 10 social workers. The authors state that the "draft scales were substantially revised on the basis of these reviews" (p. 4). The criteria for these decisions are not specified except to state that the scales were reduced from 53 to the present 26.

Data were collected on a sample of 1,158 families, which included 2,287 children. Demographics and the distribution of scores for each item are reported in the manual. Validity and reliability information is limited to a factor analysis of these scores, which resulted in a three-factor solution (i.e., Parent-Centered Risk, Child-Centered Risk, and Economic Risk) accounting for 45% of the common variance, and internal consistency reliabilities on the factor scores of "around .80" (p. 7). No information is provided on interrater reliability, test-retest reliability, or any criterion-related validity.

The manual/booklet, published by the Child Welfare League of America, may have been adequate to satisfy the requirements of the funding agencies, but it is lacking as a test manual. The information reported reflects the initial stages of scale development; it fails to provide the consumer an adequate basis for deciding on the merits of these scales for assisting in what may be life threatening/saving decisions.

The manual is unclear about how to combine scale scores. It is unclear whether the authors are recommending the use of composite factor scores, the use of separate scale ratings, or some combination of the two. Their statement that, "Family Risk Scale ratings or composite scores should never be used as the sole basis of casework decisions about a family" (p. 7) begs the question of how they are to be used in this decision process.

Until further reliability and validity information is forthcoming, the use of these scales for clinical decision making is ill advised.

Review of the Family Risk Scales by JANICE G. WILLIAMS, Associate Professor of Psychology, Clemson University, Clemson, SC:

The Family Risk Scales were designed for use by case workers in assessing a child's risk of entering foster care. The measure consists of 26 rating scales, each with 4–6 levels, with additional response categories for "not applicable" and "unknown." Each point on the rating scale has a descriptive anchor to assist in assigning a rating. The anchors give a number of examples of behaviors and conditions that are consistent with that particular rating. The authors state in the manual that a 90-minute training session should be adequate for learning to administer the scales. Ratings are to be made on the basis of factual assessment, including direct observations of the family situation, rather than inferences.

VALIDITY. The scales were constructed for content validity, based on literature review, review by expert judges, and pretesting. The manual gives little detail about the revisions that were made as a result of review and pretesting; however, attention was paid to clarity of the language and accessibility of the information. Fifty-three items were initially considered for inclusion.

A factor analysis of the items is also presented as evidence of validity. Three factors accounted for 45% of the variance in scale scores. The factors were named Parent-Centered Risk, Child-Centered Risk, and Economic Risk. The authors suggest that composite scores may be used to assess the sources of risk for a family, to match families to preventive services that will best suit their needs, and to assess change in family functioning over time. No data are presented in the manual to support these uses of the measure.

RELIABILITY. Internal consistency reliabilities are presented for the three composite scores. Coefficient alphas range from .88 for Parent-Centered Risk to .78 for Economic Risk. These estimates of reliability are adequate given the authors' cautions about use of the scores only as an adjunct to other sources of information in decision making; however, the primary focus of the test manual is on the individual scales, rather than the composite scores. Given that the ratings are based in part on observations, information about interrater reliability would be more useful for these scales. The measure could be used with more confidence if there were data suggesting that the anchors for the points on the rating scales do allow different raters to make similar ratings.

NORMATIVE SAMPLE. Comparative information for evaluating ratings comes from a sample of 1,158 families in child preventive services programs in New York City. It is instructive that, even in this sample of families already in intervention programs, ratings on many items were very low (indicating the lowest level of risk). For example, on 12 of the 26 scales, more than 50% of the sample fell into rating category 1.

Although the stated purpose of the rating scales is to assess children's risk of entering foster care, the test manual provides limited information about how the scales might be applied toward making that decision.

The manual presents descriptive results from the normative sample, but does not look directly at the relationship between Family Risk Scales ratings and other indicators of risk status such as charges of abuse or neglect. Given the paucity of psychometric data available on the scales, it is appropriate that no recommendations are given for using the measure to make predictions about risk of entering foster care.

The Family Risk Scales could appropriately be used as a systematic way to examine some aspects of family functioning that may be related to children's risk of entering foster care. Although there are not adequate data for ratings to be used in decision making, the ratings may help caseworkers to think about their observations. The Family Risk Scales have potential for further development. The measure might be useful in research in this area. Additional work on reliability and validity of the measure would add greatly to its usefulness.

Developing a measure to predict risk of entering foster care is a daunting enterprise, due to the low frequency with which this event occurs. The scales are intended for use in a population that has received a referral for service. Even in this population, it would be difficult to establish predictive validity for such a rare outcome. This measure is not going to help identify potential problems in families who are not already having obvious difficulties in functioning.

SUMMARY. The Family Risk Scales are 26 rating scales that provide a standard form for assessing aspects of family functioning, which may relate to a child's risk of entering foster care. It is intended for use in families who have been referred to child preventive services. The individual scales may be combined into three composite scores that address sources of risk for entering foster care. Internal consistency reliability and content validity appear adequate. Information about interrater reliability and predictive validity would be more helpful to potential users of the measure. Currently, there is not enough evidence about the psychometric properties of the scales to encourage its use for decision making. It does have promise for research on family functioning.

[126]
FirstSTEP: Screening Test for Evaluating Preschoolers.

Purpose: "Designed to identify preschool children who are at risk for developmental delays in the five areas mandated by IDEA (PL 99-457)."
Population: Ages 2-9 to 6-2.
Publication Dates: 1990–1993.

Scores, 7: Cognitive, Language, Motor, Composite, Social-Emotional, Adaptive Behavior, Parent/Teacher.
Administration: Individual.
Levels, 3: Ages 1–2, Ages 3–4, Ages 5–7.
Price Data, 1994: $130 per complete kit including 5 record forms each for levels 1, 2, and 3, 25 Social-Emotional/Adaptive Behavior booklets, 25 Parent booklets, manipulatives, plastic case, and manual ('93, 166 pages).
Time: (15–20) minutes.
Author: Lucy J. Miller.
Publisher: The Psychological Corporation.

Review of the FirstSTEP: Screening Test for Evaluating Preschoolers by TERRY OVERTON, Licensed School Psychologist, Learning and Behavior Therapies, Inc., and Associate Professor of Psychology, Department of Special Education, Longwood College, Farmville, VA:

This individually administered screening test for preschool-aged children requires about 15 minutes to administer. The author emphasizes that this instrument is to be used for screening only and that children who test below the expected levels should be evaluated further.

FirstSTEP contains 12 subtests, which are divided into three domains: Cognition, Communication (Language), and Motor. Each domain is assessed through 4 subtests. In addition to the direct assessment of the child, a Social-Emotional scale and an Adaptive Functioning Behavior checklist are included. The Social-Emotional is to be completed by the examiner as behaviors are observed during the assessment session. The Adaptive Behavior checklist is completed by the parent or caretaker. This instrument included all five domains required by P.L. 99-457: cognition, communication, motor, social-emotional, and adaptive behavior.

The format of the instrument is presented as a series of "games" to the preschool-age child. The games include: Money Game (Quantitative Reasoning), What's Missing? Game (Picture Completion), Which Way? Game (Visual Position in Space), Put Together Game (Problem Solving), Listen Game (Auditory Discrimination), How Many Can You Say? Game (Word Retrieval), Finish Up Game (Association), Copy Me Game (Sentence and Digit Repetition), Drawing Game (Visual-Motor Integration), Things With Strings Game (Fine Motor Planning), Statue Game (Balance), and Jumping Game (Gross Motor Planning).

The materials included in this test kit include the test manual, stimulus booklet, four-inch yellow mats, one 25-inch white shoe string, one 50-inch white shoe string, one primary pencil without eraser, one 1-inch cube with a hole in the center, four red sticks ranging from 1 to 3 inches in length, record forms and drawing booklets for three different age groups (25 each), a package of 25 Social Emotional and Adaptive Behavior checklists, and a package of 25 Parent/Teacher Scales. The examiner must supply 15 pennies, a nickel, a quarter, a ruler, a roll of masking tape, and a stopwatch.

Administration and instructions include specific directions for teaching tasks, number of trials allowed, and item termination. The record form is presented with a color coding system that easily allows the examiner to determine if the child falls within the range requiring additional assessment, is within a borderline range of possibly needing additional assessment, or is within the level expected for his/her age. Raw scores may be used on the record form to plot a profile that includes domain scores and composite scores by age groups. For the Cognitive, Language, and Motor subtests, the mean scale score is 10 with a standard deviation of 3. The average composite score is approximately 50 (ranges by age from 48.7 to 50.8).

The administration of the items to preschool-age children is quick and fairly easy. Each age group is required to complete only a few items for each of the 12 subtests. Most of the items are interesting to this age group.

The development of this instrument began with the same theoretical model as the Miller Assessment for Preschoolers, by the same author (MAP; Miller, 1988, 1982; T4:1631). The author states that some of the items for the FirstSTEP were derived from the MAP. The author includes a discussion of the development of the MAP, which spans a 15-year period of theoretical and empirical work. This author also includes a comprehensive discussion of test construction and field testing of the FirstSTEP. Pilot studies were conducted in Colorado only; however, these studies included children who were randomly selected to approximate the 1980 U.S. Census for gender, age, race/ethnicity, community size, and parent education.

Pilot research studies addressed identification of the optimal items, internal consistency reliability, item characteristics, test-retest reliability, and interrater coefficients for each item. The second pilot study included only those items "that contributed most strongly to the domain scores across all age groups

[and] had adequate item difficulty and item discrimination characteristics" (manual, p. 81). The Tryout edition was then administered to 550 children. This study included overrepresentations of four minority groups so that bias research could be conducted. The item pool was reduced by 50% during this study. The Tryout study also studied criterion-related validity using subtests and criteria of several measures (MAP, TOLD-P:2, ITPA-R, WPPSI-R, etc.). During the final phase of the Tryout studies, field researchers reviewed items for their psychometric properties and 12 child development specialists selected items based on content. The Adaptive Behavior Checklist and the Parent/Teacher Scale were studied using similar steps and techniques.

The standardization sample included 1,433 children with approximately an equal number of males and females in each of the seven age groups. The sample included all nine regions of the United States, Alaska, and Hawaii and approximated the 1988 U.S. Census. Race/ethnicity and parent education level were addressed in the study.

Reliability research seems to be comprehensive. The author states that every domain was studied using split-half reliability. Coefficients ranged from .83 to .89 with an average of .87 for Language. Coefficients ranged from .65 to .75 for Motor with an average of .71. For the Cognitive domain, coefficients ranged from .72 to .79 with an average of .75. Test-retest (1- to 2-week interval) reliability coefficients were high, with the highest domain coefficient in Language with .91. Coefficients for other domains in the test-retest study ranged from .82 to .85. The composite coefficient was .93. This instrument seems to be stable over time.

Interrater reliability was also adequate to high ranging from .77 on the Social-Emotional measure, to .96 for Cognitive and Language. The composite interrater reliability coefficient was .94.

The standard error of measurement was fairly consistent for composite scores ranging from 2.99 to 3.68. The *SEM* for age groups and by domains was less consistent, ranging from .67 to 1.77.

Validity studies included content validity; construct-related validity studies using intercorrelations of subtests; factor analysis studies using varimax rotation; and confirmatory factor analysis using one, two, three, and four factors. The Language factor seems to be the strongest measure on this instrument. Curiously, quantitative reasoning and visual position loaded most strongly on the Language factor as well as traditional language type subtests.

Criterion-related validity using classification and cutpoints for children at risk of developing Cognitive, Language, or Motor delays was assessed. This instrument appears to have a weakness in identification of false positives. As the author states, it is probably better to err on the side of false positive, indicating additional assessment is needed, than false negative resulting in a child being overlooked for additional testing. The percentage of false positives was approximately 15–21% and for false negatives was 1–3%.

Data are presented of comparison studies of the FirstSTEP with the MAP, the Wechsler Preschool and Primary Scale of Intelligence—Revised, the Bruininks-Oseretsky Test of Motor Proficiency, the Test of Language Development Primary—Second Edition, the Walker Problem Behavior Identification Checklist—Revised, and the Vineland Scales of Adaptive Behavior. These correlations range from fair to adequate. One would not expect some of these instruments to correlate highly with this particular screening instrument. For example, the Walker Problem Behavior Identification Checklist measures a more narrow band of behaviors that concern childhood pathology; a screening of skills across a wide range of domains would not be expected to correlate strongly.

Clinical studies included groups of children with language, cognitive, and motor delays as well as children with social-emotional problems. These studies were fairly impressive in that they discriminated these groups with accuracy. The various clinical groups obtained scores more than 1 standard deviation below the norm group, and in some cases, more than 2 standard deviations below (ranged from 1.67 to 2.4 standard deviations below the norm).

In summary, the FirstSTEP seems to meet adequate technical standards expected for an instrument of this nature. The author has undertaken substantial research for an instrument that is administered in about 15 minutes. This instrument will certainly find its place among the many school and preschool environments, some which must screen hundreds of students each year. Using this instrument, one should have some confidence that most students at risk will be identified for additional testing. Some may be identified who truly do not need additional assessment (false positives). But fewer will slip through without being noticed. This instrument is a welcome addition.

REVIEWER'S REFERENCE

Miller, L. J. (1982, 1988). Miller Assessment for Preschoolers (MAP). San Antonio, TX: The Psychological Corporation.

[127]
The Five P's (Parent/Professional Preschool Performance Profile) [Revised].

Purpose: Constructed as a "method for collecting information regarding the current level of functioning" and for "preparation of the child's IEP."

Population: Children with disabilities functioning between the ages of 6 and 60 months.

Publication Dates: 1982–1995.

Scores: 13 scales in 6 areas of development: Classroom Adjustment, Self-Help Scales (Toileting and Hygiene, Mealtime Behaviors, Dressing), Language Development (Communicative Competence, Receptive Language, Expressive Language), Social Development (Emerging Self, Relationships to Adults, Relationships to Children), Motor Development (Gross Motor/Balance/Coordination Skills, Perceptual/Fine Motor Skills), Cognitive Developmental Skills.

Administration: Individual.

Price Data, 1994: $125 per materials for class of 10 children including 10 sets of Five P's educational assessment booklets, 11 Five P's instructional manuals, 10 graphic profiles, 1 bound copy of The Five P's Preschool Annual Goals and Short-Term Instructional Objectives; $45 per training video (25 minutes); $6 per set of research papers (2 papers—Validity and Reliability); $75 per sample packet including PDQ (Parent Data Questionnaire), Five P's assessment packet, training video, Five P's research papers, The Five P's Preschool Annual Goals and Short-Term Instructional Objectives; $125 per set of PDQ's (10 each form for screening or evaluation: Form A for children 24–35 months, Form B for children 36–47 months, Form C for children 48–60 months, bound copy of The Five P's Preschool Annual Goals and Short-Term Instructional Objectives); $295 per computerized preschool short-term instructional objectives.

Foreign Language Edition: Spanish edition available.

Time: Administration time not reported.

Comments: Ratings by parents and teachers.

Authors: Judith Simon Bloch, John S. Hicks (technical manual), and Janice L. Friedman (technical manual).

Publisher: Variety Pre-Schooler's Workshop.

Cross References: For a review by Barbara Perry-Sheldon, see 10:116.

Review of The Five P's (Parent/Professional Preschool Performance Profile) [Revised] by ANNIE W. WARD, Emeritus Professor, University of South Florida, Daytona Beach, FL:

DESCRIPTION. The Five P's is a coordinated observation system for use by both teachers and other professionals and by parents of young children (ages 6 to 60 months). The system was developed at the Variety Pre-Schooler's Workshop, which is a well-funded school and research center for children with special needs. It is designed to serve as the basis for consultation between parents and professionals and for the development of the Individual Education Program (IEP), as well as for identifying the child's learning needs and monitoring his or her progress. An important objective of the system is to empower parents and help them to become partners in their child's education. A Spanish edition is available, and there is a Hebrew edition of an earlier form.

There are 13 scales, covering six areas of development: Classroom Adjustment, Self-Help, Language Development, Social Development, Motor Development, and Cognitive Development. The latter two scales are combined in a single booklet, so there are only five booklets. Each of these scales has some items labeled "Interfering Behaviors," which are scored separately from the other items. Except for the Classroom Adjustment scale, the scales are filled out by both parent and teacher. There are a total of 458 skills, although the parents rate only 427. Furthermore, the child is rated only on those items up to and through his or her age level except in special cases. Each child is also rated on ALL interfering behaviors, because these behaviors are not thought to be age-related.

Recently an abbreviated version of The Five P's called the PDQ has been developed for parents. There are three forms, one for each of three different age ranges. Each form of the PDQ contains approximately 120 items. The manual states that items were carefully selected for the PDQ, using as the criteria the correlation with the total score, the correlation with chronological age, and the frequency with which teachers and parents selected the Developmental Skill as an instructional objective. These are reasonable criteria, but studies should be made to ascertain that the PDQ scores are well correlated with the scores on the original scales and to establish equivalent scores.

ADMINISTRATION/SCORING. There are instructions for both parents and professionals for doing the observations, and each item is rated either Y = YES—*Always/usually true;* S = SOMETIMES—*Sometimes true;* or N = NO—*Never/rarely true.* Although the scales are called "observational scales" and the instructions emphasize that the ratings are intended to reflect the child's behavior at a specific point in time, it is obvious from the scale descriptions that the ratings actually reflect to some extent the observer's interpretation of the child's behavior, rather than simply tabulating what happens during a specific time period. A training program and video tape are available to assist parents and professionals in using The Five P's.

The teacher or school team is responsible for transcribing the parents' ratings into the teachers' booklets and preparing the graphic profile, which is used, along with clinical evaluations, in the IEP planning conference.

TECHNICAL INFORMATION. The developers of The Five P's have published numerous reports on studies using the scales and a new manual is in development, which provides a reference list for studies that helped the developers identify the behaviors that are covered in the scales.

The early studies were limited to the children at the Variety Pre-Schooler's Workshop (VPSW) but beginning in 1986 some studies have been conducted with a national sample, although the numbers are quite small. A 1988 replication study and a 1990 validation report are available from the publishers and provide a great deal of reliability and validity data. Some of these data are included in the new manual that is now under development. Unfortunately, the manual does not always differentiate between early studies done at VPSW and those using the national sample and the Ns are small for many of the tables. Factor analytic studies were done, which included both the VPSW sample and the national sample, although the small $N(370)$ makes this procedure suspect. However, the analyses yielded similar factor structures for parents and teachers except for "Toileting/Hygiene," which was a separate factor for parents but was a part of "motor skills" for teachers.

SUMMARY. The goal of including parents in the evaluation and planning for students with special needs is commendable. Also the extent of the research base for The Five P's is much more thorough than for most such instruments.

A major deterrent to the use of The Five P's is the sheer number of the ratings that must be done by both parents and professionals and the amount of time per student that will be involved. It may be that schools where this is a problem will choose to use the PDQ version, although not as much research has been done with it as with The Five P's. If the PDQ version is to be offered except for research, it should have the same kind of reliability and validity studies as the original version.

Another problem will be the extent to which both parents and teachers are able and willing to participate in the training that would be essential if the ratings are to be valid. The manual needs extensive reorganization and editing to clarify some information and make it more easily accessible.

Review of The Five P's (Parent/Professional Preschool Performance Profile) [Revised] by STEVEN ZUCKER, School Psychologist, Cherry Creek Schools, amd Honorarium Instructor, University of Colorado at Denver, Denver, CO:

The Five P's (Parent/Professional Preschool Performance Profile) [Revised] (Five P's) offers a unique, collaborative approach to the process of assessing the developmental functioning of preschoolers with disabilities. The authors take a wholistic, ecological perspective while illuminating the broad array of children's strengths and needs that must be considered to effectively translate assessment data into prescriptive, home-based and classroom support services. Their belief in the parent-professional partnership and the necessity of repeated observations across time and context provides the foundation for The Five P's assessment process. The authors seem to recognize that any instrument, in itself, can do only so much; that an effective, collaborative relationship lies at the heart of the assessment of preschool children. Although the message the authors impart is coherent and laudable, the materials (technical and otherwise) could benefit from additional tailoring and refinement. The Comprehensive Manual and Technical Reports offer a wealth of information, yet they are lacking in refinement and clarity. The value of the materials and the beauty of the message are somehow lost amidst the historical documentation, multiple forms and formats, and technical information provided. The clarity of The Five P's manual (in contrast to the Comprehensive Manual), and presumably that of The Five P's System User Manual (also "in progress ... designed for the hands-on user," p. 9) is far more succinct and user-friendly.

The field-based practitioner might view the present Comprehensive Manual as somewhat cumbersome and overwhelming (the authors do state clearly that the manual is a "work in progress"). In its current form, for example, the child's parents and teacher would complete The Five P's Educational Assessment consisting of 13 scales; the teacher alone also completes the Classroom Adjustment Scale. A classroom aide would then transfer the parent's scores to the teacher's form (and vice-versa). He or she would then combine these on an additional Share and Compare Form. Next, the scores are transcribed to a color-coded Graphic Profile Form. Following these procedures, the team begins the process of translating assessment results into behavioral objectives (specific short-term objectives and annual preschool goals), assisted by The Five P's Preschool Annual Goals and Short-Term Instructional Objectives booklet. Even with available computer-scoring programs (not reviewed), if one were to attempt the three 90-minute parent training sessions (which the authors recommend precede the assessment process) the preschool team may feel quite stretched for time.

The abbreviated Five P's Parent Data Questionnaire (PDQ), however, recommended at one point in the manual for entry level screening and evaluation purposes, and then later as only "a research edition" (p. 98), may suffice in many instances. The PDQ utilizes the technically "strongest" items from each developmental domain (e.g., items that correlated highest with domain scores; frequency with which teachers chose items to tailor short-term objectives, etc.). A similar process was used to select the Interfering Behaviors items from the PDQ. Although one may also derive specific short- and long-term goals and objectives when using the PDQ, there is not a direct correspondence between The Five P's Preschool Annual Goals and Short-Term Instructional Objectives booklet and the PDQ, as there is for the goals/objectives booklet and The Five P's Educational Assessment. Furthermore, (as addressed below) crucial psychometric data are unavailable for the PDQ.

Based on a total sample of 370 children with "varying disabilities," 20 months–7 years of age, from six U.S. states, the authors report adequate to excellent test-retest reliability (2- to 3-week intervals) on various subgroups of approximately 30–130 children (coefficients in the low .80s to mid .90s). Internal consistency reliability (Cronbach's alpha) and interrater reliability are also quite good (low .80s to mid .90s). Comparability of Parent-Teacher ratings was also evaluated (n = 264–283) and yielded only moderate correlations for the five major domains (.60–.84), with Social Development yielding the lowest agreement. Although raters' agreement increased somewhat with age, and were higher in the Spring assessment (versus initial Fall assessment), such findings suggest that parents and teachers may well view children differently (in specific domains) and that children's social-interpersonal behavior varies from one setting to the next (e.g., home versus school).

Good evidence of content validity is reported in the Comprehensive Manual and supplementary technical report. Concurrent validity is reported on a sample of 55 children with disabilities for The Five P's and "selected standardized tests" (e.g., Vineland, McCarthy) with correlations ranging from .48 to .74 (specific correlations with the Vineland, McCarthy etc., were not clarified in the manual or in the technical supplement). Attempts to validate the "Interfering Behaviors" construct with the Burks' Behavior Rating Scale proved disappointing, as the 1:1 correspondence between The Five P's and Burks' scale components are less than adequate. It may have been more fruitful to consider the use of additional convergent/discriminant validation methods (e.g., Five P's Interfering Behaviors should correlate negatively with Vineland Adaptive and/or BASC Adaptive Profile Scores etc.). Although concurrent data may be viewed as adequate, these data must be interpreted cautiously until further clarification of criterion measures can be obtained.

Factor Analyses utilizing larger sample sizes (i.e., n = 370, n = 290) reveals the relative independence of The Five P's Developmental Skills and Interfering Behaviors clusters. Additionally, there is adequate evidence to support the authors' contention that the Developmental Skill domain yields three major factors (Motor Development and Self-Help Skills; Language and Cognitive Development; and Social Development—including Classroom Adjustment). Factor analysis of the Interfering Behavior scales provided sparse evidence for the emergence of separate factors. The authors state that "further factor analytic studies will be done on the Five P's when the normalization sample is complete" (p. 83). Additional factor analytic studies (and other examinations of validity) would seem warranted. Given their preference for functional assessment data (which should be applauded), the authors might consider evaluating the validity of decision-making processes utilizing The Five P's as the ultimate hallmark of validation a test can receive (e.g., were kids well served; were outcomes satisfying to parents, productive for children, etc.).

Of significant concern to those wishing to utilize The Five P's for classification and eligibility decisions is the absence of a representative and substantive sample of normally developing children. Provisional Developmental Scale norms are reported for a sample of only 460 preschool children (across seven age ranges) as norming updates are in progress. Although The Five P's may prove beneficial in the observation, collaboration, and planning process, one should use the provisional norms with caution and with the knowledge of typical developmental patterns as a basis for instructional planning and decision making. This seems especially true when evaluating Interfering Behaviors. One should be cautious using available norms to assume "clinically significant" deviance from normal. Although provisional norms (n = approximately 400) for typically developing children are also available for the PDQ, no separate studies of reliability and validity have been conducted on the PDQ.

SUMMARY. As a tool that may structure the observation, collaboration, and instructional planning process for preschool children with disabilities, The Five P's may become an invaluable contribution. The laudable attributes and refreshing philosophical approach of The Five P's to collaboration and planning are somewhat diminished by the cumbersome documentation, excessive forms and formats, and limited psychometric adequacy. Improvements in the clarity and coherence of the Comprehensive Manual and a substantial tailoring and refinement of forms and formats would make The Five P's a more appealing and user-friendly instrument. The absence of a representative and substantive sample of normally developing children is a drawback at this time, especially for those wishing to utilize The Five P's for classification and eligibility decisions. The Five P's Partnership video is a helpful introduction to The Five P's system and philosophy of parent-partnership collaboration.

[128]
Functional Fitness Assessment for Adults Over 60 Years.

Purpose: Designed to "assess the functional fitness of adults over 60 years of age."
Population: Adults over age 60.
Publication Date: 1990.
Scores, 7: Body Composition (Body Weight, Standing Height Measurement), Flexibility, Agility/Dynamic Balance, Coordination, Strength, Endurance.
Administration: Group.
Price Data, 1993: $7.50 per manual (24 pages).
Time: Administration time not reported.
Authors: Wayne H. Osness, Marlene Adrian, Bruce Clark, Werner Hoeger, Diane Rabb, and Robert Wiswell.
Publisher: American Alliance for Health, Physical Education, Recreation and Dance.

Review of the Functional Fitness Assessment for Adults Over 60 Years by MATTHEW E. LAMBERT, Research Psychologist, Neurology Research and Education Center, St. Mary Hospital, Lubbock, TX:

The Functional Fitness Assessment for Adults Over 60 Years is a field test designed to assess the functional fitness of adults over 60 years old and developed by a committee of the American Alliance for Health, Physical Education, Recreation and Dance. Items for the assessment were drawn to meet the goals of being able to determine the functional capacity of older adults, establish age- and sex-related norms, publish test procedures and normative data, establish training for professionals completing such assessment, and then disseminate the test for professional use. A three-phase process was used to develop the battery with the first phase focusing on the needs for testing elderly populations. The second phase seeks to establish reliability and validity and the third phase emphasizes dissemination of the test and its results. Several parameters were selected for inclusion in the test: Body Composition, Flexibility, Agility/Dynamic Balance, Coordination, Strength/Endurance, and Endurance. The Body Composition parameter is calculated via the Ponderal Index using the subparameters—body weight and standing height.

The test manual provides detailed instructions for setting up and administering the test items utilizing simple, readily available equipment. Drawings are provided in the manual to help guide equipment setup. Administration of the test items is quite simple and can be easily completed by average elderly individuals. Warm-up activities are suggested prior to administering test items.

The Flexibility parameter is scored by the number of inches reached in each trial, whereas the Agility/Dynamic Balance, Coordination, and Endurance parameters are scored in terms of the time required to complete test trials. The Strength/Endurance parameter is scored for the number of repetitions completed in a 30-second interval. Average score ranges for each parameter are provided in the manual.

The manual includes 16 references related to the test's philosophical and scientific underpinnings. Nevertheless, no data are provided in the manual related to the assessment's reliability or validity. Because of the assessment's nature and nouveau status, adequate reliability and validity data are not fully available. Specific aspects of reliability and validity are available in the professional literature, however. For example, Shaulis, Golding, and Tandy (1994) examined test-retest reliability across three multiple practice sessions over a two-week interval for both men and women. Reliability correlations ranged from .89 to .99 for men and .71 to .98 for women across the five assessment parameters. Similarly, Bravo, Gauthier, Roy, Tessier, Gaulin, Dubois, and Peloquin (1994) assessed reliability and validity for elderly women. Again, test-retest reliability coefficients ranged from .54 to .94 for the five assessment parameters. Validity analysis for the cardiorespiratory endurance item was conducted by comparing the performances of exercisers and nonexerciser controls. As expected, exercisers performed significantly better than nonexerciser controls, casting support for the validity of the measure. Another analysis utilized factor analyses to develop a composite battery score and the test-retest correlation coefficient was estimated at .81 and was found to have a -.64 correlation with a measure of maximal work capacity. Other reliability and validity data can be found by further review of the literature.

The Functional Fitness Assessment for Adults Over 60 Years offers a unique method for assessing fitness in the ever-growing elderly population. Although many assessment instruments focus on pathological functioning, the fitness assessment emphasizes normal physical functioning. By implication, however, pathological performances can be understood in relation to normal abilities. The only drawback to the assessment at this time is that limited reliability and validity data are available. From a review of the literature, the assessment seems to be still in the second developmental stage, namely development of reliability and validity data. Now needed is a comprehensive reliability and validation study that assesses large groups of elderly men and women from various cultural, social, and economic backgrounds. Obtaining normative data should be a priority so as to advance the assessment to its third developmental phase. Until such data are available, the Functional Fitness Assessment for Adults Over 60 Years remains a research instrument.

REVIEWER'S REFERENCES

Bravo, G., Gauthier, P., Roy, P. M., Tessier, D., Gaulin, P., Dubois, M. F., & Peloquin, L. (1994). The Functional Fitness Assessment Battery: Reliability and validity data for elderly women. *Journal of Aging and Physical Activity, 2*, 67–79

Shaulis, D., Golding, L. A., & Tandy, R. D. (1994). Reliability of the AAHPERD Functional Fitness Assessment across multiple practice sessions in older men and women. *Journal of Aging and Physical Activity, 2*, 273–279.

Review of the Functional Fitness Assessment for Adults Over 60 Years by CECIL R. REYNOLDS, Professor of Educational Psychology & Professor of Neuroscience, Texas A&M University, College Station, TX:

The functional fitness assessment was designed as a field test to assess the functional fitness of adults over 60 years of age and was developed by a committee appointed by the Council on Aging and Adult Development. The manual for the functional fitness assessment clearly designates that it is a test and refers to it as such throughout the manual. A commonsense rationale demonstrating the need for such a test is presented adequately but without references to any literature. A number of cautions therein are also provided related to risk factors (health related) associated with physical activity when evaluating functional fitness of the elderly. The test was designed purposely to allow its administration by "semiskilled professionals" (p. 2) or paraprofessionals without the use of costly laboratory equipment. The manual makes a number of claims as to the usefulness of the functional fitness assessment but these are completely without substantiation in the manual and references in the text of the manual to supportive scientific literature are nil. If the authors did not claim the functional fitness assessment to be a test, it would not be regarded as such by most familiar with the concept of measurement.

The test consists of six distinct sets of items yielding some eight scores. Interpretation of the scores provided is neither reviewed nor substantiated in the manual. The only scores provided are raw scores and no means, standard deviations, or other parameters of the raw score distributions are noted in the manual.

The discussion of reliability and validity from the test manual is, in its entirety, stated on page v. The manual states that the "items are reliable and, in some cases, statistically valid for persons of this age" (p. v). The methods by which such reliability and validity were established are not discussed in the manual. The user is simply presented with claims of reliability and validity with no treatment whatsoever of traditional concepts of reliability and validity as related to the use of measurement devices. The intended interpretations of the test are stated in broad, sweeping terms, once again without any attempt to produce quantitative evidence to support the interpretations so designated.

There is no description of the samples used in pilot testing or in the derivation of any items. The sample size is not discussed and a discussion of error in the measurement process is not presented at any point in the manual. The manual does give the examiner some choice of particular items and instructs the examiner to only administer those items that will yield valid results. This is an appropriate admonition and given the validity data in the manual, certainly argues that no items from the functional fitness assessment should be administered to anyone for any purpose other than to investigate the reliability and validity of this so-called test.

From a psychometric standpoint, the functional fitness assessment is inadequate. There is no recognition of the basic concepts of measurement, not even at the most fundamental levels of reliability, validity, and norming. There is no consideration of potential ethnic or gender bias at any point in the manual. Standard equipment is not provided for the assessment and a considerable amount of equipment is in fact necessary. Examiners are allowed to generate their own materials assuring that administration of the items will not approximate like conditions across examiners. The functional fitness assessment has nothing to recommend it at this stage of development and is likely to result in inappropriate interpretations and potentially harmful recommendations regarding activities for adults over 60 years. Examiners are cautioned strongly not to rely upon information taken from the functional fitness assessment in determining the physical fitness of adults or in making recommendations regarding their activities.

[129]
Functional Linguistic Communication Inventory.

Purpose: "Designed to quantify the functional linguistic communication skills of moderately and severely demented individuals."
Population: Adults diagnosed with Alzheimer's disease.
Publication Date: 1994.
Acronym: FLCI.
Scores, 11: Greeting and Naming, Question Answering, Writing, Comprehension of Signs and Object-to-Picture Matching, Word Reading and Comprehension, Reminiscing, Following Commands, Pantomime, Gesture, Conversation, Total.
Administration: Individual.
Price Data, 1996: $145 per complete kit including manual (31 pages), 25 response record forms, 25 score forms, stimulus book (50 pages), and 3 objects (comb, pencil, mask); $15 per 25 response record forms; $6 per 25 score sheets; $50 per manual; $55 per stimulus book.
Time: (30) minutes.
Authors: Kathryn A. Bayles and Cheryl K. Tomoeda.
Publisher: Canyonlands Publishing, Inc.

Review of the Functional Linguistic Communication Inventory by CAMERON J. CAMP, Research Scientist, Myers Research Institute of the Menorah Park Center for the Aging, Beachwood, OH, and JENNIFER A. BRUSH, Speech-Language Pathologist, Menorah Park Center for the Aging, Beachwood, OH:

The Functional Linguistic Communication Inventory (FLCI) reports that it is designed to quantify the functional linguistic communication skills of moderately and severely demented individuals. Dementia, a progressive deterioration of abilities such as memory, judgment, and abstract reasoning, also affects one's personality and behavior. This test was standardized on individuals with Alzheimer's-type Dementia (AD), but the authors suggest that the test is appropriate for all demented persons who are beyond the mild stage. Given that dementia can have a variety of underlying causes with corresponding differences in communicative abilities, this statement is problematic.

The development and standardization of the FLCI are described in an accompanying manual. The standardization population consisted of 40 individuals screened for AD and recruited from the local community, presumably in Tucson, Arizona. In addition, 91 persons with AD, and who met the same diagnostic criteria, were tested in a 5-year longitudinal study. Approximately half the items in the FLCI came from the research battery used in the longitudinal study. Staging severity of dementia associated with AD was defined by a modified version of the Functional Assessment Stages (FAST) (Reisberg, Ferris, & Franssen, 1985). For the standardization sample, persons with AD were classified as belonging to one of five levels of modified FAST stages of dementia ranging from mild to very severe. Unfortunately, sample sizes at each level of dementia ranged from 4 to 14. Sample sizes appear inadequate for good standardization, especially if testers wish to compare results to both level of dementia and gender. The percentage of persons completing each item at each FAST stage in the standardization sample is reported, but no measures of internal consistency are given. Criteria for item selection or exclusion were not described, nor was information given on differential validity across groups. Persons in the standardization sample were described as speaking English as a first language and being literate in a premorbid state. Subtest performance is reported as mean scores of persons categorized according to FAST stage, and a profile is given on performance on the FLCI subtests of groups classified according to FAST stage. Testers can then compare the profile of an individual client to these standardized study subjects' profiles. Scoring is simple. Clear step-by-step directions are provided.

Test-retest reliability was assessed by retesting 20 of the 40 persons with AD used in the standardization study following a one-week delay. Pearson product-moment correlation coefficients (coefficients of determination) for the 10 subtests ranged from .28 to .78, with 3 having values of .7 or above. In addition, probabilities of concordance (.5 x [1 + Kendall's tau(b)]) ranged from .69 to .92, with seven subtests having values of .8 or higher.

With regard to criterion validity, 13 persons in the FLCI standardization sample were also tested with the Arizona Battery for Communication Disorders of Dementia (ABCD), which was created by the same authors (Bayles & Tomoeda, 1993), and was designed for persons with milder levels of dementia than those normally receiving the FLCI. The ABCD is reported to "correlate highly" with the MMSE (Folstein, Folstein, & McHugh, 1975), the Wechsler Block Design subtest (Wechsler, 1981), and the Global Deterioration Scale (Reisberg et al., 1985). The Pearson product-moment correlation between scores on the FLCI and the ABCD was reported as $r = .78$. The case for criterion validity would have been stronger had the authors related performance on the FLCI to tests not also created by the authors.

Those familiar with the Boston Naming Test (Kaplan, Goodglass, & Weintraub, 1983; T4:207), will be familiar with the items on the naming subtest on the FLCI (pencil, mask, knocker, comb, dart, stethoscope, hanger, harmonica, and compass). Bayles and Tomoeda do not give a rationale for the objects used in the test, nor do they reference the Boston Naming Test and its authors. The same nine items are also used in four other subtests.

The subtest that assesses an individual's ability to answer questions contains three open-ended, three multiple-choice, three two-choice, and three yes/no questions. The writing section asks the examinee to write one's name, a novel sentence about oneself, and to write the previously mentioned nine objects from dictation. With regard to comprehension of signs, the client is asked to demonstrate an understanding of a stop sign, an enter and exit sign, and restroom signs. The object-to-picture matching section includes three actual objects that the client must match with the appropriate picture given nine choices.

To evaluate word reading and comprehension, the examinee is shown one word at a time and asked to select the picture that corresponds with each word. The three incorrect choices are either phonemically, semantically, or visually similar to the correct answer.

To test reminiscing skills, the examinee is shown a picture of an old fashioned telephone and an old-style car and asked if they remember something related to each. The second author of this review administered the test to several individuals with dementia, all of whom had the ability to reminisce. However, the car and the phone were not meaningful to them, and they scored very low on this subtest.

The FLCI includes two commands to follow. This is a limited assessment of an individual's ability to comprehend directives. The pantomime section contains a picture of each of the nine previously mentioned items. The examinee is asked "Show me what you would do with this." The client does not hold the actual object. To determine if the client can communicate through gestures, the examinee is asked to wave, salute, point, and blow a kiss. The client must be able to follow directions to complete this subtest. The conversation section has four items that do not all measure the same type or level of communication, as some only require automatic responses rather than conversational contributions.

The test instructions are brief, yet clearly written and easy to understand. It took the second author of this review 30 minutes to administer. Instructions provide examples of appropriate responses and indicate when questions may be repeated. Administration is easy and requires no special training. Bayles and Tomoeda suggest that results can be used in decisions about patient management, functional maintenance programs (speech therapy), and counseling professional and personal caregivers.

The FLCI does provide useful information to caregivers and professionals about some of the abilities of AD patients. However, its psychometric properties leave much to be desired. For a thorough evaluation, this test should be used in conjunction with an assessment that examines memory, problem solving, and abstract reasoning.

REVIEWER'S REFERENCES

Folstein, M. F., Folstein, S. E., & McHugh, P. R. (1975). "Mini-mental state": A practical method for grading the cognitive state of patients for the clinician. *Journal of Psychiatric Research, 12,* 189–198.

Wechsler, D. (1981). Wechsler Adult Intelligence Scale—Revised. San Antonio, TX: The Psychological Corporation.

Kaplan, E., Goodglass, H., & Weintraub, S. (1983). The Boston Naming Test. Malvern, PA: Lea and Febiger.

Reisberg, B., Ferris, S. H., & Franssen, E. (1985). An ordinal functional assessment tool for Alzheimer's-type Dementia. *Hospital and Community Psychiatry, 36,* 593–595.

Bayles, K. A., & Tomoeda, C. K. (1993). Arizona Battery for Communication Disorders of Dementia. Tucson, AZ: Cayonlands Publishing, Inc.

Review of the Functional Linguistic Communication Inventory by WILFRED G. VAN GORP, Associate Professor of Psychology in Psychiatry and Director, Neuropsychology Assessment Program, Cornell University Medical College, White Plains, NY:

CRITIQUE. The Functional Linguistic Communication Inventory (FLCI) was designed to quantify the language difficulties and retained abilities of patients with moderate to severe dementia. The authors state that results from this assessment can guide patient management, functional maintenance programs, etc. The instrument can also be used in research on moderately to severely demented individuals, when a characterization of preserved versus impaired language functions is required.

As a means of evaluating the language skills of individuals with moderate to more severe dementia, the FLCI fills an important gap in the existing clinical tools available for language assessment. Most language batteries contain items that would be too difficult for moderately to severely demented patients, and hence, would result in "floor effects" with scores at or near 0. This reviewer knows of no other language assessment instrument designed to assess patients with dementia of this level of severity. As such, clinicians seeking assessment tools with better psychometric properties or normative data (see below) than the FLCI have few other choices, as existing language batteries will be too difficult or complex for patients with later stages of dementia to complete.

The FLCI stimuli are appropriate for the predominantly older adult population with dementia, upon which it will be administered. The stimuli are large and easily seen by older adults. Instructions are quite simple and ecologically valid, often using over-learned social conventions in speech (e.g., "What is your name?" "Hello, my name is _____"). (The examiner then records whether the patient gives an appropriate verbal response.) The manual is clearly written and easy to follow. Scoring appears to be relatively straightforward.

My greatest concern with the FLCI is the unusually small number of subjects used in the standardization sample, which consisted of only 40 individuals, all with Alzheimer's Disease (AD; the authors do not state whether they had "possible" or "probable" AD; however, page 12 of the manual implies "probable"). The test authors, in Table 4 of the manual, present demographic characteristics of the subjects in their sample, broken down by severity of dementia. Although a useful way to present these data, the 40 subjects simply do not provide a sufficient n for each of the five severity levels. For subjects with least severe dementia (modified stage "4") and most severe dementia (modified stage "8"), there are only 4 subjects per group. Other stage groupings

have between 8 and 14 subjects per group, a concerningly small number to use for clinical diagnostic (and normative) purposes.

Table 6 presents the percentage of subjects, by severity stage (4–8), who successfully completed the FLCI dichotomous items and Table 7 presents mean scores and standard deviations for the scored items, by severity stage (4–8). Some items (those in boldface type) in both tables present data from both the standardization sample of 40 subjects *and* subjects from a separate, longitudinal study of dementia, whereas other items (in regular type) present normative scores solely for the 40 subjects in the standardization sample. This is confusing, and potentially problematic in that some items have a larger and potentially more heterogeneous n than other items, within the same table. At the *very* least, the authors should present more data in the manual on the comparability of the two normative cohorts. The same criticism about the small n above applies to Tables 6 and 7 for the various stages of dementia severity.

In Figure 1, the authors present performance profiles of the AD patients in the standardization sample study, grouped according to severity of dementia. They state that "profiles for each severity group are distinguishable" (p. 12). Based upon a very small number of subjects, this approach (and conclusion) is not necessarily valid and the authors need to recruit a larger sample on which to test this assertion. Additionally, no statistical tests (such as tests of parallelism) are reported to actually determine if the pattern (and not merely level) of performance is actually distinguishable across groups.

Reliability of the FLCI was determined by retesting only 20 of the subjects, one week after initial testing, and the results are shown in Table 10 of the manual. This interval seems appropriate for this dementia population, as they would be expected to change in severity over time as the illness progresses, and the resulting correlations are acceptable for most scales (except for greeting and naming, and gesture). However, these conclusions are based upon only 20 individuals, and therefore the results on reliability must be regarded as tentative given the small sample on which these data are based.

Criterion validity was attempted to be established by also testing the least impaired subjects ($n = 13$) with a language battery for mildly impaired dementia patients. Although the authors cite a strong positive correlation ($r = .78$, $p<.002$), their results are based upon only 13 individuals. Hence, ultimate conclusions regarding criterion validity must await replication with a larger sample.

Finally, the authors state the FLCI is appropriate for individuals with "dementia," though their normative sample consists only of patients with AD. Therefore, their norms cannot necessarily be used reliably with patients with other types of dementia (such as vascular dementia, HIV-associated dementia, etc.).

In sum, the FLCI fills a needed gap in the published clinical tools available to assess patients with moderate to severe AD. Given the limited normative database, and the as-yet not fully defined psychometric properties of the instrument (including test-retest reliability and criterion validity), clinicians must be cautious in their interpretation of test scores until the psychometric properties of the instrument are better defined with larger, and more diverse, samples.

[130]
Gilliam Autism Rating Scale.

Purpose: Constructed to "help professionals diagnose autism."
Population: Ages 3–22.
Publication Date: 1995.
Acronym: GARS.
Scores: 4 subscales (Stereotyped Behaviors, Communication, Social Interaction, Developmental), plus Autism Quotient.
Administration: Group.
Price Data, 1996: $69 per complete kit including manual (45 pages) and 25 summary/response forms in storage box; $34 per 25 summary/response forms; $37 per manual.
Time: (5–10) minutes.
Comments: Ratings by teacher, teacher's aide, or parent.
Author: James E. Gilliam.
Publisher: PRO-ED, Inc.

Review of the Gilliam Autism Rating Scale by DONALD P. OSWALD, Assistant Professor of Psychiatry, Medical College of Virginia/Virginia Commonwealth University, Richmond, VA:

The Gilliam Autism Rating Scale (GARS) is a behavior checklist that is intended to assist professionals in diagnosing autism. The GARS may be used in the assessment of individuals, aged 3 through 22 years, who display severe behavior problems. The checklist may be completed by anyone who has had direct and sustained contact with the individual being assessed and requires approximately 5 to 10 minutes to complete. The GARS yields standard scores for each of four subscales and an overall Autism Quo-

tient, which indicates the probability of the subject being diagnosed autistic and provides a measure of the severity of autism.

The GARS consists of 56 items divided into four subscales: Stereotyped Behaviors, Communication, Social Interaction, and Developmental Disturbances. Each item on the first three subscales is rated according to the frequency with which it is observed in the subject, ranging from a rating of 0 (*Never Observed*) to a rating of 3 (*Frequently Observed*). Clear, objective criteria are offered in the examiner's manual regarding the frequency of behaviors corresponding to each of the ratings. The items on the fourth subscale, Developmental Disturbances, are rated either "yes" or "no" and require detailed knowledge of the subject's development in the first 36 months of life. When such information is not available, the Developmental Disturbances subscale may be omitted, and the Autism Quotient is based on the other three subscales. The GARS also includes a section entitled "Key Questions" to be used as the basis for an interview with the subject's caretaker. The "Key Questions" section elicits additional information necessary to establish a diagnosis of autism.

The Summary/Response Form includes (a) a response form for each of the subscales; (b) a cover page with identifying information, a summary and profile of scores, and an interpretation guide; (c) a response form for the Key Questions section; and (d) a brief overview of the characteristics of the GARS, intended to summarize technical information about the instrument that may be useful in explaining the results.

Items on the GARS were generated from behavioral descriptions and examples characteristic of autism found in the *Diagnostic and Statistical Manual of Mental Disorders, Fourth Edition* (American Psychiatric Association, 1994) and in the Autism Society of America's definition of autism (Autism Society of America, 1994); thus, the scale possesses considerable face validity. Items were included in the scale if they achieved significant discrimination coefficients and were at least moderately correlated with the scale's total score. Median item-total coefficients are in the acceptable range for each of the four subscales.

The normative group for the GARS is described in the examiner's manual as "a sample of 1,092 children and young adults who had been diagnosed as autistic" (p. 19). Although a sample of this size is quite impressive for the low-incidence population of persons with autism, it cannot be guaranteed to be representative, given the sample selection method. The method involved contacting teachers, other educational personnel, and parents of children with autism and requesting them to complete checklists on students diagnosed as autistic. There was, thus, no verification of diagnosis for the subjects nor any way to guard against selection bias. In spite of these limitations, the resulting sample matches the school-age population adequately with regard to race, ethnicity, and geographic area and is reasonably evenly distributed across the 3-to-22-year age span.

The GARS demonstrates quite good reliability estimates. A study of internal consistency yielded coefficient alphas ranging from .88 to .93 for the GARS subscales. The interrater reliability correlation coefficient for the Autism Quotient was reported to be .88 in one study, with a range from .73 to .82 for the subscale coefficients. A stability study produced test-retest correlation coefficients ranging from .81 to .86 for the subscales and a test-retest correlation coefficient of .88 for the Autism Quotient although the study involved a very small sample. Median item-subscale total correlations ranged from .61 to .69, offering some support for the scale's content validity. Criterion-related validity was investigated in a study of the relationship between GARS subscale scores and Autism Behavior Checklist (Krug, Arick, & Almond, 1993) subscale scores. Hypothesized relationships based on the content of subscale items were generally supported with moderate-to-strong correlations (median = .69), offering good support for the validity of the GARS. A discriminant analysis study found that the GARS Autism Quotient correctly classified 90% of a group of subjects randomly drawn from the normative study sample, further bolstering the criterion-related validity. Construct validity was supported by the finding that GARS subscale and total scores are generally unrelated to age but are moderately related to each other. Finally, GARS subscale and total scores were found to be higher in subjects with autism than in any of the comparison groups in virtually every case. In sum, the psychometric studies included in the GARS examiner's manual are quite strong for a checklist of this sort and will provide the user with reasonable confidence in the resulting data.

The scale displays some idiosyncrasies to which the user should be alerted. The examiner's manual acknowledges that many autistic subjects are mute and lack any form of augmentative communication system. Nonetheless, raters are advised to "encourage these subjects to communicate. If, after 2 weeks of effort, the subject still makes no attempt to communicate, the examiner should omit the Communication subtest" (p. 10). The Autism Quotient can be derived even if the Communication subscale is not administered, but reliability estimates generated for the full scale will not apply to abbreviated administrations.

The Likert-type scale for rating is somewhat anomalous in that a "0" rating is to be used if the rater has never observed the subject displaying the behavior and a "1" rating is used if the behavior is displayed 1 to 2 times per 6-hour period. The rating for a behavior that is displayed once or twice a day is ambiguous according to this scale.

Despite these unusual features, the GARS appears to be a sound addition to the pool of instruments available to assist in the diagnosis of autism. The test development methodology and the psychometric studies are adequate and generally more sophisticated than found for many of the alternative instruments. The manual is informative and the record form is comprehensive and conveniently laid out. The "Key Questions" sections of the scale is an interesting addition to the instrument and helps to overcome some of the deficiencies inherent in a diagnostic checklist by supplementing item ratings with interview data. The choice to print the GARS Characteristics Section on the Summary/Response Form is a creative addition that will be appreciated by users. In sum, the GARS is a welcome contribution to the field and has the potential to become a popular and valuable instrument in the diagnosis of autism.

REVIEWER'S REFERENCES

Krug, D. A., Arick, J. R., & Almond, P. J. (1993). *Autism Screening Instrument for Educational Planning* (2nd ed.). Austin, TX: PRO-ED, Inc.
American Psychiatric Association. (1994). *Diagnostic and statistical manual of mental disorders* (4th ed.). Washington, DC: Author.
Autism Society of America. (1994). Definition of Autism. *The Advocate: Newsletter of the Autism Society of America, 26,* 3.

Review of the Gilliam Autism Rating Scale by J. STEVEN WELSH, Director, School Psychology Program, Nicholls State University, Thibodaux, LA:

The Gilliam Autism Rating Scale (GARS) was developed to assist in the diagnosis of individuals suspected of autism or other serious behavioral problems, to monitor an individual's response to treatment, and to assist in the development of training goals and objectives for a student's individualized educational plan (IEP). The author also indicated that the GARS may be used as a measure of autism in research protocols. The GARS is divided into four behavioral domains: (a) Stereotyped Behaviors, (b) Communication, (c) Social Interaction, and (d)

Developmental Disturbances. In addition, the instrument yields an Autism Quotient composite score. The author describes the GARS as a norm-referenced instrument that yields a composite standard score with a mean of 100 and a standard deviation of 15. Each domain score has a mean of 10 and a standard deviation of 3. Percentile ranks are reported for each of the GARS domain areas and the Autism Quotient.

The GARS manual reported that the instrument is designed to be administered by educators, parents, educational diagnosticians, and psychologists who are familiar with the instrument. Interpretation, however, is reserved for professional examiners who have had training in psychometrics and/or experience in testing and appraisal. Two sources of data collection are available to the examiner. The examiner may directly observe the child or may solicit information from parents, teachers, or other professionals who may have reliable information about the child. Behavioral descriptors for the Stereotypical Behaviors, Communication, and Social Interaction domains are scored on a Likert-type scale ranging from (0) *Never Observed* to (3) *Frequently Observed*. The Developmental Domain is rated on a dichotomous yes/no scale indicating the behavioral descriptor was present or was not present during the developmental period (first 36 months of life). The person responding to items in this domain must have been a parent or caregiver who has had sustained contact with the child during the child's first 36 months. Raw scores for each domain are converted to derived standard scores and percentiles. The sum of the standard scores for each domain are converted to the Autism Quotient. If a primary caregiver is not available to complete the Developmental Disturbances subtest or if the examiner, after a recommended 2-week trial, is unable to observe suitable verbalizations to complete the Communication subtest, the GARS may be scored using the three domains in which adequate responses were recorded. A separate category for converting the domain scores to the Autism Quotient using three subtest scores is provided in the manual.

The GARS was normed on a sample population of 1,092 children and young adults who had previously been diagnosed as autistic. Subjects were selected from 46 states, the District of Columbia, Puerto Rico, and Canada. The age range of subjects was from 2 through 28 years. Consistent with known prevalence rates, 79% of the sample were male. The race/ethnicity of the sample was varied

with approximately 68% Caucasian (or other), 20% African American, 8% Hispanic, 4% Asian, and <1% Native American. Regional data indicated the Southern region was somewhat overrepresented with 40% of the sample. The Northeast, North Central, and West region sample each had approximately 20% of the standardization sample. More teachers ($n = 720$) than parents ($n = 372$) completed protocols in the standardization study.

Estimates of internal consistency were computed using Cronbach's coefficient alpha. Reliability estimates for the domain scores ranged from .88 to .93 with the Autism Quotient obtaining a reliability estimate of .96. Test-retest correlation coefficients (after 2 weeks) ranged from .81 to .86 with the Autism Quotient obtaining a coefficient of .88. High estimates of interrater reliability coefficients were obtained for the Autism Quotient between teachers (.94), parents (.83), and teacher-parents (.99). Individual items were derived from the definition of autism promulgated by the Autism Society of America (ASA) (1994) and the *Diagnostic and Statistical Manual of Mental Disorders: Fourth Edition* (DSM-IV; American Psychiatric Association, 1994). Item discrimination coefficients (correlations of item scores with total scores) ranged from .61 to .69 with the median coefficients for each domain statistically significant ($p < .01$). The authors represent these data as evidence supporting the content validity of GARS items. The manual cites two studies that tend to support the criterion-related validity of the GARS. Studies related to the construct validity also seem to provide evidence in support of the GARS. However, the manual is somewhat confusing regarding the nature of the standardization sample and the subject pool used to establish a measure of contrasted groups validation or the ability of the instrument to provide adequate differential diagnoses. The author stated that a sample of nonautistic subjects from the subjects in the standardization sample with diagnoses other than autism were used to assess the ability of the GARS to discriminate between autistic and otherwise disabled individuals. Earlier in the manual, the author indicated that the standardization sample consisted of 1,092 subjects previously diagnosed as autistic. This discrepancy should be clarified and corrected in future editions of the manual.

The GARS appears to be a suitable addition to the behavioral checklist genre of instrumentation available to professionals responsible for the assessment and diagnosis of individuals with autism. As with any instrument of this type, the examiner is cautioned to seek additional sources of data in order to complete a thorough and comprehensive multimodal assessment. The GARS may be useful in the diagnostic process of identifying autism and may facilitate the differential diagnosis between autism and other disabilities such as mental retardation, speech and language disorders, emotional disturbance, or neurological disorders. The author suggested that the GARS may be useful in documenting progress during behavioral treatment and to assist in the development of IEP goals. However, considering the limited number of behavioral descriptors in each domain category ($n = 14$), it is unlikely that the test items will provide sufficient behavioral specificity to facilitate development of short-term IEP objectives, behavioral therapy objectives, and/or habilitation plans, or be useful in monitoring behaviorally based treatment outcomes. This is not intended to be a criticism unique to the GARS but a characteristic common to many norm-referenced tests or behavioral checklists.

The manual appears to be well written and provides sufficient technical data affording the user adequate information regarding the reliability and validity of the instrument. A thorough introduction of autism, taken primarily from the ASA and *DSM-IV*, is provided. The GARS is intended to be used in the assessment of individuals with severe behavioral problems. The author constructed the GARS with a focus on the *DSM-IV* diagnostic criteria for autism and the instrument appears to have adequate face validity. The normative sample appears to be representative and the reliability and validity of the GARS may be considered adequate.

REVIEWER'S REFERENCES

American Psychiatric Association. (1994). *Diagnostic and statistical manual of mental disorders* (4th ed.). Washington, DC: Author.
Autism Society of America. (1994). Definition of autism. *The Advocate: Newsletter of the Autism Society of America, 26,* 3.

[131]
GOALS: A Performance-Based Measure of Achievement.

Purpose: A measure of student achievement using open-ended questions requiring reasoning skills.
Population: Grades 1–12.
Publication Date: 1992–1994.
Administration: Group.
Forms, 3: A, B, C (Form C is secure and not available through the catalog).
Levels, 11: 1–11.
Price Data, 1997: $17.50 per 25 test booklets including directions for administering; $8.50 per scoring guide;

$5.50 per directions for administering; $19.50 per 1991 norms booklet (separate by content area); $58.50 per 1992 norms booklet (all content areas); $38.50 per technical manual ('94, 114 pages); $19.50 per interpretive manual; $3.07 per Option 1 computer scoring by publisher of one domain including scoring and two copies of the Student Performance Roster; $2.45 per each additional domain; $.16 per additional copy of Student Performance Roster); $540.97 set-up charge for Option 2 computer scoring by publisher including scoring and recording of scores in test booklets; $2.45 per domain scored; $1.22 per domain for Option 3 scoring (school district scores tests and records scores on a scannable scoring sheet; publisher processes score sheets and sends two copies of Student Performance Roster; $.36 per additional domain); $1.53 per domain for Option 4 scoring (school district records scores in tests booklets; publisher sends two copies of Student Performance Roster; $.62 per additional domain); $.43 per class profile ($30.62 per order each additional copy); $.36 per school profile ($24.50 per order each additional copy); $.31 per district profile ($18.37 per order each additional copy); $.55 per administrator's data summary-school ($24.50 per order each additional copy); $.55 per administrator's data summary-district ($18.37 per order each additional copy); $.73 per administrator's data summary-school and district ($30.62 per additional copy); $.62 per student profile ($.18 per additional copy); $.49 per student record label; $.49 per master list of test results ($.16 per additional copy); $.49 per student performance roster ($.16 per additional copy); $.31 per student data diskette; $75 per reel charge for student data tape ($.31 per student); $551.27 per set-up charge for customer data input (plus cost of additional reports ordered).
Time: Approximately one class period.
Comments: Produces norm-referenced and holistic-analytic scores.
Author: Harcourt Brace Educational Measurement—the educational testing division of The Psychological Corporation.
Publisher: Harcourt Brace Educational Measurement.
a) MATHEMATICS.
Scores, 5: Content (Problem Solving [All Levels], Procedures [All Levels]), Process (Applying Mathematical Skills and Concepts to Solve Problems [Levels 1–2], Drawing Conclusions Using Mathematical Skills and Concepts [Levels 1–4], Integrating Mathematical Concepts and Skills to Solve Problems [Levels 1–8], Analyzing Problems Using Mathematical Skills and Concepts [Levels 3–11], Creating Solutions Through Synthesis of Mathematical Concepts and Skills [Levels 5–11], Evaluating Problems Using Mathematical Skills and Concepts [Levels 9–11]).
b) LANGUAGE.
Scores, 5: Content (Narrative Writing, Expository Writing), Process (Skill in Composing, Understanding of Usage, Application in Mechanics).

c) READING.

Scores, 5: Content (Narrative Text, Informational Text), Process (Global Understanding, Identification and Application of Strategies, Critical Analysis).

d) SCIENCE.

Scores, 6: Content (Life Science, Physical Science, Earth/Space Science), Process (Collecting and Recording Scientific Data, Applying Science Concepts, Drawing Conclusions).

e) SOCIAL SCIENCE.

Scores, 5: Content (Geographic/Economic/and Cultural Foundations of Society, Historical and Political Bases of Society), Process (Understanding of Basic Conceptual Social Science Frameworks, Creative Thinking and Problem-Solving Skills, Inquiry and Decision Making Using Social Science Tools).

Review of GOALS: A Performance-Based Measure of Achievement by C. DALE CARPENTER, Professor of Special Education, Western Carolina University, Cullowhee, NC:

GOALS is a series of tests in five areas of academic achievement: Language, Mathematics, Reading, Science, and Social Science. Each area has three equivalent or parallel forms of 11 level tests covering grades 1 through 12. Grades 11 and 12 are combined. With the exception of the area of Language, the tests use an open-ended format of 10 items and have a time limit of 50 minutes. Level 1 and 2 tests may be administered orally. The Language tests utilize an editing task where examinees are required to detect errors and make corrections. They are also asked to compose additional sentences and to answer questions about the passage.

Each of the tests in all areas assesses content and process. For example, the Reading tests include the content of narrative and informational text and measure the processes of global understanding, identification and application of strategies, and critical analysis. The Reading tests present passages and the examinee must answer questions about the passages. Two passages are presented at each level.

For items on some tests students can draw pictures or graphs to answer questions. Items are scored holistically according to a general rubric. Typically, a score of 3 is assigned for complete accurate responses, with 2 or 1 assigned for responses that are either less complete or less accurate. Scoring guides are detailed and comprehensive. A general rubric is explained and examples of answers and corresponding scores are provided.

One possible difficulty is that open-ended questions can have many correct answers and it is not possible to present every possible correct answer. Scorers must be careful and knowledgeable in scoring answers about which there might be some ambiguity. Without extensive experience with the test, it is not possible for this reviewer to comment on the adequacy of provided sample answers.

A similar concern with open-ended response formats and holistic scoring is interrater reliability. Reliability coefficients for interrater reliability are presented in the technical manual and the majority are in excess of .90. The scoring guide also presents sufficient information for the use of two or more scorers to evaluate a large group of tests while maintaining consistency in scoring.

Other reliability estimates are also fully documented. The manual reports internal consistency coefficients for all levels for every test. Reading, Language, and Mathematics tests have alpha coefficients that are usually .70 or higher. Science and Social Science tests have some coefficients of internal consistency as low as .50, but the majority are in the .60 to .75 range. Alternate form reliability estimates are also reported in detail and, of 110 coefficients reported, only 15 coefficients are .80 or greater indicating less than satisfactory alternate form reliability.

Validity data presented include concurrent criterion-related validity correlating scores on GOALS tests to scores on the Stanford Achievement Test (SAT) series and the Metropolitan Achievement Tests (MAT). Most validity coefficients are in the .60 to .75 range indicating substantial correlation with the SAT and MAT. Correlations with the National Assessment of Educational Progress and the Otis-Lennon School Ability Test were not as strong.

Content validity, as determined by information regarding how items were constructed and selected, is available although there is no specific information concerning why specific items were included regarding the domains sampled. For example, no information is provided stating why the number of items on the Language test measuring Application in Mechanics is more desirable than more or fewer items. Similarly, there is no information stating why Understanding of Usage items are included on the Language test. Potential users will have to judge the appropriateness of content and format for themselves. However, each of the tests seems to include items that are consistent with current curricular emphases in their respective areas. The open-ended format is certainly consistent with current trends in requiring production-type responses. A national advisory panel reviewed all items for inclusion and attended to curriculum and potential bias.

Performance on the GOALS tests may be evaluated in two ways: criterion-referenced and norm-referenced. Criterion-referenced evaluation uses the holistic rating scores for each item and for overall performance in each of the four areas. Each item receives a score of 0 to 3 (or 0 to 4 on the Language tests). Those scores are added together to get an overall performance indicator with predetermined cutoff scores indicating mastery of the content and processes measured. A wide range of norm-referenced scores is also provided including scaled scores and percentile ranks. These are based on an extensive national standardization sample.

Many consumers are familiar with norm-referenced scores and informed users are aware of the advantages and limitations of such scores as scaled scores and grade equivalents. Consumers may not be as familiar with holistic performance indicators used on the tests. For example, on the Language tests a performance indicator of 4 means that the student has "a clear understanding of the language concepts and processes," (p. 20), whereas a score of 1 indicates "some difficulty understanding the language concepts and processes" (p. 20). Combined item ratings yield similar indicators on composites such as Skill in Composing and Understanding Usage. Whether the consumer has as much confidence in these arbitrarily set standards is not clear. It would help if some correlation with teacher judgments of achievement in corresponding areas was included. There is no evidence of validation of these performance indicator explanations.

CRITIQUE SUMMARY. GOALS is an ambitious attempt to provide academic achievement assessment in a way that is consistent with the most recent trends in assessment. GOALS is performance assessment and an argument may be reasonably put forth that it is authentic assessment. Certainly the items require production in skills that are problem solving in nature and allow for more than one answer. Responses are not just right or wrong. The quality of responses can be evaluated in a way that is reasonably consistent. As a norm-referenced instrument, GOALS has adequate technical properties. The standardization sample, reliability, and validity information are well documented and are generally adequate. As a criterion-referenced instrument, GOALS is more difficult to evaluate. The worth of a criterion-referenced instrument may be how well it

indicates mastery of content or skill. The scoring system is attractive, but little evidence supports the validity of the ratings.

The manual strongly recommends use of GOALS with other assessments. In that context, it appears that potential users have a promising supplement to most traditional forms of assessment. Consumers have a well-constructed series of tests in five basic academic areas that measure a moderate range of content and processes across several grade levels. The materials are convenient, inexpensive, and attractive. GOALS provides a richer sample of student behavior than selection type test formats such as multiple-choice items.

Review of GOALS: A Performance-Based Measure of Achievement by DARRELL L. SABERS, Professor of Educational Psychology, University of Arizona, and DONNA S. SABERS, Educational Consultant, Tucson, AZ:

GOALS represents an ambitious undertaking—an attempt to provide a full range of norm-referenced scores while reflecting the standards for national curricula and assessment and providing instructional extensions. Test publishers, who have been criticized for not being in conformity with the educational reform movement (Hambleton, 1995), may be expected to produce products like GOALS to provide assessments that attempt to assess higher-level cognitive skills. GOALS "was designed to be a comprehensive response to the demand that classroom assessment mirror more closely the kinds of instruction that students receive on a daily basis" (technical manual, p. 5). By using open-ended questions, asking students to demonstrate their thinking, and awarding partial credit, these assessments appear quite different from multiple-choice tests.

Form A materials reviewed for this report include 55 test booklets (11 levels in each of five subject areas: Mathematics, Language, Reading, Social Science, and Science) plus the 55 scoring guides that accompany those booklets; five norms booklets; and six directions for administering. We also reviewed test booklets and scoring guides for Form B (Form C is secure). In addition, we reviewed the technical manual and read the description in the publisher's catalog.

TEST USE. A test should be evaluated regarding whether it is appropriate for the intended purpose (Rudner, 1994). The technical manual states, "GOALS can be used in any testing program, either as a complement to a multiple-choice achievement battery or on its own for norm-referenced or content-referenced information" (p. 5). Our efforts are focused on the usefulness of GOALS for providing norm-referenced scores and content-referenced scores.

TEST DEVELOPMENT AND CONTENT VALIDITY. When reviewing a test, one expects to find some description of the test blueprint and how items were developed or selected to fit the blueprint. The technical manual describes the goal for content coverage in each subject area, and there is a mention that blueprints were articulated across the grade levels according to instructional sequence. But there is no blueprint shown and no description of how items were selected. Also, there is no discussion of how content was assigned to levels and no evidence that opinion was sought concerning the degree to which the items reflect the desired content. It is evident that using an advisory panel to check for undesirable characteristics was a paramount concern in test development, but the same concern for checking the relevance and representativeness of content is not documented.

The technical manual states that "The GOALS emphasis on higher order thinking in a meaningful context reflects a shared commitment with the International Reading Association, National Council of Teachers of Mathematics, National Council of Teachers of English, National Science Teachers' Association, and National Council for the Social Studies" (p. 11). However, except for a statement that the five objectives of the Mathematics test came from the National Council of Teachers of Mathematics, there is no tie to these organizations for the origin of the content of the tests. The types of content covered in each area are described in the technical manual, but there is no way for the potential user to assess coverage at any specific level from those descriptions. The old dictum applies here: If you want to know what is measured by any one of these tests, take it (or examine it) yourself.

Some technical data are rendered less useful because of the similarity of test stimuli in the various levels and forms. There are three items in Science, for Level 3, that appear intact in both Forms A and B. One Reading passage at each level, 3 through 11/ 12, is identical in both Forms A and B. Although this stimulus appears each time with different specific questions, this duplication might produce some spurious correlations between forms.

Although the goal was to "assess objectives not measurable by a multiple choice format" (p. 6, norms

booklets), several of the language tasks require students to edit stimuli (letters), a skill that some multiple-choice tests assess. Student writing/composing consists of rewriting a sentence, adding a sentence, or giving reasons for titling a passage. To many educators, these limited writing samples will not provide the in-depth assessment of written expression they may seek. But the main criticism of GOALS with respect to test development and content validity is the absence of information needed to evaluate the product.

TEST DIRECTIONS. The general directions for each content area are identical for grades 1 through 12 for Reading, and for grades 3 through 12 for the other areas. There is no explanation why these directions are the same across so many levels. It seems very unlikely that one set of directions is adequate or appropriate for both primary and high school students.

The directions appear to be out of order. The student is told to open the test booklet and look at a specific page that contains a problem before the general directions are read. The student is told to read along as the administrator reads the directions, but not all the directions that are read to the student are printed in the student's booklet. A better procedure might be to provide the students with a copy of what the administrator will read, and then have the student turn to the first item when it is time to look at the item.

Directions also suggest that all tests will take 50 minutes, regardless of level and area. A uniform 50 minutes (plus 5 minutes for distributing materials and reading directions) seems questionable because there are no data presented to show what actual times were taken in the standardization.

In the directions for the Mathematics tests teachers are informed to watch students so that calculators are used only on certain items. These directions are used for all levels, even though Level 9 has no item for which a calculator should be used. However, on Level 6 Item 10 requires a calculator; it is assumed that the teacher is to watch that no student uses a calculator while working Item 9. All students are to be provided rulers with both metric and inch markings, even though not all levels require these rulers to be used. These cumbersome aspects of directions result from having one set of directions for all levels.

Some of the item directions do not make clear what the student is to do to obtain the maximum score. For example, the scoring guide suggests for one item in Level 9 in Science that a score of 3 is given for an answer that is supported by a good reason, but for that item the student is asked to draw a conclusion, not support a conclusion.

TEST SCORING. In each area except Language, there are 10 items per test with possible scores from 0 to 3. These scores are assigned by a "holistic analytic" system that offers separate scores for student performance on different objectives. In Language, there are three holistic scores (0 to 4) assigned to each of two editing categories plus two scores (0 to 3) on open-ended questions. Thus, each test has scores ranging from 0 to 30 except Language where Level 1 has 36 and Level 2 has 42 possible points. The system of scoring and the rationale underlying it are clearly described. With holistic analytic scoring, agreement may be less problematic than agreement associated with holistic scoring of longer tasks. Also, using 10 tasks per test may provide a broader coverage of content than having only one or two tasks per hour test, although some critics may argue that the authenticity is weakened by this choice.

Scorers are told that student handwriting is not important, and this is evident in the scoring guides. However, in Mathematics the length and straightness of lines in drawing a triangle are essential components of the score. Should the student be told that handwriting is not important but that drawing lines correctly is essential? On one item in Science, the rationale for not giving full credit for a response saying two reptiles are different colors is that the picture is in black and white, and therefore color cannot be known. Yet one reptile has black markings and the other has virtually none; so they are different colors.

There are numerous examples in the scoring guides where the scoring seems arbitrary and tends not to be related to the test directions. An example of arbitrary scoring is in Science where on a question about how two things feel different a student can get full credit by writing how they taste different and writing nothing about how they feel. Although the scoring guides caution that response length is not synonymous with quality, responses that give more elaboration than the directions specify do appear to receive more credit. For example, in one item a student is given information and asked to determine a time and show the answer by drawing hands on the face of a clock. Two points are given for writing the time and ignoring the face of the clock; only one point is given for drawing hands of equal lengths that point to the correct numbers on the clock. If this is the way this item is to be scored, the students should be told to write their answer before drawing the hands so that all students have equal opportunity to score.

However arbitrary one believes the scoring guides are, no modifications in scoring are permissible if the published test norms are to be used. Norms are compromised unless the standardized administration and scoring procedures are followed exactly.

CONSTRUCT VALIDITY. There is an abundance of evidence to examine with respect to construct validity for Forms B and C, and a little evidence related to Form A. This evidence leads the reader to question the construct validity of GOALS. For example, correlations of the GOALS tests with the Otis-Lennon School Ability Test (OLSAT) tend to be higher than might be desirable. The correlations with intelligence tests are about as high as the correlations with other achievement tests in the same content area. Hambleton (1995) suggested that such correlations reflect a capability to take tests regardless of content. This type of evidence supports the view that GOALS is just another ability test or that the OLSAT is just another achievement test. Some of the lower correlations with other achievement tests may result from the low reliability associated with the National Assessment of Educational Progress (NAEP) tests used as criteria, but low reliability is certainly not the cause of low correlations in Science when the Stanford Achievement Tests (Stanford 8) and Metropolitan Achievement Test (MAT7) are used as criteria.

The construct validity evidence for GOALS could provide the documentation requested by Hambleton (1995) to support the contention that the MAT7 items purported to measure higher level thinking skills do perform as expected. There are a number of correlations showing high correlations between MAT7 and GOALS that support such a position. However, if the intention was to measure different skills than multiple-choice tests do, there is little statistical evidence to support a claim of success.

APPROPRIATE SAMPLES FOR TEST VALIDATION AND NORMING. Approximately 200,000 students were involved in the research programs, although it is impossible to determine the exact number of students involved in the standardization of any particular test within the battery. The GOALS tests were not normed in the usual manner; rather, they were equated to the Stanford 8 and the MAT7. The samples and the sizes are probably appropriate for equating and for obtaining validity information. Any problems mentioned below with the norms do not reflect on the composition or sizes of the samples.

NORMS. A cursory look at the norms will reveal that GOALS should not be used for normative comparisons. There are serious problems with the ceiling and floor effects. The floor is so high for some levels that a score of a single point produces a percentile rank as high as 8 for an on-level test. In many cases the tests cannot differentiate among the lowest 5% or 6% of the students for this reason. A recurring problem is that there are not enough scores near the middle of the score distribution to have meaningful norms. In some cases, a single point can move an individual as much as 12 percentile points, with differences of 8 points near the median being very common. One should not take scores seriously for individual students when a single item can change an examinee's percentile rank by 25 points. The spread of scores near the median is likely a result of the item selection procedure used in the development of these tests. Given that there are ten 3-point items in a test, it is much more difficult to select additional items for which scores are centered near the ability level of the students. Such an item selection procedure is easy for a typical norm-referenced test such as the MAT7, or for example, in the Scaled Curriculum Achievement Levels Test (SCALE; MMY12:341) where items are selected because they are of appropriate difficulty, and the student is assigned a level of the test near his or her ability.

SCORES. Norm-references scores available are percentile ranks, stanines, and grade equivalents. Because of the spread of scores near the medians of these tests, it is difficult to support the use of any of these scores. Given the wide spread of scores throughout the distributions, there is no legitimate reason for grade-equivalent scores. How would one explain a 2-year difference in performance that results from a single score point?

In addition to the above scores, scaled scores are available that put Form A tests on the Stanford 8 scale or Forms B and C on the MAT7 scale.

Content-referenced scores available are item scores, category scores, cluster scores, total raw scores, and performance indicators. The item scores allow for full or partial credit according to the quality of the student's response, and are assigned in all content areas. Category scores are assigned for editing categories in Language; these scores also allow for full or partial credit. Item and category scores are summed to produce cluster scores and total scores, which are then transformed to performance indicators. Performance indicators are numbers from 0 to 3 (to 4 in Language) used for summarizing the student's performance when accompanied by a statement describing what the score indicates.

The tables for transforming raw scores to performance indicators do not account for the varying difficulties of the tests across levels within each subject area, and the resulting performance indicators are very misleading. A "1" for one cluster may be associated with better achievement than a "2" for another due to the second category being assessed by a less difficult set of tasks. The problem is exacerbated with total scores.

ITEM ANALYSIS. Tables 97–99 in the technical manual show a wide range of difficulty indices for the items in the tests, but do not document how many items were at any given level of difficulty. It is not clear whether any data from item analyses were used in the selection of items for the various tests. Because the problem with the data for GOALS appears to be that the items selected do not produce the proper distribution of scores, a discussion of how item data were used in the development of the tests would be welcome.

There is adequate evidence to show that all items correlate well with the criterion of total score within each test (point-polyserial correlations). There apparently is no problem with interitem consistency.

RELIABILITY. There are numerous coefficients of reliability reported in the technical manual, including coefficients of internal consistency and equivalence, generalizability coefficients, and signal-to-noise ratios. However, due to some overlap in items across levels and forms, some of these coefficients are spurious. For Form A, the median reliabilities are .80 in Reading and Language and range from .74 to .77 in the other areas. The tests are not reliable enough given that a single score point may represent a big difference in the student's standing. The standard errors of measurement exceed 2 and sometimes 3 score points in distributions where a single point corresponds to a difference of 8 or more percentile points.

The generalizability analysis and signal-to-noise ratios are limited to Forms B and C. Also, these analyses do not address important issues of dependability of scores used for interpretation; for example, there is no discussion of reliability of performance indicators even though the data indicate that these scores would be much less reliable than the raw scores for which reliability coefficients are reported.

TEST REPORTING. Although score reports generated by the publisher can be easily read, they cannot be recommended because of limitations in the scores reported. The performance indicators have serious problems due to lack of uniform difficulty among the tests, and the norm-referenced scores suffer from the limited spread of scores. It is probably impossible to avoid misinterpretation of test performance on GOALS.

TEST AND ITEM BIAS. A panel of judges was involved during test development to ensure that the test was not offensive; however, it is not clear what role the panel took in examining test bias. As Bond (1996) has explained, scoring performance assessments has implications for fairness and equity. There is no evidence that there was any examination of the scores or the scoring regarding these considerations. Our examinations of the scoring guides lead us to suspect that these issues should not have been ignored.

The combined effects of art stimuli, scoring guidelines, and test directions could be substantial, especially given the effect of a single point on the resulting score. It is not clear from the description of the test development that there was any consideration by the developers or the panel of judges concerning any issues beyond offensive items.

TECHNICAL MANUAL. The technical data are reported in a very incomplete manner. It is not possible to determine the exact sizes of the standardization samples. The terms "equating of forms" and "equating of levels" do not refer to equating studies; rather, they refer to gathering data for correlations across forms and levels. Form A was equated to the Stanford 8, and the other forms were equated to the MAT7; however, no information describes how the equating was done. No evidence of equating Form A to Form B was included, but such equating is not necessary. Form A would be used by customers who use the Stanford 8 whereas Form B would be used by customers who use the MAT7. Others can use either form. It is not clear what purpose secure Form C would serve, especially when the norms are not valid for high-stakes testing.

Technical information on interrater agreement is not very useful because of a lack of data on the training of the raters. The user interested in scoring these tests will find no description of the amount of training necessary to get scorers to an acceptable level of agreement. There is no information describing how the data for agreement were obtained or who the raters were, an omission that renders an entire appendix nearly useless. This omission of descriptive information on raters is disappointing because there is a sizable amount of information regarding the extent of agreement between scorers.

An example of user-unfriendly information is in the data comparing performance across levels, where the means are reported as raw scores. To see how comparable the scores are, the reader must use the norms booklet to convert the means. For example, Table 96 (page 110; technical manual) indicates that the on-level Social Science mean for grade 11/12 was 8.32 and the off-level mean was 15.57. If the means come from Form A, the norms booklet shows that the corresponding percentile ranks are about 43 and 82, a substantial difference. However, the reader cannot determine whether Form A norms apply due to the way in which the data are reported. Thus, these data are essentially useless for drawing any conclusion about validity or comparability of the tests.

Hambleton (1995) suggested with regard to the MAT7 that "more than one page of text in the technical manual should have been used in explaining the validity results in nine appendices" (p. 610). The same comment can be made about this technical manual. The main problem is that there is not sufficient technical documentation to evaluate several significant aspects of GOALS.

PROPOSED USE. For the classroom teacher not interested in getting norm-referenced information or using the content-referenced scores provided by GOALS, this battery represents an opportunity to evaluate how students perform on tasks requiring higher levels of thinking than are found in many classroom assessments. There is an interesting mix of item types and appealing settings over a variety of content that should encourage the student to think. There is variety in each set of 10 items, although the formats tend to repeat over levels. To obtain maximum benefits from the use of GOALS, the teacher should use the responses to gain insight into the students' thinking and the strategies they employ to solve problems. Should the teacher need a method of quantifying the qualitative responses from the students, the performance indicators are not recommended. No attempt to document growth should be used given the differences in test difficulty across levels.

Because there is no evidence to support the use of a test at the designated level, we suggest that the teacher examine adjacent levels to determine which test best fits the local objectives. To the child in a classroom, real high-stakes testing might be that which affects how the classroom teacher views the students in the class. Thus, it might be important that the teacher have a voice in choosing such instruments rather than having test selection be a state or district task.

The other legitimate use of GOALS might be a criterion for validation of the MAT7 and Stanford

8. If one agrees the GOALS tests measure higher order thinking, the correlations are high enough to indicate that the MAT7 and the Stanford 8 also measure higher order thinking.

SUMMARY. Proponents of authentic assessment may not agree that all of the items reflect instructional procedures and elicit higher order thinking. Editing others' writing and producing a single sentence does not "mirror" real life writing to the extent that some educators will advocate. Classroom activities in science may be more "hands on," whereas in GOALS Science is assessed through writing. Yet, because many of the items ask students to explain their thinking and justify their conclusions, some will agree that students are required to function at higher cognitive levels than in most classroom assessments.

Those familiar with test batteries that provide normative data will definitely not approve of GOALS based on the data in the norms booklets. The problems with the data reported are more major than the lack of technical information and interpretation in the technical manual. Although the samples are appropriate, the tests themselves do not have sufficient variations in test scores to warrant normative use of the instruments. None of the scores provided by GOALS, content-referenced or norm-referenced, can be recommended. However, it is recognized that some performance assessments currently being used are not as good as GOALS.

REVIEWERS' REFERENCES

Rudner, L. M. (April, 1994). Questions to ask when evaluating tests. *ERIC/AE Digest.* EDO-TM-94-06. Washington, DC: ERIC Clearinghouse on Measurement and Evaluation.

Hambleton, R. K. (1995). [Review of the Metropolitan Achievement Test, Seventh Edition]. In J. C. Conoley & J. C. Impara (Eds.), *The twelfth mental measurements yearbook* (pp. 606–610). Lincoln, NE: Buros Institute of Mental Measurements.

Bond, L. (1996). Unintended consequences of performance assessment: Issues of bias and fairness. *Educational Measurement: Issues and Practice, 14*(4), 21–24.

[132]
The Gordon Diagnostic System.

Purpose: Aids in the evaluation of Attention Deficit Hyperactivity Disorder. Is also used in the neuropsychological assessment of disorders such as subclinical hepatic encephalopathy, AIDS dementia complex, post concussion syndrome, closed head injury, and neurotoxicity.
Population: Children, adolescents, and adults.
Publication Dates: [1982–1996].
Acronym: GDS.
Scores: 11 tests: Standard Vigilance Task, Standard Distractibility Test, Delay Task, Preschool Delay Task, Preschool Vigilance "0" Task, Preschool Vigilance "1" Task, Vigilance "3/5" Task, Adult Vigilance Task, Adult Distractibility Task, Auditory Vigilance Task, Auditory Interference Task.
Administration: Individual.
Price Data, 1996: $1,595 per GDS III microprocessor-based portable unit including all tasks, capacity for automatic output to a printer, instruction manual ('96, 102 pages), interpretive guide, 50 record forms, 4 issues of ADHD/Hyperactivity Newsletter, and 1-year warranty; $200 plus shipping per 2-month trial rental; $299 plus shipping per GDS compatible printer; $30 per 50 GDS record forms; $399 plus shipping per optional auditory module
Time: (9) minutes per task.
Author: Michael Gordon.
Comments: A micro-processor-based unit that administers tests of attention and impulse control.
Publisher: Gordon Systems, Inc.
Cross References: See T4:1051 (6 references).

TEST REFERENCES

1. Power, T. J. (1992). Contextual factors in vigilance testing of children with ADHD. *Journal of Abnormal Child Psychology, 20,* 579-593.
2. Wherry, J. N., Paal, N., Jolly, J. B., Adam, B., Holloway, C., Everett, B., & Vaught, L. (1993). Concurrent and discriminant validity of the Gordon Diagnostic System: A preliminary study. *Psychology in the Schools, 30,* 29-36.
3. Kubiszyn, T. (1994). Pediatric psychopharmacology and prescription privileges: Implications and opportunities for school psychology. *School Psychology Quarterly, 9,* 26-40.
4. Hickey, J. E., Suess, P. E., Newlin, D. B., Spurgeon, L., & Porges, S. W. (1995). Vagal tone regulation during sustained attention in boys exposed to opiates in utero. *Addictive Behaviors, 20,* 43-59.
5. Rasile, D. A., Burg, J. S., Burright, R. G., & Donovick, P. J. (1995). The relationship between performance on the Gordon Diagnostic System and other measures of attention. *International Journal of Psychology, 30,* 35–45.
6. Reid, R. (1995). Assessment of ADHD with culturally different groups: The use of behavioral rating scales. *School Psychology Review, 24,* 537–560.

Review of the Gordon Diagnostic System by ROBERT G. HARRINGTON, *Professor of Educational Psychology and Research, University of Kansas, Lawrence, KS:*

The Gordon Diagnostic System (GDS) is a portable, solid-state, child-proof, microprocessor-based unit operating independently of a microcomputer (Post, Burko, & Gordon, 1990), designed to administer a series of three game-like tests. The GDS has been used primarily to provide a behavior-based measure of the vigilance or sustained attention span and self-control (Gordon, 1987) of children, adolescents, and adults with attention deficit/hyperactivity disorder. Vigilance and behavioral inhibition have been considered two of the central components in the diagnosis of attention deficit disorder in children and adults. The device also can be used to monitor responses to stimulant medication (Barkley, Fisher, Newby, & Breen, 1988; Brown & Sexton, 1988), as well as in the evaluation of AIDS-related complex (Saykin et al., 1990), closed head injury (Risser & Hamsher, 1990), Fragile X Syndrome (Hagerman, Murphy, & Wittenberger, 1988), and

Alzheimer's disease (Gordon, Beeber, & Mettelman, 1987). The GDS provides a reading or printout of the number of correct responses, incorrect responses, and failures to respond and comes complete with parallel forms of each task for retesting. The GDS has been cleared as a medical device by the Food and Drug Administration.

Computerized assessment of ADD/Hyperactivity has arisen as a result of concern with the unreliability of diagnostic decisions based upon subjective clinical judgments, informal interviews, and rating scales standardized on small samples of clinic-referred children (Gordon, 1986, 1987). Approximately 1,300 nonhyperactive boys and girls, 4–16 years of age, were included in the standardization. Norms also are available for college students, adults, and geriatric populations. "An additional 1100 hyperactive and nonhyperactive protocols from various subject populations, including deaf, blind, emotionally disturbed, learning disabled, and Spanish-speaking have also been gathered" (Gordon, 1987, p. 57). One limitation of this standardization sample is that the selection was limited mostly to the upstate area of New York and thus the representativeness of the sample must be called into question. Currently, research is being conducted to extend the standardization of the GDS to represent a Puerto Rican sample (Bauermeister, 1986; Bauermeister, Berrios, Jimenez, Acevedo, & Gordon, 1990). Normative data are presented in Threshold Tables, which show score ranges demarcating Normal, Borderline, and Abnormal ranges of performance by age (4–5, 6–7, 8–11, 12–16 years). The author claims that the norms are not presented by sex or socioeconomic status because these variables are not correlated with GDS performance, but this finding is curious because other research has clearly shown a much higher prevalence of ADD/hyperactivity in males than in females (Ross & Ross, 1982).

In studies conducted by the author of the GDS, tasks on the GDS have been found to have moderate but significant levels of test-retest reliability over 2 to 45 days ($r = .60$ or higher) and stability over a one-year time period ($r = .52$ or higher) (Gordon & Mettelman, 1988). The GDS also appears to correlate moderately but significantly with other neuropsychological instruments (Grant, Ilai, Nussbaum, & Bigler, 1990), behavior-based measures (McClure & Gordon, 1984), and a variety of teacher and parent ratings of attention deficit hyperactivity disorders (Gordon, Mettelman, Smith, &

Irwin, 1990). In an independent study using a sample of 119 age 6 to 12 year, 11 month-old ADHD males, only two tasks, the number of correct responses for Vigilance and Distractibility Tasks, correlated consistently with other measures (WISC-R, the WRAT-R Arithmetic, Beery Test of Visual and Motor Integration, and various sensory-motor variable from the Halstead-Reitan neuropsychological battery) (Grant, Ilai, Nussbaum, & Bigler, 1990). Gordon defends this lack of concurrent validity with other major measures used in ADD diagnosis by contending that the GDS makes a unique contribution in the measurement of attention, not assessed by more traditional tests. Gordon also argues that efforts to validate the utility of the GDS have been limited by disagreement among professionals with regard to a consensus definition of ADD/Hyperactivity (Gordon, Di Niro, & Mettelman, 1988). Despite these arguments it would seem clear that this research suggests that continuous performance tests such as the GDS may be useful, but are insufficient alone in the diagnosis of difficulties in impulsivity or sustained attention in children.

Scores from the GDS, such as the Efficiency Ratio (Gordon, 1979) and the Delay Task (McClure & Gordon, 1984; Barkley, 1991), have demonstrated some discriminant validity with regard to distinguishing accurately between groups classified as hyperactive and normal. In another study of school-referred children, the GDS discriminated among children classified as ADD and those identified as reading-disabled, overanxious, and normal (Gordon & McClure, 1983). In a recent study (Wherry et al., 1993) research failed to support the discriminant validity of any GDS score regardless of whether the Child Behavior Checklist-Teacher Report Form or the ADHD Rating Scale was used as a criterion measure. These authors concluded that teacher rating forms should remain the "gold standard" for identifying ADHD youngsters. In one recent study concerns were raised about the extent to which the GDS may underidentify children who are classified by parent and teacher reports as ADHD (DuPaul, Anastopoulos, Shelton, Guevremont, & Metevia, 1992). In fact, it has been found that although the GDS will classify a normal child as ADHD in only 2% of the cases (Gordon, Mettelman, & Di Niro, 1989), it will produce false negative classifications anywhere from 15 to 35% of the time depending on the age of the child, criteria for subject selection, and the combination of scores employed (Gordon et al.,

1989; Trommer, Hoeppner, Lorber, & Armstrong, 1988). On the other hand, the Vigilance Task Commission Score has been found to be particularly sensitive to the effects of stimulant medication, especially at higher doses (Barkley & Edelbrock, 1986). There is definitely need for further validity studies. As Gordon (1987) himself has indicated, the mere computerization of a measure does not preclude the need for "meaningful studies of validity" (p. 54). Furthermore, because many of the validity studies related to the GDS have been conducted by its developers, Barkley (1991) has suggested that there is a need for validity studies replicated by other independent researchers.

To evaluate consumer satisfaction with the GDS, Gordon (1994) sent a survey to a sample of 475 GDS users who were randomly selected from a list of 900 users. He found that the GDS was used most frequently in private practice to evaluate ADD in children and adolescents (89%) and adults (48%). Most used the GDS as part of a multifaceted test battery that included standardized behavior checklists of parents (89%) and teachers (86%), achievement and intelligence tests (75%), formal observations (50%), and interviews with the child and parent (33%). Users indicated that the GDS agreed with other clinical information in about 73% of cases and when it disagreed 92% of the clinicians saw the discrepancy as a justification for further evaluation rather than as test error. Eighty-four percent of clinicians felt that the GDS provided opportunities for direct observations of a child's actual behavior in a standardized situation that requires attention and self-control. A somewhat disconcerting finding was that half the sample used the GDS, at least in part, because its objectivity helped "sell" the diagnosis to parents and schools. Eighty percent of the respondents marked either a 4 or 5, indicating that they were likely moderately or very confident with the final diagnosis of ADD when the GDS was used for confirmation as a part of a multidisciplinary battery.

In summary, Continuous Performance Tests (CPTs) have a long history (Rosvold, Mirsky, Sarason, Bronsone, & Beck, 1956) and are playing an increasingly broader role in the assessment of attentional processes. Unfortunately, research on the ability of CPTs such as the GDS to discriminate children with ADHD from their normal counterparts or to detect stimulant drug effects is limited. Research is hampered, in part, by nuances in subject selection criteria for ADHD/Hyperactivity. "Studies employ differ-

ent rating scales, laboratory measures, observational techniques and interviews in addition to varying cutoff scores and exclusionary criteria" (p. 539, Gordon, Di Niro, & Mettelman, 1988). There is a need for a generally accepted set of research criteria in defining a sample with ADD/Hyperactivity of the sort suggested by Barkley, Fischer, Newby, and Breen (1988). Furthermore, like most other CPTs the GDS relies on visually presented stimulus materials, despite the fact that there is recent research (Baker, Taylor, & Leyva, 1995) that indicates that auditory presentations of stimuli can increase the difficulty of tasks and should be considered in the evaluation of vigilance and impulse control. Nevertheless, instruments such as the GDS may in the future provide clinically useful, objective, convenient, and relatively inexpensive measures of sustained attention and impulse control for ADHD children, adolescents, and adults. As Gordon concedes, no score on the GDS should be the sole determinant of a diagnosis of ADHD. In fact, Rasile, Burg, Burright, and Donovick (1995) found that in a sample of college students the GDS is not a substitute for other commonly used tests of visual and auditory attention, including the Digit Span, Digit Symbol, and Arithmetic subtests of the WAIS-R, Kagan's Matching Familiar Figures Test, the Visual Span Subtest of the Wechsler Memory Scale—Revised, and the Stroop. The GDS should be viewed as providing only one source of information to be integrated with other sources in reading a final diagnostic decision about the presence or absence of attentional problems. When compared to other automated CPTs on the market such as the Test of Variables of Attention (T.O.V.A., 336; Greenberg & Waldman, 1991) the GDS would appear to have a much greater amount of published research support and a longer history supporting its use in clinical settings. In conclusion, Barkley (1991) has argued that a thorough assessment of ADD/Hyperactivity should include direct observations of ADHD symptoms in their natural settings, but concedes that analogue observations such as the GDS may be more feasible. Despite this concession, Barkley (1991) has warned against claiming a lab measure as the single standard for the diagnosis of ADHD. Given this caveat, clinicians should consider the GDS to be one of the several useful tools they might employ in the determination of attentional problems of children, adolescents, and adults and researchers should find the GDS a rich source of data in studying this complex variable called attention.

REVIEWER'S REFERENCES

Rosvold, H. E., Mirsky, A. F., Sarason, I., Bronsone, E. D., Jr., & Beck, L. H. (1956). A continuous performance test of brain damage. *Journal of Consulting Psychology, 20,* 343–350.

Gordon, M. (1979). The assessment of impulsivity and mediating behaviors in hyperactive and nonhyperactive boys. *Journal of Abnormal Child Psychology, 7,* 317–326.

Ross, D. M., & Ross, S. A. (1982). *Hyperactivity: Current issues, research, and theory* (2nd ed.). New York, Wiley.

Gordon, M., & McClure, F. D. (1983). *The assessment of ADD/Hyperactivity in a public school population.* Unpublished raw data.

McClure, F. D., & Gordon, M. (1984). The performance of disturbed hyperactive and nonhyperactive children on an objective measure of hyperactivity. *Journal of Abnormal Child Psychology, 12,* 561–572.

Barkley, R. A., & Edelbrock, C. (1986, August). *Attention Deficit Disorder with and without hyperactivity: Empirical corroboration of subtypes.* Paper presented at the 94th annual convention of the American Psychological Association, Washington, DC.

Bauermeister, J. J. (1986, August). *ADD and hyperactivity in Puerto Rican children: Norms for relevant assessment procedures.* Paper presented at the meeting of the American Psychological Association, Washington, DC.

Gordon, M. (1986). Microprocessor-based assessment of Attention Deficit Disorder. *Psychopharmacology Bulletin, 22,* 288–290.

Gordon, M. (1987). How is a computerized attention test used in the diagnosis of Attention Deficit Disorder? In J. Loney (Ed.), *The young hyperactive child: Answers to questions about diagnosis, prognosis and treatment* (pp. 53–64). New York: Haworth Press.

Gordon, M., Beeber, A., & Mettelman, B. (1987). *Primary degenerative dementia and continuous performance tasks.* Unpublished manuscript. SUNY Health Science Center, Syracuse, NY.

Barkley, R. A., Fisher, M., Newby, R. F., & Breen, M. J. (1988). Development of a multimethod clinical protocol for assessing stimulant drug response in children with attention deficit disorder. *Journal of Clinical Child Psychology, 17,* 14–24.

Brown, R. T., & Sexton, S. B. (1988). A controlled trial of methylphenidate in black adolescents: Attention, behavioral and psychological effects. *Clinical Pediatrics, 27,* 74–81.

Gordon, M., Di Niro, D., & Mettelman, B. B. (1988). Effect upon outcome of nuances in selection criteria for ADHD/Hyperactivity. *Psychological Reports, 62,* 539–544.

Gordon, M., & Mettelman, B. B. (1988). The assessment of attention: I. Standardization and reliability of a behavior-based measure. *Journal of Clinical Psychology, 44,* 682–690.

Hagerman, R. J., Murphy, M. A., & Wittenberger, M. D. (1988). A controlled trial of stimulant medication in children with the Fragile X syndrome. *American Journal of Medical Genetics, 30,* 377–392.

Trommer, B. L., Hoeppner, J. B., Lorber, R., & Armstrong, K. (1988). Pitfalls in the use of a continuous performance test as a diagnostic tool in attention deficit disorder. *Developmental and Behavioral Pediatrics, 9,* 339–345.

Gordon, M., Mettelman, B. B., & Di Niro, D. (1989). *Are continuous performance tests valid in the diagnosis of ADHD/hyperactivity?* Paper presented at the 97th annual convention of the American Psychological Association, New Orleans.

Bauermeister, J. J., Berrios, V., Jimenez, A. L., Acevedo, L., & Gordon, M. (1990). Some issues and instruments for the assessment of Attention-Deficit Hyperactivity Disorder in Puerto Rican Children. *Journal of Clinical Child Psychology, 19,* 9–16.

Gordon, M., Mettelman, B., Smith, D., & Irwin, M. (1990). *ADHD profiles based upon a cluster analysis of clinic measures.* Unpublished manuscript.

Grant, M. I., Ilai, D., Nussbaum, N. L., & Bigler, E. D. (1990). The relationship between the continuous performance tasks and neuropsychological tests in children with attention-deficit hyperactivity disorder. *Perceptual and Motor Skills, 70* 435–445.

Post, E. M., Burko, M. S., & Gordon, M. (1990). Single-component microcomputer driven assessment of attention. *Behavior Research Methods, Instruments, and Computers, 22,* 297–330.

Risser, A. H., & Hamsher, DeS. (1990, February). *Vigilance and distractibility on a continuous performance task by severely head-injured adults.* Paper presented at the 18th Annual Meeting of the International Neuropsychological Society, Orlando, FL.

Saykin, A., Janssen, R., Cannon, L., Moreno, I., Spehn, G., O'Connor, B., Watson, S., & Allen, R. (1990, February). *Neurobehavioral patterns in HIV-1 infection: Relation of cognitive and affective changes and activities of daily living.* Symposium presented at 18th Annual Meeting of the International Neuropsychological Society, Orlando, FL.

Barkley, R. A. (1991). The ecological validity of the laboratory and analogue assessment methods of ADHD symptoms. *Journal of Abnormal Child Psychology, 19,* 149–178.

Greenberg, L. M., & Waldman, I. D. (1991). *Developmental normative data on the Test of Variables of Attention (T.O.V.A.).* Unpublished manuscript.

DuPaul, G. J., Anastopoulos, A. D., Shelton, T. L., Guevremont, D. C., & Metevia, L. (1992). Multimethod assessment of Attention Deficit-Hyperactivity Disorder: The diagnostic utility of clinic-based tests. *Journal of Clinical Child Psychology, 21,* 394–402.

Wherry, J. N., Paal, N., Jolly, J. B., Adam, B., Holloway, C., Everett, B., & Vaught, L. (1993). Concurrent and discriminant validity of the Gordon Diagnostic System: A preliminary study. *Psychology in the Schools, 30,* 29–36.

Gordon, M. (1994). *Clinical and research applications of the Gordon Diagnostic System: A survey of users.* DeWitt, NY: Gordon Systems, Inc.

Baker, D. B., Taylor, C. J., & Leyva, C. (1995). Continuous performance tests: A comparison of modalities. *Journal of Clinical Psychology, 51,* 548–551.

Rasile, D. A., Burg, J. S., Burright, R. G., & Donovick, P. J. (1995). The relationship between performance on the Gordon Diagnostic System and other measures of attention. *International Journal of Psychology, 30,* 35–45.

Review of the Gordon Diagnostic System by JUDY J. OEHLER-STINNETT, Associate Professor of Applied Behavioral Studies, Oklahoma State University, Stillwater, OK:

INTRODUCTION. The Gordon Diagnostic System (GDS) is a computerized instrument designed to measure sustained attention, sustained attention under a distractibility condition, and impulse control through delayed responding. The electronic device is portable, child-proof, and requires no external computer. The GDS directly measures children's ability to perform three tasks, which primarily require attention through correct responding and inhibition of incorrect responding (limited norms for adults are also available). The test is intended for use as one component of a comprehensive assessment for children experiencing difficulties in the areas of attention, impulsivity, and hyperactivity (the authors are to be commended for stressing the importance of multifactored assessment). It is also intended to aid in the diagnosis of Attention Deficit Hyperactivity Disorder (ADHD), the determination of whether stimulant medication is indicated, and the monitoring of medication response. Because of the seriousness of the diagnosis and the frequent resulting medication of children, any instrument contributing to such a diagnosis must meet the highest standard of validity including convergent, discriminant, and predictive validity.

The impetus for developing direct measures related to attention stems in part from the relative absence of such tasks in traditional psychoeducational batteries and to problems noted in using indirect measures such as behavior rating scales (e.g., respondent bias and lack of discriminant validity of the subtests purported to measure attention; see Oehler-Stinnett & Stinnett, 1995 for a comparative review of rating scales). Although many subtests of cognitive measures require considerable attention on the part of the examinee, these subtests are designed to assess such skills as perceptual organization, processing speed, and memory. The tasks also are typically power tests in which items become increasingly more difficult. Thus, although the child's attention level during tasks can be observed through behavior and used as part of an overall assessment of attentional difficulties, the scores represent more than a measure of attention. Also, most of these tasks are continuous for only about 2 minutes, so attention to a discrete task over time is not measured.

One type of measure developed to assess attention directly is the continuous performance test (CPT), which has a rich history in the research and clinical literature. Most CPTs require basic visual perception and discrimination of numbers (sometimes alternative stimuli such as pictures or auditory stimuli are also used), a motoric response to the target stimuli (through pushing a button, clicking keyboard keys/mouse, or using paper and pencil), and inhibiting responding to irrelevant stimuli. Task difficulty may be kept constant, or become increasingly more difficult by increasing presentation speed or frequency of the target stimuli. Difficulty is also increased if additional distracters are included. However, higher-order cognitive processing difficulty is minimized and remains constant. Although these steps increase the likelihood of measuring attention per se, they may also decrease the relevance of the task to examinees. Therefore, motivational issues must be considered. Length of the task in its entirety will also affect performance, with a task lasting 30 minutes more likely to show decrements across time blocks than a task lasting 5 minutes (Das, Naglieri, & Kirby, 1994).

Two of the three subtests on the GDS can be described as CPTs. The Vigilance (or sustained attention) task is a straightforward CPT that requires respondents to press a button when the target visual stimuli (a pair of numbers in the correct order) appears and to refrain from responding to any other stimuli (manual). The child version of the task lasts for 6 minutes for 4- and 5-year-olds and 9 minutes for the other age groups. This task has a standard 1/9 stimulus format and an alternate form in which the target stimulus is 3/5. The Distractibility task, which lasts 9 minutes and has norms for ages 6–16, is a version of the CPT in which distracter numbers appear in columns on either side of the column in which the target stimuli appear. These tasks require visual discrimination of numbers and detection of physical identity of the stimuli (as opposed to having to remember categorical data), sustained attention, memory for digits (minimal in that the target stimuli are only two digits), accurate responding, responding fast enough to avoid a commission error to the next stimulus, and learning to inhibit responding to the non-target stimuli (such as only one of the numbers in the pair). The Distractibility task increases the difficulty of inhibiting responding to irrelevant stimuli and may pick up impulsive responding and difficulties in selective attention when the Vigilance task does not. For both tasks, the Total Correct score is considered primarily a measure of attention, whereas the Total Commission score is considered a measure of attention and impulse control. No feedback is given to the child during the procedures on either the Vigilance or Distractibility subtests; therefore, children must sustain motivation throughout the task. Users must use good judgment as to whether motivation significantly impacts scores and may want to assess this area further if warranted, as noted in the manual. Behaviors indicative of hyper- or hypoarousal, anxiety, frustration, or anger should also be further investigated for underlying factors and/or comorbidity.

A third task, the Delay task, is designed as a more direct measure of impulsivity or ability to delay responding, and was derived through the author's doctoral work. It requires respondents to press a button after a certain time interval (at least 6 seconds for ages 6–16), which is not revealed in the instructions. However, feedback is given to the child to aid in determining the correct time interval and to sustain motivation. Thus, the child must develop a strategy to determine the correct time length, respond appropriately, and inhibit responding before the time is up. Attention during the time interval must be most directed at determining time rather than responding to visual stimuli as in the other tasks. The strategy requirements also necessitate higher level learning, planning, and problem solving in relation to the other two tasks. Efficiency Ratio (ER) or percentage of correct responses, Total Correct Responses (not usually used), and the Total Number of Responses (which might indicate hypo- or hyperarousal) scores are provided. The author states that this task may be related to the impulsivity component of ADHD such as lack of inhibition and delay of gratification, awareness of cause and effect, and deficits in time estimation and management. Given the paucity of direct measures of impulsivity, this task could add important information to the overall diagnostic picture.

NORMATIVE INFORMATION. The normative data for the GDS were derived from scores of regular education children in the Syracuse, New York, and Charlottesville, VA areas collected in the mid 1980s (technical guide). For the Delay Task there were 1,183 4–16-year-olds, for the Vigilance Task there were 1,019 4–16-year-olds, and for the Distractibility Task there were 362 6–16-year-olds. Racial and ethnic makeup of the normative sample is not described. Although these data represent an improvement over previously available CPT norms and have the advantage of being based on a nonclinical sample, the lack of a well-described national sample and the relative date of the norms are weaknesses. Norms for minority children, such as Hispanics, are in development. As other CPTs become available, the GDS will need scores based upon updated national norms to remain competitive. It would also be useful to have norms based on relevant well-defined subgroups within the clinical population (e.g., ADD versus ADHD groups). Although there were statistically significant gender differences on all three subtests, these were found to account for a clinically insignificant amount of variance; therefore, norms are collapsed across gender. The advantage of collapsed norms is that boys, who tend to be overrepresented in ADHD diagnoses, will not be missed, and girls, who tend to be underrepresented, will not be overidentified. However, the interpretative manual does state that girls will tend to score lower. Socioeconomic status effects were also considered impractical for consideration in developing the normative tables.

Age differences corresponding to developmental increases in task performance were taken into account and percentile tables are available for six different age groups (technical guide). This developmental increase in GDS performance lends support to the instrument as a measure of age-appropriate attention level. That is, a critical feature of attention/impulsivity difficulties is a perception by adults that a child exhibits behaviors that may be appropriate for younger children but are below expected levels for the child's age. The test does become less sensitive in the older age groups, and results within normal limits are interpreted more cautiously for examinees over age 14.

Two neuropsychological studies conducted by Dr. Saykin and colleagues (Saykin et al., 1995) utilized 80 and 43 normal adults, respectively. Norms based on these small samples are also made available in the interpretative manual. Until norms based on a larger, more representative sample of adults are made available, interpretation of adult scores should be conducted with extreme caution, if at all. However, the GDS does show promise in the area of neuropyschological assessment with adults, and more research is encouraged.

RELIABILITY. Because the tasks are always administered on the same device, variance that might have been due to differences in computer keyboards and monitors across administrations, as is typical with software-based CPTs, is controlled. Major strengths of the GDS are the circumvention of interscorer error through the computerized device

and the automated printout of results. The direct measure of children's performance also avoids the interrater error that hounds behavior rating scales.

Test-retest reliability was examined utilizing 32 to 90 children (technical guide). For the Delay Task, the retest interval was 30–45 days; for the Vigilance and Distractibility Tasks, 2–22 days. The average reliability coefficient was .76, with correlations ranging from a high for the Distractibility Commission Score of .85 to a low for the Delay Task ER of .60. A one-year retest interval yielded correlations between .52 and .94. The highest reliability overall is for the commission scores. Although these coefficients are acceptable given the relatively low N utilized for some analyses and the retest interval of others, these results do not meet the highest standards for test-retest reliability. The authors should stress this limitation more adamantly in the manual. For example, standard error of measurement should be calculated and utilized in the scoring and interpretation sections of the manual. Particularly on borderline cases, or those involving results that are discrepant from other findings, a second administration should be recommended.

For the Vigilance Task alternate forms, a t-test found no significant differences between groups administered one version or the other. The Vigilance Task form used was also found to have no effect on later performance on the Distractibility Task. No correlation of the alternate forms utilizing the same group of children was reported. Practice effects of the Vigilance/Distractibility Tasks have not been reported. Because the standardization was performed with the Vigilance Task first, this is the recommended administration order.

There is no Total Score yielded for the GDS, primarily because the author views the tasks as measuring different components of the attention/impulsivity constructs. It would be useful to have internal consistency data in the form of alpha coefficients reported in order to examine this issue more closely, particularly in light of the moderate intertask correlations discussed below.

VALIDITY. Although alpha coefficients are not reported in the manual, the task intercorrelations reported by Gordon and Mettelman (1988) yield some evidence of internal consistency and construct validity. In general, the highest correlations are found between the Vigilance and Distractibility commission scores and between the two Total Correct scores. Correlations between the Vigilance Total

Correct and Total Commission scores and the Distractibility Total Correct and Total Commission scores are also significant. However, the correlations are moderate, ranging from -.41 (negative due to scoring direction) to .66. This overall pattern lends support to the author's contention that the tasks and scores measure in common some components of attention/inhibition but also contribute uniquely to the profile of the child being assessed. In fact, the interpretation section reviews each task separately. Given the relationship of the scores to each other, interpretative suggestions and research studies that focus on such scores in common (i.e., profile analysis) would be useful. The Delay Total Correct score is moderately related to the other correct scores, suggesting that perhaps it, too, should be interpreted with similar scores. The ER score from the Delay Task bears little relationship to the other measures of the GDS, even the commission scores, which supposedly tap into impulsivity, suggesting that the ER measures a different subconstruct of the attention/impulsivity construct. Given currently available results, it is important to administer and interpret all tasks to best determine the functioning of children being assessed. It would be useful to have factor analytic data to better determine the task relationships.

In terms of concurrent validity, there is a large body of research relating the GDS to other measures of attention/impulsivity and to traditional behavior rating scales and psychoeducational instruments. Correlations with other direct measures of attention, such as the Intermediate Visual and Auditory Continuous Performance Test (IVA; 22), Test of Variables of Attention (T.O.V.A.; 336), or Conners Continuous Performance Test (CCPT) are not reported, making it difficult to select among these instruments or to bootstrap their construct validity. Correlations with other direct measures of children's functioning have yielded interesting results. Overall, the GDS is not highly correlated with measures of intelligence and it is safe to say that the GDS measures something other than overall intelligence (Gordon & Mettelman, 1988). However, the GDS is more related to intelligence among children with learning problems than for normal children (Carter, 1993; Rush, 1995). According to the PASS theory of intelligence (Das, Naglieri, & Kirby, 1994), arousal and attention contribute to higher order cognitive processes, so we would expect some relationships to occur between measures. Where relationships have been found, in general they are consistent with ex-

pected results. The Total Correct scores are typically more related than the other scores to intellectual measures (Grant, Ilai, Nussbaum, & Bigler, 1990). The GDS has been shown to be related to numerical fluency and memory through its correlations with measures such as the Visual-Aural Digit Span, the Freedom from Distractibility Factor of the WISC-R and WISC III, the Matching Familiar Figures test, and other visually or numerically loaded tests (e.g., Grant et al., 1990). A review of available studies indicates that the GDS adds information to a comprehensive assessment over and above that found in more traditional batteries due to reasons discussed in the introduction to this review. The traditional GDS is less related to verbal-type tasks except for correct scores. An auditory version is becoming available, and preliminary results indicate that the visual and auditory tasks discriminate different subgroups of children with attentional difficulties. These results indicate that the visual GDS alone may not identify all children with attentional difficulties.

The GDS has also been extensively compared to behavior rating scales traditionally used to identify children as ADD or ADHD (Bauermeister, Berrios, Jimenez, Acevedo, & Gordon, 1990; Kinstlinger, 1988; Mitchell & Quittner, 1996; Wherry et al., 1993; Williams-White, 1993). Unfortunately, many of the rating scales used suffer from discriminant validity problems. They may identify children as ADHD who exhibit conduct problems, aggression, and oppositional defiant disorder and miss ADD children who do not display overt hyperactivity and impulsivity. Thus, children described in the literature as "GDS false negatives" may in fact be rating scale "false positives." Even so, the GDS has been shown to be related to the appropriate subtests of the Conners Rating Scale, the ADD-H: Comprehensive Teacher's Rating Scale (ACTeRS), the Burks Behavior Rating Scale, the Achenbach Child Behavior Checklist and Teacher Report Form, and the Iowa Conners. Relating the GDS more carefully to the rating subscales that differentiate attention, hyperactivity, impulsivity, and conduct problems will likely lead to stronger results (for example, utilizing the ACTeRS or the Behavior Assessment System for Children [BASC], whose attention scales measure only attention and not using hyperactivity subtests that confound motor activity with conduct problems). Unfortunately, all the scales confound impulsivity with other constructs such as attention, hyperactivity, and conduct problems, making it difficult to use them in determining the GDS's ability to measure impulsivity. Given currently available information, the Delay Task would be a useful adjunct to behavioral rating scales in determining whether impulsivity under GDS conditions exists. It would then be up to the examiner to use the GDS results along with other data, such as observation and interview, to determine whether impulsive responding in the environment appears to be under the control of the child (conduct problems) or not (impulsivity). Intentionality is a critical component in differential diagnosis of ADHD versus conduct problems, and the GDS may aid in this decision.

It should be noted that the GDS is not a measure of hyperactivity per se, but rather of attention and impulse control in a defined situation. This fact should be considered more closely in research studies, in clinical practice, and in the interpretation section of the manual. The closest the GDS comes to measuring motor activity is in the commission score—a child who has an extremely high score may have motoric inhibition difficulties related to fine-motor hyperactivity. A child with gross motor overactivity may not be able to sit through the test, thus invalidating it, or may have overriding activity that obviously prevents attention to the tasks. This kind of problem would most likely be evident no matter what psychological test was being attempted. In fact, it may be missed during the GDS administration if the tasks are perceived as interesting enough and exacerbated by tests of the child's known weaknesses such as academics (see Roberts & Landau, 1995, for a review of curriculum-based assessment with attention problems). The manual does state that behavioral observations of overactivity during testing should be taken into account. Otherwise, the GDS scores should not be expected to diagnose "hyperactivity" but a particular type of impulsivity. Impulsive responding on the GDS may generalize to a general pattern of impulsivity, but it is more likely that it relates most strongly to impulsive responding on tasks with similar behavioral demands, such as academic tasks. Carefully differentiating attention, hyperactivity, and impulsivity, and the subconstructs of each, should also be more carefully done in the literature and in the manual in order to avoid misdiagnoses.

The GDS has also been used extensively to determine group differences (Kinstlinger, 1987; McClure & Gordon, 1984; Oppenheimer, 1988; Tucker, 1991). The strongest results come from its ability to differentiate clinical from nonclinical groups.

However, much data suggest that the GDS may not be able to discriminate subgroups of clinical problems, such as ADHD from developmental difficulties or conduct problems. Although some have stated that the equivocal group difference results limit the utility of the GDS, it is more likely that the instruments and procedures used to develop group formation in the first place (e.g., DSM diagnoses, rating scales that lack discriminant validity) led to difficulties in the GDS discriminating groups, and that the GDS is able to ferret out the children who do have an attention problem! There is also evidence that children with attentional difficulties due to depression or other internalizing disorders will show attentional deficits on the GDS, suggesting that children with ADD only or ADD comorbid with internalizing disorders will be identified on the GDS. GDS scores that are significantly different from average will identify kids with attention problems and kids with attention problems comorbid with or exacerbated by other conditions (high positive predictive ability).

Despite the ability of the scale to detect problems, the GDS is likely to produce some false negatives due to the nature of the examination process. Children who exhibit attentional/impulsivity problems in school may not display them in a clinical, one-on-one setting during a relatively entertaining task (as those who give traditional batteries often note as well). Children with auditory attentional problems may also be missed by the visual GDS, and the GDS does not measure the full range of attentional skills. It does predict generalization to the academic setting in that it is related to achievement scores, classroom behavior observations, and ratings and children's behavior in school.

Despite these limitations, the utility of the GDS has been demonstrated in medication trials (Anderson, 1990; Brown & Sexson, 1988; Fischer & Newby, 1991). Children who show mild difficulties on the GDS are more likely to be given no or low dose medication and/or be medication nonresponders. This is the strongest evidence that children showing difficulties on the GDS are "true" ADHD cases for whom medication is appropriate. The GDS also is sensitive to dosage levels and can be used in conjunction with other measures to monitor treatment regimes. It has also distinguished children in behavioral and cognitive treatment programs from controls (Poley, 1996).

SCORING AND INTERPRETATION. Scoring is relatively straightforward. The GDS yields percentile ranks that are interpreted through cutoff points determined through "statistical and clinical convention." Scores beyond the 25th percentile are described as borderline, whereas scores lower than the 5th percentile are considered abnormal. It would be useful to have in the manual a description of effects of these cutpoints on identification rates within referred populations. Use of these cutpoints yields identification of children within one standard deviation of the mean (i.e., the 16th percentile) typically considered within normal limits, as "borderline." Examination of the percentile rank tables indicates that the conversion from raw to percentile scores results in the typical exaggeration of score differences in the middle of the distribution. For example, one raw score point difference in many instances results in a large jump in the percentile rank score, and unfortunately, many of these jumps occur right around the borderline cutoff range of the 25th percentile. Use of standard scores may obviate this difficulty and allow more ready interpretative use of the standard error of measurement. In the mean time, practitioners are cautioned to be flexible in their use of the proscribed cutpoints and interpret scores in light of all available data.

The bottom line is that although the GDS cannot, by itself, discriminate children with ADD or ADHD from children with other difficulties, it can add to the diagnostic picture by helping to determine if attentional difficulties are present. Identification of GDS deficits do not rule out comorbidity with or causative factors of other conditions, such as developmental delay, depression, or conduct problems. Also, a normal GDS score alone cannot rule out attention problems. As noted by the author, the GDS should never be used alone as a diagnostic instrument, and should not even be used as the definitive instrument in a broad-based assessment. Unfortunately, despite this caution throughout the author's writings, the case examples in the manual encourage practitioners to interpret the GDS alone as diagnostic of ADHD (e.g., if the score is abnormal, then we would likely utilize an ADHD diagnosis) and pay only lip service to other instruments (e.g., if all other data ...). The author does describe several cases with comorbid conditions or underlying emotional reasons for attentional problems, and it must be noted that even the WISC computerized reports are guilty of the same single instrument interpretation.

The author's handbook on "How to Operate an ADHD Clinic or Subspecialty Practice" is a useful adjunct to the GDS manual. Although the title to this resource suggests we are looking for one type of

pathology, the introduction provides a nice overview of childhood pathology that guides practice in a general direction. The GDS should be used much like a social skills scale—just because a child has a poor social skills score, we do not label him or her as having a "social skills disorder." We assume the social skills problem is contributing to or resulting from other adjustment problems and we look for them. If the GDS shows an attention/impulsivity problem, we should look to other factors as well before assuming the child has "attention deficit disorder" only due to the limited discriminant validity. School psychologists are encouraged to expand their repertoire in ADHD assessment through the use of the GDS and other direct measures of attention in conjunction with traditional psychoeducational measures. It is hoped the price of these instruments will come down as have computerized tools in other areas. Psychologists practicing in clinics are encouraged to work with school-based practitioners in the areas of assessment and intervention rather than making a diagnosis based primarily on clinic measures without consulting school-based personnel in a meaningful way. Specifically, clinicians need to understand the limited utility of DSM classifications in the schools and utilize the expertise of school psychologists in making school-based diagnoses that meet the guidelines of the Individuals with Disabilities Education Act (IDEA) and Section 504 of the Rehabilitation Act in the school setting. One of the primary criteria is that the decision must be made by a school-based multidisciplinary team rather than a sole professional. If the GDS or clinic manual included these recommendations and examples, it would be of benefit to all who are working to help children fulfill their potential.

REVIEWER'S REFERENCES

McClure, F. D., & Gordon, M. (1984). Performance of disturbed hyperactive and nonhyperactive children on an objective measure of hyperactivity. *Journal of Abnormal Child Psychology, 12*, 561–572.

Brown, R. T., & Sexson, S. B. (1988). A controlled trial of methylphenidate in black adolescents: Attention, behavioral, and physiological effects. *Clinical Pediatrics, 27*, 74–81.

Gordon, M., & Mettelman, B. B. (1988). The assessment of attention: I. Standardization and reliability of a behavior-based measure. *Journal of Clinical Psychology, 44*, 682–690.

Kinstlinger, G. (1988). The use of the Gordon Diagnostic System for assessing attention deficit disorders as compred with traditional adppative behavior measures in the public schools. *Dissertation Abstracts International, 49*(1), 72–A.

Oppenheimer, P. M. (1988). A comparison of methods for assessing attention deficit disorders with hyperactivity in emotionally disturbed, learning-disabled and normal children. *Dissertation Abstracts International, 48*, 2610–A.

Anderson, K. C. (1990). Assessment and treatment outcomes of medicated and unmedicated groups of children with attention deficit hyperactivity disorder. *Dissertation Abstracts International, 51*, 1483–B.

Bauermeister, J. J., Berrios, V., Jimenez, A. L., Acevedo, L., & Gordon. (1990). Some issues and instruments for the assessment of attention-deficit hyperactivity disorder in Puerto Rican children. *Journal of Clinical Child Psychology, 19*, 9–16.

Grant, M. L., Ilai, D., Nussbaum, N. L., & Bigler, E. D. (1990). The relationship between continuous performance tasks and neuropsychological tests in children with attention-deficit hyperactivity disorder. *Perceptual and Motor Skills, 70*, 435–445.

Fischer, M., & Newby, R. F. (1991). Assessment of stimulant response in ADHD children using a refined multimethod clinical protocol. *Journal of Clinical Child Psychology, 20*, 232–244.

Tucker, R. L. (1991). The ability of the Gordon Diagnostic System to differentiate between attention deficit hyperactivity disorder and specific developmental disorders in children. *Dissertation Abstracts International, 51,* 4072–A.

Carter, J. D. (1993). The relationship between intelligence and attention in kindergarten children. *Dissertation Abstracts International, 54*(2), 460–A.

Wheery, J. N., Paal, N., Jolly, J. B., Adam, B., Holloway, C., Everett, B., & Vaught, L. (1993). Concurrent and discriminant validity of the Gordon Diagnostic System: A preliminary study. *Psychology in the Schools, 30,* 29–36.

Williams-White, S. C. (1993). The association of attention processes and internalizing and externalizing symptoms among inpatient boys. *Dissertation Abstracts International, 53,* 3801–B.

Das, J. P., Naglieri, J. A., & Kirby, J. R. (1994). *Assessment of cognitive processes: The PASS theory of intelligence.* Boston: Allyn & Bacon.

Oehler-Stinnett, J. J., & Stinnett, T. A. (1995). Teacher Rating Scales for Attention Deficity-Hyperactivity: A comparative review. *Journal of Psychoeducational Assessment, Monograph Series Advances in Psychoeducational Assessment: Assessment of Attention-Deficit Hyperactivity Disorders,* 88–105.

Roberts, M. L., & Landau, S. (1995). Using curriculum-based data for assessing children with attention deficits. *Journal of Psychoeducational Assessment, Monograph Series Advances in Psychoeducational Assessment: Assessment of Attention-Deficit Hyperactivity Disorders,* 74–87.

Rush, H. C. (1995). The relationship between children's attention and WISC-III IQ scores: Implications for psychoeducational assessment. *Dissertation Abstracts International, 55,* 3144.

Saykin, A. J., Gur, R. E., Shtasel, D. L., Flannery, K. A., Mozley, L. H., Malamut, B. L., Watson, B., & Mozley, P. D. (1995). Normative neuropsychological test performance: Effects of age, education, gender, and ethnicity. *Applied Neuropsychology, 2,* 79–88.

Mitchell, T. V., & Quittner, A. L. (1996). Multimethod study of attention and behavior problems in hearing-impaired children. *Journal of Clinical Child Psychology, 25,* 83–96.

Poley, J. A. (1996). Effects of classroom cognitive behavioral training with elementary school ADHD students: A pilot study. *Dissertation Abstracts International, 56,* 2616–A.

[133]
Gordon Personal Profile—Inventory [Revised].

Purpose: Constructed to assess "eight important factors in the personality domain."

Population: Grades 9–12 and college and adults.

Publication Dates: 1951–1993.

Acronym: GPP-I.

Administration: Group.

Price Data, 1995: $45 per complete kit including profile/inventory booklet, profile booklet, inventory booklet, and manual ('93, 119 pages); $69 per 25 profile/inventory test booklets; $31 per 25 test booklets (select profile or inventory); $15 per set of scoring keys (select profile or inventory); $37 per keys for hand scoring profile/inventory; $37 per manual.

Time: (20–25) minutes.

Comments: Combination of Gordon Personal Profile and Gordon Personal Inventory; separate booklet editions still available.

Author: Leonard V. Gordon.

Publisher: The Psychological Corporation.

a) GORDON PERSONAL PROFILE.

Scores, 5: Ascendancy, Responsibility, Emotional Stability, Sociability, Self-Esteem (Total).

b) GORDON PERSONAL INVENTORY.

Scores, 4: Cautiousness, Original Thinking, Personal Relations, Vigor.

Cross References: See T4:1053 (2 references); for reviews of an earlier edition by Douglas Fuchs and Alfred B. Heilbrun, Jr., see 10:128 (4 references); see also 9:444 (1 reference), T3:966 (6 references), 8:568 (34 references), 8:569 (52 references), T2:1194 (56 references), and P:93 (23 references); for reviews by Charles F. Dicken and Alfred B. Heilbrun, Jr., see 6:102 (13 references) and 6:103 (25 references); for reviews by Benno G. Fricke and John A. Radcliffe and excerpted reviews by Laurance F. Shaffer and Laurence Siegel, see 5:58 and 5:59 (16 references).

TEST REFERENCES
1. Watts, F. N., Webster, S. M., Morley, C. J., & Cohen, J. (1992). Expedition stress and personality change. *British Journal of Psychology, 83,* 337-341.

2. Kentle, R. L. (1994). Correlation of scores of the Eysenck Personality Inventory with those on the Gordon Personal Profile and Inventory. *Psychological Reports, 75,* 905-906.

3. Torres, R., Fernández, F., & Maceira, D. (1995). Self-esteem and value of health as correlates of adolescent health behavior. *Adolescence, 30,* 403-412.

4. Kentle, R. L. (1996). Intercorrelations of scores on the SONSO Personality Inventory and on the Gordon Personal Profile and Inventory. *Psychological Reports, 78,* 255-258.

Review of the Gordon Personal Profile—Inventory [Revised] by ROBERT M. GUION, Distinguished University Professor Emeritus, Bowling Green State University, Bowling Green, OH:

The 1950s saw a flurry of test and inventory construction. Psychologists who had served in military psychological research centers and had seen successes attributable to good testing continued the work as civilians. Some instruments developed during this period have faded, but some remain high on the lists of favorites. Among the latter were the Gordon Personal Profile (GPP) and the Gordon Personal Inventory (GPI), later issued together as sections of the Gordon Personal Profile—Inventory (GPP-I).

Each section measures four factor-analytically defined constructs using forced-choice tetrads. Each tetrad has one item reflecting each factor; two of them are high- and two are low-preference items, based on prior scaling. The respondent must indicate the most and the least self-descriptive items. A ninth construct, Self-Esteem, is the sum of the four scores on the Profile section. Worth noting, however, is that a sum of scores on presumably independent traits may be seen as a response set, not as a measure of a further trait (e.g., the sum of GPI scores in Kriedt & Dawson, 1961). A "Global Edition" has been developed for use (in English) in countries other than the United States; it was developed by editing items to avoid phrases likely to be misinterpreted in other cultures.

Scores are reliable enough. Coefficient alpha is the appropriate reliability estimate for factorial scales; except for one coefficient of .79, all of the coefficients alpha in three samples were in the .80s. Short-term (2 months) and long-term (up to 4-year intervals) test-retest reliabilities are reported. They vary, of course, but on average, the traits appear to be fairly stable and reliably measured by the GPP-I.

Personality and related social perceptions and stereotypes are changeable; because many people now consider separate norms for men and women politically incorrect, the new manual provides norms for male, female, and combined samples. Psychometric theory has surely changed; concepts of validity, for example, have changed from correlations with criteria, through the misguided era of division into "three kinds" of validity, to the comprehensive, multifaceted evaluation encouraged by Messick (1989). Considering such changes, one may ask if these inventories can be recommended for practical use four decades after their development.

Only the manual has been revised, not the GPP-I itself; the GPP-I manual and its implications for evaluating the instrument must be evaluated against current standards, not those of 40 years ago. In my judgment, it falls short, but no more than most other current test manuals. I perceive these shortcomings:

1. Technical data are sparse. In some tables, means are presented without variances or standard deviations. A 2-point significant difference between mean scores of black and white student teachers on Emotional Stability is the largest of four significant differences in two samples (i.e., 16 comparisons), a fact hard to interpret without knowing the relative variances of the different scales in the subgroups in these samples.

2. Some topics are documented only with old data. Bias is an important topic. One kind of bias is faking, but the most recent fakability study cited was published in 1973. Ethnic bias probably is of greater contemporary concern, but it, too, is addressed only by old studies.

3. Factor analytic bases are given superficial treatment. Both sections of the GPP-I are based on factor analytic research. Two tables show the relevant factor loadings of some items. Only some of the items are listed, and it is not clear how these particular items were chosen as no information is given about cross-loadings on the "wrong" factors. Moreover, although the factor loadings shown are indeed strong, no information is offered about the method of factor analysis and how it did or did not overcome the problem of the lack of operational independence of the variables; the ipsative nature of forced-choice measurement precludes such independence.

4. Only zero-order criterion-related validity coefficients are reported, without correction for criterion unreliability or variance restriction. The original validation samples consisted of 55 male and 63 female students living in dormitories. Criteria were peer ratings on the constructs measured by the GPP-I; validity coefficients ranged from .39 to .73. Contemporary research standards seem to require population estimates, to seek more samples, and maybe to look toward meta-analysis. Would corrected coefficients differ as greatly from scale to scale? Would they be in the same order? The manual does not say, either for the original study or for more recent ones.

Some information that would help in the manual is in the studies cited. In the originals I checked, the evidence generally supports assertions that the eight constructs (nine counting Self-Esteem) are validly measured, but the manual alone does not give enough support. It is worth noting that the manual is not limited to the old studies of GPP-I development; roughly half of the studies cited appeared throughout the 20 years preceding the manual revision.

As in earlier editions, correlations with other tests and inventories are reported. Language is a perennial problem in personality assessment; different developers use different words for basically the same construct or the same words for different constructs. Nevertheless, the score, particularly for the GPP section, converge as one would expect—further evidence of construct validity. Still more evidence comes from factor analytic reports, from the independence of these scales (except perhaps the Original Thinking scale), from cognitive abilities, and from the generally low intercorrelations among the eight scales.

The manual reports many criterion-related coefficients in a variety of educational, employment, and military settings. Many are small, many are substantial, but most are in the conventional levels of .20s and .30s.

The GPP-I has been used in employment and academic selection and in guidance and counseling, as well as in research and training programs. The individualized uses call for extensive norms, provided in 17 tables. Sample sizes for college and high school student norms are in the thousands; those for adult men and women are substantially smaller, less than 500 combined cases, and those for specific occupations smaller yet. An aggregated table of people employed in a miscellany of jobs was large, nearly 2,500 cases. The important thing about the norms, however, is not the number of tables or the sizes of the samples; it is that the norms were developed by fitting curves to empirical data rather than using raw numbers. This attention to fitting statistical or psychological theory to data has been characteristic of the GPP-I all along. Its endurance over the years seems testimony to the value of this approach.

Which brings us back to the question: Can the GPP-I be recommended for practical use after more than four decades? I think it can, and I so recommend. The basic eight constructs seem stable and validly measured; there is evidence that the scores can be valid predictors. There are other, newer personality inventories, but I have no evidence that they are better. Many of them, like the GPP-I, were based on factor-analytically derived theories. Some of them are using newer theories, such as the five-factor model. The GPP-I seems to have anticipated both the five-factor model and some objections to it; like Funder (1991) and Hough (1992), Gordon thinks the reduction to five factors obscures some important distinctions. I think it is possible that contemporary thinking in personality theory may be catching up, not surpassing the original GPP-I thinking.

REVIEWER'S REFERENCES

Kriedt, P. H., & Dawson, R. I. (1961). Response set and the prediction of clerical job performance. *Journal of Applied Psychology, 45,* 175–178.

Messick, S. (1989). Validity. In R. L. Linn (Ed.), *Educational Measurement* (3rd ed.) (pp. 13–103). New York: American Council on Education and Macmillan.

Funder, D. C. (1991). Global traits: A neo-Allportian approach to personality. *Psychological Science, 2,* 31–39.

Hough, L. M. (1992). The "big five" personality variables—construct confusion: Description versus prediction. *Human Performance, 5,* 139–155.

Review of the Gordon Personal Profile—Inventory [Revised] by ALLEN K. HESS, Distinguished Research Professor and Department Head, Department of Psychology, Auburn University at Montgomery, Montgomery, AL:

The Gordon Personal Profile—Inventory (GPP-I) is a "quasi-ipsative" amalgam of the Gordon Personal Profile (GPP) and the Gordon Personal Inventory (GPI). The GPP-I is self-administered, taking 20 to 25 minutes to complete. Four and a half decades ago the GPP was designed to contrast forced-choice and traditional questionnaire methods of personality measurement. The author reviewed Cattell's personality factor research and selected four factors to form the GPP. Four additional factors were developed to augment the taxonomy to provide a better basis for making predictions. Theoretically, the dimensions Cattell derived factorially parallel those of the "Big Five" and are represented on the combined GPP-I with the Big Five Extraversion split into the Ascendancy and Sociability scales. Thus, the GPP-I and its forbearers were intended to tap the basic "temperament domain" or dimensions of personality.

ITEM AND SCALE DEVELOPMENT. The author developed two sets of 150 items. Subjecting them to factor analysis, he developed a four-scale measure, the GPP. No item or scale inclusion criteria, such as factor loadings of items or confirmatory factor analysis for scales, are presented in the manual. The GPI apparently went through the same factor-analytic birth but no inclusion criteria for GPI items or scales are presented. The GPP has 18 tetrads (four items per tetrad for a total of 72 personality descriptors), the GPI is composed of 20 tetrads, and the combined form, GPP-I, has 38 tetrads. The respondent is asked to mark the item most like and least like himself or herself. A typical tetrad reads: "inclined to become very annoyed at people … likes to keep 'on the go' all the time … would rather not take chances or run risks … prefers work requiring little or no original thought." Each tetrad was designed to have two items that have "high-preference" value and two that have "low-preference" value. Preference values tap social desirability but the method used to equate high items and low items is not specified in the manual. The Inventory yields nine scale scores. Four of the scales were developed as the GPP: Ascendancy (A), Responsibility (R), Emotional Stability (E), and Sociability (S), and four are derived from the GPP: Cautiousness (C), Original Thinking (0), Personal Relations (P), and Vigor (V). A ninth scale, Self-Esteem (SE), is the sum of the GPS's four scales.

RELIABILITY. Split-half reliability coefficients for the GPP's A, R, E, and S scales range from .74 to .89; coefficient alphas range from .82 to .88. Stability coefficients for the GPP-I on a French employee sample (2-month retest), a U.S. Naval recruit sample (29-week retest), and a Dutch steel worker sample (4-year retest) ranged from .88 (C) to .77 (A) for the first sample, from .50 (E) to .79 (0) for the U.S. sample, and from .26 (R) to .68 (A) for the Dutch sample. Ipsative measures produce inflated correlations because the scores are dependent. That is, for one to score highly on one scale one must not endorse items on some competing scale or scales, incurring colinearity or inherent intercorrelations between scales. An ipsative measure faces a psychometric hurdle to show the items composing tetrads are equivalent in all respects. Otherwise, the content may be overridden by such irrelevant and distorting factors as ease of item endorsement in affecting item endorsement. Thus, an item of the Vigor scale in a particular tetrad may be more easily endorsed than other scale items in the tetrad or than other Vigor items in other tetrads. This results in responses that do not reflect content or personality differences. For ipsative and "quasi-ipsative" measures the burden to show such equivalence falls on the test author's shoulders.

VALIDITY. Gordon lists selection, assessment, vocational guidance, counseling, teaching and management training, and research as uses for the GPP-I. The validity chapter shows small correlations with aptitude batteries, respectable correlations between peer ratings and the GPI on Antioch College female students circa 1950, and respectable to impressive correlations with other personality tests, particularly those whose development was similarly based on factor-analytic work (e.g., Guilford-Zimmerman Temperament Survey, 16 PF, Eysenck Personality Inventory). Relationships of the GPP-I with tests composed by comparison group criteria or developed from theoretical models, particularly those not using factor analytic methods, tended to show more modest, though still statistically significant correlations.

Because the GPP-I is intended for vocational and industrial selection, it is interesting that it correlates minimally with the Holland Occupational Themes. There are some impressive correlations between the GPP-I and assessment center tasks, Peace Corps deselection, managerial advancement, and salary level years after test administration. The GPP-I manual discusses the importance of representing the personality domain in saving cost and energy in human resource allocation in an employment situation. However, there is no evidence presented regarding the GPP-I's relative efficacy in representing the personality domain in contrast to other personality tests. That is, perhaps other instruments are more predictive than the GPP-I.

Correlations with other criteria such as success on probation or peer ratings of therapeutic effectiveness of hospital service workers, physical fitness scores of physical education students, academic achievement, and teaching effectiveness are significant statistically but suffer the same two problems as most personality scales. That is, the amount of variance accounted for by a .30 correlation coefficient is less than 10%, significant but of little practical import. For example, a study comparing successful and randomly selected optometrists shows a $p < .01$ difference on Vigor, Original Thinking, Sociability, and Ascendancy (.15 to .33) accounted for 2.25% to 9.9% of the variance but yielded scale score differences of 1.7 to 2.8. Thus, creating a meaningful cutting score is not possible and an analysis of hits and misses or predictive accuracy is not presented for any of the selection uses proposed by the manual. The second problem with such a potpourri of findings is that personality scale interpretations are flexible enough that either positive or null findings can be impressively explained. Although it may appear that a successful optometrist should be vigorous, ascendant, sociable, and think original thoughts, why should we expect the successful optometrist not to be responsible, cautious, emotionally stable, and facile in personal relations; scales that do not differentiate the two groups. If the result turned out inversely, could we not explain them equally palatably? The absence of specific predictions and an incisive rationale or clear hypothesis testing leave the many statistically significant findings less digestible.

The GPP-I may have uses in settings that have used it for years and built up local norms. However, the reasons for using it over other personality devices go begging.

[134]
Grandparent Strengths and Needs Inventory.

Purpose: "To help grandparents recognize their favorable qualities and identify aspects of their family relationships in which further growth is needed."
Population: Grandparents of children 6 and over.
Publication Date: 1993.
Acronym: GSNI.
Scores, 6: Satisfaction, Success, Teaching, Difficulty, Frustration, Information Needs.
Administration: Group.
Price Data, 1993: $65 per complete kit including 20 identification forms and 20 inventory booklets each: grandparent, parent, and grandchild versions, 20 profiles, and manual (20 pages).
Foreign Language Edition: Spanish version available.
Time: Administration time not reported.
Comments: Parent and grandchild inventories included for comparison purposes.
Authors: Robert D. Strom and Shirley K. Strom.
Publisher: Scholastic Testing Service, Inc.

TEST REFERENCES
1. Strom, R., & Strom, S. (1990). Grandparent education. *Journal of Instructional Psychology, 17*, 85-91.
2. Strom, R., Collinsworth, P., Strom, S., Griswold, D., & Strom, P. (1992). Grandparent education for Black families. *Journal of Negro Education, 61*, 554-569.

Review of the Grandparent Strengths and Needs Inventory by ROGER A. BOOTHROYD, Associate Professor, Florida Mental Health Institute, University of South Florida, Tampa, FL:

DESCRIPTION. The Grandparent Strengths and Needs Inventory (GSNI) is a 60-item measure intended to "help grandmothers and grandfathers recognize their favorable qualities and identify aspects of their family relationships in which further growth is needed" (manual, p. 2). The GSNI has three versions: (a) a grandparent version, (b) a parent version, and (c) a grandchild version, for use with children over 6 years of age. For each item, a 4-point, Likert-type response format is used: *always, often, seldom,* and *never*. The authors purport that the items form six, 10-item subscales that denote: Satisfaction, Success, Teaching, Difficulty, Frustration, and Information Needs. They further suggest that three of the subscales (i.e., Satisfaction, Success, and Teaching) can be combined to represent an index of grandparent Potentials and that the remaining three subscales (i.e., Difficulty, Frustration, and Information Needs) compose an index of grandparent Concerns.

SCALE CONSTRUCTION AND ITEM SE-LECTION. Little information is reported in the manual on the development of the GSNI, although the measure seemingly evolved from grandparent education seminars conducted by the authors. No item selection criteria or item analysis information are provided. Despite a section in the manual titled "Rationale for the Subscales," which includes the authors' rationale, no literature is cited that provides a theoretical basis for the six domains included in the inventory.

SCORING AND INTERPRETATION. The GSNI is hand scored by summing the assigned response values for the items comprising each subscale. For half of the items, *Always* is assigned a value of 4 and *Never*, 1. The reverse is true for the remaining items (i.e., *Always* = 1; *Never* = 4). With respect to handling missing responses, the authors indicate that based on their experience incomplete items are uncommon but occur most frequently when the inventory is sent home and returned at a later date. They recommend using telephone follow-ups to obtain missing responses and when that is unsuccessful to eliminate incomplete inventories from the research sample.

Although the authors indicate that an item score of 2.5 should be used to differentiate between favorable and unfavorable performance and that an average score of 25 on any of the six subscales distinguishes between favorable and unfavorable ratings, there is no empirical evidence included in the manual to substantiate these claims. For example, no data are reported comparing the mean subscale scores of grandparents judged to be "successful" and "unsuccessful" that would substantiate that 25 is the critical score. The use of a contrasting groups standard setting procedure comparing grandparents judged as "favorable" and "unfavorable" could be useful as an empirical approach to set these cut scores.

The "Profile" sheet provided has little interpretive value given that the item responses of *Always, Often, Seldom,* and *Never* are simply relabeled and interpreted as *Highly Favorable, Slightly Favorable, Slightly Unfavorable,* and *Highly Unfavorable*.

Reporting and interpretation of results is somewhat confusing given that the Potentials and Concerns scores listed in Tables 1 and 2 in the manual are presented in different forms. In Table 1, for example, the Potential prescore for grandparents is reported as the average score of the 30 items comprising the scale (i.e., 2.9978) whereas the Potential prescore for grandparents presented in Table 2 is the sum of the 30 items (i.e., 89.933).

NORMS. No normative data are provided to assist in interpretation. There is no descriptive information on the grandparents, parents, or grandchildren from whom the reliability and validity data were generated.

RELIABILITY. Estimates of internal consistency and test-retest reliability are provided but the information is limited. Although the range of alphas for the subscales is presented (i.e., .82 to .93), specific subscale alphas are not reported. Similarly, the authors state that test-retest reliabilities obtained over a 6-week interval range from .70 to .85, but neglect to report the stability coefficients for specific subscales.

VALIDITY. The manual contains virtually no validity information. A limited summary of a factor analysis is offered as evidence of the inventory's validity, but it is impossible to determine from this summary the extent to which items on the empirically derived factors correspond to the authors' rationale clustering of the items on their purported subscales. A review of the article in which they published their factor analytic results, which happens to be incorrectly cited in the manual for those who try to locate it (Collinsworth, Strom, Strom, & Young, 1991) indicates that "Five of the six dimensions originally proposed by the researchers have been supported" (p. 790). One factor (i.e., Factor IV) contained "items from both the Success and Difficulty Subscales" (p. 791) indicating the authors' proposed rationale structure of the instrument may differ somewhat from the empirically derived structure. Additionally, they report that high correlations exist between items on the Success subscale and items on the Teaching and Difficulty subscales suggesting that these subscales may lack independence.

COMMENTARY. Although the GSNI represents an attempt to develop a measure to assess the strengths and needs of grandparents and may be useful in training as a way of providing personal insight for participants, the instrument is not ready for use as a research measure because too little is known about its psychometric properties. There are many important unanswered questions about this inventory. In terms of its development, there is no substantiation that the six dimensions included in the GSNI are important ones or that scores on these dimensions have any predictive validity. With respect to interpretation, empirical support is needed to back the claim that scores below 2.5 constitute an unfavorable rating. Additionally, insight is needed on how the GSNI should be interpreted when the perceptions of grandparents, parents, and grandchildren differ significantly. Gender differences also need to be explored. Do grandmothers and grandfathers typically respond in a similar fashion? Given that culture influences familial relationships, one wonders about, and should be concerned with, potential systematic response differences among cultural and ethnic subgroups. Given that the GSNI is available in Spanish, Arabic, Japanese, and Mandarin, it would be helpful to use these data to assess the similarity of grandparents' responses across diverse cultures. With respect to the GSNI's validity, one might expect that scores would reflect the grandparents' level of involvement with the grandchild or perhaps his or her age, yet no analyses are presented comparing the GSNI scores across different subpopulations of grandparents.

Finally, the items on the GSNI reflect the roles and expectations of grandparents that have been more traditionally valued such as the satisfaction item "I like how much time my son or daughter spends with my grandchild." Although this is in and of itself not a criticism, it does limit the utility of the GSNI with the increasing number of grandparents who have taken on the role of the primary caregiver for their grandchildren. In a recent study conducted in the Bronx, NY involving families with children aged 5–18 with a severe emotional disturbance (Evans, Boothroyd, & Armstrong, 1996), nearly 6% of the primary caregivers were grandparents. The strengths and needs of these grandparents extend far beyond the boundaries of this instrument.

Although the development of measures focusing on the roles and needs of grandparents is greatly needed, this inventory, in its present form, does not fill this void. Further developmental and psychometric work are necessary if this measure is going to be useful as a research tool and it is hoped this work will continue.

REVIEWER'S REFERENCES
Collinsworth, P., Strom, R., Strom, S., & Young, D. (1991). The Grandparent Strengths and Needs Inventory: Development and factorial validation. *Educational and Psychological Measurement, 51*(3), 785–792.
Evans, M. E., Boothroyd, R. A., & Armstrong, M. I. (1996). *The development and implementation of an experimental study of the effectiveness of intensive in-home crisis service for children.* Albany, NY: New York State Office of Mental Health.

Review of the Grandparent Strengths and Needs Inventory by DIANNA L. NEWMAN, Associate Professor of Educational Theory and Practice, University at Albany/State University of New York, Albany, NY:

The Grandparent Strengths and Needs Inventory is a multi-manual kit, developed by Strom and Strom, for use with grandparenting education classes. The development of the kit is based on the assumption that grandparents have a certain knowledge base and skills that are or should be shared with grandchildren. The purpose of the inventory is to assess grandparents' positive and negative qualities in relation to these skills and to identify areas in which they are in need of further growth. The inventory can be used as a starting point for educational purposes, a research tool, or an evaluation instrument for larger programs.

The kit contains five components. The first is a manual providing background information on the grandparent education movement including references, a description of the assessment tools, the rationale for subscales, psychometric properties, and administrative and scoring information. Also included in the kit are single copies of the three assessment inventories—one to be completed by the grandparent, one to be completed by the grandchild, and one to be completed by the parent of the grandchild. A Grandparent Strengths and Needs Profile Sheet is provided for use by the grandparent, educator, or researcher in identifying individual strengths and weaknesses of family relationships.

Prior to assessment, the grandparent is instructed to select one, and only one, grandchild as the focus of relationship assessment. The grandchild and parent of the grandchild forms are then completed by the corresponding individuals. Each of the three assessment inventories consists of a demographic section and 60 affective items. Demographic data reflect grandchild's gender, age, home situation, and legal and geographic relationship to grandparent, grandparent's age, education, marital status, employment, health, religious and ethnic background, and amount of time spent with child. Similar data are collected from the parent of the child and grandchild. The authors indicate that use of all three inventories is not necessary but the use of all will provide a more complete, in-depth view of the grandparents' potentials and concerns.

On each inventory, 60 affective items are used to assess six grandparenting constructs: Satisfaction, Success, Teaching, Difficulty, Frustration, and Information Needs. Each of these six constructs is composed of 10 Likert-type items utilizing a 4-point scale. The first three scales reflect positive aspects of grandparenting, identified by the authors as Grandparenting Potential. Satisfaction includes aspects of grandparenting that are pleasing (e.g., satisfaction with the grandchild's upbringing and satisfaction with the grandparent/grandchild relationship). Grandparent Success assesses perceptions of skills that grandparents might have such as grandparent-grandchild communication, reinforcement of parent values, and ability to respect and learn from the younger generation. Grandparent Teaching reflects the specific skills of teaching, focusing on "what," not "how," the grandparent can teach. Topics include goal setting, family history, religion, problem solving, etc. The last three scales, Grandparent Difficulties, Grandparent Frustration, and Information Needs, assess areas in which respondents perceive weaknesses or differences in relationship. Grandparent Difficulty reflects perceptions of difficulty related to value differences, lack of communication, and relationship issues. Frustration reflects specific areas of discontent related to activities in the grandchild's home, manner of communication, and social or emotional growth. Information Needs assesses a grandparent's desire for more knowledge about the grandchild's social, emotional, and educational experiences and pressures.

After reading each of the 60 items on the scale, respondents are asked to indicate how frequently that concept occurs. Satisfaction, Success, and Teaching are scored as positive scales with *Always* = 4, *Often* = 3, *Seldom* = 2, and *Never* = 1. Difficulty, Frustration, and Need for Information are scored inversely with *Never* = 4 and *Always* = 1. Grandchild and Parent of Grandchild scales use similar items and response forms.

Item scores may be summed to form subscales or, by combining subscales, to form two constructs (Grandparent Potential and Grandparent Concerns). According to the authors, when examining group data, a mean score of 2.5 per item is considered the cutoff point indicating need for further work. A mean of 25 on a subscale or a construct mean of 75 on the combined Potential or Concerns scale can be used for a similar purpose. No normative data are provided for these cut points.

According to the manual, individual profiles may be established by transferring the grandparent's responses to the profile sheet. When creating this profile, grandparent responses are recoded such that "Always" become "Highly Favorable" and "Never" become "Highly Unfavorable" for the three Potential constructs (and vice versa for the three Concern constructs). No psychometric background is provided for this recoding of respondent affective values. Instructions for the profile indicate how to use it for pre- and posttesting in workshop settings. No information is provided on how to compare the multigenerational information, nor is a profile sheet available that allows for comparison of the three multigenerational assessments.

Only limited reliability and validity information are available. Internal consistency alphas range from .82 to .93; test/retest (6-week interval) coefficients range from .70 to .85. Initial tests of construct validity are provided through references to factor analytic findings. Only incomplete information on these properties is provided in the manual, but references are cited. According to the manual, alternate language forms are available in Spanish, Arabic, Japanese, and Mandarin Chinese; no psychometric properties are discussed for these versions.

According to the manual, the inventory can be administered in groups or individually. Grandparents and parents can self-administer the appropriate form. It is recommended that children under 12 have assistance in completing the form and that children under 6 be excluded from assessment. The manual provides draft copies of the necessary letters of introduction and consent forms for all participants.

Overall, the Grandparent Strengths and Needs Inventory provides a tentative tool that can be used to assess perceptions relating to grandparenting education. Its best use appears to be for educational workshop purposes with self-selected or volunteer individuals. When used in these settings, it should be assumed that the respondent is seeking a closer, more involved grandparent-grandchild relationship. The items and the scoring system may be at variant with some cultural and or age-related values (for instance "learning from my son or daughter"; "taking part in activities"; and "accepting help"). The form, as currently validated, is not appropriate for curriculum offerings related to grandparents in "only adult" situations or multicultural/multiethnic relationships. The reading level of the form and the cultural laden values implied by some items (e.g., "the need for learning throughout life" and "television habits") may also make the scale inappropriate in some settings. The scale has potential for use as a research tool on grandparenting issues. No validity or norming data are yet available for use with the demographic data. Consequently, studies in these areas, as well as investigation of alternate versions and creation of multi-generational profiles, would be appropriate.

[135]
Guide to the Assessment of Test Session Behavior for the WISC-III and the WIAT.

Purpose: Assesses "whether a child's behavior during WISC-III and/or WIAT testing differs substantially from the behavior of other children of the same age."
Population: Ages 6–16.11.
Publication Dates: 1992–1993.
Acronym: GATSB.
Scores: 3 scales: Avoidance, Inattentiveness, Uncooperative Mood.
Administration: Individual.
Price Data, 1994: $59 per complete kit including 25 ready-score answer forms and manual (88 pages); $24 per 25 ready-score answer documents; $29 per manual.
Time: (5–10) minutes.
Authors: Joseph J. Glutting and Tom Oakland.
Publisher: The Psychological Corporation.

Review of the Guide to the Assessment of Test Session Behavior for the WISC-III and the WIAT by ALICE J. CORKILL, Associate Professor of Educational Psychology, University of Nevada—Las Vegas, Las Vegas, NV:

The Guide to the Assessment of Test Session Behavior (GATSB) is a rating instrument designed to help evaluate test session behavior of children administered either the Wechsler Intelligence Scale for Children—Third Edition (WISC-III; 12:412) and/or the Wechsler Individual Achievement Test (WIAT; 359). In particular, the GATSB focuses on the "ethnologically relevant expressions of children's attitudes and conduct" (manual, p. 25) during a testing session. That is, it helps the examiner determine whether there were testing behaviors that might affect the scores the examinees obtained on the WISC-III or the WIAT.

The GATSB is completed by the test administrator immediately after administering either the WISC-III or the WIAT. It consists of 29 statements that reflect three subscales: Avoidance, Inattentiveness, and Uncooperative Mood. The Avoidance subscale consists of 11 items that describe aversion to testing tasks and display of fearfulness. An example of an aversion item is, "Does not respond when queried or prompted." The Inattentiveness subscale consists of 10 items that describe poor

attention behaviors and impulse-control problems. An example of an Inattentiveness item is, "Is sensitive to minor disturbances or competing stimuli (e.g., noises, lights, visual phenomena)." The Uncooperative Mood subscale consists of 8 items that describe specific test session behaviors such as persistence or need for encouragement. An example of an Uncooperative Mood item is, "Becomes noticeably more restless as testing progresses." Each statement is coded as either *usually applies, sometimes applies,* or *doesn't apply* on a special, double-page, carbon test document. Items 1 through 14 are on one side, Items 15 through 19 are on the other. When the test document is opened (by tearing along a perforated edge of the test document and separating the pages top and bottom), the instructions for scoring the instrument are seen inside, as well as a marked scoring system. That is, the answers that were marked on the answer document are now seen on the inside of the answer document—already scored. The scale administrator only needs to transfer the circled numbers into the appropriate boxes and sum the subscale scores. This special answer document makes scoring the instrument especially easy.

GATSB scores are reported as *T* scores. Scores less than or equal to 69 indicate "test session behavior that is typical of the average child" (p. 8). Scores greater than or equal to 70 indicate that the test scores on the WISC-III or WIAT may be invalid due to one or more of the factors measured by the GATSB. When scores greater than or equal to 70 are achieved, it is recommended that the test administrator acquire information from other sources such as teachers or parents in order to determine if the test session behavior was substantially different from the child's typical behavior. The scores (standard and raw) on the GATSB are positively skewed as would be expected. The GATSB is designed to identify atypical behavior during testing sessions. The majority of examinees will cooperate, thus the skewed distribution.

The three subscales of the GATSB were identified via factor analysis. The "Development and Standardization" chapter of the test manual gives a comprehensive description of the construction of the scale, along with a detailed description of the theoretical support for each subscale, and the factor-analytic procedures used to validate the subscales. It should be noted that the instrument creators did a thorough job of validating the instrument.

The GATSB was standardized on a sample of 640 children ranging from 6.0 to 16.11 years old.

Gender, ethnicity, parent education level, and ability level information was collected on the standardization sample. All of these variables were reported to closely approximate the U.S. population. Three age groups were established for the purpose of reporting standard scores. Age Group 1 comprised subjects from 6.0 to 8.11 years of age (n = 212). Age Group 2 comprised subjects from 9.0 to 12.11 years of age (n = 211). Age Group 3 comprised subjects from 13.00 to 16.11 years of age (n = 217). These age groups were constructed based on the results of a series of analyses of variance that suggested that no significant differences in GATSB scores occurred within the identified age groups, yet significant differences in GATSB scores occurred between the identified age groups.

Extensive reliability and validity information are available in the test manual. Reliability values are reported for all three subscales as well as the total scale and for each of the three age groups. Reliabilities range from .77 (Age Group 3; Inattentiveness subscale) to .93 (Age Group 1; Total score). Validity information is presented in astonishing detail. Several factor analyses are reported, each of which clearly delineates the three subscales.

The authors of the instrument recommend caution when interpreting the GATSB. In particular, they recommend that those who interpret the results have appropriate graduate or professional training in psychological assessment. Four case studies are reported in the test manual, which should be studied before one attempts to interpret results from the GATSB. Furthermore, on the basis of exosession validity studies (the relationship between two separate testing sessions), they indicate that how an examinee responds during one test session may not relate to how he or she would respond to another testing session. The results of the GATSB should not be used to make predictions abut a child's school or home behavior.

SUMMARY. The GATSB provides a quick and easy method for assessing test session behavior for children who have taken the WISC-III or the WIAT. The instrument is remarkably well constructed and validated. It could serve as a valuable tool to professionals who are committed to reporting valid and reliable scores for children who take the WISC-III or WIAT, especially when those professionals are working with atypical populations such as students with behavior difficulties.

Review of the Guide to the Assessment of Test Session Behavior for the WISC-III and WIAT by ELEANOR E. SANFORD, Senior Testing Consult-ant, Division of Accountability Services/Testing, North Carolina Department of Public Instruction, Raleigh, NC:

The Guide to the Assessment of Test Session Behavior (GATSB) is an objective, multiscale assessment for evaluating the behavior of children during the administration of the Wechsler Intelligence Scale for Children—Third Edition (WISC-III; 12:412) and the Wechsler Individual Achievement Test (WIAT; 359). The 29-item behavior-rating instrument estimates whether a child's behavior is atypical of children of the same age and, if so, what effect does the atypical behavior have on the quality of the test scores. The GATSB is designed for use with children ages 6 years, 0 months to 16 years, 11 months and examines their behavior during the administration of an individual measure of intelligence and compares that behavior to typical behavior in and out of the classroom. In addition to a global assessment of test session behavior, three subscores are provided that indicate the child's proclivity for Avoidance, Inattentiveness, and Uncooperative Mood.

ADMINISTRATION. The GATSB ratings are based on the examiner's recall immediately after the test session of the subject's test session behavior. Examiners are cautioned that ratings should be based "only on the behavior that *you* [the examiner] observe *during the test session*" (manual, p. 6). The GATSB is easy to score and interpret. Scores are reported as *T*-scores for all three subscales and the total test. Several case studies are presented to show how the GATSB should be interpreted employing a general-to-specific approach. If atypical behavior is observed, examiners are encouraged to talk with teachers and parents to determine if the atypical behavior is situation specific or is the normal behavior. If the atypical behavior is situation specific, then the examiner must decide how the atypical behavior affects the test results. The test developers caution that the behaviors assessed by the GATSB are not the only behaviors that could affect test scores, so an examiner must consider the overall session results before making a decision whether to use the test results.

DEVELOPMENT. The GATSB is well grounded in a theoretical framework based on research examining behavioral observations, expressions of ethnologically relevant attitudes ("types of behavior that reflect a child's temperament and personality" [p. 25]), and previous test session behavior rating scales.

The test was developed through extensive item tryouts with samples of students administered the WISC-R and then the GATSB ratings were completed at the end of the session. The data were factor analyzed and the results produced the three subscales theoretically defined—Avoidance, Inattentiveness, and Uncooperative Mood. The GATSB was standardized across three age groups (6–8, 9–12, and 13–16 years). Analyses were performed that confirmed there were no significant differences in the total score or the subscale scores with age groups, but differences were observed across age groups. Three set of norms are provided for use in interpreting the test results.

RELIABILITY. The GATSB has acceptable reliability for making individual and group decisions. Test-retest correlations (average interval was 1 day) for the subscales of all three groups ranged from .71 for Uncooperative Mood to .77 for Inattentiveness; the test-retest reliability coefficient for the total test was .87. Internal consistency estimates calculated by Cronbach's coefficient alpha ranged from .84 for Inattentiveness to .88 for Uncooperative Mood; the internal consistency estimate for the total test was .92.

What has not been examined is the reliability of the scoring procedure. No research was described in the manual where an external researcher also rated each child during the test session and then both sets of ratings were correlated. The GATSB ratings are done on a scale of 0 (doesn't apply) to 2 (usually applies), with 1 indicating that the behavior "sometimes applies" to the child. Although there was discussion in the manual of why a 5-point scale was not used (to improve clinical decision making), there still needs to be some investigation concerning the consistency of the ratings by multiple raters. Even though the results of this assessment are only used to determine if the child's intelligence test scores are reflective of his or her true ability, the ratings should be validated.

Overall, the GATSB is a well-developed assessment of test session behavior and much research has gone into the development and standardization. Given the growing importance of school and student accountability in the public schools today, this assessment is very important. Many decisions based on test scores are made for an individual child that can have long-lasting effects on his or her self-confidence and future educational and vocational choices.

[136]
Hamilton Depression Inventory.

Purpose: "Designed for the evaluation of the severity of depressive symptomatology."
Population: Adults.
Publication Date: 1995.
Acronym: HDI.

Scores: Total score only.
Administration: Group.
Forms, 2: HS and Short Form.
Price Data, 1998: $79 per complete kit including manual (140 pages), 5 reusable item booklets, 25 summary sheets, 25 answer sheets, and 5 short form test booklets; $15 per 10 reusable item booklets; $29 per 25 short form test booklets; $27 per 25 answer sheets; $11 per 25 summary sheets; $38 per manual.
Time: (10) minutes.
Comments: Self-report version of the Hamilton Depression Rating Scale; computer scoring system available from publisher.
Authors: William M. Reynolds and Kenneth A. Kobak.
Publisher: Psychological Assessment Resources, Inc.

TEST REFERENCES

1. Berthiaume, M., David, H., Saucier, J-F., & Borgeat, F. (1996). Correlates of gender role orientation during pregnancy and the postpartum. Sex Roles, 35, 781–800.
2. Brown, C., Schulberg, H. C., Madonia, M. J., Shear, M. K., & Houck, P. R. (1996). Treatment outcomes for primary care patients with major depression and lifetime anxiety disorders. American Journal of Psychiatry, 153, 1293–1300.
3. Fava, M., Alpert, J. E., Borus, J. S., Nierenberg, A. A., Pava, J. A., & Rosenbaum, J. F. (1996). Patterns of personality disorder comorbidity in early-onset versus late-onset major depression. American Journal of Psychiatry, 153, 1308–1312.
4. Greenwald, B. S., Kramer-Ginsberg, E., Krishwan, K. R. R., Ashtazi, M., Aupperle, P. M., & Patel, M. (1996). MRI signal hyperintensities in geriatric depression. American Journal of Psychiatry, 153, 1212–1215.
5. Lesser, I. M., Boone, K. B., Mehringer, C. M., Wohl, M. A., Miller, B. L., & Berman, N. G. (1996). Cognition and white matter hyperintensities in older depressed patients. American Journal of Psychiatry, 153, 1280–1287.
6. Miller, M. D., Schulz, R., Paradis, C., Houck, P. R., Mazumdar, S., Frank, E., Dew, M. A., & Reynolds, C. F., III. (1996). Changes in perceived health status of depressed elderly patients treated until remission. American Journal of Psychiatry, 153, 1350–1352.
7. Musselman, D. L., Tomer, A., Manatunga, A. K., Knight, B. T., Porter, M. R., Kasey, S., Marzec, V., Harker, L. A., & Nemeroff, C. B. (1996). Exaggerated platelet reactivity in major depression. American Journal of Psychiatry, 153, 1313–1317.
8. Prudic, J., Haskett, R. F., Mulsant, B., Malone, K. M., Pettinati, H. M., Stephens, S., Greenberg, R., Rifas, S. L., & Sackeim, H. A. (1996). Resistance to antidepressant medications and short-term clinical response to ECT. American Journal of Psychiatry, 153, 985–992.
9. Raguram, R., Weiss, M. G., Channabasavanna, S. M., & Devins, G. M. (1996). Stigma, depression, and somatization in South India. American Journal of Psychiatry, 153, 1043–1049.
10. Reynolds, C. F., III, Frank, E., Kupfer, D. J., Thase, M. E., Perel, J. M., Mazumdar, S., & Houck, P. R. (1996). Treatment outcome in recurrent major depression: A post hoc comparison of elderly ("young old") and midlife patients. American Journal of Psychiatry, 153, 1288–1292.
11. Reynolds, C. F., III, Frank, E., Perel, J. M., Mazumdar, S., Dew, M. A., Begley, A., Houck, P. R., Hall, M., Mulsant, B., Shear, M. K., Miller, M. D., Cornes, C., & Kupfer, D. (1996). High relapse rate after discontinuation of adjunctive medication for elderly patients with recurrent major depression. American Journal of Psychiatry, 153, 1418–1422.
12. Roy-Byrne, P., Wingerson, D. K., Radant, A., Greenblatt, D. J., & Cowley, D. S. (1996). Reduced benzodiazepine sensitivity in patients with panic disorder: Comparison with patients with obsessive-compulsive disorder and normal subjects. American Journal of Psychiatry, 153, 1444–1449.
13. Schwartz, P. J., Brown, C., Wehr, T. A., & Rosenthal, N. E. (1996). Winter seasonal affective disorder: A follow-up study of the first 59 patients of the National Institute of Mental Health seasonal studies program. American Journal of Psychiatry, 153, 1028–1036.
14. Thase, M. E., Dubé, S., Bowler, K., Howland, R. H., Myers, J. E., Friedman, E., & Jarrett, D. B. (1996). Hypothalamic-pituitary-adrenocortical activity and response to cognitive behavior therapy in unmedicated hospitalized depressed patients. American Journal of Psychiatry, 153, 886–891.
15. Weiner, M. F., Risser, R. C., Cullum, M., Honig, L., White, C., III, Speciale, S., & Rosenberg, R. N. (1996). Alzheimer's Disease and its Lewy body variant: A clinical analysis of post mortem verified cases. American Journal of Psychiatry, 153, 1269–1273.
16. Wilens, T. E., Biederman, J., Prince, J., Spencer, T. J., Faraone, S. V., Warburton, R., Schleifer, D., Harding, M., Linehan, C., & Geller, D. (1996). Six-week, double-blind, placebo-controlled study of desipramine for adult attention deficit hyperactivity disorder. American Journal of Psychiatry, 153, 1147–1153.
17. Zanardi, R., Franchini, L., Gasperini, M., Perez, J., & Smeraldi, E. (1996). Double-blind controlled trial of sertraline versus paroxetine in the treatment of delusional depression. American Journal of Psychiatry, 153, 1631–1633.

18. Zlotnick, C., Shea, T., Pilkonis, P. A., Elkin, I., & Ryan, C. (1996). Gender, type of treatment, dysfunctional attitudes, social support, life events, and depressive symptoms over naturalistic follow-up. *American Journal of Psychiatry, 153*, 1021–1027.

19. Alexander, G. E., Furey, M. L., Grady, C. L., Pietrini, P., Brady, D. R., Mentis, M. J., & Schapiro, M. B. (1997). Association of premorbid intellectual function with cerebral metabolism in Alzheimer's Disease: Implications for the cognitive reserve hypothesis. *American Journal of Psychiatry, 154*, 165–172.

20. Alexopoulos, G. S., Meyers, B. S., Young, R. C., Kakuma, T., Silbersweig, D., & Charlson, M. (1997). Clinically defined vascular depression. *American Journal of Psychiatry, 154*, 562–565.

21. Amsterdam, J. D., Fawcett, J., Quitkin, F. M., Reimherr, F. W., Rosenbaum, J. F., Michelson, D., Hornig-Rohan, M., & Beasley, C. M. (1997). Fluoxetine and norfluoxetine plasma concentrations in major depression: A multicenter study. *American Journal of Psychiatry, 154*, 963–969.

22. Benight, C. C., Antoni, M. H., Kilbourn, K., Ironson, G., Kumar, M. A., Fletcher, M. A., Redwine, L., Baum, A., & Schnetderman, N. (1997). Coping self-efficacy buffers psychological and physiological disturbances in HIV-infected men following a natural disaster. *Health Psychology, 16*, 248–255.

23. Berger, M., Vollmann, J., Hohagen, F., König, A., Lohner, H., Voderholzer, V., & Riemann, D. (1997). Sleep deprivation combined with consecutive sleep phase advance as a fast-acting therapy in depression: An open pilot trial in medicated and unmedicated patients. *American Journal of Psychiatry, 154*, 870–872.

24. Berman, R. M., Darnell, A. M., Miller, H. L., Anand, A., & Charney, D. S. (1997). Effect of pindolol in hastening response to fluoxetine in the treatment of major depression: A double-blind, placebo-controlled trial. *American Journal of Psychiatry, 154*, 37–43.

25. Bulik, C. M., Sulivan, P. F., Carter, F. A., & Joyce, P. R. (1997). Lifetime comorbidity of alcohol dependence in women with bulimia nervosa. *Addictive Behaviors, 22*, 437–446.

26. Emamghoreishi, M., Schlicher, L., Li, P. P., Parikh, S., Sen, J., Kamble, A., & Warsh, J. J. (1997). High intracellular calcium concentrations in transformed lymphoblasts from subjects with bipolar I disorder. *American Journal of Psychiatry, 154*, 976–982.

27. Evans, D. L., Leserman, J., Perkins, D. O., Stern, R. A., Murphy, C., Zheng, B., Gettes, D., Longmate, J. A., Silva, S. G., van derHorst, C. M., Hall, C. D., Folds, J. D., Golden, R. N., & Petitto, J. M. (1997). Severe life stress as a predictor of early disease progression in HIV infection. *American Journal of Psychiatry, 154*, 630–634.

28. Fava, M., Borus, J. S., Alpert, J. E., Nierenberg, A. A., Rosenbaum, J. F., & Bottiglieri, T. (1997). Folate vitamin B12, and homocysteine in major depressive disorder. *American Journal of Psychiatry, 154*, 426–428.

29. George, D. T., Benkelfat, C., Rawlings, R. R., Eckardt, M. J., Phillips, M. J., Nutt, D. J., Wynne, D., Murphy, D. L., & Linnoila, M. (1997). Behavioral and neuroendocrine responses to m-chlorophenylpiperazine in subtypes of alcoholics and in healthy comparison subjects. *American Journal of Psychiatry, 154*, 81–87.

30. Greenberg, B. D., George, M. S., Martin, J. D., Benjamin, J., Schlaepfer, T. E., Altemus, M., Wassermann, E. M., Post, R. M., & Murphy, D. L. (1997). Effect of prefrontal repetitive transcranial magnetic stimulation in obsessive-compulsive disorder: A preliminary study. *American Journal of Psychiatry, 154*, 867–869.

31. Jenike, M. A., Baer, L., Minichiello, W. E., Rauch, S. L., & Buttolph, L. (1997). Placebo-controlled trial of fluoxetine and phenelzine for obsessive-compulsive disorder. *American Journal of Psychiatry, 154*, 1261–1264.

32. Kalayam, B., Alexopoulos, G. S., Musiek, F. E., Kakuma, T., Toro, A., Silbersweig, D., & Young, R. C. (1997). Brainstem evoked response abnormalities in late-life depression with vascular disease. *American Journal of Psychiatry, 154*, 970–975.

33. Koran, L. M., Sallee, F. R., & Pallanti, S. (1997). Rapid benefit of intravenous pulse loading of clomipramine in obsessive-compulsive disorder. *American Journal of Psychiatry, 154*, 396–401.

34. McElroy, S. L., Strakowski, S. M., West, S. A., Keck, P. E., Jr., & McConville, B. J. (1997). Phenomenology of adolescent and adult mania in hospitalized patients with bipolar disorder. *American Journal of Psychiatry, 154*, 44–49.

35. Moore, C. M., Christensen, J. D., Lafer, B., Fava, M., & Renshaw, P. F. (1997). Lower levels of nucleoside triphosphate in the basal ganglia of depressed subjects: A phosphorous-32 magnetic resonance spectroscopy study. *American Journal of Psychiatry, 154*, 116–118.

36. Neumeister, A., Praschak-Rieder, N., Hesselmann, B., Vitouch, O., Rauh, M., Barocka, A., & Kasper, S. (1997). Rapid tryptophan depletion in drug-free depressed patients with seasonal affective disorder. *American Journal of Psychiatry, 154*, 1153–1155.

37. Rabkin, J. G., Goetz, R. R., Remien, R. H., Williams, J. B. W., Todak, G., & Gorman, J. M. (1997). Stability of mood despite HIV illness progression in a group of homosexual men. *American Journal of Psychiatry, 154*, 231–238.

38. Reynolds, C. F., III, Frank, E., Houck, P. R., Mazumdar, S., Dew, M. A., Cornes, C., Buysse, D. J., Begley, A., & Kupfer, D. J. (1997). Which elderly patients with remitted depression remain well with continued interpersonal psychotherapy after discontinuation of antidepressant medication? *American Journal of Psychiatry, 154*, 958–962.

39. Sallee, F. R., Vrindavanam, N. S., Deas-Newsmith, D., Carson, S. W., & Sethuraman, G. (1997). Pulse intravenous clomipramine for depressed adolescents: Double-blind, controlled trial. *American Journal of Psychiatry, 154*, 668–673.

40. Sax, K. W., Strakowski, S. M., Keck, P. E., Jr., McElroy, S. L., West, S. A., Bourne, M. L., & Larson, E. R. (1997). Comparison of patients with early-, typical-, and late-onset affective psychosis. *American Journal of Psychiatry, 154*, 1299–1301.

41. Schofield, P. W., Marder, K., Dooneief, G., Jacobs, D. M., Sano, M., & Stern, Y. (1997). Association of subjective memory complaints with subsequent cognitive decline in community-dwelling elderly individuals with baseline cognitive impairment. *American Journal of Psychiatry, 154*, 609–615.

42. Stewart, J. W., Tricamo, E., McGrath, P. J., & Quitkin, F. M. (1997). Prophylactic efficacy of phenelzine and imipramine in chronic atypical depression: Likelihood of recurrence on discontinuation after 6 months remission. *American Journal of Psychiatry, 154*, 31–36.

43. Thase, M. E., Buysse, D. J., Frank, E., Cherry, C. R., Cornes, C. L., Mallinger, A. G., & Kupfer, D. J. (1997). Which depressed patients will respond to interpersonal psychotherapy? The role of abnormal EEG sleep profiles. *American Journal of Psychiatry, 154*, 502–509.

Review of the Hamilton Depression Inventory by EPHREM FERNANDEZ, Associate Professor of Clinical Psychology, Southern Methodist University, Dallas, TX:

The Hamilton Depression Inventory (HDI) is a recent successor to the venerable Hamilton Depression Rating Scale (HDRS; Hamilton, 1960, 1967), a semistructured clinical interview. The adoption of a paper-and-pencil forced-choice format in the HDI has resulted in greater ease of administration and better standardization of scoring than in the HDRS. More substantively, the HDI has kept abreast of the latest revisions in DSM criteria for depression. Although the original 17 items of the HDRS are still embedded in the HDI, new items have also been included to expand the breadth of assessment of depression. A short form of the instrument (the HDI-SF) is also available but is recommended only for preliminary screening purposes.

Instead of a taxonomic approach to assess subtypes of depression, it is repeatedly emphasized that the HDI aims to quantify severity of depression. However, it must be borne in mind that the qualitative features of depression are not always separable from the magnitude of depression. The greater the intensity of subjective dysphoria, the more likely that somatic and behavioral symptoms will arise.

To its merit, the HDI assesses more symptoms relevant to depression than does the Beck Depression Inventory (BDI; Beck, Ward, Mendelson, Mock, & Erbaugh, 1961). One of these is hypersomnia, which is a conspicuous omission from the BDI. However, some of the phenomena assessed (e.g., indecisiveness, indigestion, and the host of sympathetic nervous system reactions) are hardly specific to depression. On the other hand, there is one item that, although not scored, explores the subject's level of insight into his/ her condition; this is Item 16, which enquires about the subject's causal attribution of depression.

What particularly sets the HDI apart from other inventories of the same genre is the use of multiple questions (probes) to assess individual features of depression. Weight loss, for instance, is assessed using three separate questions. Thus, there are 38 questions tapping into 23 different symptoms. Wherever applicable, symptoms are further assessed using multiple parameters of intensity, frequency, and duration/latency. For example, dysphoria is probed by five separate questions, two of which pertain to subjective intensity and estimated frequency, respectively; insomnia is probed by questions pertaining to the frequency and latency of sleep onset, frequency of sleep disruption, lagtime before sleep resumption, and frequency and latency of premature sleep termination. All this boosts the confidence level in symptom identification.

There are no negatively keyed items. However, there are pairs of "opposite" items (e.g., hypersomnia versus insomnia) which, if endorsed as part of a response set, would raise questions about the validity of the data. Furthermore, some items, if answered in the negative, require the test-taker to skip the next question or next few questions; random or uncritical response patterns could thus be detected. Ascertaining the more pernicious problem of motivated responding, however, will require additional tests like the Marlowe-Crowne Scale of Social Desirability (Crown & Marlowe, 1960).

Factor analysis of the HDI has revealed a four-factor solution (five-factor for psychiatric sample) accounting for 55% of the total score variance, the bulk of this variance being explained by one factor representing depressed mood and demoralization. This is consistent with earlier results on the HDRS using a multidimensional normal item response theory model (Gibbons, Clark, & Kupfer, 1991). The lack of variance accounted for by vegetative and other symptoms of depression has raised some concern about the construct validity of the HDI. As with the HDRS, the inclusion of several somatic symptoms that are not definitive of depression may well leave the HDI vulnerable to the confounding effects of multimorbidity (Fleck, Poirier-Littre, Guelfi, Bourdel, & Loo, 1995; Linden, Borchelt, Barnow, & Geiselmann, 1995).

Other psychometric properties of the HDI are good. Criterion-related validity has been demonstrated using the HDRS because a comprehensive clinical interview of depression is regarded as the gold standard in depression assessment. Given a range from 0–73, a raw score of 19 maximizes the hit rate (98.2%), sensitivity (99.3%), and specificity (95.9%). The 1-week retest reliability is .95, and internal consistency is .89. Although these reliability coefficients are often regarded as impressive, Boyle (1985)

points out that tests of depression should have situational sensitivity (and, therefore, moderate retest reliability) that can be ascertained by administering the test under known levels of depressive induction; he further reminds us of the Catellian view that item homogeneity should not be excessive, preferably no more than .7 because high internal consistency may be an indication that the test is too narrow in scope. It should also be noted that because the HDI has multiple questions per symptom, it would be interesting to know the internal consistency of these "subtests." However, the authors of the HDI have indicated that their objective was not to develop subscales at the time of test development.

In summary, the HDI is a multifaceted test that represents an advance upon its precursor, the HDRS, in terms of conceptualization and procedure. As far as psychometric properties are concerned, there is some concern about its construct validity due to the inclusion of several symptoms that are associated, but not defining, characteristics of depression. However, this is a problem that applies to several other tests of depression, too. Among the triumphs of the HDI over other competing measures are its use of multiple probes and parameters that allow greater confidence in the detection of symptoms and measurement of depressive severity.

REVIEWER'S REFERENCES

Crowne, D. P., & Marlowe, D. (1960). A new scale of social desirability independent of psychopathology. *Journal of Consulting Psychology, 24*, 349–354.

Hamilton, M. (1960). A rating scale for depression. *Journal of Neurology, Neurosurgery, and Psychiatry, 23*, 56–62.

Beck, A. T., Ward, C. H., Mendelson, M., Mock, J., & Erbaugh, J. (1961). An inventory for measuring depression. *Archives of General Psychiatry, 4*, 561–571.

Hamilton, M. (1967). Development of a rating scale for primary depressive illness. *British Journal of Social and Clinical Psychology, 6*, 278–296.

Boyle, G. J. (1985). Self-report measures of depression: Some psychometric considerations. *British Journal of Clinical Psychology, 24*, 45–59.

Gibbons, R. D., Clark, D. C., & Kupfer, D. (1993). Exactly what does the Hamilton Depression Rating Scale measure? *Journal of Psychiatric Research, 27*, 259–273.

Fleck, M. P., Poirier-Littre, M. F., Guelfi, J. D., Bourdel, M. C., & Loo, H. (1995). Factorial structure of the 17-item Hamilton Depression Rating Scale. *Acta Psychiatrica Scandinavica, 92*, 168–172.

Linden, M., Borchelt, M., Barnow, S., & Geiselmann, B. (1995). The impact of somatic morbidity on the Hamilton Depression Rating Scale in the very old. *Acta Psychiatrica Scandinavica, 92*, 150–154.

Review of the Hamilton Depression Inventory by CARL ISENHART, *Administrative Coordinator, Addictive Disorders Section, Department of Veterans Affairs Medical Center, Minneapolis, MN:*

The Hamilton Depression Inventory (HDI) is a self-report adaptation of the Hamilton Depression Rating Scale (HDRS; a 17-item structured interview). The HDI assesses the severity and range of depressive symptoms but is not designed to make DSM-IV depressive disorder diagnoses. The HDI self-report format was developed to reduce rater variance and eliminate the time and costs associated with training clinicians to complete the HDRS structured interview format. Also, contemporary depression concepts were incorporated and "fidelity" increased by assessing select depressive domains with multiple questions. Consequently, the HDI consists of 38 questions that assess 23 areas of functioning. Additional versions include the HDI-17, a 17-item scale that parallels the 17-item HDRS; the HDI-SF, a 9-item short form; and the HDI-Mel, a 9-item subscale that assesses melancholia. The HDI-17 and HDI-Mel are calculated from the HDI protocol. The HDI instruments were designed for clinical (inpatients and outpatients) and nonclinical (college students and job applicants) adults between the ages of 18 through 89. They require a fifth grade reading level and should not be used with individuals with developmental disabilities. The HDI takes 10 to 15 minutes to complete and the HDI-SF takes 5 minutes or less. Available HDI and HDI-SF software administers and scores protocols and produces interpretive reports. The software and narrative reports are not addressed here.

ADMINISTRATION AND SCORING. Patients are provided with the HDI test booklet and a carbonless two-page answer sheet. Their responses are transferred to the bottom sheet that contains recommended cutoff scores and specific scoring instructions for the HDI, the HDI-17, and the HDI-Mel. Space is provided to record the patient's T score and percentile. This sheet also contains a section to record the patient's scores on DSM-IV depression items. In addition, seven "critical" items (e.g., suicidal ideation) are listed for which space is provided to assess each symptom's nature and intensity during a clinical interview. The scoring process is clearly described and the score sheet is well designed and easy to follow. The manual provides examples of scored protocols as guides.

The HDI-SF was developed from items that best discriminated between depressed patients, patients with other psychiatric disorders, and a community sample that yields high item-total-scale correlations. The HDI-SF assesses six of nine DSM-IV depression criteria. Interestingly, the three items not assessed were the "vegetative" symptoms: insomnia/hypersomnia, psychomotor agitation/retardation, and weight loss/appetite. Patients provide answers on a two-page carbonless sheet on which the nine items are printed. The answers are transferred to the bottom sheet that contains scoring instructions, the recommended cutoff score, and space for the raw score, T score, and percentile.

The authors stress reviewing the protocol for irregular scoring patterns (e.g., blank items and alternating responses) and examining item pairs with opposite content (e.g., Item 4 [insomnia] with Item 18 [hypersomnia]) for inconsistencies. One enhancement would be to add these contrasting item pairs to the score sheet to make this comparison a routine part of the scoring process (much like the "VRIN" scale on the MMPI-2). They recommend that protocols with five or more missing items be invalidated. Protocols with four or less blank items can be prorated to obtain an estimated full score. However, there were no reports of the accuracy of these estimates. The manual provides interpretative information and case examples. The authors recommend that inconsistencies be assessed in a clinical interview and stress that clinical reports and collateral information be included when making interpretations.

NORMS. The authors provide demographic information (age, sex, and race) and HDI scores on 510 community adults, 98 college undergraduates, and 313 psychiatric outpatients evaluated before treatment. The authors reported some statistically significant HDI score differences across age and sex; however, these differences were not clinically significant. The norms for the HDI, HDI-17, and HDI-SF were generated from the community sample and reported for the total sample and by sex. The norms are reported by sex even though the sex differences were not clinically significant because of author-cited research documenting sex differences in self-report depression instruments. The community sample was also used to calculate T scores and percentiles for each of these scales, including the HDI-Mel, which are also reported by sex.

RELIABILITY. The reliability of the HDI, HDI-17, HDI-SF, and HDI-Mel scales was assessed with internal consistency and test-retest correlations, item analysis, and calculation of standard errors of measurement. The internal consistency measures ranged from .805 to .936 in the community sample and from .724 to .905 for the psychiatric sample. One goal in the development of the HDI was to increase its fidelity over other instruments. These internal consistency measures suggest that this goal was met, but perhaps too much so. These measures suggest a high level of redundancy, even for the short form (alpha = .919 to .930), and that fewer items likely could be used to assess the same domains. The test-retest reliability measures were assessed over a 1-week interval (mean = 6.2 days and range = 2 to 9 days) using 189 subjects from the community and psychiatric samples and ranged from .918 to .958. Corrected item-total scale correlations ranged from .23 to .86. The calculated standard errors of measurement were within 2 to 3 raw score points; these data allow the test user to develop confidence intervals for obtained scales.

VALIDITY. The authors reported content, concurrent criterion-related, construct (convergent, divergent, and factorial), and contrasted groups validity estimates, and cutoff scores and measures of specificity, sensitivity, and diagnostic accuracy. Item review demonstrated that HDI content is inclusive of DSM-IV concepts of depression and supported the content validity. The criterion-related validity compared the HDI with the HDRS in 403 subjects, community and psychiatric outpatients. The correlations between the HDRS and the four HDI scales, for the total sample and by sex, ranged from .905 to .951. The authors also reported correlations ranging from .26 to .89 (with most correlations in the .70s) between HDI-17 and HDRS items. However, the reported high correlations would be expected given the HDI was developed from the HDRS. Therefore, these concurrent validity results could be strengthened by using additional depression measures.

HDI scores were correlated with the Beck Depression Inventory (BDI), the Beck Hopelessness Scale, the Beck Anxiety Inventory, the Adult Suicidal Ideation Questionnaire, the Rosenberg Self-Esteem Scale, and the Marlowe-Crowne Social Desirability Scale—Short Form to demonstrate convergent construct validity. The HDI scales demonstrated highly statistically significant correlations for the total sample and by sex with these other measures, especially the BDI (all $rs \geq .89$). All correlations were positive except for correlations with the self-esteem and the social desirability. In addition, multiple regression analysis demonstrated that the HDI scales assess depression in particular and not emotional distress in general: the HDI, HDI-17, and HDI-Mel shared the most variance with the BDI and less (though still significant) variance with the other measures. Additional multiple regression analyses used the same independent and dependent variables except that the HDRS replaced the BDI, and similar results were found. Findings of statistically significant negative correlations between the HDI scales and social desirability were used to demonstrate discriminant validity. However, it is reasonable to assume that depressed individuals may both present themselves in a socially desirable fashion and because

of associated low self-esteem, be self-deprecatory. As a result, they may produce low social desirability scores. Consequently, social desirability may be a concept related to depression, and it would be expected that high depression would be associated with low social desirability. It would have been interesting to see the correlations between self-esteem and social desirability and to have included social desirability in the multiple regression. Clearly, other unrelated concepts need to be used to assess discriminant validity. Factor analytic study of the community sample demonstrated that the HDI's factors are consistent with their model of depression: depressed mood, sleep difficulties, somatic-vegetative problems (e.g., weight loss), and agitation-disorientation. Similar findings were obtained using the psychiatric sample.

Measures of sensitivity, specificity, positive predictive power, negative predictive power, hit rate, and calculations of chi-square, phi, and kappa coefficients support the HDI's accuracy in identifying who of 140 patients met DSM-III-R diagnostic criteria for major depression. The authors provide a range of potential cutoff scores for each HDI scale. Most of the hit rates for the HDI scales were in the middle to upper .90s, all chi-squares were significant, and most of the phi and kappa coefficients were in the .80s and .90s. A contrasted groups procedure found statistically significant mean HDI scale scores between three groups: The depressed group consistently scored higher than the "other psychiatric disorder" group, which consistently scored higher than the community sample. This contrasted group procedure was repeated for individual HDI and HDI-SF items with almost identical results.

SUMMARY. The HDI scales quickly and efficiently assess depressive symptomatology. The administration and scoring procedures are straightforward and easy to follow. However, this reviewer is not convinced that increased fidelity (i.e., the use of multiple questions) justifies this instrument being used over others. Redundancy was demonstrated by high internal consistency measures and by the HDI-SF's psychometrics being comparable to the full scale. However, the scales have other strengths that may justify its use over other instruments. The authors conscientiously used multiple procedures to assess and report reliability and validity data. However, other measures of depression and more divergent concepts than the ones reported in the manual would add to the instrument's strength. Other recommendations for improvement include: better justification of why different areas are assessed by multiple items and some are not, incorporating the "validity check" of contrasting items, replications with researchers other than the authors, and clarification regarding the process by which the community sample was selected. Finally, the manual is readable and adequate enough to use the tests. However, in places it goes into more detail and justification than what is needed and it is repetitive. Even the authors seemed to notice the redundancy as the phrases "as noted through out this manual," "as noted earlier," and "as discussed earlier," occur frequently throughout the manual.

[137]
Hebrew Speaking Test.

Purpose: "Designed to evaluate the level of oral proficiency attained by English speaking learners of Hebrew."
Population: Adults.
Publication Date: 1989.
Acronym: HST.
Scores, 7: Personal Conversation, Giving Directions, Detailed Description, Picture Sequence Narration, Topical Discourse, Situational Discourse, Total.
Administration: Group.
Price Data: Available from publisher.
Time: (45–50) minutes.
Comments: Mail-in scoring.
Author: Center for Applied Linguistics.
Publisher: Center for Applied Linguistics.

Review of the Hebrew Speaking Test by MARSHA BENSOUSSAN, Senior Lecturer, Department of Foreign Languages, Haifa University, Haifa, Israel:

TEST COVERAGE AND USE. The Hebrew Speaking Test (HeST) is intended for English-speaking learners of Hebrew at proficiency levels from Intermediate-Low to Superior, on the Proficiency Guidelines developed by the American Council on the Teaching of Foreign Languages (ACTFL, 1986). The primary focus of the HeST is to assess the ability to speak Hebrew in contemporary, real-life language-use contexts according to the ACTFL (American Council on the Teaching of Foreign Languages) scale. The HeST is a semi-direct simulated oral interview (SOPI) test using relatively authentic, context-based test tasks (Shohamy & Stansfield, 1990; Stansfield, 1991; Stansfield & Kenyon, 1996).

The HeST is designed to be an alternative to the face-to-face oral proficiency interview (OPI). It uses a semi-direct format, one that has the examinee record responses on a tape for subsequent scoring. Semi-direct testing is intended to offer a standard-ized approach to oral proficiency testing in situations where it is not feasible to give an oral interview due to the unavailability of trained testing personnel, or lack of time and budget for such testing. The HeST format emulates "the OPI for intermediate and advanced level students by its various linguistic and socio-linguistic probes of examinee speaking ability" (manual, p. 20).

This criterion-referenced test is available in two versions. The USA version assumes no implicit prior experience with Israeli life, and is appropriate for students of Hebrew who have not had language training or residency in Israel. The Israeli version assumes some knowledge of Israeli life, and is appropriate for North American students who have spent some time in Israel or for English-speaking students studying in Israel. There are two parallel forms for each version. Also, each form is available in two formats: one intended for male examinees and one intended for female examinees. This is necessary because of the unique linguistic features of the Hebrew language. These accommodations made to the different background and sex of examinees are designed to reduce any bias that might otherwise be present in test tasks.

The HeST consists of multiple speaking tasks spread among four types. These are as follows: (a) personal conversation, about family, education, hobbies, etc.; (b) tasks based on drawings in the test booklet (e.g., giving directions to a friend on the phone, describing a place in detail, narrating a sequence of depicted events); (c) topic-related discourse that requires the examinee to organize and present information. Tasks include explaining a process, supporting an opinion and talking about a hypothetical situation; (d) situation-based discourse. Tasks range from making simple requests to giving an informal speech. These tasks invoke a broad range of speaking competencies, thereby making the test a measure of general oral language proficiency.

TEST USES. The Official Test Manual lists the following purposes of the test: (a) admission to and placement in a Hebrew study program, (b) exemption from a Hebrew language requirement, (c) competency testing on exit from a Hebrew program, (d) application for scholarship or appointment, (e) certification of Hebrew language proficiency for occupational purposes, (f) evaluation of a Hebrew instructional program, and (g) admission to an Israeli university (p. 3). Although these purposes include both formal and informal registers, the questions in the HeST cover the informal register more thoroughly. As reported in the manual (pp. 25–26) the

HeST, unlike the Oral Proficiency Interview (OPI), is limited in the amount of probing it is able to do, especially at the highest levels (3+ to 5) on the Interagency Language Roundtable (ILR) scale. Because the HeST is not viewed as an effective discriminator of individual differences in proficiency at these high levels, HeST scores at these levels are combined into a single rating of High–Superior.

Whereas the test is appropriate for educational purposes, there may be a problem with requiring formal, professional, academic speaking skills for Purposes 4, 5, and 7. When testing the formal register, the HeST does not probe, for example, ability to speak at a formal gathering or present an academic report—skills that may be linked to using language in certain professions or to functioning in higher education contexts. This limitation may be a by-product of the SOPI test type, which does not assess as wide a range of examinee abilities as the OPI (Stansfield, 1991, p. 207).

TEST ADMINISTRATION AND SCORING. The test takes about 45 minutes to administer and elicits a speech sample from the examinee of approximately 20 minutes in length.

The HeST may be administered in a language laboratory setting. Thus, unlike the OPI, it is suitable for large group testing. Alternatively, the HeST can be administered to individuals using two tape recorders. All test administration specifications are fully described in the test manual.

In semi-direct testing, examinees are presented with the stimulus through a test tape and a test booklet; their responses are recorded on a second tape. This HeST examinee response tape is then scored by specially trained raters using the ACTFL Proficiency Guidelines. Alternatively, it can be scored using the scale of the Interagency Language Roundtable (ILR) of the U.S. government, within the range of 1 to 3+. Each examinee receives a rating on the modified ACTFL/ILR scale. The manual describes the ACTFL Proficiency Guidelines, explaining ratings of Novice, Intermediate, Advanced, and Superior, as well as the points on the ILR scale.

TEST DEVELOPMENT. Procedures for developing the HeST were carefully carried out on two continents. Each version was field tested separately in the corresponding location, either the U.S. or Israel. The forms in the USA version were field tested using students of Hebrew as a foreign language from American schools and colleges. The Israeli versions were field tested on American students

studying Hebrew as a second language at Tel Aviv University.

The time allowed for examinee responses was carefully analyzed during the development of the instrument. When field test subjects were asked about pause length, 90% of the students in both studies rated the pause length as either "about right" or "too long," so there is clear evidence that the test is not speeded. In addition, if the examinee does not finish the response, the rater may evaluate the sample of language produced by the examinee.

RELIABILITY. Because of the standardization of the testing conditions, the SOPI format used by the HeST is highly reliable. It provides quality control, offering the same quality of interview to each examinee (Stansfield, 1991).

As is the case with any rater-scored test, the standard error of measurement (*SEM*) cannot be calculated exactly as the score depends in large part on the reliability of the individual rater. For the two raters used in each HeST validity study, the *SEM* was less than a quarter of a level on the ILR scale or less than a sublevel on the ACTFL scale. This is about the degree of variation that one would hope to find on a test that employs these two scales.

The raters used in the validation study were highly consistent in the ratings they give to the HeST speech samples. Interrater reliabilities ranged from .92 to .97 for the four forms of the test. Parallel form reliability coefficients were also high, ranging from .91 to .99. Even when different forms were scored by different raters, the correlation between the scores on the different forms remained high (.91 to .94). The data reported demonstrate that the SOPI can produce a highly reliable score, if a competent rater is available to score the test.

VALIDITY. Evidence of content validity is found in the tasks examinees are asked to perform in demonstrating oral proficiency. The tasks parallel those used in a face-to-face oral proficiency interview. In addition, for some examinees, the HeST produces a longer and more thorough examination than might be the case in an OPI, due to the number of speaking tasks and the amount of time given the examinee to respond.

Because the HeST was designed to be used as a surrogate of the OPI, by following the same format and using the same rating scale, the HeST also claims to assess the same construct as the OPI, when use of a direct interview is not practical. The authors present evidence of this in the test manual using data from the validation study they carried out.

The results were that when the HeST and the live interview were scored by the same rater, the correlations for the different forms and raters ranged from .84 to .96, with an average correlation of .92. When the HeST and the OPI were scored by different raters, the correlations ranged between .84 and .95, with an average correlation of .91. A final summary correlation that paired all 40 independent interview ratings (20 interviews, 2 raters) with the 80 independent HeST ratings (20 ratings, 2 forms, 2 raters) is .93 for the USA versions and .89 for the Israeli versions of the test. The overall correlation between all pairs of scores was .91. These high correlations support the construct validity of the HeST as a measure of oral proficiency and support its use as an alternative to the OPI.

This evidence is supported by examinee evaluations of the test gathered during the validation study. When asked whether the questions asked during the OPI and the HeST adequately probed their maximum level of speaking ability, 75% of the subjects said "Yes."

EVALUATION. The HeST appears to be a reliable and valid alternative to the face-to-face oral proficiency interview when used by a trained rater. As soon as is practical, the authors or the publisher should develop a self-instructional rater training kit to accompany it. Currently, one has to take the extensive ACTFL OPI interviewer training in order to be able to score the HeST. Because of the time and expense involved, only a handful of people can score the OPI or the HeST. Unless a self-instructional rater training kit is developed, the full potential of the HeST will not be realized.

REVIEWER'S REFERENCES

American Council on the Teaching of Foreign Languages. (1986). *ACTFL proficiency guidelines.* Hastings-on-Hudson, NY: Author.
Shohamy, E., & Stansfield, C. W. (1990). The Hebrew Speaking Test: An example of international cooperation in test development and validation. *AILA Review, 7,* 79–90.
Stansfield, C. W. (1991). A comparative analysis of simulated and direct oral proficiency interviews. In S. Anivan (Ed.), *Current developments in language testing* (pp. 199–209). Singapore: SEAMEO Regional English Language Center.
Stansfield, C. W., & Kenyon, D. M. (May, 1996). Simulated oral proficiency interviews: An update. *ERIC Digest.* Washington, DC: Center for Applied Linguistics.

Review of the Hebrew Speaking Test by MARGARET E. MALONE, Language Testing Specialist, Peace Corps, Washington, DC:

The Hebrew Speaking Test (HeST) is a semi-direct test of oral proficiency in Hebrew. It tests oral proficiency via a test tape and test booklet in place of a live interviewer, and was developed for native speakers of English learning Hebrew as a second language. Two versions of the test are available: The USA version for Americans learning Hebrew in the United States and the Israeli version for native speakers of English who have lived or studied in Israel. Each version, USA and Israeli, has two forms, A and B. The test can be administered to large groups in a language laboratory setting, or to individuals. It is scored at a later time by a trained rater according to the ACTFL (American Council on the Teaching of Foreign Language) Guidelines (1986).

The 45 minute test has six parts to which each examinee responds. The first item is a personal conversation between the examinee and a native speaker of Hebrew. This is the only part of the prerecorded test that includes spoken Hebrew. The second part requires the examinee to give directions based on a map provided. The third part requires the examinee to describe a picture in detail. The fourth part calls for more extended speech in its three items. For each item, the examinee gives a detailed description of a sequence of pictures. The next part, "Topical Discourse," has five items in which the examinee speaks about five different topics. In the last part, "Situational Discourse," the examinee responds to five items. The examinee is asked to react to real-life situations. All items are timed, and research was conducted in the pilot study on appropriate pause length for "thinking time" between the description of the item and when the examinee responds, as well as on the amount of time for the response.

No formal studies have investigated appropriate uses of the test. Instead, the test manual suggests several uses, including admission to an Israeli university, certification of language proficiency for work purposes, and admission to a Hebrew language study program, and recommends that a specific program or institution perform its own validation studies for institutional use. Nor does the test manual recommend cutoff scores or minimal scores for different types of uses; instead, the authors suggest that each program conduct a study on scores appropriate for each use. The uses mentioned in the test manual are similar to those suggested for the Oral Proficiency Interview (OPI) used by U.S. government agencies and the ACTFL.

The test has two major weaknesses: the methodology of the initial pilot study and construct validity. First, the description of the pilot study is not as detailed as it could be for potential users. The initial pilot study included 20 participants for each version, USA and Israeli. Each participant was administered the OPI in Hebrew, then each form of either the

USA or Israeli version of the HeST. The number of participants is small, and the test manual does not describe the examinees' backgrounds (this information is described in a separate article). Because of the wide variety of potential uses for the test—from classroom to occupational applications—it might be helpful to users to see how well the test discriminates among individuals from various backgrounds. In addition, the manual does not describe the variation among examinee performance. Therefore, it is not known if any participants scored at the lowest and highest levels.

In addition to information about the field test population, questions arise about possible rater bias in the pilot study. All examinees took an OPI, then each form (A and B) of the appropriate version of the HeST (USA or Israeli). At times, the OPI and both forms of the HeST were administered and scored by the same raters. Although such methodology results in high interrater reliability, it could also cause bias on the part of the HeST scorers because they would have already administered and rated an OPI before scoring some examinees' HeST tapes.

The second major issue is the test's construct validity, and this is an issue shared with the OPI. The authors state that the "construct validity of the OPI [on which the HeST is based] is high" (p. 25). However, many, including Bachman and Palmer (1981), Savigron (1985), and others have questioned the construct validity of the OPI and of the ACTFL Guidelines (1986) used for scoring it. Therefore, the construct validity of the HeST is part of a larger controversy.

However, the test has a number of positive characteristics, including its content validity, its criterion-referenced validity, its reliability, and its ease of administration. Unlike the OPI, which is administered solely in Hebrew, the directions for the HeST are solely in English. Therefore, there is no confusion between the listening and speaking domain in testing; only Hebrew speaking ability is measured. In addition, the authors conducted a rigorous study of its criterion-referenced validity with the OPI in Hebrew. As part of the pilot study, all examinees were administered the OPI, and for both versions and both forms of the HeST, reliability ranged from .84 to .96. Therefore, the HeST is a valid substitute for the OPI, and its content validity may be higher.

The test's reliability and ease of administration are its strongest features. The test's interrater reliability ranges from .92 to .97 on both versions and forms. This is perhaps because the test's contents are constant and therefore all raters are rating the same items for all examinees, unlike the OPI, which often differs in the questions asked by interviewers. The test forms, too, show high parallel form reliabilities of .91 to .99.

The test is also quite sensitive to different kinds of speakers of Hebrew: those familiar with Israeli culture and those unfamiliar with Israeli culture. In developing two versions of the test, the test developers removed the obvious bias of those who have spent time in the target culture and those who have not.

The HeST is easy to administer and does not require a trained tester for administration. The test manual includes detailed, step-by-step directions for both types of administration that are easy to replicate. It can be administered to a large group in a language laboratory, which is convenient for large-scale testing, or to an individual using two tape recorders. Because the test is tape-recorded and scored at a later time, it is an extremely efficient way of testing large groups or of testing individuals in a less commonly taught language such as Hebrew.

Though the HeST suffers from many of the same questions about construct validity as does the OPI and the ACTFL Guidelines, its benefits of practicality and content validity are favorable. The authors are clear about its intended audience—native speakers of English studying Hebrew as a second language. It is an excellent choice for large- or small-scale testing, particularly in a less commonly taught language.

REVIEWER'S REFERENCES
Bachman, L., & Palmer, A. (1981). The construct validation of the FSI Oral Interview. *Language Learning, 31,* 67–86.
Savigron, S. (1985). Evaluation of communicative competence: The ACTFC Provisional Proficiency Guidelines. *Modern Language Journal, 69,* 129–133.
American Council on the Teaching of Foreign Languages. (1986). *ACTFL proficiency guidelines.* Hastings-on-Hudson, NY: Author.

[138]
Hogan Personality Inventory [Revised].

Purpose: Measure of normal personality designed for use in personnel selection, individualized assessment, and career-related decision making.

Population: College students and adults.

Publication Dates: 1985–1995.

Acronym: HPI.

Scores: 7 primary scale scores (Intellectance, Adjustment, Ambition, Sociability, Likeability, Prudence, School Success), 6 occupational scale scores (Service Orientation, Stress Tolerance, Reliability, Clerical Potential, Sales Potential, Managerial Potential), and Validity scale score.

Administration: Group.

Price Data, 1997: $2 per 5 reusable test booklets; $12.50 per 25 answer sheets; $40 per technical manual ('95, 126 pages); $40 per specimen set including manual, sample report, reusable test booklet, and answer sheet; scoring services producing interpretive and/or graphic reports available from publisher ($30 per interpretive Personality Report; $15 per graphic; $15 per data file; $.50 per faculty research; $10 per interpretive report for Occupational Scale and Clerical, Sales, or Managerial Scales; $5 per graphic).

Time: (15–20) minutes.

Authors: Robert Hogan and Joyce Hogan (manual).

Publisher: Hogan Assessment Systems.

Cross References: See T4:1169 (7 references); for reviews of an earlier edition by James J. Hennessy and Rolf A. Peterson, see 10:140.

[Editor's Note: These reviews are based on materials received prior to the 1995 Second Edition manual.]

TEST REFERENCES

1. Hogan, J., & Hogan, R. (1989). How to measure employee reliability. *Journal of Applied Psychology, 74,* 273-279.

2. Mount, M. K., Barrick, M. R., & Strauss, J. P. (1994). Validity of observer ratings of the big five personality factors. *Journal of Applied Psychology, 79,* 272-280.

Review of the Hogan Personality Inventory (Revised) by STEPHEN N. AXFORD, Psychologist, Pueblo School District No. Sixty, Pueblo, CO, and University of Phoenix, Southern Colorado Campus, Colorado Springs, CO:

As described by its authors, the Hogan Personality Inventory (HPI) "is a measure of normal personality … primarily for use in personnel selection, individualized assessment, and career-related decision making" (p. 1, HPI manual). This seems to be an accurate description of the instrument. Examination of the HPI and its manual clearly indicates purpose and design focused on practical use within organizations.

The HPI resembles other objective personality measures such as the Minnesota Multiphasic Personality Inventory—2 (MMPI–2; T4:1645), Millon Clinical Multiaxial Inventory III (MCMI–III; 201), and Personality Assessment Inventory (PAI; 12:290), except that it is intentionally much less clinically oriented. Instead, the HPI caters to business and administrative needs, as reflected in the language and style of writing found in the HPI manual, particularly as related to test results. Also, HPI test items, compared to items from more clinically oriented personality measures, are likely to be more palatable to examinees, as such sensitive issues as sexuality and drug use are omitted. Furthermore, business professionals are likely to find the information provided by the HPI, focusing on "social outcomes" rather than psychopathology, to be more familiar and useful than that provided by perhaps better known objective measures of personality.

Despite its intended use as a measure of "normal personality," the HPI may, nevertheless, also have clinical utility, as seems to be acknowledged by the authors. For example, the School Success scale significantly and positively correlates with the MMPI–2 Pd factor (Psychopathic Deviate). In addition, the HPI Adjustment scale, according to the authors, is sensitive to "neuroticism or negative affectivity" (p. 40, HPI manual). According to the authors, regarding the Adjustment scale, individuals "with scores below the 10th percentile may be candidates for professional assistance" (p. 40). This seems to suggest that the HPI could be used as a screening instrument for mental health referral (i.e., employee assistance programs, private providers). However, additional research (i.e., discriminative validity) would be needed before extending the HPI for this use.

The HPI materials are well written and professional looking. The manual and Interpretive Report (computer generated, not unlike those for the MMPI–2, MCMI–III, and PAI) are very "user friendly" and avoid jargon that might be confusing to individuals with limited background in psychometrics and clinical theory. However, the individual well versed in psychometrics will likely find the attention given by the authors to test construction and validation to be quite adequate. The authors also succinctly but adequately address theoretical and historical issues related to personality assessment in general, underlying constructs, application, and test construction.

The HPI provides seven primary scale scores, six occupational scale scores, and a validity scale score (similar to the MMPI F validity scale) "designed to detect careless or random responding" (p. 12, HPI manual). A positive impression management response set index, the Virtuous HIC (similar to that reported for the PAI) is also provided for the HPI.

Intellectance, Adjustment, Ambition, Sociability, Likeability, Prudence, and School Success comprise the primary scale scores. Although case studies and predictive validity research studies are reviewed by the authors, an essentially ecological or systems approach for interpretation and application of these scales seems advocated by the authors. In other words, the authors seem to emphasize the need for task analysis of specific vocations and careers (job analysis) within particular settings, as this may relate to the HPI personality scales. As noted by the authors, interpretation of scale scores is situation dependent; "sometimes high scores are desirable, sometimes low scores are desirable—depending on the decision context" (p. 39, HPI manual). The authors also seem to advocate that organizations employ the HPI in their own predictive validation research, which then could be used for selection purposes. To be commended, the authors provide helpful information for conducting such research.

The six Occupational Scales, a useful, innovative, and unique component of the HPI, are designed and validated to predict outcomes "related to the performance requirements that are common to many jobs" (p. 63, HPI manual). These scales include: Service Orientation, Stress Tolerance, Reliability, Clerical Potential, Sales Potential, and Managerial Potential.

Extensive validation research is reported by the authors. The authors specifically address three areas of evidence: correlations with other validated tests, correlations with peer ratings, and correlations with measures of organizational performance. Scales from the following tests were correlated with HPI Scales: Armed Services Vocational Aptitude Battery, PSI Basic Skills Tests for Business, Myers-Briggs Type Indicator, Self-Directed Search, Inventory of Personal Motives, Interpersonal Adjective Scales, Big-Five Factor Markers, Minnesota Multiphasic Personality Inventory–2, and PROFILE.

In general, the validation studies yielded correlations of adequate magnitude and in the direction predicted, supporting the validity of the HPI. In addition, regarding the primary scales, internal consistency reliabilities (Cronbach's coefficient alpha) range between .70 (Likeability) and .89 (Adjustment), employing an N of 960. An average alpha of .80 is reported. With an average of .71, test-retest reliabilities for the primary scales range from .57 (Likeability) to .79 (School Success).

The HPI manual also contains detailed and clear information regarding administration and scoring. Included are instructions on the use of a computer on-line testing service, Keyed Data Entry (available scoring software), optical scanning for personal computer scoring, and mail-in or FAX scoring. Correlations between HPI alternative forms (On-Line, Verbal; Ns of 30 and 34, respectively) scales range from .80 to .92. Instructions for administering the HPI to disabled individuals are also provided.

In summary, the Hogan Personality Inventory appears to be a theoretically sound, carefully conceptualized, and well-validated instrument offering practical utility for organizations. It should appeal particularly to business professionals such as managers or those involved in personnel selection, organizational research, career counseling, and training. Within this context, it has advantages over more traditional objective measures of personality such as the MMPI—2, PAI, and MCMI—III.

Review of the Hogan Personality Inventory (Revised) by STEVEN G. LoBELLO, Associate Professor of Psychology, Auburn University at Montgomery, Montgomery, AL:

The Hogan Personality Inventory (HPI) is a self-report instrument consisting of 206 true-false items that make up seven orthogonal personality scales derived through factor analysis: Adjustment, Ambition, Sociability, Likeability, Prudence, Intellectance, and School Success. Each scale is composed of smaller groups of related items termed Homogeneous Item Composites (HICs). The HICs are recombined to form six occupational scales: Service Orientation, Stress Tolerance, Reliability, Clerical Potential, Sales Potential, and Managerial Potential. The HPI manual authors indicate that item responses give a sample of a person's usual style of self-presentation. Responses to the HPI and other objective inventories are likened to being interviewed. The information revealed in an interview or in responding to personality inventory questions is meant to communicate something about the image usually presented to others.

The HPI can be administered to individuals 16 years of age or older and takes about 20 minutes to complete. Reading level analysis indicates that items require about a fourth grade reading level. Over 11,000 (Editor's Note: 30,000 in 1995 manual) people were tested for norm development and the sample fairly represents men and women, as well as people of different racial groups.

The two-sided answer sheet can be optically scanned, or the data may be entered into a personal computer for scoring with appropriate software. Hogan Assessment Systems also provides for scoring by mail or fax, but there are no hand-scoring keys available. In career assessment or personnel selection, the HPI may be administered along with an occupational interest inventory. The Adjustment factor may operate as a screen for individuals with psychiatric problems, who then may be referred for additional assessment. The focus of the HPI, however, is decidedly on the adaptive, positive aspects of personality.

Test-retest reliabilities for the seven personality scales were determined by testing 150 university students with at least a 4-week interval between administrations. These reliability coefficients range from .86 (Adjustment, School Success) to .74 (Prudence) according to one table, though the values reported in the text are different (and lower). Internal consistency for the personality scales, as determined by Cronbach's alpha, range from .89 (Adjustment) to .71 (Likeability). Alpha values for the HICs are generally moderate to strong, though a few are rather low, indicating a lack of homogeneity among content-similar items.

A detailed chapter on Validity documents the relationship between the HPI and other psychological tests such as the Minnesota Multiphasic Personality—2 (MMPI-2), the Myers-Briggs Type Indicator, and the Self-Directed Search. HPI scores were also correlated with peer ratings, which show robust relationships with the personality scales.

Each personality scale is also the subject of a small section describing the results of studies related to their construct validity. For example, a study of service dispatchers is cited, which showed that the Prudence scale correlates -.40 with hours absent and -.24 with error rates.

The discussion of the occupational scales includes a table referencing numerous validation studies that can be found in the literature for three of the scales. The reported coefficients range from moderate to low, though most are in the predicted directions. Even a modest correlation can improve predictability, which may be important if the cost of errors is high. A similar table summarizing validation research on the personality scales would be helpful to anyone wishing to investigate the construct validity of these scales in greater depth.

The manual is generally user friendly, and includes norms, clear directions for administration, interpretive guidelines, and an example of a computer-generated report. Unfortunately, the sample report follows a scale-by-scale approach to interpretation and apparently does not identify some interesting patterns discussed in the manual that require the consideration of multiple scores.

The discussion in the manual strikes me as lacking focus as the authors explain how the test was developed along the lines of socioanalytic theory, how it was modeled on the California Psychological Inventory, and how it relates to the Five-Factor Model of personality. In other parts of the manual, the authors make some ambiguous statements such as: "the HPI is uniquely designed to forecast performance in real world settings" (p. 63). Do they mean to imply that other personality inventories do not strive to accomplish this? Or do they mean the HPI has more research documenting its validity than some other inventories?

In summary, the Hogan Personality Inventory is a valid and reliable test of adaptive and positive personality characteristics that is recommended for use as part of a battery in vocational and personnel selection settings. It may appeal to individuals in these nonclinical settings who want a time-efficient

measure of personality, though the absence of hand-scoring keys may be troublesome to those who do not have ready access to computers or fax machines.

[139]

House-Tree-Person and Draw-A-Person as Measures of Abuse in Children: A Quantitative Scoring System.

Purpose: "Developed to assess personality/emotional characteristics of sexually abused children."
Population: Ages 7–12.
Publication Date: 1994.
Acronym: H-T-P/D-A-P.
Scores, 4: Preoccupation with Sexually Relevant Concepts, Aggression and Hostility, Withdrawal and Guarded Accessibility, Alertness for Danger/Suspiciousness and Lack of Trust.
Administration: Individual.
Price Data, 1996: $49 per complete kit including manual (140 pages) and 10 scoring booklets; $29 per 25 scoring booklets; $42 per manual.
Time: Administration time not reported.
Comments: A projective drawing instrument; for related instruments see The Draw-A-Person, Draw A Person: A Quantitative Scoring System, Draw-A-Person Quality Scale, and Draw A Person: Screening Procedure for Emotional Disturbance (T4:813–816).
Author: Valerie Van Hutton.
Publisher: Psychological Assessment Resources, Inc.

TEST REFERENCES
1. Riordan, R. J., & Verdel, A. C. (1991). Evidence of sexual abuse in children's art products. *The School Counselor, 39,* 116–121.
2. Wilson, M. S., & Reschly, D. J. (1996). Assessment in school psychology training and practice. *School Psychology Review, 25,* 9–23.

Review of the House-Tree-Person and Draw-A-Person as Measures of Abuse in Children: A Quantitative Scoring System by E. THOMAS DOWD, Professor of Psychology, Kent State University, Kent, OH:

I am not sure if projective tests projectively assess the client variables they purport to measure or the hopes and wishes of their developers. Over the years, they have been quite controversial, with strong supporters on one hand and strong detractors on the other.

The controversy appears to be one of reliability and validity, perhaps more so the latter than the former. The author of this test acknowledges the controversy, without discussing it in any detail, and to her credit has attempted to resolve the controversy by developing a quantitative scoring system for this historic test to assess the potential for sexual abuse in children. Both by developing the quantitative system and by narrowing the focus of investigation, she has advanced the outlook for the continued use of projective tests.

The book is essentially a detailed description of the scoring system used in analyzing children's drawings. It assesses four constructs: Preoccupation with Sexually Relevant Concepts (SRC); Aggression and Hostility (AH); Withdrawal and Guarded Accessibility (WGA); and Alertness for Danger, Suspiciousness, and Lack of Trust (ADST). The rationale for the selection of these constructs has a certain face validity, though it is not explained other than by reference citations. Each of the four areas in turn is divided into additional categories of analysis including Behavioral, General, House, Tree, and Person, which in turn each have specific items for which to look (e.g., elongated feet, omission of arms, door very small). These are summarized in the appendix, along with literature citations from which each was drawn and presumably supported. The majority of the book is taken up with descriptions of each item, with illustrative examples of many. Chapters on interpretation, mostly consisting of two case examples, future directions for research, and normative data, including reliability and validity, complete the book.

Many of the individual items possess a certain face validity. For example, emphasis on bedroom and presence of genitals may suggest sexual abuse, whereas a clenched fist and oversized figure may indicate hostility. But what is one to do with the statement that *both* the drawing of a less mature *and* a more mature figure than the actual child may be taken as a sign of sexual abuse? Likewise, what is the rationale for the item that a door on the side of a building may indicate withdrawal or that a "Picasso" eye (one only) or an emphasis on the outline of eyes may indicate alertness for danger? There may be reasonable explanations in the projective literature but it is not obvious what they are. This is not just churlishness on my part but a question of ultimate validity.

The author compared three samples on the test: a normal sample of 145 children from public school and summer day camp settings, 20 sexually abused children who had documented histories of such by social service agencies, and 20 emotionally disturbed but nonabused children from a special education school. Concerning the normal sample, the author assures the reader that, "There was a high probability or certainty that these children were neither physically or sexually abused nor suffering from an emotional disturbance" (p. 102). No data are presented in support of this assertion, however.

The scoring system appears to have been carefully developed. Items that were confusing to raters or were scored with less that 80% agreement were dropped or reworded. Then, additional ratings on new drawings were conducted and further changes made. Perhaps as a result, the author reports mostly good interrater reliability for the scoring system: .96 for SRC, .97 for AH, .95 for WGA, and .70 for ADST.

Validity, which is entirely discriminant, is documented by the ability of the scoring system to differentiate the three groups. Two methods were used: a two-way ANOVA with group and gender as factors, and an examination of the accuracy of the classification of subjects into groups. Both methods demonstrated that the SRC was able to discriminate between the normal and sexually abused children with a high degree of predictive power. The emotionally disturbed children, especially females, tended to resemble normals. The classification rates for AH and WGA were only slightly better than the base rate, whereas the ADST was unable to differentiate significantly the abused from nonabused children at all. But the validity of the categories and items behind the scale remains undocumented and thus adequate validity can be said to be lacking.

It appears that the specifically constructed SRC scale can be of some assistance in discriminating those children who have been sexually abused from those who have not, though some emotionally disturbed males may resemble the sexually abused. The other scales were of minimal or no use, however. Perhaps the SRC scale can be of use in identifying children who have been abused and have difficulty talking about it. But there does not seem to be much point to administering the complete scale, at least for the purposes of identifying sexual abuse in children.

The author is to be commended in attempting to apply rigorous measurement standards to the fuzzy world of projective tests. In doing so, she has contributed to their increased respectability. But the question of ultimate validity remains.

Review of the House-Tree-Person and Draw-A-Person as Measures of Abuse in Children: A Quantitative Scoring System by HOWARD M. KNOFF, Professor of School Psychology, Department of Psychological Foundations, University of South Florida, Tampa, FL:

The House-Tree-Person and Draw-A-Person as Measures of Abuse in Children: A Quantitative Scoring System is a recent book that, with a supplemental scoring protocol, adapts the traditional House-Tree-Person (HTP) projective drawing technique, pairs it with the Draw-A-Person (DAP) projective drawing technique, and introduces a quantitative scoring system that is designed "for use with children in screening for possible child sexual abuse" (p. 1). Although Van Hutton suggests her scoring system focuses on other more general personality/emotional characteristics that are present in children and adults, this claim is unsubstantiated in that Van Hutton's scoring system was normed only with children between the ages of 7 and 12 years of age. Thus, this review will limit itself to the norming sample described and the resulting psychometric properties of the quantitative system.

As noted, the introduction and other parts of this book suggest that this HTP/DAP scoring system is intended to be used as a supplemental screening tool to help identify victims of sexual abuse and that this system is preliminary and in need of additional research. However, other parts of this book read as if this tool is ready for clinical use and that its psychometric properties and norming processes are sound. For example, the author states that "(t)he present work is designed to provide the diagnostician with an objective, quantifiable scoring system that has a well-grounded theoretical and research base" (p. 2). Unfortunately, neither of these assertions is true. This scale makes numerous, faulty assumptions as to the theoretical and research base that forms the foundation of this system, and there are many significant shortcomings in the system's norming process, its normative data, and in its psychometric properties. In the end, and at most, this system should be used only in research that is geared toward improving and validating the system *itself*. It should *not* be used in research attempting to concurrently validate other abuse-related tools, nor any research focusing on assessment or intervention with abused children. Further, the system definitely is not ready for any clinical use. And, given the validity and utility of projective assessment approaches in general (e.g., Gresham, 1993; Knoff, 1993; Knoff, Batsche, & Carlyon, 1993), perhaps there is little reason to pursue any continued work with this system at all.

Below, the development, the administration, scoring and interpretation, the norming, and the psychometric properties of the HTP/DAP system will be described and critiqued. Although attempting to describe the information and procedures as presented in the book, the critique will draw on related research as well as the principles and practices of sound test development.

UNDERLYING RATIONALE FOR THE DEVELOPMENT OF THE SCORING SYSTEM. According to the author, the HTP/DAP scoring system is based on (a) the premise that, because quantitative scoring systems with projective tests already exist, other systems "are both possible and useful" (p. 10); (b) projective drawing research that focuses specifically on abused children; and (c) other research that has identified other emotional characteristics that may be indicative of child abuse. To expand, the author discusses (chapter 2) the historical use of drawing tests and reviews the few quantitative scoring methods that have previously been developed with projective drawing approaches. Although demonstrating that quantitative scoring systems are possible, the author fails to note that none of these systems have been independently validated, that they are infrequently used, and that they have not focused on specific clinical populations (Knoff, Batsche, & Carlyon, 1993). Thus, there is no evidence that these scoring systems, or any future systems, are useful. The author then describes four studies, each over 10 years old, involving projective assessments with abused children. Significantly, the author does not provide a critical review of the subjects, geographic locations, or methods used in these studies, nor does she critique these studies such that the generalizability of their results can be established. Moreover, although acknowledging the poor technical adequacy of past projective drawing research, the author does not go far enough, failing to cite, for example, analyses (e.g., Knoff, Batsche, & Carlyon, 1993) that show that projective drawing research is largely nonempirical and case study oriented, of questionable methodological and technical integrity, and lacking in convergent and discriminant validity with most clinical populations. In the end, this HTP/DAP system is based primarily on general and specific (relative to abused children) projective assessment studies that cannot be clinically or psychometrically defended.

Finally, this system is based on four characteristics that "may be indicative of child abuse" (p. 99) chosen by the author from a sampling of studies completed with children of abuse. Without describing, critiquing, or validating these characteristics, the author uses these studies to create her system's four interpretive scales: the Preoccupation with Sexually Relevant Concepts (SRC); Aggression and Hostility (AH); Withdrawal and Guarded Accessibility (WGA); and Alertness for Danger, Suspiciousness, and Lack of Trust (ADST) scales. She then organizes numerous projective drawing indicators into these four scales without describing why they were chosen or the criteria used to "load" them onto a specific scale. Although Appendix A in the book provides citations meant to support why the various projective indicators are organized onto each scale, most of these citations involve studies that either are not data-based or have questionable research methodologies (Knoff, Batsche, & Carlyon, 1993).

Ultimately, the final HTP/DAP system presented involves a scoring process whereby House-Tree-Person and Draw-A-Person drawings are qualitatively analyzed across 90 projective indicators that are based on a child's comments and behaviors during the drawing process or on the presence of details in the house, tree, person, or combined drawings, respectively. The indicators are organized onto the four interpretive scales (31 on the Preoccupation with Sexually Relevant Concepts, 28 on the Aggression and Hostility, 21 on the Withdrawal and Guarded Accessibility, and 10 on the Alertness for Danger, Suspiciousness, and Lack of Trust scale), and the total number of indicators on each scale is converted to a percentile score based on the normative sample described. This scoring approach is based on the presence of isolated indicators (rather than clinical behaviors that are empirically correlated with abused children and situations), and it assumes that these indicators have equal impact or weighting relative to predicting abuse and that a total score of indicators has construct, discriminant, and/or convergent validity—psychometric characteristics not demonstrated by the system at this time.

ADMINISTRATION, SCORING, AND INTERPRETATION. Administration directions for this system consist of giving children two blank, unlined pieces of 8.5 x 11-inch paper and a #2 pencil, and asking them to draw a picture of a house, a tree, and a person on the first sheet of paper (the HTP) and a picture of another person on the second sheet of paper. Reportedly, the second human figure drawing is requested to insure that enough details are available for proper interpretation. The examiner then scores the system using the eight-page scoring booklet and the book that provides 59 pages of case study drawings that are supposed to exemplify the qualitative descriptions of the 90 projective indicators. An indicator is scored when it appears in either the HTP or DAP drawing. That is, an indicator need not be present in both drawings. The raw score for each of the four scales represents the total number of indicators present in the drawings. Raw scores then are converted to percentile ranks with normal scores at or below the 84th percentile, borderline

scores (indicating a possibility of sexual abuse) between the 84th and 94th percentile, and significant scores (indicating a high probability of sexual abuse) at or above the 95th percentile. Experienced clinicians reportedly were able to score protocols in approximately 4 minutes after practice and training.

By way of critique, the request for a house, tree, and person drawing on one sheet of paper is unusual and different from the typical HTP administration that uses separate pieces of paper. Although the projective drawing interpretive research is already suspect, this creates additional questions as to whether prior projective interpretations from separate HTPs can be generalized to a conjoint HTP. Relative to scoring, the author notes that the clarity and accuracy of the scoring instructions were validated by asking a master's-level clinical psychologist and counselor to independently score 30 children's drawings. Although the interrater agreements for these clinicians were acceptable, the validation of scoring criteria based on only two individuals is highly questionable. Finally, beyond the interpretation problems already noted, the failure to document or demonstrate the discriminant validity for each of the projective indicators calls the entire system into question.

THE NORMING OF THE HTP/DAP SYSTEM. The HTP/DAP system was normed using 145 children (73 males and 72 females), ages 7 through 12, drawn from public school and summer day camp settings in two unnamed metropolitan cities (chapter 5). Critically, other than gender, demographic information relative to ethnicity, socioeconomic status, and other important variables was not included. This sample was contrasted with two additional samples, one with 20 individuals who were sexually abused and another with 20 additional individuals who were emotionally disturbed but nonabused. With the interpretation of this system dependent on the norms developed, the fact that this sample is extremely small, nonrandom, unstratified, and geographically limited is of major concern (even the author noted that "comparisons with this sample should be made with caution"; p. 73). In fact, these sampling weaknesses far outweigh the statistical analyses used to generate the norms reported, rendering these norms and their use meaningless. Further, the two contrasting samples have the same limitations making any suggestion of this system's convergent and/or discriminant validity inappropriate.

Beyond these concerns, the author reported the analyses contrasting the normative sample with the two other samples resulted in significant main effects for the SRC, the AH, and the WGA scales, but not the ADST scale. She then designated the ADST scale a "research scale" (p. 103), but this designation is not found in the Scoring Booklet to prompt clinicians who either miss this brief passage in the book or do not read the book at all.

PSYCHOMETRIC PROPERTIES. Relative to the reliability of the HTP/DAP system, only interrater reliability is considered; other types of reliability, such as test-retest and internal reliability, are not reported. Critically, although the author reports interrater reliability correlations above .90 for SRC, AH, and WGA scales and .70 for the ADST scale, these ratings are based on only two clinicians, a doctoral-level child psychologist with 20 years of experience and a master's-level counselor with 5 years experience, who each scored 41 protocols from the normal, emotionally disturbed, and the sexually abused groups noted above. Clearly, additional research establishing the reliability of this system is needed given the dependence on only two clinicians for its interrater reliability and the absence of other types of reliability data.

Relative to validity, neither construct validity nor concurrent validity were addressed in the book. Significantly, construct validation is especially needed to confirm the four scales of the HTP/DAP system that were selected from the literature by the author. As noted above, one discriminant validity study was reported involving the normative sample and the samples of emotionally disturbed and sexually abused children. Although sample discriminations occurred on the SRC and AH scales and the system's cutoff scores were determined to best discriminate abused versus nonabused children, the limited sample sizes involved in this study (i.e., a clinical sample of only 20 abused children) and the lack of descriptive information about the samples preclude any conclusion that discriminant validity was demonstrated.

CONCLUSIONS. The author correctly states that "conclusions about the likelihood of sexual abuse should never be made based on the results of any one instrument ... Hence, data should be gathered from additional sources, such as clinical interviews, medical examinations, and reports from parents and teachers" (p. 75). Indeed, given the conceptual, empirical, psychometric, and other weaknesses inherent to this system, one must question whether it provides any additional information beyond what can be gathered through these other sources. In summary and because of these weaknesses, it is apparent that the

publication of this system was premature. Although significant improvements are needed relative to the system's norms, validity, and reliability, the question still remains as to whether this, or any other, projective instrument—with or without a quantitative scoring approach—can ever be sensitive and efficacious enough to be useful as a diagnostic tool in an area as complex as child abuse.

REVIEWER'S REFERENCES

Gresham, F. M. (1993). "What's wrong with this picture?": Response to Motta et al.'s review of Human Figure Drawings. *School Psychology Quarterly, 8*, 182–188.
Knoff, H. M. (1993). The utility of Human Figure Drawings in personality and intellectual assessment: Why ask why? *School Psychology Quarterly, 8*, 191–196.
Knoff, H. M., Batsche, G. M., & Carlyon, W. (1993). Projective techniques and their utility in child psychotherapy. In T. R. Kratochwill & R. J. Morris (Eds.), *Handbook of psychotherapy with children and adolescents* (pp. 9–37). Hillsdale, NJ: Lawrence Erlbaum Associates.

[140]
How Am I Doing? A Self-Assessment for Child Caregivers.

Purpose: Designed to identify areas of strength and skill development needs of caregivers of children with disabilities.
Population: Caregivers of children with disabilities.
Publication Date: 1993.
Scores: 8 sections: Arrival and Departure, Free Choice Play, Structured Group Activities, Outside Play, Meal Time, Toileting, Nap Time, Throughout the Day.
Administration: Group.
Price Data: Price data available from publisher.
Time: Administration time not reported.
Author: Irene Carney.
Publisher: Child Development Resources.

Review of How Am I Doing? A Self-Assessment for Child Caregivers by LISA G. BISCHOFF, Associate Professor of School Psychology, Indiana State University, Terre Haute, IN:

According to the manual, the How Am I Doing? A Self-Assessment for Child Caregivers was developed to identify caregiver skills needed to provide services to preschool children with disabilities and their families. It may be used by caregivers for self-assessment or by supervisors following observation of the caregiver.

The instrument is divided into eight sections including Arrival and Departure, Free Choice Play, Structured Group Activities, Outside Play, Meal Time, Toileting, Nap Time, and Throughout the Day. Each section contains two to eight statements on which the caregiver is rated using a 5-point Likert scale with anchors ranging from *I can do this well* to *I can do this with some children, but not with others* to *I don't know how to do this*. Instructions for administration, scoring, and interpretation are not provided in the manual.

It is stated in the manual that the results of assessment may be used to "help caregivers see that many of the skills needed for working with children with disabilities are the very same skills they use to provide developmentally appropriate child care for all children" (p. iv). Furthermore, results may be used to plan skill development activities for caregivers. Information regarding specific caregiver populations with which the instrument may be used are not included in the manual nor are settings in which the instrument may be used specified. I. Carney (personal communication, October, 1996) stated that the instrument was developed for use in a training project for caregivers of children with disabilities.

The manual provides no specific information regarding development of the How Am I Doing? The instrument was developed by Irene Carney, Ph.D., for Child Development Resources, Incorporated as part of SpecialCare, a 3-year model demonstration project designed to increase the number of inclusive child-care settings available for families of children with disabilities. According to I. Carney (personal communication, October, 1996), the items for the instrument were determined using a checklist for child-care providers developed by T. Harms at the Frank Porter Graham Child Development Center at the University of North Carolina. Carney reported that the How Am I Doing? was field-tested on a limited basis with students at a community college for clarity of items.

Information regarding psychometric properties of the How Am I doing? is not included in the manual. Items included appear to have some "face validity" as they are related to stated areas and to care of children with disabilities. However, reliability and validity are not addressed in the manual. According to I. Carney (personal communication, October, 1996), the instrument was developed for and has been used with a demonstration training project for child-care providers of children with disabilities. Validation studies have not been conducted on the instrument.

The How Am I Doing? is an instrument designed to assess skills of caregivers involved in delivering services to children with disabilities and their families. Although the instrument includes items related to skills relevant to the provision of child-care services to children with disabilities and their families, the lack of information regarding instrument development, validity, reliability, administra-

tion, scoring, and interpretation preclude its use as an evaluation instrument in practice. However, caregivers may find the instrument useful in training to state skills relevant to care of children with disabilities.

Review of How Am I Doing? A Self-Assessment for Child Caregivers by FREDERIC J. MEDWAY, Professor of Psychology, University of South Carolina, Columbia, SC, and KAREN FAY, Psychology Intern, Lexington County Mental Health Center, Lexington, SC:

How Am I Doing? is a rating scale to identify the skill needs of caregivers who work with young children with disabilities and their families. The scale was developed to provide an assessment of caregivers' ability in regard to specific skills presumed required during various times of the day in working with young disabled children. The author presents it for use as a caregiver self-assessment or to be used by the caregiver's supervisor following periods of caregiver skill observations. Results are to be used to improve skills in areas where the caregiver has weakness or uncertainty.

The scale has a total of 46 items divided into sections covering the routines in a typical day of preschool care such as dealing with going and coming (e.g., separation issues, dressing), outside and inside play (e.g., matching children's skills to various activities), eating and drinking, toileting, napping, and play and communication. Within the sections are items that include ability to increase children's comfort, support self-sufficiency, deal with family members, and select materials and activities. All items are scored on a 5-point scale ranging from *I can do this well* to *I don't know how to do this*, although numerical values are not assigned to the scale points.

The scale consists of one spiral-bound booklet with the test items. There are no test forms. The booklet contains no information on scale development and presumably items were chosen based on face validity. Neither the publishers or author provide information on scale development, reliability, or validity in other published sources. There is no test-retest information even though the scale is suggested to be used for periodic rechecks of caregiver skills.

There are no specific scoring procedures for the scale nor any information regarding the validity of dividing the scale into various sections. Where the author suggests reviewing the results to identify caregiver areas of strength and skill development, more specific scoring guidelines would be useful and a factor analysis of the scale is needed to confirm the stated structure.

Because of the lack of any information on test development and characteristics, How Am I Doing? must be considered a very crude measure. It might suggest areas for general staff training and could highlight areas of potential weakness for those seeking employment in working with young disabled children. However, its use as an employee performance appraisal instrument is not justified.

[141]
I-SPEAK Your Language™: A Survey of Personal Styles.

Purpose: Designed to teach employees how to identify and modify their communication style to work best with others in a variety of situations.
Population: Employees.
Publication Dates: 1972–1993.
Scores, 8: Favorable Conditions (Intuitor, Thinker, Feeler, Senser), Stress Conditions (Intuitor, Thinker, Feeler, Senser).
Administration: Group or individual.
Price Data, 1993: $45 per 10 questionnaires; $12.95 per Self-Development Exercises manual ('92, 59 pages); $12.95 per manual ('93, 46 pages); $25 per specimen set including questionnaire, manual, and Self-Development Exercises manual.
Time: (20) minutes.
Comments: Also available in Spanish (except Self-Development Exercises manual).
Author: Drake Beam Morin, Inc.
Publisher: DBM Publishing.

Review of I-SPEAK Your Language: A Survey of Personal Styles by MARY ANNE BUNDA, Professor, Educational Leadership, Western Michigan University, Kalamazoo, MI:

I-SPEAK Your Language and I-SPEAK are trademarks of Harcourt Brace Jovanovich, Inc., but the copyright to the instrument and manuals is held by Drake Beam Morin, Inc.

The manual for this instrument indicates that it was developed using the theories of Carl Jung, but nowhere in any of the materials are there citations to works used or data used in the development of the material. Those familiar with the Myers-Briggs Type Indicator (MBTI; T4:1702) will see similarities between that instrument and this one. However, this instrument does not have the wealth of research information the MBTI has. It is not the purpose of this review to comment on the quality of the MBTI. However, Pittenger (1993) in an extensive review of information on the MBTI concluded that there was insufficient evidence to support the claims of utility in work settings.

The I-SPEAK Your Language instrument consists of 18 stems each followed by four alternative statements. Each of the statements must be rated on a 4-point scale to show how much like the respondent the statement is. These ratings are then used to form the eight score scales.

The manual tries in 45 pages to explain what each of the styles are and to "show" how they can be used in business (e.g., "shows people how to determine communication styles … and teaches them to use this knowledge to foster enhanced communications that produce results" [p. 45]). Although disclaimers are presented about primary styles and situational effects, most of the manual is designed to create stereotypes that are not supported by any scientific evidence. The manual suggests that training can be provided to change styles. It suggests that characteristics such as prudence and creativity are effective applications of a particular style. It suggests that it can be used to analyze customers as well as sales. It suggests that it can be used to strengthen subordinate performance (i.e., be used as a job coaching tool). It suggests that oppositional styles may be used to strengthen teams. To say the least, the manual asks the user of the instrument to draw conclusions that are unwarranted.

Real harm can be caused by this package in what is called the "Self-Development Exercises." In this workbook, respondents are asked to guess at professions that particular styles are likely to pursue. They are given a quiz on the use of the system in sales, learning that "a Senser client-customer tends to be impatient, stubborn, demanding services 'yesterday'" (p. 11); learning how your style may "turn off" various types of customers; and learning how to use appearance of clothing as a diagnostic tool. "It is very difficult to draw conclusions from mode of dress; nevertheless, how and what a person wears does provide additional clues to one's personal style" (p. 39). Thus, it is suggested that a tie with a small pattern would likely be selected by a Thinker, whereas a Senser is likely to wear comfortable shoes. Likewise, it suggests that looking at a customer's book shelf can provide evidence that Sensers would have digests whereas Intuitors would read Toffler.

One can only marvel at the coincidence of the development of this instrument shortly after the Pittenger findings.

REVIEWER'S REFERENCE

Pittenger, D. J. (1993). The utility of the Myers-Briggs Type Indicator. *Review of Educational Research, 63,* 467–488.

Review of the I-SPEAK Your Language: A Survey of Personal Styles by KIMBERLY A. LAWLESS, Assistant Professor of Instructional Technology, Utah State University, Logan, UT:

The I-SPEAK Your Language assessment battery is a program of evaluation and study that helps individuals to identify the communication styles used by themselves and others in business settings. It also purports to teach how to use this information to enhance communication between two parties. The I-SPEAK manual claims that "understanding how individuals experience things and behave can be improved by knowing their *primary* and *back-up* [communication] styles" (p. 2). The program operates on the basic premise that individuals communicate most effectively with others who exhibit a similar communication style. As such, learning to alter your style to complement that of another will greatly increase effective communication.

The scale is based on the work of Jung, indicating the four major personality styles that people employ in work and personal situations. These styles further break down into typical behavior functions. The styles and functions, as listed in the survey manual are as follows: Intuitor (conceiving, projecting, inducing); Thinker (analyzing, ordering in logical fashion); Feeler (relating to and understanding experience through emotional reactions and responses to feelings); and Senser (experiencing mainly on the basis of one's own sensory perceptions). The scale measures individuals' communication styles under normal and stressful conditions.

The I-SPEAK questionnaire consists of 18 self-descriptive partial stems. Each of these partial stems is followed by four completer stems. The respondent is instructed to rank the four completer stems on a scale of 1 to 4. A score of 4 indicates that stem best describes their behavior, a score of 1 is least descriptive. A scoring sheet helps the respondent to create sum scores for each on the four communication styles. Two sum scores are created for each communication style, one for normal conditions, and one for stressful conditions. The highest sum score for each condition indicates the dominant communication style.

Once the dominant communication styles have been identified, the respondent or test administrator is referred to the I-SPEAK manual. The manual explains how scores are interpreted, as well as explains each type of communication style. The manual also presents a variety of applications for the I-SPEAK questionnaire, including sales training, team building, conflict resolution, management development, and personnel selection.

No studies of reliability or validity have been conducted. Because this scale has been available to the public since 1972, to neglect to perform such studies is reproachable. In the absence of such data, no judgment concerning the consistency or accuracy of the scale can be made. Some general comments about the scale format, however, are warranted.

The forced-choice format of the I-SPEAK questionnaire makes it an ipsative measure. Ipsative measures are infamously sensitive to biases resulting from social desirability (Gable & Wolf, 1993). Thus, when people are threatened or simply desire to present a particular image, "faked responses" result. In addition, Clemans (1966) argues that intercorrelations between concepts measured on ipsative scales are falsely inflated due to the summed nature of the forced-choice response format. The high interdependence of the scale scores seriously limits alpha-internal consistency reliabilities (Hicks, 1970) as well as the ability to interpret variance information for construct validity (Guilford, 1952).

Although the test manual for the I-SPEAK Your Language questionnaire provides interesting information concerning the various communications styles, from both a psychometric viewpoint and a practical viewpoint, the scale itself offers no benefits. I caution any person using this scale to be wary of the unintended ramifications of the ipsative response format. The use of this scale to make important decisions such as personnel selection and career development should be avoided.

REVIEWER'S REFERENCES

Guilford, J. P. (1952). When not to factor analyze. *Psychological Bulletin, 49,* 26–37.

Clemans, W. V. (1966). An analytical and empirical examination of some properties of ipsative measures. *Psychometric Monographs,* No. 14. Chicago: University of Chicago Press.

Hicks, L. E. (1970). Some properties of ipsative, normative and forced-choice normative measures. *Psychological Bulletin, 74*(3), 167–184.

Gable, R. K., & Wolf, M. B. (1993). *Instrument development in the affective domain* (2nd ed.). Boston, MA: Kluwer Academic Publishers.

[142]

IDEA Reading and Writing Proficiency Test.

Purpose: To provide "comprehensive assessment for the initial identification and redesignation of Limited English Proficient (LEP) students."

Population: Grades 2–12.

Publication Dates: 1992–1993.

Acronym: IPT R & W.

Scores, 8: Reading (Vocabulary, Vocabulary in Context, Reading for Understanding, Reading for Life Skills, Language Usage), Writing (Conventions, Write a Story, Write Your Own Story).

Administration: Group.
Levels, 3: Grades 2–3, Grades 4–6, Grades 7–12.
Price Data: Available from publisher.
Foreign Language Editions: English and Spanish versions available for each level.
Time: (70–115) minutes.
Comments: Used in conjunction with the IPT Oral Language Proficiency Test.
Authors: Beverly A. Amori, Enrique F. Dalton, and Phyllis L. Tighe.
Publisher: Ballard & Tighe.

Review of the IDEA Reading and Writing Proficiency Test by JAMES DEAN BROWN, Professor, Department of ESL, University of Hawaii at Manoa, Honolulu, HI:

The IDEA Reading and Writing Proficiency Test (IPT R&W) provides "comprehensive assessment for initial identification and redesignation of Limited English Proficient (LEP) students" (examiner's manual, p. 3). These tests only claim to measure reading and writing skills. They are meant to be administered in conjunction with the IDEA Oral Language Proficiency Test.

The IPT R&W contains test booklets, answer sheets, scoring templates, examiner's manuals, and technical manuals covering Level 1 (grades 2–3), Level 2 (4–6) and Level 3 (7–12). Color-coded by level to help avoid confusion, the three levels all have the same general look and organization.

The test booklets have adequate directions and appropriately large type-face and format for the age levels involved. The multiple-choice answer sheets are the machine-scorable kind, but scoring templates are also provided for hand scoring. The picture and prose prompts in the writing subtests are clear and appropriate for the age levels being tested.

The examiner's manuals (one for each level) contain sections on: the background of the test developers, the history and development of the tests, description of the test, administering the reading test, administering the writing test, scoring the reading test, rating the writing samples, scoring the writing test, summary rules for testing, and implications for instruction. The authors also furnish a number of useful appendices: item specifications, definitions of the three student designations (non-English, limited English, and competent English), diagnostic reading profiles, directions for hand scoring the reading subtests, sample writing responses, and explanations of the standardized scores along with equivalency tables.

Throughout the examiner's manuals, those instructions that proctors should read aloud to examinees are clearly indicated in contrasting blue print. The guidelines for rating the open-ended parts of the writing subtests include rubrics, abundant examples, and guidelines for rater training. These descriptions are somewhat complex so raters must study them well in advance.

Two technical manuals are available, one for Levels 1 and 2 combined, and another for Level 3. Each of these provides sections on: information about the test designers, the test rationale and test development steps, normative information, and advice on interpreting standard scores.

In more detail, the authors explain that the test specifications were based partly on California's Curriculum Frameworks for English and Language Arts "reflecting a nationwide trend toward a holistic approach to language learning" (technical manual, pp. 1–2), and partly on a survey of textbooks and achievement tests done by the authors.

The multiple-choice subtests (Reading and Writing Conventions) are discussed separately from the open-ended writing sample subtests in the technical manuals. The Level 1A and 2A multiple-choice Reading and Writing Conventions subtests were administered in 23 schools to 1,406 students in grades 2 and 3 (for Level 1) and grades 4 to 6 (for Level 2), and the Levels 3A and 3B tests were administered in 18 schools to 869 students in grades 7 to 12. The primary languages of 89% of the Levels 1 and 2 sample were English or Spanish; 84% of the Level 3 sample listed those two languages as primary. The authors provide abundant and clear information about the students' ages, genders, grades, ethnicities, district language designations, and teacher opinions of students' abilities.

The authors begin their statistical presentation with the percent correct and standard deviations for each of the items. Strangely, no discrimination index or item-total correlations are supplied to help readers understand the degree to which items discriminated between high and low achievers. Descriptive statistics and Cronbach alpha reliabilities are also reported. The alphas for the total Reading scores are .95, .91, .90, and .96 for the 1A, 2A, 3A, and 3B tests, respectively. The alphas for the various multiple-choice subtests are lower, ranging from .54 to .86, which makes sense because these subtests are considerably shorter. Smaller sample test-retest and alternative-forms reliabilities show similar patterns. The authors' discussion of reliability would have been much enhanced if they had provided an explanation of how the standard error of measurement can be used in decision making.

The authors defend content validity in tables of item specifications that list the competencies or concepts being tested in each subtest and the corresponding item numbers. In a few cases, competencies are tested by only one item. Nonetheless, these item specifications are exemplary because they openly display the content of the tests so that readers can judge for themselves if the tests are valid for their purposes.

The authors argue for construct validity by examining the intercorrelations among the subtests and similarities in subtest-total correlations, as well as by comparing the mean scores of different grade levels and types of students (as determined by amount of English language instruction). This latter discussion is fairly persuasive, but would be even more convincing if the statistical significance of the reported mean differences had been explored so that readers would know the probability that the observed differences occurred by chance alone.

The authors also explore criterion-related (concurrent) validity by examining the correlations of reading test percentile scores with the California Test of Basic Skills percentile scores at each grade level. These coefficients averaged .76 for the 1A and 2A tests, and .53 for the 3A and 3B tests. Then, the correlations with teachers' opinions are shown to range from .28 to .63.

Laudably, the authors also provide considerable advice on establishing cut scores for the non-English, limited English, and competent English reading designations.

The authors administered the Level 1A and 2A open-ended writing sample subtests in three schools to 143 students in grades 2 and 3 and grades 4 to 6. The 3A and 3B tests were administered in 13 schools to 117 students in grades 7 to 12. The primary language of 96.5% of the Levels 1 and 2 samples was English or Spanish; in the Level 3 sample, the percentage was 78.2%. Again, the demographic information is clear and complete.

The authors estimate the reliability of the writing subtests by examining interrater correlations (.90 to .98) and exact agreement between raters (79% to 86%). They explore criterion-related validity through examination of correlations between the writing subtest scores and three criterion measures: (a) teacher opinions of students' academic and writing abilities, (b) students' Writing Conventions subtest scores, and (c) norm-referenced language scores. These correlations are not very convincing; they range from .59 to .77 for Levels 1 and 2, and from .26 to .52 for Level 3. However, once again, advice is provided to help in establishing responsible cut points.

In sum, the IPT R&W tests are clearly organized, color coded, and appropriately formatted. These tests have clear administration procedures and provide considerable guidance for setting standards. The technical manual is reasonably comprehensive, but would be even more complete if it included some discussion of item discrimination and more explanation of the standard error of measurement. In addition, norms based on groups of non-natives other than Spanish speakers would have made the tests more useful in places where those other language backgrounds are prevalent. These last negative comments are simply meant to suggest ways that the IPT R&W tests could be enhanced. As they are, these tests provide a useful set of tools for making decisions about the reading and writing levels of Limited English Proficient students, especially if used in conjunction with the IDEA Oral Language Proficiency Test and other information about the students.

Review of the IDEA Reading and Writing Proficiency Test by ALAN GARFINKEL, Professor of Spanish and Education, Purdue University, West Lafayette, IN:

Federal legislation on bilingual education directs that federal funding be directed toward a process called transition. That process allows students who speak various languages to make a transition to the use of English after a start in their home language. The complexity of that process becomes clear when one considers that not all children enter schools in this country at the same level of development and that not all children are equally capable of listening, speaking, reading, and writing either their home language or English. When a student enters the mainstream of the proficient user of English, how is a school district to assess English proficiency in order to maximize student success at that point? The authors of the IDEA Reading and Writing Proficiency Test (IPT R&W) have carefully and conscientiously created a set of instruments that will make an important contribution to that assessment.

The IPT R&W is a standardized, group-administered set of tests of reading and writing in English for students at varying levels of English proficiency. The Reading subtest consists of sets of items in Vocabulary, Vocabulary in Context, Reading for Understanding, Reading for Life Skills, and Language usage. The Writing unit includes a segment on Conventions (such as punctuation), describing a set of pictures of a set of sequential events, and writing one's own story based on a picture. I was particularly impressed with the Life Skills segments because they seem to me to be challenging enough to generate a measurement without being inappropriate for the age in question.

Instructions in the administrator's manuals at each level are clear and detailed. In fact, they include a script for test administrators to use. The manuals also contain assistance in holistically grading the writing samples the test generates. Criteria for identifying stages of writing proficiency ranging from "non-expressive" to "competent" are provided along with samples of student writing. The rating of "competent" is particularly useful in the context of mainstreaming because it indicates with examples there may still be things to teach and learn.

Technical manuals for tests are complete and most helpful. Technical terms in testing and measurement are clearly explained. The data supplied about the norming populations are ample. Included is information on the age, gender, grade level, and ethnicity as well as teacher opinions and expectations. A sound theoretical and practical background is cited and reliability ratings for the reading subtest are, for the most part, exceptionally high. Validity is discussed from several points of view and very well supported.

Using the IPT R&W test is likely to yield valuable information that school administrators can use in combination with other factors to make enlightened decisions on mainstreaming children of varying English proficiencies.

[143]
Individual Service Strategy Portfolio.

Purpose: Designed to help human service organizations gather information about clients' vocational plans and to assist in creating such plans.
Population: Human service clients.
Publication Date: 1993.
Acronym: ISSP.
Scores: Total Assets and Barriers for 7 categories: Personal Considerations, Health, Work Orientation, Career Planning Skills, Job Seeking Skills, Job Adaptation Skills, Education and Training.
Administration: Individual.
Price Data: Available from publisher.
Time: Administration time not reported.

Authors: LaVerne L. Ludden (manual and portfolio), Bonnie R. Maitlen (manual and portfolio), and J. Michael Farr (portfolio).
Publisher: JIST Works, Inc.

Review of the Individual Service Strategy Portfolio by JAVAID KAISER, Senior Research and Evaluation Officer, Academy for Educational Development, Washington, DC:

The Individual Service Strategy Portfolio (ISSP) is designed to assess the employability of individuals. The ISSP also provides a structure to identify other relevant information that is useful in determining the employability status, counseling needs, and training needs of participants. The information obtained from different sources is organized in a three-part folder. The folder provides a quick look at the strengths and weaknesses of participants and serves as a remarkable tool for employment counselors and service providers. The authors claim that the ISSP is very effective in carrying out employment and training programs such as JTPA.

The ISSP organizes the information into seven areas: Participant Information, Family Situation, Work History, Assessment and Recommendations, Employability Assessment Checklist, Employability Assessment Summary Chart, and Training and Service Plan. The background information such as name, address, phone number, date of birth, gender, employment status, economic status, and vocational goal fall under the Participant Information category. Marital status, household size, child care needs, adult care needs, and family medical needs are listed under the Family Situation section. The Work History section provides space to record information about the last seven jobs. The information includes job title, start/end dates, the employer, and the address of the employer. In addition, self-management skills, skills transferable to other jobs, and skills specific to the job are also identified for each of the three most recent jobs. The Assessment and Recommendations section of the ISSP has three subsections: Assessment Methods, Assessment Outcomes, and Recommended Services. Structured interview, behavioral observation, aptitude test, paper-and-pencil test, interest/attitude surveys, basic skills test, performance tests, and career guidance inventories are listed as possible Assessment Methods. The service provider/counselor simply checks the methods used in making assessments and records the dates of assessment. The outcomes of these assessments are recorded in the Assessment Outcomes section. This section provides the space to list information about basic skills, aptitudes/abilities, job skills, vocational interests, work style and behaviors that may affect employment. The recommendations based on the results of these assessments are recorded in the Recommended Services section.

The Employability Assessment Checklist (EAC) is the fifth area of the ISSP. It consists of 84 items that are evenly divided into seven areas: Personal Issues and Considerations, Health, Work Orientation, Career Planning Skills, Job Seeking Skills, Job Adaptation Skills, and Education and Training Credentials. The items present attributes and respondents identify them as assets, barriers, or critical barriers. The assets and barriers reported under each area are counted and recorded in the employability Assessment Summary Chart, the sixth section of the ISSP. The respondents are classified as having low, medium, or high assets if the count of their assets is four or less, five to eight, or greater than eight, respectively. The same scheme is used to categorize barriers into low, medium, and high. A visual profile of assets or barriers of a participant may be obtained by connecting the points representing their respective scores. The critical barriers identified by respondents for each area are also listed in the summary chart.

The last section of the ISSP, Training and Services Plan, is used to record the vocational plan, which is tailored for the participant. The plan lists the achievement goals, actions required to achieve these goals, provider organization responsible, duration of the intervention, start/stop dates, justification of start/stop action, and the completion date. The folder also has a space where participants list their employment goals and show their preferences for hours of work, the type of business, full-time/part-time job, wage requirements, transportation arrangements, child care needs, and the technique they want to use in searching for a job. Both the provider and the participant sign the card. The way vocational plans are written helps providers in monitoring the progress of job searches, counseling sessions, and training needs of participants. It also provides ample opportunities to make modifications in vocational plans when needed.

The Employability Assessment Checklist, which is a major component of the ISSP, identifies assets and barriers of participants about their employability. Although the scale has face validity, no information is available about construct validity and reliability of the scores. Without construct validity, it is not certain that the assets and barriers identified

by the scale determine the employability of a person. Similarly, the authors have not provided any empirical evidence to suggest that scale scores are correlated with the job search or job success. In the absence of criterion-related validity, the use of scale scores to predict the employability of a participant is questionable. The authors have also failed to document how cutoff points were selected to categorize assets and barriers into low, medium, and high categories. It appears that these decisions were made arbitrarily and are not based on normative data.

The ISSP is a valuable tool for gathering and organizing information on participants who need employment counseling, occupational training, or other help in finding jobs. It, no doubt, simplifies the record keeping of employment counselors and service providers and increases the opportunities for providing quality service to participants. However, the use of the EAC scores in assessing assets and barriers of participants is questionable without validity and reliability information. In view of the significant contribution the EAC scores can make in assessing the employability of people, the authors are strongly encouraged to document its psychometric properties to make it a useful assessment tool.

Review of the Individual Service Strategy Portfolio by ALBERT OOSTERHOF, Professor of Educational Psychology, Florida State University, Tallahassee, FL:

The Individual Service Strategy Portfolio is used to collect background information about clients served by employment and training programs and to list assessment outcomes and recommended services to be provided clients. The portfolio also includes an Employability Assessment Checklist and a summary chart used to report scores on this checklist. The entire portfolio form is printed on the front and back sides of a three-panel file folder. This format allows the portfolio to be stored in a file cabinet and to contain supporting material. A separate portfolio is prepared for each client.

The Instructor's Manual that accompanies the Individual Service Strategy Portfolio identifies three goals for the portfolio: gathering the types of client data required of many employment and training programs, helping provide more effective counseling by identifying a client's employment weaknesses and strengths, and helping clients quickly define and reach career planning and employment goals. Ultimately, the service agency has to evaluate the usefulness of information collected by the portfolio form. This review describes the type of items included in the form and raises some issues to be addressed when considering its possible use.

Items on the first page of the portfolio solicit background information organized into three parts: Participant Information, Family Situation, and Work History. Information sought by many of the items is clear, such as the client's date of birth and number of dependents. A number of items are quite broad using a single question to establish information such as a client's economic status or family medical needs. An agency using the portfolio must establish the specific information to be recorded within these broad areas as the accompanying manual provides little guidance. The agency may find space provided for recording information to be inadequate for some of the items although separate paper can be used and easily inserted in the portfolio as needed.

The second page of the portfolio is titled Assessment and Recommendations. In a small portion of this page, the user enters the dates when various assessment methods were used to obtain information about the client. The various methods are described in broad terms, such as structured interview, paper-and-pencil test, and performance test. Several of the listed methods are overlapping such as aptitude tests, paper-and-pencil tests, and basic skills tests. Space is then provided to describe assessment outcomes and recommend services. The manual again provides little guidance for completing this section of the portfolio.

The third and fourth pages contain the Employability Assessment Checklist. This checklist is organized into seven sections each consisting of 12 items. The sections are titled Personal Issues and Considerations, Health, Work Orientation, Career Planning Skills, Job Seeking Skills, Job Adaptation Skills, and Education and Training Credentials. The 12 items within each section seem consistent with the respective titles. For instance, Job Adaptation Skills includes items such as good attendance, punctuality, and accepts responsibility. Within each section, the user responds to each of the 12 items by rating the characteristic as an asset or barrier with respect to the client's employability. Space is also provided to comment on any qualities judged to be a critical barrier.

The Summary Chart is then used to record the numbers of items within the checklist marked as an asset versus barrier. These tallies are recorded for each of the seven sections. The Summary Chart provides separate tallies for Assets and Barriers, which

is needlessly redundant because a higher number of assets is equivalent to a lower number of barriers and vice versa. For each section, the summary chart categorizes the number of assets (and barriers) as high, medium, or low, but provides no normative information or other rationale for these categories.

The final page of the portfolio is entitled Training and Services Plan. On this page, the user records information such as achievement goals for the client, required action, and start/stop dates for the actions. Again, the space provided for responses is limited with the caveat that a separate paper can be used as needed to record information.

As noted earlier, the service agency must evaluate the usefulness of information collected by the portfolio form. The Instructor's Manual presents what the authors call the Employability Development Model; however, the relationship of this model with research literature in social work is unclear. The model appears to guide somewhat superficially the content of the portfolio. The manual provides a telephone number through which staff training related to the use of the portfolio can be requested. The nature and cost of this training are not described.

[144]

Individual Style Survey.

Purpose: "Intended to be an educational tool for self and interpersonal development."
Publication Dates: 1989–1990.
Administration: Group.
Price Data: Available from publisher.
Time: (60–90) minutes.
Comments: Self-administered, self-scored survey.
Author: Norman Amundson.
Publisher: Psychometrics Canada Ltd. [Canada].
  a) INDIVIDUAL STYLE SURVEY.
  Population: Adults.
  Publication Date: 1989.
  Acronym: ISS.
  Scores, 14: 8 categories of behavior (Forceful, Assertive, Outgoing, Spontaneous, Empathetic, Patient, Reserved, Analytical) yielding 4 styles (Dominant, Influencing, Harmonious, Cautious) that combine to form 2 summary scores (People/Task Orientation, Introspective/Interactive Stance).
  b) MY PERSONAL STYLE.
  Population: Ages 10–18.
  Publication Date: 1990.
  Acronym: MPS.
  Scores, 14: 8 categories (Carefree, Outgoing, Straight Forward, Forceful, Precise, Reserved, Patient, Sensitive) yielding 4 styles (Influencing, Strong

Willed, Cautious, Peaceful) that combine to form 2 summary scores (People/Task Orientation, Expressive/Thoughtful Stance).

Comments: Simplified version of the Individual Style Survey for use with young people.

Review of the Individual Style Survey by JEFFREY A. ATLAS, Deputy Chief Psychologist and Associate Clinical Professor, Bronx Children's Psychiatric Center, Albert Einstein College of Medicine, Bronx, NY:

The Individual Style Survey, in its adult version, is introduced "to provide a structured activity for self and interpersonal development" (p. 1). The secondary-school youth version, like the adult booklet containing a self form as well as three others to give to friends, family, or work or teacher contacts, is introduced "to provide a way for you to find out more about yourself and others" (p. 1). These stated purposes appear to meld the aims of assessment and intervention, individually and in groups, but the Individual Style Survey (ISS) is compromised by weaknesses in construct validity and consequent real-world application.

The "Leader's Guide," in what functions as a test manual, cites foundations for the study of individual style as diverse as Jung and Adler to more current counseling and industrial psychology researchers. The theory of the behavioral descriptors draws from the earlier authors and is pictorialized in a circle bisected by people/task-oriented and thoughtful/expressive axes, evoking an image of quadrants of individual style recalling Timothy Leary's typology of personality. The implementation of the survey instrument and recommended applications draws more from the ethos of industrial psychology and counseling.

Unlike other, more straightforward career-interest inventories for adults or youth, such as the Strong-Campbell or Career Decision Making System, there are no norms for the ISS to compare individuals' self-descriptors to responses of groups in selected occupations or to comparative descriptive information by schooling. The construct, then, of "individual style" as characterized by self- or other-ascribed characteristics of, for example, "Influencing" (the quadrant comprising "Spontaneous" and "Outgoing") has face validity but poor construct validity. There are no data comparing responses to other descriptive data sources or behavioral outcomes, or indeed taking into account the linguistic issue of category naming, which would suggest some variety of factor analysis to discover if the different descriptors could meaningfully be added in equal ways to produce summary scores. The summary scores, given

weak empirical grounding, thus carry the oracular aura of an astrology reading (e.g., those scoring high in Influencing can learn that "When your influencing style is used appropriately, it can be a powerful means of moving people to action through persuasion rather than coercion. You are energetic and inspiring and confidently express your opinions. You also have a twinkle in your eye and a good sense of humor" [test booklet, p. 16]).

A question is why such an instrument should emerge now, and in this structure, given that self-assessment (updated here to individual style) has been a documented aspect of human existence since antiquity (e.g., Augustine's *Confessions*). The ISS presumes that self-descriptions are easily accessible to consciousness or may be captured by comparing them to others' observations (recalling the "I" and "me" dialectic of G. H. Mead). The notion that such aspects of personhood can be absorbed by scores on categories such as Influencing or Cautious carries a danger (or purpose?) of reification of human qualities into commodity-like items that may be combined or altered to "fit the market" (p. 17). Indeed, in the applications section of the Leader's Guide, a Board of Directors Scenario entails possible people versus task group responses given a mandated 30% reduction in labor force due to falling oil prices (e.g., one class of group responses was "lay off employees according to seniority" [p. 17]). The ISS in this way appears topical (i.e., responsive to such events as 1970s—1980s shifts in oil prices) and yet dated, dependent upon shifts in (Western) economic crises and associated changes in corporate structures and strategies.

For a person who "under uses influencing style," the Leader's Guide suggests "allow time for a response to new ideas, give advance warning of meetings" (p. 16). The ISS is less an assessment instrument than an intervention program awaiting validation (e.g., in industrial-corporate settings). Practitioners in such settings may find the ISS a useful experimental or programmatic technique to try in joint aims of facilitating worker productivity and satisfaction, as long as the projected change in styles is not overly depended upon to cover over real organizational or micropolitical problems. (Exploitative work relations are unlikely to be "harmonized" through the ISS or any other measures). In a similar vein, the ISS offers some thoughtful general approaches in self-assessment and counseling, such as with a person who overuses the cautious style ("validate the close inspection of details, but show ... action planning" [p. 16]) or who underuses the cautious style ("share the 'dream,' but slow down the process" [p. 16]). Counseling psychologists and their clients may find such leads effective but should know that changes in individual style, in or out of the workplace, are unlikely to go beneath the superficial unless change is predicated upon structural changes in the individual's lifespace or the individual's psychological means of apprehending and changing experience.

Review of the Individual Style Survey by WILL-IAM I. SAUSER, JR., Professor and Executive Director for Outreach, College of Business, Auburn University, Auburn, AL:

The Individual Style Survey (ISS) is a very simple instrument intended, according to the manual, "to be an educational tool for self and interpersonal development. Through using the survey it is possible to acquire increased understanding of self and others. This information is an important aspect of competence development … and for team building" (p. 1). The instrument clearly is intended for use within a group training or individual counseling context. An alternate form of the ISS, employing language more appropriate for adolescents, is marketed as My Personal Style (MPS).

The author indicates that the ISS arose from the tradition of personality "type" theory espoused by such writers as Jung, Kretschmer, Adler, and Leary. This reviewer noted a striking similarity of the ISS dimensions to the four types espoused by Geier (1977) in his Personal Profile System (T4:1982). The author cites Geier's instrument, as well as Anderson's (1987) Personal Style Indicator (228), as other "systems of analysis" flowing from the personality "type" tradition. Although not cited by the author, the Myers-Briggs Type Indicator (MBTI; T4:1702) is a well-known (and better constructed, researched, and documented than the ISS; see Wiggins, 1989) example of instruments of this nature.

The ISS consists of eight words accompanied by one-sentence definitions; for example, "Spontaneous: I am instinctive and act on my impulses" (p. 4). The test-taker is directed to "Read the descriptors and then choose two descriptors most like you, continuing through the list to the two descriptors least like you" (p. 3). The rank orders of the descriptors then become scores, which are summed in various ways to produce the four "style" and two "summary" scores. One new twist with this instrument is that the test-taker is instructed, after completing the "self" form, to "give the 'others' form to three

different people of your choice and ask for their honest opinions" (p. 1). Once these additional data are collected, they are melded into the scoring process as well.

The ISS is interesting and engaging, and could—in the hands of a capable trainer or counselor—be used to develop limited insight into certain characteristics and behaviors of the test-taker. The instrument itself provides some interpretive material relating to effective use, overuse, and underuse of each style. Further interpretive material is found in the manual, which draws connections between ISS styles and various styles of learning, information processing, and communicating. Unfortunately, neither the instrument nor the manual provides any definitive guidance for determining whether a certain style is being used effectively or ineffectively. The manual states, "The extent to which people are over or under using a style is a matter for individual reflection and assessment" (p. 3).

Stone (1992) rightly categorizes instruments of this ilk as "parlor games," citing their general lack of validity evidence. (Stone excepts the MBTI from this group because validation data have been presented for it.) This reviewer must agree: The author presents no shred of evidence of validity for the ISS and MPS. Furthermore, none of the standard psychometric concerns—norms, reliability evidence, test bias, reporting test results—are even mentioned in the manual. Clearly the ISS and MPS are totally inappropriate to serve as bases for decisions affecting the test-taker. Human resource professionals are warned not to use the ISS as a basis for any personnel management decisions, because it has not been demonstrated to be psychometrically sound.

The "type" approach to personality theory has some merit and enjoys considerable intuitive appeal. Although the MBTI would likely be a better choice, trainers and counselors seeking to illustrate the "type" approach might—with appropriate professional caution—use the ISS within the context of an educational module. However, given the instrument's obvious fakability, the lack of scientific rigor employed in its development, and the absence of any data documenting its psychometric quality, the Individual Style Survey should not be considered a professionally developed test, nor should it be used as a basis for any decisions regarding the test-taker. This reviewer joins Stone (1992), Wiggins (1989), and others in calling for more scientific rigor on the part of authors developing instruments from the perspective of personality "type" theory.

REVIEWER'S REFERENCES

Geier, J. G. (1977). *Personal Profile System.* Minneapolis: Performax Systems International.

Anderson, T. D. (1987). *Personal Style Indicator.* Vancouver: Consulting Resources Group.

Wiggins, J. S. (1989). [Review of the Myers-Briggs Type Indicator.] In J. C. Conoley & J. J. Kramer (Eds.), *The tenth mental measurements yearbook* (pp. 537–538). Lincoln, NE: The Buros Institute of Mental Measurements.

Stone, G. L. (1992). [Review of the Personal Style Assessment.] In J. J. Kramer & J. C. Conoley (Eds.), *The eleventh mental measurements yearbook* (pp. 287–288). Lincoln, NE: The Buros Institute of Mental Measurements.

[145]
Indonesian Speaking Test.

Purpose: "Designed to evaluate the level of oral proficiency attained by English speaking learners of Indonesian."

Population: Adults.

Publication Date: 1989.

Acronym: IST.

Scores, 6: Personal Conversation, Giving Directions, Picture Sequence Narration, Topical Discourse, Situational Discourse, Total.

Administration: Group.

Price Data: Available from publisher.

Time: (40–45) minutes.

Comments: Mail-in scoring.

Author: Center for Applied Linguistics.

Publisher: Center for Applied Linguistics.

Review of the Indonesian Speaking Test by MARGARET E. MALONE, Language Testing Specialist, Peace Corps, Washington, DC:

The Indonesian Speaking Test (IST) is an example of innovation in both oral proficiency testing and in testing the less commonly taught languages. The IST is 1 of 10 simulated oral proficiency interviews (SOPI) developed by the Center for Applied Linguistics (it is also available in Arabic, Mandarin Chinese, Hausa, Hebrew, French, German, Japanese, Portuguese, and Spanish). Because it was only the third test of this type developed, it does not benefit from many of the improvements made in future SOPIs based on research performed in the earlier tests.

The IST tests oral proficiency of native speakers of English studying Indonesian as another language. The specificity of audience (native speakers of English) is important, because all test directions and explanations of the items occur in English, and it seems necessary to have a near-native proficiency in English to understand the test directions and respond to the items.

The test has a number of potential uses, from assessment for study abroad to assessment for professional purposes. Because the test developers conducted neither specific-use validation studies nor standard-setting studies to determine appropriate scores for different uses of the test, no information is supplied about either topic.

Test administration takes 40 minutes and can be done for a large group in a language laboratory or with two tape recorders (one to play the test tape and one to record the responses) for an individual. All test directions and items are read over a test tape and are written in a test booklet. The test has five parts and an undisclosed number of items. The first part, the personal conversation, is the only part that includes any Indonesian. In this item, the examinee is asked to respond to short, personal questions in Indonesian, which are spoken on tape by a native speaker of Indonesian. In the next part, the examinee uses a drawn map to give directions in Indonesian. The next three items require the examinee to explain a sequence of four or five pictures on a page. The purpose of these three items is to elicit past, present, and future tense narration, respectively.

The next part, Topical Discourse, has six items. Examinees speak about different topic areas. Finally, in the last part, the examinee is asked to imagine that she or he is in a real-life situation and to speak accordingly. The test is sent for rating to an IST-trained rater and is scored according to the ACTFL (American Council on the Teaching of Foreign Languages) Guidelines.

The test has a number of negative and positive features. On the negative side, the sample size of pilot study participants was small and the construct validity of the test is unclear. On the positive side, the test has high interrater and parallel form reliability, as well as ease of administration and scoring. These issues are discussed in more detail below.

The size of the pilot study is small. Eight participants were students at the same university and the other 8 (for a total of 16) were from a variety of backgrounds not described in the test manual. It is unfortunate that more information is not available in the manual, because such information might help potential users to determine the test's applicability to their situation. Each participant was administered an Oral Proficiency Interview (OPI), which was scored according to the ILR (Interagency Language Roundtable) Guidelines, because there were no Indonesian-ACTFL certified testers available. Each examinee then took both forms (A and B) of the IST, which were scored by two raters. Because the OPI was administered and scored by one of the IST raters, this may have led to some bias on the rater's part.

Though this study is small, it is important to note that the sample of non-native speakers of Indonesian in the United States is also rather small.

Therefore, this possible source of error reflects a very real situation in the United States, the paucity of Indonesian language learners.

A second difficulty, inherent to the OPI, is the question of construct validity. A debate continues on the construct validity of the OPI; and the IST, because it was modeled on the OPI, therefore may also suffer from lack of construct validity.

On the positive side, the test has high reliability, content and criterion-referenced validity, and ease of administration. Two kinds of reliability were investigated: interrater reliability of the IST, across the two raters, and parallel form reliability. The interrater reliability for both forms of the test was .96 to .99. The parallel form reliability ranged from .91 to .95.

The content validity of the test is also quite high. Unlike the OPI, the SOPI gives all directions for all items in English. Therefore, there is no confusion between the listening domain and the speaking domain because the only skill tested is speaking ability in Indonesian. In addition, the criterion-referenced validity, or the correlation between the OPI and the IST, was also quite high—.93–.96.

Finally, the IST is extremely easy to administer. The test booklet supplies detailed, step-by-step directions. The test is quite sensitive to less commonly taught languages because it can be administered virtually anywhere by any language lab technician or other personnel and can be rated at a later time in a different location.

Though the IST could have profited from a larger sample of pilot study examinees and its construct validity is undetermined, it is nonetheless a reliable test of oral proficiency.

[146]
Infant-Toddler Developmental Assessment.

Purpose: Constructed as "an integrated family-centered assessment process that addresses the health and development of children."
Population: Birth to 3 years.
Publication Date: 1995.
Acronym: IDA.
Scores: 8 developmental domains: Gross Motor, Fine Motor, Relationship to Inanimate Objects (Cognitive), Language Communication, Self-Help, Relationship to Persons, Emotions and Feeling States (Affects), and Coping.
Administration: Individual.
Price Data, 1997: $394 per complete kit including 25 parent record forms, 25 health record guides, 25 record forms, foundations and study guide (223 pages), adminis-

tration manual (217 pages), readings (327 pages), manipulatives kit, and carrying case; $220.50 per complete kit without manipulatives and carrying case; $22 per 25 parent record forms; $22 per 25 Spanish parent report forms; $17 per 25 health record guides; $39 per 25 record forms; $53.50 per foundations and study guide; $53.50 per administration manual; $44 per readings; $220.50 per manipulatives kit; $52 per carrying case.
Time: Administration time not reported.
Comments: Ratings by multidisciplinary team.
Authors: Sally Provence, Joanna Erikson, Susan Vater, and Saro Palmeri.
Publisher: The Riverside Publishing Company.

Review of the Infant-Toddler Developmental Assessment by MELISSA M. GROVES, Assistant Professor of Child & Family Studies, University of Tennessee, Knoxville, TN:

The aim of the Infant-Toddler Development Assessment (IDA) is to improve early identification of children who may be in need of monitoring or intervention services. As such, the approach of the IDA is a "comprehensive, family-centered transdisciplinary approach to developmental assessment and family service planning" (manual, p. 2). The IDA is designed to be conducted by teams of at least two developmental professionals. The IDA consists of six phases of the assessment process that are described in detail in the manuals. These phases as named in the IDA material are: referral and preinterview data gathering; initial parent interview; health review; developmental observation and assessment; integration and synthesis; and share finding, completion, and report. The steps involved in the six phases are explained in detail in the manuals accompanying the IDA. The IDA also includes the Provence Profile that yields scores on the eight developmental domains. There are three manuals for the IDA: the IDA Foundations and Study Guide; the IDA Administration Manual; and the Family Centered Assessment of Young Children at Risk: The IDA Readings. The administration manual has been updated from earlier editions of the procedures manual (1985, 1987, 1991). The other manuals are new to the 1995 test edition.

A strength of the IDA is the addition of the study guide and readings manuals. These two manuals offer the beginning examiner an opportunity for self-study and to become familiar with the aim and goal of the IDA. The IDA Readings, although not specifically concerning the use of the IDA, give a theoretical foundation in child development that supports the assessment process suggested by the authors. The IDA Foundations and Study Guide contain useful examples and case studies for those individuals hoping to learn how to use the IDA. These materials provide a valuable developmental overview of the need for such a whole child, transdisciplinary approach to assessment.

The psychometric properties of the Provence Profile are discussed in the administration manual. The profile is used in the developmental observation and assessment phase of the IDA. According to the administration manual, the item scores on the profile are used to appraise a child's developmental level on the eight domains. Content validity is reported based on the review of experts and comparison of the items with other scales such as the Bayley, the Vineland, and the Learning Assessment Profile (LAP). The agreement rate on developmental age between the Provence Profile and the other developmental assessment is reported as ranging from 84% to 100%. Evidence of concurrent validity was presented by comparing classification criterion scores from the Bayley and the Vineland with the Provence Profile. This information is difficult to accept at face value given the different score structure of each instrument. Predictive validity is reported on a small sample of 15 agencies that had received IDA referrals on 57 children. Of the 12 agencies that responded to this inquiry, 10 (83%) found the report useful and appropriate to their agency. Reliability of the Provence Profile on the eight domain scores was computed using coefficient alpha. These coefficients range from .77 to .96. Interrater agreement on domain performance is reported as ranging from 91% to 95% for all the domains except Language/Communication where agreement was 81%.

Troublesome to this reviewer, however, was the lack of complete and full disclosure on some other psychometric properties of the Provence Profile and full IDA. There is no discussion of the types of children who represented the group used for development of both the Provence Profile and the complete IDA. Without such information, it is impossible to determine whether or not the IDA is representative along characteristics such as gender, family experience, and ethnicity. Without this information one could question the appropriateness of the IDA for all children. For example, although the test developers do have a Spanish Parent Report Form available, there is no indication that applicable parts of the Provence Profile can and should be administered to children in languages other than English.

Additionally, the authors report limited information on an interrater reliability analysis conducted on the full IDA process based on clinical supervisors' ratings of nine children. The interrater reliability on the subscales and full IDA process were reported as ranging from .81–.95.

In conclusion, the Infant-Toddler Development Assessment would appear to be a useful and viable instrument for the purpose for which it was designed. The psychometric properties of the Provence Profile would be appropriate for the test's purpose of identifying children who may need further services. The full IDA with its focus on collection of multiple data points and team approach to assessment make it an appealing instrument. The approach used by the IDA suggests that it may be ecologically valid. The inclusion of more information in the manuals regarding the specifics of the development of the IDA would only make the case for its use more convincing.

Review of the Infant-Toddler Developmental Assessment by E. JEAN NEWMAN, Assistant Professor of Educational Psychology, University of South Alabama, Mobile, AL:

The Infant-Toddler Developmental Assessment (IDA) was designed to aid in early identification of at-risk children ages birth to 3 years old. Eight domains are addressed by the process: Gross Motor, Fine Motor, Relations to Inanimate Objects, Language and Communications, Self-Help, Relationship to Persons, Emotions and Feeling States, and Coping Behavior. The central tool in the assessment process is the Provence Birth-to-Three Developmental Profile (Provence Profile). The standardized procedures include six steps of professional collaboration: Referral and Preinterview Data Gathering: Initial Parent Interview; Health Review; Developmental Observant and Assessment; Integration and Synthesis; and Share Findings, Completion, and Report.

The assessment requires optimally two-person teams from differing fields of expertise including mental health practitioners, medical professionals, teachers, social workers, speech and language therapists, occupational therapists, and physical therapists. The problematic facet of such a plan is that the use of two professionals (rather than assistants, students, interns, or support staff) is costly, time-consuming, and complicated by the need to coordinate services.

Another factor to be considered is the depth of training and resources required and/or available. The process must be taught only by those well trained and experienced in the administration of the procedures. The time, cost, and coordination required for training must be examined in order to maintain any sense of standardization.

THE KIT. The 23 assessment items are loosely packed in a bag similar to a laptop case. Most of the test materials are durable and washable. Some of the items (small blocks, sugar pellets) are small enough to require close supervision when assessing infants. There is no specific placement of the items in the bag, so quick location and use may be difficult.

THE MATERIALS. The Parent Report, Family Recording Guide, Health Recording Guide, and IDA Record are clear and uncomplicated. The manual provides extensive and well-written directions for administration. The protocol is scored after the session, requiring substantial reliance on memory of specifics, as well as increased time demanded for collaboration and protocol completion. Proficiency with this instrument requires experience and training. To remain facile, repetitive and continuous administration are required.

PSYCHOMETRIC PROPERTIES. A norming sample was not recruited; instead 100 cases from the files of 23 agencies using the IDA were analyzed. This does not provide an appropriate normative sample, as the cases were all volunteers, and were clients already referred to a training clinic. The sample included 52 males, 37 females and 11 children whose sex was not reported. No data were furnished regarding the spread of scores, regional or gender representation per age group, or procedures for choosing these particular 100 cases.

To assess content validity, three procedures were utilized. First, 18 professionals reviewed the content, and field tests were conducted by an unspecified number of children. Second, item comparisons were made between the Provence Profile and the Bayley Scales of Infant Development (8:206; 10:26; 29), the Hawaii Early Learning Profile (HELP; 11:157), and the Learning Accomplishment Profile (LAP; Sanford & Zelman, 1981). The manual reported the number of items in common with each scale (range 20 to 170 items), and percentage of agreement on developmental age (range 84% to 100%). However, because the Bayley instrument has separate scales for only three areas (mental, motor, and infant behavior) compared to the eight domains of the IDA, commonality of items without regard to domain does not guarantee content validity. Comparison with the HELP offers even less support of

content validity. The HELP is accompanied by virtually no psychometric information (11:37), has five domains in common with the IDA, and contains no norming information. The third step in content validation was a collaboration between the senior authors of the IDA and of the Vineland Adaptive Behavior Scale (9:1327; 10:381). There is little direct correspondence between the 13 scores of the Vineland and the eight domains of the IDA, other than fine and gross motor skills. Thus, although there may be high general agreement on content between the IDA and analogous scales, these methods of validation are not specific enough, either in domain or in statistical analysis.

An assessment of concurrent validity compared 53 children, ages .25 to 2.08, on scales of the Provence profile, the Vineland Adaptive Behavior Scales, and the Bayley Scales of Infant Development. With different criteria for eligibility, and with different areas of development, the authors readily admit that comparison is difficult and assert that further analysis is in progress.

Predictive validity was addressed by a follow-up questionnaire sent to 15 agencies involved in IDA administration. Representing 57 referrals, with 12 of 15 agencies responding, 10 agencies reported that the referrals were appropriate, one agency found the referral not useful, and one had no record of receiving a referral. It is unclear as to how many of the original 57 individual referrals were represented by these responses.

Analysis of internal consistency reliability involved using coefficient alpha to assess the homogeneity of items within each domain. For ages 1–18 months ($n = 35$), the range for alpha was .90 to .96. For ages 19–36 months ($n = 65$), the range was .77 to .96. Noting the small sample size and the range of items per domain (19 to 49), these estimates reflect an acceptably high interitem consistency. An interrater agreement analysis, involving three raters working in pairs to assess nine children, ranged from 81% to 95% agreement.

SUMMARY. The IDA is distinguished among infant development instruments by providing resources for thorough training, emphasizing relationships with all parties, and centering on the child as a whole while simultaneously providing detailed information in targeted areas. Its stated purpose as a method of gathering descriptive data does not supersede its usefulness.

There are some major concerns regarding the psychometric properties of the Provence Profile. There was no pilot test on nonreferred children, and no data are provided regarding age and gender variances within domains. Content validity was addressed, but was neither statistically supported nor specific in coverage. Likewise, criterion validity and predictive validity were assessed but with less than conclusive results. Internal reliability coefficients were acceptably high, but no evidence of test results across defined groups was provided, and tests over time consisted of 6-month reports on a limited sample. Questions still remain in the areas of content sampling, sample size, and normative comparisons.

To gather descriptive information, the IDA is conceptually and procedurally sound. For normative screening, the user may consider some combination of the following: Bayley Scales of Infant Development (10:26; 29), the Vineland Adaptive Behavior Scales (9:1327; 10:381), the Infant Mullen Scales of Early Learning (11:177), and the Brigance Diagnostic Inventory of Early Development (9:164). Albeit with some overlap, these may render a more thorough and valid assessment. Meanwhile, the IDA may be enhanced by further analysis and data collection.

REVIEWER'S REFERENCE

Sanford, A. R., & Zelman, J. G. (1981). *The learning accomplishment profile.* Winston-Salem, NC: Kaplan.

[147]
Influence Strategies Exercise.

Purpose: Designed to identify various influence strategies used by individuals.
Population: Managers and employees.
Publication Date: 1990.
Acronym: ISE.
Scores, 9: Empowerment, Interpersonal Awareness, Bargaining, Relationship Building, Organizational Awareness, Common Vision, Impact Management, Logical Persuasion, Coercion.
Administration: Group.
Parts, 2: Participant Version, Employee Version (optional).
Price Data, 1993: $60 per complete kit including 10 exercises and 10 profiles and interpretive notes (19 pages); $25 per 10 employee version exercises.
Time: (20–25) minutes.
Comments: Self-administered questionnaire.
Author: McBer & Company.
Publisher: McBer & Company.

Review of the Influence Strategies Exercise by COLLIE W. CONOLEY, Professor of Educational Psychology, Texas A&M University, College Station, TX:

The Influence Strategies Exercise (ISE) is for use in helping managers reflect upon and enhance their influence strategies with those whom they manage. The ISE is reported to "stimulate your thinking about which influence strategies you tend to use and which you can use most effectively with different people and in different situations. Knowing when and how to use each strategy is key to your success" (p. 7, Profile and Interpretive Notes). There is no manual and no information on validity or reliability. The Profile and Interpretive Notes booklet refers to unpublished studies by McBer and Company but they were not available upon telephone request.

The ISE consists of three booklets: two booklets of multiple-choice questions about influence styles and one interpretation booklet. One questionnaire booklet is for the manager's self-appraisement, and the other for the manager's supervisees. The responses are easily summed to produce scores for each of the nine influence strategies. A mean of the scores is used for multiple supervisee booklets. The manager uses the Profile and Interpretive Notes booklet to become educated about the influence strategies and understand her/his scores. The supervisees apparently do not receive any feedback.

A score from the perspective of the manager and the supervisees is profiled for the nine influence strategies: Empowerment, Interpersonal Awareness, Bargaining, Relationship Building, Organizational Awareness, Common Vision, Impact Management, Logical Persuasion, and Coercion. The categories were stated to be based upon unpublished research. The profile allows the manager to identify most and least used influence strategies. There is no suggestion to compare the absolute numbers to any other person or standard.

The booklet defines, gives examples, and outlines the times to use each of the strategies. A series of booklet questions guide the manager through understanding his/her influence strategies. There is an important section that asks the manager to validate the profile by providing examples of times when certain forms of influence were attempted. This section appears to promote a reasonable self-exploration of the manager's self-report responses. The multiple-choice questions appeared much easier for self-delusion than the provision of influence examples.

The ISE appears to have value. However, validity and reliability data from the publisher are essential. Without the data the value of the ISE is unknown.

Review of the Influence Strategies Exercise by PAUL M. MUCHINSKY, Joseph M. Bryan Distinguished Professor of Business, The University of North Carolina at Greensboro, Greensboro, NC:

The Influence Strategies Exercise (ISE) is a self-administered questionnaire designed to identify various influence strategies used by individuals in organizations. There are two versions, one for a self-assessment, the other for the assessment of a manager or colleague. The questionnaire consists of 54 behaviorally oriented items, each of which is rated on a 4-point scale of frequency. Six items are devoted to assessing each of nine influence strategies. The instrument is self-scored by summating the six scores per strategy, resulting in a nine-score profile. A Profile and Interpretive Notes guide describes how to score and interpret the profile. The guide states the profile can be interpreted from only a self-assessment perspective, or also by comparing two profiles, one based on self-assessment and the other based on average ratings of other people who assessed the target individual. Detailed definitions and examples of the nine influence strategies are presented. The user is encouraged to regard the scores as a form of multirater feedback in terms of strategies the target and others perceive as being used most and least often. Each strategy is further analyzed in terms of the conditions and situations under which it is most and least effective. The user is instructed to record situations where he or she attempted to use a particular influence strategy on the job, what the result was, and to consider what other influence strategy might have been used to produce a better result. Finally, the guide presents specific tactics of skill enhancement for each of the nine influence strategies, and outlines a goal setting plan for the reader to become more adept at using a diversity of influence strategies.

In many ways this is a more effective assessment than is typically found in organizationally based contexts. The Profile and Interpretive Notes guide is primarily a workbook, not a manual. The intent of the assessment is for individuals to enhance their own skills, skills that are highly relevant in a business environment. The guide has a very user-friendly quality to it. The theoretical foundation for the assessment rests with the classic research of French and Raven (1959) and the more recent research of Yukl and Falbe (1990). I was impressed that the authors refer to the assessment as an "exercise," which is exactly what it is. Its purpose is to make users more aware of their own behavior style, how that style is perceived by others, how they can expand their behavioral repertoire, and the conditions under which certain styles are likely to be differentially effective. This is no small task. From a validation standpoint I would have liked information relating influence strategy skill enhancement to subsequent job perfor-

mance. The guide would also benefit from normative data on use of influence tactics in business, as well as additional psychometric information. However, such information is more typically found in a test manual than in a user's workbook. Although the original research upon which this instrument is based does address these issues, I would have preferred its inclusion in an appendix to the workbook.

The ISE makes no pretentious claims or unfounded assertions. I am clearly positive in my overall evaluation of its merits. The omission of relevant psychometric information is still troublesome to me. Nevertheless, I believe the instrument delivers on its stated intentions, and can serve to enhance self-learning in an important and rarely presented facet of organizational life.

REVIEWER'S REFERENCES

French, J. R. P., Jr., & Raven, B. (1959). The bases of social power. In D. Cartwright (Ed.), *Studies in social power* (pp. 150–167). Ann Arbor, MI: Institute for Social Research.
Yukl, G., & Falbe, C. M. (1990). Influence tactics and objectives in upward, downward, and lateral influence attempts. *Journal of Applied Psychology, 75,* 132–140.

[148]

Informal Reading Comprehension Placement Test [Revised].

Purpose: "Assesses the instructional and independent comprehension levels of students from pre-readiness (grade 1) through level twelve plus (grade 12)."

Population: Grades 1–8 for typical learners and grades 8–12 remedially; adult education students.

Publication Dates: 1983–1994.

Scores, 3: Word Comprehension, Passage Comprehension, Total Comprehension.

Administration: Individual.

Price Data, 1994: $49.95 per test.

Time: (35–50) minutes for the battery; (15–20) minutes for Part 1; (20–30) minutes for Part 2.

Comments: Automatically administered, scored, and managed; for use with adults, the placements are correlated with Tests of Adult Basic Education (343); test administered in two parts; Apple II or IBM microcomputer necessary for administration.

Authors: Ann Edson and Eunice Insel.

Publisher: Educational Activities, Inc.

Cross References: For reviews by Gloria A. Galvin and Claudia R. Wright, see 11:178.

Review of the Informal Reading Comprehension Placement Test [Revised] by DIANE J. SAWYER, Murfree Professor of Dyslexic Studies, Middle Tennessee State University, Murfreesboro, TN:

The stated major objective of this inventory is to yield findings for use in prescribing a developmental, corrective, or remedial reading program for individuals (manual, p. 2). It is the opinion of this reviewer that the stated major objective cannot be achieved. This inventory was specifically designed to yield an estimate of an individual's instructional reading comprehension levels based upon a criterion level performance of 75% accuracy on word meaning tasks and questions related to content in brief passages. It is not possible to *prescribe* a reading program based upon such limited and global information. Further, it is doubtful that the scores obtained by means of this inventory have practical value for selecting material for independent reading or for instruction. At best, this inventory may be useful for screening individuals, in the intermediate grades and above, to estimate the level of other diagnostic tests or tasks to use in identifying the range of reading comprehension strategies and competencies an individual possesses. What to teach, or what must be learned about comprehending text, is not identified or defined by the grade level of difficulty assigned to words or passages.

The Word Comprehension subtest (Part I) consists of eight items per grade level (Levels 1 through 13 inclusive). Each item is presented in an analogic form (e.g., *jump* is to *up* as *sit* is to _____). The reader selects the best answer from the two options provided. The authors provide no information regarding the source of vocabulary included or the basis upon which words were assigned to a specific level of difficulty. The analogic format requires, in many instances, fairly sophisticated reasoning to arrive at the appropriate answer. This subtest does go beyond knowledge of individual word meanings and may be appropriately considered a measure of comprehension applied at the word level. There is much diagnostic *potential* for such a test but this would require a fairly large number of items at each level to tap the various word level comprehension strategies students at that level might be expected to apply. Further, an item analysis option would be needed to permit the teacher to identify individual competence with each of the types of strategies. In its current form, the Word Comprehension subtest can only provide an estimate of word knowledge with no opportunity to identify where or why reasoning about meaning breaks down.

The Passage Comprehension subtest (Part II) consists of graded passages (grades 1–13) ranging in length from about 40 words to about 250 words. Each passage is followed by four questions. Typically, one question involves a vocabulary item, one addresses main idea, one assesses recall of detail, and

one taps inferential reasoning. No information is provided by the authors regarding the source of these passages or how the grade levels of difficulty were assigned. The upper level passages (11–13) contain quite sophisticated topic-specific vocabulary. Poor performance on these passages may not accurately reflect how students will perform in typical texts or recreational material written for the grade level. No item analysis is provided to permit examination of possible patterns of errors associate with the comprehension questions.

The Informal Reading Comprehension Placement Test may be useful in estimating a student's ability to cope with grade level texts (grades 4–12). The computer software format may be especially helpful to classroom teachers (grades 4–6) and remedial teachers (assisting students in grades 4–12) in dealing with new entrants during the school year. However, the format does not seem well suited to situations such as adult literacy classes, where estimates of individual achievement levels for a large number of students must be obtained quickly. Group-administered tests are better suited to the item constraints associated with instruction in these settings. Further, among students in grades 1–3, much more relevant information regarding overall reading ability can be gained by listening to the student read aloud. At these levels, poor comprehension is frequently associated with restricted levels of word recognition or limited word attack strategies. This test can provide no further information relative to these abilities. Similarly, teachers of older students who obtain unusually poor scores on this test should consider word recognition and word analysis competencies as a possible interfering factor.

Potential users of the Informal Reading Comprehension Placement Test should be aware that the authors offer no evidence regarding validity or reliability. It is noted that "the test was validated by over 3,000 students over ten years in the Baldwin, New York public schools" (manual, p. 4). However, no description of the school system, the student population, or the validation study is provided. It appears that determination of the effectiveness of this test in accomplishing the purpose and objective for which it was developed is left entirely to the user. Potential users should carefully consider the significant limitations of this test as it is currently presented.

Review of the Informal Reading Comprehension Placement Test [Revised] by GABRIELLE STUTMAN, Consulting Psychologist, Cognitive Habilitation Services, New York City, NY:

This test attempts a brief, sequential, and reliable computerized evaluation of reading comprehension placement level for students in grades 1–12, as well as for remedial secondary, adult, and special education. The Word Comprehension Test (WCT) (Part 1) Analogies contains 96 items using an analogy format to facilitate the assessment of both word meanings and thinking skills. Each of the 12 sets of eight words is vocabulary controlled using EDL and Dolch Word Lists. The Passage Comprehension Test (PCT) (Part 2) contains 12 graded reading passages that are controlled for vocabulary and sentence length using Spache, Frye, and Dale Chall readability formulas. Four comprehension questions follow each passage to test detail, main idea, inference, and vocabulary from the context. Results are automatically scored to provide the teacher with three levels of reading functioning: an Independent Level (WCT = 99%, PCT ≥90%), an Instructional Level (WCT ≥90%, PCT ≥75%), and a Frustration Level (WCT <90%, PCT <51%). The latter is to be avoided in order to maximize student motivation and achievement. In addition, a Total Instructional level is also calculated as a composite of the WCT and PCT. These measures are intended to provide classroom, content area, resource teachers, and curriculum specialists with rapid student placement while minimizing teacher time. The student's record is maintained over time so that progress can be recorded. The teacher may access individual student's scores, or scores for the entire class, either on screen or hard copy. Both individual and class files are easily deleted.

The program is easy to operate for students who are able to follow written instructions such as, "Please type your first name and then press RETURN." Less (computer) literate students will require the aid of a teacher to begin. The test may begin at any level that the teacher wishes. Sample items are given to insure appropriate entry points, progress from level to level is smooth, and the assessment is automatically ended at the point where the student is unable to perform at 75%–80% accuracy. The publishers state that the test was validated by over 3,000 students over 10 years in the Baldwin, New York public schools. This is a very respectable sample size; however, no demographics of this sample are given, and so the user has no way of knowing the age/grade, gender, and/or English language proficiency distribution, or whether adults or remedial readers were included in the sample at all. In addition, no reliability or validity coefficients of any kind are provided. Several sections of the test have rather long runs (three in a row) of same-letter-correct choices. In a test that demands 75% competence on as few as four questions to proceed to the next level, validity may be seriously compromised by response bias. When this reviewer took the test from the beginning with a response bias of "B," she achieved reading readiness in the area of Word Comprehension. Indeed, the labels of "readiness" and "pre-readiness" at the bottom end of the assessment range are misnomers. Readiness to read is not the same thing as reading ability. Reading readiness correlates with the capacity to segregate phonemes from morphemes and/or to discriminate and recognize complex visual patterns. Pre-readiness is incompetence at making such auditory and visual discriminations. These very important aspects of developmental reading ability are not assessed, and for that reason the lowest levels would be more appropriately labeled "Nonreader" and "Beginning Reader." For beginning readers, the structure of the test response matrix may cause difficulties. The student must respond on a keyboard by pressing either an "A," "B," or "C" to indicate their choice of correct answer. Therefore, when reading the typewriter keyboard from left to right, the student must ignore irrelevant letters and deal with a letter sequence that presents itself as "A, C, B." For this reason variables of attention and confusion may interfere with the validity of the reading assessment. Changing the response alternatives to "1," "2," and "3" may enhance validity as well as ease of use. Finally, in the comprehension selection on Wild Turkeys, the word "presently" is misused to mean "currently." Usage errors such as this have no place in an educational assessment instrument. In all, although the idea of a computerized reading assessment is a very good one, much work is still to be done if this instrument is to pass muster.

[149]
INSIGHT Inventory.

Purpose: To help "participants understand how their behavior is influenced by the relationship between their personality and the environment and use the information to improve their communication with others, thereby enhancing teamwork and interpersonal relationships."
Population: Students ages 16–20, employees.
Publication Dates: 1988–1995.
Scores, 16: 8 profile scores for each area Work Style and Personal Style: Getting Your Way (Direct, Indirect), Responding to People (Reserved, Outgoing), Pacing Activity (Urgent, Steady), Dealing with Details (Unstructured, Precise).

Administration: Group.
Forms, 6: Business forms: A, B, Style Feedback Set, Interviewing with Insight; Student forms: C, D (Student Style Feedback Set).
Price Data: Price information available from publisher for inventories, preview packages, training kits, videos, technical manual, etc. These price structures available: retail, consultants, non-for-profit (schools and churches).
Time: (15–50) minutes.
Comments: Forms A, B, and Student Form are self-report behavior profiles; Business Style Feedback Set and Student Form D are feedback reports completed by others who know the participant; Form B available in German, French, Dutch, and Spanish.
Author: Patrick Handley.
Publisher: Insight Institute, Inc.

Review of the INSIGHT Inventory by SUSANA URBINA, Associate Professor of Psychology, University of North Florida, Jacksonville, FL:

INSIGHT is a simple instrument. The entire inventory consists of two lists—of 32 adjectives each—presented side by side. Both lists contain the same terms but the order in which they are arranged differs. In the list labeled "Work Style" (or "School Style"), persons completing the inventory indicate, on a 4-point scale, the extent to which the adjectives describe the way they are at work (or, for students aged 16 to 20, at school). In the second list, labeled "Personal Style," individuals indicate, in the same manner, the degree to which the words describe their "at home" or personal selves.

The purpose of this novel self-report inventory is to help people understand their personal styles of behaving at home and in the workplace. The basic idea behind INSIGHT is that such an understanding will lead individuals to more flexible and effective functioning in both settings. The instrument is self-scorable and comes with either a 16-page booklet (Form A) or a 6-page guide (Forms B and C), which can be used by test takers themselves for self-interpretation. Variations of the inventory designed for use in employment interviewing and in counseling students are available, as are forms for providing feedback to others. In addition, the publisher provides packages of support materials, such as training guides, manuals on Skill Building Exercises, and videotapes. These materials are aimed at helping trainers, teachers, or counselors to interpret and expand on the information that the inventory provides. The INSIGHT program is advertised as useful in team building, career development, and various kinds of effectiveness training. The technical

manual, however, deals only with the development and psychometric characteristics of the inventory itself as a descriptive self-report tool; it does not provide any background or support for the usefulness of the ancillary materials.

The author of INSIGHT, Patrick Handley, cites the work of Kurt Lewin, Gordon Allport, and Raymond Cattell as the source material that influenced the development of the inventory. From Lewin's field theory, Handley takes the premise that behavior is a function of the person and of the person's psychological environment; from Allport he borrows the use of adjectives for personality description, the notion of personal dispositions, and the emphasis of *insight* as a hallmark of the mature personality; Cattell is cited as an influence because he was a pioneer in the use of factor analysis for personality test development. The exposition of this "theoretical background" in the technical manual (pp. 14–20) is simple and direct, and should be understandable to most readers. For anyone familiar with the primary sources, however, the content of the manual is likely to seem exceedingly superficial and its language far too imprecise.

The development of the INSIGHT Inventory, sketchily described in the manual, began with the selection of an initial set of adjectives from Allport and Odbert's (1936) list. The criteria for selection were that the items should be words commonly used to describe behavior that is noticeably different among people, that the words should be considered neither positive nor negative, and that they should have a clearly identifiable opposite (e.g., "talkative"). After some initial modifications, the resulting list of 36 items was administered to a sample of 1,540 adults and subjected to factor analyses. Based on these analyses, the list was altered again, reduced to 32 items, and factor analyzed once more with new samples of 589 adults and 1,021 high school and college students. The resulting factor loadings were used to create four scales—each consisting of eight adjectives—representing four factors. These bipolar scales describe styles of (a) Getting One's Way (i.e., Direct versus Indirect); (b) Responding to People (i.e., Outgoing versus Reserved); (c) Pacing Activity (i.e., Steady versus Urgent); and (d) Dealing with Details (i.e., Precise versus Unstructured). Norms are presented separately for female, male, and combined gender groups of adults and students drawn from a variety of settings.

Internal consistency estimates for the four scales in each of the two modes of responding (i.e., Work/School Style and Personal Style) were obtained by means of alpha coefficients based on a sample of

1,602 adults and students. These coefficients ranged from .71 to .85, with a median of .77. Stability over a period of 6 weeks was evaluated by means of test-retest reliability coefficients derived from a sample of 90 undergraduates. The stability coefficients for the four scales in each of the two styles ranged from .54 to .82 (median = .755).

In the technical manual, the evidence of validity for INSIGHT is limited to comparisons between its scores and those of three other well-known self-report inventories, namely, the Myers-Briggs Type Indicator (MBTI), the Sixteen Personality Factor Questionnaire (16 PF), and the Self-Directed Search (SDS). The samples for all three sets of concurrent validity studies were made up of between 169 and 241 college students. Results generally reflect the patterns one would expect from an inspection of the names of the scales and of the constructs measured across the various inventories. For instance, the correlations between Factor G (Conformity) of the 16 PF and the INSIGHT scale that assesses degree of precision in Dealing with Details are .40 and .46, respectively, for the School Style and the Personal Style. Not all correlations are of this high a magnitude, and not all interscale comparisons yield meaningful results. Furthermore, both the intertest comparisons and the results of the factor analyses described earlier suggest that the four INSIGHT scales themselves are somewhat intercorrelated. Nevertheless, given the direct nature of the measures obtained through the INSIGHT inventory—namely, self-ratings on behaviorally descriptive, face valid, and unambiguous adjectives—it is not surprising to see the correlational data fall in line with expectations for convergent and discriminant validity.

SUMMARY. The INSIGHT Inventory is based on the well-accepted premise that people vary their behavior as a function of the situations in which they find themselves. This premise is not only psychologically sound, but potentially very useful. Furthermore, the very simplicity and directness of the measure are likely to increase its usefulness and appeal. Of all the applications that its author proposes, it would seem that the most appropriate would be as a starting point for a discussion about interpersonal relationships in the context of team building and other such efforts. Depending on the level of sophistication of the population involved, the inventory may also be useful as an aid in personal development or leadership training. It is important to note, however, that because this tool is so simple and face

valid, it may not contribute information beyond that which could be ascertained easily through an interview or biographical information form. In the absence of any attempt to control for socially desirable responding, the use of INSIGHT in employee selection or in any other such decision making would seem questionable. Moreover, although the packaging of INSIGHT is unique—in that it combines two modes of administration within a single protocol—there are other available tools that can be used for the same purposes. Among the most salient alternatives that may be considered—depending on the test user's purposes and constraints—are: (a) the NEO-PI-R self-report and observer-report forms (Costa & McCrae, 1992; 12:330); (b) repeated administrations of the Adjective Check List (Gough & Heilbrun, 1983; T4:93), with different sets of instructions; and (c) use of the Q sort technique, with different frames of reference.

REVIEWER'S REFERENCES
Allport, G. W., & Odbert, H. S. (1936). Trait-names, a psycholexical study. *Psychological Monographs, 47*(1, Whole No. 211).
Gough, H. G., & Heilbrun, A. B., Jr. (1983). *The Adjective Check List manual* (rev. ed.). Palo Alto, CA: Consulting Psychologists Press.
Costa, P. T., Jr., & McCrae, R. R. (1992). *Revised NEO Personality Inventory (NEO-PI-R) and NEO Five-Factor Inventory (NEO-FFI) professional manual.* Odessa, FL: Psychological Assessment Resources.

[150]
The Instructional Environment System—II: A System to Identify a Student's Instructional Needs (Second Edition).

Purpose: "Designed to assist education professionals in a systematic analysis of a target student's instructional environment, which includes both school and home contexts."
Population: Grades K–12.
Publication Dates: 1987–1993.
Acronym: TIES-II.
Scores: 12 Instructional Environment Components (Instructional Match, Teacher Expectations, Classroom Environment, Instructional Presentation, Cognitive Emphasis, Motivational Strategies, Relevant Practice, Informed Feedback, Academic Engaged Time, Adaptive Instruction, Progress Evaluation, Student Understanding), 5 Home Support for Learning Components (Expectations and Attributions, Discipline Orientation, Home Affective Environment, Parent Participation, Structure for Learning).
Administration: Individual.
Forms, 4: Instructional Needs Checklist, Parent Interview Record, Home Support for Learning Form, Instructional Environment Form.
Price Data, 1994: $47.50 per TIES-II Program Kit including 15 copies of each of the 4 forms and manual ('93, 199 pages); $19.50 per replacement forms set including 15 copies of each of the 4 forms.
Time: Administration time not reported.

Comments: Observational and interview data from teachers, parents, and students is gathered by an education professional; can be used in regular classrooms, homes, special education, and in different content areas.
Authors: James Ysseldyke and Sandra Christenson.
Publisher: Sopris West, Inc.
Cross References: For reviews by Kenneth W. Howell and by William T. McKee and Joseph C. Witt of an earlier form, see 10:149.

Review of The Instructional Environment System— II: A System to Identify a Student's Instructional Needs (Second Edition) by MICHAEL J. FURLONG, Associate Professor, Graduate School of Education, and JENNIFER A. ROSENBLATT, Doctoral Candidate, University of California, Santa Barbara, Santa Barbara, CA:

TIES-II is an extension and revision of the TIES (Ysseldyke & Christenson, 1987), which was developed to address a gap in traditional special education assessment procedures and models. Existing taxonomies of children's learning needs have typically focused on intra-child variables as critical in understanding the etiology and remediation of learning problems. The original TIES expanded assessment interest beyond the child to include conditions in the classroom environment that facilitate learning. TIES-II extends this ecological perspective to include various facilitative conditions in the child's home.

CONTENT. The authors of TIES-II extensively reviewed effective-instruction literature to identify teacher behaviors and classroom conditions found to be associated with positive learning outcomes. As such, they have not developed a formal test, but a procedure with which educators can systematically organize their own perceptions of the quality of the classroom instructional environment.

The classroom content of the TIES-II consists of 12 "components" organized into four instructional environment domains: *Planning Instruction* (#1 Instructional Match and #2 Teacher Expectations), *Managing Instruction* (#3 Classroom Environment), *Delivering Instruction* (#4 Instructional Presentation, #5 Cognitive Emphasis, #6 Motivational Strategies, #7 Relevant Practice, and #8 Informed Feedback), and *Monitoring/Evaluating Instruction* (#9 Academic Engaged Time, #10 Adaptive Instruction, #11 Progress Evaluation, and #12 Student Understanding). The fact that Managing Instruction has only one component (#3) leads one to wonder why it is not just referred to as classroom environment. This organization represents the authors' conceptualization of the essential components of effective classroom

instruction. These 12 components are identical to those included in the original TIES but in the manual the authors have updated the discussion about empirical research identifying these components as important classroom environment characteristics.

Given the second author's interest in the role that families play in the educational process, soon after the publication of TIES, Christenson and Ysseldyke (1989) began to integrate home environment factors into their ecological model of student achievement. A primary innovation of TIES-II is the inclusion of five new components (#13 to #17) examining the types of support for student learning found within the home environment itself. These five new components assess (#13) Expectations and Attributions, (#14) Discipline Orientation, (#15) Home Affective Environment, (#16) Parent Participation, and (#17) Structure for Learning. The academic and ecological focus of the TIES-II and the integration of home factors into the assessment process should be well received by teachers and parents because it addresses issues that have high relevance to a child's educational program.

TEST MATERIALS/RESOURCES. TIES-II uses six forms, four of which are used for data gathering and observations (Instructional Needs Checklist, completed by teachers; Instructional Planning Form, Direct Observation Form, and Parent Interview Record, completed by parent or guardian) and two forms for recording and organizing summary perceptions/ratings of the 17 components mentioned above (Instructional Environment Form [components #1 to #12]; and Home Support for Learning Form [components #13 to #17]).

TIES-II is intended to be used by a team of educators working collaboratively in a consultative relationship. Observation and evaluation forms can be completed by one educator, but it is clear that a more comprehensive understanding of a child's learning environment will be obtained when multiple informants are used, notably the classroom teacher and parents. The authors have a respectful tone throughout the manual with disclaimers designed to encourage parents and teachers not to be defensive about identifying conditions in the home or school that do not appear to support the child's learning. It is particularly important to seek the input of the classroom teacher because the content of the TIES-II relates directly to the use of instructional strategies and the organization he or she brings to the classroom. Thus, there is the obvious potential for misuse of TIES-II to place blame or responsibility, at least implicitly, on the teacher for any instructional component deficits that are found. Although the authors go to great lengths in the detailed manual to discourage the use of TIES-II for evaluating teacher performance, its proper use will be increased greatly if the teacher is part of the assessment team. Inasmuch as TIES-II is not a standardized test, one of its potential strengths is to encourage communication about a child's learning environment among the classroom teacher, support personnel, administrators, and parents. This obviously cannot happen unless all parties are equal partners in the assessment process.

ADMINISTRATION/SCORING. The forms intended for use by educators are well arranged and should help facilitate thinking about ways to enhance a child's learning environment; but the ratings are completely subjective. The authors offer no data showing that different raters using TIES-II and rating the same environment would produce similar outcomes. Without such information, it is impossible to know if users of TIES-II produce biased ratings that reflect their own instructional orientation and beliefs.

Consistent with the authors' theoretic orientation, some of TIES-II response scales on the Parent Interview Record form are worded behaviorally; for example, the response category "Yes" is defined as meaning that the referent behavior occurs 80% of the time (4 to 5 days per week). However, these response anchors are not repeated on each page of the record sheets and this response format is not used throughout the parent form. In other sections of the parent form, they are asked to check if conditions related to items describing a variety of home conditions and child behaviors are "fairly typical" (i.e., "happens often") of their child. These changes in response format are likely to cause confusion among some parents. In addition, although the form is called the "Parent Interview Record" it is structured much like any traditional parent self-report checklist. It is likely that this form will be given to parents to complete on their own. Given the heavy verbal loading of the form, this 98-item instrument has decreased utility for parents with limited English literacy skills. Similarly, the lack of translated versions of the Parent Interview Record further restricts its potential use. In addition, the core of the Parent Interview Record is a list of 56 items describing learning-related conditions in the home. The manner in which responses to these items are to be organized, however, is not provided. There is no psychometric analysis to verify

the content or construct validity of these items. Although TIES-II was not developed as a norm-based checklist type of instrument, this does not eliminate the responsibility of the authors to demonstrate that items included in the parent form meet minimal standards of validity and reliability. Another concern is that the items included in this portion of the parent form are wordy with multiple elements (e.g., "My child is encouraged to work hard in school, to put forth a lot of effort, and to try again"). How some items are to be interpreted is ambiguous. For example, what does it mean if a parent indicates that they do not reward their child for "good grades"? Parent responses to the aforementioned items and other TIES-II items can have multiple meanings, thus appropriate use will require at least some direct contact with the caregiver to ensure that the meanings of their responses are understood. One final point, the items are sometimes worded in the first person, "I stay informed about by child's progress," whereas other items are worded more generally, "My child has opportunities to solve problems at home." Some items are just unnecessarily vague, for example, "My child's schoolwork is viewed on a weekly basis." The authors offer no information about how these wording variations affect responses or interpretation of the instrument.

SUMMARY. The authors have done a commendable job of organizing literature about factors associated with high levels of student academic performance. This is actually a unique resource for educators because it provides them with citations to empirical research that identifies conditions in the classroom and at home that enhance student learning. As such, it offers a useful tool as part of a comprehensive assessment (see Christenson & Ysseldyke, 1989, for an example of how to use the TIES procedures as part of the instructional planning process.) This organization of a very important body of research is well worth obtaining.

Notwithstanding the potential usefulness of TIES-II, users need to be mindful of several issues. Firstly, it has demonstrated content validity because the 17 components are carefully derived from research findings. However, the presentation of information about the components was constructed by the authors and represents their own, unverified interpretation and organization of what this research says. They did not, for example, ask experts to verify that the descriptions of their components are valid and appropriate. Secondly, the authors claim a strong link to intervention, but no specific instructional suggestions are generated by the TIES-II—this level of instructional planning is left entirely to the assessment team. If one is looking to the TIES-II to offer suggestions about specific instructional activities, they will likely be disappointed. Users are told that they need to have a strong knowledge base about academic instruction and remediation before they can make optimal use of the TIES-II. However, the TIES-II does not offer specific suggestions for obtaining this knowledge. Thirdly, there is no evidence that use of this system is associated with any of a variety of positive educational outcomes, such as prevention of student placement in special education classes or enhanced academic performance. For that matter, there is no evidence to suggest that as a result of using the TIES-II, any teacher or parent actually changed their behavior to create conditions in the classroom or at home that are favorable to enhanced learning. There is a weak link between the TIES-II consultation process and procedures or skill training options that would encourage teachers and/or parents to engage in the behaviors needed to bring about improved classroom or home learning conditions consistent with the 17 TIES-II learning components. Finally, even nearly 10 years after the publication of the original TIES, the TIES-II assessment procedures have not been independently validated by other researchers, nor has it been used extensively in research studies. Until TIES-II receives additional independent reviews demonstrating that it is validated for its stated uses and purposes across diverse populations, it will not fulfill its objective of encouraging functional, ecologically focused assessments of youths' learning needs.

REVIEWERS' REFERENCES

Ysseldyke, J. E., & Christenson, S. L. (1987). The Instructional Environment Scale (TIES). Austin, TX: PRO-ED, Inc.

Christenson, S. L., & Ysseldyke, J. E. (1989). Assessing student performance: An important change is needed. *Journal of School Psychology, 27,* 409–425.

Thurlow, M. L., Ysseldyke, J. E., Wotruba, J. W., & Algozzine, B. (1993). Instruction in special education classrooms under varying student-teacher ratios. *Elementary School Journal, 93,* 305–320.

Review of The Instructional Environment System—II: A System to Identify a Student's Instructional Needs (Second Edition) by JERRY TINDAL, Associate Professor, Behavioral Research and Teaching, University of Oregon, Eugene, OR:

This instrument is designed to identify a student's instructional needs by using an observational rating scale and interview forms of teachers, students, and parents. The authors consider the five data-gathering tools to be the Observation Record, Student Interview Record, Teacher Interview Record, Parent Interview Record, and Instructional Needs Checklist. The intervention planning forms include the Instructional Environment Form, the Home Support for Learning Form, and the Intervention Planning Form.

The Instructional Environment System—II (TIES-II) has four data-gathering tools described in the manual: (a) an Observation Record that includes a focus on such issues as planning, management, delivery, and monitoring; (b) Student Interview Record, which addresses understanding of assignments, teacher expectations, and use of strategies for work completion; (c) Teacher Interview Record, which focuses on expectations, planning, instructional placement, assignments, and overall success; and (d) Intervention Planning Form.

The test also includes four additional forms that are completed with directions provided in a manual: (a) Parent Interview Record, (b) Instructional Needs Checklist, (c) Home Support for Learning Form, and (d) Instructional Environment Form.

In the Parent Interview, ratings are made on a 4-point scale regarding parents' perception of the child's proficiency-understanding in the basic skill areas, the child's difficulty areas, anecdotal observations, and specific observations that reflect self-statements of the parent.

The Instructional Needs Checklist includes directions for the teacher to note student strengths and weaknesses; description of concerns; checklists of instructional needs reflecting classroom characteristics, instructional plans, management of instructional needs, implementation of these needs, and evaluation of the needs; reflections on student responses to tasks; and checklists of instructional factors to get the student more engaged as well as use of instructional tasks and materials and modifications.

The Home Support for Learning Form reflects judgments on the part of the observer for five components; expectations and attributions, discipline orientation, home affective environment, parent participation, and structure for learning. An extensive comments section is provided for notes to be written on "ways the parents would like to assist their child's learning at home" and "other concerns" (p. 3).

The Instructional Environment Form provides a structure for documenting the referring concerns and contexts and then to pinpoint statements on 12 instructional components:

1. Instructional match (dealing with student's needs and goals).

2. Teacher expectations (to determine if they are both realistic and high).

3. Classroom environment (management techniques, time use, and climate).

4. Instructional presentation (lesson development, clarity of directions, and checking for understanding).

5. Cognitive emphasis (emphasizing thinking skills and learning strategies).

6. Motivational strategies (strategies to heighten student interest).

7. Relevant practice (opportunity to practice with appropriate and relevant materials).

8. Informed feedback (emphasizing immediate and specific information on performance that is corrective).

9. Academic engaged time (both involvement and maintenance).

10. Adaptive instruction (accommodations specific to the student's needs).

11. Progress evaluation (emphasizing direct and frequent measurement of progress).

12. Student understanding (of what is to be done and how it is to be done).

In all of these areas, the person completing the evaluation provides a rating of agreement-disagreement (on a 4-point scale) for each of two dimensions: (a) presence and (b) importance. In the manual appendix, extensive information is presented on each of these components, providing positive statements that reflect details of each construct (component).

The manual provides extensive documentation on information relevant to understanding many issues of instructional environments in five chapters that provide a rationale, methodology, integration of findings, technical considerations, and empirical basis for understanding. The rationale presents a well-written summary of research on effective teaching, and includes many of the major works to appear in the educational literature in the past 20 years. In the second chapter a very extensive review of empirical research and references is included. Chapter 3 provides directions to integrate the information from both the data-gathering tools and intervention planning forms. The perspective is holistic with an emphasis on making global, integrative judgments. Furthermore, the intervention planning process is oriented toward collaborative problem solving and a consultation-based program. In the fourth chapter, technical data are presented that include the sources for selecting items on the checklists and empirical support in the form of the following reliability and validity

information: (a) The content sampling plan is well documented and easy to follow; (b) interrater reliability coefficients are high for all 12 components; (c) validity coefficients between ratings on the 12 components and achievement measures are low-moderate; (d) several studies that reflect percentage of students with mild disabilities at various rating values; (e) comparisons of ratings for students with mild disabilities in special and general education; (f) gender differences in the ratings; and (g) differences in ratings among students with different disability categories.

In the last chapter of the manual, correlates of academic achievement are reviewed, providing extensive literature that dates back to the late 1970s and extends forward to more recent publications. This literature is presented for each of the 12 components.

In summary, TIES-II is a very extensive data-collection tool that represents a considerable and extensive literature base appearing in the professional educational literature for the past 20 years. All components of the instrument (records and forms) are well described and formatted in a manner that is clear and easy to use. Documentation is extensive. TIES-II also is a very comprehensive instrument for understanding the classroom ecology, making it a potentially difficult one to use for novice practitioners.

[151]

Instrument Technician.

Purpose: Developed to measure knowledge and skills required for instrument technician jobs.

Population: Applicants and incumbents for jobs requiring technical knowledge of instrumentation.

Publication Dates: 1989–1990.

Scores, 12: Mathematics, Digital Electronics, Analog Electronics, Schematics and Electrical Print Reading, Process Control, Power Supplies, Basic AC/DC Theory, Test Instruments, Mechanical, Computer and PLC, Chemical Processes, Total.

Administration: Group.

Price Data, 1993: $498 per complete kit including 10 reusable test booklets, 100 answer sheets, manual ('90, 13 pages), and answer key.

Time: Administration time not reported.

Author: Roland T. Ramsay.

Publisher: Ramsay Corporation.

Review of the Instrument Technician by PHILLIP L. ACKERMAN, Professor of Psychology, University of Minnesota, Minneapolis, MN:

The Instrument Technician is made up of two separate forms/manuals: IPO Test I and IPO Test II. The purposes of the two tests, according to the manuals, are identical: "for use with applicants and incumbents for jobs where technical knowledge of instrumentation is a necessary part of job activities." The manual for Test II adds that the applicable job title associated with the test is "Instrument Mechanic" from the *Dictionary of Occupational Titles*. Test I has 100 items and Test II has 122 items. The manuals lack clarity regarding how the items within the tests were constructed. For example, the "subject experts'" rankings of the importance of different areas (e.g., math, digital electronics, test instruments, etc.) were identical from one test to the other, but Test I has 8 questions on Digital Electronics and Test II has 18 questions on Digital Electronics. The test items appear to reflect a broad sampling of content within the job classification, and further appear to be presented at a high level of difficulty (which is supported by the very limited item difficulty data described below).

RELIABILITY/VALIDITY. There were minimal data provided on reliability and validity for these two tests. "Reliability" is reported for Test I as .93, based on 14 "applicants for instrument technician jobs" (pp. 7–8) and reliability for Test II is reported as .85, based on 9 "applicants for instrument technician jobs." Even ignoring the problem of such small sample sizes, such information is virtually uninterpretable, given the fact that the "kind" of reliability is not reported (e.g., test-retest, alternate form, internal consistency). Item difficulty statistics are provided, but the samples are clearly very small and the difficulty indices provoke some concern about the data sample or item design. Specifically, 9 items in Test I and 35 items in Test II have difficulty indices of 1.0, which means that they do not discriminate at all. There are no quantitative data on test validity—only an appeal to the content validity of the tests. However, there are no descriptions of how the test items were selected or developed to provide any grounding for the content validity assertion.

NORMS. The only normative information is a raw score to percentile rank conversion for each test. However, little information is provided indicating where the normative data come from (except that the data are from "instrument technician applicants"). No information is provided on even how many persons were tested for each norm group, although it appears from the numbers that the percentiles were computed on the basis of small groups of examinees, similar in size to the groups that provided the "reliability" data.

ADMINISTRATION/INTERPRETATION. The test is administered in an untimed format. No instructions or reference information are provided for the interpretation of scores from either test form.

SUMMARY. Although both Test I and Test II purport to assess "knowledge and skills required for the Instrument Technician jobs" (manual, Test I, p. 4), it is not clear whether the tests are substantially different in overall content, in scores obtained by respondents, or in the validity of the tests for particular occupations. Both tests appear to provide a broad sampling of topics relevant to electronics, mathematics, and test instruments. However, with no data for specific forms of reliability, criterion-related validity, minimal norms from job applicants, and no norms from job incumbents, it is impossible to ascertain whether either of these test forms are suitable for any particular application.

Review of the Instrument Technician by ALAN C. BUGBEE, JR., Director of Psychometric Services, The American Registry of Radiologic Technologists, St. Paul, MN:

The Ramsay Corporation Job Skills—Instrument Technician Test I and Instrument Technician Test II are group-administered achievement tests to assess whether examinees possess the necessary skills to be Instrument Technicians. According to one of the test manuals, citing the *Dictionary of Occupational Titles*, an Instrument Technician, in general, is a person who repairs instruments. More specifically, it is one who "installs, repairs, maintains, and adjusts indicating, recording, telemetering, and controlling instruments and test equipment, used to control and measure variables, ... using precision instruments, and handtools" (U.S. Department of Labor, 1991). Presumably, these are employment tests for entry into or advancement in this profession.

There are two different tests that comprise the Ramsay Corporation Job Skills—Instrument Technician, Test I and Test II. Both are Form IPO. No explanation is provided about what, if anything, IPO stands for, although a phone call to Ramsay Corporation revealed that it was used only internally by Ramsay and is neither an acronym nor does it have any special meaning beyond identification. These tests are different from one another, each having a different test manual, test booklet, and questions. Although there is no mention of it in either of the test manuals, according to a representative of Ramsay Corporation during a phone call, Test II is a more advanced version than Test I. Perhaps they are intended as being a basic or introductory test for employment as or promotion to a beginning Instrument Technician

(Test I) or as a screening instrument for an advanced Instrument Technician position (Test II). Because these tests are part of a presumably larger test series (see also reviews of Ramsay Corporation Job Skills—Mechanic Evaluation tests and others in this volume), it is possible that this is covered in some other manual. Unfortunately, no information addressing this was provided to this reviewer.

Instrument Technician Test I is a 100-question multiple-choice test. The items are presented in 11 sections: Mathematics (12 questions), Digital Electronics (8), Analog Electronics (13), Electrical Print Reading (9), Process Control (9), Power Supplies (8), Basic AC/DC Theory (17), Test Instruments (8), Mechanical (5), Computer and PLC (6), and Chemical Process (5). Instrument Technician Test II is a 122-item test that also covers the same areas, although the order of the sections is slightly different, with Mechanical coming last. Test II also has a different number of items and percentage concentration in six areas. Test II has a higher or much higher concentration than Test I in Digital Electronics, Process Control, and Computer and PLC. It is notably lower in Mathematics, Basic AD/DC Theory, and Test Instruments. It is essentially the same as Test I in the other five areas.

TEST ADMINISTRATION. Both tests are untimed, although the manual and the instructions to test takers say it should not take more than 2 hours to complete. The manual instructs the exam administrator to keep time and record completion time on the answer sheet for each test taker. No information, however, is provided about how this timing should or could be used or what relevance it might have in employee selection and promotion. This is odd because both manuals say that "time limits specified must be observed precisely as specified for each test" (manual, Test I, p. 5; manual, Test II, p. 5).

Test I and Test II have detailed instructions for the test administrator. In addition, these tests provide clear and concise written and verbal instructions for the test takers. The instructions to both the administrator and test takers are exactly the same for each test. Both manuals specify that one examiner can test up to 20 candidates and that an assistant is needed for each additional 20 test takers.

Each test has two practice questions on the front cover. The test administrators are instructed to be certain that every examinee completes the practice questions and records them on the answer sheet. Interestingly, the practice questions are numbered 1 and 2 on the answer

sheet and the regular test questions begin with the number 3 and end at 102 in Test I, and 124 in Test II. This could lead to some confusion among the test takers.

Examinees take this test using a standard two-sided answer sheet. The tests are scored through the use of hand-scoring keys (not provided to this reviewer). The score on the test is the number correct. This score is entered on the front of the answer sheet. There is an implication that these tests can be either machine scored by the user or by the Ramsay Corporation, but no information is provided about this in the manuals or on the tests. There is no subscoring. Each item is given an equal weight, although because there are not an equal number of test questions across each section, some sections are given a de facto heavier weight in the total score than others.

PSYCHOMETRIC PROPERTIES. Both of the tests for Instrument Technician suffer greatly from a lack of information about reliability, validity, item analysis, and normative information. Both manuals are mirrors of one another, using exactly the same language and only changing figures, dates, and names, as appropriate. It appears that very minimal psychometric studies were conducted on these tests.

For example, the reliability of Test I is reported as .93 with a standard error of measurement as 3.67. However, no information is provided about which type of reliability coefficient is used for this figure. More importantly, this estimate is based solely on performance by 14 job applicants for instrument technician positions in one paper plant in the Midwest. More surprisingly, the reliability estimate for Test II (.85, $SEM = 3.66$) is based upon the tests of 9 test takers, also at a Midwest paper plant. This is the extent of the information provided about these tests' reliabilities.

Both tests present the same information about validity. Under content-related validity, the manuals say "the content validity of the test is assured when the behaviors required on the test are also required on the job. It is a paper-and-pencil form of a work sample" (manual, Test I, p. 11; manual, Test II, p. 12). Both tests have had their items ranked by eight subject experts against a Maintenance Activity List (no citation given). An interrater agreement of .91 is reported for both Test I and Test II. Apparently, the Ramsay Corporation believes that this alone establishes the tests' validity as employment tests. However, "Before it is used, the test should have proven effectiveness, such as criterion-related validity" (Allen & Yen, 1979, p. 96).

The manuals very briefly address both construct and criterion-related validity, but clearly state that no studies of either of these types of validity have been undertaken. The brief descriptions of construct validity in both manuals take the position that construct validity "is attained by the procedures of development" (manual, Test I, p. 11; manual, Test II, p. 12) and that because the tests have content validity, they also have construct validity! Even if this circular logic was true, it is not sufficient evidence of the construct validity of a test. Ramsay Corporation makes no attempt to show a relationship between these tests and any others that measure the areas of skill necessary for success as an instrument technician.

The brief sections on criterion-related validity start by saying that because it is an achievement-type test, it only needs to have content validity. The manuals then go on to cite an article (Hunter, 1983) that has apparently shown a strong relationship between tests with content validity and criterion-related validity. Ramsay Corporation seems to wish to establish its test's validities through insinuation. However, "even if scores derived from criterion-referenced tests are descriptive of the objectives they are supposed to reflect, the usefulness of the scores as predictors of, say, 'job success' or 'success in the next unit of instruction' cannot be assured" (Hambleton & Rogers, 1991, p. 29). It is never sufficient for a test to rely on only content validity, regardless of how well it is established or what it may imply for other types of validity.

Information about normative data is essentially nonexistent in both tests. The manuals contain two sentences; one defines for what normative data are used; the other refers to a table of percentile equivalents relating raw scores to percentile ranks. No information whatever is provided about how these data are collected and how the percentiles were derived.

Both manuals present data, primarily in table format, about the difficulty and discrimination of the questions in the tests. The Instrument Technician Test I has nine items that everyone got right. These questions offer no useful information about the test takers. In addition, eight of the items have negative point biserial correlation coefficients ranging from -.05 to -.32. These show an inverse relationship between getting the question right and general test performance. Five of the questions, in addition to the nine that everyone got right, have very low (.04 or less) point biserials, showing almost no relationship between performance on the total test and whether or not the taker got the question right. In other words, over 20% of the questions on the examination offer little to nothing that would help

the test user select or promote candidates for a position as instrument technician.

Instrument Technician Test II has the same problems. Among the 122 questions on this test, 35 (29%) are ones everyone got right. Twenty items (16%) have a negative point biserial correlation coefficient and 4 (3%) have a low difficulty. All-in-all, 48% of the questions on this test offer little or no information related to the total test score.

Part of the problem with the item statistics for these tests is that they seem to have been acquired from the same extremely low number of test takers (14 for Test I, 9 for Test II), as was noted for the reliability statistics. Although this is not mentioned in either manual, it can be inferred from the reported difficulty of the questions. Regardless, these item statistics, in conjunction with the test statistics, call into question the usefulness of these tests to measure knowledge and skills required for instrument technician jobs.

In summary, Ramsay Corporation Job Skills Instrument Technician Test I and Instrument Technician Test II are difficult to review. Because they are so poorly constructed, it is hard to find something good to say about them. Any test manual that says that a test has "excellent reliability" when the only reliability estimate was based on a sample of nine makes one wonder about the quality of the examination and the background of the manufacturer. Perhaps these are good tests. After all, there is no information presented to show that they are not. Unfortunately, there is no information to show that they are, either. Indeed, the manuals present little information at all. These tests need to be restandardized to establish whether or not they do what they are supposed to do. That is, whether they are valid. In their current state, they cannot be recommended for use.

REVIEWER'S REFERENCES

Allen, M. J., & Yen, W. M. (1979). *Introduction to measurement theory.* Monterey, CA: Brooks/Cole.
Hunter, J. E. (1983). A causal analysis of cognitive ability, job knowledge, job performance, and supervisor ratings. In F. Land, S. Zedeck, & J. Cleveland (Eds.), *Performance measurement and theory* (pp. 257–266). Hillsdale, NJ: Lawrence Erlbaum.
Hambleton, R. K., & Rogers, H. J. (1991). Advances in criterion-referenced measurement. In R. K. Hambleton & J. N. Zaal (Eds.), *Advances in educational and psychological testing: Theory and applications* (pp. 3–43). Boston: Kluwer.
U.S. Department of Labor (1991). *Dictionary of occupational titles* (4th ed.). Washington, DC: U.S. Government Printing Office.

[152]

Integrated Assessment System.

Purpose: "A series of performance tasks that can be used independently or in combination with a norm-referenced achievement test to offer a comprehensive view of student achievement."

Population: Grades 1–9.
Publication Dates: 1990–1992.
Acronym: IAS.
Subtests: 3.
Administration: Group.
Authors: Roger Farr and Beverly Farr (Language Arts and Spanish only).
Publisher: The Psychological Corporation.
    a) IAS-LANGUAGE ARTS.
Population: Grades 1–8.
Scores, 3: Response to Reading, Management of Content, Command of Language.
Price Data, 1994: $104 per complete grade 1 package including 25 each of three student booklets and directions for administering; $182 per complete grades 2–8 package including three sets of guided-writing-activity black line masters, directions for administering, three packages of 25 response forms, and response form directions; $18 per grade 1 examination kit including student booklet, directions for administering, and one passage specific scoring rubric; $22.50 per grades 2–8 examination kit including reading passage, guided-writing-activity black line master, response form, response form directions, directions for administering, and one passage-specific scoring rubric; $26 per grade 1 activity package including 25 of one student booklet and directions for administering; $65 per grades 2–8 activity package and directions for administering; $65 per grades 2–8 activity package including 25 of one reading passage and directions for administering; $5.50 per grades 2–8 response form package; $7 per grades 1–8 directions for administering; $15.50 per grades 1–8 scoring guides; $24 per grade 1 reading passage only; $59 per grades 2–8 reading passage only; $12.50 per grades 2–8 guided-writing-activity black line masters; $35.50 per technical report ('91, 53 pages); $210.50 per scoring workshop kit including videotape, trainer's manual, 25 overhead transparencies, and masters of model papers and training papers; $130 per portfolio starter kit including classroom storage box, 25 student portfolios, and teacher's manual; $42 per student portfolio folders; $42 per teacher's manual; $63.50 per introductory videotape and viewer's guide; $4.16 per basic scoring service; $6.24 per 25 student demographic sheets.
Time: (120–240) minutes.
    1) *IAS—Language Arts, Spanish Edition.*
Scores: Same as *a* above.
Price Data: $17.50 per grade 1 examination kit including student booklet, directions for administering, and a passage specific scoring rubric; $21.50 per grades 2–8 examination kit including reading passage, guided-writing-activity black line master, one response form, response form directions, directions for administering, and passage specific scoring rubric; $25 per grade 1 activity

package including 25 copies of one student booklet and one directions for administering; $62.50 per grades 2–8 activity package including 25 copies of one reading passage, one directions for administering, and one guided-writing-activity black line master; $5.50 per grades 2–8 response form package including 25 response forms and response form directions; $1 per response form directions; $7 per grades 1–8 directions for administering; $15 per grades 1–8 scoring guides; $23 per 25 grade 1 reading passage; $57 per 25 grades 2–8 reading passage; $12 per grades 2–8 guided-writing-activity black line masters; $4.16 per basic scoring service; $6.24 per student demographic sheet.
    b) IAS-MATHEMATICS
Population: Grades 1–9.
Scores, 4: Reasoning, Conceptual Knowledge, Communication Procedures.
Price Data: $17.50 per examination kit including student booklet, directions for administering, and scoring rubric; $27 per activity package including 25 student booklets and directions for administering; $7.50 per directions for administering; $16 per scoring guides; $120 per scoring training kit including binder and overhead transparencies; $9.31 per basic scoring holistic and analytic; $6.24 per 25 student demographic sheet.
Time: (80–90) minutes.
    c) IAS-SCIENCE.
Population: Grades 1–8.
Scores, 4: Experimenting, Collecting Data, Drawing Conclusions, Communicating.
Price Data: $17.50 per examination kit including student booklet, directions for administering, and scoring rubric; $25 per activity package including 25 student booklets and one directions for administering; $7 per directions for administering; $16 per scoring guides; $30 per manipulative materials; $120 per scoring workshop kit including trainer's manual; $5.15 per basic scoring service; $6.25 per 25 student demographic sheet.
Time: (80–90) minutes.

Review of the Integrated Assessment System by GABRIEL M. DELLA-PIANA, Director of Evaluation, El Paso Collaborative for Academic Excellence, University of Texas at El Paso, El Paso, TX:

The Integrated Assessment System (IAS) is a series of performance tasks in three subject matter areas. This review focuses on Language Arts Assessment because this subtest has the greatest amount of documentation.

The purpose of the IAS-Language Arts is "to measure how well students are developing as readers and writers at the time of testing so that effective instruction can be planned" (technical report, p. 27). Elsewhere in the technical report (p. 10) two other purposes are stated: (a) to help students understand their own literacy growth and performance to guide their development as readers and writers; (b) to help administrators and other decision makers to understand how students are developing literacy skills needed to be effective citizens. The purpose of this review is to determine what we can about how well the test achieves its purposes.

Reading/Writing prompts were selected to tap the kinds of writing students are typically taught at each grade level based on a "survey … of the leading language arts instructional programs" (technical report, p. 16). Similarly, thinking skills tapped by the prompts were to be "representative of thinking students are asked to do at [each] grade level" (p. 18). Neither of these selection processes was described in sufficient detail to judge the claims made. Though the grade level selections seem appropriate in general, this rigid classification prevents seeing that all kinds of writing are possible in some form at all grade levels. For example, the kind of "if-then" thinking that can be done in kindergarten in talking about simple experiments or narratives is really the beginning of essay writing. But essay writing is first listed in the grade 4 writing products. Thus, it would be well to guide teachers to see developmental progressions of skills that are a part of different kinds of writing as stretching over the entire range of grades (1 to 8) encompassed in the assessment, rather than fixed at one grade level.

A general scoring rubric for writing was created with three dimensions. Response to Reading (addressing reading comprehension) includes amount of information from the passage used in the writing, the accuracy of the information, and the selection or relevance of the information to the task. This reviewer found the scoring guide for Response to Reading to be generally inconsistent with the writing prompts and other instructions to the writer. For example, for the passage on The Sinking of the Titanic, the student is asked to "use the facts in the passage to write a story [the directions for administering reads, in error, "write a good essay," p. 8] from the point of view of someone who might have been on the ship when it sank" (Reading Passage, p. 3). Then, in the directions for administering this passage, the teacher directs the student to that prompt in the reading passage, and adds that "it is important

that the details they use in their writing should accurately reflect what they have read" (directions for administering, p. 8). In the scoring guide, the scorer is asked to consider: "How much information from the passage does the student bring to the writing?" (p. 5). But the prompt and directions do not emphasize "how much information" is used. Again, in opposition to the prompt and directions, the scoring rubric for this passage gives a "2" (out of a possible 4 points) to a response that presents a minimal amount of information and a "4" (highest score) to one that presents "a substantial amount of information" (p. 6). Because one of the purposes of the assessment is for students to understand their own literacy growth, this scoring in opposition to directions for the writing is likely to be confusing and lacking in credibility for both student and teacher. A case in point is one "model paper" for a score of 2 on this dimension (scoring guide, p. 28). The paper was a narrative of a young couple with most of the narrative describing their getting ready for the trip on the Titanic, the waving to the family, a proposal to get married on the ship, the enjoyment of four days, and then the disaster. Some detail from the reading passage was used up to this point. More detail from the passage came in at that stage. The point is that the narrative met the criteria for the writing prompt and the additional directions during the administration of the task and did it in a way that one knew enough about the characters to have the disaster hit home. The scoring guides for the other two dimensions (management of content or organization and development of the writing and command of language or such matters as sentence structure, word choice, and mechanics) seem more appropriate to this reviewer.

A Scoring Workshop Kit (technical manual, p. 28) is available with a trainer's manual, videotape, and other supportive material (though the scoring guide does not reference it in "materials needed," p. 3). With a 6-hour training session, evidence is reported that trained scorers obtain a reasonably high agreement with "expected scores" for the training papers. Over 70% of the judgments were in exact agreement with "expected scores" and fewer than 2% differed by more than one point. In addition, independent scorers in about 25% of the cases differed by one point or more. This would make a big difference for a student who may be rated "minimal" (2) rather than "adequate" (3), or "adequate" rather than "excellent" (4). There are procedures for resolving differences, but no study is reported for focusing on what happens in these cases. The appropriateness of the level of scoring reliability for use for individual feedback to students seems questionable.

There is no apparent guidance for the test user (student, teacher, administrator, or "other decision makers") in the scoring guide or technical report with respect to making inferences from the test information and considering implications for instruction, student development, or policy level issues. Because the purposes of the test listed above focus on these test uses, the present level of development of supportive guides for interpretation and use are severely limited.

If the teacher decides not to use the "optional" Guided Writing Activity (with its specific guide to prewriting, drafting, and revising) the teacher simply takes students through those steps, presumably in whatever way she or he chooses to follow. This introduces considerable variation in administration procedures. Directions suggest to the teacher administering the test, that "you should function as a 'coach'. That is you should motivate, guide, prod, and encourage students to produce their best work without actually doing the work for them. The amount of prompting you provide can range from very little to quite a bit depending upon the needs and abilities of your students" (directions for administering, pp. 4–5). Given the ambiguity and planned variation in directions for administration, and the lack of any suggested training for administration of the test in any of the documents listed as "needed" on page 3 of the directions for administering, there will be considerable variability in test administration procedures. This lack of standardization of procedures for administration will likely play havoc with interpretation of student performance and with making sense of whatever lines of validity evidence is gathered for inferences to be made from test performance. Thus, though some validity evidence is presented, it is not considered here because of the lack of test standardization making interpretation of any findings lacking in credibility.

In spite of the limitations in standardization of procedures, the reading passages and writing tasks appear to be useful for providing in-class practice in integrated reading and writing and could provide interpretable scores if teachers agreed upon standard procedures for administration that are consistent with the scoring guides.

The IAS-Science Assessment and IAS-Mathematics Assessment both contain a useful set of performance tasks. Both are problem-solving pro-

cess and problem generating in form with an attempt to get at "real-world" (p. 15) contexts. Scoring is holistic and analytic and can be performed by the user or by the publisher. Holistic and analytic scoring are generic rather than task specific. Although the tasks appear useful for instruction and assessment, the lack of a technical report on selection of items, reliability, validity, and guides for interpretation and use make it premature to evaluate these subtests.

Review of the Integrated Assessment System by BIKKAR S. RANDHAWA, Professor of Educational Psychology, University of Saskatchewan, Saskatoon, Canada:

The Integrated Assessment System (IAS) was designed to assess student performance in Language Arts, Mathematics, and Science through a series of performance tasks. As the performance tasks in three areas are independent and also the available validation and technical information for each area varies, each assessment area is reviewed in a distinct section.

IAS—LANGUAGE ARTS PERFORMANCE ASSESSMENT. The Language Arts Performance Assessment (LAPA) series of instruments is based on a sound rationale. Changes in language arts curricula and instruction, an integration of literacy skills, a focus on constructing meaning, an emphasis on problem solving and critical thinking skills, use of collaboration and cooperative learning in classrooms, and contemporary assessment approaches that advocate performance tasks are important considerations in the development of these Language Arts Assessment tools. In my view, this system is integrated within the language arts assessment domain because reading and writing are not considered as isolated areas for instruction and assessment but rather they are viewed as an integrated whole. Proficiency in one is necessary for proficiency in the other. This is where these tools distinguish from the others in the market.

The LAPA includes for each grade (2 to 8) three booklets of reading passages. The passage in the booklet is preceded by the reading/writing prompt in a colored box. Each prompt is intended to integrate reading and writing and to engage the student in problem solving and critical thinking. For each passage for a grade there is a separate manual of directions for administering, with a specific section for each prompt. The option is available for teachers to allow a variable number of class periods for each passage. Also, consistent with a teacher's instructional approach and preference, allowance is made for permitting students to collaborate and cooperate in working on the preliminary stages of the writing activity. The final draft, however, is expected to be written and revised by each student individually. For the final draft, materials in the LAPA include a response form for each passage. An optional guided writing activity form is available for teachers to use. This focused activity guide for each prompt provides structure for the writing activity. It directs students to review the pertinent and important details about the passage, to organize the required writing, to prepare a draft of the writing required by the prompt, and to critique and rewrite a final draft. There is a separate scoring guide for each passage in the set. Scoring guides consist of an introduction to the scoring guide, six sections, and three appendices. Distinctive and prompt-specific parts of these guides are Sections 3–5 and Appendix A.

Section 1 of the scoring guides describes the type of scoring, purportedly a combination of the elements of holistic, analytic, and primary trait assessment methods. It also provides the definition of terms, the general scoring rubric, and factors to consider in assigning a score for each dimension to be scored, that is, Response to Reading, Management of Content, and Command of Language.

Section 2 deals with general procedures for scoring. It includes: following the scoring system, working with a partner, checking reliability, resolving differences, handling unexpected responses, and avoiding extraneous factors in scoring. Section 3 provides specific procedures for scoring a specific prompt. In this section, the general scoring rubric is modified to reflect the specific prompt in three dimensions to be scored.

Section 4 contains two model papers for each score point (1 to 4) for a specific prompt. Section 5 includes a sample paper to be scored by the teacher for practice and self-determination of scoring accuracy. Teachers are encouraged to use the model papers for additional practice, if deemed necessary. Each model paper is scored on only one dimension so that a teacher may use that paper to score for the other two dimensions for practice.

Section 6 is general and basically applies to three prompts for each grade. It reflects the philosophy of the assessment system and distinguishes between process and product evaluation. This section also deals with the limitations, from the authors' perspective, of the LAPA and makes useful suggestions to the users for augmenting this assessment with standardized normative tests if other purposes are intended.

The technical report for the LAPA provides extensive technical data. This includes opinions of students and teachers in the tryout samples, convergent and discriminant validity correlational tables for each prompt involving two scorers, interdimensional correlations by prompt, percentage of agreement between scorers for field test data for each prompt, interrater reliability estimates by dimension and prompt, and other descriptive statistics. However, there are several redundancies in these reported statistics as well as inappropriately derived results. For example, interdimensional correlations by prompt in Table 12 are redundant with statistics in Tables 4 to 11. Statistics in Table 12, furthermore, are slightly inflated because the data for the two scorers, I assume, are combined for calculating these statistics. On the other hand, Table 14 provides interrater reliability estimates by dimension and prompt using both Pearson and Spearman correlation procedures. It is not clear why this was done. How one is to decide which of these is appropriate for score interpretation is not explicitly stated. There are many discrepancies in the number of interrater scores for each response to a prompt reported in Tables 13 and 14.

A more serious difficulty in the reported convergent and discriminant validity evidence, Tables 4 to 11, is that for scoring a response to a prompt Scorer 1 and Scorer 2 are not two specific individuals who scored all the responses to a prompt. Multiple scorers were used and different sets of each response were scored by different pairs of scorers. Hence, the reported scores are thereby confounded and the contaminated variables might produce spuriously higher values than expected.

It is useful to have the interrater reliability evidence. However, it should be noted that it, too, is affected by the confounding of the scorer variable, as described above. For the purposes of a classroom teacher who may not have the luxury of a second reader for the student responses nor time for herself to reread the papers, this evidence serves as an assurance that scoring is reasonably robust provided instructions are strictly followed and that the teacher has undergone the type of training that the scorers of the field test responses had taken.

In summary, this set of materials is exemplary in providing classroom teachers an introduction to performance assessment in language arts. The philosophy behind the development of these materials is well articulated and the limitations of this assessment are clearly stated. The user has the responsibility to ascertain whether one short reading prompt is sufficient to provide durable evidence on the overall language ability as well as on the three components of language acquisition in the time required for the administration of each prompt. For other purposes, standardized instruments must not be ruled out as irrelevant or inappropriate.

IAS—SCIENCE PERFORMANCE ASSESSMENT. The Science Performance Assessment (SPA) system is parallel to the LAPA in that each student booklet, directions for administering, and scoring guide have the same basic structure and are based on the same philosophical orientation. At each grade level, I assume, there are two sets or forms of materials. I assumed this to be the case because there is no overall grid that orients the user to the numeric codes on each booklet, for example, 911 and 912, 921 and 922, etc. I have not quite determined the significance of the "9" in the numeric code.

For each assessment task in the SPA, one per form per grade, there are five scores available. The holistic score has a range of 0 to 6. Each of the four analytic scores, experimenting, collecting data, drawing conclusions, and communicating, has a range of 1 to 4. The scoring guide provides rubrics for each score in the holistic and analytic system. However, there is only one illustration for each holistic score, which is supposedly based on a hypothetical student response. I do not think that these responses are actual responses selected for illustration. These are transcriptions or made-up responses to demonstrate expectations for each holistic score point. Following each holistic score illustration, there is a score for that illustration for each analytic component. Only excerpts from the specific scoring rubric are provided for each analytic score assigned for the response in this illustration. Perhaps, that is sufficient for experienced scorers who have used this kind of performance assessment either in the classroom context or as a scorer in a large-scale assessment. It is not appropriate for inexperienced teachers who may only receive initial training in scoring. Such teachers need more illustrations and some unscored samples to develop consistency in scoring. The unscored samples should be followed by expert-assigned scores. Such a procedure was used in the Language Arts Assessment.

There is no evidence available for this specific performance assessment set for me to conclude that two or more independent raters would be consistent in scoring responses to these tasks. In essence, there is no technical evidence to support the use, interpre-

tation, and consequences of these assessments. Therefore, these materials, at best, could be considered supplemental instructional materials and not assessment instruments per se in the strictest sense. Validity evidence should be available before these sets are marketed as assessment materials in science.

I do not undervalue the importance of writing in any subject. Further, I appreciate the development of critical thinking and scientific attitude. These highly valued cognitive abilities and attitudes cannot exist without a sufficiently rich knowledge base (Okagaki & Sternberg, 1990). Process approaches are important but these instructional schemes must not take hostage the content of the domain. We cannot think in vacuum. Thinking must be developed in conjunction with the development of scientific content. Everything in science cannot be learned through experimentation. Reading in science involving scientific content, that is, facts, principles, and rules and the way scientists have gone about establishing those, is also critical. It appears to me that there has to be a balance. In correcting for rote learning in science in the past, a completely process and experimental approach may lead to ignorant experimentation. The experimental approach is only one of the ways that science is learned. Hence, scientific performance is more than the evidence a teacher can get by using these materials.

Teachers planning to use these materials may like to determine the authenticity of the tasks for their specific group of students in the specific community context. The relevance, everyday use, and familiarity of the tasks to their specific students are important considerations. Such evidence should be the responsibility of providers of assessment materials. In the absence of that evidence, users bear that responsibility.

IAS—MATHEMATICS PERFORMANCE ASSESSMENT. The integrated assessment system also includes the Mathematics Performance Assessment (MPA). As stated in the SPA, these assessment materials also are parallel to and use the format and description for rubrics in the LAPA. For grades 1–9, there appear to be multigrade student task booklets, directions for administering, and scoring guides. The lowest level materials are for grades 1–3; the next set for grades 2–4; and so on. There are two forms of materials for each grade range. Again, no explicit description is found to indicate that this is indeed the intended use. It was my initial inference from the numerical codes used and subsequently I confirmed this with the publisher.

Each task booklet consists of just one task, as is the case with the LAPA and SPA booklets. The format of the various booklets in this series is not the same, which is in contrast to the SPA booklets. The only change from booklet to booklet in the SPA was the specific reference to the task here and there. Therefore, the MPA booklets are not monotonous and boring. Students can be expected to be more interested and motivated if more than one task is used for assessment. However, the holistic scoring rubrics for the various levels are the same for all three domains of assessment regardless of the grade level, which in itself is rather interesting and curious. Should one not expect variability in expectations of the overall performance? Was it for convenience and expediency?

The rubrics for the analytic scoring of the four components, Reasoning, Conceptual Knowledge, Communication, and Procedures, provide for the same range of scores (1–4) as for the LAPA and SPA. However, the specific descriptions pertain to the mathematical content. These descriptions are used for scoring all the responses, grades 1–9. Teachers are expected to allow for developmental differences in scoring student responses.

The scoring guides for these materials are deficient in that they do not provide exemplars and guidance for teachers to score consistently. There are no specific illustrations of various types of student responses that are assigned different scores. There is no opportunity for teachers to assess their consistency, except if they happen to have a willing colleague. Such an expectation is not realistic considering the present structure of heavy demands of in-school and extracurricular duties on teachers. I understand that training materials for scorers are available for the school systems. In spite of that, it is important that assessment tasks are scored consistently and that consistency verification opportunities are available for teachers in the scoring guide for each performance task.

In the scoring guide for the Booklet 789, Form 2 on the task Color Spectrum, the typical student responses on page 18 that are supposedly illustrative of no serious major flaws for holistic scoring purposes are in fact indications of misreading of the chart. For each specific question asked, some holistic analysis is provided but there is no overall paper-wise assignment of various points. How the teachers are to synthesize these componential analyses for the holistic score to be assigned is not clear.

These materials, like the SPA, do not have accompanying validity evidence. Also, the content validity of just one task per booklet, even though the assessment may extend over two class periods and writing is encouraged in these tasks, may be questionable. Even if a task is expected to be and designed to be content valid and provides for the assessment in a teaching-like environment, no validity evidence is available. In conclusion, these tasks are interesting exercises that teachers may use in conjunction with their own assessment in mathematics and with their knowledge of the students from their daily experience with them. For diagnostic and prescriptive instructional purposes, teachers ought to seek out other available assessment instruments that have the required validity evidence for commercially available materials, as required in the *Standards for Educational and Psychological Testing* (AERA, APA, & NCME, 1985).

CONCLUSION. The title of this set of instruments is misleading. It gives the impression that assessment in Language Arts, Mathematics, and Science is integrated. From my view, integrated assessment means that it is linked or connected. This is not the case. There is no evidence to support interconnectedness or linking of the three areas. The only defensible claim is that assessment in Language Arts is integrated in the sense that reading and writing are assessed together using a common prompt or task. I have not seen any explicit statement regarding the integrated assessment in either Mathematics or Science.

Another impression one gets is that the tasks used in the three areas are authentic. I like to distinguish between performance assessment and authentic assessment. Performance assessment provides the student or the examinee an opportunity to show his or her competence on a job-related or applied situation. Authentic assessment, on the other hand, is more complex. It not only presents to the student peformance tasks but also ensures that tasks have clear relationship to the curriculum, instruction, and as much as possible to real-life situations a student has encountered. Tasks used in these assessments are performance tasks that assess application of knowledge and problem solving but not job-related or real-life tasks. In the Language Arts area of these measures, there is evidence on the appropriateness of the tasks for curriculum and instruction. However, many tasks are not those that students experience in their daily lives or those that have relevance for job situations.

For the Mathematics and Science assessment instruments there are no technical data. Guidance to teachers on scoring, even though scoring guides are provided, is not clear and unambiguous. It seems to me that the guides do not have actual student responses as examples of various score points that are consistent with the rubrics. Teachers are basically left to fend for themselves in terms of scoring consistency. However, an expensive scoring service from the publisher is available, but it seems to defeat the purpose of these assessments. Teachers do not gain valuable insight of student strengths and weaknesses if scoring is done by professional scorers.

Language Arts Assessment is based on technically sound evidence and is, therefore, recommended as a good source of integrated language arts performance assessment. There is a need of validity evidence for both the Mathematics and Science assessments before they are recommended for use. At present, these tasks could be used as an adjunct to a teacher's own assessment attempts for instructional decisions.

REVIEWER'S REFERENCES

American Educational Research Association, American Psychological Association, & National Council on Measurement in Education. (1985). *Standards for educational and psychological testing.* Washington, DC: American Psychological Association, Inc.

Okagaki, L., & Sternberg, R. J. (1990). Teaching thinking skills: We're getting the context wrong. *Contributions to Human Development, 21*, 63–78.

[153]
INteraction CHecklist for Augmentative Communication, Revised Edition.

Purpose: Designed to assess features of interaction between augmentative system users and their partners.
Population: Augmentative system users.
Publication Dates: 1984–1991.
Acronym: INCH.
Scores, 13: Strategies (Initiation, Facilitation, Regulation, Termination); Modes (Linguistic, Paralinguistic, Kinesic, Proxemic, Chronemic); Contexts (Familiar-Trained, Familiar-Untrained, Unfamiliar-Trained, Unfamiliar-Untrained).
Administration: Individual.
Price Data, 1993: $31 per complete kit including manual ('91, 74 pages) and 15 checklists; $8 per 15 checklists.
Time: Administration time not reported.
Comments: Behavior checklist.
Authors: Susan Oakander Bolton and Sallie E. Dashiell.
Publisher: Imaginart Communication Products.

TEST REFERENCES

1. Sutton, A. E., & Gallagher, T. M. (1993). Verb class distinctions and AAC language-encoding limitations. *Journal of Speech and Hearing Research, 36*, 1216–1226.

Review of the INteraction CHecklist for Augmentative Communication, Revised Edition by ANTHONY J. NITKO, Professor of Education, School of Education, University of Pittsburgh, Pittsburgh, PA:

The INteraction CHecklist for Augmentative Communication (INCH), Revised Edition is a clinical checklist for assessing social communication skills of persons unable to use oral speech effectively and who must use an augmentative and alternative communication (AAC) aid. The INCH does not assess general linguistic competencies or technical skills in using an AAC aid. Instead, it focuses on whether a person is able to use an AAC aid to communicate with others in typical social settings such as the home, school, work, and community.

The INCH is a list of 32 communication behaviors (called strategies) organized into four communication scales: Initiation (6 strategies), Facilitation (13 strategies), Regulation (9 strategies), and Termination (4 strategies). Assessment consists of rating a person's use of each of the 32 strategies in each of five communication modes: Linguistic (verbal language), Paralinguistic (nonverbal vocalizations, inflections), Kinesic (facial expression, body movements, gestures), Proxemic (physical positioning, distance), and Chronemic (timing, rate). A person's usage of each strategy is rated as *present* (effective without prompting), *emerging* (needs prompting, inconsistent), *absent* (or not observed), or *not applicable.*

The ratings are summarized for each of the 32 strategies and for each of the four communication scales. A strategy that receives a majority of "present" ratings across all the appropriate modalities is labeled a *strength*. Otherwise, it is a *weakness*. Each of the four communication scales receives a numerical score obtained by counting the number of strategies that were identified as "strengths." The number of "presents" also result in a score.

The INCH ratings may be completed by communication specialists and/or paraprofessionals who observe the person directly or by an interviewer who discusses the person being rated with one or more informants (family members, educators, caregivers, employers, etc.).

Once the checklist is completed, the specific strategies identified as weak are targeted for training. The manual authors describe how to translate each weakness into a statement of a specific and measurable learning target. They also describe how to prioritize learning targets in the intervention learning sequence. Examples of intervention learning activities are provided.

TECHNICAL DATA. The INCH manual contains no empirical data to support the scientific validity of using the results for diagnosis and prescription. Descriptions of how the specific strategies were developed or selected are not given. Data supporting the listed strategies as the most critical to rate are missing. Normative data on the typical INCH performance of persons with different types and degrees of disabilities, and using different types of AAC aids, would be helpful when interpreting a person's results. The amount of confidence we should have in the INCH results could be better understood if we had data supporting stability and interrater reliabilities.

SUMMARY. The use of the INCH should probably be restricted to highly skilled social communication specialists. Even so, the INCH is best seen as an informal assessment tool rather than as a scientifically grounded instrument. At this time the manual contains no data to support the argument that INCH results may be validly used for diagnosing social communication weaknesses among persons needing to use AAC aids.

Review of the INteraction CHecklist for Augmentative Communication, Revised Edition by KENNETH G. SHIPLEY, Professor and Chair of Communicative Sciences and Disorders, California State University, Fresno, Fresno, CA:

The INteraction CHecklist for Augmentative Communication (INCH) is not a test per se but, as the authors describe it, an observational tool or checklist to assess different types of interactive behavior pertinent to helping develop nonoral communication. In their words, "the authors developed the Checklist to help clinicians describe the critical features of interaction necessary for successful communication between augmentative system users and their partners" (manual, p. 3).

The one-piece scoring sheet, which folds out, contains three different sections: (a) the cover sheet containing identifying information and an assessment of entry skills; (b) the recording sheet for scoring augmentative or alternative communication system skills by four communication strategies (Initiation, Facilitation, Regulation, and Termination) across five communication modes (Linguistic, Paralinguistic, Kinesic, Proxemic, and Chronemic); and the worksheet to summarize results and begin planning intervention strategies.

Several fundamental concepts are important in understanding the INCH, its scoresheet, and what the checklist is attempting to do. A fundamental premise of the instrument is viewing communication modes within the following categories: Linguistic, or

verbal language skills; Paralinguistic, such as nonverbal vocalizations or inflection; Kinesic, such as facial expression, body movement, or gestures; Proxemic, such a physical positioning and distance; and Chronemic, or timing and rate.

These five communication modes are then evaluated across four types of communication, which are termed strategies: Initiation, such as responding to greetings or introducing self; Facilitation, such as use of eye contact or seeking help; Regulation, such as giving feedback or expanding on a message; and Terminating, such as a social farewell or indicating completion of a conversation.

A total of 32 different topics are addressed within these four areas of Initiation, Facilitation, Regulation, and Termination. As appropriate to a client, each of the 32 different topics is assessed as being *present, emerging, absent,* or *not applicable.* The effect of this scoring methodology is viewing the four communication strategies (e.g., Initiation) across five communication modes (e.g., Linguistic) by one of four response patterns (e.g., present). For example, Kinesic Initiation might be present, but Linguistic Initiation absent. The scoring sheet also allows space for clinicians to describe behaviors seen, and make a general estimate of strengths and weaknesses within each of the 32 topic areas.

The accompanying manual is subdivided into five chapters and a selected references section. The five chapters are Introduction, Components, Administration, Application and Use, and Intervention. There are relatively good descriptions of the different terminology used and definitions of the conceptual framework used found in the manual. One real strength within the manual is a number of figures to illustrate key concepts. These are highly useful for individuals without extensive experience with augmentative and alternative communication clients or methods. Chapters 4 and 5 address a number of areas pertaining to intervention, such as developing appropriate goals and procedures. Although some of the suggestions are potentially helpful, users are cautioned that some of the procedures are rather simplistic or cursory—additional training and knowledge beyond that found in the manual is advisable.

A limitation throughout the manual is the absence of appropriate literature underpinning some of the suggestions and approaches. For example, there are 16 items listed in the selected references section of the manual. However, only five of these are even cited in the text—three of these citations are listed to substantiate one thought, and one of the five citations is a dictionary. There is an absence of solid backing offered for some of the suggestions and underpinnings of the model used.

There is another point that merits consideration. Throughout the manual, the authors note that the INCH is a checklist or a tool—not a test. It is not a test per se, but it is used for assessment purposes and users do make important clinical decisions from information attained. Also, the manual authors offer a number of suggestions for interpreting results and developing treatment strategies. However, there are no data or discussions about any type of validity or reliability. There is a presumption of face validity, as well as content validity on many items contained on the checklist, but validity is not really addressed in any form. Similarly, reliability is simply not addressed. This restricts the confidence one can place in obtained results.

In summary, the INCH provides a model for looking at the needs of patients who would benefit from alternative or augmentative communication. Many of the items are highly appropriate to such an assessment. The scoring sheet is relatively easy to use, and it provides useful reference (by page number) to specific items in the manual for further clarification. As the authors have commented, the checklist should be used in combination with other materials and assessment procedures. Some of the intervention strategies and suggestions may be helpful for some clinicians. However, care should be taken not to overrely on the tool due to the fundamental validity and reliability questions that are not addressed. The user could also be more confident in the instrument if there were more thorough, appropriately cited discussions of the fundamental underpinnings of the checklist and some of the suggestions offered for intervention.

[154]

Interaction Index.

Purpose: "To identify the cause(s) of poor on-the-job relationships and prescribe steps for improvement."
Population: Adults.
Publication Date: 1989.
Scores, 8: Give Positive Strokes, Give Negative Strokes, Accept Positive Strokes, Accept Negative Strokes, Ask for Positive Strokes, Ask for Negative Strokes, Refuse to Give Positive Strokes, Refuse to Give Negative Strokes.
Administration: Group.
Price Data, 1989: $4 per one test booklet and one scoring and interpretation booklet (8 pages); $15 per Leader's Guide.
Time: (10–15) minutes.
Authors: Michalak Training Associates, Inc.
Publisher: Michalak Training Associates, Inc.

Review of the Interaction Index by KATHY E. GREEN, Professor, College of Education, University of Denver, Denver, CO:

The Interaction Index is a brief measure based on the transactional analysis ideas of giving and receiving "strokes." The index is intended to identify areas of on-the-job behavior that could be changed to allow more effective interaction. The index provides feedback to individuals about their behavior, which brings it to conscious awareness, which can lead to change. It seems to be designed for participants of business training workshops. The 24 items are marked on a *seldom* to *regularly* response scale (0–3) and ask the workshop participant to "think of a person at work with whom you have a relationship that is *not as good as you'd like it to be* ... think about how each statement applies to your relationship with the person you've chosen." The index is easily self-scored. The index is diagnostic in that ranges of scores reflecting healthy, effective relationships are given. An interpretation of scores lower and higher than this effective range is provided. The individual interprets index results and the scoring and interpretation booklet is written for the workshop participant.

The scoring and interpretation booklet is not a technical or administration manual. As such, it has little information about the rationale for the index and no information regarding reliability, validity, or any technical aspect of measure development. Suggested effective score ranges on each subscale are listed with no explanation of how the ranges were obtained.

The Interaction Index may be used to stimulate reflection and discussion but lacks the development and technical information to be considered a measure. Production of a technical manual would require explanation of the link between the measure and transactional analysis, evidence that the items actually reflect interaction, and a basis for score interpretation as well as technical evidence supporting reliability and validity. At this stage, there is no reason to give the index any more weight than a quiz found in a magazine.

Review of the Interaction Index by JAY R. STEWART, Assistant Professor and Director, Rehabilitation Counseling Program, Bowling Green State University, Bowling Green, OH:

GENERAL DESCRIPTION. The Interaction Index, a 24-item self-report inventory, is intended to determine what factors are causing poor work-related relationships and establish a plan for improving these relationships. The items are statements describing how the respondent reacts to another person with whom he or she is not having a good work relationship. The items describe on-the-job situations in which the respondent either gives, accepts, asks for, or refuses "strokes." The strokes are ways individuals may receive recognition and attention and can be viewed as positive or negative (Berne, 1964). For each item the respondent chooses among four answers, listed incrementally as to what degree or how often the respondent engages in the described behavior.

THEORETICAL MODEL. The Interaction Index is based on Eric Berne's transactional analysis, in which individuals interact by giving and receiving strokes based on their life scripts. The life scripts reflect childhood decisions intended to maximize the receiving of parental strokes (Harris, 1969). Adults fulfill their life scripts through providing or withholding strokes to themselves and others. Stroking methods reflect a basic position, how a person feels about self and others.

The Interaction Index identifies the kind and frequency of strokes given, accepted, asked for, and refused by the respondent. Depending upon the motive of the respondent, the positive stroke can be a positive reinforcement or can be used as a temporary "feel-good" for the receiver, but not genuine. The negative stroke can be constructive criticism that causes the receiver to change or can be used to make the receiver feel bad. McKenna (1974) presented stroking profiles that are apparently the basis for the Interaction Index.

Stroke giving and receiving patterns can be changed through redecisions (Goulding & Goulding, 1979). In redecisioning, persons go back to the childhood moment where decisions about their life script are made, reexperience the decision making, make new decisions, and change behaviors to reinforce their decisions. The instrument does not promote revisiting childhood decisions, but does include a contract for changing dysfunctional stroking and other behaviors.

STANDARDIZATION, RELIABILITY, AND VALIDITY. Although average score ranges are provided, a norming process was not identified in the manual. There are no indications of reliability or validity studies in the professional literature.

INSTRUMENT ADMINISTRATION AND INTERPRETATION. The instrument, intended to be administered to managers and employees in an interpersonal skills training program environment, can be given individually or in a group setting. Respondents are instructed to identify a substandard relationship with a person in their work environment. The Scoring and Interpretation Booklet, for use by the respondent, explains what strokes are, contains an index for scoring and interpreting strokes, and includes a contract for changing personal interactions.

CONCLUSIONS. The instrument appears to be useful in a relationship skills training seminar for mentally healthy and responsible workers, if the seminar trainer strictly limits the analysis of the instrument to specific types of interpersonal interactions. In this manner, workers can be made aware of statements made to others, possible motivations that prompt those statements, and adverse consequences to their statements. The instrument does not appear appropriate for resolving specific conflicts between coworkers; however, it appears to be a tool that can help uncover poor interpersonal interacting skills and relationship styles in the workplace. Finally, the instrument has no research that verifies the reliability or validity of the results.

REVIEWER'S REFERENCES
Berne, E. (1964). *Games people play.* New York: Grove Press.
Harris, T. A. (1969). *I'm OK—You're OK.* New York: Avon.
McKenna, J. (1974). Stroking profile: Application to script analysis. *Transactional Analysis, 4*(4), 20–24.
Goulding, M. M., & Goulding, R. L. (1979). *Changing lives through redecision therapy.* New York: Brunner/Mazel.

[155]
Inventory of Drinking Situations.

Purpose: "Designed to assess situations in which a client drank heavily over the past year."

Population: Ages 18 to 75.

Publication Date: 1987.

Acronym: IDS.

Scores, 8: Personal Status (Unpleasant Emotions, Physical Discomfort, Pleasant Emotions, Testing Personal Control, Urges and Temptations), Situations Involving Other People (Conflict with Others, Social Pressure to Drink, Pleasant Times with Others).

Administration: Group.

Forms, 2: IDS-100, IDS-42 (Brief Version).

Price Data, 1993: $25 per specimen set including user's guide (53 pages), 25 questionnaires, 25 answer sheets, 25 profiles; $13.50 per user's guide; $12.75 per 25 IDS-42 (Brief Version) questionnaires, 25 answer sheets, and 25 profile sheets; $14.75 per 25 IDS-100 questionnaires, 25 answer sheets, and 25 profile sheets; $140 per computer software program (50 uses); $450 per computer software program (200 uses).

Foreign Language Edition: Both forms available in French.

Time: (20–25) minutes.

Comments: IDS-42 (Brief Version) is for research use only.

Authors: Helen M. Annis, J. Martin Graham, and Christine S. Davis.
Publisher: Addiction Research Foundation [Canada].
Cross References: See T4:1265 (2 references).

TEST REFERENCES

1. Cannon, D. S., Rubin, A., Keefe, C. K., Black, J. L., Leeka, J. K., & Phillips, L. A. (1992). Affective correlates of alcohol and cocaine use. *Addictive Behaviors, 17,* 517–524.

2. Sobell, L. C., Toneatto, T., & Sobell, M. (1994). Behavioral assessment and treatment planning for alcohol, tobacco, and other drug problems: Current status with an emphasis on clinical applications. *Behavior Therapy, 25,* 533–580.

3. Sobell, M. B., Sobell, L. C., & Gavin, D. R. (1995). Portraying alcohol treatment outcomes: Different yardsticks of success. *Behavior Therapy, 26,* 643–669.

Review of the Inventory of Drinking Situations by MERITH COSDEN, Professor, Department of Education, University of California, Santa Barbara, CA:

The Inventory of Drinking Situations (IDS) is a self-report instrument designed to identify situations in which respondents drank heavily over the past year. The need for this instrument stems from the literature on relapse for clients in treatment for substance abuse. This literature indicates that certain types of situations are more likely to trigger heavy drinking than others, and that these situational "triggers" vary across individuals. The IDS can be used to understand specific drinking problems and to delineate situations under which an individual is more likely to relapse.

The IDS has 100 items that describe eight situations in which drinking is likely to occur. These situations were adapted from a taxonomy of potential relapse determinants developed by Marlatt and Gordon (1985). Five situations are defined by personal states: Unpleasant Emotions, Physical Discomfort, Pleasant Emotions, Testing Personal Control, and Urges and Temptations. The other three are social situations: Conflict with Others, Social Pressure to Drink, and Pleasant Times with Others. In developing the scale the authors considered items from extant substance abuse assessment scales as well as creating their own items based on their work with clients who were alcohol dependent. Items were reviewed by clinicians in the field and pilot tested on men in an inpatient employee assistance program.

The IDS is self-administered, and comes in paper-and-pencil and computerized formats. In either format it takes approximately 20 minutes to complete. It can be administered individually or in group settings. Correlations between paper-and-pencil and computerized versions (with a 2-week interval) of the IDS are reported for 27 clients and range from .75 to .91 across subscales. The manual notes that the IDS should not be used with individuals who are under the influence of alcohol or who are experiencing alcohol withdrawal. One concern of the reviewer is that both administration formats require the client to read and respond independently. Self-administration may be contraindicated if the client is illiterate, or if heavy drinking has impaired the client's cognitive abilities. Administration of the IDS through interview format should be considered.

Each item is rated on a 1—4 scale, as respondents indicate the frequency with which they have engaged in heavy drinking over the past year in that situation as *never, rarely, frequently,* or *almost always.* Six of the scales contain 10 items, and two of the scales, Unpleasant Emotions and Conflict with Others, contain 20 items. The manual explains all scoring procedures. Subscale scores are obtained by adding the scores for items on each subscale. Problem Index scores are derived by dividing each subscale score by the maximum possible score for that subscale and multiplying by 100. A form for graphing Problem Index scores is provided.

Scores can be interpreted in several ways. Problem Index scores, which range from 0–100, provide a general assessment of the severity of one's drinking. The manual suggests that subscale scores of 67–100 reflect a history of heavy drinking and define situations that may be risky for the client in terms of relapse. The Client Profile, consisting of the eight subscale Problem Index scores, can be used to determine patterns of drinking problems, such as whether a client drinks more in the company of others, alone, or under positive or negative affective states. Finally, a client's raw scores can be compared to the standardized scores for the normative sample.

The normative sample was originally composed of 247 clients who had received treatment for alcohol problems in a Canadian clinic. As this sample was primarily male (81.8%), an additional 96 women from the same clinic were subsequently included, resulting in a total sample of 193 males and 130 females. Education level, substance abuse history, and marital status for clients in the sample are provided in the manual, but ethnicity is not noted. Differences in subscale scores were found for men and women and as a function of age. The manual presents subscale scores by gender and three age groupings, which differ slightly for men and women. For men, the age groupings are under 36, 36–55, and over 55, and for women the groupings were under 36, 36–45, and over 45. Differences in the age groupings for men and women reflect differences in subscale score patterns by gender, as well as differences in the distribution of male and female clients in the sample by age.

The manual provides internal consistency data on each of the eight subscales. Alpha levels range from .87 to .96, reflecting high internal consistency for each subscale, whereas item-total correlations within each of the subscales was somewhat lower (.39 to .82). As noted below, there are questions raised in the literature as to whether the scale represents eight or fewer distinct situations. Other types of reliability, including interrater reliability, are not discussed in the manual.

Studies of the factor structure of the IDS do not fully support the original eight-factor structure. Initially, factors were rationally derived, based on Marlatt and Gordon's (1985) taxonomy of relapse situations. A principal components analysis was conducted separately on each of the eight subscales using scores obtained from the normative sample. Six of the eight subscales were unifactorial; the subscale labeled Conflict with Others had four factorial components, whereas Pleasant Times consisted of two factors. The nature of these subfactors was not further examined. In a subsequent study (Cannon, Leeka, Patterson, & Baker, 1990) a principal components analysis was conducted on all items based on responses by 336 male inpatients in an Alcohol Dependence Treatment Program. Three components were identified in this manner, contributing to 43% of the test variance: Negative Findings, Positive Findings, and Conflict with Others. Cannon et al. report that the authors of the IDS (Annis and her associates) were able to replicate their findings with data from the normative sample when they followed the same statistical procedures. The validity of these three subscales in relation to the validity of the original eight subscales requires further study.

The manual reports on the content validity and concurrent validity of the IDS. Content validity was evaluated by asking raters to place test items into the eight categories; they were able to do so with a high degree (92%–99%) of interrater agreement. External validity has been assessed through correlations between other measures of substance abuse, levels of drinking, and IDS subscale scores. Differences in subtest scores for heavy, moderate, and light drinkers have been noted. Integral to the significance of the IDS, however, is its ability to predict relapse situations; that is, are the situations in which clients report higher levels of drinking more likely to be those in which they experience a relapse? Studies of the predictive validity of the IDS are not available.

In addition to the original IDS, there is a computerized version for the IBM. Questions are displayed on the computer screen, and clients are asked to press the number on the keyboard that most accurately describes their behavior over the past year. The program scores the IDS, displays Problem Index scores on a bar graph, and provides a list of specific situations under which the client noted heavy drinking *frequently* or *almost always*.

A shortened form of the IDS, with 42 items, was developed as a research tool. Based on the principal components analysis of the original subscales, test items with the highest item-subscale correlations were selected for the short form. Four items were selected to represent each of the six unifactorial subscales; 18 additional items were selected to represent the two multifactorial subtests, Conflict with Others and Pleasant Times with Others; 18 additional items were selected. Internal reliability of the subscales is in the .80–.92 range, whereas correlations between the long and short form subscales range from .93 to .98. Subsequent studies (Isenhart, 1993) identified a five-factor structure for the short form of the IDS, with the five scales highly correlated with one higher-order dimension.

Although the scale specifically addresses use of alcohol, many people seeking treatment for substance abuse problems are both drug and alcohol users. Several investigators (e.g., Cannon, Rubin, Keefe, Black, Leeka, & Phillips, 1992) have used the IDS to study differences between alcohol and drug users. In doing so, Cannon et al. changed the wording of the stem in the IDS from "drank heavily" to "drank or used drugs heavily." Use of the instrument in this manner requires further psychometric study.

The IDS can provide valuable information for treatment planning for clients with drinking problems. Its strengths include its ease of administration, clinical relevance, and concurrent validity with regard to differentiating clients with moderate and heavy drinking problems. There is a need for research on the predictive validity of the instrument. Application of the IDS to populations in which both drugs and alcohol are concerns also warrants further study.

REVIEWER'S REFERENCES

Marlatt, G. A., & Gordon, J. R. (1985). Relapse prevention: Maintenance strategies in the treatment of addictive behaviors. New York: Guilford.

Cannon, D. S., Leeka, J. K., Patterson, E. T., & Baker, T. B. (1990). Principal components analysis of the Inventory of Drinking Situations: Empirical categories of drinking by alcoholics. *Addictive Behaviors, 15,* 265–269.

Cannon, D. S., Rubin, A., Keefe, C. K., Black, J. L., Leeka, J. K., & Phillips, L. A. (1992). Affective correlates of alcohol and cocaine use. *Addictive Behaviors, 17,* 517–524.

Isenhart, C. E. (1993). Psychometric evaluation of a short form of the Inventory of Drinking Situations. *Journal of Studies on Alcohol, 54,* 345–349.

Review of the Inventory of Drinking Situations by KEVIN L. MORELAND, Professor of Psychology and Chair, Fordham University, Bronx, NY:

The Inventory of Drinking Situations (IDS-100) is a 100-item questionnaire that assesses situations in which an alcohol rehabilitation client drank heavily *almost always, frequently, rarely,* or *never* during the past year. It was developed as a situation-specific measure of drinking that could be used to identify an individual client's high-risk situations for alcoholic relapse (User's Guide, p. 1). A 42-item short form of the IDS (IDS-42) is also available. The IDS-100 is recommended for clinical purposes whereas the IDS-42 may be preferable for research applications where time is at a premium. A computer-administered version of the IDS is available that shows promising congruence with the paper-and-pencil version used to develop the instrument.

The classification of drinking situations embodied in the IDS was based on the extensive efforts of Marlatt and his colleagues to determine what causes alcoholic relapse (e.g., Marlatt & Gordon, 1985). Eight expert judgment-based subscales are divided among two superordinate classes also based on expert judgment: Personal States and Situations Involving Other People. Most of the former are not "situations" in the way that term is ordinarily used to characterize the extrapersonal environment. Rather, they are subjective states such as Unpleasant Emotions (e.g., "When I was lonely"), Physical Discomfort (e.g., "When I had a headache"), Pleasant Emotions (e.g., "When I was enjoying myself"), and Testing Personal Control (e.g., "When I started to think I wasn't really hooked on alcohol"). The fourth Personal State, Urges and Temptations, includes a few subjective states (i.e., Urges like "When I remembered how good it [liquor] tasted") and a number of extrapersonal situations (i.e., Temptations like "When I passed by a bar"). Situations Involving Other People comprises subscales tapping Conflict With Others (e.g., "When someone criticized me"), Social Pressure to Drink (e.g., "When my boss offered me a drink"), and Pleasant Times with Others (e.g., "When I wanted to celebrate with a friend").

ITEM DEVELOPMENT. Suggestions for item content were drawn from a number of sources including other inventories, clinicians, persons recovering from alcoholism, and clients being treated for alcohol problems. "A draft of the resulting questionnaire was sent to five clinicians who had extensive experience working with alcoholics to solicit comments on item clarity and on item coverage .... Similar feedback was also solicited in a pilot testing ... on alcoholics" (User's Guide, p. 2). Formal psychometric considerations did not influence the final composition of the IDS-100. All of the subscales except Unpleasant Emotions and Conflict With Others comprise 10 items, the latter each comprise 20 items.

Despite the authors' extensive efforts to write good items, some potential problems are apparent. Some items are so general that they seem only to summarize the content of the remainder of the subscale (e.g., the Social Pressure to Drink item "When I was offered a drink and felt awkward about refusing"). Other items are so specific that the situations may be irrelevant to substantial numbers of persons with alcohol problems (e.g., "When my boss offered me a drink"). Still other items appear to tap more than one construct (e.g., the Unpleasant Emotions item, "When I was troubled and I wanted to think more clearly"). That item might better exemplify the category if it ended at "troubled." Interestingly and importantly, these potentially problematic items tended not to clear the psychometric hurdles necessary for inclusion in the IDS-42.

Items for the IDS-42 were selected by examining unrotated principal components within each of the eight IDS-100 subscales. Only Conflict with Others (4) and Pleasant Times (2) yielded more than one principal component with an eigenvalue greater than one. Items for the IDS-42 are those with the highest item-component correlations unless two items were judged too similar in content, in which case one was replaced by the next highest correlating item. The IDS-42 comprises four items for each of the unifactorial subscales and three items for each component of the multifactorial subscales. Correlations between the IDS-42 subscales and their IDS-100 counterparts ranged from .93 to .98.

NORMS. Normative data for the IDS-100 are based on 323 "individuals with a wide variety of alcohol-related problems who were assessed on admission" (User's Guide, p. 8). Multivariate analyses of this sample led the authors to provide separate *T*-score conversions by sex or age for every subscale except Physical Discomfort. This seems ill-advised. The total normative sample is small. Subdividing it yields some tiny subsamples (e.g., 30 men over age 55). Although it is common to study demographic variables, I believe that IDS users would be better served by studies of psychological variables (e.g., sex role identity rather than gender). Perhaps Conflict With Others *is* a curvilinear function of age, younger people tending toward more interpersonal conflict in general and the interpersonal conflicts so often generated by alcoholism eventually being somewhat off-set by the mellowing of middle age. The ability to assess these hypotheses is obscured by the use of different norms for different age groups. I suggest that users calculate a single set of norms from the data available in Appendix B of the User's Guide (pp. 33–41).

For interpretive purposes the authors emphasize a "Problem Index" score, which is simply the percentage of the maximum possible score. Although these scores are, no doubt, easier to discuss with clients than are T scores, no other justification is provided for their use. I recommend that they be used only to illustrate inferences that have been properly drawn from norm-referenced scores.

Psychometric Properties.

RELIABILITY. The eight IDS-100 subscales are very internally consistent. Cronbach alphas ranged from .87 (Urges and Temptations) to .96 (Unpleasant Emotions) in a very carefully described sample "of 247 clients who had voluntarily sought treatment ... [and] their major substance of abuse was ... alcohol" (User's Guide, p. 2). Not surprisingly, the IDS-42 subscales are slightly less reliable than their IDS-100 parents, with alphas ranging from .80 (physical Discomfort and Urges and Temptations) to .92 (Conflict with Others). The User's Guide provided no data concerning the stability of either form of the IDS.

VALIDITY. The issue of content coverage was dealt with in the section on item selection. Additionally, three undescribed raters were asked to sort the IDS-100 items into the eight subscales. Interrater agreement ranged from 92% to 99%.

The test authors presented evidence that all the IDS-100 scales are positively related to drinking behavior as indexed by variables such as scores on the Alcohol Dependence Scale (Skinner & Horn, 1984). However, as the authors noted, "research is needed ... to establish its relation to relapse episodes, and to document ... its utility as a treatment planning tool" (User's Guide, p. 9).

Intercorrelations among subscales were not provided in the User's Guide, but item-level factor loadings for the IDS-42 were. Details of the factor analytic method are not provided, although it was obviously exploratory and employed an oblique rotation; the sample is presumably the same one used to assess other psychometric properties of the IDS.

The factor structure did not completely conform to the a priori structure. Items from Unpleasant Emotions and Conflict With Others merged into one factor as did Pleasant Times With Others and

Social Pressure to Drink. Two new dimensions emerged composed mainly of items from Conflict With Others: Social Problems at Work and Problems With Intimacy. The first order factors composed two second order factors that reflected positive (e.g., Pleasant Emotions) and negative (e.g., Physical Discomfort) motivations to drink rather than the two superordinate a priori classes of Personal States and Situations Involving Other People.

SUMMARY. The authors of the IDS are clearly sophisticated clinicians and psychometricians. The IDS appears to be the best instrument of its kind. On the other hand, the User's Guide includes some interpretive advice that is, at best, hard to defend (e.g., emphasis on the Problem Index scores) and omits some critical information (e.g., intercorrelations among the scales). I hope the authors will soon update the decade-old User's Guide both to respond to critics and to inform users about new research that will improve the use of an already useful tool.

REVIEWER'S REFERENCES
Skinner, H. A., & Horn, J. L. (1984). *Alcohol Dependence Scale (ADS): User's guide.* Toronto: Addiction Research Foundation of Ontario.
Marlatt, G. A., & Gordon, J. R. (1985). *Relapse prevention: Maintenance strategies in the treatment of addictive behaviors.* New York: Guilford.

[156]
Inventory of Learning Processes—R.

Purpose: To measure learning styles of college and university students.
Population: College and university students.
Publication Dates: 1977–1992.
Acronym: ILP-R.
Scores, 14: Academic Self-Concept (Intrinsic Motivation, Self-Efficacy, Non-reiterative Processing, Self-Esteem, Total), Reflective Processing (Deep Processing, Elaborative Processing, Self-Expression, Total), Agentic Processing (Conventional, Serial Processing, Fact Retention, Total), Methodical Study.
Administration: Group.
Price Data, 1993: $3 per test booklet (includes answer sheets).
Time: Administration time not reported.
Authors: Ronald R. Schmeck and Elke Geisler-Bernstein.
Publisher: Ronald R. Schmeck (the author).

TEST REFERENCES
1. Hall, R. H., Rocklin, T. R., Dansereau, D. F., Skaggs, L. P., O'Donnell, A. M., Lambiotte, J. G., & Young, M. D. (1988). The role of individual differences in the cooperative learning of technical merit. *Journal of Educational Psychology, 80,* 172–178.
2. Albaili, M. A. (1993). Psychometric properties of the Inventory of Learning Processes: Evidence from United Arab Emirates college students. *Psychological Reports, 72,* 1331-1336.
3. Jakoubek, J., & Swenson, R. R. (1993). Differences in use of learning strategies and relation to grades among undergraduate students. *Psychological Reports, 73,* 787-793.
4. Lavelle, E. (1993). Development and validation of an inventory to assess processes in college composition. *British Journal of Educational Psychology, 63,* 489–499.

5. Albaili, M. A. (1994). Learning processes and academic achievement of United Arab Emirates college students. *Psychological Reports, 74,* 739-746.

Review of the Inventory of Learning Processes— R by KUSUM SINGH, Associate Professor, Educational Leadership and Policy Studies, College of Human Resources and Education, Virginia Tech, Blacksburg, VA:

It is important to note that the authors of this instrument have not provided a manual, and the following review is based on a published paper by the authors that was enclosed with the test. If the test user is supposed to glean the useful information on the uses, construction, and psychometric properties of the test from the article, it is a cumbersome task to say the least.

According to the authors, the Inventory of Learning Processes—R (ILP-R) is a measure of learning styles of college and university students. It is an instrument with 173 items on a Likert-type scale with six response choices ranging from 0 meaning *strongly disagree* to 5 meaning *strongly agree*. The ILP-R consists of four scales: Academic Self-Concept, Reflective Processing, Agentic Processing, and Methodical Study. Academic Self-Concept refers to the extent to which the "student has organized and emotionally invested in his or her academic skills so that a smooth flow of processing can occur without excessive self-doubt" (Schmeck, Geisler-Brenstein, & Cercy, 1991, p. 350). Academic Self-Concept has four subscales: Intrinsic Motivation, Self-Efficacy, Non-iterative Processing, and Self-Esteem. The second major scale, called Reflective Processing, includes the deep and elaborative processing statements from the original ILP along with the new items related to self-expression, self-assertion, and holistic, free-associative information processing. Reflective Processing has three subscales: Deep Processing, Elaborative Processing, and Self-Expression. Agentic Processing, the third scale, taps "elements of focus, directness and planfulness" (Schmeck et al., 1991, pp. 350–351). It includes a tendency to "technify" learning, emphasizing procedures that increase memory for details. Agentic Processing has three subscales: Conventional, Serial Processing, and Fact Retention. The fourth scale, Methodical Study, consists of traditional statements concerning study habits such as very frequent studying and careful spacing of study sessions, overlearning, and outlining all that is studied, etc.

In the accompanying article by Schmeck et al. (1991), the authors describe a conceptual framework for the development of the test and techniques used for scale development. The authors claim that the test was developed within the context of cognitive psychology, and derived from laboratory research concerned with information processing and memory. According to the authors, conceptual and empirical work suggested a distinction between depth and breadth of information processing, which is related to the learning style of the individual.

NORMING SAMPLE. Data on college students ($N = 129$) from various academic majors in two beginning psychology courses were collected to examine the construct validity of the ILP-R. The sample consisted of student volunteers. Because the sample size was small for subgroup analyses and the authors mention only one sample, more work needs to be done to develop norms for the test, using different populations of college students. No data or information are provided on the norms or samples used for testing, piloting, or validation work. It is unclear what samples (and sample sizes) were used for pilot testing, validation, and norming. When references are made to the subgroups, samples were fairly small. For example, the authors refer to splitting the sample into two groups: High self-concept and low self-concept groups. The sample size in each group was about 30 people. A large number of intercorrelations were computed on small sample sizes. No test score data are provided from a norming group for test interpretations.

RELIABILITY/VALIDITY. The authors report Cronbach alpha coefficients ranging from .65 to .93 in support of the reliability of subscales. The coefficients are reasonably high except the Methodical Study scale and Serial Processing subscale have relatively lower internal consistency (.65 and .69 respectively). The authors report several approaches to construct validity. They report the intercorrelations among the ILP-R scales and subscales, and intercorrelations between the scales and subscales of the ILP-R and three personality measures (Taylor Manifest Anxiety Scale, Coopersmith Self-Esteem Inventory, and Rotter Locus of Control Scale). These relationships were found to be theoretically consistent and as expected. The table of the intercorrelations indicates that subscales within a scale are more highly related to one another than to those on other scales with which they supposedly have an underlying common factor. To examine the construct validity further, two groups were formed using median splits (low MAS, high LOC internality, high SEI scores, and high MAS, low LOC internality, and low SEI, respectively) and interrelationships between the ILP-

R and subscales for the two groups were computed and compared to determine if correlations were as would be predicted by the theoretical framework. Intercorrelations between all ILP-R factors and subfactors were found to be consistent with the theoretical expectations for each subgroup. Mean scores on the ILP-R scales and subscales were calculated for each of the high and low self-concept groups. *T*-Tests were computed between all high-low self-concept pairs for each scale to evaluate the significance of possible differences. Significant differences found in academic self-concept subscales were considered as expected and consistent with the theoretical formulations.

SUMMARY. Despite the authors' considerable research in developing the theoretical framework and the effort in validating the constructs, this test in its present form cannot be recommended to users for several reasons. No relevant and concise information is provided on the uses and interpretations of the test and its various scales and subscales.

No manual is available to the user. Users will find it very difficult to glean the useful information from the accompanying article. Secondly, the authors give almost no information on the uses of the test. Who should use it and for what purposes? Intended uses of the test are not clearly stated. It is not clear what interpretations based on scores or score ranges can be made. There is no scoring key nor guidelines for scoring and interpretations.

The most glaring omission is that the user is not provided information on which items belong to which scale. For example, the authors mention the number of items for each scale and subscale, and then give three illustrative items for each subscale. But how about other items in a scale? How do they expect the rank and file user of the test to know which other items would fall under a particular subscale? Furthermore, the authors provide no norms for the test and no range of scores to be interpreted in any way. For example, how does a user know what range of scores would constitute high reflective processing versus low reflective processing?

No clear guidelines are provided for reporting test results, including scaled scores, subtest results, and total scores. The authors mention in passing that the test is valuable in counseling clients but they do not elaborate in what ways and for what purposes. In any case, if the purpose of the test is to understand and identify the learning processes of various students, more norming data are needed. Clearly this

work is far from complete and there are major to minor problems. For example, authors report that there are either 158 or 160 items in the instrument and the table of scales and subscales indicates 158 items but the actual test contains 173 items. Before the instrument can be readily used, much more information on its uses, norms, and scale and subscale interpretations needs to be compiled.

REVIEWER'S REFERENCE

Schmeck, R. R., Geisler-Brenstein, E., & Cercy, S. P. (1991). Self-concept and learning: The revised inventory of learning processes. *Educational Psychology, 11,* 343–362.

Review of the Inventory of Learning Processes— R by GERALD L. STONE, Professor of Counseling Psychology and Director, University Counseling Service, The University of Iowa, Iowa City, IA:

The Inventory of Learning Processes-R (ILP-R), conceptualized as a measure of individual differences in learning style, is a 173-item (although reported as both 158 and 160 items in an accompanying article) self-report questionnaire "consisting of statements regarding school-related behaviors, attitudes, opinions, and motivations" (Schmeck, Geisler-Brenstein, & Cercy, 1991, p. 352). There is a 6-point Likert scale for each item with agree-disagree as the anchors. There is no manual (in preparation), but an article (see Schmeck, Geisler-Brenstein, & Cercy, 1991) is recommended as sort of a manual.

The ILP-R has a number of scales and subscales. There are four major inventory scales (with relevant subscales in brackets): Academic Self-Concept [Intrinsic Motivation, Self-Efficacy, Non-Reiterative Processing, and Self-Esteem], Reflective Processing [Deep Processing, Elaborate Processing, and Self-Expression], Agentic Processing [Conventional, Serial Processing, and Fact Retention], and Methodical Study.

The Schmeck, Geisler-Brenstein, and Cercy article (1991) describes the evolution of the ILP-R over several years. The ILP-R is a revision of the original ILP (1977). The original ILP was based primarily on information processing and academic study skills literatures. As the original ILP was used in learning research over the years, the authors increasingly found personality and attitude dimensions (e.g., self-efficacy, self-esteem, locus of control, conformity) to relate to learning style. As a result of this research program, items were generated to assess these dimensions, resulting in the factorially more complex constructs of the ILP-R. The Academic Self-Concept Scale contains self-evaluative items from the original ILP plus new statements regarding self-efficacy, self-esteem, anxiety, and locus of control. In other words, an academic self-confidence scale has been formed. The Reflective Processing Scale includes deep ("integration of information" and "abstraction of meanings") and elaborate ("self-referenced") processing statements form the ILP along with newer ones related to self-referenced information processing. The authors' development of the deep and elaborate processing factors relied on the information-processing work of Craik and Lockhart (1972). The third scale, Agentic Processing, expanded the original seven-item Fact Retention Scale with items from the original study skills scale (Methodical Scale) on planning and focus and new items on sequential processing, conventionality, and conformity. The final division, Methodical Study, has drawn most of the traditional study habit statements from the Methodical Study Scale of the original ILP.

Schmeck et al. (1991), developers of the ILP-R, conducted a study with 129 undergraduates of various academic majors from two beginning-level psychology courses from a midwestern university. The ILP-R and three personality measures (Taylor Manifest Anxiety Scale [MAS], Rotter's Locus of Control [LOC], and Coopersmith's Self-Esteem Inventory [SEI]) were administered. Results suggest reasonable internal consistencies with Cronbach alphas ranging from .65 to .93. Subscales within a scale are more highly related to one another than to those on other scales. Intercorrelations of the ILP-R scales and subscales were also examined separately for two subsamples of students (i.e., 27 low self-concept students [low on MAS, high on LOC and SEI] and 30 high self-concept students [high on MAS, low on LOC and SEI]). Although such analysis may lead to theoretical explanations about subscale combinations and overlap, as well as possible links between personality variables and learning style, there are a number of limitations to the evidential bases of the ILP-R. Major limitations include a lack of cross-validation using multicultural samples across types of learning settings (community college versus research university versus distance learning via the internet) and disciplines (e.g., humanities versus sciences) and a need for a more adequate sample size to look at the large number of relevant intercorrelations across theoretically informed sample partitions. Although the ILP-R is a promising research instrument, it is premature to promote it as a guidance tool for students or as a sufficient basis for a theory regarding school learning. Perhaps a comprehensive manual will address some of these limitations and enable reviewers and consumers to make an informed choice among learning style inventories.

REVIEWER'S REFERENCES
Craik, F. I. M., & Lockhart, R. S. (1972). Levels of processing: A framework for memory research. *Journal of Verbal Learning and Verbal Behavior, 11,* 671–684.
Schmeck, R. R., Geisler-Brenstein, E., & Cercy, S. P. (1991). Self-concept and learning: The revised inventory of learning processes. *Educational Psychology, 11,* 343–362.

[157]

The Inventory of Positive Thinking Traits.

Purpose: "Designed to assess the attitudes of individuals in terms of their positivity and negativity."
Population: Adults and adolescents.
Publication Date: 1992.
Scores: Total score only.
Administration: Individual and group.
Price Data: Available from publisher.
Time: (10) minutes.
Author: Millard J. Bienvenu.
Publisher: Millard J. Bienvenu, Northwest Publications.

Review of The Inventory of Positive Thinking Traits by PEGGY E. GALLAHER, Assistant Professor of Psychology, Baruch College of the City University of New York, New York, NY:

This 34-item paper-and-pencil test purports to assess "attitudes of individuals in terms of their positivity and negativity" (p. 1). The test author suggests it is appropriate for use in clinical settings to supplement clinical impressions, and as a pre- and posttest instrument for measuring improvement in positive thinking after therapy or other attitude training.

No technical information is supplied with the test. Although the instrument produces a single score, a glance at the items suggests that the test may be multidimensional; this possibility should be examined via factor analysis. Without knowing something about the test-retest reliability of the instrument, it would be next to impossible to interpret change scores.

If there is a theory that guided the construction of this test, there is no mention of it in the one-page guide that accompanies the inventory. In it, the test author states that "Positive thinking strengthens the immune system," that "Individuals who are optimistic have fewer stress reactions," and that "a positive attitude also facilitates in the management of problems and crises" (p. 1). These assertions suggest a number of criteria that could be employed in validity studies of the instrument.

A one-page scoring guide is supplied with the test, but there are no test norms or instructions on test score interpretation. Without this crucial information, scores generated from the instrument are essentially meaningless. The test is not recommended.

Review of The Inventory of Positive Thinking Traits by CHOCKALINGAM VISWESVARAN, Assistant Professor of Psychology, Florida International University, Miami, FL:

A two-page guide accompanying this inventory claims that this inventory can be used to: (a) obtain additional diagnostic information to supplement a counselor's clinical observations of an individual's level of positivity; (b) provide specific suggestions for enhancing positive thinking; and (c) assess the improvement in positive thinking over the course of counseling (when used as a pre-post test instrument). The Inventory comprises 34 items with three response categories each (*yes*, if the item can be answered as happening most of the time or usually; *no*, if seldom or never; *sometimes*, if the respondent cannot answer yes or no). The responses are scored from 0 to 3. A scoring key accompanies the Inventory and indicates how many points should be given for the response chosen for each item. The sum of the points across the 34 items yields the total score, with higher scores indicating greater levels of positivity. The guide suggests that items receiving a score of zero (and to a lesser extent those receiving a score of 1) can be viewed as areas needing specific suggestions and ways for enhancing positivity.

No information is given on how the scoring key was derived (why certain responses got 3 whereas other got 2). No information is given on test development and item selection strategies. No reliability or validity data are provided. No data on normative samples are provided. No evidence of convergent and discriminant validity (in terms of correlations with other scales) is provided. No data are reported assessing the viability of this instrument to assess the effectiveness of counseling. In summary, this appears to be a scale with important applications, but the empirical evidence to evaluate the claimed usefulness was not available to this reviewer.

[158]
Inventory of Suicide Orientation-30.
Purpose: "To assess and help identify adolescents who are at risk for suicide orientation by measuring the strength of their suicide orientation."
Population: Adolescents.
Publication Dates: 1988–1994.
Acronym: ISO-30.

Scores, 2: Final Raw Score, Final Critical Item Score.
Administration: Group.
Price Data, 1997: $38.50 per handscoring starter kit including 10 answer sheets and manual ('94, 67 pages); $78 per 50 handscoring answer sheets (reorder); $15 per 25 computer scoring answer sheets; $2.60 per computer scoring report.
Foreign Language Edition: Also available in Spanish.
Time: (5–15) minutes.
Authors: John D. King and Brian Kowalchuk.
Publisher: NCS Assessments.

Review of the Inventory of Suicide Orientation—30 by GEORGE DOMINO, Professor of Psychology, University of Arizona, Tucson, AZ:

The Inventory of Suicide Orientation—30 (ISO-30) is a 30-item self-report questionnaire with an objective to help professionals identify adolescents at high risk for suicide, by measuring "the strength of their suicide orientation" (p. 2). The 10-minute questionnaire is administered individually but can be group administered. The ISO-30 is based on a theoretical model that sees suicide orientation as a three-stage progression: threat, crisis, and resolution; but its use is not tied to acceptance of this model.

The ISO-30 was empirically developed from a longer Life Orientation Inventory (LOI) that contained five "belief systems" central to suicide: hopelessness, suicidal ideation, perceived inadequacy, inability to cope with emotions, and social isolation/withdrawal.

The test development/normative sample consisted of 768 adolescents (ages 12–18) in both clinical ($n = 366$) and school ($n = 402$) settings, who completed the 113-item LOI, the Beck Hopelessness Scale (BHS), and the Suicidal Ideation Questionnaire (SIQ) and (SIQ-JR). Adolescents in clinical settings were rated by their clinician on a 7-point suicidal ideation rating form. The manual presents clear demographic data as to gender, age, type of clinical setting, and other aspects.

From each of the five domains of the LOI, the six items with the highest item-domain correlations were selected; these coefficients range from a low of .22 to a high of .63 (median r of .50). The six suicidal ideation items called "critical" were chosen because they also correlated with the SIQ and SIQ-JR, and with clinical ratings of suicidal ideation; the item total correlations for these items are somewhat higher (range from the low .40s to mid .70s) though the correlations with the two criteria are not given.

The 30 items use a 4-point response scale of "I Am Sure I Disagree," "I Mostly Disagree," "I Mostly

Agree," and "I Am Sure I Agree," scored zero through 3 (11 items are scored in reverse). Hand scoring the ISO-30 is straightforward through the use of a pressure-sensitive second page. Three scores are computed: a raw score, a critical item score, and an overall tripartite risk classification. The raw score can range from 0 to 90 and is the sum of the responses, but is complicated somewhat by omitted items. The critical item score (which can range from 0 to 6) is the number of critical items endorsed. The raw score and the critical item score are then integrated to assign the client to an overall risk classification: low (raw score less than 30 and critical score less than 3), moderate (raw score between 30 and 44 and critical score less than 3), and high (raw score of 45 or higher and critical score of 3 or higher).

RELIABILITY. Internal consistency (coefficient alpha) reliability estimates ranged from .90 to .92 for the ISO-30 raw scores, and .78 to .79 for the critical items. Test-retest reliability (3- to 4-days interval) was estimated to be .80 for the raw scores and .70 for the critical item score. These are quite acceptable, considering the brief nature of the instrument, especially the critical item score.

VALIDITY. Validity is presented only from a criterion validity point of view. Raw scores correlated .64 with the Beck scale (BHS) and .78 with the SIQ. Both sensitivity (the number of correctly identified positives) and specificity (the number of correctly identified negatives) are reported using clinical ratings as the criterion. Sensitivity equals 52% and specificity is between 75% and 82%. No significant gender or age differences were obtained.

ON THE PLUS SIDE. This is a well-designed instrument and a clearly written manual. The manual discusses suicide, suicide orientation theory, how to interpret test results, and what to do with high risk adolescents. More importantly, the manual explicitly, and repeatedly, indicates the need for the administrator to be well trained, that great caution in interpreting test results is needed, and that the test is not a substitute for clinical decision making.

ON THE MINUS SIDE. Given that the target user is an adolescent, the items seem somewhat convoluted, such as "I often think about my appearance and how I get along with people. When I see someone who's got what I don't have, I feel that it's not fair. I was cheated." Similarly, the four response categories are somewhat unusual, and not the typical Likert-like response. The manual gives no information about the parent instrument, so the interested reader needs to consult another manual. These are minor points. The major point is that much remains to be done. All the normative data, though extensive, were collected by the authors and no references to published sources that further explore the validity of the ISO-30 are given; thus commercial publication seems premature.

Clinical and rather superficial descriptions are given of high, moderate, and low risk adolescents, not based upon empirical observations such as Q sorts, adjectival correlations, or ratings. Assignment to these risk categories appears to be based on clinical judgment rather than psychometric considerations.

The items were selected on the basis of highest item-total correlations, but there is no indication of how each item correlated with the other domains. It would be helpful to present the results of a factor analysis to indicate the factorial structure of the ISO-30; is there one main factor of suicide orientation or five factors that reflect the five domains, or some other number? How do raw scores and critical scores correlate?

The authors used the BHS and the SIQ and SIQ-JR as criteria, but do not present any comparative data on these two instruments (i.e., how does the ISO-30 compare with these two in predictive validity?).

The ISO-30 is clearly geared for individual use by clinicians, with most information in the manual presented in this vein. Will the typical clinician who deals with potentially suicidal adolescents use such an instrument? My guess is no. Where the ISO-30 can be potentially more useful is in research studies or in screening situations. Most individuals involved in such efforts would want to see substantially greater psychometric information than is currently available in the manual, such as intercorrelations between the five domains, the correlation between final raw scores and critical item score, the use of regression equations to assess utility, statistical significance of the mean difference between clinical and school samples, tables of percentiles, etc.

RECOMMENDATION. Many such instruments are available, even though their titles may differ (e.g., Rothberg & Geer-Williams in Maris, Berman, Maltsberger, & Yufit [1992] identify and review 19 instruments). The ISO-30 has a reasonable chance of taking its place among the better instruments, if additional data and analyses can be generated.

REVIEWER'S REFERENCE
Maris, R. W., Berman, A. L., Maltsberger, J. T., & Yufit, R. I. (Eds.). (1992). *Assessment and prediction of suicide.* New York: The Guilford Press.

[159]

Iowa Tests of Basic Skills, Forms K, L, and M.

Purpose: "To provide a comprehensive assessment of student progress in the basic skills."

Population: Grades K–9.

Publication Dates: 1955–1996.
Acronym: ITBS.
Administration: Group.
Levels, 10: 5–14.
Forms, 3: K, L, and M; 3 batteries: Core, Complete, and Survey.
Price Data, 1997: $37.50 per Complete Battery examination kit; $32 per Survey Battery examination kit; $12 per 25 Levels 5 and 6 practice test booklets with Directions for Administration; $16 per 25 Levels 7, 8, or 9 practice test booklets with Directions for Administration; $16 per 25 Levels 9–11 or Levels 12–14 practice test booklets with answer documents and Directions for Administration; $9 per 25 Reports to Parents (English or Spanish); $20 per 25 Message to Parents (English or Spanish); $40 per Complete or Core Battery norms and score conversions booklet; $36 per Survey Battery norms and score conversions booklet; $6.50 per Preparing for Testing; $6 per Interpretive Guide for Teachers and Counselors; $20 per Interpretive Guide for School Administrators; $20 per Content Classifications with Item Norms; $14.50 per Technical Summary 1; $44 per special norms booklets (specify Large City, Catholic/Private, High Socioeconomic Status, Low Socioeconomic Status, International).
Special Editions: Braille and large-print editions available.
Comments: Part of Riverside's Integrated Assessment System.
Authors: H. D. Hoover, A. N. Hieronymous, D. A. Frisbie, and S. B. Dunbar.
Publisher: The Riverside Publishing Company.

a) LEVEL 5.
Population: Grade K.1–1.5.
Scores, 7: Vocabulary, Listening, Language, Language Total, Mathematics, Core Total, Word Analysis (optional).
Price Data: $89 per 25 Level 5 Complete Battery machine-scorable test booklets.
Time: Untimed, approximately 130 minutes (including Practice Page).

b) LEVEL 6.
Population: Grade K.8–1.9.
Scores, 10: Vocabulary, Listening, Language, Language Total, Mathematics Advanced Skills, Mathematics Total, Core Total, Word Analysis (optional), Reading Advanced Skills, Reading Total.
Price Data: $105 per 25 Level 6 Complete Battery machine-scorable test booklets.
Time: Untimed, approximately 173 minutes (including Practice Page).

c) LEVELS 7 and 8.
Population: Grade 1.7–2.6; Grade 2.5—3.5.
Scores: Complete Battery: 16 scores: Vocabulary, Reading, Reading Total, Listening Language, Language Total, Mathematics Concepts, Mathematics Problems, Mathematics Computation [optional], Mathematics Total, Core Total, Social Studies, Science, Sources of Information, Composite, Word Analysis [optional]; Survey Battery: 7 scores: Reading, Advanced Skills, Reading Total, Language Advanced Skills, Language Total, Mathematics Advanced Skills, Mathematics Total, Survey Battery Total.
Price Data: $111 per 25 Complete Battery machine-scorable test booklets; $90 per 25 Core Battery machine-scorable test booklets; $89 per 25 Survey Battery machine-scorable test booklets.
Time: Untimed, approximately 270–275 minutes for Complete Battery; approximately 100 minutes for Survey Battery.

d) LEVELS 9–14.
Population: Grades 3–8.
Scores: Complete Battery: 19 scores: Vocabulary, Reading Comprehension, Reading Total, Spelling, Capitalization, Punctuation, Usage and Expression, Language Total, Mathematics Concepts and Estimation, Mathematics Problem Solving and Data Interpretation, Mathematics Total, Mathematics Computation [optional], Core Total, Social Studies, Science, Maps and Diagrams, Reference Materials, Sources of Information Total, Composite; Survey Battery: 7 scores: Reading Advanced Skills, Rading Total, Language Advanced Skills, Language Total, Mathematics Advanced Skills, Mathematics Total, Survey Battery Total.
Price Data: $86 per 25 Complete Battery reusable test booklets; $77 per 25 Survey Battery reusable test booklets; $52 per 25 Form K reusable test booklets for Mathematics tests with Directions for Administration; $11 per Directions for Administration; $55 per 50 Listening Assessment answer folders (Levels 9–14) including Directions for Administration and score interpretation and materials needed for machine scoring (scored by Riverside); $106 per one copy Form K Complete Battery Braille Edition test, Braille administration notes, and supplement to the Directions for Administration; $88.50 per one copy Form K Survey Battery Braille Edition test, Braille administration notes, and Directions for Administration; $53 per Form K Complete Battery large-print edition including test booklet, and general instructions for testing visually impaired students; $35 per Form K Survey Battery large-print edition including test booklet and general instructions for testing visually impaired students; $34 per 50 Complete Battery answer folders including materials needed for machine scoring; $30 per 50 Survey Battery answer sheets including materials needed for machine scoring; $34 per 50 Complete Battery Forms combined ITBS/CogAT 5 answer documents including materials needed for machine scoring; $1,242 per 1,500 Complete Battery continuous-form answer docu-

ments including materials needed for machine scoring; $28 per 25 Survey Battery easy-score answer documents including class record folder; $14.50 per scoring key.

Time: 310 minutes for Complete Battery; 100 minutes for Survey Battery.

Cross References: See T4:1280 (33 references); for reviews by Suzanne Lane and Nambury S. Raju of Form J, see 11:184 (24 references); for reviews by Robert L. Linn and Victor L. Willson of Forms G and H, see 10:155 (45 references); for reviews by Peter W. Airasian and Anthony J. Nitko of Forms 7 and 8, see 9:533 (29 references); see also T3:1192 (97 references); for reviews by Larry A. Harris and Fred Pyrczak of Forms 5–6, see 8:19 (58 references); see T2:19 (87 references) and 6:13 (17 references); for reviews by Virgil E. Herrick, G. A. V. Morgan, and H. H. Remmers, and an excerpted review by Laurence Siegel of Forms 1–2, see 5:16. For reviews of the modern mathematics supplement, see 7:481 (2 reviews).

TEST REFERENCES

1. Colangelo, N., & Brower, P. (1987). Labeling gifted youngsters: Long-term impact on families. *Gifted Child Quarterly, 31,* 75–78.
2. Henderson, P. A. (1987). Effects of planned parental involvement in affective education. *The School Counselor, 35,* 22–27.
3. Moore, E. G. J. (1987). Ethic social milieu and Black children's intelligence test achievement. *Journal of Negro Education, 56,* 44–52.
4. Pink, W. T. (1987). Continuing the struggle to improve urban schools: An effective schools project revisited. *Journal of Negro Education, 56,* 184–202.
5. Boliek, C. A., Obrzut, J. E., & Shaw, D. (1988). The effects of hemispatial and asymmetrically focused attention on dichotic listening with normal and learning-disabled children. *Neuropsychologia, 26,* 417–433.
6. Hughes, G. M. (1988). The success story of Lee elementary school: A R.I.S.E. school. *Journal of Negro Education, 57,* 267–281.
7. Juel, C. (1988). Learning to read and write: A longitudinal study of 54 children from first through fourth grades. *Journal of Educational Psychology, 80,* 437–447.
8. Kaye, S. H. (1988). The impact of divorce on children's academic performance. *Journal of Divorce, 12*(2/3), 283–298.
9. Lehrer, R., Guckenberg, T., & Lee, O. (1988). Comparative study of the cognitive consequences of inquiry-based logo instruction. *Journal of Educational Psychology, 80,* 543–553.
10. Obrzut, J. E., Conrad, P. F., Bryden, M. P., & Boliek, C. A. (1988). Cued dichotic listening with right-handed, left-handed, bilingual and learning-disabled children. *Neuropsychologia, 26,* 119–131.
11. Soto, L. D. (1988). The home environment of higher and lower achieving Puerto Rican children. *Hispanic Journal of Behavioral Sciences, 10,* 161–167.
12. Stevens, R. J. (1988). Effects of strategy training on the identification of the main idea of expository passages. *Journal of Educational Psychology, 80,* 21–26.
13. Valencia, R. R. (1988). The McCarthy Scales and Hispanic children: A review of psychometric research. *Hispanic Journal of Behavioral Sciences, 10,* 81–104.
14. Vosniadou, S., Pearson, P. D., & Rogers, T. (1988). What causes children's failures to detect inconsistencies in text? Representation versus comparison difficulties. *Journal of Educational Psychology, 80,* 27–39.
15. Duffy, T. M., Higgins, L., Mehlenbacher, B., Cochran, C., Wallace, D., Gill, C., Haugen, D., McCaffrey, M., Burnett, R., Sloane, S., & Smith, S. (1989). Models for design of instructional text. *Reading Research Quarterly, 24,* 434–457.
16. Ebmeier, H., & Schmulbach, S. (1989). An examination of the selection practices used in the Talent Search Program. *Gifted Child Quarterly, 33,* 134–141.
17. Grabe, M. (1989). Evaluation of purposeful reading skills in elementary-age students. *Journal of Educational Psychology, 81,* 628–630.
18. McEvoy, R. E., & Johnson, D. L. (1989). Comparison of an intelligence test and a screening battery as predictors of reading ability in low income, Mexican American children. *Hispanic Journal of Behavioral Sciences, 11,* 274–282.
19. Obrzut, J. E., Conrad, P. F., & Boliek, C. A. (1989). Verbal and nonverbal auditory processing among left- and right-handed good readers and reading-disabled children. *Neuropsychologia, 27,* 1357–1371.
20. Peterson, P. L., Carpenter, T., & Fennema, E. (1989). Teachers' knowledge of students' knowledge in mathematics problem solving: Correlational and case analyses. *Journal of Educational Psychology, 81,* 558–569.
21. Renick, M. J., & Harter, S. (1989). Impact of social comparisons on the developing self-perceptions of learning disabled students. *Journal of Educational Psychology, 81,* 631–638.
22. Reynolds, A. J. (1989). A structural model of first-grade outcomes for an urban, low socioeconomic status, minority population. *Journal of Educational Psychology, 81,* 594–603.

23. Van Tassel-Baska, J., Willis, G. B., & Meyer, D. (1989). Evaluation of a full-time self-contained class for gifted students. *Gifted Child Quarterly, 33,* 7–10.
24. Vitek, D. J., & Schwantes, F. M. (1989). Automatic-spreading activation effects following children's reading of complete sentences. *Journal of Reading Behavior, 21,* 181–194.
25. Zabrucky, K., & Ratner, H. H. (1989). Effects of reading ability on children's comprehension evaluation and regulation. *Journal of Reading Behavior, 21,* 69–83.
26. Burns, D. E. (1990). The effects of group training activities on students' initiation of creative investigations. *Gifted Child Quarterly, 34,* 31–36.
27. Cox, B. E., Shanahan, T., & Sulzby, E. (1990). Good and poor elementary readers' use of cohesion in writing. *Reading Research Quarterly, 24,* 47–65.
28. Juel, C. (1990). Effects of reading group assignment on reading development in first and second grade. *Journal of Reading Behavior, 22,* 233–254.
29. Kelly, K. R., & Colangelo, N. (1990). Effects of academic ability and gender on career development. *Journal for the Education of the Gifted, 13,* 168–175.
30. Manning, B. H. (1990). A categorical analysis of children's self-talk during independent school assignments. *Journal of Instructional Psychology, 17,* 208–217.
31. Tracy, D. M. (1990). Toy-playing behavior, sex-role orientation, spatial ability, and science achievement. *Journal of Research in Science Education, 27,* 637–649.
32. Barnhart, J. E. (1991). Criterion-related validity of interpretations of children's performance on emergent literacy tasks. *Journal of Reading Behavior, 23,* 425–444.
33. Callahan, C. M. (1991). An update on gifted females. *Journal for the Education of the Gifted, 14,* 284–311.
34. Carr, E., Bigler, M., & Morningstar, C. (1991). The effects of the CVS strategy on children's learning. *Yearbook of National Reading Conference, 40,* 193–200.
35. Collins, C. (1991). Reading instruction that increases thinking abilities. *Journal of Reading, 34,* 510–516.
36. Fisher, P. J. L., Blachowicz, C. L. Z., & Smith, J. C. (1991). Vocabulary learning in literature discussion groups. *Yearbook of National Reading Conference, 40,* 201–209.
37. Garcia, G. E. (1991). Factors influencing the English reading test performance of Spanish-speaking Hispanic children. *Reading Research Quarterly, 26,* 371–392.
38. Henk, W. A., & Melnick, S. A. (1991). The initial development of a scale to measure "Perception of self as reader." *Yearbook of National Reading Conference, 40,* 111–117.
39. Mulholland, D. J., Watt, N. F., Philpott, A., & Sarlin, N. (1991). Academic performance in children of divorce: Psychological resilience and vulnerability. *Psychiatry, 54,* 268–280.
40. Schwantes, F. M. (1991). Children's use of semantic and syntactic information for word recognition and determination of sentence meaningfulness. *Journal of Reading Behavior, 23,* 335–350.
41. Smith, M. L. (1991). Meanings of test preparation. *American Educational Research Journal, 28,* 521–542.
42. Spears, M. W., & Gambrell, L. B. (1991). Prediction training and the comprehension and composing performance of fourth-grade students. *Yearbook of National Reading Conference, 40,* 239–245.
43. Stahl, S. A., Richek, M. A., & Vandevier, R. J. (1991). Learning meaning vocabulary through listening: A sixth-grade replication. *Yearbook of National Reading Conference, 40,* 185–192.
44. Wood, T., Cobb, P., & Yackel, E. (1991). Change in teaching mathematics: A case study. *American Educational Research Journal, 28,* 587–616.
45. Brunkhorst, B. J. (1992). A study of student outcomes and teacher characteristics in exemplary middle and junior high science programs. *Journal of Research in Science Teaching, 29,* 571–583.
46. Carver, R. D. (1992). What do standardized tests of reading comprehension measure in terms of efficiency, accuracy, and rate? *Reading Research Quarterly, 27,* 347–359.
47. Cipielewski, J., & Stanovich, K. E. (1992). Predicting growth in reading ability from children's exposure to print. *Journal of Experimental Child Psychology, 54,* 74–89.
48. Cornell, D. G., Delcourt, M. A. B., Goldberg, M. D., & Bland, L. C. (1992). Characteristics of elementary students entering gifted programs: The Learning Outcomes Project at the University of Virginia. *Journal for the Education of the Gifted, 15,* 309–331.
49. Hembree, R. (1992). Experiments and relational studies in problem solving: A meta-analysis. *Journal for Research in Mathematics Education, 23,* 242–273.
50. Malone, L. D., & Mastropieri, M. A. (1992). Reading comprehension instruction: Summarization and self-monitoring training for students with learning disabilities. *Exceptional Children, 58,* 270–279.
51. Romance, N. R., & Vitale, M. R. (1992). A curriculum strategy that expands time for in-depth elementary science instruction by using science-based reading strategies: Effects of a year-long study in grade four. *Journal of Research in Science Teaching, 29,* 545–554.
52. Thompson, P. W. (1992). Notations, conventions, and constraints: Contributions to effective uses of concrete materials in elementary mathematics. *Journal for Research in Mathematics Education, 23,* 123–147.
53. Barnett, L. B., & Durden, W. G. (1993). Educational patterns of academically talented youth. *Gifted Child Quarterly, 37,* 161–168.
54. Cunningham, J. W., & Moore, D. W. (1993). The contribution of understanding academic vocabulary to answering comprehension questions. *Journal of Reading Behavior, 25,* 171–180.
55. Duran, R., & Powers, S. (1993). Reliabilities of the Iowa Tests of Basic Skills for Hispanic- and Anglo-American students. *Psychological Reports, 73,* 64–66.
56. Garofalo, J. (1993). Mathematical problem preferences of meaning-oriented and number-oriented problem solvers. *Journal for the Education of the Gifted, 17,* 26–40.

57. Hancock, M. R. (1993). Character journals: Initiating involvement and identification through literature. *Journal of Reading, 37,* 42-50.

58. Holden, G. W., Nelson, P. B., Velasquez, J., & Ritchie, K. L. (1993). Cognitive, psychosocial, and reported sexual behavior differences between pregnant and nonpregnant adolescents. *Adolescence, 28,* 557-572.

59. Kibby, M. W. (1993). What reading teachers should know about reading proficiency in the U.S. *Journal of Reading, 37,* 28-40.

60. Lupkowski-Shoplik, A. E., & Assouline, S. G. (1993). Identifying mathematically talented elementary students: Using the lower level of the SSAT. *Gifted Child Quarterly, 37,* 118-123.

61. May, D. C., & Kundert, D. K. (1993). Pre-first placements: How common and how informed? *Psychology in the Schools, 30,* 161-167.

62. Medo, M. A., & Ryder, R. J. (1993). The effects of vocabulary instruction on readers' ability to make causal connections. *Reading Research and Instruction, 33,* 119-134.

63. Pellegrini, A. D., & Davis, P. D. (1993). Relations between children's playground and classroom behaviour. *British Journal of Educational Psychology, 63,* 88–95.

64. Roth, M., McCaul, E., & Barnes, K. (1993). Who becomes an "at-risk" student? The predictive value of a kindergarten screening battery. *Exceptional Children, 59,* 348-358.

65. Spencer, M. B., Cole, S. P., DuPree, D., Glymph, A., & Pierre, P. (1993). Self-efficacy among urban African American early adolescents: Exploring issues of risk, vulnerability, and resilience. *Development and Psychopathology, 5,* 719-739.

66. Waterman, J., & Lusk, R. (1993). Psychological testing in evaluation of child sexual abuse. *Child Abuse & Neglect, 17,* 145-159.

67. Williams, J. P. (1993). Comprehension of students with and without learning disabilities: Identification of narrative themes and idiosyncratic text representations. *Journal of Educational Psychology, 85,* 631-641.

68. Attar, B. K., Guerra, N. G., & Tolan, P. H. (1994). Neighborhood disadvantage, stressful life events, and adjustment in urban elementary-school children. *Journal of Clinical Child Psychology, 23,* 391-400.

69. Carr, M., & Kurtz-Costes, B. E. (1994). Is being smart everything? The influence of student achievement on teachers' perceptions. *British Journal of Educational Psychology, 64,* 263–276.

70. Davis, A., Clarke, M. A., & Rhodes, L. K. (1994). Extended text and the writing proficiency of students in urban elementary schools. *Journal of Educational Psychology, 86,* 556-566.

71. Flynn, J. M., & Rahbar, M. H. (1994). Prevalence of reading failure in boys compared with girls. *Psychology in the Schools, 31,* 66-71.

72. Hynd, C. R., McWhorter, J. W., Phares, V. L., & Suttles, C. W. (1994). The role of instructional variables in conceptual change in high school physics topics. *Journal of Research in Science Teaching, 31,* 933–946.

73. Lewandowski, L., & Arcangelo, K. C. (1994). The social adjustment and self-concept of adults with learning disabilities. *Journal of Learning Disabilities, 27,* 598–605.

74. Mavrogenes, N. A., & Bezrucko, N. (1994). A study of the writing of fifth-grade disadvantaged children. *Journal of Educational Research, 87,* 228-238.

75. McCormick, C. E., Stoner, S. B., & Duncan, S. (1994). Kindergarten predictors of first-grade reading achievement: A regular classroom example. *Psychological Reports, 74,* 403-407.

76. McGhee, R., & Lieberman, L. (1994). Gf-Gc Theory of human cognition: Differentiation of short-term auditory and visual memory factors. *Psychology in the Schools, 31,* 297-304.

77. Moore, W. D. (1994). The devaluation of standardized testing: One district's response to a mandated assessment. *Applied Measurement in Education, 7,* 343-367.

78. Murrell, P. C., Jr. (1994). In search of responsive teaching for African American males: An investigation of students' experiences of middle school mathematics curriculum. *The Journal of Negro Education, 63,* 556–569.

79. Renzulli, J. S., & Reis, S. M. (1994). Research related to the schoolwide enrichment triad model. *Gifted Child Quarterly, 38,* 7-20.

80. Reutzel, D. R., Hollingsworth, P. M., & Eldredge, J. L. (1994). Oral reading instruction: The impact on student reading development. *Reading Research Quarterly, 29,* 41-62.

81. Roller, C. M. (1994). Teacher-student interactions during oral reading and rereading. *Journal of Reading Behavior, 26,* 191–208.

82. Samejima, F. (1994). Nonparametric estimation of the plausibility functions of the distractors of vocabulary test items. *Applied Psychological Measurement, 18,* 35-51.

83. Stoiber, K. C., & Houghton, T. G. (1994). Adolescent mothers' cognitions and behaviors as at-risk indicators. *School Psychology Quarterly, 9,* 295-316.

84. Stone, B. J. (1994). Group ability test versus teachers' ratings for predicting achievement. *Psychological Reports, 75,* 1487-1490.

85. Strom, R., Strom, S., Strom, P., & Collinsworth, P. (1994). Parent competence in families with gifted children. *Journal for the Education of the Gifted, 18,* 39-54.

86. Waltman, K. K., & Frisbie, D. A. (1994). Parent's understanding of their children's report card grades. *Applied Measurement in Education, 7,* 223-240.

87. Wiggins, J. D., Schatz, E. L., & West, R. W. (1994). The relationship of self esteem to grades, achievement scores, and other factors critical to school success. *The School Counselor, 41,* 239–244.

88. Adams, C. M., & Callahan, C. M. (1995). The reliability and validity of a performance task for evaluating science process skills. *Gifted Child Quarterly, 39,* 14-20.

89. Armstrong, B. E., & Larson, C. N. (1995). Students' use of part-whole and direct comparison strategies for comparing partitioned rectangles. *Journal for Research in Mathematics Education, 26,* 2-19.

90. Conger, R. D., Patterson, G. R., & Ge, X. (1995). It takes two to replicate: A mediational model for the impact of parents' stress on adolescent adjustment. *Child Development, 66,* 80-97.

91. Cornell, D. G., Delcourt, M. A. B., Goldberg, M. D., & Bland, L. C. (1995). Achievement and self-concept of minority students in elementary school gifted programs. *Journal for the Education of the Gifted, 18,* 189-209.

92. Eckenrode, J., Rowe, E., Laird, M., & Brathwaite, J. (1995). Mobility as a mediator of the effects on child maltreatment on academic performance. *Child Development, 66,* 1130–1142.

93. Frisbie, D. A., & Cantor, N. K. (1995). The validity of scores from alternative methods of assessing spelling achievement. *Journal of Educational Measurement, 32,* 55–78.

94. Joshi, R. M. (1995). Assessing reading and spelling skills. *School Psychology Review, 24,* 361–375.

95. Kreitler, S., Zigler, E., Kagan, S., Olsen, D., Weissler, K., & Kreitler, H. (1995). Cognitive and motivational determinants of academic achievement and behavior in third and fourth grade disadvantaged children. *British Journal of Educational Psychology, 65,* 297–316.

96. Linn, R. L., & Kiplinger, V. L. (1995). Linking statewide tests to the National Assessment of Educational Progress: Stability of results. *Applied Measurement in Education, 8,* 135–155.

97. Majsterek, D. J., & Ellenwood, A. E. (1995). Phonological awareness and beginning reading: Evaluation of a school-based screening procedure. *Journal of Learning Disabilities, 28,* 449–456.

98. Mardell-Czudnowski, C. (1995). Performance of Asian and White children on the K-ABC: Understanding information processing differences. *Assessment, 2,* 19-29.

99. Meyer, M. J., & Zentall, S. S. (1995). Influence of loud behavioral consequences on attention deficit hyperactivity disorder. *Behavior Therapy, 26,* 351–370.

100. Qualls, A. L., & Ansley, T. N. (1995). The predictive relationship of ITBS and ITED to measures of academic success. *Educational and Psychological Measurement, 55,* 485-498.

101. Ross, S. M., Smith, L. J., Casey, J., & Slavin, R. E. (1995). Increasing the academic success of disadvantaged children: An examination of alternative early intervention program. *American Educational Research Journal, 32,* 773–800.

102. Sparks, R. L., Ganschow, L., & Patton, J. (1995). Prediction of performance in first-year foreign language courses: Connections between native and foreign language learning. *Journal of Educational Psychology, 87,* 638–655.

103. Stevens, L. J., & Bliss, L. S. (1995). Conflict resolution abilities of children with specific language impairment and children with normal language. *Journal of Speech and Hearing Research, 38,* 599–611.

104. Sweeney, N. S. (1995). The age position effect: School entrance age, giftedness, and underachievement. *Journal for the Education of the Gifted, 18,* 171-188.

105. Tur-Kaspa, H., & Bryan, T. (1995). Teachers' ratings of the social competence and school adjustment of students with LD in elementary and junior high school. *Journal of Learning Disabilities, 28,* 44–52.

106. Williams, J. E., & Montgomery, D. (1995). Using frame of reference theory to understand the self-concept of academically able students. *Journal for the Education of the Gifted, 18,* 400–409.

107. Lewis, H. A., & Kliewer, W. (1996). Hope, coping, and adjustment among children with sickle cell disease: Tests of mediator and moderator models. *Journal of Pediatric Psychology, 21,* 25–41.

108. Pungello, E. P., Kupersmidt, J. B., Patterson, C. J., & Burchinal, M. R. (1996). Environmental risk factors and children's achievement from middle childhood to early adolescence. *Developmental Psychology, 32,* 755–767.

109. Southard, N. A., & May, D. C. (1996). The effects of pre-first-grade programs on student reading and math achievement. *Psychology in the Schools, 33,* 132–142.

110. Williams, J. E. (1996). Gender-related worry and emotionality test anxiety for high-achieving students. *Psychology in the Schools, 33,* 159–162.

Review of the Iowa Tests of Basic Skills, Form K, L, and M by SUSAN M. BROOKHART, Associate Professor, Department of Foundations and Leadership, School of Education, Duquesne University, Pittsburgh, PA:

DESCRIPTION. The Iowa Tests of Basic Skills (ITBS) began in 1935 as the Iowa Every Pupil Test of Basic Skills and has taken its place as a standard in standardized assessment. Forms K and L were normed in 1992 and Form M in 1995. Form M was equated to Form K in 1995. Norming samples were large, carefully chosen, and well documented. The test is available in Levels 5 through 14, roughly corresponding to the ages of children who will take them, and is intended for use in grades K through 8. The Core Battery is composed of sections for Listening (Levels 5–8 only), Word Analysis (Levels 5–8 only), Vocabulary, Reading, Language, and Mathematics. The Complete Battery adds to this, starting with Level 7, Social Studies, Science, and Sources of Information. A Writing Assessment and a Listening Assessment are available for Levels 9 through 14. The Survey Battery is a Reading, Language, and Mathematics battery using subsets of items from the Core Battery, designed to produce a reliable overview of these basic skills using a minimum amount of testing time.

A large variety of supporting materials is available for these tests, and that is a point worth emphasizing. This reviewer has worked with districts that did not avail themselves of all the relevant information and, therefore, had more information in their students' scores than they interpreted or used. That seems a shame. In addition to the tests themselves (test booklets and answer sheets), Riverside publishes practice tests for each level, preparing for testing manuals for teachers and directions for administration and scoring, interpretive guides for school administrators, interpretive guides for teachers and counselors, content outlines, technical summaries (of test construction and reliability evidence, ceiling and floor data, etc.), norms and score conversions, and separate norms for high and low socioeconomic areas, Catholic/private schools, large cities, and international students. Taken together, this supporting information provides for a much richer interpretation of ITBS results than is often made in school districts. This reviewer recommends that districts choosing the ITBS request all the relevant supporting information and use it. The text in the manuals is quite readable.

PURPOSE AND USES. "Basic skills" means different things to different people—as does "higher-order thinking." The common public perception of basic skills—"reading, writing, and arithmetic"—is not what the ITBS purports to measure. The test authors consider "'basic skills' to be the entire range of skills a student needs to progress satisfactorily through school" (Technical Summary I, p. 15). This includes higher-order thinking skills, interpretation, classification, comparison, analysis, and inference. Questions tapping these skills are most evident in the reading, math, science, social studies, and reference sections and least evident in the language section, where the mechanics of spelling, capitalization, punctuation, and usage predominate, although there is a section on language expression.

So why do some people complain that the "basic skills" tests do not tap higher-order thinking?

This reviewer thinks it is because some people do not consider the bite-sized inferences and analyses that the ITBS items call for to be "higher-order thinking." For districts that wish to include tests that require student-constructed responses in their testing programs, constructed-response supplements (Form 1) are available for Levels 9 through 14. These are titled "Thinking about Reading," "Thinking about Language," and "Thinking about Mathematics." These test supplements come in workbook-style format, and students put their responses right in the booklets. The response "bite size" is larger for these tests than for the multiple-choice format, but it is still not the sustained construction required for long-term projects, an aspect of achievement that is outside the domain of the ITBS.

The purpose of the ITBS, along with its companion tests for older students (Tests of Achievement and Proficiency [TAP] and Iowa Tests of Educational Development [ITED; 160]), is "to provide test results that may be used to improve the quality of instruction" (Technical Summary I, p. 10). Therefore, the argument is made that the most important validity evidence is evidence of content aligned with curriculum. The authors chose the content for the ITBS after studying texts and other curriculum materials, recommendations of professional societies, and practices of school districts. Content descriptions for each section of the test are presented in the technical manual, and numbers of items in each content domain, for each form, are listed in the content specifications manuals. The content specifications provide enough detail for the kind of thorough content review that is required for each district that uses the ITBS to assure that it will be measuring skills its curriculum teaches and knowledge that it values. The manuals make it clear that it remains the responsibility of each test user to do this and this is consistent with the *Code of Professional Responsibilities in Educational Measurement* (NCME, 1995). This reviewer urges districts that use the ITBS to obtain and read the content specification manuals and discuss alignment with the curriculum with administrators and teachers. This step should not be skipped.

Specific purposes for the ITBS are listed in the Technical Summary I (p. 15), and one additional one is added in a draft report on Validity Information (p. v-4). These purposes all comport with the general purpose of making good instructional decisions. The purposes specified include decisions at both the individual and group (class, program) level, so individual scores and group averages are both units of interest. This has implications for validity studies. Purposes include: (a) to help teachers determine the extent to which individual students in their classes have the knowledge and skills needed to deal successfully with the academic aspects of the instructional program the teacher has planned; (b) to provide information to parents that will enable home and school to work together in the students' best interests [this is the one that has been added]; (c) to estimate the general developmental level of students so that teachers may adapt materials and instructional procedures to meet individual needs; (d) to identify each student's areas of greatest and least development for use in planning individual instructional goals and approaches; (e) to provide achievement information that makes it possible to monitor year-to-year developmental differences; (f) to provide information for making administrative programming decisions that will accommodate developmental differences; and (g) to identify areas of relative strength and weakness in the performances of groups (e.g., classes), which may have implications for curriculum change—either in content or emphasis—as well as for change in instructional procedures (Technical Summary I, p. 15).

The authors also prudently identify some inappropriate uses of the ITBS, all having to do with using one test to make important decisions about individuals or groups. This caution is made in the draft Validity Report and also in the Interpretive Guides for Teachers and Counselors.

OTHER VALIDITY ISSUES. These uses of ITBS score information require evidence of sound content development, provided by the publisher, and evidence of comportment with the curriculum, provided by district review. Content evidence is necessary but is not sufficient validity evidence for the purposes listed above, however. The authors have summarized some other evidence for validity, studying the nature of the "basic skills" construct by investigating subtest intercorrelations and correlations with the Cognitive Abilities Test (CogAT), a test of problem solving and reasoning; correlations with future grades and future test performance; studies of cognitive processes students use for the test, especially for problem solving; bias studies; equating studies related to score meaning; and studies of interpretation and understanding of parents and teachers. The overwhelming evidence is positive, that is, the ITBS scores provide valid measures of basic academic skills, if defined and used in the manner intended.

To the authors' credit, they also report the results of validity studies that did not fully support the validity of the test. For example, a study by Ansley and Forsyth (1990, cited in Validity Information for the ITBS and ITED, 1997, p. v-66) found that some problem-solving items tapped mostly computational skill and some tapped mostly reading. The same report cites a study by Witt (1993, cited on p. v-81) that found correlations between average analytic scores and holistic scores of direct assessments were lower than expected if these two scoring methods produced measures of the same construct. References to studies despite their level of support for the validity of inferences and uses of the various tests' scores strikes this reviewer as ethical and scientific. These studies also point to places where more work is needed and where caution in interpretation must be exercised.

One comment about the nature of evidence designed to show that "basic skills" are stable over time, and thus be evidence for construct validity, seems in order. ITBS scores are correlated with (predict) future test scores, grades, and future ITBS scores. This stability over time is considered a good thing for validity because the constructs are stable, that is, "basic skills" remain necessary for success in school. However, the intended uses are for making instructional decisions. One could argue that if ITBS scores were used as intended, that is, if districts tailored instruction and improved programs to meet student and group needs as measured by the ITBS, then the ultimate goal and a demonstration of validity of use would be to wipe out or at least attenuate relationships with future success in school. Students whose basic academic skills indicated their needs were not being met would benefit from changes in instruction and would, therefore, succeed in the future beyond what was predicted by a measure of their achievement to date.

RELIABILITY. The ITBS has high reliability coefficients for the most part. The ITBS prides itself on its reliability, claiming rightly that its reliability levels are among the highest in the testing industry. Most subtest reliabilities are in the .80s and .90s across Forms K, L, and M; in general, Levels 5–8 have lower reliabilities (around .80), and the higher levels have higher reliabilities (around .90). Core Total and Composite reliabilities are all above .90. Listening Assessment reliabilities range from .67 to .79.

The lower reliability for the younger students, although still within an acceptable range, serves as a reminder that the performance of primary level children is variable and that teacher judgment as well as a variety of kinds of performance is relevant information for any instructional decision about young children, even minor ones. Reliabilities for Science and Social Studies at Levels 7 and 8 tend to be lower (mostly in the .60s) for Forms K and L. For Form M, reliabilities for Science and Social Studies for Level 7 are slightly better (high .60s to low .70s), but reliability for the Science subtest for Level 8 is .60 for grade 2, spring, and .59 for grade 3, fall.

Standard errors are also reported for each subtest, level, and form. Some equivalent-forms reliability estimates are given, as well. The sizes of these values, as for the K-R 20s, are quite acceptable. The Writing Assessment comes with rater training material and anchor papers suitable for reaching acceptable levels of interrater reliability, given proper use.

NORMS AND SCORES. The ITBS offers a number of different kinds of scores, useful for different purposes. Status measures such as percentile ranks describe performance in terms of the norm group cohort. Developmental Standard Scores describe performance across grades on the same scale. This reviewer's experience suggests that students, teachers, districts, and community members focus on status measures and do not use the developmental measures to their full advantage. In the opinion of this reviewer, people are too busy comparing themselves to others, especially with percentile ranks, to estimate status and not nearly busy enough charting progress over time, with Developmental Standard Scores. It is the latter, it seems, that defines education. Developmental Standard Scores are not well understood generally, although the literature provided with the ITBS is complete, explanatory, and readable. This is probably because the standard score scale is more abstract than percentile ranks. Developmental Standard Scores make possible some longitudinal evaluation studies that would be most helpful for districts evaluating subject-area programs over time, for example in Reading or Math.

The accuracy of status comparisons in practice is further limited by the common use of "national norms." There are separate norms for high and low socioeconomic areas, Catholic/private schools, large cities, and international students, and local norms can be computed if the district asks for them. For some purposes, this information is more relevant than national norms. For example, the relative strengths and weaknesses of students in a high-socioeconomic area school district can better be judged with the norms for this group. Comparison to national norms may simply result in a feel-good judgment that no improvement is necessary or possible. Another common misuse of norms is to use individual percentile ranks to interpret aggregated, school-, or district-level data. The ITBS manuals clearly describe the differences between the two and provide appropriate tables for each use.

The one "score" this reviewer wishes would simply not be calculated is the grade equivalent (GE) score. A grade equivalent score is the typical score for a student in the identified grade and month of school. But the conclusions that can legitimately be made from this information can also be made from other available scores, such as percentile ranks and stanines. Grade equivalent scores perform no unique functions, but they introduce great risks for misinterpretation and misuse. It is too easy to define "grade" as the curriculum and class instruction that goes with it, because that is certainly how "grade" is experienced by students, teachers, and parents, and misinterpret GE scores to mean readiness for grade level objectives or achievement of them. "Grade" also plays into the rank and status judgments that standardized test scores can tempt people to do because the name connotes gradations of progress through the curriculum. This reviewer wishes that GE scores would magically disappear!

SUMMARY. The ITBS is one of the oldest and the best in the business. It is a set of standardized tests of basic skills that is supported by exemplary research and documentation. There are some problems with its interpretation and use in common practice; the authors are aware of these problems and are explicit in their description of them. The test is well constructed. It is reliable enough to use for both individual and group judgments. It could well form a part of a school district's routine evaluation and documentation of progress. The things this reviewer wishes for the ITBS do not inhere as problems within the test but as systemic problems in education more generally. Teacher observation and judgment and student performance on other achievements tasks must be consulted before major decisions are made about individuals or programs. Testing young children should not be done routinely, without a clear rationale for why the data are needed and for what purpose they will be used. Greater attention should be paid to charting progress over time and less to reporting status. The ITBS already has and reports these capabilities. Readers of this review are encouraged to make valid use of the information it provides.

REVIEWER'S REFERENCE

National Council on Measurement in Education. (1995). *Code of professional responsibilities in educational measurement.* Washington, DC: NCME.

Review of the Iowa Tests of Basic Skills, Forms K, L, and M by LAWRENCE H. CROSS, Associate Professor, Department of Educational Leadership and Policy Studies, Virginia Polytechnic Institute and State University, Blacksburg, VA:

The Iowa Tests of Basic Skills (ITBS) has been evolving for over 60 years. The current forms (K, L, and M) maintain its tradition of quality while introducing changes to reflect contemporary views of curriculum, instruction, and measurement. The items appear to be very well crafted and the physical appearance is excellent. Support materials describe how the development of these tests has been guided by a consideration of current instructional materials, input from textbook authors as well as other nationally recognized specialists in curriculum and measurement, sensitivity reviews to ensure cultural fairness, research studies of various types, criticisms raised by past users, and by subject-matter standards such as those set forth by the National Council of Teachers of Mathematics and by the National Council of Teachers of English. Although the publishers have made every effort to ensure that the tests reflect the scope and sequence of national trends in curricula and instructional practices, only a careful review of the tests and test items by educators at the local level can determine the extent to which scores from these tests will provide valid indicators of achievement in a given setting.

CHANGES FOR THE NEW EDITION. Although the structure of the test batteries is largely the same as for the old forms, there are some notable changes and additions. As before, each form contains a Complete Battery of tests at each of 10 levels appropriate for ages 5 through 14 (grades K through 8). Perhaps the most notable addition is the introduction of Survey Batteries as alternatives to the Complete Batteries. These are 30-minute tests in reading, language, and mathematics containing items sampled from the full-length tests. The Survey Batteries should be of considerable interest to users willing to sacrifice diagnostic information and a modest reduction in score reliability in exchange for a reduction in testing time.

Another worthwhile addition is a new Integrated Writing Skills Test available as an option only for Form M at Levels 9–14. Rather than assess language skills with separate tests of spelling, punctuation, capitalization, and usage, the Integrated Writing Skills Tests measure editing skills in these areas by requiring students to identify a mix of errors integrated within a series of passages. This test

would appear to represent a viable alternative to the four separate language tests. However, the reduction in testing time (45 minutes versus 60 minutes) is offset by a corresponding reduction in reliability estimates relative to the total language scores.

The mathematics tests have changed considerably from the previous edition, especially for Levels 9 through 14 (grades 3–8). The computation test, which was introduced with Forms 7 and 8 in 1978, is now offered only as an optional test and is no longer used in computing the composite score for the battery unless specifically requested. The Math Concepts test is now a two-part test and renamed Math Concepts and Estimation to reflect those two parts. Similarly, the Math Problem Solving test is also a two-part test and renamed Math Problem Solving and Data Interpretation to reflect those two parts. The first parts to each of these tests are similar to the old tests with the same names, but the second part to each test represents major changes. The changes made in these tests were influenced by the Standards set forth by the National Council of Teachers of Mathematics. The reading of graphs and tables, which formerly was part of the Visual Materials test, is now included in the second part of the Mathematics Problem Solving and Data Interpretation test. Whereas estimation problems were barely in evidence in the old forms, estimation is now a major component (e.g., 16 of 40 items at Level 10). However, the estimation items are given only half the score credit assigned to the concept problems, thus limiting their contribution to the scores for this test. Perhaps the reason for having so many estimation items is to provide a reasonable number of items for assessing the five subskills identified within estimation. Though the items associated with these subskills may provide instructionally useful information to teachers, the items appear to this reviewer to represent little more than problems in rounding followed by one of the four basic operations, in which case, a test half as long would suffice.

Whereas most of the tests making up the ITBS batteries use a multiple-choice format, constructed responses are used for a few optional tests. Writing assessments were introduced with the previous edition of the ITBS and are available again in the current forms (for Level 9 and above). It should be noted that extensive training materials are provided for scoring these assessments at the local level and that the score reliability and interrater reliability are characteristically modest for these assessments. In addition, there are three new constructed-response tests in reading, language, and mathematics for Levels 9 through 14, which are titled Thinking about Reading, Thinking about Language, and Thinking about Mathematics. No interpretive guides or technical information could be located in the review materials for these tests. However, it can be expected that the reliability of the scores from these short tests will be quite modest due to the limited number of items contained in each and due to the subjectivity of the hand scoring, which, judging from the writing assessment, would be done at the local level. Past research, including that reported for the writing assessments, demonstrates that scores from constructed-response and multiple-choice tests correlate very highly (often well above .90) when the correlation coefficients are adjusted for the unreliability of the tests. Nonetheless, it is understandable that the publishers have introduced constructed-response tests in an era when multiple-choice tests are being denigrated by many who advocate portfolio, performance, and other "authentic" assessments. Although the constructed-response tests have the potential to yield information that may be instructionally useful to teachers, users will have to decide whether the value added by these tests is worth the cost and time to administer and score these tests.

In addition to changes in the tests, there are two new interpretive guides, an Interpretive Guide for School Administrators and an Interpretive Guide for Teachers and Counselors (quotations from the guides will refer to page numbers given in the Interpretive Guide for School Administrators). Both provide detailed descriptions of the tests and clear explanations of the many scores and score reports provided for these tests. The Interpretive Guide for Teachers and Counselors devotes an entire section to suggested instructional uses for the test results. Unfortunately, neither guide contains any technical data regarding reliability, validity, or norms in support of the suggested uses. As noted in a cover letter that accompanied the review materials, the Manual for School Administrators for the previous edition was becoming unwieldy and was quite intimidating to many users in the schools. Although a publication entitled Research Handbook to the Iowa Tests of Basic Skills is being prepared, the absence of any technical information in the interpretive guides may send the message that such information is superfluous for effective use and interpretation of the ITBS.

PURPOSES SERVED. Both interpretive guides claim that "the primary purpose of using a standardized achievement battery is to provide information that can be used to improve instruction" (p. 11) and list seven appropriate uses of these tests for instructional planning (p. 12). It is interesting to compare this primary purpose to the motivation behind the development of the ITBS. According to Robert Ebel (personal communication, 1977), the predecessor to the ITBS, the Iowa Every-Pupil Test of Basic Skills, was instituted as an academic competition to give recognition to those high school students (and schools) in the same way athletic competition brought recognition to individuals and schools. Although athletic events that rank-order contestants and athletic teams still go unquestioned in our society, norm-referenced tests that rank-order students or schools have been severely questioned ever since criterion-referenced testing was introduced nearly 30 years ago.

CRITERION-REFERENCED INTERPRETATIONS. Not surprisingly, the publishers have turned to criterion-referenced interpretations to inform instructional decisions. The Interpretive Guides for the current forms suggest: "Even though the tests in the ITBS Battery were not developed primarily for criterion-referenced purposes, it is still appropriate for you to use the scores in those ways" (p. 57). However, there is reason to be skeptical about drawing both types of inferences from a single test. Criterion-referenced tests are generally designed to estimate whether an examinee's achievement is above or below a given point (e.g., mastery versus nonmastery) on an achievement continuum and such tests are usually built to provide maximum discrimination at that point by including items with difficulties peaked at the decision point. By contrast, the ITBS, as well as other norm-referenced tests, are designed to discriminate across the entire achievement continuum and, correspondingly, contain items with a wide range of difficulties.

The approach adopted by the ITBS is to base criterion-referenced interpretations on number-right scores provided for the subskills measured within each test. The problematic nature of making criterion-referenced interpretations can be illustrated by referring to the score report titled "Student Criterion-Referenced Skills Analysis." This report lists for each skill area the number and percentage of items the student answered correctly along with the average percent-correct score for the class and the nation. The Interpretive Guides suggest that if the teacher believes the national percent-correct is an unsatisfactory standard for judging either class or individual-student progress, the teacher could review the test items and could decide which questions her students should answer correctly to meet her standard of "satisfactory." Clearly, the performance standard associated with such a criterion-referenced judgment has no meaning beyond a teacher's personal opinion. Criterion-referenced standards are being superimposed on score distributions from tests that were not specifically designed to classify examinees into dichotomous performance levels. Nonetheless, ITBS skill level reports may provide instructionally useful information to teachers and curriculum supervisors to the extent that the skills identified for these tests are aligned with the curriculum. However, teachers are cautioned against placing much faith in skill reports for individual students. Few, if any, of the skills are measured with a sufficient number of items to yield reasonably reliable scores, nor are reliability data provided for the skill-based number-right scores. However, greater confidence can be placed in skill-based reports for classes or schools because individual errors of measurement will tend to cancel out across a group of individuals.

NORM-REFERENCED INTERPRETATIONS. In addition to the seven appropriate uses, the Interpretive Guides identify three fundamental purposes for testing, which can be served well by the norm-referenced scores of the ITBS. These purposes are listed as: (a) to describe each student's developmental level within a test area, (b) to identify students' (and groups') areas of relative strength and weakness in subject areas, and (c) to monitor year-to-year growth in the basic skills (p. 51). Clearly such uses depend upon the adequacy of the norms on which they are based. Forms K and L were normed in 1992 and Form M was normed in 1995, but users are invited to have the tests scored with either the 1995 or the 1992 norms. Norms and Score Conversion manuals are provided for each form and contain tables to convert (a) raw scores to developmental scaled scores, (b) developmental scaled scores to grade-equivalent scores, and (c) developmental scaled scores to national percentile ranks for individuals and for schools. The inclusion of tables to convert raw scores to developmental scaled scores overcomes a deficiency of the old Manual for Administrators, which focused on grade-equivalent scores and did not provide for direct conversions of raw scores to standard scores. Also available are separate norm manuals for large city schools, Catholic/private schools, high and low socioeconomic schools, and even international schools. The 1992 norms are based on a sample of 136,934 students, including 13,468 Catholic school students and 5,642 students attending private non-Catholic schools. The manuals do not indicate the number of schools participating for the 1992 norms, but the 1985 norms, involving 126,468 students, were based on 175 schools, including 55 Catholic and 29 private/non-Catholic schools. By contrast, the standardization testing for the Stanford Achievement Tests (Ninth edition, K through 12) involved approximately 250,000 students from 1,000 schools for the Spring, 1995 testing, and another approximately 200,000 students participated in the Fall, 1995 standardization. As the publishers of the ITBS note, "a carefully selected sample of reasonable size would be preferred over a much larger sample less carefully selected" (Technical Summary I, p. 50). Although there is no reason to question the adequacy of the general norm tables, one might question whether nationally representative norms can be obtained for subpopulations of schools when the entire sample was likely to involve fewer than 200 schools.

Though neither reliability or validity data are presented to support criterion-referenced scores and their interpretation, considerable evidence is offered to support the norm-referenced scores and their interpretation. Internal consistency reliability estimates (K-R 20) for raw scores from most of the individual tests tend to be between .85 and .92, with higher estimates associated with the scores from the upper level batteries. Somewhat lower estimates are reported for the capitalization test, especially in the lower level batteries. Reliability estimates for the Listening Assessments range from .67 to .79 across grades 3 through 8. Internal consistency reliability estimates for developmental scale scores are provide only for total scores in reading, language, and math, and these estimates tend to hover around .95 across levels. "Indirect estimates" of equivalent forms reliability are offered for both the Survey and Complete Batteries by adjusting the correlations between scores obtained from these two batteries when administered to the same students during the 1992 standardization. These "indirect estimates" range between .68 and .93 for the Complete Battery tests and are distinctively lower for the Survey Battery tests. The coefficients on which these equivalent forms reliability estimates are based are presented elsewhere as evidence of convergent validity. Conventional standard errors of measurement are reported for all tests as well as conditional standard errors of measurement for developmental scale scores.

A minor concern related to reliability of multiple-choice test scores is the issue of guessing. Although the Directions for Administration (Forms K and L, Levels 9–14, p. 12) admonish teachers to discourage random guessing but to permit educated guesses, the directions to examinees are silent on the issue. The next time these tests are standardized the authors are urged to provide explicit directions as to what examinees should do when unsure of an answer. Because testwise students *and teachers* recognize there is no score penalty for incorrect guesses, the only defensible practice is to advise examinees to answer all questions, even if their answers represent a random guess among all choices.

The reliability of the writing assessment was assessed with regard to consistency of scores across readers and consistency of student performance across writing prompts. The reader reliability estimates for both holistic and analytical scoring, averaged across grade levels, were somewhat less than .80. Reliability estimates associated with student performance across prompts were distinctively lower, averaging somewhat below .50. Considered together, these two sources of error should give pause to anyone drawing a strong inference about an individual student's writing ability. As noted above, no reliability data could be found in the review materials for the constructed response tests in reading, language, and mathematics, but the reliability of scores from these tests can be expected to be lower than their multiple-choice counterparts due to the subjectivity of scoring and limited number of items.

Overall, the tests of the ITBS yield scores that are as reliable as one might hope to obtain from any well-constructed achievement battery containing tests of comparable length. However, users are cautioned not to overinterpret score differences at the individual level, especially for the writing assessment and constructed-response tests, which can be expected to have more modest reliability.

It is generally recognized that content validity is of paramount concern for standardized achievement tests and this must be judged at the local level by considering how well the test reflects the curriculum. To facilitate this judgment, the publishers have provided detailed descriptions of the tests and have described the research and development program undertaken to ensure that tests reflect contemporary educational practices. In addition, the publishers have presented traditional evidence in support of the construct and criterion-related validity of these tests. Information regarding validity is summarized in a draft publication titled *Validity Information for the Iowa Tests of Basic Skills (ITBS) and Iowa Tests of Educational Development (ITED)*. This document contains tables of intercorrelations among developmental scores for the tests of the ITBS offered as evidence of the internal structure of these tests. The correlations among scores from subtests measuring the same constructs (reading, language, and mathematics), are generally somewhat higher than the correlations between scores from subtests measuring different constructs. However, the total scores in reading, language, and mathematics correlate quite highly (typically .75) with each other and with scores from the optional tests in science, social studies, and sources of information. Scores from the achievement tests also correlate quite highly with scores from the Cognitive Abilities Test (CogAT). As expected, the verbal ability scores tend to correlate highest with the total reading scores and the quantitative ability scores tend to correlate highest with the total math scores (about .80 in both cases across levels). In general, the pattern of intercorrelations among scores of the achievement tests and between scores of the achievement tests and the CogAT tend to support the construct validity of the batteries, even though one might hope to see somewhat stronger evidence of discriminant validity.

As noted above, the correlations between scores from the Survey Battery tests and scores from the corresponding tests in the Complete Batteries are offered as evidence of the concurrent validity of the Survey Battery tests and served as the basis for estimating equivalent forms reliability for both the Complete and Survey Batteries. For Forms K and L these coefficients are generally in the mid .80s across grades 2 through 8, which are quite impressive, given the reduced length of the Survey Battery tests.

No information was found in the review materials regarding the validity of the listening tests, the new integrated language tests, the writing assessments, or the constructed-response tests in reading, language, and mathematics. Moreover, evidence to support criterion-related validity was limited to a few older studies conducted in the '50s, '60s, and '80s and is less compelling today, given the ever changing nature of the ITBS. Additional and more recent evidence of validity is needed and it may be provided in the Research Handbook to the Iowa Tests of Basic Skills when it becomes available. However, content validity is the most important concern for those selecting an achievement battery, and this judgment is best left to educators at the local level.

[160]
Iowa Tests of Educational Development, Forms K, L, and M.

Purpose: "To provide objective, norm-referenced information about high school students' development in the skills that are the long-term goals of secondary education—skills that constitute a major part of the foundation for continued learning."

Population: Grades 9–12.

Publication Dates: 1942–1996.

Acronym: ITED.

Levels, 3: 15, 16, 17/18.

Scores: Complete Battery, 13 tests: Vocabulary, Content Area Reading, Reading Total, Correctness and Appropriateness of Expression Advanced Skills, Expression Total, Ability to Do Quantitative Thinking Advanced Skills, Quantitative Thinking Total, Core Total, Ability to Interpret Literary Materials, Analysis of Social Studies Materials, Analysis of Science Materials, Use of Sources of Information Composite; Survey Battery, 7 tests: Reading Advanced Skills, Reading Total, Correctness and Appropriateness of Expression Advanced Skills, Expression Total, Ability to Do Quantitative Thinking Advanced Skills, Quantitative Thinking Total, Survey Battery Total.

Administration: Group.

Forms, 3: K, L, and M; editions: Complete and Survey Batteries.

Price Data, 1997: $37.50 per Complete Battery examination kit; $32 per Survey Battery examination kit; $16 per 25 practice tests including directions for administration; $86 per 25 Complete Battery reusable test booklets including directions for administration; $77 per 25 Survey Battery reusable test booklets including directions for administration; $106 per Complete Battery Form K Braille edition test, administration notes, and Supplement to the Directions for Administration; $88.50 per Survey Battery Form K Braille edition test, administration notes, and Supplement to the Directions for Administration; $53 per Complete Battery Form K large-print edition test, including General Instructions for Testing Visually Impaired Students; $35.50 per Survey Battery Form K large-print edition test, including General Instructions for Testing Visually Impaired Students; $47 per 50 Listening Assessment answer documents including directions for administration and score interpretation and materials needed for machine scoring; $34 per 50 Complete Battery answer folders including materials needed for machine scoring; $30 per 50 Survey Battery answer sheets including materials needed for machine scoring; $34 per 50 combined answer folders including materials needed for machine scoring (to be used for testing students with the ITED and the Cognitive Abilities Test, Form 5; $28 per 25 Survey Battery Easy-Score answer documents; $14.50 per scoring key manual; $47 per Complete Battery scoring masks; $20 per 25 pretest A Message to Parents (English or Spanish); $9 per 25 posttest Report to Students and Parents (English or Spanish); $6 per Preparing for Testing manual; $10 per Directions for Administration manual; $40 per Complete Battery norms and score conversion booklet; $36 per Survey Battery norms and score conversion booklet; $44 per special norms booklet (Large City, Catholic/Private, High Socioeconomic Status, Low Socioeconomic Status); $6 per Interpretive Guide for Teachers and Counselors; $20 per Interpretive Guide for School Administrators; $20 per Content Classification with Item Norms booklet; $29 per Research Handbook.

Special Editions: Braille and large-print editions available.

Time: 235 minutes for Complete Battery; 90 minutes for Survey Battery.

Comments: Part of Riverside's Integrated Assessment System.

Authors: Leonard S. Feldt, Robert A. Forsyth, Timothy N. Ansley, and Stephanie D. Alnot.

Publisher: The Riverside Publishing Company.

a) LEVEL 15.

Population: Grade 9.

b) LEVEL 16.

Population: Grade 10.

c) LEVEL 17/18.

Population: Grades 11–12.

Cross References: See T4:1281 (4 references); for a review by S. E. Phillips of an earlier edition, see 10:156 (3 references); for reviews by Edward Kifer and James L. Wardrop of an earlier form, see 9:534 (5 references); see also T3:1193 (14 references); for reviews by C. Mauritz Lindvall and John E. Milholland of an earlier form, see 8:20 (15 references); see T2:20 (85 references); for reviews by Ellis Batton Page and Alexander G. Wesman of earlier forms, see 6:14 (23 references); for reviews by J. Murray Lee and Stephen Wiseman, see 5:17 (9 references); for a review by Eric Gardner, see 4:17 (3 references); for reviews by Henry Chauncey, Gustav J. Froelich, and Lavone A. Hanna, see 3:12.

TEST REFERENCES

1. Callahan, C. M. (1991). An update on gifted females. *Journal for the Education of the Gifted, 14*, 284–311.
2. Camilli, G., Yomamoto, K., & Weing, M. (1993). Scale shrinkage in vertical equating. *Applied Psychological Measurement, 17*, 379–388.
3. Vispoel, W. P. (1993). Computerized adaptive and fixed-item versions of the ITED vocabulary subtest. *Educational and Psychological Measurement, 53*, 779–788.
4. Vispoel, W. P., Rocklin, T. R., & Wang, T. (1994). Individual differences and test administration procedures: A comparison of fixed-item, computerized-adaptive, and self-adapted testing. *Applied Measurement in Education, 7*, 53–79.
5. Witt, E. A., Dunbar, S. B., & Hoover, H. D. (1994). A multivariate perspective on sex differences in achievement and rater performance among adolescents. *Applied Measurement in Education, 7*, 241–254.
6. Qualls, A. L., & Ansley, T. N. (1995). The predictive relationship of ITBS and ITED to measures of academic success. *Educational and Psychological Measurement, 55*, 485–498.
7. Rocklin, T. R., O'Donnell, A. M., & Holst, P. M. (1995). Effects and underlying mechanisms of self-adapted testing. *Journal of Educational Psychology, 87*, 103–116.

Review of the Iowa Tests of Educational Development, Forms K, L, and M by WILLIAM A. MEHRENS, Professor of Educational Measurement, Michigan State University, East Lansing, MI:

Various editions of the Iowa Tests of Educational Development (ITED) have been in print since 1942. The ITED is one of the most respected and long-lived nationally normed high school achievement tests. The edition reviewed here continues that long, respected tradition. Included as a part of (or supplement to) the ITED are Writing Assessments, Listening Assessments, and Constructed-Response Supplements. This current edition of the ITED is published as part of an integrated system that includes the Iowa Tests of Basic Skills (ITBS; 159), the Tests of Achievement and Proficiency (TAP), and the Cognitive Abilities Test (CogAT; 71). All of these tests were standardized together.

PURPOSE. According to the authors, "The primary reason for using a standardized achievement battery is to gather information that can be used to improve instruction" (Interpretive Guide for Teachers and Counselors, p. 7). This edition (like its predecessors) is intended to measure "skills that are important in adolescent and adult life, abilities that constitute a major part of the foundation for continued learning" (Technical Summary I, p. 36). The ITED are achievement tests in a broad sense. They are characterized (correctly, I believe) as a critical-thinking test battery. There may be some trade-off between measuring fairly general skills (rather than more specific course-based skills) and having data useful for specific instructional decision making. The information the ITED provides is certainly useful for instructional decision making, but in a general sense. Although the authors state that the information survey tests can provide is usually not specific enough to direct instruction in a highly focused way, I believe the authors could have addressed that a bit more fully. Nevertheless, the decision to measure broader skills is the correct approach for a high school standardized achievement test.

NORMS AND EQUATING. As mentioned, the ITBS, TAP, ITED, and CogAT were standardized together. The basic standardization/norming occurred in 1992. The sampling design included three primary stratifying variables: geographic regions (4), district enrollment (9 categories), and socioeconomic status of the district (5 strata). A Catholic school sample and a private non-Catholic school sample were also drawn. The standardization design is described in detail in the Technical Summary I and is exemplary. In the spring sample students took the Complete Battery of Form K of the ITED, Form 5 of the CogAT, and a scaling test to provide data for an integrated scale of the ITBS/TAP/ITED. In the fall, students took either Form K or L of the Complete Battery (allowing equating through an equivalent samples design) and the other form of the Survey Battery (allowing common student equipercentile equating and thereby eliminating any item sequencing or context effects that would be present in an IRT anchor test equating). In addition, each student took two prompts of the Writing Supplements or the Listening Supplement.

Form M was equated to Form K in the fall of 1995 via the same randomly equivalent samples design used to equate Forms K and L in 1992. The 1995 norms are described in detail in the Norms and Score Conversions manual for Form M. Although not literally a national sample, the weighting of user schools and the derivation of the 1995 norms was done in a manner to allow the authors to remove differences in "user effect" from the estimates of change in achievement over time. This process resulted in 1995 norms for Forms K, L, and M that are relatively free of the differences in score levels of users and nonusers of the tests.

In addition to the national norms, special norms exist for students using calculators for the quantitative thinking test, norms for school averages, and norms for special populations (large city norms, Catholic/private norms, high socioeconomic norms, and low socioeconomic norms). The procedures for obtaining these various special norms are well described in the technical materials and are judged by this reviewer to exceed professional standards.

In summary, the norming and equating were done very well. Norms exist for fall, midyear, and spring (midyear was interpolated) and the equating design allows users to be confident that the norms are equivalent across the form used (K, L, or M; Complete Battery or Survey).

KINDS OF SCALES. The ITED provides a developmental standard score scale (DSS) across all grade levels of the ITBS and ITED. This was produced through scaling tests administered to each student in the spring 1992 standardization. In addition to the developmental standard score, the ITED provides grade equivalent (GE) scores. It is not clear why GE scores are provided. As the Interpretive Guide for Teachers and Counselors points out, "At the secondary level, ... because of the lack of a common curriculum, the GE score loses much of its meaning" (Interpretive Guide for Teachers and Counselors, Levels 15, 16, 17/18, Form M, p. 34). In addition to the developmental scales (DSS and GE), relative position status scores—within grade percentile ranks, stanines, and normal curve equivalents—are provided. The Interpretive Guide does a fine job in explaining these relative position status scores.

RELIABILITY. K-R 20 reliability data and traditional and conditional standard errors of measurement are provided for all subtests, forms, and levels. Standard errors are also provided separately for Whites, African Americans, Hispanic Americans, females, and males. The K-R 20s are almost all in the .80s or .90s for the Complete Battery subtests. For the Survey Battery these same high coefficients generally exist, although there are some values in the .70s. The Complete Composite Battery reliability estimates are very high (.98) and the Survey Battery total reliability estimates are in the mid .90s.

The Writing Assessment reports reader reliability estimates in the .80s for both focused holistic and analytic total scoring. For the four subcategories (ideas/content, organization, voice, and conventions), the analytic scoring reader reliability estimates are typically in the .70s although there are some in the .80s. However, these reliability estimates are for the samples scored during the standardization process. One cannot necessarily infer that the reader reliability estimates would apply to any specific local district scoring process. (The publisher does provide very good instructions/training for local scoring.) Score reliabilities are estimates across prompts *within* mode of discourse. These reliability estimates are quite variable across grade levels but they generally seem to average in the .40s to .50s for focused holistic scores and slightly higher for analytic total scores.

Reliability coefficients for the Listening Assessment generally are in the .70s to .80s. Constructed-Response supplements have estimated coefficient alphas ranging from the mid .60s to the mid .80s.

In general, the reliability data are quite high and very thoroughly reported in the technical manuals. I have only one concern. The Directions for Administration and Score Interpretation for the Listening Assessment implies that the difference scores within the Listening Assessment test are reliable enough to be used with caution, but I could find no evidence of the reliability of these difference scores. I think there should have been more stress on the need for caution if such diagnostic interpretations are to be suggested at all.

VALIDITY. For achievement tests, the appropriate emphasis is on content validity evidence. The authors do not claim that the ITED measures all worthwhile educational objectives, but rather, the content of the ITED is meant to measure a carefully selected sample of tasks demanding the use of important skills that practically all adults use in daily life. The ITED is designed to measure critical thinking skills. Each of the tests' domains in the battery is described in the appropriate manuals. For example, in the Interpretive Guide for Teachers and Counselors for Form M there are 24 pages devoted to describing the tests' general domains and presenting tables of specifications for the tests—classified (for most tests) by process and content—which provide the number of questions for each subclassification. In addition, the Appendix of the guide provides tables that list the individual questions for each major objective. Certainly one can get a good idea of the content of the ITED battery by reading the information provided in the Interpretive Guide. Nevertheless, the authors appropriately stress that: "The most effective way to gain insight into the skills demanded by an achievement test is to take the test" (Interpretive Guide for Teachers and Counselors, Form M, p. 8). Although there can be some legitimate debate about what skills a high school achievement battery should assess, there is no doubt that the skills the ITED battery assesses are well described. They fit with my notion of what should be assessed in a high school achievement test.

Criterion-related validity evidence and construct-related validity evidence are also presented in the various manuals. Examples of this evidence include disattenuated correlations of the ITED with the Listening Assessment (from .68 to .79 with ITED composite); correlations between the Complete Battery and Constructed-Response Supplements (typically in the .60s to low .70s); tables showing intercorrelations for the ITED tests and the CogAT (e.g., correlations between CogAT Verbal and subtests of the ITED range from .65 to .85); and ITED correlations with the ASVAB, PLAN, Work Keys, and the ACT (for example, the correlation in grade 11 between the ITED core and the ACT composite was .86).

FAIRNESS. Steps taken to ensure fairness are described in the various manuals. These steps included what is traditionally recommended in the professional literature: an independent fairness review of each piece of stimulus material and each test question, and statistical analyses of the data. DIF analyses were conducted for the final editions of all forms. The overall percentage of items showing significant DIF was very small. For example .7% of the items favored African Americans and 1.1% of the items favored Whites. Smaller percentages were obtained for Hispanic Americans versus Whites and Females versus Males.

READABILITY, SPEEDEDNESS, AND CEILING/FLOOR EFFECTS. The various manuals report evidence on readability, speededness, and ceiling and floor effects. The Dale-Chall evidence suggests that the readability tends to be highest for the Social Studies test where the values were typically in the 9th grade range. Completion rates suggest that most of the ITED are power rather than speed tests. The evidence suggests there are not any serious ceiling or floor effects.

MANUALS AND OTHER ANCILLARY MATERIALS. The various technical and interpretative manuals for the ITED and the related Listening Assessments, Writing Assessments, and Constructed-Response supplements are very well done. A few examples of exemplary materials follow: The Directions for Administration contains an excellent section on the necessary preparations for testing; the Interpretive Guide for Teachers and Counselors contains a very thorough section presenting a number of different score reports and a discussion that facilities an understanding of these reports; a separate Interpretive Guide for School Administrators is well done; practice tests and directions for administering practice tests exist—the latter containing a very good section on how and when it might be useful to administer practice tests; there is a separate message to parents that describes the tests and gives suggestions regarding how parents can encourage students to try to do their best but not feel unnecessarily anxious; a report to students and parents gives descriptions of the test content and scores and describes the purposes of the tests; and there is an excellent manual for scoring and administering the Iowa Writing Assessment along with a set of training papers and scoring protocols.

A limitation at the time of writing this review is that a proposed ITED Research Handbook has not yet been completed. Although much of the necessary information to complete this review was available in other published material, and although the authors of the ITED provided me with draft copies of some sections of the forthcoming handbook, it would have been preferable to have had the proposed handbook in hand. The practice of publishing an achievement test prior to completing such a research handbook is a fairly common practice and certainly understandable. One wants to get an updated test on the market as soon as possible. This benefits both the company and the users. However, I hope that by the time this review appears the handbook has been published. If not, I urge the authors to proceed with great speed to accomplish this task.

SUMMARY. The ITED and related materials are an excellent integrated assessment system. The measures have high technical quality and the various users' guides are well done and should prove very useful to school personnel, parents, and students.

Review of the Iowa Tests of Educational Development, Forms K, L, and M by MICHAEL J. SUBKOVIAK, Associate Dean, School of Education, and Professor of Educational Psychology, University of Wisconsin-Madison, Madison, WI:

The Iowa Tests of Educational Development (ITED) have a very long history, which can be traced to the early 1940s, and the development of these achievement tests has been continuously guided by distinguished psychometricians such as E. F. Lindquist, Leonard A. Feldt, and others. However, the Metropolitan Achievement Tests (12:232), which date to the 1930s and the Stanford Achievement Test (292), which dates to the 1920s, represent competitors with similarly long and distinguished histories. In addition, the Classified Subject Index of the *Mental Measurements Yearbooks* lists a number of other instruments for testing high school achievement. In choosing among these alternatives, a school district should compare competing tests with respect to at least three basic characteristics: (a) validity, (b) reliability, and (c) norms. Thus, the following review will focus on the ITED as it relates to these three essential elements.

VALIDITY. The manual of "Validity Information" for the ITED would be even more useful to consumers if a more balanced presentation of evidence for content, construct, and criterion-related validity were provided. The publishers choose to give primary emphasis to content validity, and less attention to other relevant forms of validity evidence: "The final evaluation must rest primarily upon your own critical item-by-item inspection of the test itself and analysis of its content in relation to the appropriateness of the objectives for *your* pupils, teachers, school, and community" (p. v-1). The manual thus provides numerous tables describing the content knowledge and skills required on the various ITED subtests. By way of summary, the publisher characterizes the ITED content as follows: "the *ITED* was the model for the original *American College Testing*

Program (ACT) tests and the *General Educational Development (GED)* tests. The current *ACT* and *GED* tests still have many content and skills specifications the same as or similar to the *ITED*....The general abilities needed in adult life were considered to be the guiding criteria in determining the skills and concepts to be measured. To as great an extent as possible, the tests were designed to require of students the kinds of critical thinking that all educated citizens must do in daily life" (p. v-2-3).

In other words, the ITED is designed to measure general verbal and numerical "abilities needed in adult life" (p. v-3), and ITED scores should thus correlate with other academic measures and with future performance in school and on the job. Such implications invite validity evidence in addition to content validity, and the manual does provide a limited sample of such information. For example, a matrix of intercorrelations among subtests of the ITED and the Cognitive Abilities Test is provided as evidence of construct validity; and the median correlation of about .70 is substantial. Also reported are ITED subtest intercorrelations with the Armed Services Vocational Battery (median correlation .73), with the PLAN test (median correlation .75), and with the WORK KEYS test (median correlation .56). Surprisingly, factor analytic procedures are not applied to these matrices of intercorrelations to isolate and identify the common verbal and numerical factors that account for performance on the ITED. Criterion-related validity evidence, such as correlations with future GPA or with future success on the job, is also absent.

The issue of test fairness for various ethnic or gender subgroups is addressed in a peculiar fashion. Standard errors of measurement are computed separately for African Americans versus whites, for Hispanic Americans versus whites, and for males versus females; and these standard errors are shown to be similar across the subgroups being compared. However, similarity of standard errors is not convincing evidence of fairness. The numerical value of a standard error is primarily determined by a test's length and is not directly sensitive to differential functioning of test items across various subgroups. Thus, similar standard errors are to be expected across subgroups because test length (n) remains constant. A more accepted method for detecting differential item functioning across subgroups, the Mantel-Haenszel procedure, was also done.

RELIABILITY. Kuder-Richardson (K-R 20) reliability coefficients are reported for the ITED in two separate manuals: "Technical Summary I" and "Technical Summary I Supplement." This illustrates one of the challenging aspects of evaluating the ITED; information is dispersed across many separate technical manuals and handbooks and is interspersed among parallel information pertaining to two other instruments (Iowa Tests of Basic Skills and Tests of Achievement and Proficiency).

The various subtests and composite scores of the Complete Battery are generally satisfactory in terms of reliability. For example, the 235-minute Complete Battery subtests have median K-R 20s near .90; and the composite scores have K-R 20s above .95. The 90-minute Survey Battery is somewhat less reliable, as would be expected of shorter tests (e.g., median K-R 20s for subtests near .85).

Surprisingly, no parallel forms reliability coefficients are reported, although Forms K, L, and M of the ITED are available. Also, no information is reported about the reliability of differences between ITED scores, which is an issue relevant to one of the suggested uses of the scores: "permits comparisons between broad areas of achievement at each testing and also permits an assessment of student growth within each area" ("Technical Summary I," p. 37). Comparison between areas of achievement and assessment of student growth both involve computation of differences scores, which are generally quite unreliable.

NORMS. The norm groups provided by a test publisher should ideally be current, relevant, and representative. The ITED's norms are definitely current in that these reference groups were recently tested (1992–95). Because changes in general verbal and numerical abilities at the national level take place slowly, the ITED's norm groups are an appropriate basis of comparison for interpreting the scores of current students. For a general ability test like the ITED, norms are typically updated every 7–10 years.

A given student's ITED score can be compared to a number of different norm groups; the publisher provides national, large city, Catholic/private, low socioeconomic status, and high socioeconomic status norms. Of course a particular group, like Catholic/private, is relevant as a basis of comparison only if the student is a member of that subgroup. For a given subgroup, Fall, Midyear, and Spring norms by grade level are provided. There are also special norm tables for interpreting school averages.

A norm group is representative if it is a microcosm of the particular population of interest, such as all public high school students or all Catholic/private high school students. Forms K and L of the ITED were administered in 1991 to almost 14,000 pupils in grades 9–12. The participating school districts were selected to be representative of the U.S. population in terms of district enrollment, geographic region, socioeconomic status, and public versus private affiliation. Of course, representativeness is an ideal that is never totally realized in practice because randomly sampled schools sometimes decline to participate in the standardization process and must be replaced by second or third choices. However, the 1992 standardization sample of the ITED seems to be reasonably representative in terms of district enrollment, geographic region, and the other stratifying variables noted above.

Norms for 1995 are now available, and users can choose to have Forms K, L, and M scored using either 1992 or 1995 norms. The 1995 norms are not based on randomly selected schools, but rather on school districts that have elected to regularly use the ITED as part of their testing programs since 1992. Such pupils were used to calculate the average change in test performance between 1992 and 1995, and the cumulative change since 1992 is incorporated into the 1995 norms. This procedure assumes no interaction exists between the characteristics of regular users of the ITED and nonusers. The publisher claims that the 1995 norms are "relatively free from the influence of major differences in the score levels of users and nonusers of the tests" (p. v). Further evidence of this fact is needed.

SUMMARY. The Iowa Tests of Educational Development continue a long tradition of excellence. They represent valid tests of the general verbal and numerical abilities that high school students need in adult life. Estimates of the reliability of scores are generally satisfactory for most of the recommended uses. The 1992 norms are clearly recent, reasonably representative, and relevant for a number of different subgroup comparisons. As such, the ITED is one of the best alternatives available for testing high school achievement.

[161]
Iowa Tests of Music Literacy, Revised.

Purpose: Assesses "a student's comparative strengths and weaknesses in six dimensions of tonal and rhythm audiation and notational audiation" and compares these scores to the student's "music aptitude."
Population: Grades 4–12.
Publication Dates: 1970–1991.
Scores, 9: Tonal Concepts (Audiation/Listening, Audiation/Reading, Audiation/Writing, Total), Rhythm Concepts (Audiation/Listening, Audiation/Reading, Audiation/Writing, Total), Total.

Administration: Group.
Price Data, 1993: $295 per complete kit for all six levels including manual, six cassette tapes, 50 answer sheets, six record folders, and scoring masks; $75 per complete kit for one level (specify level) including manual, one cassette tape, scoring masks, 50 answer sheets, and 6 record folders; $8 per 50 tonal answer sheets; $8 per 50 rhythm answer sheets; $15 per 50 cumulative record folders; $3 per 6 class record sheets; $15 per manual; $15 per cassette tape (specify level).
Time: 36(45) minutes for Tonal Concepts; 36(45) minutes for Rhythm Concepts.
Author: Edwin E. Gordon.
Publisher: G.I.A. Publications, Inc.
Cross References: For a review by Paul R. Lehman of an earlier edition, see 8:97 (16 references); see also T2:199 (5 references) and 7:245 (2 references).

Review of the Iowa Tests of Music Literacy, Revised by RUDOLF E. RADOCY, Professor, Division of Music Education and Music Therapy, University of Kansas, Lawrence, KS:

PURPOSE. Edwin Gordon calls the Iowa Tests of Music Literacy (ITML) a basic achievement test. "Basic achievement" encompasses "audiation," the ability to comprehend musical stimuli in the absence of immediate sound. A person may audiate music in recalling previously heard tonal material, over a long term or a short term. Gordon views tonal and rhythmic audiation skills as basic to musical aptitude and achievement, and the ITML purportedly assesses basic listening, reading, and notating skills that are prerequisites for more sophisticated musical achievements. The tests are *not* tests of "literacy" in the sense of familiarity with music literature or conventions of musical interpretation.

The 1991 edition is a revision of the 1970 edition. The new version uses cassette rather than reel-to-reel recordings, a different answer sheet format, and different names for the test subsections. The auditory stimulus material is identical, and reliability, validity, and norms are based on the standardization sample for the 1970 version.

TEST CONTENT. The test battery contains two major sections, "Tonal Concepts" and "Rhythm Concepts." Each major section includes three subsections: "Audiation/Listening," "Audiation/Reading," and "Audiation/Writing." Each subsection exists at six sequential levels. Levels 1, 2, and 3 have sets of norms for grades 4-5-6, 7-8-9, and 10-11-12. The upper three levels have sets of norms for grades 7-8-9 and 10-11-12. The test levels are administratively independent; testing at one level is not a prerequisite for testing at any other level. Gordon recommends administering the "Tonal Concepts" section first, and administering the "Rhythm Concepts" section at another time during the same week. Each section requires 45 minutes for each level. As a convenience, the answer sheets, cassettes, and scoring masks are color coded for each level.

In the "Tonal Concepts: Audiation/Listening" (TC A/L) subsections, the student's basic task is to identify what Gordon calls tonality, which is what most musicians call mode. (Tonality customarily refers to organization around a tonal center to which other tones in the musical section relate. [Gordon prefers the term "keyality."] Mode refers to a pattern of whole and half steps comprising the scale upon which tonal music is built. "In what key is the music?" customarily is a question of tonality. "Is it major, minor, or some other scale organization?" is a question of mode.) The stimulus patterns are limited to major and harmonic minor modes at Levels 1 and 2; the student classifies each pattern as major or minor. At Level 3, the stimuli include dorian, phrygian, lydian, mixolydian, aeolian, and locrian modes as well as major and harmonic minor; the student responds with "yes" if the pattern is in either major *or* harmonic minor mode, or with "no" if the pattern is in neither target mode. The task remains the same at Level 4, but the stimulus material becomes more complex because it includes atonal patterns (which Gordon calls "multitonal"). At Levels 5 and 6, the student classifies each pattern as being in a major or in a harmonic minor mode. The stimuli are two-part major and minor tonal patterns for Level 5; Level 6's patterns have chordal accompaniment. At all levels, the student is encouraged to use an "in doubt" response if he or she is unsure of the answer.

For "Tonal Concepts: Audiation/Reading" (TC A/R) the basic task is to evaluate whether what is seen represents what is heard. At all levels, the student indicates "yes" if the printed notation matches the sounds, "no" if it does not, and a "?" if the student is uncertain. The patterns at Levels 1 and 2 are limited to major or harmonic minor; notation uses only the C major/A minor key signature (no sharps or flats) and the treble clef. Level 3's patterns include the additional modes found in Level 3 of TC A/L as well as pentatonic scales; notation remains in the treble clef but may employ key signatures with as many as three sharps or flats. Notation is limited identically in Level 4, but the tonal patterns are in major or harmonic minor modes or are atonal. Level 5's patterns are in two parts and may be major or

harmonic minor. Notation includes treble and bass clefs, with key signatures of up to three sharps or flats. At Level 6, major and harmonic patterns have chordal accompaniments. The corresponding notation employs treble and bass clefs as well as chord symbols; key signatures lack any sharps or flats.

"Tonal Concepts: Audiation/Writing" (TC A/W) asks the student to complete partially printed notation patterns to portray what he or she hears. The student must ignore answer spaces that are not required to portray the tonal sequence. Levels 1 through 5 employ single line patterns; the sixth level employs two-part patterns. Major and harmonic minor modes occur at all levels; Levels 5 and 6 also include atonal patterns. No sharps or flats occur in key signatures at the first, second, and sixth levels; Levels 3 and 4 employ up to three sharps or flats; Level 5 patterns use no more than one sharp or flat. Levels 1, 2, 3, and 6 employ the treble clef exclusively. Both the treble and the bass clef occur at Level 5. Level 4 is exclusively bass clef.

Whereas the "Tonal Concepts" section stimuli are sequences of synthesized tones, the stimuli in the "Rhythm Concepts" section are sequences of click-like sounds, accompanied by clicks of a slightly lower frequency and different timbre that mark "macro" beats. (What Gordon calls a "macro" beat is what most musicians would call the felt beat or *Takt*. In many musical instances, the felt beat and the notated beat are equivalent: The number of beats felt in a measure are equal to the number of notated beats. With faster or slower tempi, the felt beats may be more or less frequent: In an *adagio* 4/4 meter passage, as found in some concerti of the Classical Era, a performer might feel it and a conductor might conduct it in 8/8 meter. In an *allergro* 3/4 passage, as in a fast Viennese waltz, the felt beat likely would be one to a measure. The characteristic "swing" of a 6/8 march comes from the feeling of two beats per measure.)

In the "Rhythm Concepts: Audiation/Listening" subsections (RC A/L), the student must evaluate meter. For Levels 1 and 2, the student classifies each pattern as duple or triple meter. The stimuli are in "usual" duple or triple meter. (Gordon classifies meter as "usual duple," "usual triple," "usual combined," and "unusual." A duple-triple classification is common in standard musical vocabulary: meters that feel as if they move in twos [e.g., 2/4, 4/4, 2/2] are duple; meters that feel as if they move in threes [e.g., 3/4, 3/8] are triple. Gordon's use of the subdivision of the beat as a basis for classification is peculiar; most musicians classify meter as duple or triple on the basis of felt beats. For Gordon, 6/8 at a march tempo is triple meter; for most musicians, that is duple meter. The "usual-unusual" classification has no parallel in standard vocabulary, other than [possibly] frequency of occurrence. A "usual combined" meter is a compound meter [i.e., a meter such as 9/8 or 12/8 where the number of notated beats in a measure is multiple of 3 or 2, although 6/8 meter, a compound meter, often is a "usual triple" meter in Gordon's system]. An "unusual" meter is a mixed meter combination of duple and triple, such as 5/4 or 7/8.) Level 3 asks the student to indicate "yes" if the pattern is in either "usual" duple or "usual" triple meter, and "no" if the pattern is in neither. The stimuli are in "usual" duple, triple, and "combined" meters. At Level 4, the stimuli include "unusual" meters in addition to "usual" duple and triple meters; the student indicates "yes" for the "usual" forms and "no" for the "unusual" forms. Levels 5 and 6 require the student to indicate "yes" if the meter is a "usual combined" and "no" if it is not. The stimuli at Level 5 include "unusual" as well as "usual combined" meters. At all levels, the student is supposed to indicate a question mark if he or she is uncertain about the classification.

In the "Rhythm Concepts: Audiation/Reading" subsections (RC A/R), the student indicates whether or not the printed notation matches what is heard. Again, an in doubt response is available. Levels 1 and 2 employ the 2/4 and 6/8 meter signatures ("usual" duple and "usual" [for Gordon] triple). At Level 3, the signatures are 2/4, 4/4 (in the numerical and C form), and 2/2 ("usual" duple); 3/4, 3/8, and 6/8 ("usual" triple); and 6/4 ("combined"). Levels 4 and 5 employ the "usual" duple meters 2/4, 4/4, and 2/2; the "usual" triple meters 3/4, 3/8, 6/8, and 9/8; and the "unusual" meters 5/8, 7/8, and 11/8. Level 6's meters are 2/4, 3/4, 4/4 (as C), 6/4, 3/8, 5/8, 6/8, 7/8, 9/8, 11/8, and 2/2. These are, according to the manual (p. 15), "usual combined" and "unusual" meters; a meter that is simply "usual" in other subsections may be "combined" due to differences in the felt beat.

As with its parallel in the "Tonal Concepts" section, the "Rhythm Concepts: Audiation/Writing" (RC A/W) subsection requires the student to complete partially printed notation patterns, in this case by filling in spaces for noteheads, beams, flags, ties, or rests. The student must ignore answer spaces that are unnecessary to portray the rhythm. The first three levels employ 2/4 and 6/8 meter signatures.

(Gordon calls meter signatures "measure" signatures, perhaps in recognition of how the felt beat of identical notated meter signatures may vary with tempo.) Level 4 uses 2/4, 3/4, 4/4, 6/4, 3/8, 6/8, and 2/2 (in both the numerical and the "cut-time" form). The upper two levels use 3/4, 5/8, 7/8, 8/8, 9/8, and 11/8.

SCORES AND NORMS. Scoring, which must be done by hand, requires using four scoring masks at each level. In the TC A/L, TC A/R, RC A/L, and A/R subsections, the student's raw score is the number of pencil marks that appear in the scoring mask's appropriate windows. The raw score is converted to a standard score in accordance with a table.

Scoring the TC A/W and RC A/W subsections requires two separate overlays of scoring masks. The student receives credit for each correctly ignored blank notation segment as well as each correctly blackened notation segment, so the scorer must first count the number of correctly filled spaces in accordance with one scoring mask and then count the number of correctly *unfilled* spaces in accordance with another mask. The scorer sums the correctly filled and correctly unfilled scores; that sum is converted to a standard score.

The standard scores for TC A/L, TC A/R, and TC A/W may be combined into a TC section standard score. Similarly, the corresponding RC subsection standard scores may be combined into an RC standard score. The section standard scores may be combined into a composite standard score.

The nine standard scores obtainable from administration of any complete ITML level—six subsection scores, two section scores, one composite score—may be expressed as a percentile rank. Separate percentile rank norms exist for grades 4-5-6, 7-8-9, and 10-11-12 for the lower three levels, and for grades 7-8-9 and 10-11-12 for the upper three levels.

Gordon derived the 1970 version's standard scores and percentile ranks from a national sample of 18,680 students in grades 4 through 12, enrolled in 27 school systems in 27 states. The 1970 standardization is simply reused for the 1991 ITML. The manual (p. 58) states four reasons for not restandardizing the new edition: One is the absence of longitudinal norms. Although Gordon had hoped to follow many of the original standardization sample through school to develop longitudinal norms, that did not happen, and he did not believe a new set of cross-sectional norms was "prudent." Second, Gordon claims that music curricula have not changed in 20 years. Third, the ITML is intended to compare students with one another rather than school districts, so school districts should develop local norms. Finally, because the new version has hand scoring rather than machine scoring, allegedly done to make a more readable answer sheet, the amount of test scoring required by a standardization program would be prohibitively expensive.

RELIABILITY AND VALIDITY. According to the 1970 ITML standardization data, split-halves reliability coefficients, corrected by the Spearman-Brown prophecy formula, range from .70 through .88 for individual "Tonal Concepts" subsections, and from .70 through .85 for individual "Rhythm Concepts" subsections. Respective reliability ranges for combined "Tonal Concepts," combined "Rhythm Concepts," and the composite ITML are .80–.92, .80–.90, and .87–.94.

Content validity is presumed on the basis of the skills and knowledge necessary for doing well on the test. The manual cites various studies by Gordon's students as evidence of the 1970 version's experimental or criterion-related validity.

OVERALL EVALUATION. The ITML is a narrow measure of musical achievement, an achievement that combines specific skills requiring short-term tonal and rhythm memory, knowledge of certain vocabulary, and ability to read music. As the manual makes abundantly clear, the ITML is rooted firmly in Gordon's theories and is a measure of audiation skills. Whether this truly is musical literacy is questionable, although one could argue that any skill involving reading music and classifying it is some part of literacy. Using the test requires accepting Gordon's nonstandard vocabulary as well as his belief in audiation's importance. For a school system not using Gordon's *Jump Right In* music curriculum to use the ITML would be foolish.

Edwin Gordon firmly believes in his particular theories of instruction, musical aptitude, and musical ability. The ITML is one part of the total package, which includes his Primary (T4:2099), Intermediate (T4: 1249), and Advanced Measures of Musical Audiation (12:22), his Musical Aptitude Profile (12:251), his curriculum, and a sequentially ordered set of musical patterns. If a person advocates the Gordon approach, there is a place for the ITML.

The test's technical quality is mixed. Exhaustive statistics (albeit based on the first edition) and clear directions abound in the comprehensive manual. Exact instructions for administering and scoring the test are clear. The quality of the tapes is questionable; this reviewer was annoyed by "print through" from the Tonal

side while listening to the Rhythm side. A noticeable hiss is annoying. The cassettes may have been duplicated from long-stored master reel-to-reel tapes, subject to such problems. The Level 1 cassette's sides are mislabeled—the Tonal test is on the Rhythm side, and vice versa. The scoring procedure, although explicitly clear, is quite time-consuming and subject to mechanical errors.

In short, the ITML is valid as part of a particular belief. Despite technical shortcomings and the questionable use of nonstandard musical vocabulary, the true believer may be justified in using the test. Otherwise, the test is a reissue of a historical curiosity.

[162]
Jackson Personality Inventory—Revised.

Purpose: Designed to produce "a set of measures of personality reflecting a variety of interpersonal, cognitive, and value orientations."

Population: Adolescents and adults.

Publication Dates: 1976–1994.

Acronym: JPI-R.

Scores: 15 scales in 5 clusters; Analytical (Complexity, Breadth of Interest, Innovation, Tolerance), Emotional (Empathy, Anxiety, Cooperativeness), Extroverted (Sociability, Social Confidence, Energy Level), Opportunistic (Social Astuteness, Risk Taking), Dependable (Organization, Traditional Values, Responsibility).

Administration: Group.

Price Data, 1996: $59 per examination kit including manual ('94, 138 pages), 10 reusable test booklets, 25 answer sheets, 25 profile sheets, and one JPI-R Basic Report; $28 per 25 reusable test booklets; $17 per 25 answer sheets; $9.50 per 25 profile sheets; $6 per Basic Report; $99 per Sigma Soft trial package including 10 computer administrations (specify 5.25-inch or 3.5-inch disk); $175 per Sigma Soft full package including 25 computer administrations (specify 5.25-inch or 3.5-inch disk); $130 per renewal password including 25 computer administrations.

Foreign Language Edition: Available in French (booklets only).

Time: (35–45) minutes.

Author: Douglas N. Jackson.

Publisher: Sigma Assessment Systems, Inc.

Cross References: See T4:1296 (28 references) and T3:1203 (6 references); for reviews of an earlier edition by Lewis R. Goldberg and David T. Lykken, see 8:593 (6 references).

TEST REFERENCES

1. Arolio, B. J., & Barrett, G. V. (1987). Effects of age stereotyping in a simulated interview. *Psychology and Aging, 2*, 56-63.

2. Osborn, D. R. (1988). Personality traits expressed: Interior design as behavior-setting plan. *Personality and Social Psychology Bulletin, 14*, 368-373.

3. Ackerman, R. J. (1990). Career developments and transitions of middle-aged women. *Psychology of Women Quarterly, 14*, 513-530.

4. Howell, J. M., & Higgins, C. A. (1990). Champions of technological innovation. *Administrative Science Quarterly, 35*, 317-341.

5. Tett, R. P., & Jackson, D. N. (1990). Organization and personality correlates of participative behaviours using an in-basket exercise. *Journal of Occupational Psychology, 63,* 175-188.

6. Cornell, D. G., Callahan, C. M., & Loyd, B. H. (1991). Socioemotional adjustment of adolescent girls enrolled in a residential acceleration program. *Gifted Child Quarterly, 35,* 58-66.

7. Fish, M., Stifter, C. A., & Belsky, J. (1991). Conditions of continuity and discontinuity in infant negative emotionality: Newborn to five months. *Child Development, 62,* 1525–1537.

8. MacIntyre, P. D., & Gardner, R. C. (1991). Methods and results in the study of anxiety and language learning: A review of the literature. *Language Learning, 41,* 85–117.

9. Volling, B. L., & Belsky, J. (1991). Multiple determinants of father involvement in dual-earner and single-earner families. *Journal of Marriage and the Family, 53,* 461–474.

10. Volling, B. L., & Belsky, J. (1993). Parent, infant, and contextual characteristics related to maternal employment decisions in the first year of infancy. *Family Relations, 42,* 4-12.

11. Craig, J., Koestner, R., & Zuroff, D. C. (1994). Implicit and self-attributed intimacy motivation. *Journal of Social and Personal Relationships, 11,* 491-507.

12. Haverkamp, B. E. (1994). Using assessment in counseling supervision: Individual differences in self-monitoring. *Measurement and Evaluation in Counseling and Development, 27,* 316-324.

13. Lancaster, S. J., Colarelli, S. M., King, D. W., & Beehr, T. A. (1994). Job applicant similarity on cognitive ability, vocational interests, and personality characteristics: Do similar persons choose similar jobs? *Educational and Psychological Measurement, 54,* 299-316.

14. Lay, C. H. (1994). Trait procrastination and affective experiences: Describing past study behavior and its relation to agitation and dejection. *Motivation and Emotion, 18,* 269–284.

15. O'Leary, K. D., Malone, J., & Tyree, A. (1994). Physical aggression in early marriage: Prerelationship and relationship effects. *Journal of Consulting and Clinical Psychology, 62,* 594-602.

16. Pratto, F., Sidanius, J., Stallworth, L. M., & Malle, B. F. (1994). Social dominance orientation: A personality variable predicting social and political attitudes. *Journal of Personality and Social Psychology, 67,* 741-763.

17. Stice, E., & Shaw, H. E. (1994). Adverse effects of the media portrayed thin-ideal on women and linkages to bulimic symptomatology. *Journal of Social and Clinical Psychology, 13,* 288–308.

18. Belsky, J., Crnic, K., & Gable, S. (1995). The determinants of coparenting in families with toddler boys: Spousal differences and daily hassles. *Child Development, 66,* 629-642.

19. Wolfe, R. N., & Johnson, S. D. (1995). Personality as a predictor of college performance. *Educational and Psychological Measurement, 55,* 177-185.

20. Kashy, D. A., & DePaulo, B. M. (1996). Who lies? *Journal of Personality and Social Psychology, 70,* 1037–1051.

21. Shrauger, J. S., Ram, D., Greninger, S. A., & Mariano, E. (1996). Accuracy of self-prediction versus judgments by knowledgeable others. *Personality and Social Psychology Bulletin, 22,* 1229–1243.

Review of the Jackson Personality Inventory— Revised by DAVID J. PITTENGER, Associate Professor of Psychology, Marietta College, Marietta, OH:

Much has changed since 1976 in personality research and measurement. Notably, the advances in theory and measurement technology have softened the pejorative sting evoked by Mischel's (1968) concept of the personality coefficient. Among these advances, the development of the "Big-Five" concept has done much to renew enthusiasm for and confidence in personality measurement and research. On the surface, it would appear that the Jackson Personality Inventory (JPI-R) has evolved much in the 20 years since it was first published. Upon closer inspection, however, this revision seems to be another example of putting an old wine, of dubious vintage, into a new bottle. Although the test boasts revised scale names, a Big-Five format, new normative data, and an expanded research base, the test appears to suffer the same criticisms raised by Goldberg and Lykken (8:593) in their reviews of the first edition of the instrument. Essentially, there is scant evidence that the instrument measures the constructs it claims to measure, or that the constructs afford useful descriptions of behavior.

The JPI-R consists of 300 true-false statements. As in the earlier version of the inventory, these questions represent 15 separate personality traits. According to the manual, factor analysis of the data identified five major trait categories. The five major trait categories and their constituent components are: (a) Analytical, which includes Complexity, Breadth of Interest, Innovation, and Tolerance; (b) Emotional, which includes Empathy, Anxiety, and Cooperativeness; (c) Extroverted, which includes Sociability, Social Confidence, and energy Level; (d) Opportunistic, which includes Social Astuteness and Risk Taking; and (e) Dependable, which includes Organization, Traditional Values, and Responsibility. Each of the 15 scales consists of 20 items with an equal number of true and false keyed items. The inventory uses essentially the same questions from the first edition of the test. The exceptions are that the original validity scale was removed and several of the items in the Traditional Value scale were revised.

The manual is clear that the JPI-R was not designed for the assessment of persons with severe mental health disorders. Instead, the test serves as a general purpose personality inventory to be used with normal individuals. One of the primary recommended uses of the JPI-R is as a part of career and vocational counseling where one wishes to match a person's personality with a specific job. In addition, the author of the JPI-R recommends the instrument as a research tool. The inventory can be administered to high-school-aged and older individuals.

On the surface, the test appears to be easy to administer and score. The questions are unambiguous, and a carbonless scoring template facilitates rapid scoring of the instrument. The 15 content scales have familiar sounding names that appear to represent useful personality dimensions and the five-factor structure makes the test appear to be a member of the new generation of personality inventories. A deeper reading of the manual reveals that there is precious little to warrant the expense of using this test. Reviewing the manual quickly becomes a task of listing what is missing rather than critiquing what is present.

To begin, there are no true reliability data. The manual offers no information concerning the temporal stability of the instrument's test scores. The only reliability information provided is Cronbach's coefficient alphas and Bentler's theta, which are measures of internal consistency. Although such information is useful, they do not speak to the broader and extremely important issue of test-retest reliability. Unfortunately, the error is compounded when the coefficient alphas are converted to standard errors of measurement. This statistic is misleading because it does not represent random variation due to the passage of time. One would have hoped that in the past 20 years more convincing and essential data would have been collected and reported.

Data that attest to the construct validity are also noticeably absent. As with the previous version of the inventory, there is little rationale for the selection of the 15 personality traits. There is, however, a lengthy section describing a factor analytic study of the JPI-R and evidence to suggest that the 15 scales can be summarized by five primary personality dimensions. The manual notes that, based on the names of the individual traits, the JPI-R shares much in common with conventional measures of the Big-Five. The exceptions appear to be that the Emotional dimension embodies both Neuroticism and Agreeableness, and that the Opportunistic dimension is unique to the JPI-R. Again, there is a conspicuous absence of empirical evidence to verify these claims and there are no data to demonstrate that the JPI-R is qualitatively or quantitatively different from other Big-Five measures of personality. Although the Big-Five characterization of the JPI-R is in keeping with the current trends in personality measurement, the retention of the 15 individual constituent traits appears anachronistic. At the very least, it appears that the JPI-R violates Ockham's request that we not make distinctions beyond necessity.

Perhaps the most egregious error of omission is a clear demonstration that the JPI-R measures anything of relevance or consequence. Considering the fact that the instrument is marketed as a tool to help in career counseling, one would expect some shard of evidence that there is a meaningful relation between the measured personality traits and career selection. There is no attempt to demonstrate a meaningful link between personality profiles and various professions. Without normative data or an explicit theoretical guide, it is difficult to determine how one offers reasonable career advice using the results of the test.

The manual reports several modest, small-sample-size, correlational studies examining the relationship between the JPI-R and other assessment devices. The selection of tests is odd, however. For example, the test is compared to the Minnesota Multiphasic Personality Inventory. Given that the reader is told that the JPI-R is not designed for diagnosis of pathology, one must question the relevance of the data. There are also data relating the JPI-R and other career inventories including the Survey of Work Styles and the Jackson Vocational Interest Survey. The correlations are modest at best, and reveal no definitive rationale for why one would use the JPI-R as an alternative to these instruments. More specifically, there is no evidence that the instrument is capable of successfully matching people with jobs.

The manual contains several tables that describe the essential features of each of the 15 traits. There are also many case studies that are said to represent prototypical profiles one might find using the JPI-R. For example, there is a profile for an outstanding teacher, a suicidal student, a good nurse, and a student doing poorly in school. Although these are interesting case studies, there is no empirical evidence that these profiles are truly representative of similar cases. These cases represent little more than anecdotal instances with no empirical support.

In summary, the JPI-R has evolved little since its initial development and publication. Although the current manual appears to offer more information than the first edition, one is still left with more questions than answers about the utility and validity of this instrument. Essentially, the JPI-R offers little to suggest that it has kept pace with the times and emerged from the shadow of the personality coefficient.

REVIEWER'S REFERENCE

Mischel, W. (1968). *Personality and assessment.* New York: Wiley.

Review of the Jackson Personality Inventory— Revised by PETER ZACHAR, Assistant Professor of Psychology, Auburn University at Montgomery, Montgomery, AL:

The Jackson Personality Inventory—Revised (JPI-R) is the second edition of a test designed to measure normal personality functioning for use in schools, colleges, and universities. Its clinical application is geared toward traditional counseling psychology settings, particularly career counseling and personnel selection in industry. The 15 scales on the JPI-R are supposed to help clinicians predict future behavior. For example, knowing that a person is extremely low on a trait such as tolerance or empathy might make us reluctant to suggest that they pursue a career in social work.

The JPI-R is the product of Douglas Jackson, who has popularized what is often called a "rational" test construction strategy. In contrast to relying on actuarial-based decision making to select items, the rational strategy holds that using human judgment to select items is compatible with psychometric validity. In this view, it does not matter how items and constructs are *discovered*, what is important is how they are *justified*. As long as we can demonstrate reliability and validity, the test is a good one whether or not it was created using purely statistical decision making all the way through.

In Jackson's model, construct validity is developed by means of careful item selection aimed at making scales as unique as possible and avoiding the problems of acquiescent response sets and conceptual redundancy. The details of how this was accomplished for the JPI-R are provided in the manual. Some advantages that can be expected from a Jackson-created test are very easy scoring and a straightforward presentation of the results. Jackson's tests have been developed to compete with the major tests used by psychologists working with nonpsychiatric populations and ease of use has been one of his selling points. He does not disappoint with the JPI-R. It is extremely easy to score and conversion of raw scores to a profile is painless.

IMPROVEMENTS IN THE REVISED EDITION. Both the test and the new manual are arguably superior in their revised norms. The most important improvement is the organization of the 15 scales into five conceptually integrated clusters. These clusters are Analytic, Emotional, Extroverted, Opportunistic, and Dependable. Although it would be rather grandiose to call them the "big five," they do make the interpretation of results easier. Within each cluster, several of the 15 original scales have been renamed to better reflect the construct being measured. For example, what was formerly called "Interpersonal Affect" is now called "Empathy."

The test has also been shortened by removal of the 20-item infrequency scale. Jackson believes that the advantage of reducing the test by 20 items outweighs the disadvantage of not having an infrequency scale. Although the manual provides an alternative strategy for assessing infrequency, the directions are complicated and the calculation is time-consuming. Rules for assigning meaning to the infrequency index are also missing. The manual also addresses the issue of faking, which is important in personnel selection settings, but practical advice for actually detecting faking is absent.

Some important additions have been made to the manual itself. One of the concerns expressed in previous reviews was a lack of information on internal consistency. The manual now reports both Cronbach's alpha and Bentler's theta for the 15 basic scales. Although one might have expected them to be higher given that internal consistency is a goal of Jackson's test development methodology, they appear to be reasonably adequate (i.e., alphas generally in the .70s and .80s).

Two new aids to interpretation are also included in the edition of the test. The first is a listing of items for each scale in Appendix A of the manual. These lists can help interpreters learn how to think about each scale, providing an opportunity to go beyond basing interpretations solely on cookbook adjective lists.

The second aid is the availability of computer scoring and interpretation. These methods cut down on the work of the interpreter. Furthermore, the ability of the user to obtain information on scales that are not easy to score by hand (such as infrequency) is greatly enhanced. I was not provided the computer software so have limited information on its use. I was provided with one copy of a computer-generated report. It is as presentable as most PC-generated computer reports. It furnishes interpretive hypotheses for extreme scores on each of the 15 scales and the five clusters, but does not provide information for people who score in the average range. Although the report is written for the person taking the test, the explanation of percentiles may be overly technical for the typical test taker. A summary personality description similar to those included in other computer-generated reports is also missing.

Another addition to the current manual is presentation of evidence that the scores are normally distributed, which is important if results are going to be reported as standardized scores, like the T-scores used in the JPI-R. Jackson's numerical estimates of skewness and kurtosis indicate that the scores are probably normally distributed in the population. Finally, two new sets of norms have been added to supplement the norms for high school and college students. The new norms are for blue collar workers and white collar executives. Although new norms were also collected for college students, it does not appear that they were collected for high school students.

AREAS FOR IMPROVEMENT. One problem with the last edition of the manual was a failure to report test-retest reliabilities. This omission has not been corrected. Jackson's observation that means and standard deviations have remained stable for 20 years is not an adequate replacement for test-retest reliability. Measures of traits have little value if they cannot be shown to be stable.

Even though the five clusters make an excellent addition, it would help to know their psychometric properties. If they are going to be used in interpretation, they should also have demonstrated reliability and construct validity. These "clusters" were derived in a factor analysis and the factor solution looks like a clean one. A replication on another sample (at least) would increase my confidence in it.

Information on the validity of the test as a clinical assessment instrument is still lacking. It clearly has research potential, but more data on its ability to discriminate between groups and make predictions about specific behaviors would be helpful. This is particularly true for the Social Astuteness and Tolerance scales, which have more troubled reliability and validity than the other scales on the test.

One of the least convincing aspects of the manual is the discussion of modal profiles, which is an attempt to come up with a JPI-R typology. Unfortunately, the modal profile analysis is purely promissory. As a possible competitor to John Holland's (1978) vocational typology or even the Myers-Briggs typology, my optimism about its chances is muted for the simple reason that the JPI-R modal types do not make intuitive sense. Even if the modal profiles can be shown to distinguish between types of people, after empirical concerns are addressed, parsimony and catchiness are as responsible as anything else for a typology's usefulness. The ultimate value of modal profiles will probably involve actuarial rather than intuitive applications. Complex computer algorithms can determine if a person meets criteria for a modal profile. Then and only then, computers can suggest a personality description.

When he originally developed the JPI, reviewers criticized Jackson for lacking a theoretical rationale in choosing certain constructs. Jackson claimed that the constructs were derived from research in personality and social psychology, but he failed to provide specific references. The revised manual also indicates that some scales were created based on Dr. Jackson's personal opinion regarding their potential usefulness. Criticisms of this shortcoming, however, may have been overblown. As stated, the philosophical premise of the rational construction approach is that it does not matter how constructs are discovered, what matters is how they are justified.

Some critics also questioned whether these constructs are justified. For example, in a previous review, David Lykken (8:593) expressed a concern that these scales were not natural kinds, that they did not "carve nature at her joints." Even if that is true, the same could be said for the MMPI, the CPI, and most categories of the DSM-IV. If we take this kind of scientific realism as seriously as philosophers of science do, then the explanatory constructs of "folk psychology" (i.e., beliefs, desires, and intentions) are not natural kinds either (Churchland, 1989; Dennett, 1987). We should allow Jackson the same constructivist liberties as any proponent of psychological explanation. The immediate questions pertinent to the value of the JPI-R are conceptual and pragmatic, not ontological.

Unfortunately, lingering conceptual problems about what the JPI-R is measuring have not been eliminated. I think some scale names may be misleading. For example, if we take the Dependability cluster at its face value, creative, liberal, and educated people are undependable whereas moralism and rigidity are associated with dependability. One implication of using the JPI-R as a personnel selection instrument might be that it supports the development of an authoritarian corporate culture. At the very least, decisions about naming scales could be made more public, with advantages and disadvantages of the eventual names listed.

My major difficulty with the JPI-R concerns the attempt by personality test developers like Dr. Jackson to sell their tests as measures of normal personality as opposed to psychopathology. They do this by making an assumption that a categorical distinction can be made between the two. Although there are advantages to positively reframing certain psychiatric categories, such as calling psychopathic deviance "rebelliousness," suggesting that a personality test like the JPI-R does not tap pathology is untenable. For example, individuals taking this test can be labeled narrow, unimaginative, intolerant, dogmatic, prejudiced, cold, agitated, fearful, withdrawn, egotistical, lazy, moralistic, and rigid, to name a few. These adjectives do not conform to most psychologists' models of mental health.

Although not psychiatric syndromes, these traits can be reliable indicators of them, irrespective of what kind of test we are using. More important, there is no reason why a test like this would not be informative with respect to psychiatric populations. For example, a person with paranoid schizophrenia who is high on cognitive complexity is going to look very different from someone with the same disorder who is concrete and literal.

Dysfunctional and inflexible personality styles are not going to be limited to the study of ostensibly psychiatric populations. The reason personality psychologists need to address issues of pathology is not so that they can apply the right name to a person's *problem*, but rather just the opposite, so that they understand the limits of the labels—and educate test users about those limits. Only with the greatest effort will dysfunctional labels be avoidable when using a dimensional model of personality. Because this test is more and more geared toward employment settings, this issue needs to be addressed in the manual. Dr. Jackson may want to consider undertaking the task of typing to reframe positively all his adjectives, or address the issue of how users can think about the more dysfunctional adjectives.

My final concern about the JPI-R involves the writers' indecisiveness about the manual's intended audience. They could not decide if they were writing for an audience of psychometricians or for an audience of masters' level counselors and personnel directors. With respect to the second audience, including a glossary of technical terms was an excellent idea. Unfortunately, the definitions are so technical that most people who need to look them up will not be able to understand them. The best example of writing consistently to the second audience is found in the section on administration guidelines. These basic how-to instructions help insure the proper use of the test, no matter what the user's educational background. As with the administration guidelines section, any section of the manual written for the second audience should take comprehendibility into account.

CONCLUSIONS. Douglas Jackson has an excellent reputation in the counseling profession and this test is going to be used. Students will find it attractive for theses and dissertations. Counselors will be attracted to the nonpsychiatric focus, even though more information about its clinical utility is needed. Its psychometric properties are adequate. The personality scales are not anything special, but they are as good as many other personality scales. If this test represents a typical instrument used by mental health professionals, rethinking some of its characteristics using the sophistication of both traditional clinical and contemporary counseling psychology with respect to pathology would be beneficial. Even is one does not focus on psychiatric syndromes, studying the range of personality will still tap aspects of psychopathology.

REVIEWER'S REFERENCES

Dennett, D. C. (1987). *The intentional stance.* Cambridge, MA: The MIT Press.

Churchland, P. M. (1989). *A neurocomputational perspective: The nature of mind and structure of science.* Cambridge, MA: The MIT Press.

[163]
Job Search Inventory.

Purpose: "To help the job applicant choose realistic occupations for a job search based on a consideration of background and interests."
Population: Job applicants.
Publication Date: 1985.
Acronym: JSI.
Scores, 5: 4 ratings (Interest, Leisure, Training, Work) and Total for each work activity.
Administration: Group.
Price Data: Available from publisher.
Time: (20–60) minutes.
Comments: "For use with the occupational classification structure of the Guide for Occupational Exploration."
Author: New York State Employment Service.
Publisher: U.S. Department of Labor.

Review of the Job Search Inventory by RALPH O. MUELLER, Associate Professor of Educational Research, Department of Educational Leadership, Graduate School of Education and Human Development, The George Washington University, Washington, DC:

The Job Search Inventory (JSI) is an 81-item self-scoring instrument designed to aid job applicants in choosing employment according to their interest, leisure activities, prior training, and work experiences. It must be used in conjunction with information from the fourth edition of the *Guide for Occupational Exploration* (published by the same authors) to match obtained JSI scores to one of 66 work groups in the Guide. Two forms of the JSI are available, one designed to be used directly with the Guide, the other accompanied with an information sheet summarizing the identified work groups; according to the authors, each form should take about 50 minutes to complete.

Materials accompanying the JSI consist of a self-scoring form and an instruction sheet for administrators of the instrument. The strength of the instrument and the scoring forms is that they are both written clearly and, indeed, are self-explanatory to the job applicant. A major weakness, however, is that the information provided to administrators is insufficient. For example, no rationale is given for the incorporated items (except that they are supposed to be "typical of the occupations within a specific Work Group and unique to that Work Group" [Instruction Sheet]). Most serious, no evidence of the validity and reliability of the JSI is available. This is in clear violation of numerous standards set forth in the *Standards for Educational and Psychological Testing* (American Educational Research Association, American Psychological Association, & National Council on Measurement in Education, 1985) and should concern the potential user in search of a valid and reliable instrument to assist job applicants.

The test authors claim that completion and interpretation of JSI results "foster a more informed exploration of the occupational options of the applicant" and that it "will help insure a more realistic interpretation of the applicant's relative strengths and weaknesses in relation to occupational requirements and employment opportunities in the local labor market." In this reviewer's opinion, although possibly true for individual cases, empirical evidence should be provided before the potential user trusts this overall claim and confidently selects the JSI for a give population of job applicants.

REVIEWER'S REFERENCE

American Educational Research Association, American Psychological Association, & National Council on Measurement in Education. (1985). *Standards for educational and psychological testing.* Washington, DC: American Psychological Association, Inc.

Review of the Job Search Inventory by SHELDON ZEDECK, Chair and Professor of Psychology, Department of Psychology, University of California, Berkeley, CA:

The Job Search Inventory (JSI) is a self-assessment instrument designed to help a job applicant choose occupations for a job search based on a consideration of the applicant's background and interests. It consists of 81 short task-based statements or job titles such as "carry luggage in a hotel or airport," "settle insurance claims," or "work as a lawyer." The respondent indicates (essentially "yes" or "no") whether he or she (1) would be *interested* in doing this kind of work; (2) has ever done this in his or her *leisure* time; (3) has ever had *training* in the activity; and (4) has ever had *work experience* like the one in the activity. An accompanying document entitled Instructions for Administering and Using the Job Search Inventory informs the user that the 81 items are keyed to 66 Work Groups that compose the *Guide for Occupational Exploration* (this "guide" was not submitted for review by the test publisher nor was it available in this reviewer's library). According to the "Instructions" the "Guide" contains all the defined occupations that are described in the *Dictionary of Occupational Titles* (4th ed.). The JSI enables the applicant to use the Guide to compare his or her personal background factors to general occupational requirements and to select specific occupations for a job search.

After responding to the statements, the applicant self-scores how many of the four questions were responded to in the positive for each statement.

Because each statement is keyed to a "work group," the code of which is provided to the applicant, it is feasible to identify the five highest scoring "work groups." The applicant then reads about the five "work groups" in the "Guide" and selects one for a more specific occupational search.

No psychometric evidence is presented for the instrument. We are not told how the items were chosen, how the items were keyed to the "work groups," and why there is any expected relationship between the results of tallying responses and subsequent job performance or satisfaction. There are no norms, reliability, or validity data.

In summary, there is no way to judge whether the instrument is worth the time to take. There is no prerequisite that there be discussion of the results with any professional; this situation could leave some applicants in a state of greater confusion or uncertainty than prior to taking the inventory. If one wants to find out about potential careers, they are more likely to get better information by taking the Strong Interest Inventory (12:374).

[164]
Job Style Indicator.

Purpose: Analyzes how employers and their staff perceive a job.
Population: Adults.
Publication Date: 1988.
Acronym: JSI.
Scores, 4: Behavioral, Cognitive, Interpersonal, Affective.
Administration: Group.
Price Data, 1993: $6 per test booklet; $35 per leader's manual (80 pages); $15 per audiotape (Living and Working With Style).
Time: (30–60) minutes.
Comments: May be used in conjunction with Personal Style Indicator (228).
Authors: Terry D. Anderson and Everett T. Robinson (JSI and PSI/JSI Leader's Manual), Jonathon Clark and Susan Clark (audiotape).
Publisher: Consulting Resource Group International, Inc.

Review of the Job Style Indicator by NEAL SCHMITT, University Distinguished Professor, Psychology and Management, Department of Psychology, Michigan State University, East Lansing, MI:

The Job Style Indicator (JSI) is designed to assess the nature of job requirements on four dimensions (Behavioral, Cognitive, Interpersonal, and Affective). It is meant to be used in conjunction with the Personal Style Indicator (PSI; 228), which assesses a person's preferences on the same dimensions. Use of these instruments in conjunction with each other is meant to stimulate self-inquiry into what one likes and whether job requirements are such that they match or enhance one's preferred styles of behavior. The instruments are meant to provoke further self-exploration and self-discovery. The JSI dimensions are also thought to match tasks involving data, people, and things as described in the *Dictionary of Occupational Titles* as well as involvement with ideas in the social environment.

A manual that describes the theory underlying the PSI and JSI reviews the major theories in personality and describes how the four dimensions relate to these various theoretical approaches. The manual also claims that the use of these two instruments in conjunction with each other will "enhance the clarity of communication and planning ... can potentially improve morale and performance, decrease conflict and narrow gaps in people's expectations. It may also increase motivation on the job and improve teamwork and cooperation" (manual, p. 3).

Throughout the manual, there are numerous disclaimers regarding the psychometric nature of the instrument. The authors state that the instrument is not intended to produce psychometric evaluations. It is not designed to be predictive; it was never intended to be psychometrically rigorous or scientifically validated. Given the ipsative nature of the measures, these caveats are appropriate. The manual is devoid of any statistical evaluation of the instruments with the exception of one statement that the test-retest reliability of one of the instruments (which one is not specified) was .85 for a sample of 20–25 individuals.

The authors encourage an extensive empirical program of research on these instruments, but also recognize that any research on the instruments will be difficult given the fact that they are ipsative. One cannot use an ipsative measure to make comparative statements about individuals and the use of the usual correlational indices used to evaluate hypotheses about ipsative measures are almost always meaningless.

If one views the use of the JSI and PSI as interventions and takes seriously the claims of the authors cited above, however, there are data one could collect to ascertain whether the use of these measures results in the outcomes the manual's authors claim result from the use of the tests. For example, one would expect increased adjustment, and perhaps less turnover and absenteeism, among job applicants who have examined their own personal style and that demanded of the job as opposed to those applicants who did not engage in such self-

examination. These and other claims made for the use of these instruments have not been evaluated in any systematic manner, though several pieces of anecdotal evidence of the benefits of the use of these instruments are mentioned. It seems the authors of the test should collect and provide such evidence prior to the publication and dissemination of their instrument. The repeated disclaimers regarding the "traditional" assessments of the psychometric adequacy of these tests do not absolve the authors from presentation of evidence that supports claims that they believe are more relevant to their instrument.

The instruments themselves have apparently been revised several times to reflect comments from users about the content, reading level, and appropriateness of the items. The end result appears to be a simple, easy-to-use, and brief measure. Because the JSI represents a theory of personality, or personal style, it is also important that the authors present evidence that the theory explains and is consistent with human behavior and/or consistent with other theory and research. The manual contains an extensive review of the theoretical literature and the authors' statements about the degree to which the instrument reflects these other theories and research. The authors present no data substantiating the degree of correspondence between the constructs suggested by these other theories and their four-dimensional depiction of personal style. In terms of the JSI, it would be interesting to see how the JSI dimensions match dimensions that come out of job analyses. The important question is whether the JSI is capturing the majority of the variance in job demands, or even the important dimensions separating jobs. At this point, no evidence is available.

This is a difficult test to review. No psychometric data or evaluative data are available and the authors claim it is irrelevant. Given the test is ipsative, the authors are correct about the psychometric data. However, if the test is to be used as an intervention, which seems consistent with the authors' claims, other data evaluating the effectiveness of this intervention should be available. Other than the several anecdotes involving human resource professionals' use of the measure, no such data are reported. Users of this instrument should be aware that the only support for the use of this measure lies in the authors' claims and the anecdotal evidence collected from some users of the instrument.

Review of the Job Style Indicator by DAVID M. WILLIAMSON, Psychometrician, The Chauncey Group International, Princeton, NJ:

The Job Style Indicator (JSI) is designed to assist individuals in evaluating the personal style requirements of a particular job to facilitate an appropriate match between the individual and the demands of the job. The JSI is intended to be used in conjunction with the Personal Style Indicator (PSI; 228), with the former providing insight as to the personal style demands of the job and the latter providing insight into an individual's own personal style preferences.

The JSI is presented as a tool for the enhancement of the communication process in selection interviews, performance reviews, and career planning. In this capacity the JSI establishes a common basis (four dimensions of personal style) for discussion between employer or counselor and (potential) employee of the personal style (as opposed to knowledge, skill, and ability) requirements of a job. It is also intended to assist individuals in the process of introspection and comparison of their personal style with the behavioral styles requirements of a particular job. As it is specifically not intended as a screening or selection tool, any results shared by the individual with an employer or counselor must be voluntary and unprompted. The PSI is a purely ipsative measure for individual self-evaluation and is not intended or valid for comparisons among individuals. No data on norms or relative scoring of different jobs are reported.

The JSI is a self-administered, self-scored, and self-evaluated paper-and-pencil form consisting of 16 sets of four words or phrases that indicate types of tasks or style behaviors which may be required by a particular job. Each of the words or phrases in a set of four is representative of one of four dimensions used to describe the personal style requirements of a job. These four personal style dimensions and the general content of work tasks to which they are related are: Behavioral (things), Cognitive (data), Interpersonal (people), and Affective (ideas). Each of the four words in a set is rank ordered from that which is most descriptive of job requirements (4) to that which is least descriptive of job requirements (1). Scores on the four dimensions are the sums of the ratings of the words and phrases of that dimension across the 16 sets. These scores on the four dimensions are plotted as a bar graph.

The resultant configuration of perceived job style requirements can be compared to the perception of another individual (presumably a job incumbent or manager) as well as to the results of the PSI. Users are guided through a checklist of potential job strengths and difficulties and are encouraged to consult with coworkers or supervisors to better match their individual work style with their perception of the personal style requirements of the job.

Test-retest reliability coefficients are reported as "greater than .85 on each of the four scales" (manual, p. 37) but this assessment of reliability was performed on a very small ($N = 20$–25) and homogeneous sample with the time between administrations unreported. The reliability from this small, homogeneous sample cannot be relied upon as representative of the reliability of the instrument for the larger heterogeneous population for which the scale is intended for use. No other evidence of reliability is reported.

Personal Style Theory forms the conceptual basis of the JSI and PSI. Solely through intuition and experience as college professors and counselors Anderson and Robinson decided a "personal style" exists as one of six components of personality development. The division of personal style into four separate factors is based on informal examination of historical four-factor theories from Hippocrates to Jung and limited consideration of literature on differences in left-right brain processes and the Reticular Activating System.

Development of the JSI followed an abbreviated version of PSI development which itself consisted of entirely "informal and subjective procedures" (manual, p. 29) culminating in a scale meeting the single requirement that Anderson and Robinson felt confident that the stimulus words within each of the four factors formed a coherent group and shared a common meaning different from the stimulus words of the other factors. This process of development was conducted predominantly with college students as test subjects. As such the JSI was developed without empirical support or process and there is no basis for belief that the authors have succeeded in their intention of building a valid measure of the construct dimensions or if they have, that this validity would generalize beyond the homogeneous sample of college students used to develop the scale.

The claims of the test publisher that the JSI can provide an indication of the need for stylistic features required for a job to be performed well is unsubstantiated. Similarly, no evidence is provided to support the utility of the JSI for its stated purpose of predicting how a person is likely to behave as a result of preferences and predispositions. The dearth of evidence for validity and reliability makes the JSI inappropriate as a selection tool or as a requirement of the screening, selection, performance review, or career counseling process. Even as a means of facilitating communication the JSI offers no evidence that the dimensions used are relevant to the actual demands of the job or to the success or satisfaction of the employee.

Regardless of how accurately the four dimensions capture the personal style demands of the job, the JSI may serve a role in focusing attention on job demands that go beyond the knowledge skills, and abilities that are typically the focus of employment choices. Any benefit of the JSI may derive from the process of completing and interpreting the measure itself causing the prospective employee to consider and discuss aspects of the job that would not otherwise have been a focus of attention. Although having potential for some uses, the JSI is in need of research evaluating the validity, reliability, and utility of the measure.

In summary, Personal Style Theory, being based solely on the intuition and experience of two professors and counselors, provides a weak foundation for the JSI. No empirical evidence for the validity of the JSI, or the theory upon which it is based, is provided. The complete lack of validity evidence and the untrustworthy evidence of reliability make it impossible to recommend the JSI when other measures, such as the Strong Interest Inventory (12:374), are accompanied by a body of research demonstrating the utility of the measure for its intended purposes.

[165]
Joliet 3-Minute Speech and Language Screen (Revised).

Purpose: To "identify children with age-appropriate phonological, grammatical, and semantic structures."
Population: Grades K, 2, 5.
Publication Dates: 1983–1992.
Scores, 5: Receptive Vocabulary, Grammar (Evoked Sentences), Phonology, Voice, Fluency.
Administration: Individual.
Levels, 3: Grades K, 2, 5.
Price Data, 1994: $55 per complete kit including manual ('92, 39 pages), vocabulary plates, record-keeping manual (15 pages), 2 scoring forms, and record-keeping disk in binder.
Time: (2–5) minutes.
Authors: Mary C. Kinzler and Constance Cowing Johnson.
Publisher: The Psychological Corporation.
Cross References: For a review of the original edition by Robert E. Owens, Jr., see 9:555 (1 reference).

Review of the Joliet 3-Minute Speech and Language Screen (Revised) by MARTIN A. FISCHER, Associate Professor and Program Director, Program in Communication Disorders, Department of Human Services, Western Carolina University, Cullowhee, NC:

The Joliet 3-Minute Speech and Language Screen (Revised) is reported to have grown "out of the authors' need to quickly and accurately identify children with age-appropriate phonological, grammatical, and semantic structures" (manual, p. 3). The screen is specifically designed for individual administration to large groups of school-age children (kindergarten, second grade, and fifth grade). It is further designed to allow for complete administration in approximately 3 minutes.

The authors suggest the areas of speech and language used in this screen (receptive vocabulary, expressive syntax, and phonology) are sufficient to reflect accurately the child's language development. Assessment techniques used include a recognition vocabulary task, for Receptive Vocabulary, and an evoked imitation task, for Expressive Syntax, Phonology, Voice, and Fluency.

Specifically, Receptive Vocabulary is assessed by presenting 24 plates (8 at each grade level), with each plate containing a picture of the target vocabulary item and three foils. A vocabulary word is presented verbally along with each plate with the instructions to "point to the one I'm saying" or "point to _____." The child's response is noted on an "Individual Screen" (IS) form as correct or incorrect. The number of errors is then compared with cutoff scores listed on the IS form for grades kindergarten, second, and fifth.

Expressive Syntax is assessed through an evoked imitation task containing 10 sentences. The sentences are read from the IS form, and errors are marked. The number of errors is then compared to individual cutoff scores for each of the three grades. Areas of expressive syntax evaluated include certain auxiliary verbs, tag questions, interrogative reversals, pronouns, articles, and copular forms.

Phonology is assessed at the same time as expressive syntax by judging phonological errors that occur during the evoked sentence task. Phonemes that are to be evaluated are printed on the IS form and are circled if incorrect.

In addition to Receptive Vocabulary, Expressive Syntax, and Phonology, the authors provide a place on the IS form to record subjective judgments regarding Voice and Fluency. Guidelines are given for evaluation of each area with suggestions for follow-up evaluations and/or referral. The Joliet contains two reproducible scoring forms (an Individual Screen, and a Class Record) and a computerized record keeping program formatted for an Apple IIe computer.

STANDARDIZATION. Standardization of the screen was conducted using 2,587 children from three ethnic backgrounds, three socioeconomic classes, and three grades (kindergarten, second, and fifth). Cutoff scores were obtained from 586 children randomly selected from the above sample population.

A test of validity using the Cochran Q test (Meyers & Grossen, 1974) suggested the Grammar portion of the Joliet correlates strongly with the Carrow Elicited Language Inventory (CELI) (Carrow, 1974) at all age levels (.05 level of significance). The vocabulary portion of the Joliet correlated strongly with the Peabody Picture Vocabulary Test (PPVT) (Dunn, 1965) at grades kindergarten and 2 but tended to be more sensitive in identifying borderline high-risk vocabulary cases at grade 5. Test-retest reliability was strong with no significant differences being observed in results obtained from two test administrations 4 weeks apart.

EVALUATION. The overall structure and format of the Joliet appears to be clear and unambiguous. Each of the 24 plates used for the recognition vocabulary task contains four black-and-white illustrations, one representing the target vocabulary word and three representing foils. All drawings appear to be appropriate, nonbiased, and discriminable at the specified grade levels. Likewise, the 10 sentences used to evaluate expressive syntax and phonology contain clear and unambiguous examples of the various syntactic and phonological structures. Test administration and scoring procedures were simple and should be familiar to individuals who have administered the PPVT and the CELI, respectively.

Several concerns must be addressed regarding the Joliet. The most significant concern is related to the basic assumptions of the authors. Specifically, the authors claim the areas of receptive vocabulary, expressive syntax, and phonology are able to sample and reflect accurately the child's language development. Although there can be no doubt that all three of these areas are of primary importance to the development of appropriate language ability, it is possible that a significant number of individuals will exhibit speech and language problems in areas not addressed by the screen. I am referring in particular to children who present with pragmatic and/or language comprehension problems. Specifically, children who exhibit inappropriate discourse/narrative

ability (including the ability to follow commands or answer questions) may exhibit age-appropriate recognition vocabulary and syntactic skill and, thus, not be referred for additional testing following administration of the Joliet. Although I feel this limitation is significant, it should not be taken as a fatal criticism of the Joliet but rather as a suggestion for future revisions.

A second concern is related to the choice of the PPVT as a measure of concurrent validity. The PPVT was replaced by a revised version (PPVT-R) (Dunn, 1982) in 1982. As such, the PPVT-R should have been used as a measure of concurrent validity rather than the PPVT.

A third concern, although minor, is related to the Apple IIe format chosen for the computerized record keeping program. Although it can be argued that many public schools still use Apple II computers, the trend is rapidly moving toward Macintosh or DOS/Windows based machines. As such it would be helpful to include a program that can be used across platforms.

In summary, the Joliet appears to be a well-organized, easily administered screening tool. It can, in fact, be administered in 3 minutes and is quickly and unambiguously scored. It seems to be very effective in screening school-age children with deficits in syntax, recognition vocabulary, and/or phonology. Limitations include minimal coverage of pragmatics and language comprehension, use of an unrevised test for concurrent validity, and the inclusion of computer software that may soon become outdated.

REVIEWER'S REFERENCES

Carrow, E. (1974). Carrow Elicited Language Inventory. Chicago: Riverside Publishing Co.
Dunn, L. M. (1965). Peabody Picture Vocabulary Test. Circle Pines, MN: American Guidance Service, Inc.
Meyers, L. S., & Grossen, N. E. (1974). *Behavioral research: Theory, procedure and design.* San Francisco: W. H. Freeman.
Dunn, L. M. (1982). Peabody Picture Vocabulary Test—Revised. Circle Pines, MN: American Guidance Service, Inc.

Review of the Joliet 3-Minute Speech and Language Screen (Revised) by MALCOLM R. McNEIL, Chair, Communication Science & Disorders, University of Pittsburgh, Pittsburgh, PA and THOMAS F. CAMPBELL, Director, Audiology and Speech Pathology, Children's Hospital, Communication Science & Disorders, University of Pittsburgh, Pittsburgh, PA:

The stated purpose of the Joliet 3-Minute Speech and Language Screen is to "identify children with age-appropriate phonological, grammatical, and semantic structures" (p. 3). It is designed to be administered individually by "a certified speech-language pathologist or a carefully trained paraprofessional" (p. 4). Neither procedures for training nor criteria for establishing competence for the paraprofessional were presented other than the directions for administration and scoring provided in the manual. The examination is, as the name of the test implies, designed as a screening tool. Children who fail to meet preestablished criteria for performance "qualify for a complete speech and language evaluation" (p. 4).

CONSTRUCT VALIDITY. It is stated that the areas of "receptive vocabulary," "expressive syntax," and "phonology" provide the most accurate representation of the child's speech and language development. Although unjustified beyond this assumption, these three areas of language provide the structure for the test. Voice and fluency are also observed and scored during the administration of the grammar section.

Although there is a substantive body of literature available that debates various elicitation procedures for the evaluation of language, no theoretical motivation or clinical justification is given for the assessment of grammar through sentence repetition. The validity of this assumption is in need of support.

Criteria for failure on the Receptive Vocabulary, Grammar, Phonology, Voice, and Fluency sections of the examination are clearly stated, but are without justification. As the purpose of the screening examination is to detect children who require additional assessment, a calculation of the false positive, false negative, true positive, and true negative assignments of children is essential. These data are not reported although the authors do report the number of children from each grade level who passed and failed the examination on both the Vocabulary and Grammar sections of the test.

The criteria for failing the Phonology section of the exam is a single error of any type, even for the 5-year-old subjects. Studies on speech-sound normalization (Shriberg, Gruber, & Kwiatkowski, 1994) clearly indicate that a number of consonant sounds are not completely mastered until 6 years of age. More than 50% of the target sounds used in the screening procedure fall into the Shriberg et al. late-8 speech sound normalization group. Based on the criteria for failure, an unacceptably high probability of false positive identifications could result.

CONTENT VALIDITY. The content and procedural design of the test was constrained by the maximum administration time of 3 minutes. Within this context, Receptive Vocabulary is assessed with eight different words for kindergarten, second, and fifth grade levels. These words and the appropriate foils were selected from those that met the criteria for universality. The authors also state the words were

subjected to item analysis and found to be discriminating; however, these analyses were not presented. Although the test was designed and constrained by the administration time, it is not a timed test. The authors state that the "usual" time is approximately 3 minutes.

Ten sentences reflecting the most frequently erred syntactic and morphologic structures in the authors' own therapy programs were selected for assessment and elicited from sentence repetition. These included exemplars of auxiliary verbs, tag questions, interrogative reversals, pronouns, articles, and copular forms. It is from these sentences that the phonologic evaluation is done. Although no theoretical justification or specific methods of phonological analysis of these connected speech samples were provided, the authors stated that the sentences were "loaded with phonemic content for assessing the child's acquisition of speech sounds" (p. 3).

The vocabulary words are elicited with black-and-white, hand-drawn pictured stimuli, four pictures per plate. The pictures are well drawn and appear to be discriminable and identifiable based on their sizes, shapes, and clarity of detail.

Fluency is evaluated during the administration of the Grammar section of the examination. The authors suggest that a sample of spontaneous speech may be required if there is a question concerning the adequacy of the child's fluency observed during the Grammar section of the examination. No guidance or criteria for the elicitation or adequacy of this spontaneous sample is provided.

It is recommended that the Voice sample be audiotape recorded and judged by consensus; however, there is no indication of the number of listeners that are necessary to judge the sample. It is recommended that a history be taken from the caregiver/parent with queries about chronicity of any observed voice problem.

Using the Cochran Q Test, differences in performance on the Vocabulary section of the 3-Minute Speech and Language Screen between boys and girls; blacks and whites; Hispanic-others and white; blacks and Hispanic-others; high-mid and mid socioeconomic groups; high-mid and low socioeconomic groups; and mid and low socioeconomic groups were all significant. Differences in performance on the Grammar section between boys and girls; blacks and whites; blacks and Hispanic-others; and mid and low socioeconomic groups were nonsignificantly different. Although these differences between groups were found for the Grammar section of the examination, no differences in cutoff scores were developed.

CONCURRENT VALIDITY. Of the 2,587 children administered the examination, 586 were randomly selected to establish cutoff scores and for other concurrent validation studies. The manual authors do not indicate clearly whether these 586 children were selected because they were speech or language impaired; however, they do indicate these children "were mainstreamed for the greater part of the day" (p. 21), suggesting that they, or a portion of them may not have been impaired. These children were administered both the Joliet 3-Minute Speech and Language Screen along with the Peabody Picture Vocabulary Test (Dunn, 1965) and the Carrow Elicited Language Inventory (Carrow, 1974). The time between administrations was not specified. Significant group differences between the tests were reported using the Cochran Q statistic. The observed difference in vocabulary performance between the Joliet 3-Minute Speech and Language Screen and the Peabody Picture Vocabulary Test was significant ($p<.05$) for the fifth grade group. There were no significant differences in performance on the Grammar section of the Joliet 3-Minute Speech and Language Screen and the Carrow Elicited Language Inventory at any of the three grade levels. Correlation coefficients between the Joliet 3-Minute Speech and Language Screen and the other two measures were not reported, making direct assessment of the test's concurrent validity extremely difficult.

STANDARDIZATION. The Joliet 3-Minute Speech and Language Screen (Revised) was administered to 2,587 children from three ethnic backgrounds (black, white, and Hispanic-other), three occupation-determined socioeconomic classes (high-mid, mid, and low), and three academic grade levels (kindergarten, second, and fifth). No mention is given as to whether the proportions for each of these stratification variables matched the demographics of the general population. Using the preestablished cutoff criteria for the Vocabulary and Grammar sections of the test, it was determined that between 10.1% and 12.8% of the 2,587 children failed the examination. No specification is given as to which children failed. That is, it is unknown how many, if any, of the identified children were later found to have been accurately or inaccurately classified. Given the known prevalence and incidence of specific language and speech disorders in these populations of children (Campbell, Dollaghan, & Felsenfeld, 1995), it appears that the number identified is too high, thus suggesting inordinately high false-positive identifications.

ADMINISTRATION. The details provided in the manual for administering the test in terms of the physical environment and patient instructions for each part of the test appear to be sufficient for replicating performance (however, see reliability below). All stimuli are administered for all tasks. Repetition of the stimulus is allowed for only one stimulus in the section.

SCORING. Plus/minus scoring is used for the Receptive Vocabulary section. Cutoff scores (threshold for failure) for the Receptive Vocabulary section were set at five or more errors for all children (kindergarten, second grade, and fifth grade). As different stimuli are used for each group, the consistent criterion across groups may be appropriate.

A 2-point equal-appearing interval scale is used to evaluate the Grammar section. One point is given for omitted, substituted, unintelligible words, word additions, word transpositions, and added contractions that do not occur in the sentence. Two points are scored if a contraction is omitted. (It should be noted that the authors state in one place [p. 8] that the examiner should score 1 point if the student does not repeat an existing contraction, but in another [p. 8] that omitted contractions are scored 2 points.) Appropriately, dialectal (e.g., omitted possessive markers or copulas or substituted *be* for *have been*) differences are not scored as errors.

Phonology is scored by counting the number of omissions, substitutions, or distortions of the targeted sounds. Errors on each phoneme and each error type are scored equally. Criteria for failure is one or more sounds in error at any age level.

Abnormal fluency or "flow of speech" is, according to the authors, characterized by pauses, hesitations, interjections, prolongations, and repetitions that are obtained from a spontaneous speech sample. It is suggested that the child be rescreened if the child shows phrase or whole word repetitions, superfluous interjections, hesitation phenomena (e.g., false starts, silent pauses), or if the parent/caregiver is unconcerned with the disfluencies in the child's speech. The child should be referred for a full fluency evaluation if the child demonstrates part-word and one-syllable repetitions, prolonged sounds that occur more frequently than those considered to occur in normally disfluent children, or if the overall sample, regardless of the number disfluencies, could not be misperceived as fluent speech. Specific criteria eliciting an adequate speech sample or for judging any of these suggested observations or for determining pass/fail criteria are not given.

The voice sample is evaluated subjectively with observations directed to abnormal laryngeal tone (observing hoarseness, harshness, breathiness, pitch, loudness and flexibility pitch, and loudness). Hypernasality and hyponasality are also to be observed. Specific criteria for eliciting the speech sample or for judging "abnormal" voice in any specific parameter are not given.

RELIABILITY. *Test-Retest*: One hundred and thirteen children were retested with the 3-Minute Joliet Speech and Language Screen (Revised) 4 weeks following an initial administration. The authors report that "No significant differences were found between any of the tests at any of the grade levels" (p. 27). Only data for the Vocabulary and Grammar portions of the test are reported. These data are reported as Q Values and thus do not inform the reader about individual subject's performance between the two test administrations. It is known that as a group there were no significant differences between the children's performance on the two administrations; however, the range and standard deviation of the group's performance are not known. For example, it is not known how many children would have passed or failed the test based on the cutoff scores on either administration. It is also not known how many children changed classification from the first to the second administration. These critical omissions in the reporting of the reliability of the instrument seriously jeopardize the utility of the test.

Given the underspecified and complex perceptual judgments required on several portions of the examination (e.g., Voice and Fluency), other forms of reliability such as intra- and interjudge reliabilities are critical to have established. However, neither of these forms of reliability were reported. In addition, measures of internal consistency are not reported.

STRENGTHS AND WEAKNESSES. The strengths of the test appear to be in the test's ease and time of administration with clearly pictured stimuli used to elicit responses. Any strengths of the 3-Minute Joliet Speech and Language Screen (Revised) are, however, severely constrained by the lack of psychometric information regarding the test. The general construct validity of the test is greatly underspecified. Test procedures for eliciting the sentence repetition for the assessment of grammar, and speech samples for the assessment of fluency and voice, are poorly justified and underspecified. The derivation of the specific criteria for failure on any portion of the test is unjustified. Inter- and intrajudge reliabilities are not reported. Most importantly, the validity of the test's accurate (true positive and true negative) and inaccurate (false positive and false negative) detection of children with and without speech and language disorders has not been determined.

SUMMARY. The 3-Minute Joliet Speech and Language Screen is designed to meet an important need in the rapid identification of children K–5 that should be given formal speech and language evaluations. Its discriminant validity is, however, unproven. Therefore, I believe the test cannot be used for the purpose for which it was designed.

REVIEWERS' REFERENCES

Dunn, L. M. (1965). Peabody Picture Vocabulary Test. Circle Pines, MN: American Guidance Service, Inc.
Carrow, E. (1974). Carrow Elicited Language Inventory. Chicago, IL: Riverside Publishing Co.
Shriberg, L. D., Gruber, F. A., & Kwiatkowski, J. (1994). Developmental phonological disorders III: Long-term speech-sound normalization. *Journal of Speech and Hearing Research, 37*, 1151–1177.
Campbell, T. F., Dollaghan, C., & Felsenfeld, S. (1995). Disorders of language, phonology, fluency, and voice: Indicators for referral. In C. Bluestone, S. Stool, & M. Kenna (Eds.), *Pediatric Otolaryngology*, Vol. 2 (3rd ed.) (pp. 1595–1606). Philadelphia: W. B. Saunders.

[166]
Kaufman Functional Academic Skills Test.

Purpose: "Measure of an adolescent's or adult's ability to demonstrate competence in reading and mathematics as applied to daily life situations."
Population: Ages 15–85 and over.
Publication Date: 1994.
Acronym: K-FAST.
Scores, 3: Arithmetic Subtest, Reading Subtest, Functional Academic Skills Composite.
Administration: Individual.
Price Data, 1994: $89.95 per complete kit including manual (110 pages), test easel, and 25 record forms; $74.95 per test easel; $19.95 per 25 record forms; $26.95 per manual.
Time: (15–25) minutes.
Comments: Examinees may respond in any language.
Authors: Alan S. Kaufman and Nadeen L. Kaufman.
Publisher: American Guidance Service.

TEST REFERENCES

1. Chen, T-H., Kaufman, A. S., & Kaufman, J. C. (1994). Examining the interaction of age x race pertaining to Black-White differences at ages 15 to 93 on six Horn abilities assessed by K-FAST, K-SNAP and KAIT subtests. *Perceptual and Motor Skills, 79*, 1683–1690.
2. Kaufman, A. S., Kaufman, J. C., Chen, T. H., & Kaufman, N. L. (1996). Differences on six Horn abilities for 14 age groups between 15–16 and 75–94 years. *Psychological Assessment, 8*, 161–171.

Review of the Kaufman Functional Academic Skills Test by STEVEN R. SHAW, School Psychologist, School District of Greenville County, Greenville, SC:

The Kaufman Functional Academic Skills Test (K-FAST) measures aspects of adaptive behavior involving the application of academically acquired learning to the problems of daily living. The K-FAST is useful for examinees aged 15 to 85. The K-FAST is a supplement to traditional norm-referenced academic tests and adaptive behavior measures. Although most academic tests assess skills needed to perform in school, the K-FAST assesses reading and arithmetic skills required for daily living in society. Unlike most adaptive behavior scales, the K-FAST does not use respondents or interviews with the examinee. The K-FAST requires examinees to demonstrate skills in an individual testing situation on the K-FAST. The manual reports that the K-FAST may be used in residential settings or prisons to determine the degree of self-care an examinee can manage, for making personnel decisions, and to aid in vocational counseling.

The K-FAST consists of an Arithmetic and a Reading Subtest. There are 25 items in the Arithmetic Subtest and 29 items in the Reading Subtest. Topics in the Reading Subtest include: simple directions, signs, pictorial rebuses, labels, newspapers and magazine articles, advertisements, abbreviations, and catalog information. Unlike many reading tests, the K-FAST Reading Subtest does not emphasize pronunciation. The Arithmetic Subtest includes topics such as: counting, adding and subtracting the value of coins, grocery shopping, cooking, reading maps, understanding graphs and charts, telling time and understanding time concepts, earning money and budgeting, banking, taking trips by car or taxi, and purchasing a variety of items. The subtest scores can be combined to form a Functional Academic Skill Composite. This composite score represents overall functional academic skill development.

ADMINISTRATION AND SCORING. The K-FAST is easy and quick to administer. Items are not timed. Typical time to complete an administration of the K-FAST is 15 to 25 minutes. Yet, the manual reports that some individuals may take up to 50 minutes to complete the test. A variety of personnel may administer the K-FAST. There is no special training involved. However, examiners must be thoroughly familiar with standardized test administration, discontinuation rules, and item content. The easel format is convenient for administration. The individual test records are large and easy to follow. Tables for converting raw scores to standard scores, standard score confidence intervals, percentile ranks, and descriptive categories are straightforward. The manual contains a table presenting standard

score differences between Arithmetic and Reading Subtests required for statistical significance. The manual supplies no information on base rates of standard score differences. The K-FAST is quick to administer and convenient to score. Any professional with training and experience administering and scoring standardized tests will have minimal problems with the K-FAST.

NORMATIVE DATA. The K-FAST was constructed as part of a 28-subtest battery of approximately 1,850 items. After the tryout phase, the battery was divided into the K-FAST, the Kaufman Adolescent and Adult Intelligence Test (KAIT; 12:204), the Kaufman Brief Intelligence Test (K-BIT; 12:205), and the Kaufman Short Neuropsychological Assessment Procedure (K-SNAP; 167). The national standardization of the K-FAST involved over 2,600 participants from 27 states. The norm sample consisted of 1,424 participants. The norm samples were small for the 65–69 ($N = 81$), 70–74 ($N = 93$), and 75–85+ ($N = 103$) age groups. The sample is reasonably representative of the general U.S. population for gender, ethnic group status, and education. However, the norm sample is not representative for geographic region. The Northeast and West are underrepresented and the North Central and South are overrepresented. Data were not collected from the populous states of New Jersey, Florida, Hawaii, Arizona, South Carolina, and Virginia. For most tests, geographic representation is not a significant problem. However, Arizona and Florida are two states with large, active senior populations. As a result, it is possible that the norms for ages over 65 may not be representative of the U.S. population. Despite these minor shortcomings, the K-FAST has well-developed normative data.

RELIABILITY. The manual reports data on internal consistency and stability. Internal consistency reliability was estimated using split-half reliability corrected with the Spearman-Brown formula. The mean internal consistency reliability estimate for the Arithmetic Subtests was .88 (range .83–.94). The mean internal consistency reliability estimate for the Reading Subtest was .90. Reliability coefficients ranged from .86 to .95. For the Functional Composite, the mean internal consistency reliability estimate was .94. Reliability coefficients ranged from .92 to .97. Standard errors of measurement for Arithmetic, Reading, and the Functional Composite are 5.1, 4.7, and 3.7, respectively.

Temporal stability of the K-FAST was determined by administering the K-FAST to 116 nonhandicapped adolescents and adults. The test-retest intervals ranged from 6 to 94 days with a mean of 33 days. Correlations between the two testings, corrected for variability, were .84 for Arithmetic, .88 for Reading, and .91 for the Composite. There was also a slight practice effect. The mean gain in scores was 1.0 standard score points for Arithmetic, 2.9 for Reading, and 2.3 for the Composite. Overall, the manual clearly demonstrates that the K-FAST is a reliable and stable test for ages 15 to 85.

VALIDITY. The manual presents a variety of data supporting the validity of the K-FAST. An exploratory factor analysis of the K-FAST along with the KAIT and K-SNAP indicates that both Reading and Arithmetic load significantly on the first unrotated factor (g). Both subtests also have significant loading on Crystallized intelligence. Arithmetic has significant loadings on Fluid intelligence for persons aged 20–54 and 70–85+. The authors note age changes in performance on the K-FAST. The highest raw scores are for persons between the ages of 30 and 50. This may be due to a developmental difference in education (i.e., 15-year-olds have not completed their education) or other confounding factors. The authors conducted concurrent validity studies with the Wechsler Intelligence Scale for Children—Revised (WISC-R), the Wechsler Adult Intelligence Scale—Revised (WAIS-R), the Stanford-Binet Intelligence Scale, Fourth Edition, the KAIT, the K-BIT, the K-SNAP, and the Peabody Picture Vocabulary Test—Revised (PPVT-R). Correlations are moderate to high with all tests of intelligence. However, the K-FAST should be considered a rough estimate of general intellectual ability. The K-FAST is not an appropriate estimate of intelligence, especially with reading- or mathematics-disabled persons. Concurrent validity studies were also conducted with persons who have reading disabilities, mental retardation, severe depression, Alzheimer's disease, and neurological impairments. Validity studies employed a heterogeneous clinical sample as well. The K-FAST discriminated well between normal and most clinical populations. However, the clinically depressed sample scored higher than the nonimpaired norm sample. In sum, the validity data of the K-FAST are extensive and well presented. Most data strongly support the validity of the K-FAST for many purposes.

SUMMARY. The K-FAST is a well-developed direct measure of the academic subdomain of adaptive behavior. The test is easy to administer and score. Results from the K-FAST can be invaluable in a variety of situations such as transition planning for low functioning high school students, vocational counseling, or determining functional skill loss after stroke. The norm sample was well selected. Save some potential problems with the geographic representativeness of the sample in states with large senior populations, the test is carefully and completely normed. For such a brief test, the K-FAST has outstanding reliability. The manual delves into great detail concerning the establishment of validity data. Validity is appropriately established for a variety of purposes.

The K-FAST is an excellent test for a small niche in assessment. Most often norm-referenced academic tests, intelligence tests, or adaptive behavior measures are adequate for meeting assessment needs. The K-FAST should be used to supplement, rather than replace, tests of these domains. Yet, tests of these domains do not often consider real life applications of the above constructs. Thus, if an assessment requires a brief estimate of functional academic skills, subsets of the construct of adaptive behavior, then the K-FAST is an outstanding assessment instrument.

Review of the Kaufman Functional Academic Skills Test by ROBERT T. WILLIAMS, Professor of Education, Colorado State University, Fort Collins, CO:

The Kaufman Functional Academic Skills Test (K-FAST) follows in the tradition of many other American Guidance Services assessments. That is, it is brief, it uses the ceiling/discontinue format to be applicable with a wide range of examinees; it has explicit and clear directions for administration and scoring; it uses an easel format for task stimulus; it has a clear, legible, efficient-to-use test record; and it has an excellent manual with readable tables and extensive references.

The purpose of the K-FAST is a "measure of an adolescent's or adult's ability to demonstrate competence in reading and mathematics as applied to daily life situations" (manual, p. 1). It contains 25 arithmetic items in 11 categories and 29 reading items in 9 categories. The authors suggest that the K-FAST is to serve as a supplement, not a substitute, for popular tests of intelligence, achievement, or adaptive behavior.

The K-FAST purports to measure fluid-crystallized intelligence. From the manual, page 4, "Crystallized intelligence includes problem-solving tasks that are dependent on previously learned skills. Fluid intelligence encompasses tasks that involve novel problem-solving skills—the kind that are not acquired in formal or informal learning situations. Fluid problem solving relies heavily on flexibility, analytic ability, and adaptability. ... K-FAST Arithmetic was strongly associated with both the Fluid and Crystallized factors for most age groups." And on page 5, "the Reading Subtest measures abilities acquired from previous learning situations and through acculturation" [Crystallized].

The K-FAST was developed at the same time as the Kaufman Brief Intelligence Test (K-BIT, Kaufman & Kaufman, 1990; 12:205), the Kaufman Adolescent and Adult Intelligence Test (KAIT, Kaufman & Kaufman, 1993; 12:204), and the Kaufman Short Neurological Assessment Procedure (K-SNAP, Kaufman & Kaufman, 1994; 167). Consultants searched adaptive inventories for topics and items. The consultants are identified without reference to their qualifications. The KAIT, K-BIT, K-SNAP, and K-FAST evolved from a national tryout of 28 subtests and about 1,850 items. Six group-administered forms and one individually administered form, including a total of 148 functional reading and 67 functional arithmetic items, were used.

The sample sizes (tryout $N = 1,140$ and standardization $N = 2,600$) are appropriate. The proportionality of age, ethnic group, geographic region in the United States, and socioeconomic level (years in school completed by individual or by parents, if still in school) of the tryout and standardization sample is excellent, falling within 5 percentage points of the U.S. population on almost all categories. There is an underrepresentation of subjects for the Northeast and an overrepresentation from the South.

Reliability is estimated for split-half (by age range), test-retest ($N = 116$; $r = .87$ to .91), and interrelation of subtests. Authors use "error bands" based upon Standard Error of Measurement to "make it easier to interpret the test and help examiners avoid test abuse" (p. 49).

Content validity is documented by discussing consultants' examination of adaptive inventories and the selection of concepts and items. This procedure seems appropriate. However, the credibility of the consultants is never established. The K-FAST emerged as one of the products of an ambitious effort to develop the various assessment devices named above. The mention of Fluid/Crystallized intelligence is interesting. Although references are given, there is not enough conceptual or practical information about this construct offered for the reader to understand or evaluate the application of the construct. This reviewer would have appreciated a matrix that summarized each test item by skill category and as Fluid, Crystallized, or both. Without more discussion, this construct is lacking.

Clinical validity was evaluated by comparing clinical subjects to control subjects. There is a good effort to compare clinical samples with matched controls. Differences were significant in favor of controls except for the clinically depressed population. This is a valuable model. Grouping the total clinical sample gives a large population ($N = 137$) but the weakness of these individual studies is the small sample size ($N < 35$).

Construct validity is discussed through establishing reading and mathematics tasks applied to daily situations. Probably anyone who reads, uses, or reviews the K-FAST will identify "reading and mathematics items applied to everyday life" that are not included in the assessment. In Mathematics, the authors purport to assess survival arithmetic, numerical reasoning, computational skills, and mathematical concepts. They use 25 items for one topic. In Reading, the authors purport to assess reading survival skills, recognition and comprehension of signs and written material, and practical, nonschool tasks. They use 29 items to assess nine skills. This reviewer conducted an informal content analysis and found some mathematics and reading skills to have as few as 1 item, some to have 2 items, and some to have as many as 8 items. This reviewer feels that topic coverage has been overstated and that some skills have too few items to adequately assess abilities.

Criterion-related validity is discussed with studies and analyses conducted during K-FAST development and standardization. Age changes on the K-FAST and correlates with comprehensive intelligence tests are reported to support validity. The authors caution not to interpret the K-FAST as an intelligence test. They go on to say it "can provide a good estimate of intelligence where other test scores are unavailable" (p. 9). This is an unfortunate comment. Users may not try to get other assessments or may see the K-FAST as the same as a multifaceted assessment of intellectual ability.

The K-FAST is a user-friendly, readable, brief assessment of daily life situations in reading and mathematics, which is to be a supplement to other assessment. Claims of categories of assessment do not hold. There are too few items to accurately evaluate the several categories offered by the authors. The uses and applications made in the manual sound as if they had been written by the marketing department: Everybody can use this! A sensitive, intuitive, informed teacher, tutor, or counselor could develop an informal assessment of daily life situations that could be as useful for academic, personal, or job training planning. The Comprehensive Adult Student Assessment System (CASAS, 1992; 78) is an adult-oriented functional assessment system that measures a broad range of adult literacy skills with application in real life situations. The CASAS measures reading, writing, math, and problem-solving skills (using separate tests for each area) in the domains of consumer resources, occupational knowledge, community resources, and health. The CASAS spans a range of abilities from nonreaders to adults at the GED or high school level. The separate surveys are untimed (and may take as long as 60 minutes each) and may be administered individually or in groups. For functional and/or work place literacy or academic or career planning, this reviewer would favor the CASAS.

REVIEWER'S REFERENCES

Kaufman, A. S., & Kaufman, N. L. (1990). Kaufman Brief Intelligence Test (K-BIT). Circle Pines, MN: American Guidance Service.

CASAS. (1992). Comprehensive Adult Student Assessment System. San Diego, CA: Foundation for Educational Achievement, Inc.

Kaufman, A. S., & Kaufman, N. L. (1993). Kaufman Adolescent and Adult Intelligence Test (KAIT). Circle Pines, MN: American Guidance Service.

Kaufman, A. S., & Kaufman, N. L. (1994). Kaufman Short Neuropsychological Assessment Procedure (K-SNAP). Circle Pines, MN: American Guidance Service.

[167]
Kaufman Short Neuropsychological Assessment Procedure.

Purpose: Constructed to assess the "ability to demonstrate intact mental functioning."
Population: Ages 11 to 85.
Publication Date: 1994.
Acronym: K-SNAP.
Scores, 5: Gestalt Closure, Number Recall, Four-Letter Words, Recall/Closure Composite, K-SNAP Composite.
Administration: Individual.
Price Data, 1996: $145 per complete kit including manual (128 pages), easel, and 25 record forms; $24.95 per 25 record forms.
Time: (30) minutes.
Authors: Alan S. Kaufman and Nadeen L. Kaufman.
Publisher: American Guidance Service.

TEST REFERENCES

1. Chen, T-H., Kaufman, A. S., & Kaufman, J. C. (1994). Examining the interaction of age x race pertaining to Black-White differences at ages 15 to 93 on six Horn abilities assessed by K-FAST, K-SNAP and KAIT subtests. *Perceptual and Motor Skills, 79,* 1683–1690.

2. Kaufman, A. S., Kaufman, J. C., Chen, T. H., & Kaufman, N. L. (1996). Differences on six Horn abilities for 14 age groups between 15–16 and 75–94 years. *Psychological Assessment, 8,* 161–171.

Review of the Kaufman Short Neuropsychological Assessment Procedure by KAREN GELLER, Developmental Neuropsychologist in Private Practice, Whitehouse Station, NJ:

The Kaufman Short Neuropsychological Assessment Procedure (K-SNAP) is intended to be used as a short cognitive evaluation, as part of a comprehensive neuropsychological or intellectual assessment, or as a screening measure to aid in the decision-making process to determine who would benefit from a comprehensive examination. It includes a well-normed Mental Status test. It is easy and quick to administer and easily portable. Complete administration yields an Impairment Index, which the authors caution can be used to identify people who are likely to require follow-up evaluation, but should *not* be used to assume that follow-up is not necessary.

The test is based on A. R. Luria's conceptualization of functional units or "blocks" that are necessary for mental activity. These are (1) Arousal; (2) Receiving, Processing, and Retaining Information; and (3) Planning. The four subtests are designed to vary in level of complexity and to assess these three areas of functioning. There are two middle-level tasks, which can be combined to derive a composite. This score can then be combined with results from the most complex task to form an overall composite score. The Impairment Index is then calculated based on the overall Composite score, the descriptive category on the Mental Status Subtest, the difference between the two mid-level tests, and the difference between the actual Composite score and a predicted score based on educational level.

The norming sample of over 2,000 individuals aged 11 to 94 was based on the 1990 United States Census. The sample was stratified within each age group by gender, geographic region, socioeconomic status, and race or ethnic group. This test was normed at the same time as the Kaufman Adolescent and Adult Intelligence Test (KAIT) and the Kaufman Functional Academic Skills Test (K-FAST), so subjects were given all of the subtests that make up these three tests.

The test items were carefully evaluated to minimize bias. Test items were evaluated statistically to determine if they yielded different results within different groups and some items were subsequently eliminated. Reliability and validity data provided indicate that the K-SNAP is psychometrically sound. Internal consistency and stability are both very good. Reliability of the Impairment Index was good.

Validity studies used factor analysis of K-SNAP subtests with other similar and dissimilar tests. All tests loaded only with other measures of the construct they were hypothesized to assess. Developmental changes from age 11 to over 85 were carefully examined. Test results were then correlated with comprehensive and brief IQ tests for normal samples and for clinical samples, with excellent results. The Impairment Index was examined for its ability to discriminate between clinical and nonclinical samples. The Index was found to be able effectively to identify people with generalized cognitive impairment, but it is not sensitive to unilateral brain damage.

Test administration procedures are very simple and clearly described. The manual states that nonpsychologists can administer the test, but that the interpretation must be performed by professionals with both psychometric and clinical training.

From a technical standpoint, the K-SNAP produces highly reliable scores and is a well-normed measure. It provides a quick overview of cognitive functioning that is easy to administer, score, and interpret. It provides useful data as part of a comprehensive assessment and is especially welcome as a standardized examination of mental status. The K-SNAP is only moderately useful for documenting the need for comprehensive neuropsychological or intellectual evaluation, because although it can show reliably that follow-up is needed, it does not accurately identify those who do not need additional evaluation.

Review of the Kaufman Short Neuropsychological Assessment Procedure by MARTINE HÉBERT, Assistant Professor, Department of Counseling, Administration and Evaluation, Université Laval, Québec, Canada:

The Kaufman Short Neuropsychological Assessment Procedure (K-SNAP) is a brief, individually administered measure of the cognitive functioning of adolescents and adults. The authors intend the test to be useful across a wide range of individuals between the ages of 11 and 85 years in various settings (hospitals, nursing homes, vocational rehabilitation centers, etc.). The K-SNAP is designed to evaluate the individual's ability to demonstrate intact mental functioning at three levels of cognitive complexity, corresponding to Luria's framework of three functional units or blocks. Four subtests are included: the low-level Mental Status subtest (10 items—which is a supplementary subtest on the Kaufman Adolescent and Adult Intelligence Test [KAIT]) pertaining to measurement of attention-orientation, two medium-level complexity subtests corresponding to either sequential processing—Number Recall (16 items) or simultaneous processing—Gestalt Closure (25 items), and a Four-Letter Words subtest (23 items) aimed at evaluating higher level planning ability. Testing time averages 30 minutes.

As with other instruments developed by Kaufman and Kaufman, the material is presented in an attractive and well-constructed easel. The subtests of the K-SNAP are organized according to the order in which they are presented and administration is facilitated by the directions being noted in the easel kit. The examiner is allowed to teach an approach to solving the tasks if the client does not give an initial correct response on all K-SNAP subtests except for the Mental Status subtest. Teaching is limited to unscored sample items and to the first two scored items. Discontinue rules are specified directly on the record form. Only the Four-Letter Word subtest is timed.

Although testing procedures are easy to follow and authors state that a wide range of personnel (nonpsychologists) may administer and calculate the scores from the K-SNAP, competency in interpreting the results derived requires qualified professional training in psychometrics and clinical assessment.

Results from the K-SNAP are summarized into three subtest scores, two composite scores, a descriptive category for Mental Status (given the very negatively skewed distribution—most individuals obtaining near-perfect scores—scaled scores are not derived) and an Impairment Index. The Number Recall, Gestalt Closure, Four-Letter Words subtests, and the Recall/Closure composite, derived from the scores on the two medium complexity level subtests, yield scaled scores (mean = 10, standard deviation = 3), percentiles, and descriptive categories. A K-SNAP composite score is obtained by the combination of scaled scores from the Recall/Closure composite and the Four-Letter Word subtest and produces standard scores (mean = 100, standard deviation = 15), percentile ranks, and descriptive categories. Finally, derived scores are used with a set of four diagnostic criteria to generate an 8-point Impairment Index. Each of the following criteria is weighted from 0 to 2: (a) the standard K-SNAP Composite score; (b) the descriptive category for Mental Status; (c) the difference between the Gestalt Closure and Number Recall subtest scaled scores; and (d) the difference between the K-SNAP Composite standard score and a predicted score based on the number of years of schooling completed by the client (or the client's parents). An Impairment Index of 3 or more is used to identify clients likely to require a more comprehensive assessment.

Individual test record booklets enable the examiner to record scores, percentile ranks, and descriptive categories and to graph confidence intervals (90% or 95%) for subtest (except for Mental Status) and composite scores. As well, necessary data to verify whether differences in scaled score comparisons are significant (.05 or .01 level) and to calculate the Impairment Index are presented directly on the record booklet.

The test manual is well organized, comprehensive, and contains information required to administer, score, and interpret the K-SNAP. Chapters included also present the theoretical rationale for each subtest and composite scores as well as extensive information on the development, standardization, and the psychometric properties of the K-SNAP.

STANDARDIZATION. The K-SNAP was developed in parallel with the KAIT, the Kaufman Brief Intelligence Test (K-BIT), and the Kaufman Functional Academic Skills Test (K-FAST). The standardization sample included 2,000 subjects aged from 11 to 85 years and comprised between 100 and 250 subjects for each of the 13 age level groups used. The sample was stratified by gender, geographic region, socioeconomic status (examinee or parental education levels), and race/ethnic group based on U.S. Bureau of the Census population estimates for 1990. Comparison of the demographic characteristics of the sample to the American population reveals a close match for the variable considered. However, regarding geographic region, the standardization sample contained fewer individuals from the Northeast region whereas the West region was slightly overrepresented.

RELIABILITY. Internal consistency estimates are reported by age level for each subtest (excluding Mental Status) or composite scores. Corrected split-half coefficients are found to average in the mid .80s for the Gestalt Closure, Number Recall, and Four-Letter Words subtests. Estimates of the reliabilities of composite scores range from .75 to .92 (Mean: .85) for the Recall/Closure Composite and from .82 to .94 (Mean: .89) for the K-SNAP Composite. Standard errors of measurement are estimated to be about 1 point on the three subtests and on the Recall/Closure composite, and 5 standard score points on the K-SNAP composite score.

Test-retest (1-month interval) reliability analysis was performed on a normal sample of 132 adolescents and adults. Stability coefficients, corrected for the variability of the norm group, are lower, varying from .65 to .79 for the three different subtests and averaging in the low .80s for the two composite scores. With this normal sample, the stability coefficient obtained for the Impairment Index was marginal (.68). The stability of the Mental Status subtest was examined with a subsample (N = 54) of individuals aged 55 and older and found to be in the mid .70s. Split-half reliability coefficients for the Mental Status subtest score, computed with two clinical samples (N = 50 and N = 91) were acceptable.

VALIDITY. The manual reports an impressive set of studies supporting the validity of the K-SNAP. The initial item pool was pretested and evaluated by means of conventional item analysis and more sophisticated Rasch model analysis. As well, the Mantel-Haenszel procedure was used to investigate the possibility of item bias related to gender and race/ethnic groups. Support for the concurrent validity of the K-SNAP composite score is provided by substantial correlations with global scores on comprehensive intelligence measures (KAIT, K-ABC, SB-IV, WISC-R, WAIS-R) and moderate correlations with scores obtained on other brief cognitive ability measures (K-FAST, K-BIT, and PPVT-R) in normal samples.

Age-related changes on the subtests correspond to the expected growth patterns reported in the empirical literature. Evidence for the construct validity is further illustrated by results of joint factor analysis with the Wechsler Adult Intelligence Scale—Revised (WAIS-R), the KAIT, and the K-FAST, which revealed each K-SNAP subtest to be associated only with the hypothesized factor. Validity analyses were also performed with various small clinical samples (neurologically impaired, Alzheimer's, mentally retarded, reading disabled, and clinically depressed), results again documenting the concurrent validity of the K-SNAP.

The diagnostic validity of the K-SNAP was examined by contrasting the test results for the clinical groups and matched controls. Although the combined clinical sample obtains significantly lower subtest and composite scores than matched controls, when individual samples are considered, some of the differences disappear. The means of the right-hemisphere damaged sample, for instance, are similar to that of matched controls on the two composite scores. As well, the results from the Mental Status subtest give rise to reliable results mostly for Alzheimer's (mean raw score = 4.8) and mentally retarded (mean raw score = 6.8) patients. Although the mean raw score of brain-damaged patients (9.4) is close to a perfect score of 10, compared to matched control, the means of right-damaged and the combined brain-damaged group were significantly lower. The mean for left-damaged patients is not found to be significantly different from that of matched controls. In analyzing the validity of the Impairment

Index, data show its ability to discriminate brain-damaged from clinically depressed patients and brain-damaged from a combined group of low-functioning clients (Alzheimer's and mental retardation). Although about 90% of patients with Alzheimer's or mental retardation obtained a score equivalent to or higher than the clinical cutoff (3 points), only a third of the neurologically impaired patients did so. The majority of patients with documented brain damage thus obtained an Impairment Index within the normal range.

CONCLUSION. The K-SNAP is an interesting addition to the series of instruments developed by Kaufman and Kaufman and presents many innovative features relative to more traditional tests of cognitive functioning. The K-SNAP is a well-designed, well-normed, brief instrument, which may provide a valuable asset for professionals involved in mental and neuropsychological assessment. The K-SNAP presents many good qualities to recommend its use. It should not, however, be used as a substitute for more comprehensive instruments or diagnostic tools. Given the limitations noted, further studies with larger clinical samples are needed to substantiate claims regarding the diagnostic validity of the K-SNAP.

[168]

Khatena-Torrance Creative Perception Inventory.

Purpose: Measures of creative personality.
Population: Age 12–adult.
Publication Date: 1976.
Administration: Group.
Price Data, 1996: $53.50 per starter set including 35 WKOPAY, 35 SAM, 35 scoring worksheets, and instruction manual (70 pages); $35.25 per 35 each of WKOPAY, SAM, and scoring worksheets; $30.40 per instruction manual; $18.90 per specimen set.
Publisher: Scholastic Testing Service, Inc.
a) WHAT KIND OF PERSON ARE YOU?
Purpose: Designed to "yield an index of the individual's disposition or motivation to function in creative ways."
Acronym: WKOPAY.
Scores: 5 factors: Acceptance of Authority, Self-Confidence, Inquisitiveness, Awareness of Others, Disciplined Imagination.
Time: (5–10) minutes.
Author: E. Paul Torrance.
b) SOMETHING ABOUT MYSELF.
Purpose: Designed as an autobiographical "screening device for the identification of creative people."
Acronym: SAM.

Scores: 6 factors: Environmental Sensitivity, Initiative, Self-Strength, Intellectuality, Individuality, Artistry.
Time: (10–15) minutes.
Author: Joe Khatena.
Cross References: For a review by Philip E. Vernon, see 9:569 (3 references).

TEST REFERENCES

1. Campos, A., & González, M. A. (1994). Influence of creativity on vividness of imagery. *Perceptual and Motor Skills, 78,* 1067–1071.
2. Morse, D. T. (1994). Reliability estimates for total, factor, and group mean scores on the Khatena-Torrance Creative Perception Inventory. *Perceptive and Motor Skills, 79,* 155–162.

Review of the Khatena-Torrance Creative Perception Inventory by DAVID L. BOLTON, Assistant Professor, West Chester University, West Chester, PA:

The Khatena-Torrance Creative Perception Inventory consists of two instruments: What Kind of Person Are You? and Something About Myself. According to the manual, the purpose of both instruments is to provide a method of identifying creativity and creative personalities.

What Kind of Person Are You? consists of 50 pairs of characteristics purported to distinguish between creative and less creative individuals. Those taking the test are asked to select one of the pairs of traits. One of the traits is that of a creative person, whereas the other characterizes a noncreative person. This list of characteristics is based upon a survey conducted by one of the authors, Torrance (Torrance, 1962), of research studies on creativity. This survey found 84 characteristics that differentiated creative from noncreative individuals. Out of these 84 characteristics, 50 were selected for this instrument. These traits are paired with other traits that do not characterize creative individuals. If a person chooses the creative trait, a point is added to the overall score. This score is then compared with norms to obtain a standard score on a scale of from 1 to 9.

Something About Myself also consists of 50 items. These items were also determined using previous research. The 50 statements fall into one of three categories: personality traits, use of creative thinking strategies, and creative productions. Personality traits consist of statements describing characteristics of an individual, such as "Others consider me eccentric." Use of creative thinking strategies involve statements of problem-solving techniques, such as "I am prepared to review my judgments when new information turns up." Statements describing creative productions show ways in which the creative personality has been expressed and include such things as "I have composed a dance, song or musical piece for voice or instrument." Those taking the test are to read through the statements and check them if they feel they pertain to them. Scoring is done by counting the number of items a person has checked. This score is also compared with norms to obtain a standard score on a scale of from 1 to 8.

Reliability of both instruments was determined using interrater, internal consistency, and test-retest methods. Several studies were done for each instrument. Interrater reliability coefficients for both tests were high as would be expected for an objective test. Internal consistency methods for both tests generally showed high reliability coefficients, typically greater than .90. Test-retest (1-day to 6-week interval) reliability coefficients for What Kind of Person Are You? ranged from .71 to .97. For Something About Myself, test-retest (1-day to 4-week interval) reliability coefficients went from .77 to .98, with most of the studies showing reliability greater than .90. Overall the reliability appears to be satisfactory.

Following the development of the instruments, the authors conducted much research to support their validity. Generally this research has involved administering one of the instruments and correlating the results with other measures of creativity or other measures that are theoretically related to creativity. These instruments included Runner Studies of Attitude Patterns, Omnibus Personality Inventory, Torrance Test of Creative Thinking, Sounds and Images, and Onomatopoeia. (Both Sounds and Images and Onomatopoeia are now part of the inventory Thinking Creatively With Sounds and Words, Research Edition [T4:2830]). The instruments were also correlated with biographical factors, self-ratings, and other variables. The studies showed results for the most part in the desired directions, although the strength of the correlation varied significantly from one study to another.

A major validity issue with these types of instruments has to do with self-report. The authors point out this difficulty in their introduction to the manual, indicating the possibility that respondents might not be honest. In What Kind of Person Are You? pairs of characteristics are listed. For the most part, these pairs are of similar social desirability. However, there are some pairs in which one pair is more socially desirable. For example, one pair is "Fault-finding" and "Popular, well-liked." Given the choice, respondents are more likely to choose the socially desirable response, reducing the validity of the measure.

Also, these instruments rely upon the respondent having an accurate self-perception. To the extent that this is not the case, the instruments will lack validity. What Kind of Person Are You? requires individuals to make a forced choice between two different options. In looking at the choices, it would be expected that most individuals would accurately be able to differentiate between these options. However, in Something About Myself, individuals are asked to determine if stated characteristics pertain to them. For some of the statements, individuals may easily know if it fits them. An example of this is "I have invented a new product." However, other statements require more self-awareness. Two examples are: "I am resourceful" and "I can spot the source of a problem and define it." Because these statements require a greater sense of self-awareness, it is less likely that respondents will be able to determine accurately if these statements pertain to them.

Some of the measures with which the instruments are correlated are also self-report instruments. These are likely to evoke socially desirable responding and inaccurate self-perceptions of the respondents as well. One way of avoiding the self-report issue is to correlate the instruments with other measures of creativity that do not involve self-report. The authors do so in that they use instruments for which a creative response is required from the respondents. The Torrance Tests of Creative Thinking, Sounds and Image, and Onomatopoeia are all instruments in which an individual's responses are solicited and the response evaluated by a scorer. They are not self-report instruments. The prompts differ for these instruments. For the Torrance Tests of Creative Thinking the prompts are verbal and figural. For Sounds and Images and Onomatopoeia the prompts are primarily auditory. The correlations with these instruments support, for the most part, the validity of the instruments. For example, in the studies correlating What Kind of Person Are You?, Sounds and Images, and Onomatopoeia, the correlation ranged from .26 to .75, with the median correlation being .425.

One thing the authors fail to do is to define adequately what is being measured. The tests not only attempt to identify creative personalities (criterion-related validity), but they also appear to purport to measure creativity of individuals (construct validity). The authors, however, do not overtly define what is meant by creativity. This undermines any attempt at trying to establish construct validity. It appears that the instrument would do an adequate job at identifying creative individuals. However, because the authors fail to define a construct, it could not be said that the instruments have more than just the ability to predict.

Without a clear-cut definition of the construct being measured, the authors provide no prespecified notion of its dimensionality. Is it a unidimensional or multidimensional entity? The instrument implies that there is one overall creative self-perception score. However, the authors provide two different instruments in the inventory. When they correlated the scores from both instruments, there was a correlation of only .36. This begs the question as to what each instrument is measuring and how what each is measuring differs. And there is no explanation as to how to use the two instruments with each other.

An exploratory factor analysis is conducted on both instruments separately to determine their dimensionality. After conducting the analysis, five factors were determined for What Kind of Person Are You?: Acceptance of Authority, Self-Confidence, Inquisitiveness, Awareness of Others, and Disciplined Imagination. For Something About Myself, six factors were determined: Environmental Sensitivity, Initiative, Self-Strength, Intellectuality, Individuality, and Artistry.

It would have strengthened the instrument considerably if a more definitive definition of the construct had been formulated and confirmatory factor analysis used to test the dimensionality of the construct. It would also have been better if the responses from both instruments would have been used in one factor analysis to determine their relationship. As such, the results must be viewed as being fairly tentative. Further research would be needed to confirm these factors.

In general, there is little instruction as to how to use this inventory in practice. An extensive reference list is provided. However, it would require much effort on the part of the user to find the information needed. A major improvement to the manual would be a section describing how to use the inventory practically.

Norms were obtained for both instruments. For What Kind of Person Are You? 4,362 subjects were used, and for Something About Myself, 2,923 subjects were used. According to the manual, adult and adolescent norms were obtained, implying that there were separate norms for both. However, in the manual there are not separate norms for each group; there is only one set of norms. So it is not clear how many subjects were considered adults and how many were adolescents.

The adults used to create the norms were college students. The assumption that college students are representative of all adults for these tests is questionable. Not only is the degree of self-aware-

ness lower than many adults, the experiences of college students are not as extensive as older adults. This might be important in responding to such items as "I experiment in cooking and make new recipes," and "I have shown organizational ability." Some college students may do these things in the future, but they may not have had the opportunity to do them up to this point in their life.

For What Kind of Person Are You? the norming group is based upon students from several colleges from various parts of the United States. For Something About Myself the colleges are not as representative. There are only students from five colleges in the norming group. There are no colleges represented from the western part of the United States. The adolescents in the norming group are from junior and senior high schools from Ohio, Virginia, and West Virginia. This should not be considered a very representative group of adolescents from across the country.

The Khatena Torrance Creative Perception Inventory is an instrument that might be used to predict how well respondents will perform in situations that require creative thinking. However, it would be recommended that those using it conduct their own research to verify that it has validity for their particular situation. Because successful performance of creative tasks involves many different factors, the results of this inventory can only be used as one of the bits of information in any type of selection process.

REVIEWER'S REFERENCE

Torrance, E. P. (1962). *Guiding creative talent*. Englewood Cliffs, NJ: Prentice-Hall.

Review of the Khatena-Torrance Creative Perception Inventory by WILLIAM STEVE LANG, Associate Professor of Educational Measurement and Research, University of South Florida, St. Petersburg, FL:

The Khatena-Torrance Creative Perception Inventory (KTCPI) is an autobiographical instrument in two parts, which is designed to assess components of creativity as self-perceived. Specifically, the instrument's areas are: What Kind of Person Are You? (WKOPAY) and Something About Myself (SAM).

The WKOPAY consists of 50 items for which test takers simply check those that self-describe themselves from a pair of adjectives and descriptive phrases. A typical item is to chose between "Feels strong emotions" and "Reserved." Scoring is the simple frequency count of the items scored against a key. Scores are reported for the dimensions: Acceptance of Authority, Self Confidence, Inquisitiveness, Awareness of Others, Disciplined Imagination, and a Total Scale.

The SAM consists of 50 items. The respondent simply puts a check by the statements that are applicable to themself. The SAM is a simple frequency count to obtain a score. The six factor orientations measured are Environmental Sensitivity, Initiative, Self Strength, Intellectuality, Individuality, Artistry, and a Total Scale.

The authors suggest the instruments can be administered in groups up to size 40. Both measures can be finished in less than 45 minutes.

The manual contains an extensive discussion of the instruments. The development of the two instruments is described. The two separately developed measures were combined for the current form. Both tests were factor analyzed to determine the components.

Internal consistency, interrater, and test-retest (same day to 6-week intervals) reliability studies are reported for both parts of the KTCPI with reliability figures from approximately .7 to .98. These are very good reliability estimates for an instrument designed to measure an aspect of creativity.

The KTCPI reports on validity studies for content validity, construct validity, and criterion-related validity for both parts. The content validity section is the weakest, as the manual admits that defining the scope and sequence of creative skills or talent is difficult, which precludes a table of specifications for content validity. On the other hand, the construct validity of the KTCPI is fairly well defended with correlational studies, factor analysis, and cross-validation studies. The criterion-related validity evidence of the KTCPI includes studies where other instruments, observable behaviors, and observational judgments served as criteria.

Extensive normative data for the KTCPI were available in the manual. Tables for adults and adolescents, by school and state, and for "gifted" persons were provided with means and standard deviations. Stanines were also available in separate tables. The tables were typically complete, though disjointed and somewhat disorganized as to placement. There were 36 tables, and much of the data and table titles were confusing.

Despite the evidence that the KTCPI is technically sound, there are some weak areas a user should note. First, it is not clear that the authors' contention that "the use of autobiographical instruments as screening devices for giftedness has found support in the opinion and research of many in the field of creativity" (Instrument Manual, p. 9) is accurate. Secondly, the copyright for the KTCPI is 1976 and most of the references date from the 1950s through 1970s. There is no indication in the manual that the instrument or norms tables have been updated in the last 20 years.

Obviously, an autobiographical instrument used for screening for gifted or talented programs would be a target for false answers from the test taker who wanted to be in a program. If there is external observation or some other screening to determine placement, then why use the KTCPI? Perhaps as a first-step screening device or for guidance and counseling activities it would be appropriate but would be seriously lacking for placement decisions.

As a self-awareness tool, the KTCPI has merit, and for some students would be part of a study of potential creative abilities—again assuming the participants did not put false scores in response to hopes, halo effects, parental wishes, and competition with classmates. The authors would be well served to give specific uses of the KTCPI and research-based conclusions for its application.

A less important but significant criticism of the KTCPI is the somewhat incestuous and dated nature of many of the defenses to autobiographical instruments in lieu of more projective techniques (e.g., the Torrance Tests of Creative Thinking [T4:2849]) or observational measures. Even though the autobiographical approach is quick and easy to administer and score, the ultimate validity of the scores is subject to the perception of oneself, who also must have a clear conception of the traits measured. This is why the KTCPI needs an interpreter so that the users understand the nature of the statements presented.

The forced-choice form used by the WKOPAY is preferred to the SAM's simple checking of applicable statements. At least, there is a more projective nature to the WKOPAY. Why not use the same format for both?

In summary, the KTCPI would be useful for research, general screening with low-stakes results, and self-awareness purposes with a focus on creativity and the factors suggested by the authors. It is a useful addition to an area that does not have a large number of creativity tests available, and where validity and reliability studies are difficult. It needs defined uses and more research examination of the dependability of autobiographical views of one's own skill with this particular instrument. The manual is technically accurate, but extremely dated and poorly written.

[169]

Khatena-Morse Multitalent Perception Inventory.

Purpose: Identifies giftedness in music, art, and leadership.

Population: Ages 6 to adult.

Publication Dates: 1985–1994.

Acronym: KMMPI.

Scores, 6: Artistic, Musical, Creative Imagination, Initiative, Leadership, Versatility.

Administration: Group.

Forms, 2: A, B.

Price Data, 1996: $52.50 per starter set including 35 questionnaires (specify Form A or B) and manual ('94, 101 pages); $25.75 per 35 questionnaires (specify Form A or B); $28.88 per manual; $30 per specimen set.

Time: (30–45) minutes.

Authors: Joe Khatena and David T. Morse.

Publisher: Scholastic Testing Service, Inc.

Review of the Khatena-Morse Multitalent Perception Inventory by CAROLYN M. CALLAHAN, William Clay Parish, Jr. Professor of Education, University of Virginia, Charlottesville, VA:

Designed to assess five dimensions of talent (Artistry, Musical, Creative Imagination, Initiative, and Leadership), the Khatena-Morse Multitalent Perception Inventory (KMMPI) relies on self-report regarding participation in activities and self-evaluation of capabilities in each of the domains. The scores from the subscales may be combined to yield a "Versatility Index." The number of items on the subscales range from 4 to 13. The sentence structure is simple and the reading level is low. The implied purpose of the instrument is for assessing talent as part of the process of identifying gifted and talented students. A secondary purpose alluded to by the authors is for intra-individual comparisons of relative strengths.

Estimates of internal consistency (coefficient alpha) reliability for the subscales range from .41 to .87 for children and .41 to .92 for adults. Hence, the use of factor scores for making high-stakes decisions about individuals is not warranted, particularly for the Creative Imagination, Initiative, and Leadership scales—a caution noted by the authors who recommend using a combination of Forms A and B in these cases. However, even when the forms are combined the reliability does not exceed .80 for any scale. Therefore, appropriate application of three of the five scales requires them to be combined to achieve adequate levels of reliability. Equivalency reliability estimates and test-retest (2-week interval) reliabilities are presented for total scores only. The authors claim that these data support "the reliability of the instrument for use as a measure of multiple talents or versatility of children or adults" (p. 19). This claim raises a validity issue: What exactly is the construct of multiple talents or versatility?

Validity of the KMMPI seems to rest on the adequacy of scores on the subscales to represent talent in the five dimensions and to predict talents in these domains or success in gifted programs designed to develop these talents. The authors' claim for content validity is based on creation of items reflecting "previous research findings, some hypotheses relative to talent and creativity, and judgment of the authors" (p. 21). No evidence is provided of a sampling matrix relative to the factors assessed or to other expert judgments of the adequacy of the sample.

The evidence presented in support of construct validity is complex, but at times tangential. One study of college students used a priori rational factors (rather than the empirically derived factors used in scoring) to compare art or music majors with majors taking courses or nonmajors not taking courses. A follow-up study using the empirically derived factors provided evidence that the Artistic subscale means were significantly higher for majors, and the Musical subscale means were significantly higher for music majors. The significant differences across these groups are not surprising given the experience base of the instrument and the population selected. The usefulness of this information as validity evidence is questionable. A factor analytic analysis supports the factor structure, although clearly the artistic and musical items yield the strongest factors. In sociometric tests of the leadership scales with children, total selections by male classmates and same sex peers were *not* significantly correlated with leadership.

Correlations of the KMMPI with other measures of originality were quite low (.16–.42). Although the authors claim this is to be expected given the broad nature of the versatility scale, correlations with the Creative Imagination subscale alone are still very low. The authors claim that patterns of relationship are "congruent with the idea of a creative imagination as facilitative of production of creative ideas" (p. 39); however, little light is cast on the meaning of the versatility score. Two of the three correlations between subscales and teacher judgments of talent in art and music are at the college level.

Comparisons of gifted with nongifted populations are based on the weak premise: "to the extent that students who excel academically also distinguish[ed] themselves in these areas of talent, differences would also be anticipated" (p. 43).

Although the authors present considerably more evidence of validity than is available for most instruments of this type, evidence of validity, low reliabilities of subscales scores, the lack of a clear statement regarding the purpose of the instrument, lack of a clear definition of versatility and its relationship to the factors assessed, and lack of clear construct or predictive validity evidence make the use of scores derived from this instrument for identification or placement decision-making purposes inappropriate. At this time, the KMMPI should be used for group assessment or research purposes only.

Review of the Khatena-Morese Multitalent Perception Inventory by WILLIAM STEVE LANG, Associate Professor of Educational Measurement and Research, University of South Florida, St. Petersburg, FL:

The Khatena-Morse Multitalent Perception Inventory (KMMPI) is an autobiographical instrument in two forms which is designed to assess components of a broad concept of giftedness which are not normally measured by traditional tests of ability and aptitude. Specifically, these areas are leadership, visual art, and performing art within the broader context of creativity.

The KMMPI consists of 50 items. The test taker simply checks those items that self-describe. Others are left blank. A typical item is, "I can keep time to a tune easily." Scoring is the simple frequency count of the items checked. Scores are reported for the dimensions Artistic, Musical, Creative Imagination, Initiative, Leadership, and a Total (called Versatility).

The authors suggest the KMMPI can be administered to 10-year-olds and up without help and to younger students in school with an examiner to assist the child in identifying the characteristics possessed. The KMMPI can be administered to groups and no time limit is set, though 10 to 20 minutes is the usual completion time suggested by the authors.

The KMMPI manual contains an extensive discussion of the instrument. The selection of items from conception to final form is clear and appropriate. Large samples (up to 6,000 subjects) were used to create an item pool and to develop the final 50-item forms. Proportion correct and discrimination statistics for every item are included.

Internal consistency, alternate form, and test-retest reliability (2-week interval) studies are reported with reliability estimates from approximately .6 to .95. This is very good evidence of reliability for an instrument designed to measure an aspect of creativity and better than many other tests of musical, artistic, or leadership ability.

The KMMPI reports on validity studies for content validity, construct validity, and criterion-related validity. The content validity section is the weakest, as the manual admits that defining the score and sequence of creative skills or talent is "almost ridiculous," which precludes a table of specifications for content validity. On the other hand, the construct validity of the KMMPI is fairly well defended with correlational studies, factor analysis, and cross-validation studies. The manual admits that the Leadership subtest is the poorest in terms of construct validity, but some support is demonstrated. The criterion-related validity evidence of the KMMPI includes studies where other instruments, observable behaviors, and observed judgments served as criteria. The evidence was moderate to weak that the KMMPI has predictive power, even though most relationships were in the direction predicted by the test.

Extensive normative data for the KMMPI were available in the manual. Tables for adults and children, by grade and region, and for "gifted" persons were provided with means, percentile ranks, *SDS T* scores, and stanines. The tables were typically complete, though disjointed and somewhat disorganized as to placement.

Despite the evidence that the KMMPI is technically sound, there are some weak areas a user should note. First, it is not clear what the instrument would be best used for in the view of the authors. Obviously, an autobiographical instrument used for screening for gifted or talented programs would be a target for false answers from the test taker who wanted to be in a program. If there is external observation or some other screening to determine placement, then why use the KMMPI? Perhaps as a general first-step screening device, it would be appropriate, but it would not likely take the place of recommendations of the band directors and art teachers who are already charged with observational assessments.

As a self-awareness tool, the KMMPI has merit, and, for some students, would be part of a study of potential abilities in music, art, or leadership—again assuming the participants did not provide false scores due to hopes, halo effects, parental wishes, and competition with classmates. The authors would be well served to give specific uses of the KMMPI and research-based conclusions for its applications other than for research purposes.

A less important but significant criticism of the KMMPI is the somewhat incestuous and dated nature of many of the defenses to autobiographical instruments in lieu of more projective techniques (like the Torrance Test of Creative Thinking) or observational measures of music, art, and leadership.

Even though the autobiographical approach is quick and easy to administer and score, the ultimate validity of the scores is subject to the perception of oneself, who also must have a clear conception of the traits measured. This is why the KMMPI needs an interpreter so that younger children understand the nature of the statements presented. It is possible an adult will "understand" and respond to the statement, "I am able to hum or sing any tune easily," but may not be one that all of us would want to listen to outside of the shower! As a group, the scores make correlational sense, but, for the individual, there is probably much judgmental error.

In summary, the KMMPI would be useful for research, general screening with low-stakes results, and self-awareness purposes with a focus on creative aspects of music, art, and leadership domains. It is a useful addition to an area that does not have a large number of quality tests available, and where validity and reliability studies are almost nonexistent. It needs defined uses and more research examination of the dependability of autobiographical views of one's own skill. The manual is technically accurate, but users may be lost before getting to "Table 112 (cont.)," so a consolidation of the manual would be most welcome.

[170]
Kilmann-Saxton Culture-Gap Survey [Revised].

Purpose: Assesses "actual versus desired cultural norms."
Population: Work team members, employees.
Publication Dates: 1983–1991.
Acronym: CGS.
Scores, 4: Task Support, Social Relationships, Task Innovation, Personal Freedom.
Administration: Group.
Price Data, 1994: $6.25 per survey.
Time: (30) minutes.
Authors: Ralph H. Kilmann and Mary J. Saxton.
Publisher: XICOM, Inc.
Cross References: For reviews of an earlier edition by Andres Barona and Gargi Roysircar Sodowsky, see 11:192.

Review of the Kilmann-Saxton Culture-Gap Survey [Revised] by RUSSELL N. CARNEY, Associate Professor of Psychology, Southwest Missouri State University, Springfield, MO:

The Kilmann-Saxton Culture-Gap Survey [Revised] is a concise self-report instrument that purports to measure both the *actual* and *desired* cultural norms of one's workplace. Comparing an individual's actual and desired responses to this survey

yields what are termed "culture-gaps" in four areas. Specifying these culture-gaps serves to identify the "invisible forces in a company's culture [that] can be barriers to high performance and morale" (manual, p. 29).

ADMINISTRATION. On each of the 28 items presented in Part 1 (Actual Norms), the examinee chooses between two statements based on what he or she feels is the actual norm for the work group (e.g., "A. Encourage creativity" vs. "B. Discourage creativity," or "A. Don't develop friendships with your co-workers" vs. "B. Develop friendships with your co-workers"). As can be seen, in many instances one of the pair is clearly the ideal. Next, the employee completes Part 2 (Desired Norms), which is composed of the same 28 items (in the same order, renumbered 29–56). Here, the choice is made based on how the employee feels the work place "should be operating in order to increase performance, job satisfaction, and morale" (p. 7). Having completed these two sets of 28, a separate page pairs corresponding items into four conceptual subsets, and describes a simple self-scoring procedure. A computerized analysis is available, but no details are provided in the manual.

SELF-SCORING AND INTERPRETATION. Self-scoring of responses yields positive or negative whole number values (-7 to +7) representing culture-gap scores in four areas: Task Support, Task Innovation, Social Relationships, and Personal Freedom. These four raw scores may then be plotted on a bar graph profile provided in the administration manual. Filled bars represent positive scores, whereas unfilled bars (also plotted upward) represent negative scores. The four areas may be further conceptualized in terms of a human/technical dimension, and a short-term/long-term dimension.

Interpretative information in the manual suggests that a score of +3 or higher represents a potentially significant culture-gap. A positive score suggests "a desire for *more* task support, *more* task innovation, *more* social relationships, or *more* personal freedom" (p. 24), depending on the area. A +2 is described as borderline, and a +1 as insignificant. Negative scores are said to occur less frequently, and to suggest that *less* structure is desired (i.e., less task support, etc.). If three or four scores are found to be significant, the authors suggest that a "rather broad-based cultural problem" (p. 24) may exist.

Once the individual completes the survey and figures his or her scores, an entire work group, department, and/or organization can complete the survey to provide group-based culture-gap data. In each case, group means are calculated, and space is provided in the manual for plotting each of these as before. Toward the end of the manual, an example presents four area means for a hypothetical work group (+3.2, +5.4, +1.5, and -3.7) and discusses the implications of these culture-gaps. As a final note, the authors suggest re-administering the survey after a 6- to 12-month delay to evaluate the organization's efforts to reduce culture-gap scores.

VALIDITY AND RELIABILITY. A call to XICOM (800-759-4266) confirmed that no technical manual accompanies the administration manual. This lack of published technical information in support of the instrument is clearly problematic, as two earlier reviews have pointed out (Barona, 1992; Sodowsky, 1992). With this in mind, perhaps the most pressing question concerns the instrument's *construct validity* (e.g., Messick, 1989). Although the survey purports to measure culture gaps in four areas (Task Support, Task Innovation, Social Relationships, and Personal Freedom), *no* evidence for these constructs is ever provided. For example, we are not informed as to how the 28 item pairs were selected, nor how the items were divided into the four subsets of 7 representing the four construct areas (although face-validity is apparent). Although the current manual is mute on the subject, Barona reported that the survey was based on "more than 400 items generated through interviews and group discussions with employees from a wide range of organizations" (p. 440) and that statistical analyses were used to determine the final 28 items. Further, *no* information regarding *reliability* (e.g., the stability of the score over time, or the internal consistency of the items) is provided. Barona reported that additional technical details were available in Saxton's dissertation. If this information *is* available, the authors need to publish these important psychometric details.

ADDITIONAL CONCERNS. The manual provides *no* rationale for the authors' interpretation of culture-gap scores (e.g., that a +3 represents a potentially significant culture-gap). However, Barona (1992) again sheds some light on this, reporting that these "diagnostic guidelines derived from more than 1,000 responses from over 25 profit and nonprofit organizations" (p. 440). Publishing demographic and descriptive statistics regarding this sample (e.g., means and standard deviations per area) would be helpful in justifying the interpretative cutoffs.

Although the bar graph profile is indeed user friendly, it seems misleading on at least two counts.

First plotting negative culture-gap scores upward (as unfilled bars) is confusing because negative numbers are usually plotted downward on graphs. Further, the four areas are plotted in four adjacent cells or quadrants. The fact that they touch suggests some kind of continuum, which I do not believe is the case. Hence, it would be more appropriate to plot these four graphs on unconnected profiles. In an earlier review, Sodowsky (1992) listed several problems regarding the nature of the statements used in the survey. For example, the use of pronouns such as "you" and "your" in Part 1 items (e.g., "Live for your job or career") may elicit response sets reflecting personal reactions to the statements as opposed to the group's actual norms. Further, in Part 2, because in many of the item pairs one represents the ideal (e.g., "A. Complete all tasks in the best possible way" vs. "B. Do as little as necessary to get by"), the examinee may choose the socially acceptable response, as opposed to marking their own preference. Also, as illustrated on the final item (e.g., "A. Believe in your own values" vs. "B. Believe in the organization's values"), the two statements may not necessarily contradict each other.

SUMMARY. In closing, this survey may hold potential in terms of measuring culture-gaps among actual and desired cultural norms in the workplace. However, this revision of the Kilmann-Saxton Culture-Gap Survey continues to suffer from a lack of published technical data in regard to such fundamental test development concepts as reliability and validity. Further, because the employees and organizations who were involved in the development of the items are not described, it is difficult to specify for whom the survey is appropriate. As it stands, I cannot recommend the instrument because the technical information required by the *Standards for Educational and Psychological Testing* (AERA, APA, & NCME, 1985) is not provided. Two potential sources of information appear to be Saxton's dissertation (date and source unknown) and Kilmann's book *Managing Beyond the Quick Fix* (Jossey-Bass, 1989). If this is the case, it would seem a straightforward matter for these authors to produce a technical manual to accompany their survey. In the meantime, however, using this instrument represents a leap of faith.

REVIEWER'S REFERENCES

American Educational Research Association, American Psychological Association, & National Council on Measurement in Education. (1985). *Standards for educational and psychological testing*. Washington, DC: American Psychological Association, Inc.

Messick, S. (1989). Validity. In R. L. Linn (Ed.), *Educational measurement* (3rd ed.; pp. 13–103). New York: Macmillan.

Barona, A. (1992). [Review of the Kilmann-Saxton Culture-Gap Survey.] In J. J. Kramer & J. C. Conoley (Eds.), *The eleventh mental measurements yearbook* (pp. 439–440). Lincoln, NE: Buros Institute of Mental Measurements.

Sodowsky, G. R. (1992). [Review of the Kilmann-Saxton Culture-Gap Survey.] In J. J. Kramer & J. C. Conoley (Eds.), *The eleventh mental measurements yearbook* (pp. 440–442). Lincoln, NE: Buros Institute of Mental Measurements.

Review of the Kilmann-Saxton Culture-Gap Survey [Revised] by NORMAN D. SUNDBERG, Professor Emeritus, Department of Psychology, University of Oregon, Eugene, OR:

The Kilmann-Saxton Culture-Gap Survey (CGS) is intended to be used as a method for revealing norms within organizations. (It is not a study of individual acculturation as the name might imply.) The CGS consists of 28 paired statements similar to these: "It's all right to mix friendships with business" vs. "Don't make friends with people at work," and "Develop new ways of doing things" vs. "Avoid changing things." At first respondents choose one in the pair according to their perceptions of the actual situation within their work group; then they answer the same set of 28 pairs according to what they see as desirable. Thus, a desired-actual "culture-gap" score is created.

The CGS provides gap scores for each of four content areas (made up of mutually exclusive items): Task Support and Task Innovation (which together are called Technical Concerns) and Social Relationships and Personal Freedom (which are called Human Concerns). Splitting the other way in a fourfold table, the authors label Task Support and Social Relationships as Short Term and Task Innovation and Personal Freedom as Long Term. This procedure may be applied at different levels in an organization, such as work group, department, or the whole organization, and can be repeated to observe changes after introduction of an organizational development program. Results are plotted on bar graphs. The CGS is contained in a 28-page booklet for the company user, and covers the items, scoring, and interpretation. The interpretation (or diagnosis) for the surveyed unit depends on the size of the difference between desired and actual. Differences, whether positive or negative, over a small amount indicate organizational problems. (Apparently zero difference is desirable, though that suggests an acceptance of the status quo.)

The "manual" is very readable and seems to be written for the intelligent business person, not a professional expert. The reader is referred to Kilmann's book, *Managing Beyond the Quick Fix* (Jossey-Bass, 1989), for an "integrated program for creating and maintaining organizational success—with managing cultural norms at center stage" (p. 27). The authors are experienced professionals and consultants in organizational work. Ralph Kilmann is a Business Administration professor at the University of Pittsburgh and president of a well-known consulting firm. He has written many books and articles, and Mary Saxton has co-authored several books and articles in the management field. The Culture-Gap Survey is cleverly developed and scored to reveal some important aspects of organizations.

The potential user should be aware of several concerns and conditions: Firstly, the CGS, as presented in the booklet, is not a test in the traditional sense. The booklet is not a manual for professionals interested in research covering item analyses, norm groups, reliability, and validity. It does not meet the guidelines of the *Standards for Educational and Psychological Testing* (AERA, APA, & NCME, 1985). There are no studies of other answer formats or of influences of test-taking attitudes. The reviews of the 1983 edition by Barona and Sodowsky in the *11th MMY* do mention that diagnostic guidelines were derived from 1,000 responses but even this information is not in this "manual." Kilmann's 1989 book presents a longer exposition of the CGS, including case illustrations, but it does not cover psychometric details such as national norms or statistical evidence of change over time. The CGS seems to have face validity, but there is no research evidence of its actual utility.

Secondly, the CGS addresses only organizational norms based on reports of individuals or groups, not wider characteristics of organizations related to productivity, job satisfaction, etc. One misses studies of how culture gaps might be involved in these larger characteristics on one hand and how they fit in with observations and interviews on the other hand.

Thirdly, the word "culture" in the title may be misleading for many in these times of multicultural concerns. That word and the similar word, "climate," have been widely used and disputed in the business world. In the CGS the term has the limited reference to group norms. The CGS booklet shows no concern with problems of ethnicity, which is often implied by "culture" in the larger cross-cultural or anthropological sense. Kilmann, in his book, does caution against interpretations when using the CGS in other countries because national cultures may affect corporate cultures. This larger cultural effect would probably be particularly apparent in collectivist Asian cultures. Especially susceptible to cultural influences would be items dealing with putting individual goals ahead of the group effort.

Fourthly, the theoretical rationale behind the CGS might be questioned. For instance, the distinction between Short Term and Long Term in the four-fold table seems peculiar. The quadrant Personal Freedom is classified with Task Innovation as Long Term and Social Relations with Task Support as Short. Why are the latter two not also required in the Long Term, one wonders. Apparently, the assumptions are that innovation is Long Term only and that innovation requires personal freedom. It would be helpful to have research evidence for the underlying theoretical structure. There is also an assumption that culture-gaps are of such importance that they should set priorities for organizational development. Again, it would be good to see evidence of their importance in the larger picture of organizations.

In sum, the Culture-Gap Survey is a clever and fairly simple procedure that might be used to focus early efforts in consulting with an organization. It should have face validity with managers and would stimulate further explorations, but it does not have the status of a psychometric test.

REVIEWER'S REFERENCE

American Educational Research Association, American Psychological Association, & National Council on Measurement in Education. (1985). *Standards for educational and psychological testing*. Washington, DC: American Psychological Association, Inc.

[171]
Kohn Problem Checklist/Kohn Social Competence Scale.

Purpose: "Designed to assess the social and emotional functioning of preschool and kindergarten children through the systematic observation of classroom behavior."
Population: Ages 3–6.
Publication Dates: 1979–1988.
Acronym: KPC/KSC.
Scores, 2: Apathy—Withdrawal, Anger—Defiance.
Administration: Individual.
Price Data, 1994: $75 per complete KPC/KSC combined kit including 25 ready-score answer sheets from each test, and manual ('88, 47 pages); $77.50 per 100 KPS ready-score answer sheets; $31 per manual for both KPC and KSC.
Time: Administration time not reported.
Author: Martin Kohn.
Publisher: The Psychological Corporation.
Cross References: See T4:1369 (5 references); for reviews of the Kohn Problem Checklist by James L. Carroll and Bert O. Richmond, see 9:575 (2 references); for reviews of the Kohn Social Competence Checklist by James L. Carroll and Ronald S. Drabman, see 9:575 (5 references).
[Editor's Note: The publisher advised in December 1997 that this test is now out of print.]

TEST REFERENCES

1. Keltner, B. (1990). Family characteristics of preschool social competence among black children in a Head Start program. *Child Psychiatry and Human Development, 21*, 95-108.
2. Adalbjarnardottir, S. (1995). How school children propose to negotiate: The role of social withdrawal, social anxiety, and locus of control. *Child Development, 66*, 1739-1751.

Review of the Kohn Problem Checklist/Kohn Social Competence Scale by GLORIA MACCOW, School Psychologist, Guilford County Schools, Greensboro, NC:

The Kohn Problem Checklist (KPC) and the Kohn Social Competence Scale (KSC), published in 1988, is the research edition. The instrument had been published previously in research studies beginning in the early 1970s. A review in the *Ninth Mental Measurements Yearbook* indicates the Rating and Scoring Manual were available in mimeographed form at that time. The manual for the current, research edition is bound in 54 (6-inch x 9-inch) pages.

The KPC and KSC were designed for teachers to observe and rate the classroom behavior of children in preschool and kindergarten. The scales were designed to identify children who have, or are at risk for developing, emotional difficulties. The current edition is useful for research on the social competence and social-emotional functioning of young children. The theoretical rationale for the development of the scales is the finding that early identification of disturbed children is critical for early intervention. Furthermore, it is important to assess the children's competence as well as their problem behavior.

On the KPC, the teacher uses 49 statements to rate the student's problem behaviors. The KSC consists of 64 statements describing positive *and* negative characteristics of social-emotional functioning. (A 73-item version of the KSC, for children enrolled in full-day programs, is listed in Appendix B.) Teachers rate the items based on the frequency with which the behavior occurred during the preceding week.

The items on the KPC and KSC assess social functioning along two dimensions. The first dimension focuses on the child's interest, curiosity, and assertiveness in the classroom; the second dimension assesses the willingness or ability of the children to conform to the rules and routines of the classroom. The KPC focuses on the presence or absence of problem behaviors; the KSC measures problem behaviors as well as adaptive behaviors. The two factors on the KPC are labeled Apathy-Withdrawal and Anger-Defiance. For the KSC, these two factors form the negative end of bipolar factors. The positive end of Factor I and Factor II are labeled Interest-Participation and Cooperation-Compliance, respectively.

The manual provides explicit directions for administration and scoring. For the KPC, teachers or teacher aides are asked to rate the child's behavior during the most recent week as "Not at all typical" (0); "Somewhat typical" (1), or "Very typical" (2). The statements on the KSC are rated on a 5-point scale ranging from 1 for *Hardly Ever/Never* to 5 for *Very Often/Always.*

The manual describes specific limitations of the research edition of the KPC and KSC. Because the scales are in an intermediate stage of development, information on their technical properties is incomplete. Furthermore, studies were conducted on earlier versions of the scales, which differed from the research edition. The normative sample also is incomplete, and users are advised to develop local norms especially when the scales are used for clinical assessment.

Scoring is facilitated by Ready-Score™ Answer Sheets. For the KPC, the scores for the Factor I items are within circles. The scores for Factor II items are within triangles. The numbers in the circles are added to provide the raw score for Apathy-Withdrawal; the sum of the numbers within the triangles constitutes the raw score for Anger-Defiance. The manual cautions users to be careful in adding the numbers. Because of the arrangement of the ratings 0, 1, 2, in each of the four rows of items, it is easy to add the incorrect numbers.

A second rater's scores should be added to the first. If there is no second rater, the user should repeat the sum of the first rater's scores. The "pooled" raw score is used to enter a table to determine the standard score. Two types of standard scores are provided. The first are *T*-scores with a mean of 50 and a standard deviation of 10. The second are from Kohn's original work and have a mean of zero and a standard deviation of 100. Norms are provided for full-day programs by gender and factor and for half-day programs for boys by factor and type of rater.

Scoring of the KSC is similar to that of the KPC except that there are four different shapes: one each for the positive and negative items on each of the two factors. The numbers in each shape are added after which the negative sum for each factor is subtracted from its positive sum. The difference is either doubled or added to the difference of a second rater's scores. These numbers are used to enter the table to identify standard scores.

For the KPC, norms are provided for boys and girls in full-day programs. Norms are provided for the KSC and the KPC for boys in half-day programs.

No norms are provided for the 73-item full-day KSC. The sample used for the KPC for full-day programs is not representative of children in preschool. Although the 604 girls and 628 boys were selected randomly, they were from New York City only. The children were from lower- to lower-middle-class families; the majority were Black and from single-parent households. The data were collected in 1967 and may not reflect present-day cultural norms. The norms for the half-day programs are based on a more representative sample of boys, but the number is small ($n = 287$). The time of the ratings is not clear from the manual. Users are encouraged to develop local norms to "ensure maximum representativeness of the scale" (p. 15).

Factor analysis was used to determine the dimensions underlying the KPC and KSC. Several studies are reported to illustrate the technical properties of the scales. However, these studies were conducted on the original versions of the KPC and KSC, which differ from the current research edition.

As a research instrument, the KPC and KSC have some utility. Professionals can use the items to support reliability and validity of the scores based on the scales for a more representative sample of children. Local norms would have to be developed in order to use these scales for clinical assessment. In a 1977 study, Kohn noted similarities between the factors on the KPC and KSC and the Peterson Problem Checklist. Because the technical properties of the current Quay and Peterson's Revised Behavior Problem Checklist are established, it makes sense to use this instead of the KPC/KSC to measure personality and conduct problems in young children. Indeed, one of the reviewers in the *Ninth Mental Measurements Yearbook* identified Quay and Peterson's checklist as a formidable competitor of the KPC/KSC. That conclusion still holds today.

[172]
Language Arts Assessment Portfolio.

Purpose: To "analyze and evaluate student achievement in all areas of the language arts: reading, writing, listening, and speaking."
Population: Grades 1–6.
Publication Date: 1992.
Acronym: LAAP.
Administration: Individual.
Levels: 3 levels.
Price Data, 1993: $99.95 per complete LAAP kit Level 1, 2 or 3; $23.95 per 30 portfolio folders; $23.95 per 30 evaluation booklets; $79 per LAAP training video.

Time: Administration time not reported.
Comments: Assessment done with students' own language arts materials.
Author: Bjorn Karlsen.
Publisher: American Guidance Service, Inc.

a) LEVEL I.
Population: Grade 1.
Scores: 15–24 language arts skill areas: Reading Analysis (Reading Comprehension, Oral Reading, Decoding), Optional Reading Analysis (Silent Reading Problems, Oral Reading Problems), Writing Analysis [Process (Story Creation), Product (Sentence Structure, Story Content, Spelling, Mechanics)], Optional Writing Analysis (Spelling, Mechanics), Listening Analysis [Listening in Interaction (Attentiveness, Understanding), Listening to Teaching (Memory, Interpretation)], Optional Listening Analysis (Auditory Decoding, Rhymes and Rhythms, Phonetic Elements, Structural Elements), Speaking Analysis [Oral Interaction, Oral Presentation (Delivery)], Optional Speaking Analysis (Language Development).

b) LEVEL II.
Population: Grades 2–3.
Scores: 16–25 language arts skill areas: Reading Analysis (Silent Reading Comprehension, Oral Reading, Decoding), Optional Reading Analysis (Silent Reading Problems, Oral Reading Problems), Writing Analysis [Process (Story Creation, Process Awareness), Product (Story Content, Organization, Spelling, Mechanics)], Optional Writing Analysis [Spelling Error Analysis, Mechanics (Punctuation, Capitalization)], Listening Analysis [Listening in Interaction (Attentiveness, Understanding), Listening to Teaching (Memory, Interpretation)], Optional Listening Analysis (Auditory Decoding, Phonetic Elements, Structural Elements), Speaking Analysis [Oral Interaction, Oral Presentation (Delivery)], Optional Speaking Analysis (Language Development).

c) LEVEL III.
Population: Grades 4—6.
Scores: Same as *b* above except that Attentiveness is not included for Listening Analysis.
Cross References: See T4:1384 (1 reference).

Review of the Language Arts Assessment Portfolio by ANTHONY J. NITKO, Professor of Education, School of Education, University of Pittsburgh, Pittsburgh, PA:

The Language Arts Assessment Portfolio (LAAP) is an informal formative assessment system in reading, writing, listening, and speaking. The materials are organized in three levels: grade 1, grades 2–3, and grades 4–6. Each level contains a Teacher's Guide, Evaluation Booklet, Students' Self-Evaluation Booklets, portfolio folders, and a storage box. A teacher assesses students using local classroom materials and activities. The LAAP provides no tasks or test items.

Each language arts area is divided into two broad areas: a main analysis and an optional analysis. The main analysis assesses students in overall basic skills. The optional analysis obtains a more detailed diagnosis for students who do poorly in the main analysis. For example, the listening main analysis is organized into two broad skill areas: Listening in Interactions and Listening to Teaching. Listening to Teaching is further divided into the broad areas of Memory and Interpretation. Interpretation, in turn, is divided into five finer-grained skills. A teacher rates each student on each skill on a 5-point scale: excellent, satisfactory, needs improvement, beginning to learn, and serious problem. The author recommends rating four times during the school year. Each student's ratings are recorded along with information about the materials used for assessment and the teacher's comments. Students (and teachers) may include examples of the work evaluated in the folder (hence the portfolio aspect).

The Teacher's Guide, like the entire LAAP, is well organized. The broad skills are nicely described. Each narrower skill is described for assessment as follows: (a) "What to look for" (defines the narrow skills), (b) "How to assess it" (how to conduct an assessment of that specific skill), and (c) "Evaluating the responses" (the key performances on which to focus when rating a student). Suggestions and comments are made about expected student performance. It would have been useful to include suggestions for how to teach or remediate students after they are assessed.

TECHNICAL REVIEW. The LAAP was field-tested over a 2-year period at several sites in 19 states. Three field-tests, a telephone survey, and a focus group discussion of the materials were part of the development process. Teachers were especially trained by the LAAP developer.

It is important to note that the LAAP is an informal classroom assessment procedure. No attempt is made to standardize the materials, assessment process, assessment training, or any other assessment aspect. Thus, the LAAP should not be used for curriculum evaluation, for accountability, or for comparing students' progress from grade to grade.

Teachers need to be trained to use the LAAP system, especially in how to administer the assessment and rate students. If the LAAP is to be used in the same school by more than one teacher per grade, training on how to rate students is especially needed to assure that ratings have the same meaning across teachers. Formal studies of other portfolio assessment systems have shown very low consistency of ratings from teacher to teacher and low generalizability of a student's performance across different kinds of tasks.

SUMMARY. The LAAP is a useful informal system for organizing a teacher's ratings of students' language arts performance in reading, writing, listening, and speaking. It is designed specifically for a classroom teacher to monitor students' progress over the course of a year. To accomplish this purpose, teachers may need special inservice training in how to use the LAAP. Appropriately, the author does not recommend using the LAAP for summative student evaluation. Lest some school officials be tempted, we add that the LAAP should not be used for either student, teacher, or school accountability programs.

Review of the Language Arts Assessment Profile by RICHARD M. WOLF, Professor of Psychology and Education, Teachers College, Columbia University, New York, NY:

The Language Arts Assessment Profile (LAAP) is an amalgam of an assessment system for teachers to appraise student performance in the areas of reading, writing, listening, and speaking; a student self-evaluation form; and a record-keeping system. It is intended for use by classroom teachers to monitor student performance in each of these four language arts areas. The three levels of the system are intended for use by teachers in grade 1, grades 2–3, and grades 4–6. The Teacher's Guide for each level runs from 57 to 71 pages, depending on the level, and provides a detailed guide about the system and how to use it.

The LAAP is basically a two-pronged assessment system. For each language arts area, there is both a teacher evaluation booklet and a student evaluation booklet. Each is laid out so that as many as four assessments can be made in each area of the language arts during the school year. The items that comprise each area appear reasonable although no evidence is furnished to justify their inclusion. For teachers, ratings are supplied for each item using a five category rating code ranging from E (excellent) to P (serious problem). A sixth category for Not applicable (NA) is also provided. The Teacher's Guide provides a description of each rating code. These definitions allow considerable latitude for teachers to impose their own standards for each rating code

category. The categories seem generally reasonable although the rating of S (Satisfactory) is defined as "mastery for this level of achievement" (p. 11). Equating mastery with satisfactory performance is somewhat odd.

In addition to the teacher and student evaluation booklets, the appendix of each Teacher's Guide contains from five to eight additional forms that can be used. At grades 4–6, these are: (a) student interest survey, (b) log of contents, (c) reading log, (d) writing sample cover sheet, (e) writing peer evaluation form, (f) listening log, (g) oral presentation cover sheet, and (h) speaking peer evaluation form. Although these additional items are optional, their use could result in a very cumbersome system. Even the basic system with just the teacher and student evaluation booklets requires a good deal of management. To assist in this task, the system comes with a set of individual student folders in which to keep the records.

The LAAP underwent an extensive development process. The system was developed by the author on the basis of his experience in the field and was initially field tested in 21 sites around the United States. A second field test was carried out in 31 sites. A telephone survey of potential users and a focus group discussion were also carried out. The purpose of this work, it seems, was to work out the details of the use of the system. Unfortunately, no evidence is presented regarding the results of the field tests or the other activities carried on during the development phase. No evidence regarding either the validity or the reliability of the LAAP is provided for a potential user to judge the adequacy of the system.

One major problem in the use of the LAAP involves the determination of an overall rating in each of the four language areas. It is left entirely up to the teacher to obtain an overall rating in each language area after reviewing the specific rating of the various skills. The Teacher's Guide alerts the teacher to a possible halo effect in obtaining specific ratings but little guidance is provided on how to obtain an overall rating. In fact, the overall ratings are downplayed in the Teacher's Guide and a plea is made to use the specific ratings in a diagnostic way. If this is so, why provide for an overall rating, especially because this is what might carry considerable weight with parents?

In summary, the LAAP is a system for assessing the progress of students in the four language arts areas: reading, writing, listening, and speaking. It consists of a number of rating scales in each area for both teachers and students to use. It also includes a rather elaborate record-keeping system. Although some elementary school teachers may find the LAAP a useful way to record and store information about student progress in the language arts, others may find it cumbersome. As far as a series of measuring instruments, there is no evidence provided to establish its validity and reliability. Consequently, teachers will need to decide if the items that comprise the teacher and student evaluation booklets are relevant to their instructional goals. Use of the LAAP depends heavily on the ability of an individual teacher to find a way to use the system.

[173]
Law Enforcement Candidate Record.

Purpose: "To predict law enforcement officer success despite any manifest organizational differences."
Population: Candidates for law enforcement positions.
Publication Dates: 1986–1994.
Acronym: LECR.
Scores: 5 tests: Vocabulary, Arithmetic Reasoning, Spatial Analysis/Reasoning, Number Scanning, Memory/Recall, plus an autobiographical questionnaire.
Administration: Group.
Price Data: Available from publisher.
Time: 63(73) minutes for tests; none stated for the autobiographical questionnaire.
Author: Richardson, Bellows, Henry, & Co., Inc.
Publisher: Richardson, Bellows, Henry, & Co., Inc.

Review of the Law Enforcement Candidate Record by JIM C. FORTUNE, Professor of Research and Evaluation, Virginia Tech University, Blacksburg, VA:

INTRODUCTION AND GENERAL DESCRIPTION. The Law Enforcement Candidate Record (LECR) was developed during a time period when adverse impact was a major civil rights concern and at the time society felt a great need for adding to local police forces and for improving local police forces. Unlike the National Police Office Selection Test (12:253) developed by Standard & Associates, Inc., the Law Enforcement Candidate Record is intended to serve as a selection test rather than a simple screening device. Both tests report similar job analysis techniques and results. However, the LECR has been studied in accordance with the standard criteria for an employment test: linkage of test content to job, coverage of content, reliability, administrative ease, ability to produce results from which valid interpretations can be made, and evidence of criterion-related validity.

The LERC was developed in accordance with the *Uniform Guidelines on Employee Selection Proce-*

dures (Section 8). And, the manuals for the LERC speak of a continuing effort to develop criterion-related validity evidence.

THE JOB ANALYSIS. The job analysis was conducted and reported with a criterion-related validation study. This validation study involved two groups of 2,088 and 1,419 officers and troopers from 23 towns, cities, or agencies. The technical report for the instrument goes into detail concerning the collection of importance ratings for a menu of ability/behavior and work task elements and the derivation of a criterion-performance-measurement instrument. Demographics for these two samples are reported. One flaw of this study is the service time reported by the participants, which averages in excess of 6 years for the youngest group. It is impossible to discern whether or not some part of the predictive relationship emerged during service as opposed to the relationship of preservice abilities to in-service performances. It is true that the verbal and mathematical tests are likely not enhanced on the job, but responses on the autobiographical report may likely be influenced by on-the-job experiences.

DESCRIPTION OF THE LECR. Although the research materials create confusion with regard to the LECR selection instruments, it appears that the LECR intended for selection is composed of a 70-item multiple-choice verbal test to be completed in 10 minutes, a 144-item test of perceptual and recall skills to be completed in 9 minutes, and a personal description questionnaire to be completed without time constraints. The LECR used in the research program of the company is composed of six parts. They include: the 70-item timed tests of verbal comprehension, a 45-item multiple-choice test of arithmetic reasoning to be completed in 20 minutes, a 45-item test of spatial analysis and reasoning to be completed in 15 minutes, 100 paired items to test number scanning to be completed in 4 minutes, the 144-item test of perceptual and recall skills to be completed in 9 minutes, and the autobiographical questionnaire. The reason for variance in the battery was not given. No description for the scoring of the autobiographical data was given, and penalty for guessing was mentioned but not detailed with regard to the verbal and recall subtests.

THE ON-GOING VALIDATION STUDY. Richardson, Bellows, Henry & Co., Inc. request that participating municipalities and agencies participate in a continuing criterion-related validity study. Results for two groups of participants are reported in the technical report for the LECR. This study uses the extended LECR battery of Vocabulary, Arithmetic Reasoning, Spatial Analysis/Reasoning, Number Scanning, Memory/Recall, and the autobiographical questionnaire with two criterion instruments, a performance-criterion scale made up of a duty rating scale and an ability rating scale. Perhaps, a serious flaw in the design of the validity study is when the law officers take the LECR. Although it is not clear in the technical manual, it appears that the participants in the validity study take the LECR at the time they are assessed on the performance criteria. If this is the case, it becomes difficult to determine the extent that on-the-job experience has affected the officers' performances on the LECR.

DESCRIPTION OF THE CRITERION INSTRUMENT. The survey process through which the criterion instrument was developed is described in the technical report. The criterion instrument includes 46 behavior/abilities and 90 work elements divided into eight duty areas. These include: preparing for work, patrolling-traffic/pedestrian control, crime/accident/emergency scene procedures, investigative/arrest/arraignment procedures, court procedures, administrative procedures, community relations, and other requirements. The criterion measurement process uses three judges in assessing performance.

LECR RELIABILITY. At the time the existing documentation was developed no composite reliability information was available. A telephone call to Richardson, Bellows, Henry & Co., Inc. (personal communication, November 15, 1996) revealed that a composite reliability index had been computed. Hence, the reliability of the verbal score plus the recall score plus the scored autobiography was found to be .70. This reliability coefficient was a test-retest coefficient.

Reliability for the criterion-scores in the validation study was reported to range from .48 to .54 (Table 5-6 in technical report). The criterion assessment was made for work tasks and for abilities and behaviors. Intraclass correlations among the study samples were .79 and .76 for work tasks and .86 and .89 for abilities and behaviors. Two raters were used for each of the two study samples and their agreement produced correlations in the low .30 range.

LECR CRITERION-RELATED VALIDITY. To date the criterion-related validity was found to be $r = .28$ for the sample of 3,076. The size of this correlation represents positive validity evidence, but appears too low to serve as the single selection criterion.

ADMINISTRATIVE EASE. The administration manuals are comprehensive and easy to follow. Proctoring requirements, room configuration, and examination control procedures are spelled out in clear, concise instructions. There is some confusion between LECR requirements and participation in the criterion-related validity study.

READABILITY OF THE MANUALS. The administration manual is very readable and clear. To administer the three parts of the LECR one just follows this manual. However, confusion begins when one is also exposed to the research administration manual and the expanded battery also called the LECR. I think that it would be helpful in one manual to focus more on the selection process.

The technical manual is not complete. Missing from this manual is basic reliability information and rationale and use of the expanded LECR. The manual should include the test-retest information that was gained in the telephone call and some measure for internal consistency for the verbal and recall scales.

REVIEWER'S COMMENTARY. The LECR offers great promise in an area of high need. Exceptional work has been done to put together a criterion for police selection and to design a criterion-related validity study. The test used to complete the selection process needs to be discussed more with regard to reliability and internal consistencies of the verbal and recall scales including the processes for scoring the biographical questionnaire. The role of the battery used in the criterion-related validity needs discussion and more information is needed on the mathematical and spatial relations subtests. Perhaps, these additional scales would increase the validity coefficient obtained in the early study results.

Review of the Law Enforcement Candidate Record by MICHAEL J. ROSZKOWSKI, Associate Professor of Psychology/Director of Marketing Research, The American College, Bryn Mawr, PA:

The Law Enforcement Candidate Record (LECR) is a battery of six tests meant to be used in the selection of candidates for entry level law enforcement positions. In designing the battery, the developers aimed to create a job-related selection procedure that would adhere to the *Uniform Guidelines on Employee Selection Procedures,* minimizing differences between the races while producing validity coefficients that were at least equivalent to other, more racially adverse methods. They also wanted the selection procedure to be generalizable across jurisdictions of varying size, geographical locales, and work environments. Results reported in the manual indicate that a weighted composite score with three of the six tests produces the desired results.

The six selection tests in the battery, all multiple choice, are as follows: Verbal Comprehension (70 items, timed: 10 minutes)—Involves the selection of synonyms and antonyms. Arithmetic Reasoning (45 items, timed: 20 minutes)—Involves arithmetic word problems (e.g., How many fifty cent bullets can you buy for $2.00?). Spatial Analysis (45 items, timed: 15 minutes)—Items consist of four drawings that share a common characteristic. The examinee must select another drawing (from an array of six) that shares the same characteristic as the other four. Number Scanning (100 items, timed: 4 minutes)—Requires determining whether number pairs are the same or different (e.g., 3821 vs. 3812). Memory Recall (144 items, timed: 9 minutes)—A three-letter word to a two-digit number key is presented. The item is a word, and the examinee must pick the corresponding number from an array of four numbers. Autobiographical Questionnaire (185 items, untimed)—The questions cover experiences such as academic application, work history, physical health and activities, self-esteem, and social skills. A correction for guessing is made on all five cognitive tests.

The technical report describes the results of a study examining the relationship between the test battery and supervisory performance ratings in two consortia, representing over 20 police departments in New York, New Jersey, Michigan, Nevada, and Georgia. The samples were limited to individuals with patrol responsibilities because these are typically the entry level positions in law enforcement. Consortium I (n = 2,088) consisted primarily of state troopers and county police, whereas Consortium II (n = 1,419) was mainly composed of municipal police officers, but included railroad security personnel and corrections officers. These consortia were analyzed separately as well as in a combined sample. The consolidated sample had an average age of 33 (SD = 8), was 95% male and 87% white, with about 8 years of experience. On average, the subjects were high school graduates with some (less than 2 years) college education.

The subjects completed all six selection tests, as well as a job analysis questionnaire (Job Requirements Questionnaire for Law Enforcement Classifications) developed by the same authors. The job analysis questionnaire consisted of 90 work task elements (duties) and 46 ability-behavior elements

(skills). Each of the work tasks was rated by these officers on (a) the extent to which it was required for the job (Not, Minor, Moderate, Major) and (2) time that the individual spent performing the task relative to other police officers (less than most, about the same, more than most). The ability-behavior elements were rated only on the first dimension.

The jobs of the officers from the various jurisdictions and organizations were compared for similarity using (a) rankings of mean element scores, (b) correlating mean element scores, and (c) interclass correlations. The "time spent" and "extent required" ratings correlated highly (upper .8 to low .9 range). High agreement across organizations was found on the task requirements (interclass correlation = .79 in Consortium I and .76 in Consortium II), and even higher agreement on the ability-behavior elements (interclass correlation = .86 and .89 in Consortia I and II, respectively). The median Pearson correlation in Consortium I was .82 for tasks and .94 for ability-behavior.

The job performance of the subjects was assessed with an instrument called the Performance Evaluation Record (PER) for Law Enforcement Classifications, which consists of 34 job duty statements (Part 1) and 28 specific job-ability statements (Part 2). The PER was derived from the job analysis instrument described earlier by having a team of officers, their supervisors, and technical advisors review the job analysis data of incumbents (n = 969) and select those items that (a) constituted significant job requirements and (b) could be rated meaningfully.

All 3,507 subjects received a performance appraisal from their immediate supervisor. A second appraisal was obtained on 3,076 of them from another superior who was able to evaluate their job performance. In both instances, the ability-behavior ratings showed more variability than the task ratings. The interappraiser agreement was low in both consortia (tasks = .33 in Consortium I and .32 in Consortium II; ability-behavior = .38 in Consortium I and .37 in Consortium II).

The ratings from the two appraisers were averaged to increase reliability. No data are currently available on the test-retest (rate-rerate) reliability of the performance ratings, but a study of this type was said to be underway at the time of the publication of the technical report.

Three scoring keys were developed for the autobiographical questionnaire. The first key, consisting of 94 items, was developed on the basis of the relationship between the biodata items and performance appraisals in Consortium I. A double cross-validation check was conducted. The second scoring key consisted of 81 items and was developed from the data on Consortium II. The third key retained only those biodata items that differentiated between performance ratings in *both* Consortium I and Consortium II. As might be expected, a smaller number of items survived (65); it was felt that this key was more generalizable because it worked in two different samples.

The 28 intercorrelations that were computed among the eight predictors (five cognitive tests and three biodata scoring keys) ranged from .16 to .97 with a median of .25 in Consortium I. In Consortium II, the range was .15 to .97, with a median of .22. Not surprisingly, the highest correlations occurred among the three autobiographical keys (.91, .93, and .97 in Consortium I; .92, .94, and .97 in Consortium II). Moderate correlations were found between Scanning and Memory (.57, .58), Verbal Reasoning and Arithmetic Reasoning (.50, .46), Spatial Analysis and Arithmetic (.43, .46). The authors concluded that these three correlations were too high to consider using both members of the pair in a battery.

The correlation coefficients computed between each of the predictors and the two sections of the performance appraisal are reported for Consortium I by itself, Consortium II by itself, and both consortia combined. The relationship between the predictors and the ratings of the first appraiser, second appraiser, and the average of the two appraisers are indicated for both the tasks and the abilities sections of the performance appraisal. The correlations based on the average of the two supervisors are slightly higher than the correlations based on either appraiser alone. The correlations between the predictors and the average of the two ratings ranged from .09–.29 for the Consortium I and II sample. The authors contend that the cognitive test validity coefficients are underestimated due to a restriction in the range of talent in the predictors. I would argue that the problem could also be due, at least in part, to the unreliability of the criterion, given the low reported interrater agreement.

The authors claim that the predictors have greater value when used together in a multiple correlation. Analyses were computed using the two cognitive composites (Recall & Spatial; Recall & Spatial & Verbal) along with the autobiographical key. The multiple correlations with the Recall & Verbal composite were more stable across the samples compared to the multiple correlations using the Recall & Spatial & Verbal composite. The recommended predic-tion equation applies a weight to the autobiographical data that is three times the weight given to the Recall & Verbal composite.

The correlation between the averaged (two appraisers) duties performance ratings and the predictor (Recall & Verbal & Autobiographical) was .28 in the consolidated (Consortium I and II) sample. A correlation of .29 was obtained when the abilities performance rating served as the criterion. After they were adjusted for unreliability in the criterion, these correlations increased to .40 (tasks) and .39 (abilities).

The authors present the results of a utility analysis to counter the negative impression created by the low correlations, which they consider a misleading basis for judging the practical significance of a validity coefficient. Dividing the distribution of the predictor score into seven levels, they demonstrate that at the highest test score level, 66% of the candidates met or exceeded the total sample's average duty performance ratings, compared to only 24% at the lowest test score level. Indeed, the data producing a correlation of .28 do look much more impressive if a utility analysis is used to illustrate the possible improvements in selection.

The authors also applied the recommended scoring system to the test scores of a sample (*n* = 16,987) of White (74%), Black (12%), and Hispanic (13%) candidates from one jurisdiction to determine whether score differences between minorities and the majority group are reduced with this selection procedure. Little detail is provided about this sample. The mean scores of the Black and Hispanic candidates were lower than those for the White candidates, but the difference equaled about 6/10 of a standard deviation, which is less than the one standard deviation difference typically produced by other selection procedures. Male and female mean scores did not differ. The authors caution that these results may not generalize to other jurisdictions, but they find these results "highly encouraging" (p. 53).

The LECR had withstood a legal challenge from the Las Vegas Metropolitan Police Department, a participant in both the Consortium I (Metro police officers) and Consortium II (Metro corrections officers) studies. The Las Vegas Metropolitan Police Department contended that there is insufficient validity evidence for relying on the LECR, especially as a basis for selecting corrections officers. The court disagreed with Metropolitan's charges, contending that the LECR was developed to be job-related and that the really relevant dimension on the job analysis is the *abilities* required for success as a corrections officer, and these showed a high overlap with the police officers. The court focused on the fact that the LECR had a significant predictor-criterion correlation and that the predictor was shown, by a job analysis, to be related to important elements of the job.

I could not find any reliability data in the manual, so apparently the lack of reliability data on the individual tests forming the battery was not viewed as critical. I personally feel that although criterion-related validity is the ultimate basis for judging the value of a selection device, the authors should also present the test users with data on the reliability of the procedures. One hopes this information will be forthcoming, not just on the criterion measure (as indicated in the manual will be the case), but on the predictors as well.

The size of the samples used to develop the LECR are truly impressive. A meta-analysis of law enforcement selection procedures (Hirsh, Northrop, & Schmidt, 1986) found that the average sample size in such investigations was only 92. The magnitude of the derived validity coefficients is small, but the coefficients are higher than the average reported in the meta-analysis (i.e., .13) and the LECR does have a less adverse impact on minorities. Information on the reliability of the LECR can perhaps help in suggesting how the test battery can be fine-tuned. Increasing reliability should lead to higher validity.

If one wants to avoid using cognitive measures for selection of law enforcement personnel, biodata seems to offer a viable alternative. Another approach might be a personality measure, such as the Minnesota Multiphasic Personality Inventory (MMPI; T4:1645), but there may be some legal constraints on their use (Pallone, 1992).

REVIEWER'S REFERENCES

Hirsh, H. R., Northrop, L. C., & Schmidt, F. L. (1986). Validity generalization results for law enforcement occupations. *Personnel Psychology, 39,* 399–420.
Pallone, N. J. (1992). The MMPI in police officer selection: Legal constraints, case law, empirical data. *Journal of Offender Rehabilitation, 17,* 171–188.

[174]
Law School Admission Test.

Purpose: "To measure skills that are considered essential for success in law school."
Population: Law school entrants.
Publication Dates: 1948–1991.
Acronym: LSAT.
Scores: Total score plus unscored writing sample.
Administration: Group.
Price Data, 1993: $74 per LSAT; $44 per late registration; $22 per test center change; $22 per test date change; $164 per nonpublished test center (U.S.A., Canada,

Puerto Rico); $219 per nonpublished test center (all other countries); $27 per hand scoring; $30 per reporting renewal; $27 per former registrants score report; $75 per LSDAS subscription (12 months plus one law school report); $7 per law school report ordered at time of subscription; $9 per law school report ordered after initial subscription; $44 per LSDAS subscription renewal.
Time: 175(200) minutes per LSAT; 30(40) minutes per writing sample.
Comments: Test administered 4 times annually (June, October, December, February) at centers established by the publisher.
Authors: Law School Admission Council, administered by Law School Admission Service.
Publisher: Law School Admission Council/Law School Admission Service.
Cross References: See T4:1400 (4 references); for a review of an earlier edition by Gary B. Melton, see 9:594 (2 references); see also T3:1292 (6 references), 8:1093 (7 references), and T2:2349 (7 references); for a review by Leo A. Munday of earlier forms, see 7:1098 (23 references); see also 5:928 (7 references); for a review by Alexander G. Wesman, see 4:815 (6 references).

TEST REFERENCES

1. Alexander, R. A., Carson, K. D., Alliger, G. M., & Cronshan, S. F. (1989). Empirical distributions of range restricted SD$_y$ in validity studies. *Journal of Applied Psychology, 74,* 253-258.
2. Frisby, C. L. (1992). Construct validity and psychometric properties of the Cornell Critical Thinking Test (Level Z): A contrasted groups analysis. *Psychological Reports, 71,* 291-303.
3. Camilli, G., Wang, M., & Fisq, J. (1995). The effects of dimensionality on equating the Law School Admission Test. *Journal of Educational Measurement, 32,* 79–96.
4. Deegan, D. H. (1995). Exploring individual differences among novices reading in a specific domain: The case of law. *Reading Research Quarterly, 30,* 154–170.
5. Powers, D. E., & Leung, S. W. (1995). Answering the new SAT reading comprehension questions without the passages. *Journal of Educational Measurement, 32,* 105–129.
6. Wainer, H. (1995). Precision and differential item functioning on a testlet-based test: The 1991 Law School Admissions Test as an example. *Applied Measurement in Education, 8,* 157–186.
7. Young, J. W. (1995). A comparison of two adjustment methods for improving the prediction of law school grades. *Educational and Psychological Measurement, 55,* 558-571.
8. DeChamplain, A. F. (1996). The effect of multidimensionality on IRT true-score equating for subgroups of examinees. *Journal of Educational Measurement, 33,* 181–201.

Review of the Law School Admission Test by JAMES B. ERDMANN, *Professor of Medicine (Education) and Associate Dean, Thomas Jefferson University, Jefferson Medical College, Philadelphia, PA:*

Ample evidence exists that the Law School Admission Test (LSAT) is a highly professionally developed and administered testing program. Extensive descriptive information helping students prepare for the test is readily available. Sample tests and analyses of test questions are plentiful. Advice directed at assisting examinees to improve their test-taking strategies is also provided. It is difficult to imagine that the Law School Admission Council (LSAC) could do anything further to aid candidates in their preparation.

Admissions personnel in the law schools are treated no less lavishly. Quite explicit information about the limitations of the test, how scores should be combined with other information in making selection decisions, cautions on the use of scores obtained under nonstandard conditions and on overinterpreting small differences in scores among candidates, even a service to help individual schools determine the predictive value of test scores in their specific application and the best weighting of test scores and grades for a given school—all of these and other interpretation and use of scores decisions are quite adequately discussed and supported. There are even materials designed to help pre-law faculty answer questions of aspirants to the profession.

Though it is a bit more pedantic, information about registering for the test and all the associated mechanics of test administration and score reporting is voluminous but clear and well organized.

What a surprise, then, to learn that there is no technical manual for the test program. The very bases and foundation of the test program seems to have received relatively little attention. Little information exists on how the test specifications were prepared and by whom. If research was conducted on why the test contains the components it does and uses the item formats it does, it is at best hinted at. Something as elementary as test reliability is covered in a sentence or two. And even then the information is meager and imprecise. Suggestions are offered that one can expect reliabilities in the 90s. However, the reference makes no mention of when the data were obtained, how often the findings are replicated, and very importantly, what kind of reliability is being reported. Were the reliabilities test-retest, internal consistency, etc. measures?

The issue of validity is hardly noted. Maybe the assumption is made that the validity service offered to individual schools by the Law School Admission Service (LSAS) satisfies the need. There is no doubt that such a service is invaluable because regardless of national or program-wide experience, individual schools should be expected to conduct their individual studies to determine proper weighting of test scores and grades, and other criteria for that matter, in selection decisions. In this reviewer's opinion, however, this validity service does not absolve the program from reporting validity measures at the program level. It should be a rather simple matter, given the existence of the validity service, to report a distribution of validity indices for different types of schools. Such information would be of

invaluable assistance to the school that may be considering a policy requiring applicants to submit LSAT scores. Such information is especially critical when a new edition of the test is introduced. There is no evidence that such information was provided when the test was modified on several occasions in the recent past. Usually, in addition, there is an expectation that some evidence of construct validity be reported. Evidence of construct validity would lend credence to the assumption that the skills that are purported to be measured are in fact the skills being measured. That is, what support is there for the user to believe that the analytical reasoning test is really measuring analytical reasoning skills?

What is perhaps the tragedy in all of these matters, is that the test sponsors probably are in possession of most if not all of this information. A bibliography of research reports is available if one takes the initiative to ask. Though no abstracts of the reports are provided, the bibliography cites studies of test preparation approaches by examinees, of validity indices for repeaters, of differential predictive validity for subpopulations, a national summary of validity correlations, score differences between the sexes, studies of the dimensionality of the test—and the list goes on.

Thus, circumstantial evidence indicates that a respectable group of professionals is responsible for test quality—is actively studying various aspects of the test, is applying some of the latest techniques to meet program requirements (e.g., the use of item response theory to satisfy equating needs), and is exploring computer adaptive testing for future administrations.

In short, there is reason to believe that one can be an examinee as well as a test score user with considerable confidence. However, this confidence is based not so much on direct evidence of quality but on inference and indirect evidence. Again, it is surprising that a program that responded to assaults on standardized testing from groups like Fair Test and the New York legislature by exposing much of its test material, would not similarly feel compelled to make very explicit in published form all of the technical justification for the program and its applications.

There is one footnote. There does not seem to have been any systematic review of the writing sample and its value in the selection process. As it stands now, writing samples are not graded, but copies are distributed as submitted by the examinee to the schools receiving the test scores. Because there is inevitably additional cost associated with collecting and distributing the writing sample not only in dollars but also in testing effort, it would seem that its value should be systematically examined and a determination made as to whether this segment of the test should be modified or discontinued.

Review of the Law School Admission Test by ROBERT F. McMORRIS, *Professor of Educational Psychology and Statistics, University at Albany, State University of New York, Albany, NY, and ELIZA-BETH L. BRINGSJORD, Assistant Professor, Division of Nursing, Russell Sage College, Troy, NY, and WEI-PING LIU, Head Test Librarian, University at Albany, State University of New York, Albany, NY:*

A bride dressed in an LSAT would be wearing something both old and quite new. The Law School Admission Test (LSAT) was introduced a half century ago, and it has evolved since, with changes in format, length, types of questions, score scale, and testing time. The contemporary versions, beginning in June 1991, contain five, 35-minute sections of multiple-choice items followed by a 30-minute essay.

> Four of the 35-minute sections determine a test taker's score and include three different types of questions, organized as one reading comprehension section [RC], one analytical reasoning section [AR], and two logical reasoning sections [LR]. Questions on the LSAT are designed to measure abilities and skills such as the ability to read and comprehend complex texts with accuracy and insight, organize and manage information and draw reasonable inferences from it, reason critically, and analyze and evaluate the reasoning and argument of others. (Law School Admission Services [LSAS], 1991, p. 7)

These four sections provide a total score based on the approximately 100 five-option items. Additionally, there is another 35-minute section of multiple-choice items used for pretesting items and pre-equating tests over time plus an essay that is reproduced (unscored) for use by the law schools. Comments in this review will refer to these contemporary versions unless otherwise indicated.

The items do appear to measure abilities critical to the study of law, to measure comprehension and reasoning as their subtest titles indicate, to reflect aptitude for law school and neither the specific content learning in law expected from law school itself nor terminology associated with specific undergraduate courses, to be fair to applicants from diverse academic backgrounds, and to be of medium difficulty for competent test takers.

RELIABILITY. Reliability coefficients for the total score, estimated using an internal consistency approach, are in the low .90s. For example, for the four administrations of the test from June 1995 to February 1996, one coefficient was .92, three others .93, showing consistency for the reliability estimates.

A few comments, speculations, and cautions: The information for score interpretation, including reliability information, refers only to the total score; without a profile with multiple subscores to interpret, reliability information is simplified.

Second, these numbers do not generalize directly to stability of performance for individuals over time with independent testings. Indeed, the statement "The higher the reliability coefficient for a test, the more certain we can be that test takers would get very similar scores if they took the test again" (LSAS, 1993, p. 106) appears to stretch the interpretation of available reliability data given that internal consistency data are based on one-time testings. Some information on stability is available from a table on repeaters, that is, on performance for candidates who took the test in 1994–95 having taken the test previously (Law School Admission Council [LSAC], 1996b, pp. 18–19). The sample is based on the 17% of candidates who took the test twice and about 4% who took it more than twice. The average gain was small as were the standard deviations for the most recent LSATs given the previous LSAT score. No correlation coefficient was provided, however.

Third, judging from Wainer's (1995) concern for the nonindependence of items clustered in subsets following a common stem, reliability for the reading comprehension and analytic reasoning sections may be overestimated, although reliability for the two logical reasoning sections may be slightly underestimated. The net effect may be that the reliability coefficients are slight overestimates compared to results of alternate computational approaches used with the same data.

And fourth, as Wesman (1953) and Melton (1985) reminded us in earlier reviews, an internal consistency approach to reliability will provide an inflated estimate if the test is speeded; those reviewers differed in their estimates of the speededness of the test versions they were reviewing. The test developers suggest that the current test is not speeded based on percentage of test takers completing all items. However, accurate assessment of the extent to which the test is speeded is hampered by the developers' recommendation that test takers guess on items for which they are unsure. Perhaps a debriefing of test takers immediately following test administration would shed additional light on speededness. Nevertheless, this test must be quite reliable to support the criterion-related validity coefficients summarized later in our review.

The developers provide help for interpreting scores for individuals or pairs of individuals. Standard errors of measurement are given both for individual scores and for score differences (between people). Standard errors are approximately 2.5 to 2.8 for individuals and 3.6 to 3.9 for comparing individuals. Supporting information about reliability to aid interpretation for individuals appears quite correct (e.g., for a given true score, how the observed scores would be distributed) and at times even conservative (e.g., using 95% as well as 68% confidence intervals, and including score differences and not just an individual's scores).

VALIDITY. First, what does the test measure? Potential test takers and users/interpreters are urged to study illustrative items from past tests, easily available through LSAC. A short description of the test appears at the beginning of this review. Reading comprehension and reasoning abilities are tapped at quite a high level, and these abilities would seem consistent with the demands on law students. Intercorrelations among the multiple-choice subtests are highest for Reading Comprehension with Logical Reasoning ($r = .76$); rs for either of these variables with Analytical Reasoning were in the .50s (Stricker, 1993). Not surprisingly, when Stricker investigated discrepant subscores, the most frequent discrepancies involved Analytical Reasoning as one of the variables. For example, compared with the other two subscores, Analytical Reasoning tended to be relatively low for the older test takers but relatively high for females and Asians.

Information on the predictive value of the test is impressive. "Impressive" is considered here in terms of the magnitude of the correlations with first-year average (FYA) in law school, and then in terms of ways data are presented for an individual law school and ways data are summarized across schools. The test developers maintain an ongoing program of validation in cooperation with the law schools, which is an impressive activity itself.

Wightman (1993) summarized the predictive validity for the LSAT based on results for each of 167 schools for each of three years (1990–1992) just prior to use of the newest version of the test. The mean correlations with FYA were .41, .26, and .49 for the LSAT, undergraduate grades (UGPA), and the combination of LSAT and UGPA, respectively. Strikingly similar results were reported even more recently. Validity studies conducted during 1994 for 171 law schools showed:

correlations between LSAT scores and first-year law school grades ranged from .07 to .65 (median is .42). Correlations between LSAT scores combined with undergraduate grade-point averages and first-year law school grades ranged from .23 to .73 (median is .50). (LSAC, 1996b, p. 124)

These correlations for the LSAT as a sole predictor and for the LSAT and UGPA as joint predictors are high in at least three respects: (a) when considering that both predictors have already been used in the admissions process and therefore their ranges would be restricted, (b) when compared with results summarized in previous decades by Evans (1982) and by Schrader (1976), and (c) when compared with results summarized for other aptitude measures used to predict grades in other graduate and professional schools. We note also that for virtually every school, the test was a better predictor than was the UGPA. Additionally, there is incremental validity for UGPA; using the combination of the two predictors is superior to using either one alone. Partially because of such incremental validity, law schools are cautioned by LSAC not to use LSAT scores as the sole criterion for admission decisions.

Participating law schools can obtain free-of-charge studies of prediction for the individual school as well as summary data across schools. Information for each school includes descriptive results for each variable, predictive results for LSAT and UGPA as predictors of FYA, and results compared with the results for all participating law schools. (Results for other schools are not identified individually, thereby minimizing confrontations legal and otherwise.) The test developers further the users' understanding of the predictive situation by incorporating considerable description using summary statistics and graphical presentations of the groups' performance both on each variable and on the combinations of variables. Often information is presented not only for the most recent year but also for the most recent 3-year period, which would tend to provide additional stability for the results. Particularly interesting figures found in the report include: (a) the correlations of the predictors with the criterion measure for the individual school embedded on distributions of correlations for all the schools, and (b) performance for a prospective student on the two predictors entered in figures designed to show the probability of a FYA above, or below, certain percentiles. These latter figures may be considered particular applications of double-entry expectancy tables, and are based on data for the individual law school.

Wightman (1993) also assists the interpreter in other ways. For example, she discusses and illustrates cross validation. Further, she specifies Brogden's approach to test interpretation, simply stated as "the benefit from a selection program increases *in proportion to the validity coefficient*" (Cronbach, 1990, p. 429), which, compared with use of the old coefficient of determination, is more supportive for validity and more consistent with a decision-theoretic orientation to interpretation.

NORMING/EQUATING. When the LSAT was revised in 1991, primary goals of the revision included: (a) reducing error during the equating of test forms; (b) reducing differential impact among subsets of test-takers; and (c) improved accuracy and consistency of measurement along the score scale. Each of these three goals has been attacked, in part, through use of item response theory (IRT). Using IRT-based equating, scaled scores are intended to have the same meaning regardless of when they are obtained. That is, "for any individual, a given scaled score represents the same degree of ability regardless of when it is earned" (LSAC, 1996a, p. 1).

The test developers have quite a task, developing new forms four times a year where 140 minutes worth of the items are released to the public after one use. The remaining items are used for piloting and preequating. Even with the use of item response theory technology, the developers earn our congratulations for producing high-quality tests equated such that a score on the 120–180 scale does not have to be qualified with date-of-testing information.

Percentile ranks are available for comparisons with each of several reference groups. Comparison (norm) groups include test takers from the three most recent years, all applicants during an application year, and even applicants to a particular law school during a particular year.

The test developers will also work with individual law schools to provide an admission index based on a composite of LSAT and UGPA performances. Schools may pick weights based however they wish; multiple regression weights are among the options. The index could provide the school a basis for preliminary evaluation and sorting of candidates, and, as such, carries policy implications.

Given the test contains three distinct types of items (LR, RC, and AR), concerns arise about the use of IRT-based equating procedures with the LSAT.

A basic assumption for use of an IRT model is that items are unidimensional, that is, that they reflect a single ability. There has been some debate in the literature as to whether unidimensionality holds for the LSAT. Studies conducted by Camilli, Wang, and Fesq (1995) and Douglas, Kim, Roussos, Stout, and Zhang (1995) support two major, related dimensions to account for the item responses. Fortunately, Camilli and colleagues found this apparent multidimensionality had no substantial impact on score conversions and equating, concluding "It may appear that for the purpose of equating, the LSAT is functionally unidimensional even though, statistically, two general and a number of specific factors emerge" (Camilli et al., 1995, p. 94). However, their conclusion is qualified: As long as the two factors are highly correlated, equating is not problematic, and this high correlation was found with the two factors identified by the researchers. Further, the authors suggest that because the content of the LSAT is carefully specified (see p. 94), this correlation is likely to remain high and ensure continued adequacy for unidimensional equating models.

FAIRNESS AND DIFFERENTIAL ITEM/TEST FUNCTIONING. The developers seek fairness in the test content partially through attentive processes in item writing and editing. LSAS (n.d.) has a set of sensitivity guidelines for item writing and test development with sections on fairness, respect, and diversity. Use of these guidelines should minimize the number of items that are unfair or offensive to any group of test takers.

Studies at the level of the test or subtest have been undertaken to determine whether the test is equally appropriate for various subgroups. For example, DeChamplain (1995) considered whether LSAT equating was affected by multidimensionality differentially for subgroups of test takers. He considered subgroups of African Americans, Hispanics, and Caucasians as well as the total group. "Equating results indicated that the differences between the conversion lines obtained for the three ethnic groups and the total test-taker population were negligible" (DeChamplain, 1995, p. iii). Other studies have been done to examine comparability of validity coefficients across test-taking groups.

The test developers routinely investigate differential item functioning (DIF) to "identify items that function differentially for identifiable subpopulations" (Plake, 1995, p. 205). Every operational item of the LSAT is subjected to at least three stages of scrutiny for DIF, including pretesting and preoperational stages as well as operational. If any nontrivial DIF is detected, the item is reviewed by a DIF committee that determines the item's fate. Demographic variables of gender, ethnicity, and citizenship (Canadian and U.S.) are used in DIF analyses. Also, the technique is used to study DIF for the set of items; considering the items on a test, the further the standard deviation of the DIF values is from zero, the stronger the evidence is that the items as a whole exhibit DIF. For the LSAT, the standard deviation values are less than .40, which the developers maintain indicates a negligible DIF (see, e.g., LSAC, n.d.).

COACHING AND EXAMINEE PREPARATION. The LSAC encourages test takers to prepare for the exam. In the current Registration and Information Book, the LSAC provides item descriptions, analyses, illustrations, answers, rationales, even suggested strategies. In that book, they also provide a sample test with the recommendation for the potential test taker to simulate actual testing conditions, at least with regard to strict timing. Additional forms and explanations are available in the LSAT: Official TriplePrep series (see, for example, LSAC, 1996c).

In the past, few examinees have shunned preparation. McKinley (1993) found only 3.1% to 5.5% of the respondents to a question on test preparation checked "No preparation." The percentages varied slightly over the four testing times and were likely only slight underestimates given a response rate of 86% for the 153,000 test takers.

Given the results of coaching studies reported for various admissions tests (see, e.g., Linn, 1990), we estimate that most test takers can improve their scores by thoughtful preparation, and the LSAC provides appropriate material.

The test developers have refrained from being greedy in seeking retest takers. For example, in the current Registration and Information Book (LSAC, 1996b, pp. 18–19), they advise only those who "believe some circumstance, such as illness or anxiety, prevented them from performing as well as they might have expected" (p. 18) to consider retaking the test, and point out that 79% of the total test takers took the test only once. As noted previously (see Reliability), gains tended to be modest both in means and standard deviations. As expected given the statistical characteristics of gains and the self-selection of retakers, typically more people gained than lost points on retake for each initial score.

WRITING SAMPLE. Since June 1982, a writing sample has been administered in the last 30-minute session of the LSAT to provide information about the applicant's ability to communicate in writing (LSAS, 1991). Test takers write their essays in a self-contained two-page booklet.

> A copy of each candidate's writing sample is sent, along with his or her LSAT score, to each law school to which he or she applies. LSAS does not score the writing sample. … Writing samples are retained for a five-year period and the three most recent samples are reproduced as part of a candidate's Law School Report. (LSAS, 1991, p. 11)

Each law school has the option of deciding who evaluates whose essays on what basis. In some schools, all candidates' writing samples are evaluated, whereas in some other schools, only the writing samples of admitted students will be diagnosed (LSAS, 1991).

IN CONCLUSION. The LSAT is certainly a vital test contributing to crucial decision making in law school admissions. Considerable professional effort over half a century has led to a refined instrument with considerable information to support interpretation. As Linn (1990) noted, its title is modest, using *Admission* and not *Aptitude* or *Ability*, yet it tends to predict FYA better than does UGPA, and in combination with UGPA predicts amazingly well given that self-selection and institutional selection have reduced the variability in both predictors for individual law schools.

Support for and use of research by the LSAC has encouraged development of the test and material supporting interpretation. Topics we might expect continued within their ongoing research program would include use of subtest scores, differential functioning, development of criteria for judging the writing sample, and use of computer assisted or computer adaptive testing.

REVIEWERS' REFERENCES

Wesman, A. G. (1953). [Review of the Law School Admission Test]. In O. K. Buros (Ed.), *The fourth mental measurements yearbook* (pp. 814–816). Highland Park, NJ: The Gryphon Press.

Schrader, W. B. (1976). Summary of law school validity studies, 1948–1975 (Research Report LSAC-76-8). In *Reports of LSAC Sponsored Research, Volume III, 1975–1977* (pp. 519–550). Princeton, NJ: Law School Admission Council.

Evans, F. R. (1982). Recent trends in law school validity studies (Research Report LSAC-82-1). In *Reports of LSAC Sponsored Research: Volume IV, 1978–1983* (pp. 347–361). Newtown, PA: Law School Admission Services.

Melton, G. B. (1985). [Review of the Law School Admission Test]. In J. V. Mitchell, Jr. (Ed.), *The ninth mental measurements yearbook* (pp. 824–826). Lincoln, NE: Buros Institute of Mental Measurements.

Cronbach, L. J. (1990). *Essentials of psychological testing* (5th ed.). New York: Harper & Row.

Linn, R. L. (1990). Admissions testing: Recommended uses, validity, differential prediction, and coaching. *Applied Measurement in Education, 3,* 297–318.

Law School Admission Services. (1991). *The law school admission test: Sources, contents, uses.* Newtown, PA: Author.

Law School Admission Services. (1993). *LSAT registration and information book 1993–1994 (Canadian edition).* Newtown, PA: Author.

McKinley, R. (1993). *Summary of self-reported methods of test preparation by LSAT takers for 1990–1991 testing year* (Research Report 93-02). Newtown, PA: Law School Admission Council.

Stricker, L. J. (1993). *Discrepant LSAT subscores* (Research Report 93-01). Newtown, PA: Law School Admission Council/Law School Admission Services.

Wightman, L. F. (1993). *Predictive validity of the LSAT: A national summary of the 1990–1992 correlation studies* (Research Report 93-05). Newtown, PA: Law School Admission Council/Law School Admission Services.

Camilli, G., Wang, M., & Fesq, J. (1995). The effects of dimensionality on equating the Law School Admission Test. *Journal of Educational Measurement, 32,* 79–96.

DeChamplain, A. F. (1995). *Assessing the effect of multidimensionality on LSAT equating for subgroups of test takers* (Statistical Report 95-01). Newtown, PA: Law School Admission Council.

Douglas, J., Kim, H., Roussos, L., Stout, W., & Zhang, J. (1995). *LSAT dimensionality analysis for the December 1991, June 1992, and October 1992 administrations* (prepublication copy). Newtown, PA: Law School Admission Council.

Plake, B. S. (1995). Differential item functioning in licensure tests. In J. C. Impara (Ed.), *Licensure testing: Purposes, procedures, and practices* (pp. 205–218). Lincoln, NE: Buros Institute of Mental Measurements.

Wainer, H. (1995). Precision and differential item functioning on a testlet-based test: The 1991 Law School Admissions Test as an example. *Applied Measurement in Education, 8,* 157–186.

Law School Admission Council. (1996a). *Interpretive guide for LSAT score users.* Newtown, PA: Author.

Law School Admission Council. (1996b). *LSAT/LSDAS registration and information book 1996–1997.* Newtown, PA: Author.

Law School Admission Council. (1996c). *LSAT: The official TriplePrep Plus: With explanations.* Newtown, PA: Author.

Law School Admission Council. (n.d.). *Differential item functioning.* Newtown, PA: Author.

Law School Admission Services. (n.d.). *LSAS sensitivity guidelines for item writing and test development.* Newtown, PA: Author.

[175]
Leadership Competency Inventory.

Purpose: Measures an individual's use of four competencies related to leadership.

Population: Adults.

Publication Date: 1993.

Acronym: LCI.

Scores, 4: Information Seeking, Conceptual Thinking, Strategic Orientation, Service Orientation.

Administration: Group.

Price Data, 1993: $60 per complete kit including 10 profiles and interpretive notes (25 pages), and 10 questionnaires; $25 per 10 (employee version) questionnaires.

Time: Administration time not reported.

Comments: Self-scored questionnaire.

Author: Stephen P. Kelner.

Publisher: McBer & Company.

Review of the Leadership Competency Inventory by L. CAROLYN PEARSON, Associate Professor of Education, University of West Florida, Pensacola, FL:

The Leadership Competency Inventory (LCI) is designed to measure the degree to which an individual possesses leadership characteristics as defined by specific behaviors from the perspective of either the individual's self-report, or the individual as perceived by others. There are two versions that assess leadership skills in four areas: Information Seeking, Conceptual Thinking, Strategic Orientation, and Service Orientation. The Participant version assesses self-perceived competence in the four areas through the use of specific behaviors that are attributed to effective leadership. The Employee version assesses the same four areas and may be used simultaneously by one or more raters.

Both versions use the same 46 items and have the respondent assess to what degree they have demonstrated or seen various behaviors. For example, the Information Seeking scale inquires into such matters as asking questions or personally investigating matters; the Conceptual Thinking scale inquires into recognizing patterns or applying complex concepts. The Strategic Orientation scale inquires into such behaviors as aligning current actions with strategic goals or understanding external impact; the Service Orientation scale inquires into making oneself available or maintaining clear communication. The Likert scale used for all of the items ranges from 0, the behavior being absent, to 4, the behavior occurring extremely frequently, and is very awkward. All of the scales are composed of hierarchical levels that range from the simplest to the most complex behaviors that leaders can demonstrate, with two items measuring each level. There is no justification provided as to why some behaviors are considered to be more complex than others. Also, for three of the four scales, the first two levels are not scored and no explanation is given as to why. The scoring guide was easy to follow, but because it does not include zero it is inconsistent with the scaling used for the items; this discrepancy is confusing. Scores are then graphed to demonstrate strengths and weaknesses for each of the competency areas. There is no explanation given for minimal cut scores in demonstrating competency but the user is provided with suggestions on how the competencies may be improved.

The author provides no rationale or theoretical framework for the behaviors that are used for each of the four areas that are assessed. A leadership model is presented, but the linkage between this model and how it was derived from the leadership research was not given. There is no logical analysis presented as to how the items were developed, pretested, or selected from the research on leadership. Consequently, in terms of empirical research, no reliability or validity data are reported; therefore, it is assumed that the instrument is probably only suitable for screening purposes. The items seem to be free of bias on face value.

In conclusion, the LCI is in need of establishing the research base from which it came, especially in terms of the derivation of the model that was presented. The items have good face validity; however, there is no indication of how they were derived from the research on leadership. Evidence of the instrument's reliability, validity, and biases is yet to be done. A better alternative would be the Leadership Practices Inventory (Pfeiffer and Company International Publishers; 12:213), which has undergone extensive validation. I cannot recommend the LCI because there are no empirical studies to support it as a measure of leadership competency.

[176]
Leadership Skills Inventory [Consulting Resource Group].

Purpose: Helps individuals develop the ability to handle the "people" side of enterprise.
Population: Adults.
Publication Date: 1992.
Acronym: LSI.
Scores, 7: Transforming Leadership Principles, Awareness and Self-Management Skills, Interpersonal Communication Skills, Counseling and Problem Management Skills, Consulting Skills for Developing Groups and Organizations, Style/Role and Skill Shifting for Developing Versatility, Grand Total.
Administration: Group.
Editions, 2: Self Assessment, Other.
Price Data, 1993: $10 per test booklet (Other); $12 per test booklet (Self Assessment).
Time: (40–50) minutes.
Comments: Self-administered and self-scored; book entitled *Transforming Leadership: New Skills for an Extraordinary Future* serves as manual.
Author: Terry D. Anderson.
Publisher: Consulting Resource Group International, Inc.

Review of the Leadership Skills Inventory by MARY HENNING-STOUT, Professor of Counseling Psychology, Lewis & Clark College, Portland, OR:

The Leadership Skills Inventory was developed by T. D. Anderson as a tool for enacting his theories of leadership development as set forth in his book, *Transforming Leadership: New Skills for an Extraordinary Future*, 1992. The inventory is available in two forms, one for self-assessment and one for assessment by others. Each form includes instructions for completing the scale. The self-assessment form offers brief suggestions for ways to interpret responses and develop a personal leadership plan based on the results. In the narrative of that form, consumers are referred to Anderson's book for more thorough support in developing such a plan.

Because there was no manual accompanying the inventories, I contacted a representative of the

Consulting Resource Group International, the publisher of the inventory. The Leader of Marketing Communications, Eleanor Parkinson, provided much of the information upon which this review is based. Parkinson described the scale as useful for top-level executive teams interested in leadership development. She indicated that the scale would be inappropriate for individuals who were not ready and willing to improve themselves as leaders (e.g., if use of the scale were forced on an executive by a corporate president or general manager).

Parkinson described a new use of the scales for providing what she described as 360 degree feedback. In such instances, an individual completes a self-assessment form and three to five colleagues complete the others-assessment form with reference to the individual of focus. The results are tabulated and provided to the individual as a way for understanding how her or his leadership is seen from all angles. Parkinson indicated that it is quite difficult for any person to be unconsciously competent at all times and to all people, but that such leadership—that is, always walking one's talk—is the appropriate goal of any leader.

PSYCHOMETRIC CONSIDERATIONS. The author of this scale makes no comment on the normative or ipsative nature of this inventory, although Parkinson was clear that the scale is ipsative, completely derived from and based in Anderson's theory. These are not tests. They are not to be applied or construed as such. Rather, they are learning and communication tools. I asked Parkinson if there were any acknowledgments of the cultural limitations of this instrument and she indicated that Anderson sees his ideas as universal and noted the consistency between Anderson's theories and those of Kouzes (Kouzes & Posner, 1987).

SUMMARY. The Leadership Skills Inventory is marketed alongside the book upon which it is based. It is clear in the narrative of the self-assessment inventory form that use of these scales will support the development of a personal leadership plan and that responses to the inventory's questions will be most easily interpreted in the context of Anderson's leadership theory. This is not an assessment of skill or potential in any global sense. The inventory is marketed to top-level executives and can therefore be seen as limited, by design, to people fitting that economic class. The generalizability of the instrument across cultural and gender groups is not addressed and remains unclear.

REVIEWER'S REFERENCES

Kouzes, J. M., & Posner, B. Z. (1987). *The leadership challenge: How to get extraordinary things done in organizations.* San Francisco: Jossey-Bass.

Anderson, T. D. (1992). *Transforming leadership: new skills for an extraordinary future.* Amherst, MA: HRD Press.

Review of the Leadership Skills Inventory by GEORGE C. THORNTON III, *Professor of Psychology, Colorado State University, Fort Collins, CO:*

The Leadership Skills Inventory (LSI) is one of numerous questionnaires that have appeared in recent years that can be used to provide 360 degree feedback to managers. The readers should be aware that there is an earlier questionnaire with the same title, which has been used to assess leadership skills of high school students (Karnes, 1990). Anderson's use of this title is unfortunate. Anderson's LSI consists of a self-assessment version and an others' version that can be filled out by associates and subordinates. It is designed to provide an assessment of several leadership skills and to help the individual initiate developmental activities. The inventory is a condensed version of a self-assessment process that is embedded in a book (Anderson, 1992) that provides a detailed description of the theory and rationale behind the leadership skills covered in the questionnaire. The LSI begins with a section that asks the individual to express agreement or disagreement with 12 principles that form the basis of Anderson's theory of transforming leadership. A self-scoring guide allows the person to assess if he or she is moving in the general direction of Anderson's approach to leadership.

The next five sections of the inventory consist of sets of 8 to 12 rating scales subsumed under the general headings of Self-Management; Interpersonal Communication; Counseling and Problem Management; Consulting; and Role, Style, and Skill Shifting. The final section of the questionnaire provides a place for the individual to graph scores from the self and others' assessments. There are no norms for interpreting the meaning of scores. There is no provision to graph separately the responses of subordinates, peers, or manager, as is done with the results from other 360 degree feedback programs.

The scales within each section call for ratings on skills, processes, or interactions with others. For example, under Self-Management, scales such as "grounding" and "centering" appear. Under Interpersonal Communication, scales on "self-disclosure" and "image management" appear. Each attribute is rated on a 5-point scale ranging from "Skill is new to me, I cannot do it" to "Can do it very well, and teach others if I want to." In addition, others can respond: "This skill was not observed."

In contrast to the abstract dimensions contained in the LSI, the items that appear on other similar instruments are much more behavioral in nature. I doubt that others are able to provide accurate ratings on many of the scales of the LSI, some of which refer to the target individual's thoughts and feelings (e.g., "centering: maintains clear awareness of self in the context of external events").

The self-assessment version suggests that the individual distribute the others' version to colleagues, have them complete and score the responses, return the results, and then record the scores at the back of the self form. This process destroys the anonymity of the others' responses and is likely to diminish the validity of their assessments. At the very least, others are likely to temper any negative feedback and thus minimize the developmental benefits to the individual. A much more effective practice is to follow the procedure carried out with comparable instruments whereby a neutral third party compiles the others' responses.

No manual for the LSI is provided. Thus, there are no norms or evidence of reliability or validity. In response to my request, the author wrote "The LSI is currently undergoing initial validity research. Test-retest reliability is sound with four groups of university students (N = 30) (Terry Anderson, February 26, 1996, personal communication). None of the technical information required by the *Standards for Educational and Psychological Testing* (AERA, APA, & NCME, 1985) is provided in any source.

Before this instrument can be recommended for use, the author must provide empirical data indicating that the supposed benefits will be attained, including accuracy of assessment and effects on development of leadership skills. The complete lack of supportive data for the LSI is in sharp contrast with thorough research and supporting documentation provided by authors of comparable instruments such as Wilson's Survey of Management Practices (T4:469), the Profilor by Personnel Decisions Inc. (Davis, Skube, Hellervik, Gebelein, & Sheard, 1992), and D. Campbell's Leadership Potential Index (Clark & Clark, 1990).

In summary, although the LSI has a nice companion book to lead someone through a description of the leadership concepts underlying the questionnaire, the dearth of technical data relevant to the reliability and validity makes it difficult to recommend the LSI for applied uses.

REVIEWER'S REFERENCES

American Educational Research Association, American Psychological Association, & National Council on Measurement in Education. (1985). *Standards for educational and psychological testing.* Washington, DC: American Psychological Association, Inc.

Davis, B. L., Skube, C. J., Hellervik, L. W., Gebelein, S. H., & Sheard, J. (1992). *Successful manager's handbook: Development suggestions for today's managers.* Minneapolis, MN: Personnel Decisions, Inc.

Clark, K. E., & Clark, M. B. (Eds.) (1990). *Measures of leadership.* West Orange, NJ: Leadership Library of America.

Karnes, F. A. (1990). Leadership and youth: A commitment. In K. E. Clark & M. B. Clark (Eds.), *Measures of leadership* (pp. 563–566). West Orange, NJ: Leadership Library of America.

Anderson, T. D. (1992). *Transforming leadership: New skills for an extraordinary future.* Amherst, MA: HRD Press.

[177]
Learning and Study Strategies Inventory—High School Version.

Purpose: Designed to assist high school students "in determining their study skills strategies, problems and attitudes, and learning practices."

Population: Grades 9–12.

Publication Date: 1990.

Acronym: LASSI-HS.

Scores, 10: Attitude, Motivation, Time Management, Anxiety, Concentration, Information Processing, Selecting Main Ideas, Study Aids, Self Testing, Test Strategies.

Administration: Group.

Price Data, 1994: $2.25 per self-scored form; $2.50 per computer scored form.

Time: (25–30) minutes.

Authors: Claire E. Weinstein and David R. Palmer.

Publisher: H & H Publishing Company.

TEST REFERENCES

1. Eldredge, J. L. (1990). Learning and Study Strategies Inventory—High School Version. *Journal of Reading, 34,* 146-149.
2. Walsh, J. (1993). The promise and pitfalls of integrated strategy instruction. *Journal of Learning Disabilities, 26,* 438-442.
3. Tallent-Runnels, M. K., Olivárez, A., Jr., Candler Lotvin, A. C., Walsh, S. K., Gray, A., & Irons, T. R. (1994). A comparison of learning and study strategies of gifted and average-ability junior high students. *Journal for the Education of the Gifted, 17,* 143-160.
4. Hagborg, W. J. (1995). High school student perceptions and satisfaction with group advisory. *Psychology in the Schools, 32,* 46-51.

Review of the Learning and Study Strategies Inventory—High School Version by KENNETH A. KIEWRA, Professor of Educational Psychology, University of Nebraska—Lincoln, Lincoln, NE:

The Learning and Study Strategies Inventory—High School Version (LASSI-HS) is designed to measure learning and study strategies at the secondary school level. The LASSI-HS is an offshoot of the original LASSI, published in 1987, for use at the college level. I review the LASSI-HS with respect to (a) purpose; (b) composition; (c) administration, scoring, and interpretation; (d) test characteristics; and (e) my conclusion.

PURPOSE. The LASSI-HS is intended for use as (a) a diagnostic measure to identify strategy strengths and weaknesses; (b) a counseling tool for advising students into appropriate programs; (c) a basis for planning individual prescriptions to remedy weaknesses and enrich strengths; (d) a pre-post

achievement measure to determine a student's strategy growth, and (e) an evaluation tool to assess a program's or course's success. The instrument is appropriate for 9th through 12th grade students.

COMPOSITION. The LASSI-HS is a 76-item self-report instrument incorporating a 5-point rating scale with the endpoints "very much like me" and "not at all like me." The five choices appear atop each item column for easy referral. Items are both positively stated and negatively stated to encourage thoughtful responding and discourage uncharacteristic response patterns.

The LASSI-HS is divided into 10 scales with most comprising eight items. The 10 scales appear to fit within four important factors associated with learning and studying: cognitive (e.g., information processing and concentration), metacognitive (e.g., self-testing), motivational (e.g., motivation and time management), and affective (e.g., attitudes and anxiety), but are not based on any systematic model of studying. Still, the items are, in my estimation, reflective of important and current research and theory associated with learning and studying, and represent the best collection of items I have observed among several such inventories. The LASSI-HS, for example, assesses metacognition, motivational attributions, and organization and elaboration strategies—areas often ignored in similar instruments. However, the LASSI-HS contains some omissions. It neglects to assess, for example, whether notes are recorded adequately (completely and with examples) and whether students prepare adequately for procedural tasks (e.g., solving math word problems) by practicing problem classification and problem solving.

ADMINISTRATION, SCORING, AND INTERPRETATION. The LASSI-HS is an untimed inventory administered easily to an individual, class, or school within 20–25 minutes. Although students complete the inventory without assistance, an adult examiner is required to distribute materials, read instructions, answer student questions, and collect materials.

There are two versions of the LASSI-HS: computer scored and student scored. They are identical in content, but vary in form. The computer-scored version includes a one-page Student Directions handout and the LASSI-HS computer-scored form. This form contains the items and five "bubbles" alongside each item for recording responses.

The computer-scored forms must be checked by students and examiners so that no data are lost due to omitted items or missing student information. The completed forms are sent to the publishing company, which provides individual and class scores and graphs for each of the 10 scales within one week of receipt. The relative advantages of computer scoring are the elimination of student scoring errors and the provision of class summaries. The relative disadvantages of computer scoring are the slightly higher cost of the computer-scored forms and delayed feedback.

The student-scored version is contained within a single booklet. The booklet includes directions, test pages, scoring materials, and norming tables. The instructions appear on the booklet's front cover. Two test pages are removed from the booklet prior to testing. Students mark their responses directly on the test pages. The pressure sensitive pages transfer a student's responses onto a scoring sheet below. The scoring sheet reveals a numerical response to each item and each item's scale classification.

Students record their item score within a chart organized by the 10 scales. Next, they sum item scores to determine scale scores. These are plotted on a norming chart corresponding to their grade level (9–12). The chart provides percentile scores based on national norms. The norming data are somewhat limited and restricted; they are based on about 500–800 students at each grade level from a single southwestern city.

The test booklet and the user's manual provide brief explanations of the 10 scales to aid in interpretation. The manual also provides vague implications for remediation such as "learn techniques to enhance concentration and set priorities" (p. 15). The LASSI-HS is not equipped to remediate or enrich the behaviors measured.

TEST CHARACTERISTICS. Test characteristics are described with respect to development, reliability, and validity. The LASSI-HS was developed by adapting the original Learning and Study Strategies Inventory (LASSI). It appears that only minor modifications were made. Both forms contain the identical 10 scales and contain a nearly identical number of items (77 and 76). The adaptation was carried out by a team of experts who revised LASSI items consistent with high school vocabulary and demands. The resulting item set was field tested using 750 ninth graders although the instrument is intended for students in 9th through 12th grades. How the two forms actually differ is not mentioned.

A reliability estimate for the entire instrument was not furnished. Reliability coefficients for the 10 scales ranged from .68 (Study Aids) to .82 (Anxiety and Concentration). Reliability coefficients in this range indicate that each scale was reasonably internally consistent and adequately measured a common behavior. Intercorrelations among scale scores were not reported, however, leaving unknown the degree to which the 10 scales measure unique behaviors. My own inspection of items revealed several that might be appropriate for more than one scale. The item "I am up-to-date in my class assignments" (protocol, p. 3), for example, is included in the Motivation scale but also seems consistent with the Time Management scale. Another example is the item "I make drawings or sketches to help me understand what I am studying" (protocol, p. 4). It is classified within the Study Aid scale but represents an organization strategy that seemingly fits within the Information Processing scale.

Also not reported was test-retest reliability. Therefore, nothing is known about the stability of scores. Without this information, it is unwise to administer the inventory before and after instruction and then assume that performance changes on the inventory resulted from instruction.

No validity data are reported for the LASSI-HS. Without such data it is impossible to know whether the test scores can be interpreted as measures of learning and studying behaviors as intended. The manual provides tangential and undocumented claims for the validity of the original LASSI. No data are provided, however, relating performance on either Learning and Study Strategy Inventory to academic performance or to indices of actual learning and study behaviors (e.g., analyses of lecture notes, inspection of time logs, or teacher observations).

CONCLUSION. At face value, the LASSI-HS contains scales and items that seem to tap important learning and study behaviors. The items are the best I have seen. The lack of psychometric evidence, however, makes its use risky and premature among those demanding assurance about its construction, accuracy, and usefulness.

Review of the Learning and Study Strategies Inventory—High School Version by ROBERT T. WIL-LIAMS, Professor of Education, Colorado State University, Fort Collins, CO:

The Learning and Study Strategies Inventory—High School Version (LASSI-HS) is a 76-item, self-report, individually or group administered assessment of high school (grades 9–12) students' use of learning and study strategies and methods. There are two formats: self-scored or computer scored. The self-scored format gives immediate results.

Recording, adding, and transferring scores demands attention to detail. Computer scoring is done by the publisher. It provides class and individual reports and a computer disk (IBM compatible) of raw data.

Separate norms are given for grades 9, 10, 11, and 12. The grade 12 norms are suggested to be appropriate for first-year college students. A review of the norm tables reveals that there is little difference in raw scores (3 or less) for the 50th percentile at any grade level. In other words, there does not seem to be any difference in the way typical students in grades 9, 10, 11, or 12 respond to the items in the scales.

The 76 items are statements that assess "covert and overt thoughts and behaviors that relate to successful learning in high school *and* that can be altered through educational interventions" (manual, p. 3). The authors maintain that "these thought processes and behaviors also contribute significantly to success in college *and* can be learned or enhanced through programs and interventions in secondary educational settings" (manual, p. 3). The authors do not provide research data or references to support these propositions.

The authors suggest the LASSI-HS may be used as a diagnostic tool, a counseling tool, a basis for planning individual prescriptions for learning interventions with students, as a prepost achievement measure, and as an evaluation tool.

The inventory has 10 scales. These scales are identified and explained using words from pages 14–17 of the manual. The coefficient alpha, a measure of internal consistency reliability, is in parentheses. *Attitude*—general attitude and motivation for succeeding in school and performing the tasks related to school success (.74); *Motivation*—the degree to which students accept responsibility for performing the specific tasks related to school success (.78); *Time Management*—the degree to which students create and use schedules (.77); *Anxiety*—how tense or anxious students are when approaching academic tasks (.82); *Concentration*—ability to concentrate and direct attention to school and school-related tasks, including study activities (.82); *Information Processing*—how well students can create imaginal and verbal elaborations and organizations to foster understanding and recall (.80); *Selecting Main Ideas*—skills at selecting important information on which to concentrate for further study in either the classroom lecture or autonomous learning situations (.71); *Study Aids*—ability to use and create study aids that support and increase meaningful learning and retention (.68); *Self Testing*—importance of self-testing and reviewing

and the degree to which students use these methods (.74); *Test Strategies*—use of test-taking and test preparation strategies (.81).

The 76 items are distributed randomly within the inventory; half of the items are stated in a positive direction and half are stated in a negative direction. Students respond to the items with a 5-point Likert-type scale of *a = Not at all like me* through *e = Very much like me*. The reviewer found the scale on the Student Response Form slightly difficult to follow.

Research and development of the LASSI, from which the LASSI-HS was created, began in 1978 in the University of Texas, Austin, Cognitive Learning Strategies Project. The manual efficiently describes the several year evolution of the LASSI and the LASSI-HS through conceptual development, item pool development, pilot testing, inventory construction, and norm development.

The authors offer information about the validity of the LASSI by saying the scale scores have been compared with other assessments, that several of the scales have been validated against performance measures, and that there have been repeated tests of user validity. There is no research or reference evidence to support any of the claims. The user validity claim supported by educational practitioners in over 700 colleges and universities and the on-going evaluation at the Cognitive Learning Project is the strongest. The user is left to accept that the validity for the LASSI transfers to the LASSI-HS.

The reliability as reported by coefficient alpha is acceptable. The derivation and interpretation of the coefficient is not explained beyond the statement "The coefficient alpha is a measure of reliability" (manual, p. 13).

The norms for the LASSI-HS were developed from a sample of 2,616 students in a "mid-sized city in the southwest" (manual, p. 20) in grades 9 (N = 857), 10 (N = 500), 11 (N = 575), and 12 (N = 604) "selected to reflect a range of ethnic backgrounds, economic conditions, and academic achievement levels" (p. 20). No gender or ethnic data are given. The geographic region is limited.

In the opinion of this reviewer, the LASSI-HS has good content and construct validity and no reported concurrent validity. The norms do not appear useful because there is no meaningful difference in the performance of the grade groups and there are no gender or ethnic norms. The Inventory has intuitive value for gaining information about how to help students, for academic counseling, and for instructional planning. A guide and resource list for planning prescriptions for students would be a useful addition to the manual. This reviewer questions the usefulness of the inventory as a pre-post achievement measure or a program evaluation tool because any intervention should "teach" the students how to answer on the post-test and would not be a measure of behavior. Changes in attendance and grades could be more stable indicators for evaluation.

[178]
Learning Preference Scales.

Purpose: "Provides a measure of the preference for cooperative, competitive and individualised learning."
Publication Date: 1992.
Acronym: LPS.
Scores, 5: Cooperation, Competition, Individualism, Combined Involvement, Cooperative Involvement.
Administration: Group.
Price Data, 1993: $59.95 per complete kit including manual (54 pages) and one copy of each scale.
Time: (10–45) minutes.
Authors: Lee Owens and Jennifer Barnes.
Publisher: Australian Council for Educational Research, Ltd. [Australia].
   a) LEARNING PREFERENCE SCALES—STUDENTS.
   Population: Grades 4–12.
   Acronym: LPSS.
   b) LEARNING PREFERENCE SCALES—TEACHERS.
   Population: Elementary and secondary teachers.
   Acronym: LPST.
   c) LEARNING PREFERENCE SCALES—PARENTS.
   Population: Parents of school students.
   Acronym: LPSP.

TEST REFERENCES

1. Li,. A. K. F., & Adamson, G. (1995). Motivational patterns related to gifted students' learning of mathematics, science and English: An examination of gender differences. *Journal for the Education of the Gifted, 18,* 284-297.

Review of the Learning Preference Scales by TRENTON R. FERRO, Associate Professor of Adult and Community Education, Indiana University of Pennsylvania, Indiana, PA:

The three Learning Preference Scales—one each for Students (LPSS), Teachers (LPST), and Parents (LPSP)—are intended to provide "systematic information on the attitudes of school students, teachers or the parents of school students towards cooperative, competitive and individualised [*sic*] learning as it take place in the classroom" (p. 3). Each scale consists of a set of statements (36, 33, and 24

respectively). Each statement is followed by four spaces representing four varying reactions the person completing the scale might have toward each statement: "completely/clearly true," "sort of true" or "a bit more true than false," "sort of false" or "a bit more false than true," or "completely/clearly false." Numerical values of 4, 3, 2, and 1 are assigned to each of these responses (or, conversely, 1, 2, 3, and 4 for negatively stated items).

The statement in each Learning Preference Scale can be divided into three equal groups of 12, 11, and 8 statements, respectively. Adding together the scores for statements in each of these groups provides three subscales representing preferences for *Cooperative, Competitive,* and/or *Individualized* learning. Two composite scales can also be obtained: *Combined Involvement* is derived by adding the Cooperative and Competitive subscale scores, and *Cooperative Involvement* is obtained by subtracting the Competitive subscale score from the Cooperative subscale score. The Student scale is designed for students from grade 4 through secondary school. The scales are not recommended for use by nonreaders. Readability levels for the three instruments, based on 90% comprehension, are Year 6 for the LPSS, Year 10 for the LPST, and Year 8 (estimated) for the LPSP (roughly speaking, "year" = "grade").

The authors of the instrument present a variety of ways in which the results of each instrument might be used. Included in the recommendations are such aspects as diagnosing attitudes of students, teachers, and parents about differing learning styles and modes and toward those expressing preferences for these differing modes; planning and carrying out varying and alternative teaching/learning strategies; contributing to policy decisions; providing information for in-service training; and improving communication among students, teachers, and parents regarding matters related to learning preferences.

The manual is well designed and easy to use. In addition to providing copies of the instrument and describing their purpose and ways to use the results derived from their use, the manual provides instructions for administering and scoring the instruments and recording and reporting the results. Information is also provided on reference groups and the development of the instruments (including a discussion of versions devised for use in the United States and in England since the original development of the instruments occurred in Australia).

The three scales have been tested for reliability through several large scale administrations in New

South Wales, Western Australia, the United States, and England. Using Cronbach's alpha, the coefficients ranged from .60 to .78 on all subscales of all administrations of the LPSS, from .37 to .79 on the LPST (from .62 to .79 on the Cooperative and Competitive subscales and from .37 to .60 on the Individualized), and from .46 to .85 on the LPSP (from .71 to .85 on the Cooperative and Competitive and from .46 to .65 on Individualized). Intercorrelations among the three subscales have also been calculated using Pearson r. These findings

> support the "new theory" contention that preferences of students for Cooperative and Competitive modes of learning comprise independent dimensions. This is in contrast with the earlier "old theory" argument that preferences for Cooperative and Competitive modes were negatively related and opposed in a polar relationship. .... The data on Cooperative and Individualised [sic] preferences indicates [sic] that a moderate negative relationship prevails and that this does not vary with sex or year at school. (p. 25)

A considerable number of articles, conference papers, theses, dissertations, and research projects have been devoted to these scales and their spin-offs. However, a vast majority of this research has been done by the authors themselves and by others working with them. There is still considerable room for, and need of, testing by independent researchers. Nevertheless, the scales should certainly prove useful and valuable if they are used, as suggested by the authors, for improving teaching and learning in the classroom and for helping students, teachers, and parents better understand the variety of ways people can, and prefer to, learn. The tests are not intended to be used for individual diagnoses leading to such decisions as educational placement. Such a use would be a misuse.

Review of the Learning Preference Scales by ROBERT J. MILLER, Associate Professor of Special Education, Mankato State University, Mankato, MN:

There are three Learning Preference Scale instruments. These include the: (a) Learning Preference Scale—Students (LPSS), (b) Learning Preference Scale—Teachers (LPST), and (c) Learning Preference Scale—Parents (LPSP). The purpose of each instrument is to provide a measure for preference of the individual completing the scale for cooperative, competitive, and individualized learning. These instruments may be used separately or in combination. The Student instrument (LPSS) contains 36 items with 12 items in each of the three

subscales mixed randomly throughout the instrument. The Teacher scale (LPST) contains 33 items arranged in the same three subscales of cooperative, competitive, and individualized learning with 11 items in each subscale. The Parent scale (LPSP) contains 24 items across the three subscales.

Each instrument is largely self-administered and the instrument may be completed alone or in a group. The Student (LPSS) form takes approximately 10 to 15 minutes to complete for older students and from 25 to 45 minutes for younger students or less competent readers. Results of readability testing by the authors suggest the reading level at which these instruments could be read by the test takers with 90% comprehension was 6th grade for the LPSS (Student form), 10th grade for the LPST (Teacher form), and an estimated 8th grade for the LPSP (Parent form). The authors do not recommend the use of this instrument with students younger than 4th grade or with students after the completion of secondary school.

The test manual includes directions for administering the student instrument to a large group. It is suggested that the Teacher and Parent forms will almost always be completed on an individual basis. Directions for completing the instrument are included on the Teacher and Parent forms but not on the Student form. Directions for the Student form are designed to be provided orally and the manual provides specific directions for student participants. Each of the 36 items in the Student form (LPSS) is a simple statement of 6 to 20 words. The test taker is to read the statement, and rate their agreement or disagreement with the statement using a 4-point Likert-type scale ranging from *True, Sort of True, Sort of False, False* regarding their learning preferences. An identical Likert-type scale is used for test takers on the LPST (Teacher) and LPSP (Parent) forms of the instrument. Scoring is done manually, by a paper-and-pencil compilation. Items that are rated by the test taker as *True* of their learning preferences receive a score of 4. Items that are *Sort of True* receive a score of 3. *Sort of False* items are scored as 2, and *False* items are scored as 1. Negative items in each scale (those requiring reverse scoring) are identified in the test manual.

Interpretation of raw scores is based on percentiles with separate reference group data provided in tables in the test manual for populations of students from New South Wales (Sidney, Australia); Western Australia (Perth, Australia); Minneapolis, Minnesota (U.S.A.); and from three Midlands counties of England. Separate tables in the manual provide the quartile scores, the mean scores, and standard deviations of scores obtained by a number of smaller subgroups of these populations. Quartile scores on the LPSS are provided for each school year group by sex and on the LPST for different subject teachers, as well as for male and female teachers separately. No information is provided regarding the LPSP (Parent) form of the instrument.

The authors suggest: "By selecting an appropriate comparison group it is possible to convert a raw score for an individual into a percentile rating, indicating that the obtained score is equal to or greater than that of a certain percentage of that comparison group" (p. 13). Implied in this statement is that one would find value in comparing a subject's score to that of the comparison group. Unfortunately, the norming of this instrument is woefully inadequate and the norm sample limits the usefulness of the instrument as a diagnostic tool and also the usefulness of comparing the subject's performance to that of the comparison group. For example, information for the United States sample was collected from one senior high school, one junior high school, and two primary schools in suburban Minneapolis in 1981. This norming population was situated in "predominately white areas" (p. 12). The total United States norm sample was 1,058 school-aged children and young adults from the Minneapolis area. Although the sample has a roughly equal distribution of boys ($n = 533$) and girls ($n = 525$) and primary ($n = 486$) and secondary students ($n = 572$), the sample is from one region of the United States and the manual provides no information regarding socioeconomic status of the norming sample nor adequate information regarding minority group representation. No students from rural or urban locations were included in the United States sample. It is, therefore, difficult to gauge whether the population to which the instrument is normed is reflective of any larger population.

Alpha reliabilities were provided for each of the subscales of all three forms of the Learning Preference Scales. Three tables presented alpha reliabilities for students, teachers, and parents. The coefficients for the LPSS (Student) subscales across the international field tests of the instrument ranged as follows: (a) Cooperation subscale from .64 to .75; (b) Competition subscale from .52 to .77; and (c) Individualism subscale from .60 to .75. In all cases, the lowest reliability coefficients were found in the primary grades and the highest in the secondary grades. The alpha reliabilities for the LPSS indicate marginally adequate internal consistency.

The alpha coefficients for the LPST (Teacher) subscales of the instrument ranged as follows: (a) Cooperation subscale from .62 to .76; (b) Competitive subscale from .73 to .79; and, (c) Individualism subscale from .37 to .60. The alpha coefficients for the LPSP (Parent) subscales were as follows: (a) Cooperative subscale .71 to .82; (b) Competition subscale .78 to .85; and, (c) Individualism subscale .46 to .65. Alpha reliabilities for both the Teacher and Parent forms in the area of the Individualism subscales were low whereas all other areas were adequate.

One of the most useful types of reliability evidence for this sort of instrument is consistency over time or test-retest reliability. In the manual, the authors suggest "the LPSS seems to have been demonstrated in obtaining stable results in short-term, test-retest usage" (p. 24). However, no evidence is provided in the manual to support the test-retest reliability of this instrument. No information is provided regarding the test-retest reliability of the LPST or the LPSP.

The discussion of validity of the Learning Preference Scales provided by the authors is inadequate. Neither content validity nor predictive validity are discussed in the manual. Although construct validity is implied in the authors' discussion of the development of the instruments, no systematic evidence is provided. A discussion of validity of these instruments is needed.

The Learning Preference Scales are a set of instruments that are designed to measure the test taker's preference for cooperation, competition and individualism in the learning environment. The strength of the Learning Preference Scales is the intriguing topic of the test instruments. The weaknesses are substantial. Although the authors have collected much information on students from around the world, the end result of this huge endeavor may have been less comprehensive than the authors had hoped. The Learning Preference Scales have limited usefulness as norm-referenced instruments. For example, the norm sample in the United States is inadequate and limits the use of these instruments in comparing the subject's performance to other students. Too little information regarding the reliability and validity of the instruments is presented in the manual. Very little information was included in the manual regarding the LPSP (Parent) form of the instrument. In this reviewer's opinion, the strength of this set of instruments is the LPSS (Student) form and I would suggest its use only as a criterion-referenced instrument.

[179]
Learning Skills Profile.

Purpose: To assess the gap between personal aptitudes and critical skills required by a job.

Population: Junior high to adults.

Publication Date: 1993.

Acronym: LSP.

Scores, 36: 3 scores: Personal Learning Skill, Job Skill Demand, and Learning Gap in each of 12 skill areas: Interpersonal Skills (Leadership Skill, Relationship Skill, Help Skill), Analytical Skills (Theory Skill, Quantitative Skill, Technology Skill), Information Skills (Sense-Making Skill, Information-Gathering Skill, Information Analysis Skill), Behavioral Skills (Goal Setting Skill, Action Skill, Initiative Skill).

Administration: Group.

Price Data, 1993: $85 per complete kit including 5 workbooks and profiles, and 1 set of reusable LSP cards and instructions; $65 per 5 workbooks and profiles; $32 per reusable LSP cards and instructions.

Time: Administration time not reported.

Comments: Self-scored profile.

Authors: Richard E. Boyatzis and David A. Kolb.

Publisher: McBer & Company.

Review of the Learning Skills Profile by DAVID O. HERMAN, Associate Education Officer, Office of Educational Research, New York City Board of Education, Brooklyn, NY:

Reduced to its skeleton, the Learning Skills Profile (LSP) is a set of 12 six-item rating scales. The 12 scales represent job-related skills that may be considered as either personal characteristics of a job holder or skills demanded by the job. "Working as a member of a team" (Relationship Skill) and "Finding solutions to problems" (Goal Setting Skill) are examples of the items. Most of the item statements are simply worded, although a reference to "mathematical models" may not be clear to some users.

The user rates him or herself on all 72 items, using a 7-point scale that ranges from 1 (*No skill or experience in this area*) to 7 (*A leader or creator in this area*). Then the user rerates each item for the extent to which his or her job requires the activity. Again a 7-point scale is used, this one ranging from 1 (*Not relevant to job or career*) to 7 (*A top priority activity*). Two complete sets of total scores are obtained for the 12 learning-skill scales, with one set describing the rater ("Personal Learning Skills"), and the other describing his or her job ("Job Skill Demands").

A difference between the two scores on any scale is said to reflect a "learning gap." If the Personal Learning Skill score is less than the Job Skill Demand score, the discrepancy signifies an area in which the user needs further development; if the score difference is in the other direction, it indicates an area where the user is overskilled or overqualified for the job.

The Learning Skills Profile is a highly elaborated version of this skeleton. The 72 activity statements are printed onto two separate decks of cards. The user physically sorts one deck into seven piles to describe the self, then sorts the second deck similarly to describe the job. The numerical ratings are now transcribed, statement by statement, onto a grid on a special score sheet; this is done twice, once for the self and once for the job. Total scores for the 12 skill areas are recorded separately for the self-description and the job description, and the two sets of 12 scores are plotted on a clock-like circle graph.

The user then turns to the LSP Workbook. After reading a general introduction to the LSP, the user is directed to copy once again the two complete sets of 72 item ratings for detailed consideration. Various exercises encourage the user to reflect on the accuracy of the scores, to compare one's self-assessment with feedback from others, and to make plans to rectify any "learning gaps."

I think the Learning Skills Profile offers people, especially those in supervisory and managerial positions, an opportunity to view themselves critically and constructively. The LSP materials are so minimal, however, they cannot be judged by the usual criteria for evaluating tests. No manual or technical supplement accompanied the review kit to document, for example, the internal consistency of the scales; or whether the scale intercorrelations support the circular arrangement on the LSP graphical display (this is important because sets of scales that are adjacent on the display are said to make up supervariables or so-called "skill types"); or whether ratings are distributed about the same on all 12 scales (this is important because, in the absence of norms, interpretations of profile elevation require that a given score level have about the same meaning on all scales). The LSP offers no control for social desirability or conscious deception. It may be true that such refinements are less important with a self-evaluation exercise of this kind than with other kinds of instruments used in high-stakes settings. Nevertheless, it must be said the LSP has no known measurement characteristics.

The procedures for rating the items and interpreting the results are labor-intensive and probably tedious. Careful forms design could, I believe, place the 72 items and the two rating scales efficiently on a single sheet of paper, thus avoiding much clerical drudgery. Possibly the authors have found the recommended procedures get users deeply involved in the rating process, and thus yield more accurate results than briefer, more streamlined methods—but we do not know.

In summary, the Learning Skills Profile is rather like an elaborate, highly structured interview aimed at exploring a job holder's self-reported skills and how well they fit the demands of the job, and for planning future actions in the light of the findings. I am aware of no competition.

[180]

Learning Style Inventory [Price Systems, Inc.].

Purpose: Identifies "the conditions under which an individual is most likely to learn, remember, and achieve."
Population: Grades 3–12.
Publication Dates: 1976–1994.
Acronym: LSI.
Scores: 22 areas: Noise Level, Light, Temperature, Design, Motivation, Persistent, Responsible, Structure, Learning Alone/Peer Oriented, Authority Figures Present, Learn in Several Ways, Auditory, Visual, Tactile, Kinesthetic, Requires Intake, Evening/Morning, Late Morning, Afternoon, Needs Mobility, Parent Figure Motivated, Teacher Motivated, plus a Consistency score.
Administration: Group.
Price Data, 1993: $2.50 per 10 answer sheets for grades 3 and 4 or for grades 5 and above; $.40 per individual interpretative booklet; $9.50 per manual ('89, 95 pages); $3.25 per research report; $295 per computerized self-administered inventory program with 100 administrations ($60 per 100 additional administrations) (specify IBM or Apple); $395 per Scan and Score programs; $.60 per answer form to use with Scan and Score; $4 or less per individual profile available from publisher's scoring service; $7.50 or less per group and subscale summaries; summaries available from publisher only in addition to individual profiles.
Time: (20–30) minutes.
Comments: Apple, IBM, or IBM-compatible computer required for (optional) computerized administration; 3000, 3051 NCS, OPScan 5, Scrantron 8000, 8200, 8400, or Scanning System 380 scanner required for (optional) Scan and Score System.
Authors: Rita Dunn, Kenneth Dunn, and Gary E. Price.
Publisher: Price Systems, Inc.
Cross References: See T4:1432 (3 references); for reviews by Jan N. Hughes and Alida S. Westman, see 11:203 (6 references).

TEST REFERENCES

1. Stice, C. F., Bertrand, N. P., Leuder, D. C., & Dunn, M. B. (1989). Personality types and theoretical orientation to reading: An exploratory study. *Reading Research and Instruction, 29*(1), 39-51.
2. Reynolds, J., & Gerstan, M. (1991). Learning style characteristics of adult dependent decision makers: Counseling and instructional implications. *Career Development Quarterly, 40,* 145-154.
3. Dunn, R., Griggs, S. A., & Price, G. E. (1993). Learning styles of Mexican American and Anglo-American elementary school students. *Journal of Multicultural Counseling and Development, 21,* 237-247.
4. Cornwell, J. M., & Manfredo, P. A. (1994). Kolb's learning style theory revisited. *Educational and Psychological Measurement, 54,* 299-316.
5. Lenehan, M. C., Dunn, R., Ingham, J., Signer, B., & Murray, J. B. (1994). Effects of learning-style intervention on college students' achievement, anxiety, anger, and curiosity. *Journal of College Student Development, 35,* 461–466.
6. Yuen, C., & Lee, S. N. (1994). Applicability of the Learning Style Inventory in an Asian context and its predictive value. *Educational and Psychological Measurement, 54,* 541-549.
7. Dunn, R., Griggs, S. A., Olson, J., Beasley, M., & Gorman, B. S. (1995). A meta-analytic validation of the Dunn and Dunn model of learning-style preferences. *The Journal of Educational Psychology, 88,* 353–362.
8. Grimes, S. K. (1995). Targeting academic programs to student diversity utilizing learning styles and learning-study strategies. *Journal of College Student Development, 36,* 422–430.
9. Hong, E., & Suh, B. K. (1995). An analysis of change in Korean-American and Korean students' learning styles. *Psychological Reports, 76,* 691–699.

Review of the Learning Style Inventory [Price Systems, Inc.] by THOMAS R. KNAPP, Professor of Nursing and Education, The Ohio State University, Columbus, OH:

In her scathing review of Dunn, Dunn, and Price's Learning Style Inventory (LSI) in *The Eleventh Mental Measurements Yearbook*, Jan N. Hughes (1992) claimed that "the LSI has no redeeming values" (p. 461). Alida S. Westman (1992) was considerably kinder, but she, too, pointed out a number of weaknesses in the inventory. I am no expert on learning styles, but I agree with Hughes that this instrument is a psychometric disaster. In my review I would like to concentrate on a few shortcomings I observed that are over and above those alluded to by the previous reviewers.

Most of the items have identical wording on the two versions (one for grades 3–4, the other for grades 5–12), but there are some curious differences, apparently due to an effort to adjust the reading level. For example, Item 4 on the third and fourth grade version is "I like for my teacher to explain my assignments," whereas Item 4 on the version for the older children is "I like to be told what to do when I get an assignment." The difference between the two versions for Item 32, however, is merely the use of "It's" (grades 3–4) versus "It is" (grades 5–12).

Included in the directions on the separate answer sheet for both versions is the incredible sentence "Some of the questions are repeated to help make the inventory results more reliable." If that is the only way the authors could think of to improve the reliability of the inventory they are in real trouble! (No items are, in fact, repeated word for word. They are simply reworded. For example, Item 10 on both versions is "I usually feel more comfortable in warm weather than I do in cool weather"; Item 36 is "I usually feel more comfortable in cool weather than I do in warm weather." Such items contribute to a consistency check, as Westman mentioned in her review, and are not really concerned with reliability at all.)

The reliability coefficients reported in the 1976–1977 Research Report and in the 1989 test manual are said to be Hoyt reliabilities that are equivalent to K-R 20s, but this cannot be true because the items are not dichotomously scored for either version. (I assume that they are Cronbach's alphas.) In the two-page section of the 1989 manual headed "Reliability and Validity" there is actually no mention of validity, much less any validity data.

The LSI has been around for a long time—approximately 25 years. There appears to have been little research or development activity in the '90s and interest in using the inventory also appears to have declined. One reason for this may have been the negative reviews referred to above. It would seem that we in the measurement community have fulfilled our responsibilities with respect to this particular measuring instrument by pointing out its psychometric limitations.

REVIEWER'S REFERENCES

Hughes, J. N. (1992). [Review of the Learning Style Inventory]. In J. J. Kramer & J. C. Conoley (Eds.), *The eleventh mental measurements yearbook* (pp. 460–461). Lincoln, NE: Buros Institute of Mental Measurements.
Westman, A. S. (1992). [Review of the Learning Style Inventory]. In J. J. Kramer & J. C. Conoley (Eds.), *The eleventh mental measurements yearbook* (pp. 461–462). Lincoln, NE: Buros Institute of Mental Measurements.

Review of the Learning Style Inventory [Price Systems, Inc.] by CRAIG S. SHWERY, Assistant Professor of Teacher Education, Fort Hays State University, Hays, KS:

The Learning Style Inventory (LSI) consists of 104 items assessing elements of an individual's preferences in learning across 22 domains. Examples of the 22 domains are Noise Level, Light, Temperature, Design, etc. As reported by the authors, analysis of the results can provide prescriptive information on the type of environment, social groups, motivational factors, and instructional activities that can maximize an individual's achievement. The LSI takes approximately 20 to 30 minutes to complete and may be taken in more than one sitting by students in grades 3 through 12. At present there are also research editions of the LSI in Arabic, Brazilian, French, Hebrew, Hindi, and Spanish.

The LSI provides an individual profile of a student's preferred learning style. Standard scores are reported with a mean of 50 and standard deviation of 10. Scores of 60 or above indicate a high preference for that area whereas scores of 40 or lower indicate a

low preference for that area. The individual profile also provides a consistency score that functions as an index of students' reliability in answering the questions. High scores indicate consistency, whereas low scores may indicate lack of motivation or ability to concentrate. The LSI also provides a group summary and an area summary. The group summary yields information about students with similar preferences for learning environments, whereas the area summary provides information about which elements are least and most important for the group as a whole.

The present edition of the LSI has undergone several revisions since 1975. Not much has changed. The instrument is still plagued by issues related to its construct validity and the lack of an a priori theoretical paradigm for its development. These problems, however, relate to a greater debate, namely, the existence of aptitude-treatment interactions in learning styles. Aptitude-treatment interactions as related to learning styles have not unequivocally been demonstrated.

NORMS. The LSI provides insufficient information for the critical analysis of the normative group. No information is provided on the demographic stratification of the normative group. The authors merely state that the standard scores were based on "more than 500,000 students who had completed the LSI" (manual, p. 11). Given the paucity of information on the normative group, any interpretation of the scores is not meaningful.

RELIABILITY. Scant evidence of reliability for scores from the LSI is provided in the manual. The authors report "research in 1988 indicated that 95 percent" (p. 30) of the 22 areas for grades 5 through 12 provided internal consistency estimates of .60 or greater. The actual range is .55 to .88. Internal consistency across areas in the third to fourth grade age group ranged from .42 to .91. The internal consistency of a number of areas for the third to fourth grade age groups was low. As such, the link between the areas and justifiably making decisions about instruction in these areas is questionable. The authors also make references to "other" studies that provide "very good reliability" for the LSI (p. 28). One study did yield a test-retest reliability coefficient of .929 (approximately 1-year interval). Given the sources of measurement error that can contribute to an individual's score, one outside source of test-retest reliability is insufficient as evidence of this test's stability across administrations.

VALIDITY. The authors make numerous references to the predictive validity of the LSI. Development of the LSI was based on content and factor analytic procedures. The areas derived from the factor analysis were purported to explain 62% of the variance. No explanation, however, is provided as to the relationship between the factors derived from the analysis and the area conceptualization. Again, this is evidence of little or no a priori guiding theory. The LSI was purported to possess good predictive validity when compared with nine other instruments, yet the reader is referred to other studies to substantiate this claim.

TEST AND ITEM BIAS. No information is provided by the authors regarding examination of the test and test items for their appropriateness across various groups. To what extent can the results of the LSI be generalized across other cultural groups? The authors, do, however, report that items that "were confusing, could be interpreted in different ways or were not clear in their assessment of the defined areas" were removed or reworded (p. 29). This sparse information, however, is meaningless without elaboration.

SUMMARY. In summary, the LSI possesses a number of psychometric limitations that may derive from the lack of a clear and concise theoretical paradigm for its development. Given its widespread use among teachers, more research is needed to establish its predictive validity. In addition, the LSI's student-centered focus fails to consider the wealth of literature on teachers' beliefs and practices. Despite the LSI's limitations, this reviewer believes the LSI does provide qualitative information that can be used in tandem with teacher observation to assess a student's learning environment. For example, the LSI can highlight alternative strategies in lesson plans, a common source of stress for teachers. However, in this reviewer's opinion, the LSI should be considered as only one source of information among many when classroom instructional decisions are made.

[181]
Leisure Search Inventory.

Purpose: To identify employment opportunities related to leisure interests.
Population: Adults.
Publication Date: 1994.
Acronym: LSI.
Scores: 12 areas: Artistic, Scientific, Plants and Animals, Protective, Mechanical, Industrial, Business Detail, Selling, Accommodating, Humanitarian, Leading-Influencing, Physical Performing.
Administration: Group.
Manual: No manual.
Price Data: Available from publisher.

Time: Administration time not reported.
Comments: Self-administered and self-scored.
Author: John J. Liptak.
Publisher: JIST Works, Inc.

Review of the Leisure Search Inventory by LEO M. HARVILL, Professor and Assistant Dean for Medical Education, East Tennessee State University, Johnson City, TN:

This inventory has some potential to be a useful instrument for exploring occupational opportunities. Exploring leisure interests is certainly one approach that could be used for this purpose. The inventory seems intended for use with adults who are looking for a first career or a change in career. Examinees are provided with scores in 12 occupational clusters that were developed by the U.S. Department of Labor. The score for each cluster is derived from responses to examinee interest in eight items dealing with leisure activities. For each item, the examinee is to respond with one of five choices: *like the activity very much, like the activity a little, neither like nor dislike the activity, dislike the activity somewhat, dislike the activity very much.*

Directions for completing and scoring the inventory are adequate. The directions for interpreting the results are also appropriate. There are good suggestions provided in the inventory for resources that provide additional information concerning the initial exploration of occupational opportunities.

The inventory is not accompanied by a manual. Thus, there are a number of unanswered questions concerning this instrument:

1. How were the sets of eight items for each of the 12 clusters of occupations developed?

2. What validity evidence is available?

3. What is the test-retest or internal consistency reliability of the 12 occupational cluster scores?

The inventory lacks face validity for some sets of eight items for particular occupational clusters. For example, in the Scientific cluster of eight items, two pertain to astronomy and only one pertains to health care. In the Artistic cluster, three items pertain to reading and/ or writing and none of the eight items pertain to music. It would be of interest to know how the sets of eight items were selected for each occupational cluster and whether any factor analytic studies were conducted in the development of the inventory.

It would be very helpful to have some information concerning the reliability of the 12 scores for the inventory but none is presented in the inventory itself in the form of reliability coefficients or standard errors of measurement. Validity studies concerning the inventory would also be helpful in making decisions about using the instrument. For example, what experience has there been in the use of the inventory? How do people score on the Leisure Search Inventory who are employed in the 12 occupational cluster areas and who are satisfied with their work? Data from such a study could be useful in providing some normative information that would assist examinees in interpreting their scores from the inventory.

This inventory may possibly be useful to adults in their early search for a career choice. However, without a manual that covers, at a minimum, inventory development, reliability, and validity, use of the inventory is difficult to recommend.

Review of the Leisure Search Inventory by ELLEN WEISSINGER, Associate Dean, Teachers College, University of Nebraska-Lincoln, Lincoln, NE:

The Leisure Search Inventory (LSI) is designed to assist people in identifying employment opportunities that are related to their leisure interests. The assumption behind the test seems to be that people are happier in their work life if their job uses skills or interests that have been developed during free time activities. Although this assumption has some intuitive appeal, the authors of the test offer no empirical support or theoretical rationale for their central contention. This is a major shortcoming of the test.

The LSI consists of a single, large, multi-fold piece of paper. One brief paragraph describes the purpose of the test. Test takers are then directed to complete a section of the test that asks them to rate their "liking or disliking" of 96 leisure activities. Test takers respond by circling one of five letters (L = "Like the activity very much," l = "Like the activity a little," N = "Neither like nor dislike the activity," d = "dislike the activity somewhat," and D = "Dislike the activity very much"). This odd mix of lower and upper case letters is awkward and difficult to follow.

After responding to the 96 leisure activity items, the test taker is directed to assign numeric values to their responses by writing a small number next to the letter they circled. Responses of "L" are scored as 2 points; responses of "l" are scored as 1 point. All other responses (N, d, D) are scored as 0. Next, test takers are told to add up the scores across rows of four items each. These row scores are identified as "subtotals." Two different groups of 12 rows each are color coded and assigned subtotal labels of 1A, 1B, and so on to 12A and 12B. For example,

rows 1A and 1B seem to include arts activities (e.g., visit art galleries, take pictures/develop film), and rows 4A and 4B seem to include items related to public service activities (e.g., learn about firefighting, prevent neighborhood crime). Row subtotals can range from 0–8 (individual item scores can range from 0–2 and there are 4 items in each subtotal).

After creating row subtotals, the test taker is directed to place these numbers into spaces provided on the "LSI Interest Profile" chart. This chart enables the test taker to add up scores in 12 "occupational clusters" (for example, the subtotals for rows 1A and 1B are added to create the score for the "Artistic" occupational cluster). Occupational cluster scores can range from 0 to 16 (as they include 8 items, each of which can range from 0–2). These scores are partitioned into three categories: scores of 0–4 are labeled "Low" cluster scores, 5–11 are "Medium" cluster scores, and 12–16 are "High" cluster scores. No rationale is provided for these cluster score labels.

Next, test takers are instructed to interpret their cluster scores. "Low" scores indicate little interest in that occupational cluster, "Medium" scores indicate some interest, and "High" scores indicate a lot of interest. Test takers are encouraged to explore career options related to clusters in which they have high interest. This is facilitated by a Career Exploration Chart listing United States Department of Labor Guide for Career Exploration Interest Groups. This chart lists sample occupation and self-employment options related to each of the 12 occupational clusters. Test takers are also provided with a list of additional career exploration resources.

Finally, test takers are provided with a LSI Career Planning Guide. This "guide" is a blank template that provides room for the test takers to note their occupational interest groups, specific jobs available in that group, education or training required, pros and cons related to the occupational group, and next steps in the career exploration process.

The LSI has no test manual. Information related to the conceptual framework, reliability, validity, and norming of the test is not presented. No information is provided to explain why the leisure activities were selected, nor is the rationale for relating certain leisure activities to specified occupational clusters explained. For example, the leisure activity "research family history/genealogy" is associated with the "Business Detail" occupational cluster, and "do needlework" is placed in the "Industrial" cluster.

These shortcomings argue against using the LSI as a diagnostic assessment in educational, clinical, or therapeutic settings. The Strong Interest Inventory (12:374) is the dominant test in this area and has clear advantages over the LSI. The LSI may have value as a tool to help individuals begin a casual exploration of their leisure interests, and in turn, their employment interests. The self-administration format of the test may increase its accessibility. It seems possible that individuals could gain personal insight as a result of completing the exercises presented in the LSI.

[182]

Life Roles Inventory.

Purpose: "Designed to assess the importance of life-career values and the relative importance of five major life roles."
Population: Junior high students–adults.
Publication Date: 1985.
Acronym: LRI.
Subtests: 2 subtests.
Administration: Group.
Price Data: Available from publisher.
Foreign Language Edition: French edition ('85) available.
Authors: George W. Fitzsimmons, Donald Macnab, and Catherine Casserly.
Publisher: Psychometrics Canada Ltd. [Canada].
  a) VALUES SCALE.
  Scores, 20: Ability Utilization, Achievement, Advancement, Aesthetics, Altruism, Authority, Autonomy, Creativity, Economics, Life Style, Personal Development, Physical Activity, Prestige, Risk, Social Interaction, Social Relations, Variety, Working Conditions, Cultural Identity, Physical Prowess.
  Time: (20–25) minutes.
  b) SALIENCE INVENTORY.
  Scores, 15: 5 scores (Studying, Working, Community Service, Home and Family, Leisure) in each of 3 areas (Participation, Commitment, Role Values).
  Time: (25–30) minutes.

TEST REFERENCES

1. Brintnell, E. S., Madill, H. M., Montgomerie, T. C., & Stavin, L. L. (1992). Work and family issues after injury: Do female and male client perspectives differ. *Career Development Quarterly, 41,* 145-160.

Review of the Life Roles Inventory by RICHARD W. JOHNSON, Director of Training at Counseling & Consultation Services of the University Health Services, and Adjunct Professor of Counseling Psychology, University of Wisconsin–Madison, Madison, WI:

The Life Roles Inventory (LRI) consists of two inventories designed to measure the importance of life goals and roles for individuals living in Canada. The two inventories, the Values Scale (VS) and the Salience Inventory (SI), are very similar to the two instruments with virtually these same names developed for use within the United States (see 10:379 and 11:339). The inventories are based on research conducted by members of the Work Importance Study, an international consortium headed by Donald Super, which includes vocational psychologists from 12 countries and which was formed in 1979 to investigate the significance of major life roles in different cultural settings.

The VS consists of 100 items that measure 20 different values. Each scale has five 4-point items, three of which are common to all countries and two of which are unique to Canada. The item content includes both work and personal values. The U.S. version of the VS scale contain 21 scales, 19 of which are identical to those on the Canadian version. The two versions of the VS differ in that two of the scales on the former version (Economic Rewards and Economic Security) have been collapsed into one scale on the latter version (Economics).

The SI assesses the relative importance of life roles for individuals as described in Super's (1980) life-career rainbow model. Each of five major life roles—Study, Work, Home and Family, Leisure, and Community Service—are evaluated in terms of three aspects of importance—Participation, Commitment, and Value Expectations—to produce a total of 15 scales. The three areas of importance include measures of behavior (Participation) and affect (Commitment and Values Expectations), but not knowledge. According to the authors, Super's Career Development Inventory (48) should be used to evaluate knowledge in the area of work. The 15 scales on the two versions of the SI are identical. Both instruments contain 170 four-point items with similar content; however, the exact wording of the items frequently differs.

Both parts of the LRI (the VS and SI) have been standardized on Canadian populations. Separate norms have been established for the English and French editions of the LRI. The norms are further divided in regard to sex, type of work (professional, clerical, skilled, and unskilled), and year-in-school (postsecondary students, 12th grade students, and 10th grade students). The characteristics of the normative samples are described in some detail in the technical manual; however, it is not clear to what extent the norms are representative of the Canadian population.

In general, the SI scales have produced higher coefficients of internal consistency than the VS scales, presumably because the SI contains more items per scale than the VS. Median Cronbach alpha coefficients for the French and English adult normative samples for the 20 scales on the VS were both .80, whereas the median alphas for these same samples for the 15 scales on the SI were better than .90. Similar differences were obtained with the other normative samples. Because of such high alpha coefficients for the SI, the authors indicate that they may develop a short version of the SI for use where time is limited.

As has been noted for the U.S. versions of the VS and SI, the test-retest reliabilities of the Canadian versions of these scales run somewhat low. The test-retest reliabilities over a 4- to 6-week time period for grades 10 and 12 students ranged from .53 to .83 with a median of .65 for the French version of the LRI VS. For the English version, the reliabilities ranged from .63 to .82 with a median of .69. The test-retest reliability coefficients for the SI scales for these same students were slightly higher; however, the median rs were still only .72 and .73 for the French and English versions, respectively. These reliability coefficients indicate that one's scores could change substantially upon retesting over relatively short time periods for scales on either instrument.

Both the VS and SI exhibit content validity in the sense that the items for the scales have been selected to measure different types of values and life roles suggested by vocational theory and research in a number of cultural settings. Items for the final scales were selected on the basis of item and factor analyses.

The authors have conducted several studies to demonstrate the convergent and discriminant validities of the LRI. Their research shows that the scales on the VS and SI correlate with similar scales on other instruments. In contrast, the scales do not produce high correlations with other types of vocational measures from which they should differ. For example, correlations between scores on both the VS and SI scales and scores on interest inventory scales have been relatively low.

Research indicates that the VS significantly differentiates among students enrolled in various academic programs. In a well-conducted study of postsecondary students enrolled in three different majors (rehabilitation medicine, business, and education), the authors found the VS to be more effective than the Work Values Inventory (T4:2998) the Minnesota Importance Questionnaire (T4:1641), or the Work Aspect Preference Scale (T4:2987) in differentiating among the students.

Studies cited in the technical manual show that the SI distinguishes among individuals in different settings or circumstances in expected directions. For example, occupational therapists who were leaving the field obtained lower scores on the Commitment and Participation scales for the Work role and higher scores on the scales for the Home and Family role than did occupational therapists who had recently assumed administrative or supervisory positions. Participation, Commitment, and Role Values for Studying were rated higher by professional and skilled groups than by clerical and unskilled groups in the normative samples.

Principal component analysis of the VS indicates that five components (Personal Achievement and Development, Social Orientation, Independence, Economic Conditions, and Physical Activity and Risk) account for most of the variance in the instrument. These five components are similar to those obtained in factor analyses of work values instruments with the exception of Physical Activity and Risk, which appears to be unique to the VS. The authors conclude that some of the scales on the VS could probably be combined, a project that they suggest for further research.

In summary, the LRI contributes to the field of vocational psychology by providing measures of life roles and values that are more comprehensive than those provided by other instruments. As part of an international project, the LRI can also be used productively in cross-cultural research. It needs to be strengthened in regard to test-retest reliability. Validity data are still relatively limited.

REVIEWER'S REFERENCE

Super, D. E. (1980). A life-span, life-space approach to career development. *Journal of Vocational Behavior, 16*, 282–298.

Review of the Life Roles Inventory by S. ALVIN LEUNG, Associate Professor of Educational Psychology, The Chinese University of Hong Kong, Hong Kong:

The Life Roles Inventory (LRI) consists of two separate scales, the Values Scale and the Salience Inventory. The LRI is designed to assess what a person wants to get out of work and life (values), and the importance of work roles in relation to other major life roles. The LRI can be administered to junior and senior high school and college students and to adults with different vocational needs and concerns in career and vocational guidance, general counseling, and job placement counseling.

The LRI was the result of an international research collaboration known as the "Work Importance Study." Vocational psychologists from a number of European, Asian, and American countries, led by Donald Super, developed vocational assessment instruments aimed at measuring work values and life roles of individuals. This effort resulted in several national editions of an assessment instrument, and the LRI is the Canadian edition. The LRI has both an English and a French version. Normative and psychometric information for both language versions are provided in the administrative manual and the technical manual. A back-translations process was used to ensure comparability of the two language versions. Handscoring of the LRI can be done easily by following the procedure described in the administrator's manual. Computer scoring and interpretation is also available.

The Values Scale measures 20 values on a 4-point scale (1 = *of little or no importance,* 4 = *very important*). Each item is a statement about preference (e.g., use my skills and knowledge). Each value is measured by five items resulting in a total of 100 items. The values are Ability Utilization, Achievement, Advancement, Aesthetics, Altruism, Authority, Autonomy, Creativity, Economics, Life Style, Personal Development, Physical Activity, Prestige, Risk, Social Interaction, Social Relations, Variety, Working Conditions, Cultural Identity, and Physical Prowess. For each value scale, a raw scores is computed, which is then transformed into a percentile score using the normative table provided in the administrator's manual. A profile sheet is used to plot both the raw and the percentile scores.

The Salience Inventory uses a 4-point scale (1 = *never or rarely,* 4 = *always or almost always* or 1 = *little or none,* 4 = *a great deal*) to measure the meaning and importance of five life activities, which are Studying, Working, Community Service, Home and Family, and Leisure Activities. It consists of three sections. The first, Participation (50 items), measures current involvement in the five life activities. The second, Commitment (50 items), measures how one feels about the five life activities. The third is Role Values Grid, consisting of 70 items about an individual's long-term expectations to fulfill 14 values in each of the five life activities. The 14 values are Ability Utilization, Achievement, Aesthetics, Altruism, Autonomy, Creativity, Economics, Life Style, Physical Activity, Prestige, Risk, Social Interaction, Variety, and Working Conditions. Both raw scores and percentile scores are plotted.

Normative information is available for adults and for post-secondary and high school students. There is evidence that the samples were drawn from diverse geographic areas within Canada, and educational and occupational levels. The LRI scores are converted to percentile scores using normative data from the group that is most appropriate for the test taker.

Information on internal consistency and test-retest reliability are available. For internal consistency of the English version of the Values Scale, the range for adults was from .67 to .88, with a median of .80. The alphas for post-secondary students ranged from .68 to .91, with a median of .83. The alpha for grade 12 students ranged from .65 to .90, with a median of .79. On the French version, the alphas ranged from .64 to .84, with a median of .80. The alphas for grade 12 students ranged from .60 to .88, with a median of .74. Test-retest correlation coefficients for the Values Scale were computed for a high school sample in a 4- to 6-weeks time interval. The median correlation for the English and French versions of the Values Scale were .69 and .65, respectively. Given that values are relatively stable constructs, one would expect a higher degree of test-retest stability. Alternate forms correlation between the English and French versions ranged between .62 and .88, with a median correlation of .74. Again, one would expect a higher correlation between the two language versions if the two forms were highly equivalent.

On the Salience Inventory, the alpha coefficient estimates of internal consistency for French- and English-speaking adult samples ranged from .84 to .95. For English-speaking post-secondary students, the range was from .83 to .95, and for English and French high school students, the range was from .88 to .96. The 4- to 6-weeks test-retest correlation for the English version ranged from .66 to .81, with a median of .73. For the French version, the test-retest correlation ranged .68 to .81, with a median of .72. The correlation between the English and French versions of the Salience Inventory ranged from .59 to .84, with a median of .77. For the same reasons as in the case of the Values Scale, the test-retest and alternative-forms reliability is lower than expected.

Evidence on the validity of the LRI is summarized in the technical manual. For the Values Scale, a principal component factor analysis of the items using a varimax procedure yielded factors that were similar to 14 of the 20 a priori value scales, supporting the construct validity of the Values Scale. The Values Scale correlated significantly with similar scales measuring work values. Differences in work values were observed among students in education, business, and rehabilitation medicine. Using the Values Scale scores, students were correctly classified into one of the above three academic areas.

There is some evidence on the validity of the Salience Inventory. Students were asked to rate the importance of different academic, occupational, recreational, community, and family activities, and their ratings generally converged with their Salience Inventory scores. Occupational therapists who were actively practicing in their profession rated the work role as more important in the participation and Commitment subscales of the Salience Inventory, whereas those who were not actively practicing rated home and family roles as more important.

Although the amount of research evidence on the validity of the LRI is limited and additional research studies are needed, the LRI appears to be a carefully constructed instrument that has a sound conceptual foundation in Donald Super's theoretical work on career development. There are at least three advantages of using Super's theory. First, there is a large volume of research literature on Super's theory (e.g., see Savickas, 1994), and thus the validity and utility of the LRI are complemented by the research evidence supporting Super's theory. Second, in the process of interpreting the LRI, Super's theory can be used to help individuals understand the implications of the test scores. Third, Super's conceptual framework can be used as a basis to further research the validity of the LRI.

On a cross-cultural perspective, the LRI has two strengths. First, the instrument was conceptualized through a process of international collaboration in which the cross-cultural similarities and differences in work values and life roles were considered. Second, the Canadian LRI is in English and French, and normative information was available for both versions. To further meet the needs of an increasing multicultural society, it would be desirable for the LRI to provide additional language or normative information for other major ethnic and cultural groups in Canada, such as American Indians and Asians.

A weakness of the LRI is that both the administrator's manual and technical manual do not provide specific information on how the LRI can be used in a counseling context. A number of areas related to interpretation are not described clearly. For example, how can the LRI be used to assist individuals in different counseling situations suggested to be appropriate by the authors (career, personal, and job placement)? What information should be communicated to a test taker regarding the meaning of test scores? How can the LRI be used along with other vocational assessment instruments?

What interpretation strategies can be used for individuals with specific profiles, such as those who have high scores (i.e., an elevated profile) and those with low scores (i.e., a depressed profile)? Should raw scores or percentile scores be used in interpretation? Answers to the above questions would be helpful to users of the LRI.

The print quality of the LRI administrator's manual and technical manual is poor and should be improved. Many tables are very small and are hard to read (e.g., normative tables, and tables on reliability).

Overall, the LRI is a useful instrument to help individuals with diverse vocational concerns. The LRI can be used in conjunction with other career assessment instruments (e.g., interests inventory) to counsel individuals in different stages of career and life planning. However, additional research studies are needed to further examine the reliability and validity of the LRI, and to demonstrate that the LRI produces possible outcomes for students and adults in different counseling situations.

REVIEWER'S REFERENCE

Savickas, M. L. (Ed.). (1994). From vocational guidance to career counseling: Essays to honor Donald Super [Special issue]. *The Career Development Quarterly, 43*(1).

[183]

Life Space Analysis Profile.

Purpose: Evaluates factors that contribute to life space, including self image, home, family and work/career.

Population: Adults.

Publication Date: 1991.

Acronym: LSAP.

Scores: 18 scores in 3 major areas: Self Space (Activity, Interpersonal Relationships, Being Alone, Emotional, Body, Psychological), Home/Family Space (Financial, Leisure, Physical Environment, Origins, Mate, Offspring), Work Space (Career, Compensation, Relationships, Skills, Climate, Goals).

Administration: Individual.

Price Data, 1993: $40 for IBM software (specify 5.25-inch or 3.5-inch).

Time: (30) minutes.

Comments: PC-based; confidential.

Author: John W. Baker, II.

Publisher: XICOM, Inc.

Review of the Life Space Analysis Profile by W. DALE BROTHERTON, Associate Professor of Counselor Education, Western Carolina University, Cullowhee, NC:

The Life Space Analysis Profile (LSAP) is designed to assess the degree of balance a person has in three life space areas. The concept of life space originated from the development of Field Theory begun by Kurt Lewin (1951). Lewin maintained that a person's level of functioning depends on the interactive process between the person and the various environments she or he encounters. The areas of life space measured are Self Space, Home/Family Space, and Work Space. Each of the life space areas is broken down into six subtopics.

The LSAP is a 76-item computer-supported instrument on disk. The program allows the individual to complete the instrument twice. It is designed for persons of normal population 18 years old and older who are married and employed.

A support manual accompanies the computer disk providing a description of each of the main life space areas and the corresponding subtopic areas. With each subtopic area, there is a work sheet for a person to identify current issues, short- and long-term goals, and to begin an action plan. A self-help-oriented reading list is included at the end of the manual.

When the LSAP is completed, profiles are created which can be viewed on the screen, printed, and saved to a disk file. The person receives a component profile of the three main life space areas and a detailed profile that includes the main areas broken down by six subtopics per area. The participant can then view a written analysis by item for each of the subtopics. With the written analysis, suggestions for change are provided.

To complete the LSAP, the participant needs to be sufficiently computer literate in use of an IBM-compatible personal computer having at least 640K of memory and an MS/DOS operating system. The participant navigates through a series of on-screen menus allowing for the entering of two responses for each item. The first part asks for the person's degree of satisfaction in a specified life area. Possible choices include: *very satisfactory, almost satisfactory, somewhat satisfactory*, and *not satisfactory*. The second part asks a question relating to change. Possible responses for this question are: *unchanging and that's okay with me, changing in the desired direction, unchanging and wishing it would change*, and *changing in the undesired direction*. After both parts of each item are answered, the respondent is asked to verify the response before the next item is presented on the screen.

Scoring is done internally by the computer program once the participant has responded to all the items. No numerical scores are provided. The respondent is directed to two profiles and an analysis-by-item section. The first profile displays a bar graph

of the three major areas indicating a placement of the individual into one of four integration/polarization categories. The four categories are: highly integrated, moderately integrated, moderately polarized, and high polarized. The second profile displays a bar graph of the 18 subtopics (6 for each major area) and indicates a placement using the same integration/polarization categories. After viewing the second profile, the person is directed to the section that gives a written analysis by item as it pertains to a given subtopic.

Face validity was established using a panel of 10 psychologists who were given a description of the components, subtopics, and the 76 questions. Unanimous agreement was reached that the overall assessment tool would test a person's perception of balance in the three life space areas. The scale has undergone two field tests to determine if the profiles could be self-interpreted and if they accurately represented the participant's current life space. In the first field test the subjects ($n \sim 20$) all reported they could easily interpret the profiles and that the results were an accurate representation of their life space areas. In the second field test the subjects ($n = 140$, 83% male) were members of a corporation. They received the LSAP, an evaluation form they were to return, the results, and a group seminar follow-up. Because of the low return rate of the evaluation form (28 persons, 20% returned), it is difficult to know how the LSAP was received by the participants or the perceived accuracy of the results. The author does report that participants were able easily to interpret the information provided, and with one exception, believe the profiles to be representative of his/her current life span. Internal reliability was determined through use of four "catch questions." Reliability scores of .60 and .81 ($p = .001$) were obtained when the average score for all questions was matched with the overall catch question and the average of the three component questions. Test/retest reliability, interitem correlation, and factor analysis data were not provided.

The strength of the LSAP seems to be in its ability to provide a "snapshot" of a person's developmental place as it pertains to feeling balanced in life space areas of Self, Home/Family, and Work. Questions can be raised, however, that suggest caution in interpretation. First, are the items mutually exclusive by life space area or for each of the 18 subtopics? For instance, one might reason that a spousal relationship within the Home/Family area might impact how a person responds to items relating to Work Space. Second, can four items per subtopic provide enough information to assess each subtopic area accurately? Without a factor analysis of the LSAP the subcategories are questionable. Finally, does one's gender, social class, and/or cultural heritage bias the results? Because the LSAP was normed on predominantly white (assumed) males in a corporate setting it is unclear, for instance, whether or not a black female in a blue collar job could receive an accurate analysis as to her level of balance in the three life space areas.

The LSAP is designed for married individuals from normal adult populations who are established in the work world. Use of this instrument is limited. Human Resource Development divisions within corporations might find it useful, but the expense per person might be prohibitive. Until more normative data can be collected with women, the culturally different, and persons of varied social economic classes, caution should be used as to its wide-spread application.

REVIEWER'S REFERENCE

Lewin, K. (1951). *Field theory in social science.* New York: Harper.

Review of the Life Space Analysis Profile by ROBERT M. GUION, *Distinguished University Professor Emeritus, Bowling Green State University, Bowling Green, OH:*

The Life Space Analysis Profile is based on the idea that one's Life Space has three components (Self, Home and Family, and Work spaces), each of which can be described in more detail by six different topics. There are four questions for each topic, and four more "catch questions" for a total of 76; topic scores follow a continuum from "highly integrated" to "highly polarized." Polarization seems an odd, rather narrow choice as the opposite of integrated, but it was probably wise to narrow the scope of nonintegration, given only four dichotomous items for each score. Even so, the construct (if that is the appropriate term) is not a clear continuum; the score scale is based on a combination of satisfaction and perceptions of change related to the item and to the topic, with no indications of the degree to which these are related. Score reports are divided into four segments: highly integrated, moderately integrated, moderately polarized, and highly polarized. If the score for a topic is in the polarized region, the computer report offers advice. For example, a score indicating the polarization on the body topic (one topic in the Self Space component), is accompanied by advice that enhancing one's body image may be achieved by joining an exercise or aerobics class; those who are too focused on body image are advised to

remove most of the mirrors in their homes. No useful information is given to show either a scientific foundation or an empirical basis for these bits of advice.

LSAP also means Life Space Analysis *Program,* in which the total program includes both assessment and development components. I looked first at some materials for the development purpose, and it was not clear why this instrument was submitted for review in a mental *measurement* book. Its accompanying notebook looks more like a workbook than a test or inventory; for each topic there is space for notes on current issues related to the topic, on action plans, and on ideas for both a short- and long-term future. The Program uses the Profile as a basis for advice or workbook notes if the score is somewhere in the polarized half of the continuum, but the profile is neither a means of measuring well-defined, transitive constructs nor an instrument for "psychological or psychiatric diagnosis. It is a means of obtaining an overview of your present self-reported Life Space" (Program, p. 4). Despite that disclaimer, the values suggested by the integrated-polarized dichotomy, and the visual profile reported, seem to suggest a diagnosis of relative strengths and weaknesses, or of satisfactory and less satisfactory aspects of life space—a set of ipsative comparisons. Ipsative comparisons, of course, require good scales on a common metric. So it is, after all, reasonable to examine this offering as a psychometric device. It comes up wanting.

Development of the program stems from 1981; field testing was done in "1985, 86, and 87," and the instrument was published in 1988; computer diskettes carry a 1991 copyright date. In that time, it would seem that a useful body of technical material would have accumulated and that a technical manual would exist. Apparently, neither has happened. More-or-less technical material submitted for review consisted of (a) an unedited computer printout giving brief information about the background, author, and development history; (b) a largely handwritten report to "Jack" (presumably the author) giving a "more detailed description of what happened in the statistical analysis; and (c) a computer printout identified by hand as "LSAP Reliability Study." The first of these asserts that the assessments are based on "a validated instrument." Perhaps this was intended to be supporting evidence: "to establish face validity, the components, the ingredients, and the 76 questions were subjected to a panel of experts. These 10 independent psychologists were in unanimous agreement that the assessment tool would, in fact, test what it intended to test" (Background, p. 1). In a field test, about 20 people said that the report accurately represented their Life Space components. This is woefully inadequate evidence of validity for any purpose. Reliability data are similarly inadequate. For example, in a study the details of which can only be guessed at, correlations of .57, .60, and .81 "show high reliability."

The "report to Jack" (dated 3/17/84) used only 71 words on which to base assertions of validity and reliability. It also gave a series of frequency distributions and polygons with unclear labels. I criticize the printout of the reliability study with a red face: It is every bit as incomprehensible as many of mine where I was sure that the acronyms and abbreviated phrases would be universally understood forever. The author and data analysts in this case may still know the meaning of Variable 3, "rating by one catch," but I do not.

The kindest comment I can offer is that this is the work of people who are psychometrically naive. The basic idea may be very good, but there is no evidence that either the profile or the program has successfully captured the idea.

[184]
Life Stressors and Social Resources Inventory—Adult Form.

Purpose: "Provides an integrated picture of an individual's current life context" including "stable life stressors and social resources."
Population: Healthy adults, psychiatric patients, and medical patients.
Publication Dates: 1988–1994.
Acronym: LISRES-A.
Scores: 16 scales: 9 Life Stressor Scales (Physical Health, Home/Neighborhood, Financial, Work, Spouse or Partner, Children, Extended Family, Friends, Negative Life Events); 7 Social Resources Scales (Financial, Work, Spouse or Partner, Children, Extended Family, Friends, Positive Life Events).
Administration: Individual or group.
Price Data, 1996: $70 per complete kit including manual ('94, 40 pages), 10 reusable item booklets, and 25 handscorable answer/profile forms.
Time: (30) minutes.
Comments: May be administered using either a self-report or a structured interview format.
Authors: Rudolf H. Moos and Bernice S. Moos (manual).
Publisher: Psychological Assessment Resources, Inc.

TEST REFERENCES

1. Holahan, C. J., Moos, R. H., Holahan, C. K., & Brennan, P. L. (1995). Social support, coping, and depressive symptoms in a late-middle-aged sample of patients reporting cardiac illness. *Health Psychology, 14,* 152–163.

Review of the Life Stressors and Social Resources Inventory—Adult Form by M. ALLAN COOPERSTEIN, Clinical Psychologist/Forensic Examiner: Private Practice, Willow Grove, PA:

The Life Stressors and Social Resources Inventory—Adult Form (LISRES-A) was developed to help researchers and clinicians examine life stressors and social resources, health and well-being, and provide "an integrated picture of an individual's current life context" (p. 1). It taps eight life experience domains: physical health status, housing and neighborhood, finances, work, relationship with spouse or partner, children, extended family, and friends and social groups. Composed of 200 items in 16 scales (9 life stressors and 7 social resources), it provides global indices for positive and negative life experiences. The manual states that the inventory is appropriate for individuals from age 18 upward, including healthy adults, psychiatric, substance abuse, and medical patients.

The LISRES-A is administered individually or in groups, as a self-report questionnaire or structured interview.

ADMINISTRATION, SCORING, AND INTERPRETATION. Materials include a manual, a reusable item booklet, and hand-scorable answer forms. Instructions are clear and examples of how questions are to be answered are provided. When complete, the answer sheet is pulled away, revealing responses and scoring keys below. Profiles of life stressors and social resources are found on the back page.

The manual states that nonprofessionals can administer and score the LISRES-A as long as a qualified psychologist or counselor supervises them. Examiners should be proficient at LISRES-A administration as either a self-report or a structured interview. Test interpretation requires professional training in clinical psychology, counseling, or a related field.

Administration takes 30 minutes or less; scoring was 10–15 minutes. Although scoring instructions were clear, the keys for summing positive and negative life experience were distributed among other scores. This was visually confusing; I recommend that these be made more distinct and easily tracked.

Raw scores are converted to T scores, then transferred to the stressors and resources profiles. These provide illustrations of stress and resource areas for interpretation. It would be helpful if standard score descriptors were printed directly onto the profiles.

TEST DEVELOPMENT. Life stressors and social resources have been conceptualized as independent domains. The LISRES-A authors integrate the two domains within interpersonal contexts, contending that they are linked to health and well-being and that stable life context factors influence the assessment of life events and the choice and effectiveness of coping strategies. Among clinical groups—specifically depressed and alcoholic populations—stressors and social resources affect recovery and relapse. Life context factors are also said to be related to the psychosocial functioning of medical patients and healthy individuals.

The LISRES-A was developed empirically, based upon procedures and instruments assessing physical health, housing and neighborhood characteristics, and an individual's relationships in a variety of settings. The following stages were involved: stressor and resource domains identified with development of item pool, construction of a preliminary inventory, inventory revision based on pilot interviews, initial field trials and further revision based on interviews with specific populations, re-administration of the revised inventory as a self-report 18 months after initial field trial, a second field trial and 1-year follow-up on the self-report format with 1,884 adults participating in a study of normal and problem drinking.

NORMATIVE INFORMATION. The initial field trial consisted of four groups of 20 participants, each group identified by the following characteristics: depression, alcoholism, arthritic, or normal-drinking healthy adults. The population was largely (85%) Caucasian with a mean educational level of 14 years, average socioeconomic status, and a mean age of 48 years. In the field trial of 1,181 males and 703 females, the mean age was 61 years, the median level education was 14 years, and the population was 90% Caucasian.

RELIABILITY AND VALIDITY. In developing content and face validity, specific domain definitions were developed; items were constructed to fit constructs and selected empirically as belonging to given dimensions. Items were placed on only one dimension to increase clarity and minimize overlap. Meaningfulness, item comparability, item distribution, item interrelatedness, and scale independence were considered and built into elements.

Cronbach's alpha was used to evaluate internal consistency of stressor and social resource scales with the exception of essentially independent conditions. Re-assessed after 1 and 4 years, the scales demonstrated respectably high reliability, although correlates were weakest for negative life events (particularly for males) over time.

SUMMARY. Initially, I was favorably impressed by the LISRES-A. This was reinforced by

my taking and giving it to a patient. However, my patient and I matched the norms for age, race, education, and socioeconomic status.

There are, however, considerable threats found to internal and external validity (e.g., interactions of test with less educated and/or non-Caucasian respondents, lack of appropriate sample stratification, and overrepresentation of older, Caucasian, better-educated males). Older respondents report fewer stressors and fewer positive and negative life events, probably due to restricted variance in age in the second field trial sample.

Consequently, use of the LISRES-A with younger and/or non-Caucasian populations could provide misleading results and the universe of items might not sufficiently represent non-Caucasian, less-educated populations.

Therefore, generalizability of the LISRES-A is limited by the populations used for standardization and possibly the item pool itself. There are no indications that cultural or educational bias or ethnicity was considered by the researchers, nor was the inventory analyzed in consideration of English-language proficiency that would impact upon less well-educated respondents.

Within the parameters of the population upon which it was standardized, the LISRES-A demonstrates sufficient reliability to permit stable estimates. With a similar caveat, it appears to have predictive validity that, according to the manual, has been examined at greater length in association with alcoholism.

The LISRES-A is a well-designed and useful inventory that can, as the authors assert, assist clinicians to examine life stressors and social resources. At this stage in its development, however, it appears to be conceptually geared towards a narrowed population and purposive sample that emphasizes problem versus non-problem drinkers. Validity problems limit its overall usefulness to specific respondents corresponding with the normative populations; we should not assume that the inventory is appropriately designed for all "healthy adults, psychiatric and substance abuse patients, and medical patients" (p. 3). I hope that the authors will remedy these deficits and carry the LISRES-A development to its greater potential.

Review of the Life Stressors and Social Resources Inventory—Adult Form by RICHARD B. STUART, Professor Emeritus, Department of Psychiatry, University of Washington, and Regional Faculty, The Fielding Institute, Seattle, WA:

PROPOSED USES OF THE TEST. The Life Stressors and Social Resources Inventory—Adult

Form (LISRES-A) is recommended for use with adults 18 and older. The authors suggest that it can be used clinically: as "an integrated measure of current life stressors and social resources and can be used to describe a person's life context, to monitor its stability and changes over time, to compare individuals and programs, and to examine how new life events affect an individual's situation and functioning" (pp. 9–10). Recommended research uses include: identification of risk factors in remission and relapse by psychiatric and medical patients, delineating of sources of stress and resources for coping in normal individuals, and the development of an ecological perspective on health and well-being.

TEST FORM. The test can be administered in a self-report format to individuals or groups in about 30 minutes, or as a structured interview in 30 to 60 minutes. The final version of LISRES-A is an eight-page booklet with 200 primary questions, 38 of which may lead to supplemental questions depending on the response to the primary question. Slightly over half (97) of the primary questions are answered "Yes" or "No"; 16 are answered with the following alternatives: "Definitely Yes," "Mainly Yes," "Mainly No," and "Definitely No"; and 85 questions are answered with a 5-point frequency scale from "Never" to "Often." All supplemental questions are "Yes" or "No." Some of the subjects to whom I administered the test had difficulty in coordinating the answer categories with the questions in the test booklet and the appropriate blanks on the answer sheet. Others had difficulty choosing between dichotomous answers to questions about physical symptoms, job concerns, and the like. For example, one experienced "swollen ankles"—but only in the summer, whereas another did have "frequent headaches"—but so mild as to not warrant taking even one aspirin. For them, the test was irritating because they were concerned that their answers belied the facts.

The answer form contains carbonless scoring sheets, which provide a template for scoring. For ease of scoring, stressor items are indicated in red and resource items in blue. Although most of the subsets of items are scored either by counting the number of "Yes" and "No" responses or adding the Likert-scale values for all items in the group, others require some simple arithmetic. Although the directions are quite clear, test scorers will need practice in tabulating responses concerning extended family members. Missing data may also pose a problem. Subjects are asked to circle the number of items they choose not to answer, and to indicate others that are not appli-

cable. Scales in which fewer than half of the items are answered are unscorable. The scores of missing items on other scales are projected as an average of those that have been answered resulting in potentially misleading results. A table for converting from raw to T scores is the final element of the test booklet.

TEST DEVELOPMENT. The LISRES-A was developed with the same care its senior author has demonstrated in his creation of a series of widely used environmental measures. An initial pool of 1,200 items was developed through a review of the literature on stress and coping. Three judges subsequently reduced these to 500 items that were used in pilot interviews. After pruning an additional 100 items, the scale was administered to 40 men and 40 women, with equal numbers of depressed, alcoholic, arthritic, and normal-drinking healthy adults. A revision of the instrument was readministered to 75 of these subjects 18 months later. The present form was finally administered to a field sample of problem- and non-problem-drinking men (N = 1,181) and women (N = 703), averaging 61 years of age, 90% Caucasian, with a median of 14 years of education, and middle-class incomes. A large number of these subjects were retested at 1- and 4-year intervals. Unfortunately, operational definitions of drinking categories are not provided. And the demographic bias in this sample imposes limits on the populations it can be assumed to represent. Indeed, many of the concerns common to younger people, such as the vicissitudes of dating and finding a mate, are not addressed, and because more than 50 of the items pertain to spouses and children they are irrelevant to single respondents. The omission of some potentially potent stressors and resources, and the irrelevance of others, undermine the utility of the LISRES-A for individual treatment planning and assessment.

PSYCHOMETRICS. The scales of stressors and resources have moderate to high levels of internal consistency with Cronbach alphas ranging from .50 to .93. Intercorrelations among stress scales and among resource scales each averaged approximately .20. This suggests that each set of scales measures related aspects of respondents' life context. As expected, most stressors and resources are negatively correlated at levels ranging from -.01 to -.65. Test-retest reliability over 1- and 4-year periods were reasonable, ranging from .24 to .90 for the resource scales, and .26 to .80 for the stressors scales.

As a measure of the instrument's predictive validity, test samples were shown to display the expected demographic differences (e.g., fewer health and other problems among married men and women, fewer finance-related stressors among the better educated Caucasian respondents, and a decrease in the number of stressors as a function of age). In the same vein, differences were noted between the four clinically defined groups in the test sample. For example, problem drinkers reported more stressors and fewer resources than those whose alcohol use was deemed to pose no problem. And their spouses reported levels of stress proportionate to rises and falls in the level of use of alcohol by heavy drinkers. Scores also predicted social functioning (e.g., seeking treatment) among patients and case controls.

Concurrent validity was evaluated through two sets of analyses. LISRES-A responses correlated in the expected direction with the alcohol consumption, drinking problems, global depression, and self-confidence subscales of the similarly constructed Health and Daily Living Form (Moos, Cronkite, & Finney, 1994).

DISCUSSION. The measurement of life stress has been a holy grail of health researchers. Few challenge the hypothesized role of stress in the etiology and exacerbation of physical and mental illness. But major problems have been encountered in efforts to account for differences in the resilience or vulnerability inherent in individuals' responses to similar life events. For example, a job promotion can be a stress if it brings new responsibilities, greater time pressure, and/or a new work environment or colleagues. But it can also be a major asset for those who like change and welcome challenge. In the same vein, separation or divorce from a partner can be a health-impairing stress, or they can be joyful emancipation that is health-enhancing. Neither this instrument, nor its predecessors, solicits respondents' evaluation of the impact of the life events it addresses. Sensitive interviewing may be the only way to gain this understanding, and LISRES-A scores are unlikely to add very much at this clinical level.

On the other hand, as demonstrated by the results of the authors' research (see pp. 23–30 of the manual) the instrument may have greater utility in large-sample efforts to determine the service needs of communities or the treatment response of large cohorts of service recipients. In selecting research protocols, however, investigators might find it valuable to evaluate shorter instruments that measure various LISRES-A components such as the Social Support Apgar (Norwood, 1996). And researchers would also find it worthwhile to contrast linear

probability and logit and probit models when trying to weight the relative importance of various life events (Vilhjalmsson, 1993).

REVIEWER'S REFERENCES

Vilhjalmsson, R. (1993). Life stress, social support and clinical depression: A reanalysis of the literature. *Social Science and Medicine, 37*(3), 331–342.
Moos, R. H., Cronkite, R. C., & Finney, J. W. (1994). Health and Daily Living Form (2nd ed.). Palo Alto, CA: Center for Health Care Evaluation.
Norwood, S. L. (1996). The Social Support Apgar: Instrument development and testing. *Research in Nursing and Health, 19,* 143–152.

[185]

Life Stressors and Social Resources Inventory—Youth Form.

Purpose: "Provides an integrated picture of a youth's current life context … assesses stable life stressors and social resources as well as changes in them over time."

Population: Ages 12–18.

Publication Dates: 1990–1994.

Acronym: LISRES-Y.

Scores, 16: 9 Life Stressors Scales (Physical Health, Home and Money, Parents, Siblings, Extended Family, School, Friends, Boyfriend/Girlfriend, Negative Life Events); 7 Social Resources Scales (Parents, Siblings, Extended Family, School, Friends, Boyfriend/Girlfriend, Positive Life Events).

Administration: Individual or Group.

Editions, 2: Youth, Adult.

Price Data, 1996: $70 per introductory kit including manual ('94, 38 pages), 10 item booklets, and 25 profile forms; $21 per 10 item booklets; $32 per 25 profile forms; $28 per manual; $28 per sample set including manual, item booklet, and profile form.

Time: (45) minutes for self-report; (45–90) minutes for structured interview.

Comments: Available as self-report or structured interview; structured interview "allows an interviewer to use the inventory with youths whose reading and comprehension skills are below a sixth-grade level."

Authors: Rudolf H. Moos and Bernice S. Moos.

Publisher: Psychological Assessment Resources, Inc.

TEST REFERENCES

1. Valentiner, D. P., Holahan, C. J., & Moos, R. H. (1994). Social support, appraisals of event controllability, and coping: An integrative model. *Journal of Personality and Social Psychology, 66,* 1094–1102.

Review of the Life Stressors and Social Resources Inventory—Youth Form by KEVIN D. CREHAN, Associate Professor of Educational Psychology, University of Nevada—Las Vegas, Las Vegas, NV:

The Life Stressors and Social Resources Inventory—Youth Form (LISRES-Y) is a self-report paper-and-pencil device designed to measure stable sources of psychosocial stress as well as social resources that might influence the effect of stressors on the well-being of youth. The inventory is intended for youths 12 to 18 years of age and can be group or individually administered. The measure can also be used as a structured interview for youths with low reading skills. Nine Stressor scores and seven Social Resources scores are derived from 209 items. No special training is required for administration, but interpretation requires professional preparation in clinical or counseling psychology. Scoring is a bit arduous, especially when adjusting for missing responses. It took this reviewer over 30 minutes to complete a profile for the first time. The scoring time should decrease with practice and the authors suggest a scoring time of about 20 minutes.

The manual presents three sample profiles with interpretive narratives. The profile samples are for a depressed girl, a boy with conduct disorder, and a girl with rheumatic disease. Additional suggestions for clinical interpretation, intervention, and research applications are offered in the manual.

The norming sample totaled 400 youths composed of 197 labeled as healthy, 49 diagnosed as depressed, 58 with conduct disorder, and 96 diagnosed as pediatric rheumatoid. Norm tables allow conversion from raw scores to T-scores. Interpretations of T-score intervals are suggested (e.g., the T-score interval 41–45 is labeled "somewhat below average," p. 10). It is probably safe to say the norm sample is not representative of youths in general, based on the fact that more than half of the sample was composed of distressed youths.

The manual presents internal consistency and stability evidence of reliability. Internal consistency (alpha) for seven of the Stressor scales is judged fair to good, with a range of .69 to .92 (median = .84) for males (N = 168) and .66 to .91 (median = .81) for females (N = 206). Internal consistency estimates for Physical Health and Negative Life Events are not reported because these scales enumerate essentially independent events. The Social Resources scale alpha reliability estimates are uniformly high, with a range of .78 to .92 (median = .89) for males and .80 to .93 (median = .86) for females. The alpha reliability estimate for the Positive Life Events scale was not reported, again because of the independence among these occurrences. Scale stabilities were assessed with a 12- to 15-month interval between observations. Stressor scales had stability estimates for males (N = 102) ranging from .12 to .53 (median = .38), whereas for females (N = 141) the range was .15 to .64 (median = .49).

Intercorrelation matrices for the Stressor scales and the Social Resources scales, based on the norming sample, are reported in the professional manual. For the Stressors, the correlations for males (N = 179) ranged from -.01 to .54 (median = .26), and for females (N = 221) the range was .06 to .56 (median = .22). The highest interscale dependence was among the Parents, Siblings, and Extended Family scales and between the Friends and School scales. Intercorrelations among the Social Resources scales ranged from .10 to .51 for males (median = .34) and from -.01 to .54 (median = .29) for females. The highest observed interscale dependence ($rs > .52$) for males was between Parents and Extended Family and Parents and School. For females the highest dependence ($rs > .48$) was between Parents and Extended Family and Parents and Siblings.

Correlations between like-named Stressor and Social Resources scales exhibited high negative values for the Parents scales (-.56 for males and -.65 for females) and for the Siblings scales (-.48 for males and -.62 for females). The other correlations were somewhat lower (-.34 to -.10) and, interestingly, the Negative and Positive Life Events scales were correlated positively (.30 for males and .37 for females).

Although the construct evidence of validity is not compelling, the LISRES-Y shows promise. Evidence of validity from group differences is examined via an analysis of covariance controlling for age and gender. The contrasts comparing depressed and normal youths found higher Stressor scores on five of the scales and lower Social Resources on four scales for the depressed youths. Youths with conduct disorders also reported more stressors than normals on three scales and fewer resources from Friends. Validity evidence was also observed in differences between the groups of youths who were depressed, conduct disordered, or rheumatoid when compared to their respective sibling group.

Additional evidence of validity is derived from five measures of youth functioning administered during two field trials. These five brief measures observed depression, anxiety, substance abuse, behavior problems, and self-confidence. The most noteworthy finding from these data is the evidence that both of the LISRES-Y Parents scales had, uniformly, the highest correlations (.30 range) with the measures of youth functioning.

The LISRES-Y does not appear to have been used widely in research. A search of the literature found only a few studies that employed the LISRES-Y, and almost all of these were authored or co-authored by the instrument's developers. It is not known how extensively the LISRES-Y is used in clinical practice. The scale scores and profiles provide a range of information that a clinician should find useful. However, the time necessary for scoring and profile construction may be problematic. Perhaps a shortened and more quickly scored version of the instrument could be developed. The negative correlations between the Stressor and Resource scales, which are especially high for the Parents and Siblings scales, suggest that at least some of the like-named Stressor and Resource scales may be measuring the same trait. Combining the Stressor and Resource scales may not make sense theoretically, but the empirical evidence suggests some commonality exists between like-named Stressor and Resource scales. A shortened and machine-scored format would also improve the measure's viability as a research tool.

Review of the Life Stressors and Social Resources Inventory—Youth Form by ALBERT OOSTERHOF, Professor of Educational Psychology, Florida State University, Tallahassee, FL:

The Life Stressors and Social Resources Inventory—Youth Form (LISRES-Y) is a self-report survey designed to assess Life Stressors (physical and interpersonal problems that cause stress) and Social Resources (interpersonal relationships that provide support). According to the manual, the LISRES-Y is for use with both youth who are healthy and those experiencing psychological problems or medical disorders. The LISRES-Y includes a reusable booklet containing 209 mostly Likert-type items and a separate answer form. Directions in the booklet are clear and questions posed by items are concise. Reading level seems appropriate.

The answer form uses carbonless two-part paper with the bottom sheet becoming a template for scoring responses. The scoring (and administration) are straightforward and with proper instruction can be performed by individuals without training in psychology. Scores are obtained for nine Life Stressors scales and seven Social Resources scales. Examples of Stressors and Resources include physical health, physical conditions in the home and neighborhood, family, school, friends, and life events. Raw scores on each scale are converted to *T*-scores.

The manual indicates the LISRES-Y was field tested using 315 youth "drawn from groups of healthy youth, depressed youth, youth with conduct disorders, and youth with rheumatic disease" (p. 15). These and 85 additional youth who were assessed later served as the norm group. More information needs to be provided in order for these youth to serve

as a useful norm group. Types of questions that should be addressed include the proportion of youth coming from each of the subgroups, the distribution of their ages, and how age and group membership interact with scores on the inventory. The manual indicates the inventory was revised following the initial field test. Because most of the normative data were gathered prior to the final revision, the nature of the revision should be carefully described. Descriptive statistics suggest scores on some of the scales are skewed, maybe extremely so. If so, the nature of the distribution should be included in the discussion of normative data.

The manual wisely encourages the administrator to obtain missing responses if at all possible or to discard scales for which a large number of responses are missing. If more than half the responses to a scale were obtained, the examiner is directed to prorate missing responses from existing responses. Although this may be the only reasonable option, the manual should provide some evidence of what happens when scale scores are based on responses to a subset rather than a full set of responses to items.

The LISRES-Y manual is well organized and readable and should be carefully reviewed by the professional who will be interpreting scores on the inventory. The content of the manual is generally complete. The first of four sections within the manual briefly describes the instrument and its rationale. The second section provides clear directions concerning the administration and scoring of the inventory. Three brief case studies are included, which relate profiles on the inventory to anecdotal information.

Section 3 of the manual describes procedures used to develop the inventory and provides psychometric information. Internal consistency (Cronbach) coefficients are moderate to high, distributed evenly from approximately .70 to .90. The reliability coefficients along with raw-score means and standard deviations are reported separately for females and males. Intercorrelations among the nine Life Stressors scales and among the seven Social Resources scales are reported. Correlations are substantially lower than reliability coefficients suggesting the scales are measuring fairly distinct qualities.

Section 4 of the manual summarizes a series of published articles to help present validity evidence for the LISRES-Y. Generally, these research articles establish a relationship between scores on scales from the inventory and relevant external variables. For example, correlations between scores on stressor scales such as Home and Money, Siblings, and Friends were correlated with external measures of alcohol and drug use and reported number of behavior problems. As would be expected, most correlations are fairly low. Unfortunately, the manual often emphasizes the statistical significance of relationships more than interpreting the magnitude of correlations. (Statistical significance implies rejection of the hypothesis that the population correlation coefficient equals zero, which in itself is not strong evidence of validity.) Attention could be given to the effect attenuation has on the correlation coefficients (observed correlations are depressed by the less than perfect reliabilities of scales within the inventory and also criterion variables external to the LISRES-Y). The research studies can also be used to illustrate how the LISRES-Y provides useful albeit incomplete indications of stresses and social resources.

In summary, the construct the LISRES-Y is designed to assess is clearly specified. Evidence is provided that the content of the inventory is consistent with that construct. A series of research studies are summarized that describe the relationships between scores on the LISRES-Y and relevant variables external to the inventory. These relationships are generally low but not unexpectedly. The reliability of scale scores is generally high. Preliminary normative information is provided. Items within the inventory appear well constructed. Directions for administering the LISRES-Y are concise and appear easy to use.

[186]
Lifestyle Assessment Questionnaire.

Purpose: Provides individuals with a measurement of their lifestyle status in various wellness categories, offers a health risk appraisal component that lists the individual's top ten risks of death, projects an achievable health age, makes suggestions for lifestyle improvement, and offers a stimulus for positive lifestyle change by providing a guide to successful implementation of that change.
Population: Adults with a minimum of 10th grade education.
Publication Dates: 1978–1991.
Scores, 16: Physical (Exercise, Nutrition, Self-Care, Vehicle Safety, Drug Usage), Social/Environmental, Emotional (Emotional Awareness and Acceptance, Emotional Management), Intellectual, Occupational, Spiritual, Actual Age, Appraised Health Age, Achievable Health Age, Top 10 Risks of Death, Lifestyle Improvement Suggestions.
Administration: Group.
Price Data, 1993: $3 per literature set including questionnaire, results folder, Behavior Change Guide, and scannable answer sheet; $.25 per scannable answer sheet; $10 per individual National Wellness Processing Center scoring; $1,995 per software program and license.

Time: (45–60) minutes.
Comments: Computer scoring or scoring by National Wellness Institute available; information on up to four wellness areas included in scoring report; individual and group reports available.
Authors: Dennis Elsenrath, Bill Hettler, and Fred Leafgren.
Publisher: National Wellness Institute.
Cross References: See T4:1461 (3 references).

TEST REFERENCES

1. Smith, B. A. (1993). Physical exercise practices of Mexican-American college students. *College Student Journal, 27*, 146-156.
2. Fedorovich, S. E., Boyle, C. R., & Hare, R. D. (1994). Wellness as a factor in the selection of resident assistants in university student housing. *Journal of College Student Development, 35*, 248-254.
3. Patten, J. A. (1994). Dietary patterns of Hispanic and White college freshman. *College Student Journal, 28*, 39-45.

Review of the Lifestyle Assessment Questionnaire by MICHAEL B. BROWN, Assistant Professor of Psychology, East Carolina University, Greenville, NC:

The Lifestyle Assessment Questionnaire (LAQ) is a tool for evaluating an adult's habits and knowledge on a number of health and wellness dimensions. The questionnaire requires the respondent to answer 227 questions about demographics, lifestyle, and health risks. An additional 43 questions allow for the respondent to request additional information on a wide variety of health-related topics. Responses are made on an optical scanning sheet, which can be scored on site through a single site software license or through a scoring and interpretation service offered through the publisher.

Computer-generated individual and group reports are available. The individual report includes a wellness report, health-risk appraisal, and resources for further information on the topics requested by the user. The wellness report is considered an assessment of the individual's lifestyle in six life areas including occupational, emotional, intellectual, physical, social, and spiritual dimensions. Percentage scores are provided for the individual, the average scores of individuals in the organization with whom the individual is taking the assessment, and the average score of the same age/sex reference group. The health-risk appraisal provides an assessment of an individual's risk of death over the next decade and provides suggestions for lifestyle improvements. Results are presented for risk of death, life expectancy, and life expectancy if suggested changes are made. A behavior change guide called Making Wellness Work For You provides a systematic guide for making a specific behavior change. The personal growth resource list provides bibliographic resources for further information on specific health and wellness topics. The management group report provides a summary of lifestyle and health-risk status of the individuals in an organization. This report is intended to serve as both an organizational wellness needs assessment and an evaluation of the organization's wellness programming.

MANUAL. The LAQ software package comes with a ring-bound user's guide that is devoted to installation and use of the software package, interpretation of results, and a description of its technical characteristics. Several pages of technical information were provided in addition to that in the manual. Sample individual and group reports are also available with the manual. There are no guidelines on qualifications of users or overall strategy for the use of the instrument.

TECHNICAL CHARACTERISTICS. There are significant limitations with both the types and adequacy of technical data. Although the reference group includes a large sample of over 47,000 persons, descriptive data are provided only for age and sex. No data are provided for other relevant descriptors of the norm group, such as socioeconomic status or level of education. Although the reference group includes persons from 15 years of age and older, 23% of the sample were 18 years old. With the exception of those identified as college students, the method of selection and identification of the remainder of the reference group is not specified. Based upon these limitations, it is unclear how representative the reference group is or how well the group may represent persons of different ethnic and socioeconomic groups. Information on the derivation of health-risk data is also limited. Health risk is said to be based on data from the most recent U.S. Centers for Disease Control epidemiological data, although the exact year of the data is not specified. No information is provided for how life expectancy scores are computed, or how forecast life expectancy was calculated.

Reliability data are reported for test-retest reliability over 2-week periods for the wellness scale. Test-retest reliabilities of the wellness categories ranged from .57—.87, with an average coefficient of .76. Test-retest reliability for the subscales ranged from .81–.97. However, the two studies reported in the manual included only 15 and 39 subjects, which is an inadequate number of subjects from which to ascertain reliability. The internal consistency of the wellness subscales ranged from .67–.94. However, no information was provided from which to identify the size of the group used to determine internal consistency.

Content validity is said to have been established by a panel of experts, who are not identified

further in the manual. Later in the manual, content validity was said to be ascertained by two experts in measurement and health promotion. Factor analysis was said to be used to determine construct validity, but no data are provided that identify the factors utilized, resulting factor structure, or factor scores. Two studies are cited that are said to establish criterion validity. The first study reports that the LAQ emotional subscales can differentiate college students who are receiving psychotherapy from those who are not. Few additional details are provided on this study. The other criterion-validity study investigated the relationship between the LAQ wellness scales and objective physiological indicators of health. No relationship was found in the college students studied, although a relationship was found between the scores taken "as a whole" and "general health." There is a section that provides research citations for a number of health risks. Another section follows listing research studies that used the LAQ. Its placement here is potentially misleading, as the research cited does not study the technical characteristics of the LAQ, but uses the LAQ only as a measurement tool for research on wellness intervention.

OVERALL EVALUATION. The Lifestyle Assessment Questionnaire has inadequate technical data to support its use as a norm-referenced measurement tool. The reference group, although large, is not sufficiently described to allow a test user to be certain that users of various socioeconomic and ethnic groups are represented in the reference group. In addition, the reference group is heavily weighted to persons of college age. Reliability studies, although encouraging, are not large enough to demonstrate reliability. Validity data are not sufficiently described in the manual, and do not illuminate the meaning or predictive power of the scales. The scale scores for the wellness portion of the inventory have only face validity. The health-risk appraisal portion may be based on adequate epidemiological data, but this is not clear from the information provided. There is no information supporting the forecast life expectancy. This could be misleading to clients and unsophisticated users. The Health Risk Appraisal may be useful, although its suggestions for reducing risk are very generic and somewhat unimaginative. For example, suggestions to reduce risk of motor vehicle accidents include "obey all rules of the road" and "don't drive while tired." The Making Wellness Work For You behavior change guide is a thorough and well-constructed device that could be very helpful to persons who are motivated to change.

Review of the Lifestyle Assessment Questionnaire by WILLIAM E. MARTIN, JR., Professor of Educational Psychology, Northern Arizona University, Flagstaff, AZ:

According to an information pamphlet provided by the National Wellness Institute, Inc., "The Lifestyle Assessment Questionnaire (LAQ) is a powerful wellness tool developed in 1976 by the Board of Directors and Cofounders of The National Wellness Institute." The LAQ is intended to serve a dual purpose for assessment and education. The assessment purpose of the LAQ is to provide individuals with a measurement of their lifestyle status in the following six wellness dimensions: occupational, intellectual, spiritual, social, physical, and emotional. The measurement information generated from the LAQ provides an educational stimulus for individuals to change their lifestyles.

The LAQ is divided into four primary sections. The first of the four sections, Personal Data, comprises 12 multiple-choice questions related to age, sex, etc. The second section is the Lifestyle Inventory. The Lifestyle Inventory has 11 subsections that relate to the six wellness dimensions. However, it is not clear to me how some of the subsections would be grouped with the six wellness dimensions (i.e., self-care, vehicle safety, and drug usage and awareness). This section has 185 statements formatted with a 5-point Likert-type response ranging from *Almost never* (less than 10% of the time) to *Almost always* (90% or more of the time). The number of questions per subsection varies from 10 to 31 questions.

The third section of the LAQ is Health Risk Appraisal and consists of interlocked questions: 33 for men and 38 for women. For this section, both multiple-choice and short answer questions are used. The final section, Topics for Personal Growth, is a listing of 43 lifestyle topics. In this section, the examinee is instructed to select four lifestyle topics for which they would like to receive additional information.

The Lifestyle Inventory of the LAQ is used to generate individual reports that compare an individual's score to those of the group with which the test was taken and to group scores for all those who have taken the LAQ since 1978. The Health Risk Appraisal scores are compared to national averages for individuals of the same sex and age. Group reports are also generated to provide direction to organizations for developing wellness programs.

DEVELOPMENT OF THE SCALES. The authors state that when the LAQ was initially developed, it was reviewed by a panel of health promotion and wellness professionals to verify the validity of the instrument's content. The 11 assessment categories of the LAQ's Lifestyle Inventory were reviewed by professionals working in each of the six wellness dimensions and the Health Risk Appraisal section was developed using research data from the Carter Center at Emory University and the Center for Disease Control.

RELIABILITY AND VALIDITY. A two-page National Wellness Institute, Inc. flyer briefly described two studies that have generated test-retest reliability and internal consistency coefficients and two studies that were intended to reflect test validity of the LAQ. The first test-retest study was conducted in 1982 with 39 parents of incoming university students. For this sample, the 2-week test-retest reliability coefficients on the Lifestyle Inventory scales ranged from .57 to .87 with an "overall" coefficient of .76. The Personal Growth section yielded a .87 coefficient and a .90 test-retest reliability coefficient was reported for the Health Risk Appraisal section. A 1985 study of 15 female university students demonstrated test-retest reliability coefficients ranging from .81 to .97; however, no time interval was identified. Additionally, coefficients of internal consistency ranging from .67 to .94 were reported as part of this study. The discussion presented relative to validity studies was too brief and unclear to report with any accuracy. For example, a result of one of the studies was "there is considerable support for external validity of the physical scales." The use of the term external validity is confusing because it is a concept related to research design not measurement. It appears that the authors meant to use the term criterion-related validity.

ADMINISTRATION, SCORING, AND INTERPRETATION. Lifestyle Assessment Questionnaires are given to the individual to self-administer and can be taken in an individual or group setting. Either way, it is not necessary for a test administrator to be present. Directions are provided throughout the questionnaire and test takers respond to questions using scannable answer sheets. Completed questionnaires can be scored either by sending the materials to the National Wellness Institute Processing Center or by purchasing a software program and license. Individual and group reports (where appropriate) are generated that provide numerical information and narrative interpretation. Scores on the individual report range from 0 to 100 and represent the percent of possible points for each area. Scores and bar charts are given for wellness dimensions and subcategories.

An individual's LAQ scores are compared to those of the group (when applicable) with which the test was taken and to individuals who have taken it since 1978. The individual's Health Risk Appraisal scores are compared to a national population average for individuals of the same age and sex. Additionally, the individual report presents information concerning suggestions on increasing expected years of life, health-risk appraisal forecast information, and available resources related to various health-related topics. When a group of individuals from a shared organizational setting take the LAQ as a group, a group report is generated. The report reflects group frequency and percentage scores by dimensions and subcategories.

SUMMARY. Although the LAQ has functional use appeal, is attractively packaged, and has been used since 1978, there are technical weaknesses that must be considered in using the instrument. The first concern relates to the instrument's construct validity. Established methods in test construction appear not to have been used in the development of the LAQ scales including: (a) a theoretical grounding of the construct of wellness, (b) empirically derived factors and items, and/or (c) evidence of homogeneity in relation to the construct. Do the six dimensions of the LAQ accurately represent the construct of wellness? Do the items accurately reflect the dimensions of wellness? The validity and reliability studies presented appear weak partially because they are difficult to understand due to limited information and a lack of clarity on what is presented. Additionally, there were several methodological problems reported in the studies such as using only 15 subjects for test/restest reliability estimates and establishing content validity of the LAQ "with evaluation by two experts in measurement and health promotion." Second, there have been significant changes in knowledge of wellness since 1978. There is no evidence that the authors have adapted the LAQ to evolving research and changing knowledge about wellness. Based upon the first two concerns, it is highly recommended that a thorough literature review covering the last 20 years be completed and a factor analytic study be conducted to generate a wellness construct that is empirically derived. Then, the established steps for test construction can be followed. There is no doubt that a psychometric instrument that soundly measures a construct of wellness would be beneficial in promoting healthful practices by individuals. Accurate measurement of a valid and stable construct must, however, be demonstrated for users to have confidence in the LAQ.

[187]
Loewenstein Occupational Therapy Cognitive Assessment.

Purpose: "A cognitive battery of tests for both primary assessments and ongoing evaluation in the occupational therapy treatment of brain-injured patients."

Population: Ages 6 to 12 and brain-injured adults.

Publication Date: 1990.

Acronym: LOTCA.

Scores: 21 tests in 4 areas: Orientation (Orientation for Place, Orientation for Time), Visual and Spatial Perception (Object Identification, Shapes Identification, Overlapping Figures, Object Constancy, Spatial Perception, Praxis), Visual Motor Organization (Copying Geometric Forms, Reproduction of a Two-Dimensional Model, Pegboard Construction, Colored Block Design, Plain Block Design, Reproduction of a Puzzle, Drawing a Clock), Thinking Operations (Categorization, ROC Unstructured, ROC Structured, Pictorial Sequence A, Pictorial Sequence B, Geometric Sequence).

Administration: Individual.

Price Data, 1993: $198 per complete kit including manual (56 pages), test booklet, and other materials packed in a plastic carrying case.

Time: (30–45) minutes.

Authors: Loewenstein Rehabilitation Hospital;, Malka Itzkovich (manual), Betty Elazar (manual), Sarah Averbuch (manual), Naomi Katz (principal researcher), and Levy Rahmani (advisor).

Publisher: Maddak Inc.

Review of the Loewenstein Occupational Therapy Cognitive Assessment by ELAINE CLARK, Professor of Educational Psychology, University of Utah, Salt Lake City, UT:

The Loewenstein Occupational Therapy Cognitive Assessment (LOTCA) is a battery of tests that measure cognitive skills in patients who have suffered a brain injury. The LOTCA was intended to be used by occupational therapists who need baseline data to evaluate patient abilities and disabilities and to develop and evaluate treatment goals. Although the authors indicate that the battery was designed as a qualitative, process-oriented assessment tool, there is no information provided in the manual that would assist test users to use the LOTCA in this manner. The majority of the manual is devoted to quantifying patient responses.

The LOTCA is composed of 20 subtests that measure four areas of cognitive functioning: Orientation, Perception, Visuomotor Organization, and Thinking Operations. The rationale for including these skills and excluding others (e.g., language) is provided in the test manual. The test is intended to be concise, taking no more than 30 to 45 minutes to administer. There are no guidelines as to who might be qualified to give the test.

ADMINISTRATION AND SCORING. The instructions for administering and scoring the LOTCA are lengthy and at times confusing. Even the authors acknowledge that some of the scoring criteria and procedures are inadequate and refer examiners to an external source for further information. According to the authors, "in order to be able to administer and score the test" (manual, p. 17), referring to the Riska Object Classification (ROC) subtest, examiners need to read a 1985 book chapter by Riska and Allen. Because the chapter was not included anywhere in the battery, and the only argument for its inclusion was that it enhances the categorization operation, it is hard to imagine that anyone would bother to look for the 1985 chapter.

Unfortunately, examiners are not provided any further assistance with the scoring sheet. In fact, the scoring sheet is limited to space to mark the subtest score (this is done on a rating scale of 1 to 4, and sometimes 1 to 5) and write two or three words in the comment section. Rather than including an essentially blank sheet of paper for examiners to write in comments, the scoring sheet would best be expanded to include instructional and scoring prompts to clarify some of the confusion.

Test users will find there are a number of minor but annoying inconsistencies in the test (e.g., the scoring sheet, test manual, and test materials). There are differences in subtest titles, order of subtest administration, and the numbering of stimulus cards. Although test users are warned about the difference in card numbering, there is no explanation as to why the cards are not numbered in the order they are intended to be presented (correct numbering would have been more helpful than a footnote in the manual alerting examiners to potential problems with this). The fact the authors failed to explain these and other problems (e.g., lack of consistency in numbering subtests and failing to include information about the necessary materials for a given test) is likely to lead potential users to conclude that sufficient care was not taken with the development of the LOTCA. This is also the conclusion one would draw from careful examination of the psychometric data.

RELIABILITY AND VALIDITY. Although reliability and validity data are reported in the manual, the numbers of subjects included in these studies are either unknown or small, and the designs are poorly described. For example, the interrater reliability coefficients for the various subtests appears high (.82 to .97); however, the number of subjects is no more than 30. It is unclear from the wording, "three pairs of raters tested ten subjects" (p. 37), if this means 10 or 30 subjects were included in the analysis. Without this and other information about the raters themselves (e.g., how well they were trained to give the LOTCA) and the design of the study (e.g., how the coefficients were averaged across the six raters), it is difficult to evaluate the quality of the reported estimates. The only other interrater reliability data mentioned in the manual were based on a sample size of one, making this analysis also difficult to evaluate.

The internal consistency coefficients appear adequate for the domains of perception (.87), visuomotor organization (.95), and thinking operations (.85), and for the individual subtests. The coefficients for the subtests ranged from .40 to .80, which is adequate given the relatively short length of the subtests. As with the interrater reliability, it is unclear how many subjects were included in the analysis.

Validity was assessed using both criterion and construct methods. As with the reliability data, a small number of subjects were included in these studies. Although a correlation coefficient of .68 does not appear to be a problem, with only 20 subjects correlations can be expected to be highly unstable (a confidence band would demonstrate this point). It is unclear why so few subjects were included in this study. It is also unclear why only one domain of the battery was assessed for criterion validity, visuomotor organization, and why only one subtest of the Wechsler Adult Intelligence Scale—Revised (Block Design), was used to evaluate the domain. This raises a question of the possibility that other Wechsler scales were given to evaluate more than the one domain but the data were not favorable.

Construct validity was evaluated using a principal component factor analysis. Two groups, 96 patients and 55 controls, were used for the analysis. Although the data from the analyses support the three factors, perception, visuomotor organization, and thinking operations, a more general factor was found for the patient group. Again, the small number of subjects included in this group could be responsible for factor differences. The problem of sample size becomes particularly serious when looking at the control group data. A factor analysis with 55 subjects and 18 variables provides little meaningful data (even a group of 96 is questionable and does not meet the common standard of 10–12 subjects per variable).

Validity was also assessed by evaluating the ability of the LOTCA to differentiate between the subjects with head injuries and strokes, and between these two groups of subjects and the controls. Wilcoxon's two-sample test was used for this purpose. The results showed that all subtests except Identification of Objects differentiated the groups at a .0001 level of significance.

TEST SCORE INTERPRETATION. There are no normative data, per se; however, the data from the 55 controls and the 48 subjects with brain injuries provide comparisons. Means and standard deviations for all three groups are included in the manual. Because two sets of scores are provided for the two groups with brain injuries (one set pertaining to the first evaluation, and the other pertaining to the second evaluation), it is somewhat unclear which set is to be used for purpose of comparison. It is also unclear how useful the data will be, given the small number of subjects and the limited range of performance (3.6 to 4.0).

Data are also provided for 240 children between the ages of 6 and 12. This is the largest sample reported in the manual, although there is no indication that the LOTCA is to be used with children. From the authors' description, the purpose of including data on "normal" children was to "verify the hierarchical order of acquiring the cognitive competencies tested in the battery" (manual, p. 36). As expected, there was greater score variability for the group of "normal" children when comparing their scores to the "normal" adults; however, the degree to which the scores varied had to do with age and the skill being measured.

SUMMARY. The LOTCA has a number of problems, not the least of which pertain to the clarity of the instructions for administering and scoring the test. Some of these problems can be expected from a test that is developed out of an emergent need to evaluate large numbers of patients with brain injuries from a war, specifically the 1973 war in Israel. It is unexpected, however, to find that these and other problems were not worked out over the course of more than two decades. Although occupational therapists may find the LOTCA helpful in providing information to develop and evaluate treatment goals, users must be aware the data provided to support the reliability or the validity are limited.

Review of the Loewenstein Occupational Therapy Cognitive Assessment by STEPHEN R. HOOPER, Associate Professor of Psychiatry, University of North Carolina School of Medicine, Chapel Hill, NC:

The Loewenstein Occupational Therapy Cognitive Assessment (LOTCA) is described by the test authors "as a first attempt to offer a practical tool to the occupational therapist engaged in neurological rehabilitation" (manual, p. 4). Based upon a dynamic view of brain-behavior relationships, as well as neuropsychological and developmental theories, the LOTCA provides a set of procedures that purportedly serve as a base for a qualitative, process-oriented, and client-centered assessment for patients from age 6 years through adulthood who have sustained brain injuries. As such, the authors state the primary goals of evaluation are: to indicate what the patient's strengths and weaknesses are across the constructs of orientation, perception, visuomotor organization, thinking operations, and attention; to establish starting points for rehabilitation; to formulate specific goals; to monitor treatment effects; and to serve as a screening for further assessment. An administration time of 30 to 45 minutes is reported, with administration over multiple sessions being acceptable. The manual is clearly written, with approximately one-half of the manual being devoted to a description of the tests, administration, and scoring procedures.

The LOTCA is divided into five major domains that include Orientation, Perception, Visuomotor Organization, Thinking Operations, and Attention; however, total domain scores are not produced from the subtests within each domain. For most of the subtests contained within each domain, an individual's performance is scored on a scale from 1 (low) to 4 (high). For three of the subtests contained within the Thinking Operations Domain, the performance is scored on a scale of 1 to 5. These numbers do not represent interval level scaling but, rather, rank order data. Interrater reliability for the subtests ranged from .82 to .97, although specific reliability coefficients for each subtest were not listed. Despite these positive findings, there are a number of significant psychometric concerns about the LOTCA.

Nearly all of the basic psychometric data generated on the LOTCA were derived from 103 adults: 20 patients with a cranio-cerebral injury, 28 with a cerebro-vascular accident, and 55 normals. In addition to the small numbers upon which to base the psychometric findings, the patient groups were poorly described, and these problems likely had an impact on the psychometric data generated. For example, if the patients in the cranio-cerebral group included open head injuries, closed head injuries, and other such injuries, it is highly likely that the differing behavioral manifestations of this heterogeneous group would interfere with obtaining accurate estimates of reliability and validity for any one group, and generalization of these findings to other patient populations is of concern. Similar difficulties are likely by including the patients diagnosed with cerebro-vascular accidents (e.g., left hemisphere stroke versus right hemisphere stroke will manifest differently on many neurobehavioral measures). Further, 55 normal adults does little to address the basic psychometric issues important to a battery of this size.

Just because the LOTCA shows differences between the two brain injured groups and the normal controls does little to address the validity of this battery. Although one would expect the normal controls to perform more proficiently than a heterogeneous brain-injured group, it is not clear what was expected from the brain injured groups on the LOTCA. Meager criterion validity data also were presented for one dimension (i.e., Visuomotor Organization), although the method whereby this was generated (i.e., mean score of the visuomotor subtests) is not mentioned as a recommended procedure for scoring the LOTCA. A factor analysis also was attempted, but this was poorly done. The subjects-to-variables ratio was quite small, likely contributing to instability in the factor structure, and the results were confounded by inclusion of multiple assessments of the same patient.

Without the benefit of solid item analysis, item placement, and adequate reliability and validity, the LOTCA was administered to 240 normal children (40 at each age level between 6 and 12 years) in order to establish its utility for child populations. The sample was randomly chosen from a large urban public elementary school. Had the authors utilized similar procedures for the development of the LOTCA, its basic psychometric foundations would have been better received. The results of these procedures revealed clear developmental trends for many of the subtests, although there also were a number of subtests that did not evidence such trends (e.g., most of the perception tests). It would seem that these procedures would set the stage for making decisions about whether specific subtests should be included or excluded in the battery.

In summary, the LOTCA has been proposed as "a first attempt" (manual, p. 4) at a tool for occupational therapists to measure selected aspects of neurocognitive functioning in a rehabilitation setting. The intended uses proposed for the LOTCA appear worthwhile, and the battery itself is nicely organized with relatively clear administration and scoring procedures. Of significant practical concern, however, is that it is not clear how this measure will compete with and/or complement psychological and neuropsychological measurement with this patient population, or how the use of this battery will conflict with and/or facilitate the work of other specialists in a rehabilitation setting.

Along with these major pragmatic questions, there are a number of basic psychometric concerns that lead to questions regarding its utility in a rehabilitation setting. Despite initial findings presented in the LOTCA manual, basic reliability and validity issues have yet to be addressed in a satisfactory manner, particularly for adults. Although the basic structure of the battery remains conceptually adequate, the factor analysis provided little in the way of psychometric support. Consequently, the primary goals of the LOTCA have not been achieved from a psychometric perspective. Although a qualitative assessment approach guides this battery, it remains woefully inadequate from a psychometric perspective in its current form, and its routine use in any setting remains tenable at best. The authors have gathered interesting developmental data on their battery, and these data may provide the basis for obtaining the necessary psychometric data to bring this test up to basic testing standards.

[188]
MacArthur Communicative Development Inventories.

Purpose: "Evaluates young children's communication skills with norm-referenced parent checklists."

Population: 8–30 months.

Publication Date: 1993.

Acronym: CDI.

Scores, 16: Words and Gestures [Early Words (First Signs of Understanding, Phrases, Starting to Talk, Vocabulary Checklist), Actions and Gestures (First Communicative Gestures, Games and Routines, Actions with Objects, Pretend To Be a Parent, Imitating Other Adult Actions, Pretend Gestures)], Words and Sentences [Words Children Use (Vocabulary Checklist, How Children Use Words), Sentences and Grammar (Word Endings/Part I, Word Forms, Word Endings/Part II, Examples of the Child's Three Longest Sentences)].

Administration: Individual.

Price Data, 1994: $56.05 per complete kit including User's Guide and Technical Manual (114 pages), 20 Words and Gestures forms, and 20 Words and Sentences forms; $35.70 per User's Guide and Technical Manual; $20.35 per 20 Words and Gestures; $20.35 per 20 Words and Sentences.

Time: (20–30) minutes.

Authors: Larry Fenson, Philip S. Dale, J. Steven Reznick, Donna Thal, Elizabeth Bates, Jeffery P. Hartung, Steve Pethick, and Judy S. Reilly.

Publisher: The Psychological Corporation.

TEST REFERENCES

1. Plunkett, K., & Marchman, V. (1993). From rote learning to system building: Acquiring verb morphology in children and connectionist nets. *Cognition, 48,* 21–69.
2. Spencer, P. E. (1993). Communication behaviors of infants with hearing loss and their hearing mothers. *Journal of Speech and Hearing Research, 36,* 311–321.

3. Weismer, S. E., Murray-Branch, J., & Miller, J. F. (1993). Comparison of two methods for promoting productive vocabulary in late talkers. *Journal of Speech and Hearing Research, 36,* 1037–1050.

4. Aram, D. M., & Eisele, J. A. (1994). Limits to a left hemisphere explanation for specific language impairment. *Journal of Speech and Hearing, 37,* 824–830.

5. Mervis, C. B., & Bertrand, J. (1994). Acquisition of the novel name-nameless category (N3C) principle. *Child Development, 65,* 1646-1662.

6. Mervis, C. B., Golinkoff, R. M., & Bertrand, J. (1994). Two-year-olds readily learn multiple labels for the same basic-level category. *Child Development, 65,* 1163-1177.

7. Snow, D. (1994). Phrase-final syllabus lengthening and intonation in early child speech. *Journal of Speech and Hearing, 37,* 831–840.

8. Thal, D., & Tobias, S. (1994). Relationships between language and gesture in normally developing and late-talking toddlers. *Journal of Speech and Hearing Research, 37,* 157–170.

9. Weismer, S. E., Murray-Branch, J., & Miller, J. F. (1994). A prospective longitudinal study of language development in late talkers. *Journal of Speech and Hearing, 37,* 852–867.

10. Kehoe, M., Stoel-Gammon, C., & Buder, E. H. (1995). Acoustic correlates of stress in young children's speech. *Journal of Speech and Hearing, 38,* 338–350.

11. Mervis, C. B., & Bertrand, J. (1995). Acquisition of the novel name-nameless category (N3C) principle by young children who have Down Syndrome. *American Journal on Mental Retardation, 100,* 231–243.

12. Stahmer, A. C. (1995). Teaching symbolic play skills to children with autism using pivotal response training. *Journal of Autism and Developmental Disorders, 25,* 123–141.

13. Cronan, T. A., Cruz, S. G., Arriaga, R. I., & Sarkin, A. J. (1996). The effects of a community-based literacy program on young children's language and conceptual development. *American Journal of Community Psychology, 24,* 251–272.

14. Tyler, A. A. (1996). Assessing stimulability in toddlers. *Journal of Communication Disorders, 29,* 279–297.

Review of the MacArthur Communicative Development Inventories by CAROL WESTBY, Professor of Communicative Disorders and Sciences, Wichita State University, Wichita, KS:

The MacArthur Communicative Development Inventories are the refined product of over 20 years of research. The inventories consist of two forms: the Communicative Development Inventory (CDI) Words and Gestures, designed for use with 8- to 16-month-old infants and the CDI Words and Sentences, designed for use with children between 16 and 30 months. The infant inventory generates scores for vocabulary comprehension, vocabulary production, and use of gestures; the toddler inventory yields scores for vocabulary production, and a number of aspects of grammatical development including sentence complexity and mean length of utterance. Because many professionals are using the inventories with older, developmentally delayed children, no age designation is given on the forms.

The inventories are completed by parents following directions on the printed form. The inventories minimize the usual problems associated with parent-reporting instruments by relying on a recognition format rather than requiring parents to recall words their children use.

Each inventory has two parts. Part I of the CDI Words and Gestures Inventory has four sections. The first section asks questions to determine if a child has begun to respond to any language. Section 2 asks the informant to indicate the phrases in a 28-item list the child understands. Section 3 contains two questions, one about the child's frequency of imitating and one about the child's frequency of labeling. Section 4, the major section, is a 396-item vocabulary checklist organized into 19 semantic categories. Ten of the categories are composed of nouns. Additional categories are included for sound effects and animal sounds, games and routines, verbs, adjectives, pronouns, question words, prepositions, and locations, quantifiers, and words about time. The parent checks the words the child *understands* and the words the child *uses and understands.*

Part II of the Words and Gestures inventory consists of 63 gestures organized into five categories: (a) communicative gestures that include gestures such as pointing, showing, giving, or raising arms to be picked up; (b) games and routines such as peek-a-boo and patty cake; (c) actions with objects such as eating with a spoon, pushing a toy car, or blowing to indicate something is hot; (d) pretending to be a parent, which includes carrying out actions on dolls or stuffed animals; and (e) imitating adult actions such as sweeping, pounding with a hammer, or writing with a pencil.

Part I of the CDI Words and Sentences Inventory consists of a 680-word productive vocabulary checklist organized into 22 semantic categories (most categories of the infant inventory plus categories for helping verbs and connecting words and a separation of the noun category for outdoor things and places to go). Part II of the Words and Sentences Inventory is designed to assess morphological and syntactic development. It consists of 125 items divided into five sections. Section A asks parents questions about the child's use of plurals, possessives, progressive -ing, and past -ed morphemes. Section B asks about a child's specific use of irregular plurals and verbs. Section C is a checklist of overregularized plural nouns (e.g., teeths) and past tense verbs (e.g., sitted). Section E is a forced-choice recognition format in which parents are asked to choose which member of a pair of sentences best reflects a child's present speech level.

The technical manual for the CDI Inventories is thorough and clearly written. It provides a discussion of the history of the development of the inventories, information on the norming sample, uses for the inventories, cautions in using the inventories and in interpreting the normative data, discussion of the developmental course of each component and intercorrelations among the components, separate percentile tables for boys and girls for all sections of the inventories, and reports on studies of the reliability and validity of the inventories. The discussion is supported by extensive reference to the literature on language development and to research studies carried out with the inventories.

The inventories have particular value for research. They can be used to preselect children who are at a specific point in language acquisition or who have particular language characteristics (e.g., late talkers with good comprehension) or particular language styles (e.g., referential versus expressive referring to the proportion of the vocabulary devoted to object names). The detail provided by the inventories can ensure that research groups are initially equivalent in communicative skills.

Since their first publication, the inventories have been used to screen for language delay. The authors caution professionals about this use, however. The normative data for the inventories are based on 671 infants and 1,142 toddlers from New Haven, Seattle, and San Diego. Seventy-seven percent of the norming population had some college education or a college degree compared to 33% of the general population with this educational level. Recent research by Hart and Risley (1995) has shown that children in working class families hear twice the number of words per hour as children in welfare families, and children from professional families are exposed to three times the number of words per hour as children in welfare families. By age 3 years, children from professional families have a cumulative vocabulary that is 2 1/2 times greater than that of children in welfare families.

Because of the lack of representativeness of the norming population, the inventories should not be used to identify infants or toddlers as language delayed. They can, however, be used to document a child's present language level, to develop intervention goals for vocabulary development, and to document vocabulary changes over time.

Substantial data are presented in the technical manual that provide evidence of the reliability and validity of the CDI Inventories. All three vocabulary scales and the sentence complexity scales demonstrate high internal consistency with alpha values of .95 or greater. For test-retest reliability, 500 parents completed a second inventory within 6 weeks of the first. Pearson correlations were computed separately for each month. Pearson coefficients for vocabulary on the infant form were in the .8 to .9 range for each month (with the exception of the 12-month level where the value was .6) and exceeded .9 for each monthly level for the toddler vocabulary production. Narrow confidence limits and small standard deviations indicate that the sample sizes were sufficiently large to provide good estimates of population values.

The wide range of vocabulary sampled by the inventories provides good face validity to parents. The 20-year history of language development research behind the inventories provides them with good content validity. The items within each subscale were drawn from the developmental literature and from suggestions made by parents to earlier versions of the forms. Concurrent validity, based on the relationship between the parent report (the CDI scores) and child performance on associated laboratory measures, is substantial. Correlations between language tests such as the One Word Expressive Vocabulary Test, the Preschool Language Assessment Scale, and the Bayley Expressive Language Scale are in the .53 to .73 range. It is not surprising that the correlations are not higher because the CDI assesses a broader vocabulary range than can be assessed through picture identification tasks characteristic of these other tests. A number of studies comparing vocabulary scores at differing ages attest to the predictive power of the CDI Inventories within each inventory and across both inventories.

The CDI Inventories currently provide the most thorough means for documenting the vocabulary skills of children between 8 and 30 months. Unlike standardized tests that sample a limited number of vocabulary words, primary nouns, and verbs, for this age range, the MacArthur Inventories include words having a wide range of semantic and syntactic functions. The inventories' recognition format provides a highly reliable and valid means of using parent-report data for documenting children's language skills. The inventories have proven their value in language research. They have the potential to be particularly useful in family-centered early intervention programs that seek parental involvement in the development and implementation of intervention plans.

REVIEWER'S REFERENCE

Hart, B., & Risley, T. (1995). *Meaningful differences in the everyday experience of young American children.* Baltimore: Paul H. Brookes.

[189]

Maintest.

Purpose: "Developed to measure the mechanical and electrical knowledge and skills required for maintenance jobs."

Population: Applicants and incumbents for jobs requiring practical mechanical and electrical knowledge.

Publication Date: 1991.

Scores, 22: Hydraulics, Pneumatics, Welding, Power Transmission, Lubrication, Pumps, Piping, Rigging, Mechanical Maintenance, Shop Machines/Tools/Equipment, Combustion, Motors, Digital Electronics, Schematics and Print Reading, Control Circuits, Power Supplies, Basic AC and DC Theory, Power Distribution, Test Instru-

ments, Computers and PLC, Electrical Maintenance, Total.
Administration: Group.
Price Data, 1993: $500 per 10 instruments including manual (17 pages).
Time: (150–160) minutes.
Comments: Tests scored by publisher; percentile ranks given for local and national norms.
Author: Roland T. Ramsay.
Publisher: Ramsay Corporation.

Review of the Maintest by NAMBURY S. RAJU, Distinguished Professor and Director, Center for Research and Service, Institute of Psychology, Illinois Institute of Technology, Chicago, IL:

The Maintest (Form 1), a diagnostic test of maintenance skills, consists of 153 multiple-choice items covering 21 knowledge areas: Hydraulics, Pneumatics, Welding, Power Transmission, Lubrication, Pumps, Piping, Rigging (Light), Mechanical Maintenance, Shop Machines, Combustion, Motor, Digital Electronics, Schematics and Print Reading, Control Circuits, Power Supplies, Basic AC/DC Theory, Power Distribution, Test Instruments, Computers and PLC, and Electrical Maintenance. This test is intended for use with applicants and incumbents for jobs where mechanical and electrical knowledge and skill are necessary parts of maintenance job activities. Even though there are no specific time limits, the manual notes that no more than 2 1/2 hours should be required for taking this test.

RELIABILITY. An estimate of reliability for the Maintest was .93 (probably KR20) based on a sample of 201 applicants for maintenance jobs in a manufacturing plant. The raw score mean, standard deviation, and standard error of measurement were also reported as well as the results (*p*-values and point-biserials) from an item analysis of the Maintest. The description of the item analysis and reliability sample is much too sketchy (just a couple of short sentences in the test manual), thus making it impossible to evaluate the quality and appropriateness of the sample used. The claim in the manual that the reported reliability estimate is excellent is premature. There is no information about the test-retest and parallel form reliability estimation in the manual.

VALIDITY. The test manual does not really contain any validity information for the Maintest. Because these are work sample tests, the manual claims that the content validity of the test is assured. Although that may be true, information about what types of job analyses were performed and how the appropriateness and representativeness of test con-

tent were established is not presented. No data are presented in support of either criterion-related validity or construct validity for the Maintest. The manual notes, however, that the content validity of the Maintest should be regarded as reflecting adequate criterion-related validity (p. 13, test manual).

NORMS. Percentile ranks are available for the Maintest. The test manual does not specify which sample was used for developing the percentile data. The inadequate sample description makes one wonder about the utility of these normative data. According to the manual, normative data should "facilitate the comparisons of persons scoring at a given level with a reference group, e.g., employed workers, skilled craft workers" (p. 13). Without a detailed description of the reference group or the relationship between the reference group and the group used in developing the percentile scores, it is difficult to offer a valid comparison of an individual's performance on the Maintest to that of a reference group.

In summary, the psychometric quality of the Maintest (Form NL-1) is difficult to assess at this time because of the lack of relevant statistical data. The current test manual provides very limited information about the rationale for the test, its use, its validity, and the intended audience. The test manual notes that it is a diagnostic test for maintenance skills and yet no normative or psychometric data are offered to substantiate this claim for the 21 knowledge areas included in this test. The sample sizes are small for both reliability assessment and item analysis. Information about item tryouts and the validity of the final, operational version of the test is not available in the manual. There is also no information about differential item functioning, nor is there information about selection bias and/or adverse impact for those intending to use this test for selection and/or placement. Finally, the test manual is brief and provides very limited information about test development and test use. This is disappointing because the test has been around since 1991.

Review of the Maintest by WILLIAM J. WALDRON, Administrator, Employee Testing & Assessment, TECO Energy, Inc., Tampa, FL:

INTRODUCTION. Maintest (Form NL-1), according to its publisher, is intended for use with applicants and incumbents for jobs where practical mechanical and electrical knowledge and skill are necessary parts of maintenance job activities.

Job knowledge testing seems to be undergoing a recent resurgence, as organizations facing increasingly competitive environments focus on selecting the best employees possible. More widespread use of skills-based pay programs and promotion/progression systems based on demonstrated competence have also increased interest in objective knowledge/skills measurement. Although larger organizations may have the resources necessary to conduct their own job analyses and develop their own tests, most smaller organizations do not; tests such as Maintest can be very useful to them.

The test consists of 153 four-to-five-option multiple-choice items covering 21 knowledge areas (e.g., Hydraulics, Welding, Mechanical Maintenance, Digital Electronics, Basic AC/DC Theory); the number of questions per area ranges from 4 to 12. Within the test booklet, the items are grouped within the knowledge areas, which are labeled for the examinee. The test is untimed, although the instructions note that examinees should not require more than 2 1/2 hours to complete it.

The 17-page test manual provides very clear and detailed instructions for administering the test; this section could serve as a positive example for other test publishers.

The manual provides *some* information on the psychometric characteristics of the test. A reliability coefficient (assumed, but not specified, to be internal consistency) of .93 is reported for a group of 201 maintenance applicants in a manufacturing plant. Item difficulty and discrimination indices are provided for each item as well (on a group of employees, rather than applicants—neither the size of this group nor the reason for using employees instead of applicants is specified). Normative data (the distribution of total scores on the test) are provided for "maintenance applicants"—it is unclear whether or not this is the same group of 201 on which the reliability calculation was based. At least in this normative sample, the test has a relatively high ceiling: A raw score of 121 (or 79% correct) is sufficient to rank at the 99th percentile.

No criterion-related validity studies are reported. As noted by the publisher, the test was designed using a content-oriented validation strategy; they call it "a paper-and-pencil form of a work sample" (p. 13).

The manual states that the test is scored by the publisher; no information is given about what is reported back to the test user other than "individual test scores."

CRITIQUE. The Ramsay Corporation would do well to revise significantly the manual accompanying Maintest (Form NL-1); the current manual lacks much information that a test user would require in order to evaluate the test for potential use. Some examples:

No information is provided about the job analysis process upon which the test was based. Although the content universe (the 21 knowledge areas) the test samples is clearly specified, it is not known whether this was simply determined to be representative of typical maintenance jobs by the publisher, or whether the test was based upon an analysis of the requirements of actual jobs. Related to this, no information is provided on the reasons for weighting each area in terms of the number of questions contained on the test.

Information about the intended uses of the test would be helpful. Although the manual implies that the primary use for the test would be in selecting employees, the test is subtitled as a *diagnostic* instrument. This implies that interpretation of scores based on the specific knowledge subareas would be of value. However, this is not discussed at all in the manual, nor are data provided on the reliabilities of the subscores. These data would also be important to users whose jobs entail only a subset of the knowledge areas covered by the test. Given the wide variety of content on the test, this would appear to be a common situation. Guidance for users in such situations would be of value.

More information should be provided on the samples used in calculating reliability and in conducting the item analysis, as should more background on the normative group for which the score distribution is presented in the manual. For instance, no data on adverse impact (or lack thereof) by gender and/or race/ethnicity are mentioned. Users evaluating the test for potential use in employee selection should be provided with this information; if the sample sizes to date are not large enough for meaningful calculation of such data, the manual should say so.

SUMMARY. Maintest (Form NL-1) could serve a very useful purpose in assisting organizations to select and promote maintenance employees based upon objective demonstration of knowledge and skills. There are very few readily available tests of this type. From the data presented, the test looks to be of high psychometric quality. However, a better manual with more information about the test's development and use should be provided so that potential users can evaluate realistically the suitability of the test for their purposes.

[190]

Management Style Inventory [Hanson Silver Strong & Associates].

Purpose: To assess management style.
Population: Administrators and leaders.
Publication Date: 1981.
Acronym: MSI.

Scores: 4 Management Styles: Sensing Feeling, Sensing Thinking, Intuitive Thinking, Intuitive Feeling.
Administration: Group.
Price Data, 1990: $3 per inventory.
Time: Administration time not reported.
Comments: Previously included under title Hanson Silver Management Style Inventory (10:135).
Authors: J. Robert Hanson and Harvey F. Silver.
Publisher: Hanson Silver Strong & Associates, Inc.

Review of the Management Style Inventory by STEPHEN F. DAVIS, Professor of Psychology, Emporia State University, Emporia, KS:

The Management Style Inventory (MSI), a self-administering, self-scoring, and self-interpreting instrument, yields a description of decision-making preferences. The MSI is based on Jung's Type Theory and produces separate scores pertaining to four types of managers: The Sensing Feeling Manager, The Sensing Thinking Manager, The Intuitive Thinking Manager, and The Intuitive Feeling Manager.

The scale itself consists of 15 items (variables), each of which represents a behavior the authors believe is "common to managerial decision-making" (p. 1). Examples of these behaviors include Managerial Strengths, Orientation to Problem-Solving, Participation in Meetings, Achieving Organizational Objectives, Staff Evaluation, Stress and Pressure, Motivation, and so forth. Each of these 15 behaviors or situations is followed by four descriptive phrases indicating how this situation might be dealt with. (Each phrase corresponds to one of the four management styles.) The examinee assigns a numerical weight to the one or two (but not more than two) most important descriptors. Following completion of these 15 items, the examination booklet describes the four general management styles in detail. The examinee is then required to rank order these styles as they correspond to the individual's self-perception of his or her own style. Once this second task is completed, it is a simple matter to transfer the assigned weightings for the 15 items to the score sheet on the back page and tally the totals for each management style. Thus, the final "results" consist of the managerial style rankings and a total score for each style. Once the scores are calculated, a scale of preference values allows the examinee to determine the strength of his or her preference scores and whether a particular style is "Dominant," "Auxiliary," "Supportive," or "Least Used." Although no time limits are imposed, it would appear (based on personal administrations) that 15–20 minutes is sufficient to complete and score the MSI. Examinees will have no trouble reading and comprehending the MSI items, instructions, and interpretations.

On the surface, the MSI appears to be an instrument that has potential to add to the industrial/organizational psychologist's repertoire. Unfortunately, several omissions and deficiencies render this instrument less than optimal. The most serious problems concern the complete lack of statistical data for the MSI. For example, no measures of validity and reliability are presented. Likewise, no normative data are presented to support the preference value ranges that are used to determine the relative strength of the preference scores. Likewise, it would be helpful to report reliability and validity data for Jung's theory on which this instrument is based. Finally, the lack of standardized administration procedures will be a source of concern for potential users of the MSI.

The paucity of information concerning the uses and applications of the MSI also is a potential problem. When the MSI is completed, the examinee is left with his or her ranking of the four managerial styles and a total score that appears to reflect the perceived importance or intensity of each style. It would be helpful to provide some guidance in the interpretation and use of the final rankings and scores.

These problems and deficiencies notwithstanding, the MSI does possess some merit. It is easy to administer, not time-consuming to complete, easy to score, and easy to evaluate. The MSI appears to have potential for facilitating and stimulating appropriate dialogue between management and managerial trainees. Used under appropriately structured and guided conditions, the MSI also appears to offer an opportunity for examinees to determine, confront, and better understand their own particular management style.

Review of the Management Style Inventory by MARY A. LEWIS, Director, Human Resources, Chlor-Alkali and Derivatives, PPG Industries, Inc., Pittsburgh, PA:

The Management Style Inventory (MSI) is a self-scoring, self-report inventory designed to help an individual identify managerial strengths and needs. The inventory consists of 15 broad sets of behaviors, with four behavioral statements defining each set. The individual is asked to assign 5 points to one or two of the statements based on the strength of preference for the statement. For example, the individual may assign a 5 to one statement only, or may split preferences across two statements as a 4–1 score or a 3–2 score. There are 60 such statements, each associated with one of four potential decision-making styles. The styles are described as being based on Jung's theory of psychological types.

After completing the inventory, the individual is asked to review one-page descriptions of the four Managerial Behavior Styles: The Sensing Feeling Manager (SF), The Sensing Thinking Manager (ST), The Intuitive Thinking Manager (NT), and the Intuitive Feeling Manager (NF). These approximately one-page write-ups include a narrative description of the particular style and bulleted descriptions of the style under the headings of Assets, Liabilities, Facilitators (Turn-Ons), and Inhibitors (Turn-Offs). The individual is asked to rank order each description, based on preference.

After reviewing these descriptive narratives associated with the four styles, the individual is then instructed on self-scoring. The scoring requires the individual to transfer the preference number associated with each statement to the appropriate style column space, as indicated by the statement number. From 30 to 45 of the statement numbers may be blank and any particular statement may have an integer value from 1 to 5. The style scoring requires adding up the column of scores and then, based on the size of the number, ranking them as Dominant (highest score), Auxiliary, Supportive, and Least Used (lowest score). A five-category preference scale for these numbers is provided, which describes number ranges from Little or no preference (0–29) to Very strong preference (60–75).

The MSI is handsomely printed in a green and white motif and is easy to read. The process will have intuitive appeal to a layman, and the statements describing the styles are easy to follow. Each style is described in a positive way that will help the individual "feel good."

No references are provided to support the MSI. One Jung reference is mentioned with a date, but no citation is provided. No psychometric data of any type are provided. No reliability, no interscale correlations, and no evidence of a relationship to other scales are included. No attempt is made to provide any type of validity evidence. No means and standard deviations of scales are provided, and no support for the preference category metric is provided.

The tone of the document, with its "Turn-ons" and "Turn-offs," its lack of any psychometric evidence, and the Barnum Statement approach to the scale descriptors, properly relegates this instrument to informal uses. There are other tools, such as the Myers-Briggs Type Indicator (Myers, 1985; T4:1702),

with a solid theoretical and empirical base, which can provide developmental feedback on Management Style. These other instruments are considered more appropriate for this assessment purpose.

REVIEWER'S REFERENCE

Myers, I. B., & McCaulley, M. H. (1985). *Manual: A guide to the development and use of the Myers-Briggs Type Indicator.* Palo Alto, CA: Consulting Psychologists Press.

[191]

Manchester Personality Questionnaire.

Purpose: Designed to provide an occupational personality test with a focus on traits relevant to creative and innovative behavior.
Population: Adults.
Publication Dates: 1993–1996.
Acronym: MPQ.
Administration: Group.
Authors: CIM Test Publishers.
Publisher: CIM Test Publishers.

a) MPQ FACTOR 14.
Purpose: An assessment of 14 personality traits covering the Big Five personality factors.
Scores, 19: Big Five Factors (Creativity, Agreeableness, Achievement, Extroversion, Resilience), Originality, Rule Consciousness, Openness to Change, Assertiveness, Social Confidence, Empathy, Communicativeness, Independence, Rationality, Competitiveness, Conscientiousness, Perfectionism, Decisiveness, Apprehension.
Price Data, 1994: £40 per administration set including user's manual ('96, 72 pages), reusable questionnaire, answer sheet, and profile chart; £32.50 per user's manual; £27.50 per 5 reusable questionnaires; £15 per 25 answer sheets; £15 per 25 profile charts; £450 per MPQ Expert System.
Time: (20) minutes.

b) MANCHESTER CREATIVITY QUESTIONNAIRE FACTOR 7.
Purpose: An assessment of the personality attributes of creativity.
Scores, 9: Global Factor (Creativity), Originality, Rule Consciousness, Openness to Change, Assertiveness, Independence, Achievement, Radicalness, Response Style.
Price Data: £15 per profile chart; £30 per 25 combined questionnaire/answer sheets.
Time: Administration time not reported.

Review of the Manchester Personality Questionnaire by JACK E. GEBART-EAGLEMONT, Lecturer in Psychology, Swinburne University of Technology, Hawthorn, Victoria, Australia:

The stated purpose of the Manchester Personality Questionnaire (MPQ) is to provide a measure of occupationally relevant personality factors with the special focus on traits related to creativity. The MPQ is a self-report instrument that measures 14 primary dimensions; the second-order factors theoretically reproduce the Big Five Factor model. A measure of social desirability is also included, in the form of a Response Style scale, which reflects Impression Management. The primary dimensions are measured by eight items each and the response format is a 5-point Likert-type rating scale (*Never, Occasionally, Fairly Often, Generally, Always*). The primary scales are reducible to five major dimensions (Creativity, Agreeableness, Achievement, Extroversion, Resilience) using a simplified factor score formula in the hand-scored "paper and pencil" version and the exact factor-based formula in the computerized version. The approach to calculation of factor scores is based on a regressional method, which reflects the different contributions of the primary scales.

An autonomous part of the MPQ, the Manchester Creativity Questionnaire (MCQ; Factor 7), includes items from seven scales that loaded highly on the Creativity factor (Originality, Rule Consciousness, Openness to Change, Assertiveness, Independence, Achievement, Radicalness) and the Impression Management scale. Each scale contains seven items in a response format similar to the MPQ. Some of the items are slightly reformulated, and they form one scale (the MCQ Total Score, "Innovators-Adaptors").

TEST DEVELOPMENT. The construction of the MPQ followed the objective of measuring the Big Five personality factors. The Big Five concept refers to the replicable set of five central dimensions of personality, emerging from factor analyses of data from various personality tests. Different authors propose diverse labels for these factors, and there is some disagreement concerning the markers of the Big Five. For the MPQ, an initial set of over 500 items was generated using the Big Five factor structure as conceptualized by Goldberg (1992). The second step involved factor analysis of a pilot inventory with 182 items, reflecting 14 clusters of primary personality dimensions. A final version was factor analyzed, using the principal components method with Varimax rotation. The obvious and well-known problems with the use of the principal components method for extraction are, in the case of the MPQ, additionally complicated by an inadequate rotational method. The manual presents contradictory results, first stating that an orthogonal rotation was applied, and then reporting intercorrelations among the factors (including $r = .34$ between Extroversion and Agreeableness). If the factors are really orthogonal (which is almost never true for psychological dimensions, such as personality characteristics), they should be uncorrelated. The final 120-item version of the MPQ measures 14 dimensions that reproduce Big Five factorial dimensions in their second-order factors. In the third phase the test was subjected to validation procedures and an interpreter software was developed. The computer program provides on-line questionnaire completion and produces profiles and narrative reports.

NORMATIVE DATA. The MPQ normative sample ($N = 554$) included mainly managers and other professionals. This rather specific sample is consistent with the declared objective of the MPQ—the test is described by the publisher as "an occupational personality questionnaire" (p. 31). The normative sample for the Factor 7 (MCQ) was quite small ($N = 126$), and the composition of the sample is not disclosed. It is described vaguely in the manual as "managers and professionals spanning 28 nationalities" (p. 37). The norms for the MCQ are not presented in the manual.

RELIABILITY. Internal consistency of the MPQ scales was assessed using the Cronbach alpha reliability method. Nine scales (Originality, Rule Consciousness, Openness, Assertiveness, Empathy, Rationality, Perfectionism, Decisiveness, Apprehension) had alpha coefficients above .70, and the remaining scales (Social Confidence, Communicativeness, Independence, Competitiveness, Conscientiousness) demonstrated alpha coefficients above .60. There are no data concerning test-retest reliability.

VALIDITY. Data concerning convergent validity of the MPQ are presented in the manual. Some correlation coefficients between the MPQ scales and the NEO PI-R (Costa & McCrae, 1992) dimensions indicate a moderate level of convergent validity (Creativity with NEO PI-R Openness, $r = .47$; Achievement with NEO PI-R Conscientiousness, $r = .40$; Extroversion with NEO PI-R Extraversion, $r = .50$; Resilience with NEO PI-R Neuroticism, $r = .53$), but there seems to be a potential problem with the Agreeableness scale (low correlation with the NEO PI-R Agreeableness, $r = .14$, but much higher correlations with the remaining NEO PI-R scales). The MPQ Agreeableness factor obviously failed to demonstrate any convergent and discriminant validity, at least when using the NEO PI-R as a validating device. It should also be mentioned that the validation sample size was quite small ($N = 98$) and rather homogeneous (sales people). The scales of the MPQ were also regressed on the dimensions of the Occupational Personality Questionnaire (OPQ; Saville & Holdsworth, 1992). Multiple correlations appear satisfactory (Creativity: .47; Agreeableness: .78; Achievement: .62; Extroversion: .70; Resilience: .69), but it should be noted that this statistical approach obscures the discriminant validity component and inflates the relationships with the predictors; the zero-order correlations were not reported. A very limited attempt to demonstrate criterion validity (criterion defined as "sales performance") was undertaken with the same sample of 98 sales people. Only the Achievement scale correlated significantly with this criterion ($r = .20$, $p<.01$).

MPQ Factor 7, Creativity (Manchester Creativity Questionnaire) was validated against the Kirton Adaption-Innovation Inventory (KAI; Kirton, 1976). The MCQ total scores is correlated with the Total KAI score at the acceptable level ($r = .69$). Some of the MCQ scales show some promising correlations with the KAI's dimensions (Originality with KAI Originality, $r = .67$; Rule Consciousness with KAI Conformity, $r = .58$). The validation sample size was slightly larger ($N = 126$) than in the case of the MPQ.

CONTROL SCALE. The MPQ has one eight-item control scale, Impression Management. The manual does not show any validity data concerning this scale (such as correlations with other social desirability instruments), or concerning the relationship of this scale with the measured personality dimensions. Because the MPQ items show high levels of item transparency, the questions about the value and role of the control scale remain unanswered. Faking personality questionnaires in organizational settings, such as personnel selection, may pose a serious problem (Furnham, 1990). In evaluative situations respondents tend to shape their self-report according to their image of the expected "prototypal personality" for a given job. This includes those "who could be described as knowing dissemblers and those who are naive but honest" but their responses are still guided by their ideal image (Kirton, 1977).

SUMMARY. In comparison with the Hogan Personality Inventory (HPI; Hogan & Hogan, 1995), the MPQ's direct competitor, it appears that the potential strength of the MPQ is that it is more oriented toward measurement of creativity, including an expanded autonomous creativity scale. The idea of measuring personality for explicitly defined occupational purposes using Big Five is meritorious and should prove quite marketable. The HPI, on the other hand, is generally much better documented,

has much stronger validation data, and provides more information concerning important occupational characteristics (Service Orientation, Stress Tolerance, Reliability, Clerical Potential, Sales Potential, Managerial Potential).

Overall, the MPQ scales appear to have an acceptable level of internal consistency, and the factor structure seems clear. The inadequacies of the factor analytic solutions need to be rectified (Maximum Likelihood instead of Principal Components, and oblique rotation instead of orthogonal solutions, because the factors are quite clearly intercorrelated). The obtained factor structures could also be tested using confirmatory factor analysis, using a more contemporary analytic approach, such as LISREL (Jöreskog & Sörbom, 1989) or EQS (Bentler, 1989); this would provide some indices of the goodness of fit of the measurement model. The strong practical point of the MPQ is the interpreter software, which allows the user to administer and score the test. The program is very functional—the output includes profiles for 14 primary factors and for 5 second-order factors. The narrative interpretation produced by the program is well articulated and provides clearly structured information about the strengths and weaknesses of the testee, as well as useful developmental advice. The only problem with the MPQ software is the embarrassing presence of spelling errors in several test items.

The weak points of the test at this stage are that the convergent validity data are still quite scanty and based on comparatively small samples. Further developmental work should concentrate on validation with much larger samples, and the validity data should be reported in a less enigmatic way. One of the central weaknesses of the MPQ is limited data concerning predictive validity; more research is needed in this direction, using clearly defined occupational criteria. Also, the limited data concerning the control scale, in circumstances of an overall high item transparency, makes the MPQ open to criticism that the test may be vulnerable to response distortion, especially faking.

The MCQ (Factor 7) as a measure of personality characteristics related to creativity shows quite acceptable levels of reliability and validity. In comparison with the Kirton Adaption-Innovation Inventory, the MCQ's closest competitor, the major weak points are a small normative sample and limited validation data. The Kirton Adaption-Innovation Inventory has very impressive validation data, including studies involving more than 12,000 managers (Fleenor & Taylor, 1994), and there is strong evidence that responses to the KAI are relatively unaffected by social desirability (Goldsmith & Matherly, 1986).

In summary, the MPQ demonstrates great potential as an occupational personality test, but more research on validity is needed (including investigation of the validity and role of the control scale), especially in light of publisher's suggestions concerning the use of the MPQ in personnel selection.

REVIEWER'S REFERENCES

Kirton, M. (1976). Adaptors and innovators: A description and measure. *Journal of Applied Psychology, 61,* 622–629.
Kirton, M. (1977). Characteristics of high Lie scorers. *Psychological Reports, 40*(1), 279–280.
Goldsmith, R. E., & Matherly, T. A. (1986). The Kirton Adaption Innovation Inventory, faking, and social desirability: A replication and extension. *Psychological Reports, 58*(1), 269–270.
Bentler, P. M. (1989). *EQS Structural Equations Program manual.* Los Angeles: BMDP Statistical Software.
Jöreskog, K. G., & Sörbom, D. (1989). *LISREL 7: A guide to the program and applications.* Chicago: SPSS.
Furnham, A. (1990). Faking personality questionnaires: Fabricating different profiles for different purposes. *Current Psychology Research and Reviews, 9*(1), 46–55.
Costa, P. T., & McCrae, R. R. (1992). *NEO PI-R professional manual.* Odessa, FL: Psychological Assessment Resources.
Goldberg, L. R. (1992). The development of markers for the big-five structure. *Psychological Assessment, 4*(4), 26–42.
Saville & Holdsworth Ltd. (1992). *Handbook for OPQ Occupational Personality Questionnaires.* Surrey, U.K.: The author.
Fleenor, J. W., & Taylor, S. (1994). Construct validity of three self-report measures of creativity. *Educational and Psychological Measurement, 54*(2), 464–470.
Hogan, R., & Hogan, J. (1995). *Hogan Personality Inventory manual, second edition.* Tulsa, OK: Hogan Assessment Systems.

Review of the Manchester Personality Questionnaire by CARL ISENHART, Administrative Coordinator, Addictive Disorders Section, Department of Veterans Affairs Medical Center, Minneapolis, MN:

The Manchester Personality Questionnaire (MPQ) is an occupational personality test developed from the Big Five model of personality (McCrae & Costa, 1987) to assess creative and innovative behavior. It yields 14 "Primary Dimension" personality traits and Big Five factor scores, takes 20 minutes to complete, and provides norm-referenced scores. A companion instrument, the nine-scale Manchester Creativity Questionnaire (MCQ) "measures traits related to both the personal nature of the creative process and the essentially social nature of the innovation process" (p. 4). The manual suggests these instruments can be used in training, team development, and counseling. An available software assessment program will not be reviewed.

SCALE DEVELOPMENT. The MPQ development description was vague and confusing, as demonstrated from this description taken from the manual: Over 550 items were generated, reduced to 182 items "based on 14 groupings" and administered to "a large number of subjects" (p. 27). The 14 groups were developed from a process where "different solutions were examined by varying the number of factors specified in the analysis and by looking at different rotational methods" (p. 28). This is not an appropriate use of factor analysis; ideally, rotational methods are based on data type and the questions asked, and the number of factors to retain is determined prior to rotation. In addition, a 15th measure, the Response Style scale, was added to determine "whether the test-takers were completing the questionnaire accurately" (p. 28). However, there was no information about the scale's development or reliability and validity other than to indicate that it "correlates with the Occupational Personality Questionnaire's (OPQ; Saville & Holdsworth Ltd., 1992) Social Desirability Responding" (p. 18). Finally, limited demographic data were presented to describe the normative group; there was no information regarding racial background, educational level, or years of experience. Also, no demographic data were presented for any other subjects used in the development and analysis of these instruments.

The only MCQ development discussion was: "the MCQ represents a different statistical model of the personality characteristics covered by Factor 14 [the MPQ]. It is based on the scales which correlate highly with the MPQ Creativity factor" (p. 30).

ADMINISTRATION AND SCORING. The MPQ instructions are listed in the test booklet. The examinee indicates the extent a personality trait applies (*never, occasionally, fairly often, generally,* or *always*) and marks the appropriate selection on the two-page carbonless answer sheet. The mark is transferred to the second sheet on which is a printed scoring key. The examinee's responses are summed for each scale then placed on the answer sheet and transferred to a "Profile Chart" on which are listed the Primary Dimension and Big Five Factor scale names (and low- and high-scale score descriptions), areas to indicate the client's raw and sten scores, and a score scale on which to display the client's sten score. (A sten scale is a 10-unit modification of the 9-unit stanine scale.) The instructions then state to "work out the Sten scores for the primary scales using the norms printed on the Personality Profile Chart" (p. 6). There are no norms on the Personality Profile Chart. Actually, the conversion chart is listed in Table 7 in the manual. After the scale sten scores are calculated and placed on the profile sheet, the sten is marked on the scale. To calculate the Big Five scores, the primary scale sten scores are transferred to equations listed on the second page of the original answer sheet, multiplied by a weighting factor, and summed. These raw scores are transferred to the profile sheet and converted to sten scores (again using the unmentioned Table 7 in the manual), and the sten score marked on the sten scale. Overall, the scoring instructions are incomplete and the scoring process is tedious with a lot of shifting between the answer sheet, the profile chart, and the manual.

The administration and scoring of the MCQ is even more confusing and could not be completed with the provided material. The instructions, questions, and rating response scales are all printed on a two-page carbonless sheet. The examinee reads the personality trait description and indicates the extent it applies (*never, occasionally, fairly often, generally,* or *always*). The answer is transferred to the bottom sheet, where scoring is done by transferring the answers to equations for each scale, summing, then transferring the score to a profile chart that contains scale names (and low- and high-scale score descriptions), areas to indicate the client's raw and sten scores, and a score scale on which to display the client's sten score. Again, the examiner is instructed to convert the raw to sten scores and place those scores on the profile chart; however, this reviewer could find no conversion tables in the manual, answer sheet, or profile sheet. Thus, the profile chart could not be completed and the results were uninterpretable. Supposedly, a "global factor" creativity score is calculated from the weighted sten scores sums of Scales 1 through 5 minus the sum of Scale 7 + the number 13. However, there is no rationale for the scoring algorithm: why Scales 6 and 8 are excluded, why some scales are weighted by a factor of 3 and some by 2, and the rationale for subtracting the sum of Scale 7 and the number 13.

SEX DIFFERENCES. The manual describes sex differences between the 14 primary scales but says nothing about the Big Five factors. Six of the scales showed statistically significant differences; however, the report is incomplete. No standard deviations were reported. There was no description of how these differences were analyzed. A Bonferroni correction (.05/14) of .00357 would suggest that none of the reported differences were significant. Beyond the statistical significance, there is the question of clinical significance. In many cases the difference between the sexes is much smaller than the scale's reported standard error of measurement (*SEM*). For example, on Scale 10, the sex difference is .9 (males 22.4 and females 21.5), but the *SEM* is 2.12. Therefore, if one were to develop confidence intervals, there would be huge overlap between the sexes.

RELIABILITY. The manual reports MPQ internal consistency measures ranging from .64 (Conscientiousness) to .85 (Rule Consciousness). No other data besides *SEM*s are listed. Clearly these data are inadequate to support the reliability of this instrument. Test-retest reliability should be considered given the advisability of calculating this statistic on stable traits such as those being assessed here (Kaplan & Saccuzzo, 1993).

VALIDITY. The validity discussion focused mostly on the Big Five factors and less on the 14 primary scales. The MPQ's validity was examined by analysis of the Big Five factor structure. A scree test determined the number of factors to retain; however, the scree test likely overestimated the number of factors (Tinsley & Tinsley, 1987). Several more appropriate alternatives have been suggested (Zwick & Velicer, 1986). Some of the scales had high multiple factor loadings but were still used for one or more factors. For example, "Independence" had factor loadings of .42, -.53, and -.41 on Factors I, II, and IV, respectively. It is questionable whether these scales should be used to calculate the Big Five factors even when factor loadings are used as weights. Also, it is curious that the "Independence" scale had its second highest factor loading on Factor I (.42) in the factor analysis, but the scale is not used in the computation of the Factor I (Creativity) dimension. A confirmatory factor analysis of the individual items should be completed to assess whether the instrument assesses 14 distinct dimensions.

The manual stated that "An important requirement of a well constructed test is that the scales should be statistically independent" (p. 35). However, there is no discussion about the reported correlations and how they support the instrument's validity.

Validity was examined by correlating the MCQ (the creativity instrument) with the Kirton Adaption-Innovation Inventory (KAI; Taylor, 1989). This is inappropriate because there is no documentation of the MCQ's development or normative or reliability data.

The MPQ Big Five scales were correlated with the NEO Personality Inventory (NEO PI-R; Costa & McCrae, 1992) resulting in 170 correlations. This type of analysis and presentation is overwhelming and difficult to interpret. To complicate matters further, levels of significance were not reported. The same process was completed with the 14 MPQ scales and the NEO PI-R. This yielded a sea of 525 correlations. Again, the sheer number was overwhelming, and there were no levels of significance reported. However, even if significance levels were reported, with such a high number of correlations significant relationships would be found by chance and would have questionable meaning. A more useful process would have been to have hypothesized positive and negative relationships between specific scales based on conceptual domains and use multiple regression procedures to examine these relationships. For example, specific MPQ scales could be regressed onto selected NEO scales; this type of analysis could show convergent and discriminant validity.

Another attempt to demonstrate validity was to correlate the MPQ with the OPQ. Each separate MPQ Big Five factor was regressed on an OPQ scale that "appeared to be measuring similar personality domains" (p. 40). For example, the MPQ Agreeableness factor was regressed on the OPQ Empathy dimensions (e.g., modest, democratic, and caring). (To highlight previous comments, the subjects were described only as "a sample of managers.") Considering there was more than one OPQ dimension, it would have made more sense for the OPQ dimensions to be regressed on the MPQ dimensions. Thus, there appears to be an inconsistency between what was stated and what appears most logical. Significant multiple correlations were found; however, the direction of the regression makes the interpretation a little difficult. This type of analysis was reported for the Big Five factors only, and not the 14 primary dimensions.

Finally, the MPQ Big Five factors were correlated with job performance. The criterion was average monthly sales revenue. The largest and only significant correlation was .2; none of the other MPQ Big Five factors significantly correlated. Analysis of the 14 primary dimensions resulted in .18 as the highest significant correlation for two scales. Criterion validity is not demonstrated by an instrument sharing less than 4% of the variance with the criterion measure.

THE MANUAL. The manual was frequently confusing, vague, and incomplete; this was quite irritating to this reviewer and complicated the process of evaluating the instrument. Descriptions of the scales are provided, but they are of questionable utility given the technical problems with the instrument. There were a number of errors: missing figure captions, incorrect references, redundancy between text and tables, and references to wrong tables.

SUMMARY AND RECOMMENDATION. This reviewer is not impressed with this instrument and cannot recommend its use. Information regarding development and rationale for various procedures is incomplete and confusing, and the scoring and interpretation is cumbersome. The reliability and validity data are weak at best and frequently address the Big Five factors and not the 14 primary scale dimensions. The manual is a model of obfuscation that leaves the potential examiner bewildered and unimpressed.

REVIEWER'S REFERENCES

Zwick, W. R., & Velicer, W. F. (1986). Comparison of five rules for determining the number of components to retain. *Psychological Bulletin, 99,* 432–442.

McCrae, R. R., & Costa, P. T. (1987). Validation of the five-factor of personality across instruments and observers. *Journal of Personality and Social Psychology, 52,* 81–90.

Tinsley, H. E. A., & Tinsley, D. J. (1987). Uses of factor analysis in counseling psychology research. *Journal of Counseling Psychology, 34,* 414–424.

Taylor, W. G. K. (1989). The Kirton Adaption-Innovation Inventory: A reexamination of the factor structure. *Journal of Organizational Behaviour, 10,* 297–307.

Costa, P. T., & McCrae, R. R. (1992). *Revised NEO Personality Inventory: Professional manual.* New York: Psychological Assessment Resources, Inc.

Saville & Holdsworth Ltd. (1992). *Handbook for OPQ Occupational Personality Questionnaires.* Surrey, U.K.: The author.

Kaplan, R. M., & Saccuzzo, D. P. (1993). *Psychological testing: Principles, application, and issues* (3rd ed.). Pacific Grove, CA: Brooks/Cole Publishing Co.

[192]
Marital Check-Up Kit.

Purpose: "Designed to help couples examine their relationship and to determine ways in which it can be enriched or strengthened."

Population: Married couples.

Publication Date: 1980.

Acronym: MCK.

Scores: No scores.

Administration: Group.

Price Data: Available from publisher.

Time: Administration time not reported.

Comments: Can be administered to individuals, couples, or groups.

Author: Millard J. Bienvenu.

Publisher: Millard J. Bienvenu, Northwest Publications.

Review of the Marital Check-Up Kit by FRANK BERNT, Associate Professor of Health Services, St. Joseph's University, Philadelphia, PA:

The Marital Check-Up Kit (MCK) is designed to identify potential problems in a relationship before they reach a critical stage and to strengthen communication between spouses. Its aims are congruous with those of brief marital therapies and relationship enrichment programs, which are generally considered to have small but consistently positive effects (Hahlweg & Markman, 1988; Worthington et al., 1995).

No data relating to the MCK's validity or reliability, norms, or score calculation are provided; a computer literature review yielded no studies referring to either its quality or its use. It seems appropriate, therefore, to consider the MCK as simply a set of exercises that provides a structured sequence to follow for examining the strengths and weaknesses of a marital relationship. The remainder of this review focuses on the potential utility of the exercises for marital therapy without further comment on its utility as an assessment tool.

The MCK is designed for use by marital counselors. A two-page set of directions is provided with the MCK packet. Counselors using the MCK are instructed, if married, to complete the MCK with their spouses beforehand in order to "get a better feel for how couples experience the exercises and a deeper understanding of the overall procedure and the forms used" (p. 1, directions). No theoretical framework is provided.

Instructions are quite simple. Couples receive copies (one for each partner) of the MCK and generally complete the exercises at home, reporting back to the counselor at a future session. In cases where couples cannot talk calmly about their relationship, instructions dictate that the MCK be completed in the counselor's presence. Instructions also advise counselors to practice such therapeutic habits as reassurance, praise for openness and effort, asking for feedback, and availability. The checklist itself consists of six separate exercises that focus upon the following areas: perceptions of self and spouse, communication habits, major current events in the relationship, satisfaction with partner's qualities, perception of one's own strengths and weaknesses, and feelings about oneself. Exercises vary in number and format of items; the MCK includes checklists, rating scales, and sentence completion formats. For each exercise, marital partners are instructed to complete the items separately; then to exchange and review each other's answers; then to discuss responses to items and reactions to each exercise as a whole. If these steps are accomplished without a breakdown in communication, the couple is directed to continue on to the next exercise; if there is a communication breakdown, the couple is instructed to stop and resume at a later time.

Prior to beginning the exercises, participants read a brief paragraph that likens marriage to a large house with many rooms to be enjoyed and explored, for which effective marital communication is the key that unlocks the doors. The exercises are offered as a means of beginning to forge the key. This same metaphor is repeated at the end of the six exercises, followed by a paragraph that explains how couples have different reactions to the MCK and that it is hoped that the experience has been meaningful.

The MCK provides no theoretical framework as its basis; the sense one has in completing the exercise is not one that includes clear structure or purpose. The connection between stated aims of the MCK and the exercises themselves is not at all obvious. Estimates of the time needed to complete each exercise, plus a brief explanation prior to each exercise regarding its rationale and specific purpose, would provide respondents with a clearer sense at the beginning of what the exercises involved and of where they were leading.

There is no explanation regarding how the test was constructed or of how items and types of exercises were selected. There is no indication that a pilot was ever done, nor that the MCK has ever been refined in response to user feedback. Consisting mostly of 50 separate rating items and 47 sentence completion items, the exercises seem to be many trees in search of a forest. It is difficult to determine exactly what each exercise is "for" and how each contributes to the overall aims of the MCK.

In summary, the MCK needs work, and there is little tangible evidence that it does work. There are more widely used instruments that include information on test development, validity, and reliability and that address similar issues. Well-established instruments such as the Dyadic Adjustment Scale (T4:824), the Myers-Briggs Type Indicator (T4:1702), and The FIRO Awareness Scales (T4:982) are used in marital therapy to assess marital satisfaction, personality, and communication styles (see Filsinger, 1983 and Fredman & Sherman, 1987, for extensive reviews of such instruments). The recently developed ENRICH instrument (Hawley, 1994) facilitates exploration of the multiple facets of a marital relationship, clearly identifying 13 different areas for discussion.

Most of these instruments have been developed according to APA standards and have been analyzed psychometrically, so that their strengths and weaknesses are open to scrutiny. It may be the case that marital counselors use such instruments mainly for education and planning and that they are relatively unconcerned about whether such instruments are standardized (Boughner, Hayes, Bubenzer, & West, 1994). Be that as it may, the use of such tests presupposes a level of responsibility on the part of the author to conscientiously develop, pilot, and improve such instruments and on the part of the user to correctly interpret the responses that such instruments evoke. Some form of thoughtful development and evaluation of the MCK is needed to strengthen its credibility and to minimize the likelihood of its misuse. Until such time as the author of the MCK takes steps in this direction, the reader is advised to explore the use of alternatives that have explicit theoretical bases, data to support their quality, clear instructions to assure their appropriate administration, and wider use over time to suggest their utility.

REVIEWER'S REFERENCES

Filsinger, E. E. (Ed.). (1983). *Marriage and family assessment: A sourcebook for family therapy.* Beverly Hills, CA: Sage.

Fredman, N., & Sherman, R. (1987). *Handbook of measurements for marriage and family therapy.* New York: Brunner/Mazel.

Hahlweg, K., & Markman, H. J. (1988). Effectiveness of behavioral marital therapy: Empirical status of behavioral techniques in preventing and alleviating marital distress. *Journal of Consulting and Clinical Psychology, 56*(3), 440–447.

Boughner, S. R., Hayes, S. F., Bubenzer, D. L., & West, J. D. (1994). Use of standardized assessment instruments by marital and family therapists: A survey. *Journal of Marital and Family Therapy, 20*(1), 69–75.

Hawley, D. R. (1994). Couples in crisis: Using self-report instruments in marriage counseling. *Pastoral psychology, 43*(2), 93–103.

Worthington, E. L., McCullough, M. E., Shortz, J. L., Mindes, E. J., Sandage, S. J., & Chartrand, J. M. (1995). Can couples assessment and feedback improve relationships? Assessment as a brief relationship enrichment procedure. *Journal of Counseling Psychology, 42*(4), 466–475.

Review of the Marital Check-Up Kit by W. DALE BROTHERTON, Associate Professor of Counselor Education, Western Carolina University, Cullowhee, NC:

The Marital Check-Up Kit (MCK) consists of a battery of exercises to be completed by individuals who are wanting to strengthen and enrich their relationship with one another. The MCK is designed to identify potential problems, if any, in the relationship and to create opportunities for improved communication between partners. The MCK can be used in marital counseling or in a couple's enrichment group setting and can be completed at home under the guidance of a counselor or in the direct presence of the counselor in the counseling setting. The MCK seems to be appropriate with couples who are seeking to enrich an already satisfying relationship. Although the wording of the exercises suggests the MCK is for married couples, it is this author's opinion the exercises can be adapted to be used with nonmarried couples, with sexual orientation of the couple not being a hindrance to use of the exercises.

Counselors choosing to use the MCK should be trained in professional marriage and family counseling and maintain appropriate credentials. Because individuals in the couple relationship are not always ready to acknowledge personally, to each other, or to a counselor problems in the spousal relationship, professionals should carefully assess for severity of marital problems and the couple's ability for conflict resolution before asking couples to complete the MCK at home. In an unsupervised home environment, problems may arise and escalate unnecessarily. Couples wishing to participate in a couples group should be carefully screened as to their appropriateness for group membership and informed about group process (Association for Specialists in Group Work, 1989) before being allowed to participate.

When a couple uses the MCK, participants finish each exercise independently. After completion of an exercise, the partners share with each other their answers and discuss together differences and similarities with their responses. The MCK is meant to be self-pacing, allowing the partners to move to the next exercise when they feel ready. Most of the exercises in the MCK present to the couple a series of open-ended completion statements that ask for perceptions of how partners see each other and themselves as partners in the relationship. Although there is more emphasis placed on identifying individual and couple strengths than weaknesses, the exercises allow the partners to identify problem areas that might exist in the relationship and state what each wants from the other through the relational experience.

Two exercises in the MCK ask for partners to use a rating scale as a way of clarifying and sharing perceptions about one another. One of these exercises is about marital communication and asks for the partners to assess the frequency of identified communication behaviors exhibited by the partner and the degree of comfort the person feels with the level of sharing in the relationship. The second asks for a partner to rate his or her degree of satisfaction with the partner in 22 areas. Areas include trustworthiness, listening, affection, self-confidence, parenting, religion, and companionship.

No information could be obtained from the author as to how the MCK was normed, or the extent of its use. Because of lack of standardization, the MCK would not be appropriate as an assessment tool with couples requesting counseling or as a measure to evaluate change in the couple's relationship. More widely used instruments such as the *Couple's Therapy Workbook* by Stuart and Jacobson (1987) might be more acceptable for couples in need of counseling, whereas the MCK seems best suited as a "tune up" for couples who need only minor adjustments to a relationship that is for the most part satisfying.

REVIEWER'S REFERENCES

Stuart, R. B., & Jacobson, B. (1987). *Couple's therapy workbook.* Champaign, IL: Research Press.

Association for Specialists in Group Work. (1989). *Ethical guidelines for group counselors.* Alexandria, VA: Author.

[193]
Mathematics Topic Pre-Tests.

Purpose: "Designed as coarse screening device to help teachers find the gaps in their students' prior knowledge of particular mathematics."

Population: Form 3 (junior secondary) students in New Zealand school system.

Publication Date: 1990–1996.

Scores: 3 tests: Percentages, Integers, Measurement.

Administration: Group.

Price Data, 1996: NZ$8.10 per 20 reusable pretests (specify Percentages, Integers, or Measurement); $10.80

per 20 answer sheets; $9 per worksheet masters; $9 per teacher's manual (specify Percentages ['90, 12 pages], Integers ['90, 12 pages], or Measurement ['96, 12 pages]); $27 per specimen set.
Time: (30) minutes per test.
Authors: New Zealand Council for Educational Research, Ministry of Education, and Hamilton Region Mathematics Writing Group, and Auckland College of Education.
Publisher: New Zealand Council for Educational Research [New Zealand].

Review of the Mathematics Topic Pre-Tests by GERALD E. DeMAURO, Director, Bureau of Assessment, New Jersey State Department of Education, Trenton, NJ:

The Mathematics Topic Pre-Tests are designed to identify gaps in the mathematics knowledge of students before they encounter the topic in New Zealand Form 3 (about ninth grade in the United States). Cautions are provided against using the materials for student evaluation, because they are designed primarily to inform instruction *before* the topic is introduced, as a baseline of knowledge for further instruction.

There appears to be a great deal of flexibility in the ways in which the pretests are administered, but a 3-day model of pretesting, instructional intervention, and posttesting is provided. The two pretest topics reviewed are Percentages and Integers.

DEVELOPMENT

History. Remedial mathematics materials were first developed in 1984 for junior secondary students by educators in the Waikato/Bay of Plenty Region. The New Zealand Department of Education and the New Zealand Council for Educational research then entered a collaboration with a group that became known as the Hamilton Region Mathematics Writing Group to develop materials on percentages for Form 3 students. The materials were designed to address weaknesses in New Zealand junior secondary students that were identified in the early 1980s by the International Association for the Evaluation of Educational Achievement. Development of the integers material followed. Pools of completion-type items in both areas were developed for Forms 1–4 (grades 7–10).

Percentages. The seven objectives addressed for Percentages are: converting fractions to percentages, converting decimals to percentages, converting percentages to fractions, converting percentages to decimals, interpreting percentages from bar graphs and pie charts, expressing one quantity as a percentage of another, and calculating a given percentage of a quantity. The pretest consists of 28 items, 4 for each of the objectives.

Integers. The 10 Integer objectives addressed are: location on number lines, order of relationship, addition, subtraction, multiplication, division, knowing the addition property of zero, knowing the addition property of opposite numbers, knowing the multiplication property of zero, and knowing the multiplication property of one. The pretest consists of 32 items, 4 items for each of the first six objectives and 2 items for each of the last four objectives.

Item development. Objectives for the topics were drawn from the revised mathematics syllabus for Forms 1–4. After the above objectives were identified, they were reviewed by Form 2 mathematics teachers to assure that they were compatible with the Form 2 mathematics curriculum.

Pools of completion-type items were written by graduate mathematics students. Four test forms each for Percentages (first) and for Integers were administered to Form 2 students (Percentages) and Form 3 students (both Percentages and Integers). Item analyses were made, including identification of common errors. Students were also interviewed to provide information to help develop distractors for multiple-choice questions.

Two parallel forms each of multiple-choice pretests were developed and field tested. A final pretest and parallel posttest form were then developed from surviving items in each of the subject areas, and remedial curricula were developed based on common errors. The remedial Percentages curricula were field tested in 20 secondary schools nationwide, and the Integers remedial curricula were field tested in Auckland secondary schools. The curricula were then edited to yield two trial worksheets for each objective, 14 for the seven Percentages objectives and 20 for the 10 Integers objectives.

For all of the Percentages objectives and the first six of the Integers objectives, there are four questions per objective, covering two levels of difficulty and presented either as numerical or more abstract word problems. For the final six Integer objectives, questions alternate between numeric and more abstract word problems.

ADMINISTRATION

Each pretest topic is administered over the course of 3 days. On the first day, the pretest is administered, and students mark the papers, followed by class diagnosis and work sheet assignments on the basis of the diagnosis. On the second day, the work sheet is completed. Finally, on the third day, the posttest is administered and new work is assigned.

SCORING

Points are accumulated for items according to objective, for the type of common error, and for whether the question is a word problem or a numeric problem.

TECHNICAL CONSIDERATIONS

Reliability. In traditional American terms, the teacher's manuals provided for the pretest topics do not provide much psychometric support for the types of decisions teachers might make based on the pretest results. However, the model is similar to curriculum-based assessment models more popular in the school psychology literature in the United States. In particular, the iterative testing and identification of errors are familiar intervention elements in such models. Use of models like this depend on the inferences drawn from results by teachers. The reliability ultimately rests on the capacity of the information to consistently recommend intervention strategies, and this is best accomplished in consideration of the student's academic history and interactions with the teacher. Clearly, these instruments are not designed to make these determinations in a vacuum.

Validity. Given the original problem of poor performance in some areas of mathematics, it remains to document that the content domain is related to the weakness, and that the test items are a representative sample of that domain. Note, criticality of the sample is less important than representative sampling here, because the results are intended to advise instructional intervention. The documentation provided about how the domain was defined and sampled is an important component of test validity, and the reader could benefit from greater detail concerning the numbers of experts involved and a little more precision about the nature of their reviews.

For the purposes of construct validity documentation, it would be helpful to demonstrate that use of the materials was related to improved performance on instruments related to the Percentage and integer measures on the International Association for the Evaluation of Educational Achievement instruments.

One important element of validity that might be overlooked is the test development strategy that began with four forms each of completion-type questions and resulted in a pre- and posttest form of multiple-choice questions in each topic. The derivation of distractors, based on an analysis of the common errors from field testing, would buttress the validity of the pretest for making curricular decisions.

CONCLUSION. The Mathematics Topic Pre-Tests are an interesting approach to instructional intervention. Although much more documentation of the development and psychometric properties of the instruments might help to support their utility for the American classroom, the instruments are consistent with curriculum-based assessment models already familiar to American educators.

Review of the Mathematics Topic Pre-Tests by MICHAEL KANE, Professor of Education, University of Wisconsin, Madison, WI:

The two Mathematics Topic Pre-Tests, one on Integers and one on Percentages, are admirable in the modesty of the claims made for them in the teacher's manuals. The tests were developed for use in remedial instruction on specific topics in the mathematics curriculum. The test on Integers is designed to help students identify their strengths and weaknesses over a set of 10 objectives on integers. The test of Percentages provides feedback on 7 objectives on percentages. Each test also provides the teacher with diagnostic information on individual students and on classes.

The tests are designed as tools to be used by teachers and students in guiding instructional decisions in limited and well-defined areas of the mathematics curriculum. The test questions are clearly related to the objectives and are of high quality. The teacher's manual is short, clear, low-key, and sensible. The materials should be easy to use, and the set of materials is flexible enough to be integrated with instruction in a variety of ways.

The tests are part of a fairly comprehensive set of instructional materials including a pretest, worksheets keyed to specific pretest results, and a posttest. The packet of materials includes a copy of the pretest and a self-diagnosing answer sheet, which directs students to certain worksheets based on their pattern of errors. The manual authors suggest that students who make few errors be given alternate work or extension work, and that students with idiosyncratic error patterns be taught individually or in small groups. Students who make the common errors identified by the self-diagnosing answer sheet are to work systematically, an objective at a time, through the worksheets. The teacher's manual suggests a detailed timetable for using the materials effectively.

No information is provided on norms, reliability, or validity, and given the intended uses of the tests, this is not surprising. The emphasis is on the use of the tests within instructional modules designed for the remediation of specific weaknesses in student mastery of the topics covered. The tests are not intended for high-stakes decisions and are not proposed for use outside of the context of remedial instruction.

Within this context, the materials seem to have been very carefully developed and very well thought through. Each objective is assessed by four or more items, and therefore the diagnostic information is likely to be dependable. Each worksheet provides brief explanations, examples, and practice items. All of the materials have been designed for ease of use by classroom teachers. The overall design of the modules does reflect a very traditional approach to mathematics instruction, involving a pretest, instruction, drill and practice, and a posttest, but there is likely to be a role for this kind of focused instruction on specific skills in even the most authentic curriculum.

[194]
MDS Vocational Interest Exploration System.

Purpose: "A computer-assisted interest exploration process that facilitates the discovery of personal preferences and job opportunities."
Population: High school–adults.
Publication Date: 1991.
Acronym: VIE.
Scores: 3 steps: Selection of Jobs Based on Work Preferences, Occupational Exploration, Job Review Comparison.
Administration: Individual.
Price Data, 1992: $350 per set including computer program (IBM/Compatibles, Macintosh, and Apple), 4 VIE job manuals, instructor's manual (135 pages), 25 VIE system guides with work preference questionnaires and job review forms.
Time: Administration time not reported.
Comments: Three supplementary forms are also provided with materials: Pre-Post Job Knowledge Form, Understanding of Self and Job Questionnaire, and Vocational Goal Planning Exercise.
Authors: Lawrence T. McCarron and Harriette P. Spires.
Publisher: McCarron-Dial Systems.

Review of the MDS Vocational Interest Exploration System by DOUGLAS J. McRAE, Educational Measurement Specialist, Monterey, CA:

PURPOSE. The MDS Vocational Interest Exploration System (VIE) is a computer-assisted interest exploration program designed to facilitate the discovery of personal preferences and job opportunities.

DESCRIPTION. The MDS VIE System consists of a short Work Preference Questionnaire (WPQ, 20 items), computer software that matches WPQ responses to 100 representative jobs, four extensive job manuals with information on each of the 100 representative jobs, and Job Review Forms that facilitate comparison of the user identified top three job choices. After completing the WPQ, the computer software suggests six jobs for further review, which the user narrows to three jobs for final comparison. Also included in the system are a Pre-Post Job Knowledge form, an Understanding of Self and Job Questionnaire, and a Vocational Planning Exercise form.

RATIONALE. The MDS VIE is based on the rationale that a focused systematic approach to vocational interest exploration will assist an individual in rational career decision making. The items in the WPQ were derived from analysis of entry level skills identified in the *Dictionary of Occupational Titles*. The 100 representative jobs were selected to be representative of entry level work. The MDS VIE was developed based on extensive field testing (3,600 individuals) with regular secondary education students, young adults ages 21–35, special education students ages 12–22, and vocational rehabilitation clients ages 22–35. Special attention was given during the development process to validate the system for individuals with a variety of handicapping conditions.

TECHNICAL INFORMATION. The MDS VIE does not contain a measurement component that might be labeled an aptitude instrument or an interest inventory. Closest to a measurement component is the Work Preferences Questionnaire, which results in matches to jobs rather than scores. The system has no empirical information to either support its rationale or justify its results. The only technical information available was a very modest reliability study based on pre-post information ($N = 80$) indicating a relative stability of individual work preferences over a short period of time.

EVALUATION. The MDS VIE appears to be a useful tool for secondary school students and young adults exploring the entry job market. It is based on organization of information and convenience in targeting users to the appropriate information, rather than a theoretical or empirical rationale. It does not contain a measurement component in the traditional sense. As such, its use should be limited to individual exploration. It should not be used for high stakes individual decisions or program evaluation.

Review of the MDS Vocational Interest Exploration System by MYRA N. WOMBLE, Assistant Professor of Occupational Studies, University of Georgia, Athens, GA:

DESCRIPTION OF THE SCALE. The Vocational Interest Exploration (VIE) System for Entry Level Employment is a three-step process intended to help users examine preferences about working conditions and requirements of entry level jobs. Step 1 involves completion of a Work Preference Questionnaire and computer-assisted selection of jobs based on identified work preferences. The second step is occupational exploration and Step 3 is job review comparison. It is also intended to improve the user's ability to make realistic vocational decisions and to serve as a tool for selection of appropriate vocational education or job training sites. A four-volume set of job manuals, intended as guided references, contain photographs and basic job information for 100 jobs organized into 20 occupational clusters. Job information such as duties, working conditions, abilities, training needs, job location, estimated earnings, and vocational outlook is included.

The authors consider the VIE System appropriate for use in secondary and rehabilitation settings, with regular education students, students with special needs, and by traditional rehabilitation services. The reading level for the VIE System is approximately grade 4, which seems better suited for use with diverse populations than inventories with reading levels from grades 6–9. According to the authors, persons with diverse disabilities relate well to the VIE System procedures, with assistance.

DEVELOPMENT. The jobs selected for inclusion in the four VIE job manuals used in Step 2 were considered representative of entry level work based on 1989 U.S. Department of Labor statistical data, which indicated that young workers are concentrated in relatively few occupations. The occupations included in the VIE System are representative of jobs held by almost half of 7.9 million employed youth ages 16–24. According to the authors, the 100 entry level jobs included in the VIE System were carefully selected from 20 occupational areas to include sufficient diversity and representation of entry level jobs. Each manual contains photographs to represent concrete referents and job information such as working conditions. However, no details about how this information was developed for the jobs selected is provided. There is also no description of how the Job Review Form, used in Step 3, was developed.

The items in the Work Preference Questionnaire used in Step 1 were selected to adequately sample working conditions based on an analysis of the 1977 *Dictionary of Occupational Titles (DOT)*. Edited and expanded job descriptions were compiled into a handbook, then used to identify work preferences considered representative of working conditions found in most entry level jobs. Specific criteria used to identify work preferences and details about procedures are not provided in the VIE instructor's manual.

The norm group was randomly selected from eight states (representing each region of the U.S.) and included 2,300 regular education students (ages 12–20), 300 average adults (ages 21–35), 600 special education students (ages 12–22), and 400 vocational rehabilitation clients with a wide range of disabilities (ages 22–35). Four ethnic groups, Mexican American (20%), African American (10%), Asian (2%), and American Indian (2%), and three socioeconomic backgrounds (e.g., low, middle, upper-middle) were represented. The regional distribution, type of student, age, and ethnic demographics suggest that the norming sample is a representative cross-section of the population for which the test is designed. However, no information is provided relative to distribution of gender.

ADMINISTRATION AND SCORING. The VIE System can be used independently or administered by a teacher or counselor. However, Steps 2 and 3 require considerable reading, study, and analysis, suggesting the need for some form of guided assistance. Some users may also need guidance with additional instructional materials (e.g., pre-post job knowledge form) intended to assist in the interest exploration process.

First, users select work preference statements using the computer or written forms. Preferences for working conditions are then correlated with jobs that include the conditions, resulting in a match listing from 6–10 entry level jobs. This first step generally takes less than 5 minutes, but longer periods of time may be necessary if assistance is needed. Next, users were expected to learn more about each of the jobs listed in the VIE computer report by referring to the appropriate job manual. Finally, users complete Job Review Forms to record and compare information about their top three job choices. Benefits of Steps 2–3 are limited without review and discussion of results with a qualified person to help clarify goals, expectations, and a course of action.

When completing Step 1 of the VIE System, individual and advisor modes are available, both of which are relatively simple to use. In individual user mode, clients use the computer to respond to the same state-ments contained in the Work Preference Questionnaire. The batch processing options in advisor mode allow the examiner to assist clients by entering and storing re-sponses from any number of clients, then generating their reports.

RELIABILITY. Consistency of individual's re-sponses to the work preference items used in Step 1 was evaluated over a 3- to 5-week interval. On pre- and posttesting, 93% of the individuals ($N = 80$) obtained the same job listing, which suggests relative stability of individual work preference responses. Statistical analysis of pre- and posttest scores showed no significant differ-ence. However, a description of the clients participating in the pre- and posttesting ($N- 80$) was not provided, but would have been informative. According to the authors, responses from middle school age students and emotion-ally distressed persons were often less consistent, but supporting data were not provided. Finally, no indepen-dent content validity studies were reported. Use of the *Dictionary of Occupational Titles* and U.S. Depart-ment of Labor statistical data is prudent, but without independent sources, validity is not established.

SUMMARY. The VIE System attempts to differ-entiate itself from traditional interest inventories by in-cluding a computer search that matches individual work preferences with specific jobs learned through work experience. Also, rapid change in the workplace due to evolving technologies suggests that many of the jobs profiled may be outdated because those selected were based on 1989 labor statistics. Considerable assistance of a qualified person is needed to guide users through Steps 2–3, yet no information is pro-vided regarding administrator expertise or training. The VIE System is not recommended as a strategy to improve the user's ability to make realistic vocational decisions nor to serve as a tool for selection of appropriate vocational education or job training sites. At best, users may consider the VIE System as a way to "explore" personal interests. Use of other interest inventories such as the Strong Interest Inventory (12:374), which are more well defined and supported by psychometric information, may be a better alternative.

[195]

Measure of Achieving Tendency.

Purpose: Developed to assess achievement motivation.
Population: Ages 15 and older.
Publication Dates: 1969–1993.
Acronym: MACH.
Scores: Total score only.
Administration: Group or individual.

Price Data, 1994: $28 per complete kit including scales, scoring directions, norms, manual ('94, 8 pages), and literature review.
Time: (10–15) minutes.
Comments: Current revision also based on previous edition entitled A Questionnaire Measure of Individual Differences in Achieving Tendency.
Author: Albert Mehrabian.
Publisher: Albert Mehrabian.
Cross References: For a review by Timothy S. Hartshorne of an earlier edition, see 10:301; for a review by Jayne E. Stake of an earlier edition, see 9:682; see also T3:1442 (1 reference).

TEST REFERENCES

1. Puffer, S. M. (1989). Task-completion schedules: Determinants and consequences for performance. *Human Relations, 42,* 937–955.

Review of the Measure of Achieving Tendency by JAMES T. AUSTIN, Research Specialist 2, Vocational Instructional Materials Lab, The Ohio State University, Columbus, OH:

Researchers studying achievement need within the dominant Murray-McClelland-Atkinson tradi-tion are aware of systematic differences between fantasy-projective (implicit) and questionnaire (self-attributed) methods of measuring the construct (McClelland, Koestner, & Weinberger, 1989; Spangler, 1991; Weiner, 1978). The revised Achiev-ing Tendency Scale (MACH; Mehrabian, 1994), a questionnaire, defines the construct being assessed as an individual difference. In other writings, the author identifies the Murray-McClelland-Atkinson stream of research as influential in his conception of achieving tendency and he presents a range of evi-dence for the measure from several life domains (Mehrabian, 1994–95). Missing is consideration of work by Heckhausen (Heckhausen, Schmalt, & Schneider, 1985) of other theoretical developments (e.g., Kuhl, 1978; Revelle & Michaels, 1976; Spence & Helmreich, 1983), or of other measures of achievement needs (e.g., Cassidy & Lynn, 1989; Tziner & Elizur, 1985). The importance of other theoretical work is to improve the conceptualization of the construct, whereas other measures of the construct can help provide conver-gent validity evidence. Consider that Fineman (1977) identified 22 measures of need achievement two decades ago, ranging from subscales of objective personality bat-teries to single construct measures.

The MACH scale consists of 36 agree-dis-agree items (-4 to 0 to +4), evenly balanced to reduce response bias. The current scale represents the continuing efforts of Mehrabian since he first pub-lished separate male and female forms (Mehrabian,

1968). Shortly after publishing those separate scales, Mehrabian (1969) presented a unified version, Mehrabian and Bank (1978) revised the scales and generated additional validity evidence. The current version is called the latest and best version. Among the uses suggested for the MACH scale are personnel selection and career planning. What support is provided for such applications?

Throughout this review, one guiding principle is that all validation is construct-related (Cronbach, 1989; Messick, 1995). What constructs influence scores? What theories can be brought to bear on the focal construct? What nomological network surrounds the construct (Cooper, 1983)? What inferences are warranted on the basis of test scores? What evidence is integrated by the test developer to instill confidence in test users or test takers (Clark & Watson, 1995)? As a preliminary step and to supplement the test developer/publisher's materials, a computer search was undertaken of both library and World Wide Web (WWW) databases. In addition, previous reviews of the measure were examined (Hartshorne, 1989; Stake, 1985).

The manual is a primary source of information about the evidence supporting score inferences. There is little information available to evaluate the quality of the evidence. First, as noted by Hartshorne (1989), the explanation of the scoring remains confusing and was not changed. Then, in the section on Norms there is no information about the sample(s) used to develop the z-score norms ($M = 50$, $SD = 34$). Moving to the brief section on reliability, a single unspecified internal consistency estimate for the current version (.92) is presented and compared with its corresponding estimate (.91) for the Mehrabian and Bank (1978) revision. Again, these two estimates are presented without any sample description. In the section on validity, which is extremely brief, a series of nine statement are made about differences between high MACH scorers and low MACH scorers on a variety of variables. These statements are linked to a recent review article by Mehrabian (1994–95), but no further detail is provided. In sum, the manual appears to be inadequate when evaluated against chapter 5 of the *Standards for educational and psychological testing* (American Educational Research Association, American Psychological Association, & National Council on Measurement in Education, 1985).

Reliability and validity evidence for the measure, in addition to their inadequate reporting, can be improved. For reliability, information over and above internal consistency estimates could be provided by retest estimates, some of which are available (for example, Weiner, 1978, noted that retest estimates in the range .70 to .80 have been obtained). Generalizability theory might provide additional information about sources of variance in scores, for example that associated with variation in situations. Lastly, the standard error of measurement of the scale is required information. In terms of validity, I believe that a start has been made on what Cronbach (1989) called the "weak" program of construct validation in that a net has been cast for supporting correlations. Additional evidence could be provided in at least two ways to complete the weak program. First, correlations with conceptually relevant criteria across achievement domains are required. A second type of evidence would be provided by examining convergent and discriminant validity in comparisons with other instruments. Further, although a shift to the strong program, defined as development of a rigorous theoretical framework and testing of hypotheses, would require substantial effort by the developer, it is both desirable and possible. Embedding the need achievement construct into a well-articulated theoretical framework is required. Candidates include Mehrabian's (1996) own Pleasure-Arousal-Dominance model of temperament or a more established framework, for example Eysenck's (1981) biologically based Psychoticism-Extroversion-Neuroticism model or control theory (Lord & Levy, 1994). One profitable avenue would involve formulating and testing hypotheses about social incentives and activity incentives (McClelland et al., 1989; Spangler, 1992).

SUMMARY. On the credit side, the developer has made an effort to deal with response bias and has stimulated a fairly large body of studies that have used the MACH. On the debit side, however, several of the flaws pointed out by Stake (1985) and by Hartshorne (1989) have not been corrected. These include the inadequacy of the manual and the incomplete elaboration of a conceptual frameowrk for the construct under assessment. Thus, other instruments, developed with faceted (Tziner & Elizur, 1985) or multifactorial (Cassidy & Lynn, 1989) frameworks, may provide better content converge of the need achievement construct domain. Especially troubling to this reviewer are the claims for inferences concerning personnel selection and career planning made by the developer without adequate evidence or caution.

REVIEWER'S REFERENCES

Mehrabian, A. (1968). Male and female scales of the tendency to achieve. *Educational and Psychological Measurement, 28,* 493–502.
Mehrabian, A. (1969). Measures of achieving tendency. *Educational and Psychological Measurement, 29,* 445–451.

Revelle, W., & Michaels, E. J. (1976). The theory of achievement motivation revisited: The implications of inertial tendencies. *Psychological Review, 83,* 394–404.

Fineman, S. (1977). The achievement motive construct and its measurement: Where are we now? *British Journal of Psychology, 68,* 1–22.

Kuhl, J. (1978). Standard setting and risk preference: An elaboration of the theory of achievement motivation and an empirical test. *Psychological Review, 85,* 239–248.

Mehrabian, A., & Bank, L. (1978). A questionnaire measure of individual differences in achieving tendency. *Educational and Psychological Measurement, 38,* 475–478.

Weiner, B. (1978). Achievement strivings. In H. London & J. Exner, Jr. (Eds.), *Dimensions of personality* (pp. 1–36). New York: Wiley.

Eysenck, H. J. (Ed.). (1981). *A model for personality.* New York: Springer.

Cooper, W. H. (1983). An achievement motivation nomological network. *Journal of Personality and Social Psychology, 44,* 841–861.

Spence, J. T., & Helmreich, R. L. (1983). Achievement related motives and behaviors. In J. T. Spence (Ed.), *Achievement and achievement motives: Psychological and sociological approaches* (pp. 7–74). San Francisco, CA: Freeman.

American Educational Research Association, American Psychological Association, & National Council on Measurement in Education. (1985). *Standards for educational and psychological testing.* Washington, DC: American psychological Association, Inc.

Heckhausen, H., Schmalt, H. D., & Schneider, K. (1985). *Achievement motivation in perspective.* New York: Academic Press.

Stake, J. E. (1985). [Review of Measures of Achieving Tendency]. In J. V. Mitchell, Jr. (Ed.), *The ninth mental measurements yearbook* (pp. 943–944). Lincoln, NE: Buros Institute of Mental Measurements.

Tziner, A., & Elizur, D. (1985). Achievement motive: A reconceptualization and new instrument. *Journal of Occupational Behaviour, 6,* 209–228.

Cassidy, T., & Lynn, R. (1989). A multifactorial approach to achievement motivation: The development of a comprehensive measure. *Journal of Occupational Psychology, 62,* 301–312.

Cronbach, L. J. (1989). Construct validation after thirty years. In R. L. Linn (Ed.), *Intelligence: Measurement, theory, and public policy* (pp. 147–171). Urbana: University of Illinois Press.

Hartshorne, T. S. (1989). [Review of A Questionnaire Measure of Individual Differences in Achieving Tendency]. In J. C. Conoley & J. J. Kramer (Eds.), *The tenth mental measurements yearbook* (pp. 673–674). Lincoln, NE: Buros Institute of Mental Measurements.

McClelland, D. C., Koestner, R., & Weinberger, J. (1989). How do self-attributed and implicit motives differ? *Psychological Review, 96,* 690–702.

Spangler, W. D. (1992). Validity of questionnaire and TAT measures of need for achievement: Two meta-analyses. *Psychological Bulletin, 112,* 140–154.

Lord, R. G., & Levy, P. E. (1994). Moving from cognition to action: A control theory perspective. *Applied Psychology: An International Review, 43,* 335–398.

Mehrabian, A. (1994). *Manual for the revised Achieving Tendency Scale.* (Available from Albert Mehrabian, 1130 Alta Mesa Road, Monterey, CA 93940).

Mehrabian, A. (1994–95). Individual differences in achieving tendency: Review of evidence bearing on a questionnaire measure. *Current Psychology: Developmental, Learning, Personality, Social, 13,* 351–364.

Clark, L. A., & Watson, D. (1995). Constructing validity: Basic issues in objective scale development. *Psychological Assessment, 7,* 309–319.

Messick, S. (1995). Validity of psychological assessment: Validation of inferences from persons' responses and performances as scientific inquiry into score meaning. *American Psychologist, 50,* 741–749.

Mehrabian, A. (1996). Pleasure-arousal-dominance: A general framework for describing and measuring individual differences in temperament. *Current Psychology: Developmental, Learning, Personality, Social, 14,* 261–292.

Review of the Measure of Achieving Tendency by E. SCOTT HUEBNER, Professor of Psychology, University of South Carolina, Columbia, SC:

The current version of the Mehrabian Measure of Achieving Tendency Scale (MACH) is a 36-item self-report measure of achievement motivation. The MACH is the most recent revision of a scale described originally in Mehrabian and Bank (1978). The MACH is accompanied by a brief, four-page manual that provides a definition of the achieving tendency, scoring procedures for the MACH, and some limited technical information (norms, reliability, and validity). Additional information related to a previous 38-item version of the scale is available in Mehrabian (1995), although there is no information provided on the comparability of the two versions.

The 1993 MACH manual states that the current scale is the "best version of the measures originally reported" (p. 2). However, no information is provided as to how this version is superior to previous ones. Information is also lacking with respect to the nature of the changes and the rationale for the changes.

The scoring procedures for the 36-item MACH indicate that responses to the items are aggregated to yield a single overall achievement motivation score. In contrast to such a unidimensional framework, however, Mehrabian (1995) suggests that an earlier 184-item version revealed a multidimensional structure comprising 22 "factors," all of which are also reportedly represented on the 38-item version. Because neither the MACH manual nor Mehrabian (1995) include the results of any factor analytic procedures (e.g., factor loadings, eigenvalues, factor intercorrelations), the meaning of the MACH score is thus difficult to interpret.

The MACH manual provides no information regarding the standardization sample beyond the provision of a mean and standard deviation, presumably applicable to adults of all ages. No information is provided regarding sample size(s) or demographics (e.g., socioeconomic status, gender, ethnicity).

For scoring procedures, the author recommends the calculation of z-scores, followed by conversion to percentile ranks. The latter scores must be obtained from standard statistical tables elsewhere.

Item analysis data are not reported in the manual or the Mehrabian (1995) article. Information regarding test and/or item bias is also not presented.

Internal consistency reliability for the current version is described as .92, which is quite acceptable. Nevertheless, the procedure used to compute the coefficient is not indicated. The author states that the current reliability estimate is similar to the estimate obtained for a previous version, but it should be noted that the previous estimate was based upon a K-R 20 procedure rather than the appropriate coefficient alpha. No test-retest data are provided.

Validity data are somewhat promising, but sketchy. Based on previous versions of the scale, Mehrabian (1995) reviews a number of studies that have investigated the correlates of MACH scores. For example, the MACH has been shown to correlate in predictable ways with general trait anxiety, fear of failure, goal commitment and effort, internal locus of control, and various performance measures (e.g., GPA, clerical tasks). The MACH reportedly discriminates business owners and managers from secretaries. Age differences have also been found, with lower scores for elderly individuals. A correlation of .65 was reported between the MACH and Jackson Achievement Scale. Despite the promising nature of many of the studies, important details (e.g., description of the samples, correlation coefficients) of some of the studies are omitted in Mehrabian's summary, requiring users of the MACH to refer not only to the manual and the article but also presumably to the original articles to evaluate the validity of the scale. Thus, although the validity data offer promise for the further development of the instrument, further data (including the aforementioned factor analytic findings) should be provided.

In summary, information related to the test development, norms, reliability, and validity of the current version of the MACH is sparse. Thus, the MACH cannot be used with confidence for research or clinical purposes at the present time.

REVIEWER'S REFERENCES

Mehrabian, A., & Bank, L. (1978). A questionnaire measure of individual differences in achieving tendency. *Educational and Psychological Measurement, 38*, 475–478.

Mehrabian, A. (1995). Individual differences in achieving tendency: Review of evidence bearing on a questionnaire measure. *Current Psychology, 13*(4), 351–364.

[196]
Measures of Affiliative Tendency and Sensitivity to Rejection.

Population: Ages 15 and older.
Publication Dates: 1976–1994.
Administration: Group or individual.
Price Data, 1994: $28 per complete kit including scales, scoring directions, norms, manual ('94, 13 pages), and literature review.
Time: (10–15) minutes.
Author: Albert Mehrabian.
Publisher: Albert Mehrabian.

a) AFFILIATIVE TENDENCY.
Purpose: "Designed to measure friendliness, sociability, and social skills conducive to positive and comfortable social exchanges."
Score: Total score only.

b) SENSITIVITY TO REJECTION.
Purpose: "Designed to assess social submissiveness."
Scores: Total score only.

Cross References: For a review by Peter D. Lifton of an earlier edition, see 9:683; see also T3:1443 (1 reference).

Review of the Measures of Affiliative Tendency and Sensitivity to Rejection by SHEILA MEHTA, Assistant Professor of Psychology, Auburn University at Montgomery, Montgomery, AL:

Mehrabian designed two complementary scales to assess two related personality traits: Affiliative Tendency is defined in terms of "generalized positive expectations in social relationships," and Sensitivity to Rejection is defined in terms of "generalized negative social expectations" (Mehrabian, 1994, p. 98). The Measure of Affiliative Tendency (MAFF) and the Measures of Sensitivity to Rejection (MSR) "were designed to be independent of each other and to exhibit theoretically different (not simply inverse) patterns of relations with affiliation, conformity, and dependency behaviors" (Mehrabian, 1994, p. 98). Mehrabian and Ksionzky (1970) proposed mathematical models of how related behaviors are functions of the two traits, and more recently Mehrabian (1997) showed how these two traits are mathematically related to a network of affiliative-related traits and temperaments. Information concerning the psychometric properties of these two measures was obtained from the two manuals that accompany the measures and from the Mehrabian (1994) paper.

The scales are brief paper-and-pencil self-report measures that can be administered to groups or individuals. The MAFF has 26 items and the MSR has 24; for both scales, the test taker responds using a 9-point Likert scale, indicating degree of agreement or disagreement with each statement. The statements are balanced for response bias: Half the items are worded positively and the other half negatively. Scoring is accomplished by algebraically summing responses to the positively worded items and subtracting from this quantity the algebraic sum of the responses to the negative items. Means, standard deviations, instructions on how to compute z-scores, percentile scores, and verbal interpretations of the scores are provided in the manuals.

NORMS, RELIABILITY AND VALIDITY. The norms for both measures were based on data from 916 university students in the mid 70s. The composition of the sample, however, is not described. No information about the gender and ethnic composition or socioeconomic status is included.

Internal consistency for the MAFF, as assessed by the Kuder-Richardson-20 coefficient, is .80 and for the MSR is .83. The measures appear to be stable over time as indicated by test-retest (4-week interval) of .89 for the MAFF and .92 for the MSR. These data, together with information about a shortened version of the measures, indicate that the instruments are reliable.

The test manuals provide the bare essentials regarding the validity of the instruments, whereas an abundance of information is available in the Mehrabian (1994; 1997) papers. In terms of content validity, however, there is no mention of item selection or development. In regard to construct validity, at minimum one must identify properties of the construct and rudimentary elements of the empirical relationships into which the construct should and should not enter. Mehrabian does furnish a rationale for the constructs. He also outlines hypotheses linking the constructs to a variety of related behaviors. Furthermore, he supplies minimum evidence for discriminant validity and a plenty of evidence for convergent validity. In terms of discriminant validity, both scales correlate low with social desirability and extremely low with each other, indicating that their social desirability bias is satisfactorily low and that the two measures deal with different, not simply opposing, facets of interpersonal orientation and behavior. Regarding convergent validity, Mehrabian provides an abundance of studies demonstrating a relationship between either the MAFF or the MSR and other paper-and-pencil measures of constructs that would be expected to correlate with these interpersonal orientations. For example, the MAFF had a moderate negative correlation with a measure of social anhedonia (Leak, 1991) and a moderate positive relationship with a scale of liking people (Filsinger, 1981). Besides this type of evidence of the instruments' convergent validity, several laboratory and field studies provide further evidence. One study (Miller, Rossbach, & Munson, 1981) demonstrates cross-situational differences with the MAFF. Moreover, another provides evidence that the MAFF and MSR correlate in the expected directions with behavioral measures of affiliative behavior and social sensitivity, such as breadth and depth of self-disclosure with a stranger (Ksionzky & Mehrabian, 1980).

This last study provides an essential bit of evidence, in that it is the only piece fitting into the multimethod portion of Campbell and Fiske's (1959) multimethod-multitrait matrix. All the other evidence fully satisfies the multitrait portion of the matrix. The case proving construct validity of the MAFF and the MSR would be even stronger if there were more data about method variance.

Lifton's (1985) earlier review of the MAFF and the MSR mentions several problems, most of which have been solved by the presence of the test manuals. One drawback remains, however: Because the instruments' norms were university students, their utility beyond this population is questionable. A word about the manuals is in order: They are useful and

concise and greatly aid in scoring and interpretation of the scales' scores. They are, perhaps, too terse in that a user interested in details about the validity of the instruments would be disappointed. Also there are a few minor omissions in the MAFF manual that appear in the MSR manual, such as the age of the suitable population and the delay interval of the test-retest reliability coefficient. In conclusion, the MAFF and the MSR are of proven reliability and validity, making them useful instruments in the study of personality.

REVIEWER'S REFERENCES

Campbell, D., & Fiske, D. (1959). Convergent and discriminant validation by the multitrait-multimethod matrix. *Psychological Bulletin, 56*, 81–105.

Mehrabian, A., & Ksionzky, S. (1970). Models for affiliative and conformity behavior. *Psychological Bulletin, 74*, 110–126.

Ksionzky, S., & Mehrabian, A. (1980). Personality correlates of self-disclosure. *Social Behavior and Personality, 8*, 145–152.

Filsinger, E. E. (1981). A measure of interpersonal orientation: The liking people scale. *Journal of Personality Assessment, 45*, 295–300.

Miller, S., Rossbach, J., & Munson, R. (1981). Social density and affiliative tendency as determinants of dormitory residential outcomes. *Journal of Applied Social Psychology, 11*, 356–365.

Lifton, P. D. (1985). [Review of Measures of Affiliative Tendency and Sensitivity to Rejection.] In J. V. Mitchell, Jr., (Ed.), *The ninth mental measurements yearbook* (pp. 944–945). Lincoln, NE: Buros Institute of Mental Measurements.

Leak, G. K. (1991). An examination of the construct validity of the Social Anhedonia Scale. *Journal of Personality Assessment, 56*, 84–95.

Mehrabian, A. (1994). Evidence bearing on the Affiliative Tendency (MAFF) and Sensitivity to Rejection (MSR) scales. *Current Psychology: Developmental, Learning, Personality, Social, 13*, 97–116.

Mehrabian, A. (1997). Analysis of affiliation-related traits in terms of the PAD Temperament Model. *Journal of Psychology, 131*, 101–117.

Review of the Measures of Affiliative Tendency and Sensitivity to Rejection by SCOTT T. MEIER, Associate Professor and Director of Training, Department of Counseling and Educational Psychology, SUNY Buffalo, Buffalo, NY:

The Measures of Affiliative Tendency and Sensitivity to Rejection scales are self-report questionnaires designed by Mehrabian (1970, 1976, 1994a, 1994b) to measure traits related to social skills. The 26-item Affiliative Tendency Scale (MAFF) contains 13 positively worded and 13 negatively worded items; a similar division occurs with the 24-item Sensitivity to Rejection Scale (MSR). Mehrabian (1994a) described affiliative persons as "friendly, sociable, helpful, skillful in dealing with people" (p. 1), whereas sensitive individuals "generally feel that they lack control or influence in their social interactions" (Mehrabian, 1994b, p. 1).

Many of Lifton's (1985; 9:683) previous descriptions and criticisms of these scales still apply. Mehrabian has built a theory of affiliative behavior based on a temperament model with three dimensions of pleasure-displeasure, trait arousability, and trait dominance-submission. Because these rationally constructed scales relate to this theory, test users interested in other theoretical approaches may find the scales of limited use. Basic evidence exists for the reliability (e.g., .83 *alpha* for

MAFF, .92 4-week test-retest for MSR and validity [e.g., correlations with measures and behaviors of extroversion, conformity, social interests]) of both scales.

Although Lifton noted that no manual for the scales was available at the time of his review, Mehrabian (1994a, 1994b) has now constructed two brief manuals. They describe the measured trait, list the positively and negatively scored items, provide norms in the way of a single mean and standard deviation, list several reliability and validity estimates and references, and append the scales themselves. Mehrabian indicates that both scales require about 10 minutes to complete and that the MSR can be used with persons ages 15 and older; no age requirement is described for the MAFF. Little or no information is provided, for example, about appropriate test purposes, required reading level, or characteristics of the normative sample. Because the theory on which the items are based says little about how these constructs might change during development or in response to an intervention (cf. Meier, 1994), testing purposes would seem to be restricted to personality research and possibly selection testing.

A recent publication (Mehrabian, 1994c) provides a more adequate theoretical and empirical summary of relevant data. Here Mehrabian describes the normative sample as 916 university students. Discriminant validity is supported by a correlation of .09 between the MAFF and MSR, but the MSR is weakened by correlations in absolute value near .20 with a social desirability measure. Mehrabian summarizes theoretical work with the MAFF by suggesting that positive interpersonal expectations form a key component. Similarly, the MSR appears highly related to social submissiveness.

Personality researchers have employed the MAFF and MSR in a steady program of basic research around social temperament constructs. These scales should be considered experimental in nature and should continue to be useful in basic research (e.g., Yamaguchi, Kuhlman, & Sugimori, 1995). Mehrabian (1994c) suggested that the scales can be employed to identify overlapping measures, compare findings from different social skills domains, and further refine theory. With greater attention to developing norms, both the MAFF and MSR have potential application for selection decisions related to social skills in schools and work settings. Whether the scales' theoretical refinement can improve predictive validity compared to other measures (e.g., of vocational interests, such as the Self-Directed Search [281] or Strong Interest Inventory [12:374]) remains to be seen. In their current forms, these trait-based scales would appear to have little to offer to test users

interested in studying longitudinal development or change resulting from psychosocial interventions.

REVIEWER'S REFERENCES
Mehrabian, A. (1970). The development and validation of measures of affiliative tendency and sensitivity to rejection. *Educational and Psychological Measurement, 30,* 417–428.
Mehrabian, A. (1976). Questionnaire measures of affiliative tendency and sensitivity to rejection. *Psychological Reports, 38,* 199–209.
Lifton, P. (1985). [Review of Measures of Affiliative Tendency and Sensitivity to Rejection.] In J. V. Mitchell, Jr., (Ed.), *The ninth mental measurements yearbook* (pp. 944–945). Lincoln, NE: Buros Institute of Mental Measurements.
Mehrabian, A. (1994a). *Manual for the Affiliative Tendency Scale.* Monterey, CA: Author.
Mehrabian, A. (1994b). *Manual for the Sensitivity to Rejection Scale.* Monterey, CA: Author.
Mehrabian, A. (1994c). Evidence bearing on the Affiliative Tendency (MAFF) and Sensitivity to Rejection (MSR) scales. *Current Psychology, 13,* 97–117.
Meier, S. T. (1994). *The chronic crisis in psychological measurement and assessment: A historical survey.* New York: Academic Press.
Yamaguchi, S., Kuhlman, D. M., & Sugimori, S. (1995). Personality correlates of allocentric tendencies in individualist and collectivist cultures. Special Section: Culture and self. *Journal of Cross Cultural Psychology, 26,* 658–672.

[197]
MecTest (A Test for Maintenance Mechanics).

Purpose: "Developed to measure the mechanical knowledge and skills required for maintenance jobs."

Population: Applicants and incumbents for maintenance jobs.

Publication Dates: 1991–1993.

Scores, 10: Hydraulics and Pneumatics, Print Reading, Welding and Rigging, Power Transmission, Lubrication, Pumps and Piping, Mechanical Maintenance, Machines/Tools/Equipment, Safety, Total.

Administration: Group.

Price Data, 1993: $10 each per 20–99 self-scoring booklets (20 minimum order).

Time: (60) minutes.

Comments: Self-scored instrument.

Author: Roland T. Ramsay.

Publisher: Ramsay Corporation.

Review of the MecTest (A Test for Maintenance Mechanics) by ROBERT J. DRUMMOND, Professor of Education and Human Services, University of North Florida, Jacksonville, FL:

The MecTest (A Test for Maintenance Mechanics) (MEC) consists of 60 multiple-choice questions covering 11 areas including Hydraulics (10), Pneumatics (5), Welding (3), Power Transmission (5), Lubrication (4), Pumps (4), Piping (3), Rigging (4), Mechanical Maintenance (9), Shop Machines Tools and Equipment (9), and Print Reading (4). The manual provides directions for administering and scoring the MEC. The test can be self-scored. The answer sheet can be torn apart and the correct response counted. No time limit is mandated but the author indicates most test takers complete the MEC within an hour.

Reliability data are presented for a group of over 200 maintenance employees in a processing plant. The type of coefficient was not identified by the coefficient was reported to be .89. The *SEM* was 3.24. Item difficulty and item discrimination data are presented. The author claims the MEC has content validity and a review of the items would indicate it appears to have face validity. Missing, however, is how the KSAs (knowledge and skill areas) were identified. Were subject matter experts (*SME*s) utilized in the process? How were the number of items selected? Are the items based on a review of job descriptions of individuals hired as maintenance mechanics? Evidence for criterion-referenced validity is provided through correlations of test scores with supervisory ratings. Norms are provided in the test manual in the form of percentile ranks and are based on a sample of 201 maintenance mechanics. Only the total score is utilized. There is no profile or norms developed to help interpret the subscores.

SUMMARY. Preliminary data presented in the MecTest manual indicate that it shows promise for providing valid and reliable scores of the knowledge and skills required by maintenance mechanics. It would help if additional data on other samples were presented and cross-validation evidence presented in the manual. More discussion needs to focus on how the knowledge and skill areas were chosen. The MEC may provide a quick screen of candidates for such a position but performance assessment might get at some of the skills better than a pencil-and-paper examination. The self-scoring answer sheet makes it user friendly and easy to score. The author, however, needs to add a section in the manual on the interpretation of the MEC scores and include several case studies to demonstrate how the test results could or should be interpreted.

[198]
Mentoring Style Indicator.

Purpose: Identify particular mentoring styles and the match between mentor and protégé style preferences.
Publication Dates: 1987–1993.
Acronym: MSI.
Administration: Group.
Price Data, 1993: $20 per manual ('93, 15 pages).
Time: (45–75) minutes.
Authors: William A. Gray, Terry D. Anderson, and Marilynne Miles Gray.
Publisher: The Mentoring Institute, Inc. [Canada].
   a) MSI FOR MENTORING YOUTH.
   Population: Mentors of youth and protégés.
   Scores, 5: Prescriptive Mentoring, Persuasive Mentoring, Collaborative Mentoring, Confirmative Mentoring, Mentoring Style.
   Price Data: $4 per test booklet.

b) MSI FOR BUSINESS AND GOVERNMENT—VERSION FOR NEW HIRES.
Population: Mentors of new hires and protégés (new hires).
Scores, 5: Informational Mentoring, Guiding Mentoring, Collaborative Mentoring, Confirming Mentoring, Mentoring Style.
Price Data: $8 per test booklet.
c) MSI FOR BUSINESS AND GOVERNMENT—VERSION FOR CAREER DEVELOPMENT.
Population: Mentors of employees and protégés.
Scores: Same as for *b* above.
Price Data: $8 per test booklet.
d) MSI FOR MENTORING NEW TEACHERS.
Population: Mentors of new teachers and protégés.
Scores: Same as for *b* above.
Price Data: $4 per test booklet.
e) MSI FOR MENTORING COLLEGE STUDENTS.
Population: Mentors of college students and protégés.
Scores: Same as for *b* above.
Price Data: $4 per test booklet.
f) MSI FOR EDUCATIONAL ADMINISTRATORS.
Population: Educational administrators and protégés.
Scores: Same as for *a* above.
Price Data: $4 per test booklet.

Review of the Mentoring Style Indicator by RAOUL A. ARREOLA, Professor and Director of Educational Evaluation and Development, The University of Tennessee, Memphis, TN:

INTRODUCTION. The Mentoring Style Indicator (MSI) consists of a Leader's Guide and a set of six instruments designed to identify current preferences for different mentoring styles of both a mentor and the protégé being mentored. Designed by William A. Gray, the MSI is based on Gray's Mentor-Protégé Relationship Model, and, as noted in the supporting material accompanying the MSI, "was not developed to be a psychometric instrument which measures a stable human characteristic in a consistent or reliable way with repeated administrations (like the MBTI or MMPI)" (personal communication, letter from William Gray to Buros Institute, September 28, 1993).

The MSI defines four mentoring styles:

Informational: Reflects the one-way transmission of various types of information from the mentor to the protégé, without much interaction occurring between them.

Guiding: Reflects the mentor's greater influence while interacting with the protégé in various ways.

Collaborative: Reflects the joint input and responsibility of the mentor and protégé while interacting.

Confirming: Reflects the protégé's more active participation and responsibility, and the various ways the mentor can support the protégé.

The MSI model is reminiscent of Stuart Atkins' LIFO (Life Orientations) model (Atkins, 1985). Where the MSI identifies four mentoring styles, the LIFO identifies four life orientation styles (Supporting Giving, Conserving Holding, Adapting Dealing, and Controlling Taking). The MSI Informational style has similarities to the LIFO Controlling Taking style; the MSI Guiding Style to the LIFO Conserving Holding; the MSI Collaborative Style to the LIFO Adapting Dealing Style; and the MSI Confirming Style to the LIFO Supporting Giving Style. Although not identical in nature or intent, much in the Stuart Atkins well-documented LIFO model can serve to further illuminate the MSI.

The MSI instruments are not intended to be used in isolation to "brand" an individual with a specific mentoring style score but, rather, are intended to be used as part of a training program to prepare both mentors and protégés to participate in a successful mentoring relationship leading to a fully functional autonomous worker. The four styles of the MSI are seen as developmental and essentially sequential in nature with successful Informational Mentoring leading to Guiding Mentoring, then to Collaborative Mentoring, to Confirming Mentoring, and finally resulting in a Successful Protégé able to function autonomously and independently. Ideally, the Successful Protégé in this model is then able to serve as a mentor for the next generation.

ADMINISTRATION. The MSI is intended to be used in groups led by a trainer following the steps provided in the Leader's Guide. Detailed information in the Leader's Guide enables the trainer to administer the instruments, guide the scoring and interpretation of scores, and includes suggestions for matching mentors to protégés. Additional information is provided on training mentors and their protégés separately. Also provided is a strategy for evaluating mentor and protégé growth after training by using a post-test 6 to 9 months after the training has occurred.

The MSI contains six separate instruments, consisting of scenarios or "situations." Each instrument presents various "situations" to which the respondent must rank order four different responses with the first (number 1) being their most preferred response and their last (number 4) being their least preferred response. The test booklets are self-scoring and all but two are printed on NCR paper. However, the four MSI styles are not identified or explained until after the form is completed and scoring is under way.

Each MSI instrument is designed for use with a different group of individuals and is intended for use by either mentors or protégés. One instrument is designed for Mentoring College Students, one for Mentoring Youth, one for Mentoring Educational Administrators, one for Mentoring New Teachers, and two for mentoring individuals in Business and Government who are either (a) New Hires, or (b) existing Business and Government individuals interested in Career Development. Several of the instruments have unfortunate misspellings that detract from their professional nature. For example, in the Mentoring New Teachers instrument one of the case studies refers to a "magnate" school when what is clearly intended is "magnet" school.

The instrument for Mentoring College Students consists of six situations revolving around the new college student; the Mentoring New Teachers consists of six situations revolving around problem situations in which new teachers may find themselves if teaching in a high school setting; the Business and Government instrument for New Hires consists of six situations revolving around the individual facing new job responsibilities and duties; and the Business and Government instrument for Career Development consists of six situations revolving around mid-career decision-points. The instruments for Educational Administrators and Mentoring Youth are constructed somewhat differently and are not printed on NCR paper for ease of self-scoring. The Educational Administrators instrument consists of eight situations revolving primarily around principals and supervisors of public schools; and the Mentoring Youth instrument consists of eight situations revolving around middle or high school students. Each of the instruments results in four scores indicative of the respondent's preferences as related to the four MSI styles.

SCORING AND INTERPRETATION. Each of the six MSI instruments results in four preference scores: one representing the respondent's preference for Informational Mentoring, one for Guiding Mentoring, one for Collaborative Mentoring, and one for Confirming Mentoring. These scores are derived from the rank order numbers given to each of the four possible response statements to each situation. The total of these four scores should be 60 for those instruments with six situations and 80 for those with eight situations. Each booklet provides an interpretation table that enables the respondent to determine whether their score represents a Weak Preference, a Moderate Preference, or a Strong Preference for any given mentoring style.

The preferences of the mentor and the preferences of the protégé are intended to serve as a guide to match mentors with protégés and/or for training either the mentor or the protégé to develop flexibility in shifting from an inappropriate preference to an appropriate one depending upon the situation.

No technical information is provided on the instruments. No indication of validity or reliability studies or estimates is offered. Reference is made, however, to Gray's Mentor-Protégé Relationship Model and Anderson's Style Shift Counseling Theory as the basis for the Mentoring Style Indicator (MSI) and its six instruments. No data concerning how the table for interpreting whether a score indicates a weak, moderate, or strong preference appears in either the Leader's Guide or the other supporting material. However, references to a number of articles by the MSI author, William A. Gray, are listed although none of them deal specifically with the development and validation of the MSI.

In summary, the Mentoring Style Indicator appears to be an instrument designed primarily to be part of a training program for developing successful mentor-protégé relationships in business, government, public secondary school, and social community settings. The relative shortness of each instrument (six or eight items) and the lack of definitive evidence concerning their validity and reliability, would appear to make them of limited use. The materials provided with the MSI contain advertisements for The Mentoring Institute (TMI) and its mentoring training services. Given the listed corporate and noncorporate clients of TMI, it would seem that the MSI when used as part of a professionally designed mentor training program can be quite useful in assisting in the development of successful mentor-protégé relationships.

REVIEWER'S REFERENCE

Atkins, S. (1985). *The name of your game.* Beverly Hills, CA: Ellis & Stewart Publishers.

Review of the Mentoring Style Indicator by *RUSSELL N. CARNEY, Associate Professor of Psychology, Southwest Missouri State University, Springfield, MO:*

The Mentoring Style Indicator (MSI) is an instrument designed to help identify one's preferred mentoring style, such as Informational, Guiding, Collaborative, Confirming, or a combination of these. Respectively, the four specific styles represent a gradual decrease in the mentor's role, and increasing independence on the part of the protégé. The MSI consists of a Leader's Guide for Using the MSI and 10 different versions of the instrument targeted toward different audiences: Business and Government (new hires, 5th ed.), Business and Government (for career development, 6th ed.), Sales Training and Development (3rd ed.), Entrepreneurs (2nd ed.), Health Care Professionals (1st ed.), New Teachers (3rd ed.), College Students (4th ed.), School Administrators (3rd ed.), Youth (3rd ed.), and a new Generic Version (1st ed.) (W. A. Gray, personal communication, February 25, 1997).

ADMINISTRATION. In the current editions of the MSI, Step 1 presents six situations by way of an NCR paper booklet (this prevents the examinee from looking ahead to see what the instrument is measuring). Each situation describes a relevant mentor/protégé scenario. In the MSI for Mentoring College Students, for example, a student might be described as a freshman having difficulty with core science courses (the actual scenario is several sentences in length). Beneath the described situation, four potential mentoring responses (reflecting preferred styles) are listed—ranging from directly telling the student what they should do (i.e., Informational), to listening and encouraging the student (i.e., Confirming). Whether mentor or protégé, the examinee is asked to rate the four responses from 1 to 4, with 4 being the *most* preferred style, and 1 being the *least* preferred style, for that particular situation.

SCORING AND INTERPRETATION. When the examinee has finished rating the four responses for each of the six situations, he or she is directed to pull the NCR paper apart to reveal a copy of his or her responses and scoring instructions inside. Here, Step 2 directs examinees to first read a section dealing with the importance of mentoring style. For example, the examinee is told that effective mentors and successful protégés are able to "style shift" based on the needs of the situation. In contrast, ineffective mentors and unsuccessful protégés tend to "get stuck" (p. 8), inflexibly using one style (e.g., a mentor might routinely tell the student what to do). The various styles described are based on Gray's Mentor-Protégé Relationship Model (M -> Mp -> MP -> mP -> P). This concise model effectively characterizes the mentor/protégé style as ranging from Informational (M), to Guiding (Mp), to Collaborating (MP), to Confirming (mP), to the successful, independent protégé (P). As can be seen, a capital letter indicates that the mentor (M) or protégé (P) is playing the more directive role in the relationship, whereas a small letter (m or p) indicates a weaker role.

In Step 3 the examinee is directed to add his or her total ratings for each of the four preferred styles across the six situations. Given the parameters established by the 4-point scale, the lowest potential score for any style is 6 (i.e., all 1s), and the highest potential score is 24 (i.e., all 4s). A score ranging from 6 to 11 is described as a "Weak Preference," from 12 to 18 as a "Moderate Preference," and from 19 to 24 as a "Strong Preference." No technical rationale for these cutoffs is provided. One's "Preferred Mentoring Style" is defined as "that style of help and relationship a mentor prefers to provide— or a protégé prefers to receive" (p. 2). Three categories of mentoring style are then identified: Single Dominant Style (i.e., a *single* score in the Strong Preference range), Mixed Mentoring Style (i.e., two or three scores in the Strong Preference range), and Balanced Mentoring Style (i.e., where all four scores fall within the Moderate Preference range). In Step 4, the examinee is directed to read a section describing his or her particular preferred mentoring style. Following this, Step 5 asks individuals to "Develop a Plan for Increasing Your Mentoring Style Versatility," and provides an outline and space for this plan on the final page of the test booklet. Facilitating the development of such versatility, described as the ability to style shift as necessary, is a major goal of the MSI. After mentors and protégés have practiced style shifting for several months, the MSI can be re-administered—the expectation being that a more balanced style will have emerged for both mentor and protégé.

The MSI materials I reviewed were accompanied by a helpful letter from William A. Gray, Ph.D., co-author of the MSI, as well as several pieces of literature regarding the services provided by TMI—The Mentoring Institute, Inc. This information was updated by way of a phone call to Dr. Gray (personal communication, February 25, 1997). The MSI is a *fundamental component* of the institute's training program, as opposed to a stand-alone instrument. The MSI is usually completed prior to clients' participation in the mentoring training provided by TMI. Having identified the preferred styles of mentors and protégés, the development of more balanced styles (through style shifting) is then encouraged through several training activities.

VALIDITY. The MSI has developed over the years based on the authors' experience in conducting mentoring training with a variety of clients. The various versions of the MSI are updated as needed to keep the hypothetical situations current (e.g., one of the instruments is now in its 6th edition). Hence, it would appear that content validity has been built in as a result of the authors' direct experience in working with clients in these various areas. As described earlier, the MSI is theoretically based on Gray's Mentor-Protégé Relationship Model, which resulted from the first author's research. Although technical psychometric information regarding construct validity is not provided, the model certainly appears to identify various mentor-protégé relationship patterns.

RELIABILITY. In terms of reliability, Dr. Gray stated that the MSI "was not developed as a psychometric instrument which measures a stable human characteristic in a consistent or reliable way with repeated administrations" (personal communication, William Gray to Buros Institute, September 28, 1993, p. 1). Once examinees have worked their way through the entire MSI test booklet (which eventually labels and explains what is being measured), they would likely be affected by their new knowledge about mentoring styles if they were to retake the MSI. Further, having gone through the TMI training program, one would expect participants to exhibit more balanced mentoring styles and hence choose somewhat *different* responses on a second administration of the MSI. I believe, however, that one's "preferred style" of mentoring is viewed as a rather stable construct; otherwise, why would individuals get "stuck" in using a specific style? Hence, it would seem possible and appropriate to assess stability over time. As stated in the *Standards for Educational and Psychological Testing,* the test developer has "primary responsibility for obtaining and reporting evidence concerning reliability" (AERA, APA, & NCME, 1985, p. 19). For example, the authors could find appropriate samples for each version of the MSI, and then administer *only* the six situations. The examinees would not work through the entire test booklet, nor participate in a mentoring training program. After, for instance, a 2-week delay, participants could then be retested. As a result, descriptions of the respective samples and estimates of the instruments' test-retest reliabilities would then be available for publication with the instrument.

SUMMARY. As an integral part of the TMI training program, the MSI appears to be a useful tool for providing information regarding individuals' preferred mentoring styles in a variety of settings. The test booklet is clearly written and easily scored. Further, the booklet provides interpretive information regarding the various types of mentoring styles, with a final page providing space and direction for the development of a plan for increasing "your mentoring style versatility." I would like to see more technical data provided regarding validity, and especially test-retest reliability. Nevertheless, in the context of the TMI training program, this instrument should serve as a useful training tool by first identifying preferred mentoring styles, then fostering communication between mentor and protégé, and finally facilitating the development of mentoring style versatility.

REVIEWER'S REFERENCE

American Educational Research Association, American Psychological Association, & National Council on Measurement in Education. (1985). *Standards for educational and psychological testing.* Washington, DC: American Psychological Association, Inc.

[199]
MicroCog: Assessment of Cognitive Functioning.

Purpose: "Assesses important neurocognitive functions in adults."
Population: Ages 18–89.
Publication Date: 1993.
Scores: 9 areas: Attention/Mental Control, Memory, Reasoning/Calculation, Spatial Processing, Reaction Time, Information Processing Accuracy, Information Processing Speed, General Cognitive Functioning, General Cognitive Proficiency.
Administration: Individual.
Price Data, 1994: $150 per MicroCog kit including user's guide (120 pages), technical manual (211 pages), 3.5-inch and 5.25-inch high-density diskettes, and 4 report credits on PsyTest Use Counter; $150 per 10 report credits; $200 per PsyTest Assessment Management System Package.
Time: (50–60) minutes for Standard form; (30) minutes for Brief form.
Comments: Computer administered and scored; must be used with PsyTest Assessment Management System.
Authors: Douglas Powell, Edith Kaplan, Dean Whitla, Sandra Weintraub, and Randolph Catlin.
Publisher: The Psychological Corporation.

Review of the MicroCog: Assessment of Cognitive Functioning by CHARLES J. LONG, Professor of Psychology, and STEPHANIE L. CUTLAN, Research Assistant, Psychology Department, The University of Memphis, Memphis, TN:

The MicroCog is a computerized neurocognitive assessment instrument that was developed through the efforts of the Risk Management Foundation and The Psychological Corporation. It was designed as a screening device as well as a diagnostic tool that evaluates a number of cognitive abilities (Attention/Mental Control, Memory, Reasoning/Calculation, Spatial Processing, and Reaction Time). Two forms of MicroCog are available: the Standard Form reqires the administration of 18 subtests and requires approximately 1 hour; the Short Form contains 12 subtests and can be administered in approximately 30 minutes. This test is accompanied by a thorough, well-written manual that accomplishes many tasks, including the presentation of extensive evidence that MicroCog is a reliable and valid instrument with acceptable norms.

The MicroCog manual reports split-half and test-retest reliability coefficients. For the standard form, index scores showed internal consistency reliabilities within the .83 to .95 range. Confidence in the reliability of this instrument will be strengthened by independent studies prior to drawing firm conclusions, but preliminary research suggests that future corroboration is likely.

Other research conducted by the test authors and summarized in the manual has demonstrated criterion-related validity by using scores to classify subjects correctly into clinical and nonclinical groups. The reported correct classification rates for clinical groups with known or suspected organic etiology range from .65 for a group composed of lupus patients to .92 for a group with dementia. Sensitivity classifications range from .65 to .89, and specificity classifications are between .65 and .94. Although the classification rate for a major depression group was only .63, MicroCog scores did show a strong ability to differentiate between the depression group and the dementia group (rate of correct classification = .86).

Detailed supporting data are also provided regarding construct-related validity; several expected relationships between scores were identified. Concurrent validity was established by showing that scores were correlated as predicted with measures of particular constructs. Finally, attempts to ensure content-related validity were made as neuropsychologists, neurologists, and psychiatrists conducted reviews of the content areas during the battery's development.

The standardization sample consisted of 810 adults. Favorable attributes of this sample were that it included nine different age groups, equal numbers of females and males, three racial groups, and four geographic regions of the United States; the racial groups and geographic regions were sampled in proportion to the U.S. Census. Also notable was the attempt to stratify according to education level and thus to provide separate norms based on education. However, only three education levels (Less than High School, High School, and Greater than High School) were defined. It seems that at the very least the upper level (Greater than High School) should be further divided. (There are likely to be large differences in level of average cognitive ability between individuals who complete one semester of post-high school education and those who obtain medical or doctoral degrees.) One other shortcoming of the standardized sample is that the participation rate was not reported, limiting ability to assess the true representativeness of the sample.

On the basis of its reported reliability and validity and its relatively well-defined norms, the MicroCog appears to be a promising assessment battery. However, there are several procedural details that could be modified in order to improve the quality of this instrument. One major suggestion is that the subject be provided with more information on the speed/accuracy trade-off. The general population is perhaps not likely to carefully consider whether strategies employed should emphasize speed or accuracy, yet the particular emphasis chosen can greatly influence test performance.

There are also two problems with the "Story 1 and 2" recall subtests. First, the stories are presented visually on a continuous basis until the subject indicates that he or she desires to proceed. Nothing prohibits or even discourages a subject from reading the story numerous times, thereby inflating the apparent recall ability. Second, the wording of a portion of one story and of some of the questions is confusing and/or misleading. For example, one question requires the subject to recognize "the person's name" from a previously presented story that identified *two* people.

On the reaction time tests, subjects should be instructed on the specific location at which to anchor the responding finger. Otherwise, test-wise people may anchor the finger directly on the response key whereas others need to move the finger over space to respond.

Several changes could be made to simplify the battery for individuals who are not test-wise and for those not accustomed to working with computers. The incorporation of computer terminology in instructions should be avoided (e.g., "after entering your answer" could read "after typing your answer"). Distracting words on the answer screen (especially during immediate recall tasks such as "Numbers Forward") should be minimized. The option to pause during

administration of a subtest should be eliminated, as the subtests are short and the frequent explanation of when pausing is or is not an option is potentially confusing. Finally, the frequent opportunities for practice prior to test administration are generally desirable, although the practice sequence preceding the "Alphabet" subtest should be changed to more exactly represent the actual test. (Currently the practice presents letters simultaneously but the test does so sequentially.)

On the first page of the manual, it is stated that the MicroCog "takes into account levels of premorbid intellectual functioning by providing age- and education-level adjusted norms" (p. 1). First, it is unclear what the term "premorbid" applies to and calls into question exactly for whom the test battery is designed. Second, the ability to account for premorbid functioning by considering only age and three education groups is not likely to be highly accurate.

The results of the assessment are stored in the computer but can be printed out. The results from one subject produce 23 pages of information. Clearly there is a need for the authors to condense this information into a concise summary with additional data available by request.

In conclusion, several minor changes could be made to the MicroCog to improve its overall quality and reduce chances that subjects will experience unnecessary confusion. Nevertheless, this assessment battery appears to offer a reliable and valid means of gathering important data on several neurocognitive abilities in a short period of time. It has great potential as a powerful tool for use in the evaluation of brain-behavior relationships.

Review of the MicroCog: Assessment of Cognitive Functioning by CYNTHIA A. ROHRBECK, Associate Professor of Psychology, The George Washington University, Washington, DC:

The MicroCog is a self-administered, computer test of cognitive functioning in adults (18–89), particularly designed to identify changes in mental performance over time. Its Standard form includes 18 subtests and can be completed in about 60 minutes. The 18 subtests are combined into nine indices: Attention/Mental Control, Memory, Reasoning/Calculation, Spatial Processing, Reaction Time, Information Processing Speed, Information Processing Accuracy, General Cognitive Functioning, and General Cognitive Proficiency. (The Short form includes 12 of those subtests and takes approximately 30 minutes to complete.) The nine indices include five broad measures of mental performance (or domain index scores), two information processing measures (speed and accuracy), and two measures of global cognitive ability (functioning and proficiency). (The summary scores of information processing and cognitive ability are also referred to as summary index scores.)

The MicroCog was standardized on a nationally representative stratified sample. Individuals in the sample were included based on census percentages for geographic region (four regions), education level (three levels), race (African American, Hispanic, and White), Gender, and age group (using nine age groups). Norms are available both for the highest scoring group (individuals aged 18–34) and an individual's peer group (age group).

The program that is used to score the MicroCog is managed by the PsyTest Assessment Management System. It computes Subtest Scores for general and for selected age and education groups. The program is easily self-administered, even for those without computer experience. For example, the number of computer keys used is restricted to the numeric keyboard, the P key (for pause), and the Backspace and Enter keys.

The MicroCog was developed by a large group of clinicians, researchers, and software developers. The manual concisely and clearly explains and describes substantial evidence for the MicroCog's reliability and validity. Split-half reliability coefficients, standard errors of measurement, and test-retest scores appear to be adequate and are presented in detail in the manual. Evidence for the MicroCog's validity includes expert reviews (for content validity), exploratory factor analytic studies, correlations with other similar tests, and discriminant analyses. MicroCog has correctly classified over 90% of the individuals in Dementia groups, with lower rates (as expected) for Schizophrenic and Depressive groups. Correlations between MicroCog and measures of attention, memory, reasoning, and spatial processing have usually been significant and in the expected direction.

When interpreting one's performance on the MicroCog, comparisons of functioning in one area can be compared with functioning in other areas in order to identify strengths and weaknesses. The manual provides examples of interpretations for differences between summary index scores, domain index scores, and subtest scores, though it warns against comparisons that are spurious and therefore not meaningful when making multiple comparisons. Finally, guidelines for item-error analyses are included. As noted in the manual, the MicroCog

should be used with other tests (e.g., observations, interviews, etc.) before making a definitive diagnosis. In addition, other factors should be considered that might contribute to poor performance, such as premorbid cognitive status.

In summary, the MicroCog is a self-administered computer test that assesses a variety of neurocognitive processes. Its developers have presented solid evidence of its reliability and validity. Furthermore, the MicroCog is relatively easy to use and quick to complete and score. A large number of initial studies show its relevance with various populations. It should certainly be considered when deciding on a battery of neuropsychological or cognitive tests.

[200]
Mill Hill Vocabulary Scale.

Purpose: Provides a measure of acquired verbal knowledge.

Publication Dates: 1943–1994.

Acronym: MHV.

Scores: Total score only.

Administration: Group.

Forms, 2: A, B.

Price Data, 1994: $35.50 per 35 test booklets; $62.40 per specimen set including one of each test booklet, scoring key, and appropriate sections of the Raven's manual (Section 1–1993, 60 pages; Section 5A–1994, 38 pages).

Time: (15–40) minutes.

Comments: To be used in conjunction with the Raven Progressive Matrices (T4:2208); short-form also available.

Authors: J. C. Raven, J. H. Court, and J. Raven.

Publisher: Oxford Psychologists Press, Ltd. [England]; U.S. Distributor: The Psychological Corporation.

a) JUNIOR.

Population: Ages 11–13.

b) SENIOR.

Population: Ages 14–adult.

Cross References: See T4:1629 (51 reference); 9:705 (8 references), T3:1485 (29 references), and T2:402 (32 references); for a review of an earlier edition by Morton Bortner, see 6:471 (16 references); see also 4:303 (7 references); for a review by David Wechsler, see 3:239 (3 references).

TEST REFERENCES

1. McLeavey, B. C., Daly, R. J., Murray, C. M., O'Riordan, J., & Taylor, M. (1987). Interpersonal problem-solving deficits in self-poisoning patients. *Suicide and Life-Threatening Behavior, 17,* 33–49.
2. Newcombe, F., DeHaan, E. H. F., Ross, J., & Young, A. W. (1989). Face processing, laterality and contrast sensitivity. *Neuropsychologia, 27,* 523–538.
3. Hanley, J. R., Dewick, H. C., Davies, A. D. M., Playfer, J., & Turnbull, C. (1990). Verbal fluency in Parkinson's disease. *Neuropsychologia, 28,* 737–741.
4. Rabbitt, P., & Alison, V. (1990). "Lost and Found": Some logical and methodological limitations of self-report questionnaires as tools to study cognitive ageing. *British Journal of Psychology, 81,* 1–16.
5. Vriezen, E. R., & Moscovitch, M. (1990). Memory for temporal order and conditional associative-learning in patients with Parkinson's disease. *Neuropsychologia, 28,* 1283–1293.
6. Dewick, H. C., Hanley, J. R., Davies, A. D. M., Playfer, J., & Turnbull, C. (1991). Perception and memory for faces in Parkinson's disease. *Neuropsychologia, 29,* 785–802.

7. Garety, P. A., Hemsley, D. R., & Wessely, S. (1991). Reasoning in deluded schizophrenic and paranoid patients: Biases in performance on a probabilistic inference task. *The Journal of Nervous and Mental Disease, 179,* 194-201.

8. Scarr, S. (1992). Developmental theories for the 1990s: Development and individual differences. *Child Development, 63,* 1-19.

9. Baddeley, A., Emslie, H., & Nimmo-Smith, I. (1993). The Spot-the-Word Test: A robust estimate of verbal intelligence based on lexical decision. *British Journal of Clinical Psychology, 32,* 55-65.

10. Goldberg, T. E., Hyde, T. M., Kleinman, J. E., & Weinberger, D. R. (1993). Course of schizophrenia: Neuropsychological evidence for a static encephalopathy. *Schizophrenia Bulletin, 19,* 797-804.

11. Perfect, T. J., & Rabbitt, P. M. A. (1993). Speed and accuracy of memory decisions in older adults. *Psychological Reports, 73,* 607-610.

12. Blackwood, D. H. R., Muir, H. M., Roxborough, M. R., Walker, M. R., Townshend, R., Glaluis, M. F., & Wolff, S. (1994). "Schizoid" personality in childhood: Auditory P300 and eye tracking responses at followup in adult life. *Journal of Autism and Developmental Disorders, 24,* 487-500.

13. Davies, S., Bishop, D., Manstead, A. S. R., & Tantam, D. (1994). Face perception in children with autism and Asperger's syndrome. *Journal of Child Psychology and Psychiatry and Allied Disciplines, 35,* 1033-1057.

14. Deary, I. J. (1994). Intelligence and auditory discrimination separating processing speed and fidelity of stimulus representation. *Intelligence, 18,* 189-213.

15. Egan, V. (1994). Intelligence, inspection time and cognitive strategies. *British Journal of Psychology, 85,* 305-315.

16. McLeavey, B. C., Daly, R. J., Ludgate, J. W., & Murray, C. M. (1994). Interpersonal problem-solving skills training in the treatment of self-poisoning patients. *Suicide and Life-Threatening Behavior, 24,* 382-394.

17. Pesenti, M., Seron, X., & Van der Linden, M. (1994). Selective impairment as evidence for mental organisation of arithmetical facts: BB, a case of preserved subtraction. *Cortex, 30,* 661-671.

18. Rapee, R. M. (1994). Failure to replicate a memory bias in panic disorder. *Journal of Anxiety Disorders, 8,* 291-300.

19. Sliwinski, M., Buschke, H., Kuslansky, G., Senior, G., & Scarisbrick, D. (1994). Proportional slowing and addition speed in old and young adults. *Psychology and Aging, 9,* 72-80.

20. Van der Linden, M., Brédart, S., & Beerten, A. (1994). Age-related differences in updating working memory. *British Journal of Psychology, 85,* 145-152.

21. Wilding, J., & Valentine, E. (1994). Memory champions. *British Journal of Psychology, 85,* 231-244.

22. Wilding, J., & Valentine, E. (1994). Mnemonic wizardry with the telephone directory—but stories are another story. *British Journal of Psychology, 85,* 501-509.

23. Bradley, B. P., Mogg, K., Millar, N., & White, J. (1995). Selective processing of negative information: Effects of clinical anxiety, concurrent depression, and awareness. *Journal of Abnormal Psychology, 104,* 532-536.

24. Coney, J., & Serna, P. (1995). Creative thinking from an information processing perspective: A new approach to Mednick's theory of associative hierarchies. *The Journal of Creative Behavior, 29,* 109-132.

25. Dalgleish, T., Cameron, C. M., Power, M. J., & Bond, A. (1995). The use of an emotional priming paradigm with clinically anxious subjects. *Cognitive Therapy and Research, 19,* 69-89.

26. Deary, I. J. (1995). Auditory inspection time and intelligence: What is the direction of causation? *Developmental Psychology, 31,* 237-250.

27. McManus, I. C. (1995). Familial sinistrality: The utility of calculating exact genotype probabilities for individuals. *Cortex, 31,* 3-24.

28. Haeske-Dewick, H. C. (1996). Are perception and memory for faces influenced by a specific age at onset factor in Parkinson's disease? *Neuropsychologia, 34,* 315-320.

29. Java, R. I. (1996). Effects of age on state of awareness following implicit and explicit word-association tasks. *Psychology and Aging, 11,* 108-111.

30. Power, M. J., Comeron, C. M., & Dalgleish, T. (1996). Emotional priming in clinically depressed subjects. *Journal of Affective Disorders, 38,* 1-11.

Review of the Mill Hill Vocabulary Scale by THEODORE L. HAYES, *Senior Research Analyst, The Gallup Organization, Lincoln, NE:*

The Mill Hill Vocabulary Scale (MHV) is the verbal test component of an intellectual assessment package that includes Raven Progressive Matrices (T4:2208). The two inventories in tandem permit evaluation of the test taker's *eductive* (Matrices) and *reproductive* (MHV) mental processes. Eduction is defined as the individual's ability to evolve and understand high-level constructs, and reproduction means the individual's capacity to master, recall, and communicate a culture's store of verbal concepts. An

MHV score shows the test taker's "present cultural level relative to other people" (p. 4) in terms of verbal test performance. The MHV is purported to be a means through which to understand the individual's ability to express his/her intellectual functioning. In fact, the MHV is a verbal intelligence test.

Previous versions of the MHV have been reviewed by Wechsler (*MMY*, 3:239) and Bortner (*MMY*, 6:471). The test authors have not adequately addressed earlier commentary. They note that their concern is to move the debate away from "technicalities" (p. 1) of intelligence test construction toward the social and educational policy issues that interact with inferences from intelligence test results.

The MHV consists of 88 words equally divided between two sets (A and B). There are two test administration modes. In the Definitions or Open-Ended Form modality, the test taker is asked to explain orally the meaning of each stimulus word. The Combined Open-Ended and Multiple Choice Forms modality is intended for test takers who are able to read and write. Test takers are asked to explain the meaning of each stimulus word in Set A, and then to choose the most accurate synonym in Set B among the six provided for each stimulus word. Each modality is further subdivided into "Junior" and "Senior" levels. In the Junior level, suitable for children aged 11 to 13, the 11 most difficult words in both Sets A and B have been dropped. Conversely, the 10 easiest words in the Senior level sets have been dropped and the 11th has been maintained as a nonscored working example. Other formats of the MHV (e.g., all multiple choice; a "short form") are also available.

The 88 MHV words were chosen and keyed based on the Concise Oxford English Dictionary during the late 1940s in Britain. The authors are unclear on this point, but it seems that 85 of the 88 words in the present list have remained since then. The manual reports normative data for children and youths as of 1979 in the U.K. Corresponding 1986 U.S. norms are presented separately for the combined-response format and the multiple-choice-only format. For adults, the most recent normative data for the two response formats were gathered in the U.K. in 1992 and in the U.S. in 1993. The authors present normative tables comparing scores for the U.K. versus the U.S. samples (the U.S. sample scored lower). There is a fine set of norms for adults throughout the life span. Normative data for adults are based on untimed administrations of the MHV. Only one set of norms is presented in each case, as the authors dismiss the possibility that separate norms are needed for men and women. Scoring instructions indicate that the MHV is a "power" test, not a "speeded" test. The short form of the MHV encourages administrators to evaluate the clinical implications of responses, but this is not recommended in the scoring instructions for the combined-response formats.

The manual still does not provide clear information concerning the reliability and statistical validity of the current form of the MHV. One table of reliability analyses, based on the original form of the test, seems to show that the test-retest correlation (time interval unclear) for adult males ranges from .90 to .98 depending on age, whereas for the same group the correlations of Set A scores with Set B scores is reported as .88. For children, another confusing table shows the correlations between Sets A and B for a revised version of the MHV to range from .67 to .79 depending on age. The authors note that 16% of the variation in their results for the MHV could be explained by socioeconomic background, but they do not present separate norms for different backgrounds. Instead, they aver that it is up to the clinician to understand the remaining 84% of the variance through use of assessments such as the MHV.

It seems that the MHV lets the user assess the individual's verbal reproduction, which would help elucidate the individual's eduction capacity at least in terms of academic performance. This is a sophisticated view of what verbal fluency may be. However, the manual states that "full-length 'Intelligence' tests are primarily measures of reproductive ability" (p. G8, General Overview manual). Thus, the authors seem to want it both ways: They claim that the MHV measures a distinct, theoretically important, and potentially valuable subcomponent of intellectual functioning; but on the other hand, they claim that intelligence is equivalent to reproduction. The manual states that in factor analytic research, the MHV has high loadings on the same factors as the Wechsler Intelligence Scale for Children, the Progressive Matrices, the California Achievement Tests, and sundry other measures of mental ability. Indeed, within-age correlations of reproductive and eductive capacities are in the range of .50 to .60 (p. G8, General Overview manual). If intelligence as typically defined is reproduction, then more careful empirical investigations need to examine the relations between general mental ability, IQ, and the MHV. These "technicalities" are not presented in the test materials so that one can evaluate assessment options. More-

over, some conceptual rationale needs to be presented for why one should choose the MHV over other measures of general mental ability and/or intelligence. This serious construct validity work requires more attention to test development "technicalities" than the authors seem ready to offer.

The MHV measures a theoretically interesting facet of performance, and it may have considerable appeal in the assessment of neuropathology and intellectual functioning over the life span. However, in the end, the MHV is a measure of intelligence and/or general mental ability. One gets the sense that its authors may be letting the theoretical tail wag the empirical dog.

Review of the Mill Hill Vocabulary Scale by WILLIAM K. WILKINSON, Consulting Psychologist, Boleybeg, Barna, Co. Galway, Ireland:

The purpose of the Mill Hill Vocabulary (MHV) Scale is the measurement of reproductive ability—the ability to recall verbal knowledge. It is widely known as the "partner" of the Raven Progressive Matrices (RPM; T4:2208), the two collectively based on the components of g identified by Spearman. The RPM and MVH are now over 50 years in existence, and there is a tremendous amount of information concerning the scales. As a result, the authors have partitioned the ever-increasing knowledge base into a General Overview manual, separate manuals for the various versions and editions of the progressive matrices, MHV scale, and Crichton Vocabulary Scale, four research supplements, and a computerized data-bank containing recent test developments. An information leaflet assists the test user in selecting the correct forms and required manuals for various subject populations. Because the present review concerns the MHV scale, the General Overview Manual and the MHV manual were reviewed, as were the three Junior and Senior MVH (U.S. Edition) forms.

The General Overview Manual is well written and covers many fundamental issues regarding ability and intelligence tests. The authors' personal perspective is expounded in parts, and readers will need to make their own appraisal of the comments contained therein. For example, the authors (p. 36) state that the RPM and MHV provide "most" of the information available on longer tests of intelligence. They further cite a review study in which individual subtest analysis on longer intelligence tests is not recommended. Although this seems to imply that the RPM and MHV scale can be used instead of traditional intelligence tests, the authors then state that the RPM and MHV are frequently used after administration of full-length intelligence tests.

The latest MHV revision is the new U.S. standardization, and the associate publication of the MHV—U.S. Edition—forms. This development will certainly be welcomed by American test users. However, those keen on using the MHV in America will be wise to follow the authors' recommendation that the appropriate ethnic and regional normative samples be used for score transformation. This is especially relevant considering the authors' statement that large variations in norms were obtained depending on ethnicity and region.

What is curious about the MHV materials is the seeming mismatch between the MHV reference manual and the U.S. Edition forms. Specifically, the MHV manual is a general reference manual, and only minimal attention is given to the U.S. standardization and technical data. For example, the MHV manual consists of a brief discussion of several item revisions in the U.S. edition, a study related to the construct validation of the MHV, U.S. Edition, and general American norms for children ages 6–16 for two different MHV U.S. Edition forms.

Detailed analyses of the U.S. standardization data do exist, and the reader is referred to Research Supplement #3 (Research Supplement #4 also makes reference to American data). Although it is understandable that the authors sectioned the amount of technical information into separate sources, I do not understand why far more information in the research supplements was not aggregated into a comprehensive U.S. Edition manual. This would make the MHV materials more internally consistent—U.S. Edition forms with a comprehensive and single reference MHV (U.S. Edition) manual. It is my understanding that tests exported for international use typically provide the relevant forms and single, comprehensive technical manual specific to the targeted country. This was the source of my original curiosity. In any case, it is imperative that American test users obtain Research Supplement #3 and #4 before using the MHV in the U.S. Perhaps future packaging of the MHV will contain a single, comprehensive U.S. manual that incorporates the U.S. database.

The MHV (U.S. Edition) forms offer the test user a variety of administrative options. Indeed, there are six different forms (seven including the short-form, which will not be reviewed here), three Junior (age 11–13) and three Senior (age 14+) forms. For both Junior and Senior groups, there are parallel Forms 1 and 2, and a third, entirely multiple-choice form. The parallel U.S. Edition Forms 1 and 2 continue the MHV tradition of using both the open-ended (Set A) and multiple-choice (Set B) methods of assessing word knowledge. The open-ended set can be administered by asking the subject to define words (oral definitions) or by writing their definitions of words on the space provided. Scoring for the open-ended responses would be facilitated by the publication of detailed responses considered correct or incorrect, as is the case with the Wechsler Intelligence Scale for Children—Third Edition (WISC-III; 12:412) Vocabulary Scale. The manual does contain a scoring "key" for the open-ended sections, but it consists only of the target word and a single synonym. In case of question, the test user is instructed to use a dictionary.

Normative interpretation of MHV raw scores is accomplished via percentiles. Exact percentile rankings are not permitted for all raw score values (unless the test user wishes to interpolate), because the test authors prefer to divide the percentile distribution into five interpretive grades (e.g., "verbally average" defines scores between the 25th and 75th percentiles).

Overall, the MHV (U.S. Edition) scale appears to provide American test users a replica of an instrument widely recognized in the U.K. The most pressing point is that U.S. test users obtain the ancillary research supplements (#s 3 and 4) in order to locate appropriate norm tables and to ascertain the technical merits (e.g., reliability and validity) of the MHV (U.S. Edition) forms.

[201]
Millon Clinical Multiaxial Inventory—III.

Purpose: Designed to provide diagnostic and treatment information to clinicians in the areas of personality disorders and clinical syndromes.

Population: "Adults [18+] who are seeking [or in] mental health treatment and who have eighth-grade reading skills."

Publication Dates: 1976–1997.

Acronym: MCMI—III.

Scores, 27: Modifying Indices (Disclosure, Desirability, Debasement), Clinical Personality Patterns (Schizoid, Avoidant, Depressive, Dependent, Histrionic, Narcissistic, Antisocial, Aggressive (Sadistic), Compulsive, Passive-Aggressive (Negativistic), Self-Defeating) Severe Personality Pathology (Schizotypal, Borderline, Paranoid), Clinical Syndromes (Anxiety, Somatoform, Bipolar: Manic, Dysthymia, Alcohol Dependence, Drug Dependence, Post-Traumatic Stress Disorder), Severe Syndromes (Thought Disorder, Major Depression, Delusional Disorder).

Administration: Individual or group.

Price Data, 1997: $109 per mail-in preview package; $109 per MICROTEST Q preview package; $31.95 per prepaid interpretive mail-in answer sheet (specify English or Hispanic); $12.50 per prepaid profile mail-in answer sheet (specify English or Hispanic); $15 per 25 MICROTEST Q answer sheets (specify English or Hispanic); $30.95 per interpretive MICROTEST Q administrations; $11.50 per profile MICROTEST Q administrations; $50 per audiocassette (specify English or Hispanic); $25 per 10 handscoring test booklets; $42 per manual ('97, 196 pages); $225 handscoring starter kit including manual, handscoring user's guide, 10 test booklets, 50 answer sheets, 50 worksheets, 50 profile forms, and answer keys; $100 per handscoring reorder kit including 50 answer sheets, 50 worksheets, and 50 profile forms.

Time: [25] minutes.

Comments: Designed to coordinate with DSM-IV categories of personality disorders and clinical syndromes; revision of the Millon Clinical Multiaxial Inventory—II (11:239).

Authors: Theodore Millon, Carrie Millon, and Roger Davis.

Publisher: NCS Assessments.

Cross References: See T4:1635 (104 references); for reviews by Thomas M. Haladyna and Cecil R. Reynolds of an earlier edition, see 11:239 (74 references); for reviews by Allen K. Hess and Thomas A. Widiger of the original edition, see 9:709 (1 reference); see also T3:1488 (3 references).

TEST REFERENCES

1. Selzer, M. A., Kernberg, P., Fibel, B., Cherbuliez, T., & Mortati, S. G. (1987). The personality assessment interview: Preliminary report. *Psychiatry, 50,* 142–153.

2. Joffe, R. T., & Regan, J. J. (1989). Personality and response to tricyclic antidepressants in depressed patients. *The Journal of Nervous and Mental Disease, 177,* 745-749.

3. Reich, J. H. (1989). Update on instruments to measure DSM-II and DSM-III-R personality disorders. *The Journal of Nervous and Mental Disease, 177,* 366-370.

4. Reich, J., Noyes, R., Jr., & Yates, W. (1989). Alprazolam treatment of avoidant personality traits in social phobic patients. *The Journal of Clinical Psychiatry, 50,* 91–95.

5. Ceballos-Capitaine, A., Szapocznik, J., Blaney, N. T., Morgan, R. O., Millon, C., & Eisdorfer, C. (1990). Ethnicity, emotional distress, stress-related disruption, and coping among HIV seropositive gay males. *Hispanic Journal of Behavior Sciences, 12,* 135–152.

6. Hogg, B., Jackson, H. J., Rudd, R. P., & Edwards, J. (1990). Diagnosing personality disorders in recent-onset schizophrenia. *The Journal of Nervous and Mental Disease, 178,* 194-199.

7. Josiassen, R. C., Roemer, R. A., Johnson, M. M., & Shagass, C. (1990). Are gender differences in schizophrenia reflected in brain event-related potentials? *Schizophrenia Bulletin, 16,* 229–246.

8. Reich, J. (1990). The effect of personality on placebo response in panic patients. *The Journal of Nervous and Mental Disease, 178,* 699.

9. Weinberger, D. A., & Schwartz, G. E. (1990). Distress and restraint as superordinate dimensions of self-reported adjustment: A typological perspective. *Journal of Personality, 58,* 381–417.

10. Wetzler, S., & Dubro, A. (1990). Diagnosis of personality disorders by the Millon Clinical Multiaxial Inventory. *The Journal of Nervous and Mental Disease, 178,* 261-263.

11. Lewis, S. J., & Harder, D. W. (1991). A comparison of four measures to diagnose DSM-III-R borderline personality disorder in outpatients. *The Journal of Nervous and Mental Disease, 179,* 329-337.

12. Organista, P. B., & Miranda, J. (1991). Psychosomatic symptoms in medical outpatients: An investigation of self-handicapping theory. *Health Psychology, 10,* 427-431.

13. Wise, T. N., Fagan, P. J., Schmidt, C. W., Ponticas, Y., & Costa, D. T. (1991). Personality and sexual functioning of transvestitic fetishists and other paraphilics. *The Journal of Nervous and Mental Disease, 179,* 694-698.

14. Beasley, R., & Stoltenberg, C. D. (1992). Personality characteristics of male spouse abusers. *Professional Psychology: Research and Practice, 23,* 310–317.

15. Chambless, D. L., Renneberg, B., Goldstein, A., & Gracely, E. J. (1992). MCMI-diagnosed personality disorders among agoraphobic outpatients: Prevalence and relationship to severity and treatment outcome. *Journal of Anxiety Disorders, 6,* 193-211.

16. Craig, R. J., & Olson, R. E. (1992). Relationship between MCMI-II scales and normal personality traits. *Psychological Reports, 71,* 699-705.

17. Delamatre, J. E., & Schuerger, J. M. (1992). Personality disorder concept scales and 16 PF dimensions. *Psychological Reports, 70,* 839-849.

18. Hsu, L. M. (1992). Correcting correlations of personality scales for spurious effects of shared items. *Multivariate Behavioral Research, 27,* 31–41.

19. Hyer, L., Davis, H., Woods, G., Albrecht, J. W., & Boudewyns, P. (1992). Relationship between the Millon Clinical Multiaxial Inventory and the Millon-II: Values of scales for aggressive and self-defeating personalities in posttraumatic stress disorder. *Psychological Reports, 71,* 867-879.

20. Strauman, T. J., & Wetzler, S. (1992). The factor structure of SCL—90 and MCMI scale scores: Within measure and interbattery analyses. *Multivariate Behavioral Research, 27,* 1–20.

21. Yeager, R. J., DiGiuseppe, R., Resweber, P. J., & Leaf, R. (1992). Comparison of Millon Personality profiles of chronic residential substance abusers and a general outpatient population. *Psychological Reports, 71,* 71-79.

22. Alden, L. E., & Capreol, M. J. (1993). Avoidant personality disorder: Interpersonal problems as predictors of treatment response. *Behavior Therapy, 24,* 357–376.

23. Bishop, D. R. (1993). Validity issues in using the Millon-II with substance abusers. *Psychological Reports, 73,* 27-33.

24. Curtis, J. M., & Cowell, D. R. (1993). Relation of birth order and scores on measures of pathological narcissism. *Psychological Reports, 72,* 311-315.

25. Haller, D. L., Knisely, J. S., Dawson, K. S., & Schnoll, S. H. (1993). Perinatal substance abusers: Psychological and social characteristics. *The Journal of Nervous and Mental Disease, 181,* 509-513.

26. Hyer, L. A., Albrecht, J. W., Boudewyns, P. A., Woods, M. G., & Brandsma, J. (1993). Dissociative experiences of Vietnam veterans with chronic posttraumatic stress disorder. *Psychological Reports, 73,* 519-530.

27. Piekarski, A. M., Sherwood, R., & Funari, D. J. (1993). Personality subgroups in an inpatient Vietnam veteran treatment program. *Psychological Reports, 72,* 667-674.

28. Reich, J. H., & Vasile, R. G. (1993). Effect of personality disorders on the treatment outcome of Axis I conditions: An update. *The Journal of Nervous and Mental Disease, 181,* 475-484.

29. Siddall, J. W., & Keogh, N. J. (1993). Utility of computer interpretive reports based on counselors' ratings of the Diagnostic Inventory of Personality and Symptoms. *Psychological Reports, 72,* 347-350.

30. Szajnberg, N. M. D., Krall, V. K., Davis, P., Treem, W., & Hyams, J. (1993). Psychopathology and relationship measures in children with inflammatory bowel disease and their parents. *Child Psychiatry and Human Development, 23,* 215–232.

31. West, M., Rose, M. S., & Sheldon, A. (1993). Anxious attachment as a determinant of adult psychopathology. *The Journal of Nervous and Mental Disease, 181,* 422-427.

32. Wierzbicki, M., & Goldade, P. (1993). Sex-typing of the Millon Clinical Multiaxial Inventory. *Psychological Reports, 72,* 1115-1121.

33. Chantry, K., & Craig, R. J. (1994). Psychological screening of sexually violent offenders with the MCMI. *Journal of Clinical Psychology, 50,* 430-435.

34. Chick, D., Martin, S. K., Nevels, R., & Cotton, C. R. (1994). Relationship between personality disorders and clinical symptoms in psychiatric patients as measured by the Millon Clinical Multiaxial Inventory. *Psychological Reports, 74,* 331-336.

35. del Rosario, P. M., McCann, J. T., & Navarra, J. W. (1994). The MCMI-II diagnosis of schizophrenia: Operating characteristics and profile analysis. *Journal of Personality Assessment, 63,* 438-452.

36. Dutton, D. G., & Starzomski, A. J. (1994). Psychological differences between court-referred and self-referred wife assaulters. *Criminal Justice and Behavior, 21,* 203–222.

37. Greenwald, D. J., Reznikoff, M., & Plutchik, R. (1994). Suicide risk and violence risk in alcoholics: Predictors of aggressive risk. *The Journal of Nervous and Mental Disease, 182,* 3-8.

38. Grillo, J., Brown, R. S., Hilsabeck, R., Price, J. R., & Lees-Haley, P. R. (1994). Raising doubts about claims of malingering: Implications of relationships between MCMI-II and MMPI-2 performances. *Journal of Clinical Psychology, 50,* 651-655.

39. Guthrie, P. C., & Mobley, B. D. (1994). A comparison of the differential diagnostic efficiency of three personality disorder inventories. *Journal of Clinical Psychology, 50,* 656-665.

40. Hastings, J. E., & Hamberger, L. K. (1994). Psychosocial modifiers of psychopathology for domestically violent and nonviolent men. *Psychological Reports, 74,* 112-114.

41. Hsu, L. M. (1994). Item overlap correlations: Definitions, interpretations, and implications. *Multivariate Behavioral Research, 29,* 127–140.

42. Hyer, L., Braswell, L., Albrecht, B., Boyd, S., Boudewyns, P., & Talbert, S. (1994). Relationship of NEO-PI to personality styles and severity of trauma in chronic PTSD victims. *Journal of Clinical Psychology, 50,* 699-707.

43. Hyer, L., Davis, H., Albrecht, W., Boudewyns, P., & Woods, G. (1994). Cluster analysis of MCMI and MCMI-II on chronic PTSD victims. *Journal of Clinical Psychology, 50,* 502-515.

44. Keller, D. S., & Wilson, A. (1994). Affectivity in cocaine and opiate abusers. *Psychiatry, 57,* 333–347.

45. Loza, W., & Simourd, D. J. (1994). Psychometric evaluation of the Level of Supervision Inventory (LSI) among male Canadian federal offenders. *Criminal Justice and Behavior, 21*, 468–480.

46. Matano, R. A., Locke, K. D., & Schwartz, K. (1994). MCMI personality subtypes for male and female alcoholics. *Journal of Personality Assessment, 63*, 250-264.

47. McKee, G. R., & Klohn, L. S. (1994). MCMI profiles of pretrial defendants. *Psychological Reports, 74*, 1346.

48. Ness, R., Handelsman, L., Aronson, M. J., Hershkowitz, A., & Kanof, P. D. (1994). The acute effects of a rapid medical detoxification upon dysphoria and other psychopathology experienced by heroin abusers. *The Journal of Nervous and Mental Disease, 182*, 353-359.

49. Palmer, B. W., Boone, K. B., Chang, L., Lee, A., & Black, S. (1994). Cognitive deficits and personality patterns in maternally versus paternally inherited myotonic dystrophy. *Journal of Clinical and Experimental Neuropsychology, 16*, 784-795.

50. Prodromidis, M., Abrams, S., Field, T., Scafidi, F., & Rahdert, E. (1994). Psychosocial stressors among depressed adolescent mothers. *Adolescence, 29*, 331-343.

51. Richman, H., & Nelson-Gray, R. (1994). Nonclinical panicker personality: Profile and discriminative ability. *Journal of Anxiety Disorders, 8*, 33-47.

52. Silverstein, M. L., Daniels, L., & Feldmar, G. G. (1994). Levels of psychopathology at hospital admission and discharge: The Millon Clinical Multiaxial Inventory as a prognostic measure. *Psychological Reports, 75*, 1104-1106.

53. Terpylak, O., & Schuerger, J. M. (1994). Broad factor scales of the 16 PF Fifth Edition and Millon personality disorder scales. *Psychological Reports, 74*, 124-126.

54. Vollrath, M., Alnaes, R., & Torgersen, S. (1994). Coping and MCMI-II symptoms scales. *Journal of Clinical Psychology, 50*, 727-736.

55. Wagner, J. K., & Perrine, R. M. (1994). Women at risk for homelessness: Comparison between housed and homeless women. *Psychological Reports, 75*, 1671-1678.

56. Wetzler, S., Marlowe, D. B., & Sanderson, W. C. (1994). Assessment of depression: Using the MMPI, Millon, and Millon-II. *Psychological Reports, 75*, 755-768.

57. Wise, E. A. (1994). Personality style code type concordance between the MCMI and MBHI. *Journal of Clinical Psychology, 50*, 367-380.

58. Baggi, L., Rubino, I. A., Zanna, V., & Martignoni, M. (1995). Personality disorders and regulative styles of patients with temporo-mandibular joint pain dysfunction syndrome. *Perceptual and Motor Skills, 80*, 267-273.

59. Blais, M. A. (1995). MCMI-II personality traits associated with the MMPI-2 Masculinity-Femininity scale. *Assessment, 2*, 131-136.

60. Boone, K. B., Savodnik, I., Ghaffarian, S., Lee, A., Freeman, D., & Berman, N. G. (1995). Rey 15-item memorization and dot counting scores in a "stress" claim worker's compensation population: Relationship to personality (MCMI) scores. *Journal of Clinical Psychology, 51*, 457-463.

61. Craig, R. J. (1995). Clinical diagnoses and MCMI code types. *Journal of Clinical Psychology, 51*, 351-360.

62. Ellason, J. W., Ross, C. A., & Fuchs, D. L. (1995). Assessment of dissociative identity disorder with the Millon Clinical Multiaxial Inventory-II. *Psychological Reports, 76*, 895–905.

63. Fals-Stewart, W. (1995). The effect of defensive responding by substance-abusing patients on the Millon Clinical Multiaxial Inventory. *Journal of Personality Assessment, 64*, 540-551.

64. Flynn, P. M., McCann, J. T., & Fairbank, J. A. (1995). Issues in the assessment of personality disorder and substance abuse using the Millon Clinical Multiaxial Inventory (MCMI-II). *Journal of Clinical Psychology, 51*, 415-421.

65. Funtowicz, M. N., & Widiger, T. A. (1995). Sex bias in the diagnosis of personality disorders: A different approach. *Journal of Psychopathology and Behavioral Assessment, 17*, 145–165.

66. Grossman, L. S., & Craig, R. J. (1995). Comparison of MCMI-II and 16 PF validity scales. *Journal of Personality Assessment, 64*, 384-389.

67. Hibbard, S., Hilsenroth, M. J., Hibbard, J. K., & Nash, M. R. (1995). A validity study of two projective object representations measures. *Psychological Assessment, 7*, 432–439.

68. Hills, H. A. (1995). Diagnosing personality disorders: An examination of the MMPI-2 and MCMI-II. *Journal of Personality Assessment, 65*, 21–34.

69. Lindsay, K. A., & Widiger, T. A. (1995). Sex and gender bias in self-report personality inventories: Item analyses of the MCMI–II, MMPI, and PDQ-R. *Journal of Personality Assessment, 65*, 1–20.

70. Munley, P. H., Bains, D. S., Bloem, W. D., Busby, R. M., & Pendziszewski, S. (1995). Posttraumatic stress disorder and the MCMI-II. *Psychological Reports, 76*, 939-944.

71. Rogers, J. H., Widiger, T. A., & Krupp, A. (1995). Aspects of depression associated with borderline personality disorder. *American Journal of Psychiatry, 152*, 268-270.

72. Rudd, M. D., Joiner, T. E., Jr., & Rajab, M. H. (1995). Help negation after acute suicidal crisis. *Journal of Consulting and Clinical Psychology, 63*, 499-503.

73. Rudd, M. D., & Rajab, M. H. (1995). Specificity of the Beck Depression Inventory and the confounding role of comorbid disorders in a clinical sample. *Cognitive Therapy and Research, 19*, 51-68.

74. Swanson, S. C., Templer, D. I., Thomas-Dobson, S., Cannon, W. G., Streiner, D. L., Reynolds, R. M., & Miller, H. R. (1995). Development of a three-scale MMPI: The MMPI-TRI. *Journal of Clinical Psychology, 51*, 361-374.

75. Tran, G. Q., & Chambless, D. L. (1995). Psychopathology of social phobia: Effects of subtype and of avoidant personality disorder. *Journal of Anxiety Disorders, 9*, 489–501.

76. Ward, L. C. (1995). Correspondence of the MMPI-2 and MCMI-II in male substance abusers. *Journal of Personality Assessment, 64*, 390-393.

77. Weekes, J. R., Morison, S. J., Millson, W. A., & Fettig, D. M. (1995). A comparison of native, metis, and caucasian offender profiles on the MCMI. *Canadian Journal of Behavioural Science, 27*, 187–1908.

78. Whyne-Berman, S. M., & McCann, J. T. (1995). Defense mechanisms and personality disorders: An empirical test of Millon's theory. *Journal of Personality Assessment, 64*, 132-144.

79. Bowman, V., Ward, L. C., Bowman, D., & Scogin, F. (1996). Self-examination therapy as an adjunct treatment for depressive symptoms in substance abusing patients. *Addictive Behaviors, 21*, 129–133.

80. Derecho, C. N., Wetzler, S., McGinn, L. K., Sanderson, W. C., & Asnis, G. M. (1996). Atypical depression among psychiatric inpatients: Clinical features and personality traits. *Journal of Affective Disorders, 39*, 55-59.

81. Widiger, T. A., Cadoret, R., Hare, R., Robins, L., Rutherford, M., Zanarini, M., Alterman, A., Apple, M., Corbitt, E., Forth, A., Hart, S., Kultermann, J., Woody, G., & Frances, A. (1996). DSM–IV antisocial personality disorder field trial. *Journal of Abnormal Psychology, 105*, 3–16.

Review of the Millon Clinical Multiaxial Inventory—III by ALLEN K. HESS, Distinguished Research Professor and Department Head, Department of Psychology, Auburn University at Montgomery, Montgomery, AL:

[Editor's Note: The publisher has provided a Second Edition (1997) of the manual for this test. However, this manual was not available to this reviewer. Reviews with benefit of this manual will be included in the next *MMY*.]

THE MCMI: A BRIEF HISTORY. Because the Millon Clinical Multiaxial Inventory (MCMI) is in its third edition, it may be helpful to place this review of the MCMI-III in the context of the reviews of the previous editions. The first edition of the MCMI met with a mixture of enthusiasm and caution. Millon's theory, on which the MCMI was based, and the tie between the DSM-III and the MCMI were particular strong points (Hess, 1985; Widiger, 1985). However, concerns were raised about the lack of clarity about base rate construction methods, the collinearity problem introduced by profuse item overlap with most items on most scales appearing on at least one or two other scales, and the need for validity studies. Hess (1985) called for psychophysical scaling studies of the scales supposedly measuring the intensity of pathologies.

The MCMI-II met with a similar mix of sentiments. Haladyna (1992) was concerned about item overlap, poorly documented factor analytic work, and a manual that was difficult to follow. Yet he believed that future validity studies may show the MCMI to be the equal to or even better than the Minnesota Multiphasic Personality Inventory (MMPI). Reynolds (1992) found the differential weights assigned to items were not justified, the norming was poor, and the scaling of the MCMI-II to be troublesome. Moreover, Reynolds noted that the pathological approach (called by Hess [1985] "[the] profligate use of 'red flag' diagnostic terms"), where it seems no one taking the MCMI can appear normal, limited the MCMI's use. Thus, Reynolds warned about the pathology bias when using the

MCMI for evaluations of child custody, foster-parents, employment (particularly security personnel where one would be tempted to use a psychopathology detection device), and in criminal forensic work where the presumption of innocence might be compromised by the MCMI-II. Reynolds (1992) concluded that the "MCMI-II is a conceptual gem and psychometrically somewhere between a nightmare and an enigma."

THE MCMI-III. The MCMI-III adds a personality scale, Depressive, and a clinical syndrome scale, Post-Traumatic Stress Disorder, to the array of MCMI-II scales, and replaces 95 items with 95 new items. Both the new scales and the replaced items are intended to tie the MCMI to the DSM-IV ever more tightly. What else good can be said about the MCMI-III? Distressingly little.

Millon's theory (1969) is the presumed cornerstone of the MCMI. But the MCMI has moved more toward the DSM-IV leaving the original theory with less of an operational connection to the MCMI. There is little sense of Millon's original Reinforcement Orientation x Active-Passive schema left in the MCMI. Despite repeated hopes and warnings in the reviews for a more solid psychometric underpinning for the MCMI, the psychometric foundations of the MCMI remain gelatinous. Let us review a few of the problems.

1. Millon eschewed the normative and contrasted groups models in developing scales, opting to use base rates to anchor the MCMI scales. The base rate concept requires certain knowledge of the prior probabilities or base rates of a phenomenon. As to the MCMI-III, the use of base rates requires us to know the rates of the various psychopathologies such as sadistic personality disorder, depressive personality disorder, major depression, and dysthymia. We do not have sufficiently precise epidemiological data to determine the base rates for the diagnostic categories used in the MCMI-III, particularly when we begin to break down the data for race, gender, age, socioeconomic status, and the like. The 998 patients used to test the items is a grossly insufficient number upon which to establish base rates. Millon asked the clinician furnishing MCMI-IIIs to give an estimate as to the patient's major disorder and the next two prominent disorders. The background, experience, and educational degrees of the raters and the reliability and validity of their ratings are unknown. He used these ratings plus an unspecified adjustment based on epidemiological data to establish base rate anchors for the MCMI-III scales. The lack of epidemiological base rate data, the lack of any infor-

mation on the reliability and validity of the clinical opinions used to set the base rate cutoffs, the lack of information regarding the clinical judges rendering opinions, and the mystical adjustment lead to the conclusion that the base rate method employed on the MCMI-III is simply unsatisfactory.

2. A set of psychometric problems plagues the MCMI-III. For example, only 39 of the 175 items are keyed "False" leaving the MCMI-III vulnerable to a response style of yea-saying. Again, most of the items appear on two, three, and even four scales. This collinearity compromises any statistics generated on the scales because the scales will have built in codependencies resulting in artificially inflated correlations. Consequently, the factor analyses of the original MCMI were bizarrely inflated. The ostensible reason for the item overlap is that without such overlap many more items would have to be used, lengthening the test to MMPI-like proportions. The weights for certain items are psychometrically unjustified; unit weighting is superior in that nothing is gained for the trouble that item weighting causes. Third, the various personality disorders are theoretically correlated so, the argument is made, that the scales should have built in correlations. This is simply a fallacious argument. Perhaps years ago someone might have made this argument plausible but with the arrival of structural modeling programs available on desktop computers, we have the statistical procedures at our fingertips that allow us to assess correlated facets of personality such as the Revised NEO Personality Inventory (NEO-PI-R; 12:330) provides. The item overlap forecloses the possibility for such research.

3. Diagnosis involves differentiating among disorders. The item overlap and the resulting inflated correlations in the interscale correlation matrix preclude discriminant validity. No discriminant validity studies are presented. Cohen, Swerdlik, and Phillips (1996) reviewed studies by independent researchers who found the MCMI yielded an alarming rate of false positives and false negatives. The data provided in the MCMI-III manual concerning sensitivity and specificity are simply contrary to studies conducted on the earlier MCMIs and contrary to psychometric theory. Specifically, sensitivity is the degree to which a test identifies individuals who have a condition whereas specificity is the degree to which the nondisordered individual is identified as such. The MCMI-III data for Base Rate 75 suggest that sensitivity ranges from 12.5% for Aggressive (Sadistic) to 53.1% for Passive-Aggressiveness, with a

mean sensitivity of 36.26%. On the other hand, the MCMI-III data for specificity range from 63.5% for Dependent to 95.5% for Compulsiveness, with a mean specificity of 82.87%. For Base Rate 85, the mean sensitivity is 17.96% with the Aggressive scale having 0.0% sensitivity and Depressive having the highest efficiency at 40.8%, and the mean specificity is 92.09%, with Depressive registering 81.1% and Aggressive registering 98.9%. Thus, the data show the MCMI is poor at detecting psychopathology and excellent in detecting those without the disorder specified on a particular scale. Because the MCMI is geared to seek pathology by design, and does so according to the literature, it makes no sense that the sensitivity rates are so low. Additionally, because the literature on the MCMI series has shown no discriminant validity, because there are extraordinarily high MCMI-III interscale correlations, and because so many items are overlapping across scales, the high specificity rates are simply not credible. I wonder whether someone has mislabeled the sensitivity and specificity data sets. In any case, either the sensitivity or the specificity is sorely lacking.

CAVEAT. Given the above problems on the three editions of the MCMI, why has it continued to be purchased? There is a need for measuring the DSM and as new DSM editions are published, new MCMI editions follow. Clinicians prefer shorter batteries, particularly if the instrument promises reliability and validity. Computerized scoring and reports are appealing to many clinicians who want to maximize the use of their time and who are impressed with computer-generated reports. However, failing to consider carefully the psychometric undergirding of the instruments they use will have costs.

At a time when society has trained a critical eye on testing, when psychologists such as Dawes (1994) have likened much of clinical assessments to tarot card reading, and when psychologists are regularly called on by the courts for help, we have a duty to produce measurement instruments of the highest quality. Reviewers of the first two editions of the MCMI were appropriately critical but quite hopeful and even enthusiastic for the MCMI. The third edition represents a regression; the MCMI's promissory notes are past due. The user of the MCMI-III does so at his or her own risk.

REVIEWER'S REFERENCES

Millon, T. (1969). *Modern psychopathology: A biosocial approach to maladaptive learning and functioning.* Philadelphia: Saunders.
Hess, A. K. (1985). [Review of the Millon Clinical Multiaxial Inventory.] In J. V. Mitchell, Jr. (Ed.), *The ninth mental measurements yearbook* (pp. 984–986). Lincoln, NE: Buros Institute of Mental Measurements.
Widiger, T. A. (1985). [Review of the Millon Clinical Multiaxial Inventory.] In J. V. Mitchell, Jr. (Ed.), *The ninth mental measurements yearbook* (pp. 986–988). Lincoln, NE: Buros Institute of Mental Measurements.
Haladyna, T. M. (1992). [Review of the Millon Clinical Multiaxial Inventory-II.] In J. J. Kramer & J. C. Conoley (Eds.), *The eleventh mental measurements yearbook* (pp. 532–533). Lincoln, NE: Buros Institute of Mental Measurements.
Reynolds, C. R. (1992). [Review of the Millon Clinical Multiaxial Inventory-II.] In J. J. Kramer & J. C. Conoley (Eds.), *The eleventh mental measurements yearbook* (pp. 533–534). Lincoln, NE: Buros Institute of Mental Measurements.
Dawes, R. M. (1994). *House of cards: Psychology and psychotherapy built on myth.* New York: Free Press.
Cohen, R. J., Swerdlik, M. E., & Phillips, S. M. (1996). *Psychological testing and assessment: An introduction to tests and measurement* (3rd ed.). Mountain View, CA: Mayfield.

Review of the Millon Clinical Multiaxial Inventory-III by PAUL RETZLAFF, Professor, Psychology Department, University of Northern Colorado, Greeley, CO:

The Millon Clinical Multiaxial Inventory—III (MCMI-III) is the third generation of this widely used test of personality and psychopathology. Its use probably ranks among the top two or three clinical tests of this type. The test is not only clinically useful but psychometrically the most sophisticated of any available product.

This newest version of the test includes four validity and modifying indices including an item reading screen, Disclosure, Desirability, and Debasement. There are 11 Clinical Personality Patterns scales including Schizoid, Avoidant, Depressive, Dependent, Histrionic, Narcissistic, Antisocial, Aggressive (Sadistic), Compulsive, Passive-Aggressive (Negativistic), and Self-Defeating. There are 3 scales of Severe Personality Pathology including Schizotypal, Borderline, and Paranoid. The Basic Clinical Syndromes scales include Anxiety, Somatoform, Bipolar: Manic, Dysthymia, Alcohol Dependence, Drug Dependence, and Post-Traumatic Stress Disorder. Finally, the 3 Severe Syndromes include Thought Disorder, Major Depression, and Delusional Disorder. The 24 content scales represent an increase of 2 over the MCMI-II (11:239). The two new scales include the Depressive scale and the Post-Traumatic Stress Disorder (PTSD) scale. As can be seen from the list of scales and a reading of the items, the constructs are consistent with DSM-IV.

The 175-item, true-false test is easily tolerated by patients and is finished quickly. The items have face validity and are not aversive. A welcome part of the current revision of the test is the reduction of the number of items per scale. The MCMI-II suffered from too many of the 175 items being assigned to each scale. The MCMI-III on average has about 16 items per scale. The fewer number of items per scale as well as more focal rewriting of items should result in more specific and divergent scales. There still does remain a problem with only 175 items used to drive 24 content scales.

Base Rate scores are calculated for each scale. These scores are unique to the Millon tests. The metric represents a mapping of the Base Rate numbers to underlying diagnostic criteria. In essence, scores from 0 to 74 suggest no pathology of that type. Scores from 75 to 84 reflect that pathology at a "traits" or "features" level. Finally, scores of 85 or greater suggest that pathology is primary and most probably of diagnostic level of severity. The Base Rate scores are quite sophisticated and reflect not only the traditional normative elements of test construction but also include the critical epidemiological prevalence information.

The internal consistency reliabilities of the MCMI-III scales are the highest in the industry. They range from a low of .66 for Compulsive to .90 for Major Depression among the content scales. Of the 24 content scales, 18 have reliabilities of .80 or higher. The test-retest stability coefficients are also very high although the data in the manual are for a too brief 5–14 day period.

The validity estimates for the MCMI-III are of two types. The first includes the traditional correlations against other tests for construct validity. These are all quite high and appropriate. For example, the correlations against the Beck Depression Inventory for the Dysthymia and Major Depression scales are .71 and .74, respectively.

The second type of validity includes a Bayesian hit rate analysis against clinician diagnoses of actual patients. Here, positive predictive power of each scale is important. Positive predictive power answers the question, "What is the probability that this individual patient with a high score on this scale actually has the diagnosis?" The MCMI-II had strong positive predictive powers with most scales having statistics in the .50s to .70s. The MCMI type tests are the only major tests that even attempt to assess such validity. The MCMI-III hit rates were initially calculated on an inappropriate sample (Retzlaff, 1996) and, as such, the data in the manual are weak. A new validity study has been completed as this review goes to press and the numbers are far better.

Scoring can be accomplished by hand but this is a time-consuming and error-prone endeavor. The computer scoring that is most popular includes the new Q system from the test publisher that scores not only MCMI-IIIs but also most of the other tests published by National Computer System (NCS). The responses may be scanned into the computer or clerk entered. Scorings that have been purchased "reside" in a small device attached to the printer port. The software will score either the basic profile or can include a narrative report. The narrative report sections on personality description are excellent and the best consultation available. The actual diagnoses printed cannot take into account interview data and as such are of limited use.

The MCMI-III is a force in the industry. There is a substantial body of research available in the literature. There are, also, a number of books on the market that cover test use (Choca, Shanley, & Van Denburg, 1992), interpretation (Craig, 1993a), research (Craig, 1993b), and therapy (Retzlaff, 1995).

In summary, the MCMI-III is a clinically useful, well-constructed, and sophisticated test. It is particularly useful to diagnose the relatively difficult personality disorders.

REVIEWER'S REFERENCES

Choca, J. P., Shanley, L. A., & Van Denburg, E. (1992). *Interpretative guide to the Millon Clinical Multiaxial Inventory.* Washington, DC: American Psychological Association.
Craig, R. J. (1993a). *Psychological assessment with the Millon Clinical Multiaxial Inventory (II): An interpretative guide.* Odessa, FL: Psychological Assessment Resources.
Craig, R. J. (Ed.). (1993b). *The Millon Clinical Multiaxial Inventory: A clinical research information synthesis.* Hillsdale, NJ: Lawrence Erlbaum Associates.
Retzlaff, P. D. (Ed.). (1995). *Tactical psychotherapy of the personality disorders: An MCMI-III based approach.* Boston: Allyn & Bacon.
Retzlaff, P. (1996). MCMI-III diagnostic validity: Bad test or bad validity study. *Journal of Personality Assessment, 66*(2), 431–437.

[202]
Millon Index of Personality Styles.

Purpose: "Designed to measure personality styles of normally functioning adults."

Population: Adults.

Publication Date: 1994.

Acronym: MIPS.

Scores, 26: Enhancing, Preserving, Modifying, Accommodating, Individuating, Nurturing, Extraversing, Introversing, Sensing, Intuiting, Thinking, Feeling, Systematizing, Innovating, Retiring, Outgoing, Hesitating, Asserting, Dissenting, Conforming, Yielding, Controlling, Complaining, Agreeing, Positive Impression, Negative Impression.

Administration: Group.

Price Data, 1994: $99 per complete kit including manual (194 pages), 2 mail-in profile booklets, 2 mail-in interpretive booklets, and mailing labels; $120 per 10 mail-in profile booklets; $180 per 10 interpretive booklets; $10 per 10 scannable booklets; $25 per 25 test booklets; $59 per scoring template; $22 per 25 answer sheets; $55 per manual; $129 per Psy Test Kit including manual, user's guide, one each 3.5-inch and 5.25-inch diskettes, and 2 scannable booklets; $70 per 10 profile report credits; $130 per 10 interpretive report credits.

Time: (30) minutes.

Comments: Measure may be scored by hand, through mail-in service, or by personal computer.

Author: Theodore Millon.

Publisher: The Psychological Corporation.

Review of the Millon Index of Personality Styles by JAMES P. CHOCA, Chief, Psychology Service, Lakeside Medical Center, Department of Veterans Affairs, Chicago, IL:

In a book published more than 25 years ago, Theodore Millon proposed a theoretical grid for the classification of personality (Millon, 1969). Part of the appeal of his proposal was that it grouped together eight different personality prototypes that had been recognized by clinicians from time immemorial (Choca & Van Denburg, 1996). The scheme leading to the prototypes was eventually revised to consist of three polarities, tendencies that theoretically resulted in the distinguishing characteristics of the different personality prototypes ([pain vs. pleasure, active vs. passive, and self vs. other], Millon, 1995). The theory influenced the development of the current classification of personality disorders (American psychiatric Association, 1994), and has led to the creation of four different psychological inventories (Millon, 1977, 1993; Millon, Green, & Meagher, 1981, 1982). One of these instruments, the Millon Clinical Multiaxial Inventory (MCMI; 201) has achieved widespread use (Piotrowski, 1997).

The Millon Index of Personality Styles (MIPS) represents an extension of the Millon assessment tools into the measurement of the "normal" individuals. Designed for use in business and vocational settings, the MIPS would seemingly compete with instruments such as the Myers-Briggs Type Indicator (Briggs & Myers, 1943–1988; T4:1702) and the tools associated with the Five Factor Personality theory (e.g., the Revised NEO Personality Inventory [NEO-PI-R; Costa & McCrae, 1992; 12:330]; the Gordon Personal Profile—Inventory [GPPI; Gordon, 1993; 133]).

Millon defines personality as a "complex pattern of deeply embedded psychological characteristics" composed of traits that "comprise the individual's distinctive pattern of perceiving, feeling, thinking, and coping" (Millon & Davis, 1994, p. 80). In developing the MIPS, Millon moved his scales down from the level he used for his other inventories: Instead of measuring personalities (e.g., the histrionic personality), the MIPS scales measure the traits that make up those personalities (e.g., the active, other-oriented, extraverted, gregarious traits that are part of the histrionic personality).

The MIPS contains three groups of scales. The first group, the Motivating Aims section, consists of 6 scales designed to measure the Millon polarities noted above (e.g., pain vs. pleasure). To add to these polarity-based scales, Millon displayed his usual resourcefulness. Borrowing concepts from Freud, Jung, Sullivan, and others, he created the other two groups of scales, labeled Cognitive Modes and Interpersonal Behaviors. There are 8 scales in the Cognitive Mode group; 10 scales measure Interpersonal Behaviors. All scales are paired on a bipolar construct. For instance, the Enhancing Scale—designed to measure the construct of pleasure—is paired with the Preserving Scale—designed to measure the construct of pain. Finally, the MIPS includes 2 scales labeled Positive Impression and Negative Impression to measure the test-taking attitude of the examinee.

Replicating the methodology used for other Millon inventories, theoretically derived test items were refined through pilot studies to exclude dysfunctional items. The resulting items were then administered to two large samples, one from business settings and another one from colleges across the nation. The data obtained from the seemingly well-balanced samples were then used to further reduce the item pool, and to generate the norms for the inventory.

In further replication of the procedures used to develop the MCMI, Millon often uses the same item for more than one scale. The raw score given to an item is weighted, from a score of 1 to a score of 3, depending on the theoretical importance the item has for the particular scale. The raw scale score is then transformed into a weighted Prevalence Score that takes into account the prevalence of the particular trait in the population. These Prevalence Scores are then adjusted in accordance to the score the individual obtained on a multitude of MIPS scales.

The MIPS is very short for the number of measures included (169 items are used to derive scores for 26 scales). The test form contains a nice arrangement of the items and allows the response to be entered in a space adjacent to the item. The scoring and interpretation of the test can be accomplished through a computer-based user-friendly program. In this reviewer's opinion, the narrative produced by this program was quite readable, and described the personality traits in a way that was comprehensive and informative. The narrative included a good balance in terms of the advantages an examinee may derive from having a particular personality trait, and the liabilities that may accompany the possession of the same trait.

As can be expected with a recently published test, there is not a great deal of literature available. The MIPS manual describes several studies dealing with the selection of personnel, vocational guidance of college students, or the assessment of middle-level managers. A study on the factorial structure of the test is also available (Weiss & Lowther, 1995). Finally, a recent book on the Millon inventories includes a chapter on the MIPS (Weiss, 1997).

In designing the MIPS scales to measure traits, as opposed to personalities, Millon escaped the pejorative connotation of the clinical personality disorders. As a trait-based instrument, the MIPS scale labels are similar to those used by instruments with demonstrated success in the business and vocational markets (e.g., the Myers-Briggs or NEO-PI). Targeting the scales to the trait level also allowed the easy addition of seemingly useful concepts. There was, however, a price to be paid for that design. As a result of the lower conceptual target the MIPS scales have, the user becomes a bit lost, looking at the trees without having a clear idea what the forest looks like. The more global view offered by the other Millon inventories has been seen as an advantage over other personality instruments (see Choca & Van Denburg, 1996, for further discussion), and will unfortunately not be enjoyed by the MIPS users.

Because the MIPS was developed following the same methodology used for the MCMI, it will be subject to the same criticisms. For instance, in spite of the fact that loading single test items on more than one scale allows for the test to be shortened in a way that is theoretically sound, this practice leads to high interscale correlations, and undermines the structural soundness of the test (Gibertini & Retzlaff, 1988; Montag & Comrey, 1987; Hess, 1985; Widiger, 1985). In the case of the MIPS, several scales have a correlation of more than .80 with another scale. Even when all of the intercorrelations make theoretical sense, there is the issue of how high a correlation has to be before the two scales are seen as redundant. In the worst of the cases, the reported correlation between the Enhancing and Preserving scales (-.87 for the combined adult sample [manual, Table 4.6]) was higher than the split-half reliability coefficients of either scale (.82 and .86 respectively [manual, Table 4.1]). That finding tells us that one of those scales has as much in common with the other as it has internally with itself.

Moving on to another MCMI controversy, the weighting of the item raw score in accordance to how well the item fits the concept being measured has theoretical merit. Nevertheless, it has been shown that this practice does not contribute to the psychometric property of the scale, and the weights obviously complicate the scoring of the inventory (Retzlaff, 1991; Retzlaff, Sheehan, & Lorr, 1990; Streiner, Goldberg, & Miller, 1993; Streiner & Miller, 1989).

In a way, the above criticisms are unfair in that they look at the MIPS against psychometric ideals. When all is said and done, the crucial question will be how well the MIPS performs against similar instruments, and how useful the findings for the MIPS are for those seeking a measure of personality variables in business or vocational settings. Given the short period of time the inventory has been available and the absence of literature using this instrument, crucial questions cannot be answered yet. The many positive qualities the test offers, however, will undoubtedly make it a good contender.

REVIEWER'S REFERENCES

Briggs, K. C., & Myers, I. B. (1943–1988). The Myers-Briggs Type Indicator. Palo Alto, CA: Consulting Psychologists Press.

Millon, T. (1969). *Modern psychopathology: A biosocial approach to maladaptive learning and functioning.* Philadelphia: Saunders.

Millon, T. (1977). Millon Clinical Multiaxial Inventory. Minneapolis, MN: National Computer Systems.

Millon, T., Green, C. J., & Meagher, R. B. (1981). Millon Behavioral Health Inventory. Minneapolis, MN: National Computer Systems.

Millon, T., Green, C. J., & Meagher, R. B. (1982). Millon Adolescent Personality Inventory. Minneapolis, MN: National Computer Systems.

Hess, A. K. (1985). [Review of the Millon Clinical Multiaxial Inventory]. In J. V. Mitchell, Jr. (Ed.), *The ninth mental measurements yearbook* (pp. 984–986). Lincoln, NE: Buros Institute of Mental Measurements.

Widiger, T. A. (1985). [Review of the Millon Clinical Multiaxial Inventory]. In J. V. Mitchell, Jr. (Ed.), *The ninth mental measurements yearbook* (pp. 986–988). Lincoln, NE: Buros Institute of Mental Measurements.

Montag, I., & Comrey, A. L. (1987). Millon MCMI scales factor analyzed and correlated with MMPI and CPS scales. *Multivariate Behavioral Research, 22,* 401–413.

Gibertini, M., & Retzlaff, P. D. (1988). Factor invariance of the Millon Clinical Multiaxial Inventory. *Journal of Psychopathology and Behavioral Assessment, 10,* 65–74.

Streiner, D. L., & Miller, H. R. (1989). The MCMI-II: How much better than the MCMI? *Journal of Personality Assessment, 53,* 81–84.

Retzlaff, P. D., Sheehan, E. P., & Lorr, M. (1990). MCMI-II scoring: Weighted and unweighted algorithms. *Journal of Personality Assessment, 55,* 219–223.

Retzlaff, P. (1991, August). *MCMI-II scoring challenges: Multiweight items and site specific algorithms.* Paper presented at the annual convention of the American Psychological Association, San Francisco, CA.

Costa, P. T., Jr., & McCrae, R. R. (1992). The Revised NEO Personality Inventory. Odessa, FL: Psychological Assessment Resources.

Gordon, L. V. (1993). Gordon Personal Profile—Inventory. San Antonio, TX: The Psychological Corporation.

Millon, T. (1993). Millon Adolescent Clinical Inventory. Minneapolis, MN: National Computer Systems.

Streiner, D. L., Goldberg, J. O, & Miller, H. R. (1993). MCMI-II item weights: Their lack of effectiveness. *Journal of Personality Assessment, 60,* 471–476.

American Psychiatric Association. (1994). *Diagnostic and statistical manual of mental disorders* (4th ed.). Washington, DC: Author.

Millon, T., & Davis, R. D. (1994). Millon's evolutionary model of normal and abnormal personality: Theory and measures. In S. Strack and M. Lorr (Eds.), *Differentiating normal and abnormal personality* (pp. 79–113). New York: Springer.

Millon, T. (1995). *Disorders of personality: DSM-IV and beyond.* New York: Wiley.

Weiss, L. G., & Lowther, J. L. (1995, March). *The factor structure of the Millon Index of Personality Styles.* Paper presented at the annual meeting of the Society for Personality Assessment, Atlanta, GA.

Choca, J. P., & Van Denburg, E. (1996). *Interpretative guide for the MCMI* (2nd ed.). Washington, DC: American Psychological Association.

Piotrowski, C. (1997). Use of the Millon Clinical Multiaxial Inventory in clinical practice. *Perceptual and Motor Skills, 84,* 1185–1186.

Weiss, L. G. (1997). The MIPS: Gauging the dimensions of normality. In T. Millon (Ed.), *The Millon Inventories.* New York: Guilford.

Review of the Millon Index of Personality Styles by PETER ZACHAR, Assistant Professor of Psychology, Auburn University at Montgomery, Montgomery, AL:

The Millon Index of Personality Styles (MIPS) is a measure of normal adult personality based on a framework devised by one of psychology's most prominent theoreticians. Although it began as a downward extension of Theodore Millon's thinking about personality disorders in psychiatric nosology, it has expanded into something more comprehensive, measuring 24 separate traits in three domains.

The purpose of the MIPS is to measure latent variables of personality. The standard example of latent personality variables in psychology is the Big Five, a set of constructs that emerge in factor analysis after factor analysis of diverse sets of items. Rather than the "latent quantitative" approach as used by the developers of the NEO-PI (Revised NEO Personality Inventory, 12:330), the MIPS developers used a "latent theoretical" approach.

Dr. Millon's implicit argument for this approach is as follows: In the history of clinical psychology, certain concepts emerge in theory after theory, even though each theorist may have different names for these concepts. These sturdy concepts, important to the "classic" thinkers in psychiatry, "rediscovered" by the social behaviorists in the '60s, and central to the program of contemporary empirical psychologists, by their robustness have also earned the title "latent." The MIPS places these traits into an integrated theoretical framework.

CONCEPTUAL DESCRIPTION. As a "metapsychological" framework, the MIPS triad of Motivating Aims, Cognitive Styles, and Interpersonal Behaviors represents a sophisticated development of the standard cognitive-behavioral triad of affect, cognition, and behavior. The new triad hits all the right notes.

Although originally developed within learning biosocial theory, Millon traces his Motivating Aims back to Freud. He shares with Freud a preference for articulating personality constructs using metaphors drawn from the biological and natural sciences. In contrast to Freud's 19th century neurology, Millon's (1991) metaphors are drawn from evolutionary biology. In their shared view, motivation is governed by the polarities of pleasure versus pain, self versus other, and active versus passive adaptation. The MIPS translates these aims into bipolar scales called Enhancing versus Preserving, Individuating versus Nurturing, and Modifying versus Accommodating. Although these six constructs are end points on three continua, each end point is a separate scale on the MIPS.

Motivating Aims are organic in nature, shared by various life forms in different degrees. The pleasure versus pain and self versus other dimensions work for chimps as well as humans. What is distinct about humans is our advanced capacity for representa-

tional thought. With a representational capacity, we can leave the present, reflect on the past, and plan for the future. A model of representation or cognition is therefore important for a field like personology, which purports to explain behavior with reference to what is in the head.

Millon notes that there are individual differences with respect to how people construct their model of the world, which he calls Cognitive Styles. His original work in Cognitive Styles occurred as a part of his description of the personality disorders. In translating these psychiatric patterns into normal personality variables, Dr. Millon recognized that his model mirrored Jung's typology, so he adopted Jung's names.

In essence, the Cognitive Style rung of the MIPS triad replicates the Myers-Briggs Type Indicator (MBTI; T4:1702). It includes the well-known scales of Introversion, Extraversion, Sensing, and Intuiting. Rather than the MBTI's Judging and Perceiving poles, and more consistent with Jung's actual theory, the MIPS contains the scales Systematizing and Innovating. One advantage of the MIPS Cognitive Styles scales is that we get familiar and well-known constructs in a more ecologically integrated model, that is, situated in between motivational and interpersonal variables.

The third fork of the MIPS triad is the Interpersonal Behaviors. For interpersonal theorists, personality is expressed only in relationships with others, so any comprehensive model of personality must take relationships into account. Although he makes reference to the ground-breaking work of Meyer, Sullivan, and Leary, Millon's own interpersonal variables appear to be downward extensions of 10 of the 13 DSM-III-R personality disorders.

Although most clinicians prefer the syndrome type personality disorders of the current nosology to a five-factor dimensional reconstruction, they also recognize that personality disorders are constructed syndromes rather than fundamental in a physical/neurological sense. There are many possible personality disorder categories not a part of the original 13, such as depressive personality disorder in the DSM-IV appendix. As a result, the Interpersonal Behaviors of the MIPS are probably less latent than are the constructs in the Motivational and Cognitive forks of the triad. The MIPS operationalizes Interpersonal Behaviors into five bipolar traits or 10 scales called: Retiring versus Outgoing, Hesitating versus Asserting, Dissenting versus Conforming, Yielding versus Controlling, and Complaining versus Agreeing.

The MIPS also includes several validity scales. The Positive Impression scale is an impressive "fake good" index. The Negative Impression scale is a "fake bad" index, measuring dissimulation of moderate neurotic disturbances. There is also an Adjustment Index that allows users to screen for potential pathology. It is based on the tenable hypothesis that extreme scores on normal personality scales can be indicators of pathology. The computer reports also have a consistency index.

PSYCHOMETRIC EVALUATION. The MIPS introduces an innovation in standardized scoring, specifically the use of Prevalence Scores (PS), which constitute an elegant combination of categorical versus dimensional models of personality. The idea behind prevalence scores is that for any trait-oriented scale, we have to identify a score at which we say the person has the trait in question. For example, how many extraverted questions do you have to agree with in order to be called an "extravert"? Millon states that using median splits as cutoffs are arbitrary. We would not give people a test for paranoid personality disorder and say that whoever obtains a score greater than the median is Paranoid and we should not do that for a trait like Extraversion either.

PS scores are contingent on epidemiological studies that estimate the base rates of certain traits. If you have an adequate estimate of the prevalence of a trait like Extraversion, 65% for example, and a representative sample from the population, it is a good bet that 65% of the people in that sample are extraverts. An extravert should therefore score at or above the 35th percentile on an extraversion scale. Millon and his colleagues estimated prevalence rates for each trait measured by the MIPS. They also implemented a stratified sampling procedure to ensure that their normative group is representative of the U.S. population.

Using prevalence scores, people can be placed in one of two groups, a group that has the trait (extravert) or a group that does not (non-extraverts). People who score at PS 50 on any scale are said to have the trait. Even more important, within each category people are rated on a dimension. Not all extraverts are equally extraverted. At PS 69, one is at the 50th percentile of the extraverted group. They are either as or more extraverted than half the extraverts. At PS 89, one is at what looks like one standard deviation above the mean, being as or more extraverted than 84% of the extraverts. The extravert's extravert with a PS vale of 100 is at the 99th percentile. For the non-extravert group, PS 9 means you are as or more extraverted than only 16% of the non-extraverts.

Obviously, clinical judgment is needed to decide how to measure a true extravert or a true introvert before prevalence studies can be undertaken. Although doubtful that the authors of the MIPS have achieved God's-eye prevalence rates for each trait on the inventory, even rough estimates represent an improvement on simply using median splits to place people in categories.

My concern about the MIPS is that the scales have overlapping items. Each scale has "prototypical items," which are supposed to be face valid measures of the construct in question. An example prototypical item for the Feeling scale is "being kind-hearted is more important than being logical." Each scale also has "support items," meaning items written for other scales but placed on the scale in question because they were correlated with that scale. An example support item for the Feeling scale is "I often wait for someone else to solve my problems." Prototypical items receive a weighting of 3 points and support items receive a weighting of either 1 or 2 points.

The developers justify this strategy by claiming that it makes the operationalization of each construct more multidimensional. Furthermore, because the constructs are theoretically supposed to be related, this test development strategy guarantees correlated scales. It has also helped Millon's pathology-based personality tests gain an advantage on the competition by being much briefer and therefore easier to take.

Suspending doubt and accepting this strategy, the important psychometric properties of the MIPS look good. The internal consistency coefficients measured by Cronbach's alpha are adequate. They average in the high .70s and low .80s. The 2-month test-retest reliabilities are very good, averaging in the mid 80s. Because some of the items are vague and could easily be answered one way or the other depending on a slight shift of interpretation, these stability coefficients are impressive. Standard errors of measurement for each scale need to be provided in future revisions. Construct validity evidence as provided by correlations with related tests is also good. (Strangely, correlations with Dr. Millon's other tests are not presented.) The research reported in the manual indicates that the ability of the MIPS to make distinctions between people and predictions about future behavior looks promising.

Adopting a more critical attitude toward the practice of keying items on multiple scales, I have some concerns about the test. Dr. Millon does not believe in simple structure as a model for a test. Even though simple structure refers to a pattern in factor analysis where items load highly onto one and only one factor, it is also a standard model for more rationally developed scales as well. The idea that constructs need to be operationally distinct even if they are conceptually related is an underlying assumption of many important statistical techniques.

With extensive item overlap between scales, any kind of prediction models, especially regression models, are risky due to high multicollinearity among variables. Discriminant function analysis and a host of other bread-and-butter research analytic strategies would also be of questionable value. If researchers did use these techniques, shared items would have to be eliminated beforehand or be partialed out in the analysis. This will not please people looking for research ideas, which is a shame because the MIPS framework is attractive.

Keying items on multiple scales assures that the scales are correlated, but these autocorrelations inflate any estimate of association between constructs. When two scales are correlated at .80 and .79, as some of the scales are, I doubt that different constructs are being measured. Millon is willing to consider correlations in the .60s between the MIPS Cognitive Styles and the MBTI scales as proof that they are measuring the same constructs, but also wants to say his Extraversion and Outgoing scales, which correlated at .65, are different constructs!

From a commonsense standpoint, if correlations exist between items on the Outgoing scale and the Extraversion scale, one does not need to put Outgoing items on the Extraversion scale in order to make the scales correlated. The ability to cross-key items means the test already has the correlational virtues that cross-keying is supposed to achieve.

Using the goal of correlated scales as a justification for a latent theoretical approach versus a latent quantitative approach is also invalid. Researchers are mistaken to think that scales created by virtue of a factor analysis are uncorrelated. By necessity, the different factors in an orthogonal solution are uncorrelated, but a latent factor includes all items that load onto it. When researchers pick the items with the highest loadings and put them onto scales, those factor-based scales are not orthogonal. The scales can be correlated.

Because previous psychometric critiques have not altered Dr. Millon's test construction philosophy, let me provide a logical critique. If Nurturance and Extraversion are correlated, the most honest way to estimate that correlation would be to develop independent scales. Cross-keying items undermines any

possibility of claiming that the hypothesis "these constructs are related" could be called a risky prediction because, by necessity, there will be positive correlations between scales. Rather than testing the hypothesis, the MIPS loads the dice. In terms of the philosophy of science, Dr. Millon is using the wrong Karl. Rather than quoting Hempel, he should read Popper (i.e., a test of a theory is an attempt to prove it wrong).

I think that the latent theoretical approach outlined by Dr. Millon does have merit. Even though metaphors drawn from the physical sciences do not assure correspondence with reality, it makes sense that variables that emerge in psychological theory after theory are fundamental in some basic way. Unfortunately, some scales on the MIPS are correlated so strongly that it is almost impossible to be high on one and low on the other, which calls into question the extent to which the MIPS constructs are as fundamental as the latent theory approach suggests they should be.

Many readers may have noticed that the "multidimensionality" justification for cross-keying has survived my critique. I save it for last because it is the most puzzling aspect of the MIPS. Cross-keying flatly contradicts the MIPS framework. According to that framework, the Motivation, the Cognitive, and the Interpersonal domains are related but separate levels of analysis. During test development, Dr. Millon emphasized the importance defining Cognitive Styles with respect to cognition functions and *not* behavior. The reason for having Extraversion in the Cognitive fork and Outgoing in the Interpersonal fork is because one is a representational level variable and the other is a behavioral level variable. But this distinction is abrogated by the fact that, after prototypical items were written for any domain of the triad, the final scales are composed mostly of items drawn from the other domain. So the representational level Extraversion scale has 10 items from the behavioral level Outgoing scale. Dr. Millon needs to rethink either the test or the framework.

The manual's discussion of the validity scales would be more appropriately placed with the discussion of the other scales. The manual needs both an index and a discussion of the consistency scale. For clinicians, a section on interpretation would be very useful. The Psychological Corporation was not forthcoming with materials so I cannot comment on either hand scoring or the computer programs. As presented in the technical manual, the personal computer program looks very slick, in the positive sense, but there may be hidden costs regarding additional test management programs needed to make the disks work. I was extremely impressed with the face validity of the mail-in interpretive report that I received.

Dr. Millon has made much of the fact that this test is based on an integrated framework. That framework may be worthy of becoming a standard chapter in personality textbooks. Unfortunately, the framework is much better than the test. Cross-keying items is psychometrically suspect and research unfriendly. If the bottom line for a test is discrimination and prediction, however, the applied research in the manual indicates that the MIPS has stronger legs than these psychometric considerations acknowledge. Other than technical considerations, more support from research published in peer-review journals is an important next step for the MIPS.

REVIEWER'S REFERENCE

Millon, T. (1991). Normality: What may we learn from evolutionary theory? In D. Offer & M. Sabshin (Eds.), *The diversity of normal behavior: Further contributions to normatology* (pp. 356–404). New York: Basic Books.

[203]
Minnesota Test for Differential Diagnosis of Aphasia.

Purpose: "For the evaluation of aphasic deficit resulting from brain damage in patients."
Population: Adults.
Publication Dates: 1965–1992.
Scores, 5: Auditory Disturbances, Visual and Reading Disturbances, Speech and Language Disturbances, Visuomotor and Writing Disturbances, Disturbances of Numerical Relations and Arithmetic Processes.
Administration: Individual.
Price Data, 1993: $54.95 per complete kit including monograph, manual ('65, 23 pages), 2 sets of stimulus cards, and 25 record booklets; $12.25 per 25 record booklets.
Time: (45–120) minutes.
Author: Hildred Schuell.
Publisher: American Guidance Service, Inc.
Cross References: See T4:1653 (12 references) and T3:1511 (14 references); see also T2:2080 (4 references); for reviews by David Jones and Seymour Rigrodsky, see 7:958 (7 references); see also P:172 (8 references).

TEST REFERENCES

1. Jason, G. W. (1983). Hemispheric asymmetries in motor function: I. Left-hemisphere specialization for memory but not performance. *Neuropsychologia, 21,* 35–45.
2. Hall, P. K., & Jordan, L. S. (1987). An assessment of a controlled association task to identify word-finding problems in children. *Language, Speech, and Hearing Services in Schools, 18,* 99–111.
3. Bacon, G. M., Potter, R. E., & Seikel, J. A. (1992). Auditory comprehension of "yes—no" questions by adult aphasics. *Journal of Communication Disorders, 24,* 23–29.
4. Bloom, R. L., Borod, J. C., Obler, L. K., & Gerstman, L. J. (1993). Suppression and facilitation of pragmatic performance: Effects of emotional content on discourse following right and left brain damage. *Journal of Speech and Hearing Research, 36,* 1227–1235.
5. Nicholas, L. E., & Brookshire, R. H. (1993). A system for quantifying the informativeness and efficiency of the connected speech of adults with aphasia. *Journal of Speech and Hearing Research, 36,* 338–350.
6. Brookshire, R. H., & Nicholas, L. E. (1994). Speech sample size and test-retest stability of connected speech measures for adults with aphasia. *Journal of Speech and Hearing Research, 37,* 399–407.
7. Records, N. L. (1994). A measure of the contribution of a gesture to the perception of speech in listeners with aphasia. *Journal of Speech and Hearing, 37,* 1086–1099.
8. Windsor, J., Doyle, S. S., & Siegel, G. M. (1994). Language acquisition after mutism: A longitudinal case study of autism. *Journal of Speech and Hearing Research, 37,* 96–105.
9. Kirshner, H. S., Hughes, T., Fakhoury, T., & Abou-Khalil, B. (1995). Aphasia secondary to partial status epilepticus of the basal temporal language area. *Neurology, 45,* 1616–1618.
10. Nicholas, L. E., & Brookshire, R. H. (1995). Presence, completeness, and accuracy of main concepts in the connected speech of non-brain-damaged adults and adults with aphasia. *Journal of Speech and Hearing Research, 38,* 145–156.

Review of the Minnesota Test for Differential Diagnosis of Aphasia by MATTHEW E. LAMBERT, Research Psychologist, Neurology Research and Education Center, St. Mary Hospital, Lubbock, TX:

The Minnesota Test for Differential Diagnosis of Aphasia (Minnesota Test) is the second edition of the test originally published in 1965 and based upon Hildred Schuell's work at the Minneapolis Veterans Administration Hospital. Schuell passed away in 1970 and the current test revision was completed by Joyce W. Sefer and published in 1973. The interpretive manual, *Differential Diagnosis of Aphasia with the Minnesota Test* (Schuell, 1973) is a combination of Schuell's original data along with data collected by Sefer for two of the five original aphasia categories. Inaccessibility to Schuell's actual raw data and reliance on statistical measures calculated on that data by Schuell, however, were noted as limitations to Sefer's revision.

The Minnesota Test addresses Schuell's aphasic categories: (a) Simple Aphasia—reduction in available language without perceptual or sensorimotor impairment or dysarthria; (b) Aphasia with Visual Involvement—reduction in available language with impaired discrimination, recognition, and recall of learned visual symbols; (c) Mild Aphasia with Persisting Dysfluency—simple aphasia with persisting dysfluency; (d) Aphasia with Scattered Findings Compatible with Generalized Brain Damage—reduced available language with visual impairment and dysarthria; (e) Aphasia with Sensorimotor Involvement—reduction in available language with discrimination, producing, or sequencing phonemes difficulty; (f) Aphasia with Intermittent Auditory Imperception—aphasia characterized by impairment of auditory perception; and (g) Irreversible Aphasia Syndrome—virtual complete loss of functional language skills in all modalities. Although these categories underlie the basis for the test, evaluative items are divided into five sections: (a) Auditory Disturbances; (b) Visual and Reading Disturbances; (c) Speech and Language Disturbances; (d) Visuomotor and Writing Disturbances; and (e) Disturbances of Numerical

Relations and Arithmetic Processes with each section comprising 4 (Disturbances of Numerical Relations and Arithmetic Processes) to 15 (Speech and Language Disturbances) subtests. The number of items per subtest ranges from 5 to 32. The validity of Schuell's aphasia model, however, may not completely reflect current understanding of aphasic disorders.

Administration instructions are included in a separate manual and are recommended to be read while conducting the examination. Materials necessary for completing the test include two bound card decks provided with the test and materials obtained by the examiner. These other materials include a bell, cup, box with an easily opened lid, long and short pencils, spoon, clock face with movable hands, various coins, stopwatch, flashlight, and lined and unlined paper. Although these materials can be secured easily there is no standardization, which opens the possibility of error between administrators and test materials, thereby reducing reliability and validity. On the positive side, use of these materials allows the examiner to observe gross behaviors with real world objects as they relate to aphasic problems.

Test responses are recorded in a seven-page booklet with historical and observational data. Yet, the booklet is cumbersome and difficult to use. It is oriented to a landscape position when the examiner records responses and then rotated to a portrait orientation for use with patient-entered responses. Moreover, the form is crowded with minimal space to record either responses or observations. The item sequences in some subtests are not defined, as stimuli can be presented using either a horizontal or vertical scanning approach.

Administration time requires upwards of 2 hours; although, according to the interpretive manual, it can be shortened by starting each test section with a subtest expected to be completed errorlessly by the subject. Should the subject perform poorly then movement to an earlier subtest is recommended until an adequate floor is established. The remaining section is then to be completed to establish each subject's ceiling. Time savings might be substantial, but reliability and validity are again compromised by this approach. Moreover, important aspects of aphasic behavior could be missed in easier subtests skipped over. Additionally, the lack of precise scoring criteria may lead to idiosyncratic interpretation of subject responses. This could, in turn, result in some subtests being prematurely terminated and other producing erroneously high performances by continuation beyond the appropriate termination point. The true

nature of a patient's aphasic symptoms may then be obscured by this scoring artifact.

Test scoring consists of tabulating the errors for each subtest. No composite scores are produced to represent the five test sections nor are there scores calculated with direct association to the seven aphasia types postulated by Schuell. Interpretation is undertaken by comparing the number of subtest errors with the mean errors produced by the various aphasia type patients for each subtest. A qualitative interpretation is then formulated based upon the perceived pattern reflected in the subtest performance. Combinations of subtests reflecting particular language skills and abilities are described in the manual and can be used to assist interpretation. The difficulty with this approach, as noted in the following, is the poor interpretive reliability. Qualitative interpretations, although important to understanding nuances of aphasic disorders, should not be the first line of interpretation, rather supplementary to a more quantitative and reliable approach.

Reliability data for test-retest, split-half, alternate forms, and interrater activities are absent from the manual. It is assumed that reliability information is available in the references provided at the end of the manual. Yet this information should be part of the test's overall psychometric description provided in the manual. Moreover, the references cited in the manual are outdated with publication dates ranging from 1959 to a "forthcoming volume in 1973." To make this a viable instrument, a complete reliability analysis of the Minnesota Test needs to be undertaken with standardized testing procedures and interpretive guidelines.

Given the above reliability statements, the Minnesota Test's validity is uninterpretable. As noted, the manual contains comparative subtest error scores for nonaphasics and patients for each aphasia type. The percent or number of subjects in each group producing subtest errors is noted in the manual, but extrapolation of these data to specific diagnostic statements cannot be undertaken readily. Some attempt at concurrent validity is made through tacit relationships between test performances to global neurological, health, and demographic variables being presented in the manual. Nevertheless, no relationships between Minnesota Test performances and patients suffering specific neurological diseases are presented nor is there any discussion of performance profiles associated with specific aphasic disorders such as Wernicke's and Broca's aphasias. As with the reliability issues, a full validation effort needs to be undertaken for the Minnesota Test. All forms of validity should be assessed to make this test up-to-date with current understanding of neurological diseases, cognitive rehabilitation, and specific language disorders.

Unfortunately, there is no single statement that can be made about the Minnesota Test other than it is outdated. It provides some heuristic information about aphasic disorders, but has not kept pace with advances in understanding neurological disorders, cognitive impairments associated with those disorders, and the burgeoning area of cognitive rehabilitation. More up-to-date instruments provide complete aphasia assessments with comprehensive normative data that guide reliable assessment and intervention.

REVIEWER'S REFERENCE

Schuell, H. (1973). *Differential diagnosis of aphasia with the Minnesota Test.* Minneapolis: University of Minnesota Press.

Review of the Minnesota Test for Differential Diagnosis of Aphasia by JAMES C. REED, Chief Psychologist, St. Luke's Hospital, New Bedford, MA:

The Minnesota Test for Differential Diagnosis of Aphasia (MTDDA) has a venerable history in psychological testing stemming from its development in 1948 and its publication in 1965. Schuell died in 1970, and the revised edition in 1973, the work of James J. Jenkins, Robert Shaw, and Joyce W. Sefer, represents a change in classification and syndrome nomenclature rather than a change in the test items. Aphasia is defined as a reduction of available language that crosses all language modalities, and in the present edition the categories of aphasia are given as (a) simple aphasia, a reduction of available language in all modalities without specific perceptual or sensory motor impairment; (b) aphasia with visual involvement, a reduction of available language with coexisting impairment of discrimination, recognition, and recall of learned visual symbols; (c) mild aphasia with persisting dysfluency, resembling simple aphasia, except for the accompaniment of persisting dysfluency; (d) aphasia with findings compatible with generalized brain damage, a reduction of available language, with findings that usually include both visual involvement and some degree of dysarthria; (e) aphasia with sensory motor involvement, characterized by severe reduction of language in all modalities and accompanied by difficulty in discriminating, producing, and sequencing phonemes; (e) aphasia with intermittent auditory imperception, severe impairment of auditory perception, with some functional speech usually retained or recovered early; and (f) irreversible aphasia syndrome, characterized by an almost complete loss of functional language skills in all modalities. The MTDDA has 47 tests and for each category of aphasia the disruption of language signs or the errors characterizing the category are given along with the most discriminating tests.

Throughout the monograph, reference is made to a factor analysis that was performed when the MTDDA was being developed and five dimensions were produced. As the tests are described, their loading on each of the factors is discussed. Nowhere is the factor matrix shown with the factors representing the columns and the rows representing the tests. This method of discussing the tests and the omission of the factor matrix makes it difficult to remember which test goes with which factor(s). However, the omission may be fortunate, because the factor analysis was done on 157 aphasic patients, and many factor analysts would state that a factor analysis of a correlation matrix of 47 tests based on an N of 157 is probably quite unstable and not to be taken seriously. If the factors and the aphasia categories are viewed as a classification system that facilitates verbal communication rather than structures etched in stone, then the categories as well as the factors can serve a useful purpose.

The MTDDA may fall short on meeting certain technical criteria frequently desired by test users and consumers. For example, conventional reliability coefficients were not presented in the monograph. However, for most tests the number of subjects in the various diagnostic groups was presented along with the percentage of those subjects who made errors. For example, in a table on the performance on oral reading of words (monograph, p. 49), the number of subjects with simple aphasia was given as 12 and 25% made oral reading errors. This means that three subjects made errors in oral reading and nine did not. Because of the small N such a finding is probably unreliable, but if one looks more deeply, out of a total of 75 aphasic subjects, 81% made errors in oral pronunciation. Among nonaphasic subjects ($n = 50$), only 2% or one subject made errors. If one regards errors as a pathognomonic sign, then within any category there will be a number of false negatives, but false positives will be rare. As another illustration, in copying Greek letters (one of the visual-motor and writing tests) the median number of errors for 75 aphasics was 0, the same as for the nonaphasic, but 21% of the aphasics made errors (i.e., 15 aphasic subjects made errors and 60 did not). Again 2% of the 50 nonaphasics or one nonaphasic subject made an error in copying a Greek letter. In short, when errors occur the person making the error probably belongs to the aphasic group. By viewing the tables and research results in this light, there is solid testimony for the validity of the MTDDA. Indeed, as is discussed in the monograph, the difference between aphasic and nonaphasic language is chiefly one of degree. All normals occasionally misread, miscopy, or say the wrong word but when errors accumulate they are diagnostically significant.

As with other psychological tests, obtaining valid results will require a trained examiner. The tests are arranged in order of ascending difficulty, and it is up to the examiner to encourage the patient and to provide the reassurance that brain-damaged patients frequently require in order to obtain the best possible performance. The authors suggest it is usually better to do the testing in more than one session. This may or may not be practical.

The test booklet contains a format for the convenient recording of important data. Page 1 is a summary section for the test scores. Page 2 is for noting factors pertinent to social history, medical history, and present illness. Page 3 contains tentative guidelines for clinical ratings in comprehension, speech, reading, writing, and dysarthria, along with a suggested diagnostic scale for the degree of impairment.

In summary, the MTDDA has survived the passage of time. Further research is needed to demonstrate the stability of the factors that are listed and the validity of the aphasic categories. Nevertheless, the test is useful to determine degree of impairment for a wide range of language behaviors and to assess improvement or deterioration in language behavior over repeated evaluations. The test provides for objective findings regarding disturbances in language, and differential classification can be made by analyzing patterns of errors for groups of similar tests, even though there may be a large number of false negatives for any single one of the 47 tests. Schuell and her colleagues, through this test, have made a substantial contribution to patient assessment. In the days when hospitals, health clinics, and health providers were paid to evaluate patients the test could be highly recommended. At present, with managed care and capitation, when the same health providers are paid not to see patients, the MTDDA has a questionable future.

[204]
Motivated Skills Card Sort.

Purpose: To identify skills that are central to personal and career satisfaction and success by rank ordering skills on two dimensions: Competency and Motivation.

Population: Adults.
Publication Dates: 1981–1994.
Scores: Skills Ratings Matrix.
Administration: Group or individual.
Price Data, 1994: $12 per complete kit including manual ('91, 34 pages) and cards; $9 per manual; $5 per set of cards.
Time: (45–60) minutes.
Author: Richard L. Knowdell.
Publisher: Career Research and Testing, Inc.

Review of the Motivated Skills Card Sort by ALBERT M. BUGAJ, Associate Professor of Psychology, University of Wisconsin—Marinette, Marinette, WI:

The Motivated Skills Card Sort (MSCS) is purportedly designed to allow the taker to isolate those abilities he or she wishes to use in the work world. The manual claims it will allow the taker to "gain a vocabulary for describing your goals and qualifications" (p. 4). As a result, this will lead to "enhanced job satisfaction and success, and for your employer, high morale and productivity" (p. 4).

The manual refers to the *Dictionary of Occupational Titles*, from which it takes an analysis of three basic types of skills: functional-transferable, self-management, and work-content. It is the first of these (functional-transferable) that the MSCS is designed to measure. These are general abilities, such as the ability to counsel, negotiate, or synthesize ideas. Hence, the test does not evaluate more task-specific (work-content) abilities, which the manual describes with such examples as a mechanic's knowledge of car engines, or a surgeon's knowledge of anatomy. Another reference is made to *The Three Boxes of Life, and How to Get Out of Them: An Introduction to Life/Work Planning*. The manual states the book discusses basic skills that "can be focused in a variety of tasks" (p. 3). Basic skills are therefore equivalent to "functional-transferable" skills.

The test consists of 56 cards and a "motivated skills matrix" sheet. Forty-eight cards are "skills cards," and 8 are "category cards." The examinee arranges 5 category cards in a column (from "totally delight in using" through "like using," to "totally dislike using"). The examinee is instructed to sort the 48 skills cards by placing each one next to the category card that indicates how much the activity is enjoyed.

As an assessment of ability, a second sort is performed in which the cards are shifted into "competency categories" (highly proficient, competent, little or no skill). The results of the dual-sort are then transferred to the matrix sheet. Based on the matrix, the examinee answers 11 questions on a worksheet, designed to lead the examinee through a self-assessment of work skills, including strengths and areas for improvement, and to develop a scenario leading to career satisfaction. Eight related, supplementary activities, are included. All results are qualitative rather than quantitative in nature.

In discussing the MSCS, the term "self-assessment" cannot be mentioned too often. The manual is written primarily in second-person, being addressed to the examinee rather than a career counselor. This quickly sets the tone that self-assessment can be accurate and highly valid. No cautions are given that one could perhaps misjudge his or her skill level or work preferences. Nowhere in the manual is it suggested the examinee discuss the results with a career counselor or work supervisor. Although it is likely the test-taker *will* be discussing the results with a counselor, the danger exists the test may promote false confidence.

From a more technical viewpoint, the manual fails to report any measures of validity or reliability. Indeed, no reference is made to whether these essential aspects of test development were performed, although the test was originally published in 1981. It is therefore impossible for a test administrator to determine the stability of the test results over time. Further, without measures of predictive validity, it cannot be determined whether the MSCS adequately predicts future job satisfaction or productivity.

It is also questionable whether all the skill cards measure functional-transferable skills. Some cards refer to using carpentry abilities, or staging shows. One might argue these are not basic, general skills, but verge on more work-content-related abilities. Here, the manual fails to address the question of content validity. That is, it does not indicate how the terms for the skills cards were chosen, whether they were tested for appropriateness, and whether the terms used were exhaustive and orthogonal.

This points toward the one potential use of the MSCS—research for determining construct validity. That is, is the distinction between functional-transferable and work-content skills in itself theoretically valid and useful? Once that is determined, and the reliability, content validity, and predictive validity of the MSCS are judged, it may prove a useful tool for counselors. At present, the Motivated Skills Card Sort might be used to prompt discussion between a counselor and client, but until adequate research is performed, it should not be used for more. Although more expensive, the prediction of job satisfaction would be better performed with the Strong Interest Inventory (12:374) or the Kuder Occupational Interest Survey (T4:1375).

Review of the Motivated Skills Card Sort by GARY J. ROBERTSON, Vice President, Research & Development, Wide Range, Inc., Tampa, FL:

The Motivated Skills Card Sort Planning Kit (MSCSPK) is a set of activities designed to identify a broad base of skills that may generalize to a large number of occupations. These are the skills labeled "functional-transferable" by the *Dictionary of Occupational Titles,* meaning skills that begin to emerge at a very early age, continue to develop during the school years, and eventually transfer to adult work and leisure activities. The assumption apparently underlying the MSCSPK is that a process designed to identify these broadly applicable skills will be useful to various individuals such as those who are unemployed, those who want to make a career change, or those who are just entering the world of work. Whether the MSCSPK really facilitates the identification of these "functional-transferable" skills remains to be demonstrated.

ADEQUACY AND APPROPRIATENESS OF THE MATERIALS. The single source for information about the MSCSPK is a 34-page client workbook that provides some introductory information about the publication, instructions for performing a two-stage card sort of 48 skill cards, a Motivated Skills Matrix, a Worksheets form for summarizing results of the card sort, and eight supplementary activities. Separate supplementary directions that illustrate the six steps to follow in performing the card sort are also available from the publisher. The client workbook is organized in a clear way, though a thorough proofreading before publication would have improved the general flow and readability of the text. The cards and category labels for the two-way matrix used to sort the cards are printed on light card stock with perforations for tearing apart to make the cards. Users of the MSCSPK might benefit from having the cards printed on laminated stock and sold separately to facilitate their repeated use. If the MSCSPK is sold to individual clients by the publisher, then the present use of perforated card stock may be the most efficient, cost-effective way to supply the cards. The inadequacy of the workbook in delimiting the use and intended clientele for the MSCSPK is a source of frustration for the potential user.

THE ASSESSMENT PROCESS. The primary source of client data used in the MSCSPK is the two-stage card sort. First, the 48 skill cards are sorted into five piles representing five gradations of motivations for using the skills. Next, each of the five stacks of cards is sorted further into three levels of proficiency. The results of these two sorts are recorded in a 15-cell Skills Matrix that, in turn, is used to complete a worksheet designed to summarize and integrate the information in the Skills Matrix. The card sort by itself can be completed in about 10–15 minutes and seems an effective way to engage the interest and attention of examinees. One source of frustration for this reviewer in performing the card sort was the unevenness of fit between the category labels used in sorting and the skills contained on the cards. A mental shift was almost always required to bring the card labels into grammatical consistency with the category labels, especially for the five motivation categories (e.g., "Totally Delight in Using," "Enjoy Using Very Much," "Like Using," "Prefer Not to Use," "Strongly Dislike Using"). For example, consider the mental process needed to sort the card "INTERVIEW FOR INFORMATION" into one of the five motivation categories. The careful examinee must produce the mental transformation "TOTALLY DELIGHT IN INTERVIEWING TO OBTAIN INFORMATION" or some similar cognitive reconfiguration to reconcile the two seemingly disparate semantic units. Requiring this sort of repeated transformation during the sorting process may well penalize examinees whose lack of verbal skills prevents them from shifting verb tenses and producing semantic transformations easily. The author should have solved this editorial problem prior to publication or at least have ascertained its effect on clients. The skill cards are more easily sorted into the three proficiency levels (e.g., "Highly Proficient," "Competent," "Little or No Skill").

A hoped-for outcome of the MSCSPK is a linking of functional-transferable skills to specific jobs in which these skills can be used. The exact way in which the MSCSPK is to achieve such a result is not clear. Judging from the Worksheets section where the results of the skills sort are processed to facilitate interpretability and future action planning, the client must have considerable knowledge of occupations and their functional skill requirements. The MSCSPK seems deficient in providing a link to some comprehensive structure of occupations such as, for example, that contained in the *Dictionary of Occupational Titles.* Considerable on-the-job knowledge and experience are required to link the MSCSPK functional-transferable skills to possible jobs. This requirement restricts the use of

the MSCSPK to individuals having work experience and renders the product less suitable for use with high school and college students whose work experiences may be more restricted.

TECHNICAL ADEQUACY. A fundamental difficulty in evaluating the MSCSPK results from the lack of any technical documentation typically found in the published manual accompanying an assessment procedure. In fact, the lack of a manual containing standard technical information raises a serious question about the extent to which this instrument meets one fundamental requirement for an assessment procedure: the availability of a manual to assist with its proper use and interpretation. One area in which such a manual might help to provide information centers on the 48 skills used in the card sort. No information is provided on how the author chose to define the construct "functional-transferable skills" or how the skill universe for that construct was sampled to ensure meaningful breadth of coverage in the MSCSPK. By inspection, it is apparent that the card sort samples a broad range of skills, from those that are fairly abstract and more difficult to define operationally (i.e., "perceive intuitively," "synthesize," "evaluate") to those that are very concrete and easily communicated (i.e., "write," "use carpentry abilities," "prepare food"); however, this apparent breadth of coverage is not an adequate substitute for information about how the domain of functional-transferable skills included was defined and sampled. The absence of reliability data leaves unanswered the question of reproducibility of Skills Matrix results.

SUMMARY. The Motivated Skills Card Sort Planning Kit is a rather narrow, specialized assessment tool that may, under some conditions, offer assistance to individuals who are unemployed and wish to re-enter the world of work or who, for a variety of reasons, may wish to change careers; however, the instrument should not be used with individuals who are just beginning career exploration and have little or no work experience. Appraisal of the instrument was greatly hindered by the lack of a comprehensive manual outlining the development procedure and providing needed basic technical information. One fundamental weakness is the lack of a clear way to link the results from the MSCSPK to a comprehensive structure of new job possibilities. After completing the card sort and the follow-up activities, this reviewer was left with the distinct impression that the MSCSPK is a work-in-progress needing additional research and an informative technical manual before a judgment can be made about its real value.

[205]
Motivated Strategies for Learning Questionnaire.

Purpose: "To assess college students' motivational orientations and their use of different learning strategies for a college course."

Population: College students.

Publication Date: 1991.

Acronym: MSLQ.

Scores, 15: 3 Motivation Scales [Value Component (Intrinsic Goal Orientation, Extrinsic Goal Orientation, Task Value), Expectancy Component (Control of Learning Beliefs, Self-Efficacy for Learning and Performance), Affective Component (Test Anxiety)]; 2 Learning Strategies Scales [Cognitive and Metacognitive Strategies (Rehearsal, Elaboration, Organization, Critical Thinking, Metacognitive Self-Regulation), Resource Management Strategies (Time and Study Environment, Effort Regulation, Peer Learning, Help Seeking)].

Administration: Group.

Price Data: Available from publisher.

Time: (20–30) minutes.

Authors: Paul R. Pintrich, David A. F. Smith, Teresa Garcia, and Wilbert J. McKeachie.

Publisher: National Center for Research to Improve Postsecondary Teaching and Learning.

TEST REFERENCES

1. Pintrich, P. R., & DeGroot, E. V. (1990). Motivational and self-regulated learning components of classroom academic performance. *Journal of Educational Psychology, 82*, 33–40.

2. Pintrich, P. R., Smith, D. A. F., Garcia, T., & McKeachie, W. J. (1993). Reliability and predictive validity of the Motivated Strategies for Learning Questionnaire. *Educational and Psychological Measurement, 53*, 801–813.

3. Karabenick, S. A., & Sharma, R. (1994). Perceived teacher support of student questioning in the college classroom: Its relation to student characteristics and role in the classroom questioning process. *Journal of Educational Psychology, 86*, 90–103.

4. Lin, Y-G., & McKeachie, W. J. (1994). Learning of concepts and definitions in different disciplines. *Perceptual and Motor Skills, 79*, 113–114.

5. Pintrich, P. R., Anderman, E. M., & Klobucar, C. (1994). Intraindividual differences in motivation and cognition in students with and without learning disabilities. *Journal of Learning Disabilities, 27*, 360–370.

Review of the Motivated Strategies for Learning Questionnaire by JERI BENSON, Professor of Educational Psychology, College of Education, University of Georgia, Athens, GA:

DESCRIPTION OF THE SCALE. The Motivated Strategies for Learning Questionnaire (MSLQ) consists of 81 items grouped into 15 scales. In the instructions to the MSLQ, the student is asked to respond to the items given the class in which they are taking the questionnaire. Thus, MSLQ scores are "situation-specific." Furthermore, students respond to the MSLQ items using a 7-point Likert scale, where only the first and seventh points are anchored (*not at all true of me* to *very true of me*). It is desirable to have all response options anchored so the examinees have a common reference point to evaluate each item. Without anchoring each option, it is hard to know what "internal" scale each examinee is using and this "inconsistency" can lead to unreliability.

SCALE DEVELOPMENT. The authors describe the development of the scale, which began formally in 1986 (informally in 1982) as part of a research project on college student learning and teaching. Several waves of data were collected from 1986–1987 to revise and construct the 15 subscales of the MSLQ. Thus, the MSLQ subscales are empirically derived on the basis of item and factor analyses. Because exploratory factor analysis can be highly subjective (e.g., the determination of the number of factors to extract, the method of factor rotation etc.), it would have been helpful if the authors had described the criteria they used in coming up with the 15 subscales.

SCALE ADMINISTRATION, SCORING, REPORTING, AND NORMS. The administration of the MSLQ is straightforward, using student self-report. The MSLQ is scored by averaging the item responses for each subscale. Sample student feedback information is provided in the manual using 9 of the 15 subscales. For each of the 9 subscales, the authors provide a description of what the subscale measures and suggest the student's raw score be compared to the class mean, and the three quartile scores for the class. The authors do not recommend the use of norms, stating that motivation and learning strategies can vary by student groups and types of courses.

RELIABILITY AND VALIDATION SAMPLE. The psychometric data reported are based on a sample size of 380. Of the 380 college students, 24 attended a community college, the remaining were from a 4-year university. The rationale for including the 24 community college students was not given. It is likely these 24 students are not similar to the university students and may affect the psychometric data in unknown ways.

RELIABILITY. The types of psychometric data reported in the manual are means and standard deviations for each subscale, the correlation between each subscale item and final grade in the course, and internal consistency estimates (alpha coefficients) for each subscale. Internal consistency estimates ranged from .62 to .93 for the Motivational Scales and for the Learning Strategies Scales from .52 to .80. Considering the type of error inherent in internal consistency estimates (differences in item content only), the subscale reliability should be higher if results are provided for individual students. Only three of the Motivational Scales and five of the Learning Strategy

Scales showed internal consistency estimates greater than .75. Therefore, the dependability of what is being measured by the MSLQ is questionable.

The subscale intercorrelations range from .00 to .70, with over half of the correlations in the range .00 to .30. Thus, empirically the 15 scales seem to be weakly related. It would have been useful for the authors to comment on this finding in terms of whether this pattern was expected based on theory.

VALIDITY. The authors report one confirmatory factor analysis (CFA) as evidence of the MSLQ's validity. The CFA was specified such that each item was allowed to associate (load) with only one factor and the factors were allowed to be correlated. The authors ran separate CFA models for the Motivation Subscales, the Learning Strategy Subscales, and then all the subscales combined. The results did not meet the criteria specified prior to model testing. The authors state, "while the goodness of fit indices are not stellar, they are, nevertheless, quite reasonable" (p. 79). The authors suggest their findings are less than adequate due to a broad range of course and subject characteristics from the sample of 380 students. Furthermore, the authors claim the MSLQ shows a "sound structure" and one can claim "factor validity for the MSLQ scales" (p. 80).

This reviewer does not agree with the claim of "reasonable" model-data fit nor the suggestion the MSLQ shows factor validity. It is well known in the use of CFA that acceptable statistical model-data fit can rarely be established by testing a single model. The "models" frequently tested in measurement studies are rough approximations to reality. Furthermore, the theory underlying a measure is often not clearly understood (e.g., all aspects of the theoretical domain may not be known). Therefore, the scale used to measure the construct is an approximation. It might have been more reasonable to have tested "competing" theoretical models (Jöreskog, 1993). For example, a different number of factors could be evaluated, and if the 15-factor structure emerged as the best fitting of the set of models evaluated, some evidence for the "validity" of the structure is provided. Currently, there is very little support for the purported 15-factor model of the MSLQ.

Finally, given that validity is the process by which the test scores take on meaning, the authors need to develop studies that are not solely internally driven (e.g., traditional and confirmatory factor analysis) (Nunnally, 1978; Benson & Hagtvet, 1996). That is, what external criterion is used to substantiate the scores from the MSLQ? Studies are needed which use external criteria to evaluate the relationship between students who are known to be highly motivated or report a particular learning strategy and MSLQ scores.

SUMMARY. The authors clearly present the reliability data for each of the MSLQ subscales. However, the reliability data are weak and the validity data are very limited and not convincing of the factor structure. There is no discussion in the manual of the theoretical basis of the MSLQ, only references to several articles. Additional reliability and validity studies are needed to improve the subscale accuracy and to substantiate the dimensionality of the scale. Summaries of these studies should be incorporated into the manual.

REVIEWER'S REFERENCES
Nunnally, J. C. (1978). *Psychometric theory* (2nd ed.). New York: McGraw Hill.
Jöreskog, K. G. (1993). Testing structural equation models. In K. A. Bollen & J. S. Long (Eds.), *Testing structural equation models* (pp. 294–316). Newbury Park, CA: Sage.
Benson, J., & Hagtvet, K. A. (1996). The interplay between design, data analysis and theory in the measurement of coping. In M. Zeidner & N. S. Ender (Eds.), *Handbook of coping: Theory, research and applications* (pp. 83–106). New York: John Wiley & Sons.

Review of the Motivated Strategies for Learning Questionnaire by ROBERT K. GABLE, Professor of Educational Psychology, and Associate Director, Bureau of Educational Research and Service, University of Connecticut, Storrs, CT:

The self-report Motivated Strategies for Learning Questionnaire (MSLQ) is based on a comprehensive line of research carried out by the developers in the areas of motivation (31 items) and learning strategies (31 items), which includes a section on student management of different resources (19 items). The 81 items are responded to on a 7-point Likert scale with end-point anchors of *not at all true of me* and *very true of me*. No discussion is provided regarding the selection of this particular response scale.

ADMINISTRATION. The 15 MSLQ scales can be administered as an entire instrument in about 25 minutes. Subsections of the instrument can also be selected for use.

VALIDITY. The content validity of the MSLQ is supported through extensive literature on college student learning and teaching. Although summaries of the literature are not included in the test manual, several appropriate references to relevant work are cited. A more comprehensive description of the judgmental process used to create items reflecting the literature-based concepts would be appropriate.

Reference is made to several early appropriate empirical analyses that contributed information for selecting final items for the MSLQ. Given the confirmatory factor analysis (Pilotte & Gable, 1990) and item response theory (Wright & Masters, 1982) research on the use of positive/negative item stems, the inclusion of some "reversed scored" items is an empirically unsupported approach to instrument development. It is likely that the positive and negative stems access different aspects of the targeted affective constructs.

Data are presented for the final set of items based on a sample of 380 college students from a variety of majors. Construct validity evidence is offered through confirmatory factor analytic information presented separately for the motivation and the cognitive/metacognitive items. The authors spend time describing what information is obtained from a confirmatory analysis, but provide inadequate specific evaluative statements regarding their findings. The lambda estimates presented are typical for these types of items, but appear low for more items than the authors suggest. Several items have estimates less than .75, which is not ideal for scales defined by only four items (e.g., the four items defining Help Seeking have loadings of .20, .17, .90, and .79). The lack of a high level of model fit is evident through the fit statistics, many of which exceed commonly accepted values. The summary statement, "Overall, the models show sound structures, and one can reasonably claim factor validity for the MSLQ scales" (p. 80), is not highly supported by the data from this one sample. Clearly, data from more samples are needed before such construct validity claims can be advanced.

Criterion-related (predictive) validity evidence is presented in the form of item and scale-level correlations with final course grades. The Motivation scale-level correlations range from -.27 (Test Anxiety) to .41 (Self-Efficacy for Learning and Performance) with the average magnitude of the correlation, disregarding direction, being .22. Learning Strategies scale-level correlations range from -.06 to .32 with an average of .17. The authors state that these correlations "are significant, albeit moderate, demonstrating predictive validity" (p. 4). The coefficients can be statistically significant due to the large sample size, but are associated with small to medium effect sizes. The authors overstate the evidence for predictive validity and fail to discuss any of the individual coefficients in the context of the literature base.

RELIABILITY. Item analysis (i.e., means and standard deviations) are presented; item/scale correlations should have been included. These correlations would facilitate item-level contributions to the

Motivation scale reliabilities, which ranged from .62 to .93 (average = .78), and the Learning Strategies scale reliabilities, which ranged from .52 to .80 (average = .71). The authors refer to these reliabilities saying they are "robust, ranging from .52 to .93" (p. 4). The word "robust" does not seem appropriate for alpha reliabilities; the authors should describe the scale reliabilities in more depth and assist the user in understanding the problems with using data from scales with low reliabilities. Although most scales are associated with adequate alpha reliability levels, users should exercise caution with interpretations of Extrinsic Goal Orientation (.62) and Cognitive and Metacognitive Strategies: Organization (.64) scale scores due to the inadequate sampling of content evident in the four-item scales with low reliabilities.

SCORE INTERPRETATION. Scoring and score interpretation are described noting that norms are not provided because "students' responses to the questions might vary as a function of different courses, so the same individual might report different levels of motivation or strategy use depending on the course" (p. 5). Students do receive their individual scores, class scale means, and quartile information. In addition, scale descriptions and ways to increase motivation levels are included.

SUMMARY. The MSLQ results from a quality line of research at the University of Michigan in the areas of teaching and learning. The present version of the MSLQ should be considered a "research edition" until additional items are added to scales with low reliabilities and additional supportive construct validity information is available. In addition, users should be provided with more interpretation in the manual regarding the referenced literature base and data presented, such as the correlations of the MSLQ scales with final course grades.

REVIEWER'S REFERENCES

Wright, B. D., & Masters, G. N. (1982). *Rating scale analysis*. Chicago: Mesa Press.
Pilotte, W. J., & Gable, R. K. (1990). The impact of positive and negative item stems on the validity of a computer anxiety scale. *Educational and Psychological Measurement, 50*, 603–610.

[206]
Nelson-Denny Reading Test, Forms G and H.

Purpose: "To assess student achievement and progress in vocabulary comprehension, and reading rate."

Population: Grades 9–16 and adult.

Publication Dates: 1981–93.

Scores, 4: Vocabulary, Comprehension, Total, Reading Rate.

Administration: Group.

Price Data, 1993: $25.50 per 25 test booklets (specify form); $3 per directions for administration ('93, 13 pages); $9 per manual ('93, 53 pages); $6 per technical report ('93, 58 pages); $40.50 per 100 machine-scored answer sheets; $48 per 50 self-scorable answer sheets; $9 per class record sheet; $17.10 per student's personal record; $13.50 per examination kit.

Time: 35(45) minutes.

Authors: James I. Brown, Vivian Vick Fishco, and Gerald S. Hanna.

Publisher: The Riverside Publishing Co.

Cross References: See T4:1715 (30 references); for reviews by Robert J. Tierney and James E. Ysseldyke of Forms E and F, see 9:745 (12 references); see also T3:1568 (38 references); for reviews by Robert A. Forsyth and Alton L. Raynor of Forms C and D, see 8:735 (31 references); see also T2:1572 (46 references); for reviews by David B. Orr and Agatha Townsend and an excerpted review by John O. Crites of Forms A and B, see 6:800 (13 references); for a review by Ivan A. Booker, see 4:544 (17 references); for a review by Hans C. Gordon, see 2:1557.

TEST REFERENCES

1. Blohm, P. J. (1987). Effect on lookup aids on mature readers' recall of technical text. *Reading Research and Instruction, 26*, 77–88.
2. Frick, R. W. (1987). A dissociation of conscious visual imagery and visual short-term memory. *Neuropsychologia, 25*, 707–712.
3. Tobias, S. (1987). Mandatory text review and interaction with student characteristics. *Journal of Educational Psychology, 79*, 154–161.
4. Dixon, P., LeFeure, J.-A., & Twilley, L. C. (1988). Word knowledge and working memory as predictors of reading skill. *Journal of Educational Psychology, 80*, 465–472.
5. LeFeure, J.-A. (1988). Reading skill as a source of individual differences in the processing of instructional texts. *Journal of Educational Psychology, 80*, 312–314.
6. Baldwin, R. S., Murfin, P., Ross, G., Seidel, J., Clements, N., & Morris, C. (1989). Effects of extending administration time on standardized reading achievement tests. *Reading Research and Instruction, 29*(1), 33-38.
7. Jacobowitz, T. (1989). AIM: A metacognitive strategy for constructing the main idea of text. *Journal of Reading, 33*, 620-624.
8. Reed, K. X. (1989). Expectation vs. ability: Junior college reading skills. *Journal of Reading, 32*, 537-541.
9. Kreek, C., Lapan, R., & Goetz, E. T. (1990). Differences in the use of selective attention by more successful and less successful tenth-grade readers. *Journal of Educational Psychology, 82*, 749–759.
10. Roberts, M. S., Suderman, L., Suderman, R., & Semb, G. B. (1990). Reading ability as a performance predictor in a behaviorally based psychology course. *Teaching of Psychology, 17*, 173–175.
11. Wade, S. E., & Adams, R. B. (1990). Effects of importance and interest on recall of biographical text. *Journal of Reading Behavior, 22*, 331-353.
12. Whitney, P., Ferraro, F. R., & Kellas, G. (1990). Reading ability and semantic processing: Isolating speed of access. *Journal of Educational Psychology, 82*, 479–485.
13. Zabrucky, K. (1990). Evaluation of understanding in college students: Effects of text structure and reading proficiency. *Reading Research and Instruction, 29*(4), 46-54.
14. Clements-Davis, G. L., & Ley, T. C. (1991). Thematic preorganizers and the reading comprehension of tenth-grade world literature students. *Reading Research and Instruction, 31*(1), 43-53.
15. Grant, R., & Davey, B. (1991). How do headings affect text-processing? *Reading Research and Instruction, 31*(1), 12-21.
16. Kemp, S. G., & Sadoski, M. (1991). The effects of instruction in forming generalizations on high school students' critical thinking in world history. *Reading Research and Instruction, 31*(1), 33-42.
17. Meigs, C. B., & McCreary, R. A. (1991). Foreign films: An international approach to enhance college reading. *Journal of Reading, 35*, 306-310.
18. Pearson, J. A. (1991). Testing the ecological validity of teacher-provided versus student-generated postquestions in reading college science text. *Journal of Research in Science Teaching, 28*, 485-504.
19. Stahl, S. A., Hare, V. C., Sinatra, R., & Gregory, J. F. (1991). Defining the role of prior knowledge and vocabulary in reading comprehension: The retiring of number 41. *Journal of Reading Behavior, 23*, 487-508.
20. Steinberg, I., Bohning, G., & Chowning, F. (1991). Comprehension monitoring strategies of nonproficient college readers. *Reading Research and Instruction, 30*(3), 63-75.
21. Wineburg, S. S. (1991). On the reading of historical texts: Notes on the breach between school and academy. *American Educational Research Journal, 28*, 495-519.
22. Carver, R. P. (1992). The three factors in reading ability: Reanalysis of a study by Cunningham, Stanovich, and Wilson. *Journal of Reading Behavior, 24*, 173-190.
23. Carver, R. P. (1992). What do standardized tests of reading comprehension measure in terms of efficiency, accuracy, and rate? *Reading Research Quarterly, 27*, 347-359.
24. Hashway, R. M., Duke, I., Hammond, C., & Brooks, L. (1992). Test anxiety and reading test performance. *College Student Journal, 26*, 180-182.
25. Hodge, E. A., Palmer, B. C., & Scott, D. (1992). Metacognitive training in cooperative groups on the reading comprehension and vocabulary of at-risk college students. *College Student Journal, 26*, 440-448.
26. Schumm, J. S., Mangrum, C. T., II, Gordon, J., & Doucette, M. (1992). The effect of topic interest and prior knowledge on the predicted test questions of developmental college readers. *Reading Research and Instruction, 31*(4), 11-24.
27. Schwartz, M. D. (1992). Study sessions and higher grades: Questioning the causal link. *College Student Journal, 26*, 292-299.
28. Simpson, M. L., & Nist, S. L. (1992). Toward defining a comprehensive assessment model for college reading. *Journal of Reading, 35*, 452-458.
29. Di Vesta, F. J., & Moreno, V. (1993). Cognitive control functions of study activities: A compensation model. *Contemporary Educational Psychology, 18*, 47-65.
30. Duchein, M. A., & Mealey, D. L. (1993). Remembrance of books past ... long past: Glimpses into aliteracy. *Reading Research and Instruction, 33*, 13-28.
31. Frazier, D. W. (1993). Transfer of college developmental reading students' textmarking strategies. *Journal of Reading Behavior, 25*, 17-41.
32. Katz, L., & Goldstein, G. (1993). The Luria-Nebraska Neuropsychological Battery and the WAIS-R in assessment of adults with specific learning disabilities. *Rehabilitation Counselor Bulletin, 36*, 190–198.
33. Rankin, J. L. (1993). Information-processing differences of college-age readers differing in reading comprehension and speed. *Journal of Reading Behavior, 25*, 261-278.
34. Schraw, G., Potenza, M. T., & Nebelsick-Gullet, L. (1993). Constraints on the calibration of performance. *Contemporary Educational Psychology, 18*, 455-463.
35. Wade, S. E., Schraw, G., Buxton, W. M., & Hayes, M. T. (1993). Seduction of the strategic reader: Effects of interest on strategies and recall. *Reading Research Quarterly, 28*, 93-114.
36. Zabrucky, K., & Commander, N. E. (1993). Rereading to understand: The role of text coherence and reader proficiency. *Contemporary Educational Psychology, 18*, 442-454.
37. Beers, S. R., Goldstein, G., & Katz, L. J. (1994). Neuropsychological differences between college students with learning disabilities and those with mild head injury. *Journal of Learning Disabilities, 27*, 315–324.
38. Bell, L. C., & Perfetti, C. A. (1994). Reading skill: Some adult comparisons. *Journal of Educational Psychology, 86*, 244-255.
39. Cox, G. C., Smith, D. L., & Rakes, T. A. (1994). Enhancing comprehension through the use of visual elaboration strategies. *Reading Research and Instruction, 33*, 159-174.
40. Hayes, Z. L., & Waller, T. G. (1994). Gender differences in adult readers: A process perspective. *Canadian Journal of Behavioural Science, 26*, 421-437.
41. Heerman, C. E., & Maleki, R. B. (1994). Helping probationary university students succeed. *Journal of Reading, 37*, 654-661.
42. Lapan, R., & Reynolds, R. E. (1994). The selective attention strategy as a time-dependent phenomenon. *Contemporary Educational Psychology, 19*, 379–398.
43. Loranger, A. L. (1994). The study strategies of successful and unsuccessful high school students. *Journal of Reading Behavior, 26*, 347–360.
44. Schraw, G. (1994). The effect of metacognitive knowledge on local and global monitoring. *Contemporary Educational Psychology, 19*, 143-154.
45. Siegel, L. S. (1994). Working memory and reading: A life-span perspective. *International Journal of Behavioral Development, 17*, 109-124.
46. Smith, B. D., Miller, C., Grossman, F., & Gold, M. V. (1994). Vocabulary retention: Effects of using spatial imaging on hemispheric-preference thinking. *Journal of Research and Development in Education, 27*, 244-252.
47. Vaidya, S. R. (1994). Diagnostic assessments and consideration of learning styles and lows of control characteristics—How do they impact teaching and learning? *College Student Journal, 27*, 159-162.
48. Zabrucky, K., & Moore, D. (1994). Contributions of working memory and evaluation and regulation of understanding to adults' recall of texts. *Journal of Gerontology: Psychological Sciences, 49*(Pt. 2), P201-P212.
49. Brisbois, J. E. (1995). Connections between first- and second-language reading. *Journal of Reading Behavior, 27*, 565–584.
50. Schraw, G., Dunkle, M. E., & Bendixen, L. D. (1995). Does a general monitoring skill exist? *Journal of Educational Psychology, 87*, 433–444.
51. Sparks, R. L., Ganschow, L., & Patton, J. (1995). Prediction of performance in first-year foreign language courses: Connections between native and foreign language learning. *Journal of Educational Psychology, 87*, 638–655.
52. Chan, D., & Schmitt, N. (1997). Video-based versus paper-and-pencil method of assessment in situational judgement tests: Subgroup differences in test performance and face validity perceptions. *Journal of Applied Psychology, 82*, 143–159.

Review of the Nelson-Denny Reading Test, Forms G and H by MILDRED MURRAY-WARD, Professor of Education, California Lutheran University, Thousand Oaks, CA:

The 1993 Nelson-Denny Reading Test is the latest edition of the test initially published in 1929. This version was developed after a survey of users was completed in 1989. The results, based on a 27% return rate, were used to revise the instrument. However, the overall test format remains generally unchanged. To address the qualities of a test as old as the Nelson-Denny, comparison of the test's characteristics in previous and current versions seems relevant.

Two noticeable changes appeared in the test. First, the number of test items was changed. The Vocabulary items were reduced from 100 to 80 items, with no reduction in administration time. The number of passages was reduced from eight to seven. Questions per passage were increased from 4 to 5, with a net increase of questions from 36 to 38. Second, an extended time administration was introduced.

Most information needed to evaluate the test is available in the technical and interpretation manuals. The test is easy to use and provides clear directions. It also may be administered in one class period. However, several problems identified in the previous edition still exist.

The authors claim that the primary purpose of the test is to rank students in Vocabulary, Comprehension, and Reading Rate. They also state that the test may also be used in identifying students for advanced or developmental reading programs, predicting academic success, and diagnosing students' reading problems. Although worthy claims, little evidence for the 1993 test supports these purposes. The interpretation manual provides examples of several studies that support these claims, but the information was collected on earlier forms, not Forms G and H. Allowing for the parallel nature of the new forms, some inferences might be made for the claims.

There is empirical evidence that Forms E and F did serve some named purposes. However, there is no empirical evidence of the diagnostic function of the test. This is a serious problem because the authors have created an individual student booklet with profile analysis directions. Furthermore, low reliability levels and strict time limits limit these interpretations.

The test employs the same means for measuring reading as the 1929 edition. The reading rate procedure still ignores differences in types of text, concept load, and various purposes for reading. According to the authors, the vocabulary words were selected from various texts, and were necessary for success in the subject discipline. However, the selection procedures were not described.

The comprehension passages were taken from various texts. As with the passages in Forms E and F, these are strictly narrative. They do not reflect current reading requirements involving use of pictures, charts, tables, and the text. Interestingly, the passages were checked for readability levels using various readability formulas, but the resulting levels were not provided. Because content texts are often written at reading levels above the grade levels in which they are used, this is an important piece of information. Furthermore, passage dependency data provided for Forms E and F items were absent for Forms G and H. Finally, the questions are limited in type and are arbitrarily divided between literal and interpretative item types. Although the list of items and their classifications are provided in the interpretation manual, the diagnostic usefulness of this information is suspect because of the authors' arbitrary and vague procedures.

The test authors introduced extended time limits for selected students with the 1993 version. These were initiated because some readers' performances were affected by the strict time limits. However, the special extended-time norms mentioned in the direction booklet are not provided in the scoring manual, and their availability is not clear.

The interpretation of the test appears on the surface to be an easy process. The scoring procedures and tables for converting scores are easy to use. Detailed information on the location and composition of high schools, 2- and 4-year colleges, and police academies used in the norming procedures is located in the technical manual. However, the basis for normative comparisons is highly questionable.

Forms E and F's norm groups overrepresented small communities and failed to represent adequately large colleges and important ethnic groups. Although the authors did attempt to remedy the situation, the problems persist to some degree. They did attempt to match the 1980 U.S. Census data and update with the 1990 data. The norm communities for Forms G and H did represent more large communities and some major larger institutions. The midwest is overrepresented and the southeast and west, where most student population growth has occurred, is underrepresented. The SES of the students overemphasizes middle-income student. Hispanics and Whites are underrepresented, and African-Americans are overrepresented.

Concerning validity, content validity is questionable because of limited information provided on the sources of words and passages and the criteria for their selection. Passage readability and item passage dependence were not provided at all.

Some predictive and screening validity evidence may be inferred from the studies cited in the technical manual. However, no evidence was provided for diagnosis based on profile analysis. In fact, the section on profile analysis in the interpretation manual describes typical patterns of performance. One interpretation, in which a student has a low Vocabulary and a high Comprehension score is unlikely, because comprehension relies on knowledge of vocabulary. Such a profile may have occurred if the student were guessing wildly.

The 1993 version provides excellent information on exploration of inflammatory and statistical bias of the test for gender, Black versus White, and Hispanic versus White. Experts screened the test for inflammatory bias, and more than half of the passages in the national tryout were discarded. A total of 74 of the 592 Vocabulary and Comprehension tryout items were statistically biased, and 49 were removed. The remaining items were retained because of their essential nature and were found to be balanced in bias on each side of the comparisons made.

Reliability of the test sections is questionable. The authors use KR-20s, after making clear that this is not an acceptable statistic for the highly speeded Nelson-Denny. Later, the authors introduce alternate forms reliability. They also use *SEM* as a reliability index. Because *SEM* is calculated from an unspecified reliability index, the meaning of the *SEM* is unclear.

Overall, the Nelson-Denny is somewhat useful in testing the general reading skills of older students. It is a concise, practical assessment that is easy to score. However, examiners should not overinterpret the scores. Although the test does measure general reading, it does not measure performance on more current materials and varied reading tasks required of students. Furthermore, the validity evidence does not substantiate claims that the test can be used to diagnose specific reading problems. There is no author-generated evidence that the 1993 version is an accurate predictor of success in college. Such evidence must be determined locally. The Nelson-Denny would be best used in combination with other reading indicators such as work samples, observations, and perhaps, other reading tests.

Review of the Nelson-Denny Reading Test, Forms G and H by DOUGLAS K. SMITH, Professor and Director, School Psychology Training Program, University of Wisconsin—River Falls, River Falls, WI:

The Nelson-Denny Reading Test, Forms G and H, measures student ability in Vocabulary development, reading Comprehension, and Reading Rate. The original forms of the test were developed in 1929 and subsequently revised in 1960, 1973, 1981, and 1993. The format of the test has remained intact except for the addition of the Reading Rate measure in 1960.

The test is designed to be administered in one session requiring about 45 minutes. The Vocabulary subtest has a 15-minute time limit and consists of 80 items, with five response choices per item. The Comprehension subtest has a 20-minute time limit and presents seven reading passages with 38 questions, with five response choices per question. Reading Rate is determined by a 1-minute timing on the first reading passage. The test can be administered in an extended time format that requires 56 minutes of working time. It is recommended that it be administered in two sessions when this option is used. Separate norms are provided for this administration.

The Vocabulary and Comprehension subtests are contained in one booklet for each form. Instructions are easy to follow and three practice exercises are provided for the Vocabulary subtest and one sample reading passage for the Comprehension subtest. The Vocabulary items consist of nouns, verbs, adjectives, and adverbs. None of the words is obscure, although some may be unfamiliar to some readers. Comprehension questions are both factual and inferential. Both subtests utilize a multiple-choice response format with five choices per item. An examination of subtest content indicates that they do appear to measure vocabulary and reading comprehension.

Raw scores can be converted to percentile ranks, grade equivalents, standard scores, and stanines. A four-page booklet explaining the test and test results, including an individual's own reading profile, is available to examinees. This booklet is written in an understandable way and provides an appropriate explanation of the test and its results.

Detailed information describing subtest development, bias analyses, and norms development are reported in the Technical Report. National standardization began in Fall 1991 and norms are presented for High School (grades 9–12), Two-Year Colleges, Four-Year Colleges/Universities, and Law Enforcement Academies. The reason for including Law Enforcement Academies is not provided. The High School sample was selected on the basis of the 1980 U.S. Census data and stratified on the basis of geographic region, district enrollment, and socioeconomic status (SES) of the community. It represents 36 public and parochial schools and 11,978 students. Low SES students are significantly underrepresented (6% of sample vs. 15.2% of population) and average SES students are overrepresented (46.4% of sample vs. 31.2% of population). The college samples were stratified on the basis of geographic region and enrollment. The Law Enforcement Academy sample consisted of 16 academies and 531 trainees. Although race/ethnicity was not a stratification variable, the white sample by group ranges from 67.4% (2-year colleges) to 84.6% (law enforcement academies) and the nonwhite sample by group ranges from 15.4% to 32.6%. U.S. Census data for 1992 indicate a white percentage of 80.3 and nonwhite of 19.7. Some caution in the use of norms is recommended when applying the results to individuals from lower SES levels.

Acceptable reliability estimates are presented in the Technical Report. Although KR-20 reliability estimates are reported, the authors recommend the use of alternate forms data as the appropriate estimate of reliability. These internal consistency estimates are acceptable and include Vocabulary = .89, Comprehension = .81, Total Test = .90, and Reading Rate = .68. The Reading Rate reliability coefficient is considerably lower than the other subtests and total test. Test-retest reliability estimates are not presented.

Validity is addressed by examining the test as a screening test and in predicting academic success. Several studies by educational institutions are summarized. In these studies previous forms of the test have been used to support the use of cutoff scores from the test, and scores have been correlated with students' grades. In addition, the test has been used in studies to predict academic success. Validity studies with Forms G and H are not reported. Although the test appears to have "face" validity, there is a lack of studies examining the actual validity of Forms G and H.

The most appropriate use of the Nelson-Denny Reading Test, Forms G and H, is for screening. It is an easily administered group measure of vocabulary and reading comprehension. As such it is useful in identifying high school students who may have difficulties in these areas. The authors provide a wealth of information regarding development of the instrument, bias analyses, and item difficulties. However, the norms are somewhat dated and unrepresentative of the U.S. population today. In addition, test-retest data and current validity studies are lacking.

[207]
Neurobehavioral Assessment of the Preterm Infant.

Purpose: "Designed to measure the relative maturity of functioning in preterm infants."
Population: Age 32–37 weeks (conceptual age).
Publication Date: 1990.
Acronym: NAPI.
Scores: 7 cluster scores: Scarf Sign, Motor Development and Vigor, Popliteal Angle, Alertness and Orientation, Irritability, Cry Quality, Percent Asleep Ratings.
Administration: Individual.
Price Data, 1996: $238.50 per complete set including 25 record forms, videotape, manual (71 pages), two rattles, and set of two head supports; $83.50 per 50 record forms; $99 for the videotape; $48 per manual; $7 per set of two rattles; $64 per set of two head supports.
Time: (30) minutes.
Authors: Anneliese F. Korner and Valerie A. Thom.
Publisher: The Psychological Corporation.

TEST REFERENCES

1. Korner, A. F., Constantinou, J., Dimiceli, S., Brown, B. W., Jr., & Thom, V. A. (1991). Establishing the reliability and developmental validity of a neurobehavioral assessment for preterm infants: A methodological process. *Child Development, 62,* 1200–1208.

Review of the Neurobehavioral Assessment of the Preterm Infant by MELISSA M. GROVES, Assistant Professor of Child & Family Studies, University of Tennessee, Knoxville, TN:

The purpose of the Neurobehavioral Assessment of the Preterm Infant (NAPI) is to "measure the relative maturity of functioning in preterm infants aged 32 weeks conceptual age to term" (p. 1). Although several additional uses are identified in the test manual, two crucial assumptions for test use are given by the authors. First, the authors strongly recommend that the NAPI be best used longitudinally rather than as a single assessment. Second, that the use of the test for "prediction of future developmental progress may or may not be possible, even from repeated examinations" (p. 2).

The test consists of 41 items that yield the seven cluster scores. Cluster scores are initially reported as raw scores but are assigned as a converted score for comparison to the normative reference groups. Conversion tables printed directly on the record form make this transformation quite easy. Besides cluster scores, the test contains 30 behavioral and physiological summary ratings the examiner makes based on observation of the preterm infant's overall performance during the testing session. The summary ratings are not included in the normative tables. To administer the NAPI reliably, a videotape of a sample examination is included for examiner training. Both the manual and the videotape include detailed, descriptive information regarding overall test administration.

A strength of the NAPI is the recognition of the need for sensitive and responsive handling of the preterm infant to gain an accurate assessment. This is stressed in both the videotape and manual. The presentation of items in a sequence that invokes the best possible response from the infant is also illustrative of this strength. Conditions are not changed artificially and dramatically to assess the preterm's response.

Another strength of the NAPI is the authors' strong and implicit recognition of the test's limitations. The authors strongly state that the NAPI is not diagnostic and that interpretations should be based on repeated testing. Normative data are presented so that the examiner can, based on multiple examinations, refer a child for more sophisticated neurological testing. Given the lack of reported predictive validity information, this is an appropriate caution.

The process of the test development of the NAPI is exhaustively discussed in the manual. The authors present a conceptual framework that guided initial selection of test items. The inclusion of items was based on "developmentally, clinically, and theoretically important dimensions" (p. 6). Three cohorts of preterm infants were used to identify items for possible inclusion in the final version of the NAPI. The preterm infants included in the three test development cohorts appear representative across gender and ethnicity. Normative data are based on all three cohorts, which included 976 assessments of 521 infants. Preterm infants who had either known gross visible or internal anomalies were excluded from the cohort groups.

Single-item functional dimensions and cluster scores retained through Cohorts I and II of test development had to have a 2-day test-retest reliability coefficient of at least .6 or greater. Cohort I was administered the long form on both occasions with resulting coefficients ranging from .59 to .90. Cohort II was administered both the long and the short form with reliability coefficients ranging from .40 to .85. Subsamples from Cohorts I and II were used to report interobserver reliability on cluster scores. The Spearman rank correlations for interobserver reliability ranged from .64 to .98.

Although the norms and reliability appear adequate, the issue of NAPI's validity is not developed as fully as it could be in the manual. Given the authors' stated emphasis on the selection of items known to have "clinical significance" and stated use of items known to elicit responses that represented developmental change, it could be argued that the test has content validity. The authors offer an explanation of the establishment of developmental validity that would lend credence to this observation. However, most test users would probably find a discussion of content validity to be more helpful.

The authors stress the need for examiner qualifications and training that yield reliable administration and scoring of the test. By following the authors' suggestions for examiner training in the manual along with the repeated viewing of the accompanying training tape, reliable test administration seems adequately addressed. However, reliable scoring of the test could be more fully covered either in the manual or the tape. For example, the NAPI authors state that examiner qualifications would include familiarity with infant behavioral states. Although such states are described in the test manual, some specific inclusion of illustrative infant states on the training video would be helpful. This is especially important considering the authors' recommendation for the inclusion of half-point ratings for state assessment when the preterm infant is between two states.

An additional minor concern relates to the scoring of the summary ratings. Although the scoring of the items leading to cluster scores on the NAPI is adequately described within the test manual, the scoring on those items concerned with summary ratings is not as well defined. This is not as crucial given that summary scores are based on overall impressions of the preterm's reaction to the test, but again, examples could be useful.

In summary, the Neurobehavioral Assessment of the Preterm Infant meets its intended purpose, both in design and function. Norm sample, reliability, and validity appear adequate for its intended uses. Content validity could be more directly addressed in the manual but given the framework in which the test was developed this would be a minor issue. The manual is quite easy to follow and use, although the videotape could be updated to illustrate some issues in scoring. The NAPI fulfills an important role as an assessment for the preterm infant and has both research and applied uses. The authors' emphasis on training and cautions against misuse make this instrument one that skilled examiners could use effectively.

Review of the Neurobehavioral Assessment of the Preterm Infant by BARBARA A. ROTHLISBERG, Professor of Psychology in Educational Psychology and Director of the M.A./Ed.S. Program in School Psychology, Ball State University, Muncie, IN:

The Neurobehavioral Assessment of the Preterm Infant (NAPI) allows clinicians trained to work with preterm and normal neonates a method of gauging the capacity of medically stable preterm infants to respond to an invariant sequence of items addressing behaviors such as motor development and movement, auditory and visual orientation, and states of alertness and irritability. The NAPI is designed to afford the clinical examiner (and through the evaluation other interested parties such as parents and physicians) a means of noting maturational changes in functioning within infants 32 to 37 weeks conceptional age and to compare the infant to the progress of other infants born prematurely. Given the increase in preterm infant survival, data on the developmental progression of responses of such neonates is warranted.

The actual development of the NAPI began in the 1970s when Korner and her associates were looking for an instrument for longitudinal assessment of the results of an intervention program. Available measures focused either on the full term infant or assessed at more lengthy intervals than the project demanded. Development of the present NAPI began as a method to evaluate the subtle changes in preterm infants as they reached term age. The NAPI now purports to measure behavior in seven domains of function: Scarf Sign, Motor Development and Vigor, Popliteal Angle, Alertness and Orientation, Irritability, Cry Quality, and Percent Asleep Ratings. Several of these domains consist of single response ratings (e.g., Scarf Sign, Popliteal Angle, Cry Quality).

Although the NAPI shares items with other infant measures (i.e., Brazelton, 1984; T4:321), it varies in its conceptual and statistical design. The NAPI items were selected to be both clinically and statistically meaningful and to show clear developmental shifts toward mature infant functioning. In addition, the invariant sequence of administration and the gentle nature of the handling of the child helps to guarantee that the preterm infant is exposed to a set of circumstances that attempt to maximize the child's responsiveness and the comparability of testing conditions across assessments. The domains assessed are the result of an item selection procedure that spanned the use of three cohorts of preterm infants (N = 521). Korner and Thom emphasize in the test manual that domains display psychometric soundness and consistency. The Appendix to the manual of the NAPI offers tables that allow the clinician to chart the neonate's developmental progress in the tested neurobehavioral areas.

The NAPI is grounded in a procedure that attempts almost continuously to monitor infant behavior and psychological responsiveness during the 30-minute evaluation. At 14 points, the infant's behavioral state is rated on a 7-point scale from Quiet Sleep (1) to Crying (6) and Unclassifiable (7). Half-point ratings can also be given. The neurobehavioral items are sequenced in a way that increases the likelihood of alert behavior as the evaluation progresses. Item sequencing and administration suggestions are presented in the manual and supplemented by a helpful videotape that records the standard administration sequence. For each test item, the infant's bilateral responsiveness and movement or sensory pattern is assessed using an ordinal point scale with more points awarded for more mature performance/alertness. These ratings can then be converted to a 0- to 100-point scale that defines the maturity level of the various behaviors (100 being most competent). Because assessment of the preterm infant can occur at one-week intervals with the NAPI, neonates who show consistent developmental lags in behavior can be identified.

The clinician who administers the NAPI must be intimately aware of the developmental progression of preterm development and the normal expectations for the neurobehavioral items. A recorder should assist in the assessment because the examiner must make almost continuous judgments about visual and motor responsiveness, type of spontaneous movement displayed by the neonate, and any other behavioral or physiological responses the infant makes to handling. Parents should be present during the assessment. Observation of their child's performance may help parents gain a greater appreciation for their child's sensitivity and needs.

REVIEWER'S REFERENCE

Brazelton, T. B. (1984). Neonatal Behavioral Assessment Scale (2nd ed.). Clinics in Developmental Medicine, No. 88, S.I.M.P. London: Lavenham Press.

[208]

NOCTI Teacher Occupational Competency Test: Appliance Repair.

Purpose: Designed to measure the individual's occupational competency in appliance repair.

Population: Teachers and prospective teachers.

Publication Dates: 1986–1994.

Scores, 11: 8 scores for Written part (Total and 7 subscores), 3 scores for Performance part (Process, Product, Total).

Parts, 2: Written, Performance.

Administration: Group.

Price Data: Price information available from publisher for test materials including Written test booklet ('93, 28 pages), Performance test booklet ('93, 17 pages), examiner's copy of Performance test ('93, 31 pages), manual for administering NOCTI TOCT Performance tests ('94, 17 pages), and manual for administering NOCTI TOCT Written tests ('94, 18 pages).

Time: 180(195) minutes for Written part; 360(380) minutes for Performance part.

Comments: Test administered at least twice a year at centers approved by publisher.

Author: National Occupational Competency Testing Institute.

Publisher: National Occupational Competency Testing Institute.

Cross References: For a review by Richard C. Erickson, see 10:227. For a review of the NOCTI program, see 8:1153 (6 references).

Review of the NOCTI Occupational Competency Test: Appliance Repair by GENEVA D. HAERTEL, Senior Research Associate, EREAPA Associates, Livermore, CA:

The instrument now known as the NOCTI Experienced Worker Tests: Appliance Repair is one of a set of occupational competency tests designed to measure objectively the technical knowledge and performance skills an individual must demonstrate to be a competent tradesperson. It has been used to certify vocational teachers and to acquire academic credit from institutions that recognize performance on NOCTI as a basis for providing credit for work experience. Like other NOCTI tests, the Appliance Repair Test has a Written and Performance version.

There are 200 multiple-choice items in the Written version of the Appliance Repair Test. Each item has four options. The 200 items are categorized within the following seven topical areas: Electrical Fundamentals, 44 items; Power Tools and Small Appliances, 12 items; Major Heating Devices, 24 items; Kitchen Equipment, 31 items; Laundry Equipment, 24 items; Refrigeration, 45 items; and Electronics, 20 items. Most of these items assess an individual's recognition of knowledge in appliance repair; few assess application of knowledge, analysis, synthesis, or evaluation of a complex appliance repair problem.

The Performance test contains a total of 11 job-related tasks, including: use of a wattmeter; use of ohmmeter; writing diagram reading; basic electrical wiring; automatic washer transmission; electric dryer; refrigeration system; refrigeration tubing assembly; test, evacuate/charge refrigeration system; microwave repair; and solid state diagnosing. The performance evaluation worksheet that the examiner fills out for every examinee provides 5-point rating scales measuring the process(es) used in completing each task and 5-point rating scales measuring the product(s) generated by each task. Both processes and products are rated from A to E along a continuum ranging from "extremely skilled worker" to "inept worker." The points along the rating scale are vague and provide little clarity about differences among examinees. The accuracy of examiners' ratings would be improved if the 5-point rating scale included behaviors that distinguished, for example, among an "average worker," "below average worker," and "inept worker."

The Performance test booklet presents 11 tasks that all test takers must complete. This is a change from an earlier version of the Performance test in which all examinees were required to complete 9 of 18 mandatory tasks and an additional 4 tasks that they could choose (see Erickson, 10:227). In the earlier version, the selection of different tasks by examinees resulted in obtained Performance test scores that were not comparable for different individuals. In the current version of the Performance test, the 11 tasks are mandatory, which has corrected the problem of noncomparable Performance scores. As a final step in assessing the test taker, the examiner is asked to provide an overall Performance rating for each candidate using the 5-point scale. Space is provide for the examiner to "state an overall impression of the candidate as a worker in the field" (p. ii).

The current Written and Performance manuals for the Appliance Repair test provide no statistical information on reliability, validity, and item analysis, nor any normative data. Although the Written and Performance versions appear face and content valid, they lack statistical indices of evidence to assure potential users of their psychometric soundness. Thus, when employing this test for personnel decisions, users would want to estimate its reliability and the predictive, construct, and consequential validity of the Written and Performance versions, as well as establish local norms. Although the reviewer was not able to acquire psychometric information on this test, some statistical indices may have been calculated by NOCTI, but are not available in a form that can be readily distributed. Thus, potential users may want to inquire about the availability of such indices before they invest in estimating the statistical indices to meet their local needs.

The manuals that accompany the Written and Performance tests provide adequate instruction on examiner duties, assessment materials needed, examining room conditions, and the explicit verbal instructions needed by the test examiner. Guidelines for security during and after the administration are presented, including forms for reporting irregularities for the group and individuals.

In summary, the NOCTI Appliance Repair Written and Performance tests provide a needed measure of competency for use among aspiring tradespersons. The scope of the content presented is impressive; however, higher level thought processes are not assessed in the Written version. If this test is to fulfill its potential, the overall lack of psychometric information describing both the Written and Performance versions made available to test consumers must be redressed. Consumers must have ready access to information that will let them interpret locally obtained scores.

Review of the NOCTI Teacher Occupational Competency Test: Appliance Repair by CYRIL J. SADOWSKI, Professor of Psychology, Auburn University Montgomery, Montgomery, AL:

The NOCTI Appliance Repair Test is designed to assess knowledge and skills in this technical domain. The Written test is composed of 200 multiple-choice items covering seven areas of competency. Items are primarily factual. The Performance test is composed of 11 tasks, 6 of which address electronics and 5 of which address refrigeration systems. Performance on the electronics items are rated on 5-point scales by an evaluator. Scores on the tasks are weighted, but no description of the basis of the weights is provided. No information about the scoring of the refrigeration system tasks was available.

The test appears to contain appropriate content, but no information about the content selection is provided. Similarly, there is no information about the reliability or validity of scores from the Written test. The Performance test raises even more concerns. Evaluators at many different sites rate candidates' performance. However, there is no information about the selection or training of the evaluators. Although the Performance tasks appear to be content valid, the lack of information about the evaluators' competence is problematic.

A test manual meeting current standards is sorely needed. Such a manual should describe content selection techniques, test reliability, evaluator training, and interrater agreement. It should also provide information about validity data, cutoffs, norms, and potential adverse impact. As the NOCTI program has been in existence for many years, such documentation is long overdue.

[209]

NOCTI Teacher Occupational Competency Test: Audio-Visual Communications Technology.

Purpose: Designed to measure the individual's occupational competency in audio-visual communications technology.

Population: Teachers and prospective teachers.

Publication Dates: 1986–1994.

Scores, 12: 9 scores for Written part (Total and 8 subscores); 3 scores for Performance part (Process, Product, Total).

Administration: Group.

Parts, 2: Written, Performance.

Price Data: Available from publisher for test materials including Written test booklet ('94, 21 pages); Performance test booklet ('94, 11 pages); examiner's copy of Performance test ('94, 33 pages); manual for administering NOCTI TOCT Performance tests ('94, 17 pages); manual for administering NOCTI TOCT Written tests ('94, 18 pages).

Time: 180(190) minutes for Written part; 360(400) minutes for Performance part.

Comments: Test administered at least twice a year at centers approved by the publisher.

Author: National Occupational Competency Testing Institute.

Publisher: National Occupational Competency Testing Institute.

Cross References: For reviews by JoEllen V. Carlson and Anne L. Harvey, see 11:262. For a review of the NOCTI program, see 8:1153 (6 references).

[Editor's Note: These reviews are based on materials available as of September 1, 1996. The publisher advises that major revisions in the NOCTI tests are in process. These will be reviewed in the future.]

Review of the NOCTI Teacher Occupational Competency Test: Audio-Visual Communication Technology by PATRICIA A. BACHELOR, Professor of Psychology, California State University at Long Beach, Long Beach, CA:

The 1986–87 version of the NOCTI Teacher Occupational Competency Test: Audio-Visual Communications Technology (AVCT) was reviewed for the *Eleventh Mental Measurements Yearbook* (1992) by J. V. Carlson and A. L. Harvey. Both reviewers called for the test authors to prepare a technical manual to address critical psychometric issues related to this test. Particularly shocking is the conspicuous lack of a technical manual to accompany the 1994 version of this test. Thus, the questions raised by the earlier reviewers are still unanswered as are additional questions suggested by the current version of the AVCT.

The current version of the AVCT consists of two components—a Written assessment and a Performance appraisal. This is the same format as the earlier test. The objective (Written) component comprises 200 four-option multiple-choice items distributed over nine content areas of photography (30 questions), computer graphics (21 questions), video production (29 questions), equipment repair and maintenance (21 questions), audio production (22 questions), presentation technology (20 questions), graphic design (20 questions), project management (32 questions), and related miscellaneous information (5 questions). This represents an expansion of the 1986–87 version, which consisted of 180 objective items assessing eight content areas. The items are appropriate to assess knowledge of the content areas, with most items requiring recall of basic facts and skills rather than analytic reasoning. As in the earlier version of the test, no evaluation criteria were presented, hence, performance cannot be interpreted.

The Performance appraisal requires the examinee to demonstrate his or her ability to perform, in order, the following 8 (rather than 10) "jobs": still photography—operation of 35mm camera; still photography—film development; still photography—printing; editing and splicing audio tape; audio production studio-recording and mixing; video shooting and editing; presentation equipment usage and maintenance (including slide projection, overhead projection, monitor set-up and operation, and general troubleshooting); and operating computer graphics equipment to recreate four graphic visuals. These "jobs" represent a comprehensive array of tasks that a skilled audio-visual worker should be able to perform successfully. The examination booklet gives clear and step-by-step instructions as well as estimates of the completion time. However, it is left for the examinee to record his/her start and stop time. The examinee's performance is rated on a variety of dimensions of each job on process as well as product using a 5-point rating scale of *extremely skilled worker, above average worker, average worker, below average worker,* or *inept worker.* These anchors, as in the 1986–87 test version, are not further defined. To conclude the Performance evaluation, a Summary Score (the sum of "process" and "product" points), Subscores (the percent of maximum points obtained on process and product), an Overall Performance Rating (using the aforementioned 5-point scale), as well as a narrative summary paragraph are prepared by the examiner. This represents no change from the prior version.

Three guides accompany the test components—one booklet for each of the two test components and an Evaluator's Guide. Each booklet describes test administration procedures either for the Written assessment or the Performance appraisal. These manuals are clearly written and are thorough in the presentation of the details of various aspects of test administration, such as seating arrangements and verbatim instructions, but there are no criteria for appraisal or standards upon which a rating or outcome score is determined. Also, absent is any information about examiner qualifications. Given that this test is most likely used in job-related testing and/or certification programs, this seems particularly troublesome. Without any criteria for successful performance by a specified and qualified examiner, an examinee would have difficulty interpreting his or her performance rating. It seems that this is either a criterion-referenced test without a specified yardstick for performance or a norm-referenced test without a clearly identified comparison group.

It is disappointing that there is no technical manual to accompany the revised AVCT. The authors have revised the test but failed to share any information about test development and modification, estimates of reliability coefficients, validity studies, and/or standardization samples and norm groups. The complete lack of any psychometric data related to this test is especially problematic, given that two earlier reviews contained negative comments about this noticeable gap in what has otherwise been a comprehensively documented test. Key psychometric information is absent, thereby preventing a candid appraisal of the technical properties of this instrument. A test consumer expects and is entitled to receive such information in order to make an informed decision regarding appropriate test selection and use. The *Standards for Educational and Psychological Testing* (AERA, APA, & NCME, 1985) speak very clearly and emphatically about technical manuals and what is to be housed within. It is hoped that authors of future versions of the NOCTI test series will prepare and distribute such essential materials.

REVIEWER'S REFERENCES

American Educational Research Association, American Psychological Association, & National Council on Measurement in Education. (1985). *Standards for educational and psychological testing.* Washington, DC: American Psychological Association, Inc.

Carlson, J. V. (1992). [Review of the NOCTI Teacher Occupational Competency Test: Audio-Visual Communications Technology.] In J. J. Kramer & J. C. Conoley (Eds.), *The eleventh mental measurements yearbook* (pp. 612–613). Lincoln, NE: Buros Institute of Mental Measurements.

Harvey, A. L. (1992). [Review of the NOCTI Teacher Occupational Competency Test: Audio-Visual Communications Technology.] In J. J. Kramer & J. C. Conoley (Eds.), *The eleventh mental measurements yearbook* (p. 613). Lincoln, NE: Buros Institute of Mental Measurements.

Review of the NOCTI Teacher Occupational Competency Test: Audio-Visual Communications Technology by CONNIE KUBO DELLA-PIANA, Assistant Professor of Communication, University of Texas at El Paso, El Paso, TX:

The NOCTI Teacher Occupational Competency Test: Audio-Visual Communications Technology is a set of test materials designed to assess technical knowledge and evaluate technical skills. The test is meant for teachers and prospective teachers, as well as "industrial candidates" to verify and to demonstrate occupational competence. The test is composed of two parts: a Written test and a Performance evaluation. The Written test consists of 200 four-option, multiple-choice items covering nine areas: photography, 30 items; computer graphics, 21 items; video production, 29 items; equipment repair and maintenance, 21 items; audio production, 22 items; presentation technology, 20 items; graphic design, 20 items; project management, 32 items; and related miscellaneous information, 5 items. Items are clearly and completely stated. In general, options have approximately the same grammatical structure and length. Items appear to reflect the problems they were intended to represent. In general, items require test takers to recall information about a particular task or situation (a focus on knowledge) rather than requiring them to reason from a set of givens (a focus on intellectual abilities and skills).

The Performance assessment portion of the Audio-Visual Communications Technology Test is administered in small groups under close supervision of the examiner. The Performance test consists of eight tasks or jobs, some of which must be completed in order, that is, the product of one task or job becomes the material needed to complete the next task or job. The Performance test includes: still photography, still photography/film development, still photography/printing, editing and splicing audio tape, audio production studio, video shooting and editing, presentation equipment/usage and maintenance, and computer graphics equipment/re-create 4 graphics visuals. Each task or job has an estimated completion time and test takers must record starting and completion times. It is not clear why each task or job has a listed estimated completion time or if completion time is an important criterion for success on the job. The examiner rates both process- and product-related aspects of the task or job by checking a rating scale for specified processes and products. Possible rating include: *extremely skilled worker, above average worker, average worker, below average worker,* and *inept worker.* A description of the performance ratings is not available in the written materials accompanying the test. This is a serious oversight because test developers claim that the assessment was developed "to verify [the test takers'] experience and demonstrate [their] competency" (p. 6). In addition, there is no mention of the training required to administer the Performance portion of the test. The format of the Performance Evaluation Worksheet is clear and concise, minus descriptions of the rating scale. According to the instructions given to the examiner "different candidates may work on different jobs or complete them in a different order due to availability of machines and equipment" (p. 6). This poses major management challenges for the examiner because the examiner is responsible for familiarizing each candidate with the equipment set-up, operation, and connections prior to starting each job, timing each candidate, evaluating and observing the performance of each candidate on every task or job, maintaining a separate evaluation worksheet for each candidate, monitoring candidate test-taking behavior, and insuring standardized administering of each job/task and the testing procedures as a whole. For instance, if the examiner is evaluating and observing a candidate's performance in the darkroom, he or she cannot be observing those candidates who are working at other workstations in the lab or shop and vice versa. No suggestions are presented to guide the examiner in developing a plan to meet the demands of managing the testing procedures. Although each task or job is described in terms of materials, equipment, and tools needed for the test, the layout for the lab or shop and the number of workstations needed for the number of candidates is left unstated. Is one workstation per job or task sufficient? Does the layout of the lab or shop influence performance? Are different models of the same type of equipment equivalent? Do different models of equipment affect performance? After the Performance portion of the test is completed, examiners are required to transfer their ratings on the Performance Evaluation Worksheet to the General Purpose NCS Answer Sheet. It is not clear from the instructions if there are two answer sheets, one for the Written portion of the test and one for the Performance portion.

The examiner's manual for the Written portion of the test is thorough and well organized. The same cannot be said for the Performance assessment manual. Pages were not in order or upside down.

Reference in the Performance assessment manual to the "Evaluator's Copy of the Performance Assessment" did not match the written material accompanying the test. An "Evaluator's Guide" was included. In an attempt to document and judge the standardization of administration, examiners are required to complete a report on group irregularities and individual irregularities.

There was no technical manual included with the test material. Lack of technical information on test development, standards for scoring and administering, reliability, validity, and score interpretation severely limit the usefulness of the Audio-Visual Communications Technology Test. The use of the interpretation of test results for certification or job-related purposes is not justified based on the lack of technical information. Without technical information, the Audio-Visual Communications Technology Test should only be used as a formative evaluation tool for instructional purposes.

[210]
NOCTI Teacher Occupational Competency Test: Auto Body Repair, Forms B and D.

Purpose: Designed to measure the individual's occupational competency in auto body repair.
Population: Teachers and prospective teachers.
Publication Dates: 1973–1994.
Scores, 14: 11 scores for Written part (Total and 10 subscores), 3 scores for Performance part (Process, Product, Total).
Parts, 2: Written, Performance.
Administration: Group.
Price Data: Price information available from publisher for test materials including Written test booklet ('87, 24 pages), Performance test booklet ('87, 3 pages), examiner's copy of Performance test ('87, 6 pages), manual for administering NOCTI TOCT Performance tests ('94, 17 pages), and manual for administering NOCTI TOCT Written tests ('94, 18 pages).
Time: 180(195) minutes for Written part; 340(360) minutes for Performance part (Form B); 305(335) minutes for Performance part (Form D).
Comments: Test administered at least twice a year at centers approved by publisher.
Author: National Occupational Competency Testing Institute.
Publisher: National Occupational Competency Testing Institute.
Cross References: See 9:777 (1 reference); for a review of the NOCTI program, see 8:1153 (6 references). [Editor's Note: These reviews are based on materials available as of September 1, 1996. The publisher advises that major revisions of the NOCTI tests are in process. These will be reviewed in the future.]

Review of the NOCTI Teacher Occupational Competency Test: Auto Body Repair, Forms B & D by ROBERT J. DRUMMOND, *Professor of Education and Human Services, University of North Florida, Jacksonville, FL:*

The Teacher Occupational Competency Test: Auto Body Repair consists of both a Written and a Performance test. The Written form consists of 190 multiple-choice questions, covering Welding (16), Filling Operations (20), Repairing Sheet Metal (30), Refinishing (38), Panel Replacement (15), Unitized Frame Body Repair (26), Front End Alignment (8), Electrical and Assessory (9), Glass Trim and Hardware (11), and Estimating, Tools, and Safety Equipment (17). The Performance test provides several jobs for the candidate to complete. These are Metal Work, Filling; Metal Work, Straightening; Oxy-Acetylene Welding; MIG Welding; Spray Painting; Estimating; Electrical Troubleshooting; and Diagnosing Structural Damage. There are three performance scores based upon the values provided by a rater, a product score, a process score, and a total score. The total points that can be achieved are 1,050.

The manuals for the examiner are very detailed as to the directions that should be followed and cover dimensions such as visitor interruptions, room conditions, seating arrangements, answering candidates questions, and reporting individual candidate irregularities. On either of the examinations, there are no discussions or guidelines for testing individuals who have handicapping conditions. No information is provided in the manuals on how the results will be reported or what the scores mean. Are there cutoff scores? If so, how were they derived? When will candidates hear the results of the testing and in what form will the scores be reported? Even if this is provided in other sources by the NOCTI, it would be good information for the candidates to have.

There is no information provided in the manuals concerning the validity and reliability of either form. Although the tests appear to have face validity, no discussion is provided on how the tasks and items were identified and selected for the two tests. How were the KSAs (knowledge, skills, and abilities) identified and selected? Were Subject Matter Experts (SMEs) used? How were the weighting of the tasks and number of items selected accomplished? How reliable are the ratings? No information is presented on the reliability of the multiple-choice form or about the item difficulty or discrimination. No criterion-referenced validity is reported for either form. The candidates on the process examination are rated on a 5-point scale from "A" *extremely skilled worker* to "E" *inept worker*. It would seem that this type of judgment would be subjective. There are no illustrations of what constitutes extremely skilled performance and what constitutes inept performance. It would be hard for one rater to rate the large number of items on the Performance examination for very many candidates because the Performance test requires both process and product ratings. How are the raters selected and trained? What is the interrater reliability? How is the reliability of the ratings monitored?

In general, the multiple-choice items could be substantially improved. Many had split stems and did not have parallel construction. The questions also would be improved if the stem stated a question rather than an incomplete statement.

SUMMARY. The tests appear to provide a comprehensive assessment of the knowledge, process, and products related to auto body repair; however, without more information and evidence on the reliability and validity of the various forms it is hard to endorse the tests without a number of reservations. The multiple-choice items need to be sharpened. The manuals need to include more information for the candidate on how the results will be reported to the candidate and what the scores mean. Also, the manual for examiners could be improved by having more detailed guidelines and illustrations of each of the five levels of performance used to differentiate among the items on process and product scales. Certification and licensing examinations are high stake evaluations and need to be continuously monitored, updated, and revised in order to be fair to the population they serve.

Review of the NOCTI Teacher Occupational Competency Test: Auto Body Repair, Forms B & D by DALE P. SCANNELL, *Professor of Education, Indiana University, Purdue University—Indianapolis, Indianapolis, IN:*

The publisher of the occupational competency tests evidently provides generic manuals for administering the Written and the Performance tests in this series. The Experienced Worker Performance Assessment Manual is 17 pages of what appears to be photocopied materials. Quality control for the production of the manual is not adequate. Printing quality is uneven and although all materials can be read, the poor quality is distracting. In the copy reviewed, the page following the table of contents is page 16, an appendix item titled "Irregularity Report." Page 1 was found printed upside down on the back of page 15, facing page 17.

The instructions for administering the Performance assessment are appropriate and comprehensive, including detailed instructions for gathering most of the materials that will be needed and for setting up the room where the exam will be administered. All of the topics one would expect to find concerning arrangements and logistics are included in the manual. Common problems that could interfere with the exam are identified and helpful directions for handling those situations are provided.

Examiners are provided with the Examiner's Copy of Performance Test, which is an expanded form of the booklet given to each examinee. The Performance test comprises nine tasks of which eight are to be completed by each examinee; Tasks 4 and 5 are options and one is to be selected. Examiners are to observe the examinees as they work on each task and rate the process and product on a 5-point scale, ranging from A = *extremely skilled worker* to E = *inept worker*. Examples of the process categories are "proper use of equipment" and "proper use of hand tools" and examples of the product categories are "contour accurate" and "general appearance" (p. 1).

In the examiner's copy, the page for each task begins with a brief description of the job to be completed (i.e., "The candidate is to fill with plastic a 9-inch square dent in a door, hood, trunk lid or fender" (p. 3). This is followed by a list of materials, tools, and equipment needed. In the next section, Directions, an acceptable sequence of steps to complete the task is provided. The last section on the page is a statement about evaluation of the candidate: "Score the candidate according to the criteria shown on the Performance Evaluation Worksheet" (p. 3). Evidently this information is the total effort to seek consistency in scoring among various examiners. There is no evidence that examiners have received training in scoring the tasks, and the definition of scale points, shown above, seems inadequate to provide confidence that consistent grading occurs.

Job #1 involves repairing a dented car part. At no place in the materials provided for this review is there an indication of where the dented object is to be obtained. On page 2 of the Experienced Worker Performance Assessment Manual there is a reference to the "Evaluator's Copy of the Performance Assessment." Is this the same as the "Examiner's Copy of the Performance Test"? If it is, which seems likely, then the examiner is never told where to obtain the parts that are to be repaired (e.g., a dented car part).

During the examination, the evaluator is to observe the work and rate the performance, recording the score in the process section of the worksheet. Later these scores are transferred to an NCS answer sheet. At the completion of a job, the product is tagged for identification and later is rated; the ratings are recorded on the answer sheet. The manual for the test indicates that the Performance test is to be administered to small groups of examinees but the maximum number is not specified. Even with relatively small groups of examinees, evaluators will be spread thin in trying to observe and judge the process of examinees. Provisions for quality control and equity in assessment across examinees are insufficient.

A major weakness for this test is the absence of technical information about the reliability and validity of the test. Although the test seems to have face validity, no information is given about the method of establishing cut scores or the relationship between performance on the test and on the job.

For the Written part of the examination, two booklets are provided, a manual for the evaluator and the written test booklet. The manual provides the type of instructions one would expect about preparations, materials needed, and directions that are to be read to examinees in guiding them through the process. Extensive suggestions are provided for seating arrangements for rooms with individual arm chairs and those with tables. This manual refers to the existence of a coordinator for the test center. However, there is no indication of the duties of the coordinator or the relationship between that person and the evaluator.

The Written test booklet contains a brief set of directions for examinees and 190 multiple-choice test items. The directions appear to be generic and indicate that the time limit for the test will be announced. The time limit was not provided for this review. The 190 items cover 10 skill areas such as welding and refinishing. The shortest subtest is nine items and longest is 38. Most item stems are incomplete statements and most of the items focus on knowledge rather than higher order skills such as application of information. Distractors for individual items frequently are not parallel so that functionally the expected chance score will be greater than 1 in 4.

As noted earlier, technical information about the tests is not available. In response to correspondence, a NOCTI representative indicated that this test is being revised and the revision is in a pilot stage. The revised test will be named Collision Repair Technology.

The NOCTI Auto Body Repair test is an extensive examination of candidate knowledge about auto repair equipment and techniques and includes performance on selected, representative repair activities. In the absence of technical information about the test and the value of the scores obtained from the tests, one choosing to use the test will be relying primarily on the face validity of the instruments. The burden placed on examiners and the apparent lack of practices that could contribute to interexaminer consistency raise major questions about the reliability of the Performance test. Inconsistencies among the various booklets and poor print quality do not instill confidence in the values to be derived from the test.

[211]
NOCTI Teacher Occupational Competency Test: Automotive Technician.

Purpose: Designed to measure the individual's occupational competency in automotive technology.
Population: Teachers and prospective teachers.
Publication Dates: 1973–1994.
Scores, 12: 9 scores for Written part (Total and 8 subscores), 3 scores for Performance part (Process, Product, Total).
Parts, 2: Written, Performance.
Administration: Group.
Price Data: Price information available from publisher for test materials including Written test booklet ('92, 27 pages), Performance test booklet ('92, 18 pages), Evaluator's guide ('92, 35 pages), manual for administering NOCTI TOCT Written tests ('94, 18 pages), and manual for administering NOCTI TOCT Performance tests ('94, 17 pages).
Time: 180(195) minutes for Written part; (300) minutes for Performance part.
Comments: Previously listed as Auto Mechanics; test administered at least twice a year at centers approved by publisher.
Author: National Occupational Competency Testing Institute.
Publisher: National Occupational Competency Testing Institute.
Cross References: See 9:778 (2 references) and T3:1595 (1 reference); for a review by Charles W. Pendleton, see 8:1133. For a review of the NOCTI program, see 8:1153 (6 references).
[Editor's Note: These reviews are based on materials available as of September 1, 1996. The publisher advises that major revisions of the NOCTI tests are in process. These will be reviewed in the future.]

Review of the NOCTI Teacher Occupational Competency Test: Automotive Technician by DALE P. SCANNELL, Professor of Education, Indiana University, Purdue University—Indianapolis, Indianapolis, IN:

The publisher of the occupational competency tests evidently provides generic manuals for administering the written and the performance tests in this series. The Experienced Worker Performance Assessment Manual is 17 pages of what appears to be photocopied materials. Quality control for the production of the manual is not adequate. Printing quality is uneven and although all materials can be read, the poor quality is distracting. In the copy reviewed, the page following the table of contents is page 16, an appendix item titled "Irregularity Report." Page 1 was found printed upside down on the back of page 15, facing page 17.

The instructions for administering the Performance assessment are appropriate and comprehensive, including detailed instructions for gathering most of the materials that will be needed and for setting up the room where the exam will be administered. All of the topics one would expect to find concerning arrangements and logistics are included in the manual. Common problems that could interfere with the exam are identified and helpful directions for handling those situations are provided.

Examiners are provided with a copy of the Experienced Worker Evaluator's Guide, which is an expanded form of the booklet given to each examinee. A list of the 12 tasks that comprise the Performance test and materials needed for each are provided in the manual. Examiners are to observe the examinees as they work on each task and rate the process and product on a 5-point scale, ranging from *A = extremely skilled worker* to *E = inept worker*. Examples of the process categories are "grinding of valve seat" and "adjustment of valve height" and examples of the product categories are "valve spring tension" and "valve height." These ratings are marked on a worksheet during the test and are transferred to an NCS answer sheet after the end of the test.

In the examiner's copy, the page for each task begins with a brief description of the job to be completed (i.e., "Disc Brake Assembly Service and Wheel Bearing Adjustment," p. 7). This is followed by a list of materials, tools, and supplies that must be provided, and the final section lists the actions the candidate is supposed to perform. Estimated completion times are given for each task, and the maximum time to be provided for the entire test is 5 hours. At no place in the manual is there an indication of where the examiner obtains the automobiles or assemblies on which the candidates work. It seems likely that a coordinator of the test center has additional manuals but these were not provided for this review.

A major weakness for this test is the absence of technical information about the reliability and validity of the test. Although the test seems to have face validity, no information is given about the method of establishing cut scores or the relationship between performance on the test and on the job. Evidently the test is administered to a group of candidates simultaneously but the recommended or maximum number is not indicated. Given the complexity of the tasks and the number of processes and products to be rated, one might question how an examiner can ensure adequate observation to rate the process and provide equity among candidates. Another major question raised by the materials provided is what has the publisher done to ensure interexaminer consistency in grading.

For the Written part of the examination, two booklets are provided, a manual for the evaluator and the written test booklet. The manual provides the type of instructions one would expect about preparations, materials needed, and directions that are to be read to examinees in guiding them through the process. Extensive suggestions are provided for seating arrangements for rooms with individual arm chairs and those with tables.

The test booklet contains a brief set of directions for the candidates and 200 multiple-choice test items. The items are provided in eight sections ranging in number from 16 to 37. Responses are recorded on a general purpose NCS answer sheet. A large number of the items have incomplete stems, and the emphasis is on knowledge rather than on higher order accomplishments. Technical flaws are found in a sample of the items. For example, Item 180 has overlapping responses and Item 169 includes some responses that are not appropriate for the stem.

As noted earlier, this test seems to have face validity, but a major weakness is the absence of technical manuals reporting standard psychometric data. The degree of interexaminer consistency in rating performance has not been reported. Similarly, the publishers do not indicate how the passing score has been set or how success on the test relates to performance.

The NOCTI Automotive Technician test is a comprehensive examination of knowledge about and skill in performing a variety of repairs to automobiles. The Performance test has a time limit of 5 hours; the recommended time limit for a written test with 126–200 items is 3 hours. Even though the Performance and Written tests appear to be comprehensive and appropriate, one cannot judge the value of the test in the absence of technical information about reliability, interexaminer consistency in rating performance tasks,

methods by which satisfactory performance is established, and relationships between performance on the test and success as an automobile technician.

Review of the NOCTI Teacher Occupational Competency Test: Automotive Technician by GEORGE C. THORNTON III, Professor of Psychology, Colorado State University, Fort Collins, CO:

Quite regrettably, NOCTI continues to fail to provide adequate technical information about the psychometric properties of its tests. Despite a long string of critical reviews of other NOCTI tests in this Yearbook dating back many years, little information beyond simple means and standard deviations for small samples is provided. The potential user has no way of evaluating the adequacy of test development, reliability, or validity for intended users. Virtually none of the professional expectations for test publication codified in the *Standards for Educational and Psychological Testing* (AERA, APA, & NCME, 1985) are met. There is little basis for evaluating whether the test accomplishes any of the lofty claims.

A slick brochure proclaims NOCTI "the leader in occupational competency testing" and lists numerous benefits of skills assessment for educators, administrators, employers, trainers, and employees. The manual purports that this test assesses the knowledge and skills of teachers and prospective teachers in the area of automotive technology. No evidence is provided to support any of these claims.

The Written test, lasting 3 hours, comprises 200 multiple-choice items covering knowledge of engines, alignment and suspension, brakes, engine electrical, drive lines, fuel and emissions systems, accessories and chassis electrical, and shop management. One summary page of statistics from NOCTI covering over 50 tests provides one line of data on the automotive test, including a reliability estimate (KR 20) of .929. This ostensibly high figure must be discounted in light of the long test length: This level of internal consistency for a test of 200 items means that the average intercorrelation of the items is only about .06. In reality, the test is quite heterogeneous, despite the seemingly high reliability estimate. A much more relevant type of reliability estimate for an occupational certification test is the consistency of making the determination of "competent" or "not competent." No such data are provided.

The Performance test, lasting 5 hours, involves 12 tasks such as servicing a cylinder head, servicing a disc brake (and) assembly, and performing wheel alignment. For each task, the evaluator observes the candidate, then evaluates several dimensions of the process carried out and the product produced. For example, when evaluating the task of a fuel system pressure test, the evaluator rates the processes of connecting gauges, safety with fuel, accurate measurement, and proper use of tools, and then rates the products of familiarity with the process, power fuel pump, and manual pressure increase. In total, 56 process subtasks and 51 product attributes are evaluated. Overall process and product scores are tabulated. Unfortunately, no evidence is reported of internal consistency of these ratings and no evidence of the interrater reliability of evaluator judgments is provided.

It is standard practice in reviews like this to comment on the adequacy of the (a) theory or plan guiding test development; (b) samples used for test development, item analysis, norming, estimates of reliability, and validation; and (c) evidence provided to support the validity of the test (i.e., the various inferences that might be made from the test scores). No such information is provided in the test manual, the slim reports sent after my repeated requests to NOCTI, or any other published or unpublished reports on the test.

Writing this review posed a serious dilemma. On the one hand, the technical evidence supporting this test from NOCTI is sorely lacking. On the other hand, faced with the practical need to test the knowledge and assess the performance of automotive technicians there may be no alternatives. About all I can say on the positive side is that the items and tasks look appropriate, and there are detailed administrator's guides for both the Written and Performance tests. But, I cannot endorse the use of this test on the basis of such superficial impressions.

REVIEWER'S REFERENCE

American Educational Research Association, American Psychological Association, & National Council on Measurement in Education. (1985). *Standards for educational and psychological testing.* Washington, DC: American Psychological Association, Inc.

[212]
NOCTI Teacher Occupational Competency Test: Scientific Data Processing.

Purpose: Designed to measure the individual's occupational competency in scientific data processing.
Population: Teachers and prospective teachers.
Publication Dates: 1988–1994.
Scores, 15: 12 scores for Written part (Total and 11 subscores), 3 scores for Performance part (Process, Product, Total).
Parts, 2: Written, Performance.
Administration: Group.

Price Data: Price information available from publisher for test materials including Written test booklet ('93, 32 pages), Performance test booklet ('93, 19 pages), examiner's copy of Performance test ('93, 22 pages), manual for administering NOCTI TOCT Written tests ('94, 18 pages), and manual for administering NOCTI TOCT Performance tests ('94, 17 pages).

Time: (180) minutes for Written part; (360) minutes for Performance part.

Comments: Test administered at least twice a year at centers approved by publisher.

Author: National Occupational Competency Testing Institute.

Publisher: National Occupational Competency Testing Institute.

Cross References: For a review by William M. Bart, see 11:263. For a review of the NOCTI program, see 8:1153 (6 references).

[Editor's Note: These reviews are based on materials available as of September 1, 1996. The publisher advises that major revisions of the NOCTI tests are in process. These will be reviewed in the future.]

Review of the NOCTI Teacher Occupational Competency Test: Scientific Data Processing by JIM C. FORTUNE, Professor of Research and Evaluation, Virginia Tech, Blacksburg, VA:

INTRODUCTION AND GENERAL DESCRIPTION. The NOCTI Teacher Occupational Competency Test: Scientific Data Processing was designed to measure scientific data processing for teachers and prospective teachers of that subject. The test is a long test composed of two parts: a Written test and a Performance test. The Written test requires 3 hours for administration and the Performance test requires 6 hours for administration. The Written test is made up of a four-choice, multiple-choice examination containing 11 subtests. These include: Computer Fundamentals, Using Software Packages, Generating Documentation, Applying Numerical Analysis, Using Operating Systems, Performing Equipment Operations, Using Languages in General, Using Basic, Using Fortran, Using Pascal, and Using C. The total test involves 179 items. Subtest scores and a total score are derived from performances on the Written tests. The Performance test involves the completion of a multi-task exercise. There are four exercises of similar, if not equal, difficulty and the instructions require the examiner to assign one to each examinee. The examinee is expected to finish the assigned exercise performing all of the required tasks. Three scores are derived from the performance of the exercise: Process, Product, and Total. The tests were designed for the experienced scientific data processor.

REASON FOR THE TESTS. The tests were designed to test competency of teachers and potential teachers in scientific data processing. After having taken the Written test, it appears to me that the test examines scientific data processing competency at an experienced worker level rather than scientific data processing competency at a level required to teach the subject. Many of the multiple-choice items require memory of terms or knowledge of order of operation that are more important at a practice level than they would be in the preparation of a lesson in such. A similar observation can be made for the Performance test.

JOB ANALYSIS. None of the materials that I received described the job analysis. Review of the content suggests potential content validity and makes one believe that a job analysis was performed. I believe that the test content is valid for the practice of scientific data processing, but I question whether or not it addresses the content at a level required to teach the material. I would expect my teacher of the subject to see the big picture rather than remembering which language is called a "high level" language. None of the materials contain a table of specifications, or the relationship of item content on the test to importance of item in practice.

RELIABILITY AND VALIDITY. None of the materials that were sent me included any reliability or validity information. A telephone call to Ferris State University made contact with a friendly, helpful staff person who provided me with the existing reliability information. This information appears slim and inconclusive to me. There appeared to be no statistics for the subtests of the Written test, and the reliability for the total score on the written test was calculated on a sample of eight subjects. KR-20 and KR-21 were calculated on the total score. KR-20 was .893 and KR-21 was .851 for this very small sample. The sample group had a mean of 97.00 (I assume the number correct out of the 167 items scored for a percent correct of 58.1%) and a standard deviation of 15.22. The reliability reported for the Performance test was coefficient alphas calculated on 17 items and a sample of nine subjects. These reliabilities were .947 for process scores and .956 for product scores. The combined score reliability was .956.

No evidence of validity was reported. A simple description of the job analysis or of the table of specification would provide the content validity that I would expect for a test of this type. It appears to me that there are areas of expected staff behaviors that are omitted from the test. I would be curious as to why editing, verification, data summary, and description were not included on the test. I would think that my teacher of data processing would emphasize editing requirements, verification requirements, and subchecks. The length of both examinations would suggest to me that fatigue may be a threat to validity of the test.

ADMINISTRATIVE EASE. Length of both tests would create difficulty in administrative control. A 3-hour Written test and a 6-hour Performance test both suggest numerous bathroom breaks, fatigue, and difficulty in administrative control. There is no administration manual specifically for the Written test. Instead, directions for the Written tests are contained in the general Written test manual and are included in the Written test booklet and in an insert sheet in this booklet. Overall, the instructions for administration are very clear with regard to most instructions, materials, and in-session security requirements. One area on the insert sheet demands a selection of language areas, which seems a little inconsistent with the scoring descriptions. The general manual describes how to distribute the answer sheets and assessment booklets. Instructions for filling out demographics on the answer sheets are given. There is no penalty for guessing so examinees are instructed to answer every question on the Written test.

The manual for the Performance test is not as clear as the manual for the Written test. This perhaps is due to the increased difficulty of the monitoring process and the assignment of an exercise to an examinee. Yet, I would rate this manual as adequate. There is also a general performance assessment manual, which appears consistent with the specific assessment manual.

SUPPORTIVE MATERIALS. The Experienced Worker Performance Assessment Manual and the Experienced Worker Written Assessment Manual are general manuals to support the administration of these tests. These general manuals are high quality, but they contain some duplication of the specific performance administration manual. Lacking from these supportive materials are information on the job analysis, validation studies, and reliability information.

REVIEWER COMMENTARY. Much of the content of the Written test appeared to be testing small details, some of which is essential for data processing. I took the test and although I did not have a scoring key, I found that many items attended to minutiae and that these items might better serve

the assessment by the reduction of the length of the test. Also, I caution that many aspects of teacher competency as to the subject matter relate to the "big picture" as opposed to so much "nitty-gritty." The Performance test appears to require too large a work sample. If I were testing for job selection in data processing, I may wish a Performance test as given. But for teacher competency, I wonder what are the costs of complexity. The Performance test assesses several traits and abilities that I suspect are not included in the scoring, such as time management, focus, planning skills, organization skills, tolerance, etc. I think I would be more pleased with the tests if I could elect to use only parts of the examinations as constructed.

Review of the NOCTI Teacher Occupational Competency Test: Scientific Data Processing by MYRA N. WOMBLE, Assistant Professor of Occupational Studies, University of Georgia, Athens, GA:

DESCRIPTION OF THE SCALE. The Scientific Data Processing test is an occupational competency test intended to assess potential teachers of vocational education programs in scientific data processing at the journey-worker level. The test has both a Performance and Written component. For the Performance test, candidates are assigned one of four programming problems, each similar in complexity and involving coding, compiling, and executing a computer program. The Written test contains 159 multiple-choice questions, 40 of which pertain to four specific programming languages.

DEVELOPMENT. The test was developed in 1988 by Associated Educational Consultants, Inc. (AEC) with the intent of integrating the finished product into the National Occupational Competency Testing Institute (NOCTI) system. Information about development of the Scientific Data Processing test was not available in the assessment manuals provided, but was obtained from NOCTI. Development of the test began by identifying occupational tasks performed by journey-workers employed in scientific data processing. According to NOCTI, minor revisions were made in 1993, but no information describing the revisions was provided.

Preliminary test content was developed by AEC with assistance from a Pennsylvania Area Vocational-Technical school, largely because the scientific data processing program at the school was considered exemplary. However, criteria used to determine "exemplary" status of the school were not provided. After review and editing of several drafts, a final duty-task list was compiled and presented to a five-member Test Development Committee.

ADMINISTRATION AND SCORING. The Performance and Written assessment manuals for examiners provide adequate details about how to administer both components of the test. Candidates are allowed 6 hours to complete the Performance test and 3 hours to complete the Written test.

PERFORMANCE TEST. During the test, examiners use a Performance Evaluation Worksheet while observing each candidate's performance level in four process and four product categories. The four process and product categories evaluated are input data, use of software, operating system/languages, and programming. Each of the four process and product categories contain criteria statements and assigned maximum score values. Evaluation of both categories requires examiners to determine the candidate's skill level, and award points accordingly, using a scale ranging from A = *extremely skilled* to E = *inept worker*. Examiners also determine and report candidates' overall performance using the same range of skill levels, and provide a written overall performance evaluation. Finally, scoring of the Performance test presents a potential problem if examiners find themselves observing and evaluating several different programming languages at the same time. Making clear distinctions among five levels of performance for each criteria statement in the two performance categories, while observing performance in several different languages, may decrease examiner's ability to score objectively.

WRITTEN TEST. The Written test is divided into seven categories each containing multiple-choice questions. The first six categories include areas such as computer fundamentals and account for 139 of the questions. The seventh category includes 40 multiple-choice questions, 10 for each of four programming languages (e.g., BASIC, FORTRAN, Pascal, C). Examinees are instructed to answer all of the questions in the first six categories, then answer 20 of the questions pertaining to only two of the four programming languages.

It should be noted that although one of the performance problems allows COBOL or RPG as choices of programming languages, questions relating to COBOL and RPG are not included in the Written test. Because candidates are allowed to complete the Performance test using COBOL or RPG, these languages should also be a part of the Written test. Also, unlike the Performance test,

there is no examiner's copy of the written test. Apparently all information needed by the examiner is included in the Written Assessment Manual, but this is unclear and should be addressed. Furthermore, no information is provided regarding scoring of the written test.

VALIDITY. The Test Development Committee (TDC) included practitioners and educators with backgrounds and experiences appropriately related to scientific data processing. According to AEC, the TDC thoroughly reviewed, amended, and edited the list of competencies and further validated the list through the use of an information occupational inventory of their peers to ensure its accuracy and relevancy to the defined occupational area. Next, the AEC staff developed a rating procedure (Pertinence Index) to identify the frequency and importance of each competency. TDC members participated in this procedure to further scrutinize the list of competencies. Although this phase of the validation process provided important information (e.g., tasks to add or change), AEC's analysis procedures are not described nor easily discerned from the data tables. Therefore, the criteria used to modify the test are unknown. An independent group of experts was not used to evaluate the content validity of the Scientific Data Processing test. Instead, according to AEC, the diverse composition of the TDC provided that all identified competencies were adequately covered. AEC reviewed and edited all questions and an expert in the field, serving as a third party evaluator, reviewed and provided feedback on the structure and content of the test.

RELIABILITY. Fifteen persons participated in field testing of the Scientific Data Processing test. Participants were sufficiently knowledgeable and experienced in scientific data processing. Additional revisions to the Written and Performance tests were made based on field-test results. Because field test results were not reported, knowledge gained that led to revisions is ambiguous. Nevertheless, according to AEC, revisions made dealt with uncertainties experienced by examinees whose expertise in software and hardware was not considered in development of the questions.

National norms on a battery of NOCTI tests, of which the Scientific Data Processing test is a part, suggest that these measures have internal consistency. Reliability measures based on 1995 national norms for the Written component are KR-20 .893 and KR-21 .851 ($n = 8$). Alpha reliability coefficients based on 1991 national norms for the Performance component are process .947, product .956, and combined .956 (*n* = 9). These reliability data look promising; however, the normative data are based on too few examinees to draw any firm conclusion regarding the reliability of this scale.

SUMMARY. The rational, exhaustive approach used to develop this test suggests an attempt to establish content validity. However, because content validity is typically evaluated by independent experts in the field, the TDC's involvement in developing and validating the test items causes concern. The norm sample needs to be increased, especially considering that this test is used to assess the occupational competencies of prospective teachers. Furthermore, decreasing the length of the test and the number of programming languages allowed to complete the Performance tests should improve the usefulness and administration of this test. Also, although focus on third and fourth generation languages is laudable, consideration should be given to including object oriented programming (e.g., C++), a concept rapidly becoming a central technique in application generators. In sum, additional revisions of the scale and sufficient norming and validity data may be necessary before general use of the scale can be recommended.

[213]
Occupational Interests Card Sort.

Purpose: To identify and rank occupational interests.
Population: Adults.
Publication Dates: 1993–1994.
Scores: Interests Summary Sheet.
Administration: Group or individual.
Price Data, 1994: $18 per complete kit including manual (38 pages) and cards; $10 per manual; $10 per set of cards.
Time: (20–30) minutes.
Author: Richard L. Knowdell.
Publisher: Career Research & Testing, Inc.

Review of the Occupational Interests Card Sort by MICHAEL B. BUNCH, Vice President, Measurement Incorporated, Durham, NC:

The Occupational Interests Card Sort is not a test in the strictest sense of the word, in that it yields no scores to be compared to a norm or a fixed criterion. Rather, it is a tool to be used in externalizing one's thoughts about work. According to the author, the Card Sort is designed for adults making occupational or career decisions. It is appropriate when the user does not want to wait for tests to be sent away for machine scoring or other off-site ma-

nipulation of data. When used by a counselor as a diagnostic tool, the Occupational Interests Card Sort is an easy way to get clients to talk about interests. Several outplacement firms use the Occupational Interests Card Sort for just this purpose. The card sort format allows clients to make as many changes as they wish.

The kit contains a 38-page booklet and five perforated sheets of cards. The client tears the 113 occupation cards and 5 category cards apart and starts the sorting process. The 38-page booklet then guides the client through a series of exercises designed to clarify occupational or career goals and identify potential career paths. Some of the exercises are well designed and would likely yield very useful information for most individuals. Other exercises are not as clear, either in their intent or directions. In many instances, the content skill and vocabulary of a trained clinician are obviously necessary. For example, although the manual provides three different ways of defining the world of work and classifying occupations, the fields listed in the first sample exercise do not seem to fit into any of the three paradigms. Persons attempting to complete the exercises without assistance would be left to ponder where these categories came from and how they were to classify the occupations they had sorted into the "Definitely Interested" pile. Many of the open-ended questions and supplementary activities (e.g., dialogue with work, question spinning) were far from helpful.

Some of the exercises are quite helpful. For example, the card sort exercise itself is quite revealing and informative. The six-page employment review forces the client not only to think about all past jobs but to reflect on job satisfaction, life satisfaction, progression, patterns, and a host of other meaningful aspects of work they might not think of without prompting. The selection of occupations (113 out of thousands) seems reasonably well balanced. It is quite possible that the primary benefit of the kit would be to expose clients to a variety of occupations not previously considered. If the employment review also evokes some insights, then the entire exercise may have been well worth the effort. The effort, by the way, is likely to be much more than the 20–30 minutes listed above. That amount of time barely covers tearing the cards apart and sorting them into piles. The exercises will take another 2 to 3 hours.

This Occupational Interests Card Sort can be quite useful if the user has access to a trained counselor. As a stand-alone tool, it is unlikely to provide very many insights for the average job seeker or individual interested in changing careers. However, with some revision of the exercises after the initial card sort, it may even be useful to this audience.

Review of the Occupational Interests Card Sort by DONALD THOMPSON, Dean, and Professor of Counseling and Psychology, Troy State University Montgomery, Montgomery, AL:

The Occupational Interests Card Sort Planning Kit (OICS) is one of four card sort career guidance tools published by Career Research and Testing, Inc. Because it lacks psychometric properties such as norms, reliability, and validity data, it should not be considered a test, but rather a career guidance and planning tool. The general purpose of the card sort is to identify and rank occupational interests. The administration booklet (the only printed material available) states that the objectives of the card sort are: "1) To define and cluster occupations holding high appeal for you; 2) To identify characteristics shared in common by these occupations; 3) To identify fields holding high appeal for you; 4) To clarify degree of readiness, skill and knowledges [*sic*] needed and competency-building steps for entry into highly appealing occupations; and 5) To apply learnings from the Occupational Card Sort to your career decisions" (p. 5).

The Occupational Card Sort consists of 113 cards. Each card contains a single occupational title (e.g., physicist, farmer, florist). The user is instructed to sort the cards into one of five categories: *Definitely Interested, Probably Interested, Indifferent, Probably Not Interested,* and *Definitely Not Interested.* After sorting the cards, the user responds to an Interest Summary Sheet by listing the titles that were sorted into each category, and then answers a series of 11 questions on an Occupational Interest Worksheet. The categorized occupational titles and the answers to questions on the worksheet are designed to "enable you to clarify more specifically the kinds of work that will offer you occupational satisfaction, and to assess the steps you need to take to increase your employability in the areas" (p. 6). The instructions do not make clear how the user is to do this, and clearly some counselor intervention and assistance would be absolutely necessary to accomplish this. The three test subjects who provided feedback for this review (age range from 25 to 41) found the process fairly difficult and time consuming, but thought it did help them focus on areas of high interest, prompted them to do some in-depth thinking about job requirements, and led them to search out more information on certain occupations. They found that the card sort validated some of their own beliefs about the occupational areas that held the highest degree of interest for them.

Card sorts have been used for a variety of purposes in assessing interests, values, and personality dimensions. There appears to be considerable research regarding card sort methodology; however, no studies were located that dealt directly with this particular card sort, despite the fact that it was first published in about 1980. According to the author, the current version (copyright 1995) has only minor differences in terms of the occupation titles, and the author indicated the need to update some occupational titles (e.g., key punch operator) that are outdated. A large majority of the occupational titles are white collar and at the professional/technical level. The author indicated that he used an intuitive method (rather than some empirical process) for selecting the occupational titles included in the sort.

If used as intended, this card sort could stimulate career exploration and suggest career possibilities and broad interest areas to be explored, but it should not be used as a definitive measure of interests. Also, its use should be limited to an adult population because it relies on a knowledge of job titles that would be unfamiliar to younger persons. There is considerable research that suggests card sorts should not be used as stand-alone measures of occupational interests, but rather as part of a more comprehensive exploration of career interests.

The set of materials received for this review included the manual/user guide of 38 pages (appears to be of xerographic quality with poor resolution of some figures and print characters), and the card deck. The manual includes instructions, worksheets to help the user organize responses, and supplementary materials to help the user further explore his/her interests.

Although not stated in the manual, the author indicated in a telephone conversation that the OICS is intended for use with an adult population. Because the user is sorting occupational titles, a degree of occupational knowledge is needed for individuals to determine whether they would or would not be interested in a particular occupation. It appears to take most users between 20 to 30 minutes to complete the sort process, and considerably longer if they complete the worksheets. The OICS can be administered individually or in groups.

The three undergraduate students used as test subjects for this review indicated that they found the instructions adequate, but the process was both time consuming and not particularly stimulating. The quality of the print reproduction should be upgraded, and perhaps some colorful graphics would provide a more visually stimulating presentation. Also, the test subjects indicated that the interpretation process is not as simple as suggested, and the instructions for using the data generated in a broader exploration of career interests may be inadequate for self-administration. Only about 10% of the occupational titles require less than a college education, and there are relatively few blue collar/technical occupations.

Some of the advantages of the OICS include that it is inexpensive; a safe, nonthreatening, nontest instrument; and a good starting point to explore the interests of bright, mature adults. Also, this tool provides counselors with the necessary information to ascertain the client's level of occupational knowledge. Disadvantages include: it has no empirical evidence regarding the effectiveness as a predictor of future occupational satisfaction or success; it requires a counselor's assistance to be most useful; and it should be used only with adults who have a fairly sophisticated knowledge of the world of work, and then only for initiating a general exploration of career interests.

In summary, the Occupational Interests Card Sort is a low-tech method in an increasingly high-tech world of computer-based career counseling. This tool does not seem to have the user appeal of some of the more recent computer-based multimedia approaches to career guidance. It may be somewhat boring to subjects who have marginal motivation to complete the task. However, it could be a useful tool for initiating career exploration when it is used with older, mature, motivated, and bright clients, and in conjunction with the assistance of a counselor as part of a more comprehensive career exploration and guidance process.

[214]
Occupational Personality Assessment.

Purpose: Designed as a "computer simulation of a vocational assessment."
Population: Individuals seeking vocational counseling.
Publication Date: 1993.
Acronym: OPA.
Administration: Individual.
Price Data, 1996: $100 per start up trial set including 5 administrations and multipart manual (54 pages); $175 per complete set including 25 administrations; $100 per each additional 20 administrations.
Time: Administration time not reported.
Comments: Self-administered computerized test requires IBM or compatible Windows for administration.

Authors: Don Schaeffer and Joyce Schaeffer.
Publisher: Measurement for Human Resources.
  a) INTEREST TEST.
  Purpose: "Designed to assess what kinds of things a person would enjoy doing."
  Scores, 3: Interest Profile, Experience Profile, How Much Interest and Experience Match.
  Comments: Scores are based on Holland's RIASEC occupational codes.
  b) COMMERCIAL ORIENTATION.
  Purpose: Designed to measure "skills and attitudes related to commercial business."
  Scores, 4: Focus on Making Money, Tactical Orientation, Reading Business Tables, Total.
  c) MOTIVATION.
  Purpose: Constructed to assess "motivational preferences."
  Scores, 8: Personal Motives (Peaceful, Sensory, Acquisitive, Work Driven), Work Motives (Intellect, Beauty, Independent Authority, Pleasing Others).
  d) MANAGEMENT.
  Purpose: Designed to assess "management style."
  Scores, 7: Aggressiveness, Field Independence, Toughness, Determination, Fluctuating Salary, Fluctuating Income Tolerance, Management Style Preference.

Review of the Occupational Personality Assessment by PETER F. MERENDA, Professor Emeritus of Psychology and Statistics, University of Rhode Island, Kingston, RI:

Four diskettes, OPA for Windows, essentially comprised the Occupational Personality Assessment with the assertion that they are the self-administering assessment tool. Little or no mention is made of conducting and publishing research during the 15 years of experience in assessment practice by the senior author that led to the development of the Occupational Personality Assessment (OPA).

Six pamphlets that presumably serve collectively as a manual for administration, desk computer operation, and reporting of psychometric data, plus the results of a few unpublished research studies accompany the disks. These pamphlets, all under the general heading, *OPA for Windows Manual*, are: (a) Instructions & Technical Description; (b) Part 1: Interest and Experience; (c) Part 2: Commercial Orientation; (d) Part 3: Motivation; (e) Part 4: Management; and (f) Validity Studies.

Also accompanying the OPA is the Job Description Scale with the instructions that it is "to be used by the human resources person, the test administrator or manager who is directing the OPA" (Job Description Scale, p. 1). The objective of using this scale is to help these persons anticipate the results that they shall be expecting or desiring to observe on the OPA. The Job Description Scale is a paper-and-pencil form of four pages asking the user to respond to work behaviors on each of the four parts of the OPA.

In the six brief "manuals" the potential user is given information relative to the proper operation of the disks, the authors' rationale for developing the assessment instrument, how the items were selected and from what sources they were taken or modified, how the profiles in each part should be interpreted, and what are some of the psychometric properties of the OPA that have been found by the authors and are alleged to be sound.

On the surface it might appear to the reader of the materials that accompany the computerized OPA that the *Standards for Educational and Psychological Testing* (AERA, APA, & NCME, 1985) have been at least minimally met or approached. In this reviewer's judgment, this is not the case. Hence, much of what follows in this review focuses on the authors' failure to comply with the *Standards* to the level that is required to render an assessment instrument ready for operational use. Reference is hereby being made to errors of both commission and omission and to the paucity of research studies that are reported, both developmental and validation research.

NORMS. No normative data are specifically reported for the OPA as specified by Standards 4.3 and 4.4 (AERA, APA, & NCME, 1985). Reference is merely made, without presentation of any empirical data, to the norms derived by the authors from the tests and inventories developed by others, and comprising the OPA "battery." A true battery, in contrast to a *collection of instruments* requires the standardization and norming on common large samples representative of the intended population.

RELIABILITY. Data attesting to the reliability of the scores yielded by the instruments included in the OPA are presented ambiguously. And the data are faulty or, at best, misleading. It is claimed that split-half coefficients based on a small mixed sample of 59 business contracts and students ranged from .73–.83. It is stated that the correlations were corrected for *attenuation* by the "*Superman*-Brown" formula. Disregarding this glaring error on page 11 of the Instructions & Technical Description pamphlet, split-half coefficients reflect only one aspect of reliability (internal consistency) and do not provide evidence for stability or consistency of scores over time. To properly estimate the dependability of scores over time what is required is to investigate the internal consistency of items, stability of scores, and to calcu-

late the corresponding errors of measurement (Standards 2.1–2.7; AERA, APA, & NCME, 1985).

VALIDITY. A few brief statements relating to validity studies are scattered among four of the OPA pamphlets. In the main, the studies refer to separate parts of the OPA and most, if not all, were conducted prior to the release of the computerized OPA in 1993. The design, postulation of *predictions* as hypotheses, conduct, and reporting of findings of these studies leave much to be desired. They fall far short of presenting convincing evidences of validity *as a unitary concept* as defined in the *Standards* (AERA, APA, & NCME, 1985, p. 9) and which is set as a standard to be met for instruments released for operational use. Among the issues of questionable value raised in these reported studies are: (a) claims that the validity of the OPA has been demonstrated, rather than the inferences that emanate from the OPA profiles; (b) the inadequate and ill-defined samples used; (c) the complete dependence on drawing conclusions solely on the basis of statistical significance—no power analyses were performed; and (d) the few reported in-house unpublished studies appear to have been conducted on only selected parts of the computerized OPA and perhaps some on prior versions. Appropriate studies on the full computerized OPA, if any, should have been identified.

Further comments regarding the important psychometric property of validity relate to unwarranted statements and claims (i.e., those not supported by empirical data). Among these are: "Clients who made use of the test provided good impressionistic evidence of its validity" (p. 8); "Later research *will* [italics added] further confirm the validity of the OPA"; "In terms of statistical development, the OPA meets and surpasses the standards set by the commercially available tests for Human Resources" (p. 18).

PROMOTIONAL MATERIALS. Accompanying the OPA pamphlets is a brochure that promotes the purchase of the instrument. It is advertised as a Personality Assessment Scale that has undergone many years of development and has been *proven* to be of practical use for hundreds of persons. It is further claimed that the OPA is a *superior* screening tool. To support these wide-sweeping claims, the potential user is told that three scientific criterion validity studies, "provide forceful validation." Such claims are unwarranted and unjustified. In two of the six pamphlets, the senior author refers to his 15 years of field experience in performing psychological assessments. No mention is made of substantial test development research in the construction of the OPA.

Three unpublished validity studies are an insufficient basis for supporting the claims that are made in the promotional materials. Hence, potential users of the OPA are cautioned to be wary of the utility and validity of the instrument.

In summary, the OPA is a collection of tests and inventories originally developed by others and modified by the authors for computerized administration and processing. The authors are commended for their sustained attempts over many years in developing a computer-based system to ease the administration, scoring, and profiling of these basically traditional instruments. On the other hand, they are faulted for not conducting the necessary comprehensive developmental research to establish the sound psychometric properties of the OPA in accordance with psychometric standards. In this light, the OPA is not deemed to be ready for operational use in its present form. It is recommended that the authors embark on a large-scale research effort to produce sound norms, extensive reliability estimates, and evidences of validity of the OPA based on a unitary concept of validity. When this is accomplished the results should be presented in a comprehensive technical manual to accompany the instrument. For now, potential users are advised of the problems with the OPA that have been detected by this reviewer.

REVIEWER'S REFERENCE

American Educational Research Association, American Psychological Association, & National Council on Measurement in Education. (1985). *Standards for Educational and Psychological Testing.* Washington, DC: American Psychological Association, Inc.

[215]
Occupational Relationships Profile.

Purpose: Designed to assess a person's preferred styles of working with colleagues.
Population: Adults.
Publication Date: 1991.
Scores, 18: Core Scales (Contact at Work, Membership, Power, Responsiveness, Openness, Shyness); Composite Scales (Sociability, Proactivity); Special Scales (Team, Individual, Leadership Overall, Leadership-Coach, Leadership-Fighter, Leadership-Expert, Preferred Style of Leader Overall, Preferred Style of Leader-Coach, Preferred Style of Leader-Fighter, Preferred Style of Leader-Expert).
Administration: Individual or group.
Price Data: Available from publisher.
Time: (30) minutes.
Comments: Computer administration and scoring available.
Author: Selby MillSmith Ltd.
Publisher: Selby MillSmith Ltd. [England].

Review of the Occupational Relationships Profile by ROBERT W. HILTONSMITH, Professor of Psychology, Radford University, Radford, VA:

The stated purpose of the Occupational Relationships Profile (ORP) is to provide a measure of personality functioning that centers on relationships between people in the work setting and to evaluate preferred styles of working with colleagues. The publisher of the profile notes that the social aspects of workplace behavior have long been known to be critical to the motivation and satisfaction of people at work, yet are difficult to measure with traditional personality questionnaires. The ORP is said to be a personality questionnaire that is designed for practices and behaviors that are specific to the occupational setting.

The ORP consists of a reusable question booklet and answer sheets. These were not included in the review materials but are said by the publisher to be "interesting and attractive" (p. 2). This measure can either be administered on-screen and scored by computer using the Assessor system (developed by the publisher) or administered via pencil and paper and scored by machine. The manual for the ORP notes that the measure "benefits from being supported by a full development program, whereby users will be regularly updated with norms and additional technical data as it becomes available" (p. 3). The manual also encourages organizations to develop their own norms, and promises support for this endeavor.

The ORP consists of six core scales, two composite scales, and two "special practical" scales. All scales are said to "relate to the quality of social interactions and personal relationships which occur in a typical day-to-day work environment" (p. 6). There are also two combined scales, one for Leadership and one for Preferred type of leader, each of which has its own score. These combined scales, in turn, each comprise three subscales corresponding to Coach, Fighter, and Expert. A total of 18 scores (sten scores) can therefore be derived. Descriptions of these scales and subscales are available in the manual.

Norms for the ORP are based on a very limited sample of 42 persons who were attendees at a professional personnel conference and completed the measure on request from the test developer. This sample is obviously inadequate in terms of size and sampling characteristics. Furthermore, it appears that this norm sample was actually used to refine a preliminary form of the measure, referred to as the "first research version," which was subsequently subjected to item analysis to produce an "initial validation version" of the ORP with five scales and 102 items. It is not clear from the manual how these earlier versions of the ORP relate to the version currently available. The manual notes that these norms are "initial and will be updated as more data becomes available" (p. 13). Users were encouraged to develop norms specific to their organization, and can do so with the Assessor computer program.

Reliability and validity data are also presented in the manual but, as with the normative data, must be considered preliminary. For example, test-retest (2.5-week interval) reliability figures, although generally acceptable (.80 to .97) are based on a sample of only eight adults. Split-half internal consistency reliability is based on a larger sample of 50 adults working in the human resource field in several organizations. Correlations here are reported from .50 to .89, with most above .60. These figures are also acceptable for a test of this kind. In terms of validity data, the manual discusses face, content, construct, criterion-related, and concurrent validity. Face and content validity were judged by feedback from volunteers who were involved in the development of the instrument. Both construct and criterion-related validity were judged by correlating the ORP with the FIRO-B, which was chosen because it is "the only other Relationship questionnaire used" (p. 17). A sample of 50 adults (presumably the same sample used to derive the split-half reliability data) took both the ORP and the FIRO-B. The results show generally moderate to high correlations between the two measures. Although the issue of concurrent validity is discussed, no data are presented. This is unfortunate, because the lack of this information makes it difficult to know if scores on the ORP actually relate in any meaningful way to practices and behaviors in the workplace. As noted earlier in this review, these workplace practices and behaviors were seen by the test developer as the central focus in developing this measure.

In summary, the ORP is a self-administered measure of workplace-related personality, focusing specifically on preferred styles of working with colleagues. It is conceptually interesting in that it purports to measure aspects of personality and social behavior that would logically appear to be important in the workplace. However, at this time the ORP has only preliminary norms and very incomplete evidence of reliability and validity. Particularly distressing is the lack of concurrent and predictive validity data, making it very difficult to attach practical meaning

and significance to the scores. The publisher, however, welcomes additional reliability and validity data, and therefore, with time, the measure may be more acceptable in this regard.

[216]
Office Skills Series.

Purpose: "Designed to measure the basic skills and aptitudes required in office and commercial occupations."
Population: Applicants for clerical positions.
Publication Dates: 1983–1993.
Acronym: OSS.
Administration: Group.
Price Data: Available from publisher.
Comments: Formerly called E.I.T.S. Clerical Tests.
Author: The Morrisby Organisation.
Publisher: The Morrisby Organisation [England].
  a) SPEED AND ACCURACY.
  Scores, 3: Number Checking, Name Checking, Total.
  Time: 5(10) minutes.
  b) ARITHMETIC.
  Scores, 3: Simple Calculation, Problems, Total.
  Time: 10(15) minutes.
  c) ENGLISH USAGE.
  Scores, 3: Spelling, Grammar, Total.
  Time: 4(9) minutes.

Review of the Office Skills Series by GREGORY J. CIZEK, Associate Professor of Educational Research and Measurement, University of Toledo, Toledo, OH:

According to the manual, the Office Skills Series (OSS) is "designed to assess the basic skills and aptitudes required in office and commercial occupations" (p. 12). However, not all office and commercial occupations are addressed by the OSS; the test is designed exclusively for two specific purposes: (a) selecting applicants for clerical positions and (b) assessing the skills of existing clerical workers.

The test consists of three subtests: Speed and Accuracy, Arithmetic, and English Usage. Each of the subtests is administered in two parts.

The first part of the Speed and Accuracy subtest requires examinees to judge whether pairs of numbers are identical. The pairs range from five to nine digits in length. Examinees are allotted 2.5 minutes to evaluate the 70 pairs of numbers. The second part of the Speed and Accuracy subtest requires examinees to perform the same task, in the same amount of time, for 70 paired names of individuals and businesses.

The first part of the Arithmetic subtest presents 32 simple, constructed-response computation problems, eight each of addition, subtraction, multiplication, and division. The second part presents 18 single-step "story" problems. These constructed-response items are also quite basic. An illustrative item is: "A woman arrives at work at 8:45 a.m. and leaves at 5:15 p.m. How many hours does she spend at work?" Examinees are permitted up to 5 minutes to complete each part.

The first part of the English Usage subtest assesses recognition of correct spelling. Examinees are presented with 60 English words and must mark whether each word is spelled correctly or incorrectly. The second part presents 30 short, grammatically incorrect sentences (13 words or less) to examinees, who are instructed to "underline the one word which makes the sentence ungrammatical." Five minutes are allotted for each part of this subtest.

All three subtests are included in a separate consumable booklet, which is scored using overlay scoring keys. Separate norms tables for applicants to clerical positions and for clerical workers are provided, which permit scores for single subtests or multiple subtests to be converted into percentiles. Percentile ranges are also assigned qualitative meaning, using a familiar norm-referenced system, and grades of A through E. Approximately the top 10% of the norm group performance corresponds to an "A" grade, the next 20% a "B" grade, the middle 40% a "C" grade, and so on.

VALIDITY AND RELIABILITY. A general case is made, and seems reasonable, that selection of applicants for clerical positions can be improved by gathering knowledge about applicants' ability to perform typical clerical tasks. Specifically, the manual states that "a large proportion of [clerical] time is spent in performing activities which require perceptual speed and accuracy in noticing small details" and notes that these characteristics are of "obvious utility" (p. 3).

Validity information for the OSS consists of both convergent and discriminant evidence. First, subtest intercorrelations are reported for a sample of 1,206 OSS examinees (n = 602 male, n = 604 female) with a mean age of 25.8 years. The intercorrelations are, as would be hoped, somewhat weak, ranging from .35 between Speed and Accuracy and Arithmetic to .47 between Speed and Accuracy and English Usage.

Additionally, scores on the OSS for a sample of 45 currently employed clerical workers were correlated with their scores on the Work Attitude Scale, a verbal test, and another office skills battery. Results provided moderate validity support. For example, performance on the OSS Arithmetic subtest correlated highly (r_{xy} = .63) with Saville & Holdsworth's Numerical Alertness subtest of the Office Skills Battery, and poorly

(r_{xy} = .36) with the Saville & Holdsworth Verbal Usage subtest, although no information is provided on the criterion measure or the validation sample.

A separate sample of 7,857 applicants for clerical positions in a bank was administered both the Raven's Progressive Matrices test and the OSS. Weak to moderate correlations were observed, which increased with age. For example, a correlation of .35 was observed for examinees under 25 years of age, whereas a correlation of .49 was reported for examinees over 45 years old. Across all age groups, the correlation was .40.

Although these correlations provide some limited support for the OSS, both the information provided in the manual and information not provided suggest that the test scores be interpreted with great caution. For example, the Arithmetic and English Usage subtests of the OSS correlate nearly the same (.515 and .521, respectively) with a verbal test entitled the PTI (Verbal). Also, no indication of the OSS's predictive validity—arguably the validity evidence of greatest interest—is provided.

Separate analyses are reported under the heading "Fairness" in which potential differential functioning by gender is discussed. The authors find "expected gender fluctuations, with females performing at higher levels on tests of speed and accuracy and language, and males performing at higher levels on the second of the two arithmetic tasks" (p. 7). However, they also report that "the overall scores showed little difference between the gender groups" (p. 7). Potential users should review this section of the manual carefully in conjunction with an investigation of the extent to which any particular clerical position requires differing proportions of verbal and quantitative skills.

Additional attention to fairness was addressed in the development of the OSS by including, for example, some names of non-English origin in the Speed and Accuracy subtest, and through use of item pretesting.

Limited reliability information is also reported in the manual. Split-half reliability coefficients (corrected using Spearman-Brown) ranged from .87 for the Arithmetic subtest to .95 for the Speed and Accuracy subtest. It is unclear, however, how the tests were split. If split naturally according to part scores, the split-half results may be inaccurate. Test-retest information would be of greater interest to potential users.

MATERIALS. The materials provided with the OSS consist of an administrator's manual, a candidate's response booklet, and scoring key overlays. The manual contains all of the necessary directions for administration, norms tables, and technical information.

There are many noteworthy cautions presented in the manual; the prospective user will find these to be of great benefit in proper interpretations of test results. For example, it is recognized that non-native speakers of English may not perform as well as those for whom English is the native language. Proper use of norms tables, qualifications of test administrators, the importance of examinees understanding the purpose and directions for the test, the necessity of conducive testing conditions, guidelines for providing feedback to examinees, and the desirability of local norming are mentioned in the manual.

There were also many minor flaws and oddities in the materials. For example, the title of the test is the Office Skills Series, although some of the materials are labeled "Office Skills Profile," which might cause some confusion. Directions to examinees refer them to the "Office Skills Speed and Accuracy booklet" (p. 14), but the response booklet actually bears a different name. Although there are directions for examinees to proceed to the next page of a subtest, there are no similar indications to tell examinees to stop at the end of the subtest. The space provided for examinees to work arithmetic problems is always on an overleaf.

The language used in the test and related materials is distinctively the King's English. The usage ranges from individual words (e.g., organisation) to phrases (the directions at the ends of columns instruct the examinee to "Go straight on with this page") to units of measure (Arithmetic items use metric units for measurement; pounds and pence are used for units of currency). Examinees are instructed to "take away" as opposed to "subtract."

There are other differences that may limit the usefulness of the test. For example, long division problems are written as 9)79271, a form that might be unfamiliar to many examinees; hyphens appear before numbers in the Speed and Accuracy subtest, making them appear like negative numbers. Finally, the Spelling test requires examinees to "mark the tick" (a check mark) if a word is spelled correctly and "mark the cross" (an X) if the word is spelled incorrectly. This seems likely to result in at least occasional confusion for examinees.

There are also some concerns related to scoring. For example, all of the Arithmetic items use the constructed-response format. The manual fails to give any guidance on the numerous scoring ambiguities that arise when this format is used. In another instance, the directions for the English Usage subtest

direct the examinee to "Underline the one word which makes the sentence ungrammatical." However, one of the items—"We was ready to leave."—can be corrected in at least two ways: by changing "We" to "I" or "was" to "were."

RECOMMENDATIONS AND CAUTIONS. Overall, the Office Skills Series provides a quick method of determining relative status on a limited number of specific abilities judged to be necessary for success in clerical occupations. Many minor flaws detract from the materials provided with the OSS which are otherwise well-organized, easy to use, and complete.

Some data are presented related to the reliability of scores on the OSS and some evidence is presented related to valid interpretations of the scores. Clearly, the authors have been guided by relevant professional standards in preparing the test and documenting its psychometric properties. However, additional information could be gathered and reported regarding the stability of scores (i.e., test-retest reliability) and predictive validity. Some cautions should also be provided regarding use of the test in contexts outside the United Kingdom.

Review of the Office Skills Series by EUGENE P. SHEEHAN, Associate Professor of Psychology, University of Northern Colorado, Greeley, CO:

The Office Skills Series (OSS) is intended for use in selecting clerical personnel. There are three sections to the test: Speed and Accuracy, Arithmetic, and English Usage. Each section contains two subsections. Speed and Accuracy is composed of Number Checking and Name Checking where candidates determine whether pairs of numbers or names are the same or different. Arithmetic is composed of a Simple Calculation subsection involving addition, subtraction, multiplication, and division, and a Problems subsection in which candidates solve word problems. Spelling and Grammar subsections comprise the English Usage part. In the Spelling subsection, candidates must indicate whether or not a word is spelled correctly. Candidates must indicate which word in a sentence makes the sentence grammatically incorrect in the Grammar subsection.

Test administration is straightforward and the test can be given in a short period of time. The three test sections may be taken together or separately. Scoring procedures are easy to follow. When scoring the OSS, scores on the Problems subsection are multiplied by 2 and those on the Grammar subsection are multiplied by 1.5. No item analysis or degree of difficulty data are presented to justify the heavier weighting for the Problems and Grammar subsections.

The manual contains useful information on providing feedback to test takers—a task often forgotten by those who test large numbers of individuals.

Although the manual mentions a job analysis, it appears that this test is not based on such an analysis. Rather, the authors' understanding of the nature of clerical work provided the basis for the three parts of the test. Because clerical work is composed of a wide variety of tasks beyond those measured by this test, including coding, filing, notetaking, proofreading, and typing, the effectiveness of the OSS in assessing the different components of this type of work is in doubt. Other tests of clerical aptitude measure a broader array of abilities than the OSS. For example, the Office Skills Tests (T4:1811) comprises 12 measures of clerical ability.

The psychometric information presented in support of the OSS is lacking in several ways. Information on norms, reliability, and validity is incomplete. The test was normed on two groups: clerical workers ($N = 346$) and clerical applicants ($N = 2,321$). Unfortunately, the manual contains little descriptive information, besides age and gender, on these groups. It would, for example, be useful to know how these groups were selected and, what is more important, to know about the work experiences of both groups. The norms for both groups are described in terms of grade levels and percentiles. As would be expected, the clerical workers obtained higher scores than did the applicants. The manual encourages users to develop their own norms. Given the limited information on the normative sample, this is a good suggestion.

Reliability evidence is based on a large sample of 1,206 individuals. Again, however, beyond age and gender information, we know little about this group. We know nothing of their clerical experience. The manual contains only split-half reliability coefficients for each section of the test. These are adequate, ranging from .87 to .95. No test-retest reliability data are provided. There are statistically significant correlations between the three sections of the test. These range from .35 to .47.

Validity data are weak. The validity section summarizes correlations between the OSS and other verbal and numerical tests. Although some of the correlations are positive and statistically significant, they are based on a sample of only 45. This type of validity study should involve more subjects. The manual also contains correlations between the OSS and the Raven's Progressive Matrices. These correlations are based on a large sample ($N = 7,857$) of applicants

for clerical positions at a bank. All of the correlations are positive and statistically significant. However, these correlations are not interpreted, nor is any theoretical reason given regarding why the OSS was correlated with the Progressive Matrices. Why was a clerical test correlated with a measure of intelligence?

Lacking from the validity section is information concerning criterion-related validity. Performance on the OSS should be measured against performance on clerical tasks. This is especially critical because the purpose of the test is to aid in the selection of clerical workers. Users of the OSS should conduct their own validity studies.

Although the manual has a professional appearance, it contains several errors and omissions. On page 8 the manual states that the reader can look to the left on a table to determine the percentile level of a score. Actually, the reader needs to look to the furthest column on the right to find the percentile levels. The manual contains few references and those that are included are not in a standard format. Several references are incomplete, lacking, for example, publication dates or publication locations. One reference is missing completely.

In summary, the OSS is a quick and easily administered test. However, although it has some face validity as a test of clerical skills, the OSS does not measure the broad spectrum of these skills. The information on norms, reliability, and validity is not satisfactory. Based on these inadequacies, users would be well advised to establish psychometric properties of the test for their own situation. Without satisfactory reliability and validity data, caution should be employed in using the test to select clerical workers.

[217]
Organizational Climate Exercise II.

Purpose: "Designed to evaluate the internal environment of an organization."

Population: Work groups.

Publication Date: 1991.

Acronym: OCE.

Scores, 12: Actual Organizational Climate and Ideal Organizational Climate on 6 dimensions: Flexibility, Responsibility, Standards, Rewards, Clarity, Team Commitment.

Administration: Group.

Price Data, 1993: $60 per complete kit including 10 questionnaires and 10 profiles and interpretive notes (11 pages).

Time: Administration time not reported.

Comments: Self-scored instrument.

Authors: Stephen P. Kelner, Jr., Lyle M. Spencer, Daniel B. Hogan, Patricia Mostue, and Katherine Hubchen.
Publisher: McBer & Company.

Review of the Organizational Climate Exercise II by MARY ANNE BUNDA, Professor, Educational Leadership, Western Michigan University, Kalamazoo, MI:

The Organizational Climate Exercise II (OCE) is marketed as an instrument that can assist managers in the improvement of organizational and individual performance. This claim is not supported by data.

There was no technical manual for this instrument that provided detailed information on the development of the instrument or the norms. Potential users of this instrument will find that no information is available in the literature bases either. Several different individuals are mentioned in the scoring supplement as either contributing authors to this instrument or its predecessor. Electronic searches of ERIC, Psychology, and ABI using their names or the instrument's name produced no information on the OCE II.

The instrument contains 24 items that are rated on a 6-point Likert type scale for actually representing the climate in the organization and for a desired level of the characteristics. These ratings yield six Actual scores and six Ideal scores. The longest scale (Team Commitment) is composed of four items and five scales are composed of only two items. The reliability of the scales is reported with alpha coefficients that range from .44 to .85, but there is no indication as to whether these coefficients are for either the Actual or the Ideal scales. Also, no information is provided concerning the characteristics of the groups on which the coefficients were calculated. It is difficult to believe that scales as short as two items could have any realistic representation of the constructs that this instrument intends to measure.

The biggest problem with the instrument lies in the interpretations managers are encouraged to make with the data they collect. Even if there was reason to believe that the instrument had some content validity, there is no evidence to support other evidence of validity or generalizability of the scores. The scoring is norm referenced with no information about the characteristics of the norm group. The scoring manual indicates that "most scales are based on a sample of 1,744 managers" (manual, p. 11). Consequently, being as good as 20% of all organizations has no real meaning. But that may not stop someone from being negatively reviewed. Addition-ally, users are also encouraged to interpret difference scores derived from the instrument—either the difference between the Ideal and the Actual averages from their staff or the difference between the staff score and the manager score. No warning is given about the lack of reliability in difference scores or about the need for adequate representation for a staff average. A concomitant problem with the directions for dealing with staff scores is the identification of individuals. The directions for the instrument indicate that the data are anonymous, whereas the directions in the aid for scoring shows individual identification.

This instrument has only one safe use. It may serve as a mechanism for focusing discussion about the working relationships between managers and staff.

Review of the Organizational Climate Exercise II by ERICH P. PRIEN, President, Performance Management Associates, Memphis, TN:

Organization climate has been a focus of very considerable attention for more than three decades. It is undeniably an attractive concept for researchers and practitioners and has been a favorite target for causal attribution to explain organization functioning effectiveness. In this respect, the concept has been a tool in the kit bag of practitioners in developing and implementing strategies and tactics in organization development. As in a variety of other areas, practice continues in spite of a lack of empirical support of either the validity of attribution or of the efficacy of intervention strategies and tactics designed and intended to change organization climate characteristics and, thus, realize improvement in organization functioning criteria.

The Organizational Climate Exercise II (OCE II) is designed as a tool for practitioners in organization analysis, evaluation, and development. The instrument is for use in describing an organization's climate in terms of six dimensions identified by Litwin and Stinger (1968) and then comparing the "actual" characteristics with what a respondent judges "should be" (manual, p. 11). The instrument itself consists of 14 statements characterizing facets of the work setting related to the six factors identified by Litwin and Stringer in their research activity. The person completing the inventory responds using a 6-point agree/disagree continuum first describing the actual organization or work unit and then repeating the description of what should be the characteristics of the work setting. The way the exercise is used, persons complete the description of the work unit or organization as it actually is and as it should be. The "actually is" description is profiled and the "should be" description is profiled and it is the difference that is the focus of attention and use in conducting organization development activities. Therein lies the fatal flaw of the OCE II, which is the dependence on difference scores derived from extremely short (two items for five, four items for one) scales.

The manual provides a single table of scale reliabilities (coefficient alpha with the caveat that users requiring higher psychometric reliability should use the full Organization Climate Survey II, which is a different instrument and not reviewed here). Although reliabilities are claimed in the range of .44 to .85 for the six subscales, the reliability and, thus, the validity of the difference score would be such that in effect the user is confronted by random numbers. The subject of reliability of difference scores has been adequately treated in the literature and, in this case, is confounded by the inevitable low reliability of short subscales. With this restriction in mind, the issue of validity must be addressed and must be viewed from two perspectives. First is the basic validity of the construct in terms of the causal relationship between organization climate characteristics and organization effectiveness. The literature abounds with anecdotes and narrative statements of a causal relationship, but the empirical support remains incredibly sparse. The second aspect of validity concerns the accuracy of the obtained difference score and this is a foregone conclusion of highly questionable validity based on the above mentioned comments on subscale reliability. If two scores are each of low reliability then the difference between them is affected by both sources of unreliability. In the event that differences reach the level supporting an inference of a real effect (what are described as "whopper" differences), the utility of the instrument would simply be to provide a redundant written record in that phenomena, which would be quite obvious to any observer.

The OCE II is a very simple instrument to administer and has a good deal of face validity. The scoring is a bit cumbersome, but again not particularly difficult and recording of scores is a matter of simple arithmetic and then plotting both the "actually is" and "should be" profiles on a simple sheet of normative scales.

My overall conclusion is that the OCE II is basically a useless instrument, primarily because of its brevity and, secondly, because of the lack of convincing evidence of the validity of the constructs it claims to measure.

REVIEWER'S REFERENCE

Litwin, G., & Stringer, R. (1968). *Motivation and organizational climate.* Boston: Harvard Business School Research Press.

[218]
Parent as a Teacher Inventory [Revised].

Purpose: "Intended to help mothers and fathers of preschool and primary grade children … recognize their favorable qualities and identify realms in which further personal growth is needed."

Population: Mothers and fathers of children ages 3–9.

Publication Dates: 1978–1995.

Acronym: PAAT.

Scores, 6: Creativity, Frustration, Control, Play, Teaching/Learning, Total.

Administration: Group.

Price Data, 1996: $51.30 per starter set including manual ('95, 29 pages), 20 inventory booklets/identification questionnaires, and 20 profiles (specify English or Spanish); $19.45 per 20 inventory booklets/identification questionnaires; $18.65 per 20 profiles; $16.50 per manual; $19.90 per specimen set.

Foreign Language Edition: Spanish edition available.

Time: (30–45) minutes.

Author: Robert D. Strom.

Publisher: Scholastic Testing Service, Inc.

Cross References: See T4:1922 (6 references); for a review by Elizabeth A. Robinson of an earlier edition, see 9:917 (1 reference).

TEST REFERENCES

1. Strom, R., Daniels, S., & Leung, A. (1988). Parental expectations in Hong Kong. *Journal of Instructional Psychology, 15,* 12–16.
2. Strom, R., & Johnson, A. (1989). Hispanic and Anglo families of gifted children. *Journal of Instructional Psychology, 16,* 164-172.
3. Strom, R., Johnson, A., Strom, S., & Strom, P. (1992). Designing curriculum for parents of gifted children. *Journal for the Education of the Gifted, 15,* 182-200.
4. Strom, R., Strom, S., Wurster, S., Fisharah, F., El-Samadeny, E. I., & El-Khatib, A. (1992). Parent expectations of Egyptian children. *Journal of Instructional Psychology, 19,* 291-301.

Review of the Parent as a Teacher Inventory [Revised] by ALICE J. CORKILL, Associate Professor of Educational Psychology, University of Nevada—Las Vegas, Las Vegas, NV:

The Parent as a Teacher Inventory (PAAT) is a questionnaire that is designed to help parents understand the nature of their interactions with their children. In particular, the PAAT claims to assess (a) what a parent expects of his or her child, (b) how a parent interacts with his or her child, and (c) what types of actions a parent takes in response to specific behaviors of his or her child.

The PAAT may be administered individually or to groups. It is available from the Scholastic Testing Service in either English or Spanish. It has also been translated into 17 other languages that may be acquired from the author of the questionnaire.

The PAAT consists of 50 statements to which a parent responds on a 4-point Likert scale (*strong yes,*

yes, no, strong no). Parents are instructed to circle "Strong yes" or "Strong no" if there is no doubt in their minds as to how they feel about the statement. Otherwise, the parent is to circle "Yes" or "No." The 50 items reflect five areas (or subscales) of parent-child interaction: Creativity, Frustration, Control, Play, and Teaching/Learning. Each subscale is covered by 10 items. Items that cover Creativity are designed to determine whether the parent is accepting of the child's creativity and willing to encourage the child's creativity. An example of a Creativity item is, "I like my child to make up stories" (p. 5). Items that cover Frustration are designed to determine level of parental frustration with the child and where the frustration is focused. An example of a Frustration item is, "It gets on my nerves when my child keeps asking me to watch him or her play" (p. 5). Items that cover Control are designed to determine the parent's need for control over the child's behavior. An example of a Control item is, "I feel play must be stopped when my child becomes angry at a playmate" (p. 7). Items that cover Play are designed to determine whether the parent understands the role of play with respect to child development. An example of a Play item is, "My child learns new words when we play" (p. 7). Items that cover Teaching/Learning are designed to tap parental views about child development and to determine whether the parent is able to support learning at home. An example of a Teaching/Learning item is, "Much of my child's learning will take place before he or she enters school" (p. 5).

The questionnaire is scored according to a key included in the manual. The most desirable responses are scored 4. The least desirable responses are scored 1. The test manual reports that the level of desirability is based on child development research. The questionnaire results in six scores per respondent, one score for each of the five subscales and a total score.

The test manual provides brief descriptions of each of the five subscales of the questionnaire. The descriptions are well written and easy to understand. Although some research is cited to support each subscale, not all of the claims or suggestions about what a subscale covers are supported empirically or theoretically. For example, in the description of the Creativity subscale, research is cited to support the claim that creative individuals have a variety of abilities including the ability to accept ambiguity and make independent judgments that may contribute to success in the future. The description, however, continues and suggests that support for creativity

should begin in the early and middle childhood years without providing evidence, either empirical or theoretical in the form of research citations, to support this claim. This pattern continues through each subscale description. Furthermore, four of the five subscales (Creativity, Frustration, Play, Teaching/Learning) claim to assess two components. For example, the Frustration subscale is designed to measure level of parental frustration with the child and where the frustration is focused. The 10 items that contribute to this subscale, however, appear to focus mostly on what may be frustrating to the parent and not where the frustration is focused (toward the child or toward self—the parent).

Some reliability and validity data are reported in the test manual. The manual, however, more often refers to research listed in a "Research Considerations" section or in the "Bibliography" rather than to specific reliability or validity studies undertaken by the author of the questionnaire during questionnaire creation or validation. The test-retest reliability values reported ($r = .80$ to .90) are satisfactory. The validity studies reported suggest that the responses provided by parents to the questionnaire satisfactorily match observations made by paraprofessionals who then observed the parent interacting with his or her child.

SUMMARY. The Parent as a Teacher Inventory is a simple questionnaire that may provide modest insights into how a parent feels about interacting with his or her child. It may help parents better understand the nature of their interactions with their children or it may help them identify areas in which they could improve. It may help counselors or psychologists better focus counseling sessions or intervention plans. It should be noted, however, that the theoretical basis for the subscales is weak.

Review of the Parent as a Teacher Inventory [Revised] by RALPH F. DARR, JR., Professor Emeritus of Education, Department of Educational Foundations and Leadership, The University of Akron, Akron, OH:

The Parent as a Teacher Inventory (PAAT) [Revised] is a 50-item self-assessment instrument designed to help parents of preschool and primary grade children to become aware of their favorable child-rearing attitudes and to identify areas in which further parental development is desirable. The instrument is composed of five subscales of 10 items each: Creativity, Frustration, Control, Play, and Teaching/Learning. Six scores are provided: five subscales and Total. The Creativity subscale reveals the extent to which the respondent accepts and supports creative behavior in his or her child. The Frustration subscale attempts to identify sources of parental frustration in child rearing. The Control subscale reflects the parent's willingness to allow the child to share in the decision-making process. The Play subscale assesses the parent's readiness to participate in the child's favorite activities. The Teaching/Learning subscale seeks to identify the parent's attitude toward child development and the parent's ability to provide a supportive learning environment in the home.

The starter set has three components: a manual, 20 Inventory Booklet/Identification Questionnaires, and 20 profiles, available in English or Spanish. The manual provides information on the purpose and structure of the instrument, rationale for the subscales, instrument reliability and validity, administration procedures, scoring procedures, and considerations when using the PAAT in research. Summaries of 47 research projects that used the PAAT are provided. The Inventory Booklet/Identification Questionnaire contains an Inventory Identification Form that solicits demographic information from respondents; however, the test constructor suggests that the questionnaire be used only when conducting research as it may intimidate some parents. The remainder of the Inventory Booklet contains the inventory: 50 short statements, all of which contain the phrase "my child." The respondent chooses his or her response from four alternates: "Strong Yes," "Yes," "No," or "Strong No." Each item is scored directionally (i.e., "strongly" at the "correct" end receives maximum credit, a 4, whereas "strongly" at the other end of the continuum receives minimum credit, a 1). "Yes" and "No" always yield a score of 2 or 3, depending on whether the desired response is "Strong Yes" or "Strong No." For 23 of the 50 items "Strong Yes" is the most desired response, thus "Strong Yes" yields a score of 4, "Yes" a score of 3, "No" a score of 2, and "Strong No" a 1. For 27 of the 50 items, "Strong No" is the most desired response, thus "Strong No" receives 4, "No" a 3, "Yes" a 2, and "Strong Yes" a 1.

The instrument appears to be rooted in two basic notions. First, the development of the young child is the result of the interaction of the child and parent(s) in the home environment. Second, development is best facilitated by frequent interactions between child and parent. Thus, the more time the child spends with the parent the better.

RELIABILITY. The field test of the PAAT Inventory was conducted by the Tucson Public Schools as part of a family development intervention program. The subjects were 124 low-income minority parents. Overall alpha coefficients were high: pretest (.76) and posttest (.81). Later studies with other populations obtained high test-retest reliability as well as high internal reliability.

VALIDITY. Several studies that found high levels of consonance between parental attitudes on the PAAT Inventory and observed parenting behaviors (75% to 85%) are cited. Other studies found parent's responses on the PAAT to be related to the child's demonstrated academic skill (i.e., score on readiness tests). The responses of parents and early childhood educators on the PAAT were found to be quite comparable. Determining the instrument's content validity is somewhat elusive. Nowhere in the manual is there any mention of the source(s) of individual items, the basis for grouping particular items into the five subsets, or the rationale for particular "correct" or "best" responses.

INVENTORY ADMINISTRATION. Directions are straightforward. The options are in the same order for all 50 items: "Strong Yes," "Yes," "No," and "Strong No." The interpretation of each option is clearly stated (e.g., "Strong Yes" indicated no doubt about the desirability of the practice). There are no time limits. The PAAT may be administered individually or in groups.

SCORING. A numeric value is assigned to the parent's response on each of the 50 items. The most desired response receives a 4, least a 1. Diminishing values are assigned to the respondent's responses as they depart from the "best response" toward the "worst response" at the other end of the continuum. The PAAT may be hand or computer scored.

REPORTING RESULTS. Results may be reported in two ways. The Individual Parent Profile provides the respondent feedback on all 50 items restated in a positive format. The four possible ratings are Highly Favorable (HF)—4 points, Slightly Favorable (SF)—3, Slightly Unfavorable (SU)—2, and Highly Unfavorable (HU)—1 point. Points on items in the subscale are totaled to provide subset scores. The Group Profile provides the individual respondent an opportunity to compare his or her performance to an arbitrary group norm ("mean") for each item, each subscale, and the total. Below the "mean" is unfavorable and above the mean is favorable (e.g., individual item "mean" is 2.5, subscale is 25, and Total "mean" is 125).

SUMMARY. The PAAT Inventory is a self-report instrument designed to assess parent's attitudes toward 50 child/parent interactions. The 50 items are arranged in five subscales. Three uses for the PAAT are suggested: (a) a research tool, (b) an instrument for evaluating instructional effectiveness, and (c) a vehicle for curriculum design. In spite of the studies cited in support of the instrument, several issues are unresolved. First, no clear theoretical base for the instrument is provided. Second, content validity is ignored. Third, several items appear to be culturally biased. Fourth, the language of some items is confusing. Fifth, no real normative data are provided for individual items, subscales, or total score. Sixth, only extreme responses, "Strong Yes" or "Strong No," are given full credit, which might suggest to the naive respondent that effective child rearing is accomplished by following 50 specific rules. Last, many items ignore the realities of contemporary society. Parents are limited in the amount of time available to interact with children. Overall, most items are realistic and easily understood. However, the PAAT Inventory lacks the content validity and normative data to support its use as a research, evaluation, or curriculum development tool.

[219]
Parent Behavior Checklist.

Purpose: Provides an assessment of a family's strengths and needs.
Population: Parents of children ages 1 to 4.
Publication Date: 1994.
Acronym: PBC.
Scores, 3: Expectations, Discipline, Nurturing.
Administration: Individual or group.
Price Data: Priced data available from publisher.
Time: (10–20) minutes.
Author: Robert A. Fox.
Publisher: PRO-ED, Inc.

TEST REFERENCES

1. Platz, D. L., Pupp, R. P., & Fox, R. A. (1994). Raising young children: Parental perception. *Psychological Reports, 74,* 643-646.
2. Fox, R. A., Platz, D. L., & Bentley, K. S. (1995). Maternal factors related to parenting practices, developmental expectations, and perceptions of child behavior problems. *The Journal of Genetic Psychology, 156,* 431–441.
3. Tucker, M. A., & Fox, R. A. (1995). Assessment of families with mildly handicapped and nonhandicapped preschoolers. *Journal of School Psychology, 33,* 29-37.

Review of the Parent Behavior Checklist by MARK J. BENSON, Associate Professor of Family and Child Development, Virginia Polytechnic Institute and State University, Blacksburg, VA:

The Parent Behavior Checklist (PBC) is a 100-item, self-report questionnaire completed by a parent. The PBC presents simple, declarative statements (e.g., "I read to my child at bedtime"). Parents rate each item on a frequency scale that includes *never, sometimes, often,* and *always.*

The PBC joins a valuable pool of self-report, parenting measures (see reviews by Holden, 1995; Holden & Edwards, 1989). These measures play important roles in research and theory development in human development, family studies, family psychology, and family sociology. They also play potentially valuable roles in applied settings.

The PBC holds several advantages over other measures currently in use. Like the Block (1965) scale, the language of the PBC items is behavioral. Also, the PBC frequency responseformat coincides with behavioral assessment more closely than the typical, agree-disagree format. The astute design of the record form facilitates the remarkably efficient completion and scoring. Perhaps most importantly, the evidence for the reliability of the PBC scales is excellent. The coefficients for internal consistency and test-retest stability are: Expectations (.97, .98), Discipline (.91, .87), and Nurturing (.82, .81).

Despite these advantages, refinements are needed in the overall title and purpose of the PBC. Although identified as a "Parent" checklist, many of the items refer to the child, not the parent (e.g., "My child takes naps"). And despite its name as a behavior checklist, nearly half of the PBC items assess not parent behaviors, but parent beliefs about their child's capabilities (e.g., "My child should know three colors"). The title also implies comprehensiveness, but two scales actually assess very narrow subsets of parent belief systems and parental responses to misbehavior. Although the manual defines the purpose as assessing "family's strengths and needs" (p. v), the norms are based on individual level, not family level, responses. The manual also offers no guidance on defining or explaining "strengths and needs" (p. v).

Such changes in the title and purpose statements need to be embedded in a conceptual or theoretical foundation for the test and the scales. The current lack of a rationale for the PBC scales makes it difficult to evaluate validity claims and to interpret scores. For example, the manual fails to define the Nurturing scale, and omits reference to other similar theoretical and empirical constructs (e.g., attachment, family cohesion, parental warmth, parental acceptance, and authoritative parenting style).

Even without a theoretical touchstone for evaluation, inconsistencies within the scales raise doubts about content validity. For example, the items on the Discipline scale relate to one another, but the scale name differs from the item content. The scale assesses punitive behaviors (spanking, hitting, yelling, threatening), and overlooks more effective, appropriate, and humane methods of handling misbehavior (e.g., structuring to prevent misbehavior, understanding the causes of misbehavior, interpreting misbehavior, providing for stimulation needs, providing attention for positive behaviors, pointing out the natural consequences, encouraging effort, using logical consequences, and using time out sparingly).

On the Expectations and Nurturing scale, there are several items that lack rational coherence with other items on the scale. Nine of the Expectation items refer not to expectations, but to behavior (e.g., "My child wears diapers at bedtime"). Three items on the Nurturing scale refer not to nurturance, but to consulting with parenting books or other parents. Two items on the Nurturance scale present open-ended situations with single solutions (e.g., when child is scared—hold him/her). These single-solution items are problematic because nurturing parents could use many varied responses (e.g., humor or redirection, preparing in advance of an event, playing with the child, or modeling courage).

Besides content validity problems, the Expectations scale elicits ambiguous responses. A parent's response might reflect: personal expectations, normative expectations, or actual behavior. For illustration, consider the item, "My child should put away his/her toys." A mother might respond that she frequently expects her child to, sometimes thinks others might expect the child to at his or her age, and never actually observes her child picking up toys. Respectively, these three types of responses: personal, normative, and actual are confounded in responding to the PBC Expectation scale. Adding to this ambiguity, the respondent faces a variety of prompts to elicit expectation (e.g., "should, I expect, should know, should be able to, should be old enough"). The metacognitive processes involved in accurately reporting expectations are sufficient complex even without this ambiguous variety of prompts. Clustering the items together, standardizing the prompt, and including directions to focus only on personal expectations rather than normative expectations or actual behavior could reduce the ambiguity of the Expectations scale. In addition, ratings by experts or using a normed, developmental scale for item construction would allow comparison between actual norms for children's behavior and parent expectations.

Although the PBC presents some case examples and advises interpreting within context, the interpretation process remains vague. In particular,

the PBC's divergence between scale name and item content can lead to serious clinical misinterpretations. Case #3 in the manual displays a glaring example of one such misinterpretation. In this case, the mother achieved a low score because she did not spank, shame, slap, hit, yell, or threaten her child. In interpreting her low score, the manual states that the mother is "not setting sufficient limits" (p. 18).

A remaining problem with interpretation is that frequency response sets are expected due to few reverse-coded items. Only 6% of the items, all on the Expectations scale, are reverse-scored. Consequently, the tendency to endorse *always* or *frequently* inflates scores, and the tendency to endorse *sometimes* or *never* deflates scores. At present, assessors should consider individual response set bias in interpreting scores.

Many features of the PBC are valuable contributions. Its behaviorally worded items, the frequency response choice, the ease of administration and scoring, and the high reliability are valuable strengths. Some recommended improvements include: revising the overall title, modifying the purpose statement, revising the subscale titles, generating conceptual grounding, deleting irrelevant items, restructuring the Expectations format, adding reverse-scored items, and improving guidance on interpretation.

REVIEWER'S REFERENCES

Block, J. H. (1965). *The Child-Rearing Practices Report (CRPR): A set of Q items for the description of parental socialization attitudes and values.* Berkeley: University of California, Institute of Human Development.
Holden, G. W., & Edwards, L. A. (1989). Parental attitudes toward child rearing: Instruments, issues, and implications. *Psychological Bulletin, 106,* 29–58.
Holden, G. W. (1995). Parental attitudes toward child rearing. In M. H. Bornstein (Ed.), *Handbook of parenting: Status and social conditions of parenting* (Vol. 3; pp. 359–392). Mahwah, NJ: Erlbaum.

Review of the Parent Behavior Checklist by HINSDALE BERNARD, *Associate Professor, Department of Counseling, Administration, Supervision, and Adult Learning, Cleveland State University, Cleveland, OH:*

The Parent Behavior Checklist (PBC) seeks to identify strengths and weaknesses in parents' behaviors as they work with their children of preschool age. The author, Robert Fox, identified two essential aspects of the environmental experiences of a child that were the guiding principles in its development: (a) what parents expect of their young children and (b) how parents behave toward them.

The 100-item PBC was developed to be completed by parents or other caregivers of children between 1 year and 4 years 11 months of age. The author's claim that no particular qualifications are required for administration is justifiable in that the readability of the PBC was estimated to be at the third grade level. Scoring of the PBC seems to be straightforward in that any individual can be easily trained to obtain the raw scores and standard scores for the PBC subscales. However, the author cautions that interpretation of the PBC requires a background in child development theory as it applies to parenting.

DEVELOPMENT AND DESCRIPTION OF THE PBC. Over 300 preliminary items were generated by an interdisciplinary research team of seven professionals that included university professors, practicing psychologists, and social workers. After each member of the team independently reviewed each item using three specific criteria, the pool was reduced to 238 items. A pilot test using 100 parents with children between the ages of 1 and 5 years yielded a coefficient alpha reliability estimate of .93 and other relevant statistics. The items were further reviewed by 16 professionals with experience working with young children and by 17 parents, resulting in a further reduction to 232 items.

The revised scale was field tested using a representative sample of 1,140 mothers who had children between 1 year and 4 years, 11 months. Factor analysis and systematic item reduction strategies resulted in a 100-item instrument that clustered around the following three subscales with examples in parentheses: Expectations (E)—50 items with score range 50 to 200 (My child should be old enough to share toys); Discipline (D)—30 items with score range 30 to 120 (I send my child to bed as a punishment); Nurturing (N)—20 items with score range 20 to 80 (I praise my child for learning new things).

The PBC is accompanied by a detailed manual describing the following aspects of the instrument in four chapters: (a) Assessment of Parenting, (b) Administration and Scoring, (c) Interpretation, and (d) Psychometric Properties. There is also an appendix with normative tables for the three subscales and a listing of the final 100 items with their item factor loadings on the three factors.

ADMINISTRATION, SCORING, AND INTERPRETATION OF THE PBC. The PBC itself consists of a Record Form, a Score Grid, and an interpretation Profile Sheet. The Record Form has a demographic section, instructions for responding to the items, and the 100 items. Parents are instructed to complete the demographic portion of the PBC first. Parents with more than one child are instructed to respond to the items with only the reference child in mind, which could be a source of inaccuracy.

Straightforward instructions include a sample item, which enhances the clarity. The author estimates that the paper-and-pencil version of the PBC could be completed in about 10 to 20 minutes, whereas oral administration to a parent or a group should require more time.

The majority of items (n = 94) are scored in the positive direction on a 4-point Likert scale with 4 = *almost always/always*, 3 = *frequently*, 2 = *sometimes*, and 1 = *almost never/never*. The remaining six items are scored in the reverse direction with 1 = *almost always/always*, 2 = *frequently*, 3 = *sometimes*, and 4 = *almost never/never*. The six reversed items are all located in the Expectations subscale. The reader is left to speculate as to why there are only six reversed items in a pool of 100, and why they are all located in only one scale.

The Score Grid facilitates the summing of the three subscale scores. Because the items of the PBC are spread over five pages, provision is made for computing a subtotal score for each subscale, for each page. Subscale total scores are then standardized by converting them to T scores, which are entered into the Profile Sheet for interpretation. The manual provides three case illustrations with accompanying guidelines for interpreting these profiles of parent behavior types.

PSYCHOMETRIC PROPERTIES OF THE PBC. Although the SES level of the normative sample of 1,140 mothers turned out to be higher than the population from which it was drawn, the sample did include mothers from diverse economic backgrounds. Overall, great care was exercised in establishing reliability and validity evidence for the PBC. Principal components factor analysis was used to establish the factor structure—related more to construct validity, although these findings seemed to be misplaced in the discussion on reliability. Average factor loadings of the three subscales were in an acceptable range of .30 to .84.

Three reliability estimates were made: (a) the internal consistencies of the three PBC subscales; (b) test-retest reliability computed on a sample of 45 mothers; and (c) a comparison of 52 mothers and fathers on their developmental expectations, without revealing the distribution of mothers and fathers in this particular sample.

Content validity was rigorously examined using expert professionals and parents as well as item-construct correlations. The description did not mention whether mothers *and* fathers were involved with the process. In all cases, estimates of reliabilities and item-construct correlations were notably substantial. No instruments were available to assess the concurrent validity of the PBC. However, a 21-item Developmental Questionnaire (DQ) was developed specifically to measure parental expectations. Although the DQ was able to discriminate between parents of younger and older children, one may question its value in establishing concurrent validity of the PBC because the former contains only 21 items and a sample of only 42 mothers was used. Furthermore, there was not enough information about the representativeness of that sample. The convergent validity of the PBC was assessed by comparing it with the Adult-Adolescent Parenting Inventory (AAPI) that had four subscales: Expectations, Empathy, Physical Punishment, and Role Reversal. Low correlations between the PBC's Expectations and Nurturing subscales and the four AAPI subscales showed that the two instruments seemed to be measuring different constructs. For discriminant validity, it was found that the PBC could discriminate between parents of handicapped and nonhandicapped preschool children. The author also assessed the influence of social desirability response set on the PBC and concluded that social desirability did not appear to be a significant factor in the mothers' responses.

REVIEWER'S COMMENTS. Although it was determined that mothers and fathers possessed similar developmental expectations, this finding was based on a sample of only 52 mothers and fathers. The Parent Behavior Checklist seems to be a misnomer because it was standardized on mothers only. Therefore it sits on a psychometrically sound foundation for mothers. The PBC is fairly easy to use and score. However, the user is cautioned about the interpretation of the results stemming from the following observations. Most, if not all of the items in the Expectations subscale (half the PBC) address the behaviors of the child that are likely related to a parent's child-rearing practices—a relationship that needs to be established. Also, most of the items in the Discipline subscale seem to be stated negatively with respect to discipline (much yelling and spanking), which warrants reversing the scoring for these items and a name change for the scale (possibly Punishment). For example, it does not seem justifiable to score the following two items in the same positive direction: (20) I yell at my child for whining; (30) I plan surprises for my child (birthday parties, gifts).

It will be extremely helpful if the items (with their numbers) can be listed by subscales in Appendix B on item factor loadings. In this way, the items could appear in descending order of loading on their principal factors. Despite these technical glitches,

the PBC can still provide a practical and useful link between mother's behavior and child development. Again, the user is reminded to exercise caution in interpreting the resulting profiles.

[220]
Parent-Child Relationship Inventory.

Purpose: "Assesses parents' attitudes toward parenting and toward their children.".
Population: Parents aged 18–54.
Publication Date: 1994.
Acronym: PCRI.
Scores, 9: 7 content scales (Parental Support, Satisfaction With Parenting, Involvement, Communication, Limit Setting, Autonomy, Role Orientation), 2 validity indicators (Social Desirability, Inconsistency).
Administration: Group.
Price Data, 1997: $95 per complete kit including manual (57 pages), 25 answer sheets, and 2 prepaid mail-in answer sheets for computer scoring and interpretation; $33 per 25 answer sheets; $45 per manual; $13 per each mail-in computer scored and interpreted answer sheet; $259 per microcomputer disk; $15 per 100 microcomputer answer sheets; $9.50 each for FAX service scoring.
Time: (15) minutes.
Comments: Self-report; microcomputer edition available.
Author: Anthony B. Gerard.
Publisher: Western Psychological Services.

Review of the Parent-Child Relationship Inventory by ROGER A. BOOTHROYD, Associate Professor, Florida Mental Health Institute, University of South Florida, Tampa, FL:

DESCRIPTION. The Parent-Child Relationship Inventory (PCRI) is a 78-item self-report measure intended to assess parents' attitudes toward parenting and their children. Parents respond to each item using a 4-point, Likert scale: *strongly agree, agree, disagree,* and *strongly disagree.* The items are grouped into seven content scales: Parental Support scale (9 items), Satisfaction with Parenting scale (10 items), Involvement scale (14 items), Communication scale (9 items), Limit Setting scale (12 items), Autonomy scale (10 items), and the Role Orientation scale (9 items). The measure also contains two validity indicators. The 5 remaining items are used to assess response Social Desirability and 10 pairs of highly correlated items assess response Inconsistency. Twenty-six of the content items are keyed positively and the remaining 47 content items are negatively keyed. The PCRI can be administered to individuals or groups and reportedly takes 15 minutes to complete.

SCALE CONSTRUCTION AND ITEM SELECTION. The scale construction and item selection procedures reported are systematic and comprehensive. Development of the scales was based on the findings from prior research and on the factor analytic results from a preliminary 345-item version on the PCRI. Sets of 24 items, balanced for strength and direction, were constructed for each of the resulting 14 scales. In addition, a 9-item Social Desirability scale was constructed. This resulted in 345 items that were then: (a) rated by expert judges, (b) assessed using qualitative feedback from professionals and respondents, and (c) evaluated by empirical analysis of pilot-test data. The 78 items contained in the final version of the PCRI were selected using both empirical and rational criteria that included: (a) the elimination of high and low frequency items, (b) retaining only the expert judges' more highly rated items, (c) eliminating items with low scale correlations, (d) examining social desirability, and (e) retaining items with the greatest clinical usefulness.

SCORING. Three scoring options are available for the PCRI: hand scoring, purchase of a microcomputer scoring and report program, or computer scoring available through Western Psychological Services. Raw scores are converted to T-scores and separate norms are provided for mothers and fathers. The author provides instructions regarding the overall number of missing responses that can be present without jeopardizing the PCRI's validity but does not indicate the number of missing items that can be present within specific scales.

The microcomputer scoring program is easy to install and use and is compatible on any system running Microsoft Windows 3.1 or above. The three-page report that is generated includes: (a) client identification information, (b) an interpretation of the validity indicators, (c) a graphic display of the parent's PCRI profile, (d) a narrative interpretation of the parent's scores on each of the seven scales, (e) a list of any critical items endorsed by the parent, and (f) a summary of the item responses and response key.

The computerized report produced from the microcomputer scoring program can be a useful aid in interpretation of PCRI scores. This author evaluated the scoring program by inputting random responses to the PCRI items. The computer-generated report appropriately documented the inconsistent manner in which the PCRI items were answered. The report stated, "Based on an analysis of selected responses [i.e., items on the Inconsistency scale] ... it is highly likely that the results reflect inattentive or random responding ... [and] that the report appears to be invalid." Appropriately, the author recommends computer-generated interpretations be verified using clinical judgments and/or other available data.

The manual contains six case studies that are also useful in learning how to interpret the PCRI but, unfortunately, the cases presented depict only individuals in the midst of some form of personal strife such as lack of finances, divorce, custody dispute, and potential domestic violence. Although the scores and interpretations provided are intuitively consistent with the situations portrayed, it would be helpful to demonstrate that the PCRI can accurately profile parents who are not experiencing strained relationships with their child.

NORMS AND STANDARDIZATION. Normative data were collected on over 1,100 parents identified through schools and day-care centers responding to the author's solicitation letter. Response to this letter was poor as only 4.4% of the 2,000 schools and day-care centers canvassed agreed to participate. The limited response resulted in a normative sample that was better educated and less diverse than the U.S. population as a whole.

A sample of 240 individuals stratified by race and education to approximate the U.S. population was used to examine the effects of race and education. Despite the fact that black parents' scores on the Satisfaction and Autonomy scales were significantly lower than white parents' responses to which the author states "In both instances these differences appear to be substantive" (manual, p. 24), separate norms were not generated because this finding "does not ... constitute evidence of systematic differences in parenting between blacks and whites" (manual, p. 25). Similarly, even though parents with 4 or more years of college had significantly higher scores on the Support and Autonomy scales, separate norms were decided against.

Separate norms were developed for mothers and fathers, which is important given that significant mean differences were present on five of the seven scales. Raw scores are converted to T-scores (which have been normalized) and some percentile equivalents are provided to assist in interpretation.

RELIABILITY. Internal consistency and test-retest reliability estimates were generated using data collected from the standardization sample. Individual scale alphas are good, ranging from .70 on the Parental Support scale to .88 on the Limit Setting scale. The median value alpha is .80. The test-retest reliabilities from two studies are reported. The first study, based on a small number of individuals ($n = 22$) who completed the original 345-item version of the PCRI a second time after approximately a one-week interval, produced test-retest reliability estimates ranging from .68 on the Communication scale to .93 on the Limit Setting scale. In the second study, 82 parents who participated in the standardization study completed the PCRI a second time after 5 months. Results were predictably lower with test-retest estimates ranging from .44 on the Autonomy scale to .71 on both the Parental Support and Role Orientation scales.

VALIDITY. A large initial pool of items reviewed by expert judges combined with a multi-stage item selection process during scale development should ensure the PCRI has sufficient content validity. The author has also employed a variety of construct validation procedures that span from examination of internal consistency to an analysis of interscale relationships to the cross validation of confirmatory factor analysis models used to assess potential gender or cultural bias in the inventory. The results of these analyses suggest the PCRI is relatively free of gender and cultural bias.

Item-scale correlations are provided in the manual. An examination indicates that for five of the seven scales, most items are more highly correlated with their own scale total scores than they are with the score totals from the other scales. This is not the case, however, for the Parental Support scale in which six of the nine items have higher item-scale correlations with other scale total scores and for the Involvement scale in which 13 of the 14 items have stronger correlations with other scale totals. The intercorrelations between the PCRI Satisfaction and Involvements scales (.64), the Satisfaction and Limit Setting scales (.65), and the Limit Setting and Autonomy scales (.64) suggest that the constructs assessed by these scales may be somewhat redundant.

Three studies are summarized to support the PCRI's predictive validity. In the first study the PCRI was administered to 35 couples undergoing court-ordered custody mediation in conjunction with the Personality Inventory for Children (PIC). Examination of the T-scores from both measures converged as both were substantially below the means of their respective standardization samples, indicative of the distress and disruption experienced by families during a divorce. The author does over interpret the PCRI and PIC interscale correlations by suggesting a causal relationship exists. The second study exam-

ined the relationship between PCRI and parents' discipline styles. A shortened version of the PCRI was administered to 174 parents who also reported the frequency with which they used various discipline practices. Support of the PCRI's predictive validity was claimed because parents who had higher scores on the PCRI communication scale were more likely to use reasoning as a method of discipline and negatively correlated with spanking. In the third study, 26 adolescent mothers considered as representing an at-risk population completed the PCRI. As predicted, PCRI scale scores for this group were depressed and in no instance exceeded the mean of the standardization sample. Although these studies provide support for the PCRI's predictive validity, the interpretation of some of the findings from these studies seem somewhat overstated.

COMMENTARY. The PCRI manual is well written and contains useful and comprehensive information regarding the development, administration, scoring, and interpretation of this measure. The development of the PCRI employed sound psychometric procedures and the reliability and validity estimates provided support its utility. Overall, this author considered the PCRI to be a sound measure.

Despite the many positive aspects of the measure, several concerns do exist. Although post data collection efforts were used to produce a representative norming sample, the 4.4% response rate to the initial solicitation letter and the subsequent nonrepresentativeness of the standardization sample present some reason for caution.

Although the author proposes using the PCRI in making custody recommendations, none of the previous work on custody determinations is cited in the manual. The work conducted by individuals such as Robert Felner, Gary Melton, and Lois Weithorn, to name a few, should be reviewed. Additionally, Grisso's (1986) review of measures relevant to divorce custody cases is also not mentioned. In particular, the *Children's Report of Parental Behavior* (Schaefer, 1965), a child-reported measure of his/her feelings about or perception of the parent, would provide a contrasting perspective against which to compare PCRI results.

Finally, the use of the word parent in today's world does not provide a clear understanding of an adult's relationship with a child. The word parent, for example, may represent a biological relationship (i.e., natural parent), a reconfigured relationship (e.g., stepparent, adoptive parent), or a custodial relationship (e.g., foster parent). It is uncertain as to the extent to which the PCRI provides a stable assessment of a "caregiver's" relationship with a child independent of whether the relationship is biological, reconfigured, or custodial. Given that the author offers no guidance on this issue, it is unclear as to whether the PCRI can be used in families where two biological parents are not present.

REVIEWER'S REFERENCES
Schaefer, E. (1965). Children's reports of parental behavior: An inventory. *Child Development, 36*, 413–424.

Grisso, G. (1986). *Evaluating competencies: Forensic assessments and instruments.* New York: Plenum.

Review of the Parent-Child Relationship by GREGORY J. MARCHANT, Associate Professor of Educational Psychology, and SHARON E. PAULSON, Associate Professor of Educational Psychology, Ball State University, Muncie, IN:

The Parent-Child Relationship Inventory (PCRI) is a 78-item self-report questionnaire completed by parents (mothers and/or fathers). Only one child in the family is targeted when completing the measure. The Likert-type items of agreement are written at the fourth grade level and the instrument takes approximately 15 minutes to complete through individual or group administration. The purpose of the measure is to evaluate parents' attitudes toward parenting and their children. Scores can be obtained on seven parenting scales: Parental Support (9 items on the level of emotional and social support a parent receives), Satisfaction with Parenting (10 items concerning the amount of pleasure derived from parenting), Involvement (14 items about the level of a parent's interaction with and knowledge of his or her child), Communication (9 items on the effectiveness of parental communication with the child), Limit Setting (12 items regarding parental discipline of the child), Autonomy (10 items concerning the ability of parents to promote the child's independence), and Role Orientation (9 items concerning attitudes about gender roles in parenting).

The measure can be used in both research and clinical settings to identify specific areas of difficulty between parents and their children. Practitioners might choose to use the measure in assessing the parenting of a target child who has been referred for poor academic performance, behavior problems, or emotional problems; or in conjunction with assessments related to marital problems, divorce/custody cases, or general family problems. It is advised that the instrument be used and interpreted in conjunction with other assessment tools.

SCORING AND INTERPRETATION. Scaled scores (*T*-scores and percentiles) are based on a sample of 1,139 parents with higher scores on each scale indicating better parenting. Scores falling one standard deviation below the mean are indicative of possible problematic parenting and scores falling two standard deviations below the mean are indicative of possible serious problems. Patterns of scores on the seven parenting scales are also considered in the interpretation. Two protocol validity scales are included. A five-item Social Desirability scale determines if parents are responding in a manner that makes themselves "look good." An Inconsistency scale (consisting of 10 highly correlated pairs of items) determines if parents are responding randomly or inattentively.

The instrument may be scored manually by mailing or faxing to WPS, or by using the microcomputer software. The PC software is a very user-friendly program that allows the instrument to be completed, scored, and interpreted at the computer with a report generated that includes a simple narrative and a bar chart of *T*-scores. Minor installation difficulties occurred on two of the three computers on which the software was tested, and each disk is limited to 25 administrations.

PSYCHOMETRIC PROPERTIES AND NORMING. The instrument went through a rigorous development process, which resulted in well-designed items. Scale reliability was determined by internal consistency (Cronbach's alpha; median alpha = .82) and test-retest correlations (mean scale autocorrelation = .81). However, the content and construct validity of the instrument are more questionable. It is not clear whether the scales reflect an accurate picture of the parenting dimensions most commonly explored in research. Although the author suggests that the items were developed based on a review of the literature, an overview of that literature is not included. In determining construct validity, only internal characteristics of the scales were assessed (e.g., item-scale correlations and intercorrelations of the scales). Such analyses provide little information regarding the ability of the scale to define the construct being measured. Very little empirical evidence regarding what is being measured by the instrument is provided.

The scales were normed using a sample of 1,139 mothers and fathers; a relatively small sample considering the range of demographics (ethnicity, education, geographic region, parent age, relation to child, sex of child, and age of child) considered in generating a representative sample. Each of the subscales differed significantly on at least two of the demographic characteristics. Demographic differences on the scales found within the sample suggest that the demographic variables might be considered when interpreting scores for individuals. Based on the analyses, separate norming and scoring are used for mothers and fathers. Although many of the other differences are statistically significant, the author suggests that they probably do not constitute a significant threat to generalizing from the sample. However, the literature clearly shows that parenting differs considerably by age of child and by ethnic group. This raises concerns that the "normalcy" of parenting a 5-year-old child, for example, is determined by a comparison to the average parenting of children ages 3–15.

Additionally, the sample tends to underrepresent young parents, Blacks and Hispanics, less educated parents, and the western and midwestern United States. The literature shows that the dimensions of parenting that have been found in white, middle-class families may not accurately reflect what occurs in minority families, especially those of African-Americans. To compare the parenting of an African-American child to a norm based on white, middle-class parents represents a bias in the judgment of what constitutes "good" parenting. It is also unclear how many of the parents are from intact families and how many single-parent families are represented. Therefore, any comparisons to the norms determined by this sample should be interpreted cautiously.

Finally, the validity of a standardized parenting score is questionable. Parenting is highly variable and highly contextual. An average score on parenting based on any representative sample does not imply that the level of parenting is necessarily "good." What score represents "good" parenting might better be determined by an empirical investigation exploring relations with positive developmental outcomes. This measure allows a comparison of parenting with "average" parenting, but may not provide an accurate picture of "good" parenting.

SUMMARY. In general, the instrument is well conceived and well developed, and fills a much needed role in both research and clinical assessment. A focus on the role of parenting in any type of family assessment has historically been missing. Overall, the dimensions reflect a reasonable picture of parenting and the interpretation of the scores makes reasonable assumptions about the nature of parenting (although

caution should be exercised in relying on the norms provided). The manual is well organized and provides good, comprehensive information regarding the measure (including case study examples). Instructions are precise and easy to follow and the instrument is well constructed, easy to administer, and easy to score. The use of the PCRI can be recommended in a variety of settings and researchers should be encouraged to further explore its psychometric properties.

[221]
Parenting Stress Index, Third Edition.

Purpose: To identify stressors experienced by parents that are related to dysfunctional parenting.
Population: Parents of children 12 years old or younger.
Publication Dates: 1983–1995.
Acronym: PSI.
Scores, 15: Child Domain (Adaptability, Acceptability, Demandingness, Mood, Hyperactivity and Distractibility, Reinforces Parent), Parent Domain (Depression, Attachment, Restrictions of Role, Sense of Competence, Social Isolation, Relationship with Spouse, Parental Health), Life Stress, Total Score.
Administration: Group or individual.
Forms, 2: Full Length, Short Form.
Price Data, 1997: $95 per introductory kit including 10 reusable item booklets, 25 hand-scorable answer sheet/profile forms, and manual ('95, 32 pages); $65 per Short Form kit including 25 hand-scorable answer sheet/profile forms, and manual; $34 per 10 reusable item booklets; $34 per 25 Short Form hand-scorable questionnaire/profile forms; $34 per 25 hand-scorable answer sheet/profile forms; $41 per manual; $450 per PSI3 Plus Software system including unlimited-use scoring/reporting for paper-and-pencil administrations, 10 software test booklets, 10 software Short Form test booklets, manual ('95, 87 pages), and key disk with 5 free administrations; $125 per key disk with 25 administrations; $18 per 25 software test booklets—Short Form; $27 per 25 Long Form test booklets.
Time: (20–30) minutes.
Comments: Self-scoring; also can be computer administered (requires IBM XT or better or compatible with 2 disk drives and color monitor).
Author: Richard R. Abidin, PAR Staff (software system), and Noriel Ona (software program design and manual).
Publisher: Psychological Assessment Resources, Inc.
Cross References: See T4:1933 (22 references); for reviews of an earlier edition by Frank M. Gresham and Richard A. Wantz, see 10:271 (2 references).

TEST REFERENCES
1. Webster-Stratton, C. C. (1989). The relationship of marital support, conflict, and divorce to parent perceptions, behaviors, and childhood conduct problems. *Journal of Marriage and the Family, 51,* 417-430.

2. Wallace, P. M., & Gotlib, I. H. (1990). Marital adjustment during the transition to parenthood: Stability and predictors of change. *Journal of Marriage and the Family, 52,* 21–29.

3. DeMaso, D. R., Campis, L. K., Wypji, D., Bertram, S., Lipshitz, M., & Freed, M. (1991). The impact of maternal perceptions and medical severity on the adjustment of children with congenital heart disease. *Journal of Pediatric Psychology, 16,* 137–149.

4. Frank, S. J., Olmsted, C. L., Wagner, A. E., Laub, C. C., Freeark, K., Breitzer, G. M., & Peters, J. M. (1991). Child illness, the parenting alliance, and parenting stress. *Journal of Pediatric Psychology, 16,* 361–371.

5. Teti, D. M., & Gelfand, D. M. (1991). Behavioral competence among mothers of infants in the first year: The mediational role of maternal self-efficacy. *Child Development, 62,* 918–929.

6. Whipple, E. E., & Webster-Stratton, C. (1991). The role of parental stress in physically abusive families. *Child Abuse & Neglect, 15,* 279-291.

7. Eiserman, W. D., Weber, C., & McCoun, M. (1992). Two alternative program models for serving speech disordered preschoolers: A second follow-up. *Journal of Communication Disorders, 25,* 77–106.

8. Kelley, S. J. (1992). Parenting stress and child maltreatment in drug-exposed children. *Child Abuse & Neglect, 16,* 317-328.

9. Quittner, A. L., DiGirolamo, A. M., Michel, M., & Eigen, H. (1992). Parental response to cystic fibrosis: A contextual analysis of the diagnosis phase. *Journal of Pediatric Psychology, 17,* 683–704.

10. Rhodes, J. E., Ebert, L., & Fischer, K. (1992). Natural mentors: An overlooked resource in the social networks of young, African American mothers. *American Journal of Community Psychology, 20,* 445-461.

11. Tannock, R., Girolametto, L., & Siegel, L. S. (1992). Language intervention with children who have developmental delays: Effects of an interactive approach. *American Journal on Mental Retardation, 97,* 145-160.

12. Black, M., Schuler, M., & Nair, P. (1993). Prenatal drug exposure: Neurodevelopmental outcome and parenting environment. *Journal of Pediatric Psychology, 18,* 605–620.

13. Cuccaro, M. L., Holmes, G. R., & Wright, H. H. (1993). Behavior problems in preschool children: A pilot study. *Psychological Reports, 72,* 121-122.

14. DeGangi, G. A., Wietlisbach, S., Goodin, M., & Scheiner, N. (1993). A comparison of structured sensorimotor therapy and child-centered activity in the treatment of preschool children with sensorimotor problems. *The American Journal of Occupational Therapy, 47,* 777-786.

15. Eisenstadt, T. H., Eyberg, S., McNeil, C. B., Newcomb, K., & Funderburk, B. (1993). Parent-child interaction therapy with behavior problem children: Relative effectiveness of two stages and overall treatment outcome. *Journal of Clinical Child Psychology, 22,* 42-51.

16. Ethier, L. S., & LaFrenière, P. J. (1993). Le stress des mères monoparentales en relation avec l'aggressivité l'enfant d'âge préscolaire. *International Journal of Psychology, 28,* 273–289.

17. Hutcheson, J. J., Black, M. M., & Starr, R. H., Jr. (1993). Developmental differences in interactional characteristics of mothers and their children with failure to thrive. *Journal of Pediatric Psychology, 18,* 453–466.

18. Krauss, M. W. (1993). Child-related and parenting stress: Similarities and differences between mothers and fathers of children with disabilities. *American Journal on Mental Retardation, 97,* 393-404.

19. MacTurk, R. H., Meadow-Orlans, K. P., Koester, L. S., & Spencer, P. E. (1993). Social support, motivation, language, and interaction: A longitudinal study of mothers and deaf infants. *American Annals of the Deaf, 138,* 19-25.

20. Passino, A. W., Whitman, T. L., Borkowski, J. G., Schellenbach, C. J., Maxwell, S. E., Keogh, D., & Rellinger, E. (1993). Personal adjustment during pregnancy and adolescent parenting. *Adolescence, 28,* 97-122.

21. Rhodes, J. E., Fischer, K., Ebert, L., & Meyers, A. B. (1993). Patterns of service utilization among pregnant and parenting African American adolescents. *Psychology of Women Quarterly, 17,* 257-274.

22. Summers, M., Summers, C. R., & Ascione, F. R. (1993). A comparison of sibling interaction in intact and single-parent families. *Journal of Divorce & Remarriage, 20*(1/2), 215-227.

23. Black, M. M., Nair, P., & Harrington, D. (1994). Maternal HIV infection: Parenting and early child development. *Journal of Pediatric Psychology, 19,* 595-616.

24. Campbell, S. B. (1994). Hard-to-manage preschool boys: Externalizing behavior, social competence, and family context at two-year followup. *Journal of Abnormal Child Psychology, 22,* 147-166.

25. Chan, Y. C. (1994). Parenting stress and social support of mothers who physically abuse their children in Hong Kong. *Child Abuse & Neglect, 18,* 261-269.

26. Girolametto, L., & Tannock, R. (1994). Correlates of directiveness in the interactions of fathers and mothers of children with developmental delays. *Journal of Speech and Hearing, 37,* 1178–1192.

27. Kazdin, A. E., & Mazurick, J. L. (1994). Dropping out of child psychotherapy: Distinguishing early and late dropouts over the course of treatment. *Journal of Consulting and Clinical Psychology, 62,* 1069-1074.

28. Kobe, F. H., & Hammer, D. (1994). Parenting stress and depression in children with mental retardation and developmental disabilities. *Research in Development Disabilities, 15,* 209-221.

29. Owen, M. T., & Mulvihill, B. A. (1994). Benefits of a parent education and support program in the first three years. *Family Relations, 43,* 206-212.

30. Sheebar, L. B., & Johnson, J. H. (1994). Evaluation of a temperament-focused, parent-training program. *Journal of Clinical Child Psychology, 23,* 249-259.

31. Stoiber, K. C., & Houghton, T. G. (1994). Adolescent mothers' cognitions and behaviors as at-risk indicators. *School Psychology Quarterly, 9,* 295-316.

32. Szatmari, P., Archer, L., Fisman, S., & Streiner, D. L. (1994). Parent and teacher agreement in the assessment of pervasive developmental disorders. *Journal of Autism and Developmental Disorders, 24,* 703-717.

33. Wall, J. E., & Holden, E. W. (1994). Aggressive, assertive, and submissive behaviors in disadvantaged, inner-city preschool children. *Journal of Clinical Child Psychology, 23,* 382-390.

34. Abidin, R. R., & Brunner, J. F. (1995). Development of a Parenting Alliance Inventory. *Journal of Clinical Child Psychology, 24,* 31-40.

35. Black, M. M. (1995). Failure to thrive: Strategies for evaluation and intervention. *School Psychology Review, 24,* 171–185.

36. Burrell, B., Thompson, B., & Sexton, D. (1995). Measurement characteristics of the Perceived Adequacy of Resources Scale. *Educational and Psychological Measurement, 55,* 249-257.

37. Chisholm, K., Carter, M. C., Ames, E. W., & Morison, S. J. (1995). Attachment security and indiscriminately friendly behavior in children adopted from Romanian orphanages. *Development and Psychopathology, 7,* 283-294.

38. Dumas, J. E., & Wekerle, C. (1995). Maternal reports of child behavior problems and personal distress as predictors of dysfunctional parenting. *Development and Psychopathology, 7,* 465–479.

39. Eiserman, W. D., Weber, C., & McCan, M. (1995). Parent and professional roles in early intervention: A longitudinal comparison of the effects of two intervention configurations. *The Journal of Special Education, 29,* 20–44.

40. Ethier, L. C., Lacharité, C., & Couture, G. (1995). Childhood adversity, parental stress, and depression of negligent mothers. *Child Abuse & Neglect, 19,* 619–632.

41. Golombok, S., Cook, R., Bish, A., & Murray, C. (1995). Families created by the new reproductive technologies: Quality of parenting and social and emotional development of the children. *Child Development, 66,* 285-298.

42. Meadow-Orlans, K. P., Smith-Gray, S., & Dyssegaard, B. (1995). Infants who are deaf or hard of hearing with and without physical/cognitive disabilities. *American Annals of the Deaf, 140,* 279–286.

43. Messer, S. C., & Gross, A. M. (1995). Childhood depression and family interaction: A naturalistic observation study. *Journal of Clinical Child Psychology, 24,* 77-88.

44. Onufrak, B., Saylor, C. F., Taylor, M. J., Eyberg, S. M., & Boyce, G. C. (1995). Determinants of responsiveness in mothers of children with intraventricular hemorrhage. *Journal of Pediatric Psychology, 20,* 587–599.

45. Volenski, L. T. (1995). Building school support systems for parents of handicapped children: The parent education and guidance program. *Psychology in the Schools, 32,* 124–129.

46. Baker, B. L., & Heller, T. L. (1996). Preschool children with externalizing behaviors: Experience of fathers and mothers. *Journal of Abnormal Child Psychology, 24,* 513–532.

47. Dukewich, T. L., Borkowski, J. G., & Whitman, T. L. (1996). Adolescent mothers and child abuse potential: An evaluation of risk factors. *Child Abuse & Neglect, 20,* 1031–1047.

48. Ligezinska, M., Firestone, P., Manion, I. G., McIntyre, J., Ensom, R., & Wells, G. (1996). Children's emotional and behavioral reactions following the disclosure of extrafamilial sexual abuse: Initial effects. *Child Abuse & Neglect, 20,* 111–125.

49. Manion, I. G., McIntyre, J., Firestone, P., Ligezinska, M., Ensom, R., & Wells, G. (1996). Secondary traumatization in parents following the disclosure of extrafamilial child sexual abuse: Initial effects. *Child Abuse & Neglect, 20,* 1095–1109.

50. Radcliffe, J., Bennett, D., Kazak, A. E., Foley, B., & Phillips, P. C. (1996). Adjustment in childhood brain tumor survival: Child, mother, and teacher report. *Journal of Pediatric Psychology, 21,* 529–539.

51. Hughes, J. N., Cavell, T. A., & Grossman, P. B. (1997). A positive view of self: Risk or protection for aggressive children? *Development and Psychopathology, 9,* 75–94.

Review of the Parenting Stress Index by JULIE A. ALLISON, Associate Professor of Psychology, Pittsburg State University, Pittsburg, KS:

The Parenting Stress Index is a 120-item self-report measure developed to identify stress levels in parent-child systems. Specifically, the PSI is intended to identify potentially dysfunctional parent-child relationships that may place a child at risk for emotional disturbance. The PSI, which could be a valuable tool for both researchers and clinicians, is available in both a 7-page item booklet (with hand-scorable PSI answer sheet) and a computerized version. Items on the PSI are simple and direct; respondents (parents) generally take about 20 minutes to circle the number that best reflects their perceptions using a 5-point Likert scale. (A shortened version of the PSI, which takes less than 10 minutes, is also available.) For each version of the PSI, immediate results are obtainable, in both raw and normative forms. An extensive manual is provided with the PSI that provides both information related to the development and utility of the PSI as well as some interpretational guidelines.

The development of the PSI was based on four assumptions. First was that the development of the PSI would be based on already existing empirical research (Assumption 1) and integrated with clinical issues related to parent-child systems (Assumption 2). The third assumption is more theoretically specific to the stress: that is, the idea that stressors or sources of stress are additive. The final assumption underlying the development of the PSI is that stressors vary in source and in kind. Specifically, three areas of stress were identified: (a) child characteristics, (b) parent characteristics, and (c) situational/demographic life stress. Given these assumptions, items on the PSI may be divided into two domains: *child* and *parent*. Each of these domains is then further subdivided into subscales.

THE CHILD DOMAIN. The 47-item child domain assumes that child characteristics have a significant impact on how easily parents are able to fulfill their parental roles. The *child domain* consists of six subscales. Four of these subscales relate to the temperament of the child and include Adaptability (AD), Demandingness (DE), Mood (MO), and Distractibility/Hyperactivity (DI). Although responses on each of these four dimensions are subject to the perceptions of the parents, the remaining two subscales are more directly impacted by parental perceptions: Acceptability (AC) refers to the match between child characteristics and parental expectations for child characteristics, and Reinforces Parent (RE) measures the extent to which the parent experiences the child as a positive reinforcement (or not).

THE PARENT DOMAIN. The parent domain consists of 54 items and includes seven subscales. Three of these subscales measure Depression (DP) levels of the parent, the parent's sense of Competence (CO) with their parenting skills, and Attachment (AT) or the level of motivation the parent may have about fulfilling their role as parent. The remaining four subscales are more related to situational aspects of the parent: the support of Spouse (SP), the parent's Health (HE), the level of Role Restriction (RO) the parent is experiencing due to the parenting role, and the level of social Isolation (IS) the parent is experiencing.

The remaining 19-item Life Stress scale is optional, and offers an index of how much stress a parent may be experiencing outside the parent-child relationship. Although this scale was not intended to be a direct measure of parenting stress, such life stress may intensify the total stress of an individual. High scores on this scale should be considered a "red flag" and merit consideration of referral for professional help.

The PSI demonstrates strong validity. Ninety-five percent of the original PSI's items were directly related to at least one research study that provided evidence for the importance of the attribute measured by the item to parental stress. Modifications of the original scale were based on suggestions from both professionals and data obtained from parents. Research documents that the relationships between PSI scores and theoretically relevant variables are quite robust. For example, PSI scores have been found to be related to children's development, behavior problems, childhood disabilities and illnesses, at-risk families, parent characteristics, family transition issues, and marital relationships.

The PSI manual reports satisfactory internal consistency reliability data. The reliability for each of the domains is strong, yielding scores of .90 for the child domain, .93 for the parent domain, and a strong .95 for the total scale. Scores are generally lower, yet acceptable, for the subscales, ranging from .70–.83 for the child domain and .70–.84 for the parent domain. Test-retest reliabilities on Total Stress score range from .65 for a 1-year interval to .96 for an interval of 1–3 months. These data are consistent with expected patterns reflecting the situational nature of parental stress.

Perhaps the biggest weakness of the PSI stems from its standardization, and its resulting normative data. The sample (N = 2,633) used for normative purposes was not random nor was it stratified. The resulting normative data, therefore, should be used with caution. The interpretation of scores using any labels or diagnoses, for example, does not seem appropriate.

Keeping in mind the limitations of its normative data, the potential uses of the PSI are wide and varied. The PSI will be helpful for anyone interested in the evaluation or assessment of children and parents within a systems context. More specifically, it could be used as a screening tool, to identify children who may be at-risk for emotional or behavioral problems, as well as parents who may be in need of parent education or professional assistance. In addition to identifying child-parent system vulnerabilities, the PSI could also be an appropriate tool for the development of prevention strategies.

Review of the Parenting Stress Index, Third Edition by LAURA L. B. BARNES, Associate Professor of Educational Research and Evaluation, School of Education Studies,, and JUDY J. OEHLER-STINNETT, Associate Professor of Applied Behavioral Studies, Oklahoma State University, Stillwater, OK:

PSI-LONG FORM: TEST COVERAGE AND USE. The Parenting Stress Index (PSI) is intended to measure stress in the parenting system from the perspective of a parent (typically the mother). Three source domains of stress measured with the instrument are those sources associated with the child's characteristics, those associated with parent characteristics, and life event stressors. Begun in the 1970s, item development for the PSI was reported to be grounded in clinical experience and the professional literature on infant development, parent-child interaction, attachment, child abuse and neglect, child psychopathology, child bearing practice, and stress. Although a rational/theoretical approach with a content analysis is a starting place for such an instrument, it would have been useful to use statistical procedures more carefully for final development of the scale. A more careful discussion of the stress construct would also be useful. Many of the items appear to measure overall adjustment/pathology in both parents and children. Path analytic work on the stress model reported in the manual would shed more light on the interactions of the many facets of adjustment the scale attempts to capture.

Within the child domain, four child temperament variables are said to be measured by the PSI—Adaptability, Mood, Demandingness, and Distractibility/Hyperactivity subtests. Some of the items on these scales ask about child behavior in an absolute sense (e.g., kicks and squirms a lot); others ask about the child's behavior in reference to the parent's expectations (e.g., more active than I expected; cries more than most children) or the impact of the behavior on the parent (e.g., child is so active it exhausts me). The author states that the purpose of these PSI scales is not to measure temperament directly but to measure the parent's perception of these temperament characteristics. The two other child domain sources of stress—Acceptability and Child Reinforces Parent—are interactive types of variables involving impacts on the parent's personality and sense of self.

Within the parent domain are three "personality/pathology" variables—Sense of Competence in parenting role, Depression, and Parental Attachment. The other four parent stress variables are situational in nature: Relationship with Spouse, Social Isolation, Parental Health, and Role Restriction. The Life Stress scale measures stress due to events such as death of a close friend or family member, beginning a new job, divorce, marital reconciliation, etc.

Subscale scores within the child domain are additive to form a Child Domain score, likewise within the parent domain. A Total Stress score is the sum of the Parent and Child domain scores. The Life Stress scale does not contribute to the Total Stress score.

Unlike previous forms of the PSI, each item in the current form (Form 6) contributes to only one subscale score and domain. In developing the new form, the manual states that both statistical and content considerations were involved in decisions regarding the deletion of items from previous forms and the assignment of items to subscales. Item-total correlations and factor analytic results were reported as the basis for statistical considerations. However, as will be discussed in more detail, factor analysis results do not seem to support the current structure of the PSI.

NORMATIVE DATA. The PSI was normed on 2,633 mothers recruited from well-child care centers, public school day care centers, private and public pediatric clinics, and health maintenance programs. Ninety-six percent of the sample came from the east coast of the United States, primarily Virginia. Ethnic composition of the sample was 76% white, 11% African American, 10% Hispanic, and 2% Asian. Children who were the focus of the PSI ranged from 1 to 12 years of age. For about 4% of the sample, the target child was a clinical referral. The bulk of the norms were obtained between 1983 and 1989. The only normative data available for father respondents are based on the responses of 200 fathers. Data suggest their stress scores are somewhat lower than that for mothers.

Separate norms are provided for those taking a Spanish translation of the PSI based on an Hispanic sample of 223 parents recruited from "among the pediatric clinics of a major medical center in New York City" (p. 25). An earlier version of the PSI manual described this sample as being "a low SES sample with a low level of occulturation [*sic*]" (Abidin, 1990, p. 55). The domain scores and Total Stress scores appear to be somewhat higher for the Hispanic sample than for the normative sample.

Appendix A contains percentile norms for Total Stress and the domain scores. The norms are broken down by age of target child with over 200 cases for each age category. Subscale norms contained on profile sheets are not age-based. Hispanic norms are also presented and are not age-based.

ADMINISTRATION, SCORING, AND INTERPRETATION. The PSI is a paper-and-pencil scale completed by the parent respondent. Most of the items are on a 5-point Likert-type scale with anchors ranging from *strongly agree* to *strongly disagree*. However, a few items are in a multiple-choice format, and three items have only a 4-point anchor. It is unclear from reviewing the items as to the need to vary the format; this shift in responding requirements may make it more difficult and/or time consuming to complete the scale. Items that are scored on a particular subtest are grouped together on the protocol. Although this may contribute to ease in scoring, it could also contribute to a response set on the part of the parent. The Life Stress section requires yes or no responding.

Scoring can be accomplished by hand or through computer software, both of which are relatively easy. No standard scores are reported. Raw scores are converted to percentile ranks only; percentiles and a profile analysis can be plotted on the scoring form. Percentiles are reported in 5-point intervals only. Also, typical problems with percentile ranks are evident in that differences in raw scores in the middle of the distribution translate into greater changes in percentile ranks than do differences at the extremes of the distribution. For example, a raw score of 26 on the Child Distractibility/Hyperactivity subscale yields a percentile of 65, and a raw score of 27 yields a percentile of 75. At the extremes where diagnostic discriminations are made, it takes a 2-point jump in the raw score (29 to 31) to yield a 5-point difference in the percentile (85 to 90). Given that cutpoints for such important decisions as suspicion of child abuse are described in the manual, these tables should be more carefully constructed and standard scores should be utilized. The 85th percentile is recommended as a cutpoint for referral, with the manual suggesting this is based on clinical and research experience. A more careful description of these studies, with percent classification based on different cutpoints, should be in the manual. With the 85th percentile being close to only a one-standard deviation cutoff, it would also be useful to discriminate a two-standard deviation cutoff for more severe difficulties.

There are also comparative interpretive statements regarding referral. For example, the manual suggests that if the Child Domain score is high but the Total Stress score is below 70 for parents of children with handicaps, then referral is "not necessary." These statements are not qualified by references to reliability or validity limitations of the scale, or by significant reference to multifactored assessment in which other data would also be utilized to determine the severity of the difficulties parents are facing. Raw score cutpoints are also given. For example, the manual provides specific recommendations "When the Total Stress raw score is at or above 260" (p. 6). Unfortunately, this raw score cutpoint translates into a percentile anywhere from the 80th to the 90th percentile, and it is unclear why a raw score interpretation is recommended. There are also a multitude of profile analyses reported in the manual; given the low reliabilities of the subtests and the problematic factor analysis, it cannot be ascertained that subtest profiles across clinical groups are stable or valid enough for this type of interpretation. The most support is for the global scores utilized in conjunction with other data.

RELIABILITY. Internal consistency reliabilities reported in the manual were computed on the norm group of 2,633 cases. Coefficient alphas for the child subscales ranged from .70 to .83 (median = .77). For the parent subscales, alphas ranged from .70 to .84 (median = .81). The Child Domain and Parent Domain score alpha reliabilities were .90 and .93, respectively, and the Total Stress score reliability was reported to be .95. Internal consistency reliabilities reported for a cross-cultural sample ($n = 435$ parents) were similar to those reported on the norming sample, though subscale reliabilities tended to be lower, ranging from .57 to .79.

Temporal stability reliabilities from four studies were reported. A study based on 15 cases reported Spearman coefficients of .82 and .71 for Child and Parent Domain scores over a 3-week interval. Two studies investigated stability over a 3-month period. Pearson coefficients of .63 and .77 for the Child Domain, .91 and .69 for the Parent Domain, and .96 and .88 for the Total Stress scores were reported for studies based on 30 and 54 cases, respectively. One-year stability coefficients of .55, .70, and .65 for Child Domain scores, Parent Domain scores, and Total Stress scores were reported for a sample of 37 cases. No stability information was provided for the subscale scores.

Internal consistency reliabilities for the domain scores and the Total Stress score appear to be high and stable across samples. These scores also appear to possess good, but not excellent, stability over time. The manual suggests that "the Total Stress score is of primary importance in guiding professional judgments as to whether or not professional intervention might be necessary or appropriate" (p. 6) and that the domain scores and Life Stress score be used to help guide the professional to explore the sources of stress. The Total Score and Domain score reliabilities are certainly high enough to support this use, though no reliability information is reported for the Life Stress scale. The internal consistency of the subscale scores, however, tends to fluctuate across samples and is, in some cases, quite low. The manual suggests a profile approach to interpreting subscale scores (i.e., "the various scores are considered in relation to each other" [p. 5]). Users need to be cautious about interpreting subscale score differences given the low reliability of some of the subscales and the fairly substantial correlations among some of the subscales. Unfortunately, the manual makes no reference to standard errors of measurement, confidence bands, or test reliability in discussing interpretive issues.

VALIDITY. Sixteen pages of abstracts of research studies investigating the validity of the PSI for various purposes and populations are presented in the manual. These articles examined various correlates of parental stress (e.g., child illness, marital dissatisfaction, difficult temperament, social isolation, child behavior problems). Reference citations for 92 measures with which the PSI has been correlated are listed in Appendix C. These include, for example, the Achenbach Child Behavior Checklist, the Bayley Scales of Infant Development, Beck Depression Inventory, Child Abuse Potential Inventory, and Infant Temperament Questionnaire. For example, correlations of .56 and .40 were found between the Achenbach Child Behavior Checklist and the PSI Child Domain score and Parent Domain score respectively. One rather strange finding was that, in a sample of 60 mothers of nursery school children, the PSI Total Score correlated .84 with the Trait Anxiety scale of the State-Trait Anxiety Inventory and .71 with State Anxiety. This result suggests that the scale may tap more than stress related to parenting. The PSI has also been used as an outcome measure to show the effects of various stress-reduction interventions. The instrument has been studied cross-culturally with a wide variety of populations, including Bermudan, Puerto Rican, and Israeli mothers. Mothers of children with various types of disabilities have also been studied. Other studies have focused on using the PSI in the prediction of potentially abusive parenting. Several abstracts indicated that scores on the PSI have been shown to discriminate between abusive and nonabusive mothers. A separate appendix includes reference citations for research

with special populations. Although this compendium is impressive, the fact remains that basic reliability and validity weaknesses may have contributed to some of the discrepancies in the literature on parental stress.

The weakest link in the evidence for the validity of the PSI is information presented in the manual to support its factor structure. The factor analytic results reported in the manual do not support the interpretation of Child or Parent subscales. Of the 47 Child domain items, 53% had loadings less than .30 on their designated scales; 19% had loadings less than .20; and 13% of the items had loadings less than .10. Similarly in the Parent domain, 44% of the 54 items loaded under .30; 30% loaded under .20; and 15% had loadings of .10 or smaller on designated Parent domain subscales. Such disconfirmatory results ought to prompt further investigation. Moreover, on the Sense of Parenting Competence scale, the two highest loading items are mother's and father's level of education. Though parents' education level may be a correlate of stress, it should not be considered an indicator of stress and these items should not contribute to the computation of stress scores. In general, the internal structure and meaning of the subscales is questionable.

Overall, the PSI represents an attempt to measure important components of family and child adjustment and difficulties. Because so few such instruments exist, it has been utilized extensively. Use of the scale as a screening instrument and/or for interview purposes to follow up on specific difficulties noted is warranted. However, much more caution is needed in interpreting scores and predicting adjustment and behavior in parents and children. The scale is correlated to a multitude of constructs and high scores may indicate anything from parental personal maladjustment to the presence of a child with a handicapping condition to the parent having a bad day when they completed the scale. Use of specific cutpoints to make unsupported assumptions about families is not recommended. Use of the global score as a screening indicator, with consideration for measurement error, can be justified in situations where time precludes full interview with parents by medical personnel. Diagnostic decisions should only be based on a full multifactored assessment.

PSI—SHORT FORM. The PSI-Short Form (PSI-SF) consists of 36 items selected from the long form and takes about 10 minutes to administer. It was developed in response to requests for a shorter instrument. The PSI-SF is based on a three-factor interpretation of the PSI items—maternal esteem, parent-child interaction, and child self-regulation. The three scales corresponding to these factors are Parental Distress (PD) with items coming from the Parent Domain scales. Parent-Child Dysfunctional Interaction (P-CDI) for which items come from both the Child and Parent Domain, and Difficult Child (DC) with items coming from the Child Domain.

The fact that the scales of this short version are based on factor-analytic techniques suggests that it has future promise and may avoid some of the psychometric problems of the longer scale. It is still unclear that the scale primarily measures parental-related stress. Examination of the Parental Distress subscale shows that 7 of the 12 items are descriptive of general maladjustment/depression. The Parent-Child Dysfunctional Interaction subscale includes items suggestive of internalizing difficulties or developmental delays on the part of the child, rather than disturbed interaction per se. The Difficult Child subscale does seem to measure this construct, with many of the items descriptive of externalizing difficulties of childhood.

Alpha reliabilities for the three scales are .87, .80, and .85, respectively and .91 for the 36-item Total Stress score. Correlations of the PSI-SR with the PSI show strong relationship between the total stress scores ($r = .94$), between the PD and Parent Domain scores ($r = .92$), and between the DC and Child Domain scores ($r = .87$). The P-CDI scale correlates more strongly with Child Domain scores than with Parent Domain scores. The PSI-SF has a well-defined factor structure supporting the scales and it was replicated in a second sample. The defensive responding scale is also available on the short form. Norms for the PSI-SR are based on 800 mothers of children from a well-child clinic in Virginia. No independent validity literature exists yet for the PSI-SF; however, it appears to be a promising instrument worthy of further study.

PSI—COMPUTER-BASED VERSION. The PSI and PSI-SF can be administered and scored by computer. Alternatively, item-level data obtained from paper-pencil administration can be entered manually via the software's editor. Data may be exported to other sources such as databases or other programs for statistical analysis; reports may also be exported to other word processors. The program automatically handles missing data in the same way as recommended for the paper-pencil version (mean substitution). The software provides graphic profiling and a narrative interpretation which includes a score summary; indications of defensive responding; a clinical description of the respondent's perception of his or her stress; diagnostic hypotheses for DSM-IV Axis I and Axis II disorders; recommendations relevant to diagnosis, treatment planning, and management; and a list of test items the professional may wish to review with the client. Additional information is the calculation of a statistical coefficient indicating the degree of fit between the respondent's PSI profile and various clinical reference groups. An impressive reference list of published and unpublished research indexed by clinical population is available and easy to obtain.

Although comprehensive, the computerized report represents overinterpretation of the scale not warranted by its basic psychometric properties. It certainly was not developed for, and has not been validated for, making DSM diagnoses, and the difficulties with the subscales make use of profiles for clinical classification questionable. It also represents overreliance on one instrument for making diagnosis and treatment recommendations.

SUMMARY. The PSI represents one of several scales, developed for clinical use, which has gained much popularity. The perception of its usefulness has been enhanced by the many studies correlating it with other measures of child and adult adjustment. These studies actually point to the discriminant validity difficulties of the instrument. It is most likely a measure of overall child and/or parent maladjustment rather than stress per se. Other notable problems include poor support for subtest organization and profile analyses (based on factor analytic studies), reliance on percentile rank interpretation, and a lack of descriptions of test limitations and use within a multifactored assessment. Cautious users would use global scores, within the context of other data, for screening purposes only.

[222]
Parker Team Player Survey.

Purpose: "Helps individuals identify their primary team player styles."

Population: Employees.

Publication Date: 1991.

Acronym: PTPS.

Scores, 4: Contributor, Collaborator, Communicator, Challenger.

Administration: Group or individual.

Time: (15) minutes.

Comments: Self-scored.

Author: Glenn M. Parker.

Publisher: XICOM, Inc.

a) PARKER TEAM PLAYER SURVEY.
Price Data, 1993: $5.50 per test booklet/manual (23 pages).
b) PTPS: STYLES OF ANOTHER PERSON.
Price Data: $4 per test booklet/manual (12 pages).

TEST REFERENCES

1. Kirnan, J. P., & Woodruff, D. (1994). Reliability and validity estimates of the Parker Team Player Survey. *Educational and Psychological Measurement, 54,* 1030-1037.

Review of the Parker Team Player Survey by GARY J. DEAN, Associate Professor and Chairperson, Department of Adult and Community Education, Indiana University of Pennsylvania, Indiana, PA:

GENERAL COMMENTS. The purpose of the Parker Team Player Survey (PTPS) and the Parker Team Player Survey: Styles of Another Person is to assess a person's style as a team player. Four styles are identified in the two instruments: Contributor, Collaborator, Communicator, and Challenger. The PTPS consists of a 22-page booklet, which includes the survey and information on scoring and interpretation. The Styles of Another Person is a 10-page booklet consisting of a survey and a section on scoring.

Both instruments consist of 18 forced-choice items. Each item has a stem and four responses that are rated by the respondent on a scale of 1 to 4, with 4 = *most applicable to you* (*them*, on the Styles of Another Person), 3 = *second most applicable statement*, 2 = *third most applicable statement*, and 1 = *least applicable statement*. Each response to the items represents one of the four team player styles. The ranking of the responses indicates which style the respondent would consider most appropriate for the situation posed in the item.

TECHNICAL INFORMATION. No information regarding the development of the instruments is provided in either of the booklets and there is no technical manual to accompany the booklets. Calling the publisher resulted in obtaining a reprint of an article (Kirnan & Woodruff, 1994) in which several studies regarding the validity and reliability of the PTPS were reported. According to Kirnan and Woodruff, further details of the origins of the styles are presented in a book by Parker (1991).

According to Kirnan and Woodruff, two studies were conducted to establish validity and one study was conducted to establish reliability for the PTPS. The first validity study consisted of correlating self-ratings on the PTPS for 95 employees with the ratings of them by co-workers using the PTPS Styles of Another Person. The Pearson product-moment correlation coefficients for this study ranged from .18 to .46. The second validity study involved 35 college students who performed an item sort on the PTPS. The 72 responses from the survey (18 items x 4 responses each) were typed onto slips of paper and assigned by the students to one of the four styles. The results of this study were reported as the median percent correct assignment (that is, the median percent of the students whose assignment of the responses to the styles agreed with Parker's assignment for each style). The median percents ranged from 63.5 to 85.5. The range of percents for each style was considerable, however, with a low of 9% agreement to a high of 100%. The reliability study was based on college students (*n* = 47) and employees (*n* = 62) and involved the test-retest method with a 3-week interval for the college students and a 4- to 6-week interval for the employees. Correlation coefficients ranged from .43 to .75. Cronbach's alpha calculations for the same study ranged from .20 to .65.

Kirnan and Woodruff (1994) report that the moderate levels of reliability for the PTPS reflect the low number of items and Parker's assertion that many people tend to exhibit more than one style. Also, it should be noted that the results from the item-sort study would have been clearer if means and standard deviations for the percents were reported rather than median percents. If there was a negative skew for the distribution of the agreements by the students, then a median score may, in fact, present an inflated figure for the level of agreement. The moderate correlations from the comparison of self to other ratings and the range of percents in the item sorting indicate that the validity studies also appear to have mixed results. One might question the extent to which the four styles are independent concepts of one another. Also not discussed is the extent to which the four styles are related to other measures of personality such as the Myers-Briggs Type Indicator (T4:1702). The preliminary data suggested by the Kirnan and Woodruff studies indicate that the PTPS may hold some promise, but much additional work is needed to establish the validity and reliability of the instrument.

ADMINISTRATION AND SCORING. Administration of the two instruments is relatively easy. It is designed to be self-administered. The directions are clear and an example of how to respond to the items is provided. The forced-choice format may prove uncomfortable for some people (this is acknowledged in the directions). Scoring is also relatively simple: One transfers the ranking of each response for each item to a grid. The only drawback is that the order of the responses for each item is not the same. For example, the responses for Item 1 are recorded a, b, c, d, whereas the responses for Item 2 are recorded d, a, b, c. This problem aside, scoring is relatively simple and the resulting score for each column in the grid is readily assigned to one of the four team player styles. The highest score designates the person's primary team player style.

INTERPRETATION. There are four sections on interpretation in the PTPS booklet, one section for each of the following: one primary style, two primary styles, three primary styles, and a uniform pattern. The author provided a definition of each of the four team player styles in the section entitled "Understanding and Interpreting the Results if You Have One Primary Style" (p. 9). Contributors are task oriented and provide the team with technical data although they may become bogged down in detail and lose sight of the big picture. Collaborators are goal-oriented people who see the mission of the team and are flexible and open to new ideas but may not give enough attention to basic team tasks and needs of other individuals on the team. Communicators are process and people oriented and are also conflict resolvers, but sometimes lack task orientation or fail to confront others on the team when necessary. Challengers question the goals, methods, or even the ethics of the team and are valued for their openness and candor but may become self-righteous. The sections on two and three primary styles simply reflect a combination of the positive and negative attributes of each style. The section on a uniform pattern merely mentions that a person has strengths from each of the four styles but that person's impact in the team may be diffused because of the lack of a strong preference for one style.

Interpreting the Styles of Another Person is accomplished by comparing a respondent's self-ratings to the ratings given to that person by others. A grid is provided for this purpose. The grid allows the respondent to record the scores of others for each of the four styles, average those scores, and then compare the average of the others' scores to their own score for each style.

CONCLUSION. The PTPS and Styles of Another Person are easy to take and score, with the caveat that some people may find the forced-choice format difficult. The potential applications in organizations would appear to make the instrument a valuable tool. The lack of persuasive data for reliability and validity, however, limit the usefulness of the

instrument at this time. Additional studies are needed, especially in the area of establishing the independence of the four styles. Provided that the instrument is used for self-exploration and growth, it may provide some useful insights.

REVIEWER'S REFERENCES
Parker, G. M. (1991). *Team players and teamwork: The new competitive business strategy.* San Francisco: Jossey-Bass.
Kirnan, J. P., & Woodruff, D. (1994). Reliability and validity estimates of the Parker Team Player Survey. *Educational and Psychological Measurement, 54*(4), 1030–1037.

Review of the Parker Team Player Survey by RICHARD B. STUART, Professor Emeritus of Psychiatry, University of Washington, and Regional Faculty, The Fielding Institute, Seattle, WA:

In using the Parker Team Player Survey, respondents are asked to describe their own behavior and that of members of their team using an 18-item instrument. Each item consists of a descriptor (e.g., "During team meetings he or she usually ..." [p. 2] or "When necessary, this person is able to ..." [p. 3]) followed by four alternatives: "provides the team with technical data or information," "keeps the team focused on our mission or goals," "makes sure everyone is involved in the discussion," and "raises questions about our goals and methods" (p. 2). Respondents are asked to rank the applicability of each alternative to the teammate being evaluated, using a 4-point scale from "least applicable statement" (p. 1) to "most applicable to them" (p. 1). Protocols are scored by entering the number assigned to response alternative on a score sheet with four columns. By totaling the columns, relative scores are obtained for the extent to which each team member is seen as displaying each of four characteristics. "Contributors" are defined as being task-oriented; "Collaborators" as goal-oriented; "Communicators" as process-oriented; and "Challengers" as question-oriented. Space is also provided for open-ended assessments of respondent's or teammate's strengths, performance enhancing and impeding actions, and areas of needed improvement. The manual implies that teammates' rating of each target individual can be averaged. Instructions are given for displaying transparencies that convey the ratings received by each named participant.

In two manuals consisting of 12 pages and 22 pages with large type, no theory of organizational or group behavior is presented as a rationale for the selection of the four team player styles. Rather, each is described in general terms, noting that the relevant behaviors have both positive and negative implications. Accordingly, no claim can be made that these types either exhaust the range of group-member attributes or that they represent the most salient of attributes. The manuals suggest that the strengths of teams be assessed along these four lines, with indications that certain styles may be missing, overly dominant, or inflexibly utilized in the group.

In the same vein, data are not presented on the reliability or validity of members' ratings of their own and each others' characteristics. Nor are data presented on the results one might expect when using this instrument in various types of organizations. Public presentation of the scores received by each member in this essentially sociometric assessment is a technique that definitely should have been evaluated because of its potentially disruptive effects.

The low cost and easy administration of this instrument, coupled with its rather simplistic array of performance characterizations, makes its use appealing. However, its use in groups that are moderate to high in conflict is unwise unless it is administered by a highly skilled group leader who has prepared protocols for dealing with varied types of feedback and the potential for negative as well as positive impact. At best, this instrument might be used as an "ice breaker" in group-based approaches to organizational consultation to facilitate team members' thinking about their peers' performance in concrete terms, which can either be reinforced or changed. But even this use is not without its risks. If the feedback to any individual is either strongly negative or discordant with that person's self-perception, it can result in resentment and/or alienation. Those interested in assessing team effectiveness in particular, or organizational effectiveness in general, might profit from a review of other approaches (e.g., Harrison, 1987).

REVIEWER'S REFERENCE

Harrison, M. I. (1987). *Diagnosing organizations: Methods, models, and processes.* Newbury Park, CA: Sage Publications.

[223]
The Patterned Elicitation Syntax Test with Morphophonemic Analysis.

Purpose: Designed to determine "whether a child's expressive grammatical skills are age appropriate."
Population: Ages 3–0 to 7–6.
Publication Dates: 1981–1993.
Acronym: PEST.
Scores, 13: Articles, Adjectives, Auxiliaries/Modals/Copulas, Conjunctions, Negatives, Plurals, Possessives, Pronouns, Questions, Verbs, Subject/Verb Agreement, Embedded Elements, Total.
Administration: Individual.

Price Data, 1994: $51 per complete kit including manual ('93, 18 pages), stimulus picture book, and 10 data form booklets.
Time: (15–20) minutes.
Comments: Previously titled The Patterned Elicitation Syntax Test.
Authors: Edna Carter Young and Joseph J. Perachio.
Publisher: Communication Skill Builders.
Cross References: For a review by Carolyn Peluso Atkins, see 9:921.

TEST REFERENCES

1. Eiserman, W. D., Weber, C., & McCoun, M. (1992). Two alternative program models for serving speech disordered preschoolers: A second follow-up. *Journal of Communication Disorders, 25,* 77–106.
2. Plante, E., & Vance, R. (1994). Selection of preschool language tests: A data-based approach. *Language, Speech, and Hearing Services in Schools, 25,* 15–24.

Review of the Patterned Elicitation Syntax Test with Morphophonemic Analysis by CLINTON W. BENNETT, Professor of Communication Sciences and Disorders, James Madison University, Harrisonburg, VA:

The Patterned Elicitation Syntax Test (PEST) presents a unique deviation from most tests of expressive grammatical skills in children; it uses a delayed imitation task and two scoring methods (criterion and norm referenced). The PEST is a screening instrument of 44 grammatical structures from Standard English. Twelve specific classes of grammatical structures are evaluated: Articles; Adjectives; Auxiliaries, Modals, and Copulas; Conjunctions; Negatives; Plurals; Possessives; Pronouns; Questions; Verbs; Subject/Verb Agreement; and Embedded Elements.

The child listens to three consecutively modeled sentences with common syntactic patterns with varied vocabulary while looking at simple black-on-white line drawings. The child then repeats the three sentences, with only the third sentence being scored. However, the authors note that the child's consistency across the three sentences can be used to draw conclusions about mastery of the grammatical structure.

The PEST stimulus items are arranged in ascending order of difficulty; therefore basal and ceiling levels were established. Three-year-olds and children suspected of significant language delays begin with Item #1 and older children begin with Item #11 and are credited with Items 1 through 10. Administration of the test is terminated after the child commits six consecutive errors.

The PEST also includes an optional morphophonemic interpretation that allows for determination of whether a child's omission of morphological markers is due to lack of morphemic knowledge or a restricted phonological system. This screening tool consists of 50 words that require the production of final consonants or consonant clusters to form plurals, possessives, and verb tenses.

The PEST normative population was only 651 children between the ages of 3-0 and 7-6 from homes where Standard English was spoken. Only children "who had no identified disability that would preclude normal language development" (p. 4) were included. The number of children per 6-month age group ranged from 51–100.

Two measures of reliability are presented in the manual: Temporal reliability was assessed by testing 106 children twice within a 2-week period. The Pearson Product Moment correlation of .94 indicates that the PEST has excellent test-retest reliability. Internal consistency was measured using split-half coefficients, which ranged from .93 to .99 across the nine age groups.

Three types of test validity are presented in the manual. Item validity was assessed to determine if the PEST is developmental (i.e., are higher scores a function of age). A series of t-tests yielded an acceptable pattern of significance between age groups, indicating that this test is developmental in its structure. Content validity was evaluated by contrasting the PEST scores with results of a spontaneous language-sample analysis from 10 normal-language and 30 language-impaired children. Correlations of .86 and .88, respectively, suggest an acceptable relationship between performance on the PEST and spontaneous use of the morphological structures assessed by the PEST. Predictive validity was used to determine if PEST performance would identify children with expressive language impairment. Thirty-five children diagnosed as language impaired from results of a full battery of diagnostic language tests and experienced clinician judgments served as subjects. The PEST scores for 34 of the 35 language-impaired children fell below the recommended cutoff (10th percentile). The remaining child was between the 10th and 25th percentile. Interestingly, 33 of 35 language-impaired children also scored below two standard deviations from the mean for their age group. These findings would indicate that a cutoff of two standard deviations from the mean would still accurately identify language-impaired children and would not identify children in the low normal range as impaired (which the 10th percentile cutoff does).

Performance on the PEST is interpreted as criterion referenced (which morphological structures were and were not successfully produced) and/or age referenced (comparison of this score to that of normal-language peers).

Criterion-referenced interpretation may be useful in determining remedial targets and documenting progress. Transferring errors from the Response Sheet to the Assessment Sheet (both in each data form booklet) allows evaluation of the 44 structures scored plus 144 additional structures which are not scored.

Age-referenced scoring can be interpreted through percentile ranks or in terms of the score's deviation from the mean for the child's age. The authors seem to favor the use of percentile ranks: "The examiner should be most interested in identifying children who score in the lowest quartile, because this represents performance out of the normal range. Children who score below the 10th percentile are almost certainly candidates for therapy" (p. 12).

Application of these recommendations will result in the overidentification of children as language-impaired. The normative population for standardization of the PEST excluded any child suspected as being "disabled"; therefore, using the lowest quartile as a cutoff would identify 25% of normal children as being language impaired; similarly, with the 10th percentile as the cutoff, 10% of normal children are found to be impaired. Because the normative sample included only normals, a cutoff using the age group mean minus two standard deviations which, theoretically, would still identify 2% of "normals"—would seem to be more clinically relevant than the authors' recommendation.

Each data form booklet is complete, containing a response sheet, in-depth assessment sheet, interpretation of morphophonemic errors, and tables for interpretation of scores (age groups, means, standard deviations, and percentile ranks). The PEST manual is user friendly with pertinent information presented in an easy-to-understand manner.

LIMITATIONS. The restricted normative sample appears to be truncated so that a 10th percentile cutoff is likely to overidentify low normal children as language impaired; the delayed-imitation task may be difficult for young children (particularly the questions forms); and use of the published norms are not appropriate for speakers of nonmainstream dialect (which the authors indicated).

CONCLUSION. The PEST is a valid and reliable screening tool for children with suspected syntactic problems. It also may serve as a probe for determining therapeutic targets and progress. However, identifying children in the lowest quartile (<25th percentile) or even below the 10th percentile will overidentify children as language impaired. The PEST is best used as a criterion-referenced measure.

Review of the Patterned Elicitation Syntax Test with Morphophonemic Analysis by SHEILA R. PRATT, Assistant Professor of Communication Science & Disorders, University of Pittsburgh, Pittsburgh, PA:

The goal of the Patterned Elicitation Syntax Test (PEST) is to assess expressive syntactic and morphophonemic skills of children within a limited period of time. The authors indicated that the PEST is primarily a screening tool that can be used to determine if children need more extensive assessment of expressive language. They also indicated that it can be used as a criterion-referenced test, as a component of a speech-language and educational assessment battery, or it can be used prescriptively. That is, they believed that the structure and analysis scheme of the PEST is useful in identifying linguistic structures that are in need of remediation.

TEST DESCRIPTION. The PEST was developed for children ages 3 to 7.5 years and includes a range of common syntactic structures and a sample of final bound morphemes. The authors indicated that the test represents structures that typically occur in children's speech but little explanation was given for why specific items were selected. The test items (a total of 44) consist of phrases and sentences that are arranged in order of increasing complexity and difficulty. With some of the items, specific words and phrases are targeted within utterances whereas with others entire sentences are targeted. Each test item is associated with a plate of three pictures. The pictures depict three structurally similar utterances. When administering the PEST, an examiner produces an utterance for each picture and then asks the child also to describe all three pictures. However, only the last utterance produced by the child is scored, thereby making the procedure a delayed imitation task.

Two analysis formats are included in the PEST—one syntactic, the other morphophonemic. The syntactic portion is the primary component of the test and the morphophonemic portion is largely supplementary. In the syntactic portion the children's productions are scored for syntactic correctness in a binary plus-minus fashion. The number of correct productions are totaled and compared to age-based norms. In the morphophonemic portion of the PEST, a number of the final bound morphemes

(single consonants and clusters that form verb tenses, plurals, and possessives) are sampled from all of the utterances produced (not just the third or target productions) and are analyzed for phonological correctness. These morphophonemic results are not, however, included in the calculation of the raw test score or associated with the norms or normative process. The implication is that the morphophonemic results are to be viewed descriptively. Further, when the morphophonemic analysis is used, some type of phonological assessment is required in order to determine if errors are morphological rather than phonological in nature. This analysis needs to occur offline from an audio recording of the test session, in part, because it and the syntactic analysis are performed on two different portions of the score sheet making response recording cumbersome if done online.

The instructions in the manual for the syntactic portion of the PEST are reasonably clear. They are vague for the morphophonemic analysis, although clarified somewhat by the directions on the score sheet. The instructions for interpreting the syntactic results are acceptable but limited relative to the morphophonemic results. In addition, not all of the required information for administration and interpretation is located where expected in the manual.

VALIDITY. One major weakness of the PEST is that the delayed imitation task on which it was based has only limited empirical support and justification. The authors suggested that the delayed imitation task reduces some of the limitations of immediate imitation such as the effects of short-term memory, restricted context, and limited communicative intent. They also indicated that language behaviors produced in a delayed imitation task may be more representative of a child's spontaneous language than immediate imitation. In addition, the PEST was described as more controlled, quicker, and less labor intensive than analyzing expressive language via spontaneous language samples. Although there may be truth in these claims, particularly the claim of control and speed, the supportive evidence is not presented in the test manual. Context and communicative intent are limited with the PEST and may not be substantively greater than that provided by direct imitation tasks. In addition, memory may play an even greater role with a delayed imitation task than direct imitation in that the amount of information presented per item is greater and the time in working memory also is likely longer. Further, the influence of producing two structurally similar sentences prior to a third target utterance was not sufficiently addressed.

The authors provided three measures of validity. They assessed content validity by comparing performance on the PEST with the production of similar structures in spontaneous speech samples from a group of children with expressive language impairment and a smaller group with normal language. The correlations between performance on the PEST and spontaneous productions were reported as .88 for the language-impaired group and .86 for the normal-language group. However, the sample size ($n = 10$) for the normal-language group was insufficient to produce a stable correlation. In addition, the procedures used to collect and analyze the language samples were poorly described. These procedures may have impacted the results. It also was unclear why only the syntactic structures sampled by the PEST were evaluated in the language sample. Information relative to predictive validity would have been obtained if the syntactic results of the PEST had been compared to the overall results of the language sample. That is, was poor performance on a language sample consistent with poor performance on the PEST?

Predictive validity was assessed by administering the PEST to 35 children previously diagnosed with expressive language impairment. Using the 10th percentile as the failure criterion, the sensitivity of the PEST was measured. Thirty-four of the 35 children tested were true failures, which is reasonably high; but because the group was restricted to only language-impaired children the results were of limited usefulness. Without testing children with a range of language skills, specificity could not be determined nor was it clear whether the high degree of predictability was a function of a biased sample. The use of the PEST as a screening tool should be questioned due to the lack of adequate sensitivity and specificity data.

As an additional measure of validity the authors evaluated the developmental nature of the test. The items were arranged in order of difficulty as reflected in the performance of their normative group, which begs the question of whether the order of the items was changed after the norms were established. If such was the case, the normative data are invalid for use with the PEST. To document that the PEST was developmental in nature, the authors tested for differences between the age groups (6-month intervals) of their normative sample. They indicated that all of their comparisons were significant although the comparisons were not specified. The manual includes a table of means, standard deviations, and t-scores for each age level but the arrangement of the data in the table suggests that all of the comparisons were made to the youngest group, which is of only limited value. In addition, for each age group the items were viewed according to percentage of correct responses to determine if the sequence of difficulty held for each age group. Although the authors said that the trend tended to hold across the groups, more formal analyses were not reported.

RELIABILITY. The reliability of the PEST was assessed with a test-retest method to measure temporal stability and a split-half procedure to measure internal consistency. Test-retest reliability was assessed with 106 children from the normative sample. The children were tested by the same examiner 2 weeks after the initial test. The resulting correlation was .94 indicating sufficiently high temporal stability. The split-half reliability was determined by correlating the scores derived from the odd items with scores from the even items for each age level. The correlations ranged from .93 to .99 with no apparent age-related differences. Therefore, the reliability of the PEST appeared to be quite acceptable.

NORMATIVE SAMPLE. The normative sample consisted of 651 children between the ages of 3.0 and 7.5 years. The number of children in each age group was not consistent. The smallest group size was 51 and the largest was 100 with the younger groups having fewer members. The normative sample comprised 324 males and 327 females. None of the children had obvious disabilities that would have interfered with normal language development although no preliminary measures were used to document normal development or normal language. The children were English speaking and came from homes in which standard American English was spoken. The children were largely from the eastern portion of the United States but the specific setting (urban vs. rural) varied. Approximately 75% of the children were from middle-class families as determined by the family breadwinner's occupation (Warner, Meeker, & Eells, 1949).

SUMMARY OF STRENGTHS. The PEST is a novel approach to assessing syntactic and morphophonemic productions and may prove to be an effective means of screening for expressive language impairment although this needs further verification. The test materials are straightforward and easy to use. The organization of the response form is structured to facilitate error analysis. In addition, instructions and norms are included on the response form, which assists with administration and interpretation. The normative sample was of sufficient size and the reliability of the test is reasonably high.

SUMMARY OF WEAKNESSES. The major weakness of the PEST is its inadequate documentation of validity. In particular, the authors did not sufficiently substantiate the validity of the delayed imitation approach upon which the test was based. Also, characterization of the performance of the PEST as a screening tool is inadequate. Further, verification of its use as a prescriptive tool is lacking as is the use of the supplementary morphophonemic component of the test. No measures of validity or reliability are supplied for the morphophonemic portion, which weakens its applicability.

REVIEWER'S REFERENCE

Warner, W. L., Meeker, M., & Eells, K. (1949). *Social class in America: A manual of procedure for the measurement of social status.* Chicago: Science Research Associates.

[224]
Pediatric Early Elementary Examination—II.

Purpose: Designed "to help generate a narrative description of a child's neurodevelopmental profile."
Population: Ages 6–9.
Publication Dates: 1983–1992.
Acronym: PEEX-II.
Scores: 8 major sections: Fine Motor Function, Ratings of Selective Attention, Behavior and Affect/Language, Gross Motor Function, Memory, Visual Processing, Delayed Recall, Task Analysis.
Administration: Individual.
Price Data, 1993: $39.70 per 12 record forms and 12 response booklets; $11.65 per stimulus booklet; $8.85 per examiner's manual ('90, 45 pages); $9.40 per specimen set including 1 record form and examiner's manual.
Time: (50–60) minutes.
Comments: Publisher suggests should represent one contribution to a multifocal assessment process.
Author: Educators Publishing Service, Inc.
Publisher: Educators Publishing Service, Inc.
Cross References: For reviews by J. Jeffrey Grill and Neil H. Schwartz of the earlier edition, see 10:272.

TEST REFERENCES

1. Schneck, C. M. (1991). Comparison of pencil-grip patterns in first graders with good and poor writing skills. *The American Journal of Occupational Therapy, 45,* 701–706.

Review of the Pediatric Early Elementary Examination—II by DENISE M. DeZOLT, Assistant Professor of Counseling Psychology, Lewis and Clark College, Portland, OR:

RATIONALE. The Pediatric Early Elementary Examination (PEEX-II) Pilot Edition is de-

signed to contribute to the neurodevelopmental profile of 6- through 9-year-old children as part of a multidimensional evaluation process that includes (a) physical, sensory, and neurological examinations; (b) developmental history; (c) parent and teacher questionnaires; and (d) prior assessment data. The PEEX-II assesses functioning across several domains including Fine and Gross Motor Functioning, Language, Memory, Delayed Recall, and Visual Processing. In addition, the examiner systematically notes Selective Attention, Behavior, and Affect at specified "checkpoints" (p. 12) throughout administration. According to the developers, the PEEX-II contains items representative of current developmental trends and knowledge such as phonological awareness. The PEEX-II consists of an examiner's manual, stimulus booklet, record form, and response booklet.

ADMINISTRATION AND SCORING. The PEEX-II materials provide (a) an individual rationale for each section; (b) specific instructions for item administration and verbatim instructions; and (c) specific scoring instructions. Items are similar to many neurodevelopmental tasks and easily administered. Selective Attention, Behavior, and Affect ratings are conducted periodically during administration of the PEEX-II. Although the manual provides guidelines for examiners' ratings, these are the most subjective components of the PEEX-II because they rely more on clinical judgment and require expertise in normative child development and testing behaviors. Because the narrative layout of the manual is cumbersome, in future versions the developers should consider a more technical layout to facilitate ease of administration. The PEEX-II is administered by a professional and in the presence of the parent(s).

Although each item provides an obtained score that may be compared to a particular age level (6–9 years), no overall total or subtests scores are obtained. Rather, task analysis and the presence of recurring themes form the basis for any specific conclusions drawn. Thematic and task analyses are conducted based on item performance across domains. The task analysis component is included in the record form.

TECHNICAL QUALITIES. No empirical support for this scale is provided in the manual. Rather, the developers view this as a work in progress and are compiling normative, reliability, validity, and interobserver agreement data typically associated with such instruments.

CONCLUSIONS AND RECOMMENDATIONS FOR USE. In summary, the PEEX-II is best used by professionals and researchers with pediatric neurodevelopmental expertise who are interested primarily in contributing to the developers' normative, reliability, validity, and interobserver agreement data base. With appropriate empirical support, this instrument has promise as a neurodevelopmental screen. Given the lack of empirical support, the PEEX-II should only be used as an ancillary part of a thorough pediatric neurodevelopmental evaluation. No conclusions or recommendations relative to normative developmental status should be made on the basis of this instrument.

Review of the Pediatric Early Elementary Examination—II by CARL J. DUNST, Research Scientist, Orelena Hawks Puckett Institute, Asheville, NC:

The Pediatric Early Elementary Examination—II (PEEX-II) is a neurodevelopmental assessment instrument for use with children ages 6 to 9. The instrument is one of several developed by the author and his colleagues for evaluating the neurodevelopmental functioning of children and adolescents between ages 3 and 15. The manual and accompanying test booklet and record forms assume not only knowledge of these other instruments but also familiarity with the author's conceptual and clinical work regarding learning disabilities and neurodevelopmental functioning. Potential users of the PEEX-II should therefore be prepared to devote time to information gathering about the evolution of the author's perspective for defining and measuring learning disorders, and the history of instrument development leading to the publication of the PEEX-II. The PEEX-II examiner's manual includes a limited amount of information about its development and none regarding the conceptual or theoretical bases of the instrument. A strength of the examiner's manual, however, is detailed interpretative descriptions of the meaning of different response patterns.

The PEEX-II measures neurodevelopmental functioning in multiple areas including Fine Motor/Graphomotor, Language, Gross Motor, Memory, Visual Processing, and Delayed Recall. The item sets are scored in a number of different ways depending on the neurodevelopmental functions being evaluated. The Fine Motor/Graphomotor, Language, and Visual Processing areas also include methods for assessing a number of aspects of child attention related to task performance. The PEEX-II additionally includes procedures for capturing a number of dimensions of child affect, behavior, strategy use, minor neurological indicators, physical health, and growth/maturation.

Collectively, the information gathered about behavior functioning in the neurodevelopmental areas and the supplemental assessment domains are used to produce a "description of a child's development and functional neurological status" (manual, p. 1) contributing to the ability to "create highly specific profiles of [children's] neurodevelopmental strengths and weaknesses" (manual, p. 42). Aggregate information from a PEEX-II examination together with other available information is used to complete a profile summary of an individual examiner's impressions of child performance and capabilities. The validity of the profiles as well as other scoring methods, however, are questionable for the reasons given next.

The major shortcoming of the instrument is the lack of psychometric data concerning either its reliability or validity. The test developer (personal communication) indicates that normative data were collected on just over 100 children and that predictive validity studies are underway. None of these data are presented in the test manual. Although this information would be extremely helpful in judging the adequacy of the PEEX-II, it would not be sufficient evidence strictly to support claims about the diagnostic value of the instrument. For example, the lack of interrater reliability for individual scale items not only raises questions about possible differences in how individual children might be evaluated by different scorers, but also raises more serious questions about the profiling of strengths and weaknesses using data having no reliability information. Overall, judgments about the possible value of the PEEX-II for evaluating neurodevelopmental functioning related to learning disorders awaits the availability of necessary psychometric evidence.

According to the test developers, the value of the PEEX-II rests on its ability to inform pediatricians and other health care professionals about areas of neurodevelopmental concern that require further attention. If the instrument is found useful for this purpose, on a case-by-case basis, perhaps the instrument has some utility. However, if the PEEX-II is found to have test sensitivity and specificity problems similar to those of its predecessor (Kenny, Gaes, Saylor, et al., 1990), clinical impressions based on the instrument findings may be misleading. The PEEX-II, therefore, is best thought of as an instrument still in the development and validation phases of scale construction, and the publication of the revised version of the scale appears to have been premature.

REVIEWER'S REFERENCE

Kenny, T., Gaes, G., Saylor, W., Grossman, L., Kappelman, M., Chernoff, R., Toler, S., & Majer, L. (1990). The Pediatric Early Elementary Examination: Sensitivity and specificity. *Journal of Pediatric Psychology, 15,* 21–26.

[225]

Personal Experience Inventory for Adults.

Purpose: Designed to yield "comprehensive information about an individual's substance abuse patterns and problems."

Population: Age 19 and older.

Publication Dates: 1995–1996.

Acronym: PEI-A.

Scores, 37: Problem Severity Scales (Personal Involvement with Drugs, Physiological Dependence, Effects of Use, Social Benefits of Use, Personal Consequences of Use, Recreational Use, Transsituational Use, Psychological Benefits of Use, Preoccupation, Loss of Control, Infrequency—1, Self-Deception, Social Desirability—1, Treatment Receptiveness), Psychosocial Scales (Negative Self-Image, Psychological Disturbance, Social Isolation, Uncontrolled, Rejecting Convention, Deviant Behavior, Absence of Goals, Spiritual Isolation, Peer Drug Use, Interpersonal Pathology, Estrangement in the Home, Infrequency—2, Social Desirability—2), Problem Screens (Suicide Risk, Work Environment Risk, Past Family Pathology, Other Impulse-Related Problems, Significant Other Drug Problem, Sexual Abuse Perpetrator, Physical Abuse Perpetrator, Physical/Sexual Abuse Victim, Need for Psychiatric Referral, Miscellaneous).

Administration: Group.

Parts, 2: Problem Severity Scales, Psychosocial Scales.

Price Data, 1996: $135 per kit including 5 prepaid mail-in answer booklets and manual ('96, 100 pages); $18.50 or less per mail-in answer booklet; $275 or less per IBM microcomputer scoring disk (25 uses; 3.5-inch); $19.50 or less per 10 microcomputer answer booklets for use with microcomputer disk; $17.50 each for FAX scoring service.

Time: (45–60) minutes.

Comments: Untimed self-report inventory; computer scored only.

Author: Ken C. Winters.

Publisher: Western Psychological Services.

Review of the Personal Experience Inventory for Adults by MARK D. SHRIVER, Assistant Professor, University of Nebraska Medical Center, Omaha, NE:

The stated purpose of the Personal Experience Inventory for Adults (PEI-A) is to function as "a comprehensive, standardized self-report inventory to assist in problem identification, treatment referral, and individualized planning associated with addressing the abuse of alcohol and other drugs by adults" (p. 3). It is designed to yield "comprehensive information about an individual's substance abuse patterns and problems [and] …also helps to identify the psycho-social difficulties of the referred individual" (p. 3). The PEI-A is developed from, and an extension of, the PEI (1989) which is a self-report measure of drug and alcohol use for adolescents ages 12 to 18 (see *Mental Measurements Yearbook* (1992) 11:284 for reviews by Tony Toneatto and Jalie A. Tucker).

The manual states that the PEI-A "was designed primarily as a clinical descriptive tool for use by addiction professionals" and that it "is intended to supplement a comprehensive assessment process" (p. 5). Specifically, the PEI-A was developed to measure the following characteristics:

1. The presence of the psychological, physiological, and behavioral signs of alcohol and other drug abuse and dependence.

2. The nature and style of drug use (e.g., consequences, personal effects, and setting).

3. The onset, duration, and frequency of use for each of the major drug categories.

4. The characteristics of psychosocial functioning, especially factors identified as precipitating or maintaining drug involvement and expected to be relevant to treatment goals.

5. The existence of behavioral or mental problems that may accompany drug use (e.g., sexual abuse or co-addiction).

6. The sources of invalid response tendencies (e.g., "faking bad," "faking good," inattention, or random responding).

The appropriate use of any measure for its intended purposes is dependent on its sample representation, reliability, and validity. This information is reviewed respective to the PEI-A's stated purposes described above.

TEST ADMINISTRATION. The manual provides easy-to-read instructions on test administration, which will assist with increasing standardization of the administration. The manual states that the reading level of the measure is approximately sixth grade (p. 7), and the test may be read to clients with lower reading abilities. No discussion is presented, however, regarding whether this type of administration occurred during norming of the test, or how this type of administration may affect the reliability or validity of the self-report measure, as the examiner is directly involved with administration, which runs counter to one of the intended goals for test development (p. 29).

The test is scored by computer, either through a mail-in service, a FAX service, or by computer disk. The mail-in service typically requires approximately 3–5 working days to return scores (p. 75). This may be too long in some clinical settings. Interpretations of each scale are provided in the computer-generated report.

TEST DEVELOPMENT. The content of the PEI-A is largely derived from the PEI. A panel of experts is reported to have examined the items on the PEI and made changes where necessary to adapt the items to an adult population. The panel of experts was composed of "Groups of researchers and drug treatment service providers" (p. 30), but no further indication is provided in the manual about who these individuals are, where they are from, and what respective experience/expertise they have in item/test development. Item selection and scale development proceeded on a "rational basis" (p. 30). In addition to the PEI, a drug use frequency checklist adapted from adolescent and adult national survey instruments was incorporated into the drug consumption section of the PEI-A.

The initial items and scales of the PEI-A were examined with a sample of 300 drug clinic subjects (150 males, 150 females) for internal scale consistency (alpha coefficients) and interscale correlations. Correlations between Problem Severity Scales "were somewhat higher than desired for scales intended to contribute substantial unique and reliable information about the respondent, ranging from .55 to .92" (p. 33). Alpha correlations of individual scales were good, typically within the .75 to .93 range (pp. 32–33). Following examination of the correlations on this initial sample of subjects "only minor adjustments in item assignment" were made in scales (p. 33).

The content of the Problem Severity Scales is described as "multidimensional, oriented around signs and symptoms of drug abuse and dependence, and not anchored in any single theoretical model" (p. 30). Review of the items on the measure suggests that the content appears appropriate for the purposes listed above. Review of the empirical evidence for sample comparisons, reliability, and validity will help determine if items originally developed for adolescents and refined for adults based on unknown expert opinion are truly valid for adults.

The test items were not analyzed statistically for possible bias. The test was examined for differences in internal consistency across gender and race, and significant differences were not found; however, predictive validity and differential decision making across gender and race have not yet been examined. Differences in primary language of the subjects was not discussed and it is difficult to determine how language (i.e., not primarily English) might affect responses (written or oral) on the PEI-A.

SAMPLES FOR TEST VALIDATION AND NORMING. Three samples were chosen for test norming: 895 drug clinic clients from Minnesota, Illinois, Washington, California, Missouri, and Ontario, although specific numbers from each state are not provided; 410 criminal offenders, most from Minnesota; and 690 nonclinical participants, all from Minnesota. All sample subjects were volunteers. No discussion is provided in the manual regarding the possible impact on client self-report due to the sample selection process, and whether valid interpretation of the results can be made with individuals who may be tested under some type of coercion such as for court-ordered treatment. Sample demographic information is provided in the manual regarding mean age, age range, gender, minority, percent in prior treatment, marital status, employment status, and education (p. 36).

Scores from the measure are compared with the drug clinic sample in the form of T scores; however, score comparisons (T scores) are also provided at the end of the computerized report for the nonclinic sample. Given the restricted geographic sampling of the nonclinic group, it is difficult to determine if this comparison provides useful information for individuals who are not from Minnesota. It is also unclear if the nonclinic sample participated by mail as described on page 35 of the manual or through group testing as described on page 36 of the manual. Both contexts for test taking are somewhat different from the typical administration (e.g., individualized, in drug clinic) described in the manual and may limit score interpretations even further.

The drug clinic sample is described in terms of two groups: outpatient and residential treatment. Only 37.5% of the outpatient drug clinic sample is female (approximately 188). Only 36.3% of the residential drug clinic sample is female (approximately 143). Separate T scores are provided for male and female samples (p. 36). Only approximately 113 members of the outpatient drug clinic sample are of an ethnic minority status, and approximately 68 members of the residential drug clinic sample are of an ethnic minority status. Minority is not defined further (e.g., African American, Hispanic, Native American), although it is conceivable that minority status may differentially impact drug use. In addition, although the gender representation may be an accurate reflection of general population drug use, the small sample size for females limits normative comparisons. Reported drug use patterns may also differ by gender.

Information is not provided on whether the norm groups come from rural or urban settings. A rural or urban context may impact drug use (i.e., availability of drugs). Also, specific numbers are not provided relative to the geographic regions from which the drug clinic samples originate, and as indicated by the authors (p. 36), geographic region may impact reported drug use (i.e., higher cocaine use in California and Washington reported relative to Midwest states and Ontario).

In summary, caution is advised in using the PEI-A with females, minorities, and individuals from geographic regions other than those sampled. In addition, the comparison with nonclinic population may not be useful for individuals outside of Minnesota. The test norms appear to be useful for comparing Caucasian males with possible drug use history with the drug clinic sample.

RELIABILITY. Internal consistency reliabilities are provided (coefficient alpha) for the entire sample and provided for male, female, white, and minority samples (pp. 37–41). In addition, test-retest reliabilities are presented for one week and for one month using the drug clinic sample, although there was some intervening treatment between pre- and posttest scores (pp. 42–43). Only reliabilities for the drug clinic and nonclinic samples will be discussed as these represent the primary comparative groups for examinees.

Coefficient alphas are generally good for the Problem Severity Scales (median .89 range .72 to .94) and the Psychosocial Scales (median .81 range .67 to .91). The coefficient alphas are low for the Validity Scales (median .63 range .58 to .77) (p. 37). The authors claim the validity reliability estimates compare favorably with other instruments, and this may be true; however, these values are just acceptable given the use to be made of these scores.

Median test-retest reliabilities at one week (70 individual) were as follows: Problem Severity scales .71 (.60 to .88), Psychosocial scales .66 (.55 to .87), and Validity Indices .52 (.40 to .57). One-month test-retest reliabilities were lower as expected given intervening treatment (pp. 42–43). Given that some subjects were provided intervening treatment in the one-week test-retest group also, it can reasonably be said that test-retest reliability has not been adequately examined and no conclusions can be drawn regarding temporal stability of the test. This makes it less useful pre- and post-treatment as it is difficult to determine if changes in scores are due to treatment or lack of score stability. This is in conflict with the authors' conclusions, however, that scores can be compared pre- and posttreatment (p. 43).

In summary, the internal consistency estimates of the Problem Severity Scales and the Psychosocial Scales range from good to acceptable. More research

is definitely needed on the stability of the test scores (test-retest) before conclusions can be drawn regarding the test's usefulness pre- and posttreatment.

VALIDITY. One potential use of this instrument is to determine appropriate treatment options for individuals. Drug clinic subjects ($N = 251$) were classified into three referral categories: no treatment, outpatient treatment, and residential treatment based on clinical staff ratings. Mean scores on the PEI-A Problem Severity Scales were examined and expected differences in scores were found for the three groups (p. 46). Future researchers, however, may want to look at the contribution the PEI-A provides above and beyond other information used in making referral decisions. In other words, are these mean score differences useful? Also, significant differences in mean scores according to sample group membership (nonclinical, drug clinic, and criminal offender) were also found (p. 46). Again, an empirical examination as to how this information contributes as part of a comprehensive assessment would be useful.

Seven of the Problem Screens were compared with staff ratings to determine sensitivity and specificity of the screens, essentially the degree of agreement regarding the existence of problems (p. 48). For the total sample, there were significant correlations ($p<.05$) for agreement between the PEI-A and staff ratings for negative ratings (i.e., individual not identified with having problem), but not for positive ratings (i.e., individual identified as having problem) (p. 49).

The Validity Indices were found to correlated as expected with Minnesota Multiphasic Personality Inventory (MMPI) Validity scales (p. 48).

To assess the construct validity of the scale, correlations with tests purported to measure similar constructs were examined. Moderate correlations were found between the Problem Severity Basic Scales scores and the Alcohol Dependence Scale (.41–.66; p. 44; ADS; Horn, Skinner, Wanberg, & Foster, 1982). In addition, correlations are also provided for Problem Severity Scale scores and the Drug Use Frequency Checklist; however, the Drug Use Frequency Checklist is actually part of the PEI-A so the usefulness of this information for construct validity is weakened. The Psychosocial Scales of the PEI-A were found to correlate significantly with MMPI scales, suggesting the psychosocial Scales are measuring psychopathology to some extent (p. 45), but there does not appear to be much differentiation between the PEI-A scales as all but Rejecting Convention and Spiritual Isolation correlate highly with each of the MMPI scales. Finally, information is provided that "select" PEI-A scales (p. 45) correlate significantly with a Significant Other Questionnaire. However, the Significant Other Questionnaire is also developed from PEI-A items, which again attenuates the meaningfulness of this relationship.

In summary, the validity evidence presented in the manual does not appear to address specifically the intended purposes/applications of the test noted above. The content looks good, but much more empirical research is needed on the validity of this instrument specifically related to the applications for which it is intended. Future research should address whether this instrument contributes significantly (above and beyond other information in a comprehensive assessment) to decision making involved in assessing and treating individuals with alcohol and drug use problems.

SUMMARY. The PEI-A may be most useful for examining alcohol and drug use in white males who are compared with a drug clinic sample. Results of this test are intended to tell the clinician whether an individual is similar to individuals in the drug clinic sample and to provide some information on the impact of drugs on the individual's life. Caution is urged in using the PEI-A with females and minorities given the small sample sizes. Geographic region and urban-rural differences may also impact reports of drug use and should be considered by the test user. In addition, this test may not be useful for individuals whose primary language is not English. The use of the nonclinic scores for comparisons is questionable for individuals outside Minnesota. Estimates of the internal consistency reliability of the scales and content appear good. Additional research on test-retest reliability is needed. More research on the validity of the PEI-A as part of a comprehensive assessment is needed. The PEI-A looks promising, but users are encouraged to heed the test author's statement that this test should only be used as part of comprehensive assessment.

REVIEWER'S REFERENCES

Horn, J. L., Skinner, H. A., Wanberg, K., & Foster, F. M. (1982). Alcohol Dependence Scale (ADS). Toronto: Addiction Research Foundation.

Toneatto, T. (1992). [Review of the Personal Experience Inventory.] In J. J. Kramer & J. C. Conoley (Eds.), *The eleventh mental measurements yearbook* (pp. 660–661). Lincoln, NE: Buros Institute of Mental Measurements.

Tucker, J. A. (1992). [Review of the Personal Experience Inventory.] In J. J. Kramer & J. C. Conoley (Eds.), *The eleventh mental measurements yearbook* (pp. 661–663). Lincoln, NE: Buros Institute of Mental Measurements.

Review of the Personal Experience Inventory for Adults by CLAUDIA R. WRIGHT, Professor of Educational Psychology, California State University, Long Beach, CA:

The Personal Experience Inventory for Adults (PEI-A) is a standardized self-report instrument for use by service providers in the substance abuse treatment field to assess patterns of abuse and related problems in adult clients (age 19 or older). The two-part, 270-item PEI-A is made up of 10 problem severity scales and 11 psychosocial scales, 5 validity indicators, and 10 problem screens; it parallels in content and form the two-part, 300-item Personal Experience Inventory (PEI; 11:284) developed for use with adolescents (age 18 or younger). A broad theoretical framework, influenced by Alcoholics Anonymous, social learning, and psychiatric models, underlies the development of both inventories. The manual presents a thorough treatment of test development, standardization, and validation procedures along with clear test administration and computer-scoring guidelines and useful strategies for score interpretation. The inventory is written at a sixth-grade reading level. No provisions are made for non-English-speaking test takers.

NORMING PROCEDURES. Norm tables were constructed separately for males and females in two standardization samples (clinical and nonclinical). Normative data were obtained primarily from Midwestern Whites, raising concerns about the generalizability of score interpretations to clients classified as nonwhite. Demographic information presented in the PEI-A manual indicates that 20% of the clinical sample ($n = 895$) was classified as minority. Clinic respondents attended outpatient and residential Alcoholics Anonymous-based programs at 12 sites (located in 3 midwestern and 2 western states and 1 Canadian province). No rationale was provided for site selection. A total of 690 Minnesota residents comprised the nonclinical sample; 11% were classified as minority. A sample of 410 criminal offenders (77% were male; 68% of the sample was nonwhite) was used to provide data for some validation analyses.

Caution is warranted in applying the PEI-A norms to members of nonwhite groups in either clinical or nonclinical settings. The test developer is to be commended for briefly acknowledging this limitation. Sampling that includes more regions, broader ethnic representation, and types of treatment program sites is essential.

RELIABILITY. For 1,995 respondents, median Cronbach alphas were (a) Problem Severity Scales = .89 (range: .81–.93); (b) Psychosocial Scales = .80 (range: .75–.88); and (c) three of the five Validity Indicators = .70 (range: .65–.73). When subsamples were broken out by gender, ethnicity (white or minority), and setting (nonclinical, drug clinic, or criminal offender), patterns of reliability estimates were comparable to those obtained with the total sample. One-week (n = 58; .42–.78, mdn = .69) and one-month (n = 49; .39–.72, mdn = .52) stability indexes for problem screens were lower than desired due to respondents' exposure to treatment programs during the test-retest intervals.

CONTENT VALIDATION. Common content validation procedures were followed. Researchers and treatment providers rated PEI items intended for inclusion in the PEI-A with respect to clinical relevance and importance to adult substance abuse. Based upon rater feedback, minor item modifications were made.

CRITERION-RELATED VALIDITY. Concurrent validity evidence for the PEI-A was provided by data comparisons examining the effects on scale scores of (a) treatment history for substance abuse among drug clinic clients (no sample size reported); (b) referral recommendation (no treatment, outpatient, or residential) (N = 251); (c) setting (nonclinical, drug clinic, or criminal offender) (N = 1,978); and (d) *DSM-III-R* (American Psychiatric Association, 1987) diagnosis of abuse or dependence upon alcohol or drugs (N = 244). The observed group differences obtained from scores on the 10 Problem Severity Scales supported the view that individuals referred to treatment settings (outpatient or residential) had greater problems with higher substance use, dependence, and related consequences of usage compared to those for whom no drug treatment was recommended. The 11 Psychosocial Scales fared less well in distinguishing among the three groups with only three scales (Negative Self-Image, Deviant Behavior, and Peer Drug Use) yielding statistically significant differences. In a separate analysis, scores obtained from a nonclinical subsample (n = 687) were significantly lower on each of the 21 scales (all p < .01) when compared with those from drug clinic (n = 887) and offender (n = 404) groups. For the *DSM-III-R* Diagnosis comparison, clients identified as dependent on alcohol or drugs had significantly higher scores on the 5 Basic Scales when compared to those classified as abusing these substances.

Although the measure is purportedly used to assist in treatment referral, no predictive validity information was presented linking referral decisions based upon standing on the PEI-A scales and outcome success.

CONSTRUCT VALIDITY. Only modest to moderate levels of construct validity evidence were presented based on correlations between PEI-A Prob-lem Severity Basic scale scores and performance on the Alcohol Dependence Scale (ADS; Horn, Skinner, Wanberg, & Foster, 1982) and the PEI-A Drug Use Frequency Checklist. Moderate coefficients were obtained for a sample of 89 clients indicating that the 5 Basic Scale scores were somewhat related to ADS scores (.52–.63, mdn = .59) and Checklist scores (.41–.66; mdn = .55). For a sample of 213 clinic respondents, correlations among the 11 PEI-A Psychosocial Scales and 9 Minnesota Multiphasic Personality Inventory (MMPI) Scales yielded 62 out of 99 possible coefficients ranging from .20–.69, mdn = .38 (all p < .001) indicating, for the most part, only modest levels of shared variance (4% to 48% explained, mdn = 14%). Moderate coefficients (above the median) were associated with PEI-A scales that deal with personal adjustment issues (e.g., Negative Self-Image, Psychological Disturbance, Social Isolation, and Absence of Goals). PEI-A scale scores dealing with personal values and environmental influences (e.g., Rejecting Convention and Spiritual Isolation) yielded negligible correlations with the MMPI. PEI-A and MMPI validity indicators also were moderately correlated.

Inspection of intercorrelations among the 10 Problem Severity Scales revealed moderate to strong coefficients posing a multicollinearity problem. It is evident from data reported in the manual that the statistical contribution of unique variance to score interpretation associated with each of the 5 Clinical Scales adds little or no unique information (r_{xy}s ranged from .04 to .09, mdn = .05). This outcome was consistent with that reported for the same 10 scales of the PEI. The 5 Clinical Scales were retained "because users have found these scales helpful" (manual, p. 33). The retention of redundant scales requires more detailed explanation than that provided in the manual. For future research and test development purposes, targeting items from scales that contribute unique information for provider applications and removing redundant items would strengthen this section of the inventory.

Intercorrelations among the Psychosocial Scales revealed patterns of coefficients more distinctive of a multidimensional scale (as intended) with proportions of unique variance ranging from .18 to .57 (mdn = .29). However, lower reliability estimates and the inability of these scales to distinguish between referral groups is of concern.

SUMMARY. The Personal Experience Inventory for Adults (PEI-A) offers a beginning point to the service provider for assessment. Most PEI-A scale scores demonstrate adequate levels of reliability and distinguish between clinical and nonclinical groups. Current norms may be too restrictive for some settings. Based upon validity evidence provided, caution is warranted in all testing with use of scores from the Clinical Scales, which are redundant with the Basic Scales and with scores from the Psychosocial Scales, which have shown only low to moderate relationships with related constructs. PEI-A computer-generated recommendations for individual clients should be considered in light of these limitations and decisions made in conjunction with other measures.

REVIEWER'S REFERENCES

Horn, J. L., Skinner, H. A., Wanberg, K., & Foster, F. M. (1982). *Alcohol Dependence Scale (ADS)*. Toronto: Addiction Research Foundation.
American Psychiatric Association. (1987). *Diagnostic and statistical manual of mental disorders* (3rd ed.). Washington, DC: Author.

[226]
Personal Skills Map.

Purpose: "Offers a means for the self-assessment of personal skills."
Population: Ages 13–19.
Publication Date: 1993.
Acronym: PSM.
Scores: 14 scales: Self-Esteem, Growth Motivation, Change Orientation, Interpersonal Assertion, Interpersonal Aggression, Interpersonal Deference, Interpersonal Awareness, Empathy, Drive Strength, Decision Making, Time Management, Sales Orientation, Commitment Ethic, Stress Management.
Administration: Group or individual.
Forms, 3: The Personal Skills Map, The Personal Skills Survey, Teacher Observation Test.
Price Data, 1994: $125 per 10 Personal Skills Map; $62.50 per 25 Personal Skills Survey (specify grades 3–5 or 6–12); $60 per 25 Teacher Observation Test.
Time: (30–40) minutes for Personal Skills Map; (20–25) minutes for Personal Skills Survey; (10–15) minutes for Teacher Observation Test.
Comments: Part of Becoming a Champion program; Personal Skills Survey and Teacher Observation Test are components derived from the Personal Skills Map.
Author: People Builders International, Inc.
Publisher: Chronicle Guidance Publications, Inc.

TEST REFERENCES

1. Kingdon, M. A., & Blimline, C. A. (1987). Evaluating the effectiveness of career development training for women. *Career Development Quarterly, 35*, 220-227.

Review of the Personal Skills Map by DELWYN L. HARNISCH, Director, Office of Educational Testing, Research & Service, and Associate Professor of Educational Psychology, University of Illinois at Urbana—Champaign, Champaign, IL:

The purpose of the Personal Skills Map (PSM) is to offer a means for the self-assessment of personal skills and self-awareness for students in grades 6–12. After having taken the Personal Skills Map, students are allowed to enroll in a program entitled, "Becoming A Champion," which is centered on the "concept that a person can change and develop creatively as he or she learns and practices new skills under the guidance of a skilled counselor or teacher" (p. 2). The authors emphasize the goals for a positive approach to self-assessment and recommend that each individual in the program "focuses on Skills to Develop/Change Areas in acquiring new information and effectiveness in building skills" (p. 2). Two components are derived from the Personal Skills Map, the Personal Skills Survey and the Teacher Observation Test.

ADMINISTRATION AND SCORING. The PSM includes two forms (PSM-E for elementary and PSM-A for adults) that may be administered to individuals and groups by psychologists, counselors, and teachers. Group administration of the PSM-E is not recommended below grade 3. The current version of the PSM was standardized in the English language with the manual published only in English. Student information from the PSM provides 14 scales in three major dimensions of personal effectiveness. This information highlights the extent to which the individual possesses 14 skills and interpersonal communication style and readiness for change.

Directions for each form request the respondent to circle the response that is most like them at work: "Most descriptive (M), sometimes descriptive (S), or least descriptive (L)" according to an "honest response of how you describe yourself." The respondent is then asked to transfer the number to the box to the right of each statement that corresponds to their response. Subtotals are created for each column and added to the remaining item scores to arrive at the total score. All total scores are then transferred to the personal map and plotted with lines connecting all score points to show one's personal assessment profile for each of the scales on the four major dimensions of personal skills: Intrapersonal skills are made up with scales of self-esteem (confidence) and growth motivation (future oriented); Interpersonal skills are made up with scales of assertion, interpersonal awareness (appropriateness), and empathy: Career/Life skills are made up with scales of drive strength (goal setting), decision making, time management, sales orientation, commitment ethic, and stress management (self-care); and Communication styles are made up of scales for interpersonal assertion, interpersonal aggression, and interpersonal deference. Raw scores are then converted to standard scores (*T*-scale) and categorized as "in need of development" if below 40, "enhanced" if above 60, and as "a strength" if score is between 40 and 60. Administration time ranges from 30 to 50 minutes. Each item on the PSM requires an independent response that has no bearing on any other items.

TEST DESCRIPTION. The individual may enter a program oriented toward the acquisition of personal skills. The 14 areas include Self-Esteem, Growth Motivation, Change Orientation, Interpersonal Assertion, Interpersonal Aggression, Interpersonal Deference, Interpersonal Awareness, Empathy, Drive Strength, Decision Making, Time Management, Sales Orientation, Commitment Ethic, and Stress Management.

RELIABILITY. The manual contains information on reliability studies conducted for the original PSM. Test-retest reliability coefficients for a sample of 24 undergraduate students with one week separating the two administrations of the test ranged from .64 (Empathy scale) to .94 (Sales Orientation scale). The authors note that because many variables can impact personal skills, reliability may not remain stable or fixed over long periods of time. No mention is made of the number of items that make up each scale in the manual. No internal consistency measures of reliability are found in the manual.

No reliability data were available on the Teacher Observation Test (TOT), the Personal Skills Survey (PSS), and the Computerized Personal Skills Map System (CPSMS) rating scales.

VALIDITY. The manual points out that an important test of the validity of the PSM was to determine whether the instrument could effectively differentiate between normal, healthy students possessing personal skills and other individuals functioning with below-average personal skills. The authors chose to administer the test to three carefully selected research groups. The first group consisted of 100 skilled professional aides in the behavioral sciences. Most were doctoral and master's degree students. The second (*n* = 99) consisted of individuals randomly selected from a "normal" population. The third group (*n* = 122) was a voluntary group who had sought counseling and psychotherapy services. PSM scale means, mean differences, and *t* ratios were computed for comparisons among the groups. Tables are given in the manual depicting the results. The

results show that the PSM does differentiate among the three groups and suggested that the PSM may be useful in clinical settings.

Evidence for concurrent validity is provided by comparing the correlations among the derived PSM scales with measures from standardized personality inventories that include the Personal Orientation Inventory (Shostrom, 1962), Edwards Personal Preference Schedule (Edwards, 1953), Sixteen Personality Factor Questionnaire (Cattell, 1956), and Minnesota Multiphasic Inventory by Hathaway and McKinley (1943). The small samples used for these concurrent validity studies (*n* = 40, 28, 22, and 17) are only suggestive of what these relationships are likely to be. Additional research is needed to further evaluate the validity of the PSM scales.

No validity data were available for scores from the Teacher Observation Test (TOT), the Personal Skills Survey (PSS), and the Computerized Personal Skills Map System (CPSMS) with the Personal Skills Map scales or other external measures.

NORMS. The test administration manual provides data and tables about norms and standardization samples. The sample included 1,157 adolescents ages 13–19 enrolled in public and private secondary schools. A variety of students were sampled from large urban, suburban, and rural schools, as well as a group of juvenile offenders. The standardization sample included Africa-American, Hispanic, and white students. The authors recommend local norming of the PSM to increase the validity of scores within a specific setting. They suggest attending to grade level and gender distinctions. Based on the standardization sample, adolescent norms consisting of means and standard deviation on each of the scales are provided along with individual tables by sex and also for gender groups at the two levels of age (13–15 vs. 16–19-year-olds).

The manual provides normative data consisting of means and standard deviations for an adult sample of 1,400 on each of the PSM scales. No information is available in the manual to describe the normative sample. Correlations among the PSM scales are based on the research and standardization sample of 359. Limited demographic data are presented on the standardization samples and no normative data are provided on culturally diverse groups.

The authors state that the PSM is effective as a program development model for use with diverse cultural groups. Caution must be emphasized when applying an instrument without any normative data for culturally diverse groups. Further work is needed to document the reliability and validity of scores from the scales in multiple-language versions before blindly using it for cross-cultural research and program development.

SUMMARY. The PSM is a very interesting battery that provides potentially useful information about adolescents' personal skills, communication style, and motivation toward change. The items have been carefully researched and developed. The Personal Skills Map can serve as a tool for use by counseling programs or special needs programs. It has potential to be useful to administrators, counselors, teachers, parents, and students in making choices about the future, building personal development programs, structuring individual or group counseling, or selecting specific support services for young people. The validity data for the Personal Skills Map show the need for examining the performances relative to age and gender groups but the personal map profile of personal skills disregards factors such as age and sex. This is a serious omission and needs to be corrected in the next edition. The norm groups are not well described and appear to lack generalizability. The authors also provide little evidence to support the culture-free status of these inventories. Despite these problems, the authors should be commended for developing an instrument that focuses on providing a positive approach to formulating a change program for the individual or group.

[227]
Personal Style Assessment, Jung-Parry Form.

Purpose: To assess an individual's relative strength on Jung's four personal styles, or "psychological types."
Population: Adults.
Publication Date: 1992.
Scores, 4: Thinker, Intuitor, Sensor, Feeler.
Administration: Group or individual.
Manual: No manual.
Price Data, 1992: $80 per set of 20 including tests, answer sheets, and interpretation folder.
Time: (20–30) minutes.
Comments: Self-administered; self-scored.
Author: Scott B. Parry.
Publisher: Training House, Inc.

Review of the Personal Style Assessment, Jung-Parry Form by VICKI S. PACKMAN, Senior Assessment Analyst, Salt River Project, Phoenix, AZ:

The Personal Style Assessment (PSA) was developed by Scott B. Parry to assess an individual's relative strength on Jung's four personal styles or "psychological types." It is self-administered, self-

scored, and is applicable for both individual and group administrations. The PSA has four scores: Sensing, Intuition, Thinking, and Feeling.

The PSA consists of a two-page Assessment Exercise, a two-page mark-sensitive answer sheet, and an eight-page Interpretation Sheet. The Assessment Exercise consists of 16 item stems with four responses that are ranked on a 4-point scale. Examples of items include: When solving a problem, I tend to; My idea of a pleasant vacation is to, and; I like to read books that deal with.

The reviewer found the forced ranking of item responses to be tedious. The directions require you to assign numbers 4 through 1 to each of the four statements that follow each item. The numbers mean: "4" most like you; "3" next most like you; "2" next most like you; and "1" least like you. This method forces the test taker to dictate four distinct preferences for each item. Assigning the number "1" and "4" was usually fairly easy but discriminating between a "2" and a "3" for the remaining responses was very tiresome for some items.

The squares for writing the ranked responses on the answer sheet are small and awkward to use. Scoring the PSA is just as tedious as the ranking. The second page of the mark-sensitive answer sheet has the words "Feeler," "Intuitor," "Thinker," or "Sensor" preprinted next to each square. These descriptors appear in different sequences and the test taker searches out the 16 numbers they have assigned to each descriptor and adds these numbers for a total. The total is then divided by 1.6 and the four totals should sum to 100. The scoring would be greatly simplified if the second page of the answer sheet branched into four columns, one for each personality style.

The Interpretation Sheet is written in a very easy-to-read style that relates personality traits to the hand of cards we are dealt at birth. This sheet does a nice job of explaining how behavior patterns can be perceived as both effective and ineffective by different personality types and how our behavior patterns can be both assets and liabilities. The author encourages readers to develop their awareness and sensitivity to the styles of others and adjust or "flex" their style "to meet others on their own wavelength" (Interpretation Sheet, p. 2). Suggestions for successfully interacting with different styles are provided.

The PSA has some serious deficiencies regarding technical properties. There is no manual nor any published studies that address evidence of the validity and reliability for this instrument. The technical soundness of the PSA is unsubstantiated and the instrument fails to meet the *Standards for Educational and Psychological Testing* (AERA, APA, & NCME, 1985). The PSA cannot be recommended for assessing Jung's personal styles or psychological types. The Myers-Briggs Type Indicator (MBTI; T4:1702) is a superior instrument for this function. It assesses the same four psychological types plus four additional ones. The MBTI has an excellent manual, has withstood rigorous research over time, and has documented evidence of validity and reliability.

SUMMARY. The Personal Styles Assessment holds promise but lacks scientific evidence of validity and reliability. Until these deficiencies are remedied the reviewer recommends that the Myers-Briggs Type Indicator be utilized for measuring Jung's personal styles or psychological types.

REVIEWER'S REFERENCE
American Educational Research Association, American Psychological Association, & National Council on Measurement in Education. (1985). *Standards for Educational and Psychological Testing.* Washington, DC: American Psychological Association, Inc.

[228]
Personal Style Indicator.

Purpose: Designed to increase mutual understanding, acceptance and communication among people and to increase self-awareness.
Population: Adults.
Publication Dates: 1988–1989.
Acronym: PSI.
Scores, 4: Behavioral Action, Cognitive Analysis, Interpersonal Harmony, Affective Expression.
Administration: Group.
Price Data, 1993: $12 per test booklet; $10 per interpretations booklet ('89, 32 pages); $15 per audiotape (Living with Style); $35 per PSI/JSI Leader's manual ('88, 75 pages).
Time: (90) minutes.
Comments: Self-administered, -scored, -interpreted.
Authors: Terry D. Anderson (test and audiotape), Everett T. Robinson, Jonathan Clark (audiotape), and Susan Clark (audiotape).
Publisher: Consulting Resource Group International, Inc.

Review of the Personal Style Indicator by JAMES T. AUSTIN, Research Specialist 2, Vocational Instructional Materials Lab, The Ohio State University, Columbus, OH:

The Personal Style Indicator (PSI) is published by a self-described "human resource development and change management consulting company" (p. i). The instrument is presented for self-report, self-scoring, and self-interpretation. Its stated objective is to "provoke further self-exploration and self-discovery" (p. iii) by respondents, as individuals or in groups. According to the leader's manual, this goal is attained by providing respondents with a "subjective self-appraisal" of their profile across modes of response to the environment. Personal styles are behavioral, affective, cognitive, and interpersonal. A six-step procedure for understanding one's personal style follows the PSI. The authors state in multiple places that the scale is not intended for evaluation, is not predictive, and that it was "never intended to be a psychometrically rigorous, scientifically validated instrument" (p. 3). I concur with that self-assessment.

For this review I conceptualize assessment within a system involving, at a minimum, publishers, users, and individuals completing the measure. Further, I am guided by the principle that all validation is construct related (Cronbach, 1989; Guion, 1980; Messick, 1995). What constructs influence scores? What inferences are warranted on the basis of test scores? What evidence is integrated by the test developer to give confidence to test users? There is now adequate guidance in the literature on scale construction and validation (e.g., Clark & Watson, 1995). After receiving the measures and documentation, I conducted a search to supplement the references provided by the publisher. My search covered library and World Wide Web (WWW) databases. In addition to material placed on the Web by the publisher, I found an unpublished dissertation by Cotroneo (1987). Its database abstract stated that an earlier version of the PSI (five style dimensions) was given to a sample of adults across eight occupational areas. A three-item job satisfaction measure was also administered. Predicted differences between occupational areas and a positive correlation between PSI scale scores and job satisfaction scores were confirmed. (Because there are other measures that have the same name, there is some question about the PSI used in this unpublished dissertation and the PSI reviewed here.)

A positive feature is that the conceptual framework within which the PSI rests, the Personal Style Theory, is outlined on pages 7–9. According to this framework, behavior is viewed as a transaction between person and environment. Compare this treatment with the treatment of person-environment-behavior provided by Bandura (1978). An individual's profile across the four personal styles is one of six factors that influence behavior. Three of the factors, bio-physical, self-worth, and personal styles are internal, whereas the remaining three, social learning, environment, and traumatics are external.

Then the authors present the Personal Style Model (pp. 9–14). It is unclear if any distinctions are drawn between the theory and the model. There are three bipolar dimensions; extroversion-introversion, people-task orientation, and verbal-nonverbal. The model was created by aggregating facets of existing personality theories (e.g., Fromm, 1964; Horney, 1942; Jung, 1928; Lewin, 1936) with speculation about neuropsychology, in particular the reticular activating system and brain hemispheric specialization. But there is no evidence that any effort was made to integrate these separate perspectives on individual differences. The number of styles may be based on how many types were (a) identified in previous theories, and (b) utilized in popular personality type indicators. The authors insist that styles and types are not equivalent. At one point they declare that style is but one factor affecting the broader construct of personality and its development (p. 7), and then at a later point they declare that style is a broad term encompassing the complexities of the concept of personality (p. 23). The quadrants of personal style identified by the authors are Behavioral (action), Affective (expression), Cognitive (analysis), and Interpersonal (harmony). The dimensions were apparently named via the authors' intuitions, experiences with students and clients, and feedback from workshop participants.

The PSI consists of 16 items in which four words are rank ordered by respondents in terms of self-descriptiveness. Scoring is accomplished with a carbon sensitive sheet immediately following the scale and a scoring key is provided on page 30 of the leader's manual. The response sheet is composed of 64 primary descriptor adjectives arranged in 16 rows of 4. All four personal style dimensions are randomized within each row. The scale is ipsative, meaning that it measures intraindividual variance, and requires nonstandard statistical treatment (a point noted by the authors on p. 38). Each of the answer options consists of a primary descriptor with three subdescriptors listed beneath it. Although this arrangement may be an adequate design, there apparently has been no statistical analysis of the primary adjectives or the subdescriptors. The primary descriptors were selected "through informal and subjective procedures of item analysis" (p. 29). How the subdescriptors were selected is not reported. The idea of giving subdescriptors to assist the selection of the primary adjective may be a positive addition to the design of such instruments—but only if the subdescriptors have been selected using adequate statisti-

cal tests or a conceptual rationale. If they do not correlate strongly with their primary descriptor and the style dimension they are subdescribing, as well as correlate weakly with all other primary descriptors and style dimensions, they may invalidate responses.

Two documents accompany the PSI, itself a 16-page document. One is the leader's manual and the other is In-Depth Interpretations. The manual, which addresses the PSI and a companion titled the Job Style Indicator (JSI; 164), begins with a preface that makes several key points. Among them are that the PSI and JSI are intended for developmental purposes, rigorous psychometrics were not a primary emphasis of development, and that further research is required and welcomed by the authors.

According to the leader's manual, scale development was based upon overcoming difficulties one of the developers (Anderson) had encountered with other self-appraisal instruments. Although the authors insist that the PSI is not scientific, the description of it attached to the response sheet states clearly that it was "scientifically developed" (p. 2).

Concerning the psychometric adequacy of the instrument, the evidence is sparse. The retest reliability of the instrument as reported in the manual was estimated on a sample of 20 or 25 respondents with an unknown lapse of time. A correlation of "+.85 on each of the four scales" (p. 37) was reported. This information does not give an adequate basis for any conclusions about reliability other than the need for additional study. There is no validity evidence presented to a test user other than the dissertation noted above. Due to the lack of evidence for validity of the Personal Style Theory and the PSI, the In-Depth Interpretations included with the response sheet are difficult to evaluate. The extensive description of how the in-depth interpretations were prepared cannot hide their clinical and subjective nature. Even when an instrument is based upon theory and constructed utilizing pertinent psychometric principles, the validity of interpretations of this sort require substantial support. This requirement is especially important when any sort of developmental diagnosis and intervention is undertaken, whether for self or another.

SUMMARY. The authors of the PSI confidently categorize their instrument as developmental, as a learning tool. The classification is then used to minimize psychometric standards that apply to all interpretations of measurement, whether scores are designed for developmental or other purposes. It does not serve the assessment community well when such arguments are used to dispense with the need for careful research into score interpretations. In addition, it appears that there were multiple opportunities for the developers to conduct research while they prepared the PSI. For example, the Personal Style Model and the authors' experience could have been used to create hypotheses concerning the likely effects of different developmental strategies suggested on the basis of PSI profiles. Measurement of multiple criteria and follow-up with clients could have evaluated such hypotheses. Moreover, the in-depth interpretations are hypotheses of a different sort, and are capable of empirical evaluation. Disappointingly to this reviewer, there is extensive discussion about the mechanics of conducting workshops based on the PSI, material which seems oriented at consulting applications of the instrument that do not appear warranted. It is curious to read multiple caveats about the instrument but then to see materials that facilitate applied use of the instrument by untrained individuals. I cannot recommend this instrument without much more evidence supporting score interpretations.

REVIEWER'S REFERENCES

Jung, C. G. (1928). *Contributions to analytical psychology.* (H. G. Baynes & C. F. Baynes, Trans.). New York: Harcourt Brace.

Lewin, K. (1936). *Principles of topological psychology.* New York: McGraw-Hill.

Horney, K. (1942). *Self-analysis.* New York: Norton.

Fromm, E. (1964). *The heart of man: Its genius for good and evil.* New York: Harper & Row.

Bandura, A. (1978). The self-system in reciprocal determinism. *American Psychologist, 33,* 344–358.

Guion, R. M. (1980). On trinitarian doctrines of validity. *Professional Psychology, 11,* 385–398.

Cotroneo, K. J. (1987). *A validity study of the Personal Style Indicator.* Unpublished doctoral dissertation, University of Georgia.

Cronbach, L. J. (1989). Construct validation after thirty years. In R. L. Linn (Ed.), *Intelligence: Measurement, theory, and public policy* (pp. 147–171). Urbana, IL: University of Illinois Press.

Clark, L. A., & Watson, D. (1995). Constructing validity: Basic issues in objective scale development. *Psychological Assessment, 7,* 309–319.

Messick, S. (1995). Validity of psychological assessment: Validation of inferences from persons' responses and performances as scientific inquiry into score meaning. *American Psychologist, 50,* 741–749.

Review of the Personal Style Indicator by KUSUM SINGH, Associate Professor, Educational Leadership and Policy Studies, College of Human Resources and Education, Virginia Tech, Blacksburg, VA:

According to the authors, the Personal Style Indicator (PSI) is designed to identify a person's basic style of responding to people and tasks. Although the authors further claim that the instrument will assist in increasing mutual understanding, acceptance, and communication among people and would increase self-awareness, they do not offer any empirical evidence to support these claims.

The PSI is self-administered, self-scored, and self-interpreted. The PSI is intended to be an informal, descriptive self-report questionnaire. It uses a forced-choice format to yield a subjective self-appraisal of a person's typical mode of responding to people and to the environment. The four subscores are calculated for each respondent: Behavioral Action, Cognitive Analysis, Interpersonal Harmony, and Affective Expression. The PSI response sheet presents 16 rows of words, each row consisting of four descriptive words. Three clarifying definitions are provided under each descriptive word. The respondent gives a ranking of 4, 3, 2, and 1 to each word according to how close the word comes in describing the person, 4 being the most descriptive and 1 being the least descriptive. Based on the scores in four categories—Behavioral Action, Cognitive Analysis, Interpersonal Harmony, and Affective Expression—a respondent can graph his or her personal style. The individual respondent can assess his or her personal style following the steps provided in the manual. In the first step the respondent reads about the four main personal styles based on earlier research and theories of personality. In the second step, the respondent graphs his or her personal style based on the scores in four corresponding areas. As a third step, general style tendencies with general orientations, typical strengths, and common difficulties of each style are discussed. The reader/respondent is appropriately warned against simplistic thinking and the dangers of pigeonholing oneself and others in tight categories. Step four involves reading the interpretive summary of the individual's style. Step five provides guidelines to become more flexible, and to adopt style shifting to become more effective in interpersonal relationships and in task performance. In step six the respondent is asked to write short responses to indicate what they have learned through the PSI. The authors state that the PSI adopts an innovative approach to self-assessment, employing an interpretive perspective of personality evaluation.

According to the authors the PSI is a learning tool. Its purpose is to help people to understand themselves better, both their uniqueness as individuals and their similarities with other people. Although the authors state that the PSI is intended to facilitate increased awareness and improved communication among people, they cite no evidence that it does that. In absence of any data, it is hard to evaluate these claims.

The PSI user is provided with a leader's manual and a manual of in-depth interpretations. The manuals are not technical manuals and do not provide information in such areas as samples used in piloting, testing, and validation; psychometric properties of test reliability and validity; and norms, etc. Instead, the manuals present guidelines for the use of the PSI, the theoretical foundations the test is built on, and how it can be suitably used. In the leader's manual, the authors provide a detailed description of the theory of personal style and present comprehensive interpretations of the personal styles. The manual also comments on how the personal style affects personality development and individual behavior patterns. But no empirical or anecdotal evidence is provided for its so-called beneficial effects.

SAMPLE. The authors are careful in pointing out that the PSI is not a psychometric instrument so they have not provided systematic information on samples and sample sizes in piloting, testing, and validation. The authors categorize the PSI as a learning tool—a sort of self-help exercise. It is stated that the development work on the PSI was done using samples of college students, counselors, and social service workers. The authors also indicate that the descriptive words in the instrument and the three clarifying definitions for every descriptive word were selected after much field testing and repeated work with groups of people. Despite such references to field testing to develop the instrument, the authors have not provided any precise information on the samples used and sample sizes. It was not intended to produce normative data and should not be viewed as a standardized personality test. The scores of the individuals cannot be compared with each other.

RELIABILITY/VALIDITY. The authors of the PSI note that it is not a psychometric, scientifically validated instrument supported by evidence from empirical research. The PSI was developed based on earlier research in personality types and reflects a synthesis of previous theories of personality but also on "observations and interviews with hundreds of people over significant periods of time" (p. 37). The authors acknowledge that the PSI needs empirical investigation to support its reliability and validity, and future research may establish reliability and validity of its scores. In absence of any data on reliability and validity, it is not possible to make any evaluation of the PSI's psychometric properties. Although the authors do not cite any systematic evidence in support of its reliability and validity, they do mention their continuous and considerable efforts in increasing the instrument's reliability by field testing the word list repeatedly and by including the clarifying definitions of the words that were also extensively field-tested for meaning, ambiguity, and

misinterpretations. No data are provided on the construct validation of the PSI although the authors present considerable work on creating a conceptual framework and synthesis of earlier theories of personality. This logical approach to construct development is mentioned by the authors. The authors also present a detailed list of the uses of the PSI for individuals, families, counselors, educators, and organizations.

SUMMARY. The PSI is a self-assessment of an individual's personal style of responding to people and to environment. The authors claim many additional benefits such as increased awareness, better communication, and improved interpersonal relations but they cite no evidence, empirical or otherwise, to support these claims. The PSI cannot be evaluated from the conventional psychometric perspective because the authors provide no relevant information in this regard. They acknowledge that future empirical research may provide data to support the reliability and validity of the PSI's scores. It is evident that considerable research was carried out in the development of the four dimensions of the personal style and the PSI reflects the synthesis of earlier research and theories of personality. Manuals are well written and provide step-by-step guidelines for self-appraisal and in-depth interpretations in general orientations, strengths, and common difficulties of each style. The manual also provides information on the appropriate uses of the PSI and warns against simplistic pigeonholing of individuals into tight categories. To sum, the PSI may be exactly what its authors characterize it to be: a "stimulant," an exercise that stimulates thinking and discussions among individuals and groups. But in absence of relevant data, its other stated goals cannot be evaluated.

[229]
Personal Styles Inventory [PSI-120].

Purpose: Provides a comprehensive assessment of normal personality characteristics.
Population: Adults.
Publication Dates: 1990–1994.
Acronym: PSI-120.
Scores, 24: Styles of "Expressing Emotions" (Sympathetic, Enthusiastic, Expansive, Confronting, Self-Willed, Reserved, Modest, Patient); Styles of "Doing Things" (Agreeing, Affiliating, Excitement-Seeking, Venturing, Restless, Solitary, Self-Restrained, Regulating); Styles of "Thinking" (Traditional, Dedicated, Imaginative, Inquiring, Individualistic, Skeptical, Practical, Focused).
Administration: Group or individual.
Price Data, 1994: $55 per introductory kit including 20 inventories, 20-use scoring diskette (specify 5.25-inch

or 3.5-inch IBM diskette), and manual; $47.50 per 20 inventories and 20-use scoring diskette; $155 per 100 inventories and 100-use scoring diskette; $22.50 per manual.

Time: (20–30) minutes.

Authors: Joseph T. Kunce, Corrine S. Cope, and Russel M. Newton.

Publisher: Educational & Psychological Consultants, Inc.

Cross References: See T4:1993 (4 references).

TEST REFERENCES

1. Kunce, J. T., & Angelone, E. O. (1990). Personality characteristics of counselors: Implications for rehabilitation counselor roles and functions. *Rehabilitation Counselor Bulletin, 34,* 4–15.

2. Holliday, G. A., Koller, J. R., & Kunce, J. T. (1996). Personality attributes of high IQ/high achieving gifted adolescents: Implications of the personal styles model. *Journal for the Education of the Gifted, 20,* 84–102.

Review of the Personal Styles Inventory [PSI—120] by PAUL A. ARBISI, Assessment Clinic Director, Psychology Service, Minneapolis Veterans Affairs Medical Center, Minneapolis, MN:

The development of the Personal Styles Inventory—120 (PSI—120) is based on the proposition that the adaptive valance of personality characteristics is situationally defined. That is, under certain circumstances the manifestation of specific personality traits can be adaptive or maladaptive. Thus, the PSI—120 eschews an evaluative determinant (normal vs. pathological) and purports to indicate the probability of occurrence of a behavior or set of behaviors within three broad subsystems of human experience: emotional, behavioral, and cognition. Unlike other so called "normal" personality inventories (e.g., the NEO-PI [Costa & McCrae, 1985]), the PSI—120 embraces a two-factor resolution rather than the prevailing Big Five. Also, when compared to the NEO-PI, the PSI—120 does not share the wealth of data supporting the underlying structure or clinical utility of the five-factor model (Costa & Widiger, 1994). Be that as it may, clinical case examples provided in the manual illustrate the effectiveness of the PSI—120 in establishing treatment goals for a troubled poly-substance-abusing adolescent, providing vocational counseling to a dissatisfied 40-year-old salesman, making decisions regarding the formation of a management team, and resolving conflict arising within an existing management team. Moreover, examples of PSI—120 applications within medical settings, career counseling, interpersonal interactions, and clinical assessments are also provided. This remarkable array of applications threatens to make the PSI—120 one of the most widely used instruments in the clinicians' assessment repertoire.

Unfortunately, the weight of the evidence suggests that the PSI—120 should remain an experimental instrument and without further revision must stay out of the clinic or counseling office.

TEST MATERIALS. As mentioned above, the manual details several examples of applications for the PSI—120 across a broad range of settings. Great attention is given to the configural interpretation of scores and an impressive range of descriptors are provided to assist in the generation of a meaningful interpretation. Administration of the PSI—120 can occur either individually or in a group. Responses are directly recorded in the booklet to reduce errors, then, apparently, the client's responses are keyed into a computer scoring program that yields the scored results. Results are produced in several formats: (a) a narrative Summary Report that contains brief interpretations about "key" personality traits and styles as well as statements about job activities suited to an individual possessing such traits; (b) a Detailed Report that provides scores and interpretations for the eight traits and 24 personal styles; (c) a Linear Report that presents the same data in a graph format and facilitates rapid identification of differences in personal style between the subsystems of affect, behavior, and cognition; and (d) a Scores-Only Report that lists raw and adjusted scores.

The manual contains a single vague and fleeting mention of basic qualifications for users of the PSI—120. In the section dealing with validity indicators, the manual suggests that "a professional level of expertise" (manual, p. 18) is required to assess the validity of a profile. The failure to provide guidelines for user credentials and training does not adhere to the *Standards for Educational and Psychological Testing* (AERA, APA, & NCME, 1985). Equally troubling is the way in which the validity rules were derived. Apparently 25 client profiles deemed valid on the basis of clinical impression and client feedback and 25 profiles generated by responses drawn from a table of random numbers were compared. The resulting four rules for establishing profile validity are based on the distribution of responses within each subsystem, the presence of outliers, and the (mean?) correlation between the basic style and current styles. Because the test is being marketed as a tool for personal selection as well as counseling, it is important not only to detect and quantify what the person is saying about him or herself, but also to determine how the person approached the test (Ben-Porath & Waller, 1992). The validity strategy described above does not allow one to determine anything beyond the fact that the item responses were not generated randomly. Because the instrument is used in clinical decision making (Kunce & Newton, 1989) as well as in personal selection, it would seem prudent to provide some means of detecting a response bias and quantify that bias because failure to do so would have significant consequences for the predictive validity of the instrument in such settings. This problem is amplified when dealing with special populations. For example, managerial applicants competing for a highly competitive job or alcohol dependent clients seeking access to a valued treatment program could reasonably be expected to minimize or exaggerate their self-report respectively (see Butcher & Han, 1995 and Berry, Wetter, & Baer, 1995 for a discussion of the issue). The PSI—120 currently has no mechanism by which to detect these response distortions.

THE CIRCUMPLEX MODEL AND PSYCHOMETRIC LEGERDEMAIN. According to the theoretical model within which the PSI—120 is embedded, the relationship of personality styles or traits across affective, behavioral, and cognitive domains is determined by two major bipolar personality dimensions: the ubiquitous, extroversion-introversion dimension, and a stability—change dimension. This model defines a circumplex of eight personality traits with Extroversion versus Introversion representing the vertical axis and Stability versus Change representing the horizontal axis. Rotating clockwise from the Extroversion pole, the personality traits are as follows: #2, Encouraging/Facilitating; #3, Promoting/Inspiring; #4, Innovating/Designing; #5, Improvising/Inventing; #6, Evaluating/Analyzing; #7, Assembling/Constructing; #8, Organizing/Systematizing; and #1, Supporting/Preserving. As measured by the PSI—120, each trait is then expressed as a "personal style" within each behavioral subsystem. For example, the trait of Encouraging/Facilitating, which falls along the Extroversion/Introversion dimension, is expressed in the affective subsystem as Enthusiasm, behaviorally as Affiliation, and cognitively as Dedication. Consequently, the PSI—120 yields 24 personal styles constructed from eight personality "traits" across the three subsystems of human behavior. Finally, the PSI—120 allows one to obtain scores across each trait within each subsystem that represents the individual's inherent (true?) personality style and scores that represent the current style, presumably representing "what the person has learned to be, needs to be, or wants to be" (manual, p. 9). Differences between so-called basic behavior (inherent) and current behavior may represent sources of stress and foci for treatment or intervention.

The construction of an earlier PSI version containing 274 items (10 unique items for each basic scale, an additional 24 items representing current behaviors, and 10 experimental items) was based on a Q-factor analysis of unpublished MMPI, Rorschach, and Personality Research Form data. No description of this process is discussed or referenced in the manual. Further, "as a consequence of requests from consumers" (manual, p. 102), a short form of the PSI was developed containing 120 items. Apparently, each of the basic 24 personal style scales contain 4 items answered on a 3-point scale. The reliabilities were increased for these scales by including 6 more items from adjacent scales to increase the scale to 10 items. Each corresponding personal style scale for current behavior contains a single item and is answered along a 5-point scale from *definitely like me* to *definitely unlike me*. No rationale is offered for use of the shortened version nor is incremental validity data provided in support of the shortened version over the 274-item PSI. Although the manual discusses the rationale used for item development in the 274-item version, no discussion ensued regarding the retention of items for the PSI—120. Somewhat inexplicably, data that are provided in the manual often refer to the 274-item version rather than the PSI—120 without explicitly stating which instrument is referenced. Clearly this is problematic because there is no evidence presented that establishes the equivalency of the two versions let alone argues for the superiority of the PSI—120.

The adjacent scales are highly intercorrelated because there is substantial overlap of items (on average 33%). Item overlap may serve to complicate interpretation of scales because one needs to take into account the spurious correlations between some scales in addition to whatever empirical correlation exists between scales (Helmes & Reddon, 1993). This becomes an even greater interpretive nightmare when one realizes that the scale scores are adjusted by averaging the means between two adjacent scales, thereby creating a single scale containing 17 items, 6 of which are shared by adjacent scales. This issue is blithely ignored as the manual suggests that "If several personal styles in a circumplex are adjacent and robust, the characteristics of each are amplified" (manual, p. 27) and therefore, interpreted accordingly. Clearly the use of the plural "styles" is suspect in this situation.

WHERE ARE THE NORMS? The interpretation of each personal style scale is based on raw scores. For example, a score of 50 indicates that the individual answered half the items as true. "Most individuals have mean scores between 35 and 75" (manual, p. 19). The meaning of this statement is unclear. After careful examination of the manual and the accompanying normative data, the average scores cited above appear to be based on two separate samples of college students ($n = 137$ and $n = 238$, respectively). Even the most basic demographic characteristics of these two samples are missing (e.g., gender, age, year in school, racial composition). The absence of this type of information is critical. For example, gender may reasonably affect mean score across the affective personal style of confronting or excitement-seeking, yet males and females are lumped together with no attempt to ascertain whether, indeed, there is an effect of gender on these personal styles. Furthermore, given that interpretation is based on an average number of items answered and these scores are not normalized, it would be useful to provide tables containing the item endorsement frequency for each personal style score. Given the fact that the normative samples are at best homogeneous and the PSI—120 is represented as having utility across broad age, gender, education, and vocational domains, inclusion of this type of data would be helpful in determining the appropriateness of the instrument to certain populations.

Internal consistency (Cronbach's alpha) for personal scale scores ranges from modest to poor and in some cases differs considerably across the two "normative" samples. Median reliabilities of .67 and .65 are reported for the two samples. The use of the median tends to obscure the fact that some of the scales continue to need work. The issue of scale surgery becomes even more evident when the basic style scales are correlated with the current scores, a procedure alleged to be an indication of "face validity" (manual, p. 105). In the two samples, 17% of the scales correlated less than .35. In sample one, 50% of the personal style scales within the cognitive subsystem correlated less than .35, in the second sample, 37.5% correlated less than .35. This raises troubling issues if one is called upon to defend an employment selection decision based on an applicant's augmented (the basic score is below 40 and the current score is above 60) or inhibited (basic score is above 60 and the current score is below 40) profile within the cognitive subsystem of behavior. In addition, much is made of differences between current behavior and basic behaviors in counseling applications; however, no normative data are provided regarding the meaning of the differences (i.e., clinical vs. statistical) or the frequency with which a difference of a certain magnitude occurs within a particular population.

Finally, chapter IV of the manual is entitled "Useful Constructs for Interpretation." Some of these constructs have been mentioned previously, but it is important to highlight the lack of empirical evidence supporting the use of these terms within the interpretive framework proposed in the manual. The term "masking" is described as a significant factor in interpersonal interactions and is operationally defined as a "robust" personal style in one of the three behavioral subsystems that can "mask" robust styles in another subsystem (manual, 1994, p. 27). For example, a generally extroverted emotional style can mask an introverted behavioral style. But, is any evidence given for this assertion? Again, no correlation matrices are provided establishing the "normative" relationship of personal styles across the affective, behavioral, and cognitive subsystems. It is not hard to imagine that "masking" would not occur very often because traits such as extroversion should manifest equally across the three domains. Further, when masking does occur, questions regarding the "true" meaning of the differences remain. Given that error accounts for 40% or more of the variance in 1/3 of the personal styles scales across the two normative samples, the use of differences in scale scores across these subsystems in any substantive fashion is ethically dangerous.

SUMMARY. The PSI—120 is a substantially shortened version of the Personal Styles Inventory (PSI) developed to assess "normal" personality traits within three broad subsystems of human experience. Additionally, by examining differences between scores based on estimates of the basic traits and scores based on estimates of current behaviors, inference can be made regarding the degree to which the individual's current presentation is representative of underlying tendencies or an adaptive or maladaptive response to "stress." The authors claim that the instrument has a myriad of applications including: psychotherapy, vocational counseling, management consultation, and employee selection. Unfortunately, little evidence is provided in the manual or the accompanying material to justify such claims for the PSI—120. The vast majority of cited studies refer to findings using the original 274-item version. Sufficiently broad and representative normative data are lacking for the PSI—120 and scale reliabilities, as well as psychometric concerns, temper any enthusiasm for the shortened instrument. Based on findings in alcohol treatment settings (Kunce & Newton, 1989; Pfost, Newton, Kunce, Cope, & Greenwood, 1993), there is reason to encourage further research, including the establishment of appropriate norms, refinement of scales, and demonstration of the instrument's efficacy in employment selection decisions. Until such time, the PSI—120 should be considered experimental and not used independently to reach clinical or employment decisions.

REVIEWER'S REFERENCES

American Educational Research Association, American Psychological Association, & National Council on Measurement in Education. (1985). *Standards for educational and psychological testing.* Washington, DC: American Psychological Association, Inc.

Costa, P. T., Jr., & McCrae, R. R. (1985). *The NEO Personality Inventory manual.* Odessa, FL: Psychological Assessment Resources.

Kunce, J. T., & Newton, R. M. (1989). Normal and psychopathological personality characteristics of individuals in alcohol rehabilitation. *Journal of Counseling Psychology, 36,* 308–315.

Ben-Porath, Y. S., & Waller, N. G. (1992). "Normal" personality inventories in clinical assessment: General requirement and the potential for using the NEO Personality Inventory. *Psychological Assessment, 4,* 14–19.

Helmes, E., & Reddon, J. R. (1993). A perspective on developments in assessing psychopathology: A critical review of the MMPI and MMPI-2. *Psychological Bulletin, 113,* 453–471.

Pfost, K. S., Newton, R. M., Kunce, J. T., Cope, C. S., & Greenwood, G. (1993). A model for individualizing interventions for alcohol abuse/dependence using basic personality dimensions. *Psychotherapy, 30,* 334–343.

Costa, P. T., Jr., & Widiger, T. A. (Eds.). (1994). *Personality disorders and the five-factor model of personality.* Washington, DC: American Psychological Association.

Berry, T. R., Wetter, M. W., & Baer, R. A. (1995). Assessment of malingering. In J. N. Butcher (Ed.), *Clinical personality assessment: Practical approaches* (pp. 236–250). New York: Oxford University Press.

Butcher, J. N., & Han, K. (1995). Development of an MMPI-2 scale to assess the presentation of self in a superlative manner: The S scale. In J. N. Butcher & C. D. Spielberger (Eds.), *Advances in personality assessment* (vol. 10; pp. 25–47). Hillsdale, NJ: LEA Press.

Review of the Personal Styles Inventory [PSI—120] by MARY HENNING-STOUT, Professor of Counseling Psychology, Lewis & Clark College, Portland, OR:

The Personal Styles Inventory—120 (PSI—120) is a brief version of the original PSI (Kunce, Cope, & Newton, 1986), a 274-item instrument designed to reflect commonplace personality characteristics that are both enduring (basic) and situational (current). The longer version is now discontinued in favor of the more efficient format of the PSI—120. As with its precursor, the PSI—120 is intended for use in supporting clinical diagnosis and treatment, psychotherapy, career counseling, and research.

The authors' apparent objective is to provide a reliable and valid reflection of an individual's basic and current personal style that is descriptive rather than evaluative. They suggest that assessment of pathology alone is insufficient for treatment planning and implementation and offer the PSI—120 as an addition to any personality assessment, in particular for providing a measure of the personality assets of individuals with clinical diagnoses. The authors describe their goal as, "develop[ing] an inventory that measures recognizable behaviors described in terms of commonplace behaviors, not problem behaviors" (manual, p. 101). Because of the descriptive nature of this inventory, the authors suggest the data can be shared directly with clients and can be used for guiding numerous therapeutic interventions.

PSYCHOMETRIC PROPERTIES. The PSI—120 was derived from the earlier version of the scale. The psychometric properties for the short version were based on two samples of university students at two large state universities (manual, p. 105), a total of 375 students. These data were used to determine Cronbach alpha internal consistency reliability (ranging from .48–.81 on the 24 basic personal style categories; from .71–.85 on the 8 basic personality traits), and to correlate current and basic traits for purposes of establishing what the authors term, face validity (ranging from .18–.79 on the 24 style categories; from .66–.81 on the traits). As reported in the manual, concurrent validity has been demonstrated with the 16PF, the Myers-Briggs, the MMPI, and the Jesness. However, no numeric data are provided to support these contentions, although one published study on MMPI correlates is cited.

The methods used by the authors to establish scoring are unclear. The manual gives no indication of use of the norm samples as a basis for scoring. Instead, scoring appears based in theory (Kunce & Anderson, 1976) and standardized only by the techniques (ipsative) imposed by the required computer scoirng of responses. All in all, the holes are more numerous than the evidence to address whether or not the PSI—120 is a psychometrically sound instrument.

CONSIDERATIONS AND CONCERNS. In general, the weak demonstration of this scale's psychometric basis is cause for concern. Information on the techniques used for developing and selecting items and for establishing scoring techniques would enhance the credibility of this instrument.

ITEM CONSTRUCTION. Several of the items are phrased in questionable ways. The language seems needlessly complex on some items, words like *always* and *relatively* are used, and endorsement of some items might or might not indicate what the authors theorize. Without additional explanation of the item selection techniques underlying this scale, interpretation, even with computer scored protocols and narrative summaries, seems unnecessarily ambiguous.

APPROPRIATENESS FOR ADOLESCENT POPULATIONS. Except for the reference to sixth grade or lower reading level on page 15 of the manual, there was no indication of the appropriate lower age limit for administration of the PSI—120. In an article on the PSI, Kunce, Cope, and Newton (1991) indicated a reading level of eighth grade or lower (p. 336) and later indicated the instrument was not recommended for use with individuals younger than 14 years of age or with individuals who have an IQ (Intelligence Quotient) of less than 85 (p. 338). The samples of university students referred to in the manual yielded data the authors interpreted tentatively based on developmental considerations, but there is no clear guidance offered for interpretation in light of developmental status.

GENERALIZABILITY ACROSS GENDER AND ETHNICITY. In one of the reviews of literature on the PSI, there were several references to studies with men (e.g., police officers and veterans). There was also a suggestion that part of one study involved nurses, a professional group still predominantly women. Other than that, however, it is unclear how applicable this instrument or its predecessor is for women. Coupled with the concerns mentioned above regarding age, the authors offer no guidance or data on the use of this instrument with girls. Related to this concern is the complete absence of consideration by the authors of cross-cultural variables. In its current form, the validity of the PSI—120 for people of culturally or linguistically diverse groups, and for women, is either unproven or unclear.

SUMMARY. The PSI—120 attempts to provide an assessment of everyday personality from both state and trait perspectives. As such, it is a step toward taking more than identified pathology into account when planning and implementing therapeutic programs for individuals with varying needs and concerns. However, the scale lacks sufficient psychometric grounding as currently described in its manual. In addition, there is little to no evidence of attention to issues of generalization across gender, ethnicity, and economic class. Finally, the scale is limited by its intrapsychic rather than social-psychological focus. Assessment of social and emotional functioning is most helpful when individual characteristics or tendencies are considered in social context.

REVIEWER'S REFERENCES

Kunce, J. T., & Anderson, W. P. (1976). Normalizing the MMPI. *Journal of Clinical Psychology, 32,* 776–780.
Kunce, J. T., Cope, C. S., & Newton, R. M. (1986). The Personal Styles Inventory. Columbia, MO: Educational and Psychological Consultants.
Kunce, J. T., Cope, C. S., & Newton, R. M. (1991). Personal Styles Inventory. *Journal of Counseling and Development, 70,* 334–341.

[230]
Personal Values Questionnaire.

Purpose: Measures individuals' "values related to achievement, affiliation, and power."
Population: Adults.
Publication Date: 1991.
Acronym: PVQ.
Scores, 3: Achievement, Affiliation, Power.
Administration: Group.
Price Data, 1993: $60 per complete kit including 10 questionnaires and 10 profiles and interpretive notes (10 pages).
Time: Administration time not reported.

Comments: Self-scored profile.
Authors: Joni Jay Fink and Richard Mansfield (profile and interpretive notes).
Publisher: McBer and Company.

Review of the Personal Values Questionnaire by BRIAN F. BOLTON, University Professor, Rehabilitation Research and Training Center, University of Arkansas, Fayetteville, AR:

The Personal Values Questionnaire (PVQ) is a self-report inventory that measures three value orientations: Achievement, Affiliation, and Power. The PVQ consists of 36 brief statements that are rated by the respondent using a standard 6-point format. The anchors range from *not important to me* to *extremely important to me.* Completion time is 10 minutes.

A brief document titled *Profile and Interpretive Notes* accompanies the PVQ. Included are a scoring key, a graph for plotting the score profile, and seven pages of explanatory material covering these topics: Understanding Your Personal Values, Distinguishing Between Values and Motives, Comparing Your Values and Job Requirements, and How Can You Change Your Values? The interpretive material consists mostly of commonsense discussions that reflect the PVQ item content.

The Personal Values Questionnaire evolved from an unpublished instrument named the Personal Motives and Values Questionnaire developed by David C. McClelland (1988) of Harvard University. The authors claim that the PVQ measures values related to three social motives prominent in McClelland's well-known research (i.e., need for achievement [n-ach], need for affiliation [n-aff], and need for power [n-pow]). In fact, McClelland's research demonstrated that nonconscious motives assessed with projective methodology operate much differently in explaining behavior than do cognitively based value choices.

The scores calculated for the three value scales are simply averages of the 10 items that compose each of the three scales. In other words, the scale scores are interpreted with reference to the 6-point anchored-response format. The absence of normative data constitutes a serious limitation to the use of the PVQ. Also absent is any description of the development of the instrument, as well as reliability and validity information. Unbelievably, there is no published technical manual, even though the PVQ has been marketed since 1991. Staff at McBer and Company did send some unpublished psychometric data, but these were insufficient to support any applications of the PVQ.

In summary, the Personal Values Questionnaire purports to measure three value orientations that emerged from the research of Harvard psychologist David C. McClelland. The authors of the PVQ do not provide any information about the development of the instrument, nor are any published norms, reliability data, or validity information available at this time. No test or inventory should be distributed without an accompanying technical manual. It must be concluded that there is no evidence to support the use of the PVQ in organizational consulting or career counseling.

REVIEWER'S REFERENCE

McClelland, D. C. (1988). *Personal Motives and Values Questionnaire*. Cambridge, MA: Department of Psychology, Harvard University.

Review of the Personal Values Questionnaire by GARY J. DEAN, Associate Professor and Chairperson, Department of Adult and Community Education, Indiana University of Pennsylvania, Indiana, PA:

GENERAL COMMENTS. The purpose of the Personal Values Questionnaire (PVQ) is to measure three values based on the work of David McClelland: Achievement, Affiliation, and Power. The instrument is self-administered, scored, and interpreted. The material consists of two parts: a three-page booklet containing a 36-item questionnaire and a 10-page booklet, the *Profile and Interpretive Notes*, for scoring and interpretation.

The questionnaire is prefaced with a brief introduction and easy-to-follow instructions. The actual questionnaire consists of 36 statements, which the respondent is asked to rate based on their importance. A 6-point scale is used to rate each item with 0 = *Not important to me*; 1 = *Of little importance to me*; 2 = *Of some importance to me*; 3 = *Important to me*; 4 = *Very important to me*; and 5 = *Extremely important to me*. Respondents mark their responses directly in the questionnaire booklet.

TECHNICAL INFORMATION. No validity or reliability data were provided with the instrument. A call to the publisher yielded several articles on both the theories of David McClelland and the reliability and validity of the PVQ. Two brief handouts (which did not contain authors, dates, or other publication information) provided some psychometric data. A handout entitled *Personal Values Questionnaire (PVQ)* stated that the PVQ was derived from an instrument called the Personal Motives and Values Questionnaire developed by David McClelland in the late 1980s. No further information was provided on the origin of the PVQ. Two studies are mentioned (without citations) in the same handout which describe the reliability and validity data. Alpha coefficients for the three values (based on a sample of 147) are Achievement = .82, Affiliation = .77, and Power = .84. A validity study was also mentioned in which the PVQ was compared to the Organizational Climate Survey Questionnaire (OCSQ) and the Management Styles Questionnaire (MSQ), two other instruments published by McBer. In this study (based on samples of 121 to 123), Achievement on the PVQ showed statistically significant convergent validity with the Rewards scale from the OCSQ and showed statistically significant discriminant validity from the Conformity scale of the OCSQ and the Affiliation scale on the MSQ. Affiliation on the PVQ showed statistically significant convergent validity with the Affiliation scale on the MSQ and showed statistically significant discriminant validity from the Coercive scale of the MSQ. There were no references to the Power scale on the PVQ. It is noted in the handout that these are preliminary data and that further study is needed.

Although the reliability coefficients are respectable, the validity studies are weak. Both reliability and validity are based on studies that are inadequately reported: All of the information cited above was contained in a three-page handout. Establishing convergent validity of the PVQ with the OCSQ and MSQ does not enhance the user's confidence in the PVQ. Both Adler (1989) and Bernardin and Pynes (1989) note that the MSQ has significant psychometric inadequacies that detract from its usability. A review of the last five *Mental Measurements Yearbooks* (Eighth through the Twelfth) did not yield a review of the OCSQ, and technical data on this instrument were not available. These factors indicate that the concurrent validity of the PVQ with the MSQ and the OCSQ is questionable.

ADMINISTRATION AND SCORING. Scoring the PVQ is relatively easy. Instructions for scoring and interpreting the questionnaire are contained in the *Profile and Interpretive Notes*. Each item is assigned a point value based on the response given to that item (i.e., *Not important to me* = 0 points for that item). Each value (Achievement, Affiliation, and Power) is measured by 10 items (6 items are presumably filler items, but this is not explained in the booklet). A final score is reached by dividing the total points for the 10 items for each of the three values by 10, resulting in a score on the original scale of 0 to 5. The final score for each of the three values is plotted in a grid so that a visual comparison can be made of the three scores.

INTERPRETATION. Interpreting the results of the PVQ is contained in four sections of the *Profile and Interpretive Notes:* Understanding Your Personal Values Profile (two pages), Distinguishing between Values and Motives (one page), Comparing Your Values and Job Requirements (two pages), and How Can You Change Your Values (two pages).

Although the 36 items on the questionnaire are general and address many different life situations, the interpretation of the instrument in the booklet is entirely related to the work environment. It is emphasized that the questionnaire measures values and not motives. The differences between values and motives are described as motives being natural drives, which are unconscious and more difficult to change than values. Comparing values to job requirements is accomplished through a 2 x 2 matrix, which juxtaposes a respondent's values that are high and low in importance to job requirements that are high and low. Although not stated any place in the booklet, it is presumed that a value is high for an individual if it is rated 3.0 (important) or higher. A value is considered high in a job if it is necessary and low if it is not necessary. It is recommended to the respondent that "By discussing your thoughts with your manager, you may get an even clearer conception of your job requirements" (p. 7). Beyond this, no clear directions are given for determining if the three values are necessary or not for a job. Four scenarios are provided to illustrate different combinations of personal values and job requirements: high value-high job requirement, high value-low job requirement, low value-low job requirement, and low value-high job requirement. One of the three values is described for each scenario as an example. The booklet concludes with a section that describes conditions under which it may be necessary to change one's personal values.

CONCLUSION. The PVQ has several positive features. First, the instrument is well designed and has a professional appearance and it is easy to administer and score. Second, interpreting the instrument for personal understanding is also readily accomplished; most people will be able to understand and apply the three values to themselves. There are several factors, however, that limit the usability of the PVQ. First, the validity and reliability studies reported are weak: They are based on small samples and the attempts to establish construct validity with the MSQ and OCSQ can only be considered very preliminary data. Second, there is a lack of formal and accessible data on the development and validity/reliability of the PVQ. Third, there are no clear guidelines for applying values to a person's job. Normative data establishing the three values for different types of jobs would not only aid in interpretation but also in establishing the validity of the instrument. Fourth, there is a lack of references to theory and the development of the PVQ. The distinction between values and motives presented in the booklet is written in understandable terms but is insufficient for a full understanding of the concepts measured by the PVQ. Fifth, the publisher should provide a technical manual that would contain all of the needed information enhancing the interpretability and usefulness of the PVQ.

REVIEWER'S REFERENCES
Adler, S. (1989). [Review of the Managerial Styles Questionnaire.] In J. C. Conoley & J. J. Kramer (Eds.), *The tenth mental measurements yearbook* (pp. 461–463). Lincoln, NE: The Buros Institute of Mental Measurements.
Bernardin, H. J., & Pynes, J. E. (1989). [Review of the Managerial Style Questionnaire.] In J. C. Conoley & J. J. Kramer (Eds.), *The tenth mental measurements yearbook* (pp. 463–465). Lincoln, NE: The Buros Institute of Mental Measurements.

[231]
Personality Inventory for Youth.

Purpose: "Assesses emotional and behavioral adjustment, family character and interaction, and school adjustment and academic ability."

Population: Ages 9–18.

Publication Date: 1995.

Acronym: PIY.

Scores, 37: Validity, Inconsistency, Dissimulation, Defensiveness, Cognitive Impairment (Poor Achievement and Memory, Inadequate Abilities, Learning Problems, Total), Impulsivity and Distractibility (Brashness, Distractability and Overactivity, Impulsivity, Total), Delinquency (Antisocial Behavior, Dyscontrol, Noncompliance, Total), Family Dysfunction (Parent-Child Conflict, Parent Maladjustment, Marital Discord, Total), Reality Distortion (Feelings of Alienation, Hallucinations and Delusions, Total), Somatic Concern (Psychosomatic Syndrome, Muscular Tension and Anxiety, Preoccupation with Disease, Total), Psychological Discomfort (Fear and Worry, Depression, Sleep Disturbance, Total), Social Withdrawal (Social Introversion, Isolation, Total), Social Skill Deficits (Limited Peer Status, Conflict with Peers, Total).

Administration: Group.

Price Data, 1997: $225 per complete kit including administration and interpretation guide, technical guide, 100 answer sheets, 1 set of scoring templates, 100 profile forms (male and female), 100 critical items summary sheets (male and female), 2 WPS TEST REPORT mail-in answer sheets for computer scoring, 2 reusable administration booklets, and audiotape; $26 per reusable administration booklet; $18.50 per Spanish Research Edition reusable administration booklet; $18.50 per 100 answer

sheets; $24.50 per 25WPS AUTOSCORE answer sheets; $18.50 per 100 profile forms; $18.50 per 100 critical items summary sheets; $32.50 per set of scoring templates; $12.50 per audiotape; $45 per administration and interpretation guide; $49.50 per technical guide.
Time: (45) minutes.
Authors: David Lachar and Christian P. Gruber.
Publisher: Western Psychological Services.

Review of the Personality Inventory for Youth by LIZANNE DESTEFANO, Professor of Educational Psychology, University of Illinois at Urbana-Champaign, Champaign, IL:

INTRODUCTION. The purpose of the Personality Inventory for Youth (PIY) is to assess, through self-report, the emotional and behavioral adjustment, family character and interaction, school adjustment, and academic ability of children and adolescents 9 through 18 years of age. Responses are scored along four validity scales (Inconsistency, Validity, Dissimulation, and Defensiveness) that indicate whether the child has produced results that are inaccurate or atypical. The nine clinical scales (Cognitive Impairment, Impulsivity and Distractibility, Delinquency, Family Dysfunction, Reality Distortion, Somatic Concern, Psychological Discomfort, Social Withdrawal, and Social Skills Deficits) represent a "broad array of adjustment difficulties" (p. 2). Twenty-four subscales provide more detailed, though technically limited, clinical information. The first 80 items of the PIY can be used as a screening assessment, resulting in a general measure of adjustment called the Classroom Screening (CLASS) scale.

The parent report items and scales of the Personality Inventory for Children—Revised (PIC-R; T4:1998) (Wirt, R. D., Lachar, D., Klinedinst, J. E., Seat, P. D., & Broen, W. E., 1984) were used as the basis of the 270 items that make up the PIY and the nine PIY clinical scales correspond to the PIC-R scales. Thus, the PIY and the parent report portion of the PIC-R can be used together in a complementary, additive, or confirmatory manner in a multisource assessment.

ADMINISTRATION, SCORING, AND INTERPRETATION. The PIY comprises 270 true-false statements written at a third grade reading level and presented in a spiral-bound administration booklet. Examinees are required to read and make an "X" in the box showing the appropriate response for each item on the answer form. An audiotape is available for youths who may have difficulty reading the items. Individual and group administration are possible. Administration of a full PIY takes from 30 to 60

minutes. Both hand- and computer-scoring services are available. Hand scoring is labor intensive. It requires transfer of information from one form to another and is highly prone to error. Computer-scoring software is available for the PC. Mail and fax scoring are available from the publisher. Given the number of scales and the complexity of scoring, computer assistance is highly recommended. The first volume of the PIY manual is the Administration and Interpretation Guide. It provides a clear, thorough description of administration and scoring procedures. The visuals that accompany the scoring directions are particularly well done and necessary to negotiate the complex hand-scoring process and obtain the PIY Profile.

The PIY Profile and the Critical Item Endorsement serve as the basis for test interpretation. In forming the PIY Profile, raw scores are converted to *T*-scores and displayed for validity scales, clinical scales, and subscales. Critical items are analogous to those identified in the Personality Inventory for Children and the Minnesota Multiphasic Personality Inventory. They suggest clinical issues that should be examined in greater detail and provide a basis for summarizing the content of an examinee's response. The manual presents a very clear five-step interpretation process. Primary and secondary profile elevations are defined using *T*-score ranges. Descriptions of typical behaviors and likely problems are provided for three levels of *T*-score elevation for each clinical scale and for one level for each subscale. These descriptions were developed through a series of validity studies to demonstrate relationships between PIY *T*-scores and other estimates of adjustment and functioning such as self-report measures, PIC-R scale scores, clinical ratings, and performance on tests of cognitive ability and academic achievement. The descriptions are very substantive and well written, and could serve as the basis of a rich description of adolescent adjustment. Strategies are presented for comparing PIY scales and the parent report section of the PIC-R, but not enough is said about the complexity of integrating similarities and differences between student self-report and parent report to enable the reader to conduct such a comparison on their own. The manual ends with the presentation of 15 well-chosen and effectively presented case studies selected to illustrate common symptomatology and diagnoses.

STANDARDIZATION AND PSYCHOMETRIC PROPERTIES. The second volume of the PIY manual is a Technical Guide. The volume contains detailed information on the standardization, validation, and assessment of psychometric properties of the PIY. The Administration and Interpretation Guide provides a brief guide to interpreting PIY scales and the Technical Guide contains an explanation of the empirical grounding for cut points, confidence intervals, the relationship among scales, and other bases of interpretation. The technical information is packaged separately for the user's convenience; unfortunately, relegating it to a second volume greatly increases the likelihood that the technical information will remain on the shelf while the examiner uses the Administration and Interpretation Guide as the primary tool for scoring and interpretation. The authors responsibly advise that competent users should be aware of the technical aspects of the test, but there is little else to encourage them to do so. The Technical Guide is rarely referenced in the Administration and Interpretation Guide and vice versa.

The PIY was constructed by transforming the 280 parent-report items of the PIC-R into first person statements that were developmentally appropriate for the intended population. The development and standardization of the PIY was conducted using two samples, one of 2,327 students in regular education classes and the other of 1,178 clinically referred students. The authors report that the data were collected in group administrations in geographically diverse sites. The regular education sample deviated from U.S. Census demographics in terms of gender, ethnic background, geographic region, and parent's educational level. However, after examining the results of a special study using a demographically representative subsample of 709 subjects, the authors concluded that demographic differences were unlikely to affect the accuracy of standard scores and the decision was made to generate standard scores (separately by gender) using the entire regular education sample. They were so confident about the instrument's stability across ages and ethnic groups that they stated, "when clinical judgment suggests that the content coverage of the PIY is appropriate for a tested individual, the PIY can be used with individuals whose age or demographic backgrounds are somewhat outside of the formal range of standardization" (Administration and Interpretation Guide, p. 5). It is generally unwise to advocate for use of an instrument outside the group represented by the standardization sample and particularly inappropriate to suggest that the PIY might be used with an even younger age group. There were very limited numbers of

examinees at the lower age levels (<9) in the standardization ($N = 70$) and clinical sample ($N = 32$) and the readability of the instrument was targeted at the third grade level, so younger examinees might have trouble reading the items.

The PIY norms were based on the full regular education sample. The nine clinical scales demonstrated moderate rates of skewness that were consistent across scales, therefore, linear T-scores were created. The validity scales and clinical subscales demonstrated much higher skewness and are subject to more cautious interpretation. Data from the clinically referred sample were used extensively in scale construction and in reliability and validity analysis. Internal consistency and test-retest reliability studies were conducted with both regular and clinical samples. The authors rightly point out that because items and scales refer to behaviors and thoughts that are relatively infrequent in normal populations and that the primary use of the PIY will be with clinical populations, the findings for the clinical sample are essential for evaluating the appropriateness of this measure. In both the clinical (median = .82) and regular education samples (median = .85), internal consistency estimates for the nine clinical scales fell within the acceptable range for an instrument of this kind. On the 24 shorter subscales, alphas were more variable and generally lower for both regular (median = .70) and clinical (median = .73) samples. Two of the four validity scales had acceptable internal consistency (range = .79 to .84). The remaining two scales were not intended to be homogenous in content; therefore, internal consistency was not a relevant indicator. Test-retest reliability studies (time interval 7–10 days) indicated that the clinical scales demonstrated acceptable stability over time for both the regular (median = .85) and clinical (median = .83) samples. These studies were quite limited in terms of sample size (86 for the clinical sample) and age range (16 to 19 years for the regular sample), however, and although they support the stability of the scales over time, additional study is warranted. Subscales were less reliable over time than the scales, providing additional evidence that subscale scores should not be reported or used heavily as a basis for interpretation.

Volume 2, the Technical Guide, reports extensively on the content, construct, concurrent, and criterion-related validity of the instrument. Chapter 2, Development and Validation of the Clinical Scales and Subscales, defines each scale and subscale and lists each item contained and their endorsement rates for both samples as an indication of the content dimensions addressed. Next, a matrix showing the correlation of the scale under discussion and all other scales and subscales of the PIY is presented as evidence of construct validity. Correlations of the PIY scales and subscales with the PIC-R and the MMPI and other measures of ability, personality, achievement, and adjustment further substantiate the concurrent validity of the instrument. Specific analyses evaluate the relationship between clinical evaluations on PIY scales and clinical evaluations on the scales of other instruments. Although the sample sizes of the validity studies are small and the samples are not well described in the text, it is an impressive array of validity information. The available data indicate that the PIY effectively differentiates among normal and clinical samples and identifies a broad range of psychological and behavioral characteristics.

SUMMARY. The PIY offers a carefully developed and psychometrically sound option for broadly evaluating personality functioning in young people through self-report. Given the shortcomings of projective testing and parent report for this age group, the PIY is a welcome addition to clinical assessment batteries for children ages 9 through 18. The scales of the PIY meet generally accepted standards for internal consistency and test-retest reliability. Considerable evidence exists to support the content, construct, concurrent, and criterion-related validity of the PIY profile. The subscales are technically limited, however, and should not be used as a basis of reporting and interpretation.

REVIEWER'S REFERENCE

Wirt, R. D., Lachar, D., Klinedinst, J. E., & Seat, P. D. (1984). *Multidimensional description of child personality: A manual for the personality inventory for children.* Los Angeles: Western Psychological Services.

Review of the Personality Inventory for Youth by GREGORY J. MARCHANT, Associate Professor of Educational Psychology, Ball State University, Muncie, IN, and T. ANDREW RIDENOUR, Post-Doctoral Fellow, Washington University, St. Louis, MO:

Frequently young people are overlooked as a major source of information about themselves in research studies and even clinical practice. When identifying behaviors, perceptions, and even personality, records are consulted and parents questioned, but there are few simple instruments designed to solicit responses from children. This suggests a real need, especially in light of evidence that a weak agreement often exists between parent and child reports (Achenbach, McConaughy, & Howell, 1987).

There is also evidence that it is the perceptions of the child that are tied to important outcomes like school achievement, rather than the perceptions of the parents (Paulson, 1994). The Personality Inventory for Youth (PIY) represents an effort to fill an important need in the area of self-perceptions of children which yield personality profiles.

The PIY is a self-report instrument for 9- to 18-year-olds. Although the authors describe adequate comprehension for individuals with low- to mid-third grade reading level and 90% or above comprehension for those with low- to mid-fourth grade reading ability, it is suspected that some children at the lower age range may experience some confusion. It was developed by modifying items from the parent-report Personality Inventory for Children—Revised (PIC-R). Items that could not be modified were deleted and replaced by items that would reflect response sets and validity concerns associated with self-report instruments. PIY validity scales were developed to identify defensiveness, exaggeration, extreme responses, and inattention or inadequate comprehension.

NORMATIVE SAMPLE. The PIY normative sample of over 2,000 students was drawn from five states (none from the east or southeast). There appeared to be a slight overrepresentation of females and those from higher socioeconomic status families, and a possible underrepresentation of children from single parent families. A more demographically balanced subsample was identified ($n = 709$) to test for the possible effect of gender, SES, age, ethnicity, region, and guardianship. Statistical differences were found for at least one scale for each of the variables tested; however, separate norm conversions were only deemed necessary for gender.

INSTRUMENT AND SCALE DEVELOPMENT. Although it is clear that the authors have followed appropriate, and arguably exhaustive, efforts to use statistical analyses to assist in establishing the instrument and its scales, the reporting of the analyses is at times a bit loose. For example, the early sample size ($N = 585$) made factor analysis to confirm the scales impractical; however, a factor analysis was conducted on the sample of over 3,000, but the manual implies that the results may not have been rigorously followed. The authors chose to focus on "clinical content and pragmatic psychometric issues" and used the term "factor-guided" (p. 5) to describe the process. Subscale correlations were described as "for the most part ... insignificant" and "relatively independent" with significant correlations only identified in the tables when meeting the slightly more demanding level of $p<.04$, instead of more traditional $p<.05$. The fact that only 5 of the 270 items are reverse coded suggests the possibility of a response pattern that could lead to higher interitem and scale correlations. The scales did demonstrate adequate test-retest reliability (7- to 10-day interval).

VALIDITY. The majority of the PIY items were derived directly from the PIC-R, which is a well-accepted instrument successfully used in clinical practice and research studies. In a study, the PIY subscales were able to differentiate PIC profile types (Lachar, Kline, Green, & Gruber, 1996). Concurrent validity for the scales was demonstrated through correlations with other appropriate instruments (such as the WISC-R, PPVT-R, and MMPI). The PIY was able to differentiate successfully between children diagnosed as conduct disordered and those suffering from major depression (Lachar, Harper, Green, Morgan, & Wheeler, 1996).

TEST ADMINISTRATION AND INTERPRETATION. The PIY is administered with a reusable administration booklet containing the items and either computer- or hand-scoring sheets for the respondents to indicate whether each item is true or false for them. Raw scores are converted to T-scores for each subscale and a profile chart can be created. Interpretation guidelines suggest cutoff scores for each scale. A series of case studies provided demonstrate the interpretation and usefulness of the PIY scales.

An 80-item abbreviated form of the PIY was created for large-scale screenings and for when the length of the complete PIY could be prohibitive. The primary scale for the Abbreviated PIY is the Classroom Screening (CLASS) scale, which contains 32 items identifying noncompliance, psychological discomfort, poor interpersonal adjustment, and unclassified traits. Three items represent each of the nine original scales. The three response validity scales are also included in reduced format. The CLASS scale has demonstrated the ability to detect adolescents at risk for psychosocial behaviors (Ziegenhorn, Tzelepis, Lachar, & Shubiner, 1994).

CONCLUSION. The minor concerns in this review should not overshadow the potential contribution this instrument can make to research and clinical practice. Overall this is a very well-developed instrument and a worthy descendant of the PIC. Seldom does a self-report instrument enter the field with the background of the PIY. At this writing a large data set that includes the PIC, PIY, clinical review, and a teacher rating form is being collected that will provide an additional validation study of the PIY.

REVIEWERS' REFERENCES

Achenbach, T. M., McConaughy, S. H., & Howell, C. T. (1987). Child/adolescent behavioral and emotional problems: Implications of cross-informant correlations for situational specificity. *Psychological Bulletin, 101*, 213–232.

Paulson, S. E. (1994). Relations of parenting style and parent involvement with ninth-grade students' achievement. *Journal of Early Adolescence, 14*, 250–267.

Ziegenhorn, L., Tzelepis, A., Lachar, D., & Shubiner, H. (1994, August). *Personality Inventory for Youth: Screening for high-risk adolescents.* Paper presented at the annual meeting of the American Psychological Association, Los Angeles, CA. (ERIC Document Reproduction No. ED 379 545)

Lachar, D., Harper, R. A., Green, B. A., Morgan, S. T., & Wheeler, A. C. (1996, August). *The Personality Inventory for Youth: Contributions to diagnosis.* Paper presented at the annual meeting of the American Psychological Association, Toronto, Ontario.

Lachar, D., Kline, R. B., Green, B. A., & Gruber, C. P. (1996, August). *Contributions of self-report to PIC profile type interpretation.* Paper presented at the annual meeting of the American Psychological Association, Toronto, Ontario.

[232]
Personnel Reaction Blank.

Purpose: "Aids in hiring dependable, conscientious employees."

Population: Ages 15 to adult.

Publication Dates: 1972–1988.

Acronym: PRB.

Scores: Total score only.

Administration: Group.

Price Data, 1993: $21 per sampler set including manual ('72, 12 pages) and test booklet; $15 per 25 test booklets; $24 per scoring keys; $14 per manual.

Restricted Distribution: "Sold only to companies that employ personnel psychologists or retain consultants qualified to use and interpret psychological tests."

Time: (10–15) minutes.

Authors: Harrison G. Gough and Richard Arvey.

Publisher: Consulting Psychologists Press, Inc.

Review of the Personnel Reaction Blank by DONNA L. SUNDRE, Associate Assessment Specialist/ Associate Professor of Psychology, James Madison University, Harrisonburg, VA:

GENERAL. The Personnel Reaction Blank (PRB) is "intended to assess what might be called the 'dependability-conscientiousness' personality factor" (p. 2), and is purported to be useful in "any setting where dependability, conscientiousness, diligence, and restraint are relevant to the quality of work" (p. 2). The intended users of the instrument are individuals making employment selection decisions for companies. Given the massive corporate losses due to blue and white collar crime, nonproductivity, and costs associated with personnel turnover, many companies need instruments to guide difficult employee selection decisions. The manual (1977) contains evidence suggesting the construct measured by the PRB is "more relevant to effective job performance in routine, non-managerial situations" (p. 2). A listing of work groups for which the PRB has provided useful information is provided; however, very little additional information concerning these applications and no information concerning what constitutes usefulness is ever mentioned. The instrument contains 90 items, of which only 42 are scored, producing a single total score.

ADMINISTRATION AND SCORING. The instrument can be administered to either groups or individuals considered literate and aged 15 and over. The manual authors indicate individuals with reading disabilities should have the items read aloud while the administrator observes to assure the respondent records the answers in the correct spaces. Administration should take no more than 15 minutes. The scoring of the instrument involves using a confidential key and manually lining up the item numbers on the key with those on the test booklet and scoring one point for each occasion in which an X occurs in an indicated column. This is a very tedious procedure, and if a large number of instruments were to be scored at one time, the likelihood of scoring error is fairly high. Scorers are cautioned to be very careful during this process and to score each test twice to assure accuracy. A stencil scoring methodology would probably provide more reliable scoring, particularly if sections of the test were scored separately and then added to form the final score, rather than having the scorer "count the correct responses in his head" (p. 4) as advised by the manual authors.

NORMS. Norms are intended to provide information regarding the performance of a defined group; however, the PRB norming group is not specified in any way other than sample size and mention of involvement of "many different cities and states" (p. 5). Several different groups are listed in a table in the appendix; however, the selection methods and participation rates of these individuals and the degree of representativeness to the intended population(s) cannot be determined on the basis of the evidence provided.

RELIABILITY. The manual contains a two-paragraph section on reliability. Two forms of reliability evidence were provided. The internal consistency of the items comprising the test was estimated using split-half reliability coefficients corrected using the Spearman-Brown procedure. The resulting reliability coefficients were quite high for delinquent samples: $r = .97$ and $.95$ for males and females respectively, but much less impressive for college samples: $r = .73$ and $.65$ for males and females respectively, and $r = .73$ for female office workers.

Study of stability of PRB scores for a very small ($N = 26$) sample of medical college students over a 5-year delay resulted in a stability coefficient of $r = .56$. This is a fairly impressive coefficient given the length of delay; however, additional evidence of stability of scores over time with larger and more appropriate samples is needed. This test is not intended to assess the conscientiousness of medical doctors. Because the test is intended to be used to assist in making decisions regarding individuals, computation and reporting of the standard error of measurement (*SEM*) is an important and necessary attribute. The test developer should report these estimates for potential test users. Given the great fluctuation in reliabilities for different samples, the *SEM*s will vary dramatically.

VALIDITY. Inadequate evidence is provided in support of the validity of the PRB. I would have liked to see a manual section that described the instrument's content validity via a discussion of the rationale behind the development and design of the instrument as well as the writing and selection of items. The authors indicate that scores resulting from administration of the instrument fall on a continuum labeled "responsibility" with low scores indicative of the "negative, asocial pole" and high scores related to the "positive, conforming end" of this continuum. This, in and of itself, requires thoughtful explication; further, the relationship between these qualities and the content of the items composing the instrument is not readily apparent. For instance, of the 90 items comprising the instrument, 30 seek information about work preferences, though only 12 are used for scoring. Of the 12 items used, it is not apparent how indifference or liking for work as a teacher and indifference and dislike for work as an accountant, life insurance salesperson, or short order cook would be indicative of greater responsibility, and thus, higher scores on the "dependability-conscientiousness" personality factor. Of the 60 personal reactions items, 30 are used for scoring. These items sometimes defy a relationship to the proposed responsibility continuum as well. For example, how an item such as "I have very sensitive eyes" discriminates asocial and conforming respondents on the responsibility continuum really needs to be explained.

Within the validity section, correlations are provided between PRB scores and ratings of work performance; the source of these ratings and the operationalization of "effectiveness or quality of work" are not provided. The correlations are fairly weak, ranging from $r = .20$ to $r = .33$. These low validity coefficients (median = .25) are defended with the observation that "dependability-conscientiousness is only one of the many factors entering into the overall criterion of job performance" (p. 7). It would seem that the appropriate validity investigation would be to correlate PRB scores with some measure of dependability and conscientiousness, rather than a more global construct. Although correlations of PRB scores with about 60 personality traits as measured by standardized tests are provided in the appendix, there is no discussion of the theoretical expectations specified by the developers for these comparisons.

Considerable evidence exists that scores on this instrument can discriminate between both male and female delinquents and nondelinquents. If the user is satisfied that membership in delinquent or nondelinquent status is an appropriate surrogate for dependability and conscientiousness, they might find this instrument useful. There are probably more efficient means of discovering membership in this population. The manual also includes evidence the instrument is susceptible to faking. This is an important admission for potential users. A sample of college student examinees were requested to take the PRB twice, first honestly and then with instructions to fake responses so as to provide an ideal employment applicant. The results indicate significantly higher scores under the faking condition for both males and females. There is no question of the differential motivation of job applicants to "look good" to potential employers. Here again, the lack of information provided about the norm group(s) and conditions under which the instrument was administered call into question the generalizability of the results reported, including the potential cut-scores and score classifications presented. This conclusion is supported by results reported in the appendix, Table 2, in which descriptive statistics from various samples used for norming are presented. Data provided by department store applicants, the only group identified as seeking employment, were the highest means reported for both males and females.

SUMMARY. Throughout the manual, the authors provided cogent advice to users on the creation of local norms, and decision-theoretic model data analysis, such as the comparison of scores of applicants who leave or are dismissed with those whose work is deemed satisfactory. Because this is the necessary evidence of the predictive validity of inferences users are most likely to want to make, this is precisely the information potential users should be able to review in order to determine if the test can meet their needs. In addition, the *Standards for Educational and Psychological Testing* (AERA, APA, & NCME, 1985) state explicitly that the "principal obligation of employment testing is to produce reasonable evidence for the validity of such predictions and decisions" (p. 59). If the test developers and publisher cannot follow their own good advice, I have difficulty recommending use of the instrument. Although many employers legitimately concerned with employee theft have used "integrity tests," such tests have generated considerable controversy due to misclassification errors and intrusiveness. Some of these tests have demonstrated considerable reliability but validity has been lacking. The PRB demonstrates neither. If an employer was desirous of such an assessment, perhaps the Employee Reliability Inventory (12:137) should be considered, because it has been subjected to more current and ongoing technical and validation study.

REVIEWER'S REFERENCE

American Educational Research Association, American Psychological Association, & National Council on Measurement in Education. (1985). *Standards for educational and psychological testing.* Washington, DC: American Psychological Association, Inc.

[233]
Pharmacy College Admission Test.

Purpose: Designed to measure general academic ability and scientific knowledge needed to begin the study of "pharmacy school curriculum."
Population: Pharmacy college applicants.
Publication Dates: 1976–1994.
Acronym: PCAT.
Scores, 5: Verbal Ability, Quantitative Ability, Biology, Chemistry, Reading Comprehension.
Administration: Group.
Restricted Distribution: Distribution restricted and test administered at licensed testing centers; details may be obtained from publisher.
Price Data: Available from publisher.
Time: (210–215) minutes.
Author: The Psychological Corporation.
Publisher: The Psychological Corporation.

Review of the Pharmacy College Admission Test by MARK ALBANESE, Associate Professor, Preventive Medicine and Director, Office of Medical Education Research and Development, University of Wisconsin—Madison, Madison, WI:

The Pharmacy College Admission Test (PCAT) is sponsored by the American Association of Colleges of Pharmacy (AACP). The AACP is the only organization representing the interests of pharmaceutical education and educators and is composed of approximately 3,000 faculty members from 75 schools and colleges of pharmacy in the United States and Puerto Rico. The PCAT is administered three times during the year in over 100 testing centers in the United States and Canada. It is clearly a high stakes admissions test that adheres to exacting testing standards.

The PCAT contains 270 items, which are scored for number correct. Examinees are advised to guess if they have no other means to arrive at an answer. Items are developed by subject matter expert consultants and staff. Both traditional test statistics and Item Response Theory statistics are used to determine the difficulty and discriminating power of each question. Scores are reported on a scale with a median of 200 and range from approximately 100 to 300. A composite scaled score is reported that consists of an unweighted average of the five subtest scores (Verbal Ability, Quantitative Ability, Biology, Chemistry, and Reading Comprehension).

NORMING SAMPLE. The PCAT scaled scores and percentile ranks are based on a norm group of 2,637 applicants to colleges of pharmacy who took the test on the October, 1992 PCAT administration. The norming sample is clearly not a random sample by any definition of the term. Whether it is representative of the entire population of examinees who took the PCAT in 1992 or in prior years (or in years since) cannot be determined from the information provided in the technical manual.

INSTRUCTIONS. The instructions to examinees are very clear and even provide suggestions for preparing for the exam in a manner that will enhance one's chances of optimal performance. The instructions for the test administrators are very clear and extremely detailed. Common questions asked and responses are provided to help the test administrators to field questions.

RELIABILITY AND VALIDITY. Test statistics are reported for over 3,400 examinees who took the PCAT in February 1993. Scaled score means ranged from 199.2 to 208.6 on the five sections. The standard deviations ranged from 25.2 to 31.4. Internal consistency reliability (KR20) values ranged from .82 to .89 with the reliability of the composite being .96. Intercorrelations between the section scores ranged from .32 to .71. Verbal Ability and Quantitative Ability had the smallest correlation. Verbal Ability and Reading Comprehension had the largest correlation. Although the reliabilities of the section scores are on the low side for interpreting individual examinee scores, they are probably adequate for most

purposes. The composite score represents the highest fidelity score and should probably be given the most weight in any high stakes decision to be made about an examinee.

The data from the reliability study were also analyzed to determine how the influence of a prior course in biology and chemistry influenced PCAT scores. A prior course in either subject area increased scores on that specific subject area; however, there was not a great deal of collateral advantage obtained for scores in the other sections. For instance, examinees who had increasingly greater exposure to college biology had lower mean scores on the Verbal, Reading Comprehension, and Quantitative Ability sections. There are many reasons this could occur without reflecting on the validity of the test; however, these results should probably be explored further.

Analyses of scores based on linguistic background (English vs. other) showed non-English speakers had means on the Verbal Ability and Reading Comprehension test that were more than one standard deviation below the means of their English-speaking counterparts. Scores on the Biology section were also lower for non-English speakers, however, only by about one-fifth standard deviation. Gender, regional, ethnic, and other subgroup differences in performance were never addressed—leaving issues of test and item bias to be potential problems.

The technical manual also provides 16 abstracts from studies published between 1976 and 1985 (a 1990 abstract was a review article) that have investigated various aspects of the PCAT. One study reported the PCAT alone predicted 25% of the variability in pharmacy school grades. Another study found the PCAT accounted for an additional 5% variance in pharmacy school grades after a battery of other predictors were already in the regression model. Although these abstracts provide support for the predictive validity of the PCAT, a more complete description of a subset of the studies in the technical report would help prospective test users interpret the results. Also, the overwhelming majority of the studies were published over 15 years ago. Studies with more recent data would provide users with confidence that the examination retains its validity as test content, examinees, and the health care environment undergo changes.

SUMMARY. Generally, the PCAT is a well-crafted examination for which composition is in alignment with recent advances in health professions high-stakes admission testing. Test security is well-maintained and multiple forms of the exams are available. Administration conditions are clearly described and test administrator instructions are very detailed. Although the internal consistency reliabilities of the section scores are lower than would be desired, the composite score reliability of .96 is well within the desired range for such tests. Predictive validity studies have found the PCAT effectively augments all other information available in predicting performance in pharmacy school. However, the normative data provided in the technical manual is not adequately described, research on the predictive validity of the PCAT needs to be updated with more recent studies, and information on test and item bias according to gender, race, ethnic origin, geographic region, and other factors are currently inadequate. Thus, although the PCAT generally appears to be an effective examination that meets the needs for which it was developed, caution should be exercised in interpreting the norms and using it for making decisions about underrepresented groups.

Review of the Pharmacy College Admission Test by LEO M. HARVILL, Professor and Assistant Dean for Medical Education, East Tennessee State University, Johnson City, TN:

The Pharmacy College Admission Test (PCAT) is a national examination program sponsored by the American Association of Colleges of Pharmacy to provide college admission committees with comparable information about the abilities of applicants. The technical manual states that it is designed to measure achievement in areas critical to the commencement of study in pharmacy and includes not only abilities measured by most standardized admissions tests, but also scientific subject matter in chemistry and biology. It is the opinion of this reviewer that this test does accomplish what it was designed to do.

The Credentialing and Postsecondary Education Division of The Psychological Corporation is responsible for the development, administration, and monitoring of the PCAT.

The PCAT consists of five test sections. Candidates receive separate scores for each test section and a composite score. All items are multiple choice. The Verbal Ability section contains 50 questions, 25 asking for antonyms of words and 25 seeking analogy completions. The Quantitative Ability section contains 65 questions, 25 nonverbal items in the arithmetic fundamentals of problem solving, decimals, and percentages and 40 items that sample various types of problem solving, including applications of

algebra and geometry. The Chemistry section consists of 60 questions that require knowledge and understanding of basic inorganic and organic chemistry. The Biology section contains 50 questions that measure examinee knowledge and understanding of principles and concepts in basic biology with emphasis on human biology. The Reading Comprehension section is made up of 45 questions that measure the ability to comprehend, analyze, understand, and interpret the contents of reading passages dealing with scientific topics. Examinees are given one-half day to respond to the 270 test questions.

Materials furnished for this review were a copy of the PCAT (1987), the PCAT Manual of Directions for Examiners (1991), the PCAT Candidate Information Booklet with Application (1991), and the PCAT Technical Manual (1993). The format for the PCAT is excellent; the items are easy to read. The PCAT Manual of Directions for Examiners is a professional document that covers all aspects of test administration. The PCAT Candidate Information Booklet is very informative and complete.

The Technical Manual provides a good overview and description of the PCAT. There is a brief, adequate description of the development of the test. There is also a section in the manual that explains the interpretation of the test results with examples of the score reports provided for the schools and the individual examinees. There is a presentation of normative data that would be useful to deans, admission officers, and faculty in pharmacy schools in making admission decisions about examinees. It is important to note that the technical manual emphasizes more than once that the PCAT is only one tool to be used with other kinds of information in making admission decisions.

Internal consistency (Kuder Richardson 20) reliability coefficients and standard errors of measurement (*SEM*) are presented for each test section score and the composite score for the February, 1993 test administration. The section reliability coefficients range from .82 to .89, whereas the composite score coefficient is .96. The manual reports that these are satisfactorily high; the reviewer would concur with that. *SEM*s are reported in raw score units in the manual. Because the sections vary in terms of the number of items, the reviewer has calculated *SEM*s as percentages of the number of items in the section. Those values range from 5.3% to 6.2% whereas the *SEM* for the composite score is 2.7% (7.29 items on a 270-item test). These *SEM*s are good values for a test that is used to make important decisions about individual examinees.

Intercorrelations among the section scores are also presented; these lend credence to the statement that each section was designed to measure different skills. Those correlations range from a low of .32 (Verbal Ability with Quantitative Ability) to a high of .71 (Verbal Ability with Reading Comprehension). Additional validity data are presented that compare PCAT scores by level of education, number of years of college biology, number of years of college chemistry, test repeater status, and linguistic background.

The final section of the Technical Manual provides an annotated bibliography of the research studies that have been published related to the validity of the PCAT as a predictor of performance in the first year of pharmacy school. The manual states that "Research has shown that the PCAT is one of the strongest predictors of first year pharmacy grade-point average and is therefore a valid tool in the admissions process" (p. 25). The reviewer concurs with this statement. The manual further states that "The Psychological Corporation and The American Association of Colleges of Pharmacy plan to conduct periodic research on the validity and use of the PCAT. In addition, independent efforts by local institutions are encouraged and supported" (p. 25). In light of this statement, it is somewhat discouraging to note that 12 of the 15 research studies listed were published shortly after the initial development of the test (1976 to 1980); the most recent publication was dated 1990. Perhaps more recent validity studies have been published since the publication of the technical manual in 1993 but, if not, there is a need for new validity studies using the PCAT and other possible predictors of success in the first year of pharmacy school.

In summary, the PCAT is an excellent admission test that is useful in making admission decisions in pharmacy schools. All of the publications reviewed were of excellent quality. There may be a need for further validity studies that will update those published in the late 1970s.

[234]
The Play Observation Scale.

Purpose: To assess children's free play preferences.
Population: Preschool children.
Publication Date: 1989.
Acronym: POS.
Scores: 27 possible ratings: 6 Non-Play (Transition, Unoccupied, Onlooker, Aggression, Teacher Conversation, Peer Conversation); 18 Play, 6 ratings (Functional, Exploratory, Reading, Constructive, Dramatic, Games) in each of 3 areas (Solitary, Parallel, Group); 3 Affective (Positive, Negative, Neutral).

Administration: Individual.
Price Data, 1993: $8 per complete kit including manual (19 pages).
Time: (4–5) minutes per observation.
Author: Kenneth H. Rubin.
Publisher: Kenneth H. Rubin [Canada].

TEST REFERENCES

1. Asendorpf, J. B. (1991). Development of inhibited children's coping with unfamiliarity. *Child Development, 62,* 1460–1474.
2. Rubin, K. H., Both, L., Zahn-Waxler, C., Cummings, E. M., & Wilkinson, M. (1991). Dyadic play behaviors of children of well and depressed mothers. *Development and Psychopathology, 3,* 243-251.
3. Coplan, R. J., Rubin, K. H., Fox, N. A., Calkins, S. D., & Stewart, S. L. (1994). Being alone, playing alone, and acting alone: Distinguishing among reticence and passive and active solitude in young children. *Child Development, 65,* 129-137.
4. Minnett, A., Clark, K., & Wilson, G. (1994). Play behavior and communication between deaf and hard of hearing children and their hearing peers in an integrated preschool. *American Annals of the Deaf, 139,* 420-429.
5. Fox, N. A., Rubin, K. H., Calkins, S. D., Marshall, T. R., Coplan, R. J., Porges, S. W., Long, J. L., & Stewart, S. (1995). Frontal activation asymmetry and social competence at four years of age. *Child Development, 66,* 1770–1784.
6. Rubin, K. H., Coplan, R. J., Fox, N. A., & Calkins, S. D. (1995). Emotionality, emotion regulation, and preschoolers' social adaptation. *Development and Psychopathology, 7,* 49-62.

Review of The Play Observation Scale by DENISE M. DeZOLT, Assistant Professor of Counseling Psychology, Lewis and Clark College, Portland, OR:

RATIONALE. The Play Observation Scale (POS) is an observational system designed to facilitate evaluation of young children's social, cognitive, and nonplay behaviors. Social play includes solitary, parallel, and group play, and considers the target child relative to peers in terms of proximity and attentiveness. Functional, constructive dramatic, and games-with-rules play comprise cognitive play. To select the appropriate cognitive play code, the observer is required to determine intention/purpose of the target child's activity. Nonplay activities include exploratory behavior, reading, unoccupied behavior, onlooker behavior, transition, active conversation, aggression, and rough-and-tumble behaviors. The manual contains brief descriptors with examples of each behavior and a summary page outlining the goal or intent of each codable category within the social, cognitive, and nonplay options. Though not stated specifically in the manual, the POS appears to be designed to assess the play skills of 2–6-year-olds. Little information is provided in the manual regarding the specific purpose and uses of the POS.

ADMINISTRATION AND SCORING. The observer using the POS is instructed to observe the target child for 30 seconds prior to beginning actual recording to familiarize oneself with contextual aspects related to the child's behaviors. Then the target child is observed in 10-second intervals after which the observer codes the predominant behavior in the designated column on an easy-to-use coding sheet.

If there are multiple behaviors observed in any 10-second interval, the observer codes the longest lasting behavior. If there are multiple behaviors of equal length, the most mature of the social and cognitive behaviors are coded. To enhance validity of the observations, the author recommends that the child be observed for no longer than 5 minutes per session, suggesting the importance of multiple observations, perhaps in different settings. In addition to the play categories, affective categories based on the type of interactions the target child has with playmates, including positive, negative, and neutral interactions, also are coded. The manual contains brief descriptors of each category and essentially the observer must rely on her or his own judgment of the target child's affective state. Although the manual provides no specific instructions for total scoring, it appears that the predominant behaviors coded, as noted in a total score, are indicative of the target child's current level of functioning as defined by these social and cognitive categories.

TECHNICAL QUALITIES. Limited empirical support for this scale is provided in the manual. Interobserver reliability data (percent agreement from 80%–95%) are available from published materials not included in the manual. In selected publications the author and colleagues have used this scale in several studies examining age, sex, socioeconomic status, and ecological considerations in relation to children's play behaviors.

CONCLUSIONS AND RECOMMENDATIONS FOR USE. In summary, the POS may be a useful observational tool when used primarily by professionals or trained paraprofessionals with expertise in child development and play. For example, it might best be used by members of a transdisciplinary or multidisciplinary team to gather pre- and postdata on a specific child's play skills and for development of appropriate goals and objectives related to specific skill enhancement. It may also be useful in assessing pre- and postfunctioning of children participating in a play skills enhancement group. Use of the POS in isolation is not encouraged. Rather, it may contribute information as part of a more comprehensive multifaceted assessment of social functioning. Given the lack of technical data regarding reliability and validity of the POS, caution is imperative when drawing conclusions relative to normative developmental social and cognitive play status and when making recommendations. In addition, supportive reliability and validity data regarding the POS should be included in the manual when available.

Review of The Play Observation Scale by MARK H. FUGATE, Associate Professor of School Psychology, Alfred University, Alfred, NY:

The Play Observation Scale is a direct observation system for measuring a variety of play and nonplay behaviors. The scale appears to be well grounded in relevant theory regarding children and the purposes or value of play. As a result, the scale appears to be useful for a variety of assessment, intervention, and research purposes.

The current edition of the Play Observation Scale was revised in 1989. This scale was developed by Kenneth Rubin, a well-respected author and researcher in the social and cognitive aspects of child development.

Play is an important childhood activity. As children mature socially and cognitively, specific characteristics of play will reflect these changes. Rubin constructed the Play Observation Scale as an objective measure for assessing the various social and cognitive components of play for children across a broad range of developmental levels. The manual contains a brief explanation of the theory behind the scale. However, a more extensive review of the developmental aspects of play can be found easily in a number of outside sources authored by Rubin (e.g., Rubin, Fein, & Vandenberg, 1983).

In the Play Observation Scale, the quality of play is recorded across three levels: the level of social interaction, the cognitive level of play, and the affective impact of play. The three social levels of play are identified as solitary, parallel, or group play. At the cognitive level, play is coded as either functional play, constructive play, dramatic play, or games with rules. The affective qualities of play are recorded relative to their positive, neutral, or negative implications. Categories of nonplay include: exploratory behavior, reading, unoccupied behavior, onlooker behavior, transition, active conversation, and aggression. Play behaviors are coded at 15-second intervals, allowing 10 seconds for observation and 5 seconds for scoring the observed behavior.

The value of any system for direct observation lies in its ability to estimate effectively the occurrence of actual events. This practical utility is a function of the clarity and relevance of behavior definitions and the appropriateness of the method of interval recording for capturing the behaviors of interest. In this regard the utility of the Play Observation Scale is quite good. Directions for use of the definitions and coding are easy to follow. The definitions of target behaviors are clear and appropriately relevant. Similarly, the method for recording the behaviors generally appears to capture effectively the occurrence of target behaviors. However, it is important to note the recording system may at times underestimate the occurrence of some behaviors.

According to the directions for recording behaviors, in most circumstances only one behavior may be recorded per 10-second interval. If more than one behavior occurs the behavior of longest duration is to be coded. If behaviors occur for equal amounts of time, there is a hierarchical system for coding the most mature social and/or cognitive behavior. This system for recording the occurrence of behavior provides adequate estimates of sustained play or nonplay activities; however, the process may result in underestimates of short duration, but potentially important, behaviors.

Although the Play Observation Scale appears to be a useful tool with potentially broad applicability, the accompanying manual is incomplete and somewhat inadequate. On the positive side, the manual provides the observer with clear definitions of the behaviors to be coded, explicit directions for scoring behaviors, and a number of "helpful hints" for improving coding accuracy.

On the other hand, the manual is generally lacking in psychometric information, and the scoring protocol is poorly designed and presented. Discussion of the psychometric properties of the scale is limited to two sentences regarding the reliability of the measure. In this short paragraph it is reported that interobserver agreement ranges from approximately 80% to 95% and that kappas are uniformly high. Additionally, a bibliography is provided for further reference. Although the manuscripts listed in the bibliography are quite useful for substantiating the psychometric properties of the observation scale, conducting the review of this literature is laborious. It would be helpful if the author would provide a more detailed summary of the reliability and validity information in the manual.

The structure of the scoring protocol is the primary weakness of the Play Observation Scale. Essentially the observation coding sheet provides six rows in which to code the various play and nonplay activities. It appears the form can be used to record only six intervals (1 minute) of play observation. Thus, if one is to observe a child for the recommended maximum of 10 minutes, it will require 5 coding sheets. Managing this amount of paper in an observation session can be unwieldy and inefficient. The poor organization of the coding form is complicated by absence of discussion of its use in the manual.

In general, the Play Observation Scale is an instrument that can be used to measure effectively the play activity of children. Although one must look beyond the manual for psychometric information, the scale appears to have adequate validity and reliability (as estimated by measures of interobserver agreement). The Play Observation Scale will be useful to both researchers and clinicians. Researchers should find the scale valuable for evaluating the social and cognitive development of children as evidenced in their play behavior. Clinically, the scale could be useful as a mechanism for assessing the social development of children and monitoring the effectiveness of therapeutic interventions. However, users of this instrument may need to set aside some time initially to reconstruct the coding sheet to their purposes.

REVIEWER'S REFERENCE

Rubin, K. H., Fein, G. G., & Vandenberg, B. (1983). Play. In E. M. Hetherington (Ed.), *Handbook of child psychology, (vol. 4), Socialization, personality, and social development* (pp. 693–774). New York: Wiley.

[235]
Power Base Inventory.

Purpose: Assesses the techniques individuals use to influence others.
Population: Work team members, leaders, managers, supervisors.
Publication Dates: 1985–1991.
Acronym: PBI.
Scores, 6: Information, Expertise, Goodwill, Authority, Reward, Discipline.
Administration: Group or individual.
Price Data, 1994: $5.25 per inventory.
Time: (15) minutes.
Comments: Self-scored.
Authors: Kenneth W. Thomas and Gail Fann Thomas.
Publisher: XICOM, Inc.

Review of the Power Base Inventory by JUDY L. ELLIOTT, Research Associate, National Center for Educational Outcomes, University of Minnesota, Minneapolis, MN:

PURPOSE. The Power Base Inventory (second edition) was designed to assess the techniques leaders or group members use to influence others.

CONTENT/OVERVIEW. The Power Base comprises one self-administered, forced-choice 30-item inventory. Item statements describe why members of a team or colleagues might be influenced by the rater. Raters choose between two forced-choice statements (A) and (B). Reading level is not indicated.

Inventory scores are used to create a profile of power bases or sources of power. The quickly hand-scored profile is created by circling the letters (A or B) for each of the 30 items. The letters fall across one of six categories: Information, Expertise, Goodwill (referent), Authority (legitimate), Reward, and Discipline (coercive).

The number of items circled in each column is totaled. These numbers, in turn, are graphed on the percentile chart. The percentile ranks are based on scores of "managers" who have already taken the inventory. (No other information about this ranking is given.) Percentile ranks are divided by upper and lower 25% and middle 50%. However, the authors note that "extreme scores are not necessarily bad" (p. 9) because some situations may require the use of extreme power bases.

The final section of the user's manual is a guide to interpreting the profile of scores. The six power bases are highlighted by Source of Power, Power Base, Influence Effect, Ideal Situation, and Practical Reality. Each is described in detail. The six power bases are discussed in terms of use, warning signals, and requirements for increasing their use.

RELIABILITY/VALIDITY. There is no formal analysis or discussion of either reliability or validity. As an inventory, the Power Base presents itself as a self-awareness tool that could be situationally based. The authors' comment of caution about interpreting extreme scores raises the issue of situationally based scores. Hence, the profile of scores is likely to be situational instead of a reliable indicator of a consistently used power base. This is in fact very similar to the Thomas-Kilmann Conflict Mode Instrument (T4:2831) previously published by one of the authors. Similarly, raters are asked to select one of two options. Thus raters' scores of this instrument also change with time and situation. It is important for users to be aware of this possible shifting in scores and what has caused them.

In summary, the Power Base Inventory is a self-directed instrument that screens styles of influence used by people as managers, team members, chairpersons, parents, or corporate presidents. Profile scores are placed on percentile ranks and interpreted according to the six power bases deemed relevant to creating influence on others.

[236]
Pre-Referral Intervention Manual [Revised and Updated Second Edition].

Purpose: To identify learning and behavior problems and provide appropriate intervention strategies.

Population: K–12 students.
Publication Dates: 1988–1993.
Acronym: PRIM.
Scores: Ratings in 13 areas: Memory/Abstractions/Generalizations/Organization, Listening, Speaking, Reading, Writing, Spelling, Mathematical Calculations, Academic Performance, Interpersonal Relationships, Depression/Motivation, Inappropriate Behavior Under Normal Circumstances, Rules and Expectations, Group Behavior.
Administration: Individual.
Price Data, 1993: $85 per complete kit including pre-referral intervention manual ('93, 504 pages), 50 pre-referral checklist forms, and 50 pre-referral intervention strategies documentation forms; $30 per pre-referral intervention manual; $30 per 50 pre-referral checklist forms; $25 per 50 pre-referral intervention strategies documentation; $190 per computerized pre-referral intervention manual.
Time: Administration time not reported.
Authors: Stephen B. McCarney, Kathy Cummins Wunderlich (manual, and Angela Marie Bauer (manual).
Publisher: Hawthorne Educational Services, Inc.

Review of the Pre-Referral Intervention Manual [Revised and Updated Second Edition] by ANTHONY W. PAOLITTO, Assistant Professor, School Psychology Program, Ohio State University, Columbus, OH:

The Pre-Referral Intervention Manual (PRIM) was developed as a response to the common perception and practice that a referral for special education virtually ensures the student being declared eligible for some level of special services. The intended consequence of instituting formalized prereferral procedures in schools is to provide screening and intermediate intervention to ultimately reduce the number of students "formally" referred and consequently receiving services. The PRIM purports to provide intervention strategies for common learning and behavior problems encountered by regular classroom teachers, which, if employed consistently by all teachers working with an individual student, is likely to result in enhanced success for the student outside of the special education context.

The Pre-Referral Intervention Manual is composed of 13 different "problem areas" relevant to differential aspects of learning and behavior (Memory, Abstractions, Generalizations, and Organization; Listening; Speaking; Reading; Writing; Spelling; Mathematical Calculations; Academic Performance; Interpersonal Relationships; Depression/Motivation; Inappropriate Behavior under Normal Circumstances; Rules and Expectations; Group Behavior). Each individual area may include as few as 7 and as many as 26 specific problems characteristic of their respective area. Overall, this results in a total of 219 specific problems, which the authors describe as "the most common learning and behavior problems" (p. 10). For example, the problem area of Reading includes the specific problems of "loses place when reading" and "fails to demonstrate word attack skills" (p. 3) as well as others. The problem area of Interpersonal Relationships includes "fights with other students" and "has little or no interaction with teachers" (p. 5). For each of the 219 specific problems there are approximately 25 to 45 or more individual interventions that relate specifically to the identified problem. The interventions are brief and concise, usually one or two sentences in length. To illustrate utilizing the behavior problem "has little or no interaction with teachers" (p. 261), suggestions from the pool of interventions include "offer the student assistance frequently throughout the day" (p. 264), "call on the student often in order to encourage communication" (p. 264), "do not force the student to interact" (p. 266), plus many others for this specific problem.

The record form for the PRIM, labeled the Pre-Referral Checklist, has instructions to the teacher completing the form to simply check off each behavior they have observed the student in question demonstrate during the last month. The form mirrors the structure of the manual contents described above. It lists the 219 learning and behavior problems over five pages in the order they appear in the manual (without the interventions). The 13 problem areas are also included, marking off those items specific to their heading. Also included is a Pre-Referral Intervention Strategies Documentation form, which simply lists the individual interventions selected relating to the specific problems identified, the dates interventions were tried, and the success or lack of success for certain interventions. Neither guidelines on which or how many interventions should be tried nor how their effectiveness might be evaluated are included.

Instructions for using the PRIM are nonelaborative and informal. Generally, any teacher who is working with a specific child may complete the record form checklist, subjectively selecting any of the 219 problems. The severity or frequency of occurrence is not considered in the instructions. Ideally, checklists are to be completed by as many educators as possible who work with the child and feel they are familiar enough with him or her to identify different behaviors. Although the child can apparently be rated by just one individual, the authors state that they hope multiple raters will derive a consistent set of interventions, which when addressed would contribute to the likeliness of the student achieving success. Although specific guidelines are not offered regarding which or how many behaviors should be targeted for intervention based upon individual or group ratings for a particular child, a consensus model is implied.

Although not specifically stated by the authors, it can be logically inferred that the Pre-Referral Intervention Manual is not intended as a psychometrically based tool, but rather as a practical resource guide or handbook. Thus, it is the practical aspects of the PRIM that will be evaluated. In addition to the 219 specific problems and their corresponding lists of interventions, the actual PRIM handbook ("Manual") includes less than three pages of supporting information including instructions, development, and applications. Although this volume is referred to as the "Revised and Updated Second Edition," there is no mention of the first edition or what changes were incorporated. Specific guidelines related to the appropriate grade or ages for which the interventions are intended are not included. The authors state that the 219 specific problems they have included are "the most common learning and behavior problems encountered by regular educators in their classroom" (p. 10). Methodology on how this was determined or any other supporting data are not provided. However, both the breakdown of the 13 problem areas as well as the high number of specific problems included indicates good face validity.

With regard to the specific interventions accompanying each problem, the authors again claim that the strategies they have included are those that "special education and regular education personnel have found most effective with students in need of more success in regular education" (p. 10). No information supporting how such decisions were derived or compiled, or by whom, are offered. Although many of the interventions appear to have face validity relevant to their specific problem behavior, no explanation is presented on criteria necessary for the interventions they chose to include, presumably at the exclusion of others. The interventions themselves include much variation in sophistication and applicability, which would allow educators to customize their choice of interventions to meet the needs of the individual child. However, one must be cautioned that there is no empirical support presented for treatment outcomes, leaving the user the responsibility of selecting interventions and monitoring their success.

In summary, the PRIM may be best regarded as an "idea generator," a term intended in a complimentary manner. With several thousand interventions listed relevant to over 200 learning and behavior problems, it would be difficult for the PRIM not to stimulate an educator's thinking in order to develop practical interventions and/or recommendations for a variety of children. Those who might like to utilize the PRIM more rigorously will be disappointed, however, due to the lack of information and validity concerning treatment success. Other than face validity, there is no psychometric information on which to base the merits of this instrument. Although easy to use, more detail regarding development and applications certainly would be desirable and would enhance the scope of this instrument. However, the PRIM can still be a useful and helpful generator of qualitative information, as long as its use is not extended for screening, diagnostic, or placement decisions.

Review of the Pre-Referral Intervention Manual [Revised and Updated Second Edition] by GABRIELE van LINGEN, Lecturer, Department of Psychology, The University of Hong Kong, Hong Kong:

The Pre-Referral Intervention Manual (PRIM) is designed for a school's prereferral team (e.g., Teacher Assistance Team, Child Study Team) in proposing interventions for use by regular classroom teachers with students who demonstrate learning and/or behavior problems. Its intent is to allow students to achieve success in the least restrictive environment, to reduce the need for testing, to assist in the identification for and placement in special education, and to increase regular education teachers' skills in handling students' learning and behavior problems. As such, the PRIM cannot be considered an assessment instrument, and the manual makes no psychometric claims.

To meet its purposes, the PRIM provides 219 sequentially numbered descriptions of learning or behavior problems, organized into 13 categories. The descriptions range from very general (e.g., "behaves in a manner inappropriate for the situation") to more specific (e.g., "fails to correctly solve math problems requiring regrouping"). A prereferral checklist that may relate to these descriptions can be acquired separately. The manual does not contain a copy of the checklist and does not refer to it or explain its development or use. It would seem that an independent assessment of a student's problems must be conducted before appropriate descriptions of problems can be identified and relevant interventions can be selected.

Although using a clear format for presentation, the PRIM does not describe the system used for selecting categories nor for assigning particular problems to a category. Although there is evidence of face validity for the categorization of many of the problems, some assignments can be questioned. For example, under the category "Inappropriate Behavior Under Normal Circumstances," one finds "cannot fasten articles of clothing" (p. 397). There also appears to be no particular system of organization for either the categories or the problems within categories. Developmental or instructional sequences do exist for the categories of Listening, Speaking, Reading, Writing, Spelling, and Mathematical Calculations, but the authors do not seem to have applied them in their sequential listing of problems within those areas.

Each of the 219 problem areas has a list of interventions. The number listed differs for each problem, ranging from 12 to 73 interventions per problem. The PRIM states that the basis for their inclusion was that they "were found most effective with students in need of more success in regular education classrooms" (p. 10) by both regular and special education personnel. The method for making this determination is not described. Moreover, no empirical studies are cited that provide information on the effectiveness of any of the interventions in remedying learning or behavior problems. The interventions tend to consist of general instructional practices and techniques for individualizing instruction and for classroom management as presented in introductory educational psychology textbooks. They usually include the use of multiple modalities for presenting information, various types of peer assistance, reinforcement for academic success or appropriate behavior, methods for communicating with parents, etc. Although the PRIM claims to cover K–12 students' needs, the interventions listed seem most appropriate to elementary students. For instance, "abstract concepts" are limited to items such as larger/smaller, left/right, square, triangle, etc. Moreover, the limited approach to individual learning styles, based solely on modalities, and the lack of innovativeness of the interventions were striking. Similar to the listing of categories and problems, the listing of interventions lacks a systematic approach. This lack results in redundancies both across and within problem areas.

The PRIM contains an appendix with sample lists and forms related to reinforcers, point systems, schedules and assignment sheets, study aids and organizers, classroom rules, contracts, methods for parent communication, and similar items. These can be useful to the beginning teacher.

In summary, the PRIM can be useful to the beginning teacher, who may need assistance in applying the techniques learned in an educational psychology course to students with learning or behavioral problems. It would be much more valuable if the descriptions of student problems were clearly tied to assessment, the problems and interventions were organized in a systematic manner and followed available developmental sequences, and the interventions were extended to middle and secondary students and incorporated recent research results and innovations for working with problem students.

[237]
Preschool and Kindergarten Behavior Scales.
Purpose: "A behavioral rating instrument for use in evaluating social skills and problem behavior patterns of preschool and kindergarten-aged children."
Population: Ages 3–6.
Publication Date: 1994.
Acronym: PKBS.
Scores, 12: Social Cooperation, Social Interaction, Social Independence, Social Skills Total, Self-Centered/Explosive, Attention Problems/Overactive, Antisocial/Aggressive, Externalizing Problems, Social Withdrawal, Anxiety/Somatic Problems, Internalizing Problems, Problem Behavior Total.
Administration: Group.
Price Data, 1996: $39 per complete kit including manual ('94, 65 pages) and 20 test forms; $17 per 20 test forms; $24 per manual; $24 per specimen set including test manual and 1 test form.
Time: (8–12) minutes.
Comments: Ratings by individual who has interacted with and known child for at least 3 months; optional additional information section.
Author: Kenneth W. Merrell.
Publisher: PRO-ED, Inc.

Review of the Preschool and Kindergarten Behavior Scales by DAVID MACPHEE, Associate Professor of Human Development and Family Studies, Colorado State University, Fort Collins, CO:

The Preschool and Kindergarten Behavior Scales (PKBS) are meant to be used as (a) a screening tool for the early detection of social-emotional problems, (b) a multiaxial battery for classifying children with behavioral problems, (c) a basis for interventions to ameliorate social skills deficits or problem behaviors, and (d) a research tool. More generally, the PKBS was developed to fill a gap for instruments that

can be used with preschoolers. Federal legislation has created a need for screening and intervention services for young children, yet few tools have been devised specifically for this age group.

DEVELOPMENT. Conceptually, the PKBS draws from research on peer and adult-related social skills, and on internalizing and externalizing disorders. The initial item pool was generated from the literature on preschool children's normal and atypical behavior. The 76 items on the final PKBS include many that duplicate either the Social Skills Rating System (Gresham & Elliot, 1990; 12:362) or the Child Behavior Checklist (Achenbach, 1992; 55), especially the Aggressive subscale for 4-to-5-year-olds. In terms of both theory and content, then, the PKBS strongly parallels existing measures of early social behavior.

The standardization sample included 2,855 preschoolers, 312 of whom had a developmental disability. Even though recruiting was selective—through private and public preschools, and pediatric clinics—the demographics were well representative based on 1980 census data. Few demographic differences in PKBS scores were observed, although the author's analytical approach minimized the chances that any would be found. For instance, parent occupation was collapsed into four categories and then was correlated with PKBS scores.

Another difficulty with the standardization sample is ambiguity in the unit of analysis. For example, some teachers may have rated multiple children, especially for test-retest reliability. If so, stability could be due to children's reputations and rater characteristics rather than actual child behavior (Cairns & Green, 1979), and the children's ratings would not represent independent units. As well, at least 102 children were rated by multiple informants; it is not clear which raters' data were used to derive norms.

In contrast to the Child Behavior Checklist and related measures, the PKBS does not present separate standard score tables for boys and girls. This decision is notable because, as the author notes, "there is a substantial body of research suggesting that ... girls ... [have] better social skills and [exhibit] fewer problem behaviors than boys" (p. 51). Indeed, the PKBS manual presents ample evidence supporting this conclusion, especially for externalizing behaviors. Thus, it is curious that the norm-referenced tables are subdivided by age but not gender, given similar group differences for these two variables.

PSYCHOMETRIC PROPERTIES. The PKBS has high enough alpha reliabilities (alpha ≥ .90), with the exception of the two Internalizing Problems subscales, to permit use for individual decision making. Test-retest reliabilities are high for the problem behavior area scores (Externalizing = .87; Internalizing = .80) and are adequate for the three social skills subscales (.66 to .70 over 3 months). Interrater reliability was adequate when raters knew children in the same setting, but was weak when examined across contexts: Teacher and teacher aide ratings were correlated .48 for Social Skills and .59 for Problem Behaviors; teacher-parent agreement was .38 for the Social Skills Total score and .16 for the Problem Behavior Total.

Regarding validity, factor analyses of the social skills items yielded the three subscales of Cooperation, Interaction, and Independence. A separate factor analysis of the problem behaviors produced a muddled pattern, with the broad-band solution (i.e., externalizing, internalizing problems) being the most sensible. The narrow-band subscales are less defensible in terms of their factor loadings, lower reliabilities, high correlations with broadband scores, and absence of data on clinical utility. Factoring social skills and problem behaviors as separate item sets also obscures relations between the two constructs. For instance, Social Independence contains many items related to peer popularity (e.g., "Is accepted and liked by other children" [p. 2, record form]) that appear to be mere inverses of the Antisocial/Aggressive subscale (e.g., teases, calls people names, bothers other children). Correlations between the Social Skills Problem Behavior subscales are not given, although the two total scores are correlated -.56. And though one would expect these two subscales to be related strongly to sociometric status, such evidence was not reported.

Convergent validity was demonstrated in part by comparing the PKBS to the Social Skills Rating System. The Social Skills Total scores were highly correlated (r = .76) as were the two Problem Behavior scores (r = .83). In addition, the PKBS Problem Behavior Total score was correlated with the Hyperactivity (r = .85) and Conduct Problems (r = .83) scales of the Conners Teacher Ratings. These results are not surprising given the overlap in item content, but they do raise questions about the unique niche filled by the PKBS.

UTILITY. The norms and validity data for the PKBS do not support its use for screening. Age-graded tables list raw score ranges that correspond to functional levels (e.g., the extreme 5th percentile represents significant deficits in social skills or behavior problems, and children between the 5th and 20th percentiles have moderate deficits). However, there is no technical analysis and rationale for establishing these cut points (cf. Standard 6.9; AERA, APA, & NCME, 1985). The best defense against inappropriately labeling children is to relate classification to diagnostic criteria, yet the PKBS manual describes these functional levels only in general terms: Children with average or better scores have "probably developed adequate social skills" and "tend to be well-liked" whereas those at the extreme "may be likely to exhibit social skills deficits" (p. 22). The manual notes that these cutoffs may produce some false-positive errors, yet no data are presented on sensitivity and specificity nor is there a discussion of how misclassification rates vary with the number of individuals in each category (cf. Standard 1.23; AERA, APA, & NCME, 1985).

Criterion validity has only been assessed relative to concurrent disability status. Children with a disability had significantly lower social skills scores and more problem behaviors, although developmental level was not controlled. The PKBS also discriminated between children in special education and those in regular classrooms, with 90.2% correctly classified. This validity coefficient is impressive, yet one should bear in mind that accuracy in classifying diagnosed students cannot be generalized to screening undiagnosed populations, especially with low-base rate childhood behavior problems. Further, the manual does not provide a rationale for using special education status as a criterion variable—adaptive behavior is only one part of the placement decision—nor were the diagnostic attributes of the criterion defined (cf. Standards 1.12 and 1.13; AERA, APA, & NCME, 1985). More defensible criteria might include peer sociometric status or *DSM-IV* diagnoses.

The PKBS also is recommended as a tool to guide intervention programs, and to monitor subsequent behavior changes, but no data related to this purpose have been gathered. Such information could support its construct validity, and would be theoretically useful in determining whether enhancing social skills concomitantly reduces problem behaviors.

SUMMARY. The PKBS is most similar in content and target age to the Social Skills Rating System (SSRS) and the Child Behavior Checklist (CBC). The PKBS has more peer-related items than the SSRS, but the latter has more items and scales pertinent to social skills. The CBC for young children does not assess social skills but it does have more problem-behavior items and narrow-band scales than the PKBS. All three instruments have excellent reliabilities, though the CBC's internal reliabilities are better for problem behaviors. The primary considerations favoring the SSRS and CBC, then, are their validity and better norms. The PKBS has minimal data on its utility for screening and diagnosis whereas the SSRS and especially CBC have extensive information on cut scores and concurrent validity. The PKBS manual presents no data on sensitivity and specificity, predictive validity, nor test item bias. The Preschool and Kindergarten Behavior Scales ultimately may prove useful in early screening and diagnosis, but only if additional research supports their validity for these purposes.

REVIEWER'S REFERENCES

Cairns, R. B., & Green, J. A. (1979). How to assess personality and social patterns: Observations or ratings? In R. B. Cairns (Ed.), *The analysis of social interactions: Methods, issues, and illustrations* (pp. 209–226). Hillsdale, NJ: Erlbaum.

American Educational Research Association, American Psychological Association, & National Council on Measurement in Education. (1985). *Standards for educational and psychological testing.* Washington, DC: American Psychological Association, Inc.

Gresham, F. M., & Elliot, S. N. (1990). *Social Skills Rating System: Manual.* Circle Pines, MN: American Guidance Service.

Achenbach, T. M. (1992). *Manual for the Child Behavior Checklist/2–3 and 1992 profile.* Burlington, VT: University of Vermont Department of Psychiatry.

Review of the Preschool and Kindergarten Behavior Scales by T. STEUART WATSON, Associate Professor of Educational Psychology, Mississippi State University, Starkville, MS:

PURPOSE AND RATIONALE. The Preschool and Kindergarten Behavior Scales (PKBS) was designed as (a) "a screening tool for identifying preschool and kindergarten-aged children who are at risk for developing serious behavioral, social, and emotional problems"; (b) "a part of a multi-axial assessment battery for formally identifying and classifying children with severe behavioral and emotional problems"; (c) "a tool for assessing social skills deficiencies and behavioral problems for the purpose of identifying appropriate interventions"; and (d) "a research instrument for studying the developing social-behavioral patterns of young children" (p. 1). The test is very similar in format (i.e., conceptualization and design) to the School Social Behavior Scales (Merrell, 1993; 277). The rationale provided by the author for developing yet another behavior rating scale is that, despite the impetus from federal legislation that mandates services for the preschool population, there is a lack of psychometrically sound instruments specifically designed to assess and screen children in this age range.

TEST CONTENT. The PKBS consists of 76 items rated on a 4-point (0–3) Likert-type scale across two broad dimensions, Social Skills (34 items) and Problem Behavior (42 items), to reflect the author's view that children's behavioral development

is best understood by these dimensions. The Social Skills dimension was designed to assess social behavior directed toward peers and adults. This dimension is divided, based on factor analysis, into three subscales: Social Cooperation (reflects "adult-related social adjustment"); Social Interaction (reflects the peer-related social behaviors of making friends); and Social Independence (reflects peer-related social behaviors that allow one to achieve independence within one's peer group). Although never explicitly stated, it seems that items were included on a factor if their loadings were .40 or higher and factors were retained if their eigenvalues exceeded 1.00. In looking at the items that comprise each of the three subscales, there does not appear to be a clear delineation between the specific social skills being measured (a point acknowledged by the author on page 4 of the manual). For example, although the Social Cooperation subscale is "more strongly connected to adult-related social adjustment" (p. 4), at least 4 of the 12 items seem to involve peer interactions (e.g., "shares toys and other belongings") and two items are more ambiguous ("shows self-control" and "uses free time in an acceptable way," p. 6). This is not a criticism of this test per se, but a demonstration of the difficulty in summarily explaining commonality between items that happen to load on the same factor.

The Problem Behavior scale was derived a bit differently than the Social Skills scale. First, a two-factor solution was specified prior to conducting the final factor analysis because previous exploratory factor analyses yielded uninterpretable results. Then, a factor analysis was conducted for each of the two factors, labeled Internalizing and Externalizing problems. Three narrow band factors and two narrow band factors emerged from the factor analyses of the Externalizing and Internalizing Scales, respectively. The three narrow band factors of the Externalizing Scale were labeled Self-Centered/Explosive, Attention Problems/Overactive, and Antisocial/Aggressive. The two narrow band factors of the Internalizing Scale were labeled Social Withdrawal and Anxiety/Somatic Problems. Despite empirical support for these two problem areas, the distinction between the two is not clear. Although there are significant correlations within items on scales that are labeled "Internalizing" or "Externalizing," there is also significant correlation, on this test and others, between items on each of the scales (e.g., McConaughy & Skiba, 1993). Thus, separation of specific behavior problems into one of these two categories seems a bit artificial, although certainly not unusual.

STANDARDIZATION. The standardization sample appears to be generally adequate as 2,855 children (1,484 males and 1,323 females) were recruited from 16 states representing the four major geographical regions of the country. The manual provides information on subjects regarding sex, age, ethnic status, and parent's occupation. Three-year-old males and females were underrepresented in the sample (n = 110, n = 89, respectively) when compared with the number of 4-, 5-, and 6-year-olds. Ethnic status of children in the sample was very consistent with 1990 U.S. Census data. For the most part, occupation of the subject's parents closely matched the percentage found in the U.S. population. However, children of unemployed parents were underrepresented and children of "operators, fabricators, and laborers" (p. 37) were overrepresented. Eleven percent of the sample were identified as either having a developmental disability (8.4%) or being evaluated for a developmental disability or delay (2.6%), which is consistent with national figures for preschool and kindergarten children. This section of the manual could be improved by presenting stratified data instead of percentages falling within nominal categories across several different variables.

Although it is a minor point, the author concludes on page 36 of the manual that socioeconomic status has minimal effects on a child's ratings on the PKBS. This assertion is based on low Pearson product moment correlations between PKBS scores and occupational status scores that were recorded into four socioeconomic divisions (high, middle, lower, lowest). Given the ordinal nature of the socioeconomic data, a more accurate estimate of the relationship between PKBS scores and socioeconomic status would have been obtained using a Spearman rho correlation.

ADMINISTRATION AND SCORING. The test requires no special skills in terms of administration. It is completed by someone who is familiar with the child for at least 3 months preceding the rating period, most commonly parents and teachers, and is subject to the same biases as other rating scales. The protocol is designed to facilitate reduced error and ease of scoring in that the scoring key appears in a vertical, color-shaded column beside the items. Scoring is simple and straightforward in that raw scores are summed and converted to percentile ranks, standard scores, and functional levels. Standard scores, percentile ranks, and functional levels are available for the Social Skills total, Externalizing Problems, Internalizing Problems, and Problem Behavior Total

scores. Only functional levels are available for each of the subscale scores. Because the functional levels for Social Skills (e.g., high functioning, average, moderate deficit, and significant deficit) and Problem Behavior (e.g., no problem, average, moderate problem, significant problem) are merely verbal descriptors that correspond to the percentile ranks, they do not provide any additional meaningful information, such as importance of the problem or distress caused by the problem.

RELIABILITY. Internal reliability, the degree to which items on a scale measure a single concept, was estimated by both coefficient alpha and Spearman-Brown split-half methods and ranged from .81 (Anxiety/Somatic Problems, using Spearman-Brown) to .97 (Externalizing Problems, using coefficient alpha). The corresponding standard error of measurement scores were low, all of which suggest that the various scales and dimensions of the PKBS have high internal reliability and low standard deviations. Test-retest reliability was estimated at 3-week and 3-month intervals. Coefficients at 3 weeks ranged from .58 (Social Skills Total) to .87 (Self-Centered/Explosive and Externalizing Problems) and at 3 months ranged from .36 (Anxiety/Somatic Problems) to .78 (Externalizing Problems and Problem Behavior Total). These test-retest coefficients suggest that the ratings on the PKBS are relatively stable over time. Two separate studies were conducted to assess interrater reliability. One compared ratings of 82 children, ages 3–5, by their preschool teachers and classroom aides and the other compared ratings of 102 children, ages 3–5, by their preschool teachers and one parent. Correlations between teachers and aides ranged from .36 (Social Independence) to .63 (Externalizing Problems), and between teachers and parents ranged from .13 (Internalizing Problems) to .57 (Social Cooperation). These correlation coefficients are weak to moderate with the Social Independence, Social Withdrawal, and Anxiety/Somatic Problems subscales and the Internalizing Problems dimension being especially susceptible to source and/or setting variance. That is, some of the scores may depend as much on who is completing the rating form as the child's actual behavior. It is not clear if source variance is a problem for this test or whether the low interrater reliability is an accurate reflection of variability in the child's behavior in the presence of different adults and in different settings.

VALIDITY. Content validity appears to be adequate as the items bear a relationship to the conceptual dimensions of the test and correlate at a minimum level (at least .30) with the appropriate subscale and scale totals. Construct validity was demonstrated by the moderate to high item-scale and item-total correlations, the moderate intercorrelations between scale scores, and the relatively robust factor structure across sex, age, and disability categories. In addition, significant group differences were found for sex, age, and disability categories, which were consistent with expectations based on the social skills and problem behavior literature, thus providing further evidence for construct validity. Convergent/divergent validity, a form of construct validity, was investigated by correlating scores on the PKBS with scores on the Social Skills Rating System (*n* = 86), the Matson Evaluation of Social Skills with Youngsters (*n* = 116), and the Conners Teacher Rating Scale-39 (*n* = 46). In general, high correlations were found between scores measuring similar constructs and low to moderate correlations were found between scores measuring dissimilar constructs. In terms of concurrent criterion-related validity, the PKBS correctly predicted group membership for 90.18% of special education students in the standardization sample, with the Social interaction subscale being the best predictor.

MANUAL. The author is to be commended for compiling such an organized, understandable, and user-friendly manual. The purpose and rationale of the test are clearly described as is the relationship between the test content and current research in the areas of social competence and behavioral development/psychopathology. All technical terms (e.g., discriminant analysis) are explained so that even novice test consumers can gain an understanding of complex psychometric concepts. The section on "Issues in Using Behavior Rating Scales" is a thorough primer for those who are unfamiliar with the uses, limitations, and best practices in using rating scales. In addition, the author takes the refreshing position throughout most of the manual of not going beyond the presented data in touting the test or in reaching premature conclusions about the usefulness of the test.

SUMMARY AND CONCLUSIONS. Overall, the PKBS seems to be a theoretically and psychometrically sound screening instrument for children ages 3–6. There are some noticeable weaknesses in the test (e.g., stratified standardization data, interrater reliability), but none so overwhelming as to render the test useless. With respect to its stated purposes, the PKBS appears to be appropriate as a screening measure for children at risk of developing social or behavioral problems, as part of an assessment battery

for identifying and classifying children with behavior problems, and as a research tool for studying behavioral and social development. It is much less useful for identifying appropriate interventions. It may assist in identifying broad classes of target behaviors, but because the focus is on topography of behavior and not on function, it does not allow identification of potentially effective interventions. The most obvious strengths of this test are its brevity and the fact that it was designed specifically for use with young children.

REVIEWER'S REFERENCES
McConaughy, S. H., & Skiba, R. J. (1993). Comorbidity of externalizing and internalizing problems. *School Psychology Review, 22,* 421–436.
Merrell, K. W. (1993). School Social Behavior Scales. Brandon, VT: Clinical Psychology Publishing Company.

[238]
Preschool Development Inventory.

Purpose: A brief screening inventory "designed to help identify children with developmental and other problems that may interfere with the child's ability to learn."
Population: Ages 3–6.
Publication Dates: 1984–1988.
Acronym: PDI.
Scores: General Development Score, Possible Problems List (24); 3 ratings: Child Description, Special Problems or Handicaps, Parent's Questions or Concerns.
Administration: Individual.
Price Data, 1993: $7 per manual ('88, 25 pages); $9 per 25 question/answer sheets.
Time: (15) minutes.
Comments: Ratings by parents; replaces the Minnesota Preschool Inventory (aka Minnesota PreKindergarten Inventory) (9:720) and the Preschool Developmental Inventory (10:291).
Author: Harold Ireton.
Publisher: Behavior Science Systems, Inc.
Cross References: See T4:2079 (1 reference); for a review by R. A. Bornstein of an earlier edition, see 10:291.

Review of the Preschool Development Inventory by LENA R. GADDIS, Associate Professor of Educational Psychology, Northern Arizona University, Flagstaff, AZ:

The Preschool Development Inventory (PDI) is a developmental screening measure for children aged 3 to 6 that relies on the report of a parent regarding the developmental course of his or her child. It is divided into five sections, with the first consisting of 60 items addressing skills in language comprehension, expressive language, fine and gross motor, self-help, and personal-social. The second section (24 items) is designed to identify behavioral symptoms (e.g., sensory, speech, language, comprehension, physical, emotional) in young children. The 84 items contained within these sections are responded to in a yes/no format. The remaining sections are in an open-ended format and request that the parents provide a description of the child, describe special problems or handicaps possessed by the child, and note any questions or concerns regarding the child. The author notes that the PDI is best used along with a directly administered developmental screening test, but that it may also be used as a prescreening instrument. The manual appropriately cautions the test consumer that the latter mentioned use is risky in that some children may go unidentified if parents are unaware of normal development or fail to report problem areas. The author notes that the scale is more sensitive to general developmental delays as opposed to delays in specific developmental areas. It is particularly insensitive to gross motor delays and to social-emotional problems unless they are extreme.

The record form consists of two pages, with directions to the parent clearly presented on the front page. Scoring of the General Development section is accomplished by obtaining a total of the "yes" responses and comparing that score with the mean total score obtained by children 25% younger (i.e., a 4-year-old's performance would be compared to that of 3-year-old). Children obtaining total scores below the cutoff score, found in a table, indicates a child with a "possible major problem." The number and kind of items endorsed in this section by the parent guides the user to identify possible "problems" and "major problems." The parent's description of the child is judged by the evaluator as "primarily positive," "primarily negative," or "very negative." Finally, problem conditions and concerns as identified by the parent are considered. From the above results, the evaluator(s) determine if follow-up evaluation is needed.

The manual does not provide a clear and thorough description of the psychometric data. The norm sample consists of 220 children from South Saint Paul, Minnesota, with approximately equal numbers of boys and girls being included. The children ranged in age from 3 years, 6 months to 4 years, 9 months, which is interesting given that it is clearly stated elsewhere in the manual that the PDI may be used for children 3 to 6 years of age. Other than by gender, there is no indication as to how diversified the sample was. It is clear, however, that the sample is quite small and is likely not representative of the U.S. population in most respects. The small sample is further divided into subsamples ac-

cording to age and gender, resulting in cell sizes ranging from 10 to 35.

No reliability data are provided in the manual. Likewise, content validity is not addressed. In fairness to the author, the PDI is an outgrowth of over two decades of work in development of similar, but more extensive, instruments, including the Minnesota Child Development Inventory (Ireton & Thwing, 1974) and the Minnesota Preschool Inventory (Ireton, 1984). Nonetheless, the author is remiss through failure to include such data in the manual.

Data in support of the criterion-related validity of the PDI are presented. The validity studies were based on the 220 children comprising the norm sample or subsamples thereof. In addition to the PDI, the participants were administered the Developmental Indicators for the Assessment of Learning (DIAL), which served as the basis of the screening decisions. Three studies were reported. The first revealed that those referred for further evaluation obtained significantly lower mean General Development Scale raw scores than did nonreferred children. Study two focused on the 41 children identified (in study one) to be in need of further evaluation. Results indicated that the mean PDI score for the group of children placed in preschool special education programs was significantly lower than those not placed. The last study reported the results of a 2-year follow-up of 100 of the original 220 participants in which kindergarten teachers were asked to rate each child's overall school performance on a 5-point scale (1 = poor, 5 = superior), as well as to identify those children considered to have "significant problems." Here again, significantly lower PDI scores were noted for kindergarten children rated by their teacher to be performing in the "poor" and "below average" ranges. The author surmises that a "low General Development Scale score is a strong indicator of a developmental problem and a potential educational problem" (p. 15).

The test developer is commended for the above validity studies, which focus on decisions made with the PDI; many screening instruments lack such documentation of validity. However, further development is needed before the PDI could be recommended for use. First, the norms provided are inadequate; the invested test consumer may wish to develop local norms. Also, discussions of content validity and test reliability are warranted and necessary. These criticisms are especially pertinent given the many psychometrically sound, multifaceted instruments currently on the market. The prudent test user would do well to investigate instruments such as the AGS Early Screening Profiles (Harrison et al., 1990; 12:24) or FirstSTEP (Miller, 1993; 126). Although parents may offer critical information about their child's development and that information should be sought out, current best practice would mandate that multiple sources of information be gathered in an evaluation process, whether it be screening, placement, or program planning. Thus, use of the PDI (or any instrument of its type) as the sole source of data is discouraged. In sum, although the PDI is inadequate for decision-making purposes, it may prove useful to gather general information regarding the perceptions of the parent.

REVIEWER'S REFERENCES

Ireton, H., & Thwing, E. (1974). Minnesota Child Development Inventory. Minneapolis: Behavior Science Systems.

Ireton, H. (1984). Preschool Development Inventory. Minneapolis: Behavior Science Systems.

Harrison, P., Kaufman, A., Kaufman, N., Bruininks, R., Rynders, J., Ilmer, S., Sparrow, S., & Cicchetti, D. (1990). AGS Early Screening Profiles. Circle Pines, MN: American Guidance Service.

Miller, L. J. (1993). FirstSTEP. San Antonio, TX: The Psychological Corporation.

Review of the Preschool Development Inventory by DIANE J. SAWYER, Murfree Professor of Dyslexic Studies, Middle Tennessee State University, Murfreesboro, TN:

The Preschool Development Inventory (PDI) was developed to elicit parental reports of behavior observed in their preschool child. Its purpose is to provide information about a child's functioning that, when added to information gathered through more typical screening instruments and procedures, assists in identifying those preschoolers whose profiles suggest the need for in-depth assessment of possible developmental difficulties. The author reports that the tool is standardized and norm referenced, with guidelines for interpretation provided.

The PDI is divided into five sections: General Development (60 items), Possible Problems (24 items), Child Description (narrative), Special Problems or Handicaps (narrative), and Questions or Concerns (narrative). It is recommended for use in screening children ages 3 to 6 prior to kindergarten. Results for each section "can be interpreted as showing no evidence of any problems, raising concern about a possible problem, or suggesting a possible problem" (manual, p. 2).

The General Development section is an abbreviated form of that scale as it previously appeared on the Minnesota Child Development Inventory. The author reports that these 60 items were among the most age-discriminating of those appearing on the earlier test. These 60 items address seven areas of development: language comprehension, expressive language, fine motor, self-help, personal-social, situation comprehension, and gross motor. However, an item analysis is not provided.

The total score on the General Development of this scale may reportedly be used to identify low-functioning children. This is possible by comparing a given child's score to that of a predetermined "cutoff score" provided in the table of norms. Below-age expected development may be indicated if the score obtained is lower than the cutoff scores. This score is said to be equal to the average score for a child who is 25% younger (e.g., the score of one at 60 months that is more like that of one who is 42 months). Separate cutoff scores are provided for boys and girls at each age level as well as cutoff scores for boys and girls combined.

The Possible Problems section of the PDI lists symptoms and behavior problems taken from the Minnesota Preschool Inventory. Fourteen items describe sensory, speech, language, comprehension, physical, and quasi-physical symptoms. Ten other items address immaturity, behavioral problems, hyperactivity, and emotional problems. The parent responds yes or no to having observed listed behaviors. The author indicates that starred items (e.g., "Seems to have trouble seeing") and double-starred items (e.g., Slow to "catch on") are considered most important because of their relationship to developmental disabilities and school learning. Again, no item analysis is provided.

The remaining three sections—Description of Child, Special Problems or Handicaps, and Parent's Questions or Concerns—are intended to elicit parental reports that permit use of their own terms to comment about the child from their perspective. Parent responses are rated on a 3-point scale: 1 = positive description; no problems or questions reported; 2 = primarily negative description; some problem or question reported; and 3 = very negative description; possible major problem or concern. A brief Child Study is provided to illustrate how to use scores and ratings obtained to interpret results of the PDI across the five sections.

It appears that recommended interpretation of the PDI is rooted in a study of 220 children (114 girls and 106 boys) representing a subsample of 283 who were screened about 16 months prior to kindergarten entrance. They ranged in age from 3 years 7 months to 4 years 9 months. Children referred for follow-up assessment were noted as were those who subsequently received preschool special education services (N = 25 of the 41 assessed). Two years later, kindergarten teachers were asked to rate all students at the end of the year. Of this group, 100 had participated in the original screening. The manual provides primarily descriptive information regarding performance of these students including mean scores obtained for different age groups, the percent obtaining scores and rankings suggestive of "at-riskness" as defined by the author, the frequency distribution of scores obtained on the General Development section, outcomes of assessment and kindergarten performance for those 100 followed to the end of kindergarten, as well as predictive probability for below average kindergarten performance based on specific problems noted by parents on the Possible Problems section and for General Development plus Possible Problems information combined. Power to predict later identified developmental difficulties or school learning problems was assigned by comparing the PDI to the Developmental Indicators for Assessment of Learning (DIAL). The two instruments appeared to address different and essentially independent aspects of development.

Although the PDI appears to be standardized with respect to administration and with respect to scoring the first two objective sections, a fair amount of personal interpretation can creep into rankings of parental narratives for Sections 3 through 5. The author does not address the issue of minimal expected preparation of those responsible for coding and summarizing the responses elicited.

With respect to the normative data provided, it is perhaps most appropriately viewed as an *estimate of* the *potential* of the PDI to screen for developmental disabilities or to supplement other screening tools. The "cut-off scores" are most problematic. Given the limited sample size, drawn from one relatively homogenous suburb (with respect to ethnicity, S.E.S., and education) there is significant likelihood of overidentifying or underidentifying children for subsequent developmental assessment.

The PDI focuses attention on parents as significant informants regarding individual child development as this relates to age. Although the content of the instrument can yield valuable information for use by one who is skilled in interpreting the variety of developmental indicators it reveals, the normative data provided probably do not generalize beyond the reference group. Caution is urged in applying this information when screening children drawn from other kinds of populations.

[239]
Preschool Developmental Profile.

Purpose: "Designed to be used to write an individualized education program and to serve as a way of measuring a child's developmental progress."
Population: Children with handicaps who function at the 3–6 year age level.
Publication Dates: 1977–1991.
Scores, 10: Perceptual/Fine Motor, Cognition (Classification, Number, Space, Seriation, Time), Speech and Language, Social Emotional, Self-Care, Gross Motor.
Administration: Individual.
Price Data: Available from publisher.
Time: (50–60) minutes.
Comments: See Early Intervention Developmental Profile (107) for younger ages.
Authors: Diane B. D'Eugenio, Martha S. Moersch, Sara L. Brown, Judith E. Drews, B. Suzanne Haskin, Eleanor Whiteside Lynch, and Sally J. Rogers.
Publisher: The University of Michigan Press.

Review of the Preschool Developmental Profile by DOREEN WARD FAIRBANK, *Assistant Professor of Psychology, Director, Meredith College Autism Program, Meredith College, Raleigh, NC:*

The Developmental programming for Infants and Young Children—Volumes 1–3 was published in 1977 by the University of Michigan Press as a developmental assessment instrument for children birth to 36 months. Volume 4—Preschool Assessment and Application and Volume 5—Preschool Developmental Profile are the latest volumes in this family of assessment instruments. The Preschool Developmental Profile addition is an assessment-based programming instrument that was designed to write an individualized education program and to serve as a way of measuring a child's development progress. The profile provides information for planning comprehensive developmental programs for children with all types of disabilities who function between the 3- and 6-year-old age level. The profile is intended to supplement, not replace, standard psychological, social, academic, motor, and language evaluation data.

The Preschool Developmental Profile is a preschool programming assessment with 213 items that are divided into six sections intended to represent a developmental approach and order: Perceptual/Fine Motor, Cognition, Language, Social, Self-Care, and Gross Motor development. The manual authors suggest the profile items are based on current research and theory in the various areas of development. The Language section reflects semantic theory of language development; the Cognition section provides landmarks of the preoperational stage of thought, "specifically focusing on the concepts of classification, seriation, number, space, and time; the motor sections look at the continuing development of precise neuromotor control; and the social section focuses on the cultural and environmental aspects of social functioning and contains items which center on the child's developing sexuality" (p. 2).

The profile can be administered in an hour by an experienced evaluator or a multidisciplinary team (teacher or psychologist, an occupational or physical therapist, and a speech and language therapist). The evaluator, according to the manual, should begin the administration of each section of the profile at the age level she or he thinks is appropriate for the child. The manual authors further state this can be determined from observations of the child's spontaneous play, from background information, or from watching the child's play with objects that are scorable at several levels on the profile. Each profile item is scored Pass (P) if the criteria stated on that item are met or Fail (F) when the child's behavior on an item clearly does not meet the scoring criteria. When the evaluator is unable to determine if the child's behavior meets the criteria or if the relevant behaviors are in a developing or emerging stage a Pass-Fail (PF) score is used. An Omitted (0) code is used when an item is not administered due to the nature of the child's disability. The scores are then graphed on the back cover of Volume 5 to provide a visual portrayal of the child's strengths, weaknesses, and general developmental pattern in each of the six sections.

In combination, the Preschool Assessment and Application—Volume 4 and the Preschool Developmental Profile—Volume 5 consists of an assessment manual, a Preschool Developmental Profile, and a series of sample sheet pictures and cards to be used in the assessment. The assessment manual contains Preschool Assessment and Application—Volume 4, a short history of the development of the instrument, the research findings, the theoretical concepts behind the assessment, and a description for administration and scoring of each assessment item. The item-by-item specifications are sufficiently detailed and should enhance the consistency of administration. The manual also contains a section on how to use the assessment findings to develop a program of behavioral objectives. This section should prove to be a rich and useful source of information for developing an individualized education program for a child with a disability.

The Preschool Developmental Profile—Volume 5 provides a systematic method of evaluating a child's skills, selecting appropriate objectives, designing an appropriate individualized educational program, and graphing a developmental profile. The profile is designed to be administered up to four times a year for a single child. The series of sample sheet pictures and cards consists of the picture items that are necessary in the administration of certain items.

A minor limitation of the Preschool Assessment and Application—Volume 4 is that it does not provide all of the materials needed to complete the assessment. The manual contains a list of the materials needed. The materials should be assembled in advance in a small suitcase or kit.

The manual authors describe the various changes and modifications made during the development and subsequent iterations of this profile. Several research projects that were completed during a field testing and validation phase are also described. However, the manual does not contain any information on the psychometric properties of the instruments, such as interrater and test-retest reliability of the instrument or the validity of the instrument.

The specific aims of the Preschool Assessment and Application—Volume 4 and the Preschool Developmental Profile—Volume 5 are to provide the evaluator and/or multidisciplinary team with a developmental preschool programming instrument that can (a) assess a child with a disability, functioning between 3 and 6 years old; (b) appropriately design an individual educational program relevant to the child's needs; and (c) provide follow-up assessments to determine the child's development. These additional volumes, Preschool Assessment and Application—Volume 4 and the Preschool Developmental Profile—Volume 5, of the original Developmental Programming for Infants and Young Children are an important aspect in accomplishing these aims.

Review of the Preschool Developmental Profile by DAVID MACPHEE, Associate Professor of Human Development and Family Studies, Colorado State University, Fort Collins, CO:

This instrument is to be used in writing individualized educational programs (IEPs) and to monitor children's progress toward goals in the IEP. The Preschool Developmental Profile is not a standardized instrument, and should not be used for diagnosis or prediction. Instead, it is meant to supplement information from formal disciplinary evaluations. Ideally, a transdisciplinary team (see Bergen, 1994) assesses a child's strengths and weaknesses in various domains, as well as the family's needs, and then uses the Preschool Developmental Profile to gain an integrated picture of the child as well as to formulate effective interventions. The strengths of the Profile are the synthesis of information on multiple facets of development and the focus on emergent skills as a basis for programming. Many of its items are redundant, however, with preschool diagnostic tests, meaning that a child may have to endure repetitive testing.

The Profile contains 213 items unevenly distributed across six domains; for example, Self-Care has 17 items whereas Gross Motor contains 56. Some items, especially those related to social and self-care skills, can be passed by parent report. Items were selected initially if: (a) they appeared on at least two standardized tests for preschoolers, (b) developmental research indicated their importance, or (c) the authors' personal experience indicated their relevance to programming. For instance, most items on the Cognition scale are unique to the Profile, and were based on Piagetian research and the authors' work with young children. A Piagetian approach reflects the zeitgeist of 1981 but it is out of step with the contemporary emphasis on information processing approaches. This is not a trivial issue. Information processing strategies are the foundation for academic skills (Siegler, 1991), whereas the authors note that, "The items on the cognition section, [which emphasize] understanding of the physical world, do not assess the typical school readiness skills found in most preschool scales" (p. 19). Research supports Piaget's skepticism about the malleability of preoperational thinking, yet the authors do not defend the relevance of a Piagetian approach to early intervention (cf. Standard 1.6; AERA, APA, & NCME, 1985). In other domains, however, the Profile's content is current and utilitarian. For example, the Language section focuses on semantics, consonant with recent research with younger children (Fenson et al., 1994), although pragmatic skills are largely omitted.

The Preschool Developmental Profile does not have a substantial data base to bolster either its construction or psychometrics. Most items were placed in ordinal sequence, in 6-month bands, based on expected ages for comparable items on other tests and on field testing with 92 preschoolers in Missouri for the Cognition section. Scalogram analyses of the Cognition section supported the ordinal sequence for three of the five areas. The small number of children in each age band, and the emphasis on "what is pertinent and vital to a specific child [rather] than ...

what [is] applicable to all children" (p. 36), are problematic for an instrument that purports to tap normative sequences of developmental skills. If items are out of sequence, basal and ceiling levels cannot be determined accurately. On a related note, each child's profile is based on "the highest item number of a sequence of passes the child earned on each of the sections" (p. 8), which is not necessarily the ceiling (i.e., failure of all items in a band). Finally, the 6-month bands include as few as 1 and as many as 15 items. Therefore, the Profile may be less discriminating or sensitive to emergent skills than other tests that include more items per age level, and the ceiling could vary with the number of items in a band or how one defines a sequence of passes.

The Profile manual has no empirical information on reliability or validity. This omission is appropriate for instruments that are intended as curriculum guides but the Profile also is meant to estimate developmental levels and progress. Concurrent validity could have been determined, but was not, because the Slosson was administered to some preschoolers in the field trials. Sixty-eight participants in intervention programs were given the Profile on at least two occasions but no analyses were conducted of 3-month stability nor of treatment impact. Goal-attainment scaling could be used to determine whether the Profile is valid for monitoring children's developmental progress toward IEP objectives.

One section of the manual is a description of how to use the Profile to develop specific IEP objectives. This synopsis of best practice is a strength of the Preschool Developmental Profile. Users are encouraged to examine competencies underlying various items rather than to write objectives that would train a child to perform well on a single splinter skill. The authors also recommend a focus on the whole child—both strengths and weaknesses—rather than treatment for deficits. A holistic approach minimizes labeling, provides the child with some successes, and better prepares a child for school entry. In comparison to the Humanics National Child Assessment Form (11:170), the Profile's stance is more holistic and contextual. However, the Humanics Form does have more detailed treatment plans, especially learning activities and observational exercises that can be implemented by parents.

In sum, the Preschool Developmental Profile synthesizes information on preschoolers' competencies in six domains, which then provides a basis for writing treatment plans. The Profile predates mandates for family service plans and a transdisciplinary team approach, yet its holistic orientation and emphasis on collaborative programming are contemporary. Improvements could be made, however, in terms of its data base and intervention guidelines. Specifically, the ordinal arrangement of items is critical to assessing emergent skills and monitoring progress toward treatment goals, yet age placements were based on a patchwork of intuition, other tests, and field testing with small samples of children. If a primary purpose is to monitor progress toward IEP goals, then validity data on the Profile's sensitivity to intervention should be provided. Finally, the Profile would be helpful in writing behavioral objectives for IEPs but practitioners may need supplementary resources, such as the Humanics National Child Assessment Form, for more detail on intervention strategies. In its present form, the Preschool Developmental Profile is a jack of all trades but a master of none. It lacks the psychometrics to be an adequate diagnostic tool, although it is meant to identify emergent skills and developmental profiles, and it does not have sufficient detail to write in-depth curricula for preschoolers with disabilities.

REVIEWER'S REFERENCES

American Educational Research Association, American Psychological Association, & National Council on Measurement in Education. (1985). *Standards for educational and psychological testing.* Washington, DC: American Psychological Association, Inc.

Siegler, R. S. (1991). *Children's thinking* (2nd ed.). Englewood Cliffs, NJ: Prentice Hall.

Bergen, D. (1994). *Assessment methods for infants and toddlers: Transdisciplinary team approaches.* New York: Teachers College Press.

Fenson, L., Dale, P. S., Reznick, J. S., Bates, E., Thal, D. J., & Pethick, S. J. (1994). Variability in early communicative development. *Monographs of the Society for Research in Child Development, 59* (Serial No. 242).

[240]
The Preschool Evaluation Scale.

Purpose: Designed to assess behavior related to developmental delays.
Population: Birth–72 months.
Publication Dates: 1991–1992.
Acronym: PES.
Scores, 7: Large Muscle Skills, Small Muscle Skills, Cognitive Thinking, Expressive Language, Social/Emotional, Self-Help Skills, Total.
Administration: Individual.
Levels, 2: Birth–35 months, 36–72 months.
Price Data, 1992: $60 per complete kit including technical manual ('92, 41 pages), 50 birth–35 months rating forms, and 50 36–72 months rating forms; $25 per 50 birth–35 months ratings forms; $25 per 50 36–72 months rating forms; $12 per computerized quick score; $10 per technical manual.
Time: (20–25) minutes.
Comments: Ratings by parents or child care providers.
Author: Stephen B. McCarney.
Publisher: Hawthorne Educational Services, Inc.

Review of The Preschool Evaluation Scale by MARY MATHAI CHITTOORAN, *UC Foundation Assistant Professor of School Psychology and Special Education, The University of Tennessee at Chattanooga, Chattanooga, TN:*

The Preschool Evaluation Scale (PES) is a rating scale designed to assess educators' perceptions of developmental delays in children between birth and 72 months. Based on the cognitive, physical, language and speech, psychosocial, and self-help areas of deficits identified by P.L. 99-457, the PES may be used to identify children with developmental delays who would benefit from intervention, and to define appropriate curricular goals and practices.

The standardization sample consisted of 2,893 children from birth to 6 years, with approximately equal numbers of males and females. Children were enrolled in 94 public school systems and were rated by 472 educators. The sample was designed to be geographically and ethnically representative and identified students by their residence and parental occupation. The sample was further subdivided into 14 standardization groups by age and/or gender.

Content validity of the PES was established on the basis of a literature review as well as the recommendations of early childhood educators and diagnosticians. The inclusion of items (94 at the birth through 2-year level and 85 at the 3- to 6-year level) was determined on the basis of adequate content validity, discriminative power of items (item/subscale score correlations greater than .49), and item/total score correlations (.33 to .91).

According to McCarney, the PES was designed to "measure the construct of early childhood development" (p. 14). Evidence of "diagnostic validity" was demonstrated by administering the PES to two groups of children ($N = 242$); children with previously identified developmental delays obtained significantly lower scores on all subscales. Construct validity was established by examining item/total score correlations (.33 to .91). Statistically significant correlations were obtained by comparing performance on the PES to the Early Learning Accomplishment Profile Developmental Kit (.58 to .71 at the birth through 2-year level) and the Learning Accomplishment Profile—Revised (.61 to .80 at the 3- to 6-year level).

Studies of test-retest reliability at 30-day intervals ($N = 391$) yielded correlations between .80 and .92 for subscales and .88 for the total score. Interrater reliability, obtained with 142 pairs of raters and 428 children, averaged .84 across all age ranges. Coefficient alpha estimates of reliability for the PES ranged from a low of .85 to a high of .96. Standard error of measurement ranged from 4.61 at the 3- through 5-year level to 5.49 at the birth through 2-year level. Subscale correlations between .55 and .92 are provided as evidence for the distinctiveness of each subscale.

Ratings on the PES are provided by "educators with primary observational opportunities" (p. 19). A rating of 0 means that a child "cannot perform the behavior" (p. 18), a 1 signifies that the child "performs the behavior successfully but on an inconsistent basis" (p. 18), and a 2 indicates that the child "performs the behavior successfully and independently" (p. 18). Performance on each of the six subscales is reported as raw scores, which are converted to subscale standard scores ($x = 10$; $SD = 3$) and an overall percentile score. A subscale standard score between 5 and 7 indicates a "significant need for attention" and a score below 4 indicates "an extreme need for attention" (p. 24).

The PES is easy to administer, score, and interpret, and the accompanying test profile is convenient. It can yield useful information about the functioning of young children as perceived by their teachers and provides evidence of skill attainment in specific areas. Internal consistency and test-retest reliability estimates appear to be good; however, interrater reliability, as expected with a rating scale of this kind, is not as impressive. There is a commendable effort to relate this test to the construct of developmental delay as defined by P.L. 99-457 but, generally, additional evidence in support of validity needs to be provided. Information about the predictive ability of the PES would appear to be critical but is lacking. The percentile score might have been supplemented by another global index of functioning such as a standard score; further, no interpretive guidelines—other than the obvious ones—are offered for the percentile score. The manual is a flimsy 41-page paperback that fell apart in the hands of this unfortunate reviewer the first time it was used.

Although the standardization sample is large and attempts to represent the population of interest, there is no evidence that it was randomly selected. Further, the test limits the norm group to those children already in school, a point of concern because many children with developmental delays, especially those under the age of 3, and therefore the most likely candidates for early intervention, are not *yet* in school. A further concern relates to the fact that children with developmental delays were included in the sample, but information about specific areas of deficit is not provided. The addition of norms for these children would be desirable, as would norms for different cultural groups. Norms for a greater number of age ranges would also be a welcome addition to the PES. Children change so rapidly in these critical years that 4- to 6-month intervals (under the age of 3) and 11- to 12-month intervals (over the age of 3) are hardly adequate to describe developmental changes. There also seems to be a disproportionate number of 5- and 6-year olds in the sample; in fact, children at this age range outnumber infants and toddlers two to one.

Another issue relates to the nature and number of items on each subscale; for example, the limited number of items on each subscale are unlikely to allow for adequate discrimination between children of differing ages and ability levels. Further, there are relatively few easy items within each subscale but a large number of difficult items. It is very possible that the PES will discriminate against children with moderate to severe delays and those from culturally and linguistically diverse groups, and that this will result in too many false positives.

A significant concern relates to the quantifiers used in rating. The test protocol reminds the rater not to leave any item blank and to score 0 any items for which the child "cannot perform the behavior." Elsewhere in the manual, the reader is advised that a score of 0 is appropriate if the rater *does not have knowledge* of the child's having engaged in a behavior. Several 0s, therefore, might mean one of three things: The child, in fact, cannot perform the task; the child performs the task but the rater does not know it; or the child can perform the behavior but for some reason does not. It would be desirable to have additional quantifiers to distinguish between these types of answers. Alternatively, a change from "cannot perform" to "does not perform" might be helpful. Further, a response category like *No Opportunity to Perform* would help identify a child who *could* perform a task if given the opportunity. The inclusion of a *Don't Know* response might also be a useful indicator of the usefulness of the informant.

McCarney's use of language on the PES is often problematic and occasionally inaccurate. For example, the term "preschool," used in P.L. 99-457 to refer to children between ages 3 and 6, is used by McCarney to refer to children from *birth* to 6 years. The definition of "criterion validity" is incomplete and the term "diagnostic validity" is confusing. The descriptions associated with quantifiers, such as "successful," "inconsistent," and "independent," are open to interpretation. An explanation of these terms is provided in the technical manual but might have been more profitably added to the test protocol where the rater could see it. Although McCarney offers brief examples for clarification, the PES is still sprinkled with several vague phrases such as "a fairly straight line," "enjoys" activities, and "knows" information. Responses to "can use a pencil sharpener independently" can vary depending on whether the sharpener is the manual or electric variety, and a child who does not say "mama" and "dada" but uses other, equally appropriate terms to refer to his or her parents, might be penalized. An expanded scoring guide with clear criteria would be an excellent addition to the PES.

Overall, this measure has some good features and several rather undesirable ones. At this point, the PES is probably best used as a screening measure of functioning in young children, as an adjunct to other measures like the Battelle Developmental inventory (T4:263), the Bayley Scales of Infant Development, Second Edition (29), and the Early Learning Accomplishment Profile (ELAP; Glover, Preminger, & Sanford, 1988), or as a starting point for the development of instructional objectives. In any event, results obtained with this measure should be interpreted with some caution.

REVIEWER'S REFERENCE
Glover, M. E., Preminger, J. L., & Sanford, A. R. (1988). Early Learning Accomplishment Profile. Winston-Salem, NC: Kaplan.

Review of The Preschool Evaluation Scale by LENA R. GADDIS, Associate Professor of Educational Psychology, Northern Arizona University, Flagstaff, AZ:

As stated in the technical manual, the Preschool Evaluation Scale (PES) was "developed to identify those preschoolers who deviate enough from the norm to require special services or a modified program in order to develop to maximum capacity" (p. 3). Stated uses for the PES include screening, diagnosis, and development of goals and objectives. The developmental constructs assessed by this measure were designed to coincide with the domains of developmental delays identified by P.L. 99-457, which mandates provision of services to children with special needs between the ages of 3 and 5 years and offers substantial incentives for services rendered to infants and toddlers who are significantly delayed or are at risk for becoming so. Specifically, the six subscales of the PES are Cognitive Thinking, Large Muscle, Small Muscle, Language, Social/Emotional, and Self-Help. The format of the PES is that of a rating scale that relies on observational reports by "professional educators" in a school environment. The manual clearly delineates the "qualifications" for those completing the PES.

There are two forms available, one for children birth to 35 months and the other for those 36 to 72 months. The PES consists of 85 or 94 items, depending on the form, in which the rater evaluates the child's mastery of the skills listed as "cannot perform the behavior," "performs the behavior successfully but on an inconsistent basis," or "performs the behavior successfully and independently." These descriptors are referred to as "quantifiers," and are operationally defined in the manual.

The norm sample consists of 2,893 children from 94 public school systems in 24 states. The sample is representative of the general population with regards to sex, race, and geographic region. Both developmentally delayed and nondelayed children were reportedly included in the sample, although the proportion of each in the sample is not identified by the constructors. A total of 472 professional educators completed the ratings. Parental occupations included both blue and white collar professions. Norms tables are provided for eight different age groups between the ages birth and 35 months. For the older age levels, separate norms are presented for males and females.

Standard scores (mean = 10, standard deviation = 3) and percentile ranks are yielded from the raw scores. A standard score of two or more standard deviations from the mean is said to reflect a "serious concern" on the given area. Inspection of the norms table indicates that there is not sufficient floor to identify children functioning two standard deviations below the mean at the two youngest age levels (0 to 8 months); the same is true for portions of the next age level (9 to 16 months). Floor problems are also noted for norms for both males and females 36 to 47 months of age, primarily in the area of Small Muscle development. Otherwise, the distribution of scores is adequate.

Types of reliability reported are test-retest, interrater, and internal consistency. All estimates revealed adequate to good levels for reliability. Content validity is well documented via a careful review of the literature and input from diagnosticians and early childhood professionals regarding item development and retention. Evidence provided for the support of construct validity included significantly lower PES scores being obtained for a group of children previously identified as developmentally delayed. Additionally, the subscales of the PES were found to be intercorrelated, indicating that subscales measure a unified construct related to child development. Further, evidence of item validity is provided. With regard to criterion-related validity, PES scores were found to be positively and significantly correlated with the Preschool Evaluation Scale and the Early Learning Accomplishment Profile. It is worthy of note, however, that these concurrent validity studies were based solely on developmentally delayed children, thus limiting the generalizability of the results to the population at large.

In conclusion, the PES may be considered psychometrically sound, although further establishment of criterion-related validity is desirable. The standardization sample is large and representative. Administration and scoring are easily accomplished, and the manual is well written. Some caution is warranted concerning the use of the instrument with infants and young toddlers. As clearly stated by the test constructor, the PES is not intended as a sole measure for either screening or diagnosis. It, and other measures of its type, need to be used concurrently with direct assessment of the child. Given that best practice mandates multisetting, multirater, and multitest format be used in the assessment process, the PES would be a nice addition to the evaluation of young children.

[241]
Preschool Language Scale—3.

Purpose: "Measures young children's receptive and expressive language ability."

Population: Ages 0 to 6–11.

Publication Dates: 1969–1992.

Acronym: PLS-3.

Scores, 3: Auditory Comprehension, Expressive Communication, Total Language Score.

Administration: Individual.

Price Data, 1994: $98 per complete kit including 12 record forms, picture book, and manual ('92, 177 pages); $22 per 12 record forms (English or Spanish); $59 per picture book; $32 per English manual; $12.50 per Spanish edition manual.

Foreign Language Edition: Spanish edition available.

Time: (20–50) minutes.

Authors: Irla Lee Zimmerman, Violette G. Steiner, and Roberta Evatt Pond.

Publisher: The Psychological Corporation.

Cross References: See T4:2084 (24 references); for an excerpted review by Barton B. Proger of an earlier edition, see 8:929 (3 references); see also T2:2024 (1 reference); for a review by Joel Stark and an excerpted review by C. H. Ammons, see 7:965.

TEST REFERENCES

1. Zagar, L. L., & Locke, J. L. (1986). The psychological reality of phonetic features in children. *Language, Speech, and Hearing Services in Schools, 17,* 56–62.

2. Dale, P. S., & Henderson, V. L. (1987). An evaluation of the Test of Early Language Development as a measure of receptive and expressive language. *Language, Speech, and Hearing Services in Schools, 18,* 179–187.

3. Hargrove, P. M., Roetzel, K., & Hoodin, R. B. (1989). Modifying the prosody of a language-impaired child. *Language, Speech, and Hearing Services in Schools, 20,* 245–258.

4. Handleman, J. S., Harris, S. L., Kristoff, B., Fuentes, F., & Alessandri, M. (1991). A specialized program for preschool children with autism. *Language, Speech, and Hearing Services in Schools, 22,* 107–110.

5. Wilson, K. S., Blackmon, R. C., Hall, R. E., & Elcholtz, G. E. (1991). Methods of language assessment: A survey of California public school clinicians. *Language, Speech, and Hearing Services in Schools, 22,* 236–241.

6. Eiserman, W. D., Weber, C., & McCoun, M. (1992). Two alternative program models for serving speech disordered preschoolers: A second follow-up. *Journal of Communication Disorders, 25,* 77–106.

7. Loeb, D. F., & Allen, G. D. (1993). Preschoolers' imitation of intonation contours. *Journal of Speech and Hearing Research, 36,* 4–13.

8. Thornburg, D. G. (1993). Intergenerational literacy learning with bilingual families: A context for the analysis of social mediation of thought. *Journal of Reading Behavior, 25,* 323–352.

9. Fazio, B. B. (1994). The counting abilities of children with specific language impairment: A comparison of oral and gestural tasks. *Journal of Speech and Hearing Research, 37,* 358–368.

10. McGregor, K. K., & Leonard, L. B. (1994). Subject pronoun and article omissions in the speech of children with specific language impairment: A phonological interpretation. *Journal of Speech and Hearing Research, 37,* 171–181.

11. Nellis, L., & Gridley, B. E. (1994). Review of the Bayley Scales of Infant Development—Second Edition. *Journal of School Psychology, 32,* 201–209.

12. Owen, M. T., & Mulvihill, B. A. (1994). Benefits of a parent education and support program in the first three years. *Family Relations, 43,* 206–212.

13. Plante, E., & Vance, R. (1994). Selection of preschool language tests: A data-based approach. *Language, Speech, and Hearing Services in Schools, 25,* 15–24.

14. Rollins, P. R., Pan, B. A., Conti-Ramsden, G., & Snow, C. E. (1994). Communicative skills in children with specific language impairments: A comparison with their language-matched siblings. *Journal of Communication Disorders, 27,* 189–206.

15. Shriberg, L. D., & Kwiatkowski, J. (1994). Developmental phonological disorders I: A clinical profile. *Journal of Speech and Hearing, 37,* 1100–1126.

16. Sommers, R. K., Fragapane, L., & Schmock, K. (1994). Changes in maternal attitudes and perceptions and children's communication skills. *Perceptual and Motor Skills, 79,* 851–861.

17. Yoder, P. J., Davies, B., & Bishop, K. (1994). Adult interaction style effects on the language sampling and transcription process with children who have developmental disabilities. *American Journal on Mental Retardation, 99,* 270–282.

18. Yoder, P. J., Davies, B., Bishop, K., & Munson, L. (1994). Effect of adult continuing wh-questions on conversational participation in children with developmental disabilities. *Journal of Speech and Hearing Research, 37,* 193–204.

19. Eiserman, W. D., Weber, C., & McCan, M. (1995). Parent and professional roles in early intervention: A longitudinal comparison of the effects of two intervention configurations. *The Journal of Special Education, 29,* 20–44.

20. Guralnick, M. J., Connor, R. T., & Hammond, M. (1995). Parent perspective of peer relationships and friendships in integrated and specialized programs. *American Journal on Mental Retardation, 99,* 457–476.

21. Guralnick, M. J., Connor, R. T., Hammond, M., Gottman, J. M., & Kinnish, K. (1995). Immediate effects of mainstreamed settings on the social interactions and social integration of preschool children. *American Journal on Mental Retardation, 100,* 359–377.

22. Janzen-Wilde, M. L., Duchan, J. F., & Higginbotham, D. J. (1995). Successful use of facilitated communication with an oral child. *Journal of Speech and Hearing Research, 38,* 658–676.

23. Yoder, P. J., Spruytenberg, H., Edwards, A., & Davies, B. (1995). Effect of verbal routine contexts and expansions on gains in the mean length of utterance in children with developmental delays. *Language, Speech, and Hearing Services in Schools, 26,* 21–32.

24. Ross, G., Lipper, E., & Auld, P. A. M. (1996). Cognitive abilities and early precursors of learning disabilities in very-low-birthweight children with normal intelligence and normal neurological status. *International Journal of Behavioral Development, 19,* 563–580.

25. Yairi, E., Ambrose, N. G., Paden, E. P., & Throneburg, R. N. (1996). Predictive factors of persistence and recovery: Pathways of childhood stuttering. *Journal of Communication Disorders, 29,* 51–77.

26. Guralnick, M. J. (1997). Peer social networks of young boys with developmental delays. *American Journal on Mental Retardation, 101,* 595–612.

Review of the Preschool Language Scale—3 by J. JEFFREY GRILL, Associate Professor of Special Education, Athens State College, Athens, AL:

The third edition of the Preschool Language Scale (PLS–3) is a norm-referenced instrument, for use with children between birth and 6 years–11 months. The PLS–3 includes an examiner's manual, and an easel-style picture manual containing uncluttered, full-color drawings as stimuli for specific items. A record booklet provides space for recording and scoring responses, a task analysis checklist and profile, a clinician's worksheet, and supplemental measures including an articulation screener, space for a language sample and checklist, and a family information and suggestions page. Also needed, but not included are: a sheet of cellophane, a teddy bear, a ball, a shoe box, keys on a key ring, 3 plastic spoons and cups, a child's white sock, a watch with a second hand, and a few age-appropriate toys or books.

The examiner's manual contains especially clear, concise, and thorough administration and scoring directions, supplemented with abundant examples, and instructions for modifying procedures for special populations. Score interpretation is thoroughly discussed, with particular attention to age-equivalent scores.

Each of two 48-item subscales, Auditory Comprehension (AC) and Expressive Communication (EC), includes 4 items (tasks) at each of 12 age levels. Age levels span 6 months, except the last two, which span 12 months. However, raw score conversion tables include four age levels of 3 months each for children in the first year of life.

The test focuses on four language aspects: language precursors (attention, vocal development, social communication); semantics (vocabulary, and concepts including quality, quantity, spatial, and time/sequence); structure (morphology, syntax); and integrative thinking skills. Appropriately, language precursor tasks are found among items for children below 30 months and integrative thinking skills tasks are among those for older children. Many tasks may be scored "pass" if spontaneously performed by the child at any time during testing, even if failed initially. Of 30 such items, 25 are in the EC subscale, and all are clearly identified. In contrast to this flexibility in scoring, the distribution of test items (4 per subscale per age level) is rigidly symmetrical.

The authors carefully describe development of the PLS–3, and field testing of 236 initial items with a national sample of 451 subjects. Yet they offer no data or criteria in the manual to support the selection of the final 96 items, and no explanation for using 48 items for each subscale. More items, not necessarily equally distributed over subscales or across age levels, might more accurately reflect the normal, asymmetrical, and explosive course of language development in young children.

Standard score and percentile rank equivalents for raw scores are provided in 3-month age intervals for children from birth to 11 months, in 6-month intervals for 1- through 4-year-olds, and in 12-month intervals for 5- and 6-year-olds for the AC and EC subscales and a Total Language (TL) composite. Age equivalents for AC, EC, and total raw scores are also provided. However, linguistically superior 5- and 6-year-olds may reach a maximum raw score of 48, but attain a scaled score less than two SDs above the mean of 100 (5-year-olds) or in the average range (6-year-olds). This suggests that the test may not be appropriate for children of these ages, or that more items are needed for these age groups.

Norms are based on the performances of 1,200 children, between the ages of 2 weeks and 6 years-11 months. Although not randomly selected, the sample (stratified using the 1986 update of 1980 U.S. Census data) approximates the U.S. population for parent education level, geographic region, and race, but not for other variables. Excluded were children identified as: language-disordered; receiving language remediation; younger than 2 weeks of age; born at less than 35 weeks gestation; and those who had "difficulties at birth." About 100 children per age level participated, except for the four 3-month intervals that included about 50 children each. Although equal numbers of boys and girls participated, the authors do not indicate that this equality was maintained within each age interval.

Four types of reliability data are reported. Internal consistency, reported as coefficients alpha, ranged from .47 to .94 across age intervals and subscales. The AC and EC subscales evidenced adequate internal consistency (i.e., coefficients of at least .80) for age groups from chronological age 1–6 through 4–5, and from 1–0 through 4–11, respectively. Total Language (TL) composite coefficients were adequate for age groups above 8 months. Standard errors of measurement, reported in standard score units, varied in consonance with internal consistency coefficients. Test-retest reliability coefficients ranged from .81 to .94 for AC, EC, and TL scores in a study of about 30 subjects each at age intervals 3–0 to 3–5, 4–0 to 4–5, and 5–0 to 5–11. Interrater reliability is reported as 89% agreement between two raters rating the open-ended EC subscale items from a random sample of 80 norm-group protocols (20 each from 3-, 4-, 5-, and 6-year-old subjects). This result from only one pair of raters is not adequate evidence of interrater reliability.

Three types of validity are discussed. Scope and sequence of PLS–3 tasks are offered as support for content validity. Construct validity was investigated via discriminant analysis to determine if the PLS–3 could differentiate between language-disordered and non-language-disordered children. Analyzing the hits and misses results of the discriminant analysis, the authors report accuracy of 66%, 80%, and 70%, respectively, for groups of fewer than 60 3-, 4-, and 5-year-olds. A correlation between AC and EC subscale standard scores of .64 is also offered as construct validity evidence. Three studies of concurrent validity, relating PLS–3 to the Denver II, the PLS-Revised Edition, and the Clinical Evaluation of Language Fundamentals—Revised (CELF—R) are reported. Of 28 infants involved in the Denver II study, all (an unspecified number) who earned a "normal" rating on the Denver II, scored within 1.5 SDs of the mean on the PLS–3. Without more information, this result is meaningless. A correlational study of the PLS–R and PLS–3, involving 29 3-year-olds, yielded coefficients of .66, .86, and .88 for the AC, EC, and TL scores. This apparent support is diminished by small sample size, restricted age range, and the criterion instrument itself. The correlational study of the PLS–3 and CELF-R, involving 58 5- to 7-year-olds, yielded coefficients of .69, .75, and .82. However, the PLS–3's questionable reliability for these age groups and limited number of items undercut this support.

In summary, the PLS–3 examiner's manual is especially valuable with clear, concise, usable information on assessing young children's language. But the test is flawed. More items, more naturally distributed over the targeted age ranges, might resolve reliability and validity problems. The PLS–3 may be used best as a quick language assessment tool for 3-, 4-, and 5-year-old children, but should not be used alone to obtain a thorough language evaluation.

Review of the Preschool Language Scale—3 by JANET A. NORRIS, Professor of Communication Sciences and Disorders, Louisiana State University, Baton Rouge, LA:

The Preschool Language Scale—3 (PLS-3) is the third edition of this standardized instrument designed to assess receptive and expressive language skills with infants and young children. The test comprises two standardized subscales (i.e., Auditory Comprehension and Expressive Communication), and three optional supplemental measures (i.e., Articulation Screener, Language Sample Checklist, and Family Information and Suggestion Form). The results of the two standardized subscales are combined to create the Total Language Score. The changes in the third revision include the three supplemental measures, expanded norms, tasks that target social or interactive communication skills and integrative thinking skills, more tasks covering basic concepts, simplified scoring, and removal of articulation tasks from the standardized Expressive Communication subscale, now assembled as the Articulation Screener supplemental measure.

The precursors of receptive language skills evaluated within the Auditory Comprehension subtest focus on attention abilities. These include measures of attention to objects, attention to people, and attention to language, assessed through tasks such as eliciting a head turn to localize a sound, or following the parent's gaze. At older ages, the Auditory Comprehension subscale assesses vocabulary; concepts of quantity, quality, space, and time; sentence structure (morphology and syntax); and integrative thinking skills such as making inferences. The precursors of expressive language skills evaluated within the Expressive Communication subscale include tasks that measure the progression of vocal behaviors from undifferentiated sound productions through inflected strings of syllables. At older ages, the Expressive Communication subscale measures the expressive productions of language abilities that parallel those on the receptive subscale.

The Auditory Comprehension and Expressive Communication subscales are standardized for ages 2 weeks through 6 years 11 months. The information obtained is recommended for use in identifying language disorders; determining the severity of the disorder; evaluating relative strengths, emerging skills, and weaknesses in language; and identifying areas of language in need of more extensive testing. The supplementary tests are designed to provide additional information about articulation, syntax and morphology used in spontaneous speech, and family, medical, and educational history that can be used when making diagnostic or treatment decisions. The results of the PLS–3 are to be combined with other formal and informal assessment procedures to get a more complete and accurate view of a child's speech and language abilities, and to plan therapy goals.

The test manual contains a detailed discussion of test administration and scoring, test interpretation, standardization, additional test instruments that may be used to explore specific language abilities in greater depth when conducting follow-up testing or planning intervention, and adaptations that may be made for children who are difficult to test. Unfortunately, no modifications in scoring are suggested to accommodate for language differences related to dialectical variations even though many of the items on both the receptive and expressive subscales would be biased against nonstandard dialects. Children from different racial/ethnic groups are included in the normative sample, but because dialectical differences would be scored as errors, they would simply be overrepresented in the lower range of the normal distribution. The manual is clearly written and sufficiently detailed to provide anyone knowledgeable about language and principles of assessment with enough information to administer, score, and interpret the test.

The normative sample on which the standard scores were derived was representative of most important dimensions. More than 1,900 children from 40 states stratified for age, gender, race/ethnicity, geographic region, and mother's educational level were included in the sample. The recommended number of 100 subjects per age interval (Salvia & Ysseldyke, 1988) was maintained for all but the four infant age intervals. However, the sample population was not representative of a normal range of language abilities. Children were ineligible for participation in the standardization testing if they were previously identified as language disordered, were receiving any language remediation services, were at-risk because of prematurity, had any condition such as Down's syndrome known to cause a language disorder, or who had difficulties at birth that placed them at-risk for normal language development. The population that was tested, therefore, did not represent the normal range of language abilities, but rather only a distribution of typically developing children. Because these were distributed along the normal curve, those children falling 2 standard deviations or more below the mean actually were average in language ability. The resulting norms, therefore, do not accurately reflect the performance of children with language disorders compared to normally developing peers. This problem should result in the overidentification of children as language disordered, when in fact their development is normal.

This predicted overidentification was not, however, the outcome of a study evaluating the construct validity of the PLS–3. In this study, the performance of 85 children with language disorders was compared to 85 matched children with no identified disorders.

Standard scores correctly classified all but two of the children with typically developing language as non-language-disordered using a criterion of performance within 1.5 standard deviations from the mean. This contributed to the manual author's calculations of a range from 66% to 80% correct classification of children for the three age levels tested. However, even this moderate success represented an overestimate of the test's effectiveness. Performance on the PLS–3 selected fewer than half of the children tested (i.e., 40 out of 85) who had identified language disorders. The test correctly classified only 36%, 61%, and 45%, respectively, of the groups of 3-, 4-, and 5-year-olds with language disorders. Consequently, the test cannot be confidently used for the purposes for which it was developed, including identifying children with language disorders, and determining eligibility for treatment or special services programs. This is a particularly problematic finding, because children with disorders should have performed far below the criterion level because they were not represented in the normative sample.

This finding suggests that there may be serious problems with the construction of the PLS–3. Examination of the instrument reveals that no coherent model or theory of language was used to support the development of the PLS–3. Rather, each component of language included on the test is described according to a relatively discrete sequence of skill acquisitions. The research supporting this sequence is briefly reviewed. The criteria used for item selection during test construction, and the procedures for selecting and ordering items included on the final version of the test are briefly described. This information is used to support the content validity of the test. However, this content may not reflect the abilities that are actually used by diagnostic teams to identify children with language disorders. Furthermore, no attempt was made to determine how children with language disorders would respond to test items or tasks because this population was purposely eliminated from the field testing. It would seem that in designing a test to identify children with language disorders and to delineate their strengths and weaknesses in language, it would be important to actually include the target population in the development and validation of the test items.

The standard error of measurement (*SEM*) for the subscales is fairly large, particularly at the extreme age intervals (infants and children older than 4 years). The resulting standard score confidence bands, or the range of scores within which a child's "true" score may fall is more than one standard deviation at most of the age intervals. For example, identification of a moderate language disorder (at or greater than -1.5 standard deviations from the mean) is equivalent to a percentile rank of 6 or below. At all age intervals, the normative tables show a percentile rank of 6 could place the child anywhere between the category of a severe disorder (-2 standard deviations) to average language ability (within ±1 standard deviation) because the confidence band typically ranged from approximately 2—19 in percentile rank. Consequently, the results of the test must be interpreted cautiously when making decisions about whether a child who receives a low score actually has a language disorder.

The reliability of the PLS–3 was assessed for internal test consistency and test-retest reliability. Internal consistency was measured by assessing the degree of homogeneity between items within the two subscales. For most age intervals, the reliability coefficients were .79 or above. A sample of 85 children was employed to measure test-retest reliability. The Total Language Score at all three age intervals tested met the minimum .90 criterion recommended for diagnostic decisions (Salvia & Ysseldyke, 1988). At most age intervals, the stability coefficients for the Auditory Comprehension and Expressive Communication subscales also were acceptably high.

The concurrent validity of the PLS–3 was assessed by comparing scores on the PLS–3 with the scores of three other tests of language. Correlations between performance on the PLS–3 compared to the two other standardized instruments ranged from .66 to .88. These results suggest that the PLS–3 measured similar but not identical skills. No information is provided regarding the validity of the comparison tests, and so all that can be said is that the tests are eliciting fairly similar performance results.

Test materials are well constructed and thoughtfully designed. Pictures are colorful and attractive to preschool-aged children. Children from a range of race/ethnic groups are depicted in the drawings. The record form is well organized with many features designed to maximize the accuracy and efficiency of test administration and scoring. Several methods of summarizing and analyzing test responses and derived scores are provided to assist in test interpretation.

In summary, the PLS–3 has many positive features in its test design and scoring. Considerable effort was made to create a language test that could reliably make initial decisions regarding the presence or absence of a language disorder in preschool children. However, findings of construct validity suggest that the test may not adequately discriminate between populations of children with and without language disorders, rendering this test of limited use for its stated purposes.

REVIEWER'S REFERENCE

Salvia, J., & Ysseldyke, J. E. (1988). *Assessment in special and remedial education* (4th ed.). Boston: Houghton Mifflin.

[242]
Productivity Environmental Preference Survey.

Purpose: Identifies "how adults prefer to function, learn, concentrate and perform in their occupational or educational activities."

Population: Adults.

Publication Dates: 1979–1993.

Acronym: PEPS.

Scores, 20: Sound, Light, Temperature, Design, Motivated/Unmotivated, Persistent, Responsible, Structure, Learning Alone/Peer-Oriented Learner, Authority-Oriented Learner, Several Ways, Auditory Preferences, Visual Preferences, Tactile Preferences, Kinesthetic Preferences, Requires Intake, Evening/Morning, Late Morning, Afternoon, Needs Mobility.

Administration: Group.

Price Data, 1992: $6 per 60 answer sheets with questions; $4 or less per individual profile (produced when sent in for computer scoring); $.40 per individual interpretative booklet; $9 per manual ('91, 75 pages); $295 per computerized self-administered PEPS survey (specify IBM or Apple, including 100 administrations); $11 per specimen set including answer sheet, interpretative booklet, and manual.

Time: (20–30) minutes.

Comments: Computer scored.

Authors: Gary E. Price, Rita Dunn, and Kenneth Dunn.

Publisher: Price Systems, Inc.

Cross References: See T4:2114 (2 references); for reviews by Craig N. Mills and Bertram C. Sippola, see 11:306 (9 references).

TEST REFERENCES

1. Reynolds, J., & Gerstan, M. (1991). Learning style characteristics of adult dependent decision makers: Counseling and instructional implications. *Career Development Quarterly, 40,* 145-154.
2. Nelson, B., Dunn, R., Griggs, S. A., Primavera, L., Fitzpatrick, M., Bacilious, Z., & Miller, R. (1993). Effects of learning style intervention on college students' retention and achievement. *Journal of College Student Development, 34,* 364-369.
3. Reynolds, J., & Werner, S. C. (1993). An alternative paradigm for college reading and study skills courses. *Journal of Reading, 37,* 272-278.
4. Murray-Harvey, R. (1994). Conceptual and measurement properties of the Productivity Environmental Preference Survey as a measure of learning style. *Educational and Psychological Measurement, 54,* 1002-1012.
5. Murray-Harvey, R. (1994). Learning styles and approaches to learning: Distinguishing between concepts and instruments. *British Journal of Educational Psychology, 64,* 373–388.
6. Dunn, R., Griggs, S. A., Olson, J., Beasley, M., & Gorman, B. S. (1995). A meta-analytic validation of the Dunn and Dunn model of learning-style preferences. *The Journal of Educational Psychology, 88,* 353–362.

Review of the Productivity Environmental Preference Survey by JAVAID KAISER, Senior Research and Evaluation Officer, Academy for Educational Development, Washington, DC:

The Productivity Environmental Preference Survey (PEPS) is a self-report instrument designed to identify productivity and learning styles of adults. The authors claim that the information gained through this survey may be used to provide situations, settings, and environments to maximize the performance of individuals. Other intended uses include the selection of individuals and formation of groups when all group members need to have similar productivity styles. Authors caution that the legitimate purpose of the instrument is to identify the learning and productivity styles and not to draw inferences about the underlying psychological factors such as motivation, attitudes, value systems, and ability levels of individuals. The test manual defines the productivity style as a product of the interaction of biological and developmental set of learning characteristics.

The instrument consists of 100 5-point Likert-type items. The response choices are *strongly agree, agree, uncertain, disagree,* and *strongly disagree.* Items can be administered in one of several ways: Present all items at once on an opscan sheet; read the questions to the respondent in an interview setting; play the cassette of prerecorded items; present items on an IBM, IBM-compatible, or Apple microcomputer. Answer sheets can be scanned for scoring. The software needed for scoring is available from the authors. When the instrument is administered on a computer, the results are immediately available for viewing and printing. The test may be completed in multiple sittings. Respondents are advised to give their first response to items and avoid serious detailed deliberations on questions. The estimated time to complete the instrument is 20–30 minutes.

The instrument collects information in four areas: Immediate Environment, Emotionality, Sociological Needs, and Physical Needs. Immediate Environment deals with environmental characteristics such as temperature, light, sound, and formal/informal setting called design. Motivation, responsibility, persistence, and structure (completely defined tasks versus less specifically defined tasks or assignments) fall under Mmotionality. Sociological Needs determine whether a person is self-oriented, peer-oriented, authority-oriented, or uses more than one of these modes (several ways). Physical Needs include elements such as perceptual preference, time of the day, intake, and mobility. The raw scores on each of these 20 areas are converted to a standard score with a mean of 50 and a standard deviation of 10. The area scores are interpreted when respondents score 40 or less or when the scores are 60 or higher ($\pm$ 1 standard deviation). The interpretations for low and high scores in all areas are clearly spelled out.

Scores are reported in the form of an individual profile along with raw and standard scores. In case of group testing, two group summaries are also prepared; one lists individuals who score 60 or higher and the other lists individuals who score 40 or less. An asterisk is placed under areas in which individuals qualified to be on the list. An individual can be included in both summaries if some of his/her area scores are 40 or less and others are 60 or higher. In addition to group summaries, two area summaries are also produced. One area summary lists all individuals by areas in which they scored 40 or less. The second area summary is also organized by areas and lists individuals who scored 60 or higher. These group summaries identify individuals who have similar preferences for learning and productivity styles.

The development of the PEPS started with the identification of research variables followed by item writing. The instrument was developed, revised, and then administered to 589 adults representing different states and work settings. Factor analysis of this data revealed 31 factors with eigenvalues greater than 1 and explained 65% of the total variance. Items of certain factors remained cross-loaded after rotation. Certain variables, which were believed to be independent, loaded on the same factors. Although the instrument was revised again after reviewing these results, the authors have not reported factor analysis on the revised instrument. It is, therefore, not clear if the 20 areas reported in the manual are orthogonal factors or if the problem of cross loadings persisted. The size and the representativeness of the sample on which the final version was tested is also unknown. The test manual also fails to disclose the literature source from where the research variables (areas) were selected.

The reliability on the 20 scales (areas) ranges from .39 to .87. Areas representing Motivation, Authority-oriented Learning, Learning in several ways, Tactile, and Kinesthetic have reliabilities of less than .60. The authors have not reported how these reliabilities were computed. To be safe, one must consider the reported reliabilities as liberal estimates of true internal consistencies.

The authors did not provide any information about the content, construct, or predictive validity for scores from the PEPS but have listed in the manual a number of studies which used this instrument. These studies have their own technical problems, which make them less useful to the PEPS. Several studies used a very small sample size. The statistical analyses in most of the studies were inappropriate: Used univariate analysis when multivariate was needed, used discriminant analysis when logistic regression was desired, ran several posthoc tests when orthogonal contrasts were more suitable, and showed complete disregard to the ratio of sample size to the number of predictors in the regression analysis. Moreover, the studies are reported in an inconsistent manner. Some are explained in unnecessary detail whereas others are just a paragraph. The reporting of results is also inconsistent; some are missing sample size whereas others did not report the significance level of findings. Many of the reported studies are missing bibliographic references. Notes like "data contributed by Dunn" (p. 23) are assumed sufficient substitutes of missed references. Some citations in the text have no entry in the bibliography. It is very difficult to locate the cited studies for an independent review. In addition, the reported studies are appended one after the other and provide no direction to the reader about the purpose of their inclusion in the manual. The authors should report only those studies that support the content, construct, or predictive validity of the PEPS and should make this relationship obvious for readers. Just listing the studies in which the PEPS was used does not add to its psychometric properties.

The review of listed studies did not render any support to the validity of the PEPS. Although some of the reported studies (citations cannot be provided because some were missing references) demonstrated the implications of mixing people with mismatched productivity styles, they failed to provide any evidence of the construct validity. Likewise, studies predicting college success using the PEPS could not support the predictive validity of the PEPS because of specification errors caused by ignoring the important variables such as motivation, persistence, ability, and difficulty of the material. These studies provided no comparisons of the PEPS scores with other variables to demonstrate that the PEPS scores are better predictors of college success. Other studies that compared the productivity styles among various groups (field dependent vs. field independent, left vs. right cerebral dominants, on-campus vs. off-campus

living, males vs. females, young vs. elderly, Asians vs. Caucasians) provided no valuable psychometric information except for describing the groups. No productivity related data were collected to establish the relationship between the PEPS area scores and the criterion variables. Without a theory that explains how 20 PEPS areas are related to each other and to other constructs of interest, full benefits of the PEPS cannot be reaped. It is much more practical to devise interventions that would enable individuals to adjust their learning and productivity styles comfortably when they encounter noncomplimentary environments than to expect an employer to maintain different levels of light and sound to accommodate their style differences. The underlying theory, once developed, will make the PEPS a more valuable instrument and will provide a clear direction for future research for the purpose of collecting validity, reliability, and normative data.

The authors are commended for extending the work on learning styles to include productivity styles for work-related environments. However, the available information does not provide enough support to the construct and predictive validity for scores from the PEPS. The reliability estimates are also poor and normative data are missing. The PEPS is not recommended for use until more evidence about its validity and reliability is obtained.

Review of the Productivity Environmental Preference Survey by THADDEUS ROZECKI, Assistant Professor, University of Northern Iowa, Cedar Falls, IA:

The Productivity Environmental Preference Survey (PEPS) is an instrument designed to measure adult preference in learning style and conditions that would enhance individual productivity in a working or learning environment. It purports to measure how an individual views both internal and external variables that would facilitate his or her highest level of productivity. The authors make no claim that this instrument is a strong measure of underlying psychological motivation for achievement or that it clearly delineates an individual's inherent skill level in either a work or academic environment. They stress, instead, that the PEPS should only be used to classify specific environmental, emotional, sociological, and physical factors that could then be used to identify environments that would be most conducive in meeting the preference of individuals within various organizational environments.

The PEPS consists of 100 items in a Likert-style format (strongly disagree, disagree, undecided, agree, strongly agree) with a 20- to 30-minute estimated time for completion. Individuals may be given the inventory in writing, on tape, or orally. The inventory need not be completed in one sitting but it is recommended that a personal interview could be valuable when held in conjunction with administration of the inventory in order to enhance insight into the subject's needs not best assessed through the written responses. Sample items include: "I prefer working in bright light; I usually finish what I start; I really enjoy television; I am most alert in the evening."

A combination of high scores on various items are purported to indicate an Analytic (sequential) or Global (holistic) processing style. There are 20 concentration areas, which correlate to scores used in the development of an individual's overall profile. These concentration areas include: Sound, Warmth, Persistent, Structure, Evening/Morning, Tactile Preference, and Needs Mobility. The authors indicate that grouping individuals with similar profiles might be beneficial in establishing working environments more conducive in meeting the preferential needs of organizational members.

Interpretation information is obtained from computer printout information provided by the publisher, a computer-assisted program for use on site available for purchase or a machine-scorable version available for those sites having access to a scanner. Except for the scanned version that focuses specifically on an individual's score, an individual and group summary profile are provided for each test taker. The individual profile reveals location on a scale for each of the 20 concentration areas in a graphed format. The group summaries provide a way to cluster individuals who have taken the test and indicate similar preferences on one or more of the concentration issues. A standard score in each concentration area (mean of 50, standard deviation of 10) provides an overall preference summary with scores below 40 or above 60 indicating a low or high preferential disposition toward the specific concentration areas. Short interpretive statements are provided for both low and high scores within each area. Hand-scored versions of the measure are not available.

The PEPS was developed by identifying research variables that appeared to describe the way individuals prefer to learn or work and were analyzed using a factor analytic method. The authors did not mention the specific research variables that were initially investigated except in a general sense. These initial variables were the foundation of the instrument that was administered to 589 adults from several states and from various academic and industrial settings. Demographic information concerning this original group is not provided and procedures used in the selection of this norm group are not clear. Further factor analytic procedures were carried out, which revealed 31 factors that accounted for 65% of the total variance on the PEPS. The actual determination of the 20 specific concentration areas is adequately explained by the authors in the test manual.

The authors provide reliability information for each of the 20 specific concentration areas but fail to mention the characteristics of the norm group ($n = 900$) to whom the test was administered. Reliability coefficients range from .39 to .87. The authors report that 75% of the reliabilities are equal to or greater than .60, including the concentration areas of "noise level, light, temperature, design, persistent, responsible, structure, learning alone/peer oriented, auditory, visual, intake, learning/working in evening/morning, late morning, afternoon, and mobility" (p. 20). Reliability coefficients for the areas of "authority figures present, learning in several ways, tactile, and kinesthetic" (p. 20) fell below .60. The manual provides a brief description of the reasons the authors believe respondents produced scores with low reliability in these areas.

Validity information for the PEPS is clearly lacking. Although the authors cite theoretical principles upon which productivity style is based, there is no specific mention in the test manual concerning validity except in relation to a number of studies that were presented concerning the use of the PEPS with various populations. It can be assumed that the authors expect that validity information for the instrument can be gleaned through a specific examination of these studies.

The manual provides 16 abstracts of studies in which the PEPS was used. These cover the general headings of cognitive style, college undergraduates, ethnic differences, gender differences, instructional style, life span changes, personnel and management, structure, and study skills. Although there is a great deal of information presented, it is difficult to ascertain in which context the PEPS can be most effectively employed.

Because of the interest that has been generated over the past 10 years in the identification of learning styles, especially in school settings, the PEPS appears to be an assessment tool that can offer a clearer assessment strategy than more simplistic methods that are often utilized by teachers, administrators, and personnel managers. It highlights specific environmental conditions and preferences that often impact work or learning performance and can serve as a guide for structuring groups that might increase their performance by being clustered together. Information on the overall reliability and validity of this instrument needs to be more clearly delineated, especially in relation to the formulation of the concentration areas and interpretation of the results. It does not appear that this measure should be used in the diagnostic assessment of an individual's ability to succeed in a particular work or academic environment, but only as an indication of tasks or environments the individual believes to be important. The authors' suggestion that a personal interview accompany the administration of this instrument appears prudent in light of the reliability and validity issues.

[243]
Profile of Aptitude for Leadership.

Purpose: To measure an individual's relative strength in each of four leadership styles (or types of leader).
Population: Adults.
Publication Date: 1991.
Acronym: PAL.
Scores, 4: Manager (Administrator), Supervisor (Coach), Entrepreneur (Leader), Technician (Specialist).
Administration: Group or individual.
Manual: No manual.
Price Data, 1991: $80 per 20 each of test, answer sheet, and interpretation folder.
Time: (20) minutes.
Comments: Self-administered; self-scored.
Author: Training House, Inc.
Publisher: Training House, Inc.

Review of the Profile of Aptitude for Leadership by JACK E. GEBART-EAGLEMONT, Lecturer in Psychology, Swinburne University of Technology, Hawthorn, Victoria, Australia:

The Profile of Aptitude for Leadership (PAL) is a 12-item self-report, self-scored instrument that allows the respondents to express their preferences for different leadership styles, defined as Manager, Supervisor, Entrepreneur, and Technician. The response format requires the respondent to rate different styles by distributing 6 points among four options available for each item (for example, 0-6-0-0, or 2-0-4-0). The scores representing each leadership style are then summed up and the respondent can interpret the results using a simple table of leaders' characteristics. The interpretations are presented in elementary, everyday language. The tables of characteristics include Leadership Style, Looks For (goals), Values, Desires, Conditions, Time Frame, Negative Consequences, Slogan, Orientation, and Proactive/Reactive. For example, the slogan of the Technician is: "Getting everything done ... if you want a job done right, do it yourself" (p. 3). The interpretation tables are followed by narrative vignettes describing the four prototypal leadership styles. There is no manual, and subsequently there is no information concerning the theory behind the leadership styles taxonomy used by the PAL. The origin of the test items is not explained and there are no indications of psychometric procedures usually involved in test development. Because the items do not include any control scales (such as social desirability or lie scales), the entire exercise is very vulnerable to response distortions.

In light of these deficiencies it appears that the Profile of Aptitude for Leadership does not measure any dimensions related to "aptitudes." The concept of aptitudes is considered to be related to abilities, capabilities, and human potential, and none of these dimensions appear to be measured by the PAL items. The instrument merely allows the respondent to structure his/her own self-perceptions concerning his/her preferences for different leadership roles. The simple scoring system is devised to roughly quantify these self-perceptions. At best, it can be stated that the PAL responses reflect attitudes toward different leadership styles, and therefore the use of the word "aptitude" in the title is not justified. The entire exercise is based on the assumed face validity of the items, and there is no attempt to control for the response styles or social desirability. Even as a self-assessment exercise (as indicated by the publisher), the PAL does not meet the most basic psychometric requirements. The accompanying materials lack any normative data, and no indices of reliability or validity of the PAL are available. This reviewer cannot recomend this product for any diagnostic application. Because the instrument is not supported by any psychometric data, and therefore there is no information concerning reliability and validity, any self-diagnostic conclusions based on the PAL would be unsubstantiated. The exercise may be used casually in training groups, as educational material, with the objective of helping respondents to structure their cognitions and attitudes concerning the various elements of leadership roles. Any other use, especially promising a delivery of an "aptitude profile," would be misleading. Because there are no norms, the construction of any meaningful "profiles" is objectionable.

This reviewer feels that much work is needed in order to analyze the validity and reliability of the

PAL. The items appear to have face validity, which makes them useful as a starting point for test development. It seems that the number of items is too low to measure any meaningful latent variables representing psychological concepts. The purpose of the PAL items is very obvious and transparent (high face validity), which makes the scales very vulnerable to response styles reflecting social desirability. Most measures used in organizational settings are susceptible to faking (Furnham, 1990). The testees tend to pattern their responses following their ideal image of the "prototypal personality." The social desirability scales (or Lie scales) should be included in tests in order to control for these tendencies.

Unfortunately, in its present form, the PAL is a relatively naive product and should not be recommended for any professional use. Although the publishers adequately labeled the PAL as "a self-assessment exercise," the distinctions between "exercises" and "tests" are often unclear within the areas of organizational consulting, development, and training, which results in a well-known persistent pattern of using unvalidated tests. The publishers of the PAL express a peculiar attitude toward the normalized devices: "They yield scores on such dimensions as the degree to which you are Theory X or Theory Y" [sic] (cover page). Following this, the publishers emphasize the virtues of the PAL: "This assessment is different. ... The leadership scores that you generate will enable you to examine the appropriateness [sic] of the different behaviour patterns that combine to make up your leadership style" (cover page). The test materials supplied for this review do not present any references concerning published research supporting such claims. After extensive computerized searches, this reviewer could not find any research indicating the validity or reliability of the PAL. Potential users will be better served if any diagnostic statements, profiles, or aptitude assessments are based on results obtained using professionally constructed psychological tests. There are several well-established and normalized professional instruments that supply validated measurement of dimensions related to leadership capability. For example, in terms of interest structures, the Jackson Vocational Interest Survey provides separate scales assessing Dominant Leadership, Stamina, Accountability, Independence, Planfulness, and Interpersonal Confidence (Jackson, 1977; T4:1297). Another approach to the assessment of leadership abilities is based on the use of specialized scales developed for normalized and validated multidimensional personality instruments such as the California Personality Inventory subscale measuring Managerial

Potential (Gough, 1984), or the Sixteen Personality Factor subscales measuring Managerial/Leadership dimensions (Bolton, 1985; Bolton, 1992; Harrell, 1992). Also, there are several simple unidimensional specialized instruments developed and validated with the sole purpose of measuring specific traits related to leadership, such as Power and Influence (Bennett, 1988), or Managerial Potential (Novelli & Gryskiewicz, 1991).

REVIEWER'S REFERENCES

Jackson, D. N. (1977). *Jackson Vocational Interest Survey Manual.* London, Ontario: Research psychologists Press.

Gough, H. G. (1984). A Managerial Potential Scale for the California Psychological Inventory. *Journal of Applied Psychology, 69,* 233–240.

Bolton, B. (1985). Discriminant analysis of Holland's occupational types using the Sixteen Personality Factor Questionnaire. *Journal of Vocational Behavior, 27,* 210–217.

Bennett, J. B. (1988). Power and influence as distinct personality traits: Development and validation of a psychometric measure. *Journal of Research in Personality, 22,* 361–394.

Furnham, A. (1990). Faking personality questionnaires: Fabricating different profiles for different purposes. *Current Psychology: Research and Reviews, 9*(1), 46–55.

Novelli, L., Jr., & Gryskiewicz, N. (1991). Reliability and factor structure of the Mangerial Potential Scale. *Educational and Psychological Measurement, 51,* 227–229.

Bolton, B. (1992). [Review of the California Psychological Inventory, Revised Edition]. In J. J. Kramer & J. C. Conoley (Eds.), *The eleventh mental measurements yearbook* (pp. 138–139). Lincoln, NE: Buros Institute of Mental Measurements.

Harrell, T. H. (1992). [Review of the Vocational Personality Report for the 16PF—Form E]. In J. J. Kramer & J. C. Conoley (Eds.), *The eleventh mental measurements yearbook* (pp. 830–831). Lincoln, NE: Buros Institute of Mental Measurements.

Review of the Profile of Aptitude for Leadership by NEAL SCHMITT, *University Distinguished Professor, Psychology and Management, Department of Psychology, Michigan State University, East Lansing, MI:*

The Profile of Aptitude for Leadership (PAL) is a 12-item instrument, each item consisting of four statements representing four leadership styles (Manager, Supervisor, Entrepreneur, and Technician) regarding the actions of a leader or beliefs about appropriate leader behavior. The respondent is asked to divide 6 points among each of the four statements in each item in a way that reflects their beliefs about leadership. A simple rank order of the four statements (i.e., 0, 1, 2, 3) would produce a sum equal to 6, but the respondent is not restricted to this response. All 6 points could be assigned to one of the options. This format makes the scores on this test totally ipsative and is this test's most important feature.

The properties and limitations of ipsative measurement have been well known for at least three decades (Hicks, 1970). The sums of the four scores on this measure will total 72 for all respondents. The average intercorrelation between scores on the four scales will be -.33. The average validity of the four scales in predicting external behavior will be zero. It should be noted that the author of the test specifically and correctly states that the instrument should not be used for selection or similar decision making. Its use should be restricted to self-examination of one's views about leadership and what they imply. Accordingly, the self-scoring instructions include a lengthy description of the four dimensions measured by the test.

Although use of the measure for self-examination or training purposes only does make the statistical limitations moot, there remain parallel interpretive limitations. Because the scores of persons on each of the scales are determined by the persons' scores on other scales, not by comparison to other respondents or a normative data base, the relative strength of a person's standing on these dimensions cannot be determined. So a person's score on the Entrepreneur scale may reflect real strength of beliefs on this dimension relative to others or it may be that it reflects relatively weak beliefs on the dimension because the respondent really has no strong feelings about any of the dimensions. Given the directions, the person has to make choices if by no other means than tossing a coin. The only base of comaprison is internal to the respondent; if the entrepreneurial score is high, it only means that when given these four options, the person will pick the entrepreneurial option.

The test is accompanied by no data on reliability, validity, or norms, so there was nothing to review or on which to comment regarding the adequacy of the data base supporting the test's use.

The author states that the PAL was developed for use in training programs dealing with managment development, leadership, and empowerment. As such, scores on the four scales noted above are relevant and my personal reading of the items suggests they have face validity. As such, they may be useful "icebreakers" in training programs. They are likely to stimulate thought, conversation, and self-examination of points of view about leadership. As psychometric instruments, however, these scales are unsupported by any data made available to me and the ipsative format of the test is associated with statistical and interpretive problems.

REVIEWER'S REFERENCE

Hicks, L. E. (1970). Some properties of ipsative, normative, and forced-choice normative measures. *Psychological Bulletin, 74,* 167–184.

[244]
Profiles of Problem Solving.

Purpose: "An assessment of mathematical problem solving designed for children in upper primary school."
Population: Grades 4–6.
Publication Date: 1993.
Acronym: POPS.
Scores, 5: Correctness of Answer, Method Used, Accuracy, Extracting Information, Quality of Explanation.
Administration: Group.
Price Data, 1993: A$75 per manual (64 pages) and photocopiable masters.
Time: [32]40 minutes.

Authors: Kaye Stacey, Susie Groves, Sid Bourke, and Brian Doig.
Publisher: Australian Council for Educational Research Ltd. [Australia].

Review of the Profiles of Problem Solving by MARY J. McLELLAN, Assistant Professor of Educational Psychology, Northern Arizona University, Flagstaff, AZ:

The Profiles of Problem Solving (POPS) is an assessment of mathematical problem solving for upper primary level school children. It is published by the Australian Council for Educational Research and is part of the Guideposts in Mathematics. Published in 1993, this assessment of problem-solving skills provides an approach to evaluating individual students and entire classrooms. The intended users of the POPS are classroom teachers. Although there would be valuable information gained from this evaluation tool in the process of an individualized psychoeducational evaluation, the emphasis is on classroom instruction.

The POPS comes in a nicely packaged portfolio-style pamphlet, including a manual and a set of photocopy master sheets. The master sheets are the actual assessment sheets provided to the students who complete the evaluation. In addition, student profile and score sheets are also photocopy ready. The manual provides clear and concise administration directions, as well as comprehensive scoring guidelines. The POPS takes approximately 40 minutes to complete. The timing is quite precise because students are guided through the test and provided a limited amount of time (5–7 minutes) to work on each problem. The examiner ensures that all the children engaged in the task are given the same amount of time to work on each problem.

Scoring is centered around understanding the student's approach to the task. This involves five aspects of problem solving: Correctness of Answer, Method Used, Accuracy, Extracting Information, and Quality of Explanation. Students are expected to provide their responses and an explanation of how they arrived at their answer for all of the questions. Each of the six responses the child gives are scored according to these preset criteria. Explanations of scoring criteria for each of the six problems are provided in the manual. Scores are 0, 1, or 2 for most of the questions and categories. Not all of the six questions have specific criteria in each of the aspects of problem solving. Profiles are created for each student by totaling scores from each question and scoring criteria. Each student then has a profile sheet that identifies them as falling into the category of a beginning, developing, or advanced problem solver.

The process of development of the POPS is described in the "Background Information on POPS" (p. 47) section of the manual. This section provides an impressive description of the development of the POPS and the theoretical rationale involved. A discussion of the development of assessment of mathematical problem skills and its importance to instruction left this reviewer convinced that the POPS was developed based on sound reasoning and has a useful purpose.

A limitation of the POPS is the consumable nature of the product. The authors acknowledge that the actual questions developed may not be used again due to the practice effect that would be involved. The manual does, however, provide information to users that could assist in the development of additional questions for students. The authors also point out that the POPS is designed as an assessment strategy for teachers and a research tool. There are also "suggestions for further learning" (p. 31) that provide specific strategies and methods teachers may consider when planning to improve the problem-solving skills of their students.

The number of children used in the development of this assessment tool is impressive, considering the individual involvement required from each child and the depth of analysis applied to each child's performance. The rationale provided for using the lock-step method of administration is an example of careful evaluation of the subjects' performance on this test. The authors are to be commended for careful consideration of these details.

In conclusion, the POPS is a limited scope assessment of mathematical problem-solving skills of upper primary grade students (grades 4–6). The limit of applicable subjects is offset by the depth of information available for each student who completes the POPS. A teacher has an impressive amount of information about how each student in a class approaches mathematical problem solving once the student's tests are analyzed. The authors point out that assessment typically influences the importance placed on any aspect of instruction; therefore, the assessment of problem-solving strategies specifically could direct the emphasis of instruction to problem solving, rather than rote instruction. The authors provide an excellent justification for the development of this assessment tool and the strengths and limitations of the POPS are discussed in a clear and concise fashion. As a research tool, the POPS provides a well-developed, thorough instrument that would be a valuable addition to a research protocol.

Review of the Profiles of Problem Solving by MARIA MEDINA-DIAZ, *Assistant Professor of Educational Measurement and Evaluation, School of Education, University of Puerto Rico, Rio Piedras, PR:*

The convenient case of materials for the Profiles of Problem Solving (POPS) includes a test manual; a test booklet (containing a sample question, the six test questions with illustrations, and a student score sheet); an Individual Profile blank card (including three levels of performance with their point scale and descriptions); and a double-sided card for completing a Group Profile and Group Strategies. These materials are prepared in a photocopy master sheet that can be copied for administering to a group of students. A good quality copy machine is needed to do the reproduction work of the test, particularly for capturing the details of the figures and pictures included in some items (i.e., Question 3—Houses).

POPS' six items (the authors called them "questions": Question 1—Medicine, Question 2—Coin Machine, Question 3—Houses, Question 4—Light Weight, Question 5—Dice, and Question 6—Ladders) were designed to assess mathematical problem-solving performance of 4th, 5th, and 6th graders in five broad categories: Correctness of the Answer, Method Used, Accuracy, Extracting Information, and Quality of Explanation. These are problems that require more than one step and strategy for finding a solution, and they cover content concerning whole number and money operations, estimation, patterns, geometry, and measurement. Information about students' problem-solving performance in seven specific strategies (identifying numerical relationships, listing possibilities, estimating, working systematically, visualizing, finding and using patterns, and generalizing) can be extracted. The intention for the POPS was "to measure those aspects of problem solving which involve general thinking skills, used in interaction with well-absorbed mathematical knowledge on realistic tasks" (p. 48). This may be true to some extent but limitations will be noted.

To what extent the categories and skills of problem solving measured in the items represent adequately those general thinking skills is not well established. The vocabulary employed in referring and describing these skills is part of the confusion. Are these "general thinking skills" (p. 48) equivalent to "broad aspects" (p. 47) or "broad categories of problem solving" (p. 49) measured in POPS? The classification of the student performance in each of the five categories of problem solving measured should be done with caution. The authors also recognize this lack of information for describing completely the student's process of problem solving.

The content and construct validity evidence presented is not sufficient to determine the correspondence and representation in the items of the problem-solving categories proposed. The content validity evidence based on the responses of 15 teachers to a five-item questionnaire is somewhat weak for supporting the five broad categories and the seven specific strategies of problem solving measured. However, in developing POPS as described in the manual, an analysis of the mathematical content of the problems and of the problem-solving process employed by a sample of 60 students was done. Such brief information in the manual is not enough evidence for test validity. Some attention should be given to the match between the meanings of the categories of problem solving measured (e.g., Method Used and Quality of Explanation) and the specific descriptions included in the scoring-rubrics for the test questions.

Although the authors indicate the POPS' problem solving categories and process are parallel to others (e.g., Polya, 1957; Charles & Lester, 1982), there is no empirical evidence to support either a statistical or a logical correspondence among them. Neither is there information about the relationship of the POPS with other mathematics problem-solving tests. Additional evidence for the construct validity of the test is the correlation between the items and problem-solving categories. The authors report that "most scores relating to one item were highly correlated" (p. 58) with Pearson correlations ranging from .35 to .80. Correlations between total item scores were not so high (ranging from -.03 to .46); correlations between total scores in the problem-solving categories ranged from .60 to .85; and correlations of scores for the same categories on different items were between 0 and .41. Based on these results, the construct validity of the test is not so well supported. More detailed evidence, and a logical scheme between what is measured and how it is measured, are needed for sustaining claims for the POPS.

Also, no demographic information is provided about the sample of students who participated in the interview phase ($N = 60$) as well as in the test trial using the lock step method ($N = 200$). The number of students for each grade in the trial sample is not reported. Mean scores of the trial sample are reported for categories and items, categories by sex and grade, and item scores by sex and grade. The test mean score of the trial sample was 28.2 out of 53, and the highest mean scores were in the categories of extracting information (6.2 out of 8) and correctness of answer (7.8 out of 13). Typically, there was a slight increment by grade levels in the mean scores of the items (however, "accuracy" decreased from grades 5–6 and extracting information decreased from 4–5) and of all problem-solving categories. The female students obtained higher mean scores than the males for all of the five categories of problem solving, in every question of the test (except for "Dice"). According to the authors, these results were similar to others reported by Australian researchers. No further explanation and evidence about possible item bias is presented. The generalization of the results of the POPS to other populations is limited because of the sample size, the weakness of sampling procedures, and the lack of representativeness of the diversity of students in Australia. There is no basis for norms interpretations, and in fact, only limited normative data are shown.

Limited information about inter- and intrarater reliability is reported. A sample of 50 student responses was scored by five judges (three authors of the POPS and two teachers). Values of intrarater consistency greater than .95 in the whole test are mentioned but Pearson's correlation results are incomplete. Nor are the exact value of the correlations by categories of problem solving provided. The values of the intrarater coefficients are also not reported. In addition, there are no reliability data regarding the different groups of test takers. Therefore, the authors' claim about high raters' consistency in using the scoring scheme has partial support. Measures of the internal consistency between the items and categories are reported; but they are not organized in a detailed fashion. More specific and organized data about all the test's reliability estimates are needed in order to appraise the quality of the test items in assessing students' problem-solving performance.

The POPS is group administered using a format labeled "lock-step" (p. 11). This means that all students are working on the same problem at the same time and move through the problem together. After each problem is read aloud by the teacher, the students are given 5 minutes to work on each of the first five problems and 7 minutes for the last one. The trial results of the lock-step format were slightly higher than of the "free" (p. 50) format of administration. According to the authors, benefits of the lock-step procedure are a reduction of reading and comprehension difficulties, encouragement of explanation by providing reminders throughout the test, and more time to write explanations.

This test was not designed to be a self-administered test but rather is one that can be designated as a "teacher-guided test"—the test-specific directions depend heavily on the teacher. The structure of the questions and the lack of clarity and precision of the students' instructions in the test stimulate this dependency. This gives to the teacher some space and flexibility to indicate to the students what to do and further, permits students to raise doubts each time a test item is read. The test manual suggests the teacher should address them in an appropriate manner. Obviously, the kind of administration procedures suggested are too distant to be standardized. Students' comments and doubts can disturb the classroom environment for the test administration.

Another issue is that a 5-minute answering period for most of the problems can limit the extent and quality of the students' answers. Why should the students not know the amount of time they can dedicate to work in each problem? Test instructions do not mention that the teacher should indicate the time allotted to answer each question but only when the time allowed for answering each test problem is finished (after 5 or 7 minutes).

The students can have (depending on the teacher) the opportunity to review and complete "a few" (p. 16) questions. How many are few? What about a student who does not have time to do all the questions and needs extra time to think and work them out? The administration time suggested is 32 minutes for testing and 40 minutes as total time. But the real time that students of different grade levels (grades 4, 5, and 6) will need to answer them appropriately should be noted. A minor point is where to write the answers. Each item includes a rectangle labeled "answer" (except in Items 4 and 5) inside which the students should write their response. In Items 4 ("Light weight") and 5 ("Dice) a drawing is requested as an answer. These rectangles guide the examinees to highlight the answer to the question.

The authors claim that a unique feature of the POPS is that the students have to explain their method of solution and in order to facilitate this the lock-step administration format is used. The test manual indicates the teacher should emphasize that the student's work should be clearly presented but that neatness and spelling will not count. Also, in some items the teacher should emphasize the need for explanations (Questions 3, 4, and 6). A main concern is what the authors mean by a written explanation, its extension and characteristics, and what they mean by "worked out the answer" (p. 15). They point out the importance of the explanation but do not provide specific information and examples about what is expected.

Six tables including the scoring rubrics for each problem are supplied. The answers are totally or partially scored in terms of the five categories of problem solving measured. Although the rubrics are adequate in describing the features of the expected answers, some additional explanation may be needed about how to use them appropriately. Another issue in the scoring procedure is that all five categories are not used in some questions. This problem is exacerbated when each rubric shows specific meanings or descriptions for the categories. An example in the manual may help to see the scoring mechanics and the use of the rubrics, particularly in cases involving a combination of different scores in the five categories.

Each of the problem-solving categories differ in the number of points assigned (13, 14, 10, 8, and 8, respectively) and also in the spread of the scores along a continuum. This is determined by the difficulty of the category. The individual's scores are recorded on the Student Score Sheet, the totals for each of the five categories calculated, and then the results transferred to the Individual Profile form. The student's total scores across the problem-solving categories are joined in order to give a visual picture of her or his position in the three levels of "development" (p. 25) in problem solving: beginning, developing, and advanced. A description of each level is included on the back of the Individual Profile. A Group profile can be constructed from each individual's profile. Also, the answers to the POPS questions can be scored according to the seven specific strategies of problem solving proposed. Due to the limited data available for each student, the authors recommend that only group data should be collected for these strategies.

SUMMARY. The POPS represents an important attempt to measure general aspects of mathematical problem-solving performance. Despite the conceptual and technical flaws mentioned, it seems more suitable for classroom use and teaching purposes than for large-scale testing. Using the results with caution, mathematics teachers can use the POPS for screening students' problem-solving approaches. Its diagnostic information is limited. A valuable asset of the POPS is a section of suggestions for instructional activities related to the specific problem-solving categories measured, and a list of references and resources. The three criteria for selecting the problems (i.e., multi-step, familiarity, and time-on-task) should be closely checked for the users of this test with particular populations of students inside and outside of Australia because of the variety of their school experiences, and of the language and context of the problems.

REVIEWER'S REFERENCES

Polya, G. (1957). *How to solve it: A new aspect of mathematical method.* Garden City, NY: Doubleday.
Charles, R., & Lester, F. (1982). *Teaching problem solving: What, why and how.* Palo Alto, CA: Dale Seymour.

[245]
Progressive Achievement Test of Listening Comprehension [Revised].

Purpose: "Intended ... to assist teachers in determining levels of development attained by their students in the basic skills of listening comprehension."
Population: Standards 1–4 and Forms 1–4 (ages 7–14) in New Zealand school system.
Publication Dates: 1971–1994.
Acronym: PAT: Listening Comprehension.
Scores: Total score only.
Administration: Group.
Levels: 8 overlapping levels labeled Parts 1–8: Primary: Parts 1–4 (Standards 1–4); Intermediate: Parts 5–6 (Forms 1–2); Secondary: Parts 7–8 (Forms 3–4).
Price Data, 1995: $1.53 per Primary, Intermediate, or Secondary test booklet; $4.05 per Primary, Intermediate, or Secondary teacher's script; $.72 per scoring key; $1.35 per 10 answer sheets; $8.10 per Intermediate audiotape; $9 per Secondary audiotape; $5.85 per teacher's manual ('94, 32 pages).
Time: (55) minutes.
Comments: 2 forms (A & B) available (Form A is used in odd-numbered years and Form B is used in even-numbered years); this test was specifically developed for use in New Zealand schools.
Authors: Neil A. Reid, Ian C. Johnston, and Warwick B. Elley.
Publisher: New Zealand Council for Educational Research [New Zealand].
Cross References: See T4:2140 (2 references) and T3:1910 (1 reference); for a review by Roger A. Richards, see 8:453 (2 references).

TEST REFERENCES

1. Chapman, J. W. (1988). Cognitive-motivational characteristics and academic achievement of learning disabled children: A longitudinal study. *Journal of Educational Psychology, 80,* 357–365.

Review of the Progressive Achievement Test of Listening Comprehension [Revised] by SHERWYN MORREALE, Chair, Center for Excellence in Oral Communication, University of Colorado at Colorado Springs, Colorado Springs, CO, and PHILIP BACKLUND, Associate Dean and Professor of Speech Communication, Communication Department, Central Washington University, Ellensburg, WA:

The introduction to this test clearly states its general purpose, to assist teachers in the New Zealand school system in assessing students' listening comprehension skills. The test is limited in that it can only be used in New Zealand, though it could be tested for use elsewhere or could act as a format for developing other tests. Five specific functions for the instrument include: identifying children with inadequate listening skills; locating areas of weakness and strength within a class; helping teachers and students recognize the importance of listening skills and the need for instruction; providing a broad estimate of reading expectancy; and providing a measure of general verbal ability. The last two applications must be considered indirect functions of this test. Adequate rationale for the instrument is grounded in the academic literature on listening. The description of the test indicates a careful process of development that has resulted in a well-structured assessment instrument. The testing materials are thorough, well organized, well written, and relatively easy to use.

Procedural instructions for administering and scoring the test are comprehensive, clarifying its use exactly. Cautions are included for the user to replicate the procedures with precision to avoid invalidating the results. Similar cautions for interpreting the test results suggest that no test score is perfectly accurate and scores only estimate students' ability. Given these cautions, ample instructions and materials for interpreting students' scores on this test are provided. Students' raw scores indicate their level of achievement on an 11-point scale, ranging from very limited ability to a very advanced degree of competency in listening comprehension. Students' raw scores can be converted to percentile rank norms that indicate how that score compares with other students of the same age and of the same class level. Excellent guidelines are outlined for reporting test results to students and parents and for using test results of listening levels in a class to redirect teaching. More cautions for using the test suggest that: Results obtained are only estimates; national norms provided are benchmarks to inform teaching, not absolute standards expected of all students; results should be used to improve instruction and measure growth; the instrument assesses skills attainment, it does not diagnose individual weaknesses; and, the results should not be used to evaluate teaching effectiveness.

The present version of the Progressive Achievement Test of Listening Comprehension (PAT: Listening Comprehension) is the result of a careful process of development, construction, revision, and item selection that began in 1969. An array of panels and review committees, teachers, advisers, and specialists in reading and language contributed to the construction and revision processes. The only shortcoming in an otherwise careful development process would be the lack of involvement of scholars with specific background in listening and speech communication.

In 1992, the present version of the instrument was tested in 76 different schools in New Zealand and then subjected to item analyses, which resulted in two equivalent forms of the tool for each of eight class levels. The development process was followed by other investigations and surveys, the results of which were used to revise the test before its standardization. For example, to more closely approximate the real-life listening experiences of students, the final version of the instrument was revised to contain less formal material, more material from radio and TV, and more peer-originated material.

The size and representativeness of the sample used to obtain nationally standardized norms for this test were both satisfactory. The test was administered to a systematically selected, representative sample of 1,000 students at each of the eight class levels. Class percentile rank norms were calculated by class and sex. Age percentile rank norms were calculated at each level in half-year age groups.

Reliability, the stability and consistency of this test, was examined using appropriate statistical methods and yielded satisfactory findings. The reliability of the relationship between two forms of the test was examined for all eight levels. Reliability coefficients for equivalent forms ranged between .77 and .84. The internal consistency of the tool was examined by calculating split-half reliability coefficients that ranged between .85 and .90. Another estimate of internal consistency, based on the difficulty level of each item, yielded coefficients ranging from .81 to .88. The mean scores of these three reliability estimates were used to calculate standard errors of measurement for both forms of the instrument at each of the eight levels. These estimates, of the extent to which the score obtained on the test would differ from a hypothetical true score, ranged from 2.6 to 3.3.

Validity, the extent to which this test measures what it intends, also was examined satisfactorily. The content validity of the test is supported by the manner in which it was planned and constructed. It is argued that the test assesses listening skills and abilities widely accepted as important by a representative group of teachers and advisers. Also the test's items were scrutinized by practicing teachers and reading and language specialists. Consensus of informed opinion is used to speak to the high content validity of the tool. The concurrent validity of the test is supported by studies that indicate the PAT: Listening Comprehension test correlates highly with tests of a similar kind developed in other countries, despite differences in emphasis and cultural background. The PAT: Listening Comprehension test correlated positively with tests of listening comprehension and scholastic abilities such as the Stanford Achievement Test ($r = .78$ and $r = .82$); and the Test of Scholastic Abilities ($r = .70$, $r = .62$, $r = .50$). Finally the construct validity of the PAT: Listening Comprehension test was investigated during various stages of its development. Those tests consistently supported the convergent-discriminant validity of the tool.

Item bias checks of the PAT: Listening Comprehension test related to gender, ethnicity, and other types of bias. Two approaches to detecting item bias took place during the trial testing phase of test development in 1992. A subjective review of the test's items was conducted by teacher/specialist panels to examine possible bias in language, subject matter, and the representation of people in ways that might be offensive or discriminatory. Any suspect passages or items were either modified or rejected. Objective statistical analysis of ethnic item bias was also conducted. The tentative final forms of the test were administered to samples of students in different parts of the country known to have significant ethnic mix. The two approaches to item bias frequently identified different items as differentiating between ethnic groups but most differences were marginal and not consistent across class levels.

The above examinations for reliability, validity, and bias were conducted with care. The results suggest that the PAT: Listening Comprehension test measures, with stability and accuracy, that which it claims to measure, doing so without any detected bias. Additionally, the presentation of these examinations in the teacher's manual is clear and easy to understand. The only recommendations that might be offered are minor. For example, longitudinal data, measuring the instrument's predictive ability, are not reported. And the examination of the instrument's construct validity began on an early version of the instrument, an instrument that underwent changes before reaching its final form. Bias analysis was performed on the items during the instrument's development. A study of ethnic bias, related to the instrument's use, also would be informative. Other than these minor concerns, this instrument is to be lauded for its careful development and thorough presentation to the user.

[246]
Project Implementation Profile.

Purpose: To identify and measure behavioral variables that may be related to project success.
Population: Project managers and team members.
Publication Date: 1992.
Acronym: PIP.
Scores, 11: Project Mission, Top Management Support, Project Schedule, Client Consultation, Personnel, Technical Tasks, Client Acceptance, Monitoring and Feedback, Communication, Trouble-Shooting, Overall Performance.
Administration: Group.
Price Data, 1993: $6.50 per profile (32 pages).
Time: (20) minutes.
Authors: Jeffrey K. Pinto and Dennis P. Slevin.
Publisher: XICOM, Inc.

Review of the Project Implementation Profile by SALLY KUHLENSCHMIDT, Associate Professor of Psychology, Western Kentucky University, Bowling Green, KY:

The purpose of the Project Implementation Profile (PIP) is to assess the status of key elements for completing a project successfully. Instructions for administration of the test are clear. The project manager and/or team members complete the PIP. The instrument consists of two parts, critical factors and project performance. The items measuring the 10 critical factors are scored on a Likert scale from 1 (*strongly disagree*) to 7 (*strongly agree*) with agreement indicating a successful project. The format assumes that the 5 items within each factor are measuring a single quality and are of equal weight. Research is necessary to know if this is an accurate assumption. Scores on each subscale are compared with "a database of 409 projects" (p. 16). Test-takers are to interpret percentiles below 50 as critical and the manual provides self-evaluation questions for "Low" scores. Half the manual consists of interpretive aids with no rationale or efficacy evidence for the interpretations. There is also a 12-item Project Performance scale.

TEST COVERAGE AND USE. The irony of the PIP is that a measure attempting to identify successful project implementation falls short in its own implementation as a project. The manual is completely inadequate, given well-established standards for tests. It includes no information on item or test development. After reading it, I still had questions concerning under what circumstances I would use this test and, more important, why. A review of several publications by the authors (e.g., Slevin & Pinto,

1987) revealed that the PIP is based on a well-articulated theory of project success. The manual ought to include the theory to aid users in interpreting the roles and relationships of the various factors and how to apply the PIP in their particular circumstances. The manual only lists the 10 "factors" or scales. These "factors" are the result of either a literature review (Schultz, Slevin, & Pinto, 1987) or a brief study (Pinto & Slevin, 1987). In the study, 52 management students who were full-time employees generated five actions they could take that would "substantially help implementation success" (p. 24) for a project. The authors then classified the 236 responses into 10 categories. Interrater agreement (percent) was .50, a very low level for percent agreement.

COMPARISON SAMPLE. The complete manual description of the standardization sample is as follows: "a database of 409 projects" (p. 16). Again, the authors have failed in the execution stage (to use their terminology) to provide information to the consumers about their product. Information from Pinto and Slevin (1989) suggests that the sample of projects was obtained by mailing a questionnaire to 585 members of the Project Management Institute. Members responded with 409 projects of which 159 were R & D projects, such as new drug or chemical process development, aerodynamic engineering research, or software/hardware development. The projects ranged in size from a "$5,000 pilot study to a $2.5 billion government-funded research grant" (p. 33) and included Fortune 500 businesses and smaller companies. The version of the PIP used with this sample included four external factors not included in the published PIP. The wording of the items makes it clear that the PIP is intended for use with engineering or technical projects, and would require moderate adaptations for use with human service projects, for example.

RELIABILITY AND VALIDITY. No reliability data are presented in the manual. The authors do recommend the PIP be administered at repeated intervals to evaluate project improvement. This recommendation is contrary to sound research principles (change scores are unstable) and made in the absence of information on the effect of repeated testing on the scores. An examination of the table used to convert raw scores to percentile scores reveals a strong client tendency to agree with items. Selecting the midpoint for all five of the questions within a scale will place the person in the bottom 10% on four of the scales and bottom 20% on another five scales. With this restriction of range in scoring comes a reduction in correlational measures of reliability and validity and difficulty in meaningfully discriminating among test takers. In addition, the authors use cutoff points for the labels "critical," "fair," and "good" project performance without providing justification for those cutoffs.

The only validity information provided is a brief comment that the 10 factors were "uncovered as the result of a series of in-depth studies and interviews with practicing project managers" (p. 2). As previously indicated, the manual does not include any information on the theoretical or research basis for these 10 factor scores or their relationship to each other or to real world criteria. Without this information, interpretation of PIP results is an exercise in speculation, although elegantly structured speculation.

OTHER CONSIDERATIONS. Beyond the psychometric shortcomings of this test, the social psychology literature on peer pressure and group thinking suggests that group dynamics could significantly influence the reliability and validity of the data. The authors should recommend safeguards (e.g., confidentiality procedures) for reducing such influences. Based on the items, the PIP is clearly designed for large, complex, long-term team projects involving multiple people and multiple levels of action for completion. Adapting the scale for use by smaller groups or even creating a checklist for success would be simple to accomplish. Some items would benefit from review and rewriting by a person not invested in the particular terminology of project management. Also, communication is primarily portrayed as flowing to the client (7 items), rather than from the client (2 items).

RECOMMENDATIONS. A consultant who frequently worked with projects in crises might find the PIP useful for structuring client understanding about projects. Administration of the test is easy to understand and the questions concerning problem areas are thought provoking. The objective of this test appears to be potentially useful and is worthy of careful development and research, particularly given the well-articulated theory detailed in other sources. Psychometrically, the information in the manual fails to meet minimal standards, including a thorough description of the comparison sample, an explication of its reliability as a measure, and, ultimately, evidence that scores actually relate to anything meaningful. Without this research basis carefully and completely detailed, I cannot recommend this test as more than a checklist of some issues to consider in project implementation. With a good research foundation, the PIP could fill an important niche.

REVIEWER'S REFERENCES

Pinto, J. K., & Slevin, D. (1987). Critical factors in successful project implementation. *IEEE Transactions on Engineering Management, EM-34*, 22–27.

Schultz, R., Slevin, D., & Pinto, J. (1987). Strategy and tactics in a process model of project implementation. *Interfaces, 17*(3), 34–46.

Slevin, D., & Pinto, J. (1987). Balancing strategy and tactics in project implementation. *Sloan Management Review, 29*(1), 33–41.

Pinto, J. K., & Slevin, D. P. (1989). Critical success factors in R & D projects. *Research Technology Management, 32*(1), 31–35.

Review of the Project Implementation Profile by KIMBERLY A. LAWLESS, Assistant Professor of Instructional Technology, Utah State University, Logan, UT:

The Project Implementation Profile (PIP) was developed as a diagnostic instrument for project managers. The scale is based on a conceptual model that outlines the essential critical factors for the successful management and implementation of a project over its life cycle. It is intended to allow project managers to formulate both an in-depth and overall picture of the current status of a project. Information from the PIP can then be used to better allocate time and other resources to ensure that all critical success factors are being addressed.

A 10-factor model of project implementation was developed by polling a pool of participants who recently had some project involvement. Participants were asked to place themselves in the role of project manager, and indicate variables that substantially impacted categories. These categories served as fodder for the conceptual model, and the participants' individual responses became the basis for the item stems. The 10 factors as listed in the PIP manual are: (a) *Project Mission,* Initial clarity of goals and general mission; (b) *Top Management Support,* Willingness of top management to provide the necessary resource and authority/power for project success; (c) *Project Schedule/Plan,* A detailed specification of the individual action steps required for project implementation; (d) *Client Consultation,* Communication, consultation, and active listening to all impacted parties; (e) *Personnel,* Recruitment, selection, and training of the necessary personnel for the project team; (f) *Technical Tasks,* Availability of the required technology and expertise to accomplish the specific technical action steps; (g) *Client Acceptance,* The act of "selling" the final project to its ultimate intended users; (h) *Monitoring and Feedback,* Timely provision of comprehensive control information at each stage in the implementation process; (i) *Communication,* The provision of an appropriate network and necessary data to all key actors in the project implementation; and (j) *Trouble-Shooting,* Ability to handle unexpected crises and deviations from the plan. In addition to the 10 factors, an overall Project Performance subscale is included.

In total, the survey contains 62 items. Each critical factor subscale contains 5 items, and the Project Performance subscale contains 12 items. All responses are rated on a 7-point bounded, Likert-type scale, where a score of 1 represents *strongly disagree,* and a score of 7 represents *strongly agree.* Items focus on both hard (i.e., technical, operational) and soft (i.e., behavioral, humanistic) implementation skills.

Information concerning reliability and validity of scores from the PIP was provided via an unpublished doctoral dissertation (Pinto, 1986). A reliability study was conducted on 42 MBA students and 55 industry representatives. Both item-total correlations and Cronbach's alpha were calculated for scores from each five-item critical factor scale. Both indices suggest strong score reliability, with alpha estimates ranging from a low of .70 for Trouble-Shooting to a high of .86 for Top Management Support. Average reliability across the 10 factors was .78. No reliability information was identified for the overall Project Performance scale.

A separate pool of 418 project managers was collected as validity data. Scores from these individuals were entered into a factor analysis. Using a varimax rotation, 10 significant factors emerged, explaining approximately 67% of the total score variance. Eigenvalues for each of the factors ranged from 1.18 for Trouble-Shooting to 13.27 for Monitoring and Feedback. Although analysis of eigenvalues indicates a solid 10-factor structure, item analysis indicates several instances where items double loaded. Inspection of the factor loadings suggested that the structure proposed by the conceptual model may not be well exemplified by the created scale structures. Several items load more highly on alternate factors, indicating some problems with model fit.

Additional validity evidence is provided from a study of the ability of the 10 PIP critical factors to predict actual project implementation success (Pinto & Slevin, 1988). Over 400 project managers from a variety of occupational backgrounds responded to the questionnaire. Each of the critical success factors from the PIP was tested independently against project success. All 10 factors were shown to be significantly related to project success at the .01 probability level.

The PIP test guide is well laid out. It first provides a very brief introduction, containing utility and general application information. Instructions for completing the scale are easy to follow and accomplish. Essentially, project managers and related staff complete the profile. A summed score for each of the 10 critical factors and the performance subscales is created. Each total score is then turned into a percentage score indicating the percent of individuals scoring lower. This chart of percentages was calculated from a pool of 409 projects (no additional information concerning this project database is provided or could be located). Percentages are then transferred onto a visual chart that classifies each of the percentages as Critical (0–50%), Fair (50–80%), or Good (80–100%). Project teams are to review this chart and evaluate areas that fall within the critical range as targets for improvement. Once these areas for improvement have been identified, the PIP manual provides some probing questions to help the team develop a plan of action for project betterment.

Overall, the Project Implementation Profile provides a quick, feasible way to assess project status and enhance project growth. The conceptual model underlying the tool seems well researched and practical for project leaders. I do, however, hold some reservation concerning the psychometric properties of this scale. The reliability sample is low in number, and the factor structure may not be accurate. Additional reliability and validity information is needed before many of the application implications of this survey are understood. If used within the parameters of a diagnostic tool (i.e., to improve a current project and inform project leaders), I recommend the use of the PIP. However, if the intent of its use is for determining future project success, project procurement, or team evaluation, I would suggest using another scale that is more specifically targeted for this type of evaluation.

REVIEWER'S REFERENCES

Pinto, J. K. (1986). *Project implementation: A determination of its critical success factors, moderators, and their relative importance across the project life cycle.* Unpublished doctoral dissertation, University of Pittsburgh.

Pinto, J. K., & Slevin, D. P. (1988). Clinical success factors across the project life cycle. *Project Management Journal,* 67–75.

[247]
PSC—Survey ADT.

Purpose: "Evaluates a job applicant's attitudes toward companies, business, work and trust attitudes."

Population: Job applicants.

Publication Date: 1987.

Scores, 4: Alienation, Trustworthiness, Total, False Positives.

Administration: Group or individual.

Price Data, 1994: $7.50 (or less) per survey.

Time: (15–20) minutes.

Comments: On-site scoring available.

Authors: Alan L. Strand and Mark L. Strand.

Publisher: Predictive Surveys Corporation.

Review of the PSC—Survey ADT by CHANTALE JEANRIE, Assistant Professor, Measurement and Evaluation, University Laval, Quebec, Canada:

The PSC—Survey ADT is a 100-item questionnaire measuring Alienation and Trustworthiness in a work context. The scale is considered a short version of three separate scales: Leniency and Trustworthiness (LT); Attitudes Towards Alcohol and Drugs (AD); and Motivation, Attitude Towards Work, Supervisors, etc. (MA). Although the information document (hereafter called "manual") presents the test as a condensed version of these three scales, the AD content has been retrieved from the test, in accordance with the American Disability Act. Scoring of the test is easily done with a built-in correction grid. The scoring key provides two subscale scores as well as overall and "don't know (?)" scores. Scale scores are obtained by summing the so-called "incorrect" answers. (To have no opinion is considered incorrect!) The degree of "virtue" attained by the respondent is then inversely related to his/her score.

The purpose of the Survey is to serve in lieu of the banned lie detector or tests asking invasive questions about the subject's past. In this perspective, the scale must be considered as an honesty or an integrity test, despite the opposite claim of the publisher. Based upon attitudes towards theft, honesty, supervisors, etc., the Survey is consistent with the "opinion" and "personality" approaches to integrity testing. If such tests have successfully been linked to job performance (Ones, Viswesvaran, & Schmidt, 1993), their relation to counterproductive behaviors is less clear (Sackett & Wanek, 1996). The controversy over tests of this kind remains (Lilienfeld, Alliger, & Mitchell, 1995), however, and does not rest upon that sole instrument. The theoretical background provided by the test publisher does not provide much to help in clearing the issue. Providing a very succinct and selective synthesis of some earlier (1935 to 1974) studies, the manual recognizes that alienated attitudes are not fixed or innate and can appear as a consequence of the working environment but fails to consider that such influences could possibly pull on the opposite direction.

The major drawback of the Survey, however, comes from the lack of convincing evidence that the test score reflects a valid measure of the psychological characteristic of interest. An inspection of item content suggests that one can obtain an incorrect response for reasons that are not related to positive work attitudes. For example, it is unclear to the

author of this review why disagreeing with "Little jobs lead to better jobs, if one does a good job" (p. 2) should be a sign of alienation when one considers the present job market and the situation of many working in "entry level positions." Many other items as well do not seem to be only related to the respondent's Alienation or Trustworthiness.

Another problem with the construct validity of the test lies in the way the test scores are computed. First, the scoring procedure mentions that any question left unanswered should be counted as incorrect although no explanation for this is provided. Because the Survey ADT is a timed test, this creates a problem of validity. Being a slow reader or a slow decision maker does not make one alienated or not worthy of trust. The treatment of "?" responses is also questionable. Although the test instructions suggest to minimize the choice of "?" responses, the scoring and interpretation guides suggest that too few of these reflect a deceptive attitude and that too many are a potential sign of a troublesome and hostile employee. It is not explained why being undecided about something leads to the inference that one is alienated or not worthy of trust. Finally, scores from the two scales can be combined into a global score. The use of a composite score should be supported by some empirical evidence.

The manual includes some data about the items of the original full-length scales and of the Survey ADT. The editors' approach to item analysis employed a contrasted groups (low and high scores on the test) procedure. Not only does this form of analysis overemphasize the relation between the items and the test but it also reduces considerably the number of subjects available for analysis and could then lead to very unstable results. Many details about the decisions that were made in the development of the scales are missing (e.g., samples size, rationale for *high* and *low* group cut-scores, etc.).

The criterion-related validity data form the former AD, LT, and MA scales are included as, apparently, reliability and validity evidence about the Survey ADT. The information is sometimes hard to follow because the purpose of the included studies is not stated and the information is often incomplete and poorly presented. A reliability study is provided for the AD scale only and consists of split-half analysis. The choice of this analysis is questionable (an alpha coefficient would have seemed a more conservative choice). No such information is presented about the Survey ADT, nor about the LT and MA scales. The main validity argument presented about the Survey ADT consists of correlations between the three longer scales and their condensed version included in the Survey ADT. Correlations obtained range from $r = .93$ to $r = .96$, with sample sizes varying from $n = 55$ to $n = 143$. The correlations are so high that there seems to be no question about the equivalence of the scores obtained with the long and short versions. One would have been more comfortable, though, if the tests had been administered to a single sample, allowing for correlations between scales. The criterion-related studies are interesting although much more detail would be needed in order to reach a conclusion of validity about the Survey ADT as well as about the AD, MA, and LT scales. For example, a study ($n = 129$) presents the score of the 20 employees with 2 or more years of tenure. The publisher suggests that these employees' average score is 31% lower than the recommended cutoff (not average) but fails to mention the average of the other 109 employees. In another study done with 253 employees, only the data from the 32 employees with 2 years or more of tenure are presented. The conclusion is that, because the average score of these 32 people is lower than the national average (which value is associated with a percentile of about 36 on the evaluation chart), "it is clear that lower scores tend to increase the probability of tenure of two years or more" (p. 79). This kind of conclusion is, to say the least, a little overstated. Consequently, the results of the studies cannot be seen as conclusive. Considering that the ADT Survey was published 10 years ago, this lack of reliability and validity evidence for the Scale appears to be a very serious deficiency.

In summary, the PSC—Survey ADT is an attitude scale designed to serve as an integrity test. Although the validity of many integrity tests is acknowledged by scientific researchers, the direct and indirect reliability and validity evidences provided with the Survey ADT are too thin or too incomplete to recommend its use as a personnel selection device. As a short-term project, the publisher should consider putting together a more complete manual containing more detailed information about the analyses that were used to develop the Survey ADT. Long-term efforts needed include more thorough, complete, and appropriate studies to collect reliability and validity evidences for the scale.

REVIEWER'S REFERENCES

Ones, D. S., Viswesvaran, C., & Schmidt, F. L. (1993). Comprehensive meta-analysis of integrity test validities: Findings and implications for personnel selection and theories of job performance. *Journal of Applied Psychology, 78*(4), 679–703.

Lilienfeld, S. O., Alliger, G., & Mitchell, K. (1995). Why integrity testing remains controversial. *American Psychologist, 50*(6), 457–458.

Sackett, P. R., & Wanek, J. E. (1996). New developments in the use of measures of honesty, integrity, conscientiousness, dependability, trustworthiness, and reliability for personnel selection. *Personnel Psychology, 49*(4), 787–829.

PSC Survey-SA.

Purpose: "Measures attitudes toward the position of supervisor for selection or promotion."
Population: Job applicants or current employees.
Publication Date: 1987.
Scores, 6: Attitudes Toward Companies and Business, Attitudes Toward Managers and Executives, Attitudes Toward Peers and Associates, Attitudes Toward Being a Supervisor, Attitudes Toward Subordinates, Total.
Administration: Group or individual.
Price Data, 1994: $7.50 (or less) per survey.
Time: (10–15) minutes.
Authors: Alan L. Strand and Mark L. Strand.
Publisher: Predictive Surveys Corporation.

Review of the PSC Survey-SA by L. CAROLYN PEARSON, Associate Professor of Education, University of West Florida, Pensacola, FL:

The Supervisory Attitude survey (PSC Survey-SA) is intended to aid in the selection of mid-level managers and supervisors and is advised for use in the screening of employees who are being considered for advancement. The five scales measure attitudes toward upper management; toward being a supervisor; toward the company and business in general; toward peers; and toward subordinate workers.

The SA comprises 60 items that have the respondent assess whether they agree, are uncertain, or disagree with statements that reflect each of the five areas. Those who have positive attitudes towards upper management, for example, relate well and trust their motives; whereas those who have negative attitudes are distrustful of and feel exploited by management. All of the items are written to reflect such positive and negative attitudes. The survey is scored by adding the answers that were contained within boxes hidden behind the instrument. The scale totals are then graphed and converted to percentile ranks directly below on the scoring form. Scoring was easy, and the graph is then used to indicate strengths and weaknesses of the applicant. The authors provide no explanation of what the scores mean or how the corresponding percentiles were derived, only that a lower score is better and that a slight difference in scores does not indicate much difference in the applicants.

The authors provide no rationale or theoretical framework for the five areas that are included on the SA. General principles for supervisors are outlined, and the items are clustered under them; yet, no explanation was given as to how this was done. The clustered items do not directly translate to the five scales on the instrument. The literature presented seems logical, but the reader is left with no indication of the sources. The authors also give no logical analysis of how the items were developed, tested, or selected from the research on management. In terms of empirical studies to establish reliability of the scales and their construct validity, no data are reported. The items seem to be free of bias on face value; yet, along with the instrument's psychometric properties, this has not been determined.

In conclusion, the SA is in need of establishing the research base from which it came, especially because the authors present general principles for supervisors that provide the basis on which the items are clustered. With no empirical work to support reliability, validity, and freedom from biases, the instrument offers little in terms of usefulness. In its current state, the SA may prove useful only as a screening tool and certainly should not be used in any final decisions as the authors advise. Somewhat more useful alternatives would be the Styles of Leadership Survey (12:379; Teleometrics International) or the Styles of Management Inventory (12:380; also from Teleometrics International), or even better, the Leader Behavior Analysis II (12:212; Blanchard Training & Development, Inc.) or the Leadership Practices Inventory (12:213; Pfeiffer & Company International Publishers), which have undergone extensive empirical investigation. I cannot recommend the SA because there are no empirical studies to support it as a reliable and valid measure of supervisory attitudes.

Review of the PSC Survey-SA by E. LEA WITTA, Assistant Professor, Educational Leadership and Research, University of Southern Mississippi, Hattiesburg, MS:

The PSC Survey-SA is a 60-item questionnaire for use in selecting applicants for direct line managerial or supervisory positions. Applicants may respond "yes," "no," or "?" to statements measuring attitude in five categories: company and business, managers and executives, peers and associates, supervisors and trainees, and subordinates. Negative responses for each category are summed and placed in a quality probability scale. A lower number of negative responses indicates a more favorable attitude. This provides an approximate percentile for each category and the total survey. The reported highest probability for success for the total survey is designated as between 5 and 13 negative responses. The survey may be administered in a group or individually. Approximately 15 minutes is required to complete the instrument. Scoring consists of counting negative responses in each category and placing the resulting sum in the quality probability profile.

The publisher emphasizes that this instrument is not to be used as the sole criteria, but as a method of screening otherwise qualified applicants. The publisher suggests ranking applicants based on number of negative responses. Then individual negative responses may be used as probing questions in subsequent interviews with applicants.

Evidence for the use of attitude scales in screening employees is provided in a manuscript provided by the publisher. Cited in the literature review are studies and texts such as the Hawthorne Study (Roethlisberger & Dickson, 1939), Productivity and Attitude toward Supervisor (Lawshe & Nagle, 1953), and *Industrial Psychology* (Gilmer, 1966). This manuscript is not, however, automatically supplied with the survey instrument. Purchasers of this survey may receive the manuscript by asking for it. The manuscript contains additional information concerning this instrument including evidence of reliability and validity from various samples. Based on this manuscript, the standardization sample consisted of 72 females and 97 males. It was assumed this sample provided the percentile ranking for the quality probability scale. Split-half reliability, established on a total sample of 172, was .74.

Concurrent validity of .72 was estimated on a sample of 15 by comparing scores from the PSC-Survey SA with supervisor ratings. Predictive validity was determined by recording the SA scores when hired for 42 men and 10 women. This was followed up 6 months later by recording supervisor ratings of these hires. Unfortunately, the correlation coefficient was not reported. However, calculating by data provided in the manuscript yielded a validity coefficient of .75. It is assumed in both these instances that only applicants with low negative scores were employed. Thus, the range of scores was attenuated. The only evidence of construct validity for the five categories of attitude measured is face validity.

In addition, some items on the instrument may be suspect. As reported in the manuscript, when comparing a low negative response scoring group (<10) to a high scoring group (>15), questions 35, 40, and 59 produced a higher proportion of negative responses in the low rather than the high scoring group. For these questions the group with the higher probability of success (the low scoring group) had more negative responses than those with a low probability of success. Sample size was not reported for these results.

In addition, based on a sample of 99 males and 72 females, 41% (n = 41) of the males scored 10 or below. Only 23% (n = 18) of the females scored 10 or below. When the cut-score is 15 or below, 61% (n = 61) of the males and 60% (n = 46) of the females meet the criteria. If applicants are rank ordered for interviews based on scale scores using 10 as the cut-score, this instrument may be biased in favor of males. Mean score for 71 females was 14.57. Mean score for 97 males was 14.35.

There is no question that attitude is a key ingredient in success. The PSC Survey-SA appears to be a useful tool in measuring attitude for screening applicants for first-line supervisory positions. It is easy to administer and score. Although the sample selection procedures for groups cited in the manuscript are unknown, it is assumed participants are those for whom the survey was designed. Adequate reliability and validity coefficients were produced by these attenuated samples. Users of this screening device, however, need to be aware of the possibility of bias toward females. If ranking of applicants is done, the cut-score should be 15 or higher rather than 13 (highest score for high probability of success). In addition, all users should obtain the listing of the proportion of item responses for low and high scoring groups from the manuscript. Further study using one of the structural equation modeling programs (i.e., LISREL, AMOS) is needed to confirm the constructs measured by this instrument.

REVIEWER'S REFERENCES

Roethlisberger, F. J., & Dickson, W. J. (1939). *Management and the worker: An account of a research program conducted by the Western Electric Company, Hawthorne Works, Chicago.* Cambridge, MA: Harvard University Press.
Lawshe, C. H., & Nagle, B. F. (1953). Productivity and attitude toward supervisor. *Journal of Applied Psychology, 37,* 159–162.
Gilmer, B. H. (1966). *Industrial psychology.* New York: McGraw-Hill.

[249]
Questionnaire Measure of Trait Arousability (Or Its Converse, Stimulus Screening).

Purpose: Designed to measure individual differences in positive and/or negative emotionality, emotional sensitivity, or emotional reactivity.
Population: Ages 15 and older.
Publication Dates: 1976–1994.
Scores: Total score only.
Administration: Group or individual.
Price Data, 1994: $28 per specimen set including manual ('94, 8 pages) and literature review.
Time: (10–15) minutes.
Comments: Previously known as Questionnaire Measure of Stimulus Screening and Arousability.
Author: Albert Mehrabian.

Publisher: Albert Mehrabian.
Cross References: For a review by James J. Jupp of the earlier edition, see 9:1025.

Review of the Questionnaire Measure of Trait Arousability (Or Its Converse, Stimulus Screening) by ROBERT A. LEARK, Clinical Professor of Psychology, Pacific Christian College, Fullerton, CA:

RATIONALE FOR TEST. In the manual, the test author sets forth the ideas and background that formulated this instrument. The rationale presented is "for a questionnaire measure of individual differences in stimulus screening—namely, individual differences in automatic (i.e., not conceptual or intentional) screening of irrelevant stimuli, and rapid habituation to distracting, irrelevant stimuli" (manual, p. 1). The questionnaire is an attempt by the author to measure the *inverse* of arousal response. The author maintains that there are two distinct types of responders: screeners and nonscreeners. The questionnaire, itself, seeks to distinguish between the two response types.

In the theoretical development of the questionnaire, the manual provides the reader with a review of information theory, including the arousal, orienting reflex (response aspect) and habituation. The review of information theory itself bears comment. The author does a better than reasonable job of presenting the reader rather complex information. The author also does a good job of including research from the former Soviet Union (on classical conditioning) and correlating Eysenck's research on neuroticism.

As stated by the author, the aim of the test and its research anchored upon "the initial amplitude of the orienting reflex, the slower rate of habituation, general arousability, and 'weakness' of the nervous system are intercorrelated aspects of human response to novel, intense, or unpredictable (i.e., high information rate) stimuli and that consistent individual differences along this dimension constitute a major component of some of the most important personality dimensions" (manual, p. 4). It is in this vein that the author connects the research to Eysenck. The questionnaire is the author's attempts to use a verbal questionnaire (the items are read to the subject) to correlate to physiological measures of arousability. The measure is an attempt to quantify the arousability component of anxiety and neuroticism.

The original questionnaire of 119 items was then cut to 60 items following the preliminary standardization. These 60 items were then reduced to the current version's 40 items.

PSYCHOMETRIC PROPERTIES. The questionnaire is composed of 40 items that are read to the subject by the examiner. The subjects then rate themselves using a 9-point Likert scale. Subject responses range from +4 (very strong agreement) to -4 (very strong disagreement), a zero (0) response is used to identify neither agreement nor disagreement. One-half of the items are worded such that agreement shows high trait arousability, the other half of the items are worded such that disagreement shows the same high trait arousability.

To obtain a total score the examiner sums responses to all 20 of the agreement items and then subtracts from this value the sum of the disagreement items (total score = [positive worded sum] - [negatively worded sum]). The norms for the test are based upon a mean score of 24 with a standard deviation of 39.

The manual provides a summary table, which converts the total raw score into z-score equivalents and percentile rankings.

A Kuder-Richardson reliability coefficient is stated as being .92, indicating high internal consistency reliability for the 40-item questionnaire. Test-retest reliability coefficients are not provided in the manual. Nine factors comprise the questionnaire. These factors are: low general arousability, rapid habituation, low arousability to sudden changes and events, thermal screening, low arousability in novel or changing settings, auditory screening, tactual and kinesthetic screening, olfactory screening, and low arousability in multicomponent or complex settings. Intercorrelations between factors range from .13 (tactual and kinesthetic screening to low arousability in multicomponent or complex settings) to .66 (low general arousability to low arousability to sudden changes and events).

The manual provides construct validity data indicating a -.54 correlation to the Eysenck and Eysenck (1968) measure of neuroticism and a -.49 correlation to the Spielberger, Gorsuch, and Lushene (1970) State-Trait Anxiety measure. These correlations provide support for the author's contention that the test is measuring arousal components of neuroticism and anxiety.

Test and item bias were handled in the development of the items themselves. The items are constructed for one half of the items such that a positive agreement reflects identification to the measure, and the other half are written such that a negative agreement (i.e., a disagreement) reflects positive identification to the measure. This allows for subjects to react to items, yet, the reaction counteracts other reactions to test items.

The specimen kit provides the manual, test items, and subject response form, along with a table to convert total raw scores to z scores and percentile rankings.

COMMENTS. The specimen kit itself is misleading. The manual is actually a stapled photocopy of the author's manuscript. It is not a manual in the sense of a comprehensive bound tome. The manuscript contains handwritten changes, which further distract from the cosmetic appearance of the product. All total, the photocopied manuscript includes about 48 pages.

The research on the test was originally conducted in the early to mid 1970s. It has not been updated or revised since then. The psychometric properties of the test itself are sound as it is reported to have high internal reliability (.92 Kuder Richardson coefficient) and mixed validity (-.49 and - .54) correlating the test to measures of trait anxiety and neuroticism. Test item bias was handled in the development of the items themselves, with reactivity to the items counteracting each other.

The original norming study of 35-plus college students leaves question to generalizability to other samples. Further, the normative data raise some questions. For example, the test mean is 24, but the test has a standard deviation of 39! This means that the variability within the normative data is extensive, greater than one and one-half that of the test mean. No standard error of measurement (*SEM*) is given, but is expected to be great, given the size of the standard deviation. Thus, meaningful interpretation of the subject's raw data is limited.

Use of the questionnaire itself is questionable. Little psychotherapy is guided along arousability theory, even biofeedback or cognitive behavioral work. I cannot imagine continued use of the instrument by most practitioners as the questionnaire will not provide information useful to them. This does not distract from the author's work on linking arousal to neuroticism and anxiety. Rather, the usefulness of the information is the issue. Theoretical issues of neuroticism have been replaced by movement away from dynamic personality and personality trait theory. Thus, the test does not provide the current practitioner or researcher with information timely to today's research and theoretical issues.

REVIEWER'S REFERENCES

Eysenck, H. J., & Eysenck, S. B. (1968). *Manual for the Eysenck Personality Inventory.* San Diego: Educational and Industrial Testing Service.
Spielberger, C. D., Gorsuch, R. L., & Lushene, R. E. (1970). *Manual for the State-Trait Anxiety Inventory.* Palo Alto, CA: Consulting Psychologists Press.

[250]

Quick Informal Assessment.

Purpose: To "informally assess a student's stage of language acquisition."

Population: Grades K–12.

Publication Date: 1992.

Acronym: QIA.

Scores: Total score only.

Administration: Individual or group.

Forms, 6: 6 alternate forms A–F.

Price Data: Available from publisher.

Time: (5) minutes.

Comments: Students classified into one of four stages of language acquisition: (a) preproduction, (b) early production, (c) speech emergence, (d) intermediate fluency.

Author: Constance Olivia Williams.

Publisher: Ballard & Tighe.

Review of the Quick Informal Assessment by ALAN GARFINKEL, Professor of Spanish and Education, Purdue University, West Lafayette, IN:

The Quick Informal Assessment (QIA) is a unique product designed to enable the classroom practitioner to make reasonably accurate judgments about a learner's stage of new language acquisition for a number of daily needs. There is nothing quite like it in published form. Most teachers devise their own, usually less valid means of making the decisions they need to make. These may include placement, assessment for inclusion in one program or another (study abroad, for example), or any other situation that requires a quick assessment. It is true that the QIA makes no claims to any more than face validity, but some of the quickly formed devices used by many teachers cannot even claim face validity. It would be a pleasure to have a set of the QIA Spanish test on hand for the numerous assessments that faculty members at all levels are asked to make.

Because the QIA is likely to be used with considerable frequency in the very busy context of the language classroom, its physical characteristics must also be considered. The publishers have put the instructions and six forms in a sturdy bound folder. The pictures used to generate responses for all forms are printed on thick pasteboard and bound. The set, packaged in a substantial plastic bag with a locking strip, will last a while, even with frequent use.

The QIA is the only test of its particular kind. Teachers of new languages at all levels will find it useful and practical. Considering the test's very special purpose, one can say that is has no self-evident shortcomings. Therefore, one would be well advised to acquire the QIA for each faculty member

that teaches ESL or Spanish in particular and all languages in general.

Review of the Quick Informal Assessment by ALFRED P. LONGO, Supervisor of Humanities, Holmdel Township School District, Holmdel, NJ:

According to the authors, Williams and Bussing, The Quick Informal Assessment (QIA) is designed "to provide teachers and paraprofessionals with an easy-to-administer instrument that will informally assess a student's stage of language acquisition in the most rapid, yet accurate, way possible" (p. 1). It is the intent of the authors that proper utilization of the QIA "will enable the examiner to identify the stage of language acquisition of each individual student for appropriate pupil placement into an English Language Development Program" (p. 1). The QIA can assess oral language development. If desired, the examiner may also choose to assess written language development through the administration of a coordinated writing sample. Both the written and oral assessments may be translated to informally evaluate primary development in a language other than English.

The QIA contains six alternate forms. This permits the examiner to use the instrument as a placement tool; it also can be utilized to track performance as part of a formative evaluation of progress. The authors make it clear that the QIA is not designed to replace standardized and more formal assessments; rather, a good use of this instrument would be its potential support of more formal and standardized instruments. It can give a teacher a quick "snapshot" of an individual's language development.

The QIA comprises three distinct components: an examiner's manual, a test picture booklet, and a pad of class profiles. The six forms (A through F) each contain 20 questions, five of which are focused on the four stages of language acquisition. The test picture booklet serves as the impetus for deriving an appropriate response. The class profile pad serves as tangible record of the results.

After selecting one of the forms, the examiner begins with the first question and stops after five questions. The examiner then proceeds to the next five questions only if the examinee has answered three of the previous five questions accurately. Questions 1 to 10 are objective and it is suggested that the examiner score the items + or 0 to signify correct or incorrect responses, respectively. Questions 11 to 20 are subjective in nature and responses to them should be evaluated according to grammatical correctness, quality and variety of vocabulary, length, complexity, and spontaneity of response.

Based on the results of the administration, students are then classified into four categories of language acquisition: Preproduction, Early Production, Speech Emergence, or Intermediate Fluency. According to the authors, in light of the results, the teacher can plan an instructional program. Without the correlation of QIA results with a more formal assessment of language development, it would seem that the QIA alone is not sufficient, on its own merit, for the planning of an instructional program.

The theoretical and instructional foundation of the QIA, Terrell's Natural Approach and Asher's Total Physical Response (TPR) together with a concordance with Krashen's stages of language acquisition make for a sound theoretical basis for the QIA. Despite its informal quality the QIA does address the four stages of second-language acquisition and does make some sound suggestions for the design of an instructional program. The Language Acquisition Chart that accompanies the assessment is predicated on the same sound scholarship as seen above and lists characteristics, student behaviors, teacher strategies, timelines, and suggested instructional programs.

For students at Stage III (Speech Emergence) and IV (Intermediate Fluency) of language development the QIA's Literacy Forms may be used to assess reading and writing skills.

Pictures from the oral assessment and a brief reading are used to elicit a written response. Students are to view the picture, read the paragraph, and construct a second paragraph related to the idea expressed in the picture and the paragraph. The directions for the examiner in terms of the writing component are simply to encourage the student to write a second paragraph. The directions could be more precise in order to produce a more standardized result. The writing is scored using a holistic scoring rubric that evaluates both content and form. The rubric, although appropriate for an informal assessment, is not well defined and seems to leave much to the discretion of the individual examiner. The result of the literacy assessment may be adversely affected by the student's ability to read.

In sum, it is difficult to recommend the use of an instrument that is not standardized or formalized. Although the ability to quickly assess a stage of language development can be a worthy goal, the quality of the result should be guaranteed. The results of the QIA can only be truly meaningful when viewed in conjunction with performance on a more standardized instrument. The Language Assessment Battery (T4:1385) created by the New York City Public Schools and The Maculaitis Assessment Program: A Multi-Purpose Test for Non-Native Speakers of English (T4:1497) are standardized batteries that have defined predictive value. Yet, the theoretical underpinnings of the QIA, its ease of administration, and timeliness speak to its utility as a quality informal assessment. It is, in effect, what it purports to be.

[251]
Quickview Social History.

Purpose: Assists in the collection and reporting of client information.
Population: Ages 16 and older.
Publication Dates: 1983–1992.
Administration: Individual.
Price Data, 1994: $45 per preview package including user's guide ('92, 33 pages), hardcover test booklet, and 3 answer sheets; $24.95 per hardcover test booklet; $2.40 per soft cover test booklet; $8 per computer-scored report.
Time: (30–90) minutes
Author: Ronald A. Giannetti.
Publisher: NCS Assessments.

a) BASIC REPORT.
Scores: 8 areas of inquiry: Demographic Data, Developmental History, Family of Origin, Educational History, Marital History, Occupational History/Financial Status, Legal History, Military History.
Comments: The report also has a follow-up summary that includes contradictory responses, indeterminate responses, and client-requested follow-up sections.

b) CLINICAL SUPPLEMENT.
Scores: Includes 8 areas of inquiry listed in Basic Report, plus Physical and Psychological Symptom Screens including: Adult Problems (Substance Use, Psychotic Symptoms, Mood Symptoms, Anxiety Disorders, Somatoform Symptoms, Psychosexual Disorders, Sleep and Arousal, Antisocial Personality, Other Current or Past Potential Adult Problems/Stressors), Developmental Problems (Activity Level/Lability, Conduct Problems, Anxious/Avoidant, Eating/Weight, Tic/Elimination/Sleep, Other Disorders/Delays, Other Potential Developmental Problems/Stressors).

Review of the Quickview Social History by DAVID N. DIXON, Professor and Doctoral Training Director, Department of Counseling Psychology, Ball State University, Muncie, IN:

The Quickview Social History is an effort to gather social history data using a self-report format.

Two types of narrative, computer-generated reports are available based on the questions completed. The Basic Report is generated from limited option responses by the client to a 130-item set and is organized in eight sections (i.e., Introduction, Developmental History, Family of Origin, Educational History, Marital History, Occupational History/Financial Status, Legal History, and Military History). The Clinical Supplement includes an additional 105 items providing information about past and present physical and psychological issues. Both the Basic Report and the Clinical Supplement forms include sections designed to assist the clinician in asking follow-up questions.

The advantages of the Quickview Social History are that it frees the clinician from the time-consuming tasks of directly gathering social history data and writing narrative reports; it standardizes the set of questions presented to all clients; and it facilitates descriptive analyses of client characteristics. A strength of the reports is the Contradictions section, which points out logical inconsistencies found in the response patterns (e.g., indicating on one response that father was actively involved in parenting and on another response that he was deceased).

Disadvantages appear to be numerous with this product. The most serious limitation is that it makes little use of available technology. Branching programming is little used in this paper-and-pencil product. Computer-administered formats offer much greater opportunities for clarification and follow-up questions. For example, Item #31 of the Basic Report asks, "What forms of nonphysical punishment did she [woman who raised you] use? Mark any that apply" (p. 7). Sixteen response options are offered for this item including: "yelled at you," "embarrassed or humiliated you," and "threatened to kill you." With no follow-up questions, the client for which these experiences were daily occurrences is indistinguishable from the client who experienced these infrequently. A format that allows for a more interactive inquiry process could greatly enrich the information base.

The Clinical Supplement report attempts to organize data to assist the clinician with diagnostic decision making. The report is organized according to DSM-III-R diagnostic categories, a system now outdated.

No psychometric information is provided in support of the Quickview Social History. An "About the Author" section describes how the author became involved in the development of the procedure, but no conceptual rationale is given for the content of the history, no comparisons are made with existing social history procedures, and no reliability and validity data are reported.

Because it is not possible to evaluate this procedure on its development and psychometric properties, the evaluation of the product is forced to rely heavily on the two sample reports found in the User's Guide. And both of them are shallow and suffer from very stiff prose. The reports mechanically parrot back responses to items with major aspects of information missing. An example is the paragraph, "The client was raised by his natural mother. The client was not raised by his natural father because his mother and father separated. The client reports having brothers and sisters" (p. 18). Questions such as—When did his parents separate? How many brothers? How many sisters? Birth order? Contact with noncustodial parent? Did the parent(s) remarry?—are not asked and result in the omission of crucial information.

If social histories are perfunctorily required by the agency and not reviewed or used in subsequent decision making, then this procedure may satisfy the need. But if social histories are viewed as an important part of the clinical decision process, then this procedure is inadequate. Self-report methods for gathering social history information are certainly possible, but they would need to use interactive technology to allow for more thorough elaboration and follow-up.

Review of the Quickview Social History by EDWARD R. STARR, Assistant Professor of Counseling Psychology, State University of New York at Buffalo, Buffalo, NY:

In these latter days of increasing concern for making psychological services more economical and amenable to external evaluation, the Quickview Social History is introduced as a reasonable way to respond to the demands imposed by managed care that has at least the potential actually to improve the quality of care. Although not a psychological measure per se, the Quickview Social History is a comprehensive psychosocial inventory that assists clinicians in collecting and reporting routine social history data. Self-report data provided by clients on a computer scan sheet are compiled into a narrative report that not only organizes information pertinent to initial client interviews, but indicates potential issues for follow-up. According to the manual, it is appropriate for use with clients at least 16 years old and with at least a 6th grade level reading ability, making it fairly widely applicable to most adult clinical settings.

The Quickview is intended as an adjunct to an initial clinical interview, allowing the therapist more opportunity to use the initial contact to establish rapport with clients. It is divided into two discrete sections: the Basic Report, yielding a comprehensive general social history; and a Clinical Supplement, consisting of information pertaining specifically to psychological and medical concerns. This feature allows for greater flexibility in its use. The Basic Report section can be administered without the Clinical Supplement, if desired, but the Clinical Supplement items must always accompany the Basic Report.

The Basic Report includes sections related to general Demographic Data, Developmental History, Family of Origin, Educational History, Marital History, Occupational History and Financial Status, Legal History, and Military History. The report also includes a Contradictions section as a check on internal validity, indicating any client responses that are logically incompatible. These are recommended as areas for further investigation.

The Clinical Supplement comprises sections dealing with Adult Problems (subsections include Substance Use and Abuse, Psychotic Symptoms, Mood Symptoms, Anxiety Disorders, Somatoform Symptoms, Psychosexual Disorders, Sleep and Arousal, Antisocial Personality, and Other Current or Past Potential Adult Problems/Stressors), and Developmental Problems (subsections include Activity Level/Lability, Conduct Problems, Anxious/Avoidant, Eating/Weight, Tic/Elimination/Sleep, Other Disorders/Delays, and other Potential Developmental Problems/Stressors). Items in these sections, although not grouped according to any particular diagnostic scheme, relate to various categories of psychopathology in the *DSM-III*. The author cautions against overreliance on this data for purposes of diagnosis, advising diagnosticians to obtain additional information. Data from the Clinical Supplement also enrich the information in the Developmental History and Family of Origin sections and append an additional Symptom Screen to the Basic Report.

A convenient Follow-Up Interview Summary, not considered part of the actual report, is provided at the end of the narrative as a clinician's reference to issues pertinent to future interviews. It essentially flags client responses to the Basic Report and Clinical Supplement sections that may require clarification. This summary consists of Indeterminate Responses (i.e., items endorsed as "other") and Client-Requested Follow-Up details (i.e., issues or concerns that clients indicated they would like to discuss with the therapist).

The Quickview Social History reflects fairly extensive research on reliable and valid methods of computerized psychosocial assessment. It was developed based on refinements to the GOLPH (Giannetti On-Line Psychosocial History) and GOLPH 2.0 psychosocial histories (Giannetti, 1987; Giannetti, Klinger, Johnson, & Williams, 1976), one of the first reliable on-line assessment systems. The on-line option is an economical and very convenient means of accomplishing a task that can otherwise consume inordinate amounts of clinicians' time and energy. When used on an institution-wide basis, it has the potential to help clinics realize what may amount to substantial financial savings.

The manual is clear and informative, although fairly brief in its discussion of the development of the inventory and lacking in detail with respect to the dimensions of assessment reflected in the various sections. The several illustrative narrative reports provided give a clear example of how client data are compiled and what actual outputs look like.

Because, unlike most other approaches to history taking, it comprises a standardized set of items in a consistent format, the Quickview also has the advantage of allowing for descriptive and comparative analyses of client characteristics. Analyses can be conducted for program planning, resource allocation, quality assurance evaluations, and other research purposes. It can also be immensely valuable for reporting to funding sources, external evaluators, accrediting bodies, and third-party reimbursers. This is a clear improvement over laborious chart reviews by hand.

Another strength of the Quickview Social History is its inclusion of a section dealing with military experience. This, in my experience, is a frequently overlooked yet often important dimension of initial history taking. It also makes the Quickview an especially invaluable aid to psychological and psychiatric units in Veteran's Administration and other veteran's services programs.

Although the major strength of the Quickview Social History is that it can be used on-line, this is also, unfortunately, its primary limitation. Despite the apparent ubiquity of computer applications in contemporary clinical settings, not all clinics have this advantage. Many other clinics face severe limitations in computer resources. Still others may not be convinced of the advantages of providing computer support to clinical personnel. Although users of the Quickview are provided the option of a mail-in service, this option is likely to compromise the real cost and time advantages that accrue to on-line users.

REVIEWER'S REFERENCES
Giannetti, R. A., Klinger, D. E., Johnson, J. H. & Williams, T. A. (1976). The potential for dynamic assessment systems using on-line computer technology. *Behavior Research Methods and Instrumentation, 8,* 101–103.
Giannetti, R. A. (1987). The GOLPH psychosocial history: Response-contingent data acquisition and reporting. In J. N. Butcher (Ed.), *Computerized psychological assessment* (pp. 124–144). New York: Basic Books, Inc.

[252]
Ramsay Corporation Job Skills—Health Care Reading Test.

Purpose: "To measure the reading skills required for health care workers."
Population: Adults.
Publication Date: 1992.
Scores: Total score only.
Administration: Group.
Price Data, 1992: $200 per complete kit including 10 reusable test booklets, 100 answer sheets, manual (11 pages), and scoring key.
Time: (30–40) minutes.
Author: Roland T. Ramsay.
Publisher: Ramsay Corporation.

Review of the Ramsay Corporation Job Skills— Health Care Reading Test by BETTY BERGSTROM, Director of Research and Psychometric Services, Commission on Dietetic Registration, The American Dietetic Association, Chicago, IL:

The Ramsay Corporation Job Skills (RCJS) Health Care Reading Test consists of 40 multiple-choice items based on five reading passages. Of the five reading passages, three are based on health care themes, one on general safety with machines, and one on telephone procedures. The test manual provides standard directions for administering the examination including testing conditions, preparation of materials, general directions, and timing (30 minutes).

The test is specified as appropriate for applicants and incumbents for jobs where reading is a necessary part of training or job activities. Further information on the appropriateness of the test for specific categories of health care workers is not given.

Although a readability level is indicated for each reading passage, no reference is provided for the readability formula used or for the development of the scale. An estimated reliability coefficient, estimated mean raw score and standard deviation, and estimated standard error of measure are provided.

Item level data (item difficulty and point biserial discrimination index) are estimated for the three reading passages related to health care themes. Item level data from a small sample of workers in fields other than health care (261 metal processing applicants and 82 post-high school business school stu-

dents) are provided for the other two reading passages.

Description of content is limited to a listing of the general topic of the reading passage. Content validity is not established. The manual specifically states that the test has not been part of a criterion-related validation study, nor have formal studies of construct validity been constructed. No information is given as to how to interpret the meaning of the scores.

No information is provided on actual test development. There is no indication that the test was pilot tested or normed by a sample of health care workers. Percentile ranks are given for a similar test (Ramsay Corporation Job Skills—Office Reading).

Overall, documentation meeting the *Standards for Educational and Psychological Testing* (AERA, APA, & NCME, 1985) is clearly not given for this test. No actual validity evidence is presented. No normative data are presented. Even more problematic is the presentation of "estimated" data and data for "similar" tests. Presentation of these statistics implies that the test scores are valid and reliable when, in fact, no evidence to substantiate these claims is supplied. Statements found in the manual such as "The data in Table 3 above indicate very good reliability" (p. 7) are extremely misleading; although it is true that the reliability coefficient presented in Table 3 does indicate adequate reliability, the statistic was not based on any analysis of data from the Health Care Reading Test.

The test appears to be one of several Ramsay Job Skills Reading tests available for different occupations. Little attempt appears to have been made to ensure validity of the Health Care Reading Test by adequate piloting and norming with an appropriate sample of health care workers.

The health care field is broad and an adequate level of reading comprehension varies for different occupations. Test users who wish to determine whether the level of reading comprehension is adequate for a particular health care occupation would be better served by (a) determining the level of reading comprehension necessary for adequate job performance and (b) selecting a valid and reliable reading comprehension test that covers the appropriate range of ability.

REVIEWER'S REFERENCE
American Educational Research Association, American Psychological Association, & National Council on Measurement in Education. (1985). *Standards for educational and psychological testing.* Washington, DC: American Psychological Association, Inc.

Review of the Ramsay Corporation Job Skills— Health Care Reading Test by CRAIG S. SHWERY,

Assistant Professor of Teacher Education, Fort Hays State University, Hays, KS:

The Ramsay Corporation Job Skills—Health Care Reading Test Form HC-1 (RCJS-HCRT) was designed as a part of a series of skills tests by the Ramsay Corporation. Specifically, the RCJS-HCRT was designed to assess the reading skills required for health care workers. According to the author, this test is intended for use with applicants and others where reading is necessary as part of their job or training. The RCJS-HCRT consists of 40 multiple-choice items across five domains: Safety with Machines (8), Care of Patients' Belongings (8), Communication (8), Cardiopulmonary Resuscitation (8), and Telephone Procedures (8). The test is to be taken within a 30-minute time limit. The test manual provides sufficient information on testing conditions, preparations, general directions to the examiner, and specific direction to the examinees.

No information is provided in the test manual as to the representation or nature of the norming sample nor item selection. Although the test appears to have face validity, no information is provided as to how the domains were selected, nor how the items within the domains were identified. Was there a panel of experts in the health care field used to identify the items? The manual does provide some "estimated" information on item analysis on what appears to be three different data sets. This analysis is tentative at best. Percentile ranks are provided; however, nowhere in the manual is there information or discussion on how the scores should be interpreted or conveyed to the examinees.

RELIABILITY. Interval consistency reliability of the RCJS-HCRT was estimated at .86. This coefficient suggests good internal consistency. No information is provided on other forms of reliability. Could individuals have been expected to rank the same on an alternate form of the test? An alternate-form reliability coefficient could have provided valuable information regarding the contributions of measurement error related to the content of the test. To what extent could the scores on one administration of the test generalize across different occasions? What is the contribution to error variance that could be attributed to random fluctuation of performance from one testing situation to another? This question could have been answered with test-retest reliability information.

VALIDITY. Validation information about the RCJS-HCRT is quite sparse. Limited information regarding criterion-related, construct, and content validity is provided. The author makes vague reference to "significant" criterion-related reliability; however, the reader is left with many unanswered questions. For example, what criterion could performance on this test be checked against? Are there any direct and independent measures of that which the test is designed to predict? Although no information is provided regarding construct validity, the author makes a weak attempt to suggest that the construct being measured is reading as "observed in many jobs involving supervisor tasks" (p. 9). This is hardly sufficient as evidence of a test's construct validity. Finally, although the author alludes to the test's content validity, there is no information regarding the systematic examination of the test's content to assess whether it covers a sample of the domains to be measured.

ITEM INFORMATION. The developer of the RCJS-HCRT provides no evidence of a sensitivity to the demographics of potential test takers. The paucity of information regarding differential item functioning and predictive validity for various groups is a serious concern. Considering the intent of this test, the lack of this information is indefensible. Can people be reliably expected to perform similarly regardless of group membership? Conceivably, a number of items could function differentially based on one's sociocultural membership.

In summary, the scope of coverage of technical information concerning the norming procedures, reliability, and validity of the RCJS-HCRT is not acceptable. At its minimum the RCJS-HCRT does not meet the *Standards for Educational and Psychological Testing* as recommended by the American Educational Research Association, the American Psychological Association, and the National Council on Measurement in Education joint committees (1985). Potential users of this instrument are encouraged to consider carefully the utility of this instrument for its intended purpose.

REVIEWER'S REFERENCE

American Educational Research Association, American Psychological Association, & National Council on Measurement in Education. (1985). *Standards for educational and psychological testing.* Washington, DC: American Psychological Association, Inc.

[253]
Ramsay Corporation Job Skills—Machinist Test.

Purpose: "To measure the knowledge and skills required in the area of machine shop jobs."
Population: Machinist job applicants.
Publication Dates: 1981–1992.
Scores: Total score only.

Administration: Group.
Price Data, 1992: $498 per complete kit including 10 reusable test booklets, 100 answer sheets, manual ('92, 15 pages), and scoring key.
Time: (100–120) minutes.
Author: Roland T. Ramsay.
Publisher: Ramsay Corporation.

Review of the Ramsay Corporation Job Skills—Machinist Test by JOHN PETER HUDSON, JR., Manager, Organization and Management Development, PepsiCo, Inc., Purchase, NY:

The Ramsay Corporation Job Skills—Machinist Test is designed to assess the machining knowledge and skills of job applicants or incumbents for jobs where such knowledge and skills are necessary parts of job activities.

TEST INSTRUMENT. The test items are well written, with a clear, consistent format and writing style. Many of the items are associated with drawings or schematic diagrams—these graphics are professionally drawn and are straightforward to understand and use. Although items themselves appear well written, the test layout has opportunities for improvement. The distinction between item categories, and sets of items that belong to a single drawing, could be made more salient to examinees. Also, test items are crowded onto pages—more white space would make the test more user friendly. The instructions on the cover could be updated and polished to make the language more crisp and clear to test takers.

TEST DEVELOPMENT. The test appears to have been developed on the basis of a single organization's need for assessment capabilities in machining domains. In building content-relevant evidence for the test, the author presents a list of knowledge and skill dimensions for each domain, but does not describe how these dimensions were derived. Nor was there an explanation of how items were written, or what research or evaluative efforts were undertaken to identify the items to be included in the final instrument. The author presents item-level difficulties and item-total correlations, but does not explain if and how these results were used to assess the psychometric qualities of the items and the instrument as a whole. It becomes the responsibility of the user to ascertain whether the domain dimensions and the item content are relevant for the specific application; such as evaluation would be assisted by a more thorough and comprehensive explanation of how the instrument was developed.

RELIABILITY AND VALIDITY EVIDENCE. There is little evidence presented to assure the user of the reliability and validity of this test. Reliability for scores from this test was computed from a single administration with small sample sizes. The argument for the content-related evidence for the validity of this test is not well articulated. The author could take the opportunity to buttress the claim of content validity by spending more time reviewing how the knowledge and skill domains were derived, and how items were developed to sample those domains.

ADMINISTRATION. Although the instructions page on the cover of the test could use some polish, the administration instructions in the technical manual are altogether comprehensive, detailed, and complete. The test user and examinee would have a clear understanding of the test administration procedures. However, there are some concerns related to administration. Instructions indicate to collect sex and date of birth information from examinees—such information is sensitive to collect during an employment testing situation because it may increase the user organization's risk of litigation under equal employment opportunity law. The administration section tells the administrator to mark the time taken to complete the test, but does not given an explanation of how that information is used. A number of items require calculations; the manual does not specify whether calculators can be used.

TECHNICAL MANUAL. On the whole, the technical manual is not well written. Several tables of data are presented, but without sufficient explanation of how they are to be used. There exist deficiencies in areas related not only to test development and validity research, but also gaps on recommendations related to test security, retest policy, and so forth.

TEST USE. There is no information on how test scores are to be used for making inferences related to any of a variety of potential test uses—hiring, promotion, workforce assessment, training assignment, and so forth. The norm data presented are not very useful because they are based on small sample sizes, with little explanation of the samples themselves. Finally, there is no information provided on the fairness of the test and its impact on legally protected subgroups.

SUMMARY. This reviewer's impression is that this test was developed specifically for use in a single organization. The content domains were established and items were written by small groups of job experts, with oversight by the author. The effort likely met the organization's needs quite well—it was probably a well-conceived test development and application project based on content-relevant validity evidence. However, the test and supporting research presented in the technical report are deficient when offered as a generic assessment of machining knowledge and skill. Although the items themselves are well written and appear promising, the author needs to conduct and present a more comprehensive and orthodox test development program to provide the test user with the appropriate information upon which to make an informed decision. As it stands now, the user has the bulk of the burden in determining whether or not the test is a sound assessment tool meeting the standards for high-quality test development and use.

Review of the Ramsay Corporation Job Skills— Machinist Test by JAMES W. PINKNEY, Professor of Counselor and Adult Education, East Carolina University, Greenville, NC:

The Ramsay Corporation Job Skills—Machinist Test (MT) is an untimed paper-and-pencil assessment of machining knowledge that is typically completed in less than 2 hours. The MT manual claims the instrument also addresses machining skills, but this is not true. The 121 multiple-choice items (including two practice items) all deal with various aspects of machining knowledge, and there is no assessment of the physical aspects of machine work. There is no explanation of why three of the items have five response options and the rest have four response options.

The items (number of items per topic) cover the following knowledge areas: machine tools (29), print reading (20), layout (14), tools/materials/equipment (19), steel/metals/materials (8), mechanical principles and repair (12), rigging (7), heat-treating (4), and lubrication (6). These nine knowledge areas are in descending order of importance as ranked by six maintenance supervisors. The manual provides no other information about these "six subject experts" (p. 3). A tenth area, safety, is claimed to be embedded in the nine knowledge areas, but inspection of the items suggests this area is a matter of opinion. There are no reported subscales for the MT. The single percentile equivalency table, based on only 27 participants, is for the total number of correct responses.

The complete and detailed directions in the manual are mildly contradictory in that the instructions given to the applicants state there is no time limit for the assessment, but the needed materials for the examiner include a stopwatch. The instructions are supportive of the applicant's doing his or her best. The examiner is encouraged to minimize distractions and note any potential limiting factors such as reading difficulty, English as a second language, or misunderstanding the directions.

The MT has serious problems with the supporting reliability and validity data. These problems would argue against using the MT for employment decisions. A related issue is the lack of information about how the items of the MT were selected, who selected the items, and where the items came from. This lack of domain and selection information means a potential user would certainly want to carefully inspect the actual items before using the MT.

The reported "reliability" (without clarification) of the MT is high (.89), but based on a sample of 27 "manufacturing applicants" (p. 7). Both the size and descriptive vagueness of the sample do not allow a reasonable estimation of how appropriate the MT would be for specific situations and real life hiring or promotion decisions.

A single, small sample may easily have a spuriously high reliability coefficient. For example, many of the applicants might have attended the same local technical college or vocational high school. This would mean that this small group of applicants was exposed to the same knowledge base in school and/or the same instructors. It could then be expected that those applicants would get many of the same items right (or wrong), which would inflate the reliability estimate.

The absence of better reliability data makes the usefulness of the MT highly questionable for employment decisions, research, or evaluation. Because the MT is a knowledge test, test-retest data would be appropriate and useful to the potential user. The lack of such readily attainable data, or split-half coefficients, further weakens the MT's case as an assessment tool of machining knowledge.

The test manual of the MT presents no evidence for the instrument's validity. There is a consistent theme in the manual that the MT relates to machining skills. This is not true. The MT is strictly an untimed assessment of knowledge learned. Repeated references to "skill" do not change the fact that the MT is an assessment of the knowledge (and calculations) that machinists use in their various jobs. In fact, the MT approximates a comprehensive final examination for coursework that machinists would reasonably be expected to take in a technical college.

Another troublesome issue with the MT is the percentile equivalency table. This table was derived from the same 27 manufacturing applicants that were used for the reliability coefficient, a far less than desirable practice. The range for these applicants is

96 to 39 correct answers out of 120 items with a reported mean of 68.7. When the top score of a knowledge test is 80%, and the mean is less than 60%, the items and how they were selected or created becomes an important issue for the potential user. Comparing job applicants to a small and vaguely defined norm group with less than stellar performance on an assessment instrument is unlikely to improve employment decision making.

In summary, the use of the MT is not supported by this reviewer based on some severe shortcomings. The apparently high reliability is based on a single, very small, and vaguely defined sample. Much more data from clearly defined samples are needed. There is no support presented for the MT's validity, and it is strictly a test of knowledge. There is no assessment of skill even though machinist jobs typically involve precise physical involvement with tools and materials. Finally, no information is provided on the process of item selection, who selected the items, or the rationale behind the selection of items.

[254]

Ramsay Corporation Job Skills—Mechanic Evaluation Test.

Purpose: To measure the knowledge and skills required for mechanics.
Population: Mechanic job applicants.
Publication Date: 1992.
Scores: Total score only.
Administration: Group.
Levels, 3: C Mechanic, B Mechanic, A Mechanic.
Price Data, 1992: $498 per complete kit including 10 reusable test booklets, 100 answer sheets, manual (A: 13 pages; B: 14 pages; C: 14 pages), and scoring key.
Time: (100–120) minutes.
Author: Roland T. Ramsay.
Publisher: Ramsay Corporation.

Review of the Ramsay Corporation Job Skills— Mechanic Evaluation Test by DAVID O. ANDERSON, Senior Measurement Statistician, Educational Testing Service, Princeton, NJ:

The Ramsay Corporation Job Skills—Mechanic Evaluation Test was first developed in 1987 and revised in 1992 for three levels of mechanics—C, B, and A. The tests are intended for use with applicants and incumbents for jobs where mechanical knowledge and skills are a necessary part of job activities. However, their application to specific uses—hiring, placement, promotion, or training—is not explained; the appropriateness of the tests to each

of these functions is up to the potential test user. The tests are untimed, although 2 hours is the suggested maximum time for each test. The three-test series consists of paper-and-pencil test booklets containing four-option, multiple-choice questions, manuals, answer sheets, and scoring keys. The manuals accompanying the test booklets contain a list of materials needed for the test and standardized administration directions.

TEST CONTENT. The C Mechanic test contains 116 items, divided into 11 content areas: Welding (11 items), Plumbing (5), HVAC (5), Pneumatics (10), Shop (11), Lubrication (12), Print Reading (5), Electrical (20), Mechanical (23), Rigging (7), and Miscellaneous (7). The B Mechanic test has 117 items in 9 areas: Welding (9), Plumbing (11), HVAC (10), Pneumatics (4), Shop (9), Lubrication (17), Print Reading (4), Electrical (28), and Mechanical (25). The 125 items on the A Mechanic test are divided into 9 areas: Welding (12), HVAC (18), Pneumatics (12), Shop (11), Lubrication (9), Print Reading (10), Electrical (23), Mechanical (24), and Miscellaneous (6).

SCORING AND REPORTING. The tests are hand scored resulting in a number-right total score. Within each test, because items for each content area are grouped together, it is possible to calculate number-right subscores for the content areas. No formal score reports are available. To facilitate the interpretation of total scores, normative data in the form of percentile rank tables are provided for the original tests. However, because the sizes of the reference groups are small (52 to 58 people) and the reference groups are not adequately described, and because the tests have been revised (especially the A Mechanic test), caution is advised when using the percentile rank tables.

VALIDITY AND RELIABILITY. The content of the tests was determined by having two maintenance supervisors independently rank the knowledge areas considered necessary for the positions of C, B, and A Mechanic, using the Maintenance Activity List (no reference), and estimate the percent of time spent in each area. Overall, interrater reliability was .67. No criterion-related validation studies have been conducted. In addition, there was no mention of the appropriateness of the reading level of the items to the intended test takers.

Using data from the original forms of the tests, reliability coefficients for the three tests range from .90 (C Mechanic) to .75 (A Mechanic); their standard errors of measurement are 4.64 and 5.02, respectively (based on sample sizes of 52 to 58). Reliability coefficients of .75 and above are considered very good for this type of test.

During the 1992 test revision, 5 of the 116 items (4%) on the C Mechanic test were replaced, 10 of 117 items (9%) on the B Mechanic test, and 35 of 125 items (28%) on the A Mechanic test. Some, but not all, of the original items with negative or low discrimination indexes were either altered or replaced. Using item analysis data from several different samples, the item difficulties in the revised C Mechanic test range from .09 to 1.00, with a mean of .56. The point biserial correlations (a measure of discrimination between high and low scorers) on that test range from -.19 to .79, with a mean of .30. Even after replacing poor items, 28 items (over 24%) still have point biserial correlations below .20, a commonly accepted cutoff for this index. Similarly, the item difficulties in the revised B Mechanic test range from .05 to .91, with a mean of .49. The point biserial correlations range from -.24 to .72, with a mean of .25. Forty-three items (over 36%) have point biserial correlations below .20. The A Mechanic test has item difficulties ranging from .08 to 1.00, with a mean of .40. The point biserial correlations, ranging from -.18 to .57, have a mean of .20. Over 36% of the items (47) have point biserial correlations below .20. Clearly, up to one third of the items on these tests are contributing little or nothing to the accurate measurement of the candidate's mechanical knowledge as indicated by a single total score. The reviewer would suggest that the test publisher at least reanalyze the data using content area scores and that these serve as the bases for the point biserial correlations. Items that continue to have low or negative point biserial correlations should be dropped or replaced in future editions of the tests.

SUMMARY. This series of tests appears to measure adequately the mechanical knowledge of three levels of mechanics; however, the appropriateness of the tests for hiring, placement, promotion, and training needs to be carefully considered by the test user. The tests could be shortened, perhaps by a third, without diluting the measurement accuracy of the total scores. Because of the 1992 revisions to the tests, caution is advised when using the out-dated percentile rank tables.

Review of the Ramsay Corporation Job Skills—Mechanic Evaluation Test by ALAN C. BUGBEE, JR., Director of Psychometric Services, The American Registry of Radiologic Technologists, St. Paul, MN:

Nearly every large building that is used in private, quasi-public, and public business needs some-

one who can keep it operating. Such a worker serves an omnibus role, having to know how to operate, maintain, and repair most of the everyday equipment used in that building. This includes such diverse areas as HVAC (heating, ventilation, air conditioning), electrical repair, mechanical repair, blueprint reading, and a variety of other tasks. Naturally, when hiring someone for such a position, it is helpful to know whether the candidate possesses the necessary knowledge and skills. This is what the Ramsay Corporation Job Skills—Mechanic Evaluation Tests are intended to do.

The Ramsay Corporation Job Skills series contains A Mechanic Evaluation Test, B Mechanic Evaluation Test, and C Mechanic Evaluation Test. Each test is based around the Maintenance Activity List (no source provided), which presumably is a standard for jobs of this kind. Each test covers the general areas of Welding, Plumbing, HVAC, Pneumatics, Shop, Lubrication, Print Reading, Electrical, and Mechanical.

The number of items or percent coverage on these topics varies from test to test. Some areas of mechanic knowledge are only covered by one or two of the tests. The subject of Plumbing is only on the C and B tests. Rigging, the use of equipment for support and movement, is only covered in the C test. Both the A test and the C test have a category of Miscellaneous, appearing at the end of the test, to cover items that, although important, do not fit with any other category. All of the tests cover Safety, although they have no section on this topic. According to the manuals, this topic pervades all of the other categories.

All three tests are group administered, consist of multiple-choice questions, and are untimed. They utilize machine-scorable answer sheets, although no information is provided about machine scoring. It would seem that these different tests may be administered at the same time because the verbal and printed instructions to the test takers are exactly the same. Even the two practice questions on the front of each test booklet are the same.

C Mechanics Evaluation Test, the lowest skill level test of this group according to a representative of the Ramsay Corporation during a telephone call, has 116 questions. The items are presented in 11 sections, plus Safety, which pervades the other items. Topics, in order of presentation, include Welding (9.5%), Plumbing (4.3%), HVAC (4.3%), Electrical (17.2%), Pneumatic (8.6%), Shop (9.5%), Rigging (6.0%), Lubrication (10.3%), Mechanical (19.8%), Print Reading (4.3%), and Miscellaneous (6.0%).

B Mechanic Evaluation Test, assessing intermediate level knowledge and skills for this field, has 117 questions. The questions are presented in nine sections plus the underlying factor of Safety. Topics include Welding (7.7%), Electrical (23.9%), Mechanical (21.4%), Pneumatic (3.4%), HVAC (8.5%), Print Reading (3.4%), Shop (7.7%), Plumbing (9.4%), and Lubrication (14.5%).

A Mechanic Evaluation Test, the most advanced knowledge and skill assessment instrument in this test series, has 125 questions. Like the B test, it also has 9 sections, with the 10th, Safety, permeating the entire test. The sequence of topics is as follows: Shop (8.8%), HVAC (14.4%), Mechanical (19.2%), Welding (9.6%), Lubrication (7.2%), Pneumatics (9.6%), Print Reading (8.0%), Electrical (18.4%), and Miscellaneous (4.8%).

The instructions for the test administrator are clear and concise. These tests have no time limit, but the instructions in the manual and those read to the test takers say that no more than 2 hours should be required to complete the test. The exam administrator is required to keep time for each test taker. This information is to be written above the examinee's name on the answer sheet. No information is provided in the test manuals about how this test time information could or should be used. Whether speed of answering the questions has any relevance is never mentioned in the manuals.

These tests are hand scored by the use of a key that presumably can be laid over the answer sheet (no copy of an answer sheet or scoring key was provided to this reviewer). The score of the test is the total number of questions (not counting the practice questions) minus the number of questions answered incorrectly or omitted. Each test manual has a percentile equivalent chart for raw scores, which provides the sole interpretive information for these tests. No subscores about performance on the sections of these tests are provided. Each question is given an equal weight in the total score, even though the questions are not equally distributed across areas covered by these tests. Presumably, the number of questions covered for each area was set by that area's importance in determining the degree of knowledge and skills test takers have as a mechanic or maintenance worker.

RELIABILITY. All three of the Mechanic Evaluation tests use exactly the same three-line statement about what reliability means and how it is presented in the manual. Interestingly enough, the reliability estimates (coefficient used is not identified)

are based on Form H-3 (A test), Form H-2 (B test), and Form H-1 (C test). Whether these are the same as the forms used on the current tests—Form A-1, Form B-1, and Form C-1—is not specified. It seems from latter information under the Item Analysis section of the manual that they are not. The reported reliabilities and standard errors of measurement are: A test, $r = .75$, $SEM = 5.02$, $N = 52$; B test, $r = .85$, $SEM = 4.79$, $N = 57$; C test, $r = .90$, $SEM = 4.64$, $N = 58$. Information is not provided about where the samples for these estimates came from, how they were selected, how they represent the population of interest, or what the range of talent, ability, skill, and/or knowledge is in this group. There are, of course, many sources of variation of scores on a test that may or may not be accounted for by the reliability estimates for these tests. The usefulness of the scores is limited due to the lack of information about the test takers.

VALIDITY. Three different types of validity are mentioned. The two sentences on content validity assert that "the content validity of the test is assured when the behaviors required on the test are also required on the job. It is a paper-and-pencil form of a work sample" (manual, A test, p. 11; manual, B test, p. 11; manual, C test, p. 11). This extremely optimistic view seems to be derived from the interrater ranking of test questions against the specifications in the previously mentioned Maintenance Activity List. The ranking was performed by two maintenance supervisors for each test and showed an interrater agreement of .67 in all cases. No information is provided about whether the same subject matter experts performed the rankings for each of the three tests. No information is provided about the Maintenance Activity List other than the general areas, presumably from that list, which are covered by items on each particular test.

The manuals also briefly mention criterion-related validity and construct validity. On criterion-related validity, the manuals mention that this type of validity study has not been conducted, but it hypothesizes that the tests would be predictive of job performance in mechanical maintenance. This allegation is based solely on an article by J. E. Hunter (1983), also the sole reference source in the manuals, which "reports that content-related valid tests usually reflect excellent criterion-related correlation coefficients" (manuals, A, B, C, p. 11). In effect, the argument is that although there is no attempt to establish the validity of these instruments in relation to an external criterion, if it was done, it would be excellent. To call this wishful thinking is an understatement.

The section on construct validity (four sentences) first defines this type of validity. It then states that no studies of this have been conducted, but asserts that construct validity is established by "the procedures of development" (manuals, A, B, C, p. 11). Needless to say, these mechanic evaluation tests have not established that they measure what they purport to measure.

NORMATIVE DATA. As was the case with the reliability studies, the forms reported for normative data are different from the forms shown on the test booklets. No information is provided for converting raw scores to percentile ranks. This is the sole extent of interpretive information provided.

ITEM STATISTICS. Information about the questions used in these tests is provided in tabular format in the manuals. The tables provide item difficulty and point biserial correlation coefficients for each of the questions. The reported item statistics are not all from the same administration or sample. The manual mentions that the test was revised in February 1992 (Form B-1, the form of the test reviewed) and that 96% of the questions are the same as the older one. Perhaps the developers have confused classical measurement statistics with those of item response theory in concluding that these item parameter estimates are invariant.

Even if these statistics were invariant, there are problems with the quality of the items in each test. A Mechanic Evaluation Test has 1 item that everyone got right, 26 items with a point biserial correlation coefficient less than or equal to zero, and 2 with a difficulty value between 0 and .10. Twenty items have no information at all. Apparently, sufficient data for item analysis have not been available because this test was revised in October 1992 and these items were added. Forty eight items (38%) in this test have either no statistics or statistics that show that the item is not optimal for accomplishing the purpose of the test.

Among the 117 questions on the B Mechanic Evaluation Test, 15 have a point biserial value between 0 and .10 and 14 have point biserial values less than or equal to zero. Three items have difficulty values less than .10 (one of these also has a negative point biserial value). In all, 32 questions (27%) do not appear to aid in helping test users assess the skills and knowledge of applicants for positions in the area of mechanic maintenance.

In comparison with the A and B tests, the C Mechanic Evaluation Test is the best, at least from the item analysis point of view. Seventeen items (14.6%) do not fulfill a desired statistical quality (too

easy—1, too difficult—1, poor discrimination—15) and one has no information. Equally important, this test has a number of questions with both moderate difficulty (.30 to .70) and good discrimination (.24 to .79), characteristics that are highly desirable in a test that is to be used in employment selection. Unfortunately, the information reported for this test includes data for three questions that were taken from three different test (or item) administrations.

SUMMARY. The Ramsay Corporation Job Skills—A Mechanic Evaluation Test, B Mechanic Evaluation Test, and C Mechanic Evaluation Test are intended to be used in the selection and promotion of persons for positions in charge of maintaining buildings and their various mechanical operations, such as electricity, air conditioning, heating, etc. Whether they accomplish their purpose is uncertain. At best, the information about these tests and their items is minimal. At worst, it is nonexistent. With rigorous standardization and studies of reliability and validity, these tests might be good at accomplishing their stated purpose. At present, they cannot be recommended for use.

REVIEWER'S REFERENCE

Hunter, J. E. (1983). A causal analysis of cognitive ability, job knowledge, job performance, and supervisory ratings. In F. Landy, S. Zedek, & J. Cleveland (Eds.), *Performance measurement and theory* (pp. 257–266). Hillsdale, NJ: Lawrence Erlbaum.

[255]
Ramsay Corporation Job Skills—Office Arithmetic Test.

Purpose: "To measure the arithmetic skills required to perform office and clerical jobs."
Population: Adults.
Publication Date: 1990.
Scores: Total score only.
Administration: Group.
Price Data, 1992: $200 per complete kit including 10 test booklets, 100 answer sheets, manual (10 pages), and scoring key.
Time: (30–35) minutes.
Author: Roland T. Ramsay.
Publisher: Ramsay Corporation.

Review of the Ramsay Corporation Job Skills— Office Arithmetic Test by FREDERICK BESSAI, Professor of Education, University of Regina, Regina, Saskatchewan, Canada:

This is a 40-item multiple-choice test (also including 5 practice exercises) designed to measure basic arithmetic computation skills. There is an approximately even distribution of items for each of addition, subtraction, multiplication, and division. The last eight items are word problems that require reference to a table and one or more calculations to arrive at the correct answer. The test yields a single raw score. The introduction in the test manual is somewhat brief and does not state what levels of arithmetic skills the test is designed to measure, or the kind of employee selection settings in which the test would be useful. The instructions for administering and scoring the test are clear and explicit.

The information on reliability and validity given in the manual is scant. Kuder Richardson (Formula 20) coefficients of .87 and .88 are reported. These were derived from the test results of two groups of post high school students—one group of 52 and another of 65 students. No standard errors of measurement are given, although there is a heading in the table for these data. [Editor's note: Publisher advises the standard errors of measurement was inadvertently omitted from the 6/96 edition because of a printer's error. They were included in the 5/97 edition but the reviewer had the 6/96 edition.] The content validity appears satisfactory and the claims for construct validity made by the authors are based on office-related content. The norms are given in percentiles only and are based on the test results of 65 students: 22 males and 43 females. No further information regarding the norming sample is given and hence the percentiles are not very useful.

The test appears to be a good instrument to assess basic office arithmetic skills but more research is required, particularly in the areas of content- and criterion-related validity. More adequate norming samples and extensive norming procedures are also needed before the test can be recommended for general use.

Review of the Ramsay Corporation Job Skills— Office Arithmetic Test by ANITA TESH, Assistant Professor, School of Nursing, University of North Carolina at Greensboro, Greensboro, NC:

This instrument is composed of 5 practice items and 40 test items. The test includes eight problems in each of the basic arithmetic operations: addition (of two- and three-digit numbers and decimal fractions), subtraction (of two- and three-digit numbers and decimal fractions), multiplication (of two-digit numbers by one- and two-digit numbers, and by two-decimal fractions), and division (of two- and three-digit numbers and two-decimal fractions by one- and two-digit numbers). Decimal fractions are often presented as small sums of money. No items involve common fractions or ratio/proportion problems. The test also includes eight word prob-

lems representing situations such as purchasing supplies or planning expenses for a trip. Some involve reading charts or tables, and use of more than one operation (e.g., multiplication and addition). The test is to be completed without use of a calculator.

All items are in multiple-choice format, with four distractors in addition to the correct answer. Distractors are chosen to represent errors commonly made in hand calculations such as misplaced decimals and failure to carry or borrow appropriately. Use of four distractors (rather than three) should decrease the number of items answered correctly due to guessing.

The test manual includes clear directions for administering the test. Qualifications of the examiner are not discussed, but administering the test does not seem to require any special skills or training. Scoring is done by hand (using a key) by the test user.

RELIABILITY. The consistency of a test's performance is referred to as reliability. The *Standards for Educational and Psychological Testing* (AERA, APA, & NCME, 1985) cite as a primary standard that estimates of reliability be provided in sufficient detail for "the test user to judge whether scores are sufficiently accurate for the intended use of the test" (p. 20). The test manual for the Ramsay Corporation Job Skills—Office Arithmetic Test (Form CA 8/90-01) gives information on internal consistency reliability obtained from two studies that used a prior version of the test (Form 9/88-02). Those internal consistency reliability estimates were adequate (KR-20s of .88 and .87, respectively) but cannot be applied directly to the current form of the test. Further, the studies used small samples ($n = 52$ and 65, respectively) of "post high school students in Pennsylvania" (manual, p. 6). The test is intended for use with adult applicants for clerical and office jobs, and these "post high school students" may differ in important ways from the typical applicant pool.

Internal consistency reliability addresses only the degree of consistency among items that constitute the test. Other measures of the consistency of a test's performance are assessed by other types of reliability estimates, such as temporal stability (i.e., test-retest reliability) and alternate-form reliability. The *Standards for Educational and Psychological Testing* (AERA, APA, & NCME, 1985, p. 21) state as a primary standard that evidence of internal consistency reliability should not be interpreted as a substitute for these other forms of reliability unless specific evidence supports this conclusion. The test manual presents no evidence of temporal stability or alternate-form reliability of the test.

VALIDITY. Validity refers to the appropriateness of conclusions that can be drawn from test results, and thus is the paramount consideration in evaluation of a test. The test manual presents scant evidence of validity of the Office Arithmetic Test. In support of content validity, the test manual states that the test "is a paper-and-pencil form of work encountered in many office and clerical jobs" (manual, p. 8). This statement appears to be the opinion of the test developers rather than a panel of experts in office and clerical job skills, and, as such, may actually represent only face validity. For example, in an actual office setting the problems might be performed on a calculator rather than by hand; or calculations involving common fractions or ratios might be important. In such cases, the test would not have content validity.

The test manual presents no statistical evidence of criterion-related validity or construct validity of the test. The manual states that similar tests have been shown to be predictive of success in office work, but this contention does not directly support the usefulness of this test.

NORMS. The test manual presents raw score percentile equivalents for a previous version of the test, determined using "22 male and 43 female students" (p. 8). These may be the same persons referred to as "post-high school students" in an earlier section of the manual (p. 6). Because consistency of measurement between the two forms of the test has not been demonstrated, and this sample may differ substantially from the persons with whom the test will be used, the usefulness of these norms is unclear.

OTHER CONSIDERATIONS. This is a timed test. No information regarding speededness of the test is presented in the test manual, but the time allowed appears to this reviewer likely to be adequate for most English-speaking applicants for clerical and office jobs.

No information is presented in the manual regarding analysis for test or item bias. The language of the items seems unlikely to be offensive to any groups, and the possibility of cultural dependency is minimal. No personal names or gender references are used in test items.

SUMMARY. Although the Office Arithmetic Test seems a well-thought-out test of basic computational skills, the test manual provides scant evidence for reliability and validity of the test. When this information is not provided by the test developer, test users assume sole responsibility for ensuring that the decisions they make based on test results are warranted. Although crucial in weighty matters such as employment decisions, this may be beyond the resources of some potential test users.

REVIEWER'S REFERENCE

American Educational Research Association, American Psychological Association, & National Council on Measurement in Education (Joint Committee). (1985). *Standards for educational and psychological testing.* Washington, DC: American Psychological Corporation, Inc.

[256]
Ramsay Corporation Job Skills—Office Reading Test.

Purpose: "To measure the reading skills required for office workers."
Population: Adults.
Publication Date: 1990.
Scores: Total score only.
Administration: Group.
Price Data, 1992: $200 per complete kit including 10 test booklets, 100 answer sheets, manual (11 pages), and scoring key.
Time: (30–40) minutes.
Author: Roland T. Ramsay.
Publisher: Ramsay Corporation.

TEST REFERENCES

1. Campion, M. A., Campion, J. E., & Hudson, J. D., Jr. (1994). Structured interviewing: A note on incremental validity and alternative question types. *Journal of Applied Psychology, 79,* 998-1002.

Review of the Ramsay Corporation Job Skills— Office Reading Test by LAURA L. B. BARNES, Associate Professor of Educational Research and Evaluation, School of Education Studies, Oklahoma State University, Stillwater, OK:

The Office Reading Test consists of five reading passages relating to office or business procedures, each followed by eight multiple-choice comprehension questions. The test manual states that the test is to be used in employee selection and the instructions to the examinees state "We are asking you to take these exercises so that we can compare your skills with those required to learn and perform the jobs." This statement implies at least two things missing from this test—evidence that the reading skills measured by this test are job relevant and that adequate normative data are available.

Though appearing to have adequate internal consistency reliability (KR20 = .84 computed on the norming sample), absolutely no validity evidence is provided. What passes for a description of "specific content" is the name of each passage, followed by the item numbers for that passage. There is no description of how the test was developed though the author claims construct validity for the test by virtue of the procedures of test development. In the manual the author states that, although no formal construct validity studies have been conducted, the construct measured by the test (ability to read, comprehend, and answer written questions based on a printed passage) "has been observed in many jobs involving clerical or office procedures. Where reading comprehension is required, the test is useful" (p. 9). Under criterion-related validity, the author states that significant correlation coefficients have been found "for an industrial reading test (The Psychological Corporation) with grades in vocational training programs" (p. 9), but no correlation coefficients are provided. Presumably, we are to accept this test on its face (i.e., depend on face validity, which is not validity).

The Percentile norms given are for a total sample of 29 male and 53 female post-high school business school students in Pittsburgh—far too few to provide stable normative comparisons. The test manual provides no information about the characteristics of the normative group that would allow a prospective user to determine the relevance or representativeness of the norm data. The average raw score mean was 34.39 (86% average difficulty) for the normative group and their score distribution was extremely negatively skewed. These characteristics would be consistent with a test designed to identify poor readers except for two things. First, many of the test questions could be answered by someone with office experience or training without referring to the passages—for example, the section on operating a computer contains questions that anyone with computer experience should be able to answer. In fact, a subsample of computer management students had the highest scores of any reported. Thus, the validity of the test as a measure of reading comprehension is questionable and it is likely biased against job applicants who do not have prior office experience—both because their raw scores will be lower than applicants who have experience and because the norms are inflated given that the norming sample was made up of business students. Second, the reading level of the test passages may be higher than necessary for a test that presumably should be useful for a range of office jobs. The SMOG grade-equivalent reading levels reported in the manual range from 10 to 13, with an average of 11.4. This seems rather high for a test presumably designed to help select individuals for a wide range of office positions. However, analyses of three passages conducted for this review using the Flesch-Kincaid, Coleman-Lian, and Bormuth formulas show somewhat lower reading levels than those reported in the manual (averages of 8.3, 9.2,

and 9.1 for the three formulas, respectively). Though the comprehensibility level of the texts may be within expected ranges, normative interpretations of raw scores must take into consideration that the norm group is likely reading at a higher level than would many pools of job applicants.

In summary, this test has a number of serious weaknesses. Validity is particularly problematic: To what extent is the test measuring reading comprehension versus knowledge of office procedures? The reading level may be higher than necessary for a range of office jobs. The norming sample is too small, may not be relevant for many applicant pools, and is not described in enough detail to enable employers to determine its applicability. I would not recommend that the test be used for any purpose until additional information is provided.

Review of the Ramsay Corporation Job Skills—Office Reading Test by STEVEN J. OSTERLIND, Professor, University of Missouri-Columbia, Columbia, MO:

The Ramsay Corporation Job Skills—Office Reading Test is authored by Roland T. Ramsay and published by Ramsay Corporation. This review is of Form G. The stated purpose for the test is "to measure the reading skills required for office workers." The test consists of five reading passages, each about 150 words long, and 40 multiple-choice items that are assigned in groups of eight to each reading passage. The passages cover general office activities, such as operating a copier and making travel arrangements. The test is scored as right versus wrong, with the total number correct as the examinee's score. It may be group administered to adults (the manual recommends about 10 in a group) and takes about 30 to 40 minutes to complete. Materials included with the test are a scoring key and a brief pamphlet that serves as a test administrator's manual. This test manual includes a few sentences on the test's development and limited technical information.

The *Standards for Educational and Psychological Testing* (American Educational Research Association, American Psychological Association, & National Council on Measurement in Education, 1985) identifies three participants in the testing process, including the test developer, the examinee, and the user of a test's scores. From any of these points of view, one is astonished at the poor quality of the Ramsay Corporation Job Skills—Office Reading Test, and this reviewer recommends that the instrument be immediately withdrawn from use. It is seemingly ill-conceived and is developed with an evident disregard for technical standards of professional test development. Regretfully, tests of this ilk give antitesting critics bountiful ammunition. In this instance, to be direct is merciful.

Although the stated purpose for the test is to assess reading skills required for office workers, there is only cursory description of what is meant by "reading skills" (i.e., the test "was developed to evaluate the ability of office or clerical workers to read and comprehend the material read," manual, p. 6). And, there is not a word of description about the difficulty level of reading for these office or clerical workers. One is left completely in the dark even about the fundamental purpose of the test.

The manual does offer a table showing a SMOG readability index for each of the five passages, but it is presented without context or corroborating information. Reading specialists are keenly aware of the shortcomings of such readability formulas, and without additional information, the table is useless.

The test manual offers no information on how these particular passages were developed or selected. What information each passage is supposed to contribute to the assessment of reading is unreported. No test content specifications are provided, and one fears that none were used in making this test.

An examination of the test's 40 items is a study in how not to prepare test questions. They seem merely to be random questions about the content of a given passage. They are not consistent in format (i.e., irregular use of capitals and periods), and some even contain grammar errors. Percent correct values (overall approximately 86%) and point-biserial indices are given for the items.

Internal reliability coefficients are reported from .49 to .87, for four different groups of examinees (Ns from 24 to 82). By itself, the widely different internal reliability coefficients should tip off the knowledgeable test developer to a problem worthy of further investigation.

The test manual offers a few sentences on validity. But the information provided in the brief description is so immature as to be uninformative. For example, in a two-sentence section called "Construct Validity" the author reports, "This skill or ability [sic] has been observed in many jobs involving clerical or office procedures. Where reading comprehension is required, the test is useful" (p. 9).

There is no information provided on interpreting the scores yielded by the test—an inexcusable omission.

In sum, one could possibly be better served by merely asking the job applicant to read a randomly selected article from a daily newspaper or from some work sample rather than the Ramsay Corporation Job Skills—Office Reading Test. It is recommended that the test be withdrawn from use and the author become acquainted with standards for test development and professional responsibility as articulated in three primary sources: (a) *Standards for Educational and Psychological Testing,* (b) *Code of Fair Testing Practices in Education,* and (c) *Code of Professional Responsibility in Educational Measurement.*

REVIEWER'S REFERENCE

American Educational Research Association, American Psychological Association, & National Council on Measurement in Education. (1985). *Standards for educational and psychological testing.* Washington, DC: American Psychological Association, Inc.

[257]
Ramsay Corporation Job Skills—Reading Electrical Drawings & Schematics.

Purpose: "To measure the skills required to learn and perform jobs involving electrical print reading skills."
Population: Adults.
Publication Date: 1992.
Acronym: RCJS—Reading Electrical Drawings & Schematics.
Scores: Total score only.
Administration: Group.
Price Data, 1993: $498 per complete kit including 10 test booklets, 100 answer sheets, manual (10 pages), and scoring key.
Time: (35–40) minutes.
Author: Roland T. Ramsay.
Publisher: Ramsay Corporation.

Review of the Ramsay Corporation Job Skills— Reading Electrical Drawings & Schematics by DAVID O. ANDERSON, Senior Measurement Statistician, Educational Testing Service, Princeton, NJ:

The Ramsay Corporation Job Skills Test: Reading Electrical Drawings & Schematics, Form A, consists of a paper-and-pencil test booklet containing 38 four-option, multiple-choice questions covering the following content categories: View and Surfaces (6 items), Basic Electrical Symbols (11), and Wiring Diagrams (21). The time limit is 35 minutes. Answer sheets are provided, as is a scoring key. The manual accompanying the test booklet contains a list of materials needed for the test and standardized administration directions.

SCORING AND REPORTING. The test is hand scored with a number-right total score. Because information is provided about which items are in each content category, calculation of category scores is possible.

VALIDITY AND RELIABILITY. The test materials appear to have face validity; however, no information is presented concerning formal studies of job relevance or criterion-related validity, test development, establishment of norms, reliability, standard error of measurement, or score interpretation. A spokesperson from Ramsay Corporation indicated that too few answer sheets had been returned to perform the above studies.

SUMMARY. This test could be an adequate device to measure the ability to read electrical drawings and schematics; however, the lack of any technical information regarding job relevance, test development, score interpretation, and reliability data severely limits this test's usefulness.

[258]
Ramsay Corporation Job Skills—Reading Prints & Drawings.

Purpose: To measure the skills required to learn and perform jobs involving reading mechanical prints and drawings.
Population: Adults.
Publication Date: 1990–1993.
Acronym: RCJS-Reading Prints & Drawings.
Scores: Total score only.
Administration: Group.
Price Data, 1993: $498 per complete kit including 10 test booklets, 100 answer sheets, manual ('93, 12 pages), and scoring key.
Time: (30–35) minutes.
Authors: Roland T. Ramsay.
Publisher: Ramsay Corporation.

Review of the Ramsay Corporation Job Skills— Reading Prints & Drawings by JAMES W. PINKNEY, Professor of Counselor and Adult Education, East Carolina University, Greenville, NC:

The Reading Prints and Drawings (RPD) instrument is intended to assess a job applicant's skill in reading and understanding mechanical drawings and production type blueprints. The paper-and-pencil RPD is a timed assessment (30 minutes) intended for use with groups of applicants. The RPD consists of 33 multiple-choice items and two practice items about the three traditional top, side, and front views of three objects and two blueprint type drawings of two separate metal objects. Of the 33 items comprising the RPD, 4 ask the applicant to identify surfaces represented by lines in the three views shown, 27 ask that various distances (dimensions) on parts of the drawings be identified, and 2 items ask the applicant to give the number of holes in an object or the number of finished surfaces. There are no subscales, and the total score is the sum of correct answers for the RPD.

The 1993 test manual states that the 1988 RPD was revised in 1990 when two items were changed. About a third (four pages) of the test manual has specific directions for giving the RPD in a group setting. The directions are thorough and emphasize the importance of standardizing the administration, offer suggestions for helping put the applicants at ease so they can do their best, and note options such as using scratch paper and avoiding distractions.

Percentile equivalents for total scores are included in the manual for technical institute students (199) and manufacturing inspectors and applicants for such jobs (23). It presents some conceptual problems to find that first through fourth term technical students soundly outscore the employed inspectors and applicants. One would logically assume that field experience (inspectors) and completion of career preparation (applicants) would improve the skill of reading blueprints and mechanical drawings. According to the table on reliability coefficients, the mean for students was 25.48 versus 15.04 for the inspectors and applicants. This suggests the RPD may be heavily slanted toward information learned in a classroom rather than through experience. This is disturbing for an instrument that claims to assess skills needed to perform jobs that require reading and understanding technical prints and drawings.

Reliability is reported in the form of Kuder-Richardson-20 (KR-20) coefficients from the scores of the technical institute students and manufacturing inspectors and applicants who make up the percentile equivalency table. Although the author claims the overall coefficients (both .83) "indicate excellent reliability" (p. 7), there are some issues that argue against that claim. First, the coefficients for subgroups of the students vary widely from .82 down to .37. A potential user would want to examine carefully both the coefficients for the various subgroups and the size of the subgroups. The smallest subgroup coefficient is based on five students in a building maintenance program.

The manual directly states that of the 27 items dealing with dimensions, 10 concern simple drawings, 7 use an intermediate drawing, and 10 relate to a complex drawing. The KR-20 may be inappropriate for items sequenced in a progression of difficulty. This issue becomes even more confusing because the item analysis does not show a consistent progression of difficulty. Finally, the manual notes that the RPD is "rather easy" and a ceiling effect would tend to inflate the apparent reliability of the instrument.

The manual's presentation of validity is less than convincing. The fact that students (some in the first term of technical college) outscore experienced workers in the field is disconcerting. No data or studies are presented to support the manual's assertion that the RPD measures the ability to read prints and mechanical drawings. Basically, the manual uses logic and assertion as a substitute for validity-oriented data. The potential user is asked to accept the RPD's validity solely as a matter of face validity—the RPD's items concern reading mechanical drawings and blueprints. Therefore, logic suggests, it is relevant to jobs that require this skill. This is extremely difficult to believe given the reported scores. The percentile equivalencies presented would argue that it is difficult if not impossible to determine what the RPD is measuring or if it is validly measuring anything useful for making employment or educational decisions.

In summary, Reading Prints and Drawings is a questionable assessment instrument and potential users should consider very carefully what they want the RPD to do for their decision-making needs. The manual's directions for administration are well done, but the technical information is of little use to the potential user. The lack of validity data and the minimal reliability data leave much to be desired. Perhaps most damaging for the RPD are the conceptually confusing differences in mean scores reported. When beginning students soundly outscore working inspectors it is difficult to know what is being assessed.

Review of the Ramsay Corporation Job Skills—Reading Prints & Drawings by NAMBURY S. RAJU, Distinguished Professor and Director, Center for Research and Service, Institute of Psychology, Illinois Institute of Technology, Chicago, IL:

The Ramsay Corporation Job Skills—Reading Prints & Drawings (RPD) test consists of 33 multiple-choice items, classified into four categories: Views and Surfaces (4 items), Simple Drawings (10 items), Intermediate Drawings (7 items), and Complex Drawings (12 items). This test was first developed in 1988 as part of a series of skills tests, and the current version, Form A, was issued in 1990. It is a timed test with a 30-minute time limit.

RELIABILITY. The Kuder-Richardson Formula 20 (KR-20) estimates are separately reported for the 1988 and 1990 versions of the RPD test. For the 1988 version, the KR-20 estimates of reliability were .73, .74, and .83, respectively, for Sample 1 (Technical Institute A), Sample 2 (Technical Institute B), and the two samples combined. The combined sample size was 199, with 157 cases for Sample 1 and 42 cases for Sample 2. The KR-20 estimate for the 1990 version was .83, and this estimate was based on a sample of 23 incumbents and applicants for inspector jobs in a manufacturing plant. Also reported are the raw score means, standard deviations, and standard errors of measurement for both versions of the test. The same samples were also used to conduct traditional item analyses. Item difficulties (*p*-values) and item-test correlations (point-biserials) were reported separately for the two versions.

Even though the reported KR-20 estimates of reliability appear to be acceptable for the total samples, the sample sizes are much too small, which raises concerns about their stability. The stability of the item analysis data should also be a concern for the same reason. Besides the sample sizes being small, the description of the item analysis and reliability samples as given in the test manual is very brief. The reliability estimates should by no means be considered excellent, as claimed at the bottom of Table 2 on page 7 of the test manual. There is no mention of test-retest and parallel form reliability estimates in the manual.

VALIDITY. The test manual does not contain any validity information for the RPD test. Because these are work sample tests, the manual claims that the content validity of these tests is assured. Although that may be true, information about what types of job analyses were performed and how the appropriateness and representativeness of test content were established is not presented in the test manual. No data were presented in support of either criterion-related validity or construct validity. It was noted, however, that tests similar to the RPD test were found to be valid in studies conducted by the U.S. Department of Labor.

NORMS. Normative data (percentile scores) were presented for the RPD test. For the 1988 version, the percentile scores were based on a sample of 199 cases, the same sample that was used for item analysis and reliability assessment. The percentile scores of the 1990 version of the RPD test was based on a sample of 23 cases. As previously noted, there is hardly any information in the manual about the sample used for developing the percentile ranks, nor is there an explanation of how to interpret the percentile ranks. One must question the practical utility of empirically derived percentile ranks with a sample of 23 cases on a test with a possible range of 34 score points.

In summary, the psychometric quality of the RPD test is difficult to assess at this point because of the unavailability of relevant statistical data. The current manual provides very limited information about the rationale for the test, its use, its validity, and the intended audience. The sample sizes are small for both reliability assessment and item analysis. The manual does not offer sufficient information about item tryouts and the validity of the final, operational version of the test. There is also no information to the potential users about differential item functioning, nor is there information about selection bias and/or adverse impact for those intending to use this test for selection and/or placement. Finally, the test manual is brief and provides very limited information about test development and test use.

[259]
Ramsay Corporation Job Skills—Supervisory Reading Test.

Purpose: "To measure the reading skills required for supervisors."
Population: Adults.
Publication Date: 1992.
Scores: Total score only.
Administration: Group.
Price Data, 1992: $200 per complete kit including 10 reusable test booklets, 100 answer sheets, manual (10 pages), and scoring key.
Time: (30–40) minutes.
Author: Roland T. Ramsay.
Publisher: Ramsay Corporation.

Review of the Ramsay Corporation Job Skills—Supervisory Reading Test by JUDITH A. MONSAAS, Associate Professor of Education, North Georgia College & State University, Dahlonega, GA:

According to the author, the Ramsay Corporation Job Skills (RCJS)—Supervisory Reading Test was developed to evaluate the ability of supervisory personnel to read and comprehend the material read. It is designed for use with applicants and supervisors in positions where reading is a necessary part of training or job activities. This is all the rationale that is provided for this instrument. Presumably, the type of business or industry in which the applicant or employee is involved does not matter. The content of the test, which includes five passages, is fairly diverse (e.g., a passage on lubrication and another on

operating a computer). The 40 items are fairly easy in that 85% or more of a sample of 259 candidates for Operator Trainee jobs at a metal processing plant answered all of them correctly. A readability grade level of 10–14 for the test passages and easiness of the items suggests that most of the Operator Training candidates can answer literal comprehension questions about reading passages written at the high school level. I question the need for a reading test when most candidates seem to have the reading skills measured by the test. Conversely, the candidates may have answered the questions correctly because the information in the questions was taken verbatim from the passages. Despite the high school readability of the passages, it is hard to see how any adult with minimal reading skills could not do well on the test.

ADMINISTRATION AND SCORING. The test booklet is well designed and attractive with clear instructions and sample problems. The test manual provides detailed directions for the test administrator including a script to follow and specific time limits (30 minutes).

The results form the RCJS—Supervisory Reading Test can be reported as raw scores or percentile ranks. Unfortunately, according to the manual, the normative data are reported on a similar, but different Ramsay Corporation Job Skills Test. These percentiles are clearly not appropriate for this test. Even if they were appropriate, the other test is so easy that a perfect score puts the examinee at the 85th percentile, incorrectly answering one item drops the individual to the 55th percentile, missing two items puts an examinee at the 32nd percentile, and getting 37 out of 40 correct is equivalent to a percentile rank of 19. Clearly, if missing one item can drop the examinee up to 30 percentile points, the norms are of little use. Maybe the test should be treated as a criterion-referenced test with a minimal passing score determined.

RELIABILITY. The reliability evidence is inadequate. An estimated KR20 reliability coefficient of .84 is provided. No information is provided regarding the size or characteristics of the sample. The table states that the "estimated group" is male and female supervisors. What was the *actual group* used for estimating the test's reliability? The coefficient of .84 for the total test is a bit low for a test used for making decisions about individuals, though it is hard to see how the authors obtained (or even estimated) a .84 with such little variability in test scores.

VALIDITY. No validity data are provided although sections labeled validity are included in the manual. The content validity section states that "the content validity of the test is assured when the behaviors required on the test are also required on the job" (manual, p. 9). The content of the passages is cited as the content of the test rather than describing the reading skills that the test is supposed to measure as the content-related validity evidence. No evidence (descriptive or otherwise) is provided supporting any reading skills tested. No criterion-related evidence is provided for the RCJS—Supervisory Reading Test, but a summary of evidence for a totally different industrial reading test published by The Psychological Corporation is cited, presumably to suggest that this *type* of test has some predictive validity. The industrial test referred to is reported to be correlated with grades in vocational training programs—not job performance, supervisory or otherwise.

According to the *Standards for Educational and Psychological Testing* (AERA, APA, & NCME, 1985), construct validity is the most important type of validity evidence. The manual reports that no studies of construct validity have been conducted but the skills measured by the test have been observed in many jobs involving supervisory tasks. Observed by whom? Because the manual states that the construct measured is the "ability to read, comprehend and answer written questions based on a printed passage" (manual, p. 9) some support for the frequent observation of these skills in the work place would seem appropriate.

SUMMARY. This test is purported to measure reading skills needed by supervisors. No data are cited to support the need for such a test (other than personal observation) or to demonstrate that the test measures the purported skills (content validity evidence), much less what inferences one can make from these scores (construct evidence). The items are so easy that if one is to accept the normative data provided, a careless marking error on one item could drop one's scores from considerably above average to considerably below average. In short, until more adequate substantive and technical data are provided to support the use of this test, this test should not be used.

REVIEWER'S REFERENCE

American Educational Research Association, American Psychological Association, & National Council on Measurement in Education. (1985). *Standards for educational and psychological testing*. Washington, DC: American Psychological Association, Inc.

Review of the Ramsay Corporation Job Skills—Supervisory Reading Test by ROBERT WALL, Graduate Professor of Education, College of Education, Towson State University, Towson, MD:

This reviewer is hard pressed to find something good to write about this test. However, the 1995 manual (Ramsay, 1995) is more professional in appearance than the 1992 manual (Ramsay, 1992). The Ramsay Corporation representative very quickly sent the 1995 manual when this reviewer requested an updated version of the 1992 manual that provided inadequate information. Unfortunately, the 1995 version corrected few substantive deficiencies.

The 14-page manual (Ramsay, 1995) provided no evidence that the author conducted any formal studies of construct validity, criterion-related validity, or content validity.

The reported reliability (KR20 = .89) and standard error of measurement (SEm = 1.66) estimates are based on a small group of 44 supervisors at a manufacturing plant. Apparently the same group of 44 is the source of the normative data. The reported mean raw score for this group is 35.77 out of 40 questions for a difficulty level of 89%. Why the author considers this a "moderately difficult" test (p. 10) is unknown. Item analysis revealed item difficulties ranging from .70 to 1.00 and point biserial index values from -.01 to .83 with 26 of 40 values below .50. The normative group scores are negatively skewed with 70% between 36 and 40. The raw scores range from 18 to 40. The skewed distribution in combination with the 1.66 standard error of measurement create score interpretation problems. Using a 95% confidence band of 3.25 (1.96 SEm) an individual scoring 38 (51st %ile) has a 95% probability of a true score falling between 35 (27th %ile) and 40 (93rd %ile). Using the same 95% confidence band when interpreting differences between two scores would require approximately a 6.5-point difference for true differences (e.g., no true score differences between 40 [93rd %ile] and 34 [26th %ile]). Using this criterion only the extreme scores exhibit true differences, thereby reducing the test's usefulness.

The results of the item analysis and KR20 reliability estimates must be considered as highly tentative because of the small sample, skewed distribution of normative group scores, .89 difficulty level, and timed nature of test. Given the quality of known technical information concerning this test, perhaps it is fortunate no cutoff scores or suggestions about how to interpret scores are provided.

This reviewer recommends that before a corporation spends $200 for this test of unknown validity and tentative reliability, it consider using a random representative sample of its communications (electronic and hard copy) to give supervisors as the basis of its screening device. One appropriate use for this test might be to use it as a class project for a graduate level measurement and assessment class. It is the reviewer's opinion that although the test author may be familiar with the *Standards for Educational and Psychological Testing* (AERA, APA, & NCME, 1985) this test does not meet them.

REVIEWER'S REFERENCES

American Psychological Association, American Educational Research Association, & National Council on Measurement in Education. (1985). *Standards for educational and psychological testing.* Washington, DC: American Psychological Association, Inc.
Ramsay, R. T. (1992). *Test manual: Supervisory Reading Test, Form A (9/92).* Pittsburgh, PA: Ramsay Corporation.
Ramsay, R. T. (1995). *Ramsay Corporation Job Skills: Supervisory Reading Test, Form A (9/92). Manual for administration and scoring.* Pittsburgh, PA: Ramsay Corporation.

[260]
Relating to Each Other: A Questionnaire for Students.

Purpose: "Designed to provide information about students' perceptions and experiences concerning the other sex."
Population: College students.
Publication Date: 1989.
Scores: No scores.
Administration: Group.
Manual: No manual.
Price Data, 1994: $3 per questionnaire.
Time: Administration time not reported.
Author: Project on the Status and Education of Women, Association of American Colleges.
Publisher: Center for Women Policy Studies.

Review of Relating to Each Other: A Questionnaire for Students by COLLIE W. CONOLEY, Professor of Educational Psychology, Texas A&M University, College Station, TX:

The assessment is designed to examine campus environment by using students' reports of classroom and campus life as it pertains to relating to the other sex. The focus is on sexual harassment that includes both men and women. The introduction invites faculty to adapt or expand the survey to cover minority issues, or other groups that might experience harassment. There are other resources on sexual harassment and climate suggested on the questionnaire.

The results provide information about harassment on campus as well as whether respondents know what sexual harassment is and if they know what to do if it occurs. The measure can be used at the classroom or college level as a needs assessment or a stimulus for discussion. Although there are no norms, Fitzgerald et al. (1988) suggest that comparing groups is legitimate and helpful.

The current questionnaire's sections are demographic information, personal definition of sexual harassment, personal and observed experiences of sexual harassment from students and faculty, places avoided on campus, responses to inappropriate behaviors, differential classroom responsiveness to males and females, campus climate toward women, and awareness of grievance procedures. The respondents can be women or men.

The questionnaire comes with no manual. There is a reference to the Fitzgerald, Shullman, Bailey, Richards, Swecker, Gold, Ormerod, and Weitzman (1988) article that provides information on the development and validation of an earlier version of the questionnaire. The questionnaire states that there are minor differences between the assessment, "Sexual Experiences Questionnaire," used in the study and the questionnaire now available. However, there appear to be many differences.

Fitzgerald et al. (1988) report that the five levels of sexual harassment assessed in the original version are based upon Till (1980). The levels are gender harassment (sexist remarks and behavior), seductive behavior (inappropriate sexual advances), sexual bribery (solicitation of sexual activity for reward), sexual coercion (solicitation of sexual activity by threat), and sexual assault. A factor analysis found a three-factor solution that combined the categories of bribery and coercion, and seduction and assault (Fitzgerald & Shullman, 1985).

Fitzgerald et al.. report Cronbach's coefficient alpha of internal consistency at .92 for the 28 items addressing harassment ($N = 1,395$). For a 2-week test-retest stability measure, a reliability of .86 was reported ($N = 46$). They report split-half coefficients for the five scales ranging from .42 to .86, averaging .75 ($N = 1,395$).

Fitzgerald et al (1988) report content validity because the scale was based upon Till's (1980) findings. One criterion item is used in the Fitzgerald et al. version but not in the current published version: "I have been sexually harassed." The items are correlated with the criterion item for validity purposes. The correlations were from .15 to .37. The low number was attributed to the low occurrence of positive responses to the questions about forced sex.

The reliability and validity coefficients cannot be considered accurate because they are based upon an earlier, different version. However, the measure appears to provide a productive step in addressing sexual harassment and has psychometric promise.

REVIEWER'S REFERENCES

Till, F. J. (1980). *Sexual harassment: A report on the sexual harassment of students.* Washington, DC: National Advisory Council on Women's Educational Programs.
Fitzgerald, L. F., & Shullman, S. L. (August, 1985). *The development and validation of an objectively scored measure of sexual harassment.* Paper presented to the convention of the American Psychological Association, Los Angeles.
Fitzgerald, L. F., Shullman, S. L., Bailey, N., Richards, M., Swecker, J., Gold, Y., Ormerod, M., & Weitzman, L. (1988). The incidence and dimensions of sexual harassment in academia and the workplace. *Journal of Vocational Behavior, 32,* 152–175.

Review of Relating to Each Other: A Questionnaire for Students by SCOTT T. MEIER, Associate Professor and Director of Training, Department of Counseling and Educational Psychology, SUNY Buffalo, Buffalo, NY:

Relating to Each Other (REO) is a self-report questionnaire for college students intended to explore their personal experiences of sexual harassment and gender discrimination. Although the questionnaire's title and instructions indicate that it is concerned with interpersonal perceptions of men and women—a more general and therefore, less reactive topic—most of the 14 items clearly tap content related to sexual harassment.

Although the publisher provides no information about the development of REO items, it appears to be a derivation of other sexual harassment instruments, including the Sexual Experiences Questionnaire (SEQ; Fitzgerald et al., 1988). The REO begins with demographic items and then asks respondents to indicate their campus experiences around harassment. Students rate the frequency of such behaviors as hearing "sexually suggestive stories, jokes, or humor" and experiencing "forced sexual intercourse" from other students or from faculty. Other items invite students to rate faculty's differential elicitation of male and female students' class participation, the campus climate for women students, and their awareness of grievance procedures. Unfortunately, no manual is provided for the REO, and no other information is available to describe such basics as norms, reliability, and validity.

Some information is available, however, for the SEQ. Fitzgerald et al. (1988) describe items as based on Till's (1980) content analysis of a national survey of college women. That analysis produced five categories, including gender harassment (e.g., sexist remarks), seductive behavior (e.g., sanction-free sexual advances), sexual bribery (e.g., soliciting sex with rewards), sexual coercion (e.g., soliciting sex with punishment), and sexual assault (e.g. gross imposition of sex). In a pilot study with 1,395 undergraduate students, Fitzgerald et al. (1988) report that the resulting 28-item test had a coefficient alpha of .92. Test-retest reliability with a sample of 46 students over a 2-week period equalled .86. Fitzgerald et al. (1988) reported support for SEQ item validity in terms of correlation with a criterion item ("I have been sexually harassed") and significant differences between male and female students. An SEQ modified for university faculty and staff evidenced comparable reliability (e.g., alpha = .86). Although more

detailed normative data are not provided by Fitzgerald et al. (1988), they do include tables showing the percentage of their samples endorsing SEQ items by educational status, gender, and type of employee.

The widespread experience of gender harassment found by Fitzgerald et al. (1988) and others in their samples of women apparently prompted the publication of Relating to Each Other by the Association of American Colleges. The REO appears to be best used as a survey to promote class discussion of these issues. However, a search of the PsycLit database found no references for the REO, although work with the SEQ has continued (e.g., Barak, Pitterman, & Yitzhaki, 1995; Fitzgerald, Gelfand, & Drasgow, 1995; Gelfand, Fitzgerald, & Drasgow, 1995). In general, then, researchers interested in investigating sexual harassment, as well as administrators seeking to assess their campus climate, would seem better advised to employ the SEQ than the REO.

REVIEWER'S REFERENCES

Till, F. J. (1980). *Sexual harassment: A report on the sexual harassment of students.* Washington, DC: National Advisory Council on Women's Educational Programs.

Fitzgerald, L. F., Shullman, S. L., Bailey, N., Richards, M., Swecker, J., Gold, Y., Ormerod, M., & Weitzman, L. (1988). The incidence and dimensions of sexual harassment in academia and the workplace. *Journal of Vocational Behavior, 32,* 152–175.

Barak, A., Pitterman, Y., & Yitzhaki, R. (1995). An empirical test of the role of power differential in originating sexual harassment. *Basic & Applied Social Psychology, 17,* 497–517.

Fitzgerald, L. F., Gelfand, M. J., & Drasgow, F. (1995). Measuring sexual harassment: Theoretical and psychometric advances. *Basic & Applied Social Psychology, 17,* 425–445.

Gelfand, M. J., Fitzgerald, L. F., & Drasgow, F. (1995). The structure of sexual harassment: A confirmatory analysis across cultures and settings. *Journal of Vocational Behavior, 47,* 164–177.

[261]

Relating with Colleagues: A Questionnaire for Faculty Members.

Purpose: "Designed to examine some aspects of the day-to-day campus environment" with respect to sex-based discrimination.

Population: College faculty.

Publication Date: 1989.

Scores: No scores.

Administration: Group.

Manual: No manual.

Price Data, 1994: $3 per questionnaire.

Time: Administration time not reported.

Author: Project on the Status and Education of Women, Association of American Colleges.

Publisher: Center for Women Policy Studies.

Review of Relating with Colleagues: A Questionnaire for Faculty Members by RAOUL A. ARREOLA, Professor and Director of Educational Evaluation and Development, The University of Tennessee, Memphis, TN:

PURPOSE OF THE INSTRUMENT. Relating with Colleagues: A Questionnaire for Faculty

Members is published by the Association of American Colleges and is a revision of a questionnaire originally authored by the Committee on the Status of Women and the Office of Education Research at St. Olaf College in Minnesota. The purpose of the questionnaire, as stated by the authors, is to examine aspects of the day-to-day campus environment as it relates to subtle and obvious forms of sex-based discrimination. It is intended to be an all-inclusive questionnaire that can be used with both men and women to assist in determining whether current policies and practices relative to sex-based discrimination are effective and whether new programs are needed. The authors also indicate that the questionnaire can be adapted for use in recruiting, hiring, promotion, tenure, and assessing issues of concern to members of minority groups and disabled persons.

ADMINISTRATION. The instrument contains 16 items on a two-sided 11-inch x 17-inch paper folded in half to make a simple 8 1/2-inch x 11-inch booklet of two, two-sided pages. Respondents are to indicate their answers by marking small boxes next to the response options of each item. The first five questions concern the demographics of the respondent (sex, rank, employment status, length at institution, and race/ethnic origin); the next six questions ask the respondent to rate their experience with, or perceptions of, sexual harassment; the next four questions ask the respondent to indicate their perceptions of the general campus climate as to support for women and grievance procedures; and the last question is an open-ended request for comments. Considerable revision of the questionnaire would need to be conducted before it could be used for the variety of purposes for which the authors state it can be used.

Although some effort to make the items usable by males and females is evident, the questionnaire appears to be intended almost exclusively for use by women concerning the frequency of observed or perceived sexual harassment by male colleagues or supervisors. No item in the questionnaire addresses elements of discrimination based on racial, ethnic, or disabled status. There are no instructions as to how, when, or to whom the questionnaire should be administered although the structure of the items appears to be oriented primarily toward female respondents.

RELIABILITY AND VALIDITY. The structure of the instrument suggests it may have been designed to measure two factors: frequency of sexual harassment by males, and perceived campus support of women. However, no scoring key and no normative or other interpretive data are provided. No manual is provided with the questionnaire to indicate whether validity or reliability studies were conducted or what their results might have been. However, the brevity of the instrument and the structure of the items make reliability and validity of scores from the instrument extremely suspect. The questionnaire uses a different response scale for virtually every item intended to measure one of the two apparent factors of sexual harassment and campus support of women. Some items contain three choices, some four, and one contains five choices. For questions that require a simple "Yes" or "No" answer a middle position of "Sometimes" is provided. Questions that require frequency of observation responses use a scale with undefined, subjective responses such as "a few times" and "often" mixed with more objectively defined choices such as "never" and "once."

CONCLUSION. The issue of addressing sexual discrimination on college campuses, as well as that of creating and maintaining a supportive environment for a diverse and broad spectrum of faculty, is a critical one in American higher education. There is need for well-designed measures and procedures for assessing campus practices and processes associated with sexual harassment and minority concerns. This is not one of those measures. The entire instrument appears negative and intended to serve some political purpose rather than to provide valid and reliable scores for use in assessing campus organizations, policies, and practices relative to sexual discrimination in the workplace. It looks like what it is, a questionnaire constructed by a committee, and appears to have been constructed without any apparent effort to meet even basic minimal professional standards of questionnaire design and development.

[262]
Retirement Activities Card Sort Planning Kit.

Purpose: "To introduce a new perspective on adult development and a model of understanding the process of change as it relates to retirement; to stimulate personal thinking on handling retirement; and to assist participants to identify and begin planning for avenues of new growth or expanded satisfaction in retirement living."

Population: Retired adults or adults who plan to retire.

Publication Dates: 1992–1994.

Scores: Item scores only.

Administration: Group or individual.

Price Data, 1994: $12 per complete kit including manual (33 pages) and Retirement Activities Card Sort.

Time: (75–120) minutes.

Comments: 8 supplementary activities included.

Author: Richard L. Knowdell.

Publisher: Career Research & Testing, Inc.

Review of the Retirement Activities Card Sort Planning Kit by M. ALLAN COOPERSTEIN, Clinical Psychologist/Forensic Examiner: Private Practice, Willow Grove, PA:

According to Cronbach (1970) a test "is a systematic procedure for observing a person's behavior and describing it with the aid of a numerical scale or a category-system" (p. 26). Not a mental measurement, the Retirement Activities: Card Sort Planning Kit (RA) is more an exploration and workbook used in the identification and development of coping resources among individuals who are (or will be) facing retirement.

Designed primarily for use by counselors and group facilitators, the RA's purpose is to stimulate participants' development of coping skills for retirement, while identifying potential weaknesses, problem areas, and, finally, assisting in the planning and development of new growth directions to enhance personal satisfaction and adjustment in retirement.

ADMINISTRATION, SCORING, AND INTERPRETATION. The RA protocol, a 33-page booklet, was designed for groups, trios, and quartets. The entire process is said to take 1.25—2 hours. Composed of three phases, an orientation to retirement is presented first. The second phase involves the use of a card sort of present and preferred activities. In the third phase, activity worksheets are completed. The amount of time for each phase is presented.

Examples of worksheets describe present and preferred activities arranged according to how frequently they are performed. These worksheets aid participants by making them aware of the activities they have performed and the positive and negative values they attach to them. By rearranging the configurations of these activities, participants become more aware of their ordinary activity patterns and the many alternatives that may be present in their retirement.

Supplementary exercises are provided that can be done by the participant during personal time or within a group. This encourages participants to reflect upon the meanings they associate with aging, retirement, retirement readiness, residence, allocation of time, and preferred activities. Options for the management of retirement time are also generated as a result. Small group discussion is part of the process and retirement readiness scales help participants visualize where, on a numeric scale, their attitudes toward select issues would fall. The 5-point scales could also be used at a later point to assess whether positive changes have occurred.

THEORETICAL BACKGROUND AND DEVELOPMENT. Neither a theoretical background nor history of development of the instrument was provided.

NORMATIVE INFORMATION. There is no attempt to gather, standardize, or provide normative data. Neither descriptive nor categorical information is presented.

RELIABILITY AND VALIDITY. Reliability and validity are not addressed. Responses and card-sort arrangements could vary from administration to administration depending upon mood, level of disclosure, how the group is constituted, and the effect of the counselor or facilitator upon the individual or group. Arrangements would then be subject to nonsystematized interpretations that could vary from counselor to counselor, group to group.

SUMMARY. The author states that the objective of the RA is to advance an innovative view of adult development and provide a model for understanding the change process as it applies to retirement. In exploring the materials and having others try it, the RA proved useful neither in explaining developmental issues associated with aging nor in providing a model of the change process in dealing with retirement.

The RA process encourages reflection and self-disclosure. This may reveal undisclosed or unrecognized personal indecision, insecurity, anxiety, or depression. Handled sensitively, the bringing to light of these issues within a supportive setting facilitated by a competent counseling staff could assist in a better adjustment to retirement and greater clarity within participants facing this major life change.

The organization of the RA could be potentially disadvantageous unless counselors and facilitators are aware of and sensitized to the limitations of this workbook and understand the psychology of aging. By tapping feelings and attitudes associated with retirement, staff should be prepared to identify and manage reactions among group members. Powerful existential and life-change issues could arise, such as fears of death, abandonment, helplessness, dependency, infirmity, and unresolved family issues.

Negative reactions could be elicited by provocative questions found among the supplementary retirement activities. These ask participants to imagine the "penalties" of growing older, their personal "nightmare" of old age, the most frightening aspects of retirement and a retirement that has been forced upon them due to illness or company policy. Elicitation of the emotions associated with retirement and its multitude of meanings could result in an upsurge of strongly charged reactions for which staff should be trained and prepared. The author should review and reconsider modifying these wordings, evaluating their possible untoward effects on the reader population.

Within prescribed limits and recognizing the above caveats, the RA could be of some limited use for counselors working with retirement or preretirement populations. Other instruments exist, however, that better assess similar dimensions of experience with greater sophistication and empirical grounding. Some examples are: Coping Inventory for Stressful Situations (Endler & Parker, 1990), Memorial University of Newfoundland Scale of Happiness (Kozma & Stones, 1980), and Quality of Life Dimensions (Flanagan, 1980). As an alternative to the use of either the RA or the above measures alone, both could be combined in an exploratory and counseling process.

REVIEWER'S REFERENCES

Cronbach, L. J. (1970). *Essentials of psychological testing* (3rd ed.). New York: Harper & Row.

Flanagan, J. C. (1980). Quality of Life Dimensions. *Education, 100,* 194–202.

Kozma, A., & Stones, M. J. (1980). Memorial University of Newfoundland Scale of Happiness. *Journal of Gerontology, 35,* 906–912.

Endler, N. S., & Parker, J. D. A. (1990). Coping Inventory for Stressful Situations. North Tonawanda, NY: Multi-Health Systems, Inc.

Review of the Retirement Activities Card Sort Planning Kit by ROBERT B. FRARY, Professor and Director Emeritus, Office of Measurement and Research Services, Virginia Polytechnic Institute and State University, Blacksburg, VA:

This product is designed to facilitate a group activity devoted to exploring potential retirement activities and to giving retirees or potential retirees new or revised perspectives for planning retirement. It could also be used with an individual. Administration time is estimated at 75 to 120 minutes.

The kit consists of a manual for the group leader and a set of cards, each specifying and describing an activity area potentially of interest to retirees. In addition, the manual contains samples of forms for the participants to fill out in the course of the group activity. Neither the forms nor the card deck appears to be available separately from the publisher and would have to be duplicated for distribution to participants. The manual and cards, however, are copyrighted, so permission to copy them would be required. Purchasing a manual and card deck for each participant might be considered undesirable due to the cost ($12) and due to material in the manual not intended for participants.

The card set also contains cards designating frequency of the activities: Daily, Regularly, Occasionally, Seldom, and Never. The participants are asked to lay out the frequency cards and sort the activity cards according to how frequently they currently participate in each of the activity areas and then to write the activities in the frequency columns of a form entitled Present Activities Summary Sheet. The next step is to rearrange the cards according to how often the participants would prefer to participate in each activity. These preferences are also transferred to a form entitled Preferred Activities Summary Sheet. Next, participants fill out an Activities Worksheet based on the preceding two summaries. This worksheet asks, for example, what "meaningful life patterns are you already living and want to maintain" (p. 13). Then the participants identify "underlying elements that characterize these activities" (p. 13). The worksheet moves on to preferred activities and how these differ from the present ones and culminates with a request for what the potential retiree plans to do as a result of the exercise. The manual recommends group interaction during this process (e.g., people presenting what they consider the "underlying elements" in their lists or telling what they plan to do).

Though work with the card deck is the central feature of the Planning Kit, the latter part of the manual contains forms to be used for eight other group exercises. Topics include reflections on adult life and growing older, how to conduct retirement research, role options in retirement, and retirement living options. Advice on how to conduct these sessions is not provided, and, again, it would be necessary to duplicate the forms for distribution to participants.

From a psychometric standpoint, there is very little that can be said about this instrument. The participants' responses, if these can be said to constitute measurements, are of use only at the intraindividual level. No scores are produced and the responses are not designed to be compared across individuals. How effective or useful the activities might be is, of course, of concern but would surely vary widely according to the effectiveness of the facilitator and the characteristics of the participants. No information is given in the manual with respect to these concerns nor, indeed, any information about actual experience using the Planning Kit. At the least, it seems likely to this reviewer that use of the Planning Kit would be effective only with fully literate and articulate participants. A search of literature data bases revealed no report on use of or evaluation of the Planning Kit. Also not discussed in the manual are the qualifications required for the facilitator. The manual does contain a brief essay on retirement, perhaps to get the facilitator into the right frame of mind, or perhaps to be provided to the participants.

These points aside, potential users of the Planning Kit should consider whether the activity areas on the cards are appropriate for their anticipated participants. The list of 48 activities, though fairly comprehensive, is a bit idiosyncratic, and the activity areas vary greatly in specificity. Some of the activity areas are rather esoteric, such as "Massage," "Conduct a survey," or "Meditate." The more commonplace activities such as "Entertain friends" or "Watch television" may be more functional for some groups. Perhaps, for some groups of participants, inappropriate cards could be deleted from the deck or substitute cards provided. Notably, none of the cards refers to any use of computers. "Read newspapers and magazines" is included, but there is no mention of reading books. Activities devoted to personal care (beauty or barber shop, grooming, etc.) are not covered. The manual does not specify any basis for the selection of the 48 activity areas.

The Retirement Activities Card Sort Planning Kit appears not to have any broadly based empirical underpinnings. Therefore, potential users should employ caution, testing the Planning Kit initially on small groups of trial participants and evaluating the results.

[263]
Revised Hamilton Rating Scale for Depression.

Purpose: Designed as a clinician-rated scale for evaluating individuals already diagnosed with depressive illness.
Population: Depressed individuals.
Publication Date: 1994.
Acronym: RHRSD.
Scores, 22: General Screening, Depressed Mood, Feelings of Guilt, Suicide, Insomnia, Nocturnal Waking, Early Morning Waking, Work and Activities, Sexual Symptoms, Loss of Insight, Retardation, Agitation, Worry, Somatic Anxiety, Gastrointestinal Somatic Symptoms, General Somatic Symptoms, Hypochondriasis, Loss of Weight, Diurnal Variation, Obsessive-Compulsive Symptoms, Paranoid Symptoms, Depersonalization/ Derealization.
Administration: Individual.
Price Data, 1997: $65 per kit including 10 AutoScore clinican forms, 10 AutoScore self-report problem inventories, and manual (62 pages); $32.50 per 25 AutoScore clinician forms; $32.50 per 25 AutoScore self-report problem inventories; $47.50 per manual; $215 or less per 25-use IBM scoring interpretive software (3.5-inch); $15 per 100 microcomputer answer sheets; $9.50 each per FAX report service.
Time: (5–10) minutes.
Comments: A self-report scale is also provided.
Author: W. L. Warren.
Publisher: Western Psychological Services.
Cross References: See T4:2261 (10 references).

TEST REFERENCES

1. La Rue, A., D'Elia, L. F., Clark, E. O., Spar, J. E., & Jarvik, L. F. (1986). Clinical test of memory in dementia, depression, and healthy aging. *Psychology and Aging, 1,* 69-77.
2. Hart, R. P., Kwentus, J. A., Hamer, R. M., & Taylor, J. R. (1987). Selective reminding procedure in depression in dementia. *Psychology and Aging, 2,* 111-115.
3. Barlow, D. H., Craske, M. G., Cerny, J. A., & Klasko, J. S. (1989). Behavioral treatment of panic disorder. *Behavior Therapy, 20,* 261–282.
4. Blanchard, E. B., Kolb, L. C., Taylor, A. E., & Wittrock, D. A. (1989). Cardiac response to relevant stimuli as an adjunct in diagnosing post-traumatic stress disorder: Replication and extension. *Behavior Therapy, 20,* 535–543.
5. Kennedy, S. H., Craven, J. L., & Roin, G. M. (1989). Major depression in renal dialysis patients: An open trial of antidepressant therapy. *The Journal of Clinical Psychiatry, 50,* 60–63.
6. Lahmeyer, H. W., Reynolds, C. F., III, Kupfer, D. J., & King, R. (1989). Biologic markers in borderline personality disorder: A review. *The Journal of Clinical Psychiatry, 50,* 217–225.
7. Miller, I. W., Norman, W. H., Keitner, G. I., Bishop, S. B., & Dow, M. G. (1989). Cognitive-behavioral treatment of depressed inpatients. *Behavior Therapy, 20,* 25–47.
8. Sachs, G. S., Gelenberg, A. J., Bellinghausen, B., Wojcik, J., Falk, W. E., Farhadi, A. M., & Jenike, M. (1989). Ergoloid mesylates and ECT. *The Journal of Clinical Psychiatry, 50,* 87–90.
9. Anderson, I. M., Parry-Billings, M., Newsholme, E. A., Poortmans, J. R., & Cowen, P. J. (1990). Decreased plasma tryptophan concentration in major depression: Relationship to melancholia and weight loss. *Journal of Affective Disorders, 20,* 185-191.
10. Barry, S., & Dinan, T. G. (1990). Neuroendocrine challenge tests in depression: A study of growth hormone, TRH and cortisol release. *Journal of Affective Disorders, 18,* 229-234.
11. Baumgartner, A., & Sucher, N. (1990). The influence of physical activity and posture on the antidepressant effect of sleep deprivation in depressed patients. *Journal of Affective Disorders, 20,* 93-99.
12. Beasley, C. M., Jr., Sayler, M. E., Cunningham, G. E., Weiss, A. M., & Masica, D. N. (1990). Fluoxetine in tricyclic refractory major depressive disorder. *Journal of Affective Disorders, 20,* 193-200.
13. Benson, K. L., King, R., Gordon, D., Silvan, J. A., & Zarcone, V. P., Jr. (1990). Sleep patterns in borderline personality disorder. *Journal of Affective Disorders, 18,* 267-273.
14. Brainard, G. C., Sherry, D., Skwerer, R. G., Waxler, M., Kelly, K., & Rosenthal, N. G. (1990). Effects of different wavelengths in seasonal affective disorder. *Journal of Affective Disorders, 20,* 209-216.
15. Craighead, W. E. (1990). There's a place for us: All of us. *Behavior Therapy, 21,* 3–23.
16. Danish University Antidepressant Group. (1990). Paroxetine: A selective serotonin reuptake inhibitor showing better tolerance, but weaker antidepressant effect than clomipramine in a controlled multicenter study. *Journal of Affective Disorders, 18,* 289-299.
17. Frank, E., Kupfer, D. J., Bulik, C. M., & Levenson, J. A. (1990). Imipramine and weight gain during the treatment of recurrent depression. *Journal of Affective Disorders, 20,* 165-172.
18. Fudge, J. L., Perry, P. J., Garvey, M. J., & Kelly, M. W. (1990). A comparison of the effect of fluoxetine and trazodone on the cognitive functioning of depressed outpatients. *Journal of Affective Disorders, 18,* 275-280.
19. Garvey, M., DeRubeis, R. J., Hollon, S. D., Evans, M. D., & Tuason, V. B. (1990). Does 24-h urinary MHPG predict treatment response to antidepressants? II. Association between imipramine response and low MHPG. *Journal of Affective Disorders, 20,* 181-184.
20. Garvey, M., Hollon, S. D., DeRubeis, R. J., Evans, M. D., & Tuason, V. B. (1990). Does 24-h urinary MHPG predict treatment response to antidepressants? I. A review. *Journal of Affective Disorders, 20,* 173-179.
21. Garvey, M., Noyes, R., Jr., & Cook, B. (1990). Comparison of panic disordered patients with high versus low MHPG. *Journal of Affective Disorders, 20,* 7-12.
22. Gelenberg, A. J., Wojcik, J. D., Falk, W. E., Baldessarini, R. J., Zeisel, S. H., Schoenfeld, D., & Mok, G. S. (1990). Tyrosine for depression: A double-blind trial. *Journal of Affective Disorders, 19,* 125-132.
23. Hagman, J. O., Buchsbaum, M. S., Wu, J. C., Rao, S. J., Reynolds, C. A., & Blinder, B. J. (1990). Comparison of regional brain metabolism in bulimia nervosa and affective disorder assessed with positron emission tomography. *Journal of Affective Disorders, 19,* 153-162.
24. Haug, H.-J., & Fähndrich, E. (1990). Diurnal variations of mood in depressed patients in relation to severity of depression. *Journal of Affective Disorders, 19,* 37-41.
25. Hubain, P. P., Castro, P., Mesters, P., De Maertelaer, V., & Mendlewicz, J. (1990). Alprazolam and amitriptyline in the treatment of major depressive disorder: A double-blind clinical and sleep EEG study. *Journal of Affective Disorders, 18,* 67-73.
26. Ingram, R. E., Atkinson, J. H., Slater, M. A., Saccuzzo, D. P., & Garfin, S. R. (1990). Negative and positive cognition in depressed and nondepressed chronic-pain patients. *Health Psychology, 9,* 300-314.
27. Kasper, S., Rogers, S. L. B., Madden, P. A., Joseph-Vanderpool, J. R., & Rosenthal, N. E. (1990). The effects of phototherapy in the general population. *Journal of Affective Disorders, 18,* 211-219.
28. Korner, A., Nielsen, B. M., Eschen, F., Moller-Madsen, S., Stender, A., Christensen, E. M., Aggernaes, H., Kastrup, M., & Larsen, J. K. (1990). *Journal of Affective Disorders, 20,* 143-149.

29. Kräuchi, K., Wirz-Justice, A., & Graw, P. (1990). The relationship of affective state to dietary preference: Winter depression and light therapy as a model. *Journal of Affective Disorders, 20,* 43-53.

30. Kravitz, H. M., Edwards, J. H., Fawcett, J., & Fogg, L. (1990). Challenging the amphetamine challenge test: Report of an antidepressant treatment study. *Journal of Affective Disorders, 20,* 121-128.

31. Maes, M., Jacobs, M.-P., Suy, E., Leclerq, C., Christiaens, F., & Raus, J. (1990). An augmented escape of B-endorphins to suppression by dexamethasone in severely depressed patients. *Journal of Affective Disorders, 18,* 149-156.

32. Maes, M., Schotte, C., Scharpé, S., Martin, M., & Blockx, P. (1990). The effects of glucocorticoids on the availability of L-tryptophan and tyrosine in the plasma of depressed patients. *Journal of Affective Disorders, 18,* 121-127.

33. Maes, M., Vandewoude, M., Schotte, C., Martin, M., & Blockx, P. (1990). Suppressive effects of dexamethasone on hypothalamic-pituitary-thyroid axis function in depressed patients. *Journal of Affective Disorders, 20,* 55-61.

34. Mobayed, M., & Dinan, T. G. (1990). Buspirone/prolactin response in post head injury depression. *Journal of Affective Disorders, 19,* 237-241.

35. Moller, S. E., Bech, P., Bjerrum, H., Bojholm, S., Butler, B., Folker, H., Gram, L. F., Larsen, J. K., Lauritzen, L., Loldrup, D., Munk-Andersen, E., Odum, K., & Rafaelsen, O. J. (1990). Plasma ratio tryptophan/neutral amino acids in relation to clinical response to paroxetine and clonsipramine in patients with major depression. *Journal of Affective Disorders, 18,* 59-66.

36. Monteleone, P., Maj, M., Iovino, M., & Steardo, L. (1990). GABA, depression and the mechanism of action of antidepressant drugs: A neuroendocrine approach. *Journal of Affective Disorders, 20,* 1-5.

37. Monti, J. M., Alterwain, P., & Monti, D. (1990). The effects of moclobemide on nocturnal sleep of depressed patients. *Journal of Affective Disorders, 20,* 201-208.

38. Morphy, M. A., Fava, G. A., Pedersen, R. C., Zielezny, M., Sonino, N., & Brownie, A. C. (1990). Effects of metyrapone and dexamethasone upon pro-gamma-MSH plasma levels in depressed patients and healthy controls. *Journal of Affective Disorders, 19,* 183-189.

39. Neimeyer, R. A., & Feixas, G. (1990). The role of homework and skill acquisition in the outcome of group cognitive therapy for depression. *Behavior Therapy, 21,* 281-292.

40. Nelson, J. C., Mazure, C. M., & Jatlow, P. I. (1990). Does melancholia predict response in major depression? *Journal of Affective Disorders, 18,* 157-165.

41. Nierenberg, A. A., Price, L. H., Charney, D. S., & Heninger, G. R. (1990). After lithium augmentation: A restrospective follow-up of patients with antidepressants-refractory depression. *Journal of Affective Disorders, 18,* 167-175.

42. Oei, T. P. S., Wanstall, K., & Evans, L. (1990). Sex differences in panic disorder with agoraphobia. *Journal of Anxiety Disorders, 4,* 317-324.

43. O'Neill, B., & Leonard, B. E. (1990). Abnormal zymosan-induced neutrophil chemiluminescence as a marker of depression. *Journal of Affective Disorders, 19,* 265-272.

44. Pande, A. C., Grunhaus, L. J., Haskett, R. F., & Greden, J. F. (1990). Electroconvulsive therapy in delusional and non-delusional depressive disorder. *Journal of Affective Disorders, 19,* 215-219.

45. Russ, M. J., Ackerman, S. H., Banay-Schwartz, M., Shindledecker, R. D., & Smith, G. P. (1990). Plasma tryptophan to large neutral amino acid ratios in depressed and normal subjects. *Journal of Affective Disorders, 19,* 9-14.

46. Sheehan, D. Y., Raj, A. B., Harnett-Sheehan, K., Soto, S., & Lewis, C. P. (1990). Adinazolam sustained release formulation in the treatment of generalized anxiety disorder. *Journal of Anxiety Disorders, 4,* 239-246.

47. Stinson, D., & Thompson, C. (1990). Clinical experience with phototherapy. *Journal of Affective Disorders, 18,* 129-135.

48. Tsujimoto, T., Yamada, N., Shimoda, K., Hanada, K., & Takahashi, S. (1990). Circadian rhythms in depression. Part II: Circadian rhythms in inpatients with various mental disorders. *Journal of Affective Disorders, 18,* 199-210.

49. van den Burg, W., Bouhuys, A. L., van den Hoofdakker, R. H., & Beersma, D. G. M. (1990). Sleep deprivation in bright and dim light: Antidepressant effects on major depressive disorder. *Journal of Affective Disorders, 19,* 109-117.

50. Volz, H.-P., Mackert, A., Stieglitz, R.-D., & Müller-Oerlinghausen, B. (1990). Effect of bright white light therapy on non-seasonal depressive disorder. Preliminary results. *Journal of Affective Disorders, 19,* 15-21.

51. Agosti, V., Stewart, J. W., & Ouitkin, F. M. (1991). Life satisfaction and psychosocial functioning in chronic depression: Effect of acute treatment with antidepressants. *Journal of Affective Disorders, 23,* 35-41.

52. Besson, J. A. O., Holland, J., Wheeldon, T., & Ebmeier, K. P. (1991). Red blood cell NMR proton relaxation times in ill and recovered patients with unipolar and bipolar affective disorders. *Journal of Affective Disorders, 21,* 89-92.

53. Bouhuys, A. L., Jansen, C. J., & van den Hoofdakker, R. H. (1991). Analysis of observed behaviors displayed by depressed patients during a clinical interview: Relationships between behavioral factors and clinical concepts of activation. *Journal of Affective Disorders, 21,* 79-88.

54. Bouhuys, A. L., & van den Hoofdakker, R. H. (1991). The interrelatedness of observed behavior of depressed patients and of a psychiatrist: An ethological study on mutual influence. *Journal of Affective Disorders, 23,* 63-74.

55. Brodaty, H., Peters, K., Boyce, P., Hickie, I., Parker, G., Mitchell, P., & Wilhelm, K. (1991). Age and depression. *Journal of Affective Disorders, 23,* 137-149.

56. Deltito, J. A., Moline, M., Pollak, C., Martin, L. Y., & Manemmani, I. (1991). Effects of phototherapy on non-seasonal unipolar and bipolar depressive spectrum disorders. *Journal of Affective Disorders, 23,* 231-237.

57. Fedoroff, J. P., Lipsey, J. R., Starkstein, S. E., Forrester, A., Price, T. R., & Robinson, R. G. (1991). Phenomenological comparisons of major depression

following stroke, myocardial infarction or spinal cord lesions. *Journal of Affective Disorders, 22,* 83-89.

58. Goetz, R. R., Puig-Antich, J., Dahl, R. E., Ryan, N. D., Asnis, G. M., Rabinovich, H., & Nelson, B. (1991). EEG sleep of young adults with major depression: A controlled study. *Journal of Affective Disorders, 22,* 91-100.

59. Grigoroiu-Serbânescu, M., Christodorescu, D., Mâgureanu, S., Jipescu, I., Totoescu, A., Marinescu, E., Ardelean, V., & Popa, S. (1991). Adolescent offspring of endogenous unipolar depressive parents and of normal parents. *Journal of Affective Disorders, 21,* 185-198.

60. Günther, V., & Kryspin-Exner, I. (1991). Ergopsychometry in depressive patients. *Journal of Affective Disorders, 23,* 81-92.

61. Hooijer, C., Zitman, F. G., Griez, E., Tilburg, W. V., Willemse, A., & Dinkgreve, M. A. H. M. (1991). The Hamilton Depression Rating Scale (HDRS): Changes in scores as a function of training and version used. *Journal of Affective Disorders, 22,* 21-29.

62. Jarrett, R. B., Giles, D. Z., Gullion, C. M., & Rush, A. J. (1991). Does learned resourcefulness predict response to cognitive therapy in depressed outpatients? *Journal of Affective Disorders, 23,* 223-229.

63. Knott, V., Lupierre, Y., Griffiths, L., de Lugt, D., & Bakish, D. (1991). Event-related potentials and selective attention in major depressive illness. *Journal of Affective Disorders, 23,* 43-48.

64. Lex, B. W. (1991). Some gender differences in alcohol and polysubstance users. *Health Psychology, 10,* 121-132.

65. Lykouras, L., Markianos, M., Hatzimanolis, J., & Stefanis, C. (1991). Effects of ECT course on TSH and prolactin responses to TRH in depressed patients. *Journal of Affective Disorders, 23,* 191-197.

66. Maes, M., Bosmans, E., Suy, E., Vandervorst, C., DeJonckheere, C., & Raus, J. (1991). Antiphospholipid, antinuclear, Epstein-Barr and cytomegalovirus antibodies, and soluble interleukin-2 receptors in depressive patients. *Journal of Affective Disorders, 21,* 133-140.

67. Maes, M., DeJonckheere, C., Vandervorst, C., Schotte, C., Cosyns, P., Raus, J., & Suy, E. (1991). Abnormal pituitary function during melancholia: Reduced alpha-melanocyte-stimulating hormone secretion and increased intact ACTH non-suppression. *Journal of Affective Disorders, 22,* 149-157.

68. Maes, M., Vandewoude, M., Scharpé, S., Clercq, L. D., Stevens, W., Lepoutre, L., & Schutte, C. (1991). Anthropometric and biochemical assessment of the nutritional state in depression: Evidence for lower visceral protein plasma levels in depression. *Journal of Affective Disorders, 23,* 25-33.

69. Magnusson, A., & Kristbjarnarson, H. (1991). Treatment of seasonal affective disorder with high-intensity light. *Journal of Affective Disorders, 21,* 141-147.

70. Meesters, Y., Lambers, P. A., Jansen, J. H. C., Bouhuys, A. L., Beersma, D. G. M., & van den Hoofdakker, R. H. (1991). Can winter depression be prevented by light treatment? *Journal of Affective Disorders, 23,* 75-79.

71. Nagayama, H., Nagano, K., Ikezaki, A., & Tashiro, T. (1991). Prediction of efficacy of antidepressant by 1-week test therapy in depression. *Journal of Affective Disorders, 23,* 213-216.

72. Nagayama, H., Sasaki, M., Ichii, S., Hanada, K., Okawa, M., Ohta, T., Asano, Y., Sugita, Y., Yamazaki, J., Kohsaka, M., Kotorii, T., Maeda, K., Okamoto, N., Ishizuka, Y., Takahashi, K., Honda, Y., & Takahashi, S. (1991). Atypical depressive symptoms possibly predict responsiveness to phototherapy in seasonal affective disorder. *Journal of Affective Disorders, 23,* 185-189.

73. Noguera, R., Altuna, R., Alvarez, E., Ayuso, J. L., Casais, L., & Udina, C. (1991). Fluoxetine vs. clomipramine in depressed patients: A controlled multicentre trial. *Journal of Affective Disorders, 22,* 119-124.

74. O'Hanlon, M., Barry, S., Clare, A. W., & Dinan, T. G. (1991). Serum thyrotropin response to thyrotropin-releasing hormone in alcohol-dependent patients with and without depression. *Journal of Affective Disorders, 21,* 109-115.

75. Parker, G., Hadzi-Pavlovic, D., Hickie, I., Boyce, P., Mitchell, P., Wilhelm, K., & Brodaty, H. (1991). Distinguishing psychotic and non-psychotic melancholia. *Journal of Affective Disorders, 22,* 134-148.

76. Rupprecht, R., Kornhuber, J., Wodarz, N., Lugauer, J., Göbel, C., Riederer, P., & Beckmann, H. (1991). Lymphocyte glucocorticoid receptor binding during depression and after clinical recovery. *Journal of Affective Disorders, 22,* 31-35.

77. Takahashi, K., Asano, Y., Kohsaka, M., Okawa, M., Sasaki, M., Honda, Y., Higuchi, T., Yamazaki, J., Ishizuka, Y., Kawaguchi, K., Ohta, T., Hanada, K., Sugita, Y., Maeda, K., Nagayama, H., Kotorii, T., Egashira, K., & Takahashi, S. (1991). Multi-center study of seasonal affective disorders in Japan. A preliminary report. *Journal of Affective Disorders, 21,* 57-65.

78. Thase, M. E., Bowler, K., & Harden, T. (1991). Cognitive behavior therapy of endogenous depression: Part 2: Preliminary findings in 16 unmedicated patients. *Behavior Therapy, 22,* 469-477.

79. Thase, M. E., Simons, A. D., Cahalane, J. F., & McGeary, J. (1991). Cognitive behavior therapy of endogenous depression: Part 1: An outpatient clinical replication series. *Behavior Therapy, 22,* 457-467.

80. Thase, M. E., & Wright, J. H. (1991). Cognitive behavior therapy manual for depressed inpatients: A treatment protocol outline. *Behavior Therapy, 22,* 579-595.

81. Theodorou, A. E., Lawrence, K. M., Healy, D., Whitehouse, A. M., White, W., Wilton-Cox, H., Kerry, S. M., Horton, R. W., & Paybel, E. S. (1991). Platelet alpha-sub-2-adrenoceptors, defined with agonist and antagonist ligands, in depressed patients, prior to and following treatment. *Journal of Affective Disorders, 23,* 99-106.

82. Wehr, T. A., Giesen, H. A., Schulz, P. M., Anderson, J. L., Joseph-Vanderpool, J. R., Kelly, K., Kasper, S., & Rosenthal, N. E. (1991). Contrasts between symptoms of summer depression and winter depression. *Journal of Affective Disorders, 23,* 173-183.

83. Winter, P., Philipp, M., Buller, R., Delmo, C. D., Schwarze, H., & Benkert, O. (1991). Identification of minor affective disorders and implications for psychopharmacology. *Journal of Affective Disorders, 22*, 125-133.

84. Wodarz, N., Rupprecht, R., Kornhuber, J., Schmitz, B., Wild, K., Braner, H. U., & Riederer, P. (1991). Normal lymphocyte responsiveness to lectins but impaired sensitivity to in vitro glucocorticoids in major depression. *Journal of Affective Disorders, 22*, 241-248.

85. Anderson, D. N., Abou-Saleh, T., Collins, J., Hughes, K., Cattell, R. J., Hamon, C. G. B., Blair, J. A., & Dewey, M. E. (1992). Pterin metabolism in depression: An extension of the amine hypothesis and possible marker of response to ECT. *Psychological Medicine, 22*, 863-869.

86. Arnold, E., Fineberg, N., Hannah, P., Glover, V., Pitt, B., & Sandler, M. (1992). Is the tyramine test for depressive illness useful in elderly patients? *Journal of Affective Disorders, 26*, 1-6.

87. Austin, M. P., Dougall, N., Ross, M., Murray, C., O'Carroll, R. E., Moffoot, A., Ebmeier, K. P., & Goodwin, G. M. (1992). Single photon emission tomography with 99mTc-exametazime in major depression and the pattern of brain activity underlying the psychotic/neurotic continuum. *Journal of Affective Disorders, 26*, 31-44.

88. Austin, M.-P., Ross, M., Murray, C., O'Carroll, R. E., Ebmeier, K. P., & Goodwin, G. M. (1992). Cognitive function in major depression. *Journal of Affective Disorders, 25*, 21-30.

89. Banki, C. M., Karmacsi, L., Bissette, G., & Nemeroff, C. B. (1992). Cerebrospinal fluid neuropeptides in mood disorder and dementia. *Journal of Affective Disorders, 25*, 39-46.

90. Barlow, D. H., Rapee, R. M., & Brown, T. A. (1992). Behavioral treatment of generalized anxiety disorder. *Behavior Therapy, 23*, 551-570.

91. Bellini, L., Gatti, F., Gasperini, M., & Smeraldi, E. (1992). A comparison between delusional and non-delusional depressives. *Journal of Affective Disorders, 25*, 129-138.

92. Bench, C. J., Friston, K. J., Brown, R. G., Scott, L. C., Frackowiak, R. S. J., & Dolan, R. J. (1992). The anatomy of melancholia—focal abnormalities of cerebral blood flow in major depression. *Psychological Medicine, 22*, 607-615.

93. Birtchnell, J., Falkowski, J., & Steffert, B. (1992). The negative relating of depressed patients: A new approach. *Journal of Affective Disorders, 24*, 165-176.

94. Bouhuys, A. L., & Albersnagel, F. A. (1992). Do interactional capacities based on observed behaviour interfere with improvement in severely depressed patients? A longitudinal study. *Journal of Affective Disorders, 25*, 107-116.

95. Bouman, T. K., de Vries, J., & Koopmans, I. H. (1992). Lithuim prophylaxis and interepisode mood. *Journal of Affective Disorders, 24*, 199-206.

96. Brand, E., & Clingempeel, W. G. (1992). Group behavioral therapy with depressed geriatric inpatients: An assessment of incremental efficacy. *Behavior Therapy, 23*, 475-482.

97. Brand, A. N., Jolles, J., & Wied, C. G-d. (1992). Recall and recognition memory deficits in depression. *Journal of Affective Disorders, 25*, 77-86.

98. Brown, K. W., & White, T. (1992). Sub-syndromes of tardive dyskinesia and some clinical correlates. *Psychological Medicine, 22*, 923-927.

99. Butler, J., O'Halloran, A., & Leonard, B. E. (1992). The Galway study of panic disorder II: Changes in some peripheral markers of nonadrenergic and serotonergic function in DSM-III-R panic disorder. *Journal of Affective Disorders, 26*, 89-100.

100. Carlson, G. A., Rapport, M. D., Pataki, C. S., & Kelly, K. L. (1992). Lithium in hospitalized children at 4 and 8 weeks: Mood, behavior and cognitive effects. *Journal of Child Psychology and Psychiatry and Allied Disciplines, 33*, 411-425.

101. Cassano, G. B., Akiskal, H. S., Savino, M., Musetti, L., & Perugi, G. (1992). Proposed subtypes of bipolar II and related disorders: With hypomanic episodes (or cyclothymia) and with hyperthymic temperament. *Journal of Affective Disorders, 26*, 127-140.

102. Celada, P., Dolera, M., Alvarez, E., & Artigas, F. (1992). Effects of acute and chronic treatment with fluroxamine on extracellular and platelet serotonin in the blood of major depressive patients. Relationship to clinical improvement. *Journal of Affective Disorders, 25*, 243-250.

103. Daimon, K., Yamada, N., Tsujimoto, T., & Takahashi, S. (1992). Circadian rhythm abnormalities of deep body temperature in depressive disorders. *Journal of Affective Disorders, 26*, 191-198.

104. da Roza Davis, J. M., Sharpley, A. L., Solomon, R. A., & Cowen, P. J. (1992). Sleep and 5-HT$_2$ receptor sensitivity in recovered depressed patients. *Journal of Affective Disorders, 24*, 177-182.

105. Delvenne, V., Kerkhofs, M., Appleboom-Fondu, J., Lucas, F., & Mendlewicz, J. (1992). Sleep polygraphic variables in anorexia nervosa and depression: A comparative study in adolescents. *Journal of Affective Disorders, 25*, 167-172.

106. Eastman, C., Lahmeyer, H. W., Watell, L. G., Good, G. D., & Young, M. A. (1992). A placebo-controlled trial of light treatment for winter depression. *Journal of Affective Disorders, 26*, 211-222.

107. Fahy, T. J., O'Rourke, D., Brophy, J., Schazmann, W., & Sciascia, S. (1992). The Galway study of panic disorder I: Clomipramine and lofepramine in DSM-III-R panic disorder: A placebo controlled trial. *Journal of Affective Disorders, 25*, 63-76.

108. Fava, M., Rosenbaum, J. F., Cohen, L., Reiter, S., McCarthy, M., Steingard, R., & Clancy, K. (1992). High-dose fluoxetine in the treatment of depressed patients not responsive to a standard dose of fluoxetine. *Journal of Affective Disorders, 25*, 229-234.

109. Frank, E., Kupfer, D. J., Buhari, A., McEachran, A. B., & Grochocinski, V. J. (1992). Imipramine and weight gain during the long-term treatment of recurrent depression. *Journal of Affective Disorders, 26*, 65-72.

110. Gann, H., Riemann, D., Hohagen, F., Dressing, H., Müller, W. E., & Berger, M. (1992). The sleep structure of patients with anxiety disorders in comparison to that of healthy controls and depressive patients under baseline conditions and after cholinergic stimulation. *Journal of Affective Disorders, 26*, 179-190.

111. Gastpar, M., Gilsdorf, U., Abou-Saleh, M. T., & Ngo-Khac, T. (1992). Clinical correlates of response to DST. The Dexamethasone Suppression Test in depression: A World Health Organisation collaborative study. *Journal of Affective Disorders, 26*, 17-24.

112. Hickie, I., & Parker, G. (1992). The impact of an uncaring partner on improvement in non-melancholic depression. *Journal of Affective Disorders, 25*, 147-160.

113. Irwin, M., Lacher, U., & Caldwell, C. (1992). Depression and reduced natural killer cytotoxicity: A longitudinal study of depressed patients and control subjects. *Psychological Medicine, 22*, 1045-1050.

114. Jagadeesh, H. N., Gangadhar, B. N., Janakiramaiah, N., Subbakrishna, D. K., & Jain, S. (1992). Time dependent therapeutic effects of single electroconvulsive therapy (ECT) in endogenous depression. *Journal of Affective Disorders, 24*, 291-296.

115. Johnson-Sabine, E., Reiss, D., & Dayson, D. (1992). Bulimia nervosa: A 5-year follow-up study. *Psychological Medicine, 22*, 951-959.

116. Koeter, M. W. J., & van dem Brink, W. (1992). The relationship between depression and anxiety: Construction of a prototypical anxiety and depression scale. *Psychological Medicine, 22*, 597-606.

117. Lam, R. W., Buchanan, A., Mador, J. A., Corral, M. R., & Remick, R. A. (1992). The effects of ultraviolet-A wavelengths in light therapy for seasonal depression. *Journal of Affective Disorders, 24*, 237-244.

118. Lanczik, M., Spingler, H., Heidrich, A., Becker, T., Kretzer, B., Albert, P., & Fritze, J. (1992). Post partum blues: Depressive disease or pseudoneurasthenic syndrome. *Journal of Affective Disorders, 25*, 47-52.

119. Leibenluft, E., Noonan, B. M., & Wehr, T. A. (1992). Diurnal variation: Reliability of measurement and relationship to typical and atypical symptoms of depression. *Journal of Affective Disorders, 26*, 199-204.

120. Loas, G., Salinas, E., Guelfi, J. D., & Samuel-Lajeunesse, B. (1992). Physical anhedonia in major depressive disorder. *Journal of Affective Disorders, 25*, 139-146.

121. Maes, M., Scharpé, S., Van Grootel, L., Uyttenbroeck, W., Cooreman, W., Cosyns, P., & Suy, E. (1992). Higher a-sub-1-antitrypsin, haptoglobin, ceruloplasmin and lower retinal binding protein plasma levels during depression: Further evidence for the existence of an inflammatory response during that illness. *Journal of Affective Disorders, 24*, 183-192.

122. Maes, M., Stevens, W. J., DeClerck, L. S., Bridts, C. H., Schotte, C., & Cosyns, P. (1992). A significantly increased number and percentage of B cells in depressed subjects: Results of flow cytometric measurements. *Journal of Affective Disorders, 24*, 127-134.

123. Mitchell, P., Parker, G., Jamieson, K., Wilhelm, K., Hickie, I., Brodaty, H., Boyce, P., Hadzi-Pavlovic, D., & Roy, K. (1992). Are there any differences between bipolar and unipolar melancholia? *Journal of Affective Disorders, 25*, 97-106.

124. Möller, H. J., & Volz, H. P. (1992). Brofaromine in major depressed patients: A controlled clinical trial versus imipramine and open follow-up of up to one year. *Journal of Affective Disorders, 26*, 163-172.

125. Muir, W. J., St. Clair, D. M., Blackwood, D. H. R., Roxburgh, H. M., & Marshall, I. (1992). Eye-tracking dysfunction in the affective psychoses and schizophrenia. *Psychological Medicine, 22*, 573-580.

126. O'Keane, V., McLoughlin, D., & Dinan, T. G. (1992). D-fenfluramine-induced prolactin and cortisol release in major depression: Response to treatment. *Journal of Affective Disorders, 26*, 143-150.

127. Peselow, E. D., Fieve, R. R., & DiFiglia, C. (1992). Personality traits and response to desipramine. *Journal of Affective Disorders, 24*, 209-216.

128. Quintana, J. (1992). Platelet serotonin and plasma tryptophan decreases in endogenous depression. Clinical, therapeutic, and biological correlations. *Journal of Affective Disorders, 24*, 55-62.

129. Rybakowski, J., & Plocka, M. (1992). Seasonal variations of the dexamethasone suppression test in depression compared with schizophrenia: A gender effect. *Journal of Affective Disorders, 24*, 87-91.

130. Steinmeyer, E. M., & Möller, H. J. (1992). Facet theoretic analysis of the Hamilton-D scale. *Journal of Affective Disorders, 25*, 53-62.

131. Stuart, S., Simons, A. D., Thase, M. E., & Pilkonis, P. (1992). Are personality assessments valid in acute major depression? *Journal of Affective Disorders, 24*, 281-290.

132. Wetzel, R. D., Murphy, G. E., Carney, R. M., Whitworth, P., & Knesevich, M. A. (1992). Prescribing therapy for depression: The role of learned resourcefulness, a failure to replicate. *Psychological Reports, 70*, 803-807.

133. Wilson, D. A., Mulder, R. T., & Joyce, P. R. (1992). Diurnal profiles of thyroid hormones are altered in depression. *Journal of Affective Disorders, 24*, 11-16.

134. Wodarz, N., Rupprecht, R., Kornhuber, J., Schmitz, B., Wild, K., & Riederer, P. (1992). Cell-mediated immunity and its glucocorticoid-sensitivity after clinical recovery from severe major depressive disorder. *Journal of Affective Disorders, 25*, 31-38.

135. Anton, R. F., Jr., & Burch, E. A., Jr. (1993). Response of psychotic depression subtypes to pharmacotherapy. *Journal of Affective Disorders, 28*, 125-131.

136. Bench, C. J., Friston, K. J., Brown, R. G., Frackowiak, R. S. J., & Dolan, R. J. (1993). Regional cerebral blood flow in depression measured by positron emission tomography: The relationship with clinical dimensions. *Psychological Medicine, 23*, 579-590.

137. Berman, K., Lam, R. W., & Goldner, E. M. (1993). Eating attitudes in seasonal affective disorder and bulimia nervosa. *Journal of Affective Disorders, 29*, 219-225.

138. Bouhuys, A. L., & Van den Hoofdakker, R. H. (1993). A longitudinal study of interaction patterns of a psychiatrist and severely depressed patients based on observed behaviour: An ethological approach of interpersonal theories of depression. *Journal of Affective Disorders, 27*, 87-90.

139. Boyce, P., Hickie, I., Parker, G., Mitchell, P., Wilhelm, K., & Brodaty, H. (1993). Specificity of interpersonal sensitivity to non-melancholic depression. *Journal of Affective Disorders, 27,* 101-105.

140. Brown, T. A., Moras, K., Zinbarg, R. E., & Barlow, D. H. (1993). Diagnostic and symptom distinguishability of generalized anxiety disorder and obsessive-compulsive disorder. *Behavior Therapy, 24,* 227–240.

141. Channon, S., Baker, J. E., & Robertson, M. M. (1993). Working memory in clinical depression: An experimental study. *Psychological Medicine, 23,* 87-91.

142. Danish University Antidepressant Group. (1993). Moclobemide: A reversible MOA-A-inhibitor showing weaker antidepressant effect than clomipramine in a controlled multicenter study. *Journal of Affective Disorders, 28,* 105-116.

143. Dassa, D., Kaladjian, A., Azorin, J. M., & Giudicelli, S. (1993). Clozapine in the treatment of psychotic refractory depression. *British Journal of Psychiatry, 163,* 822-824.

144. Dunn, G., Sham, P., & Hand, D. (1993). Statistics and the nature of depression. *Psychological Medicine, 23,* 871-889.

145. Feighner, J. P., Cohn, J. B., Fabre, L. F., Jr., Fiere, R. R., Mendels, J., Shrivastara, R. K., & Dunbar, G. C. (1993). A study comparing paroxetine placebo and imipramine in depressed patients. *Journal of Affective Disorders, 28,* 71-79.

146. Flick, S. N., Roy-Byrne, P. P., Cowley, D. S., Shores, M. M., & Dunner, D. L. (1993). DSM-III-R personality disorders in a mood and anxiety disorders clinic: Prevalence, comorbidity, and clinical correlates. *Journal of Affective Disorders, 27,* 71-79.

147. Frank, E., Kupfer, D. J., Perel, J. M., Cornes, C., Mallinger, A. G., Thase, M. E., McEachran, A. B., & Grochocinski, V. J. (1993). Comparison of full-dose versus half-dose pharmacotherapy in the maintenance treatment of recurrent depression. *Journal of Affective Disorders, 27,* 139-145.

148. Fu, Z. F., Amsterdam, J. D., Kao, M., Shankar, V., Koprowski, H., & Dietzschold, B. (1993). Detection of borna disease virus-reactive antibodies from patients with affective disorders by western immunoblot technique. *Journal of Affective Disorders, 27,* 61-68.

149. Gangadhar, B. N., Ancy, J., Janakiramaiah, N., & Umapathy, C. (1993). P300 amplitude in non-bipolar, melancholic depression. *Journal of Affective Disorders, 28,* 57-60.

150. Gangadhar, B. N., Janakiramaiah, N., Subbakrishna, D. K., Praveen, J., & Reddy, A. K. (1993). Twice versus thrice weekly ECT in melancholia: A double-blind prospective comparison. *Journal of Affective Disorders, 27,* 273-278.

151. Goodwin, G. M., Austin, M-P., Curran, S. M., Ross, M., Murray, C., Prentice, N., Ebmeier, K. P., Bennie, J., Carroll, S., Dick, H., & Fink, G. (1993). The elevation of plasma B-endorphin levels in major depression. *Journal of Affective Disorders, 29,* 281-289.

152. Goodwin, G. M., Austin, M.-P., Dougall, N., Ross, M., Murray, C., O'Carroll, R. E., Moffoot, A., Prentice, N., & Ebmeier, K. P. (1993). State changes in brain activity shown by the uptake of 99mTc-exametazine with single photon emission tomography in major depression before and after treatment. *Journal of Affective Disorders, 29,* 243-253.

153. Jolly, J. B. (1993). A multi-method test of the cognitive content-specificity hypothesis in young adolescents. *Journal of Anxiety Disorders, 7,* 223-233.

154. Jolly, J. B., Aruffo, J. F., Wherry, J. N., & Livingston, R. (1993). The utility of the Beck Anxiety Inventory with inpatient adolescents. *Journal of Anxiety Disorders, 7,* 95-106.

155. Jorge, R. E., Robinson, R. G., Arndt, S. V., Starkstein, S. E., Forrester, A. W., & Geisler, F. (1993). Depression following traumatic brain injury: A 1 year longitudinal study. *Journal of Affective Disorders, 27,* 233-243.

156. Katon, W., Sullivan, M., Russo, J., Dobie, R., & Sakai, C. (1993). Depressive symptoms and measures of disability: A prospective study. *Journal of Affective Disorders, 27,* 245-254.

157. Katona, C. L. E., Healy, D., Paykel, E. S., Theodorou, A. E., Lawrence, K. M., Whitehouse, A., White, B., & Horton, R. W. (1993). Growth hormone and physiological responses to clonidine in depression. *Psychological Medicine, 23,* 57-63.

158. Keller, M. B., Lavori, P. W., Goldenberg, I. M., Baker, L. A., Pollack, M. H., Sachs, G. S., Rosenbaum, J. F., Deltito, J. A., Leon, A., Shear, K., & Klerman, G. L. (1993). Influence of depression on the treatment of panic disorder with imipramine, alprazolam, and placebo. *Journal of Affective Disorders, 28,* 27-38.

159. Letemendia, F. J. J., Delva, N. J., Rodenburg, M., Lawson, J. S., Inglis, J., Waldron, J. J., & Lywood, D. W. (1993). Therapeutic advantage of bifrontal electrode placement in ECT. *Psychological Medicine, 23,* 349-360.

160. Levitt, A. J., Joffe, R. T., Brecher, D., & MacDonald, C. (1993). Anxiety disorders and anxiety symptoms in a clinical sample of seasonal and non-seasonal depressives. *Journal of Affective Disorders, 28,* 51-56.

161. Maes, M., Meltzer, H. Y., Suy, E., Minner, B., Calabrese, J., & Cosyns, P. (1993). Sleep disorders and anxiety as symptom profiles of sympathoadrenal system hyperactivity in major depression. *Journal of Affective Disorders, 27,* 197-207.

162. Marin, R. S., Firinciogullari, S., & Biedrzycki, R. C. (1993). The sources of convergence between measures of apathy and depression. *Journal of Affective Disorders, 28,* 117-124.

163. Meesters, Y., Jansen, J. H. C., Beersma, D. G. M., Bouhuys, A. L., van den Hoofdakker, R. H. (1993). Early light treatment can prevent an emerging winter depression from developing into a full-blown depression. *Journal of Affective Disorders, 29,* 41-47.

164. Meesters, Y., Jansen, J. H. C., Lambers, P. A., Bouhuys, A. L., Beersma, D. G. M., & van den Hoofdakker, R. H. (1993). Morning and evening light treatment of seasonal affective disorder: Response, relapse, and prediction. *Journal of Affective Disorders, 28,* 165-177.

165. Moeller, F. G., Gillin, J. C., Irwin, M., Golshan, S., Kripke, D. F., & Schuckit, M. (1993). A comparison of sleep EEGs in patients with primary major depression and major depression secondary to alcoholism. *Journal of Affective Disorders, 27,* 39-42.

166. Moller, S. E., & Danish University Antidepressant Group. (1993). Plasma amino acid profiles in relation to clinical response to moclobemide in patients with major depression. *Journal of Affective Disorders, 27,* 225-231.

167. Moore, R. G., & Blackburn, I. (1993). Sociotropy, autonomy and personal memories in depression. *British Journal of Clinical Psychology, 32,* 460-462.

168. Nolen, W. A., Haffmans, P. M. J., Bouvy, P. F., & Duivenvoorden, H. J. (1993). Hypnotics as concurrent medication in depression. A placebo-controlled, double-blind comparison of flunitrazepam and lormetazepam in patients with major depression, treated with a (tri)cyclic antidepressant. *Journal of Affective Disorders, 28,* 179-188.

169. Nolen, W. A., Haffmans, P. M. J., Bouvy, P. F., & Duivenvoorden, H. J. (1993). Monoamine oxidase inhibitors in resistant major depression. A double-blind comparison of brofaromine and tranylcypromine in patients resistant to tricyclic antidepressants. *Journal of Affective Disorders, 28,* 189-197.

170. Papadimitriou, G. N., Christodoulou, G. N., Katsouyanni, K., & Stefanis, C. N. (1993). Therapy and prevention of affective illness by total sleep deprivation. *Journal of Affective Disorders, 27,* 107-116.

171. Pardoen, D., Bauwens, F., Tracy, A., Martin, F., & Mandlewicz, J. (1993). Self-esteem in recovered bipolar and unipolar out-patients. *British Journal of Psychiatry, 163,* 755-762.

172. Pedersen, C. A., Stern, R. A., Pate, J., Senger, M. A., Bowes, W. A., & Mason, G. A. (1993). Thyroid and adrenal measures during late pregnancy and the puerperium in women who have been major depressed or who become dysphoric postpartum. *Journal of Affective Disorders, 29,* 201-211.

173. Petty, F., Steinberg, J., Kramer, G. L., Fulton, M., & Moeller, F. G. (1993). Desipramine does not alter plasma GABA in patients with major depression. *Journal of Affective Disorders, 29,* 53-56.

174. Rosenfarb, I. S., Burker, E. J., Morris, S. A., & Cush, D. T. (1993). Effects of changing contingencies on the behavior of depressed and nondepressed individuals. *Journal of Abnormal Psychology, 102,* 642-646.

175. Roxborough, H., Muir, W. J., Blackwood, D. H. R., Walker, M. T., & Blackburn, I. M. (1993). Neuropsychological and P300 abnormalities in schizophrenics and their relatives. *Psychological Medicine, 23,* 305-314.

176. Roy, A. (1993). Features associated with suicide attempts in depression: A partial replication. *Journal of Affective Disorders, 27,* 35-38.

177. Savino, M., Perugi, G., Simonini, E., Soriani, A., Cassano, G. B., & Akiskal, H. S. (1993). Affective comorbidity in panic disorder: Is there a bipolar connection? *Journal of Affective Disorders, 28,* 155-163.

178. Senra, C., & Polaino, A. (1993). Concordance between clinical and self-report depression scales during the acute phase and after treatment. *Journal of Affective Disorders, 27,* 13-20.

179. Simons, A. D., Angell, K. L., Monroe, J. M., & Thase, M. E. (1993). Cognition and life stress in depression: Cognitive factors and the definition, rating, and generation of negative life events. *Journal of Abnormal Psychology, 102,* 584-591.

180. Spangler, D. L., Simons, A. D., Monroe, S. M., & Thase, M. E. (1993). Evaluating the hopelessness model of depression: Diathesis-stress and symptoms components. *Journal of Abnormal Psychology, 102,* 592-600.

181. Steinberg, J. L., Orsulak, P. J., Raese, J. D., Gregory, R. R., Zielinski, M. H., & Wittman, P. D. (1993). Effects of tricyclic antidepressant treatment on tyramine-o-sulfate excretion in depressed patients. *Journal of Affective Disorders, 27,* 29-34.

182. Swann, A. C., Secunda, S. K., Katz, M. M., Croughan, J., Bowden, C. L., Koslow, S. H., Berman, N., & Stokes, P. E. (1993). Specificity of mixed affective states: Clinical comparison of dysphoric mania and agitated depression. *Journal of Affective Disorders, 28,* 81-89.

183. van Hoof, J. J. M., Hulstijn, W., van Mier, H., & Pagen, M. (1993). Figure drawing and psychomotor retardation: Preliminary report. *Journal of Affective Disorders, 29,* 263-266.

184. Wu, J. C., Buchsbaum, M. S., Johnson, J. C., Hershey, T. G., Wagner, E. A., Teng, C., & Lottenberg, S. (1993). Magnetic resonance and positron emission tomography imaging of the corpus callosum: Size, shape and metabolic rate in unipolar depression. *Journal of Affective Disorders, 28,* 15-25.

185. Wu, L. H., & Dunner, D. L. (1993). Suicide attempts in rapid cycling bipolar disorder patients. *Journal of Affective Disorders, 29,* 57-61.

186. Yazici, O., Ariciogłu, F., Gürvit, G., Ücok, A., Tastaban, Y., Canberk, Ö., Özgüroglu, M., Durat, T., & Sahìn, D. (1993). Nonadrenergic and serotoninergic depression? *Journal of Affective Disorders, 27,* 123-129.

187. Antony, M. M., Meadows, E. A., Brown, T. A., & Barlow, D. H. (1994). Cardiac awareness before and after cognitive-behavioral treatment for panic disorder. *Journal of Anxiety Disorders, 8,* 341-350.

188. Asmundson, G. J. G., & Stein, M. B. (1994). Selective processing of social threat in patients with generalized social phobia: Evaluation using a dot-probe paradigm. *Journal of Anxiety Disorders, 8,* 107-117.

189. Basoglu, M., Marks, I. M., Kilic, C., Swinson, R. P., Noshirvani, H., Kuch, K., & O'Sullivan, G. (1994). Relationship of panic, anticipatory anxiety, agoraphobia, and global improvement in panic disorder with agoraphobia treated with alprazolam and exposure. *British Journal of Psychiatry, 164,* 647-652.

190. Bauer, M. S., Whybrow, P. C., Gyulai, L., Gonnel, J., & Yeh, H-S. (1994). Testing definitions of dysphoric mania and hypomania: Prevalence, clinical characteristics and inter-episode stability. *Journal of Affective Disorders, 32,* 201-211.

191. Beck, J. G., & Zebb, B. J. (1994). Behavioral assessment and treatment of panic disorder: Current status, future directions. *Behavior Therapy, 25,* 581–611.

192. Bodnar, J. C., & Kiecolt-Glaser, J. K. (1994). Caregiver depression after bereavement: Chronic stress isn't over when it's over. *Psychology and Aging, 9,* 372-380.

193. Brown, R. G., Scott, L. C., Bench, C. J., & Dolan, R. J. (1994). Cognitive function in depression: Its relationship to the presence and severity of intellectual decline. *Psychological Medicine, 24,* 829-847.

194. Chouinard, G., Saxena, B. M., Nair, N. P. V., Kutcher, S. P., Bakish, D., Bradwejn, J., Kennedy, S. H., Sharma, V., Remick, R. A., Kukha-Mohamad, J. A., Belanger, M. C., Snaith, J., Beauclair, L., Pohlmann, H., & D'Souza, J. (1994). A Canadian multicentre placebo-controlled study of a fixed dose of brofaromine, a reversible selective MOA-A inhibitor, in the treatment of major depression. *Journal of Affective Disorders, 32,* 105-114.

195. Clark, D. A., Steer, R. A., & Beck, A. T. (1994). Common and specific dimensions of self-reported anxiety and depression: Implications for the cognitive and tripartite models. *Journal of Abnormal Psychology, 103,* 645-654.

196. Cowen, P. J., Power, A. C., Ware, C. J., & Anderson, I. M. (1994). 5-HT_{1A} receptor sensitivity in major depression: A neuroendocrine study with buspirone. *British Journal of Psychiatry, 164,* 372-379.

197. Devanand, D. P., Nobler, M. S., Singer, T., Kiersky, J. E., Turret, N., Rouse, S. P., & Sackeim, H. A. (1994). Is dysthymia a different disorder in the elderly? *American Journal of Psychiatry, 151,* 1592-1599.

198. Dew, M. A., Reynolds, C. F., III, Monk, T. H., Buysse, D. J., Hoch, C. C., Jennings, J. R., & Kupfer, D. J. (1994). Psychological correlates and sequelae of electroencephalographic sleep in healthy elders. *Journal of Gerontology: Psychological Sciences, 49*(Pt.1), P8-P18.

199. D'Hondt, P., Maes, M., Leysen, J. E., Gommeren, W., Scharpè, S., & Cosyns, P. (1994). Binding of [H]paroxetine to platelets of depressed patients: Seasonal differences and effects of diagnostic classification. *Journal of Affective Disorders, 32,* 27-35.

200. Dolan, R. J., Bench, C. J., Brown, R. G., Scott, L. C., & Frackowiak, R. S. J. (1994). Neuropsychological dysfunction in depression: The relationship to regional cerebral blood flow. *Psychological Medicine, 24,* 849-857.

201. Dulit, R. A., Fyer, M. R., Andrew, C. L., Brodsky, B. S., & Frances, A. J. (1994). Clinical correlates of self-mutilation in borderline personality disorder. *American Journal of Psychiatry, 151,* 1305-1311.

202. Ebert, D., & Martus, P. (1994). Somatization as a core symptom of melancholic type depression. Evidence from a cross-cultural study. *Journal of Affective Disorders, 32,* 253-256.

203. Esterling, B. A., Kiecolt-Glaser, J. K., Bodnar, J. C., & Glaser, R. (1994). Chronic stress, social support, and persistent alterations in the natural killer cell response to cytokines in older adults. *Health Psychology, 13,* 291-298.

204. Fava, M., Rosenbaum, J. F., McGrath, P. J., Stewart, J. W., Amsterdam, J. D., & Quitkin, F. M. (1994). Lithium and tricycic augmentation of fluoxetine treatment for resistant major depression: A double-blind, controlled study. *American Journal of Psychiatry, 151,* 1372-1374.

205. Fear, C. F., Littlejohns, C. S., Rouse, E., & McQuail, P. (1994). Propofol anaesthesia in electroconvulsive therapy. *British Journal of Psychiatry, 165,* 506-509.

206. Franchini, L., Gasperini, M., & Smeraldi, E. (1994). A 24-month follow-up study of unipolar subjects: A comparison between lithium and fluroxamine. *Journal of Affective Disorders, 32,* 225-231.

207. Gallagher-Thompson, D., & Steffen, A. M. (1994). Comparative effects of cognitive-behavioral and brief psychodynamic psychotherapists for depressed family categories. *Journal of Consulting and Clinical Psychology, 62,* 543-549.

208. Garvey, M. J., Hollon, S. D., & DeRubeis, R. J. (1994). Do depressed patients with higher pretreatment stress levels respond better to cognitive therapy than imipramine? *Journal of Affective Disorders, 32,* 45-50.

209. Gunderson, J. G., Phillips, K. A., Triebwasser, J., & Hirschfeld, R. M. A. (1994). The diagnostic interview for depressed personality. *American Journal of Psychiatry, 151,* 1300-1304.

210. Hiss, H., Foa, E. B., & Kozak, M. J. (1994). Relapse prevention program for treatment of obsessive-compulsive disorder. *Journal of Consulting and Clinical Psychology, 62,* 801-808.

211. Hofmann, P., Gangadhar, B. N., Probst, Ch., Koinig, G., & Hatzinger, R. (1994). TSH response to TRH and ECT. *Journal of Affective Disorders, 32,* 127-131.

212. Holzer, J. C., Goodman, W. K., McDougle, C. J., Baer, L., Boyarsky, B. K., Leckman, J. F., & Price, L. H. (1994). Obsessive-compulsive disorder with and without a chronic tic disorder. *British Journal of Psychiatry, 164,* 469-473.

213. Keijsers, G. P. J., Hoogduin, C. A. L., & Schaap, C. P. D. R. (1994). Prognostic factors in the behavioral treatment of panic disorder with and without agoraphobia. *Behavior Therapy, 25,* 689–708.

214. Kugler, J., Seelbach, H., & Kruskemper, G. M. (1994). Effects of rehabilitation programmes on anxiety and depression in coronary patients: A meta-analysis. *British Journal of Clinical Psychology, 33,* 401-410.

215. Lonnqvist, J., Sihvo, S., Syvälahti, E., & Kiviruusu, O. (1994). Moclobemide and fluoxetine in atypical depression: A double-blind trial. *Journal of Affective Disorders, 32,* 169-177.

216. Lykouras, L., Christodoulou, G. N., Malliaras, D., & Stefanis, C. (1994). The prognostic importance of delusions in depression: A 6-year prospective follow-up study. *Journal of Affective Disorders, 32,* 233-238

217. Lyness, S. A., Eaton, E. M., & Schneider, L. S. (1994). Cognitive performance in older and middle-aged depressed outpatients and controls. *Journal of Gerontology: Psychological Sciences, 49*(Pt.1), P129-P136.

218. Maes, M., Meltzer, H. Y., Stevens, W., Cosyns, P., & Blockx, P. (1994). Multiple reciprocal relationships between in vivo cellular immunity and hypothalamic-pituitary-adrenal axis in depression. *Psychological Medicine, 24,* 167-177.

219. Moffoot, A. P. R., O'Carroll, R. E., Bennie, J., Carroll, S., Dick, H., Ebmeier, K. P., & Goodwin, G. M. (1994). Diurnal variation of mood and neuropsychological function in major depression with melancholia. *Journal of Affective Disorders, 32,* 257-269.

220. Moreno, J. K., Selby, M. J., Fuhriman, A., & Laver, G. D. (1994). Hostility in depression. *Psychological Reports, 75,* 1391-1401.

221. Nolen-Hoeksema, S., Parker, L. E., & Larson, J. (1994). Ruminative coping with depressed mood following loss. *Journal of Personality and Social Psychology, 67,* 92-104.

222. O'Brien, J. T., Desmond, P., Ames, D., Schweitzer, I., Tuckwell, V., & Tress, B. (1994). The differentiation of depression from dementia by temporal lobe magnetic resonance imaging. *Psychological Medicine, 24,* 633-640.

223. O'Brien, J. T., Schweitzer, I., Ames, D., Mastwyk, M., & Colman, P. (1994). The function of the hypothalmic-pituitary-adrenal axis in Alzheimer's disease. Response to insulin hypoglycaemia. *British Journal of Psychiatry, 165,* 650-657.

224. Oren, D. A., Teicher, M. H., Schwartz, P. J., Glod, C., Turner, E. H., Ito, Y. N., Sedway, J., Rosenthal, N. E., & Wehr, T. A. (1994). A controlled trial of cyanocobalamin (Vitamin B12) in the treatment of winter seasonal affective disorder. *Journal of Affective Disorders, 32,* 197-200.

225. O'Sullivan, G. H., Noshirvani, H., Basoglu, M., Marks, I. M., Swinson, R., Kuch, K., & Kirby, M. (1994). Safety and side-effects of alprazolam: Controlled study in agoraphobia with panic disorder. *British Journal of Psychiatry, 165,* 79-86.

226. Peselow, E. D., Sanfilipo, M. P., & Fieve, R. R. (1994). Patients' and informants' reports of personality traits during and after major depression. *Journal of Abnormal Psychology, 103,* 819-824.

227. Ravindran, A. V., Chudzik, J., Bialik, R. J., Lapierre, Y. D., & Hrdina, P. D. (1994). Platelet serotonin measures in primary dysthymia. *American Journal of Psychiatry, 151,* 1369-1371.

228. Ravindran, A. V., Welburn, K., & Copeland, J. R. M. (1994). Semi-structured depression scale sensitive to change with treatment for use in the elderly. *British Journal of Psychiatry, 164,* 522-527.

229. Rickels, K., Schweizer, E., Clary, C., Fox, I., & Weise, C. (1994). Nefazodone and imipramine in major depression: A placebo-controlled trial. *British Journal of Psychiatry, 164,* 802-805.

230. Rifai, A. H., George, C. J., Stack, J. A., Mann, J. J., & Reynolds, C. F. (1994). Hopelessness in suicide attempters after acute treatment of major depression in late life. *American Journal of Psychiatry, 151,* 1687-1690.

231. Ring, H. A., Bench, C. J., Trimble, M. R., Brooks, D. J., Frackowiak, R. S. J., & Dolan, R. J. (1994). Depression in Parkinson's disease. A positron emission study. *British Journal of Psychiatry, 165,* 333-339.

232. Rohde, P., Lewinsohn, P. M., & Seeley, J. R. (1994). Responses of depressed adolescents to cognitive-behavioral treatment: Do differences in initial severity clarify the comparison of treatments? *Journal of Consulting and Clinical Psychology, 62,* 851-854.

233. Sahs, J. A., Goetz, R., Reddy, M., Rabkin, J. G., Williams, J. B. W., Kertzner, R., & Gorman, J. M. (1994). Psychological distress and natural killer cells in gay men with and without HIV infection. *American Journal of Psychiatry, 151,* 1479-1484.

234. Schlager, D. S. (1994). Early-morning administration of short-acting beta blockers for treatment of winter depression. *American Journal of Psychiatry, 151,* 1383-1385.

235. Schrader, G. (1994). Natural history of chronic depression: Predictors of change in severity over time. *Journal of Affective Disorders, 32,* 219-222.

236. Smith, J., Williams, K., Birkett, S., Nicholson, H., Glue, P., & Nutt, D. J. (1994). Neuroendocrine and clinical effects of electroconvulsive therapy and their relationship to treatment outcome. *Psychological Medicine, 24,* 547-555.

237. Sobell, L. C., Toneatto, T., & Sobell, M. (1994). Behavioral assessment and treatment planning for alcohol, tobacco, and other drug problems: Current status with an emphasis on clinical applications. *Behavior Therapy, 25,* 533–580.

238. Soloff, P. H., Liss, J. A., Kelly, T., Cornelius, J., & Ulrich, R. (1994). Risk factors for suicidal behavior in borderline personality disorder. *American Journal of Psychiatry, 151,* 1316-1323.

239. Sullivan, P. F., & Joyce, P. R. (1994). Effects of exclusion criteria in depression treatment studies. *Journal of Affective Disorders, 32,* 21-26.

240. Szádóczky, E., Fazekas, I., Rihmer, Z., & Arató, M. (1994). The role of psychosocial and biological variables in separating chronic and non-chronic major depression and early-late onset dysthymia. *Journal of Affective Disorders, 32,* 1-11.

241. Thase, M. E., Reynolds, C. F., Frank, E., Jennings, J. R., Nofzinger, E., Fasiczka, A. L., Garamoni, G., & Kupfer, D. J. (1994). Polysomnographic studies of unmedicated depressed men before and after cognitive behavioral therapy. *American Journal of Psychiatry, 151,* 1615-1622.

242. Ulrich, G., Haug, H.-J., & Fähndrich, E. (1994). Acute vs. chronic EEG effects in maprotiline- and in clomipramine-treated depressive inpatients and the prediction of therapeutic outcome. *Journal of Affective Disorders, 32,* 213-217.

243. van Os, J., Fahy, T. A., Bebbington, P., Jones, P., Wilkins, S., Sham, P., Russell, A., Gilvarry, K., Lewis, S., Toone, B., & Murray, R. (1994). The influence of life events on the subsequent course of psychotic illness. *Psychological Medicine, 24,* 503-513.

244. Vaughan, K., Wiese, M., Gold, R., & Tarrier, N. (1994). Eye-movement desensitisation: Symptom change in post-traumatic stress disorder. *British Journal of Psychiatry, 164,* 533-541.

245. Wilkinson, A. M., Anderson, D. N., Abou-Saleh, M. T., Wesson, M., Blair, J. A., Farrar, G., & Leeming, R. J. (1994). 5-Methyltetrahydrofolate level in the serum of depressed subjects and its relationship to the outcome of ECT. *Journal of Affective Disorders, 32,* 163-168.

246. Albus, M., Scheibe, G., & Scherer, J. (1995). Panic disorder with or without concomitant depression 5 years after treatment: A prospective follow-up. *Journal of Affective Disorders, 34,* 109-115.

247. Altshuler, L. L., Curran, J. G., Hauser, P., Mintz, J., Denicoff, K., & Post, R. (1995). T2 hyperintensities in bipolar disorder: Magnetic resonance imaging comparison and literature meta-analysis. *American Journal of Psychiatry, 152,* 1139–1144.

248. Arana, G. W., Santos, A. B., Laraia, M. T., McLeod-Bryant, S., Beale, M. D., Rames, L. J., Roberts, J. M., Dias, J. K., & Molloy, M. (1995). Dexamethasone for the treatment of depression: A randomized, placebo-controlled, double-blind trial. *American Journal of Psychiatry, 152,* 265-267.

249. Armitage, R., Hudson, A., Trivedi, M., & Rush, A. J. (1995). Sex differences in the distribution of EEG frequencies during sleep: Unipolar depressed outpatients. *Journal of Affective Disorders, 34,* 121-129.

250. Baer, L., Cukor, P., Jenike, M. A., Leahy, L., O'Laughlen, J., & Coyle, J. T. (1995). Pilot studies of telemedicine for patients with obsessive-compulsive disorder. *American Journal of Psychiatry, 152,* 1383–1385.

251. Baran, S. A., Weltzin, T. E., & Kaye, W. H. (1995). Low discharge weight and outcome in anorexia nervosa. *American Journal of Psychiatry, 152,* 1070-1072.

252. Barge-Schaapveld, D. Q. C. M., Nicolson, N. A., van der Hoop, R. G., & DeVries, M. W. (1995). Changes in daily life experience associated with clinical improvement in depression. *Journal of Affective Disorders, 34,* 139-154.

253. Basoglu, M., Marks, M., Sengun, S., & Marks, I. M. (1995). The distinctiveness of phobias: A discriminant analysis of fears. *Journal of Anxiety Disorders, 9,* 89-101.

254. Bench, C. J., Frackowiak, R. S. J., & Dolan, R. J. (1995). Changes in regional cerebral blood flow in recovery from depression. *Psychological Medicine, 25,* 247-261.

255. Benjamin, J., Levine, J., Fux, M., Aviv, A., Levy, D., & Belmaker, R. H. (1995). Double-blind, placebo-controlled, crossover trial of inositol treatment for panic disorder. *American Journal of Psychiatry, 152,* 1084-1086.

256. Bent-Hansen, J., Lauritzen, L., Clemmesen, L., Lunde, M., & Korner, A. (1995). A definite and a semidefinite questionnaire version of the Hamilton/ Melancholia (HDS/MES) scale. *Journal of Affective Disorders, 33,* 143-150.

257. Berlanga, C., & Ortega-Soto, H. A. (1995). A 3-year follow-up of a group of treatment-resistant depressed patients with a MAOI/tricyclic combination. *Journal of Affective Disorders, 34,* 187-192.

258. Blatt, S. J., Quinlan, D. M., Pilkonis, P. A., & Shea, M. T. (1995). Impact of perfectionism and need for approval on the brief treatment of depression: The National Institute of Mental Health Treatment of Depression Collaborative Research Program revisited. *Journal of Consulting and Clinical Psychology, 63,* 125-132.

259. Brodsky, B. S., Cloitre, M., & Dulit, R. A. (1995). Relationship of dissociation to self-mutilation and childhood abuse in borderline personality disorder. *American Journal of Psychiatry, 152,* 1788–1792.

260. Brown, C., Schulberg, H. C., & Madonia, M. J. (1995). Assessing depression in primary care practice with the Beck Depression Inventory and the Hamilton Rating Scale for Depression. *Psychological Assessment, 7,* 59-65.

261. Brown, S. A., Inaba, R. K., Gillin, J. C., Schuckit, M. A., Stewart, M. A., & Irwin, M. R. (1995). Alcoholism and affective disorder: Clinical course of depressive symptoms. *American Journal of Psychiatry, 152,* 45-52.

262. Bruce, T. J., Spiegel, D. A., Gregg, S. F., & Nuzzarello, A. (1995). Predictors of alprazolam discontinuation with and without cognitive behavior therapy in panic disorder. *American Journal of Psychiatry, 152,* 1156–1160.

263. Carter, M. M., Hollon, S. D., Carson, R., & Shelton, R. C. (1995). Effects of a safe person on induced distress following a biological challenge in panic disorder with agoraphobia. *Journal of Abnormal Psychology, 104,* 156-163.

264. Carton, S., Morand, P., Bungenera, C., & Jouvent, R. (1995). Sensation-seeking and emotional disturbances in depression: Relationships and evolution. *Journal of Affective Disorders, 34,* 219-225.

265. Castillo, C. S., Schultz, S. K., & Robinson, R. G. (1995). Clinical correlates of early-onset and late-onset poststroke generalized anxiety. *American Journal of Psychiatry, 152,* 1174–1179.

266. Claghorn, J. L., & Lesem, M. D. (1995). A double-blind placebo-controlled study of ORG 3770 in depressed outpatients. *Journal of Affective Disorders, 34,* 165-171.

267. Clark, C. P., Gillin, J. C., & Golshan, S. (1995). Do differences in sleep architecture exist between depressives with comorbid simple phobia as compared with pure depressives? *Journal of Affective Disorders, 33,* 251-255.

268. Coplan, J. D., Papp, L. A., Martinez, J., Pine, D., Rosenblum, L. A., Cooper, T., Liebowitz, M. R., & Gorman, J. M. (1995). Persistence of blunted human growth hormone response to clonidine in fluoxetine-treated patients with panic disorder. *American Journal of Psychiatry, 152,* 619-622.

269. Craske, M. G., Glover, D., & DeCola, J. (1995). Predicted versus unpredicted panic attacks: Acute versus general distress. *Journal of Abnormal Psychology, 104,* 214-223.

270. Danion, J., Kauffmann-Muller, F., Grange, D., Zimmermann, M., & Greth, P. (1995). Affective valence of words, explicit and implicit memory in clinical depression. *Journal of Affective Disorders, 34,* 227-234.

271. Deicken, R. F., Fein, G., & Weiner, M. W. (1995). Abnormal frontal lobe phospitorous metabolism in bipolar disorder. *American Journal of Psychiatry, 152,* 915-918.

272. Deicken, R. F., Weiner, M. W., & Fein, G. (1995). Decreased temporal lobe phosphomonoesters in bipolar disorder. *Journal of Affective Disorders, 33,* 195-199.

273. Evans, D. L., Leserman, J., Perkins, D. O., Stern, R. A., Murphy, C., Tamul, K., Liao, D., van der Horst, C. M., Hall, C. D., Folds, J. D., Golden, R, N., & Petitto, J. M. (1995). Stress-associated reductions of cytotoxic T lymphocytes and natural killer cells in asymptomatic HIV infection. *American Journal of Psychiatry, 152,* 543-550.

274. Freeman, E. W., Rickels, K., Schweizer, E., & Ting, T. (1995). Relationships between age and symptom severity among women seeking medical treatment for premenstrual symptoms. *Psychological Medicine, 25,* 309-315.

275. Friedman, L., Jesberger, J. A., Siever, L. J., Thompson, P., Mohs, R., & Meltzer, H. Y. (1995). Smooth pursuit performance in patients with affective disorders of schizophrenia and normal controls: Analysis with specific oculomotor measures, RMS error and qualitative ratings. *Psychological Medicine, 25,* 387-403.

276. Friedman, R. A., Markowitz, J. C., Parides, M., & Kocsis, J. H. (1995). Acute response of social functioning in dysthymic patients with desipramine. *Journal of Affective Disorders, 34,* 85-88.

277. Friedman, R. A., Mitchell, J., & Kocsis, J. H. (1995). Retreatment for relapse following desipramine discontinuation in dysthymia. *American Journal of Psychiatry, 152,* 926-928.

278. Gilley, D. W., Wilson, R. S., Fleischman, D. A., Harrison, D. W., Goetz, C. G., & Tanner, C. M. (1995). Impact of Alzheimer's type dementia and information source on the assessment of depression. *Psychological Assessment, 7,* 42-48.

279. Golomb, M., Fava, M., Abraham, M., & Rosenbaum, J. F. (1995). Gender differences in personality disorders. *American Journal of Psychiatry, 152,* 579-582.

280. Grant, G. M., Salcedo, V., Hynan, L. S., Frisch, M. B., & Poster, K. (1995). Effectiveness of quality of life therapy for depression. *Psychological Reports, 76,* 1203–1208.

281. Johnson, J. G., Williams, J. B. W., Rabkin, J. G., Goetz, R. R., & Remien, R. H. (1995). Axis I psychiatric symptoms associated with HIV infection and personality disorder. *American Journal of Psychiatry, 152,* 551-554.

282. Kato, T., Shioiri, T., Murashita, J., Hamakawa, H., Takahashi, Y., Inubushi, T., & Takahashi, S. (1995). Lateralized abnormality of high energy phosphate metabolism in the frontal lobes of patients with bipolar disorder detected by phase-encoded 31P-mrs. *Psychological Medicine, 25,* 557–566.

283. Keitner, G. I., Ryan, C. E., Miller, I. W., Kohn, R., Bishop, D. S., & Epstein, N. B. (1995). Role of the family in recovery and major depression. *American Journal of Psychiatry, 152,* 1002-1008.

284. Kotrla, K. J., Chacko, R. C., Harper, R. G., & Doody, R. (1995). Clinical variables associated with psychosis in Alzheimer's disease. *American Journal of Psychiatry, 152,* 1377–1379.

285. Kotrla, K. J., Chacko, R. C., Harper, R. G., Jhingran, S., & Doody, R. (1995). SPECT findings on psychosis in Alzheimer's disease. *American Journal of Psychiatry, 152,* 1470–1475.

286. Kranzler, H. R., Burleson, J. A., Korner, P., Del Boca, F. K., Bohn, M. J., Brown, J., & Liebowitz, N. (1995). Placebo-controlled trial of fluoxetine as an adjunct to relapse prevention in alcoholics. *American Journal of Psychiatry, 152,* 391-397.

287. Kuch, K., Cox, B. J., & Direnfeld, D. M. (1995). A brief self-rating scale for PTSD after road vehicle accident. *Journal of Anxiety Disorders, 9,* 503–514.

288. Lam, R. W., Gorman, C. P., Michalon, M., Steiner, M., Levitt, A. J., Corral, M. R., Watson, G. D., Morehouse, R. L., Tam, W., & Joffe, R. T. (1995). Multicenter, placebo-controlled study of fluoxetine in seasonal affective disorder. *American Journal of Psychiatry, 152,* 1765–1770.

289. La Rue, A., O'Hara, R., Matsuyama, S. S., & Jarvik, L. F. (1995). Cognitive changes in young-old adults: Effect of family history of dementia. *Journal of Clinical and Experimental Neuropsychology, 17,* 65-70.

290. Leibenluft, E., Clark, C. H., & Myers, F. S. (1995). The reproductibility of depressive and hypomanic symptoms across repeated episodes in patients with rapid-cycling bipolar disorder. *Journal of Affective Disorders, 23,* 83-88.

291. Lerer, B., Shapira, B., Calev, A., Tubi, N., Drexler, H., Kindler, S., Lidsky, D., & Schwartz, J. E. (1995). Antidepressant and cognitive effects of twice- versus three-times weekly ECT. *American Journal of Psychiatry, 152,* 564-570.

292. Lizardi, H., Klein, D. N., Ouimette, P. C., Riso, L. P., Anderson, R. L., & Donaldson, S. K. (1995). Reports of the childhood home environment in early-onset dysthymia and episodic major depression. *Journal of Abnormal Psychology, 104,* 132-139.

293. Malone, K. M., Haas, G. L., Sweeney, J. A., & Mann, J. J. (1995). Major depression and the risk of attempted suicide. *Journal of Affective Disorders, 34,* 173-185.

294. Malone, K. M., Szanto, K., Corbitt, E. M., & Mann, J. J. (1995). Clinical assessment versus research methods in the assessment of suicidal behavior. *American Journal of Psychiatry, 152,* 1601–1607.

295. Markowitz, J. C., Klerman, G. L., Clougherty, K. F., Spielman, L. A., Jacobsberg, L. B., Fishman, B., Frances, A. J., Kocsis, J. H., & Perry, S. W. (1995). Individual psychotherapies for depressed HIV-positive patients. *American Journal of Psychiatry, 152,* 1504–1509.

296. Mavissakalian, M. R., Hamann, M. S., Haidar, S. A., & De Groot, C. M. (1995). Correlates of DSM-III personality disorder in generalized anxiety disorder. *Journal of Anxiety Disorders, 9,* 103-115.

297. McDougle, C. J., Barr, L. C., Goodman, W. K., Pelton, G. H., Aronson, S. C., Anand, A., & Price, L. H. (1995). Lack of efficacy of clozapine monotherapy in refractory obsessive-compulsive disorder. *American Journal of Psychiatry, 152,* 1812–1814.

298. Meltzer, H. Y., & Okayli, G. (1995). Reduction of suicidality during clozapine treatment of neuroleptic-resistant schizophrenia: Impact on risk-benefit assessment. *American Journal of Psychiatry, 152,* 183-190.

299. Mendelberg, H. E. (1995). Inpatient treatment of mood disorders. *Psychological Reports, 76,* 819–824.

300. Migliorelli, R., Teson, A., Sabe, L., Petracchi, M., Leiguarda, R., & Starkstein, S. E. (1995). Prevalence and correlates of dysthymia and major depression among patients with Alzheimer's Disease. *American Journal of Psychiatry, 152,* 37-44.

301. Nair, N. P. V., Amin, M., Holm, P., Katona, C., Klitgaard, N., Ng, Y. K. N. M. K., Kragh-Sorensen, P., Leek, C. A., & Stage, K. B. (1995). Moclobemide and nortriptyline in elderly depressed patients. A randomized, multicentre trial against placebo. *Journal of Affective Disorders, 33,* 1-9.

302. Nierenberg, A. A., Grossbard, S. J., Fava, M., & Rosenbaum, J. F. (1995). Social adjustment does not predict depression relapse during continuation fluoxetine therapy. *Journal of Affective Disorders, 34,* 73-77.

303. Nierenberg, A. A., McLean, N. E., Alpert, J. E., Worthington, J. J., Rosenbaum, J. F., & Fova, M. (1995). Early nonresponse to fluoxetine as a predictor of poor 8-week outcome. *American Journal of Psychiatry, 152,* 1500–1503.

304. Nofzinger, E. A., Reynolds, C. F., Thase, M. E., Frank, E., Jennings, R., Fasiczka, A. L., Sullivan, L. R., & Kupfer, D. J. (1995). REM sleep enhancement by bupropion in depressed men. *American Journal of Psychiatry, 152,* 274-276.

305. Nugent, D. F., Dinan, T. G., & Leonard, B. E. (1995). Further characterization of the inhibition of platelet aggregation by a plasma factor(s) in unmedicated unipolar depressed patients. *Journal of Affective Disorders, 33,* 227-231.

306. O'Carroll, R. E., Rogers, A., Lawrie, S. M., Murray, C., Van Beck, M., Ebmeir, K. P., Walker, M., Blackwood, D., Johnstone, E. C., & Goodwin, G. M. (1995). Laterality of visuo-spatial attention in acute and chronic schizophrenia, major depression and in healthy controls. *Psychological Medicine, 25,* 1091–1095.

307. O'Dwyer, A.-M., Lightman, S. L., Marks, M. N., & Checkley, S. A. (1995). Treatment of major depression with metyrapone and hydrocortisone. *Journal of Affective Disorders, 23,* 123-128.

308. Ogles, B. M., Lambert, M. J., & Sawyer, J. D. (1995). Clinical significance of the National Institute of Mental Health Treatment of Depression Collaborative Research Program Data. *Journal of Consulting and Clinical Psychology, 63,* 321-326.

309. O'Leary, D., Gill, D., Gregory, S., & Shawcross, C. (1995). Which depressed patients respond to ECT? The Nottingham results. *Journal of Affective Disorders, 33,* 245-250.

310. Otto, M. W., Pollack, M. H., Fava, M., Uccello, R., & Rosenbaum, J. F. (1995). Elevated Anxiety Sensitivity Index scores in patients with major depression: Correlates and changes with antidepressant treatment. *Journal of Anxiety Disorders, 9,* 117-123.

311. Pandey, G. N., Pandey, S. C., Dwivedi, Y., Sharma, R. P., Janicak, P. G., & Davis, J. M. (1995). Platelet serotonin-2A receptors: A potential biological marker for suicidal behavior. *American Journal of Psychiatry, 152,* 850-855.

312. Parker, G., Hadzi-Pavlovic, D., Austin, M.-P., Mitchell, P., Wilhelm, K., Hickie, I., Boyce, P., & Eyers, K. (1995). Sub-typing depression, I: Is psychomotor disturbance necessary and sufficient to the definition of melancholia. *Psychological Medicine, 25,* 815–823.

313. Parry, B. L., Cover, H., Mostofi, N., Leveau, B., Sependa, P. A., Resnick, A., & Gillin, J. C. (1995). Early versus late partial sleep deprivation in patients with premenstrual dysphoric disorder and normal comparison subjects. *American Journal of Psychiatry, 152,* 404-412.

314. Paykel, E. S., Ramana, R., Cooper, Z., Hayhurst, H., Kerr, J., & Barocka, A. (1995). Residual symptoms after partial remission: An important outcome in depression. *Psychological Medicine, 25,* 1171–1180.

315. Perez, J., Zanardi, R., Mori, S., Gasperini, M., Smeraldi, E., & Racagni, G. (1995). Abnormalities of cAMP-dependent endogenous phosphorylation in platelets from patients with bipolar disorder. *American Journal of Psychiatry, 152,* 1204–1206.

316. Perkins, D. O., Leserman, J., Stern, R. A., Baum, S. F., Liao, D., Golden, R. N., & Evans, D. L. (1995). Somatic symptoms and HIV infection: Relationship to depressive symptoms and indicators of HIV disease. *American Journal of Psychiatry, 152,* 1776–1781.

317. Perna, G., Barbini, B., Cocchi, S., Bertani, A., & Gasperini, M. (1995). 35% CO_2 challenge in panic and mood disorders. *Journal of Affective Disorders, 33,* 189-194.

318. Pine, D. S., Trautman, P. D., Shaffer, D., Cohen, L., Davies, M., Stanley, M., & Parsons, B. (1995). Seasonal rhythm of platelet [^{3}] imipramine binding in adolescents who attempted suicide. *American Journal of Psychiatry, 152,* 923-925.

319. Poynton, A. M., Kartsounis, L. D., & Bridges, P. K. (1995). A prospective clinical study of steretactic subcaudate tractotomy. *Psychological Medicine, 25,* 763–770.

320. Priebe, S., & Gruyters, T. (1995). The importance of the first three days: Predictors of treatment outcome in depressed in-patients. *British Journal of Clinical Psychology, 34,* 229-236.

321. Prigerson, H. G., Frank, E., Kasl, S. V., Reynolds, C. F., Anderson, B., Zubenko, G. S., Houck, P. R., George, C. J., & Kupfer, D. J. (1995). Complicated grief and bereavement-related depression as distinct disorders: Preliminary empirical validation in elderly bereaved spouses. *American Journal of Psychiatry, 152,* 22-30.

322. Ramana, R., Paykel, E. S., Cooper, Z., Hayhurst, H., Saxty, M., & Surtees, P. G. (1995). Remission and relapse in major depression: A two-year prospective follow-up study. *Psychological Medicine, 25,* 1161–1170.

323. Rechlin, T., Weis, M., & Kaschka, W. P. (1995). Is diurnal variations of mood associated with parasympathetic activity? *Journal of Affective Disorders, 34,* 249-255.

324. Rechlin, T., Weis, M., Schneider, K., Zimmermann, U., & Kaschka, W. P. (1995). Does bright-light therapy influence autonomic heart-rate parameters? *Journal of Affective Disorders, 34,* 131-137.

325. Reynolds, W. M., & Kobak, K. A. (1995). Reliability and validity of the Hamilton Depression Inventory: A paper-and-pencil version of the Hamilton Depression Rating Scale clinical interview. *Psychological Assessment, 7,* 472–483.

326. Riemann, D., Kammerer, J., Low, H., & Schmidt, M. H. (1995). Sleep in adolescents with primary major depression and schizophrenia: A pilot study. *Journal of Child Psychology and Psychiatry and Allied Disciplines, 36,* 313-326.

327. Riley, W. T., McCormick, M. G. F., Simon, E. M., Stack, K., Pushkin, Y., Overstreet, M. M., Carmona, J. J., & Magakian, C. (1995). Effects of alprazolam doses on the induction and habituation processes during behavioral panic induction treatment. *Journal of Anxiety Disorders, 9,* 217-227.

328. Rogers, J. H., Widiger, T. A., & Krupp, A. (1995). Aspects of depression associated with borderline personality disorder. *American Journal of Psychiatry, 152,* 268-270.

329. Rothschild, A. J. (1995). Selective serotonin reuptake inhibitor-induced sexual dysfunction: Efficacy of a drug holiday. *American Journal of Psychiatry, 152,* 1514–1516.

330. Rubenstein, C. S., Altemus, M., Pigott, T. A., Hess, A., & Murray, D. L. (1995). Symptom overlap between OCD and bulimia nervosa. *Journal of Anxiety Disorders, 9,* 1-9.

331. Rush, A. J., Laux, G., Giles, D. E., Jarrett, R. B., Weissenburger, J., Feldman-Koffler, F., & Stone, L. (1995). Clinical characteristics of outpatients with chronic major depression. *Journal of Affective Disorders, 34,* 25-32.

332. Sakamoto, K., Nakadaira, S., Kamo, K., Kamo, T., & Takahashi, K. (1995). A longitudinal follow-up study of seasonal affective disorder. *American Journal of Psychiatry, 152,* 862-868.

333. Schittecatte, M., Garcia-Valentin, J., Charles, G., Machowski, R., Pena-Othaitz, M-J., Mendlewicz, J., & Wilmotte, J. (1995). Efficacy of the "Clonidine REM Suppression Test (CREST)" to separate patients with major depression from controls: A comparison with three currently proposed biological markers of depression. *Journal of Affective Disorders, 33,* 151-157.

334. Scott, J., Williams, J. M. G., Brittlebank, A., & Ferrier, I. N. (1995). The relationship between premorbid neuroticism, cognitive dysfunction and persistence of depression: A 1-year follow up. *Journal of Affective Disorders, 33,* 167-172.

335. Senra, C. (1995). Measures of treatment outcome of depression: An effect size comparison. *Psychological Reports, 76,* 187-192.

336. Sharma, R. P., Bissette, G., Janicak, P. G., Davis, J. M., & Nemeroff, C. B. (1995). Elevation of CSF somatostatin concentrations in mania. *American Journal of Psychiatry, 152,* 1807–1809.

337. Silk, K. R., Lee, S., Hill, E. M., & Lohr, N. E. (1995). Borderline personality disorder symptoms and severity of sexual abuse. *American Journal of Psychiatry, 152,* 1059-1064.

338. Simons, A. D., Gordon, J. S., Monroe, S. M., & Thase, M. E. (1995). Toward an integration of psychologic, social, and biologic factors in depression: Effects on outcome and course of cognitive therapy. *Journal of Consulting and Clinical Psychology, 63,* 369-377.

339. Small, G. W., La Rue, A., Komo, S., Kaplan, A., & Mandelkern, M. A. (1995). Predictors of cognitive change in middle-aged and older adults with memory loss. *American Journal of Psychiatry, 152,* 1757–1764.

340. Sobin, C., Sackeim, H. A., Prudic, J., Devanand, D. P., Moody, B. J., & McElhiney, M. C. (1995). Predictors of retrograde amnesia following ECT. *American Journal of Psychiatry, 152,* 995-1001.

341. Southwick, S. M., Yehuda, R., & Giller, E. L. (1995). Psychological dimensions of depression in borderline personality disorder. *American Journal of Psychiatry, 152,* 789-791.

342. Streichenwein, S. M., & Thornby, J. I. (1995). A long-term double-blind, placebo-controlled crossover trial of the efficacy of fluoxetine for trichotillomania. *American Journal of Psychiatry, 152,* 1192–1196.

343. Tarbuck, A. F., & Paykel, E. S. (1995). Effects of major depression on the cognitive function of younger and older subjects. *Psychological Medicine, 25,* 285-296.

344. Teasdale, J. D., Taylor, M. J., Cooper, Z., Hayhurst, H., & Paykel, E. S. (1995). Depressive thinking: Shifts in construct accessibility or in schematic mental models? *Journal of Abnormal Psychology, 104,* 500–507.

345. Teicher, M. H., Glod, C. A., Oren, D. A., Schwartz, P. J., Luetke, C., Brown, C., & Rosenthal, N. E. (1995). The phototherapy light visor: More to it than meets the eye. *American Journal of Psychiatry, 152,* 1197–1202.

346. Thakore, J. H., & Dinan, T. G. (1995). Effect of fluoxetine on dexamethasone-induced growth hormone release in depression: A double-blind, placebo-controlled study. *American Journal of Psychiatry, 152,* 616-618.

347. Wallace, A. E., Kofoed, L. L., & West, A. N. (1995). Double-blind, placebo-controlled trial of methylphenidate in older, depressed, medically ill patients. *American Journal of Psychiatry, 152,* 929-931.

348. Weizman, A., Burgin, R., Harel, Y., Karp, L., & Gavish, M. (1995). Platelet peripheral-type benzodiazepine receptor in major depression. *Journal of Affective Disorders, 33,* 257-261.

349. West, S. A., McElroy, S. L., Strakowski, S. M., Keck, P. E., & McConville, B. J. (1995). Attention deficit hyperactivity disorder in adolescent mania. *American Journal of Psychiatry, 152,* 271-273.

350. White, P. D., Grover, S. A., Kangro, H. O., Thomas, J. M., Amess, J., & Clare, A. W. (1995). The validity and reliability of the fatigue syndrome that follows glandular fever. *Psychological Medicine, 25,* 917–924.

351. Zettle, R. D., & Herring, E. L. (1995). Treatment utility of the sociotropy/autonomy distinction: Implications for cognitive therapy. *Journal of Clinical Psychology, 51,* 280-289.

352. Aarsland, D., Cummings, J. L., Yenner, G., & Miller, B. (1996). Relationship of aggressive behavior to other neuropsychiatric symptoms in patients with Alzheimer's disease. *American Journal of Psychiatry, 153,* 243–247.

353. Amsterdam, J. D., Fava, M., Maislin, G., Rosenbaum, J., & Hornig-Rohan, M. (1996). TRH stimulation test as a predictor of acute and long-term antidepressant response in major depression. *Journal of Affective Disorders, 38,* 165–172.

354. Bagby, R. M., Schaller, D. R., Levitt, A. J., Joffe, R. T., & Harness, K. L. (1996). Seasonal and non-seasonal depression and the five-factor model of personality. *Journal of Affective Disorders, 38,* 89–95.

355. Beats, B. C., Sahakian, B. J., & Levy, R. (1996). Cognitive performance in tests sensitive to frontal lobe dysfunction in the elderly depressed. *Psychological Medicine, 26,* 591–603.

356. Cloitre, M., Cancienne, J., Brodsky, B., Dulit, R., & Perry, S. W. (1996). Memory performance among women with parental abuse histories: Enhanced directed forgetting or directed remembering? *Journal of Abnormal Psychology, 105,* 204–211.

357. Cooke, R. G., Robb, J. C., Young, L. T., & Joffe, R. T. (1996). Well-being and functioning in patients with bipolar disorder assessed using the MOS 20-ITEM Short Form (SF-20). *Journal of Affective Disorders, 39,* 93–97.

358. Corbitt, E. M., Malone, K. M., Haas, G. L., & Mann, J. J. (1996). Suicidal behavior in patients with major depression and comorbid personality disorders. *Journal of Affective Disorders, 39,* 61–72.

359. Fava, M., Abraham, M., Alpert, J., Nierenberg, A. A., Pava, J. A., & Rosenbaum, J. F. (1996). Gender differences in Axis I comorbidity among depressed outpatients. *Journal of Affective Disorders, 38*, 129–133.

360. Frank, E., Tu, X. M., Anderson, B., Reynolds, C. F., Karp, J. F., Mayo, A., Ritenour, A., & Kupfer, D. J. (1996). Effects of positive and negative life events on time to depression onset: An analysis of additivity and timing. *Psychological Medicine, 26*, 613–626.

361. Gatti, F., Bellini, L., Gasperini, M., Perez, J., Zanardi, R., & Smeraldi, E. (1996). Fluvoxamine alone in the treatment of delusional depression. *American Journal of Psychiatry, 153*, 414–416.

362. Heuser, I. J. E., Schweiger, U., Gotthardt, U., Schmider, J., Lammers, C.-H., Dettling, M., Yassouridis, A., & Holsboer, F. (1996). Pituitary-adrenal system regulation and psychopathology during amitriptyline treatment in elderly depressed patients and normal comparison subjects. *American Journal of Psychiatry, 153*, 93–99.

363. Jacob, R. G., Furman, J. M., Durrant, J. D., & Turner, S. M. (1996). Panic, agoraphobia, and vestibular dysfunction. *American Journal of Psychiatry, 153*, 503–512.

364. Jeste, D. V., Heaton, S. C., Paulsen, J. S., Ercoli, L., Harris, M. J., & Heaton, R. K. (1996). Clinical and neuropsychological comparison of psychotic depression with nonpsychotic depression and schizophrenia. *American Journal of Psychiatry, 153*, 490–496.

365. Joffe, R., Segal, Z., & Singer, W. (1996). Change in thyroid hormone levels following response to cognitive therapy for major depression. *American Journal of Psychiatry, 153*, 411–413.

366. Klemm, E., Grünwald, F., Kasper, S., Menzel, C., Broich, K., Danos, P., Reichmann, K., Krappel, C., Rieker, O., Briele, B., Hotze, A. L., Moller, H.-J., & Biersack, H.-J. (1996). [123 I] IBZM SPECT for imaging of striatal D2 dopamine receptors in 56 schizophrenic patients taking various neuroleptics. *American Journal of Psychiatry, 153*, 183–190.

367. Knott, V. J., Telner, J. I., Lapierre, Y. D., Browne, M., & Horn, E. R. (1996). Quantitative EEG in the prediction of antidepressant response to imipramine. *Journal of Affective Disorders, 39*, 175–184.

368. Maes, M., Smith, R., Christophe, A., Cosyns, P., Desnyder, R., & Meltzer, H. (1996). Fatty acid composition in major depression: Decreased omega 3 fractions in cholesteryl esters and increased C20: 4 omega 6/C20: 5 omega 3 ratio in cholesteryl esters and phospholipids. *Journal of Affective Disorders, 38*, 35–46.

369. Maes, M., VanGastel, A., Blockx, P., Martin, M., Cosyns, P., Scharpe, S., Ranjan, R., & Desnyder, R. (1996). Lower serum transcortin (CBG) in major depressed females: Relationships with baseline and post dexamethasone cortisol values. *Journal of Affective Disorders, 38*, 47–56.

370. Mann, J. J., Malone, K. M., Diehl, D. J., Perel, J., Cooper, T. B., & Mintun, M. A. (1996). Demonstration in vivo of reduced serotonin responsivity in the brain of untreated depressed patients. *American Journal of Psychiatry, 153*, 174–182.

371. Monroe, S. M., Roberts, J. E., Kupfer, D. J., & Frank, E. (1996). Life stress and treatment course of recurrent depression: II. Postrecovery associations with attrition, symptom course, and recurrence over 3 years. *Journal of Abnormal Psychology, 105*, 313–328.

372. Rush, A. J., Gullion, C. M., Basco, M. R., Jarrett, R. B., & Trivedi, M. H. (1996). The Inventory of Depressive Symptomatology (IDS): Psychometric properties. *Psychological Medicine, 26*, 477–486.

373. Schleifer, S. J., Keller, S. E., Bartlett, J. A., Eckholdt, H. M., & Deloney, B. R. (1996). Immunity in young adults with major depressive disorder. *American Journal of Psychiatry, 153*, 477–482.

374. Slaap, B. R., van Vliet, I. M., Westenberg, H. G. M., & Den Boer, J. A. (1996). Responders and nonresponders to drug treatment in social phobia: Differences at baseline and prediction of response. *Journal of Affective Disorders, 39*, 13–19.

375. Sluzewska, A., Rybakowski, J. K., Sobieska, M., & Wiktorowicz, K. (1996). Concentration and microheterogeneity glycophorms of alpha-l-acid glycoprotein in major depressive disorder. *Journal of Affective Disorders, 39*, 149–155.

376. Spalletta, G., Troisi, A., Saracco, M., Ciani, N., & Pasini, A. (1996). Symptom profile, Axis II comorbidity and suicidal behavior in young males with DSM–III–R depressive illnesses. *Journal of Affective Disorders, 39*, 141–148.

377. Spanier, C., Frank, E., McEachran, A. B., Grochocinski, V. J., & Kupfer, D. J. (1996). The prophylaxis of depressive episodes in recurrent depression following discontinuation of drug therapy: Integrating psychological and biological factors. *Psychological Medicine, 26*, 461–475.

378. Strakowski, S. M., McElroy, S. L., Keck, P. E., Jr., & West, S. A. (1996). Racial influence on diagnosis in psychotic mania. *Journal of Affective Disorders, 39*, 157–162.

379. Strakowski, S. M., McElroy, S. L., Keck, P. E., Jr., & West, S. A. (1996). Suicidality among patients with mixed and manic bipolar disorder. *American Journal of Psychiatry, 153*, 674–676.

380. Vitaliano, P. P., Russo, J., Scanlan, J. M., & Greeno, C. G. (1996). Weight changes in caregivers of Alzheimer's care recipients: Psychobehavioral predictors. *Psychology and Aging, 11*, 155–163.

381. Watkins, P. C., Vache, K., Verney, S. P., Muller, S., & Mathews, A. (1996). Unconscious mood-congruent memory bias in depression. *Journal of Abnormal Psychology, 105*, 34–41.

382. Young, L. T., Li, P. P., Kamble, A., Siu, K. P., & Warsh, J. J. (1996). Lack of effect of antidepressants on mononuclear leukocyte G-protein levels or function in depressed outpatients. *Journal of Affective Disorders, 39*, 201–207.

Review of the Revised Hamilton Rating Scale for Depression by PAUL C. BURNETT, Senior Lecturer, School of Learning and Development, Queensland University of Technology, Kelvin Grove, Queensland, Australia:

The Revised Hamilton Rating Scale for Depression (RHRSD) is a revision of the Hamilton Rating Scale for Depression, which was originally designed by Hamilton (1960) as a rating scale for clinicians to use with individuals already experiencing a depressive illness. It also includes items to assist clinicians to confirm a diagnosis of depression and for evaluating the impact of the illness on an individual's everyday life and functioning. The RHRSD has two forms designed to be used with adults. The Clinician Rating Form is completed by a clinician during or after a patient interview; the 76-item Self-Report Problem Inventory is completed by the patient and provides the clinician with information parallel to that contained in the clinician's form. Both forms provide information about 22 clusters of depressive symptoms.

The 63-page manual is extensive and comprehensive. Clear instructions and suggestions for utilizing both forms of the scale are presented. Both forms have autoscoring and examples of the scoring processes used for each form are included and discussed. Each of the 22 symptoms are described and specific examples of the questions that can be used to tap these dimensions in an interview situation are given. A good discussion of interpretation issues is presented in the manual with three different levels described. At the general level, the clinician considers the validity of the ratings and evaluates overall symptom severity. At the next level, symptom clusters are matched against the diagnostic criteria from the *DSM-IV* to diagnose a depressive or allied illness. At the most discrete level ratings from the individual symptom levels are considered.

The verification sample described in the manual consisted of 202 depressed patients of which 76% were inpatients, 24% outpatients, and 69% were female. The manual states the demographics of this sample appeared to be a fair reflection of depressed patients in general although no data are provided to support this statement. Additionally, no information regarding the procedures used to select this sample is provided. The means and standard deviations for both forms are provided by patient type.

Internal consistency estimates were found to be .79 and .81 for the clinical and self-report forms respectively, indicating moderate reliability. Other studies found that internal consistency coefficients ranged from .45 to .95, which the manual states are consistent with the results from the verification sample. However, an internal consistency coefficient of .45 cannot be considered to be consistent with figures of .79 and .81 and does not represent "quite good" (p. 37) internal consistency.

Evidence of the RHRSD's concurrent validity is provided by citing the results of some 50 studies that have correlated Hamilton scores with scores from other instruments measuring depression (e.g., Beck Depression Inventory, Zung Self-Rating Depression Scale, MMPI Depression). The mean correlation for these studies was .67.

The correlations between the clinician and self-report forms of the RHRSD was found to be .66 for the inpatients in the verification sample and .70 for outpatients. A full matrix correlating the clinician's scores with the self-report score for the 17 main symptoms is presented. The results of a principal components analysis (with varimax rotation) using the verification's total scores for the 17 main symptoms are presented and compared with Hamilton's (1960) original factor structure. Five factors were found for the verification sample whereas Hamilton found only four. No factor analyses were completed using the scores on the items although Rasch item difficulty estimates are presented for the Self-Report Problem Inventory.

In summary, the RHRSD is a sound revision of its predecessor. The manual is well written and clearly describes the administration, scoring, and interpretation procedures. The two scales have moderate internal consistency, sound concurrent validity, and relatively consistent and stable factor structures. The manual includes an extensive overview of studies that have used the previous version. Data from these studies are utilized to demonstrate the sound psychometric properties of the instruments. The verification sample is small and is not adequately described in terms of how it was selected.

REVIEWER'S REFERENCE

Hamilton, M. (1960). A rating scale for depression. *Journal of Neurology, Neurosurgery, and Psychiatry, 4,* 561–571.

Review of the Revised Hamilton Rating Scale for Depression by BARBARA J. KAPLAN, Psychologist, Western New York Institute for the Psychotherapies, Orchard Park, NY:

Hamilton, a psychiatrist at the University of Leeds, first published the Rating Scale for Depression in 1960 with a revised form in 1967. The original ratings were determined through clinical interviews with depressed patients and their families. It was only subsequent to the interview that two clinicians would independently determine the ratings for Hamilton's scales. The goal of the instrument

was to provide the means for quantifying clinicians' appraisal of patient symptomatology. Hamilton's concern was that the rating scales available for evaluating depression inadequately represented the patterns of symptoms found in clinically significant depressions. It is difficult to know whether Hamilton foresaw the enormous impact his rating scales would have. The Hamilton Rating Scales have been widely used in the evaluation of depression in the construction of other instruments with both clinical and nonclinical populations and in measuring the outcome of a wide range of treatments and interventions where depression may be primary, or secondary to some other disorder or condition. More than 30 years after its publication, the *Social Science Citations Index* and *Science Citations Index* for 1995 and 1996 show more than 1,000 citations of Hamilton's 1960 and 1967 work.

It is rare that a test revision maintains sufficient similarity to the original to allow for comparisons between scores on earlier and later versions of the instrument. Warren's revision of the Hamilton Rating Scale for Depression (RHRSD) is elegant in its continuity and comparability to the original scale. Consistent with Hamilton's desire to go beyond a checklist, a clinician rating form is completed after interviewing the patient (the RHRSD) and a self-report scale is completed by the patients (RHRSD Problem Inventory). Scores on the RHRSD are based on Hamilton's original 17 items, and the overall score reflects only these items. Warren's comparison of the factor structure of the earlier scale and the revision strengthens the validity of the revision. Eight new items screen for *DSM-IV* (American Psychiatric Association, 1993) criteria for a diagnosis of Major Depressive Disorder or other depressive syndromes. These items address the extent of impairment in daily functioning and duration of symptoms. Four other new items on diurnal variation, obsessive-compulsive characteristics, paranoia, and depersonalization and derealization are included so that additional inquiry can determine differential diagnoses. Subscores on melancholic features and anticipated patient response to tricyclic antidepressants can be used to look at differing depressive patterns.

Evaluation of the reliability and validity for the RHRSD is limited in that a large normalization sample is not reported (the largest sample contains 202 people). Warren does address the relation of her revised scale to Hamilton's original scale and other widely used instruments, and reports reliability for the revision and correlations of clinicians' ratings with RHRSD self-reports. The decades of research carried out with Hamilton's scale contribute a great deal to our understanding of this instrument and its validity in clinical assessment and treatment planning; however, there is a need for additional research into the validity of the scores and symptoms profiles when the RHRSD is administered to different populations (e.g., ethnic groups, gender, age) and as a predictive measure for responsiveness to SSRIs (selective serotonin reuptake inhibitors) and multi-drug medications.

REVIEWER'S REFERENCES

Hamilton, M. (1960). A rating scale for depression. *Journal of Neurology, Neurosurgery, and Psychiatry, 23,* 56–62.

Hamilton, M. (1967). Development of a primary rating scale for depressive illness. *British Journal of Social and Clinical Psychology, 6,* 278–296.

American Psychiatric Association. (1993). *Diagnostic and statistical manual of mental disorders DSM-IV* (4th ed.). Washington, DC: American Psychiatric Association.

[264]
Revised PSB—Aptitude for Practical Nursing Examination.

Purpose: Designed as a "method of selection, placement, guidance and counseling of incoming [practical/vocational nursing] students."

Population: Applicants for admission to practical/vocational nursing schools.

Publication Dates: 1961–1990.

Scores, 8: Academic Aptitude (Verbal, Numerical, Nonverbal, Total), Spelling, Natural Sciences, Judgment in Practical Nursing Situations, Vocational Adjustment Index.

Administration: Individual or group.

Price Data, 1996: $10 per test booklet; $15 per technical manual ('90, 86 pages); $20 per specimen set including test booklet, answer sheet, and administrator's manual ('90, 4 pages); $10 per student for scoring and reporting services.

Time: (135) minutes.

Comments: Earlier edition, now known as Original PSB—Aptitude for Practical Nursing Examination, is still available.

Authors: Anna S. Evans, Phyllis G. Roumm, and George A. W. Stouffer, Jr., with technical assistance from Psychological Services Bureau, Inc.

Publisher: Psychological Services Bureau, Inc.

Review of the Revised PSB—Aptitude for Practical Nursing Examination by MARK ALBANESE, Associate Professor, Preventive Medicine and Director, Office of Medical Education Research and Development, University of Wisconsin-Madison, Madison, WI:

The PSB—Aptitude for Practical Nursing Examination (PSB-APNE) was revised in 1991. The test itself dates from 1959 and is designed to aid schools of Practical Nursing in selecting from among their applicants those with the highest likelihood of success in the program. U.S. Bureau of Labor Statistics project rapid growth in the demand for Practical Nurses, suggesting that the Revised PSB-APNE may be in even greater demand if the number of applicants to practical nursing schools increases in a like manner.

The Revised PSB-APNE reports scores derived from simply summing the number of items answered correctly on five subtests. The examination was revised in 1991 to incorporate suggestions derived from research conducted over the 30 years since its conception. The revised examination has fewer items than the older version (370 vs. 450) and two of the five subscores have been redefined, although they bear substantial similarities to the earlier version.

The technical report states that "studies indicate that better than 90% of the examinees will complete the test within the limits of the time allowed for each test" (p. 14). The authors do not support unlimited testing time because the educational program expects students to "assimilate a large body of knowledge in a rather limited length of time" (p. 15). Thus, unlimited testing time was considered "inimical to the purposes of the testing" (p. 15). This position may be difficult to sustain in the face of students with learning disabilities and mandates under the Americans With Disabilities Act.

The test itself is a relatively radical departure from the typical admissions test to a health professions school. Rather than the usual battery of science-related subtests coupled with a reading and quantitative section (and perhaps a writing sample), this examination approaches its task from a very different angle. A Spelling test in which the examinee is to select the word with the proper spelling from among a list of three different spellings of the word is used to estimate verbal fluency. This is an obvious departure from the more common verbal analogies approach and seems somewhat simplistic.

Perhaps the most innovative aspect of the examination is the Judgment and Comprehension in Practical Nursing Situations subtest. The objective of this subtest is to "measure the ability of the individual to arrive at wise decisions and to behave with discretion and discernment" (p. 19). Questions in this section pose a nursing situation such as a patient telling the "practical nurse" they have pain and would like some pain medication. The examinee is then asked to select which of four courses of action would be best. The questions in this section have a logical feel about them and the correct answers seem to have detectable features; however, it is not clear how the correct answers were decided upon.

A problem with questions that ask examinees to exercise judgment is that there may not be total agreement among content experts about what constitutes the "best" answer. In the test description, it is not clear how the correct answer was determined. At the very least, a test of this type should demonstrate evidence of agreement among experts that the correct answer is indeed the "best" approach to a situation.

The Vocational Adjustment Index is another innovative component of this examination. The 90 statements that ask the examinee to agree or disagree purport to "provide insight into the examinee's characteristic life style—their feelings, attitudes and opinions" (p. 20). The questions were based upon factors listed by program administrators, supervisors, and instructors, which were "felt to be desirable and important for the practical nurse to possess during the education period and, subsequently, in the working situation" (p. 20). This process (and more information on the details of this process would be helpful) led to eight factors being identified: (a) Attitude Toward Cooperation with Others, (b) Concern for the Welfare of Others, (c) Freedom for Nervous Tendencies, (d) Attitude Toward Authority, (e) Attitude Toward Health, (f) Occupational Stability, (g) Leadership Ability, and (h) Self-reliant. The only data reported supporting the validity of the Vocational Adjustment Index is a correlation of .73 with scores on the ETSA 8A Personal Adjustment Index based on 48 examinees. Given that there were eight factors used in developing the scale, it would be very helpful to have factor analysis data that would support reporting a single overall score; however, none is reported.

NORMING DATA. The authors (in personal communication) report "tentative" norming data from a sample of 3,669 examinees who were selected to be representative of: (a) nine regions into which the United States was divided, (b) urban and rural areas, (c) differing cultural and socioeconomic settings, and (d) differing ethnic and racial composition. The norming sample from 71 nursing programs constituted approximately 6% of approximately 1,128 schools/programs of practical nursing in the United States. According to the test developers, only tentative data are provided in the norms in the technical manual in order to keep users from simply copying the exam and using it without purchasing the materials. Judging from subsequent reports of data, the tentative norms in the technical manual have means that are substantially below that of the actual norms. Updated norms are periodically sent to user schools/programs.

The technical report provides results from a series of reliability studies conducted with random subsamples from the norming group. Test-retest reliability (stability) for a subsample of 126 with a time interval ranging from 10 to 30 days between successive testing were between .89 and .98 for the various subtests. Internal consistency reliability values ranged from .91 to .98 for a subsample of 155 examinees. Intercorrelations among the various subtests ranged from .05 to .27 for a subsample of 126 examinees. Comparisons of the random samples to the larger norming sample showed that there was over twice the percentage of the sample drawn from the 16–20-year-old age group than for the larger norming sample (41.2% vs. 19.4%), suggesting some bias may be present.

The technical report also summarizes results of a series of criterion-related validity studies. Concurrent validity coefficients between the Verbal subtest and the Arithmetic subtest (two parts of the academic aptitude score) correlated with comparable scales on School and College Ability Test .86 and .81, respectively, for 83 examinees. Scores for Academic Aptitude correlated .92 with scores from the Wechsler Adult Intelligence Scale for 48 examinees. Correlations of each of the Revised PSB-APNE scores with cumulative GPA in 11 Practical Nursing schools produced mean predictive validity coefficients ranging from .61 to .83. Correlations between the Revised PSB-APNE subtests and Licensing Examination Scores of a sample of 64 examinees (the Licensing Examination was taken 5 years after the Revised PSB-APNE was taken) ranged from .34 to .58. Correlations between the Revised PSB-APNE subscores and the graduating class rank of 29 examinees ranged from .46 to .63. The authors report a study of minority and majority examinees, which produced means that were not different by a statistically significant margin. There were also no statistically significant gender differences reported.

CRITIQUE. The Revised PSB-APNE is an updated version of a test that has seen valuable use for over 30 years. The authors have made a laudable attempt to address earlier weaknesses in the norming sample and in improving test items that were ambiguous and in some cases obsolete. The various scores derived from the examination have a great deal of common sense value about them, although some seem to be simplistic (e.g., spelling). The Judgment and Comprehension in Practical Nursing Situations and Vocational Adjustment Index are impressive attempts to include more than just cognitive abilities into the selection criteria. However, interjudge agreement for the keyed responses on the former exam and a factor analysis of data demonstrating support for the reporting of a single score for the latter exam would help improve their credibility. The internal consistency and test-retest reliability values reported for the various subtests meet or exceed most accepted thresholds for standardized tests. The relative lack of intercorrelation between the subtest scores suggest they are relatively independent of one another. The criterion-related validity data presented suggests that the examination predicts to a surprisingly high degree the school performance that it is attempting to anticipate. It even predicts licensing examination performance 5 years later to a surprisingly high degree. Studies reporting little differences in scores according to gender and minority status are also impressive strengths of the examination.

Although the examination has considerable strengths, there are some concerns. First, the directions to test administrators are relatively sparse and are not organized in a cohesive manner. A significant omission is what to do about examinees who come late. The lack of multiple forms may become or may already be a problem. If the examination is used by any school as a mechanism to exclude applicants, it becomes a high stakes examination for some students. As a consequence, security becomes an issue and the need for multiple forms and tight controls on administration become important. If schools are only using it as a mechanism for assessing readiness for portions of the curriculum and whether students should engage in remedial work prior to beginning the program, the need for multiple forms and security measures is less critical. However, even if there is no current need for security, it may be necessary in the future. Any school using the examination needs to give thought as to whether security is an issue for them and whether this examination is sufficiently secure.

The lack of data on interjudge agreement on the key for the Judgment and Comprehension Subscale and factor analysis to support the construct validity of the Vocational Adjustment Scale are weaknesses that need to be remedied.

The test and the technical bulletin have the look of an old examination (50s–70s). The technical bulletin has some typographical errors and would be more impressive if it had the appearance of being typeset, instead of being typed on a manual typewriter (on the first page the type font changed at midpage). The authors have rigorously applied classical test theory procedures to the development of the examination; however, it would give a more polished presentation if some of the more recently developed testing theory models were also incorporated, such as generalizability theory.

The credibility of the normative data presented and the research data regarding reliability and validity is compromised by the fact that the authors present only "tentative" norming data in the technical manual. Reporting norming data that are not accurate in the technical manual creates several problems. First, the illustrative normative data are substantially different from the data reported in the substudies that are described as being drawn from the normative sample. For instance, on the test-retest reliability data for 126 examinees, the mean on the Judgment and Comprehension Practical Nursing Situations was 37.60 (SD = 6.1). For the norming data, the median was 29.5. Because the distribution of the norming data was stated to be symmetric, the mean should be close to this value, suggesting that the sample used to obtain the reliability data was substantially different from the norm data. The technical manual states that the reliability subsamples were "a random sample of 126 examinees in the total number of examinees participating in the norming program" (p. 50), making these discrepancies raise serious questions about veracity of the studies reported in support of the reliability and validity of the examination. Results from the various other substudies also show means that are quite markedly different from one another as well as the norming data (means differing by more than 1 standard deviation), raising further questions about the reliability and validity data.

The technical manual needs to be more clear about the fact that the normative data are not related to the studies that are subsequently reported upon and in fact are quite different from the actual norms and should absolutely not be used in interpreting scores that are reported. Perhaps "sample" should be printed diagonally across the page to reinforce the footnote that indicates that the tabulated data are illustrative. The danger in having users actually use the tentative norms for interpreting scores is that the means are substantially lower than must be the case for the real norms. This would give the impression that applicants were performing at much higher levels than they actually were. Thus, an admissions officer who inadvertently misplaced current norms and turned to the technical manual for interpreting raw scores from an applicant pool could be deluded into believing the applicant pool is substantially better than it is in actual fact. This could lead the admissions committee to make decisions they would later regret.

SUMMARY. The Revised PSB-APNE appears to be a very useful instrument for appropriate placement, advisement, and for use in the establishment of realistic goals for students entering practical nursing programs. Over 30 years of research have resulted in a test that produces scores with high internal consistency and test-retest reliabilities, relatively low intercorrelations, and impressive predictive validity estimates. However, the lack of multiple forms, relatively weak security, misleading tentative norms in the technical bulletin, and inconsistent data reported across studies raise questions about its appropriate use for high stakes admissions and selection.

Review of the Revised PSB-Aptitude for Practical Nursing Examination by ANITA TESH, Assistant Professor, School of Nursing, University of North Carolina at Greensboro, Greensboro, NC:

The Academic Aptitude test (90 items; 45 minutes) contains three types of items: (a) items in which the examinee is to determine which word in a set differs most in meaning from four others, (b) arithmetic items, and (c) items on relationships among geometric forms.

The 50-item Spelling test (15 minutes) includes some words of specialized medical vocabulary, with which applicants with high aptitude but limited medical exposure might be unfamiliar (e.g., adenoid, dyspeptic).

The Natural Sciences test (90 items; 30 minutes) includes some items that are not science per se (e.g., history of physics), and some items with little direct relationship to the practice of nursing, such as knowledge about seismic waves and the relative conductivity of metals.

The Judgment test (50 items; 30 minutes) is intended to measure the ability to "use good judgment and common sense" (technical manual, p. 19), and includes items on patient care situation, study habits, interviewing, and personal characteristics.

The Vocational Adjustment Index is composed of 90 statements (15 minutes) about the nature of work, human nature, and personal characteristics, with which the examinee must either "agree" or "disagree" (no intermediate responses). Statements are intended to assess cooperativeness, concern for others, freedom from nervous tendencies, attitudes toward authority, attitudes toward health, occupational stability, leadership, and self-reliance. Although the instructions indicate that there are "probably no 'right' or 'wrong' answers" (test booklet, p. 17) many of the items have one answer that is clearly

socially desirable. These items may assess examinees' acumen regarding social expectations rather than their true attitudes.

ADMINISTRATION AND SCORING. Scoring is done by the test developer. Raw and percentile scores are reported to test users and examinees. A set of specimen questions without correct answers is available to potential examinees.

Thorough directions for administering the Revised PSB-Aptitude for Practical Nursing Examination (RPSB-APNE) are provided in the administrator's manual. No special training is necessary. The technical manual directs test users to contact the publishers for special procedures when testing the handicapped. The technical manual does not recommend a minimum score to be used for program admission, but notes that some programs prefer applicants who score at or above the 25th percentile.

NORMS. Initial norms were established in 1990 with 3,669 applicants to 71 programs of practical nursing, representing 45 states, the District of Columbia, and three Canadian schools. It is not clear whether stratified random sampling or quota sampling was used to select the programs. The technical manual contains information on age, education, and sex of the norm group. The technical manual states that norms are periodically updated, but presents no information on the schedule or procedures (p. 37). Potential test users should verify that norms are current, because composition of the applicant pool has been changing over recent years.

RELIABILITY. The technical manual includes information of the standard error of measurement for each test (but not the subtests of the Academic Aptitude test) derived from the original norm group. Other information on reliability is derived from small studies with limited representativeness.

Test-retest reliability coefficients, obtained from 126 examinees with 10 to 30 days between testings, ranged from .98 for the Spelling test to .89 for the Vocational Adjustment Index. Split-half (Odd/Even) reliabilities for 155 examinees ranged from .98 for the Academic Aptitude test to .91 for the Vocational Adjustment Index. No information is given on reliabilities of the subtests of the Academic Aptitude test. Lack of such reliability data is not in accordance with a primary standard of the *Standards for Educational and Psychological Testing* (AERA, APA, & NCME, 1985, p. 20).

VALIDITY. The technical manual (p. 53) states that content validity has been endorsed by expert judgment, but no information is given on the numbers or qualifications of experts consulted. The technical manual further asserts that the test reflects content based upon courses of study and texts, and knowledge and skills necessary during the educational period, but there are items in the Natural Sciences test that seem to this reviewer to have little relationship to practical nursing education. The technical manual states that the methods of construction of the test have ensured construct validity, but no statistical evidence of this is presented.

As evidence of concurrent criterion-related validity, the technical manual cites three small studies examining correlations between components of the RPSB-APNE and other instruments. No information is given on characteristics of the samples used in these studies. Correlations of .86 between the Verbal subtest of the RPSB-APNE and the School and College Ability Test (SCAT Series II, published by Educational Testing Service), and .81 between the Arithmetic subtest and the SCAT, are reported based on a sample of 83. Based on a sample of 48, a correlation of .92 between the Academic Aptitude Test and The Wechsler Adult Intelligence Scale is cited. A correlation of .73 between the Vocational Adjustment Index and the ESTA 8A Personal Adjustment Index, also based on a sample of 48, is reported. No evidence of concurrent validity of other components of the RPSB-APNE is presented.

As evidence of predictive validity, the technical manual cites correlations between students' scores on the RPSB-APNE and their subsequent cumulative grade-point averages in a nonrandom sample of 11 educational programs. Correlations were: .81 for the Academic Aptitude test, .63 for the Spelling test; .83 for the Natural Sciences test, .79 for the Judgment test, and .61 for the Vocational Adjustment Index. Because all data were obtained from students admitted to practical nursing programs, these correlations are likely attenuated by restriction of range. In a study in a single program (n = 29), correlations between the RPSB-APNE and graduating class rank were found to range from .46 for the Vocational Adjustment Index to .63 for the Academic Aptitude test. Information on predictive validity of the subtests of the Academic Aptitude test, required by the *Standards for Educational and Psychological Testing* (AERA, APA, & NCME, 1985, p. 14), is not provided.

In further support of predictive validity, the test manual presents data from two unorthodox studies. In one (n = 64, 1 program) licensing examination scores were correlated with scores on the RPSB-APNE obtained 5 years after graduation. Correlations ranged from .34 for the Vocational Adjustment Index to .58 for the Natural Sciences test. Another (n = 39, 1 program) examined the relationship between final grade-point average and scores on the RPSB-APNE taken at graduation. Correlations ranged from .41 for the Vocational Adjustment Index to .60 for the Natural Sciences test. Because the RPSB-APNE is intended to predict subsequent performance in an educational program, the value of this information is unclear.

The *Standards for Educational and Psychological Testing* (AERA, APA, & NCME, 1985, p. 13) state that "evidence of validity should be presented for the major types of inferences for which the use of a test is recommended." No evidence is presented regarding validity of the RPSB-APNE for guidance and counseling, two of the stated uses of the test.

OTHER CONSIDERATIONS. The technical manual states that comparative studies have revealed no evidence of racial or gender bias. Limited details of these studies are presented. The technical manual also states that the developers have attempted to minimize cultural dependency of items, but it seems likely that some cultural dependency exists in exposure to vocabulary words, items of natural science, and situations presented in the Vocational Adjustment Index and the Judgment test.

Although timed, the technical manual states that the RPSB-APNE primarily tests power rather than speed. Time allowances are stated to be adequate for examinees able to complete the test questions (p. 14).

SUMMARY. The RPSB-APNE provides information that potentially may be useful in selecting among a pool of applicants for practical nursing education programs. Only very limited information is available on the reliability and validity of the RPSB-APNE, so potential test users should carefully assess the appropriateness of the test for their programs before using it in making admission decisions. Potential test users should bear in mind that existing validity estimates for the various components of the RPSB-APNE differ dramatically, so some parts of the test may be more appropriate to use than others. Potential users should keep in mind that scores on the test may depend on exposure to certain educational or life experiences, rather than solely on aptitude. The test manual encourages test users to develop local norms to determine the relationship of test scores to success in their programs.

Potential test users should also evaluate whether the RPSB-APNE provides more useful information than alternative sources of data, such as the College Board SAT Program (T4:581), Enhanced ACT Assessment (12:139), high school GPAs, or scores on an alternative nationally normed test such as the "NLN Assessment and Evaluation Pre-Admission Examination for Practical Nursing" (National League for Nursing, 1994). Use of the RPSB-APNE for guidance and counseling, beyond possibly counseling on choice of practical nursing as a career, does not appear to be warranted.

REVIEWER'S REFERENCES

American Educational Research Association, American Psychological Association, & National Council on Measurement in Education. (1985). *Standards for Educational and Psychological Testing*. Washington, DC: American Psychological Association, Inc.

National League for Nursing (NLN). (1994). Pre-admission Examinations for Schools of Nursing. New York, NY: National League for Nursing.

[265]
Revised PSB—Health Occupations Aptitude Examination.

Purpose: Measures "abilities, skills, knowledge, and attitudes important for successful performance of students in the allied health education programs."

Population: Candidates for admission to programs of study for the allied health occupations.

Publication Dates: 1978–1992.

Scores, 8: Academic Aptitude (Verbal, Numerical, Nonverbal, Total), Spelling, Reading Comprehension, Information in the Natural Sciences, Vocational Adjustment Index.

Administration: Group or individual.

Price Data, 1997: $10 per test booklet; $10 per answer sheet including scoring and reporting service; $15 per technical manual ('92, 106 pages); $20 per specimen set including test booklet, answer sheet, and administrator's manual ('92, 6 pages).

Time: (135) minutes.

Comments: Earlier edition, now known as Standard PSB-Health Occupations Aptitude Examination, is still available.

Authors: Staff of the Psychological Service Bureau with consultant contributions.

Publisher: Psychological Services Bureau, Inc.

Cross References: For reviews by Stephen B. Dunbar and Lawrence M. Rudner of the earlier edition, see 11:312.

Review of the Revised PSB-Health Occupations Aptitude Examination by BETTY BERGSTROM, Director of Research and Psychometric Services, Commission on Dietetic Registration, The American Dietetic Association, Chicago, IL:

The Revised PSB-Health Occupations Aptitude Examination, a battery of tests including Academic Aptitude (measured by three subtests: Verbal Concepts, Arithmetic Concepts, and Nonverbal Concepts), Spelling, Reading Comprehension, Information in the Natural Sciences, and a Vocational Adjustment Index, is designed to predict whether a student will be successful in an allied health education program. An administrator's manual provides directions for administering the test and a detailed technical manual is provided.

The test publisher indicates that program directors of differing health education programs had input into the revised edition of the examination. The test publisher also indicates that content has been updated and readability improved from the earlier PSB-Health Occupations Aptitude Examination. A stated goal of the revised version is to provide adequate and appropriate measurement of older applicants.

The technical manual provides considerable information on test development including the source and piloting of items. Descriptive information is provided for each of the tests and subtests. On the Academic Aptitude test, the Verbal subtest consists of 30 synonym/antonym vocabulary items; the Arithmetic subtest consists of 30 items designed to test whether examinees can compute arithmetic problems rapidly and accurately; the Nonverbal subtest consists of 30 items designed to measure examinees' ability to identify rapidly similarities and differences in visual configurations. Testing time is 45 minutes and the test is admittedly speeded for low ability examinees. Verbal, Arithmetic, and Nonverbal items are spiraled in the test booklet, a procedure that may confound individual subtest scores.

The Spelling test, presented in a multiple-choice format, requires examinees to recognize the correct spelling of 60 words; test time is 15 minutes. The Reading Comprehension test consists of 50 questions related to four reading passages; test time is 30 minutes. The Information in the Natural Sciences test purports to measure a "core" of natural science health-related information including biology, microbiology, chemistry, physics, pharmacology, anatomy, psychology, earth science, life science, and health and safety. Test time is 30 minutes for 90 multiple-choice items.

The Vocational Adjustment Index consists of 90 statements designed to provide a composite estimate of eight personality behaviors such as "Attitude Toward Authority" and "Attitude Toward Health." The construct being measured is less well defined than for the other tests. No evidence is provided related to the unidimensionality of the construct and thus the meaning of a score derived from this test is not clear.

The examination was initially normed on a sample of 3,960 applicants to 198 allied health occupations education programs representing 39 different allied health occupations from nine distinct geographic regions. The technical manual states that norms used for scoring and reporting are periodically updated to remain current. Raw scores and percentile ranks for each of the five tests and three subtests are reported to examinees in graphical format.

Reported test-retest (10–30 day interval) reliability ranges from .88 to .98; reported split-half reliability ranges from .91 to .98.

Content of the Revised PSB-Health Occupations Aptitude Examination is reportedly based on a wide variety of sources including: review of textbooks in current use, courses of study, allied health education program curricula, and expert judgment. Validity studies, using scores earned on the Revised PSB-Health Occupations Aptitude Examination by applicants accepted for admission to a number of different allied health education programs indicated that the test results significantly predicted GPA. Sample sizes for these studies were small, ranging from 19 to 39 students.

Overall, the purpose, development, and usefulness of the Revised PSB-Health Occupations Aptitude Examination is well documented. Considerable effort seems to have been made to target the test for its intended audience. It appears that, at least for educational programs for the 39 allied health occupations used for norming, the test may be a useful tool for applicant screening.

Review of the Revised PSB-Health Occupations Aptitude Examination by HILDA WING, Personnel Psychologist, Federal Aviation Administration, Washington, DC:

The Revised PSB-Health Occupations Aptitude Examination (PSB-HOAE) is similar to the Standard PSB-HOAE and the reader is encouraged to read both of the reviews (Dunbar, 1992; Rudner, 1992) of the prior version. Although there have been changes, these reviews remain apt.

The battery includes tests of Academic Aptitude (with subscores of Verbal, Numerical, and Nonverbal, as well as Total), Spelling, Reading Comprehension, and Information in the Natural Sciences. The final "test" provides the Vocational Adjustment Index. Each of the five major parts is separately timed; the directions for each test are printed at the top of the page followed by the test items. This would appear to make the exactitude of the time limits somewhat problematical. The three parts of Academic Aptitude are not separately timed. Rather, the item types are spiraled (one Verbal, one Numerical, one Nonverbal, followed by one Verbal, etc.). Dunbar (1992) noted the potential speededness of this test in particular; the test manual provides some justification but no supporting data.

The manual states "The purpose of the VOCATIONAL ADJUSTMENT INDEX [*sic*] is to provide insight into the applicant examinee's manifest personality" (p. 23). Eight factors are named, which are "felt to be important to the successful allied health professional as a student and as a practitioner" (p. 23). With no accompanying statistics for support, it is awkward to accept the manual's claim that a single score could be used for counseling as well as selection. I personally distrust the combining of aptitude or maximum effort test scores with those from nonaptitude, typical-use survey scores. It would be possible to convince me with data, but there are none. Also, the manual suffers from occasional and distracting typos and ungrammatical expressions. In the copy of the test proper, one typo in the choices for one test item popped out; this does not reassure me about the rest of the examination.

Prior reviews faulted the Standard battery on its normative data, and now new statistics are given. For the Revised edition 3,960 applicants in nine regions of the United States were tested, covering 40 health occupations. These applicants were to represent over 95,000 students enrolled in allied health training programs during the same year. That the manual stresses local studies and does not provide norms for small groups is in its favor. For only the Radiographer occupation were there enough candidates to provide separate norms. The manual includes a number of tables to describe various subgroups (gender, age, formal education) of the norms sample. Although the percentage splits are informative, I prefer having the sample sizes as well.

Information about the reliability of the test parts was obtained from the total norms sample as well as two additional subgroups, and appears adequate. For one of these subgroups, with 176 applicants, the intercorrelations among the five test parts were minimal. I would expect the Vocational Adjustment Index to be minimally related to the others; I was surprised by the low intercorrelations of the four maximum effort tests.

I counted eight criterion-related validity studies, each showing the test parts to be sizably related to criteria such as cumulative GPA, National Registry examination scores, and class rank. The sample sizes available are very small, ranging from 19 to 35. That is, the test scores are reliably related to achievement in training, which the battery was developed to predict. The manual requests cooperative studies from test users, a good idea. The publishers should be encouraged to have a validity generalization database, which would, I predict, show that this battery is significantly and importantly related to performance in training. The manual also recommends, wisely, that there is no prescribed or universal cut score to be applied; these depend on local usage.

Finally, the manual describes the difference between the Standard and Revised versions of the HOAE. Sixty-five percent of the items in the Revised version are new, and 20% of the remaining 35% were modified. A sample of 59 administered both forms yielded equivalency correlations ranging from .638 to .892. Again, the small sample resulted in large standard errors.

This is probably a useful test battery for the stated purpose. I have concern abut many of the conclusions stated in the manual because of the absence of supporting data and statistics. This could leave a test user vulnerable if challenged. However, the development of the battery and the display of the data that were available suggest the battery would be a useful tool for selecting students for training in the allied health professions. I am much less confident about using this battery as a counseling tool because the presented information is insufficient for that activity.

REVIEWER'S REFERENCES

Dunbar, S. B. (1992). [Review of the PSB-Health Occupations Aptitude Examination]. In J. J. Kramer & J. C. Conoley (Eds.), *The eleventh mental measurements yearbook* (pp. 716–718). Lincoln, NE: Buros Institute of Mental Measurements.
Rudner, L. M. (1992). [Review of the PSB-Health Occupations Aptitude Examination]. In J. J. Kramer & J. C. Conoley (Eds.), *The eleventh mental measurements yearbook* (pp. 718–719). Lincoln, NE: Buros Institute of Mental Measurements.

[266]
Revised PSB—Nursing School Aptitude Examination (R.N.).

Purpose: Predicts "readiness or suitability for specialized instruction in a school/program of professional nursing."

Population: Prospective nursing students.

Publication Dates: 1978–1988.

Scores, 8: Academic Aptitude (Verbal, Arithmetic, Nonverbal, Total), Spelling, Reading Comprehension, Information in the Natural Sciences, Vocational Adjustment Index.

Administration: Individual or group.

Price Data, 1997: $10 per test booklet; $10 per answer sheet including scoring and reporting service; $15 per technical manual ('88, 59 pages); $20 per specimen set including test booklet, answer sheet, and administrator's manual ('88, 6 pages).

Time: (105) minutes.

Comments: Earlier edition, now known as Classic PSB—Nursing School Aptitude Examination (R.N.), is still available.

Authors: Anna S. Evans, Phyllis G. Roumm, and George A. W. Stouffer, Jr.

Publisher: Psychological Services Bureau, Inc.

Cross References: For reviews of the earlier edition by Kurt F. Geisinger and James C. Impara, see 11:313.

Review of the Revised PSB—Nursing School Aptitude Examination (R.N.) by MARK H. DANIEL, Senior Scientist, American Guidance Service, Circle Pines, MN:

This is a battery of five multiple-choice subtests designed for use in selecting students for nursing training (diploma and associate-degree programs). Four of the subtests are designed to measure abilities thought to be important for success in nursing training. The fifth, Vocational Adjustment, is described as a measure of "significant personality characteristics" and "characteristic life style" (p. 8) and is intended as a counseling tool rather than for selection.

Although this is a high-stakes examination, there is only one form. One would expect the publisher to protect test security by producing multiple forms. Furthermore, the content and the appearance of the test are dated, suggesting that this single form has been in use for many years, exacerbating the security problem.

The Academic Aptitude, Reading Comprehension, and Natural Sciences subtests are appropriate for a test designed to predict success in nursing training. The value of measuring Spelling ability is questionable. No convincing reason is given for including the Vocational Adjustment Index in the selection battery if it is not intended for use in selection. One suspects that, despite the manual's disclaimer, some schools use the Vocational Adjustment Index in their selection decisions in order to reject applicants with personality problems or poor work habits. If such is the case, the manual should advise users on the benefits and problems inherent in using a self-report personality scale for selection, and should offer considerably more guidance on interpretation.

The Academic Aptitude subtest consists of Verbal, Arithmetic, and Nonverbal items in spiral omnibus format. Each verbal item consists of five words, one of which is different in meaning from the others. Many of the words are extremely difficult (above college level), and some are arcane. The

Arithmetic items are mainly word problems; although their content is fairly basic, several are heavily computational. Some of the Arithmetic content seems to need updating. The Nonverbal items are figural analogies that rely heavily on orientation (rotation and reversal); the manual indicates that these items are designed to assess the ability to "manipulate things mentally" (p. 10). The artwork for these items is hand-drawn and occasionally unclear.

On the Spelling subtest, the examinee indicates which of three spellings of a word is correct. The words are more suitable in difficulty for high-level college graduates than nursing-school applicants. Item layout is poor, with all 50 items being packed together on a single page.

Reading Comprehension uses just three passages as the basis for 40 questions, causing excessive dependency among items. The passages are archaic in content and style. Two are articles written in 1949 and 1952 (by one of the test's authors), and the third is from an 1877 medical textbook. Nevertheless, all are treated at face value rather than as historical documents. The passages are lengthy and contain out-of-date terms. A number of the questions are redundant, some are very subtle if not ambiguous, and some employ convoluted wording. The time allowed for this subtest (15 minutes) was insufficient for this reviewer to reach all the questions.

The Natural Sciences subtest covers material likely to be included in high-school science courses. Some questions are awkwardly worded, but otherwise the content is straightforward.

The Vocational Adjustment Index consists of self-descriptive statements to which the examinee responds "Agree" or "Disagree." The items are a mix of positive and negative statements regarding depression, work habits and attitude toward work, somatic complaints, emotional instability, self-assurance, and similar dimensions. Many items are transparent and could easily be manipulated to create a positive impression. The authors deal with this problem by saying that by the end of the test the examinee is "drained physically, mentally, and emotionally and no longer has the reserve resources or is willing to spend the time in an attempt to 'steer' his or her responses" (manual, p. 15). Needless to say, this is not an adequate treatment of the problem. Statements in the introduction to this inventory that "this is not a test" and "there are probably no 'right' answers nor 'wrong' answers" may mislead examinees if Vocational Adjustment scores are in fact being used for selection.

There are a number of undesirable features in how the test is presented and formatted. The instructions and sample items are not set off from the actual test items themselves, and it would be easy for the examinee to accidentally respond to the sample items by marking the answer sheet in the spaces intended for actual items. Examinees read the subtest directions on their own, without opportunity to ask questions, and do not start reading the directions until the timed administration period for the subtest has begun. Thus, examinees who are familiar with the test have an advantage. Finally, the item layout is generally poor. All of the subtests are densely packed, making it easy to lose one's place.

TECHNICAL CHARACTERISTICS. The manual gives a general description of how the test was developed but does not indicate when this development occurred, saying only that it extended over a period of years. Prospective items were piloted on high-school seniors, college students, nurses, and nursing students. They were then administered to beginning nursing students, and the better-discriminating items were retained. Items for the Vocational Adjustment Index were selected according to their ability to discriminate between the general population and samples of neurotic and personality-disordered individuals.

Items in the final test have p values (proportion of examinees who answer an item correctly) between .10 and .75, with average values ranging from .43 (Spelling and Arithmetic) to .57 (Natural Sciences). These numbers are consistent with the previous observation that the subtests are very difficult. Spelling is particularly difficult, with the average item p value only slightly above the value obtained from guessing (.33).

Percentile and stanine norms for the five subtests and for the three subsections of the Academic Aptitude subtest are based on applicants and are continually updated by the publisher. The manual presents illustrative norms based on 3,984 applicants to about 80 schools, matched to the regional distribution of nursing training programs in the United States. The cases range in age from 16 to 61, most have completed 12 or 13 years of schooling, and 89% are females.

Reliability was estimated using the test-retest method with an interval of 10 to 30 days. The sample of 137 cases is not described. The retest reliabilities are extraordinarily high, ranging from .94 to .98 for the ability subtests and .89 for the Vocational Adjustment Index. Reliabilities are inflated by very high variances compared with the norm sample.

In striking contrast, for the same sample the ability-subtest intercorrelations range from .18 to .57, with a median of only .33. It is very unusual for reliable measures of academically related abilities to have such little overlap. Adding to the puzzlement is the fact that the Vocational Adjustment Index correlates from .21 to .75 (median = .32) with the four ability subtests. How can Academic Aptitude correlate .75 with Vocational Adjustment but only .56 with Reading Comprehension?

No specific information is provided on how content was selected, so there is little basis for a claim of content validity. The manual reports predictive validity studies in which the test scores of applicants were correlated with their academic performance after 6 months or more of nursing training. Criteria included grade point average, instructor ratings, and scores on licensing examinations. In what appears to be the largest study, correlations between admission test scores and subsequent GPA were computed at each of a number of schools, and these within-school correlations were averaged. The results are predictive validities of .79 for Academic Aptitude, .61 for Spelling, .81 for Reading Comprehension, .76 for Natural Sciences, and .59 for Vocational Adjustment. Other predictive studies using samples ranging in size from 48 to 182 students report similar correlations. These are astoundingly high values for the prediction of non-test variables, particularly when one considers the poor reliability of course grades and instructor ratings and the fact that the samples were restricted in range as a result of selection based on the test scores. These results raise as many questions as they answer, and for that reason one cannot draw conclusions from them about the test's actual predictive validity.

SUMMARY. The Revised PSB—Nursing School Aptitude Examination (R.N.) has serious weaknesses as a selection instrument: a single form that appears to have been in use for a considerable time; dated, arcane, and excessively difficult item content; poor typography and presentation; a personality self-report scale that is not intended for use in selection, and that is not appropriately explained; and questionable validity, intercorrelation, and reliability data that are not adequately documented. The abilities measured by this test can be assessed by a number of other well-developed, up-to-date instruments that would be superior choices for selecting nursing students.

Review of the Revised PSB—Nursing School Aptitude Examination (R.N.) by WILLIAM B. MICHAEL, Professor of Educational Psychology and Psychology, University of Southern California, Los Angeles, CA:

Intended for use in making decisions regarding the admission of students to schools of nursing awarding either the associate degree or diploma in nursing, this examination battery consists of five tests of which four assess cognitive and educational skills (Academic Aptitude, Spelling, Reading Comprehension, and Information in the Natural Sciences) and the last one, entitled the Vocational Adjustment Index, which covers a number of affective characteristics. For each of the five measures just cited, the respective working time is 30, 15, 15, 30, and 15 minutes for a total of 105 minutes as compared with nearly 3 hours for an earlier edition. Within the Academic Aptitude test, three subtests each consisting of 30 multiple-choice items with five alternatives are titled Verbal (vocabulary), Numerical (verbally presented problems requiring arithmetic computations and reasoning), and Nonverbal (representing figural material involving spatial relations and visualization abilities). The items in this test are presented in triads such that the first, second, and third items portray the Verbal, Numerical, and Nonverbal components, respectively. The Spelling test comprises 50 items (for each there is one correct spelling and two incorrect spellings). The examinee is directed to select the spelling that is correct. The third test of Reading Comprehension comprises 40 items, each with four alternative responses that are anchored to three different paragraphs with a health-related theme. The fourth cognitive test of Information in the Natural Sciences consists of 90 items, each with five alternative responses. These items also sample content that appears to have a satisfactory degree of face and content validity within a health sciences context. In the affective domain, the fifth test, called the Vocational Adjustment Index, contains 90 items to which the respondent indicates either agreement or disagreement. It covers a wide variety of noncognitive behaviors that would indicate its high degree of factorial complexity or multidimensionality.

This reviewer holds some reservations regarding just how relevant the Spelling test might be in the selection of nursing students, as many of the words are not related to health care. Moreover, the presentation of incorrect spellings may actually confuse the examinee and may possibly lead one to internalize a misspelling for a correct spelling of a word. The Spelling test could well be omitted from the battery. Another possible omission would be the Vocational Adjustment Index test. This reviewer suggests that a separate scale in the noncognitive domain be developed in which there would be separate subscales reflecting a number of different affective dimensions that could be employed in a counseling rather than in an admissions context. Such a measure could be administered in a separate booklet at the same, or a different, time from the cognitive tests. Omission of both the Spelling and Vocational Adjustment Index tests would still leave a potentially useful measure requiring a shorter administration time: 1 hours and 15 minutes.

TEST CONSTRUCTION AND STANDARDIZATION. Considerable effort was expended by the authors to select items that could be judged as content valid. In addition to meeting with administrators and faculty members of schools and programs of professional nursing, they interviewed students, practicing professional nurses, and significant others. A careful analysis of relevant curricula, research literature in the field, text books in current use, and student records afforded information that directed the process of test development. Pilot testing was also conducted.

A diligent effort was made to obtain a standardization sample that would appear to be representative of the populations of nursing students in associate degree and diploma programs throughout nine broad geographical areas within the United States. Data from 3,984 applicants to schools and programs of nursing were employed to provide percentile scores and stanine values on all five tests. The manual provides information concerning the age distribution of the respondents, the amount of prior education completed, and the distribution of the associate degree and diploma schools and/or programs of nursing in the nation and in the standardization sample.

RELIABILITY DATA. For a sample of 137 examinees, test-retest reliability estimates of scores and standard errors of measurement were recorded. The reliability estimates of scores on the four cognitive subtests, which ranged from .94 to .98, appeared to be exceptionally high. There was the strong possibility of correlated errors from the pretest to the posttest with the time interval of only 10 to 30 days between successive administrations. The reliability estimate for the Vocational Adjustment Index was .89.

Intercorrelations among the four cognitive subtests varied between .18 and .57 with the highest intercorrelations of .56 and .57, respectively, being between scores on the Academic Aptitude test and those on the Reading Comprehension test and between scores on the Academic Aptitude test and those on the Information in the Natural Sciences test. Somewhat surprisingly, a correlation coefficient

of .75 appeared between scores on the Academic Aptitude measure and those on the Vocational Adjustment Index test. It is difficult to explain why such a high correlation was obtained, especially in view of the item content of the affective measure. The other correlation coefficients between scores on the affective measure and those on the three remaining cognitive tests ranged between .21 and .36.

Another point of concern was the occurrence of very high reported reliability coefficients of difference scores for pairs of tests which ranged from .81 to .93. It was not clear from the manual whether these difference scores were associated with differences in standard scores between pairs of tests for the pretest administration or the posttest administration. Ordinarily, one would anticipate that the presence of relatively high or even moderate correlations between standard scores on two tests would be associated with relatively low reliabilities in the differences of their standard scores.

VALIDITY DATA. Supplementing the efforts that had been made to achieve both content and face validity, the test authors reported a number of predictive validity studies in which scores on the five tests were correlated with academic performance, rank in graduating class, licensing examination scores, ratings of students by instructors in the same five areas as those covered by the tests, and subsequent state board examination scores, which probably reflected in some instances licensing scores. For the most part, the validity coefficients seemed to be unusually high, as typically they exceeded .60 and often exhibited values as high as those ranging from the low to mid .80s. It was not altogether clear what the source of the samples was for which the validity coefficients were obtained. Certainly, additional validity studies conducted by other professional psychologists are needed in a variety of nursing training institutions to cross-validate the results obtained by the authors of this examination.

ADMINISTRATION AND SCORING. The directions for administration of the examination are provided in a clear manner in the administrator's manual as well as in the test booklets. In fact, illustrative examples are given to the examinees at the beginning of each of the five tests. Specific information is furnished to examinees concerning how to record their answers on a special answer sheet. A helpful feature to the test taker has been the distribution in advance of a practice set of items similar to those appearing in each of the five tests. Thus, the examinee should have had substantial prior orientation to what the examination will include and what the nature of its format will be.

Scoring of the examination is provided by the Psychological Services Bureau, Incorporated (publishers of the test) by optical scanning equipment. There is no mention in the manual concerning the time lapse between the receipt of the answer sheets and the reporting of scores to the participating institution.

OVERALL EVALUATION. In summary, the authors of the test have made a conscientious effort to achieve content validity and to obtain a representative sample of examinees to generate meaningful test norms. Additional work needs to be done to acquire reliability coefficients of test scores, which for the one sample employed were unrealistically high as were the predictive validity coefficients of the test scores against a variety of criterion measures. Some effort might also be expended to check for potential item or test bias. It would appear to this reviewer that the battery could be somewhat shortened by eliminating the Spelling test and by issuing as a separate measure one that indicates the multidimensionality of affective qualities. Such a scale might be useful not only in forecasting nursing success in hospital wards or clinical settings but also in furnishing valuable information in counseling situations. It seems that in its existing form, the total examination might not be altogether cost effective. It would be advisable to have responsible research personnel at each school or program carry out their own studies to check on the reliability and validity of the scores on each of the tests. Despite its limitations, the instrument shows promise and may be expected to provide some useful information in the process of selecting student nurses.

[267]
Revised PSB—Reading Comprehension Examination.

Purpose: "To reveal the examinee's comprehension or understanding of what he or she reads."
Population: Secondary and postsecondary students applying or enrolled in terminal vocational or occupational programs, general population.
Publication Dates: 1978–1993.
Scores: Total score only.
Administration: Group or individual.
Price Data, 1998: $10 per test booklet; $8 per student for answer sheet and scoring and reporting service; $15 per technical manual ('93, 92 pages); $15 per specimen set including test booklet, answer sheet, and administrator's manual ('93, 5 pages).
Time: (60) minutes.

Comments: Earlier edition, now known as Premier PSB—Reading Comprehension Examination, is still available.
Authors: Psychological Services Bureau, Inc., with consultant contributions.
Publisher: Psychological Services Bureau, Inc.
Cross References: For reviews of an earlier edition by Joseph C. Ciechalski and by Brandon Davis and John A. Glover, see 11:314.

Review of the Revised PSB—Reading Comprehension Examination by RAY FENTON, Supervisor of Assessment and Evaluation, Anchorage School District, Anchorage, AK:

The Revised PSB—Reading Comprehension Examination is an expansion of an earlier instrument, which was primarily for the purpose of screening individuals entering post high school health-related vocational programs. The new instrument is expanded to include 11 constructed reading passages followed by 90 multiple-choice questions that are presented during a 60-minute examination period.

The purpose of the standardized, norm-referenced test is "to measure or evaluate the examinee's ability to comprehend what is read … to take in or assimilate the meaning, nature, or importance of what is read" (technical manual, p. 8). The authors indicate that the test is not designed to be a diagnostic test and that the instrument should only be considered as one element in considering placement or acceptance of an individual into an academic or vocational program.

According to the Technical Manual that accompanies the test, the 11 reading passages have been rated on a "Readability Index" (p. 13). These ratings range from grade level 6.3 to 16.4. Most of the individuals participating in the norming sample were between 16 and 30 years of age and reported a highest grade level achieved between grades 11 and 14.

Information is not provided on individual test items or on similar types of items that are related to each of the 11 passages. Passages vary in length from 212 to 422 words and are presented in from one to three paragraphs. The number of items that are related to each passage vary from 5 to 15 with more questions being asked about longer reading passages. Some items call for the finding or direct recall of facts. Other more sophisticated items call for drawing conclusions and making inferences from information that is separated by a number of sentences. It is noted that 90% of the examinees finish the test.

Norms are reported for (a) general, (b) secondary and post secondary, and (c) practical, vocational/

nursing samples collected over a 3-year period. These are based on substantial numbers of 7,190; 3,656; and 5,237 examinees. Various characteristics of the norming groups are discussed without much exact detail as to the circumstances under which individuals were tested or their motivation for participating in the norming study. The differences in performance among the three norming groups are notable.

Evidence is presented to support the reliability and validity of the Revised PSB—Reading Comprehension Examination for each of the three types of groups for which there are norms. Test-retest reliability appears to be good (.89 to .94) over a time period varying from 25 to 35 days and estimates of split-half reliability are high (.89 to .94) with small groups of selected individuals that range in size from 112 to 135. There is an extensive discussion of the face validity of the test and a number of additional validity studies are reported though detail is somewhat limited.

It is reported that substantial differences are not found in the performance of men and women or various ethnic/cultural groups though the authors are still attempting to collect information on minority group members and request that users assist them in updating their data base. Information on the differential performance of groups of individuals on the 11 reading passages and 90 items is not reported.

Test users may contract with Psychological Services Bureau for the development of local norms, which are encouraged because "Sections of the country, occupational groups, and schools differ widely in the United States" (p. 55). Users are promised that they will be provided with updated norms as they are produced.

CONCLUSION. The Revised PSB—Reading Comprehension Examination appears to yield valid measures of reading comprehension based on passages constructed to reflect different types of writing and levels of reading difficulty. The measure is designed as a norm-referenced standardized test useful for the ranking of individuals rather than as a diagnostic test. Substantial numbers of individuals participated in the norming of the test and it appears to be an adequate measure for screening individuals who are making application to vocational programs. More information is needed on the performance of individuals with diverse linguistic and cultural backgrounds. Potential users might want to consider carefully the degree to which the reading passages constructed for the Revised PSB—Reading Comprehension Examination conform to what their students will be asked to read.

Review of the Revised PSB—Reading Comprehension Examination by FELICE J. GREEN, Professor of Education, University of North Alabama, Florence, AL:

The Revised PSB—Reading Comprehension Examination is designed "primarily for the measurement of reading comprehension of individuals who have progressed to the secondary level in their formal education program and are seeking additional educational opportunities in secondary or postsecondary occupational programs" (p. 9).

The test consists of 11 reading passages ranging from Level 6 to Level 16 (college). The time limit for reading the 11 passages and answering the questions is 60 minutes, which seems to be an adequate amount of time for most examinees to complete the test.

The standardization population appears adequate for the test's purpose. The age ranges were from 16 to 84. An effort was made to include a representative sample of African-Americans, Asians, Native Americans (American Indian), and Hispanics. Various socioeconomic levels were obtained by including areas with a high population of the different levels. There was also an adequate representation of males and females. There was a problem with obtaining older participants in the standardization, as older people are reluctant to participate in activities that are a "waste" of time. Urban and rural samples were also included. The total number in the standardization population was 7,190.

For potential examiners who do not have a thorough understanding of terms such as "validity," "reliability," and "standard error of measurement," the test manual gives easy-to-understand definitions. It was particularly refreshing to see that the explanation of validity included that a test is valid if it tests the skills the user desires to have tested.

The test-retest reliability (25–35-day interval) coefficients for the Revised PSB—Reading Comprehension Examination ranged from .89 to .94. The standard error of measurement ranged from 2.36 to 4.02 (reported in raw scores).

Scores for this test are reported in percentiles and stanines only, which are both more meaningful than grade level scores. An excellent explanation is given for both of these scores. Tests are scored by the publisher, Psychological Services Bureau.

The directions for administering the test are clearly stated, and so are the directions for the examinee. Administering the test poses no problems.

Unfortunately, some of the test items have serious problems. Passage One states in the first sentence, "A study of a few days ago, found that beards made men seem older and less friendly than men without beards." The introductory phrase indicates that the purpose of the study was to investigate "a few days ago." Of course, the purpose of the study was to investigate how people view the facial features of others. The first sentence (possibly a typographical error) is confusing for the reader.

The first two "sentences" of Passage Two are likewise confusing. In fact, they are fragments: "Rain with a pH that makes it 'acid rain.' Shampoo advertised as 'pH balanced.'" If the first two "sentences" were intended to be fragmented quotes from another source, they should be enclosed in quotation marks, which they are not. This would cause the reader to reread in order to try to make sense of the "sentences" before going on to read the rest of the passage.

There is a minor problem with Passage Three. The fourth sentence of the first paragraph says, "As an example a few years ago, although only a very few people knew it, the gases in spray cans ..." There should be a comma after the word "example." The absence of a comma could cause the examinee to have to reread.

Passage Seven also has an error. The first sentence of the second paragraph states, "for variously skilled clerical works including cashiers, computer operators." The word "works" should clearly be "workers."

There is a subject-verb disagreement in Passage Eight. The second sentence of the first paragraph states, "There has been, over the centuries, many controversies concerning the 'father' of the scientific method." The word "controversies" is the subject (plural), which should, therefore, have a plural verb, "have" instead of "has." It is not likely that the examinee would have to reread due to this error, but passages in reading tests should be well written.

Although, as stated earlier, 60 minutes should be an adequate amount of time for most examinees to complete all of the passages, the errors in the passages pose an extra burden. Rereading is necessary sometimes to understand a passage even for excellent readers, but one should not have to reread to make sense of poorly written passages in a test. Needless to say, this takes extra time, and, furthermore, poorly written passages in a reading test are unacceptable.

The test also purports to have ample questions to measure higher order thinking, which it fails to do. Most of the questions are on the literal level.

In conclusion, this test is seriously flawed, mainly due to poorly written reading passages.

[268]
Riverside Curriculum Assessment System.

Purpose: An item bank consisting of multiple choice and performance items to assist in the development of tests of achievement in reading, language arts, mathematics, social studies, and science.
Population: Grades K–12.
Publication Date: 1991.
Acronym: RCAS.
Administration: Group.
Price Data, 1992: $15 per Test Builder's Handbook (62 pages); $42 per 100 answer sheets; price varies by quantity per reusable or performance-based test booklet, minimum order 300; price varies by quantity per machine-scorable test booklets, minimum order 1,000; other price data available from publisher.
Authors: Riverside Publishing Co. staff and consultants.
Publisher: The Riverside Publishing Co.
  a) PERFORMANCE TEST EXERCISES.
  Scores, 3: Reading, Writing, Mathematics.
  Price Data: $15 per Performance Test Exercises catalog.
  Time: (25–90) minutes.
  b) MATHEMATICS OBJECTIVES.
  Scores: Total score only.
  Price Data: $15 per Mathematics Objectives catalog.
  Time: Administration varies according to number of items selected.
  c) READING AND LANGUAGE ARTS OBJECTIVES.
  Scores: Total score only.
  Price Data: $15 per Reading and Language Arts Objectives catalog.
  Time: Administration time varies according to number of items selected.
  d) SOCIAL STUDIES AND SCIENCE OBJECTIVES.
  Scores: Total score only.
  Price Data: $15 per Social Studies and Science Objectives catalog.
  Time: Administration time varies according to number of items selected.
[Editor's Note: The publisher advised in September 1997 that this test is now out of print.]

Review of the Riverside Curriculum Assessment System by MICHAEL HARWELL, Associate Professor of Psychology in Education, University of Pittsburgh, Pittsburgh, PA:

Reviewers sometimes find that much of the salient information about a test comes from what is not reported in the test manual. This appears to be true for the Riverside Curriculum Assessment System (RCAS), a testing system available to schools that allows customized achievement tests to be constructed for reading and language arts, mathematics, social studies, and science for grades K—12. According to the manual, the advantage for schools is the availability of a large pool of professionally written items that permits tests to be constructed that match the local curriculum.

There are several steps in using the RCAS, which are clearly laid out in The Test Builder's Handbook. The first and most crucial step is deciding whether the user-constructed tests are to be norm-referenced (NRT) or criterion-referenced (CRT). The manual points out that the RCAS is oriented toward CRTs but that the same tests can be used as NRTs. The manual does a good job of helping users understand the key differences between these two kinds of tests. Next, users must decide whether multiple-choice or performance assessment-type items will be used. For multiple-choice items, users order catalogs for the subject areas to be assessed. The catalogs contain descriptions of performance objectives that are tied to specific grades. For example, the Reading/Language Arts catalog has a section entitled reading readiness containing 28 performance objectives covering auditory discrimination, visual discrimination, letter names and forms, logical relationships, and performances. Users interested in assessing reading readiness would choose among these 28 objectives. Each performance objective has a code that is used when ordering, enabling items that assess that objective to be selected from the RCAS item bank. The manual states that every objective has at least 3 items associated with it (out of an average of 6). There are approximately 3,000 performance objectives and 18,000 items available. If performance assessment-type items (e.g., written response, open-ended) are to be used, users must order the Performance Test Exercise catalog. This catalog contains descriptions of the assessments available for the subject areas Reading, Writing, and Mathematics for grades 1–12. Each performance assessment contains 3–10 performance objectives. The choices made by a school are then sent to the publisher, along with other information such as the number of test forms needed. In the end, the school receives a ready-made achievement test.

EVOLUTION OF THE RCAS. It is useful to trace briefly the evolution of the RCAS. According to the manual, the earliest version (around 1972) of what eventually became the RCAS was the School Curriculum Objectives-Referenced Evaluation (SCORE), which was expanded to include new objectives and items and renamed MULTISCORE in 1984. The addition of 13,000 new items to the MULTISCORE item bank prompted it being renamed the RCAS. However, additional items were drawn from Forms B and C of Riverside's The 3-R's Test (nationally normed in 1980), the Life Skills Tests (standardized in 1978), and from proficiency tests developed by the Houston Independent School District (HISD) (item data obtained in 1987). The manual notes that the pool of performance objectives and items is constantly being expanded.

SELECTING PERFORMANCE OBJECTIVES AND PERFORMANCE ASSESSMENTS. One obvious concern is the number of multiple-choice items selected. The manual suggests that at least three items be selected to assess each objective, but is silent on the dangers of selecting too few items for broadly defined objectives (e.g., one item per objective). The presentation in the manual is elementary, presumably in recognition of the fact that the school officials and staff involved in constructing the tests may have limited psychometric training. Combine this with the fact that choosing more items means greater costs and that schools would probably want to minimize such costs, and it seems likely that some schools might be tempted to choose too few items to obtain psychometrically useful information. The manual does say that narrowly defined objectives can probably be satisfactorily measured with one item and that broadly defined objectives require more items. The manual also says that the publisher can assist users in deciding on the number of items to be selected. Still, it would be helpful if the manual highlighted warnings of the potential dangers of selecting too few items to assess some objectives. It would also be helpful if information about selecting mastery cutoffs was included.

One other concern is the usefulness of Table 4 in the manual, entitled "Possible Error Due to Guessing." The manual states that "Table 4 shows how various mastery criteria influence the accuracy of measurement with different numbers of items. This table indicates the probability of appearing to master an objective by guessing or marking items randomly" (p. 17). So, for example, users learn that the probability of marking two out of two items correctly for four-choice items is $.0625 = .25^2$. The purpose is to give users a sense of how likely it is that an examinee would achieve mastery status (e.g., two out of two items correct, two our of three correct) by guessing for a given number of items. These numbers do not seem very useful because they assume that an examinee is truly guessing when available evidence in the psychometric literature suggests that it is more reasonable to assume that examinees are able to eliminate some of the multiple-choice options and are only partially guessing. It is probably safe to conclude that in practice the probabilities are higher than those reported in Table 4.

ADMINISTRATION. The sample tests provided in the manual suggest that teachers should have little problem in administering the tests. The directions are clear and estimates of how long it should take examinees to finish a test in a particular subject area are given. Of course, testing time will vary according to the number of items selected. The manual emphasizes that, strictly speaking, the tests are untimed, although it notes that in practice some time limit is often imposed. Users are advised that a useful rule of thumb is to allow an average of one minute per item. For the multiple-choice tests, decisions about how many subject area tests to offer in a day are left to users, whereas for performance assessments, the manual provides estimates of how long it will take examinees (25 to 90 minutes for each performance assessment). Each Writing assessment is administered in two sessions on separate days whereas each Reading and Mathematics assessment is administered in a single session.

SCORING. The multiple-choice items are scored right-wrong and yield total-correct scores for each subject area. The range of possible scores will depend on how many items have been selected for the assessment of a particular subject area. Tests can be scored by the publisher or done locally. The manual suggests that the performance assessments be scored by the teachers administering the tests, either individually or in groups. Each performance assessment has a scoring guide. The manual suggests that teachers often score the assessments of their students, but, in general, this seems like a bad idea. The subjective nature of this kind of scoring suggests that at least two teachers should score each assessment response. Even if two or more teachers are used to score assessments, there is no guidance on how discrepancies in scoring should be resolved or the importance of reaching some minimal level of interscorer consistency. Of course, this is likely to be time-consuming as well as tedious, but that is the price for administering performance assessments. The fact that these may be high-stakes tests requires more attention to their scoring.

NORMS. No normative data are given. If the customized tests are interpreted as CRTs then, of course, norms are irrelevant. The problem is that the manual states that a customized test can be interpreted as an NRT if desired. The manual goes on to say that normative data are not available until the customized test(s) are administered, leaving users in a Catch-22 situation in the sense that users who desire an NRT must create their own norms before such interpretations are possible. Put another way, users can use the RCAS to customize their own NRT but must then customize (i.e., construct) their own norms. Because the creation of a useful normative database is no small undertaking, users who desire an NRT should, at the least, consider other available NRTs. These tests may lack the customizing possible with the RCAS but at least they have well-defined norms.

RELIABILITY. Once again the CRT and NRT distinction creates some confusion. If the RCAS is primarily intended to construct CRTs, then it seems natural to expect that the reliability evidence would be oriented toward CRTs. Unfortunately, this is not so, and what is worse is that there is little reliability evidence of any kind presented. The manual does report summaries of item difficulty and discrimination statistics based on the standardization of the MULTISCORE items in Reading/Language Arts and Mathematics in 1976, along with KR-20 reliability coefficients and standard errors of measurement. Unfortunately, these statistics are aggregated across items (e.g., median standard error of measurement for a 15-item test for second graders). The total standardization sample size is given as 19,121 students in grades 2, 3, 5, 7, and 9 from over 100 schools and 31 cities. The standardization of The 3-R's Test in Reading/Language Arts and Mathematics occurred in 1980 and used a probability sample of the national school population involving 118,134 students in grades K–12. No item statistics or reliability coefficients are reported. The Life Skills Test of basic reading and mathematics skills was standardized in 1978 with more than 10,000 students in grades K–12. Although the manual notes that approximately 2,000 institutionalized individuals in 22 state penal institutions participated in the standardization, no further explanation is offered. No item statistics or reliability information are reported. Finally, items from the proficiency tests developed by the HISD are included in the RCAS item bank. These items cover English, language arts, mathematics, science, and social studies. The manual says simply that "All items were subjected to item analyses following administration to a large number (several hundred to several thousand) of students" (pp. 57–58). No specific information about numbers of students, their demographic makeup, or reliability is reported. Reliability of the performance assessment items would focus on the consistency with which these items are scored by two or more scorers. No information of this sort appears in the manual.

VALIDITY. Without exception, validity evidence relies on content validity. With some variation, the validation process for the MULTISCORE test, The 3-R's test, and the HISD proficiency tests involved a committee of content experts (e.g., curriculum specialists, instructional supervisors, teachers, professional test developers) who wrote the performance objectives and items and then evaluated the items on several criteria, including how well they matched the objectives with which they were associated. Development of the performance assessments followed much the same process. As with much content validity evidence, there is little with which to quarrel. There appears to have been a careful attempt to define the domains to be tested, to write performance objectives that are consistent with that domain and items that assess specific objectives, etc. What is missing is empirical evidence of validity, which should be routinely provided for both NRTs and CRTs. It is difficult to understand why a representative sample of objectives and items has not been sampled and piloted, allowing validity and reliability evidence to be obtained.

The description of the development of the RCAS in the manual and the reported reliability and validity evidence suggests the following conclusions: (a) It is not clear how many items the MULTISCORE, 3 R's, Life Skills, and HISD proficiency tests contributed to the RCAS pool of objectives and items. The pool of performance objectives and items for Reading/Language Arts and Mathematics areas appear to have come largely from the MULTISCORE test. More specific information about how much each of these tests contributed to the RCAS would be helpful (e.g., approximately 20% of the RCAS items come from Test A). (b) The detailed information reported in the manual documenting the representativeness of the sample of examinees and the reliability of MULTISCORE test items is not reported for any of the other tests. (c) The NRT/CRT distinction is clearly defined at the beginning of the manual but becomes increasingly murky as information about the test construction process and reliability and validity evidence are described. (d) With the exception of the HISD items, items from the remaining tests are taken from standardizations that are somewhat dated (e.g., 1976, 1980). (e) The fact that some of the standardizations involved what appear to be nationally representative

samples does not ensure that examinee responses will be independent of race, gender, etc. The manual reports that a panel of experts was convened to ensure that items for The 3-R's Test showed no bias, but is silent about this issue for items from MULTISCORE, the Life Skills Test, and the HISD proficiency tests. But even the report of the investigation of bias for The 3-R's Test raises a few flags. In general, the psychometric community has been in agreement for some time that differential item functioning (DIF) and item bias are different things. Simply put, DIF is usually indicated when different demographic groups (e.g., males, females) show differences in their performance on an item; an item is considered biased if the DIF can be attributed to extraneous characteristics or features of the item (e.g., the item uses all male characters). In defense of the description in the manual, the DIF/bias distinction was not nearly as accepted when the panel convened (1978) as it is today. However, this suggests that 1978 standards for evaluating bias were applied to a test published in 1991.

It is quite possible that these concerns are attributable to the brevity of the description of the test construction process in the manual. Still, the manual is all that users have to rely on. If explanations for these (and similar) questions exist, the publisher should include a source potential users can use to obtain more detailed information about the MULTISCORE test, The 3-R's test, the Life Skills Test, and the HISD proficiency tests.

SUMMARY. For users interested in customizing a CRT the RCAS has much to recommend it. Its primary strengths are the ability of schools to select performance objectives that match their curriculum and a pool of professionally developed items available to assess the objectives. Several subject areas are available, and both multiple-choice and performance assessment-type items are available. Still, there are three problem areas for the RCAS that potential users should consider. One is that there is too little information about the tests whose objectives and items found their way into the RCAS. If this information is available but has not included in The Test Builder's Manual users should have the option of requesting it. Second, the suggestion that the same customized test can be treated as either a CRT or an NRT is suspect. After stating that the RCAS is intended to produce CRTs, the manual reports a hodgepodge of reliability and validity evidence that is sometimes oriented toward CRTs and sometimes toward NRTs. Users would be better served if the scope of test use was narrowed to CRTs. At the least, users interested in an NRT should consider more traditional NRTs with available norms. Third, published reliability and validity results are somewhat dated, and it is hard to understand why more recent evidence has not been obtained. Until such evidence is available, it will be more difficult for users to evaluate the psychometric properties of the RCAS items than it should be.

[269]
Rothwell Miller Interest Blank (Revised).

Purpose: "Designed primarily to give an assessment of vocational interests as an aid to a career interview ... other applications include company selection and promotion, and clinical and rehabilitation counselling."
Population: Ages 13 and over.
Publication Dates: 1958–1994.
Acronym: RMIB.
Scores, 12: Outdoor, Mechanical, Computational, Scientific, Persuasive, Aesthetic, Literary, Musical, Social Service, Clerical, Practical, Medical.
Forms, 3: A, B, and C.
Administration: Individual or group.
Price Data: Available from publisher.
Time: (15–30) minutes.
Comments: In addition to main task of ranking occupations in order of preference, there is an opportunity for free choice responses; can be used in conjunction with the complementary values measure Choosing a Career—Rothwell Miller Values Blank.
Authors: J. W. Rothwell (original test), K. M. Miller (original test and revisions), and B. Tyler (1994 revision).
Publisher: Miller & Tyler, Ltd. [England].
Cross References: For reviews by A. W. Heim and Clive Jones of an earlier edition, see 7:1034 (2 references).

Review of the Rothwell Miller Interest Blank (Revised), British Edition by RICHARD E. HARDING, Senior Vice President, The Gallup Organization, Lincoln, NE:

The Rothwell Miller Interest Blank (British Edition) (RMIB) was originally developed in Australia in 1958. It underwent a revision in 1968, and subsequently underwent a second revision in 1994, which is the version evaluated. The RMIB was designed to help individuals understand their vocational interests and how that relates to stereotypical ideas of work involved in various occupations. The Blank consist of nine blocks of 12 job titles with each block containing one representative job from 12 job interest categories. Those job interest categories are: Outdoor (e.g., farmer), Mechanical (e.g., civil engineer), Computational (e.g., accountant), Scientific (e.g., analytical chemist), Persuasive [Personal Contact] (e.g., sales manager), Aesthetic (e.g., artist), Literary (e.g., journalist), Musical (e.g., orchestral musician), Social Service (e.g., psychologist), Clerical (e.g., bank clerk), Practical (e.g., furniture upholsterer), and Medical (e.g., doctor).

The respondent is asked to rank 1 through 12 each of the 12 occupations within each of the nine blocks. The ranking form is well laid out and easy to use and score. The occupations for each of the nine blocks are presented in a different order. There is no time limit to the test, and it is reported that most respondents complete the Interest Blank in less than 20 minutes, with almost all doing so between 10 and 30 minutes. The Interest Blank is intended for use with individuals 13 years of age and older.

This revision of the Interest Blank contains three forms. Form A is a unisex version, Form B is used for males, and Form C is used for females. An example of differences across blocks for the three forms (A, B, and C) would be that for Form A, the unisex version, metal engraver is used as an example for the Practical category, but for Form B, the male version uses carpenter; and for Form C, the occupation of curtain maker is utilized.

The manual further indicates that, when the original version was developed between 1954 and 1958, it was felt to be impractical at that time to produce a unisex version. The manual also indicates that there has been pressure from society for a unisex form. Furthermore, Form Z, the unisex version, was developed with considerable difficulty. To develop the Unisex Blank, raters were drawn from tertiary students and adults, with 300 or more males and females in each group in the United Kingdom. These individuals were given two tasks: First was to take each job title and classify that job title into one of the categories; and secondly, to classify each job as to whether it was equally desirable for males and females, or more desirable for males or females. These ratings were done by individuals in the U.K. as well as verified by Australian data.

Once the Unisex Blank was developed, further developmental efforts were completed during the same time period in both the U.K. and Australia. Australian data were used where comparable British data were not available, which, in the manual, is indicated in some of the reliability tables. The sample was 2,223 cases, grouped into three categories: secondary school students ($n = 659$), tertiary students ($n = 849$), and adults (employed or seeking employment, $n = 715$). The samples are adequately described in the manual.

Various analyses were completed to study the Unisex Form with regard to gender differences and age relationships. Across the three groups: school, tertiary, and adult, there were significant differences listed between males and females with regard to the various job categories. Not every job category was significantly different between males and females across all three samples; for example, within the Persuasive category, no significant differences were detected between males and females across the three subsamples.

Test-retest reliability estimates were obtained with time differences between tests ranging from 2 weeks to 8 months across the three subsamples. The reliability estimates for the school group ranged from .69 (Persuasive category) to .96 (Medical category). For the tertiary group, the range is from .58 (Mechanical category) to .90 (Aesthetic category). For the adult subsample, the range is from .68 (Persuasive category) to .91 (Outdoor category).

Internal consistency estimates were also obtained, utilizing males and females combined, and separately, for the secondary school group and for the adult group. This reliability estimate ranges from .57 to .92 (median = .87) for males and females combined in the total school group, whereas for the total adult group, the range is from .66 to .92 (median = .88).

Validity evidence was obtained with regard to item validity (i.e., content validity, independence of categories, factor analysis, and concurrent validity). Some of this work is not based on the Unisex Blank, but is based on data from the 1968 manual.

Concurrent validity evidence was also obtained by correlating the Interest Blank to the SHL Advanced Occupational Interest Inventory. This was done on a sample of 28 respondents from a bank. The conclusion in the manual is that the relationship of the SHL to the Interest Blank does not measure the same constructs. And, it goes on to say that both instruments could appropriately be used together as complementary measures.

Normative data are provided, broken out by age and by sex; some data are from very small samples (i.e., 27 respondent males, ages 13 to 14), so they are of limited value. There are also four case studies presented in the manual with complete data and analyses that one would find quite helpful in a counseling setting.

It would seem that the greatest utility for the Interest Blank is for career or vocational counselors to help individuals explore categories of jobs (a) they have expressed interest in, and indeed, in which they have measurably more interest (according to the Interest Blank); and (b) to not rule out any categories for which little or no interest was expressed. The author correctly states that little or no interest, as measured by the Interest Blank, may translate to inadequate knowledge or a stereotypical attitude about a specific job.

Thus, the Interest Blank provides a logical place to start someone in learning or exploring various occupational fields of work. With the well-written manual, scoring keys, and interpretation guides, the Interest Blank has great utility for vocational counselors in helping individuals explore the various jobs and categories of jobs available to them. In fact, the manual indicates the RMIB has been used in a group discussion format after all in the group have completed the Interest Blank, used in Guidance Programs to help students identify their main area of interest, in personal counseling, for selection and placement, and for outplacement. This reviewer feels that those are appropriate uses of the Interest Blank as long as the Blank is not the sole source of information used in these situations.

Review of the Rothwell Miller Interest Blank (Revised), British Edition by WILLIAM K. WILKINSON, Consulting Psychologist, Boleybeg, Barna, County Galway, Ireland:

The Rothwell Miller Interest Blank (RMIB) was originally developed in Australia in the 1950s as a means of measuring career interests. It was revised in the 1960s to include British norms, British job titles, and to expand the 9 occupational scales to 12. The current revision is the development of a new "unisex" Form A. The separate gender forms are retained (Forms B and C), but with updated job titles. These developments were designed to "modernize" the RMIB, an especially worthy goal given the everchanging economic, social, and political forces that affect careers.

These significant revisions aside, the RMIB remains much the same as its predecessors regarding purpose, administration, scoring, and interpretation. For example, the RMIB still contains 12 occupational scales (e.g., Outdoor, Scientific, etc.), each comprising nine job titles (e.g., farmer, chemist, etc.). Further, as with the earlier version, the respondent is requested to rank 12 job listings in each of the nine blocks. Finally, the scoring and interpretation of the RMIB are unaltered. Therefore, earlier *Mental Measurements Yearbook* reviews remain generally applicable (cf. Heim, 7:1034; Jones, 7:1034).

With the development of Form A, the RMIB now consists of this primary form and the two separate gender forms. What confuses this reviewer is how one evaluates the new status of Forms B and

C. It is clear that the updated manual is devoted to supplying norms and technical information regarding Form A. And, in the development of Form A, it was clear that Form A job titles were partial to those with advanced training and qualifications. Thus, Forms B and C are said to "complement" Form A, being most useful for "younger school learners and older people who do not have academic or professional qualifications" (manual, p. 7). This makes it clear when to use Forms B and C, but nowhere could I evaluate the technical merit (e.g., reliability, validity) of the revised Forms B and C. Perhaps it is assumed that the 1968 manual will provide ample support for these forms, but this would be so only if the forms were not revised. In addition, the current manual only supplies norms for Form A, but not B and C. I gather that the test user relies predominately on Form A as the first choice. Revised Forms B and C meet particular examinee needs, but compared to Form A, are relatively limited interpretively and technically.

The remainder of this review focuses on the following questions: (a) How was Form A developed, (b) what norms apply to this form, and (c) what technical data exist to support Form A. How was Form A developed? Two fundamental tasks were involved—specifying the new content domain by which occupations would be sampled, and developing a procedure to quantify empirically the degree to which each occupation was in fact "unisex" verus "separate sex." Regarding the content domain, I was unable to find a specific reference that pointed to the exact "population" source by which the occupations were sample. The manual contains an appendix that includes a "directory of jobs in occupational fields" and the actual occupations contained on the form closely approximate the title in the appendix. I assume this is the "large pool of job titles" the authors refer to on page 23 of the manual, but it would be preferable to make direct reference to this "pool" at that point in the manual. This is important for those who are interested in assessing the content validity of the RMIB, namely its relatedness to alternative "pools" of occupational titles.

As for the empirical study of "unisex," criteria for item inclusion in Form A are presented in Appendix I of the manual. The results of a "classification" study are reported where men and women separately rated whether the job titles were equally suited to both sexes. For example, it was noted that 80% of the men and women in the classification sample reported that most of the job titles in Form A were equally suited to both sexes. It was subsequently stated that the minimum criterion for inclusion of items in Form A is at least 50% of one sex, and

35% of the other finding the item equally suited to both sexes. The information provided is somewhat vague because there is no summary table of the separate gender ratings for each job. Further, a summary table would help the "inquiring" test user quantify statements like "most of the job titles" as well as the number of jobs that met decreasing standards of inclusion.

What norms apply to Form A? The standardization sample reported in the manual was drawn from the U.K. and consists of 2,223 individuals grouped into three categories: secondary school students, students in tertiary education (e.g., University, Polytechnic, etc.), and an adult sample, consisting predominantly of professional and managerial groups (a detailed analysis of the adult sample was not available at the time the manual was submitted for review). The RMIB was developed for use in Britain, and it is referred to as the "UK unisex RMIB." The authors should be commended for not overstating the intended audience of the instrument.

What technical data exist to support Form A? One must be realistic and understand that technical support is like a "bottomless pit"—there can never be enough data. The RMIB manual covers most of the major categories of reliability and validity, and the supportive evidence for Form A is encouraging. There are isolated weak spots, such as the internal consistency reliability of the outdoor scale (R = .57 school; R = .66 adult), and RMIB users should be wary of the respondent's score on this scale.

In summary, the RMIB seems to meet its revision goals, namely the development of the new unisex Form A. The present manual contains norms for this form, and adequate technical support for its use. Although Forms B and C may be useful for certain respondents, they seem in "limbo," lying somewhere beyond revision and before norms and technical support. Thus, test users are wise to use the separate gender forms cautiously.

[270]
Rust Inventory of Schizotypal Cognitions.

Purpose: Constructed to assess "the schizotypal cognitions associated with the positive symptoms of acute schizophrenia and schizotypal personality disorder."

Population: Age 17 and over.

Publication Date: 1989.

Acronym: RISC.

Scores: Total score only.

Administration: Individual or group.

Price Data, 1994: $63 per complete kit; $40.50 per 25 record forms (specify English or Spanish); $29 per handbook (57 pages).

Time: (4–8) minutes.
Author: John Rust.
Publisher: The Psychological Corporation.
Cross References: See T4:2303 (3 references).

TEST REFERENCES

1. Rust, J. (1988). The Rust Inventory of Schizotypal Cognitions (RISC). *Schizophrenia Bulletin, 14,* 317–322.
2. Claridge, G. (1994). Single indicator of risk for schizophrenia: Probable fact or likely myth? *Schizophrenia Bulletin, 20,* 151–168.
3. Lenzenweger, M. F. (1994). Psychometric high-risk paradigm, perceptual aberrations, and schizotypy: An update. *Schizophrenia Bulletin, 20,* 121–135.

Review of the Rust Inventory of Schizotypal Cognitions by GREGORY J. BOYLE, Professor of Psychology, Bond University, Gold Coast, Queensland, and Department of Psychiatry, University of Queensland, Herston, Queensland, Australia:

The Rust Inventory of Schizotypal Cognitions (RISC) is a brief 26-item self-report questionnaire purported to measure schizotypal ideation. The RISC is prefaced on the assumption that positive schizotypal cognitions vary on a continuum within normal populations, ranging from mild to severe. The RISC is intended to detect ostensibly normal individuals who may be at risk for developing schizotypal and/or schizophrenic disorders (see Brabender, 1992). The inventory takes only a few minutes to administer, and scoring is straightforward, using a carbonized response sheet.

According to the handbook, an initial item bank of 300 cognitive personality items, which accorded with DSM-III criteria for schizotypal and schizophrenic thought disorders, was administered to a sample of 183 predominantly mature-age University of London students, using a dichotomous agree/disagree scoring system. The resultant item intercorrelations were factor analyzed producing no fewer than 10 separate factors. Three factors pertained to paranoid symptoms (paranoia, delusions of grandeur, and secretiveness), three to other positive schizophrenic symptoms (hallucinations, derealization and depersonalization, and thought direction), three to defense mechanisms (maintaining personal identity, avoiding uncomfortable thoughts, and avoiding uncomfortable situations), and one factor related to ritualistic thinking.

Insufficient details were provided in the handbook as to the factor analytic procedures employed. In any event, the initial sample size was inadequate for exploratory factor analysis (MacCallum, 1985, reported that at least 300 observations are generally required to have a 50% chance of deriving replicable factors). Because this initial factor analysis served as the starting point for all subsequent refinements, the psychometric adequacy of the RISC was necessarily constrained. Further analyses yielded second order dimensions pertaining to paranoid, schizoid, and experiential ideation. The third factor was dropped. Following crosscultural (principal axis) factor analyses, and comparison of adjusted item correlations with a projection scale (based on the first two factors), a greatly reduced schizotypal scale was finally derived.

The RISC was normed on diverse samples of Hong Kong, Venezuelan, British, and U.S.A. students (ranging from school children through adult university students), along with adults from diverse occupational backgrounds who were in the waiting room of a medical clinic, various schizophrenic groups and their relatives, as well as several different occult groups.

The handbook reported Cronbach alpha coefficients ranging from .68 to .82 (median = .80), suggesting moderate to high item homogeneity possibly indicative of some item redundancy (see Boyle, 1991). The test-retest reliability was reported as being .87 (over a broad retest interval ranging from 2 weeks to 3 months). However, no empirical data were provided for immediate or short-term test-retest (dependability), as opposed to longer-term retest (stability), so that it is unclear whether or not the RISC is operating as a state or a trait measure— or hybrid combination thereof (cf. Boyle, 1987).

With regard to predictive validity, the absence of a high score cannot rule out the possibility of schizotypal ideation, because an individual may choose to falsify his/her item responses (Brabender, 1992). As a self-report inventory with a high level of item transparency, the RISC is necessarily plagued by problems of motivational distortion and response sets (cf. Boyle, 1985). The attempt to camouflage the true purpose of the inventory by implying that it measures creativity can only compound the problem of response distortion, leading respondents to assent to schizotypal items more readily than they otherwise would do. In fact, low correlations ranging from .19 to .28 were reported between RISC scores and the I.P.A.T. Comprehensive Ability Battery scores on spontaneous flexibility, ideational fluency, and originality, suggesting a creative dimension to schizotypal cognition.

The handbook also reported that RISC scores correlated on average .52 with psychiatric ratings of schizophrenic samples, .12 with the Eysenck Personality Questionnaire (EPQ) psychoticism (P) scale, .38 with the Neuroticism (N) scale, and -.19 with the Lie (L) scale, supporting the view that response distortion may be problematic for the RISC. The low correlation with the P-scale may be indicative of inadequate concurrent validity of the RISC, the P-scale, or both. However, Boyle (in press), and Claridge et al. (1996) reported that the P-scale lines up with Claridge's STB scale at one end of a bipolar factor, with the L-scale at the other end, suggesting that the P-scale measures general psychotic disorder rather than schizotypal ideation, per se.

A serious limitation is that the RISC focuses exclusively on positive rather than negative schizotypal symptomatology, and therefore may permit less discriminative validity than would be the case if negative symptoms were also measured. Because negative symptoms typically appear earlier than the more pronounced positive symptoms, measurement of positive symptomatology alone may be unduly restrictive, providing inadequate predictive power (Brabender, 1992).

Another difficulty is that the handbook provides no indication as to how elevated RISC scores might be interpreted, and does not rule out other contributory variables, raising further doubts about predictive validity. As well, little is known about the long-term stability of the instrument, and there is an urgent need to investigate its concurrent, discriminative, construct, and long-term predictive validity in much greater detail than is currently provided in the handbook. Also, the handbook provides insufficient detail on psychometric issues such as factor analytic methodology, administration procedures, as well as discussion of the limitations of the RISC and its potential misapplications in various contexts (cf. Brabender, 1992).

Despite the limited information about the psychometric properties of the RISC, the final section of the handbook includes a useful theoretical discussion about schizotypal cognition and its relationship to schizotypal personality disorder and schizophrenia.

REVIEWER'S REFERENCES

Boyle, G. J. (1985). Self-report measures of depression: Some psychometric considerations. *British Journal of Clinical Psychology, 24*, 45–59.

MacCallum, R. (1985, July). *Some problems in the process of model modification in covariance structure modeling.* Paper presented at the European Meeting of the Psychometric Society, Cambridge, England.

Boyle, G. J. (1987). Review of the (1985) "Standards for educational and psychological testing: AERA, APA and NCME." *Australian Journal of Psychology, 39*, 235–237.

Boyle, G. J. (1991). Does item homogeneity indicate internal consistency or item redundancy in psychometric scales? *Personality and Individual Differences, 12*, 291–294.

Brabender, V. (1992). [Review of the Rust Inventory of Schizotypal Cognitions.] In D. J. Keyser & R. C. Sweetland (eds.), *Test critiques* (Vol. 9, pp. 438–446). Austin, TX: PRO-ED, Inc.

Claridge, G., McCreery, C., Mason, O., Bentall, R., Boyle, G., Slade, P., & Popplewell, D. (1996). The factor structure of "schizotypal" traits: A large replication study. *British Journal of Clinical Psychology, 35*, 103–115.

Boyle, G. (in press). Schizotypal personality traits: An extension of previous psychometric investigations. *Australian Journal of Psychology.*

Review of the Rust Inventory of Schizotypal Cognitions by GEORGE DOMINO, Professor of Psychology, University of Arizona, Tucson, AZ:

According to the test author, the Rust Inventory of Schizotypal Cognitions (RISC) assesses the "schizotypal cognitions associated with the positive symptoms of acute schizophrenia and schizotypal personality disorder" (p. 2), but is designed to "tap this cognitive schizotypal dimension on the normal population" (p. 2). Such schizotypal cognitions include suspicion, magical ideation, and self-delusion.

The RISC is a self-report inventory of 26 items (e.g., "Sometimes I feel I am ugly, and at other times that I am attractive"), to be responded with a Likert-type scale with no midpoint. Administration takes less than 10 minutes, can be group administered, and the RISC is easily hand scored through the use of a carbon-sensitive second page. Half of the items are positively keyed and half negatively keyed. Raw scores are transformed, through the use of a table, into stanine scores.

The RISC was developed in three stages. In Stage 1 a pool of 300 items was developed along various theoretical lines. These items were administered to 183 mature, part-time students at London University. A factor analysis indicated 10 factors. These results, plus item analyses, and various additional psychometric concerns, resulted in a 120-item questionnaire. In Stage 2, these items were administered to British education students to determine reliability and other psychometric properties. A factor analysis indicated a three-factor solution, but only two factors were considered: paranoid ideation and schizoid ideation—the third factor, experiential ideation, was inexplicably dropped from further consideration. In Stage 3, the 120-item version was administered to three groups representing speakers of English as a first language, Chinese speakers with English as a second language, and Spanish speakers. Items were then reduced by "classical item analysis" including omitting items that correlated with religiosity, or showed gender or cultural biases.

Although the manual contains substantial statistical data, including brief mentions of the use of discriminant function analyses to check for linearity of RISC items, there are also some glaring gaps. For example, there is no factor analysis of the final 26-item scale, nor exactly what was done in the "classical item analysis." There is no indication whether and how the 26 items cover the six symptom categories of the *Diagnostic and Statistical Manual*, or the multiple areas (listed under three headings in the manual, p. 14), that apparently provided the theoretical blueprint by which items were generated, or the 10 subscales that were generated in the Stage 1 development.

RELIABILITY. Split-half reliability is reported as .71, and Cronbach alphas for five samples range from .68 to .82; test-retest reliability with an interval of 2 weeks to 3 months, is .87.

VALIDITY. The manual presents the results of various studies that address the construct validity of the RISC: (a) a comparison of schizophrenic patients who scored significantly higher than normal controls; (b) significant but modest correlations of the RISC with the Neuroticism, Psychoticism, and Lie scales of the Eysenck Personality Questionnaire, in a sample of Venezuelan university students, with the author concluding that the two instruments are measuring "rather different constructs"; (c) a comparison of the RISC with the Minnesota Counseling Inventory (a derivative of the MMPI), which shows that high RISC scorers tend to have poor emotional stability, poor social relations, and are nonconforming; (d) a correlation of .52 in a sample of chronic schizophrenic patients, with psychiatrists' ratings of schizotypal symptomatology; (e) significant RISC score differences between acute and chronic schizophrenic patients; (f) significant group mean differences in two religious sects and seven "occult" groups; (g) significant correlations in a U.S. sample of college students with measures of "creativity."

As the author indicates, this instrument seems of potential interest to those "who wish to investigate the relationship between normal cognitive functioning and the very particular forms of cognitive dysfunction found in schizophrenia and its schizotypal borderline" (p. 33). It would also seem of potential interest to investigators in the area of creativity, particularly those interested in the interface of "genius and madness."

CRITICISMS. The manual presents considerable evidence on the reliability and construct validity of this measure; quite clearly the author has done his homework. On the one hand, the statistical procedures used are quite sophisticated and current, and probably overwhelming to the average reader. On the other hand, most of the samples seem to be captive samples of convenience (e.g., why Venezuelan university students?) rather than chosen for their theoretical import, or representative aspect. Some of the samples are quite small (e.g., 17 relatives of schizophrenics), but most are adequate in size.

The major problem for me is the construct of "schizotypal cognition." Despite the extensive data and theoretical discussion, it was difficult for me to get a handle on exactly what the RISC measures.

The manual gives a rather long discussion of the theoretical basis of schizotypy with an emphasis on cognitive theories, but that did not help. It is not clear to this reader what the construct is and what is being measured by the RISC. The author indicates that the RISC is designed to measure the "cognitive schizotypal dimension" in the normal population. Yet much of the validity evidence focuses on psychiatric patients, and most of the references cited are on schizophrenia. It is not clear whether, in fact, the RISC is a diagnostic measure to identify schizotypal personality disorder, a personality inventory that attempts to tap a rather unique construct, or something else.

Finally, the manual was published in 1989 and needs to be updated. If the RISC is intended as a research instrument for use with normal populations, then additional data need to be presented. For example, in the one sample that explored the topic of creativity, no means or standard deviations are given. The stanine scores are okay, but other transformations such as T scores or percentiles would be more useful.

[271]
Sales Style Indicator.

Purpose: To assist individuals and sales teams to identify strengths and weaknesses, and to help develop a plan to increase sales style flexibility.

Population: Sales personnel.

Publication Date: 1991.

Acronym: SSI.

Scores, 4: Behavioral Action, Cognitive Analysis, Interpersonal Harmony, Affective Expression.

Administration: Group.

Price Data, 1993: $15 per test booklet; $10 per interpretations booklet (41 pages).

Time: (90) minutes.

Comments: Self-administered, self-scored, self-interpreted.

Authors: Terry D. Anderson and Bruce R. Wares.

Publisher: Consulting Resource Group International, Inc.

Review of the Sales Style Indicator by WAYNE J. CAMARA, Executive Director and Senior Scientist, Office of Research and Development, The College Board, New York, NY:

The authors of the Sales Style Indicator describe it as a "scientifically, self-administered, self-scored, self-interpreted, learning and communications instrument. *It is not a test* [emphasis added]" (test booklet, p. 2). Apparently, this last statement is meant to justify the lack of any empirical data on the instrument and any description of how the instrument has been developed and its scores and interpretative statements derived.

The Sales Style Indicator is designed for use by individuals currently engaged in sales or considering a career in sales for self-reflection and greater understanding of *their* behaviors and personal styles, which may affect their interactions with prospects and clients. It is not designed for use by third parties in evaluating, selecting, or counseling others. That is, it should not be used by managers or supervisors for the selection, appraisal, evaluation, or counseling of subordinates. The intended and stated uses of the Sales Style Indicator are in areas where there is minimal risk of harmful consequences. On the positive side, the lack of any test manual, supporting validity, or description of how the interpretations have been developed will probably not be harmful to individuals because of its designed uses. However, on the negative side, no evidence is available to support the use of the Sales Style Indicator for any purpose—including its intended use for self-assessment of sales behaviors. Instruments such as this inventory, designed for use for self-guidance, are still required to produce some evidence of validity, documentation on how they have been developed, normative data, and information on how interpretive statements have been established (AERA, APA, & NCME, 1985). No such evidence is available for this instrument according to the test publisher, Consulting Resource Group International, Inc.

The test taker is asked to "describe the way you see yourself most of the time with most prospects or clients in most sales situations" (test booklet, p. 2). The inventory has only 16 items, each consisting of four words with a short definition attached to each word. Individuals rank order each set of four words that come closest to describing themselves. For example, the individual would chose among "high-roller, technical, friendly, and expressive" in the sample item. Completing this instrument would only require a few minutes of time.

Responses are completed on a one-sheet form and are easily scored on the attached scoring sheet. Individuals add the rankings (e.g., 4, 3, 2, 1) they have given to words that correspond to four scales or dimensions. Boxes having different shapes represent the four dimensions to facilitate the scoring. A grand total for all items (16 items scored 4+3+2+1) is 160 points, which is divided among the four dimensions:

Behavioral ACTION (B)—pursue a focused track, employ direct sales methods, forcefully persuade prospects.

Cognitive ANALYSIS (C)—attend to details, precision, and use logical analysis to stay in control of the sales situation.

Affective EXPRESSION (A)—use creative approaches to speaking, gesturing, or writing to intuitively interact and persuade prospects, focus on prospects' emotions.

Interpersonal HARMONY (I)—sensitive of words and actions of prospects and seek to be personally liked and respected by prospect, make prospects comfortable.

After adding ratings and computing a total score for each dimension, individuals mark their four-dimension score on a bar graph provided in the test booklet. Test takers are next instructed to read the summary of sales tendencies corresponding to the two dimensions with the highest scores located in a one-page table. This table simply has a few short statements about the general orientation, sales strengths, and sales difficulties associated with a high score on the dimension.

Dimensions with scores above 40 indicate a definite preference for style behaviors and tendencies, whereas scores below 35 indicate a tendency not to prefer the style behaviors or tendencies typical of the dimension. The instructions state that scores between 35 and 40 should be considered as a dimension of style that is sometimes preferred. The next step in interpretation is somewhat more complex as the test taker must determine which score pattern best represents their scores, such as a single dimension (B, C, A, or I), dual dimensions (e.g., A & I, B & C), a triple high score (e.g., B, C & A) or an undifferentiated profile with near equal scores on all dimensions. The test taker can refer back to their scores as plotted on the bar graph to match their profile to various possible profiles in the test booklet. There are a total of 21 possible interpretive patterns or combinations of dimensions. Once the test taker determines their profile they are instructed to both read the interpretive summaries of the profile (e.g., B, B & I) in the test booklet and to gather "deeper" interpretative meaning from a 42-page guide to "In-Depth Interpretations" (In-Depth Interpretations manual, p. 7).

The In-Depth Interpretive Guide contains about one and a half pages of text on each profile including: (a) strengths, (b) common areas of difficulty, (c) reactions to stress, (d) sales team functioning and compatibility with other styles, (e) leadership implications, and (f) recommendations to increase sales effectiveness. The overall instructions, scoring, profiles, and interpretations for the Sales Style Indicator are similar to those of dozens of other self-selection instruments, the most well known of which is the Self-Directed Search (SDS; Holland, 1985; 281). Unlike the SDS and other self-administered, self-assessments used for various self-guidance purposes, the

Sales Style Indicator is a relatively unknown instrument with no available research or additional documentations according to its publisher. Because it is a "communications instrument … not a test" the publisher and authors may believe there is no additional responsibility to validate the interpretations and statements that are made about the various profiles. However, without additional documentation and evidence a user has no way of determining whether these statements have any bearing to reality or are simply a reflection of clinical interpretation.

The In-Depth Interpretations does state that interpretative information "has been developed and refined over a period of more than half a decade, after thousands of people have read them and have given feedback as to their accuracy and usefulness … more than 90% of the comments contained in each pattern are perceived to have greater than 90% accuracy for the average sales people" (In-Depth Interpretations manual, introduction). Unfortunately, this statement, as well as the description of this as a "scientifically developed instrument" are misleading and simply not supported by any materials that were available from the publisher to this reviewer. The above claim of accuracy does not meet even the most basic requirements for a test or similar instrument. Without some documentation it appears this instrument has no appropriate use for any purpose including self-assessment and self-reflection.

REVIEWER'S REFERENCES

American Educational Research Association, American Psychological Association, & National Council on Measurement in Education. (1985). *Standard for educational and psychological testing.* Washington, DC: American Psychological Association, Inc.

Holland, J. L. (1985). *The Self-Directed Search: Professional manual—1985 revision.* Odessa, FL: Psychological Assessment Resources, Inc.

Review of the Sales Style Indicator by GERALD A. ROSEN, Consulting Psychologist, Huntingdon Valley, PA:

The Sales Style Indicator is a 16-item questionnaire intended for use by sales personnel. The instrument is self-administered, self-scored, and self-interpreted. Neither reports on the development of the Sales Style Indicator nor information on its reliability or validity are available.

The instrument consists of a test booklet containing a brief introduction, test administration instructions, questionnaire, and a six-step guide to test scoring, understanding results, and applying results to sales situations. A second booklet containing "in-depth interpretations" accompanies the test booklet. The 16 questionnaire items are each composed of four descriptors that respondents rank from 4 (most like me in a sales situation) to 1 (least like me in a sales situation). Each of the four descriptors is further defined by three additional words placed below it. One problem is that some of the additional words are not apparently consistent with their descriptors. For example, the descriptor "constrained" is further illuminated by "restrictive," "disapproving," and "blaming."

The Sales Style Indicator yields scores on four variables called sales styles: B—Behavioral (Action); A—Affective (Expression); C—Cognitive (Analysis); and I—Interpersonal (Harmony). A respondent's sales style is the variable with the highest score. A respondent's general style tendency is composed of all the styles, highest score first, where a score of 40 or above is obtained. It is represented by a code using the first letters of the respective styles. Styles with scores in the band just below the mean, 35–40, are said to be acted on less frequently or with hesitation. Styles with scores in the corresponding band above the mean, 40–45, are simply considered high with no special interpretation given to them.

The test booklet contains interpretative comments on the four sales styles and for all two and three variable combinations of general style tendency codes. Thus, a person whose highest score is on "C" (Cognitive) and who has a second 40 or above score on "I" (Interpersonal) would have a general sales tendency of CI, which is termed "Efficient." After reading the interpretive comments on the Cognitive sales style, the respondent then reads the comments for the "Efficient" general sales tendency. The authors encourage respondents to "cross out interpretative comments which you feel do not apply to you" (p. 7).

The second booklet containing in-depth interpretations presents additional comments and longer descriptions of the sales styles and general sales tendencies. It also contains the only information on test development. The authors state, "Much of the information in the in-depth interpretations has been developed and refined over a period of more than half a decade … now more than 90% of the comments contained in each pattern are perceived to have greater than 90% accuracy for the average sales people who have read the patterns which most closely match their scores." No information is provided on the number of persons from whom data were collected or on the definition of "average sales person." As with the interpretations in the test booklet, respondents are encouraged to ignore comments they feel do not apply to them.

SUMMARY. The Sales Style Indicator is a self-administered, scored, and interpreted personality test for use by sales personnel who wish to gain greater understanding and control of their behavior in sales situations. It yields scores on four variables, but does so on the basis of responses to only 16 items. No information is available on test development, reliability, or validity. It is unlikely that the instrument possesses acceptable levels of either reliability or validity given the paucity of items and apparent inconsistencies in the construction of at least a few of them. The in-depth descriptions of the personality types, called sales styles and general style tendencies, appear to follow from some conception of the relationship between personality and behavior is sales situations, but it is impossible to say on what theory and/or research those conceptions are based. In the absence of technical information, it is equally impossible to examine the relationship between the instrument and any underlying theory. Finally, the fact that users of the Sales Style Indicator are encouraged to ignore conclusions with which they disagree, for whatever reason, renders the instrument more like a parlor game than a standardized test. These facts make the use of the Sales Style Indicator, given as an instrument for self-study among sales persons, highly questionable.

[272]
The Scales for Effective Teaching.

Purpose: "To assist administrators and teachers to work together to improve teaching."
Population: Teachers.
Publication Date: 1989.
Acronym: SET.
Scores: 15 scales: Learning Outcomes, Utilization of Instructional Materials, Instructional Techniques/Strategies, Academic Learning/Engaged Time, Positive Reinforcement of Responses, Correction of Academic Responses, Classroom Discipline, Instructional Style, Instructional Efficiency, Monitoring Student Progress During Lesson, Monitoring Student Progress After Lesson, Communication, Teaming, Organizational Commitment, Professional Development.
Administration: Individual.
Price Data, 1993: $29 per complete kit including manual (42 pages) and evaluation forms.
Time: (136–168) minutes.
Comments: Utilizes both observation and interview data.
Authors: Stevan J. Kukic, Susan L. Fister, Donald P. Link, and Janet L. Freston.
Publisher: Sopris West, Inc.

Review of The Scales for Effective Teaching by FREDERICK BESSAI, Professor of Education, University of Regina, Regina, Saskatchewan, Canada:

The Scales for Effective Teaching (SET) are more of a structured means of assessing and improving individual teacher practice than a set of scales. The authors have sought not only to provide a means of developing a comprehensive picture of a teacher's professional practice, but have also provided suggestions for the improvement of practice. In general, it is an attempt to apply the current knowledge of effective classrooms and effective teaching to teacher evaluation.

The scales are to be used in a four-phase evaluation process that includes preparation for interview and observation, the collection and recording of data, a data analysis and synthesis procedure, and finally, a data interpretation phase during which the evaluator and the teacher discuss the ratings on each of the scales, identify areas of excellence, and select areas for improvements to a higher level of performance. The latter includes selecting activities to improve performance and setting a date for future evaluation. Data are collected by observation and by interviewing the teacher. Scales 1, 2, 3, and 7 require an interview as well as a period of observation. Clear instructions are given on how to conduct the interview and several sample questions are given for each scale. Rules and suggestions are also given for observation with particular attention to objective recording before any evaluation or rating is made. After data collection, the observations are matched to a set of five behavioral statements in each scale. These represent successively higher levels of performance. For example, Scale 1 on Learning Outcomes has the statement, "conducts lessons without communicating learning outcomes" (p. 28) as the lowest level (1) and the highest level (5) includes communication of learning outcomes, checking to ensure that students understand expectations, responding to their feedback, providing a rationale, and focusing them on learning outcomes. The manual is generally clear and well written but is difficult to follow in places. The five points on each of the 15 scales are identified on the teaching profile form with numbers from 5 to 1 as headers but in the body of the form they are each filled in with the letters T-E-A-C-H. This can be confusing to the user and surely serves no statistical purpose. The same letters are also used to identify the five levels of behavioral statements for each scale in the manual and the evaluation forms. The letters have no apparent relationship to the content in either case and could be omitted. The authors mention a training program for potential users but do not state where and how it can be obtained.

One of the main strengths of the SET is that it is clearly based on identifiable teacher behaviors and these are described quite extensively with sample indicators. What is needed is more research on reliability, particularly interrater reliability, and discriminant validity. Generally, the SET can be recommended for use in clinical supervision. The scales represent a positive step toward overcoming some of the subjectivity and potential omissions and biases that are perennial problems in evaluating something as complex and multifaceted as effective teaching.

Review of The Scales for Effective Teaching by TRENTON R. FERRO, Associate Professor of Adult and Community Education, Indiana University of Pennsylvania, Indiana, PA:

The Scales for Effective Teaching (SET) is an observation and interview guide intended for use by educational administrators to evaluate efficiently and effectively the quality of teachers' teaching and to provide constructive feedback for teacher improvement. Based on the effective schools literature, the SET defines teaching in 15 areas. Each area is represented by a scale that has two components: "A set of *behavioral statements* describes five levels of effectiveness for each scale, and a set of *behavioral indicators* is provided to assist the rater in determining a level of effectiveness" (p. 5). The 15 scales cover Learning Outcomes, Utilization of Instructional Materials, Instructional Techniques/Strategies, Academic Learning/Engaged Time, Positive Reinforcement of Responses, Correction of Academic Responses, Classroom Discipline, Instructional Style, Instructional Efficiency, Monitoring Student Progress During Lesson, Monitoring Student Progress After Lesson, Communication, Teaming, Organizational Commitment, and Professional Development.

Following a brief pre-observation meeting to schedule times for conducting the observation and interview and for collecting pre-observation information, the evaluator collects and records observation data for scales 1–10 and interview data for scales 1, 2, 3, 7, and 11–15. Sample indicators and sample questions are provided as guides for both processes. The evaluator then analyzes and synthesizes the collected data by applying them to the SET rating scales (included in the manual accompanying the instrument) and developing a Teaching Profile. Finally, the evaluator and teacher meet to share the analysis and synthesis (a procedure the authors call "counsel for improvement") and to set improvement goals. The entire procedure requires at least 2 to 2 1/2 hours to complete.

The instructions for the entire procedure are quite clear and helpful. The instrument is well developed, providing a focus for, and consistency in, data collection and analysis. The well-designed manual contains ample supporting material to assist the evaluator in accomplishing her or his task. However, the users must be very familiar with the rating scales so that they will be able to collect appropriate, accurate, and adequate data and will be able to use the scales effectively when analyzing the data. Some elements of the process may require even more time than the authors allow, especially by those first learning to use the SET. Those experienced in using the process and working with the instrument should be able to reduce the time needed to complete some aspects of the process. However, the full amount of time suggested should always be given to observation and the interview for data collection. As the authors emphasize, teachers and administrators must be trained in the conceptual background and use of the SET. Failure to do so will diminish greatly the potential effectiveness of the SET.

In addition to the content described above, the manual also contains the philosophical bases and belief system underlying the development and use of the SET. "The final result should be a negotiated set of professional goals for improving teaching. These goals can serve as the basis for staff development activities for teachers and administrators. This focus promotes improvement and is the focus of SET" (p. 3). This emphasis is the strength of both the instrument and the entire process. If, then, this is the SET's primary function, careful consideration needs to be given to a second claim of utility: "The authors of SET firmly believe that evaluation and supervision are not antithetical concepts, but rather believe that sound evaluation serves as the basis for supervision" (p. 3). Herein lies the major philosophical rub. Although ideal, this perspective does not square with reality. Many situations, due to politics and labor relations, are not conducive to administrators being the best person to help with staff improvement. Those who use this instrument should have a very clear understanding of *why* they are using it— what their purposes and goals are. That, in turn, will determine *how* they use it—to improve teaching or to make personnel decisions. As this reviewer has emphasized, the instrument can serve both purposes, but interpersonal and political realities would suggest that both objectives cannot be met by the same evaluator in a single situation. In this reviewer's estimation, peer evaluation would ultimately be the most helpful and productive way to work toward the improvement of teaching. Use of the instrument by administrators should be reserved for making decisions related to retention, promotion, and tenure.

On another point, the authors claim to use the "clinical supervision" (p. 2) model, which they describe as "designed to provide fair and comprehensive feedback by minimizing subjectivity in data collection and analysis" (p. 5). However, evaluation, by definition, requires making decisions and judgments. The use of well-developed scales, protocols, and other observation and interview guides leads to consistency, but evaluation, even based on extensive data collection, is still a subjective activity; the evaluator is also an instrument, especially in analyzing data and drawing conclusions from those analyses. Ultimately, the evaluator will need to make decisions and offer suggestions. That is why the choice of who will observe and provide the feedback is so important. A "subjective" decision (which, by definition, evaluation requires) based on well-collected and analyzed data is much better than an "objective" decision (which, by definition, cannot be done) based on poorly collected and analyzed data. There is a clear need to distinguish among the various steps or elements: data collection, data analysis, and making decisions based on the analysis of the data. The strength of this instrument is that it provides a framework and process for collecting and analyzing such data. However, it cannot remove from the evaluator the ultimate requirement of making judgments and decisions.

[273]

Scales of Cognitive Ability for Traumatic Brain Injury.

Purpose: To "provide a systematic method of assessing cognitive deficits associated with traumatic brain injury."
Population: Patients with acquired brain damage.
Publication Date: 1992.
Acronym: SCATBI.
Scores, 46: Perception and Discrimination (Sound Recognition, Shape Recognition, Word Recognition [no distraction], Word Recognition [with distraction], Color Discrimination, Shape Discrimination, Size Discrimination, Discrimination of Color/Shape/Size, Discrimination of Pictured Objects, Auditory Discrimination [real words], Auditory Discrimination [nonsense], Total); Orientation (Premorbid Questions, Postmorbid Questions, Total); Organization (Identifying Pictured Categories, Identifying Pictured Category Members, Word Associations, Sequencing Objects [size], Sequencing Words [alphabetical], Sequencing Events [time of year], Sequencing Events [pictured task steps], Sequencing Events [recall task steps], Total); Recall (Memory for Graphic Elements, Naming

Pictures, Immediate Recall of Word Strings, Delayed Recall of Word Strings, Cued Recall of Words, Cued Recall of Words in Discourse, Word Generation, Immediate Recall of Oral Directions, Recall of Oral Paragraphs, Total); Reasoning (Figural Reasoning: Matrix Analogies, Convergent Thinking: Central Theme, Deductive Reasoning: Elimination, Inductive Reasoning: Opposites, Inductive Reasoning: Analogies, Divergent Thinking: Homographs, Divergent Thinking: Idioms, Divergent Thinking: Proverbs, Divergent Thinking: Verbal Absurdities, Multiprocess Reasoning: Task Insight, Multiprocess Reasoning: Analysis, Total).
Administration: Individual.
Price Data: Available from publisher.
Time: Administration time not reported.
Authors: Brenda Adamovich and Jennifer Henderson.
Publisher: Applied Symbolix.

Review of the Scales of Cognitive Ability for Traumatic Brain Injury by CHARLES J. LONG, Professor of Psychology, and FAITH GUNNING, Research Assistant, Psychology Department, The University of Memphis, Memphis, TN:

The Scales of Cognitive Ability for Traumatic Brain Injury (SCATBI) is designed to assess cognitive functioning in adult patients who have sustained a closed head injury. The test was designed to provide clinicians a time effective tool that can be used to evaluate patients and design a treatment plan based on the individual's performance. The authors began their development of the SCATBI by selecting 39 subtests from commercially available instruments and administering them to traumatic brain injury (TBI) patients before treatment and monthly thereafter. Their initial study was based on data collected from 14 head-injured subjects and 9 normal controls. Subtests that make up the SCATBI were modeled after those subtests from the original 39 that were found to best discriminate between head-injured and non-head-injured individuals. The authors also mention the influence of models of child development in developing the test but do not clarify how specific models of cognitive development were used.

The instrument consists of five subtests (Perception/Discrimination, Orientation, Organization, Recall, and Reasoning) and requires an average of 2 hours to administer. Each subtest is composed of multiple testlets. A testlet is a group of items related to a single content area. The SCATBI was designed in a hierarchical fashion with tasks becoming increasingly difficult within each testlet. The items are presented either visually or auditorially to sample both modes of processing. The authors state that although a one-session administration is ideal, the scale can be administered in multiple sessions.

The testing stimulus manual, the stimulus audio tape, and the stimulus cards are very functional. Directions for administering and scoring of the SCATBI are in both the manual and the record form. Overall the directions are clear and easy to follow for both the administration and the scoring of items. One exception to this is on page 11 of the manual where testers are instructed to administer all items to each patient but the authors later say that subtests can be discontinued if the first three testlets are failed. In addition, the authors fail to provide guidelines regarding the use of the test when circumstances limit an individual's ability to complete portions of subtests (i.e., hearing loss, expressive or receptive language problems, etc.). Given the nature of the population targeted with this instrument, it is imperative that such guidelines be provided.

Raw scores are obtained for each of the five subtests by summing the scores on each testlet within a specific subtest. These raw scores are converted to standard scores for each subtest by referring to Norms Table 2 in the appendix. The standard scores from all five subtests can be converted into a Total Composite score by adding the standard scores and referring to Norms Table 3. However, if the examiner does not administer all five subtests a standard score can be obtained for what the authors refer to as the Lower Functioning Composite score (comprising Perception/Discrimination, Orientation, and Organization) or the Higher Functioning Composite score (composed of Recall and Reasoning). Finally, a severity rating (ranging from average normal to severe) can be obtained from the Total Composite. It is unclear from the manual whether or not a severity rating can be obtained for either the Higher Functioning Composite or the Lower Functioning Composite.

The authors indicate that the SCATBI may provide useful information for patients with "primary cognitive deficits secondary to right brain damage, anoxia, brain tumors, or subcortical brain lesions" (p. 5). This statement implies that this instrument is not indicated for the assessment of individuals with left-sided cortical damage. Due to the diffuse nature of many traumatic brain injuries this restriction would seriously limit the utility of the scale. In addition, the standardization sample is composed, in part, of 164 brain-injured individuals whose injuries are not reported to be limited to the right side of the brain.

The test was normed on 244 head-injured patients from 26 sites in the United States and Canada. The sites included both acute care facilities and rehabilitation facilities. In addition, a total of 78 non-brain-injured adults were drawn from the same sites. Of the 244 head-injured patients, 164 suffered closed head injuries. The authors conducted analyses and failed to find reasons to break the norms down by variables such as age or gender. Because the test was normed on inpatients, the scores obtained may not be applicable to individuals who are not receiving inpatient treatment.

Test-retest reliability measures were obtained by testing a group of 33 head-injured patients on two separate occasions, with the mean time between testing being 60 days. These reliabilities ranged from .69 to .90 on the five scales. Interitem consistency was calculated using coefficient alpha; the reliabilities on the five subtests range from .9 to .95. The authors fail to report studies of interrater reliability; instead they suggest that examiners can achieve high reliability if they carefully study the manual and work in teams to assess differences in scoring.

A major limitation of the SCATBI is the authors' failure to address the ability to predict patients' future performance using this instrument; however, they do provide limited evidence of concurrent validity by comparing performance on the SCATBI to patients' Rancho Levels. In addition, the authors fail to provide convincing evidence for the content validity of the test because the authors chose the items using data from a study with an inadequate sample size ($N = 23$) along with unspecified input from child development theories. Factor analyses of the items do not support construct validity for the five subtests, but do support the division between higher and lower functions. Finally, no supporting research was found based on data obtained in other facilities.

In summary, the SCATBI appears to be a collection of item types taken from various other tests frequently used in assessing cognitive functioning in brain-injured individuals. Neither the test construction, the statistical properties, nor the average administration time warrant the use of the SCATBI in place of more traditional neuropsychological tests. However, the SCATBI may serve as a useful tool for clinicians treating inpatients who do not meet the training qualifications required for the administration and interpretation of such traditional neuropsychological tests.

Review of the Scales of Cognitive Ability for Traumatic Brain Injury by DEBORAH D. ROMAN, Director, Neuropsychology Laboratory, and Assistant Professor, Department of Physical Medicine and Rehabilitation and Neurosurgery, University of Minnesota, Minneapolis, MN:

The Scales of Cognitive Ability for Traumatic Brain Injury (SCATBI) is intended primarily for use with head injury patients, though the authors feel it is appropriate for the assessment of patients with other forms of brain injury. Administration time is 2 hours for the entire battery, less if only select scales are given. The scale content is rationally derived and is designed to evaluate the major cognitive areas commonly adversely affected by head injuries.

The SCATBI consists of five scales: Perception and Discrimination, Orientation, Organization, Recall, and Reasoning. There are 2–11 "testlets" (similar items measuring common traits or subdomains) in each scale. Raw scores for each scale are converted into percentiles and standard scores (with a mean of 100 and standard deviation of 15). The battery also yields three composite scores: (a) Lower Functioning Composite (derived from the Perception and Discrimination, Orientation, and Organization scales); (b) Higher Functioning Composite (derived from the Recall and Reasoning scales); and (c) Total Composite, reflecting overall performance. Norms for the five scales and three composite scores are based on the performance of a group of 164 head injury subjects. Finally, severity scores are available for the three composite scores (mean: 10; standard deviation: 3). Severity ratings range from normal to severely impaired. The normative group for the severity ratings includes the 164 head injury patients plus a group of 78 normals.

The manual is well written, thorough, and fairly complete. It includes demographic data on the standardization sample and technical information pertaining to test validity and reliability.

A total of 244 brain injured patients from 26 sites in the United States and Canada were tested. They ranged in age from 15 to 88 (median: 30); males outnumbered females two to one. Only 164 of these patients, those with traumatic brain injuries, were used for the normative sample. In addition, 78 non-brain-injured patients from the same sites were tested; details are not provided regarding the nature of their injuries, and it is unclear whether they were screened to rule out prior neurological disease.

The SCATBI seems to be sufficiently valid and reliable for use with head injury patients. Discriminant analysis using the five scales on a group of head injury patients and demographically matched controls correctly classified 96% of the controls and 79% of the patients. Using a sample of 125 head injury patients, modest positive correlations (.40 to .60) were found between the five SCATBI scales and Rancho Los Amigos Levels of Cognitive Functioning.

Cronbach's alpha (interitem consistency) ranged from .9 to .95 for the five subtests ($n = 164$). Standard Errors of Measurement ranged from 1.6 to 3.7. Test-retest scores for 33 subjects showed improvements (higher scores on the second administration), as expected given their likely recovery across time. Correlations between the initial and second test scores (retest was within 8 months) were fairly high, however, ranging from .69 to .90.

Overall, this is a useful screening instrument. It is most appropriate for use with patients who have acute or more severe closed head injuries because the items are all fairly easy. As the authors acknowledge, the battery may not be sufficiently sensitive in assessing milder head injuries, or in evaluating individuals with above average premorbid abilities (who may score within normal limits despite a significant cognitive decline). It remains to be seen whether the SCATBI is useful in assessing patients with other forms of brain pathology, as the authors suggest. No data have been provided in this regard, and I question whether the battery would be sufficiently sensitive to the deficits encountered in patients with discrete focal lesions (e.g., neoplasms, multiple sclerosis, arteriovenous malformations) or static lesions (e.g., stabilized strokes).

The SCATBI is designed to assess a broad range of functions in a reasonable period of time. As such, it should not be considered a comprehensive measure of any of these abilities. Other neuropsychological measures would be more appropriate if a detailed assessment of language, memory, attention, information processing speed, or executive abilities is called for. This may be necessary in fine tuning rehabilitation treatment interventions or in making other clinical decisions. Unlike the SCATBI, many of these conventional neuropsychological measures permit a direct comparison with normal. For milder head injuries, measures such as the Paced Auditory Serial Addition Test (PASAT; Gronwall, 1977) or more demanding memory tests (such as the Rey Auditory Visual Learning Test [Schmidt, 1996], or the Rey-Osterrieth[Rey, 1991]) would be more sensitive.

REVIEWER'S REFERENCES

Gronwall, D. M. A. (1977). Paced Auditory Serial—Addition Task: A measure of recovery from concussion. *Perceptual and Motor Skills, 44,* 367–373.

Rey, A. (1991). Psychological examination of traumatic encephalopathy. *Archives de Psychologic, 28,* 286–340; sections translated by I. Corwin & F. W. Bylsma, *The Clinical Neuropsychologist,* 1993, 4–9.

Schmidt, M. (1996). Rey Auditory Verbal Learning Test. Los Angeles: Western Psychological Services.

[274]

SCAN-A: A Test for Auditory Processing Disorders in Adolescents and Adults.

Purpose: Used to identify adolescents and adults who have auditory processing disorders and who may benefit from intervention.

Population: Ages 12 to adult.
Publication Dates: 1986–1994.
Acronym: SCAN-A.
Scores, 6: Filtered Words, Auditory Figure-Ground, Competing Words, Competing Sentences, Total Test, Competing Words Ear Advantage.
Administration: Individual.
Price Data, 1994: $84.50 per complete kit including manual ('94, 69 pages), test audiocassette, and 12 record forms; $11 per 12 record forms; $37 per manual; $47.50 per test audiocassette.
Time: (20–25) minutes.
Author: Robert W. Keith.
Publisher: The Psychological Corporation.

Review of the SCAN-A: A Test for Auditory Processing Disorders in Adolescents and Adults by WILLIAM R. MERZ, Sr., Professor, School Psychology Training Program, Department of Special Education, Rehabilitation, and School Psychology, School of Education, California State University, Sacramento, Sacramento, CA:

The "SCAN-A is an upward extension of the SCAN: A Screening Test for Auditory Processing Disorders" (p. 1) designed to be used to identify auditory processing difficulties in children 3 to 11 years of age. The SCAN-A, designed for individuals 12 years or older, takes 20 minutes to administer, and is intended to do three things: "(a) describe auditory processing abilities for planning vocational, educational, and remediation goals for adolescents and adults with learning disabilities and/or language disorders; (b) describe central auditory abilities, monitor recovery, and provide a framework for counseling families of individuals who have suffered a head injury or stroke, and; (c) describe functional impairment or study that effects of medical treatment of individuals with chronic central nervous system disease" (manual, p. 1).

The test is intended for use by audiologists, speech and language pathologists, and others trained to identify auditory processing disorders for further assessment. There are four subtests: Filtered Words, Auditory Figure-Ground, Competing Words, and Competing Sentences, that are referenced to a four-page description of "What Is an Auditory Processing Disorder" (p. 4). The material includes descriptions of sensitized speech tests and dichotic (involving the simultaneous presentation of different acoustic stimuli to each ear) listening tests. The SCAN-A requires special equipment: a stereo cassette player with a speed of 1 7/8 ips (4.75 cm./sec.) and four tracks along two stereo channels. The equipment must have a frequency response of +6 db, 63-8000 Hz with a signal to noise ratio of 52 dB, a Wow and flutter of .2%, and a single volume control. Those participating in the

SCAN-A testing had pure tone thresholds of 20dB at HL at any of four frequencies (500, 1000, 2000, and 4000). The field tests were conducted at 21 sites in four major regions of the country. A breakdown of those participating is presented by age, gender, and race. Examiners at university clinics, in private practice, and at military facilities participated in the trials. Twenty-three trial sites were located in 11 states and Canada where 52 audiologists administered the test. One hundred twenty-five people participated in the field trial; equal numbers were included across five age groups that were collapsed across ages to develop norms. Raw score means and standard deviations across all four subtests varied slightly, so they were transformed to z-scores. The z-scores were, in turn, transformed nonlinearly to subtest scaled scores with a mean of 10 and a standard deviation of 3 and total scores with a mean of 100 and a standard deviation of 15.

Cronbach's alpha internal consistency reliability estimates ranged from .46 to .69 for subtest scores to .77 for total scores; the test-retest reliability for total test score for three age groups collected from 1 day to 5 months was .69 resulting in a standard error of measurement of 2.8. Individual subtests had differences that ranged from 1 to 7 points; therefore variation in scores was too small for meaningful correlations. Evidence for content validity was presented to demonstrate that the tasks included ware typical of procedures used to assess auditory processing skills. Discriminant analysis, contrasting the skills of these with normal auditory processing abilities with those who have central auditory processing disorders, is presented as evidence of construct-related validity. Intercorrelations among subtests are presented as evidence of construct validity and range between .004 and .507 suggesting unique and common aspects of measurement. However, with small mean differences among subtests and restricted ranges these data must be interpreted very conservatively. Studies of left and right ear advantage are offered to demonstrate the lack of significant differences between left and right ear scores in people with normal auditory processing and people with central auditory processing disorders. Concurrent evidence of validity is presented through correlations of the scores of 29 youths 12 to 18 years old on the SCAN-A and the SCAN; the correlation corrected for attenuation is .59.

Reporting and interpretation of test scores are amply covered in 16 pages of the manual. Included is interpretation of total score, subtest scores, and subtest differences. Behavioral observations and ear advantage are emphasized in this section of the manual. Implications and recommendations for remediation are quite detailed and appear to be a strong part of the manual. No test and item bias studies are presented.

Overall, the SCAN-A offers a useful addition to the diagnosis and treatment of learning disabilities among adults. Although the norm groups are small and reliability and validity studies are rudimentary, the data presented are promising. Finding contrasting groups for validity studies is quite difficult for tasks identifying individual disability; the authors do a creditable job in the studies reported in the manual. Having auditory and visual processing assessment devices is critical for adequately diagnosing learning disability. The SCAN-A is a good start as an adequate auditory processing screening device for adults.

Review of the SCAN-A: A Screening Test for Auditory Processing Disorders in Adolescents and Adults by JACLYN B. SPITZER, Chief, Audiology and Speech Pathology Service, VA Connecticut Healthcare System, West Haven, CT, and Associate Clinical Professor, Department of Surgery (Otolaryngology), Yale University School of Medicine, New Haven, CT:

The SCAN-A is a screening tool for central auditory processing disorders (CAPD). It is a test normed for adolescents and adults, an extension of work in diagnosis of CAPD in children, using the original version of SCAN described by Keith (1986). The test provides rapid insight, administered in approximately 20 minutes, into the functional status of the central auditory pathway.

The SCAN-A may be applied to describe central auditory function of persons with CAPD or learning disabilities, or to monitor the alteration in processing over time produced by treatment or recovery from insult. A most significant use of the test is to determine the need for referral for more detailed central evaluation.

The four subtests of the SCAN-A are: Filtered Words, Auditory Figure-Ground, Competing Words, and Competing Sentences. Each of these subtests reflects an accepted approach to the evaluation of CAPD applied in the more intensive examination of processing. The intent of the Filtered Words and Figure-Ground subtests is to examine the examinee's ability to perceive signals in a background of noise or under adverse listening conditions. The Competing Words and Competing Sentences subtests are dichotic measures that assess hemispheric specialization. The use of degraded speech and dichotic measurement has a tradition in the assessment of lesions of the central nervous system. For adult patients, the SCAN-A is an appropriate screening tool when central dysfunction is suspected or needs to be ruled out. Furthermore, in cases of known lesions, such as post-cerebral vascular accident, recovery may be monitored via serial SCAN-A measurement.

CAPD in adolescents may be manifested by learning or reading difficulties or by behavioral disruption. Thus, application of such central measures as the SCAN-A in adolescents (the majority of whom do not have central lesions) may be useful in determining rehabilitative approaches necessary to improve classroom performance or to modify the learning environment.

The SCAN-A materials consist of an examiner's manual, record forms, and audiocassette. The manual is clearly written and emphasizes the need for controlled administration using adequate quality stereo equipment and headphones to obtain valid results. The test environment should be free of distractions. Further, the requirement for symmetrical hearing within normal limits and normal middle ear function implies that hearing assessment should precede SCAN-A administration. Test administration is greatly aided by recorded instructions prior to each subtest. Scoring of the test is straightforward.

The SCAN-A reflects careful development in its normative study (Keith & Grant, 1993). Thorough standardization data are contained in the manual. The internal consistency of the total test, estimated using Cronbach's alpha, is .77, with the subtests varying from .46 (for Auditory Figure-Ground) to .69 (for Competing Words). Thus, it is preferable to use the test in its entirety rather than to rely on any subtest individually. Test-retest reliability (time intervals from 1 day to 5 months) for the total test is .69, acceptable for clinical repeated measures.

In summary, the SCAN-A is a useful screening tool that meets the requirements for speed and ease of presentation, high internal consistency, and test-retest reliability. Its application in clinical populations has indicated that it has high hit, low miss, and low false alarms rates, making the SCAN-A a test that could be appropriately applied in adolescent and adult CAPD screening.

REVIEWER'S REFERENCES

Keith, R. W. (1986). *SCAN: A Screening Test for Auditory Processing Disorders.* San Antonio, TX: The Psychological Corporation.
Keith, R. W., & Grant, G. (1993). *Standardization of SCAN-A: A Test for Auditory Processing Disorders in Adolescents and Adults.* Presentation to the American Academy of Audiology Annual Convention, Phoenix, AZ.

[275]
School Archival Records Search.

Purpose: "Designed to overlay existing school records so that they can be coded and quantified systematically."
Population: Grades 1–12.

Publication Date: 1991.

Acronym: SARS.

Scores: 11 archival variables: Demographics, Attendance, Achievement Test Information, School Failure, Disciplinary Contacts, Within-School Referrals, Certification for Special Education, Placement Out of Regular Classroom, Receiving Chapter I Services, Out-of-School Referrals, Negative Narrative Comments.

Administration: Group.

Price Data, 1993: $35 per complete kit including user's guide, technical manual (86 pages), and 50 instrument packets.

Time: Administration time not reported.

Authors: Hill M. Walker, Alice Block-Pedego, Bonnie Todis, and Herbert H. Severson.

Publisher: Sopris West, Inc.

TEST REFERENCES

1. Campbell, F. A., & Ramey, C. T. (1994). Effects of early intervention on intellectual and academic achievement: A follow-up study of children from low income families. *Child Development, 65,* 684–698.

Review of the School Archival Records Search by JOHN CRAWFORD, Director of Planning and Evaluation, Millard Public Schools, Omaha, NE:

The School Archival Records Search (SARS) is a system that is intended to guide school staff through a process of coding and tracking variables designed to predict future "at risk" status of students. Specifically, the SARS is described in the manual as a screening system for elementary age students to aid in the identification of those students who are at risk for developing later behavior disorders and who have elevated risk for dropping out of high school.

About two-thirds of the manual is devoted to procedures regarding application of the SARS coding system. The only "instruments" as such are summary sheets for recording the critical indicators. There is a four-page set of questions the person carrying out the records search completes; this information can then be summarized on the two-page "Student Profile Form." The manual contains coding procedures for the recording and the summarizing of the information.

The SARS system is relatively straightforward and should be easy to implement. The information required to represent the indicators would be reasonably easy to come by in most schools. The indicators include: demographic information (name, grade, teacher, as well as the reason for being evaluated), number of schools attended, days absent, achievement, (prior) in-grade retention, within-school referrals, special education status, out-of-classroom placement, Chapter 1 (Title 1) status, out-of-school referrals, discipline contacts, and "negative" narrative

comments from staff. In addition, much of the system usage and validation requires an assessment of whether the student's behavior pattern is primarily "externalizing" (e.g., aggressive, hyperactive, rule-breaking) or "internalizing" (excessive shyness, withdrawn, nonparticipative, depressive). Although in several places in the manual the SARS is referred to as the last stage of screening in another set of procedures (the Systematic Screening for Behavior Disorders), this review attends to the SARS as a stand-alone system.

There is some information presented on the issue of agreement among different raters. Most of the indicators are well defined and objective in nature, and therefore, one would expect high, near-perfect agreement among different raters who were performing scans of the same student records. For example, whether the student is currently verified as special education (and has an IEP), whether the student is receiving Chapter 1 services, and the number of in-grade retentions are variables that should not vary from one coder to another. There is some subjectivity in the determination of whether narrative comments regarding the student in his or her file qualify as "negative." The manual contains three pages of description and examples of "negative" narrative comments and has a practice exercise with correct answers. The authors do report data from five raters who judged 263 narrative comments, yielding an overall mean agreement level of 85% agreement.

However, it is a significant problem that the authors have not assessed stability of these indicators over time and did not show a zero-order intercorrelation matrix. At least half of the 11 indicators have a direct or indirect connection to special education classification. The study by Shaywitz, Escobar, Shaywitz, Fletcher, and Makuch (1992) found such instability in the primary method of identifying special education students (the "discrepancy" model that relies on the achievement vs. IQ difference) that they concluded what was often labeled a special education condition was nothing other than performance on the low end of an achievement continuum. Their data showed that only about one-fourth of elementary age students *remained* special education classified (with dyslexia) over a period as short as a three-grade span. If the SARS authors intend that their system be used as an elementary grade screening tool to anticipate high school age problems such as dropping out, then there should be serious study of stability over time of the indicators. Also, an intercorrelation matrix based on a sample representative of a normative population should be presented so the user could directly examine what appears to be significant multicolinearity. Factor loadings in the technical manual allow one to infer these correlations, but the correlation matrix might make it clear that it is really unnecessary to go to the trouble of computing factor scores. For example, "current IEP" is an indicator, and so is "nonregular classroom placement"; as is "academic/behavioral referrals" and "referral out" of the home school. In addition, the factor analyses presented are somewhat difficult to interpret because individual variable loadings are broken out by sample location (Oregon and Washington), and many non-trivial differences are evident in the data (between locations).

The issue of predictive validity is related to the question of stability of indicators over time. A careful reading of the manual is required to determine that a true predictive validity study was not done. The general impression given is that the tracking of these 11 indicators in elementary school will allow school staff to accurately predict students who will likely drop out in high school. The study by Block-Pedego (1990)—also the second author of the user's manual—was actually a *retrospective* study. That is, high school dropouts were identified and then their elementary records were examined. This is very much different from applying the screening tool to a large number of elementary age students, forming a prediction of which ones will be at risk in high school (while the students are still in elementary grades), and then following those students into high school age to determine the accuracy of the predictions. The retrospective "accuracy" rates cited for the elementary record scan for 11th/12th graders who drop out (as well as the rates for the grade 7–10 record scan) are surely higher than they would be in the kind of study described above. See Waldie and Spreen (1993) for an example of a longitudinal study that followed subjects from ages 8–12 to adulthood to analyze the relationship between learning disability and contact with police.

Still, reliability and validity issues notwithstanding, the system could provide help to school staff—as an organizing tool and in conjunction with other information—to identify youngsters potentially in need of attention. Especially if a student's profile completed once at the end (or beginning) of a year, for *several years in a row*, began to appear stable or as an increasing "at risk" function, one could have confidence in taking action. Most schools have access to computers and database programs now. Automating the system would make it even more helpful to staff.

REVIEWER'S REFERENCES

Block-Pedego, A. (1990). Early identification and prediction of students at risk for dropping out of school using the school archival records search (SARS). *Dissertation Abstracts*. Ann Arbor, MI.

Shaywitz, S. E., Escobar, M. D., Shaywitz, B. A., Fletcher, J. M., & Makuch, R. (1992). Evidence that dyslexia may represent the lower tail of a normal distribution of reading ability. *The New England Journal of Medicine, 326*(3), 145–150.
Waldie, K., & Spreen, O. (1993). The relationship between learning disabilities and persisting delinquency. *Journal of Learning Disabilities, 26*(6), 417–423.

Review of the School Archival Records Search by ROBERT FITZPATRICK, *Consulting Psychologist, Cranberry Township, PA:*

The School Archival Records Search (SARS) uses school records to aid in identifying and making decisions about elementary-age children "at serious risk for developing behavior disorders" or "at elevated risk for later school dropout" (p. 3). Behavior disorders are characterized as "externalizing (conduct problems) or internalizing (personality)" (p. 7) disorders.

The 11 "variables" were "derived after extensive pilot testing," in a research program called Systematic Screening for Behavior Disorders (SSBD). Although the manual contains essentially no rationale for the selection of the variables, they appear to be appropriate. However, it is confusing to find the variables are named and described somewhat differently in different parts of the manual. "Demographics," for example, is scored only for and frequently referred to as "Number of different schools attended."

The idea of seeking a standardized and quantifiable way of reviewing school records relevant to behavior disorders is intuitively attractive, and the association of the SARS with the SSBD research program seems a favorable sign.

Three scoring options are described in the manual. The first option is to evaluate each of the variables separately, as indicating whether the pupil is positive (at risk) or negative (not at risk) for a behavior disorder. For example, if a student scores below the 41st percentile on national norms for an achievement test, that student is scored positive for Achievement Test Information. Results for all 11 variables are then compared with "characteristic" profiles for externalizers, internalizers, dropouts, and normals. No justification is provided for the cutoffs; no doubt the authors have evidence to support the choice of the 41st percentile and other cutoffs, but they do not report that evidence in the manual.

The second scoring option is based on factor analytic identification of three factors, called DISRUPTION, NEEDS ASSISTANCE, and LOW ACHIEVEMENT. A "domain" score is derived for each factor, by determining if two or more of the variables that load most strongly on that factor are positive. The choice of two variables seems arbitrary, and is not explained in the manual.

The third scoring option involves the calculation of factor scores with mean of 0 and standard deviation of 1. The authors describe the calculations and provide examples and a self-test for the user. Unfortunately, many of the sample calculations are in error (or else the instructions are incorrect). On one (unnumbered) page in Appendix B, 14 of 30 results are inconsistent with the relevant instructions or formulas. The user is advised to distrust the numbers in the sample calculations.

Some evidence is provided to show the SARS scores succeed in identifying children who are at risk for behavior disorders, distinguishing between externalizing and internalizing types, and predicting later school dropout. However, there are problems with the evidence. The manual is poorly organized and lacks many details needed to understand and evaluate the evidence. In most cases, the effects seem modest; for example, in one of the two major studies reported, only 36% of the pupils rated by teachers as externalizers were identified by the SARS as DISRUPTIVE. A pervasive problem is that much of the evidence is circular; the SARS was originally developed in part as a criterion measure for other parts of the SSBD, and the validity of the SARS is defended because it is somewhat consistent with teacher judgments obtained with those other SSBD procedures.

Interrater reliability information is provided for small samples of raters and scorers. Although the data indicate reasonable levels of reliability, they are insufficient for evaluation of the instrument. More data on more types of reliability are needed.

Norms are also limited and poorly presented. In addition, the suggestions in the manual for their use are dubious.

The SARS is a promising instrument and the authors indicate further information about it will be forthcoming. The SARS is not yet suitable for routine implementation, but independent research and cautious applications are to be encouraged.

[276]
School Effectiveness Questionnaire.

Purpose: Assesses variables that have an impact on school effectiveness.
Population: Students, teachers, parents.
Publication Date: 1993.
Scores, 11: Effective Instructional Leadership, Clear and Focused Mission, Safe and Orderly Environment, Positive School Climate, High Expectations, Frequent Assessment/Monitoring of Student Achievement, Emphasis on Basic Skills, Maximum Opportunities for Learning, Parent/Community Involvement, Strong Professional Development, Teacher Involvement in Decision Making.

Administration: Group.
Forms, 4: Level 1 Students (Elementary), Level 2 Students (High School), Teachers, Parents.
Price Data, 1994: $8 per 10 reusable questionnaires (Teacher Form); $20 per 10 reusable questionnaires (Level 1, Level 2, Parent Forms); $10.50 per manual (45 pages); $50 per 100 Type 2 machine-scorable answer sheets; $14 per examination kit including manual, one each of all four questionnaires, and one answer document.
Time: (15–20) minutes.
Comments: Optional data analysis software available from publisher.
Authors: Lee Baldwin, Freeman Coney III, Diane Färdig, and Roberta Thomas.
Publisher: The Psychological Corporation.

Review of the School Effectiveness Questionnaire by ROBERT FITZPATRICK, Consulting Psychologist, Cranberry Township, PA:

How should we measure the effectiveness of schools? One approach is to test the product: What have the students learned? Alternatively, we can check the process, to determine if the schools are doing the right things (supposing that we know what the right things are). The School Effectiveness Questionnaire (SEQ) represents the latter approach. It is a set of questionnaires intended to measure school effectiveness across 11 dimensions. Teachers, parents, elementary students, and high school students complete separate questionnaires. The responses of teachers contribute to all 11 summary scores, of parents to 9, and of students to 7.

The questionnaires contain from 36 (elementary students) to 70 (teachers) statements to which each respondent is asked to indicate extent of agreement. Each statement requires a judgment or calls for an opinion about the way a school functions. Some of the judgments seem quite difficult. For example, parents are to indicate whether they agree that teachers are taking time and using techniques needed for effective instruction.

The SEQ was developed in a single large school district. A committee of educational administrators, along with representatives of parents and community, reviewed literature on school effectiveness, produced the listing and definition of the 11 characteristics thought to constitute school effectiveness, and formulated initial versions of the questionnaires. After a pilot test, the questionnaires were revised and administered to "nearly 30,000 students, teachers and parents" (p. 8). Later, some further changes, not specifically described in the manual, were made prior to publication for general use. It is not clear to me whether the data reported in the manual were derived from one or more of the earlier versions of the questionnaires or from the final versions.

Although the characteristics of effective schools chosen for measurement on the SEQ are intuitively reasonable, no data are reported linking scores on this set of questionnaires with other indicators of effectiveness. Further, some users might argue for the inclusion of other characteristics as important to measure on a school effectiveness scale. Scant attention is paid to these concerns in the SEQ manual.

Coefficient alpha reliabilities, all in the high 90s for teachers and parents, and in the 70s and 80s for students are reported. According to the manual authors, these data imply that "each characteristic is represented by a highly homogeneous set of statements on specific aspects of school effectiveness" (p. 16). But some of the coefficients are not as high as might be desired, and users are not told the size or source of the sample on which the coefficients are based. No other information about reliability or generalizability of the scales is provided.

Intercorrelations among the 11 characteristics are reported for 86 teachers, 151 elementary students, and 190 secondary students. No parent data are reported. The intercorrelations for teachers are relatively high, ranging from .52 to .83, whereas those for students are lower, with values from .16 to .72. The manual argues that this is good news, in that these coefficients are lower than the alphas but not too low. Some factor analytic information would be helpful. Lacking that, the pattern of results constitutes rather weak evidence for the construct validity of the questionnaires.

Inspection of items in corresponding scales for the four questionnaires suggests that the scales for different respondent groups may function somewhat differently. For example, Parent/Community Involvement may mean quite different things to teachers, parents, and students.

The manual contains no norms. The authors may have supposed that normative information is not needed, but do recommend comparing scores to identify relative strengths and weaknesses of the schools under study. This recommendation raises some difficulties in interpretation of item or scale score mean differences. For example, achieving high scores on some of the characteristics may be quite difficult whereas other characteristics of effectiveness may be approached more loosely. Differences among the scores may reflect a daunting goal as well as a school profile. Without norms, users will not be able to understand possible scale differences. Hence, it seems there is a need for norms,

and they are lacking. Even with norms, it is well to exercise caution in interpreting profiles of scores, a caution not expressed in the manual.

Manual authors also recommend comparison of scale means across groups of schools within a district, across grade levels, and in a before-and-after style to evaluate programs intended to improve school functioning. No guidance is provided as to the size of difference in means that might indicate meaningful change. Once again the lack of normative data creates interpretive difficulties.

The authors are inconsistent in describing the SEQ as a means to evaluate individual schools. They both caution against such use and suggest that schools with high or low scores be identified. It seems naive to suppose that comparisons and evaluations would not be made by administrators, school boards, and the public.

The SEQ is well packaged and appealing. If a school district or school determines that its content is appropriate, it could constitute a ready-made set of instruments for measuring educational effectiveness from a process point of view. However, its validity for general use is at best unproven, norms are nonexistent, needed data and analyses are lacking, and some of the comparisons suggested in the manual are of questionable suitability. Educators are advised to be cautious about adopting the SEQ.

Review of the School Effectiveness Questionnaire by MICHAEL HARWELL, Associate Professor of Psychology in Education, University of Pittsburgh, Pittsburgh, PA:

The School Effectiveness Questionnaire (SEQ) is a new instrument used to assess variables that have an impact on school effectiveness. Parents, teachers, and students respond to 11 subscales reflecting characteristics of school effectiveness: Instructional Leadership, Clear and Focused Mission, Safe and Orderly Environment, Positive School Climate, High Expectations, Frequent Assessment and Monitoring of Student Achievement, Emphasis on Basic Skills, Maximum Opportunities for Learning, Parent/Community Involvement, Strong Professional Development, and Teacher Involvement in Decision Making. Each of these characteristics is described in the manual and a few references are provided for interested readers. The manual authors wisely state that SEQ information should be used in conjunction with other indicators of school effectiveness, such as standardized test scores, class grades, etc. The authors go on to state that "The School Effectiveness Questionnaire is not intended to be used to judge whether any particular school is good or bad. Instead, it is simply an instrument that yields a profile of school effectiveness that emerges from the attitudes and opinions of the people surveyed" (p. 12).

After examining SEQ scores, three tasks are identified for users that should precede any programmatic interventions: (a) Investigate what there is about the school environment that produced a particular pattern of responses; (b) design programs that will address less favorable conditions and sustain positive conditions; and (c) oversee the implementation of the designed program.

On the one hand, then, the SEQ is described as a data collection instrument the purpose of which is simply to describe; on the other hand, users are told that there are tasks to be accomplished after viewing SEQ results, tasks that use the SEQ to judge whether certain characteristics of a school are good or bad. These two purposes (describe versus evaluate) are vastly different and this ambivalent structure runs throughout the manual. Despite the claims in the manual, it is hard to imagine how any instrument purporting to assess school effectiveness would not be used for comparative purposes and have a prescriptive function.

EASE OF USE. All forms of the questionnaire are administered in groups or by mail and most respondents should have little trouble following the written directions. (Directions for younger respondents, for example, students in first grade, are read aloud.) There are no time limits. Teachers will usually administer the SEQ to students. The manual contains detailed instructions on how to do so. The administration of the teacher form is fairly unstructured. The manual authors suggest using a faculty meeting or workshop setting in which to administer the SEQ, but provide no guidance on how questions about the form might be dealt with or that teachers should probably not talk with one another while filling out the questionnaire. Parents are typically mailed the questionnaire and may fill it out jointly. No advice is given on what parents should do if they have questions or on how long they have to return the form. The manual authors do touch on a few of the obvious difficulties, for example, the likelihood of a response bias in the returned questionnaires from parents, but more information about questionnaire and survey methods would be useful. There is a substantial survey research literature to draw on to offer advice to those administering the SEQ. The manual authors indicate the reading level for the

Level 1 form (grades 5–8) is 5th grade and for Level 2 (grades 9–12) is 8th grade, and that the reading level for the parent form is 10th–11th grade.

CHOOSING RESPONDENTS. The size of many schools will require that some sort of sampling scheme be employed. The authors suggest consulting someone knowledgeable in this area to construct a sampling plan. No advice is offered for what constitutes too small a sample. There is also a misstatement in the manual that "In schools of small or moderate size, a survey of all students (5th through 12th grades), all teachers, and all parents would yield the most reliable, valid, and meaningful results" (p. 20). The validity and meaningfulness of the results do not depend on attempting to sample the entire population, but, rather, on the accuracy of the inferences made from the responses. If, for example, items comprising the Instructional Leadership subscale had little to do with instructional leadership, it would not matter whether the entire population was sampled or not. The manual authors correctly note the critical issue in sampling is that the sample should be representative of the school or district population. This deserves more than a simple note; it should probably be put in boldface letters two inches high.

SCORING. Teachers, parents, and students are given varying numbers of Likert-type items to respond to; grades 5–8 respond to 36 items, each with a range of 1–3 (1 = *Disagree*, 2 = *No Opinion*, 3 = *Agree*); grades 9–12 respond to 48 items each scored 1—5 (1 = *Strongly Disagree*, 5 = *Strongly Agree*); parents respond to 44 items and teachers to 70 (both scored on the same 1–5 scale as grades 9–12). According to the manual, higher scores suggest more effective schools. The manual contains advice on machine scoring of the responses and on what descriptive statistics to calculate. Software for analyses of responses is available for purchase from the publisher. The authors recommend computing both individual item summaries as well as subscale scores (one for each characteristic) using valid responses. What constitutes an invalid response is not mentioned.

NORMS. No norms are presented, presumably because schools or school districts are complex organizations that defy attempts to produce interpretable averages. This seems quite defensible. For example, the meaning of an average Instructional Leadership score would probably show great variation across schools in ways that would make normative interpretations very difficult. Put another way, an average score for Instructional Leadership in one school might imply something quite different from a similar score in another school.

Norms would also promote the comparison of one school's scores with another school's, which should be avoided. However, the lack of norms places an additional burden on the scoring system, because there are no external (normative) data to guide score interpretations.

RELIABILITY. According to the manual, a committee-developed form of the SEQ was piloted using students, parents, and teachers in 10 schools, with all grade levels represented. Unfortunately, no information about the pilot study, such as the group sample sizes and relevant demographic information, is reported. Coefficient alpha reliabilities are reported for these data for each group of respondents on each subscale as well as a total score (apparently computed as the sum of the individual subscale scores). These coefficients are quite high ($\geq .94$) for parents and teachers and noticeably lower for students ($\geq .77$). Intercorrelations among the subscales are also reported for teachers ($N = 86$) and are said to be representative of the patterns observed for students; no reliability information is reported for the parent form. The description of these correlations, which generally range between .16–.83, is misleading. The authors state, "These intercorrelations indicate that the characteristics are related and can be considered facets of school effectiveness" (p. 17). Nonsense. Nonzero correlations among the subscales in no way indicates that they are facets of school effectiveness, which would require, among other things, validity evidence. Another misstatement is, "The pattern of intercorrelations is indicative of the desired relative independence of the characteristics" (p. 17). What the authors apparently mean is that the correlations suggest that the characteristics do not overlap much, although some correlations in the .70s and .80s suggests there is a good bit of overlap. There is no such thing as relative independence.

A total of 30,000 students, parents, and teachers were surveyed with the revised instrument and their responses led to the final form of the SEQ. Why such a huge sample size was used and why the reported summary statistics in the manual are not based on 30,000 is not explained. Regardless of the sample size, what is missing here is stronger evidence the subscales do or do not overlap substantially, such as might be provided with a factor analysis or item response theory approach.

VALIDITY. No validity evidence is reported in the manual, even though such evidence is badly needed. The last section of the manual is entitled "Using the Results to Improve School Effectiveness" (p. 41) and suggests that SEQ scores can guide efforts to improve school effectiveness. What empirical evidence is offered that these 11 characteristics and the chosen scoring scheme provide valid prescriptive information? The answer is none. Could such information be obtained? Of course, by studying schools that have used the SEQ to identify strengths and weaknesses (such as those associated with the sample of 30,000). As an example, suppose five schools that had used the SEQ had each found something less than a positive school climate, and then designed, implemented, and evaluated programs intended to promote a positive school climate. Asking the respondents in these studies to answer a different questionnaire that also assesses school climate and correlating the two sets of scores would provide validity evidence. Examining whether SEQ results agreed with the perceptions of one or more independent consultants hired to assess school climate would also provide validity evidence (and so on). Until validity evidence is presented, users cannot have much confidence in SEQ scores.

INTERPRETING THE RESULTS. The information and advice offered in the interpretation section is critically flawed. Users are first told, "The primary use of the School Effectiveness Questionnaire involves studying the profile of the 11 characteristic means derived from the survey" (p. 37). The authors go on to suggest that users "Look for dimensions of school effectiveness with very low (unfavorable) means. Improvement is probably needed in these areas" (p. 37). This (and similar comments) is poor advice. Because the scoring has no natural zero point and there are no norms, what would constitute an unfavorable or favorable mean? (The authors do point out the SEQ could be used for the same school over time, which would allow within-subscale, over-time comparisons.)

Most troublesome of all is the suggestion that SEQ results can be used to "Compare the characteristic means of different groups (e.g., of schools within the district or grades within a school) to see whether their perceptions of school effectiveness differ" (p. 37). It is one thing to compare different grades within a school and quite another to use the SEQ to make between-school comparisons, even if the schools are in the same district. Whatever the difficulties of assessing a single school's effectiveness, they are compounded many times over when comparing schools, and there is *nothing* in the manual to suggest the SEQ can validly and reliably be used for this task. Put another way, the authors offer no statistical or psychometric evidence that justifies the use of the SEQ to compare schools.

ADDITIONAL ISSUES. The authors fail to acknowledge what is obvious to any educator: That indicators of school effectiveness are high-stakes statistics. This failure may be responsible for the inattention given to several related issues, such as (a) How can anonymity of responses be preserved to ensure honest answers? This deserves more attention than it receives because it is easy to conceive of settings in which maintaining anonymity would be difficult. (b) Who are the results to be reported to or made available to? Are SEQ results primarily intended for administrators? (c) What motivation would students, parents, and teachers have for participating in a thoughtful way in a survey? Another issue the SEQ authors ignore is the limitation of any paper-and-pencil questionnaire assessing a high-stakes topic like school effectiveness. Clearly, the use of the SEQ should be in conjunction with information obtained from structured interviews with members of the affected groups.

The various problems with the SEQ are exacerbated by the caliber of the psychometric and statistical work reported in the manual, which is uniformly low. For example, no item analyses, either classical or based on item response theory, are reported. A list of analyses that should have been done as part of the construction of the instrument would include, but not be limited to, factor analyses to investigate the factor structure underlying the 11 subscales, item analyses that investigate possible response sets for the items, validity evidence that inferences from the subscale scores are accurate, and suggestions that users employ various statistical procedures to examine subscale means. For descriptive analyses, users would be well advised to employ now-standard robust indicators of center and spread. The suggestion that subscale means can be compared across demographic groups provides another example of questionable advice. How are these means to be compared? Descriptively, or using inferential procedures? And what of the issue of whether a sample or an entire population is represented in the data? It might be argued that prescribing appropriate statistical analyses is outside the scope of the manual. The authors do offer advice on analyzing the responses and computing and interpreting statistics such as means, standard deviations, and frequency tables, but offer no similar advice on performing inferential analyses when comparing demographic groups. At the least, it would be helpful if the authors advised users with minimal statistical training to consult someone knowledgeable in this area.

SUMMARY. Overall, the SEQ cannot be recommended to assess school effectiveness. It clearly has a prescriptive function but the authors fail to provide validity evidence. Without such evidence no inferences can be made about schools with various scores on the 11 characteristics of school effectiveness. The manual is also riddled with highly questionable advice. Perhaps the most egregious example is the suggestion that the SEQ can be used to compare schools. In the section on choosing respondents the authors advised users to consult with someone knowledgeable about sampling. The authors would also benefit from consultation from someone knowledgeable about psychometrics and statistics in the hope of upgrading the quality of this questionnaire.

[277]
School Social Behavior Scales.

Purpose: Provides rating of both social skills and antisocial problem behaviors.
Population: Grades K–12.
Publication Date: 1993.
Acronym: SSBS.
Scores, 8: Social Competence (Interpersonal Skills, Self-Management Skills, Academic Skills, Total), Antisocial Behavior (Hostile-Irritable, Antisocial-Aggressive, Disruptive-Demanding, Total).
Administration: Individual.
Price Data, 1993: $29.95 per specimen kit including manual (38 pages) and 20 test booklets; $19.95 per manual; $12 per 20 test booklets.
Time: (5–10) minutes.
Author: Kenneth W. Merrell.
Publisher: PRO-ED, Inc.
Cross References: See T4:2369 (1 reference).

TEST REFERENCES

1. Merrel, K. W., Cedeno, C. J., & Johnson, E. R. (1993). The relationship between social behavior and self-concept in school settings. *Psychology in the Schools, 30,* 293-298.
2. Demaray, M. K., Ruffalo, S. L., Carlson, J., Busse, R. T., Olson, A. E., McManus, S. M., & Leventhal, A. (1995). Social skills assessment: A comparative evaluation of six published rating scales. *School Psychology Review, 24,* 648–671.

Review of the School Social Behavior Scales by STEPHEN R. HOOPER, *Associate Professor of Psychiatry, University of North Carolina School of Medicine, Chapel Hill, NC:*

The School Social Behavior Scales (SSBS) were designed to be used by teachers and other school personnel in evaluating both positive (i.e., Social Competence) and negative (i.e., Antisocial Behavior) patterns of elementary and secondary students. The SSBS is somewhat unique in that it attempts to divide the constructs of Social Competence and Antisocial Behavior into separate scales and, by design, it does not contain items pertaining to frank psychiatric conditions and disturbances. Additionally, the SSBS attempts to provide estimates of teacher-related versus peer-related adjustments, and these items are interspersed among the Social Competence and Antisocial Behavior scales. The foundation for the SSBS is based on conceptual models of social competence and problem behavior, although a specific operational model is not specified.

Administration and scoring procedures for the SSBS are simple and clear. The SSBS is individually completed by teachers on individual students. The manual states that the SSBS can be completed by other school personnel who know the student well; however, it is not clear how well "other school personnel" fit with the normative data. The SSBS requires approximately 5 to 10 minutes for completion, thus making the ascertainment of these ratings somewhat faster than those gained by other similar instruments. According to the manual, each item must be completed in order to calculate a standard score. Gender and grade-level comparisons also can be made, although the manual notes that such comparisons should not be used for screening or placement decisions because of the relatively small sizes of these subsamples.

In addition to the standard scores, the SSBS generates descriptive levels of social functioning; however, there seem to be some developmental issues with respect to the scores needed to fall within these social functioning levels. For example, an older child (i.e., grades 7–12) could receive a score of 33 on the Interpersonal Skills Subscale on the Social Competence Scale, which would place him/her within the average range; however, a younger child (i.e., grades K–6) receiving the same score would fall within the Moderate Deficit level. A similar scenario occurs on the Self-Management Subscale, and there are developmental differences on the Academic Skills Subscale. On the Antisocial Behavior Scale, there are relatively few developmental differences between the older and younger age groups. Further, there appear to be ceiling and floor effects for the Total Scores on the Social Competence and Antisocial Behavior scales, respectively, for both younger and older age groups. These effects are in the normal direction, thus not hindering the screening goal of this rating scale, but these qualities will provide little to the user in terms of strengths in the area of social competence. Relatedly, given that one of the primary goals of this rating scale is to be a screening tool for behaviorally at-risk children, there are limited sensitivity or specificity data reported. Consequently, it is unclear how well this instrument performs for one of its intended purposes.

The development of the SSBS followed basic psychometric guidelines and principles. The item pool was generated via a number of appropriate sources (e.g., reviews of the literature on social competence, social skills training curricula, and existing rating scales). External expert reviews of these items provided initial guidance with respect to item revision and selection, and subsequent point-biserial correlations also revealed good relationships between items and their respective scales. All of the items on the Social Competence Scale are written in a positive direction and all of the items on the Antisocial Behavior Scale in a negative direction, thus setting up potential rater response bias in each of these domains.

The normative sample was large, consisting of over 1,800 students from regular and special education classrooms, and represented the major geographic regions in the United States. There is some racial diversity in the normative sample, but it is underrepresented. Although the manual notes that this should not cause inordinate problems with interpretation, especially once the effects of social class have been considered, it may create problems in screening certain populations (e.g., inner city schools with a higher representation of minority students), or in general clinical use with single subjects. A similar concern also is present for the socioeconomic status of the normative sample where the Laborer group is overrepresented.

The author elected to break the scores into two large age bands (elementary versus secondary). Although the author states that this is most desirable, this division did not appear to be founded on any psychometric basis, and likely contributed to the lack of any developmental effect across the scales.

The reliability of the SSBS was variable. The SSBS showed strong internal consistency, falling within the .90s, although temporal stability (3-week interval) and interrater reliability estimates were significantly lower, falling within the .60 to .82 range and the .53 to .83 range, respectively. The Standard Error of Measurement also is provided, although it would have been more user friendly to transform these data into test scaling indices. The lowest reliability coefficients tended to occur on the Antisocial Behavior Scale, with the interrater reliability being the lowest across the scales. Although the author attempts to address this concern via discussions pertaining to source and setting variance, this remains of considerable concern given that one of the stated purposes of this tool is to design intervention plans. How will such a plan be evaluated if the interrater reliability is poor and the temporal stability is weak?

The content validity evidence for the SSBS appears adequate, and the concurrent validity information also seems satisfactory. This latter type of validity was examined by comparing the SSBS to the Waksman Social Skills Rating Scale, Conners' Teacher Rating Scale, Walker-McConnell Scale of Social Competence and School Adjustment, and Child Behavior Checklist—Direct Observation Form, and a high degree of association was found for the SSBS for all of these measures. The SSBS does seem able to discriminate between normal students and special education students, and it seems capable of discriminating between children with behavioral and emotional problems and other children with special needs; however, the degree of this predictive accuracy was not reported in the manual. Factorial validity also was found to be satisfactory, with replication procedures confirming the overall factor structure proposed, but the intercorrelation between all of the scales of the SSBS is not reported. This latter observation is important in that the relative independence of each of the primary scales remains unknown at present.

In summary, the SSBS is a teacher rating scale designed to measure positive and negative social behaviors of students. It is quick and simple in its administration, and scoring is straightforward. The manual is clearly written and nicely organized. Loosely based on theoretical models of social competence, most of the psychometric qualities of this tool are satisfactory; however, there were concerns raised with respect to its temporal stability and interrater reliability. Although the normative data appear representative, there are ceiling and floor effects, largely limiting statements about strengths that an individual may have in social-behavioral domains. Also, from a scoring perspective, there is little psychometric justification for the younger and older age bands into which the instrument is divided. The validity of the SSBS also seems adequate; however, there are few data on the sensitivity and specificity of the SSBS, thus limiting our knowledge on the screening capabilities of this tool. Although this tool holds promise for screening social competence and antisocial behavior in the school setting, its ultimate usefulness for the school-based practitioner remains unknown.

Review of the School Social Behavior Scales by LESLEY A. WELSH, Associate Professor of Education, West Chester University, West Chester, PA:

The School Social Behavior Scales (SSBS) was designed to evaluate social competence and antisocial behavior of school-age children (K–12). The SSBS is a rating scale that may be administered by teachers and other school personnel for use in school settings. This assessment is not designed for clinical or psychiatric settings and does not contain descriptions of low-incidence behaviors. The author describes the purposes as:

1. a screening tool for identifying students who are behaviorally at-risk,

2. a component in an assessment battery for determining program eligibility and designing appropriate intervention programs, and

3. a research instrument for studying social competence and antisocial behavior patterns.

The SSBS is composed of 65 items; 32 address Social Competence and 33 address Antisocial Behavior. A unique characteristic of this instrument is that both of these scales were normed on the same population; thus, meaningful comparisons may be made about scores on the two scales. The Social Competence Scale is subdivided into Interpersonal Skills (14 items), Self-Management Skills (10 items), and Academic Skills (8 items). The Antisocial Behavior Scale is subdivided into Hostile-Irritable (14 items), Antisocial-Aggressive (10 items), and Disruptive-Demanding (9 items). The subscales are empirically derived. The author of the SSBS describes the Hostile-Irritable scale as other-directed in nature, the Anti-Social scale as likely to lead to negative social consequences such as peer-rejection, and the Demanding-Disruptive scale as likely to result in a strained relationship with the teacher.

ADMINISTRATION AND SCORING. This rating scale may be completed by school personnel who have had an opportunity to observe the student for a minimum of 6 weeks. Typically the rating scale takes between 5 and 10 minutes to complete. There is a student information section and a rater information section that should be completed to aid in interpreting the information. The test author suggests that all items should be completed, even if the rater is not exactly sure how to rate a specific item, as missing data make conversion and meaningful interpretation difficult, if not impossible. However, inaccurate estimates of student behaviors would be a serious concern when interpreting results.

Raters are asked to judge the frequency of specific behaviors on a 5-point scale (1 = *Never*, 3 = *Sometimes*, and 5 = *Frequently*). A Social Competence example is "Remains calm when problems arise"; an example of Antisocial Behavior is "Blames other students for problems."

Raw scores are calculated for each subscale, which combine into total scores for each of the scales (Social Competence and Antisocial Behavior). Raw subscale scores are converted into Social Functioning Levels for elementary (K–6) and middle/secondary (7–12) students. Raw subscale and total scale scores on the Social Competence Scale may be used to classify students as High Functioning, Average, Moderate Deficit, or Significant Deficit. Raw subscale and total scale scores on the Antisocial Scale may be used to classify students as Average, Moderate Problem, or Significant Problem. Gender and grade-level descriptive statistics are available for additional comparisons although the test user is cautioned by the test author not to use gender or grade-level comparisons for screening or placement decisions due to the low number of subjects in these groups.

The section in the manual on interpreting SSBS scores is unclear and contains inconsistencies that make it difficult to read. For example, the manual states, "The High Functioning Level includes raw scores that are above 80% of the norm groups scores for Social Competence or below 20% of the norm group scores for Antisocial Behavior" (p. 10). However, there is no High Functioning Level listed for Antisocial Behavior. The Social Competence Scale tables report in terms of "deficit," whereas the Antisocial Scale tables report in terms of "problem." However, the author uses "problem" when describing both Competence and Antisocial.

The author states (manual, p. 15) that subscales standard scores and percentile levels are not included due to nonstandard distribution of scores. He states that conversion of subscale scores could easily lead to faulty conclusions about the meaning of the scores. However, descriptive labels are provided as a general framework to assist interpretation. Yet previously the descriptive labels were defined in terms of the associated percentile rankings. If the percentiles would lead to faulty conclusions, the associated functioning levels would lead to exactly the same faulty conclusions.

The manual reports transformation of total scores for Scale A (Social Competence) and Scale B (Antisocial Behavior) into standard scores (mean of 100 and standard deviation of 15) and corresponding percentile ranks. However, examination of the conversion tables for Antisocial Behavior has a percentile of approximately 65, rather than the expected 50, corresponding with the standard score of 100. Total scores of approximately one standard deviation in the least desired direction from the mean suggests the need for further screening or assessment. Students whose total scores on both Scales are at the Significant Problem level and have other corroborating assessments should be considered seriously for placement in special education programs or other means

of delivering specially designed social-behavioral intervention (manual, p. 14).

NORMATIVE SAMPLE. The sample used to gather normative data comprised 1,858 K–12 public school students (1,025 males and 833 females). Six hundred and eighty-eight teachers completed the ratings (2.7 ratings per teacher) at 22 sites. Forty percent of the sample was from the West, 19% from the North Central, 27% from the Northeast, and 14% from the South. The ethnic composition of the sample was predominantly white (87%); African-American (8%), Hispanic (2.7%), Asian-American (.9%), and Native American (.6%) students complete the sample. Approximately half of the sample provided data to determine socioeconomic status (SES). The sample appears to have an overrepresentation of students from families identified as laborers. Grade level sample size ranges from 79 to 195. Tables are provided for gender and grade level interpretations of results; however, the author cautions that the sample size may be too small to make this type of interpretation. Approximately 88% of the sample are from regular education; the remaining 12% are from various categories of special education.

PSYCHOMETRIC CHARACTERISTICS. Internal consistency reliability estimates for the two scales ranged from .96 to .98. The internal consistency reliabilities of the subscales ranged from .91 to .96. Three-week test-retest estimates ranged from .60 to .82. Interrater reliability estimates were obtained for 40 elementary-aged learning-disabled students. However, the author does not provide information about the number of teachers this sample of students represents. Teachers and classroom aides rated the students within a 2-week period. The reliability estimates ranged from .53 to .83. The level of interrater reliability is a concern and the author strongly recommends multiple methods, multiple settings, and multiple sources of assessment of student behaviors. The author reports standard error of the estimates derived from the high internal consistency reliability estimates, rather than the more conservative test-retest reliabilities.

Content validity was established through examination of the literature, of existing behavioral and social skills scales, and of the contents of training programs and interventions. The resulting items were revised after being previewed by educators, graduate students, and parents. Concurrent criterion-related validity was examined for a sample of 39 elementary students who were administered the SSBS and the Waksman Social Skills Rating Scale. The coefficients for the various subscales ranged in magnitude from .55 to .93. The total scores had validity coefficients of .87 and -.78. Forty-one elementary students were administered the SSBS and the Conners' Teacher Rating Scale; the validity coefficients ranged in magnitude from .25 to .91.

Forty secondary students took the SSBS and the Walker-McConnell Scale of Social Competence and School Adjustment; the magnitude of the validity coefficients on the social competence scales on the SSBS ranged from .62 to .94. Validity coefficients from concurrent direct observations using the Child Behavior Checklist (CBC) were more problematic. They ranged in magnitude from .01 to .52. Apparently SSBS and direct observation using CBC are not assessing the same characteristics.

SSBS scores indicated significantly different levels of social and behavioral functioning for a normative sample and samples of students with emotional, behavioral, or other disabilities. In another study SSBS scores indicated that high performing students had significantly higher levels of social and behavioral functioning. Factor analysis was used to assign items to subscales. Stability of the factor structure was examined by performing factor analysis on randomly selected subsets of the normative sample. The author states that there was a great deal of similarity and obtained congruence coefficients between .98 and .99. However, stability of the factor structure should be examined with a different sample than the one used to determine the factor structure.

In summary, the SSBS is a 65-item rating scale intended to be used as a screening tool for identifying students who are behaviorally at-risk, as a component in an assessment battery for determining program eligibility and designing appropriate intervention programs, and as a research instrument for studying social competence and antisocial behavior patterns. The manual contains inconsistencies in the section on scoring. These inconsistencies make it difficult to have confidence in the meaning of the SSBS scores. The normative sample is predominantly white, which suggests that more data need to be gathered before using this scale to make determinations concerning nonwhite students. Internal consistency reliability is strong; however, interrater reliability is somewhat problematic. There is evidence of content validity; concurrent validity is demonstrated with several similar scales. However, the magnitude of the validity coefficients using the Child Behavior Checklist, a direct observation method, range from only .01 to .52. SSBS scores are significantly different among groups expected to have different levels of social competence and anti-social behavior.

This scale demonstrates promise, but additional samples should be more representative, interrater reliability needs further analysis, and the scoring section in the manual needs to be rewritten before it is used for identification of behaviorally at-risk students or to determine program eligibility and intervention programs.

[278]
Secondary & College Reading Inventory, Second Edition.

Purpose: "To help ... place students in appropriate reading materials."
Population: Grades 7 through college.
Publication Dates: 1981–1990.
Scores, 9: 3 reading level scores (Independent, Frustration, Instructional) for each of 3 subtests (Word Recognition in Isolation, Word Recognition in Context, Comprehension).
Administration: Individual or group.
Forms, 2: A, B.
Price Data: Available from publisher.
Time: Administration time not reported.
Author: Jerry L. Johns.
Publisher: Kendall/Hunt Publishing Co.

TEST REFERENCES

1. Michel, P. A. (1989). Secondary and College Reading Inventory. *Journal of Reading, 33,* 308-310.

Review of the Secondary & College Reading Inventory, Second Edition by HOI K. SUEN, Professor of Educational Psychology, Pennsylvania State University, University Park, PA:

The Secondary & College Reading Inventory, Second Edition is an informal reading inventory (IRI) consisting of two forms. Each form contains seven 25-word graded word lists such that each of the seven lists is appropriate for one of the grade levels from the 7th grade through college. In other words, for each form, there is a combined total sample of 175 words for 7th grade through college. This sample was drawn randomly from a 1979 published text on core vocabulary. Additionally, each form contains seven half-page graded reading passages, again with each passage being appropriate for one of the grade levels from the 7th grade through college. For each reading passage, there are 10 follow-up multiple-choice questions. The grade levels of the reading passages were evaluated based on a 1948 readability formula, a 1985 readability formula, and the author's judgment.

Based on performance, a student is categorized into either an "independent," an "Instructional," or a "Frustration" level. The criteria used to categorize students into these three levels were based on a system developed by Emmett Betts in 1954. Through this system, a student is categorized into one of the three levels for each grade. The highest grade level for which a student is classified as "independent" is the student's Independent reading level. Similarly, the highest grade level for which a student is classified as "instructional" is the student's Instructional reading level. The level beyond the student's Instructional level would be the beginning of the student's Frustration levels. In essence, the Instructional levels are the grade levels most appropriate for reading instruction for a student. The Independent levels are too low and the Frustration levels are too high for the student. Should the pattern become inconsistent, such as in a case where a student is classified as Instructional or Frustration at a lower grade level but is classified as being at an Independent level at a higher grade, the authors suggested that the teacher should use his/her best judgment.

Perhaps because this is an IRI, no attempts have been made to gather data regarding the reliability of the scores and classification decisions. Nor were there any attempts to gather validation evidence to support its interpretation, classification, and instructional uses. Nor were there attempts to validate the criteria used to determine the readability levels and the cut score criteria use for classifications. Given this lack of supportive evidence, this inventory should not be used for any high-stake decisions. That is, this inventory should not be used for student placement, program admission, grade assignment, diagnosis, classification, nor for identification of strengths and weaknesses; nor as a research tool. That is, it should not be used for decisions that may have a serious impact on the student.

The value of this inventory lies in its ability to inform instruction. This inventory can be viewed as a resource in addition to workbooks and other reading materials in a reading program. Its value lies less in the ability to determine exactly where a child's reading level is or how the child compares against other children; rather it is useful as a source of information in addition to the teacher's own sense of where things are and what to focus on next in his/her instruction. As long as there is sufficient flexibility in the reading instruction such that, should the teacher discover other indications later that the grade level for a particular student based on this inventory is not accurate, the instruction can be readjusted without any detrimental effects, this inventory can be a useful addition to the teacher's instructional took kit.

Even as an instructional/assessment tool, IRIs like this inventory should never be used alone without other sources of information regarding a child's reading ability. The risk with using this inventory alone for either assessment is the potential inadequacy, or even bias, of the chosen sample of words and the chosen sample of passages. Given the rapid changes in standards and the continuous acceptance of many new words and technical terms as part of the standard English vocabulary in the past two decades, a random sample of a 1979 vocabulary is unlikely to be an adequate representation of the reading abilities of 7th grade through college students. As for the reading passages, they are inherently context-dependent. A sample of seven reading passages may be a limited representation of contexts. As such, the scores of a child on this inventory may provide a very limited snapshot of the child's reading ability and that picture may not be generalizable to other contexts or words not represented in the 1979 vocabulary. Furthermore, the limited snapshot picture may very well be blurry. However, given the lack of reliability and validity information, we have no way to judge whether this snapshot picture is clear or blurry.

In sum, as an informal reading inventory, this inventory should not be used for important decisions about an individual child. It can be used as a valuable instructional tool along with other sources of information. As an informal assessment, the results of the assessment should be treated as a limited snapshot picture relative to a particular set of contents and contexts and by no means a complete representative photo album. Caution must be taken not to generalize too far beyond the sample of words and passages.

Review of the Secondary & College Reading Inventory, Second Edition by SANDRA WARD, Assistant Professor of Education, College of William and Mary, School of Education, Williamsburg, VA:

Two purposes of the Secondary & College Reading Inventory are clearly stated in the manual: (a) "to help teachers place students in appropriate reading materials" (p. 3), and (b) to diagnose reading abilities of individual students and groups. The inventory consists of graded word lists, graded reading passages, and two sets of comprehension questions for each reading passage. The two forms of the test can be useful for pretest/posttest purposes or silent/oral reading comparisons. The test includes two important aspects in the evaluation of reading skills: oral reading ability and comprehension.

The graded word lists were randomly selected from a published core vocabulary. The reading passages were evaluated by two readability formulas that are referenced but not provided. In addition, the results of field testing in conjunction with the author's judgment were used to assign grade levels. Specific information on the test development is not given. For example, a detailed description of the field testing, including the samples and procedures used, is necessary to evaluate the appropriateness of assigned grade levels. Because the clinical judgment of the author was also used, a description of his decision rules would clarify the important criteria in drawing conclusions.

A related issue is the lack of any reliability and validity data. Although the inventory is clearly a criterion-referenced measure, reliability coefficients could be computed on the comprehension questions for each passage. Because no information is provided on the development of these questions, the user needs to know how consistently the questions measure comprehension. Additionally, miscue analysis is applied to determine strengths and weaknesses. The author gives a detailed review of the procedures to be followed in an appendix; however, there is no evidence of interrater reliability in the use of these procedures. This represents an important detail considering the difficulty in accurately recording miscues. Given the author's intended purpose of diagnosing reading strengths and weaknesses, information on reliability is critical to support the use of the test.

In tests that are used to measure how well an individual has mastered a specific skill, support of content validity is necessary to determine whether the inventory covers a representative sample of behavior. The Secondary & College Reading Inventory provides no such information. Specifically, data should be presented that inform the user of the appropriateness and representativeness of the test content. Evidence of concurrent validity would also be valuable in assessing the inventory's diagnostic value.

The Secondary & College Reading Inventory can be administered to a group or individually. The procedures are well explained so that users precisely understand them. Scoring procedures can be readily applied based on the author's directions. The percentage correct on comprehension questions and reading rate are used to determine Independent, Instructional, and Frustration reading levels. However, the cutoff criteria are arbitrary because there is no justification for defining these levels. To determine strengths and weaknesses, the test user can analyze the types of comprehension questions answered incorrectly. However, the lack of reliability and validity

data regarding these questions render conclusions tentative. With respect to interpretation of the scores on this test, the authors strongly recommend the consideration of other data to support conclusions.

The Secondary & College Reading Inventory is an easily administered informal assessment of reading ability. The directions for administration and scoring are clearly described and easy to follow. Specific data on the development of the inventory as well as evidence of reliability and validity would strengthen the test's utility in diagnosing strengths and weaknesses. Without such data, the inventory is not recommended for diagnostic purposes. This inventory may be helpful to classroom teachers in determining appropriate reading levels, but test administrators should heed the cautions provided by the authors. Most importantly, other data should be used to support any conclusions regarding reading level, strengths, and weaknesses.

Selby MillSmith Adaptive Ability Tests.

Purpose: "For use in the selection, training, and career development of personnel in the UK."
Population: Junior school–adult.
Publication Dates: 1988–1990.
Administration: Individual.
Price Data: Available from publisher.
Time: [15] minutes per subtest.
Comments: All subtests are computer administered.
Author: Selby MillSmith Limited.
Publisher: Selby MillSmith Ltd. [England].

    a) NUMERIC ABILITY TEST.
    Purpose: "To assess basic numeracy and numerical skills at all levels of the organisation."
    Scores: Total score only.
    b) LANGUAGE ABILITY TEST.
    Purpose: "Assesses the individual's range and clarity in the use of vocabulary."
    Scores: Total score only.
    c) ADMINISTRATIVE ABILITY TEST.
    Purpose: "To assess the speed and accuracy of an individual's administrative capabilities."
    Scores, 3: Numbers, Addresses, Codes.

Review of the Selby-MillSmith Adaptive Ability Tests by COLIN COOPER, Lecturer, School of Psychology, The Queen's University of Belfast, Belfast, United Kingdom:

These three measures (Numeric Ability Test, Language Ability Test, and Administrative Ability Test) claim to be the "first commercially available adaptive ability tests" (manual, p. 1), and the test manual explains that they are derived from tests used to select soldiers for the British army. The tests share a common "feel," common adaptive algorithms, and a common manual, and so this review falls naturally into three sections. The first describes the content of the tests and their implementation. The second part considers their psychometric properties: their reliability, validity, norms, and freedom from bias. As the tests are adaptive (presenting items that are appropriate to the estimated ability of each individual candidate), the quality of this procedure is also examined in the third part of this review.

The tests are well presented and very easy for nonspecialists to use: Testing simply involves inserting the appropriate floppy disk and typing one command. Test administrators are given standard answers to some commonly asked questions. Each copy-protected PC/MS-DOS disk contains two suites of programs, one which administers the tests and one which allows candidates' norm-related scores (stens) to be displayed or printed and narrative reports to be produced.

Candidates' responses are made using a standard keyboard and the candidates' instructions include some training in locating the keys that will be used to make responses. This hardly seems to be the most ergonomic arrangement. In one test, candidates have to choose between five alternatives using keys a–e on the standard QWERTY keyboard: All tests are speeded, and so familiarity with the position of these keys will surely have an effect on test scores. It would have been much better had the program used function keys or a keyboard mask, or if a Windows version of the programs were developed so that the mouse could be used.

The content of the Language Ability Test came as rather a surprise to this reviewer. It comprises just one subtest, requiring the solution of up to 34 verbal analogies (e.g., "cat is to kitten as dog is to (a) calf (b) puppy (c) bitch (d) bark (e) cat"). According to the manual this one test taps "the range and clarity of a person's vocabulary as well as their ability to use the language" (manual, p. 4) and "a low score on this test is not an indicator of low intelligence" (p. 4). Carroll's (1993, ch. 5 & 6) scholarly review of the ability literature casts doubt on both these claims as it classifies verbal analogy problems as measures of *reasoning* rather than of language ability. The other tests are broader in scope, with the Numeric Ability Test having about 10 different kinds of problems (e.g., identifying missing operators, rounding, adding fractions). However, the precise nature of the problems presented depends on the candidate's ability: Only the high-ability candidates see the more demanding types of problems, with the lower-ability ones staying on simple "four-rule" items. The instructions informed candidates that they could use a calculator if they chose to do so (the manual suggests that a calculator should be made available). The Administrative Ability Test looks like other standard tests of clerical ability and includes tests of perceptual speed (accuracy in comparing strings and matching addresses) and a WISC-like coding task.

The test norms given in the manual are not extensive, and the computer program used to generate results or reports does not seem to offer any way of choosing between several sets of normative data. The graduate norms comprise a sample of 445 graduates drawn from 11 U.K. universities: No further detail is given except that "the majority of the sample was aged between 20 and 22" (p. 17). The clerical norms consist of between 139 and 256 "employers [sic] from a large securities company in [the] UK" (p. 16). The uncertain makeup of these samples and their small size limits the usefulness of the test in identifying the potential of individual applicants.

Test-retest reliability (approximate 2-week interval) is given for a sample of 16 people (of unknown composition): These figures are therefore of little value. The internal consistency reliability of untimed versions of the subtests from 179 "of our clients" is of the order of .8–.9: Similar results are found in a sample of 68 11-year-olds. The tests correlate .52–.66 with Saville & Holdsworth tests measuring verbal, numerical, and checking skills in tiny (N<25) samples for which the makeup and ability range are unclear: It is thus unwise to generalize these findings to the general population. The tests also correlate with children's public examination grades, but the sample sizes and makeup are not shown. Without this information the tables are of little value. There is no study in which the tests are correlated with "standard" measures (e.g., the WISC) using a carefully constructed sample. Nor is there any evidence for any of the tests' predictive validity in any area. No mention is made of internal or external bias, or of group differences.

Unlike conventional tests, candidates taking adaptive tests do not all take the same items. Instead, a computer selects items from a large bank of items for which properties (difficulty levels, discrimination power, etc.) were previously established. Items are chosen so as to provide the most information about each individual candidate's ability, and, provided that the responses to the items follow a specified mathematical model (such as the two-parameter logistic model), it is possible to compare candidates' abilities even though they may have been given completely different sets of items. Programs to develop and administer such tests have been available for a decade, and it is not obvious why the Selby-MillSmith tests do not use them. These tests are much less sophisticated. Examinees' performance on the first 10 items in each subtest seems to determine whether candidates are subsequently presented with a block of items of low, moderate, or high difficulty. It is clearly vital to ensure that people whose true ability is directly on the borderline between two of these levels (and for whom the decision as to which block is selected is essentially arbitrary) would obtain precisely the same score whichever block they were administered. The manual does not show this. Nor does it go into detail how, precisely, the scores of the blocks have been "equated"—that is, how it is known which score on the "medium difficulty" block corresponds to which score on the "easy" block, and how much measurement error is associated with this equating. Finally, it is not obvious how the trade-off between time and performance operates.

With the exception of the verbal scale, these tests would probably be quite acceptable paper-and-pencil measures of ability if they were properly normed and validated. However, the problems with the tests' ergonomics, adaptive procedures, norms, and validation make them difficult to recommend in their present form.

REVIEWER'S REFERENCE

Carroll, J. B. (1993) *Human cognitive abilities: A survey of factor-analytic studies.* Cambridge, England: Cambridge University Press.

Review of the Selby MillSmith Adaptive Ability Tests by GLEN FOX, Chartered Occupational Psychologist, Occupational Psychology Services Ltd., Sevenoaks, Kent, United Kingdom:

This battery comprises three tests that are similar to many others on the market used in assessing clerical level staff (verbal ability, numeracy, checking tasks). However, two features distinguish the battery from others: It is computer administered, and it is claimed that it can be used for all levels from production operatives up to senior management. This is just one of a number of claims for which evidence is either weak or absent.

The tests are likely to have some face validity, with candidates below junior management level in an organization, as assessing what many would see as basic skills. However, one would be likely to encounter some resistance from those in the upper levels of an organization if they were presented with the tests in any selection or development context.

One might reasonably argue that computerized administration of the tests is more relevant in today's IT-rich (Information Technology) work en-vironment; however, performance on at least two of the three administrative tests would appear to be affected by familiarity with a keyboard and, in one of the tests, typing speed. The MS-DOS format is also becoming less appropriate as Windows-based packages become more prevalent.

These are minor points, as it is the accompanying manual and user guide that provides the real bases for concern. The present manual was last revised in March 1990, and although the publishers say that they will produce a new revision in the near future, it is surprising that it has taken this long. The more detail-conscious test user might be irritated by a crop of spelling errors, missing words, and basic errors of punctuation, but that irritation could be excused if the manual provided substantial evidence that would justify use of the tests.

As it is, the manual makes a number of claims for which no real evidence can be found. The introduction outlines the key benefits of the tests, the most convincing of which relate to the consistency and ease of administration due to the computer format. One of the more far-reaching claims is that the tests were developed specifically for use in the U.K. and Europe, followed immediately by the statement that the tests were developed wholly in the U.K. (no other mention of Europe is made in the manual).

The second section describes the test modules, and states that they were designed for all types of company personnel, from operatives to management. Test users may find such breadth to be confusing, especially as no other guidance as to the intended use of the tests (e.g., selection or development) is provided. Again, a number of unsubstantiated claims are made such as "high scores on this test [the language test] would be essential for positions which require sophisticated communication skills" (p. 4).

The adaptive nature of the tests means that each test consists of three blocks of items that can be drawn from different ability levels; if candidates are performing better than average on one of the blocks, they will move on to the next block at a higher level of difficulty, so removing the need for redundant items. The "Holy Grail" of adaptive testing is to evaluate and adapt difficulty following each item, but in practice this has proved difficult, and so these tests make calculations after every 2–3 items. This approach is more realistic, although the score distributions for the development samples indicated that too few people got to the upper levels to give reliable assessment at that end of the ability spectrum.

The manual deals with test administration in a fairly standard and reasonably competent manner, although it does not include details of the one (and only one) section in the Administrative test in which lowercase letter responses are not accepted. No guidance is given to the candidate in this respect, and this can have a substantial effect in a test in which difficulty levels are determined in part by speed of response.

Helpful guidance is provided on answering candidates' questions, and is most useful on the more practical matters; however, the administrator is invited to make the same unsubstantiated claims about the tests' development, validity, and fairness on more technical issues.

The norms provided in the manual fall into two levels: operative and graduate. The operative norm samples range (for the different subtests) from 139 to 256; however, no details are given on the sample beyond the fact that they were all drawn from one U.K.-based company. The graduate sample size is 445, and is drawn from a number of U.K. universities.

No breakdown is provided on the basis of gender, ethnic background, age, or any other demographic information, and one of the most serious concerns about the manual is that no information at all is given on the fairness (or otherwise) of the tests, either in terms of group differences in performance, validity, or even the composition of the development populations.

Reliability information presented in the manual is inadequate for the purposes of evaluating the tests' true worth. Test-retest figures have been calculated on samples of 5 and 16, and although the manual acknowledges that these are preliminary, the user might reasonably ask why such figures were published at all.

Other internal consistency figures are provided based on some samples that are as high as 235, but in which 55% of the samples are lower than 40 (to quote, "results below a sample size of 10 must be considered to be unreliable" [p. 27]). The manual uses the measuremeter statistic, which would be unfamiliar to most test users, and as no indication is given of an "acceptable" measuremeter, there is a lot of information (much of it estimated) that will be virtually meaningless to most users.

Regarding validity, the manual details three studies. The first correlates test scores with performance on other similar tests produced by Saville & Holdsworth Ltd. (SHL). All results are based on inadequate sample sizes ranging between 17 and 21. One must, however, applaud the honesty in reporting that the Language and Administrative tests both correlate higher with the SHL Numerical Computation test than with their respective SHL verbal and checking counterparts.

The other studies "validate" test performance against previous educational attainment at 16 and 18 years of age, using a sample (unspecified in number or composition) of second and third year university students. How this relates to the population of operatives for whom the tests are claimed to be appropriate is unclear.

Indeed, the data provided give little justification to the claims made in the manual or, more worrisome, in the narrative reports intended for the candidate, which state that the modules are highly predictive of work performance. The narrative reports also appear to cross into the field of occupational personality (e.g., "it is likely that you will be attracted to work which involves a broader brush approach to topics").

In summary, it would be difficult to recommend use of the tests based on the available information, and it would be even more difficult to establish the context in which the tests might be used, until adequate reliability, validity, and equal opportunities analyses are presented. As is often the case, it is not possible to say that the tests themselves are ineffective, but there is simply not enough useful evidence to justify selecting them ahead of other instruments.

[280]
Self-Description Questionnaire—I, II, III.

Purpose: To measure aspects of self-concept.
Population: Ages 5–12, 13–17, 16–Adult.
Publication Dates: 1987–1992.
Acronym: SDQ.
Administration: Group.
Price Data, 1992: $110 per complete kit including SDQ—I manual ('92, 171 pages), SDQ—II manual ('92, 118 pages), and SDQ—III manual ('89, 114 pages), master copy of each instrument, master copy of each scoring profile, and scoring program; $85 per materials for two instruments; $50 per materials for one instrument.
Comments: Self-report measures.
Author: Herbert W. Marsh.
Publisher: SDQ Instruments, Publication Unit [Australia].
a) SELF-DESCRIPTION QUESTION-NAIRE—I.
Population: Ages 5–12.
Scores, 11: Academic (Mathematics, Reading, General—School, Total), Non-Academic (Physical Abilities, Physical Appearance, Peer Relations, Parent Relations, Total), Global (General—Self, Total—Self).

Time: (15–20) minutes.

b) SELF-DESCRIPTION QUESTION-NAIRE—II.

Population: Ages 13–17.

Scores, 12: Academic (Mathematics, Verbal, General—School), Non-Academic (Physical Abilities, Physical Appearance, Same Sex Peer Relations, Opposite Sex Peer Relations, Parent Relations, Emotional Stability, Honesty/Trustworthiness), Global (General—Self, Total—Self).

Time: (20–25) minutes.

c) SELF-DESCRIPTION QUESTION-NAIRE—III.

Population: Ages 16–Adult.

Scores, 14: Academic (Mathematics, Verbal, Problem-Solving, General—Academic), Non-Academic (Physical Abilities, Physical Appearance, Same Sex Peer Relations, Opposite Sex Peer Relations, Parent Relations, Spiritual Values/Religion, Honesty/Trustworthiness, Emotional Stability), Global (General—Self, Total—Self).

Time: (20–25) minutes.

TEST REFERENCES

1. Marsh, H. W. (1989). Age and sex effects in multiple dimensions of self-concept: Preadolescence to early adulthood. *Journal of Educational Psychology, 81,* 417–430.

2. Marsh, H. W., & Gouvernet, P. J. (1989). Multidimensional self-concepts and perceptions of control: Construct validation of responses by children. *Journal of Educational Psychology, 81,* 57–69.

3. Schneider, B. H., Clegg, M. R., Byrne, B. M., Ledingham, J. E., & Crombie, G. (1989). Social relations of gifted children as a function of age and school program. *Journal of Educational Psychology, 81,* 48–56.

4. Marsh, H. W. (1990). Confirmatory factor analysis of multitrait-multidimensional data: The construct validation of multidimensional self-concept responses. *Journal of Personality, 58,* 661–692.

5. Marsh, H. W. (1990). The structure of academic self-concept: The Marsh/Shavelson model. *Journal of Educational Psychology, 82,* 623–636.

6. Marsh, H. W., & Holmes, I. W. M. (1990). Multidimensional self-concepts: Construct validation of responses by children. *American Educational Research Journal, 27,* 89–117.

7. Byrne, B. M. (1991). The Maslach Burnout Inventory: Validating factorial structure and invariance across intermediate, secondary, and university educators. *Multivariate Behavioral Research, 26,* 583–605.

8. Lau, S., & Leung, K. (1992). Relations with parents and school and Chinese adolescents' self-concept, delinquency, and academic performance. *British Journal of Educational Psychology, 62,* 193–202.

9. Obiakor, F. E. (1992). Self-concept of African-American students: An operational model for special education. *Exceptional Children, 59,* 160–167.

10. Charlton, T., Mitchell, E., & Elcock, J. (1993). Inferred and expressed self-concepts of undergraduates: Comparison of self-other ratings on a multidimensional measure of self-image. *Psychological Reports, 73,* 471–475.

11. Coleman, J. M., & Minnett, A. M. (1993). Learning disabilities and social competence: A social ecological perspective. *Exceptional Children, 59,* 234–246.

12. Hatzichristou, C. (1993). Children's adjustment after parental separation: Teacher, peer and self-report in a Greek sample: A research note. *Journal of Child Psychology and Psychiatry and Allied Disciplines, 34,* 1469–1478.

13. Hymel, S., Bowker, A., & Woody, E. (1993). Aggressive versus withdrawn unpopular children: Variations in peer and self-perceptions in multiple domains. *Child Development, 64,* 879–896.

14. Marsh, H. W. (1993). The multidimensional structure of academic self-concept: Invariance over gender and age. *American Educational Research Journal, 30,* 841–860.

15. Marsh, H. W., & Byrne, B. M. (1993). Confirmation factor analysis of multitrait-multimethod self-concept data: Between-group and within-group invariance constraints. *Multivariate Behavioral Research, 28,* 313–349.

16. Strein, W. (1993). Advances in research on academic self-concept: Implications for school psychology. *School Psychology Review, 22,* 273–284.

17. Tashakkori, A. (1993). Gender, ethnicity, and the structure of self-esteem: An attitude theory approach. *The Journal of Social Psychology, 133,* 479–488.

18. Tashakkori, A., & Kennedy, E. (1993). Measurement of self-perception in multi-racial context: Psychometric properties of a modified Self Description Questionnaire. *British Journal of Educational Psychology, 63,* 337–348.

19. Thompson, T. (1993). Characteristics of self-worth protection in achievement behaviour. *British Journal of Educational Psychology, 63,* 469–488.

20. Bracken, B. A., & Mills, B. C. (1994). School counselors' assessment of self-concept: A comprehensive review of 10 instruments. *The School Counselor, 42,* 14–31.

21. Crain, R. M., & Bracken, B. A. (1994). Age, race, and gender differences in child and adolescent self-concept: Evidence from a behavioral-acquisition, context-dependent model. *School Psychology Review, 23,* 496–511.

22. Dew, T., & Huebner, E. S. (1994). Adolescents' perceived quality of life: An exploratory investigation. *Journal of School Psychology, 32,* 185-199.

23. Huebner, E. S. (1994). Preliminary development and validation of a multidimensional life satisfaction scale for children. *Psychological Assessment, 6,* 149-158.

24. Klingenspor, B. (1994). Gender identity and bulimic eating behavior. *Sex Roles 31,* 407-431.

25. Meltzer, L., & Reid, D. K. (1994). New directions in the assessment of students with special needs: The shift toward a constructivist perspective. *The Journal of Special Education, 28,* 338–355.

26. Montgomery, M. S. (1994). Self-concept and children with learning disabilities: Observer-child concordance across six context-dependent domains. *Journal of Learning Disabilities, 27,* 254–262.

27. Skaalvik, E. M. (1994). Attribution of perceived achievement in school in general and in maths and verbal areas: Relations with academic self-concept and self-esteem. *British Journal of Educational Psychology, 64,* 133–143.

28. Skaalvik, E. M., & Rankin, R. J. (1994). Gender differences in mathematics and verbal achievement, self-perception and motivation. *British Journal of Educational Psychology, 64,* 419–428.

29. Vispoel, W. P., Rocklin, T. R., & Wang, T. (1994). Individual differences and test administration procedures: A comparison of fixed-item, computerized-adaptive, and self-adapted testing. *Applied Measurement in Education, 7,* 53-79.

30. Watkins, D., & Mpofu, E. (1994). Some Zimbabwean evidence of the internal structure of the Self Description Questionnaire-I. *Educational and Psychological Measurement, 54,* 967-972.

31. Bell, S. M., & McCallum, R. S. (1995). Development of a scale reasoning student attributions and its relationship to self-concept and social functioning. *School Psychology Review, 24,* 271–286.

32. Chapman, J. W., & Tunmer, W. E. (1995). Development of young children's reading self-concepts: An examination of emerging subcomponents and their relationship with reading achievement. *Journal of Educational Psychology, 87,* 154-167.

33. Flannery, W. P., Reise, S. P., & Widaman, K. F. (1995). An item response theory analysis of the general and academic scales of the Self-Description Questionnaire II. *Journal of Research in Personality, 29,* 168-188.

34. Marsh, H. W., Chessor, D., Craven, R., & Roche, L. (1995). The effects of gifted and talented programs on academic self-concept: The big fish strikes again. *American Educational Research Journal, 32,* 285–319.

35. Orr, E., & Dinur, B. (1995). Actual and perceived parental social status: Effects on adolescent self-concept. *Adolescence, 30,* 603–616.

36. Skaalvik, E. M., & Rankin, R. J. (1995). A test of the internal/external frame of reference model at different levels of math and verbal self-perception. *American Educational Research Journal, 32,* 161–184.

37. Tam, A. S. F., & Watkins, D. (1995). Towards a hierarchical model of self-concept for Hong Kong Chinese adults with physical disabilities. *International Journal of Psychology, 30,* 1–17.

38. Tay, M. P., Licht, B. G., & Tate, R. L. (1995). The internal/external frame of reference in adolescents' math and verbal self-concepts: A generalization study. *Contemporary Educational Psychology, 20,* 392–402.

39. Thompson, T., Davidson, J. A., & Barber, J. G. (1995). Self-worth protection in achievement motivation: Performance effects and attributional behavior. *Journal of Educational Psychology, 87,* 598–610.

40. Vispoel, W. P. (1995). Self-concept in artistic domains: An extension of the Shavelson, Hubner, and Stanton (1976) model. *Journal of Educational Psychology, 87,* 134-153.

41. Byrne, B. M., & Gavin, D. A. W. (1996). The Shavelson model revisited: Testing for the structure of academic self-concept across pre-, early, and late adolescents. *Journal of Educational Psychology, 88,* 215–228.

42. Byrne, B. M., & Shavelson, R. J. (1996). On the structure of social self-concept for pre-, early, and late adolescents: A test of the Shavelson, Hubner, and Stanton (1976) model. *Journal of Personality and Social Psychology, 70,* 599–613.

Review of the Self-Description Questionnaire—I, II, III by JEFFREY A. ATLAS, Deputy Chief Psychologist and Associate Clinical Professor, Bronx Children's Psychiatric Center, Albert Einstein College of Medicine, Bronx, NY:

Measurement of the "self," in contrast to other mental measurements, brings forth some unique onto-logical, epistemological, and theoretical difficulties. Specifically these concern the ontological definition of "self," the epistemological dilemma of a self-as-agent measuring itself through self-report, and the theoretical question of relating subjectively-derived data to more consensually-derived assessment of the self by others.

The Self-Description Questionnaire (SDQ) offers itself as a measure of children's self-concept, but in the manual it is stated that it assesses "self-perceptions," a more accurate descriptor inasmuch as the SDQ is mainly aimed at measuring students' perceptions of their academic capabilities. Researchers and practitioners in child psychology who are interested in the relationship of *experience of a self* to such phenomena as the childhood psychoses (Atlas, 1985) would do well to look elsewhere for measurement devices. The present instrument presumes the ontological integrity of a self (sometimes known as a noumenal, inner, or true self, or ego) and is aimed at demonstrating its phenomenal structure in multidimensional aspects of academic, nonacademic, and general self scales. The model is analogous to efforts at portraying intelligence as a multifactorial structure in which numerous abilities, moderately correlated, contribute to an overall *g* (general) factor. A basic problem in the SDQ model is that the test constructor's multidimensional factors correlate weakly with one another and poorly with the general self-concept. In fact, the measure's general self-concept scale draws heavily from the much-used Rosenberg Self-Esteem Scale, and practitioners less interested in *academic* self-concept per se might turn to the Rosenberg Scale (Rosenberg, 1965) with greater focus and less expense. Practitioners interested in academic self-concept will need to consider the degree to which the SDQ can marshal such knowledge in a valid way.

Marsh and colleagues present much research evidence in the manual pointing to discrepancies between others' (such as teachers), appraisals of students' academic self-concepts and students' "internal" assessments. In fact, the content of many scale items varies internal and external frames of reference ("I enjoy studying for mathematics"; "I do badly in tests of mathematics"). Construct validity is linked to research results showing disjunctures between internal and external assessments (e.g., teachers attributing a high mathematics self-concept to academically capable girls, whereas their mathematical self-concept turns out low), which for other tests would point to problems in convergent validity. The SDQ authors construe this positively, however, connecting results of this internal-external (I/E) model with the author's "intuition" that children experience this lowered self-perception, the author hinting that it may be due to sociological factors, differentially reinforcing mathematics achievement for boys over girls, for instance, at certain ages. If this is accurate it would suggest political and pedagogical interventions to help students improve their self-perceptions and, presumably, better actualize their potentialities.

Absent other more compelling sources of convergent validity, however, one cannot confidently say that the findings reflect true phenomena versus problems in the instrumentation of the SDQ (nonlinearity within scales and different distributions of scores across scales).

The theoretical questions of the relations between perceptions of the self by the self versus by others, and between different academic self-perceptions, and finally their nesting or inherence in a more general self-concept, remain nebulous inasmuch as measures of the separate self-perception components may be artifacts of the design of the scale. The most compelling evidence emerging from the three rather long and detailed (and, in the case of the SDQ-III, "draft," typographical-error filled) manuals is that children's academic self-concepts, and possibly achievement, may be inversely related to the academic level of the surrounding environment. ("Big fish may do better in smaller ponds.") Although this is a result worth pondering in educational planning, it is a large-scale result derived from a high number of students, with questionable implications for assessment of an individual student's self-concept.

In summary, the SDQ offers a reasonable definition of academic self-concept or self-perception. It appears less successful in demonstrating the veridicality of components of the self-concept and thus the relation of these to assessment of academic self-concept by others. It offers some intriguing predictions and findings concerning particular populations (girls versus boys, students in high versus low achievement settings). The SDQ is indeed packaged like a set of ongoing research findings (users are urged to contribute to the database). Researchers and policy makers may find this instrument useful in educational planning, but practitioners in guidance who want to rely on a database with already validated norms might do well to rely on one or more focused and established instruments.

REVIEWER'S REFERENCES

Rosenberg, M. (1965). *Society and the adolescent self-image.* Princeton, NJ: Princeton University Press.

Atlas, J. A. (1985). Self-other differentiation and symbolization in the psychoses. *New Ideas in Psychology, 3,* 177–182.

Review of the Self-Description Questionnaire—I, II, III by ROBERT K. GABLE, Professor of Educational Psychology, and Associate Director, Bureau of Educational Research and Service, University of Connecticut, Storrs, CT:

The three levels of the SDQ (I, II, and III) provide self-report of self-concept for preadolescents (ages 5–12), adolescents (ages 13–17), and late adolescents/young adults (ages 16–adult). Important specific Academic (e.g., Mathematics) and Non-Academic (e.g., Peer Relations), as well as Global (e.g., Total-Self) aspects of self-concept are assessed. All three levels employ Likert response formats. The 76-item SDQ-I uses a 5-point (i.e., *False, Mostly False, Sometimes False/Sometimes True, Mostly True, True*) response format, whereas the 102-item SDQ-II attempts to distinguish more around the "neutral point" by employing a 6-point scale with the third and fourth steps labeled "*More False than True*" and "*More True than False.*" Finally, the SDQ-III has two sections; Section 1 contains 136 statements responded to on a 8-point scale (i.e., *Definitely False, False, Mostly False, More False Than True, More True Than False, Mostly True, True,* and *Definitely True*). The use of finer gradations and distinctions in the response format is very appropriate for the increasing age levels. The second section of the SDQ-III contains 12 statements (e.g., I am good at sports and physical activities) responded to for accuracy and importance using 9-point Likert scales ranging from "*very inaccurate*" to "*very accurate*" and "*very unimportant*" to "*very important.*"

ADMINISTRATION. The author suggests reasonable administration times around 15–25 minutes per form. Detailed and efficient administration procedures are described in the three manuals.

VALIDITY. The content validity of the SDQ is highly supported through its foundation in the Shavelson, Hubner, and Stanton (1976) multifaceted, hierarchical model of self-concept. In addition to the comprehensive, theoretical, and empirical work available from Shavelson, the SDQ series author provides users with a separate package of abstracts of approximately 80 published articles dating from the early 1980s. With few exceptions, the SDQ author was the senior author and has contributed extensively to a clearly articulated theoretical understanding of the facets of self-concept.

Construct validity empirical evidence receives special attention in the form of several exploratory and confirmatory factor analyses designed to examine the structure of self-concept and provide a strong empirical foundation for the measures. Additional construct validity evidence is presented through theoretically sound relationships with such variables as academic achievement (including gender differences in self-concept/achievement relationships), self-efficacy for academic success/failure, age, gender, reading ability, study skills, test anxiety, study processes, and masculinity/femininity. In addition, research describing the use of the SDQ measures to assess self-concept enhancement interventions are presented.

Most of the empirical validity evidence for the SDQ measures was driven by confirmatory factor analyses and simple correlational indices. This reviewer would be pleased to see a parallel line of empirical research based on latent trait item-response theory models such as the Rasch model. Additional item and person model fit statistics would contribute much to understanding how the statements and respondents fit the proposed statistical models. Such research would also be of value to examine empirically the accuracy of the multi-steps employed in the various response format options used in the three SDQ forms.

The author acknowledges the potential problems with the use of both positive and negative item statements. Several studies by the author and colleagues examine the problem of the cognitive demands of negative items for especially young children; the existence of factors created by negatively stated items in self-concept research is also acknowledged. It is surprising, though, that the author has employed both positive and negative statements in all three SDQ forms. Perhaps this was an early decision that could not be easily reversed. This area is another topic for which item-response theory techniques would be of value for providing additional empirical evidence regarding how the negative statements function in defining the targeted constructs. Although the author's theoretically based construct validity work is comprehensive, impressive, and supportive, there remains a window of empirical opportunity using item-response research for continual understanding and refinement of the SDQ item functioning and score meaning.

RELIABILITY. Comprehensive item analysis data (e.g., means, standard deviations, item-intercorrelations) are presented along with supportive alpha internal consistency reliability estimates and standard errors of measurement for each of the SDQ measures. Most of the alpha reliability estimates for the scales are in the .80s and .90s, with a minor exception found for the SDQ-III Honesty/Trustworthiness scale (.76). These high levels of reliability lend support to the adequacy of item sampling within each scale and explain the low standard error of measurement indices. Stability estimates in some cases over four time periods (see SDQ-III, p. 70) are impressive with many in the .70s and .80s for the SDQ-II and III measures; estimates for the younger SDQ-I samples are lower, but still respectable with a mean of .61 reflecting the systematic change in self-concept over the 6-month period. Overall, the internal consistency and stability estimates presented for the three different age levels for self-concept assessment are commendable and suggest accurate data will result.

SCORING AND SCORE INTERPRETATION. Scoring of the SDQ forms is accomplished using a Scoring and Profile Booklet and an optional scoring program for the mainframe version of SPSS. The booklet and manual describe an easy process to obtain raw scores and standard scale (T) scores for the separate scales and total scores. The manuals contain sections describing score interpretation in the context of the theory underlying the measures.

Normative data from Australian samples are presented in the form of percentiles and T scores for the SDQ-I. Data for a total of 3,562 students are presented for all scales except the recently added General-Self scale. For the SDQ-II version, norms for 2,658 males and 2,836 females are available. The norm sample for the SDQ-III consists of 2,436 sets of responses by Australians between the ages of 13 and 48 (mean = 20.9). For this group 1,093 different respondents were assessed as many as four times over a 22-month period. Given the large age range and differing number of observations per respondent, these norms should be used with caution.

SUMMARY. The series of SDQ measures of self-concept are clearly models for instrument development in the affective domain. The constructs assessed are thoroughly grounded in a theoretical model; the methodologies employed in the development, statistical analyses, reporting, and manuals are outstanding. Although more attention could have been given to the use of item-response theory techniques during instrument development and revision, this lack does not deter from the overall high quality of these measures.

REVIEWER'S REFERENCE

Shavelson, R. J., Hubner, J. J., & Stanton, G. C. (1976). Self-concept: Validation of construct interpretations. *Review of Educational Research, 46*, 407–441.

Review of the Self-Description Questionnaire—I, II, III by STEVEN ISONIO, Research/Assessment Advisor and Psychology Instructor, Golden West College, Huntington Beach, CA:

The Self-Description Questionnaire—I, II, III are three measures for the assessment of self-concept from mid-childhood through early adult populations. The measures were developed in response to a perceived lack of strong, comprehensive measures of the construct. This perception was largely correct, with the possible exception of the availability of the Coopersmith Self-Esteem Inventory (T4:647) and the Sears Self-Concept Inventory (available from ERIC/ETS Test Collection). The Self-Description

Questionnaire (SDQ) is based on the Shavelson (Shavelson, Hubner, & Stanton, 1976) model of self-concept, which emphasizes a multifaceted, hierarchical view of self-concept. Internal consistency measures for scale scores are adequate, and correlations between scale scores are low, indicating that they are distinct, yet related components. Factor analyses lend further support to the underlying Shavelson theoretical model. In short, the theoretical foundation is very sound, and the measures are based on rigorous empirical procedures. The SDQ is a part of a thorough program of research into the nature of self-concept, which is well documented by numerous publications.

Each test has its own manual, and each manual is somewhat imposing. The SDQ-I manual, as an example, consists of 171 single-spaced, number-packed pages with more than 160 references to other technical publications. Although all users have an obligation to be informed about the underlying theoretical and empirical foundation of the tests, nontechnically oriented users are likely to be overwhelmed with details of the many rather complicated analyses described in the manual. This information, most of which has been published elsewhere, might best be placed in a separate "technical manual," with the more practical, user-oriented details being placed in a "user manual." Such improvements might be feasible because, according to page 2 of the SDQ-III, the manual is an "*interim* [italics added] test manual and a research monograph."

A more serious concern relates to cross-cultural validity. Norms for the three tests are from large Australian samples. Although evidence is presented to show factorial invariance across age and sex samples within the Australian samples, questions about the effects of culture and nationality remain unanswered. Chapter 12 in the SDQ-I manual, entitled "Cross-National Comparisons," describes investigations in England that indicated general appropriateness of the tests for those English samples. The authors note several limitations to this effort, however, including the probable lack of representativeness on these samples, the many cultural similarities between Australia and England thereby not really testing the generality issue, and that similar factor structures and group average scores between the samples might have resulted from self-concept processes. In short, the important issue of cross-cultural validity has been largely unaddressed. As the authors rightfully conclude, "further research is needed to determine if these results generalize to other English-speaking Western countries and to other countries where language and cultural differences are more substantial" (SDQ-I manual, p. 128). This is indeed a serious shortcoming for potential users of the SDQ.

The SDQ-I is directed at children in grades 4 through 6. It includes components assessing four non-academic and three academic factors, in addition to a general factor. Additionally, "control scores" (for response validity checks) are available. The process for calculating scores is not difficult, but could become cumbersome, particularly if many tests are to be scored. The authors present evidence suggesting that the underlying factor structure is invariant across age and sex groups. The measure is oriented to address context-balancing internal and external frames of reference ("big fish little pond effect") for one's self-concept. The SDQ-II was designed for persons in grades 7 through 10. It includes the same scales as the SDQ-I, plus a "peer scale" and an Emotional Stability/Honesty-Trustworthiness scale. The SDQ-III is designed for adults (the manual indicates ages 16–25; many issues relevant to self-concept of older persons are not addressed by the SDQ-III). As with the SDQ-I and SDQ-II, hand scoring of the SDQ-III is the only true option. Again, this process can be quite cumbersome. On page 8 of the SDQ-III manual, a promising statement is made: Responses to the SDQ-III can either be hand scored or computer scored. The promise is short-lived, however. On page 9 of the same manual, we learn that although a detailed program has been developed, it "is not yet available." A diskette labeled "SDQ Scoring Program" was included with the review materials. It contains SPSS-X program files for reading existing ASCII datasets and computing scale scores and other analyses. However, it alone is likely to be of little value to users who would benefit from a scannable answer sheet and customized scoring and reporting software.

To summarize, the SDQ is a theoretically and empirically sound measure of self-concept. Because of an imposing manual and difficult scoring procedures, it is not "user-friendly." Also, more research assessing its cross-national validity is needed.

REVIEWER'S REFERENCES
Shavelson, R. J., Hubner, J. J., & Stanton, G. C. (1976). Self-concept: Validation of construct interpretations. *Review of Educational Research, 46*, 407–441.

[281]
The Self-Directed Search, Form E—1990 Revision.

Purpose: Provides a "complete career assessment for those with limited reading skills."

Population: Adults and older adolescents with lower education levels.
Publication Dates: 1970–1994.
Acronym: SDS-Form E.
Scores, 6: Realistic, Investigative, Artistic, Social, Enterprising, Conventional.
Administration: Group.
Price Data, 1996: $90 per complete kit including professional user's guide ('94, 101 pages), technical manual ('94, 92 pages), user's guide ('90, 7 pages), 25 assessment booklets, 25 Jobs Finders, 25 You and Your Job booklets; $20 per professional user's guide; $20 per technical manual; $49 per 25 sets of assessment booklets and Jobs Finders; $42 per 25 Educational Opportunities Finders; $27 per 25 assessment booklets; $27 per 25 Jobs Finders; $21 per 25 You and Your Job booklets.
Foreign Language Editions: Spanish and Canadian (English) editions available.
Time: (40–60) minutes.
Author: John L. Holland.
Publisher: Psychological Assessment Resources, Inc.
Cross References: See T4:2414 (23 references); for reviews of an earlier edition by M. Harry Daniels and Caroline Manuele-Adkins, see 10:330 (19 references); also for a review of an earlier edition by Robert H. Dolliver, see 9:1098 (12 references); see also T3:2134 (55 references); for a review by John O. Crites and excerpted reviews by Fred Brown, Richard Seligman, Catherine C. Cutts, Robert H. Dolliver, and Robert N. Hansen, see 8:1022 (88 references); see also T2:2211 (1 reference). [Editor's Note: These reviews are based on 1990 materials. The reviewers did not have the 1994 user's guide and technical manual. The revision of this test will be reviewed in an upcoming *MMY*.]

TEST REFERENCES
1. Maddux, C. D., & Cummings, R. E. (1986). Alternate form reliability of the Self-Directed Search—Form E. *Career Development Quarterly, 35*, 136-140.
2. Walsh, W. B., Bingham, R. P., & Sheffey, M. A. (1986). Holland's theory and college educated working Black men and women. *Journal of Vocational Behavior, 29*, 194-200.
3. Abler, R. M., & Sedlacek, W. E. (1987). Computer orientation by Holland type and sex. *Career Development Quarterly, 36*, 163-169.
4. Gault, F. M., & Meyers, H. H. (1987). A comparison of two career planning inventories. *Career Development Quarterly, 36*, 332-336.
5. Johnson, J. A. (1987). Influence of adolescent social crowds on the development of vocational identity. *Journal of Vocational Behavior, 31*, 182-199.
6. Miller, M. J. (1987). Career counseling for high school students, grades 10–12. *Journal of Employment Counseling, 24*, 173–183.
7. Pazy, A., & Zin, R. (1987). A contingency approach to consistency: A challenge to prevalent views. *Journal of Vocational Behavior, 30*, 84-101.
8. Sandler, S. B. (1987). Dislocated workers: A response. *Journal of Employment Counseling, 24*, 146–148.
9. Strahan, R. F. (1987). Measures of consistency for Holland-type codes. *Journal of Vocational Behavior, 31*, 37-44.
10. Vandergoot, D. (1987). Review of placement research literature: Implications for research and practice. *Rehabilitation Counseling Bulletin, 30*, 243–272.
11. Wiggins, J. D. (1987). Effective career exploration programs revisited. *Career Development Quarterly, 35*, 297-303.
12. Greenlee, S. P., Damarin, F. L., & Walsh, W. B. (1988). Congruence and differentiation among Black and White males in two non-college-degreed occupations. *Journal of Vocational Behavior, 32*, 298-306. 13. Miller, M. J., Springer, T. P., & Wells, D. (1988). Which occupational environments do black youths prefer? Extending Holland's typology. *The School Counselor, 36*, 103–106.
14. Jones, L. K., Gorman, S., & Schroeder, C. G. (1989). A comparison between the SDS and the Career Key among career undecided college students. *Career Development Quarterly, 37*, 334-344.
15. Mazen, A. M. (1989). Testing an integration of Vroom's instrumentality theory and Holland's typology on working women. *Journal of Vocational Behavior, 35*, 327-341.

16. Alvi, S. A., Khan, S. B., & Kirkwood, K. J. (1990). A comparison of various indices of differentiation for Holland's model. *Journal of Vocational Behavior, 36,* 147-152.

17. Khan, S. B., & Alvi, S. A. (1990). A study of the validity of Holland's theory in a non-Western culture. *Journal of Vocational Behavior, 36,* 132-146.

18. Matsui, T., & Tsukamoto, S-I. (1990). Relation between career self-efficacy measures based on occupational titles and Holland codes and model environments: A methodological contribution. *Journal of Vocational Behavior, 38,* 78-91.

19. McKee, L. M., & Levinson, E. M. (1990). A review of the computerized version of The Self-Directed Search. *Career Development Quarterly, 38,* 325-333.

20. Meir, E. I., Melamed, S., & Abu-Freha, A. (1990). Vocational, avocational, and skill utilization congruences and their relationship with well-being in two cultures. *Journal of Vocational Behavior, 36,* 153-165.

21. Nordvik, H. (1990). Work activity and career goals in Holland's and Schein's theories of vocational personalities and career anchors. *Journal of Vocational Behavior, 38,* 165-178.

22. Schuttenberg, E. M., O'Dell, F. L., & Kaczala, C. M. (1990). Vocational personality types and sex-role perceptions of teachers, counselors, and educational administrators. *Career Development Quarterly, 39,* 60-71.

23. Khan, S. B., & Alvi, S. A. (1991). The structure of Holland's typology: A study in a nonwestern culture. *Journal of Cross-Cultural Psychology, 22,* 283-292.

24. Gade, E. M., Hurlburt, G., & Fuqua, D. (1992). The use of the Self-Directed Search to identify American Indian high school dropouts. *The School Counselor, 39,* 311–315.

25. Humes, C. W. (1992). Career planning implications for learning disabled high school students using the MBTI and SDS-E. *The School Counselor, 39,* 362–368.

26. Jagger, L., Neukrug, E., & McAuliffe, G. (1992). Congruence between personality traits and chosen occupation as a predictor of job satisfaction for people with disabilities. *Rehabilitation Counselor Bulletin, 36,* 53–60.

27. Leung, S. A., Conoley, C. W., Scheel, M. J., & Sonnenberg, R. T. (1992). An examination of the relation between vocational identity, consistency, and differentiation. *Journal of Vocational Behavior, 40,* 95-107.

28. Meir, E. I., & Navon, M. (1992). A longitudinal examination of congruence hypotheses. *Journal of Vocational Behavior, 41,* 35-47.

29. Miller, M. J., & Knippers, J. A. (1992). Jeopardy: A career information game for school counselors. *Career Development Quarterly, 41,* 55-61.

30. Miller, M. J., Newell, N. P., Springer, T. P., & Wells, D. (1992). Accuracy of the college majors finder for three majors. *Career Development Quarterly, 40,* 334-339.

31. Tracey, T. J., & Rounds, J. (1992). Evaluating the RIASEC circumplex using high-point codes. *Journal of Vocational Behavior, 41,* 295-311.

32. Harrington, T. F., Feller, R., & O'Shea, A. J. (1993). Four methods to determine RIASEC codes for college majors and a comparison of hit rates. *Career Development Quarterly, 41,* 383-392.

33. Jones, L. K. (1993). Two career guidance instruments: Their helpfulness to students and effect on students' career exploration. *The School Counselor, 40,* 191-200.

34. Rounds, J., & Tracey, T. J. (1993). Prediger's dimensional representation of Holland's RIASEC circumplex. *Journal of Applied Psychology, 78,* 875-890.

35. Borget, M. M., & Gilroy, F. D. (1994). Interests and self-efficacy as predictors of mathematics/science-based career choice. *Psychological Reports, 75,* 753-754.

36. Brown, S. D., & Gore, P. A., Jr. (1994). An evaluation of interest congruence indices: Distribution characteristics of and measurement properties. *Journal of Vocational Behavior, 45,* 310-327.

37. Chung, Y. B., & Harman, L. W. (1994). The career interests and aspirations of gay men: How sex-role orientation is related? *Journal of Vocational Behavior, 45,* 223-239.

38. Levinson, E. M., Rafoth, B. A., & Lesnak, L. (1994). A criterion-related validity study of the OASIS-2 Interest Schedule. *Journal of Employment Counseling, 31,* 29-37.

39. Meir, E. I. (1994). Comprehensive interests measurement in counseling for congruence. *Career Development Quarterly, 42,* 314-325.

40. Strack, S. (1994). Relation Millon's basic personality styles and Holland's occupational types. *Journal of Vocational Behavior, 45,* 41-54.

41. Thompson, J. M., Flynn, R. J., & Griffith, S. A. (1994). Congruence and coherence as predictors of congruent employment outcomes. *Career Development Quarterly, 42,* 271-281.

42. Tokar, D. M., & Swanson, J. L. (1994). Evaluation of the correspondence between Holland's vocational personality typology and the five-factor model of personality. *Journal of Vocational Behavior, 46,* 89-108.

43. Eagan, A. E., & Walsh, W. B. (1995). Person-environment congruence and coping strategies. *Career Development Quarterly, 43,* 246-256.

44. Meir, E. I., Melamed, S., & Dinur, C. (1995). The benefits of congruence. *Career Development Quarterly, 43,* 257-266.

45. Tokar, D. M., & Swanson, J. L. (1995). Evaluation of the correspondence between Holland's vocational personality typology and the five-factor model of personality. *Journal of Vocational Behavior, 46,* 89-108.

46. Mahalik, J. R. (1996). Client vocational interests as predictors of client reactions to counselor intentions. *Journal of Counseling and Development, 74,* 416–421.

47. Ohler, D. L., Levinson, E. M., & Barker, W. F. (1996). Career maturity in college students with learning disabilities. *The Career Development Quarterly, 44,* 278–288.

48. Shivy, V. A. Phillips, S. D., & Koehly, L. M. (1996). Knowledge organization as a factor in career intervention outcome: A multidimensional scaling analysis. *Journal of Counseling Psychology, 43,* 178–186.

Review of The Self-Directed Search, Form E— 1990 Revision by JOSEPH C. CIECHALSKI, Associ- ate *Professor of Counselor and Adult Education, East Carolina University, Greenville, NC:*

The 1990 Revision of The Self-Directed Search (SDS) Easy Form (Form E), like the 1985 edition of Form E, was developed as an alternate form of the regular version of the SDS. Form E was specifically designed for adolescents and adults with at least a fourth-grade reading level. It is a self-administered, self-scored, and self-interpreted interest inventory based on Holland's theory of vocational choice. Holland's theory assumes that most persons can be categorized into one of six personality and environmental types: Realistic, Investigative, Artistic, Social, Enterprising, or Conventional.

The 1990 Revision of Form E contains 192 items (11 less than the 1985 edition of Form E). A total of 73 items were replaced in the 1990 edition. Replacement items were selected from a pool of 188 new items generated by three psychologists. The resulting 73 replacement items for the 1990 Revision were selected based on item analyses and on the endorsement of at least 5% of the males and females in the sample. Like the 1985 edition, the 1990 edition of the assessment booklet is divided into six sections. These sections include: Jobs You Have Thought About (up to five jobs can be listed), Activities (liked or disliked), Skills (skills you have/want or do not have/want), Jobs (liked or disliked), and Rating Your Abilities (best to poorest). The final section is a scoring section in which a two-letter summary (rather than a three-letter) code is obtained.

The directions for self-administering Form E have been revised for added ease and better comprehension. For example, in the section on Jobs, brief definitions follow each job listed. Examinees respond to items in the assessment booklet. A separate answer sheet is not required. Therefore, errors in transferring responses to an answer sheet are eliminated.

Scoring the 1990 edition of Form E is easy. Except for the Jobs You Have Thought About section, examinees simply total all their scores and record their top two scores in the spaces provided in the assessment booklet. Although Form E is self-scored, this reviewer suggests that the counselor check the scoring to guarantee accuracy of the results.

Next, examinees refer to the newly revised Jobs Finder to discover jobs that correspond to their two-letter Holland code. This edition of the Jobs Finder lists 797 occupations according to two-letter Holland codes. Each occupation is identified by a single digit number (ED) that indicates the training or schooling needed for the job. For example, the numbers 1 and 2 identify jobs that can be performed by someone who has graduated from grade school, the number 3 identifies jobs in which a high school diploma or some high school is needed, and the number 4 identifies jobs in which high school and possibly some other training is needed. In addition, a nine-digit *Dictionary of Occupation Titles (DOT)* number following each occupation can be used to locate more information about the occupation.

In addition to the Jobs Finder, the author has revised You and Your Job and the Professional User's Guide. The 1990 edition of You and Your Job is divided into six sections: You and Your Job, The Six Types of People (explains the six personality types in easy to understand language), Finding Your Type, Types of Jobs, Finding More About the Job (suggestions for using the Job Finder and *DOT*), and Choosing a Job. Examinees must read You and Your Job in order to understand their results. Again, this reviewer believes that examinees with low reading abilities should be assisted in understanding and using their results by their counselors.

The 1990 edition of the Professional User's Guide is well written and contains information on the reliability and equivalence between the 1985 and 1990 versions of Form E. Using Cronbach's alpha, the internal consistency was essentially unchanged for both versions. All correlations for section scales were above .80 and above .95 for the summary scales. A pairwise correlation of the summary scales was calculated and the results indicated that the correlations were consistent across both versions. In addition, frequency counts of the first letter of Holland's code between both versions were calculated. The frequency of the first letter is unchanged and in 76% of the cases, the two-letter codes were the same. Therefore, the author concluded that the 1990 and 1985 versions were equivalent.

Validity of the 1990 Revision was not addressed specifically in the Professional User's Guide. In earlier editions of the SDS, information about the predictive and concurrent validity was included in the 1985 edition of the Professional Manual. At this time, a 1990 edition of the Professional Manual was not available.

The 1990 Revision of Form E reflects the author's dedication to improving on an already popular and well-established instrument. Items have been replaced along with major revisions of the Professional User's Guide and You and Your Job. A new Jobs Finder was written especially for those individuals seeking jobs requiring a high school education or

less. I hope a new edition of the Professional Manual will be published soon that, like the 1985 edition, will address the validity of the instrument. Although Form E is self-scored, examinees may need assistance from their counselor. Nevertheless, Form E remains an excellent interest instrument.

Review of The Self-Directed Search, Form E— 1990 Revision by ESTHER E. DIAMOND, Educational and Psychological Consultant, Evanston, IL:

The 1990 revision of The Self-Directed Search (SDS), Form E, described as an equivalent form of the 1985 version, is intended for test-takers 16 years of age or older with at least a fourth-grade reading ability.

The development of the 1990 revision and the determination of its equivalence to the 1985 SDS is described in a helpful Professional User's Guide. Like the 1985 revision, the 1990 version is based on Holland's RIASEC typology—the theory that most persons can be categorized as one of six personality types: Realistic, Investigative, Artistic, Social, Enterprising, and Conventional. The six personality types are matched by six types of environments on the premise that people search for environments where there are others like themselves, who share their skills, abilities, and interests. The SDS scales estimate a person's resemblance to each of the six personality types by exploring his or her experiences and preferred activities.

The 1990 version of the SDS differs from the 1985 edition in the following principal ways: All section scales—Likes, Skills, Jobs—have new items; instructions are simpler and more clear; and a new version of the Jobs Finder, which lists 797 (300 more than the earlier version) has been developed. The changes represent Holland's responses to suggestions and surveys of users of the 1985 form who wanted the items to more closely reflect the types of activities and interests of the intended test-takers. They suggested, for example, that the Jobs Finder focus more exclusively on occupations at lower levels of educational preparation.

Replacement items for consideration were generated by three psychologists considered experts in Holland theory. Unanimous agreement of all three was required for adding the items to the item pool; 188 new items were generated. Possible replacement items for each of the six RIASEC scales in the 18 section scales comprising Activities, Skills, and Jobs ranged from 2 to 32. Some involved only minor rewording of existing items. No changes were proposed for the ability ratings in the Self-Estimates section.

To study the equivalency of the 1990 Revision and the 1985 Form E, an experimental Form E booklet was developed and administered to 145 individuals ranging in age from 16 to 65, with an educational level ranging from no high school education to a high school education and some technical training—similar to the target test-taker population. Sixty-five percent of the sample were females. The sample appeared to be similar to the target test-taker population.

For each item identified for possible replacement, a replacement item was selected on the basis of its correlation with the total scale as well as its mean and standard deviation. The item also had to be endorsed by at least 5% of the males and 5% of the females in the sample. Scale replacement items were found for each section; 73 items of the total of 192 were replaced, and the six original self-rating items were retained, adding an item to each summary scale. The competencies section of the test booklet, however, contains two items that appear to be outdated—one involving use of a slide rule and another involving use of a keypunch.

A number of criteria determined the equivalence of the 1985 Form E and its 1990 Revision. Internal consistency reliability coefficients (Cronbach's alpha) were essentially unchanged across the two versions. Means and standard deviations for each of the section and summary scales showed only trivial differences. Particularly important was the requirement that each scale correlate with its adjacent, alternate, and opposite scale, as depicted on the RIASEC hexagon, in a consistent way across the two forms. Still another criterion required consistency in the appearance in the first letter of the Holland code across forms. Frequency of the first letter of the code was virtually unchanged in the 1990 version. Changes in the two-letter codes occurred in approximately 34% of the cases, but in 75.9% the two letters of the code were the same across forms. (It should be noted that two-letter Holland codes are used in the 1990 revision rather than the three-letter codes in use in earlier forms.)

A number of resource materials are designed to help in the interpretation and use of the 1990 Revision of the SDS Form E. You and Your Job introduces the program briefly, explaining the purpose of the SDS, how to find out about jobs, and choosing a job. The 1990 Assessment Booklet asks the test-takers about their likes and dislikes, the skills they have or want to learn, jobs they like or think they might like, and how they rate their competencies from best to least, on a six-letter scale. They also figure out their two-letter summary code, easier to compute than the usual three-letter code. It is suggested that they then look at the Jobs Finder (JF), which now has descriptions of 797 jobs representing a wide variety of industries and occupational groups. The jobs are categorized by Holland and *Dictionary of Occupational Titles (DOT)* codes and all require a high school education or less. Educational levels required are also listed. Additional resource materials, not specifically designed for the 1990 SDS, include The Leisure Activities Finder and the *Dictionary of Holland Occupational Codes*.

Clearly, much work has been done with the 1990 Revision to respond to users' needs, criticisms, and suggestions, and the revision is fully equivalent to the 1985 Form E. Several problems persist, however. Holland still maintains that gender influences career choice and that accurate assessment of all the influences that affect career choice would promote rather than prohibit that choice. In his favor is the inclusion of an item about sewing machines as a Realistic choice in the Skills section of the Assessment Booklet, and the recognition that some individuals may never have been exposed to certain jobs or activities in the Assessment Booklet. At least they have the chance to indicate that they "might like" or "want to learn to" do a given activity or job.

Holland has been criticized for his use of raw scores rather than standard scores to determine total test scores for each personality/occupational type and the summary code in earlier versions of the SDS. The scales used to determine the total test score did not have the same number of items in each of the RIASEC areas contributing to it. In the 1990 version, however, an equal number of items contributes to each scale—32 plus 1 each for the self-rating scales, and an equal number of items for each scale contributes to the summary score.

Still another criticism is directed against the emphasis on self-administration, scoring, and interpretation of the results. However, the various resource materials mention sources of help, including counselors, so that the criticism would appear to be minimized.

In summary, the 1990 Revision of the SDS Form E has overcome many of the earlier Form E problems. Questionable items have been changed, the reading level has been dropped to fourth grade, the questions in the Assessment Booklet are uncomplicated, and the two-letter Holland code simplifies the scoring system. The resource materials should be particularly helpful and appealing to counselors as well as test-takers. Remaining criticisms, accompanied by constructive, feasible suggestions, should elicit a response from Holland for future revisions, as they have in the case of the 1990 Revision.

Self Worth Inventory.

Purpose: "Helps respondents increase their understanding of self-worth and how it is developed."
Population: Adults.
Publication Date: 1990.
Acronym: SWI.
Scores, 8: Self, Family, Peers, Work, Projected Self, Self-Concept, Self-Esteem, Self-Worth.
Administration: Group.
Manual: No manual.
Price Data, 1993: $10 per inventory.
Time: Administration time not reported.
Comments: May be self-administered.
Author: Everett Robinson.
Publisher: Consulting Resource Group International, Inc.

Review of the Self Worth Inventory by JAYNE E. STAKE, Professor of Psychology, University of Missouri, St. Louis, MO:

The purpose of the Self Worth Inventory is to communicate a set of key concepts about self-perceptions and to give test-takers insight into their own self-views. The inventory pamphlet includes 40 questionnaire items and, in addition, information about the implications of self-perceptions for adjustment and healthy functioning. The inventory is designed to be self-administering and may be used in group and individual counseling settings to stimulate discussions about counselees' self-evaluations. The content and reading level of test items is appropriate for late adolescents and adults.

The author rationally derived the test items based on his understanding of self-worth and his experience as a counselor. He makes a distinction between self-concept, which he defines as self-cognitions, and self-esteem, which he defines as affective reactions to the self. Items that refer to thoughts and feelings about the self form separate scales of Self-Concept and Self-Esteem, respectively. The same test items are divided also into five content scales: Self, Family, Peers, Work, and the Projected Self. No assessments of internal consistency, distinctiveness, and stability of the seven scales have been made. In regard to the Self-Esteem and Self-Concept scales, the definitions of the constructs on which the scales are based are not generally accepted by theorists and researchers in the area of self-evaluation. There is no empirical support for the purported cognitive/affective distinction in self-perceptions, and in fact, cognitions and affective reactions

to the self normally coincide. Hence, it is likely that scores on the two scales do not provide meaningfully distinct information. In regard to the five content scales, the wording of items on the first four appears to fit the stated categories; however, items on the Projected-Self scale overlap with the other four scales and do not appear to represent a separate domain of self-evaluation.

The general instructions for the inventory will be understandable to those with a ninth grade reading level or above. However, the wording of some items is likely to cause confusion about what response is expected. First, some items from the Family scale refer to family of origin whereas others refer only to family. On the latter items, test-takers who have a spouse and children may not recognize that they are expected to give their responses in reference to their family of origin and not in reference to their spouse and children. Second, some items have a complex construction that leads to problematic rating situations for some participants. For example, people cannot meaningfully rate themselves on the item, "I think I can be successful if I work harder," if they already see themselves as successful at their current level of performance. Confusion created by the wording of test items likely affects the reliability and validity of test scores.

Instructions for the inventory guide participants to sum their ratings for each scale and to interpret these scores based on arbitrary score range categories that are designated as high, medium, and low. These score ranges give the impression that normative data have been gathered for the scales, but such is not the case. There is no information available on what may, in fact, be a high, medium, or low score for any normative group. Hence, the validity of these score ranges is not known. More generally, there is no empirical support for the construct or predictive validity of the inventory.

In sum, the psychometric properties of the Self-Worth Inventory have not been evaluated. The primary intent of the author was to develop an instrument that would communicate ideas about self-worth to counselees. The inventory may be somewhat useful as a means of initiating discussion in small group and individual counseling settings. However, until more is known about the psychometric properties of this measure, it is not a good choice for use in research or in making decisions about individuals. Instead, if a psychometrically sound measure of overall perceptions of self-worth is needed for research purposes, the Rosenberg Self-Esteem Scale is recommended (Rosenberg, 1989). For assessment of general self-worth in clinical settings, subscales from the California Psychological Inventory (Gough, 1987; T4:361) and the Minnesota Multiphasic Personality Inventory—2 (Hathaway & McKinley, 1989; T4:1645), such as Self-Acceptance and Ego-Strength, would be helpful. If a measure of self-perceptions within a specific content area is needed, one can select among a large variety of available self-concept measures. Each is unique in what information it can provide about the individual's self-perceptions; test selection should be based on the aspect of self-perceptions under consideration.

REVIEWER'S REFERENCES

Gough, H. G. (1987). *Manual for the California Psychological Inventory.* Palo Alto, CA: Consulting Psychologists Press.
Hathaway, S. R., & McKinley, J. C. (1989). Minnesota Multiphasic Personality Inventory—2. University of Minnesota Press.
Rosenberg, M. (1989). *Society and the adolescent self-image.* Middletown, CN: Wesleyan University Press.

Review of the Self Worth Inventory by NORMAN D. SUNDBERG, Professor Emeritus, Department of Psychology, University of Oregon, Eugene, OR:

Robinson's Self Worth Inventory (SWI) is not a test by psychological standards. It appears to be intended as an adjunct for counseling or personal growth. The subtitle implies this orientation: "A learning and communication tool for understanding and developing self worth."

The eight-page booklet is addressed to a reader who is assumed to be evaluating himself or herself. It starts with two pages about the meaning of self-worth in lay terms. One page presents the "inventory" itself, asking for choices on 40 items using 5 degrees of agreement. Examples of the items are "I think I am an interesting person," "My friends would say I am successful," and "I feel proud of who I am." The respondent then scores himself or herself on responses in five categories, each with 8 items: Self, Family, Peers, Work, and Projected Self. (The last refers to how you think others see you.) There are also scores for Self-Concept thoughts and Self-Esteem feelings using 16 items each; these are mostly the same items as those in the five categories. Then a SWI booklet gives an interpretation of each of these features for the reader, and finally there are 10 recommendations about improving one's self-worth, such as "Learn more about who you really are," "Develop your spiritual life," and "Forgive yourself for past mistakes and failures" (pp. 7–8).

There is none of the information one would expect of the usual inventory or a test—no instructor's manual, no norms, no studies of reliability or validity, no concern for test-taking attitudes or faking of the very obvious items, and no item analysis. There is no recognition of possible differences in gender, age, and cultural and ethnic aspects of self-image. There are no references to research on similar concepts such as self-esteem and depression or a factor analysis justification for the five categories of items. The SWI has face validity, but the booklet gives no theoretical justification for the nature of the items or the suggested interpretations. The SWI is more sophisticated, but it is still not far from the take-it-yourself evaluations in the *Reader's Digest* or other magazines. Perhaps the SWI might be read as a bibliotherapy to help people with low self-worth.

So this is not a test or what psychologists usually call an inventory. Probably it should not be included in a mental measurements compendium, except as an example of what is not measurement.

Is it then to be considered something else—a self-help or therapeutic procedure? Clearly there is a place for informal, nonstandardized self-evaluations in such psychological activities. But then the procedure should be evaluated in a different way. Intervention techniques should be subjected to the scrutiny given therapy and counseling procedures: Are they logical and do they conform to a coherent theoretical approach? Are they effective in meeting their goals, using criteria of satisfaction and improvement? Perhaps the Self Worth Inventory is useful, but what is there to prove it?

[283]
The Senior Apperception Technique [1985 Revision].

Purpose: A projective instrument to gather information on forms of depression, loneliness, or rage in the elderly.
Population: Ages 65 and over.
Publication Dates: 1973–1985.
Acronym: S.A.T.
Scores: No scores.
Administration: Individual.
Price Data, 1993: $19.75 per manual ('85, 12 pages) and set of picture cards.
Time: Administration time not reported.
Author: Leopold Bellak.
Publisher: C.P.S., Inc.
Cross References: See T3:2148 (2 references); for a review by K. Warner Schaie, see 8:676 (1 reference).

Review of the Senior Apperception Technique by PAUL A. ARBISI, Assessment Clinic Director, Psychology Service, Minneapolis Veterans Affairs Medical Center, Minneapolis, MN:

Henry Murray (1943) conceived the Thematic Apperception Test (T.A.T.) as a mean of divining the underlying dynamics of personality: the "needs" and "press" of an individual's life. A primary assumption underlying a projective technique such as the T.A.T. is that in the process of creating a story, the client identifies with a particular character depicted in the stimuli and the conflicts, wishes, fear, or desires attributed to the character in the story reflect those of the client (Lindzey, 1952). Within the context of apperception techniques, effort has been made to increase the degree to which the client will identify with the characters by varying the characteristics of the stimuli. The desire to increase the identification with a character in the stories by modifying the appearance of the central character was prompted by Murray himself who suggested administering at least one card of the T.A.T. showing a figure who is approximately the same age and sex as the subject (Murray, 1943). On the other hand, too great an identification with a central character may not be altogether desirable because unacceptable or unpleasant desires are projected with less anxiety if the central character is different from the subject and perhaps a more suitable source of these censurable desires or needs (Piotrowski, 1950). For better or worse, the Senior Apperception Technique (S.A.T.) is one such extension of the T.A.T. and joins the Gerontological Apperception Test (G.A.T.) and the Projective Assessment of Aging Method (P.A.A.M.) in attempting to plumb the depths of the aged-psyche by depicting the central characters as elderly and, thus, the older adult can identify with them more easily.

STIMULUS. Impressive attempts have been made to extend the T.A.T. by varying the stimuli in order to increase the projective identification of the central character (for review see Murstein, 1965). Examples include the Thompson (1949) alteration where the figures in the T.A.T. cards are depicted as African Americans to be used with African American clients, the depiction of characters as either blue collar or white collar workers to better pull for vocationally determined identifications, and finally, in the ultimate attempt to maximize identification, actual photographs of client's heads have been superimposed onto the T.A.T. cards (Murstein, 1965). The S.A.T. contains 16 cards depicting elderly individuals that "pull" for themes that are relevant to the geriatric client, based on the authors' clinical experience or their reading of the gerontological literature. The themes vary from commonly identified issues relating to somatic concerns, institutionalization, and loss of loved ones to the less frequently addressed themes of sexual feeling of the elderly toward younger

individuals. The stimuli were ostensibly designed to reflect the thoughts and feelings of the elderly yet there is only minimal information in the manual regarding how these themes were chosen or how often the cards "pull" for a stated theme. By the same token, a determined effort was made to broaden the thematic content by occasionally depicting happy or pleasant scenes rather than dour or obviously unpleasant situations. In terms of other alterations to the stimuli, the cards were designed in a larger format than the T.A.T. in hopes of compensating for the failing eyesight and presbyopia found in the elderly. The authors contend that the figures are ambiguous for sex. This assertion is not at all apparent on examination of the stimuli and one wonders why it is necessary to state something that has unclear relevance and is so evidently incorrect. Perhaps the authors wish to tap the sexual bimodality of late life. If so, it would be useful to state this goal explicitly. On the whole, the stimuli are cartoonishly rendered line drawings of situations that pull for a wide range of themes. Unlike the T.A.T., there is little ambiguity or evocative richness in the depiction of situations likely to elicit themes related to aging.

TEST OR TECHNIQUE? The authors insist that the S.A.T. is not a test, but a "technique that lends itself to many different uses" (p. 345, Bellak, 1986). Moreover, according to the authors, the S.A.T. constitutes a variation of the interview question, what ails you? This sense of semantic ambiguity may save paper by eliminating the normative tables and demographic charts that ordinarily appear in test manuals, but in this case definitional ambiguity is the first step on the road to perdition and has implications for the training and credentials of those deemed qualified to use the instrument. With regard to user qualifications, it is assumed that the prior training of the user will limit the conclusions or inferences drawn from the "technique." This thinking appears to be based upon the assumption that blind squirrels never find any acorns. This premise, of course, is absurd. Thus, the authors would have us affirm the following logical construction: If the user happens to be someone who has absolutely no training in psychometric methods or unconscious processes, then the user will only be able to facilitate the communication process and make no further inferences regarding more salient themes or underlying dynamics. It follows, alternatively, that if the user is a trained psychologist or psychiatrist familiar with projective techniques and the unconscious, then the user will be able to make meaningful inferences regarding the dynamic processes of the elderly. The manual is no more specific regarding the qualifications of users and relies upon the user to limit appropriately their inference based on the users' discretion. Apparently, a reliance upon the honor system is sufficient for the authors and publishers, but the American Psychological Association embodied in *The Standards for Educational and Psychological Testing* (AERA, APA, & NCME, 1985) finds this approach to the issue to be substandard.

Perhaps, as a means of bolstering the proposition that blind squirrels never find nuts, the manual contains few guidelines and limited suggestions regarding the interpretation of each card and no hard data to support the inferences drawn from each card or the technique *in toto*. There is nothing even approximating normative data or an adequate description of the 100 elderly subjects used to develop the "technique." As suggested by the manual author, a perusal of the acknowledgments was the only way to determine the source of these subjects. By a simple count of the acknowledged individuals and their institutional association, it appears a significant number of subjects were residents of nursing homes in New York. The homogeneous nature of the sample has implications for the generalizability of the "technique." For example, a 75-year-old resident of a nursing home who, by definition, requires significant care and attention may respond quite differently than a 75-year-old who is living independently and actively consulting to a Fortune 500 company. To be fair, the manual makes no claims for statistically sophisticated validity and reliability. The data that are presented in support of the reliability and validity of the S.A.T. consist of two pilot studies cited in the manual with two further studies cited in *The T.A.T., C.A.T., and S.A.T. in Clinical Use, Fourth Edition* (Bellak, 1986). These meager studies do little to aid in establishing the validity of the "technique" and provide nothing more than intriguing possibilities for interpretation. The empirically minded clinician is troubled by the glaring lack of data supporting the use of the S.A.T. in elderly populations.

SUGGESTIONS. (a) More explicit criteria for test users should be codified in the manual. It is alarming to imagine a group of untrained individuals administering and interpreting the T.A.T. Why should it be less alarming to imagine the same scenario with the S.A.T.? (b) Despite the authors' insistence that the S.A.T. is not a test, but a "technique," more attention needs to be paid to issues of reliability and validity. W. Grant Dahlstrom (1995),

on being awarded the Bruno Klopfer Distinguished Award by the Society for Personality Assessment, described his experience in the summer of 1947 upon attending a 2-week institute offered by Bruno Klopfer on the Rorschach "technique." Dahlstrom came away with the distinct impression that Klopfer had developed an internal interpretive process whereby Rorschach-related "signs" were tabulated until a certain threshold was achieved. At that point Klopfer would assign the individual to a particular category and provide an interpretation based on the rich correlate-base of that type. In essence, an empirically driven interpretive process was applied to a projective technique that allowed for full and reasonably accurate inferences. This covert process was made overt through John Exner's system and his empirically driven interpretive strategy for the Rorschach (Exner, 1993). A bit of this type of thinking would go a long way toward improving the S.A.T. Even the most rudimentary normative data would be helpful. Would, for example, the young-old respond differently than the old-old to Card 13? More fundamentally, does the S.A.T. present an improvement over the T.A.T. for elderly populations? These questions should be addressed before this technique can be recommended, until then, *caveat emptor.*

SUMMARY. The S.A.T. is one of many variants of the T.A.T. designed to improve the projective "yield" by using stimuli that depict the characters as physically similar to the elderly client. The authors insist that the S.A.T. is not a "test" but a "technique" and accordingly provide little validity or reliability data in the manual. Thus, it is difficult to evaluate the merits of the S.A.T. by any but the most obvious means. With face validity in mind, at best the S.A.T. could facilitate communication between an elderly client and an empathetic therapist. At worst, the S.A.T. represents an ageist and extraneous method of assessing the elderly that does not provide an improvement over the T.A.T., an age-irrelevant instrument with infinitely more clinical data to support it.

REVIEWER'S REFERENCES

Murray, H. A. (1943). *Thematic Apperception Test manual.* Cambridge: Harvard University Press.

Thompson, C. E. (1949). The Thompson modification of the thematic apperception test. *Rorschach Research Exchange and Journal of Projective Techniques, 13,* 469–478.

Piotrowski, Z. A. (1950). A new evaluation of the thematic apperception test. *Psychoanalytic Review, 37,* 101–127.

Lindzey, G. (1952). Thematic apperception test: Interpretive assumption and related empirical evidence. *Psychological Bulletin, 49,* 1–21.

Murstein, B. I. (1965). The stimulus. In B. I. Murstein (Ed.), *Handbook of projective techniques* (pp. 509–546). New York: Basic Books.

American Educational Research Association, American Psychological Association, & National Council on Measurement in Education. (1985). *Standards for educational and psychological testing.* Washington, DC: American Psychological Association, Inc.

Bellak, L. (1986). *The T.A.T., C.A.T., and S.A.T. in clinical use* (4th ed.). Orlando, FL: Grune & Stratton.

Exner, J. E. (1993). *The Rorschach: A comprehensive system. I: Basic applications* (3rd ed.). New York: Wiley.

Dahlstrom, W. G. (1995). Pigeons, people, and pigeon-holes. *Journal of Personality Assessment, 64*, 2–20.

Review of the Senior Apperception Technique by MICHAEL G. KAVAN, *Associate Dean for Student Affairs and Associate Professor of Family Practice, Creighton University School of Medicine, Omaha, NE:*

The Senior Apperception Technique (S.A.T.) is a projective "technique" originally designed to "elucidate the problems of elderly individuals" (Bellak & Bellak, 1986, p. 341). More specifically, it is an apperceptive method designed to elicit a person's "meaningfully subjective interpretation of a perception" (Bellak, 1986, p. 17). The S.A.T. consists of 16 black-and-white pictures featuring one or more elderly persons in various situations. These pictures are meant to elicit themes and psychological problems in the elderly. These themes, which were derived from the gerontological literature and the authors' personal clinical experience, concern matters such as social interaction, familial issues, loneliness, anxiety, and, of course, sex. The S.A.T. is seen by the authors as a necessary extension of the Thematic Apperception Technique (T.A.T.; Morgan & Murray, 1935) due to the necessity to assess the growing number of elderly persons in the United States. Other than summarizing additional studies using the S.A.T. no changes are noted between the 1985 revision and its predecessor.

ADMINISTRATION AND SCORING. The S.A.T. may be administered by persons from a variety of professions. Qualifications of those administering the pictures depend only on how they intend to use the technique. The clinician is instructed to hand each picture to the elderly person for viewing. Beyond this, the only specific instructions provided within the manual for the administration of the S.A.T. pictures are for Picture #16, which includes these special instructions: "Here is the picture of a sleeping person having a dream. Tell me in some detail what the dream might be about—make it a lively dream" (p. 6). Also, the following statement is recommended for occasions in which there is a lack of response: "Maybe we will come back to this one" (p. 5). One is left to assume that methods similar to instructions provided for the T.A.T. or Children's Apperception Technique (Bellak, 1986) are to be used for the remaining S.A.T. pictures as well. It is recommended that no more than 5 minutes be given per picture and that each interview last no more than one-half hour, which would appear to be difficult if the maximum time is allowed for each picture (i.e., 5 minutes x 16 pictures = 80 minutes). Instructions are given that there is no need to administer all pictures to each person. Responses may be written or tape recorded by the administrator. No information regarding scoring is provided within the manual. The manual does contain a summary of typical themes seen in response to the various pictures. Because the S.A.T. is considered a technique as opposed to a test, the authors claim that it does nothing more than "facilitate the process of communicating one's feeling and thoughts by responding to standard stimuli rather than to standard clinical questions" (p. 9). It is recommended that if one is to make inferences about preconscious and unconscious processes, then this type of interpretation can be accomplished by methods described by Bellak (1975) for the C.A.T. and T.A.T.—information that is not included in the S.A.T. manual.

RELIABILITY AND VALIDITY. No reliability or validity data are provided within the manual. Several studies conducted with the S.A.T. are summarized and suggest: (a) The elderly did not differ substantially from a control group of students in regard to responses involving despair, death, and other negative images; (b) sex continued to be a major theme in elderly responses; (c) elderly and female responses were noted as more positive than those of younger and male subjects; (d) the S.A.T. was effective in discriminating between emotionally cognitively impaired and nonimpaired nursing home residents; and (e) affiliation was the most important content theme. A section on suggestions for future research is also included within the manual, but interestingly, does not include any recommendations to develop a scoring system or to establish reliability, validity, and/or normative data.

NORMS. No normative data are provided within the manual. Bellak (1986) indicates that normative data on a technique such as this are "hardly very useful" because the clinician is interested primarily in the responses characteristic of the "individual" (p. 39).

SUMMARY. The S.A.T. is an apperceptive technique meant to elicit concerns held by the elderly. Its construction is based on a review of the gerontological literature, the authors' personal clinical experiences, and a subjectively based method of paring down and revising the pictorial stimuli. The manual contains limited information about test construction, administration, scoring, interpretation, reliability, validity, and norms. As such, the S.A.T. comes nowhere close to being a test as defined by the *Standards for Educational and Psychological Testing* (American Educational Research Association, American Psychological Association, & National Council on Measurement in Education, 1985). Instead, it is, as the authors admit, "only a slight variation on the clinical technique of asking people to tell us what ails them" (p. 9). In light of this admission, the authors should, at least, be given credit for realizing that the S.A.T. is nothing more than a collection of pictures meant to facilitate the communication of feelings and thoughts by the elderly. As such, it should be used for this purpose only. Potential users of the S.A.T. are cautioned against using the S.A.T. in research and clinical settings beyond this limited purpose of the technique.

REVIEWER'S REFERENCES

Morgan, C. D., & Murray, H. A. (1935). A method for investigating phantasies: The Thematic Apperception Test. *Archives of Neurology and Psychiatry, 34,* 289–306.

Bellak, L. (1975). *The T.A.T., C.A.T., and S.A.T. in clinical use* (3rd ed.). Orlando, FL: Grune & Stratton.

American Educational Research Association, American Psychological Association, & National Council on Measurement in Education. (1985). *Standards for educational and psychological testing.* Washington, DC: American Psychological Association, Inc.

Bellak, L. (1986). *The T.A.T., C.A.T., and S.A.T. in clinical use* (4th ed.). Orlando, FL: Grune & Stratton.

Bellak, L., & Bellak, S. S. (1986). The S.A.T. In L. Bellak (Ed.), *The T.A.T., C.A.T., and S.A.T. in clinical use* (4th ed.; pp. 341–360). Orlando, FL: Grune & Stratton.

[284]
Sensory Evaluation Kit.

Purpose: "Designed to increase functional performance through the primary use of smell."
Population: Ages 2 to adult.
Publication Date: 1991.
Scores, 20: Motor, Tactile, Visual, Auditory, Olfactory, Gustatory, Problem Solving, Attention Span, Directions (2-Step, No Cuing), Interpretation of Signs/Symbols, Memory, Body Scheme (Body Parts, R/L Discrimination), Motor Planning, Stereognosis, Figure/Ground, Color Perception, Form Constancy, Position in Space.
Administration: Individual.
Price Data: Available from publisher.
Time: Administration time not reported.
Author: Bonnye S. Klein.
Publisher: Maddak, Inc.

Review of the Sensory Evaluation Kit by J. JEFFREY GRILL, Associate Professor of Special Education, Athens State College, Athens, AL:

The Sensory Evaluation Kit is intended for use "as an assessment tool and/or treatment activity … to increase functional performance through the primary use of smell" (manual, p. 5). Motor, sensory, perceptual, cognitive, psychological, and social functions may be assessed and treated, although just how this may be accomplished is not well explained. According to the anonymous author, the kit may be used with individuals with various diagnoses, including

but not limited to those with cardiovascular accident, Alzheimer's disease, developmental disabilities, mental retardation, head trauma, sensory impairments, psychiatric impairments, cerebral palsy, terminal cancer, and AIDS, as well as with general pediatric and geriatric populations. The author claims the kit may have applications in "life review, sensory stimulation, group skills, interpersonal skills, and general learning" (manual, p. 5).

The kit contains 27 "Scratch & Sniff" scents, with six peel-off discs for each scent on a separate sheet. The peel-off discs are to be separated and stored in the 27 plastic, screw-top jars, with one scent disc peeled off and placed on the jar top. Each scent is depicted by a cartoon-type representation of the nonsticky side of the disc. Also included in the kit is a six-page manual, as well as two mini-decks of cards from the Peabody Picture Collection (AGS®), depicting full color images of prepared foods and of fruits and vegetables, several one page scoring sheets, and a plastic carrying case.

The basic procedure for using the kit is to select scents that the client will be asked to identify. Initially, the examiner is to select one scent familiar to the client (and to which the client is not allergic) and two cards (one of which represents the scent) from the appropriate deck. The client is not to see the jar or its lid while the two cards are placed face down before him/her. The examiner then scratches the scent disc on the lid of the jar, turns the cards face up, places the jar under the client's nose, and instructs the client to indicate what he/she has smelled. The indication (i.e., of one of the two cards) may be given orally, by pointing, or by eye contact.

Variations on the task, to engage other senses, may include having the client touch the object represented by the scent, or permitting the client to taste the object (such as a fruit). Grading the assessment (i.e., varying the apparent difficulty level of the task) may be accomplished by having the client choose from more than two pictures, or by using black-and-white pictures (not provided). The manual includes brief suggestions for assessing a variety of motor characteristics and five sensory, eight cognitive, seven perceptual, and four psychological characteristics. Scores represent the percentage of assistance needed by the client (apparently to complete the task, though this is never directly stated), and are recorded as I (Independent—0%), MIN (Minimal—25%), MOD (Moderate—50%), MAX (Maximum—75%), D (Dependent—100%), or NA (Not Appropriate). The one-page scoring sheet includes space to rate the enumerated characteristics, and to note comments, including the number and types of scents used.

The brief, almost cryptic manual offers little direction for standard use of the kit, and virtually no criteria for scoring a client's performance. Although no claim is made for the validity or reliability of the kit, some supporting evidence for its usefulness should be provided. None is offered.

The principal elements, the scents, are not all clearly identified and nowhere is a list of scents provided. Instead, a cartoon depiction and a word or phrase on each disc serve to identify the scent. For example, red-and-white striped candy canes and the phrase "PEPPY MINTS" identify what is probably intended as a peppermint scent. But, neither a laughing ghost with the word, "BOO" nor a snowman with the phrase, "Mighty Fine" gives a clue to the scents intended for these two discs, respectively, and, with no other identifying information, these discs and many others are useless.

Other shortcomings are the poor quality of the scents. A few seem to approximate the apparently intended scent, but most are simply too faint or too sweet to be of any real use. Further, the discs do not adhere well to the jar tops, and the scents tend to blend together after being stored in a closed container (the carrying kit) after a short time.

In summary, although the purpose of the Sensory Evaluation Kit seems legitimate—to provide a non-threatening tool that an experienced clinician can use to assess, however subjectively, a client's functioning in several areas—the kit falls far short of usefulness. Its chief component, "Scratch & Sniff" scents, are utterly ineffective, and the poorly written manual is devoid of supportive documentation. Simply stated, the Sensory Evaluation Kit should be avoided. As an assessment or treatment instrument, it serves no legitimate purpose, but it reeks of rip-off.

Review of the Sensory Evaluation Kit by ELLEN WEISSINGER, Associate Dean, Teachers College, University of Nebraska-Lincoln, Lincoln, NE:

The stated purpose of the Sensory Evaluation Kit (SEK) is to "increase functional performance through the primary use of smell" (p. 5). The test manual contends that the SEK can be used as an assessment tool or treatment activity "in a variety of settings with a variety of people" including individuals with Alzheimer's, developmental disabilities, head trauma, terminal cancer, and AIDS, as well as general pediatric and geriatric populations. The test includes descriptions of 20 functional areas that may be evaluated or treated with the Kit, and the test manual notes that possible applications include "as-

sessment and treatment of motor, sensory, perceptual, cognitive, psychological and social functions" (p. 5).

Unfortunately, the test manual provides absolutely no theoretical rationale for these claims, nor does it present any empirical data as evidence of the claims. Given the breadth of contentions made by the test developers, this complete lack of theoretical or empirical justification for the test is a significant shortcoming.

The SEK consists of a plastic brief case containing a test manual, 27 small plastic jars with screw tops, two decks of cards each containing 44 cards depicting different kinds of food and four cards listing the consonant or vowel sounds in each food name, 27 sheets each containing six scratch-and-sniff peel-off stickers, and 10 copies of a "sample scoring sheet." The test manual directs test users to select one of the stickers that contains the target scent. The sticker is placed on the top of the small bottle (the remaining five stickers with the same scent are placed inside the bottle for storage). Two of the picture cards are placed face down before the client. The client is then given a sniff of the scent and the two cards are turned over to show two different food pictures (one of which correctly depicts food associated with the target scent). The client is then asked to select the correct picture.

Variations of this basic procedure are offered in the test manual. For example, to include the "tactile and gustatory senses" the client can hold and taste the actual food item. To assess or treat motor characteristics, the client can be asked to point at or reach for the card or food object. The test manual makes several vague claims concerning the 20 functional areas that can be assessed or treated with the SEK. For example, the manual notes that "problem solving ability" is assessed with the SEK because "The client will either plan what he is going to point to, or use the trial and error approach when unable to distinguish the scents and/or picture" (p. 7). And the test can assess or treat "emotional control" because "some of the scents could bring back memories from the client's past, long or short term memory" (p. 9).

Some of the claims are poorly written and difficult to comprehend. For example, the explanation as to how the SEK can test or treat "body scheme" is as follows: "To test for body scheme, the client will or will not be able to point to the pictures which include the elements of both motor planning and proprioception, and/or to discriminate any right/left directions. If the client cannot point to the picture without any physical indications, a more complete body scheme test would be indicated" (p. 8).

The manual provides very little guidance concerning use of the "sample scoring sheet." At the end of the explanation of the test's use in the 20 functional areas, a chart entitled "Scale: This scale is used for testing" appears. The scale includes five levels: Independent—0%, Minimal—25%, Moderate—50%, Maximum—75%, and Dependent—100%. No explanation is given concerning how these percentages result from the test procedures. There is a cryptic footnote that says "grading scale is the percentage of assistance needed by the client from the tester for correct response" (p. 7).

In summary, the SEK is offered as a test that does many sophisticated assessments and can serve as a therapeutic intervention for many complex areas of human functioning. Yet the test is completely without conceptual basis, and completely without empirical support. The test manual makes unsubstantiated and irresponsible claims. The manual is poorly written, disjointed, confusing, and inadequate. The test is, simply put, useless. It cannot be recommended for use in any setting, with any population, for any purpose.

[285]
Sex-Role Egalitarianism Scale.

Purpose: "Developed to measure attitudes toward the equality of men and women."
Population: High school to adult.
Publication Date: 1993.
Acronym: SRES.
Scores, 6: Marital Roles, Parental Roles, Employment Roles, Social-Interpersonal-Heterosexual Roles, Educational Roles, Total.
Administration: Group.
Price Data, 1993: $27 per examination kit including manual (58 pages), 10 question/answer documents, and 10 profile sheets; $18 per manual; $33 per 25 question/answer documents; $9.50 per 25 profile sheets.
Time: (25–35) minutes.
Comments: Two full forms, B and K; two abbreviated forms, BB and KK.
Authors: Lynda A. King and Daniel W. King.
Publisher: Sigma Assessment Systems, Inc.

TEST REFERENCES

1. Brutus, S., Montei, M., Jex, S., King, L., & King, D. (1993). Sex role egalitarianism as a moderator of gender congruence bias in evaluation. *Sex Roles, 29,* 755-765.
2. King, L. A., King, D. W., Carter, D. B., Surface, C. R., & Stepanski, K. (1994). Validity of the Sex-Role Egalitarianism Scale: Two replication studies. *Sex Roles, 31,* 339-348.

Review of the Sex-Role Egalitarianism Scale by CAROL COLLINS, Director, Family Counseling and Research Center, Caldwell, ID:

The Sex-Role Egalitarianism Scale (SRES) by Lynda A. King and Daniel W. King is a 95-question self-report instrument designed to measure attitudes about the equality of men and women. The authors suggest the test would be useful to researchers who may want to study gender-based stereotyping and discrimination as they relate to educational, career, or job opportunities. Those studying sexual harassment, abuse, or heterosexual violence should also find the test useful. The SRES would be a useful tool in evaluating programs where sex-role attitude change is an outcome goal of intervention. The authors caution that the test was not intended for clinical assessment or psychological evaluation. It may, however, be useful to the therapist furnishing supplementary information about attitudes that affect interpersonal relationships between men and women.

The test package includes alternate full forms, Form B and Form K. Domains of content within each form include: Marital Roles, Parental Roles, Employment Roles, Social-Interpersonal-Heterosexual Roles, and Educational Roles. Alternate short forms of 25 questions are also available.

ADMINISTRATION AND SCORING. Respondents are presented a list of 95 questions designed to reflect attitudes about sex-role egalitarianism. A selection of five responses follows a Likert-type scale, ranging from *Strongly Agree* to *Strongly Disagree.* Respondents are asked to circle the choice that best describes their own personal opinion. They include such questions as: "Women are just as capable as men to run a business," and "A husband should leave the care of young babies to his wife." Directions are printed on the testing form and the manual indicates the test may be self-administered. The test can be given to individuals or groups.

The manual thoroughly describes methods of scoring. It is scored by hand, and is easy and straightforward. Scores are obtained for the five differential domains, as well as a total score.

NORMING INFORMATION. Detailed tables of normative data are included in the test. Separate tables are available for males and for females, as well as a combined table of both males and females. Each table also displays scores pertaining to the five domain measures for Forms B and K. The SRES is not designed to categorize an individual by fitting him or her into a level, such as "very traditional," "moderately egalitarian," "highly egalitarian," etc., but measures differences between groups, or differences between an individual and a particular group. *T*-scores are provided for each raw score.

Comparative sample groups were drawn from students at colleges and universities in the eastern, midwestern, and western United States and western Canada. Approximately 3,000 students make up the norm pool. Representativeness of the population of college students in North America was not attempted, nor achieved. The authors refer to this fact in warranting caution in interpreting SRES scores normatively.

RELIABILITY. Internal consistency of total scores was .97. Test-retest reliability (3–4-week interval) was .88 and .91 for Forms B and K. The data provide strong support for the reliable measurement of the test. A table of internal consistency reliability estimates is provided for the various sample groups, which are essentially the different colleges and university groups where respondents attended.

VALIDITY. All the subjects included in the norming of the test were college students. Therefore, it is not possible to extrapolate to general populations. There is no evidence in support of predictive validity. It would not be wise to assume the likelihood or probability of any specific behavior, such as risk of domestic violence, based on a "traditional" view of male and female equality. Several studies have confirmed a correlation of this test with other tests that measure gender-role attitudes. The Attitudes Toward Women Scale (AWS) was found to have a correlation of .86 in a study of predominantly female college students.

SUMMARY. The Sex-Role Egalitarianism Scale (SRES) can be useful to researchers attempting to determine if a group of subjects hold traditional male/female role attitudes, or if they are alike or different from any other group of subjects. It could be useful in evaluating programs where change of attitude is the expected outcome. In comparing scores to test norms, however, it is important to recognize that the groups on which the test was normed are all college students and may not represent the population at large.

The test is easy to administer and score, and sufficient information is provided for efficient interpretation of results. The authors do not make inappropriate claims for the test, and are lavish in their suggestions for further research. Keeping the previous cautionary statements in mind, this reviewer believes the SRES is a satisfactory and useful instrument for many specific circumstances.

[286]
Shapiro Control Inventory.

Purpose: Designed to "categorize, refine, and articulate a person's state of consciousness regarding control."
Population: Ages 14–88.
Publication Date: 1994.
Acronym: SCI.
Scores, 9: General Domain (Overall Sense of Control, Positive Sense of Control, Negative Sense of Control), Modes of Control (Positive Assertive, Positive Yielding, Negative Assertive, Negative Yielding), Domain-Specific Sense of Control, Overall Desire for Control.
Administration: Group.
Price Data: Available from publisher.
Foreign Language Editions: Spanish, Japanese, and Polish editions under development.
Time: (20–30) minutes.
Author: Deane H. Shapiro, Jr.
Publisher: Behaviordyne, Inc.

Review of the Shapiro Control Inventory by WESLEY E. SIME, Professor of Health and Human Performance, University of Nebraska-Lincoln, Lincoln, NE:

The Shapiro Control Inventory (SCI) is a nine-scale, 187-item standardized assessment tool designed to aid in diagnosis and treatment planning for control-based psychotherapy and clinical health care intervention. It takes about 25 minutes to complete the instrument. The authors contend that this instrument is applicable to both psychiatric and normal populations citing several thousand case examples representing a broad range of: normative groups (age 14–88 years), at-risk populations (Adult Children of Alcoholics, prisoners), psychiatric populations (major depressions, border-line, anxiety, and eating disorders), medical populations (cardiac rehabilitation, breast cancer), and a group of mediators with varied history of practice. In addition, the SCI appears to be appropriate for assessment of the person's current sense of control, whether she or he would like to change, and a differential diagnosis citing the dimensions of control that are most deviant from the psychologically healthy profile.

I agree with the author's contention that deficiencies in sense of control or extreme need for control are central features in many clinical problems including depression, addictions, eating, anxiety, and stress disorders. In addition, it may be a salient element in the prevention and treatment of heart disease, cancer, and diabetes. Although the concept of control has been featured in several other theories (learned helplessness, self-efficacy, and need for control), it has not been measured effectively by existing instruments (Rotter's Locus of Control [1966]) and Wallston's Health Locus of Control [Wallston, Wallston, & DeVellis, 1978]) in a comprehensive manner with specific focus on several unique domains. The SCI addresses sense of control on 25 different parameters (e.g., eating, exercise, substance use, interpersonal relationships, career, etc.) and features two contrasting modes of control (assertive, problem-focused mastery of the situation versus learning to accept self or yielding to the situation). It is notable that the SCI supercedes the Rotter and the Wallston instruments by assessing "whether" the person currently feels a sense of control, in addition to his/her "motivation" for control and the specific "agency" for control (self, others, and environment). I find the distinction between self and others to be very helpful noting specifically that cancer patients might benefit greatly in their expectation for recovery (positive outlook influencing disease state) in either of two divergent situations: (a) they feel that they have a "personal" sense of control over the disease, or (b) they believe in the doctor as a powerful, benevolent, expert "outsider" who dictates control of the therapy. On the other hand, the first few times I looked at the profile summary sheet, I did not find the agency to control to be inherently logical or self-explanatory. The term "agency" does not fit comfortably into our clinical vocabulary when explaining the SCI to clients or to fellow researchers.

The output of the SCI analysis includes both a research report and a narrative interpretation (12–15 pages) together with graphs and a computer generated statement. The latter item provides: (a) a complete profile presented concisely on a single-page sheet; (b) a 2–3-page summary highlighting each of the domains of control together with an extremely succinct criterion of "healthy" versus "somewhat impaired" responses; and (c) a detailed narrative report (8–10 pages). I did not find the brief summary to be particularly helpful in understanding the client without looking further into the detailed narrative. Several examples of statements drawn from the instrument illustrate features of control (either positive or negative) to help the therapist reinforce the strengths of the client as well as to confront problem areas that might be causing some of the clinical problems. In addition, under the heading of "sense of control" a nice feature includes specific behaviors such as eating, physical exercise, physical appearance, and body weight categorized separately in one section, whereas cognitive items feature such terms as concentration, relationships, sexuality, career, and environment.

I found the domain "mode of control" to be the most difficult part of this instrument to understand. For example, there are no clear examples given in the report or the manual as to how a positive, assertive responder is distinguished from a negative, yielding responder. Descriptive words such as rational, independent, leading, and self-explorative are provided to describe each category, but I needed to search extensively to find a sense of relevance for the client in regard to this information. On the other hand,

regarding the domain, "desire for control," there is an interesting assessment of overcontrol, illustrating several negative consequences for the therapist and the client to consider. I found this to be inherently logical, provocative, and helpful to both the client and the therapist in structuring change strategy.

The scale development for the SCI was different for each domain but did include empirical, inductive, and deductive methods in accordance with accepted procedures for personality inventory construction. Regarding the mode of control, the authors used predetermined criteria to create the four quadrants (positive assertive, negative assertive, positive yielding, and negative yielding), which seems somewhat arbitrary. On the other hand there were over 2,000 mental health professionals who provided confirmatory evidence in rating the final 87 words and factor analysis revealed substantially high accountability for variation (e.g., 29%–34%) in some but not all of the four quadrants.

I was more concerned about the interrater reliability, which was determined using six experts in pairs (male and female) who were knowledgeable and experienced in three specific areas: Type A behavior, East-West psychology, and sex-role psychology. I was pleased to see that the author found 83% agreement (five of six raters) for 49 of the original words selected in the initial factor analysis. Those 49 words were the only items selected to be used in "mode of control." Reliability was demonstrated for internal consistency of items as well as for test-retest (5-week interval) reproducibility (ELSA = .70–.89 and test-retest r = .67–.93, consecutively).

The validity of the instrument was based on the citation of 12 or more different studies conducted on various different populations as listed previously. I was most familiar with the data relating "control" to heart disease and coronary prevention. This research shows that although the link between Type A personality and heart disease is currently focused on hostility and time urgency, both of these tend to emanate from manifestations of either very "possessive persons," or from the feeling of being "out of control" (i.e., having a sense of insecurity and inadequate self-esteem). Thus, control-related interventions may serve well in the therapeutic applications with heart disease patients as well as for coronary-prone persons. Similar research with the SCI shows that personal control is predictive of level of anxiety, depression, and recovery among cancer patients. This demonstrates to me that the SCI has a fairly high level of face validity in several important areas of health psychology.

In summary, the SCI is a highly sophisticated instrument with substantial validity and reliability that also provides provocative and interesting results for the client as well as for the therapist. It is appropriate for use with a broad population of both normal and clinical participants. In addition, it is equally useful for research as well as clinical applications and it is the only modern instrument that measures "control" comprehensively across several important domains.

REVIEWER'S REFERENCES

Rotter, J. (1966). Generalized expectancies for internal versus external control of reinforcement. *Psychological Monographs, 80* (Whole No. 609).

Wallston, K. A., Wallston, B. S., & DeVellis, R. (1978). Development of the Multidimensional Health Locus of Control (MHLC) Scales. *Health Education Monographs*, 6(2), 160–170.

Review of the Shapiro Control Inventory by CLAUDIA R. WRIGHT, Professor of Educational Psychology, California State University, Long Beach, CA:

The nine-scale, 187-item Shapiro Control Inventory (SCI) is a self-administered, computer-scored, standardized, multidimensional inventory that was designed for use by mental health professionals to facilitate the assessment of both general and specific areas of control-related problems and strategies employed by the client and to assist the therapist in identifying effective interventions. The SCI is divided into four general areas: (a) General Domain—Sense of Control (Scales 1–3), (b) Specific Domains of Control (Scale 4), (c) Modes of Control (Scales 5–8), and (d) Desire for Control (Scale 9). The instrument yields seven subdomain scores derived from Scale 4 (body, mind, interpersonal relationships, career, self, environment, and other) and five additional control indicators that are based upon responses to selected SCI items (mode satisfaction—desire for change, level of satisfaction—concern, preferred response style, self as source of control, and other as source of control). The inventory has been written at an eighth-grade reading level.

The manual provides a relatively clear and thorough treatment of the problem and need for a comprehensive approach to measuring control. Although an adequate presentation of conceptual and theoretical foundations is made, summaries of subsequent studies presented as validation efforts lacked critical rationales to support hypothesis testing and scale interpretations.

SCALE DEVELOPMENT. Item statements for SCI Scales 1–4 and 9 were derived from carefully constructed theoretical rationales, examined for clinical utility, and piloted for clarity and accuracy with respect to content. Mode of Control Scales 5–8 were constructed on the basis of a careful and extensive content analysis obtained from the responses of 706 mental health professionals and supported empirically through a series of factor analyses.

TEST ADMINISTRATION AND SCORING. Guidelines are presented for administration of the SCI in a group setting. Focus is on handling queries about specific words or concepts and on facilitating preparation of the machine-scored scantrons. Although not included in the testing directions, test administrators might be encouraged to emphasize test-taking instructions to assist those examinees who are not test wise to manage a different response format for each scale (7-, 6-, 4-, or 3-point Likert type response scale each with a different set of anchors) and three different statement types (complete sentences, phrases, or words).

A data block has been incorporated into the first page of the inventory to allow for the inclusion of demographic information specific to a given research program or to clinic needs. Specialized blocks require advance arrangements with the test publisher.

Comprehensive computer-generated profiles and interpretative reports are available only to licensed professionals from the publisher. A sample report is presented in the manual. The profile is made up of 14 indicators with an extensive, interpretative report of the findings clearly displayed and written in an easy-to-understand style. Appropriate cautions are made against making decisions based solely upon information obtained from this report.

NORMING PROCEDURES. Each profile analysis is contrasted with responses from "healthy" normal respondents. However, it is not clear from the text or the appendices whether this comparison is based upon responses from a group of psychiatrically screened normals ($n = 14$), and unscreened normals ($N = 2,369$) made up primarily of U.S. mental health professionals (and includes 147 unscreened normals tested in Spain), or some subsample of unscreened normals.

Means and standard deviations for each of the nine SCI scales and each of the seven domain specific areas are presented in the manual for both normal and clinical groups. The lack of detailed information on sampling procedures and demographics for many subsamples coupled with the relatively small sample sizes employed in several studies raise serious concerns about the representativeness of these norm groups to the targeted populations. For example, no ethnic breakdowns of samples were provided. Apparently, Spanish, Japanese, and Polish editions of the instrument are under development but no corresponding reliability and validity data, to date, are reported for these test forms in the technical manual.

RELIABILITY. Reported reliability estimates in the form of internal consistency (alpha) coefficients and 5-week test-retest rs were limited to scores obtained from 67 undergraduate students (unscreened normals). For the nine SCI Scales, alphas ranged from .70 to .89 (mdn = .77) and test-retest rs ranged from .67 to .93 (mdn = .81).

DISCRIMINANT VALIDITY. Three studies were cited as providing discriminant validity evidence for the SCI. In the first study, a sample of 167 respondents comprising five groups classified as either psychometrically-screened normals or with a clinical diagnosis of borderline, depression, panic disorder, or generalized anxiety were administered the SCI, Rotter's (1966) Internal/External Locus of Control (LOC) Scale, and Wallston's Multidimensional Health Locus of Control Scales (Internal, External Other, and Chance) (Wallston, Wallston, & DeVellis, 1978). Based on analysis of variance (ANOVA) procedures, SCI Scales 1–4 (General and Specific Domains) provided the strongest differentiation between normals and each of the clinical groups. Scale 7 (Negative Assertive) produced differences between normal and borderline and generalized anxiety groups. Only the comparison between the normal and borderline groups on Scale 9 (Desire for Control) was statistically significant. Overall, the SCI's performance in differentiating among groups was superior when compared to that for the LOC or Wallston's measure.

In the second study, SCI scale scores for 34 at-risk adult children of alcoholics were compared to those of two groups of sex- and age-matched unscreened normals. ANOVAs revealed that SCI Scales 1–2 differentiated between the groups. Scale 4 data, broken down by each of the seven areas, produced statistically significant differences in five of the seven domains (Body, Mind, Interpersonal, Self, and Career). In the third study, SCI scale scores for 23 clients with eating disorders were compared with matched unscreened normals, SCI Scales 1–4 differentiated between the groups. Also, in an examination of the seven domains, the eating-disorder group obtained significantly lower scores than did normals in three of the seven areas including Body, Interpersonal, and Self. Again, selection and sampling size is of concern.

CONSTRUCT-RELATED VALIDITY. Construct validity efforts focused upon the relationships between respondents' performance on the SCI scales and theoretically related measures, neurobiological correlates, and other behavioral indicators.

SUMMARY. Clearly, the strongest validity support for the SCI is in the ability of scores to discriminate among normal and various clinical groups. Also, as a measure of control, it would appear that the SCI makes a contribution to the field by providing an assessment of a control construct not previously tapped by popular measures like Rotter's LOC or Wallston's inventory. However, in general, additional support for reliability and both criterion-related and construct validities are needed in which special attention is paid to issues of representativeness (including both normal and clinical samples, regions, gender, and ethnicity) and sample size.

REVIEWER'S REFERENCES

Rotter, J. (1966). Generalized expectancies for internal versus external control of reinforcement. *Psychological Monographs, 80* (Whole No. 609).

Wallston, K. A., Wallston, B. S., & DeVellis, R. (1978). Development of the Multidimensional Health Locus of Control (MHLC) Scales. *Health Education Monographs, 6*(2), 160–170.

[287]
Short Employment Tests, Second Edition.

Purpose: "Measures verbal, numerical, and clerical skills."
Population: Adults.
Publication Dates: 1951–1993.
Acronym: SET.
Scores, 4: Verbal, Numerical, Clerical, Total.
Administration: Group or individual.
Forms, 4: 1, 2, 3, 4.
Price Data, 1994: $60 per 25 test booklets including manual ('93, 71 pages), test booklet, and key; $20 per keys; $22 per examination kit (Form 1); $28 per examination kit (Forms 2, 3, 4).
Time: 5(10) minutes.
Comments: Distribution of Form 1 restricted to banks which are members of the American Banking Association.
Author: George K. Bennett and Marjorie Gelink.
Publisher: The Psychological Corporation.
Cross References: See T4:2456 (3 references); for reviews of an earlier edition by Samuel Juni, Ronald Baumanis, and Leonard J. West, see 9:1124 (1 reference); see also T3:2180 (1 reference); for reviews by Ronald N. Taylor and Paul W. Thayer, see 8:1037 (4 references); see also T2:2151 (6 references); for a review by Leonard W. Ferguson, see 6:1045 (9 references); for a review by P. L. Mellenbruch, see 5:854 (16 references).

Review of the Short Employment Tests, Second Edition by CAROLINE MANUELE-ADKINS, Professor, Department of Educational Foundations and Counseling Programs, Hunter College, City University of New York, New York, NY:

The Short Employment Tests (SET) were designed to help employers select people for clerical and lower-level administrative jobs. They consist of three 5-minute, timed aptitude tests and include a 50-item Verbal test (V) of general vocabulary; a 90-item Numerical test (N) of basic arithmetic (addition, subtraction, multiplication, and division); and a Clerical Aptitude test (CA) of 60 items that involves alphabetical ordering, coding, and selecting tasks. These tests have been around for a long time (1951) but The Psychological Corporation, its publisher, has paid attention to updating and revising it over the years. Prior test reviews are informative about these efforts and other basic aspects of the tests.

A revised test manual with new normative data accompanies this edition of the SET (1993). It has a "face lift" in that the test booklet covers were redesigned for a more updated look, scoring keys are color coded to the test booklet, and Directions for Administering the test are on a separate sheet to make "administration less cumbersome" (p. 5). The basic tests, however, have not been changed.

The most important feature of the latest revision is the inclusion of combined group norms that include 20 new norm groups and some 5,482 cases, which means that the test developers have made a serious effort to respond to the Civil Rights Act of 1991, which legislates against the use of selective normative data that differentiate group scores according to "race, color, religion, sex or national origin" (p. 5). The new combined group norms include males and females, whites and minorities. Some of the older within group data have been collapsed with new sample data to produce these new norms.

Scoring of the SET battery is done with hand-scoring keys and the score for each test is the number of questions answered correctly. To understand how an individual's score compares to other applicants for similar positions, the test user needs to consult the norm tables where raw scores on the SET have been converted to percentile scores. Norms are available for samples of airline clerks, oil company clerks, bank clerks and tellers, accounting applicants, reservation agents, utility and financial corporation clerks, and others. The manual suggests that these norms be used only as guides if the test is used for personnel decisions. Because most users would be using the SET for this purpose it would be important for users to develop, as the manual recommends, their own local norms. This is also important in that the manual does not provide any information about cutoff scores for selection purposes.

The original development of the four equivalent forms of the SET was done by its authors in cooperation with the American Banking Association to "provide an alternative to a lengthy test battery" (p. 6). Items of general vocabulary, arithmetic problems, and clerical aptitude tasks are thus presumed to be selected with attention to their relevance for predicting performance in clerical and administrative jobs. Given the massive "sea change," driven by the computer, in all clerical occupations, questions about the relevance of these items for predicting performance in these occupations need to be raised. All of the criterion-related validity studies are old and have not been updated in the same way the normative samples were. We are thus looking at correlations between scores on the SET and Job Performance (Supervisor's Ratings) that are quite old. These need to be revisited if the user is to have more confidence in the test's ability to predict job performance or aptitude in today's computer-organized world.

The SET manual presents criterion-related validity evidence in the form of some 99 to 134 separate analyses that correlate scores on the SET with criterion measures that include supervisory ratings, salary increases, and final grades in training programs. The correlations are not very substantial. For example, correlations for the "V" test alone indicate that out of 111 tests, 24 correlations are in the .30 to .49 range and 63 are below .30. The correlations are slightly higher when all three scales (total scores) are used in the analyses. The overreliance on supervisor's ratings as a criterion measure may be the major issue here as they are affected by problems of halo effect, lack of objective criteria, different rating scales, etc. Future criterion-validity studies need to focus more on less subjective measures of worker productivity and performance.

Construct validity evidence for the SET is more robust. The test correlates highly with other tests measuring similar constructs such as the General Clerical Test or the Minnesota Clerical Test. In the 60 analyses presented in the manual where the SET is correlated with these and similar tests, 31 are above 50 indicating that the SET is measuring constructs similar to other tests of these aptitudes.

Early reliability studies of the SET include alternative form reliability, which is important for a test that has four different forms, and test-retest reliability. The studies indicate that the four forms are equivalent and that the tests given to a sample after 2 years on the job included rs of .84 for the Verbal Test, .75 for Numerical, and .71 for Clerical Aptitude. All of these studies were done in 1956. It would be important to understand how stable and accurate the test is with today's labor market.

Employers will continue to have a need for tests such as the SET to select applicants who demonstrate the most promise for clerical work. The SET appears to be efficient for this purpose in that the tests are short, easily administered, and easily scored. It includes validity and reliability data and has new updated norms. If the SET is to continue to be useful for these purposes, however, the test developer really needs to anchor the tests more in our new technological world. Additional criterion-related validity studies are needed to demonstrate relationships between performance on the SET and job performance that includes computer-related skills. And although reliability estimates are satisfactory, new analyses in this area would be a welcome addition. In the future, a computer edition of the SET would most likely be a valuable contribution.

Review of the Short Employment Tests, Second Edition by BERT W. WESTBROOK, Professor of Psychology, North Carolina State University, and MICHAEL C. HANSEN, Graduate Research Assistant in Psychology, North Carolina State University, Raleigh, NC:

The Short Employment Tests (SET) are "designed to assist in the selection of employees for clerical jobs, lower-level administrative jobs, or other jobs that require verbal ability, rapid and accurate computational skills, and accurate coding and retrieval of information" (manual, p. 7). It consists of three speeded tests: (a) Verbal—word knowledge and vocabulary, which is, the authors claim, an efficient indicator of cognitive ability; (b) Numerical—arithmetic problems involving addition, subtraction, multiplication, and division of whole numbers; and (c) Clerical Aptitude—storing and retrieving all types of information. The SET may be administered to individuals or groups of people. The time required for administration is about 20 minutes, 5 minutes for each of the three tests plus several minutes for instructions. Sample problems are provided on the cover of each test. The manual clearly describes the administration and explicitly delineates (with bold print) what the administrator must say throughout test administration.

The manual provides normative data categorized into the following occupations: General Clerical, Banking and Financial, Business and Sales, Utilities, Management, and Miscellaneous. Of the 31 samples used for normative data, 25 are samples of

applicants, 4 are samples of incumbents, and 2 are samples of both applicants and incumbents. Normative data are presented in both tables of combined-group norms and within-group norms, for which data are grouped by gender and/or ethnic group. Raw scores are presented in the normative tables with 23 percentile values, each value representing a zone five percentile units wide (zones are not as wide at the extremes).

Scores for each of the three tests are expressed as raw scores, the number of questions answered correctly. The Total Score is the sum of the raw scores for the three tests. Normative data tables are provided by occupation to establish percentile ranks for an achieved raw score in a variety of administrative jobs. Each test has sufficient reliability to be used alone, but the authors advise employers to use all three tests to obtain a profile of aptitudes, which facilitates placement. The SET utilizes hand-scoring keys. One key is provided for each test and form of the SET. Each test is easily checked by hand, and the keys are sturdy enough for repeated administration.

The SET is composed of a Verbal test: 50 items for which the examinee must choose one of four words that means or most nearly means the same as the test word (multiple choice); a Numerical test: 90 short arithmetic problems (addition, subtraction, multiplication, division); and a Clerical Aptitude test: 60 items requiring examinee to locate a name in an alphabetical listing, then read and code a dollar figure associated with that name. All three are speed tests, including simple problems requiring basic solutions. Speed and accuracy are important factors in the level of performance.

The authors do not report item analysis data, but they do present intercorrelations suggesting that the Verbal, Numerical, and Clerical Aptitude tests are measuring separate abilities. Although the authors provide no scientific evidence of content validity, they do report evidence for criterion-related validity accumulated in the 1956, 1972, and 1978 editions of the manual, which is summarized in extensive tables organized by categories. The proportion of statistically significant correlation coefficients for the Verbal test is 35 out of 111, or 31.5%. The proportion of significant correlations for the Numerical test is 48 out of 134 (35.8%), and for the Clerical Aptitude test, 47 out of 128 (36.7%). For the Total Score, 45 out of 99 (45.5%) correlations were statistically significant.

The authors use these data to support their contention that a profile of scores provided by the three tests used in conjunction tends to have the strongest validity. However, those statistics hide a somewhat positively skewed distribution. Inspecting Table 7 in the manual, it is clear that although 37.8% (Verbal), 23.8% (Numerical), 25% (Clerical Aptitude), and 28.3% (Total score) of the validity coefficients fall below $r = .10$, only 11.7% (Verbal), 14.9% (Numerical), 13.3% (Clerical Aptitude), and 21.2% (Total) of the validity coefficients have $r = .40$ or better. Although the SET has impressive predictive potential, the actual data indicate the tests may often have minimal criterion-related validity. This may be a result of the characteristics (age, education) of the testing sample or the characteristics of the job.

It is unclear whether the increased proportion of significant coefficients for the Total Score indicate that a cumulative score had generally stronger criterion-related validity, or if it is an artifact of the use of all three tests, which creates a more detailed profile of criterion-related aptitudes. In other words, did employers make selection decisions based on Total score alone (a single-score system), or did they use any combination of three test scores to make their decisions (a compensatory selection system)? The tables, although thorough in statistics, do not report how the tests were used (compensatory or single-score).

To support the construct validity of the SET, the authors measured the relationships between the SET and other clerical tests. They note that 55 of 63 reported correlations were significant at the .05 significance level or higher. The highest correlations were between the Clerical Aptitude test and similar tests.

The SET suffers from a paucity of validation studies conducted by persons other than the authors. Contemporary validation is necessary. The two studies reported here were published shortly after the first publication of the SET in 1951. Wilkinson (1953) reported that the SET did not correlate with the semi-annual ratings, but was related to job level. These results are quite opposite from what one would expect. Although some efforts of objectivity were taken, this study predates research on rater biases. Job level is also a very suspect form of criterion; in particular, promotion opportunities were much better for males than females prior to the equal rights movement of the 1960s and 1970s.

The second study provided much more interesting results. Hughes and McNamara (1955) compared the SET and the General Clerical Tests (GCT) to determine the effectiveness of the SET for people from two different educational backgrounds. It was found that the two tests were more highly correlated (.87) for a group of clerical applicants with only high school diplomas than

for a group of secretarial and stenographic applicants who had some college training (.77). In addition, the distribution of the SET-Verbal scores for the secretarial applicants was negatively skewed, suggesting the Verbal test was too easy for the more highly educated.

Alternate-forms reliability coefficients are reported. Each of three groups ($N = 268, 231, 210$) of young female candidates for nursing school admission were divided into fourths, each fourth given all forms of one of the tests. Results indicated no significant difference in raw scores for any of the tests, and thus all forms are roughly equivalent, based on these samples. The coefficients were .92, .92, and .86 for the Verbal, Numerical, and Clerical Aptitude, respectively. For test-retest reliability, 72 bookkeepers and proof machine operators were administered the SET as applicants and 2 years later as incumbents. The reliability estimates were .84, .75, and .71 for the Verbal, Numerical, and Clerical Aptitude, respectively. The time lapse testifies to stability. The authors believe that experience on the job leads to higher employee scores for the Clerical Aptitude test and thus a lower reliability coefficient.

The SET is sorely in need of updating. The revisions for the 1993 publication were made exclusively to the manual to facilitate administration. We believe that the criterion-related validity of the SET in general, and the content validity of the Verbal Test should be examined psychometrically. The low level of difficulty of the Verbal Test would suggest a ceiling effect, limiting its predictiveness with examinees with higher education. Second, spelling, in addition to vocabulary, may be important for clerical jobs. This, of course, goes beyond simple emendations, but a new conception of verbal aptitude bears consideration.

The 1993 revisions were beneficial. The more current normative data are very helpful. However, we recommend establishing local norms, particularly if the sample in question is markedly different than the normative data provided in the manual. The Short Employment Tests are fairly efficient testing devices, making them valuable tools for selection in clerical jobs, which often have considerable turnover and limited training needs. It may also serve as a screening device. The SET's brevity requires some sacrifices in criterion-related and construct validity but revisions may reduce some of the psychometric deficiencies.

REVIEWERS' REFERENCES
Wilkinson, B. (1953). Validity of Short Employment Tests. *Personnel Psychology, 6,* 419–425.
Hughes, J. L., & McNamara, W. J. (1995). Relationship of Short Employment Tests and General Clerical Tests. *Personnel Psychology, 8,* 331–337.

[288]
Situational Confidence Questionnaire.

Purpose: Designed to help clients identify high-risk drinking relapse situations.

Population: Adult alcoholics.

Publication Dates: 1987–1988.

Administration: Group.

Editions, 2: Computerized, print.

Authors: Helen M. Annis and J. Martin Graham.

Publisher: Addiction Research Foundation [Canada].

a) SITUATIONAL CONFIDENCE QUESTIONNAIRE.

Acronym: SCQ-39.

Scores, 9: Unpleasant Emotions/Frustrations, Physical Discomfort, Social Problems at Work, Social Tension, Pleasant Emotions, Positive Social Situations, Urges and Temptations, Testing Personal Control, Average.

Price Data, 1993: $14.75 per 25 questionnaires; $13.50 per user's guide ('88, 49 pages); $70 per 50 uses software edition (includes user's guide); $225 per 200 uses software edition (includes user's guide); $25 per specimen set including user's guide and 25 questionnaires.

Time: (10–15) minutes.

b) ALCOHOL CONFIDENCE QUESTIONNAIRE.

Acronym: ACQ-16.

Scores: Total score only.

Time: Administration time not reported.

Comments: Brief version of the Situational Confidence Questionnaire; test items listed in SCQ user's guide.

Cross References: See T4:2467 (1 reference).

TEST REFERENCES

1. Heather, N., Tebbutt, J., & Greeley, J. C. (1993). Alcohol cue exposure directed at a goal of moderate drinking. *Journal of Behavior Therapy and Experimental Psychiatry, 24,* 187–195.

2. Miller, K. J., McCrady, B. S., Abrams, D. B., & Labouvie, E. W. (1994). Taking an individualized approach to the assessment of self-efficacy and the prediction of alcoholic relapse. *Journal of Psychopathology and Behavioral Assessment, 16,* 111–120.

3. Sobell, L. C., Toneatto, T., & Sobell, M. (1994). Behavioral assessment and treatment planning for alcohol, tobacco, and other drug problems: Current status with an emphasis on clinical applications. *Behavior Therapy, 25,* 533–580.

4. Sobell, M. B., Sobell, L. C., & Gavin, D. R. (1995). Portraying alcohol treatment outcomes: Different yardsticks of success. *Behavior Therapy, 26,* 643–669.

Review of the Situational Confidence Questionnaire by MERITH COSDEN, Professor, Department of Education, University of California, Santa Barbara, CA:

The Situational Confidence Questionnaire (SCQ-39) is a self-report measure of self-efficacy for being able to control one's drinking. The scale is based on the premise that cognitive factors, including self-efficacy, play a role in relapse and relapse prevention. The SCQ was designed to determine self-efficacy for controlled drinking across potential drinking situations, and to assess domains in which clients

with substance abuse problems are most likely to relapse.

The 39 items on the SCQ are linked to items on the revised Inventory of Drinking Situations (IDS; 155) by the same authors (see Cosden, this volume, for a critique). On the IDS, individuals are asked to rate the frequency with which they have engaged in heavy drinking under specific situations; on the SCQ, they are asked about their confidence in being able to resist the urge to drink heavily in these same situations.

Thus, the items and subscales used on the SCQ were derived from the items and subscales of the IDS. Initially, the IDS was composed of 100 items fit into eight subscales. Five subscales described personal states that might result in drinking (i.e., Unpleasant Emotions, Physical Discomfort, Pleasant Emotions, Testing Personal Control, and Urges and Temptations), and three subscales described social situations that could promote drinking (i.e., Conflict with Others, Social Pressure to Drink, and Pleasant Times with Others). These situations were derived from a review of literature on factors related to relapse for men with drinking problems. An early version of the SCQ had 100 items, which were matched to each of the 100 original IDS items.

The number of items on the IDS was reduced by selecting the 42 items that had the highest item-subscale correlations. These 42 items include four items in each of the six original subscales, which were found to be unifactorial, and 18 items from the original Conflict with Others and Pleasant Times with Others subscales, which were found to be multifactorial. In a subsequent confirmatory factor analysis, three items were found to be strongly related to more than one variable and dropped, resulting in the current 39 items. A second confirmatory factor analysis, based on the 39 items, resulted in a model with eight different subscales, reflecting a regrouping of items. A final, confirmatory factor analysis conducted on the new model was satisfactory, supporting the following factors: Unpleasant Emotions/Frustration, Physical Discomfort, Social Problems at Work, Social Tension, Pleasant Emotions, Positive Social Situations, Urges and Temptations, and Testing Personal Control. A series of confirmatory factor analyses conducted on the first order correlation matrix determined the best second order factor structure. Although the model for the IDS placed all subscales into two categories, the best fit for the SCQ data was a three-factor model; the first four subscales were grouped under a factor labeled Negative Affect

Situations, the second two subscales were grouped under a factor called Positive Affect Situations, and the last two subscales were grouped under a factor named Urges and Testing.

The normative sample for the 42-item SCQ consisted of 424 clients in two Canadian substance abuse treatment facilities. The gender (27% female, 73% male), age (average 41 years, range from 18–76), educational history (44% completed high school), and alcohol abuse histories (average 8 years of problem drinking) were provided. Neither ethnicity nor history of abuse of other drugs were described, however.

The construct validity of the SCQ was assessed by correlating subscale scores with measures of problem drinking. In the manual, significant correlations are reported between number of drinks, number of days spent drinking, and all subscale scores. There is little differentiation between subscale scores with one exception: Only Positive Social Situations was significantly correlated with time drinking with others, indicating that clients who reported less confidence in their ability to restrain from heavy drinking in positive social situations also reported drinking more in social situations. In a study of construct validity, Miller, Ross, Emmerson, and Todt (1989) found significant differences between clients with long-term and short-term sobriety on all subscales of the SCQ except Testing Personal Control. Few studies to date have attempted to assess the predictive validity of the SCQ. Two unpublished studies by Solomon and Annis and Annis and Davis are cited in the manual. In the first study, SCQ scores obtained at intake to a substance abuse program failed to predict frequency of relapse (drinking episodes) and only weakly predicted the amount of drinking that occurred during these episodes. In the second study, the authors reported that clients tended to have a serious relapse under the two conditions (reflected in lower subscale scores) in which they rated themselves as having the least amount of control.

The SCQ can be administered as a paper-and-pencil questionnaire or electronically using an IBM computer. It can also be administered individually or in small groups. The manual includes an estimate that it takes 10–15 minutes to complete the SCQ. Clients are asked to imagine themselves in a situation and rate their confidence in their ability to abstain from heavy drinking in that situation. Heavy drinking is not objectively defined, and is left to the client's perception. A scale ranging from 0% (not at all confident) to 100% (completely confident) is presented with each item. Subscale scores are obtained

by calculating the mean confidence ratings for all items in a subscale. Clinically, subscale scores can be considered alone, or as part of a client profile. The manual also has tables that can be used to translate raw scores into standard scores for comparison with the normative sample.

The SCQ has been modified across studies to fit the needs of subgroups of substance abusers. Miller et al. (1989), for example, used the SCQ to assess the needs of clients in an abstinence-oriented program. Thus, they changed the stem to ask clients about their ability to avoid drinking altogether rather than their ability to avoid drinking heavily. In addition, they modified the rating scale to present alternatives in 10-point, rather than 20-point, increments. Despite these changes, the authors report similar subscale findings to those found on the original scales. In a further derivation from the original scale, Barber, Cooper, and Heather (1991) developed a Situational Confidence Questionnaire (Heroin) to assess the needs of heroin users. They changed the stem on the original SCQ to ask respondents about their confidence in resisting the urge to use heroin, but otherwise maintained the content and format of the questions. The impact of these changes on the reliability and validity of the scale requires further evaluation.

The authors of the SCQ have also developed a shorter form of the scale, called the Alcohol Confidence Questionnaire (ACQ). The ACQ has 16 items, 2 from each of the eight subscales. The manual presents a Cronbach alpha of .95 for the ACQ, whereas scores on the ACQ showed a correlation of .99 with scores on the SCQ. These psychometric properties of the ACQ suggest that it is a promising, if untested, measure of self-efficacy.

The authors note limitations to the SCQ, including the possibility that clients may fake responses in order to appear to be progressing in treatment. A major limitation noted by this reviewer is the lack of utility of the subscale scores. In most reported studies, problem drinking is associated with lower confidence ratings across most, or all, situations (subscales). There is little support for the use of individual subscales in determining specific relapse situations. This is not surprising, as psychometrically, the subscales have not been stable across studies. The SCQ appears most effective in providing a global measure of clients' perceptions of their ability to resist heavy drinking. Future use of the scale should focus on its utility as a global correlate and predictor of self-efficacy for drinking, or in developing more stable subscales, which can be used to predict specific relapse situations.

REVIEWER'S REFERENCES

Miller, P. J., Ross, S. M., Emmerson, R. Y., & Todt, E. H. (1989). Self-efficacy in alcoholics: Clinical validation of the Situational Confidence Questionnaire. *Addictive Behaviors, 14*, 217–224.

Barber, J. G., Cooper, B. K., & Heather, N. (1991). The Situational Confidence Questionnaire (Heroin). *The International Journal of the Addictions, 26*, 565–575.

Review of the Situational Confidence Questionnaire by CECIL R. REYNOLDS, Professor of Educational Psychology & Professor of Neuroscience, Texas A&M University, College Station, TX:

The Situational Confidence Questionnaire (SCQ) was "developed as a tool for therapists to monitor the development of a client's self-efficacy in relation to drinking situations over the course of treatment" (p. 1). It is also intended to be a measure of alcohol-related self-efficacy (not defined) for researchers interested in treatment outcomes and alcohol relapse. The original conceptualization of the instrument is modeled around the work of Albert Bandura in the area of self-efficacy. The authors believe the SCQ will be useful in repeat administrations during treatment and as an indication of treatment response. The various scores provided by the SCQ were derived through a series of factor analyses including exploratory and multiple confirmatory analyses with adjustments made in various criteria for defining factors until the authors arrived at the eight subscales they prefer.

The manual presents a 10-page discussion of the psychometric properties of the SCQ that include its normative and developmental samples, reliability evidence, validity evidence, scaling, and suggestions for interpretation. The recommended uses and description of the population for which the test is intended are presented appropriately in the manual although user qualifications are neglected.

The sample used for test development and norming is not of adequate size and is not sufficiently representative to substantiate the item selection, to establish appropriate norms, and to support conclusions regarding the use of the instrument for the intended purposes. The samples were, in fact, samples of convenience and although appearing to be a large N (424), the age range of the sample (from 18 years to 76 years) and the presence of clear age differences in responses to the SCQ renders the samples inadequate. The test development sample and norming sample were the same. Changes in items and item selection are not discussed in the manual. It is not known if any changes in items were made based upon the responses of the sample or what item selection procedures were applied.

Items on the SCQ are rated by examinees on a 6-point scale. Reliability estimates for the subscales are provided for the entire age range. This would likely inflate the reliability of various subscales because there are clear age effects. It would be desirable for reliability coefficients to be reported separately by age level. When age effects are present and reliability coefficients in the form of Cronbach's alpha are reported across the entire age range, spurious inflation of reliability estimates occurs as item variances are increased disproportionately to total test variance. The reliability coefficients reported are incredibly high, with some subscales consisting of only three items having reliability coefficients as high as .93. Standard errors of measurement are reported in raw score format although standard scores are provided for interpretation, thus complicating considerably the application of the standard errors of measurement to the interpretation of standard score reporting of individual performance.

The authors provide a good discussion of the validity of the SCQ particularly providing evidence of concurrent validity and some limited predictive validity data. The authors overinterpret the outcome of these studies, however. When applied to prediction of alcohol use in certain situations and during treatment, no validity coefficients in excess of .24 are reported. The authors interpret Pearson correlations of this magnitude as providing strong predictions of behavior. The SCQ shows a variety of weak to moderate relationships to external variables and certainly does not possess adequate validity to substantiate interpretations of the performance of any individual patient. Although it may be useful in evaluating treatment outcomes based on large samples, clinical decisions about an individual patient clearly are not substantiated on the basis of evidence provided.

The scaling of the SCQ is inadequately described. A table of T-scores is provided and the discussion in the manual leads one to believe these are normalized T-scores. The manual refers to the percentage of individuals falling within one standard deviation of the mean when T-scores are normal yet an examination of the tables reveals the T-scores provided clearly are not normalized. This is misleading in the application and interpretation of these T-scores and needs clarification. This is largely characteristic of much of the information provided in the manual. The psychometric discussions are quite brief with particular methods mentioned but not described (with the exception of some of the factor analytic studies).

No data regarding test and item bias are provided with regard to ethnicity, gender, language, geographic region, or other factors. No item analyses for possible bias were conducted and the methods by which items were selected for inclusion for the final version of the test are not described.

Directions for administration and scoring of the SCQ are relatively straightforward and easily accomplished in the test booklets provided. This represents a plus for the SCQ. Another strength is its derivation from a clear theory for which the authors are to be lauded. From a psychometric perspective, however, the SCQ has many weaknesses, rendering it unusable except in large research projects. From a clinical perspective, it certainly should not be used in any way to make decisions about treatment compliance, intervention, or predicted outcomes for an individual patient.

[289]
Skills Inventory for Teams.

Purpose: To aid early intervention practitioners to "evaluate their ability to work as part of a team."
Population: Early intervention practitioners.
Publication Dates: 1978–1992.
Acronym: SIFT.
Scores, 12: Clarity of Purpose, Cohesion, Clarity of Roles, Communication, Use of Resources, Decision Making/Problem Solving, Responsibility Implementation, Conflict Resolution, View of Family Role, Evaluation, External Support, Internal Support.
Administration: Group.
Price Data, 1993: $24.95 per administration guide and inventory ('92, 66 pages) (volume discount available).
Time: Administration time not reported.
Comments: Previously called Skills Inventory for Teachers; self-administered inventory.
Authors: Corinne Garland, Adrienne Frank, Deana Buck, and Patti Seklemian.
Publisher: Child Development Resources.

Review of the Skills Inventory for Teams by ROBERT JOHNSON, Assistant Professor of Educational Research, University of South Carolina at Columbia, Columbia, SC:

The Skills Inventory for Teams (SIFT) provides early intervention practitioners with two measures of team effectiveness: an assessment of the functioning of a team and a self-administered assessment of the skills of individual team members. To this end, the manual is divided into two sections: (a) Team Screening and Assessment and (b) Individual Team Member Screening and Assessment. In each assessment a screening scale is completed to globally assess needs in 12 areas of team functioning: Clarity of Purpose, Cohesion, Clarity of Roles, Communication, Use of Resources, Decision-Making/Problem-Solving, Responsibility/Implementation, Conflict Resolution, View of Family Role, Evaluation, External Support, and Internal Support. The results from the screening scale indicate which areas need to be explored in greater detail in a checklist of specific skills associated with team functioning.

In the Team Screening and Assessment section, each member of a team completes a 12-item screening scale to describe the functioning of the team. Each item uses a 5-point rating scale with descriptors at each extreme to elicit team members' judgments. Members of the team select the rating most closely associated with the descriptors that characterize the team. For example, for the area of Clarity of Roles the descriptor: "Our roles on the team are unclear, and/or members are not committed to roles as defined by the team" is associated with a rating of 1, and the descriptor: "Each team member's role is clearly defined and understood by all; each member is highly committed to his/her role" is associated with a rating of 5. Team member responses to each item are summarized by calculating the range of responses and the mean for each item. To establish the standard for determining areas for closer review by the team, the authors wrote: "Items with an extreme range and/or a mean less than 3 are areas in need of further assessment" (p. 12). The authors did not elaborate on how these criteria were developed: whether practitioners in the early intervention field reviewed the items to determine levels where the functioning of the team could be considered proficient or whether the levels were established by the authors.

Those areas where the proficiency of the team is questionable are further explored in a Team Assessment Checklist; the checklist is composed of the 12 areas with specific skills and procedures listed under each team function. In a group discussion, the team completes only those areas of the checklist where the screening information indicated a need. For example, if Clarity of Roles were an area of concern, then team members would complete the checklist for that area to determine if the team needed to: (a) define membership, (b) define roles of members, or (c) specify roles and responsibilities. A 3-point rating scale is used to indicate whether the team feels each skill or procedure listed under the area of need is of low, medium, or high priority. The section concludes with the team creating an action plan based on the "high priority" needs identified on the checklist.

The Individual Team Member Screening and Assessment section follows the procedures established in the Team section. Using a 5-point rating scale, individual team members complete a screening scale to assess their skills in each of the team-functioning areas. Ratings of 1 or 2 on the screening scale indicate areas for closer review on the Team Member Assessment Checklist. Again, no elaboration was offered about how the standard (i.e., scores of less than 3 indicating an area of need) was established. The checklist repeats the format established in the Team Assessment Checklist. The section concludes with the individual creating an action plan based on the "high priority" needs identified in the checklist.

The authors described the SIFT as: "an inventory of skills needed to function as part of an early intervention team" (p. 3). The manual, however, provided little information to support the claim that the instrument assesses essential team-functioning competencies. Discussion about the development of the instrument was limited to a statement about the instrument deriving from the Team Effectiveness Scale of Neugebauer (1983). No additional information was provided about theoretical frameworks or empirical studies that would support the inclusion of specific skills in the assessment. A resource list of 30 sources on team-building is included in the manual, but it was not clear if these sources informed the construction of the instrument. In this authors' correspondence with Child Development Resources, A. Frank wrote that: "The SIFT instrument was developed from a variety of sources and the literature on team development and leadership. Those sources are referenced in the product" (personal communication, April 30, 1997).

One stated purpose of the SIFT is: "To specify, for personnel decision makers and supervisors, the specific skills needed by persons providing early intervention services in a team setting" (p. 2). The authors also stated: "Teams may choose to use the SIFT as one part of a system of personnel evaluation and staff development that addresses key competencies for working in a team setting" (p. 3). Use of the SIFT in personnel decision-making (e.g., evaluation or as a diagnostic tool in career development) was not supported in the manual with any documentation about the reliability or validity of the inventory. In addition, Frank (personal communication, April 30, 1997) stated that no reliability or validity information is available for the SIFT. The lack of reliability or validity data seriously undermines the use of the SIFT as a tool to make judgments about team-effectiveness skills needed by teams and individuals.

The issue of team effectiveness is highly relevant to the current focus on integrated services for family support. The SIFT provides a useful framework for educating members of a team about skills that contribute to team efforts. Supervisors, however, should not rely on this assessment for making decisions about work-related skills. The lack of validity and reliability information precludes making personnel decisions based on the standards outlined in the *Standards for Educational and Psychological Testing* (AERA, APA, & NCME, 1985). If Child Development Resources plans to continue offering the SIFT as an assessment tool, then future editions of the manual should include information about the theoretical basis for the content of the instrument. The development of the assessment could be enhanced by conducting studies of the SIFT's reliability and validity with clients who are using the instrument.

REVIEWER'S REFERENCES

Neugebauer, R. (1983, November). Team effectiveness rating scale. *Child Care Information Exchange*, p. 4.
American Educational Research Association, American Psychological Association, & National Council on Measurement in Education. (1985). *Standards for educational and psychological testing*. Washington, DC: American Psychological Association, Inc.

Review of the Skills Inventory for Teams by E. LEA WITTA, Assistant Professor, Educational Leadership and Research, University of Southern Mississippi, Hattiesburg, MS:

The Skills Inventory for Teams consists of a manual containing several screening scales and checklists. The purpose is to provide early intervention teams with a method of assessing their current team work and individual skills as well as skills needed. The instrument is designed to facilitate a developmental sequence. Publishers emphasize it should not be the only instrument used as it does not address clinical skills. A series of screening scales for teams and team members are used. Results are then assessed and further screening scales or checklists used based on the consensus of the team. As such, teams assess shortcomings, make collective decisions, and plan corrective measures. This is not a standardized test. It is an instrument to be used for formative evaluation. As a result, there is no norming group for comparison. There is no information on validity or reliability of the instrument. There are no in-depth scoring procedures.

The inventory begins by asking team members to complete the Team Performance screening scale. Members rate on a scale of 1 (low) to 5 (high) 12 aspects that influence team functioning: Clarity of Purpose, Cohesion, Clarity of Roles, Communication, Use of Resources, Decision Making/Problem Solving, Responsibility Implementation, Conflict Resolution, View of Family Role, Evaluation, External Support, and Internal Support. Results are then summarized to determine areas of strength and weakness. Areas needing further work are specified as items with an extreme range or a mean less than 3 (neutral). Team members then proceed to the Team Assessment Checklist. Using only aspects identified as needing further work, members discuss those sections of the assessment checklist. Specific needs are identified and prioritized as high, medium, or low. From this members proceed to the Team Action Plan. Three or four goals are developed. For each goal an action is decided, members responsible are determined, and dates are set for review or completion. This includes all materials or activities needed.

The inventory profiles a need's assessment, reaching consensus, pinpointing specifics, and plan for remediation. The manual provides similar activity for individual team member assessment and development. Each of the activities is geared to developing skills. No administrative time is reported for this instrument—nor could one be determined. The time required is determined by answers to the first screening scale and the procedures that must follow it.

The team approach, which is now formalized within Part H of the Individuals with Developmental Disabilities Education Act (IDEA), is currently recognized as the best practice for early intervention services. Few early intervention practitioners, however, are trained to work as team members. The authors of this instrument have recognized this problem and have taken research into team functioning (e.g., Baker, 1980; Buchholz & Roth, 1987; Dyer, 1987) in an attempt to help teams identify problems, find solutions, and function together. This is not a quick fix solution, but a long process. Usefulness of this instrument can only be determined by the team members.

REVIEWER'S REFERENCES

Baker, R. R. (1980). *Manual: Planning for effective team functioning.* Houston, TX: Training and Measurement Systems Corporation.

Buchholz, S., & Roth, T. (1987). *Creating the high performance team.* New York: John Wiley & Sons, Inc.

Dyer, W. G. (1987). *Team building: Issues and alternatives* (2nd ed.). Reading, MA: Addison-Wesley Publishing.

[290]

Small Business Assessment.

Purpose: Provides information "about how people in the company work together."
Population: Small businesses.
Publication Date: 1984.
Acronym: SBA.

Scores: 4 areas: Organizational Climate, Supervisory Leadership, Peer Relationships, Outcomes.
Administration: Group.
Price Data, 1994: $250 for 1–25 respondents (including SBA questionnaires, tabulations, and feedback packages); $10 additional for 26–50 respondents; $500 for 1–75 respondents plus $8 for each respondent over 50; $700 for 1–100 respondents plus $4 for each respondent over 75.
Time: Administration time not reported.
Comments: Scored by publisher.
Author: Rensis Likert Associates, Inc.
Publisher: Rensis Likert Associates, Inc.

Review of the Small Business Assessment by ROBERT W. HILTONSMITH, Professor of Psychology, Radford University, Radford, VA:

The Small Business Assessment (SBA) is a 60-item questionnaire targeted for use with small businesses employing fewer than 100 persons. The SBA is adapted from the 1980 edition of the Survey of Organizations (SOO; T4:2659), developed and marketed by the same publisher. According to the questionnaire, the SBA is designed to collect information about "how people in your company work together." It goes on to state that the SBA's purpose is to "provide information to help make your work situation more satisfying and productive" (information sheet, p. 1). An information sheet directed at potential client companies notes that the SBA measures areas that are "critical for effective operation of small businesses" and can be used to "diagnose problems with your company."

The SBA is group administered. The 60 questions are answered by each respondent using several similar five-choice Likert-type formats. There is also room at the end of the answer sheet for 15 supplemental questions that can be tailored specifically for the client company. These are scored at no extra charge. Though the administration time is not reported, it would appear that the SBA could be completed in less than 20 minutes. Most questions are written clearly and should be able to be answered with a minimum amount of reflection. The test publisher's basic processing and scoring fees provide confidential feedback packages and an interpretation manual for each supervisor/manager with three or more subordinates. Included here is a "comparison of results with norms," though no information is provided on the normative sample. Additional consulting services are also available from the publisher, including survey administration, a diagnostic report, presentation of results, training in participative management concepts and skills, and facilitated feedback for work groups.

The SBA purports to measure the four major areas noted above in the test description. Within each of these four major areas are two to five subareas. In addition, one major area (Organizational Climate) not only has three subareas (Guidance System, Job Design, and Shape) but either two or three additional areas for each of these three subareas. It is not clear what kinds of scores are derived for each of these areas and subareas. It is assumed, but not stated directly, that these areas and subareas bear a strong resemblance to those on the SOO, from which the SBA was derived.

The materials for the SBA that were made available to this reviewer did not include evidence for the reliability and validity of this measure. The information sheet on the SBA notes that it is "a reliable, valid, and affordable employee survey," but no reference to corroborating evidence is included. The materials also allude to norms, but no information is provided. One might assume that normative data and evidence of reliability and validity are based on the SOO, from which the SBA is derived. Potential users are strongly advised to contact the test publisher for current information on norming, reliability, and validity before using the SBA.

In summary, the Small Business Assessment (SBA) is a group-administered questionnaire targeted at small businesses who would like to learn more about employee perceptions of organizational climate, supervisory leadership, peer relationships, group functioning, and overall job satisfaction. The intent in developing the SBA was to extend the basic approach of the Survey of Organizations (SOO), an existing measure used with large corporations, to businesses employing less than 100 persons. The questionnaire consists of 60 Likert-style items that seem straightforward and clearly written. The SBA appears promising, but it is essential that potential test users first contact the test publisher for any available information on norming, reliability, and validity. Without this information, the SBA scores are virtually impossible to interpret.

[291]
Spanish Assessment of Basic Education, Second Edition.

Purpose: "Designed to measure achievement in the basic skills ... with students for whom Spanish is the language of instruction."

Population: Grades 1.0–1.9, 1.6–2.9, 2.6–3.9, 3.6–4.9, 4.6–6.9, 6.6–8.9.
Publication Dates: 1991–1994.
Acronym: SABE/2.
Administration: Group.
Price Data, 1993: $9.45 per 35 practice tests (select level); $29 per 100 student diagnostic profiles (select level); $9.45 per 35 parent reports (select level); $1.20 per class record sheet; $8.35 per examiner's manual ('91, 41–57 pages) (select level); $11.45 per user's guide ('91, 64 pages); $11.45 per technical report ('94, 43 pages); $8.35 per norms book ('94, 159 pages); scoring service available from publisher.
Author: CTB Macmillan/McGraw-Hill.
Publisher: CTB Macmillan/McGraw-Hill.
a) LEVEL 1.
Population: Grades 1.0–1.9.
Scores, 11: Word Attack, Vocabulary, Reading Comprehension, Mechanics, Expression, Mathematics Computation, Mathematics Concepts and Applications, Total Reading, Total Mathematics, Total Language, Total Battery.
Price Data: $99.75 per 35 machine-scorable consumable test books; $71.75 per 35 hand-scorable consumable test books.
Time: (205) minutes.
b) LEVEL 2.
Population: Grades 1.6–2.9.
Scores: Same as *a* above.
Price Data: Same as *a* above.
Time: (219) minutes.
c) LEVEL 3.
Population: Grades 2.6–3.9.
Scores: Same as *a* above.
Price Data: Same as *a* above.
Time: (255) minutes.
d) LEVEL 4.
Population: Grades 3.6–4.9.
Scores, 12: Vocabulary, Reading Comprehension, Spelling, Mechanics, Expression, Mathematics Computation, Mathematics Concepts and Applications, Study Skills, Total Reading, Total Mathematics, Total Language, Total Battery.
Price Data: $71.75 per 35 reusable test books; $22 per 50 answer sheets (for CompuScan® or hand-scoring); $31.95 per set of 3 hand-scoring stencils.
Time: (249) minutes.
e) LEVEL 5.
Population: Grades 4.6–6.9.
Scores: Same as *d* above.
Price Data: Same as *d* above.
Time: (260) minutes.
f) LEVEL 6.
Population: Grades 6.6–8.9.
Scores: Same as *d* above.
Price Data: Same as *d* above.
Time: (259) minutes.

Review of the Spanish Assessment of Basic Education, Second Edition by MARIA PRENDES LINTEL, Assessment Coordinator, Lincoln Family Practice Program, Lincoln, NE:

The Spanish Assessment of Basic Education, Second Edition (SABE/2) is a series of norm-referenced tests for grades 1 through 8. These tests are designed to provide valid measurement of academic skills in reading, mathematics, spelling, language, and study skills for students receiving instruction in these subjects in Spanish. The intended use of the SABE/2 is initial screening and placement, instructional planning, and the reclassification of students into English-language educational programs. According to the manual, it is also useful in the placement of Spanish-speaking immigrant students in American schools.

It is assumed that teachers in bilingual programs are to administer the SABE/2 but this is not clearly stated in the manual. Teachers are warned that they should carefully evaluate the content of the levels they intend to administer making sure the levels are appropriate for the age and maturity of the students. This warning is particularly important when the level of the test used is more than two grades above or below the student's actual grade. In determining the appropriate test level to administer, the examiner must know the number of years of instruction in reading and mathematics the students received in Spanish, and the number of years of such instruction in the United States or in another country. Word Attack, Spelling, and Language tests were developed around the unique aspects of Spanish and are therefore not linked to the Comprehensive Test of Basic Skills, Forms U and V (CTBS U and V) and the California Achievement Test, Forms E and F (CAT E and F). Thus, for these tests only, normative information is indicated using raw scores. This information is available only for students tested with materials corresponding to their current grade. Functional grade level norms are available for the Reading and Mathematics tests.

The SABE/2 manual reviews the theoretical model on which Bilingual Education programs are based. This theory considers language as having two different types of proficiency. The first level of proficiency is unique to a language. In SABE/2, Word Attack, Spelling, and Language tests are used to measure these unique skills in Spanish. The second level of language proficiency involves the cognitive ability to process abstract and context-reduced information. This aspect of proficiency is common across languages. These skills were developed in the primary language and can be applied and transferred to academic tasks in a secondary language. This is a key concept in Bilingual Education and is assessed in SABE/2 through Reading and Mathematics testing. The use of this model and a unique research design in test development allows for a meaningful comparison between students tested with the SABE/2 and the achievement of English-language students tested with CTBS (U and V) and CAT (E and F). This design also allows for comparison of SABE/2 scores with a national reference group of Spanish-dominant students.

NORMATIVE DATA. Comparison betweem the SABE and SABE/2 indicates that the SABE/2 is a revised edition, which was expanded to include testing in the areas of spelling, language mechanics, language expression, and study skills. The SABE/2 was normed on a Spanish-dominant sample of over 10,000 students in grades 1 through 12. The majority of the norm-referenced groups were Mexican American (Spring 79%, Fall 78%), Puerto Rican (Spring 5%, Fall 8%), and Central and South American (Spring 4%, Fall 4%). Students from 142 schools in Arizona, California, Illinois, Massachusetts, Michigan, New Mexico, New York, Oregon, and Texas were represented. No other breakdown of norms was given. It is appropriate that the Mexican-American sample comprised the largest sample of the norm-referenced group. However, it is unfortunate that, with the exception of Puerto Ricans, no other Caribbean samples (e.g., Cuban, Dominican Republic) were represented. Further, Florida was not represented despite having a large population of Hispanics. This was perplexing because the developers went out of their way to include reviewers from Cuban-American, Mexican-American, and Puerto Rican backgrounds to evaluate all Spanish-language test items. Nevertheless, the sample size and the norming population continues to be a strength of the test and appropriate to the majority of the population for whom this test was intended. Because the SABE/2 was designed to measure basic academic skill in Spanish, only students who received Spanish reading instruction were included in the norming sample. Additionally only students with a relatively uninterrupted academic history of enrollment in bilingual programs were included. A monolingual-English-speaking-students sample consisting of 6,000 students in grades 1 through 8 was also gathered and used to calibrate the SABE/2 items to the CTBS/4.

CONTENT VALIDITY. According to the manual, the development of the SABE/2 included an extensive curricular review of state educational and regional school curricula as well as Spanish basal textbooks and Spanish-language criterion-referenced tests. Commonly identified skills to most curricula were compared to the objectives of the CTBS/4.

The test developer reported creating up to two times as many needed items. These items were reviewed for content, editorial accuracy, linguistic appropriateness, and ethnic and linguistic bias in the following manner. Individuals from Mexican-American, Puerto Rican, and Cuban-American backgrounds reviewed and evaluated all test items for appropriateness of language difficulty at each test level and for regional nuances that might be biased. Review of each test item was also conducted by experienced professionals in bilingual education whose specific duty was to focus on format, content, level of instructional difficulty, and fit to current methods and curricula in Bilingual Educational programs. The third group was experts in Bilingual Education research whose focus was the research design of the SABE/2. In all, a team of 10 experts and professional bilingual consultants in education were listed in the manual as content and linguistic reviewers for the SABE/2.

Most of the items were developed for use in the SABE/2. There were some items that were adaptations of English items from the CTBS U and V and the CTBS/4. Accordingly, the manual suggests these were used only when the items were culturally appropriate and relevant to reading, math, and study skills in Spanish. As a result of the Spanish-developed items and the adapted items, two types of items were identified. The Spanish tryout items developed originally from Spanish and the Spanish anchor items developed to establish the link between SABE/2, CTBS U and V, and CAT E and F. The development of these items is well explained in the manual and involved development of one Spanish and one English anchor item. These anchor items were written to measure the same skill and to have equivalent content at the same difficulty level. The anchor items were further evaluated by a panel of bilingual experts and were revised accordingly. Anchor items were then administered in both Spanish and English to the bilingual sample. Items on which the bilingual sample performed in a similar manner were used as final anchor items. The tryout and anchor items used in final selection were based on the statistics of the Spanish dominant sample.

DISCRIMINATION VALIDITY. Item Response Theory and a three-parameter statistical model were implemented. Each item underwent a discrimination,

guessing difficulty, and model fit indices consideration. Comparison performance amongst the various cultural groups comprised in the norming sample were reviewed to eliminate any item indicating bias. According to the manual, items with the best statistical qualities with maximum discrimination that also met the established content criteria were chosen for final selection.

RELIABILITY. The Kuder-Richardson Formula 20 was applied to the SABE/2. The internal consistency reliability for the subtests at various grade levels fell between .97 and .67, with most falling in the high .80s and low .90s. Standard error is discussed at length. Range bands are used to report scores.

The interpretations of results and scores are fully discussed in the manual. Scores are well organized and presented in either machine-scored report forms or hand-scored report forms. The forms are useful in reporting test results to the students and parents. The manual explains the different scores and reports available. The Objective Performance Report is particularly useful and identifies the student's strengths and specific needs.

In conclusion, the SABE/2 merits the attention of those who are engaged in Bilingual Education programs. The sample is fairly representative and the theory behind the test is sound. The instrument represents a welcome advancement in the field of Bilingual Education.

Review of the Spanish Assessment of Basic Education, Second Edition by EMILIA C. LOPEZ, Assistant Professor, Educational and Community Programs, Queens College of the City University of New York, Flushing, NY:

The second edition of the Spanish Assessment of Basic Education (SABE/2) is useful in determining Spanish-speaking students' instructional needs and/or planning for their transition to English-only instructional programs. The test is also appropriate for the purposes of program evaluation (e.g., evaluation of bilingual education programs).

Although large sample sizes were utilized for the piloting and the norming of the test, the characteristics of the norming sample are not clearly described. To illustrate, the manual states that the students who participated in the norming were chosen only if they had received Spanish reading instruction. However, information is not provided related to the students' history of reading instruction or levels of reading achievement in Spanish. The SABE/2 also measures achievement in the areas of mathematics, language, and writing in Spanish, but the norming sample is not described in terms of their exposure to Spanish instruction in these areas. In addition, the manual states that students were not included in the norming sample if they demonstrated a relatively uninterrupted academic history of enrollment in bilingual programs but a clear definition of "uninterrupted academic history" (p. 7) is missing. Data are also absent for such variables as the children's socioeconomic background and the parents' educational background. Of major concern is that there was no control for variables such as Spanish-language proficiency and number of years exposed to the Spanish and English languages.

The split-half reliability was reported as a measure of internal consistency. The reliability coefficients ranged from medium to high. Reliability coefficients were reported as follows: For Level 1, they ranged between .67 and .95; for Level 2, they ranged between .78 and .96; for Level 3, they ranged between .75 to .96; for Level 4, they ranged between .75 to .97; for Level 5, the reliability ranged between .72 and .96; and finally, for Level 6, the reliability ranged between .67 and .97. No other measures of reliability were reported. The standard error of measurement ranged from 1.24 to 6.95.

A major weakness of the SABE/2 is in the area of validity. Although numerous steps were taken to establish the test's content validity, data were not available in terms of the test's ability to predict the future achievement of Spanish-speaking children (i.e., predictive validity). Construct validity data are also not provided. One positive feature of the SABE/2 is that all items were reviewed for ethnic, age, and gender bias by expert panels that included individuals from various Hispanic cultural and linguistic groups.

Another advantage of this tool is that it was developed to allow comparisons of the reading and mathematics achievement of students tested by the SABE/2 in Spanish and of students tested with the Comprehensive Tests of Basic Skills, Forms U and V (CTBS) and the California Achievement Tests, Forms E and F (CAT) in English. The authors utilized samples of Spanish-dominant students, English-dominant students, and bilingual students to develop test items with similar content and difficulty levels. The items in the reading and mathematics subtests in the SABE/2 scale were then calibrated to the CTBS and norms were developed based on the calibration. Linkage is also provided with the CTBS and the CAT through the use of similar reading, math, spelling, and study skills objectives in the SABE/2.

The information provided by the authors in the area of test administration is comprehensive and clear. The practice tests are intended to help the students practice test-taking skills and should also be helpful for administrators to practice their test-administration skills.

Norm-referenced scores provided by the SABE/2 include scale scores; percentile ranks (converted to reference group percentiles reflecting the performance of [a] the Spanish-speaking children in the norming sample or [b] an English-speaking norm group); normal curve equivalents; stanines; and grade equivalents. The scoring instructions appear adequate for experienced test administrators but more details should be provided for the benefit of individuals with no previous scoring experiences (e.g., case study explaining steps for scoring). The test can be machine scored by CTB/McGraw-Hill. Additional information on test interpretation would also be helpful in the manual (e.g., case study with scores, discussion of test interpretation, and sample report) given that a number of different normed scores can be used for the purposes of test interpretation.

In addition to normed scores, the SABE/2 also provides criterion-referenced data for individual students as well as for an entire class. For example, the manual provides a list of criterion objectives for each level of the test. Each objective is accompanied by an Objective Performance Index (OPI) or an indicator of the student's level of mastery. The OPI represents the estimated probability that a given student would respond correctly to a randomly chosen item from the hypothetical pool of all possible items measuring the objective. Nonmastery is indicated if the student received an OPI of less than .50 for any objective. Graphic displays of OPI scores are available with bands for confidence levels. Items in which students reach a nonmastery level or a partial knowledge level can be targeted as potential curriculum goals.

Students' normed scores and criterion-referenced scores are available in the form of individual test records and class records. A parent report can also be generated for individual students. An evaluation summary is available for program evaluation purposes providing such data as means, medians, and quartile distributions. These reports seem helpful for descriptive purposes (e.g., providing normed scores) as well as for planning curriculum changes for individual children and groups of students (e.g., providing criterion-referenced scores).

To summarize, the SABE/2 appears to be a promising achievement tool. However, more reliability and validity studies are needed at this time to establish its utility with Spanish-speaking students. The manuals accompanying the test need to provide more extensive information in areas such as characteristics of norming sample, process of item selection, development of anchor items, calibration procedures, scoring procedures, and interpretation of scores.

[292]
Stanford Achievement Test, Ninth Edition.

Purpose: Measures student achievement in reading, language, spelling, study skills, listening, mathematics, science, and social science.

Population: Grades K.0–13.0.

Publication Dates: 1923–1997.

Acronym: Stanford 9.

Forms, 5: Multiple Choice (Complete Battery, Form S; Complete Battery, Form SA; Basic Battery, Form S; Abbreviated Battery, Form S); Open-Ended.

Administration: Group.

Levels, 12: Stanford Early Achievement Test 1, Stanford Early Achievement Test 2, Primary 1, Primary 2, Primary 3, Intermediate 1, Intermediate 2, Intermediate 3, Advanced 1, Advanced 2, Stanford Test of Academic Skills 1, Stanford Test of Academic Skills 2.

Comments: A variety of assessment options are available including full-length and abbreviated batteries, customized content modules (with locally developed items), and open-ended assessments.

Author: Harcourt Brace Educational Measurement.

Publisher: Harcourt Brace Educational Measurement.

a) STANFORD EARLY ACHIEVEMENT TEST 1.

Population: Grades K.0–K.5.

Acronym: SESAT 1.

Scores, 6: Reading (Sounds and Letters, Word Reading, Total), Mathematics, Listening to Words and Stories, Environment.

Price Data, 1996: $24 per Exam Kits (Forms S and SA) including Complete Battery Test Booklet, Directions for Administration, and Practice Test with Directions; $12 per 25 Practice Tests, Forms S and SA; $90 per Complete Battery Type 1 Machine-Scorable Test Booklets (Forms S and SA); $60 per 25 Complete Battery Hand-Scorable Test Booklets, Form S; $25 per Side-by-Side Keys for Scoring Hand-Scorable Booklets, Forms S and SA (hand-scoring requires Norms Books); $20 per Response Keys, Forms S and SA: $50 per Norms Book including scoring tables for both Multiple-Choice and Open-Ended Assessments (all levels; separate Norms Book published for fall and spring); $9.50 per Directions for Administering (Forms S and SA); $15 per 25 Multiple-Choice Complete Battery Preview for Parents; $15 per Understanding Test Results, appro-

priate for all forms and batteries; $3.50 per Class Records, appropriate for all forms and batteries; $4 per 25 Stanford Markers for all levels, appropriate for all forms and batteries; $16 per Compendium of Instructional Objectives, Forms S and SA, all levels; $20 per Strategies for Instruction: A Handbook of Performance Activities, appropriate for all forms and batteries; $24 per Guide for Organizational Planning, all levels, appropriate for all forms and batteries; $12 per Guide for Classroom Planning, appropriate for all forms and batteries; $3.50 per Directions for Administering Practice Tests, Forms S and SA; $45 per Technical Data Report for all levels, Forms S and SA; price for Technical Data Report ('97, 480 pages) available from publisher.

Time: (105) minutes for Basic Battery; (135) minutes for Complete Battery.

b) STANFORD EARLY ACHIEVEMENT TEST 2.

Population: Grades K.5–1.5.

Acronym: SESAT 2.

Scores, 7: Reading (Sounds and Letters, Word Reading, Sentence Reading, Total), Mathematics, Listening to Words and Stories, Environment.

Price Data: Same as *a* above.

Time: (140) minutes for Basic Battery; (170) minutes for Complete Battery.

c) PRIMARY 1.

Population: Grades 1.5–2.5.

1) *Multiple-Choice and Abbreviated Multiple-Choice.*

Scores, 11: Reading (Word Study Skills, Word Reading, Reading Comprehension, Total), Mathematics (Mathematics: Problem Solving, Mathematics: Procedures, Total), Language Form S, Spelling, Listening, Environment.

Price Data: Same as *a* above; $24 per Exam Kit, Multiple-Choice Assessment Abbreviated Battery, Form S including Abbreviated Battery Test Booklet, Directions for Administering, Practice Test with Directions and Open-Ended Assessment Preview Brochure; $12 per 25 Practice Tests, Form S; $70 per 25 Multiple-Choice Abbreviated Battery Type 1 Machine-Scorable Test Booklets, Forms S and SA; $20 per Multiple-Choice Abbreviated Battery Response Keys, Form S; $3.50 per Directions for Administering Practice Tests, Form S; $8 per Directions for Administering, Form S.

Time: (260) minutes for Basic Battery; (290) minutes for Complete Battery; (143) minutes for Abbreviated Battery.

2) *Open-Ended.*

Scores, 4: Reading, Mathematics, Science, Social Science.

Price Data: Same as *a* above; $8 per Open-Ended Reading Exam Kit including Open-Ended

Test Booklet and Directions for Administering; $8 per Open-Ended Mathematics Exam Kit including Open-Ended Test Booklet and Directions for Administering; $8 per Open-Ended Science Exam Kit including Open-Ended Test Booklet and Directions for Administering; $8 per Open-Ended Social Science Exam Kit including Open-Ended Test Booklet and Directions for Administering; $20 per 25 Open-Ended Reading Test Booklets, Form S including Directions for Administering; $20 per 25 Open-Ended Mathematics Test Booklets, Form S including Directions for Administering; $20 per 25 Open-Ended Science Test Booklets, Form S including Directions for Administering; $20 per 25 Open-Ended Social Science Test Booklets, Form S including Directions for Administering; $16 per Scoring Guide for Open-Ended Reading Assessment; $16 per Scoring Guide for Open-Ended Mathematics Assessment; $16 per Scoring Guide for Open-Ended Science Assessment; $16 per Scoring Guide for Open-Ended Social Science Assessment; $6 per Directions for Administering Open-Ended Reading Assessment; $6 per Directions for Administering Open-Ended Mathematics Assessment; $6 per Directions for Administering Open-Ended Science Assessment; $6 per Directions for Administering Open-Ended Social Science Assessment.

Time: (50) minutes.

d) PRIMARY 2.

Population: Grades 2.5–3.5.

1) *Multiple-Choice and Abbreviated Multiple-Choice.*

Scores, 11: Reading (Word Study Skills, Reading Vocabulary, Reading Comprehension, Total), Mathematics (Mathematics: Problem Solving, Mathematics: Procedures, Total), Language Form S, Spelling, Listening, Environment.

Price Data: Same as *a* and *c1* above.

Time: (290) minutes for Basic Battery; (290) minutes for Complete Battery; (137) minutes for Abbreviated Battery.

2) *Open-Ended.*

Scores, 4: Reading, Mathematics, Science, Social Science.

Price Data: Same as *a* and *c2* above.

Time: (50) minutes.

e) PRIMARY 3.

Population: Grades 3.5–4.5.

1) *Multiple-Choice and Abbreviated Multiple-Choice.*

Scores, 11: Reading (Reading Vocabulary, Reading Comprehension, Total), Mathematics (Mathematics: Problem Solving, Mathematics:

Procedures, Total), Language Form S, Spelling, Listening, Science, Social Science.

Price Data: Same as *a* and *c1* above; $74 per 25 Complete Battery Hand-Scorable Test Booklets including Science and Social Science, Form S subtests; $74 per 25 Complete Battery Reusable Test Booklets, Form S including Science and Social Science subtests; $74 per 25 Complete Battery Reusable Test Booklets, Form SA including Alternate Language Science and Social Science subtests (does not include separate Spelling and Study Skills subtests); $57.50 per 25 Abbreviated Battery Reusable Test Booklets, Form S; $35 per Stencil Keys for Scoring Hand-Scorable Answer Documents, Form S; $30 per Overlay keys for Scoring Machine-Scorable Answer Documents, Form S; $55 per 100 Complete Battery Type 1 machine-Scorable Answer Documents, Forms S and SA; $750 per 1,250 Continuous Form Type 1 Machine-Scorable Answer Documents, Form S; $18 per 25 Hand-Scorable Answer Folders, Form S; $45 per 100 Abbreviated Battery Type 1 Machine-Scorable Answer Documents, Form S.

Time: (250) minutes for Basic Battery; (300) minutes for Complete Battery; (123) minutes for Abbreviated Battery.

2) *Open-Ended.*

Scores, 5: Reading, Mathematics, Science, Social Science, Writing.

Price Data: Same as *a* and *c2* above; $8 per Writing Exam Kit including 1 Prompt each of Descriptive, Narrative, Expository, and Persuasive, Directions for Administering, and Response Form; $20 per Writing Prompts: Descriptive, Form S including 25 Writing Prompts, 25 Response Forms, and Directions for Administering; $20 per Writing Prompts: Narrative, Form S including 25 Writing Prompts, 25 Response forms, and Directions for Administering); $20 per Writing Prompts: Expository, Form S (including 25 Writing prompts, 25 Response Forms, and Directions for Administering); $20 per Writing Prompts: Persuasive, Form S including 25 Writing Prompts, 25 Response Forms, and Directions for Administering; $16 per Scoring Guide for Writing Assessment, all forms and levels; $16 per Anchor Papers, Descriptive, Form S; $16 per Anchor Papers, Narrative, Form S; $16 per Anchor Papers, Expository, Form S; 16 per Anchor Papers, Persuasive, Form S; $6 per Directions for Administering, Descriptive, Form S; $6 per Directions for Administering, Narrative, Form S; $6 per Directions for Administering, Expository, Form S; $6 per Directions for Administering, Persuasive, Form S.

Time: (100) minutes.

f) INTERMEDIATE 1.
Population: Grades 4.5–5.5.

1) *Multiple-Choice and Abbreviated Multiple-Choice.*

Scores, 12: Reading (Reading Vocabulary, Reading Comprehension, Total); Mathematics (Mathematics: Problem Solving, Mathematics: Procedures, Total), Language Form S, Spelling, Study Skills, Listening, Science, Social Science.

Price Data: Same as *a, c1,* and *e1* above.

Time: (275) minutes for Basic Battery; (325) minutes for Complete Battery; (121) minutes for Abbreviated Battery.

2) *Open-Ended.*

Scores, 5: Same as *e2* above.

Price Data: Same as *a, c2,* and *e2* above.

Time: (100) minutes.

g) INTERMEDIATE 2.
Population: Grades 5.5–6.5.

1) *Multiple-Choice and Abbreviated Multiple-Choice.*

Scores, 12: Same as *f1* above.

Price Data: Same as *a, c1,* and *e1* above.

Time: (275) minutes for Basic Battery; (325) minutes for Complete Battery; (121) minutes for Abbreviated Battery.

2) *Open-Ended.*

Scores, 5: Same as *e2* above.

Price Data: Same as *a, c2,* and *e2* above.

Time: (100) minutes.

h) INTERMEDIATE 3.
Population: Grades 6.5–7.5.

1) *Multiple-Choice and Abbreviated Multiple-Choice.*

Scores, 12: Same as *f1* above.

Price Data: Same as *a, c1,* and *e1* above.

Time: (275) minutes for Basic Battery; (325) minutes for Complete Battery; (121) minutes for Abbreviated Battery.

2) *Open-Ended.*

Scores, 5: Same as *e2* above.

Price Data: Same as *a, c2,* and *e2* above.

Time: (100) minutes.

i) ADVANCED 1.
Population: Grades 7.5–8.5.

1) *Multiple-Choice and Abbreviated Multiple-Choice.*

Scores, 12: Same as *f1* above.

Price Data: Same as *a, c1,* and *e2* above; $20 each per Strategies for Instruction: A Handbook of Performance Activities for Reading, Mathematics, Language/Spelling/Listening, and/or Science/Social Science.

Time: (270) minutes for Basic Battery; (320) minutes for Complete Battery; (120) minutes for Abbreviated Battery.

2) *Open-Ended.*

Scores, 5: Same as *e2* above.

Price Data: Same as *a, c2,* and *e2* above.

Time: (100) minutes.

j) ADVANCED 2.
Population: Grades 8.5–9.9.

1) *Multiple-Choice and Abbreviated Multiple-Choice.*

Scores, 12: Same as *f1* above.

Price Data: Same as *a, c1, e1,* and *i1* above.

Time: (270) minutes for Basic Battery; (320) minutes for Complete Battery; (119) minutes for Abbreviated Battery.

2) *Open-Ended.*

Scores, 5: Same as *e2* above.

Price Data: Same as *a, c2,* and *e2* above.

Time: (100) minutes.

k) STANFORD TEST OF ACADEMIC SKILLS 1.
Population: Grades 9.0–9.9.
Acronym: TASK 1.

1) *Multiple-Choice and Abbreviated Multiple-Choice.*

Scores, 9: Reading (Reading Vocabulary, Reading Comprehension, Total), Mathematics, Language Form S, Spelling, Study Skills, Science, Social Science.

Price Data: Same as *a, c1, e1,* and *i1* above; $70 per 25 Complete Battery Reusable Test Booklets, Form S including Science and Social Science subtests; $70 per Complete Battery Reusable Test Booklets, Form SA including Alternate Language, Science, and Social Science subtests (does not include separate Spelling and Study Skills subtests).

Time: (185) minutes for Basic Battery; (225) minutes for Complete Battery; (95) minutes for Abbreviated Battery.

2) *Open-Ended.*

Scores, 5: Same as *e2* above.

Price Data: Same as *a, c2,* and *e2* above.

Time: (100) minutes.

l) STANFORD TEST OF ACADEMIC SKILLS 2.
Population: Grades 10.0–10.9.
Acronym: TASK 2.

1) *Multiple-Choice and Abbreviated Multiple-Choice.*

Scores, 9: Same as *k1* above.

Price Data: Same as *a, c1, e1, i1,* and *k1* above.

Time: Same as *k1* above.

2) *Open-Ended.*

Scores, 5: Same as *e2* above.

Price Data: Same as *a, c2,* and *e2* above.

Time: (100) minutes.

m) STANFORD TEST OF ACADEMIC SKILLS 3.
Population: Grades 11.0–13.0.
Acronym: TASK 3.

1) *Multiple-Choice and Abbreviated Multiple-Choice.*

Scores, 9: Same as *k1* above.

Price Data: Same as *a, c1, e1, i1,* and *k1* above.

Time: Same as *k1* above.

2) *Open-Ended.*

Scores, 5: Same as *e2* above.

Price Data: Same as *a, c2,* and *e2* above.

Time: (100) minutes.

Cross References: For reviews of the Stanford Achievement Test—Abbreviated—8th Edition by Stephen N. Elliott and James A. Wollack and by Kevin L. Moreland, see 12:371; for information on an earlier edition of the Stanford Achievement Test, see T4:2551 (44 references); for reviews by Frederick G. Brown and Howard Stoker, see 11:377 (78 references); for reviews by Mark L. Davison and Michael J. Subkoviak and Frank H. Farley of the 1982 Edition, see 9:1172 (19 references); see also T3:2286 (80 references); for reviews by Robert L. Ebel and A. Harry Passow and an excerpted review by Irvin J. Lehmann of the 1973 edition, see 8:29 (51 references); see also T2:36 (87 references); for an excerpted review by Peter F. Merenda of the 1964 edition, see 7:25 (44 references); for a review by Miriam M. Bryan and an excerpted review by Robert E. Stake (with J. Thomas Hastings), see 6:26 (13 references); for a review by N. L. Gage of an earlier edition, see 5:25 (19 references); for reviews by Paul R. Hanna (with Claude E. Norcross) and Virgil E. Herrick, see 4:25 (20 references); for reviews by Walter W. Cook and Ralph C. Preston, see 3:18 (33 references). For reviews of subtests, see 9:1173 (1 review), 9:1174 (1 review), 9:1175 (1 review), 8:291 (2 reviews), 8:745 (2 reviews), 7:209 (2 reviews), 7:527 (1 review), 7:708 (1 review), 7:802 (1 review), 7:895 (1 review), 6:637 (1 review), 5:656 (2 reviews), 5:698 (2 reviews), 5:799 (1 review), 4:419 (1 review), 4:555 (1 review), 4:593 (2 reviews), 3:503 (1 review), and 3:595 (1 review); for a review of the Stanford Test of Academic Skills [1982 Edition] by John C. Ory, see 9:1182; see also T3:2298 (3 references); for reviews by Clinton I. Chase and Robert L. Thorndike of an earlier edition, see 8:31.

TEST REFERENCES

1. Ebmeier, H., & Schmulbach, S. (1989). An examination of the selection practices used in the Talent Search Program. *Gifted Child Quarterly, 33,* 134–141.

2. Gettinger, M. (1989). Effects of maximizing time spent and minimizing time needed for learning on pupil achievement. *American Educational Research Journal, 26,* 73-91.

3. Hersberger, J., & Wheatley, G. (1989). Computers and gifted students: An effective mathematics program. *Gifted Child Quarterly, 33,* 106–109.

4. Walczyk, J. J., & Hall, V. C. (1989). Is the failure to monitor comprehension an instance of cognitive impulsivity? *Journal of Educational Psychology, 81,* 294–298.

5. Burns, D. E. (1990). The effects of group training activities on students' initiation of creative investigations. *Gifted Child Quarterly, 34,* 31-36.

6. Finn, J. D., & Achilles, C. M. (1990). Answers and questions about class size: A statewide experiment. *American Educational Research Journal, 27,* 557-577.

7. Fuchs, D., Fuchs, L. S., & Bahr, M. W. (1990). Mainstream assistance teams: A scientific basis for the art of consultation. *Exceptional Children, 57,* 128-139.

8. Fuchs, D., Fuchs, L. S., Bahr, M. W., Fernstrom, P., & Stecker, P. M. (1990). Prereferral intervention: A prescriptive approach. *Exceptional Children, 56,* 493–513.

9. Konopak, B. C., Martin, S. H., & Martin, M. A. (1990). Using a writing strategy to enhance sixth-grade students' comprehension of content material. *Journal of Reading Behavior, 22,* 19-37.

10. Meloth, M. S. (1990). Change in poor readers' knowledge of cognition and the association of knowledge of cognition with regulation of cognition and reading comprehension. *Journal of Educational Psychology, 82,* 792–798.

11. Shefelbine, J. L. (1990). Student factors related to variability in learning word meanings from context. *Journal of Reading Behavior, 22,* 71-97.

12. Skinner, E. A., Wellborn, J. G., & Connell, J. P. (1990). What it takes to do well in school and whether I've got it: A process model of perceived control and children's engagement and achievement in school. *Journal of Educational Psychology, 82,* 22–32.

13. Sowell, E. J., Zeigler, A. J., Bergwall, L., & Cartwright, R. M. (1990). Identification and description of mathematically gifted students: A review of empirical research. *Gifted Child Quarterly, 34,* 147-154.

14. Andrews, J. F., & Mason, J. M. (1991). Strategy usage among deaf and hearing readers. *Exceptional Children, 57,* 536-545.

15. Bear, D. R., Templeton, S., & Warner, M. (1991). The development of a qualitative inventory of higher levels of orthographic knowledge. *Yearbook of National Reading Conference, 40,* 105-110.

16. Dole, J. A., Valencia, S. W., Greer, E. A., & Wardrop, J. L. (1991). Effects of two types of prereading instruction on the comprehension of narrative and expository text. *Reading Research Quarterly, 26,* 142-159.

17. Englert, C. S., Raphael, T. E., Anderson, L. M., Anthony, H. M., & Stevens, D. D. (1991). Making strategies and self-talk visible: Writing instruction in regular and special education classrooms. *American Educational Research Journal, 28,* 337-372.

18. Felson, R. B., & Trudeau, L. (1991). Gender differences in mathematics performance. *Social Psychology Quarterly, 54,* 113-126.

19. Freppon, P. A. (1991). Children's concepts of the nature and purpose of reading in different instructional settings. *Journal of Reading Behavior, 23,* 139-163.

20. Fuchs, L. S., Fuchs, D., Hamlett, C. L., & Stecker, P. M. (1991). Effects of curriculum-based measurement and consultation on teacher planning and student achievement in mathematics operations. *American Educational Research Journal, 28,* 617-641.

21. Henk, W. A., & Melnick, S. A. (1991). The initial development of a scale to measure "Perception of self as reader." *Yearbook of National Reading Conference, 41,* 111-117.

22. Konopak, B. C., Williams, N. L., Granier, D. M., Aveh, S., & Wood, K. E. (1991). Elementary students' use of imagery in developing meaning in literary text. *Yearbook of National Reading Conference, 40,* 247-254.

23. Pezaris, E., & Casey, M. B. (1991). Girls who use "masculine" problem-solving strategies on a spatial task: Proposed genetic and environmental factors. *Brain and Cognition, 17,* 1-22.

24. Purcell-Gates, V. (1991). On the outside looking in: A study of remedial readers' meaning-making while reading literature. *Journal of Reading Behavior, 23,* 235-253.

25. Deci, E. L., Hodges, R., Pierson, L., & Tomassone, J. (1992). Autonomy and competence as motivational factors in students with learning disabilities and emotional handicaps. *Journal of Learning Disabilities, 25,* 457–471.

26. Ewoldt, C., Israelite, N., & Dodds, R. (1992). The ability of deaf students to understand text: A comparison of the perceptions of teachers and students. *American Annals of the Deaf, 137,* 351-361.

27. Jarvis, P. A., & Justice, E. M. (1992). Social sensitivity in adolescents and adults with learning disabilities. *Adolescence, 27,* 977-988.

28. Kluwin, T. N., & Kelly, A. B. (1992). Deaf adolescents who drop out of local public schools. *American Annals of the Deaf, 137,* 293-298.

29. Kluwin, T. N., & Kelly, A. B. (1992). Implementing a successful writing program in public schools for student who are deaf. *Exceptional Children, 59,* 41-53.

30. Light, J., & Lindsay, P. (1992). Message-encoding techniques for augmentative communication systems: The recall performances of adults with severe speech impairments. *Journal of Speech and Hearing Research, 35,* 853–864.

31. Madison, C. L., & Wong, E. Y. F. (1992). Use of the Clark-Madison Test of Oral Language with the hearing-impaired: A content validity and comparative study. *Journal of Communication Disorders, 25,* 241–250.

32. McClelland, D. C., & Franz, C. E. (1992). Motivational and other sources of work accomplishments in mid-life: A longitudinal study. *Journal of Personality, 60,* 679–707.

33. Roberts, C., Ingram, C., & Harris, C. (1992). The effect of special versus regular classroom programming on higher cognitive processes of intermediate elementary aged gifted and average ability students. *Journal for the Education of the Gifted, 15,* 332-343.

34. Schumm, J. S., Vaughn, S., & Saumell, L. (1992). What teachers do when the textbook is tough: Students speak out. *Journal of Reading Behavior, 24,* 481-503.

35. Siegel, L. S. (1992). An evaluation of the discrepancy definition of dyslexia. *Journal of Learning Disabilities, 25,* 618–629.

36. Alvarez, M. C. (1993). Imaginative uses of self-selected cases. *Reading Research and Instruction, 32(2),* 1-18.

37. Braeges, J., Stinson, M. S., & Long, G. (1993). Teachers' and deaf students' perceptions of communication ease and engagement. *Rehabilitation Psychology, 38,* 235–246.

38. Coleman, J. M., & Dover, G. M. (1993). The RISK screening test: Using kindergarten teachers' ratings to predict future placement in resource classrooms. *Exceptional Children, 59,* 468-477.

39. Ginsburg, G. S., & Bronstein, P. (1993). Family factors related to children's intrinsic/extrinsic motivational orientation and academic performance. *Child Development, 64,* 1461-1474.

40. Hauck, A. L., & Finch, A. J., Jr. (1993). The effect of relative age on achievement in middle school. *Psychology in the Schools, 30,* 74-79.

41. Hirschhorn, D. B. (1993). A longitudinal study of students completing four years of UCSMP mathematics. *Journal for Research in Mathematics Education, 24,* 136-158.

42. Holt, J. A. (1993). Stanford Achievement Test—8th Edition: Reading comprehension subgroup results. *American Annals of the Deaf, 138,* 172-175.

43. Howerton, D. L., Enger, J. M., & Cobbs, C. R. (1993). Locus of control and achievement for at-risk adolescent black males. *The High School Journal, 76,* 210-214.

44. Kelly, L. P. (1993). Recall of English function words and inflections by skilled and average deaf readers. *American Annals of the Deaf, 138,* 288-296.

45. Kibby, M. W. (1993). What reading teachers should know about reading proficiency in the U.S. *Journal of Reading, 37,* 28-40.

46. Kluwin, T. N. (1993). Cumulative effects of mainstreaming on the achievement of deaf adolescents. *Exceptional Children, 60,* 73-81.

47. Mehrens, W. A., & Clarizio, H. F. (1993). Curriculum-based measurement: Conceptual and psychometric considerations. *Psychology in the Schools, 30,* 241-254.

48. Reynolds, R. E., Trathen, W., Sawyer, M. L., & Shepard, C. R. (1993). Casual and epiphenomenal use of the selective attention strategy in prose comprehension. *Contemporary Educational Psychology, 18,* 258-278.

49. Schirmer, B. R. (1993). Constructing meaning from narrative text. *American Annals of the Deaf, 138,* 397-403.

50. Uhry, J. K., & Shepherd, M. J. (1993). Segmentation/spelling instruction as part of a first-grade reading program: Effects on several measures of reading. *Reading Research Quarterly, 28,* 219-233.

51. Vaughn, S., Schumm, J. S., & Kouzekanani, K. (1993). What do students with learning disabilities think when their general education teachers make adaptations? *Journal of Learning Disabilities, 26,* 545–555.

52. Wood, E., Willoughby, T., Bolger, A., Younger, J., & Kasper, V. (1993). Effectiveness of elaboration strategies for grade school children as a function of academic achievement. *Journal of Experimental Child Psychology, 56,* 240-253.

53. Alberti, E. T., & Witryol, S. L. (1994). The relationship between curiosity and cognitive ability in third- and fifth-grade children. *The Journal of Genetic Psychology, 155,* 129-145.

54. Allinder, R. M., & Fuchs, L. S. (1994). Alternative ways of analyzing effects of a short school break on students with and without disabilities. *School Psychology Quarterly, 9,* 145-160.

55. Andrews, J. F., Winograd, P., & DeVille, G. (1994). Deaf children reading fables: Using ASL summaries to improve reading comprehension. *American Annals of the Deaf, 139,* 378-386.

56. Blennerhassett, L., Strohmeier, S. J., & Hibbett, C. (1994). Criterion-related validity of Raven's Progressive Matrices with deaf residential school students. *American Annals of the Deaf, 139,* 104-110.

57. Desselle, D. D. (1994). Self-esteem, family climate, and communication patterns in relation to deafness. *American Annals of the Deaf, 139,* 322-328.

58. Epstein, K. I., Hillegeist, E. G., & Grafman, J. (1994). Number processing in deaf college students. *American Annals of the Deaf, 139,* 336-347.

59. Flynn, J. M., & Rahbar, M. H. (1994). Prevalence of reading failure in boys compared with girls. *Psychology in the Schools, 31,* 66-71.

60. Holt, J. (1994). Classroom attributes and achievement test scores for deaf and hard of hearing students. *American Annals of the Deaf, 139,* 430-437.

61. Kluwin, T. N. (1994). The interaction of race, gender, and social class effects in the education of deaf students. *American Annals of the Deaf, 139,* 465-471.

62. Kluwin, T. N., & Gaustad, M. G. (1994). The role of adaptability and communication in fostering cohesion in families with deaf adolescents. *American Annals of the Deaf, 139,* 329-335.

63. McCutchen, D., & Crain-Thoreson, C. (1994). Phonemic processes in children's reading comprehension. *Journal of Experimental Child Psychology, 58,* 69-87.

64. Meyer, L. A., Stahl, S. A., & Wardrop, J. L. (1994). Effects of reading storybooks aloud to children. *The Journal of Educational Research, 88,* 69–85.

65. Rittenhouse, R. K., Kenyon, P. L., & Healy, S. (1994). Auditory specialization in deaf children. *American Annals of the Deaf, 139,* 80-85.

66. Zimmerman, B. J., & Bandura, A. (1994). Impact of self-regulatory influences on writing course adjustment. *American Educational Research Journal, 31,* 845-862.

67. Baker, J. M. (1995). Inclusion in Minnesota: Educational experiences of students with learning disabilities in two elementary schools. *The Journal of Special Education, 29,* 133–143.

68. Banerji, M., & Dailey, R. A. (1995). A study of the effects of an inclusion model on students with specific learning disabilities. *Journal of Learning Disabilities, 28,* 511–522.

69. Cosden, M., Zimmer, J., Reyes, C., & Gutierrez, M. (1995). Kindergarten practices and first-grade achievement for Latino Spanish-speaking, Latino English-speaking, and Anglo students. *Journal of School Psychology, 33,* 123-141.

70. Haager, D., & Vaughn, S. (1995). Parent, teacher, peer, and self-reports of the social competence of students with learning disabilities. *Journal of Learning Disabilities, 28,* 205–215, 231.

71. Holt, J. (1995). Efficiency of screening procedures for assigning levels of the Stanford Achievement Test (Eighth Edition) to students who are deaf or hard of hearing. *American Annals of the Deaf, 140,* 23–27.

72. Joshi, R. M. (1995). Assessing reading and spelling skills. *School Psychology Review, 24,* 361–375.

73. Kelly, L. P. (1995). Processing of bottom-up and top-down information by skilled and average deaf readers and implications for whole language instruction. *Exceptional Children, 61,* 318–334.

74. Kindlon, D., Mezzacappa, E., & Earls, F. (1995). Psychometric properties of impulsivity measures: Temporal stability, validity and factor structure. *Journal of Child Psychology and Psychiatry and Allied Disciplines, 36,* 645-661.

75. Shull-Senn, S., Weatherly, M., Morgan, S. K., & Bradley-Johnson, S. (1995). Stability reliability for elementary-age students on the Woodcock-Johnson Psycho-Educational Battery—Revised (Achievement Section) and the Kaufman Test of Educational Achievement. *Psychology in the Schools, 32,* 86–92.

76. Turner, J. C. (1995). The influence of classroom contexts on young children's motivation for literacy. *Reading Research Quarterly, 30,* 410–441.

77. Brown, R., Pressley, M., Van Meter, P., & Schuder, T. (1996). A quasi-experimental validation of transactional strategies instruction with low-achieving second-grade readers. *Journal of Educational Psychology, 88,* 18–37.

78. Miserandino, M. (1996). Children who do well in school: Individual differences in perceived competence and autonomy in above-average children. *Journal of Educational Psychology, 88,* 203–214.

79. Stinson, M. S., Whitmire, K., & Kluwin, T. N. (1996). Self-perceptions of social relationships in hearing-impaired adolescents. *Journal of Educational Psychology, 88,* 132–143.

80. Swanson, S., & Howell, C. (1996). Test anxiety in adolescents with learning disabilities and behavior disorders. *Exceptional Children, 62,* 389–397.

Review of the Stanford Achievement Test, Ninth Edition by RONALD A. BERK, Professor of Biostatistics and Measurement, School of Nursing, Johns Hopkins University, Baltimore, MD:

The ninth edition of the Stanford Achievement Test (Stanford 9) is the latest version of a test that began in 1923. The decision by the publisher to produce this edition was based primarily on three considerations: (a) significant changes that have occurred in the school curriculum, (b) need to update norms and interpretative materials, and (c) need to provide for the continuous assessment of achievement in the major skill areas. The tests also reflect changes in the testing technology since the eighth edition, particularly in terms of the performance assessment movement that has permeated every level of educational assessment. This edition is distinguished in both substance and form from its predecessors. A few of the key differences are the use of "extended" multiple-choice items, inclusion of open-ended constructed-response assessments, alignment of items with national content standards, projects, and models, and the use of a four-tier performance standard structure to interpret the scores.

CONTENT SPECIFICATIONS. The specifications or blueprint for building this edition of the Stanford were derived from analyses of the most recent editions of major textbook series in relevant subject areas, the most recent state and district school curricula and objectives, and the most important trends in education according to national professional organizations in reading, mathematics, language, writing, science, and social science. Further, these new specifications were aligned with national standards and projects, such as the National Assessment of Educational Progress (NAEP), Curriculum and Evaluation Standards for School Mathematics (NCTM), Writing Process Model, National Science Education Standards (NRC), and National Council for the Social Studies Curriculum Standards. Despite these efforts by the publisher to specify content and objectives reflective of national core standards, only test users in schools and school districts can judge the congruence of these standards with their own. This criterion should be a primary consideration in reviewing the Stanford 9.

ITEM DEVELOPMENT. Consistent with the trends toward multiple forms of assessment, real-world assessment experiences, and higher order complex cognitive processes, the items for this edition consist of a combination of multiple-choice and open-ended formats. "Enhanced" multiple-choice items were generated from the specifications to reflect classroom or real-life situations, integrate process with knowledge, and elicit actual performance. The distribution of items measuring basic understanding and thinking skills is reported in the technical manual for all subtests and levels. The extremely comprehensive multiple-choice test battery is complemented with an open-ended battery in Reading, Mathematics, Science, and Social Science, in addition to Writing. These assessments include grade-appropriate selections, questions, and problems to measure reasoning abilities. It is intended that teachers score these items so that they can witness their students' thinking and reasoning processes within the content areas. A holistic/analytic scoring system is used whereby the questions are double classified according to process and content. Detailed and very clearly prescribed guidelines for scoring are provided. Functionally, items are scored from 0–3. Scoring rubrics and sample student responses along with annotated anchor papers are given with the explicit point scoring for every answer.

Although the publisher intended the multiple-choice and open-ended batteries to be used separately as well as in combination, their technical quality and relationships between the different tests (described later in this review) suggest the batteries are very different, both in content and format, and should be considered as complementary rather than as alternatives to furnish a more complete assessment of a student's skills. However, the test user must review the items in the batteries in conjunction with the content specifications to determine the appropriateness of the Stanford 9 for local applications. If mismatches occur between what needs to be measured and what the Stanford 9 measures, the publisher offers customized test construction services to tailor the Stanford 9 to individual school or district requirements.

The national field-testing of all items followed a traditional classical test theory model of item analysis. It included p-values (item difficulty) and biserial correlations (item discrimination) of at least .35 (item-subtest r). Given the history of the Stanford 9, this model is appropriate, although others, such as item response theories, might be considered in future editions. One such theory, the Rasch model, was used to equate the various test forms and levels of the batteries.

STANDARDIZATION AND NORMS. Standardizations of the Stanford 9 were based on stratified random samples of 250,000 students from 1,000 school districts during spring of 1995, and another 200,000 students during the fall. A separate sample of 80,000 students was selected to participate in the equating study of levels, forms, and the Stanford, Eighth Edition. The stratification variables were socioeconomic status, urbanicity, and ethnicity. Students attending Catholic schools and other private schools were systematically oversampled to report separate norms for these groups. The acceptance rates to the standardization invitations were 20% and 30% for the spring and fall, respectively. A total of 49 states and the District of Columbia were represented in the standardizations.

Normative derived scores reported for these standardization samples include: (a) scaled scores, which are equivalent across forms and levels of the same subtest and domain total; (b) individual percentile ranks and stanines; (c) grade equivalents; (d) normal curve equivalents; (e) achievement/ability comparisons (discrepancy score tables based on the standard error of the difference score would be much easier to use and more precise); and (f) group percentile ranks and stanines. Objective-referenced information is also given for subskills as content clusters within a subtest or domain and as process clusters representing thinking and reasoning skills in each content area. This analysis of performance can be used to identify students' strengths and weaknesses in specific objectives within a content area. Item p-values (percent correct) are reported to compare item difficulty values of a local group with those of the national sample. Performance indicators are 0–3 scores, available as item, cluster, and total scores for the open-ended assessments.

PERFORMANCE STANDARDS. In addition to all of the preceding derived scores developed for the Stanford 9, four levels of performance standards were set: (a) less than partial mastery, (b) partial mastery, (c) solid academic performance, and (d) superior performance. A psychometrically defensible modified Angoff procedure employing iterations and impact data was executed using a national representative sample of 200 teachers, divided into 16 standard-setting panels. Standards were set over a 3-week series of meetings for grade level/subject area combinations, including both multiple-choice and open-ended subtests. Normative comparisons are also possible against percentages of students in the standardization sample that met each performance standard.

RELIABILITY. Reliability is the degree to which test scores are consistent, dependable, or repeatable, that is, free of errors of measurement. Several indices are reported: (a) Kuder-Richardson Formula 20 (K-R20) coefficients and standard errors of measurement for the multiple-choice battery and alpha coefficients for the open-ended assessments and multiple-choice/open-ended composite scores; (b) Kuder-Richardson Formula 21 coefficients and standard errors of measurement for all multiple-choice clusters, subtests, and totals; (c) alternate-forms coefficients and standard errors of measurement for the multiple-choice battery; and (d) interrater coefficients using the Pearson correlation and the Spearman-Brown Prophecy formula for the descriptive, expository, narrative, and persuasive writing assessments only.

Based on the intended uses of the scores for individual decisions about students, the K-R20 coefficients were in the acceptable range of the mid .80s to .90s for most tests and subtests of the full multiple-choice battery (spring and fall standardization samples). Only the Listening, Language, Science, and Social Science coefficients were in the .70s to low .80s for several grade levels. Caution should be exhibited in interpreting these specific test scores.

The alpha coefficients for the open-ended assessments in Reading, Mathematics, Science, and Social Science were considerably lower than their multiple-choice counterparts. Most were in the .60s to low .80s with a few even lower. Coefficients at these magnitudes are not unusual for the types of tasks and scoring rubrics included in these tests. When both the multiple-choice and open-ended assessments were combined, the alpha coefficients for composite scores were in the mid .80s to .90s. Unfortunately, the majority of the coefficients for the Language Composites were a few notches lower in the .70s to mid .80s. These coefficients on the open-ended assessments indicate that the scores should not be used alone for any high-stakes individual decisions. They should be interpreted in conjunction with the multiple-choice assessments and incorporated into classroom instructional activities and, perhaps, even included in a student's portfolio, as suggested by the test publisher.

Consistent with the K-R20 coefficients for the multiple-choice batteries are the K-R21 coefficients for subtests, which typically range from the .70s to the .90s. The coefficients for the clusters within each subtest, however, are considerably lower. The score profile reports for the clusters should be used to guide instructional decisions.

The alternate-forms coefficients estimated from the equating of the Form S and Form T sample for the multiple-choice assessment were in the .80s for most of the Total Reading, Total Mathematics, and Language tests, and in the .70s or lower for the remaining tests and Reading and Language subtests. The coefficients for the open-ended assessment were in the .60s and .70s for most assessments, except Writing, which ranged from the .30s to the .60s.

The final set of reliability coefficients reported in the technical manual were interrater coefficients for the open-ended writing assessments only, which are extremely important to evaluate the objectivity-subjectivity involved in the scoring process. The simple correlations ranged from the .50s to mid-.80s and the Spearman-Brown estimates generally ranged from the .70s to mid-.90s. This evidence provides borderline usefulness of the separate writing assessments for individual decisions, although such coefficients for holistically scored verbal prompt formats are not unusual. There are no other assessment techniques that can directly measure prewriting, composing, and editing skills much more reliably.

In summary, all of the reliability evidence currently available on this edition of the Stanford indicates that the multiple-choice batteries and multiple choice/open-ended composite scores yield high levels of score reliability. The open-ended assessments are considerably less reliable and should not be used alone for any individual high-stakes decisions. These assessments and the cluster scores should be used to guide instructional decisions. Reliability coefficients not reported but important for teacher decisions are interrater coefficients for all of the open-ended assessments other than writing and decision-consistency coefficients for the performance standards recommended for criterion-referenced interpretations. The estimates would have been very useful in judging the quality of the "new" open-ended assessments in this test edition.

VALIDITY. Validity is the degree to which a certain inference from a test is appropriate or meaningful. Evidence on the three traditional categories of validity are described in the technical manual: (a) content, (b) criterion-related, and (c) construct. The most important pertains to content-related validity. The items on the Stanford 9 were reviewed during the development phase for content, style, and appropriateness for measuring the instructional objectives by a panel of content experts, editors, measurement specialists, and teachers. However, because validity is contingent on the specific test use and application, the test user in the school or school district must review the test content and compare the Stanford 9 Compendium of Instructional Objectives with the objectives of their school's or district's curriculum. Once these reviews are completed at the local level, the extent to which the curriculum is taught in the school(s) should be evaluated to determine whether students have the opportunity to learn the content and answer all of the questions. The publisher provides the user with completion rates as a guide for all multiple-choice subtests at every level. For most tests (Forms S & T) these rates are in the 90s. Only in Mathematics and Science did the rates drop lower than the other tests for grades 9 and above. These rates need to be estimated by the user to furnish evidence of the appropriateness of the tests as measures of power rather than speed.

Related to content validity is bias and/or stereotyping in the item content in terms of gender, ethnicity, culture, socioeconomic status, and geographic region. The entire battery was scrutinized by an advisory panel of prominent minority-group educators to identify objectionable items, which were subsequently eliminated or revised. In addition to these appropriate "judgmental" procedures, comprehensive quantitative analyses using the Mantel-Haenszel statistic were conducted for gender and Caucasian, African-American, and Hispanic student sample comparisons. Items flagged by this differential item functioning (DIF) method were reviewed and possibly excluded from the final test forms. All of these analyses are required to assure that the items are valid for all examinees.

Evidence of criterion-related validity was reported in the forms of item statistics, including median p-values and biserial correlations, means and standard deviations of scaled scores, correlations between the eighth and ninth editions, and correlations between the multiple-choice and open-ended assessments. The latter correlations, in particular, are the most interesting. For the majority of tests and subtests (both forms), the multiple-choice and open-ended assessments have less than 60% in common in

terms of the content they measure and large percentages of unique content measured by each assessment format. Consequently, one assessment should not be used in lieu of the other. Each provides significantly different information on a student's performance in each content area.

Construct validity evidence is reported as correlations between the multiple-choice subtests and subtests of the Otis-Lennon School Ability Test, which demonstrate the interrelationships between school achievement and ability, and between the multiple-choice subtests at adjacent grade levels, which demonstrate the continuity of the content being measured across different levels. Correlations between the Stanford battery and other popular achievement batteries, such as the California Achievement Tests (40) and Iowa Tests of Basic Skills (159), would have been more informative of the constructs measured by those achievement tests and subtests.

SUMMARY. This latest edition of the Stanford Achievement Test Series is the most comprehensive and psychometrically studied of any edition. It builds on its long tradition of excellence to include "enhanced" multiple-choice items, open-ended items in all major content areas, multiple-level performance standards, conormed achievement/ability comparisons, and extensive and appropriate analyses of bias, reliability, and validity. Schools and school districts searching for an up-to-date achievement assessment series should give the Stanford 9 serious consideration.

Review of the Stanford Achievement Test, Ninth Edition by THOMAS M. HALDYNA, Professor of Educational Psychology, College of Education, Arizona State University West, Phoenix, AZ:

The Stanford Achievement Test, Ninth Edition (Stanford 9) is one of the most popular and well developed of a small number of published, standardized, survey achievement tests available to school districts and states. The Stanford was introduced in 1923 and continues to provide high quality information about student achievement in a variety of subject matters.

TEST CONTENT. The stated intent of this publisher is to reflect the result of extensive curriculum review and analysis in addition to large-scale research programs. References were provided for textbooks series and other sources of content. The technical manual for the Stanford 9 is very extensive and provides a rich source of statistical and procedural evidence that was used in this review. The rationale for the Stanford 9 is three-fold: (a) reflecting changes in school curricula, (b) updating norms, and (c) providing for a continuous scale that crosses many grade levels. Indeed, the publishers have been successful in accomplishing all three objectives. The Stanford 9 reflects the consideration of standards of leading professional organizations and the content emphases of many textbook series. The introduction of the performance items (in earlier versions of the Stanford) has created the versatility to measure a variety of student outcomes, some of which are not well suited to the multiple-choice format.

COMPARABILITY/EQUATING. Correlations between comparable forms of Stanford 9 and Stanford 8 scores were about as high as reliability permitted, showing the strong relationship between content tested on the prior and present forms. Correlations between a mental ability test (the Otis Lennon) and Stanford 9 scores were fairly high. The high degree of relationship among all measures suggests a dominant factor, namely mental ability, that pervades all tests. These results seemed consistent at all levels of the Stanford 9.

SCALING. The scaled scores ranged from the low 400s to about 700. Means were reported for each grade level for each test and major subtest. These means can provide useful benchmarks, standards, or targets for school districts or states intending to show progress. However, users might want to avoid subscore scales as the amount of growth can be very small and less reliably measured from grade level to grade level.

ITEM QUALITY. Item quality is a complex construct. First we should consider the procedures followed to develop the item and then consider statistical data arising from field testing. Some of the issues to be considered in this section are the formats used, the content of items, the type of mental behaviors exhibited, whether the item received reviews by content experts, and whether bias or sensitivity reviews were done, and the degree to which the items received editing for clarity. In the technical manual, the publishers stated that items were developed, reviewed, and edited appropriately. The item development effort focused on two kinds of items: basic understanding and thinking skills. Rather than work with the cumbersome Bloom taxonomy, the publishers have sensibly used this two-level system that will be easier to understand and apply to classroom teaching and testing.

A sampling of performance and multiple-choice items were evaluated in terms of clarity, cognitive level elicited from students, editorial quality, use of graphics, bias/sensitivity, and adherence to item-writing rules. Both the multiple-choice and performance items reflected all the necessary steps used in high quality testing programs. Items were generally clearly presented and engaging. Graphics were very effectively used in both item formats. The use of four-option and occasionally five-option multiple-choice items seems disappointing in light of research showing that most test items have only two or three "working" options. No data were offered about the frequency of choice for distractors or their discriminating ability. This would be a source of possible improvement for the Stanford 10. Some of the performance items could be presented in a multiple-choice format. In other words, the cognitive behavior underlying the item was identification with a clear right answer. Research has not yet clearly demonstrated that the information gained from such performance items is very different from information obtained by multiple-choice in these circumstances. Many of these performance items seem to reflect what can be measured with less expensive multiple-choice.

To address the issue of the information gained from performance items in the Stanford 9, reliability and correlational data for multiple-choice, open-ended, and composite test scores were assembled from the technical manual for three comprehensive batteries: Primary 1, Intermediate 1, and Advanced 1. When correlations between multiple-choice and open-ended scores were corrected for attenuation, results were generally in the .80s, suggesting that a good overlap existed between the two sets of scores (multiple-choice and open-ended) but some variance was unique to the format.

Statistical qualities of the multiple-choice items were what you would expect from a high quality survey achievement test; difficulties ranged appropriately from .40s to .80s with a few exceptions. Median biserial correlations between item and total test performance (a measure of item discrimination) were very high.

For the performance items, both difficulty and discrimination values were reported for all items. Median item-total correlations were consistently high.

RELIABILITY. Reliability coefficients for the multiple-choice parts of the Stanford 9 are consistently in a very high range. Because these test scores are often reported as group means (for example, by class, school, district, or state), the reliability of group means is often much higher than for individuals. Therefore, users should have a good deal of confidence in test scores they receive from the multiple-choice parts of the Stanford 9.

The reliability of performance tests ranged from .61 to .88. Interrater consistency is very high.

Although the performance-based reliability coefficients are not as good as multiple-choice reliability coefficients, these indexes are high enough to suggest that when scores are grouped by class, school, district, or state, reliability will be very high. High-stakes decisions on the basis of performance tests should NOT be done or done with extreme caution.

Writing score reliabilities were unreported but by inference must be very low, because composite reliabilities (multiple-choice and performance) were often lower than multiple-choice alone. Composite score reliabilities for other tests were high, but not as high as one might expect. Coefficients ranged from .68 to low .90s. Some of the coefficients for multiple-choice tests were nearly as good or even better than the composite reliabilities, thus attesting to the inferior reliabilities of the open-ended tests.

Subscale reliabilities were predictably low. One should never report or use subscores at the individual level, but the reliability of these subscores at the class, school, district, or state levels would be more reliable, hence usable. It would be helpful for the publishers to present the reliabilities of group means so consumers have more confidence in their use. It is not clear why KR-21s are reported when the more desirable KR-20 coefficients are easily computed. The alternate forms reliability coefficients are impressive after we consider that the reliabilities of the alternate forms provides a ceiling for the correlation of alternate forms scores.

TEST ADMINISTRATION IRREGULARITIES. Speededness did not seem to be a problem in these timed tests. Completion rates were fairly high for most tests, with a median in the 90%–100% range. The few tests that have a lower completion rate will cast suspicions on test scores. Is the time allotment too little or student motivation inadequate?

CONCLUSIONS. The tests that comprise the Stanford 9 are staggering in number, measuring a stack over 3 feet high, including technical manuals and other accompanying materials. Any review of this series will probably be inadequate from the standpoint of thoroughness. Thus, these conclusions are tempered by the enormity of the task undertaken by this reviewer.

The publishers of the Stanford 9 should be commended for developing a survey achievement test battery that addresses the needs of school districts and states. The availability of practice tests, full length batteries, abbreviated versions of the full length batteries, and the added performance options makes the Stanford 9 very versatile in terms of the needs of consumers. Differences in orientation to curriculum,

learning theory, instruction, and sequence of learning can be addressed using the customization feature of the Stanford 9.

Some limitations are reported. Foremost, in the crucial area of test use, the publishers have been circumspect instead of direct. Although testing specialists have written volumes about misinterpretation and misuse of test results, this publisher, like many other publishers, avoids this conflict and continues to provide test results that are often inappropriately used.

For school districts and states wanting dependable test information about students for the purposes of evaluating curriculum, instructional programs, and making decisions about resource allocations to improve student learning, the Stanford 9 offers quite a bit. But these school districts and states will have to be very careful about matching the tests they choose to the intended interpretations and uses. Careful curriculum review and evaluation of these options in the Stanford 9 series should help school districts and states make good choices about how the Stanford 9 can satisfy their information needs.

A word of caution is offered about the open-ended tests. Although some evidence was presented for the extra information available with open-ended items, the cost and benefits of such assessment must be evaluated by anyone considering adopting the Stanford 9 with the open-ended tests. With the writing tests, potential users need to be very cautious and ask the publisher for more data supporting its use. In particular, reliability may be a problem.

All things considered, the Stanford 9 measures up very well to testing standards. Once again the Stanford series appears to be one of the best, most comprehensive, standardized survey achievement tests available.

[293]
Stanford Diagnostic Mathematics Test, Fourth Edition.

Purpose: Designed to measure "competence in the basic concepts and skills that are prerequisite to problem solving in mathematics."

Publication Dates: 1976–1996.

Acronym: SDMT.

Administration: Group.

Parts, 2: Multiple Choice, Free Response.

Forms: 1 for Red, Orange, and Green levels; 2 (J, K) for Purple, Brown, and Blue levels.

Price Data, 1997: $27 per examination kit including multiple-choice test booklet and free-response test booklet (specify level) and directions for administering for each, answer document, practice test and practice test directions for administering, and ruler/marker; $12 per 25 practice tests and directions (specify level); $85.50 per 25 machine-scorable multiple-choice test booklets (specify Red, Orange, or Green level); $59 per 25 hand-scorable multiple-choice test booklets (specify Red, Orange, or Green level), directions for administering, and class record; $59 per 25 free-response test booklets (specify Red, Orange, or Green level) and directions for administering; $85.50 per hand-scorable multiple-choice/free-response combination kit including 25 hand-scorable multiple-choice test booklets and directions for administering, 25 free-response test booklets and directions for administering, and class record (specify Red, Orange, or Green level); $107 per machine-scorable multiple-choice/free response combination kit including 25 machine-scorable multiple-choice test booklets and directions for administering and 25 free-response test booklets and directions for administering (specify Red, Orange, or Green level); $59 per 25 reusable multiple-choice test booklets and directions for administering (specify Purple, Brown, or Blue level and Form J or K); $59 per 25 free response test booklets and directions for administering (specify Purple, Brown, or Blue level and Form J or K); $85.50 per reusable multiple-choice/free-response combination kit including 25 reusable multiple-choice test booklets and directions for administering and 25 free-response test booklets and directions for administering (specify Purple, Brown, or Blue level and Form J or K); $11 per set of response keys for multiple-choice tests (specify level and form); $11 per side-by-side keys for hand-scorable test booklets including blackline master of student record form (specify Red, Orange, or Green level); $11 per scoring guide for free-response tests including blackline master of student record form (specify level and form); $16 per stencil keys for hand-scorable answer documents (specify Purple, Brown, or Blue level and Form J or K); $21.50 per 25 hand-scorable answer documents with blackline master of student record form and class record (specify Purple, Brown, or Blue level); $27 per 25 Purple/Brown/Blue level machine-scorable answer documents type I; $4.50 per 25 ruler/markers; $37.50 per Fall ('96, 166 pages) or Spring ('96, 166 pages) multilevel norms booklet; $16 per teacher's manual for interpreting (specify Level Red/Orange ['96, 61 pages], Green/Purple ['96, 64 pages], or Brown/Blue ['96, 63 pages]); $7.50 per directions for administering (specify multiple-choice or free-response, and Level Red, Orange, Green, or Purple/Brown/Blue); $4.50 per practice test directions for administering (specify Red, Orange, Green, Purple, or Brown Level); $4.50 per class record (specify Red, Orange, Green, or Purple/Brown/Blue level); prince information for various scoring services available from publisher.

Author: Harcourt Brace Educational Measurement.

Publisher: Harcourt Brace Educational Measurement.

a) RED LEVEL.

Population: Grades 1.5–2.5.

Scores, 9: Concepts and Applications (Number Systems and Numeration, Patterns and Functions,

Graphs and Tables, Problem Solving, Geometry and Measurement, Total), Computation (Addition of Whole Numbers, Subtraction of Whole Numbers, Total).

Time: 65 minutes for multiple choice; 90 minutes for free response.

b) ORANGE LEVEL.

Population: Grades 2.5–3.5.

Scores, 9: Same as for Red level.

Time: Same as for Red level.

c) GREEN LEVEL.

Population: Grades 3.5–4.5.

Scores, 11: Concepts and Applications (Number Systems and Numeration, Patterns and Functions, Graphs and Tables, Problem Solving, Geometry and Measurement, Total), Computation (Addition of Whole Numbers, Subtraction of Whole Numbers, Multiplication of Whole Numbers, Division of Whole Numbers, Total).

Time: Same as for Red level.

d) PURPLE LEVEL.

Population: Grades 4.5–6.5.

Scores, 12: Concepts and Applications (Number Systems and Numeration, Statistics and Probability, Graphs and Tables, Problem Solving, Geometry and Measurement, Patterns and Functions [free response only], Total), Computation (Addition of Whole Numbers, Subtraction of Whole Numbers, Multiplication of Whole Numbers, Division of Whole Numbers, Total).

Time: 65 minutes for multiple choice; 80 minutes for free response.

e) BROWN LEVEL.

Population: Grades 6.5–8.9.

Scores, 15: Concepts and Applications (Number Systems and Numeration, Patterns and Functions [free response only], Statistics and Probability, Graphs and Tables, Problem Solving, Geometry and Measurement, Total), Computation (Addition and Subtraction of Whole Numbers, Multiplication of Whole Numbers [multiple choice only], Division of Whole Numbers [multiple choice only], Multiplication and Division of Whole Numbers [free response only], Operations with Fractions and Mixed Numbers, Operations with Decimals and Percents, Equations, Total).

Time: Same as Purple level.

f) BLUE LEVEL.

Population: Grades 9.0–13.0.

Scores, 12: Concepts and Applications (Number Systems and Numeration, Patterns and Functions [free response only], Statistics and Probability, Graphs and Tables, Problem Solving, Geometry and Measurement, Total), Computation (Operations with Whole Numbers, Operations with Fractions and Mixed Numbers, Operations with Decimals and Percents, Equations, Total).

Time: Same as Purple level.

Cross References: See T4:2554 (5 references); for reviews by Bruce G. Rogers and Lorrie A. Shepard of an earlier edition, see 9:1177 (2 references); see also T3:2291 (1 reference); for reviews by Glenda Lappan and Larry Souder, see 8:292.

Review of the Stanford Diagnostic Mathematics Test, Fourth Edition by IRVIN J. LEHMANN, Professor of Measurement, Michigan State University, East Lansing, MI:

Whereas traditional achievement tests are designed to measure the strengths and weaknesses of individuals in a variety of content areas, diagnostic tests are primarily concerned with measuring skills or abilities that subject-matter specialists believe are essential in learning a particular subject and are important for diagnosis or remediation. In other words, whereas an arithmetic achievement test is designed to measure a student's knowledge of arithmetic, a diagnostic arithmetic test is designed to learn what difficulties a student may have, for example, in addition and carrying. Therefore, diagnostic tests place more emphasis on the lower achiever who is having problems. Thus, they contain more easy questions than do general mathematics achievement tests, which are intended to measure the broad range of ability of the entire student population.

The primary purpose of the Stanford Diagnostic Mathematics Test, Fourth Edition (SDMT 4) "is to determine specific areas in which each student is having difficulty. Once these problem areas have been identified, students can be given help that will enable them to make satisfactory progress in the instructional sequence" (teacher's manual for interpreting, p. 7). The former illustrates the diagnostic purpose of the SDMT 4 whereas the latter is aligned with the test's instructional purpose. This reviewer has no argument with the test's primary purpose (i.e., "assisting students who lack some of the essential mathematical skills," multilevel norms booklet, p. 7). What does concern me are some of the other claims made concerning the test's purpose. For example, why should a diagnostic test be used "to challenge students who are doing well" (multilevel norms booklet, p. 7)? Would it not be more appropriate to use an out-of-level achievement test? Is it not conceivable that a good student *might* think that she or he knows more about those concepts measured than is true?

The SDMT 4 authors imply that the test results can also be used for program evaluation, to measure change, identify the mathematical ability of a district's students, and the like. I question using the results of a diagnostic test in these ways because these tests are quite focused in their coverage of specific instructional areas. In my opinion, a survey achievement test would be more appropriate.

CONTENT COVERAGE. The SDMT 4 has six levels ranging from grade 1.5 through community college. There is a single form for each of the three lower levels (1.5–4.5). For each of the three upper levels (grade 6 to community college) there are two forms. At all levels, "two interrelated areas of mathematical competence—Concepts and Applications, and Computation" (teacher's manual for interpreting, p. 43) are measured in two formats—multiple choice and free response. Because the NCTM Standards recommended that problem solving be the focus of curriculum, instruction, and assessment, the SDMT 4 emphasizes problem solving and problem solving strategies while maintaining a traditional computation subtest. The test authors claim that many of the items in both formats may be classified as enhanced or enriched.

As in previous editions, the SDMT 4 is a well-developed criterion-referenced test that also provides norm-referenced information. The procedures described in the manual reflect sound conventional test development techniques: developing the test specifications, item development and review, and national item tryouts.

DEVELOPING TEST SPECIFICATIONS. The development process began with careful analyses of "the most recent literature in the field of mathematics education in general and of diagnosis and instruction in particular, the most recent state and district school curricula and educational objectives and the most important trends and directions in mathematics education according to recommendations ... of the NCTM Standards" (multilevel norms booklet, p. 7). Concurrent with these steps was a thorough analysis of the SDMT 3 to determine which aspects of its content coverage and format should be retained. These analyses and reviews "resulted in recommendations for areas and objectives to be measured, number of test levels necessary for effective coverage [the number of levels increased from four for SDMT 3 to six for SDMT 4], types of assessment formats, number and kinds of items to be included, and testing times desired for the final forms" (multilevel norms booklet, p. 7). The other minor change made was that although the upper level of the SDMT 3 was community college, it was the first semester of college for the SDMT 4. Why this was done is unclear to this reviewer unless it was for marketing purposes.

ITEM DEVELOPMENT AND REVIEW. The SDMT 4 differs from most achievement tests in that it "contains more easy questions ... [this] means that even very low-achieving students are likely to experience some success ... [and measurement of] below-average students is more precise when a test is not too difficult for them" (teacher's manual for interpreting, p. 7). This reviewer commends the test publisher and authors for this approach because nothing can be more frustrating for an examinee (especially one who is below average) than to encounter failure on the majority of items.

NATIONAL ITEM TRYOUT. About 27,000 students from about 150 districts from 32 states and the District of Columbia were selected to be representative of the national school population. Each student took the new SDMT 4 items and an appropriate set of items from the SDMT 3 to compare the achievement of the tryout sample with the SDMT 3 standardization sample and to calibrate the SDMT 4 items on a common difficulty scale across forms and levels.

Conventional procedures were used to develop the final forms "to eliminate clues from item to item, similarity of pictures, and repetition or overlap of content" (multilevel norms booklet, p. 9). In addition, an advisory panel of minority group individuals reviewed all the test items for potential bias.

MANUALS AND REPORTS. For each level, the SDMT 4 is accompanied by a manual that is attractive, well-organized, and color-coded to match the appropriate test booklet. Instructions for administration are clear and easy to follow. Teachers are constantly reminded to make certain that the pupils understand WHAT/HOW/WHERE they are to do. The manuals provide clear, succinct descriptions of the types of test scores reported, give suggestions on which test score is appropriate/inappropriate for various purposes, and provide sample diagnostic reports to guide the user in interpreting the test results. The manuals suggest how teachers can use the results for instructional purposes such as grouping students for instruction, developing an IEP for Low Achievers, and establishing instructional emphases. In addition, some very valuable diagnostic insights and their relationship to instruction are offered. Throughout this section is a discussion of how the SDMT 4 clusters link to the NCTM Standards. Administrators are also shown how to use the results for administrative purposes such as comparing local with national performance and measuring change. This reviewer questions this use. However, the test authors recognize the problems associated with measuring change and advise administrators involved in, or who intend to become

involved in, program evaluation but are deficient in statistical procedures to consult with an expert.

There are four reports available. Three of them—the Class Summary Report, the Individual Diagnostic Report, and the School and District Summaries—are routinely furnished as part of the Basic Scoring Service. The other one—Group Roster Summary—is available as an optional service. With these reports, teachers are able to obtain numeric, graphic, and verbal information about the performance of the whole class as well as being able to compare the performance of their class with that of the national standardization sample. In addition, summary information is available for both the school and the district and can be compared with that of the national standardization sample as is true for most tests, this reviewer would like to see more discussion of material to assist the user in interpreting test results. Some case studies could prove to be invaluable, especially for teachers who lack sufficient training in testing and measurement. The authors are commended for cautioning prospective test users against overinterpreting small differences. For example, they suggest that only when the percentile bands do not overlap or when scores are at least two stanines apart should teachers consider them as being significantly different.

The authors also caution prospective users regarding testing students with special needs. However, it is questionable whether the norm-referenced information is of much value because the norms were developed on students who were tested under standardized conditions and were *not* accommodated. Similar cautions are given for testing students out-of-level especially with respect to using the progress Indicators (PI). Because PIs are provided only for those grades included in the norming sample, they should *not* be used for these purposes. Instead, the PI should be estimated using the PI for the highest grade available for the level used.

With 918 items on the eight tests, one would be surprised to find nothing to say about the quality of the items, the directions for administration and scoring, the quality of the diagrams, and maybe even the quality of the paper. Most of the items seem to be appropriate and clear. Some general comments are in order to see whether suggestions made by reviewers of the third edition have been considered by the SDMT 4 authors. Because all the items are new in the SDMT 4, I will confine my remarks to such things as clarity of directions, quality of illustrations, and format. Concerns about the new test, per se, are discussed elsewhere.

For the Red Level, most of the concerns raised by reviewers of the SDMT 3 have been corrected. For example:

1. The direction "First we are going to find out how much you know about" which could have caused anxiety in some students has been replaced by "I am going to give you a booklet that has many interesting things to do in it."

2. As before, students are encouraged to answer the practice items orally but *now are also told to mark their answers in the test booklet*. In the SDMT 3, they were not told to answer to themselves once the test actually began.

3. The text of the questions is now in the test booklet whereas in the SDMT 3 it was absent. The teacher, however, still reads the text as before.

4. The pictures and drawings are generally of high quality except that the drawings of the coins, most notably the size of the 50-cent piece is not that much different from the size of the 25-cent piece in both editions.

5. A previous reviewer of the SDMT 3 felt that having a "NOT HERE" as a foil was not advisable "because it does not correctly *answer* the item" (Lappan, p. 436). This reviewer disagrees. It is true that having foils such as "none of the above" or "all of the above" are not acceptable to some item writers, but they are acceptable if such a foil is the correct answer in some instances and the incorrect answer in other items. If there is some question about the "NOT HERE" option, it is that there should be some questions where this foil is the correct answer and that it not be a foil in every question.

Although some comments made by previous reviewers of the SDMT 3 dealing with such things as the appropriate placement of items, the number of items per cluster, and the attention or lack of attention paid to certain skills such as interpreting graphs or tables could be addressed here, this reviewer will leave those matters to subject-matter specialists and mathematics teachers and educators who have a better handle on the NCTM Standards.

STANDARDIZATION SAMPLE. The methods used to construct a nationally representative sampling frame were appropriate. A stratified random sampling technique was used to obtain a sample that was representative of the national school population. The stratification variables were geographic region, SES, urbanicity, and ethnicity. There was both a Fall and Spring standardization. Comparisons made between the demographic characteristics of the standardization sample with the 1990 U.S. Census data show favorable agreement, more so for the Fall standardization program sample than for the Spring standardization sample. Two major differences in sample characteristics were on the ethnicity and urbanicity variables.

We are told that for the Fall Standardization about 41,500 students from 425 school districts participated and for the Spring Standardization 40,000 students were used. However, we have no information about the number of school districts invited. This is a common fault for test publishers. It is conceivable that the sample finally used may be biased.

TYPES OF SCORES. The SDMT 4 provides several types of scores such as content-referenced scores (raw scores and progress indicators), scaled scores, and norm-referenced scores (percentile ranks, stanines, normal curve equivalents, and grade equivalents). Technical terms are clearly explained in both the norms booklets and the Teacher's Manual For Interpreting with appropriate caveats, such as "scaled scores are not equivalent across subtests [or] ... across types of assessments" (teacher's manual for interpreting, p. 14). The authors provide a simple but technically accurate summary table of the characteristics and applications of the various score types.

Progress indicators (PIs) are cut scores established for each SDMT 4 cluster and subcluster separately for the multiple-choice and free-response tests for both the Concepts/Applications and Computation subtest. In the SDMT 3 a "+" or "-" was used to indicate whether the student met or fell short of the designated cutoffs. On the Individual Diagnostic Report for the SDMT 4, to indicate that the student's score is at or above the cutoff score, the "+" sign was replaced by a shaded box and an oval for the multiple-choice and free-response tests, respectively. What is significant about the PIs is their susceptibility of misinterpretation despite the appropriate caveats furnished by the authors and how they were set. It should be recognized at the outset that the PI is *not* a *mastery* score but is only an indication that satisfactory progress has been made on the topic and the student is ready for regular grade-level instruction on the topic instead of remediation or other instructional modifications. Also, we must recognize that the PIs were established by the authors (using the judgment of mathematics educators) who state they were guided by the "relative importance of each skill to mathematics; the location of these skills in the developmental sequence; and the performance of students at different achievement levels on the items measuring these skills" (multilevel norms booklet, p. 15). Regrettably, this is the only information given in the manual. Recognizing the importance of standards and cutoff scores and the debates surrounding them, it would have been most beneficial to have more description about this procedure than the 45 words in the manual. Users should carefully examine the PIs to determine how validly they reflect local instructional objectives. It should also be noted that PIs are not available for out-of-level testing.

TECHNICAL INFORMATION. Reliability estimates are reported as KR20, KR21, alternate-forms, and standard errors of measurement in raw score units for the Fall Standardization sample. Depending upon the reliability estimate used, the data are reported for all subtests, clusters, and subclusters for the Fall Standardization sample. In addition, interrater reliability coefficients are reported for the free-response or open-ended questions.

The major subtest reliability estimates are sufficiently high to be used for making decisions about individual pupils. The alternate-forms reliabilities are in the .70s and above for all the subtests, with the exception of the free-response computation subtest of the Brown level (grade 6–8) where it is only .51. Why this anomaly exists is unclear because the alternate-form reliabilities for the Purple and Blue levels are .78 and .81, respectively.

The problem with reliability indicators is the high correlations among the subtests, a fault that also existed with the SDMT 3. Although one might say that this supports the test's overall reliability, it also suggests that the subtests are redundant. Granted, some overlap on what is being measured by various subtests of a mathematics test are to be expected, but this reviewer feels that there is too much overlap to attach much importance to differences, something that is *essential* in a diagnostic test.

Evidence of test validity includes content validity, construct validity, and criterion-related validity. Content validity is the sine qua non of any achievement test. If the content of a test does not reflect the instructional objectives of the user, it should not be used. The table of specifications clearly shows the SDMT 4's instructional objectives, which are based on the NCTM Standards. As long as a school's instructional objectives match those of the Standards, the SDMT 4 most likely has content validity.

Construct validity evidence was studied by computing intercorrelations among the SDMT 4 subtests and the Otis-Lennon School Ability Test,

Sixth Edition. Despite the fact that these correlations are high, this reviewer feels that these findings lend little support to construct validity. Why should a high relationship between one's performance on a diagnostic test and on a general ability test substantiate construct validity? If anything, one might expect the intercorrelations to be quite low. In addition, the authors report correlations between corresponding subtests and total at adjacent levels to provide "further evidence for the construct validity … these data demonstrate the continuity of SDMT 4 across levels and the extent to which the levels are consistent in measuring the same aspects of mathematics achievement" (multilevel norms booklet, p. 24). Again, this reviewer is perplexed as to how such findings attest to construct validity.

Criterion-related validity evidence for the SDMT 4 was based on correlations between pupils' performance on the SDMT 3 and SDMT 4. This reviewer might be inclined to accept this approach to substantiate criterion-related validity if the validity of the SDMT 3 was substantiated. If it is, then the authors have an obligation to present this evidence. If I wanted to provide evidence of criterion-related validity, I would *not* use an earlier edition. Rather, if evidence could be presented to show that the test successfully identified particular areas where remedial instruction resulted in improved performance, I would be satisfied. Regrettably, such evidence was not presented for the SDMT 4.

SUMMARY. The SDMT 4 is a very well-developed content-referenced mathematics test that also provides norm-referenced information. Although many specific scores are provided, the "diagnostic" value may be questionable. Even though the content is limited and the test is easier than a traditional achievement test, this does not necessarily qualify as a diagnostic test. This is possible but there are some serious limitations. For example, it should *not* be used to assess the strengths and weaknesses of average or above average pupils. Nor should it be used as a major criterion for grouping students into instructional groups on the basis of their stanine score. Also, it should *not* be used to test students with special needs. And it should not be used to measure change of average or above-average groups. This reviewer feels that the construct and criterion-related evidence presented poses a serious deficiency.

On the other hand, there are some positive features of the SDMT 4. The care with which the table of specifications was constructed and the quality of the items are both pluses. The content validity and the reliability of the test are acceptable. The norms are adequate.

So then, do we have a "thumbs up/down" situation? I would give the SDMT 4 a qualified "thumbs-up" provided users focus its use on the below-average student, are cognizant of the criterion-related and construct validity inadequacies, and satisfy themselves that the content matches local instructional objectives.

REVIEWER'S REFERENCE

Lappan, G. (1978). [Review of the Stanford Diagnostic Mathematics Test.] In O. K. Buros (Ed.), *The eighth mental measurements yearbook* (pp. 436–437). Highland Park, NJ: Gryphon Press.

Review of the Stanford Diagnostic Mathematics Test, Fourth Edition by PHILIP NAGY, Professor, Measurement and Evaluation, The Ontario Institute for Studies in Education of the University of Toronto, Toronto, Ontario, Canada:

The strengths and weaknesses reported by other reviewers of earlier versions of the Stanford Diagnostic Mathematics Test (SDMT) remain in Version 4, largely due to difficulties inherent in what the test tries to accomplish. The test attempts to be both diagnostic and normative, and does not fully succeed at either. Subtests selected for homogeneity of content are quite short, resulting in scores accurate enough for diagnosis at the group level only.

MATERIALS. The SDMT is designed to be marketed to those in a great variety of circumstances. Thus, the consumer must (or, more positively, may) choose from a large and at times confusing range of options. For each of six levels, there is a multiple-choice (MC) test, a free-response (FR) test, and the recommended combination. There are eight separate administration booklets, three different interpretation books, and two norms books. Both machine-scorable and hand-scorable answer forms are available, as well as various reporting and recording forms. There are practice tests, with their own administration booklets for each level. None of the materials I received set out the plethora of options in a straightforward manner.

CONTENT AND PURPOSES. The test attempts content-based diagnosis combined with norm-based comparison. The result is less than might be desired, although all that should be expected. Content emphasis is on material prerequisite to later topics. The manual makes it clear that, because of this, average to good students find the test easy (mean scores on computation are over 80%). Some important topics are omitted. As earlier reviews have suggested, these features compromise the normative information available. Reliance on this test for instructional guidance would also lead to an impoverished curriculum, especially for more able students. If the goal is normative rather than diagnostic, better tests, some from the same publisher, are available. As a diagnostic instrument, difficulties arise when we consider the breadth of the curriculum compared to the available testing time.

The first problem is the number of items available for diagnosis of difficulties at the subtest level. There are two main subtests. Concepts and Applications, and Computation, each with substructure. If the FR or MC test is used alone, scores are available based on as few as three items. The reliabilities of subtest scores are low, due to the shortness of the subtests. For example, for the spring norms of the Red version (Form J), subtest KR-20s range from .29 to .70, with a median value of .54. These subtest scores are not accurate enough for use at the individual level.

Reliabilities are provided also for combined FR and MC items on the same subtopic, raising the minimum number of items to 6. Using both tests, sufficient accuracy can be achieved on longer subtests to justify low-stakes decisions about individuals. However, shorter combined subtests of up to 10 items still cannot be used with any confidence at the individual level. For example, a typical score of 7 of 10 items on Subtraction of Whole Numbers (Green level) reflects, at best, a true score between 5 and 9, which is not accurate enough for individual diagnosis. The manual does caution that scores on this test ought never to be used in isolation from other information on the student.

The second problem is the level of detail in the definitions of the subtests. In general, the Computation subtests are sufficiently narrowly and precisely defined (e.g., "Find 2-digit differences with regrouping and 3- and 4-digit differences without regrouping"; pp. 23–24) to be of diagnostic value. However, the Concepts and Applications subtests are not as specific, due to the nature of the content (e.g., "identify the properties of numbers and relationships among numbers"; p. 42). Although instructional consequences of low scores on Computation subscores are relatively clear, this is not the case for similar scores on Concepts and Applications subtests.

PROGRESS INDICATORS. One of the features of this test is "progress indicators." For each subtest, cut scores have been selected to "identify those students who have demonstrated sufficient competence in specific areas to make satisfactory progress in the regular developmental mathematics program" (p. 13, Green/Purple teacher's manual). For example, if grade 3 students (spring) get 1 of 3 items correct in Geometry (Green, MC), or 5 of 8 in Whole Numbers, they should be deemed to be progressing at a satisfactory rate. There are two serious problems with this conception. First, the idea of cut scores is presented independently of any notion of error in the scores. Second, very strong assumptions need to be made about the nature of the curriculum the child has been and will be exposed to. Without access to what the child has been taught, the test developers are not in a position to offer the kind of detailed curricular diagnosis that these cut scores imply.

OTHER SCORE TYPES. The variety of score types offered reflects the confusion between the normative and diagnostic goals of this test. Raw scores, which are the only viable basis for diagnosis, are presented, along with progress indicators, as just one of several score types, all the others being normative. Scaled score interpretations ("you no longer need to be concerned with level of test"), are presented in direct antithesis of diagnosis. Grade equivalents are presented with so many (quite appropriate) disclaimers that one wonders why they are presented at all.

INTERPRETATION. The instructional advice offered in the manual is good common sense, but naturally very general, in keeping with the general nature of the information available. There is a caution not to overinterpret small differences. In the reporting forms, the only indication of error is through use of bands to indicate national percentile placing.

SUMMARY. This test is best used to diagnose progress at the group (that is, classroom) level. The best interpretations can be achieved by inspection of the actual items asked of the students. Because the test does not reflect a balanced curriculum appropriate for the wide range of students, normative uses should be avoided.

Review of the Stanford Diagnostic Mathematics Test, Fourth Edition by G. MICHAEL POTEAT, Associate Professor of Psychology, East Carolina University, Greenville, NC:

The Stanford Diagnostic Mathematics Test, Fourth Edition (SDMT-4) is both an elaborate measure of mathematics achievement and a diagnostic mathematics test. The SDMT-4 has six levels ranging from Red (for grades 1 to 2) to Blue (grades 9 to 12 and community college). The three upper levels also have alternate forms. There are two response formats: multiple choice and free-response. At each of the six levels, there are 32 multiple-choice questions on Concepts and Applications, and 20 multiple-choice questions on Computation. There are also 30 free-response questions on Concepts and Applications, and 20 free-response questions on Computation. The content focus of the items varies among levels but the overall coverage of mathematical operations is relatively complete. As an example: on Concepts and Applications at the Purple Level (for grades 6 and 7), there are 10 multiple-choice items on Numeration, 8 items on Problem Solving, 4 items involving Graphs and Tables, 4 items on Statistics and Probability, and 6 items on Geometry and Measurement. Computation items at the Purple Level include 4 items on the addition of whole numbers, 4 items on the subtraction of whole numbers, 3 items on multiplication facts, 3 items on multiplication operations, 3 items on division facts, and 3 items on division operations. The breakdown of the free response items is similar. Overall, the range and number of items appears to be adequate. The multiple-choice and free-response items can be used separately, but it is recommended that the two formats be combined.

The test can be administered to a single subject or to a small group of selected subjects. A practice test is provided for each level and should be administered during the week preceding the test administration. Total test time for the Green Level (grade 3 to 4), not including the practice test, is 205 minutes in five different test settings. Because of the amount of time involved, most examiners will want to use the SDMT-4 to test groups of children. The test instructions are very explicit and administration does not require any special training other than familiarization with the instructions.

The SDMT-4 provides a variety of norms and standard scores. Two multilevel norm books are provided for either Spring or Fall administration. The tests may be either hand scored or mailed for computer scoring. Because of the complexity of the norms, I suggest that group testing be computer scored to avoid the probability of errors. If hand scoring is used, then the individual using the various norms will need to have some familiarity with tests and measurements. Raw scores are converted to scaled scores, and then scaled scores can be converted to stanines and percentile ranks. Scaled scores can also be converted to grade equivalents. A progress indicator "cut score" is also provided to indicate if a student is making sufficient progress to be placed in regular mathematics instruction. The "cut score" is a form of criterion-reference score. Computer-generated reports for both groups and individual subjects provide some additional information including national normal curve equivalents and comparisons with local norms. A teacher's manual for interpreting scores is provided and includes information on interpreting the test scores and using the results for instructional development.

Psychometrically, the SDMT-4 is an example of thoughtful test development. The Fall standardization involved over 40,000 students in more than 400 school districts. A similar sample was obtained in the Spring. Both normative samples are comparable to the U.S. school population in terms of geographical region, ethnicity, SES status, and type of community (urban, suburban, or rural). Interrater reliability for scoring free-response items is excellent (>.95 in all comparisons). Measures of internal consistency are generally above .80 and most are closer to .90. Alternate form reliability for the Purple, Brown, and Blue Levels ranges from satisfactory to good. Efforts were also made to eliminate items that reflected ethnic, gender, or other sources of bias, and statistical methods (based on differential item functioning) were also employed to identify and eliminate items that showed statistical evidence of bias. Some evidence for validity is found in the correlations obtained between the SDMT-4 and the Otis-Lennon School Ability Test. The statistics vary but generally the correlations among subtests on the two instruments are in the .60s and .70s.

In summary, the SDMT-4 is an impressive instrument. It is primarily designed to be a diagnostic test and I do not recommend it for use if the goal is simply to obtain achievement test norms. As a diagnostic instrument, it provides a great deal of information and the free-response format will allow for a more detailed analysis of students' mathematical skills. The SDMT-4 has good to excellent psychometric characteristics, and the obtained scores can be used with confidence. A minor criticism is that the test information should be better organized. However, the materials provided to teachers are very complete and should foster better mathematical instruction. The content of the test is good overall, but students who have mastered 8th grade mathematics will have few difficulties with items on the SDMT-4. It is not a test that would be useful in diagnosing problems in algebraic operations. I would recom-

mend the SDMT-4 for use in grades 1 through 8 and with older students who have deficits in mathematics. It is also recommended for use in both regular and special education programs, and can be used by individual teachers or adopted by an entire school or school system.

[294]
Stanford Diagnostic Reading Test, Fourth Edition.

Purpose: "Intended to diagnose students' strengths and weaknesses in the major components of the reading process."
Publication Dates: 1978–1996.
Acronym: SDRT4.
Administration: Group.
Forms, 2: J, K (for Purple, Brown, and Blue levels).
Price Data, 1996: $25 per examination kit including multiple-choice test booklet and directions for administering, practice test and directions for administering, answer document, class record form, Reading Questionnaire, Reading Strategies Survey, Story Retelling (Story and Response Form), and directions for each (specify level); $11 per 25 practice tests and directions for administering (specify Red, Orange, Green, Purple, or Brown level); $80 per 25 machine-scorable test booklets type 1 and directions for administering (specify Red, Orange, or Green level); $55 per 25 hand-scorable test booklets, directions for administering, and class record (specify Red, Orange, or Green level); $55 per 25 reusable test booklets and directions for administering (specify Purple, Brown, or Blue level and Form J or K); $25 per 25 Reading Questionnaires and directions for administering (specify level and form); $25 per 25 Reading Strategies Surveys and directions for administering (specify Level Red/Orange, Green/Purple, or Brown/Blue); $30 per Story Retelling manual ('95, 15 pages) and 25 Story and Response forms (specify Level Red/Orange, Green/Purple, or Brown/Blue); $25 per 25 machine-scorable answer documents type 1 (for Purple/Brown/Blue levels); $20 per 25 hand-scorable answer documents with blackline master of student record form and class record (for Purple/Brown/Blue levels); $10 per side-by-side keys for hand-scorable test booklets including blackline master of student record form (specify Red, Orange, or Green level); $10 per response keys (specify level and form); $15 per stencil keys for hand-scorable answer documents (specify Purple, Brown, or Blue level and Form J or K); $4 per class record (specify Level Red, Orange, Green, or Purple/Brown/Blue); $4.50 per 25 row markers; $35 per Fall or Spring Multilevel norms booklet ('96, 103 pages); $15 per teacher's manual for interpreting (specify Level Red/Orange ['96, 67 pages], Green/Purple ['96, 68 pages], or Brown/Blue ['96, 62 pages]); $7 per test directions for administering (specify Level Red, Orange, Green, or Purple/Brown/Blue); $4 per practice test directions for administering (specify Level

Red, Orange, Green, Purple, or Brown); $4 per Reading Questionnaire directions for administering; $4 per Reading Strategies Survey directions for administering; $6 per Story Retelling manual; price information for scoring services available from publisher.

Authors: Bjorn Karlsen and Eric F. Gardner.

Publisher: Harcourt Brace Educational Measurement.

a) RED LEVEL.

Population: Grades 1.5–2.5.

Scores, 19: Phonetic Analysis (Consonants-Single, Consonants-Blends, Consonants-Digraphs, Consonants Total, Vowels-Short, Vowels-Long, Vowels Total, Total), Vocabulary (Word Reading, Listening Vocabulary, Nouns, Verbs, Others, Total), Comprehension (Sentences, Riddles, Cloze, Total), Paragraphs with Questions.

Time: 105(110) minutes.

b) ORANGE LEVEL.

Population: Grades 2.5–3.5.

Scores, 19: Phonetic Analysis (Consonants-Single, Consonants-Blends, Consonants-Digraphs, Consonants Total, Vowels-Short, Vowels-Long, Vowels Total, Total), Vocabulary (Listening Vocabulary, Reading Vocabulary, Synonyms, Classification, Total), Comprehension (Cloze, Total), Paragraphs with Questions, Recreational Reading, Textual Reading, Functional Reading.

Time: 100(105) minutes.

c) GREEN LEVEL.

Population: Grades 3.5–4.5.

Scores, 22: Phonetic Analysis (Consonants-Single, Consonants-Blends, Consonants-Digraphs, Consonants Total, Vowels-Short, Vowels-Long, Vowels-Other, Vowels Total, Total), Vocabulary (Listening Vocabulary, Reading Vocabulary, Synonyms, Classification, Word Parts, Content Area Words, Total), Comprehension, Paragraphs with Questions, Recreational Reading, Textual Reading, Functional Reading, Initial Understanding, Interpretation, Critical Analysis and Reading Strategies.

Time: 100(105) minutes.

d) PURPLE LEVEL.

Population: Grades 4.5–6.5.

Scores, 16: Vocabulary (Reading Vocabulary, Synonyms, Classification, Word Parts, Content Area Words, Total), Comprehension, Paragraphs with Questions, Recreational Reading, Textual Reading, Functional Reading, Initial Understanding, Interpretation, Critical Analysis, Reading Strategies, Scanning.

Time: 85(90) minutes.

e) BROWN LEVEL.

Population: Grades 6.5–8.9.

Scores, 16: Same as Purple Level.

Time: 85(90) minutes.

f) BLUE LEVEL.

Population: Grades 9.0–12.9.

Scores, 16: Same as Purple Level.

Time: 85(90) minutes.

Cross References: See T4:2555 (24 references); for reviews by Robert J. Tierney and James E. Ysseldyke of an earlier edition, see 9:1178 (7 references); see also T3:2292 (15 references); for a review by Bryon H. Van Roekel, see 8:777 (13 references); see T2:1651 (2 references); for a review by Lawrence M. Kasdon of Levels 1–2 of an earlier edition, see 7:725 (3 references).

TEST REFERENCES

1. Borkowski, J. G., Weyhing, R. S., & Carr, M. (1988). Effects of attributional retraining on strategy-based reading comprehension in learning-disabled students. *Journal of Educational Psychology, 80,* 46–53.

2. Thames, D. G., & Readence, J. E. (1988). Effects of differential vocabulary instruction and lesson frameworks on the reading comprehension of primary children. *Reading Research and Instruction, 27,* 1–12.

3. McKenna, M. L., & Layton, K. (1990). Concurrent validity of cloze as a measure of intersentential comprehension. *Journal of Educational Psychology, 82,* 372–377.

4. Vogel, S. A., & Adelman, P. B. (1992). The success of college students with learning disabilities: Factors related to educational attainment. *Journal of Learning Disabilities, 25,* 430–441.

5. Graham, S., Schwartz, S. S., & MacArthur, C. A. (1993). Knowledge of writing and the composing process, attitude toward writing, and self-efficacy for students with and without learning disabilities. *Journal of Learning Disabilities, 26,* 237-249.

6. Aaron, P. G. (1995). Differential diagnosis of reading disabilities. *School Psychology Review, 24,* 345–360.

7. Baker, S. K., & Good, R. (1995). Curriculum-based measurement of English reading with bilingual Hispanic students: A validation study with second-grade students. *School Psychology Review, 24,* 561–578.

8. Joshi, R. M. (1995). Assessing reading and spelling skills. *School Psychology Review, 24,* 361–375.

9. Kaminski, R. A., & Good, R. H., III. (1996). Toward a technology for assessing basic early literacy skills. *School Psychology Review, 25,* 215–227.

Review of the Stanford Diagnostic Reading Test, Fourth Edition by GEORGE ENGELHARD, JR., Professor of Educational Studies, Emory University, Atlanta, GA:

The purpose of the Stanford Diagnostic Reading Test, Fourth Edition (SDRT4) is to diagnose students' strengths and weaknesses in the major components of the reading process. The specific components measured by the SDRT4 are Phonetic Analysis, Vocabulary, Comprehension, and Scanning. The SDRT4 includes six levels designed to assess reading skills of examinees from the end of grade 1 through the first semester of college. The teacher's manual also provides some suggested activities for teaching reading, as well as some additional material to aid teachers that are not reviewed here (reading questionnaire, reading strategies survey, story retelling, and performance assessments).

In addition to diagnosing students' strengths and weaknesses, the authors recommend that the SDRT4 be used to "challenge students who are doing well and provide special help for others who lack some of the essential reading skills" (p. 7). The authors also recommend the SDRT4 for identifying trends in reading levels of students in school districts, providing information regarding the effectiveness of instructional programs, measuring changes that have taken place over an instructional period, and keeping the community and school board informed about student progress in reading. Before using the SDRT4 for any of these additional purposes, the user should carefully consider the differences between diagnostic instruments and other more general tests of reading achievement. As stressed in the manual, diagnostic tests have two important differences from reading achievement tests: (a) diagnostic tests provide more detailed coverage of reading skills as compared to the broader coverage of a range of skills with less detail, and (b) diagnostic tests place a greater emphasis on measuring the skills of low achieving students, and therefore diagnostic tests include easier items than general achievement tests. Both of these differences should be taken into account when using the results of the SDRT4 for purposes in addition to diagnostic testing.

The SDRT4 provides both norm-referenced and criterion-referenced information on reading skills. The norm-referenced scores are based on normative data collected during the fall of 1994 (approximately 33,000 examinees) and the spring of 1995 (approximately 20,000 examinees); the norms for college freshman were based on approximately 2,000 students. A very detailed comparison of the demographic characteristics (geographic location, SES, urbanicity, ethnicity, handicapping conditions, and school type: public, non-public) of the Total U.S. School Enrollment with the fall and spring norms is provided in the manual. Both normative samples have an excellent match to the Total U.S. School Enrollment statistics with the possible exception of the spring standardization sample that appears to have an overrepresentation of rural students and an underrepresentation of urban students. The specific norm-referenced scores provided are scaled scores, percentile ranks, stanines, normal curve equivalents (NCEs), and grade equivalents. The authors provide a very nice description for teachers regarding the appropriate uses of these various scores.

The criterion-referenced scores (called content-referenced scores in the manual) include raw scores and Progress Indicator Cut (PIC) scores. The PIC scores are used to classify students who have demonstrated "sufficient competence in specific areas to make satisfactory progress in regular developmental reading programs" (teacher's manual, p. 14). These PIC scores should be used, if at all, with great caution because insufficient detail is provided on how these cut scores were set and by whom. Further, the PIC scores are set for some subtests with as few as three or four items, and given the precision of scores based on such a limited sample of the domain, the PIC scores should not be used for the subtests on the SDRT4. No validity evidence is provided in support of the recommended uses for the PIC scores.

The psychometric research conducted in support of the SDRT4 included both traditional methods of data analysis and the application of Rasch model techniques. The manual only reports the results of the traditional methods (e.g., KR20 and KR21), and does not report any Rasch-related statistics, such as model-data fit statistics (e.g., mean square error statistics), item and person separation statistics, etc. Without information regarding model-data fit, it is difficult to evaluate the psychometric quality of the SDRT4. Also, if the Rasch model was used to equate, calibrate, and develop scale scores across forms and levels, as well as equating the SDRT4 to SDRT3, no details are provided on how these activities were accomplished.

In support of the reliability of scores on the SDRT4, the manual provides estimates of KR20, KR21, alternate-form reliability, and standard errors of measurement for the fall and spring standardization samples. The KR20 coefficients range from .79 to .94 for the four major components of the SDRT4, and KR20 coefficients range from .95 to .98 for the total scores; the KR21 coefficients are comparable. Some of the KR21 coefficients for the subtests are quite low, and the use of the shorter subtests for the diagnosis of an individual's strengths and weaknesses is not recommended; for example, the subtest designed to measure student skills related to "long vowels" has a KR21 of .59. The alternate-form reliability coefficients for the components range from .62 to .82, and they range from .86 to .88 for the total scores. Rasch person separation indices are not reported. No evidence of the stability of the scores over time, such as test-retest reliability coefficients are provided.

In support of the content-related validity of the SDRT4, the authors provide a clear and detailed description of the objectives and items included in the SDRT4. Potential users have enough information to make a decision regarding the appropriateness of the SDRT4 for their intended uses. The correlations of scores on the SDRT4 with the Otis-Lennon School Ability Test, Sixth Edition and the SDRT3, as well as intercorrelations of subtest and total scores within the SDRT4 are also reported. These correlations are typical of what would be expected for these types of tests.

The manuals provided clear and detailed instructions for test administration. The score reports that are provided are described fully in the manuals along with appropriate cautions. Even though there are some concerns regarding the interpretation of the subtest scores with a small number of items, the score reports include the number of items in each subtest for the teachers' information. Score reports include national percentile bands, and standard errors of measurement for the other types of scores should be added. Given the low reliabilities of the subtest scores, the highlighting of subtests with scores below the PIC scores should be discontinued.

The content of the SDRT4 was reviewed for bias by an advisory panel of minority group educators. The Mantel-Haenszel procedure was used to examine statistically differential item functioning. More detailed information concerning item and test bias should be provided in the manual. Because the SDRT4 is recommended for use with low achieving students, and given the current structure of American schools, it is likely that many of the students tested with this instrument will be members of minority groups. Therefore, it is essential to have additional psychometric information regarding how well the SDRT4 measures reading skills for various groups. For example, separate reliability coefficients and standard errors of measurement should be reported for different groups of examinees.

In summary, the SDRT4 reflects sound professional test development, administration, and scoring strategies, and appears to offer a useful measure of reading. The traditional psychometric information is adequate, although the precision of some of the subtest scores is quite low, and should not be used for individual diagnosis. The omission of information regarding the use of the Rasch measurement model makes it difficult to evaluate the overall psychometric quality of the SDRT4. The SDRT4 appears to offer a fairly standard and traditional view of reading achievement. Of course, this is not necessarily a weakness, given the recent debates over reading instruction, but the user should be aware of the philosophical orientation undergirding the instrument and consider whether or not it matches the local views of reading held by teachers, other educators, parents, and various stakeholders.

Review of the Stanford Diagnostic Reading Test, Fourth Edition by MARK E. SWERDLIK, Professor of Psychology, and JAYNE E. BUCY, Assistant Professor of Psychology, Illinois State University, Normal, IL:

The SDRT4 represents a major revision of the third edition published in 1986. The SDRT4 con-

sists of six levels with two alternate forms at each of the upper three levels. The test is based on a developmental view of reading as a process involving the four components of decoding or Phonetic Analysis (assessed at only the lower three levels of grades 1.5–4.5), Vocabulary, Comprehension, and Scanning (i.e., the ability to scan material quickly for important information), which is assessed at only the upper three levels (grades 4.5–13). Consistent with the more recent emphasis of reading instruction on comprehension and away from phonics, beginning at Level 2 (grade 2.5), comprehension of various types of text (Recreation, Textual, and Functional) and various modes of comprehension (e.g., Interpretation) are assessed.

The SDRT4 was designed for primary use with low achieving students. It was constructed with a greater number of easy questions as compared to general reading achievement tests and "where appropriate and not impossible due to other constraints, difficult items are interspersed throughout the test and are 'cushioned' by easier items immediately preceding and following" so as to reduce the level of frustration experienced by low achieving students.

In addition to diagnosing the strengths and weaknesses in the reading skills of individual students, the SDRT4 was designed to be useful in program planning and evaluation related to assessing the effectiveness of instructional programs for individual students and of remedial reading programs as a whole. The authors also suggest that the SDRT4 can be useful in identifying trends related to reading performance of students district-wide with reading levels from grade 1 through first semester in college. However, it is unclear how useful the SDRT4 will prove to be for this latter purpose as it was developed to assess more thoroughly the skills of weaker students.

The SDRT4 also includes three optional informal assessments. The Reading Questionnaire assesses a student's attitudes towards reading, reading habits and interests, and familiarity with topics and important concepts involved in the reading comprehension subtest. The Reading Strategies Survey is a self-report measure of a student's use of desirable and counterproductive reading strategies. The Story Retelling subtest assesses comprehension ability by having students reconstruct a story either orally or in writing. These informal assessments allow the test user to diagnose more fully a student's strengths and weaknesses in conjunction with the more formal standardized component of the SDRT4 or other standardized reading tests.

A Multilevel Norms Book and Technical Information and a Teacher's Manual for Interpreting are available for each level of the test. Each manual is clearly written. In addition to administration, scoring, and general instructions for interpreting scores related to the performance of individual students, general and specific teaching suggestions are also described. However, references to the current literature on reading instruction are not provided and so the research base of these interventions is unclear.

All components of the SDRT4 are easy to administer in a group or individual format and score by either the classroom teacher or reading specialist. The SDRT4 can be either hand or machine scored, except for the three informal assessments, which can only be hand scored. Identical information can be obtained from either scoring format. Guidelines for interpretation are also clearly written and include appropriate cautions.

The SDRT4 yields a variety of scores to aid in both norm-referenced and criterion-referenced interpretation. These scores are grouped into content-referenced and norm-referenced scores and include raw scores, percentile ranks, stanines, normal curve equivalents, grade equivalents, scaled scores, and progress indicators. Progress indicator scores, which are actually cutoff scores, are available for each of the SDRT4 skill or item clusters and the Scanning subtests and can be used to identify students with demonstrated sufficient competence in specific areas of reading to make satisfactory progress in the regular developmental reading program. These cut scores were determined by taking into account a number of factors including the relative importance of the skill to the reading process, where the skill fell in the developmental sequence, and the performance of students at different levels of achievement on items measuring these skills. They cannot be interpreted without taking into account the teachers' own instructional objectives and expectations regarding the students' performance.

The use of the content-referenced scores allows the test user to assess a student's performance on specific test questions related to particular reading objectives/skills. Scaled scores can be compared across all six levels for the same subtest and can be useful for assessing change over a period of instruction. However, these scaled scores are not equivalent across subtests and cannot be compared across subtests.

The test development and national standardization process was ambitious. The national standardization was based on the 1990 U.S. Census and consisted of approximately 33,000 students from 400 school districts in the fall and another 7,000 students in the three equating programs (equating of forms, equating of levels, and equating for the SDRT4 and SDRT3) and another 20,000 were part of the spring standardization, all of which are fully described in the manual. The sample was collected using a stratified random sampling technique based on geographical region, socioeconomic status, urbanicity, ethnicity, handicapping condition, and nonpublic schools (Catholic versus private) to be representative of the national school population. The authors were successful in having the fall and spring standardization samples approximate the national school population on most variables. However, the fall standardization sample is overrepresented with students attending private schools (double the national percentage) and underrepresented with Hispanic students for both the spring and fall norming. The spring standardization sample is underrepresented with urban school districts and overrepresented with rural school districts (almost double the national percentage). No descriptive information on the 2,000 college freshman comprising the fall norms is provided, leading the test user to be more cautious in using these norms.

Efforts were undertaken to eliminate/reduce bias in the SDRT4. The content of the items in the final forms of the SDRT4 was balanced in the number and nature of the appearance of particular minority group members. An "expert panel" of nine minority educators also reviewed each item to eliminate or revise those that reflected ethnic, gender, socioeconomic, cultural, or regional bias or stereotyping. In addition, all items from the national tryout were analyzed statistically to expose those on which majority group members functioned differentially from focal (minority) group members (males/females, Whites/African-Americans, Whites/Hispanics). Items detected using these procedures were further reviewed and either revised or eliminated.

Internal consistency measures (Kuder Richardson Formula #20 and Kuder Richardson Formula #21, which provide the lower limits of reliability) are reported. However, it is unclear if the assumption for using KR#21 (i.e., test items have the same degree of difficulty) has been met. KR#20 estimates exceed .85, for all but the Vocabulary subtest at grade 2, suggesting that these SDRT4 subtest and total scores are of sufficient reliability to pinpoint specific domains of reading strengths and weaknesses. However, several item clusters at particular levels (Consonants, Vowels, Listening Comprehension, and Comprehension) have reliability coefficients (KR#21) well below .85 suggesting that they are too unreliable to assess strengths or weaknesses. These low internal consistency estimates of reliability are due to the small numbers of items comprising these clusters. Standard errors of measurements are also provided. Alternate-forms reliability estimates for grades, 4, 6, and 8, a more rigorous estimate, were obtained during the Equating of Forms program and are within acceptable ranges. No test-retest reliability estimates are provided to determine how stable test performance is over time. Further, no reliability data are provided for the three informal assessments.

The authors report evidence for three types of validity. Related to content validity, the SDRT4 measures most important concepts and skills that are part of most reading curricula. Selection of items was based, in part, on a review of the recent literature related to reading education, diagnosis, and instruction; the most recent state and district school curricula and educational objectives; surveys of reading teachers and reading specialists; and a review of trends and directions in reading education as articulated by the International Reading Association and the National Council of Teachers of English. The authors appropriately caution that test users must determine the extent to which the SDRT4 test reflects their own local curricular content. The authors facilitate this process by providing a listing of objectives, including numbers of items by objective, measured at all levels. In addition, standardization data show growth from year to year for the same subtests supporting the relevance of the SDRT4 to the instructional sequence.

Criterion-related validity evidence provided includes high correlations between performance on the SDRT4 and the Third Edition. However, no data are presented correlating the SDRT4 with other well-accepted measures of reading achievement. It would not be unexpected that the SDRT4 and the Third Edition would be highly correlated as the Fourth Edition represents a revision of this criterion measure.

Moderate intercorrelations among the SDRT4 subtests and correlations between these subtests and the Otis-Lennon School Ability Test, Sixth Edition, provide evidence of the construct validity of the SDRT4. No validity data are provided related to the effectiveness of using SDRT4 scores in developing reading interventions for students. Further, no validity data are provided for any of the three informal assessment measures.

SUMMARY. The SDRT4 is a generally well-developed diagnostic measure to assess reading strengths and weaknesses of students experiencing reading difficulties in grades 1 through 12. The college norms, which are not adequately described, should be interpreted with caution as should the three informal assessments as no reliability or validity evidence is provided. The test user should also avoid interpreting some areas of strength and weakness due to the low reliability of some clusters. Despite these limitations, the SDRT4 could prove particularly useful for classroom teachers and reading specialists who want to evaluate large numbers of students and want to assess the effectiveness of instructional programs. As is true of most diagnostic reading tests, the usefulness of the SDRT4 in developing effective interventions for students experiencing reading difficulties is yet to be documented. In addition, as is also true of all diagnostic reading tests, test users must carefully assess the correspondence of the test content to the reading curriculum in which their students were instructed and if a close match does not exist the use of the SDRT4 would not be recommended.

[295]
Stanford Writing Assessment Program, Second Edition.

Purpose: Provides for the direct assessment of written expression in four modes: Descriptive, Narrative, Expository, Persuasive.

Population: Grades 3–12.

Publication Dates: 1982–1991.

Scores: 4 writing modes: Descriptive, Narrative, Expository, Persuasive.

Administration: Group.

Levels, 9: Primary 3, Intermediate 1, Intermediate 2, Intermediate 3, Advanced 1, Advanced 2, TASK 1, TASK 2, TASK 3.

Forms, 2: J, K.

Price Data, 1997: $48.50 per 25 answer sheets, directions for administering, and 25 writing prompts; $4.50 per directions for administering; $31 per manual for interpreting; $38.50 per national norms booklet; $6.42 per prompt administered for basic holistic scoring service ($5.67 additional for analytic scoring) (includes two master lists and master list summaries); $.56 per student narrative; $.56 per individual student report; $.56 per student record label; $.40 per additional master list.

Time: 30(35) minutes.

Comments: Holistic and analytic scoring available; computer scoring available; Form K is a secure form.

Author: Harcourt Brace Educational Measurement—the educational testing division of The Psychological Corporation.

Publisher: Harcourt Brace Educational Measurement.

Review of the Stanford Writing Assessment Program, Second Edition by PHILIP NAGY, Professor, Measurement and Evaluation, The Ontario Institute for Studies in Education of the University of Toronto, Toronto, Ontario, Canada:

This testing program is aimed at assessing the writing skills of students from grades 3–12 within each of four modes: Descriptive, Narrative, Expository, and Persuasive. What the customer is purchasing is standardized scoring and access to norms. The test itself is simply a verbal prompt, an editing checklist, and a writing booklet that allows machine reading of student information. The writing space is four pages of newsprint quality paper. The space and 35-minute time limit do not vary across grades.

The program is based on two flawed but common premises: that we can engage in process rather than product evaluation in an external assessment, without involving the teacher in scoring and in formative dialogue with the student; and that we can accurately assess writing ability from a single sample. These flaws are shared by all writing assessments based on a single sample and externally scored. The accountability need for evidence of achievement beyond teacher judgment is often taken, at least implicitly, as justification for ignoring these problems. Individual diagnosis should not be done on the basis of scores on this test alone, although a test score is legitimate as additional information on an individual. Group average scores (in normal curve equivalents) are sufficiently accurate for use.

There is an administration manual, an interpretation manual, and a norming manual with technical information. For each mode, 9 different prompts cover the grades. Holistic and analytic scores are available. For holistic, two judges score on a 6-point scale, disagreements of more than 1 point are resolved, and a score out of 12 is reported. For analytic, scores on three 4-point scales for Sentence Formation, Word Usage, and Writing Mechanics, each from one judge, are provided. For holistic scoring, four different standards (scoring rubrics) are used depending on prompt and grade. For analytic scoring, three standards are used. Reporting is by point-scores, with no mention of confidence intervals.

There is an option to purchase training for local scoring. One of the benefits of within-district scoring is professional development of staff. This option helps to deal with the problem of lack of teacher involvement, and may be the best use of this test.

The analytic scores are criterion referenced. There are no norms, and no discussion of accuracy, although only one judge is used, and agreement on analytic scores is just as elusive as on holistic scores. Interpretation is through verbal descriptions. For example, a score of 3 on Sentence Formation means "Basically adequate sentence structure. Few errors but little variety in length and form." For the holistic scores, each prompt has been normed for both fall or spring administration in the same or adjacent grades. Tables allow conversion of raw scores to percentiles, stanines, NCEs, and scaled "growth" scores. The stanine scores are broad enough to reflect the low reliability of such data, whereas the three-digit "growth" scores invite indulgence in false accuracy.

The interpretation manual is informative. It contains cursory cautions with respect to the flaws identified above. It explains the benefits of process evaluation, and discusses how the characteristics of writing within each mode change across grades. There is a long, although generic, section on how to improve student writing.

The norming/technical manual gives too much unimportant and too little important information. Thirty-eight of 143 pages are spent showing that the norming group was equivalent to the group used to norm the Stanford Achievement Test, and another 47 on largely unnecessary and unwise procedures for out-of-level testing.

Important data are missing. There are two kinds of error in writing assessment. One is judge disagreement. The other is that students do not perform consistently on different prompts, even within a single mode. Users need to know the confidence with which we can generalize from a score to "narrative writing ability on this particular prompt" and then the next step to "narrative writing ability in general." Neither of these issues is addressed in a transparent manner in the manual. Fortunately, data are provided that allow appropriate calculations (with sensible assumptions), but the test user should not be expected to take the time to do so.

With respect to agreement between judges, median values of judge intercorrelations yield a 95% confidence interval around an estimate of *writing ability on this particular prompt*. A score on the 2–12-point scale should be taken as plus or minus 2 points. For a typical score of 6, depending on the prompt and mode, this range runs from about the 20th to 80th percentile. This range raises a red flag with respect to individual scores on this test. However, it is no wider than is found with any other single-sample writing test.

The data on student consistency across prompts give confidence intervals for the broader generalization beyond the particular prompt. Again using median values, the 95% confidence interval for generalizations across prompts within modes should be plus or minus 4. This covers virtually the entire range of the 2–12-point score scale. So, it is quite impossible to generalize to writing ability for an individual, even within a mode, from a single writing sample.

In summary, as with most such tests, individual scores are tentative enough that they should be treated with extreme caution. Scores for group averages are much more accurate. For a typical class size, the confidence interval around the class average would be in the order of plus or minus less than 1 point. Testing groups for accountability purposes is a legitimate use of this test. The manual would be enhanced by information that would put a class or school average score in an appropriate context.

Review of the Stanford Writing Assessment Program, Second Edition by WAYNE H. SLATER, Associate Professor of Curriculum and Instruction, University of Maryland, College Park, MD:

The Stanford Writing Assessment Program, Second Edition, provides a direct measure of writing achievement for students in grades 3 through 12 within four modes of written discourse: Narrative, Descriptive, Expository, and Persuasive. Proficiency in any of the four modes can be assessed at any grade level (3–12). This allows the user the flexibility to test narrative writing at grade 3, for example, or persuasive writing at grade 9. At the same time, users have the option to assess several modes at a particular grade level to determine students' overall achievement in writing and proficiency within specific modes. Two parallel forms, J and K, are available for each mode at each level. Form K, a secure form, is offered only through special arrangement. Both holistic and analytic scoring are available through The Psychological Corporation's Writing Assessment Center. Users also have the option of selecting local scoring in which case The Psychological Corporation provides information about appropriate training for raters. In addition, if users desire a more comprehensive evaluation, the Stanford Writing Assessment Program can be used in combination with the Stanford Achievement Test language and spelling subtests.

Basing their efforts, in part, on insights derived from modern developmental psychology (Piaget, Vygotsky, and Erikson), the authors of this assessment cite an impressive research base to define and warrant the use of the four modes selected for assessment (Britton, Burgess, Martin, McLeod, & Rosen, 1979; Cazden, 1992; Corbett, 1990; Kinneavy, 1980; Lindemann, 1995; Mullis et al., 1994; Perelman & Olbrechts-Tyteca, 1969) and at the same time, manage to strike a middle ground on current thinking on these issues (Hillocks, 1986; Kellogg, 1994).

It takes approximately 45 minutes to administer the Stanford Writing Assessment Program. Identical administration procedures are used for all grade levels and modes of writing. Prompts and directions are distributed and read aloud to students. The 35-minute writing time includes time for planning (a space on the answer sheet is provided for this purpose). When 10 minutes remain, students are advised so they can use the editing checklist (provided) as a guide to proofread their completed writing sample.

Although the test administrator manuals are straightforward and the topics for writing are field tested and sufficiently generic to meet the needs of most students, a number of writing experts might question the validity of the writing sample collected by this assessment because of the limited time provided for the student writing response, 35 minutes (White, 1994). Given current thinking on the writing process (prewriting, drafting, reflecting, revising) and its recursive properties, the time issue cannot be ignored (Flower & Hayes, 1980; Hillocks, 1986; Kellogg, 1994; Lauer & Asher, 1988). The authors state that the Stanford Writing Assessment Program system of scoring allows for the fact that a large-scale writing assessment can provide enough time for only a rough draft response. Because there is not a great deal of time for editing or substantial revision, the readers do not expect to score papers that are final drafts. In addition, the authors argue convincingly that their assessment provides an estimate of a student's achievement at one point in time and that results must be considered in relation to other information gathered about students' writing from additional sources such as in-class writing assignments, homework, reports, and special projects.

The students' written responses are scored both holistically and analytically. The Writing Assessment Program system for holistic scoring involves two independent raters who judge the overall merit of a student's paper. Strengths and weaknesses of a student's paper are considered in light of general characteristics of good writing, including organization, detailed clarification/development of ideas, attention to audience, and fluency. Each rater assigns the paper a score, based on a 6-point scale. The lowest possible score is 1; the highest possible score is 6. The 6-point scale allows for more fine-tuned discriminations among score points and is particularly useful for distinguishing levels of quality in papers. The ratings are done independently. The student's raw score is the sum of the two independent ratings. Thus, the total score scale is 2–12. If the readers' ratings differ by more than 1 score point, a third (resolution) reader is used. The score assigned by the third reader must be within 1 score point of one of the first two scores, or a second resolution reader is required. The raw score for the paper is the sum of either the two closest scores or the two higher scores, if equidistant. To account for the developmental nature of student writing, the Writing Assessment Program has developed scoring standards. These standards are grade-level groupings (Standard I: 3.5–5.5; Standard II: 5.5–7.5; Standard III: 7.5–9.9; Standard IV: 9.0–12.9) that allow students' writing to be judged according to developmental levels of achievement. Student papers are scored with reference to a set of anchor papers. These anchor papers were selected during a National Standardization Program by a panel consisting of writing scoring specialists, classroom teachers, language arts curriculum specialists, and representatives of the test publisher. In addition, scoring guidelines were developed for each prompt to clarify for scorers the level of proficiency typical at each score point. The scoring guidelines are generalizations about the characteristics of the anchor papers for a particular score point. The development of standards and scoring guidelines helps to ensure reasonable and consistent criteria for scoring (Anastasi, 1996).

Analytic scoring is considered a complement to holistic scoring by the authors of the Writing Assessment Program. Taken together, holistic and analytic scoring offer a powerful direct measure of a student's writing performance (Bereiter & Scardamalia, 1987; Braddock, Lloyd-Jones, & Schoer, 1963; Cooper & Odell, 1977; Mosenthal, Tamor, & Walmsley, 1983; Kellogg, 1994). A 4-point scale is used for analytic scoring, which is sufficient to describe a student's achievement in using syntax, word choice, spelling, and the conventions of language. A separate analytic score is reported for each of the three analytic categories: writing mechanics, sentence formation, and usage. Because there is a single reader for analytic scoring, the lowest possible ana-

lytic score for any of the three categories is 1; the highest possible score is 4. Like the Writing Assessment Program's holistic scoring, the analytic scoring uses scoring standards based on developmental considerations. Three standards, or developmental levels, have been established for analytic scoring (Standard I: 3.5–5.5; Standard II: 5.5–7.5; Standard III: 7.5–12.9). As with the holistic scoring, papers are scored using anchor papers and scoring criteria guides. Again, the development of standards and scoring guidelines helps to ensure reasonable and consistent criteria for scoring.

Users can obtain several types of scores from the Standard Writing Assessment Program. These scores can be grouped into two categories: raw scores and norm-referenced scores. The raw scores are related to specific prompts at the various levels, whereas the norm-referenced scores are used to compare a student's performance to the performance of students representing a particular reference group. The characteristics, applications, and limitations of each type of score are presented in a straightforward manner in order to help users determine which scores are needed for their particular purposes.

The authors of the Stanford Writing Assessment Program provide two extraordinarily complete, user-friendly manuals: The Stanford Writing Assessment Program: Manual for Interpreting and the Stanford Writing Assessment Program: National Norms Booklet. In the Manual for Interpreting, the user is provided with information that includes an overview of the Writing Assessment Program, scoring principles and procedures, interpreting test results, and improving students' writing. In the National Norms Booklet, the user is presented with precise technical information on the National Standardization Programs used to obtain normative data descriptive of writing performance in the nation's schools and to establish the statistical reliability and validity of the Writing Assessment Program. The programs involved four separate phases: Spring Standardization, Fall Standardization, Equating of Levels, and Equating of Forms. For the Spring Standardization, approximately 64,400 students participated in the standardization, with another 68,600 in the equating programs. For the Fall Standardization, approximately 35,200 students participated in the program. Approximately 400 school districts from across the nation were represented in the research program. The Writing Assessment Program was normed concurrently with the Stanford Achievement Test Series, Eighth Edition. A two-stage sampling procedure was employed. During the first stage, a nationally representative sample was selected to take the Stanford battery. Participants were selected to represent the national student population in terms of geographic region, socioeconomic status, urbanicity, and ethnicity. In the second stage, a stratified random subsample was selected to participate in the standardization of the Writing Assessment Program. The subsample was also selected to represent the national student population with respect to socioeconomic status and ethnicity. In this reviewer's judgment, these manuals set a standard of excellence for thoroughness and comprehensibility.

To conclude, this reviewer would highly recommend the use of the Stanford Writing Assessment Program, Second Edition, as an important part of any school district's efforts to develop valid and reliable assessments of its students' writing achievement. If the results from the Writing Assessment Program are used in concert with other information gathered about students' writing such as in-class writing assignments, homework, reports, and special projects, users will have a powerful data source that will allow them to map the development of their students' writing achievement and to create writing instructional programs targeted to meet the needs of their students.

REVIEWER'S REFERENCES

Braddock, R., Lloyd-Jones, R., & Schoer, L. (1963). *Research in written composition.* Champaign, IL: National Council on Teachers of English.

Perelman, C., & Olbrechts-Tyteca, L. (1969). *The new rhetoric: A treatise on argumentation* (J. Wilkinson & P. Weaver, Trans.). Notre Dame, IN: University of Notre Dame Press.

Cooper, C. R., & Odell, L. (1977). *Evaluating writing: Describing, measuring, judging.* Urbana, IL: National Council of Teachers of English.

Britton, J., Burgess, T., Martin, N., McLeod, A., & Rosen, H. (1979). *The development of writing abilities (11–18).* London: Macmillan Education Ltd.

Flower, L. S., & Hayes, J. R. (1980). The dynamics of composing: Making plans and juggling constraints. In L. W. Gregg & E. R. Steinberg (Eds.), *Cognitive processes in writing.* Hillsdale, NJ: Lawrence Erlbaum.

Kinneavy, J. (1980) *A theory of discourse.* New York: W. W. Norton.

Mosenthal, P., Tamor, L., & Walmsley, S. A. (Eds.). (1983). *Research on writing: Principles and methods.* New York: Longman.

Hillocks, G., Jr. (1986). *Research on written composition: New directions for teaching.* Urbana, IL: National Conference on Research in English and ERIC Clearinghouse on Reading and Communication Skills.

Bereiter, C., & Scardamalia, M. (1987). *The psychology of written composition.* Hillsdale, NJ: Lawrence Erlbaum.

Lauer, J. M., & Asher, J. W. (1988). *Composition research: Empirical designs.* New York: Oxford University Press.

Corbett, E. P. J. (1990). *Classical rhetoric for the modern student* (3rd ed.). New York: Oxford University Press.

Cazden, C. B. (Ed.). (1992). *Whole language plus: Essays on literacy in the United States and New Zealand.* New York: Teachers College Press.

Kellogg, R. T. (1994). *The psychology of writing.* New York: Oxford University Press.

Mullis, I. V. S., Dossey, J. A., Campbell, J. R., Gentile, C. A., O'Sullivan, C., & Latham, A. S. (1994, July). *National Center for Education Statistics: Report in brief: NAEP 1992 trends in academic progress: Achievement of U.S. students in science, 1969 to 1992; mathematics, 1973 to 1992; reading, 1971 to 1992; writing, 1984 to 1992: Report No. 23-TR01.* Washington, DC: U.S. Department of Education, Office of Educational Research and Improvement.

White, E. M. (1994). *Teaching and assessing writing* (2nd ed.). San Francisco: Jossey-Bass Publishers.

Lindemann, E. (1995). *A rhetoric for writing teachers* (3rd ed.). New York: Oxford University Press.

Anastasi, A. (1996). *Psychological testing* (7th ed.). New York: Macmillan Publishing Company.

[296]
State-Trait Anger Expression Inventory, Revised Research Edition.

Purpose: To provide "concise measures of the experience and expression of anger."
Population: Ages 13 and over.
Publication Dates: 1979–1991.
Acronym: STAXI.
Scores, 8: State Anger, Trait Anger, Angry Temperament, Angry Reaction, Anger-in, Anger-out, Anger Control, Anger Expression.
Administration: Individual or group.
Forms, 2: HS, G.
Price Data, 1996: $79 per complete kit including manual ('91, 27 pages), 50 item booklets, and 50 rating sheets; $31 per 50 item booklets; $31 per 50 rating sheets; $27 per manual; scoring service offered by publisher.
Time: (10–12) minutes.
Comments: Test booklet title is *Self-Rating Questionnaire.*
Author: Charles D. Spielberger.
Publisher: Psychological Assessment Resources, Inc.
Cross References: See T4:2562 (12 references); for reviews by Bruce H. Biskin and Paul Retzlaff of an earlier edition, see 11:379 (8 references).
[Editor's Note: The following reviews are based on materials received in 1995. The 1996 edition will be reviewed in the next *MMY.*]

TEST REFERENCES

1. Anderson, N. B., Lane, J. D., Taguchi, F., & Williams, R. B., Jr. (1989). Patterns of cardiovascular responses to stress as a function of race and parental hypertension in men. *Health Psychology, 8,* 525–540.

2. Armstead, C. A., Lawler, K. A., Gorden, G., Cross, J., & Gibbons, J. (1989). Relationship of racial stressors to blood pressure responses and anger expression in Black college students. *Health Psychology, 8,* 541–556.

3. Deffenbacher, J. L., & Shepard, J. M. (1989). Evaluating a seminar on stress management. *Teaching of Psychology, 16,* 79-81.

4. Ditto, B., France, C., & Miller, S. (1989). Spouse and parent-offspring similarities in cardiovascular response to mental arithmetic and isometric hand-grip. *Health Psychology, 8,* 159–173.

5. Riley, W. T., Treiber, F. A., & Woods, M. G. (1989). Anger and hostility in depression. *The Journal of Nervous and Mental Disease, 177,* 668-674.

6. Woodall, K. L., & Matthews, K. A. (1989). Familial environment associated with type A behaviors and psychophysiological responses to stress in children. *Health Psychology, 8,* 403–426.

7. Czajkowski, S. M., Hindelang, R. D., Dembroski, T. M., Mayerson, S. E., Parks, E. B., & Holland, J. C. (1990). Aerobic fitness, psychological characteristics, and cardiovascular reactivity to stress. *Health Psychology, 9,* 676-692.

8. Folingstad, D. R., Wright, S., Lloyd, S., & Sebastian, J. A. (1991). Sex differences in motivations and effects in dating violence. *Family Relations, 40,* 51-57.

9. Welsh, W. N., & Gorden, A. (1991). Cognitive mediators of aggression: Test of a causal model. *Criminal Justice and Behavior, 18,* 125–145.

10. Denollt, J., & De Potter, B. (1992). Coping subtypes for men with coronary heart disease: Relationship to well-being, stress and type A behaviour. *Psychological Medicine, 22,* 667-684.

11. Dolan, C. A., Sherwood, A., & Light, K. C. (1992). Cognitive coping strategies and blood pressure responses to real-life stress in healthy young men. *Health Psychology, 11,* 233–240.

12. Johnson, E. H., Collier, P., Nazzaro, P., & Gilbert, D. C. (1992). Psychological and physiological predictors of lipids in black males. *Journal of Behavioral Medicine, 15,* 285-298.

13. Jorgensen, R. S., Gelling, P. D., & Kliner, L. (1992). Patterns of social desirability and anger in young men with a parental history of hypertension: Association with cardiovascular activity. *Health Psychology, 11,* 403–412.

14. Kroner, D. G., & Reddon, J. R. (1992). The Anger Expression Scale and State-Trait Anger Scale: Stability, reliability, and factor structure in an inmate sample. *Criminal Justice and Behavior, 19,* 397–408.

15. Landsbergis, P. A., Schnall, P. L., Deitz, D., Friedman, R., & Pickering, T. (1992). The patterning of psychological attributes and distress by "job strain" and social support in a sample of working men. *Journal of Behavioral Medicine, 15,* 379-405.

16. Mendes deLeon, C. F. (1992). Anger and impatience/irritability in patients of low socioeconomic status with acute coronary heart disease. *Journal of Behavioral Medicine, 15*, 273-284.

17. Ballard, M. E., Cummings, E. M., & Larkin, K. (1993). Emotional and cardiovascular responses to adults' angry behavior and to challenging tasks in children of hypertensive and normotensive parents. *Child Development, 64*, 500-515.

18. Burns, J. W., & Katkin, E. S. (1993). Psychological, situational, and gender predictors of cardiovascular relativity to stress: A multivariate approach. *Journal of Behavioral Medicine, 16*, 445-465.

19. Linden, W., Chambers, L., Maurice, J., & Lenz, J. W. (1993). Sex differences in social support, self-deception, hostility and ambulatory cardiovascular activity. *Health Psychology, 12*, 376-380.

20. Semenchuk, E. M., & Larkin, K. T. (1993). Behavioral and cardiovascular responses to interpersonal challenges among male offspring of essential hypertensives. *Health Psychology, 12*, 416-419.

21. Suarez, E. C., Harlan, E., Peoples, M. C., & Williams, R. B. (1993). Cardiovascular and emotional responses in women: The role of hostility and harrassment. *Health Psychology, 12*, 459-468.

22. Clark, M. E. (1994). Interpretive limitations of the MMPI-2 anger and cynicism content scales. *Journal of Personality Assessment, 63*, 89-96.

23. Comunian, A. L. (1994). Anger, curiosity, and optimism. *Psychological Reports, 75*, 1523-1528.

24. Deffenbacher, J. L., Thwaites, G. A., Wallace, T. L., & Oetting, E. R. (1994). Social skills and cognitive-relaxation approaches to general anger reduction. *Journal of Counseling Psychology, 41*, 386-396.

25. Dreman, S., & Aldor, R. (1994). A comparative study of custodial mothers and fathers in the stabilization phase of the divorce process. *Journal of Divorce & Remarriage, 21*(3/4), 59-79.

26. Dreman, S., & Aldor, R. (1994). Work or marriage? Competence in custodial mothers in the stabilization phase of the divorce process. *Journal of Divorce & Remarriage, 22*(1/2), 3-22.

27. Ferrari, J. R., & Olivette, M. J. (1994). Parental authority and the development of female dysfunctional procrastination. *Journal of Research in Personality, 28*, 87-100.

28. Greene, A. F., Jones, C. J., & Johnson, E. H. (1994). Psychopathology and anger in interpersonal violence offenders. *Journal of Clinical Psychology, 50*, 906-912.

29. Haaga, D. A. F., Davison, G. C., Williams, M. E., Dolezal, S. L., Haleblian, J., Rosenbum, J., Dwyer, J. H., Baker, S., Nezami, E., & DeQuattro, V. (1994). Mode-specific impact of relaxation training for hypertensive men with Type A behavior pattern. *Behavior Therapy, 25*, 209-223.

30. Hains, A. A. (1994). The effectiveness of a school-based, cognitive-behavioral stress management program with adolescents reporting high and low levels of emotional arousal. *The School Counselor, 42*, 114-125.

31. Law, A., Logan, H., & Baron, R. (1994). Desire for control, felt control, and stress inoculation training during dental treatment. *Journal of Personality and Social Psychology, 67*, 926-936.

32. Marshall, G. N., Wortman, C. B., Vickers, R. R., Jr., Kusulas, J. W., & Hervig, L. K. (1994). The five-factor model of personality as a framework for personality-health research. *Journal of Personality and Social Psychology, 67*, 278-286.

33. Pugh, D. N. (1994). Revision and further assessment of the Prison Locus of Control Scale. *Psychological Reports, 74*, 979-986.

34. Siblerud, R. L., Motl, J., & Kienholz, E. (1994). Psychometric evidence that mercury from silver dental fillings may be an etiological factor in depression, excessive anger, and anxiety. *Psychological Reports, 74*, 67-80.

35. Smyth, N. J., Ivanoff, A., & Jang, S. J. (1994). Changes in psychological maladaptation among inmate parasuicides. *Criminal Justice and Behavior, 21*, 357-365.

36. Clay, D. L., Wood, P. K., Frank, R. G., Hagglund, K. J., & Johnson, J. C. (1995). Examining systematic differences to chronic illness: A growth modeling approach. *Rehabilitation Psychology, 40*, 61-70.

37. Deffenbacher, J. L., Oetting, E. R., Huff, M. E., & Thwaites, G. A. (1995). Fifteen-month follow-up of social skills and cognitive-relaxation approaches to general anger reduction. Journal of Counseling Psychology, 42, 400-405.

38. Dunkley, D. M., Blankstein, K. R., & Flett, G. L. (1995). Self-criticism and dependency in relation to anger. *Psychological Reports, 76*, 1342.

39. Eckhardt, C. I., Kassinove, H., Tsytsarev, S. V., & Sukhodolsky, D. G. (1995). A Russian version of the State-Trait Anger Expression Inventory: Preliminary data. *Journal of Personality Assessment, 64*, 440-455.

40. Epps, J., & Kendall, P. C. (1995). Hostile attributional bias in adults. *Cognitive Therapy and Research, 19*, 159-178.

41. Foa, E. B., Riggs, D. S., Massle, E. D., & Yacczower, M. (1995). The impact of fear activation and anger on the efficacy of exposure treatment for posttraumatic stress disorder. *Behavior Therapy, 26*, 487-499.

42. Goldman, L., & Haaga, D. A. F. (1995). Depression and the experience and expression of anger in marital and other relationship. *The Journal of Nervous and Mental Disease, 183*, 505-509.

43. Saam, R. H., Hodtke, K. H., & Hains, A. A. (1995). A cognitive reduction program for recently unemployed managers. *The Career Development Quarterly, 44*, 43-51.

44. Snell, W. E., Jr., Gum, S., Shuck, R. L., Mosley, J. A., & Hite, T. L. (1995). The Clinical Anger Scale: Preliminary reliability and validity. *Journal of Clinical Psychology, 51*, 215-226.

45. Sutker, P. B., Davis, J. M., Uddo, M., & Ditta, S. R. (1995). Assessment of psychological distress in Persian Gulf troops: Ethnicity and gender comparisons. *Journal of Personality Assessment, 64*, 415-427.

46. Vitaliano, P. P., Russo, J., & Niaura, R. (1995). Plasma lipids and their relationships with psychosocial factors in older adults. *Journal of Gerontology: Psychological Sciences, 50B*, P18-P24.

47. Blazina, C., & Watkins, C. E., Jr. (1996). Masculine gender role conflict: Effects on college men's psychological well-being, chemical substance usage, and attitudes toward help-seeking. *Journal of Counseling Psychology, 43*, 461-465.

48. Deffenbacher, J. L., Lynch, R. S., Oetting, E. R., & Kemper, C. C. (1996). Anger reduction in early adolescents. *Journal of Counseling Psychology, 43*, 149-157.

49. Deffenbacher, J. L., Oetting, E. R., Thwaites, G. A., Lynch, R. S., Baker, D. A., Stark, R. S., Tacker, S., & Elswerth-Cox, L. (1996). State-trait anger theory and the utility of the Trait Anger Scale. *Journal of Counseling Psychology, 43*, 131-148.

50. Kopper, B. A., & Epperson, D. L. (1996). The experience and expression of anger: Relationships with gender, gender role socialization, depression, and mental health functioning. *Journal of Counseling Psychology, 43*, 158-165.

51. Newman, A. L., & Peterson, C. (1996). Anger of women incest survivors. *Sex Roles, 34*, 463-474.

52. Schafer, J., & Fals-Stewart, W. (1997). Spousal violence and cognitive functioning among men recovering from multiple substance abuse. *Addictive Behaviors, 22*, 127-130.

Review of the State-Trait Anger Expression Inventory, Revised Research Edition by DAVID J. PITTENGER, Associate Professor of Psychology, Marietta College, Marietta, OH:

Spielberger developed the State-Trait Anger Expression Inventory (STAXI) as an empirical measure of anger experience and expression. The goals for the test are to provide a means for assessing anger reaction within normal and clinical populations, and to examine the link between anger and various medical conditions. The revised edition provides the potential user with a more broad and comprehensive collection of psychometric information concerning the performance of the test.

The STAXI consists of 44 questions ranging in length from "I am furious" to "If someone annoys me, I'm apt to tell him or her how I feel." Responses for each statement are coded on a 4-point Likert scale. The hand-scored version of the test requires a series of simple computations for each of the eight subscales. A machine-scored version of the test is also available. Appendix A of the manual provides a comprehensive collection of tables, representing different normative samples, for converting the raw scores of each of the scales into T-scores and percentiles. Specifically, this appendix includes tables for male and female adults, college students, and adolescents. Appendix B contains normative tables for special populations including, for example, medical and surgical patients, prison inmates, and military recruits. Separate tables for males and females of each population are included.

As the title implies, the instrument attempts to measure State and Trait Anger. State Anger refers to reactions to specific events in time whereas Trait Anger measures the general disposition for anger. The Trait Anger scale is further subdivided into two separate components labeled Angry Temperament and Angry Reaction. Angry Temperament refers to persons who express their anger with little or no provocation. Angry Reaction refers to persons who become angered when criticized. The four additional scales consist of Anger-In, Anger-Out, Anger Control, and Anger Expression. The Anger-In and Anger-Out scales attempt to measure the degree to which a person withholds expression of anger, or directs anger towards others. The Anger Control scale measures the frequency with which the person attempts to control his or her expression of anger. Anger Expression is a measure of the frequency with which the person expresses anger.

The manual is clearly written and provides much necessary information. The author takes pains to note that the instrument is a research tool and should not be used indiscriminately or used by persons without professional training in psychometrics. In addition, the author notes that clinical interpretations should be made with caution. The author urges clinical users of the test to develop local norms for the scales.

Test scores are interpreted by converting the scale raw scores to percentiles. As a generality, persons scoring above the 75th percentile may have levels of anger expression that interfere with their lives. As with other parts of the manual, the author provides clear interpretations of scores for persons scoring high on each of the subscales.

The manual contains basic descriptive statistics about each of the scales including mean, standard deviations, and coefficient alphas for each of the scales. Reviewing the tables in the two appendices, it is apparent that the scales have considerable skew. Given the sizable nature of the skew, the use of empirically derived percentiles in the interpretation of the data is imperative.

The only reliability information is coefficient alphas for the various scales. There is no information concerning the temporal stability of the scale scores. As Cronbach (1990) made clear, different reliability indices estimate a different source of variation due, for example, to sampling or measurement error. Because the experience and expression of anger may be ephemeral phenomena, test-retest reliability data would be greatly appreciated.

The wording of the questions makes clear the purpose of the instrument. However, the STAXI does not contain a mechanism for assessing the veracity of the individual's responses. Similarly, the manual does not report the relation between scale scores and measures of social desirability or other indices that indicate an individual's propensity to provide a less-than-honest set of responses.

The manual provides a detailed review of attempts to demonstrate the validity of the inventory. For example, assessment of coefficient alphas and factor analysis indicate justification for the various scales. Additionally, the coefficient alphas for the State and Trait Anger scales range from .82 to .93 for normal populations. High factor loading corroborates the independence and unique character of the two scales. Correlations of the STAXI and other measures of anger and psychopathology reveal evidence of convergent and discriminant validity.

There is also a report of empirical studies relating scores on the STAXI with various cardiovascular disorders. For example, there is a moderate correlation between the Anger-In scale and increased levels of systolic and diastolic blood pressure. Most of this research was conducted in the 1980s, however. Unfortunately, the concurrent and predictive validity of the STAXI have not been extensively studied since the publication of the revised manual. The initial research successes portend future uses and refinements of the instrument.

Although the manual is well written and provides the reader with useful information, the layout of the manual leaves much to be desired. The font, pitch size, and layout of the manual created much eye strain for me. I can read without glasses; therefore, I pity the reader whose eyesight is challenged.

In summary, the STAXI appears to offer what it advertises. The instrument is a research tool that can be used effectively to measure components of an important emotion. As with any measurement tool, the STAXI requires and will benefit from continued empirical analysis and refinement. Presently, the instrument appears to offer many opportunities for future insights into the relation between an individuals' expression of anger and the biological and social consequences of those behaviors.

REVIEWER'S REFERENCE

Cronbach, L. J. (1990). *Essentials of psychological testing* (5th ed.). New York: Harper Collins.

Review of the State-Trait Anger Expression Inventory, Revised Research Edition by ALAN J. RAPHAEL, President, International Assessment Systems, Inc., and Adjunct Associate Professor of Psychology, University of Miami, Miami, FL:

Published solely as a research tool in 1979, 1986, 1988, 1989, and 1991 by Psychological Assessment Resources, Inc. (PAR), the State-Trait Anger Expression Inventory (STAXI) is a 44-item self-rating inventory based on the six scales and two subscales developed by the author as a byproduct of two long-term personality assessment research projects. This began in 1966 to measure both the experience and expression of two of the major components of anger: trait and state anger.

The STAXI was designed as an easily and objectively used research measure of anger experience and anger expression for individuals ages 13 through 67 who possess at least a fifth grade reading level.

The author's definition of State anger is "An emotional state marked by the subjective feelings that vary in intensity from mild annoyance or irritation to intense fury and rage. State anger is generally accompanied by muscular tension and arousal of the autonomic nervous system" (manual, p. 6). The definition of Trait anger is "The disposition to perceive a wide range of situations as annoying or frustrating and the tendency to respond to such situations with more frequent elevations in State anger. Individuals high in trait anger experience state anger more often and with greater intensity than individuals low in trait anger" (p. 6).

Anger expression is viewed as containing three separate components: The expression of anger towards other people or objects (Anger-out); anger expressed inwardly or the holding in or suppressing anger (Anger-in); and the degree to which a person attempts to control the expression of anger (Anger Control).

For the user, this model of classification is essentially consistent with the prevailing major theories of affect and thus would be considered valid from a theoretic standpoint. The author has continued to upgrade and improve the measure since its introduction in 1979.

The 44-item inventory considers three separate scales that include "How I feel right now," "How I generally feel," and "How I react or behave when angry or furious." Although the 44 items reflect a wide range of self-statements, a larger number of stimuli examples would enhance the inventory's applicability.

Like most self-report instruments, this measure has no validity scale or method of controlling for test-taking attitude or external influences such as secondary gain motivation, psychosis, deception, depression, self-serving behavior, lack of understanding, denial, or random responding. This is particularly significant for research with forensic and inpatient psychiatric patient populations.

This measure, like all self-report measures, is limited because it relies on the veracity, forthrightness, self-awareness, motivation, and comprehension of the test taker. This is particularly significant for its self-described special interest groups, including prison inmates, military recruits, and general medical and surgical patients.

Although the 1991 STAXI manual still represents the test as a research edition, the test is well normed with T scores and percentiles generated for a wide number of diverse populations. Users should be careful to select the appropriate norms group for a specific client. The author has made several sets of norms available for consideration.

Although there are a wide range of normative samples available, each sample is limited and can be critiqued in terms of gender makeup, geographic sampling, and generalizability. Issues of ethnicity and culture are also not addressed in the manual. Thus, comparisons to these samples should be limited as closely as possible to the characteristic of the groups collected in the normative studies, although many specifics of each sample are missing in the manual. These deficiencies clearly limit the potential uses of this test in many populations until further data or identifying information are supplied by the author. However, some of the needed data can be obtained from the published literature.

The manual itself presents an extensive list of research articles dealing directly with the validity of the test despite its relative newness. There appear to be at least 40 additional research articles published in the literature from 1991–1996.

The author provides extensive data on concurrent validity with such instruments as the MMPI, BDNI, and EPQ as well as other psychological dimensions including anxiety and curiosity. Correlations with blood pressure in one study are also presented in the manual. These data provide strong information on the convergent and divergent validity of the scales, which appear to hold up well. Research regarding the relationship between Anger Expression and medical symptoms appears especially strong and potentially very useful to the researcher.

Data are presented for the State and Trait scales as well as the Anger Expression scales. However, there is little information presented on test-retest reliability across populations. The scales themselves were developed with an aim towards maximizing internal consistency reliability using factor analytic techniques.

A major limitation in the published research data to date is the lack of replication outside of the author's students, although we are now beginning to see such studies appearing in the literature. Also, it should be emphasized that this measure is clearly designated as a research measures and has not been released for general clinical use. Clinical uses of the test, such as with forensic or employment populations, are also less clear, as is the impact of malingering or other self-serving or deviant response styles.

Overall, from an empirical viewpoint there is much this instrument has to offer to the researcher. Despite some of the cultural and normative deficits and the expected limits of most self-report inventories (i.e., the absence of a validity scale), this measure is a valuable tool in the hands of a personality assessment researcher or medical researcher interested in the focalized measurement of the self-reported affect of anger. Its use for general clinical measurement remains untested.

The data presented in the manual clearly show that the author is well aware of the standards for psychological tests, thus, it is quite likely that this test will withstand the evaluation of time. It is clearly a well-thought-out, soundly researched instrument equal to or better than other similar measures.

[297]
State Trait Depression Adjective Check Lists.

Purpose: "Measures depressed mood and feelings in a form that neither implies pathology nor is judgmental."
Population: Ages 14 and older.
Publication Dates: 1967–1994.
Acronym: ST-DACL.
Scores, 6: State-Positive Mood, State-Negative Mood, State Mood-Total, Trait-Positive Mood, Trait-Negative Mood, Trait Mood-Total.
Administration: Group.
Forms, 4: 1, 2, A-B, C-D.
Price Data, 1996: $75 per introductory kit including manual ('94, 117 pages), 25 Forms 1 & 2, 25 Forms A-B, 25 Forms C-D, and 25 profile forms; $13 per 25 check lists for Forms 1 & 2, A-B, or C-D; $17 per 25 profile forms; $35 per manual; $22 per bibliography.
Time: (8) minutes per list (A–G).
Comments: Developed from the Depression Adjective Check Lists (T4:742); Forms 1 and 2 are used to measure state and trait depressed mood, Forms A-B and C-D are used to measure only state depressed mood.
Author: Bernard Lubin.
Publisher: Psychological Assessment Resources, Inc.
Cross References: See T4:742 (79 references); see also 9:315 (21 references), T3:681 (46 references), 8:536 (20 references), and T2:1154 (2 references); for reviews of the earlier edition by Leonard D. Goodstein and Douglas M. McNair, see 7:65 (3 references); see also P:57 (4 references).

TEST REFERENCES

1. Deutscher, S., & Cimbolic, P. (1990). Cognitive processes and their relationship to endogenous and reactive components of depression. *The Journal of Nervous and Mental Disease, 178,* 351-359.
2. Kamen-Siegel, L., Rodin, J., Seligman, M. E. P., & Dwyer, J. (1991). Explanatory style and cell-mediated immunity in elderly men and women. *Health Psychology, 10,* 229-235.
3. Katz, R. (1991). Marital status and well-being: A comparison of widowed, divorced, and married mothers in Israel. *Journal of Divorce & Remarriage, 14*(3/4), 203-218.
4. Grimmell, D., & Stern, G. S. (1992). The relationship between gender role ideals and psychological well-being. *Sex Roles, 27,* 487-497.
5. Hatch, J. P., Moore, P. J., Bocherding, S., Cyr-Provost, M., Boutros, N. N., & Seleshi, E. (1992). Electromyographic and affective responses of episodic tension-type headache patients and headache-free controls during stressful task performance. *Journal of Behavioral Medicine, 15,* 89-112.
6. Pop, V. J., Komproe, I. H., & van Son, M. J. (1992). Characteristics of the Edinburgh Post Natal Depression Scale in the Netherlands. *Journal of Affective Disorders, 26,* 105-110.
7. Sung, H., Lubin, B., & Yi, J. (1992). Reliability and validity of the Korean Youth Depression Adjective Check List (Y-DACL). *Adolescence, 27,* 527-533.
8. Teichman, Y., Rabinovitz, D., & Rabinovitz, Y. (1992). Gender preferences of pregnant women and emotional reaction to information regarding fetal gender and postpartum: An examination of Freud's view about motivation for motherhood. *Sex Roles, 26,* 175-195.
9. Andrews, J. A., Lewinsohn, P. M., Hops, H., & Roberts, R. E. (1993). Psychometric properties of scales for the measurement of psychosocial variables associated with depression in adolescence. *Psychological Reports, 73,* 1019-1046.
10. Lubin, B., & Turnbull, C. M. (1993). Measuring depressive affect in chemically dependent persons using the Depression Adjective Check Lists. *Psychological Reports, 72,* 251-257.
11. Lubin, B., Whitlock, R. V., Schemmel, D. R., & Swearingin, S. E. (1993). Evaluation of a brief measure of depressive mood for use in a university counseling center. *Psychological Reports, 72,* 379-385.
12. Lubin, B., Whitlock, R. V., Swearingin, S. E., & Seever, M. C. (1993). Self-assessment of state and trait depressive affect by college students: Reliability and validity of an adjective check list. *Journal of College Student Development, 34,* 249–255.
13. Sayers, S. L., Baucom, D. H., & Tierney, A. M. (1993). Sex roles, interpersonal control, and depression: Who can get their way? *Journal of Research in Personality, 27,* 377-395.
14. Whitley, B. E., Jr., & Gridley, B. E. (1993). Sex role orientation, self-esteem, and depression: A latent variable analysis. *Personality and Social Psychology Bulletin, 19,* 363-369.
15. Lubin, B., & McCollum, K. L. (1994). Depressive mood in black and white female adolescents. *Adolescence, 29,* 241-245.
16. Lubin, B., McCollum, K. L., Van Whitlock, R., Thummel, H., Powers, M., & Davis, V. (1994). Measuring trait-depressive mood in adolescents with the Depression Adjective Check Lists. *Adolescence, 29,* 193-206.
17. Lubin, B., & Van Whitlock, R. (1994). Development of a critical item scale for the Depression Adjective Check Lists. *Journal of Clinical Psychology, 50,* 841-846.
18. Lubin, B., Van Whitlock, R., McCollum, K. L., Thummel, H., Denman, N., & Powers, M. (1994). Measuring the short-term mood of adolescents: Reliability and validity of the state form of the Depression Adjective Check Lists. *Adolescence, 29,* 591-604.
19. De Beurs, E., van Balkom, A. J. L. M., Lange, A., Koele, P., & van Dyck, R. (1995). Treatment of panic disorder with agoraphobia: Comparison of fluvoxamine, placebo, and psychological panic management combined with exposure and of exposure in vivo alone. *American Journal of Psychiatry, 152,* 683-691.
20. Grayson, P., Lubin, B., & Van Whitlock, R. (1995). Comparison of depression in the community-dwelling and assisted-living elderly. *Journal of Clinical Psychology, 51,* 18-21.
21. Riesenmy, K. R., Lubin, B., Van Whitlock, R., & Penick, E. C. (1995). Psychometric characteristics of the trait version of the Depression Adjective Check Lists (DACL) in adult psychiatric outpatients. *Journal of Clinical Psychology, 51,* 13-17.

Review of the State Trait—Depression Adjective Check Lists by ANDRÉS BARONA, Professor of Educational Psychology and School Psychology Program Training Director, Arizona State University, Tempe, AZ:

The State Trait—Depression Adjective Check Lists (ST-DACL) represent an extension of the Depression Adjective Check Lists (DACL) developed by Lubin (1967; 1981). Whereas the original version measured only State-Mood, the most recent version includes measures of both State-Mood and Trait-Mood.

DEVELOPMENT. The ST-DACL was developed by conducting two separate item analyses on a pool of 171 adjectives from the initial responses of 95 neuropsychiatric patients previously diagnosed as markedly or severely depressed (Goodstein, 1972; ST-DACL professional manual, p. 19) and a control group matched for age and education. All 171 items were administered to 48 female neuropsychiatric patients with a diagnosis of marked or severe depression and 179 normal women. This first item analysis resulted in 128 adjectives that differentiated the two groups; depressed subjects checked 88 items more frequently than normal subjects and normal subjects checked 40 items more frequently than depressed subjects. From these 128 adjectives four lists (A, B, C, and D), each consisting of 22 negative and 10 positive adjectives, were developed.

To conduct the second item analysis, all 171 items also were administered to 47 male patients diagnosed as markedly or severely depressed and 100 normal men. This analysis yielded 108 adjectives, 72 negative and 36 positive, that differentiated the two groups. Three additional lists (E, F, and G), each consisting of 22 negative and 12 positive adjectives, were developed from these 108 adjectives.

In developing the Trait-Mood scales of the ST-DACL, Lubin thought it important to use the same pool of adjectives used to develop the State-Mood scales. Thus, the only difference between the State-Mood and Trait-Mood lists lies in the instructions provided. The instructions for the ST-DACL Trait-Mood lists state, "check the words that describe how you generally feel," instead of "check the words that describe how you feel now—today" (manual, p. 20).

TEST MATERIALS AND PSYCHOMETRIC PROPERTIES. The ST-DACL materials include an examiner's manual and three single-page, color-coded checklists. The first includes ST-DACL Forms 1 and 2 printed in burgundy lettering on opposite sides of the same sheet. Forms 1 and 2 are considered equivalent measures. Each form contains 34 State-Mood items and 34 Trait-Mood items placed side by side with separate instructions. Form 1 consists of S-list E and T-list F; and Form 2 consists of S-list E and T-list G. The State-Mood form asks clients to "Check the words that describe how you feel now—today" and the Trait-Mood form asks clients to "Check the words that describe how you generally feel" (manual, p. 6).

ST-DACL Forms A and B, printed in blue letters on opposite sides of the same sheet, also are considered equivalent forms but measure State-Moods only. The third ST-DACL checklist consists of Forms C and D, is similarly formatted, and also measures State-Mood. Forms A—B and C—D are the original forms from the earlier version (DACL) of the instrument whereas Forms 1—2 include the newer Trait-Mood format.

A color-coded ST-DACL scoring and profile sheet for the three checklists also is provided. The scoring and profile sheet with scoring keys for each checklist is color coded for ease of use and can accommodate up to four repeated administrations of the State-Mood lists.

Two separate sections of the manual are devoted to an extensive presentation of descriptive data, reliability, and validity studies of both the State-Mood and Trait-Mood lists, respectively. State-Mood means, standard deviations, and standard errors of measurement are provided for: (a) adolescents in grades 7 to 12, (b) adults between the ages of 18 and 62, and (c) elderly adults between the ages of 63 and 89. Alpha coefficients are reported for various samples and range from a low of .82 for elderly adults to a high of .94 for adults. Split-half reliabilities also are reported and range from .67 for a group of counseling clients to .95 for adolescents. These moderate to high alpha coefficients and split-half reliability coefficients reported for various samples indicate high internal consistency for the State-Mood checklists. In addition, a number of studies cited in the manual provide evidence of the face, construct, and predictive validity of the State-Mood checklists.

Trait means, standard deviations, and standard errors of measurement for adolescents, young adults, and elderly adults are provided in the manual. Cronbach's alpha, a measure of internal consistency for the Trait-Mood check lists ranged from a low of .79 on T-list D for young adults to a high of .93 on all three T lists (E, F, G) for a state hospital sample. Split-half reliabilities ranged from a low of .60 on T-list D for a referred group to a high of .92 for T-list D for young adults. Additional psychometric studies present evidence of face, construct, and predictive validity of the ST-DACL checklists.

ADVANTAGES AND USE. One major advantage of the ST-DACL is its ease of administration and scoring. Administration is straightforward and the ST-DACL can be self-administered or group-administered in less than 3 minutes. Scoring and profile development is reported to take only 5 minutes, allowing for an entire administration, scoring, and profiling of both the State-Mood and Trait-Mood lists in less than 10 minutes. Instructions for administration are clear and brief for either self or group administrations. This simplicity of administration allows for training a broad range of individuals to administer, *but not to interpret,* the ST-DACL. Previous research on the DACL suggested no significant differences between self-administered and examiner-administered checklists (Lubin, Marone, & Nathan, 1978).

A second advantage is the ST-DACL's applicability to a broad age range and diversity of clientele. The ST-DACL has been used with clients ages 14 to 89, college students, normal and depressed adults, the elderly, and other clinical samples. In addition, the clinical studies by Christenfeld, Lubin, and Satin (1978), Lubin and Whitlock (1993b; 1994a; 1994b), and Lubin, Whitlock, Dale, and Riesenmy (1994), coupled with the addition of the Trait-Mood check lists, suggests the ST-DACL (1994) overcomes the previous criticism that it was primarily useful for research and group categorization but weak in clinical and individual diagnostics.

WEAKNESSES. Although the State-Mood lists have been thoroughly researched, the Trait-Mood lists are relatively new and have not yet been thoroughly examined. Moreover, although factorial and construct validity studies typically have supported the construct validity of the instrument, it still is difficult to determine exactly what the ST-DACL measures. For example, when compared to other measures of depression such as the Beck Depression Inventory (Beck, Ward, Mendelson, Mock, & Erbaugh, 1961), the Zung Depression Scale (Zung, 1965), and the Minnesota Multiphasic Personality Inventory (MMPI) scale scores (Christenfeld, Lubin, & Satin, 1978), only modest correlations ranging from a low of .27 to a high of .44 are reported. One final weakness, perhaps unfounded, is that it appears much of the research aimed at examining both the original DACL and the more recent ST-DACL has been conducted by the author, although to his credit he encourages others to conduct research on all forms of the ST-DACL and appears more than willing to provide information for investigators.

SUMMARY. The DACL (State-Mood) lists have been thoroughly reviewed and scrutinized objectively by Lubin and others for more than two decades. The more recent Trait-Mood component, although not as thoroughly examined as the State-Mood component, appears to be psychometrically sound. The new ST-DACL continues to be useful for both group categorization and research purposes. Moreover, the addition of the Trait-Mood component coupled with more recent clinical studies suggests an increase in the ST-DACL's usefulness in clinical settings and diagnosis as well as for research and group categorizations. Factor analytical studies coupled with the ST-DACL's face validity support the notion of a two-factor solution measuring both depressive and positive moods.

In sum, the extension of the DACL to include a Trait-Mood component represents an improvement in an already well-known instrument. This addition coupled with its reasonable price and ease of administration and scoring suggest the ST-DACL will continue to stimulate and generate much research on the measurement and evaluation of depression.

REVIEWER'S REFERENCES

Beck, A. T., Ward, C. H., Mendelson, M., Mock, J., & Erbaugh, J. (1961). Inventory for measuring depression. Archives of General Psychiatry, 4, 561–571.
Zung, W. W. K. (1965). A self-rating depression scale. Archives of General Psychiatry, 12, 63–70.
Lubin, B. (1967). Depression Adjective Check Lists. San Diego, CA: Educational and Industrial Testing Service.
Goodstein, L. D. (1972). [Review of the Depression Adjective Checklists—DACL]. In O. K. Buros (Ed.), The seventh mental measurements yearbook (vol. 1, pp. 132–133). Highland Park, NJ: Gryphon Press.
Christenfeld, R., Lubin, B., & Satin, M. (1978). Concurrent validity of the Depression Adjective Check Lists in a normal population. American Journal of Psychiatry, 135, 582–584.
Lubin, B., Marone, J. G., & Nathan, R. G. (1978). A comparison of self-administered and examiner-administered Depression Adjective Check Lists. Journal of Consulting and Clinical Psychology, 46, 584–585.
Lubin, B. (1981). Depression Adjective Check Lists: Manual (2nd ed.). San Diego, CA: Educational and Industrial Testing Service.
Lubin, B., & Whitlock, R. V. (1993). Diagnostic efficiency of the Depression Adjective Checklists. Journal of Clinical Psychology, 49, 695–901.
Lubin, B., & Whitlock, R. V. (1994a). Development of a critical item scale for the Depression Adjective Checklists. Journal of Clinical Psychology, 50, 841–843.
Lubin, B., & Whitlock, R. V. (1994b). Levels of depression on the ST-Depression Adjective Checklists as defined by the BDI, the MMPI-D scale, and the CES-D scale. Manuscript submitted for publication.
Lubin, B., Whitlock, R. V., Dale, T. M., & Riesenmy, K. R. (1994). Further study of the diagnostic and screening efficiency of the ST-Depression Adjective Check Lists. Manuscript submitted for publication.

Review of the State Trait—Depression Adjective Check Lists by JANET F. CARLSON, Associate Professor, and BETSY WATERMAN, Assistant Professor, Counseling and Psychological Services Department, State University of New York at Oswego, Oswego, NY:

The State Trait—Depression Adjective Check Lists (ST-DACL) was designed to measure depressed mood. This expanded and revised version follows the first two editions of the Depression Adjective Check Lists published in 1967 and 1981. Historically, the DACL has focused on state (current) symptoms of depression but now includes two forms that measure trait depression. The original and current editions include alternative forms, which have made it more useful as a research tool than other, single-form, measures.

The ST-DACL consists of three pairs of lists: Forms 1 and 2 each include a State list and a Trait list; Forms A—B and C—D each include two State lists. Forms 1 and 2 comprise 34 adjectives designed to elicit information about State (how you feel now—today) depression and 34 adjectives designed to elicit information about Trait (how you generally feel) depression. Forms 1 and 2 are suggested for use in initial or final therapy sessions, as part of a psychological battery, or as part of a single therapeutic or research session. Forms A—B and C—D are made up of two lists each of 32 adjectives. These lists are suggested for use in repeated testing. Each list is estimated to take approximately 3 minutes to complete. Reading level of the words is reported to be at the eighth grade level.

The ST-DACL is recommended for use as (a) a periodically administered instrument for evaluating client's progress in counseling or psychotherapy at various points in time, (b) a screening tool for groups of students or adults who are depressed, (c) an outcome measure in research, (d) a means of identifying people who may be at-risk for engaging in poor coping behaviors, and (e) a method for conducting community surveys where measures of depression or psychological distress are needed. The ST-DACL is designed for use with individuals or groups of individuals between the ages of 14 and 89 from either psychiatric or nonpsychiatric populations. Use with special populations (i.e., recent immigrants, individuals for whom English is a second language, nonreaders, or physically or visually disabled persons) is discussed briefly.

Administration and scoring procedures are outlined in the manual, including standardized verbal instructions. Testing administration is generally straightforward and requires only the checking of words that the individual feels describe his or her feelings at this particular point in time (State) or in general (Trait). It was not clearly stated, but assumed, that the test administrator would administer only one list at any given point in time. Some discussion related to the validity of the measure with a particular individual (e.g., if the individual marked an exceedingly high or low percentage of adjectives) was discussed but no specific criteria were presented to assist in making this determination. Administration of this measure with special populations was cursorily outlined and included several deviations from the typical administration such as providing synonyms for adjectives that an individual may not understand. Such deviations may appear to make using this measure more flexible but it is unclear how these may impact the reliability or validity of results. Of particular concern here is the use of this instrument with individuals from different language or cultural backgrounds. The risk of misunderstood terms, even if appropriate synonyms are provided, seems to be high and inaccurate interpretations possible.

Scoring on all forms is accomplished by referring to a scoring key included on the profile forms. This key identifies those terms defined as negative or positive and, to determine the raw score, the test administrator simply counts the number of positive (e.g., "great") and negative (e.g., "lifeless") adjectives that are marked by the individual. Raw score totals for State depressed mood are achieved by adding the number of positive adjectives that were not marked (a measure of "absence of positive mood") to the number of negative adjectives that were marked. On Forms 1 and 2, totals for Trait depressed mood also can be determined in the same manner as that described for State-Total. Raw scores are converted to standard scores (T-scores) and percentiles using the tables provided in the appendices. Separate tables exist for males and females at three age levels— Adolescent 14–18 years), Young Adult (19–62 years), and Elderly Adult (63–89) years). A shaded area of the grid indicates where State Mood-Total and Trait Mood-Total scores reach the clinically significant range.

Interpretation of test data is suggested across several levels—respondent's behavior, review of specific adjectives marked, comparison with normative group, comparison of state and trait mood scores, and interpretation of the complete configuration of scores. The use of both quantitative and qualitative information in interpretation is encouraged.

Norms were developed in the early 1990s. It is difficult to ascertain the precise number of subjects used in the standardization sample from the information provided in the test manual. The total sample size appears to be adequate, exceeding 1,000. Evidence from an earlier study conducted in 1980 by the author and his associates indicates that no age trends were noted in a national sample. Based on this finding, the current norms for the Young Adult group were developed and based entirely on the responses of college students at an unspecified number of sites. Demographic data about the normative samples are incomplete, although they usually include information about sex and age.

Psychometric properties are reported in separate chapters for state and trait components. Data related to previous editions are intermingled with data pertaining exclusively to the current edition, although this is not readily apparent in the test manual. The author presents extensive information concerning reliability and validity. However, the manner of presentation leaves much to be desired, as information to which a potential test user must have ready access is obfuscated by information of questionable relevance or utility.

Internal consistency reliability is addressed using alpha reliability coefficients and split-half reliabilities. Among nonreferred samples, alpha coefficients for the State scale ranged from .82 to .94 across lists and age groups (median value .89). As expected, split-half reliabilities were slightly lower, on average, with a median value of .86. Somewhat lower reliability coefficients are reported for two clinic populations. Alternate forms reliability coefficients ranged from .77 to .93 across lists and age groups (median value .86) among nonreferred samples. Comparable coefficients are reported for two clinic populations. Test-retest reliability coefficients for the State scale are reported. Because the scale is designed to assess mood at the moment the respondent replies rather than over a period of time, coefficients were, predictably and understandably, low.

For the Trait scale, alpha coefficients ranged from .79 to .91 across lists and age groups (median value about .86) among nonreferred samples, and split-half reliabilities were slightly lower, on average (median value .81). The test manual also reports internal consistency reliabilities for several referred groups. Alternate forms reliability coefficients were between .73 and .93 across lists and age groups (median value about .86) among nonreferred samples. Test-retest reliability coefficients for the Trait scale are reported, using intervals from 5 days to 7 weeks. Across lists and age groups, correlation coefficients ranged from .44 to .84, with a median coefficient of .62.

Validation evidence for the State scale is provided in the test manual under the headings of construct, factorial, and predictive validity. Correlation coefficients between the ST-DACL State scores and the Beck Depression Inventory (BDI), Self-Rating Depression Scale (SDS), Children's Depression Inventory (CDI), The Center for Epidemiologic Studies—Depression Scale (CES-D), and the Geriatric Depression Scale (GDS) demonstrated median values of .59, .60, .49, .51, and .34, respectively. A variety of additional validation evidence is summarized in the test manual.

Factorial validity of the State scales is addressed by the presentation of the results of factor analyses, which suggest that there are two factors—depressed mood and elated mood. Only the primary factor pattern is presented in the test manual. As the minimum factor loading was .30, sizable secondary loadings are possible and may be important, but these are not presented in the test manual. Similar results for factorial validity of the Trait scales are reported.

Predictive validity of the State scale was assessed by administering two of the lists to 229 newly enlisted United States Air Force recruits and con-

ducting discriminant function analyses to determine whether the lists would differentiate recruits who were discharged prior to graduation from those who graduated. Mean differences between the groups were observed and were in the predicted direction. However, insufficient base rate information appears to make the results concerning prediction and correct classification rates suspect.

Validation evidence for the Trait scale is presented in terms of construct and factorial validity. Construct validity, in the form of convergent validity, is based on correlation coefficients between the ST-DACL and the BDI, CDI, SDS, CES-D, and the GDS. Median coefficients were .62, .57, .65, .52, and .56, respectively. Further evidence of construct validation is provided in the test manual, where additional instruments or subscales therein are used to draw comparisons and contrasts with the ST-DACL Trait scale.

Evidence concerning the reliability and validity of the State and Trait subscales (State-Positive Mood, State-Negative Mood, Trait-Positive Mood, and Trait-Negative Mood) also is presented in the test manual. Other issues related to validity of the State and Trait scales (e.g., response sets, faking, social desirability, psychiatric diagnoses, and assessment of suicide risk) are discussed and research bearing on these issues and their relevance to the ST-DACL is noted. The author, appropriately, acknowledges that several of these issues will require further investigation.

The ST-DACL is an easy and quick-to-administer check list that appears to be sensitive to dysphoric mood state. It is reported for use across a wide age range (14—89) and with various special populations although appropriate norm comparison groups were not always included in the norming sample. The inclusion of alternative forms is useful for research applications. The author appropriately suggests that this instrument be interpreted only by trained clinicians. Such a caution appears particularly important given the highly subjective, almost "look-see," approach to administration and interpretation. The author acknowledges the need for additional studies of the ST-DACL particularly relating to issues of faking, response set, and social desirability.

Intermingling of data from earlier editions with data from the present editions leads to unnecessary confusion and extra work for the test user. Descriptive labels of the tables could be more accurate and clear (e.g., few people would think of a 62-year-old person as a young adult and most test users would prefer ages listed on the tables). The normative sample is restricted, particularly for those between the ages of 19 and 62. The lists themselves were constructed about 30 years ago and may be in need of revamping.

In the absence of a theory or clear definition of how the author conceptualizes depression one must make the assumption that state and trait symptomology or experiences are distinct from each other, something that may or may not be true. The author states that this instrument is designed to measure one critical aspect of the symptom picture of depression (i.e., dysphoric mood), but then encourages use in much broader ways. The levels of validity that the author is presenting support the use of this instrument as a possible screening instrument or research measure. If clinical applications are made, such applications should be accompanied by additional (i.e., multiple) measures as has been suggested elsewhere (Petzel, 1985).

REVIEWER'S REFERENCE

Petzel, T. P. (1985). Depression Adjective Checklists. In D. J. Keyser & R. C. Sweetland (Eds.), *Test critiques* (vol. III. pp. 215–220). Kansas City, MO: Westport.

[298]
The Stieglitz Informal Reading Inventory: Assessing Reading Behaviors from Emergent to Advanced Levels.

Purpose: Designed to provide educators with information about students' reading behaviors.
Population: Grades 1–9.
Publication Date: 1992.
Acronym: SIRI.
Scores, 7: Graded Words in Context (Independent, Instructional, Frustration), Graded Reading Passages (Word Recognition, Oral Comprehension, Prior Knowledge, Interest).
Administration: Individual.
Price Data: Available from publisher.
Time: (20–30) minutes.
Author: Ezra L. Stieglitz.
Publisher: Allyn and Bacon.

Review of The Stieglitz Informal Reading Inventory: Assessing Reading Behaviors from Emergent to Advanced Levels by KORESSA KUTSICK MALCOLM, School Psychologist, Augusta County Public Schools, Fisherville, VA:

The Stieglitz Informal Reading Inventory was designed to provide professionals who are involved in the diagnosis of reading skills and behaviors a more comprehensive test than has been available previously. In the manual, the author provides a summary of reading inventories research that highlights the strengths and weaknesses of these tests. The rationale for the development of the Stieglitz Inventory was to incorporate the positive attributes, and address the weaknesses of, this form of reading assessment.

The author contends the Stieglitz Inventory differs from other tests of its kind in several ways. The test incorporates the standard practice of evaluating a reader's knowledge of basic sight words as well as obtaining information regarding the informal, instructional, and frustration reading levels of students. In addition to these, Stieglitz has included materials and procedures to measure an individual's skill at reading words in context as well as those needed to assess the prereading skills of young or nonreading subjects. This second assessment strategy involves analysis of a subject's dictated story, which includes review of the student's reading of his or her own story, identifications of words in that story, and review of the subject's general awareness of oral and written communication. One very positive feature of the Stieglitz Inventory is that it allows examiners to obtain more subjective information about a student's reading history (i.e., familiarity with particular topics), which can be incorporated into the interpretation of the individual's reading performance. Another interesting feature of the Stieglitz Inventory is that it provides for the assessment of the differences between a subject's reading of narrative and expository text. This difference could be useful in determining types of reading materials that would be of most interest, or of most necessity, to subjects involved in remedial reading activities.

One of the most positive aspects of the Stieglitz Inventory is that it provides for a rather detailed analysis of a student's reading skills. Examiners may select the extent to which they want to examine an individual's reading skills based on the amount of time they have available to assess subjects, as well as on the level of analysis needed to design instructional programs for those subjects. Comprehensive information is provided which allows extensive error analysis. The scoring codes utilized in this process may be somewhat difficult for examiners to master; however, the recommendation to tape record reading sessions should help first time users to obtain accurate analyses of subjects' readings.

Reading materials necessary to administer the Stieglitz Inventory are included in the manual. Examiners may photocopy particular sets of materials to fit their evaluation needs. Users of this test would be encouraged to obtain their own three-ringed binder to keep the materials in order, as the presented format of the manual would not hold up well with extensive wear. Lamination of the reading materials might also be necessary for this same reason. Other materials, such as carbon paper and a tape recorder or computer screen/word processing program, must be supplied by the test user.

Reading difficulties of the presented passages of the Stieglitz Inventory were obtained by two different techniques. The Spache Readability Formula was applied to the grade 1 through grade 3 passages and the Fry Readability Graph was applied to the grade 4 through grade 9 passages. The author did not provide great detail on how the passages were selected, with the exception that some were obtained from children's literature and magazines, whereas others were written specifically for this inventory. It was noted that attempts were made to find high interest materials, although again, no specific information was presented that indicated whether or not the passages would actually be of interest to intended readers.

Almost no statistical reliability or validity data were provided for this inventory. This is a common problem with reading inventories. Users of the Stieglitz Inventory are not provided information as to how well the obtained reading levels might correlate with other measures of reading (such as standardized measures found in most achievement batteries) or with actual reading performances of students in an applied setting. This does limit the application of this inventory for comparison of reading levels between students or to a norm, which is often required in the diagnosis of reading difficulties for special services eligibility.

Overall, the Stieglitz Informal Reading Inventory seems to represent good progress in the development of reading inventories. Information regarding the reliability and validity of this test should be obtained and reported before examiners could use it for identification of reading problems. If used just to analyze a particular subject's strengths and weaknesses in reading, examiners might find the Stieglitz Informal Reading Inventory to be a user-friendly instrument with good potential.

Review of The Stieglitz Informal Reading Inventory: Assessing Reading Behaviors from Emergent to Advanced Levels by STEPHANIE STEIN, *Associate Professor of Psychology, Central Washington University, Ellensburg, WA:*

The primary purpose of the Stieglitz Informal Reading Inventory (SIRI) is to assist educators in placing students in basal readers and diagnosing strengths and weaknesses in areas such as word recognition and comprehension. It appears the main way the SIRI differs from most published informal reading inventories (IRIs) is in its comprehensiveness.

The SIRI provides the traditional informal reading measure of graded word passages for determining students' independent, instructional, and frustration reading levels. In doing so, however, the SIRI looks at student performance on both narrative and expository passages as well as assessing passage comprehension on literal and interpretive-level questions. This inventory also assesses students' prior knowledge about and interest in the passage topic to provide further information in interpreting test results. In determining the appropriate level to begin testing in the graded word passages, the SIRI uses lists of graded words in sentences to determine how well the student identifies words in context, rather than the traditional use of words in isolation. Lists of graded words in isolation are also provided as an option to assess sight word recognition and decoding.

To obtain information on "emergent" readers (those students whose base reading level on the graded words in context is below first grade), the SIRI provides guidelines on using a dictated story assessment strategy. The students are shown a photograph, dictate a story to the examiner about the photograph, and then attempt a variety of tasks such as reading their dictated story, identifying words in isolation, and copying their story. This assessment strategy is based on the "language experience approach" (LEA), a controversial method of teaching reading to young children. For those educators who believe in the LEA, this may be a useful tool. Most examiners will probably have difficulty, however, translating the results of this measure into practical instructional information.

The entire SIRI test and manual are combined in a single wire-bound booklet with perforated pages that can be torn out if necessary and photocopied. Two sets of graded words in context, two sets of graded words in isolation, four sets of graded passages, and 10 photographs for the dictated story assessment are provided for 11 levels in reading: preprimer, primer, and 1st through 9th grade. Each word list and passage has a student copy (large print for the lower levels) and a teacher copy.

The SIRI has some notable strengths. The author provides very detailed information regarding the administration, scoring, and interpretation of the numerous tests and diagnostic procedures. Many diagnostic options are described in the manual. Case examples are provided to assist the examiner in learning about the instrument. The four sets of equivalent forms enable teachers to monitor student progress over time with less worry about practice effects. Finally, the author specifies how most of the materials were developed (through review of the literature and other IRIs, consultation with experts, and some field testing).

One of the limitations of this instrument may be its ambitiousness. It purports to measure many skills. The scoring and testing procedures appear to be more complicated than many other IRIs and might require extensive practice to master. However, the main limitation of the SIRI is similar to that of most other published IRIs—an insufficient degree of technical information on reliability, validity, and norms. As with most IRIs, there are no norms to speak of, though I see very little reason why this trend must continue. The author refers to field testing of different parts of the instrument with various numbers of students in grades 1–12 in Rhode Island and the surrounding vicinity. However, there are no data about the breakdown of students at each grade level tested or the demographics of the students.

To the author's credit, the SIRI manual contains some information addressing reliability and validity issues rather than ignoring them altogether. Some evidence of alternative forms reliability is provided in that 80% to 85.7% of the 48 students in a study were given identical placements regardless of the graded reading passage form used.

The author also attempts some arguments in favor of the validity of the SIRI. All four forms of the graded reading passages were administered to 240 students (no grade level given) and the composite results were compared to teacher estimates of students' instructional levels. A little over half of the students (56.3%) were given identical placements with both methods. Although the author states that "this comparison was significant beyond the .001 level" (p. 276), it still seems disconcerting that almost half of the comparisons resulted in *different* placements, ranging from 28.3% off by one grade level to 4.6% off by as much as three grade levels. The remainder of the validity evidence relates to practice effects and interest level. Finally, the author indicates that, on Forms A and B, "the higher-order questions were, as expected, more difficult for students to answer than lower-order questions" (p. 279) with incorrect responses on literal comprehension questions ranging from 14.3% to 21.5% and ranging from 29.4% to 32.6% on interpretive questions.

In summary, the SIRI is one of the more comprehensive informal reading inventories on the market. It is probably not as easy and convenient to use as many other similar measures but it does provide more types of reading information than most and might be particularly attractive to reading specialists who have the time and interest to learn the instrument. Although the psychometric support for the SIRI is weak in terms of reliability and validity, it is frankly better than many other informal reading inventories. However, the author should still be encouraged to provide further psychometric support for the SIRI as well as more detailed information about the demographics of the students involved in the field testing of the instrument.

[299]
Stokes/Gordon Stress Scale.

Purpose: Developed to measure stressors in healthy individuals over age 65.
Population: Healthy individuals over age 65.
Publication Date: 1987.
Acronym: SGSS.
Scores: Total stress score.
Administration: Group.
Price Data, 1993: $30 per 100 scales.
Time: (15–30) minutes.
Comments: Self-administered in person or by mail.
Authors: Shirlee A. Stokes and Susan E. Gordon.
Publisher: Lienhard School of Nursing.
Cross References: See T4:2572 (1 reference).

Review of the Stokes/Gordon Stress Scale by SHARON L. WEINBERG, Professor and Head, Program of Quantitative Methods, School of Education, New York University, New York, NY:

The Stokes/Gordon Stress Scale (SGSS) is conceptually based on Selye's (1956) definition of stress as "the state manifested by the specific syndrome which consists of all the nonspecifically induced changes within a biologic system" (p. 311), and Lazarus' (1977) expanded view that "an event or situation is interpreted and evaluated by an individual as stressful in light of the person's past history and experience" (Stokes & Gordon, 1988, p. 16). The SGSS, designed to measure stress in healthy individuals in the age group 65 years or older, defines a stressor as an event or situation, ranging from a daily hassle to a major life event, that occurs in this age group. In addition, it defines healthy as living in one's home, possessing the ability to care for oneself, and being able to leave the home when desired.

The SGSS consists of 104 items (stressors) derived from a review of the literature, interviews with individuals 65 years or older, and consultation with experts in the field of gerontology. Examples of scale items are: death of a son or daughter (unanticipated or unexpected), death of a son or daughter (anticipated or expected), change in residence by moving to an institution, illness or injury of husband or wife, going to jail, not enough visits to or from family members, concern about elimination, decreasing number of friends or losing old friends, making out a will, feeling of being taken advantage of by "the system," and pressure for increased socialization.

In the instructions for completion printed on the scale itself, respondents are asked to "place an X next to any event or situation [they] are currently experiencing" (p. 1). A total stress score is obtained as a sum of weights corresponding to the items the respondent has checked. The weights assigned to each stressor range from 100 (most stressful) to 59 (least stressful) and reflect the perceptions of a convenience sample of 43 healthy individuals who are predominantly female and married with an age range of 65 to 85 years. For example, the item, "death of a son or daughter (unanticipated or unexpected)" is assigned a weight of 100, whereas the item, "change in your sexual activity" is assigned a weight of 59. The higher the total score on the scale, the greater the respondent's stress is reported to be. The SGSS can be administered in person or by mail, and, according to the manual, it requires approximately 15 to 30 minutes to complete.

As noted by the authors, the SGSS has been submitted only to initial psychometric evaluation by virtue of the small convenience samples used in the evaluation process. Test-retest reliabilities were obtained on three convenience samples of size 11, 23, and 18 with a testing interval of 2 weeks. These reliability estimates are .98, .91, and .90, respectively. Cronbach alpha internal consistency reliability, obtained on another convenience sample of 63 individuals was estimated to be .86. Evidence for validity also comes from small convenience samples. The correlations between the SGSS and two other measures of stress, the Schedule of Recent Events (SRE) and the Geriatric Social Readjustment Rating Scale (GSRRS) were found, on a sample of size 11, to be .81 and .65, respectively. Furthermore, on another convenience sample of 46 individuals, the SGSS score, obtained at the beginning of the year, correlated statistically significantly, yet low, with the onset of illness for the total year ($r = .36$).

Of particular concern is the use of a limited convenience sample (43 predominantly female and married healthy individuals with ages from 65 to 85 years) on which to calibrate item weights. Because the scale is conceptualized on Lazarus' (1977) thinking that an individual's past history or experience, one must question to what extent the calibrated weights based on such a limited sample generalize to individuals other than those in or represented by the calibration sample. The authors themselves note that "[i]t is possible that subpopulations [other than those represented by the calibration sample] would assign different weights to the items, thus resulting in altered forms of the SGSS appropriate to the subpopulations" (Stokes & Gordon, 1988, p. 18). Another concern is that norm data are not currently available to help in the interpretation of test scores.

In summary, the SGSS is simple to administer and score. Given its apparent content validity, the SGSS may have the potential to serve as an effective measure of stress in older adults. Such potential can only be realized, however, if we can place greater confidence in the psychometric properties of the scale, and in particular, in the appropriateness of weights assigned to the individual items, through additional research that utilizes a greater number of individuals sampled from a broader spectrum of populations.

REVIEWER'S REFERENCES
Selye, H. (1956). *The stress of life.* New York: McGraw-Hill Book Co.
Lazarus, R. S. (1977). Cognitive and coping processes in emotion. In A. Monat & R. S. Lazarus (Eds.), *Stress and coping: An anthology* (pp. 145–158). New York: Columbia University Press.
Stokes, S. A., & Gordon, S. E. (1988). Development of an instrument to measure stress in the older adult. *Nursing Research, 37,* 16–19.

[300]
Stress Indicator & Health Planner.

Purpose: "Assists people to identify their present health practices, pinpoint problem areas and plan for improved health, productivity and well-being."
Population: Adults.
Publication Dates: 1990–1993.
Acronym: SIHP.
Scores, 10: Physical Distress, Psychological Distress, Behavioral Distress, Total Distress Assessment, Interpersonal Stress Assessment, Nutritional Assessment, Health

Assessment, Total Wellness Assessment, Time-Stress Assessment, Occupational Stress Assessment.
Administration: Group.
Price Data, 1993: $12 per test booklet; $12 per Professional's Guide ('93, 12 pages); $15 per Releasing Relaxation: Mind and Body audiotape.
Time: (30) minutes for Basic; (180–360) minutes for Facilitated/Advanced.
Comments: Self-administered and self-scored.
Authors: Gwen Faulkner and Terry Anderson.
Publisher: Consulting Resource Group International, Inc.

Review of the Stress Indicator & Health Planner by DENNIS C. HARPER, Professor of Pediatrics and Rehabilitation Counseling, University of Iowa Hospitals and Clinics, Iowa City, IA:

The Stress Indicator and Health Planner (SIHP) is a "Self-assessment and planning tool for managing stress, developing wellness and improving performance" (booklet cover), designed by Faulkner and Anderson. The SIHP is presented as a concise guide to review the following five aspect of human functioning: Personal Distress, Interpersonal Stress, Wellness Assessment, Timed-Stress Assessment, and Occupational Stress Assessment. The first section of the SIHP is the Stress Indicator. The authors indicate this is not a psychometric test but a self-assessment and learning tool to promote an individual's awareness of personal stress, coping style, and lifestyle habits. The second section of the SIHP is the Health Planner. The Health Planner is a series of questions providing feedback and educational information in relation to coping and problem-solving skills. Test administration is either individual or in small groups. Administration times are approximately 20 minutes for the Stress Indicator. Use of the Health Planner is an individual process and can range from half an hour to 2.5 hours depending upon how the facilitator or user wishes to structure the experience of progressing through the information in the Health Planner.

The authors indicate the development of the instrument was in response to the need in the fields of health psychology, health promotion, and corporate wellness for a brief and comprehensive self-assessment tool. From a theoretical standpoint the authors note that self-awareness of perceived stress, coping abilities, and lifestyle habits is beneficial in improving health. Health is defined from a "holistic" perspective. Active participation in health planning is reported to increase well-being.

The Stress Indicator and Health Planner profile consists of a 15-page self-administered docu-

ment. It is easily read, well organized, and well presented graphically. The Professional's Guide to the Stress Indicator and Health Planner contains interpretive material, use and application, theoretical and practical understanding of the impact of stress, and description of the limitations of the Stress Indicator and Health Planner. Data are also presented in this manual on interpretation of scores, reliability and validity, and appropriate disclaimers of liability. Specific stress and wellness resources are presented.

The application of the Stress Indicator and Health Planner is as an aid to individuals who wish to gain knowledge about their stress levels and health habits. The authors suggest the material be presented by a trained professional experienced in health psychology to maximize impact. No other information is offered regarding the credentials of trainers. The authors assert the SIHP has been used by a variety of consumers and professionals in disciplines including medicine, psychology, sociology, nursing, and health science. The authors further assert that hospitals and corporations have found the SIHP useful in improving their awareness of stress and assessing harmful lifestyle habits.

After the profile is completed specific scores are compared to data presented in the profile planner. Scores are characterized in terms of Low Stress, Moderate Stress, and High Stress. Specific cautions are offered in the Professional's Guide in terms of the limitations of the materials as well as their particular interpretations. For example, transitory stress problems should be understood as potentially inflating scores, the SIHP is not intended as a substitute for competent medical/professional assessment of health. Each individual section of the SIHP consists of a series of specific questions where the respondent is requested to indicate a number from 1 through 5 reflective of the severity/frequency/intensity of the particular question. Total scores represent a weighted score in each of the five areas. Normative data are not presented for the test's interpretive section. In fact, little information is presented describing exactly how to score and interpret the normative outcome. The authors report some brief reliability and validity information. A 1-week test-retest reliability project was attempted with 26 college students completing the SIHP. Correlation coefficients greater than +.88 on all five scales are reported. Face validity was described following a study of 152 college students completing the SIHP rating the extent that they found the scores on the SIHP to be accurate on a 5-

point Likert scale. The average score for the group was 4.36. No other specific information was given on the psychometrics of scale construction or scale development.

The SIHP is, as the authors intend, a guide for examining stress and health issues. It reflects the personal bias of the two particular authors, it has some face validity, but lacks any theoretical support or empirical psychometric data. It is read easily, presented clearly, but moderately to highly priced per booklet. The utility of this instrument probably lies heavily on its face validity. The authors' assertions that the instrument assist people to identify their present health practices, pinpoint problem areas, and plan for improved health, productivity, and well-being are certainly not supported by available data.

Review of the Stress Indicator & Health Planner by BARBARA L. LACHAR, Assistant Professor of Psychiatry (Psychology), Baylor College of Medicine, Houston, TX:

The Stress Indicator and Health Planner (SIHP) is a self-assessment and planning instrument designed for individual or group administration. The authors state the SIHP is not a psychometric test, but an instrument designed to promote self-awareness of personal stress, coping style, and life style habits. Behavioral change is also a goal. However, in order to fulfill these functions, any assessment instrument must be developed and evaluated in accordance with psychometric standards.

STRESS INDICATOR. Part One, the Stress Indicator (SI) is divided into five sections: Personal Distress, Interpersonal Stress, Wellness, Time-Stress, and Occupational Stress. Individuals rate their physical symptoms, emotional symptoms, feelings, behaviors, interpersonal difficulties, and job satisfaction. These ratings are combined to produce scores on the five sections.

Users rate items on a Likert scale anchored by numbers from 1 to 5. Descriptors of percentage time (10 to 90%), and adjectives ranging from "rarely" to "almost always" are also provided. Numerical ratings are summed across the items in each section, and plotted on a scale for interpretation as "low," "moderate" or "high stress." There is no further explanation of the meaning of these levels, nor are there recommendations to accompany specific assessment results. The Professional's Guide, a 12-page booklet, contains little information relevant to administration or the interpretation of results.

The SI is defined as an evaluation of stress, but assesses physical symptoms, emotional symptoms,

behavioral problems, and health behaviors. There is no clear delineation between stress and illness. For example, the Personal Distress dimension is a combination of a checklist of both somatic and psychological complaints. Many of the physical symptoms, such as shortness of breath, chest pain, and headache pain may be signs of serious illness requiring medical attention. Similarly, items concerning psychological distress such as "feelings of hopelessness or helplessness" and "thoughts of suicide as a way out" may be more diagnostic of a depressive disorder. Appropriate recommendations for medical attention are not provided in either the SIHP booklet or the Professional's Guide.

HEALTH PLANNER. Following the self-assessment, users complete Part Two, the Health Planner (HP), which consists of five parts of educational text titled: Stress Management, Effective Communication, Health Practices, Time Management, and Occupational Stress. The first section, Stress Management, fails to provide a definition of stress, but includes a brief section on irrational thinking as a source of stress. However, no directions or opportunities are provided for the user to assess thinking. There are also no instructions on how to modify irrational thoughts to produce less stress. Similar comments apply to other sections as there is no self-appraisal for Communication Techniques nor specific exercises for altering perceived communication problems. The sections on Aerobic Exercise, Relaxation, and Smoking Cessation similarly are lacking specific examples of recommended exercise, guidance for how to practice relaxation, and instructions for breathing exercises.

Although there are sound recommendations that can serve to educate users, some statements in the HP appear superficial, limited, or unsubstantiated. The authors make recommendations and report global conclusions from research without support. Examples include "experts estimate 60-90% of all diseases are stress and lifestyle related" (test booklet, p. 13) and "Studies have shown that many times smokers have quit during transition times in their lives so that the required motivation and time are best known by the specific smoker" (test booklet, p. 16). These statements lack an appropriate supporting reference in either the SIHP or Professional's Guide. There are six sections titled "New Directions for Growth" containing four blank lines that appear to serve as opportunities for users to plan their behavioral changes, but these plans do not readily follow from the results of the SI assessment.

PROFESSIONAL'S GUIDE. The Professional's Guide is described as providing the theoretical background and rationale for the development of the SIHP. It is the only manual available. The guide presents a brief discussion of stress and health, but no coherent theory is offered as the basis for the SIHP. Neither is there a rationale for the selection of either the dimensions or their items. Measures of situational stressors, including stressful life events, daily hassles, safety, and financial insecurity are noticeably lacking. Even where citations are made, the appropriate reference is not always provided.

The guide authors state the SIHP has been used in a variety of settings including hospitals, businesses, and government agencies. No norms are provided and no data regarding results are offered.

Test-retest reliability for all five scales of the SIHP is estimated to be at least .88 based on a study of 26 college students retested after a 1-week interval. Additionally, the authors claim that they have established face validity by having 152 college students rate their scores on the SIHP for accuracy. Results indicate that none of the students rated their results as inaccurate. As this is the only evidence offered of reliability and validity, there is a need for studies to establish the construct validity of this tool as a measure of stress and wellness. Suggested studies include internal consistency reliability, factor analysis, and correlations of SI dimension scores with alternative measures of stress, anxiety, depression, and wellness. Additionally, scores of individuals with different physical diagnoses such as headache, lumbar strain, and coronary artery disease could be compared with those of a control group. It is also recommended that data be analyzed to obtain correlations between scores and job performance, productivity, absences, and health care costs. Studies reporting the percentage of users who make behavioral changes resulting in measurable health improvements are also required to support the validity of this instrument.

Health and stress appraisals have the potential to contribute to individual education and behavior change. The SIHP attempts to measure a variety of dimensions relating to stress and health, in addition to motivating behavioral change. However, the SIHP lacks the documentation, careful construction, and research effort necessary to support claims of utility and to justify its cost.

[301]
Stress Resiliency Profile.

Purpose: Designed to identify some ways individuals unintentionally contribute to their own stress levels.
Population: Employees.
Publication Date: 1992.
Acronym: SRP.

Scores, 3: Deficiency Focusing, Necessitating, Skill Recognition.
Administration: Group or individual.
Price Data, 1993: $5.50 per test booklet/manual (23 pages).
Time: (15) minutes.
Comments: Self-administered and self-scored.
Authors: Kenneth W. Thomas and Walter G. Tymon, Jr.
Publisher: XICOM, Inc.

Review of the Stress Resiliency Profile by JOHN A. MILLS, Professor/Psychologist, Counseling and Student Development, Indiana University of Pennsylvania, Indiana, PA:

The Stress Resiliency Profile (SRP) is a self-report measure designed to assess ways in which people unintentionally contribute to their own stress levels. Three scores are developed, which lead to lessons for the individual to interpret the results. The booklet for the instrument presents the items, a method for scoring, and interpretive lessons. The instructions are simple, clear, and easy to follow. The normed scores are simply plotted, though one of the scores is plotted in the opposite direction of the others. The lessons for interpretation are interesting as they stand and the concepts clearly defined, but the theoretical constructs or empirical support for the specific scale content and scope are not presented and are not evident. The booklet does not provide information about development of the instrument or any of its psychometric properties. The booklet does indicate that the examinee's score is a comparison to people who have taken the instrument, but there is no description of the comparison group or the significance of specific scale scores. This reviewer finds the instrument useful only as a potential stimulus for self-reflection or discussion, and does not find the timbre or substance of the interpretive lessons to lead to useful change. The lack of substantial normative information makes it useless for significant interpretation or intervention planning.

Review of the Stress Resiliency Profile by WILLIAM R. MERZ, SR., Professor, School Psychology Training Program, Department of Special Education, Rehabilitation, and School Psychology, School of Education, California State University, Sacramento, Sacramento, CA:

The Stress Resiliency Profile is an 18-item questionnaire designed to assess a respondent's cognitive responses to stressful incidents in everyday life. It yields three subscales of six items each; these scales are labeled Deficiency Focusing, Necessitating, and Skill Recognition. The respondent rates a reaction to a response on a 7-point scale between extremes labeled *strongly disagree* and *strongly agree*. Responses are plotted on a profile giving the percentile of the scale value. The percentiles are referenced to the responses of 300 managers in the private and public sectors. This occupies 7 pages of the 21-page profile booklet; the remaining pages assist the respondent to apply the results to changing cognitive responses to stress.

The profile and the pages on interpretation are nicely presented. Unfortunately, the authors present no information on the rationale behind the profile, item construction, the norm group, or evidence of reliability and validity. The whole profile and interpretation process appear much more like a set of cognitive-behavioral exercises than an assessment of response to stress.

The Standards for Educational and Psychological Testing (AERA, APA, & NCME, 1985) require authors of instruments to provide statements of recommended test coverage and use, appropriate samples for test validation and norming, evidence of reliability and validity, and description of intended use for information generated. This device has none of those statements. As a result, it is difficult to know how to use the information and how confident you can be that the information generated is valid, reliable, and interpretable. Six item scales are too brief to yield reliable scores, even with the best techniques of construction. Eighteen items is so restricted in number that it would be difficult to show that the domain labeled "stress resilience" is adequately sampled so that the generalizations can be made with a degree of confidence.

No matter how nicely the material is put together, it must have this technical information if it is to be used with confidence. Until that information is presented, the material is an interesting exercise built on common sense and cognitive-behavioral theory. One cannot state with any degree of surety that the information generated is accurate, interpretable, or generalizable. The authors would be well advised to provide the information required by the *Standards* so that consumers can be informed about the issues of accuracy, interpretability, and generalizability of the constructs assessed by the Profile. Until that time, caution is the best course.

REVIEWER'S REFERENCE

American Educational Research Association, American Psychological Association, & National Council on Measurement in Education (1985). *Standards for educational and psychological testing*. Washington, DC: American Psychological Association, Inc.

[302]
Student Goals Exploration.

Purpose: "Designed to help researchers better understand the academic goals of college students."
Population: College.
Publication Date: 1990.
Acronym: SGE.
Scores: 46 scales in 7 sections: Goals in Attending College (Prepare for Career and/or Graduate Professional School, Acquire a General Education, Nondirected), Educational Purpose (Social Change, Effective Thinking, Systematic Instruction, Vocational Orientation, Personal Enrichment, Great Ideas, Values Clarification), General Academic Orientation (Develop Creativity, Increase Self-Understanding, Improve Speaking Skills, Improve Reasoning Skills, Develop a Life Philosophy, Understand the World Around Me, Work for Social Causes, Develop Scientific Inquiry Skills, Prepare for a Career, Gain Expertise, Develop Human Relations, Improve Numerical Ability, Understand Cultural Diversity, Value Learning for Its Own Sake, Improve Basic Skills), Subject-Specific Goals (English, History, Sociology, Psychology, Biology, Mathematics, Fine Arts, Romance Languages, Introductory Business, Universally Endorsed), Feelings About Studying (Goal Time Frame [Long-Range], Goal Time Frame [Short-Range], Goal Clarity, Goal Source [Expectations], Goal Source [Self], Expectations and Study Skills (Self-Confident Scholar, Anxious Student), Types of Activities Scales (Relates and Applies Coursework, Interacts About Coursework, Explores Beyond Assignments, Concentrates on Task).
Administration: Group.
Forms, 6: Version IR-1 (to be completed early in academic term); Version IR-2 (to be completed late in academic term); Version IR-M (for students who have chosen a field of study); Version CR-1 ("examines goals that students bring to their college courses"); Version CR-2 ("examines students' goals as they complete college courses"); Version CR-M ("examines goals that students hope to achieve in their chosen major").
Price Data, 1993: $15 per user's manual (Institutional Research Guide, 1991, 149 pages; Classroom Research Guide, 1991, 117 pages) and 300 forms; $.50 per additional copy.
Time: (45) minutes for SGE-IR version; (30) minutes for SGE-CR version.
Authors: Joan S. Stark, Malcolm A. Lowther, Kathleen M. Shaw, and Paula L. Sossen.
Publisher: National Center for Research to Improve Postsecondary Teaching and Learning.

Review of the Student Goals Exploration by ROBERT D. BROWN, Carl A. Happold Distinguished Professor Emeritus of Educational Psychology, University of Nebraska-Lincoln, Lincoln, NE:

The Student Goals Exploration (SGE) scales are well designed and carefully validated to accomplish their stated purpose (i.e., "to help researchers better understand the academic goals of college students"). Individual users at the institutional or classroom level will have to decide if using the instruments serves any utilitarian purpose for them.

Two user's manuals describe the inventories. The Institutional Research Guide includes information on the development of the inventories and their psychometric properties. The Classroom Research Guide contains some technical information but is aimed more at the faculty member who may be less interested or familiar with test development issues. Both Guides describe the intent of the multiple scales and the versions that can be used in a pre-post manner at the beginning and end of a term. The scales focus on general academic goals and subject-specific goals. The post-scales also include items asking for reports of activities (e.g., books read, discussions with other students). A Faculty Version of the scales makes it possible to develop faculty profiles for comparison with student profiles.

The scales focus almost exclusively on academic goals, though the authors recognize that students are influenced by other goals as well. The utility of the scales might have been enhanced if they included an additional scale devoted to assessing the students' non-academic reasons for attending college (e.g., social, athletic, fulfilling family expectations) so that these could be used as a context in which to interpret the academic goals.

The authors provide sufficient support for their arguments that the scales discriminate among student attending different types of institutions and among students enrolled in different academic majors. One reported concurrent validity study provides correlations between the SGE and other inventories assessing need for cognition, learning and grade orientation, and goal instability. With few exceptions the correlations are low, but the general pattern appears supportive. For either institutional research or for classroom research, each user will want to examine the scales and the items comprising the scales as to their relevance for his or her institution or class.

Except for scales with relatively few items (e.g., Activities Scales and Feelings About Studying), indices of reliability, primarily Cronbach alphas, are sufficiently high (median in the mid .80s) for use in interpreting group scores. There is overlap of items among the scales, however, and this would inflate the

reliability indices. The authors recommend using profiles to report scores rather than using means and standard deviations.

In both Guides, the authors include a section describing possible uses of the SGE for institutional research or classroom research. The message is that the more institutions and faculty members know about student goals the better they will be able to interact with students to discuss their goals and to adopt institutional policies and instructional practices that will best benefit students. Discussions among faculty members, administrators, and students, in my estimation, are essential to successful use of the SGE at an institutional or classroom level. Clearly, the SGE can be a useful tool for researchers studying students' motivation and aspirations as they relate to the host of other variables, such as student outcomes. If the SGE is to be used for purposes of institutional change or faculty development, however, careful planning on how the results will be used is required. The manuals provide relevant examples of uses of the SGE at institutional and classroom levels, but with incomplete illustrations of the dynamics or possible courses of action dependent on different outcomes.

In conclusion, the Student Goal Exploration scales appear to be psychometrically sound for purposes of research on student goals. Strong arguments can be made for the utility of these scales for stimulating discussions among students, faculty, and administrators about institutional and classroom expectations and activities. Institutions that have a commitment to examine reflectively their missions and outcomes and have accompanying funding support for such studies will find these scales highly useful.

Review of the Student Goals Exploration by STEVEN R. SHAW, School Psychologist, School District of Greenville County, Greenville, SC, and NICHO-LAS BENSON, Counselor, Illinois State University, Normal, IL:

The purpose of the Student Goals Exploration (SGE) is to assess the goals of college students so institutions of higher education, individual college instructors, and departments within colleges can best respond to student goals. The authors of the SGE state that student goals are neglected because no useful assessment instruments have been developed. The authors developed the SGE to fill this niche. However, the SGE is "not intended to be used as a source of data for counseling or advising individual students" (p. 9). The SGE is designed so that overall means can be interpreted. Thus, the intent of the SGE is to assess the goals of groups of students to help institutions of higher learning in course content, curricular change, and major field course selection requirements. The SGE has two versions: The Classroom Research version (SGE-CR) and the Institutional Research version (SGE-IR). The SGE-CR also has a version to asses faculty perspectives on the goals of students. Both classroom and institutional versions have forms for general college students. Each version also has a parallel form so that by administering Form 1 and, later, Form 2, some measure of change in goals can be determined.

The SGE is primarily a research and evaluation instrument. The manual suggests several purposes for the SGE: (a) "to help understand the goals of groups of students newly enrolled in courses, including the special goals of any existing subgroups of students" (p. 8); (b) "to assess changes in the goals of a group of students during a semester or year of enrollment in a course (or a program) of study" (p. 8); (c) "to assist a faculty group in planning courses that will capitalize on student goals" (p. 8); (d) "to measure student goals as a mediating variable between intended student outcomes and actual outcomes" (p. 9); and (e) "to explore the relationships between students' course-level goals and their feelings about studying, their expectations and study skills" (p. 8). While advocating keeping all current items the authors of the SGE encourage potential users of this test to modify items, administration procedures, or create new items to achieve appropriate classroom and institutional goals.

The SGE consists of several sections and scales. Section 1 consists of 19 items for assessing Goals in Attending College. Three scales comprise this section: Prepare for Career and/or Graduate Professional School, Acquire a General Education, and Nondirected. Section 2 is Education Purpose. This section contains seven items representing students' beliefs about the purpose of college. Section 3 is General Academic Orientation. This section consists of 15 separate small scales. These scales contain as few as 3 items (e.g., Improve Speaking Skills, Improve Numerical Ability) or as many as 11 items (e.g., Improve Reasoning Skills scale). Section 4 assesses subject-specific goals. There are 10 academic subject-specific goal scales (e.g., English, History, Mathematics). Each scale includes items typically endorsed as useful by individuals studying that academic subject. Section 5 is Feelings About Study-

ing. These 18 items measure students' attitudes concerning expectations and goals concerning academic work. Section 6 is Expectations and Study Skills. These 18 items differentiate Self-Confident Scholars from Anxious Students. Student demographic information, career goals, academic preparation, and student activities can also be assessed.

ADMINISTRATION AND SCORING. All versions of the SGE can be administered in a group or individual format. Items are multiple choice and are untimed. The SGE takes less than 45 minutes to complete. Many items represent a student goal. The examinee is to respond to the importance of these goals on a 4-point scale. Although the manual provides information for hand scoring only, many universities have the resources to convert the SGE into an optically scanned, computer-scored instrument. Examiners may administer the SGE to students during class, at home and returned later, or even completed through mail. Examiners may choose to create local items, eliminate some existing items, and administer only parts of the test. There is limited information on how these variations in administration affect reliability.

STANDARDIZATION DATA. There are no norms for the SGE because "there are no 'right' goals for students and teachers to hold" (p. 10). It is possible for schools, departments, or teachers to develop local norms. Authors developed items via interviews with students, responses from teaching faculty, and developments of goal statements by the authors. Seven universities and approximately 5,500 students were involved in the standardization of the SGE. Data from the four versions of the test were used to select quality items, calculate reliability coefficients, and to conduct exploratory factor analyses. The seven cooperating 4-year universities may not be representative of college students nationwide. Four of these colleges are in the Midwest, one in the South, and two in the Eastern U.S. The standardization sample includes no community colleges, a potentially useful audience for the SGE. Because of the potentially nonrepresentative standardization sample, the items selected and factor analytic data may not generalize to a wide population of college students.

RELIABILITY. The manual reports internal consistency reliability estimates for all scales. Kuder-Richardson 20 internal consistency coefficients range from .33 (Goal Source (Self) in the Feelings about Studying section) to .92 (Improve Numerical Ability in the General Academic Orientation section). The manual provides no reliability data for the overall scale. Given that items can be regrouped, deleted, or added; and administration instructions can be changed to suit the need of the examiner, the reliability of the SGE is questionable. However, when used as a research instrument, results can be attenuated for unreliability. We recommend this procedure when conducting research with any section or scale of the SGE.

VALIDITY. The sections and scales of the SGE were correlated with the Need for Cognition (NFC) scale (Cacioppo, Petty, & Kao, 1984), the LOGO II Student Survey (Eison, 1981), and the Goal Instability Scale (Robbins & Patton, 1985). The manual states that correlations between the SGE and the three scales provide evidence of concurrent validity. Yet, none of the 112 correlation coefficients among the scales are greater than .48. Many of the correlations are negative and most are less than .20. It is unclear whether the SGE, LOGO II Student Survey, NFC, and Goal Instability scale assess similar constructs.

The Subject Specific section of the SGE appears to discriminate among students of different majors (e.g., English majors endorse the importance of classes on literature more than students with other majors). However, detailed analyses and descriptions of the methods used lack detail.

SUMMARY. The SGE is not an assessment instrument. It is a carefully thought out item bank of questions pertaining to the goals of college students. The SGE is not to be used for advisement or counseling of individual students. Classrooms and universities may find the various forms of the SGE useful in evaluating the needs and goals of the student body. Faculty perception of the students' goals can also be assessed to determine congruence between students and faculty. Colleges or departments then can adjust the curriculum to meet the students' goals. With many universities being held accountable for the value of a college education, incoming freshmen may take the SGE Form I and outgoing seniors may take the SGE Form II. In this fashion, universities can demonstrate that students' educational goals and beliefs changed while attending college. The authors selected items based on pilot data from nonrepresentative samples. Reliability is not clearly established. Validity of the SGE appears to depend a great deal on the local needs of the user. The manual does not provide strong evidence of validity. The SGE may be a good first step for colleges wishing to conduct research to learn about the needs and goals of their students.

REVIEWERS' REFERENCES

Eison, J. (1981). A new instrument for assessing students' orientations towards grades and learning. *Psychological Reports, 48*, 919–924.

Cacioppo, J. T., Petty, R. E., & Kao, C. F. (1984). The efficient assessment of need for cognition. *Journal of Personality Assessment, 48*, 306–307.

Robbins, S. B., & Patton, M. J. (1985). Self-psychology and career development: Construction of the superiority and goal instability scales. *Journal of Counseling Psychology, 32*, 221–231.

[303]
Student Self-Concept Scale.

Purpose: Designed as a "multidimensional self-report measure of self-concept and related psychological constructs."

Population: Grades 3–12.

Publication Date: 1993.

Acronym: SSCS.

Scores, 13: Self-Confidence (Self-Image, Academic, Social, Lie, Composite), Importance (Self-Image, Academic, Social, Lie), Outcome Confidence (Self-Image, Academic, Social, Composite).

Administration: Group.

Levels, 2: Grades 3–6, grades 7–12.

Price Data, 1993: $30 per 25 record booklets (specify Level 1 or Level 2); $35 per manual (82 pages).

Time: (20–30) minutes.

Authors: Frank M. Gresham, Stephen N. Elliott, and Sally E. Evans-Fernandez.

Publisher: American Guidance Service, Inc.

Review of the Student Self-Concept Scale by JERI BENSON, Professor of Educational Psychology, College of Education, University of Georgia, Athens, GA:

DESCRIPTION OF THE SCALE. The Student Self-Concept Scale (SSCS) consists of 72 items that measure Self-Image, Academic, and Social aspects of oneself. Scores are obtained across these areas for Confidence, Importance, and Outcome Confidence. A Lie Scale is included to detect faking. All items are rated on a 3-point scale.

The authors suggest that the SSCS is helpful in screening, classifying, and planning interventions with children and adolescents. The manual contains many useful features such as information on preparing student interventions, extensive sections on score interpretation (including a case study), limitations of the SSCS, and issues in the use of self-report measures with children. No specific user training is required beyond knowledge of proper test use and interpretation.

SCALE DEVELOPMENT AND STANDARDIZATION. A very desirable feature of the SSCS is that its development is strongly tied to the research literature. The authors present operational definitions of such terms as self-concept, self-efficacy, and self-esteem and link their definitions to the research literature. Scale development began in 1988 and after several psychometric studies resulted in 75 items. The 75 items were used in the standardization of the current 72-item SSCS (3 items were dropped based on item analysis). The standardization sample was nationally representative and consisted of 2,151 elementary students and 1,435 secondary students from 19 states stratified by gender, ethnicity, region, and community size with special emphasis on including students with disabilities. Numerous tables provide breakdowns of the standardization sample compared to census data in each demographic category.

ADMINISTRATION, SCORING, AND NORMS. The SSCS is self-administered on forms that can be easily scored and raw scores converted to standard scores (with confidence bands) or percentiles for the Self-Confidence and Importance ratings of Self-Image, Academic, and Social. Descriptive behavioral levels are provided for the Outcome Confidence scores because of low reliability. The norms are highly representative of the U.S. and fairly recent, being gathered in Spring of 1988.

RELIABILITY. The types of psychometric data reported in the manual are internal consistency estimates (alpha coefficients) for each subscale, test-retest reliability estimates, and the standard error of measurement. Internal consistency estimates ranged from .55 to .92. The internal consistency estimates for the composite scores of Self-Confidence and Outcome Confidence are quite high (median = .90 and .81 respectively). The three subscales from the Outcome Confidence domain showed the lowest reliability, less than .75 across the elementary and secondary students.

The stability of the SSCS scores was based on a 4-week interval, and ranged from .35 to .72 (median .58) for elementary students and .52 to .82 (median .73) for secondary students. The lower stability coefficients were from the same subscales that had low internal consistency estimates mentioned above. The authors provide relevant cautionary comments for the Outcome Confidence subscales due to the lower reliabilities and offer only descriptive behavioral levels rather than standard scores for these subscales.

The standard error of measurement (based on internal consistency) is given for all subscales/composites with either a 68% or 95% level of confidence. The *SEM* ranges from a low of 5 to a maximum of 16 depending on the level of confidence. The use and interpretation of the *SEM* is carefully described for the practitioner.

VALIDITY. The authors' claim the SSCS is a valid measure of students' self-concept is based on multiple sources of information. They report the SSCS items were "selected" based upon ratings of experienced researchers and practitioners as evidence of content validity. However, no specific information was provided on: who the "experts" were, how they were selected, nor how many experts were involved.

The results of several criterion-related validity studies are reported. This includes correlations of the SSCS with related measures such as the Social Skills Rating System (SSRS) and the Child Behavior Checklist and with other measures of self-concept (e.g., Coopersmith, Tennessee, Pier-Harris, SDQ). Overall, the correlations are quite variable ranging (in absolute value) from .00 to .76. Many of the correlational data are hard to interpret due to the sheer number of correlations presented with little or no link to theory in terms of expected correlational patterns. The sample sizes for these studies were in the 40s for the self-concept measures to over 1,000 for the SSRS, which was a part of the standardization.

Finally, evidence of construct validity is presented in the form of subscale intercorrelations, developmental and gender differences, confirmatory factor analysis, and comparisons of groups known to differ on the trait. The confirmatory factor analysis result is not convincing because only one model is tested and the overall model—data fit are not very strong. Factor intercorrelations are also not presented. The developmental and gender differences data are supportive in that no differences in these two areas are predicted by theory and none are found with the SSCS. The potentially most powerful set of analyses are the comparison of groups expected to differ based on theory. The groups are students with learning disabilities ($n = 75$), and other disabilities ($n = 34$) who are compared to nondisabled students ($n = 586$). It appears the SSCS does differentiate aspects of self-concept for these groups, but as the authors indicate, more research needs to be done with larger samples and better defined groups of disabled children.

SUMMARY. The manual is a useful guide to the proper use and interpretation of the SSCS. Considerable effort went into development and standardization and thus the norms are highly representative of the U.S. The separate subscales and composite scores of the SSCS are generally highly reliable and slightly more stable for adolescents than for younger children. The validity data are promising in terms of empirically demonstrating the relationship between the SSCS and other measures of self-concept. However, linking the strong theory that supported the development of the SSCS with tightly designed and focused validity studies in the future could ensure the SSCS as being one of the foremost measures of students' self-concept.

Review of the Student Self-Concept Scale by FREDERICK T. L. LEONG, *Associate Professor of Psychology, The Ohio State University at Columbus, Columbus, OH:*

The Student Self-Concept Scale (SSCS) is an excellent addition to the repertoire of self-concept measures. It has undergone a rigorous development and the authors have expended considerable efforts in ensuring that adequate validation and normative work has been conducted prior to its publication. The SSCS is also based on sound theoretical information and models such as Bandura's model of self-efficacy and Robert White's model of effectance motivation. The authors are also to be commended for preparing a very thorough test manual that provides the conceptual and theoretical basis for the scale, an overview of the development process, and most of the necessary technical and psychometric information.

The strengths of the Student Self-Concept Scale are that it is a well thought out, carefully validated, and extensively normed instrument. The Scale actually measures three different domains of self-concept including self-image, the academic, and social domains. These domains are assessed across three dimensions including self-confidence, importance, and outcome confidence. The measure of the subjective task value and the rating of the importance of a particular task are unique features of the current scale. In developing this scale, the authors provide a linkage between the extensive self-concept literature and the burgeoning literature on self-efficacy. Other strengths of the Student Self-Concept Scale include strong evidence of reliability and validity. More specifically, the internal consistency and the test-retest reliability estimates were all within the acceptable ranges with the exception of one or two subscales that were in the mid-50s range. The authors have also done very thorough work in providing evidence of the validity of this scale by examining both the content and the criterion-related validity of the scale. The authors have also examined the concurrent validity of the scale by correlating it with other measures such as the Coopersmith Self-Esteem Inventory, the Piers-Harris' Children's Self-Concept Scale, and the Achenbach Child Behavior Checklist. A particularly unique feature of the Student Self-Con-

cept Scale is the inclusion of the salience, or what the authors have labeled as the importance dimension, which is an important moderator to take into account when developing self-concept scales. The authors also used other measures to examine theoretically expected developmental trends as another aspect of construct validity. They also used the contrasted group approach to evaluate the discriminant validity of the Student Self-Concept Scale. Finally, the authors have identified a normative sample for the current scale that is a cross-section representative of the United States in terms of gender and racial/ethnic breakdown.

There are a few limitations to this extremely well-developed test that need to be pointed out. The first limitation is a conceptual one. As mentioned by the authors, self-esteem needs to be conceptualized within domains that are culturally valued. The authors' assumption, and I believe it to be a correct one, is that there are likely to be cultural variations in some domains such that individuals possess high or low self-esteem. Despite recognizing this very important point, the authors provide no discussion of subculture variations in the United States in terms of what domains and dimensions may exhibit cultural variations in levels of self-esteem. There is considerable evidence, some of which is quite controversial, that there are subcultural variations in the levels of self-esteem among racial/ethnic minority youth in this country as well as what characteristics or traits are valued among these different groups of adolescents. For example, African-American and Hispanic- or Asian-American children may not value the same traits or may not consider the same dimensions as equally salient to their self-esteem and self-concept.

Whether it is simply sufficient to collect normative data from a representative sample of the United States and not examine subcultural variations remains a debated issue. For example, the National Institute of Mental Health, in recognizing the importance of cultural differences, now routinely requires grant applicants to collect data on racial and ethnic minorities and to analyze those data separately for possible cultural variations. Grant applicants who choose not to do this are required to provide a written rationale and justification. Some would argue that requiring a similar standard for test developers would be too extreme. However, the authors of the current scale in recognizing and conceptualizing self-concept as embedded within a cultural context were therefore obligated to examine this issue of cultural validity. There is sufficient research on ethnic minority psychology that suggests we can no longer assume an instrument has cultural validity until proven otherwise. This failure to address potential cultural variations is unfortunate because the authors have collected information on African-American and Hispanic samples and could have done some analysis to determine if the Student Self-Concept Scale is indeed vulnerable to cultural variations. If no such cultural variations are found, it suggests that cultural validity may not be a problem. Obviously, just as construct validity cannot be demonstrated with one or two studies, neither can cultural validity be fully resolved in one or two datasets. On the other hand, if significant and systematic cultural variations are found, the authors may be able to offer certain caveats to psychologists and other test users when administering and interpreting the Student Self-Concept Scale with racial and ethnic minority populations.

One other limitation to the Student Self-Concept Scale, which appears quite common among newly developed scales, is the authors' failure to provide a discussion of how their self-concept scale is similar to or different from the already well established measures of self-concept such as the Coopersmith (T4:647), Piers-Harris (T4:2030) and the Tennessee (320) scales. For example, it would have been useful for the authors to provide some information on whether the Student Self-Concept Scale provides incremental validity to the other measures. As a multidimensional measure of self-concept, a discussion of the unique and different dimensions in the Student Self-Concept Scale as contrasted with other measures also would have been useful. Without such information, it is somewhat difficult for test users to compare and select the best self-concept scale to use to achieve their specific goals.

In summary, with the exception of a few limitations, the Student Self-Concept Scale is a sound and rigorously developed and validated measure which should prove to be a useful instrument in its domain. It has the advantage of a representative normative sample as well as the integration of recent theoretical developments in the area of self-efficacy theory to the traditional literature in self-esteem and self-concept.

[304]

Stuttering Severity Instrument for Children and Adults, Third Edition.

Purpose: "Measures stuttering severity for both children and adults."
Population: School-age children and adults.

Publication Dates: 1980–1994.
Acronym: SSI-3.
Scores, 8: Frequency, Duration, Physical Concomitants (Distracting Sounds, Facial Grimaces, Head Movements, Movements of the Extremities, Total), Total.
Administration: Individual.
Forms, 2: Reading, Nonreading.
Price Data, 1994: $64 per complete kit; $29 per 50 test record and frequency computation forms; $37 per examiner's manual ('94, 48 pages) and picture plates.
Time: Administration time not reported.
Comments: Tape recorder necessary for speech sample.
Author: Glyndon D. Riley.
Publisher: PRO-ED, Inc.
Cross References: See T4:2613 (5 references).

TEST REFERENCES

1. Pindzola, R. H., & White, D. T. (1986). A protocol for differentiating the incipient stuttering. *Language, Speech, and Hearing Services in Schools, 17,* 2–15.
2. Runyan, C. M., & Runyan, S. E. (1986). A fluency rules therapy program for young children in the public schools. *Language, Speech, and Hearing Services in Schools, 17,* 276–284.
3. Pindzola, R. H., Jenkins, M. M., & Lokken, K. J. (1989). Speaking rates of young children. *Language, Speech, and Hearing Services in Schools, 20,* 133–138.
4. Watson, B. C., Pool, K. D., Devous, M. D., Freeman, F. J., & Finitzo, T. (1992). Brain blood flow related to acoustic laryngeal reaction time in adult developmental stutterers. *Journal of Speech and Hearing Research, 35,* 555–561.
5. Ramig, P. R. (1993). High reported spontaneous stuttering recovery rates: Fact or fiction? *Language, Speech, and Hearing Services in Schools, 24,* 156–160.
6. Wolk, L., Edwards, M. L., & Conture, E. G. (1993). Coexistence of stuttering and disordered phonology in young children. *Journal of Speech and Hearing Research, 36,* 906–917.
7. Berkowitz, M., Cook, H., & Haughey, M. J. (1994). A non-traditional fluency program developed for the public school setting. *Language, Speech, and Hearing Services in Schools, 25,* 94–99.
8. Blood, G. W., Blood, I. M., Bennett, S., Simpson, K. C., & Susman, E. J. (1994). Subjective anxiety measurements and cortisol responses in adults who stutter. *Journal of Speech and Hearing, 37,* 760–768.
9. Brin, M. F., Stewart, C., Blitzer, A., & Diamond, B. (1994). Laryngeal botulinum toxin injections for disabling stuttering in adults. *Neurology, 44,* 2262–2266.
10. Caruso, A. J., Chodzko-Zajko, W. J., Bidinger, D. A., & Sommers, R. K. (1994). Adults who stutter: Responses to cognitive stress. *Journal of Speech and Hearing, 37,* 746–754.
11. Kelly, E. M. (1994). Speech rates and turn-taking behaviors of children who stutter and their fathers. *Journal of Speech and Hearing, 37,* 1284–1294.
12. Throneburg, R. N., & Yairi, E. (1994). Temporal dynamics of repetitions during the early stage of childhood stuttering: An acoustic study. *Journal of Speech and Hearing, 37,* 1067–1075.
13. Watson, B. C., Freeman, F. J., Devous, M. D., Chapman, S. B., Finitzo, T., & Pool, K. D. (1994). Linguistic performance and regional cerebral blood flow in persons who stutter. *Journal of Speech and Hearing, 37,* 1221–1228.
14. Zebrowski, P. M. (1994). Duration of sound prolongation and sound/syllable repetition in children who stutter: Preliminary observations. *Journal of Speech and Hearing Research, 37,* 254–263.
15. Blood, G. W. (1995). A behavioral-cognitive therapy program for adults who stutter: Computers and counseling. *Journal of Communication Disorders, 28,* 165–180.
16. Blood, G. W. (1995). POWER2: Relapse management with adolescents who stutter. *Language, Speech, and Hearing Services in Schools, 26,* 169–179.
17. Dietrich, S., Barry, S. J., & Parker, D. E. (1995). Middle latency auditory responses in males who stutter. *Journal of Speech and Hearing Research, 38,* 5–17.
18. Kelly, E. M. (1995). Parents as partners: Including mothers and father in the treatment of children who stutter. *Journal of Communication Disorders, 28,* 93–105.
19. Zebrowski, P. M. (1995). The topography of beginning stuttering. *Journal of Communication Disorders, 28,* 75–91.
20. Blood, I. M. (1996). Disruptions in auditory and temporal processing in adults who stutter. *Perceptual and Motor Skills, 82,* 272–274.
21. McCauley, R. J. (1996). Familiar strangers: Criterion-referenced measures in communication disorders. *Language, Speech, and Hearing Services in Schools, 27,* 122–131.

Review of the Stuttering Severity Instrument for Children and Adults, Third Edition by RONALD B. GILLAM, Assistant Professor of Communication Sciences and Disorders, The University of Texas at Austin, Austin, TX:

The Stuttering Severity Instrument for Children and Adults, Third Edition (SSI-3) is the second revision of the Stuttering Severity Instrument (Riley, 1972; 1980). Like the two preceding versions, the purpose of the SSI-3 is to measure and quantify stuttering severity objectively. The author suggests the SSI-3 should be used to augment information from patient interviews, speech samples, and other speech and language tests in evaluating the severity of stuttering in children and adults.

When the SSI-3 is administered to children with less than a third grade reading level, examiners rate conversation samples. Black-and-white line drawings of a farm scene, a dinosaur scene, a ship yard scene, and a space scene are provided for use in eliciting speech during conversations with the examiner. A sample dialogue is provided in the manual. Examiners are also advised to obtain and analyze a sample of the child's speech at home.

Examiners analyze speech samples for frequency of stuttering, duration of stuttering events, and physical concomitants of stuttering. Frequency of stuttering is assessed by summing repetitions, audible prolongations, and silent prolongations of sounds or syllables and dividing this value by the total number of syllables contained in the speech samples. This percentage is converted to a Frequency score. Duration of stuttering is assessed by measuring the length of the three longest stuttering events. The average duration is converted to a Duration score. Physical events that accompany stuttering are assessed by qualitative judgments of the degree of noticeability/distractibility of nonspeech sounds, abnormal facial movements or tension, head movements, and movements of the extremities that accompany stuttering. Each type of physical concomitant is rated according to a 6-point Likert scale that ranges from 0 (none) to 5 (severe and painful-looking). Values for the four judgments are summed to yield a Physical Concomitants score.

When the SSI-3 is administered to children or adults who read at or above a third-grade level, examiners obtain speech samples in reading and conversation contexts. Two reading passages that vary in length between 160 and 228 syllables are provided at third-grade, fifth-grade, seventh-grade, and adult reading levels. The conversation sample is obtained while the patient and the examiner converse about familiar topics such as school, jobs, recent holidays, favorite TV shows, or current movies. Separate tables are provided for scoring stuttering frequency during speaking and reading tasks, and the Frequency score is derived by summing the two task scores. Duration and Physical Concomitants scores are derived in the same manner as described previously for nonreaders.

Frequency, Duration, and Physical Concomitants scores are summed to yield a Total Overall score that is converted into percentile and severity ratings. Conversion tables are available for preschoolers (ages 2-10 to 5-11), school-age children (ages 6-1 to 16-11), and adults (ages 17-0 and up).

Intra- and interexaminer reliability figures are based on extremely small samples, but appear to be adequate for clinical purposes. Unfortunately, measures of the stability and internal consistency of the SSI-3 are not reported. Therefore, no judgments can be made concerning the stability of the SSI-3 across times or situations, and there is no way to estimate the standard error of measurement.

Criterion-related validity was assessed by correlating the Total Overall score to the Frequency score. Correlations are within the acceptable range. However, a better approach would have been to correlate Overall scores with percentages of stuttered syllables. Reports of construct validity are not convincing. At minimum, the author should have correlated overall scores with stuttering history, (in months), and he should have used factor analysis to support the constructs of frequency, duration, and physical concomitants as separate factors.

Unfortunately, there are numerous other difficulties with this test, many of which are related to insufficient information concerning procedures and norms. For example, examiners are encouraged to analyze samples of children's speech collected in their homes, but guidelines for collecting and selecting these samples are too vague to insure that the collected samples are similar in nature to samples that were collected for the norming group. Additionally, there are no guidelines for selecting reading passages. Readability affects reading fluency and should also affect speech fluency while reading aloud. Precise instructions about methods for assigning and selecting reading passages are needed to control for potential confounding effects related to reading fluency.

There are also problems with scoring the SSI-3. Ratio-level measures of frequency and duration are converted to ordinal-level scores, but the author does not provide information about how the "stanine intervals" (p. 15) were derived. Additionally, Likert scale values are summed to obtain a Physical Concomitants score. These procedures serve to dilute discrete measures of complex behaviors into numeric values that have little specific meaning and even less discriminating power.

Finally, there are problems with interpreting the SSI-3. Percentile and severity ratings are based on relatively small samples of stutterers from one state who span wide age ranges (72 preschoolers, 139 school-age children, and 60 adults). Unfortunately, no information is provided about the criteria for including subjects in the normative sample or the exact ages of the individuals. Additional interpretation problems are related to reliability and validity. Because stuttering is a highly variable behavior, it is surprising that the author does not provide information about test-retest reliability or internal consistency. Stability across time and conditions is a necessary prerequisite for determining whether a test actually measures what it purports to measure. It is difficult, therefore, to judge the validity of the SSI-3.

In summary, there are a number of flaws in the SSI-3 that limit its usefulness. Lack of necessary information about procedures for collecting speech samples, scoring conversions that decrease power, a small and undefined normative sample, and lack of critical reliability data interfere with the interpretability of test results. Perhaps the author says it best when he notes, "Reliance on quantifiable test scores, which are limited by their definitions of the behaviors and by their reliability, may lead to conclusions that are incomplete and incorrect" (p. 1). This test would make a poor substitute for clinical insight. At best, beginning clinicians and speech and language clinicians with relatively little experience with stutterers might use the SSI-3 as a partial means for calibrating and/or confirming clinical impressions of stuttering in conversation and/or reading contexts. This would comprise a very small part of a comprehensive stuttering evaluation.

REVIEWER'S REFERENCES

Riley, G. D. (1972). A stuttering severity instrument for children and adults. *Journal of Speech and Hearing Disorders, 37,* 314–322.

Riley, G. G. (1980). Stuttering Severity Instrument for Children and Adults (Revised). Austin, TX: PRO-ED, Inc.

Review of the Stuttering Severity Instrument for Children and Adults, Third Edition by REBECCA McCAULEY, Associate Professor, Communication Sciences, University of Vermont, Burlington, VT:

TEST STRUCTURE. The Stuttering Severity Instrument for Children and Adults (SSI-3) is designed to assess stuttering severity for clinical and research purposes among preschool children (ages 2-10 to 5-11), school-aged children (6-1 to 16-11), and adults (17-0 and older). There are two versions of the instrument—one for readers and one for non-readers (i.e., children who read below the third grade

level). Both versions require assessment of stuttering frequency, duration, and physical concomitants, that are combined to provide a single score with an associated 5-point descriptive severity level ranging from "very mild" to "very severe" (p. 11).

TEST ADMINISTRATION AND INTERPRETATION. The instrument requires at least two 200-syllable speech samples for assessment. Because children are thought to be more affected by the clinical setting, one of their samples consists of a video- or audio-taped conversation recorded at home with (usually) a parent. For older children and adults, one sample consists of a conversation with the examiner and the other, the reading of an age-appropriate passage. During the conversation in which she or he participates, the examiner is instructed to "interject questions, interruptions, and mild disagreements to simulate the pressures of normal conversation at home and elsewhere" (p. 7)—an instruction likely to introduce considerable variability in the nature of samples obtained.

Three subtest scores are calculated from the speech samples—the percentage of syllables stuttered, the mean duration of the longest three stutters, and a rating for the presence of physical concomitants in four areas: Distracting Sounds, Facial Grimaces, Head Movements, and Movements of the Extremities. Stuttering examples are given during the description of percentage of syllables stuttered calculation, but no other explicit definitions are provided, thus making the approach used in this instrument one that might be described as involving a perceptual definition of stuttering.

Although specific scoring procedures for each subtest measure are stated, the range of variables possibly affecting both the stuttering behavior itself and the possible reliability of the examiner are alarmingly numerous and include the immediacy of measurement (on-line versus from a recorded sample) and type of recording used (audio versus video).

NORMS. Norms consist of group means and standard deviations. For two of the three age groups, sample sizes were generally smaller than a desirable 100 per group (i.e., $n = 72$ for preschoolers, 139 for school-age children, and 60 for adults). The normative population is insufficiently described: The reader is told only they came from a variety of clinical and public school sources and, if older than 8 years of age, had generally received stuttering treatment. Despite the disappointing nature of these norms, however, they constitute the best available for standardized severity measures of stuttering.

Interpretation of test results consists primarily of the assignment of a percentile score and associated severity label using the norms for each group but there is no justification for the specific percentile intervals used.

RELIABILITY. The methods used to document reliability depart from those typically reported for standardized measures, probably because of the considerable difficulty reported in the research literature of obtaining acceptable levels of agreement for at least some of the measures included in this scale (Cordes & Ingham, 1994). The author notes that "a special procedure" was used "to improve reliability of stuttering measurements" (p. 15), which consisted of using stanine values for percentage and duration measures. This procedure is problematic given that test interpretation is not based on those same values. In addition, percentage of agreement was calculated by dividing the smaller score by the larger score for each judgment pair—a measure of agreement that has been termed "one of the least stringent" of such measures (Cordes & Ingham, 1994). Additional problems with the reported agreement data include a lack of clarity, from my perspective, concerning what units were used as "judgment pairs" in the calculation of agreement and a lack of information concerning agreement for live versus off-line scoring of some measures. Thus, despite a reported "intra/interexaminer reliability" averaging from 82 to 93% for experienced raters (manual, p. 16) and despite appropriate suggestions that examiners calculate and seek to improve their self-agreement as a means of improving reliability, users of this instrument should be skeptical about its overall reliability.

VALIDITY. Three types of *criterion-related evidence* for validity are presented. Two of these, however, involve correlations to highly related measures sharing the same author—one between the SSI-3 and one of its subtests, SS%, and the other (Yaruss & Conture, 1992) between an earlier version of the SSI-3, the SSI-R (Riley, 1980) and the Stuttering Prediction Instrument (Riley, 1981), a "companion instrument to the SSI-3" (manual, p. 17). As the third source of criterion-related evidence, the author unconvincingly and somewhat unclearly argues from the previously discussed reliability data.

Hypotheses studied to provide evidence of *construct validity* were "tested" on a single set of data, namely, part-whole correlation matrices for the three age groups. These hypotheses were that severity would "increase with the length of time the individual has stuttered" (p. 17) and that subtests would be "related to each other, because they are parts of the overall construct of severity" (p. 17). Unfortunately, whereas the second hypothesis was somewhat supported by low to moderate correlations between subtests, the first hypothesis was not really tested, but advanced through a restatement of the descriptive statistic values.

SUMMARY. This is a widely used measure of stuttering severity, designed to be used for individuals ages 2 and above. Methods vary depending upon client age and reading ability, but include the assessment of stuttering Frequency, Duration, and Physical Concomitants, which are combined to derive a 5-point severity rating. Norms, reliability, and validity data provided are unsatisfactory. Nonetheless, this instrument represents the only standardized measure of its kind. Consequently, clinicians should use this measure cautiously and consider the development of local norms and the assessment of their own reliability as necessary to its use in quality clinical service.

REVIEWER'S REFERENCES
Riley, G. (1980). Stuttering Severity Instrument for Children and Adults (Revised). Austin, TX: PRO-ED, Inc.
Riley, G. (1981). Stuttering Prediction Instrument. Austin, TX: PRO-ED, Inc.
Yaruss, J., & Conture, E. (1992). Relationship between mother-child speaking rates in adjacent fluent utterances. *ASHA, 34,* 210.
Cordes, A. K., & Ingham, R. J. (1994). The reliability of observational data: II. Issues in the identification and measurement of stuttering events. *Journal of Speech and Hearing Research, 37*(2), 279–294.
Lewis, K. E. (1995). Do SSI-3 scores adequately reflect observations of stuttering behaviors? *American Journal of Speech-Language Pathology, 4,* 46–59.

[305]
Styles of Conflict Inventory.

Purpose: "Designed to aid in the assessment of couples' conflict."

Population: Heterosexual couples.

Publication Date: 1993.

Acronym: SCI.

Scores, 6: Appraisal of Conflict, Styles of Conflict, Comparison of Partners' Styles of Conflict, Differences Between Behaviors and Perceptions, Critical Items, Total.

Administration: Group.

Price Data, 1993: $29 per sampler set including manual (83 pages), test booklet, and answer sheet; $72 per 10 test booklets and answer sheets; $25 per manual.

Time: (15–20) minutes.

Comments: Self-administered test; mail-in scoring.

Author: Michael E. Metz.

Publisher: Consulting Psychologists Press, Inc.

Review of the Styles of Conflict Inventory by JULIE A. ALLISON, Associate Professor of Psychology, Pittsburg State University, Pittsburg, KS:

The Styles of Conflict Inventory (SCI) assesses conflict among couples, and was intended to aid either clinicians or educators conducting relationship workshops to help couples understand their relationship conflict and how each of the individuals deals with their conflict. Test booklets are formatted on computer scantron sheets where both questions are provided and responses are given. Partners are first asked to provide basic demographic information, and then to complete the 138-item SCI. The SCI items are simple and direct; all responses are provided on either 5-point or 7-point Likert scales. The SCI may be administered easily, is understandable, and does not take long to complete (15–20 minutes).

Part I of the SCI is called "Appraisal of Conflict" and collects information regarding each of the partner's perceptions about the general quality of their relationships. Although this section was not based on any strong theoretical basis, the assessment of these constructs is important and provides meaningful information, which may provide a context for interpreting the results obtained from subsequent sections of the scale.

The development of Parts II and III of the SCI were based on various theories of conflict. The primary premise of the theoretical basis is that there are two basic orientations to relationship conflict: engagement and avoidance. Each of these approaches is further subdivided into specific actions (or nonactions), and may be viewed as lying on a continuum from most engaging to most avoiding, including aggression, assertion, adaptation, submission, denial, and withdrawal. Items for the SCI were developed to reflect these various styles of dealing with conflict in two separate ways: cognitively and behaviorally. Respondents are asked, then, to indicate both the frequencies of having particular thoughts in response to threat (e.g., "I want to resolve our disagreement") *and* of behaving in particular ways (e.g., "Yield to your partner"). These categories comprise Sections IIA (30 items) and IIB (48 items), respectively.

The final section of the SCI, Part IIC (48 items) uses this same theoretical continuum, but asks respondents to indicate their perceptions of how their *partner* behaves when conflict is experienced. Because the SCI measures several different possible styles of conflict within three different domains (cognitions, behaviors, and perceptions of partner's behaviors) results from these sections are quite complex, and yield 20 different scores for each of the partners. Consequently, the results of the SCI yield numerous scores and will require sufficient time for the administrator to interpret before sharing the results with the couple. The interpreter should also consider the fact that all data obtained from the SCI are self-report in nature.

Responses to the SCI are to be returned to the administrator, who in turn must send in the test booklets to be scored by Consulting Psychologists Press. Hence, one drawback to this procedure is that the results may be costly and are not immediately available for interpretation. The computer-generated report is easy to read, however, and provides the results in the form of respondent's average frequency scores, as well as in bar graphs that show how the respondent compares to a normative sample (through *T*-scores). The SCI manual is also helpful in aiding interpretation. Part 1 provides a description of how both individuals appraised conflict in their relationship, and also provides brief interpretive statements about how the partners may be perceiving such conflict differently. Part 2 helps to develop a profile of each individual's style of conflict. In Part 3, these profiles are presented side-by-side so that any patterns in the relationship may be revealed. Finally, Part 4 reports on any differences between behavior and perceptions of behavior between the two individuals. It should be noted that although the standardized scores provided may be quite useful to both the interpreter and the couple, the normative sample used to develop standardized scores is quite limited: 98% of those in the heterosexual sample were Caucasian with a mean annual income of $49,000.

Given that the SCI was intended to be concise, with 3–7 items for each subsection of Parts II and III, reliability scores are generally acceptable. Internal consistency scores ranged from .61–.88, with most scores ranging from .73–.80. Test-retest reliability coefficients were less stable, ranging from .22–.93. This large range may be understandable, given the considerable impact that both situations and time may have on conflict and conflict styles, but does raise questions about the temporal stability of any results. The test-retest data were also based only on 2- and 4-week intervals; expanding this time interval may be useful in identifying the parameters of SCI results.

The validity data of the SCI are quite solid. The developer of this scale went to great lengths to gather evidence for both face and content validity. Though some modifications were made based on factorial analyses (i.e., verbal and physical aggression are each scored separately), results of these analyses provide support that SCI items fit the theoretical constructs intended to be measured. Concurrent validity appears to be established through expected correlations between SCI scores and scores obtained from several different theoretically relevant scales, including the Dyadic Adjustment Scale, Marital Adjustment Scale, and the Conflict Tactics Scale. Although most correlation coefficients are in the expected direction, not all are statistically significant, and the statistical significance of some correlations are not reported. However, given the extremely large number of significant correlations that were obtained, this does not seem to be a serious problem. The SCI has good discriminant validity, with successful discrimination between various types of couples (e.g., satisfied vs. dissatisfied) ranging between 69% to 98%.

Overall, the SCI will be a useful inventory for couples seeking to understand their relationship conflict. This tool would be most useful as an initial scaling device that could open up important dialogue for a couple with the help of a therapist or counselor, particularly toward understanding the various conflict patterns that may be present in the relationship, and individual differences that exist in conflict styles. This scale may also be helpful in identifying any abusive relationships. However, the SCI would be less helpful for relationships already identified as abusive. The strongest asset of the SCI may be in its simplicity: Despite all of the subscales of this inventory, it does do a good job of uncomplicating the complicated.

Review of the Styles of Conflict Inventory by JUDY L. ELLIOTT, Research Associate, National Center for Educational Outcomes, University of Minnesota, Minneapolis, MN:

PURPOSE. The Styles of Conflict Inventory (SCI) comprises a self-report measure designed to facilitate the assessment of couples' conflict. The SCI was designed to provide an initial screen of relationship conflict interaction patterns. It gathers both cognitive and behavioral responses between couples and gives a general screen of interactions. Its purpose is to assist in diagnosing, treatment planning, monitoring, and outcome evaluation for working with couples in conflict.

OVERVIEW/CONTENT. The SCI is a neutral-gendered inventory designed to assist in the assessment of couples' conflict. It is intended for adults aged 18–82. It is a self-administered questionnaire designed to assess cognitions, behaviors, and perception of couples in conflict. The SCI has a reported reading level of approximately grade 5. Norms for the SCI are available for heterosexual and homosexual (gay and lesbian) couples. Two basic orientations to relationship conflict have been identified—Engagement and Avoidance. The SCI measures both styles using three different scales. Engaging responses to conflict are measured via Assertion, Aggression, and Adaptation scales. The avoiding responses are measured on Withdrawal, Submission, and Denial scales. The SCI was designed for use in clinical settings with couples in a significant personal relationship confronted with conflict.

The SCI comprises two questionnaires. The Part I Appraisal of Conflict form consists of a 12-item Likert-style inventory to assess cognitive dimensions (i.e., efficacy and outcome expectancies, attributions of power, etc.) of conflict. The Appraisal of Conflict yields a rating of overall relationship satisfaction, frequency, intensity, and quality of conflict, perception of partner and self-responsibility for conflict, attribution of blame, optimism about the future conflict resolution, perception of one's own and partner's power, rating of one's own and partner's distress over relationship conflict, and motivation for change.

Part II of the SCI is a three-section Styles of Conflict form. It consists of 126 items that assess the prevalence or frequency of responses to thoughts (cognitions), actions (behaviors), and impressions of the partner's actions (perceptions). Additionally, Part II measures the discrepancy between respondent's perceptions and partner's self-reported behavior.

The SCI is computer scored and produces a summary that highlights the amount and intensity of relationship conflict. The report provides a profile of each partner's cognitive, behavioral, and perceptual response styles. The cognitive scales comprise the following: Assertion, Aggression, Submission, and Denial. The cognitive scales yield standardized scores that can be used to compare corresponding behavioral scores to assess the consonance between an individual's cognitions and behaviors.

The behavioral and perceptual scales consist of eight subscales each. Each of the eight scales produces three sets of scores—individual's self-rating, partner's perception of the other person's behavior, and a discrepancy between the self-rating and the partner's perception. Individual data are provided through the use of graphic profiles of both the individual's self-rated behavior and the partner's perceptions.

Five case studies illustrating the use of the SCI are provided in the inventory's manual. Each case study includes a brief clinical history, the couple's initial presenting problem, and describes the SCI results for each partner as well as the couple as a unit. Results are interpreted in the context of the relationship and conflict management issues. Outcomes of each case study (if known) are shared.

ADMINISTRATION AND SCORING. The SCI is a self-administered paper-and-pencil inventory. Administration is estimated at 15–20 minutes. Forms for Part I and Part II of the SCI are provided in duplicate so that each partner can fill out both questionnaires.

Results are composed of six sections: Section 1, Appraisal Conflict, describes the general climate of the relationship and conflict and summarizes each partner's rating of the conflict; Section 2, Style of Conflict, summarizes the conflict response styles for each partner in the areas of Thoughts, Behaviors, and Perceptions; Section 3, Comparison of Partner's Style of Conflict, contrasts partner's scores on each of the four cognitive, eight behavioral, and eight perceptual scales; Section 4, Difference Between Behaviors and Perceptions, compares each individual's behavior with the partner's perception of that behavior, included in this section is a Difference Score indicating the discrepancy that exists between each partner's self-reported behavior and the other partner's view of that behavior; Section 5, Critical Items, lists all the items for which either partner rated a score of 5 (Very Often); and Section 6, Raw Scores.

Scores on the SCI are reported as *T*-scores (mean of 50, standard deviation of 10) and provide the capacity to compare the scores of an individual to the scores of a norm group. Hence, the SCI profile scores have comparability across scales. As long as the norm group is used as the reference point, an individual's scores on one scale can be compared with that individual's score on other remaining scales.

Finally, the interpretation section in the SCI manual advises that professionals conduct validity checks by asking partners to recall how they felt when they gave their answers. Several guidelines and strategies for interpretation and clinical use of the SCI are provided.

NORMS AND STANDARDIZATION PROCEDURES. The norm group for the SCI consisted of 156 heterosexual couples who were residents of several counties in metropolitan Minneapolis, Minnesota. Couples were recruited from a primary-care physician's list. These patients were reported as those "not acutely ill" (p. 24). All couples who were on a physician's patient billing list were invited to participate in the procedure. Not all the couples were legally married. SCI scale statistics for heterosexual couples are provided. Results for all heterosexual couples taking the SCI are compared with this norm group for deriving standard scores. Separate norms for homosexual couples are provided. The heterosexual norm group is composed of a broad range for age and length of relationship; it is, however, not representative of all heterosexual couples. This sample used for development of the SCI was reported to be predominantly homogenous, white, middle-class, and college-educated adults. Therefore, the ability to generalize results to other ethnic or minority groups cannot be easily done. Additionally, differences in cultural attitudes, means of approaching conflict, and general reactions and responses to assessment situations cannot be overlooked.

ITEM SELECTION. Items for the SCI were derived to measure conflict response styles with a goal of achieving face validity. Negative test items were avoided to reduce confusion and variance in language ability. Negative items were thought to describe an absence of cognition or behavior rather than providing an accurate picture of their existence. Items were developed to elicit quick responses instead of those requiring slow pondered thought. The latter was thought to yield ambiguous and less valid data.

Item content validity was developed by seven "expert" raters. The raters were assigned the 56 items from the original pool of cognitions and behaviors, to Assertion, Aggression, Withdrawal, Submission, or Denial. As a result of the rating process, 47 items (21 cognition items and 26 behavior items) were retained because they met preset criterion that category rating be consistent among at least six of the seven raters. The initial rating resulted in 38 of the items (81%) receiving 100% rater agreement and 9 items (19%) receiving agreement from six of seven raters. The 26 rated behavior items were then restated to form 26 corresponding items for Part 2-C, to tap the respondent's perception of the partner's behavior. Hence, the SCI has 73 items: 21 cognitions—Part 2A, 26 behavior—Part 2B, and 26 perception's of the partner's behavior—Part 2C. Each scale is composed of 4 to 7 items, with no scale overlap. The scales of the SCI were evaluated using two studies that investigated internal consistency reliability, test-retest reliability, and factorial validity.

RELIABILITY. The author presented estimates for two types of reliability: (a) internal consistency, and (b) test-retest. Internal consistency reliability estimates the extent to which the items in a given scale measure a unitary construct. For example, the cognitive dimension of the SCI includes a subscale called *aggression*; a high internal consistency reliability coefficient alpha (i.e., >.70) would indicate that the items in this scale are all measuring something similar. The technical manual reports Cronbach's alpha coefficients for each subscale of the SCI on male and female samples separately and together. All but a few scales meet traditionally acceptable levels of internal consistency reliability (alpha >.70). Such high alphas are particularly noteworthy given that most subscales contain only three items (everything being equal, the greater the number of items the higher the value of alpha). In the Behavior dimension, internal consistency reliability estimates for both the Assertion scale and the Submission scale are lower than .70. It is important to note that reliability is not a property of an instrument, but is affected by the particular sample used and the intended interpretation of the scores. In any event, the addition of one to two well-constructed items to both scales would likely boost reliability to acceptable levels. Corrected item-total correlations would be helpful to determine whether every item is contributing positively to the internal consistency reliability.

The technical manual also provides information on test-retest reliability. Samples were separated into clinical and nonclinical couples and by gender. The clinical couples were retested 2 weeks later, whereas the nonclinical couples were retested 4 weeks later. Test-retest correlations for all groups were moderate (clinical $.60 < r < .90$; nonclinical $.59 < r < .88$). The clinical group was retested after 2 weeks of a therapeutic intervention. One may expect that couples receiving an effective intervention would tend to score at a more similar level, and thus become a more homogenous group. Other things being equal, this would likely result in a fairly low test-retest correlation, and oddly, the test-retest correlations were fairly high. A more thorough examination of this phenomenon may be needed.

VALIDITY. The technical manual includes information that enables examination of several aspects of validity: (a) content validity, (b) construct validity, and (c) criterion-related validity. Content validity was evaluated by having seven experts assign (assumed independently) the SCI items into their designated scales. The author reports agreement on 95% of the items. Thus, there is evidence that the scale designators sufficiently differentiate the content of the items.

The second type of validity presented is construct validity. Construct validity commonly includes such concepts as factorial validity, and convergent and discriminant validity. There is no single quantitative index of construct validity. Rather, construct validity is evaluated by the accumulation of evidence. Although the author provides factor analytic results and numerous tables of correlations between scores on SCI scales and scores on other more established instruments, the presentation of information is at once chaotic and incomplete. First, the author presents what he believes is evidence of factorial validity. Factorial validity is demonstrated by running a factor analysis on scores on scales from different instruments (the one of interest and another more established instrument). Rather, the author ran a factor analysis on the SCI alone. This is not what is meant by factorial validity. The issue becomes further confused by presentation of separate factor analyses on subcomponents of the SCI (e.g., verbal and physical aggression items from the aggression behavior scale).

The amount of data gathered to evaluate convergent and discriminant validity is admirable, but again, the presentation is unfocused. Eight tables with well over 100 correlations are provided. Although many of the associations between SCI scales and scales from other instruments are moderate and significant, there is little rationale provided to interpret the meaning of various associations.

The author also reports data used to evaluate criterion-related validity. One way of demonstrating this type of validity is to show that test scores differ substantially for groups that would be expected to differ. Scores were compared for contrasting groups along four dimensions: satisfaction/dissatisfaction, adjusted/distressed, nonclinical/clinical, and sexual dysfunction versus sexual offender. T-tests on scores obtained on each scale for each group were used to assess group differences. Many significant differences were obtained for each of the contrasted groups.

SUMMARY. The SCI is a self-administered inventory designed to assist in the assessment of couples' conflict. The SCI is intended to be a brief screening instrument and as a result has a small number of items per scale. However, an outcome of quick and efficient is to raise many cautions. All information on the SCI is self-reported and is open to distortion on the part of the respondents. Clinical observation and other assessments should be used to corroborate as well as to supplement the SCI. A computer-scored profile is provided that reports several aspects of individual's self-rating, partner's perception of the other person's behavior, and a discrepancy between the self-rating and partner's perception. The profile also includes cognitive, behavioral, and perceptual response styles. Standardized scores are reported in *T*-scores and norms for heterosexual and homosexual couples are provided. Although the analysis of reliability and validity is vast, such vastness sometimes creates confusion in understanding the purpose and use of some of the analyses.

[306]
Substance Abuse Relapse Assessment.

Purpose: Designed to assess and monitor relapse prevention and coping skills.
Population: Adolescents and adults.
Publication Date: 1993.
Acronym: SARA.
Scores: 4 parts: Substance Abuse Behavior, Antecedents of Substance Abuse, Consequences of Substance Abuse, Responses to Slips.
Administration: Individual.
Price Data, 1996: $75 per introductory kit including 25 interview record forms, 25 each of 3 relapse prevention planning forms, and manual (31 pages) with stimulus card; $27 per 25 interview record forms; $11 per 25 relapse prevention planning forms (specify Form 1—Pretreatment, Form 2—Current, or Form 3—Relapse); $28 per manual with stimulus card.
Time: (60) minutes.
Authors: Lawrence Schonfeld, Roger Peters, and Addis Dolente.
Publisher: Psychological Assessment Resources, Inc.

Review of the Substance Abuse Relapse Assessment by MICHAEL G. KAVAN, Associate Dean for Student Affairs and Associate Professor of Family Practice, Creighton University School of Medicine, Omaha, NE:

The Substance Abuse Relapse Assessment (SARA) is a structured interview designed to assist in developing relapse prevention goals and monitoring the achievement of these goals within substance abuse treatment programs. The major aim of the SARA is to identify the antecedents and consequences of pretreatment alcohol and/or drug use and to use this information to develop individualized treatment plans. The SARA is based on, and therefore, similar to, several drinking profiles (e.g., Drinking Profile [Marlatt, 1976], Comprehensive Drinker Profile [Marlatt & Miller, 1984], Gerontology Alcohol Project Drinking Profile [Dupree, Broskowski, & Schonfeld, 1984]). It consists of a manual with stimulus card, a four-part interview record form, and three relapse prevention planning forms. The interview record form consists of questions regarding substance abuse behavior, antecedents and consequences of use, and responses to slips. The relapse prevention planning forms allow the examiner to identify the client's substance abuse behavior chain, pretreatment skills used to avoid relapse, and current relapse prevention goals.

ADMINISTRATION AND SCORING. The SARA is designed to be administered individually to adolescents and adults who have a history of substance abuse, whose ability to avoid substance abuse relapse is in question, or who are involved in substance abuse treatment programs. It may be administered by any professional with appropriate training in substance abuse assessment and intervention. It is recommended that examiners should also have experience in the use of structured interviews and in the development of individualized treatment plans. Instructions for the interview record form are fairly clear and easy for examiners to follow. However, some clients may have difficulty keeping track of the multiple response options read to them for certain questions. For these questions, it may have been more useful to allow the examiner to show the client the various response options listed in the interview record form or present a stimulus card to the client. A stimulus card is used to identify client feelings associated with the relapse and to determine how confident the client is regarding his or her ability to avoid substance use. The examiner may request additional information throughout the interview to clarify responses or information that is contradictory.

Once the interview record form is completed, the interviewer uses this information to complete the relapse prevention planning forms, which identify behavior chain(s) (i.e., antecedents, behaviors, and consequences) associated with substance use as well as various pretreatment and proactive coping skills. Those working with the client can then use this information to discuss relapse prevention issues during treatment. It is also recommended that these forms be revised as new information is disclosed by the client during the course of treatment. No other information is provided within the manual regarding the scoring of the SARA. Administration time is approximately one hour.

RELIABILITY AND VALIDITY. No data are provided within the manual regarding reliability or validity. The manual does provide a sample case illustration for "Joe," which highlights how the various components of the SARA can be used to develop a treatment plan for a client. Limited guidelines are provided regarding how to systematically apply the information from the relapse prevention planning forms to a treatment plan. Of importance to note is that no data are provided regarding the impact of such planning on outcome.

NORMS. The SARA was "field tested" with 101 inmates (63 males and 38 females; ages 17 to 47 years) in a sheriff's office substance abuse treatment program in Tampa, Florida. Limited data are provided from this field test. Information is provided on the inmates' major problem substances, major locations of use, persons with whom the inmates have used substances most frequently, and various antecedents to use for this group. The authors indicate that this preliminary study indicated that emotional and situational events were the major precipitants of alcohol and drug use. As such, it is recommended that treatment plans be designed to address various negative emotional, interpersonal conflicts, and peer pressure through skills training, behavioral rehearsal, and practice situations. Beyond these, the manual contains no other normative information.

SUMMARY. The SARA is a structured interview designed to assist in developing relapse prevention goals and monitoring the achievement of these goals within substance abuse treatment programs. The major goal of the SARA, which is to identify the antecedents and consequences of pretreatment alcohol and/or drug use and to use this information to develop individualized treatment plans, is admirable and desirable. However, the SARA provides no data regarding its ability to accomplish this feat. Likewise, no information is provided within the manual regarding the SARA's ability to influence treatment outcomes. In fact, the only data provided within the manual relate to a field test of 101 inmates in a Florida county jail. Surely, these are not the only persons with substance abuse problems that could possibly benefit from the SARA. Additional studies with more diverse groups are certainly necessary. Another problem with the SARA is that it fails to incorporate useful relapse prevention issues such as the quality of the client's social support network, the quality of the client's primary intimate relationships (Marlatt, 1985), and self-attribution for behavior change (Annis, 1991) into the interview process. In addition, the Interview Record Form is based on recall, which is subject to a variety of biases. Until these problems are addressed, the SARA is unfortunately relegated to only a somewhat useful, structured method for obtaining information about substance use and relapse; nothing more.

REVIEWER'S REFERENCES

Marlatt, G. A. (1976). The Drinking Profile: A questionnaire for the behavioral assessment of alcoholism. In E. J. Mash & L. G. Terdal (Eds.), *Behavior therapy assessment: Diagnosis, design, and evaluation* (pp. 127–137). New York: Springer.

Dupree, L. W., Broskowski, H., & Schonfeld, L. (1984). The Gerontology Alcohol Project: A behavioral treatment program for elderly alcohol abusers. *The Gerontologist, 24,* 510–516.

Marlatt, G. A., & Miller. W. R. (1984). The Comprehensive Drinker Profile. Odessa, FL: Psychological Assessment Resources, Inc.

Marlatt, G. A. (1985). Situational determinants of relapse and skill training interventions. In G. A. Marlatt & J. R. Gordon (Eds.), *Relapse prevention: Maintenance strategies in the treatment of addictive behaviors* (pp. 77–127). New York: Guilford.

Annis, H. M. (1991). A cognitive-social learning approach to relapse: Pharmacotherapy and relapse prevention counseling. *Alcohol and Alcoholism (Supplement), 1,* 527–530.

Review of the Substance Abuse Relapse Assessment by JEFFREY S. RAIN, Assistant Professor and Chairman, Industrial/Organizational Psychology Program, School of Psychology, Florida Tech, Melbourne, FL:

The Substance Abuse Relapse Assessment (SARA) was designed to assess and monitor relapse prevention and coping skills. Setting aside debates between medical, psychodynamic, and behavioral approaches to alcohol, tobacco, and other drug (ATOD) treatment and debates over abstinence versus relapse prevention, the SARA appears to be a very comprehensive, theory-driven, practical guide for identifying relapse risk potential and assisting in treatment planning. Whereas the SARA purports to excel in these areas, except for a limited field test, it lacks research studies specific to the instrument itself.

Addressing psychometric criteria first, the SARA is a very new instrument and lacks empirical evidence of support. In fact, statistical documentation is nonexistent. The only data presented in the manual are the descriptions of the original sample of 101 inmates of a law enforcement substance abuse treatment program in Florida. Data on reliability, validity, bias, administration, and other standard criteria for psychometric quality are not presented. Evaluations of the majority of the technical aspects of the SARA are thus precluded from this review.

With the psychometric deficits stated, a number of potentially very strong positives emerge on the SARA's practical and administrative side. The Professional Manual primarily consists of a description of the SARA and its administration as well as a case illustration and sample treatment plan. Instructions are comprehensive and easy to follow. Particularly helpful is the detailed sample case illustration, which provides clarification for instances where the administrator is unclear exactly how to complete the SARA.

Another positive feature of the SARA is the ability of this instrument to provide a good foundation on which to build treatment plans. Twelve-step programs, if used, also appear to integrate well with the SARA. Additionally, the SARA recognizes the reality of multiple-substance abuse and does not limit itself to a single substance. It does have the flexibility to consider a primary ATOD focus as well as secondary ATOD foci.

Whereas the time frame of the SARA is a 30-day reporting period, the authors acknowledge the changing nature of substance abuse relapse prevention. Therefore, the SARA should be considered a dynamic instrument requiring regular updating. At a minimum it is designed to be used before, during, and after treatment. Given the frequency of updating and the detail involved, the authors' stated caution for conditions potentially precluding the completion of the SARA cannot be overstated. Depending on the situation, the SARA may require multiple sessions to complete. Some of the effort may be reduced by having portions of the updating completed by clients as "homework" (p. 6). However, it should be noted that the detail of information requested places a heavy burden on both client and practitioner. Clients may not be capable of contributing fully to the SARA or be able to complete homework assignments with sufficient detail.

From a theoretical standpoint, the SARA is very well supported by a behavior-based approach. Applying functional analysis to substance abuse identifies a chain of behaviors (i.e., antecedents, behaviors, and consequences or ABCs) that have an impact on the abuse (e.g., Cummings, Gordon, & Marlatt, 1980). The functional analysis approach is a cornerstone of behavior therapy and, therefore, may not be readily adopted by all practitioners, but has been shown to be an effective treatment approach for substance abuse (e.g., Baer, Marlatt, & McMahon, 1993).

On the whole, the theoretical foundations give the SARA clear clinical application. Wholesale endorsement of the SARA must be reserved until its individual research base is more fully established. Still, the SARA is very user friendly, though administratively demanding. Data from the SARA appear to be highly generalizable to various traditional treatment programs (e.g., 12-step programs) as well as other alcohol, tobacco, and other drug (ATOD) cases. The proof of the SARA will be in the research but the theoretical base, instructions, and case illustrations are a solid beginning.

REVIEWER'S REFERENCES

Cummings, C., Gordon, J. R., & Marlatt, G. A. (1980). Relapse: Prevention and prediction. In W. R. Miller (Ed.), *The addictive behaviors* (pp. 291–321). Oxford, UK: Pergamon Press.

Baer, J. S., Marlatt, G. A., & McMahon, R. J. (Eds.) (1993). *Addictive behaviors across life span: Prevention treatment and policy issues.* Newbury Park: Sage.

[307]
Substance Abuse Screening Test.

Purpose: "Designed to screen-out those students who are unlikely to have a substance abuse problem."
Population: Ages 13—adult.
Publication Date: 1993.
Acronym: SAST.
Scores: Total Level of Risk.
Administration: Group.
Forms, 2: Response Form, Observation Report.
Price Data, 1996: $55 per complete kit including 50 Response Forms, 50 Observation Reports, and manual (34 pages); $22 per 50 Response Forms; $14 per 50 Observation Reports; $25 per manual.
Time: (5) minutes.
Authors: Terry Hibpshman and Sue Larson.
Publisher: Slosson Educational Publications, Inc.

Review of the Substance Abuse Screening Test by MARY LOU KELLEY, Professor of Psychology, Louisiana State University, Louisiana State University Medical Center, Baton Rouge, LA:

The Substance Abuse Screening Test (SAST) was developed to aid in the screening of adolescents and young adults (ages 13–30) who are and are not at risk for substance abuse. The authors explicitly state that the measure is not intended for diagnosis or labeling and thus, provide an appropriately conservative statement of purpose and test limitations. The primary test consists of a 30-item questionnaire requiring the respondent to indicate whether or not each statement is true of their feelings or behavior. Items range in content from those that explicitly ask about alcohol or drug use to those tapping perceptions of loneliness, family conflict, and general mood states, among other characteristics assumed to be associated with substance abuse risk. The authors do not distinguish between alcohol and illicit drug use/abuse as they believe abusers represent a heterogeneous sample that is not functionally differentiated by the type of substance abused. However, most of the items that specifically tapped substance abuse asked about drinking rather than drug use. The authors purport that the items represent those that differentiate abusers from nonabusers. However, statistical data supporting this conclusion were not provided in the technical manual.

The test materials also include an Observation Report form for the evaluator to record observations in response to several open-ended questions as well as to provide general comments. The authors indicate that the Observation Report allows for the personalization of the screening but that, as with the SAST, the instrument is not to be used diagnostically.

The administration, scoring, and test interpretation procedures were described succinctly and clearly. The scoring involves simply summing the number of endorsed items. Three procedures are provided to aid in score interpretation. Raw scores can be placed in one of four risk levels, converted to standardized scores with a mean of 100 and standard deviation of 15; or entered into a Bayesian table for estimating substance abuse likelihood. All interpretation procedures are relatively easy to use although it is unclear how the authors determined the cutoff levels for the classification system.

Discussions of the psychometric characteristics of the test and the technical development of the instrument were often lacking in important details. For example, the authors identified the states from which the standardization sample came and the age range; however, there was no mention of the number of subjects, SES, gender, or racial composition of the sample, nor the number of individuals included who had a substance abuse problem. In contrast, the authors did provide data on mean test scores of substance abusers, nonabusers, and a variety of comparison groups as well as means based on respondent age, race, and gender. The authors did report significant differences between groups, which supported the validity of the instrument. The authors provided data on the item-total correlation coefficients, the magnitudes of which were acceptable. The authors concluded that test-retest reliability was not applicable because test stability was not a desired feature of the instrument because an individual's score should improve with treatment. This conclusion regarding test stability is wholly inaccurate as most tests assessing clinical symptomatology are potentially sensitive to treatment effects. Overall, the psychometric properties of the instrument are impossible to interpret given the lack of information on the standardization sample as well as the limited reliability data.

The test developers do not provide information on the relationship of the test scores to other measures of substance abuse. Also, it appeared that the authors included a sample of known substance abusers in, or about to enter, treatment. It is not clear how treatment resistant or denying substance abusers would respond to the questionnaire. It would have been useful had the authors included a lie scale as a component of the instrument to assess the influence of social desirability. It appears the measure would not be very useful in detecting substance abusers who are reticent in reporting about their patterns of use.

In summary, the Substance Abuse Screening Test is a short, easily administered and scored instrument for assessing drug and alcohol use. The test is intended for screening only and is not diagnostic. The authors reported that items differentiated abusers from nonabusers. Although the test has some positive features, I cannot recommend use of the instrument as a screening measure at this point given the limited psychometric data. Specifically, additional data are needed addressing the reliability and content validity of the instrument. Furthermore, it is unclear how substance abusers not interested in treatment would score on the instrument. It is my concern that the test would lead to excessive numbers of false negatives given the direct nature of many of the items.

Review of the Substance Abuse Screening Test by MARIELA C. SHIRLEY, Assistant Professor of Psychology, University of North Carolina at Wilmington, Wilmington, NC:

The Substance Abuse Screening Test (SAST) was developed as a brief measure to identify individuals "who may be at risk of substance abuse" (manual, p. 7), and to help with referral decisions (manual, p. 1). Although it is questionable whether true risk can be determined in a format other than a longitudinal design, the SAST's goal is consistent with screening tests focused on the early identification of individuals with possible substance abuse problems who require further evaluation (Connors, 1995; Miller, Westerberg, & Waldron, 1995). This test comprises two parts: (a) a 30-item self-report response form, and (b) an optional 5-item qualitative Observation Report. The SAST can be administered either individually or in a group format by staff with little training in addictions or assessment. The Observation Report should be completed by an examiner who is familiar with the individual being screened, particularly when self-report is suspect. Potential for bias in observer reporting is not addressed.

The SAST was not intended to be a diagnostic instrument; it was designed to screen out individuals who do not have substance abuse problems. However, 12 of the 30 items significantly overlap with *DSM-IV* criteria for dependence (i.e., alcohol). In adolescents, questions on withdrawal and tolerance may not be appropriate. SAST items were developed using a rational approach based on the test developers' experience and a literature review, and the test includes items that directly and indirectly assess for substance abuse (problem areas assessed include: aggression, conduct disorder/antisociality, parental conflicts, school problems, self-esteem, alienation, affect, attention/concentration, and mild cognitive impairment). Age of onset of use and family history of substance abuse are not assessed. An initial pool of 181 items was reduced to 30 by using the following approaches: (a) a rational approach, (b) by how well items discriminated between individuals with and without substance abuse problems based on item correlation with the total test score and diagnostic type (r range .49 to .77), and (c) by elimination of items considered to be redundant (where their correlation was lower than the similar retained item). A coefficient alpha of .895 was obtained as an estimate of internal consistency reliability. Principal components factor analysis was used on the final items to determine unidimensionality (manual, p. 15), with the first principal component dominating other factors in the analysis.

The standardization sample was obtained from samples in Kentucky, New York, Nebraska, and Kansas. No information is provided in the test manual regarding how the sample was obtained, its size, or characteristics (e.g., socio-demographics, sample size by age range, percentage of substance users vs. nonsubstance users, etc.). The age range selected (13–30) is arbitrary and confounds adolescents with adults. The authors indicate that the test discriminates well: (a) between individuals who have/do not have substance use problems (manual, p. 3); and (b) between substance abusers and individuals with other types of problems (e.g., psychiatric disorders, learning problems, behavior disorders, and physical disabilities). Scores were developed based on the probability that an individual will have a problem given the score and individual demographic characteristics (manual, p. 4). However, no data on sampling information are provided despite inferences that there were no differences for gender and race or for presence/absence of a substance use problem.

According to the authors, the SAST has strong face validity. However, whether *risk* (i.e., individuals without current substance use problems who are at risk for developing problems) for the development of a substance use disorder (risk reduction screening) vs. *need* for further assessment in individuals who already have a substance abuse problem (disease detection screening) is measured (construct validity) is open to question (Cooney, Zweben, & Fleming, 1995). Overall, the test appears to assess *deviance* (where one behavioral problem area could be substance abuse). If so, the Problem Oriented Screening Instrument for Teenagers (POSIT) is a better measure that assesses multiple behavior problem areas and discriminates between adolescents in treatment and school settings (Rahdert, 1991). Concurrent or convergent validity relative to other widely used measures in the field that screen for potential substance abuse problems (e.g., Adolescent Drinking Index [12:17], Adolescent Alcohol Involvement Scale [Mayer & Filstead, 1979] Personal Experience Screening Questionnaire [Winters, 1992], Drug Use Screening Inventory [Tarter, 1990; Tarter & Hegedus,1991], Problem Oriented Screening Instrument for Teenagers [Rahdert, 1991], Rutgers Collegiate Substance Abuse Screening Test [Bennett et al., 1993]) or a reference test (e.g., Michigan Alcoholism Screening Test [Selzer, 1971]) is not provided. Strong agreement between the total score and known history of substance abuse is claimed, yet poor documentation is provided. In an attempt to develop a test to assess *risk* the authors appear to confuse concurrent validity with predictive validity. In determining risk, predictive validity is more appropriate as the question would be "What is the likelihood that … will develop a substance abuse problem?" Further cautions of the impact of positive screens should be provided (i.e., on employability, insurability, scholarships, etc.).

Scoring is based on categorical yes/no responses with most substance abuse items requiring endorsement if the individual "ever or usually" had these symptoms. This may not be congruent with their "current" situation. In a review of special considerations in evaluating adolescents, Miller, Westerberg, and Waldron (1995) emphasized that although 90% of adolescents experiment with substances, many mature out after age 21. Interpretation of raw scores can be done in one of three ways: (a) risk level range, (b) standardized scores, and (c) Bayesian table of the likelihood that a problem exists.

Risk level cutoffs were based on efforts at maximizing sensitivity while minimizing specificity. A total score of 1–9 or 1–11 (for ages 13–18 and over 18 respectively) is unremarkable. Borderline risk is based on a score of 10–14 or 12–17 (for ages 13–18 and over 18 respectively). Moderate risk requires a score of 15–18 or 18–20, and high risk scores are 19–30 or 21–30 (for ages 13–18 and over 18 respectively for each of these risk ranges). Data are not provided on how cutoff scores were devised and what methods were used to link these to risk levels. At least 12 items bear some direct relationship to *DSM-IV* criteria (e.g., Item 20: "Once I start drinking it is hard for me to stop"). Presumably, one could endorse 9 of the 12 items yet be considered "unremarkable."

Standard scores use a mean of 100 (*s.d.* = 15) and are based on a sample of individuals who do not have a substance abuse problem and excludes substance abusers or individuals with other disorders. Standard scores were calibrated so that higher scores indicate lower risk and lower scores indicate higher risk (manual, p. 9). Again, there is no information on the sample used to derive these standard scores.

Finally, Bayesian tables are provided to help determine the likelihood that the SAST will accurately identify individuals with known problems using population baserates (manual, p. 25). Professionals utilizing these tables need to know the baserates of the community in which they live; this is often not the case as population estimates are usually given for much larger groupings of cities or socio-demographic categories. In addition, baserates for particular sample characteristics (e.g., blacks in rural communities, certain professions, etc.) are not always available. Even if baserate information were available, it is questionable how this would be utilized in a clinical setting or in facilitating a referral for further assessment. No test-retest or interrater reliability estimates are presented.

In summary, construct validity and other psychometric properties of the SAST are questionable. Although screening for substance use problems in adolescents is important, this measure is poorly developed, poorly documented, and offers no advantage over other screening instruments. Studies are needed to further evaluate its predictive validity.

REVIEWER'S REFERENCES

Selzer, M. L. (1971). The Michigan Alcoholism Screening Test: The quest for a new diagnostic instrument. *American Journal of Psychiatry, 127*, 1653–1658.

Mayer, J., & Filstead, W. J. (1979). The Adolescent Alcohol Involvement Scale: An instrument for measuring adolescents' use and misuse of alcohol. *Journal of Studies on Alcohol, 40*, 291–300.

Tarter, R. E. (1990). Evaluation and treatment of adolescent substance abuse: A decision tree method. *American Journal of Drug and Alcohol Abuse, 16*, 1–46.

Rahdert, E. R. (Ed.). (1991). *The Adolescent Assessment/Referral System manual.* Rockville, MD: U.S. Department of Health and Human Services.

Tarter, R. E., & Hegedus, A. M. (1991). The Drug Use Screening Inventory: Its application in the evaluation and treatment of alcohol and other drug abuse. *Alcohol Health and Research World, 15*, 65–75.

Winters, K. C. (1992). Development of an adolescent alcohol and other drug abuse screening scale: Personal Experience Screening Questionnaire. *Addictive Behaviors, 17*, 479–490.

Bennett, M. E., McCrady, B. S., Frankenstein, W., Laitman, L. A., Van Horn, D. H. A., & Keller, D. S. (1993). Identifying young adult substance abusers: The Rutgers Collegiate Substance Abuse Screening Test. *Journal of Studies on Alcohol, 54*, 522–527.

Connors, G. J. (1995). Screening for alcohol problems. In J. P. Allen & M. Columbus (Eds.), *Assessing alcohol problems: A guide for clinicians and researchers* (pp. 17–29) NIAAA Treatment Handbook Series 4 (NIH Publication No. 95-3745). Rockville, MD: National Institute on Alcohol Abuse and Alcoholism.

Cooney, N. L., Zweben, A., & Fleming, M. F. (1995). Screening for alcohol problems and at-risk drinking in health care settings. In R. K. Hester & W. R. Miller (Eds.), *Handbook of alcoholism treatment approaches: Effective alternatives* (2nd ed.; pp. 45–60). Boston, MA: Allyn & Bacon.

Miller, W. R., Westerberg, V. S., & Waldron, H. B. (1995). Evaluating alcohol problems in adults and adolescents. In R. K. Hester & W. R. Miller (Eds.), *Handbook of alcoholism treatment approaches: Effective alternatives* (2nd ed.; pp. 61–88). Boston, MA: Allyn & Bacon.

Substance Use Disorder Diagnosis Schedule.

Purpose: Designed to elicit information related to the diagnosis of substance use disorders.

Population: Suspected alcohol or drug abusers.

Publication Date: 1989.

Acronym: SUDDS.

Scores: Scores for 12 substances (Alcohol, Marijuana, Cocaine, Sedatives, Tranquilizers, Stimulants, Heroin, Other Opioids, Hallucinogens, PCP, Inhalants, Other/Mixed); ratings for Stress; and a Depression Screen.

Administration: Individual.

Price Data: Available from publisher.

Time: (30–45) minutes.

Comments: Structured diagnostic interview; also available as a computer-administered interview.

Authors: Patricia Ann Harrison and Norman G. Hoffmann.

Publisher: New Standards, Inc.

TEST REFERENCES

1. Veneziano, C., & Veneziano, L. (1992). Psychological characteristics of persons convicted of driving while intoxicated. *Psychological Reports, 70*, 1123-1130.

2. Watson, D., Weber, K., Assenheimer, J. S., Clark, L. A., Strauss, M. E., & McCormick, R. A. (1995). Testing a tripartite model: I. Evaluating convergent and discriminant validity of Anxiety and Depression Symptom Scales. *Journal of Abnormal Psychology, 104*, 3-14.

Review of the Substance Use Disorder Diagnosis Schedule by ANDRÉS BARONA, Professor of Educational Psychology and School Psychology Program Training Director, Arizona State University, Tempe, AZ:

The Substance Use Disorder Diagnosis Schedule (SUDDS) is a structured diagnostic interview used to obtain information about specific events and behaviors useful for corroborating *DSM-III* and *DSM-III-R* diagnoses of alcohol and/or other drug dependencies. Development of the SUDDS was based on a perceived need for a structured diagnostic interview for the specific purpose of detecting substance use disorder. The 1989 version of the SUDDS represents changes and revisions of the Diagnostic Interview Schedule (DIS; Robins, Helzer, Ratcliff, & Seyfried, 1982) and the Substance Abuse Modified Diagnostic Interview (SAMDIS; Hoffman & Harrison, 1984).

The SUDDS consists of 99 items that address general background information; exposure to life events that may lead to stress or depression; and use of coffee, tobacco, alcohol, and other drugs. A "fixed-phrasing" format is used in which the examiner first elicits affirmation (yes/no) or occurrence responses on the alcohol section without probing positive responses. A follow-up of positive responses occurs at the end of the alcohol section. This two-stage process also is used to inquire about other substance use. In instances of multiple substance use, initial administration of the SUDDS is aimed at determining if a lifetime pattern of substance-use disorder can be established. Positive responses are further queried in a second administration to determine if the behavior(s) have occurred within the past year. In most instances a trained interviewer can administer the SUDDS in approximately 30 minutes. However, a history of multiple drug use will significantly increase administration time.

Information obtained from the interview is coded onto one of two diagnostic checklists (*DSM-III; DSM-III-R*) designed to assist in determining if the respondent meets the respective *DSM* criteria for substance use disorder. Positive substance use and symptomology are coded as current (i.e., occurring within the past year) or lifetime (i.e., occurring prior to the past year). The *DSM-III-R* checklist additionally provides guidelines to classify positive responses into *DSM* symptom categories and facilitate diagnoses.

A computer-assisted version of the SUDDS also is available to facilitate ease of administration for some clients and available evidence suggests that interviewer-administered and computer-administered versions are equally effective (Davis, Hoffman, Morse, & Luehr, 1992).

ADVANTAGES. The SUDDS provides clinicians an efficient way to obtain sufficient/comprehensive information to make diagnoses regarding substance use disorder according to *DSM-III* and *DSM-III-R* criteria. Use of the more fully developed *DSM-III-R* Diagnostic checklist, which includes a listing of *DSM-III-R* psychoactive Substance Use Disorder Diagnoses Codes, allows for quick reference and diagnosis. The structured format eliciting information about numerous observable events and behaviors related to substance use permits the clinician to defend objectively the diagnosis and to verify when necessary the veracity of responses by interviews with family members and other collateral sources.

WEAKNESSES. Given its length (many of the 99 items have multiple subsections), the detailed nature of the questions, and the authors' description of the instrument, the SUDDS seems most useful as a confirmatory measure. In spite of its reported quick and easy administration, it may be limited in its usefulness as a screening instrument or with populations in which drug use has not been a priori established. Although adequate for providing useful information for diagnosing substance use disorder, the SUDDS provides limited information to help clinicians determine if other diagnoses are warranted.

Similarly, behaviors useful for developing treatment regimens are not included in the interview. The fixed-phrasing format limits clinical interaction and may require additional meetings to obtain information useful in developing therapeutic interventions. In addition, although the authors clearly do not consider the SUDDS to be a psychometric instrument but rather a diagnostic aid, it is questionable whether most interviewers will use it in this manner. Finally, the SUDDS-IV, which covers the key content of the *DSM-IV*, either is already available or in final stages of development. This newer version is designed to provide "clear documentation of specific events and behaviors which can be used to support a diagnosis or demonstrate that the individual denies the occurrence of events frequently associated with abuse or dependence" (N. G. Hoffman, personal communication, February 21, 1996). Although field trials have not been completed and normative data is not yet available, it is likely that the more current SUDDS-IV will have greater clinical utility.

SUMMARY. The SUDDS is a structured fixed-format interview designed to obtain data about specific events and behaviors indicative of a *DSM-III* or *DSM-III-R* diagnosis of substance use disorder. As a clinical measure, it appears useful for corroborating and formulating specific diagnoses involving substance use disorders. The SUDDS is likely to provide clinicians with sufficient documentation to satisfy the requirements of various agencies (e.g., mental health facilities, insurance companies), as well as to defend a diagnosis made on the basis of *DSM-III* or *DSM-III-R* descriptors. Moreover, it provides an opportunity for clinicians to verify the veracity of data critical to accept or rule out a specific diagnosis.

Psychometric data involving the SUDDS are not available. Normative and additional research data involving the SUDDS and its newer version, the SUDDS-IV, would be useful in better determining the psychometric utility of the instrument. However, as an interview technique, the measure is useful in systematically collecting information related to substance use and is likely to be useful with populations where the incidence of abuse is relatively high.

REVIEWER'S REFERENCES

Robins, L. N., Helzer, J. E., Ratcliff, K. S., & Seyfried, W. (1982). Validity of the Diagnostic Interview Schedule, Version II: DSM-III diagnoses. *Psychological Medicine, 12,* 855--870.

Hoffmann, N. G., & Harrison, P. A. (1984). Substance Abuse Modified Diagnostic Interview Schedule (SAMDIS). *Psychological Documents, 14,* 10.

Davis, L. J., Jr., Hoffmann, N. G., Morse, R. M., & Luehr, J. G. (1992). Substance Use Disorder Diagnostic Schedule (SUDDS): The equivalence and validity of a computer-administered and an interview-administered format. *Alcoholism Clinical and Experimental Research, 16*(2), 250–254.

Review of the Substance Use Disorder Diagnosis Schedule by STEVEN I. PFEIFFER, Professor, Graduate School of Education, Kent State University, Kent, OH:

The Substance Use Disorder Diagnosis Schedule (SUDDS) is a structured interview for documenting the diagnosis for alcohol and other drug dependencies. The instrument was developed from an earlier version called the Substance Abuse Modified Diagnostic Interview Schedule (SAMDIS) (Hoffman & Harrison, 1984).

The interview consists of a wide range of questions within seven areas: general demographic data, psychosocial stressors, a brief screen for depression, coffee consumption and smoking habits, and alcohol and drug use. Administration time can be as brief as 30 minutes with a client with minimal alcohol use to as long as 60 minutes for a client with extensive and longstanding drug involvement.

The manual states that the SUDDS is designed to assist in the diagnosis of substance use disorders. It is not recommended as a screening device, but rather is described as an in-depth inquiry with individuals already identified as likely alcohol and drug users.

The authors are to be commended for their thoughtful attention to providing detailed and clear instructions that facilitate administration and ensure a standardized interview process. The manual also provides helpful guidelines that assist in establishing *DSM-III-R* diagnoses—a useful feature of the test.

As mentioned earlier, the manual describes the test as a revision of the SAMDIS, which was based on *DSM-III* diagnostic criteria and "other widely used criteria sets" (p. 11). However, no information is provided on the procedures followed in the development of the SUDDS, including no description of how items were selected, which "widely used (diagnostic) criteria sets" (p. 11) were used, or if a pilot phase occurred.

Face validity appears acceptable, and item coverage is extensive. Nevertheless, the manual provides no evidence that any research was conducted to determine representative content coverage or construct validity. For example, no panel of experts were invited to validate the content of the SUDDS, no inter-item correlation or factor analyses were performed, and no studies were undertaken comparing the SUDDS with other substance use instruments.

Equally surprising and disappointing is the fact that the authors provide no evidence of reliability. It is critical for a clinical tool to be sufficiently reliable for use in individual decision making; the SUDDS, unfortunately, does not furnish any information on

interrater, test-retest, or internal consistency. Relatedly, no effort was made to evaluate item or test bias. This is a particularly telling weakness in that one might expect interview questions on a substance use scale potentially to be influenced by culture, gender, ethnicity, SES, and geographic region.

Although the manual offers guidelines for making a *DSM-III-R* diagnosis, there are no standardization data or norms. The test user is not provided cut scores or thresholds for making a diagnosis, apparently because the authors did not undertake any validation studies before publishing the SUDDS. It is unknown, for example, what the sensitivity or specificity of the SUDDS might be for different groups of high-risk substance using populations.

The SUDDS is a structured interview for documenting suspected alcohol and drug dependency. The test has acceptable face validity and extensive item coverage, including questions on psychosocial stressors and depressive symptoms associated with substance abuse. Unfortunately, the test falls far short in omitting information on test development, norming, reliability, and validity. The manual does not provide cut scores to aid in interpreting test results, and until these weaknesses are addressed in a revised manual, the SUDDS should only be used as a research tool or in clinical practice to help formulate hypotheses but not make differential diagnoses.

REVIEWER'S REFERENCE

Hoffman, N. G., & Harrison, P. A. (1984). Substance Abuse Modified Diagnostic Interview Schedule (SAMDIS). *Psychological Documents, 14*, 10.

[309]

SUP'R Star Profiles.

Purpose: Designed to identify an individual's dominant personality type.
Population: Adults.
Publication Date: 1994.
Scores: 4 personality types: Self-Reliant, Upbeat, Patient, Reasoning.
Administration: Group.
Price Data, 1994: $5.95 per test; price information for user's guide available from publisher.
Time: (15–20) minutes.
Author: James H. Brewer.
Publisher: Associated Consultants in Education.

Review of the SUP'R Star Profiles by JEFFREY B. BROOKINGS, Professor of Psychology, Wittenberg University, Springfield, OH:

The SUP'R Star Profiles, Form 1 was designed to identify an individual's dominant personality type:

Self-Reliant (S), Upbeat (U), Patient (P), or Reasoning (R). The identification of type is accomplished by having the assessee select 20 sets of adjectives (each set contains three adjectives)—from a pool of 80 sets—that best describe him or her. The test form is a tear-off sheet that, when removed, indicates the dimension or type on which each adjective set is scored. The assessee then counts the number of adjective sets selected for each dimension, and the dimension on which they selected the most sets is their dominant personality type.

An interpretive guide accompanies the test form. However, there is no manual, so the theoretical rationale for the four personality types is unknown, and there is no information on the development of the instrument, normative data, or psychometric properties. Consequently, the test fails to meet the criteria set forth in the *Standards for Educational and Psychological Testing* (AERA, APA, & NCME, 1985), technical review of the test is not possible, and this reviewer therefore cannot recommend its use.

REVIEWER'S REFERENCE

American Educational Research Association, American Psychological Association, & National Council on Measurement in Education. (1985). *Standards for educational and psychological testing.* Washington, DC: American Psychological Association, Inc.

Review of the SUP'R Star Profiles by CAROL COLLINS, Director, Family Counseling and Research Center, Caldwell, ID:

The SUP'R Star Profiles was developed by James H. Brewer for the purpose of identifying personality types and assessing the strengths and weaknesses of one's personality profile. Positive benefits stated by the author include relating better to others, as one comes to understand others' personality types. With increased knowledge about self and others, it is stated that an individual can predict how others will react to oneself, thereby improving interpersonal relationships.

DESCRIPTION. The test consists of 80 sets of words with three words in each group. Examples include "Correct, Accurate, Right," "Cheerful, Enthusiastic, Excited," and "Good Speaker, Talker, Believing." Subjects are asked to select from the list 20 word groups that best describe them. A profile of a personality type then emerges as the score is tabulated.

SCORING. The SUP'R Star Profiles can easily be administered to groups or individuals. Scoring is simply a matter of adding the number of choices that fall into each of four categories: Self-Reliant, Upbeat, Patient, or Reasoning. The highest number of like letters represents the dominant personality type.

RELIABILITY. No reliability information is provided. The test writer attempts to correlate personality type to favorite colors; for example, patient people like browns, self-reliant prefer red, upbeat people like blue, and reasoning types prefer green. Nothing in the test packet supports these contentions with research data.

VALIDITY. No validity data are reported.

STRENGTHS OF TEST. The SUP'R Star Profiles is extremely easy to administer, and can be hand scored by the individual taking the test. Interpretation and description of the four personality types is provided and no special expertise is required to interpret and understand the results. Although the test is overly simplistic and includes statements that may have no basis in research, it can give an individual a quick indication of his or her manner of interacting with the world and other people. The test writer encourages the subject to seek balance between the types and suggests ways each can improve interpersonal functioning by modifying one's behavior when appropriate. For example, the self-reliant individual is cautioned to listen more and pay attention to details.

WEAKNESSES OF TEST. The most salient weakness of the SUP'R Star Profiles is the lack of information relating to reliability and validity. Without more supporting data, the test cannot be considered useful, other than to indicate a general trend of personality preference. Some inconsistency exists in the text of the profile. The caveat is made that "we must avoid stereotyping" (p. 1), yet the test does just that (i.e., "Upbeat [people] like blue") (p. 3). The author states that one is born with a personality tendency and "your personality *stays the same throughout life* [italics added]" (p. 1). However, the subject is encouraged to "Be a Sup'R Star and *modify your personality* [italics added]" (p. 3). These statements seem confusing and contradictory.

A general criticism of personality surveys that attempt to categorize all people into four types is that they are extremely limiting and the subject has no alternative but to become a "stereotype." It is true there are only four major compass points: north, south, east, and west, but innumerable directions exist between those four points.

SUMMARY. The SUP'R Star Profiles can be useful in very limited circumstances, if appropriate caution is taken not to overinterpret the results. The test could easily be misused if employees or individuals in other work groups were "typed," especially in such an oversimplistic manner as color preference. In the extreme, one could simply ask an individual to name his or her favorite color, then jump to the conclusion that one knows that individual's personality type. Great danger exists to confine interactions to the expected, rather than work toward more effective communication and understanding between people. Based on the lack of data supporting reliability and validity, and the potential for misuse, this reviewer does not see the SUP'R Star Profiles as a suitable assessment tool in most circumstances.

[310]
Survey of Organizations.

Purpose: "Describes conditions and practices" in an organization "to determine specific opportunities for improvement."
Population: Employees.
Publication Dates: 1967–1988.
Acronym: SOO-2000.
Scores, 28: Organization Climate (Communication Flow, Decision Making Practices, Concern for People, Influence and Control, Job Challenge, Job Reward, Job Clarity, Organization of Work, Absence of Bureaucracy, Coordination, Work Interdependence), Supervisory Leadership (Support, Team Building, Goal Emphasis, Work Facilitation, Encouragement of Participation, Interpersonal Competence, Involvement, Administrative Scope), Peer Relationships (Support, Team Building, Goal Emphasis, Work Facilitation), End Results (Group Functioning, Goal Integration, Satisfaction, Group Performance, Individual Performance).
Administration: Group.
Price Data, 1990: $500 per 25 questionnaires including instructions for coding and administration, tabulations and comparison of results to norms, optional supplemental questions, confidential feedback package, and interpretation manual ('87, 57 pages) for each supervisor/manager; price data for additional reports and tabulations available from publisher.
Foreign Language Edition: Available in Spanish, French, Finnish, Norwegian, and Swedish.
Time: Administration time not reported.
Comments: For measurement of groups rather than individuals.
Author: Rensis Likert Associates, Inc.
Publisher: Rensis Likert Associates, Inc.
Cross References: See T3:2369 (2 references); for reviews by Robert Fitzpatrick and Stephan J. Motowidlo, and an excerpted review by John Toplis of an earlier edition, see 8:985 (12 references).

Review of the Survey of Organizations by JOHN M. ENGER, Professor of Education, Arkansas State University, State University, AR:

The Survey of Organizations is produced by a company (Rensis Likert Associates, Inc.) whose founder is a popular name in the behavioral sciences. In a 1932 analysis of an attitudinal instrument, Likert introduced a parallel, much simpler analysis that correlated .99 with the more difficult rendition (Likert, 1932). Researchers now use the Likert scale, where numerical values are assigned to attitudinal characteristics under the assumption that the data results in an interval scale. This concept is utilized in the object of this review, the Survey of Organizations.

The Survey of Organizations was originally developed in the 1960s and 1970s and has been marketed in close to its present form since 1980. Developed for organizations representing various kinds of industry, education, government, etc., the Survey of Organizations is a 120-item questionnaire meant to be administered to various work groups and levels within an organization.

The completed questionnaires are returned to the publisher who performs the analysis based on 100 of the items. (Twenty items are descriptive or nonindex items omitted from the analysis.) Results are reported in four broad categories: Organizational Climate, Leadership, Peer Relationships, and Outcomes. These categories are further broken down into subcategories. Item scores are also reported. As an example, three items constitute "Communication Flow," which is part of a subcategory called "Guidance System," which is part of the broad category "Organizational Climate."

Analyses are made based on a 5-point Likert scale, with all items coded with 5 as the optimum response. Along with percent answering at each response level (such as "to a very little extent"), item means are reported as are the normative comparisons.

The publisher offers a variety of normative comparisons, by type of organization and by type of position within the organization. There are five categories of norms for organizational level: top management, middle management, first-line supervision, nonsupervisory white collar, and nonsupervisory blue collar. There are 22 function norm categories, such as general production, purchasing, etc. Internal norms can be provided to compare groups within an organization; for this option there must be 20 or more work groups within the organization. For additional analyses, there are special norm sets for some 20 occupational groups, such as automotive, health care, etc.

Some analyses contrast respondents' ratings of how the organization is now versus how they would like the organization to be. (Of the 100 items analyzed, 21 are such paired items.) Organizational strengths are identified by items scoring at or above the 60th percentile. Potential problems are identified by items scoring at or below the 40th percentile. However, it was not reported how these cutoff points for strengths and weaknesses were determined.

After receiving the results of the survey, organizations are advised to share the findings in group meetings where strengths and weaknesses are identified, reasons are elicited for these identified strengths and weaknesses, and action plans are discussed. In discussing the results, groups are advised to explain why the high scores are high (i.e., what are we doing right) and why the low scores are low (i.e., what are we doing wrong). The concept behind the Survey of Organizations is straightforward and the presentation is easy to comprehend. (The instrument has a reported 11th grade readability level.)

The form of Survey of Organizations made available for this review was dated 1988; however, the technical information, including norms, was undated and perhaps outdated. Although the reported subscale reliability coefficients appear quite adequate for a measure of this type, the documentation was quite old, the size of the sample was not noted, and the group was never defined. Questions would also arise on the reliability of measures based upon so few items.

The publisher claims the data gathered for this survey are based on descriptions, not perceptions of the workplace—because respondents are asked for the extent to which something exists. It is said that the results provide a "snapshot" of the organization based on the past 6 months to 1 year; however, no substantiation is provided for this statement. (From another source in the documentation, this snapshot was said to be for the past 6 to 8 months.)

The value of the Survey of Organizations is highly dependent on the organization leadership's ability to interpret and utilize the results with its membership. Other providers of similar organizational surveys generally offer consulting services of trained professionals to tailor the results to the organization.

Overall, the Survey of Organizations could be an effective tool for an organization wanting a mechanism to look at itself and involve the membership in identifying various strengths and weaknesses to prompt discussion on the organization's present and future.

REVIEWER'S REFERENCE

Likert, R. (1932, June). A technique for the measurement of attitudes. *Archives of Psychology*.

Review of the Survey of Organizations by JOHN W. FLEENOR, Director of Research, Mediappraise Corp., Raleigh, NC:

Based on Rensis Likert's theory of organizations, the Survey of Organizations (SOO) is a 120-item questionnaire developed to capture perceptions of employees about the organizations in which they work. The SOO was designed to measure four domains of organizational effectiveness, using 28 scales. These domains are Organization Climate (11 scales), Supervisory Leadership (8 scales), Peer Relationships (4 scales), and End Results (5 scales). The domains focus primarily on the respondent's work group and supervisor, rather than on physical working conditions. The authors recommend that the SOO be used for organizational assessment and diagnosis, benchmarking, survey feedback, and employee development.

The initial version of the SOO was developed in 1965 at the Institute of Social Research at the University of Michigan. In 1967, the questionnaire was converted to opscan scoring—one of the first surveys to use this technology. The instrument was revised again in 1969 and 1974. In 1980, content from the closely related Organizational Survey Profile was incorporated into the SOO. The current edition was published in 1988. Two reviews (Fitzpatrick & Motowidlo, 8:985) of the 1974 version of the SOO appeared in *The Eighth Mental Measurements Yearbook*.

MANUALS. A comprehensive technical manual (Taylor & Bowers, 1972) was developed for the 1969 edition of the SOO. The 1988 version of the technical manual, however, provides only sketchy information concerning the administration of the instrument, and the reliability and validity of its scores. To conduct a complete evaluation of the SOO, it would be necessary to refer extensively to the 1972 manual.

The 1988 edition of the instrument also includes a supervisor's handbook, which provides detailed information about interpreting the feedback report and conducting feedback sessions with employees. Possibly in response to criticism from earlier reviews, the authors have tried to make the SOO documentation more practitioner oriented, which resulted in less emphasis on the psychometric aspects of the instrument.

ADMINISTRATION AND SCORING. The instructions for coding and administration are included with the SOO processing package, and are not covered in the manuals (and were not included in the review package). The 1972 manual included detailed standardized instructions for administering the SOO. One would hope that these detailed instructions are still being provided to users of the 1988 edition.

SOO items are rated on a 5-point scale, with anchors that change from scale to scale. The anchors are clearly defined, so switching from one set of anchors to another should not disturb test takers.

In addition to the 120-items on the survey, the SOO provides the option of adding up to 80 supplemental items. These items can be used to collect data on issues specific to the organization that are not covered by the survey items. No allowance is made for open-ended responses.

Confidential feedback reports are provided to each supervisor with three or more employees who complete the survey. The feedback reports compare each supervisor's results to the appropriate norm group through the use of percentile plots. The feedback report also compares the results to appropriate job function norms, and to internal norms if available. Additionally, for each item, the percentage of respondents in each response category is presented (i.e., the percent of individuals who rated the item as a "1," etc.).

NORMS. According to the technical manual, SOO norms were developed using a nationwide data bank of over 14,000 groups, and the norms are updated periodically. Separate norms are available for various organizational levels (nonsupervisory to top management), job functions (e.g., engineering, marketing, manufacturing, etc.), and industries (e.g., automotive, health care, utilities, etc.). Organizations may also create their own internal norms for the SOO.

RELIABILITY. The technical manual reports alpha coefficients for the 26 SOO scales. These reliabilities range from .58 (Job Clarity) to .92 (Supervisory Encouragement of Participation), with a mean of .82. One other scale (Influence and Control) has a reliability below .70. Sample sizes for the alpha coefficients are not reported. No other evidence of reliability is reported.

VALIDITY. Previous reviews of the SOO called for more evidence of validity for its scales; that is, evidence that the mean SOO scores reflect actual conditions in the organization. The reviewers also expressed hope that researchers would continue to revise, refine, and validate the scales. Although some additional work has been done in this area, several questions regarding the validity of the SOO remain unanswered.

To some extent the 1988 edition of the SOO has been revised based on additional validity studies, but the information provided in the technical manual is not adequate to judge the quality of these studies. According to the manual, all archived SOO data (sample size not reported) were subjected to factor analysis, smallest space analysis, cluster analysis, and multidimensional scaling. These four methods generally confirmed the domain structure of the instrument. The four factors of the supervisory leadership domain were replicated, and a new scale, Encouragement of Participation, was added. The factors of the Peer Relationships domain were replicated, but some clustering weaknesses were found in the Goal Emphasis scale. The factors representing the outcome domain scales were replicated and remained unchanged; however, the scales on the Organization Climate domain were restructured into three subdomains (guidance system, job design, and shape).

The technical manual also states that several studies have demonstrated that the SOO scales are related to objective measures of organizational performance, but details of these studies are not provided.

CONCLUSION. The SOO represents one of the first efforts to measure employees' perceptions of their organizations with a standardized instrument. At one time, the SOO was probably one of the best instruments available for this purpose. The SOO documentation and feedback reports are not flashy, resulting in a relatively low cost compared to other organizational surveys. Unfortunately, research and development on the SOO has not kept up with the times—the instrument has not been revised in almost 10 years. Without more recent and more complete evidence of its reliability and validity, the SOO cannot be recommended without reservation.

REVIEWER'S REFERENCE

Taylor, J., & Bowers, D. (1972). *Survey of Organizations: A machine-scored standardized questionnaire instrument.* Ann Arbor, MI: Institute for Social Research.

[311]
Survey of Work Styles.

Purpose: A "measure of six components of the Type A behavior pattern."
Population: Adults.
Publication Dates: 1988–1993.
Acronym: SWS.
Scores, 8: Impatience, Anger, Time Urgency, Work Involvement, Job Dissatisfaction, Competitiveness, Scale A, Total.
Administration: Group.
Price Data, 1993: $41 per complete kit including 50 handscorable question/answer sheets, 50 scoring sheets, and one set of templates; $10 per manual ('93, 22 pages);

$5 per basic reports including machine-scorable question/answer sheet and computer report.

Time: (15–20) minutes.

Authors: Douglas N. Jackson and Anna Mavrogiannis Gray.

Publisher: Sigma Assessment Systems, Inc.

Cross References: See T4:2664 (1 reference).

TEST REFERENCES

1. Tett, R. P., Bobocel, D. R., Hafer, C., Lees, M. C., Smith, C. A., & Jackson, D. N. (1992). The dimensionality of Type A behavior within a stressful work simulation. *Journal of Personality, 60*, 533–551.

Review of the Survey of Work Styles by PEGGY A. HICKS, School Psychologist, Hand Q Consultants, Richmond, VA:

Motivation, competitiveness, and immersion in one's job, attributes measured by the Survey of Work Styles (SWS), are recognized as characteristics essential for success in corporate America. Unfortunately, these same attributes also carry increased risk for coronary heart disease (CHD), medical problems, psychological problems, and interpersonal concerns. Designed to identify triggers and quantify intensity, frequency, and duration of behaviors consistent with Type A behavior pattern, this 96-item self-report instrument profiles Type A behavioral patterns from a multidimensional perspective. The SWS is designed to provide an economical, convenient, and objective alternative to the Rosenman Structured Interview (Rosenman, Brand, Jenkins, Friedman, Straus, & Wurm, 1975). Characteristics of the Type A individual (Impatience, Anger, Work Involvement, Time Urgency, Job Dissatisfaction, and Competitiveness) are addressed in six subscales of the Survey of Work Styles. In addition to scores from the six subtests listed above, authors of the SWS suggest a global Type A score can be derived by adding equally weighted subtest scores, using the results of Scale A, or defining a dichotomous classification of global scores distinguishing Type A (high-scoring) from Type B (low-scoring) individuals. The authors also suggest that a modal profile analysis using multivariate procedures could be used.

It should be noted that the SWS is identified as a research instrument with a limited norming population. The test authors, Jackson and Gray, suggest the SWS for studies of coronary heart disease, related medical conditions, health maintenance behaviors such as smoking and alcohol use, work-related stress, and individual differences in the concomitants of stress. Interpersonal factors such as group performance, conflict and cooperation, negotiation, and supervisory styles can also be sampled

with the SWS. The SWS also has potential in studies investigating psychological factors influencing employee performance such as ability to adjust to retirement, quality of marital relations, maintenance of self-esteem, responses to task failure, and reactions to environmental stressors. Other recommended uses of the Survey of Work Styles include research designed to address employee selection, job placement, job performance, job satisfaction, employee turnover, promotability, and absenteeism.

The Survey of Work Styles manual is primarily focused on TABP theory and reads more like a journal article than a test manual. The manual provides a comprehensive review of theoretical constructs that serve as the foundation for the Survey of Work Styles. Administration of the SWS is fairly straightforward, but limited press is given to test scoring and interpretation of results. Even the experienced evaluator is likely to find hand-scoring procedures for the SWS cumbersome and time-consuming. The cryptic explanation of hand-scoring procedures is insufficient and increases the opportunity for scoring errors. The process for deriving scores for the six subscales is not addressed in the manual. Approaches for deriving global scores described on page 9 of the manual appear to be suggestions rather than procedures founded in psychometric theory and are cryptic and unclear.

Test questions and answer sheets for the Survey of Work Styles are combined on a computer scan sheet that is a plus for the examinee and decreases the opportunity for clerical errors. The design of the scoring templates, that provides no place for recording scores, is not user friendly. The hand-scoring worksheet emphasizes the importance of reversed (R) and unreversed (U) items but R and U responses are not mentioned in the manual. There is a discrepancy between the manual, which indicates that the respondent is asked to indicate degree of agreement using a 5-point scale (*strongly agree* to *strongly disagree*) and the response sheet, which asks the examinee to determine if the statements are *extremely characteristic, moderately characteristic, neutral, moderately uncharacteristic,* or *extremely uncharacteristic* of themselves. Guidelines and resources for interpreting test results are limited. The SWS does not provide a profile sheet that is useful in providing feedback to employee or employer. Although the SWS manual indicates that batch scoring is available from the publisher, there are no directions for procuring this service. The manual refers to an IBM-compatible scoring program but does not elaborate. This reviewer did not have the opportunity to review the compuscore program or a computer-generated feedback form.

The SWS norming sample of 133 females (mean age 49) and 233 males (mean age 55) was drawn from the greater metropolitan district of Boston. The pilot study, which addressed provisional items and scales, was based on 227 male and female university students. Jackson and Gray acknowledge the need for a larger sample with expanded regional representation and indicate that the collection of norming data is continuing. Table 2, page 10 in the manual, provides a gender-based summary of means and standard deviations for the six subtests, Scale A, and Overall Type A. Scale A consists of 35 items found to be most predictive of the Rosenman Structured Interview. The coefficient alpha reliability coefficient for the SWS scales based upon two separate samples ranges from a low of .71 on Anger to a high of .91 on Overall Type A. The interscale correlation matrix (Table 3 on page 11) shows the six subscales to be moderately related in the expected way. With the exception of Work Involvement and Job Dissatisfaction, examinees who score higher on one subscale usually have higher scores on other subscales. As expected, the authors report a negative correlation between Work Involvement and Job Dissatisfaction indicating that people who are more involved with their work are less dissatisfied with their job. Impatience (.77) and Anger (.69) are the best indicators of Type A behavior pattern and Job Dissatisfaction (.40) is the weakest index. A comparison of the respondents' performance on the SWS and the Framington Type A scale yielded a correlation of at least .85 across all six scales and .76 for Total scores. Cross-validation procedures using discriminant function analysis documented that 83% of Type A managers were correctly identified by the SWS in relation to the Rosenman Structured Interview. An extensive review of theory and prior research in the area of Type A behavior patterns supported by item analysis provides evidence of content validity.

Recognizing that this is a research tool, many of the concerns voiced by this reviewer may be addressed as the SWS evolves. Users of Research Edition II of the Survey of Work Styles who plan to hand score this instrument need to be prepared for poorly designed transparent scoring templates, vague scoring direction, and limited guidelines for interpretation.

REVIEWER'S REFERENCE

Rosenman, R. H., Brand, R. J., Jenkins, D. C., Friedman, M., Straus, R., & Wurm, M. (1975). Coronary heart disease in the Western Collaborative Group Study: Final follow up experience of 8 1/2 years. *JAMA, 233*, 872-877.

[312]
Swanson-Cognitive Processing Test.

Purpose: Designed to assess "different aspects of mental processing ability and potential."
Population: Ages 5 to adult.
Publication Date: 1996.
Acronym: S-CPT.
Scores: 11 subtest scores: Rhyming Words, Visual Matrix, Auditory Digit Sequence, Mapping and Directions, Story Retelling, Picture Sequence, Phrase Recall, Spatial Organization, Semantic Association, Semantic Categorization, Nonverbal Sequence; 3 composite scores: Semantic, Episodic, Total; 4 component scores: Auditory, Visual, Prospective, Retrospective; 4 supplementary scores: Strategy Efficiency Index, Processing Difference Index, Instructional Efficiency Index, Stability Index.
Administration: Individual.
Price Data, 1995: $169 per complete kit including manual (183 pages), 25 profile/examiner record booklets, picture book, card decks, and strategy cards in storage box; $49 per 25 profile/examiner record booklets; $49 per manual; $19 per picture book; $38 per card deck; $19 per strategy cards.
Time: (120) minutes.
Author: H. Lee Swanson.
Publisher: PRO-ED, Inc.

Review of the Swanson-Cognitive Processing Test by CAROLYN M. CALLAHAN, William Clay Parrish, Jr. Professor of Education, University of Virginia, Charlottesville, VA:

The stated purpose of the Swanson-Cognitive Processing Test (S-CPT) is to measure "dynamic working memory" and the "sensitivity of a test-related intervention that is sufficient to administer within a normal testing period" (manual, p. 4) with the ultimate goal of assessing "processing potential" (p. 1). The subtests of the instrument are described and identified by type of information assessed, whether the errors in memory reflect errors in retrospective memory or prospective memory, as measures of semantic or episodic memory, and whether the task requires primarily auditory or visual-spatial processing. The technical manual for the test provides an extensive discussion of the theoretical framework underlying working memory and the development of this particular instrument.

According to the author, the test can be administered in its entirety or the examiner may select five or six subtests to administer in abbreviated form. Further, it can be administered under static or dynamic conditions. In the dynamic condition, the examiner compares performance before and after hints for remembering the stimulus are presented and also assesses the degree to which the level of performance after intervention is maintained. Administration of only the "static" dimension of the test would yield only a measure of aptitude, which is equated by the author to an intelligence test. [All data supporting reliability and validity are based on administration of the full test "requiring more than 2 hours of testing per subject" (p. 121).] If the user of the test were making a decision to use only the static assessment, a Wechsler Intelligence Scale for Children, Third Edition (WISC-III; 12:412) or Wechsler Adult Intelligence Scale (WAIS; T4:2937) would be a more appropriate instrument.

Numerous scores are calculated from the numbers of correct responses under each condition. These include Initial, Gain, and Maintenance scores in the categories of a total composite score, Semantic and Episodic Memory scores, Auditory, Visual, Prospective, and Retrospective scores. Supplemental scores in Strategy Efficiency, Processing Difference, Instructional Efficiency, and each of the subtest scales are also calculated. The primary set of scores are expressed as scores with a mean of 100 and a standard deviation of 15, likening them to intelligence test scores.

The administration and scoring of the instrument are complex, confusing at some points and vague at others. The examiner who wished to use this instrument would need to spend considerable time practicing for administration and have considerable experience with individuals of the examinee's age level, as well as significant knowledge and understanding of the literature on cognitive processing, episodic and semantic memory, and their relationships to the learning process.

Although the test was normed on 1,611 persons from four geographic regions in the U.S. and two in Canada, the sample appears to be one of convenience rather than representing a carefully stratified, purposeful sample. Sample sizes of the six age groups used for assigning standard scores range from 61 (4.11 to 6.00) to 590 (9.10 to 13.00). The author notes the overrepresentation of Hispanics and underrepresentation of African-Americans.

The reliability and validity data presented are complex and extensive; however, the complexity of the information presented does not contribute to a clear understanding of the stability of the measure or exactly which constructs are supported by the data. The estimates of internal consistency are high, but are presented across all age groups assessed, with little information about reliabilities when used with particular age groups. Although the scale is a Guttman scale, there is no evidence of scaleability.

The factor analysis of the subtests does not begin with any indication that the subtests are, in fact, scales themselves that should be interpreted as such. The factors derived from the analysis support the existence of a Semantic and an Episodic Memory scale, but do not support the computation of the many other scores that are derived from the testing. The evidence of convergent and/or criterion validity is very difficult to interpret given an unclear statement of expected relationships. Discriminant validity evidence in two cases is not really evidence of discriminant validity as traditionally designated in measurement. In these cases, the only evidence is of the test's ability to discriminate among groups of learners. In the third case, the discriminant validity evidence is quite weak. A convergent/discriminant matrix is not presented (presumably because of the differing samples on which each validity study was completed).

Although the author claims that the scores are measures of processing ability, the use of a total composite score so parallel to traditional intelligence test scaled scores will most likely suggest to most with only passing familiarity with the test that these are measures of intellectual aptitude. The author agrees with this interpretation for the initial composite score. The other two scores are assumed to assess Vygotsky's zone of proximal development (Composite Gain Score) and the examinee's ability to incorporate instructional clues to sustain performance (Maintenance Composite Score). Although the face validity of the test would seem to suggest that this is the case, the empirical validity is lacking. In fact, the correlations with achievement and intelligence assessments presented as validity evidence suggest equally strong correlations of the three scales with those instruments.

The interpretation of discrepancies between these scores is based on an assumption that "scores that show at least a 15-point discrepancy are clinically important" (p. 83). Evidence supporting this assumption was not presented.

At this point, the Swanson-Cognitive Processing Test should be used only for research purposes. The evidence of its usefulness in helping clinicians explain performance or to analyze processing problems and suggest interventions is not yet established. The complexity of the instrument makes it impractical for anyone but highly skilled examiners to use.

Review of the Swanson-Cognitive Processing Test by RALPH F. DARR, JR., Professor Emeritus of Edu-

cation, Department of Educational Foundations and Leadership, The University of Akron, Akron, OH:

GENERAL DESCRIPTION. The Swanson-Cognitive Processing Test (S-CPT) is an individually administered battery of 11 subtests designed to measure various aspects of mental processing. The battery may be administered in a complete (all 11 subtests) or an abbreviated (5 or 6 subtests) version. The S-CPT is designed to be used with individuals ages 5 to adulthood. Subtest 1: Rhyming Words assesses the respondent's ability to recall similar sounding words. Subtest 2: Visual Matrix assesses one's ability to remember visual sequences within a matrix. Subtest 3: Auditory Digital Sequence measures the individual's ability to recall numerical information embedded in a short sentence. Subtest 4: Mapping and Directions uses an unmarked map to determine whether the respondent can remember a sequence of directions given orally by the examiner. Subtest 5: Story Retelling assesses the respondent's ability to recall a series of events presented in a paragraph read by the examiner. Subtest 6: Picture Sequence assesses the examinee's ability to remember shapes in a sequence of increasing spatial complexity. Subtest 7: Phrase Sequence measures the individual's ability to recall isolated phrases. Subtest 8: Spatial Organization assesses the examinee's ability to remember the spatial organization of a series of cards with pictures on them. Subtest 9: Semantic Association evaluates the respondent's ability to make semantic associations. Subtest 10: Semantic Categorization assesses the examinee's ability to recall word associations by categories. Subtest 11: Nonverbal Sequencing assesses one's ability to sequence a series of cards with pictures of nonsense shapes with no organization cues provided by the examiner. The 11 S-CPT subtests are designed to evaluate both episodic and semantic memory. Episodic memory subtests (e.g., 5: Story Retelling and 6: Picture Sequence) are designed to measure static memory of events and relationships. Semantic memory subtests (e.g., 7 Phrase Sequence, 9 Semantic Association, and 10 Semantic Categorization) assess the individual's ability to organize existing information.

THEORETICAL FRAMEWORK. The S-CPT is rooted in the information processing model of skill acquisition and learning. The battery is specifically designed to distinguish between the respondent's passive short term memory and dynamic working memory system. Focus is on assessment of the examinee's working memory rather than the more traditional static measures of intelligence (e.g., recall or recognition of synonyms and antonyms).

ADMINISTRATION. To administer subtests 1, 2, 3, 4, 6, 7, 9, and 11, the examiner begins with an item judged to be appropriate for the respondent's age and level of development. For Subtests 5, 8, and 10 all items are administered. The total battery requires a minimum of 2 hours. The author recommends two sessions for the full administration. Two shorter administration formats are possible. Method 1: Run through the entire battery asking each question once without using the probes that encourage the examinees to rethink their responses. This method would yield only an Initial Score for each subtest. Method 2: Use five or six subtests obtaining all of the scores possible. Usually the following Subtests are used: 2 Visual Matrix, 3 Auditory Digit Sequence, 4 Mapping and Directions, 8 Spatial Organization, 9 Semantic Association, and 10 Semantic Categorization. The scores on the six subtests can be tallied to estimate Composite and Component scores on the full battery. Either shortened method reduces administration time to about 45 minutes.

In order to obtain reliable, valid, and generalizable results on the S-CPT, the author recommends that the examiner have prior experience administering and scoring individual test batteries and have practiced giving the instrument 10 to 15 times. The author recommends that examiners get examinees actively involved in the testing process by probing respondents' thought processes with cueing and questioning (i.e., dynamic testing conditions).

SCORING. The S-CPT scoring process is complex. The instrument yields subtest, component, and composite scores. Each subtest provides at least four scores. The Initial Score is the number of correct responses without cueing from the examiner. Thus, it reflects static performance (recall). If the item is missed, the examiner provides a series of top-down cues or probes that focus on the types of errors the respondent made. The Gain Score represents the highest number of items correctly recalled with the assistance of the examiner. It suggests the examinee's potential ability when helped. The Probe Score represents the number of hints necessary to produce the Gain Score (i.e., the maximum level of achievement). The Maintenance Score is obtained by the examiner's readministering the highest item on the subtests for which Gain Scores have occurred. The Maintenance Score assesses the degree to which the respondent is able to retain recent learning. If the examinee maintains the same level of performance, the Maintenance Score and Gain Score are the same for that subtest. If the examinee misses the item on the retest, then the individual's Maintenance Score and Initial Score are the same for that subtest. A Strategy Efficiency Score is computed for Subtests 3, 4, 7, 8, 10, and 11. This score assesses the type of strategy the respondent applied to the four-choice picture array. Component and Composite scores are obtained by adding the scores of various combinations of subtests. Component Scores reflect various aspects of the examinee's working memory. The Total Composite Score reflects the respondent's ability to acquire, retain, and retrieve information. Raw scores are converted to scale and standard scores. Tables are provided for converting raw scores to scale scores and scale scores to standard scores. Standard scores have mean of 100 and a standard deviation of 15.

STANDARDIZATION. The standardization sample was composed of 1,611 subjects from 10 western states and two Canadian provinces between 1987 and 1994 (ages 4.5 to 78.6; 45% female and 55% male; 10% special education students; 72% Anglo, 13% Hispanic, 9% African-American, 5% Asian, 1% other; 35% low income, 65% middle income; 89% English as first language, 11% English as second language). Tables of means and standard deviations of scores for standardization sample by age, gender, and disability category are provided.

RELIABILITY. Because of the probing techniques used in the dynamic administration process, test-retest coefficients of reliability were not computed. The Cronbach alpha procedure with age effects partialed out was used to assess reliability. The total alpha score (sum of scores across subtests for initial gain and maintenance conditions) was found to be highly reliable ($r = .96$). Initial, Gain, and Maintenance Scores were found to be correlated across all subtests ($r = .72$ to $.89$).

VALIDITY. Construct validity was established by (a) correlating the various subtests with common experimental measure of working memory and (b) testing whether Initial Scores conform to the working memory model. Factor analysis of Initial Scores of the 11 subtests identified two factors: semantic memory (four subtests) and episodic memory (four subtests). Three subtests loaded on both factors. Various abbreviated formats were found to fit the two-factor model.

Criterion validity was established by assessing the degree of relationship between scores on the S-CPT and various static psychometric measures, both achievement and aptitude. Composite Initial, Gain, and Maintenance Scores on the S-CPT were found to be correlated with other psychometric measures. However, the dynamic S-CPT measures of Processing Differences, Instructional Efficiency, and Stability and Strategy Efficiency were found to be unrelated to examinees' scores on intelligence and achievement tests.

SUMMARY. The S-CPT is an individually administered test designed to assess the different facets of mental processing in subjects ages 5 through adulthood. The instrument is grounded in information processing theory. Its tasks require both recall (episodic memory) and operation on recalled information (semantic memory). The standardization process was carefully executed. The standardization norms should be useful for working special populations. Acceptable reliability and validity is demonstrated. However, the S-CPT has many of the problems associated with other individually administered measures of intelligence. Administrators need special training. The instrument is time-consuming to administer and score. At least two separate testing sessions are required to administer all 11 subtests. Respondents' answers are open to interpretation by the examiners. Calculating the many types of scores will take time. Also, interpreting the various types of scores to consumers (i.e., parents, students, and teachers) may be difficult and time-consuming.

[313]
Systematic Screening for Behavior Disorders.

Purpose: To screen and identify students at risk for developing serious behavior problems.
Population: Grades K–6.
Publication Dates: 1990–1992.
Acronym: SSBD.
Administration: Group.
Price Data, 1993: $195 per complete kit including technical manual ('92, 80 pages), user's guide ('92, 151 pages), observer training manual ('92, 136 pages), videotape, and 25 sets of classroom screening forms.
Authors: Hill M. Walker and Herbert H. Severson.
Publisher: Sopris West, Inc.
  a) STAGE I.
  Scores: 2 rankings: Internalizing, Externalizing.
  Time: (30–45) minutes.
  Comments: Rankings by teacher.
  b) STAGE II.
  Scores, 6: 3 scores: Total Critical Events, Total Adaptive Behavior, Total Maladaptive Behavior in two areas: Internalizing, Externalizing.
  Time: (30–45) minutes.
  Comments: Ratings by teachers.

c) STAGE III.

Scores, 11: Academic Engaged Time (Total); Peer Social Behavior (Social Engagement, Participation, Parallel Play, Alone, No Code, Social Interaction, Negative Interaction, Positive Interaction, Total Positive Behavior, Total Negative Behavior).
Administration: Individual.
Time: (60) minutes.
Comments: Observations by trained staff member.

Review of the Systematic Screening for Behavior Disorders by MARY LOU KELLEY, Professor of Psychology, Louisiana State University, Louisiana State University Medical Center, Baton Rouge, LA:

The Systematic Screening for Behavior Disorders (SSBD) is a three-stage, multiple-gating screening procedure for use in the identification of children with significant behavior problems. Both internalizing and externalizing behavior disorders are identified with the use of classroom teachers as informants. The three-stage screening process begins with a minimally time-consuming, teacher nomination procedure and ends with a detailed, objective account of student behavior in two naturalistic settings. The overall screening process is logical, practical, and well supported by research.

Stage I requires classroom teachers to rank order their students on externalizing and internalizing behavioral dimensions. The authors provide operational definitions of the dimensions evaluated along with concrete examples. Ten students who exhibit the greatest symptomatology along each dimension are identified. Students may be listed only once and cannot appear among the top 10 on both externalizing and internalizing dimensions.

The purpose of Stage II is to evaluate the specific behavior problems exhibited by the top three children on the teachers' lists. Teachers are required to complete two rating scales: the Critical Events Checklist and the Combined Frequency Index for Adaptive and Maladaptive Behavior. Teachers complete slightly different forms for the internalizing and externalizing children, with both having identical questionnaire formats and number of items. The Critical Events Checklist asks teachers to indicate whether the top rated children (or any other child in their classroom) exhibit any of 33 behaviors. The behaviors vary in severity from "Has tantrums" to "Sets fires," "Is self-abusive," or "Shows evidence of drug use." The Combined Frequency Index for Adaptive and Maladaptive Behavior requires teachers to rate the top three internalizing and externalizing students along a 5-point, Likert-type scale on 12 appropriate and 11 inappropriate interpersonal social and classroom behaviors.

The directions for Stage I and Stage II are very clear and the authors suggest that both screening phases be completed consecutively in a group format. The authors indicated that the entire procedure can be completed within about an hour and thus, provides an efficient, easy-to-administer screening tool. The criteria for determining whether a student passes the "screening gates" from Stage II to Stage III are well operationalized and based on scores obtained on the measures. Although well defined, the cutoff scores for continuing in the assessment process appear to be rather arbitrary and the rationale for the cutoff points was not evident.

Stage III consists of direct observation of identified students on the playground and in the classroom by school personnel other than the classroom teacher. The procedures require trained observers to evaluate academic engaged time and peer social behaviors using operationally defined code categories. The author recommends at least two observations in each setting. The coding procedure is well supported by research and extensive normative data are available. The specific observational procedures are well defined and clearly described in the manual.

The technical manual presents detailed rationales for the SSBD and the research supporting the instruments. The authors have carefully considered empirical, theoretical, and clinical reasons for item selection and measurement format. The measures are carefully and thoughtfully constructed and reflect contemporary views on child psychopathology and behavioral assessment procedures. The authors have devoted considerable attention to establishing the psychometric properties of the SSBD. The instrument is supported by adequate internal consistency, test-retest reliability, and good interrater agreement. Furthermore, concurrent, discriminant, criterion-related, and predictive validity studies support the utility of the instrument.

Overall, the SSBD is a well-constructed, practical instrument with good evidence of reliability and validity. The authors have carefully considered logistical, theoretical, and clinical research in their construction of the three-part screening measure. The measure fills a void in the school-based assessment of behavior-disordered children and adds empiricism to an identification process that routinely has relied on subjective impressions from teacher or other, poorly operationalized methods. Furthermore, the authors offer flexibility in determining cutoff scores for identification of children as well as other practical considerations, which adds to the utility of the instrument in a wide array of school settings and communities. I know of no other measure equal to the SSBD in comprehensiveness, practicality, and psychometric soundness for use in identifying behavior-disordered children.

Review of the Systematic Screening for Behavior Disorders by LELAND C. ZLOMKE, Director of Clinical Psychology, Beatrice State Developmental Center, Beatrice, NE, and ROBERT SPIES, Doctoral Candidate, University of Nebraska-Lincoln, Lincoln, NE:

The Systematic Screening for Behavior Disorders (SSBD) was developed to identify students in first through sixth grades with behavior problems by means of a three-stage, multiple-gating screening system. This instrument's potential role in assessment is to "make this process [the identification of behavioral disorders] substantially more objective, systematic, and precise" (Walker et al., 1990, p. 44).

Stage I of the SSBD requires the teacher to identify students in the classroom most characterized by internalizing or externalizing behaviors. After the top 10 students are chosen in each category, teachers rank order students from the most to the least on these two dimensions. The top three internalizing and externalizing students progress to the next stage.

During Stage II, the teacher completes two questionnaires designed to provide statistical support for the classification decision. The Critical Events Index (CEI) is a 33-item checklist of specific behaviors (e.g., steals, sets fires) requiring only notation of the presence or absence of the behavior. The 23-item Combined Frequency Index (CFI) lists 12 adaptive and 11 maladaptive behaviors to be ranked according to a 5-point scale ranging from *never* to *frequently*. From these scales, a total adaptive and maladaptive score for the six selected students is determined. The manual estimates total teacher time for Stage I and II would be "an hour to an hour and one half" (User's Guide and Administration Manual, p. 3).

Stage III begins a process of systematic student observation for individuals exceeding the criteria on either the CEI or the CFI. In contrast to the first two stages, the third stage requires the participation of school personnel other than the classroom teacher "such as the school psychologist, counselor, resource teacher and others who have been trained to use these observations codes" (User's Guide and Administration Manual, p. 19). During Stage III, student observations are conducted in two different settings (classroom and playground) during four separate 15-minute interval recording sessions. Analysis of student behavior is summarized into academic engaged time and peer social behavior. Decision rules are again employed to pass students through Stage III into the formal referral process.

STANDARDIZATION SAMPLE. The SSBD national standardization was conducted with 4,463 students (Stage II) and 1,275 students (Stage III). No standardization data were provided for Stage I. Despite finding significant correlations with grade at Stage II, the authors assert that "the low range of magnitude did not justify the creation of separate samples and distributions based on grade and sex" (technical manual, p. 66).

The national standardization sample was drawn from eight states and 18 school districts across the United States. The western states were overrepresented, with over 58% of the Stage II sample and almost 70% of the Stage III sample derived from the states of Washington, Oregon, and Utah. No data were presented on the breakdown between urban, suburban, and rural school populations. Ethnicity and socioeconomic status were addressed in the standardization sample only by breakouts from the total school enrollment as "non-white enrollment" and "low income enrollment."

RELIABILITY AND VALIDITY. A number of studies were presented in the manual to support the development and validation of the SSBD. Overall, Stage I test-retest reliabilities are lower than desirable. During the trial testing of Stage I, test-retest rank order correlations (1-month retest) averaged .76 for externalizers and .74 for internalizers. Of the top three students with externalizing and internalizing behavior, 69% were listed among the top three students 1 month later. During Stage II trial testing of the CFI, test-retest reliabilities improved to .88 for adaptive behaviors and .83 for maladaptive behaviors. Measures of internal consistency on the Stage II CFI were similar to test-retest reliabilities. The coefficient alphas averaged .86 on the adaptive scale and .84 on the maladaptive scale. Due to low frequencies of positively checked items on the Stage III CEI, analyses were not conducted during trial testing.

Interrater agreement ratios for the Stage III five-category PSB code (using 10-second interval recording) consistently were within the .80 to .90 range. Interrater reliability for the Stage II measure, however, had not been estimated at the time of initial printing.

The authors dedicated a large section of the technical manual to a discussion of validity studies, including subsections on item validity, factorial analysis, and criterion-related, construct, predictive, concurrent, and discriminant validity. Research on discriminant validity generally supports the use of the SSBD in areas such as classifying group membership assignments and discriminating between externalizers and internalizers.

Predictive validity data were much less persuasive. On Stage I measures, only 52% of internalizers and 69% of externalizers from the previous year were listed among the top three ranked students in the subsequent year. The Stage II index ranged from .32 (Critical Events Index) to .70 (Maladaptive Rating Scale) and shared with the Stage III measure classification efficiencies "in the low to moderate range" (technical manual, p. 56).

Concurrent validity was addressed by correlating the total score on the Stage II ratings with two other measures designed by the first author (the Walker-McConnell Scale of Social Competence and School Adjustment). Although these results provided some support for the Stage II measures, most scores also were in the low to moderate magnitude range.

CONCLUSIONS. The SSBD is a three-stage, multiple-gating instrument proposed as a partial battery of tests for the screening and identification of behaviorally disturbed elementary school students. The stages have intuitive appeal and will provide some face validity for student classification decisions. As a screening instrument, the SSBD insures both internalizing and externalizing disorders will be addressed by the classroom teacher. One published study (Walker et al., 1994) suggests that the SSBD is favorably rated by the majority of psychologists and teachers who have used it. The separate manual and videotape used for Stage III observer training is clear and concise without oversimplifying the challenges of direct observation. These attributes likely will enhance its overall attraction to psychologists and educators. As the manual suggests, however, the SSBD is not to be used in isolation. If the certification of behavioral disturbance is required, the manual recommends a variety of more specific instruments be used in conjunction with the SSBD. The SSBD is not to be used as the sole measure for classifying behaviorally disturbed students.

Less apparent to these reviewers are the psychometric advantages of the SSBD over other instruments traditionally used but not specifically designed for screening. As a method of selecting students with behavioral disorders, the SSBD requires the expenditure of significant amounts of teacher time to determine if a student fits into successive referral stages.

The authors justify this time requirement based upon their review of research indicating that behaviorally disturbed students, particularly internalizing students, are less likely to be referred by general education teachers than students with academic problems. In addition, Walker et al. (1994) have provided some evidence that the SSBD is at least comparable (and perhaps marginally better) in terms of administrative cost to traditional assessment procedures in the state of Utah. This cost differential, however, is likely to vary dramatically depending upon state regulations.

In summary, low to moderate levels of reliability and validity in some stages is an obvious concern with this instrument. Standardization is limited for the most part to western states, and data on ethnicity and socioeconomic status need to be expanded. Nevertheless, the SSBD has been sufficiently developed to be considered for the screening purpose for which it has been designed.

REVIEWER'S REFERENCES

Walker, H. M., Severson, H. H., Todis, B. J., Block-Pedego, A. E., Williams, G. J., Harring, N. G., & Barckley, M. (1990). Systematic Screening for Behavior Disorders (SSBD): Further validation, replication, and normative data. *Remedial and Special Education, 11*(2), 32–46.
Walker, H. M., Severson, H. H., Nicholson, F., Kehle, T., Jenson, W. R., & Clark, E. (1994). Replication of the Systematic Screening for Behavior Disorders (SSBD) procedure for the identification of at-risk children. *Journal of Emotional and Behavioral Disorders, 2*, 66–77.

[314]

Tapping Students' Science Beliefs: A Resource for Teaching and Learning.

Purpose: Designed to "assess the belief students have about certain natural phenomena and permits appropriate learning experiences to be planned."

Population: Primary grade level students.

Publication Date: 1993.

Acronym: TSSB.

Scores, 5: Skateboard News, What Happened Last Night, The Day We Cooked Pancakes in School, Children's Week, Our School Garden.

Administration: Group.

Price Data, 1993: A$90 per complete kit including manual (77 pages), 5 unit tests with 1 student score sheet and 1 group profile sheet per unit.

Time: (30) minutes per unit.

Authors: Brian Doig and Ray Adams.

Publisher: Australian Council for Educational Research Ltd. [Australia].

Review of Tapping Students' Science Beliefs: A Resource for Teaching and Learning by JERRILYN V. ANDREWS, Assistant for Assessment and Data Collection, Office of School Administration, Montgomery County Public Schools, Rockville, MD:

Tapping Students' Science Beliefs (TSSB) consists of five exercises designed to help elementary school teachers assess their students' scientific sophistication regarding certain natural phenomena. The logic behind the TSSB is that if beliefs and misconceptions can be identified, then teachers can tailor instruction to help students develop as scientific thinkers. It is clear from the manual that the TSSB is intended to be only a diagnostic instrument. The authors caution that TSSB scores are not achievement scores, that growth in conceptual development "may be quite haphazard" (p. 56), and that, therefore, a reassessment that does not show an increased level of sophistication "does not necessarily indicate a worsening situation, but rather may indicate the natural process of concept development and refinement" (p. 3). With those limitations, the estimated 2.5 hours of classroom time to give the TSSB, plus the additional time for scoring, the instructional benefits that could be derived from the assessment could not come close to equalling the costs.

All items in each exercise require the student to produce an answer; sometimes a written response is requested and sometimes a picture. For each item there are between 2 and 5 possible score points. For each score point the manual provides a one- or two-sentence description and often one or two examples. Unfortunately, many of the examples simply restate part of the description. Further, the examples may not be actual student-produced responses. In addition, for some items that require the student to draw a picture, the manual includes only a verbal description and no examples. These scoring instructions do not appear adequate to ensure reasonable reliability among scorers. An example will illustrate the potential scoring difficulties. One item states "When things dissolve, the total volume may not increase. Draw and label a picture that explains what happens when things dissolve." The description of the highest score point for that item is "The response use[s] the particulate model to explain how the particles of sugar can become suspended in between the particles of the liquid" (p. 27). One of the lowest score points reads, "The response simply states that the sugar mixes in. There is no explanation of the mixing process that blends the sugar and liquid" (p. 27). For this item, the manual provides no examples to help teachers score elementary school students responses. Scoring reliability is never mentioned.

Although the ideas behind the instrument are rooted in current thinking about teaching and learning science, the manual contains no evidence regarding the instrument's technical properties. The user is given only cursory information about how the assessments were developed and the score points and descriptions determined. No reliability or validity data are included. There are no norms or even examples to indicate what the performance of children in a given grade or age group might look like. The five exercises are interesting and could be used as the basis for classroom instruction. A section of the manual contains good ideas for thought-provoking science instruction. However, the total lack of technical information and the inadequate scoring instructions make this unsuitable for use as an assessment.

Review of Tapping Students' Science Beliefs: A Resource for Teaching and Learning by JAMES P. VAN HANEGHAN, Associate Professor of Behavioral Studies and Educational Technology, College of Education, University of South Alabama, Mobile, AL:

Assessing the development of science concepts in a way that touches everyday experience has always been a difficult task for teachers. Tapping Students' Science Beliefs (TSSB) is a tool for tapping children's understanding of some basic notions of physical science and living things. It consists of a set of five structured scenarios for school-age children. The scenarios are comic book representations that embed questions about the concepts. Some are in the form of short stories, whereas others are simulated situations. Because the scenarios touch on different concepts, their scoring and administration are done separately. The authors suggest carrying out a TSSB assessment prior to teaching a set of concepts. The goal is to identify student misconceptions and levels of development.

The first scenario, *Skateboard News*, examines issues surrounding gravity, force, and motion. It is in the form of a newsletter that engages children by asking them how a skateboard works. For example, one question asks why the skateboard will eventually stop if the person riding does not apply a force to it.

The second scenario, *What Happened Last Night*, involves questions about the earth, moon, and sun. They are posed in the guise of a story about an alien landing on earth and requesting information about the earth, moon, and sun.

The third scenario, *The Day We Cooked Pancakes in School*, concerns matter and its various forms. The characters in this story have an ongoing discussion of matter as they make pancakes and lemonade. They touch on issues such as condensation on the lemonade pitcher, and the mixing together of liquids, solids, and gas to make the batter.

The fourth scenario, *Children's Week*, involves simulation of a "Children's Week" celebration where the assessed children are asked to teach younger children about the concept of light. This scenario involves questions and descriptions of the younger children's responses to the questions. The responses the children give are elaborations and corrections of the younger children's knowledge of light and vision.

The last scenario, *Our School Garden*, involves a conversation between two children creating a garden. The main concepts addressed involve plant and animal life. For example, one question asks whether plants are living things.

The scenarios are in a written booklet-like form copied from masters. Responses are written and drawn in the booklet, although oral presentation and response to the questions could be used with younger or less literate children. There are no age limits suggested, although some of the concepts are mastered early in the elementary school years, whereas others may not be mastered by adults who have shied away from science. There is not much information in the manual about typical age levels where these concepts are mastered or understood, although some references are provided for test users.

The scenarios present a good mixture of situations that children from a variety of backgrounds would be interested in exploring; however, the "Children's Week" celebration may not be sufficiently widespread to use as a "hook" for this scenario. It might have been better had the authors used another guise.

Overall scenario and individual item scores are generated. Individual items within scenarios are generally scored on 3- or 4-point scales. The scoring key includes examples of answers that correspond to individual scores, but usually only one or two examples are presented, and some items do not have representative responses included. Individual item scores are added together to come up with an overall scenario score. Scores for each item and the overall score are placed into an individual profile that can help the teacher examine specific elements of children's understanding.

The overall scenario scores are categorized as prescientific, developing scientific, or scientific. Along with this general description of score level, three to five verbal descriptions of what ranges of scores for the concepts mean are presented. A group profile can also be set up for each scenario to determine who in a class has scientific, developing scientific, or prescientific understanding.

Ideas on how to use scores to improve instruction are included in the manual. The test manual, however, provides little *specific* evidence for the reliability and validity of the TSSB. The TSSB was based on a study assessing 3,000 Australian students' science concepts, so the authors had adequate data for scaling purposes. From the manual's brief description of test development, the Rasch scaling model they used seems appropriate for their scale. The ordering of concepts seems consistent with the literature, and thus, there is some evidence for content validity and the reliability of the scaling. On the other hand, no data are presented on interrater reliability, test-retest reliability, or criterion-related validity.

Interrater reliability information would help determine how easy it is to score a scenario. The manual does not suggest what background knowledge is needed to use the TSSB well. Although one might presume that teachers should be capable of scoring the TSSB, some teachers may require additional training. The concepts covered by the scenarios are nicely described with references to research; however, there are no training materials presented other than the criteria for scoring and a few examples. In some cases there are no sample responses associated with the criterion for an item.

Test-retest reliability data would provide information about the stability of scores. Such information is important to making inferences about changes in scores related to instruction. The authors do note that changes from instruction may not always be in the positive direction. For example, a child may shift from a developing scientific to a prescientific concept when faced with evidence that refutes the developing scientific concept. However, one would expect good instruction to eventually alter children's misconceptions, and thus, data on the stability of concepts over time would be of interest.

The issue of changes related to instruction leads to the question of why the authors did not develop parallel forms of the TSSB. There are other scenarios from everyday life that could be used to assess these various concepts. The concepts are not so idiosyncratic that the development of alternative scenarios would present a problem. Additionally, it is important to know how the assessment context influences scores on the various concepts.

The need to consider the stability of the concepts across contexts suggests that data on the concurrent validity of TSSB scenarios with other measures are important. The test manual does not include such evidence, although one of the authors reported a strong correlation ($r = .77$) between scores on *Skateboard News* and other measures of force and motion in a sample of 40 students (Brian Doig, personal communication, October 25, 1996). Further data on predictive validity and the utility of TSSB scores for instruction are also needed.

Overall, the TSSB is a unique tool for assessing children's ideas about scientific concepts. Aside from some Piagetian tasks (e.g., see Voyat, 1982), there are few systematic assessments of physical concepts such as these. It is unique in that it assesses these concepts using everyday scenarios. However, the data supporting its reliability and validity need to be bolstered. Additionally, more training materials and more scenarios would increase the utility of the TSSB as a classroom assessment tool.

REVIEWER'S REFERENCE

Voyat, G. E. (1982). *Piaget systematized*. Hillsdale, NJ: Lawrence Erlbaum Associates.

[315]
Taylor-Johnson Temperament Analysis [1992 Edition].

Purpose: Measures personality traits which influence personal, interpersonal, scholastic, and vocational functioning and adjustment.

Population: Adolescents and adults (individuals, couples).

Publication Dates: 1941–1992.

Acronym: T-JTA.

Scores: 9 traits: Nervous vs. Composed, Depressive vs. Lighthearted, Active-Social vs. Quiet, Expressive-Responsive vs. Inhibited, Sympathetic vs. Indifferent, Subjective vs. Objective, Dominant vs. Submissive, Hostile vs. Tolerant, Self-Disciplined vs. Impulsive (plus Test-Taking Attitude Scale); computer report scales—partial listing (Adequacy of Self-Image [Self-Esteem], Emotional Pressure [Stress], Leadership Potential, Potential for Successful Marital Adjustment, Potential for Successful Parenting.

Administration: Group.

Price Data, 1994: $110 per basic package, Option A including 5 question booklets (choice of Regular, Non-Criss-Cross, Secondary), 50 answer sheets, 50 profiles (Shaded, Shaded Without Zone Designations, Sten), handscoring stencils, pen set, ruler, and manual ('92, 114 pages); $130 per expanded basic package, Option B including 10 question booklets (choice of Regular, Non-Criss-Cross, Secondary), 100 answer sheets, 100 profiles (Shaded, Shaded Without Zone Designation, Sten), handscoring stencils, pen set, ruler, and manual; $140 per comprehensive basic and secondary package, Option C including 5 Regular question booklets, 5 secondary question booklets, 100 handscoring answer sheets, handscoring stencils, 50 student sten profiles, 50 profiles (Shaded,

Shaded Without Zone Designation, or Sten), pen set, ruler, student sten norms, and manual; $75 per computer scoring package, Option D including 10 question booklets (choice of Regular, Non-Criss-Cross, Secondary), 50 computer answer sheets, and manual; $120 per basic package, Option S including 5 Spanish question booklets (Regular Edition), 50 Spanish profiles (Shaded, Shaded Without Zone Designations, or Sten), 50 Spanish answer sheets, handscoring stencils, pen set, ruler, Spanish norm tables, and Spanish manual; $30 per military scoring training packet; $12 per 10 reusable question booklets (Regular, Non-Criss-Cross, or Secondary); $17.50 per 100 handscoring or PPI computer scoring service answer sheets; $34.50 per set (6) of handscoring stencils; $52.50 per set (6) of military handscoring stencils; $17.50 per 100 profiles (choice of Shaded, Shaded Without Zone Designations, Regular Sten, Student Sten); $3.50 per percentile and sten locator per ruler; $1.50 per pen; $65 per manual; $25 per handbook; $17.50 per student sten norms; $16.50 per practice scoring training packet; $12 per copy of "The AWOL Syndrome"; $25 per norms for Spanish Speaking Americans; $75 per Spanish test manual; $5 per research and reference list; computer scoring, profiling and interpretive reports available from publisher: $5 per answer sheet (self test) or $20 per 4 answer sheets (Criss-Cross) for scoring and profiling report, Option 1; $10 per answer sheet (self test) or $30 per 4 answer sheets (Criss-Cross) for brief reports including scoring and profiling, Option 2; $20 per answer sheet (self test) or $50 per 4 answer sheets for interpretive reports including scoring and profiling, Option 3.

Foreign Language Edition: Spanish, German, French, and Portuguese editions available.

Time: (30–45) minutes.

Authors: Original edition by Roswell H. Johnson, revision by Robert M. Taylor, Lucille P. Morrison (manual), W. Lee Morrison (handbook and secondary edition question booklet and statistical consultant), Richard C. Romoser (statistical consultant); and James C. Berbiglia ("The AWOL Syndrome").

Publisher: Psychological Publications, Inc.

a) REGULAR EDITION.

Population: Adults and college students (reading level grade 8 and over).

Publication Dates: 1941–1992.

b) SECONDARY EDITION, FORM-S.

Population: Secondary school students and adult poor readers (minimum grade 5 reading level).

Publication Dates: 1972–1992.

Comments: Used only for self-testing.

Cross References: See T4:2690 (3 references); for reviews by Cathy W. Hall and Paul McReynolds, see 10:357; see also T3:2396 (1 reference); for a review by Robert F. Stahmann, see 8:692 (18 references); see also T2:840 (3 references); for a review by Donald L. Mosher of an earlier edition of *a*, see 7:572 (1 reference); see also

P:264 (3 references) and 6:130 (10 references); for a review of the original edition by Albert Ellis, see 4:62 (6 references); for a review of the original edition by H. Meltzer, see 3:57.

Review of the Taylor-Johnson Temperament Analysis [1992 Edition] by JEFFREY A. JENKINS, Attorney and Counselor at Law, Albuquerque, NM:

The Taylor-Johnson Temperament Analysis (T-JTA) provides a measure of nine common personality characteristics. These are described in the T-JTA manual as Nervous (vs. Composed), Depressive (vs. Lighthearted), Active-Social (vs. Quiet), Expressive-Responsive (vs. Inhibited), Sympathetic (vs. Indifferent), Subjective (vs. Objective), Dominant (vs. Submissive), Hostile (vs. Tolerant), and Self-Disciplined (vs. Impulsive). The T-JTA consists of 180 items in a question format, such as "Does _____ prefer to be alone rather than with people?" The examinee responds by indicating "+" ("decidedly yes" or "mostly so"), "-" ("decidedly no" or "mostly not so"), or "Mid" (undecided). Respondents can work quickly through the clearly presented list of questions, completing the 180 items in 30 to 45 minutes. The descriptive nature of the items regarding personal characteristics and life activities helps to maintain the interest of the respondent. A unique characteristic of the instrument is that it may also be used in a "criss-cross" fashion, allowing the examinee to describe the perceived characteristics of another person. This approach is useful in family, marital, or other relationship counseling situations. The instrument can be sent to the publisher for computer processing, or handscored using scoring stencils provided with the test kit. Results are reported on a profile showing percentile or sten scores for each of the nine personality traits.

First reviewed in the *Mental Measurements Yearbook* as the Johnson Temperament Analysis, the T-JTA underwent extensive revision in 1967. Norms and scoring procedures were updated in 1984 and, most recently, in 1992. A form for use with adolescents was developed in 1972 by simplifying the language used in the items to a fifth grade reading level. The present version of the regular form of the instrument does not differ from the original 1967 revision, except that scoring is accomplished using the 1992 norms. Comprehensive reviews of the instrument and the 1984 norms were provided by Cathy W. Hall and Paul McReynolds (10:357). The reader is also referred to previous reviews of the T-JTA, which have discussed the technical characteristics of the instrument (Stahmann, 8:692; Mosher, 7:572). With respect to the reliability and validity of the T-JTA, suffice it to say that reliability coefficients for the trait scores appear to be adequate (internal consistency estimates range from .71 to .90 for the nine traits) and, although some early support for the construct validity of the T-JTA is reported in the T-JTA manual, the publishers should provide users with a summary of more current research involving the T-JTA, which may provide further support for the instrument's validity. This is particularly important given the lack of a strong theoretical basis for the underlying personality traits the T-JTA purports to measure and the significant strides taken in the field of psychological measurement since the early 1960s.

The 1992 version of the T-JTA differs from the 1984 edition by its updated norms and scoring procedures. The current norms do little to increase the user's confidence in the validity of individual results. Unfortunately, sparse information about the norms groups is provided in the T-JTA manual, and the information given raises serious questions about the adequacy of the norms.

The population groups used for the 1992 norms have been redefined in terms of age alone. Specifically, the comparison groups are not Adolescent (ages 13–17), Young Adult (ages 18–25), General Adult (ages 26–54), and Senior Adult (age 55 and over). In contrast, the groups used for the 1984 norms were defined as General Population, College Students, and Secondary. Although the new classifications seem appropriate, the justification provided by the publishers for the new Young Adult category seems peculiar: "As social and cultural changes have made college students and non-college population of the same age virtually indistinguishable, the College Student group has been redefined and replaced by the Young Adult group" (manual, p. A-i). No additional explanation or support is given for this conclusory statement that college students and non-college young adults are "virtually indistinguishable."

The norm groups are described in the T-JTA manual as "gathered from the Psychological Publications Scoring Service and includes data from 804 counselors in 46 U.S. states and from 8 counselors from various cities in Canada" (p. A-i). Although the percentage of the total norm sample from each state is provided, such percentages for the specific norm groups are not. Moreover, nearly a third of the norm sample is from California. It appears that little or no attempt was made to reflect the general population in the norm sample. In addition, the sample sizes for the Adolescent norms (Male, $N = 256$; Female, $N = 198$) and the Senior Adult Norms (Male, $N = 459$, Female, $N = 314$) seem insufficient for scoring and interpreting responses by examinees in these age groups.

More important, however, is that the selection process for norm group respondents raises questions about generalizability to the general population of scores derived from such norms. Specifically, the subjects included in the norm groups were presumably only those individuals who were seeing counselors. Although nothing is known about the reasons for seeking counseling services or the service provider's background or credentials (e.g., psychologist, unlicensed therapist, minister), it is clear that groups thus chosen would differ in numerous respects from the general population. Thus, scores from the present version of the T-JTA can only be interpreted in comparison to individuals who are undergoing counseling. The meaning to be placed upon such scores is left in doubt without more information about the reference groups. Some rationale for employing this norm group should be given or, at a minimum, a caveat regarding interpretation of scores derived from these limited norms. Both are absent from the T-JTA manual.

In addition, the data used for creation of the norms include only responses sent in by counselors for computerized scoring. One can only speculate about differences between respondents whose counselors employ computerized scoring versus handscoring, but the cost of scoring or time constraints on the counselor may be factors that could raise questions about whether the norms are generalizable.

Given the shortcomings with the 1992 norms, the T-JTA cannot be recommended as a general diagnostic tool for personality assessment. However, the T-JTA continues to have utility in the research setting, as well as for helping respondents, with the assistance of a counselor, begin to discuss issues that might otherwise remain uncovered.

Review of the Taylor-Johnson Temperament Analysis [1992 Edition] by BARBARA J. KAPLAN, Psychologist, Western New York Institute for the Psychotherapies, Orchard Park, NY:

The Taylor-Johnson Temperament Analysis (T-JTA), first published as the Johnson Temperament Analysis (JTA) in 1941, underwent substantive revisions in 1967 and 1984. Updated and population-specific norms have been added since the 1967

revision (e.g., adolescents, college students, and senior adults). This questionnaire provides scores for nine dimensions of personality: Nervous vs. Composed, Depressive vs. Lighthearted, Active-Social vs. Quiet, Expressive-Responsive vs. Inhibited, Sympathetic vs. Indifferent, Subjective vs. Objective, Dominant vs. Submissive, Hostile vs. Tolerant, Self-Disciplined vs. Impulsive. Factor analysis demonstrates the relative independence of these traits as measured by the T-JTA, but the selection of the traits themselves was derived from Johnson's clinical experience rather than from a theory of personality. Although the T-JTA has been subsequently validated by correlational comparisons with scores on the Minnesota Multiphasic Personality Inventory (Dahlstrom, Welsh, & Dahlstrom, 1960) and the Sixteen Personality Factor Questionnaire (Cattell, Eber, & Tatsuoka, 1970), the JTA was originally validated by psychologists' ratings of clients whose personalities they knew well. The test manual suggests that these ratings were "substitutes for pure criterion measures" (p. 23). It is in the area of criterion and predictive validity that the T-JTA is weakest.

The authors present data demonstrating that the instrument does measure personality as it is currently conceptualized. Scores are fairly stable over 1 to 3 weeks' time (.71 to .90). Individuals' scores were also compared with others' ratings (mostly spouses and other family members) and "significant positive correlations" are mentioned in the validity findings for the 1984 edition; however, the results themselves are not reported. However, no data show change on the T-JTA as a result of counseling, identify the test profiles of individuals who may be expected to benefit most from counseling, or suggest what combinations of profiles for couples or family members are most able to alter their relationship in a positive direction. Professionals examining the T-JTA might reasonably look for information of this sort because the test authors state that the purpose of the instrument is the measure of "common personality variables or attitudes and behavioral tendencies which influence personal, social, marital, parental, family, scholastic, and vocational adjustment" (p. 1). The latter part of this statement is presumably the reason one should use the T-JTA.

It is difficult to know why one would choose this assessment over some other standardized measure of personality, other than its historical origin in a counseling setting and the explicit suggestion that comparison of self-ratings with others' ratings ("crisscross" ratings) may be of interest. Certainly, the difference between self-perceptions and others' perceptions remains a perplexing and tantalizing question for psychology; however, this instrument adds little theoretically or empirically to the answer.

A large number of clients have been assessed with the JTA and the T-JTA. It does function in the counseling setting as an easy opening for discussion of personality and the client's present concerns. In this context, the T-JTA may be selected to enhance the counseling environment. There are, however, other widely used and well-validated personality measures that would serve just as well.

REVIEWER'S REFERENCES
Dahlstrom, W. G., Welsh, G. S., & Dahlstrom, L. F. (1960). *An MMPI handbook*. Minneapolis: University of Minnesota Press.
Cattell, R. B., Eber, H. W., & Tatsuoka, M. M. (1970). *Handbook for the Sixteen Personality Questionnaire*. Champaign, IL: Institute for Personality and Ability Testing.

[316]
Team Development Survey.

Purpose: A brief assessment tool for work teams.
Population: Work team members.
Publication Date: 1992.
Acronym: TDS.
Scores, 12: Clear Purpose, Informality, Participation, Listening, Civilized Disagreement, Consensus Decisions, Open Communication, Clear Roles and Work Assignments, Shared Leadership, External Relations, Style Diversity, Self-Assessment.
Administration: Group.
Price Data, 1993: $40 per complete kit including leader's guide (18 pages), scoring form, and 10 team member surveys.
Time: Administration time not reported.
Author: Glenn M. Parker.
Publisher: XICOM, Inc.

Review of the Team Development Survey by GREGORY J. CIZEK, Associate Professor of Educational Research and Measurement, University of Toledo, Toledo, OH:

The Team Development Survey (TDS) was designed to provide a structured way of collecting information about characteristics believed to be necessary for effective functioning of work groups ("teams") in corporate settings. The manual indicates that the survey is appropriate for teams engaged in activities such as "product development, quality improvement, customer service, cost reduction, systems development, as well as traditional business teams" (p. 1). The manual also states that the survey can be used with different types of teams, including permanent teams, ad hoc teams, and cross-functional teams.

The TDS was developed "in response to a need for a brief assessment tool for teams" (p. 1). Four intended uses of the TDS are suggested: (a) data collection as part of an assessment of a team, (b) a tool for training needs assessment, (c) an exercise workshop on team effectiveness, and (d) a tool for evaluating a team building or training program.

MATERIALS. The complete kit consists of three components: Leader's Guide, Team Member Survey, and Team Scoring Form. The Leader's Guide provides an introduction to the survey and procedures for administering the TDS for each of the four intended uses.

The Team Members Survey form consists of 12 statements—one for each of 12 team functioning characteristics—and space for respondents to circle their reactions to the statements according to two 5-point Likert scales. Brief, clear instructions also appear on the form.

The two scales address "Description" (the degree to which the statement accurately describes the respondent's work team), and "Importance" (the extent to which the characteristic is judged to be important for the success of the team). For example, one of the characteristics is "Participation." This characteristic is defined by the statement, "There is a lot of discussion and everyone is encouraged to participate." After reading the statement, a respondent simply circles a Description rating from 1 (Strongly Disagree) to 5 (Strongly Agree) corresponding to their opinion of how accurately the statement describes their work team. Then the respondent circles an Importance rating from 1 (Unimportant) to 5 (Critically Important) corresponding to their opinion of how necessary the characteristic is to the success of the team. Space is also provided for respondents to supply comments on each characteristic.

The third part of the survey is a Team Scoring Form. The form provides a place to compile the individual ratings of up to 10 respondents. Ratings of each respondent are summed for each characteristic and the mean is interpreted as the team's standing on each characteristic. Results can be graphed onto a 2x2 classification matrix depicting high and low standing on team "strengths," "improvement opportunities," "untapped resources," and "unknowns."

RELIABILITY AND VALIDITY. Despite the intuitive appeal of the 12 characteristics, no evidence is provided to support the validity of the TDS for assessing team functioning or for any of the suggested uses indicated in the manual. One paragraph in the manual implies some construct validity, claiming that: "The list of 12 characteristics grows out of earlier work by McGregor (1960) and Likert (1961)" (p. 1) and that it was "influenced by Blake and Mouton's work on leadership styles (1964)" (p. 1). However, a review of these sources reveals little overlap in the characteristics assessed in the TDS and the characteristics described in those references. It seems implausible also that an assessment on the relatively new concept of work teams could be grounded in literature more than 30 years old.

The TDS does bear a strong relationship, however, to the more recent work of its author, presented in *Team Players and Teamwork: The New Competitive Business Strategy* (Parker, 1990). In fact, the TDS is identical to a survey presented in chapter 2 of that reference, although no empirical support for its validity is presented there either. Neither is any support provided for the classifications resulting from summing TDS scores ("strength," "improvement opportunity," etc.). The user cannot determine if the suggested mean cutoff of 3.0 for "high" classification was simply arbitrarily selected.

Similarly, no evidence is provided for the reliability of scores or classifications.

RECOMMENDATIONS AND CAUTIONS. The TDS may have value for stimulating discussion about roles for workers functioning in teams, or as an aid in understanding the perceptions of team members on various topics. The manual contains a framework for organizing such discussions, which users may find helpful. Consequently, the TDS might best be viewed as an instructional adjunct.

However, because no evidence is available to users regarding the adequacy of the assessment, it cannot be recommended as adequate for any assessment purpose. The manual fails to incorporate—or even acknowledge—relevant assessment guidelines, such as those in the *Standards for Educational and Psychological Testing* (AERA/APA/NCME, 1985). The author notes that validation studies for a companion instrument, the Team Player Survey, have been designed. Similar studies of the TDS should be designed, conducted, and reviewed before the instrument can be used for any critical classifications, decisions, or diagnoses related to team functioning.

REVIEWER'S REFERENCES

McGregor, D. (1960). *The human side of enterprise.* New York: McGraw-Hill.
Likert, R. (1961). *New patterns of management.* New York: McGraw-Hill.
Blake, R. R., & Mouton, J. S. (1964). *The managerial grid.* Houston, TX: Gulf.
American Educational Research Association, American Psychological Association, & National Council on Measurement in Education. (1985). *Standards for educational and psychological testing.* Washington, DC: American Psychological Association, Inc.
Parker, G. M. (1990). *Team players and teamwork: The new competitive business strategy.* San Francisco: Jossey-Bass.

Review of the Team Development Survey by LYNN R. OFFERMANN, *Associate Professor of Psychology, George Washington University, Washington, DC:*

Given the proliferation of concerns about teamwork in organizations, a well-designed instrument measuring team performance would indeed be useful. The Team Development Survey largely draws its conceptual base from McGregor's (1960) classic and well-regarded thinking about characteristics of effective work teams. In fact, of the 12 characteristics represented on the survey, 10 items address characteristics presented by McGregor (with at least two of these overlapping with work by Likert, 1961), one was suggested by the work of Hastings, Bixby, and Chaudhry-Lawton (1987) on the importance of external relations to teams, and one characteristic of style diversity was drawn from Parker's own work (1990) on team player styles. Evidence for the content validity of the instrument is based on its derivation from these sources.

Team members score themselves on 5-point scales on each of these 12 characteristics, both in terms of how well the characteristic describes their team, and how important the characteristic is to team success. Team members are also asked to record observations as to the strengths of the team and areas for improvement. A team scoring form is provided to permit individual team member responses on each item to be summed and divided by the number of team members to yield a team mean for each of the 12 dimensions, both for Description and Importance (24 scores). The author suggests, without presentation of supportive data, that means of 3.0 or higher be considered "high" and those below "low." The description and importance means for each item can then be paired and graphed into one of four boxes: "High description/High importance" (Strengths), "High description/Low importance" (Untapped Resources), "Low description/High importance" (Improvement Opportunity) and "Low description/Low importance" (Unknown). Results are to be analyzed by examining the contents of each box, and an action plan developed through the assistance of guided questions for each dimension.

The leader's guide suggests five potential uses for the survey: as a data collection tool as part of a team assessment, as a team building activity, as a tool for training needs assessment, as an exercise in a workshop on team effectiveness, and as a tool for evaluating a team building effort or training program (pre/post test use). The guide provides absolutely no information about normative samples or evidence of reliability and validity beyond content validity based on the sources from which the instrument was derived, nor is such information available from the publisher. The lack of such information seriously limits the usefulness of the instrument for many of the purposes suggested. Although extensive validation work is often scarce for instruments of this type, there are other team assessment instruments such as the Team Performance Inventory by Drexler, Sibbet, and Forrester (1993) (which assesses a team's stage of development but incorporates some of the same characteristics) or the Wilson Our Team instrument (1993) (based on Wilson's Task Cycle model) which do at least provide some comparative normative data. Wilson also presents some evidence of adequate scale reliabilities for his instrument.

In sum, the Team Development Survey is useful only as a quick informal self-assessment of how a team sees itself at a given point in time. It might be useful in a training environment to generate discussion around relevant team issues and for developing action plans where follow-up measurement is not planned. Given the lack of comparative normative samples and reliability and validity evidence, the instrument is clearly not appropriate at this time for pre/post comparisons of any particular team's performance, for comparative assessment of teams, for predicting team performance on the job, for selecting particular teams for assignments, or any other purpose for which satisfactory psychometric evidence of reliability and validity should be in evidence.

REVIEWER'S REFERENCES

McGregor, D. (1960). *The human side of enterprise*. New York: McGraw-Hill.
Likert, R. (1961). *New patterns of management*. New York: McGraw-Hill.
Hastings, C., Bixby, P., & Chaudhry-Lawton, R. (1987). *The superteam solution*. San Diego, CA: University Associates.
Parker, G. M. (1990). *Team players and teamwork: The new competitive business strategy*. San Francisco: Jossey-Bass.
Drexler, A., Sibbet, D., & Forrester, R. (1993). The Team Performance Inventory. North Potomac, MD: Quality Team Performance Inc.
Wilson, C. L. (1993). Survey of Our Team. Silver Spring, MD: Clark Wilson Group, Inc.

[317]

The Team Leadership Practices Inventory.

Purpose: Focuses on the behaviors and actions of high-performing teams and self-directed work groups.
Population: Managers.
Publication Date: 1992.
Acronym: LPI.
Scores, 15: 3 scores: Self-Average, Team-Average, Total in each of 5 areas: Challenging the Process, Inspiring a Shared Vision, Enabling Others to Act, Modeling the Way, Encouraging the Heart.

Administration: Group.
Price Data, 1993: $34.95 per trainer's package including 3 booklets, self-assessment, and observer and trainer's manual (47 pages); $59.95 per deluxe trainer's package including the leadership challenge, self-assessment and analysis, and trainer's manual; $195 per IBM scoring program including manual (12 pages); $8.95 per instrument and participant's manual.
Time: (20–140) minutes.
Comments: Self-scored inventory.
Authors: James M. Kouzes and Barry Z. Posner.
Publisher: Pfeiffer & Company International Publishers.

Review of The Team Leadership Practices Inventory by JEFFREY B. BROOKINGS, Professor of Psychology, Wittenberg University, Springfield, OH:

The Team Leadership Practices Inventory (TEAM-LPI) is a 30-item inventory designed to assess variations in specific behaviors of work groups or teams. The conceptual foundation of the TEAM-LPI—and its predecessor, the LPA (12:213)—is Kouzes and Posner's (1987) model of leadership behavior, which identifies five "key" leadership practices: (a) Challenging the Process (e.g., risk-taking, experimentation); (b) Inspiring a Shared Vision (e.g., shaping a common understanding of team goals and their congruence with larger organizational objectives); (c) Enabling Others to Act (e.g., goal setting and team planning, communication and information-sharing); (d) Modeling the Way (e.g., accountability, modeling appropriate team behaviors); and (e) Encouraging the Heart (e.g., providing feedback and recognition of group achievements). The test form includes six descriptive statements (e.g., "We look for innovating ways to improve what we do in this organization") for each of the five leadership practices; respondents rate the extent to which each statement describes their work team on a scale ranging from 1 (*Rarely or Very Seldom*) to 5 (*Very Frequently or Almost Always*).

Work team members complete the TEAM-LPI individually; then, the tests are scored and interpreted as part of a "workshop" of approximately 2–4 hours duration. In these workshops, team members discuss individual and group scores on the items comprising each leadership dimension, and identify specific leadership practices in which team improvement would be desirable. Finally, "Action Planning Work Sheets" are used to list specific actions needed to achieve the agreed-upon leadership improvement goals.

To date, there are no published studies of the psychometric properties of the TEAM-LPI. Evidence for its reliability and validity is assumed from its similarity to the more extensively studied LPI (the two measures are essentially identical in item format and content). In addition, the authors cite split-half reliabilities ranging from .83 to .91 for the five TEAM-LPI subscales, and significant correlations of the instrument with measures of "work-team effectiveness," as evidence of its reliability and predictive validity, respectively. However, because these findings are not published in professional journals, and no details on the research sample, methodology, and criterion measures are provided, the psychometric soundness of the TEAM-LPI has not been established. Furthermore, because no norms are provided, potential users have no basis for interpreting their results.

In summary, the absence of relevant psychometric data makes it impossible to render a technical evaluation of the TEAM-LPI. The instrument may be useful for initiating discussion of leadership behaviors in small-group settings. However, until more extensive evidence on its measurement properties is available, its use as a measure of work-team leadership dimensions cannot be recommended.

REVIEWER'S REFERENCE

Kouzes, J. M., & Posner, B. Z. (1987). *The leadership challenge: How to get extraordinary things done in organizations.* San Francisco: Jossey-Bass.

Review of The Team Leadership Practices Inventory by WILLIAM J. WALDRON, Administrator, Employee Testing & Assessment, TECO Energy, Inc., Tampa, FL:

INTRODUCTION. The Team Leadership Practices Inventory (TEAM-LPI) is designed to measure leadership within work teams—that is, peer leadership rather than that displayed by a formal leader. It is ideally suited for use with self-directed work teams. The instrument is part of an extensive ongoing research program conducted by the authors (Kouzes & Posner, 1987). The TEAM-LPI is an adaptation of the Leadership Practices Inventory (LPI; 12:213), which was designed to measure the leadership behavior of supervisors and managers (Posner & Kouzes, 1988).

In developing the TEAM-LPI, the authors translated their leadership framework, which is based upon and supported by a good deal of empirical research, to the peer/team level. It measures five key team member attitudes and activities:

1. Challenging the Process "entails being willing to take risks, exploring new alternatives, experimenting, learning from mistakes, and supporting one another in these efforts."

2. Inspiring a Shared Vision means having "a common understanding of what the team is trying to accomplish, realizing how team members' efforts are aligned with larger organizational goals, and using values to guide further actions."

3. Enabling Others to Act means being actively involved "in setting goals and planning projects, establishing cooperative objectives, sharing information and keeping one another informed, and demonstrating respect for one another's ideas and competencies."

4. Modeling the Way entails "translating shared values into actions, being accountable to one another, influencing by example, and breaking tasks into manageable steps so that people can experience small 'wins' on the way to achieving goals."

5. Encouraging the Heart means "feeling emotionally connected to the team, providing one another with timely feedback, pointing with pride to team accomplishments, and celebrating together the achievement of milestones." (manual, pp. 1–2)

Each of these five factors is measured by six 5-point Likert type items, so that scores on each factor can range from 5–30. The items are responded to in terms of how often the team engages in each behavior or activity. Each individual completes the instrument independently.

The TEAM-LPI is designed to be used as part of a team development workshop; it is sold as part of a package also including workbooks for the team members and a Trainer's Manual for the workshop facilitator. No "test manual" is available, although the Trainer's Manual provides a good deal of information regarding the background and development of the instrument.

It is intended that the TEAM-LPI typically be self-scored as part of a workshop; however, it can also be scored manually by the facilitator in advance or, optionally, using software available from the publisher to produce a team report. During the workshop, the participants review and discuss the distribution of their team ratings on each of the five factors; the average member score is taken as the team's score on each factor.

CRITIQUE. The quality of the Trainer's Manual is very high. In addition to clear information about the development of the instrument, it provides very thorough step-by-step instructions for using the TEAM-LPI as part of a 4-hour workshop (ideally conducted over two sessions).

Quite often, materials intended for organizational trainers as opposed to selection and testing professionals are of substandard quality in terms of information about instrument development, as compared to typical test manuals. That is not the case for the TEAM-LPI. Although, understandably, it does not go into extensive detail about psychometric issues, the fact that such data are covered at all distinguishes this instrument. Although as a new instrument the data available are not extensive, the data discussed in an Appendix indicate that the TEAM-LPI factors demonstrate excellent reliability (both internal consistency and retest over short periods), that the instrument structure is supported by factor analysis, and that scores on the instrument are strongly related to independent measures of team effectiveness.

Although measurement professionals would like more details presented about the psychometric underpinnings, there really is little to criticize, given the intended audience for the manual. The authors have demonstrated a willingness to publish such data for the related (LPI) instrument (references to these studies are provided in the manual), and it would be expected that the same will be done for this measure as data become available.

One addition, however, would be useful. The psychometric data provided in the Appendix are based upon the responses of individuals; this is, of course, how such research is typically done. Because the TEAM-LPI is intended to measure characteristics of *groups*, however, some indication of the degree to which it does so would be useful—at minimum, data about within-group rater agreement.

SUMMARY. The TEAM-LPI is a high quality instrument, developed with a sound empirical and theoretical background. It measures behaviors and activities that are extremely important in many modern organizations. The care taken in its construction distinguishes the TEAM-LPI from many other instruments marketed for similar purposes. Organizations who have instituted work teams would do well to consider its use.

REVIEWER'S REFERENCES

Kouzes, J. M., & Posner, B. Z. (1987). *The leadership challenge: How to get extraordinary things done in organizations.* San Francisco: Jossey-Bass
Posner, B. Z., & Kouzes, J. M. (1988). Development and validation of the Leadership Practices Inventory. *Educational and Psychological Measurement, 48, 483–496.*

[318]
Technician Electrical Test—Form A2.

Purpose: "To measure the knowledge and skills required for electrical jobs."
Population: Electrical workers and applicants for electrical jobs.
Publication Dates: 1987–1994.
Scores: Total score only.
Administration: Group.

Price Data, 1993: $498 per 10 reusable test booklets, administration manual ('94, 13 pages), scoring key, and 100 blank answer sheets.
Time: (120) minutes.
Author: Roland T. Ramsay.
Publisher: Ramsay Corporation.

Review of the Technician Electrical Test—Form A2 by JOHN GEISLER, Professor, Department of Counselor Education and Counseling Psychology, Western Michigan University, Kalamazoo, MI:

The Technician Electrical Test (TET)—Form A2 is a group-administered, 132-item, paper-and-pencil, multiple-choice answer test originally published in 1989 by the Ramsay Corporation. It is a refinement of Form A, which was published in 1987. The test manual was published in 1992. It is designed to measure the knowledge of persons who are seeking positions as electricians. Fifteen content areas are covered on the TET.

The directions for administration are clear and precise and are read verbatim. One administrator can manage 20 examinees. Additional proctors are needed for every additional 20 examinees. The test is untimed and hand scoring is the only scoring option. The scoring directions indicate that the raw scores are derived by subtracting the number of incorrect and unanswered questions from the total number of test items (132). All unanswered items are therefore scored as wrong answers. As examinees turn in their answer sheets, the administrator is requested to mark the time it took to complete the tests although no rationale is provided for this request and the time element does not enter the scoring procedure.

Reliability was determined by Kuder-Richard Formula #20 and was reported as .95 ($n = 70$). This coefficient was computed on Form A, not Form A2, which is being reviewed here. Although the difference between the two forms is minor, the authors need to conduct additional reliability studies on Form A2 with larger samples and report other reliability coefficients (alpha, test-retest, split-half, etc.). Although .95 is certainly very acceptable, additional data are needed to support reliability claims.

The authors report that the test has not been validated with appropriate criterion-related studies. They indicate that the test does have content validity and therefore should probably correlate well with job performance. However, no evidence is provided to support this claim. This is the most glaring weakness of this instrument. There is no indication that the TET has content, predictive, concurrent, or construct validity. There is no information on how the items were selected. There is no history, rationale, or background provided. There is no evidence provided as to whether or not the items are from work-related situations. No predictive research studies are cited. There is no evidence that this instrument has any correlation with other instruments in the field or with any other work-related criteria (supervisors' ratings, work production, etc.). The use of this test for employee selection cannot be supported until empirical evidence is forthcoming.

Normative data in the form of percentile ranks are provided for Form A (not Form A2). There is no information on the composition of the norm group, the number in the norm group, or the characteristics of the norm group. This is a serious flaw and must be corrected before meaningful comparisons can be made.

The TET must be seen as an experimental instrument that is in need of field testing and additional study before it can be recommended for use. Content, predictive, and concurrent validation research needs to be conducted and additional reliability studies need to be reported. Hand scoring the answer sheet may lead to scoring error and should be corrected by developing a computer-scored answer sheet. Norm group information needs to be added. The instrument has some promise, but the number of flaws that need to be corrected auger against its general use at this time.

Review of the Technician Electrical Test—Form A2 by KEITH HATTRUP, Assistant Professor of Psychology, San Diego State University, San Diego, CA:

The Technician Electrical Test—Form A2 is a paper-and-pencil test of electrical knowledge. It includes 132 multiple-choice items designed to assess 15 separate knowledge areas, including motors, digital electronics, analog electronics, schematics, AC/DC theory, power distribution, etc. The test is not timed, but examinees are instructed they should complete the test within 2 hours. According to the test manual, the test should be administered individually or in groups of up to 20 examinees per examiner.

Internal consistency reliability of the 132 items is high (alpha = .95), as might be expected given the large number of items. Item-total correlations ranged from -.03 to .70, with an average of .38. The test manual also reports the standard error of measurement; however, the manual does not describe how the SEM should be interpreted or used in constructing and evaluating confidence intervals. This in-

formation would be a useful addition to any test manual. Additional evidence of this test's retest reliability would contribute to supporting inferences about the consistency of test scores across time and testing situations.

The test was developed to provide a content valid measure of achievement in the area of electrical knowledge. A panel of five subject matter experts (electrical maintenance supervisors) independently rated the amount of time job incumbents spend using each of several categories of electrical knowledge. An attempt was then made to write relatively more items for more important categories of electronics knowledge. As a result, the test development contributes to the test's content validity as a general test of knowledge of job-relevant electrical facts and principles. Unfortunately, the test manual does not indicate the job types or levels for which the knowledge assessed by the test is most applicable. The items assess a level of knowledge that is clearly above that of most high school graduates, but it is not clear from the manual how much extra training is required to answer test items correctly. None of the items assesses abstract, content-free, or fluid reasoning abilities; instead, the items all measure crystallized intelligence that must be developed through systematic training. Unfortunately, the population of examinees for whom this test is most appropriate is poorly defined in the manual.

Assuming an appropriate population of examinees could be identified, the objectivity and specificity of the measure as a test of advanced electrical knowledge probably represent both the most significant strengths and limitations of the instrument. On one hand, the large number of clear factual items, and the research conducted to document the job-relevance of knowledge assessed by the measure, contribute to arguments supporting the instrument's content validity. However, the difficulty of the test and its reliance on factual information about electrical systems and principles means that the instrument is likely to be relevant in only a limited number of circumstances. Hunter (1983) has shown that one of the best predictors of job performance is an incumbent's job-specific knowledge. However, it is only appropriate to test and screen for high levels of job knowledge among applicants if the job requires newly hired incumbents to perform tasks with little job-specific training. A more general test of cognitive ability would be far more useful in selecting job applicants who would be expected to develop high level electronics knowledge on the job. In other words, the Technician Electrical Test would be appropriate for testing and selection of already-trained applicants for jobs requiring high levels of electronics knowledge, whereas a test of general mental ability would be more appropriate for use in selecting applicants who would be expected to benefit from job-relevant training. Some discussion of these issues in the test manual would help test users evaluate the trade-offs between testing for high-level job-specific knowledge versus more general reasoning and learning abilities.

Aside from evidence supporting the test's content validity, no studies have been conducted to assess criterion-related validity or other aspects of the test's construct validity. Criterion-related validity coefficients, correlations of the test with other achievement and aptitude tests, and correlations with other psychological and demographic variables would contribute to a better understanding of the sources of variance contributing to scores on the Technician Electrical Test. Studies of mean differences, adverse impact, and differential prediction across sex and race groups would also help support inferences about the test's appropriateness when used for members of diverse groups. It should also be noted that 30 of the 132 items are also included in the Electronics Test—Form G2 by the same publisher. Some discussion of the similarities and differences of these two tests would help test users choose between them, particularly given the high degree of similarity in the constructs measured by the instruments.

The test manual provides clear and detailed recommendations for test administration and hand scoring of test responses. Experienced test administrators should have no difficulty setting up, administering, and scoring the Technician Electrical Test. Interpretation of test scores is likely to prove much more difficult. The only normative information provided in the test manual are the means, standard deviations, and percentile equivalents of observed scores for a sample of 70 "electrical maintenance applicants" (manual, p. 8). Unfortunately, the normative data are for an earlier version of the Technician Electrical Test (Form A), rather than the present test (Form A2), which retained approximately 92% of the original items from the earlier form. From the information presented in the manual, it is impossible to determine the education, job experience, and demographic backgrounds of the 70 "electrical maintenance applicants" who were included in the norming and reliability studies. Therefore, it is impossible to determine whether the normative data presented in the manual are representative of what might be observed in any particular setting. Normative information for various demographic groups (e.g., sex, race, geographic region, education, etc.) and various job levels or types (e.g., recent graduates, entry-level trainees, apprentices, journey-level trades workers, different industries, etc.) would also be helpful. Users of this test are urged to collect evidence supporting the test's reliability and validity in the setting in which it is to be used.

In summary, the Technician Electrical Test—Form A2 was carefully developed based on an analysis of the electrical knowledge needed in the performance of jobs that involve electrical work. The factual nature of the items and their representativeness in sampling a well-defined knowledge domain provide support for the test's content validity. Much more detailed information is needed about the norming sample and the population of examinees for whom the test is appropriate to guide test users in selecting this test and evaluating test scores. Until additional psychometric evidence is made available, use of the Technician Electrical Test—Form A2 can only be recommended for applications in which psychometric issues are secondary, such as in facilitating the identification of training needs or training content. Additional research, either done locally by test users or by the test authors, is needed to support the test's use in employment decision making.

REVIEWER'S REFERENCE

Hunter, J. E. (1983). A causal analysis of cognitive ability, job knowledge, job performance, and supervisory ratings. In F. Landy, S. Zedeck, & J. Cleveland (Eds.), *Performance measurement and theory* (pp. 257–275). Hillsdale, NJ: Lawrence Erlbaum.

[319]

Technician Mechanical Test—Form A2.

Purpose: Measures "knowledge and skill in the mechanical area."

Population: Mechanical workers and applicants for mechanical jobs.

Publication Dates: 1987–1994.

Scores: Total score only.

Administration: Group.

Price Data, 1993: $498 per 10 reusable test booklets, administration manual ('94, 16 pages), scoring key, and 100 blank answer sheets.

Time: (120) minutes.

Author: Roland T. Ramsay.

Publisher: Ramsay Corporation.

Review of the Technician Mechanical Test—Form A2 by WILLIAM M. VERDI, Manager, Employment Testing & Validation, Long Island Rail Road, Middle Village, NY:

The Technician Mechanical Test—Form A2 is intended to measure the mechanical knowledge and skill of a trained or experienced individual. It is not intended to measure someone's mechanical ability and it is not intended to be taken by an inexperienced or naive individual with regard to mechanical ability.

It measures knowledge of hydraulics, pneumatics, print reading, welding, power transmissions, lubrication, pumps, piping, light rigging, and mechanical mainte-nance. The test is untimed, but the publisher suggests a 2-hour maximum to answer the 124 questions. There are no subscores. The only score is based upon the total number of items answered correctly. Perusing the items shows that the publisher has taken great care to cover many aspects of the mechanical realm. Unfortunately, the test falls short on several basic levels and this could be problematic for some users.

Content validation procedures have been used. This means that instead of showing a relationship between test scores and some indicator of mechanical knowledge or skill, the publisher opted to show that the test's content is representative of the mechanical knowledge content area. An interrater agreement of .76 was shown with six subject matter experts. No construct or criterion validation efforts have been reported. This makes it difficult for a personnel manager to utilize the test for skills assessment and/ or development or for selection purposes.

Reliability information on the Technician Mechanical Test was described as "excellent" by the test manual. But the manual failed to specify what type of reliability indicator was computed. Also missing was a description of the sample used and its relevancy or characteristics. Such frequent gaps in information leave the user continually wanting more relevant information. For a less experienced user such information would become critical.

Item difficulty information, reliability, content valid-ity, and normative data are all reported for Form A. Form A2 is currently being reviewed. The publisher states that 90% of Form A2's content comes from Form A and the difference stems from modifications made based upon the item difficulty information collected for Form A. It would have been nice to see data collected examining how the other 10% in Form A2 helps the test assess mechanical knowledge and skills.

Researchers, personnel managers, and hiring departments will have difficulty using this test with-out conducting their own criterion validation study. A criterion validation study helps provide informa-tion that demonstrates the relationship between test performance and a job/performance related criteria. Unfortunately, no criterion-related validity informa-tion or normative data are provided. With the ever-growing need to demonstrate that a test is valid and fair to all ethnic, racial, and gender groups, potential users will have to answer the validity and fairness questions on their own. Subgroup scores or validity information are not provided.

Once additional normative and validity data are collected for Form A2 then a better assessment of the test's usefulness and predictive ability can be made. Right now a definitive statement regarding the test's usefulness cannot be made. Currently, potential users should have their own mechanical experts examine the test's content for applicability and use it only after they have conducted a proper validation effort. Given the price of the test and its lack of basic validity and normative information, potential users should use this test with caution.

[320]
Tennessee Self-Concept Scale, Second Edition.

Purpose: Designed as a multidimensional self-concept assessment instrument.
Population: Ages 7 to 90.
Publication Dates: 1964–1996.
Acronym: TSCS: 2.
Scores, 15: Validity scores (Inconsistent Responding, Self-Criticism, Faking Good, Response Distribution); Summary scores (Total Self-Concept, Conflict); Self-Concept scales (Physical, Moral, Personal, Family, Social, Academic Work); Supplementary scores (Identity, Satis-faction, Behavior).
Administration: Group.
Price Data, 1998: $130 per kit including 20 AutoScore™ Answer Forms (10 for Adults; 10 for Chil-dren), manual, and 4 WPS TEST REPORT prepaid mail-in answer sheets (for computer scoring/interpreta-tion); $32.50 per 20 AutoScore™ Answer Forms; $52.50 per manual; $13.50 per mail-in answer sheets; $225 per microcomputer disk (IBM) (25 uses; 3.5-inch); $15 per 100 TSCS microcomputer answer sheets; $9.50 fax scor-ing charge.
Time: (10–20) minutes.
Comments: Self-administered; WPS TEST REPORT Service available for computerized scoring and test inter-pretation.
Authors: W. H. Fitts and W. L. Warren.
Publisher: Western Psychological Services.
  a) TSCS:2 ADULT FORM.
  Population: Ages 13 and older.
  b) TSCS:2 CHILD FORM.
  Population: Ages 7–14.

c) TSCS:2 SHORT FORM.

Population: Adults (13 and older); child (7–14).

Comments: The Short Form consists of the first 20 items on the adult and child forms.

Cross References: See T4:2723 (32 references); for reviews by Francis X. Archambault, Jr. and E. Thomas Dowd, see 11:424 (89 references); see also 9:1236 (60 references); T3:2413 (120 references); 8:693 (384 references), and T2:1415 (80 references); for reviews by Peter M. Bentler and Richard M. Suinn and an excerpted review by John O. Crites of an earlier edition, see 7:151 (88 references); see also P:266 (30 references).

TEST REFERENCES

1. Buri, J. R., Louiselle, P. A., Misukanis, T. M., & Mueller, R. A. (1988). Effects of parental authoritarianism and authoritativeness on self-esteem. *Personality and Social Psychology Bulletin, 14,* 271–282.
2. Livneh, H. (1988). Assessing outcome criteria in rehabilitation: A multicomponent approach. *Rehabilitation Counseling Bulletin, 32,* 72–94.
3. Peterson, A. V., & Peppas, G. J. (1988). Trained peer helpers facilitate student adjustment in an overseas school. *The School Counselor, 36,* 67–73.
4. Earls, C. M., & David, H. (1989). A psychosocial study of male prostitution. *Archives of Sexual Behavior, 18,* 401–419.
5. Janos, P. M., Robinson, N. M., & Lunneborg, C. E. (1989). Markedly early entrance to college: A multi-year comparative study of academic performance and psychological adjustment. *Journal of Higher Education, 60,* 495–518.
6. Nelson, R., & Lignugaris/Kraft, B. (1989). Postsecondary education for students with learning disabilities. *Exceptional Children, 56,* 246–265.
7. Walsh, J. A., Wilson, G. L., & McLellarn, R. W. (1989). A confirmatory factor analysis of the Tennessee Self-Concept Scale. *Criminal Justice and Behavior, 15,* 465–472.
8. Renneberg, B., Goldstein, A. J., Phillips, D., & Chambless, D. L. (1990). Intensive behavioral group treatment of avoidant personality disorder. *Behavior Therapy, 21,* 363–377.
9. Dadds, M., Smith, M., Webber, Y., & Robinson, A. (1991). An exploration of family and individual profiles following father-daughter incest. *Child Abuse & Neglect, 15,* 575–586.
10. Magill-Evans, J. E., & Restall, G. (1991). Self-esteem of persons with cerebral palsy: From adolescence to adulthood. *The American Journal of Occupational Therapy, 45,* 819–825.
11. Norvell, N., Martin, D., & Salamon, A. (1991). Psychological and physiological benefits of passive and aerobic exercise in sedentary middle-aged women. *The Journal of Nervous and Mental Disease, 179,* 573–574.
12. Raskin, R., Novacek, J., & Hogan, R. (1991). Narcissism, self-esteem and defensive self-enhancement. *Journal of Personality, 59,* 19–38.
13. Schultz, N. C., Schultz, C. L., & Olson, D. H. (1991). Couple strengths and stressors in complex and simple stepfamilies in Australia. *Journal of Marriage and the Family, 53,* 555–564.
14. Beaty, L. A. (1992). Adolescent self-perception as a function of vision loss. *Adolescence, 27,* 707–714.
15. Buri, J. R., Murphy, P., Richtsmeier, L. M., & Komar, K. K. (1992). Stability of parental nurturance as a salient predictor of self-esteem. *Psychological Reports, 71,* 535–543.
16. Holdnack, J. A. (1992). The long-term effects of parental divorce on family relationships and the effects on adult children's self-concept. *Journal of Divorce & Remarriage, 18*(3/4), 137–155.
17. Obiakor, F. E. (1992). Self-concept of African-American students: An operational model for special education. *Exceptional Children, 59,* 160–167.
18. Super, J. T., & Block, J. R. (1992). Self-concept and need for achievement of men with physical disabilities. *The Journal of General Psychology, 119,* 73–80.
19. Bat-Chava, Y. (1993). Antecedents of self-esteem in deaf people: A meta-analytic review. *Rehabilitation Psychology, 38,* 221–234.
20. Garzarelli, P., Everhart, B., & Lester, D. (1993). Self-concept and academic performance in gifted and academically weak students. *Adolescence, 28,* 235-237.
21. LaConte, M. A., Straw, D., & Dunn, I. (1993). The effects of a rational-emotive affective education program for high-risk middle school students. *Psychology in the Schools, 30,* 274–281.
22. Möller, A. T., Kotzè, H. F., & Sieberhagen, K. J. (1993). Comparison of the effects of auditory subliminal stimulation and rational-emotive therapy, separately and combined, on self-concept. *Psychological Reports, 72,* 131–145.
23. Ortiz, L. P. A., & Farrell, M. P. (1993). Father's unemployment and adolescent's self concept. *Adolescence, 28,* 937-949.
24. Silliman, M. E. (1993). Self-esteem and locus of control of women who report sexual-abuse during childhood. *Psychological Reports, 72,* 1294.
25. Waterman, J., & Lusk, R. (1993). Psychological testing in evaluation of child sexual abuse. *Child Abuse & Neglect, 17,* 145-159.
26. Bracken, B. A., & Mills, B. C. (1994). School counselors' assessment of self-concept: A comprehensive review of 10 instruments. *The School Counselor, 42,* 14–31.
27. Christensen, M. J., Brayden, R. M., Dietrich, M. S., McLaughlin, F. J., & Sherrod, K. B. (1994). The prospective assessment of self-concept in neglectful and physically abusive low income mothers. *Child Abuse & Neglect, 18,* 225-232.
28. Finkenberg, M. E., Shows, D., & Dinucci, J. M. (1994). Participation in adventure-based activities and self-concepts of college men and women. *Perceptual and Motor Skills, 78,* 1119-1122.
29. Gabriel, M. T., Critelli, J. W., & Ee, J. S. (1994). Narcissistic illusions in self-evaluations of intelligence and attractiveness. *Journal of Personality, 62,* 143–155.
30. Leddy, M. H., Lambert, M. J., & Ogles, B. M. (1994). Psychological consequences of athletic injury among high-level competitors. *Research Quarterly for Exercise and Sport, 65,* 347–354.
31. Lewandowski, L., & Arcangelo, K. C. (1994). The social adjustment and self-concept of adults with learning disabilities. *Journal of Learning Disabilities, 27,* 598–605.
32. Post, P., & McCoard, D. (1994). Needs and self-concept of runaway adolescent. *The School Counselor, 41,* 212–219.
33. Salokun, S. O. (1994). Positive change in self-concept as a function of improved performance in sports. *Perceptual and Motor Skills, 78,* 752-754.
34. Conte, H. R., Plutchik, R., Picard, S., Clutz, K., & Karasu, T. B. (1995). Development of a self-report conflict scale. *Journal of Personality Assessment, 64,* 168-184.
35. Kanakis, D. M., & Thelen, M. H. (1995). Parental variables associated with bulimia nervosa. *Addictive Behaviors, 20,* 491–500.
36. Tam, A. S. F., & Watkins, D. (1995). Towards a hierarchical model of self-concept for Hong Kong Chinese adults with physical disabilities. *International Journal of Psychology, 30,* 1–17.
37. Worling, J. R. (1995). Adolescent sibling-incest offenders: Differences in family and individual functioning when compared to adolescent nonsibling sex offenders. *Child Abuse & Neglect, 19,* 633–643.
38. Compton, W. C., Smith, M. L., Cornish, K. A., & Qualls, D. L. (1996). Factor structure of mental health measures. *Journal of Personality and Social Psychology, 71,* 406–413.
39. Onyeneje, E. C., & Eyo, I. E. (1996). Custodial status and self-concepts of Nigerian inmates remanded to prison custody. *Perceptual and Motor Skills, 82,* 209–210.
40. Guanipa, C., Talley, W., & Rapagna, S. (1997). Enhancing Latin American women's self-concept: A group intervention. *International Journal of Group Psychotherapy, 47,* 355–372.
41. Levy-Shiff, R., Zoran, N., & Shulman, S. (1997). International and domestic adoption: Child, parents, and family adjustment. *International Journal of Behavioral Development, 20,* 109–129.

Review of the Tennessee Self-Concept Scale, Second Edition by RIC BROWN, Associate Vice President, Research and Graduate Studies, California State University, Sacramento, Sacramento, CA:

For many years, the "Tennessee" has been synonymous with the measurement of self-concept. Published in the 1960s, the Tennessee Self-Concept Scale (TSCS) was originally developed to provide a multidimensional description of self-concept. The manual for the second edition states that by the time the 1988 edition of the TSCS was published, over 200 references annually could be found in publications in education, psychology, and the social sciences. Self-concept is defined by the authors as "who am I," versus self-esteem, which is defined as "how do I feel about myself." The authors report that the two constructs are more highly correlated at older ages.

There are two forms of the TSCS-2: an 82-item Adult form and a 76-item Child form. Respondents rate the items on a 5-point scale from *always false* to *always true*. The measure takes 10 to 20 minutes to complete, either in a group or individual settings. The TSCS-2 has been streamlined to 15 scales, with 13 of the 34 scales from the 1988 edition retained. New scales for Faking Good and Academic/Work self-concept have been added. A validity score is also provided to check social desirability, and there is a 20-item short form with only a total score calculated. Equivalence studies for the two versions are provided; thus, existing literature can be utilized in support of the current scales.

The manual that accompanies the test is very complete including sections on development, administration, scoring, interpretation, restandardization, and psychometric properties. The TSCS-2 can be scored by hand in 10 minutes and includes a profile sheet to graph results. For the computer-scored version, a test report is generated, which plots each scale in T scores and provides a 7-page, customized summary. The computer version can be sent for scoring via disk, mail, or fax.

A very clear and detailed chapter is provided for interpretation and application of the TSCS-2. Each individual scale is explained with examples and a variety of profile patterns are discussed. Norm tables are provided for ages 7 through 90.

Reliability has been estimated using Cronbach's alpha with internal consistencies ranging from a low of .73 on the Social Self-Concept scale to a high of .93 on Total Self-Concept. Test-retest reliability (over a period of 1 to 2 weeks) for both the Adult and Child Forms are slightly lower, with ranges from .47 to .82 for the Adult form, and .55 to .83 on the Child form. An extensive section of the manual provides adequate evidence of the construct validity in the form of principal components analysis. Concurrent validity information shows acceptable levels of correlations of the TSCS with other psychological measures. As would be expected with any measure of self-concept, these correlations are low to moderate.

As a measure of self-concept the TSCS-2 probably has no equal. It is a well-developed scale with much data to support its use. As with all measures of constructs that are ambiguous in definition, it should be recognized that the measurement of self-concept is tenuous at best. However, a researcher using the Tennessee Self-Concept Scale will maximize chances to find relationships between self-concept and other constructs of interest.

Review of the Tennessee Self-Concept Scale, Second Edition by JOHN HATTIE, Chair, Educational Research Methodology, University of North Carolina at Greensboro, Greensboro, NC:

The Tennessee Self-Concept Scale (TSCS) was one of the first scales offering a broad multidimensional set of self-concept dimensions. The present (2nd) edition includes a Child (76 items) and Adult

form (82 items) based on six substantive scales: Physical, Moral, Personal, Family, Social, and a new Academic/Work scale. These six substantive dimensions can be grouped into a Total score, and a Conflict score (the degree to which the person has a "balanced self-view" and thus is not in conflict). The first 20 items can be used as a short form (which correlates >.90 with the longer version). Within each scale the items are grouped into Identity ("Who am I"), Satisfaction ("I am fine just the way I am"), and Behavior ("This is how I act") domains. There are also four validity scores: Inconsistent Responding compares responses to nine pairs of similarly worded items, Self-Criticism relates to eight negatively worded and mildly derogatory items, Faking Good is based on seven desirable items (e.g., "I feel good most of the time"), and response distribution is the number of extreme responses (i.e., 1s and 5s). As each substantive scale includes three types of items, there are also three supplementary scores: Identity, Satisfaction, and Behavior. The total number of scores from the TSCS is a marked reduction from the 34 scores obtainable from the previous edition. Changes from the previous version include dropping some scales (e.g., Psychopathology, General Maladjustment), reducing the number of items (100 to 80), including a Child (7–14 years) and Adult version (13 to 90 years), renorming using 1,944 adults and 1,396 children, and providing substantially improved guidance for interpreting the scores. It is claimed that there are no sex, ethnic, education, or socioeconomic differences in the means, although the scores increase with age (with a marked changing occurring at age 18; hence the Adult and Child versions). The estimates of reliability (both internal and test-retest) are mostly in an acceptable range and thus the standard errors are low (T-scores approximately 4–6 points).

The validity information is primarily based on the accumulated studies from previous versions. Within each scale of the second edition, a principal component solution clearly indicates two factors based on the positively and negatively worded items. The manual then presents factor analyses of each scale separated by the positive and negative items. There is evidence of a single factor for positive and for negative Academic and Family in the Child form, and Physical, Moral, Family, and Academic in the Adult form, but less clear factorial distinctiveness for the remaining scales. My own maximum likelihood solution indicates a single factor underlying the six substantive scales (with 60% of the variance explained). The separation into positively and negatively worded items is troublesome, as it is not clear whether this is substantively defensible or the consequences of linguistic differences—irrelevant method effects. Although all tables in the manual are based on separating the positive and negative items, the correlations between the positive and negative items within each scale are not provided.

This test will retain its popularity, especially because this new edition removes the more complicated scoring methods, simplifies the scales, and provides excellent interpretative resources. It is not as encompassing as the Marsh Self-Description Questionnaire (SDQ; 280) battery, and the manual could include more information on construct validity. The problems relating to the positive and negative factors very much are in need of further research.

[321]

Test of Academic Achievement Skills—Reading, Arithmetic, Spelling, and Listening Comprehension.

Purpose: Measures a child's reading, arithmetic, spelling, and listening comprehension skills.
Population: Ages 4–0 to 12–0.
Publication Date: 1989.
Scores, 6: Spelling, Total Reading (Letter/Word Identification, Listening Comprehension, Total), Arithmetic, Total.
Administration: Individual.
Price Data, 1990: $46.95 per complete kit including 25 test booklets, manual (74 pages), and card; $23.95 per 25 test booklets; $16.95 per manual; $8.95 per card; $17.95 per specimen set including manual and one test booklet.
Time: (15–25) minutes.
Author: Morrison F. Gardner.
Publisher: Psychological & Educational Publications, Inc.

Review of the Test of Academic Achievement Skills—Reading, Arithmetic, Spelling, and Listening Comprehension by C. DALE CARPENTER, Professor of Special Education, Western Carolina University, Cullowhee, NC:

The Test of Academic Achievement Skills—Reading, Arithmetic, Spelling, and Listening Comprehension (TAAS-RAS) is a simple academic achievement screening instrument measuring basic skills for children ages 4 to 12. It is meant to be individually administered and the directions and materials are straightforward. This is an untimed instrument.

The Spelling subtest uses a dictation format and appears to use more regular than irregular words in the way they are spelled. Reading actually consists of two subtests: Letter/Word Identification and Listening Comprehension. The first uses the standard format of requiring students to read a graded word list whereas Listening Comprehension consists of the examiner reading a short passage to the student and orally asking five–six questions about the passage. The 6–12-year-old Arithmetic subtest is a computational test. Subtests for younger children down to the age of 4 are slightly different, including some number identification, number comparison, and simple computational problems.

TECHNICAL CHARACTERISTICS. The test was standardized on 899 children ages 4 through 11. Besides being approximately equally divided between males and females, no other information is available. The only estimate of reliability provided is internal consistency calculated using the Kuder-Richardson 20 formula. Median coefficients ranged from .72 for Listening Comprehension to .93 for Reading Word Identification. Criterion-related validity is reported by showing correlations between TAAS scores and scores on such tests as the Test of Kindergarten/First Grade Readiness Skills (328) and subtests of the Wide-Range Achievement Test—Revised (10:389) and the Wechsler Intelligence Scale for Children—Revised (9:1351) among others. Correlations are generally low. Higher correlation coefficients were reported when correlating TAAS scores with the Test of Auditory-Perceptual Skills (324).

To determine content validity, items on each subtest must be examined. The format of the Spelling subtest is preferred to multiple-choice tests. However, the list of words seems heavily weighted toward phonetically regular words and no explanation of the source of the word list is provided except to say that all items were submitted by teachers and went through piloting and item analysis. For the reading words used, there is also no more elaboration on source of list. Although the Listening Comprehension subtest format has an advantage of tapping comprehension not confounded by reading ability, the questions are limited. There are no main idea questions or questions requiring inferences or questions about vocabulary. Furthermore, neither of the Reading subtests measures reading comprehension, considered by many experts to be the most important component of reading. Likewise, the Arithmetic subtest does not measure mathematical reasoning. Content validity for the TAAS lacks a comprehensive approach to academic achievement.

SUMMARY. The Test of Academic Achievement Skills is at best a screening option for children aged 4 through 12. Lacking acceptable technical properties and offering nothing that other instruments do not have, there appears little reason to choose this instrument. It is much like the Wide Range Achievement Test (WRAT3; 12:414), which is more popular and based on a larger standardization sample. More comprehensive academic achievement tests such as the Wechsler Individual Achievement Test (359), Woodcock-Johnson Psycho-Educational Battery (12:415), and the Kaufman Test of Educational Achievement (T4:1348) appear to be better choices.

Review of the Test of Academic Achievement Skills—Reading, Arithmetic, Spelling, and Listening Comprehension by STEVE GRAHAM, Professor of Special Education, University of Maryland, College Park, MD:

The Test of Academic Achievement Skills—Reading, Arithmetic, Spelling, and Listening Comprehension (TAAS-RAS) is designed to assess preschool to preteen children's mastery of basic academic skills. The instrument provides professional examiners, such as psychologists, teachers, therapists, and counselors, information about a child's academic achievement, strengths, and weaknesses in reading, spelling, and arithmetic. According to the author, results from the test can be used to determine a child's readiness for school, promotion to the next grade, or need for remedial assistance.

The test is given individually and takes 30 minutes or less to administer. Reading achievement is assessed by examining the child's ability to name letters and words presented on a laminated card (Letter/Word Identification score) and answer questions about stories read aloud by the examiner (Listening Comprehension score). A child's performance on the Letter/Word Identification and Listening Comprehension scales are used to calculate a Total Reading score. Spelling is assessed by asking the child to write letters and words presented orally by the examiner. Arithmetic is measured by assessing the child's skill in naming written numbers, identifying the larger or smaller of two numbers, determining the number before or after a specific number, calculating simple oral word problems, and answering a variety of computational problems (e.g., 43 - 14 = ____).

The TAAS-RAS is easy to administer and score. A minor inconsistency between the manual and the test

booklet, however, may cause some confusion concerning the administration of the easiest items in each domain to students who are 6 years old. The manual indicates that the easiest items, such as saying or writing letters, are administered to 4- and 5-year-olds, whereas the test booklet indicates that they are to be given to children 4 to 6 years of age.

Raw scores obtained for each academic domain are converted to scaled scores, percentile ranks, and age-equivalent scores. The sum of the scaled scores is used to obtain a percentile rank and an academic quotientfor the test as a whole. A median academic age is obtained by computing the average between the next to highest and next to lowest age-equivalent scores on the four subtests. The author should be commended for providing appropriate cautions in the text of the manual on the use of age-equivalent scores. Recommendations or procedures for computing confidence intervals, however, are notably absent. The standard error of measurement for each measure by age is provided in the test manual.

One significant drawback to the TAAS-RAS is that the test items do not adequately represent the knowledge, behaviors, and skills involved in reading, spelling, and arithmetic. To specify the content of these domains, preschool through sixth-grade teachers were asked to indicate what children were expected to learn in each area. Unfortunately, this approach resulted in a very narrow conceptualization of the content underlying each domain. In the area of Reading, for example, phonological awareness, word attack skills, fluency, and reading comprehension are not assessed.

Inadequate procedures were also used in norming the TAAS-RAS. The instrument was standardized on a small sample of 899 students, attending just nine schools. No information on the race, ethnicity, SES, or locale of the students in the normative sample is provided. Purposefully excluded from the normative sample were children with learning problems and other special needs. This is a curious omission, as the test is most likely to be used with children experiencing problems in school.

The author of the TAAS-RAS does not present a strong or convincing case regarding the reliability and validity of the instrument. Only one measure of reliability was established. The Kuder-Richardson 20 formula was used to estimate the internal consistency of the various subtests at ages 4 through 11. On the basis of this single measure, it does not appear that the Listening Comprehension or Arithmetic subtests are reliable enough to be used to make decisions about individual students (all but one reliability estimate was below .90). The Spelling and Word Recognition subtests, however, were reliable enough to warrant individual decision making for most children ages 7 to 11 (all but one reliability estimate was greater than or equal to .90).

Similarly, information on the validity of the instrument is quite meager. For students in the normative sample, correlations between subtests at each age level were computed, resulting in low to moderate associations—suggesting that each subtest assesses a unique aspect of academic achievement. Validity was further evaluated by examining the relationship between scores on the TAAS-RAS and other measures of academic achievement. Performance on the TAAS-RAS was only moderately correlated to performance on the Test of Kindergarten/First Grade Readiness Skills (328) and the Wide Range Achievement Test—Revised (10:389). Despite the claim by the author that the test can be used to make decisions about readiness for school or promotion to the next grade, data on the predictive validity of the test is conspicuously absent.

It should be noted that several of the stories for the Listening Comprehension subtest present scenarios that provide a poor match to the backgrounds of many school-age children. One story, for instance, involves a vacation ending with a visit with the family friend, the senator! Furthermore, all of the stories included in this subtest are stilted and uninteresting, and the comprehension questions students are asked focus exclusively on the recall of factual information (e.g., "What color is the cat?").

In summary, the TAAS-RAS should not be used to make decisions about a child's readiness for school or promotion, as there is currently no evidence on the predictive validity of the instrument. The test also provides limited information on a child's academic achievement and strengths and weaknesses, as it does not sample adequately the domains of reading, spelling, or arithmetic.

[322]
Test of Academic Performance.

Purpose: Developed to assess achievement in four curriculum areas: Mathematics, Spelling, Reading, and Writing.
Population: Grades K–12.
Publication Date: 1989.
Acronym: TOAP.
Scores, 6: Basic subtests (Mathematics, Spelling, Reading Recognition, Reading Comprehension), Optional subtests (Written Composition, Copying Rate).

Administration: Individual and group.
Price Data, 1997: $82 per complete set including examiner's manual (182 pages), 25 student response forms, 25 record forms, and package of four reading stimulus cards.
Time: 15(20) minutes for Mathematics subtest; 7.5(12.5) minutes for Spelling subtest; 7.5(12.5) minutes for Reading Recognition subtest; 20(25) minutes for Reading Comprehension subtest; 10(15) minutes for Written Composition subtest; 1(6) minutes for Copying Rate subtest.
Authors: Wayne Adams, David Sheslow, and Lynn Erb.
Publisher: The Psychological Corporation.

Review of the Test of Academic Performance by STEVE GRAHAM, *Professor of Special Education, University of Maryland, College Park, MD:*

The Test of Academic Performance (TOAP) is designed to provide an estimate of a child's academic achievement, identify above-average or below-average performance, and measure changes in performance over time. The instrument samples content in reading, writing, and mathematics from kindergarten to grade 8. The test can be administered, however, to students in grades 9 through 12, as norms are also provided for high school students. Although the authors do not specifically indicate for whom the test is designed or the particular situations where it should be applied, it is most likely to be used with children experiencing difficulty in school, especially those being tested for special education placement or receiving special education services.

The TOAP includes a battery of six subtests. The two reading subtests, Reading Recognition and Reading Comprehension, are given individually and measure, respectively, the ability to name words presented on a laminated card and answer questions about stories read silently. The other four subtests are administered either individually or in a group. The Mathematics subtest assesses the ability to answer increasingly difficult computation problems during a set period of time. The Spelling subtest measures the ability to write correctly words presented orally by the examiner. Written Composition, an optional subtest for children age 8 and above, evaluates the quality of a composition produced during a 10-minute period. Copying Rate, another optional subtest for kindergarten through grade 8, assesses the number of words the child copies in 1 minute.

It should be noted the TOAP is a power or speed test—all of the subtests involve completing tasks under timed conditions. The time requirements for the Spelling, Reading Recognition, and Reading Comprehension subtests require extra vigilance on the part of the examiner, as items on each must be completed in a specific period of time. On the Reading Comprehension subtest, for example, the child has 30 seconds to answer each comprehension question posed by the examiner.

According to the authors, a primary goal in designing the TOAP was to develop an instrument that could be administered quickly and easily. Although the first part of this goal was actualized, the second part was not. The full test takes about 45 minutes to an hour to give, and the administration time can be reduced by 12 to 15 minutes if the two optional subtests are not included. Nevertheless, examiners using the test for the first time are likely to be frustrated by the complexity of the administration rules, including ceiling criteria that change from subtest to subtest as well as time limits that vary depending upon the age of the child and the subtest under consideration.

Scoring procedures for Mathematics and Reading Comprehension are also unnecessarily complicated, as two different methods for scoring each subtest are provided. Written Composition is the most challenging subtest to score, however, requiring the examiner to count the number of words produced and rate on a 3-point scale three attributes of both form and content. Although the manual contains practice exercises for scoring six compositions, some examiners may require more practice and guidance in order to use the two rating scales reliably and validly. Furthermore, the rationale underlying the procedures for scoring the Copying Rate subtest are unclear. The examiner is directed to count the number of words copied, scoring as correct any word in which half of the letters were copied. A more precise measure would simply be to count the number of letters copied.

With the exception of the two optional subtests, raw scores are converted to scaled scores, standard scores, percentiles, and grade-equivalent scores. Confidence intervals are established for either standard scores or percentiles. Norms for both age and grade are included in the manual. The authors are to be commended for providing appropriate cautions on the interpretation of the results from the overall test and on specific types of scores.

For the two optional subtests, Written Composition and Copying Rate, raw scores are converted to an index that shows a child's standing (high, medium, or low) at a particular grade level. More traditional indices were not developed for these two subtests, because there was considerable overlap of score ranges between grade levels for students participating in the standardization process.

In constructing the TOAP, the authors indicated their goal was to construct a measure that would accurately match curricula in today's schools. At each grade level, they reportedly selected a small number of critical, instructional objectives from the broad range of possible objectives. One or more items for each of the selected objectives were then developed and field tested. Although the authors provide a detailed description on the methods used for field testing, it is not clear how instructional objectives at each grade level were selected. It is obvious, however, that the authors' goal of constructing a measure that would match today's curricula was only partially met. In the area of mathematics, for example, methods for computing various operations were emphasized, but the applications of these operations were not. Similarly, important aspects of reading such as phonological awareness, word attack skills, and fluency were not assessed.

The standardization sample was drawn from six school districts in six states, with at least one district in each major region of the United States. Approximately 300 students per grade were tested, except in grades 9 through 12 where number of students per grade averaged 99. With a few exceptions, the standardization sample was similar to national norms on sex, race, and residence. Children of Spanish origin appeared to be underrepresented in the standardization sample, whereas students from the South were overrepresented. Although mainstreamed students with disabilities were included in the testing, students in self-contained classes were not. This is an unfortunate omission, as the test is likely to be used with these students.

The authors of the TOAP do not present a strong or convincing case regarding the reliability or validity of the instrument. No reliability data were provided for the Copying Rate subtest. Test-retest reliability was established at only two grade levels for the other five tests, and neither the Mathematics or Written Composition subtests were reliable enough to be used to make decisions about individual students. Interrater reliability for scoring the Written Composition subtest was only .76. Finally, the authors erroneously used internal consistency coefficients as a measure of reliability for the four basic subtests. Internal consistency coefficients produce artificially high estimates when used with speeded tests.

Data on the validity of the instrument were limited to intercorrelations between the subtests, and correlations between grade level items in Mathematics and Spelling and corresponding performance on the complete subtest. Although the data from these analyses were consistent with the conceptual framework underlying the instrument, additional research is clearly needed.

In summary, the TOAP provides a quick, but not necessarily easy-to-administer estimate of a child's academic achievement. At the present time, the instrument appears to be best suited for experimental work. Further refinement as well as additional evidence supporting the reliability and validity of the test are needed before the TOAP can be recommended as an instrument for estimating a child's academic performance or monitoring changes in achievement.

Review of the Test of Academic Performance by CLEBORNE D. MADDUX, Professor of Special Education and Educational Technology, University of Nevada, Reno, NV:

The Test of Academic Performance (TOAP) is yet another attempt to provide a quick achievement test of basic academic subjects to compete with the Wide Range Achievement Test Revision 3 (WRAT3; Wilkinson, 1993; 12:414). The TOAP includes subtests in similar format to the format of the WRAT3 in Mathematics, Spelling, and Reading Recognition. Unlike the WRAT3, however, the test also includes a Reading Comprehension subtest and two supplementary subtests (Written Composition and Copying Rate). Raw scores can be converted to scaled scores, standard scores (based on age or grade), percentile ranks, and grade equivalents. Instructions for calculating confidence intervals for standard scores are included.

The manual authors suggest the test is useful only for screening. They further suggest the two reading subtests must be administered individually, and the other four may be used in a group setting.

The test manual is lengthy and can be confusing due to separate sets of instructions in Mathematics and Spelling, depending on whether the examiner chooses to administer the entire subtests or use the basal/ceiling procedures. The manual contains guidelines for deciding when to choose each procedure, but novice examiners who are likely to use the test will find them vague and ambiguous on this topic. Making the decision calls for considerable judgment and expertise on the part of the examiner. It would have been advisable for the test authors to decide when each procedure was to be used and to offer hard and fast rules based on the child's age or grade.

All answers are found in the Examiner's Record Form, a separate booklet from the Student Response Form. The former is poorly designed and visually confusing because it employs very small print and a crowded, busy format. This separation means the two forms must be kept together to allow others both to see student responses and review results. This is a disadvantage, and the two forms could be consolidated if the subtest answers were moved to the Examiner's Manual.

MATHEMATICS. There are 45 arithmetic calculation items in this subtest. The majority are mechanical addition, subtraction, multiplication, or division algorithms. No discussion of the rationale for this algorithm approach to mathematics was found in the manual.

READING RECOGNITION. The Reading Recognition subtest includes 45 words that the student is asked to read aloud until four out of five in a single row are incorrectly pronounced.

READING COMPREHENSION. The Reading Comprehension subtest consists of seven short silent reading passages of increasing difficulty. Students are given 3 minutes to read each passage and four questions are asked about each passage after it is removed from sight. Entry point is determined by performance on the Reading Recognition subtest, and ceiling rules are provided on the Examiner's Record Form.

COPYING RATE. This optional subtest consists of two sentences for the student to copy. Printing or cursive is acceptable and the number of words correctly copied is the raw score. A word is considered correctly copied if more than half the letters are correct.

WRITTEN COMPOSITION. This optional subtest consists of asking examinees above second grade to write for 10 minutes after being asked to "Explain what is best and worst about a rainy day and why" (p. 14). A subjective scoring system requires the examiner to judge both content and form as low, middle, or high. A score for length is also calculated, and the three scores are aggregated to produce one score up to 18 points.

NORMATIVE DATA. The TOAP was normed in 1984 and 1985 on 3,216 students in six school districts in six states. After gathering the sample and recording grade, age, sex, race, Spanish origin, and region, 1980 U.S. Census data were consulted and the sample was weighted "to approximate even more closely the observed percentages of the population represented by each of these demographic groups" (examiner's manual, p. 14). There was at least one school district from each of the four main geographic regions in the United States. Each school district contributed a class at each grade from kindergarten through eighth grade. Three hundred ninety-six students were in grades 9 through 12 but the authors give no information as to how these students were selected.

RELIABILITY. Test-retest reliability data are reported only for students in grades 3 and 7. Correlations between the two administrations 3 to 4 weeks apart range from .94 and .95 for grades 3 and 7 in Reading Recognition to .31 and .51 for grades 3 and 7 in Reading Comprehension. Test-retest correlations are poor, with only two of the six subtest administrations exceeding .90 at the third grade level, and only one exceeding .90 at the seventh grade level. Internal consistency of subtests are reported by age level and are unacceptably low when the short form of each subtest is administered. Internal consistencies are acceptable for complete Mathematics and Spelling subtests and for Reading Recognition, but are low for Reading Comprehension (.40 for age 5, and .75 for ages 14–18).

VALIDITY. The manual contains sketchy information related to face and content validity, stating only that all items "were either reviewed, revised, or written by teachers familiar both with the K–8 mathematics, reading, and language arts curricula and with standardized test development" (p. 81). A research study is referred to but no details or reference are provided.

Subtest intercorrelations at grades 1, 3, 5, and 7 are presented as evidence of construct validity. These vary in size but are all significant beyond the .001 level. No data or discussion of criterion-related or concurrent validity appear in the manual.

SUMMARY. The TOAP is a norm-referenced achievement test probably intended as an alternative to the WRAT3. The manual is confusing and poorly organized, and the student and examiner forms should be consolidated.

Authors of the TOAP are to be commended for attempting to measure Reading Comprehension in addition to simple word recognition skills. Internal consistency of this subtest indicates that further development is needed.

Information on reliability and validity is incomplete, but it appears that use of the short form of the various subtests is not supported.

The TOAP shows some potential, particularly with regard to utility as a screening instrument that includes a measure of Reading Comprehension. Further

development is needed, however, before the TOAP can be considered a serious competitor for the WRAT3.

REVIEWER'S REFERENCE

Wilkinson, G. S. (1993). The Wide Range Achievement Test 3. Wilmington, DE: Jastak Associates/Wide Range.

[323]
Test of Adolescent and Adult Language, Third Edition.

Purpose: Designed "(a) to identify adolescents and adults whose scores are significantly below those of their peers and who might need interventions designed to improve language proficiency; (b) to determine areas of relative strength and weakness across language abilities; (c) to document overall progress in language development as a consequence of intervention programs; and (d) to serve as a measure for research efforts designed to investigate language characteristics of adolescents and adults."

Population: Ages 12-0 to 24-11.

Publication Dates: 1980–1994.

Acronym: TOAL-3.

Scores, 8: 8 subtest scores (Listening/Vocabulary, Listening/Grammar, Speaking/Vocabulary, Speaking/Grammar, Reading/Vocabulary, Reading/Grammar, Writing/Vocabulary, Writing/Grammar); 10 composite scores (Listening, Speaking, Reading, Writing, Spoken Language, Written Language, Vocabulary, Grammar, Receptive Language, Expressive Language).

Administration: Individual in part.

Price Data, 1994: $114 per complete kit including 50 answer booklets, 10 test booklets, 50 summary/profile sheets, and examiner's manual ('94, 111 pages); $39 per 50 answer booklets; $24 per 10 test booklets; $19 per 50 summary/profile sheets; $36 per examiner's manual; $79 per Apple or IBM software scoring system; $89 per Macintosh software scoring system.

Time: (60–180) minutes.

Authors: Donald D. Hammill, Virginia L. Brown, Stephen C. Larsen, and J. Lee Wiederholt.

Publisher: PRO-ED, Inc.

Cross References: See T4:2738 (9 references); for reviews by Allen Jack Edwards and David A. Shapiro of an earlier edition, see 10:365; for a review by Robert T. Williams of an earlier edition, see 9:1243.

TEST REFERENCES

1. Caskey, W. E., & Franklin, L. D. (1986). The test of adolescent language (TOAL) and WISC-R IQ scores: A caveat. *Language, Speech, and Hearing Services in Schools, 17,* 307–311.
2. Catts, H. W., & Kamhi, A. G. (1986). The linguistic basis of reading disorders: Implications for the speech-language pathologist. *Language, Speech, and Hearing Services in Schools, 17,* 329–341.
3. Mack, A. E., & Warr-Leeper, G. A. (1992). Language abilities in boys with chronic behavior disorders. *Language, Speech, and Hearing Services in Schools, 23,* 214–223.
4. Scott, C. M., & Stokes, S. L. (1995). Measures of syntax in school-age children and adolescents. *Language, Speech, and Hearing Services in Schools, 26,* 309–319.
5. Sabers, D. L. (1996). By their tests we will know them. *Language, Speech, and Hearing Services in Schools, 27,* 102–108.
6. Wiig, E. H., Jones, S. S., & Wiig, E. D. (1996). Computer-based assessment of word knowledge in teens with learning disabilities. *Language, Speech, and Hearing Services in Schools, 27,* 21–28.

Review of the Test of Adolescent and Adult Language, Third Edition by JOHN MacDONALD, School Psychologist, North Kitsap School District, Kingston, WA:

The authors intend to assess semantic and syntactic understanding and production of spoken and written language. Phonology, morphology, pragmatics, and proxemics are excluded. Although the title includes "adult," norms only extend the usable age range to near 25. New norms were collected only for ages 18 to 25, and no items were revised.

Norms for the Test of Adolescent and Adult Language, Third Edition (TOAL-3) include data from 3,056 people, but most are from the TOAL and TOAL-2 norming. About 60% of the data for ages 12 to 18 were collected in 1980, the remainder in 1987. Norms for ages 18 to 25 were collected in 1993 from 587 people representative of the 1990 U.S. Census.

Scores on intellectual ability tests have risen since 1980. If a similar rise has occurred in traits measured by the TOAL-3, it will produce scores 5 points higher than tests normed in 1997. This is a bigger problem than it seems. If getting speech and language services depends on getting a score of 70 or below, examiners will miss 60% of eligible students using the TOAL-3 rather than a test with 1997 norms.

Subtests and composites are internally consistent (coefficient alpha median values .84 to .98), and have acceptable test-retest reliability (average between .80 and .96 for 2-week interval) and acceptable interrater agreement (.70 to .99).

On Listening and Reading items, examinees choose two correct answers from four alternatives—a novel format for many. The manual instructs examiners to ensure that examinees choose two alternatives. On Reading subtests the alternatives remain in plain sight, but for Listening tests the examinee must remember all alternatives and then choose two that mean the same.

Speaking and Writing subtests require examinees to produce products, and the manual provides scoring guides. Scoring is straightforward for the expressive grammar tests, but scoring expressive vocabulary tests is difficult. The examinee produces a sentence using the given word. Vague content is scored correct as long as the sentence is syntactically correct—"he improvised" is correct for "improvised" (p. 23). This seems to be tapping a superficial understanding of vocabulary.

Speaking/Grammar requires repeating sentences word-for-word. Does a low score indicate poor syntactic understanding or difficulty with verbal working memory?

The Speaking/Grammar subtest seems particularly prone to bias when testing minority dialects. The authors state that item difficulties are similar for members of different racial and gender groups, but this does not eliminate bias concerns completely. There may be regional dialects within ethnic groups that will lead to different scores. Unless a sentence is reproduced exactly as the examiner said it, the item is wrong, even if the response would be syntactically correct within that linguistic community.

Listening/Grammar requires an examinee to say which two of three sentences mean the same. It may measure syntactic understanding, but performance also seems to depend on short-term verbal memory.

The manual reports moderate correlations between TOAL subtests and similar measures. Listening/Vocabulary correlates .49 with the Peabody Picture Vocabulary Test (PPVT) and Reading/Vocabulary correlates .82 with Total Reading from the Comprehensive Tests of Basic Skills. The manual reports similar correlations with the Clinical Evaluation of Language Fundamentals, the Test of Written Language, the Fullerton Language Test for Adolescents, and the Screening Test of Adolescent Language.

Some relationships are surprising: The PPVT correlates more highly with Speaking/Vocabulary (.73) than Listening/Vocabulary (.49), a test with more similar content and format. The Test of Language Development—Intermediate Listening correlates more highly with TOAL Expressive (.75) than with TOAL Receptive (.62). Because these are all moderate and not differentiated, could TOAL subtests all be measuring general ability?

The manual reports only one study relating intellectual ability to TOAL performance. Correlations with the California Short-Form Test of Academic Aptitude ranged from .36 for Speaking/Grammar to .75 for Reading/Vocabulary and .79 with the General Language Quotient. Principal components analysis yielded a single factor. Given the high correlation between TOAL-3 performance and intellectual ability, it would be useful to know what information this test provides beyond intelligence in assessing language skills. If an intelligence test has already been done, why spend 100 minutes to give the TOAL-3?

The TOAL-3 correctly classifies 89% of 28 Language Learning Disabled (LLD) and 86% of 28 non-LLD students, but the manual does not report how the LLD group was identified. The manual reports lower TOLD-3 scores for learning disabled, mentally retarded, emotionally disturbed, poor reader, and juvenile delinquent samples. It is not surprising that these groups should obtain lower scores on the TOAL-3; they are likely to also score lower on tests of general ability. How do individual TOAL-3 subtests vary with different language problems? Surprisingly, poor readers did better on the TOAL-3 Reading quotient (87) than on Listening (81) or Writing (79).

The TOAL-3 has outdated norms, likely resulting in underidentification of students with language disorders. Norms currently extend only to age 25. The TOAL-3 is reliable, but what it measures is questionable: Is it language proficiency, intellectual ability, or verbal short-term memory? It does not assess phonology or pragmatics. It takes a long time to give for so little. A competent speech and language pathologist will get more useful information from informal conversation with the student.

Review of the Test of Adolescent and Adult Language, Third Edition by ROGER A. RICHARDS, Adjunct Professor of Communication, Bunker Hill Community College, Boston, MA, and Consultant, Massachusetts Department of Education, Malden, MA:

The latest edition of the Test of Adolescent and Adult Language (TOAL-3) is attractively presented, complete with an examiner's manual with impressive-looking tables; test booklet, answer booklet, record form; and software scoring and report system. Unfortunately, the test offers less than meets the eye.

The authors state that the most significant improvement of the third edition has been "extending the normative data upward from 18-0 years through 24-11 years of age" (p. vi).

The TOAL-3's most troubling deficiency is the lack of a sound theoretical base. The authors describe "The TOAL-3 Test Model" (p. 4) as a three-dimensional model of communication, which shows spoken and written communication, receptive and expressive systems, and semantics and syntax as linguistic features.

That is an interesting model but it does not quite fit what this test attempts to do. Its biggest shortcoming is that it yields two artificial constructs that do not correspond to anything in the real use of language: "Listening/Grammar" and "Reading/Grammar." What are they? What do we tell students we are doing in the subtests that bear these designations; that we are measuring how well you use grammar when you listen and read?

The manual gives the impression that the authors looked for interesting testing strategies and

then forced them to fit what was an inappropriate model to begin with.

The fuzziness of the theoretical underpinnings sets the tone for many other aspects of the test. The instructions for administration, spread over two chapters, are not well thought out. The administration is complicated at best. Because the test is partially an individual test and partially a group test, the techniques of both are combined.

The directions mix a script "[Say, 'I AM GOING TO SAY A WORD THAT RELATES TO TWO OF THE FOUR PICTURES']" (p. 15) with general suggestions "[Describe the format of the test]" (p. 15). The instructions are often vague; for example, "When administering to groups, testing is begun with Item 1 on every subtest and continued *until the examiner is relatively certain most of the examinees have reached a ceiling*" (p. 10, emphasis added). No guidance is offered as to how the examiner can divine that moment. The time required to give the test to a class of 25 students would be out of proportion to the value derived. If the TOAL-3 is to be accepted as a standardized instrument, the methods for administration must be uniform.

The authors use basals and ceilings in administering and scoring the test, but there is no reason for them with the written subtests, which are quite short. In an example in the manual, a test taker who completed all 35 items on Listening/Vocabulary answered 20 items correctly but through the application of basals and ceilings is awarded a score of 23. Such manipulation amounts to little more than a gimmick.

The treatment of norms is sketchy and the norms are of limited usefulness. The manual tells us that "TOAL-3 was normed on a sample of 3,056 persons residing in 26 states" (p. 47) over a period of 14 years. Half of the subjects were tested in 1980. The upward extension of the norms in 1993 was based on the testing of a mere 587 subjects in the 18-0 through 24-11 age group.

We discover the identity of school systems in which the normative testing was done only accidentally by reading the acknowledgments, where the school systems and individuals involved are thanked. But we have no idea how many students in any school system were tested, only that "the majority of standardization cases were obtained" from schools in Mobile, Alabama; Berthoud, Colorado; Hibbing, Minnesota; Kansas City, Missouri; Dover, Oklahoma; Moore, Oklahoma; Beaverton, Oregon; and Erie, Pennsylvania (p. vii)—hardly a cross section of the United States! The norms seem to have little relevance to students in big-city school systems. Because a high concentration of students with language deficiencies is to be found in the major urban centers, their exclusion from the norming of a test purporting to identify them is of concern.

By reporting correlations of item-difficulty statistics for different subgroups, the authors present convincing statistics to buttress their claim that the test is neither gender-biased nor race-biased. Whether or not these statistics would hold up in testing a more heterogeneous population should be investigated by the authors.

Although the manual consists of 104 pages, it does not tell us very much about some of the things we need to know. Information on item difficulties is missing—crucial data when basals and ceiling are used. And it has not been carefully edited. A thorough proofreading is needed to eliminate passages like the following:

> The examiner says a word and asks the person being tested to select from four pictures the *one* [emphasis added] that best goes with the stimulus word. For example, in response to hearing the word *palm*, he or she would select *two* [emphasis added] of the following pictures. (p. 5)

Ultimately, the test must stand or fall on the quality of the eight subtests. These are generally not of high quality.

SUBTEST 1: LISTENING/VOCABULARY. The examinee identifies two of four drawings which are "most representative" of a word spoken by the examiner. This subtest is of dubious validity, however, because of the poor quality of the items. The authors appear to have been too easily satisfied; a bit more rigor would have yielded more defensible items. A few drawings are difficult to identify. Some items are weak because the words used do not lend themselves to pictorial representation: *apprehend, rampant* as an adverb, *absorbed, bellows* as a verb, *bolster* as a verb. And a number of esoteric stimulus words seem not to tap general vocabulary but rather special kinds of experience, such as a *rampant*, an *arabesque* (two forms!), a *grapple*, a weaving *shuttle*, a *capital* as an architectural feature, and *tack* in equestrian and nautical contexts. In what is intended as a basic screening device to identify individuals with gross language deficiencies, these more esoteric items are inappropriate. It would be interesting to know the basis on which the words were selected.

SUBTEST 2: LISTENING/GRAMMAR. Identifying the two of three given sentences that

"mean almost the same thing" (p. 16) is a useful technique for assessing listening comprehension. But are there not other techniques that would assess different grammatical elements of speech?

A couple items are debatable in that no two of the sentences mean the same thing (e.g., Item 28. A. If we leave, Carolyn will return; B. We will leave when Carolyn returns; C. If Carolyn returns, we will leave. Item 35. A. It is the one we want if it is not put away; B. If it is the one we want, put it away; C. If it is not the one we want, do not put it away). (One suspects that the best students would have the most difficulty with these items.) Moreover, the subtleties involved require more deliberation than is possible in oral presentation.

SUBTEST 3: SPEAKING/VOCABULARY. Requiring a word to be used correctly in a sentence is a valid test of an individual's understanding of the word's meaning. However, the directions specify that the sentence must "use the word exactly as it is given" (p. 18). Many of the suggested unacceptable responses are rejected by the authors because of errors of form rather than meaning. For example, the response "I missed many episodes" (p. 18) is keyed as incorrect for the word *episode*.

SUBTEST 4: SPEAKING/GRAMMAR. Examinees are asked to repeat verbatim "grammatically correct sentences spoken by the examiner" (p. 20). The sentences are arranged in approximate order of length, from 7 words in Item 1 to 29 words in Item 30. This subtest appears to be a measure of short-term memory much more than of grammatical understanding. Its validity is therefore dubious. The scoring directions for this subtest unrealistically require the scorer to differentiate between "variations common to normal speech" (p. 21) and "local nonstandard dialect" (p. 21).

SUBTEST 5: READING/VOCABULARY. "The examinee silently reads three stimulus words, all of which are related to a common concept. Next, from four printed words, he or she selects the two words that are closely associated with the three stimulus words" (p. 6). This technique seems overly complex; in each item, the test-taker must deal with seven different words. The lack of knowledge of just one of them can make the correct answer impossible. A simpler, more direct measure of word comprehension is needed.

SUBTEST 6: READING/GRAMMAR. The same technique is used here as for the Listening/Grammar subtest, except that five choices are supplied instead of only three. The use of a single technique for both Reading/Grammar and Listening/Grammar implies that there is no difference between listening and reading and prevents the tapping of other elements of grammatical knowledge.

SUBTEST 7: WRITING/VOCABULARY. The same technique is used here as in Speaking/Vocabulary with the same resultant difficulties, except that the answer key is better.

SUBTEST 8: WRITING/GRAMMAR. Sentence combining in this subtest is appropriate for measuring grammatical understanding in an interesting format but is time-consuming and subjective.

Four different studies related to reliability are presented. The most convincing is the internal consistency reliability of the subtests and composite scores by age level; the results are primarily in the high .80s and .90s. Interscorer agreement statistics are promising, but they are based on only six scorings of 15 test booklets. Test-retest reliability coefficients range from the high .70s to .90s for two groups (twice at 2-week intervals), students at a parochial school and college students. A fourth study involved scoring the same test protocols with and without a few items added at the lower levels of the subtests and finding a high correlation between the two scores—which represented basically the same performance.

In a lengthy treatment of validity, the authors present a variety of statistical analyses, but as with the items in the test, they appear to have been too easily satisfied. Many of the tables raise more questions than they answer.

The Test of Adolescent and Adult Language must be considered a work in progress. Now in its third edition, it should be more of a finished product than it is. We can be reasonably confident that someone who does very well on the test has more highly developed language skills than someone who does poorly, but any conclusions beyond that would be problematic.

[324]
Test of Auditory-Perceptual Skills.

Purpose: "To measure a child's functioning in various areas of auditory perception."
Population: Ages 4–12.
Publication Date: 1985.
Acronym: TAPS.
Scores, 7: Auditory Number Memory, Auditory Sentence Memory, Auditory Word Memory, Auditory Interpretation of Directions, Auditory Word Discrimination, Auditory Processing (Thinking and Reasoning), Hyperactivity Index.

Administration: Individual.
Price Data, 1994: $69.50 per complete package including manual (79 pages) and 35 test booklets; $54.50 per 35 English test booklets; $39 per 25 Spanish test booklets; $16.95 per manual; $18.50 per specimen set including manual and sample form.
Foreign Language Edition: Spanish version available.
Time: (15–25) minutes.
Comments: The Hyperactivity Index is a parental questionnaire developed by C. Keith Connors.
Author: Morrison F. Gardner.
Publisher: Psychological and Educational Publications, Inc.

TEST REFERENCES

1. Jirsa, R. E. (1992). The utility of the P3 AERP in children with auditory processing disorders. *Journal of Speech and Hearing Research, 35,* 903–912.
2. McFadden, T. V. (1996). Creating language impairments in typically achieving children: The pitfalls of "normal" normative sampling. *Language, Speech, and Hearing Services in Schools, 27,* 3–9.

Review of the Test of Auditory-Perceptual Skills by ANNABEL J. COHEN, Associate Professor of Psychology, University of Prince Edward Island, Charlottetown, Prince Edward Island, Canada:

There are numerous tests of individual auditory skills (e.g., Cherry, 1980; Rosner & Simon, 1971). As an aid to zeroing in on a particular deficit, a battery of tests that taps various auditory skills within a short time period has practical advantages. As its title suggests, the Test of Auditory-Perceptual Skills (TAPS) by Morrison F. Gardner might serve such a purpose.

The TAPS was standardized on 808 children, 4–12 years of age, in the San Francisco Bay area. The published median raw subtest scores increase with age. Subtest scores are also presented scaled with a mean of 10 and standard deviation of 3. A finer gradation of scaled scores across ages is provided through interpolation, at 4-month intervals for ages 4 through 6 years and, at 6-month intervals for ages 7 through 9 years. An auditory quotient (AQ) based on the scaled subtest scores has a mean of 100 and standard deviation of 15. Percentile ranks are also provided.

To examine the current relevance of published norms of this proposed culture-free test, the reviewer oversaw the administration of the TAPS by a senior student to a sample of 90 children, 15 in each of six age groups, from a small metropolitan community in Eastern Canada. The test was straightforward to administer, taking the predicted 15 to 25 minutes per child. Mean raw scores for each age group increased with age, with the exception of the oldest group, on two subtests. Also with one exception, mean raw subtest scores for each age group fell within one *S.D.*

of the published values. Thus, the TAPS is relevant to other geographical and cultural milieus more than 15 years after its publication. Nevertheless, there are several concerns.

The Auditory Word Discrimination subtest measures the ability to discriminate words on the basis of sound. Fourteen of the word pairs sound identical and the remainder differ in one or more phonemes. Only the scores for *different* pairs are counted. The *same* scores provide information about validity, with a cutoff of 10 correct for ages 5 and 6 years and 14 correct for the 7- to 12-year-olds. The latter criterion (100%) seems unfairly strict, especially if the examiner happens to say the two members of a *same* pair detectably differently, in which case the response *different* is correct. Presentation of recorded audio materials would solve this problem. In our sample, none of the youngest age groups had invalid responses by the published criterion whereas typically 20% of the older age group's responses were invalid. No child scored less than 12 out of 14. The manual does not say what to do if the criterion is exceeded. The manual points out that the Auditory Word Discrimination task "reveals something of a child's cognitive functioning—a child has to be able to understand the meaning of words, such as *same* and *different*" (p. 10). Thus, if the child does poorly on this task it is not clear whether the problem is one of understanding or discrimination. To eliminate this discrepancy, the test could include several nonauditory examples, such as picture discrimination, providing evidence that the child understands the nature of a *same/different* task. Fewer items focusing on more difficult discrimination could reduce test time. Of all seven subtests, this one produces the least correlation with age (correlation of .42) and seems to be the least interesting to the children.

The Auditory Number Memory subtest is very similar to the Wechsler Intelligence Scale for Children (WISC) digit span, though scoring differs (forward and reversed are distinguished only in the TAPS). The author claims that the digits reversed task "taps a child's ability to concentrate and to perform an activity requiring mental control" (p. 9); presumably "in the auditory realm" is implied. Errors arise if a number is repeated out of sequence, or if a number is incorrectly substituted. Scoring does not distinguish these two types of errors. Thus, a child may recall all the numbers and receive no credit. The manual states that "since this is a sequencing test, it is wise to note if the child changes the sequence, but remembers the numbers correctly" (p. 26). The manual provides no indication of what to do with this information that is "wise to note." This situation is common in the reversed condition.

Unlike the previous subtest, in the Auditory Word Memory subtest, the order of report of individual items (words) is not relevant to the score. The instructions suggest ("it is a good plan …") that the examiner face away from the child so that visual cues are not provided. For purposes of standardization, these instructions should be specific. The cognitive demands on the examiner may be quite high for longer sentences, as the examiner must draw a line through words repeated incorrectly, circle words omitted, write out all mispronounced and substituted words above stimulus words, and indicate where possible sequencing errors occur, though the latter are not included in the score.

In the Auditory Sentence Memory subtest, the child must repeat a sentence verbatim. The ceiling is established when the child makes one or more errors in two consecutive sentences. There are no exceptions allowed such as change of order of presentation of the words, or provision of a synonym. In contrast, for the Auditory Interpretation of Directions subtest, the child must repeat a list of directions with respect to their meaning only. This entails translating the sentence from the heard second singular person (you) to the first person (I). The task relies on auditory short-term memory and sequencing but in addition requires understanding, grammatical knowledge, and interpretation of the information. Ceiling is reached when the child makes one or more substitutions, insertions, omissions of key words, phrases, and errors in sequencing that change meaning in each of two consecutive responses. Once again, the examiner records the child's verbatim response.

For the Auditory Processing (Thinking and Reasoning) subtest the child is presented verbally with a problem and is asked for the solution. The task requires understanding of the question and the ability to convert an idea into speech. The examiner records verbatim responses of the child. There is some leeway given the examiner in scoring, though this is vague. "Examiners should adhere to the scoring criteria as shown in Appendix A, but (based on professional experience) may determine a questionable response correct if the response shows close association to the responses given in Appendix A" (p. 30). Poor performance could stem from several sources, some not directly related to auditory perceptual skill. For example, the task is highly correlated with the WISC Vocabulary Subtest (.49) (Table 10, p. 52). Although the items are supposedly culture free, over the last decade it is possible that some of what was standard knowledge in the 1980s is no longer so. For example, one question asks how to boil an egg? With the preponderance of microwaves and ready made processed foods, boiled eggs are less likely a common menu item. Answers to other types of questions may indicate deep understanding yet fail to match the prescribed answer. For example, for the question: "why does a knife cut," the correct answer is "sharp." The different answer "to share" indicates understanding and cognitive development. In this task, the youngest age group scored more than one *S.D.* above the mean, perhaps resulting from greater world knowledge through media and education than was typically available at the time of standardization. Many of the difficult items received higher scores than the earlier easier items, although test items are to increase in difficulty. Less than half the 6-year-olds and 8-year-olds were correct on the question about boiling an egg; one half of the 8-year-olds and 11-year-olds did not know what pulls a train, which is an early (easy) question. Many children missed Items 27 (What causes night?) and 28 (If a person can't hear, that person can't what?) but almost all were correct on Items 29 to 31 (e.g., 30, From what is cotton cloth made?). A new item-analysis and updating of items might be in order for this test. Moreover, the correlation with general intelligence should be obtained.

The Hyperactivity Index Scale (parent's questionnaire) helps to account for poor performance that is nonauditory in origin because most of the subtests require the child's total attention, concentration, and motivation. The examiner also completes a brief assessment of temperament. It would be reassuring if some data were provided that showed that the parent's assessment correlated with that of the examiner. Of course, if it did, then one would wonder whether the added Hyperactivity Index was necessary. In our sample, almost all returned Indexes indicated low (i.e., normal) hyperactivity. Parents may have been reluctant to return forms indicating their child as hyperactive and hence have declined to participate in the study, as not all parents returned forms permitting their children to be given the TAPS.

TEST DEVELOPMENT. The theoretical basis underlying the development of the TAPS is unclear. Although there are over 35 references to

related literature, none (excluding that of the test author) is dated more recently than 1974, a decade before the publication of the test. In the last 20 years there has been an enormous growth in research in auditory perceptual deficits and developmental language disorders (e.g., Tallal, Stark, Kallman, & Mellits, 1980, 1981), and it would be useful to have placed the TAPS within a more current theoretical framework. Comparison with other batteries such as the Goldman-Fristoe-Woodcock Test of Auditory Discrimination (Goldman, Fristoe, & Woodcock, 1970; T4:1046) would be useful. Never is the term auditory perceptual skill defined and it is unclear to what extent the test author proposes that the battery is in any way comprehensive.

RELIABILITY. Reliability obtained through the examination of internal consistency was calculated using the Kuder-Richardson Formula 21 values. The total group reliabilities ranged from .79 to .89, with reliabilities for individual age groups ranging from .51 to .91. Cronbach's alpha scores were calculated for 2 of the tests. Standard error of measurement (*SEMS*) are also provided but test-retest reliabilities are not.

THE MANUAL. The 75-page manual is easy to read. It contains useful appendices of scoring examples and criteria and 15 tables of statistics. Language ages for each subtest are provided but their origin is not clear. According to the author "a language age score is a familiar and convenient index of an individual's TAPS performance" (p. 18).

Directions are explicit in regard to how the child is treated during the test, that is with encouragement and at his/her own pace. There are several small errors. On page 15 "Fifty (50) items were selected for the Auditory Word Discrimination subtest, and 35 items were selected for the Auditory Processing subtest—14 of them involved same words and 36 involved different words." The last clause is misplaced, referring to the Auditory Processing subtest rather than the Word Discrimination subtest. In general, two places of decimal are used in the tables, so it is odd to see one entry with three places of decimal in Table 6. In Table 9, two tests are incorrectly named (e.g., AWM-F should be ANM-F; AWM-R should be ANM-R). Some information seems irrelevant. For example, the reader probably is not interested in knowing that the test author cannot assess how long it took to develop the TAPS (p. 8).

VALIDITY. The content validity was evaluated through reviews of items by teachers (kindergarten through sixth grade) who were asked to confirm the appropriateness of test items with respect to age, culture, region, ethnicity, and gender. According to the author "The six subtests, when taken together, provide a comprehensive sampling of an individual's auditory-perceptual skills" (p. 20). Why certain skills were included and others not, however, is not addressed by the author.

The items selected for the test met criteria of item discrimination. (These criteria were that an item had to be correlated with the total test score of its subtest, with the sum of the subtest scores, and with chronological age. Finally, the correlation with the subtest had to exceed its correlation with any other subtest.) Items were arranged in general in terms of increasing order of difficulty, as measured by Spearman rank order correlation calculated between item order and item difficulty (range -.71 to -.88) for tests entailing multiple-choice items. This permits stopping testing after the child has made a series of incorrect responses. In some subtests, however, some later items seem easier than earlier ones (e.g., Auditory Processing) as shown in our data.

According to the author, the diagnostic validity for the TAPS is concerned with the ability of the test to detail unique characteristics of auditory perception and to identify individuals with auditory perceptual deficits. A table is provided of the median intercorrelation across age groups of each test with each other. These range from .15 to .52 (AID and AWM). It is not clear how many numbers are represented by the median (eight age groups for eight numbers?). What correlation value constitutes evidence of independence? Higher correlations of the subtest means with the total scores are not surprising because over 14% of the total score is directly contributed to by the subtest. Perhaps an additional valuable index would be the correlation of each subtest with the total of the remaining six scores. The author writes that further studies are needed to determine whether the TAPS effectively identifies individuals with deficits in auditory perception. The author invites users of the test "to submit studies that pertain to its validity." The invitation is made twice in the manual (pp. 21 and 22). No such studies had been submitted as of June 1996 (personal communication, Morrison Gardner). The test reviewer found at least one study (Jirsa, 1992) reported use of the TAPS in determining the effects of auditory training in 10 children with central auditory processing disorders. Scores on five of seven TAPS measures increased with auditory therapy. Changes were also noted in an auditory evoked response potential (AERP, a physiological measure, the main purpose of Jirsa's study) and performance on several other auditory tasks. It is noted that Jirsa (1992) used the test as a measure of auditory central processing, without considering the meaning of the individual tests, and without considering the overall Auditory Quotient.

The TAPS performance with chronological age led to correlations ranging from .42 to .80. It appears that chronological age was measured in terms of eight age categories rather than by months; the latter would lead to a more sensitive index. The highest correlation was for Auditory Processing. The lowest correlation with age was for Auditory Word Discrimination, likely resulting from a ceiling on this ability early in life coupled with the insensitivity of the test. Tables of correlations are also provided of the TAPS scores with the Vocabulary subtest of the Wechsler Preschool and Primary Scale of Intelligence (WPSI) and Wechsler Intelligence Scale for Children—Revised (WISC-R), and a test of expressive language (Expressive One-Word Picture Vocabulary Test, EOWPVT) that had been administered concurrently with the TAPS. Correlations range from .17 to .56 and the author consequently states that the TAPS shows a significant amount of unique variance and appears to assess aspects of auditory perception that are not addressed by these tests. In our own laboratory, 10 subjects from each of six age groups who had been administered the TAPS also received a subtest of the Culture Fair Intelligence Test (T4:699), and an original test of sequential auditory memory for up to five animal sounds (Cohen & O'Connor, 1994; Graham & Cohen, 1996). Correlations with the TAPS subtests were obtained for these two measures. The intelligence test correlated highly (.49) with the Auditory Interpretation of Directions, for ages 5–8 years, once again suggesting that this subtest includes a large nonauditory component. Our animal sound memory test correlated highly with the TAPS Digits Forward subtest (.62) (but also highly with Interpretation of Directions and Auditory Processing, both at .60), moderately with Word Memory (.52) and most poorly with Word Discrimination (.28). Thus, the TAPS proved useful in helping to isolate what aspect of auditory perceptual skill a new auditory test measures.

SUPPLIED PROFILE AND OTHER FEATURES. The test comes with a profile form that facilitates the recording of data. For example, it provides rows and columns for computation of the child's age in years and months. Two of the subtests have been adapted for Spanish (Word Memory and Discrimination).

SUMMARY. I have no hesitation in recommending the TAPS to a speech therapist or psychologist working for a school board. Practically speaking, the test is short, easy to administer, and provides an overview of performance on several auditory perceptual skills. Exactly what is and what is not covered by the TAPS is not clear, but low performance on one or more subtests could help to direct more sensitive testing. The TAPS could be improved and updated; and it is my understanding that the test is currently in revision and undergoing standardization with a more representative sample (personal communication, Gardner, May 1996). To increase standardization, reliability, and validity, the subtest stimuli could be presented on separate audio or video cassettes. At the very least, a demonstration audiotape could provide auditory examples of how the sound stimuli should be presented with respect to timing and accent. Finally, most of the subtests depend on the examiner's ability to record verbatim what the child has said and to detect errors in repetition. Given the possible limitations of the examiner's own short-term memory, auditory skills, and divided attention, it could be helpful to have an auditory tape of the session itself. A tape-recorded session, however, would more than double the work of the examiner (current scoring time is approximately 10 minutes) but would assure accuracy and standardization and provide a good chance to measure interobserver reliability.

REVIEWER'S REFERENCES

Goldman, R., Fristoe, M., & Woodcock, R. (1970). *Manual for Goldman-Fristoe-Woodcock Test of Auditory Skills.* Circle Pines, MN: American Guidance Service.

Rosner, J., & Simon, D. P. (1971). The auditory analysis test: An initial report. *Journal of Learning Disabilities, 4,* 40–48.

Cherry, R. S. (1980). *Selective auditory attention test.* St. Louis: Auditec of St. Louis.

Tallal, P., Stark, R. E., Kallman, C., & Mellits, D. (1980). Developmental dysphasia: Relation between acoustic processing deficits and verbal processing. *Neuropsychologia, 18,* 273–284.

Tallal, P., Stark, R., Kallman, C., & Mellits, D. (1981). A reexamination of some nonverbal perceptual abilities of language-impaired and normal children as a function of age and sensory modality. *Journal of Speech and Hearing Research, 24,* 351–357.

Jirsa, R. E. (1992). The clinical utility of the P3 AERP in children with auditory processing disorders. *Journal of Speech and Hearing Research, 35,* 903–912.

Cohen, A. J., & O'Connor, J. (1994). Development of memory for sequences of nonverbal sounds. *XXII International Congress of Audiology (Abstracts). Halifax,* p. 199.

Graham, P., & Cohen, A. J. (1996). Development of memory for sequences of animal sounds: Relation to digit-span and language ability. *Canadian Acoustics, 24,* p. 66.

Review of the Test of Auditory-Perceptual Skills by ANNE R. KESSLER, Audiologist, VA Connecticut Healthcare System, Newington, CT; and JACLYN B. SPITZER, Chief, Audiology and Speech Pathology Service, VA Connecticut Healthcare System, West Haven, CT and Associate Clinical Professor, Department of Surgery (Otolaryngology), Yale University School of Medicine, New Haven, CT:

The Test of Auditory-Perceptual Skills (TAPS) was developed by a psychologist, Morrison F. Gardner, in order to measure a child's performance on a variety of auditory perception tasks. Prior to the TAPS, the author reported that several different tests were required to assess the seven subtests (Auditory Number Memory, Auditory Sentence Memory, Auditory Word Memory, Auditory Interpretation of Directions, Auditory Word Discrimination, Auditory Processing, and the Hyperactivity Index Scale) incorporated in this one test. The development of this battery appears to be comprehensive and well thought out. Each of the seven subtests was subjected to appropriate reliability and validity measures. The presentation and scoring of the test are relatively fast and easy. The final results give individual subtest scores with percentile ranks and stanines as well as a sum of scaled scores giving an overall percentile rank and median language age.

After an informal survey of more than 20 professionals (both speech-language pathologists and audiologists) in the university setting, elementary school setting, and pediatric hospital setting, it was difficult to find anyone who had used the TAPS test on more than one or two occasions. After locating several professionals who had used it, the comments about the test were of a similar vein. They felt it was a somewhat useful test that was easy to administer and score. Most felt that the test was primarily beneficial after an auditory processing problem has been diagnosed. The TAPS would then allow one to determine which specific areas of processing were affected. This knowledge allows for a more tailored intervention program.

One major drawback of the TAPS is that because the test is administered orally, the child's score appears to be highly influenced by receptive language skills. One professional even stated that the Auditory Word Discrimination subtest was not really testing auditory discrimination at all but really language ability. Another problem with the oral/live-voice administration is standardization. Because speakers and presenters differ, live presentation introduces variability into the presentation.

Regular users of the TAPS considered the Auditory Word Memory and Auditory Number Memory subtests to be the most useful. In contrast, none of the professionals reported using the Hyperactivity Index Scale. The Auditory Processing portion seemed the most questionable in terms of actually testing its target skill. This section asks open-ended questions of the child (e.g., "What pulls a train?" and "What causes night?" [Protocol, p. 11]). The tester is told to mark the answers as correct or incorrect. It would appear that there are several answers to many of the questions and several ways to interpret the questions leading to judgmental scoring of this section. In addition, the TAPS seems to test cognitive and reasoning skills rather than solely auditory processing.

Given that the development of this battery appears to be comprehensive and well thought out, some of the limitations reported by professionals in the field may be reasons it appears to be underused. Knowing these limitations, the TAPS would appear to have two major applications: (a) as a screening tool for speech-language pathologists to use in the school to identify children who need a referral for further testing and (b) as an intervention tool to be used following a diagnosis of auditory processing deficit. Used in this manner, the TAPS allows one to determine if the deficit is on the word or sentence level.

[325]
Test of Cognitive Skills, Second Edition.

Purpose: "Designed to assess the academic aptitude of students in Grades 2–12."
Population: Grades 2–3, 4–5, 6–7, 8–9, 10–11, 11–12.
Publication Dates: 1981–1992.
Acronym: TCS/2.
Scores, 5: Sequences, Analogies, Memory, Verbal Reasoning, Total (Cognitive Skills Index).
Administration: Group.
Price Data, 1994: $9.45 per 35 practice tests; $32 per 100 individual record sheets for hand scoring; $1.15 per class record sheet for hand scoring; $8.35 per norms book ('92, 50 pages); $11.75 per test coordinator's handbook ('92, 41 pages); $11.75 per technical bulletin ('93, 62 pages); $8.35 per examiner's manual ('92, 29 pages) (select Levels 1, 2–6); $12.60 per test organizer; scoring service available from publisher.
Authors: CTB/Macmillan/McGraw-Hill.
Publisher: CTB/Macmillan/McGraw-Hill.
  a) LEVEL 1.
  Population: Grades 2–3.
  Price Data: $50.05 per 35 hand-scorable consumable test books; $63.35 per 35 CompuScan machine-scorable consumable test books.
  Time: 50(55) minutes.
  b) LEVEL 2.
  Population: Grades 4–5.
  Price Data: $63.35 per 35 machine-scorable consumable test books; $50.05 per 35 hand-scorable or reusable test books; $13 per 50 CompuScan answer sheets; $23 per 50 hand-scorable answer sheets; $17

per 25 SCOREZE answer sheets; $9.60 per hand-scoring stencil.
  Time: 54(59) minutes.
  c) LEVEL 3.
  Population: Grades 6–7.
  Price Data: $45.15 per 35 reusable test books; answer sheet prices same as *b* above.
  Time: Same as *b* above.
  d) LEVEL 4.
  Population: Grades 8–9.
  Price Data: Same as *b* above.
  Time: Same as *c* above.
  e) LEVEL 5.
  Population: Grades 10–11.
  Price Data: Same as *b* above.
  Time: Same as *c* above.
  f) LEVEL 6.
  Population: Grades 11–12.
  Price Data: Same as *b* above.
  Time: Same as *c* above.
Cross References: See T4:2745 (4 references); for reviews by Timothy Z. Keith and Robert J. Sternberg of an earlier edition, see 9:1248; for a review by Lynn H. Fox and an excerpted review by David M. Shoemaker of the Short Form Test of Academic Aptitude, see 8:202 (9 references).

TEST REFERENCES
1. Chernick, R. S. (1990). Effects on interdependent, coactive, and individualized working conditions on pupils' educational computer program performance. *Journal of Educational Psychology, 82,* 691–695.
2. Hoge, D. R., Hanson, S. L., & Smit, E. K. (1990). School experiences predicting changes in self-esteem of sixth- and seventh-grade students. *Journal of Educational Psychology, 82,* 117–127.
3. Luchman, A., & Michels, K. A. (1990). NDN: An outlet for exemplary programs. *Journal for the Education of the Gifted, 13,* 156–167.
4. Vallicorsa, A. L., & Garriss, E. (1990). Story composition skills of middle-grade students with learning disabilities. *Exceptional Children, 57,* 48–54.
5. Stahl, S. A., Hare, V. C., Sinatra, R., & Gregory, J. F. (1991). Defining the role of prior knowledge and vocabulary in reading comprehension: The retiring of number 41. *Journal of Reading Behavior, 23,* 487–508.
6. Janelle, S. (1992). Locus of control in nondisabled versus congenitally physically disabled adolescents. *The American Journal of Occupational Therapy, 46,* 334–342.
7. Kuschè, C. A., Cook, E. T., & Greenberg, M. T. (1993). Neuropsychological and cognitive functioning in children with anxiety, externalizing, and comorbid psychopathology. *Journal of Clinical Child Psychology, 22,* 172–195.
8. Spencer, S. L., & Fitzgerald, J. (1993). Validity and structure, coherence, and quality measures in writing. *Journal of Reading Behavior, 25,* 209–231.

Review of the Test of Cognitive Skills, Second Edition by RANDY W. KAMPHAUS, Professor of Educational Psychology, The University of Georgia, Athens, GA:

The Test of Cognitive Skills, Second Edition, (TCS/2) is a group-administered academic ability (i.e., intelligence) test that is designed to assess general ability via a Cognitive Skills Index (CSI). The CSI is composed of four subtests: one verbal, two nonverbal, and one memory. A nonverbal composite is also produced. The TCS/2 is a carefully developed academic ability measure that uses state-of-the-art test production methods.

The administration procedures for the TCS/2 are top notch. The guidelines for examiners are clear and succinct. Moreover, the test stimuli seemed unambiguous and well organized in the response booklets.

The test content of the TCS/2 is also laudatory in that the developers went to unusual lengths to limit the influences of prior achievements on TCS/2 performance. The Memory subtest, for example, cleverly uses nonsense words as stimuli. The Verbal Reasoning test attempts to use highly familiar English-language stimuli. The content blueprint for the four subtests was thoughtfully conceived to include only items that are conceptually consistent with the construct(s) measured by each subtest.

Evidence of careful test development procedures can be found throughout the 150-page Technical Report. The TCS test development procedures benefit heavily from survey level achievement testing technologies. The items proceeded through several screens prior to final selection including editorial reviews, extensive statistical and judgmental bias reviews, item factor analyses, distractor analyses, and item calibration using a three-parameter IRT model.

The Technical Report also reveals careful study of several issues that are often ignored in test manuals. The effects of speed (versus power) on test performance, and the ability to differentiate samples of exceptional students from the norm are discussed.

In some cases, however, the presentation of data takes precedence over thorough discussion of the results. In the Technical Report, for example, less than a page of text is devoted to a discussion of item factor analysis results. In direct contrast, roughly 80 pages are devoted to the presentation of intercorrelation matrices and factor analytic solutions. Several aspects of the factor analyses could have benefited from further discussion or analysis. Specifically, because the TCS/2 is described primarily as a measure of general cognitive ability, it seems curious that an unrotated principal component was not extracted or reported in order to assess this hypothesis.

The Test Coordinator's Handbook is also thorough and well written. The glossary of measurement terms and interpretive information is helpful and logically presented. It seems that all of the important caveats associated with the interpretation of ability tests are presented. The developers could do more, however, to assist the test user. There must, for example, be an interpretive implication associated with the factor analytic finding (p. 12 of the Technical Report) that the verbal items tended to have significant secondary loadings on the nonverbal factor. The

authors give some examples of individualized interpretations but more would be helpful. In reality, parents often request such interpretations from teachers and others with whom they discuss these results.

A reviewer could quibble about the minutia associated with any test. A citation was missing in the Technical Manual reference list (i.e., Burket, 1974). It also seems unlawful for a cognitive ability test to have so little theoretical discussion of the constructs being measured and, consequently, such a brief reference list. Surely the assumptions that underlay the construction of the TCS/2 can be traced to the century-old tradition of intelligence testing. A final detail—the KR-20 reliability coefficients for the subtests yielded more values in the .60 to .70 range than I expected.

The overall value of the TCS/2, however, should not be lost in the details. The field of individually administered ability (intelligence) testing would progress significantly if it were to adopt many of the test development procedures used for the TCS/2. The TCS/2 sets a high standard with respect to diligent and thoughtful test development procedures for academic ability testing.

[326]
Test of Early Written Language, Second Edition.

Purpose: "Measures early writing ability in children."
Population: Ages 3–0 to 10–11.
Publication Dates: 1988–1996.
Acronym: TEWL—2.
Scores, 3: Basic Writing, Contextual Writing, Global Writing.
Administration: Individual or group.
Forms, 2: A, B.
Price Data, 1996: $134 per complete kit including manual ('96, 116 pages), 10 each Form A and Form B student workbooks, 10 each Form A and Form B profile/record booklets in storage box; $34 per 10 student workbooks (specify Form A or B); $16 per 10 profile/record booklets (specify Form A or B); $39 per manual.
Time: (30–45) minutes.
Authors: Wayne P. Hresko, Shelley R. Herron, and Pamela K. Peak.
Publisher: PRO-ED, Inc.
Cross References: See T4:2754; for a review of an earlier edition by Patricia Wheeler, see 11:430.

Review of the Test of Early Written Language, Second Edition by DAVID P. HURFORD, Director of the Center for the Assessment and Remediation of Reading Difficulties and Associate Professor of Psychology and Counseling, Pittsburg State University, Pittsburg, KS:

The Test of Early Written Language, Second Edition (TEWL-2) evaluates writing ability in young children aged 3-0 to 10-11. The TEWL-2 is composed of two subtests: the Basic Writing Subtest, used to assess the mechanical aspects of writing, and the Contextual Writing Subtest, used to measure a student's ability to produce quality writing with the use of a writing sample. Each subtest has two forms (A and B), which are comparable. The authors believe that both subtests should be given to obtain the Global Writing Quotient, which allows for a more complete understanding of the child's writing abilities. Along with reading assessments, evaluations of written language help to define a student's literacy development. Literacy skills, particularly reading, are crucial to a child's academic success. It has been said that children first learn to read and then read to learn. Examination of written language early in a child's literacy development would help to identify weaknesses that could be rectified so that literacy will develop appropriately. In this regard, the authors contend that tests of early written language are quite important and useful.

The TEWL-2 was developed from a conceptual framework derived from the reading and writing literature. The philosophy for the TEWL-2 is that assessment of children's writing must include the child's ability to transcribe, which is assessed with the Basic Writing Subtest, and to communicate thoughts, use correct standards and conventions for writing, and use creativity of expression, which are assessed with the Contextual Writing Subtest. As the authors indicate, the reading and writing literature is quite vast with research examining writing being the smaller of the two areas. One of the difficulties with the writing literature is a lack of instruments designed specifically to assess writing skills. Written language difficulties are indicative of literacy difficulties, broadly defined. It is in this regard that the TEWL-2 was designed. The TEWL-2 has four purposes:

1. To identify students who are significantly beneath their peers in writing.

2. To determine the strengths and/or weaknesses of a student's writing ability.

3. To document change in a student's writing ability as a result of an intervention.

4. To provide a research vehicle for the assessment of children's writing abilities.

The TEWL-2 is intended to be used as a measure of the basic components of written language. The TEWL-2 is probably not the best measurement device to assess highly competent writers, nor was it intended to do so. It was designed for the purposes stated above, particularly to identify children who could benefit from some type of intervention.

The Basic Writing Subtest taps knowledge and skills related to the writing process and comprises 57 items; each scored as 1 for correct or 0 for incorrect. The subtest progresses in a developmental fashion, earlier items are most relevant for younger children or children who have less developed writing skills. For example, early items have to do with drawing pictures of a favorite television character and telling about that picture, pointing to different writing utensils, showing the direction of writing across the page, and writing the child's name (spellings that are phonetically correct is appropriate). Later items on the subtest have the student constructing sentences from words that are haphazardly strung together.

The student produces a writing sample during the Contextual Writing Subtest. The child is shown a picture and is asked to write a story about the stimulus material. For the younger students (ages 5-0 to 6-11), a simple scenario is provided in which there are three pictures depicting a sequential scene (a woman and a small boy with an ice cream cone for Form A and a boy inflating balloons for Form B). For students aged between 7-0 through 10-0 a complex scene is provided (a birthday party with several children, a birthday cake, presents, and a piñata for Form A, and a playground scene with several children and play equipment for Form B). The writing samples are scored with reference to 14 different criteria: use of objects in story, recognizable words, almost spelling, recognizable sentences, sentence structure, use of pronouns, recognizable theme, topic sentences, five letters correct (the number of words five letters or longer that are spelled correctly), beginning and end (the story should have a recognizable beginning and ending), sequence of events, beyond the picture (elaboration of the story beyond the picture), main and secondary characters, and monologue or dialogue. The writing sample is scored from 0 (an absence of the particular ability) to 3 (the specific writing ability is sufficiently developed). A scoring key is provided to assist the test scorer in determining the appropriate score for each writing feature, although prior knowledge with the assessment of written language would be very useful.

The TEWL-2 has no time limit; however, under most circumstances the test probably will not take more than 50 minutes. Unlike many standardized tests, the child has the opportunity to review and modify his or her answer. If the child does, the modified answer is the response that is scored. The TEWL-2 uses basals and ceilings for the Basic Writing Subtest. Both are simple to determine; the basal is the highest five consecutively correct items and the ceiling is the lowest five consecutively incorrect items. The manual provides suggested starting items for each age level. The total correct is the raw score.

The profile/record booklet provides information concerning various demographic information including age at the time of testing and conditions at the time of administration (number of sessions, administration time, place of administration, noise level, interruptions, distractions, lighting, temperature, energy level, attitude toward test, rapport, and perseverance). These issues are important in reporting test scores because they very well may play important roles in the nature of the score. The actual test scores can be reported in terms of raw scores, which are not comparable across subtests, and percentiles, normal curve equivalents, standard scores (quotients; BWQ—Basic Writing, CWQ—Contextual Writing, and the GWQ—Global Writing, which combines the two subtests), which are comparable across the two subtests. The TEWL-2 also reports age equivalent scores for administrative purposes; however, the authors strongly advise against using these scores due to the general inadequacies of age equivalents with regard to statistical properties and the possibility that the scores may be misleading.

The TEWL-2 was standardized on a sample of 1,479 students aged 3-0 to 10-11 from 41 states and British Columbia, Canada. The sample was stratified according to age, gender, race, ethnicity, residence (urban or rural), and geographic region. Norms are also available for learning disability, speech/language disorder, mental retardation, and others. The inclusion of disability status variables is quite helpful and is consistent with the intended purposes of the test, (i.e., to identify students who are significantly beneath their peers in writing and to determine the strengths and/or weaknesses of a student's writing ability).

Reliability of the TEWL-2 was examined with internal consistency, test-retest, and interscorer reliabilities. Internal consistency was evaluated with Cronbach's coefficient alpha over the various age groups. The coefficients ranged from .90 to .99 (M = .948). The interval between administrations of the test was 14 to 21 days. Both test forms were used in the determination of the test-retest reliabilities. Some

of the students received the same form at both times of testing whereas other received two different forms. Reliabilities ranged from .82 to .94 (M = .890). The range of coefficients for the interscorer reliabilities was between .92 and .99 (M = .952).

Issues regarding validity were examined with respect to content validity, criterion-related validity, and construct validity. The tasks involved in the TEWL-2 reflect the domains involved with writing. The content of the test includes items pertaining to directionality (the progression of print; left to right), awareness of letter features, metalinguistic knowledge, spelling, punctuation, capitalization, proofing, sentence combining, logical sentences, contextual vocabulary (semantics), syntactic maturity, and thematic maturity. Test items were also assessed for potential bias. Four individuals (three females, one male; two Caucasian, one Hispanic, and one African American), who successfully completed two advanced measurement courses, reviewed each item for bias. In addition, delta values (differences in difficulty across groups) were generated for the test items. Any items that had an item difficulty difference between groups of .10 were modified or removed from the test. Concurrent validity was considered by examining the relationship between the scores from the TEWL-2 and several other tests tapping similar abilities (Test of Early Written Language [TEWL], Comprehensive Scales of Student Abilities, Diagnostic Achievement Battery, Peabody Individual Achievement Test—Revised, Preschool Language Scale—3, Quick Score Achievement Test, Test of Early Language Development—2, Test of Written Spelling—2, Wechsler Individual Achievement Test, Woodcock-Johnson Psycho-Educational Battery—Revised, Wide Range Achievement Test—Revised, etc.). The coefficients ranged from .24 to .90 (M = .490). Predictive validity was explored by comparing scores from the TEWL with later scores from the TEWL-2. Two studies were performed yielding correlations between the two tests at different times of measurement of .69 and .62, respectively. Construct validity was assessed by comparing the relationship between TEWL-2 scores and tests that tap cognitive functioning. Generally, the relationship between these scores was weak to modest and ranged between .31 and .71 (M = .47). Although it could be argued that the TEWL-2 measures cognitive ability, differences in patterns of variability between TEWL-2 scores and tests that tap cognitive ability are not surprising. Modest correlation coefficients would be expected, and for the most part, were obtained. The TEWL-2 scores were also used to determine disability group membership. The standard scores from various disabled students (n = 22 to 45) were reported in the TEWL-2 manual. Each disabled group had significantly below average standard scores (M = 70 to 85). Although the test may have potential in identifying at-risk or disabled students, much more needs to be done to insure validity and reliability (e.g., discriminant analysis between TEWL-2 scores and group membership, etc.).

In summary, the TEWL-2 appears to provide reliable and valid scores measuring early written language. It was developed to identify students who are significantly beneath their peers in writing, to determine the strengths and/or weaknesses of a student's writing ability, to document change in a student's writing ability as a result of intervention, and to provide a research vehicle for the assessment of children's writing abilities. The test was carefully constructed to assess the developmental status of written language in children between the ages of 3-0 to 10-11. The manual is well written and user friendly. Although developing a test that assesses written language skills is a formidable task, the TEWL-2 provides an excellent conceptual framework and content-appropriate items.

Review of the Test of Early Written Language, Second Edition by MICHAEL S. TREVISAN, Assistant Professor, Department of Educational Leadership and Counseling Psychology, Washington State University, Pullman, WA:

The Test of Early Written Language (TEWL-2) was first published in 1988 as a screening and research measure of early writing skills of young children. Now in its second edition, the TEWL-2 has been expanded and refined to provide detailed information about the writing strengths and weaknesses of a child and the additional feature of providing impact data for program evaluation.

The authors of the TEWL-2 are to be commended for heeding reviewer concerns about the first edition of the test and taking action to address the issues. (See the examiner's manual for a list of previous criticisms and how they were addressed.) Notable changes to the test include the development of two forms, the addition of a subtest that requires students to provide a sample of their writing, and detailed information regarding student writing skills. In addition, psychometric enhancement of the test has been conducted, meeting professional standards of test development.

The test now has two subtests. The first, the Basic Writing Subtest, consists of 57 items scored 1 or 0 and presented in developmental sequence. The subtest measures the use of conventions, linguistics, and conceptualization. Information from the subtest can be use to construct a diagnostic profile of a child's writing strengths and weaknesses. The second, referred to as the Contextual Writing Subtest, is composed of 14 items scored 0 to 3. Scores are obtained by presenting a child with one of two pictures (depending on the age of the child) and asking the child to write about what he or she sees. Each item prompts the scorer to evaluate aspects of the writing relative to specific scoring criteria. This subtest provides a holistic measure of the same three components measured by the Basic Writing Subtest.

A previous criticism of the test was that scoring guidelines were not clear for some of the items. This has been corrected in the TEWL-2. Scoring and administration guidelines are straightforward. Scoring criteria for the 14 items on the Contextual Writing Subtest are well written, fostering consistent scoring decisions by professionals administering the test.

Percentiles, TEWL-2 quotients for each subtest, a Global Writing Quotient, normal curve equivalents (NCE), and age equivalents are derived scores available with the TEWL-2. These scores are easily obtained from conversions tables in the examiner's manual. Performance descriptions for quotient and NCE score ranges are also provided to aid in communicating test performance.

The addition of the NCE score provides a ready means of evaluating program impact, such as a writing program. Mean NCE scores, pre and post, can be computed with their difference providing an aggregate measure of impact. Given the national focus and expectation for program evaluation in social and education programs, many will find this feature of the TEWL-2 quite useful and worth its purchase.

The TEWL-2 is designed to be individually administered, although the Contextual Writing Subtest can be administered to a group of children. Both subtests must be administered in order to obtain the Global Writing Quotient.

Reliability data for scores from the test are provided for each age tested. This includes data regarding content sampling, time sampling, and scorer differences. All reliability estimates are above .80 and many are above .90, illustrating that consistent decisions can be made from test data obtained from proper test administration and scoring. In general, obtaining uniformly high reliability estimates is not a simple matter. It can be particularly difficult when test scores are computed across dichotomous items and tasks scored relative to scoring criteria as in the TEWL-2. The high reliability estimates of scores from the TEWL-2 exemplify the rigor with which the test was developed.

Perhaps the defining feature of the TEWL-2 is the thoughtfulness with which the validity of data from the test was established. The content validity, for example, is couched within the research literature of what it means to write well. Items and tasks are directly developed from this writing. Data from the TEWL-2 correlate well with data from similar measures, establishing concurrent validity. Two predictive validity studies were conducted, providing solid evidence for predicting future writing performance from TEWL-2 test data. Constructs measured by the TEWL-2 were identified and logical hypotheses were generated from these constructs, which were subsequently verified by validity studies. Thus, evidence of construct validity is also provided.

As the authors continue to refine the TEWL-2 it is recommended that the validity of test data continue to be examined and reformulated. Establishing a validity framework as suggested by Shepard (1993), rather than providing discrete categories of validity evidence, will further improve the TEWL-2 and align its development and refinement with current thinking with regard to validity. Along these lines, establishing and testing falsifying hypotheses will bolster the validity argument (Cronbach, 1989).

In summary, this author recommends the TEWL-2 without reservation. This measure has been developed with professional expertise. The authors have shown willingness to address previous criticisms of the instrument, which in the end has produced a better measure. Use of the TEWL-2 will surely aid personnel in the screening of writing skills of young children or those conducting research in this field.

REVIEWER'S REFERENCES

Cronbach, L. J. (1989). Construct validation after thirty years. In R. L. Linn (Ed.), *Intelligence: Measurement theory and public policy* (pp. 147–171). Urbana: University of Illinois Press.
Shepard, L. A. (1993). Evaluating test validity. In L. Darling-Hammond (Ed.), *Review of research in education* (vol. 19, pp. 405–450). Washington, DC: American Educational Research Association.

[327]
Test of Inference Ability in Reading Comprehension.

Purpose: "Designed to provide diagnostic information about the inference ability of students."
Population: Grades 6–8.

Publication Dates: 1987–1989.
Scores: Total score only.
Administration: Group.
Forms, 2: Multiple-choice, Constructed-response.
Price Data, 1993: $35 per 35 tests (specify multiple-choice or constructed-response); $10 per manual ('89, 24 pages); $12 per technical report ('89, 58 pages).
Time: (40–45) minutes per form.
Authors: Linda M. Phillips and Cynthia C. Patterson (multiple-choice format).
Publisher: Linda M. Phillips [Canada].

Review of the Test of Inference Ability in Reading Comprehension by DOUGLAS K. SMITH, Professor and Director, School Psychology Training Program, University of Wisconsin—River Falls, River Falls, WI:

The Test of Inference Ability in Reading Comprehension "is designed to provide diagnostic information about the inference ability of students in grades 6, 7, and 8 and information to support instructional improvement" (manual, p. 3). Inferring is defined "as a constructive thinking process whereby a reader expands knowledge by proposing and evaluating hypotheses about the meaning of text" (manual, p. 4). Detailed information on the rationale of the test and differences between inference ability and reading comprehension are provided in the manual.

Two formats are available: a multiple-choice format and a constructed-response format. With both formats, students read three stories and answer questions about them. Administration time (individual or group) is about 45 minutes, although there are no strict time limits. Detailed administration instructions are presented in the manual. Administration of the test is quite easy and verbatim directions are provided.

Scoring of the multiple-choice format is easily accomplished. Each question has four response choices that are scored 0, 1, 2, or 3, producing a possible range of scores from 0 to 108 for the 36 items. Each response to the 34 items on the constructed-response format is assigned an appropriate value. A rationale for scoring and sample responses for the 34 questions are provided. For each item, sample responses range from minimum (score of 0) to the maximum (score of 3).

Norms for the multiple-choice format are based on a sample of 999 students in grades 6, 7, and 8 from schools across Canada including Southern Alberta, Western Newfoundland and Labrador, Northern Nova Scotia, and Southern Ontario. The students are divided into four groups with rather general descriptions such as "Group 4: 66 grades 6, 7, and 8 students from a large urban area in Southern Ontario. The students were from a wide range in economic levels, and many from single parent homes" (manual, p. 8). Means and standard deviations are presented by group and grade and by age and sex within grade for each of the four groups. Due to the limited nature of the standardization sample, extreme caution should be used in interpreting results for individual students.

Reliability data include K-R 20 reliability estimates for each story and the total test. These are at moderate levels and range from .49 to .77 for the three stories with a Total Test reliability coefficient of .79. Test-retest data are not reported.

Very limited validity data are presented. Each item on the test was given to 95 students (selection criteria are not provided) and students were asked to select the appropriate response and explain the reasoning for their choice. This procedure yielded a reading score and a thinking score. Two independent raters assigned the thinking scores for each item and the thinking score and reading score for each item were correlated and provided an average correlation of .55. Although the technical report (Phillips, 1989) provides in-depth information on the theory behind the test and describes the development of the test in detail, additional validity studies are not reported.

This instrument is probably best used in a research setting or as an instructional instrument. The narrow age range (grades 6–8) and limited norms preclude widespread use of the test. The test should not be used for placement decisions as the norm sample is limited in size (n = 999) and region (four regions in Canada). In addition, selection criteria for the norm sample are not provided.

REVIEWER'S REFERENCE

Phillips, L. M. (1989). *Developing and validating assessments of inference ability in reading comprehension*. Urbana-Champaign, IL: Center for the Study of Reading Technical Report No. 452.

Review of the Test of Inference Ability in Reading Comprehension by ROBERT WALL, Graduate Professor of Education, College of Education, Towson State University, Towson, MD:

The 36-item power test has the narrowly focused diagnostic function of measuring 6th–8th grade students' ability to make inferences from reading material. Anyone planning a complete reading assessment program will need more than this test. As the manual points out, this test is not a criterion-referenced but rather a norm-referenced test. However, most prospective users must conduct their own validity and reliability studies because the norms provided in the manual are based on moderate sized, 1987 mid-year samples of Canadian school children from rural and urban settings. The final test data were provided by 999 Canadian students in grades 6, 7, and 8.

Prospective test users must first determine if the test's norming sample and objectives are appropriate for their needs. They must also evaluate the similarity of background information of their student population with that of the norming sample. According to the test manual, "background knowledge [is] a necessary part of inferential reasoning" (p. 3). The lack of appropriate background information may have a major effect on test scores and consequently the test's validity for a specific student population.

In this time of shrinking budgets and increased clamor for more "bang for the buck" there are several questions that must be asked. How appropriate is this test for my specific student population? How much time and money do I have available to conduct a pilot study to determine the test's appropriateness? What is the proper balance between time for assessment and time for instruction? Will this approximately 45-minute test provide enough new information to justify its administration? How can I use information from this norm-referenced diagnostic test? What instructional changes will this test information promote?

The authors appear to have expended much time and effort constructing and gathering validity data for a test available in both multiple-choice and constructed-response formats. However, the manual very legitimately points out that, "Insufficient data is available at this time to make claims that the two formats are parallel" (p. 8). Unfortunately, no norms are provided for the constructed-response format. Also this reviewer could find no evidence in the manual of interrater reliability for constructed-response reading scores although interrater reliabilities were reported for total and individual thinking scores. The scoring schema of awarding 0 through 3 points for responses to each item creates problems for the computation and interpretation of item difficulty levels and internal consistency values. The range of reported correlations between individual test items and overall test performance was in the low to moderate positive range, -.01 to .48.

According to the technical report (Phillips, 1989) analysis of variance of the final test data revealed statistically significant differences for the major effects of grade and age, and the interactions of sex by grade and grade by age. The difference in means for grades and ages reflects positively upon the test's validity; however, the statistically significant findings for the two interactions raises some troubling questions and indicates the need for research in this area.

The directions for the administration of the test seem well thought out with examples and suggestions although there are no suggestions for special needs students.

This test represents a pioneering attempt to measure the inferring ability of grade 6–8 students. Before adopting this test one must be willing to conduct their own reliability, validity, and usability tests.

REVIEWER'S REFERENCE

Phillips, L. M. (1989). *Developing and validating assessments of inference ability in reading comprehension.* Urbana-Champaign, IL: Center for the Study of Reading Technical Report No. 452.

[328]
Test of Kindergarten/First Grade Readiness Skills.

Purpose: "To assess a child's readiness for kindergarten or for first grade."
Population: Ages 3–6 to 7–0.
Publication Date: 1987.
Acronym: TKFGRS.
Scores, 3: Reading, Spelling, Arithmetic.
Administration: Individual.
Price Data, 1994: $37.95 per complete kit including manual (32 pages), 25 record booklets, and 8 cards; $15 per manual; $19.50 per 25 record booklets; $5.95 per 8 cards; $16 per specimen set including manual and samples.
Time: (20–25) minutes.
Author: Karen Gardner Codding.
Publisher: Psychological & Educational Publications, Inc.

Review of the Test of Kindergarten/First Grade Readiness Skills by D. JOE OLMI, Assistant Professor, School Psychology Program and Director, School Psychology Service Center, Department of Psychology, University of Southern Mississippi, Hattiesburg, MS:

The Test of Kindergarten/First Grade Readiness Skills (TKFGRS) is a norm-referenced instrument that was designed by its author to be used by instructional personnel and assessment specialists to determine a child's preacademic and academic readiness for kindergarten or first grade in reading, spelling, and arithmetic. Additionally, the instrument was designed to determine "areas of low functioning" (p. 5).

The TKFGRS was normed on 373 children from 3 to 7 years of age at 6-month intervals. Information about normative sampling procedures was absent from the technical portions of the manual. Approximately equal numbers of males and females comprised each 6-month age interval. Statements of ethnic diversity of the normative sample were made, but the manual included no demographic breakdown, other than by age and gender. It is assumed by this reviewer that the author's sample was either limited in demographics or was a sample of convenience because no other information was made available.

Each academic section has certain "domains of activities" (p. 8), for example, within the Reading section, domains include letter identification (matching either uppercase letters with lowercase letters, saying the presented letter, or completing a sequence of letters), phonetic identification, word identification, and story comprehension. Likewise, the Spelling and Arithmetic sections have specific domains of activity. The instrument offers 43 Reading items, 22 Spelling items, and 31 Arithmetic items. All items must be administered to a child, and each item is scored plus (correct) or minus (incorrect). Information in the manual indicated that all items were free from bias, although no procedures for making such determinations were suggested.

Performance on the TKFGRS results in raw scores that are converted to age equivalents, scaled scores, percentile ranks, and stanines. The scaled scores have a mean of 100 with a standard deviation of 15.

Item selection was based on content validity, item difficulty, item-to-test correlations, and criterion-related validity. The measures against which the TKFGRS was compared for validity purposes were the Wechsler Preschool and Primary Scale of Intelligence (WPPSI) Vocabulary and Arithmetic scores, the Wechsler Intelligence Scale—Revised (WISC-R) Vocabulary and Arithmetic scores, and the Test of Auditory-Perceptual Skills (TAPS) scores. The correlations were less than adequate, ranging from .14 between the Spelling section of the TKFGRS and the WPPSI Vocabulary score to .54 between the TAPS Auditory Processing score and the Reading section. The average correlation between sections and any of the validity measures was .39. The author should have attempted to establish validity of a preacademic/academic assessment device using other measures of academic ability as opposed to measures of cognitive ability and auditory perception. Normatively and psychometrically, the TKFGRS is lacking.

The TKFGRS contains a technical and administration manual, test cards for each section, and a record booklet. The administration of the TKFGRS is simple and the record booklet is user friendly. Training requirements for administration are minimal. Administration time was not indicated other than it would take longer to administer the instrument to older children than younger children. A shortcoming of the administration guidelines is that all items must be administered. Given that the sampling of academic behaviors of the TKFGRS is rather small to begin with, this would seem an unnecessary requirement which will more than likely result in frustration for younger children who are academically deficient.

In summary, this reviewer would not advise the use of the TKFGRS. At best, it is a poor screener of academic abilities for preschool and early elementary children. Many other strategies could be more functional to the instructional or assessment specialist including teacher-constructed criterion-related measures or other more sound assessment strategies. The instrument is plagued by shortcomings associated with normative sampling, item selection, and validity procedures. It was unclear to this reviewer whether the instrument is intended to be used for screening or diagnosis. In either case, the TKFGRS falls short on all accounts.

Review of the Test of Kindergarten/First Grade Readiness Skills by J. STEVEN WELSH, Director, School Psychology Program, Nicholls State University, Thibodaux, LA:

The purpose of the Test of Kindergarten/First Grade Readiness Skills (TKFGRS) is to provide educators, counselors, and psychologists a criterion measure of academic readiness of young children entering kindergarten or the first grade. The manual author states that the instrument will assist professionals in determining areas of academic deficiency or "low functioning" in children. The manual author suggests the test may be used with children age 3.6 years old to 7.0 years old and measures academic skill development in Reading, Spelling, and Arithmetic.

The norm sample included 373 children ranging from 3 years to 7 years of age. Children were enrolled in either public or private elementary schools. None of the children in the standardization sample had learning disabilities, hearing impairments, or visual impairments. Subjects were divided by age into seven groups in 6-month increments. The sample was 53.4% male and 46.6% female. Unfortunately, the manual does not provide the reader data regarding the racial/ethnic makeup of the sample, geographic region of the sample, at what point in the academic year data were collected, and the ratio of children in public schools to private schools. Children who had not had exposure to "readiness skills" and non-English-speaking children were eliminated

from the standardization group. The manual does not specifically define "exposure to readiness skills" (p. 7) or by what manner children were assessed and eliminated from the sample.

The Reading section of the TKFGRS assesses letter identification by having the child match upper and lower case letters, respond to a visually presented letter stimulus and say the correct letter, and complete a sequence of letters with the next correct letter. Stimuli of letter items are presented to the child on a 4-inch x 8-inch card. Phonetic identification is accomplished by having the child produce the sounds of six letter pairs. The examiner says the letter to the child and then asks the child to produce the sound of the letter. The manual does not indicate if the letter is identified only for the sample item or for all letters in the subtest. Word identification requires a child to read from a list of nine words. Story comprehension is a measure of listening comprehension that requires a child to answer a series of questions after the examiner has read the passage. The Spelling section requires the child to write individual letters or words from dictation. The Arithmetic section requires the child to write numbers from dictation, complete written computations, verbally respond to orally presented problems, tell time, and correctly identify numbers within a sequence of numbers.

The manual provides very limited information regarding the reliability and validity of the TKFGRS. Estimates of internal consistency using Cronbach's alpha were provided for the Reading, Spelling, and Arithmetic subtests. Coefficients for the Reading section on the instrument ranged from .87 to .93 with an overall reliability coefficient of .96. The Spelling section reliability coefficients ranged from .66 to .91, with an overall coefficient of .95. Reliability estimates for the Arithmetic section ranged from .69 to .91 with an overall section coefficient of .94. The manual does not report data regarding split-half or test-retest reliability. No data regarding a child's scores on this instrument and subsequent performance in school were included in the manual.

Content validity is addressed in the manual and is discussed in terms of how the items on the TKFGRS are analogous to the items of tests that purport to measure the same ability. The manual goes on to indicate that "within each test section, different kinds of items were used in measuring the stated behaviors" (p. 10). The manual indicated that the items that were included in the final pool had item difficulty ranges from .185 to .858 for Reading, .09 to .563 for Spelling, and .029 to .853 for Arithmetic.

Criterion-related validity was established by correlating readiness section scores to a child's performance on the Wechsler Intelligence Test for Children (WISC-R) or the Wechsler Preschool and Primary Scale of Intelligence (WPPSI) Vocabulary subtest for the TKFGRS Reading and Spelling sections. The WISC-R or WPPSI Arithmetic subtest scores were used to establish criterion validity of the TKFGRS Arithmetic section. The scores for each TKFGRS subtest were also correlated to performance on the Test of Auditory-Perceptual Skills (TAPS). Correlation coefficients were uniformly low with the WISC-R Vocabulary score and TKFGRS Reading section correlation of .33. The correlations between the WISC-R or the WPPSI with the Spelling section were .23 and .14 respectively. The correlations between the WISC-R or WPPSI with the Arithmetic section were .43 and .45. Correlations between the TAPS and the Reading, Spelling, and Arithmetic sections of the TKFGRS were .54, .43, and .52 respectively. The manual leads the reader to believe that the author considered these low correlations sufficient to establish adequate criterion-related validity. It is not clear if it was the intent of the author to establish that the TKFGRS was measuring constructs that differ from those traditionally associated with achievement measures, namely intellectual functioning. Other technical data comparing TKFGRS and other measures of academic readiness or achievement were not reported in the manual.

The TKFGRS manual indicated that the instrument yields standard scores with a mean of 100 and a standard deviation of 15. However, these data are not provided in the tables. Scaled scores are reported in a range from 1 to 19 with an apparent mean of 10. The manual does not provide estimates of the standard error of measurement for overall scores or for the various age categories. Age equivalents, percentiles, and stanine score are reported in table form in the manual.

Considering the dearth of information provided about the standardization sample, limited technical data regarding the reliability and validity of the TKFGRS, and confusing tables, it is recommended the potential user proceed with caution if screening and school placement decisions will be made based on a child's performance on this instrument. The wisdom of dropping children without exposure to academic readiness skills from the standardization sample for an instrument designed to assess academic readiness skills is questionable. Assessment of this type is typically accomplished to identify at-risk children who may not be prepared for entering school and who might benefit from programs to help them become "ready." Head Start is an example of such a program. It would seem that including a percentage of these "non exposed children" in the standardization sample might positively improve the predictive validity of the instrument. The TKFGRS does not appear to offer a particularly robust measure of academic readiness and should not be used as a diagnostic tool. Future editions of the TKFGRS will certainly be improved if more precise technical data are presented in the manual. Additionally, the test would be further strengthened if other nonacademic factors of school readiness such as developmental and social-emotional readiness factors are included.

[329]
Test of Mathematical Abilities, Second Edition.

Purpose: "A measure of math ability."
Population: Ages 8-0 to 18-11.
Publication Dates: 1984–1994.
Acronym: TOMA-2.
Scores, 6: Vocabulary, Computation, General Information, Story Problems, Attitude Toward Math, Total.
Administration: Group.
Price Data, 1994: $64 per complete kit including 25 Profile/Record forms and Examiner's Manual ('94, 51 pages); $34 per 25 Profile/Record forms; $34 per Examiner's manual.
Time: (120–130) minutes.
Authors: Virginia L. Brown, Mary E. Cronin, and Elizabeth McEntire.
Publisher: PRO-ED, Inc.
Cross References: For a review by Mark L. Davison of the earlier edition, see 9:1263.

TEST REFERENCES
1. McCloskey, M., Aliminosa, D., & Macaruso, P. (1991). Theory-based assessment of acquired dyscalculia. *Brain and Cognition, 17*, 285-308.

Review of the Test of Mathematical Abilities, Second Edition by DELWYN L. HARNISCH, Director, Office of Educational Testing, Research & Service, and Associate Professor of Educational Psychology, University of Illinois at Urbana—Champaign, Champaign, IL:

The Test of Mathematical Abilities, Second Edition (TOMA-2) is the second edition of the Test of Mathematical Abilities (TOMA). The Test of Mathematical Abilities (TOMA) was introduced in 1984 and was designed to identify students (using a norm-referenced interpretation) who are significantly below or above their age peers in their mathematical abilities so that they can receive special intervention. The Second Edition, while retaining most of the items from TOMA, improved the technical adequacy of the test instrument as follows: (a) Increased the reliability of the instrument; (b) increased the size of the normative sample at the lower and upper age brackets; (c) stratified the normative sample so as to conform to the 1990 U.S. Census population; (d) included studies showing the absence of racial and gender bias; (e) improved the quality of the items; and (f) rewrote the administrative procedures to make them easier to implement.

TOMA-2 is a measure of math ability designed for use with students in the 8–18 age group. In addition to the story problems and computations, it also provides standardized information about attitudes, vocabulary, and general cultural applications of mathematical information to assist administrators not only to identify individuals who are weak in math, but also to understand better the nature of those problems.

SUBTEST DESCRIPTION. The Vocabulary (VO) subtest contains 25 mathematical terms (e.g., fraction, decimal, pi, hypotenuse) that relate to size, shape, measurement, and position in time and space. The student is asked to write a brief meaning, as used in the mathematical sense, for each of the terms. The examiner's manual provides illustrations of correct and incorrect responses with the final judgment involving subjectivity to determine the status of response. The goal is to test students' mastery of mathematics vocabulary with less of an emphasis on spelling and punctuation. Mastery of the mathematical vocabulary is assumed to help students in math comprehension.

The Computation (CO) subtest contains 30 items ranging in difficulty from simple one-digit addition problems to complex mathematical problems involving the use of fractions, decimals, money, and percentages. The test measures students' problem-solving ability because mastery of mathematical computations is one of the goals of mathematics instruction.

The General Information (GI) subtest contains 30 phrases, read by the examiner, about common everyday situations. Mastery of general math concepts provides information about the child's range of information in mathematics, alertness to the use of these concepts in their daily environment, and social and cultural background. It is expected that because students encounter these items in their daily experiences, they do not have to do any computations or mental mathematical reasoning to answer the item. The student

can either answer the questions orally or write the answers on the profile/record form. Some of the items are clearly mathematical, "asking the students to tell you what the numbers 5 feet, 6 inches tells you," whereas other items are less mathematical, "what does it mean to 'subscribe' to a newspaper or magazine."

The Story Problem (SP) subtest, often known as "Word Problems," consists of a total of 25 items in a story format and is based on classroom activities and teacher-made tests. The student reads the story and solves the mathematical problem related to the text. The problems are arranged in easy-to-difficult order. It is not clear whether this basic procedure of organizing items from easiest to hardest is followed on any of the other subtests. Given the scoring rule of stopping item administration once a student misses three consecutive items suggests that this may be true but no evidence was found in the manuals to document this.

The 15-item Attitude Toward Math (AT) subtest measures student's attitudes towards math. Positive attitude toward math is often associated with students with higher achievement in math. Each item describes a math situation (e.g., "I'm better at math than most of my friends," and "I like math competitions or contests"). The student is given a choice of four options: "yes, definitely!; closer to yes; closer to no; or no, definitely!" to reflect their feelings about the statements. The items were constructed from The Estes Attitude Scales (1981). The format of this subtest allows for the examiner and/or the student to read the test.

TEST ADMINISTRATION AND SCORING. The examiner's manual recommends assessment training for the examiners by taking a course in assessment at a college. The examiners are also advised to be familiar with the school policies, local and state regulations, and the use of the test results. The examiner's manual includes a set of 14 simple rules for the examiners to follow to assure a reliable administration of the test. These rules are based on common sense and are very practical to test administrators. The manual describes the "Entry points and Ceiling" procedures, with simple examples for both the individual and group situations, to calculate the raw score. Each subtest comes with its own set of information on the ceiling, test instructions, and an answer key.

NORMATIVE PROCEDURES. The TOMA-2 was normed on 2,082 students between 8–18 years of age from four major school districts covering 26 states in the U.S. Schools with demographic characteristics matching one of the four major census districts were selected. Trained personnel conducted normative data collection and actual testing. The demographic characteristics of the normative sample match with the school age population of the U.S. as reported in the 1990 Statistical Abstract of the United States.

The TOMA-2 results are reported for each subtest in terms of standard scores, composite math quotient, and age and grade equivalent. The standard score is derived from the cumulative frequency distribution of the raw scores of students in the normative sample and has a mean of 10 and a standard deviation of 3. The Math Quotient is derived by adding the standard scores of Vocabulary, Computation, General Information, and Story Problems subtests. For the benefit of guidance staff and school administrators, the manual includes separate tables to convert raw scores into percentiles and to calculate age and grade equivalent estimates.

TEST RELIABILITY. Internal consistency reliability estimates (Cronbach's coefficient alpha) and standard errors are given on each subtest and math quotient for each age and subtest. The reported reliabilities ranged from .73 (Vocabulary subtest for 8-year-olds) to .96 (Vocabulary subtest for 18-year-olds) with over 55% of the reliabilities above a value of .90. The reliability coefficients averaged for all the age groups and for the math quotient all exceed .84. The stability-over-time reliability was conducted using the test-retest method for 198 students from New Orleans, Louisiana with a 2-week period between testing. The test-retest reliabilities were all good (above .80) for reported ages 10 through 14, with the exception of Attitudes Toward Math (average .70).

TEST VALIDITY. Evidence for content validity is based on an item analysis using the point biserial correlation technique that was performed on the normative sample during the development stage of TOMA-2. The median item discrimination coefficients are included in the handbook and range from .34 (Computation test—age 9) to .70 (General Information—age 17).

Evidence for criterion-related validity was evaluated with concurrent student test scores from the KeyMath Diagnostic Arithmetic Test (1971), Peabody Individual Achievement Test (1970), and Wide Range Achievement Test (1965). These criterion-validity studies are based on a sample of 38 children with learning disabilities who were between the ages of 9 and 17 and took the tests. The correlation coefficients, corrected for age, ranged from .27 to .56 for the subtests and between .34 to .46 for the Math Quotient. The correlation coeffi-

cient of the standard scores between TOMA-2 and SRA Achievement Series (1992) ranged between .38 and .72 for the subtests and .61 for the Math Quotient based on a sample of 290 students attending schools in Illinois and Louisiana. The validity coefficients of TOMA-2 with SRA tend to be higher than those shown with the KeyMath, Peabody Individual Achievement Test, or the Wide Range Achievement Test. These differences may be due to the greater test length found with SRA for Computation and Story Problems.

Evidence for construct validity is found in the correlation of the core subtests with age. The four core subtests correlated highly with age of the individuals in the entire normative sample, ranging from .61 for Vocabulary to .36 for Story Problems. The coefficient is negative (-.26) for the Attitude Towards Math subtest, indicating that as children get older they like math less and less.

The four core subtests are highly intercorrelated ranging from .55 to .62. The intercorrelations among the core subtests and the Attitude Towards Math is low (ranges from .09 with Vocabulary to .21 for Computation and Story Problems). In short, the TOMA-2 aptitude subtests correlate as highly with the general academic ability measures (WISC full scale IQ and Slosson Intelligence Test IQ) as with the three math tests. These results are consistent with the review of the earlier edition of the TOMA (Davison, 1985).

To test the group differentiation capabilities of this test, the test was administered to a sample of 38 students with disabilities. The average standard scores ranged between 6 and 9 compared to a score of 10 expected from a typical student. The low scores on the subtests as well as on the math Quotient indicate that the TOMA-2 is able to discriminate students with varying abilities.

Bias studies of the TOMA-2 were conducted. Formats for the items on the test were reviewed to reduce cultural loadings on test items. The reported correlation values between Delta values for race and gender on TOMA-2 subtests are very high ranging from .95 and above indicating low or no gender and race bias in the TOMA-2.

TEST MANUAL. The authors estimate that each subtest takes 30 minutes or less to administer. The examiner's manual is well written and informative. The test comes with the profile/record form for recording the students' score profile information on testing condition, data from nontest sources such as teacher's local assessment program, and diagnostic comments of the examiner regarding the interpretations and recommendations. Separate norms are provided for all subtests and the Math Quotient for various age groupings (8-0 through 8-11; 9-0 through 9-11; … 18.0 through 18.11). The TOMA-2 approximates the national normative group on several important features: proportion of males and females; whites, blacks, and others; ethnicity categories; four U.S. geographical regions; and disabling condition.

SUMMARY. In summary, the overall quality of the TOMA-2 has increased estimates of reliability on the subtests dues to improved test design and development considerations. The revisions and norming procedures were carefully crafted; reliability coefficients are relatively high. If the test were to be used outside of the U.S.A. the content and wording of some of the items would require revision and appropriate norms would need to be developed. However, a concern that still remains is the scale range to qualify a wide range of abilities and ages. Davison (1985) described this as "coarseness" and suggested that it may be due to the size of the norm group. Even with the revised normative sample, the "coarseness" still remains but not to the same degree as noted by Davison (e.g., a 3-point raw score increase from 16–18 on the General Information subtest for children aged 11-0 through 11-11 does not change a child's percentile rank, but a 1-point raw score increase from 24 to 25 will raise the percentile rank 7 percentage points in contrast to a 12-point increase on the earlier edition). The high correlations among the subtests and with other IQ tests (WISC and Slosson) leaves one in a quandary as to whether this test is measuring math achievement, aptitude, or general academic ability.

REVIEWER'S REFERENCES

Estes, T. H., Estes, J. J., Richards, H. C., & Roettger, D. M. (1981). Estes Attitude Scales. Austin, TX: PRO-ED, Inc.

Davison, M. L. (1985). [Review of Test of Mathematical Abilities.] In J. V. Mitchell, Jr. (Ed.), *The ninth mental measurements yearbook* (pp. 1578-1579). Lincoln, NE: Buros Institute of Mental Measurements.

Review of the Test of Mathematical Abilities, Second Edition by ROSEMARY SUTTON, Associate Professor, College of Education, Cleveland State University, Cleveland, OH:

The Test of Mathematical Abilities, Second Edition (TOMA-2) has four purposes: identify students who are significantly below or above their age peers, determine strengths and weaknesses of students, evaluate students' progress, and provide researchers with a nontraditional measure of mathematics. To fulfill these purposes the authors devised

five subtests. Two of these, Computation and Story Problems, are traditionally found in mathematics achievement tests, whereas the other three, Vocabulary, General Information, and Attitude Towards Math, are not.

The Computation subtest contains 30 items. It begins with basic addition and subtraction problems (e.g., 5+4), moves to more difficult arithmetic problems including fractions and decimals, and ends with geometry and algebra problems. The Story Problems subtest contains 25 items. An easy item is "Tom has 1 yellow boat. He had one red car. He has 1 blue car, too. How many cars does Tom have?" A harder item is "A ten-foot fence casts a shadow that is 6 feet long. An adjacent building is 20 yards away. Its shadow is 40 feet long. About how tall is the building?"

On the General Information subtest the examiner reads the questions to the student who replies orally or in writing. Sample questions from the 30 items include ones that are clearly mathematical (e.g., "How many pennies in a dime?") as well as others that are not as clearly mathematical (e.g., "What does it mean to 'subscribe' to a newspaper or magazine?"). The Vocabulary subtest contains 25 words, which the student reads and then writes a definition. Examples of words include "dozen" and "ellipse." For both of these subtests the manual provides scoring rules.

The Attitude Towards Math scale is an optional subtest that contains 15 items such as "It's fun to work math problems" and "The teacher makes math easy for me to understand." Students respond on a 4-point scale. Students may read this subtest or have it read to them by the examiner.

Because the TOMA-2 test is devised to assess mathematical abilities for a wide age range (8-0 years to 18-11 years) the use of ceilings is employed. On the Vocabulary, Computation, General Information, and Story Problems subtests, testing always begins at the first item but stops after the student misses three in a row. The use of ceilings assumes that the items are in increasing order of difficulty, and that this order is consistent across groups. The authors used item discrimination techniques to place the items in increasing levels of difficulty, but did not examine possible regional differences. Students' ability to answer many questions, especially those on the Vocabulary subtest, will be dependent, in part, on what is taught in the schools they have attended. This problem is particularly serious because of the definition of ceiling. In other tests, ceilings are more flexible (e.g., three out of four items are failed).

The TOMA-2 was normed on 2,082 students from 26 states. The demographic data of the norming sample are given clearly in the manual and are representative of the U.S.A. in terms of gender, race, ethnicity, region, and disability. Because this test covers 10 years of age the norming subsample for each year varies in size (from 77 to 316) and is too small for some age groups (e.g., age 18). The authors included three types of data in their norming sample: data from the first edition or TOMA; data the authors or trained staff collected from select schools on the TOMA-2; and data from customers who were willing to collect tests from 10 to 50 students. This means that administration of the test was not standardized for all students, which raises issues about the utility of the norms. Additional concerns about the norms arise because two of the subtests (General Information and Attitudes Towards Math) can be administered orally by the examiner or read by the students but the authors do not provide data documenting the effect these various testing conditions have on test scores and norms.

The authors provide clear evidence about the reliability of the subtest scores and the Math Quotient (sum of standard scores of the four subtests: Vocabulary, Computation, General Information, and Story Problems) for various age levels. Internal consistency coefficients (Cronbach's alpha) range from .73 to .96 for the subtests, and .94 to .98 for the Math Quotient. Test-retest data are provided based on 198 students, aged 10–14, in New Orleans over a 2-week period. The coefficients range from .66 to .87 for the subtests and .91 to .93 for the Math Quotient. Standard errors of measurement for each age level and subtest are also provided.

The manual contains evidence related to content, construct, and predictive validity for each subtest. Two types of content validity evidence are given. First, the authors provide a logical rationale for the content of each subtest and for all subtests (except General Information) identify a test containing similar content. However, all the identified tests have publication dates that precede the introduction of the NCTM (National Council of Teachers of Mathematics) standards (1989) and there is no discussion of the possible impact of the standards on the content validity. Second, the authors describe the process of item analysis and present item discrimination coefficients for all age groups. The values of these coefficients range from .34 to .70, which indicates that the items in each subtest are relatively homogeneous. Contrary to the assertion in the manual, this does not provide validity evidence (Anastasi, 1988).

The criterion-related evidence presented in the manual is very weak. First, the authors argue that the correlation coefficients between the subtests of the TOMA and the TOMA-2 are so high (greater than .85) that they will use "the acronym TOMA-2 … to refer to both TOMA and TOMA-2 because the tests are almost identical" (p. 34). This is extraordinarily misleading as they then present criterion-related data based on the original TOMA and label it TOMA-2. These data are old, based on only 38 students with learning disabilities, aged 9 to 17, and have been criticized by previous reviewers (e.g., Howell, 1989–90). A more recent study compared the scores of 290 students from Illinois and Louisiana on the SRA Achievement Series (Naslund, Thorpe, & Lefever, 1992) with the TOMA or TOMA-2 (the manual is unclear). The correlations (corrected for attenuation) ranged from .58 to .72 for the achievement subtests.

The authors include a variety of construct validity evidence. First, they demonstrate that there are positive correlations between age and test scores on the four core subtests. Second, intercorrelations among the subtests are reported and the four core subtests have moderate to high correlations but, as predicted, the correlations with Attitudes Towards Math are much lower. Third, correlations between the subtests and two intelligence tests are moderate to high. However, the correlation (.71) between the total Math Quotient score and one of the intelligence tests (Slosson, Nicholson, & Hibpshman, 1990) is higher than any of the correlations between the Math Quotient score and the mathematical achievement tests (ranging from .34 to .61). This suggests that the TOMA-2 may be closer to an intelligence test than a traditional mathematics test. The authors need to examine discriminant validity evidence as well as convergent validity evidence (Campbell & Fiske, 1959).

In the manual, the authors state that in developing the second edition of the TOMA they sought to overcome the deficiencies documented by earlier reviewers. Although some improvements have been made, including a more representative norming sample, more discussion of validity evidence, and data on test bias, there are still serious issues associated with the standardization of the conditions in establishing norms and with the validity evidence presented. I recommend that, if possible, users select alternative instruments to measure mathematics achievement and attitudes towards mathematics.

REVIEWER'S REFERENCES

Campbell, D. T., & Fiske, D. W. (1959). Convergent and discriminant validation by the multitrait-multimethod method. *Psychological Bulletin, 56*(2), 81–105.
Anastasi, A. (1988). *Psychological testing* (6th ed.). New York: MacMillan.

Howell, K. W. (1989–90). Test of mathematical abilities (TOMA). *Diagnostique, 15*(1–4), 210–217.

National Council of Teachers of Mathematics. (1989). *Curriculum and evaluation standards for school mathematics.* Reston, VA: Author.

Slosson, R. L., Nicholson, C. L., & Hibpshman, T. H. (1990). Slosson Intelligence Test for Children and Adults (rev. ed.). East Aurora, NY: Slosson Educational Publishers.

Naslund, R. A., Thorpe, L. P., & Lefever, D. W. (1992). SRA Achievement Series. New York: CTB/MacMillan/McGraw-Hill.

[330]
Test of Memory and Learning.

Purpose: For "evaluating children or adolescents referred for learning disabilities, traumatic brain injury, neurological diseases, serious emotional disturbance, Attention Deficit-Hyperactivity Disorder."

Population: Ages 5 to 19.

Publication Date: 1994.

Acronym: TOMAL.

Scores, 25: 9 Verbal subtest scores (Memory for Stories, Word Selective Reminding, Object Recall, Digits Forward, Paired Recall, Letters Forward, Digits Backward, Letters Backward, Total); 7 Nonverbal subtest scores (Facial Memory, Visual Selective Reminding, Abstract Visual Memory, Visual Sequential Memory, Memory for Location, Manual Imitation, Total); 4 composite scores (Verbal Memory Index, Nonverbal Memory Index, Composite Memory Index, Delayed Recall Index); 5 Delayed Recall scores (Memory for Stories, Facial Memory, Word Selective Reminding, Visual Selective Reminding, Total).

Administration: Individual.

Price Data, 1994: $159 per complete kit including examiner's manual (105 pages), picture book, 25 record forms and administration booklets, 25 supplementary analysis forms, facial memory picture book, 15 facial memory chips, visual selective reminding test board, and a set of delayed recall cue cards; $32 per examiner's manual; $49 per picture book; $34 per 25 record forms and administration booklets; $11 per 25 supplementary analysis forms; $19 per facial memory picture book; $5 per visual selective reminding test board; $12 per delayed cue card set; $79 per software scoring and report system.

Time: (40–45) minutes.

Authors: Cecil R. Reynolds and Erin D. Bigler.

Publisher: PRO-ED, Inc.

TEST REFERENCES

1. Farmer, J. E., & Peterson, L. (1995). Pediatric traumatic brain injury: Promoting successful school reentry. *School Psychology Review, 24,* 230–243.

Review of the Test of Memory and Learning by KAREN GELLER, Developmental Neuropsychologist in Private Practice, Whitehouse Station, NJ:

The Test of Memory and Learning (TOMAL) is an attempt to fill a significant gap in standardized assessment of children's memory. The TOMAL is an improvement over the Wide Range Assessment of Memory and Learning (WRAML; T4:2957), its only major competitor, in some respects. It is much more comprehensive, eliminates graphomotor demands, provides useful delayed recall measures, and uses visual stimuli that do not generally lend themselves easily to verbal labels. Conversely, the WRAML is much more attractive to children and has a delayed recognition measure for story paragraphs, which can help to discriminate between weakness in storage versus retrieval.

The test is designed for use with children who are exhibiting difficulty in learning or who are known to have certain conditions that place the child at risk for memory impairment (e.g., epilepsy). The authors provide an excellent overview of the history of memory assessment and the need for a comprehensive battery for children. They appropriately caution examiners against using test results to attempt localization of brain lesions and provide suggestions for interpreting children's memory performance within a meaningful context. Within the manual, there is a clear and cogent overview of memory functioning and neuroanatomy. The authors recommend that examiners should have a base of knowledge about children's memory in order to adequately interpret test results.

The norming sample is based on the 1990 and 1992 United States Census. Population proportionate sampling was used, with consideration of age, gender, ethnicity, socioeconomic status, geographic region of residence, and urban/rural residence. The manual states that standardization examiners were trained in TOMAL administration via a training tape produced by the authors and publisher of the test. The publisher's staff and the authors were also actively involved in supervising data collection.

The test items were carefully selected to minimize bias. Test items were evaluated statistically to determine if they yielded different results within different groups. Item functioning was found to be highly consistent across gender and ethnic groups. The authors state that the Verbal Memory subtests should be restricted to use with proficient speakers of English.

Reliability and validity data provided indicate that the TOMAL is psychometrically sound. Internal consistency is quite strong. Test-retest reliability, based on a small sample (35 children tested between 4 and 9 weeks apart), was also very good. The manual describes content validity, construct validity, and criterion-related validity at length. Concurrent validity is addressed only by describing a small study (41 subjects) of children with learning disabilities, but more evaluation is necessary in this area to determine whether or not the TOMAL accurately identifies children with impairments in memory and learning. Predictive validity is not addressed.

The TOMAL provides many ways to analyze performance. Besides the Verbal Memory, Nonverbal Memory, and Total Memory indices, there is a Delayed Memory index and there are several supplemental indices (i.e., Learning Index, Associative Recall Index, Free Recall Index, Sequential Recall Index, and Attention/Concentration Index). Standard scores are reported at 1-year intervals. The Supplementary Analysis Form provides a graphic format for comparison of memory performance with IQ and achievement, as well as comparing current performance to a baseline. Normal learning curves are provided for comparison as well.

The test eliminates a common confound for visual memory tasks, errors due to weakness in visual-motor integration, by not requiring the child to write or draw their responses. Recall of verbal and visual information following a delay is formalized and standardized. The WRAML does not assess delayed recall of visual information at all and delayed verbal recall assessment is based on the difference between number of details recalled initially and after a delay, regardless of the level of initial learning. In addition, the TOMAL authors have attempted to develop visual memory tasks that are difficult to encode verbally, so that they would truly assess visual processing. This goal was achieved for most of the visual memory subtests, but the Abstract Visual Memory subtest stimuli are fairly easy to label verbally.

Test administration procedures are generally quite clear and thorough, with one significant omission. The manual does not indicate the frequency of presentation of stimuli in either the Word Selective Reminding or Visual Selective Reminding subtests. The Abstract Visual Memory subtest, which has a higher starting point for older children, requires the examiner to return to the beginning of the subtest to establish a basal, but this is not indicated on the test form and it is easy for the examiner (especially one with less experience with this test) to forget to do this and thus render this subtest's results invalid.

There were a few problems with test materials and items. I have found that some older children are confused on the Paired Recall subtest because one of the words used in a sample word pair (i.e., boy-girl) is used again as a test stimulus (i.e., girl-flag). On Memory for Stories Delayed, one of the stories is labeled for the child in a manner that they often do not recognize (i.e., the Toy Store story). The test is quite difficult for children at younger ages and may overestimate performance on several subtests; how-ever, when composite scores are computed children with very poor memory are clearly identified. In addition, the child can easily see through the pages in the administration booklet, sometimes revealing the objects that they are to remember. According to Dr. Bigler, this was corrected in the second printing, but those of us who purchased the test before this was fixed must still block these pages. Because this flaw can materially affect children's test performance, I feel that it would have been appropriate for the publisher to replace the administration books of those who bought tests from the first printing.

I have administered this test to more than 20 children and adolescents. In my experience, children find it long and tedious. Most of them complain particularly about being presented with three learning tasks in a row, with eight presentations of items on the first two and then five on the third.

From a technical standpoint, the TOMAL is a highly reliable and well-normed measure. The Visual Memory subtests provide a substantial improvement over previously available measures. Further investigation of the TOMAL's sensitivity and ability to correctly differentiate children with memory difficulties is necessary.

In sum, as an attempt to fill a gap in standardized assessment of children's memory the TOMAL is only partially successful. There is still a need for a psychometrically sound, child-friendly memory battery that can predict which children will need additional assistance and training in memory skills.

Review of the Test of Memory and Learning by SUSAN J. MALLER, *Assistant Professor of Educational Measurement and Research, University of South Florida, Tampa, FL:*

The Test of Memory and Learning (TOMAL) was constructed to provide a standardized measure of memory function for children and adolescents with memory deficits due to a variety of reasons such as learning disabilities, traumatic brain injury, neurological disorders, serious emotional disturbances, and attention deficit-hyperactivity disorder. The "standard" or "core" battery consists of 10 subtests forming two Memory Indexes, Verbal (VMI) and Nonverbal (NMI), which combine to form the Composite Memory Index (CMI). Two supplementary indexes, Associate Recall and Learning, may also be computed based on the 10 core subtests. Four more supplementary subtests (three Verbal and one Nonverbal) are included in the computation of the Sequential Recall, Free Recall, and Attention/Concentration Indexes. A Delayed Recall Index (DRI) is available, comprising modifications of two VMI and two NMI subtests, and is designed to assess memory decay. The manual presents a historical and theoretical overview of the evaluation of memory but does not provide a clear theoretical rationale outlining the TOMAL test constructs.

The manual states that the TOMAL should be administered by a qualified examiner with formal training in assessment who has consulted their school or agency and professional organization policies regarding the diagnosis of "handicapping" conditions and subsequent placement. The TOMAL is individually administered, requiring approximately 45 minutes for the standard battery and 15 minutes for the supplementary subtests. Basal rules are determined by age, whereas ceiling rules are used to shorten administration time. Examiners must supply a stopwatch and clipboard (for the record form). Test materials include a picture book, used with several of the subtests, which is not in easel form. It is highly recommended that an easel be used, because stimulus materials are printed on each side of the booklet and can be distracting for the examinee. Furthermore, the manual recommends the purchase of an easel, such as the one available from the publisher.

The scoring system used for several of the subtests, including Digits Forward, Digits Backward, Letters Forward, and Letters Backward, is awkward, because examiners are to award one point for each digit or letter repeated in the correct position. However, it is unclear how the examiner should score digits or letters correctly repeated subsequent to an omitted digit or letter. Traditionally, these tasks are scored as one item comprising the entire sequence (e.g., the Digit Span subtest in the Wechsler Scales).

The standardization sample (N = 1,342), which included children ages 5-0-0 to 19-11-30, was representative of the 1990 U.S. Census, and was "later corrected based on updated reports through 1992" (p. 51). The sample included approximately equal numbers of males and females, and was stratified in terms of ethnicity and urban versus rural residence. Individuals' socioeconomic status (SES) data were not collected; however, school sites were chosen in part based on their "SES and related demographic constituency" (p. 52). Because the standardization sample data did not match the U.S. Census in terms of geographical region of residence, "a small amount of weighting was done" (p. 52) in order to correct for the lack of representativenes.

Age-based norms are provided at one-year intervals. These norms were created with most sample sizes (9 of the 15 age intervals) consisting of less than 100 children. Percentiles and standard scores were obtained by normalizing raw score distributions and smoothing.

Raw scores are converted to standard scores for the subtests (M = 10, SD = 3) and Indexes (M = 100, SD = 15). Index scores may be prorated when only four of five subtests are administered. The manual advocates the use of profile analysis of subtest scores and provides a case example. Without empirical studies regarding the prevalence and predictive validity of specific profiles, the validity of the suggested interpretive method is questionable.

The reliability of the instrument was determined using internal consistency, reported by age, and test-retest methods. Median internal consistency coefficient alphas across age ranged from .84–.97 for the Verbal and Nonverbal subtests and .67–.88 for the Delayed Recall subtests. The median Core Index reliabilities ranged from .85 to .96, whereas the median Supplemental Indexes ranged from .90 to .99. Test-retest (4–9 week interval) reliability coefficients were reported using a sample that was not representative of the norm sample (30 White and 5 Hispanic children, ages 8 to 11, from a southern urban location). Standard errors of measurement (*SEMs*), based on the internal consistency reliability coefficients, were reported by age level for all subtests and indexes.

The validity evidence is limited. Content validity was determined by the test authors. The manual states that several tasks were eliminated during tryout versions of the test using an "iterative process," but specific details are not provided. According to the manual, the items were developed based on the "scrutiny of the authors, consulting reviewers at the office of the test publisher, commentary from other practitioners in the field, and the ultimate tests of reliability and validity" (p. 61). This statement is somewhat vague, because (a) the test does not appear to be based on any clear theoretical framework; (b) the manual does not specify the methods used to ensure content validity, such as the development of a table of specifications; and (c) empirical justification for item selection seems to be lacking, because item analyses results (using either classical or item response theory methods) were not reported.

Evidence of construct validity was obtained by reporting (a) moderate correlations for subtest raw scores with age and (b) test structure using factor analytic methods. The factor structure does not support the "expert-determined" scales (i.e., indexes). Thus, no empirical justification was made for the computation of the index scores. Confirmatory factor analytic methods would have been preferable in light of the authors' "expert-determined" scales. Criterion-related validity evidence is likewise discouraging. The samples used in the validity studies were not representative of the standardization sample; samples were generally unbalanced in terms of gender and reported to be from middle class SES groups. Small numbers of children representative of minorities (the authors use the term "Nonwhites") were used without further investigations of differential predictive validity. Low to moderate correlations of the TOMAL subtest and index scores with both intelligence and achievement test scores were reported. The authors minimized the lack of criterion-related validity by stating that their test measures unique information not measured by other tests, without providing correlations of the TOMAL with other tests of memory. Although the authors reported the results of one study involving children with learning disabilities, the sample included only children from an upper-middle class suburban school district and the determination of learning disabilities was vague (e.g., qualifications of the examiner were not reported and "severe" discrepancy was not defined explicitly). Because the authors claimed that the TOMAL is useful in the assessment of children with memory deficits due to a variety of etiologies, a section reporting the results of validity studies using the method of contrasting clinical groups seems to be a critical omission.

The method used in the assessment of item and test bias for groups (males/females, "White/Nonwhite," and "Anglo/Non-Anglo") is outdated. The authors justified their use of this method by citing Cole and Moss (1989), and claimed that the method tends to overestimate the presence of bias. Cole and Moss (1989) actually cited Camilli and Shepard's (1987) argument that the method ignores differences between groups in item discrimination, which may give a false impression of the presence or absence of bias by only examining item difficulty. The method used by the TOMAL authors is influenced by the ability distributions of the samples, whereas more current methods to detect differential item functioning match groups on ability. Investigations of test bias, such as differential prediction or factor structure invariance, as advocated by Reynolds (1982), were not reported.

In conclusion, evidence is lacking regarding the stability of test scores and the psychometric properties of the TOMAL when administered to minority populations. The TOMAL may, as the authors claim, add unique information to the assessment process, but sufficient evidence has not been presented regarding the nature (i.e., test constructs) and predictive validity of that information, especially for the clinical populations for whom the test was designed.

REVIEWER'S REFERENCES

Reynolds, C. R. (1982). The problem of bias in psychological assessment. In C. R. Reynolds & T. B. Gutkin (Eds.), *The handbook of school psychology* (pp. 178–208). New York: John Wiley.
Camilli, G., & Shepard, L. A. (1987). The inadequacy of ANOVA for detecting test bias. *Journal of Educational Statistics, 12*, 87–99.
Cole, N. S., & Moss, P. A. (1989). Bias in test use. In R. L. Linn (Ed.), *Educational measurement* (3rd ed.) (pp. 201–219). New York: American Council on Education & Macmillan.

[331]
Test of Oral and Limb Apraxia.

Purpose: "Designed to identify, measure, and evaluate the presence of oral and limb apraxia in individuals with developmental or acquired neurologic disorders."
Population: Ages 20–99.
Publication Date: 1992.
Acronym: TOLA.
Scores, 5: Limb, Oral, Pictures, Command, Imitation, Total.
Administration: Individual.
Price Data: Available from publisher.
Time: (15–20) minutes.
Author: Nancy Helm-Estabrooks.
Publisher: The Riverside Publishing Co.

Review of the Test of Oral and Limb Apraxia by PEGGY A. HICKS, School Psychologist, Hand Q Consultants, Richmond, VA:

Designed to identify and quantify deficits in the ability to perform purposeful motor activities in the absence of paralysis or other sensory or motor deficits, the Test of Oral and Limb Apraxia (TOLA) is an appropriate diagnostic tool for use when the neurological condition is developmental or acquired. Specifically, apraxia is a disturbance in the ability to program, sequence, and execute purposeful gestures through imitation or on command when failure to execute is not due to muscle weakness, incoordination, confusion, or inattention. Target populations include persons who have encephalopathy secondary to traumatic brain injury, strokes, congenital disorders, anoxia, brain tumors, infections of the central nervous system, and progressive neurological syndromes such as dementia of the Alzheimer's type. A test of ideomotor apraxia, the TOLA assesses Oral

Apraxia (nonrespiratory vs. respiratory), Limb Apraxia (distal vs. proximal and transitive vs. intransitive) and Pictures (proximal, distal, and oral). Designed for adults, the TOLA norming sample ranges from 20 to 99 years of age.

By design, the TOLA can be administered by any clinician with specialized training in assessing individuals with neurologic disorders. Test format allows for convenient administration at the beeside or in the treatment room. In order to administer the TOLA, the evaluator needs the test protocol, the stimulus cards, and a pencil. The manual suggests videotaping the test administration. According to the manual, administration on average takes 15 minutes with scoring requiring less than 5 minutes. However, an experienced clinician could score the test during the administration. TOLA Windows scoring software is available.

The Test of Oral and Limb Apraxia is a userfriendly, normed instrument developed by a clinician for clinicians. Recognizing that target populations frequently include individuals with hemiplegia, hemiparesis, and/or oral comprehension problems, subjects are required to use their nondominant hand and all items are administered with both verbal commands and gestural imitation. The arrangement of TOLA subtests reflects hierarchy of praxis task difficulty including the body part and motor pathway involved in the movement and the symbolic or conceptual complexity of a target gesture. The TOLA is useful when determining the types and severity of oral and limb apraxia, and tracking patterns of natural recovery. Practically, the TOLA can be used to infer the competence of gestural communications in formal testing by other healthcare professionals and in the natural environment. It is compatible with treatment planning, providing a basis for development of goal and objectives as well as providing a standardized measure of treatment effects. Sensitivity to small changes in patients' behavior and the absence of practice effects make this test a useful test-retest instrument for monitoring incremental changes in functioning.

Both the manual and the test protocol are user friendly. Recognizing the problems with using professional jargon, terms are clearly defined to prevent confusion. The manual makes good use of white space that is especially important whether learning a new test or reviewing to assure standardized administration. As reflected in the tables delineating the specific descriptors of the standardization population, special consideration has been given to assuring

that the norming sample is representative of individuals likely to be tested with this instrument. This information can be helpful to case managers negotiating lengths of stay with third party payers. Pages 7 and 8 of the manual clearly delineate behavioral criteria for each score on the 4-point rating scale (normal [3], adequate [2], partially adequate [1], and inadequate [0]). Norm tables are easily accessed and uncluttered. Tables present means and standard deviations for patients and normal subjects for TOLA part scores and subtests and percentile and standard scores for subtests and composite scores. The manual also provides guidelines for interpreting test results.

The TOLA's user-friendly test protocol and quick score format makes good use of professional time and allows for timely feedback. In addition to raw scores, results are reported in percentile ranks, a descriptive measure that can easily be explained to patients and families, and standard scores that provide equal-interval units for comparison across test administrations and assessment instruments. The protocol includes all information needed to administer the test. General instruction, notes to the evaluator, and scoring criteria are included in the protocol. Standardized directions for administration are presented at the beginning of each new subtest. Responses are easy to record, a space by each item is provided for notes, and subtotals are easy to calculate. Transferring subtotals to the score summary is uncomplicated. Space is provided for recording other important observations. Recognizing that the assessment is not finished until the paperwork is done, this test lends itself well to both dictation and word-processing. Scores are easily accessed, information is organized in a manner that facilitates oral reporting to treatment teams, and item format provides at-your-fingertips information for behaviorally based narrative summaries thereby increasing efficiency and decreasing turnaround time.

The norming sample for the Test of Oral and Limb Apraxia included a total of 176 brain-injured patients and an additional 21 normal subjects from 34 sites in the United States and Canada. With a median age of 70 and 75% of the normative population being 60 years or older, the sample is most certainly skewed. Some of the cells are also poorly represented. The author does note that age is not considered to be a predictor for aphasia. Because apraxia is typically evident when damage involves language-dominant left cerebral hemisphere and often occurs concurrent with aphasia, patients were included if they had incurred strokes or other brain injury typically associated with aphasia. In order to explore the relationship between apraxia and aphasia, the Aphasia Diagnostic Profiles (ADP) were also administered. The ADP Elicited Gestures was also administered for the purpose of investigating construct validity. Based on discriminant analysis, the TOLA measures what it purports to measure indicated by accurately classifying 84% of 127 patients and normals studied. Cronbach's alpha values (ranging from .96 to .99 for raw scores on all subtests and composite scores) indicate a high interitem consistency. Considering the substantial improvement in patients over an 11-day mean interval, the test-retest coefficient of .64 was also quite high.

In summary, the TOLA is a user-friendly and pragmatic assessment tool that rules out the presence of apraxia, defines the degree of involvement for an individual patient, and compares a patient's performance to a similar normative population. Sensitivity to incremental changes in behavior and lack of practice effect means that this instrument can be administered at varying points in the course of rehabilitation. Thus, the TOLA can be very helpful for initial treatment planning and monitoring progress for adults with developmental and acquired encephalopthy.

Review of the Test of Oral and Limb Apraxia by MICHAEL LEE RUSSELL, Director, Neuropsychology Fellowship, Tripler Regional Medical Center, Honolulu, HI:

There are two well-established traditions in neuropsychological testing. One follows from the psychometric traditions of psychology, with empirical construction, item analysis, and large and representative normative samples. The other follows from the traditions of neurology and is essentially an attempt to standardize portions of a behavioral neurologists' clinical examination. Many of these tests have both limited validity data and normative samples. The Test of Oral and Limb Apraxia (TOLA) falls under the latter general category.

The TOLA is a very specialized instrument, designed to "identify, measure, and evaluate the presence of oral and limb apraxia in individuals with developmental or acquired neurologic disorders" (manual, p. 1). Apraxia generally results from a lesion to the dominant parietal lobe of the brain (Adams & Victor, 1989), is a disorder of skilled movement, and in its purest sense is seen in the absence of weakness, ataxia, or loss of primary modes of sensation (Lezak, 1995). Neurologists typically elicit information on apraxia by asking a patient to perform a series of complex actions, most commonly to demonstrate how they brush their teeth, comb their hair, and hammer a nail. There are examples of these simple apraxia tests in most neurology and neuropsychology text books. A question, then, is what advantage is to be had with purchasing this test over using those common procedures available at no charge? Assessment for apraxia is also a part of most standard neuropsychological test batteries.

The TOLA is more specifically a test of Ideomotor Apraxia, one of the several categories of apraxia in general use (Adams & Victor, 1989; Lezak, 1995). This begs the question of why the TOLA is not expanded to be a more general measure of apraxia rather than a single subset of apraxia. It would not be possible to use this test in isolation from other measures of aphasia and language function, as many of the subtests assume adequate receptive language ability for which the TOLA cannot alone assess. For example, one of the items: "Pretend you are in the army. How would you salute?" which is to be delivered without example picture or gesture, is grammatically complex, requires sufficient abstract thought to be able to "pretend," and requires a fairly intact memory. As the author herself points out, failure to salute after this command cannot be interpreted as apraxia unless all of these other factors have been ruled out.

The test itself consists of a slender manual (34 pages) and 16 stimuli cards, which are line drawings of common objects. There is a total of 75 questions on the TOLA. The manual suggests the TOLA be videotaped for later scoring, but notes that "skilled clinicians can score the TOLA as the test is being administered" (p. 1).

Scoring is problematic, as each item is graded on a 4-point scale of 0, 1, 2, 3. There is no problem defining what constitutes a "3: completely normal performance," (p. 7) nor a "0: Inadequate, no response or a response that lacks any crucial component of the target" (p. 7). However, I am frankly confused as to what differentiates a "2: Adequate performance" from a "3: Normal Performance," and where the line is drawn for a "1: Partially Adequate" response. To get decent interrater reliability on the TOLA would require exhaustive examples for scoring each item, which the manual does not provide. I fear this is an effort to extract more numerical data from the items than is really justified: Although a 3-point scale would be justified (pass, partial credit, fail), a 4-point scale is not. The 75 questions should thus have a total possible range of 0–150, rather than 0–225.

The standardization sample and norms are not good. Only 21 normal subjects were tested in the normative sample, and thus the "standard score" the TOLA gives is based upon a sample of 145 patients with various degrees of "brain damage." A standard score relative to assorted apraxic patients in various stages of recovery is not a useful reference point, and the manual cannot answer how "close to normal" a patient is, or even how much "spontaneous apraxia" is expected in a nonpatient sample. The TOLA reports difference scores for limb, oral, and gestural apraxias; however, these scales are so highly intercorrelated (.72 to .85) that there appears little justification to state they measure different things at all.

The Test of Oral and Limb Apraxia is a very specialized instrument for certain aspects of apraxia, rarely seen in isolation from other disorders of speech and language. For this reason it is best seen as a "test fragment" that would be better used as a subtest of a more general assessment of aphasia with an instrument like the Boston Diagnostic Aphasia Examination (T4:207) or the Western Aphasia Battery (T4:2949). It is hard to imagine using this test in isolation, but it could be used as a supplement to a weak aphasia test, such as the Reitan Indiana test used in the Halstead Reitan Battery (T4:1119). The TOLA, however, lacks meaningful norms, and its scoring system is problematic. The author suggests it has application in pre-post testing of rehabilitation efforts of apraxic patients, and test forms could be mined for useful apraxia interview items. However, the TOLA itself has major flaws, and very limited application.

REVIEWER'S REFERENCES

Adams, R. D., & Victor, M. (1989). *Principles of neurology* (4th ed.). New York: McGraw-Hill.
Lezak, M. D. (1995). *Neuropsychological assessment* (3rd ed.). New York: Oxford.

[332]
Test of Orientation for Rehabilitation Patients.

Purpose: Measures orientation to person and personal situation, place, time, schedule, and temporal continuity.
Population: Adult and adolescent inpatient rehabilitation patients.
Publication Date: 1993.
Acronym: TORP.
Scores, 6: Person and Personal Situation, Place, Time, Schedule, Temporal Continuity, Total Test.
Administration: Individual.
Price Data, 1993: $29.95 per 25 test booklets; $99 per complete kit including 25 test booklets, manual (100 pages), and laminated response cue cards.
Time: Administration time not reported.

Comments: "Designed to be administered and scored by a variety of rehabilitation personnel."
Authors: Jean Deitz, Clara Beeman, and Deborah Thorn.
Publisher: The Psychological Corporation.
[Editor's Note: The publisher advised in November 1996 that this test is now out of print.]

TEST REFERENCES

1. Deitz, J. C., Tovar, V. S., Thorn, D. W., & Beeman, C. (1990). The Test of Orientation for Rehabilitation Patients: Interrater reliability. *The American Journal of Occupational Therapy, 44*, 784-790.
2. Ottenbacher, K. J., & Tomchek, S. D. (1993). Reliability analysis in therapeutic research: Practice and procedures. *The American Journal of Occupational Therapy, 47*, 10-16.

Review of the Test of Orientation for Rehabilitation Patients by JAMES K. BENISH, School Psychologist, Helena Public Schools, Adjunct Professor of Special Education, Carroll College, Helena, MT:

The Test of Orientation for Rehabilitation Patients (TORP) is an individually administered criterion-referenced test of orientation to Person and Personal Situation, Place, Time, Schedule, and Temporal Continuity. Designed for adult and adolescent patients, "it was created to assess patients who are believed to be confused or disoriented secondary to traumatic head injury, cerebrovascular accident, seizure disorder, brain tumor, or any other neurological condition resulting in such symptoms" (manual, p. 3). This measurement tool is designed to screen patients or monitor patient progress over time. The TORP contains 46 test items grouped within five domains, and each item serves as either an open-ended or auditory recognition task question. The recognition task questions are used when a patient cannot recall the answer to an open-ended question. Recognition task questions have the correct answer randomly placed within a group of three distractors, which includes an alternate distractor in the event one of the original distractors is the correct answer. The TORP was developed to "(a) aid in diagnosis; (b) facilitate management, care, and planning; (c) facilitate the evaluation of treatment effectiveness; and (d) be useful as a research measure" (manual, p. 21).

Instructions for administering the TORP are clearly described in the test manual. "Examiner Response Procedure" cards are supplied to allow for quick reference during testing. There are no time limits specified in the manual, but total test time is to be recorded on the score sheet. It is recommended that testing be completed in one session, whenever possible. A training module is included that provides detailed steps to facilitate testing continuity. Authors suggest that training is best accomplished with a partner. Scoring is accomplished by converting domain and total test raw scores to percentage points. The score sheet allows for corrected scores based on the number of items administered. There are separate daily and weekly graphs to display total test corrected scores. Patient progress can be monitored fairly easily with these graphs.

TEST DEVELOPMENT. Test items were developed through an extensive review of literature based on the premise there was a specific need to assess patients with brain injuries in an inpatient rehabilitation setting. The authors selected items for the TORP by administering them to brain-injured and non-brain-injured patients. Test items were then reviewed by an interdisciplinary group composed of researcher, educators, and clinicians. A content validity study served to determine the 46 items that were grouped into respective domains. This process was described in detail in the manual.

STANDARDIZATION SAMPLE. It was unclear how many patients were assessed during test item development. However, subject numbers were given for construct validity and interrater reliability studies. Items selected for the final version were "piloted on patients with brain injuries and patients without brain injuries" (manual, pp. 21–22). It was also unclear as to the category breakdown of individuals studied by age, gender, type of brain trauma, etc. used in the study.

RELIABILITY AND VALIDITY. Test-retest reliability was good, with intraclass correlation coefficients of .85 for the non-brain-injured and .95 for the brain-injured groups, respectively, for total scores. Intraclass correlations for domain scores ranged from .72 to a respectable .92. An interrater reliability study comparing 34 brain-injured patients with 35 non-brain-injured patients suggested excellent reliability for both domain and total test scores. The authors noted that studies of concurrent and predictive validity would add value to test research. Such studies would enhance the standardization of this criterion-referenced test.

SUMMARY. The Test of Orientation for Rehabilitation Patients (TORP) is an easily administered measure of orientation to Person and Personal Situation, Place, Time, Schedule, and Temporal Continuity. It is designed for adolescent to adult populations receiving inpatient rehabilitation services. The manual and test protocol are clearly and concisely written. Practice modules are included to help increase consistency in test administration among rehabilitation personnel. Aside from limited statistical and research data found in the manual, the TORP could prove worthwhile for rehabilitation personnel either as a screening tool to determine deficiencies due to brain injury or to monitor progress in an inpatient setting.

Review of the Test of Orientation for Rehabilitation Patients by ELAINE CLARK, Professor of Educational Psychology, University of Utah, Salt Lake City, UT:

The Test of Orientation for Rehabilitation Patients (TORP) measures orientation in adolescent and adult rehabilitation patients. The TORP was designed to provide a more thorough, quantifiable, reliable, and valid assessment of orientation than other tests afford. The TORP is more comprehensive than most of its competitors. It consists of 46 items that measure five orientation domains. In addition to assessing whether the patient knows who and where they are, and what the current time-frame is (Person, Place, and Time), the TORP assess the patient's awareness of discrete events in their current schedule and the passage of time (Schedule and Temporal Continuity).

The TORP is designed to be administered by a variety of rehabilitation personnel, including speech and language pathologists, psychologists, occupational therapists, nurses, and physicians. The test authors recommend that examiners have prior experiences with rehabilitation patients and knowledge of general testing principles and specific TORP procedures. A well-designed training module is included that will help with TORP administration and scoring; however, examiners should heed the advice of experience working with rehabilitation patients. Problems can be anticipated whenever a test not only starts with the question, "what is your first name," but gives credit for it. Examiners need to be well prepared if they intend to ask 46 questions to patients who are not only disoriented but potentially agitated. Examiners may want to make sure their rehabilitation experience is also with patients who are in the early stages of recovery from brain injury.

ADMINISTRATION AND SCORING. The test manual and test form are clearly written and will answer most of the questions that examiners will have about administering and scoring the TORP. Detailed instructions are presented in two sections—one a section that pertains to the preparation for administrating the test, and the other a section pertaining to actual test administration and scoring. General guidelines and specific examples make these manual sections very helpful. Issues regarding scheduling (e.g., what to do if the patient cannot complete the test in one sitting) and testing environment (e.g., insuring that prompts such as clocks and calendars are not in view) are some of the issues discussed. The test form also provides scoring guidelines and prompts for most of the test instructions. Because some key instructions are omitted (e.g., discontinue the test if Item #1 is failed and timing of the test), examiners will definitely need to review the manual thoroughly. In addition to administration instructions on the test form itself, laminated examiner response procedure charts are provided to help examiners make decisions about questionable patient responses (e.g., when the patient gives two answers, one that is correct and the other that is incorrect).

Test items are scored as the test is administered. A separate score sheet is provided for this purpose. Each item is scored as spontaneously correct (SC), recognition correct (RC), or incorrect (I). Like the test booklet itself, the score sheet is easy to use. In addition to providing information about individual items, the SC, RC, and I scores are calculated for each domain and the total test (percentage scores are also calculated using conversion tables included in the manual). A data sheet is also included to calculate domain corrected scores and the total test corrected scores (corrected scores take into account items that are not administered to a particular patient). Daily and weekly graphs are included for repeated test administrations. These graphs are helpful in evaluating progress over time.

TRAINING MODULE. The training module is likely to clear up any remaining questions about giving and scoring the TORP. The module consists of filling out two case protocols and passing two competency tests. The cases provide good examples of rehabilitation patients and give the more novice interviewer a sense of what might be found in the patient's chart (e.g., history of injury, therapy evaluations, progress notes, and daily schedules). The cases also provide an opportunity to practice the administration and helpful hints for scoring. Although the multiple-choice competency tests allows examiners to receive further feedback about testing procedures and gives further information about the test itself, examiners are likely to find this exercise laborious, and for the more experienced tester, unnecessary.

RELIABILITY AND VALIDITY. Limited content and construct validity data are provided. Content validity was studied by having 11 "experts" judge the items. An index of item-objective congruence was used to study the items and Lu's (1971) coefficient of agreement was used to study the five behavioral domains. These analyses supported the inclusion of 46 of the 49 original items. Construct validity was evaluated by comparing the TORP scores of 25 rehabilitation patients with brain injuries and 25 rehabilitation patients without brain injuries. Although current thought on construct validity is that it be more broadly defined to include other types of support (e.g., concurrent and criterion validity), more support than what the authors have provided is expected. The fact that rehabilitation patients with brain injuries scored lower than those without does not provide adequate evidence that the test measures orientation. It is obviously feasible that these two groups of patients could be discriminated by a number of functions besides orientation.

Interrater and test-retest reliability data were collected. Interrater reliability was based on the test protocols of 34 subjects with brain injury and 35 without. The coefficients for the total test score were .98 and .99, respectively, for the subjects with and without brain injury. The reliability coefficients for the individual domains were similarly adequate with coefficients for the subjects with brain injury ranging from .89 to 1.00 for orientation to Place and orientation to Time, respectively. Coefficients for subjects without brain injury were also high: .94 for orientation for Person and Personal Situation, and .99 for orientation to Time, Schedule, and Temporal Continuity.

Test-retest data were collected over a 3- to 5-day period. For total test scores, subjects with brain injuries had a coefficient of .95 and for those without brain injuries, a coefficient of .85. Domain stability coefficients for the brain injury group ranged from .72 (orientation to Schedule) to .92 (orientation to Place). There was greater variability for the group without brain injury. Domain coefficients ranged from .25 (orientation to Place) to .86 (orientation for Person and Personal Situation). The magnitude of test and retest score differences for the subjects without brain injuries, however, suggests that the problem is a lack of score variability not stability.

TEST SCORE INTERPRETATION. The normative sample for the test includes 35 rehabilitation patients without brain injuries. Examinees' total and domain corrected scores are compared to the high and low scores and the percentile scores of this group of subjects. It should be noted that 90% of the standardization subjects missed five items or less, and 50% missed one or two items or less. The range of total scores for the normative sample was 1.76 to 2.00 (possible range is 1.00 to 2.00). A total test cutoff score of 1.24 is used to indicate problems with orientation (each domain has its own cutoff score). Without describing how this very small normative sample was selected and what their characteristics are (e.g., why were they in rehabilitation), it is difficult to interpret the meaning of the cutoff scores. Demographics of this sample are limited to information about their sex (16 males and 19 females), age (15 to 87), and socioeconomic background ("varied"). Such a limited sample makes it difficult to know how orientation is distributed among a "normal" population.

SUMMARY. The authors have provided a more comprehensive evaluation of orientation than most other tests on the market; however, this may be at a cost. Administering 46 two-part items to disoriented and potentially agitated patients is likely to be perceived by overburdened rehabilitation personnel as too time-consuming and discarded in favor of shorter measures of orientation. The problem of length is a very serious concern given the fact that TORP is intended to be given more than once to assess progress over time. Although the authors should be commended for their efforts in designing well-written and well-organized test materials, including a training module, they have failed to provide adequate data that would convince users that the time invested in this test is worth it. In addition to providing support for reliability, which the authors have done, support must be provided for the validity of the test and the usefulness of the test scores. A small and poorly defined normative sample will not convince the test users the authors intended to convince, that is, those with knowledge about tests and measurement. Although the authors acknowledge the need for additional data that describe the performance of rehabilitation patients without brain injuries, it would have been better to have provided such data before publishing the test.

REVIEWER'S REFERENCE

Lu, K. H. (1971). A measure of agreement among subjective judgments. *Educational and Psychological Measurement, 31,* 75–84.

[333]
Test of Phonological Awareness.

Purpose: "Measures young children's awareness of individual sounds in words."
Population: Ages 5–8.
Publication Date: 1994.
Acronym: TOPA.
Scores: Total score only.
Administration: Group.
Editions, 2: Kindergarten, Early Elementary.
Price Data, 1994: $98 per complete kit including examiner's manual (38 pages), 25 kindergarten student booklets, 25 early elementary student booklets, 25 kindergarten profile/examiner forms, and 25 early elementary profile/examiner forms; $27 per examiner's manual; $29 per 25 student booklets (specify kindergarten or early

elementary); $9 per 25 profile/examiner forms (specify kindergarten or early elementary).
Time: (15–20) minutes.
Authors: Joseph K. Torgesen and Brian R. Bryant.
Publisher: PRO-ED, Inc.

TEST REFERENCES
1. Catts, H. W. (1993). The relationship between speech-language impairments and reading disabilities. *Journal of Speech and Hearing Research, 36,* 948–958.
2. Foster, K. C., Erickson, G. C., Foster, D. F., Brinkman, D., & Torgesen, J. K. (1994). Computer administered instruction in phonological awareness: Evaluation of the Daisy Quest program. *Journal of Research and Development in Education, 27,* 126–137.
3. Felton, R. H., & Pepper, P. P. (1995). Early identification and intervention of phonological deficits in kindergarten and early elementary children at risk for reading disability. *School Psychology Review, 24,* 405–414.

Review of the Test of Phonological Awareness by STEVEN H. LONG, *Assistant Professor of Communication Sciences, Case Western Reserve University, Cleveland, OH:*

The Test of Phonological Awareness (TOPA) measures young children's ability to match words with same or different phonemes in initial or final position. Its major purpose is in identifying during the early school years children who are at risk for reading difficulties.

TEST MATERIALS. The TOPA comes in two versions, one intended for administration to kindergarten (age 5–6) students and the other for early elementary (6–8) students. Both versions consist of two forms: (a) a booklet with black-and-white line drawings that the student marks in response to test stimuli; and (b) a record form used to score the responses from the booklet. The graphics style and layout of the student booklet is reminiscent of the Boehm Test of Basic Concepts—Revised (Boehm, 1986; T4:314). Procedures for administering and scoring the TOPA are given in an accompanying manual.

TEST ADMINISTRATION. The TOPA can be administered individually or to groups of children. The kindergarten version consists of two tasks, each performed with 10 items. In the first task, the examiner speaks a stimulus word, then speaks three response words. Each of the four words is pictured in the child's booklet. The child is asked to mark the response word that begins with the same sound as the stimulus word. In the second task, the examiner speaks four words. The child is asked to mark the word that has a different first sound than the other three. The only difference in the early elementary version of the TOPA is that the child is asked to identify words with same or different final sounds.

Because the TOPA is administered with live voice it is important that the examiner possess "speech that is sufficiently clear" (p. 5). According to the manual, this disqualifies individuals with articulation deficits and also ones who speak in a dialect different from that of the students. In multicultural environments, the latter requirements must be carefully noted.

The TOPA is scored simply by counting the number of items marked correctly. Normative tables can then be consulted in the manual.

PSYCHOMETRIC ADEQUACY. The TOPA is described as a measure of analytic phonological awareness; that is, it determines whether children can group or contrast words based on phonemic differences. The content validity of the test derives from the belief that such phonological awareness facilitates early reading acquisition.

Stimulus items for the TOPA were selected after an analysis of word familiarity and articulatory ease. Items were then tested with children in the targeted age range and final selections were made from items that had an average pass rate between 58% and 83%. No analysis was performed to assess possible cultural bias in the items selected. The unfamiliarity of words, such as hut, jack, and bulb to children from less mainstream backgrounds could pose a problem for test validity.

Test-retest reliability was calculated with and without an adjustment for internal consistency of response. The kindergarten version showed a test-retest correlation of .84–.94 (6-week interval); the early elementary version was .69–.77 (8-week interval). The lower coefficient of the early elementary version is attributed to the influence of reading instruction during first and second grade, which produces more rapid change in phonological awareness.

The standardization group for the kindergarten version was 857 students; for the early education version it was 3,654 students. Both groups were reasonably evenly distributed across regions of the United States, gender, and core ethnic groups. No indication is given of the language background (monolingual, bilingual) or socioeconomic status of the standardization groups.

Norms are reported in 6-month intervals for the ages 5-0 to 6-11 and yearly intervals for the ages 6-0 to 8-11. Different norms are given for 6-year-olds enrolled in kindergarten and enrolled in first grade at the time of testing. The manual notes that kindergartners in the standardization group were tested during the second half of the school year. This timing should be followed, if the norms are to be applied equitably.

SUMMARY. The TOPA examines children's abilities to differentiate the initial and final sounds of words. From this performance, it is suggested, an inference can be made about a child's readiness for reading. The test format is simple and administration should be completed rapidly in most instances. The TOPA's most apparent shortcoming is that it is at risk for bias if the dialect of the examiner does not match that of the students or if a child's cultural background does not include certain of the lexical items on the test.

REVIEWER'S REFERENCE

Boehm, A. E. (1986). Boehm Test of Basic Concepts—Revised. San Antonio, TX: The Psychological Corporation.

Review of the Test of Phonological Awareness by REBECCA McCAULEY, *Associate Professor, Communication Sciences, University of Vermont, Burlington, VT:*

TEST STRUCTURE. This test was designed for group assessment of children's abilities to isolate individual speech sounds in spoken words for purposes of identification, general screening, and research. The test consists of two forms: The TOPA— Kindergarten, designed for children in kindergarten, and the TOPA—Early Elementary, designed for children in grades 1 and 2. The TOPA—Kindergarten focuses on children's awareness of initial sounds, requiring children to indicate which word from a set of three words contains the same initial sound as the stimulus word (the Initial Sound-Same Subtest) and which word from a set of four words contains a different initial sound from the other three (the Initial Sound-Different Subtest). The TOPA— Early Elementary focuses on children's awareness of final sounds, requiring children to perform assessments comparable to those required by children in the TOPA— Kindergarten, except on final rather than initial sounds.

TEST ADMINISTRATION AND INTERPRETATION. The test may be given by professionals who have a background in educational assessment and whose speech is precise and matches the dialect of the children being tested. Its directions are clear and comprehensive for both forms of the test, an important achievement in light of the test's use with groups of children who are likely to be prereaders. In their discussion of test score interpretation and norms, the authors caution users about the sensitivity of the test to the time during the school year in which it is administered (because the test's norms were collected in the Spring) and about its relative insensitivity to differences among children with higher levels of phonological awareness. Test scores are reported as raw scores, percentiles, and several standard scores.

NORMS. Relatively large groups of children were used to standardize the two forms of the test; specifically, 857 children for the TOPA—Kindergarten and 3,654 for the TOPA—Early Elementary form. The resulting normative samples were nationally representative in terms of race, ethnicity, gender, and geographic location. Most subgroup sample sizes fell beyond a desirable 100 per cell. Several subgroups fell below these levels, including 5-year-olds tested using the TOPA—Kindergarten (e.g., N = 38 for African American, 23 Hispanic, 3 Native American, and 6 Oriental subgroups).

RELIABILITY. High internal consistency was found when the test results for 100 children at each age level were examined. Those data are reported both as correlation coefficients and as standard errors of measurement. Test-retest reliability was examined using a procedure recommended by Anastasi (1988), in which a standard test-retest paradigm is followed by a procedure designed to remove the error associated with internal consistency. When both forms of the test were examined in this way, a very high adjusted stability estimate of .94 was obtained for the TOPA—Kindergarten; whereas only a "high" adjusted correlation of .77 was obtained for the TOPA—Early Elementary. The authors speculate that the lower performance of the TOPA—Early Elementary may have been due to the use of a longer test-retest interval (8 weeks instead of 6) or to the greater response of the older children to their ongoing reading instruction.

VALIDITY. The content validity evidence provided by the test authors consists of a relatively detailed review of the existing literature on the emergence of phonological awareness in children and an impressive account of the test's development, which included two item tryouts preceding standardization and a final item analysis following standardization. Because the test focuses on the identification of children with possible problems rather than the measurement of phonological awareness abilities across both high and low levels of performance, items were selected with higher levels of difficulty than might usually be the case in a norm-referenced test.

Both concurrent and predictive criterion-related validity evidence are provided. Direct evidence of concurrent validity consists of moderate to high positive correlations between one or both versions of the test with the Word Analysis and Word Identification subtests of the Woodcock Reading Mastery Tests (Woodcock, 1987) and three measures of phonological awareness (i.e., a measure of sound isolation, a measure of sound segmentation, and a set of five different phonological tasks taken from a computer-adaptive test, Undersea Challenge [Foster, Erickson, Foster, & Torgesen, in press]). Predictive

validity was examined only for the TOPA—Kindergarten. That evidence consists of moderate correlations between TOPA scores obtained during kindergarten and children's performance in alphabetic reading on the Word Analysis subtest of the Woodcock Reading Mastery Test and the finding that 18 of 23 children who fell in the lowest quartile on the TOPA also fell below the median in alphabetic reading skills in first grade.

Evidence of construct validity for this test begins with the careful elaboration of the construct being tested (which was provided in the description of item selection) and of other aspects of the test's development. It is further supported not only by the other evidence of validity described above, but also by three explicit arguments. First, the authors cite work by Stanovich and his colleagues (1984) and by Wagner and his colleagues (in press) in which the types of tasks used in the TOPA were shown to be closely related to a variety of other phonological awareness tasks. Second, the authors describe a training study examining the relationship between performance on the TOPA and children's response to a 12-week training in phonological awareness. Results of that study indicated that children who performed best initially on the TOPA also showed the greatest gains in training. As a third type of evidence, the authors discuss research demonstrating that children's performance on the TOPA items was unlikely to have been due to their responding to global phonological similarity, a possible confound suggested in the literature.

SUMMARY. The TOPA makes a substantial contribution to the group assessment of phonological awareness in young school-age children. For children in kindergarten through grade 3 (ages 5 to 8-11), its merit as a screening tool is attested by a strong history of test development and validation. Test-retest reliability for the TOPA—Early Elementary fell a bit below a recommended level of .80, but appears likely to have been affected by the length of test-retest interval and by ongoing training on related skills. Other evidence of reliability and validity is generally quite adequate. The provision of predictive validity evidence for the TOPA—Early Elementary version is particularly impressive given probable uses of the test.

REVIEWER'S REFERENCES

Stanovich, K. E., Cunningham, A. E., & Cramer, B. B. (1984). Assessing phonological awareness in kindergarten children: Issues of task comparability. *Journal of Experimental Child Psychology, 38*, 175–190.
Woodcock, R. (1987). Woodcock Reading Mastery Tests—Revised. Circle Pines, MN: American Guidance Service.
Anastasi, A. (1988). *Psychological testing* (6th ed.). New York: Macmillan.
Foster, K. C., Erickson, G. C., Foster, D. F., & Torgesen, J. K. (in press). *Undersea challenge*. Unpublished software, Adventure Learning Software, Orem, UT.

Wagner, R. K., Torgesen, J. K., & Rashotte, C. (in press). The development of reading-related phonological processing abilities: New evidence of bi-directional causality from a latent variable longitudinal study. *Developmental Psychology.*

[334]
Test of Reading Comprehension, Third Edition.

Purpose: Designed to "quantify the reading comprehension ability of individuals."

Population: Ages 7-0 to 17-11.

Publication Dates: 1978–1995.

Acronym: TORC-3.

Scores: 9 subtests: General Vocabulary, Syntactic Similarities, Paragraph Reading, Sentence Sequencing, Supplementary (Mathematics Vocabulary, Social Studies Vocabulary, Science Vocabulary, Reading the Directions of Schoolwork), Reading Comprehension Quotient.

Administration: Group.

Price Data, 1996: $134 per complete kit including 10 student booklets, 50 answer sheets and subtest 8, 50 profiles, and manual ('95, 91 pages) in storage box; $29 per 10 student booklets; $34 per 50 answer sheets and subtest 8; $19 per 50 profiles; $41 per manual.

Time: (60) minutes.

Authors: Virginia L. Brown, Donald D. Hammill, and J. Lee Wiederholt.

Publisher: PRO-ED, Inc.

Cross References: See T4:2785 (3 references); for reviews by James A. Poteet and Robert J. Tierney of an earlier edition, see 10:372 (4 references); for reviews by Brendon John Bartlett and Joyce Hood of the original edition, see 9:1270; see also T3:2456 (1 reference).

TEST REFERENCES

1. Misulis, K. E. (1989). Test of Reading Comprehension (TORC)—Revised Edition. *Journal of Reading, 33,* 228-229.
2. Wolery, M., Cybriwsky, C. A., Gast, D. L., & Boyle-Gast, K. (1991). Use of constant time delay and attentional responses with adolescents. *Exceptional Children, 57,* 462-474.
3. Bromet, E. J., Schwartz, J. E., Fennig, S., Geller, L., Jandorf, L., Kovasznay, B., Lavelle, J., Miller, A., Pato, C., Ram, R., & Rich, C. (1992). The epidemiology of psychosis: The Suffolk County Mental Health Project. *Schizophrenia Bulletin, 18,* 243–255.

Review of the Test of Reading Comprehension, Third Edition by FELICE J. GREEN, Professor of Education, University of North Alabama, Florence, AL:

The Test of Reading Comprehension, Third Edition (TORC-3) is designed to test children between the ages of 7-0 to 17-11 who can read English. It is not appropriate for nonreaders. The results are useful in analyzing reading strengths and weaknesses.

The TORC-3 consists of eight subtests. Four of the subtests are grouped under the General Reading Comprehension Core, and four are grouped under the Diagnostic Supplements.

The four subtests under the General Reading Comprehension Core are General Vocabulary, Syntactic Similarities, Paragraph Reading, and Sentence Sequencing. The Diagnostic Supplements contain three subtests that measure content area vocabularies: Mathematics, Social Studies, and Science. The last subtest under Diagnostic Supplements is Reading the Directions of Schoolwork.

The title "General Vocabulary" for Subtest 1 is misleading in that the subtest does not just measure general vocabulary. It requires that the examinee make analogies. Its stated purpose in the manual is to measure "the reader's understanding of sets of vocabulary items that are all related to the same general concept" (p. 6). This is a very difficult task for 7-, 8-, or 9-year-old children. Even older children may have problems with this task. Although children should learn to do analogies in school, too often this is not a part of the curriculum. The potential test user needs to be aware that if students have not had previous experiences with analogies, the examinees may make a low score not due to lack of knowledge of the meanings of the words, but due to the inability to do analogies. There are two example items given before the test, but this could hardly make up for several learning activities on analogies.

The Paragraph Reading subtest is far superior to many other tests of this type. There are five questions for each of the six paragraphs in this test. Two of the five questions require the reader to make inferences, which is a higher order thinking-reading skill not covered well in many tests.

It is good that content areas are included in this test, as a general reading test (narrative passages and general vocabulary) cannot assess how well a student can read in the content areas. This test is supposed to measure "the reader's understanding of words associated with specific school subject matter" (p. 7). The content areas included are, as stated earlier, Mathematics, Social Studies, and Science. Unfortunately, the content area subtests have the same format as the General Vocabulary. The reader must first determine how three stimulus words are related and then choose two words from among four choices that are related to the three stimulus words. Again, younger readers may do poorly on these subtests due to lack of prior experiences with analogies. Even junior and senior elementary education majors (although preservice teachers) who were asked to take the test by the reviewer considered the task too difficult for young readers.

The formats of the Syntactic Similarities and Sentence Sequencing subtests should pose no problems for readers of any age. The reader must choose from among five sentences the two sentences that most closely convey the same meaning in the Syntactic Similarities subtest. The Sentence Sequencing subtest requires the reader to put five randomly ordered sentences in the proper sequence to relate a meaningful paragraph or story.

The Reading Directions of Schoolwork subtest is excellent and very useful. It is designed to be used with young and remedial readers to determine their understanding of written directions found in schoolwork. The reader is required to read 25 written commands and carry them out directly on the answer sheet. One example command is "Write the numbers between 1 and 5."

There were 1,962 persons in the norming sample of the TORC-3 from 19 states in the Northeast, North Central, South, and West geographic regions. There was an adequate representation of sexes, urban and rural residents, and races/ethnicities. There were also children in the sample with learning disabilities, speech and language disorders, and other disabilities, which means test administrators can use the TORC-3 with children exhibiting these problems with some level of confidence.

The TORC-3's overall reliability ranges from .89 to .97. A reliability score of .80 is acceptable if the test is administered for the purpose of screening. If the purpose for the test is to make decisions about placing students in programs such as Title I/Chapter 1, the reliability should be at least .90. With the aforementioned in mind, the reliability is adequate depending on the purpose for giving the test.

The format of the TORC-3 affects the validity of some of the subtests negatively. As mentioned earlier, the analogy format of the General Vocabulary, Mathematics Vocabulary, Social Studies Vocabulary, and Science Vocabulary subtests may pose a problem for 7- and 8-year-old readers, possibly even 9-year-old readers. The areas covered in these subtests are ones that most examiners want to test, so in that respect those subtests would be valid. The tests would not be valid if the examiner does not wish to determine the readers' ability to see relationships. The manual indicates this is a good (valid) way to test these areas, but many young readers simply have not had enough practice with analogies to use the format to measure their vocabulary knowledge. The other subtests have good construct and content validity.

The test is untimed. The average time for administration is about 1 hour, varying from 30 minutes to an hour and a half. The test may be used with individuals or groups. Administering the test to an individual yields more diagnostic information, as the examiner can observe the examinee closely.

The TORC-3 Profile/Examiner Record Form, which is to be filled out for each examinee, has a section titled "Administration Conditions." This section has subsections for the examiner to rate the characteristics of the examinee and the conditions of the test environment. It also has a subsection for the examiner to write notes about such things as "Departure from Directions in Examiner's Manual" and "Special Motivation or Reinforcements." These features are very helpful for recording observations. Other sections of the Profile/Examiner Record Form are for recording test results, interpretation of results, and recommendations.

Overall, the TORC-3 would be a good test for middle school children and older, but it may not be a suitable testing instrument for primary students. There are subtests that would be suitable for school-aged children, but potential users of this test must look carefully at the individual subtests to determine whether the students they work with have had experiences performing tasks that are required on the TORC-3.

Review of the Test of Reading Comprehension, Third Edition by CAROLE PERLMAN, Director of Student Assessment, Chicago Public Schools, Chicago, IL:

The Test of Reading Comprehension, Third Edition (TORC-3) is an untimed silent reading test for students aged 7-0 to 17-11. It is based on "a constructivist orientation that focused on holistic, cognitive and linguistic aspects of reading" (manual, p. v). The authors list four purposes for the TORC-3: "to quantify the reading comprehension ability of individuals and to compare their scores with those of age-mates" (manual, p. 8); to determine an individual's areas of strength and weakness; to evaluate progress in reading programs; and in research.

The TORC-3 items are identical to those of the 1978 and 1986 editions. New in TORC-3 are normative data collected in 1993–94; descriptive information about the norming population; additional reliability, validity and bias information; and grade-equivalent scores.

The 25 items in the General Vocabulary subtest begin with three words that are related in some way (e.g., color names). The student must decide which two of the four answer choices are related to the initial set of words; this format was selected in part to minimize the effect of guessing. Syntactic Similarities consists of 20 items that require the student to select which two of the five sentences presented mean the same thing. Paragraph Reading presents the student with a paragraph and five multiple-choice items, two of which measure literal comprehension and three that require inference. All of the paragraphs are written in narrative form and purposely include no vocabulary from mathematics, science, or social studies. The same six, very brief, selections are used for students from 7-0 to 17-11 years of age and comprise the only material longer than a sentence that the student is ever asked to read. Sentence Sequencing has 10 items, each consisting of five randomly ordered sentences, which the student must place in correct sequential order. These four subtests comprise the General Reading Comprehension Core and yield a composite score, the Reading Comprehension Quotient (RCQ).

There are four optional Diagnostic Supplement subtests. The vocabulary tests, each 25 items long, use the same format as the General Vocabulary Test and cover vocabulary in mathematics, science, and social studies. Reading the Directions of Schoolwork, which is intended for "young and remedial readers," has 25 items, each of which asks the student to follow a simple direction.

The authors take pains to point out that their holistic, constructivist orientation is consistent with whole language approaches to literacy. Nonetheless, a whole language adherent would probably be troubled by a test that assesses decontextualized vocabulary and asks multiple-choice questions about clumsily written, paragraph-length passages that could hardly be characterized as "authentic."

Students may mark their answers on a separate answer sheet or in the test booklet, both of which might pose some problems for some younger students or those with perceptual or fine motor problems. A more judicious use of shading and increased spacing would be helpful. Particularly problematic is the Reading the Directions of Schoolwork subtest, which is printed in two columns down the page, but lacks either a line or sufficient space between the columns to demarcate adequately where one column ends and the other begins; the eye is drawn across the entire page, rather than down the columns.

With a few exceptions, the instructions for administering and scoring the test are generally adequate. The tests may be administered individually or in a group setting. In the group administration, students in grades 2–5 take only a subset of the items. In individual administrations, testing continues until the student reaches a ceiling, which for most subtests is getting three successive items wrong. This means that for younger students and very poor readers, an individually administered subtest might consist of only a few items. In fact, it is questionable how much useful information the TORC provides for younger students, particularly those being tested because there is reason to believe they may have difficulty reading. For example, a student from age 7-0 to 7-5 who gets one item right on the General Vocabulary, Syntactic Similarities, and Paragraph reading subtests scores at the 25th, 50th, and 25th percentiles on those subtests, respectively. The limited number of items, combined with floor effects and the small norming sample for that grade ($N = 111$), suggest that the test might be more appropriate for older students or better-than-average younger ones.

Given the authors' holistic orientation, it is not surprising that the diagnostic information provided is not related to specific skills; suggestions for remedial activities are quite general. As the authors correctly point out, TORC-3 results should be used in combination with other sources of information about the student.

Scores are recorded on the Profile/Examiner Record Form. Subtests are reported chiefly as standard scores with a mean of 10 and a standard deviation of 3, although percentile ranks, grade-equivalents (in 3-month increments), and age-equivalents are also provided. The composite Reading Comprehension Quotient (RCQ) has a mean of 100 and standard deviation of 15. The authors recommend converting scores from other tests to that scale and plotting them alongside the TORC-3 subtest scores and RCQ to form a profile. Missing from the profile form, however, is any mention of standard error or guidance on what might constitute significant differences between subtest scores.

STANDARDIZATION. The TORC-3 was normed in 1993–94 on a sample of 1,962 persons aged 7 to 17 years. Although all students tested attended general classes, no information is given on how the students came to be selected and it is not clear whether students might have been sent to the testing centers because they had reading problems. The norming sample *as a whole* approximates the school-age population of the U.S. in gender, race, geographic area, type of community, ethnicity, and disability status (no information is provided about SES or students whose first language is not English). This is also true for age groups (7–9, 10–12, 13–15, and 16–17). However, normative comparisons are made within a single age and no breakdowns are provided except in the 3-year intervals noted above. It is therefore hard to evaluate how representative the sample is at each age. A major weakness is that the number of students tested at each age is extremely small (median = 178), with a low of only 111 students in the national norming sample for 7-year-olds.

RELIABILITY. Internal consistency reliabilities are generally above .90. Test-retest reliabilities for the TORC-3 subtests, based on 15–17-year-old subjects tested and retested after a 2-month interval, were not especially high, ranging from .79 to .88. It is not clear why only older students were involved in this study and whether the results would generalize to younger students, whose scores might be influenced more by instruction, which would tend to lower the test-retest reliabilities. Interrater reliabilities ranged from .87 to .98.

VALIDITY. The authors' evidence for content validity takes the form of an extensive rationale for their theoretical model and for the selection of various item types; it also includes median point-biserial correlations for each subtest at each age. The median point-biserials are, for the most part, well above .40. Exceptions include science vocabulary, sentence sequencing, and paragraph reading for the youngest students.

Several of the TORC-3 items seem dated; mothers are occupied with food preparation and "rock" is the current music of interest. Despite the claim on the profile/examiner record form that "[i]tems were built using reviews of current content-area textbooks," the content area vocabulary words are drawn from texts published in the early to mid-1970s. For those who value reading in the content areas, the lack of content area vocabulary in the reading passages and the absence of nonfiction passages would be a drawback.

Of the six different studies cited as evidence of criterion validity, four used TORC-1, one used TORC-2, and only one used TORC-3. Although the items have remained unchanged since the first edition, the norming has changed, so it is not possible to determine whether the correlations between earlier editions of the TORC-3 and other reading tests (the criterion measures) would have been the same using new norms. The studies are described only briefly and it is not always possible to tell the age or grade of the subjects, whether the test was individually or group administered, or whether the students had disabilities, and if so, what kind. The studies based on students in grades 2–5 generally exhibited moderate correlations (mostly between .50 and .65) between the TORC-3 subtests and the CAT and CTBS reading tests. The two studies known to have used adolescent subjects showed higher correlations

with the criterion variables, but both had small *N*s and were based on disabled students; it is hard to know how well these results generalize to disabled elementary students or adolescents without disabilities. The discussion of criterion validity yielded no information on the correlation between other reading measures and the Reading Comprehension Quotient (RCQ), which the authors call "the most reliable, valid and useful measure of reading comprehension that is derived from TORC-3" (p. 31). In fact, the only correlation presented involving RCQ is a correlation with the Wechsler Intelligence Scale for Children—Revised (WISC-R) for a sample of learning disabled students of unknown age. That correlation, a very substantial .81, is provided as evidence of construct validity, but it could also be interpreted as suggesting that the TORC-3 is more of an intelligence measure than a reading test. Other evidence of construct validity consists of mean scores of 10 samples of students, including some low-achieving and disabled populations. Although these data are potentially helpful, they are difficult to interpret without standard errors.

How well does the TORC-3 accomplish the authors' stated purposes? The limited size of the norming population and floor effects for 7–8-year-old students (especially those with reading problems) suggest that this test might be best used with older students, if at all. Clearly the authors' rather unusual operationalization of "reading comprehension" with only a handful of narrative, paragraph-length passages will make some users uncomfortable and the validity information is incomplete and far from unambiguous. Combined with other assessment data, the TORC-3 could be helpful, perhaps as a screening device, rather than as a diagnostic measure. It may be of some use in research, assuming that the authors' view of "reading comprehension" is consistent with that of the researcher and that the researcher feels adequate validity evidence has been provided for whatever inferences are to be drawn. Its use in program evaluation may be limited for the reasons stated above and the lack of a parallel form.

[335]

Test of Understanding in College Economics, Third Edition.

Purpose: To measure college students' understanding of college economics.

Population: Introductory economics students.

Publication Dates: 1967–1991.

Acronym: TUCE III.

Scores: Total score only.
Administration: Group.
Editions, 2: Microeconomics, Macroeconomics.
Price Data: Available from publisher.
Time: (40–45) minutes per test.
Author: Phillip Saunders.
Publisher: National Council on Economic Education.
Cross References: See T2:1970 (10 references); for a review by Christine H. McGuire, see 7:902.

Review of the Test of Understanding in College Economics, Third Edition by JOSEPH C. CIECHALSKI, Associate Professor of Counselor and Adult Education, East Carolina University, Greenville, NC:

The third edition of the Test of Understanding in College Economics (TUCE III) was designed to assess a student's ability to understand and apply microeconomic and macroeconomic terms, concepts, and principles. Like its two predecessors, the TUCE III was developed by the American Economic Association's Standing Committee on Economic Education and the Joint Council on Economic Education. Unlike previous editions, the TUCE III consists of a single-form macroeconomics test and a single-form microeconomics test.

Both the macroeconomics and microeconomics test booklets contain 33 multiple-choice items. The last 3 items on each test deal with international economic concepts and may be omitted at the discretion of the examiner. Only 3 items on the macroeconomics test and 4 questions on the microeconomics test of the TUCE III have the same wording as the TUCE II. All of the remaining items of the TUCE III are either completely new, revised, or edited versions of the items on the TUCE II.

The TUCE III is easy to administer. Examinees are instructed to read the directions on the front of the test booklets. The directions are clear, and important points are printed in boldface type and underlined. Examiners need to inform the examinees whether they are to answer all 33 items or to skip the last three (international) items and answer 30 items. Responses to the items are made on separate answer sheets. However, answer sheets are not provided in the test package. Instead, answer sheets in use at the examiner's institution can easily be adapted for use on the TUCE III. Examiners may use different colored answer sheets or have examinees indicate the form of the test they are taking on their answer sheet.

The macroeconomics and microeconomics tests may be either hand or machine scored. Instructions for developing a hand-scoring stencil or scoring by machine are explained in the test manual. The score for each test is the total number of correct responses. Total scores may be converted to either percentiles or *T*-scores using conversion tables. Conversion tables for those who answered 30 items or all 33 items are provided in the manual. These conversion tables include pre- and posttest results for those who will administer the TUCE III before and after instruction.

The norming sample for the TUCE III consisted of 2,724 students who took the 30-item macroeconomics test and 2,726 students who took the 30-item microeconomics test at the beginning and end of the course. In addition, a norming sample consisting of those tested on all 33 items of the macroeconomics and microeconomics tests was described in the manual. This norming sample consisted of 1,324 students for the 33-item macroeconomics test and 1,426 students for the 33-item microeconomics test. Separate norming tables are provided in the manual for those taking either the 30-item or the entire 33-item test. The author of the manual points out that neither the macroeconomics test nor the microeconomics test samples are random. Unlike the previous editions, the norming group for TUCE III included students attending 2-year colleges. Thus, the TUCE III sample is larger and more representative of higher education institutions than the two previous editions.

Reliability coefficients for the microeconomics and macroeconomics tests were calculated using the Kuder-Richardson 20 formula and the results are reported in Table 5 of the test manual. For the microeconomics test, the reliability coefficients are .80 for the 30-item test and .81 for the entire 33-item test. According to the manual, these coefficients are higher than those of previous editions of TUCE for the micro forms. For the macroeconomics test, the reliability coefficients are .77 for the 30-item test and .75 for the entire 33-item test. The author claims that these results are comparable to most of the previous macroeconomics forms, but not as high as TUCE II Macro Form A. The standard error of measurement for TUCE III ranged from a low of 2.50 for the 33-item micro test to a high of 2.53 for the 33-item macro test.

Evidence of content validity is provided in Tables 1 and 2 of the test manual. Table 1 classifies each of the 33 macroeconomics items into one of six content areas and into one of three cognitive categories (Recognition and Understanding; Explicit Application; and Implicit Application items) covering basic terms, concepts, and principles and Table 2 does the same for each of the 33 microeconomics items. The purpose of the content categories is to ensure adequate coverage of the basic content of college principles courses. The purpose of the cognitive categories is to ensure that the items measure beyond simple recall and recognition. According to the manual, two-thirds of the items on both tests of TUCE III are application items.

The TUCE III reflects the Joint Council on Economic Education's commitment to provide a quality instrument to assess the principles of macroeconomics and microeconomics. It is an easy instrument to administer, score, and interpret. The test manual is comprehensive and well written. In addition, the manual describes the test's strengths and limitations in detail. Those who have used any of the previous editions of the TUCE will find the TUCE III to be even better. Those who have not are advised by this reviewer and the author of the test manual to order a specimen set and decide for themselves whether the content of their courses is congruent with the content sampled by the TUCE III.

Review of the Test of Understanding in College Economics, Third Edition by JENNIFER J. FAGER, Assistant Professor, Education and Professional Development, Western Michigan University, Kalamazoo, MI:
DESCRIPTIVE INFORMATION. The Joint Council on Economic Education published the third edition of the Test of Understanding in College Economics (TUCE III) to join three additional economics-focused tests to complete a comprehensive examination of economic understanding. Although this review does not focus on the other exams, it should be noted that the publishers are aware of the need for economic understanding at the elementary, middle, and high school levels and they have met that need by providing exams to assess this understanding.

Like previous editions of this exam, the authors of the Test of Understanding in College Economics, Third edition (TUCE III) consulted with a group of economists representing the many professions impacted by economics. These consultants provided input into the constructs represented in the TUCE III that led to its current format varying from previous editions. Changes in the format of the TUCE III represent changes in college course foci. The TUCE III has a single-form microeconomics test and a single-form macroeconomics test and each test includes questions on international economics to respond to the variations in university course content.

The authors suggest that international economics is an unsettled issue in economics departments. Some departments teach the content in microeconomics and others in macroeconomics, thus the questions are represented on each test version.

The TUCE III has two primary objectives, according to the authors: (a) to serve as an instrument for measuring specific outcomes in introductory economics courses at the college level; and (b) to enable instructors to compare their students to national norms (p. 1). Each of the two tests in the TUCE III includes 33 multiple-choice questions. Each of the 33 questions on the macro test represent content from six broad categories and three cognitive categories. The same holds true for the micro test questions. The international economics test questions are at the end of each test allowing the instructor to include or eliminate them depending on the course content.

Macroeconomics questions are classified into the following categories: measuring aggregate economic performance, aggregate supply, productive capacity, and economic growth, income and expenditure approach to aggregate demand and fiscal policy, monetary approach to aggregate demand and monetary policy, policy combinations, and international economics. The micro content categories include: the basic economic problem; markets and the price mechanism; costs, revenue, profit maximization, and market structure; market failures, externalities, government intervention and regulation; and income distribution and government redistribution policies, and international economics. In addition to focusing on content, the authors prepared a cognitive structure to ensure attention was given to the application of the content constructs. Although the authors concede that students may not use mental processes to apply knowledge they have learned, they have reduced the likelihood that memorization will be the sole reason for success on the TUCE III.

The questions on both forms of the test are clear, well formulated, and relatively free from psychometric error. Administration of each test requires 45 minutes unless both tests are given during the same session—then 90 minutes should be set aside. A school's individual multiple-choice answer sheets may be used, thus reducing costs and the need to send responses away for scoring. The procedure for collecting norming data is purposefully broader than for previous TUCE editions. The authors recognized the large number of students taking economics courses at 2-year institutions and data collected from these schools were included for the first time. In all, 53 schools representing scores from 2,724 (macroeconomics) or 2,726 (microeconomics) students were used to prepare the norm tables. Test users should be satisfied with the scales available in the examiner's manual for comparison purposes.

Previous editions of the TUCE reported reliability information for tests that included micro and macro questions. Since separating the questions into two distinct tests, the authors are able to report reliability information more accurately. The K-R 20 reliability estimate for the micro test is .80 when the international economics questions are excluded and .81 for the 33-item test. Reliability coefficients for the macro test are .77 for the 30 items and .75 for the 33 items. It is likely that these reliability scores can be attributed to the low number of test items per content category. As a result, the authors note that the TUCE III is designed to be a norm-referenced test to be used to discriminate across a broad range of student ability and is not to be substituted for teacher-made tests (p. 7).

The manual that accompanies the test deserves a separate note. The authors attended to detail when creating the examiner's manual for the TUCE III. It is explicit in the directions provided and allows little room for misinterpretation or misuse of the test. Specific uses are provided at the end of the opening section. The intentions for TUCE III use include evaluation, controlled experiments, and individual student evaluation, as well as a teaching aid. Specific cautions are given for each of these uses that will prevent the economics instructor from inaccurate use of the test results.

If the TUCE III is used as it is intended, economics instructors will be provided with information useful for measuring the economic understanding of their students. It is a highly convenient instrument for evaluating students' knowledge of broad economic constructs in both micro- and macroeconomics.

[336]
Test of Variables of Attention.

Purpose: For screening, diagnostic evaluation, and monitoring treatment of children and adults with attention deficit disorder.
Population: Ages 4 and over.
Publication Dates: 1988–1993.
Acronym: T.O.V.A.
Scores: 7 variables: Errors of Omission, Errors of Commission, Response Time, Variability, Anticipatory Responses, Multiple Responses, Post-Commission Response Time.
Administration: Individual.

Price Data: Available from publisher.
Time: [11 and 22.5] minutes.
Comments: Available for Apple IIe, Macintosh, and IBM or compatible computers; formerly called the Minnesota Computer Assessment.
Authors: Lawrence M. Greenberg (test and manuals) and Tammy Rose Dupuy (manuals).
Publisher: Universal Attention Disorders, Inc.
[Editor's Note: The following reviews are based on test materials received prior to August 1996. Version 7.0 will be reviewed in the next *MMY*.]

TEST REFERENCES

1. Greenberg, L. M., & Waldman, I. D. (1993). Developmental normative data on the Test of Variables of Attention. *Journal of Child Psychology and Psychiatry and Allied Disciplines, 34,* 1019-1030.

Review of the Test of Variables of Attention by ROSA A. HAGIN, Professor Emeritus, Fordham University—Lincoln Center, New York, NY, and PETER DELLA BELLA, Instructor in Psychiatry, Department of Psychiatry, New York University School of Medicine, New York, NY:

The Test of Variables of Attention (T.O.V.A.) is a standardized, visual, continuous performance test designed for use in diagnosing and monitoring medication in children and adults with attention deficit disorders. This 23-minute fixed-interval computerized test is available for Macintosh and IBM/IBM-compatible computers and has modest system requirements. It requires no use of language, no right-left discrimination, nor recognition of numerals or letters. Two easily discriminated visual stimuli (a square containing a small square adjacent to the top or bottom edge of the larger square) are presented for 100 milliseconds at 2-second intervals. The stimulus within the inner square adjacent to the top edge is the designated target. The T.O.V.A. presents two 11-minute test conditions: frequent and infrequent presentation of targets. The first condition, which is an infrequent presentation of targets (target to non-target ratio of 1:3.5), is designed to measure attention; the second condition, which is a frequent presentation of targets (target to nontarget ratio of 3.5:1), is designed as a measure of impulsivity. Scores on seven variables are produced. The author defines and interprets these variables as follows:

1. Errors of omission (failures to respond to a target), which are interpreted as an indication of inattention.
2. Errors of commission (responding inappropriately to a nontarget), which are interpreted as an indication of impulsivity or disinhibition.
3. Mean correct response times, which are interpreted as measures of processing speed.

4. Standard deviations of response times, which are interpreted as measures of variability.

5. Anticipatory response (responses made before the two stimuli can be differentiated), which can be used to determine whether the subject followed the instructions.

6. Post-commission mean correct response times (mean times of correct responses immediately following a commission error), which may help to differentiate subjects with behavior disorders from subjects with attentional problems.

7. Multiple responses (more than one response per stimulus), which may be interpreted to reflect immaturity or neurological dysfunction.

The T.O.V.A. kit consists of a computer disk, microswitch/scorebox, and manuals for installation of software and interpretation of test results. Purchasers receive five free computerized test interpretations initially; thereafter, full interpretations are offered for a fee. Licensed clinical psychologists may purchase, in addition to the kit, raw data scorings for a one-page "self scoring" at the cost of $5.00 for each test administration.

Two well-designed videotapes demonstrate how the T.O.V.A. can be used by the clinician for several major purposes: to screen for Attention Deficit Hyperactivity Disorder (ADHD) in schools, to diagnose the disorder, to predict response to medication, to establish optimal dosage, and to monitor the psychopharmacotherapy over time. The test may also be used to compare responses to different doses of the same medication and, presumably, it may also be used to compare responses to different medications.

A major component of the T.O.V.A. is the challenge test, which assesses peak drug effect an hour and a half after the baseline test has been completed. According to the interpretation manual, comparisons of baseline scores (while not on medication) with those earned in the challenge test (on medication) enable the clinician to determine not only whether the subject has ADHD, but also to make some hypotheses concerning dosage. Detailed clinical instructions for dosage adjustment procedures are contained in the interpretation manual.

A psychiatrist might find that utilizing a laboratory paradigm like the challenge test to measure the effects of medication on the pertinent psychophysiologic parameters would be advantageous. Because there is a prompt dose-dependent relationship between stimulant medication and improvement of the symptoms of ADHD, treatment may involve a stepwise adjustment of dosage upwards over several visits and simultaneously reassessing the client's progress with each increase in dose. This is often accomplished through parent, teacher, and patient reports. The process is laborious and often hampered by reliance on consistent and timely completion and return of behavior rating scales. The response to scales is further beset by such threats to validity as nonblindness to treatment and fatigued raters, who may complete their ratings for the week at one moment in time. The use of a laboratory measure, such as the T.O.V.A., although it should not be used as a substitute for more global measures of clinical status, nevertheless introduces a welcome measure of objectivity into the evaluation.

On the other hand, the impression of objectivity inherent in the numerical values can also be misleading in focusing both diagnosis and treatment. Medication remains the standard and, too often, the only approach to treatment of ADHD. The knowledgeable clinician includes medication as part of a *multimodal approach* that aims at ameliorating and reversing the collateral damage of ADHD and its frequently encountered concomitants.

To his credit, T.O.V.A.'s author points out in the videotapes, manuals, and reports the need to relate the laboratory values of the T.O.V.A. to all relevant clinical information including interviews, physical examinations, psychological testing, and behavior ratings. Much less emphasis is given to treatment techniques that might be alternatives or adjuncts to medication. For example, the case studies in the interpretation manual did not deal with any related clinical information, but were confined to discussion of T.O.V.A. parameters. Of the 15 cases presented in the interpretation manual, all but 2 resulted in a trial of medication.

Individuals diagnosed with ADHD are often found to have other comorbid conditions such as learning disorders, oppositional-defiant disorder, conduct disorders, or tic disorders. They may additionally suffer from academic problems, low self-esteem, ostracism by their peers, and the psychological effects of avoidant or exasperated parents and teachers who have been compelled to set limits on their behaviors. Problems such as low self-esteem can be dealt with through individual child therapy; out-of-control behaviors can be dealt with through parent training and behavior therapy; socialization difficulties can be addressed in individual and group therapy and also through social skills training; children may often need educational intervention and close consultation between the clinician and the teacher; family therapy can be a useful adjunct to help parents and other family members adjust to the demands created by the disorder. All of these interventions need to be considered as well as medication.

Viewed in terms of the standards for psychological tests, the T.O.V.A. manuals and supporting documents raise questions about the independent use of this measure in making decisions about children and adults. The three manuals received for review appear to have been collated from unpublished papers and few actual research publications. One manual is undated, so that it is not possible to relate the manuals to each other in the development of the instrument. The proofing errors, errors in paging, and near duplication of whole paragraphs within the text do not build confidence in the data presented.

Norms for the test variables appear in two of the manuals, the T.O.V.A. Interpretation Manual and the Test of Variables of Attention Computer Program, which appears to be a technical manual for computer installation. Both of these manuals contain 1989/93 copyright dates, but the norms tables are dated 7/94. Separate norms, based on a total of 1,590 subjects are provided for males and females, ages 4 through 80 plus years grouped in 2-year intervals for ages 4–19 and 10-year intervals thereafter. The normative sample is not otherwise identified, except in the installation manual, which describes the subjects as "normal." In view of the many factors that influence scores on continuous performance tests—experience with computer games; motivation; IQ levels; effects of caffeine and nicotine; presence of psychostimulant, anticonvulsant, or antidepressant medications; comorbid conditions such as depression—this is a serious lack of information.

Nor is adequate evidence of test-retest reliability provided. An undated manual refers to test-retest results with 33 randomly selected normal children, 40 ADHD subjects, and 24 normal adults, producing no significant differences in paired t-tests, except for a decrease in commission errors on the first half of the test from the first to second test. No citation for this study is given, nor is more conventional evidence of reliability provided. With the recommended use of repeated challenge tests for recommending or adjusting dosage of medication, this lack of evidence of reliability is also serious.

Questions of validity are also not dealt with in a straightforward fashion. The major issue is one of content validity (i.e., whether this small sample of behavior is a valid estimate of characteristic behavior of the individual under study). The test author has

broad clinical insights in work with people with attentional problems, but there is a very limited research data base and/or detailed longitudinal case studies for many of the broad generalizations and detailed interpretations of the test variables.

Finally, there is a marked commercial tone in the supporting materials provided by the publisher. For example, the publisher sent a sample mathematical calculation showing that purchasers will recoup the cost of the equipment in the first five tests and earn a net income of $255 in addition. Another memo from the publisher inquires whether the purchaser wished to be placed on the publisher's referral list. Still another advertises the publisher's computerized interpretation service that provides immediate results based on over 10,000 protocols, an amazing number in that the published norms are based on 1,500 records. Finally, a memo addressed to health care providers (HMOs) indicates that the T.O.V.A. can be administered by a nurse or specially trained technician, providing an immediately generated report for the clinician. It states that "With the report in hand, the clinician can present findings to the parent. Results are presented in a simple, easy to understand format and demonstrates [sic] clearly the neurological basis of ADD. This helps the clinician by increasing parent compliance and reducing time spent with explanations and data collecting from outside sources." This kind of advertising seems contrary to ethical standards for the distribution of tests to qualified purchasers and the professional cautions recommended in the T.O.V.A.'s own manuals.

In summary, the T.O.V.A. holds promise in contributing to the diagnosis and management of individuals with attentional disorders. It draws upon the work of a child psychiatrist who shares his extensive clinical knowledge. The test equipment itself is well designed and its use is well explained in the manuals. However, existing manuals do not provide adequate information about the nature of the normative sample, the test's research foundations, and technical characteristics of reliability and validity. It is to be hoped that the author and publisher will remedy these gaps in order to insure ethical distribution and professionally responsible use of the test materials.

Review of the Test of Variables of Attention by MARGOT B. STEIN, Clinical Assistant Professor of Psychiatry, University of North Carolina School of Medicine, Chapel Hill, NC:

The Test of Variables of Attention Computer Program (T.O.V.A.), formerly called the Minnesota

Computer Assessment (MCA) and authored by Lawrence M. Greenberg, is a fixed-interval, visual continuous performance test, used to assess attention deficit disorders and monitor medication treatment. It has three principal clinical uses with regard to Attention Deficit Disorders: to screen students suspected of having attention deficits and students referred for learning disability assessments; as a diagnostic tool used as part of a multifaceted, multidisciplinary assessment of children, adolescents, and adults who may have an attention deficit; and to help determine the dosage level and monitor the use of medication over time. This 22.5-minute computerized test, which is nonlanguage based and uses geometric shapes rather than alphanumeric stimuli, can be used with IBM or IBM-compatible and Macintosh computers. The test requires no right-left discrimination and is said to have negligible practice effects. The T.O.V.A. variables include *errors of omission* (interpreted as a measure of inattention), *errors of commission* (interpreted as a measure of impulsivity), *mean correct response times* (interpreted as a measure of processing and response time), *standard deviations* of response times (interpreted as a measure of variability or consistency of performance), *anticipatory responses* (used to determine whether the subject followed the instructions), *post-commission mean correct response time* (which, the authors state, may help to differentiate conduct disordered from ADD subjects), and *multiple responses* (which, the authors believe, can indicate neurological immaturity).

The installation and administration of the T.O.V.A. are straightforward and require little background knowledge on the part of the consumer. The system is easily installed on the computer using the T.O.V.A. disk (available in both 3.5-inch and 5.25-inch sizes) and microswitch/scorebox. The subject then sits before a computer screen on which flash target stimuli at fixed 2-second intervals, and presses the hand-held microswitch when he or she perceives the target stimulus. The test instrument includes a practice test of 2.25 minutes, followed by the 22.5-minute test for clients above age 5 (4- and 5-year-olds take a shorter version of the test that lasts 11 minutes). The instrument contains two different test situations. In the first two quarters of the test, the target (a colored square containing a small square near the top edge) is presented once every three and a half nontargets. These two quarters are characterized by the "infrequent" presentation of the target, the most commonly utilized form of continuous

performance test, and one that generates boredom and, relatedly, errors of omission. A unique feature of the T.O.V.A. is that during the second half of the test the target is present three and a half times to every nontarget presentation. This type of presentation sets up an expectation in the subject and a rhythm that makes errors of commission more common than in the first half of the test.

Two manuals are provided with the T.O.V.A. software package that also includes a microswitch, modem, and two T.O.V.A. videos. The Installation Manual contains information necessary to install and administer the test, and the Interpretation Manual contains information about the test results, variables, interpretations, and case examples. They are detailed, well organized, and clearly written with respect to administration and scoring. The author presents a plausible rationale for the T.O.V.A., particularly for its use in adjusting (titrating) stimulant medication dosages. However, the reference section is brief, and relies heavily on the research of the author and his collaborators. The manual has a succinct introductory review of attention deficit disorders that points out the complex etiology of attentional dysfunction, particularly when it involves hyperactivity. The author also emphasizes the importance of providing multisituational, multiobserver, and multiinstrument assessments for clients with possible attention deficits, including standardized behavior ratings completed by both parents and teachers in conjunction with the T.O.V.A., in order to arrive at a valid diagnosis. The author also reminds the consumer that appropriate interventions for attention deficits are not limited to medication, but also should include parental counseling that draws on behavior modification techniques, as well as environmental adjustments.

The T.O.V.A. is scored and interpreted either by the staff administering the test using hand calculations, or by a Certified T.O.V.A. Interpreter using the software program and microswitch. There is a charge for each computer scoring and interpretation, raw data, scores (standard deviations, standard scores, percentile scores and T scores), written interpretation, and graphics. An appendix contains the normative tables arranged by 15 bands. Eight of these are 2-year age bands for ages 4–5 through 18–19, six 10-year age bands (20–79), and one 80+ age band.

It should be noted, however, that a full summary of the normative data on the T.O.V.A. is not available in either manual, although these data can be found in a journal article and unpublished manuscript form (Greenberg & Waldman, 1993; Greenberg & Crosby, 1992). The manual makes brief mention of developmental normative data on 1,500 normal children and adults (ages 4–80+) on which the norms listed in the appendix are based. Male and female norms are available, but there is no mention of other variables such as race/ethnicity or socio-economic class. Greenberg also refers to research on the effects of psychostimulant medication on the T.O.V.A. performance of children with attention deficits both pre-treatment and on-medication and on varying amounts of stimulant medication.

The T.O.V.A.'s statistical properties are not presented in much detail for analysis in the manuals, although the manual does refer to high test-retest reliability for 33 randomly selected normal children, 40 ADD subjects, and 24 normal adults. With regard to sensitivity and specificity, the author cites his study of 73 youngsters with ADD with and without hyperactivity and matched (age, sex) normals, in which 85% of normal and 72% of the ADD subjects were correctly classified using a standardized score of T.O.V.A. False positives and false negatives were somewhat high (15% and 28% respectively). The author states in the T.O.V.A. Computer Program Manual that "preliminary results suggest respectable specificity for the T.O.V.A. in combination with the CPTQ-A [Conners Parent-Teacher Questionnaire]" (p. 6).

The purpose and design of the T.O.V.A. invite comparisons with another fixed-interval, visual continuous performance test, the Gordon Diagnostic System (GDS; 1986; 132), which also has been computerized and standardized. The T.O.V.A. is distinguished by a number of features including the use of nonsequential geometric stimuli (rather than alphanumeric stimuli), two test conditions (target infrequent and target frequent) built into the same test, and the use of a specially designed hand-held microswitch (rather than a button on the computer) with an insignificant error of measurement (20 msec) and which minimizes muscular fatigue. The duration of the T.O.V.A. (11 and 22.5 minutes) also is longer than the GDS (8 minutes). Both instruments measure the performance of persons age 4 through adulthood. GDS norms include socioeconomic class variables using the Hollingshead Index, but not race/ethnicity variables. Unlike the GDS, Greenberg reported a significant correlation between standardized IQ scores and performance on the T.O.V.A. Unlike the GDS, the T.O.V.A. offers computerized

individual scoring (standard deviations, standard scores, percentile scores, and T-scores) and interpretation (at additional cost).

In summary, the T.O.V.A. is primarily a nonlanguage-based continuous performance test designed for use in the diagnosis and treatment of children and adults in combination with standardized behavior ratings, a thorough developmental history, and other data. At this time, perhaps the most appropriate use of the T.O.V.A. is as a pre-post measure to predict pharmacotherapy outcome and to titrate dosage levels to psychostimulants. Apparently, it is also used by clinicians to screen large populations, such as schoolchildren, for ADD. However, this test probably should be used with caution for this purpose, until more inclusive normative data, including information about socioeconomic status and race/ethnicity, are available.

REVIEWER'S REFERENCES
Gordon, M. (1986). The Gordon Diagnostic System. DeWitt, NY: GSI, Inc.
Greenberg, L. M., & Crosby, R. D. (1992). *A summary of developmental normative data in the T.O.V.A.: Ages 4–80+.* Unpublished manuscript.
Greenberg, L. M., & Waldman, I. D. (1993). Developmental normative data on the Test of Variables of Attention (T.O.V.A.). *Journal of Child Psychology and Psychiatry and Allied Disciplines, 34,* 1019–1030.

[337]
Test of Visual-Motor Skills.

Purpose: To assess a child's visual-motor functioning.
Population: Ages 2–13.
Publication Date: 1986.
Acronym: TVMS.
Scores: Total score only.
Administration: Group or individual.
Price Data, 1994: $35 per 15 test booklets and manual (72 pages); $23.50 per 15 test booklets; $14.95 per manual; $15.50 per manual and sample of test designs.
Time: (3–5) minutes.
Author: Morrison F. Gardner.
Publisher: Psychological and Educational Publications, Inc.
Cross References: See T4:2791 (1 reference).

TEST REFERENCES
1. Carr, S. H. (1989). Louisiana's criteria of eligibility for occupational therapy services in the public school system. *The American Journal of Occupational Therapy, 43,* 503–506.
2. Goldstein, D. J., & Britt, T. W., Jr. (1994). Visual-motor coordination and intelligence as predictors of reading, mathematics, and written language ability. *Perceptual and Motor Skills, 78,* 819–823.

Review of the Test of Visual-Motor Skills by DEBORAH ERICKSON, *Professor of Counseling, Niagara University, Niagara University, NY:*

The Test of Visual-Motor Skills (TVMS) was designed to assess visual perception and visual motor integration skills of children from ages 2 to 13. The test requires the child to visually perceive and replicate with his or her hand, nonlanguage forms. If used in conjunction with the Test of Visual-Perceptual Skills (Non-Motor) (TVPS; T4:2798), published in 1982 by Special Child Publications, an examiner can determine if a child has the ability to perceive forms correctly or if the child has difficulty due to poor visual-motor functioning.

The TVMS consists of 26 forms, with specific characteristics that allow for measurement of various types of motor functioning. The designs are purported to be free from cultural and gender bias and the figures are common to children living in all parts of the United States and other countries. The manual is clearly written and directions for administration and scoring are adequate. There is a slight amount of judgment necessary for scoring; however, this is true with most tests of visual-motor skill that require a child to draw figures (e.g., Bender Gestalt Test; T4:291).

The test development was reported clearly in the manual. Item analysis was thorough, and the final forms were developed from a stimulus pool of 140 forms and reduced by a panel of teachers and psychologists and actual administration to students. Standardization of the test included 1,009 children considered to be normally functioning and residing in the San Francisco Bay area. The item difficulties ranged from .37 to .98, with a median value of .63. The item/total test score correlations ranged from .34 to .86 with a median value of .78. Test development would have been enhanced if the standardization procedure could have occurred in various geographic locations with more students at each age level.

Test reliability indicates a consistent test. Cronbach's coefficient alpha, reflecting internal consistency of the test for children at each age level, was from .31 to .90, with a median value of .82. Except for the .31 reliability coefficient, which occurred at the 2-0 to 2-11 age level, the scores were within the range acceptable for a reliable and consistent measurement. The SEMs ranged from .88 to 2.99 with a median value of 2.08.

Test validity, indicating that the test measures what it is supposed to measure, was evaluated through content validation, item validation, and criterion-related validation strategies. Professionals in the field of psychology and testing reviewed the items selected for the test to ascertain the degree to which the items were similar to those used in other tests of visual-motor skills (content validity). The relationship between an individual item and a criterion (item validity) was assessed by correlating the test with the

Developmental Test of Visual Motor Integration Test (VMI; 12:111) and the manual states only those items correlating highly with the VMI were selected. Criterion-related validity was evaluated by correlating the total TVMS score with the scores from the Bender Visual-Motor Gestalt Test (T4:291) and the VMI. Correlation's between the Bender and the TVMS ranged from .48 to .77 with an overall correlation of .75. The correlation between the VMI and TVMS ranged from .25 to .76 with an overall correlation between the two tests of .92.

Interpretive scores for the TVMS can be obtained through standard scores, scaled scores, percentile ranks, and stanines—all corresponding to the raw scores by chronological age.

In summary, the TVMS is a well-constructed test and can be used with confidence for assessing a child's level of visual-motor functioning. If used in conjunction with the Test of Visual-Perceptual Skills (Non-Motor) (TVPS), an examiner can assess both "how a child visually perceives non-language forms (TVPS) … and how a child translates with his or her hand what is visually perceived (TVMS)" (p. 5).

Review of the Test of Visual-Motor Skills by JANET E. SPECTOR, Assistant Professor of Education, University of Maine, Orono, ME:

The Test of Visual-Motor Skills (TVMS) assesses a student's ability to reproduce by hand a series of geometric designs. According to the test's author, the TVMS is useful in identifying students who might have "fine-motor problems of one kind or another—such as difficulty in writing letters and words with good legibility; directional confusion; slow psychomotor speed; etc." (p. 5). In addition, the measure is designed as a companion to the author's (non-motor) Test of Visual-Perceptual Skills (TVPS; Gardner, 1982; T4:2798). Gardner claims that when used together, the TVMS and the TVPS help the examiner to distinguish between poor visual-motor performance due to visual-perceptual problems and poor performance due to fine-motor difficulties. Unfortunately, the manual provides no data to support this claim.

The TVMS comprises a series of 26 designs, each of which is presented as a bold, black-lined drawing on white paper. The measure is similar in content and procedure to the Developmental Test of Visual-Motor Integration (VMI; Beery & Buktenica, 1989; 12:111). Unlike the VMI, however, each TVMS item is included on a separate page. This feature is particularly advantageous when testing young children who might be distracted by the presence of multiple stimuli. Furthermore, the use of white rather than green paper (as on the VMI) makes the test more suitable for children who have visual impairment.

Although the TVMS is easily administered, scoring is apt to be difficult for the novice examiner. For 24 of the 26 items, three scores are possible; 2 (the design is copied with precision), 1 (the design is copied with minor errors), and 0 (the design is copied incorrectly). On the one hand, the provision of partial credit is an improvement over the VMI, where slight errors result in total loss of credit. On the other hand, scoring guidelines are problematic on four counts. First, Designs 2 (horizontal line) and 4 (diagonal line) are scored only as 1 or 0, but the rationale for this exception is not discussed. Second, the number of scoring examples is insufficient for many designs. Design 1 (circle) includes at least four examples for each possible score (i.e., 0, 1, or 2), but 18 of the designs include only one example of a 2. Third, some of the guidelines are unnecessarily vague. For instance, on Design 5, a score of 2 requires that lines be of "equal length," whereas a score of 1 specifies that lines be "similar in length" (p. 24). If a line is off by 1/16 of an inch, is it considered "equal" or "similar"? Such ambiguity could easily be eliminated by providing more precise guidelines. Fourth, the size of the reproduction relative to the stimulus affects scoring on some (e.g., Design 2), but not all, designs (e.g., Design 10). It is not clear why this is the case, particularly because the only corrective feedback permitted is on Design 1, which does not require that the drawing be similar in size to the stimulus.

A major weakness of the test is its norms, a shortcoming that undermines its viability as a norm-referenced device. The manual claims that "the norms for the TVMS were derived from groups which are representative of the population of children from age 2 through 12 years, 11 months" (p. 12). However, the test was standardized in one geographic region (San Francisco Bay area), using a sample of 1,009 children from 13 schools and a hospital. No information regarding race or socioeconomic status is provided. Furthermore, the number of students sampled at the youngest ($n = 38$) and oldest ($n = 54$) age levels is small and the proportion of males and females is imbalanced at some ages.

Another problem area is reliability. According to the manual, test reliability was estimated using only one approach, internal consistency. Cronbach's alpha ranged from .31 at age 2 to .90 at age 5, with a median reliability of .82. Clearly, the test should not be used with 2-year-olds. At most other ages, the test fails to meet the recommended standard (i.e., .9) for use in high-stakes decisions regarding an individual student (Salvia & Ysseldyke, 1995). Furthermore, the manual includes no mention of test-retest reliability. In the absence of information about test stability over time, the TVMS falls short even as a screening instrument.

Interrater reliability was assessed in a sample of 217 children in grades 1, 3, and 5 and 41 kindergartners, using two raters (registered occupational therapists). Across the ages, interrater reliability ranged from .80 to .89. These estimates are lower than those reported for the most recent version of the VMI, in which examiners received from 2 to 5 hours of training. The TVMS's author does not indicate the type of training that scorers received prior to participating in his scoring study, so it is difficult to determine whether the results in the manual will generalize to other scorers, particularly those who are not occupational therapists.

Finally, the manual includes a brief discussion of "item validity," content validity, and criterion validity. What the author calls "item validity" (the correlation between each item and total test score) would be more appropriately considered as evidence of reliability (i.e., internal consistency). Other validity data generally support the claim that the test is primarily a measure of design copying skill and that it assesses a construct similar to that of the VMI. However, the author fails to show that performance on the test correlates with performance on fine-motor tasks other than design copying (e.g., handwriting, drawing) or that it is predictive of future performance. It is therefore not clear why examiners would want to identify students who do not do well on this test.

Overall, the TVMS is a quick and easily administered measure of design copying skill that might be of interest to teachers or occupational therapists who need to assess the progress of children who have difficulty with fine-motor tasks. However, given the limitations of the standardization sample and the results of reliability studies, the test should not be used at all at age 2 or for high-stakes decision making at other ages (e.g., determination of eligibility for special services). Until the author provides evidence regarding test-retest reliability and predictive validity, the test is not recommended as a screening measure.

REVIEWER'S REFERENCES

Gardner, M. F. (1982). Test of Visual-Perceptual Skills (Non-Motor). San Francisco: Special Child Publications.
Beery, K. E., & Buktenica, N. A. (1989). The Developmental Test of Visual-Motor Integration (3rd rev.). Cleveland: Modern Curriculum Press.
Salvia, J., & Ysseldyke, J. E. (1995). Assessment (6th ed.). Boston: Houghton Mifflin Company.

[338]
Test of Word Knowledge.

Purpose: Developed to "assess a student's skill in the reception and expression of ... semantics."

Population: Ages 5–17.

Publication Date: 1991–1992.

Acronym: TOWK.

Scores, 11: Expressive Vocabulary, Receptive Vocabulary, Word Opposites, Word Definitions, Synonyms, Multiple Contexts, Figurative Usage, Conjunctions and Transition Words, Receptive Composite, Expressive Composite, Total.

Administration: Individual.

Levels, 2: Ages 5–8, Ages 8–17.

Price Data, 1992: $119.50 per complete kit including stimulus manual, examiner's manual (118 pages), and 12 record forms; $62.50 per stimulus manual; $43.50 per examiner's manual; $22 per 12 record forms

Time: (31) minutes for Level 1; (65) minutes for Level 2.

Authors: Elisabeth H. Wiig and Wayne Secord.

Publisher: The Psychological Corporation.

TEST REFERENCES

1. Nippold, M. A. (1995). School-age children and adolescents: Norms for word definition. *Language, Speech, and Hearing Services in Schools, 26*, 320–325.

2. Byrne, M. E., Crowe, T. A., Hale, S. T., Meek, E. E., & Epps, D. (1996). Metalinguistic and pragmatic abilities of participants in adult literacy programs. *Journal of Communication Disorders, 29*, 37–49.

3. Wiig, E. H., Jones, S. S., & Wiig, E. D. (1996). Computer-based assessment of word knowledge in teens with learning disabilities. *Language, Speech, and Hearing Services in Schools, 27*, 21–28.

Review of the Test of Word Knowledge by RICK LINDSKOG, Professor of Psychology, Pittsburg State University, Pittsburg, KS:

This instrument cites an initial standardization copyright of 1990, and the reviewed materials reveal a 1992 copyright. The Test of Word Knowledge (TOWK) is an individually administered test developed to assess semantic skills in expressive and receptive areas. The intent is to provided information regarding the semantic (word meaning) skills. This identification of strengths and weaknesses, according to the authors, provides information pertaining to developmental levels, and appropriate educational programs. The target population is persons with communication disorders, head traumas, developmental disabilities, and Non-English-speaking students.

The test consists of two levels: ages 5–8 (Level 1) and ages 8–17 (Level 2). Each has two expressive and two receptive subtests. Level 1 Language tasks are referential and relational in nature, assessed by the two expressive subtests of Expressive Vocabulary and Word Definitions, and the two receptive subtests of Receptive Vocabulary and Word Opposites. Level 1, developed for children ages 5–8, contains one supplemental receptive subtest (Synonyms).

Level 2 (ages 8–17) addresses relational and metalinguistic tasks. The core subtests for expressive skills are Word Definitions and Multiple Contexts, and receptive subtests are Synonyms and Figurative Usage. This level also contains four supplementary subtests, which are designed to: "explore deficits in word and concept knowledge beyond the areas and tasks provided in the Core Battery" (p. 4). The single supplemental subtest that measures expressive skills is Expressive Vocabulary, and receptive skills are measured by Receptive Vocabulary, Word Opposites, and Conjunction and Transition Words subtests.

The theoretical foundation of the instrument is based on semantic development. One of the test authors has published in this area (Wiig, 1989). The instrument allows for developmental age differences in linguistic skills.

Instructions for each subtest are accompanied by stimulus materials to avoid taxing auditory memory. Items are scored 1 or 0. The start points are based on chronological age, and the basal and discontinuation rules are constant across all of the subtests (five items each).

The national standardization was preceded by a pilot test and a national item tryout. The national item tryout was extensive, involving 340 examiners and 2,866 students, 552 of whom were receiving special education. A group of 167 diagnosed as language-learning disabled were also selected for separate study.

Analyses were conducted to detect developmental growth in subtest scores, and to see if the items could differentiate between educational classifications.

The standardization sample consisted of 1,570 students in 26 states. There were equal numbers of males and females for age groups using one-year increments. The groups for ages 5-0 to 13-11 years old each had 130 students and the 14-0 to 17-11 year age groups each had 100 students. The 1980 Census of Population was used to guide representative sampling. The sites were instructed to exclude self-contained special education classroom students, and include students from "mainstreamed" program services in language instruction. The gender, racial identification, and parent education align well with the Census Data; however, the standardization sample for the Northeast U.S. was about 10% underrepresented and the North Central region was approximately 12% overrepresented.

The norms were developed in an uncommon way, and the authors did not provide justification as to why the standard scores were derived by converting mid-interval percentile scales to z scores, then converted to standard scores. This reviewer wondered why a more traditional method was not utilized. Raw score means and standard deviations were provided by age group for each subtest. The authors also explain the methods they used to derive age equivalent scores. The following derived norm-based scores are provided in the manual: standard scores for raw scores (by age for each subtest); age equivalents for raw scores; receptive and expressive composite standard scores; total standard scores; percentile ranks, normal curve equivalents (NCEs); and stanines.

The content validity of the test was initially measured by assessing how well the instrument discriminates between identified and nonidentified individuals with language learning disabilities (LLD). The TOWK demonstrated 67% accuracy. The instrument had more false negatives than false positives errors in this study. The authors speculate this was due to the fact that the TOWK only measures semantics and a student could be deficient in other language areas. Construct validity was measured by examining the intercorrelations between the subtests. The range was .51 to .61 for Level 1 and .57 to .74 for Level 2.

The factor analytic studies support the underlying theory of expressive and receptive skills as factors at both levels of the TOWK.

To assess concurrent validity, the TOWK was correlated with the Clinical Evaluation of Language Fundamentals-R (CELF-R). The correlation was .64. In another study with the Wechsler Intelligence Scale for Children—Third Edition (WISC-III), the composite correlation was .76. Internal consistency reliability was estimated as .84 to .92 for composite scores across all age groups on Level 1, and .85 to .94 for all age groups across Level 2. Test-retest stability coefficient (1–4-week interval) were (for all groups) .89 (receptive), .92 (expressive), and .94 (composite).

In addition, the manual provides charts to facilitate interpretation of subtest and composite score differences (i.e., is the difference statistically significant, and what percent of the population might be expected to demonstrate this difference?).

In summary, this reviewer was positively impressed with the authors' attempt to generate an instrument that assesses semantics as a central component of the language process. The instrument is well constructed, and the materials consist of straightforward achromatic line drawings. A pilot version and national item tryout were done, and the stan-

dardization sample was representative of the 1980 U.S. Census for region, gender, ethnicity, and parent education (with the exception of a slight imbalance between the North Central and Northeast regions).

Estimates of internal consistency reliability are of adequate magnitude, ranging from .84 to .95 (both levels), and the average stability coefficient was .94 for Level 2. The interscorer reliability correlation ranged from .90 to .99.

Evidence presented to support concurrent validity was adequate, but it must be noted there is no standard assessment instrument for measuring semantic process. There is a basis to interpret two factors (expressive semantics, and receptive semantics) as postulated by the authors. This instrument showed some facility in discriminating identified LLD from non-LLD students (67% accuracy). It is noted that there were more false negative errors, indicating that the TOWK would underidentify the LLD in any given population. Furthermore, the manual does not address a continuing flaw of linguistic process tests, namely their inability to isolate a weakness (in this instance receptive and expressive semantics) that can be remedied and subsequently be linked to an outcome (such as increases in reading skills or written language).

This reviewer believes the TOWK can be a useful tool for assessing a child's language strengths and weaknesses. It is well conceptualized and statistically defensible. Additionally, it would seem to be an excellent tool for research with regard to language function and remediation/intervention efforts.

REVIEWER'S REFERENCE

Wiig, E. H. (1989). *Steps to language competence: Developing metalinguistic strategies.* San Antonio, TX: The Psychological Corporation.

[339]

Test of Written Expression.

Purpose: Constructed as a "norm-referenced test of writing."

Population: Ages 6–6 to 14–11.

Publication Date: 1995.

Acronym: TOWE.

Scores, 2: Items, Essay.

Administration: Individual or group.

Price Data, 1996: $109 per complete kit including manual (58 pages), 25 profile/examiner record forms, and 25 student booklets in storage box; $34 per 25 student booklets; $39 per profile/examiner record forms; $39 per examiner's manual.

Time: (60) minutes.

Authors: Ron McGhee, Brian R. Bryant, Stephen C. Larsen, and Diane M. Rivera.

Publisher: PRO-ED, Inc.

TEST REFERENCES

1. Ehrler, D. J. (1996). Test of Written Expression: A critical review. *Journal of School Psychology, 34*, 387–391.

Review of the Test of Written Expression by MILDRED MURRAY-WARD, *Professor of Education, California Lutheran University, Thousand Oaks, CA:*

According to the authors, the Test of Written Expression (TOWE) serves four main purposes: to identify students with writing difficulties, to reveal writing strengths and weaknesses, to document student writing progress, and to aid in writing research.

The Test of Written Expression uses two formats to assess student generated writing. The first is a set of 76 "contrived" items in which the students are asked to produce a letter, word, or sentence in response to a stimulus from the examiner. The second component is a brief "on demand" writing exercise in which students complete a story read to them by the examiner.

The TOWE is an interesting contrast to other writing tests. Many commercial writing assessments use multiple-choice formats in which students recognize errors in usage, punctuation, grammar, and spelling. Others use recognition of good writing through sentence-combining exercises in which students choose the best combined sentence from a set of options. Recently, commercial writing assessments have focused on student writing production, as well.

The authors suggest that writing assessment should explore students' backgrounds, the writing processes they use, and the writing products they create. The TOWE examines only the writing products. The test's analytic writing approach also contrasts with the holistic one used by many states and schools. Although useful in a general writing assessment, holistic scoring does not provide diagnostic information to teachers. In analytic scoring, aspects of writing are examined in isolation and used to help students improve their writing in specific areas.

Overall, the TOWE exhibits quite a bit of variation in its technical qualities. The items were created through study of language arts programs, teacher-made writing activities, and examination of writing skills taught in elementary and junior high schools.

The administration and scoring procedures are complex, but are well described in the examiner's manual. For each grade level, the test sets a specific entry point in the 76 items and employs basal and ceiling levels. The items are hierarchically arranged. However, the authors provide no information explaining how item arrangement was determined.

The manual provides detailed directions for administering and scoring each of the 76 items to arrive at an overall score. An informal analysis of the students' performances on scoring dimensions is also provided. However, validity evidence for this analysis is not provided.

The writing sample is scored using an analytic rubric that determines presence or absence of a characteristic with 1 or a 0. The sample is also checked for complexity as defined by the number of seven-letter words and correctly structured sentences. The scoring seems superficial because the quality of each characteristic is not assessed.

The score interpretations are based on the age of students. This procedure assumes that writing is developmental. It ignores the background and instructional experience of children discussed in an earlier section of the manual. The manual also provides many suggestions for profiling students' writing with other tests by converting scores to common scales. Although an interesting procedure, the test comparisons may not be valid because they may not tap the same trait. Furthermore, no empirical evidence exists for interpreting discrepancies among students' test scores. The authors do suggest making comparisons, but with little discussion of acceptable ones. Interestingly, inappropriateness is illustrated in a subsequent statement that discrepancies occur even in children with no learning problems.

Once the raw score is attained, the procedures for converting the scores are described. The chronological age is used to convert raw scores to scaled scores. These are used to obtain percentile ranks and grade equivalents. All necessary tables are provided in the manual.

The authors used current curricula to create items. These were tried out and standardized with a nationally representative norm group. The sample matched the 1990 U.S. Census on race, ethnic, gender, community type, and geographic region. No SES information was provided, an important omission considering the influence of family circumstances on achievement. Furthermore, the entire norming sample was quite small, with 1,355 children from 21 states. A few heavily populated states were not included, and the small total sample resulted in small numbers of children for each age level. For example, 114 12-year-olds were included in the sample. Assuming that this group adequately represented each racial group, only 13 African American students were involved in norming for that age level, placing serious doubts on score interpretations.

The authors conducted elaborate procedures to assure valid and reliable results. The reliability procedures were well designed, but were completed with very small numbers of students on which the authors provided little information. Internal consistency reliabilities were excellent, and the alternate forms reliability quotients were acceptable for group interpretations, but not individual ones. The interjudge reliabilities were excellent, but completed with only two raters. The item difficulties and the discriminations were good overall, but were lower at the lower age levels.

Validity studies were quite thorough covering content, construct, and criterion validity. However, these efforts suffered from the same problems as the reliability studies, with small groups of poorly described students. The resulting correlations for these studies were all in the moderate range. Finally, the authors provided evidence only for the identification of students with writing problems.

Few validation studies are presented to support other stated purposes. No evidence was provided for the claims of diagnosing strengths and weaknesses of students. The profiling suggestions were not explored in any empirical studies. The purpose of helping educators evaluate educational progress was not adequately explored, because no studies of instructional sensitivity were completed. As a research tool, it is doubtful that researchers could adequately evaluate the appropriateness of the TOWE for research on a specific population because of omissions in the norming sample description.

Assuming that examiners accept the TOWE writing assessment approach, it is a good choice. It follows a more current model of writing assessment, and the authors used good content validity procedures. In addition, the authors made excellent efforts to explore the test's technical qualities. However, the small numbers in the sample and test validity studies limit the interpretability of the scores. The TOWE should only be used with other writing assessment evidence, such as writing samples and observation. The scores should be viewed as general indicators of writing ability and not be overinterpreted through profiles of TOWE subtests or profiles comparing students' results with other tests.

Review of the Test of Written Expression by CAROLE PERLMAN, Director of Student Assessment, Chicago Public Schools, Chicago, IL:
The Test of Written Expression (TOWE) is a norm-referenced writing assessment for ages 6-6 to 14-11. It has four purposes: "to identify students who have writing problems" (manual, p. 5), to diagnose areas of strength and weakness, to evaluate progress in school, and to serve as a research measure.

The TOWE consists of two distinct parts. The first part includes 76 items that measure vocabulary, capitalization, punctuation, spelling, ideation, semantics, and syntax. A few of the questions are multiple choice, but most are short constructed response items. Not all students take all items; individual testing proceeds from a basal level to a ceiling and group administrations cover a subset of the items that depends on grade level. If a student fails to achieve a basal or ceiling in a group administration, some additional individual testing is necessary.

The second part of the TOWE is a writing sample in which the student is given 15 minutes to write a narrative essay in response to a "story starter." The story is rated on 12 attributes, such as structure and organization, descriptive detail, length, spelling, punctuation, capitalization, and usage. The essay is intended for students age 8 and above.

Instructions for administration and scoring are, with a few exceptions, generally good. The authors do not specify how much help, if any, can be provided the student. This is particularly a concern when the student is confronted with an unfamiliar item format (e.g., an analogy) for which no sample items are given. Is it permissible to ask a student to rewrite an illegible response? The manual does not say. Although it is not mentioned in the section on examiner qualifications, in order to score the test the tester needs to know precisely what compound words and compound sentences are, yet those terms are never defined and no examples are given. Testers should also be cautioned to have a dictionary available.

The student booklet is generally well laid out, with one major exception: Test items do not always appear in numerical order (e.g., Item 13 appears at the top of a new page, whereas Item 14 appears at the bottom of the preceding page). This could be confusing, especially for a group-administered test and one wonders why the items were not simply renumbered.

Scoring of items is on an "all or none" basis, even though a given item might require the student to exercise several different skills. However, it is possible to do an informal analysis of item performance that gives more detailed diagnostic information than the overall score alone.

Scores on the two parts are expressed as standard scores (mean = 100, standard deviation = 15), grade equivalents, and percentile ranks. The standard scores are preferable to the rather crudely derived grade equivalents.

STANDARDIZATION. The TOWE was standardized on 1,355 students residing in 21 states. The norming sample *as a whole* approximates the school-age population of the U.S. in gender, race, geographic area, type of community, and ethnicity. This is also true for age groups (6–8, 9–11, and 12–14). However, normative comparisons are made within a single age and no breakdowns are provided except in the 3-year intervals noted above. One, therefore, cannot tell how representative the sample is at each age. In any case, the number of students tested at each age is exceedingly small (median = 129), with a low of only 81 six-year-olds in the national norming sample. No information is given on whether any members of the norming population were disabled or whether there were any whose first language was not English.

RELIABILITY. Internal consistency (coefficient alpha) reliabilities range from .88 to .95 for the items. For the essay, the range is from .78 at age 8 to .93 for age 14; from ages 11–14 all internal consistency reliabilities are at least .90. Interrater reliabilities, based on 30 protocols, were .98 for the Items and .89 for the Essay.

VALIDITY. In developing items for the TOWE, the authors reviewed published language arts programs, scope-and-sequence charts, and teacher-made activities. Median point biserial correlations are also provided as evidence of content validity. For the test items, the point biserials are not especially high, ranging between .20 and .32 at ages 7–14, and extremely low (median = .00) at age 6. Median point biserials for the essay ranged from a low of .15 age 8 to between .42 and .57 for ages 9–14.

To provide evidence of criterion validity, the authors present correlations between TOWE Item and Essay scores and other measures of writing, spelling, punctuation, capitalization, and usage, including the ITBS and CTBS language subtests and the Woodcock-Johnson—Revised writing test. The correlations are quite substantial, mostly between .60 and .80 for the Items and between .50 and .70 for the Essay. However, the descriptions of the study populations do not include the subjects' ages, so it is not clear that there is good criterion validity across the entire range of ages. More information on how well the TOWE predicts performance on writing performance assessments (as opposed to multiple-choice tests of grammar and the like) would also be helpful.

The TOWE correlates moderately with other achievement measures and with intelligence. The authors cite a study in which 186 learning disabled students (ages unspecified) took the TOWE and received an average standard score of 86.5 for the Items and 86.7 for the Essay. Standard errors were not provided.

BIAS. Gender and racial (white vs. nonwhite) bias were examined using the correlations between delta values for the two groups in question. Little evidence of either type of bias was shown. No information was provided on students whose first language was not English.

SUMMARY. The TOWE's strength is that it includes both test items and a writing sample for ages 8 and above (though the reliability of the essay at age 8 is marginal). Its weaknesses are a very small norming sample and limited information on special populations. The TOWE, in combination with other assessment data, can provide some helpful information for students age 9 or above. According to the manual, TOWE results "should be treated as an indicator of problem areas to be investigated further" (p. 27) by observations, additional testing, or teacher reports. "The point is especially critical when decisions are to be made about placement in a special education or remedial program" (p. 27).

[340]
Test of Written Language—Third Edition.

Purpose: Designed to "(a) identify students who perform significantly more poorly than their peers in writing and who as a result need special help; (b) determine a student's particular strengths and weaknesses in various writing abilities; (c) document a student's progress in a special writing program; and conduct research in writing."
Population: Ages 7-0 to 17-11.
Publication Dates: 1978–1996.
Acronym: TOWL-3.
Scores: 8 subtest scores (Vocabulary, Spelling, Style, Logical Sentences, Sentence Combining, Contextual Conventions, Contextual Language, Story Construction) plus 3 composite scores (Contrived Writing, Spontaneous Writing, Overall Writing).
Administration: Individual or group.
Forms, 2: A, B.
Price Data, 1996: $159 per complete kit including manual ('96, 134 pages), 25 student response booklets Form A, 25 student response booklets Form B, and 50 profile/story scoring forms in storage box; $39 per 25 A or B student response booklets; $37 per 50 profile/story scoring forms; $48 per manual; $98 per Windows or Macintosh PRO-SCORE System; $89 per IBM DOS PRO-SCORE System.
Time: (90) minutes.

Authors: Donald D. Hammill and Stephen C. Larsen.
Publisher: PRO-ED, Inc.
Cross References: See T4:2804 (2 references); for reviews of an earlier edition by Stephen L. Benton and Joseph M. Ryan, see 11:444 (6 references); for reviews of the original edition by Edward A. Polloway and Robert T. Williams, see 9:1278.

TEST REFERENCES

1. Graham, S., & Harris, K. R. (1989). Improving learning disabled students' skills at composing essays: Self-instructional strategy training. *Exceptional Children, 56*, 201–214.
2. Koenig, L. A., & Biel, C. D. (1989). A delivery system of comprehensive language services in a school district. *Language, Speech, and Hearing Services in Schools, 20*, 338–365.
3. Graham, S. (1990). The role of production factors in learning disabled students' composition. *Journal of Educational Psychology, 82*, 781–791.
4. Jacobson, J. E. (1991). Test of Written Language-2 (TOWL-2). *Journal of Reading, 34*, 663–665.
5. Parker, R. I., Tindal, G., & Hasbrouck, J. (1991). Progress monitoring with objective measures of writing performance for students with mild disabilities. *Exceptional Children, 58*, 61-73.
6. Graham, S., MacArthur, C., Schwartz, S., & Page-Voth, V. (1992). Improving the compositions of students with learning disabilities using a strategy involving product and process goal setting. *Exceptional Children, 58*, 322-334.
7. Berninger, V. W., & Hooper, S. R. (1993). Preventing and remediating writing disabilities: Interdisciplinary frameworks for assessment, consultation, and intervention. *School Psychology Review, 22*, 590-594.
8. Berninger, V. W., & Whitaker, D. (1993). Theory-based branching diagnosis of writing disabilities. *School Psychology Review, 22*, 623-642.
9. Roberts, G. I., & Samuels, M. T. (1993). Handwriting remediation: A comparison of computer-based and traditional approaches. *Journal of Educational Research, 87*, 118-125.
10. Arehole, S., Augustine, L. E., & Simhadri, R. (1995). Middle latency response in children with learning disabilities: Preliminary findings. *Journal of Communication Disorders, 28*, 21–38.
11. Benton, S. L., Corkill, A. J., Sharp, J. M., Downey, R. G., & Khramtsova, I. (1995). Knowledge, interest, and narrative writing. *Journal of Educational Psychology, 87*, 66–79.
12. Graham, S., MacArthur, C., & Schwartz, S. (1995). Effects of goal setting and procedural facilitation on the revising behavior and writing performance of students with writing and learning problems. *Journal of Educational Psychology, 87*, 230-240.
13. Johnson, C. J. (1995). Expanding norms for narration. *Language, Speech, and Hearing Services in Schools, 26*, 326–341.
14. Zigmond, N. (1995). Inclusion in Kansas educational experiences of students with learning disabilities in one elementary school. *The Journal of Special Education, 29*, 144–154.
15. Berninger, V., Whitaker, D., Feng, Y., Swanson, H. L., & Abbott, R. D. (1996). Assessment of planning, translating, and revising in junior high writers. *Journal of School Psychology, 34*, 23–52.
16. Wiig, E. H., Jones, S. S., & Wiig, E. D. (1996). Computer-based assessment of word knowledge in teens with learning disabilities. *Language, Speech, and Hearing Services in Schools, 27*, 21–28.

Review of the Test of Written Language—Third Edition by JOE B. HANSEN, Executive Director, Planning, Research and Evaluation, Colorado Springs School District Eleven, Colorado Springs, CO:

The Test of Written Language—Third Edition (TOWL-3) is represented as a comprehensive test of written language. As the third edition of a test first published in 1978, the TOWL-3 is substantially improved from earlier versions. Improvements include reduced length of time for administering and scoring, a tighter and more logically defensible conceptual model of writing, improved norms, improved reliability and validity, and a bias study.

PURPOSE AND USE. The TOWL-3 is a diagnostic and formative evaluation tool, developed to meet better the stated assessment needs of identifying students who need special help, documenting students' strengths and weaknesses, and monitoring the effectiveness of programs designed to improve writing skills. The test is designed for students from 7 years to 17 years and 11 months of age.

The underlying model of writing upon which the TOWL-3 is based incorporates three writing components, *conventional, linguistic,* and *cognitive* and two writing sample formats, *contrived* and *spontaneous* to assess different sets of skills essential to effective and efficient writing. Contrived Writing, in which predetermined stimuli are given to the student and he or she selects or provides the correct responses, is used to assess Vocabulary, Spelling, Style (which includes punctuation and grammar), Logical Sentences, and Sentence Combining. Spontaneous Writing uses student-generated writing samples to assess Contextual Conventions, Contextual Language, and Story Construction. Three composite scores are produced: Spontaneous Writing, Contrived Writing, and Overall Writing (a combination of the other two composite scores). This separation of writing into two discrete components with an overall score enables the educator to ascertain how well the individual student understands the conventions and forms of written language as well as how he or she actually writes. This key feature of the TOWL-3 is, to my knowledge, unique among written language assessments and should be considered a definite strength.

The authors are thorough and clear in their description of appropriate uses of the test. The TOWL-3 seems to be appropriate for its intended uses and audiences.

ADMINISTRATION AND SCORING. Although it is clearly designed to be individually administered, the TOWL-3 can be used as either an individually or group administered test. Persons who administer, score, and interpret the test require training in these areas and in evaluation. They should also be knowledgeable about the rules governing English language usage (p. 9, examiner's manual). The examiner's manual contains sample stories and instructions on how to score them. These can be used for examiners to practice. Nine rules for administering the test are provided. If adhered to, these rules provide at least a minimal level of guidance to ensure valid interpretation of scores. An entire chapter of the examiner's manual is dedicated to instruction on how to score each of the eight subtests. Although the TOWL-3 is intended to be untimed, a convenient chart in the manual provides timing guidelines for administering and scoring the test. Special instructions are provided for group administration.

Scoring instructions are clear and easy to follow, using the tables in the appendix. Nevertheless, the number of steps involved in the process could be daunting to many classroom teachers. Given the complex nature of this test and the administration and scoring procedures, it should not be used by the classroom teacher without training and practice. It would be more appropriate for an assessment professional, evaluator, or school psychologist to be responsible for the administration and scoring. At the very least, such a person should conduct training and set high performance standards for those who would administer and score the test. The cumbersome nature of manual scoring also limits the appeal of this test.

Although the TOWL-3 is substantially improved over previous versions, a degree of subjectivity remains in the scoring procedures, especially for Subtest 8, Story Construction. This subjectivity appears in the relatively low mean interscorer reliability for this subtest (.83 across Forms A and B). Some subjectivity is also observable in Subtest 6, Contextual Conventions. Both subtests employ rating scales that ask for scorer judgments of "poor," "average," or "good"; or "immature," "boring," or "interesting." Such judgments are inherently subjective and are likely to provide a significant source of error.

Raw scores, age and grade equivalents, percentiles, subtest standard scores, and composite quotients comprise the scores available from the TOWL-3. To the authors' credit, they issue strong caveats regarding the use of age and grade equivalents, indicating that they have chosen to include them among the available scores only because some legal and administrative jurisdictions require their use. A procedure is provided for converting scores from other tests to TOWL-3 percentiles and quotients, but no information is provided on how to use these data once the conversions have been made.

RELIABILITY AND VALIDITY. An abundance of data on reliability and validity are provided in the examiner's manual. Also included are clear and concise definitions and explanations of each type of reliability and validity, sources of error variance, and the procedure used to gather the evidence. This instructive aspect of the documentation is commendable.

Four types of reliability coefficients are provided: coefficient alpha, alternate forms (immediate administration), test-retest (time-interval not specified), and interscorer. Although most reliability

statistics are within industry standards, the Contextual Conventions subtest provides a notable exception. The average coefficient alpha coefficient for this subtest is a mere 70, with a range from .60 to .77. Alternate form reliability is .71 and time sampling (test-retest) yields .75. This subtest "measures the ability to spell words properly and to apply the rules governing punctuation of sentences and capitalization of words in a spontaneously written composition" (manual, p. 38). Further research should be conducted by the authors to investigate possible sources of error in this subtest and correct the problem. One such source was mentioned above in the subjectivity of the scoring guide.

Three types of validity data: content, criterion related, and construct, are provided. Evidence for content validity is present in the form of a strong, clear, logical rationale for each subtest. Classical item analysis is used as a means of screening items. An item inclusion criterion of .3 plus statistical significance was used for point-biserial coefficients. Nevertheless, median discrimination indices for age groups 7 and 8 are unacceptably low for all five contrived subtests. This finding renders the TOWL-3 relatively useless for primary grade students.

A DIF item bias analysis was conducted using a Delta Scores analysis procedure. This analysis yielded DIF coefficients in the high 90s across all subtests and dichotomous groups (male/female, white/nonwhite, Hispanic/non-Hispanic). Criterion-related validity data are provided in the form of correlations with writing scale scores on the Comprehensive Scales of Student Abilities (Hammill & Hresko, 1994), a teacher rating scale of a wide range of academic abilities including writing. The data, collected from 76 students in a single elementary school, reveal "moderate" correlations in the range of .34 to .69, which the authors claim "are large enough to support the criterion-related validity of the TOWL-3" (p. 72). It should be noted, however, that the data provided by the authors contain observable differences between alternate forms, favoring Form B. ANOVA data on differences by form, type of test, and subtest would be helpful in ascertaining whether there are significant differences in criterion-related validity between forms or subtests. Strong and convincing evidence is provided for construct validity through logical analysis, correlational analysis, and factor analysis.

NORMATIVE INFORMATION. The norming sample, comprising 2,217 students in 25 states, was tested in 1995. Two approaches were taken in collecting normative data. First, a site was selected in each of the four major U.S. Bureau of Census regions: Northeast, North Central, South, and West. A total of 970 students in general classes were tested in the four sites. Second, 54 volunteers, selected from among TOWL-2 test users, tested an additional 1,247 students. Data comparing the demographic characteristics of the norming sample to Census data support the representativeness of the sample overall. However, the small size of the sample should raise questions about its representativeness for each of the age groups covered by the test. Age group Ns range from 105 (age 7) to 350 (age 10). Data are provided on stratification by age group for geographic region, gender, race, urban-rural residency, and ethnicity. Census Bureau data enabling a comparison of proportionality of age groups by each of these variables is not provided. The norming sample is marginally adequate for the purposes it supports. A larger sample, with data showing proportionality of the subgroups to population statistics, would be helpful.

SUMMARY. The TOWL-3 is substantially improved from earlier versions. As a diagnostic and formative evaluation tool, it is most useful in identifying student writers who are performing substantially below their peers. Strengths of this test include: a strong conceptual model of writing, generally acceptable levels of subtest reliabilities (with the exception of Contextual Conventions subtest), and generally good evidence of validity. Its weaknesses include: complex and time-consuming manual scoring and interpretation procedures, a need for user training, subjectivity in some of the scoring procedures (especially for Story Composition), poor discrimination for ages 7–8, and marginally adequate norms.

REVIEWER'S REFERENCE

Hammill, D. D., & Hresko, W. P. (1994). Comprehensive Scales of Student Abilities. Austin, TX: PRO-ED, Inc.

Review of the Test of Written Language—Third Edition by JAYNE E. BUCY, Assistant Professor of Psychology, and MARK E. SWERDLIK, Professor of Psychology, Illinois State University, Normal, IL:

The Test of Written Language—Third Edition (TOWL-3) was designed to provide a comprehensive, diagnostic assessment of written language in children ages 7-0 to 17-11. The TOWL-3's stated purposes are to (a) provide normative means of identifying children with writing difficulties, (b) diagnose strengths and weaknesses in written language, (c) measure student progress in response to intervention efforts, and (d) provide a research tool. It represents a major revision of the TOWL-2 by shortening administration and scoring time, including easier items for younger students, and providing updated norms, additional reliability and validity information, and both age and grade equivalent scores. The authors report that the test can be administered in approximately 65 minutes. Scoring is estimated to take 15 minutes, which might be an underestimate for less experienced examiners. It may be administered to individuals or groups. Two parallel test forms are provided. Computer scoring is available in Windows, Mac, and DOS versions.

The TOWL-3 is made up of eight subtests. All items are untimed, making the measure more fair to children with disabilities. Five subtests (Spelling, Style, Vocabulary, Sentence Combining, and Logical Sentences) follow a contrived writing format requiring the student to demonstrate writing skills in isolation, such as incorporating a word into a sentence, spelling from dictation, and combining sentences in a logical manner. The three remaining subtests (Contextual Conventions, Contextual Language, and Story Construction) incorporate a spontaneous writing format. For these subtests, the student produces a spontaneous writing sample (a story), which is evaluated for specific criteria such as vocabulary, grammar, plot, and punctuation. The Spontaneous Writing Sample is generated by asking students to write a story about a picture. The stimulus pictures are black and white and unchanged from the TOWL-2. Form A shows a futuristic scene of astronauts, space ships, and construction activity. For Form B, the stimulus is a prehistoric scene of people in animal skins hunting a prehistoric mammal. These pictures would seemingly hold limited appeal to some children, though the authors do not provide evidence that motivation or interest will not adversely influence test performance.

Age standard scores and percentiles are available for each subtest. Three composite standard scores (called quotients) may also be computed. The Overall Writing Composite represents performance on all eight subtests and is described as "the best estimate of a person's general ability in written language" (manual, p. 37). Composite scores may also be computed for Contrived Writing and Spontaneous Writing subtests. Subtest raw scores may be converted to age and grade equivalents.

Examiner qualifications include training in educational assessment, proficiency in use of the English language, and familiarity with the instrument. Basic administration and scoring procedures (individual and group) are furnished. The authors provide 12 sample stories with scoring that will allow the novice examiner to reach an acceptable level of scorer reliability. The manual also provides useful information explaining test interpretation, providing cautions in the use of age and grade equivalents, testing of limits, and explaining test results to others and use of local norms.

Normative data for the TOWL-3 were acquired from a representative sample of 2,217 students in grades 2 through 12 residing in 25 states. The sample size is adequate with sufficient representation at each age level (range of sample sizes across age levels is 105–350). The sample is designed to be representative of the 1990 U.S. Census. Demographic characteristics are provided and are also stratified by age, geographical region, gender, race, residence, and ethnicity. Students with disabilities comprise 10% of the standardization sample and include children with learning disabilities (6%), speech-language disorders (3%), mental retardation (1%), and other disabilities (1%). Distribution of the disability group on characteristics such as age and gender is not provided.

A limitation of this measure is that a scale score can be computed from raw scores of zero. This is most clearly a problem at younger ages when, for example, a 7-year-old scoring zero in Sentence Combining earns a Subtest Standard Score of 9. Guidance is needed from the authors when scoring and interpreting protocols of students who obtain subtest raw scores of zero.

Test reliability for the TOWL-3 was provided in three ways. Internal consistency (coefficients alpha) was estimated for each subtest and composite score at the 11 ages (7–17 years). For all ages, composite scores for Contrived Writing and Spontaneous Writing of both test forms meet minimal standards (.90) for purposes of educational decision making with individual students. Coefficients alpha for the Overall Writing Composite (.97) for both forms meets a desirable standard at all ages. Internal consistency for some subtests approaches or meets the desired standards at certain ages, although other subtests are unacceptable at all ages (Contextual Conventions, Contextual Language) suggesting that the test user cannot interpret these subtest strengths and weaknesses. Coefficients alpha for selected subgroups of gender, ethnicity, and disability status show a similar pattern for subtests. Reliability coefficients for these subgroups for composite scores are not provided and would be useful.

Alternate forms reliability was provided, though specific procedures such as time between administrations, order and format of administration (individual or group), and sample size are absent. Reliability coefficients at each age level were acceptable for Spontaneous Writing (.76–.89), Contrived Writing (.86–.95), and Overall Writing (.83–96). Subtest group means and standard deviations for the forms were essentially identical.

A study of test/retest reliability (2 weeks delay) was conducted, though with only 27 second graders and 28 twelfth graders as subjects. The groups were administered both forms at each interval. Subtest coefficient estimates are in the .70s and .80s with composite coefficients in the .80s to .90s. With a few exceptions, these estimates did not meet the minimally acceptable range of .90 for individual decision making.

Interscorer reliability was reported as acceptable for all composites and four of the eight subtests (Vocabulary, Spelling, Style, and Contextual Conventions). This was obtained by PRO-ED staff scoring 38 randomly selected protocols. Staff training was not described, therefore it is impossible to determine if this level of interscorer reliability can be expected among typical test users.

Three types of validity evidence (content, criterion, and construct) are presented. The authors provide a plausible argument for the content validity of the TOWL-3 by describing the underlying rationale of each subtest. Test content is reasonable for the stated purposes of the test. In addition, the evidence of item discrimination for most subtests (Vocabulary, Spelling, Style, and Sentence Combining) was satisfactory in both forms for children 9–17 years of age. Logical Sentences, Contextual Language, and Story Construction are generally satisfactory at all ages. Care should be taken when using the TOWL-3 with younger children (7 and 8 years) because the index discrimination may be an artifact of the small number of accessible items at these ages. The authors described their efforts to minimize test bias. Subgroup comparisons for gender and race evidenced little or no item bias.

Criterion validity evidence included a study with 76 elementary students. Moderate correlations were reported between TOWL-3 scores and the results of a teacher rating scale of academic abilities (Comprehensive Scales of Student Abilities; Hammill & Hresko, 1994). Additional studies with larger samples, at all ages and with different criterion measures, are needed.

Evidence of construct validity was provided in an examination of test performance at each age level (7–17) and in correlations of subtest scores to age.

The TOWL-3 also differentiates between children with disabilities (learning disabled and speech impaired) and children without disabilities, and between low and high achievers. Moderate correlations with nonverbal intelligence were also found. Additional validity studies with measures of verbal intelligence and larger and more representative samples are needed.

The authors provide suggestions for remediation techniques based on TOWL-3 test results. These recommendations do not appear to be based on most recent research relating to instructional practices. In addition, there is no evidence presented for the usefulness of utilizing TOWL-3 performance for developing effective interventions for students.

In summary, the TOWL-3 represents a comprehensive revision of the TOWL-2. Changes include reduced administration and scoring time. Despite the addition of easier items for younger students with academic difficulty, the test is likely to be too difficult for this group. Age and grade equivalents are now provided. The entire instrument was renormed on a representative sample of subjects ages 7 through 17. Studies support the reliability of this measure for diagnostic purposes, though interpretations at the subtest level are ill advised. Additional validity studies are needed. Notwithstanding these limitations, the TOWL-3 meets a need for a measure of written language for both diagnostic and research purposes.

REVIEWER'S REFERENCE

Hammill, D. D., & Hresko, W. P. (1994). Comprehensive Scales of Student Abilities. Austin, TX: PRO-ED, Inc.

[341]
Test of Written Spelling, Third Edition.

Purpose: To assess spelling skills across different types of words.

Population: Ages 6-0 to 18-11.

Publication Dates: 1976–1994.

Acronym: TWS-3.

Scores, 3: Predictable Words, Unpredictable Words, Total.

Administration: Group.

Price Data, 1993: $46 per complete kit including manual ('94, 52 pages) and 50 answer sheets; $29 per examiner's manual; $19 per 50 answer sheets.

Time: (15–25) minutes.

Authors: Stephen C. Larsen and Donald D. Hammill.

Publisher: PRO-ED, Inc.

Cross References: See T4:2805 (4 references); for reviews by Deborah B. Erickson and Ruth M. Noyce of an earlier edition, see 10:374; for reviews by John M. Bradley and Deborah B. Erickson of an earlier edition, see 9:1279 (1 reference).

TEST REFERENCES

1. Klesius, J. P., Griffith, P. L., & Zielonka, P. (1991). A whole language and traditional instruction comparison: Overall effectiveness and development of the alphabetic principle. *Reading Research and Instruction, 30*(2), 47-61.
2. Lewis, B. A., & Freebairn, L. (1992). Residual effects of preschool phonology disorders in grade school, adolescence, and adulthood. *Journal of Speech and Hearing Research, 35*, 819-831.
3. Gettinger, M. (1993). Effects of error correction on third graders' spelling. *Journal of Educational Research, 87*, 39-45.
4. Reid, R., & Harris, K. R. (1993). Self-monitoring of attention versus self-monitoring of performance: Effects on attention and academic performance. *Exceptional Children, 60*, 29-40.
5. North, K., Joy, P., Yuille, D., Cocks, N., Mobb, E., Hutchins, P., McHugh, K., & deSilva, M. (1994). Specific learning disability in children with neurofibromatosis type 1: Significance of MRI abnormalities. *Neurology, 44*, 878-883.

Review of the Test of Written Spelling, Third Edition by ALFRED P. LONGO, Supervisor of Humanities, Holmdel Township School District, Holmdel, NJ:

The Test of Written Spelling (TWS-3) is a norm-referenced test that has been designed to assess the spelling proficiency of students in grades 1 to 12. In response to previous reviews of the second edition of this instrument, the authors have developed the third edition of the TWS. In so doing, they have attempted to address the criticisms contained in those prior reviews.

The TWS-3 comprises two subtests. Each subtest utilizes a dictated word format. Based upon an analysis of phoneme/grapheme rules and English orthography, the instrument divides its assessment of spelling proficiency along the lines of "predictable words" (words that conform to orthographic rules) and "unpredictable words" (words that do not). In their test design the authors have properly considered this duality of English spelling by attempting to assess proficiency in the spelling of both rule-governed and "irregular" words. The research they cite in this regard (Hanna, Hanna, Hodges, & Rudorf [1966]) is sound, yet dated. By allowing potential users to isolate specific error patterns in spelling they provide teachers with a valid means of diagnosing particular weaknesses in a student's spelling. Most other spelling tests do not offer this level of distinction.

Also, unlike most other spelling tests, on the TWS-3 the test taker does not respond to a forced choice between the correct and incorrect spelling of a given word; rather, he or she must definitively write down the proper spelling of the dictated word. This further differentiates the ability to spell from the ability to edit or to recognize an error.

The TWS-3 was developed for use in a school setting. The clear and well-designed test manual gives straightforward administration and scoring procedures. The test can be administered in individual settings in about 15 to 25 minutes. Because of the clarity and completeness of the directions, the administration is simple. It should also be noted that the authors have considered such items as the comfort of the examinee in their notes on administration.

In the administration of the test the examiner says a word in isolation, uses a sentence from the manual that contains that word in context, and then repeats the word. In order to establish a basal threshold, five consecutive words must be spelled correctly. If the examinee does not accomplish this, the examiner tests "downward" until five consecutive words are spelled correctly. This procedure makes the instrument difficult to administer in a group setting and also may cloud the establishment of basals and ceilings for performance when used in that manner. This may be the most limiting aspect of the TWS-3.

Normative procedures seem to be comprehensive. The normative sample has been composed with two samples; the sample of 3,805 students used to norm the TWS-2 in 1986 was enhanced with 855 new cases in 1993 to form a combined sample of 4,760. [Editors Note: 3,805 + 855 = 4,660. However, 4,760 is the number given on page 15 of the examiner's manual.] The authors explain that the merging of the two samples is justified, for the means of the two groups are not significantly different at any age interval and the fact that only 7 years lapsed between the testings. It is also noted that the items on the tests were identical. In response to previous criticisms, the current manual contains information on how the subjects in the sample were selected. For each characteristic of gender, race, geographic region, age, ethnicity, etc. the sample's percentages were compared to those reported in *The Statistical Abstract of the United States* that had been keyed to the 1990 Census. Four of the samples' variables (geographic region, gender, race, and ethnicity) are further delineated in a chart that stratifies those variables by age intervals. The entire process seems to be reasonable, complete, and responsive to previous reviewers' concerns. In light of the changes in Language Arts instruction (e.g., whole language) and in the passage of time since the initial sampling, it is suggested that, if other editions are planned, an entirely new sample be selected.

Using a reliability analysis dependent on Anastasi's (1988) three sources of test error (content, time, and interscorer reliability) the authors demonstrate reliability by showing mean reliability of .98 for total words. In addition, the specific data supplied on coefficient alphas, time sampling, and interscorer reliability show mean scores in each category from .92 to .97. These easily exceed the minimally acceptable standard of .80.

Content validity is demonstrated in two ways: a rationale, predicated on the findings of Hanna et al. (1966), first utilized in the creation of the first TWS in 1976; and an item analysis. The TWS-3 demonstrates a strong correlation between the words it tests and words appearing in five basal readers produced by major publishers (Follett, Silver-Burdett, McGraw-Hill, Houghton Mifflin, and Scott-Foresman). For the upper levels of the test (above grade 8) *The EDL Core Vocabulary in Reading, Mathematics, Science and Social Science* was utilized. The changes in current reading series, the movement to true literature, may signal a revision in the words that can be considered core. Is the TWS-3's content as valid when one considers the changes in popular reading series?

The TWS-3 correlates well with other standardized measures of spelling. A mean correlation coefficient of .88 is reported as a result of comparison with scores on the *Durrell Analysis of Reading Difficulty, Wide Range Achievement Test, California Achievement Test,* and the *SRA Achievement Series.*

The TWS-3 is a spelling test that has a firm theoretical foundation in its evaluation of a student's ability to spell both "predictable" and "unpredictable" words. Its limitations may lie in the fact that other factors besides direct instruction in spelling rules and the memorization of irregular words account for spelling proficiency. Also, its application in the large group environment can be questioned both in the awkwardness of administration in that setting and, therefore, its diagnostic and instructional value for numbers of students. On the other hand, the authors attempts on this latest edition to add to, and clearly define, the normative sample, to demonstrate the absence of racial and gender bias, and the discussion of the limitations of spelling ages and grade level equivalents are all positive enhancements to this test.

The test manual is clear, comprehensive, and precise. The technical data presented are complete and present an instrument that has strong validity and reliability when used to address an individual student's spelling ability.

Finally, and most noteworthy, is the test's continued reliance upon the examinee writing the correct spelling of a given word. This represents an authentic, true assessment of spelling ability, not an artificially contrived editing exercise.

REVIEWER'S REFERENCES

Hanna, P. R., Hanna, J. S., Hodges, R. G., & Rudorf, E. H. (1966). *Phoneme-grapheme correspondences to spelling improvement.* Washington, DC: Office of Education, United States Department of Health, Education, and Welfare.
Anastasi, A. (1988). *Psychological testing* (6th ed.). New York: Macmillan.

Review of the Test of Written Spelling, Third Edition by HOI K. SUEN, Professor of Educational Psychology, Pennsylvania State University, University Park, PA:

The Test of Written Spelling, Third Edition (TWS-3) is a 100-word spelling test consisting of two 50-word subtests. One subtest contains 50 "predictable" words, the spellings for which conform to phonic rules. The other subtest contains 50 "unpredictable" words that do not follow phonic rules. The test is administered in a dictation format, in that the examiner pronounces a word in isolation, followed by a sentence in which the word is used, and then followed by the single word again. The child is to spell the word on paper. This process is repeated for all 100 words. The number-correct raw scores is then converted to either a norm-referenced normalized standard score for ages 6-0 through 18-11 or a grade-equivalent score for grades 5 through 11.5.

The normative sample used for scaling was excellent. A combined sample of 4,760 children residing in 23 states was used. The composition of the sample in terms of gender, race, age, ethnicity, and geographic representation was close in approximation to that of the U.S. population in general. A rather comprehensive set of results of various classical psychometric analyses were presented to support score reliability and the validity of the intended score interpretation. Except for a few relatively minor technical imperfections (e.g., inappropriate z-transformation of Cronbach's alpha, separate reliability estimates instead of a single generalizability analysis, evidence of relevance to basal series but not of representativeness), the results of the psychometric analyses, which included various approaches to estimating reliability, item analyses, statistical correlations with other spelling tests, and various hypothesis-testing studies in support of the nomological net, were comprehensive, meticulous, and compelling. When the totality of evidence is considered, it is cogently clear that the scores on the TWS-3 are valid indicators of a child's relative level of spelling proficiency.

A new feature of the TWS-3, not otherwise available in previous versions, was a series of studies the purposes of which were described as "controlling for bias" (p. 31). The study of potential race/gender/ethnic bias in important if the TWS-3 is to be used for high-stakes decisions. The authors' attempts in this direction have filled a gap in previous versions of this test. Unfortunately, these attempts were not entirely successful in that the data were analyzed through the correlations

between delta values, a method not quite appropriate for the stated purpose. The delta method does not "control" for bias nor does a high correlation between delta values indicate the absence of biased items. The delta-plot method was designed to detect biased items by isolating outlier items. This method is generally considered uninformative and can give an inappropriate picture of bias. There are quite a few better alternatives to the delta method, generally grouped under the term differential item functioning, including the Mantel-Haenszel method, the IRT method, and the chi-square method. The analyses would have been more conclusive had any of these better methods been used.

Reviewers for the second edition had criticized TWS-2 as not appropriate for the purpose of building spelling programs or diagnosing specific error patterns. In response, the authors added materials that "spell out clearly the uses of the TWS-3 results and their limitations" (p. vi). However, there is no evidence to support the proposed uses of the test thus spelled out. Specifically, the authors proposed that the TWS-3 could be used to identify persons who are deficient in spelling ability, that it is clinically useful in analyzing intraindividual differences, and can be used to evaluate progress in remedial and developmental programs. Unfortunately, there is no direct evidence to support any of these claims. For example, to support the first claim would require evidence of utility, perhaps through a Bayesian analysis or such statistics as positive predictive power and negative predictive power. To support the second and third claims would require evidence that these purposes can in fact be realized through the use of the TWS-3. For example, whether the TWS-3 can be used to document overall progress in spelling as a consequence of an intervention program can be expected to depend on whether the contents of the intervention program correspond to the contents of the TWS-3, the most effective intervention being an extreme and questionable one in which the spelling of these 100 specific words are directly taught. Also, a lack of progress may or may not be "a consequence of intervention program" (p. 3). The claim that the TWS-3 is useful to determine areas of strength and weakness is somewhat exaggerated. Basically, there are only two areas: Predictable Words and Unpredictable Words. To the extent that a difference exists between the two areas, a child is either weaker in "unpredictable" words or weaker in "predictable" words. What exactly may be the utility of this knowledge of a weaker area is not clear. The authors claimed that this knowledge would be useful in planning additional assessment procedures but were not clear on exactly how this could be useful; nor was there evidence that this is really useful. In addition, both the second and third claims require the use of difference scores. As such, the reliabilities of difference scores need to be investigated. It should be noted that the authors did appropriately warn users of the TWS-3 not to use the test for the purposes of instructional planning.

To the extent an overall ability to spell unspecified English words correctly in general remains a concern in the age of spell checkers, contrived commercial words, and an explosion of technical words, the TWS-3 provides a meaningful and appropriate measure of the spelling proficiency of a child relative to his/her normative peers. However, as the claimed purposes for using the TWS-3 lack supportive evidence, the usefulness of the TWS-3 remains unclear. In sum, the TWS-3 is a psychometrically excellent test in search of a useful, practical function.

[342]
Test on Appraising Observations.

Purpose: Designed to test one aspect of critical thinking: judging credibility.
Population: Grade 10 to adult.
Publication Dates: 1983–1990.
Administration: Group.
Price Data: Available from publishers.
Authors: Stephen P. Norris (multiple-choice format and constructed-response format) and Ruth King (multiple-choice format).
Publisher: Faculty of Education, Memorial University of Newfoundland [Canada].
    a) MULTIPLE-CHOICE FORMAT.
    Publication Date: 1983.
    Scores: Total score only.
    Parts, 2: A, B.
    Time: (40–45) minutes.
    b) CONSTRUCTED-RESPONSE VERSION.
    Publication Date: 1986.
    Scores, 2: Answer-Choice, Justification.
    Time: (40–45) minutes.
Cross References: See T4:2806 (1 reference).

Review of the Test on Appraising Observations by MICHAEL KANE, *Professor of Education, University of Wisconsin, Madison, WI:*

Both forms of the Test on Appraising Observations, the multiple-choice version and the constructed-response version, have a very specific interpretation, focusing on a particular part of critical thinking, the appraisal of observation reports. The proposed interpretation is stated in the title of the test, it is suggested by the content of the test and the scoring key, and it is emphasized in the manual. The clarity and specificity of the proposed interpretation contributes to the value of the test in various contexts by making misuse and misinterpretation less likely.

NORMS. The norms data are very limited, and at best provide a very rough indication of what scores mean in a norm-referenced sense. The manual authors state the test is designed primarily for senior high school students but is useful at the junior high and college levels. Percentiles for eight relatively small convenience samples are reported in the manual. The largest group consists of 287 students in grades 10, 11, and 12, "in a wealthy neighborhood in southern Ontario," and the smallest group consists of "48 non-academic grade 10 students taking general science in a large metropolitan area in Canada's Atlantic Provinces" (p. 6). Although one would not want to base a norm-referenced interpretation on any of these samples, they do provide some indication of how different groups might be expected to perform, and therefore add to the interpretability of the scores.

VALIDITY. The section on validity in the manual is organized in terms of three kinds of evidence: criterion-related, content-related, and construct-related, with most of the space devoted to criterion evidence. However, the most convincing validity evidence is based on the close relationship between the tasks included in the test and the intended interpretation.

The authors propose to interpret the test scores in terms of the ability to appraise observations and see this ability as a psychological construct. They expand on this interpretation in the section on construct-related evidence. Based on their previous work and other sources, the authors present a fairly detailed outline of principles for judging the credibility of observations, and argue that, for purposes of the Test on Appraising Observations, good thinking be defined as thinking in accordance with these principles. The test items, which are keyed to the principles, provide a thorough sampling of the list of principles, and the manual and Norris (1992) contain evidence indicating that students who answer items correctly generally do so by using the appropriate principles. This argument is quite persuasive.

However, there are some possible counterarguments that are not addressed in the manual. In addition to concerns about generalizability, which are discussed below, response bias represents a potentially serious threat to validity. Each item is embedded in a story and includes two contradictory statements made by different characters in the story. The instructions suggest that there are three possible answers to each item: (a) that there is more reason to believe the first statement, (b) that there is more reason to believe the second statement, and (c) that there is no reason to believe either statement over the other. In fact, however, one of the two statements is always the keyed answer, and the third option is always incorrect. The test is forced-choice, but the instructions state that it is not forced-choice. Now, when two witnesses flatly contradict each other (as they do in each of the items) and there is no material evidence to support either of the two accounts, there is good reason to suspect both accounts, and therefore, a cautious student might pick the third option. The cautious student who can appraise observations effectively could thereby get a low score.

The section in the manual on validity begins with a fairly lengthy discussion of correlations between the Test on Appraising Observations and several general tests of critical thinking (e.g., Watson-Glaser) for a group of 172 students in grades 10 to 12, from a large metropolitan school district in Canada. These correlations, which are presented as criterion-related evidence, range from .20 to .62 for the multiple-choice version, and from .06 to .25 for the constructed-response version. Unfortunately, it is not clear what these results mean. The tests being used as criteria cover much more than the ability to appraise observations; and therefore, correlations with these criteria are at best marginally relevant to the validity of the specific interpretation being proposed for the Test on Appraising Observations.

RELIABILITY. The data on reliability in the manual are limited to alpha coefficients (with values between .54 and .80) for the eight norms groups mentioned earlier. No data on interrater reliability or test-retest reliability are reported.

The alpha reliabilities are hard to interpret for at least two reasons. First, the items are presented within the context of long stories. The constructed-response version includes 25 items in one story, and the multiple-choice version includes 50 items within two stories. The instructions to examinees state that, for each item, examinees can use information from previous items, but should not use information from later items. The lack of independence among the items resulting from the nesting of items within stories would tend to inflate the alpha coefficients.

On the other hand, the convenience samples used to estimate the alpha coefficients would tend to be more homogeneous than the target population as a whole, and this restriction of range would tend to lower the alpha coefficients. The alpha coefficients are subject, therefore, to conflicting biases of unknown magnitude.

A more thorough analysis of the generalizability of the scores is needed. The interpretation of the scores in terms of ability to appraise observations would suggest generalization over items, over the contexts in which the observations are set, and over occasions, and for the constructed-response format, over scorers. The alpha coefficients address generalization over items, but no data are provided on the potential impact of variation over occasions, over the context of the items, or over scorers.

OVERALL EVALUATION. The Test on Appraising Observations has a very clear and focused interpretation, and the two forms of the test were systematically developed to yield scores consistent with this interpretation. The potential uses of the test discussed in the manual are generally quite reasonable. The test should prove useful for research purposes and for formative and summative evaluation of programs that include the appraisal of observations among their goals. The test could also be used for the formative evaluation of student progress. The use of group performance on particular items to diagnose specific deficiencies in reasoning for the group, as suggested in the manual, is not justified because the items have not been shown to be of equal difficulty in any sense, and it is reasonable to expect that some items may call for more subtle judgments than other items. Given the limited evidence for generalizability and the possibility of response bias, the test should not be used for high-stakes decisions.

REVIEWER'S REFERENCE

Norris, S. P. (1992). A demonstration of the use of verbal reports of thinking in multiple-choice critical thinking test design. *The Alberta Journal of Educational Research, 38,* 155–176.

Review of the Test on Appraising Observations by JEFFREY K. SMITH, *Professor of Educational Psychology and Associate Dean, Graduate School of Education, Rutgers, The State University of New Jersey, New Brunswick, NJ:*

The Test on Appraising Observations measures secondary school students' ability to judge correctly the credibility of reports of observations. That is, how good are the examinees in judging which of two reports of an event is more credible based on principles of judging credibility (e.g., if one person has no preconceived notion about how the observation will turn out, then that person's observation will be more credible than a person who does have such preconceived notions). The authors argue that this ability is a component of overall observation ability and that observation ability is in turn a component of critical thinking.

There are two forms of the test, one multiple choice and one constructed response. The multiple-choice format is based on two scenarios that involve individuals making statements based on observations. It allows examinees to choose from one of three options: The first statement is more credible, the second statement is more credible, or there is no reason to believe that either statement is more credible. The constructed response format uses only the first of the two scenarios, but requires the examinee to provide a justification for the response given. The constructed response format can be scored either for right answers or for valid justifications.

The Test on Appraising Observations has much to recommend it. The theoretical development of the measure appears to be sound. The technical documentation provided in the manual that accompanies the test is clear, thorough, and modest in its claims. The test is easy to administer and score. Professional literature is available that supports the use of the measure, in particular the multiple-choice form of the measure (Norris, 1992; 1990).

There are also some problems with the measure. First, the reliability and validity data reported for the measure are not particularly strong, especially with regard to the constructed response format. For the multiple-choice version, reliabilities across seven different samples range from .58 to .76; for the constructed response version the reliabilities in two studies were .54 and .80 for the right answer scoring and .71 and .74 for the justification scoring. Criterion-related validity was investigated by correlating the measure with seven established indicators of critical thinking such as the Watson-Glaser Critical Thinking Appraisal and the Cornell Critical Thinking Test. Validity coefficients ranged from .22 to .62 for the multiple-choice format, and from .06 to .25 for the constructed response format. The multiple-choice format and the constructed response format correlate at .42, suggesting substantial differences across the two formats. The data suggest that the multiple-choice version of the measure is much stronger than the constructed response format.

A second problem is that the measures purport to address only a fairly limited component of the overall concept of critical thinking ability. Most of the validity and reliability studies were conducted on high school students, but it is somewhat difficult to imagine what practical applicability there is for the instrument at the high school level except for research purposes.

Overall, the Test on Appraising Observations appears to be a useful tool for measuring a limited aspect of critical thinking. Although there are some problems with reliability, the validity for the multiple-choice version of the test seems reasonable, and validity is the key issue. One should keep in mind, however, there are a host of critical thinking measures available that are more comprehensive than what is presented here. The question for a potential user of the measure is whether this aspect of critical thinking is what is needed in a given situation.

REVIEWER'S REFERENCES

Norris, S. P. (1990). Effect of eliciting verbal reports of thinking on critical thinking test performance. *Journal of Educational Measurement, 27,* 41–58.
Norris, S. P. (1992). A demonstration of the use of verbal reports of thinking in multiple-choice critical thinking test design. *The Alberta Journal of Educational Research, 38,* 155–176.

[343]
Tests of Adult Basic Education, Forms 7 & 8.

Purpose: Designed to measure achievement of basic skills commonly found in adult basic education curricula and taught in instructional programs.

Acronym: TABE.

Administration: Group.

Levels, Editions, and Parts: 2 Forms: 7 & 8, each with 2 editions: Complete Battery and Survey, and 5 Levels: L, E, M, D, A.

Price Data, 1994: $19.08 per review kit including product overview, complete battery test book Levels L, M-7, and A-7, and Survey test book Levels E-8 and D-8, Practice Exercise and Locator test, 2 examiner's manuals ('94, 63 pages [complete battery] and 36 pages [survey battery]), individual diagnostic profile Level M, marker item booklet, examinee record book Level L, SCOREZE answer sheet, CompuScan answer sheet; $30 per 25 Practice exercise and Locator Test booklets; $25 per 25 Complete Battery Test booklets Level L; $54.50 per 25 Complete Battery and Survey Test books E, M, D, and A; $15 per Large Print Edition Practice Exercise and Locator Test; $15 per large print Complete Battery Test book Level L; $31.75 per large print edition Complete Battery or Survey Tests Levels E, M, D, or A; $30.21 per 50 answer sheets; $19 per 25 hand-scorable SCOREZE answer sheets; $15 per 50 machine-scorable answer sheets— Scantron Option 2; $15 per 50 CompuScan 48-column Practice Exercise and Locator Test or Survey Levels E, M, D, A; $29.50 per 50 CompuScan 48-column Complete Battery Levels E, M, D, or A; $11 per scoring stencil for hand-scoring CompuScan answer sheets for Practice Exercise and Locator Test stencil; $22 per scoring stencil for hand-scoring CompuScan answer sheets for Complete Battery and Survey Levels E, M, D, A;

$11.95 per word list; $20 per 25 marker item booklets; $8 per individual diagnostic profile Complete Battery and Survey Levels E, M, D, A; $27 per test user's handbook; $9.75 per norms book, Form 7 & 8 ('95, 90 pages); $1.75 per group record sheet; $11 per technical report ('96, 72 pages); $9.75 per Complete Battery or Survey manual; $14 per 25 examinee record book Level L.

Foreign Language Edition and Other Special Editions: Form 7 is available in a large print edition; TABE Español is available.

Comments: Level L is the same for both the Complete Battery and the Survey editions; an interview checklist, a word list to assist determination of appropriate TABE level, and an Individual Diagnostic Profile are available; a Practice Exercise is available in the same booklet as the Locator Test.

Authors: CTB/McGraw-Hill.

Publisher: CTB Macmillan/McGraw-Hill.

a) FORMS 7 & 8.

Population: Adults in Adult Basic Education programs, vocational-technical centers, and correctional facilities, first and second year college students.

Publication Dates: 1957–1996.

Scores: Level L: 3 scores: Pre-Reading, Reading Skills, Total Reading; Levels E, M, D, and A: 7 scores: Reading, Math Computation, Applied Math, Total Mathematics (Math Computation plus Applied Math), Language, Total Battery, Spelling.

Price Data: $25 per 25 Level L Test books; $54.50 per 25 E, M, D, or A test books; $15 per large print edition test book, Level L; $31.75 per large print edition test book, Levels E, M, D, or A; $30.21 per 50 large print answer sheets; $19 per 25 hand-scorable SCOREZE answer sheets; $29.50 per 50 CompuScan 48-column answer sheets; $22 per scoring stencil for hand-scoring CompuScan answer sheets; $8 per 25 individual diagnostic profiles; $9.75 per manual ('94, 63 pages).

Time: 154–164 (209) minutes for Levels E, M, D, and A; 35 (65) minutes for Level L.

1) *Locator Test.*

Purpose: "Used to determine the appropriate level of TABE to administer to each examinee."

Scores, 3: Reading, Mathematics, Language (optional).

Time: (35–40) minutes for Reading and Mathematics; (50–55) minutes for Reading, Mathematics, and Language.

b) SURVEY FORM.

Population: Adults in Adult Basic Education programs, vocational-technical centers, and correctional facilities, second year college students.

Publication Dates: 1987–1996.

Scores: Level L: 3 scores: Pre-Reading, Reading Skills, Total Reading; Levels E, M, D, and A: 5 scores: Reading, Mathematics Computation, Applied Mathematics, Language, Spelling.

Price Data: $54 per 25 test books; $31.75 per large print test book; $30.21 per 50 large print answer sheets; $19 per 25 hand-scorable SCOREZE answer sheets; $15 per 50 machine-scorable answer sheets or CompuScan 48-column answer sheets; $11 per survey stencil for hand-scoring CompuScan answer sheets; $9.75 per manual ('94, 36 pages).

Time: (112) minutes.

1) *Locator Test* (same as *a* above).

Cross References: For reviews by Robert W. Lissitz and Steven J. Osterlind of an earlier edition, see 11:446 (2 references); for reviews by Thomas F. Donlon and Norman E. Gronlund of an earlier edition, see 8:33 (1 reference); for a review by A. N. Hieronymus and an excerpted review by S. Alan Cohen of an earlier edition, see 7:32.

Review of the Tests of Adult Basic Education, Forms 7 & 8 by MICHAEL D. BECK, President, Beck Evaluation & Testing Associates, Inc., Pleasantville, NY:

Forms 7 and 8 of the Tests of Adult Basic Education (TABE) comprise the latest edition of this widely used achievement battery for adults. Normed in 1994, these forms are designed "to meet the needs of diverse adult education programs" (p. 1). The publisher claims that the TABE measures "achievement of basic skills commonly found in adult basic education curricula" (p. 1). Available in five overlapping levels—L (Literacy), E (Easy), M (Medium), D (Difficult), and A (Advanced)—the tests assess Reading, Mathematics, and Language/Spelling at all levels except L, which includes only prereading and beginning reading skills. Two versions of the TABE are available for the four highest levels—a Complete Battery and a shorter Survey version.

In reviewing a test series such as the TABE, it is instructive to start with the instrument's stated purposes or the publisher's claims for the product. In the case of the TABE, these claims and purposes include provision of both norm- and criterion-referenced information; the assessment of "basic skills" as generally defined in adult curricula; and test content with "subject matter of high interest to adults" (p. 1). These are addressed below, in addition to reactions to the instrument's content and technical adequacy.

CONTENT DEVELOPMENT. The TABE content development is sketchily described in the Technical Report. Descriptors such as "rigorous and systematic procedures," "carefully reviewed," "comprehensive curriculum review," "comprehensive" evidence of construct validity, "significant innovations," and "precisely" measured skills pervade the Technical Report, though few such promotional claims are supported with either written descriptions or data. It is not even possible from the supportive materials to determine how much of the content of this edition of the TABE is new and what proportion was carried forward from the earlier edition. (The Technical Report states that "many new test items" [p. 8] were tried out.) It is unfortunate that the materials do not provide a more extensive rationale for the test content and a more complete description of the test plan and content outline. This is especially bothersome due to the broad range of educational curricula and programs for which the TABE is intended.

The published items are generally sound and well edited. Test booklets are attractive, well-formatted, and clearly presented. Test instructions presented in an Examiner's Manual are clear, direct, and easy to follow. The Practice Exercise and sample items are clear and helpful. With the exception of Level L, test timing, directions, and numbers of items per subtests are identical across levels, making it possible for a single proctor to administer all levels concurrently. Subtest timing is described in a curious way, however. Although essentially a power test, the TABE was normed with specific time limits for each subtest. Test proctors are even advised to use a stopwatch or watch with a second hand. However, the Examiner's Manual describes the time limits as "suggested times" and, for each subtest, advises proctors to "allow *about*" X minutes. In order for TABE norms to apply, the time limits should be adhered to specifically. A similar curiosity applies to timing of the Locator Test. The Examiner's Manual states that this test takes "approximately 35 minutes to administer" (p. 15). Yet the following specific subtest directions for student working time alone total 48 minutes, not including time for directions and samples.

The Locator Test, used to select the most appropriate TABE level for each examinee, is a potentially valuable component. It apparently was used during the norming program though this was not stated in published materials. A concern about this component relates to the cut points used to make TABE level decisions. The Examiner's Manual describes the cut scores as being based on "preliminary" research, the supposed final such cut scores are to be available on an addendum sheet. This raises concerns about how the preliminary cuts were set and, more seriously, the appropriateness of revising such cut scores after norming.

Overall, test development should be better described, especially because of the varied potential audiences for the TABE. However, the test materials are of high professional quality. As would be the case for any achievement test, prospective users must assess test content relative to the instructional program to determine whether the TABE provides an adequate match to the content and focus of the curriculum assessed. The publisher claims that the TABE measures "basic skills commonly found in adult basic education curricula" (p. 1); it is the user's task to determine whether this claim is correct for each intended use of the instrument.

NORM- AND CRITERION-REFERENCED DATA. The Technical Report contains almost no support for criterion-referenced use of the TABE. Such interpretation focuses primarily on "Objectives Mastery" information in which examinee performance on various global objectives (e.g., recall information, fractions, geometry, or writing conventions) is summarized. Most such global objectives are assessed by a minimum of 4 test items—some with more than 10 items. However, no theoretical or technical rationales are provided to justify the nonmastery/partial mastery/mastery cutoffs used for each objective. Such promoted uses of the TABE, although not unique to this instrument, are of limited interpretive or instructional value and of questionable psychometric defensibility.

The norm-referenced data from the TABE are almost certainly the primary interpretive information desired by users. Norms are provided for four groups: Adult Basic Education (ABE), Adult and Juvenile Offender, Vocational/Technical training, and College. Unfortunately, this reviewer would strongly discourage norm-referenced use of the TABE for at least two, and possibly all of the four normative groups. For example, consider these unexplained and regrettable characteristics of the normative samples:

The "College" norms are based on a complete sample of only 307 students drawn from only four institutions. Worse, the Technical Report provides almost no description of this sample: what age, what year of college, what type of college, what college program/major, etc.? For a major test publisher to provide normative data based on such an indefensibly described and grossly inadequate sample is lamentable.

The TABE normative data were drawn from a total of 415 institutions. However, the total sample was fewer than 7,000 examinees. (Data in the Technical Report make it impossible to determine the exact number.) Therefore, the typical institution contributed fewer than 20 test takers. This calls into question *who* these test takers were and how representative they were of either their institutions or the reference group. For example, the entire Vocational/Technical norms group totals just over 500, yet these were drawn from 71 institutions. How were the handful of students chosen at each of these locations? The Technical Report descriptions are inadequate.

The Adult/Juvenile Offender sample is larger (over 1,500), but is similarly weakly described. This group, curiously for an *adult* test, includes offenders as young as age 14. No information is provided concerning the distributions of ages or formal schooling of this sample.

Norms data were developed by pooling cases across all TABE levels. Therefore, empirical norms for any single level of the TABE are based on a significantly smaller (unstated) number of cases. Although the latent-trait procedures used to develop TABE norms may make such a pooling psychometrically possible, the same sizes per test level per reference group are very small. This is especially a concern when objective- or item-level data are used.

Even the ABE sample, which makes up well over one-half of the TABE norming group, is inadequately described. The only information provided is a breakdown of the sample by sex and ethnic group. No information regarding age, prior schooling, curriculum program or status, demographics, or the like is provided. Prospective users are given less-than-adequate information upon which to decide the appropriateness of the norms.

Overall, this reviewer could recommend only the ABE norms for the TABE. Even for this group, prospective users would need to obtain additional unpublished information about the characteristics of this sample to ascertain the appropriateness of this reference group. The TABE normative samples and publisher descriptions of the same are disappointing.

OTHER TECHNICAL DATA. The publisher conducted an equating study between this edition of the TABE and its predecessor edition. Reported correlations between comparable subtests ranged from .52 to .73, with a median of approximately .60. These low correlations lead to the suggestion that users of the previous version of the TABE very carefully consider the content and statistical relationships between the old and new editions before adopting TABE 7 or 8.

Users concerned primarily with the accuracy of the normative data would probably best be advised to use Form 7, the only form used for norming. Form 8 was equated to Form 7 a year later. The Technical Report unfortunately provides no data indicating the statistical relationships between Forms 7 and 8 or between the Complete Battery and the shorter Survey. The Survey battery is, curiously, only 40 items longer than the Locator Test. It omits the Spelling test and, although it includes 15 Math Computation items, no norms for this subtest are provided. The explanation for this omission is that 15 items "are too few to yield a reliable score" (p. 2). Although the Computation items are included in the Total Mathematics Survey scale, this sloppiness in test construction is regrettable.

A similar lack of sufficient content occurs on Level L, the new basic literacy level. No norms are provided for the 23-item "pre-reading skills" subtest. The publisher's passing statement that these skills can be interpreted only via raw scores strikes this reviewer as another unfortunate aspect of the tests.

Reliability data for the Complete Battery are generally consistent with those reported for other soundly developed tests. It is unfortunate that only internal-consistency reliability estimates are provided, especially because a separate forms-equating study was conducted. Similarly, no data are reported for either the Total Mathematics or Total Battery scales. Given that the Technical Report contains 10 full pages of IRT standard error curves, it is difficult to explain such omissions of important data routinely included in TABE reporting. Reliability data reported for the Survey tests are, as would be expected, significantly lower than those for the Complete Battery. Users of the Survey should be very cautious if using such data to assess the performance of individual test takers.

The Technical Report contains summary raw score data and item-by-item p values by form, level, type of battery, and reference group. Unfortunately, the source of these data is not adequately described. The data appear to apply to the imputed performance of *all* test takers in the norming sample, regardless of the TABE level used. The data as presented are potentially highly misleading and are unlikely to be correctly interpreted by other than the most sophisticated user. Grade equivalents (GE) by subtest were developed via an equating study to the California Achievement Test. The median GEs in Reading and Mathematics were approximately mid-grade 5, indicating that the typical TABE test taker in the norms sample performed similarly to a typical school-age 5th grader. Prospective users must assess how appropriate such a level is for their needs. Curiously, the median Language TABE GE was *below* grade 5, and for Spelling, the median was above grade 7. No explanation for these irregularities is provided.

Finally, the Technical Report contains several assertions concerning TABE validity ("evidence of construct validity is comprehensive," "compilation of multiple sources of validity evidence supports the construct validity," "scores that are valid for most types of educational decision making," [p. 3] etc.). However, almost no data are presented to assess such claims. Nearly the entire validity section either describes the subtest content or outlines in a general way the major steps of test development. Although it may not be surprising to find little, if any, data evidencing a test series' validity, it *is* surprising to find *claims* of validity in a technical publication without accompanying data. It would seem incumbent on the publisher to provide the data that support the claims.

SUMMARY. TABE 7 and 8 is a disappointing product. It is a widely used test, now in "middle age," published by one of the country's most respected houses. Its content appears to be well conceived and of professional quality. Yet its technical underpinnings are both inadequately presented and generally weak. The series will undoubtedly continue to be a popular one. However, other than limited use of the ABE norms for the Complete Battery, this reviewer would not recommend the TABE.

Review of the Tests of Adult Basic Education, Forms 7 & 8 by BRUCE G. ROGERS, Professor of Educational Psychology, University of Northern Iowa, Cedar Falls, IA:

The Tests of Adult Basic Education (TABE) were designed to measure achievement in the types of competencies that are likely to be encountered in basic education programs for adults. Those competencies are assessed in the content areas of Reading, Language, Mathematics, and Spelling. The Language and Spelling components are indirect measures of the types of skills needed to accomplish writing tasks commonly required in most occupations.

The TABE has been a widely used test battery in the field of adult assessment for several years. Originally a revision of the California Achievement Test, it was criticized by the *MMY* reviewers as not being applicable for an adult population. Subsequently the publishers have issued Forms 7 and 8 with completely new items that incorporate practical suggestions from users and technological innovations from measurement theorists. A significant characteristic of the battery is its division into two versions.

The shorter Survey version is intended to provide global information, whereas the Complete Battery is designed to provide more specific diagnostic information. They can be used alone or together as a pretest and a posttest. For each of the two versions, both norm-referenced interpretations and objective-based interpretations are given to facilitate decision making. Each version has subtests in the content areas of Reading, Language, and Mathematics (with Spelling as an optional subtest). As stated in the manual, the intent of the test is to evaluate "true skills in working with real-life test stimuli" (p. 4) by using examples such as written descriptions of job interviews and floor plans of houses.

The assessment ranges from skills taught in the early elementary grades upward through those at the high school level. Each subtest is available in four overlapping skill levels, namely, Easy, Medium, Difficult, and Advanced. (In addition, there is a Literacy level, which focuses on prereading and beginning reading skills.) Each skill level represents a range of two or three grade levels. To produce estimated grade-equivalent scores, the test was equated with the California Achievement Test, using sound test-equating procedures. In order to determine which of the test levels is appropriate for a student, a 50-item Locator test is used as the initial instrument. The results obtained from that instrument are interpreted by the administrator, using a chart, to select the appropriate level of either the Survey version or the Complete Battery. Because this is a very positive feature of the TABE, some readers will likely desire to know how the Locator test scores were matched with the test levels. Such information would be a useful addition to the technical manual.

The test can be administered with booklets and answer sheets (hand scored or machine scored) or with a microcomputer (which can then score the responses). Because this reviewer was provided with the booklets, this review is limited to that format. The booklets are easy to read. On each page, items are neatly arranged with adequate white space. The print style and size appear to be appropriate for each grade level.

DEVELOPMENT. The construction of the TABE reflects a professional approach toward the measurement of basic skills. Curriculum guides and textbooks were analyzed and educational experts were consulted. As is customary for tests of this type, content validity was the main consideration. Toward that goal, the test manual states that the items were designed to represent essential instructional objectives. The manual also states that the content was aligned toward the GED tests; but readers could have more confidence in the alignment process if the technical manual contained data to substantiate the correspondence between the GED and the TABE.

The manuals for the tests show the level at which each objective is assessed. In addition, very detailed charts are given to show the correspondence between the items and the objectives. These will be found valuable to the user in evaluating the content validity. Because some of the steps in the test development process involved the analysis of data, it would be helpful to have a summary of the results of that data analysis. In the construction and selection of the test items, much consideration was given to the factor of test bias because minority groups were found to be in the majority among users of TABE. Item writing guidelines were followed, items were reviewed by members of ethnic and gender groups, and item tryout data were obtained from ethnic and gender groups. An examination of the items themselves appears to confirm that the tests do meet the goal of bias reduction. A variety of statistical procedures were employed in the process of item selection, including the item response theory model (three-parameter IRT). The use of these procedures appears to be consistent with professional test development.

Many tests in the past have shown their items classified according to thinking skills. Users of the TABE will see an example of this in the charts showing the items classified into six categories according to the Rankin-Hughes Framework of Thinking Skills. At all four levels of the tests, two patterns are evident. First, for both the Mathematics Computation and the Spelling subtests, the modal classification is the lowest category, Gather Information. Second, for the Reading, Language and Applied Mathematics subtests, the modal classification is the third category, Analyze Information. These detailed classification charts provide useful evidence related to the content validity of the tests and show a very professional approach by the publishers.

DESCRIPTION. Each of the subtests begins with one or two practice problems, which are followed by a series of multiple-choice questions. The Reading test emphasizes the construction of meaning by testing vocabulary, critical thinking skills, and the use of reference materials. Vocabulary is assessed by presenting words in the context of simple sentences and testing for meaning. Other skills are tested with a sequence of interpretive exercises, each containing a reading passage followed by six or seven questions. Within each exercise, some of the questions are factual and others are inferential. The Mathematics Computation test is designed to focus on the four basic operations applied to whole numbers and fractions. It is expected that the typical student will be able to do most of the problems with mental arithmetic; however, for some of the problems, students may want to use scratch paper. Of the five options given, one is "None of the above," a strategy designed to reduce guessing and encourage actual computation. Sometimes the options are arranged in numerical order, but not always. Some test takers may find the exceptions to be distracting, hence, administrators might appreciate having a rationale in the Administrator's Manual or the Technical Manual. The Applied Mathematics test was designed around current trends in mathematics curriculum and reflects a strong influence from the NCTM Standards (National Council of Teachers of Mathematics, 1995). Among the skills tested are estimation, pattern recognition, and problem solving. The focus is upon concepts rather than computation. The Language test presents several types of exercises, some requiring the identification of errors in grammar, punctuation, and capitalization, whereas other exercises require comprehension in order to properly combine sentences, all of which are intended to measure skills used in revising a piece of writing. The optional test, Spelling, presents a brief sentence with a missing word followed by four options showing variant spellings of the word. An examination of the items in each subtest indicates that a large majority of them require thought processes beyond the memorization of facts.

Reliability data in the manuals are based on the internal consistency measures from a single administration of each test using Kuder-Richardson Formula 20 (KR20) values. Standard error of measurement values are generated as a function of the scale scores. The emphasis in the manual on the interpretation of score bands is commendable. However, the "Microcomputer-Produced Scoring Report" shows point estimates but not confidence intervals. Perhaps that option will be considered in the future. It is generally considered desirable to also show evidence of reliability from parallel forms, but, as of yet, that information is not in the Technical Manual. The manual does state that Forms 7 and 8 were later equated by administering both tests to the same sample of students. Data of that type might be used to generate parallel form reliability measures.

In addition to the discussion on content validity, it would be useful to have evidence about criterion-related validity. Correlations with grades in basic education courses and with GED scores would also be useful information. Because previous reviewers have questioned whether the TABE actually measures what adults need to know, finding relationships between the test scores and job performance would yield relevant information.

STANDARDIZATION AND NORMS. The sample for the national norming study was drawn from institutions that offered some type of basic education program for adults. Although the sampling procedure could not be technically described as a random sampling procedure, it did seek for representativeness by involving over 400 institutions in 49 states. It would appear that users can be confident that the normative data reflect reasonable estimates of the abilities for the population of persons who enroll in basic education courses.

Several types of derived scores are available to users, including national percentiles, stanines, and grade equivalents. For each of these, both proper uses and limitations are discussed. To generate grade equivalent scores, students were administered both the TABE and the California Achievement Test (CAT). Each subtest was equated and grade-equivalent tables were produced. Although this is a commendable procedure, the estimated GE scores should be interpreted with much caution. Because the importance of the concept of standard error of measurement is brought out in the Technical Manual, it might be useful to report those values for the GE scores.

A scoring sheet is provided for criterion-referenced score interpretation. For each objective, the scores on the relevant items are added and the resulting sum is graded as Nonmastery, Partial Mastery, or Mastery. Information on how these gradations were determined was not found in the Technical Manual, but it would be useful for the interpretation of the mastery scores.

MANUALS AND SUPPORTING LITERATURE. Four types of manuals are available for users of the TABE: (a) The Examiner's Manual, which provides basic information about the TABE, along with directions for administering the tests. (b) The Norm booklet, which contains tables for converting raw scores to percentiles, grade equivalents, and stanines, along with directions for using the tables. (c) The Technical Report, which discusses the topic of validity, reliability, and norms, along with other detailed information on the technical aspects of the test. This manual is very clear and complete; it can

serve as a good model for the developers of other tests. (d) The User's Manual (also called the Coordinator's Manual), which contains very detailed descriptions of the test materials and interpretive information. It provides sample items and information for preparing students to take the test. Also discussed is how the items were classified into thinking skills. This document provides a very positive orientation to the proper use of tests.

SUMMARY. The TABE series is a relatively new addition to the many existing achievement tests, because only recently have there been strong programs for teaching basic skills to adults. It therefore fills a definite need in our culture. The items are well written, the booklets have an attractive appearance, and the manuals provide good explanations with directions for those who administer the tests. For scores on the subtests, the norm-referenced interpretations are supported by data from meaningful norm groups. The criterion-referenced scores might be useful for remedial work, but they would benefit from more empirical support. The evidence on reliability and validity is preliminary and should be expanded. Overall, this test is constructed in a professional manner. Those educators who work with adults in basic skills courses should give careful consideration to adopting the Tests of Adult Basic Education as part of their evaluation program.

REVIEWER'S REFERENCE

National Council of Teachers of Mathematics. (1995). *Assessment standards for school mathematics.* Reston, VA: The Council.

[344]

Tests of Adult Basic Education Work-Related Foundation Skills.

Purpose: "To provide pre-instructional information about an examinee's level of achievement on basic skills, … to identify areas of weakness … measure growth, … and involve the examinee in appraising his or her learning needs to assist … [in preparing] an instructional program to meet the examinee's individual needs."

Population: Adults in vocational/technical programs, students in adult basic education programs 2-year colleges, and secondary school ROP & JTPA programs.

Publication Date: 1994–1996.

Acronym: TABE WF.

Scores, 6: Reading, Math Computation, Applied Math, Total Mathematics (Math Computation and Applied Math), Language, Total Battery.

Administration: Group.

Forms, 4: General, Business/Office, Health, Trade/Technical.

Price Data, 1994: $17.97 per review kit including general test book, trade/technical test book, health test book, business/office test book, examiner's manual ('94, 30 pages), and individual diagnostic profile; $30 per manual and 25 locator tests; $54.50 per manual and general trade technical, health, or business/office test book; $14.50 per 25 locator test SCOREZE answer sheets; $19 per general trade/technical, health, or business/office SCOREZE answer sheets; $15 per 50 CompuScan answer sheets; $15 per 50 Scantron Opt. 2 answer sheets; $8 per 25 individual diagnostic profiles; $11 per hand-scoring stencil; $1.75 per group record sheet; $9.75 per examiner's manual; $9.75 per norms book; $8.85 per technical bulletin; price data for technical report ('96, 33 pages) for use with this test and the TABE Work-Related Problem Solving available from publisher.

Time: 120(160) minutes.

Authors: CTB Macmillan/McGraw-Hill.

Publisher: CTB Macmillan/McGraw-Hill.

Review of the Tests of Adult Basic Education Work-Related Foundation Skills by KURT F. GEISINGER, Professor of Psychology and Academic Vice President, LeMoyne College, Syracuse, NY:

This test is the current version of a series of instruments used to assess basic academic skills that are primarily useful either in vocational-technical academic institutions (whether secondary or post-secondary) or private industry. In the case of its industrial uses, these measures are employed primarily for purposes of assessing the skill levels of employees and assessing training needs. The instrument is particularly geared to evaluate the "opportunity to learn" or "ability to benefit" (p. 2) criterion that is required of post-secondary institutions by the U.S. Federal Government with regard to Guaranteed Student Loans. The reader of the examiner's manual is also very correctly reminded that scores emerging from the Tests of Adult Basic Education Work-Related Foundation Skills (TABE WRFS) instruments should not be used by themselves, especially for any kind of high-stakes assessment (e.g., hiring decisions). The instrument measures levels of achievement in three broad areas: Reading, Mathematics Computation and Reasoning, and Language Use. Goals of the instrument include assessing basic skills, identifying basic academic weaknesses, helping instructors and curriculum planners to properly adjust instruction to the level of the students, and showing improvements due to such training. In that there are four forms of the instrument, the last use (above) is aided because the test can be used in a "pretest, posttest" design to evaluate the effects of an instructional program.

The test plan or intended content of this examination was determined by "compiling information from various state and district adult education curricula, and by studying the outcomes and competency frameworks of adult programs throughout the country" (technical report, p. 8), but neither the nature nor the results of this needs assessment-type research has been presented in either the examiner's manual (1994) or the technical report (1996). As such, the TABE WRFS includes four subtests measuring the three above-mentioned areas. The four subtests cover (a) Reading, (b) Mathematics Computation, (c) Applied Mathematics, and (d) Language. All of the tests are composed solely of multiple-choice test questions. The examiner's manual rightly reminds the reader, especially in regard to the Language subtest, that neither oral nor written skills are measured and that a more complete assessment should include evaluations of these skills.

Four forms of the test are available; three of these are oriented to specialized uses and the fourth is a general form to cover the remaining situations, as well as to serve as a pretest or posttest in conjunction with one of the specialized forms. The four forms are Health, Trade/Technical, Business/Office, and General. The subtests, the number of multiple-choice test items for each subtest, and the testing time for each subtest are all identical for the four forms. All of the test forms have been pitched in terms of grade level for the range from 6.6 to 8.9. In that they measure general academic skills, this range both appears appropriate and well operationalized in terms of the test items. The items for each of the three specialized forms of the test are written using realistic examples from the respective domains and are highly face valid in the opinion of this test reviewer. In particular, the graphics in the examinations are excellent and make the test especially realistic. In that these test items appear remarkably authentic and tied to job skills that might be expected of vocational-technical students, employees, and those in training programs, they should enjoy a maximum acceptance from test takers and test users alike.

The Reading subtest (40 questions in 40 minutes) covers recognition of words in context, recollection of information found in brief reading passages, interpretation of graphics, and both inferring meaning from text and extending the meaning to new situations. A number of questions involve interpretation of down-to-earth graphs and figures. The items on the Mathematics Computation subtest (20 questions in 15 minutes) cover addition, subtraction, multiplication, division, percentages, fractions, and other very basic mathematical manipulations. Unlike the other three subtests, the items on the Mathematics Computation subtest contain five (rather than four) options; the fifth option is always "None of these" so that test takers who do not find the answer that they compute may elect that option (and alternatively, are not cued in that they have not correctly solved the question). These Mathematical Computation items are not written using "job relevant" words; they are simply presented as pure mathematical items, with a minimum of reading involved. The Applied Mathematics items (35 questions in 35 minutes) involve questions containing both written stems and conceptual questions. Test takers must read and understand the questions and draw conclusions, reach interpretations, and employ computation, data interpretation, geometry, and both pre-algebra and algebra skills. Items are once again written in a face-valid manner, and graphic information presented in the items continues to be extremely well done. The Language subtest (35 questions in 30 minutes) contains items assessing language usage, and assesses the test taker's ability to identify proper sentences, paragraphs, and other conventions of writing. In that it is multiple choice in format, it is what many consider a test of editing ability rather than writing ability per se, although it is likely to be correlated with writing ability. Test takers are asked to select words to insert in sentences; to identify correct sentences; to identify problematic words, phrases, and sentences; to combine related concepts into a single sentence; and so on.

Three answer sheets are available and the test may be scored using hand scoring or either of two optical scanning options. Such flexibility is both unusual and highly customer sensitive.

The examiner's manual is excellent. It is clearly written and explains the concepts of test administration in an understandable yet conceptually rich manner. Certainly, more information on the research that led to the test plan would be useful. The total testing time is 130 minutes, although the manual suggests that about 2 1/2 hours are needed for the entire process. There appears generally to be enough time to take the tests; they are primarily power tests.

ANALYTIC INFORMATION. The development of this measure would appear to be an example of the finest test construction practices in the industry today. Although more information could be contained in both the examiner's manual and the technical report, these documents present an overview of what appears to have been an excellent test development process. The steps taken to build the measure are described in the technical report; they are presented conceptually rather than in detail. It is reported that the test plan was developed based on research (neither the research results nor the test plan are presented), items were written and reviewed, a tryout sample of 84 institutions and about 3,400 test takers took the examination as well as a previous version of the instrument so that items could be calibrated, item analyses were performed, items were selected for the final version of the form, and norms were developed on a sample of nearly 5,000 test takers. The description of the tryout sample provided is quite brief and, although the sample is relatively large, the description does not permit an assessment of whether this sample is representative of the ultimate population of test takers. A three-parameter logistic item-response theory model (Hambleton, Swaminathan, & Rogers, 1991) was used to analyze data both for the test development and the calibration model. In general, the model was applied in a sophisticated manner. It is not clear to this reviewer, however, the extent to which the domain underlying performance in these basic skills fits the three-parameter model of test performance. Some of the restrictions (e.g., that data be unidimensional) might be questioned and no data supporting the fit of the data to the model are presented in the manuals. Items were selected for use on the test to maximize the information conveyed by the test and to increase reliability (i.e., internal consistency). The standardization sample was larger still and was reputed to be representative, but no information was provided to permit the reader to assess its representativeness. The manual reports the numbers of men and women in the sample (with approximately two-thirds being women) and an ethnic breakdown. The data appear to overrepresent African- and Hispanic-Americans in the sample. Such oversampling is often well advised, especially if the test publishers are concerned about any possible biases.

The test publisher reports having engaged in several activities to limit any potential bias present in the examination. Early in the test development process, items were reviewed and edited for possible bias both by editors at CTB/McGraw-Hill and by professionals from the educational community. Subsequently, as part of the item analysis stage using data from their tryout of the test, analyses of differential item functioning (item bias) were performed. Performance on individual items was compared between men and women; and Blacks, Hispanics, Asians, and a group labeled Other were all compared to the majority group. The technical report states, "The selection of potentially biased items for the final version of each test was minimized, and the final version of the test was required to have a lower average bias rating than the pool of items from which it was selected" (technical report, p. 3). Why the publisher would have selected any items that appeared biased, if they did, should be questioned.

The KR-20 index of internal consistency reliability is reported for each of the four subtests on each of the four forms. Reliability coefficients for the Health, Trade/Technical, Business/Office, and General tests range from .86–.91, .82–.89, .82–.91, and .85–.89, with median reliability coefficients of .90, .87, .89, and .89, respectively. These coefficients would appear quite appropriate as long as the test is used for the purposes for which it is intended. No information on either correlations across forms or temporal stability of the measures is presented. Research on practice effects would be especially useful in that the test publisher recommends its use in pretest, posttest training program evaluations.

All of the subtests on each of the four test forms have been equated both to previous versions of the TABE series and a version of the California Achievement Test. Grade equivalent scores as well as other scale scores are available.

The validity of the instruments is largely based upon content validation. However, in that no clear test plan is presented in the technical report, it is not clear how representative of the domains in question the various subtests are. The technical report refers to a TABE user's manual, but it is not listed among the references. The technical report also states that to ensure content validity, "CTB/McGraw-Hill developers conducted a comprehensive curriculum review and met with educational experts to determine common educational goals and the knowledge and skills emphasized in today's curricula" (p. 5). More details on the nature of this work and its implementation would be useful for those using (or reviewing) the test. Correlations with other similar tests would be a useful supplement to this information on the content validity of the examination. It would also be useful to show the correlations among the four subtests for each test form.

AN EVALUATION OF THIS INSTRUMENT. The authors of the test manual rightly consider this instrument a norm-referenced measure. It is a well-normed measure that would appear appropriate for the uses suggested by the test publisher. Yet the test publisher also describes it as a criterion-referenced measure for some interpretations, but provides no data supportive of such interpretations. Validation evidence generally would be helpful. For this measure to be applied properly, local validations of the use of the measure would be essential.

Very little information on score interpretation is provided in the test manual. It may be available in the user's manual for the TABE series.

The test publisher has employed sophisticated methodological procedures to calibrate the test and to select items to compose it. More information on the appropriateness of those procedures (e.g., are assumptions of the models met?) is needed. Although rigorous procedures were used to review, edit, and analyze the items for potential bias, it appears possible that an item flagged for bias could nonetheless be placed in the examination. If this situation is indeed possible, it would appear that changes should be made in the next version in this series.

Review of the items themselves is extremely positive. This test is one that is thoroughly professional from the perspective of item writing and production. It is one of the most face-valid instruments this reviewer has ever seen. It indeed appears to be a fine instrument with the potential for effective use.

REVIEWER'S REFERENCE

Hambleton, R. K., Swaminathan, H., & Rogers, H. J. (1991). *Fundamentals of item response theory.* Newbury Park, CA: Sage Publications.

Review of the Tests of Adult Basic Education Work-Related Foundation Skills by JEFFREY A. JENKINS, Attorney and Counselor at Law, Albuquerque, NM:

The Tests of Adult Basic Education (TABE) Work-Related Foundation Skills (WRFS) is one of the TABE series of achievement tests. The WRFS is an instrument for assessing "skills that an individual needs in order to function in the workplace and in society" (examiner's manual, p. 1). The goal of the WRFS is to provide a measure of an individual's basic skills and is designed to provide either a pre-instructional summary of such skills or an outcome measure following instruction. The WRFS is a norm-referenced achievement test in the areas of reading, mathematics, and language. While covering these content areas, the items were written to reflect different workplace environments, resulting in four different test forms: Health, Trade/Technical, Business/Office, and General. These contexts should allow an examinee a level of comfort while responding to items in an area of familiarity, and provide a degree of relevance to a prospective area of employment or instructional program. The work-related context is adopted for a companion TABE instrument, Work-Related Problem Solving (WRPS) reviewed separately herein (345).

Each form of the WRFS consists of 40 Reading items, 20 Mathematics Computation items, 35 Applied Mathematics items, and 35 Language items, for a total of 130 multiple-choice test items. The total testing time is 2 hours. Each subtest within the test booklet is identified with a heading at the beginning of the section, and a sample question precedes the actual test items. The items are presented appropriately on each page in a clear and readable format. The allotted testing time appears to be more than adequate for the number and difficulty level of items on all of the subtests. Test scores are reported on an Individual Diagnostic Profile, which summarizes total scores, subscale scores, and mastery of objectives. Scores share a common scale with other TABE instruments.

The reading subtest focuses on the examinee's comprehension skills, including simple recall of facts as well as the ability to draw reasonable inferences from a text. For example, one item type presents a completed employment application which the examinee must review before answering specific questions about the information contained in the application, such as the length of previous employment or hourly wages in a particular job. Another series of items in each of the forms requires the examinee to understand instructions contained in a passage describing a specific job task.

The Mathematics portion of the test is divided into two subtests, addressing math concepts and computational skills. The computational subsection is straightforward, covering basic math operations, decimals, fractions, integers, percents, and money. The items are of the type generally found on computational skills tests, such as "11.112 - 10.021 = _____" and "80% of 200 = _____." The applied math subtest involves math problems set within the context of a particular work setting. For example, some items involve application of math knowledge to the information contained within a chart or graph such as a payroll record or a cash register tally sheet, whereas others involve the everyday problem-solving skills needed by workers in a particular field (e.g., "An electrician has 8 feet of wire. Solve for x to find how many more feet she needs for a job that requires 64 feet").

The Language subtest includes a variety of typical multiple-choice language item types such as sentence completion ("Choose the word or phrase that best completes the sentence"), grammatical correctness ("Choose the sentence that is written correctly"), sentence combination ("Read the underlined sentences. Then choose the sentence that best combines the sentences into one"), paragraph development ("Choose the answer that best develops the topic sentence"), and proofreading ("Choose the answer that shows the best capitalization, punctuation, spelling, and usage").

The technical characteristics of the WRFS are described in detail in a separate technical report, which discusses the test development and characteristics of both the WRFS and the WRPS. The technical report summarizes the process undertaken in development of the WRFS, including item writing, review, tryout, and analysis. The procedures used reflect the publisher's adherence to modern test development practices involving rigorous item review, the employment of empirical data and statistical item response models, and attention to potential item bias.

The content validity of the WRFS appears to be adequate, based upon a description of the test development procedures and the clearly defined skill objectives set out in the technical report. The technical report states that the "subtest and objective structures were determined by compiling information from various state and district adult education curricula, and by studying the outcomes and competency frameworks of adult programs throughout the country" (p. 8). Such is an acceptable approach to assuring content coverage and, along with the care taken in drafting and reviewing the items themselves, addresses many content validity concerns. The technical report also notes that many items require more than simple recall of facts, such as the ability to "analyze situations, make interpretations, look for connections, synthesize information, predict outcomes, and generate ideas" (p. 10). Although no specific support for measurement of these varied skills is provided, a review of the items suggests that the WRFS does call upon these more advanced abilities.

Internal consistency reliability coefficients (KR20) of the WRFS are reported for each of the content areas and are generally acceptable for instruments of this type, ranging from .82 to .91. Standard Errors of Measurement (*SEM*) for each subtest are also provided, as well as Standard Error Curves showing the variation in *SEM* across the range of scale scores. The latter indicates that measurement error for the WRFS increases at the extremes of the scoring scale, but within generally acceptable ranges.

The development of norms for the WRFS was done as part of a study to equate the WRFS to

TABE 7, which shares the same score scale. The WRFS was administered to reference groups in the areas of health, trade/technical, and business/office, corresponding to the forms of the test. Care was taken to obtain a cross-section of ethnic and age group representation. Unfortunately, however, neither the technical report nor norms book provides more description regarding the source of the examinees. For example, it is not reported whether the examinees in the norms group constitute a national cross-section or whether they come from private or public schools, training programs, or work settings. Such an oversight should be remedied for what appears to have been an otherwise careful norms development process. The norms book provides tables for score conversions along with a clear description of converting raw (number correct) scores for each subtest and the total battery. Tables allow conversion of raw scores to scale scores, grade equivalents, percentile ranks, and stanines.

The WRFS accomplishes its measurement goal of assessing basic skills needed to function in the work place. The WRFS has particular utility for measuring the achievement of students in adult basic education programs or in technical or vocational training programs. Although not intended as a placement test by employers, the WRFS also provides a useful measure of basic skills possessed by workers in the employment setting. Overall, the WRFS benefits from the publisher's adherence to contemporary test development procedures, and represents an assessment instrument that can be used with confidence in work-related areas.

[345]
Tests of Adult Basic Education Work-Related Problem Solving.

Purpose: "Designed to help employers, educators, and training professionals diagnose how an examinee deals with the different aspects of problem solving."

Population: Students in secondary schools, vocational education programs, adult basic education programs, and junior colleges, and employees in industry.

Publication Date: 1994–1996.

Acronym: TABE-PS.

Scores, 5: Competency scores (Employs Reading and Math Skills to Identify and Define a Problem, Examines Situations Using Problem-Solving Techniques, Makes Decisions About Possible Solutions, Evaluates Outcomes and Effects of Implementing Solutions), Total Number Correct Score.

Administration: Group.

Forms, 2: 7, 8.

Price Data, 1994: $11.50 per review kit including examiner's manual/scoring guide ('94, 56 pages), and test book; $32 per 25 test books with 1 manual; $19 per 50 practice exercises; $8 per 25 hand-scorable individual diagnostic profiles; $15 per 50 machine-scorable individual diagnostic profiles; $9.75 per examiner's manual/scoring guide; price data for technical report ('96, 33 pages) for use with this test and the TABE Work-Related Foundation Skills available from publisher.

Time: 70(75) minutes for Form 7; 60(65) minutes for Form 8.

Comments: May be administered alone or in conjunction with other TABE materials; test includes a Practice Exercise which was included in the norming studies and so should be administered along with the test; includes Individual Diagnostic Profile, and Interview/Interest Questionnaire.

Authors: CTB Macmillan/McGraw-Hill.

Publisher: CTB Macmillan/McGraw-Hill.

Review of the Tests of Adult Basic Education Work-Related Problem Solving by GALE M. MORRISON, Professor, Graduate School of Education, University of California, Santa Barbara, Santa Barbara, CA:

The construction of these tests responds to the America 2000 goals that call for workers who are skilled at job-related problem solving. It addresses the need for employers to know about specific aspects of problem solving related to on-the-job tasks. These tests address this need through use of problem-solving test items that are authentic and realistic.

The tests are designed as "constructed-response tests"; that is, the examinee constructs his or her own response to problem situations that may require several steps toward eventual problem solution. The visual presentation of the items provides a clear structure within which the respondent can construct the responses.

The items are designed to elicit responses that represent various aspects of general problem-solving process such as defining the problem, examining the problem, suggesting possible solutions, evaluation solutions, and generalizing solutions to other problem situations. Examinee performance on these generic problem-solving components is reflected in Competency Scores.

The test was designed to measure problem-solving skills, as opposed to reading and writing abilities; therefore, the manual suggests that reading and mathematics levels of approximately 6.6 to 8.9 grade range are required for nonconfounded measurement of problem-solving skills.

The test materials (individual booklets for Forms 7 and 8) are easy to understand and use. Administration directions are clear, and appropriate practice is provided to examinees prior to the start of the test.

Scoring is easily accomplished by either sending test results to the publishers or through use of the Scoring Guide and the Individual Diagnostic Profile. The scoring guide, located in the test manual, provides the correct response for each problem step and solution. For some items, "other acceptable" responses are provided. Clear notations are provided when only one response is considered acceptable and when the response must meet specific criteria in order to be considered correct. As each item is scored, the Individual Diagnostic Profile provides a hand scoring chart on which to record the scores. The Competency Scores and the Total Number-Correct Score can then be easily calculated.

The Individual Diagnostic Profile provides several indices for anchoring or comparing the Total Number-Correct Scores. Mastery levels (needs development, developing, proficient) for each of the Competency Scores are provided. The total scores also may be converted to standard scores, percentiles, and stanines. Standard error of measurement (SEM) estimates are also provided.

A "Technical Report" is available for the Work-Related Foundation Skills and Problem Solving parts of the TABE. This report gives extensive information about the general approach taken to test development methods ranging from item analysis to norms development to validity and reliability. However, the specific information available for the Work-Related Problem Solving tests is limited. The validity evidence presented essentially addresses content validity and hinges on the review by "educators in various disciplines who are familiar with assessment." There are no methods reported that attempt to address criterion-related concurrent, predictive or construct validity.

Information is available on two standardization samples. The first included approximately 1,700 adult learners of unspecified ethnic, age, and gender characteristics. Percentile norms presented in the Individual Diagnostic Profile are derived from this sample.

The authors of the "Technical Report" describe a second study completed with 1,100 examinees from four types of programs (general education development, vocational/technical training, adult basic education, and regional occupational programs). Data are presented on the gender, age, and ethnic breakdown of this group. It is stated that these cases were pooled to provide data to generate the reference group norms that consisted of an undifferentiated (by gender, age or ethnicity) scale score summary for Forms 7 and 8 combined and number-correct summary statistics for Forms 7 and 8, separately. Information is presented on item difficulty and reliability. Internal consistency coefficient alphas for Forms 7 and 8 were .89 and .84, respectively.

Thus, information on the technical aspects of the TABE Work-Related Problem Solving Skills is somewhat limited. The test user is left without any information about criterion-related or construct validity. Further, the user does not have detailed information on the norming sample from which the standard scores, SEM, percentiles, and stanine were derived. Although information is available from a second norming study, the question can be raised about how comparable the sample for some technical data (the standard scores, SEM, percentiles, and stanine) is to the sample for other technical data (scale score summaries, item difficulties, and reliability). Specific information is not available on the geographic location or ability level of either sample, limiting test user considerations about these variables.

Related to validity and norming limitations, although the idea of having Mastery level indicators, such as "needs development, developing, proficient" is attractive, the lack of information on how these levels were derived and validated renders such distinctions meaningless.

In summary, despite the good intentions and great potential of a measure of this nature, the limitations of technical information undermines its utility. The user is provided with materials that are easy to use; however, the validity of interpretations about results for individuals or groups is restricted.

Review of the Tests of Adult Basic Education Work-Related Problem Solving by JERRY TINDAL, Associate Professor, Behavioral Research and Teaching, University of Oregon, Eugene, OR:

Tests of Adult Basic Education (TABE) Work-Related Problem Solving is intended for use with secondary and post secondary students to help make diagnostic decisions about work-related problem-solving skills, viewed by the authors as a trait that reflects an ability to use complex thinking skills while synthesizing information across various disciplines.

An Individual Diagnostic Profile is included in the materials to document mastery of competencies. In the second chapter, a rather extensive description of administrator preparation is presented; it is suggested that the test be given to a maximum group size of 15 students. Other topics include testing cautions, timing and scheduling, and test materials. In the third chapter, general directions are provided for ensuring standard test conditions, with specific directions presented in chapter 4. Finally, scoring the test is described in chapter 5, with a reduced copy of the test presented on the left side of each page and corresponding scoring steps (with specific point values) listed on the right side. Although the authors note that the range of answers is quite varied, the validity of the response depends on the justification of the examinee. In general, guides are given for acceptable, unacceptable, and other acceptable responses. It is noted that all answers are scored for the concepts rather than language conventions (spelling and punctuation errors). The final score for examinees is the total number correct and recorded on the cover sheet of the form, indexed by the letter N (Needs Development), D (Developing), and P (Proficient). A note appears on the test booklet that "normed scores will be printed in a space on the form by Aug., 1994." No such information was available at the time the test was reviewed (June, 1996). [Editors note: This information was provided by the publisher in November 1996.]

The problem-solving competency and skill structure includes: (a) using reading and math skills to identify and define a problem; (b) examining problems by asking the right question, judging relevance of information, using appropriate models, recognizing relationships, and understanding criteria for making judgments; (c) making decisions involving determining whether a decision can be made, considering consequences selecting among alternatives, and explaining reasons for a decision; and (d) evaluating outcomes including extending the meaning, integrating solutions, demonstrating learning, and suggesting possible next steps.

On the back of the Individual Diagnostic Profile is an interview form and interest inventory that addresses issues such as work experience, interests, skill self-analysis, perceptions of jobs, need for more training, and some demographic questions.

The following problem-solving tasks are included in the test:

1. Improving pet shop operations is the practice exercise. This Practice Exercise is included to orient the students to both the content and the format of the test; it is suggested that it be administered along with the test to ensure reliable results.

Actual testing time is approximately 60 minutes with the following tasks from one of the forms.

2. How should the menu be changed?
3. Graphing sales.
4. Improving the production of gears.
5. Finding the right person for the job.

The TABE Work-Related Problem Solving has four to five interesting work situations: The problems are realistic and the solutions offered as part of the scoring key (and for which students are given 1 point for each step) appear reasonable. At the same time, absolutely no technical information is provided about the reliability or validity of the test. Many assertions are made about the adequacy of the test but no specific information is presented about content sampling, expert judgments, criteria validation, mastery vindication, administration variation, scoring consistency, or decision making about instruction or improvement. Although the authors suggest that the test can be used to plan instruction or measure growth, no data support this contention.

The TABE Work-Related Problem Solving is intended to include work-related problems that address competencies and foundation skills assembled by a vague reference to a review of curriculum and consultation with employers, without any supporting documentation or specific references. No information is provided about the content sampling plan. The test purportedly "measures the ability to diagnose and understand the different aspects of problem solving: defining the problem, examining the problem, suggesting possible solutions, evaluating solutions, and extending the meaning of the solution to related situations … it measures the steps used in solving a broad spectrum of problems" (p. 2). The authors report that the skills assessed are useful in planning instructional programs based on test results. Although it is not intended to assess basic skills of reading, writing, and math, the test uses a constructed response and, therefore, clearly requires such literacy. Reference also is made to the careful expert review of the competency framework and tasks used to define the skills within the framework, including a pilot test of the prototype tasks; no specific information or empirical support is presented for these assertions. Other efforts to avoid ethnic, gender, or age bias are reported with equal sincerity and concurrent lack of evidence or specificity. Finally, a norming study is reported to "place the Work-Related Problem Solving tasks on a scale" (p. 3) and to ensure that the two forms are linked statistically. Other than the authors stating that the two forms are alternate forms statistically and represent comparable coverage and "the forms may be used in a pretest/posttest situation to show growth in the mastery of the problem-solving competencies" (p. 3), no data are presented to support these assertions. Likewise, the difficulty level supposedly was held to a grade range of 6.6 to 8.9, "to ensure that reading and mathematics skills would not interfere with the ability to measure these competencies" (p. 3). Support for this statement is not presented.

In summary, the authors expect purchasers of this test to buy on faith and promises of good work. The test is best used to clinically sample behavior and make no serious judgments or high stakes decisions about individual students. Technical information needs to be forthcoming; at the very least, promises of best practice as if they were full accounting of best practice should be excised from the manual.

[346]
TestWell: Health Risk Appraisal.

Purpose: "Designed to provide an awareness of how current behaviors and physical health measurements impact health risks."

Population: Adults with a minimum of 10th grade education.

Publication Date: 1992.

Scores, 5: Appraised Age, Achievable Age, Positive Lifestyle Behaviors, Top 10 Risks of Death, Suggestions for Improvement.

Administration: Group.

Manual: No manual.

Price Data, 1993: $99.95 per interactive version, single user license; $329.95 per interactive version, multiuser license; $279.95 per group/batch version; $.50 per group/batch entry questionnaire booklet; $390 per reproduction rights (educational institutions only); $395 per scanner support capability.

Time: (20) minutes.

Comments: Requires IBM or compatible computer hardware.

Author: National Wellness Institute, Inc.

Publisher: National Wellness Institute, Inc.

Review of the TestWell: Health Risk Appraisal by BARBARA L. LACHAR, Assistant Professor of Psychiatry (Psychology), Baylor College of Medicine, Houston, TX:

INTRODUCTION. National Wellness Institute's TestWell: Health Risk Appraisal is one of many health-risk appraisal instruments that have become available since the 1970s. A health-risk appraisal is an assessment that relates an individual's identifying information, physiological measurements, family medical history, and health behaviors to available mortality statistics and epidemiological data. These appraisals are designed to provide education and promote favorable health behaviors by emphasizing risk. The majority of such measures use self-report data, often a questionnaire, to assess individual risk factors. Answers to these questions are used to calculate the estimated risk of death and potential decrease in risk from national mortality statistics. Mathematical calculations produce results in terms of the risk of death per 100,000 individuals of the same age and sex. Feedback consists of a chart that displays the risk of mortality from the 10 leading causes of death and information concerning ways to reduce the risk. Appraisals have many common characteristics, but they differ according to target group and amount and type of information collected.

Health-risk appraisals have been criticized, in general, for their inability to predict mortality for any one individual although they are presumed statistically accurate for large groups. In general, their ability to actually contribute to changes in individual behavior or longevity has not been proven. Health promotion is a laudable goal, but the extent to which these interventions alter behavior or outcome is unknown. Counseling is recommended as an accompaniment to feedback of health-risk results in order to increase the likelihood of health behavior change.

DESCRIPTION. The TestWell: Health Risk Appraisal is available as a software program designed to inform users how current behaviors, family health history, and physical health measurements relate to health risks. Both an interactive individual version and a group/batch software version are available. IBM or IBM-compatible hardware, with a minimum of 640K RAM and 4 megabytes, is required as well as DOS versions of 3.3 or later. Graphics-supporting monitors and printers are also recommended, although monochrome monitors and dot matrix printers are compatible. Scoring by scanner is an option.

Assessments are completed either interactively online or by questionnaire for group/batch administration. Item content differs for males and females. There are 39 questions for males, which include 4 specific questions dealing with risk of testicular and prostate cancer. Women respond to 44 questions, 9 of which are specific to female health risks. Administration time is approximately 10 to 20 minutes. Information on specific disease states, such as a personal history of cancer, a previous myocardial infarction, autoimmune illness, or renal dysfunction are excluded. There are six questions relating to use of tobacco, two questions on use of alcohol and drinking and driving, two concerning diet, and one on exercise. Family history is limited to diabetes, breast cancer, and early mortality due to heart attack.

REPORTS. The individual report lists the actual age, appraised risk age, and achievable risk age. The appraised risk age is the age of the relevant demographic group that matches the individual's calculated health risks. Positive lifestyle behaviors or strengths are highlighted. The top 10 risks of death per 100,000 for a group with similar responses are displayed, in tabular and bar chart form, in comparison to the risks for an individual's demographic group. Next, each of the 10 risk factors is listed with specific health- or safety-promoting recommendations. An achievable risk age is calculated and presented with suggestions for attainment. The proportion of risk, for example, .39 years, that could be eliminated or "gained" is provided for each recommendation.

The program allows the maintenance of separate group files and permits data from groups to be merged, as well. The group profile report provides an analysis of specific group results and is divided into seven sections, including group demographics. The first section, the Management Summary, presents a chart of modifiable group risk behaviors with the number of individuals and percentage endorsing each risk. The second section, Group Health Age looks at the actual health age, the appraised health age, and the achievable health age for both men and women. The appraised age is defined as the age equivalent to the risk of dying for the average person in the group and the achievable age indicates the improvement that could be attained with health-promoting behavioral changes. Group demographics and health-related characteristics, such as weight, blood pressure, cholesterol, and exercise behavior are displayed according to age and sex. The data regarding men's and women's health concerns are displayed separately. The final section reports on quality of life indicators such as ratings of health status and life satisfaction. Although security is protected by required logon information, confidentiality of results could be a concern of users and may need to be addressed.

RELIABILITY AND VALIDITY. There is no technical manual describing the theory, item construction, development, validity or reliability of this instrument. Although a psychometric test may be judged by the quality of its manual, health-risk appraisals are not typical psychometric tools and many do not make these statistics available. However, no information is provided concerning the currency of the epidemiological data, the specific reference groups, nor the validity of the predictions. It is not known whether data from relevant age and ethnic groups are used to calculate the estimated health risk age.

SUMMARY. The TestWell: Health Risk Appraisal is a cost-efficient, brief health promotion tool that can be used for individual education or to aggregate group health status information for organizations. Administration may be accomplished by paper-and-pencil questionnaire or by personal computer. The program is capable of producing both individualized reports and management summaries. Results are provided in terms of a health risk age and an achievable health age as well as the chance of death per 100,000 individuals for 10 leading causes of death in the next 10 years.

STRENGTHS. This health-risk appraisal can be used by individuals of varying ages and ethnicity. The program utilizes current health information such as blood cholesterol level and blood pressure but accepts default values if these are unknown. Processing is immediate and tailored education information is provided. Health risks are rank ordered and quantified. The relative advantages of behavioral change are presented and prioritized along with quantitative measures of risk reduction.

WEAKNESSES. Accuracy of prediction of information for any one individual is unknown as are the source, timeliness, and composition of the epidemiological data. There is no way of incorporating current information on past or present disease states, nor are risks of Human Immunodeficiency Virus (HIV) included in the calculations.

The TestWell: Health Risk Appraisal shares many of the strengths and weaknesses of other health appraisal instruments. It appears to have broad appeal and applicability. Its usefulness may be to rapidly disseminate health education information and to summarize data on group health risks. These data can provide baseline information to both stimulate and evaluate the extent of behavioral change when employed as pre and post measures.

REVIEWER'S REFERENCE

Beery, W., Wagner, E. H., Graham, R. M., Karon, J. M., & Pezzullo, S. (1984). *Description, analysis and assessment of health/hazard risk appraisal programs.* Springfield, VA: National Technical Information Service.

Review of the TestWell: Health Risk Appraisal by STEVEN G. LoBELLO, Associate Professor of Psychology, Auburn University at Montgomery, Montgomery, AL:

The TestWell: Health Risk Appraisal, produced by the National Wellness Institute, is designed to give an estimate of risk of dying of the 10 leading causes of death for a given age group. The program also calculates an "appraised health age" and an "achievable age." The former is an expression in years of a person's age given their risk factors (e.g., a 35-year-old who smokes and drinks heavily may have an appraised health age of 44 years); the latter gives an estimate in years of risk if lifestyle changes are made.

The printed questionnaire consists of 44 items for women and 39 questions for men that ask about a variety of health-related issues. A separate answer sheet is used, although a copy was not available for examination. Item content deals with smoking and alcohol consumption, safe driving practices, blood pressure, dietary practices and cholesterol level, and preventive health care behaviors such as frequency of breast self-examination for women and testicle self-examination for men.

A computer program is needed to score the completed questionnaire, or the items can be answered directly on the computer. When the questionnaire is taken from the computer, the program automatically presents the appropriate questions for men and women. Another option is to process questionnaires from a number of respondents to produce a group profile of health risk. The program is easy enough to use, although the computer graphics are rather primitive. Menu options allow users to view their health risk profile and read recommendations on-screen, or print out a paper copy. With on-screen viewing users see a graph or two that may not reproduce on paper with all printers.

The manual for the Health Risk Appraisal gives general information on how to load and use the computer software. There is little documentation about how risk is evaluated or how the program was developed. An appendix contains the items that are used to calculate risk. For some diseases there are no questions on the inventory that assess individual risk. Instead, the program reports a population risk for an individual's age and sex. For example, there are no questions about sexual practices or intravenous (IV) drug use, but because HIV/AIDS is a relatively high risk for some age groups, one's personal risk is given as the population risk. Although there are statements acknowledging this program peculiarity, it is possible for people to be misled by the data. For HIV/AIDS, someone who practices safe sex and refrains from IV drug use would have a lower risk than the population base-rate, whereas someone who engages in these behaviors would be at higher risk than indicated by the program.

There are no validity or reliability data reported but there are warnings that such an assessment is not a substitute for a medical examination. In addition, it is not recommended for use in people who already have been diagnosed with cancer, heart disease, kidney disease, or other serious health problems. After risk has been assessed, a list of recommendations for improving chances of survival is provided. Some of the recommendations are sensible, such as those dealing with weight reduction and eating a low-fat diet. Others are inane. For individuals judged to be at risk for death by homicide, it is recommended that they "avoid arguments with people you don't know."

Another problem with the inventory is the user must be able to report systolic and diastolic blood pressure, serum cholesterol level, and low and high density lipoprotein levels. Recognizing that most people are not aware of these numbers, the program automatically enters default values. Of course, when this is done, accuracy of risk appraisal is sacrificed.

The TestWell: Health Risk Appraisal is the sort of instrument seen at health fairs and other activities designed to raise individual and community awareness of health-related issues. It does not meet the minimal standards of psychological tests and probably should not be regarded as one. Rather, it is better regarded as an information source, and not a very accurate one at that.

One danger with devices of this type is that an employer could introduce it into the workplace and gain access to employee health data under the guise of providing a "health benefit." An unscrupulous employer looking to minimize insurance costs might use this instrument to sort out high-risk from low-risk employees. (This is unlikely, but possible.) And although it does not meet the usual standards of psychological tests, it would probably be wise to control its distribution to minimize the chance of such mischief.

[347]
TestWell: Wellness Inventory.

Purpose: Designed to promote awareness of wellness.
Population: Adults with a minimum of 10th grade education.
Publication Date: 1992.
Scores, 11: Physical Fitness and Nutrition, Social Awareness, Medical Self-Care, Spirituality and Values, Emotional Management, Intellectual Wellness, Environmental Wellness, Safety, Occupational Wellness, Sexuality and Emotional Awareness, Total.
Administration: Group.
Manual: No manual.

Price Data, 1993: $59.95 per interactive version, single user license; $249.95 per interactive version, multiuser license; $189.95 per group/batch version; $.50 per group/batch entry questionnaire booklet; $750 per reproduction rights (educational institutions only); $395 per scanner support capability.
Time: (20) minutes.
Comments: Requires IBM or compatible computer hardware.
Author: National Wellness Institute, Inc.
Publisher: National Wellness Institute, Inc.
Cross References: See T4:2821 (1 reference).

TEST REFERENCES

1. Jones, J. P., & Frazier, S. E. (1994). Assessment of self-esteem and wellness in health promotion professionals. *Psychological Reports, 75,* 833-834.

Review of the TestWell: Wellness Inventory by WILLIAM W. DEARDORFF, *Clinical Faculty, U.C.L.A. School of Medicine, Los Angeles, CA:*

TestWell: Wellness Inventory is a wellness assessment based on the six dimensions of wellness: physical, emotional, social, intellectual, occupational, and spiritual (manual, p. 20). The assessment provides information on how successful a person or group is at achieving well-being in each of the above-listed areas.

The test consists of 100 questions, which are answered with a number between 1 (*almost never*) to 5 (*almost always*), representing relative degrees of frequency relating to the behavior described in the question. There are 10 sections consisting of 10 questions each: Physical Fitness and Nutrition, Medical Self-Care, Safety, Environmental Wellness, Social Awareness, Sexuality and Emotional Awareness, Emotional Management, Intellectual Wellness, Occupational Wellness, and Spirituality and Values.

The assessment is a self-report format and can be administered individually or in a group. Administration of the test can be done either by paper and pencil, or interactively by computer and can take up to 20 minutes to complete.

The test is computer scored and minimum hardware requirements are an IBM-compatible computer, DOS 3.3 or later, 640K of RAM, a hard drive with at least two megabytes of space, a monochrome monitor, and a printer. The software does support the use of a scanner.

Two different types of reports can be generated: individual or group. The individual report shows the percentage of total possible points for each of the 10 sections along with an overall composite score and the overall balance in each of the six wellness dimensions. Results are interpreted in terms of "excellent," "good," and "room for improvement."

The printout concludes with a recommendation paragraph, along with a brief suggestion for reading resources.

The group report is designed to be used in employment settings, among others. It gives an overview of a group's overall strengths and weaknesses relating to wellness. The information is purported to help design and implement a wellness program. The results are similar to the individual report, except they are presented based on the group average. Additional results include scores by age range and sex.

Prices range from $59.95 (single user license) to $249.95 (multi-user license). The test appears useful in providing descriptive information about a group's strengths and weakness in the various areas of wellness. There is no information on how well a person's scores on the scales actually correlate to the wellness behaviors being assessed.

Review of the TestWell: Wellness Inventory by THEODORE L. HAYES, *Senior Research Analyst, The Gallup Organization, Lincoln, NE:*

The TestWell: Wellness Inventory is published by the National Wellness Institute, Inc. Materials included a flyer listing the questions, promotional materials, a 3.5-inch diskette containing a computerized version of the Wellness Inventory, and some computer documentation. Computer support personnel were helpful in answering installation questions.

The inventory contains 100 items measuring "the six dimensions of wellness," each of which is presented sui generis (i.e., constituting a class alone): Physical, Social, Emotional, Intellectual, Occupational, and Spiritual. Seven additional subcomponents (Physical Fitness, Nutrition, Self-care and Safety, Environmental Wellness, Social Awareness, Sexuality and Emotional Awareness, and Emotional Management) are evaluated as part of the inventory. The publisher defines wellness in these materials as "a continuous, active process—not a single goal or achievement" (p. 20). The idea is to become aware both of the areas of one's life as reflected in this inventory and that investments in one area may come at the expense of investments in another area. The inventory is designed to indicate the balance each individual has attempted between these areas so that one can make "choices that will help you attain a higher level of health and well-being" (p. 20). The inventory's publisher clearly intends it to be useful to employers in assessing employee wellness as part of establishing corporate wellness programs. The test materials include a bibliography of wellness products and resources—available from the National Wellness Institute—for interested consumers.

It is impossible to say how appropriate the Wellness Inventory measures are because the publisher provides no rationale for their inclusion in this inventory. Some consumers may believe that short shrift is given to some areas (for example, Spiritual or Occupational) or that the Wellness Inventory dimensions do not readily map onto conceptual models from other sources of wellness information. Also, the inventory's content and premises may not reflect new findings from nationally known wellness programs operating in conjunction with many major schools of public health (e.g., Harvard, Cal-Berkeley).

Though the dimensions measured in this inventory may seem more or less appropriate, I found the item content to be highly selective and the wording to be stilted. For example, "well" people may be described as "aware," "tolerant," "concerned," "informed," and as having high-fiber diets. Interestingly, it is not necessary to enjoy life to be "well." In fact, I could find no more than three items that reflected any joie de vivre. It seems that "well" people are constantly worrying. Meanwhile, I was left with the impression that "less well" people drive sport utility vehicles, smoke cigars, eschew educational television, and keep their houses above 68° F in the winter.

The Wellness Inventory comes wholly without psychometric information. One cannot determine how internally consistent these measures are, or whether they have any statistical validity. Furthermore, it is likely that test scores would be highly influenced by two important sources of error variance. Because wellness is more of a journey than an achievement, scores may change from time to time due to temporary life circumstances or even the season of the year (transient error). Some consumers may be influenced in their answers due to peculiarities in item wording (specific error). Because test-retest reliability is not provided, there is no point in looking for changes in wellness scores over time because many changes could simply be due to measurement error.

Probably the most serious problem is the lack of demographically based normative values. I think it is indisputable that "wellness" for a 26-year-old suburban pregnant woman may be completely different than "wellness" for a 62-year-old urban-dwelling man, yet the inventory allows the user no way to distinguish between scores generated from these two individuals (not to mention that changes in scores for these individuals may need to be evaluated in different ways). Finally, it is clear from the item content that individuals with physical or developmental disabilities will probably score lower on these dimensions. I would be particularly concerned about the use of this inventory for those individuals.

The Wellness Inventory would not be passable as a Master's thesis project. It is an example of what is known in economics as Gresham's Law, to wit, bad measurement drives out good measurement. There are no theoretical or conceptual bases for its dimensions, and no measurement basis for interpretations and inferences. There may be issues related to invasion of privacy when using this inventory in worksite wellness programs, as responses to many of the items and dimensions could easily be misconstrued and/or misused by incautious managers. I find this inventory completely unacceptable as a professional assessment instrument.

In summary, the TestWell: Wellness Inventory purports to measure the progress one has made in balancing several important areas of one's life. The supposition is that those with higher scores have been better able to make personal decisions that are consonant with a higher level of health and well-being. However, there is no rationale presented to assess the content validity of its measures. Many of the inventory's items seem stilted and selective. The technical information that would be necessary to evaluate the consistency or stability of scores, or even if the scores relate to any outcomes at all, is not provided. Finally, there are no norms provided for score interpretation and so it is impossible to determine whether the same scores from different individuals (e.g., men and women) mean the same thing. This inventory is currently lacking many components that would be necessary to recommend its use.

[348]
TestWell: Wellness Inventory—College Version.

Purpose: "Designed to address lifestyle choices facing today's college students."
Population: College students.
Publication Date: 1993.
Scores, 11: Physical Fitness, Nutrition, Social Awareness, Self-Care and Safety, Emotional and Sexuality, Intellectual Wellness, Environmental Wellness, Emotional Management, Occupational Wellness, Spirituality and Values, Total.
Administration: Group.

Manual: No manual.
Price Data, 1993: $89.95 per interactive version, single user license; $299.95 per interactive version, multiuser license; $249.95 per group/batch version; $.50 per group/batch entry questionnaire booklet; $750 per reproduction rights (for educational institutions only); $395 per scanner support capability.
Time: (20) minutes.
Comments: Requires IBM or compatible computer hardware.
Author: National Wellness Institute, Inc.
Publisher: National Wellness Institute, Inc.

Review of the TestWell: Wellness Inventory—College Version by DAVID L. BOLTON, Assistant Professor, West Chester University, West Chester, PA:

TestWell is a computer-based test that purports to provide information about wellness and helps measure success in achieving well-being. The test helps one gain knowledge about enhancing one's wellness. Wellness is defined by the authors of the test as a "process of becoming aware of the different areas in your life, identifying the areas that need improvement, and then making choices that will help you attain a higher level of health and well-being" (manual, p. 20). The manual lists and briefly defines six dimensions of wellness on which the test is based: Physical, Emotional, Social, Intellectual, Occupational, and Spiritual.

The test consists of a series of 100 statements. Students have to react to these statements on a 5-point scale. These statements fall into 1 of 10 areas: Physical Fitness, Nutrition, Self-care and Safety; Environmental Awareness, Social Awareness; Emotional Awareness and Sexuality, Emotional Management, Intellectual Wellness, Occupational Wellness, and Spirituality and Values. Each area is measured using 10 statements. Individual scores are obtained for each of the 10 areas for each person, as well as an overall score.

There is a paper-and-pencil version of this test as well as a computerized version of the test. The computerized version allows for administration to groups of students. One way of doing this is to administer the test on paper to a large group and then batch-feed into the computer. Or it can be administered on the computer individually with the group results being compiled once all in the group have taken the test. A group identifier can be set up and scores compiled for that group. The way it is set up allows one to keep track of the results of groups of large numbers of students. These scores are then visually represented using bar graphs and pie charts.

The manual does not provide any theory- or research-based justification for the definition of wellness or for the six dimensions of wellness. At a casual glance, they appear to have face validity. However, there needs to be stronger justification for the definition of wellness. And there need to be empirical data justifying the six-category breakdown.

The manual does not explain why there are six dimensions of wellness in the definition, but 10 categories on the test. By looking at the test questions, it appears that Physical is broken down into three categories, Physical Fitness, Nutrition, and Self-care and Safety, Social is divided down into Environmental Awareness and Social Awareness, and Emotional Wellness is divided down into Emotional Awareness and Sexuality and Emotional Management.

For the most part, the breakdowns make sense, with one notable exception. The questions under the category Self-care and Safety do not fit together very well. For example, one question has to do with riding in vehicles with drivers who are under the influence of alcohol. Another has to do with flossing teeth.

If one is going to break down the categories on the test, it makes more sense to define the underlying construct that way. Environmental Awareness appears to be distinctly different from Social Awareness. Why not speak in terms of environmental wellness? Emotional Awareness and Sexuality really focuses on sexual wellness.

There is no explanation as to how the questions were derived. There are also no data on the reliability of the test provided in the manual and no norms are provided.

There are a couple of statements that could be construed to be value-laden. One statement in the category Spirituality and Values has to do with spending time each day in prayer, meditation, and/or personal reflection. On the other side of the spectrum under Emotional Awareness and Sexuality, another statement has to do with respecting the rights of others who have different sexual orientations. However, for the most part the statements are relatively value-neutral or value-mainstream.

When installing the test on my Windows 3.1 PC computer, there was a message at the start indicating that the computer system was not compatible with the TestWell: Wellness Inventory. In spite of the message, the test appeared to install properly on the computer. However, it would not install on a Windows95 system. It simply froze up the computer. Although it may be possible to get the program to run on a Windows95 system, it would require technical assistance.

Although the test allows for administrators to identify a group by assigning a group identifier, it did not appear to allow one to input individual identifiers. When someone starts the test, he or she is required to input the group identifier as well as an individual identifier. There are no menu options, so the person needs to know this information before starting the test. The person also must type age and gender. It is not clear why this is important because this information does not appear to be used in scoring or in compiling group results.

The person taking the test responds to each statement using the same scale. The scale consists of numbers from 1 to 5. Each point also has a descriptor, as well as a percentage associated with it. The descriptors for the scale going from 1 to 5 are "Almost Never," "Seldom," "Often," "Very Often," and "Almost Always." A major problem with this scale is that the wording of the descriptors does not represent evenly spaced points on the scale. Some descriptors describe points that are very close together. The descriptors Often, Very Often, and Almost Always are all so close it would be hard to distinguish between them. Almost Never and Seldom have the same problem. And there is a big gap in the middle of the scale between Seldom and Often, with nothing in between. In taking the test, it was frequently difficult to find an appropriate match that fit the desired response. Generally people respond more in the middle, but there was no possibility for such a response.

Having one scale for all statements does not work well. It would be better to have a distinct scale for every statement specifically addressing the statement. At times, the scale used seems to fit the question only awkwardly. For example, one statement on the test is worded "I include whole grain breads and/or cereals in my diet every day" (p. 2). As stated, there is only a yes or no response possible for this statement.

The scores provided are minimal. The only score provided is a percent score. It is not explained how the percent is derived. If the middle score, 3, is chosen for all statements in a category, the score is 60%. This is equivalent to dividing 3 by 5, the maximum score. It is assumed that all questions are scored equally. A percent score is provided for all 10 categories, as well as an overall score. Acceptable ranges are provided for the overall score. No mini-

mally acceptable scores are provided for each of the categories.

What is provided is a bar graph with the scores from the 10 categories displayed. Presumably, one is able to compare the scores from various categories to determine relative weaknesses. A bar graph and pie chart are provided comparing the scores for the six wellness categories as well. It is not stated how the scores are combined for the six wellness categories. By looking at the chart one is to determine areas that need to be improved. All these diagrams can be derived for a group of students, allowing one to determine areas of group weakness.

The lack of norming data raises questions about the interpretation of test scores. If the student were to score in the middle of the scale, it is not clear if that is due to a weakness in that area, or whether that is a high score relative to other people taking the test.

As stated above, one of the purposes of the test is to make people aware of areas in need of improvement. However, in the current format the test relies upon the person's own self-awareness in taking the test and in their willingness to be forthright with their self-awareness. For example, one question under Social Awareness is "My behavior reflects fairness and justice" (test, p. 3). This requires a knowledge of what fairness and justice are. It also requires that the person be aware of his or her possession of this characteristic. And finally, it requires that the person who does not possess such a behavior has a willingness to admit such. A breakdown in any of these areas can significantly reduce the validity of the test.

Because of required self-awareness, the results of any test should be viewed skeptically, particularly in some areas such as the social and emotional areas, which require a lot of self-awareness. A person taking the test may have a high (or low) score simply due to the fact that the person may lack self-awareness and therefore falsely respond to the statements.

An instrument such as this is best used in conjunction with a wellness education program. Persons could then become familiar with what wellness is and be more self-aware. Without this basic understanding, the responses to the test are suspect. Having developed an education program, it would be easy to create a similar test on one's own that could fulfill the very same function.

Review of the TestWell: Wellness Inventory— College Version by RICHARD E. HARDING, Senior Vice President, The Gallup Organization, Lincoln, NE:

The user manual for the TestWell: Wellness Inventory—College Version contains no information on either validity or reliability. Rather, the manual concentrates on providing information about how to install and run the computer program provided. The test is an interactive program designed to address choices in life style that college students are facing. As such, the test defines six dimensions of wellness, which are Physical, Social, Emotional, Intellectual, Occupational, and Spiritual. These are defined in the computer program as well as in the user's manual.

The test itself is composed of 100 statements configured around 10 areas (10 items each area) designed to measure the six dimensions of wellness. Those 10 areas are: Physical Fitness, Nutrition, Self-Care and Safety, Environmental Wellness, Social Awareness, Emotional Awareness and Sexuality, Emotional Management, Occupational Wellness, Intellectual Wellness, and Spirituality and Values.

The goal of the program is for individuals to understand themselves well enough on these areas so that they can make appropriate choices to increase their wellness. The statements are scaled on a 5-point scale, from "1" *almost never* (less than 10% of the time) to "5" *almost always* (90% or more of the time). The middle scales are *occasionally* (approximately 25% of the time), *often* (approximately 50% of the time), and *very often* (approximately 75% of the time). The test is arranged so that the respondent answers 10 questions on Physical Fitness, then 10 questions on Nutrition, then 10 questions on Self-Care and Safety, etc. How the statements were chosen and placed into the 10 areas was not stated in the manual. It does not appear that this was done using any empirical methods.

The program was easy to run with well-designed screens. After responding to each statement, the individual has a chance to review his/her scores and graphs, look at helpful suggestions, or read some fun suggestions. The scores and graphs give information on how well the individual scored on each of the 10 sections. This is on a percentage point level, with the scale going from 200 to 1,000; 850 to 1,000 is determined to be *excellent*, 700 to 850 is *good*, and less than 700 indicates *room for improvement*. What category you would be in if your score was 850, however, is not easily determined. How these score ranges were determined and the subsequent descriptors attached (excellent, good, room for improvement) are not delineated in the user's manual or in any of the associated documentation. And, the overlap of score 850 raises even more questions.

After viewing the individual scores through the use of a pie chart or bar graphs, one is taken to a screen called "Helpful Suggestions." In this screen, each of the 10 areas are listed as being low, medium, or high and suggestions are given for improvement in the low areas. Some of those suggestions seemed rather obvious, such as you need to improve your level of wellness. Also listed with this are books and other software by Testwell to raise awareness in these areas.

In the third section one can go to fun suggestions, and accompanied by music, little rectangles with suggestions in them appear on the screen—suggestions, such as take 10 deep breaths, laugh, watch the sunset, take a walk, visit a museum are used.

There are also provisions in the program to look at group data and determine various levels of wellness regarding the types of groups in a study. Within the group information, one is provided with information on age ranges and on gender.

With no information available on reliability, validity, or normative evidence, this reviewer called the Testwell Wellness Institute. Officials at the Institute indicated that some studies are ongoing but at this time they are not complete. This reviewer was not made aware of the types of studies that are currently being undertaken and whether or not they will address any issues of reliability, validity, and/or provide normative evidence based on age and gender.

From this, one should apply caution in the use of this test. At this point, it seems the most appropriate use of this test would be for an individual in a counseling situation or on his/her own to use this test to examine the 100 statements (i.e., behaviors presented in the test) and his/her response to these behaviors. The individual could determine whether or not his/her responses are acceptable or whether he/she should target that individual behavior for further study and/or change. In this absence of any kind of supporting data, one should be very cautious in using the score range that is part of the report format.

[349]

Tool Room Attendant.

Purpose: "Developed to measure the knowledge and skills required for maintenance jobs."
Population: Applicants for maintenance jobs.
Publication Dates: 1991–1993.
Scores: Total score only.
Administration: Group.
Price Data, 1993: $498 per complete kit including manual ('93, 12 pages), scoring key, 10 reusable test booklets, and 100 answer sheets.

Time: (100–120) minutes.
Author: Roland T. Ramsay.
Publisher: Ramsay Corporation.

Review of the Tool Room Attendant by
STEPHEN L. KOFFLER, Executive Director, Edu-
cational Testing Service, Princeton, NJ:

The Tool Room Attendant Test (Form WCS [4/91]) was developed for use with applicants and incumbents for jobs where knowledge and skill in the maintenance area are necessary parts of job activities. The test consists of 100 four- to five-choice items. It is an untimed paper-and-pencil test; however, the directions indicate that examinees should need no longer than 2 hours to complete the test.

OVERALL EVALUATION. It is difficult to offer any evaluation of this test because of the paucity of information provided for it. The test lists a 1991 copyright date; however, the test manual (copyright 1993) provides sparse, if any, information about validity, reliability, scoring, norms, or interpretation of scores. Considerable additional information is needed before this test can be adequately evaluated for the appropriateness of its use for the purpose for which it was developed.

TEST DEVELOPMENT. The Tool Room Attendant Test measures knowledge in 10 areas (Electrical; Hydraulics & Pneumatics; Print Reading; Tools, Materials, and Equipment; Power Transmission; Pumps and Piping; Rigging; Maintenance Records; Mobile Equipment Operation; and Safety). The test manual does not specify how these areas were selected or their job relevance although it alludes to an expert-opinion type of job analysis. The manual indicates that the areas were independently ranked by five subject experts (maintenance supervisors) and that the interrater agreement was .90 for the raters using the Maintenance Activity List. Further, subject experts (presumably the same five) estimated the percent of time spent in each category to determine the percentage of the 100 items that would measure each area.

Basing a job analysis and determination of test specifications only on five experts is tenuous at best. Further, even if this approach were appropriate, the manual does not provide the qualifications or background of the five raters. Thus, there is question about the sufficiency of the job analysis and the specifications upon which the test is based.

There also is no information to describe the item development process and no data to support the quality of the items themselves. There is an empty table in the test manual related to item difficulties and point biserial correlation indices. The author states that "Form WCS (4/91) test data for maintenance employees will be gathered and run on SPSS when available" (manual, p. 8).

SCORING/NORMS. According to the test manual, this test is to be hand scored and the score provided is a rights-only, raw score. However, there are neither criterion-referenced (e.g., a cut score) nor norm-referenced data provided to interpret the scores. Presumably the type of interpretation the author suggests is norm referenced because a table is provided that relates raw scores to percentile ranks. However, the table is empty and the manual indicates that the table will be completed when the data are available.

VALIDITY. The test manual discusses content, criterion-related, and construct validity in general, but provides no validity evidence for the interpretation of the test scores.

For content validity, the manual states, "The content validity of the test is assured when the behaviors required on the test are also required on the job. It is a paper-and-pencil form of a work sample" (p. 10).

For criterion-related validity, the manual states "Because the test is an achievement or skill test, the appropriate model for validity is content validity. Although the test has not been part of a criterion-related validation study, the hypothesis is that it would be predictive of job performance measures in jobs requiring maintenance knowledge and skills. Hunter (1983) reports that content-related valid tests usually reflect excellent criterion-related correlation coefficients" (p. 10).

For construct validity, the manual provides that "The construct measured by Tool Room Attendant Test is knowledge and skill in the maintenance area." The manual also indicates that no formal studies of construct validity have been conducted, but it states that "construct validity is attained by the procedures of development. This skill or ability has been observed in many jobs in maintenance. Where knowledge or skill in maintenance is required, the test is useful" (p. 10).

This approach to providing evidence about the validity of the test is inadequate.

RELIABILITY. The only data provided in the test manual are an estimated KR-20 reliability index (.85), estimated standard deviation (10.0), and estimated standard error of measurement (4.0). The test manual states that these data indicate "excellent reliability" (p. 8). However, the manual does not provide the source of the data upon which these estimates are based. Clearly, the data source is needed before one can draw inferences about the reliability of the test. It also is peculiar that there is a KR-20 estimate provided but no item statistics.

SUMMARY. Much more information is needed about the validity, reliability, and usefulness of the scores from the test for its intended population. When all of the analyses are completed for the Tool Room Attendant Test—although there is no indication of the date by when the necessary analyses are to be conducted—it might turn out that the test does provide valid, reliable, defensible, and usable scores. However, until such time as those details are provided and it can be determined that the test does meet the principles of measurement called for in the *Standards for Educational and Psychological Testing* (AERA, APA, & NCME, 1985), the test cannot be recommended for use.

REVIEWER'S REFERENCE

American Educational Research Association, American Psychological Association, & National Council on Measurement in Education. (1985). *Standards for educational and psychological testing.* Washington, DC: American Psychological Association, Inc.

Review of the Tool Room Attendant by EUGENE (GENO) PICHETTE, Assistant Professor in the Division of Rehabilitation Psychology and Counseling, University of North Carolina at Chapel Hill, Chapel Hill, NC:

The Tool Room Attendant Test Form WCS was designed as an instrument to assess knowledge and skills of applicants and/or incumbents for occupations in the maintenance area. According to the author, the test was developed by the Ramsay Corporation as part of the development of a series of skills tests. This test requires a person to answer a series of exercises by reading each test question in the test booklet and placing the answer on the Tool Room Attendant Test Form WCS answer sheet.

The Tool Room Attendant Test Form WCS instrument measures knowledge and skills for nine different maintenance areas. These include: Electrical; Hydraulics and Pneumatics; Print Reading; Tools, Materials, and Equipment; Power Transmission; Pumps and Piping; Rigging; Maintenance Records; and Mobile Equipment Operation. The 100-item test was divided by knowledge areas and each knowledge area has a different number of test questions assigned. This was derived at using five maintenance experts who estimated the percentage of time spent in each of the different maintenance areas. According to the author, the

interrater agreement was .90 for the five experts using the Maintenance Activity List. The test is untimed; however, the manual states that the test should not need more than 2 hours to complete. It is group administered and is hand scored. According to the manual, the test can be administered to up to 20 examinees at a time by one examiner. The manual does suggest, however, that if there are more than 20 examinees, an assistant is to assist in the test administration.

Although the test is easily administered with clear, simple-to-follow instructions, the manual offers very limited information on scoring and test interpretation. Specifically, the manual instructs the examiner to hand score using the scoring keys. A raw score is derived by subtracting the number incorrect from the total possible (100 items). The manual provides no basis for score interpretation, other than obtaining a total score.

A significant weakness of this test is the lack of any normative data. The manual states that normative data will facilitate the comparison of a person's score to an established specific group (e.g., employed workers, skilled craft workers, etc.). Subsequently another problem area of the test is the lack of any validity information. The manual provides a cursory descriptive review regarding definitions of content, criterion, and construct validity. However, no data are provided.

Test reliability indicates consistency of measurement. The manual provides limited information regarding the reliability of this instrument. Accordingly, an estimated reliability coefficient (KR 20) was listed as .85. Other basic psychometric properties were listed. Included were the estimated standard deviation of 10.00 and the estimated standard error of measurement of 4.00. The manual indicates that test data for maintenance employees will be gathered and an item analysis will be conducted at a future date.

In summary, a number of weaknesses of the test are evident. A major shortcoming is the obvious lack of normative data. Accordingly, no validity information is available and nothing more than a raw score can be obtained by this test. Another problem area is reliability. The manual reports "excellent reliability" (p. 8). Accordingly, The Tool Room Attendant Test Form WCS has an estimated reliability coefficient of .85; however, the manual lacks information about the test stability over time. Due to the lack of adequate normative data, resulting in no validity information and limited reliability data, the test falls short as an adequate screening device for employee selection.

Generally, the test is a relatively quick, easily administered instrument designed as an employee screening test for maintenance occupations. With only a raw score derived from the test, the test has limited use at this stage of development. Many of the test items appear to have face validity, which is a desirable feature of tests. In practical situations, face validity can offer the appearance of what is measured for examinees. However, the author mentions little if anything regarding validity in the manual. Until additional evidence is produced regarding reliability and validity, the test is not an adequate screening instrument for applicants and/or incumbents for jobs where knowledge and skill in the maintenance area are important for job activities.

[350]
Total Quality Management Readiness Index.
Purpose: Identifies whether an individual or work group is ready to successfully organize and implement change.
Population: Managers and work groups.
Publication Date: 1993.
Acronym: TQMRI.
Scores, 14: Managerial Style (Authoritative, Affiliative, Democratic, Coaching), Competencies (Achievement Orientation, Analytical Thinking, Customer Service Orientation, Directing Others, Initiative, Team Orientation), Climate (Standards, Clarity, Rewards), Total.
Administration: Group.
Price Data, 1993: $59 per complete kit including 10 questionnaires and 10 profiles and interpretive notes (19 pages).
Time: Administration time not reported.
Author: McBer & Company.
Publisher: McBer & Company.

Review of the Total Quality Management Readiness Index by PAUL M. MUCHINSKY, Joseph M. Bryan Distinguished Professor of Business, The University of North Carolina at Greensboro, Greensboro, NC:

The Total Quality Management Readiness Index (TQMRI) purports to assess the degree of fit between managerial styles and competencies and organizational climate for the purpose of gauging readiness to implement organizational change through TQM. The packet of material I was asked to review consisted of three items: The TQMRI Questionnaire, the TQMRI Scoring Instructions & Interpretive Notes, and a one-page TQMRI Profile. The questionnaire consists of 26 questions of a behavioral nature, which the respondent is to rate on a 4-point scale of frequency. The respondent can either render a self-assessment or an other-assessment. The 26

questions reflect 13 scorable dimensions: 4 assess Managerial Style, 6 assess Managerial Competencies, and 3 assess Organizational Climate. Thus, each dimension is measured by two questions. The 10 Managerial Style and Managerial Competency scores are averaged to yield a single score, whereas the 3 Climate scores are similarly averaged to yield an organization score. The two averaged scores are then plotted on the TQMRI Profile, which is a three-color grid. If the pair of scores fall in the lower (red-colored) quadrant, "the person should 'stop' and review climate, competencies and managerial styles before proceeding with TQM" (p. 1). If the pair of scores fall in the upper (green-colored) quadrant, "'go' ahead with TQM-based change efforts" (p. 1). If the pair of scores fall anywhere within the yellow area, "use 'caution' in implementing TQM, as it may be impeded by existing climate problems" (p. 1). The green area represents about 5% of the grid, the red area represents about 20% of the grid, and the yellow area represents the remaining 75%.

The Scoring Instructions & Interpretive Notes is what passes for a manual. It is here that the deficiencies of the TQMRI become most apparent. There is no construct definition of "readiness" or manifestations of it. The sum total of the validation evidence is described as deriving from "a study of managers across different industries who successfully implemented TQM" (p. 6). There is no empirical criterion-related validity evidence. There is no reliability evidence. No norm-based test score data are presented. There is no explanation of how the questions were derived, other than they reflect factors associated with "measurable savings" achieved by TQM work teams over a period of 2 to 8 years. Who these teams were, where they were located, what work they did, etc., is not specified. There is no statement about the questionable validity of psychological constructs being assessed by *two* items each. There is no statement about how the cut scores were determined to produce the green, yellow, and red outcome decisions. There is no consideration given to the measurement of the respondents providing self- versus other-assessments.

The most useful part of the Scoring Instructions & Interpretive Notes is a narrative description of various managerial styles and competencies. Presumably this material could be used to make individuals more aware of their own behavior, and how their behavior relates to implementing TQM. The value of this instrument thus lies in the narrative material, which could serve as a coaching device, but one could obtain such information from other sources without having to endure the TQMRI. The final page of the scoring guide lists five other publications by the author "if you wish to pursue a more in-depth analysis of climate or managerial style" (p. 19). However, I surmise based on the titles that these other sources only strengthen the narrative coaching material, and do little or nothing to enhance the woeful psychometric integrity of the TQMRI.

Organizations can benefit from assessments that guide decision making about moving toward a TQM-based system of organizational change. Such decisions, given the magnitude of organizational commitment required, should not be undertaken lightly. I fail to see how the TQMRI assists in this process. More harm can potentially come from its use than its absence. To utilize a metaphor of the author, my assessment of the TQMRI is a bold, red STOP! It does not even warrant a yellow caution.

Review of the Total Quality Management Readiness Index by VICKI S. PACKMAN, Senior Assessment Analyst, Salt River Project, Phoenix, AZ:

The Total Quality Management Readiness Index (TQMRI) was developed by McBer & Company to identify whether an individual or work group is ready to successfully organize and implement change. It is self-administered, self-scored, and is applicable for both individual and group administrations.

The TQMRI consists of a 5-page Questionnaire, a 1-page Profile, and a 19-page Scoring Instructions & Interpretive Notes. The Questionnaire consists of 26 items and can be used as either a self-assessment or to assess others. Examples of items include: Makes a special effort to explain to subordinates the purpose of their work (p. 2); Works with a long-term perspective toward the customer (p. 4); and Creates new opportunities (p. 4). Items are rated on a 4-point scale on which the numbers mean: 4 = *Very Frequently*; 3 = *In Some Situations*; 2 = *Not Very Often*; and 1 = *Never*.

The directions state that individual scores can be averaged to yield composite scores for managers but there is no worksheet to assist the test taker in accomplishing this.

The TQMRI has 13 scales and a Total. There are exactly two items for each of the 13 scales. Basing scales that purportedly assess managers in terms of Styles, Competencies, and Climate factors on only two items seems precarious at best.

The anchors utilized by the 4-point scale are unusual and lack continuity. The term *Never* is extreme and limiting. Even the worst managers might have demonstrated the behaviors measured at least once or twice. This anchor may discourage use and inadvertently reduce the scale to 3 points. "Rarely" might be a preferable anchor. The scale appears to jump from *Very Frequently* to *In Some Situations*. The authors might consider revising their anchors to "Very Frequently," "Frequently," "Sometimes," and "Rarely" or something similar.

Ratings are recorded in the Questionnaire in columns that denote scales. Columns are totaled and sums are recorded for scales on a Scoring Worksheet in the scoring Instructions & Interpretive Notes. Scales 1 through 10 are summed and divided by 10 to determine the Management Readiness Index. Scales 11 through 13 are summed and divided by 3 to determine the Climate Index. These two indexes are plotted on the TQMRI Profile to determine whether to stop and review before proceeding, proceed with caution, or proceed with TQM-based change efforts.

The TQMRI Profile is very attractive and colorful yet misleading. A perfect score on all of the scales of the Questionnaire would result in scores of 4.0. However, on the graph on which the scores are plotted, both axes plot out to roughly 4.2. The graph consists of one large square that contains two smaller squares. The squares are colored to represent their diagnosis; red = "Stop," yellow = "Caution," and green = "Go." These diagnoses translate into the following scores: Stop = 0 to 2.5, Caution = 2.5 to 3.5, and Go = 3.5 to 4.0. There can, of course, be overlap when one axis plots in one diagnosis and the other in another. The graph is plotted so that most individuals and groups will receive diagnoses of "Stop" or "Caution" rather than "Go." The rationale for this is not documented.

The Scoring Instructions & Interpretive Notes is very easy to read and comprehend. It does a nice job of defining the Managerial Styles, Competencies, and Climate factors measured by the questionnaire. It also contains suggestions on how to effectively utilize the styles and competencies and lists suggestions for applying these styles to improve the climate dimensions.

The TQMRI has some serious deficiencies regarding technical properties. There is no manual and no published studies that address the validity and reliability of this instrument. The technical soundness of the TQMRI is unsubstantiated and the instrument fails to meet the *Standards for Educational and Psychological Testing* (AERA, APA, & NCME, 1985). The TQMRI cannot be recommended for assessing individual or organizational readiness to implement change. The reviewer could not find another instrument with this same purpose to recommend in place of the TQMRI. The TQMRI might prove effective for initiating discussions regarding implementing change but should not be taken seriously until appropriate evidence of validity and reliability is presented.

SUMMARY. The Total Quality Management Readiness Index is an interesting instrument that lacks evidence of validity and reliability. Until these deficiencies are remedied the reviewer recommends that this instrument be utilized only as a vehicle for initiating discussions regarding implementing change.

REVIEWER'S REFERENCE

American Educational Research Association, American Psychological Association, & National Council on Measurement in Education. (1985). *Standards for educational and psychological testing.* Washington, DC: American Psychological Association, Inc.

[351]
The Trait Pleasure—Displeasure Scale.

Purpose: One of three fundamental dimensions of temperament in Mehrabian's Temperament Model; provides a general assessment of psychological adjustment-maladjustment.
Population: Ages 15 and older.
Publication Dates: 1978–1994.
Scores: Total score only.
Administration: Group or individual.
Price Data, 1994: $28 per complete kit including scale, scoring directions, norms, manual ('94, 10 pages), and literature review.
Time: (10–15) minutes.
Author: Albert Mehrabian.
Publisher: Albert Mehrabian.

TEST REFERENCES

1. Mehrabian, A., & Stefl, C. A. (1995). Basic temperament components of loneliness, shyness, and conformity. *Social Behavior and Personality, 23,* 253–264.

Review of the Trait Pleasure—Displeasure Scale by THADDEUS ROZECKI, Assistant Professor, University of Northern Iowa, Cedar Falls, IA:

The Trait Pleasure—Displeasure Scale is a brief instrument that attempts to highlight an individual's typical level of pleasure or displeasure regarding a representative variety of life situations. This instrument is based on the premise that scores on the pleasure/displeasure dichotomy of temperament reveal an underlying psychological adjustment and mental health as opposed to an overall maladjustment and dysfunction within a specific individual.

The scale consists of 47 items presented in a semantic differential format. For each item a pair of descriptive contrasting adjectives is presented separated by nine spaces. The subject is requested to consider the two adjectives that appear for each item and place a check mark on one of the nine spaces that separate the adjectives. The subject is requested to mark a space that most closely describes his or her feeling toward the adjective descriptors. The closer the check mark appears to the descriptor presented, the more strongly the subject feels it best reveals his or her own temperament toward the contrasting adjectives presented for each item. Adjective pairs include: affectionate/nasty; happy/tyrannical; wide-awake/spiteful; affectionate/spiteful; and angry/activated. The author estimates that 15 minutes are required for completing this instrument.

In order to mask which adjective pairs are being measured the author has included 23 adjective pair items that are not included in the final analysis. Only 24 items are used in developing the final individual score. They are linguistically similar to the masking or buffer items. Buffer items are interspersed with operational items throughout the entire measure. The subject is requested to mark each item by providing an accurate individual judgment of the balance between the two feelings (adjectives) across most everyday life situations.

The instrument is scored by obtaining a total raw score, which can then be converted to both z scores and percentiles for comparison to the normative sample. The total score is obtained by a comparison of positive and negative summations corresponding to the adjective pairs considered. The author of the instrument has determined which feeling identified in the adjective word pairing possesses either a positive or negative ranking (mean = 45, standard deviation = 20). There is no specific information provided in the manual about the normative sample to which the subject is being compared. There is no indication of how the normative sample was obtained or the number of persons who have taken the measure. Interpretations of the overall score range from "very extremely high" to "very extremely low" but it is unclear what these terms describe. Without accompanying demographic and normative information the test user is left to make his or her own interpretations of the scores.

Reliability data are extremely sparse. The author indicates that this measure has a high internal consistency reliability (.91.) but offers no indication in the manual regarding the procedure used in obtaining this figure. No test/retest reliability information is provided by the author, which seems to mirror the lack of normative population information. The author does cite an external source that speaks to the question of reliability for this measure.

Information related to the validity of this instrument is also very weak. The author suggests that there are significant positive correlations with various personality scales that assess psychological adjustment in personal relationships, sentience, and achievement but offers no statistical information nor specific analysis to supplement these claims. Even if the issue of concurrent validity is partially addressed through an introduction of these statements, information concerning construct and predictive validity are nonexistent. There appears no strong evidence that this instrument does, in fact, measure an individual's predisposition toward a positive or negative state in reviewing general life situations and thus a correlated psychologically functional or dysfunctional posture.

The Trait Pleasure—Displeasure Scale appears to be lacking in both reliability and validity. There is no clear indication provided by the author for which group of individuals the instrument is intended nor the reasons for using the measure in general. Interpretations of the results are suspect and do not clearly indicate a diagnostic or research preference. Without additional information it would be difficult to ascertain how this measure could be used effectively with its inclusion in an assessment battery. The test manual does provide some supplementary bibliographic resources but does not delineate in specific terms how test results can be used in a clinical or research environment.

Review of the Trait Pleasure—Displeasure Scale by CHOCKALINGAM VISWESVARAN, Assistant Professor of Psychology, Florida International University, Miami, FL:

The Trait Pleasure—Displeasure Scale was designed as a measure of "a person's characteristic or typical level of pleasure versus displeasure over time and across a representative variety of life situations" (manual, p. 2). The scale comprises 24 items consisting of a pair of adjectives, 12 of which are reverse scored. The 12 positively and 12 negatively scored items alternate, and 23 buffer items (8 of which were originally developed to assess trait arousal and the other 15 for trait dominance) are placed such that there is a buffer item between any two of the 24 items. The scale used is a 9-point semantic differen-

tial scale. The scores on the 12 negatively directed items are summed and subtracted from the sum of the scores on the 12 positively directed items to yield one total score. The higher the total score, the greater the tendency to experience pleasure.

Although the manual gives no information on the test development process or the item selection strategies used, based on published journal articles cited in the manual, the following information was gathered. The process started with 250 emotion-denoting terms rated by 30 subjects on pleasantness, arousal, and dominance. Forty-five pairs of emotion-denoting terms that were matched on arousal and dominance were administered to 200 University of California undergraduates. Based on item-total correlations, 22 items were retained. Adding an additional set of 64 pairs, the 86 pairs were administered to another group of 357 University of California undergraduates. Again based on item-total correlations, 40 items were collected into a scale, which was administered to another sample of 142 University of California undergraduates. The final scale retained 24 items. It should be noted that in all three stages additional emotion-denoting term pairs (differing in either dominance or arousal but matched on pleasantness and either arousal or dominance) were also included as buffer items. Finally, a fourth sample of 274 University of California undergraduates was used to assess the psychometric properties of the final 24-item scale.

The KR-20 reliability estimate of the scale was reported in the manual as .91 on a sample of 274 University of California undergraduates. Further, in a published study employing this scale, a KR-20 reliability estimate of .97 has been reported (Mehrabian & de Wetter, 1987). Another published study (Mehrabian & Bernath, 1991) had employed this scale with 253 University of California undergraduates, but no reliability values were reported.

Given that the score obtained from this scale is a continuous scale (24 to 216), coefficient alpha should be reported (not just KR-20). Further, given that this scale is designed to assess a person's typical level of pleasure *over time*, coefficients of stability (i.e., test-retest) should be reported.

Although not reported in the manual, the scale correlates .36 ($N = 211$ University of California undergraduates) with Crowne and Marlowe's social desirability scale. The scale correlates .32 with Eysenck's measure of extroversion, and .50 with the affiliation scale of Jackson's PRF. The scale correlates -.03 with the autonomy scale of Jackson's PRF. The Trait Pleasure—Displeasure scale has been correlated with 34 other measures but neither the manual nor the published journal articles I retrieved reported the zero-order correlations (only regression weights where the 24-item measure is one of three independent variables have been reported).

Although claims are made that this scale predicts behavior, validity coefficients are not reported. Specifically, correlations between scale scores and behavioral measures of adjustment are needed. Contrasted groups design showing differences in scale scores between normal individuals and patients will also help. Also useful would be more information on test administration time (how was the 10–15 minutes range established?).

Score norms are reported in the manual (mean = 46 and SD = 20), but no information is given about the norming sample. However, Mehrabian (1978) reports on a sample of 274 University of California undergraduates with a mean of 43 and standard deviation of 20. Considering that the manual reports a KR-20 of .91 based on 274 University of California undergraduates, a question arises whether the mean reported contains a typographic error (either in the manual or in Mehrabian, 1978). Normative data have not been provided for different ages, races, and between gender. Thus, no evaluation of item bias or differential validity across demographic groups is possible. No data are reported on non-English-speaking samples.

In summary, the scale has been meticulously developed and appears to have adequate evidence of reliability and construct validity. The manual provided to me for review was not compiled according to professional guidelines, and needs to be revised. Data should be collected on test-retest reliability and on the predictive validity of this scale for predicting behavior. The manual should be revised to report coefficient alphas, normative data broken down by demographic groups, and the zero-order correlations with the 34 measures of personality with which this scale has been correlated.

REVIEWER'S REFERENCES

Mehrabian, A. (1978). Measures of individual differences in temperament. *Educational and Psychological Measurement, 38,* 1105–1117.

Mehrabian, A., & de Wetter, R. (1987). Experimental test of an emotion-based approach to fitting brand names to products. *Journal of Applied Psychology, 72,* 125–130.

Mehrabian, A., & Bernath, M. S. (1991). Factorial composition of commonly used self-report depression inventories: Relationships with basic dimensions of temperament. *Journal of Research in Personality, 25,* 262–275.

[352]
Transdisciplinary Play-Based Assessment, Revised Edition.

Purpose: Constructed as a multidimensional approach to identifying service needs, to developing intervention plans, and to evaluating progress in children.

Population: Children developmentally functioning between infancy and 6 years of age.
Publication Date: 1993.
Acronym: TPBA.
Scores: 4 domains: Cognitive, Social-Emotional, Communication and Language, Sensorimotor Development.
Administration: Individual
Price Data, 1995: $48 per manual (347 pages).
Time: (60–90) minutes.
Comments: Ratings by transdisciplinary team.
Author: Toni W. Linder.
Publisher: Paul H. Brookes Publishing Co., Inc.

Review of the Transdisciplinary Play-Based Assessment by TERRY OVERTON, Licensed School Psychologist, Learning and Behavior Therapies, Inc., and Associate Professor of Psychology, Department of Special Education, Longwood College, Farmville, VA:

This instrument was designed to provide structure for professionals charged with the task of evaluating children between birth and age 6 years. The focus of the evaluation is structured and unstructured play accompanied by systematic observation. The domains assessed include Cognitive, Social-Emotional, Communication and Language, and Sensorimotor. The author states that any number of professionals or nonspecialized personnel and parents may participate in the assessment process. The purpose of this instrument is to assist professionals in the development of a program plan for specific interventions for children in early childhood programs.

This assessment involves many play situations and all are recommended to occur in an early childhood type setting. No materials, other than the manual, are included with this instrument.

The assessment is completed in six phases. During Phase I, the child participates in unstructured play in which the child leads or initiates play with the examiner. Phase II is structured and incorporates specific play tasks that the child did not initiate in Phase I. Phase III provides the opportunity for the child to interact with a peer. During Phase IV, the child and parent participate in structured and unstructured play. Phase IV also includes situations in which the parent is asked to leave so that separation and reunion behaviors may be observed. Phase V involves structured and unstructured motor play. Phase VI, the final phase, includes a snack which the author states allows for screening of oral motor difficulties and other developmental observations.

The Transdisciplinary Play-Based Assessment manual provides guidelines for each of the domains assessed. These guidelines aid the examiner in formulating appropriate questions and tasks as the child is assessed across the domains. Worksheets, which are sold separately by the publisher, are available to use as a method of organizing the specific behaviors and categories observed during play. The manual provides a framework for determining which of the observed skills are strengths and which ones are to be included in the program as skills the child is ready to learn.

Each domain assessed is presented in a separate chapter of the manual. A comprehensive treatment of each domain is provided and rationale is given for the domain construct as it is related to play assessment. These chapters are the strength of this assessment technique. The explanations and descriptions provided will assist any early childhood professional in analyzing play behavior and using the information to design appropriate interventions. Following each of the domain chapters are guidelines used to structure the observation and assessment of the specific domain and developmental age ranges. The age ranges are "adapted" from several sources, some of which are quite well known. The scores within age ranges are not noted to have been normed in any manner. These age ranges may serve only as very limited guidelines and not, as the author stated, to "permit team members to document developmental skill levels for specific milestones" (p. 4) or as a reference for skill acquisition.

Once the assessment has been completed, seven steps are suggested for the team to follow as they develop a program plan for the child. One of the steps suggested is a review of the videotaped play session. This allows the team members to discuss their observations and reach conclusions as a team.

The manual includes a comprehensive case study to illustrate the use of this instrument for assessment and program planning. Sample worksheets are completed for this case study. A final chapter discusses how parents can be involved in the assessment process and the changing role of parents.

The development of this assessment technique was begun by this author in the 1980s. The original Transdisciplinary Play-Based Assessment was published in 1990 and this second edition was published 3 years later. The author has subsequently written an accompanying book on intervention: *Transdisciplinary Play-Based Intervention*. The author's expertise seems to be functional assessment and intervention.

The weakness of this assessment technique is within the technical quality of the instrument. There is very little discussion about the design of the instrument and even less about reliability and validity. The author cites a single unpublished doctoral dissertation as the reliability and validity evidence gathered thus far. In presenting content validity, the author mentions that "experts" supported the developmental guidelines. The author does not describe how this was determined. A brief mention of concurrent validity is included by saying only that this instrument was compared with some standardized measures and found to be accurate in determining which students needed special services. Test-retest reliability was mentioned in one study of "a group" of children who were tested and retested within 6 weeks yielding "similar outcomes" (p. 5). Interrater reliability was "well supported" by "several independent raters" viewing videotapes. Again, no details are provided in the manual.

This assessment process seems to be rich in content and construct validity, but this has not been adequately researched. It would appear to have the qualities of an instrument with some predictive and discriminant validity; this has not been researched either. The quality of the descriptive and explanatory work by this author is to be admired. One only wishes that the technical adequacy was half as thorough. This instrument would be useful to many more professionals if norm-referenced data were included. Although this instrument was designed to be an alternative to norm-referenced standardized assessment, it would be useful in the field of professional psychology, as well as education, if it met the rigors of this type of assessment.

Review of the Transdisciplinary Play-Based Assessment, Revised Edition by GARY J. STAINBACK, Senior Psychologist I, Department of Pediatrics, East Carolina University School of Medicine, Greenville, NC:

The Transdisciplinary Play-Based Assessment (TPBA) is not a formal psychometric instrument, but rather a list of developmental skills observed through play for children from infancy through 6 years of age. Four developmental domains are explored: Cognitive, Social-Emotional, Communication and Language, and Sensorimotor. It is also intended by the author that the TPBA be utilized by a transdisciplinary team whose goal is to help identify areas where specialized services are warranted, and help provide guidance for goals and objectives in the development of an individualized Education Plan (IEP) or Individualized Family Service Plan (IFSP). The author recommends the TPBA be utilized for both formative (ongoing) as well as summative (year-end) evaluations of children. The TPBA is implemented by a team consisting of parents and professionals who are very knowledgeable of development in young children. Unlike some multidisciplinary assessment approaches where each developmental professional (e.g., physical therapist, occupational therapist, speech pathologist, psychologist, etc.) utilizes a developmental instrument of each professional's choosing, the TPBA's scales are intended to be used by the entire team. Furthermore, the team has specific responsibilities during the assessment.

There is a play facilitator who will interact with the child during the evaluation. This is the central person to interact with the child except during times another professional may need to have "hands on" time with the child (e.g., assessment of muscle tone by a physical therapist).

Secondly, there is a parent facilitator who interacts with the parents, providing interpretation of observations and securing evidence to the consistency of the observations. There is also a videocamera operator who tapes the session for later viewing and scoring by team members.

Finally, there are other team members who observe and record their observations utilizing the TPBA format. The TPBA is intended to last 60–90 minutes, consisting of six phases that incorporate both unstructured as well as structured play, parent-child and child-child interactions, motor play, and a snack being observed.

The role of the parent is emphasized in the TPBA, and the author makes a point of stressing that any child functioning between infancy and 6 years of age can be assessed. Certainly modifications in the play environment will be needed for physically disabled children; however, there is no specific listing of toys or equipment given in order to direct the team in designing the play environment. It is recommended that a large preschool classroom be utilized, with the room divided into visibly distinct areas (e.g., house, block, art, sand or water table, and gross motor areas). A "variety of colorful toys and equipment" (p. 46) are utilized that would entice the child of various ages to interact with the play facilitator or toy.

During this time when the child, through unstructured as well as structured play, interacts with the toys, parent, or another child, team members are recording their observations on the Observation Guidelines, which are designed in a qualitative format (e.g., How did the child accomplish the task?) rather than simply yes/no responses. Or team members may record observations on the Observation Worksheet. Whichever approach is utilized, team members need to be familiar with the guidelines for all domains and not only with their specialty. These observational recordings may be completed during the actual assessment phase or when reviewing the videotape of the session. A Summary Sheet, filled out after each domain has been completed, addresses relative strengths and weaknesses, present level of functioning, and areas where the child needs further assistance as well as areas in need of further evaluation. These steps are performed by team members working cooperatively together and who are thoroughly familiar with the developmental functioning levels of normal and handicapped young children.

The role of traditional assessment versus play-based assessment is addressed by the author, as well as limitations of TPBA. These limitations include the fact that states may require standardized testing before identification of children for special services is considered. Some areas of development may need further assessment in order to assess adequately (e.g., receptive language, motor handicaps, sensory-motor integration, etc.). Excellent thought and organization has been given to the TPBA, and it has drawn considerable attention from multidisciplinary teams that evaluate preschool age children for developmental handicapping conditions. Often young children do not have the stamina to perform in an arena assessment where different professionals are interacting with the child during a similar time session. These children may also not have the temperament to interact in an examiner-lead format ("do what I say or do what I do"). These children are certainly more cooperative during "play" during which many of their developmental skills can be observed. Considering the role of team members, areas they need to address, and the extensive range of play from infancy to 6 years of age that is covered, from handicapped to normal degrees of functioning, the role of a developmental team member appears quite massive and different from the training he/she may have received. Consequently selections of team members should not be taken lightly.

Lacking from the TPBA is evidence of the reliability or validity of this assessment approach. Normative data are based on previous research in different areas of play in the four domains. The use of a number of scales incorporated into one assessment procedure addressing several domains of development, and involving a number of professionals, certainly makes the TPBA worthy of attention.

However, the lack of evidence regarding the instrument's reliability and validity seriously affects the recommendation that the TPBA be utilized in the assessment of young children. Research on the reliability and validity of this approach is direly needed. Presently it can help provide information for children that standardized assessment approaches would offer limited guidance. It can also be utilized effectively for reevaluation of children where the team needs further insights on how to work more effectively with the child.

[353]
Uniform Child Custody Evaluation System.

Purpose: Constructed as a "uniform custody evaluation procedure."
Population: Professionals involved in custody evaluation.
Publication Date: 1994.
Acronym: UCCES.
Scores: No scores.
Administration: Individual.
Forms, 25: General Data and Administrative Forms (UCCES Checklist, Initial Referral Form, Chronological Record of all Case Contacts Form, Case Notes Form, Consent for Psychological Services to Child(ren) Form, Authorization to Release Information Form, Suitability for Joint Custody Checklist, Collateral Interview Form, Consent for Evaluation of Minor(s) Form, UCCES Summary Chart), Parent Forms (Parent's Family/Personal History Questionnaire, Parent Interview Form, Parenting Abilities Checklist, Suitability for Joint Custody Interview, Analysis of Response Validity Checklist, Behavioral Observations of Parent-Child Interaction Form, Home Visit Observation Form, Agreement Between Parent and Evaluator Form, Explanation of Custody Evaluation Procedures for Parents and Attorneys), Child Forms (Child History Questionnaire, Child Interview Form, Child Abuse Interview Form, Abuse/Neglect Checklist, Child's Adjustment to Home and Community Checklist, Parent-Child Goodness of Fit Observation Form and Checklist).
Price Data, 1996: $110 per complete kit including manual (47 pages), 2 sets of Parent Forms, 2 sets of Child Forms, and 1 set of Administrative and Data Forms; $79 per replacement kit including all the materials in the complete kit except the manual; $19 per set of forms (specify Administrative and Data, Parent, or Child); $30 per manual.
Time: Administration time not reported.
Authors: Harry L. Munsinger and Kevin W. Karlson.
Publisher: Psychological Assessment Resources, Inc.

Review of the Uniform Child Custody Evaluation System by STEVEN ZUCKER, School Psychologist, Cherry Creek Schools, and Honorarium Instructor, University of Colorado at Denver, Denver, CO:

The Uniform Child Custody Evaluation System (UCCES) was designed to standardize the data-gathering process in child custody evaluation procedures. The UCCES provides a common, systematic platform from which clinical inferences are derived, and forms the basis for decision-making processes and recommendations regarding child custody. By providing a uniform, systematic process for gathering, transcribing, and organizing data, the authors hope to focus the court's attention on the recommendations and opinions of the professionals involved, not upon the processes and procedures that underlie those opinions. Although there are no reliability, validity, or normative data provided in the manual, the UCCES does provide a useful, well-integrated approach for organizing objective data and clinical impressions.

The UCCES manual provides a succinct, historical overview of the research, legislation, and philosophical imperatives regarding questions of child custody. As there is little uniformity regarding qualifications and experience for experts the court may recognize, the need for a uniform approach to gathering pertinent data is clearly underscored. The UCCES provides 25 forms to assist the evaluator in organizing and managing a broad range of essential information and in assessing the overall degree of response validity across the range of information obtained. It would seem that several of these forms could be combined and/or bound together, to enhance manageability of data (e.g., Case Contacts/Case Notes—Forms 4 and 5; Parents Family/Personal History Questionnaire/Parent Interview—Forms 10 and 12). There are additional instances in which greater succinctness and integration would facilitate the attainment of a more coherent picture of the overall case dynamics. Although the forms would seem to facilitate managing the case, one must still manage the forms.

Several of the interview forms, and much of the interview processes, are highly prone to bias and response sets. Fortunately, the authors do provide several forms (#23, Analysis of Response Validity Checklist and #25, UCCES Summary Chart) and numerous recommendations/considerations to help the evaluator assess the degree of validity or confidence one may infer from client responses. However, normative data would be helpful here, to assist the evaluator (the novice evaluator in particular) as he or she considers the degree of confidence to place in potentially biased responses. For example, how many checkmarks are typical for the Analysis of Response Validity Checklist (#23); how many blank spaces indicate substantial deviance from the norm, etc. Also, developmental norms would prove helpful on the Child History Questionnaire (Form 11) for evaluators unfamiliar with typical ranges for developmental milestones. This would assist in determining accuracy and/or potential biases in responses and would also alert the evaluator to potentially significant neurodevelopmental considerations. Ultimately, such norms would improve the overall utility, and likely the validity, of the UCCES.

There seem to be assumptions made regarding appropriate interpretation of "projective" data (e.g., Kinetic Family Drawing; responses to hypothetical "what-ifs," etc.) which would benefit from empirically derived interpretive and/or normative guidelines. For example, there is only modest (and quite tenuous) empirical support for conclusions regarding psychological bonds based on the measured distance between child and respective parent in a kinetic family drawing. One would hope for solid empirical data if such indicators are to guide one's decision-making process. Finally, the UCCES might benefit from normative data addressing the discriminative value of the Suitability for Joint Custody Interview Form/Suitability for Joint Custody Checklist (Forms 21 and 22). Although the evaluator's clinical and practical judgments are primary in making recommendations for joint custody, there would be great value in gathering predictive outcome data to guide the decision-making process (again, especially helpful for the novice evaluator).

Overall, the forms provided have been carefully constructed and reflect a healthy respect for, and sensitivity to, the needs of children and their families in such difficult proceedings. In practice, it is likely that evaluators will depart from the scripted sequences provided for in the Child Interview forms (there is a stilted feel to many of the scripted questioning sequences). Still, there may be room for additional questions/considerations on the forms themselves. For example, in the spirit of best interests of the child, it is often helpful in such cases to ask the child if there are any wishes he or she would like conveyed directly to the judge. In custody hearings the court often appreciates this type of information.

Child custody evaluators will likely appreciate the manual's description of UCCES rationale, interpretation, and preparation for court. It would, however, likely prove beneficial to include some of the normative data reported in the "Rationale" chapter on the respective forms that assess the associated variables. For instance, norms regarding the validity of, and confidence to place in, reports of sexual abuse; the incidence of mental health concerns for parents

experiencing separation and divorce, etc., would be helpful when evaluating the impact of specific reports and observations. The authors remind us that decision making in child custody cases is "rife with uncertainty" (p. 13). They only imply, however, that the validity and utility of the decision-making process (even when adhering to the UCCES) is predicated on the clinical competence, sensitivity, and integrity of the clinician making the judgments.

SUMMARY. The Uniform Child Custody Evaluation System (UCCES) is a useful tool for gathering and organizing data in child custody procedures. The UCCES can provide a coherent platform from which clinical inferences and recommendations may be derived. Although the manual is clear, succinct, and well organized, the number of forms seems excessive and could be organized more efficiently. The absence of normative data is a detriment in particular situations. The lack of reliability and validity data is equally disconcerting. Nevertheless, for the evaluator seeking a systematic method for gathering, organizing, and evaluating data in child custody cases, the UCCES will be a valuable tool.

[354]
USES General Aptitude Test Battery for the Deaf.

Purpose: Used "in vocational counseling and occupational placement."
Population: Hearing impaired adults.
Publication Dates: 1984–1990.
Acronym: GATB for the Deaf.
Scores: Scores are the same as for the USES General Aptitude Test Battery, see 9:1304.
Administration: Group or individual.
Price Data: Available from publisher.
Time: (150–160) minutes.
Comments: Adaptation of the USES General Aptitude Test Battery.
Author: U.S. Department of Labor.
Publisher: U.S. Department of Labor.

Review of the USES General Aptitude Test Battery for the Deaf by RALPH G. LEVERETT, Professor of Education/Special Education, Union University, Jackson, TN:

This government publication is an assessment of aptitude for prevocational and vocational counseling. No stated age range is given; however, it is presumably for those considering a career initially or those considering a career change. Information to be given to the examinee states that "this is *not* a test of what you learned in school. It shows how well you can learn to do different jobs" (manual, p. 7). Test results are to be "used to 'screen' a handicapped applicant *into* rather than out of, a job" (manual, p. 9). The term "handicapped" is used in the manual as well as the term "deaf." Current preferred terminology would likely discourage the use "handicapped." The test was designed with two primary goals: to simplify the reading level of the standard version of the test and to provide directions and explanations that are "inaudible to deaf applicants" (p. 1).

The test consists of 12 subtests that can be grouped into language, mathematical, visual discrimination, and performance categories. These designations, however, are not listed in the manual. All tests, even those that are performance in nature, require comprehension of the tasks. As such, even these are language-dependent tasks.

Materials included with the test include two test booklets for each of the two forms (A and B) and two answer sheets for Part 8. The materials provided to this reviewer did not include separate answer sheets for Part 8. In a discussion on "Adapting Test Material," the examiner is instructed that the test booklets and Part 8 "have been prepared with instructions blocked out and are available from the USES test materials supplier" (p. 5). No such modifications were made to the booklets supplied with the test for review.

Additional materials required include stopwatches, scratch paper, two pegboards, three fingerboards, and a set of cards for administration of the General Aptitude Test Battery (GATB). No separate cards were provided to this reviewer. The test manual includes card-like boxes with instructions. Each of these cards is numbered. It is uncertain from the manual whether the examiner is to photocopy, cut, and mount these cards for use with the test. Use of the cards as they are printed in the manual would be cumbersome and probably confusing to the examinee. Also confusing is the manual's reference to the "examinee's card." In another apparent oversight, the list of materials required makes no mention of the rivets and washers necessary for completion of Subtests 11 and 12. Perhaps these accompany the standard version of the GATB, but the examiner cannot determine that information from the manual for the adapted version.

Although a manual for administration, scoring, and interpretation is included with test booklets, scoring and interpretation require the manual for the standard version of this test battery. No actual application of test results is possible using the information in the manual for the adapted version.

No rationale is provided for the development of the test format or specific test items. Although this information may be included in the standard manual, the user of the adapted version would profit from this information as well. It would appear that the examiner should be thoroughly familiar with the standard version of the GATB because the information provided in the manual for the adapted version is inadequate to provide confidence to the user in its current form.

To the test's credit is the detail provided for administration of the test. Care is taken to inform the examinee of the nature and purpose of the test. Additionally, the examiner is prompted in interacting with the persons who have hearing loss. Candidates for the test must be able to read at the sixth-grade level. This caution is necessary considering the generally depressed reading scores of many persons with hearing loss. The manual notes that administration of the entire test may "not always be feasible for this reason, but no firm rule has been established" (p. 3).

This test may be administered in group or individual format. Group administration utilizes sign language, finger spelling, and simplified directions on cards. Individual administration does not require knowledge of sign language by the examiner. Simplified directions on cards and hand printed notes are used. The simplified test booklets are appropriate for either testing format. Group administration is considered "more efficient and may be preferred by deaf examinees" (p. 1). The complete test may require up to 2 1/2 hours.

SUMMARY. At face value, this test appears to be useful to professionals serving clients with hearing loss. Technically, however, the test appears limited in both its lack of a stated research base and in its practical application.

[355]
The Values Scale, Second Edition.

Purpose: "A cross-cultural measure of values in various life roles."

Population: Junior high school to adult.

Publication Dates: 1986–1989.

Acronym: VS.

Scores, 21: Ability Utilization, Achievement, Advancement, Aesthetics, Altruism, Authority, Autonomy, Creativity, Economic Rewards, Life Style, Personal Development, Physical Activity, Prestige, Risk, Social Interaction, Social Relations, Variety, Working Conditions, Cultural Identity, Physical Prowess, Economic Security.

Administration: Group.

Price Data, 1993: $31 per sampler set including manual, test booklet, answer sheet, and report form; $15 per 25 reusable test booklets; $14 per 25 non-prepaid answer sheets; $15 per 25 report forms; $30 per manual.

Time: (30–45) minutes.
Author: Dorothy D. Nevill and Donald E. Super.
Publisher: Consulting Psychologists Press, Inc.
Cross References: See T4:2876 (1 reference); for reviews by Denise M. Rousseau and Robert B. Slaney of an earlier edition, see 10:379.

TEST REFERENCES

1. Drummond, R. J. (1988). Test review. *Journal of Employment Counseling, 24,* 136–138.
2. Krau, E. (1989). The transition in life domain salience and the modification of work values between high school and adult employment. *Journal of Vocational Behavior, 34,* 100-116.
3. Sverko, B. (1989). Origin of individual differences in importance attached to work: A model and a contribution to its evaluation. *Journal of Vocational Behavior, 34,* 28-39.
4. Carter, R. T., Gushue, G. V., & Weitzman, L. M. (1994). White racial identity development and work values. *Journal of Vocational Behavior, 44,* 185-197.

Review of The Values Scale, Second Edition by KATHY E. GREEN, Professor, College of Education, University of Denver, Denver, CO:

The Values Scale, Second Edition was designed to measure intrinsic and extrinsic values individuals seek in life roles, with emphasis on the importance of work as values expression relative to general values. It is intended for use in research associated with occupation, cultural differences, socialization, and life stage, and in career commitment evaluation. The authors suggest its use as a counseling tool should be further explored but also state the instrument is "ready for more extended, individual use in career counseling" (p. 12), with "either ipsative or normative interpretation" (p. 15). Combinations of the 21 values scores can be reported in five groupings (Inner-Oriented, Group-Oriented, Material, Physical Prowess, and Physical Activity). Responses to 105 items are obtained with a 4-point (*little or no importance* to *very important*) scale; one additional item is used only for cross-national scoring. Scoring is accomplished by hand or by sending payment to the publisher. The Values Scale has been used with upper elementary students to adults in semiskilled, skilled, clerical, sales, professional, and managerial occupations. The Values Scale comprises two pages of items that are easily read and can be answered quickly. The individual report form is presented in an easy-to-read profile format.

The Values Scale was developed by an international consortium of vocational psychologists from over a dozen European, American, and Asian countries beginning in 1978. Values were defined and agreed upon following panel review. Items were developed, reviewed, and revised by international teams. The Values Scale resulted from the contributions of people with varied cultural, religious, and economic perspectives. A 1980 version of the Values Scale contained 10 items per scale which were reduced to the 5 best with consortium advice. Although the manual provides norms for the United States sample, The Values Scales has been used in Australia, Belgium, Canada, Italy, Portugal, and the former Yugoslavia.

NORMS AND STANDARDIZATION. Until 1985, convenience samples were used. Since then data from high school samples designed to be representative of socioeconomic, gender, and population density levels; university samples designed to represent arts, letters, science, and technical students from major regions of the country; adult samples representing all Holland-type occupations and "literate socioeconomic levels" have been obtained. These samples provide the norming data for the three groups, with data from approximately 3,000 high school students, 2,000 university students, and 2,000 adults.

The sampling designs are not specified nor are the sampling methods, so the test user may question whether the norms are representative on a national basis though the sample sizes certainly exceed those of some other test developers claiming normative data. As The Values Scale profile is suggested to provide only one of multiple pieces of information used in career counseling, a question regarding the precision of norms may be a minor point. Nevill and Super suggest The Values Scale to be a "particularly appropriate instrument for cross-cultural research as it was developed by a multinational team" (p. 13). But, as Walsh et al. (1996) point out, Values Scale norms are based on age and grade but ignore the multicultural composition of the United States. Walsh et al. examined Values Scale scores for 323 ethnic minority students and suggest scores on some scales differ for those groups. Further specification of sampling methods and cultural differences of samples would be useful in judging the appropriateness of the norms provided in the manual for any particular individual. However, ipsative interpretation may still prove useful.

PSYCHOMETRIC PROPERTIES. The first edition of the Values Scale was reviewed by Rousseau and by Slaney in 1989 for *The Tenth Mental Measurements Yearbook* and several points of criticism they identified have not been addressed by the second edition. Specifically, no theoretical model underlying The Values Scale scores is provided nor are the definitions agreed upon by the international consortium provided. Scale reliabilities (in the .6 to .8 range for internal consistency and .5 to .8 for test-retest) support group use but not use of scales for individuals. Reliabilities of the five groupings of scales are not reported.

Values Scale validity is questionable at this time for the following reasons. First, although face validity is supported by measure construction methods, it is impossible to determine whether the measure addresses aspects of values central to theory because the underlying theory is absent. Second, most of the studies conducted by the authors and their colleagues are reported in conference or unpublished papers and so are not readily available. Third, the authors report scale differences in accord with expectation but do not justify the expectation. For example, it is unclear why gender differences on some scales are expected at the high school level but not at the college level. I would argue that expected gender, educational level, and socioeconomic differences support validity but do not "assure" it, as the authors state. Fourth, exploratory factor analyses across age levels were conducted with similar factors emerging. Invariance testing with confirmatory factor analysis would evaluate whether the factor structure was actually stable across age levels and could also be conducted for gender and cultural groups to examine bias as well as invariance. Fifth, correlations with alternative measures are cited as significant but the coefficients are not furnished. Finally, and most compelling, no predictive validation has as yet been accomplished. The authors note this shortcoming and their intent to remedy it when such longitudinal data are available.

CONCLUSION. Lack of evidence of sample representativeness and moderate reliability levels limit interpretation of scores for individual use. However, group use of scores seems warranted if used with literate groups. Evidence supporting validity would strengthen the utility of The Values Scale for group interpretation as would presentation of the underlying theory and its association with measure content. Future studies might address the stability of construct definition across cultural groups and investigate bias and differential validity.

REVIEWER'S REFERENCE

Walsh, B. D., Vacha-Haase, T., Kapes, J. T., Dresden, J. H., Thomson, W. A., & Ochoa-Shargey, B. (1996). The Values Scale: Differences across grade levels for ethnic minority students. *Educational and Psychological Measurement, 56,* 263–275.

Review of The Values Scale, Second Edition by PATRICIA SCHOENRADE, Professor of Psychology, William Jewell College, Liberty, MO:

To assist in career direction, the counselor will, ideally, know something about the client's values both with respect to work and more generally. Such is the information that The Values Survey (VS) helps to identify. Although the instrument is designed to assess values particularly relevant to the work situation, the authors recognize that work-related values are not independent of one's overall value system. Thus, the scales assessing 21 different values include both work-specific and more general statements. Values, for the authors, are "the objectives sought in behavior" (p. 3). The VS includes both intrinsic values, in which the objective is attained while engaging the behavior, and extrinsic values, in which the objective is the result of the behavior. Examples of the former include Autonomy and Creativity; examples of the latter are Economic Rewards and Prestige.

The VS is composed of 106 items and takes about 30–45 minutes to administer. For each of the 21 values assessed, a five-item scale includes at least two work-related statements and at least two more general statements. (The additional item is included because of a substitution required in cross-national administration.) The respondent indicates the degree to which "It is important for me now or will be in the future to" (attain each objective). The 21 scales are interspersed throughout the inventory; the response sheet provides for easy hand scoring. Computer scoring and profiling are also available.

Among the particular strengths of the VS is its cross-national development. A consortium of vocational psychologists from some 12 countries (the Work Importance Study group) participated, and the VS is available in 10 different languages. The manual provides tables of norms for samples from several of the participating countries, often with tables for high-school students, college students, and/or adults.

The cross-national development process appears to have been more empirical than theoretical, including reviews of the literature on values, identification of specific values, particularly those not assessed by existing scales, preparation of definitions, and writing and testing of sample items. The process is described in some detail in the manual, though the criteria for inclusion of items are not always clear.

The 21 scales possess reasonably good internal consistency, with alphas ranging from .67 to .87 (for adult samples; slightly lower for university and high school samples). Only university samples were available for test-retest studies, where correlations ranged from .52 to .82. Appropriate cautions are offered for the three scales for which both internal consistency and test-retest reliability consistently fall below .7 (Ability Utilization, Life Style, and Personal Development).

A rich base of normative data appears in the manual, with means and standard deviations broken down by age group, gender, and career group. The normative samples are generally quite large (1000+). Tables for conversions to standard scores are included, and instructions for both ipsative and normative interpretation are provided.

The case for the content validity of the VS is strong owing to the expertise and cross-cultural makeup of the consortium. The argument for construct validity could, perhaps, be more clearly presented. Gender differences and interscale correlations are described as showing "expected relationships," but the basis for these expectations is not made clear. Relationships between certain VS scales and psychological constructs measured by other scales are described, but the actual correlations are not reported. Factor analyses of the items add to the evidence for construct validity by demonstrating that items from a given scale frequently load together.

The authors readily acknowledge the need for data on predictive validity, and indicate their intention to begin gathering the longitudinal data necessary. They wisely observe that criteria in these predictive validity studies should include "satisfaction, stability, and occupational discrimination data" (p. 26).

The manual offers helpful suggestions for use of the VS in both research and career guidance contexts. Research possibilities including occupational, cultural, and life stage differences are suggested. The outline of a model for career counseling is presented, and a readable case-study is included as an example.

The Values Survey appears so well-suited to applications in career counseling and vocational research that it seems a bit curious that its title suggests nothing specific to work or career. Used in these contexts, however, it can serve to quantify and focus expectations, ambitions, and objectives that may otherwise be vaguely stated or missed. The 21 scores, and perhaps individual items, may be the basis of fruitful discussion between client and counselor.

[356]
Vocational Assessment and Curriculum Guide.

Purpose: "Designed to assess and identify skill deficits in terms of competitive employment expectations; to prescribe training goals designed to reduce identified deficits; to evaluate program effectiveness by reassessing the worker after training."
Population: Mentally retarded employees.
Publication Dates: 1982–1993.
Acronym: VACG.

Scores, 10: Attendance/Endurance, Independence, Production, Learning, Behavior, Communication Skills, Social Skills, Grooming/Eating, Reading/Writing, Math.
Administration: Group.
Price Data, 1994: $12 per complete kit including manual (5 pages), 10 test booklets, curriculum guides, and summary profile sheets; $8 per set of 10 extra forms.
Time: (15–20) minutes.
Authors: Frank R. Rusch, Richard P. Schutz, Dennis E. Mithaug, Jeffrey E. Stewart, and Deanna K. Mar.
Publisher: Exceptional Education.
Cross References: See T4:2898 (1 reference).

Review of the Vocational Assessment and Curriculum Guide by HINSDALE BERNARD, Associate Professor, Department of Counseling, Administration, Supervision, and Adult Learning, Cleveland State University, Cleveland, OH:

As an extension of the Prevocational Assessment and Curriculum Guide (Mithaug, Mar, & Stewart, 1978; 12:304), the Vocational Assessment and Curriculum Guide (VACG) was developed to assist vocational evaluators, teachers, trainers, coordinators, and administrative personnel in the development of effective training programs for handicapped persons to become competitive in light industrial, food service, janitorial, and maid service occupations. Its primary functions are:

1. To assess and identify skill deficits in terms of competitive employment expectations,
2. To prescribe training goals designed to reduce identified deficits, and
3. To evaluate program effectiveness by reassessing the worker after the training. (manual, p. 1)

DESCRIPTION AND ADMINISTRATION OF THE VACG. The VACG is designed to assess Worker Behaviors, Interaction Skills, Self-Help Skills, and Academic Skills that most supervisors consider important for entry into competitive employment. The Worker Behaviors include: Attendance/Endurance, Independence, Production, Learning, and Behavior. The Interaction Skills include: Communication Skills and Social Skills. The Self-Help Skills consist of seven personal Grooming/Hygiene Skills. The Academic Skills include: Reading/Writing and Math Skills. The skills are all broken down into their several components. For example, the following skills appear under the Independence aspect of the Worker Behaviors: working alone; working independently from coworkers, supervisors and others; working without being distracted; working safely; and getting to work independently.

There are four parts to the VACG, namely, the manual, inventory, Curriculum Guide, and Summary Profile Sheet. The manual is a separate booklet that describes the purpose and rationale for using the VACG. It details the content and usage of the VACG with instructions for administering and scoring the inventory. The manual also provides information on how to identify skill/behavior deficits, how to use the Curriculum Guide to identify training needs, and how to plot the worker's VACG scores against expected levels on the Summary Profile Sheet. Appropriate concrete examples help to clarify these activities. Validity and reliability of the VACG are discussed briefly in the manual.

The 49-item inventory consists of the following 10 categories that reflect the skills already mentioned: Attendance/Endurance (3 items), Independence (5 items), Production (5 items), Learning (5 items), Behavior (7 items), Communication Skills (11 items), Social Skills (2 items), Grooming/Eating (7 items), Reading/Writing (2 items), and Math (2 items). The inventory comes in a separate 3-page booklet and the 49 questions appear in the 10 categories: 20 items are multiple choice and 29 items require a "yes/no" response.

The VACG is designed to be administered to workers by their supervisors or persons familiar with the behavior of the workers such as classroom teachers, workshop trainers, or prevocational coordinators. As such, the VACG itself comes with no instructions for its completion. This is also the case for the curriculum guide and the summary profile sheet. The curriculum guide is a compilation of goals that mirror the inventory items in the 10 categories. The goals are intended to serve as the basis for developing a worker's individualized total service plan (Rusch & Mithaug, 1980). The profile sheet is designed to chart an individual's performance in the 10 categories as well as suggest areas for improvement. Up to four different evaluations may be superimposed on the same profile sheet so that a worker's progress may be followed. The inventory, curriculum guide, and profile sheet all ask for the worker's name and birth date, the trainer's name, and the evaluation date(s). No demographic information about the worker is requested. Such information can be useful for research purposes.

TEST CONSTRUCTION AND PSYCHOMETRIC PROPERTIES. The authors adapted items from the list of procedures for assessing prevocational competencies in severely handicapped young adults developed by Mithaug and Hagmeier (1978). A noticeable omission was a description of the original list

of procedures because changes to that list were made by a panel of "representative community employers" (p. 3) to form a 47-item questionnaire—the precursor of the VACG. This 47-item instrument was pilot tested on two separate occasions (Rusch, Schutz, & Agran, 1982; Schutz, 1983) on two similar samples of service industry employers (55 and 53, respectively) in six midwestern communities. No information was provided on how these studies were conducted, the actual sample sizes on whom the data were collected, and what kinds of data were actually gathered. Significant correlation coefficients (.66 and .63) were quoted without any mention of the variables that were compared.

The combined results of the two pilot tests (referred to as surveys) provided the basis for selecting items to be included in the VACG. An item was retained in the VACG if 80% or more of the "combined respondents" (p. 4) considered its contents to satisfy the entry requirements for competitive employment. The authors' claims that the instrument reflected concurrent validity and test-retest reliability (Menchetti, 1983) beyond the .001 level of significance are somewhat questionable. The method used to establish *concurrent* validity seemed to apply to *discriminant* validity. And, even so, the dependent variables used to discriminate between the three levels of work experiences among the mentally retarded persons were not mentioned. A couple questions also arose concerning the test-retest reliability measures. How many subjects were retested in the three groups? How much time elapsed between the tests?

REVIEWER'S COMMENTS. Although the VACG seems to have face validity in that on the surface it deals with some minimum competency skills for handicapped persons, the content validity was not adequately addressed. A number of issues needed clarification. Who comprised the panel of "representative community employers"? How many persons were on this panel? What was the definition for "handicapped persons"? How many handicapped persons, if any, were used in the samples for the two pilot tests? In other words, was the VACG normed on employers or employees? What were the demographic compositions of these samples? Under what conditions were the surveys conducted? Who were the "respondents" who conducted the screening of the items? What kinds of midwestern communities were involved in the pilot tests? These questions bear direct relevance to the norms established for the VACG Summary Profile Sheet.

Despite the many unanswered questions in the description of the VACG, the user may still find this checklist of skills to be useful for identifying skill deficits in handicapped employees. What may remain in doubt is an accurate interpretation of competency levels from the profile sheets.

REVIEWER'S REFERENCES

Mithaug, D. E., & Hagmeier, L. D. (1978). The development of procedures to assess prevocational competencies of severely handicapped young adults. *AAESPH Review, 3*, 94–115.

Mithaug, D. E., Mar, D. K., & Stewart, J. E. (1978). *The Prevocational Assessment and Curriculum Guide.* Seattle, WA: Exceptional Education.

Rusch, F. R., & Mithaug, D. E. (1980). *Vocational training for mentally retarded adults: A behavior analytic approach.* Champaign, IL: Research Press.

Rusch, F. R., Schutz, R., & Agran, M. (1982). Validating entry-level survival skills for service occupations: Implications for curriculum development. *The Journal of the Association for the Severely Handicapped, 7*(3), 32–41.

Menchetti, B. (1983). *Assessing the nonsheltered employment survival skills of mentally retarded adults.* Doctoral dissertation, University of Illinois, Campaign, IL.

Schutz, R. (1983). *Assessing light industrial employers' expectations for competitive employment.* Doctoral dissertation, University of Illinois, Campaign, IL.

Review of the Vocational Assessment and Curriculum Guide by GERALD R. SCHNECK, Professor of Rehabilitation Counseling, Mankato State University, Mankato, MN:

The Vocational Assessment and Curriculum Guide (first published in 1982) is listed as an extension of the previously developed Prevocational Assessment and Curriculum Guide (Mithaug, Mar, & Stewart, 1978; 12:304). This instrument was developed from information provided about employers' expectations of workers entering into light industrial, food service, janitorial service, and maid service occupations. Emphasis of the instrument and the accompanying curriculum guide is upon assisting educators and other vocational and rehabilitation professionals "in the development of effective training programs for handicapped persons who are preparing for competitive employment" (p. 1). Its primary functions are to: (a) identify skill deficits regarding competitive employment expectations; (b) prescribe training goals to remediate identified skills deficits; and (c) evaluate program effectiveness through post-training assessment of the worker. Assessed are four primary worker capability areas: Work Behaviors, Interaction Skills, Self-Help Skills, and Academic Skills. A total of 49 items, assessing skills in these four areas, are included in the VACG under 10 categories: Attendance/Endurance (3 items); Independence (5 items); Production (5 items); Learning (5 items); Behavior (7 items); Communication Skills (11 items); Social Skills (2 items); Grooming/Eating (7 items); Reading/Writing (2 items); and Math (2 items).

Completion of the VACG "must be completed by someone familiar with the behavior of the worker" (p. 2), such as a teacher, trainer, or prevocational coordinator at a professional or para-professional level. Information provided through completion of the inventory can then be utilized by others (i.e., vocational evaluator, aide, administrator, etc.) to complete the VACG Curriculum Guide and Summary Profile Sheet. The manual for the VACG recommends that the evaluator review each item in the inventory and "note any assessment items which might require new arrangements of task materials and classroom conditions in order to make reliable judgments about behaviors being assessed" (p. 2). Raters must answer several questions pertaining to each of the categories included in the VACG, by selecting one of the several answers that are offered for each question, regarding how the worker "characteristically responds in class/work situations" (p. 2). Each of the alternative answers is weighted for subsequent use in identifying skill/behavior deficits and completing the VACG Summary Profile Sheet. Those answers which are checked as being characteristic responses of the worker/student being assessed may be considered as skill/behavior deficits of the worker/student.

Vocational training goals for each item in the inventory are listed within the VACG Curriculum Guide. From this list, individual goals are to be selected for inclusion in the individual worker/student individualized total service plan. It is suggested by the VACG authors that the worker/student VACG Summary Profile Sheet can be utilized to monitor the individual's progress at regular intervals.

Initial survey items were derived from Mithaug and Hagmeier's (1978) list of items that were utilized in a survey of sheltered employment entry requirements. Subsequently, the original list was modified using the results of a "panel of representative community employers" (p. 3). An initial survey of 55 service industry employers (i.e., food service and janitorial occupations) in "six Midwestern communities" (p. 3), was followed by a second survey of 53 light industrial employers located in "the same six Midwestern communities" (p.3), which resulted in similar information being provided about the worker behaviors and skills employers considered important for entry into their businesses. Validity coefficients (Pearson's *r*) of .66 and (Spearman's rho) of .63 (which were both significant at the .001 level) were obtained. Items included in the finalized version of the VACG Inventory were taken from both of these surveys, wherein 80% or more of the combined employers considered the skill/behavior to be entry level requirements for competitive employment.

Menchetti (1983) conducted a study of the VACG in terms of its concurrent validity and instrument discrimination ability, both with groups of workers who were mentally retarded who had differing levels of work experience and vocational success, and with those workers without identified mental impairment who had successfully been employed in a competitive work setting. He found that the VACG discriminated between these groups of workers, particularly those who were competitively employed and those who were not. In addition, Menchetti (1983) also estimated the reliability of VACG scores for the three groups of individuals diagnosed with mental retardation, finding test-retest reliability (time interval not specified) median reliability coefficients (r) estimates of .877, .879, and .842, respectively.

This instrument was developed and initially published at a time (the early 1980s) when community-based supported employment options were utilized on a limited basis by education and rehabilitation programs. When compared to current practices of first placing persons with severe physical and mental impairments in a competitive work environment and then training them in the necessary skills of the work they are to perform, the Vocational Assessment and Curriculum Guide (VACG) appears to hold considerable promise in providing an objective means of assessing an individual's skill and behavior training needs. Also, this instrument can be utilized in monitoring the individual's progress towards training goals designed to remediate skill and behavior deficits of the worker/student. The format of the Vocational Assessment and Curriculum Guide (VACG) manual, VACG inventory, VACG Curriculum Guide, and VACG Summary Profile Sheet are easily understandable and practical. They provide for rapid integration of the assessment information into training and supported employment settings by either professional or paraprofessional staff who have had a short orientation to the materials and who have had some training in at least the basics of behavioral assessment.

However, given the results of the studies that were performed to develop the VACG instrumentation, including its predecessor, and those studies performed by Manchetti (1983) to determine the discrimination power, validity, and reliability of instrumentation, some questions should be raised regarding its applicability to those occupational areas originally included in item formation and norming, and the types of students/trainees with which the materials should be utilized. Concerns include the limited nature of employers surveyed in the initial content determination studies, particularly in that they represent only those industrial and service occupations that are often stereotypic for individuals with disabilities. Skill and behavior expectations of workers entering and capable of maintaining competitive employment should be broadened to include those that employers in a much wider variety of businesses and industries would consider as important. Also, because we have shifted from an assess-train-place approach conducted initially in a segregated setting (e.g., special or vocational special needs classroom, sheltered workshop, day activity center, etc.) to a place-assess-train-support approach in a more natural employment setting for the vocational preparation of individuals with disabilities, assessment and training instruments such as the VACG will need to be modified to accommodate for other entry-level options, such as minimum skills/behaviors that are needed to enter into a supported employment setting with considerable job-coaching support, at differing levels of job-coach support and skill/behavioral interventions, along with the competitive level of employment being identified. Items included in the VACG and similar instruments, as well as their inherent reliability and validity, will need to be reassessed as to their usefulness in addressing the skill/behavior deficits, training needs and goals, and readiness for entry into community-based employment at various levels, for those individuals with physical and mental impairments other than solely those with mental retardation. At this time, the manual and instrumentation for the VACG only mention in passing within the limited discussion of research results, that all research for development of the instrument and its use focused on workers/students who were mentally retarded. Considerable effort should be devoted to refinement of VACG instrumentation for broader application to persons with other physical and mental disabilities, in community-based supported employment programs, and in more diverse business and industry settings. It is also suggested that there be procedures for the development of local norms, useful in cross-validating the outcomes of service delivery programs and those of consumers with disabilities who are or have received placement/training services. Modifications to item content will likely be necessary to accommodate these essential and current practice application needs, but the basic foundation for the development of such skill and behavior assessment and analysis are found in existing instruments such as the VACG. Although this and most other published assessment instruments are guilty of these shortfalls, they continue to offer a more objective basis for development of appropriate employment training and placement opportunities for persons with disabilities than could be achieved with lesser skill and behavior rating methods.

REVIEWER'S REFERENCES

Mithaug, D. E., & Hagmeier, L. D. (1978). The development of procedures to assess prevocational competencies of severely handicapped young adults. *AAESPH Review, 3,* 94–115.

Mithaug, D. D., Mar, D. K., & Stewart, J. E. (1978). The Prevocational Assessment and Curriculum Guide. Seattle, WA: Exceptional Education.

Menchetti, B. (1983). *Assessing the nonsheltered employment survival skills of mentally retarded adults.* Doctoral dissertation, University of Illinois, Champaign, IL.

[357]
Vocational Interest Inventory—Revised.

Purpose: "Measures the relative strength of an individual's interest in eight occupational areas."

Population: High school juniors and seniors.

Publication Dates: 1981–1993.

Acronym: VII-R.

Scores, 8: Service, Business Contact, Organization, Technical, Outdoor, Science, General Culture, Arts and Entertainment.

Administration: Group.

Price Data, 1996: $79.50 per complete kit including manual ('93, 63 pages), 4 test reports and mail-in answer sheets; $45 per manual; $9.80 (or less) per test report; $150 or less per microdisk (IBM; 25 uses).

Time: (20–25) minutes.

Comments: Based on Ann Roe's occupational classifications.

Author: Patricia W. Lunneborg.

Publisher: Western Psychological Services.

Cross References: For reviews by Jo-Ida Hansen and Richard W. Johnson, see 9:1339 (2 references).

TEST REFERENCES

1. Lunneborg, C. E., & Lunneborg, P. W. (1991). Who majors in psychology? *Teaching of Psychology, 18,* 144–148.

2. Tracey, T. J., & Rounds, J. (1994). An examination of the structure of Roe's eight interest fields. *Journal of Vocational Behavior, 44,* 279–296.

Review of the Vocational Interest Inventory— Revised by DAVID O. HERMAN, Associate Education Officer, Office of Educational Research, New York City Board of Education, Brooklyn, NY:

The Vocational Interest Inventory—Revised (VII-R), a forced-choice interest inventory, is designed to help students in the upper high school grades to focus their thinking on college majors and vocations that are consonant with their interest patterns. Scores are produced on eight scales, each corresponding to a broad group of occupations.

The first 56 items present pairs of occupational titles (e.g., Police Chief, Draftsperson), and the student is to indicate the one that would interest him or her more. The second 56 items all offer a choice of two activities (e.g., Baby-sit, Talk people into voting for our schools) of which the respondent chooses the more interesting. All of the items are said to have been written at the 10th grade level, yet one must wonder if most high school students know the nature and duties of some of the jobs (e.g., "theatrical speculator" and "library page"). And surely "hand typesetter" is a vanishing occupation with little general relevance today.

The VII-R items are printed on both sides of a single scannable answer document, and students mark their responses directly on the sheet. (The print is quite small, but should be readily legible for most high school students.) The marked answer document is sent to the publisher for scoring and reporting. The inventory may also be administered on-line to a student seated at a microcomputer; in this case, the necessary scoring and reporting software is available from the publisher. Details of the scoring procedures, such as scoring keys, norms, and the algorithm for selecting interpretive statements are considered proprietary information, and are not available to users.

The computer-produced test report is extensive. It begins with a general introduction and a description of the eight scales, and presents a profile of percentile scores with a special interpretation of those at or above the 75th percentile, including a list of jobs related to the highest score or scores. These job titles are grouped separately according to whether they require only high school graduation or a bachelor's degree or greater. Following is a list of 25 college majors ranked according to the similarity of the student's profile to the mean profiles of people who graduated in those majors. Students who intend to continue their education beyond high school are likely to find this information helpful in their planning.

The two choices offered by each of the 112 items represent different scales. Early versions of the inventory were subjected to several rounds of tryout and revision between 1969 and 1978. The 1978 version is the one in use today. Items were redrafted when necessary to avoid options with extreme endorsement rates (greater than 80% or less than 20%), options that correlated higher with scales other than the one for which they were intended, and options that correlated more than .15 with sex. Thus, the forced-choice format made possible some level of control at the item level for sex bias, and the author felt that separate-sex norms for interpreting raw scores were unnecessary. Yet the strategy was only partly successful, for sex differences still remain on some of the scales; some of the reported mean scores of males and females differ by about one standard deviation.

Norms for the VII-R are based on the performance of more than 27,000 high school juniors and seniors. They were tested in 1987 in the state of Washington, as part of a statewide pre-college testing program. Although very large, the sample has this severe geographic limitation. Sample members intended to obtain more post-high school education than do typical students in the United States (i.e., all but 6% of the sample planned to get at least a 2-year college degree). Although the resulting norms *may* resemble those that would be developed from a representative national sample, the manual contains no evidence that they do. Furthermore, nearly all of the developmental work on the inventory was carried out on similar samples tested in the same state about 20 years ago; if response tendencies are different in other parts of the country, or if they have shifted appreciably over time, not only could the norms be misleading but also the controls for sex bias and for item-endorsement rates could be compromised.

The manual contains internal-consistency estimates of reliability; split-half reliability coefficients range from .40 (Technical) to .80 (Scientific). These statistics reflect not only the homogeneity of the eight scales, but also the validity of the corresponding occupational categories used in developing the inventory—in this case, categories proposed by Anne Roe in the 1950s. Thus, the alpha of the .40 may mean that the author developed the Technical scale inadequately, or that Roe's Technical group is inherently disparate, or both. Six-month retest coefficients are also available, and range from .66 (Technical) to .85 (Scientific).

Several types of validity evidence for the VII-R are reported in the manual. Collectively, the studies show, for example, that both the VII-R scale with the highest score and the entire profile have been found associated with high school students' intended college majors, and with the college majors or vocational/technical programs that they actually chose later on; and that the VII-R scales that correlated highest with scores on Holland's Vocational Preference Inventory and the Strong-Campbell Interest Inventory were generally as predicted. Factorial studies are supportive of the scale's theoretical structure—and of Roe's scheme for organizing occupations. The VII-R is clearly measuring in a domain that is relevant to its stated purpose.

SUMMARY. The Vocational Interest Inventory—Revised appears to have been competently and

conscientiously assembled. The interpretive printout impresses me as thorough and helpful. A great deal of information relevant to validity is reported in the manual.

This review has mentioned a few relatively minor concerns, for example, some isolated items that may mystify high school students, and the low reliability of some scales (which is of less concern with this kind of instrument than with one used for high-stakes selection and placement). The major obstacle to recommending the VII-R for general use, however, is the homogeneous group on which it has been developed and normed—college-bound students in Washington. At the very least, national norms will be essential if the publisher wishes to see the inventory used more widely. In the meantime, other well-developed instruments such as the Vocational Preference Inventory (T4:2910) and the Strong Interest Inventory (12:374) offer very strong competition.

Review of the Vocational Interest Inventory—Revised by JOSEPH G. LAW, JR., Associate Professor of Behavioral Studies and Educational Technology, University of South Alabama, Mobile, AL:

The Vocational Interest Inventory—Revised (VII-R) contains 112 forced-choice items and is designed to help high school students select a college major. Half of the items focus on activities and half on occupational titles. Computerized reports are available that compare the respondent's profile to Anne Roe's eight interest areas. The test items are written at the 10th grade level and the inventory is designed to be both self-administered and interpreted. The manual contains a brief introductory chapter, a chapter on interpretation, a chapter on test development and standardization, and a fourth chapter on technical issues related to reliability and validity.

The VII-R has a number of positive characteristics for the career counselor. At 112 items, it is fairly quickly administered. The one-page (front and back) computer answer sheet is easy to complete. The computer-generated report contains easy-to-read narrative and graphical feedback to the student. One unique feature is the use of same-sex norms. The manual author notes that any item with a phi coefficient greater than +.15 or -.15 with gender was rewritten or removed. Items with endorsements greater than 80% or less than 20% were removed to correct for social desirability. The manual contains numerous tables with data on the norm group as well as case studies to assist in interpretation.

The 1993 edition of the VII-R has the same 112 items as the original edition, although new norms on 27,444 high school students in Washington State were collected in 1987. Stable norms are a plus, but the limited geographical sampling is a weakness. Although 14% of the sample consists of minorities, only 2% were Black—significantly affecting the VII-R's applicability for that population of students. Most students in the norm group planned to complete at least 4 years of college. Only 2% planned to stop with a high school diploma, only 4% to attend vocational/technical school, and 6% to get a 2-year college degree. The VII-R's lack of focus on predicting occupational choice limits its usefulness for counselors who work with clients who are not college-bound.

The 1990 Strong Interest Inventory (SCII; 12:374) is a good benchmark with which to compare the VII-R's psychometric qualities. The median alpha for the SCII Basic Interest Scales was .91 for females, .92 for males, and .90 for both genders on General Occupational Themes (Worthen, 1995). Alpha coefficients ranging from .41 to .80 (median r = .65) for the eight full scales in a study of 670 high school juniors are reported in the manual. The median alpha for split-half reliability was .66. Test-retest correlations between the two instruments are more difficult to compare because of differing intervals. However, the median test-retest correlation of .87 for the SCII over a 3-year period exceeds the median correlation of .76 for the VII-R over a 6-month interval. Correlations between the Vocational Preference Inventory and the VII-R reported in the manual range from .30 to .60 and offer some support to the construct validity of the test.

Unfortunately, the limitations of the VII-R that were noted in its predecessor (Hansen, 1985) are still largely present. The VII-R is based on a limited and nonrepresentative norm group. The 10th grade reading level and emphasis on predictive validity for selecting college majors limits its usefulness with non-college-bound students. Test-retest reliability reported in the manual is limited to a 6-month interval. Its merits include ease of use and interpretation and adherence to Anne Roe's well-known typology. The VII-R's stability and validity do not compare favorably to venerable instruments such as the Strong, but may be a useful tool for college counselors who want an inventory with mixed sex norms based on high functioning students.

REVIEWER'S REFERENCES

Hansen, J. I. (1985). [Review of the Vocational Interest Inventory.] In J. V. Mitchell, Jr. (Ed.), *The ninth mental measurements yearbook* (pp. 1677–1678). Lincoln, NE: Buros Institute of Mental Measurements.
Worthen, B. R., & Sailor, P. (1995). [Review of the Strong Interest Inventory, 4th Edition.] In J. C. Conoley & J. C. Impara (Eds.), *The twelfth mental measurements yearbook* (pp. 999–1002). Lincoln, NE: Buros Institute of Mental Measurements.

[358]
Watson-Glaser Critical Thinking Appraisal, Form S.

Purpose: Designed to help "select employees for any job requiring careful, analytical thinking."
Population: Adults with at least a ninth grade education.
Publication Date: 1994.
Acronym: WGCTA Form S.
Scores: Composite score derived from following content areas: Inference, Recognition of Assumptions, Deduction, Interpretation, Evaluation of Arguments.
Administration: Group.
Price Data, 1995: $38.50 per complete kit including Form S test booklet, answer document, and manual (87 pages); $70 per 25 test booklets; $27 per 25 scannable answer documents; $18 per key for hand scoring scannable answer documents; $35 per manual; $4 per Directions for Administering.
Time: (30–40) minutes.
Comments: Developed as a shorter version of the WGCTA Form A; Form S norms are developed from norms of original WGCTA (T4:2933).
Authors: Goodwin B. Watson and Edward M. Glaser.
Publisher: The Psychological Corporation.
Cross References: For information on the original edition of the WGCTA, see T4:2933; for reviews by Allen Berger and Gerald C. Helmstadter, see 9:1347 (4 references); see also T3:2594 (15 references), 8:822 (49 references), and T2:1775 (35 references); for excerpted reviews by John O. Crites and G. C. Helmstadter, see 7:783 (74 references); see also 6:867 (24 references); for reviews by Walker H. Hill and Carl I. Hovland of an earlier edition, see 5:700 (8 references); for a review by Robert H. Thouless and an excerpted review by Harold P. Fawcett, see 3:544 (3 references).

Review of the Watson-Glaser Critical Thinking Appraisal, Form S by KURT F. GEISINGER, Professor of Psychology and Academic Vice President, LeMoyne College, Syracuse, NY:

The Watson-Glaser Critical Thinking Appraisal (WGCTA) has a long history, has been frequently reviewed (e.g., Berger, 1985; Helmstadter, 1985; Woehlke, 1985) and is used with regularity. A number of forms of the Watson-Glaser Critical Thinking Appraisal (WGCTA) have appeared since the instrument was first published in 1942. Form S represents a short form of Form A of the instrument. Form A is a one-hour examination composed of 80 test items following 16 scenarios, whereas Form S consists of 40 test items and may be given untimed or in 30 minutes. The goal of Form S is to be a shorter, more quickly administered and updated version of the WGCTA. All of the items and almost all of the research supporting the use of Form S was taken from data sets that were based on individuals who had taken Form A. The authors of the manual report that outdated items were eliminated in this form. In that Modjeski and Michael (1983) faulted the measure stating that some items and scenarios were beginning to become a problem with respect to their datedness, this change is indeed appropriate.

The measure is intended for those with at least a ninth grade education. Form S continues to have five subtests: (a) Inference, (b) Recognition of Assumptions, (c) Deduction, (d) Interpretation, and (e) Evaluation of Arguments. Each subtest is separated in the instrument and is based on approximately eight items. The manual for Forms A and B urges users not to use individual subtest scores. The manual for Form S simply states that they should not be used. Certainly, the reliability and validity of these individual scales is such that they should not be used except for the most rudimentary of research. Some of the items are based on emotionally charged scenarios and others involve neutral scenarios, under the premise that emotions may interfere with critical thinking, so to test it most validly, some emotionally charged critical thinking items are needed.

It is stated in the manual that because the test is "intended as a test of power rather than speed, the WGCTA may be given in either timed or untimed administrations" (p. 11). This reviewer was surprised that the manual later suggests that "WGCTA norms are appropriate for both timed and untimed administration" (p. 19), especially in that it would (a) appear that norms were in large measure based upon timed administrations of Form A and (b) the very small pretesting of Form S (N = 42) indicated that some 10% of the sample (N = 4) did not finish responding to the instrument in a 30-minute test period. Furthermore, no indication that the pre-test sample is representative is made. In addition, the manual does not appear to provide any guidance with regard to the nature of those situations that would suggest timed versus untimed test administrations. Analyses indicate that the reading level of the examination was maintained at the ninth grade level.

All of the items are objective questions in which the test taker selects an answer. As such, Form S may be either hand scored or scored using an optical scanner. Scores are raw number correct scores with no adjustment for guessing. The lack of a correction for guessing is somewhat surprising in that

33 of the items, all of the items except for the Inference items, have only two choices. (The Inference items have five choices.) Other scoring issues are reported in the Analytic Information section below.

Norms for 17 groups based upon a total of 4,571 cases are provided. Almost all of these data were collected using Form A and then reanalyzed using those items that survive on Form S. These norm groups include five levels of management and two job areas for managers, two groups in sales and marketing, two groups in banks, two religious groupings (ministers and seminary students), and four specific occupations.

Proper uses of the measure represents an interesting issue. The manual cites uses for employment settings, employment-related training, and career and vocational counseling. Certainly, with the offering of many college-level classes stressing critical thinking, the measure is used in educational evaluations, needs assessments, and for educational research with some regularity. Most of the validation studies that are reported in the manual are correlational studies performed in educational settings, most typically with grade-point average or grades in individual courses as the criterion. Results of other studies that correlate the measure with other tests, generally tests of intelligence and other general cognitive skills, are also provided.

ANALYTIC INFORMATION. The authors of the manual report that they had five primary goals in selecting items from Form A for Form S (p. 25). These include: maintaining the five-subtest structure and the scenario-based format, selecting psychometrically sound scenarios and items, continuing test reliability, sustaining the reading level of the examination, and enhancing the currency of the test. The publisher appears to have succeeded in meeting these criteria in the process.

Scores are reported in 23 bands. It is not surprising, given that the majority of the items have only two options, that score distribution appears quite skewed. There are 41 possible scores (from 0–40), yet the fifth percentile for either Clergy or Mid-level Management applicants is a score of 27 correct. For most other groups, the fifth percentile ranges from 23–25. Thus, 95% of the norm group is spaced over only approximately 15 score points. This restriction in range of most of the responses is yet more problematic when considered with regard to the standard error of measurement. No norming information is available depending upon the sex, ethnicity, or language of the test takers.

The internal consistency reliability (coefficient alpha) of the measure was .81, down from the corresponding value for Form A. Coefficient alpha reliability coefficients for 21 groupings are provided in the manual (p. 34). Coefficient alphas within specific groups, where the variability of ability levels is more limited, is likely to reduce the apparent reliability of the measure. The numbers of individuals in each group ranges from 23–909, and the median reliability coefficient is .76. This degree of reliability is probably acceptable, even for a personnel selection measure, assuming that the measure is used in consort with other measures. It should not be used alone to make such decisions. A test-retest reliability analysis was performed using a small sample of 42 with a 2-week period intervening between testings. A reliability coefficient of .81 resulted from this analysis.

Standard errors of measurement vary by group ranging from 2.05 to around 2.3 raw score points. Given the relative paucity of test scores at the lower end of the distribution, when we look at the range within which one would likely score if one took the test again, the percentile rank interpretation becomes quite difficult. For example, consider an Executive Management applicant whose raw score of 34 places her at the 60th percentile rank. If this individual takes the test again, about 68% of the time, her score would fall between 31.8 and 36.2, ranging between the percentile ranks of approximately 33 and 86, respectively. To be 95% certain of the individual's score, the range of scores is from 29.7 to 38.3, with associated percentile ranks of approximately 19 and 99, respectively. This huge amount of uncertainty is frankly unacceptable. The instrument would appear therefore incapable of making fine score distinctions reliability. Similarly, within some norm groups, answering a single additional question correct can have a significant impact on a score. Consider an applicant for a Lower to Upper-Level Management position whose score is 33 (equivalent to the 55th percentile rank). Should this individual have answered a single additional question correct, his score would have become 34, with an associated percentile rank at the 70th percentile.

One source of validation information concerns the relationship between this measure and the longer form from which it was created. Part-whole correlations were computed between Form S and Form A, from which it came. These analyses were performed using data from a single administration of Form A. Form S scores were computed from these data, as were Form A scores. This "part-whole correlation" represents an overestimate of independent correlations (based upon an alternate-forms analysis with two separate test administrations). The correlation that emerged (based upon the sample of 3,727) was a .96.

One of the strengths of the WGCTA and its manual is the voluminous amount of research that has been performed with the measure. The results of many validation studies are presented in tables in the manual, and still others are referenced in the manual. Tables presenting dozens of validity coefficients are presented. Most if not all of these correlations are based upon the use of earlier forms of the WGCTA, not Form S. These coefficients exhibit a pattern that suggests the measure appears to be a valid measure of cognitive skills. The publisher wisely advises users to perform local validation studies.

Additional information pertaining to the construct validity of the measure is provided in the manual. Students who are further along in their educational paths do better on the exam. Likewise, considerable evidence is provided that scores are positively affected by instructional experiences such as critical thinking classes and laboratory-centered science classes.

The test publisher neither reports on item selection activities related to removing biased items from the examination, if any, nor on score differences across racial or ethnic groups. This reviewer would certainly prefer to see such information.

AN EVALUATION OF THIS INSTRUMENT. Modjeski and Michael found this measure to be one of the finest measures of critical thinking available. Since the time of their work, however, considerable work in critical thinking has transpired (e.g., Halpern, 1966; Moore & Parker, 1992) and critical thinking has become, especially in higher education, one of the primary concerns in general education programs. The WGCTA measure comes with a long history of successful use in instructional and evaluation research in such programs and courses. The validation evidence for Forms A, B, and previous forms presented in the manual is quite impressive. The evidence of the results of its use in industry is more limited.

This short form does appear to continue to represent the long history of the Watson-Glaser Critical Thinking Appraisal successfully. It is sufficiently reliable and should be expected to be approximately as valid as one would expect given the shorter length. Standard formulae exist for estimating the reductions in criterion-related validation coefficients based on the reduction in reliability associated with the shortening of the form. (See, for example, Magnusson, 1966, p. 151.)

That 33 of 40 items are essentially two-option multiple-choice items is certainly problematic. Two overall reliability coefficients were both found to be .81 (internal consistency and test-retest), but reliability coefficients within specific groups are likely to be reduced. Use of Form S in individual decision making is limited by this marginally acceptable reliability, although the form could certainly be used effectively in conjunction with other measures. Its shortened administration time makes it perhaps more useful in such batteries.

Perhaps the biggest issue faced by the measure relates to its distribution, as noted above. The publishers should attend to this apparent problem. However, it is not clear whether the same issues have been present in previous, longer versions of the instrument. If so, they have not been mentioned heretofore in the literature and they have not impeded the validity of the longer forms of the measure, which have been rather impressive. Additional research (and recommendations for users) is also needed with respect to the untimed administration.

The evaluation of any shortened version of a well-established measure will depend on the extent to which users find it beneficial. The advantages as well as any special disadvantages need to be assessed. It should be clear, for example, that subtest scores should not be used. The measure is nevertheless likely to attract a following given its relatively quick administration time and the long, successful history of the measure.

REVIEWER'S REFERENCES

Magnusson, D. (1966). *Test theory.* Reading, MA: Addison-Wesley.

Modjeski, R. B., & Michael, W. B. (1983). An evaluation by a panel of psychologists of the reliability and validity of two tests of critical thinking. *Educational and Psychological Measurement, 43,* 1187–1197.

Berger, A. (1985). [Review of the Watson-Glaser Critical Thinking Appraisal]. In J. V. Mitchell, Jr. (Ed.), *The ninth mental measurements yearbook* (pp. 1692–1693). Lincoln, NE: Buros Institute of Mental Measurements.

Helmstadter, G. C. (1985). [Review of the Watson-Glaser Critical Thinking Appraisal]. In J. V. Mitchell, Jr. (Ed.), *The ninth mental measurements yearbook* (PP. 1693–1694). Lincoln, NE: Buros Institute of Mental Measurements.

Woehlke, P. L. (1985). [Review of Watson-Glaser Critical Thinking Appraisal]. In D. J. Keyser & R. C. Swetland (Eds.), *Test critiques* (vol. 3) (pp. 682–685). Kansas City, MO: Test Corporation of America.

Moore, B. N., & Parker, R. (1992). *Critical thinking* (3rd ed.). Mountain View, CA: Mayfield.

Halpern, D. F. (1996). *Thought & knowledge: An introduction to critical thinking* (3rd ed.). Mahwah, NJ: Lawrence Erlbaum.

Review of the Watson-Glaser Critical Thinking Appraisal, Form S by STEPHEN H. IVENS, Vice President, Research & Development, Touchstone Applied Science Associates, Brewster, NY:

Form S of the Watson-Glaser Critical Thinking Appraisal (WGCTA), derived from the longer Form A published in 1980, is a measure of critical thinking designed for use with adults in a variety of settings from predicting performance in educational and/or training programs to selection for employment. Prospective users of this instrument need to first understand how the publisher defines critical thinking and then how this definition gets translated into an operational test form. The discussion of critical thinking in the manual is brief, but sufficient to provide a context for potential users to evaluate the utility of the instrument.

The WGCTA, Form S, is composed of five subtests: Inference, Recognition of Assumptions, Deduction, Interpretation, and Evaluation of Arguments. Each subtest of Form S consists of reading passages followed by a series of exercises. The reading passages are classified as neutral or controversial. Neutral selections are those for which people typically do not hold strong opinions, whereas controversial topics are those that tend to evoke strong feelings. With the exception of the Inference subtest, which uses five-option, multiple-choice items, the subtests employ two-option, multiple-choice items. Given the number of items on each of these subtests, the publisher correctly notes that only the composite score should be used as a reliable measure of critical thinking.

There is some confusion regarding whether Form S is to be administered as a timed or untimed test. The manual states that Form S can be given in either timed or untimed administrations. As a timed test, the manual indicates the time limit should be "based on the amount of working time required to finish the test by the majority of examinees in test tryouts" (p. 11). Users, however, are not provided with this information. In the directions for administration, a time limit of 30 minutes is given. The normative data presented for specific reference groups of test takers do not indicate whether the data were obtained under timed or untimed administrations. Given this ambiguity, it is hard to understand why anyone would administer the test under timed conditions.

Reference group normative data are available for employees in a variety of settings. Although such data may serve as a guide for prospective users of the instruments, the publisher correctly notes that such data are of limited usefulness and that local norms should be established whenever possible.

Information to help test takers understand the instrument and become familiar with the directions and format of the test are not available.

The manual reports internal consistency coefficients (Cronbach's alpha) generally in the mid .70s to low .80s. These are acceptable as long as the instrument is used as one component in a more complex employee selection process. Equivalence between Form S and the longer Form A, from which Form S was derived, is acceptable. Evidence of validity for Form S is primarily limited to predictive validity studies involving college and graduate students. Limited information is provided regarding the validity of the instrument as an employee selection tool. This is not a particularly serious problem, however, because the responsibility for assessing the utility and validity of the instrument for a particular purpose ultimately has to reside with the user.

Form S of the Watson-Glaser Critical Thinking Appraisal is a short, practical measure of critical thinking. Prospective users should opt for the longer forms of the instrument, however, if testing time is not a constraint.

[359]
Wechsler Individual Achievement Test.

Purpose: For assessing educational achievement of children and adolescents.
Population: Ages 5–19.
Publication Date: 1992.
Acronym: WIAT.
Administration: Individual.
Comments: Standardized with Wechsler Intelligence Scale for Children—III (12:412).
Author: The Psychological Corporation.
Publisher: The Psychological Corporation.
  a) WIAT SCREENER.
  Scores, 4: Basic Reading, Mathematics Reading, Spelling, Screener Composite.
  Price Data, 1994: $80 per complete WIAT Screener kit including 25 record forms, stimulus booklet 1, and screener manual; $27 per 25 record forms; $27 per screener manual; $59 per stimulus booklet 1.
  Time: (10–18) minutes.
  b) WIAT.
  Scores, 13: Basic Reading, Reading Comprehension, Total Reading, Mathematics Reasoning, Numerical Operations, Total Mathematics, Listening Comprehension, Oral Expression, Total Language, Spelling, Written Expression, Total Writing, Total Composite.
  Price Data: $198 per complete WIAT kit including 25 WIAT record forms, 5 screener record forms, 25 response booklets, stimulus booklet 1, stimulus booklet 2, and manual (387 pages); $29.50 per 25 record forms; $10.50 per 25 response booklets; $59 per stimulus booklet 1, $85.50 per stimulus booklet 2; $43 per manual.
  Time: (30–75) minutes.

TEST REFERENCES

1. Berninger, V. W., & Hooper, S. R. (1993). Preventing and remediating writing disabilities: Interdisciplinary frameworks for assessment, consultation, and intervention. *School Psychology Review, 22*, 590-594.

2. Cotugno, A. J. (1993). The diagnosis of Attention Deficit Hyperactivity Disorder (ADHD) in community mental health centers: Where and when. *Psychology in the Schools, 30*, 338-344.

3. Flanagan, D. P., & Alfonso, V. C. (1993). Differences required for significance between Wechsler verbal and performance IQs and WIAT subtests and composites: The predicted achievement method. *Psychology in the Schools, 30*, 125-132.

4. Flanagan, D. P., & Alfonso, V. C. (1993). WIAT subtest and composite-predicted-achievement values based on WISC-III verbal and performance IQs. *Psychology in the Schools, 30*, 310-320.

5. Glutting, J. J., McDermott, P. A., Prifitera, A., & McGrath, E. A. (1994). Core profile types for the WISC-III and WIAT: Their development and application in identifying multivariate IQ-achievement discrepancies. *School Psychology Review, 23*, 619–639.

6. Slate, J. R. (1994). WISC-III correlations with the WIAT. *Psychology in the Schools, 31*, 278-285.

7. Aaron, P. G. (1995). Differential diagnosis of reading disabilities. *School Psychology Review, 24*, 345–360.

8. Felton, R. H., & Pepper, P. P. (1995). Early identification and intervention of phonological deficits in kindergarten and early elementary children at risk for reading disability. *School Psychology Review, 24*, 405–414.

9. Gentry, N., Sapp, G. L., & Daw, J. L. (1995). Scores on the Wechsler Individual Achievement Test and the Kaufman Test of Educational Achievement—Comprehensive Form for emotionally conflicted adolescents. *Psychological Reports, 76*, 607-610.

10. Joshi, R. M. (1995). Assessing reading and spelling skills. *School Psychology Review, 24*, 361–375.

11. Ricard, R. J., Miller, G. A., & Heffer, R. W. (1995). Developmental trends in the relation between adjustment and academic achievement for elementary school children in mixed-age classrooms. *School Psychology Review, 24*, 258–270.

12. Schuerholz, L. J., Harris, E. L., Baumgardner, T. L., Reiss, A. L., Freund, L. S., Church, R. P., Mohr, J., & Denckla, M. B. (1995). An analysis of two discrepancy-based models and a processing-deficit approach in identifying learning disabilities. *Journal of Learning Disabilities, 28*, 18–29.

13. Sullivan, G. S., Mastropieri, M. A., & Scruggs, T. E. (1995). Reasoning and remembering: Coaching students with learning disabilities to think. *The Journal of Special Education, 28*, 310–322.

14. Weiss, L. G., & Prifitera, A. (1995). An evaluation of differential prediction of WIAT achievement scores from WISC-III FSIQ across ethnic and gender groups. *Journal of School Psychology, 33*, 297–304.

15. Berninger, V., Whitaker, D., Feng, Y., Swanson, H. L., & Abbott, R. D. (1996). Assessment of planning, translating, and revising in junior high writers. *Journal of School Psychology, 34*, 23–52.

16. Donders, J. (1996). Cluster subtypes in the WISC-III standardization sample: Analysis of factor index scores. *Psychological Assessment, 8*, 312–318.

17. Webster, R. E., Hall, C. W., Brown, M. B., & Bolen, L. M. (1996). Memory modality differences in children with Attention Deficit Hyperactive Disorder with and without learning disabilities. *Psychology in the Schools, 33*, 193–201.

Review of the Wechsler Individual Achievement Test by TERRY ACKERMAN, Associate Professor, Department of Educational Psychology, University of Illinois, Champaign, IL:

PURPOSE. This test is intended to be a comprehensive individually administered achievement battery. It is designed for grades K through 12 or ages 5 years, 0 months to 19 years, 11 months. It is particularly suited to investigate ability-achievement discrepancies in children aged 6 to 16. The Wechsler Individual Achievement Test (WIAT) was purposively designed to be a highly reliable achievement test that is specific to educational curriculum trends and instructional objectives, that parallels areas in which a child could be identified as learning disabled, and that provides a link to IQ test scales.

The WIAT is composed of eight subtests: Basic Reading (covers picture recognition, vocabulary, and word reading ability; 55 items), Spelling (requires subjects to spell dictated words; 50 items), Reading Comprehension (requires subjects to read a passage, listen to questions and respond orally; 38

items), Mathematics Reasoning (presents items orally, though some include visual stimuli, and the subject responds orally; 50 items), Numerical operations (includes 10 sets of four simple algebraic equations, which subjects must solve manually; 40 items), Listening Comprehension (requires subjects to read a passage that accompanies a figure and then respond to questions orally; 36 items), Oral Expression (requires subjects to define words and orally describe a scene; 16 items), and Written Expression (requires subjects to respond to an essay prompt for 15 minutes). Subtests are best used collectively rather than individually.

The WIAT is the only achievement test that can be directly linked to the Wechsler IQ tests, namely the Wechsler Intelligence Scale for Children—Third Edition (WISC-III; 12:412), the Wechsler Preschool and Primary Scale of Intelligence—Revised (WPPSI-R; T4:2941), and the Wechsler Adult Intelligence Scale—Revised (WAIS-R; T4:2937). The test also provides comprehensive coverage for learning-disabled children following the guidelines suggested by PL 94-142.

The test is designed to be used primarily in school clinics or residential treatment settings. WIAT scores should be used in concert with other relevant information to make recommendations for placement and classification decisions and the diagnosis and treatment of children. Practitioners are strongly cautioned not to base decisions solely upon the WIAT scores but within the context of the total history of the child. In the technical manual a warning is also given not to use the results as a measure of giftedness in adolescents (p. 7), despite the fact that an example is shown for using the WIAT test to determine academic giftedness for a child (technical manual, p. 31).

ADMINISTRATION DIRECTIONS. For each subtest explicit directions for administering, recording answers, and scoring are furnished. These include starting points for different grade levels, a reverse rule in case a suggested starting point is too difficult for a child, and a discontinue rule, indicating when a subtest should be terminated. For the Listening Comprehension and the Oral Expression subtests, examples of correct and incorrect responses are supplied to guide the examiner.

Test administrators of the WIAT should have graduate school training in individually administered assessment instruments. Practice is recommended so as to be sufficiently familiar with them during an actual administration, although no formal training is required. Explicit administration directions and diagrams showing the positions of the examinee and the examiner, as well as the set-up of the test materials are provided. Ideally, the test should be administered in a classroom or school office.

Administration times for the entire complement of tests vary. For grades K–2 the testing time ranges from 30–50 minutes, and for grades 3–12 the time ranges from 55–60 minutes. A screening subsection of the test involving only the Basic Reading, the Mathematics Reasoning, and the Spelling subtests can be administered in 10 minutes to students in kindergarten and in 15–18 minutes for students in grades 1–12.

SCORING. Explicit scoring guides are furnished for each subtest. All subtests are dichotomously scored, (0 = incorrect, 1 = correct) except for the Written Expression subtest, which is scored on a 1–4 Likert type scale. Results can be expressed on any one of five different types of score scales: a standard score scale ($M = 100$, $SD = 15$); a percentile rank (by age and by grade); age and grade equivalent scores; normal curve equivalent (NCE) scores ($M = 50$, $SD = 21.06$); and stanine scores.

In the Written Expression subtest directions are presented for both analytic and holistic scoring. The authors give an excellent, lucid description of how to score this section properly. For each score type, scoring rubrics and actual writing examples with corresponding annotated scores are provided. However, standard scores and normative information are provided only for the analytic scoring.

Oftentimes school personnel need to know if there is a significant difference between the scores from different content areas. Statistical techniques to determine if there is a significant difference between a single subtest score and an average of subtest scores or between subtest scores are described and corresponding tables are provided in the appendix of the technical manual. It is here that the authors of the technical manual use the terms *significance* and *confidence* interchangeably. Statistically, however, the two terms have quite different meanings and are not synonymous. The authors write about differences at the .05 and .15 levels of "confidence" (pp. 146, 147, 363) when in reality they mean levels of significance. Not only is this a miswording, but rarely if ever is the .15 level of significance used in tests of statistical significance; nominal levels are usually .05 or the more conservative approach of .01.

RELIABILITY. Several different types of reliability coefficients are presented in the technical manual. To measure internal consistency, split-half reliability estimates were computed. Unfortunately the technical manual does not indicate what the halves were (e.g., odd vs. even, first half vs. second half). Perhaps a better approach would have been to compute coefficient alpha, which is the mean of all possible split-half coefficients. Their coefficients and the corresponding standard error of measurement are given for each age group (5–17 years) and for each grade level (K–12) (for Fall and Spring testings) for each subtest and each composite. The coefficients for the most part are quite high, ranging from .59 (Basic Reading, Kindergarten, Fall) to .94 (Basic Reading for Grades 2, Fall, and Grades 1–3, Spring). The reliabilities tend to be higher for the Spring testing than for the Fall testing. This is understandable because of the effect of instruction.

Test-retest stability coefficients were computed for a sample of 367 students drawn from five grades (1, 3, 5, 8 and 10) from the standardization sample. The median interval between the two test administrations was 17 days. Means and standard deviations are reported for each subtest and composites, for each grade, for each administration. Results are quite consistent. Coefficients averaged across grades range from .76 (Listening Comprehension) to .94 (Basic Reading and Spelling). Oral Expression has the lowest stability coefficients, ranging from .49 (grade 10) to .79 (grade 1). For the most part the coefficients tended to range from the mid .80s to the low .90s.

For tests that require scorer judgment (Reading Comprehension, Listening Comprehension, Oral Expression, and Written Expression), interscorer agreement was examined. In two separate studies, 50 protocols (15 from K–3; 17 from grades 4–7, and 18 from 8–12) were randomly selected from the standardization sample. The ratings of four scorers on all of these subtests were analyzed. The first study examined the dichotomously scored subtests (Reading Comprehension and Listening Comprehension); the average of the six possible pairs was .98. In the second study the multipoint criteria scoring of the Oral and Written Expression subtests were inspected. Intraclass correlations ranged from .79 (Prompt 2, Written Expression) to .93 (Oral Expression).

NORMS. The effort to obtain a representative sample of the U.S. population is to be lauded. The sample consisted of 4,252 children, ages 5 to 19, enrolled in kindergarten through grade 12. The sample consisted of an approximately equal number of males (2,092) and females (2,160). The percent-ages by race/ethnicity, by geographic region, and by parent educational level match those of the 1988 U.S. Census very closely. Complete standardization information is provided in the technical manual.

VALIDITY. Two different measures of content validity are supplied: one empirical, a content analysis, and one nonempirical, an item analysis. The WIAT developers went to great lengths to make use of curriculum experts in reading, mathematics, speech, and language arts. The test specifications including content, item format, and subtest designs paralleled those used for the 1992 Stanford Achievement Test Series—Eighth Edition. Care was given to match curriculum objectives at each grade level. Detailed descriptions of the item content are provided for each subtest by grade level.

Item analyses information for both the tryout and standardization samples is discussed but details are not given. Item response theory analyses using the one-parameter Rasch model (which assumes items only differ in difficulty) were conducted; however, no rationale for this particular model versus the two-parameter model (which assumes items differ in both difficulty and discrimination) or detail of the IRT analysis is presented. It would have been interesting to employ the IRT information function to examine where along the ability scale each test is best measuring ability.

Items were checked substantively and statistically for differential item functioning (DIF) to insure that there is no bias favoring either gender or any ethnic groups(s). No details about the statistical procedures are provided, leaving this analysis suspect. Standard procedures that are commonly used such as the Mantel-Haenszel (Holland & Thayer, 1988) or SIBTEST (Shealy & Stout, 1993) were not used. This is unfortunate because SIBTEST will enable one to examine not only item-level DIF but also the collective effect of items of a particular type.

Evidence of construct validity is also provided. These include intercorrelations among the subtests, correlation with various Wechsler IQ tests (WPPSI-R, WISC-III, and the WAIS-R), and patterns of increasing scores with age and grade level that are commonly observed in quality standardized achievement tests. Multitrait-multimethod validity was also considered using scores from students who had taken both the WIAT and the Stanford Achievement Test, Seventh Edition Plus (SAT7+; Gardner et al., 1987), or the WIAT and the Iowa Test of Basic Skills, Form G, (ITBS-G; Hieronymous, Hoover, &

Lindquist, 1986), or the WIAT and the California Achievement Test, Form E (CAT-E; CTB Macmillan/McGraw-Hill, 1988). Correlations between pairs of scores measuring the same construct across the test batteries provide evidence of convergent validity.

Criterion-related evidence is presented by correlating results between the WIAT and scores on other achievement tests (both group and individually administered), school grades, and diagnosed classifications such as gifted, mentally retarded, and learning disabled. Individually administered achievement test results that were correlated with the WIAT include the Basic Achievement Skills Individual Screener (BASIS; The Psychological Corporation, 1983) (rs ranged from .75 to .90 for grades 3 and 8); the Woodcock-Johnson Psycho-Educational Battery—Revised, Tests of Achievement (WJ-R; Woodcock & Johnson, 1989) (rs ranged from .68 to .88); the Wide Range Achievement Test—Revised (WRAT-R; Jastak & Wilkinson, 1984) (rs ranged from .69 to .87); the Kaufman Test of Educational Achievement (K-TEA; Kaufman & Kaufman, 1985) (rs ranged from .73 to .87); the Differential Ability Scales (DAS; Elliott, 1990) (rs ranged from .42 to .86); and the Peabody Picture Vocabulary Test—Revised (PPVT-R; Dunn & Dunn, 1981) (rs ranged from .68 to .75).

For group-administered achievement tests three areas were correlated including reading, mathematics, and spelling. For similar content areas WIAT results were correlated with the SAT7+E/F, the ITBS-GH/J, the CAT-E/F, the Comprehensive Test of Basic Skills, Forms U and V (CTBS-U/V) or the CTBS/4 (CTB Macmillan/McGraw-Hill, 1989), the SAT8-J/K, and the Metropolitan Achievement Test, Sixth Edition, Form L/M (MAT6-L/M; Prescott, Balow, Hogan, & Farr, 1985).

Overall, the WIAT tends to correlate moderately high (.70s to .80s) with the established individually administered achievement tests and less well (.50s to .70s) with established group administered achievement tests.

Several studies were conducted with special populations, specifically the gifted, the mentally retarded, the emotionally disturbed, children with learning disabilities, children with attention-deficit hyperactivity disorder, and children who are hearing impaired. A special version implementing the American Sign Language was created for this last group. Also, a sample of 93 students ranging in age from 7–

17 and classified as gifted (using both achievement tests—such as the CTBS/4, the ITBS, and the WISC-III FSIQ—and parental/teacher evaluations) was administered the WIAT. Results and implications are discussed in the technical manual.

SUMMARY COMMENTS. The WIAT appears to be a quality instrument. The content coverage and scoring guides are well thought out. The links that have been made with other traditional achievement tests should help practitioners anchor the WIAT within the myriad of standardized achievement tests. It also has strong ties with established IQ scales and thus provides a means for researchers to further explore the relationship between aptitude and achievement. However, given that the WIAT is relatively new, empirical evidence supporting its effectiveness needs to be gathered.

REVIEWER'S REFERENCES
Dunn, L. M., & Dunn, L. M. (1981). Peabody Picture Vocabulary Test—Revised. Circle Pines, MN: American Guidance Service.
The Psychological Corporation. (1983). Basic Achievement Skills Individual Screener. San Antonio, TX: Author.
Jastak, S., & Wilkinson, G. S. (1984). Wide Range Achievement Test—Revised. Wilmington, DE: Jastak Associates.
Kaufman, A. S., & Kaufman, N. L. (1985). Kaufman Test of Educational Achievement. Circle Pines, MN: American Guidance Service.
Prescott, G. A., Balow, I. H., Hogan, T. P., & Farr, R. C. (1985). Metropolitan Achievement Test, Sixth Edition. San Antonio, TX: The Psychological Corporation.
Hieronymus, A. N., Hoover, H. D., & Lindquist, E. F. (1986). Iowa Test of Basic Skills, Forms G and H. Chicago: The Riverside Publishing Company.
Gardner, E. F., Madden, R., Rudman, H. C., Karlsen, B., Merwin, J. C., Callis, R., & Collins, C. S. (1987). Stanford Achievement Test, Seventh Edition Plus. San Antonio, TX: The Psychological Corporation.
CTB Macmillan/McGraw-Hill. (1988). California Achievement Tests, Forms E and F. Monterey, CA: Author.
Holland, P. W., & Thayer, D. T. (1988). Differential item functioning and the Mantel-Haenszel procedure. In P. W. Holland & H. Wainer (Eds.), Differential item functioning: Theory and practice (pp. 129–145). Hillsdale, NJ: Lawrence Erlbaum.
CTB Macmillan/McGraw-Hill. (1989). Comprehensive Tests of Basic Skills/4. Monterey, CA: Author.
Woodcock, R. W., & Johnson, M. B. (1989). Woodcock-Johnson Psycho-Educational Battery—Revised, Tests of Achievement. Allen, TX: DLM Teaching Resources
Elliott, C. D. (1990). Differential Ability Scales: Introductory and technical handbook. San Antonio, TX: The Psychological Corporation.
Shealy, R., & Stout, W. F. (1993). An item response theory model for test bias and differential test functioning. In P. W. Holland & H. Wainer (Eds.), Differential item functioning: Theory and practice (pp. 197–239). Hillsdale, NJ: Lawrence Erlbaum.

Review of the Wechsler Individual Achievement Test by STEVEN FERRARA, Director of Research and Psychometrics, Center for Educational Assessment, American Institutes for Research, Washington, DC:

Although it is not explicitly stated in the user's manual, one of the main focuses for the design and development of the Wechsler Individual Achievement Test (WIAT) is to meet requirements in the 1977 federal law PL 94-142, "Education for All Handicapped Children Act," for determining if a school age child has a specific learning disability. The WIAT can be used with the Wechsler intelligence scales to determine if a child demonstrates a severe discrepancy between achievement and intellectual ability in several areas related to learning and functioning in schools. Currently, some theorists, researchers, and practitioners express dissatisfaction with this approach to determining the presence of a specific learning disability. They cite two concerns with this approach: (a) It provides only a broad indication of areas of relative strength and weaknesses and little information to guide design of instruction; and (b) it tends to overlook the largest disability category, children with average and above IQs but with reading disabilities that may have been initially manifested as phonological problems (Lyon, 1996). Unless regulations for re-authorization of federal special education law changes this diagnostic criterion for determining the presence of a specific learning disability, psychoeducational batteries like the WIAT-Wechsler intelligence scale combination will continue to be widely used.

INTENDED USES, USERS, AND TARGET EXAMINEES. The WIAT is explicitly intended for assessing the educational achievement of children in kindergarten through grade 12. The WIAT, used by itself provides norm-referenced educational achievement scores. It can also be used, as stated throughout the manual, for meeting requirements of PL 94-142 because it provides ability-achievement discrepancy scores when used with one of the Wechsler (or other) intelligence scales and because the WIAT subtests parallel exactly the educational achievement areas in which discrepancies are expected to occur in learning disabled children, according to the law. It is also explicitly *not* designed as a measure of academic giftedness in adolescents (manual, p. 7). The publisher permits use of the WIAT by professionals involved in educational or psychological testing with graduate level training in the use of individually administered assessment instruments.

DESIGN, DEVELOPMENT PROCEDURES, AND CONTENT COVERAGE. Based on descriptions in the manual, the authors of the WIAT have followed standard procedures for test design and development, item try-out and selection (including item "bias" analyses), and standardization and norming. The framework for the WIAT's eight subtests is provided by the content areas specified in PL 94-142. These subtests represent both traditional and unique features for an educational achievement battery. The Reading Composite score includes two subtests: Basic Reading (e.g., examinee

matches words to pictures or pronounces printed words) and Reading Comprehension (i.e., examinee orally answers comprehension questions). The Mathematics Composite score includes two subtests: Numerical Operations (i.e., examinee performs arithmetic computations) and Mathematics Reasoning (e.g., examinee solves word problems related to money, time, numerical order, graphs). The Language Composite score includes the Listening Comprehension (i.e., examiner reads a word or passage, examinee identifies a corresponding picture or answers comprehension questions) and Oral Expression (e.g., examiner provides a definition corresponding to an illustration, examinee provides a word; examinee describes objects in an illustration) subtest scores. Finally, the Writing Composite score includes two subtests: Spelling (i.e., examinee writes a letter or word) and Written Expression (i.e., examinee writes an essay in response to a prompt).

On the positive side, the WIAT subtest design reflects some modern views of educational achievement and some preferred approaches to assessing achievement. For example, in the spelling test examinees write dictated words rather than point to the correct spelling, and writing is assessed directly (i.e., via an essay rather than through multiple-choice items). In addition, the WIAT assesses all four facets of literacy and communication (i.e., reading, writing, speaking, and listening). On the negative side, however, the publisher's claims regarding a match between what is tested in the WIAT and "curriculum elements found in school instructional programs" (manual, p. 2) is weak. For example, the Basic Reading subtest requires examinees to pronounce given words but does not directly assess phonics and other word attack skills, a necessary part of instruction for all young children and often a major weakness for students with learning disabilities. Also, reading difficulty in the Reading Comprehension subtest is often manipulated by the use of "big words" (e.g., "concatenation") and esoteric concepts (e.g., a literary "trope") rather than by the sources of reading difficulty in typical school texts (e.g., amount of prior knowledge required by a reading assignment); the Numerical Operations subtest includes no division with remainders, even though it includes some simple algebra items; and many of the Mathematics Reasoning subtests contain only simple, one-step problems. Naturally, any test designed to be administered in 60–75 minutes would be constrained in coverage of school curricula. However, the narrowness of the educational achievement constructs represented by these subtests limits the usefulness of the WIAT for instructional planning.

TEST ADMINISTRATION, ITEM SCORING, AND EASE OF USE. The examiner displays the WIAT test materials to the examinee in easy-to-use table top easels. The materials are bright and attractive and scripted directions to examinees and written administration directions to examiners are clear and simple. Although the WIAT can be administered in a short time, users should consider the additional administration time for the Wechsler intelligence scales (50–90 minutes). As is the case for other individual screening and achievement tests, scoring examinee responses is an important consideration in relation to time, cost, and accuracy. The more open-ended Written and Oral Expression and Reading and Listening Comprehension subtests probably are the most time-consuming and difficult to score accurately. The scoring guide for the Written Expression subtest does not provide sufficient support to ensure accurate scoring (e.g., a training protocol and scoring accuracy tests), especially compared to large scale essay examination programs. Scoring of examinee responses in the other, less open-ended subtests is more straightforward but still requires time and effort for accurate scoring.

NORMING. Two standardization samples and norming procedures are important for valid interpretations from an instrument like the WIAT: the sample on which normative scores are based and the "linking" sample on which the ability-achievement discrepancy scores are based. Users can interpret WIAT scores with reasonable confidence as long as they keep in mind minor limitations of the standardization samples. In general, the national norming sample is reasonably large, compared to other nationally normed individual achievement tests, and reasonably representative. The sampling frame and procedures resulted in final norming sample demographics that match 1988 U.S. Census demographics reasonably well after case weighting, although the number of examinees in the South seems a bit high and the number in the Northeast seems a bit low. Information about participation and replacement of schools and students is not provided and no final sample information about numbers of students in urban, suburban, and rural areas is provided. Because 4,252 examinees comprise the final total norming sample, on average 250–350 examinees comprise each age/grade subgroup. Of particular note, 5% of the U.S. public school population is identified as learning disabled (Lyon, 1996), and 6% of the norming sample is identified as learning disabled or with speech/language, emotional, or physical disabilities. An additional 1.4% of the norming sample is identified as mildly mentally retarded.

WIAT ability-achievement discrepancy scores are based on linking samples that were administered both the WIAT and the appropriate Wechsler intelligence test by trained examiners. The linking samples include 1,284 examinees, or on average approximately 100 per age group for the WIAT/WISC-III/WAIS-R linking samples for ages 6–16, plus 84 5-year-olds in the WIAT/WPPSI-R, sample and 82 examinees ages 17–19 years in the WIAT/WAIS-R sample. Although these numbers are reasonable for the regression analyses used to create the predicted achievement scores (but marginal for ages 5 and 17–19), no regression accuracy information is given (i.e., standard error of estimate, R-square, description of residual plots). Overall, the linking sample matches 1988 U.S. Census demographics reasonably well. The publisher adjusted the linking sample mean IQ scores to approximately 100 (i.e., the Wechsler scale means), but does not indicate whether similar adjustments were made to standard deviations. The publisher provides no information on percentages of learning disabled students in the linking samples.

EVIDENCE FOR SCORE VALIDITY. Score reliability evidence for the WIAT is incomplete but positive. As would be expected for a commercially produced achievement test, most of the age- and grade-based internal consistency (i.e., split-half) coefficients for composite scores are .88 or higher. Also of note, most subtest coefficients are in the .70–.90 range, age-based coefficients tend to be higher than grade-based coefficients, grade-based coefficients are higher in spring than in fall, and kindergarten and Written Expression coefficients are lowest. Internal consistency coefficients of .71–.87 for the Written Expression subtest—a one-item essay test—are surprisingly high and warrant explanation by the publishers. The publishers report standard errors and confidence intervals in standard score units and provide details on how each is calculated. Corrected test-retest reliabilities (median time interval of 17 days) in studies of 367 students in five grades are mostly in the .80–.95 range for subtests and in the .85–.95 range for most composite scores. However, several subtests reflect a practice effect (e.g., the Listening Comprehension second testing means are

3–5 points higher) whereas the Written expression subtest second testing means suggest a fatigue/motivation effect, both of which are cause for concern about score reliability and validity. Correlations among scores assigned by four scorers in a special study of the Reading and Listening Comprehension and Oral and Written Expression subtests using 50 WIAT examinee protocols are high (i.e., .79 and .89 for Written Expression, .89–.99 for all others). However, this evidence by itself is insufficient. It indicates that scorers rank examinees similarly but does not indicate if any of the scorers scored accurately. The publishers do provide information relevant to the reliability of WIAT-Wechsler intelligence scale difference scores. This information is in the form of difference score magnitudes required for a statistically significant difference (at .85 and .95 levels of confidence). Also useful is the information on base rates for composite score differences; that is, the frequency with which various composite score differences occur in the norming sample. This information is helpful in determining whether a statistically significant difference score is clinically significant because of its rarity, similar to a criterion for making psychiatric and medical diagnoses. Base rates for subtest score differences would be helpful as well.

Score validity evidence for the WIAT is insufficient, but generally positive. The evidence on content validity, described earlier in this review, suggests a combination of positives (e.g., assessment of Written Expression using an essay) and negatives (e.g., Mathematics Reasoning is somewhat simplistic). Construct validity evidence is not extensive. Convergence and divergence evidence includes WIAT subtest intercorrelations and correlations with Wechsler Full Scale IQs, most of which are moderate to high (i.e., .3–.7), as expected. A brief discussion is provided of a "multitrait-multimethod study" (manual, p. 150) for reading, mathematics, and spelling, but it includes no discussion of divergence and no evidence for the other WIAT subtests. Criterion-related validity evidence is limited by the constraints on examinee samples, including oversampling of males and unknown percentages of special education students. The evidence includes correlations of WIAT scores with scores from group and individually administered educational achievement tests, primarily in reading, spelling, and mathematics. These correlations, mostly in the .6–.9 range, provide good validity evidence for WIAT scores. The publishers wisely provide results from studies with special examinee groups as validity evidence. Despite sometimes severe sample limitations, this evidence is promising. For example, WISC-III scores accurately predicted WIAT scores for 17 gifted and talented students and 44 mildly retarded examinees. In addition, samples of emotionally disturbed (n = 15), ADHD (n = 22), hearing impaired (n = 10), and learning disabled (n = 48 across ages 6–16) examinees exhibited expected patterns of WIAT-Wechsler intelligence score discrepancies. However, the sample of learning disabled students in particular is too small (and includes only 24% girls), because ability-achievement score discrepancies for these students is among the most important evidence for validating the primary use of the WIAT. Further, the publishers should have provided information on the accuracy with which the WIAT identifies examinees as disabled and nondisabled, in the form of both classification consistency and classification accuracy. Finally, analysis of whether separate male-female norms are necessary for valid interpretations could have been provided.

In conclusion, although validity evidence for WIAT scores is limited, the available results suggest a positive picture of the reliability and validity of WIAT scores for their intended uses.

SCORE CONVERSION, SCORE REPORTING, INTERPRETATION, AND USE. Instructions in the manual for converting, reporting, and interpreting WIAT scores, like the test materials themselves, are easy to use. Specifically, the steps for conducting ability-achievement discrepancy analyses are straightforward and should be easy for most WIAT users to follow. The manual is filled with helpful hints and caveats for those who read it closely (e.g., a warning against using WIAT scores independent of other evidence, cautions about interpreting scores for young children and older adolescents, cautions about modifying administration conditions for severely handicapped examinees). In other cases, the manual provides no guidance to the user (e.g., which base rates to use for interpreting differences between a subtest score and the average of all other subtest scores, how much modification in administration conditions would invalidate score interpretation). As is true for any test, users should examine norms tables for relative differences in scale increments that can inform score interpretation (e.g., some subtest raw score changes of 1 point correspond to 2–4-point standard score changes).

CONCLUSION. The WIAT has been designed, field tested, and normed according to conventional technical procedures. The contents of the subtests reflect both modern and traditional features; score conversion is straightforward, although accurate item scoring is challenging and time-consuming; norming and linking samples appear adequate; and score reliability is adequate, although validity evidence is promising but limited. Educators and clinicians do have at least one other choice. In addition to the WIAT-Wechsler intelligence scales combination, one of the most popular instruments for identifying ability-achievement discrepancies is the Woodcock-Johnson Psycho-Educational Battery—Revised (WJ-R; 12:415). One major difference between these two choices is that the Wechsler intelligence scales are empirically selected whereas the WJ-R cognitive ability scales are model-based (i.e., on the Horn-Cattell model of intellectual processing). A second major difference is that the WIAT can be used with school-age children (i.e., ages 5–19) whereas the WJ-R can be used with examinees of any age (i.e., ages 2–90). Educators and clinicians are urged to compare the WIAT-Wechsler intelligence scale combination, the WJ-R, and other options with due consideration for their purposes for assessing, the examinees they will assess, and other contextual factors.

REVIEWER'S REFERENCE

Lyon, G. R. (1996). Learning disabilities. *The Future of Children: Special Education for Children with Disabilities, 6*(1), 54–76.

[360]

Welding Test.

Purpose: "Measures knowledge and skills in welding areas."
Population: Welding job applicants.
Publication Dates: 1984–1990.
Scores: Total score only.
Administration: Group.
Price Data, 1993: $498 per complete kit including 10 test booklets, 100 answer sheets, manual ('90, 13 pages), and scoring key.
Time: (100–120) minutes.
Author: Roland T. Ramsay.
Publisher: Ramsay Corporation.

Review of the Welding Test by JOHN PETER HUDSON, JR., Manager, Organization and Management Development, PepsiCo, Inc., Purchase, NY:

The Ramsay Corporation Job Skills Series—Welding Test is designed to assess the welding knowledge and skills of job applicants or incumbents for jobs where such knowledge and skills are necessary parts of job activities.

TEST INSTRUMENT. The test items are well written, with a clear, consistent format and writing style. Many of the items are associated with drawings or schematic diagrams—these graphics are professionally drawn and are straightforward to understand and use. Although items themselves appear well written, the test layout has opportunities for improvement. The distinction between item categories, and sets of items that belong to a single drawing, could be made more salient to examinees. Also, test items are crowded onto pages—more white space would make the test more user-friendly. The instructions on the cover could be updated and polished to make the language more crisp and clear to test takers.

TEST DEVELOPMENT. The test appears to have been developed on the basis of a single organization's need for assessment capabilities in welding domains. In building content-relevant evidence for the test, the author presents a list of knowledge and skill dimensions for each domain, but does not describe how these dimensions were derived. Nor was there an explanation of how items were written, or what research or evaluative efforts were undertaken to identify the items to be included in the final instrument. The author presents item-level difficulties and item-total correlations, but does not explain if and how these results were used to assess the psychometric qualities of the items and the instrument as a whole. It becomes the responsibility of the user to ascertain whether the domain dimensions and the item content are relevant for the specific application; such an evaluation would be assisted by a more thorough and comprehensive explanation of how the instrument was developed.

RELIABILITY AND VALIDITY EVIDENCE. There is little evidence presented to assure the user of the reliability and validity of scores from this test. Reliability was estimated from a single administration with small sample sizes. The argument for the content-related evidence for the validity of this test is not well articulated. The author could take the opportunity to buttress the claim of content validity by spending more time reviewing how the knowledge and skill domains were derived, and how items were developed to sample those domains.

ADMINISTRATION. Although the instructions page on the cover of the test could use some polish, the administration instructions in the technical manual are altogether comprehensive, detailed, and complete. The test user and examinee would have a clear understanding of the test administration procedures. However, there are some concerns related to administration. Instructions indicate to collect sex and date of birth information from examinees—such information is sensitive to collect during an employment testing situation because it may increase the user organization's risk of litigation under equal employment opportunity law. The administration section tells the administrator to mark the time taken to complete the test, but does not give an explanation of how that information is used. A number of items require calculations; the manual does not specify whether calculators can be used.

TECHNICAL MANUAL. On the whole, the technical manual is not well written. Several tables of data are presented, without sufficient explanation of how they are to be used. There exist deficiencies in areas related not only to test development and validity research, but also gaps on recommendations related to test security, retest policy, and so forth.

TEST USE. There is no information on how test scores are to be used for making inferences related to any of a variety of potential test uses—hiring, promotion, workforce assessment, training assignment, and so forth. The normative data presented are not very useful because they are based on small sample sizes, with little explanation of the samples themselves. Finally, there is no information provided on the fairness of the test and its impact on legally protected subgroups.

SUMMARY. This reviewer's impression is that this test was developed specifically for use in a single organization. The content domains were established and items were written by small groups of job experts, with oversight by the author. The effort likely met the organization's needs quite well—it was probably a well-conceived test development and application project based on content-relevant validity evidence. However, the test and supporting research presented in the technical reports are deficient when offered as a generic assessment of welding knowledge and skill. Although the items themselves are well written and appear promising, the author needs to conduct and present a more comprehensive and orthodox test development program to provide the test user with the appropriate information upon which to make an informed decision. As it stands now, the user has the bulk of the burden in determining whether or not the test is a sound assessment tool meeting the standards for high-quality test development and use.

Review of the Welding Test by DAVID C. ROBERTS, Consultant, Personnel Decisions International, Dallas, TX:

The Welding Test was designed for use as an employee selection and placement tool for jobs in which welding knowledge and skills are required. One hundred multiple-choice items cover the following content categories: Print Reading (26 items), Welding (33), Welder Maintenance and Operation (13), Tools, Machines, Material, and Equipment (14), Mobile Equipment and Rigging (6), and Production Welding Calculations (8). An item related to safety is included for each content area.

Test administration and scoring instructions are provided in the manual. There is no time limit for the test; however, the manual states that most examinees can finish the test in 120 minutes or less. The multiple-choice answer sheet is scored by hand, producing a single score that represents number of correct answers.

The manual lists areas and subareas of knowledge and skill identified by the publisher as required in electrical maintenance jobs and used as a starting point for item development. Four managers served as subject matter experts to provide "percent of time spent" (p. 3) and relative importance ratings of the knowledge and skill areas; no demographic, organizational, or industry information is provided for the sample of SMEs. These ratings were used to determine the number of test items written to cover each area. No other information on item development is provided.

The test was administered to a sample of 38 examinees (no other information about this sample is reported) and items statistics calculated. Item difficulty ranged from .29 to 1.0 (mean = .81); point biserial discrimination coefficients ranged from -.22 to .71 (mean = .27). Internal consistency (KR20) of the test in this sample was .88, with a standard error of measurement of 3.4 (mean = 81.37, SD = 9.91); no information regarding test-retest reliability is reported. Raw score to percentile equivalents are reported for a sample of applicants for welding jobs at an equipment company (sample size or other descriptive information is not reported); this is the only normative information provided in the manual.

The manual provides no information regarding construct or criterion-related validity of the test; the publisher argues that a content validation strategy be used to support test use. No adverse impact or fairness evaluations are reported.

The items comprising this test could be useful in assessing the requisite knowledge and skill required in electrical maintenance jobs. The items demonstrate face validity: Some require mathematical operations, spatial ability, and knowledge of technical terms that are required in welding jobs. However, given the insufficient information regarding relevance across jobs or organizations, psychometric properties across samples, or criterion-related validity, its use without supporting work should be avoided. Given the publisher's content-driven argument for the test's job relevance, it is especially disconcerting that limited information is provided regarding the job analyses that drove item development. The information that is provided would be inadequate in determining if the test is appropriate for welding jobs in organizations other than the one(s) involved in test development. Organizations considering use of the test should, at a minimum, ensure its job relevance through a confirmatory task analysis and establish locally derived norms using a sample of sufficient size to ensure stability.

Although test development sample sizes are small enough to question stability of the data, the trends that are reported indicate further development work with this test would allow for a better instrument. Eight items have negative point biserial correlations with total score; an additional 32 have point biserial correlations of .20 or lower (4 have a correlation of zero and difficulty of 1.0). Furthermore, preliminary item difficulty statistics and mean score in the item development sample indicate that the ceiling of the test may not be high enough. If these trends hold in additional samples, the test could be strengthened by replacing the poorly performing items with more difficult, construct-related items. In addition, the usefulness of the test in organizations might be expanded if investigation of the instrument's internal structure were undertaken. Identification and scoring of subscales assessing specific knowledge areas would provide more diagnostic insight about incumbent or applicant knowledge and skills. This information could be used to guide targeted training or remediation of distinct competencies that fall under the welding knowledge and skill domains.

[361]
Wiig Criterion Referenced Inventory of Language.

Purpose: "Designed to assist speech-language pathologists and special and regular educators in the diagnosis of children with language disorders and language delays."
Population: Grades 1–8 with Diagnosis of a Language Disorder.

Publication Date: 1990.
Acronym: Wiig CRIL.
Scores: 4 modules: Semantics, Morphology, Syntax, Pragmatics.
Administration: Individual.
Price Data, 1994: $198 per complete kit including Professional's Guide (63 pages), all 4 stimulus manuals and 10 each of all four record forms; $54.50 per module package (specify Semantics, Morphology, Syntax, or Pragmatics) including stimulus manual and 10 record forms; $30 per 20 record forms (specify Semantics, Morphology, Syntax, or Pragmatics); $25 per Professional's Guide.
Time: Untimed.
Author: Elisabeth H. Wiig.
Publisher: The Psychological Corporation.

Review of the Wiig Criterion Referenced Inventory of Language by CLINTON W. BENNETT, Professor of Communication Sciences and Disorders, James Madison University, Harrisonburg, VA:

The Wiig Criterion Referenced Inventory of Language (Wiig CRIL) is designed to complement norm-referenced assessment results of the semantic, morphemic, syntactic, and pragmatic abilities of children with impaired language. The Wiig CRIL is a series of selected probes, formatted in four expressive language modules: Semantic (8 probe sets: semantic relations and referential terms for quantitative, spatial, and temporal concepts); Morphology (19 probes; noun plurals, noun possessives, regular past tense, and noun and verb irregular forms); Syntax (18 probes: basic structures, coordinated and subordinated phrases, and subject-object relative clauses); and Pragmatics (13 probes: social interaction, joint attention, and behavior regulation speech acts). Each probe, which consists of 10 items, relates to one selected concept of oral language and a curriculum-referenced objective for English literacy. Probes require expressive language responses which, as the author noted, require language comprehension and "represent the skills expected of the student in both natural- and school-language interactions" (p. 6). The testing format involves picture naming, sentence completion, parallel production (termed closure by some), and speech act elicitation.

The Wiig CRIL is not designed to be used as a diagnostic tool or assessment for eligibility. Rather, after a child has been identified as language impaired, probe sets would be selected based upon the child's performance on other assessment instruments. This inventory has three major purposes: (a) extension testing for baseline data for levels of success/failure in specific expressive language skills; (b) establishing intervention targets (assist in developing IEP objectives or classroom curriculum-based objectives); and (c) assessing habilitative progress using portions of the inventory as pre- and posttests.

The norm-reference extension testing is recommended when a child's performance is below normal—defined by the author as 1 or 1.5 standard deviations below the mean or below the 16th percentile for the child's age. Application of these recommendations may result in the overidentification of children as language impaired. I believe a cutoff using minus two standard deviations from the mean for age would be more clinically relevant than the author's recommendation. [Editor's note: *The Standards for Educational and Psychological Testing* (AERA, APA, & NCME, 1985) recommend setting cutscores based on local norms rather than routinely using publisher's recommendations.] Other bases for selecting specific probes are areas of weakness from standardized subtests and existing relationships between standardized tools and this inventory. Of particular use to clinicians might be the appendices in the Wiig CRIL establishing relationships between this measure and the subtests of the Clinical Evaluation of Language Fundamentals—Revised (CELF-R; T4:521) and Clinical Evaluation of Language Fundamentals—Preschool (67). The manual also includes five developed appendices that relate literacy objectives to spoken language usage so that probes can be selected based upon the child's performance of curriculum objectives.

Being a criterion-referenced measure, Wiig appropriately recommended interpretation of performance: 80%–100% is mastery; 60%–80% indicates a transition stage of linguistic development in which the students need further instruction to more fully develop the concept; 30%–60% performance is the emergence stage in which the student has limited linguistic control of the concept; and below 30% is indicative of random performance or no awareness of the concept. Using these criterion levels, the clinician can establish baselines and prioritize language habilitation goals and have reference points for therapeutic progress.

Validity and reliability are not discussed in the manual. Rationales for the linguistic concepts tested are not presented; however, the scope of the concepts assessed in the four modules appear to be sufficiently broad with the exception of pragmatics, which seems limited. The combined number of concepts addressed in the semantics, morphological, and syntactic modules is 45.

Each individual record form booklet is complete, containing the linguistic concept assessed in each probe, a response sheet for each probe, and results summaries in chart and graph forms for a 3-year period. The Wiig CRIL manual is user friendly with pertinent information presented in an easy-to-understand manner. The author presents a sound theoretical basis and the administration and scoring instructions are clear and concise. An appendix of acceptable dialectal variations of Black English, Appalachian English, Southern White Nonstandard English, General American Nonstandard, and influences of Spanish will be of use to clinicians.

The Wiig CRIL is the best available instrument of its kind. Its strength is as probes for determining therapeutic targets and documenting progress.

Review of the Wiig Criterion Referenced Inventory of Language by JUDITH R. JOHNSTON, Professor of Audiology and Speech Sciences, University of British Columbia, Vancouver, British Columbia, Canada:

The Wiig Criterion Referenced Inventory of Language (CRIL) is intended to aid speech-language pathologists and educators in their assessment of a child's language competence. It is meant for in-depth description following an initial diagnostic decision that the child's language development is below age expectations. The various CRIL modules consist of sets of pictures and questions designed to elicit specific language patterns in four domains: Morphology, Syntax, Semantics, and Pragmatics. Each language pattern/category (e.g., *Noun + Verb* or *progressive verb ending -ing*) is sampled by 10 items that are scored as a separate subtest. Evaluators can present whichever subtests are suggested by standardized test performance. The manual suggests that results can be used to document current knowledge, plan educational/intervention programs, and assess progress.

Description of a child's knowledge of specific language patterns is essential to the assessment process, and many speech language pathologists and educators would welcome elicitation probe materials for this purpose. Features of the CRIL, however, raise concerns about validity and thus limit its value. First, elicited language responses may not provide a valid picture of a child's language knowledge. Elicitation tasks often require high level, "metalinguistic" abilities, and responses are not motivated by self-generated communicative intentions. For these reasons, performance on elicitation probes can substantially underestimate the real-life language abilities of young children. In the CRIL Subordinate Clauses subtest, for example, the child is asked "Can you tell about both things [pictured events] in one sentence? Use the word 'when'" (p. 157). Normal acquisition data indicate that children who would have difficulty understanding these directions could nevertheless be using constructions with "when." Likewise, the Pragmatics module requires children to assume the speaking role for a series of pictured characters and to imagine what they might say in the illustrated situations. Children who would not yet be capable of such role playing should still be able to use language for real-life Greetings and Farewells.

Discrepancies of this sort would seem to compromise the utility of CRIL data in setting goals for educational programs. Samples of spontaneous language would provide a more valid basis for teaching. Although Language Sampling may be inefficient when evaluating specific content vocabulary, most of the CRIL syntactic and morphological patterns are easily evaluated with this technique. Data on the predictive relationships between CRIL performance and spontaneous language could identify the language levels and patterns where elicitation probes would be most valid, but the manual does not provide this information.

The CRIL also raises concerns about content validity. This "Inventory of Language" is understandably selective in its coverage, but the manual provides no discussion of why certain patterns were selected for testing, nor does it discuss the presumed nature of these patterns. For example, 7 of the 18 Syntax subtests focus on the use of conjunctions, but there are no subtests for phrasal and sentential verb complements (e.g., "John told *Joey to stop hitting him*" or "The boy learned *how to build a kite*"). Moreover, 4 of the conjunction subtests actually test the same syntactic patterns, differing only in the specific conjunctions that are required. Similar shortcomings are found in the Pragmatics module where 5 of 13 subtests focus on the same communicative purpose (i.e., to request information), and differ primarily in the specific question words that are needed. Also, there is no coverage of children's ability to construct multisentence texts such as narratives or explanations despite the large literature showing that this is an area of difficulty for school-age language-disordered children. In the Semantics module, many subtest labels imply that relational structures are being tested (e.g., "Action-Object"), when, in fact, the child need only supply single-word answers to questions such as

"What is she doing." These, and other, facts about the scope and content of the CRIL appear to require considerable justification, but none is provided.

A third concern is presented by the CRIL claim that probe sets "are arranged, as closely as possible, in order of emergence in natural language or in relative order of difficulty" (p. 8). The research behind particular sequences is not referenced, however, and a number of sequence decisions seem dubious. For example, reversible full passives are listed prior to coordination of noun phrases, and noun derivatives are listed prior to subject pronouns. A more thorough search of the child language literature would have strengthened this aspect of the Inventory.

In summary, the CRIL is well intended but poorly designed. A set of elicitation tasks could be a valuable adjunct to standardized language tests in an assessment process that was oriented towards educational planning. However, such materials would need to be well motivated in scope and sequence, and to make appropriate task demands. They would focus on those aspects of language knowledge that are the most difficult to infer from samples of spontaneous speech, and on relatively advanced language patterns where metalinguistic competence is no longer at issue. The CRIL does not meet these criteria.

[362]
Wonderlic Basic Skills Test.

Purpose: "A short form measure of adult language and math skills ... designed to measure the job-readiness of teenagers and adults."

Population: Teenagers and adults.

Publication Dates: 1994–1996.

Acronym: WBST.

Scores, 9: Test of Verbal Skills (Word Knowledge, Sentence Construction, Information Retrieval, Total), Test of Quantitative Skills (Explicit Problem Solving, Problem Solving, Interpretive Problem Solving, Total), Composite Score.

Subtests, 2: Test of Verbal Skills, Test of Quantitative Skills.

Administration: Group or individual.

Forms: 2 equivalent forms for each subtest: VS-1, VS-2 for Test of Verbal Skills; QS-1, QS-2 for Test of Quantitative Skills.

Price Data, 1996: $80 per 25 tests, manual ('96, 92 pages), and necessary software for either the Verbal or Quantitative subtests; $110 per composite set including 25 Verbal subtests, 25 Quantitative subtests, manual, and necessary software; price information for User's Manual for Ability-to-Benefit Testing ('96, 83 pages) available from publisher.

Time: 20 (25) minutes for each subtest.

Comments: The Verbal and Quantitative Skills subtests may be administered together or separately, and are available as separate booklets; scoring requires using IBM-compatible PC; the WBST has been approved by the U.S. Department of Education for use in qualifying postsecondary students for Title 10 Federal financial assistance and schools using the WBST for this purpose must follow special procedures and guidelines published in the User's Manual for Ability-to-Benefit Testing.

Authors: Eliot R. Long, Victor S. Artese, and Winifred L. Clonts.

Publisher: Wonderlic Personnel Test, Inc.

Review of the Wonderlic Basic Skills Test by THOMAS F. DONLON, *Director, Test Development and Research, Thomas Edison State College, Trenton, NJ:*

The Wonderlic Basic Skills Test (WBST) is a brief, multiple-choice test intended to measure the language and math skills of adults, and to be used in assessing the job-readiness of teenagers and adults. As stated in the user's manual: "Job readiness means having sufficient language and math skills to successfully handle the written and computational requirements of the job" (p. 4).

Each form of the WBST comes in two booklets, the Test of Verbal Skills and the Test of Quantitative Skills. Each test booklet is attractively designed and presents its material with a clear type face and an open, clean-looking, layout. There are 50 questions in a Verbal test, 45 in a Quantitative test, and all tests have a 20-minute time limit. The questions are in ascending order of difficulty and the subject is told this up front and is advised not to skip around, but to continue with each question in order.

Actually, each test is composed of three subtests, called GED 1, GED 2, and GED 3, presented sequentially in that order, and extensive use is made of the subscores that these yield. Generally, more test content is given to measuring at GED Level 2 than the others.

The reference to GED levels is a reference to a Department of Labor (DOL) system for describing job requirements in terms of six levels of ability, covering all ability levels through the completion of college, and on three dimensions: Reasoning, Mathematics, and Language. The WBST Verbal and Quantitative scales are obvious analogs to DOL Language and Mathematics scales, and so, for example, Computer Operator is said to require Level 3 mastery in Verbal, and a Level 2 mastery in Quantitative, in the eyes of the Department of Labor. The

WBST Composite Score, which is based on all of the items, both verbal and quantitative, is offered as an estimator of the Reasoning dimension of the Department of Labor schema.

Brief DOL descriptions of the meanings of the math and verbal levels are presented. In these, typical statements are "Add and subtract two digit numbers" (Level 1, p. 26); "Add, subtract, multiply, and divide all units of measure" (Level 2, p. 26). These brief and general DOL descriptions have essentially been operationally defined as the test content of the WBST, using the judgment of consultant-experts. The WBST is thus considered to be tied to the DOL scales, and to provide a description of individuals in terms of their DOL level of attainment. The test is aimed at workers in jobs that can be described within the first three levels of the scales, spanning the skills taught in primary school and up through 10th grade. The publisher states: "The job title, the required language and math skills, and WBST test performance can all be linked through the GED scales" (p. 4).

The 95 items that an examinee confronts are really worked over: The WBST Individual Score Report provides an opportunity for 18 scaled score results, all expressed on a scale from 0 to 500. There are Total scores on the Verbal, Quantitative, and Composite scales; there are nine GED subscale scores (three levels by three kinds of score, Verbal, Quantitative, and Composite), and there are six special additional scales, three for the Verbal test, three for the Quantitative Skills test. For each GED subscale, a score of 265 is considered to be a required minimum for succeeding at that level, whereas a score of 350 or more indicates "mastery" (p. 25). The manual states that "A score of 265 is representative of correctly responding to approximately 65% of the test content at that level" (p. 25). It also states that "Like the GED Level scores, subscale scores of 265 indicate modest success with the materials in that skill area" (p. 25).

The three scales that slice the verbal material in a different way yield scores in Word Knowledge, Sentence Construction, and Information Retrieval, and the three scales that slice the mathematical material in a different way yield scores in Explicit Problem Solving, Applied Problem Solving, and Interpretive Problem Solving. This additional scale information is intended to guide the interpretation of generally low level scores on the basic GED level scales, by providing another opportunity for the subject to demonstrate strength.

All of the scales are defined using Item Response Theory (IRT) methodology, and a part of the user's manual is devoted to a presentation concerning this methodology. The manual notes that IRT has been a fairly recent introduction in educational and psychological assessment. Because of this recency, there is as yet no widely agreed-upon set of standards for describing the operations that are carried out in the development. The descriptions of the development of the WBST scales appeared to this reviewer to fall short of the mark. Calls to appropriate persons in the Wonderlic organization were rewarded with careful, patient, and clarifying discussion, but a substantial part of what was being said could have been presented in the manual. The largest focus was on the logical basis for holding that 265 on a WBST scale constitutes "minimum competency" (p. 25) and 350 is "mastery" (p. 25) in the sense of defining the GED level meanings. Basically, this logical basis is derived from the extensive item development by Wonderlic, both from a content and an internal statistical point of view. The concepts and language of the Department of Labor work were used to make the test. The test is not "linked" to the GED scale system in any empirical or statistical way. There is no demonstration that DOL rating scales are accurately reflected in WBST operations.

It seemed to this reviewer that the internal statistical steps could have been more fully described. Important decisions, such as the decision to restrict GED scale estimation to the subset of items that define that scale, are not mentioned in the manual. It is clear from the presentation of scale overlap in Figure 5 on page 40 that one could make cross-scale estimations, improving the Level 1 estimate by incorporating information from Level 2 and 3 items. The present practice was defended as safeguarding the interpretations of the scales, pointing to the spectre of an examinee who can succeed on GED Levels 2 and 3, and would get a handsome Level 1 estimate from these, but who cannot, in fact, do the Level 1 material. The point is not that the procedures used are in error; it is that they are insufficiently described in the manual.

A potentially useful set of median WBST scores for various occupations is being developed, enabling employers to gauge the general levels of scaled scores attained by the typical worker in a job. As noted in the manual, this can provide a practical benchmark to use in areas where the employer's experience is not sufficient.

No data concerning reliability or score precision derived from the IRT development are reported. Test-retest alternate-form correlations for Verbal were .86 (46 cases) and .79 (64 cases), and for Quantitative they were .90 (38 cases) and .84 (58 cases). In a shift from IRT, internal consistency reliabilities (Cronbach's alpha) of about .92 are reported for the two verbal and the two quantitative tests. The inflating character of speededness for these results is acknowledged, but the failure to provide any summary of the IRT information on the accuracy of the score estimates, via graphical or tabular presentation, seems an error. The score report itself does generate an IRT error statement, bracketing the observed score with a "Probable Score Range," but this guide to score interpretation comes too late to be useful in test selection.

This reviewer took the tests, but selected answers so that only every fourth item was answered correctly. This yielded a score, but the score was asterisked to a warning that the response pattern was "significantly different than expected" and that "Retesting this examinee may be appropriate." This is an excellent feature. The use of IRT and computer administration in this way is a significant advance, and the move by Wonderlic to incorporate it has to be commended.

The lack of any data on the precision of the scores is exacerbated by the large number of scales. Scales made up of 11 or 12 items will not demonstrate high levels of precision even when IRT methods are being used to generate the score. We are assured that the scale score ranges were constrained to intervals where the change in the standard error of measurement was no greater than the change in scale score. But test users are somewhat at sea in making score comparisons.

The relationship between WBST median score and grade level is used to develop a table of Grade Level Equivalent Scores for grades 6 to 12. This work draws upon a 1,404-person within-school sample, spanning grades 8 through 12, and a 4,043-person adult (over 21) group, in the workforce. Although not considered "a national sample" (p. 30), the fairly large groups were examined from a number of demographic standpoints, and considered closely similar to national samples. The comparison of the student data and the adult data indicated that youngsters presently in 8th grade scored higher than adults in the work force whose reported last grade was the 8th grade. Accordingly, the adults were considered to have an associated grade level one year prior to the year they left school, and these "shifted" (p. 32) adult results were used to smooth, extrapolate, and develop the equivalents. The processes seem judgmental and approximate. The manual states that "Grade equivalent scores are commonly required for qualifying students for training programs. They are also used for counseling students" (p. 30), but it is unclear whether these "students" are also "adults" or not. Over the years, quite a bit of measurement scar tissue had developed through debates on the merits and limits of grade equivalent scores. The development here presumably meets someone's practical needs, but it is difficult to evaluate it.

The Wonderlic Basic Skills Test seems in general to be a practical route to a set of descriptions of workforce personnel that are carefully based on a comprehensive and detailed content foundation logically related through expert judgment to the GED levels. As such, it could guide effective decisions about the subjects. The use of warning signals associated with the scores derived from response records that are internally inconsistent must be applauded. But the multiplicity of scales and the absence of summary accuracy information could lead some users to rely on results of indifferent value. IRT does not miraculously cure the likely unreliability of a score derived from 11 items. The WBST is presented as a work in progress, with the promise of additional data over time. This promise is a welcome one.

Review of the Wonderlic Basic Skills Test by GERALD S. HANNA, Professor of Educational Psychology and Assessment, Kansas State University, Manhattan, KS:

Designed to measure the job-related verbal and math skills of adults and teenagers seeking entry-level employment or entering vocational training programs, the Wonderlic Basic Skills Test (WBST) is intended for use in career counseling and applicant selection. It surveys those language and quantitative skills identified as necessary for jobs classified in the lower three levels of the six-level General Education Development (GED) scales of the U.S. Department of Labor.

The computer-generated Individual Score Report compares the examinee's scores with the skill-level requirements of the job designated on the answer sheet. In addition, it reports grade equivalent scores and the GED skill levels achieved. Also reported are percentile ranks with respect to adults at work and with respect to those employed in the job in question. Although scoring is complex, owing to its reliance on Item Response Theory (IRT), it can be done locally by means of a IBM-compatible PC and publisher-furnished diskette.

NORMATIVE AND DEVELOPMENTAL DATA. The User's Manual provides age, sex, and race demographic information for the developmental samples. However, the reference groups that were subsequently used to provide the various kinds of normative data are not described in as much detail as this reviewer would wish in order to judge the extent to which they are representative of the respective national populations of students in school and adult workers.

VALIDITY. This reviewer judges the developmental history of the test, particularly, its linkage to the job and skill descriptions in the *Dictionary of Occupational Titles,* to be consistent with its purposes. In particular, the decision to focus test content on skills identified as job requirements (in contrast to curriculum taught) seems very sound and the content seems to be appropriate for the instrument's purpose. Items are well written, varied, and balanced in both content and format. Moreover, they are clearly relevant to the world of work without being job specific, gender specific, or subculture specific. Content-related validity evidence is, therefore, judged very favorably.

The user's manual commendably points out that the WBST does not assess all job-relevant attributes, only verbal and quantitative skills. Likewise, readers are warned that it does not provide detailed diagnostic information.

As is often the case with new instruments, predictive validity studies have not, to date, been reported. Because this is the kind of validity evidence that would merit the most weight in judging the utility of the test, its absence—although understandable—is unfortunate.

Confidence in the WBST would be enhanced by the presence of more construct-related validity evidence. Although grade-progression data support the instrument's validity, and a good discussion describes how item ordering minimized the impact of speededness upon scores, other kinds of construct-related evidence would be desirable. For example, this reviewer would have appreciated reports of studies concerning test wiseness, sensitivity to coaching, context dependence, and discriminant validity of subscores.

To amplify on the latter, three subscores are provided for each of verbal and math skills. This seems questionable on two grounds. First if, as the user's manual reports, each subtest measures one dominant factor, then how meaningful are subfactors? This question could have been addressed by reporting the intercorrelations among the three subscores of each major part of the WBST. Yet no evidence of the subscores' discriminant validity is offered.

RELIABILITY. Test-retest reliability coefficients are reported both for (a) same form and (b) alternate forms. Findings are reported for time interval of (a) the same day, (b) within the next 30 days, and (c) after 30 days. These coefficients vary from .83 to .93. The variation in these two dimensions of research design is highly commendable. Yet, these samples are not described in terms of means and standard deviations. Hence, the findings are, at best, difficult to interpret.

Internal consistency coefficient alphas reported in the 1996 User's Manual range from .90 to .95. Unfortunately the means and standard deviations are not reported for these samples either, so it is not possible to judge the generalizability of the findings.

Although the WBST subtests are somewhat speeded, internal consistency findings are, as noted above, reported. The 1996 User's Manual also reports alphas for untimed administration, and the resulting coefficients are slightly *higher*. Yet the absence of descriptive data for the samples renders the findings impossible for meaningful comparison.

On a positive note, the use of IRT enabled standard errors of measurement to vary with score level—a desirable feature that is uncommon.

The User's Manual reports a sufficient amount and variety of reliability information but fails to report the minimum information essential to an informed assessment of the utility of the data that are reported. In particular, variability of reliability samples is essential to their informed interpretation.

SUMMARY. The WBST is a short instrument designed to assess selected areas of achievement as they apply to the workplace. It resulted from a sophisticated developmental program. Its content is judged very favorable; however, other validity data are meager. Its reliability has not been adequately reported. It is to be hoped that new editions of the User's Manual will soon correct most of these deficits.

[363]
Woodcock-McGrew-Werder Mini-Battery of Achievement.

Purpose: Constructed as a "brief, wide-range test of basic skills and knowledge."
Population: Ages 4–90.
Publication Date: 1994.
Acronym: MBA.
Scores, 5: Basic Skills (Reading, Writing, Mathematics, Total), Factual Knowledge.
Administration: Individual.

Price Data, 1997: $156 per complete kit including test book including examiner's manual (37 pages), 25 test records with subject worksheets, and 5.25-inch and 3.5-inch computer disks; $24 per 25 test records and subject worksheets; $138 per MBA computer disk (specify IBM, Apple, or Macintosh).
Time: (25–30) minutes.
Authors: Richard W. Woodcock, Kevin S. McGrew, and Judy E. Werder.
Publisher: The Riverside Publishing Company.

Review of the Woodcock-McGrew-Werder Mini-Battery of Achievement by WILLIAM B. MICHAEL, Professor of Educational Psychology and Psychology, University of Southern California, Los Angeles, CA:

Designed for use as a measure of developed abilities or achievement from age 4 through elderly adulthood, the individually administered Mini-Battery of Achievement (MBA) is intended to be employed in educational, clinical, vocational, or research settings. The Reading test consists of three parts: Part A, Identification, assesses skills in identifying isolated letters and words presented in large type on the examinee's side of the test book; Part B, Vocabulary, requires the examinee to state a word opposite in meaning to the one presented; and Part C, Comprehension, taps a variety of skills needed for reading comprehension with most items directing the examinee to supply a missing word in a sentence. The Writing test consists of two subtests: Part A, Dictation, measures skill in furnishing written responses to a variety of items requiring "knowledge of letter forms, spelling, punctuation, capitalization, and word usage" (p. 220) and Part B, Proofreading, assesses the ability to identify an error in a typewritten passage and to indicate how to correct the error—the error being in punctuation, capitalization, word usage, or spelling. The Mathematics test has two major sections: Part A, Calculation, assesses skill in carrying out basic mathematical operations ranging from simple arithmetic to problems in calculus and Part B, Reasoning and Concepts, reflects the ability to analyze and to solve practical problems in mathematics as well as one's knowledge of concepts and vocabulary in mathematics. These three tests afford a composite score referred to as Basic Skills. The fourth test, entitled Factual Knowledge, measures one's familiarity with information about science, social studies, and the humanities (literature, music, and art).

TEST CONSTRUCTION AND STANDARDIZATION. Conventional procedures in test development were followed including determination of test specifications, development and selection of test items by educational and testing specialists, and completion of item analysis studies. More sophisticated methods derived from latent trait theory followed by an analysis of the data using the Rasch model were employed. Items were placed in order of difficulty level, which was highly correlated with the age of the examinee.

Norms for the MBA were derived from a comprehensive and representative sample of 6,026 subjects from age 4 to 95 years. More than 100 geographically and demographically diverse communities throughout the United States were represented from which the examinees were randomly chosen through use of a stratified sampling design intended to control for 10 community and subject variables. Norms central to the use of the MBA Scoring and Reporting Program were based on the distribution of scores at the examinee's chronological age or grade placement.

ADMINISTRATION AND SCORING. To administer the test, the examiner consults a chart in the manual to ascertain the precise grade placement of the examinee and then follows the directions given in the test pages of the easel book to determine where to start posing questions to the examinee. From that starting point, items are presented until the subject fails four consecutive questions. If the starting point is too high, a backward procedure is followed on page after page until the four items with the lowest numbers are answered correctly.

All items are scored 1 or 0 with some latitude being provided in responses given in the Vocabulary and Comprehension subtests. The MBA is scored through use of a computer program that provides typically a one-page report of the scores of the examinee on all tests with information on each test regarding age (grade) equivalent, percentile rank, standard score (mean of 100 and standard deviation of 15), normal curve equivalent (NCE) score, and T score (with the conventional mean and standard deviation of 50 and 10, respectively). This report sheet does not communicate to its interpreter what the NCE or T scores mean. Appropriate caution is communicated in the manual concerning the interpretation of scores and the conditions that might influence test results.

RELIABILITY DATA. Internal consistency estimates of scores and accompanying standard errors of measurement are presented for all four tests as well as for the basic skills cluster over a range of ages from early childhood to late adulthood. These samples ranged between 125 and 715 examinees for the four

tests. Beyond the age of 6 these coefficients typically varied between .82 and .98 with the median value being in the vicinity of .92. For samples of 52 grade 6 pupils, 53 college students, and 56 adults, test-retest (one-week) reliability estimates varied between .85 and .97 with a median value approximating .89. These coefficients could be judged as being quite satisfactory and comparable to those found for competing instruments.

VALIDITY DATA. The previously presented information about test construction is excellent evidence in support of content validity. That most of the items were either open-ended or free-response in their characteristics also serves to reduce substantially the occurrence of guessing, which could confound the interpretation of test scores such as those derived from multiple-choice examinations.

Extensive evidence was furnished concerning the concurrent validity of scores on the various tests of the MBA with comparable measures from other test batteries of achievement such as the Wide Range Achievement Test—Revised (Jastak & Wilkinson, 1984), the Kaufman Tests of Educational Achievement (Kaufman & Kaufman, 1985), the Peabody Individual Achievement Test—Revised (Markwardt, 1989), and the Woodcock-Johnson Psycho-Educational Battery—Revised (Woodcock & Johnson, 1989). Although one would not anticipate an identical match of the content from one instrument to another, a relatively high degree of correspondence would be expected across various content areas. The concurrent validity coefficients between scores on any of the MBA tests and those representing various content areas in other achievement test batteries typically ranged from about .50 to .70. In the instance of the Woodcock-Johnson Psycho-Educational Battery—Revised (WJ-R), validity coefficients for an adult sample on essentially corresponding sections between scores on the MBA and those on the WJ-R for Reading, Writing, Mathematics, Factual Knowledge, and Basic Skills were .75, .85, .88, .77, and .88, respectively. On the three other test batteries cited, coefficients of scores on comparable segments varied between .69 and .87 for the same adult sample. From the standpoint of concurrent validity these coefficients could be considered quite satisfactory and indicative of a favorable competitive position for the MBA.

Of additional interest would be the intercorrelations of scores among the four tests of the MBA at different age levels. These intercorrelations varied between .42 and .88 with a median value approximating .68. It is evident that the scores on the various tests of the MBA probably represent the presence of a general factor of intellectual or cognitive achievement.

OVERALL EVALUATION. In summary, the authors have developed a relatively short battery of achievement tests that reflect a satisfactory degree of reliability and concurrent validity of their scores, especially in relation to parallel data for other widely known test batteries. The normative data also appear to be comprehensive and representative of the performance of individuals over a wide age range. The apparent requirement for scoring with the computer program that comes with the test and the seeming lack of more detailed information on the interpretation of test scores in the report form provided the consumer may constitute potential limitations in the use of the MBA. One would want to make certain that an experienced examiner would administer the MBA, as considerable judgment is needed in the scoring of many of the responses. This reviewer would consider the MBA to be a practical measure requiring a relatively short time (about 30 minutes) to administer and in light of the supporting reliability and validity data would recommend its use.

REVIEWER'S REFERENCES

Jastak, S. R., & Wilkinson, G. S. (1984). Wide Range Achievement Test—Revised. Wilmington, DE: Jastak Associates, Inc.
Kaufman, A. C., & Kaufman, N. L. (1985). Kaufman Tests of Educational Achievement. Circle Pines, MN: American Guidance Service.
Markwardt, F. C. (1989). Peabody Individual Achievement Test—Revised. Circle Pines, MN: American Guidance Service.
Woodcock, R. W., & Johnson, M. B. (1989). Woodcock-Johnson Psycho-Educational Battery—Revised. Itasca, IL: Riverside Publishing.

Review of the Woodcock-McGrew-Werder Mini-Battery of Achievement by ELEANOR E. SANFORD, Senior Testing Consultant, Division of Accountability Services/Testing, North Carolina Department of Public Instruction, Raleigh, NC:

The Mini-Battery of Achievement (MBA) is a brief, wide-range test of basic skills and knowledge. The assessment consists of four tests—Reading (identification, vocabulary, and comprehension), Mathematics (calculation, and reasoning and concepts), Writing (dictation and proofreading), and Factual Knowledge (science, social studies, and humanities). The Reading, Writing, and Mathematics test scores can be combined and reported as a Basic Skills Cluster score. All of the tests are presented in an open-ended or free-response format and are appropriate for use with individuals from 4 years to 90+ years.

The examiner's manual describes many uses for the MBA results, but the most appropriate is as a screening measure that "yields results that help identify the need to use a more in-depth diagnostic instrument" (p. 222). Many other uses of the MBA are presented such as "the tests can be used in kindergarten screening programs to determine developmental levels" and "to give information about literacy levels" (pp. 222–223). Although on the surface the results from the MBA appear to be able to make these kinds of inferences, no data or studies are presented to support making these types of inferences.

ADMINISTRATION AND SCORING. Each test of the MBA is presented as one series of items, ordered by difficulty, with several suggested starting points based on the subject's estimated achievement. The subject is asked to respond to items in the series until four items in a row are missed. The examiner is cautioned to note any behaviors by the subject or any modifications of the test administration procedures that may affect the MBA results. The examiner's manual also states that because the tests are presented in an open-ended format, the examiner may not be able immediately to score an item correct or incorrect. Possible correct and incorrect answers are presented, but there are many more correct responses for some items on several of the tests. The examiner may need to refer to additional sources of information. No information is given as to how often this situation typically arises and if it arose during the standardization process and the impact of subject scores because of this.

The MBA assessment is easy to administer and the whole battery can be administered in approximately 30 minutes. Raw scores are calculated by the examiner and then input into a micro-computer program, along with background information describing the subject, to generate age/grade scores, standard scores, percentiles, NCEs, and *T*-scores. A brief interpretative report is also generated by the computer program.

DEVELOPMENT. The overall plan for the development of the items for the MBA is presented (objectives for the development of the MBA, use of the one-parameter IRT model [Rasch model], method for equating MBA scores with Woodcock-Johnson Psycho-Educational Battery—Revised [WJ-R] scores), but none of the specific information related to the development of the MBA is presented. The MBA items are subsets of items from the item pools used to develop the WJ-R and psychometric information regarding the development and standardization of these items is presented in the WJ-R technical manual (McGrew, Werder, & Woodcock, 1991). Test specifications are mentioned as matching the objectives for the MBA development and content specification was guided by the basic skills content areas included in typical school curricula. More information needs to be presented to better understand how the three areas of the Factual Knowledge test are weighted and how the proportions of dictation items and proofreading items on the writing test were specified. Pilot studies and full-scale item analyses using the Rasch model are mentioned but not described. Summary statistics are presented for each of the tests and the Basic Skills Cluster score for nine selected age levels. All of the tests seem to show an increase across the ages 5 years to 18 years, the scores level off for ages 18 years to 39 years, and then decrease for age groups 50–59 and 70–79. The MBA may be better for discriminating development at the younger and older ends of the scale than in the middle of the scale.

RELIABILITY. The MBA has acceptable reliability for making individual decisions—corrected split-half estimates ranged from .70 to .98, with medians for each of the tests and the Basic Skills Cluster score ranging from .87 for Factual Knowledge to .94 for Reading. As noted above, the tests discriminate better at some parts of the distribution as compared to other ranges. The standard errors of measurement generally are smallest for the categories 9 and 13 years. The standard errors of measurement are larger at age 5 years on all of the scales, but this is to be expected due to the developmental changes going on at this age. The MBA also exhibits adequate test-retest reliability over one week (tests—correlations range from .85 to .94; Basic Skills Cluster score—correlations range from .94 to .97).

VALIDITY. Scores from the MBA have been correlated with a variety of wide-range achievement tests at three age levels (grade 6, college students, and adults). The MBA tests correlate highly with tests measuring similar skills on other tests. For example, the Reading test for the grade 6 sample correlates .79 with the WJ-R: Broad Reading score, .82 with the Peabody Individual Achievement Test—Revised (PIAT-R): Total Reading score, and .64 with the Wide Range Achievement Test—Revised (WRAT-R): Reading score. Although these correlations are high, the MBA Reading Test also correlates even higher with the total score from each of these tests

(.84 with the WJ-R; .86 with the PIAT-R; and .70 with the WRAT-R). A hierarchical factor analysis should be performed to examine the relative sizes of the unique factors (separate tests) over and above the general factor for the test (possibly represented by the basic Skills Cluster score). The MBA has not been validated with any measures specifically designed to measure only one skill, such as reading comprehension or computation.

In general, the Mini-Battery of Achievement appears to be a good measure of overall achievement that can be easily administered to a wide range of subjects. The Writing test is more a measure of writing skills than of the ability to write a meaningful piece of text. This assessment is intended to be a separate assessment from the Woodcock-Johnson Psycho-Educational Battery (12:415), thus, information describing the development, standardization, and validation of intended uses of the test is summarized in the examiner's manual that is packaged with the test.

REVIEWER'S REFERENCE

McGrew, K. S., Werder, J. K., & Woodcock, R. W. (1991). *WJ-R technical manual*. Itasca, IL: Riverside Publishing.

[364]

Woodcock-Muñoz Language Survey.

Purpose: "Designed for measuring cognitive-academic language proficiencies."
Population: Ages 4–adults.
Publication Date: 1993.
Acronym: LS-E; LS-S.
Scores, 7: Picture Vocabulary, Verbal Analogies, Letter-Word Identification, Dictation, Oral Language, Reading-Writing, Broad Ability.
Administration: Individual.
Editions, 2: LS-E (English language); LS-S (Spanish language).
Price Data, 1997: $175 per complete battery including manual (117 pages), scoring, and reporting software (3.5-inch disks), specify English or Spanish edition and IBM or Macintosh; $24 per 25 test forms.
Foreign Language Edition: Available in English and Spanish.
Time: (15–20) minutes.
Authors: Richard W. Woodcock and Ana F. Muñoz-Sandoval.
Publisher: The Riverside Publishing Co.

Review of the Woodcock-Muñoz Language Survey by LINDA CROCKER, Professor of Foundations of Education, University of Florida, Gainesville, FL:

This battery was designed for measurement of cognitive-academic language proficiency (CALP), allowing examinees to be classified into one of five levels of proficiency. The battery is designed to be administered in Spanish and/or English so that an examinee's proficiency in either/or both languages can be assessed and compared. The manual suggests the following uses for test scores: (a) determining eligibility for bilingual services; (b) classifying students by language ability for instruction; (c) assessing progress or readiness for English-only instruction; (d) evaluating ESL program effectiveness; (e) classifying subject's English or Spanish language proficiency; and (f) assessing language proficiency of subjects in research studies. Scores of the four subtests of the battery can be combined to yield three cluster scores; thus, a total of seven scores altogether are available for interpretation.

The test format, easel booklet, and layout facilitate administration. Instructions for scoring and administration in the comprehensive manual are clear. A "plus feature" for potential users is the chapter on examiner training featuring guidelines, accompanied by practice exercises and the examiner checklists. Obviously, it is desirable for the administrator to be fluent in English and/or Spanish because correct pronunciation of vocabulary words by the examiner and interpretation of correctness of examinee-oral responses in both languages are required if an examinee is to receive a language proficiency score in both English and Spanish. The English and Spanish versions of the test have completely separate manuals. One shortcoming in the instructions is the omission of instructions for administering both versions of the test to the same examinee, although that usage is suggested by the illustrative score interpretations. The authors do not mention practical considerations such as time between testings, order of administration, practice effects, or differential administrator effects if both language versions are administered.

Scores may be reported as age equivalents, grade equivalents, relative proficiency indices, percentile ranks, including NCEs, and W scores based on Rasch logits. CALP levels are based on W score differences between the examinee and the population median at that age or grade level. Ranges of W score differences are associated with CALP levels, which are intended to indicate the language demands of monolingual instruction at an age or grade level. An examinee may be tested with either the Spanish or the English version of the test and receives a separate customized score report for each form, generated by a microcomputer program included with the test kit.

Reliability estimates are reported for seven test and cluster scores for eight different age levels, including four adult age groupings. Reliability estimates were calculated for the Language Survey in English using odd-even, split-half coefficients with Spearman Brown correction. Coefficients generally fell in the .80 and .90 range. Given the arrangement of items in order of difficulty within subtests and the use of basal-ceiling rule for administration, odd-even split-half coefficients are likely to be higher than other types of reliability estimates that could have been reported. Users should recognize that reliability of CALP scores would be expected to be lower than the reliability of the English scores alone, given psychometric theory about the reliability of difference scores. Commendably, the authors have reported different standard errors of measurement for different score ranges within each subtest. However, reliability of classifications into the five proficiency levels is not addressed.

The manual contains sections entitled Content, Criterion-Related, and Construct Validity, but the evidence of these score characteristics presented therein is fragile. For example, the Content Validity section merely refers to an earlier section where item selection was sketchily described. There appears to have been no validation by an external panel of experts and there is no description of the qualifications of experts whose opinions were used in item selection. Criterion-related validity evidence is limited to examination of correlations with other test scores from various small-scale studies. Construct validity evidence is offered in the form of intercorrelations among subtests with no attempt to explore or confirm underlying traits that account for observed patterns.

The norming sample for the English form of the test seems substantial and reasonably representative; however, the Achilles heel of this measurement system may lie in the equating method used to link the English and Spanish versions. A subset of items from the English test were translated into Spanish, then administered to a Spanish-speaking sample. Item difficulties were obtained via Rasch calibration for each sample separately, then adjusted to a common scale. Such an equating rests upon assumptions that all items measure a unidimensional trait, that translation of the items did not affect their underlying dimensionality, and that all items were equal in discrimination. Meaningful comparisons of an examinee's performance in English and Spanish rests upon the validity of these assumptions.

In summary, a test that allows an examinee's language proficiency to be assessed simultaneously in both English and Spanish and readily compared with a technological, but user-friendly, scoring system should have high user appeal. The danger is that these features may lull potential users into a state of confidence in the "scientific respectability" of the scores and computer-generated interpretation that is unwarranted based on psychometric evidence.

Review of the Woodcock-Muñoz Language Survey by CHI-WEN KAO, Assistant Assessment Specialist and Assistant Professor of Psychology, Office of Student Assessment, James Madison University, Harrisonburg, VA:

The Woodcock-Muñoz Language Survey, with English (LS-E) and Spanish (LS-S) versions, was designed to measure individuals' cognitive-academic language proficiency (CALP) (Cummins, 1984) in English and Spanish, and to classify subjects into five CALP levels ranging from Advanced to Negligible English or Spanish. The surveys are "an integral part of the more comprehensive English and Spanish batteries ... the Woodcock-Johnson Psycho-Educational Battery—Revised (WJ-R) (Woodcock & Johnson, 1989) and the Bateria Woodcock-Muñoz—Revised [(BATERIA-R)] (Woodcock & Muñoz, 1996)" (p. 5). The Survey consists of four subtests: Picture Vocabulary, Verbal Analogies, Letter-Word Identification, and Dictation, which were previously included in the WJ-R and BATERIA-R.

The Picture Vocabulary requires the examinee to "say" the object of the picture in each item pointed to by the examiner who asks a question, such as "What is this?" Verbal Analogies requires the examinee to "say" a word that would complete a logical relationship of a concept when three key words are given by the examiner. For example, "A bird flies; a fish ...." These two tests intend to measure oral language ability. In the Letter-Word Identification test, the examinee is required to "read" words that are presented one at a time. The examinee is scored based on whether the word is read correctly. However, the test authors note that a correct response does not imply an understanding of the meaning of the word. In the Dictation test, the examinee responds to measures of handwriting readiness (e.g., drawing lines), spelling, punctuation, capitalization, and word usage by "writing" out the answer. These two tests intend to measure the subject's reading-writing ability. A combination of the four tests is claimed to measure broad English/Spanish ability.

The survey requires individual administration, and generally takes about 15 to 20 minutes for the examinee to complete the four tests. The basal-ceiling guideline is used in the testing procedure, whereby the examinee's ability level is addressed by administering items suitable to his/her level without wasting time on the too easy or too difficult items. The details of administration procedures are clearly explained in the manual, which also includes exercises for examiner training. The test booklets of the Survey are in an easel format with the question stem facing the examinee and the instructions and answers facing the examiner. The procedures for scoring are simple and also clearly explained in the manual. Scoring can be done by hand or microcomputer. If done by microcomputer, a narrative report about the examinee's ability is generated.

Examinees' abilities are estimated through use of the Rasch item response theory model. Reported scores are W scores, which are a transformation of Rasch logistic ability scale scores. One advantage of using the Rasch model is that a unique *SEM* is given to each possible ability score. Ability scores other than the W scores include: CALP levels, age equivalent scores, grade equivalent scores, percentile ranks, standard scores including NCEs, and relative proficiency index (RPI).

NORMING. The norms for the English version of the Survey were collected through a stratified sampling design and are the same data for the WJ-R (1989) involving a total of 6,359 subjects aged from 2 to 90+ years old. The sampling technique was designed to produce the proportions in 10 demographic variables (e.g., gender, ethnicity, education levels, community, etc.) of the sample consistent with that of the American population. In their design, data were continuously collected through the year, a positive feature. By this method, score growth throughout the year is taken into account and the grade equivalent scores can be more accurate than those produced by interpolation.

The equating data for the Spanish version of the Survey were gathered from more than 2,000 Spanish-speaking subjects aged from 2 to the age of college students from several Spanish-speaking countries and the United States. However, no information about sampling procedures and composition of this equating sample was reported. It was claimed that the item difficulty of the Spanish test was scaled to the levels of the English test, and an examinee's proficiency can be compared to his or her English proficiency and interpreted in the same way. However, the manual descriptions explaining the equating procedures for the two tests were unclear and confusing. It was not clear which equating design was used for data collection (for example, random groups or common item nonequivalent groups designs). This reviewer would assume that the common item nonequivalent groups design was used because of the mention of common items in both tests for equating, and because the English- and Spanish-speaking subjects are two different groups. However, when items in English were translated into Spanish, they were no longer the same items. How could they be used as common items?

RELIABILITY. The split-half procedure corrected by the Spearman Brown formula, dividing odd items from even items, was employed to estimate reliability coefficients for the English (LS-E) test. The reliability estimates of the four subtests and three broad language clusters are only reported across several selected age groups such as 4, 6, 9, 13, 18, 30–39, 50–59, and 70–79 years old. The reported reliability coefficients in the high .80s and mid .90s are satisfactory. Unfortunately, reliability coefficients are not reported for the Spanish test. *SEM*s for each Spanish score are reported.

VALIDITY. Information reported about the content validity is insufficient. The survey simply lacks evidence of procedures for conducting content validity. Although the authors emphasized that the tests were designed to assess cognitive and academic level proficiency, it would seem imperative to know how the domain of CALP was defined or at least that a panel of content experts have agreed on the representation of test items relative to the CALP domain.

In defending concurrent validity, empirical evidence from seven studies is presented that correlate the Survey with the Woodcock Language Proficiency Battery—Revised (WLPB-R) (Woodcock & Johnson, 1991), another WJ-R family product, and with other standardized tests. Each of these studies focuses on different aspects of language proficiency (oral language, reading, and/or writing) for different subsample groups. When the empirical data are carefully reviewed, even a person with advanced psychometrics training would find the information overwhelming and difficult to be summarized. It is very unfortunate that the clarity of writing previously mentioned did not extend to this critical section of the manual. Comments about the reported concurrent validity are as follows. First, the English version of the Survey showed a strong correlation with the

WLPB-R. The median correlation in each of the English language clusters was high in the .90s. However, because the WLPB-R is a WJ-R product, WLPB-R and the Survey should be correlated to some satisfactory extent. Second, very little information was reported for the concurrent validity of the Spanish test. Only two out of the seven studies examined the correlation of the Spanish test with several other tests. One of these studies involved 70 preschool kids and the other included 120 second and third graders. Third, some of the studies focus on only one aspect of language proficiency of the Survey, for example, the oral language ability in Alvarado's study (p. 58 in the manual), with other established criterion measures. However, it is not clear whether the subtest or the total test of a particular criterion measure is used for the correlation study. At the same time, when oral language is the focus of the study, the tables also present correlation coefficients as discriminating information relative to the reading and writing scales with the criterion. The same pattern of the data presentation was repeated in several other studies, and that is one of the main reasons that the concurrent validity information appears to be overwhelming and difficult to summarize.

As for the construct validity, the authors present intercorrelation information among the Survey tests and three language clusters across selected age levels as evidence. The correlations between the total scores and each of the other subscores were consistently high for older subjects (e.g., aged 30–39, 50–59, 70–79), ranging from a low of .79 to the high .90s. However, the correlation between the total scores and each of the other subscores did not appear consistently high for younger kids (e.g., aged 4 to 18), ranging from low .50s to .90s. Another kind of construct validity is provided by correlating the three Survey language proficiency clusters with five measures of school achievement in reading, writing, mathematics, content knowledge, and total achievement for different age groups. Again, these criterion measures were WJ-R subtests. The median correlation coefficients ranged from .53 to .86 for the English test and from .57 to .83 for the Spanish test. The correlation for subjects beyond 11th graders is missing for the Spanish test.

In examining the nature of the item types in the Survey, it is found that the examinees do not need to express their answers beyond "vocabulary" level. None of the items require examinees to express an answer at sentence level. When measuring reading ability, even the manual authors admit that the nature of the item type does not guarantee that examinees know the meaning of words when they read. The Survey claims to be a measure of oral language, reading, and writing, but the nature of the item type does not appear to access the cognitive process that the survey claims to measure.

SUMMARY. The English version of the Survey has merits, such as its well-established norms, and satisfactory reliability coefficients across age groups. The Spanish version of the Survey, however, has insufficient information about its calibration and reliability. Content validity was missing. One kind of concurrent validity for the English version of the Survey presented by correlating the English Survey with the WLPB was satisfactory; the same kind of information for the Spanish version of the Survey was missing. This reviewer found that the suggested purposes (listed in Chapter 2 of the manual) of the Survey were misleading in that many had no evidence of validity in exploration. For example, the validity of using the CALP cut-scores for determining eligibility for bilingual service, or for providing information about program effectiveness, etc. was not addressed, yet users are encouraged to use the instrument for these purposes. The manual authors continuously recommended use of other WJ-R family tests for more in-depth and broader information for diagnosing individual language problems. These continuous self-endorsements seem to suggest a very limited use and application for the Survey. This reviewer wonders who would need a test that could classify subjects into CALP levels but could not provide substantial validity evidence of the CALP cut-scores and inferences made concerning those scores.

REVIEWER'S REFERENCES

Woodcock, R. W. (1982). Bateria Woodcock Psico-Educativa en Español. Itasca, IL: The Riverside Publishing Co.
Cummins, J. (1984). *Bilingualism and special education: Issues in assessment and pedagogy.* San Diego, CA: College-Hill Press.
Woodcock, R. W., & Johnson, M. B. (1989). Woodcock-Johnson Psycho-Educational Battery—Revised. Itasca, IL: The Riverside Publishing Co.
Woodcock, R. W., & Johnson, M. B. (1991). Woodcock Language proficiency Battery—Revised. Itasca, IL: The Riverside Publishing Co.

[365]
Work Adjustment Inventory.

Purpose: "Designed to evaluate adolescents' and young adults' temperament toward work activities, work environments, other employees, and other aspects of work."
Population: Adolescents and young adults.
Publication Date: 1994.
Acronym: WAI.
Scores, 7: Activity, Empathy, Sociability, Assertiveness, Adaptability, Emotionality, WAI Quotient.

Administration: Group.
Price Data: Available from publisher.
Time: (15–20) minutes.
Author: James E. Gilliam.
Publisher: PRO-ED, Inc.

Review of the Work Adjustment Inventory by MARK J. BENSON, Associate Professor of Family and Child Development, Virginia Polytechnic Institute and State University, Blacksburg, VA:

The Work Adjustment Inventory (WAI) is easy to administer and score. Its 80 items employ simple vocabulary in short, declarative statements (e.g., "I have a lot of energy"). For each statement, the respondent circles a frequency alternative from among five choices: *almost never* (1), *seldom* (2), *sometimes* (3), *usually* (4), and *almost always* (5). The subtest scores are derived by simply summing the item scores for each subscale. Each item scores on only one subscale with the number of items per subscale ranging from 10 to 20: Activity (20), Empathy (15), Sociability (15), Assertiveness (10), Adaptability (10), and Emotionality (10).

Besides ease of administration and scoring, the size of the norming sample is impressive ($N = 7,399$). And the demographic proportions in the norming sample are nearly identical to the 1990 U.S. Census proportions for gender, race, geographic area, and family income.

A further advantage of the test is the evidence for reliability. The test-retest (2-week interval) reliability coefficients across the six subscales are good (.72 to .89). Similarly, the internal consistency estimates are sufficiently high to justify use. The estimates are particularly solid in the 13–19-year age range, as none of the scales have an interval consistency reliability less than .67 for males or females.

Though these positive features suggest utility for adolescent research, the test is inadequate for its intended audience of teachers, counselors, psychologists, or employers. The main flaw is not merely the lack of demonstrated validity, but the available information suggests invalidity regarding the intended purpose of assessing temperament in the work situation.

In reading the items, potential users will find that most items are not specific to the work situation. Only 10% of the items refer to work, and most of them are on one scale called "Activity." The developers could enhance validity by linking the measure to careers or career groupings. Leading career interest and aptitude inventories exemplify prototypes that match scores with career clusters. Such inventories include the Strong Interest Inventory (12:374), the Kuder Occupational Interest Survey (12:209), and the Occupational Aptitude Survey and Interest Schedule (12:263; 12:264).

Beyond inadequate links to work, the WAI also fails to validly assess temperament by standard definitions, including the definition in the manual. According to the brief literature review in the WAI manual, temperament is present early in life, biologically based, genetically determined, stable across situations, and stable across time. Nothing in the manual, however, supports that the scales measure something biologically based, genetically determined, or stable over time. The closest evidence for stability over time is a mere 2-week test-retest. Moreover, temperament implies that the assessed behavior exhibits cross-situational consistency. The test focuses, however, on assessing only one narrowly defined situation—work. Assessing a single domain and labeling it temperament reflects a myopic assessment of the cross-situational traits implied by the temperament construct.

If the "temperament" and "work" claims are omitted from the test purpose, then the measure represents six personality subscales. These subscales were derived from factor analysis of a large pool of items. Although the factor matrices are not identical, there are some similarities between the factors generated in the WAI and previous factor analytic research of personality items. For example, extroversion, neuroticism, agreeableness, and conscientiousness factors identified from the big-five personality constructs (Goldberg, 1990) are similar, respectively, to the Sociability, Emotionality, Adaptability, and Activity subscales of the WAI. The WAI appears not to measure the openness-intellect trait of the big-five. Instead, two additional factors emerge in the WAI, Assertiveness and Empathy.

Because the scales were constructed based on factor analysis, the items have empirical coherence within the subscales. The conceptual coherence is apparent for most items. For several scales, however, some items diverge from the subscale name. For example, the Empathy subscale includes items such as, "I like things neat and orderly" (p. 2) and "I am a predictable person" (p. 4). Eliminating items that lack conceptual similarity to the subscale would improve the test validity.

Although the subscales have some merit, the overall WAI quotient is meaningless. The manual claims that the quotient "provides an overall or summary score about an individual's temperament toward work" (p. 7). Not only is there no evidence for this, but the items themselves are questionable. For example,

endorsing *almost always* to "I am a moody person" (p.4); "I get angry when things go wrong" (p. 2) increases the WAI quotient. Even casual observers of work environments are unlikely to see these characteristics as positively associated with work adjustment. More dangerous, however, are interpretations of low scores on the quotient. The manual states, "Persons with low scores discount their qualities. They may be insecure, overly critical of themselves, or lacking insight into their true feelings" (p. 17).

A problem with interpreting the overall score or any subscale score is the lack of correction for response set bias. None of the test items are reverse scored. Consequently, the tendency to endorse *usually* or *almost always* inflates scores. Conversely, individuals who conservatively apply self-referent labels, by indicating *seldom* or *never*, artificially deflate their scores. The negatively skewed normative distributions for every scale magnify the risk of inaccurate negative inferences for conservative responders. For example, on the Sociability scale, 90% of the norm sample score above the theoretical midpoint. An 18-year-old scoring at the theoretical midpoint for Sociability falls in the 2nd percentile.

Although not recommended for educational or clinical use, the WAI has some utility for research purposes. Often researchers will select more established measures in selecting comprehensive personality inventories such as the Sixteen Personality Factor Questionnaire (12:354) and the Revised NEO Personality Inventory (12:330). The focus on adolescents in designing the WAI, the substantial normative data, and the novel dimensions such as empathy and assertiveness imply potential in future research.

REVIEWER'S REFERENCE

Goldberg, L. R. (1990). An alternative "description of personality": The big-five factor structure. *Journal of Personality and Social Psychology, 59*, 1216–1229.

Review of the Work Adjustment Inventory by **WAYNE J. CAMARA,** *Executive Director and Senior Scientist, Research and Development, The College Board, New York, NY:*

Recently, there has been a resurgence of interest in measures of personality for predicting success at work. Reviews of literature have concluded that measures of temperament are systematically related to job performance criteria (Barrick & Mount, 1991). The Work Adjustment Inventory (WAI) is an 80-item, self-report instrument designed to evaluate the temperament of adolescents or young adults who are preparing for work.

Temperament is generally considered a stable and central component of one's personality; it is similarly described as one's natural disposition or characteristic of an individual's emotional nature and strength. Measures of temperament have been incorporated into clinical personality tests and often several different constructs or components of temperament have been identified. The WAI author reports deriving the conceptual framework and six scales of the WAI from major theoretical and empirical work in personality. The WAI differs from many such broad-based personality tests in focusing on young adults' job-related temperament. It also differs from pre-employment personality tests in that it has not been validated for individual decisions regarding selection. Three major uses are given for this test: (a) to assess an individual's job-related temperament, (b) to provide information about how an individual is likely to fit in with other employees and supervisors in generic work environments, and (c) for research on work-place temperament. It appears most suited for broad vocational assessment of young adults preparing for work entry. It may be used effectively with career/interest inventories by vocational and school counselors evaluating one's preparedness ("goodness of fit" to generic work environments) for work.

The inventory states "this is a survey about how people see themselves" (p. 8) and instructs test takers to read each statement carefully and circle the number that best describes them, and it informs them that there are no right or wrong answers. The test taker uses a 5-point scale to classify each statement as *almost never, seldom, sometimes, usually,* and *almost always.* The WAI is an untimed test, with very brief instructions, and is written at a third-grade reading level. It is appropriate to administer the WAI individually or in groups and testing time is 15 to 20 minutes. Six scale scores and a WAI Quotient (composite) score are computed.

Six scales, representing components of temperament, comprise the test. They are: (a) Activity, with 20 statements reflecting ideas, values, and attitudes about work activities; (b) Empathy, with 15 items concerning sensitivity and concern for others; (c) Sociability, describing one's ability to interact with others and one's outgoingness, is measured with 15 items; (d) Assertiveness, composed of 10 items that reflect one's willingness to express their thoughts and feelings, as well as one's propensity to stand up for themselves; (e) Adaptability, has 10 items focusing on an individual's capacity to deal with change, job stress, and diversity in the workplace; and (f) Emotionality, composed of statements describing one's feelings or affect through 10 items. Scale items are randomly ordered on the inventory. The record form includes the statement, five values for each item (1–5 scale), and six columns, corresponding to the six scales. The examiner transposes the circled item value to the corresponding scale. The examiner then adds the numbers in each scale column and enters the raw scale scores on the front of the record form. The examiner is instructed to not score any scale where one or more items have been omitted. This appears to be a major drawback for this inventory and it is quite possible that several scales could be invalidated for a sizable number of test takers who may be unwilling to respond to a few items. Interpolation or other mechanisms should be considered so that useful data are not so easily discarded.

Raw scores have no inherent value and must be converted to standard, norm-referenced scores and percentiles for interpretation. Separate norms are provided for each scale by gender and age. Normative tables contain between two and six different age ranges. For example, six age ranges are used for the Assertiveness male scale (12, 13, 14–15, 16–17, 18, 19–22) and only two age groupings are used for the Assertiveness female scale (12–16, 17–22). Ages were reportedly combined if means and standard deviations were similar; however, there is inadequate explanation of the exact decision rules used to combine or distinguish age groupings. The examiner is instructed to identify the correct table (i.e., Empathy: female), then find the appropriate age range (i.e., 16–17) and determine the percentile rank and the standard score. These values are transposed to a table at the front of the record form. A quotient score is computed in a separate table by summing all scaled scores and dividing by the number of scales that were scored (there are six scales but omitted items would invalidate a scale requiring a lower number of scale scores to be used for this composite score).

A norming study conducted in 1990 indicated that males and females performed differently on all scales and age differences were also found. This study was conducted with a respectable sample of 7,399 students between the ages of 12 and 22 and was generally representative of the population of youth in terms of gender, race, ethnicity, geographic area, and family income. Approximately 87% of the sample were between the ages of 12–18 and the proportion of the sample at ages 19–22 drops off sharply. Less than 250 students are represented at each of the latter ages, whereas approximately 700 to 1,300 cases are represented at each age between 13–18. The mean scale scores for ages 20–22 appear less stable than those at other age ranges—possibly reflecting the instability of the smaller sample for these ages. Performance by ethnicity is not reported.

The raw score distributions were converted to standard scores, smoothed to reduce random variability across ages, and have a mean of 10 and a standard deviation of 3. The standard error of measurement (*SEM*) was 1 for about half of the scale scores for each gender and age group and 2 for another half of the scale scores. An *SEM* of 2 on these scales indicates questionable levels of reliability for the scale. The Adaptability and Emotionality scales were substantially less reliable than other scales in this regard. The WAI Quotient score has a mean of 100 and a standard deviation of 15, with an *SEM* of 4 for males and 5 for females (across all scales).

Internal consistency reliability was computed (Cronbach's coefficient alpha) for all seven scores (six scale scores and WAI Quotient score) for each gender and age range. Reliability for the Quotient score exceeds .90 for 18 of 22 groups. Again, the Adaptability and Emotionality scales had the lowest internal consistency. The manual does not state explicitly that reliability used the entire normative sample, but that is the assumption the reader draws from the discussion. However, test-retest reliability was computed on a sample of 20 college students at 2-week intervals. The test-retest reliabilities are adequate, yet the sample is much too small and nonrepresentative of the intended test-taking population to make any meaningful inferences. An additional test-retest study is required.

There are few empirical data to support claims for construct or criterion-related validity of the total test and independent scales. One study is reported where scores from the WAI Quotient were compared to a total score on a 10-item questionnaire that asked external raters to determine the individuals' temperament in the work environment. Eighty-seven students in Texas were subjects in this study and the correlation between the WAI Quotient and a total score on the rating scale was .39. There is insufficient information on this study and the rating scale to make any solid estimates about the validity of the scale and the WAI. Construct and criterion-related validity could be better determined by comparing student scores on the WAI scales with their performance on other more established personality and temperament inventories or other job-related criteria (e.g., supervisor ratings). The WAI is not intended for pre-employment screening and the administrative manual should clearly indicate that such uses are not appropriate, thus reducing the potential for misuse by less informed test users. There are several personality inventories designed for employment selection that could serve this purpose and that have substantial empirical data (see the Personnel Decision Inc. Employment Inventory, the Personnel Reaction Blank (232), and the Hogan Personnel Selection System).

Intercorrelations among WAI scales and a factor analysis were conducted to confirm the structure of the test. The intercorrelations were conducted with a subsample of 120 subjects from the normative sample. There is no explanation why the total normative sample was not used for this analysis because the data were already available from the normative tables. Several scales had high intercorrelations (e.g., Empathy and Sociability .61; Assertiveness and Adaptability .66) questioning the distinctiveness of the six subscales contained in the test. Finally, a factor analysis was conducted to examine the factor structure of the measure, but insufficient details of this analysis are provided to fully confirm the results.

The WAI is a norm-referenced, self-report inventory designed to evaluate adolescents' temperament toward work activities and environment, used for vocational, career counseling, and research purposes. The test comprises 80 short positive statements, with five responses reflecting how the individual perceives himself or herself. It has been developed to reflect the solid theoretical framework concerning temperament. Six separate scale scores and a WAI Quotient can be derived. The test is easily administered, directions are clear, and the test manual contains adequate instructions for scoring and interpretation. The WAI is one of several available measures of workplace temperament used exclusively for vocational and research purposes. It lacks strong evidence of criterion-related and construct validity, but does contain extensive normative data on a large sample of test takers. There are several preferable instruments if individual pre-employment selection is desired (e.g., PDI Employment Inventory, and the Hogan Personnel Selection System). Other similar instruments designed for vocational and research uses include the Temperament and Values Inventory (T4:2717) and Thurstone

Temperament Schedule (T4:2833). A variety of alternative instruments developed for such purposes and which appear to provide more direct measures of workplace attitudes and adjustment are also available. However, these measures are primarily based on work skills and behaviors and unlike the WAI, they do not attempt to provide a broader measure of temperament.

REVIEWER'S REFERENCE

Barrick, M. R., & Mount, M. K. (1991). The Big Five personality dimensions and job performance: A meta analysis. *Personnel Psychology, 44*, 1–26.

[366]
The Work Adjustment Scale.

Purpose: "A measure of a student's behavioral readiness for employment."
Population: Junior and senior high school students.
Publication Date: 1991.
Acronym: WAS.
Scores, 4: Work Related Behavior, Interpersonal Relations, Social/Community Expectations, Total.
Administration: Individual.
Price Data, 1992: $51 per complete kit including technical manual (27 pages), 50 rating forms, and intervention manual (171 pages); $10 per technical manual; $25 per 50 rating forms; $16 per intervention manual.
Time: (12–15) minutes.
Comments: Ratings by teachers.
Author: Stephen B. McCarney.
Publisher: Hawthorne Educational Services, Inc.

Review of The Work Adjustment Scale by RIC BROWN, Associate Vice President, Research and Graduate Studies, California State University, Sacramento, Sacramento, CA:

The Work Adjustment Scale (WAS), formerly known as the Transition Behavior Scale, is reported to measure behaviors in society in general, and in employment specifically. The author indicates that the WAS is based on the premise that individual behavior that is acceptable is a basic requirement for employment success. It is further stated that inappropriate behavior, despite other skill deficits or attainments, most likely will lead to the loss of a job. The Work Adjustment Scale relies on documenting behavior patterns of high school students that are thought to be predictive of behavior in employment. One goal is the screening of students with particular problems so that assistance might be successful. A manual is included in the text packet with goals, objectives, and strategies for behavioral intervention activities.

The scale itself consists of 54 questions that are divided into three areas: Work Related, Interpersonal Relations, and Social/Community Expecta-

tions. The Work Related subscale deals mostly with task completion, the ability to follow instructions, and so on. The Interpersonal subscale considers communication skills and working cooperatively. The Social/Community Expectation subscale involves following rules, as well as displays values such as honesty and punctuality.

For 3 months in late Fall 1986, 47 individuals including guidance counselors, education personnel, and some employers (no descriptive information or numbers of each given) responded to a request to indicate a list of those behaviors they considered most common to predict success in employment situations and/or transitions to society. From those "hundreds" of questions, 83 were selected by the author and then returned to the original respondents. From that second review, 54 behavioral indicators were ultimately used. The items were then completed by 2,665 students, from 70 school districts, across 23 states representing four regions of the United States. This standardization sample compares quite well to the 1980 U.S. Census in terms of gender, race, and parental occupation. However, the sample is much more rural than the national average, with a larger percentage coming from the North Central area of the United States. The scale is to be completed by teachers and employers who have primary observational opportunities for the individual rated. The raters of the individuals use a 3-point scale that includes, "does not perform the behavior, performs the behavior inconsistently, performs the behavior consistently" (technical manual, p. 16). It takes about 15 minutes to complete and the author suggests that ratings of each student be done by at least three individuals (it does not suggest which of the three ratings or whether an average of the ratings should be used). The technical manual provides relatively clear information on administering and scoring the scale. Once a student has been given a score on each of the three scales, a percentile is developed from a raw score conversion table, based on the standardization sample.

In terms of reliability, fairly strong internal consistency, test retest (30 days), and interrater coefficients for each scale are presented. Validity information is presented in terms of correlations of the Work Adjustment Scale with a behavior evaluation scale, as well as discriminating between regular high school seniors in the standardization sample compared to another group who had been previously identified as having behavioral problems.

SUMMARY. The mechanical strengths of the Work Adjustment Scale include a relatively easy-to-follow form, both in terms of rating an individual student as well as a methodology for compiling the scale scores and comparing them to the percentiles of the standardization sample. Certainly, the Work Adjustment Scale is a measure of behavioral characteristics, and if they are found acceptable by a user, the scales provide a concise and organized way to offer feedback to an individual student. If some of the behaviors are deemed unacceptable, the use of the intervention manual would allow school authorities to work with students to improve those behaviors.

However, a great deal of caution must be exercised because of the general lack of any predictive validity. Although the authors indicate that the scale can be used to assess workplace behaviors, there is absolutely no evidence that those behaviors are in fact predictive of workplace performance or responsibilities. An individual might know where they scored in relationship to the norm sample, now 7 years old, but there are no standards by which one can decide if the behaviors identified have any meaning in terms of scores necessary for success in the workplace. The usefulness of the scale would have been immensely strengthened had the author rated individuals in job settings to identify criterion scores of a successful employee or conversely predict failure in the workplace beyond skill level performance. The 1985 Standards for Educational and Psychological Testing (AERA, APA, & NCME) indicate that for predictive validity, a criterion measure needs to be used as well as a cut point established.

Although the title of the instrument indicates work adjustment, there is no specific evidence reported for job-related behaviors. The use of teachers, guidance counselors, and some employers might perhaps indicate more perception than reality. Items on the scale that need to be rated such as: is dependable, is attentive, follows the rule of the classroom, etc., have face appeal, but there is no evidence presented as to how many of these appropriate behaviors are necessary to compete in the workplace. For example, can a particular individual with somewhat less than appropriate behaviors overcome those behaviors by having a skill that is valued highly?

A problem with all scales that attempt to access appropriate behaviors is that the term "appropriate" is so value laden. Clearly the items on the WAS come from a value system of a work ethic. Values such as loyalty, sharing, following rules, following directions from superiors, honesty, turning the other cheek, etc., are prevalent. Sometimes such values are con-tradictory. How can working cooperatively with peers and sharing materials be highly valued, but at the same time being independent is also valued? One item of major concern involves the rating of "responds appropriately to typical physical exchanges with peers (e.g., being bumped, touched, brushed against, etc.)" (p. 20). What is the appropriate response if the peers are male and female? Scale scoring and the intervention manual indicate that the appropriate response is *not* to overreact. Yet, many sexual harassment policies use the same behaviors to describe a potentially hostile work environment.

REVIEWER'S REFERENCE

American Educational Research Association, American Psychological Association, & National Council on Measurement in Education. (1985). *Standards for educational and psychological testing.* Washington, DC: American Psychological Association, Inc.

Review of The Work Adjustment Scale by CHANTALE JEANRIE, *Assistant Professor, Measurement and Evaluation, University Laval, Quebec, Canada:*

The Work Adjustment Scale (WAS) is designed to measure those students' behaviors assumed to be predictors of success in both employment and independent living, although the former objective is more frequently mentioned throughout the manual. The author states that the WAS is a shortened and revised version of the previously published Transition Behavior Scale but no information is provided as to the changes that occurred between the two versions. The WAS is an observer rating standardized grid to be completed by teachers or others having a regular and extensive contact with the student. Evaluators rate students on 54 items, assessing whether behaviors are performed consistently, inconsistently, or at all. The items measure dependability and conscientiousness for three subscales: (a) Work Related Behaviors (23 items), (b) Interpersonal Relations (11 items), and (c) Social/Community Expectations (20 items). The test is handscored and provides an overall score in addition to three subscale scores.

The technical manual contains psychometric information and rating guidelines. The conceptual framework presented in Chapter 1 (rationale and overview) consists of a brief and narrow overview of the link between school behaviors and later problems in societal transitions, and of descriptive information that is repeated over 2 1/2 pages. The "development and technical characteristics" chapter is relatively detailed and easy to read, but, in some sections statistical details are explained somewhat more obscurely. Along with the technical manual, an intervention guide provides goals and objectives meant to assist in preparing students for the transition to employment, as well as an extended list of possible interventions to improve each of the 54 behaviors. The list is said to include interventions that "have been found to be more successful ... on helping students" (intervention guide, p. 4) but presents no theoretical or empirical grounds for such a statement. Proposed interventions are numerous (from 21 to 61 for each behavior) but some rely so much on common sense (e.g., "reinforce the student," "present a task in the most attractive and interesting manner possible," etc.) that their presence raises questions about the credibility of the other proposed interventions.

The strength of the WAS, developed in 1991, lies in its norms. Large in size (n = 2,665), the standardization sample matches rather closely the United States 1980 Census data on categories such as sex, race, geographic area, etc. Scores are provided for the general sample and by gender. These can be considered a notable asset. The interpretation of the normative scores, however, is not supported by any kind of material. Besides the facts that each item rated 0 or 1 is considered as a potential source for intervention and that standardized subscores smaller or equal to 6 can be associated with the lowest 15%–20% of the distribution, the test user is left with only the insight that the distribution is highly skewed (i.e., that most students comply with the positive behaviors examined by the scale). More thorough interpretive information should be included in the manual.

Reliability of the scale has been assessed carefully, using internal consistency, test-retest, and interrater indexes. Test-retest reliability was tested over a 30-day period and the coefficients obtained are very satisfactory (r = .87 to .92, p<.01). Reliability of judges' ratings across teachers is also very high (r = .87 to .92, p<.01), as is the interrater agreement between teachers and employer (r= .77 to .80, p<.01). Although the author recommends that all students be observed by more than one person, no information is provided as to how their ratings should be combined. Measures of internal consistency are also extremely high (alpha = .93 to .97), perhaps even too high if one takes the stand that behavioral assessment need not rely on consistency and stability as much as trait theory does. The concern raised by the high level of internal consistency is made more acute by the correlations obtained between subscales (r = .846 to .878). Considering that the author selected the four-factor solution but then retained only three of those

factors as being "theoretically satisfactory," it seems somewhat overstated to conclude that "While extremely high correlations indicate that the subscales measure the same domains, the principal components analysis ... supported the interpretability of the three distinct subscales" (technical manual, p. 13).

Evidences of content, concurrent, and construct validity are presented. Content validity rests on the involvement of 47 educational diagnosticians, guidance counselors, education personnel, and employers in the production of indicators. Proportion of employers in the sample, however, is not known. The concurrent validity of the WAS was tested against three related subscales of the Behavior Evaluation Scale and led to moderate to high correlations (r = .48 to .69, p<.001). Construct validity was tested by a contrasted groups approach, comparing 263 high school students from the normative sample to as many students identified as having behavior/adjustment problems. Results suggest that the scale can efficiently discriminate between the two groups (percentile difference of approximately 30 points, p<.001), providing an interesting evidence of construct validity. Nevertheless, a major criticism can still be expressed about the validity studies: Despite the scale's title, no attempt is made to link the scores with on-the-job behaviors. To rely upon a very narrow piece of the scientific literature of the 1950s to claim that a scale involving school behaviors rated by teachers ought to be a strong predictor of success in employment is simply not convincing.

In summary, the Work Adjustment Scale can be considered a valuable behavior rating scale of work-related behaviors in a school context although its interpretation should be limited to the overall score because the distinctiveness of the three subscales has not been well established. Its use as an employment screening tool, however, is not warranted at this point, due to insufficient theoretical and empirical support. Test editors would be well advised to conduct a concurrent and/or predictive study using on-the-job behaviors as a criterion.

[367]
Work Performance Assessment.

Purpose: Designed to assess "work-related social/interpersonal skills."
Population: Job trainees.
Publication Dates: 1987–1988.
Acronym: WPA.
Scores: 19 supervisory demands: Greet Each Trainee, Direct Trainee to Work Station and Explain Nature of Work, Provide Vague Instructions, Explain Supervisory

Error, Provide Detailed Instructions, Observe Trainees Working, Stand Next to Trainee, Create a Distraction, Show New Way to Work, Introduce Time Pressure, Criticize Trainee's Work, Compliment Trainee's Work, Ask Trainees to Switch Tasks, Ask Trainees to Socialize, Direct Trainees to Work Together, Ask Trainees to Criticize Each Other, Ask Trainees to Compliment Each Other, Observe Trainees Completing the Task Together, Socialize with Each Trainee, yielding a Total Score.

Administration: Group.

Price Data, 1993: $5 per manual ('87, 41 pages); $15 per 25 scripts and rating forms.

Time: (60–70) minutes.

Comments: Ratings by supervisor.

Authors: Richard Roessler, Suki Hinman, and Frank Lewis.

Publisher: Arkansas Research & Training Center in Vocational Rehabilitation.

Review of the Work Performance Assessment by CAROLINE MANUELE-ADKINS, Professor, Department of Educational Foundations and Counseling Programs, Hunter College, City University of New York, New York, NY:

The Work Performance Assessment (WPA) consists of one test booklet, which includes a description of 19 assessment situations involving supervisors, workers, and co-workers, that need to be set up, acted out, and conducted by the test administrator. Accompanying each situation are criteria for rating and recording trainee behavior in such situations as receiving vague instructions from a supervisor, being distracted by a co-worker, or being criticized by a supervisor for poor work performance. According to the manual, the purpose of the WPA is to assess work-related social/interpersonal skills for rehabilitation trainees who, based on WPA results, may be recommended for vocational training and placement, entry-level employment, or further work-adjustment services.

Administering the WPA is no simple task as it involves setting up real work samples and work station situations where trainees have to physically sort items in a bag, put items on trays, or reorganize food service materials. Directions for setting up these samples are difficult to follow as they are incomplete in the test booklet and confusing in the test manual where the information is scattered in different locations. In addition to setting up testing situations, the test administrator acts out a role in the simulations, provides directions to trainees, and observes and rates behavior. This is quite a juggling act for the test administrator who follows a script that includes complicated "demand/demeanor" and "dialog/directions"

instructions further complicated by the fact that there are two different sets (for assessing two trainees at the same time).

The manual discusses different methods for scoring the WPA, which involves completing an 83-item behavior rating form that is included in the appendix of the manual, checking the presence or absence of specified behaviors in the test booklet, or videotaping each administration of the WPA with independent raters viewing and scoring it. Whichever method is used, the score is a simple calculation involving the proportion or percentage of the number of criterion behaviors that were demonstrated in a range of possible scores of 0 to 83. The major problem with the mechanics of the scoring system relates back to how the test is administered. It seems highly likely that the administrator may miss observing and recording the demonstration of relevant behavior because he or she is so involved in the required role playing. The videotaped scoring method would thus be the most advisable one to use even though it is more time-consuming and labor intensive.

We have no information about the meaning or interpretation of these scores. The test manual makes no mention of what a high, average, or low score is or how scores are diagnostically different for different groups of trainees. Missing also from the manual is any description of samples used for norming the measure on appropriate populations. The authors of the WPA have been imprecise in defining for whom the measure was really designed. It could be the entire rehabilitation population in that clients are referred to in very general terms (e.g., rehabilitation trainees, job placement clients, vocational adjustment clients). One reliability study uses clients with traumatic brain injury but other than that we do not know if its intended use is with retarded populations, emotionally disturbed, physically disabled, special education students, or others. Norming the measure on different subgroups in the rehabilitation population is essential in any future development of the WPA.

The major problem with the WPA, however, is the absence of any validity data and the reporting of reliability data that is very limited. The problem begins with the development of the test where brief mention is made by the authors about first reviewing existing literature in social/interpersonal elements of job keeping behavior and employability instrumentation then defining specific behaviors with broad categories of job keeping behaviors. No experts are cited as being employed to make a judgment about content validity and no studies are reported that would link scores on the WPA to real work performance or to other relevant constructs such as dealing with authority, I.Q., education and vocational skill levels, or nature of disability. More information is needed about the WPA's validity before we can have confidence in its usefulness for determining a client's ability to handle the interpersonal demands of stable employment.

Reliability data for the WPA consist primarily of reporting on studies that examined interrater reliability between different scoring methods: "in vivo" by the person who administered the test and by using raters who viewed videotaped recordings of trainees as they performed in the WPA situations. Interrater reliability for these scoring methods was reported to be .61 and .77 in one study and .88 and .92 in a second study. The authors conclude that the WPA can be reliably scored by administrators "in vivo" or from videotape by trained raters. The two interrater reliability studies are robust and appropriate and of sufficient depth and coverage. The problem is that they address only one aspect of reliability. Test-retest reliability is not addressed and no information is provided about internal consistency reliability.

To summarize, the WPA needs more development before the user can have confidence in its ability to assess rehabilitation clients' capacity to cope with work-related demands. Basic validity studies, different types of validity analyses, and information about the test's performance on different norming groups are needed. To begin with, the developers need to design a test booklet that is less complicated to follow; they need to include clear descriptions of how to set up relevant work sample situations and they need to decide on a scoring method that is reliable and easy to use. Information about different target populations' performance on the WPA is essential for both interpreting the test results and for understanding for which rehabilitation clients it is most suitable. The WPA appears to be a curriculum that was initially used to teach clients these skills. The test developers need to turn a clear editorial eye to the manual and the accompanying test booklet deciding how to turn this curriculum into a valid assessment device.

Review of the Work Performance Assessment by GERALD R. SCHNECK, Professor of Rehabilitation Counseling, Mankato State University, Mankato, MN:

The Work Performance Assessment (WPA) was developed by the authors, as an "efficient alternative" to multi-week situational assessment methods. Through the use of three work samples (all of which involved the sorting of food service items), an evaluator would assess two trainees at a time on their

responses to 19 "common work demands." These work demands fell into four categories: responding to supervision, completing job tasks, cooperating with other workers, and socializing on the job. Estimated time to complete the assessment of two trainees was 1 hour. Scoring of the WPA can be performed by the evaluator by means of completing (a) an 83-item behavior rating form, or (b) the Work Personality Profile, which is available on computer disk from the Arkansas Research and Training Center in Vocational Rehabilitation. Employment strengths and limitations on 58 behaviors result from administration and scoring of the WPA.

The authors state that the interrater reliability of the WPA rating form is acceptable, but recommend that users perform multiple ratings/administrations for attaining the most reliable performance estimates. Research performed during the development of the WPA identified that administrator effects on WPA scores were possible, emphasizing the need for careful administrator training. Reported research results from a study performed with 24 individuals, who were clients of a rehabilitation facility serving persons with traumatic brain injury, indicated that the WPA discriminated between adjustment and work-ready clients, although similar results were not obtained from a comparable study that was performed at a large rehabilitation center. The manual indicated that when data collected from multiple raters and components were analyzed, "learning effect (the order in which WPA components were administered) was minimal, and parallel form reliability approached an acceptable level" (p. 11). However, a number of problems were also identified, particularly the impacts of two factors on WPA scores. These factors included evaluator differences in ratings and the failure of the instrument and approach to discriminate between those individuals assigned directly to training and those recommended for work adjustment. Further, several problems with validity criteria were noted in the research appendix to the manual, which focused on the failure of the criteria to show relationship to other work adjustment measures or to completion of the rehabilitation center program. Participants in the latter study were 24 individuals, all of whom had been determined eligible for rehabilitation services, were identified as ready for vocational training or work adjustment, and represented a variety of physical, emotional, and intellectual impairments.

During the administration of the WPA, the evaluator utilizes a script that specifies the work demand that is being placed on the individual trainee, dialog that is required to deliver the commands, special instructions and/or materials needed, and the behavioral criteria on which the trainees are to be evaluated. A booklet is provided, which includes the Script & Rating Form, within which all instructions and subsequent trainee rating items are provided.

Within the WPA manual, background information pertaining to the development of the WPA, summaries of research studies performed on the WPA, and more detailed setup, administration, and scoring instructions are provided. Specific items needed for each of the three work samples that are administered to each of the two trainees are identified in a figure within the WPA manual, but are not replicated in the separate Script & Rating Form. Likewise, administration instructions, observation and rating considerations, and critical precautions for administration, scoring, and interpretation of WPA outcomes are provided in the manual for the instrument, but not replicated in the separate Script & Rating Form.

The WPA manual emphasized that additional research on and refinement of the WPA was necessary to improve the reliability and validity of the instrument and procedures. Further, substantial emphasis was placed on the fact that in-depth training of staff members, use of multiple raters in administration, and multiple administrations for each trainee were essential to ensure that the best outcomes would be attained in assessment of participating trainees. A significant number of recommendations were provided by the WPA developers regarding the need for overcoming administration effects, additional evidence of satisfactory reliability and validity being attained, and in improving the discriminatory capabilities of the procedure and outcomes. Although the manual indicates interest of the authors in collaborating with users of the WPA, in further research and refinement activities related to the instrument and procedure, no updated information is provided regarding the attempts to remedy the deficiencies noted, even though a decade has passed since it was originally published. Further, although the computerized Work Personality Profile (WPP) was identified as an alternative to using the WPA Script & Rating Form for trainee assessment, no specific information regarding the content of the WPP was provided, nor was there any discussion provided regarding the benefits or limitations of the alternative rating approaches and the relationship, or lack thereof, between outcome scores on each measure.

Observation of this reviewer is that although the developers of the WPA were attempting to improve upon previous work sample approaches to the assessment of training and work readiness of trainees with severe cognitive impairments, the methods by which they attempted to improve administration efficiency and assessment results are deficient in a number of ways. Much of assessment practice has turned from an assess-train-place approach to one in which more natural environments are being used to place-assess-train-maintain for even those individuals with severe and multiple physical, cognitive, and emotional impairments. Community-based training, rehabilitation, and supported employment programs have expanded over the past two decades to more effectively integrate these individuals into society, particularly within the workplace and independent living settings. Use of work samples and other more intensive assessment approaches, which are often conducted in simulated and isolated settings, have been abandoned or significantly reduced in their utilization, given their technical and practical limitations, particularly at this point of development of more inclusive and naturalistic approaches to the provision of training and employment services for persons with disabilities. The extremely limited range of work activity included within the WPA work sample segments is very stereotypic of the sorting tasks that were most typically associated with rehabilitation services for individuals with severe disabilities, particularly those who were being served in residential programs, sheltered workshops, day activity centers, or in isolated special education classrooms. Although some improvements that would have been essential to the improvement of procedures and outcomes for the WPA and similar work samples and behavior rating approaches would have been considered important prior to the evolution of supported employment and community-based service philosophy and approaches, they have very limited application to current "natural" assessment approaches and service provision settings. There are numerous other behavioral observation and analysis instruments and approaches available that are readily applicable to a wide variety of natural training and employment settings for persons with a much wider range of vocational and functional impairments, particularly in addressing the needs of the persons we are attempting to better serve.

[368]

Work Temperament Inventory.

Purpose: Identifies "personal traits" of the worker that are then matched to suitable occupations.
Population: Workers.
Publication Date: 1993.
Acronym: WTI.

Scores: 12 scales: Directive, Repetitive, Influencing, Variety, Expressing, Judgments, Alone, Stress, Tolerances, Under, People, Measurable.
Administration: Group.
Price Data, 1993: $30 per complete set including manual (39 pages), software, and 50 forms; $5 per manual; $20 per software (5.25-inch disk); $7.50 per 50 forms.
Time: (15–20) minutes.
Authors: Brian Bolton and Jeffrey Brookings.
Publisher: Arkansas Research & Training Center in Vocational Rehabilitation.

Review of the Work Temperament Inventory by PETER F. MERENDA, Professor Emeritus of Psychology and Statistics, University of Rhode Island, Kingston, RI:

According to the authors, the Work Temperament Inventory (WTI) is a self-report measure of 12 work temperaments originally formulated in the early 1950s within the U.S. Employment Service. The inventory was designed and developed for use in the vocational counseling and job placement of adult workers who respond either *Like* or *Dislike* to 134 job task activities. Raw scores for each of the 12 job temperament scales are obtained by summing the "Like" responses, which are then converted to percentiles derived from the normative sample.

The WTI is accompanied by a technical manual in accordance with the guidelines posited in Section 5 of the *Standard for Educational and Psychological Testing* (AERA, APA, & NCME, 1985). The review that follows is based primarily on the standards put forth in the AERA et al. (1985) publication with which test authors, publishers, and users are expected to comply. In this review, attention is focused on the psychometric properties of the instrument and the procedures used by the authors in obtaining them.

NORMS. In obtaining unbiased norms for instruments, authors must take precautions to reduce biasing effects in the sampling both of items and of subjects. The 134 items were selected from an item pool of 170 statements and then were, as stated in the manual, "arranged in random order, subject to the restriction that items from each of the 12 scales were spaced equally throughout the instrument" (pp. 5–6). Inspection of the scoring key (Appendix 7) reveals that the latter was accomplished, but there is evidence that the order is not random. The systematic (not random) placement of the items, therefore, raises the question of whether bias has been introduced into the norms from this source.

The normative samples for instruments should be large and represent clearly described groups (Standard 4.3, AERA et al., 1985). The normative sample for the WTI is small and ill-defined as to representativeness. The sample consists of only 329 subjects of whom at least two out of three are female for the 261 for whom gender is reported. The sample was composed of college students (57%), secretarial/administrative university employees (23%), and rehabilitation clients (20%). Hence, the norms are based on a sample that is unacceptably small for normative purposes and not representative of a meaningful population. Yet the authors state in the manual that, "the total normative sample is a broadly representative composite group" (p. 7). Potential users of the WTI are hereby cautioned to seriously consider the nature of the population upon which they intend to apply the inventory.

RELIABILITY. Very little is reported in the manual regarding the important psychometric property of reliability. Only internal consistency coefficients (alphas) are reported for the 12 scales, and except for Scales R, I, and E, their magnitudes are not impressive. In fact, four scales (D, J, S, and U) border on homogeneity and Scale V shows more heterogeneity than homogeneity. These observations are made on the combination of alpha coefficients and item-total correlations reported in revised Table 6. The authors make the unwarranted and misleading statement, "The retest coefficients for several of the scales (V, J, and U, in particular) would probably be somewhat higher" (p. 7). Such a statement, cautioned against by Standard 2.6 (AERA et al., 1985), implies that internal consistency coefficients are being used as substitutes for coefficients of stability. It raises the question as to why the authors failed to investigate the full reliability of the WTI and report the errors of measurement for the 12 scales in accordance with Section 2 of the *Standards* (AERA, APA, & NCME, 1985, pp. 19–20).

VALIDITY. The *Standards* (AERA, APA, & NCME, 1985) state rightfully that "Validity is the most important consideration in test evaluation." Validity is defined as a *unitary concept* and as such requires that evidences to support the inferences to be made from the protocols be accumulated over a sustained period of time. These evidences are to be accumulated through the conduct by authors and/or publishers of instruments of content-related, criterion-related, and construct-related validity studies. The section purporting to report validity evidences is the weakest section of the WTI manual.

The reporting is also faulty and confused with psychometric properties of reliability and structure of the instrument. Of the three categories of validation, only content-related validity is mentioned but as a validation strategy used by the U.S. Department of Labor in the 1950s and then followed by the authors in the development of the WTI. However, the correctional data reported in Tables 7, 8, and 9 relate to criterion-related concurrent validity, not content-related validity. The correlations were run between the 12 WTI scales and the 12 USES Inventories. No data are reported for the more important construct-related validity and criterion-related predictive validity. Hence, the validity evidence that is presented in the manual falls far short of demonstrating validity as a unitary concept for the WTI (see pp. 9–13; AERA, APA, & NCME, 1985).

FACTOR (COMPONENT) STRUCTURE. The 12 WTI scales were subjected to Principal Component Analysis (PCA) for two purposes, as stated by the authors: (a) to investigate the structure of the instrument; and (b) to relate the structure to the "Big-Five" personality dimensions. It is this reviewer's opinion that it was the second objective of the factor analysis that led the authors to extract five components for the 12 scales, whereas the PCA results do not appear to justify that many "real" components. The scree plot of the eigenvalues given on page 10 of the manual suggests only two components, which account for 62.2% of the total variance; not five accounting for 83.2% of the total variance. To be reconciled also from what is presented to the reader in Table 4 (Intercorrelations of the 12 scales) and Table 5 (Varimax Loadings and Communalities for the five components) are issues raised by the analyses that the authors performed.

First, it is stated that the five components that were retained were rotated twice; once obliquely (oblimin) and secondly orthogonally (varimax). This is considered to have been a wise decision by this reviewer. However, the authors state that they chose the orthogonal rotation in revealing the component structure because the average intercorrelation of the five components was only .24. Yet the scale intercorrelations of Table 4 range from .00 to .77, with a median of .42. Hence, substantial overlap among the components is present. This fact is confirmed by inspecting Table 5 for complexity of scales (D, V, J, T, U). In factor analysis when variables overlap substantially, oblique transformation of the reference axes is normally performed.

Second, the correspondences between the WTI and "Big-Five" structures claimed by the authors are open

to serious question. Because there are so many complex scales on the WTI (5 of 12), it is difficult enough to attach proper meaning to these five scales, let alone interpret them in relation to the "Big-Five" dimensions. Potential users of the WTI who are also interested in measuring the "Big-Five" personality dimensions are advised to use the Revised NEO Personality Inventory (NEO-PI-R; Costa & McCrae, 1992; 12:330) separately rather than accepting the authors' claims of correspondence between the two instruments.

SUMMARY. The Work Temperament Inventory (WTI) is a self-report measure of 12 work temperaments, at least 5 of which are substantially overlapping in the purported five-dimensional structure of the instrument. The origin of these 12 work temperaments goes back to more than 40 years of developmental research in the U.S. Employment Service. The developers of the WTI, based on the earlier work within the Department of Labor, have devoted much work themselves in the development of this instrument. They are to be commended for their efforts. However, much more work needs to be done for the instrument to become ready for operational use. In order to comply with the *APA Standards* (AERA, APA, & NCME, 1985), the psychometric properties of norms, reliability, validity, and factor structure need to be further investigated and established as being sound according to psychometric principles. Until then, users are cautioned to apply the instrument with care, keeping in mind the issues that have been raised in this review.

REVIEWER'S REFERENCES

American Educational Research Association, American Psychological Association, & National Council on Measurement in Education. (1985). *Standards for educational and psychological testing*. Washington, DC: American Psychological Association, Inc.

Costa, P. T., Jr., & McCrae, R. R. (1992). *Revised NEO Personality Inventory (NEO-PI-R) and NEO Five-Factor Inventory (NEO-FFI) professional manual*. Odessa, FL: Psychological Assessment Resources, Inc.

Review of the Work Temperament Inventory by ALAN J. RAPHAEL, *President, International Assessment Systems, Inc. and Adjunct Associate Professor of Psychology, University of Miami, Miami, FL:*

Published in 1993 by the Arkansas Research and Training Center in Vocational Rehabilitation, the Work Temperament Inventory (WTI) is based on the 12 temperamental requirements derived from a 1959 publication on the rating of temperament requirements of various jobs. The authors are trying to resuscitate a 50-year-old assessment of these traits and would be better off beginning anew.

The definition of work temperament used by the authors is "the adaptability requirements made on the worker by specific types of jobs" (p. 1), which is restated as "the personal traits required of the worker by the job situation" (p. 1). Unfortunately for the user, this model of classification is essentially obsolete. Today's and tomorrow's workers, managers, and executives face constantly changing, multi-faceted job situations with ever-changing technology and the issue of personal traits is better addressed vis-à-vis aptitude measurement and behavioral propensity measurement. Both EEOC and ADA guidelines frown on potential discriminatory personality measures that are not job specific. Of the 11 references supplied in the manual, none is more recent than 1992 and 9 of the 11 were published between 1946 and 1988.

The 134-item Inventory considers 134 job tasks that workers perform and many of these functions are currently operational. However, many are also obsolete and many current employment functions are not included. For example, there are no tasks that clearly require computer literacy, programming, or information system capabilities. The scope of this inventory is too limited to be of much use to most 21st century vocational counselors.

Like many self-report instruments, this measure has no method of controlling for test-taking attitude or external influence like depression, deception, or random responding. This is particularly significant for vocational measures that are often involved in rehabilitation matters where secondary gain matters like financial compensation abound.

Reliability data on the test are scarce in the manual. Measures of internal consistencies (alpha) are generally below .80, a minimum level of consistency if we are to assume that the scales are measuring a single construct. A more relaxed criteria of .75 would still find half of the scales as failing to meet the criteria. The authors state that their estimates would be higher if test-retest methodology was used. No test-retest data were included.

Validity of the test is also questionable. The authors themselves state "all analyses for this research entailed internal (or inter- and intra-instrument) criteria. A different picture might emerge in analyses of external criteria, such a job performance, retention, accidents, absenteeism, etc." (p. 20).

The normative data used are questionable as well. The representative sample mix is primarily college students (186/329) who are 66% female, 75 university employees (status unknown) who are 88% female, and 68 medically disabled clients who are 69% male. This sample appears to be a sample of

convenience rather than representing any specific or meaningful population likely seen by clinicians.

The authors perform a factor analysis purporting to show five factors, which they argue represent the five basic personality factors. Examination of their data shows only three meaningful factors with eigenvalues greater than one. Both the analysis and the interpretation appear forced to fit with the authors' a priori assumptions about what results they should get.

Overall, from an empirical viewpoint, there is very little presented in the manual to support the use of the test or the computer program. Although further research may support the use of the instrument, its current use could easily be challenged for inadequate validity and reliability data. For those seeking a measure of temperament, the Temperament and Values Inventory (TVI; T4:2717), by Charles B. Johansson and Patricia L. Webber, distributed by NCS, is recommended. Frankly, any well-researched, valid, and reliable measure would be preferential to the WTI.

[369]
Writing Process Test.

Purpose: "Measures the quality of students' written products."
Population: Grades 2–12.
Publication Dates: 1991–1992.
Acronym: WPT.
Scores, 14: Development [First Pass (Purpose/Focus, Audience, Vocabulary, Style/Tone, Total), Second Pass (Support/Development, Organization/Coherence, Total)], Fluency [Third Pass (Sentence Structure/Variety, Grammar/Usage, Capitalization/Punctuation, Spelling, Total)], Total.
Administration: Group.
Editions, 2: Individual, Classroom.
Price Data, 1997: $139 per complete kit including test manual ('92, 144 pages), technical manual ('92, 40 pages), 25 analytic scales, 25 Form A first draft booklets, and 25 revision booklets; $50 per test manual; $16.50 per 25 analytic record forms; $18 per 25 first draft booklets; $12 per 25 revision booklets; $33 per technical manual; $55 per scoring videotape.
Time: [45] minutes (+30 minutes for revision).
Authors: Robin Warden and Thomas A. Hutchinson.
Publisher: Applied Symbolix.

TEST REFERENCES
1. Hutchinson, T. A. (1996). What to look for in the technical manual: Twenty questions for users. *Language, Speech, and Hearing Services in Schools, 27,* 109–121.

Review of the Writing Process Test by ERNEST W. KIMMEL, Executive Director, Office of Public Leadership, Educational Testing Service, Princeton, NJ:

The Writing Process Test (WPT) clearly reflects the shift in the teaching of composition that has occurred over the past decade. It conceptualizes writing as a recursive process that requires a writer to use a variety of cognitive processes to reflect on, evaluate, and revise his or her own writing. The goal of the authors was "to directly measure the quality of students' written products and their perceptions or misperceptions of strategic processes related to effective writing" (p. 1). Consequently, the WPT will be of particular interest to teachers and schools that emphasize the writing process in their language arts program. The WPT is designed to assess a student's writing competence in the context of a realistic activity that requires them to create a meaningful composition and then to evaluate both the product and the processes by which the product was created. The authors are to be commended for providing a rationale for the design of the test that articulates the relationship of the test and scoring process to the underlying research evidence.

The WPT is designed to be administered in a two-phase procedure. During the first phase (45 minutes) a student is asked to (a) plan and draft a composition, (b) complete a self-report about the frequency and use of specific planning and drafting strategies, and (c) reread the composition and to evaluate its effectiveness in relationship to particular criteria. The second phase (30 minutes—to be administered at least one day after the first phase) provides an opportunity for a student to (a) edit and revise the first draft and (b) complete another self-report about the use of revision strategies. Unfortunately, this second phase is optional. Much of the value of the test and its link to the recursive nature of the writing process will be lost if the second phase is omitted.

The heart of the WPT is the well-elaborated analytical scoring process. The authors have gone to considerable length to help the users score the student responses in a systematic, reliable fashion. A training video is provided in addition to written directions and sets of training and calibration compositions for each of the two forms (prompts). Particularly helpful are the rationales for the scores assigned to each of the sample compositions. These rationales highlight the writing features that distinguish the five score levels for each of the 10 analytical scales. If the training and calibration compositions are worked through and discussed among a group of scorers, they should be able to achieve and maintain a satisfactory level of interrater agreement and to calibrate their scores to the criteria used in the standardization of the WPT.

The scoring of the WPT involves rating 10 different features of writing competence using a 5-point scale of: 4 = Sophisticated, 3 = Competent, 2 = Partly Competent, 1 = Not Yet Competent, 0 = Problematic. The 10 analytic scales are clustered as follows to reflect the student's *Development* of the topic and the *Fluency* with which language structures and mechanical conventions are used. Development: (a) *Purpose/Focus*—addressing the requirements of the task; (b) *Audience*—using techniques and making the necessary adjustments and choices to engage the reader; (c) *Vocabulary*—using words to precisely communicate purpose and style; (d) *Style/Tone*—using ideas and language structures and conventions to communicate the writer's individuality; (e) *Support/Development*—providing original and interesting details to support ideas; (f) *Organization/Coherence*—adhering to a discernible plan throughout the composition. Fluency: (g) *Sentence Structure/Variety*—using a variety of structurally correct sentence patterns and lengths; (h) *Grammar/Usage*—using correct subject-verb and gender agreement, tense sequence, and word formation; (i) *Capitalization/Punctuation*—using correct mechanical conventions; (j) *Spelling*—using phonetic rules and conventions to spell common, difficult, and unusual words.

This set of scales is used to analyze student compositions at all grades. The scores assigned to the features are summed to produce Development and Fluency raw scores as well as a Total Analytic Raw Score. Tables are provided for converting these three raw scores into grade or age-based percentile ranks. A table is provided for converting the percentile ranks, in turn, to any of five different standard score equivalents (e.g., stanines).

The technical manual demonstrates that the authors recognize the difficulties in using traditional indicators of reliability and validity when dealing with what is essentially a single-item test. They provide substantial evidence of inter- and intrarater agreement in scoring the WPT. Coefficient alpha estimates of the internal consistency of raters' scores are in the .77–.89 range for the three raw scores. A variety of indicators of the validity of the WPT are presented. Several factor analytic studies make evident that the WPT is not a unidimensional measure of writing. This evidence suggests that the Development and Fluency raw scores are measuring somewhat different things. The score assigned to the 10 writing features may be helpful to a teacher in determining where individual students need help.

The authors caution that the students' self-reports on the process strategies employed in writing the composition should be used with care in guiding instructional decisions because there is little empirical evidence about the accuracy or consistency of these self-reports. It seems likely that the student self-reports after first draft and revision are most useful as instructional activities to reinforce the range of strategies that writers can use to reflect on and evaluate their own writing.

The publisher, authors, and users should continue to gather evidence of the validity of the scores deriving from the WPT scoring process. The concurrent validity evidence presented in the technical manual is very limited. Because of the complex, multifaceted nature of good writing, it would be very useful to have studies relating WPT performance to other test results, teacher judgments, etc. At the secondary school level, in particular, it would be helpful to study the WPT in relation to other widely used tests, which include direct measures of writing such as NAEP Writing, SAT-Writing, or the Advanced Placement English Language examination. In view of the changing demography of American schools, it is also important to gather evidence regarding any performance differences among gender, racial, or ethnic groups. Of particular interest would be evidence of how English-as-a-Second-Language students perform on the WPT.

One may also question the appropriateness of a relatively short composition as the sole measure of writing proficiency. The authors would better serve the language-arts community if they developed an extended writing prompt that could be scored using the same analytical framework. The self-reports on the use of writing process strategies would seem to be even more applicable to an extended piece of writing than they are to the brief compositions evoked by the current prompts and time limits.

The Writing Process Test is an important example of a measurement instrument that reflects recent cognitive-process research and theory and is supportive of newer modes of instruction. With its well-developed set of scoring criteria and exemplar compositions, it should be helpful when used as a guide and tool for the teaching and practice of the writing process; the evidence is inadequate to justify its use for high-stakes decisions about students (or their teachers). As the authors acknowledge, "In fact, the greatest value of the test may be that it gives students a tool for self-evaluation and monitoring and gives teachers and students a common language for discussing both writing process and specific features of the written product" (technical manual, p. 38).

Review of the Writing Process Test by SANDRA WARD, Assistant Professor of Education, College of William and Mary, School of Education, Williamsburg, VA:

The Writing Process Test (WPT) is designed to assess students' written products and their perceptions of strategic processes related to effective writing. The authors do not provide a clear statement regarding the test's intended uses. However, they do refer to the WPT as an authentic assessment of writing that can be used to discriminate between effective and ineffective writing.

The WPT was developed based on a cognitive-process model for teaching composition. However, the relationship between this model and the test items is not fully explained. It represents a two-phase assessment procedure. During the first phase students plan and write a composition, complete a self-report on the use of strategies, and evaluate the composition on 10 dimensions (writer score). The test administrator also evaluates the composition on the same 10 dimensions (rater score). During the optional second phase students edit, revise, and complete another self-report on the use of strategies. The 10 scales for evaluating the written product were developed and refined based on administrations to students, however, there is no mention of any specific analyses. An overriding concern of the authors was to maximize interrater reliability. Six of these 10 features are determined to reflect "development," whereas four reflect "fluency." There is no justification for this division. The self-report aspect relies heavily on metacognition. Given that metacognitive awareness is developmental, it is questionable how accurate younger children in elementary school will report such strategies. Furthermore, the use of strategies is often unconscious and may not be subject to recall. Consequently, the scoring and interpretation of reported strategy use should be considered with respect to this evidence.

The test was standardized on 5,000 students in grades 2–12. Comparisons were made with the U.S. population; however, the year from which the U.S. Census data were obtained is not cited. With respect to geographic region, the south was underrepresented and the northeast was overrepresented. Students in the norm sample of Spanish origin were underrepresented, but the percentages of black and white children closely matched the U.S. population. Additionally, only 11 school districts were included in the norm sample because the authors sampled entire classrooms rather than a few children from each classroom. The lack of correspondence with U.S. Census data, the limited number of school districts represented, and failure to include socioeconomic status as a demographic variable severely limits the generalization of the norms.

The WPT produces scores for the Development and Fluency scales as well as a total score. Standard score equivalents based on percentile ranks are produced for the rater's and writer's analyses. Additionally, standard score equivalents and stanines are available for the difference between the rater and writer scores. Although the evidence provided shows a developmental trend for the rater scores, no such trend is evident in the writer scores. The authors caution interpreting the writer scores as measures of the writers' ability. Instead they suggest that test users interpret the difference between rater and writer scores. However, little information is offered as to the meaning of differences and how they might assist in instruction.

The authors present substantial data as evidence of reliability. The internal consistency coefficients for raters' scores represents adequate reliability for group-administered tests. However, the internal consistency coefficients for writers' scores are considerably lower and raise concerns about the consistency of writers' evaluations of their compositions. The coefficients for interrater reliability (ranging from .40 to .84) are lower than expected considering the importance that was given to interrater reliability in developing the scales. The reliability coefficients across forms indicate that Form B is more difficult, so they are not parallel forms of the test.

The authors also provide a great deal of data to support validity of the WPT. Although a detailed explanation of the reasons for including elements of the test is provided, there is no description of any specific procedure for ensuring content validity. Preliminary evidence for concurrent and predictive validity is presented; however, the studies are limited with respect to sample size and scope. The factor analysis consistently yielded a 5-factor solution; however, there was no support for the Fluency/Development dichotomy the authors emphasize in scoring and interpreting performance.

The test manual is clearly written and easy to follow. Directions for administration and scoring are complete and easily understood. The authors do an exceptional job of training test administrators in scoring the responses, which is labor-intensive. The directions are comprehensive and replete with examples and exercises. This is supplemented with a video that portrays teachers administering and scoring the test. Unfortunately, the interpretation of scores is confusing and not supported with evidence.

SUMMARY. The WPT assesses the quality and process of written products. Directions for administration and scoring are straightforward and supplemented with examples. The standardization sample is inadequate for generalizing norms. Reliability coefficients do not meet accepted criteria (.80) for group-administered tests. Preliminary evidence for validity is provided, but more research is needed. The Development/Fluency dichotomy is not supported in the factor analysis, which raises concerns about the meaningfulness of these scores. Furthermore, interpretation of scores is questionable. I believe the most appropriate use of the WPT is within a curriculum-based assessment of writing skills that emphasizes intraindividual differences. The use of norm-based scores for making interindividual comparisons and diagnostic decisions is not supported by evidence in the technical manual.

CONTRIBUTING TEST REVIEWERS

PHILLIP L. ACKERMAN, Professor of Psychology, University of Minnesota, Minneapolis, MN

TERRY ACKERMAN, Associate Professor, Department of Educational Psychology, University of Illinois, Champaign, IL

MARK ALBANESE, Associate Professor, Preventive Medicine, and Director, Office of Medical Education Research and Development, University of Wisconsin-Madison, Madison, WI

JULIE A. ALLISON, Associate Professor of Psychology, Pittsburg State University, Pittsburg, KS

DAVID O. ANDERSON, Senior Measurement Statistician, Educational Testing Service, Princeton, NJ

JERRILYN V. ANDREWS, Assistant for Assessment and Data Collection, Office of School Administration, Montgomery County Public Schools, Rockville, MD

PAUL A. ARBISI, Assessment Clinic Director, Psychology Service, Minneapolis Veterans Affairs Medical Center, Minneapolis, MN

RAOUL A. ARREOLA, Professor and Director of Educational Evaluation and Development, The University of Tennessee, Memphis, TN

PHILIP ASH, Director, Ash, Blackstone and Cates, Blacksburg, VA

JEFFREY A. ATLAS, Deputy Chief Psychologist and Associate Clinical Professor, Bronx Children's Psychiatric Center, Albert Einstein College of Medicine, Bronx, NY

JAMES T. AUSTIN, Research Specialist 2, Vocational Instructional Materials Lab, The Ohio State University, Columbus, OH

STEPHEN N. AXFORD, Psychologist, Pueblo School District No. Sixty, Pueblo, CO, and University of Phoenix, Southern Colorado Campus, Colorado Springs, CO

GLEN P. AYLWARD, Professor of Pediatrics, Psychiatry, and Behavioral and Social Sciences, Southern Illinois University School of Medicine, Springfield, IL

PATRICIA A. BACHELOR, Professor of Psychology, California State University at Long Beach, Long Beach, CA

PHILIP BACKLUND, Associate Dean and Professor of Speech Communication, Communication Department, Central Washington University, Ellensburg, WA

LAURA L. B. BARNES, Associate Professor of Educational Research and Evaluation, School of Education Studies, Oklahoma State University, Stillwater, OK

ANDRÉS BARONA, Professor of Educational Psychology and School Psychology Program Training Director, Arizona State University, Tempe, AZ

MICHAEL D. BECK, President, Beck Evaluation & Testing Associates, Inc., Pleasantville, NY

PETER DELLA BELLA, Instructor in Psychiatry, Department of Psychiatry, New York University School of Medicine, New York, NY

JAMES K. BENISH, School Psychologist, Helena Public Schools, Adjunct Professor of Special Education, Carroll College, Helena, MT

CLINTON W. BENNETT, Professor of Communication Sciences and Disorders, James Madison University, Harrisonburg, VA

JERI BENSON, Professor of Educational Psychology, College of Education, University of Georgia, Athens, GA

MARK J. BENSON, Associate Professor of Family and Child Development, Virginia Polytechnic Institute and State University, Blacksburg, VA

NICHOLAS BENSON, Counselor, Illinois State University, Normal, IL

MARSHA BENSOUSSAN, Senior Lecturer, Department of Foreign Languages, Haifa University, Haifa, Israel

BETTY BERGSTROM, Director of Research and Psychometric Services, Commission on Dietetic Registration, The American Dietetic Association, Chicago, IL

RONALD A. BERK, Professor of Biostatistics and Measurement, School of Nursing, Johns Hopkins University, Baltimore, MD

HINSDALE BERNARD, Associate Professor, Department of Counseling, Administration, Supervision, and Adult Learning, Cleveland State University, Cleveland, OH

FRANK M. BERNT, Associate Professor of Health Services, St. Joseph's University, Philadelphia, PA

FREDERICK BESSAI, Professor of Education, University of Regina, Regina, Saskatchewan, Canada

LISA G. BISCHOFF, Associate Professor of School Psychology, Indiana State University, Terre Haute, IN

LISA BLOOM, Associate Professor of Special Education, Western Carolina University, Cullowhee, NC

BRIAN F. BOLTON, University Professor, Rehabilitation Research and Training Center, University of Arkansas, Fayetteville, AR

DAVID L. BOLTON, Assistant Professor, West Chester University, West Chester, PA

ROGER A. BOOTHROYD, Associate Professor, Florida Mental Health Institute, University of South Florida, Tampa, FL

GREGORY J. BOYLE, Professor of Psychology, Bond University, Gold Coast, Queensland, and Department of Psychiatry, University of Queensland, Herston, Queensland, Australia

ELIZABETH L. BRINGSJORD, Assistant Professor, Division of Nursing, Russell Sage College, Troy, NY

SUSAN M. BROOKHART, Associate Professor, Department of Foundations and Leadership, School of Education, Duquesne University, Pittsburgh, PA

JEFFREY B. BROOKINGS, Professor of Psychology, Wittenberg University, Springfield, OH

W. DALE BROTHERTON, Associate Professor of Counselor Education, Western Carolina University, Cullowhee, NC

JAMES DEAN BROWN, Professor, Department of ESL, University of Hawaii at Manoa, Honolulu, HI

MICHAEL B. BROWN, Assistant Professor of Psychology, East Carolina University, Greenville, NC

RIC BROWN, Associate Vice President, Research and Graduate Studies, California State University, Sacramento, Sacramento, CA

ROBERT D. BROWN, Carl A. Happold Distinguished Professor Emeritus of Educational Psychology, University of Nebraska-Lincoln, Lincoln, NE

JENNIFER A. BRUSH, Speech-Language Pathologist, Menorah Park Center for the Aging, Beachwood, OH

JAYNE E. BUCY, Assistant Professor of Psychology, Illinois State University, Normal, IL

ALBERT M. BUGAJ, Associate Professor of Psychology, University of Wisconsin—Marinette, Marinette, WI

ALAN C. BUGBEE, JR., Director of Psychometric Services, The American Registry of Radiologic Technologists, St. Paul, MN

MICHAEL B. BUNCH, Vice President, Measurement Incorporated, Durham, NC

MARY ANNE BUNDA, Professor, Educational Leadership, Western Michigan University, Kalamazoo, MI

PAUL C. BURNETT, Senior Lecturer, School of Learning and Development, Queensland University of Technology, Kelvin Grove, Queensland, Australia

CAROLYN M. CALLAHAN, William Clay Parish, Jr. Professor of Education, University of Virginia, Charlottesville, VA

WAYNE J. CAMARA, Executive Director and Senior Scientist, Office of Research and Development, The College Board, New York, NY

CAMERON J. CAMP, Research Scientist, Myers Research Institute of The Menorah Park Center for the Aging, Beachwood, OH

THOMAS F. CAMPBELL, Director, Audiology and Speech Pathology, Children's Hospital, Communication Science & Disorders, University of Pittsburgh, Pittsburgh, PA

KAREN T. CAREY, Associate Professor of Psychology, California State University, Fresno, Fresno, CA

JANET F. CARLSON, Associate Professor, Counseling and Psychological Services Department, State University of New York at Oswego, Oswego, NY

JoELLEN CARLSON, Director of Testing Standards, New York Stock Exchange, Inc., New York, NY

RUSSELL N. CARNEY, Associate Professor of Psychology, Southwest Missouri State University, Springfield, MO

C. DALE CARPENTER, Professor of Special Education, Western Carolina University, Cullowhee, NC

MARY MATHAI CHITTOORAN, UC Foundation Assistant Professor of School Psychology and Special Education, The University of Tennessee at Chattanooga, Chattanooga, TN

JAMES P. CHOCA, Chief, Psychology Service, Lakeside Medical Center, Department of Veterans Affairs, Chicago, IL

JOSEPH C. CIECHALSKI, Associate Professor of Counselor and Adult Education, East Carolina University, Greenville, NC

GREGORY J. CIZEK, Associate Professor of Educational Research and Measurement, University of Toledo, Toledo, OH

ELAINE CLARK, Professor of Educational Psychology, University of Utah, Salt Lake City, UT

ANNABEL J. COHEN, Associate Professor of Psychology, University of Prince Edward Island, Charlottetown, Prince Edward Island, Canada

CAROL J. COLLINS, Director, Family Counseling and Research Center, Caldwell, ID

COLLIE W. CONOLEY, Professor of Educational Psychology, Texas A&M University, College Station, TX

COLIN COOPER, Lecturer, School of Psychology, The Queen's University of Belfast, Belfast, United Kingdom

M. ALLAN COOPERSTEIN, Clinical Psychologist/Forensic Examiner: Private Practice, Willow Grove, PA

ALICE J. CORKILL, Associate Professor of Educational Psychology, University of Nevada—Las Vegas, Las Vegas, NV

MERITH COSDEN, Professor, Department of Education, University of California, Santa Barbara, CA

JOHN CRAWFORD, Director of Planning and Evaluation, Millard Public Schools, Omaha, NE

KEVIN D. CREHAN, Associate Professor of Educational Psychology, University of Nevada—Las Vegas, Las Vegas, NV

DIANA CRESPO, Research Assistant, Trenton State College, Trenton, NJ

LINDA CROCKER, Professor of Foundations of Education, University of Florida, Gainesville, FL

LAWRENCE H. CROSS, Associate Professor, Department of Educational Leadership and Policy Studies, Virginia Polytechnic Institute and State University, Blacksburg, VA

STEPHANIE L. CUTLAN, Research Assistant, Psychology Department, The University of Memphis, Memphis, TN

AYRES G. D'COSTA, Associate Professor, The Ohio State University, Columbus, OH

MARK H. DANIEL, Senior Scientist, American Guidance Service, Circle Pines, MN

RALPH F. DARR, JR., Professor Emeritus of Education, Department of Educational Foundations and Leadership, The University of Akron, Akron, OH

BRANDON DAVIS, School Psychologist, Arbor Clinic, Muncie, IN

STEPHEN F. DAVIS, Professor of Psychology, Emporia State University, Emporia, KS

GARY J. DEAN, Associate Professor and Chairperson, Department of Adult and Community Education, Indiana University of Pennsylvania, Indiana, PA

WILLIAM W. DEARDORFF, Clinical Faculty, U.C.L.A. School of Medicine, Los Angeles, CA

CONNIE KUBO DELLA-PIANA, Assistant Professor of Communication, University of Texas at El Paso, El Paso, TX

GABRIEL M. DELLA-PIANA, Director of Evaluation, El Paso Collaborative for Academic Excellence, University of Texas at El Paso, El Paso, TX

GERALD E. DeMAURO, Director, Bureau of Assessment, New Jersey State Department of Education, Trenton, NJ

LIZANNE DESTEFANO, Professor of Educational Psychology, University of Illinois at Urbana-Champaign, Champaign, IL

DENISE M. DeZOLT, Assistant Professor of Counseling Psychology, Lewis and Clark College, Portland, OR

ESTHER E. DIAMOND, Educational and Psychological Consultant, Evanston, IL

DAVID N. DIXON, Professor and Doctoral Training Director, Department of Counseling Psychology, Ball State University, Muncie, IN

BETH DOLL, Associate Professor of School Psychology, University of Colorado at Denver, Denver, CO

GEORGE DOMINO, Professor of Psychology, University of Arizona, Tucson, AZ

THOMAS F. DONLON, Director, Test Development and Research, Thomas Edison State College, Trenton, NJ

E. THOMAS DOWD, Professor of Psychology, Kent State University, Kent, OH

ROBERT J. DRUMMOND, Professor of Education and Human Services, University of North Florida, Jacksonville, FL

JUDY R. DUBNO, Professor, Department of Otolaryngology and Communicative Sciences, Medical University of South Carolina, Charleston, SC

CARL J. DUNST, Research Scientist, Orelena Hawks Puckett Institute, Asheville, NC

JUDY L. ELLIOTT, Research Associate, National Center for Educational Outcomes, University of Minnesota, Minneapolis, MN

GEORGE ENGELHARD, JR., Professor of Educational Studies, Emory University, Atlanta, GA

JOHN M. ENGER, Professor of Education, Arkansas State University, State University, AR

JAMES B. ERDMANN, Professor of Medicine (Education) and Associate Dean, Thomas Jefferson University, Jefferson Medical College, Philadelphia, PA

DEBORAH ERICKSON, Professor of Counseling, Niagara University, Niagara University, NY

JENNIFER J. FAGER, Assistant Professor, Education and Professional Development, Western Michigan University, Kalamazoo, MI

DOREEN WARD FAIRBANK, Assistant Professor of Psychology, Director, Meredith College Autism Program, Meredith College, Raleigh, NC

XITAO FAN, Assistant Professor of Psychology, Utah State University, Logan, UT

RICHARD F. FARMER, Assistant Professor of Psychology, Idaho State University, Pocatello, ID

KAREN FAY, Psychology Intern, Lexington County Mental Health Center, Lexington, SC

RAY FENTON, Supervisor of Assessment and Evaluation, Anchorage School District, Anchorage, AK

EPHREM FERNANDEZ, Associate Professor of Clinical Psychology, Southern Methodist University, Dallas, TX

STEVEN FERRARA, Director of Research and psychometrics, Center for Educational Assessment, American Institutes for Research, Washington, DC

TRENTON R. FERRO, Associate Professor of Adult and Community Education, Indiana University of Pennsylvania, Indiana, PA

MARTIN A. FISCHER, Associate Professor and Program Director, Program in Communication Disorders, Department of Human Services, Western Carolina University, Cullowhee, NC

ROBERT FITZPATRICK, Consulting Psychologist, Cranberry Township, PA

JOHN W. FLEENOR, Director of Research, Mediappraise Corp., Raleigh, NC

JIM C. FORTUNE, Professor of Research and Evaluation, Virginia Tech University, Blacksburg, VA

GLEN FOX, Chartered Occupational Psychologist, Occupational Psychology Services Ltd., Sevenoaks, Kent, United Kingdom

ROBERT B. FRARY, Professor and Director Emeritus, Office of Measurement and Research Services, Virginia Polytechnic Institute and State University, Blacksburg, VA

PATRICIA K. FREITAG, Assistant Professor of Educational Research, Department of Educational Leadership, Graduate School of Education and Human Development, The George Washington University, Washington, DC

MARK H. FUGATE, Assistant Professor of School Psychology, Alfred University, Alfred, NY

MICHAEL J. FURLONG, Associate Professor, Graduate School of Education, University of California, Santa Barbara, Santa Barbara, CA

ROBERT K. GABLE, Professor of Educational Psychology, and Associate Director, Bureau of Educational Research and Service, University of Connecticut, Storrs, CT

LENA R. GADDIS, Associate Professor of Educational Psychology, Northern Arizona University, Flagstaff, AZ

PEGGY E. GALLAHER, Assistant Professor of Psychology, Baruch College of the City University of New York, New York, NY

RONALD J. GANELLEN, Director, Neuropsychology Service, Department of Psychiatry, Michael Reese Hospital and Medical Center, and Associate Professor, Northwestern University Medical Center, Chicago, IL

ALAN GARFINKEL, Professor of Spanish and Education, Purdue University, West Lafayette, IN

JACK E. GEBART-EAGLEMONT, Lecturer in Psychology, Swinburne University of Technology, Hawthorn, Victoria, Australia

KURT F. GEISINGER, Professor of Psychology and Academic Vice President, LeMoyne College, Syracuse, NY

JOHN GEISLER, Professor, Department of Counselor Education and Counseling Psychology, Western Michigan University, Kalamazoo, MI

KAREN GELLER, Developmental Neuropsychologist in Private Practice, Whitehouse Station, NJ

RONALD B. GILLAM, Assistant Professor of Communication Sciences and Disorders, The University of Texas at Austin, Austin, TX

BERT A. GOLDMAN, Professor, School of Education, University of North Carolina at Greensboro, Greensboro, NC

STEVE GRAHAM, Professor of Special Education, University of Maryland, College Park, MD

FELICE J. GREEN, Professor of Education, University of North Alabama, Florence, AL

KATHY E. GREEN, Professor, College of Education, University of Denver, Denver, CO

FRANK M. GRESHAM, Professor, School of Education, University of California—Riverside, Riverside, CA

J. JEFFREY GRILL, Associate Professor of Special Education, Athens State College, Athens, AL

MELISSA M. GROVES, Assistant Professor of Child & Family Studies, University of Tennessee, Knoxville, TN

ROBERT M. GUION, Distinguished University Professor Emeritus, Bowling Green State University, Bowling Green, OH

FAITH GUNNING, Research Assistant, Psychology Department, The University of Memphis, Memphis, TN

GENEVA D. HAERTEL, Senior Research Associate, EREAPA Associates, Livermore, CA

ROSA A. HAGIN, Professor Emeritus, Fordham University—Lincoln Center, New York, NY

THOMAS M. HALDYNA, Professor of Educational Psychology, College of Education, Arizona State University West, Phoenix, AZ

KARL R. HANES, Consultant Psychologist, and Director, Vangard Publishing, Carlton, Victoria, Australia

GERALD S. HANNA, Professor of Educational Psychology and Assessment, Kansas State University, Manhattan, KS

JOE B. HANSEN, Executive Director, Planning, Research and Evaluation, Colorado Springs School District Eleven, Colorado Springs, CO

MICHAEL C. HANSEN, Graduate Research Assistant in Psychology, North Carolina State University, Raleigh, NC

RICHARD E. HARDING, Senior Vice President, The Gallup Organization, Lincoln, NE

DELWYN L. HARNISCH, Director, Office of Educational Testing, Research & Service, and Associate Professor of Educational Psychology, University of Illinois at Urbana—Champaign, Champaign, IL

DENNIS C. HARPER, Professor of Pediatrics and Rehabilitation Counseling, University of Iowa Hospitals and Clinics, Iowa City, IA

ROBERT G. HARRINGTON, Professor of Educational Psychology and Research, University of Kansas, Lawrence, KS

PATTI L. HARRISON, Professor and Chair, Educational and School Psychology Program, The University of Alabama, Tuscaloosa, AL

LEO M. HARVILL, Professor and Assistant Dean for Medical Education, East Tennessee State University, Johnson City, TN

MICHAEL HARWELL, Associate Professor of Psychology in Education, University of Pittsburgh, Pittsburgh, PA

JOHN HATTIE, Chair, Educational Research Methodology, University of North Carolina at Greensboro, Greensboro, NC

KEITH HATTRUP, Assistant Professor of Psychology, San Diego State University, San Diego, CA

THEODORE L. HAYES, Senior Research Analyst, The Gallup Organization, Lincoln, NE

SANDRA D. HAYNES, Assistant Professor of Human Services, Metropolitan State College of Denver, Denver, CO

MARTINE HÉBERT, Assistant Professor, Department of Counseling, Administration and Evaluation, Université Laval, Quebec, Canada

CARLEN HENINGTON, Instructor in Educational Psychology, Mississippi State University, Starkville, MS

MARY HENNING-STOUT, Professor of Counseling Psychology, Lewis & Clark College, Portland, OR

DAVID O. HERMAN, Associate Education Officer, Office of Educational Research, New York City Board of Education, Brooklyn, NY

ALLEN K. HESS, Distinguished Research Professor and Department Head, Department of Psychology, Auburn University at Montgomery, Montgomery, AL

PEGGY A. HICKS, School Psychologist, Hand Q Consultants, Richmond, VA

ROBERT W. HILTONSMITH, Professor of Psychology, Radford University, Radford, VA

STEPHEN R. HOOPER, Associate Professor of Psychiatry, University of North Carolina School of Medicine, Chapel Hill, NC

TE-FANG HUA, Ph.D. Candidate, University of Hawaii at Manoa, Honolulu, HI

ANITA M. HUBLEY, Assistant Professor of Psychology, University of Northern British Columbia, Prince George, British Columbia, Canada

JOHN PETER HUDSON, JR., Manager, Organization and Management Development, PepsiCo, Inc., Purchase, NY

E. SCOTT HUEBNER, Professor of Psychology, University of South Carolina, Columbia, SC

DAVID P. HURFORD, Director of the Center for the Assessment and Remediation of Reading Difficulties and Associate Professor of Psychology and Counseling, Pittsburg State University, Pittsburg, KS

CARL ISENHART, Administrative Coordinator, Addictive Disorders Section, Department of Veterans Affairs Medical Center, Minneapolis, MN

STEVEN ISONIO, Research/Assessment Advisor and Psychology Instructor, Golden West College, Huntington Beach, CA

STEPHEN H. IVENS, Vice President, Research & Development, Touchstone Applied Science Associates, Brewster, NY

CHANTALE JEANRIE, Assistant Professor, Measurement and Evaluation, University Laval, Quebec, Canada

JEFFREY A. JENKINS, Attorney and Counselor at Law, Albuquerque, NM

RICHARD W. JOHNSON, Director of Training at Counseling & Consultation Services of the University Health Services, and Adjunct Professor of Counseling Psychology, University of Wisconsin–Madison, Madison, WI

ROBERT JOHNSON, Assistant Professor of Educational Research, University of South Carolina at Columbia, Columbia, SC

JUDITH R. JOHNSTON, Professor of Audiology and Speech Sciences, University of British Columbia, Vancouver, British Columbia, Canada

KEVIN M. JONES, Assistant Professor of Psychology, Eastern Illinois University, Charleston, IL

GERALD A. JUHNKE, Assistant Professor of Counseling and Educational Development, School of Education,

The University of North Carolina at Greensboro, Greensboro, NC

SAMUEL JUNI, Professor, Department of Applied Psychology, New York University, New York, NY

JAVAID KAISER, Senior Research and Evaluation Officer, Academy for Educational Development, Washington, DC

RANDY W. KAMPHAUS, Professor of Educational Psychology, The University of Georgia, Athens, GA

MICHAEL KANE, Professor of Education, University of Wisconsin, Madison, WI

CHI-WEN KAO, Assistant Assessment Specialist and Assistant Professor of Psychology, Office of Student Assessment, James Madison University, Harrisonburg, VA

BARBARA J. KAPLAN, Psychologist, Western New York Institute for the Psychotherapies, Orchard Park, NY

ALAN S. KAUFMAN, Senior Research Scientist, Psychological Assessment Resources, Inc. (PAR), Odessa, FL

NADEEN L. KAUFMAN, Professor of Clinical Psychology, California School of Professional Psychology, San Diego, CA

MICHAEL G. KAVAN, Associate Dean for Student Affairs and Associate Professor of Family Practice, Creighton University School of Medicine, Omaha, NE

PATRICIA B. KEITH, Assistant Professor of School Psychology, Alfred University, Alfred, NY

MARY LOU KELLEY, Professor of Psychology, Louisiana State University, Louisiana State University Medical Center, Baton Rouge, LA

ANNE R. KESSLER, Audiologist, VA Connecticut Healthcare System, Newington, CT

KENNETH A. KIEWRA, Professor of Educational Psychology, University of Nebraska—Lincoln, Lincoln, NE

ERNEST W. KIMMEL, Executive Director, Office of Public Leadership, Educational Testing Service, Princeton, NJ

RICHARD T. KINNIER, Associate Professor, Counseling Psychology Program, Arizona State University, Tempe, AZ

JEAN POWELL KIRNAN, Associate Professor of Psychology, Trenton State College, Trenton, NJ

HELEN KITCHENS, Associate Professor, Division of Counseling, Education, and Psychology, Troy State University—Montgomery, Montgomery, AL

THOMAS R. KNAPP, Professor of Nursing and Education, The Ohio State University, Columbus, OH

HOWARD M. KNOFF, Professor of School Psychology, Department of Psychological Foundations, University of South Florida, Tampa, FL

STEPHEN L. KOFFLER, Executive Director, Educational Testing Service, Princeton, NJ

DAMON KRUG, University Professor, College of Education, Governors State University, University Park, IL

SALLY KUHLENSCHMIDT, Associate Professor of Psychology, Western Kentucky University, Bowling Green, KY

ANTONY JOHN KUNNAN, Assistant Professor of Education, Division of Educational Foundations and Interdivisional Studies, California State University, Los Angeles, CA

KWONG-LIEM KARL KWAN, Assistant Professor of Educational Studies, College of Education, Purdue University, West Lafayette, IN

BARBARA L. LACHAR, Assistant Professor of Psychiatry (Psychology), Baylor College of Medicine, Houston, TX

MATTHEW E. LAMBERT, Research Psychologist, Neurology Research and Education Center, St. Mary Hospital, Lubbock, TX

WILLIAM STEVE LANG, Associate Professor of Educational Measurement and Research, University of South Florida, St. Petersburg, FL

JOSEPH G. LAW, JR., Associate Professor of Behavioral Studies and Educational Technology, University of South Alabama, Mobile, AL

KIMBERLY A. LAWLESS, Assistant Professor of Instructional Technology, Utah State University, Logan, UT

ROBERT A. LEARK, Clinical Professor of Psychology, Pacific Christian College, Fullerton, CA

STEVEN W. LEE, Associate Professor & Coordinator, School Psychology Program, Department of Educational Psychology and Research, University of Kansas, Lawrence, KS

IRVIN J. LEHMANN, Professor of Measurement, Michigan State University, East Lansing, MI

FREDERICK T. L. LEONG, Associate Professor of Psychology, The Ohio State University at Columbus, Columbus, OH

S. ALVIN LEUNG, Associate Professor of Educational Psychology, The Chinese University of Hong Kong, Hong Kong

RALPH G. LEVERETT, Professor of Education/Special Education, Union University, Jackson, TN

MARY A. LEWIS, Director, Human Resources, Chlor-Alkali and Derivatives, PPG Industries, Inc., Pittsburgh, PA

RICK LINDSKOG, Professor of Psychology, Pittsburg State University, Pittsburg, KS

MARIA PRENDES LINTEL, Assessment Coordinator, Lincoln Family Practice Program, Lincoln, NE

WEI-PING LIU, Head Test Librarian, University at Albany, State University of New York, Albany, NY

STEVEN G. LoBELLO, Associate Professor of Psychology, Auburn University at Montgomery, Montgomery, AL

CHARLES J. LONG, Professor of Psychology, The University of Memphis, Memphis, TN

STEVEN H. LONG, Assistant Professor of Communication Sciences, Case Western Reserve University, Cleveland, OH

ALFRED P. LONGO, Supervisor of Humanities, Holmdel Township School District, Holmdel, NJ

EMILIA C. LOPEZ, Assistant Professor, Educational and Community Programs, Queens College of the City University of New York, Flushing, NY

LESLIE EASTMAN LUKIN, Assessment Specialist, Lincoln Public Schools, Lincoln, NE

GLORIA MACCOW, School Psychologist, Guilford County Schools, Greensboro, NC

JOHN MacDONALD, School Psychologist, North Kitsap School District, Kingston, WA

DAVID MacPHEE, Associate Professor of Human Development and Family Studies, Colorado State University, Fort Collins, CO

CLEBORNE D. MADDUX, Professor of Special Education and Educational Technology, University of Nevada, Reno, NV

KORESSA KUTSICK MALCOLM, School Psychologist, Augusta County Public Schools, Fishersville, VA

SUSAN J. MALLER, Assistant Professor of Educational Measurement and Research, University of South Florida, Tampa, FL

MARGARET E. MALONE, Language Testing Specialist, Peace Corps, Washington, DC

CAROLINE MANUELE-ADKINS, Professor, Department of Educational Foundations and Counseling Programs, Hunter College, City University of New York, New York, NY

GREGORY J. MARCHANT, Associate Professor of Educational Psychology, Ball State University, Muncie, IN

GARY L. MARCO, Executive Director, Educational Testing Service, Princeton, NJ

WILLIAM E. MARTIN, JR., Professor of Educational Psychology, Northern Arizona University, Flagstaff, AZ

REBECCA McCAULEY, Associate Professor, Communication Sciences, University of Vermont, Burlington, VT

MARY J. McLELLAN, Assistant Professor of Educational Psychology, Northern Arizona University, Flagstaff, AZ

ROBERT F. McMORRIS, Professor of Educational Psychology and Statistics, University at Albany, State University of New York, Albany, NY

MALCOLM R. McNEIL, Chair, Communication Science & Disorders, University of Pittsburgh, Pittsburgh, PA

DOUGLAS J. McRAE, Educational Measurement Specialist, Monterey, CA

MARIA MEDINA-DIAZ, Assistant Professor of Educational Measurement and Evaluation, School of Education, University of Puerto Rico, Rio Piedras, PR

FREDERIC J. MEDWAY, Professor of Psychology, University of South Carolina, Columbia, SC

WILLIAM A. MEHRENS, Professor of Educational Measurement, Michigan State University, East Lansing, MI

SHEILA MEHTA, Assistant Professor of Psychology, Auburn University at Montgomery, Montgomery, AL

SCOTT T. MEIER, Associate Professor and Director of Training, Department of Counseling and Educational Psychology, SUNY Buffalo, Buffalo, NY

PETER F. MERENDA, Professor Emeritus of Psychology and Statistics, University of Rhode Island, Kingston, RI

WILLIAM R. MERZ, Sr., Professor, School Psychology Training Program, Department of Special Education,

Rehabilitation, and School Psychology, School of Education, California State University, Sacramento, Sacramento, CA

WILLIAM B. MICHAEL, Professor of Educational Psychology and Psychology, University of Southern California, Los Angeles, CA

ROBERT J. MILLER, Associate Professor of Special Education, Mankato State University, Mankato, MN

JOHN A. MILLS, Professor/Psychologist, Counseling and Student Development, Indiana University of Pennsylvania, Indiana, PA

JUDITH A. MONSAAS, Associate Professor of Education, North Georgia College & State University, Dahlonega, GA

KEVIN L. MORELAND, Professor of Psychology and Chair, Fordham University, Bronx, NY

SHERWYN MORREALE, Chair, Center for Excellence in Oral Communication, University of Colorado at Colorado Springs, Colorado Springs, CO

GALE M. MORRISON, Professor, Graduate School of Education, University of California, Santa Barbara, Santa Barbara, CA

PAUL M. MUCHINSKY, Joseph M. Bryan Distinguished Professor of Business, The University of North Carolina at Greensboro, Greensboro, NC

RALPH O. MUELLER, Associate Professor of Educational Research, Department of Educational Leadership, Graduate School of Education and Human Development, The George Washington University, Washington, DC

MILDRED MURRAY-WARD, Professor of Education, California Lutheran University, Thousand Oaks, CA

PHILIP NAGY, Professor, Measurement and Evaluation, The Ontario Institute for Studies in Education of the University of Toronto, Toronto, Ontario, Canada

DIANNA L. NEWMAN, Associate Professor of Educational Theory and Practice, University at Albany/State University of New York, Albany, NY

E. JEAN NEWMAN, Assistant Professor of Educational Psychology, University of South Alabama, Mobile, AL

ANTHONY J. NITKO, Professor of Education, School of Education, University of Pittsburgh, Pittsburgh, PA

JANET A. NORRIS, Professor of Communication Sciences and Disorders, Louisiana State University, Baton Rouge, LA

SALVADOR HECTOR OCHOA, Assistant Professor of Educational Psychology, Texas A&M University, College Station, TX

JUDY J. OEHLER-STINNETT, Associate Professor of Applied Behavioral Studies, Oklahoma State University, Stillwater, OK

LYNN R. OFFERMANN, Associate Professor of Psychology, George Washington University, Washington, DC

BILLY T. OGLETREE, Assistant Professor of Communication Disorders, College of Education and Allied Professions, Western Carolina University, Cullowhee, NC

D. JOE OLMI, Assistant Professor, School Psychology Program and Director, School Psychology Service Center, Department of Psychology, University of Southern Mississippi, Hattiesburg, MS

ALBERT OOSTERHOF, Professor of Educational Psychology, Florida State University, Tallahassee, FL

STEVEN J. OSTERLIND, Professor, University of Missouri-Columbia, Columbia, MO

DONALD P. OSWALD, Assistant Professor of Psychiatry, Medical College of Virginia/Virginia Commonwealth University, Richmond, VA

TERRY OVERTON, Licensed School Psychologist, Learning and Behavior Therapies, Inc., and Associate Professor of Psychology, Department of Special Education, Longwood College, Farmville, VA

STEVEN V. OWEN, Professor of Educational Psychology, University of Connecticut, Storrs, CT

VICKI S. PACKMAN, Senior Assessment Analyst, Salt River Project, Phoenix, AZ

KATHLEEN D. PAGET, Division Director, The Center for Child and Family Studies, College of Social Work, University of South Carolina, Columbia, SC

ANTHONY W. PAOLITTO, Assistant Professor, School Psychology Program, Ohio State University, Columbus, OH

SHARON E. PAULSON, Associate Professor of Educational Psychology, Ball State University, Muncie, IN

L. CAROLYN PEARSON, Associate Professor of Education, University of West Florida, Pensacola, FL

CAROLE PERLMAN, Director of Student Assessment, Chicago Public Schools, Chicago, IL

CHARLES A. PETERSON, Director of Training in Psychology, Department of Veterans Affairs, Minneapolis Medical Center, and Associate Clinical Professor of Psychology, University of Minnesota, St. Paul, MN

STEVEN I. PFEIFFER, Professor, Graduate School of Education, Kent State University, Kent, OH

LeADELLE PHELPS, Professor of School Psychology, Department of Counseling and Educational Psychology, State University of New York at Buffalo, Buffalo, NY

EUGENE (GENO) PICHETTE, Assistant Professor in the Division of Rehabilitation Psychology and Counseling, University of North Carolina at Chapel Hill, Chapel Hill, NC

WAYNE C. PIERSEL, Associate Professor of Educational Psychology, University of Nebraska—Lincoln, Lincoln, NE

JAMES W. PINKNEY, Professor of Counselor and Adult Education, East Carolina University, Greenville, NC

DAVID J. PITTENGER, Associate Professor of Psychology, Marietta College, Marietta, OH

MARCEL O. PONTON, Director, Neuropsychology Clinic, Harbor-UCLA Medical Center, and Assistant Clinical Professor, Department of Psychiatry, UCLA School of Medicine, Los Angeles, CA

G. MICHAEL POTEAT, Associate Professor of Psychology, East Carolina University, Greenville, NC

SHEILA R. PRATT, Assistant Professor of Communication Science & Disorders, University of Pittsburgh, Pittsburgh, PA

ERICH P. PRIEN, President, Performance Management Associates, Memphis, TN

RICHARD C. PUGH, Professor of Education, and Director of Education Technology Services, Indiana University, Bloomington, IN

RUDOLF E. RADOCY, Professor, Division of Music Education and Music Therapy, University of Kansas, Lawrence, KS

JEFFREY S. RAIN, Assistant Professor and Chairman, Industrial/Organizational Psychology Program, School of Psychology, Florida Tech, Melbourne, FL

NAMBURY S. RAJU, Distinguished Professor and Director, Center for Research and Service, Institute of Psychology, Illinois Institute of Technology, Chicago, IL

BIKKAR S. RANDHAWA, Professor of Educational Psychology, University of Saskatchewan, Saskatoon, Canada

ALAN J. RAPHAEL, President, International Assessment Systems, Inc. and Adjunct Associate Professor of Psychology, University of Miami, Miami, FL

JAMES C. REED, Chief Psychologist, St. Luke's Hospital, New Bedford, MA

ROBERT C. REINEHR, Professor of Psychology, Southwestern University, Georgetown, TX

PAUL RETZLAFF, Professor, Psychology Department, University of Northern Colorado, Greeley, CO

CECIL R. REYNOLDS, Professor of Educational Psychology & Professor of Neuroscience, Texas A&M University, College Station, TX

ROGER A. RICHARDS, Adjunct Professor of Communication, Bunker Hill Community College, Boston, MA, and Consultant, Massachusetts Department of Education, Malden, MA

T. ANDREW RIDENOUR, Post-Doctoral Fellow, Washington University, St. Louis, MO

DAVID C. ROBERTS, Consultant, Personnel Decisions International, Dallas, TX

GARY J. ROBERTSON, Vice President, Research and Development, Wide Range, Inc., Tampa, FL

BRUCE G. ROGERS, Professor of Educational Psychology, University of Northern Iowa, Cedar Falls, IA

CYNTHIA A. ROHRBECK, Associate Professor of Psychology, The George Washington University, Washington, DC

DEBORAH D. ROMAN, Director, Neuropsychology Laboratory, and Assistant Professor, Departments of Physical Medicine and Rehabilitation and Neurosurgery, University of Minnesota, Minneapolis, MN

GERALD A. ROSEN, Consulting Psychologist, Huntingdon Valley, PA

JENNIFER A. ROSENBLATT, Doctoral Candidate, University of California, Santa Barbara, CA

MICHAEL J. ROSZKOWSKI, Associate Professor of Psychology/Director of Marketing Research, The American College, Bryn Mawr, PA

BARBARA A. ROTHLISBERG, Professor of Psychology in Educational Psychology and Director of the M.A./Ed.S. Program in School Psychology, Ball State University, Muncie, IN

THADDEUS ROZECKI, Assistant Professor, University of Northern Iowa, Cedar Falls, IA

HERBERT C. RUDMAN, Emeritus Professor of Measurement and Quantitative Methods, Michigan State University, East Lansing, MI

MICHAEL LEE RUSSELL, Director, Neuropsychology Fellowship, Tripler Regional Medical Center, Honolulu, HI

DARRELL L. SABERS, Professor of Educational Psychology, University of Arizona, Tucson, AZ

DONNA S. SABERS, Educational Consultant, Tucson, AZ

CYRIL J. SADOWSKI, Professor of Psychology, Auburn University Montgomery, Montgomery, AL

JONATHAN SANDOVAL, Professor and Acting Director, Division of Education, University of California, Davis, Davis, CA

ELEANOR E. SANFORD, Senior Testing Consultant, Division of Accountability Services/Testing, North Carolina Department of Public Instruction, Raleigh, NC

WILLIAM I. SAUSER, JR., Professor and Executive Director for Outreach, College of Business, Auburn University, Auburn, AL

DIANE J. SAWYER, Murfree Professor of Dyslexic Studies, Middle Tennessee State University, Murfreesboro, TN

DALE P. SCANNELL, Professor of Education, Indiana University, Purdue University—Indianapolis, Indianapolis, IN

WILLIAM D. SCHAFER, Associate Professor of Measurement, Statistics, and Evaluation, University of Maryland at College Park, College Park, MD

FRANK SCHMIDT, Professor, College of Business, University of Iowa, Iowa City, IA

NEAL SCHMITT, University Distinguished Professor, Psychology and Management, Department of Psychology, Michigan State University, East Lansing, MI

GERALD R. SCHNECK, Professor of Rehabilitation Counseling, Mankato State University, Mankato, MN

PATRICIA SCHOENRADE, Professor of Psychology, William Jewell College, Liberty, MO

GENE SCHWARTING, Project Director, Early Childhood Special Education, Omaha Public Schools, Omaha, NE

STEVEN R. SHAW, School Psychologist, School District of Greenville County, Greenville, SC

EUGENE P. SHEEHAN, Associate Professor of Psychology, University of Northern Colorado, Greeley, CO

KENNETH G. SHIPLEY, Professor and Chair of Communicative Sciences and Disorders, California State University, Fresno, Fresno, CA

MARIELA C. SHIRLEY, Assistant Professor of Psychology, University of North Carolina at Wilmington, Wilmington, NC

MARK D. SHRIVER, Assistant Professor, University of Nebraska Medical Center, Omaha, NE

CRAIG S. SHWERY, Assistant Professor of Teacher Education, Fort Hays State University, Hays, KS

WESLEY E. SIME, Professor of Health and Human Performance, University of Nebraska-Lincoln, Lincoln, NE

KUSUM SINGH, Associate Professor, Educational Leadership and Policy Studies, College of Human Resources and Education, Virginia Tech, Blacksburg, VA

WAYNE H. SLATER, Associate Professor of Curriculum and Instruction, University of Maryland, College Park, MD

DOUGLAS K. SMITH, Professor and Director, School Psychology Training Program, University of Wisconsin—River Falls, River Falls, WI

JANET V. SMITH, Assistant Professor of Psychology and Counseling, Pittsburg State University, Pittsburg, KS

JEFFREY K. SMITH, Professor of Educational Psychology and Associate Dean, Graduate School of Education, Rutgers The State University of New Jersey, New Brunswick, NJ

JANET E. SPECTOR, Assistant Professor of Education, University of Maine, Orono, ME

ROBERT SPIES, Doctoral Candidate, University of Nebraska-Lincoln, Lincoln, NE

JACLYN B. SPITZER, Chief, Audiology and Speech Pathology Service, VA Connecticut Healthcare System, West Haven, CT and Associate Clinical Professor, Department of Surgery (Otolaryngology), Yale University School of Medicine, New Haven, CT

GARY J. STAINBACK, Senior Psychologist I, Department of Pediatrics, East Carolina University School of Medicine, Greenville, NC

JAYNE E. STAKE, Professor of Psychology, University of Missouri, St. Louis, MO

EDWARD R. STARR, Assistant Professor of Counseling Psychology, State University of New York at Buffalo, Buffalo, NY

MARGOT B. STEIN, Clinical Assistant Professor of Psychiatry, University of North Carolina School of Medicine, Chapel Hill, NC

STEPHANIE STEIN, Associate Professor of Psychology, Central Washington University, Ellensburg, WA

JAY R. STEWART, Assistant Professor and Director, Rehabilitation Counseling Program, Bowling Green State University, Bowling Green, OH

TERRY A. STINNETT, Associate Professor of Applied Behavioral Studies in Education, Oklahoma State University, Stillwater, OK

GERALD L. STONE, Professor of Counseling Psychology and Director, University Counseling Service, The University of Iowa, Iowa City, IA

RICHARD B. STUART, Professor Emeritus of Psychiatry, University of Washington, and Regional Faculty, The Fielding Institute, Seattle, WA

GABRIELLE STUTMAN, Consulting Psychologist, Cognitive Habilitation Services, New York City, NY

MICHAEL J. SUBKOVIAK, Associate Dean, School of Education, and Professor of Educational Psychology, University of Wisconsin-Madison, Madison, WI

RICHARD R. SUDWEEKS, Associate Professor of Instructional Science, Brigham Young University, Provo, UT

HOI K. SUEN, Professor of Educational Psychology, Pennsylvania State University, University Park, PA

NORMAN D. SUNDBERG, Professor Emeritus, Department of Psychology, University of Oregon, Eugene, OR

DONNA L. SUNDRE, Associate Assessment Specialist/Associate Professor of Psychology, James Madison University, Harrisonburg, VA

ROSEMARY SUTTON, Associate Professor, College of Education, Cleveland State University, Cleveland, OH

MARK E. SWERDLIK, Professor of Psychology, Illinois State University, Normal, IL

ANITA TESH, Assistant Professor, School of Nursing, University of North Carolina at Greensboro, Greensboro, NC

DONALD THOMPSON, Dean, and Professor of Counseling and Psychology, Troy State University Montgomery, Montgomery, AL

NORA M. THOMPSON, Neuropsychologist, Center on Human Development and Disabilities, University Hospital, Seattle, WA

GEORGE C. THORNTON III, Professor of Psychology, Colorado State University, Fort Collins, CO

JERRY TINDAL, Associate Professor, Behavioral Research and Teaching, University of Oregon, Eugene, OR

MICHAEL S. TREVISAN, Assistant Professor, Department of Educational Leadership and Counseling Psychology, Washington State University, Pullman, WA

SUSANA URBINA, Associate Professor of Psychology, University of North Florida, Jacksonville, FL

NICHOLAS A. VACC, Professor and Chairperson, Department of Counseling and Educational Development, School of Education, The University of North Carolina at Greensboro, Greensboro, NC

WILFRED G. VAN GORP, Associate Professor of Psychology in Psychiatry and Director, Neuropsychology Assessment Program, Cornell University Medical College, White Plains, NY

JAMES P. VAN HANEGHAN, Associate Professor of Behavioral Studies and Educational Technology, College of Education, University of South Alabama, Mobile, AL

GABRIELE van LINGEN, Lecturer, Department of Psychology, The University of Hong Kong, Hong Kong

WILLIAM M. VERDI, Manager, Employment Testing & Validation, Long Island Rail Road, Middle Village, NY

DOLORES KLUPPEL VETTER, Professor of Communicative Disorders, University of Wisconsin—Madison, Madison, WI

CHOCKALINGAM VISWESVARAN, Assistant Professor of Psychology, Florida International University, Miami, FL

WILLIAM J. WALDRON, Administrator, Employee Testing & Assessment, TECO Energy, Inc., Tampa, FL

ROBERT WALL, Graduate Professor of Education, College of Education, Towson State University, Towson, MD

NIELS G. WALLER, Associate Professor of Psychology, University of California, Davis, CA

ANNIE W. WARD, Emeritus Professor, University of South Florida, Daytona Beach, FL

SANDRA WARD, Assistant Professor of Education, College of William and Mary, School of Education, Williamsburg, VA

BETSY WATERMAN, Assistant Professor, Counseling and Psychological Services Department, State University of New York at Oswego, Oswego, NY

T. STEUART WATSON, Associate Professor of Educational Psychology, Mississippi State University, Starkville, MS

SHARON L. WEINBERG, Professor and Head, Program of Quantitative Methods, School of Education, New York University, New York, NY

ELLEN WEISSINGER, Associate Dean, Teachers College, University of Nebraska-Lincoln, Lincoln, NE

J. STEVEN WELSH, Director, School Psychology Program, Nicholls State University, Thibodaux, LA

LESLEY A. WELSH, Associate Professor of Education, West Chester University, West Chester, PA

PAUL D. WERNER, Professor, California School of Professional Psychology, Alameda, CA

BERT W. WESTBROOK, Professor of Psychology, North Carolina State University, Raleigh, NC

CAROL WESTBY, Professor of Communicative Disorders and Sciences, Wichita State University, Wichita, KS

RICHARD G. WHITTEN, Clinical Assistant Professor of Psychiatry, University of South Dakota Medical School, Sioux Falls, SD

WILLIAM K. WILKINSON, Consulting Psychologist, Boleybeg, Barna, Co. Galway, Ireland

JANICE G. WILLIAMS, Associate Professor of Psychology, Clemson University, Clemson, SC

ROBERT T. WILLIAMS, Professor of Education, Colorado State University, Fort Collins, CO

DAVID M. WILLIAMSON, Psychometrician, The Chauncey Group International, Princeton, NJ

HILDA WING, Personnel Psychologist, Federal Aviation Administration, Washington, DC

JOSEPH C. WITT, Professor of Psychology, Louisiana State University, Baton Rouge, LA

E. LEA WITTA, Assistant Professor, Educational Leadership and Research, University of Southern Mississippi, Hattiesburg, MS

KRISTEN WOJCIK, Research Assistant, Trenton State College, Trenton, NJ

RICHARD M. WOLF, Professor of Psychology and Education, Teachers College, Columbia University, New York, NY

MYRA N. WOMBLE, Assistant Professor of Occupational Studies, University of Georgia, Athens, GA

MICHELLE WOOD, Researcher, Graduate School of Education, University of California, Santa Barbara, Santa Barbara, CA

BLAINE R. WORTHEN, Professor of Psychology, Utah State University, Logan, UT

CLAUDIA R. WRIGHT, Professor of Educational Psychology, California State University, Long Beach, CA

PETER ZACHAR, Assistant Professor of Psychology, Auburn University at Montgomery, Montgomery, AL

SHELDON ZEDECK, Chair and Professor of Psychology, Department of Psychology, University of California, Berkeley, CA

LELAND C. ZLOMKE, Director of Clinical Psychology, Beatrice State Developmental Center, Beatrice, NE

STEVEN ZUCKER, School Psychologist, Cherry Creek Schools, and Honorarium Instructor, University of Colorado at Denver, Denver, CO

INDEX OF TITLES

INDEX OF ACRONYMS

This Index of Acronyms refers the reader to the appropriate test in The Thirteenth Mental Measurements Yearbook. *In some cases tests are better known by their acronyms than by their full titles, and this index can be of substantial help to the person who knows the former but not the latter. Acronyms are only listed if the author or publisher has made substantial use of the acronym in referring to the test, or if the test is widely known by the acronym. A few acronyms are the registered trademarks (e.g., SAT); where this is known to us, only the test with the registered trademark is referenced. There is some danger in the overuse of acronyms, but this index, like all other indexes in this work, is provided to make the task of identifying a test as easy as possible. All numbers refer to test numbers, not page numbers.*

CLASSIFIED SUBJECT INDEX

The Classified Subject Index classifies all tests included in The Thirteenth Mental Measurements Yearbook into 18 major categories: Achievement, Behavior Assessment, Developmental, Education, English, Fine Arts, Foreign Language, Intelligence and Scholastic Aptitude, Mathematics, Miscellaneous, Neuropsychological, Personality, Reading, Science, Sensory-Motor, Social Studies, Speech and Hearing, and Vocations. Each category appears in alphabetical order and tests are ordered alphabetically with each category. Each test entry includes test title, population for which the test is intended, and the test entry number in The Thirteenth Mental Measurements Yearbook. All numbers refer to test entry numbers, not to page numbers. Brief suggestions for the use of this index are presented in the introduction.

ACHIEVEMENT

Achievement Test for Accounting Graduates; Accounting job applicants or employees, see 5

Aprenda: La Prueba De Logros en Español; Grades K.5–1.5, 1.5–2.5, 2.5–3.5, 3.5–4.5, 4.5–5.5, 5.5–6.5, 6.5–8.9, see 12

California Achievement Tests, Fifth Edition; Grades K.0–K.9, K.6–1.6, 1.6–2.2, 1.6–3.2, 2.6–4.2, 3.6–5.2, 4.6–6.2, 5.6–7.2, 6.6–8.2, 7.6–9.2, 8.6–10.2, 9.6–11.2, 10.6–12.9, see 40

Canadian Achievement Tests, Second Edition; Grades 2.6–12.9, see 44

Collegiate Assessment of Academic Proficiency; Students in the first 2 years of college, see 74

Comprehensive Testing Program III; Grades 1–2, 2–3, 3–4, 4–6, 6–8, 8–12, see 83

CTB Portfolio Assessment System; Grades 1 & 2, 3, 4, 5 & 6, 7 & 8, see 87

Diagnostic Achievement Test for Adolescents, Second Edition; Ages 12–0 to 18–11, see 98

GOALS: A Performance-Based Measure of Achievement; Grades 1–12, see 131

Integrated Assessment System; Grades 1–9, see 152

Iowa Tests of Basic Skills, Forms K, L, and M; Grades K.1–1.5, K.8–1.9, 1.7–2.6, 2.5–3.5, 3, 4, 5, 6, 7, 8–9, see 159

Iowa Tests of Educational Development, Forms K, L, and M; Grades 9–12, see 160

Kaufman Functional Academic Skills Test; Ages 15–85 and over, see 166

Riverside Curriculum Assessment System; Grades K–12, see 268

Spanish Assessment of Basic Education, Second Edition; Grades 1.0–1.9, 1.6–2.9, 2.6–3.9, 3.6–4.9, 4.6–6.9, 6.6–8.9, see 291

Stanford Achievement Test, Ninth Edition; Grades K.0–13.0, see 292

Test of Academic Achievement Skills—Reading, Arithmetic, Spelling, and Listening Comprehension; Ages 4–0 to 12–0, see 321

Test of Academic Performance; Grades K–12, see 322

Tests of Adult Basic Education, Forms 7 & 8; Adults, see 343

Tests of Adult Basic Education Work-Related Foundation Skills; Adults in vocational/technical programs, students in adult basic education programs 2-year colleges, and secondary school ROP & JTPA programs, see 344

Wechsler Individual Achievement Test; Ages 5–19, see 359

Wonderlic Basic Skills Test; Teenagers and adults, see 362

Woodcock-McGrew-Werder Mini-Battery of Achievement; Ages 4–90, see 363

BEHAVIOR ASSESSMENT

DEVELOPMENTAL

EDUCATION

ENGLISH

FINE ARTS

FOREIGN LANGUAGES

INTELLIGENCE AND SCHOLASTIC APTITUDE

MATHEMATICS

MISCELLANEOUS

NEUROPSYCHOLOGICAL

PERSONALITY

READING

SCIENCE

SENSORY-MOTOR

SOCIAL STUDIES

SPEECH AND HEARING

VOCATIONS

PUBLISHERS DIRECTORY AND INDEX

This directory and index give the addresses and test entry numbers of all publishers represented in The Thirteenth Mental Measurements Yearbook. *Please note that all numbers in this index refer to test entry numbers, not page numbers. Publishers are an important source of information about catalogs, specimen sets, price changes, test revisions, and many other matters.*

Ablin Press Distributors, 700 John Ringling Blvd., #1603, Sarasota, FL 34236-1504: 103

Addiction Research Foundation, Marketing Services, 33 Russell Street, Toronto, Ontario M5S 2S1, Canada: 10, 16, 104, 155, 288

Allyn & Bacon, Department 894, 160 Gould Street, Needham Heights, MA 02194-2310: 113, 298

American Alliance for Health, Physical Education, Recreation, & Dance, 1900 Association Drive, Reston, VA 22091: 128

American College Testing, 2201 North Dodge Street, P.O. Box 4060, Iowa City, IA 52243-4060: 73, 74

American Guidance Service, Inc., 4201 Woodland Road, Circle Pines, MN 55014–1796: 34, 166, 167, 172, 203, 303

American Psychiatric Press, Inc., 1400 K Street, N.W., Suite 1101, Washington, DC 20005: 77

Applied Symbolix, 800 N. Wells St., Suite 200, Chicago, IL 60610: 11, 76, 273, 369

Arkansas Research & Training Center in Vocational Rehabilitation, P.O. Box 1358, Hot Springs, AR 71902: 367, 368

Associated Consultants in Education, P.O. Box 875, Suffern, NY 10901: 37, 309

Australian Council for Educational Research Ltd., 19 Prospect Hill Road, Private Bag 55, Camberwell, Victoria 3124, Australia: 8, 38, 178, 244, 314

Ballard & Tighe Publishers, 480 Atlas Street, Brea, CA 92821: 142, 250

Barrett and Associates, Inc., 500 West Exchange Street, Akron, OH 44302–1428: 23

Behavior Science Systems, Inc., P.O. Box 580274, Minneapolis, MN 55458: 56, 238

Behaviordyne, Inc. [Address Unknown]: 286

Bienvenu, Millard J., Northwest Publications, 710 Watson Drive, Natchitoches, LA 71457: 157, 192

Paul H. Brookes Publishing Co., Inc., P.O. Box 10624, Baltimore, MD 21285-0624: 352

Arnold R. Bruhn and Associates, 7910 Woodmont Avenue, Ste. 1300, Bethesda, MD 20814: 109

C.P.S., Inc., P.O. Box 83, Larchmont, NY 10538: 58, 112, 283

Canadian Test Centre, Educational Assessment Services, 85 Citizen Court, Suites 7 & 8, Markham, Ontario L6G 1A8 Canada: 44, 45

Canyonlands Publishing, Inc., 141 S. Park Avenue, Tucson, AZ 85719: 129

Career Research and Testing, Inc., 2005 Hamilton Avenue, Suite 250, San Jose, CA 95125: 53, 204, 213, 262

CASAS, 8910 Clairemont Mesa Blvd., San Diego, CA 92123-1104: 78

Center for Applied Linguistics, 1118-22nd Street, N.W., Washington, DC 20037: 62, 63, 137, 145

Center for Architecture and Urban Planning Research, P.O. Box 413, University of Wisconsin—Milwaukee, Milwaukee, WI 53201–0413: 106

Center for Creative Leadership, One Leadership Place, P.O. Box 26300, Greensboro, NC 27438–6300: 94

Center for Women Policy Studies [Address Unknown]: 260, 261

CFKR Career Materials, 11860 Kemper Road, Unit 7, Auburn, CA 95603: 50

Child Behavior Checklist, University Medical Education Associates, 1 South Prospect Street, Room 6434, Burlington, VT 05401-3456: 55

Child Development Resources, P.O. Box 280, Norge, VA 23127-0280: 140, 289

Child Welfare League of America, Inc., Publications Department, 440 First Street NW—Suite #310, Washington, DC 20001-2085: 125

Chronicle Guidance Publications, Inc., Aurora Street, P.O. Box 1190, Moravia, NY 13118–1190: 226

CIM Test Publishers, 23 Dunkeld Road, Ecclesall, Sheffield S11 9HN, United Kingdom: 191

Clinical Psychometric Research, Inc., P.O. Box 619, Riderwood, MD 21139: 93

The College Board, 45 Columbus Ave., New York, NY 10023–6992: 4

Communication Skill Builders, 555 Academic Court, San Antonio, TX 78204-2498: 102, 223

Consulting Psychologists Press, Inc., 3803 East Bayshore Road, P.O. Box 10096, Palo Alto, CA 94303: 48, 232, 305, 355

Consulting Resource Group International, Inc., #386 — 200 West 3rd Street, Sumas, WA 98295–8000: 120, 164, 176, 228, 271, 282, 300

CTB Macmillan/McGraw-Hill, 20 Ryan Ranch Road, Monterey, CA: 93940-5703: 40, 54, 57, 87, 88, 291, 325, 343, 344, 345

DBM Publishing, 100 Park Avenue, New York, NY 10017: 141

Educational & Psychological Consultants, Inc., 601 East Broadway, Suite 301, Columbia, MO 65201: 229

Educational Activities, Inc., P.O. Box 392, Freeport, NY 11520: 148

Educational Records Bureau, 345 East 47th Street, 14th Floor, New York, NY 10017: 122

Educational Testing Service, Publication Order Services, P.O. Box 6736, Princeton, NJ 08541–6736: 83

Educators Publishing Service, Inc., 31 Smith Place Cambridge, MA 02138–1089: 224

Exceptional Education, 18518 Kenlake PL NE, Seattle, WA 98155: 356

Faculty of Education, Memorial University of Newfoundland, St. John's, Newfoundland, A1B 3XB, Canada: 342

G.I.A. Publications, Inc., 7404 S. Mason Avenur, Chicago, IL 60638: 161

Gordon Systems, Inc., P.O. Box 746, DeWitt, NY 13214: 132

H & H Publishing Co., Inc., 1231 Kapp Drive, Clearwater, FL 34625: 177

Hanson Silver Strong & Associates, Inc. [Address Unknown]: 190

Harcourt Brace Educational Measurement, 555 Academic Court, San Antonio, TX 78204-2498: 131, 292, 293, 294, 295

Robert J. Harvey, 200 Woodbine, Blacksburg, VA 24060: 75

Hawthorne Educational Services, Inc., 800 Gray Oak Drive, Columbia, MO 65201: 105, 117, 236, 240, 366

Health Prisms, Inc., 130 Pleasant Pointe Way, Fayetteville, GA 30214: 84

Hogan Assessment Systems, Inc., P.O. Box 521176, Tulsa, OK 74152: 138

Imaginart, 307 Arizona Street, Bisbee, AZ 85603: 153

Insight Institute, Inc., 7205 N.W. Waukomis Drive, Kansas City, MO 64151: 149

Institute for Personality and Ability Testing, Inc., Test Services Division, P.O. Box 1188, Champaign, IL 61824-1188: 60

Invest Learning, Worldwide Development Headquarters, 4660 S. Hagadorn Rd., Suite 520, East Lansing, MI 48823-5353: 14

JIST Works, Inc., 720 North Park Avenue, Indianapolis, IN 46202-3431: 49, 143, 181

Keeler Instruments, Inc., 456 Parkway, Broomall, PA 19008: 65

Kendall/Hunt Publishing Company, 4050 Westmark Drive, P.O. Box 1840, Dubuque, IA 52004–1840: 278

Law School Admission Council/Law School Admission Service, Box 40, Newtown, PA 18940–0040: 174

Learnco Incorporated, Box L, Exeter, NH 03833: 101

Lienhard School of Nursing, Pace University, Pleasantville/ Briarcliff Campus, Bedford Road, Pleasantville, NY 10570: 299

Life Insurance Marketing and Research Association, Inc., P.O. Box 208, Hartford, CT 06141: 17, 52

Maddak Inc., Industrial Road, Pequannock, NJ 07440– 1993: 187, 284

Madison Geriatric Research, Education, and Clinical Center, VA Medical Center, 2500 Overlook Terrace, Madison, WI 53705: 20

Sigma Assessment Systems, Inc., Research Psychologists Press Division, 511 Fort Street, Suite 435, P.O. Box 610984, Port Huron, MI 48061–0984: 162, 285, 311

Simon & Schuster, Higher Education Group, 200 Old Tappan Road, Tappan, NJ 07675: 123

Slosson Educational Publications, Inc., P.O. Box 280, East Aurora, NY 14052–0280: 307

Sopris West, Inc., 1140 Boston Avenue, P.O. Box 1809, Longmont, CO 80502-1802: 150, 272, 275, 313

Stoelting Co., Oakwood Center, 620 Wheat Lane, Wood Dale, IL 60191: 35

Touchstone Applied Science Associates (TASA), Inc., Fields Lane, P.O. Box 382, Brewster, NY 10509: 90

Training House, Inc., P.O. Box 3090, Princeton, NJ 08543–3090: 13, 227, 243

TRT Associates, 65 Eagle Ridge Drive, Highland, NC 28741: 26

U.S. Department of Labor, Employment and Training Administration, 200 Constitution Avenue, N.W., Washington, DC 20210: 163, 354

Universal Attention Disorders, Inc., 4281 Katella Avenue, #215, Los Alamitos, CA 90720: 336

The University of Michigan Press, 839 Green Street, P.O. Box 1104, Ann Arbor, MI 48106–1104: 107, 239

Variety Pre-Schooler's Workshop, 47 Humphrey Drive, Syosset, NY 11791–4098: 127

Western Psychological Services, 12031 Wilshire Blvd., Los Angeles, CA 90025-1251: 220, 225, 231, 263, 320, 357

Dale E. Williams, Department of Psychology, John Carroll University, University Heights, OH 44118: 61

Wonderlic Personnel Test, Inc., 1509 N. Milwaukee Avenue, Libertyville, IL 60048-1387: 362

XICOM, Inc., 60 Woods Road, Tuxedo, NY 10987-3108: 119, 170, 183, 222, 235, 246, 301, 316

INDEX OF NAMES

Barry, C. T.: ref, 55(226)
Barry, S.: ref, 263(10,74)
Barry, S. J.: ref, 304(17)
Bart, W. M.: rev, 212
Bartelstone, J. H.: ref, 31(666)
Barthel, D. W.: ref, 20r
Bartko, J. J.: ref, 31(136), 55(109)
Bartl, G.: ref, 31(479)
Bartlett, B. J.: rev, 334
Bartlett, J. A.: ref, 263(374)
Bartusch, D. J.: ref, 55(365)
Baryza, M.: ref, 55(266)
Basco, M. R.: ref, 31(969), 263(373)
Basoglu, M.: ref, 31(422,423,667,668), 263(190,226,254)
Bass, J. D.: ref, 29(85)
Basu, J.: ref, 112r
Bat-Chava, Y.: ref, 320(19)
Bates, E.: test, 188; ref, 239r
Bates, J. E.: ref, 55(143,144,209,252,270,271,295,495)
Bates, M. A.: ref, 31(438)
Batsche, G. M.: ref, 58r, 139r
Battaglia, M. M.: ref, 31(927)
Battersby, R. D. E.: ref, 31(863)
Battle, M. A.: ref, 31(579)
Baucom, D. H.: ref, 296(13)
Bauer, A. M.: test, 236; ref, 21r
Bauer, E. A.: rev, 118
Bauer, M. S.: ref, 263(191)
Bauer, R. H.: ref, 40(20,31)
Bauermeister, J. J.: ref, 132r
Baum, A.: ref, 31(283,910), 136(22)
Baum, J. G.: ref, 31(115)
Baum, S. F.: ref, 263(317)
Bauman, K. E.: ref, 40(9)
Baumanis, R.: rev, 287
Baumgardner, T. L.: ref, 55(446,530), 359(12)
Baumgartner, A.: ref, 263(11)
Baumgartner, H.: ref, 15r
Baumgartner, M.: ref, 55(229)
Bauserman, S. A. K.: ref, 31(669)
Bauwens, F.: ref, 263(172)
Baxter, A.: ref, 29(64)
Baxter, G.: ref, 87r
Bayles, K. A.: test, 129; ref, 129r
Bayley, N.: test, 29; ref, 99r, 107r
Bazin, N.: ref, 31(424)
Beach, J.: ref, 55(504)
Beach, R.: ref, 122r
Beach, S. R. H.: ref, 31(92,94,183,201,425)
Beale, M. D.: ref, 263(249)
Beals, J.: ref, 55(53,130)
Beamesderfer, A.: ref, 31r
Bean, R. M.: ref, 40(10,32)
Bear, D. R.: ref, 292(15)
Beardsall, L.: ref, 55(273)
Beardslee, W. R.: ref, 31(992,993), 55(542)
Beasley, C. M.: ref, 136(21)

Beasley, C. M., Jr.: ref, 263(12)
Beasley, M.: ref, 180(7), 242(6)
Beasley, R.: ref, 201(14)
Beats, B. C.: ref, 263(356)
Beatty, S.: ref, 31(670)
Beatty, W. W.: ref, 31(499,671)
Beaty, L. A.: ref, 320(14)
Beauclair, L.: ref, 31(446), 263(195)
Beauvais, F.: ref, 18r, 104r
Bebbington, P.: ref, 263(244)
Bech, P.: ref, 263(35)
Beck, A. J.: ref, 30(47), 31(739)
Beck, A. T.: test, 30, 31, 32, 33; ref, 30r, 30(1,4,16,21,22,
    57,58,59,63), 31r, 31(41,293,294,332,399,449,451,
    500,585,626,848,849,901), 32r, 32(26,30), 33r, 136r,
    263(196), 297r
Beck, C. K.: ref, 32(59)
Beck, J. G.: ref, 30(17), 31(426), 263(192)
Beck, J. S.: ref, 30(21,57), 31(293,449), 32(26)
Beck, L. H.: ref, 132r
Beck, M. D.: rev, 343
Beck, N. C.: ref, 55(293)
Beck, R. W.: ref, 31r
Beck, S. J.: ref, 31(776)
Becker, J.: ref, 31(2,602,603)
Becker, J. T.: ref, 36(45), 42(37)
Becker, J. V.: ref, 31(116)
Becker, R. E.: ref, 31(73)
Becker, T.: ref, 263(118)
Becker-Lausen, E.: ref, 31(827)
Beckham, J. C.: ref, 31(117,872)
Beckman, P.: ref, 107(1)
Beckmann, H.: ref, 263(76)
Bédard, F.: ref, 31(1002)
Bédard, P. J.: ref, 31(1002)
Bederman, J.: ref, 55(82)
Bedi, G.: ref, 55(181)
Bedinger, S. D.: ref, 40(77)
Bedrosian, J. L.: ref, 68(1)
Beebe, D. W.: ref, 31(672)
Beeber, A.: ref, 132r
Beehr, T. A.: ref, 162(13)
Beeman, C.: test, 332; ref, 332(1)
Beer, J.: ref, 31(202,203,211,238), 33(1,2)
Beers, S. R.: ref, 42(17), 206(37)
Beersma, D. G. M.: ref, 31(107,152,357,358), 263(49,
    70,164,165)
Beerten, A.: ref, 200(20)
Beery, K. E.: ref, 337r
Beery, W.: ref, 346r
Begin, A.: ref, 31(156)
Begley, A.: ref, 31(963), 136(11,38)
Beidel, D. C.: ref, 55(372,485)
Beitchman, J. H.: ref, 55(42)
Beitman, B. D.: ref, 31(51)
Belanger, M. C.: ref, 31(446), 263(195)
Bell, J. E.: rev, 58

Braimen, S.: ref, 31(111)
Brainard, G. C.: ref, 263(14)
Braith, J. A.: ref, 31(84,85,560,561)
Bramlett, R. K.: ref, 40(78)
Brand, A. N.: ref, 263(97)
Brand, E.: ref, 31(208), 263(96)
Brand, E. F.: ref, 31(684)
Brand, R. J.: ref, 311r
Brand, S.: ref, 40(101)
Brandsma, J.: ref, 201(26)
Brandt, H. A.: ref, 31(209)
Brandt, J.: ref, 31(998), 32(80), 36(30,34,58,65)
Brandt, J. P.: ref, 36(13)
Brandt, P.: ref, 29(22), 55(83)
Braner, H. U.: ref, 263(84)
Brant, R.: ref, 55(188)
Brantley, D. C.: ref, 40(54)
Braswell, L.: ref, 201(42)
Brathwaite, J.: ref, 159(92)
Brauer, S.: ref, 55(69)
Braun, C. M. J.: ref, 42(12)
Braungart, J. M.: ref, 29(55)
Braungart-Rieker, J.: ref, 55(374)
Braver, S. L.: ref, 55(112)
Bravo, G.: ref, 128r
Bray, J. H.: ref, 55(19)
Brayden, R. M.: ref, 320(27)
Brazelton, T. B.: ref, 207r
Breault, C.: ref, 93r
Brecher, D.: ref, 263(160)
Brédart, S.: ref, 200(20)
Breen, M. J.: ref, 55(78), 132r
Breier, A.: ref, 31(529)
Breitbart, W.: ref, 31(893), 32(73)
Breiter, H. C.: ref, 30(19), 31(434)
Breitzer, G. M.: ref, 221(4)
Brennan, J. M.: ref, 31(766,942)
Brennan, P. L.: ref, 184(1)
Brennan, R. L.: ref, 88r
Brenneman, L. M.: ref, 68(32)
Brent, D.: ref, 71(21)
Brent, D. A.: ref, 31(296)
Breslau, N.: ref, 31(53)
Breuer, P.: ref, 31(715)
Brewer, B. W.: ref, 31(297)
Brewer, J. H.: test, 37, 309
Brewerton, T. D.: ref, 31(209)
Brewin, C. R.: ref, 31(537)
Breyer, M.: ref, 29(11)
Brichácek, V.: ref, 29(117)
Bridges, M. W.: ref, 31(610)
Bridges, P. K.: ref, 263(319)
Bridts, C. H.: ref, 263(122)
Bridwell, L. S.: ref, 122r
Briele, B.: ref, 263(366)
Brier, N.: ref, 55(257)
Briere, J.: ref, 55(422)

Brieter, H. C.: ref, 31(816)
Briggs, C.: ref, 30(33), 31(543)
Briggs, K. C.: ref, 202r
Briggs, M.: ref, 55(339)
Briggs-Gowan, M. J.: ref, 55(488)
Brin, M. F.: ref, 304(9)
Bringsjord, E. L.: rev, 40, 174
Brinker, R. P.: ref, 29(64,65)
Brinkman, D.: ref, 333(2)
Brintnell, E. S.: ref, 182(1)
Brinton, B.: ref, 68(2,5,33)
Brisbois, J. E.: ref, 206(49)
Britt, D. M.: ref, 31(729)
Britt, T. W., Jr.: ref, 337(1)
Brittlebank, A.: ref, 263(334)
Britton, J.: ref, 122r, 295r
Broadnax, S.: ref, 31(463), 32(35)
Brodaty, H.: ref, 263(55,75,123,139)
Brodsky, B.: ref, 263(357)
Brodsky, B. S.: ref, 32(36), 263(201,259)
Brodzinsky, A. B.: ref, 55(84)
Brodzinsky, D. M.: ref, 55(84)
Brogan, D.: ref, 31(327), 55(178)
Broich, K.: ref, 263(366)
Brokaw, B. F.: ref, 112r
Bromberger, J. T.: ref, 31(433,894)
Bromet, E. J.: ref, 32(18), 334(3)
Bromfield, E. B.: ref, 31(565), 42(25)
Bronsone, E. D., Jr.: ref, 132r
Bronstein, P.: ref, 55(152,489), 292(39)
Brookhart, S. M.: rev, 159
Brookhouser, P. E.: ref, 55(135)
Brooking, J.: ref, 31(493)
Brookings, J.: test, 368
Brookings, J. B.: rev, 309, 317
Brookmeyer, R.: ref, 36(65)
Brooks, D. J.: ref, 263(231)
Brooks, J. D.: ref, 31r
Brooks, L.: ref, 206(24)
Brooks-Gunn, J.: ref, 29(40,56), 55(153,308)
Brookshire, B. L.: ref, 55(398)
Brookshire, R. H.: test, 102; ref, 203(5,6,10), 102r
Brophy, J.: ref, 31(223), 263(107)
Broskowski, H.: ref, 306r
Brotherton, W. D.: rev, 183, 192
Brouwers, P.: ref, 29(95)
Brower, C. A.: ref, 55(504)
Brower, P.: ref, 159(1)
Browers, P.: ref, 29(78,119)
Brown, B. S.: ref, 31(110)
Brown, B. W., Jr.: ref, 207(1)
Brown, C.: ref, 31(685), 102r, 136(2,13), 263(260,345)
Brown, D.: ref, 29(110)
Brown, E.: ref, 55(211)
Brown, E. J.: ref, 31(686)
Brown, F.: rev, 281
Brown, F. G.: rev, 292

Burns, D. D.: ref, 31(369,438,439)
Burns, D. E.: ref, 159(26), 292(5)
Burns, G. L.: ref, 31(175)
Burns, J. W.: ref, 296(18)
Burrell, B.: ref, 221(36)
Burright, R. G.: ref, 132r, 132(5)
Burrows, R.: ref, 31(58), 64r, 64(1)
Burt, D. B.: ref, 29(100)
Burton, J.: ref, 31(131)
Burton, S. D.: test, 95
Busby, K.: ref, 89(7)
Busby, R. M.: ref, 201(70)
Buschke, H.: ref, 200(19)
Bush, N. F.: ref, 31(929)
Busse, J.: ref, 71(23)
Busse, R. T.: rev, 55; ref, 55(171), 277(2)
Busto, U.: ref, 30(56)
Butcher, J. N.: ref, 31r, 229r
Butler, B.: ref, 263(35)
Butler, J.: ref, 263(99)
Butler, L. D.: ref, 31(440)
Butler, L. S.: ref, 29(64)
Butler, R. W.: ref, 55(490)
Butler, S. M.: ref, 55(375)
Butters, N.: ref, 31(221,853), 32(20), 42(2,27,38,40,41,48)
Buttolph, L.: ref, 136(31)
Buttolph, M. L.: ref, 31(50,579)
Buxton, W. M.: ref, 206(35)
Buysse, D. J.: ref, 136(43,38), 263(198)
Buytenhuijs, E. L.: ref, 42(18)
Bwibu, N.: ref, 29(21)
Bylsma, F. W.: ref, 36(30,34)
Byrne, A.: ref, 32(75)
Byrne, B. M.: ref, 31(298), 280(3,7,15,41,42)
Byrne, M. E.: ref, 338(2)
Bzoch, K. R.: ref, 107r

Cacioppo, J. T.: ref, 302r
Caddell, J. M.: ref, 31(23)
Cadoret, R.: ref, 201(81)
Cahalane, J. F.: ref, 31(181), 263(79)
Cahan, S.: ref, 71(19)
Cairns, R. B.: ref, 237r
Calabrese, J.: ref, 263(161)
Calamari, J. E.: ref, 31(86,441)
Calarco, M. M.: ref, 31(703)
Caldararo, R.: ref, 42(37)
Caldwell, B. M.: ref, 55(255), 106r
Caldwell, C.: ref, 263(113)
Caldwell, C. B.: ref, 31(56), 32(8)
Caldwell, D. S.: ref, 31(117)
Calev, A.: ref, 263(291)
Calhoun, K. S.: ref, 31(75)
Calkins, S. D.: ref, 55(445,507), 234(3,5,6)
Callahan, C. M.: rev, 169, 312; ref, 159(33,88), 160(1), 162(6)
Callahan, T.: ref, 31(323)

Callis, R.: ref, 359r
Camara, W. J.: rev, 271, 365
Cameron, C. M.: ref, 31(706), 200(25)
Cameron, R. P.: ref, 31(745,895)
Camilli, G.: ref, 40(55), 160(2), 174r, 174(3), 330r
Camp, C. J.: rev, 20, 129
Campbell, A.: test, 123
Campbell, D.: test, 43; ref, 55(225), 196r
Campbell, D. T.: ref, 31r, 329r
Campbell, F. A.: ref, 29(66,101), 275(1)
Campbell, J. D.: ref, 31(524)
Campbell, J. R.: ref, 122r, 295r
Campbell, S. B.: ref, 55(20,259,376,491), 221(24)
Campbell, T. A.: ref, 55(174)
Campbell, T. F.: rev, 165; ref, 165r
Campbell, T. L.: ref, 31(292)
Campion, J. E.: ref, 256(1)
Campion, M. A.: ref, 256(1)
Campis, L. K.: ref, 55(48), 221(3)
Campling, G. M.: ref, 31(653)
Campos, A.: ref, 168(1)
Campos, J.: ref, 29(28,55)
Campos, J. J.: ref, 29(99)
Canadian Test Centre, Educational Assessment Services: test, 44, 45
Canberk, Ö.: ref, 263(186)
Cancienne, J.: ref, 31(454), 263(356)
Candler Lotvin, A. C.: ref, 177(3)
Cannon, D. S.: ref, 155r, 155(1)
Cannon, L.: ref, 132r
Cannon, W. G.: ref, 31(858), 201(74)
Cantor, N. K.: ref, 159(93)
Cantrell, J. K.: ref, 2r
Cantwell, D. P.: ref, 55(96)
Capaldi, D. M.: ref, 55(45,85)
Caplan, G.: ref, 89r
Capps, L.: ref, 24(2)
Caprara, G. V.: ref, 55(483)
Capreol, M. J.: ref, 201(22)
Capuano, F.: ref, 55(111)
Caraballo, L.: ref, 55(395)
Carbonell, J. L.: ref, 25r
Cardon, L. R.: ref, 36(46)
Carey, K. T.: rev, 1, 65; ref, 22r
Cargo, A. P.: ref, 55(158)
Carlson, E.: ref, 29(124), 55(168)
Carlson, E. A.: ref, 55(377)
Carlson, G. A.: ref, 263(100)
Carlson, J.: rev, 3, 5; ref, 277(2)
Carlson, J. F.: rev, 31, 296
Carlson, J. V.: rev, 209; ref, 209r
Carlson-Greene, B.: ref, 55(378)
Carlsson, S. G.: ref, 31(960)
Carlyon, W.: ref, 58r, 139r
Carmelli, D.: ref, 36(46,55)
Carmichael, M. S.: ref, 31(442)
Carmona, J. J.: ref, 30(55), 263(327)

Dadds, M. M.: ref, 55(484)
Dagon, E. M.: ref, 31(375)
Dahl, A. A.: ref, 112r
Dahl, K. L.: ref, 40(38)
Dahl, R. E.: ref, 263(58)
Dahlquist, L. M.: ref, 31(309,906)
Dahlstrom, L. F.: ref, 315r
Dahlstrom, W. G.: ref, 31r, 283r, 315r
Dail, P. W.: ref, 125(3)
Dailey, R. A.: ref, 292(68)
Daimon, K.: ref, 263(103)
Dalack, G. W.: ref, 31(705)
Dalakas, M. C.: ref, 31(452)
Dalal, M.: ref, 31(1015)
Dale, J. K.: ref, 31(270)
Dale, P. S.: test, 188; ref, 239r, 241(2)
Dale, T. M.: ref, 297r
Daleiden, E. L.: ref, 55(469)
Dalessio, A. T.: ref, 52r
Daley, S. E.: ref, 31(741,907)
Dalgleish, T.: ref, 31(706,769,961), 200(25,30)
Dalton, E. F.: test, 142
Daltroy, L. H.: ref, 55(90)
Daly, E.: ref, 68(18)
Daly, R. J.: ref, 32(4,42), 200(1,16)
Damarin, F.: rev, 29
Damarin, F. L.: ref, 281(12)
Damasio, A. R.: ref, 36(5,13)
Damasio, H.: ref, 36(5,13)
Damos, D. L.: ref, 31(465), 42(20)
Danforth, J. S.: ref, 55(326)
Daniel, M. H.: rev, 101, 266
Daniels, L.: ref, 201(52)
Daniels, M. H.: rev, 281
Daniels, S.: ref, 218(1)
Danion, J.: ref, 263(270)
Danish University Antidepressant Group: ref, 263(16, 142,166)
Danos, P.: ref, 263(366)
Dansereau, D. F.: ref, 156(1)
Daoust, P. M.: ref, 24(1)
D'Ari, A.: ref, 55(489)
Darnell, A. M.: ref, 136(24)
Darr, R. F., Jr.: rev, 218, 312
Dartigues, J. F.: ref, 36(14,63)
Darwish, T. A.: ref, 31(576)
Das, J. P.: ref, 82r, 132r
Dashiell, S. E.: test, 153
Dassa, D.: ref, 263(143)
Daston, S.: ref, 111r
D'Attilio, J. P.: ref, 31(285)
Dauber, S. L.: ref, 40(52)
Davey, B.: ref, 206(15)
David, A. S.: ref, 31(310)
David, H.: ref, 31(17,890), 136(1), 320(4)
Davidson, C. E.: ref, 55(167)
Davidson, D. A.: ref, 29(102)

Davidson, F.: ref, 63r
Davidson, J. A.: ref, 280(39)
Davidson, J. M.: ref, 31(363,442)
Davidson, K. C.: ref, 55(398)
Davidson, R. J.: ref, 31(503,636)
Davies, A. D. M.: ref, 200(3,6)
Davies, B.: ref, 29(96, 97,114), 241(17,18,23)
Davies, F.: ref, 31(707)
Davies, K.: ref, 42(51)
Davies, M.: ref, 31(111), 33(14), 263(318)
Davies, O. S.: ref, 112r
Davies, S.: ref, 200(13)
Davila, J.: ref, 31(741,907)
Davis, A.: ref, 159(70)
Davis, B.: rev, 28, 110, 267
Davis, B. J.: ref, 72r
Davis, B. L.: ref, 176r
Davis, C. S.: test, 155
Davis, D. R.: rev, 124
Davis, E. Z.: ref, 31(713)
Davis, H.: ref, 201(19,43)
Davis, J. M.: ref, 31(856,857,908), 263(311,336), 296(45)
Davis, L. J., Jr.: ref, 308r
Davis, P.: ref, 55(224), 201(30)
Davis, P. D.: ref, 159(63)
Davis, R.: test, 201
Davis, R. D.: ref, 202r
Davis, S. F.: rev, 120, 190
Davis, V.: ref, 296(16)
Davis-Sacks, M. L.: ref, 89r
Davison, G. C.: ref, 296(29)
Davison, M. L.: rev, 292, 329; ref, 329r
Daw, J. L.: ref, 359(9)
Dawes, R. M.: ref, 201r
Dawson, G.: ref, 29(80)
Dawson, K. S.: ref, 31(331), 201(25)
Dawson, R. I.: ref, 133r
Dax, E. M.: ref, 31(110)
Day, A.: ref, 42(4)
Day, D. M.: ref, 55(269)
Day, L. S.: ref, 68(21)
Dayson, D.: ref, 263(115)
D'Costa, A. G.: rev, 52
De Avila, M. E.: ref, 31(809)
De Beurs, E.: ref, 31(708), 296(19)
De Bruyn, E. E.: ref, 55(538)
De Bruyn, E. E. J.: ref, 55(553)
de Groot, A.: ref, 55(496)
De Groot, C. M.: ref, 31(785), 263(296)
De Guire, M. J.: ref, 55(100)
de Lugt, D.: ref, 263(63)
De Maertelaer, V.: ref, 263(25)
de Paúl, J.: ref, 55(384)
De Potter, B.: ref, 296(10)
de Sonneville, L. M. J.: ref, 36(9)
de Vries, H.: ref, 55(258)
de Vries, J.: ref, 263(95)

Dyer, K.: ref, 29(12)
Dyer, W. G.: ref, 289r
Dykens, E. M.: ref, 55(389)
Dykman, B. M.: ref, 31(288,913,923)
Dykman, R. A.: ref, 30(29), 55(148,166,245,246)
Dykstra, S. P.: ref, 31(64)
Dyssegaard, B.: ref, 221(42)
Dywan, J.: ref, 36(37)
D'Zurilla, T. J.: ref, 93(3)

Eagan, A. E.: ref, 281(43)
Earleywine, M.: ref, 55(314)
Earls, C. M.: ref, 31(17), 320(4)
Earls, F.: ref, 292(74)
East, T. D., IV: ref, 55(121)
Easterbrooks, M. A.: ref, 29(128), 55(167)
Eastman, C.: ref, 263(106)
Eastman, K. L.: ref, 55(475)
Eaton, E. M.: ref, 31(553), 42(24), 263(217)
Eaton, H. M.: ref, 55(90)
Eaton, W. O.: ref, 29(20)
Eaton, W. W.: ref, 77(3)
Eaves, D. M.: ref, 29(68)
Eaves, L. C.: ref, 29(68)
Eaves, L. J.: ref, 55(344)
Ebel, R. L.: rev, 292
Eber, H. W.: ref, 315r
Ebert, D.: ref, 263(202)
Ebert, L.: ref, 221(10,21)
Ebmeier, H.: ref, 40(11), 159(16), 292(1)
Ebmeier, K. P.: ref, 263(52,87,88,151,152,219)
Ebmeir, K. P.: ref, 263(306)
Eckardt, M. J.: ref, 136(29)
Eckblad, G.: ref, 55(93)
Eckblad, G. F.: ref, 55(234)
Eckenrode, J.: ref, 31(255), 159(92)
Eckert, E. D.: ref, 31(448)
Eckhardt, C. I.: ref, 296(39)
Eckhardt, M. J.: ref, 31(713)
Eckholdt, H. M.: ref, 263(373)
Eddowes, E. A.: ref, 55(274)
Edelbrock, C.: ref, 31(114), 55r, 55(390), 132r
Edelman, R. E.: ref, 32(37)
Edelsohn, G.: ref, 40(62,102)
Ediger, E.: ref, 31(924)
Ediger, J. M.: ref, 31(192,269)
Edmonds, J.: ref, 31(624)
Edson, A.: test, 148
Educational Records Bureau: test, 83, 122
Educational Technologies, Inc.: test, 14
Educational Testing Service: test, 123
Educators Publishing Service, Inc.: test, 224
Edwards, A.: ref, 29(114), 241(23)
Edwards, A. J.: rev, 323
Edwards, B. C.: ref, 31r
Edwards, J.: ref, 55(421), 68(24), 201(6)
Edwards, J. A.: ref, 31(645)

Edwards, J. H.: ref, 263(30)
Edwards, K. J.: ref, 112r
Edwards, L. A.: ref, 219r
Edwards, M. C.: ref, 31(130), 55(49)
Edwards, M. L.: ref, 304(6)
Edwards, P.: ref, 55(345)
Edwards, R.: ref, 18r
Edwards, R. P.: ref, 2r
Ee, J. S.: ref, 320(29)
Eells, K.: ref, 223r
Efran, J. S.: ref, 31(656)
Egan, V.: ref, 200(15)
Egashira, K.: ref, 263(77)
Egeland, B.: ref, 29(82,124), 31(65,583,584), 55(24,168,169,327,391,499), 96(2,3)
Ehi, M. K.: ref, 32(59)
Ehlers, A.: ref, 31(471,714,715,748)
Ehrhardt, A.: ref, 36(12)
Ehrler, D. J.: ref, 339(1)
Ehrlich, R. M.: ref, 29(36)
Eichelberger, T.: ref, 40(32)
Eigen, H.: ref, 221(9)
Einarsson-Backes, L. M.: ref, 29(27)
Eisdorfer, C.: ref, 201(5)
Eisdorfer, C. E.: ref, 36(25)
Eisele, J. A.: ref, 188(4)
Eisenberg, J. M.: test, 100
Eisenson, J.: test, 124
Eisenstadt, T. H.: ref, 55(170), 221(15)
Eiserman, W. D.: ref, 221(7,39), 223(1), 241(6,19)
Eison, A. R.: ref, 55(417)
Eison, J.: ref, 302r
Eitel, P.: ref, 31(716)
Ekern, M. D.: ref, 31(448)
Ekwall, E. E.: test, 113
El-Khatib, A.: ref, 218(4)
El-Samadeny, E. I.: ref, 218(4)
El-Sheikh, M.: ref, 55(275,276,500,501)
Elazar, B.: test, 187
Elcholtz, G. E.: ref, 68(7), 241(5)
Elcock, J.: ref, 280(10)
Eldredge, J. L.: ref, 159(80), 177(1)
Eldredge, K.: ref, 31(413,655)
Elger, C. E.: ref, 36(49)
Elias, J. W.: ref, 31(540)
Eliason, M. J.: ref, 29(69)
Elie, R.: ref, 31(43)
Eliot, J.: ref, 55(333)
Elizor, A.: ref, 31(860)
Elizur, D.: ref, 195r
Elkin, I.: ref, 31(989), 136(18)
Ellason, J. W.: ref, 201(62)
Ellenbogen, M. A.: ref, 31(427)
Ellenwood, A. E.: ref, 159(97)
Elley, W. B.: test, 245
Ellington, S.: ref, 31(39)
Elliot, D. J.: ref, 55(25)

Gilliam, J. E.: test, 130, 365
Gillin, J. C.: ref, 31(807,815), 42(2,41), 263(165,261, 267,313)
Gillis, J. S.: ref, 31(325)
Gillis, M. M.: ref, 30r, 30(46)
Gillman, I.: ref, 31(133)
Gillon, G.: ref, 68(22)
Gilmer, B. H.: ref, 248r
Gilroy, F. D.: ref, 281(35)
Gilsdorf, U.: ref, 263(111)
Gilvarry, K.: ref, 263(243)
Gingas, J.: ref, 31(1016)
Ginsburg, G. S.: ref, 292(39)
Ginter, G. G.: ref, 31(728)
Gipson, M. T.: ref, 31(743)
Girionas, I.: ref, 31(661)
Girolametto, L.: ref, 221(11,26)
Giroux, B.: ref, 55(195)
Giudicelli, S.: ref, 263(143)
Giunta, L. C.: ref, 30(41), 31(659), 32(54)
Givens, T.: ref, 2r
Gladstone, T. R. G.: ref, 31(992,993), 55(542)
Glaluis, M. F.: ref, 200(12)
Glanz, L. M.: ref, 32r
Glaser, E. M.: test, 358
Glaser, R.: ref, 263(203)
Glass, D. C.: ref, 31(787)
Glass, T. A.: ref, 92(1)
Glassman, A. H.: ref, 31(705,1000)
Gleason, J. R.: ref, 108r
Gleason, R.: ref, 31(171)
Gleckman, A. D.: ref, 31(235)
Glennerster, A.: ref, 31(918)
Gleser, G. C.: test, 89; ref, 89r
Glod, C.: ref, 263(224)
Glod, C. A.: ref, 263(345)
Glover, D.: ref, 263(269)
Glover, H.: ref, 31(490)
Glover, J. A.: rev, 267
Glover, M. E.: ref, 240r
Glover, V.: ref, 263(86)
Glowacki, J. M.: ref, 31(503)
Glue, P.: ref, 31(93), 263(236)
Glutting, J. J.: test, 135; ref, 359(5)
Glymph, A.: ref, 31(397), 159(65)
Gnys, J. A.: ref, 55(402)
Göbel, C.: ref, 263(76)
Godding, P. R.: ref, 31(729)
Godlewski, M. C.: ref, 36(44)
Godovy, J. F.: ref, 31(641)
Goering, P.: ref, 77(7,13)
Goetz, C. G.: ref, 263(278)
Goetz, E. T.: ref, 206(9)
Goetz, R.: ref, 32(14,47), 263(233)
Goetz, R. R.: ref, 31(753), 32(81), 136(37), 263(58,281)
Goevremont, D. C.: ref, 31(199), 55(79,81)
Gold, A.: ref, 29(127), 55(549)

Gold, J. M.: ref, 42(22)
Gold, M.: ref, 42(43)
Gold, M. V.: ref, 206(46)
Gold, R.: ref, 31(640), 263(244)
Gold, Y.: ref, 260r
Goldade, P.: ref, 201(32)
Goldberg, A. E.: ref, 104r
Goldberg, E.: ref, 42(1)
Goldberg, J. O.: ref, 202r
Goldberg, L. R.: rev, 162; ref, 121r, 191r, 365r
Goldberg, M. D.: ref, 55(265), 159(48,91)
Goldberg, S.: ref, 29(93,127), 55(403,549)
Goldberg, S. J.: ref, 31(9)
Goldberg, T. E.: ref, 42(13,22), 200(10)
Goldbloom, D. S.: ref, 77(7)
Golden, R. N.: ref, 136(27), 263(273,316)
Goldenberg, I. M.: ref, 263(158)
Goldfried, M. R.: ref, 31(695)
Golding, L. A.: ref, 128r
Goldman, B. A.: rev, 49, 71
Goldman, B. D.: ref, 29(30)
Goldman, L.: ref, 31(730), 296(42)
Goldman, R.: ref, 324r
Goldner, E. M.: ref, 263(137)
Goldschmid, M. L.: rev, 71
Goldsmith, D. F.: ref, 31(731)
Goldsmith, H. H.: ref, 55(546)
Goldsmith, L. A.: ref, 112r
Goldsmith, R. E.: ref, 191r
Goldstein, A.: ref, 31(214), 201(15)
Goldstein, A. J.: ref, 30(26), 31(98,491), 320(8)
Goldstein, D.: ref, 29r
Goldstein, D. E.: ref, 55(293)
Goldstein, D. J.: ref, 337(1)
Goldstein, G.: ref, 42(17), 206(32,37)
Goldstein, M. G.: ref, 30(62), 31(892)
Goldstein, M. J.: ref, 31(229)
Goldstein, S.: ref, 31(132), 36(12)
Golin, A. K.: ref, 40(50)
Golinkoff, R. M.: ref, 188(6)
Golomb, M.: ref, 263(279)
Golombok, S.: ref, 31(732), 221(41)
Golshan, S.: ref, 31(815), 263(165,267)
Gommeren, W.: ref, 263(199)
Gonman, J.: ref, 31(326)
Gonnel, J.: ref, 263(190)
Gonzales, C.: ref, 42(11)
Gonzalez, J.: ref, 31(721)
González, G.: ref, 31(578)
González, M. A.: ref, 168(1)
Good, G. D.: ref, 263(106)
Good, G. E.: ref, 31(504)
Good, R.: ref, 294(7)
Good, R. H., III: ref, 294(9)
Goodale, T. S.: ref, 31(492)
Goodglass, H.: ref, 129r
Goodin, M.: ref, 55(164), 221(14)

Haskell, W. L.: ref, 31(25,344)
Haskett, M. E.: ref, 55(411)
Haskett, R. F.: ref, 136(8), 263(44)
Haskin, B. S.: test, 239
Haslam, N.: ref, 31(332,500)
Hastings, C.: ref, 316r
Hastings, J. E.: ref, 201(40)
Hastings, J. T.: rev, 292
Hatch, D. R.: ref, 31r
Hatch, J. P.: ref, 31(230), 296(5)
Hatchett, L.: ref, 31(716)
Hathaway, S. R.: ref, 282r
Hatt, C. V.: rev, 58
Hattie, J.: rev, 44, 320
Hattori, M.: ref, 89(4)
Hattrup, K.: rev, 116, 318
Hatzichristou, C.: ref, 280(12)
Hatzimanolis, J.: ref, 263(65)
Hatzinger, R.: ref, 263(211)
Hauck, A. L.: ref, 292(40)
Haug, H.-J.: ref, 263(24,242)
Haugen, D.: ref, 159(15)
Haughey, M. J.: ref, 304(7)
Haun, D. M.: ref, 55(207)
Hauser, G.: ref, 31(445)
Hauser, P.: ref, 263(247)
Hauser, W. A.: ref, 36(17)
Haverkamp, B. E.: ref, 162(12)
Haviland, M. G.: ref, 31(139)
Hawken, L.: ref, 31(910)
Hawkins, C. A.: ref, 31(1007)
Hawley, D. R.: ref, 192r
Hawton, K.: ref, 31(291)
Haxby, J. V.: ref, 68(18)
Hay, D. F.: ref, 31(231)
Hay, P.: ref, 31(826)
Hayes, A. M.: ref, 31(695,820)
Hayes, D. P.: ref, 102r
Hayes, J. R.: ref, 295r
Hayes, M. T.: ref, 206(35)
Hayes, S. F.: ref, 192r
Hayes, T. L.: rev, 200, 347
Hayes, Z. L.: ref, 206(40)
Hayford, J. R.: ref, 29(74), 55(215,306)
Hayhurst, H.: ref, 31(805,814,859), 263(314,322,344)
Hayne, C.: ref, 31(28)
Hayne, C. H.: ref, 31(140)
Haynes, N. M.: ref, 40(3)
Haynes, S. D.: rev, 64, 111
Haynes, S. N.: ref, 31(942)
Hays, R. D.: ref, 32(59)
Hayslip, M. A.: ref, 16r
Haythronthwaite, J.: ref, 31(142)
Hayward, P.: ref, 31(501)
Hazzard, A.: ref, 55(412,492)
Healy, B.: ref, 31(132)
Healy, C. C.: ref, 48(13)

Healy, D.: ref, 263(81,157)
Healy, J.: ref, 31(295)
Healy, J. M., Jr.: ref, 55(183)
Healy, S.: ref, 292(65)
Heath, A. C.: ref, 77(12)
Heather, N.: ref, 288r, 288(1)
Heaton, R.: ref, 42(40)
Heaton, R. K.: ref, 42(52), 263(364)
Heaton, S. C.: ref, 42(52), 263(364)
Heber, R.: ref, 1r, 2r
Hébert, M.: rev, 45, 167
Heckhausen, H.: ref, 195r
Hedeker, D.: ref, 31(59)
Hedlund, S.: ref, 31(744)
Heefner, A. S.: ref, 31(841)
Heeren, T. J.: ref, 31(763)
Heerman, C. E.: ref, 206(41)
Heffer, R. W.: ref, 34r, 359(11)
Hegar, R.: ref, 55(413)
Hegar, R. L.: ref, 31(495)
Hegedus, A. M.: ref, 307r
Hegel, M. T.: ref, 31(502)
Heger, A.: ref, 55(191)
Heidrich, A.: ref, 263(118)
Heigl, E. A.: ref, 112r
Heilbrun, A. B.,Jr.: rev, 133; ref, 149r
Heilman, K. M.: ref, 42(4,43)
Heim, A. W.: rev, 269
Heimberg, R. G.: ref, 31(73,435,686)
Heindel, W.: ref, 42(2,41)
Heindel, W. C.: ref, 31(853), 42(27)
Heinz, A.: ref, 77(6)
Heinze, M. C.: ref, 58(4)
Heiskanen, O.: ref, 36(43)
Heiss, G. E.: ref, 31(428)
Heist, E. K.: ref, 31(267)
Hekmat, H.: ref, 31(155)
Helkala, E.-L.: ref, 36(53)
Hellawell, D. J.: ref, 36(19)
Heller, K. W.: ref, 29(103)
Heller, T. L.: ref, 55(415,482), 221(46)
Hellervik, L. W.: ref, 176r
Hellström, K.: ref, 30(8), 31(159,257)
Helm-Estabrooks, N.: test, 11, 39, 331; ref, 39r
Helmes, E.: ref, 229r
Helmreich, R. L.: ref, 195r
Helmstadter, G. C.: rev, 358; ref, 358r
Helmstaedter, C.: ref, 36(49)
Helwig, S.: ref, 29(77)
Helzer, J. E.: ref, 308r
Hembree, R.: ref, 159(49)
Hemsley, D. R.: ref, 31(750), 200(7)
Henderson, D.: ref, 2(3)
Henderson, J.: test, 273; ref, 31(413,655)
Henderson, M. C.: ref, 31(657)
Henderson, P. A.: ref, 159(2)
Henderson, V. L.: ref, 241(2)

Lemerond, J.: ref, 31(362), 32(27), 33(5)
Lemery, K. S.: ref, 55(546)
Lemoine, H. E.: ref, 44(1)
Lenane, M.: ref, 55(32)
Lenane, M. C.: ref, 55(510)
Lenehan, M. C.: ref, 180(5)
Leng-Shiff, R.: ref, 55(184)
Lengua, L. J.: ref, 55(515)
Lennings, C. J.: ref, 31(546)
Lenz, J. W.: ref, 31(351), 296(19)
Lenzenweger, M. F.: ref, 31(145,547,806,904), 270(3)
Leo, R.: ref, 31(278)
Leon, A.: ref, 263(158)
Leon, A. C.: ref, 31(615)
Leonard, B. E.: ref, 263(43,99,305)
Leonard, B. R.: ref, 24(1)
Leonard, L. B.: ref, 241(10)
Leong, F. T. L.: rev, 8, 303
Leos, N.: ref, 55(204)
Lepoutre, L.: ref, 263(68)
Lerer, B.: ref, 263(291)
Lerner, M. S.: ref, 31(78), 32(10)
Lesage, A.: ref, 31(43,837)
Lesanics, D.: ref, 31(783), 55(425)
Lesem, M. D.: ref, 31(209), 263(266)
Leserman, J.: ref, 136(27), 263(273,316)
Lesko, L. M.: ref, 55(125)
Leslie, M. I.: ref, 30(6), 31(216)
Lesnak, L.: ref, 281(38)
Lespérance, F.: ref, 31(724)
Lesser, I. M.: ref, 31(267), 136(5)
Lester, D.: ref, 31(247,348,349,350,468,505,548,773, 774,946), 320(20)
Lester, F.: ref, 244r
Lester, J. M.: ref, 30(41), 31(659), 32(54)
Letarte, H.: ref, 30(43), 31(711)
Letemendia, F. J. J.: ref, 263(159)
Letenneur, L.: ref, 36(63)
Letourneau, P. K.: ref, 31(62,63), 32(9)
Lettenneur, L.: ref, 36(14)
Leuder, D. C.: ref, 180(1)
Leun, H. S.: ref, 39r
Leung, A.: ref, 218(1)
Leung, F.: ref, 31(400)
Leung, K.: ref, 280(8)
Leung, S. A.: rev, 118, 182; ref, 281(27)
Leung, S. W.: ref, 174(5)
Leveau, B.: ref, 31(807), 263(313)
Levendosky, A. A.: ref, 55(322)
Levengood, R. A.: ref, 42(46)
Levenson, J. A.: ref, 263(17)
Levenson, R. L., Jr.: ref, 29(76)
Levenson, R. W.: ref, 25r
Leventhal, A.: ref, 277(2)
Leventhal, J. M.: ref, 55(506)
Leverett, R. G.: rev, 102, 354
Levin, H. S.: ref, 36r

Levin, J. R.: ref, 40(2)
Levin, R.: ref, 31(742)
Levine, J.: ref, 263(255)
Levine, M. N.: ref, 2r
Levine, R. E.: ref, 31(363)
Levinson, E. M.: ref, 48(15), 281(19,38,47)
Levitt, A. J.: ref, 31(144,197,770), 263(160,288,354)
Levitt, M.: ref, 31(697)
Levy, B. A.: ref, 44(1)
Levy, B. M.: ref, 55(520)
Levy, D.: ref, 263(255)
Levy, D. L.: ref, 31(904)
Levy, P. E.: ref, 195r
Levy, R.: ref, 263(355)
Levy-Shiff, R.: ref, 320(41)
Lewandowski, L.: ref, 71(14), 159(73), 320(31)
Lewin, K.: ref, 183r, 228r
Lewin, T. J.: ref, 31(958)
Lewinsohn, P. M.: ref, 31(79,217,218,598), 55(33,88,404), 263(232), 296(9)
Lewis, B. A.: ref, 68(10,11), 341(2)
Lewis, C. A.: ref, 31(559)
Lewis, C. P.: ref, 31(101), 263(46)
Lewis, D. A.: ref, 31(157)
Lewis, F.: test, 367
Lewis, H. A.: ref, 159(107)
Lewis, K. E.: ref, 304r
Lewis, K.R.: ref, 29(100)
Lewis, M.: ref, 29(32,60), 55(221,505)
Lewis, M. A.: rev, 37, 190
Lewis, M. H.: ref, 31(1015)
Lewis, N. D. C.: rev, 124
Lewis, P. D. R.: ref, 31(533)
Lewis, R.: test, 8; ref, 8r
Lewis, S.: ref, 263(243)
Lewis, S. J.: ref, 201(11)
Lex, B. W.: ref, 263(64)
Ley, T. C.: ref, 206(14)
Leysen, J. E.: ref, 263(199)
Leyva, C.: ref, 132r
Lezak, M. D.: ref, 36r, 331r
Li, A. K. F.: ref, 178(1)
Li, D.: ref, 36(10)
Li, P. P.: ref, 136(26), 263(382)
Li, Y. C.: ref, 63r
Liang, M. H.: ref, 55(90)
Liao, D.: ref, 263(273,316)
Liaw, F.: ref, 29(40), 55(153,308)
Licht, B. G.: ref, 280(38)
Lidberg, A.: ref, 31(516)
Liddell, D. L.: ref, 31(649)
Liddle, P. F.: ref, 31(290)
Lidsky, D.: ref, 263(291)
Liebenaver, L. L.: ref, 55(243)
Lieber, J.: ref, 107(1)
Lieberman, L.: ref, 159(76)
Liebowitz, M. R.: ref, 36(8), 263(268)

Losch, M.: ref, 31(48)
Loss, N.: ref, 31(776), 41(2)
Lothar, S. S.: ref, 55(196)
Lothman, D. J.: ref, 55(328)
Lottenberg, S.: ref, 263(184)
Louis, B.: ref, 29(32)
Louiselle, P. A.: ref, 320(1)
Louks, J.: ref, 31(28)
Louks, J. L.: ref, 31(140)
Lovelace, L.: ref, 29(118)
Loveland, K. A.: ref, 29(100)
Lovett, B. B.: ref, 55(423)
Lovett, D. L.: ref, 2(1)
Lovette, G. J.: ref, 31(870)
Lovibond, S. H.: ref, 30r
Low, B. P.: ref, 55(230)
Low, H.: ref, 263(326)
Lowe, C. F.: ref, 31(81,444)
Lowenbraun, P. B.: ref, 30(10)
Lowry, C. B.: ref, 55(244)
Lowther, J. L.: ref, 202r
Lowther, M. A.: test, 302
Loyd, B. H.: ref, 162(6)
Loza, W.: ref, 201(45)
Lozoff, B.: ref, 29(104)
Lu, K. H.: ref, 332r
Lubin, B.: test, 296; ref, 31(277,352,552), 296(7,10,11,
    12,15,16,17,18,20,21), 297r
Lublin, F.: ref, 42(11)
Luborsky, L.: ref, 31(665,880)
Lucas, F.: ref, 263(105)
Lucas, H.: ref, 29(67)
Lucas, J. A.: ref, 31(146), 36(11)
Luce, S. C.: ref, 29(12)
Lucente, S.: ref, 31(475)
Luchman, A.: ref, 325(3)
Ludden, L. L.: test, 143
Ludgate, J. W.: ref, 32(42), 200(16)
Luehr, J. G.: ref, 308r
Luetke, C.: ref, 263(345)
Lugauer, J.: ref, 263(76)
Luhtanen, R.: ref, 31(463), 32(35)
Lukin, L. E.: rev, 44, 119
Lumley, M. A.: ref, 55(197)
Lumley, T.: ref, 63r
Lunde, M.: ref, 263(256)
Lundy, A.: ref, 31(777)
Lunneborg, C. E.: ref, 320(5), 357(1)
Lunneborg, P. W.: test, 357; ref, 357(1)
Lupierre, Y.: ref, 263(63)
Lupkowski-Shoplik, A. E.: ref, 40(64), 159(60)
Lushene, R. E.: ref, 249r
Lusk, R.: ref, 31(406), 55(239), 60(2), 159(66), 320(25)
Lustig, J. L.: ref, 55(112)
Luthar, S. S.: ref, 55(309,424)
Luzzo, D. A.: ref, 48(7,9,11,12,14)
Lyketsos, C. G.: ref, 77r

Lyketsos, G. C.: ref, 77r
Lykken, D. T.: rev, 162
Lykouras, L.: ref, 263(65,216)
Lyman, R. D.: ref, 55(321)
Lynam, D.: ref, 55(86)
Lynch, B.: ref, 62r
Lynch, B. K.: ref, 63r
Lynch, E. W.: test, 107, 239
Lynch, M.: ref, 29(38), 55(157)
Lynch, M. E.: ref, 31(327), 55(178)
Lynch, P. M.: ref, 31(29)
Lynch, P. S.: ref, 55(459)
Lynch, R. S.: ref, 31(909), 296(48,49)
Lynch, S.: ref, 40(22)
Lynch, S. J.: ref, 40(64)
Lyness, S. A.: ref, 31(553), 42(24), 263(217)
Lynn, G.: ref, 2r
Lynn, R.: ref, 55(348), 195r
Lynn, S. J.: ref, 89(12)
Lyon, G. R.: ref, 359r
Lyon, H. M.: ref, 31(554)
Lyons-Ruth, K.: ref, 29(15,43,128)
Lytle, C.: ref, 55(191)
Lyubomirsky, S.: ref, 31(778)
Lywood, D. W.: ref, 263(159)

Maag, J. W.: ref, 40(84,92)
Mabe, P. A.: ref, 55(113)
MacArthur, C.: ref, 340(6,12)
MacArthur, C. A.: ref, 40(60), 294(5)
Macaruso, P.: ref, 329(1)
MacCallum, R.: ref, 270r
Maccow, G.: rev, 91, 171
Macdiarmid, J. I.: ref, 31(779), 111(2)
MacDonald, A. W., III: ref, 55(481)
MacDonald, C.: ref, 31(144), 263(160)
MacDonald, J.: rev, 68, 323
MacDonald, V. V.: ref, 55(533)
Maceira, D.: ref, 133(3)
MacGillivray, R. G.: ref, 31(555)
MacGregor, D.: ref, 29(93)
Machalow, S.: ref, 115r
MacHarg, R. A.: ref, 40(43)
Machida, S.: ref, 55(64)
Machowski, R.: ref, 263(333)
MacIntyre, P. D.: ref, 162(8)
Mack, A. E.: ref, 68(13), 323(3)
Mackay, S.: ref, 31(304)
Mackay, S. A.: ref, 55(375)
Mackenzie, T. B.: ref, 31(448)
Mackert, A.: ref, 263(50)
Mackie, B.: ref, 113(1)
MacKinnon-Lewis, C.: ref, 31(249)
MacLean, W. E., Jr.: ref, 55(114)
MacLeod, A. K.: ref, 31(556,780), 32(40,62,75)
Macmann, G. M.: ref, 55(198)
MacMillan, D. L.: ref, 2r

Mindes, E. J.: ref, 192r
Mindry, D.: ref, 36(12)
Miner, M. E.: ref, 55(398)
Minichiello, W. E.: ref, 31(50), 136(31)
Ministry of Education: test, 193
Miniutti, A. M.: ref, 68(6)
Minkonas, D. V.: ref, 55(243)
Minner, B.: ref, 263(161)
Minnett, A.: ref, 234(4)
Minnett, A. M.: ref, 280(11)
Mintun, M. A.: ref, 263(370)
Mintz, J.: ref, 31(253,603), 263(247)
Mintz, L. I.: ref, 31(253)
Mirabella, R. F.: ref, 31(483)
Miranda, J.: ref, 31(369,795), 201(12)
Mireault, G.: ref, 55(263)
Mirsky, A. F.: ref, 29(2), 132r
Mischel, W.: ref, 162r
Miserandino, M.: ref, 292(78)
Mislevy, R. J.: test, 123
Misukanis, T. M.: ref, 320(1)
Misulis, K. E.: ref, 334(1)
Mitchell T. W.: ref, 52r
Mitchell, D. R.: ref, 42(11)
Mitchell, E.: ref, 280(10)
Mitchell, E. S.: ref, 31(45)
Mitchell, J.: ref, 263(277)
Mitchell, J. E.: ref, 31(448)
Mitchell, K.: ref, 247r
Mitchell, P.: ref, 77(4), 263(55,75,123,139,312)
Mitchell, T. V.: ref, 132r
Mithaug, D. E.: test, 356; ref, 356r
Mitropoulou, V.: ref, 31(1017)
Mitrushina, M.: ref, 31(572)
Mizes, J. S.: ref, 31(239)
Mizuta, I., 55(519)
Mobayed, M.: ref, 263(34)
Mobb, E.: ref, 68(19), 341(5)
Mobley, B. D.: ref, 201(39)
Mock, J.: ref, 31r, 32r, 136r, 297r
Mock, L. O.: ref, 55(186)
Modjeski, R. B.: ref, 358r
Moeller, F. G.: ref, 263(165,173)
Moersch, M. S.: test, 107, 239
Moes, D.: ref, 31(254)
Moffitt, T. E.: ref, 29(48), 55(86,299,365,527)
Moffoot, A.: ref, 263(87,152)
Moffoot, A. P. R.: ref, 263(219)
Mogg, K.: ref, 31(683,792), 200(23)
Mohr, J.: ref, 55(446), 359(12)
Mohr, J. P.: ref, 36(17,18)
Mohs, R.: ref, 263(275)
Moilanen, D. L.: ref, 31(793)
Moilanen, I.: ref, 58(3)
Mok, G. S.: ref, 31(71), 263(22)
Molchan, S.: ref, 31(631)
Molfese, V. J.: ref, 29(77,118,129)

Moline, M.: ref, 263(56)
Moller, H.-J.: ref, 263(366)
Moller, S. E.: ref, 263(35,166)
Möller, A. T.: ref, 320(22)
Möller, H.-J.: ref, 263(124,130)
Moller-Madsen, S.: ref, 263(28)
Molloy, M.: ref, 263(248)
Molock, S.: ref, 55(185)
Molock, S. D.: ref, 31(566), 33(8)
Momose, T.: ref, 36(16)
Mongrain, M.: ref, 31(679)
Monk, T. H.: ref, 263(198)
Monroe, J. M.: ref, 31(393), 263(179)
Monroe, S. M.: ref, 31(396,844,954), 263(180,338,371)
Monroe-Blum, H.: ref, 31(1011)
Monsaas, J. A.: rev, 90, 259
Monsch, A. U.: ref, 42(38,48)
Montag, I.: ref, 202r
Montague, M.: ref, 55(203)
Montei, M.: ref, 285(1)
Monteleone, P.: ref, 263(36)
Montgomerie, T. C.: ref, 182(1)
Montgomery, D.: ref, 159(106)
Montgomery, J. W.: ref, 68(26)
Montgomery, M. J.: ref, 55(116)
Montgomery, M. S.: ref, 280(26)
Monti, D.: ref, 263(37)
Monti, J. M.: ref, 263(37)
Moody, B. J.: ref, 263(340)
Mooney, A.: ref, 29(5,6)
Moore, B. D.: ref, 55(520)
Moore, B. H.: ref, 40(16)
Moore, B. N.: ref, 358r
Moore, C.: ref, 55(82)
Moore, C. M.: ref, 136(35)
Moore, D.: ref, 206(48)
Moore, D. W.: ref, 159(54)
Moore, E. E.: ref, 36(29)
Moore, E. G. J.: ref, 159(3)
Moore, G.: ref, 55(491)
Moore, G. T.: test, 106; ref, 106r
Moore, J. R.: ref, 55(1)
Moore, K. J.: ref, 55(318)
Moore, M. W.: ref, 40(50)
Moore, P. J.: ref, 31(230), 296(5)
Moore, R. G.: ref, 31(361,567,955), 263(167)
Moore, W. D.: ref, 159(77)
Moos, B. S.: test, 184, 185
Moos, R. H.: test, 184, 185; ref, 31(90), 55(229), 184r, 184(1), 185(1)
Moote, G. T.: ref, 125(4)
Moran, M.: ref, 42(51)
Moran, P. B.: ref, 31(255)
Morand, P.: ref, 263(264)
Morano, C. D.: ref, 31(362), 32(27), 33(5)
Moras, K.: ref, 31(439), 263(140)
Morehouse, R. L.: ref, 31(770), 263(288)

Netemeyer, R. G.: ref, 31(751)
Neugebauer, R.: ref, 289r
Neukrug, E.: ref, 281(26)
Neumann, C.: ref, 29(21)
Neumeister, A.: ref, 136(36)
Nevels, R.: ref, 201(34)
Nevill, D.: ref, 48(3)
Nevill, D. D.: test, 355
New York State Employment Service: test, 163
New Zealand Council for Educational Research: test, 193
Newbrough, J. R.: ref, 55(141)
Newby, K.: ref, 55(491)
Newby, R. F.: ref, 132r
Newcomb, K.: ref, 55(170), 221(15)
Newcomb, M. D.: ref, 55(351)
Newcombe, F.: ref, 200(2)
Newcomer, P.: ref, 98r
Newcomer, P. L.: test, 91, 98; ref, 91r
Newcorn, J. H.: ref, 55(181,294)
Newell, N. P.: ref, 281(30)
Newhouse, P. A.: ref, 31(631)
Newlin, D. B.: ref, 55(414), 132(4)
Newman, A. I.: ref, 296(51)
Newman, C. F.: ref, 31(293), 32(26)
Newman, D. L.: rev, 134
Newman, D. R.: ref, 40(31)
Newman, E. J.: rev, 21, 146
Newman, J.: rev, 36
Newman, M. G.: ref, 31(748)
Newsholme, E. A.: ref, 31(49), 263(9)
Newsom, G.: ref, 112r
Newsum-Davis, J.: ref, 31(918)
Newton, J. E. O.: ref, 55(246)
Newton, R. M.: test, 229; ref, 229r
Nezami, E.: ref, 296(29)
Nezu, A. M.: ref, 31(796)
Nezu, C.: ref, 31(796)
Ng, Y. K. N. M. K.: ref, 263(301)
Ngo-Khac, T.: ref, 263(111)
Niaura, R.: ref, 30(62), 31(892,903), 296(46)
Nich, C.: ref, 31(443,691)
Nicholas, L. E.: test, 102; ref, 102r, 203(5,6,10)
Nicholas, M.: ref, 39r
Nicholls, J.: ref, 55(361,471)
Nichols, G. T.: ref, 55(137)
Nichols, M. E.: ref, 36(29)
Nichols, R. C.: rev, 71
Nichols, S. L.: ref, 41(1)
Nicholson, C. L.: ref, 329r
Nicholson, F.: ref, 313r
Nicholson, H.: ref, 263(236)
Nicholsonne, M. R.: ref, 40(4)
Nicolson, N. A.: ref, 263(252)
Niederche, G.: ref, 31(34)
Nields, J. A.: ref, 31(474)
Nielsen, B. M.: ref, 263(28)
Nielsen, S. L.: ref, 32r

Niemi, K. A.: ref, 40(107)
Nierenberg, A. A.: ref, 136(3,28), 263(41,302,303,359)
Nihira, K.: test, 1, 2; ref, 1r, 2r
Nimmo-Smith, I.: ref, 200(9)
Nippold, M. A.: ref, 80(1), 338(1)
Nirenberg, T. D.: ref, 31(156)
Nist, S. L.: ref, 206(28)
Nitko, A. J.: rev, 40, 153, 172
Nitko, A. J.: rev, 159
Nixon, C. D.: ref, 31(364)
Nixon, G. W. H.: ref, 31(163)
Nixon, S. J.: ref, 31(499)
Njiokiktjien, C.: ref, 36(9)
Noam, G. G.: ref, 55(67), 89(2,9)
Nobler, M. S.: ref, 263(197)
Nofzinger, E.: ref, 31(634), 263(241)
Nofzinger, E. A.: ref, 31(365), 263(304)
Noga, K.: ref, 31(672)
Noguera, R.: ref, 263(73)
Noh, S.: ref, 32(38)
Nolan, R.: ref, 31(574)
Nolen, W. A.: ref, 263(168,169)
Nolen-Hoeksema, S.: ref, 31(127,440,778), 263(221)
Noll, R. B.: ref, 31(320), 55(172)
Noonan, B. M.: ref, 263(119)
Noor, N. M.: ref, 31(797)
Nora, A.: ref, 74(1,2,3)
Norcross, C. E.: rev, 292
Nordvik, H.: ref, 281(21)
Nores, A.: ref, 42(55)
Norman, D.: ref, 55(82)
Norman, R. M. G.: ref, 31(557)
Norman, W. H.: ref, 31(33,879), 263(7)
Norring, C.: ref, 31(40)
Norris, J. A.: rev, 67, 241
Norris, S. L. W.: ref, 31(560,561)
Norris, S. P.: test, 342; ref, 342r
North, K.: ref, 68(19), 341(5)
North, R. D.: rev, 40
Northam, E.: ref, 55(119)
The Northern California Neurobehavioral Group: ref, 39r
Northrop, L. C.: ref, 173r
Norton, G. R.: ref, 30r, 30(24), 31(458)
Norvell, N.: ref, 320(11)
Norwood, S. L.: ref, 184r
Noshirvani, H.: ref, 31(422), 263(189,225)
Nostadt, A.: ref, 31(224)
Nouwen, A.: ref, 31(1016)
Novacek, J.: ref, 320(12)
Novalany, J.: ref, 31(881)
Novelli, L., Jr.: ref, 243r
Novelly, R. A.: ref, 42(1)
Novotny, P.: ref, 112r
Noyce, R. M.: rev, 108, 341
Noyes, R., Jr.: ref, 201(4), 263(21)
Nugent, D. F.: ref, 263(305)
Nugent, J. K.: ref, 29(18)

Rifai, A. H.: ref, 30(35), 31(593), 263(230)
Rifas, S. L.: ref, 136(8)
Riggs, D. S.: ref, 31(264,723), 296(41)
Riggs, P. D.: ref, 55(535), 77(15)
Rigrodsky, S.: rev, 203
Rihmer, Z.: ref, 263(240)
Riksen-Walraven, J. M.: ref, 29(120)
Riley, A. W.: ref, 55(51)
Riley, G.: ref, 304r
Riley, G. D.: test, 304; ref, 304r
Riley, G. G.: ref, 304r
Riley, W. T.: ref, 30(55), 55(113), 263(327), 296(5)
Ring, H. A.: ref, 263(231)
Rinne, J. O.: ref, 31(939)
Riordan, H.: ref, 42(8)
Riordan, R. J.: ref, 139(1)
Ripple, C. H.: ref, 55(309)
Rise, S.: ref, 31r
Riskind, J. H.: ref, 30r
Risley, T.: ref, 188r
Riso, L. P.: ref, 31(94), 32(72), 263(292)
Risser, A. H.: ref, 132r
Risser, R. C.: ref, 136(15)
Rissmiller, D. J.: ref, 30r, 31(626)
Ritchie, K. L.: ref, 159(58)
Ritenour, A.: ref, 263(360)
Ritsma, S.: ref, 72r
Rittenhouse, R. K., 292(65)
Ritter, C.: ref, 31(745,895)
Rivelli, S.: ref, 31(705)
Rivera, D. M.: test, 339
Rivera-Stein, M. A.: ref, 36(8)
Riverside Publishing Company staff and consultants: test,
    268
Rizzi, L. P.: ref, 55(490)
Rizzo, M.: ref, 36(33)
Robb, J. C.: ref, 263(357)
Robbins, P. R.: ref, 31(594)
Robbins, S. B.: ref, 302r
Roberts, C.: ref, 292(33)
Roberts, D. C.: rev, 114, 360
Roberts, G. I.: ref, 340(9)
Roberts, J. E.: ref, 31(954,965), 55(443), 76(1), 263(371)
Roberts, J. M.: ref, 263(248)
Roberts, M. A.: ref, 55(434)
Roberts, M. L.: ref, 132r
Roberts, M. S.: ref, 206(10)
Roberts, M. W.: ref, 55(104)
Roberts, R. E.: ref, 55(526), 296(9)
Roberts, R. W.: ref, 55(1)
Roberts, W. C.: ref, 31(84,85,560,561)
Robertson, G. J.: rev, 46, 204
Robertson, I. H.: ref, 36(19)
Robertson, M. M.: ref, 31(301), 263(141)
Robertson-Tchabo, E. A.: ref, 36r
Robinett, R.: test, 50
Robins, C. J.: ref, 31(820)

Robins, L.: ref, 201(81)
Robins, L. N.: ref, 308r
Robins, R. W.: ref, 55(299,527)
Robinson, A.: ref, 320(9)
Robinson, B. B. E.: ref, 31(966)
Robinson, B. F.: ref, 29(121)
Robinson, E.: test, 282
Robinson, E. A.: rev, 218
Robinson, E. T.: test, 164, 228
Robinson, J.: ref, 29(28,55), 55(541)
Robinson, M. A.: ref, 55(8)
Robinson, M. E.: ref, 31(227)
Robinson, N. M.: ref, 55(381), 71(20,23), 320(5)
Robinson, N. S.: ref, 55(444)
Robinson, P. J.: ref, 31(265)
Robinson, R. G.: ref, 31(103), 263(57,155,265)
Roche, L.: ref, 280(34)
Rock, D. A.: test, 123; ref, 62r
Rockert, W.: ref, 31(577)
Rocklin, T. R.: ref, 156(1), 160(4,7), 280(29)
Rodenburg, M.: ref, 263(159)
Rodin, G. M.: ref, 31(80)
Rodin, J.: ref, 296(2)
Rodoletz, M.: ref, 31(952)
Rodrigue, J. R.: ref, 31(472), 55(214)
Roehlke, H. J.: ref, 31(504)
Roelandt, J. T. C.: ref, 55(233)
Roemer, L.: ref, 31(595)
Roemer, R. A.: ref, 201(7)
Roesler, T. A.: ref, 31(596,597)
Roessler, R.: test, 367
Roethlisberger, F. J.: ref, 248r
Roettger, D. M.: ref, 329r
Roetzel, K.: ref, 241(3)
Rogers, A.: ref, 263(306)
Rogers, B. G.: rev, 40, 87, 293, 343; ref, 40r
Rogers, D.: ref, 40(105)
Rogers, H. J.: ref, 151r, 344r
Rogers, J. H.: ref, 31(821), 201(71), 263(328)
Rogers, M. P.: ref, 55(90)
Rogers, P. J.: ref, 31(736)
Rogers, R. W.: ref, 31(100)
Rogers, S. J.: test, 107, 239; ref, 29(46), 107r
Rogers, S. L. B.: ref, 263(27)
Rogers, T.: ref, 159(14)
Rogg, J.: ref, 42(49)
Rogler, L. H.: ref, 77(1)
Roglic, G.: ref, 31(370)
Rogoff, B.: ref, 31(731)
Rogosch, F.: ref, 55(130)
Rogosch, F. A.: ref, 55(127,157)
Rohde, P.: ref, 31(598), 263(232)
Rohena-Diaz, E.: ref, 80r
Rohrbeck, C. A.: rev, 36, 199
Roid, G. H.: ref, 29(47)
Roin, G. M.: ref, 31(24), 263(5)
Roitman, G.: ref, 31(991)

Rubin, K. H.: test, 234; ref, 31(165), 55(445,507), 234r, 234(2,3,5,6)
Rubin, R. T.: ref, 31(267)
Rubino, I. A.: ref, 201(58)
Rubinow, D. R.: ref, 31(385)
Rudd, M. D.: ref, 31(822,823,931,932), 32(11,60,66,67), 201(72,73)
Rudd, R. P.: ref, 201(6)
Rude, S.: ref, 31(438)
Rude, S. S.: ref, 31(381,744,824)
Ruderman, M. N.: test, 94; ref, 94(1,2)
Rudman, H. C.: rev, 50, 123; ref, 359r
Rudner, L. M.: rev, 265; ref, 131r, 265r
Rudolph, K. D.: ref, 31(741)
Rudorf, E. H.: ref, 341r
Ruef, A. M.: ref, 25r
Ruffalo, S. L.: ref, 277(2)
Rugle, L.: ref, 31(382)
Rulon, P. J.: ref, 18r
Rund, B. R.: ref, 55(528)
Rundell, J. R.: ref, 31(541)
Runyan, C. M.: ref, 304(2)
Runyan, S. E.: ref, 304(2)
Rupprecht, R.: ref, 263(76,84,134)
Rusch, F. R.: test, 356; ref, 356r
Rush, A. J.: ref, 31(141,517,969), 263(62,249,331,372)
Rush, H. C.: ref, 132r
Ruskin, E.: ref, 29(106)
Russ, M. J.: ref, 263(45)
Russell, A.: ref, 263(243)
Russell, M. L.: rev, 39, 331
Russell, R. J. H.: ref, 31(878)
Russell, V.: ref, 89(7)
Russo, J.: ref, 31(45,108,604), 263(156,380), 296(46)
Russo, M. F.: ref, 40(93), 55(338)
Rust, J.: test, 270; ref, 270(1)
Rustin, L.: ref, 68(28)
Rutemiller, L. A.: ref, 55(433)
Rutherford, M.: ref, 201(81)
Ruttenberg, B. A.: test, 35
Rutter, M.: ref, 29(34)
Rutter, M. L.: ref, 55(344)
Ryan, C.: ref, 31(989), 136(18)
Ryan, C. E.: ref, 263(283)
Ryan, C. M.: ref, 31(985)
Ryan, J. M.: rev, 340
Ryan, K.: ref, 63r
Ryan, L.: ref, 31(853), 36(32), 42(40)
Ryan, N. D.: ref, 263(58)
Ryan, R. M.: ref, 31(825), 55(343)
Ryan, S. M.: ref, 55(484)
Rybakowski, J.: ref, 263(129)
Rybakowski, J. K.: ref, 263(375)
Ryder, R. J.: ref, 159(62)
Rynders, J.: ref, 238r
Rysberg, J. A.: rev, 29, 56
Ryser, G. R.: ref, 6r

Saam, R. H.: ref, 296(43)
Saayman, G. S.: ref, 55(39)
Sabe, L.: ref, 36(56,57), 263(300)
Sabers, D. L.: rev, 83, 131; ref, 27r, 68(35), 323(5)
Sabers, D. S.: rev, 131
Saccuzzo, D. P.: ref, 31(74), 191r, 263(26)
Sachdev, P.: ref, 31(826)
Sachs, G. S.: ref, 30(9), 31(36), 31(258), 263(8,158)
Sackeim, H. A.: ref, 136(8), 263(197,340)
Sackett, P. R.: ref, 247r
Sacks, L. A.: ref, 31(383)
Saddler, C. D.: ref, 31(383)
Sadoski, M.: ref, 206(16)
Sadowski, C. J.: rev, 17, 208
Safran, J. D.: ref, 31(509)
Safran, J. S.: ref, 96(4)
Safran, S. P.: ref, 96(4)
Sagar, H. J.: ref, 31(166,306,307,863)
Sahakian, B. J.: ref, 263(355)
Sahin, D.: ref, 31(423), 263(186)
Sahs, J. A.: ref, 32(47), 263(233)
Saigal, J.: ref, 55(225)
Saigh, P. A.: ref, 31(970)
Sailor, P.: ref, 357r
Saint-Cyr, J. A.: ref, 42(5)
Saitoh, T.: ref, 42(38)
Saitzyk, A. R.: ref, 55(95)
Sakai, C.: ref, 263(156)
Sakamoto, K.: ref, 263(332)
Sakurai, Y.: ref, 36(16)
Salamero, M.: ref, 31(605)
Salamon, A.: ref, 320(11)
Salazar, A. M.: ref, 31(388,541,920)
Salcedo, V.: ref, 31(734), 263(280)
Salinas, E.: ref, 31(248), 263(120)
Salkovskis, P.: ref, 31(801)
Salkovskis, P. M.: ref, 30r, 30(23), 31(159)
Sallee, F. R.: ref, 31(1018), 136(33,39)
Salmela-Aro, K.: ref, 31(1019)
Salmon, D. P.: ref, 31(853), 41(1), 42(27,38,40,48)
Salokun, S. O.: ref, 320(33)
Salt, P.: ref, 31(992,993), 55(542)
Saltstone, R.: ref, 16r
Salvia, J.: ref, 29r, 34r, 67r, 82r, 241r, 337r
Salzberg, A. D.: ref, 55(511)
Salzinger, S.: ref, 55(217,395)
Samejima, F.: ref, 159(82)
Sameroff, A. J.: ref, 29(65)
Samson, D.: ref, 31(260)
Samson, J.: ref, 31(354)
Samson, J. F.: ref, 29(92)
Samuel-Lajeunesse, B.: ref, 31(248), 263(120)
Samuels, M. T.: ref, 340(9)
Sanchez-Bernardos, M. L.: ref, 31(268)
Sandage, S. J.: ref, 192r
Sandberg, D. E.: ref, 55r, 55(218)
Sandel, M. E.: ref, 36(35)

Schery, T. K.: ref, 29(37)
Schiffman, E.: ref, 36(8)
Schill, M. T.: ref, 55(529)
Schill, T.: ref, 31(611)
Schilling, K. M.: ref, 121r
Schindler, A. W.: rev, 40
Schinka, J. A.: ref, 42(34)
Schinkel, A. M.: ref, 55(100)
Schirmer, B. R.: ref, 292(49)
Schittecatte, M.: ref, 263(333)
Schlaepfer, T. E.: ref, 136(30)
Schlager, D. S.: ref, 263(234)
Schlechte, J. A.: ref, 31(157)
Schleifer, D.: ref, 31(987), 136(16)
Schleifer, S. J.: ref, 263(373)
Schlicher, L.: ref, 136(26)
Schloss, P. J.: ref, 68(29)
Schlosser, S. S.: ref, 31(995)
Schlundt, D. G.: ref, 31(754,868)
Schluter, J. L.: ref, 30(53), 31(804)
Schmalt, H. D.: ref, 195r
Schmeck, R. R.: test, 156; ref, 156r
Schmider, J.: ref, 263(362)
Schmidt, C. W.: ref, 201(13)
Schmidt, F.: rev, 37
Schmidt, F. L.: ref, 173r, 247r
Schmidt, K. L.: ref, 31(519)
Schmidt, L. A.: ref, 55(507)
Schmidt, L. G.: ref, 77(6)
Schmidt, M.: ref, 42(16), 273r
Schmidt, M. H.: ref, 29(73), 263(326)
Schmidt, N. B.: ref, 31(831)
Schmidt, P. J.: ref, 31(385)
Schmidt, U.: ref, 31(37)
Schmitt, N.: rev, 164, 243; ref, 206(52)
Schmitz, B.: ref, 263(84,134)
Schmitz, J. B.: ref, 31(910)
Schmitz, S.: ref, 55(541)
Schmock, K.: ref, 241(16)
Schmulbach, S.: ref, 40(11), 159(16), 292(1)
Schnall, P. L.: ref, 296(15)
Schnayer, R.: ref, 55(3)
Schneck, C. M.: ref, 224(1)
Schneck, G. R.: rev, 356, 367
Schneider, A. M.: ref, 31(320), 55(172)
Schneider, B.: ref, 31(832)
Schneider, B. H.: ref, 280(3)
Schneider, K.: ref, 195r, 263(324)
Schneider, L. S.: ref, 31(553), 42(24), 263(217)
Schneider, M. S.: ref, 31(167)
Schneider, P.: ref, 68(36)
Schneider, S. G.: ref, 32(15)
Schnetderman, N.: ref, 136(22)
Schnoll, S. H.: ref, 31(331), 201(25)
Schoenfeld, D.: ref, 31(71), 263(22)
Schoenrade, P.: rev, 119, 355
Schoer, L.: ref, 122r, 295r

Schofield, P.: ref, 77(4)
Schofield, P. W.: ref, 36(66), 136(41)
Schofield, W.: rev, 36
Scholte, E. M.: ref, 55(132)
Schomer, D.: ref, 55(520)
Schonfeld, L.: test, 306; ref, 306r
Schonholtz, J.: ref, 55(241)
Schorr, S.: ref, 31(62,63), 32(9)
Schotte, C.: ref, 31(386), 263(32,33,67,122)
Schrader, G.: ref, 32(48), 263(235)
Schrader, W. B.: ref, 174r
Schram, M.: test, 20; ref, 20r
Schrank, F. A.: ref, 27r
Schraw, G.: ref, 206(34,35,44,50)
Schreiber, G.: ref, 31(991)
Schreiber, G. S.: ref, 31(833)
Schreibman, L.: ref, 31(254)
Schroeder, C. G.: ref, 281(14)
Schroeder, C. M.: ref, 31(952)
Schroeder, P. J.: ref, 112r
Schubert, D. S. P.: ref, 32(28)
Schuckit, M.: ref, 263(165)
Schuckit, M. A.: ref, 77(14), 263(262)
Schuder, T.: ref, 292(77)
Schuell, H.: test, 203; ref, 203r
Schuerger, J. M.: ref, 201(17,53)
Schuerholz, L. J.: ref, 55(446,530), 359(12)
Schuerman, J. A.: ref, 31(871)
Schulberg, H. C.: ref, 31r, 31(685), 136(2), 263(261)
Schuldberg, D.: ref, 31(497)
Schuler, M.: ref, 221(12)
Schuller, D. R.: ref, 31(197)
Schulman, P.: ref, 31(738), 32(58)
Schulte, L. E.: ref, 55(135)
Schultz, C. L.: ref, 320(13)
Schultz, G.: ref, 31(387)
Schultz, N. C.: ref, 320(13)
Schultz, R.: ref, 246r
Schultz, S. K.: ref, 263(265)
Schulz, P. M.: ref, 263(82)
Schulz, R.: ref, 136(6)
Schumaker, J. F.: ref, 31(833)
Schuman, W. B.: ref, 55(219)
Schumm, J. S.: ref, 40(75), 206(26), 292(34,51)
Schunk, D. H.: ref, 40(18)
Schuri, U.: ref, 36(28), 42(15)
Schut, H.: ref, 31(979)
Schutte, C.: ref, 263(68)
Schuttenberg, E. M.: ref, 281(22)
Schutz, J.: ref, 55(368)
Schutz, R.: ref, 356r
Schutz, R. P.: test, 356
Schwab, K.: ref, 31(388,920)
Schwab-Stone, M.: ref, 55(280,339,488)
Schwantes, F. M.: ref, 159(24,40)
Schwarting, G.: rev, 95, 99
Schwartz, C. E.: ref, 55(531)

Shapiro, A. P.: ref, 31(985)
Shapiro, D.: ref, 31(328)
Shapiro, D. A.: rev, 68, 323; ref, 31(613,629,838,851,852)
Shapiro, D. H., Jr.: test, 286
Shapiro, E. G.: ref, 29(88)
Shapiro, E. S.: ref, 59r
Shapiro, M. F.: ref, 32(59)
Sharma, R.: ref, 205(3)
Sharma, R. P.: ref, 263(311,336)
Sharma, V.: ref, 31(446), 55(181,294), 263(194)
Sharp, J. M.: ref, 40(97), 340(11)
Sharp, M.: ref, 31(611)
Sharpe, M. J.: ref, 31(839)
Sharpley, A. L.: ref, 31(220,653), 263(104)
Shaulis, D.: ref, 128r
Shavelson, R.: ref, 87r
Shavelson, R. J.: ref, 19r, 113r, 280r, 280(42)
Shaw, B. F.: ref, 31(956)
Shaw, D.: ref, 159(5)
Shaw, D. G.: ref, 31(139)
Shaw, D. S.: ref, 31(391,526,614,840,973), 55(340,341, 449,532)
Shaw, H. E.: ref, 162(17)
Shaw, K. M.: test, 302
Shaw, S. R.: rev, 166, 302
Shawcross, C.: ref, 263(309)
Shaywitz, B. A.: ref, 275r
Shaywitz, S. E.: ref, 275r
Shea, M. T.: ref, 31(678), 263(258)
Shea, T.: ref, 31(989), 136(18)
Shealy, R.: ref, 359r
Shean, G. D.: ref, 31(841)
Shear, K.: ref, 263(158)
Shear, M. K.: ref, 31(454,615,963), 136(2,11)
Shear, P. K.: ref, 42(10)
Sheard, J.: ref, 176r
Shearer, S. L.: ref, 32(49)
Shearing, C. H.: ref, 31(170)
Sheebar, L. B.: ref, 55(342), 221(30)
Sheehan, D. Y.: ref, 31(101), 263(46)
Sheehan, E. P.: rev, 94, 216; ref, 202r
Shefelbine, J. L.: ref, 292(11)
Sheffey, M. A.: ref, 281(2)
Shek, C. C.: ref, 31(246)
Shek, D. T. L.: ref, 31(271), 32(68)
Shekhar, A.: ref, 31(919), 55(401)
Shekim, W.: ref, 55(96)
Sheldon, A.: ref, 201(31)
Shell, D. F.: ref, 40(109)
Shelton, R. C.: ref, 31(693), 263(263)
Shelton, T. L.: ref, 55(79), 132r
Shenk, J. L.: ref, 31(749)
Shenson, H. L.: test, 120
Shepard, C. R.: ref, 292(48)
Shepard, J. M.: ref, 296(3)
Shepard, L.: ref, 40(112)
Shepard, L. A.: rev, 293; ref, 326r, 330r

Shepherd, M. J.: ref, 292(50)
Shepherd, R. W.: ref, 31(384)
Sheppard, B. H.: ref, 31(5)
Sher, K. J.: ref, 31(726)
Sherbenou, R. J.: test, 95; ref, 82r, 98r
Sherman, M. F.: ref, 31(551)
Sherman, R.: ref, 192r
Sherman, S. J.: ref, 31(194)
Sherrod, K. B.: ref, 320(27)
Sherry, D.: ref, 263(14)
Sherwood, A.: ref, 296(11)
Sherwood, R.: ref, 201(27)
Sheslow, D.: test, 322; ref, 41r
Sheu, W. J.: ref, 10r
Shide, D. J.: ref, 111(3)
Shields, A. M.: ref, 55(343)
Shimoda, K.: ref, 263(48)
Shindledecker, R. D.: ref, 263(45)
Shine, J.: ref, 77(4)
Shioiri, T., 263(282)
Shiota, J.: ref, 36(61)
Shipley, K. G.: rev, 153
Shirk, S. R.: ref, 55(392)
Shirley, M. C.: rev, 93, 307
Shivy, V. A.: ref, 281(48)
Shoemaker, D. M.: rev, 325
Shoemaker, O. S.: ref, 31(85)
Shohamy, E.: ref, 137r
Shohdy, A.: ref, 31(576)
Shor, H.: ref, 31(860)
Shores, J. H.: rev, 40
Shores, M. M.: ref, 31(321), 263(146)
Shorkey, C. T.: ref, 32(29)
Shortz, J. L.: ref, 192r
Showers, C. J.: ref, 31(974)
Shows, D.: ref, 320(28)
Shrauger, J. S.: ref, 162(21)
Shriberg, L. D.: ref, 165r, 241(15)
Shrivastara, R. K.: ref, 263(145)
Shriver, M. D.: rev, 59, 225
Shtasel, D. L.: ref, 132r
Shubiner, H.: ref, 231r
Shuck, R. L.: ref, 296(44)
Shuckers, P. L.: ref, 31(445)
Shull-Senn, S.: ref, 292(75)
Shullman, S. L.: ref, 260r
Shulman, C.: ref, 24(3)
Shulman, I.: ref, 31(143)
Shulman, S.: ref, 8r, 320(41)
Shurtleff, D. B.: ref, 55(176)
Shwery, C. S.: rev, 180, 252
Shybunko, D. E.: ref, 55(4)
Sibbet, D.: ref, 316r
Siblerud, R. L.: ref, 31(272,616), 296(34)
Sichel, A. F.: ref, 55(427), 96(6)
Sidanius, J.: ref, 162(16)
Siddall, J. W.: ref, 201(29)

Smallish, L.: ref, 31(114)
Smallman, E.: ref, 48(17)
Smeraldi, E.: ref, 136(17), 263(91,206,315,361)
Smit, E. K.: ref, 325(2)
Smith, B.: ref, 31(256), 55(117)
Smith, B. A.: ref, 186(1)
Smith, B. D.: ref, 206(46)
Smith, C. A.: ref, 31(644), 311(1)
Smith, D.: ref, 132r
Smith, D. A.: ref, 31(536), 55(59)
Smith, D. A. F.: test, 205; ref, 205(2)
Smith, D. K.: rev, 206, 327
Smith, D. L.: ref, 206(39)
Smith, D. W.: ref, 31(976)
Smith, G. P.: ref, 263(45)
Smith, J.: ref, 31(28), 263(236)
Smith, J. C.: ref, 159(36)
Smith, J. E.: ref, 31(394)
Smith, J. J.: test, 100
Smith, J. K.: ref, 40(24)
Smith, J. K.: rev, 74, 342
Smith, J. V.: rev, 91
Smith, K.: ref, 31(4), 55(125)
Smith, L. J.: ref, 159(101)
Smith, M.: ref, 320(9)
Smith, M. H.: ref, 20r
Smith, M. L.: ref, 40(112), 159(41), 320(38)
Smith, P. K.: ref, 55(477)
Smith, R.: ref, 31(947), 263(368)
Smith, R. L.: ref, 29(53)
Smith, S.: ref, 159(15)
Smith, S. S.: ref, 31(169)
Smith, T. E.: ref, 112r
Smith, T. W.: ref, 31(57,102,447,617)
Smith, W. P.: ref, 31(845)
Smith, Y. N.: ref, 40(96)
Smith-Gray, S.: ref, 221(42)
Smits, R. C. F.: ref, 42(30)
Smouse, P. E.: ref, 20r
Smyth, N. J.: ref, 31(515,618), 32(39,50), 33(7), 296(35)
Snaith, J.: ref, 31(446), 263(194)
Snell, W. E., Jr.: ref, 296(44)
Snider, E. C.: ref, 31(949)
Snidman, N.: ref, 55(531)
Snow, C. E.: ref, 241(14)
Snow, D.: ref, 30(63), 31(901), 188(7)
Snow, M. E.: ref, 55(464)
Snow, W. G.: ref, 42(55,56)
Snyder, C. R.: ref, 31(843)
Snyder, D.: ref, 55(278)
Snyder, J.: ref, 55(70,345)
Snyder, J. J.: ref, 55(450)
Snyder, R. D.: ref, 31(937,938)
Sobell, L. C.: ref, 30(36), 31(619), 36(41), 42(31), 77(5), 155(2,3), 263(237), 288(3,4)
Sobell, M.: ref, 30(36), 31(619), 36(41), 42(31), 77(5), 155(2), 263(237), 288(3)

Sobell, M. B.: ref, 155(3), 288(4)
Sobieska, M.: ref, 263(375)
Sobin, C.: ref, 263(340)
Sobotková, D.: ref, 29(117)
Sodoro, J.: ref, 68(12)
Sodowsky, G. R.: rev, 170; ref, 170r
Sohlberg, S.: ref, 31(40)
Sokol, L.: ref, 30(1), 31(41)
Sokol, R. J.: ref, 29(41), 31(340)
Solberg, V. S.: ref, 72r
Solis, S.: ref, 93r
Soloff, P. H.: ref, 31(395,620), 263(238)
Solomon, A.: ref, 30(37), 31(621)
Solomon, J.: ref, 55(451)
Solomon, R. A.: ref, 31(131,220), 263(104)
Solomon, S.: ref, 31(846,975)
Solomonica-Levi, D.: ref, 24(3)
Solovitz, B. L.: ref, 55(526)
Somer, G.: ref, 30(56)
Somlai, A.: ref, 31(759)
Sommerfeldt, L.: ref, 31(59)
Sommers, R. K.: ref, 241(16), 304(10)
Sommerville, K. W.: ref, 36(24)
Song, L-Y.: ref, 55(346)
Sonino, N.: ref, 263(38)
Sonneborn, D.: ref, 30(64), 31(926)
Sonnenberg, R. T.: ref, 281(27)
Sorbara, D. L.: ref, 29(36)
Sörbom, D.: ref, 191r
Sorensen, J. L.: ref, 31(795)
Soriani, A.: ref, 263(177)
Sossen, P. L.: test, 302
Soto, L. D.: ref, 159(11)
Soto, S.: ref, 31(101), 263(46)
Souder, L.: rev, 293
Southard, N. A.: ref, 40(113), 159(109)
Southwick, S.: ref, 31(142)
Southwick, S. M.: ref, 263(341)
Souza, F. G. M.: ref, 31(170)
Sowa, C. J.: ref, 48(17)
Sowell, E. J.: ref, 40(27), 292(13)
Spaccarelli, S.: ref, 55(452,453)
Spalletta, G.: ref, 31(977). 263(376)
Spangler, D. L.: ref, 31(396), 263(180)
Spangler, W. D.: ref, 195r
Spanier, C.: ref, 263(377)
Spar, J. E.: ref, 36(1), 263(1)
Sparks, R. L.: ref, 159(102), 206(51)
Sparrow, S.: ref, 2r, 238r
Sparrow, S. S.: ref, 2r
Spears, M. W.: ref, 159(42)
Speciale, S.: ref, 136(15)
Speck, C.: ref, 40(71)
Specker, S. M.: ref, 31(448)
Spector, J. E.: rev, 337
Speece, D. L.: ref, 71(6,8)
Spegg, C.: ref, 77(7)

Steinberg, J.: ref, 263(173)
Steinberg, J. L.: ref, 263(181)
Steiner, M.: ref, 31(770), 263(288)
Steiner, V. G.: test, 241; ref, 67r
Steingard, R.: ref, 55(82), 263(108)
Steinherz, P.: ref, 31(783), 55(425)
Steinmeyer, E. M.: ref, 263(130)
Steketee, G.: ref, 31(104,174)
Stemerdink, N.: ref, 55(537)
Stender, A.: ref, 263(28)
Stepanski, K.: ref, 285(2)
Stephens, G. C.: ref, 31(628)
Stephens, S.: ref, 136(8)
Stephenson, S.: ref, 31(302)
Sterling, R. C.: ref, 31(777)
Stern, G. S.: ref, 296(4)
Stern, R. A.: ref, 136(27), 263(172,273,316)
Stern, Y.: ref, 36(12,17,18,51,52,66), 136(41)
Sternberg, R. J.: rev, 325; ref, 45r, 152r
Sternberger, L. G.: ref, 31(175)
Stetner, F.: ref, 31(705,1000)
Stevens, D. D.: ref, 292(17)
Stevens, L. J.: ref, 159(103)
Stevens, R. J.: ref, 40(39,110), 159(12)
Stevens, W.: ref, 263(68,218)
Stevens, W. J.: ref, 263(122)
Stevens-Ratchford, R. G.: ref, 31(402)
Stevenson, J.: ref, 55(63)
Stewart, A.: ref, 31(630)
Stewart, A. J.: ref, 55(183)
Stewart, B. J.: ref, 55(8)
Stewart, B. L.: ref, 30(47), 31(739)
Stewart, C.: ref, 304(9)
Stewart, G. W.: ref, 55(29)
Stewart, J. E.: test, 356; ref, 356r
Stewart, J. R.: rev, 33, 154
Stewart, J. W.: ref, 136(42), 263(51,204)
Stewart, K. B.: ref, 29(27)
Stewart, M. A.: ref, 263(261)
Stewart, S.: ref, 234(5)
Stewart, S. L.: ref, 234(3)
Stewart, S. M.: ref, 29(90), 55(228)
Stice, C. F.: ref, 180(1)
Stice, E.: ref, 55(222,456), 162(17)
Stieglitz, E. L.: test, 298
Stieglitz, R.-D.: ref, 263(50)
Stiffman, A. R.: ref, 31(42), 55(13)
Stifter, C. A.: ref, 29(14), 31(740), 162(7)
Stiles, W. B.: ref, 31(629,851,852)
Stilwell, B.: ref, 55(401)
Stinnett, T. A.: rev, 2, 60; ref, 132r
Stinson, C.: ref, 31(333)
Stinson, D.: ref, 31(105), 263(47)
Stinson, M. S.: ref, 292(37,79)
Stitzer, M. L.: ref, 31(177)
Stocker, C. M.: ref, 55(457)
Stoddard, K.: ref, 40(73)

Stoel-Gammon, C.: ref, 188(10)
Stoiber, K. C.: ref, 159(83), 221(31)
Stokes, H.: test, 97; rev, 292
Stokes, J. L.: ref, 42(50)
Stokes, P. E.: ref, 263(182)
Stokes, S. A.: test, 299; ref, 299r
Stokes, S. L.: ref, 68(30), 323(4)
Stolberg, A. L.: ref, 55(6,50,227)
Stoll, M. F.: ref, 55(152)
Stollak, G. E.: ref, 89(3,8)
Stoltenberg, C. D.: ref, 201(14)
Stone, B. J.: ref, 71(18), 159(84)
Stone, G. L.: rev, 156; ref, 144r
Stone, J.: ref, 31(568)
Stone, L.: ref, 263(331)
Stone, L. J.: rev, 58
Stone, P.: ref, 55(206)
Stoner, S. B.: ref, 31(492), 71(16), 159(75)
Stones, M. J.: ref, 262r
Stoolmiller, M.: ref, 55(352)
Stoppard, J. M.: ref, 31(633)
Storandt, M.: ref, 31(417), 36r
Stormshak, E. A.: ref, 55(534)
Stotland, S.: ref, 31(176)
Stouffer, G. A. W., Jr.: test, 264, 266
Stout, J.: ref, 42(40)
Stout, J. C.: ref, 31(853), 42(27)
Stout, J. D.: ref, 52r
Stout, W.: ref, 174r
Stout, W. F.: ref, 359r
Stouthamer-Loeber, M.: ref, 40(74), 55(46,86,195,223, 299,365,527)
Strack, F.: ref, 31(52)
Strack, S.: ref, 281(40)
Strahan, R. F.: ref, 281(9)
Strain, E. C.: ref, 31(177)
Strain, J. J.: ref, 31(72)
Strakowski, S. M.: ref, 136(34,40), 263(349,378,379)
Strand, A. L.: test, 247, 248
Strand, M. L.: test, 247, 248
Stranger, C.: ref, 55(556)
Strassberg, Z.: ref, 55(458)
Strauman, T. J.: ref, 31(8), 201(20)
Straus, R.: ref, 311r
Straus, S. E.: ref, 31(270)
Strauss, E.: ref, 36r
Strauss, J. P.: ref, 138(2)
Strauss, M. E.: ref, 30(61), 31(874), 32(69), 42(32), 308(2)
Stravynski, A.: ref, 31(43)
Straw, D.: ref, 320(21)
Street, S.: ref, 72(1)
Streichenwein, S. M.: ref, 31(854), 263(342)
Strein, W.: ref, 280(16)
Streiner, D. L.: ref, 31(404,858), 201(74), 202r, 221(32)
Stricker, L. J.: ref, 174r
Stringer, R.: ref, 217r
Stritzke, P.: ref, 42(8)

Szuszkiewicz, T. A.: ref, 55(442)
Szymanski, M. L.: ref, 31(694)

Tacker, S.: ref, 31(909), 296(49)
Tager-Flusberg, H.: ref, 67(2), 68(20)
Taguchi, F.: ref, 296(1)
Tait, R. C.: ref, 31(13)
Takahashi, K.: ref, 263(72,77,332)
Takahashi, N.: ref, 36(61)
Takahashi, S.: ref, 263(48,72,77,103,282)
Takahashi, Y.: ref, 263(282)
Takeda, K.: ref, 36(16)
Talajic, M.: ref, 31(724)
Talbert, S.: ref, 201(42)
Talbot, F.: ref, 31(1016)
Talken, T. R.: ref, 72(3)
Tallal, P.: ref, 42(10), 324r
Tallent-Runnels, M. K.: ref, 177(3)
Talley, J. L.: ref, 41r
Talley, W.: ref, 320(40)
Tam, A. S. F.: ref, 280(37), 320(36)
Tam, W.: ref, 31(770), 263(288)
Tamma, F.: ref, 31(67)
Tamor, L.: ref, 122r, 295r
Tamul, K.: ref, 263(273)
Tan, C.: ref, 55(125)
Tan, J. C. H.: ref, 31(633)
Tanaka, J. S.: ref, 55(5)
Tanar, M. E.: ref, 31(274)
Tancer, M. E.: ref, 31(136)
Tanck, R. H.: ref, 31(594)
Tandy, R. D.: ref, 128r
Tang, C. S.: ref, 31(106)
Tannenbaum, A.: ref, 29(39)
Tanner, C. M.: ref, 263(278)
Tannock, R.: ref, 221(11,26)
Tanrikut, C.: ref, 31(980)
Tantam, D.: ref, 200(13) .
Tarbuck, A. F.: ref, 31(556), 32(40), 263(343)
Tarico, V. S.: ref, 55(230)
Tariot, D. N.: ref, 31(631)
Tarnowski, K. J.: ref, 55(25)
Tarrier, N.: ref, 31(640), 263(244)
Tartaglini, A.: ref, 31(116)
Tarter, R.: ref, 18r
Tarter, R. E.: ref, 55(314), 104r, 307r
Tasca, G. A.: ref, 89(7)
Tashakkori, A.: ref, 280(17,18)
Tashiro, T.: ref, 263(71)
Taska, L. S.: ref, 31(601)
Tastaban, Y.: ref, 263(186)
Tata, S. P.: ref, 72r
Tate, R. L.: ref, 280(38)
Tatemichi, T. K.: ref, 36(17,18)
Tatsuoka, M. M.: ref, 18r, 315r
Taub, E.: ref, 31(309)
Taub, K.: ref, 31(62,63), 32(9)

Tautermannová, M.: ref, 29(117)
Tay, M. P.: ref, 280(38)
Taylor, A. E.: ref, 31(11,677), 42(5), 263(4)
Taylor, C.: ref, 77(2)
Taylor, C. B.: ref, 31(25,48,212,344)
Taylor, C. J.: ref, 132r
Taylor, H. F.: test, 84
Taylor, H. G.: ref, 55(136,226,461), 68(31)
Taylor, H. S.: ref, 36(29)
Taylor, J.: ref, 310r
Taylor, J. R.: ref, 263(2)
Taylor, M.: ref, 31(853), 32(4), 42(27,40), 200(1)
Taylor, M. J.: ref, 31(859), 221(44), 263(344)
Taylor, R.: ref, 55(305)
Taylor, R. M.: test, 315
Taylor, R. N.: rev, 287
Taylor, S.: ref, 30(71), 31(178,981), 55(118), 191r
Taylor, S. E.: ref, 32(15,46,78)
Taylor, W. G. K.: ref, 191r
Teachman, J.: ref, 55(71)
Teasdale, G.: ref, 39r
Teasdale, J. D.: ref, 31(859), 263(344)
Tebbutt, J.: ref, 288(1)
Teddlie, C.: ref, 40(98)
Teicher, M. H.: ref, 263(224,345)
Teichman, Y.: ref, 31(860), 296(8)
Tein, J. Y.: ref, 55(130)
Teja, S.: ref, 55(227)
Telch, C. F.: ref, 31(403,412,413,655)
Telch, M. J.: ref, 31(146), 36(11)
Tellegen, A.: ref, 31r, 55(177), 96(5)
Telner, J. I.: ref, 263(367)
Temoshok, L. R.: ref, 31(541,771)
Temple, C. M.: ref, 36(62)
Templer, D. I.: ref, 31(858), 201(74)
Templeton, S.: ref, 292(15)
Tems, C. L.: ref, 55(228)
Teng, C.: ref, 263(184)
Tenke, C. E.: ref, 31(116)
Teo, A.: ref, 29(124)
Terenzini, P. T.: ref, 74(2,3)
Terepa, M.: ref, 30(60), 31(850)
Terkuile, M. M.: ref, 32(31)
Terman, L. M.: ref, 2r
Terpylak, O.: ref, 201(53)
Terrill, D. R.: ref, 30(47), 31(739)
Terry, D. J.: ref, 31(982)
Terwilliger, J.: ref, 83r
Tesh, A.: rev, 255, 264
Teson, A.: ref, 36(57), 263(300)
Tesón, A.: ref, 36(56)
Tess, D. E.: ref, 31(235)
Tessier, D.: ref, 128r
Teti, D. M.: ref, 31(179,861), 221(5)
Tett, R. P.: ref, 162(5), 311(1)
Thackston-Williams, L.: ref, 32(51)
Thakore, J. H.: ref, 263(346)

SCORE INDEX

This Score Index lists all the scores, in alphabetical order, for all the tests included in The Thirteenth Mental Measurements Yearbook. *Because test scores can be regarded as operational definitions of the variable measured, sometimes the scores provide better leads to what a test actually measures than the test title or other available information. The Score Index is very detailed, and the reader should keep in mind that a given variable (or concept) of interest may be defined in several different ways. Thus the reader should look up these several possible alternative definitions before drawing final conclusions about whether tests measuring a particular variable of interest can be located in the* 13th MMY. *If the kind of score sought is located in a particular test or tests, the reader should then read the test descriptive information carefully to determine whether the test(s) in which the score is found is (are) consistent with reader purpose. Used wisely, the Score Index can be another useful resource in locating the right score in the right test. As usual, all numbers in the index are test numbers, not page numbers.*

Code of Professional Responsibilities in Educational Measurement

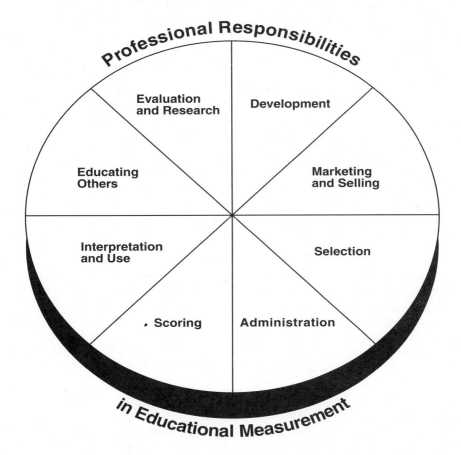

Prepared by the NCME Ad Hoc Committee on the Development of a Code of Ethics:

Cynthia B. Schmeiser, ACT—Chair
Kurt F. Geisinger, State University of New York
Sharon Johnson-Lewis, Detroit Public Schools
Edward D. Roeber, Council of Chief State School Officers
William D. Schafer, University of Maryland

Preamble and General Responsibilities

As an organization dedicated to the improvement of measurement and evaluation practice in education, the National Council on Measurement in Education (NCME) has adopted this Code to promote professionally responsible practice in educational measurement. Professionally responsible practice is conduct that arises from either the professional standards of the field, general ethical principles, or both.

The purpose of the Code of Professional Responsibilities in Educational Measurement, hereinafter referred to as the Code, is to guide the conduct of NCME members who are involved in any tinge of assessment activity in education. NCME is also providing this Code as a public service for all individuals who are engaged in educational assessment activities in the hope that these activities will be conducted in a professionally responsible manner. Persons who engage in these activities include local educators such as classroom teachers, principals, and superintendents; professionals such as school psychologists and counselors; state and national technical, legislative, and policy staff in education; staff of research, evaluation, and testing organizations; providers of test preparation services; college and university faculty and administrators; and professionals in business and industry who design and implement educational and training programs.

This Code applies to any type of assessment that occurs as part of the educational process, including formal and informal, traditional and alternative techniques for gathering information used in making educational decisions at all levels. These techniques include, but are not limited to, large-scale assessments at the school, district, state, national, and international levels; standardized tests; observational measures; teacher-conducted assessments; assessment support materials; and other achievement, aptitude, interest, and personality measures used in and for education.

Although NCME is promulgating this Code for its members, it strongly encourages other organizations and individuals who engage in educational assessment activities to endorse and abide by the responsibilities relevant to their professions. Because the Code pertains only to uses of assessment in education, it is recognized that uses of assessments outside of educational contexts, such as for employment, certification, or licensure, may involve additional professional responsibilities beyond those detailed in this Code.

The Code is intended to serve an educational function: to inform and remind those involved in educational assessment of their obligations to uphold the integrity of the manner in which assessments are developed, used, evaluated, and marketed. Moreover, it is expected that the Code will stimulate thoughtful discussion of what constitutes professionally responsible assessment practice at all levels in education.

The Code enumerates professional responsibilities in eight major areas of assessment activity. Specifically, the Code presents the professional responsibilities of those who:

1) Develop Assessments
2) Market and Sell Assessments
3) Select Assessments
4) Administer Assessments
5) Score Assessments
6) Interpret, Use, and Communicate Assessment Results
7) Educate About Assessment
8) Evaluate Programs and Conduct Research on Assessments

Although the organization of the Code is based on the differentiation of these activities, they are viewed as highly interrelated, and those who use this Code are urged to consider the Code in its entirety. The index following this Code provides a listing of some of the critical interest topics within educational measurement that focus on one or more of the assessment activities.

General Responsibilities

The professional responsibilities promulgated in this Code in eight major areas of assessment activity are based on expectations that NCME members involved in educational assessment will:

1) protect the health and safety of all examinees;
2) be knowledgeable about, and behave in compliance with, state and federal laws relevant to the conduct of professional activities;
3) maintain and improve their professional competence in educational assessment;
4) provide assessment services only in areas of their competence and experience, affording full disclosure of their professional qualifications;
5) promote the understanding of sound assessment practices in education;

6) adhere to the highest standards of conduct and promote professionally responsible conduct within educational institutions and agencies that provide educational services; and

7) perform all professional responsibilities with honesty, integrity, due care, and fairness.

Responsible professional practice includes being informed about and acting in accordance with the Code of Fair Testing Practices in Education (Joint Committee on Testing Practices, 1988), the Standards for Educational and Psychological Testing (American Educational Research Association, American Psychological Association, National Council on Measurement in Education, 1985), or subsequent revisions, as well as all applicable state and federal laws that may govern the development, administration, and use of assessments. Both the Standards for Educational and Psychological Testing and the Code of Fair Testing Practices in Education are intended to establish criteria for judging the technical adequacy of tests and the appropriate uses of tests and test results. The purpose of this Code is to describe the professional responsibilities of those individuals who are engaged in assessment activities. As would be expected, there is a strong relationship between professionally responsible practice and sound educational assessments, and this Code is intended to be consistent with the relevant parts of both of these documents.

It is not the intention of NCME to enforce the professional responsibilities stated in the Code or to investigate allegations of violations to the Code.

Since the Code provides a frame of reference for the evaluation of the appropriateness of behavior, NCME recognizes that the Code may be used in legal or other similar proceedings.

Section 1:
Responsibilities of Those Who Develop Assessment Products and Services

Those who develop assessment products and services, such as classroom teachers and other assessment specialists, have a professional responsibility to strive to produce assessments that are of the highest quality. Persons who develop assessments have a professional responsibility to:

1.1 Ensure that assessment products and services are developed to meet applicable professional, technical, and legal standards.

1.2 Develop assessment products and services that are as free as possible from bias due to characteristics irrelevant to the construct being measured, such as gender, ethnicity, race, socioeconomic status, disability, religion, age, or national origin.

1.3 Plan accommodations for groups of test takers with disabilities and other special needs when developing assessments.

1.4 Disclose to appropriate parties any actual or potential conflicts of interest that might influence the developers' judgment or performance.

1.5 Use copyrighted materials in assessment products and services in accordance with state and federal law.

1.6 Make information available to appropriate persons about the steps taken to develop and score the assessment, including up-to-date information used to support the reliability, validity, scoring and reporting processes, and other relevant characteristics of the assessment.

1.7 Protect the rights to privacy of those who are assessed as part of the assessment development process.

1.8 Caution users, in clear and prominent language, against the most likely misinterpretations and misuses of data that arise out of the assessment development process.

1.9 Avoid false or unsubstantiated claims in test preparation and program support materials and services about an assessment or its use and interpretation.

1.10 Correct any substantive inaccuracies in assessments or their support materials as soon as feasible.

1.11 Develop score reports and support materials that promote the understanding of assessment results.

Section 2:
Responsibilities of Those Who Market and Sell Assessment Products and Services

The marketing of assessment products and services, such as tests and other instruments, scoring services, test preparation services, consulting, and test interpretive services, should be based on information that is accurate, complete, and relevant to those considering their use. Persons who market and sell assessment products and services have a professional responsibility to:

2.1 Provide accurate information to potential purchasers about assessment products and services and their recommended uses and limitations.

2.2 Not knowingly withhold relevant information about assessment products and services that might affect an appropriate selection decision.

2.3 Base all claims about assessment products and services on valid interpretations of publicly available information.

2.4 Allow qualified users equal opportunity to purchase assessment products and services.

2.5 Establish reasonable fees for assessment products and services.

2.6 Communicate to potential users, in advance of any purchase or use, all applicable fees associated with assessment products and services.

2.7 Strive to ensure that no individuals are denied access to opportunities because of their inability to pay the fees for assessment products and services.

2.8 Establish criteria for the sale of assessment products and services, such as limiting the sale of assessment products and services to those individuals who are qualified for recommended uses and from whom proper uses and interpretations are anticipated.

2.9 Inform potential users of known inappropriate uses of assessment products and services and provide recommendations about how to avoid such misuses.

2.10 Maintain a current understanding about assessment products and services and their appropriate uses in education.

2.11 Release information implying endorsement by users of assessment products and services only with the users' permission.

2.12 Avoid making claims that assessment products and services have been endorsed by another organization unless an official endorsement has been obtained.

2.13 Avoid marketing test preparation products and services that may cause individuals to receive scores that misrepresent their actual levels of attainment.

Section 3:
Responsibilities of Those Who Select Assessment Products and Services

Those who select assessment products and services for use in educational settings, or help others do so, have important professional responsibilities to make sure that the assessments are appropriate for their intended use. Persons who select assessment products and services have a professional responsibility to:

3.1 Conduct a thorough review and evaluation of available assessment strategies and instruments that might be valid for the intended uses.

3.2 Recommend and/or select assessments based on publicly available documented evidence of their technical quality and utility rather than on unsubstantiated claims or statements.

3.3 Disclose any associations or affiliations that they have with the authors, test publishers, or others involved with the assessments under consideration for purchase and refrain from participation if such associations might affect the objectivity of the selection process.

3.4 Inform decision makers and prospective users of the appropriateness of the assessment for the intended uses, likely consequences of use, protection of examinee rights, relative costs, materials and services needed to conduct or use the assessment, and known limitations of the assessment, including potential misuses and misinterpretations of assessment information.

3.5 Recommend against the use of any prospective assessment that is likely to be administered, scored, and used in an invalid manner for members of various groups in our society for reasons of race, ethnicity, gender, age, disability, language background, socioeconomic status, religion, or national origin.

3.6 Comply with all security precautions that may accompany assessments being reviewed.

3.7 Immediately disclose any attempts by others to exert undue influence on the assessment selection process.

3.8 Avoid recommending, purchasing, or using test preparation products and services that may cause individuals to receive scores that misrepresent their actual levels of attainment.

Section 4:
Responsibilities of Those Who Administer Assessments

Those who prepare individuals to take assessments and those who are directly or indirectly involved in the administration of assessments as part of the educational process, including teachers, administrators, and assessment personnel, have an important role in making sure that the assessments are administered in a fair and accurate manner. Persons who prepare others for, and those who administer, assessments have a professional responsibility to:

4.1 Inform the examinees about the assessment prior to its administration, including its purposes, uses, and consequences; how the assessment information will be judged or scored; how the results will be kept on file; who will have access to the results; how the results will be distributed; and examinees' rights before, during, and after the assessment.

4.2 Administer only those assessments for which they are qualified by education, training, licensure, or certification.

4.3 Take appropriate security precautions before, during, and after the administration of the assessment.

4.4 Understand the procedures needed to administer the assessment prior to administration.

4.5 Administer standardized assessments according to prescribed procedures and conditions and notify appropriate persons if any non-standard or delimiting conditions occur.

4.6 Not exclude any eligible student from the assessment.

4.7 Avoid any conditions in the conduct of the assessment that might invalidate the results.

4.8 Provide for and document all reasonable and allowable accommodations for the administration of the assessment to persons with disabilities or special needs.

4.9 Provide reasonable opportunities for individuals to ask questions about the assessment procedures or directions prior to and at prescribed times during the administration of the assessment.

4.10 Protect the rights to privacy and due process of those who are assessed.

4.11 Avoid actions or conditions that would permit or encourage individuals or groups to receive scores that misrepresent their actual levels of attainment.

Section 5:
Responsibilities of Those Who Score Assessments

The scoring of educational assessments should be conducted properly and efficiently so that the results are reported accurately and in a timely manner. Persons who score and prepare reports of assessments have a professional responsibility to:

5.1 Provide complete and accurate information to users about how the assessment is scored, such as the reporting schedule, scoring process to be used, rationale for the scoring approach, technical characteristics, quality control procedures, reporting formats, and the fees, if any, for these services.

5.2 Ensure the accuracy of the assessment results by conducting reasonable quality control procedures before, during, and after scoring.

5.3 Minimize the effect on scoring of factors irrelevant to the purposes of the assessment.

5.4 Inform users promptly of any deviation in the planned scoring and reporting service or schedule and negotiate a solution with users.

5.5 Provide corrected score results to the examinee or the client as quickly as practicable should errors be found that may affect the inferences made on the basis of the scores.

5.6 Protect the confidentiality of information that identifies individuals as prescribed by state and federal laws.

5.7 Release summary results of the assessment only to those persons entitled to such information by state or federal law or those who are designated by the party contracting for the scoring services.

5.8 Establish, where feasible, a fair and reasonable process for appeal and rescoring the assessment.

Section 6:
Responsibilities of Those Who Interpret, Use, and Communicate Assessment Results

The interpretation, use, and communication of assessment results should promote valid inferences and minimize invalid ones. Persons who interpret, use, and communicate assessment results have a professional responsibility to:

6.1 Conduct these activities in an informed, objective, and fair manner within the context of the assessment's limitations and with an understanding of the potential consequences of use.

6.2 Provide to those who receive assessment results information about the assessment, its purposes, its limitations, and its uses necessary for the proper interpretation of the results.

6.3 Provide to those who receive score reports an understandable written description of all reported scores, including proper interpretations and likely misinterpretations.

6.4 Communicate to appropriate audiences the results of the assessment in an understandable and timely manner, including proper interpretations and likely misinterpretations.

6.5 Evaluate and communicate the adequacy and appropriateness of any norms or standards used in the interpretation of assessment results.

6.6 Inform parties involved in the assessment process how assessment results may affect them.

6.7 Use multiple sources and types of relevant information about persons or programs whenever possible in making educational decisions.

6.8 Avoid making, and actively discourage others from making, inaccurate reports, unsubstantiated claims, inappropriate interpretations, or otherwise false and misleading statements about assessment results.

6.9 Disclose to examinees and others whether and how long the results of the assessment will be kept on file, procedures for appeal and rescoring, rights examinees and others have to the assessment information, and how those rights may be exercised.

6.10 Report any apparent misuses of assessment information to those responsible for the assessment process.

6.11 Protect the rights to privacy of individuals and institutions involved in the assessment process.

Section 7:
Responsibilities of Those Who Educate Others About Assessment

The process of educating others about educational assessment, whether as part of higher education, professional development, public policy discussions, or job training, should prepare individuals to understand and engage in sound measurement prac-

tice and to become discerning users of tests and test results. Persons who educate or inform others about assessment have a professional responsibility to:

7.1 Remain competent and current in the areas in which they teach and reflect that in their instruction.

7.2 Provide fair and balanced perspectives when teaching about assessment.

7.3 Differentiate clearly between expressions of opinion and substantiated knowledge when educating others about any specific assessment method, product, or service.

7.4 Disclose any financial interests that might be perceived to influence the evaluation of a particular assessment product or service that is the subject of instruction.

7.5 Avoid administering any assessment that is not part of the evaluation of student performance in a course if the administration of that assessment is likely to harm any student.

7.6 Avoid using or reporting the results of any assessment that is not part of the evaluation of student performance in a course if the use or reporting of results is likely to harm any student.

7.7 Protect all secure assessments and materials used in the instructional process.

7.8 Model responsible assessment practice and help those receiving instruction to learn about their professional responsibilities in educational measurement.

7.9 Provide fair and balanced perspectives on assessment issues being discussed by policymakers, parents, and other citizens.

Section 8:
Responsibilities of Those Who Evaluate Educational Programs and Conduct Research on Assessments

Conducting research on or about assessments or educational programs is a key activity in helping to improve the understanding and use of assessments and educational programs. Persons who engage in the evaluation of educational programs or conduct research on assessments have a professional responsibility to:

8.1 Conduct evaluation and research activities in an informed, objective, and fair manner.

8.2 Disclose any associations that they have with authors, test publishers, or others involved with the assessment and refrain from participation if such associations might affect the objectivity of the research or evaluation.

8.3 Preserve the security of all assessments throughout the research process as appropriate.

8.4 Take appropriate steps to minimize potential sources of invalidity in the research and disclose known factors that may bias the results of the study.

8.5 Present the results of research, both intended and unintended, in a fair, complete, and objective manner.

8.6 Attribute completely and appropriately the work and ideas of others.

8.7 Qualify the conclusions of the research within the limitations of the study.

8.8 Use multiple sources of relevant information in conducting evaluation and research activities whenever possible.

8.9 Comply with applicable standards for protecting the rights of participants in an evaluation or research study, including the rights to privacy and informed consent.

Afterword

As stated at the outset, the purpose of the Code of Professional Responsibilities in Educational Measurement is to serve as a guide to the conduct of NCME members who are engaged in any type of assessment activity in education. Given the broad scope of the field of educational assessment as well as the variety of activities in which professionals may engage, it is unlikely that any code will cover the professional responsibilities involved in every situation or activity in which assessment is used in education. Ultimately, it is hoped that this Code will serve as the basis for ongoing discussions about what constitutes professionally responsible practice. Moreover, these discussions will undoubtedly identify areas of practice that need further analysis and clarification in subsequent editions of the Code. To the extent that these discussions occur, the Code will have served its purpose.

To assist in the ongoing refinement of the Code, comments on this document are most welcome. Please send your comments and inquiries to:

Dr. William J. Russell
Executive Officer
National Council on Measurement in Education
1230 Seventeenth Street, NW
Washington, DC 20036-3078

Supplementary Resources

The following list of resources is provided for those who want to seek additional information about codes of professional responsibility that have been developed and adopted by organizations having an interest in various aspects of educational assessment.

American Association for Counseling and Development (now American Counseling Association). (1988). *Ethical standards of the American Counseling Association.* Alexandria, VA: Author.

American Association for Counseling and Development (now American Counseling Association) & Association for Measurement and Evaluation in Counseling and Development (now Association for Assessment in Counseling). (1989). *Responsibilities of users of standardized tests: RUST statement revised.* Alexandria, VA: Author.

American Educational Research Association, American Psychological Association, & National Council on Measurement in Education. (1985). *Standards for educational and psychological testing.* Washington, DC: Author.

American Educational Research Association. (1992). Ethical standards of the American Educational Research Association. *Educational Researcher, 21*(7), 23-26.

American Federation of Teachers, National Council on Measurement in Education, & National Education Association. (1990). *Standards for teacher competence in educational assessment of students.* Washington, DC: Author.

American Psychological Association. (1992). *Ethical principles of psychologists and code of conduct.* Washington, DC: Author.

American Psychological Association President's Task Force on Psychology in Education. (in press). *Learner-centered psychological principles: Guidelines for school redesign and reform.* Washington, DC: Author.

Joint Advisory Committee. (1993). *Principles for fair assessment practices for education in Canada.* Edmonton, Alberta: Author.

Joint Committee on Testing Practices. (1988). *Code of fair testing practices in education.* Washington, DC: Author.

Joint Committee on Standards for Educational Evaluation. (1988). *The personnel evaluation standards: How to assess systems for evaluating educators.* Newberry Park, CA: Sage.

Joint Committee on Standards for Educational Evaluation. (1994). *The program evaluation standards: How to assess evaluations of educational programs.* Thousand Oaks, CA: Sage.

National Association of College Admission Counselors. (1988). *Statement of principles of good practice.* Alexandria, VA: Author.

Index to the Code of Professional Responsibilities in Educational Measurement

This index provides a list of major topics and issues addressed by the responsibilities in each of the eight sections of the Code. Although this list is not intended to be exhaustive, it is intended to serve as a reference source for those who use this code.

Topic	Responsibility
Advertising:	1.9, 1.10, 2.3, 2.11, 2.12
Bias:	1.2, 3.5, 4.5, 4.7, 5.3, 8.4
Cheating:	4.5, 4.6, 4.11
Coaching and Test Preparation:	2.13, 3.8, 4.11
Competence:	2.10, 4.2, 4.4, 4.5, 5.2, 5.5, 7.1, 7.8, 7.9, 8.1, 8.7
Conflict of Interest:	1.4, 3.3, 7.4, 8.2
Consequences of Test Use:	3.4, 6.1, 6.6, 7.5, 7.6
Copyrighted Materials, Use of:	1.5, 8.6
Disabled Examinees, Rights of:	1.3, 4.8
Disclosure:	1.6, 2.1, 2.2, 2.6, 3.3, 3.7, 4.1, 5.1, 5.4, 6.2, 6.3, 6.4, 6.6, 6.9, 8.2, 8.4, 8.5
Due Process:	4.10, 5.8, 6.9
Equity:	1.2, 2.4, 2.7, 3.5, 4.6
Fees:	2.5, 2.6, 2.7
Inappropriate Test Use:	1.8, 2.8, 2.9, 3.4, 6.8, 6.10
Objectivity:	3.1, 3.2, 3.3, 6.1, 6.5, 7.2, 7.3, 7.9, 8.1, 8.2, 8.5, 8.7
Rights to Privacy:	1.7, 3.4, 4.10, 5.6, 5.7, 6.11, 8.9
Security:	3.6, 4.3, 7.7, 8.3
Truthfulness:	1.10, 2.1, 2.2, 2.3, 2.11, 2.12, 3.2, 4.6, 7.3
Undue Influence:	3.7
Unsubstantiated Claims:	1.9, 3.2, 6.8